THE
PUB
GUIDE
2015

Published by AA Publishing, a trading name of AA Media Limited, whose registered office is Fanum House, Basing View, Basingstoke RG21 4EA. Registered number 06112600.

18th edition September 2014.
© AA Media Limited 2014.

Assessments of AA inspected establishments are based on the experience of the Hotel and Restaurant Inspectors on the occasion(s) of their visit(s) and therefore descriptions given in this guide necessarily contain an element of subjective opinion which may not reflect or dictate a reader's own opinion on another occasion. See pages 8–9 for a clear explanation of how, based on our Inspectors' inspection experiences, establishments are graded. If the meal or meals experienced by an Inspector or Inspectors during an inspection fall between award levels the restaurant concerned may be awarded the lower of any award levels considered applicable.

AA Media Limited strives to ensure accuracy of the information in this guide at the time of printing. Nevertheless, the Publisher cannot be held responsible for any errors or omissions, or for changes in the details given in this guide, or for the consequences of any reliance on the information provided by the same. This does not affect your statutory rights. Due to the constantly evolving nature of the subject matter the information is subject to change. AA Media Limited will gratefully receive any advice from our readers of any necessary updated information.

Please contact:
Advertising Sales Department: advertisingsales@theAA.com
Editorial Department: lifestyleguides@theAA.com
AA Hotel and B&B Scheme Enquiries: 01256 844455

Website addresses are included in some entries and specified by the respective establishment. Such web sites are not under the control of AA Media Limited and as such AA Media Limited has no control over them and will not accept any responsibility or liability in respect of any and all matters whatsoever relating to such web sites including access, content, material and functionality. By including the addresses of third party web sites the AA does not intend to solicit business or offer any security to any person in any country, directly or indirectly.

Photographs in the gazetteer are provided by the establishments.

Typeset/Repro: Servis Filmsetting Ltd, Stockport.
Printed and bound by Printer Trento SRL, Trento
Directory compiled by the AA Lifestyle Guides Department and managed in the Librios Information Management System.

Pub descriptions have been contributed by the following team of writers: Phil Bryant, Neil Coates, David Halford, Jon Oxtoby and Mark Taylor.

Maps prepared by the Mapping Services Department of AA Publishing.

Maps © AA Media Limited 2014.

Contains Ordnance Survey data © Crown copyright and database right 2014.

Information on National Parks in England provided by the Countryside Agency (Natural England).

Information on National Parks in Scotland provided by Scottish Natural Heritage.

Information on National Parks in Wales provided by The Countryside Council for Wales.

A CIP catalogue for this book is available from the British Library.

ISBN: 978-0-7495-7618-9

Contents

Welcome to the AA Pub Guide 2015

We aim to bring you the country's best pubs, selected for their atmosphere, good beer and great food. Updated every year, this popular and well-established guide includes lots of old favourites, plus many new and interesting destinations for drinking and eating across England, Scotland and Wales.

Who's in the guide?

We make our selection by seeking out pubs that are worth making a detour for – 'destination' pubs – where publicans show real enthusiasm for their trade and offer a good selection of well-kept drinks and good food. We also choose neighbourhood pubs which are supported by locals and prove attractive to passing motorists or walkers. Our selected pubs make no payment for their inclusion in the guide*; they appear entirely at our discretion.

That special place

We find pubs that offer something special: pubs where the time-honoured values of a convivial environment for conversation while supping or eating have not been forgotten. They may be attractive, interesting, unusual or in a good location. Some may be very much a local pub or they may draw customers from further afield, while others appear because they are in an exceptional place. Interesting towns and villages, eccentric or historic buildings, and rare settings can all be found within this guide.

Tempting food

We look for menus that show a commitment to home cooking, that make good use of local produce wherever possible, and offer an appetising range of freshly prepared dishes. Pubs presenting well-executed traditional dishes like ploughman's or pies, or those offering innovative bar or restaurant food, are all in the running. In keeping with recent trends in pub food, we are keen to include those where particular emphasis is placed on imaginative modern dishes. Occasionally we include pubs that serve no food, or just snacks, but are distinctive in other ways.

Pick of the Pubs

Some of the pubs included in the guide are particularly special, and we have highlighted these as Pick of the Pubs. For 2015, over 650 pubs have been selected using the personal knowledge of our editorial team, our AA inspectors, and suggestions from our readers. These pubs have a more detailed description, and this year over 150 have chosen to enhance their entry by purchasing two photographs to create a full-page entry.

Beer and cider festivals

As well as keeping their ales and ciders in tip-top condition throughout the year, many of the pubs in this guide hold beer and cider festivals, either just one a year or on several occasions. If they have told us that they do, we have indicated these events in the pub entries, and where possible have also mentioned the month/s of the year or bank holidays when they are held. You'll find lists of these festivals at the back of the guide.

Tell us what you think

We welcome your feedback about the pubs included, and about the guide itself. We would also be pleased to receive suggestions about good pubs you have visited that do not feature in this guide. A Readers' Report form appears at the back of the guide, so please write in or email us at **lifestyleguides@theaa.com**.

* Once chosen for the guide, pubs may decide to enhance their text entry or include advertising for which there is a charge

How to use the guide

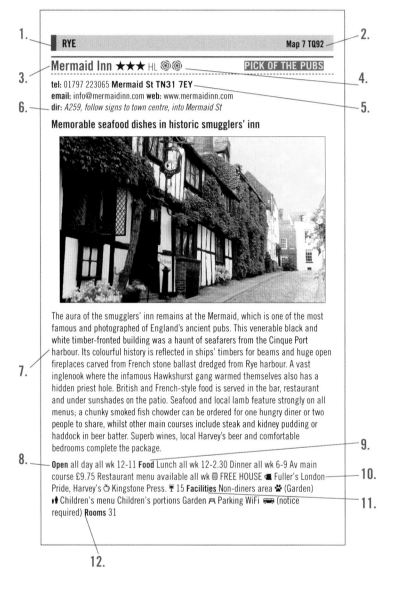

1.

RYE   Map 7 TQ92

2.

3.

Mermaid Inn ★★★ HL ◉◉   PICK OF THE PUBS

4.

tel: 01797 223065 **Mermaid St TN31 7EY**
email: info@mermaidinn.com **web:** www.mermaidinn.com
dir: *A259, follow signs to town centre, into Mermaid St*

5.

6.

Memorable seafood dishes in historic smugglers' inn

The aura of the smugglers' inn remains at the Mermaid, which is one of the most famous and photographed of England's ancient pubs. This venerable black and white timber-fronted building was a haunt of seafarers from the Cinque Port harbour. Its colourful history is reflected in ships' timbers for beams and huge open fireplaces carved from French stone ballast dredged from Rye harbour. A vast inglenook where the infamous Hawkshurst gang warmed themselves also has a hidden priest hole. British and French-style food is served in the bar, restaurant and under sunshades on the patio. Seafood and local lamb feature strongly on all menus; a chunky smoked fish chowder can be ordered for one hungry diner or two people to share, whilst other main courses include steak and kidney pudding or haddock in beer batter. Superb wines, local Harvey's beer and comfortable bedrooms complete the package.

7.

9.

Open all day all wk 12-11 **Food** Lunch all wk 12-2.30 Dinner all wk 6-9 Av main course £9.75 Restaurant menu available all wk ⊕ FREE HOUSE ◀ Fuller's London Pride, Harvey's ♻ Kingstone Press. ♈ 15 **Facilities** Non-diners area ♥ (Garden) ♦♦ Children's menu Children's portions Garden ⊓ Parking WiFi ▭ (notice required) **Rooms** 31

8.

10.

11.

12.

1. Location
Guide order Country; county; town or village. Pubs are listed under their town or village name alphabetically within their county, within their country. There is a county map at the back of the guide. Some village pubs prefer to be listed under the nearest town, in which case the village name appears in their address.

2. Map reference
Each town or village is given a map reference – the map page number and a two-figure reference based on the National Grid. For example: **Map 7 TQ92**
7 refers to the page number of the map section at the back of the guide
TQ is the National Grid lettered square (representing 100,000sq metres) in which the location will be found
9 is the figure reading across the top and bottom of the map page
2 is the figure reading down at each side of the map page
London Maps: A Central London map and a Greater London map follow the map section at the back of the guide. The pub location will either appear on Plan 1 or Plan 2.

3. Pub name
Where the name appears in italic type the information that follows has not been confirmed by the pub for 2015.

4. AA ratings/designators/awards
★★☆ Star rating under AA Hotel or B&B Schemes (see pages 8–9) followed by a designator (i.e. HL) which shows the type of hotel or B&B.

AA Rosette award for food excellence (see page 9).

PICK OF THE PUBS (see page 5)

5. Address and contact details

6. Directions
Brief details are given on how to find the pub.

7. Description

8. Opening times
Times are given for when the pub is open, and also closed.

9. Food
Indicates the days and times that food can be ordered, followed by the average price of a main course (as supplied to us by the pub). Please be aware that last orders could vary by up to 30 minutes. We also show if a separate restaurant menu is offered and on what days it is available.

10. Brewery and Company
indicates the name of the brewery to which the pub is tied, or the company that owns it. FREE HOUSE is shown if the pub is independently owned and run.
indicates the principal beers sold by the pub. The pub's top cask or hand-pulled beers are listed. Many pubs have a much greater selection, with several guest beers each week.

indicates the real ciders sold by the pub.
the number of wines available by the glass.

11. Facilities
indicates that the pub serves food outside
indicates that the pub has told us they are happy to be described as dog friendly. If possible we also show whereabouts the dogs are accepted (i.e. bar, restaurant, garden and/or outside area).
indicates that the pub welcomes children and if they offer a children's menu and/or children's portions. Further information in this section shows if the pub has a non-diners' area; holds a beer festival and/or a cider festival; has a children's play area, a garden or outside area; if parking is available; if they accept coach parties, and if prior notice is required; if WiFi is available.

12. Rooms
The number of bedrooms is only shown if the pub's accommodation is rated by the AA.

Notes
As so many establishments take one or more of the major credit or debit cards, we only indicate if a pub does not accept any cards.

Key to Symbols

★★★	Accommodation rating. See explanation on pages 8 & 9
U	Accommodation rating not yet confirmed
	Rosettes – The AA's food award. See explanation on page 9
	Name of Brewery; Company; Free House
	Principal beers sold
	Real ciders sold
	At least eight wines available by the glass. The number of wines may be shown beside the symbol
	Dog-friendly pubs: dogs can be accepted in bar, restaurant, garden and/or outside area
	Children welcome
	Outside eating area
	Coach parties accepted; pre-booking may be required
	Credit and debit cards not accepted
NEW	Pubs appearing in the guide for the first time

AA classifications and awards

Many of the pubs in this guide offer accommodation. Where a Star rating appears next to an entry's name in the guide, the establishment has been inspected by the AA under common Quality Standards agreed between the AA, VisitBritain, VisitScotland and VisitWales. These ratings are for the accommodation, and ensure that the establishment meets the highest standards of cleanliness, with an emphasis on professionalism, proper booking procedures and prompt and efficient services. Some of the pubs in this guide offer accommodation but do not belong to an AA rating scheme; in this case reference to the accommodation is not included in their entry.

AA recognised establishments pay an annual fee that varies according to the classification and the number of bedrooms. The establishments receive an unannounced inspection from a qualified AA inspector who recommends the appropriate classification. Return visits confirm that standards are maintained; the classification is not transferable if an establishment changes hands.

The annual *AA Hotel Guide* and *AA Bed & Breakfast Guide* give further details of recognised establishments and the classification schemes. Details of AA recognised hotels, guest accommodation, restaurants and pubs are also available at theAA.com, and on AA apps.

AA hotel classification

Hotels are classified on a 5-point scale, with one star ★ being the simplest, and five stars offering a luxurious service at the top of the range. The AA's top hotels in Britain and Ireland are identified by red stars. (★) In addition to the main **Hotel** (HL) classification which applies to some pubs in this guide, there are other categories of hotel which may be applicable to pubs, as follows:

Town House Hotel (TH) – A small, individual city or town centre property.

Country House Hotel – (CHH) Quietly located in a rural area.

Small Hotel (SHL) – Owner managed with fewer than 20 bedrooms.

AA Guest Accommodation

Guest accommodation is also classified on a scale of one to five stars, with one ★ being the most simple, and five being more luxurious. Gold stars (★) indicate the very best B&Bs, Guest Houses, Farmhouses, Inns, Restaurant with Rooms and Guest Accommodation in the 3, 4 and 5 star ratings. A series of designators appropriate to the type of accommodation offered is also used, as follows:

Inn (INN) – Accommodation provided in a fully licensed establishment. The bar will be open to non-residents and food is provided in the evenings.

Bed & Breakfast (B&B) – Accommodation provided in a private house, run by the owner and with no more than six paying guests.

Guest House (GH) – Accommodation provided for more than six paying guests and run on a more commercial basis than a B&B. Usually more services, for example dinner, provided by staff as well as the owner.

Farmhouse (FH) – B&B or guest house rooms provided on a working farm or smallholding.

Restaurant with Rooms (RR) – Destination restaurant offering overnight accommodation. The restaurant is the main business and is open to non-residents. A high standard of food should be offered, at least five nights a week. A maximum of 12 bedrooms. Most Restaurants with Rooms have been awarded AA Rosettes for their food.

Guest Accommodation (GA) – Any establishment which meets the entry requirements for the Scheme can choose this designator.

U A small number of pubs have this symbol because their Star classification was not confirmed at the time of going to press.

Rosette awards

Out of the thousands of restaurants in the British Isles, the AA identifies, with its Rosette Awards, around 2,000 as the best. What to expect from restaurants with AA Rosette Awards is outlined here; for a more detailed explanation of Rosette criteria please see theAA.com

ⓖ Excellent local restaurants serving food prepared with care, understanding and skill and using good quality ingredients.

ⓖⓖ The best local restaurants, which consistently aim for and achieve higher standards and where a greater precision is apparent in the cooking. Obvious attention is paid to the selection of quality ingredients.

ⓖⓖⓖ Outstanding restaurants that demand recognition well beyond their local area.

ⓖⓖⓖⓖ Amongst the very best restaurants in the British Isles, where the cooking demands national recognition.

ⓖⓖⓖⓖⓖ The finest restaurants in the British Isles, where the cooking stands comparison with the best in the world.

AA Pub of the Year

The prestigious annual awards for the AA Pub of the Year for England, Scotland and Wales have been selected with the help of our AA inspectors and we have chosen three very worthy winners. These pubs stand out for being great all-rounders, combining a convivial atmosphere, well-kept beers and ciders, excellent food, and of course, a warm welcome from the friendly and efficient hosts and their staff.

ENGLAND

THE PHEASANT ★★★★★ ◉

GESTINGTHORPE, ESSEX page 188

Situated on the Essex and Suffolk border and surrounded by lovely countryside, The Pheasant is definitely a place worth seeking out. Owners, James and Diana Donoghue have gained a strong reputation and a loyal following at their stylish gastro-pub. Before his new career here, James was an award-winning garden designer (gaining a medal at the Chelsea Flower Show) and he has used his skills to great effect in the one-acre garden. By creating raised vegetable beds and building polytunnels, a steady supply of seasonal, organic fruit and vegetables is readily available for the busy kitchen. They keep chickens and bees too, and the output from the smokehouse is prolific. James actively encourages visitors to explore the garden and hosts many village events throughout the year; the summer beer festival is an excuse to quaff a pint or two of ale or cider, enjoy good food and admire the vintage steam traction engines that trundle their way to the front door. Inside the charming pub you'll find original low beams and warming log fires alongside an extensive range of real ales and imaginative menus. If you decide to stop over after an enjoyable evening meal, there are elegant en suite bedrooms in the Coach House; each named after a notable local person – artists Gainsborough and Constable, Antarctic explorer Captain Oates, silk mill owner Courtauld and botantist Catesby. Overall this is a place that inspires many, and is a worthy winner.

SCOTLAND

THE BRIDGE INN ★ ★ ★ ★
RATHO, CITY OF EDINBURGH   page 599

Arrive by boat, on foot or by car at this inn beside the tree-lined Union Canal east of Edinburgh. Back in the 19th century The Bridge was frequented by navvies digging the canal, but today the hospitality and dedication to customer care would be unrecognisable to them. The award-winning food is supported by a good range of Scottish cask ales including brews from the Cairngorm Brewery in the Highlands, Dark Island in Orkney and Isle of Skye and Isle of Arran Breweries; all the wines, including some of the owners' personal favourites, are available by the glass which makes trying something new an easy option. Such is their commitment to offering fresh ingredients on their menus, The Bridge keeps chickens, ducks and Saddleback pigs and cultivates fruit and vegetables, and even nettles, in their walled garden that's just 200 yards along the towpath. Beyond that they source all the meat and all the fish from Scotland. The interior areas are stylish, contemporary spaces and on fine days there's an outside terrace for eating a leisurely meal or just enjoying a drink. The pub has two restaurant barges which can be booked for lunch, afternoon tea or dinner; they travel as far as the Almondell Aqueduct which is suspended over the River Almond. If needing somewhere to stop overnight, The Bridge has four individually designed bedrooms, each with a view of the canal. Everyone visiting here receives a warm welcome from the friendly and helpful staff.

WALES

THE BUNCH OF GRAPES
PONTYPRIDD, RHONDDA CYNON TAFF   page 645

'The Bunch' as it's known locally, fulfils all expectations of a well-run, traditional pub – good beer, good food, warm hospitality and a commitment to engaging with the local community and drawing in a wider circle of followers. It's played a part in Pontypridd's history for over 160 years, being built originally to slake the considerable thirsts of the employees of the Brown Lenox chain works who became parched by the extreme heat generated by the furnesses. Today, the forward-thinking pub owners are still enthusiastic about real ales, not least because of their own microbrewery – Otley Brewing Co. A pint of the flagship brew, O2 Croeso, is well worth trying. Complementing the range of real ales on tap you'll find continental and American imported beers, fruit beers, lagers and an increasing number of Welsh ciders and perries. Look to their blackboards for the daily-changing dishes created by the young kitchen team who are dedicated to sourcing sustainable produce from local suppliers. Beer events are held regularly and include food and beer parings, meet the brewer evenings and themed ale festivals; The Bunch Beer Academy keeps aficionados in touch with what's going on. To take a little bit of Welsh produce home with you, look no further than the pub's own popular deli, where bread, cheeses, chutneys and a whole lot more seasonal items can be found. There's always something interesting going on at The Bunch of Grapes.

Swine and dine

by Phil Bryant

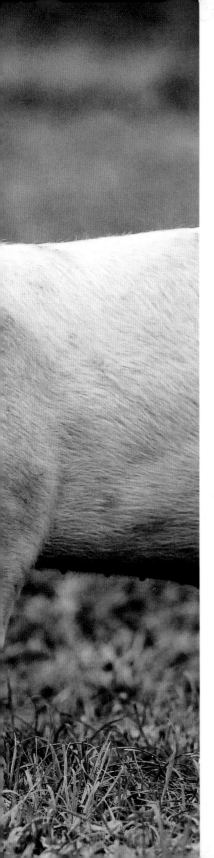

They say you can eat everything from a pig except its oink. Our writer set out to discover if this is true and how some pubs go 'the whole hog'.

"All pigs are intelligent, emotional, and sensitive souls," wrote naturalist Sy Montgomery. She also said that they desire contact and comfort, have a wonderful sense of mischief and seem to enjoy music. Perhaps not something to dwell on as you tuck into a pork chop or read about some of the dishes mentioned in this guide.

If you're a vegetarian it may be best to stop reading now. If you're not, carry on, because you'll appreciate the well-known saying: "You can eat everything from a pig except its oink." How true that almost is, the only real exceptions being the hair and the bones.

Pubs that raise their own pigs, mostly rare-breed, are pretty thorough when it comes to using what lies twixt snout and tail. Certain dishes, of course, appear on most, if not all, menus, including the ever-popular roast pork and pork belly. But there's a lot more to a pig than its best known recipies.

Take The Wellington Arms, once the Iron Duke's hunting lodge, at Baughurst near the Hampshire/Berkshire border. In their field owners Jason King and Simon Page keep four Tamworth pigs with pedigree Jacob sheep, rare-breed and rescue hens, and two hives full of bees. Depending on the day's menu, diners may choose from a wide range of porcine treats, such as prosciutto, rillettes and occasionally pig's-head terrine, which involves boiling the head for eight hours to loosen the flesh.

Simon acknowledges that sending their own pigs to slaughter can be an emotional business: "Sad? Yes, every time, but we have them to use on our menu, so we try very hard not to become too attached." A dispassionate pig-naming policy – One, Two, Three, Four, etc. – probably helps.

Pig Heaven

In Blaisdon, Gloucestershire, Sharon Hookings takes a different approach. Landlady of The Red Hart Inn, a family-owned free house, she names only her breeding sows, the current mum being Princess. She borrows dads-to-be from a nearby farm and always calls them Roger (don't ask!), the lucky boar then doing his duty in a field fittingly called Pig Heaven.

Once her piglets have been weaned, Sharon feeds them on raw vegetable waste, spent brewery grain and apple pulp from a cider maker. The four fattest then go to the abbatoir. "The first time we sent pigs off it was hard," she recalls. "They trusted me and followed me into the trailer, but I now remind myself that they've led a good, if short, life."

Sharon's local butcher cures the hams and makes sausages, while her kitchen team prepares dishes such as slow-roasted belly pork with black pudding and celeriac mash, and pork tenderloin with mushroom Marsala wine sauce. They even cook the ears for Sharon's springer spaniel, Jay.

"We wanted to do more than just be on the local-produce bandwagon."

Linda Gotto and Lucinda Parks own The Parrot Inn at Forest Green, in the Surrey Hills; Linda also has a farm where she raises about two hundred Middlewhite and Saddleback pigs. "They are absolutely fascinating to keep," she says, "but I don't name the sows and saying goodbye is not an issue. We have our own butchery and use all parts of the carcass to make charcuterie, black puddings and sausages, and to cure bacon and ham. Our menu changes with what's available, pork belly being a firm favourite. Scratchings are always popular, too."

Opposite the village green in Dial Post, near Horsham, in West Sussex, is The Crown Inn, a gastro-pub run by James Middleton Burn and his wife Penny, whose grandparents owned it in the late 60s and early 70s. James for many years travelled the world combining his twin loves of skiing and fine cooking, until eventually settling here, where he makes excellent use of the pigs (and lambs) reared on a nearby farm by Penny's sister Jo.

Many different breeds

No doubt rather tired of it being pointed out – so apologies for doing it again – Garry Cook is the aptly-named chef at another Crown Inn, a 15th-century, one-time smugglers' haunt in Snape, Suffolk. On its five acres he and his wife Teresa raise Old Spots and Large Whites, as well as quail, poultry, Suffolk lambs and Anglo-Nubian goats. "We wanted to do more than just be on the local-produce bandwagon," explains Garry, whose neighbouring butcher prepares the carcasses. In addition to the usual cuts, heads are used for potted pork, and trimmings and offal for terrines, chorizo and pancetta.

Picturesque Broughton Gifford near Melksham in Wiltshire, is where Alex and Jodanna Geneen run The Fox, behind which a smallholding accommodates their chickens, ducks and pigs. Alex recalls the time when some piglets escaped and within minutes had completely rooted up the neighbouring pub garden.

"We've had many different types – Saddlebacks, Welsh, Old Spots, Large Blacks and British Lops," says Alex. "We use everything from 'nose to tail' and make charcuterie, air- and wet-cured hams, sausages and even bacon. The end product is so good. It would be considerably cheaper to buy in whole beasts, but the quality is not even close, except that from a few select suppliers."

Not too far away, at The Bath Arms Hotel on the Longleat Estate, landlord Jason Thorley took delivery in early 2014 of ten boisterous Saddleback piglets, born locally to a sow from a previous litter. They live in the hotel grounds, where, as manager Tracey Penny says: "Our guests love visiting them. It's important for children to understand where their food comes from. We use the whole pig – nothing is wasted."

She remembers trying to feed some piglets one day in torrential rain, but had been able to find only size-12 wellies. As she climbed into the pen they all ran at her and, helpless in her huge boots, she fell over in the mud as she tried to escape.

More than just the money

Wiltshire has at least one more member of the pig-owning pub club, the early 17th-century Red Lion, a free house just off the Thames Path in historic Cricklade. Owner Tom Gee alternates between Saddlebacks and Oxford Sandy and Blacks, which he keeps on a neighbour's land a hundred yards from his pub's front door.

Tom doesn't raise pigs to make money, explaining, "The pork costs us more to produce than it would to buy, but with people increasingly aware of what they are eating, to be able to offer rare-breed pork from our own pigs is another string to our bow and I think the benefits outweigh the negatives."

It takes twelve months to air-dry the hams, while a local butcher makes sausages to a pub recipe featuring beer from Tom's own micro-brewery. His "healthy but delicious take on scratchings" are pig quavers, skin with the fat removed, oven dried and then cooked very hot so that it puffs up.

In Oxfordshire lies the semi-wetland bird sanctuary and farming community of Otmoor, encircled by the 'Seven Towns' (but picture villages). One of these is Murcott where, at The Nut Tree Inn – the one with three thatched piglets on the roof, and known locally as 'the pig pub' – Mike and Imogen North keep Old Spots and Tamworths.

Last spring Doris, one of their two sows (the other is Ethel), gave birth to five piglets, courtesy of Tinie Tempah, their boar. "We'll see what the meat's like and if it's good we'll keep going with him," promises Imogen. "We use everything – pigs' hearts on toast are surprisingly popular. Our butcher makes us sausages and we have a smoker made from an old drinks fridge."

In the grounds of The Bridge Inn in Ratho, just west of Edinburgh, Graham and Rachel Bucknall's Saddlebacks are looked after by all the family, in

"We give only our sows names, as they're unlikely to end up on the plate..."

support of their belief that a happy pig produces the tastiest meat. Their menus feature pork loin, fillet, belly, sausages and crackling, as well as the occasional pig's cheeks and crispy ears, home-made popcorn with pork seasoning and, on Bonfire Night, slow-roasted suckling pig.

By the time this guide is published, The Bridge Inn's menus should also feature home-cured bacon and snout terrine, served with glazed ear and home-grown salad. "And in 2015 we hope to be serving dry-cured hams, although we have to be very patient," explains Rachel. "We give only our sows names, as they're unlikely to end up on the plate. Our first, Nellie, was utterly gorgeous and probably the hardest to say goodbye to, although she did die of old age."

For more than 200 years, The Alice Hawthorn has stood at the heart of Nun Monkton in North Yorkshire. Three Saddleback-Old Spots crosses and six Tamworths live in the grounds, partly so that the management team can look after them, but also so that customers can see them.

"We name them after pub team members, so everyone has a pig," says general manager, Karen Metcalfe. "We're passionate about field-to-fork, from getting our piglets at ten weeks old to fattening them up for dishes such as our best-selling slow-roasted belly pork with braised pig cheek and ham hock."

Is it difficult to say goodbye? "Not as far as our chefs are concerned, because they're excited about what they can make," she suggests, "but ask one of the waitresses and they'll probably say 'Yes!'"

New pigs on the block

For our final piggy pub we head back to the appropriately-named village of Ham in Gloucestershire and The Salutation Inn, aka The Sally, a rural free house close to the Severn Estuary. On Monday evenings the cooking is done by guest chefs Polly and Craig, who raise Old Spots, Middle Whites and Saddlebacks on their smallholding in the next village. Among the monikers resulting from their no-holds-barred naming policy have been Fatty-Fatty-Pig-Pig, Psycho-pig and Sneaky McSneakerson.

Says landlord Peter Tiley: "Polly and Craig like Old Spots because they have a great temperament. As well as having strong personalities, they look good, grow well and produce a nice layer of fat on the meat, which has a wonderful sweet flavour." He serves every part of the pig at The Sally – 'Going The Whole Hog', as he calls it – from trotters to devilled kidneys, from faggots to smoked pulled shoulder, and from slow-roasted belly to salamis, prosciutto and speck. He even claims that pig fat is good for waterproofing walking boots!

Plans to bring the pigs on-site to The Sally are in hand, so it'll soon be time for Ham-made ham.

So, fans of eating all things pork can rejoice in the fact that there are many excellent pub owners throughout the land who are dedicated to giving their home-reared pigs a fine and fitting send off.

17

The water of life

by Mark Taylor

What makes whisky such a popular and enduring favourite? We've been finding out from pubs around the country.

Strolling into the award-winning Clachaig Inn in the heart of Glencoe and ordering a 'wee dram' of Scotch whisky is not as straightforward as it sounds.

Popular with walkers, mountaineers and tourists from around the world, the pub is set against the stunning mountains of the Highlands and it's an ideal spot to sip a glass of Scotland's famous amber spirit. However, the choice is overwhelming, stretching to more than 300 different malts alone.

"As a business in the Scottish Highlands, we have always promoted the very best of Scotland's produce," says manager Gordon Keppie, who admits to having a soft spot for Speyside malts, which he says are lighter, sweeter and offer 'a lot more body and power' thanks to being aged in heavily sherried casks.

Although a comparatively small region, Speyside has 84 working distilleries, including some of the world's best-sellers, iconic global brands such as The Glenlivet, Glenfiddich and The Macallan – the tipple of choice for James Bond in the film *Skyfall*.

At the Clachaig Inn, there is a comprehensive whisky menu complete with distillery information and tasting notes. As well as popular everyday whiskies, it serves a range of vintage malts including the highly-prized Glen Grant 1951 at £36 a nip.

For a product that starts out with the basic ingredients of grain and water, Scotch whisky is a complex drink that has become one of the biggest assets to the UK's economy. Employing more than 10,000 people in Scotland, the Scotch whisky industry is now worth more than £4 billion a year and accounts for a quarter of all UK food and drink exports.

The term 'whisky' comes from the Gaelic *uisge beatha*, meaning 'water of life' and the first written record of a Scotch whisky's distillation can be traced back to King James IV in 1494. Little has changed in the production of Scotch whisky over the past 200 years, with traditional methods still employed alongside more efficient and modern production techniques.

The early stages of whisky making are similar to the making of beer. Like any other alcohol, whisky is the result of natural chemical alterations of sugar so the process starts by changing the starches in the barley into sugar to produce malt. The malt is dried and ground into a coarse, flour-like substance called grist, which is mixed with hot water in a mash tun to extract sugar. The result is wort, which is transferred to vessels called wash backs, where yeast is added to start the fermentation process and then the fermented liquid is distilled in heated copper stills to separate the alcohol from water and other substances.

Scotch is double distilled and, once it has been cooled in a condenser, it is transferred to oak casks which have often previously been used to store sherry, bourbon or port, which can impart an additional fragrance to the Scotch.

The ageing process takes a minimum of three years from start to finish and if the distilled spirit hasn't stayed in an oak cask for that length of time, it can not legally call itself whisky.

"Whisky is enjoying a renaissance in high-end bars and pubs as a new generation discovers it"

What's in a whisky?

The minimum percentage of alcohol for whisky is 40%, although some are much higher, and Scotch can be aged for up to 20 years in the cask. Unlike wine, whisky doesn't age in the bottle so a whisky that has been aged in casks for 12 years stays a 12-year-old Scotch from the point when it is bottled. To be classed as 'Scotch', whisky must be both distilled and matured in Scotland and it is sold as 'single malt', 'pure malt' or 'blended'.

Scotch whiskies are made only from malted barley, water and yeast, and no additives or enhancers are allowed, although a small amount of caramel can be added for colour at the point of bottling. Blended whisky created from several different malts – anything from 15 to 50 single whiskies – accounts for the majority of Scotch consumed.

Single malt whisky is made only from malt whiskies from a single distillery and classified by their area of origin, namely Speyside, Highland, Lowland, Islay, the Islands and Campbeltown.

The rarest Scotch, produced by only a handful of distilleries, is single grain Scotch made in a single distillery from unmalted barley, corn or wheat, water and barley.

Like wine regions, Scotland's whisky-producing areas each offer their own qualities and characteristics, depending on location, climate and the skills and experience of the distillers.

Malts produced in the Islands and Islay are famous for their 'peaty, maritime' aromas, whilst whiskies made in the Highlands have a reputation for being 'smooth and floral'.

Speyside malts are described as 'fruity and delicate', the rolling fields of the Lowlands produce 'light and fresh' malts and Campbeltown whiskies offer a mix of 'smoky and salty' character profiles.

It's these regional variations and unique characteristics that make Scotch an increasingly popular tipple for an ever-widening cross-section of drinkers.

The Nobody Inn in Doddiscombsleigh, Devon, sells more than 260 different whiskies, something that started with the previous owners and continues with new licensee Sue Burdge and bar manager Tim Hamilton.

Sue says, "I think whisky has always been a source of interest to young people and we have noticed a definite increase in women enjoying a dram – there is a whisky for everyone.

"Our whiskies are chosen by conducting research, customer requests and after visiting distilleries and discovering new ones. We don't think our customers favour a particular style of whisky and are happy to be guided by us. We try to establish the flavours and finish they are seeking and from that recommend an appropriate whisky."

Diversity

Although the UK market for Scotch fell 3% in 2013, whisky is enjoying a renaissance in high-end bars and pubs as it is discovered by a new generation.

"The Scotch whisky industry is in excellent shape," says Rosemary Gallagher of the Scotch Whisky Association. "Exports are worth around £4.3 billion annually and Scotch is exported to about 200 countries worldwide. Producers are very optimistic about the future.

"There seem to be more specialised whisky bars opening, and bars that offer a wider range of whiskies. Some bars, restaurants and hotels are putting a lot of effort into educating staff on the types of Scotch whisky available and about the different tastes and regions.

"There is a wide range of Scotch whisky producers in the industry – from smaller, family-owned businesses to international companies. Such diversity is an important part of the industry. The fact that at least 20 new distilleries are planned shows that there is optimism and confidence in the future of the industry."

Beyond Scotland

And it's not just Scotland that's benefiting from the boom in whisky. Although it's not allowed to call itself Scotch, there is now award-winning Welsh malt being produced at the tiny Penderyn distillery in the foothills of the Brecon Beacons and there are new whisky distilleries in Cumbria, Cornwall, Norfolk, Suffolk and London.

The latest to open is The Cotswolds Distillery at Shipston-on-Stour, which started distilling in the summer of 2014 and will have its first limited edition batch of Cotswolds Single Malt Whisky ready for release in 2017. American-born founder Daniel Szor has enlisted Scottish master distiller Harry Cockburn and consultant Jim Swan to help develop the distillery and its products.

Szor says, "Behind our vision of establishing a distillery of worldwide renown, there is long-term investment and a considerable commitment of skills and resources.

"We intend all our products to be worthy ambassadors for the region and certainly aim to produce a flagship single malt that is characteristic of the region's heritage, and every bit as good and intriguing as whisky neighbours to the north."

Whisky trails

Whether it's from south or north of the border, whisky is an increasingly important tourist attraction thanks to distillery tours and whisky trails. The Malt Whisky Trail in Speyside features behind-the-scenes 'barrel to bottle' tours of seven working distilleries including 'nosing and tasting' sessions and even a visit to the only working cooperage in the UK where skilled craftsmen make whisky barrels using traditional tools and methods.

At The Brook House Inn at Boot in Cumbria, licensee Gareth Thornley has noticed more and more tourists willing to try whiskies and with 180 available at this Lake District country pub, there's something for everybody who walks through the door. Scotch even appears on the food menu at this inn, perhaps in the shape of chicken ballotine with whisky and mustard sauce, which might be followed by whisky and lemon pannacotta.

"We cater a lot for the holiday trade so our list needs to be balanced between malts priced for the everyday drinker alongside some rarer bottlings for the connoisseur or special occasions. We sell a lot more malt whisky than we do blended ones, and over the years we have helped introduce many people, young and old, to the delights of malt whisky.

"Although we are well known for our beer and the pub has won awards for the range of ales, we have a growing number of people coming because of the whisky."

Back at the Clachaig Inn in Glencoe, manager Gordon Keppie holds regular whisky-tasting masterclasses and staff are sent on courses at local distilleries. He says it's all part of making Scotch more accessible to his customers.

"Over the years, whisky has shaken off its 'old man with a wee heavy and a half pint' image and has become more acceptable to both female and younger customers. I'm sure this is partly down to clever marketing, but also we find that people interested in whisky really appreciate the history behind the bottle and are likely to be more adventurous when choosing malt whisky.

"Scottish whisky is an iconic international product and yet for many its secrets remain a black art. Our aim is to change this view, bringing a little knowledge, so that you can take on the 300 or so malts on our shelves with a renewed confidence.

"Our customer base is wide and varied and includes regular visitors, all season mountain climbers, walkers, locals and holiday tourists from all over the world. Despite occasional trends we find our customers are reasonably well informed and may well have a favourite.

"For those on the fence, our staff are on hand to help with their choices. The curiosity factor usually leads people to sample something they haven't tried before and you will find amongst our collection some unusual whiskies from England, Wales, Ireland, Japan and India."

There is little doubt that the popularity of whisky remains undiminished, indeed its unique qualities are now appreciated by more customers around the globe than at any time its long, illustrious history.

"Over the years, whisky has shaken off its 'old man with a wee heavy and a half pint' image"

England

BEDFORDSHIRE

BEDFORD
Map 12 TL04

The Embankment

tel: 01234 261332 **6 The Embankment MK40 3PD**
email: embankment@peachpubs.com
dir: *From M1 junct 13, A421 to Bedford. Left onto A6 to town centre. Into left lane on river bridge. Into right lane signed Embankment. Follow around St Paul's Square into High St, into left lane. Left onto The Embankment*

Mock-Tudor riverside pub with a hospitable atmosphere

On the edge of Bedford's beautifully landscaped Embankment gardens, this imposing pub sits behind an outdoor terrace overlooking the River Great Ouse. Dating from 1891, the building has been renovated and its Victorian features brought back to life: the open fire, antique mirrors, vintage tables, sofas in racing green and silk lampshades. Food choices range from deli boards to full meals, such as wood pigeon Kiev with pomegranate and bacon salad, followed by sun-dried tomato gnocchi, confit peppers, basil purée and a parmesan crisp, and finishing with pineapple upside down cake.

Open all day all wk Closed 25 Dec **Food** Lunch all wk 12-6 Dinner all wk 6-10 Av main course £15 Set menu available ⊕ PEACH PUBS ◼ Wells Eagle IPA & Bombardier, Young's ♂ Aspall. ♟ 16 **Facilities** Non-diners area ❄ (Bar Outside area) ♦ Children's portions Outside area ⊼ Parking WiFi ▦ (notice required)

NEW The Knife and Cleaver ★ ★ ★ ★ INN

tel: 01234 930789 **The Grove, Houghton Conquest MK45 3LA**
email: info@theknifeandcleaver.com web: www.theknifeandcleaver.com
dir: *A6 from Bedford towards Luton. In 5m right to Houghton Conquest. Or B530 from Bedford towards Ampthill left to Houghton Conquest*

Food and drink all day every day

A short hop from Woburn Abbey and Safari Park, The Knife and Cleaver sits in an idyllic rural spot opposite England's largest Grade I listed church. The neatly laid-out bar and All Saints Restaurant welcome customers and their children for resuscitation at any time of day, seven days a week, whether it's just for a pint of Wells Eagle, a bar snack, or a full à la carte meal. Here you are spoilt for choice: starters include shredded Peking-style duck. Next, try chicken Amsterdam (stuffed with asparagus and covered with cheese sauce), and finish with a home-made dessert – Baileys profiteroles dipped in Belgian chocolate perhaps.

Open all day all wk **Food** Lunch all day Dinner all day Av main course £7.50 Set menu available Restaurant menu available all wk ⊕ CHARLES WELLS ◼ Eagle IPA, Courage Directors, Guest ale ♂ Symonds. ♟ 35 **Facilities** Non-diners area ♦ Children's menu Children's portions Family room Garden Outside area ⊼ Parking WiFi ▦ (notice required) **Rooms** 9

The Park Pub & Kitchen
PICK OF THE PUBS

tel: 01234 273929 **98 Kimbolton Rd MK40 2PA**
email: info@theparkbedford.co.uk
dir: *M1 junct 14, A509 follow Newport Pagnell signs, then A422, A428 onto A6. Right into Tavistock St (A600). Left into Broadway, 1st left into Kimbolton Rd. Pub 0.5m*

Smart, bright and spacious, a stylish mix of old and new

Built in the 1900s, this fine-looking pub is a stone's throw from Bedford Park, just a little way out of town. The smartly decorated exterior promises a similarly well cared for interior, and you won't be disappointed – fireplaces, flagstone floors and beamed ceilings combine to create a traditional welcoming atmosphere. Beyond the wrap-around bar are a spacious restaurant, relaxing conservatory and airy garden room; this leads to an outdoor area where heaters permit comfortable drinking and dining if there's a chill in the air. Eagle IPA and Bombardier from the town's Wells and Young's brewery are served in the bar, along with over 30 wines sold by the glass. Most of the pub's suppliers are proudly detailed on the menu, while the

kitchen team produces the pub's own bread, pasta, ice creams and chutneys. In addition, snacks and sandwiches with home-cut chips are served from Tuesday to Sunday, 3pm to 6pm.

Open all day all wk **Food** Lunch Mon-Sat 12-3, Sun 12-8 Dinner Mon-Sat 6-10, Sun 12-8 Restaurant menu available all wk ⊕ CHARLES WELLS ◼ Bombardier, Eagle IPA ♂ Symonds. ♟ 33 **Facilities** Non-diners area ❄ (Bar Garden) ♦ Children's portions Garden ⊼ Parking WiFi ▦ (notice required)

The Three Tuns

tel: 01234 354847 **57 Main Rd, Biddenham MK40 4BD**
email: info@threetunsbiddenham.com
dir: *On A428 from Bedford towards Northampton 1st left signed Biddenham. Into village, pub on left*

Thatched pub with food of a high standard

In a pretty village, this stone-built pub has a large garden with a patio and decking, and a separate children's play area. Owner Chris Smith worked for celebrity chef Jean-Christophe Novelli for a number of years and now produces dishes such as white onion and cumin soup; creamy chicken, bacon and ale pot pie; and pineapple carpaccio with coconut and tarragon sorbet and lime jelly. Each dish on the à la carte is matched with a recommended wine. The two-course set menu is excellent value. In the garden is a long-disused, possibly haunted, morgue, the oldest building hereabouts.

Open all wk 12-3 5.30-late (Fri-Sat all day Sun 12-6) **Food** Lunch Tue-Sun 12-2.30 Dinner Tue-Sat 6-9.30 Set menu available Restaurant menu available Tue-Sun ⊕ GREENE KING ◼ IPA, Guinness, Guest ale ♂ Aspall. ♟ 16 **Facilities** Non-diners area ♦ Children's portions Play area Garden ⊼ Parking WiFi ▦ (notice required)

BOLNHURST
Map 12 TL05

The Plough at Bolnhurst ⊛
PICK OF THE PUBS

tel: 01234 376274 **Kimbolton Rd MK44 2EX**
email: theplough@bolnhurst.com
dir: *On B660, N of Bedford*

Tudor inn with notable food and wine

Six miles north of Bedford, this whitewashed 15th-century country inn has a fresh, country-style decor coupled with original features such as thick walls, low beams and great open fires. The impressive choice of real ales and inspired wine list are matched by a delicious menu prepared by Raymond Blanc-trained Martin Lee and his team of skilled chefs. The menu is driven by the freshest local and regional produce and specialist foods gathered from all corners. The result is an ever-changing choice of unique dishes, which have gained The Plough an AA Rosette. Start with spinach and smoked haddock soup and poached free-range egg; or Denham Estate venison carpaccio with pickled quince; follow up with slow-cooked Jimmy Butlers' pork cheeks, wok-fried bok choi, sautéed sweet potato, chilli, pickled ginger and coriander. Rum baba makes a tempting dessert but do leave room for the cheeseboard, with its astonishing choice of British, Italian and French varieties.

Open Tue-Sat 12-3 6.30-11 (Sun 12-3) Closed 1 Jan, 2wks Jan, Mon & Sun eve **Food** Lunch Tue-Sun 12-2 Dinner Tue-Sat 6.30-9.30 Set menu available ⊕ FREE HOUSE ◼ Adnams Southwold Bitter, Potton Village Bike, Fuller's London Pride, Hopping Mad Brainstorm, Church End Goat's Milk ♂ Aspall Harry Sparrow. ♟ 13 **Facilities** Non-diners area ❄ (Bar) ♦ Children's portions Garden Parking WiFi ▦

HARROLD Map 11 SP95

The Muntjac

tel: 01234 721500 **71 High St MK43 7BJ**
email: muntjacharrold@hotmail.co.uk
dir: *Phone for detailed directions*

Free house with an Indian restaurant

This 17th-century former coaching inn in a pretty village has a lot on offer. Six real ales on handpump, 30 gins and 13 vodkas for a start; a real fire in the winter, pool table and Sky Sport TV for the big matches. Attached to the pub is Harrolds Indian Cuisine that offers an extensive range of traditional dishes cooked to order, to eat in or take away; you can even 'challenge the chef' to create your own dish if you ask.

Open all wk Mon-Thu 5.30-11 (Fri 12.30-12 Sat 12-12 Sun 12.30-10.30)
Food Contact pub for details ⊕ FREE HOUSE ◀ Regularly changing ales.
Facilities Non-diners area ♦ Children's portions Garden Parking ⇔ (notice required) **Notes** ⊛

IRELAND Map 12 TL14

The Black Horse

tel: 01462 811398 **SG17 5QL**
email: ctaverns@aol.com **web:** www.blackhorseireland.com
dir: *From S: M1 junct 12, A5120 to Flitwick. Onto A507 by Redbourne School. Follow signs for A1, Shefford (cross A6). Left onto A600 towards Bedford*

Traditional and modern comfortably combined

Original beams, slate floors, inglenook fireplaces, original artwork and low ceilings combine to create a chic and modern interior in this family-run, 17th-century inn. The flower-rich garden and courtyard offer alfresco dining in the warmer months. Grab a pint of Adnams, or choose from the excellent wine list, and settle down in comfort to appreciate the tempting seasonally inspired dishes made from locally sourced produce – maybe smoked trout and horseradish pâté with apricot and ginger chutney; spiced roasted duck leg, Puy lentils, with light chicken and orange jus; or griddled Dingley Dell pork chop with sage and apple sauce.

Open all wk 12-3 6-12 (Sun 12-6) Closed 25-26 Dec, 1 Jan **Food** Lunch Mon-Sat 12-2.30, Sun 12-5 Dinner Mon-Sat 6.30-10 Av main course £11.95 Set menu available ⊕ FREE HOUSE ◀ Adnams, Sharp's Doom Bar, Fuller's London Pride ♂ Westons Mortimers Orchard. ♟ 16 **Facilities** Non-diners area ♦ Children's portions Garden ⇱ Parking WiFi ⇔ (notice required)

KEYSOE Map 12 TL06

The Chequers

tel: 01234 708678 **Pertenhall Rd, Brook End MK44 2HR**
email: chequers.keysoe@tesco.net
dir: *On B660, 7m N of Bedford. 3m S of Kimbolton*

Classic pub grub in a tranquil country pub

This peaceful 15th-century country pub has been in the same safe hands for over 25 years. No games machines, pool tables or jukeboxes disturb the simple pleasures of well-kept ales and great home-made food. The menu offers pub stalwarts like ploughman's; home-made steak and ale pie; pan-fried trout; glazed lamb cutlets and a variety of grilled steaks; and a blackboard displays further choice plus the vegetarian options. For a lighter option try the home-made chicken liver pâté or soup, fried brie with cranberries, or plain or toasted sandwiches.

Open Wed-Sun 11.30-2.30 6.30-11 Closed Mon & Tue **Food** Lunch Wed-Sun 12-2 Dinner Wed-Sun 6.30-9 ⊕ FREE HOUSE ◀ Hook Norton Hooky Bitter, Fuller's London Pride ♂ Westons Stowford Press. **Facilities** Non-diners area ♦ Children's menu Children's portions Play area Family room Garden Parking ⇔ (notice required) **Notes** ⊛

LEIGHTON BUZZARD Map 11 SP92

NEW The Heath Inn ★★★ INN

tel: 01525 237816 **76 Woburn Rd, Heath and Reach LU7 0AR**
email: enquiries@theheathinn.com **web:** www.theheathinn.com
dir: *Phone for detailed directions*

Great cask ales in a traditional setting

This privately-owned free house on the outskirts of the charming market town of Leighton Buzzard hosts live music throughout the year. The wood-beamed bar is cosy with an open fire; or take your refreshments out to the pretty courtyard garden in summer, where children are well catered for with swings and a slide in the play area. Cask ales are well represented from the likes of Tring, Hopping Mad and Marston's, ably supported by cider from Westons, draft lagers and quality wines. Food served in the bar or in Balens Restaurant follows traditional lines, from ploughman's and jackets to grills and Sunday roasts.

Open all day all wk **Food** Lunch all wk 12-2.30 Dinner Mon-Sat 6-9 Av main course £10 ⊕ FREE HOUSE ◀ Tring, Marston's, Hopping Mad ♂ Westons Stowford Press. **Facilities** Non-diners area ♦ Children's menu Children's portions Play area Outside area ⇱ Parking WiFi ⇔ (notice required) **Rooms** 16

LINSLADE Map 11 SP92

The Globe Inn

tel: 01525 373338 **Globe Ln, Old Linslade LU7 2TA**
email: 6458@greeneking.co.uk
dir: *N of Leighton Buzzard*

Canalside pub that's a hive of activity

A very homely old pub, creaking with the character of the small Georgian farmhouse and stables it once was; beams, log fires, partial weatherboarding and a wrinkly roof line. Fronting the Grand Union Canal at the end of a no-through lane, it's a marvellous place to linger watching boating activity, supping on Greene King beers and choosing from a Pandora's Box of meals, varying from traditional meaty favourites like grilled pork chop to chicken fajitas; vegetable and cashew paella; and smoked salmon and king prawn salad. There's a well-appointed restaurant, and children are made welcome with a play area in the tree-shaded garden.

Open all day all wk 11-11 **Food** Lunch all wk 11-11 Dinner all wk 11-11 Av main course £5.95 Set menu available ⊕ GREENE KING ◀ Abbot Ale & IPA, Morland Old Speckled Hen ♂ Aspall. ♟ 16 **Facilities** Non-diners area ♣ (Bar Garden) ♦ Children's menu Children's portions Play area Garden ⇱ Beer festival Cider festival Parking WiFi ⇔ (notice required)

NORTHILL
Map 12 TL14

The Crown

tel: 01767 627337 **2 Ickwell Rd SG18 9AA**
email: info@crownnorthill.co.uk
dir: *In village centre, adjacent to church*

Greene King pub with a wide-ranging menu

A delightful 16th-century pub with smart, modern interior decor. A number of guests ales are very well kept, and make a delightful companion to almost anything on the menu. Dig into sharing deli boards or sub rolls and panini with fillings such as brie and bacon, or fish fingers and ketchup. Or how about mains such as roasted cod loin with bacon mustard leeks and poached egg, or soy and honey marinated duck with spiced vegetable and noodle stir-fry? The garden has plenty of tables for alfresco eating, and a children's play area.

Open all day all wk **Food** Lunch Mon-Fri 12-3, Sat 12-10, Sun 12-6 Dinner Mon-Fri 6.30-10, Sat 12-10, Sun 12-6 ⊕ GREENE KING ◀ IPA & Abbot Ale, Morland Old Speckled Hen, Hardys & Hansons Olde Trip, Guest ales ♂ Aspall. ♀ 9 **Facilities** Non-diners area ❀ (Garden) ♦ Children's menu Children's portions Play area Garden Parking WiFi ➡

OAKLEY
Map 11 TL05

NEW Bedford Arms

tel: 01234 822280 **57 High St MK43 7RH**
email: bedfordarmsoakley@btconnect.com
dir: *From A6 N of Bedford follow Oakley signs*

Pretty village inn specialising in fresh fish dishes

Bounded on three sides by the River Ouse in the heart of the pretty village of Oakley, this 16th-century inn is surrounded by beautiful countryside but only a short drive from Bedford. Enjoy a pint of Charles Wells Eagle in the cosy, traditional beamed bar or head to the large garden and decked alfresco dining area for a meal. Fresh fish is a speciality here, and the fish board changes daily to reflect the very best at the market that day; typical dishes include white crabmeat and smoked salmon tagliatelle, and roast rump of lamb with buttered spinach and mint hollandaise. Just let them know if gluten-free dishes are required and they will make sure a wide range is available.

Open all day all wk **Food** Contact pub for details Restaurant menu available Mon-Sat ⊕ CHARLES WELLS ◀ Wells Eagle IPA, Courage Directors, Guest ale ♂ Aspall. ♀ 35 **Facilities** Non-diners area ❀ (Bar Garden) ♦ Children's menu Children's portions Garden ⋈ Parking WiFi ➡ (notice required)

RAVENSDEN
Map 12 TL05

NEW The Horse & Jockey

tel: 01234 772319 **Church End MK44 2RR**
email: horseandjockey@live.com
dir: *N of Bedford. Phone for detailed directions*

Quiet country pub with a caring approach

Sarah Smith's friendly staff ensure a happy welcome at this quiet country pub, which sits atop a hill next to the village church. Locals and visitors feel equally at home, enjoying an Adnams ale or Stowford Press cider in the bar, or relaxing in the peaceful garden where birdsong is all that can be heard; the pub supplies fleece blankets for cooler evenings. Sarah's husband Darron runs the kitchen, and is

passionate in his distinctly British approach to food. Expect the likes of lobster macaroni to start, chargrilled sirloin or rib-eye steaks to follow, and caramel cheesecake with walnut praline to finish.

Open all wk 12-3 6-11 **Food** Lunch 12-2 Dinner 6-9.30 Set menu available Restaurant menu available Mon-Sat ⊕ FREE HOUSE ◀ Adnams Southwold Bitter, Sharp's Doom Bar ♂ Westons Stowford Press. ♀ 26 **Facilities** Non-diners area ❀ (Bar Garden) ♦ Children's portions Garden ⋈ Parking WiFi ➡ (notice required)

SALFORD
Map 11 SP93

The Swan
PICK OF THE PUBS

tel: 01908 281008 **2 Warendon Rd MK17 8BD**
email: swan@peachpubs.com
dir: *M1 junct 13, follow signs to Salford*

Smart gastro-pub that appeals to everyone

Located in a pretty village, the tile-hung, Edwardian-era Swan, run by an enthusiastic team, has a lively bar with comfy leather armchairs that make you feel instantly at home, as does the eating area, where the big French doors can be thrown open to the garden. Peer through the feature window into the kitchen to watch the chefs preparing dishes from the best, locally supplied or own-grown ingredients. Sandwiches, snacks and deli boards are available throughout the day. The pub has its own smokehouse so the likes of home-smoked pork loin and home-smoked mackerel appear on the deli boards. Main courses include seared acorn squash strudel, Wensleydale and endive salad with cranberry dressing; or roast Tidenham duck breast, duck fat potatoes with carrot and vanilla purée. Puddings are very tempting- who could resist Valrhona dark chocolate and banana brownie with honeycomb ice cream? The restored barn with a large central dining table can be used for a private dinner. There's a busy social calendar of events.

Open all day all wk 11am-mdnt (Sun 12-10.30) Closed 25 Dec **Food** Lunch all wk 12-6 Dinner Mon-Sat 6-9.45, Sun 6-9.30 Restaurant menu available all wk ⊕ PEACH PUBS ◀ Sharp's Doom Bar ♂ Aspall. ♀ 12 **Facilities** Non-diners area ❀ (Bar Garden) ♦ Children's portions Garden ⋈ Parking WiFi ➡

SOULDROP
Map 11 SP96

The Bedford Arms

tel: 01234 781384 **High St MK44 1EY**
email: thebedfordarms@tiscali.co.uk
dir: *From Rushden take A6 towards Bedford. In 6m right into Stocking Lane to Souldrop. Pub 50mtrs on right*

Children welcome at this village free house

The time-honoured hallmarks of low beams, open fireplace, horse brasses, tankards and bar skittles are all present and correct in this over 300-year-old pub. On the bar counter, pump badges declare the presence of, among others, Hopping Mad Brainstorm from Olney and Evershed's real cider. Shelves are laden with china, and artworks are for sale in the cottage-style dining room, where a good selection of pub dishes includes pork valentine; vegetable tikka masala; Whitby scampi; and signature dishes of steak and ale pie, and leek and Stilton bread and butter pudding. Play boules in the garden.

Open 12-3 6-11 (Fri-Sat 12-11 Sun 12-10) Closed Mon (ex BHs) **Food** Lunch Tue-Sat 12-2, Sun 12-4 Dinner Tue-Sat 6.30-9 Av main course £9.95 ⊕ FREE HOUSE ◀ Phipps NBC Red Star, Greene King IPA, Black Sheep, Hopping Mad Brainstorm, Guest ale ♂ Evershed's Cider, Thatchers Gold. ♀ 13 **Facilities** Non-diners area ❀ (Bar Garden) ♦ Children's menu Children's portions Garden ⋈ Parking WiFi

SOUTHILL
Map 12 TL14

The White Horse

tel: 01462 813364 **High St SG18 9LD**
email: thewhitehorse1@live.com
dir: *Phone for detailed directions*

Pub with family appeal in pretty village

A country pub with traditional values, happily accommodating the needs of children in the large patio gardens, and those who like to sit outside on cool days enjoying a well-kept pint (the patio has heaters). Offering traditional English food, fish, vegetarian and children's dishes, grilled steaks are a big draw in the restaurant but other main courses from the extensive menu include rack of barbecue spare ribs; home-made game or fisherman's pie; plus choices from the chef's specials board. Salads, ploughman's, sandwiches, baguettes and wraps are also available.

Open all wk 11.30-3 6-11 (Sat 11.30-11 Sun 12-10.30) Closed 26 Dec **Food** Lunch Mon-Fri 12-2, Sat-Sun all day Dinner Mon-Fri 6-9.30, Sat-Sun all day ⊕ ENTERPRISE INNS ◆ Greene King IPA, Sharp's Doom Bar Ö Thatchers Gold. ♈ 8
Facilities Non-diners area ◆ Children's menu Play area Garden ⌂ Parking WiFi ▦ (notice required)

STANBRIDGE
Map 11 SP92

The Five Bells

tel: 01525 210224 **Station Rd LU7 9JF**
email: fivebells@fullers.co.uk
dir: *A505 from Leighton Buzzard towards Dunstable, turn left to Stanbridge*

Relaxed village pub with large garden

This whitewashed 400-year-old village inn has been delightfully renovated and revived. The bar features lots of bare wood as well as comfortable armchairs and rustic wood and tiled floors. The modern decor extends to the bright, airy 75-cover dining room with its oak beams and paintings. The inn uses local suppliers where possible to offer farm-assured chicken and beef, and sustainable seafood. The menu typically includes dishes such as beer battered cod and chips, and steak and ale suet pudding, which are complemented by light lunches, blackboard daily specials and Sunday roasts. There's also a spacious lawned garden and patio.

Open all day all wk 11-11 (Sun 12-10.30) **Food** Lunch Mon-Sat 12-10, Sun 12-9 Dinner Mon-Sat 12-10, Sun 12-9 ⊕ FULLER'S ◆ Fuller's London Pride, George Gale & Co Seafarers, Guest ale Ö Aspall, Westons Stowford Press. ♈ 8
Facilities Non-diners area ❤ (Bar Garden) ◆ Children's menu Children's portions Garden ⌂ Parking WiFi ▦ (notice required)

STUDHAM
Map 11 TL01

The Bell in Studham

tel: 01582 872460 **Dunstable Rd LU6 2QG**
email: info@thebellinstudham.co.uk **web:** www.thebellinstudham.co.uk
dir: *M1 junct 9, A5 towards Dunstable. Left onto B4540 to Kensworth, B4541 to Studham*

Over 500 years old with fine garden views

Landlords Phil and Nikki have been in the licensed trade for years; not so their dog Jazz, but she already understands that being nice to customers' dogs in the Study Bar is good for business. Phil was once a butcher, so expect quality steaks; fresh fish is another speciality. Hearty, home-made dishes include fish and triple-cooked chips; pie of the day; marinated rack of ribs; sea bass fillet with tomato and oregano; and Sunday roasts. A weekday set lunch of chicken goujons and chilli dip, and a fresh-dough margarita pizza costs under a tenner. There is a beer and cider festival in the summer.

Open all day all wk **Food** Lunch Mon-Fri 12-2.30, Sat-Sun all day Dinner Mon-Fri 6-9.30, Sat-Sun all day Set menu available ⊕ FREE HOUSE ◆ Greene King IPA, Guest ales Ö Thatchers Gold & Heritage. ♈ 10 **Facilities** Non-diners area ❤ (Bar Garden) ◆ Children's portions Garden ⌂ Beer festival Cider festival Parking WiFi ▦ (notice required)

SUTTON
Map 12 TL24

NEW The John O'Gaunt

tel: 01767 260377 **Sutton Rd SG19 2TP**
email: thejohnogauntsutton@hotmail.co.uk
dir: *From A6001 in Biggleswade take B1040 towards Potton. Turn right to Sutton*

Village pub in good hands

Jago and Jane Hurt used to have a pub at Old Warden a few miles away before coming here. Set back from the road, their new acquisition was built in the 18th century as three cottages - the trio of gables gives the game away - near an ancient packhorse bridge. Holding court in the bar are Woodforde's Wherry and Adnams Ghost Ship, with a real cider back-up of Aspall Harry Sparrow. Home-cooked meals from local ingredients include white mushroom risotto; braised pork belly with parsnip purée and butter mash; goujons of lemon sole; and sirloin steak with pepper sauce.

Open 12-3 6-11 Closed Mon **Food** Lunch all wk 12-3 Dinner all wk 6-11 Av main course £12.50 ⊕ FREE HOUSE ◆ Woodforde's Wherry, Adnams Ghost Ship Ö Aspall Harry Sparrow. ♈ **Facilities** Non-diners area ❤ (Bar Garden) ◆ Children's menu Children's portions Garden ⌂ Parking WiFi

TILSWORTH

Map 11 SP92

The Anchor Inn

tel: 01525 211404 **1 Dunstable Rd LU7 9PU**
dir: *Exit A5 at Tilsworth. In 1m pub on right at 3rd bend*

Classic Victorian country dining pub with a garden that's great for kids

The only pub in a Saxon village, The Anchor dates from 1878. Alan the landlord and his son, Vincent the chef, pride themselves on their fresh food and well-kept beers and guest ales. An acre of garden includes patio seating for alfresco dining, an adventure playground and a barbecue. A current menu lists the likes of sausage and mash; Thai chicken curry; pan-fried salmon steak; gnocchi and button mushrooms; and pie of the day. Also available are a selection of tortilla wraps and baguettes.

Open all day all wk 12-11.30 **Food** Lunch Tue-Sat 12.30-2.30, Sun & BHs 12-4 Dinner Tue-Sat 5.30-8.30 ⊕ GREENE KING ◀ Rotating Guest ales Ö Aspall. **Facilities** Non-diners area ◀ Children's menu Children's portions Play area Garden ╦ Parking WiFi ☞ (notice required)

WOBURN

Map 11 SP93

The Birch at Woburn

tel: 01525 290295 **20 Newport Rd MK17 9HX**
email: ctaverns@aol.com **web:** www.birchwoburn.com
dir: *Phone for detailed directions*

Serious about good, locally sourced food

Close to Woburn Abbey and the Safari Park, this smart family-run establishment is located opposite Woburn Championship Golf Course and a short hop from junction 13 of the M1. The pub has built its reputation on friendly service and freshly cooked food; the kitchen team is passionate about sourcing ingredients from local farms and estates. The menu offers a range of English and continental dishes, and there is a griddle area where customers can select their steaks and fish, which are then cooked to your liking by the chefs.

Open 12-3 6-12 Closed 25-26 Dec, 1 Jan, Sun eve **Food** Lunch all wk 12-2.30 Dinner Mon-Sat 6-10 ⊕ FREE HOUSE ◀ Sharp's Doom Bar, Adnams. ♀ 14 **Facilities** Non-diners area ◀ Children's portions Outside area ╦ Parking ☞ (notice required)

The Black Horse

tel: 01525 290210 **1 Bedford St MK17 9QB**
email: blackhorse@peachpubs.com
dir: *In town centre on A4012*

Georgian coaching inn serving seasonal fare

Right in the middle of the pretty village of Woburn, this 18th-century inn cuts an elegant figure. Behind the Georgian frontage, the original coaching inn feel of the cosy bar has been retained and complemented with a chic, relaxed dining area where seasonal, locally sourced food drives the all-day menus. Cornish mack bap, lettuce and tartare sauce sandwich makes a light lunch or start with smoked Cotswold chicken terrine or devilled lamb's kidneys on toast with crispy bacon before sea trout supreme with new potatoes, hispy cabbage and caper and lemon butter, and iced banoffee parfait with stem ginger shortbread to finish.

Open all day all wk 11-11 (Sat 11am-11.30pm) Closed 25 Dec **Food** Lunch all wk 12-6 Dinner all wk 6-9.45 Av main course £15 ⊕ PEACH PUBS ◀ Greene King IPA & Abbot Ale, Morland Old Golden Hen, Guest ale Ö Aspall. ♀ 10 **Facilities** Non-diners area ❖ (Bar Garden) ◀ Children's portions Garden ╦ WiFi ☞ (notice required)

BERKSHIRE

ALDERMASTON

Map 5 SU56

Hinds Head

tel: 0118 971 2194 **Wasing Ln RG7 4LX**
email: hindshead@fullers.co.uk
dir: *M4 junct 12, A4 towards Newbury, left on A340 towards Basingstoke, 2m to village*

Charming pub with many original features

This 17th-century inn with its distinctive clock and bell tower still incorporates the village lock-up, which was last used in 1865. The former brewhouse behind the pub creates an additional dining area. The menu features home-made British choices with international influences. Dishes range from a meze board to share; country pie of the week; rice noodle salad with prawns; leek and cheese crumble; honey-glazed roast salmon; and lunchtime jackets and sandwiches.

Open all wk Mon-Thu 11-11 (Fri-Sat 11am-mdnt Sun 11-10.30) **Food** Lunch Mon-Sat 12-3, Sun 12-6 Dinner Mon-Sat 6-9, Sun 12-6 ⊕ FULLER'S ◀ London Pride & ESB, Guest ales Ö Aspall. ♀ 12 **Facilities** Non-diners area ❖ (Bar Garden) ◀ Children's menu Children's portions Family room Garden ╦ Parking WiFi

ALDWORTH

Map 5 SU57

The Bell Inn

tel: 01635 578272 **RG8 9SE**
dir: *Just off B4009 (Newbury to Streatley road)*

Well-kept local ales in timewarp setting

Beginning life as a manor hall in 1340, The Bell has reputedly been in the same family for 200 years: ask landlady Mrs Macaulay, she's been here for over 75 years. A 300-year-old, one-handed clock still stands in the taproom 'keeping imperfect time', and the rack for the spit-irons and clockwork roasting jack are still over the fireplace. One might be surprised to discover that an establishment without a restaurant can hold its own in a world of smart gastro-pubs. But The Bell survives thanks to hot, filled rolls and cracking pints of Arkell's or a West Berkshire brew or a monthly guest ale plus local farmhouse ciders.

Open Tue-Sat 11-3 6-11 (Sun 12-3 7-10.30) Closed 25 Dec, Mon (open BH Mon L only) **Food** Lunch Tue-Sat 11-2.30, Sun 12-2.30 Dinner Tue-Sat 6-9.30, Sun 7-9 ⊕ FREE HOUSE ◀ Arkell's Kingsdown Special Ale & 3B, West Berkshire Old Tyler & Maggs' Magnificent Mild, Guest ales Ö Upton's Farmhouse, Tutts Clump, Lilley's Pear & Apple. **Facilities** Non-diners area ❖ (Bar Garden) ◀ Garden ╦ Parking Notes ⊗

PICK OF THE PUBS

The Hinds Head ✿✿✿

BRAY Map 6 SU97

tel: 01628 626151
High St SL6 2AB
email: info@hindsheadbray.com
web: www.hindsheadbray.com
dir: *M4 junct 8/9 take Maidenhead Central exit. Next rdbt take Bray/Windsor exit. 0.5m, B3028 to Bray*

Old-English fare with a modern twist

Heston Blumenthal's younger sibling to his eponymous Fat Duck restaurant has, not surprisingly, become a gastronomic destination, yet the striking 15th-century building remains very much a village local. Its origins are a little obscure, with some saying it was used as a royal hunting lodge and others as a guest house for the local Abbot of Cirencester. What is known is that Queen Elizabeth II dined with European royalty at the pub in 1963. Expect an informal atmosphere in the traditional bar, with its beams, sturdy oak panelling, log fires, leather chairs, and pints of Rebellion available at the bar. On the ground floor is the main restaurant, while upstairs are two further dining areas, the Vicars Room, and the larger Royal Room. Having worked alongside the team in the Tudor kitchens at Hampton Court Palace, Heston rediscovered the origins of British cuisine, and has reintroduced some classic recipes that echo the pub's Tudor roots. Top-notch ingredients are used in gutsy dishes that are cooked simply and delivered in an unfussy manner by head chef Kevin Love. Take bar snacks or starters like devils on horseback; or soused mackerel and grapefruit dressing, with main courses taking in fish pie with 'sand and sea'; or duck fillet, beetroot, barley, turnips and duck sauce. Room should be left for a memorable pudding, perhaps Quaking pudding, or chocolate wine 'slush' with millionnaire shortbread. Well selected, widely sourced wines complete the picture. The two- and three-course set menus are good value. Booking for meals is recommended. Dogs are welcome in the bar area.

Open all wk 11.30-11 (Sun 12-7) Closed 25 Dec **Food** Lunch Mon-Sat 12-2.30, Sun 12-4 Dinner Mon-Sat 6.30-9.30 Set menu available ⊞ FREE HOUSE ◀ Rebellion IPA & Seasonal ales, Windsor & Eton Seasonal ale ♂ Tutts Clump. ☘ 15 **Facilities** Non-diners area ❖ (Bar) ♦ Children's menu Parking 🚌 (notice required)

ASCOT
Map 6 SU96

The Thatched Tavern

tel: 01344 620874 **Cheapside Rd SL5 7QG**
email: enquiries@thethatchedtavern.co.uk
dir: *Follow Ascot Racecourse signs. Through Ascot 1st left (Cheapside). 1.5m, pub on left*

Modern grub in a historic pub

En route to Windsor Castle, Queen Victoria's carriage was allegedly sometimes spotted outside this 400-year-old, flagstone-floored, low-ceilinged pub, while what the history books call 'her faithful servant' John Brown knocked a few back inside. The sheltered garden makes a fine spot to enjoy a Fuller's real ale, a glass of wine and, for lunch, perhaps sausage and red onion marmalade ciabatta or a ploughman's. For something more substantial try warm mackerel fillet, pickled winter vegetables and home-made guacamole, then lemon and thyme marinated corn-fed chicken breast, rustic ratatouille and dauphinoise potatoes.

Open all wk Mon-Thu 12-3 5.30-11 (Fri-Sun all day) **Food** Lunch Mon-Sat 12-2.30 ⊕ FREE HOUSE ◀ Fuller's London Pride, Guinness Ö Westons Stowford Press. ¶ 11 **Facilities** Non-diners area ◀❙ Children's portions Garden Parking WiFi

ASHMORE GREEN
Map 5 SU56

The Sun in the Wood

tel: 01635 42377 **Stoney Ln RG18 9HF**
email: suninthewood@wadworth.co.uk
dir: *From A34 at Robin Hood Rdbt left to Shaw, at mini rdbt right then 7th left into Stoney Ln. 1.5m, pub on left*

Country pub surrounded by woodland

The Sun is a country pub and restaurant surrounded by beautiful mature woodland. In the lounge bar and restaurant, the beams and tables were stripped back to their natural hue. The menu proffers sandwiches and sharing boards and reliable starters such as duck liver and cognac terrine with red onion chutney; and deep-fried brie with cranberry sauce; a typical main course might be Walter Rose butcher's sausages, mash and onion gravy; or sesame chicken breast with creamy curry sauce. Coconut and honey cheesecake, or sticky toffee pudding make a great way to finish.

Open all wk 12-3 6-11 (Sun 12-5) **Food** Lunch Mon-Sat 12-2.30, Sun 12-5 Dinner Mon-Sat 6-9.30 Av main course £12 ⊕ WADWORTH ◀ 6X, Henry's Original IPA, The Bishop's Tipple Ö Westons Stowford Press. ¶ 15 **Facilities** Non-diners area ✿ (Bar Garden) ◀❙ Children's menu Children's portions Play area Garden ⌂ Parking WiFi ⌷

BOXFORD
Map 5 SU47

The Bell at Boxford

tel: 01488 608721 **Lambourn Rd RG20 8DD**
email: paul@bellatboxford.com
dir: *M4 junct 14, A338 towards Wantage. Right onto B4000 to x-rds, signed Boxford. Or from A34 junct 13 towards Hungerford, right at rdbt onto B4000. At x-rds right to Boxford. Pub signed*

Seafood specials in a pretty setting

At the heart of the lovely Lambourn Valley, close to Newbury Racecourse, this mock-Tudor country pub, boasts a period main bar in the part of the building dating back to the 17th century, and the very occasional visit from Mr Merritt, the resident ghost. Alfresco dining in flower-laden heated terraces offers hog roasts and barbecues and there's a good range of local ales, and now also Stowford Press cider on draught; all 60 wines on the list are available by the glass. Feast on seafood specials (whole lobster available if the season's right); tiger prawn linguine; duck egg, black pudding and hollandaise; and mushroom risotto.

Open all day all wk **Food** Lunch Mon-Sat 12-2 (pizza Mon-Sat 2.30-10.30), Sun 12-9 Dinner Mon-Sat 7-10.30 (pizza 6.30-10.30), Sun 7-9.30 Set menu available Restaurant menu available all wk ⊕ FREE HOUSE ◀ Wadworth The Bishop's Tipple, 6X & Henry's Original IPA, Guinness, West Berkshire Good Old Boy Ö Westons Stowford Press, Lilley's Apples & Pears. ¶ 60 **Facilities** Non-diners area ✿ (Bar Garden) ◀❙ Children's portions Garden ⌂ Parking WiFi ⌷ (notice required)

BRAY
Map 6 SU97

The Crown Inn ◉◉
PICK OF THE PUBS

tel: 01628 621936 **High St SL6 2AH**
dir: *M4 junct 8, A308(M) signed Maidenhead (Central). At next rdbt, right onto A308 signed Bray & Windsor. 0.5m, left onto B3028 signed Bray. In village, pub on left*

Cosy, Thames-side village inn

Half-timbered outside, this Tudor building explodes with the character of days long gone, with heavy beaming, open fires and all the trimmings. It's been an inn for several centuries; its name possibly derives from regular visits made by King Charles II when visiting Nell Gwynn nearby. Assignations today are firmly rooted in the desire to enjoy the dishes that have gained this Heston Blumenthal-owned pub two AA Rosettes for the distinctively traditional English menu. Diners (restaurant bookings essential, but not for bar meals) may commence with a starter such as Morecambe Bay shrimp, shrimp butter and cucumber salad, setting the standard for mains the like of roasted fillet of Loch Duart salmon; or chargrilled Hereford sirloin steak, marrowbone sauce and fries, finishing with 'Duffy Sheardown' chocolate parfait, blackberry and vanilla. The enclosed courtyard is sheltered by a spreading vine, and there's a large garden in which to quaff Caledonian XPA.

Open all day all wk **Food** Lunch Mon-Fri 12-2.30, Sat 12-3, Sun 12-8 Dinner Mon-Thu 6-9.30, Fri-Sat 6-10, Sun 12-8 ⊕ STAR PUBS & BARS ◀ Courage Best & Directors, Caledonian Flying Scotsman & Golden XPA. ¶ 19 **Facilities** Non-diners area ✿ (Bar Garden Outside area) ◀❙ Children's menu Children's portions Garden Outside area ⌂ Parking WiFi ⌷ (notice required)

The Hinds Head ◉◉◉
PICK OF THE PUBS

See Pick of the Pubs on page 29

BURCHETT'S GREEN
Map 5 SU88

The Crown

tel: 01628 824079 **Burchett's Green Rd SL6 6QZ**
email: info@thecrownburchettsgreen.com
dir: *From Maidenhead take A4 towards Reading. At mini rdbt right signed Burchett's Green. Pub in village centre*

Village pub in spirited new hands

Now a free house, following its acquisition from a brewery by chef-landlord Simon Bonwick, this early-Victorian village local reflects his delightfully quirky persona. Take, for example, his declaration that, although there's no table service in the bar or eating areas, he promises, despite being virtually a one-man band, "to continuously look after you in a friendly manner, like the pubs of yesterday!" Or that, in the bar, dogs are welcome, "apart from pit bulls, Rottweilers and other belligerent animals like lions and tigers". His starters include stuffed goose neck with sherry-dressed lentils, and among his mains are crispy salmon with winkle, cockle and shrimp butter; slow-roast Blackface lamb with tomato and mint; and truffle polenta, squash pickle and salted chestnut. Children are not allowed in the bar, but Simon happily serves smaller portions of his 'really nice grub'. Abbot is the real ale bar staple, with regularly-changing guests and craft beers.

Open 6pm-11pm (Sun 12-4) Closed Mon L **Food** Lunch Sun 12-3 Dinner Summer Mon-Sat 6-9, Winter Wed-Sat 6-9 Restaurant menu available Mon-Sat ⊕ FREE HOUSE ◀ Greene King Abbot Ale, Guest ales. **Facilities** Non-diners area ◀❙ Children's portions Garden ⌂ Parking

CHIEVELEY
Map 5 SU47

The Crab at Chieveley ★★★★ RR ⊛⊛

tel: 01635 247550 **North Heath, Wantage Rd RG20 8UE**
email: info@crabatchieveley.com web: www.crabatchieveley.com
dir: *M4 junct 13. 1.5m W of Chieveley on B4494*

Experience fresh seafood without a trip to the coast

This lovely old thatched dining pub has an award-winning seafood restaurant, which makes it the perfect place to break a tedious M4 journey or chill out at on a summer evening. Specialising in fish dishes and with fresh deliveries daily, the continuously-changing menu in the maritime-themed restaurant offers mouth-watering starters such as Carlingford Loch oysters, followed by catch of the day, venison loin, bouillabaisse or Cornish lobster thermidor. The interesting dessert menu has treacle and pistachio tart with apricot purée and pistachio anglaise. Boutique bedrooms complete the package. Dogs are welcome.

Open all day all wk 11am-mdnt ⊕ FREE HOUSE ◀ Sharp's Doom Bar, Greene King Abbot Ale, Shepherd Neame Spitfire ♂ Savanna. **Facilities** ☻ (Bar Garden) ◖ Children's menu Children's portions Garden Parking WiFi **Rooms** 14

COLNBROOK
Map 6 TQ07

The Ostrich

tel: 01753 682628 **High St SL3 0JZ**
email: enquiries@theostrichcolnbrook.co.uk
dir: *M25 junct 14 towards Poyle. Right at 1st rdbt, over next 2 rdbts. Left at sharp right bend into High St. Left at mini rdbt, pub on left*

900 years of hospitality and still going strong

Close to Heathrow and just minutes from the motorway, stands, surprisingly, one of England's oldest pubs. Dating from 1106 and once a coaching inn on the old London-Bath road, the vast and rambling Ostrich oozes history (some tales are particularly gruesome), with its heavily timbered façade, cobbled courtyard and an interior filled with wonky oak beams, massive fireplaces and crooked stairs. Cross Oak Inns have designed it in contemporary style, so expect glass doors, a steel bar, chunky furnishings and vibrant colours. Equally modern, the menu takes in chicken terrine with rustic bread, pork belly with cider jus, and milk chocolate fondant.

Open all wk 12-3 5-11 (Sun all day) **Food** Lunch Mon-Sat 12-2.30, Sun 12-9 Dinner Mon-Sat 6-9.30, Sun 12-9 ⊕ FREE HOUSE ◀ Hogs Back TEA, Abbot Ale, Wells Bombardier, Guest ales ♂ Thatchers. ☗ 10 **Facilities** Non-diners area ◖ Children's menu Children's portions Garden ⌂ Parking WiFi ▦ (notice required)

COOKHAM
Map 6 SU88

The White Oak ⊛⊛

tel: 01628 523043 **The Pound SL6 9QE**
email: info@thewhiteoak.co.uk
dir: *From A4 E of Maidenhead take A4094 signed Cookham. Left into High St (B4447) signed Cookham Rise/Cookham Dean. Pass through common. Left at mini rdbt, pub on right*

Seasonal menus and accomplished cooking

The arrival of chef Clive Dixon (ex-Blumenthal's Hinds Head) at this Thames Valley gastro-pub took the menu and cooking to another level and it's now the favoured eaterie in this affluent Berkshire village. In a cool, contemporary, yet relaxed setting discerning diners can tuck into some accomplished modern British dishes, accompanied by some select wines, or a pint of Abbot Ale. Daily menus brim with seasonal produce, so perhaps start with oak-smoked pollock with crab mayonnaise, shaved fennel and lemon, then choose Cornish lamb fillet with garlic greens and mustard mash, or lobster and crab burger. To finish, try the hot brioche doughnuts with raspberry purée and vanilla sauce.

Open all wk **Food** Lunch Mon-Sat 12-2.30, Sun 12-3.30 Dinner Mon-Sat 6.30-10, Sun 5.30-9 ⊕ GREENE KING ◀ Abbot Ale, Morland Old Speckled Hen ♂ Aspall. ☗ 24 **Facilities** Non-diners area ◖ Children's menu Children's portions Garden ⌂ Parking WiFi

COOKHAM DEAN
Map 5 SU88

The Chequers Brasserie
PICK OF THE PUBS

tel: 01628 481232 **Dean Ln SL6 9BQ**
email: info@chequersbrasserie.co.uk
dir: *From A4094 in Cookham High St towards Marlow, over rail line. 1m on right*

Historic pub with an established brasserie

Tucked away between Marlow and Maidenhead, The Chequers is in one of the prettiest villages in the Thames Valley. Striking Victorian and Edwardian villas around the green set the tone, whilst the surrounding wooded hills and dales have earned Cookham Dean a reputation as a centre for woodland walks. Wooden beams, an open fire and comfortable seating welcome drinkers to the small bar, perhaps to sample Rebellion's fine ales. Dining takes place in the older part of the building, or in the conservatory; a private dining room can be reserved for parties. The menus of expertly prepared dishes are based on fresh, quality ingredients enhanced by careful use of cosmopolitan flavours. A starter of seared scallops with pea purée, pancetta and chopped hazelnuts could be followed by pan-fried salmon fillet with crayfish risotto and confit fennel; or open ratatouille lasagne with rocket pesto and parmesan shavings. Dogs are welcome in the garden only.

Open all wk Mon-Fri 10-3 5.30-11 (Sat-Sun all day) **Food** Lunch all wk 12-2.30 Dinner Sun-Thu 6.30-9.30, Fri-Sat 6.30-10 Set menu available Restaurant menu available all wk ⊕ FREE HOUSE ◀ Rebellion IPA ♂ Westons Stowford Press. ☗ 14 **Facilities** Non-diners area ◖ Children's portions Garden ⌂ Parking WiFi ▦ (notice required)

CRAZIES HILL
Map 5 SU78

The Horns
PICK OF THE PUBS

tel: 0118 940 6222 **RG10 8LY**
email: enquiries@thehornscrazieshill.co.uk
dir: *Follow signs from A321 NE of Wargrave towards Henley-on-Thames*

Pretty black timbered pub with barn restaurtant

Head to the secluded garden for summer alfresco options In the peaceful village of Crazies Hill, The Horns is a beautifully restored 16th-century pub with oak beams, terracotta walls and stripped wooden floors. There are three interconnecting rooms full of old pine tables, warmed by open fires; the main dining room is in an elegantly converted barn, which was added 200 years ago. The tranquil atmosphere makes it a great place to enjoy a pint of Oxford Gold or one of the dozen wines offered by the glass. Alternatively, you can eat and drink outside in the secluded garden when the weather is fine. The evening menu might offer starters of ham hock terrine, crispy duck salad or smoked mackerel pâté, while main courses encompass favourites such as slow-braised shin of beef with mash; roasted cod with braised baby gem and sautéed wild mushrooms; or guinea fowl wrapped in Parma ham with Puy lentils and fondant potatoes.

Open all wk 12-3 5-11 (Sat-Sun all day) **Food** Lunch Mon-Sat 12-2, Sun 12-3.30 Dinner Tue-Sat 6-9 ⊕ BRAKSPEAR ◀ Bitter, Oxford Gold ♂ Thatchers Gold. ☗ 12 **Facilities** Non-diners area ☻ (Bar Garden) ◖ Children's menu Children's portions Play area Family room Garden ⌂ Parking WiFi ▦

CURRIDGE
Map 5 SU47

NEW The Bunk Inn

tel: 01635 200400 **RG18 9DS**
email: info@thebunkinn.co.uk
dir: *M4 junct 13, A34 N towards Oxford. Take 1st slip road. At T-junct right signed Hermitage. In approx 1m right at mini rdbt into Long Ln, 1st right signed Curridge*

Village tavern handy for Newbury Racecourse

One of the oldest village buildings, the inn was lovingly refurbished in 2013 by Upham Brewery, whose tasty beers populate the handpulls on the bar. The log fire-warmed village snug remains a comfy focus for chatter or contemplation, whilst an airy restaurant with eye-catching decor or a heated patio offer alternative locations to sit, sup and study the compact, well-balanced menu. The chefs home-in on local suppliers and create dishes such as confit bacon with smoked mash and black cabbage; or Rosary goats' cheese and herb risotto. Specials may feature game from the local estates and woods that characterise this green heart of Berkshire.

Open all day all wk **Food** Lunch Mon-Fri 12-2.30, Sat 12-3, Sun 12-3.30 Dinner Mon-Sat 6.30-9.30, Sun 6.30-9 Av main course £13-£15 Restaurant menu available Mon-Sat ⊕ UPHAM BREWERY ◀ Punter, Tipster, 1st Drop & Stakes ♂ Orchard Pig. ♥ 9 **Facilities** Non-diners area ❖ (Bar Garden) ♦️ Children's menu Children's portions Family room Garden ⊼ Beer festival Parking WiFi ⬛ (notice required)

EAST GARSTON
Map 5 SU37

The Queen's Arms Country Inn ★★★★ INN
PICK OF THE PUBS

tel: 01488 648757 **RG17 7ET**
email: info@queensarmshotel.co.uk web: www.queensarmshotel.co.uk
dir: *M4 junct 14, 4m onto A338 to Great Shefford, then East Garston*

Stylish pub in the heart of racehorse country

Pleasantly located in the Lambourn Valley, home to over 2,000 racehorses and more than 50 racing yards, this charming pub acts as a quasi-headquarters for British racing with owners, trainers and jockeys among its clientele. The inn's oldest part was a farmer's cottage in the 18th century; its name derives from being licensed around 1856, the year of Queen Victoria's Silver Jubilee. The welcome is warm and the setting stylishly traditional. So with a glass of Doom Bar in hand, and a listening ear tuned for an indiscreet racing tip, choose from the menu: a sandwich? Kelmscott Farm cured bacon with roasted tomato and wholegrain mustard mayo perhaps. A pub favourite? Smoked chicken, ham and leek pie served with skinny chips and pea purée. After a gallop two courses could be called for: try spiced and sweetened crispy pork cheeks with baby watercress and chipotle peppers, followed by whole lemon sole with roasted courgettes and lemon butter.

Open all day all wk 11am-mdnt Closed 25 Dec **Food** Lunch Mon-Sat 12-2.30, Sun 12-3.30 Dinner Mon-Sat 6.30-9.30 Av main course £15 ⊕ FREE HOUSE ◀ Wadworth Henry's Original IPA, Sharp's Doom Bar, Guinness, Guest ales ♂ Westons Stowford Press. **Facilities** Non-diners area ❖ (Bar Garden) ♦️ Children's portions Garden ⊼ Parking WiFi ⬛ (notice required) **Rooms** 8

FRILSHAM
Map 5 SU57

The Pot Kiln ◉◉
PICK OF THE PUBS

tel: 01635 201366 **RG18 0XX**
email: admin@potkiln.org
dir: *From Yattendon follow Pot Kiln signs, cross over motorway. 0.25m, pub on right*

Recommended for their locally sourced game dishes

Game and wild food has long fascinated Mike Robinson, a passion that lies behind the success he and his wife Katie enjoy at their 18th-century pub, a former kiln-workers' beerhouse. Down narrow lanes, it can be a bit elusive, but when you find it - and you will - the bar will be ready with a choice of West Berkshire Brewery real ales and Cotswold's real cider. A big draw is the food, especially venison from the deer herd that Mike manages nearby. Once out of the pot, they are served in various ways, such as muntjac ragout with rosemary tagliatelle as a starter and, as a main course, fallow deer venison with dauphinoise potatoes, garden kale and slow-roast shallots. Other signature dishes include twice-baked shoulder of lamb with glazed root vegetables; and roast hake with Palourde clam broth. River Kennet trout and crayfish may also feature. On summer Sunday evenings, pizzas are cooked in a wood-fired oven in the garden.

Open Mon & Wed-Fri 12-3 6-11 (Sat-Sun 12-11) Closed 25 Dec, Tue **Food** Lunch Wed-Mon 12-2.30 Dinner Wed-Mon 6.30-8.30 Restaurant menu available Wed-Mon ⊕ FREE HOUSE ◀ Brick Kiln, West Berkshire Mr Chubb's Lunchtime Bitter & Maggs' Magnificent Mild ♂ Thatchers, Cotswold. **Facilities** Non-diners area ❖ (Bar Garden) ♦️ Children's menu Children's portions Play area Garden ⊼ Parking WiFi ⬛ (notice required)

HERMITAGE
Map 5 SU57

The White Horse of Hermitage

tel: 01635 200325 **Newbury Rd RG18 9TB**
email: whoh@btconnect.com
dir: *5m from Newbury on B4009. From M4 junct 13 follow signs for Newbury Showground, right into Priors Court Rd, left at mini rdbt, pub approx 50yds on right*

A refurbishment and a warm welcome

A family friendly pub dating back at least 160 years, The White Horse has achieved a solid reputation for its pub food, using the freshest and finest local produce to create a daily menu. As we went to press we understood that a refurbishment was underway, and unfortunately up-to-date menus were not available. Outside you choose between the Mediterranean-style patio or the large garden.

Open all day summer (Mon 5-11 Tue-Thu 12-3 5-11 Fri-Sat 12-11 Sun 12-10 winter) Closed Mon L (ex BHs) ⊕ GREENE KING ◀ Abbot Ale & IPA, Guinness, Guest ales ♂ Westons Stowford Press. **Facilities** ❖ (Bar Garden) ♦️ Children's menu Children's portions Play area Garden Parking WiFi

HOLYPORT
Map 6 SU87

The Belgian Arms

tel: 01628 634468 **SL6 2JR**
email: reservations@thebelgianarms.com
dir: *M4 junct 8, A308(M). At rdbt take A330 signed Ascot. At Holyport village green left signed Bray & Windsor. 1st left into Holyport Rd. Belgian Arms on right*

Earthy decor, friendly staff and classy food

The name of this wisteria-draped village pub, just off the green and overlooking the pond, begs the question - what's the connection with Belgium? Apparently, during the First World War many local men fought in Flanders and so its name was changed from The Eagle as a tribute to them. Today's reputation is founded on executive chef Dominic Chapman's British food, featuring fresh, daily-delivered produce, often from artisan suppliers. Menus typically feature steak béarnaise; stews; roast Berkshire roe deer; Scottish salmon and mussel pie; and Sunday roasts.

Open all day all wk 11-11 (Sun 12-6) **Food** Lunch Mon-Sat 12-2.30, Sun 12-3.30 Dinner Mon-Thu 6.30-9.30, Fri-Sat 6-10 Set menu available Restaurant menu available all wk ⊕ BRAKSPEAR ◀ Brakspear Best, Marston's Pedigree Ö Symonds. ▼ 12 **Facilities** Non-diners area ❧ (Bar Garden) ♦♦ Children's menu Children's portions Garden ⋒ Parking WiFi

The George on the Green

tel: 01628 628317 **SL6 2JL**
email: natalie@thegeorgeonthegreen.com
dir: *M4 junct 8/9, at rdbt 2nd exit onto A308(M). At rdbt 3rd exit onto A308. At rdbt take 2nd exit signed Holyport. Pub in village centre*

Traditional landmark inn on the village green

Facing the vast, eponymous green, this low-beamed 16th-century pub may possibly have played host to Charles II and Nell Gwynne when the actress lived locally. Today's locals can look forward to great beers from Rebellion Brewery in nearby Marlow Bottom coupled with a selective, well thought-out menu; maybe baked crab gratin to start, then smoked chicken, leek and butternut squash risotto, or slow-roasted half shoulder of lamb with sweet potato boulangère. From outside tables, views stretch across the green to the tree-shaded village duck pond.

Open 12-3 5-11 (Sat 12-11 Sun 12-6) Closed Mon **Food** Lunch Tue-Fri 12-2.30, Sat-Sun 12-4 Dinner Tue-Fri 5.30-9, Sat-Sun 6-9 ◀ Rebellion, Fuller's London Pride Ö Thatchers Gold. **Facilities** Non-diners area ♦♦ Children's portions Garden Parking ⬛

HUNGERFORD
Map 5 SU36

The Pheasant Inn

tel: 01488 648284 **Ermin St, Shefford Woodlands RG17 7AA**
email: info@pheasantinnlambourn.co.uk
dir: *M4 junct 14, A338 towards Wantage. Left onto B4000 towards Lambourn*

Welcoming atmosphere, chic interior and good food

Originally called The Paraffin House because it was licensed to sell fuel alongside ale, this old drovers' retreat in the Lambourn Valley is a notable food pub. Its interior retains original features such as beams, wood-panelling and a stone floor. Food choices include sharing boards crammed with the likes of houmous, tzatziki, olives and pitta bread, or full meals such as crispy salt and pepper squid with garlic mayonnaise followed by chicken and leek pie with mash and green vegetables, with ginger pannacotta and poached rhubarb for dessert. Wash it down with Ramsbury Gold or Symonds Founders Reserve cider.

Open all day all wk Closed 25 Dec **Food** Lunch all wk 12-2.30 Dinner Mon-Sat 6.30-9.30, Sun 6.30-8.30 Av main course £13.50 Restaurant menu available all wk ⊕ FREE HOUSE ◀ Ramsbury Gold, Upham Punter Ö Symonds Founders Reserve. ▼ 12 **Facilities** Non-diners area ❧ (Bar Restaurant Garden) ♦♦ Children's portions Garden Parking WiFi ⬛

The Swan Inn ★★★★ INN
PICK OF THE PUBS

tel: 01488 668326 **Craven Rd, Lower Green, Inkpen RG17 9DX**
email: enquiries@theswaninn-organics.co.uk **web:** www.theswaninn-organics.co.uk
dir: *S on Hungerford High St, past rail bridge, left to Hungerford Common, right signed Inkpen*

Village free house in fine walking country

Up in the North Wessex Downs, just below Combe Gibbet, is this 17th-century beamed pub with open fires. Owners Mary and Bernard Harris are organic beef farmers; their beers are organic too, principally Butts Traditional and Jester Bitter from nearby Great Shefford. Almost everything on the menu is prepared using the Harrises' own fresh produce: all beef comes from their farm and is butchered on the premises, although their chicken comes up from Devon's Otter Valley. Most pasta is freshly made on the premises, maybe appearing on the plate as ravioli di manzo, spaghetti marinara or beef lasagne. Traditional English favourites include award-winning home-made sausages and mash (the Swan is a proud member of the British Sausage Appreciation Society); beef Stroganoff with basmati rice; and poached salmon with lemon and grapefruit dressing. A farm shop is attached to the pub, and there is an attractive terraced garden. Ten en suite bedrooms are available.

Open all wk 12-2.30 7-11 (Sat 12-11 Sun 12-4) Closed 25-26 Dec **Food** Lunch all wk 12-2.30 Dinner Mon-Sat 7-9.30 Av main course £10 Restaurant menu available all wk ⊕ FREE HOUSE ◀ Butts Traditional, Jester & Blackguard Porter, Guest ales. **Facilities** Non-diners area ♦♦ Children's menu Children's portions Play area Garden Outside area ⋒ Parking WiFi ⬛ (notice required) **Rooms** 10

HURLEY
Map 5 SU88

The Olde Bell Inn ★★★★★ INN ◉◉
PICK OF THE PUBS

tel: 01628 825881 **High St SL6 5LX**
email: oldebellreception@coachinginn.co.uk **web:** www.theoldebell.co.uk
dir: *M4 junct 8/9 follow Henley signs. At rdbt take A4130 towards Hurley. Right to Hurley, inn 800yds on right*

Ancient inn widely known for its good food

As long ago as 1135, pilgrims visiting the now-ruined Hurley Priory (although the nave survived to become today's parish church) would stay here in what was its guest house. In truth, not all of it is quite that ancient, but let's not split hairs - it claims to be the country's oldest still-operating inn and its nooks, crannies and crooked floors strongly suggest that it's a fair claim. Age apart, attractions include the accomplished food, backed by two AA Rosettes, with daily-changing menus based firmly on produce from local farms and suppliers. Grilled herring with sweet pepper escabeche and horseradish cream; and Crottin goats' cheese with celery and shallot salad often appear as starters. And, quite likely appearing as mains, are sirloin of Dedham Vale beef with hand-cut chips; and pan-roasted whole plaice with anchovies, buttered potatoes, and lemon and caper noisette sauce. The terrace and wildflower-meadow beer garden are delightful.

continued

HURLEY continued

Open all day all wk 11am-mdnt (Sun 11-11) **Food** Lunch Mon-Sat 12-2.30, Sun 12.30-3.30 Dinner Mon-Sat 6-9.30, Sun 6.30-9 Av main course £10 Set menu available Restaurant menu available all wk ⊕ FREE HOUSE ◖ Rebellion, Theakston ♻ Burrow Hill. ♟ 10 **Facilities** Non-diners area ♣ (Bar Garden) ♦ Children's menu Children's portions Play area Garden ⊟ Parking WiFi ⊟ **Rooms** 48

HURST
Map 5 SU77

The Green Man

tel: 0118 934 2599 **Hinton Rd RG10 0BP**
dir: From Workingham on A321 towards Twyford. Right after Hurst Cricket Club cricket ground on right into Hinton Rd

Ever reliable village retreat

A homely half-timbered cottage pub situated close to the village cricket pitch and with a capable change of hands at the helm. Older parts of the building predate its first licence granted in 1602; thick beams were recycled from Tudor warships and offer a memorable interior in this appealing rustic retreat. The Brakspear Brewery leased the inn for 1000 years from 1646; their bitter and seasonal ales still keep drinkers happy. Diners can anticipate a seasonally adjusted, solidly British menu with mains like chicken, rabbit and bacon stew with bread and butter pudding to follow. There's a tree-shaded beer garden with serene country views and the pub is very dog friendly.

Open all day all wk **Food** Lunch all wk 12-3 Dinner Mon-Fri 6-9.30, Sat-Sun all day Av main course £12 ⊕ BRAKSPEAR ◖ Bitter & Seasonal ales, Wychwood Hobgoblin ♻ Addlestones. ♟ 20 **Facilities** Non-diners area ♣ (Bar Garden) ♦ Children's menu Children's portions Play area Garden ⊟ Parking WiFi

KNOWL HILL
Map 5 SU87

Bird In Hand Country Inn
PICK OF THE PUBS

tel: 01628 826622 & 822781 **Bath Rd RG10 9UP**
email: info@birdinhand.co.uk
dir: On A4, 5m W of Maidenhead, 7m E of Reading

Friendly country pub

When George III lived at Windsor Castle, he sometimes stopped off at this part 14th-century inn. Today it's run by Caroline Shone, one of the third generation of her family to do so. The choice of real ales in the wood-panelled bar, the oldest part of the pub, runs to five guests and that's in addition to Binghams locally brewed Twyford Tipple. The 50-bin wine list includes a white and a rosé from nearby Stanlake Park vineyard. In the attractive restaurant, which overlooks a courtyard and fountain, the menu (this also applies in the bar) offers light meals such as meze with taboula, falafel, fatouch, houmous and a pitta, or filled omelette. Classic mains include steak and kidney pudding; Thai chicken curry; and cod and chips. There are also grill options and a selection of home-made desserts. Beer festivals take place in June and November.

Open all day all wk **Food** Lunch all wk 12-10 Dinner all wk 12-10 Set menu available ⊕ FREE HOUSE ◖ Binghams Twyford Tipple, 5 Guest ales ♻ Thatchers. ♟ 20 **Facilities** Non-diners area ♣ (Bar Garden) ♦ Children's menu Children's portions Garden ⊟ Beer festival Parking WiFi ⊟ (notice required)

LECKHAMPSTEAD
Map 5 SU47

The Stag

tel: 01488 638436 **Shop Ln RG20 8QG**
dir: 6m from Newbury on B4494

A great spot after a country walk

The white-painted Stag lies just off the village green in a sleepy downland village, close to the Ridgeway long-distance path and Snelsmore Common, home to nightjar, woodlark and grazing Exmoor ponies. Inside old black-and-white photographs tell of village life many years ago. Surrounding farms and growers supply all produce, including venison, pheasant and fresh river trout. So you might find venison and redcurrant sausages with butternut squash mash; pork loin with creamy mushroom sauce; or traditional beer-battered fish and chips with mushy peas on the menu. There are around 20 red and white wines, among them varieties from Australia, California and France.

Open 12-3 6-11 Closed Sun eve & Mon **Food** Lunch Tue-Sat 12-2, Sun 12-2.30 Dinner Tue-Sat 6-9 ⊕ FREE HOUSE ◖ Morland Original, West Berkshire Good Old Boy, Guest ales ♻ Aspall. **Facilities** Non-diners area ♣ (Bar Garden Outside area) ♦ Children's menu Children's portions Garden Outside area ⊟ Parking WiFi ⊟ (notice required)

MARSH BENHAM
Map 5 SU46

The Red House

tel: 01635 582017 **RG20 8LY**
email: info@theredhousepub.com
dir: From Newbury A4 towards Hungerford. Pub signed. in approx 3m. Left onto unclassified road to Marsh Benham

Thatched country pub with gluten-free menu specialities

Tucked away in the verdant Kennet Valley, trim thatched roofs cap this tranquil retreat just a modest stroll (dog walkers welcome) from the Kennet & Avon Canal. Indulge in a beer from the respected West Berkshire brewery whilst contemplating views from the sheltered beer garden, or slumber beside the log fire, anticipating your choice from the kitchen overseen by experienced French chef-patron Laurent Lebeau. His essentially British menu might include braised ox cheeks in red wine with celeriac mash or, from the thoughtful gluten-free menu, south coast bream fillets and roasted root vegetables. As for the wines, Laurent chooses well.

Open all day all wk **Food** Lunch all wk 12-10 Dinner all wk 12-10 Av main course £14 Set menu available ⊕ FREE HOUSE ◖ West Berkshire Good Old Boy & Mr Chubb's Lunchtime Bitter, Guest ales ♻ Westons Stowford Press. **Facilities** Non-diners area ♣ (Bar Garden) ♦ Children's menu Children's portions Garden ⊟ Parking WiFi ⊟ (notice required)

MONEYROW GREEN
Map 6 SU87

The White Hart

tel: 01628 621460 **SL6 2ND**
email: admin@thewhitehartholyport.co.uk
dir: *2m S from Maidenhead. M4 junct 8/9, follow Holyport signs then Moneyrow Green. Pub by petrol station*

Perfect stop for Windsor visitors

The close proximity to the M4 makes this traditional 19th-century coaching inn a popular spot for those heading to nearby Maidenhead and Windsor. The wood-panelled lounge bar is furnished with leather chesterfields, and quality home-made food and award-winning real ales can be enjoyed in a cosy atmosphere with an open fire. Typical mains are mushroom Stroganoff; tuna niçoise salad; and baked sea bass. Sandwiches, baguettes and jacket potatoes are offered at lunchtime. There are large gardens to enjoy in summer with a children's playground and petanque pitch. Time a visit for the annual summer cider and beer festival.

Open all day all wk **Food** Lunch all wk 12-2.30 Dinner all wk 6-9 Av main course £8.95 ⊕ GREENE KING ◀ IPA, Morland Old Speckled Hen, Guest ales Ŏ Westons Stowford Press. **Facilities** Non-diners area ♣ (Bar Garden) ⋆♦ Children's portions Play area Garden ⊨ Beer festival Cider festival Parking WiFi ⊶ (notice required)

OAKLEY GREEN
Map 6 SU97

The Greene Oak ◉

tel: 01753 864294 **SL4 5UW**
email: info@thegreeneoak.co.uk
dir: *M4 junct 8, A308(M) signed Maidenhead Central. At rdbt take A308 signed Bray & Windsor. Right into Oakley Green Rd (B3024) signed Twyford. Pub on left*

Thriving gastro-pub near Windsor

The first of Henry Cripps's trio of gastro-pubs stands close to Windsor and draws an affluent dining crowd. They love the relaxed feel of the stylish and contemporary surroundings and are wowed by the imaginative modern food on the daily-changing menus, and the excellent choice of wines. Kick off a memorable meal with seared pigeon breast with braised leg and wild mushroom fricassée, follow with pan-fried monkfish with pea and bacon risotto and parmesan, or beef Wellington for two with fat chips and jus, leaving room for pear and almond tarte Tatin with caramel sauce.

Open all wk **Food** Lunch Mon-Sat 12-2.30, Sun 12-3.30 Dinner Mon-Sat 6.30-9.30, Sun 5.30-9.30 ⊕ FREE HOUSE ◀ Greene King IPA & Abbot Ale, Morland Old Speckled Hen Ŏ Aspall. ♚ 26 **Facilities** Non-diners area ⋆♦ Children's menu Children's portions Garden ⊨ Parking WiFi ⊶ (notice required)

PALEY STREET
Map 5 SU87

The Royal Oak Paley Street ◉◉◉ `PICK OF THE PUBS`

tel: 01628 620541 **Littlefield Green SL6 3JN**
email: reservations@theroyaloakpaleystreet.com
dir: *M4 junct 8/9A, A308(m) signed Maidenhead (central)*

Award-winning food in celebrity-owned village pub

It's 14 years since TV chat-show host Sir Michael Parkinson and son Nick first set eyes on this 17th-century, oak-beamed pub. Although Dad wasn't convinced, Nick saw the untapped potential of running this unloved village pub and how right he was; his celebrity father is now a regular here. Its genteel serenity is partly due to the artworks on the walls, and partly to the white pebbles and waterfall in the garden. The food is certainly award-winning, expect dishes such as roast Cornish skate wing with cockles, cucumber and parsley sauce; wild Berkshire rabbit and bacon pie; and butternut squash and goats' curd ravioli with sage, pine nuts and parmesan. Desserts have a high comfort factor: steamed butterscotch pudding; and rhubarb crumble with custard, for instance. Fuller's real ales are on tap alongside 25 wines by the glass. Please note only children over three are welcome.

Open all wk 12-3 6-11 (Sun 12-4) **Food** Lunch Mon-Sat 12-3, Sun 12-4 Dinner Mon-Sat 6-11 Restaurant menu available all wk ⊕ FULLER'S ◀ London Pride, George Gale & Co Seafarers. ♚ 25 **Facilities** Non-diners area ⋆♦ Garden Parking WiFi

PEASEMORE
Map 5 SU47

The Fox at Peasemore

tel: 01635 248480 **Hill Green Ln RG20 7JN**
email: info@foxatpeasemore.co.uk **web:** www.foxatpeasemore.co.uk
dir: *M4 junct 13, A34 signed Oxford. Immediately left onto slip road signed Chieveley, Hermitage & Beedon. At T-junct left, through Chieveley to Peasemore. Left at phone box, pub signed*

Clear proof that village pubs can be successful

The awards Philip and Lauren Davison have won between them over the years would fill several mantelpieces. Admittedly, some were earned before they came to The Fox, but the way things are going more display space will soon be needed. Charmingly rustic, with elegant modern touches, they didn't just refurbish the pub, they transformed it. The bar, warmed by a log-burner, serves Good Old Boy and Butts Traditional, plus Tutts Clump cider. On the main menu are grilled medallions of beef fillet with mushrooms and bordelaise sauce; home-made fishcakes with chunky hand-cut chips and mushy peas; and goats' cheese, mushroom and Mediterranean vegetable tart with tomato provençale sauce. Pub classics are on a blackboard, and sandwiches, baguettes and ploughman's are available too. Outside seating overlooks beautiful countryside - great for a traditional Sunday roast, subject inevitably to Britain's roller-coaster weather.

Open 12-3 6-11 (Sat-Sun 12-late) Closed Mon **Food** Lunch Tue-Sun 12-2 Dinner Tue-Sun 6-9 Av main course £11.50 Set menu available Restaurant menu available Wed-Sun ⊕ FREE HOUSE ◀ Butts Traditional, West Berkshire Good Old Boy Ŏ Tutts Clump. ♚ 14 **Facilities** Non-diners area ♣ (Bar Garden Outside area) ⋆♦ Children's menu Children's portions Garden Outside area ⊨ Parking WiFi ⊶ (notice required)

See advert on page 36

READING
Map 5 SU77

The Flowing Spring

tel: 0118 969 9878 **Henley Rd, Playhatch RG4 9RB**
email: info@theflowingspringpub.co.uk
dir: *3m N of Reading on A4155 towards Henley*

Cosy country pub at the edge of the Chilterns

Unusually this pub is on the first floor, which slopes steeply from one end of the bar to the other; the verandah overlooks Thames Valley countryside. The pub has been recognised for its well-kept ales and cellar, and the menu of no-nonsense pub favourites is backed by a comprehensive range of vegetarian, vegan and gluten-free and dairy-free options. The pub hosts beer festivals, astronomy nights, outdoor live music, stand-up comedy nights and many other exciting events throughout the year. The huge garden is bounded by streams.

Open all day Closed Mon **Food** Lunch Tue-Sun 12-2.30 Dinner Tue-Sat 6-9 ⊕ FULLER'S ◀ London Pride & ESB, George Gale & Co Seafarers, Guest ale Ö Aspall. ♟ 10 **Facilities** Non-diners area ❀ (Bar Restaurant Garden) ♦♦ Children's portions Play area Garden ☷ Beer festival Cider festival Parking WiFi 🚐 (notice required)

The Shoulder of Mutton

tel: 0118 947 3908 **Playhatch RG4 9QU**
email: shoulderofmutton@hotmail.co.uk
dir: *From Reading follow signs to Caversham, take A4155 to Henley-on-Thames. At rdbt left to Binfield Heath, 1st pub on left*

Village pub that is true to its name

Close to Caversham Lakes and the River Thames; a pleasant walled cottage garden, beams and open fire grace this long-established local favourite in tiny Playhatch. Beer lovers pop in for ales brewed just up the road by Loddon Brewery, whilst diners travel from afar to indulge in chef-patron Alan Oxlade's astonishing mutton dishes. The 7-hour roasted shoulder of mutton is famous; the 5-hour shepherd's pie deserves equal consideration; reserve a seat in the airy conservatory and indulge. The wider menu is equally impressive; braised venison and beef pie cooked with beetroot-infused gravy, or the 6-hour cooked Gressingham duck in the 'River and Orchard' dish (with roast almond, sour cherry and port sauce) cases in point.

Open 12-3 6-11 (Mon & Sun 12-3 Sat 12-3 6.30-11) Closed 26 Dec, 2 Jan, Sun eve, Mon eve **Food** Lunch all wk 12-2 Dinner Tue-Sat 6.30-9 Restaurant menu available Tue-Sat ⊕ GREENE KING ◀ Abbot, IPA, Loddon Hoppit & Hullabaloo Ö Aspall. **Facilities** Non-diners area ♦♦ Children's portions Garden ☷ Parking 🚐 (notice required)

RUSCOMBE
Map 5 SU77

Buratta's at the Royal Oak

tel: 0118 934 5190 **Ruscombe Ln RG10 9JN**
email: enquiries@burattas.co.uk
dir: *From A4 (Wargrave rdbt) take A321 to Twyford (signed Twyford/Wokingham). Straight on at 1st lights, right at 2nd lights onto A3032. Right onto A3024 (Ruscombe Rd which becomes Ruscombe Ln). Pub on left on brow of hill*

Relaxed pub with its own antiques shop

Originally a one-bar pub, the Royal Oak has been extended over the years and the old cottage next door is now the kitchen. With Binghams Brewery and Fuller's London Pride as resident ales, the relaxed restaurant offers a wide range of meals, from hearty bar snacks and sandwiches to regularly changing à la carte choices such as crayfish cocktail followed by pan-fried sea bass with sautéed garlic, balsamic tomatoes and chive mash. The large garden, complete with resident ducks, is dog friendly. The pub even has its own antiques shop and nearly everything in the pub is for sale.

Open Tue-Sat 12-3 6-11 (Sun-Mon 12-3) Closed Sun eve & Mon eve **Food** Lunch all wk 12-2.30 Dinner Tue-Sat 7-9.30 ⊕ ENTERPRISE INNS ◀ Fuller's London Pride, Binghams, Guest ales. ♟ 12 **Facilities** Non-diners area ❀ (Bar Restaurant Garden) ♦♦ Children's menu Children's portions Garden ☷ Parking WiFi 🚐 (notice required)

SINDLESHAM
Map 5 SU76

The Walter Arms

tel: 0118 977 4903 **Bearwood Rd RG41 5BP**
email: mail@thewalterarms.com
dir: *A329 from Wokingham towards Reading. 1.5m, left onto B3030. 5m, left into Bearwood Rd. Pub 200yds on left*

Welcoming pub with interesting menu of global dishes

A typically solid Victorian building built about 1850 by John Walter III, grandson of the man who founded *The Times* newspaper. The idea was that it should be a working men's club for the workers on the Bearwood Estate, where Walter lived. Now a popular dining pub, the seasonal menus offer traditional English dishes, such as pan-roasted rump of lamb, and beer-battered sustainable haddock; as well as pasta, stone-baked pizzas and oriental- and Arabian-style 'smörgåsbord'. The beer garden is a good spot for a pint of Twyford Tipple or Courage Best.

Open all day all wk 12-11 (Sat 12-12 Sun 12-10) **Food** Lunch Mon-Fri 12-2.30, Sat 12-10, Sun 12-9 Dinner Mon-Fri 6-9.30, Sat 12-10, Sun 12-9 ⊕ FREE HOUSE ◀ Courage Best, Binghams Twyford Tipple, Guest ale Ŏ Westons Stowford Press. **Facilities** Non-diners area ♦ Children's menu Children's portions Garden ☠ Parking

SONNING
Map 5 SU77

The Bull Inn

tel: 0118 969 3901 **High St RG4 6UP**
email: bullinn@fullers.co.uk
dir: *From Reading take A4 towards Maidenhead. Left onto B4446 to Sonning*

Welcoming olde-worlde inn

Two minutes' walk from the River Thames in the pretty village of Sonning, this black-and-white timbered inn can trace its roots back 600 years or so; it can also boast visits by former owner Queen Elizabeth I and a mention in Jerome K Jerome's classic novel *Three Men in a Boat*. With Fuller's ales on tap, comfy leather chairs and log fires in the grate, The Bull charms locals and visitors alike. It's a great place to eat too, with an interesting menu of British and world cuisine. Dishes could include a slow braised blade of beef; roasted pheasant stew; Greek meze platter; jerk spiced ham; butternut squash gnocchi and chicken fajita wraps.

Open all day all wk 11-11 **Food** Lunch all wk 10-9.30 Dinner all wk 10-9.30 Av main course £15 Set menu available Restaurant menu available all wk ⊕ FULLER'S ◀ London Pride, Chiswick Bitter, Discovery & Organic Honey Dew, George Gale & Co HSB, Guest ale. ♟ 24 **Facilities** Non-diners area ♣ (Bar Garden) ♦ Children's portions Garden ☠ Parking WiFi ▄▄ (notice required)

STANFORD DINGLEY
Map 5 SU57

The Old Boot Inn

tel: 0118 974 4292 **RG7 6LT**
email: johnintheboot@hotmail.co.uk
dir: *M4 junct 12, A4/A340 to Pangbourne. 1st left to Bradfield. Through Bradfield, follow Stanford Dingley signs*

Peaceful situation and well known for good food

Oak beams and half-timbering feature inside this cottagey inn remote along lanes in the peaceful Pang Valley. The rustic theme continues with log fires and an enormous beer garden rolling back to merge with pastureland backed by wooded hills. The modern conservatory restaurant is light and airy; just the place to moor up with a pint of local Dr Hexters beer and seek inspiration on the menus. Old

school bar meals are the tip of the iceberg, complemented by an à la carte selection and robust specials, perhaps roast chump of lamb with black pudding, red wine jus and seasonal vegetables.

Open all wk 11-3 6-11 (Sat-Sun all day) **Food** Lunch all wk 12-2 Dinner all wk 6-9 ⊕ FREE HOUSE ◀ Bass, West Berkshire Dr Hexters, Fuller's London Pride Ŏ Westons Stowford Press. ♟ 10 **Facilities** Non-diners area ♣ (Bar Garden) ♦ Children's menu Children's portions Play area Garden ☠ Parking WiFi ▄▄ (notice required)

STOCKCROSS
Map 5 SU46

NEW The Lord Lyon ⓤ

tel: 01488 657578 **Ermin St RG20 8LL**
email: lordlyon@arkells.com **web:** www.lordlyon.co.uk
dir: *A4 from Newbury towards Hungerford. At rdbt take B4000 signed Stockcross. Pub on left*

Just the place after a day at the races

Lord Lyon was a famous racehorse, but older villagers still call the pub The Nag's Head, its original name. Equine connections, especially its location close to Newbury Racecourse, make it popular with trainers and jockeys. As an Arkell's house, it serves the brewery's Moonlight and Wiltshire Gold, as well as 13 wines by the glass. Pub food includes the Lord Lyon beefburger with onion rings and spicy tomato and onion chutney; beer-battered cod and chips; American-style chicken breast marinated in barbecue sauce with bacon and cheese; and spinach and mushroom lasagne. There are weekly specials too.

Open 11.30-3 5.30-11.30 (Sat 12-12 Sun 12-6) Closed Sun eve **Food** Lunch Mon-Sat 12-2.30, Sun 12-3 Dinner Mon-Sat 6-8.30 Av main course £6.95 ⊕ ARKELL'S ◀ Moonlight & Wiltshire Gold Ŏ Westons Stowford Press. ♟ 13 **Facilities** Non-diners area ♣ (Bar Garden Outside area) ♦ Children's menu Children's portions Family room Garden Outside area ☠ Parking WiFi ▄▄ (notice required) **Rooms** 5

SWALLOWFIELD
Map 5 SU76

The George & Dragon
PICK OF THE PUBS

tel: 0118 988 4432 **Church Rd RG7 1TJ**
email: dining@georgeanddragonswallowfield.co.uk
dir: *M4, junct 11, A33 towards Basingstoke. Left at Barge Ln to B3349 into The Street, right into Church Rd*

Friendly country pub dating back to the 17th century

Formerly a farm, this country pub and restaurant looks very much the part with its low, stripped beams, log fires, rug-strewn floors and warm earthy tones. It has been under the same ownership for the last 20 years, and regular customers know what to expect from the internationally inspired seasonal menus, sourced extensively from local suppliers. Starters that may be available are herbed spinach and button mushroom pancake with mornay sauce; and soy- and chilli-braised octopus with pineapple, orange and tomato salsa. Typical main courses include local venison loin steak with haggis mash and redcurrant jus; baked meatballs in a rich Barolo wine tomato sauce, with zesty gremolata and pasta; and monkfish on sweet potato bubble-and-squeak. The garden overlooks beautiful countryside and makes a great place to head for after walking the long-distance Blackwater Valley Path, which follows the river from its source in Rowhill Nature Reserve to Swallowfield.

Open all day all wk **Food** Lunch Mon-Sat 12-2.30, Sun 12-3 Dinner Mon-Sat 7-9.30, Sun 7-9 ⊕ FREE HOUSE ◀ Ringwood Best Bitter, Sharp's Doom Bar, Guest ale Ŏ Thatchers Gold. **Facilities** Non-diners area ♣ (Bar Garden) ♦ Children's menu Children's portions Garden ☠ Parking

WALTHAM ST LAWRENCE

Map 5 SU87

The Bell

tel: 0118 934 1788 **The Street RG10 0JJ**
email: info@thebellwalthamstlawrence.co.uk
dir: *On B3024 E of Twyford. From A4 turn at Hare Hatch*

Good ciders and beers at very old inn

This 14th-century free house is renowned for its ciders and an ever-changing range of real ales selected from small independent breweries. The building was given to the community in 1608 and profits from the rent still help village charities. Iain and Scott Ganson have built a local reputation for good food where everything possible is made on the premises, including all charcuterie and preparation of game. Start with yellow split pea soup with Bell beer bread or Welsh rarebit, then continue with pan-fried trout with Puy lentils, rainbow chard and horseradish dressing; or confit of pork belly with fondant potato, haricot beans, spinach and salsa verde. Don't miss the annual summer beer festival.

Open all wk 12-3 5-11 (Sat 12-11 Sun 12-10.30) **Food** Lunch Mon-Fri 12-2, Sat-Sun 12-3 Dinner all wk 6-9.30 ⊕ FREE HOUSE ◀ Binghams Twyford Tipple, 5 Guest ales Ō Pheasant Plucker, Westons Old Rosie. ₱ 19 **Facilities** Non-diners area ❖ (Bar Restaurant Garden) ⦁ Children's menu Children's portions Garden ⊫ Beer festival Parking

WHITE WALTHAM

Map 5 SU87

The Beehive

tel: 01628 822877 **Waltham Rd SL6 3SH**
email: beehivepub@aol.com
dir: *M4 junct8/9, A404, follow White Waltham signs*

A cracking country local in an idyllic village setting

With a smart, contemporary interior, this red-brick pub features an extension which gives easy access to the front patio overlooking the cricket pitch. Renowned for its relaxing atmosphere and choice of real ales, which includes a local Loddon brew, The Beehive is also a great place to eat. In addition to its lunchtime bar menu of burgers, jackets, salads and sandwiches, fresh seasonal dishes may feature smoked haddock with mash, spinach, poached egg and beurre blanc; chicken supreme with whisky, wild mushroom and bacon sauce; and Thai-style salmon fishcakes with sweet chilli dipping sauce.

Open all wk 11-3 5-11 (Sat 11am-mdnt Sun 12-10.30) Closed 26 Dec **Food** Lunch Mon-Fri 12-2.30, Sat 12-9.30, Sun 12-8.30 Dinner Mon-Fri 5-9.30, Sat 12-9.30, Sun 12-8.30 Restaurant menu available all wk ⊕ ENTERPRISE INNS ◀ Fuller's London Pride, Greene King Abbot Ale, Rebellion, Brakspear, Loddon guest ale Ō Symonds. ₱ 14 **Facilities** Non-diners area ❖ (Bar Garden) ⦁ Children's menu Children's portions Garden ⊫ Parking WiFi ▭ (notice required)

WINKFIELD

Map 6 SU97

NEW The Winning Post

tel: 01344 882242 **Winkfield St SL4 4SW**
email: info@winningpostwinkfield.co.uk
dir: *M4 junct 6, at rdbt 1st exit onto A355. 3rd exit at rdbt into Imperial Rd (B3175). Right at lights into Saint Leonards Rd (B3022). At 2nd rdbt 2nd exit into North Street signed Winkfield. Through Winkfield, at sharp left bend turn right into Winkfield St. Pub 200yds on right*

Tranquil village pub popular with the racing fraternity

A short canter from Ascot and Windsor racecourses, this charming 18th-century pub has long been a favourite with the equine-inclined. The Winning Post is off the beaten track and surrounded by stunning Berkshire countryside but it's a convenient pitstop for Heathrow Airport. Newly refurbished, the open fire and stone floors retain the building's original character and the beer garden offers alfresco

opportunities. Enjoy a pint of Tipster & Punter ale as you order from an enticing menu that might offer venison terrine with prune and fig chutney; and sea trout fillet with sauté new potatoes, curly kale and sauce vierge.

Open all day all wk **Food** Lunch Mon-Thu 12-9.30, Fri-Sat 12-5.30 Dinner Mon-Thu 12-9.30, Sun 7-9 Restaurant menu available Mon-Sat ⊕ UPHAM PUB CO ◀ Tipster & Punter Ō Thatchers. ₱ **Facilities** Non-diners area ❖ (Bar Garden) ⦁ Children's menu Garden ⊫ Parking WiFi

WINTERBOURNE

Map 5 SU47

The Winterbourne Arms

tel: 01635 248200 **RG20 8BB**
email: mail@winterbournearms.com
dir: *M4 junct 13 into Chieveley Services, follow Donnington signs to Winterbourne. Right into Arlington Ln, right at T-junct, left into Winterbourne*

Idyllic pub with large gardens

Steeped in 300 years of history, warmth and charm, yet only five minutes from the M4, this pretty village pub once housed the village bakery and shop. The Winterbourne's real ales may include local Whistle Wetter, while 16 wines served by the glass and 20 more by the bottle make for a comprehensive list. The traditional and modern British menus and daily-changing specials offer starters like deep-fried butterfly prawns or pan-fried wild mushrooms, followed by chicken fillet filled with garlic herb butter or slow braised flaked ham hock with butter beans, which can be enjoyed by candlelight or alfresco in summer. Local game is served in season.

Open all wk 12-3 6-11 (Sun 12-10.30) **Food** Lunch all wk 12-2.30 Dinner all wk 6-10 Av main course £8.50 Restaurant menu available all wk ⊕ FREE HOUSE ◀ Winterbourne Whistle Wetter, Ramsbury Gold, Guinness Ō Symonds. ₱ 12 **Facilities** Non-diners area ❖ (Bar Garden) ⦁ Children's portions Garden ⊫ Parking ▭ (notice required)

WOOLHAMPTON

Map 5 SU56

The Rowbarge

tel: 0118 971 2213 **Station Rd RG7 5SH**
email: rowbarge@brunningandprice.co.uk
dir: *From A4 (Bath Rd) at Midgham into Station Rd, signed to station & pub. Over rail crossing, over canal, pub on right*

Traditional pub by the Kennet Canal

This early 18th-century pub that sits alongside a busy lock on the Kennet & Avon Canal retains its traditional character; the large garden runs down to the canal towpath so cyclists and walkers can easily pop in for a pint. The bar serves half a dozen cask ales – King John and Saxon Archer among them – Aspall cider and 16 wines by the glass. For something light, try smoked haddock kedgeree, or a rump steak sandwich; main meals include calves' liver and bacon; baked salmon Wellington; and pan-fried parmesan gnocchi.

Open all day all wk 11-11 (Sun 11-10.30) **Food** Lunch Mon-Sat 12-10, Sun 12-9.30 Dinner Mon-Sat 12-10, Sun 12-9.30 ⊕ FREE HOUSE ◀ Original, Andwell, Three Castles, Guest ales Ō Aspall. ₱ 16 **Facilities** Non-diners area ❖ (Bar Garden) ⦁ Children's menu Children's portions Garden ⊫ Beer festival Parking WiFi ▭ (notice required)

PICK OF THE PUBS

The Royal Oak Hotel

YATTENDON   Map 5 SU57

tel: 01635 201325
The Square RG18 0UG
email: info@royaloakyattendon.com
web: www.royaloakyattendon.co.uk
dir: *M4 junct 12, A4 (Newbury,) right at 2nd rdbt (Pangbourne) then 1st left. From junct 13, A34 N 1st left, right at T-junct. Left then 2nd right to Yattendon*

Village pub with pretty garden

Yattendon doesn't make much of a footprint on the Berkshire countryside, but although small, it's a delightful village. It once had a castle, but this was wrecked during the Civil War, and locals tell a story of a wealthy family who fled the village after having first hidden a vast fortune in gold down a deep well. The search goes on. Forming part of a row of 16th-century cottages, the pub offers log fires in the bar, oak beams, and quarry-tiled and wooden floors in the adjoining lounge and dining rooms. Not surprisingly, owner Rob McGill serves real ales from the village's West Berkshire Brewery, including Good Old Boy and Mr Chubb's Lunchtime Bitter. Abundant local produce from top suppliers helps head chef Toby Barrett create unfussy seasonal dishes that have gained recognition in many a foodie guide. Consider, for example, a set lunch of chicory, walnut and Stilton salad; salmon and basil fishcake with wilted spinach; and lemon posset with shortbread. Other ideas from the regularly changing carte include roast Berkshire pork belly with beetroot gratin, swede mash and grain mustard sauce; and grilled sea bass with steamed clams, fennel, Pernod and saffron butter. Popular desserts are chocolate and almond tart and ice cream; and red wine-poached pear, hazelnut caramel and cinnamon Chantilly. Gather a party of eight, give four days' notice, and a feasting menu enables you to dine on roast suckling pig, roast rib of beef, venison Wellington or whole roasted sea bass. French windows lead to a walled rear garden with a vine-laden trellis. Quizzes are held fortnightly, and there are rib and crab nights, seafood weekends, local bands playing and weekend barbecues in the summer.

Open all day all wk **Food** Lunch Mon-Fri 12-2.30, Sat-Sun 12-3 Dinner Mon-Thu 6.30-9.30, Fri-Sat 6.30-10, Sun 6.30-9 ⊕ FREE HOUSE ◀ West Berkshire Good Old Boy & Mr Chubb's Lunchtime Bitter, Guest ales ♂ Westons Stowford Press. ▢ 10 **Facilities** Non-diners area ❧ (Bar Restaurant Garden) ♦ Children's menu Children's portions Garden ⊟ Parking WiFi

WOKINGHAM
Map 5 SU86

The Broad Street Tavern

tel: 0118 977 3706 **29 Broad St RG40 1AU**
email: broadstreettavern@wadworth.co.uk
dir: *In town centre, adjacent to Pizza Express*

Town pub with interesting food options

Housed in a handsome detached period building fronted by elegant railings, this town-centre watering hole offers a friendly and relaxed atmosphere and both large indoor and outdoor seating areas. In good weather the garden, with a summer bar and BBQ area, is just the place to catch the sun and enjoy a drink and food that ranges from tapas to traditional pub grub such as sausage and mash; and gammon, egg and chips. Please note children are only allowed in on Sundays between noon and 5pm.

Open all day all wk Closed 25 Dec **Food** Lunch all wk 12-2.30 Dinner all wk 6-9.30 ⊕ WADWORTH ◀ Swordfish, Horizon, 6X, Henry's Original IPA, The Bishop's Tipple Ö Westons Old Rosie. ☗ 15 **Facilities** Non-diners area ✿ (Bar Garden) Garden ⌖ Beer festival WiFi ▱ (notice required)

YATTENDON
Map 5 SU57

The Royal Oak Hotel
PICK OF THE PUBS

See Pick of the Pubs on page 39

See Pick of the Pubs on page 39

BRISTOL

BRISTOL
Map 4 ST57

The Albion

tel: 0117 973 3522 **Boyces Av, Clifton BS8 4AA**
email: info@thealbionclifton.co.uk
dir: *From A4 take B3129 towards city centre. Right into Clifton Down Rd. 3rd left into Boyces Ave*

Popular from brunch time through to the evening

This handsome Grade II listed coaching inn dates from the 17th century. Owned by the St Austell Brewery, it's a popular place to enjoy West Country ales and ciders, as well as being a gastro-pub. In the enclosed courtyard you can order jugs of Pimm's in summer or sip mulled cider under heaters in the winter. The modern British cooking uses local produce in dishes such as braised pork belly, scallops and chorizo purée; pan-fried hake with sauerkraut, gnocchi, champagne velouté and clams. Brunch and Sunday lunch menus are also available. There is an annual cider festival in May.

Open all day 12-12 (Sat 11am-mdnt Sun 11-11) Closed 25-26 Dec, Mon L **Food** Lunch Tue-Fri 12-3, Sat 11-3, Sun 11-3.30 Dinner Tue-Sat 7-10 ⊕ ST AUSTELL BREWERY ◀ Otter Bitter, Proper Job, Tribute, Black Prince Ö Thatchers Cheddar Valley, Thatchers Gold. ☗ 12 **Facilities** Non-diners area ✿ (Bar Outside area) ♦♦ Children's portions Outside area ⌖ Cider festival WiFi ▱ (notice required)

NEW The Alma Tavern & Theatre

tel: 0117 973 5171 **18-20 Alma Vale Rd, Clifton BS8 2HY**
email: info@almatavernandtheatre.co.uk
dir: *Phone for detailed directions*

Good food in a traditional pub with its own theatre

Down a leafy side street in the heart of Clifton, this bustling Victorian pub has the unique and added attraction of a small theatre upstairs. The team here continues to draw in the theatre crowd and maintain a pubby atmosphere for the locals, while also enticing others with their good food offering. As well as an appealing lunchtime menu of sandwiches and light bites, the bar menu offers pub classics

and a carte that might include pan-fried wild wood pigeon, bacon, black pudding, herb salad and red wine jus; and herb-crusted hake with Dorset crab and dill risotto.

Open all day all wk **Food** Lunch Mon-Fri 12-3, Sat-Sun 12-5 Dinner Mon-Sat 6-9.30 Av main course £10 Set menu available Restaurant menu available Mon-Sat ⊕ SPIRIT ◀ Bath Ales Gem, Sharp's Doom Bar, St Austell Tribute Ö Addlestones, Thatchers Heritage & Gold. ☗ 12 **Facilities** Non-diners area ✿ (Bar Garden) ♦♦ Children's menu Children's portions Garden ⌖ Beer festival Cider festival WiFi ▱ (notice required)

Cornubia

tel: 0117 925 4415 **142 Temple St BS1 6EN**
email: philjackithecornubia@hotmail.co.uk
dir: *Opposite Bristol Fire Station*

One of Bristol's best kept secrets

Hidden among tall office buildings in the centre of Bristol, this welcoming Georgian pub was originally built as two houses. The pub's name is the Latinised version for Cornwall. Local workers love it, not just because of its convenience, but also for its choice of changing real ales, including its own Cornubia, two draught ciders and a serious collection of malts and bottled beers. Weekday lunchtime bar snacks include baguettes, specials of the day, and the pub's famous pork pies. There is a raised decking area at the front and live entertainment every week.

Open all day 12-11 Closed 25-26 Dec, 1 Jan, Sun ⊕ FREE HOUSE ◀ Cornubia, Guest ales Ö Thatchers Cheddar Valley & Gold, Guest ciders. **Facilities** ✿ (Bar Garden) Garden Parking WiFi

Highbury Vaults

tel: 0117 973 3203 **164 St Michaels Hill, Cotham BS2 8DE**
email: highburyvaults@youngs.co.uk
dir: *A38 to Cotham from inner ring dual carriageway*

Ever popular unpretentious city escape

A classic little city pub which oozes the character of a Victorian drinking house; lots of dark panelled nooks and crannies, dim lighting, impressive original bar and a cosmopolitan crowd of locals, many of whom retreat from their labours in academia and medicine at this corner of the university area of Bristol. Condemned Victorian prisoners took their last meals here; today's crowd are more fortunate, revelling in beers such as Bath Ales and chowing down on no-nonsense pub fare like fish pie, sausage and mash or burgers. Other benefits include no music or fruit machines and a heated garden terrace.

Open all day all wk 12-12 (Sun 12-11) Closed 25 Dec eve, 26 Dec L, 1 Jan L **Food** Lunch Mon-Fri 12-2, Sat 12-2.30, Sun 12-3 Dinner Mon-Fri 5.30-8.30 Av main course £7.50 ⊕ YOUNG'S ◀ London Gold & Bitter, Bath Gem, St Austell Tribute, Guest ales Ö Addlestones, Thatchers Gold. **Facilities** Non-diners area ♦♦ Garden ⌖ WiFi ▱ (notice required) **Notes** ☺

The Kensington Arms
PICK OF THE PUBS

tel: 0117 944 6444 **35-37 Stanley Rd BS6 6NP**
email: info@thekensingtonarms.co.uk
dir: *From Redland Rail Station into South Rd, then Kensington Rd. 4th right into Stanley Rd*

Buzzy backstreet local with a reputation for good food

On a tucked away corner in the leafy backstreets of Bristol's desirable Redland district, this Victorian pub still attracts discerning drinkers but the food has a strong local following. The dining room is packed with mismatched antique furniture, Victorian prints and views into the open kitchen. The modern British food utilises the very best local produce and the menu changes daily, with meat from the region's farms and fish delivered daily from Cornwall. In the bar, try a salt beef sandwich or pollock goujons with tartare sauce with your pint of Old Golden Hen.

Typical restaurant dishes in the evening are starters of pig's head croquette and sauce gribiche; or warm lentil salad and wild mushrooms. These might be followed by chicken and trotter pie with curly kale or beef rib bourguignon and parsnip mash. Finish with lemon curd doughnuts; salted caramel ice cream or a selection of artisan cheeses.

Open all day all wk Closed 25 & 26 Dec **Food** Lunch Mon-Fri 12-3, Sat 10-3 Dinner Mon-Sat 6-10 Av main course £11 Restaurant menu available all wk ⊕ GREENE KING ◼ Morland Old Golden Hen, Hardys & Hansons Olde Trip ♻ Westons Stowford Press, Thatchers Gold. ♟ 14 **Facilities** Non-diners area ❧ (Bar Restaurant Outside area) ♦ Children's portions Outside area ⋒ WiFi ⛟ (notice required)

BUCKINGHAMSHIRE

AMERSHAM
Map 6 SU99

Hit or Miss Inn

tel: 01494 713109 **Penn Street Village HP7 0PX**
email: hit@ourpubs.co.uk
dir: M25 junct 18, A404 (Amersham to High Wycombe road) to Amersham. Past crematorium on right, 2nd left into Whielden Ln (signed Winchmore Hill). 1.25m, pub on right

A dining pub that is certainly a hit

Overlooking the cricket ground from which its name is taken, this is an 18th-century cottage-style dining pub. It has a beautiful country garden with lawn, patio and picnic tables for warmer days, while inside you'll find fires, old-world beams, Badger ales and a warm welcome from landlords Michael and Mary Macken, who have been running the pub for over ten years. Options on the menu range from tempting sandwiches and baked potatoes to dishes like confit duck leg, red cabbage, walnuts and spinach sauce. There are daily specials, Sunday roasts and a children's menu, too. There is a village beer festival in mid-July.

Open all day all wk 11-11 (Sun 12-10.30) **Food** Lunch Mon-Fri 12-2.30, Sat 12-3, Sun 12-8 Dinner Mon-Sat 6.30-9.30, Sun 12-8 ⊕ HALL & WOODHOUSE ◼ Badger Dorset Best, Tanglefoot, K&B Sussex, Badger Firkin Fox ♻ Westons Stowford Press. ♟ 14 **Facilities** Non-diners area ❧ (Bar Restaurant Garden) ♦ Children's menu Children's portions Garden ⋒ Beer festival Parking WiFi ⛟ (notice required)

AYLESBURY
Map 11 SP81

The King's Head

tel: 01296 718812 **Market Square HP20 2RW**
email: info@farmersbar.co.uk
dir: Access on foot only. From Market Square access cobbled passageway. Pub entrance under archway on right

Brewery tap for the Chiltern microbrewery

Henry VIII reputedly wooed Anne Boleyn when staying at this well-preserved coaching inn dating from 1455. Today, The King's Head is the award-winning brewery tap for the Chiltern Brewery, one of the oldest microbreweries in the country. In addition, there is a special weekly gravity beer, served from a wooden cask atop the bar. Enjoy a pint in the ancient cobbled courtyard; or dine on porter glazed ham, wild mushroom and goats' cheese Wellington, club sandwich or beef in beer stew. Rothschild's supplies the wines from its former family seat at nearby National Trust-owned Waddesdon Manor. Contact the pub for details of the beer festivals.

Open all day all wk 11-11 (Sun 12-10.30) Closed 25 Dec **Food** Lunch Mon-Fri 12-2, Sat-Sun 12-3 ⊕ FREE HOUSE/CHILTERN BREWERY ◼ Beechwood Bitter, Chiltern Ale, 300s Old Ale ♻ Westons Stowford Press & Wyld Wood Organic. ♟ 11 **Facilities** Non-diners area ♦ Children's menu Children's portions Garden ⋒ Beer festival ⛟ (notice required)

BEACONSFIELD
Map 6 SU99

The Red Lion Knotty Green

tel: 01494 680888 **Penn Rd, Knotty Green HP9 2TN**
email: info@myredlion.com
dir: M40 junct 2, A355 signed Beaconsfield. At 2nd mini rdbt right onto A355 signed Amersham. Over railway, left into Ledborough Ln signed Penn. At T-junct right on B474 Haslemere & Penn. Pub on left

Delightful country pub with a literary past

The gallery of original Noddy prints and library of Enid Blyton books in the Snuggery is explained by the fact that the famous children's author lived most of her life in the hamlet, and this old pub was her local. From a menu declaring, somewhat tongue in cheek, "The finest food in all of Knotty Green!", dining possibilities include salmon and watercress Wellington; spicy Mexican chicken; mushroom or seafood risotto; a selection of pizzas; lemon sponge pudding and Belgian waffles. At the front, there's decking with tables and chairs.

Open all wk 12-3 5-11 (Mon 5-11, Fri 12-3 5-1am, Sat 12-12, Sun 12-8) **Food** Lunch Tue-Fri 12-3, Sat 12-9, Sun 12-5 Dinner Tue-Thu 5-8.30, Fri 6-9.30, Sat 12-9, Sun 12-5 Av main course £9 Restaurant menu available Tue-Sun ⊕ PUNCH TAVERNS ◼ Young's, Wells Bombardier ♻ Westons Stowford Press. ♟ 10 **Facilities** Non-diners area ❧ (Bar Garden) ♦ Children's menu Children's portions Garden ⋒ Beer festival Parking WiFi ⛟ (notice required)

The Royal Standard of England
PICK OF THE PUBS

tel: 01494 673382 **Brindle Ln, Forty Green HP9 1XT**
email: theoldestpub@btinternet.com
dir: A40 to Beaconsfield, right at church rdbt onto B474 towards Penn, left into Forty Green Rd, 1m

Historic inn renowned for its beers and game dishes

Tucked away in The Chilterns on a site where ale has been provided since Saxon times, this is said to be the oldest freehouse in England. Many people visit this gabled, idyllic pub to quaff the ales flowing from the pub's own microbrewery, complementing other beers brewed in the surrounding chalk hills and a range of Somerset farm ciders and Herefordshire perry. Hearty food is the order of the day on the quality menus, served amid the leaded windows, quirky artefacts, ancient pillars and beams and flagstone floors, warmed in winter by log-burners and an inglenook. Comforting pub classics include Welsh lamb's liver and bacon with mash and onion gravy or steak and kidney suet pudding, followed perhaps by hot chocolate fondant and ice cream. Keep an eye on the specials boards for seasonal game, rabbit, pigeon or venison dishes. There's a bank holiday beer and cider festival in August.

Open all day all wk 11-11 **Food** Contact pub for details ⊕ FREE HOUSE ◼ Chiltern Ale, Brakspear Bitter, Britannia IPA & Lion, Guest ales ♻ The Orchard Pig, Westons Perry, Bridge Farm Artisan Cider. ♟ 11 **Facilities** Non-diners area ❧ (Bar Restaurant Garden) ♦ Children's portions Family room Garden Beer festival Cider festival Parking WiFi ⛟

Read all about whisky in our feature on page 18

PICK OF THE PUBS

The Royal Oak

BOVINGDON GREEN Map 5 SU88

tel: 01628 488611
Frieth Rd SL7 2JF
email: info@royaloakmarlow.co.uk
web: www.royaloakmarlow.co.uk
dir: *A4155 from Marlow. 300yds right signed Bovingdon Green. 0.75m, pub on left*

Successful pub strong on seasonality

'Dogs, children and muddy boots welcome' is the friendly motto at this little old whitewashed pub, just up the hill from town on the edge of Marlow Common. It stands in sprawling, flower-filled gardens and is one of the well-regarded Salisbury Pubs mini-empire in and around the Chilterns.* Inside, it's spacious yet cosy, with dark floorboards, rich fabrics, and a wood-burning stove. All this sets the tone for early evening regulars gathered round a challenging crossword with a pint of Rebellion from Marlow, or Tutts Clump draught cider from West Berkshire. The imaginative modern British and international menu, put together with good food ethics in mind, is designed to appeal to all, beginning with 'small plates', such as potted smoked haddock and salmon with brown butter vinaigrette and corn bread; and beetroot pannacotta with Colston Bassett Blue, walnuts and crispy horseradish ice cream. Main courses cover ground from maple syrup

glazed pork belly with sea salt crackling, black pudding, celeriac mash and apple gravy; herb-crusted Cornish hake fillet with parsley gnocchi, field mushrooms, pearl onions and crispy bacon; to spiced chickpea, sweetcorn and onion burger with fat chips. Perhaps treat yourself to New York style lemon cheesecake with blueberry muffin ice cream to finish. An exclusively European wine list has 24 by the glass and a wide choice of pudding wines, including one from Worcestershire. Outside there's a sunny summer terrace, pétanque piste and, if you're lucky, red kites wheeling around in the sky.

*Alford Arms, Hemel Hempstead, Hertfordshire; and in Buckinghamshire, The Swan Inn, Denham; The Old Queens Head, Penn.

Open all day all wk 11-11 (Sun 12-10.30) Closed 25-26 Dec **Food** Lunch Mon-Fri 12-2.30, Sat 12-3, Sun all day Dinner Mon-Thu 6.30-9.30, Fri-Sat 6.30-10, Sun all day Av main course £14.75 ⊕ SALISBURY PUBS LTD ◀ Rebellion IPA, Smuggler ♨ Westons Mortimers Orchard, Tutts Clump. ♟ 24 **Facilities** Non-diners area ♣ (Bar Garden) ♦♦ Children's portions Garden ⊼ Parking WiFi

BLEDLOW
Map 5 SP70

The Lions of Bledlow

tel: 01844 343345 **Church End HP27 9PE**
web: www.lionsofbledlow.co.uk
dir: *M40 junct 6, B4009 to Princes Risborough, through Chinnor into Bledlow*

Lovely old pub often in the spotlight

This lovely old free house dates back to the 1500s and is often used as a filming location for dramas such as *Midsomer Murders, Miss Marple* and *Restless*. Low beams and careworn flooring give the pub a timeless feeling, underlined by the steam trains chugging past on the heritage railway beyond the village green. Ramblers who drop down from the wooded Chiltern scarp can fill up on generously filled baguettes and rustic home-made meals like beef lasagne with garlic bread; and hot smoked mackerel fillets with salad and boiled potatoes, boosted by daily-changing specials.

Open all wk 11.30-3 6-11 (wknds all day) **Food** Lunch all wk 12-2.30 Dinner Mon-Sat 6.30-9.30, Sun 7-9 ⊕ FREE HOUSE ◄ Wadworth 6X, Guest ales ♂ Westons Stowford Press. ₹ 12 **Facilities** Non-diners area ◄┇ Children's menu Children's portions Family room Garden ⊟ Parking ☞

BLETCHLEY
Map 11 SP83

The Crooked Billet ◉
PICK OF THE PUBS

tel: 01908 373936 **2 Westbrook End, Newton Longville MK17 ODF**
email: john@thebillet.co.uk
dir: *M1 junct 13, follow signs to Buckingham. 6m, signed at Bottledump rdbt to Newton Longville*

A high-end destination dining pub

Just down the road from the Bletchley Park is this thatched village pub. Timbers from a sailing vessel surplus to requirements around the time of Sir Francis Drake were recycled to create the core of the building. The soul of the once rural alehouse remains; crackling winter log fires (the house bacon is smoked in the inglenook) cast flickering shadows across oak beams; and there are huge lawned gardens. Top sommelier John Gilchrist and wife/chef Emma took on the run-down Billet more than a decade ago. Emma's menus are based on the finest, freshest ingredients from small, local specialist producers and suppliers, and the emphasis is on taste and modern presentation; a cosmopolitan mix of contemporary and classical with English and French influences. The carte selection reads like a gastronome's wish list; all meals are matched to particular wines. Typical dishes could be pan-fried scallops with sweet potato purée; and crispy suckling pig and bacon.

Open 12-2.30 5.30-11 (Sun 12-4 7-10.30) Closed 27-28 Dec, Mon **Food** Lunch Tue-Sat 12-2, Sun 12-3 Dinner Tue-Thu 7-9, Fri-Sat 7-9.30 ⊕ GREENE KING ◄ Ruddles Best, Abbot Ale, IPA, Guest ales ♂ Aspall. ₹ 200 **Facilities** Non-diners area ◄┇ Children's portions Garden ⊟ Parking

BOVINGDON GREEN
Map 5 SU88

The Royal Oak
PICK OF THE PUBS

See Pick of the Pubs on opposite page

BRILL
Map 11 SP61

The Pheasant Inn

tel: 01844 239370 **Windmill St HP18 9TG**
email: info@thepheasant.co.uk
dir: *In village centre, by windmill*

Stunning views from Brill's popular inn

Occupying a fine hilltop position on the edge of Brill Common, with impressive views over the Vale of Aylesbury and the Chilterns, this 17th-century beamed inn stands next to Brill Windmill, one of the oldest postmills in the country. A simple menu offers hearty modern pub dishes, including starters of chicken liver pâté with apple and ale chutney, and main courses like roasted lamb rump with celeriac and rosemary dauphinoise; and confit pork belly with cabbage and bacon, black pudding mash and apple purée. Salads, filled baps and ploughman's lunches are served at lunchtime – best enjoyed in the garden in summer.

Open all day all wk 12-11 (Fri-Sat 12-12 Sun 12-10.30) **Food** Lunch Mon-Sat 12-2, Sun 12-6 Dinner all wk 6.30-9 ⊕ FREE HOUSE ◄ A Very Pleasant Pheasant Ale (pub's own) & Guest ales ♂ Westons Family Reserve. **Facilities** Non-diners area ◄┇ Children's portions Garden ⊟ Cider festival Parking WiFi ☞ (notice required)

BUCKINGHAM
Map 11 SP63

The Old Thatched Inn

tel: 01296 712584 **Main St, Adstock MK18 2JN**
email: manager@theoldthatchedinn.co.uk **web:** www.theoldthatchedinn.co.uk
dir: *A413 from Buckingham towards Aylesbury. Approx 4m left to Adstock*

Spacious pub with plenty of original character

Once called the Chandos Arms, this lovely 17th-century thatched inn still boasts traditional beams and inglenook fireplace. The spacious interior consists of a formal conservatory and a bar with comfy furniture and a welcoming, relaxed atmosphere. Using the freshest, seasonal ingredients from local and regional suppliers, the evening menu takes in smoked mackerel rillette with cucumber and dill salad; and braised lamb neck fillet with roasted root vegetables and minted red wine gravy. Typical lunchtime dishes include pan-fried fillet of pollock with chorizo and potato hash; and Cumberland sausages with mash and onion gravy.

continued

BUCKINGHAM *continued*

The Old Thatched Inn

Open all day all wk Closed 26 Dec **Food** Lunch Mon-Fri 12-2.30, Sat 12-3, Sun 12-9 Dinner Mon-Sat 6-9.30, Sun 12-9 Set menu available Restaurant menu available all wk ⊕ FREE HOUSE ◄ Hook Norton Hooky Bitter, Morland Old Speckled Hen, Fuller's London Pride, Timothy Taylor Landlord, Sharp's Doom Bar ♂ Aspall. ♛ 14 **Facilities** Non-diners area ♣ (Bar) ♦ Children's menu Children's portions Outside area ⊟ Parking WiFi

See advert on opposite page

CHALFONT ST PETER   Map 6 TQ09

The Greyhound Inn   PICK OF THE PUBS

tel: 01753 883404 **SL9 9RA**
email: reception@thegreyhoundinn.net
dir: *M40 junct 1/M25 junct 16, follow signs for Gerrards Cross, then Chalfont St Peter*

Good food from Savoy-trained chef

Over the centuries, this old coaching inn has welcomed many a traveller, Oliver Cromwell and Winston Churchill among them. Judge Jeffreys presided over some of his famous assize courts here, often sending miscreants to the gallows overlooking the adjacent River Misbourne. Much of the pub's 14th-century character survives, particularly the massive beams, huge brick chimneys, and imposing panelled and flagstoned bar. The newly-refurbished restaurant specialises in English and Continental dishes devised by Savoy Hotel-trained head chef Nana Akuffo. Try the chicken, ham and leek pithivier with spring vegetables, fresh morels and mash; gently-spiced kedgeree with free-range poached egg; loin of lamb with kofte, boulangère potatoes and three-bean side dish; or wild mushroom Wellington with celeriac, potato purée and truffle sauce. For lunch there are sandwiches, salads, venison sausages and cod and chips. Nana's sherry trifle, and passionfruit crème brûlée will both prove tempting desserts.

Open all day all wk Mon-Wed 6.30am-10.30pm (Thu 6.30am-11.30pm Fri-Sat 6.30am-1am Sun 8.30am-10.30pm) **Food** Lunch Mon-Sat 12-2.30, Sun 12-6 Dinner Mon-Sat 6-9.30 ⊕ ENTERPRISE INNS ◄ Fuller's London Pride, Sharp's Doom Bar, Adnams. ♛ 10 **Facilities** Non-diners area ♣ (Bar Garden) ♦ Children's menu Children's portions Garden ⊟ Parking WiFi

CHENIES   Map 6 TQ09

The Red Lion   PICK OF THE PUBS

tel: 01923 282722 **WD3 6ED**
email: theredlionchenies@hotmail.co.uk
dir: *Between Rickmansworth & Amersham on A404, follow signs for Chenies & Latimer*

A true local with good food

Mike and Heather Norris like to describe their white-painted, 17th-century, Chess Valley village pub as 'autarkic'. It's a real word, meaning self-sufficient, which, as

a privately-run free house, it is. Expect a simply furnished main bar, and a charming dining area in the original cottage to the rear, with a tiled floor, inglenook and rustic furniture. Mike is an expert custodian of his beers, from Rebellion in Marlow, Vale in Brill, Wadworth in Devizes, and guest ales. Heather cooks everything, including lamb's kidneys in creamy mustard and cayenne pepper sauce on toast; fresh daily pies - try the chicken and haggis; chilli con carne; the day's grilled flat fish; and chef's risotto. Daily specials are chalked up, along with home-made puddings. Heather also prepares light meals, sandwiches and filled jacket potatoes. Outside, on the pub's sunny side, is a small seating area.

Open all wk Mon-Fri 11-2.30 5.30-11 (Sat 11-11 Sun 12-10.30) Closed 25 Dec **Food** Lunch Mon- Fri 12-2, Sat 11-10, Sun 12-9 Dinner Mon-Fri 7-10, Sat 11-10, Sun 12-9 ⊕ FREE HOUSE ◄ Wadworth 6X, Rebellion Lion's Pride, Vale Best Bitter, Guest ales ♂ Thatchers Gold. ♛ 10 **Facilities** Garden Outside area ⊟ Parking

CHESHAM   Map 6 SP90

The Black Horse Inn

tel: 01494 784656 **Chesham Vale HP5 3NS**
email: enquiries@black-horse-inn.co.uk
dir: *A41 from Berkhamsted, A416 through Ashley Green, 0.75m before Chesham right to Vale Rd, at bottom of Nashleigh Hill, 1m, inn on left*

Traditional Chilterns' pub without modern intrusions

This 500-year-old pub is set in some beautiful valley countryside and is ideal for enjoying a cosy, traditional environment without electronic games or music. During the winter there are roaring log fires to take the chill off those who may spot one of the resident ghosts. An ever-changing menu includes an extensive range of snacks, while the main menu features hearty lamb casserole; baked fillet of sea bass with prawns in garlic butter; home-made pies; and steaks. In summer, why not eat in the large garden?

Open 12-3 6-11 (Sun 12-6) Closed Sun eve **Food** Lunch Mon-Sat 12-2, Sun 12-3 Dinner Mon-Sat 6-9 Set menu available ⊕ PUNCH TAVERNS ◄ Tring Side Pocket for a Toad, Fuller's London Pride, 2 Guest ales ♂ Westons Stowford Press. **Facilities** Non-diners area ♣ (Bar Garden) ♦ Children's portions Garden ⊟ Beer festival Parking WiFi ▭ (notice required)

The Swan

tel: 01494 783075 **Ley Hill HP5 1UT**
email: swanleyhill@btconnect.com
dir: *1.5m E of Chesham by golf course*

A warm welcome and a cosy fire

Set in the delightful village of Ley Hill, this beautiful 16th-century pub this was once the place where condemned prisoners would drink a 'last and final ale' on the way to the nearby gallows. During World War II, Glen Miller and Clark Gable cycled here for a pint from the Air Force base at Bovingdon. These days, it is a free house offering a warm welcome, real ales and good food, plus a large inglenook fireplace and original beams. Fillet of salmon with crayfish; chicken and chorizo tagliatelle; and home-made steak and kidney pie are typical choices. Look out for the Bank Holiday beer festival in August.

Open 12-2.30 5.30-11 (Sun 12-4) Closed Mon **Food** Lunch Tue-Sat 12-2.30 Dinner Tue-Sat 6.30-9.30 ⊕ FREE HOUSE ◄ St Austell Tribute, Timothy Taylor Landlord, Tring Side Pocket for a Toad, Guest ales. **Facilities** Non-diners area ♣ (Garden) ♦ Children's menu Garden ⊟ Beer festival Parking ▭ (notice required)

CUBLINGTON
Map 11 SP82

The Unicorn ◉◉

tel: 01296 681261 **High St LU7 0LQ**
email: theunicornpub@btconnect.com
dir: *2m N of A418 (between Aylesbury & Leighton Buzzard). In village centre*

Top Aylesbury Vale village free house

That the 17th-century Unicorn overflows with character is not surprising, given its low-beamed bar, wooden floors and real fires. Even the mismatched furniture plays its part. Relax, maybe in the secluded garden, with a pint of Sharp's Doom Bar or Long Crendon's XT. Two AA Rosettes recognise the inventive dishes on the seasonal menus, such as white onion, garlic and potato soup; pan-fried pollack with garlic new potatoes; or roasted field mushrooms with baked sage dumplings and mustard cream sauce. Finish with lemon meringue Eton Mess with kiwi sorbet perhaps. Events include quiz nights and May and Summer Bank Holiday beer festivals featuring 12 real ales and ciders.

Open all day all wk 10.30am-11pm (Fri-Sat 10.30am-mdnt) **Food** Lunch Mon-Sat 12-2, Sun 12-3 Dinner all wk 6.30-9 Restaurant menu available all wk ⊕ FREE HOUSE ◀ Sharp's Doom Bar, Timothy Taylor Landlord, Long Crendon XT ♂ Westons Stowford Press, Thatchers. **Facilities** Non-diners area ❖ (Bar Garden) ♦♦ Children's menu Children's portions Play area Garden ⊫ Beer festival Parking WiFi ▦ (notice required)

CUDDINGTON
Map 5 SP71

The Crown
PICK OF THE PUBS

tel: 01844 292222 **Spurt St HP18 0BB**
email: david@djbbars.com
dir: *From A418 between Thame & Aylesbury follow Cuddington signs. Pub in village centre*

Atmospheric pub offering a modern menu with international influences

This thatched and whitewashed listed pub sits in the picturesque village of Cuddington. The Crown's atmospheric interior includes a locals' bar and several low-beamed dining areas lit by candles in the evening. Fuller's London Pride, Adnams and guest ales are on tap, and there's also an extensive wine list, with 12 by the glass, and Symonds cider. The well thought out menu might include lamb koftas, tzatziki and pitta bread to start, followed by seared tuna steak with stir-fried vegetables, sunblush tomato and basil dressing; and salmon streak with citrus cream cheese and filo pastry crust, orange salad and new potatoes. Seafood is a big draw here. Among other modern options are belly pork, black pudding and apple hash, Parmentier potatoes, apple and cider sauce; and Gressingham duck breast, celeriac purée, roast potatoes, blackberry compôte and parsnip crisps. Look to the blackboard for daily specials or the set menu for good value options. A compact patio area provides outside seating.

Open all wk 12-3 6-11 (Sun all day) **Food** Lunch all wk 12-2.15 Dinner Mon-Sat 6.30-9.15 ⊕ FULLER'S ◀ London Pride & ESB, Adnams, Guest ales ♂ Symonds. ♀ 12 **Facilities** Non-diners area ♦♦ Children's portions Outside area ⊫ Parking WiFi ▦ (notice required)

DENHAM
Map 6 TQ08

The Falcon Inn ★★★★ INN

tel: 01895 832125 **Village Rd UB9 5BE**
email: mail@falcondenham.com web: www.falcondenham.com
dir: *M40 junct 1, follow A40/Gerrards Cross signs. Approx 200yds, right into Old Mill Rd. Pass church on right. Pub opposite village green on left*

The heart and soul of a conservation village

Barely 17 miles as the crow flies, yet central London seems light years away from this lovely 16th-century coaching inn opposite the village green. Expect well-kept Brakspear, Timothy Taylor and Wells real ales. Brasserie food includes pan-fried sea bass; stuffed chicken with chorizo; and steak and Merlot pie with chips and seasonal vegetables. The menu also lists pub classics such as beer-battered cod; and ham, egg and chips; check the daily specials too. Other attractions are a south-facing terraced garden and four bedrooms, two of which have original oak beams.

Open all day all wk **Food** Lunch Mon-Sat 11-3, Sun 12-6 Dinner Mon-Sat 5-9.30, Sun 12-6 Restaurant menu available Mon-Sat ⊕ ENTERPRISE INNS ◀ Timothy Taylor Landlord, Wells Bombardier, Brakspear ♂ Westons Stowford Press. ♀ 10 **Facilities** Non-diners area ❖ (Bar Garden) ♦♦ Children's portions Family room Garden ⊫ Beer festival Cider festival WiFi ▦ (notice required) **Rooms** 4

The Swan Inn
PICK OF THE PUBS

See Pick of the Pubs on opposite page

DORNEY
Map 6 SU97

The Palmer Arms

tel: 01628 666612 **Village Rd SL4 6QW**
email: chrys@thepalmerarms.com
dir: *From A4 take B3026, over M4 to Dorney*

Community pub with a suntrap garden

Built in the 15th century with wooden beams and open fires, this family-friendly pub in the pretty conservation village of Dorney is just a short stroll from the Thames Path and Boveney Lock. The interior is contemporary and the menu combines both modern and classic British dishes, which can be accompanied by wines from the comprehensive list. Scottish salmon gravad lax may precede a main of pan-fried venison medallions. There is a lighter lunch menu, roasts on Sundays and tasting menu evenings. A summer beer festival features local beers and ciders.

Open all day all wk 11am-11.30pm (Sun 12-10.30) **Food** Contact pub for details ⊕ GREENE KING ◀ Abbot Ale & IPA, Guinness ♂ Aspall. ♀ 18 **Facilities** Non-diners area ❖ (Bar Garden) ♦♦ Children's menu Children's portions Play area Garden ⊫ Beer festival Parking ▦ (notice required)

EASINGTON
Map 5 SP61

Mole and Chicken
PICK OF THE PUBS

tel: 01844 208387 **HP18 9EY**
email: chef@themoleandchicken.co.uk
dir: *M40 juncts 8 or 8a, A418 to Thame. At rdbt left onto B4011 signed Long Crendon & Bicester. In Long Crendon right into Carters Lane signed Dorton & Chilton. At T-junct left into Chilton Rd signed Chilton. Approx 0.75m to pub*

Almost in the middle of nowhere, but really worth finding

The whimsical sign outside Steve and Suzanne Bush's pub shows both creatures in silhouette enjoying a clearly bibulous meal. The name recalls two long-gone landlords, 'Moley' and 'Johnny Chick'. On the Oxfordshire-Buckinghamshire border, it was built in 1831 as housing for estate workers, later becoming the village store and beer and cider house. The views across what must be half a county from its high terraced garden are magnificent, while inside it's a combination of exposed beams, flagged floors and smart, contemporary furniture. Village-brewed XT and Vale brewery's Easington Best are on tap, alongside Long Crendon cider. From a British and eastern Mediterranean-influenced menu, a typical meal would be seared scallops, samphire risotto and black pudding, then braised shoulder of lamb, creamed spinach, Heritage potatoes and fresh mint; ending with sticky toffee pudding and caramel ice cream. Bar dishes include flaked chicken and noodle laksa, an Asian spicy noodle soup.

Open all day all wk Closed 25 Dec **Food** Lunch Mon-Sat 12-2.30, Sun 12-4 Dinner Mon-Sat 6.30-9.30, Sun 6-9 Av main course £12 Restaurant menu available all wk ⊕ FREE HOUSE ◀ XT4, Easington Best (pubs own) ♂ Long Crendon Ciders. **Facilities** Non-diners area ♦♦ Children's menu Children's portions Play area Garden ⊫ Parking WiFi ▦

PICK OF THE PUBS

The Swan Inn

DENHAM   Map 6 TQ08

tel: 01895 832085
Village Rd UB9 5BH
email: info@swaninndenham.co.uk
web: www.swaninndenham.co.uk
dir: *A40 onto A412. 200yds follow 'Denham village' sign. Through village, over bridge, last pub on left*

Good beer and good food both prove a draw

In the picturesque village of Denham, this Georgian, double-fronted inn covered in wisteria feels tucked away in the country and yet it's surprisingly close to London and motorways. It's one of the well-regarded Salisbury Pubs mini-empire in and around the Chilterns.* The traditional country inn's large log fire and collection of rather interesting pictures picked up at auction give it a really homely feel. Outside, a secluded terrace and large gardens are ideal for families. Locals help to maintain a thriving bar trade, drawn in by well-kept Marlow Rebellion IPA and guests, perhaps Caledonian's Flying Scotsman. However, the food also attracts a following: fresh seasonal produce underpins a menu and daily specials that feature more than a few old favourites, some with a twist. For a starter, look to the 'small plates' section of the menu for slow cooked duck faggot, caramelised rhubarb and honey braised beetroot. Then, among the 'big

plates' you'll find plenty of variety, perhaps pan-fried skate wing with buttered samphire, crispy capers and new potatoes; Rebellion IPA beer-battered whiting fillet with pea purée and hand-cut chips; roasted red pepper, Somerset brie and black olive puff pastry tart; or slow-cooked English beef cheek cottage pie with cheddar mash and sautéed sprout tops. Among the puddings are brioche apple doughnuts and custard dip; and warm dark chocolate brownie with mint ice cream. An exclusively European wine list includes 24 by the glass and a wide choice of pudding wines. A private dining room is also available.

*Alford Arms, Hemel Hempstead, Hertfordshire; and in Buckinghamshire, The Royal Oak, Bovingdon Green; The Old Queens Head, Penn

Open all day all wk 11-11 (Sun 12-10.30) Closed 25-26 Dec **Food** Lunch Mon-Fri 12-2.30, Sat 12-3, Sun all day Dinner Mon-Thu 6.30-9.30, Fri-Sat 6.30-10 Av main course £14.75 ⊕ SALISBURY PUBS LTD ◖ Rebellion IPA, Caledonian Flying Scotsman ♂ Westons Mortimers Orchard. ♟ 24 **Facilities** Non-diners area ♣ (Bar Garden) ♦ Children's portions Garden ♫ Parking WiFi

---

FARNHAM COMMON
Map 6 SU98

The Foresters

tel: 01753 643340 **The Broadway SL2 3QQ**
email: info@theforesterspub.com
dir: *Phone for detailed directions*

Well-chosen dishes in an eclectic setting

This handsome 1930s building has an interior where old meets new – crystal chandeliers and log fires, real ales and cocktails, glass-topped tables and wooden floors, chesterfields and velvet thrones. Opt for a starter of English asparagus with poached egg and hollandaise sauce, or one of the 'mini dishes' – perhaps prawn popcorn with sweet and sour sauce, or tempura green beans with sake dip. Typical main dishes include sea bream stuffed with aromatic herbs, under a sea salt crust with fennel salad; and pulled pork and cider risotto with crispy sage leaves and 'petty pommes'. Choose something sweet from the list of dessert tapas. There are front and rear gardens.

Open all day all wk **Food** Lunch all wk 12-3 Dinner all wk 6.30-10 Av main course £16.50 Set menu available Restaurant menu available all wk ⊕ PUNCH TAVERNS ◀ Fuller's London Pride, Young's, Sharp's Doom Bar, Guest ales Ŏ Thatchers Gold. ☻ 16 **Facilities** Non-diners area ❧ (Bar Garden) ◆◆ Children's menu Children's portions Garden ⊭ Parking WiFi ⟴ (notice required)

FARNHAM ROYAL
Map 6 SU98

The Emperor

tel: 01753 643006 **Blackpond Ln SL2 3EG**
email: bookings@theemperorpub.co.uk
dir: *Phone for detailed directions*

A pub for all seasons

Off the beaten track, this village inn with an attractive whitewashed façade is over 100 years old. Polished wood floors and original beams run through the bar, conservatory and front, and there is a log fire in winter and alfresco tables in the summer. Owned by actor Dennis Waterman and his friend Martin Flood, The Emperor has continued to be a friendly local pub with traditional values. British favourites based on fresh seasonal fare, together with a handful of pizzas, drive the daily specials and à la carte menus, which might include pigeon breast, black pudding with a crispy poached egg followed by Cornish fillet of sea bass fillet, crayfish and crab risotto. Contact the pub for details of their beer festival.

Open all day all wk **Food** Lunch Mon-Sat 12-3, Sun 12-6 Dinner Mon-Sat 6-10, Sun 12-6 ⊕ ORIGINAL PUB CO LTD ◀ Fuller's London Pride, Rebellion, 3 Guest ales. ☻ 8 **Facilities** Non-diners area ❧ (Bar Garden) ◆◆ Children's menu Children's portions Garden ⊭ Beer festival Parking WiFi ⟴ (notice required)

FRIETH
Map 5 SU79

The Prince Albert

tel: 01494 881683 **RG9 6PY**
dir: *4m N of Marlow. Follow Frieth road from Marlow. Straight across at x-rds on Fingest road. Pub 200yds on left*

A peaceful retreat and traditional pub grub

There's no television, jukebox or electronic games in this cottagey Chiltern Hills pub. What you get instead, surprise, surprise, is just good conversation, probably much as when it was built in the 1700s. In the bar, low beams, a big black inglenook stove, high-backed settles and lots of copper pots and pans; an alternative place to enjoy a pint of Brakspear is a seat in the garden, while admiring the woods and

fields. A short menu sources locally for traditional pub food: sandwiches; filled jacket potatoes; Hambleden Valley sausages and mash; gammon steak, egg and chips; and smoked salmon with prawn salad.

Open all day all wk 11-11 (Sun 12-10.30) **Food** Lunch Mon-Sat 12.15-2.30, Sun 12.30-3 Dinner Fri-Sat 7.30-9.30 ⊕ BRAKSPEAR ◀ Bitter, Seasonal ales. ☻ 9 **Facilities** Non-diners area ❧ (Bar Garden) ◆◆ Children's portions Garden ⊭ Parking

---

GERRARDS CROSS
Map 6 TQ08

The Three Oaks

tel: 01753 899016 **Austenwood Ln SL9 8NL**
email: info@thethreeoaksgx.co.uk
dir: *From A40 at lights take B416 (Packhorse Rd) signed Village Centre. Over railway. Left signed Gold Hill into Austenwood Ln. Pub on right*

Contemporary gastro-pub with relaxed feel

Part of a small gastro-pub group in the Thames Valley, The Three Oaks is in the heart of affluent Gerrards Cross. Like the other two 'Oaks' (the White Oak & Greene Oak in Berkshire), it is a stylish dining venue with a smart, contemporary feel, yet the vibe is relaxed and informal. Drop by for a pint of local Rebellion Ale or a glass of unoaked Chardonnay and tuck into the cracking value set lunch menu, or perhaps potted salt beef, pickled heritage carrots and horseradish cream, followed by Cornish lamb rump, tzatziki, spiced red cabbage purée, kale potato terrine, and then lemon crémeux and blackcurrant sorbet. There's a super terrace for alfresco dining, and don't miss the summer beer festival.

Open all wk **Food** Lunch Mon-Sat 12-2.30, Sun 12-6 Dinner Mon-Sat 6.30-9.30 Av main course £15 Set menu available Restaurant menu available all wk ⊕ ENTERPRISE INNS ◀ Fuller's London Pride, Rebellion & IPA Ŏ Aspall. ☻ 24 **Facilities** Non-diners area ◆◆ Children's menu Children's portions Garden ⊭ Beer festival Parking WiFi ⟴ (notice required)

GREAT HAMPDEN
Map 5 SP80

The Hampden Arms

tel: 01494 488255 **HP16 9RQ**
email: louise.lucas@outlook.com
dir: *M40 junct 4, A4010, right before Princes Risborough. Great Hampden signed*

Home-cooked food at lovely countryside inn

The large garden of this mock-Tudor free house on the wooded Hampden Estate sits beside the common, where you might watch a game of cricket during the season. Chef-proprietor Constantine Lucas includes some Greek signature dishes such as kleftiko and Greek salad alongside more traditional choices such as fish crumble; aubergine and tomato lasagne; and duck breast with a wild mushroom and brandy sauce; blackboard specials add to the choices. The pub has a secure beer garden, ideal for private functions.

Open all wk 12-3 6-12 **Food** Lunch Mon-Sat 12-2, Sun 12-3 Dinner Mon-Sat 6-9.30, Sun 7-9.30 Set menu available Restaurant menu available all wk ⊕ FREE HOUSE ◀ Fuller's London Pride, Chiltern, Rebellion, Guest ales Ŏ Addlestones. **Facilities** Non-diners area ◆◆ Children's menu Children's portions Family room Garden ⊭ Beer festival Parking WiFi

---

GREAT MISSENDEN
Map 6 SP80

The Nags Head ★★★★ INN ⊛   **PICK OF THE PUBS**

See Pick of the Pubs on opposite page

PICK OF THE PUBS

The Nags Head ★★★★ INN 🌹

GREAT MISSENDEN   Map 6 SP80

tel: 01494 862200
London Rd HP16 0DG
email: goodfood@nagsheadbucks.com
web: www.nagsheadbucks.com
dir: *N of Amersham on A413, left at Chiltern hospital into London Rd signed Great Missenden*

Charming rural pub with excellent Anglo-French cooking

The late Roald Dahl used to be a regular here and the dining room is decorated with limited edition prints by the children's author, who drew inspiration from the pub for his famous book *Fantastic Mr Fox*. Originally three small workers' cottages whose inhabitants made spindles for chairs, the Nags Head became a coaching inn in the 16th-century and was a popular stop for travellers and their horses commuting from the midlands to London. Tucked away in the sleepy valley of the River Misbourne in the picturesque Chiltern Hills, the pub has been restored by the Michaels family, who sprinkled similar magic dust on sister pub the Bricklayers Arms in Flaunden, Hertfordshire. The family has helped the Nags Head to gain a formidable reputation for food and hospitality. Low oak beams and an inglenook fireplace have been carefully retained as a backdrop for the stylish new bar, where drinkers can enjoy one of the real ales, perhaps from the Tring

brewery. Food is taken seriously here, and executive head chef Claude Paillet sources the finest ingredients from local suppliers wherever possible, for a menu fusing English with French. Lunch and dinner menus may offer starters like poached egg cocotte, Swiss chard with Stilton cream; or goose rillette with pear chutney and toast. Main courses range from pan-fried pink trout with crayfish and parsley sauce; to slow-cooked beef bavette in red wine. Leave room for warm apple and rhubarb tart or chocolate and honey fondant with pistachio ice cream. In summer, relax over a drink or a meal whilst gazing out across the Chiltern Hills from the pub's lovely garden. Alternatively, stay overnight in one of the five beautiful bedrooms.

Open all day all week Closed 25 Dec
Food Lunch Mon-Sat 12-2.30, Sun 12-3.30 Dinner Mon-Sat 6.30-9.30, Sun 6-8.30 Set menu available, Restaurant menu available all week. ⊕ FREE HOUSE
🍺 Rebellion, Tring, Vale, Sharp's Doom Bar 🍎 Aspall. ♟ 19 **Facilities**
Non-diners area 🐾 (Bar Garden)
👪 Children's portions Garden 🪑 Parking
WiFi **Rooms** 5

GREAT MISSENDEN *continued*

The Polecat Inn | PICK OF THE PUBS

tel: 01494 862253 **170 Wycombe Rd, Prestwood HP16 OHJ**
email: polecatinn@btinternet.com
dir: *On A4128 between Great Missenden & High Wycombe*

The large garden is a big draw here

The Polecat, with its flower baskets and partial timber framing, dates back to the 17th century, and the beautiful three-acre garden, set amidst rolling Chilterns' countryside, is part of its great attraction. John Gamble bought the run down property over 20 years ago, then renovated and extended it to create an attractive free house that still retains many original features. The small low-beamed rooms radiating from the central bar give many options when it comes to choosing where to eat or sup a pint of Adnams Broadside. Dishes are prepared from local ingredients, including herbs from the garden. Lunchtime snacks are backed by a menu with plenty of choices, from a starter of Portobello mushroom, garlic and cream on onion bread crostini; to main courses such as salmon en croûte with watercress sauce; chicken forestière; and Cumberland sausage with onion gravy and cheddar bubble-and-squeak; and for pudding, vanilla sponge cheesecake with mulled berries. Daily blackboard specials add to the choices.

Open 11-2.30 6-11 (Sun 12-3) Closed 25-26 Dec, 1 Jan, Sun eve **Food** Lunch all wk 12-2 Dinner Mon-Sat 6.30-9 Av main course £12 ⊕ FREE HOUSE ◀ Brakspear Bitter, Ringwood Best Bitter, Skinner's Betty Stogs, Adnams Broadside ♂ Thatchers Gold. ⬤ 16 **Facilities** Non-diners area ♦♦ Children's portions Play area Family room Garden ⋒ Parking ⬛ (notice required)

GROVE | Map 11 SP92

Grove Lock

tel: 01525 380940 **LU7 OQU**
email: grovelock@fullers.co.uk
dir: *From A4146 (S of Leighton Buzzard) take B4146 signed Ivinghoe & Tring. Pub 0.5m on left*

Perfect atmosphere in summer and winter

This pub is situated next to Lock 28 on the Grand Union Canal, and is less than a mile from the scene of the 1963 Great Train Robbery. Its lofty open-plan bar has leather sofas, assorted tables and chairs and canal-themed artworks. The restaurant, once the lock-keeper's cottage, serves breaded chicken Caesar salad; butternut squash risotto; sausages and mash; and smoked belly of pork. Plenty of outdoor seating means you can watch the barges, while enjoying a pint of Fuller's. Catch a summer barbecue and hog roast.

Open all day all wk Mon-Sat 11-11 (Sun 11-10.30) **Food** Lunch Mon-Sat 12-9 Dinner Sun 12-7 ⊕ FULLER'S ◀ London Pride, Chiswick Bitter, Organic Honey Dew ♂ Aspall. ⬤ 14 **Facilities** Non-diners area ♦♦ Children's menu Children's portions Garden ⋒ Parking WiFi

HAMBLEDEN | Map 5 SU78

The Stag & Huntsman Inn ★★★★ INN

tel: 01491 571227 **RG9 6RP**
email: jaxon@thestagandhuntsman.co.uk web: www.thestagandhuntsman.co.uk
dir: *5m from Henley-on-Thames on A4155 towards Marlow, left at Mill End towards Hambleden*

Lovingly restored inn retaining old world charm

Close to the glorious beech-clad Chilterns, this 400-year-old brick and flint village pub has featured in countless films and television series. Ever-changing guest ales are served in the public bar, larger lounge bar and cosy snug. Food is available in the bars as well as the dining room, from an extensive menu of home-made pub favourites prepared with local seasonal produce. Opt for the likes of pan-fried fillet of salmon; rib-eye steak; or oven-roasted peppers filled with spiced couscous. Hambleden Estate game features strongly when in season, and there is a pizza and barbecue menu to enjoy in the garden during the summer months.

Open all wk 11-11 **Food** Lunch all wk 12-2.30 Dinner all wk 6-9 ⊕ FREE HOUSE ◀ Rebellion, Sharp's, Loddon, Guest ales ♂ Westons Stowford Press. **Facilities** ❀ (Bar Garden) ♦♦ Garden ⋒ Parking ⬛ **Rooms** 9

HEDGERLEY | Map 6 SU98

The White Horse

tel: 01753 643225 **SL2 3UY**
dir: *Phone for detailed directions*

One for the beer festival follower

An ale drinker's paradise if ever there was one, parts of which date back 500 years. With three beer festivals a year (Easter, Spring Bank Holiday and Summer Bank Holiday) and barely a pause between them, this pub can almost claim to run a single year-long celebration, with over 1,000 real ales consumed annually. Real cider and Belgian bottled beers augment the already mammoth range. A large well-kept garden at the rear hosts summer barbecues; otherwise the menu of home-cooked pub favourites ranges from a salad bar with quiches, sandwiches and ploughman's, through to curries, chilli, pasta dishes, pies and steaks (lunchtime only).

Open all wk 11-2.30 5-11 (Sat 11-11 Sun 11-10.30) **Food** Lunch Mon-Fri 12-2, Sat-Sun 12-2.30 ⊕ FREE HOUSE ◀ 8 rotating ales ♂ 3 guest ciders. ⬤ 10 **Facilities** Non-diners area ❀ (Bar Garden) ♦♦ Children's portions Family room Garden ⋒ Beer festival Parking ⬛

HIGH WYCOMBE
Map 5 SU89

The Sausage Tree

tel: 01494 452204 **Saffron Rd HP13 6AB**
email: sausagetreepub@hotmail.co.uk
dir: *M40 junct 4, A404 signed Town Centre & Amersham. At rdbt 2nd exit signed Beaconsfield, Amersham, A404. At rdbt 2nd exit signed Beaconsfield. Left into Stuart Rd, left into Easton Terrace, left into Saffron Rd*

Chilterns' pub specialising in sausages

For a mind-boggling choice of sausages made from exotic meats or unusual ingredients, perhaps, pork, banana and honey, then look no further than this pub on the outskirts of High Wycombe. Deciding just which types of sausage to tuck into is difficult: pheasant and whisky; hot garlic; tipsy turkey, or kangaroo are just a few examples. Maybe plump instead for one of the 100 speciality beers on offer, or a pint of local Rebellion Ale, with a 16oz rump steak or a seafood kebab cooked at your table on fearsomely hot volcanic rock platters.

Open all wk 12-3 5-11 (Sun 12-6) Closed Sat L **Food** Lunch Mon-Fri 12-3, Sun 12-6 Dinner Mon-Sat 6-9.45 Av main course £14 Restaurant menu available all wk ⊕ ENTERPRISE INNS ◀ Rebellion Ales. ♥ **Facilities** ♦ Children's portions Outside area ⏞ Parking WiFi

LACEY GREEN
Map 5 SP80

The Whip Inn

tel: 01844 344060 **Pink Rd HP27 0PG**
dir: *1m from A4010 (Princes Risborough to High Wycombe road). Adjacent to windmill*

Traditional pub popular with walkers and cyclists

Standing high above the Vale of Aylesbury in the heart of the Chiltern Hills, the beer garden of this 200-year-old pub overlooks the Lacey Green windmill. Ramblers on the Chiltern Way join locals in appreciating some of 800 different real ales offered each year, as well as real Millwhites cider. A robust menu of home-made classic favourites such as ham, egg and chips and chargrilled steaks seals the deal at this rustic, music- and fruit-machine-free country inn. The Whip holds a beer festival twice a year in May and September.

Open all day all wk **Food** Lunch Mon-Sat 12-2.30, Sun 12-3 Dinner Mon-Sat 6.30-9 ⊕ FREE HOUSE ◀ Over 800 guest ales a year Ŏ Thatchers, Millwhites. ♥ 22 **Facilities** Non-diners area ♦ Children's menu Children's portions Garden ⏞ Beer festival Parking

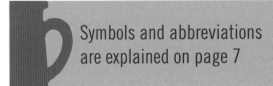
Symbols and abbreviations
are explained on page 7

LANE END
Map 5 SU89

Grouse & Ale

tel: 01494 882299 **High St HP14 3JG**
email: info@grouseandale.co.uk **web:** www.grouseandale.com
dir: *On B482 in village*

Smart pub with modern menus

For nearly a century before a major refurbishment a few years ago this had been The Clayton Arms, named after Sir Robert Clayton who, in 1679, built it to live in on becoming Lord Mayor of London. One of the draws is the cosy bar and dining area, where you can relax with the papers and a pint of Adnams Broadside or Caledonian Deuchars. The menu lists modern pub food such as chicken saltimbocca; beer-battered haddock; pork tenderloin; and spiced lentil and root vegetable hotpot. Daily specials supplement the main menu. The suntrap courtyard can be a good place to eat.

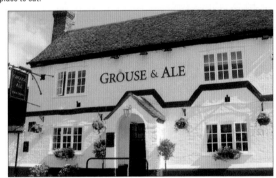

Open all day all wk **Food** Lunch Mon-Sat 12-2.30, Sun 12-4 Dinner Mon-Sat 6-9.30 ⊕ STAR PUBS & BARS ◀ Adnams Broadside, Caledonian Deuchars IPA, Courage. ♥ 27 **Facilities** Non-diners area ❀ (Bar Outside area) ♦ Children's menu Children's portions Outside area ⏞ Parking WiFi

LITTLE KINGSHILL — Map 6 SU89

The Full Moon

tel: 01494 862397 **Hare Ln HP16 0EE**
email: email@thefullmoon.info
dir: *SW of Great Missenden, accessed from either A413 or A4128*

Perfect for post-walk ales and meals

A popular post-ramble refuelling stop, especially as both dogs and children are warmly welcomed inside, this pub has a wealth of wonderful walks through the Chiltern Hills radiating from its doorstep. It is noted for its tip-top Fuller's London Pride and the weekly-changing guest ales, and the pub throngs during the mid July beer festival. Walking appetites will be satisfied with one of the sharing platters, a chargrill steak sandwich or hearty mains like char-grilled pork fillet with Dijon mustard and carrot sauce; whole baked sea bass with green pesto, new potatoes and green beans; or chicken, bacon and pepper skewers with basmati rice.

Open all day all wk **Food** Lunch all wk 12-3 Dinner all wk 6-10 ⊕ PUNCH TAVERNS ◀ Fuller's London Pride, Young's, Adnams, Guest ale ♂ Aspall. ♥ 21 **Facilities** Non-diners area ♣ (Bar Garden) ♦♦ Children's menu Children's portions Play area Garden ⋔ Beer festival Parking ☎ (notice required)

LITTLE MARLOW — Map 5 SU88

NEW The Queens Head

tel: 01628 482927 **Pound Ln SL7 3SR**
email: tqhlittlemarlow@yahoo.co.uk
dir: *From A404 take Marlow exit towards Bourne End. Approx 1m, right by church into Church Rd. Approx 100mtrs right into Pound Ln*

A rose-clad gem of a pub

Dating from the 16th century and called 'Marlow's little secret', this is a pretty collection of buildings from three different periods. Standing opposite the manor house, its beamed, open fire-warmed interior feels immediately welcoming. Since it's just a tankard's throw from the Marlow Rebellion Brewery, expect IPA and from November to January, Roasted Nuts (surely the only real ale named after a bar snack). Modestly priced light lunches include barbecue chicken and mayo ciabatta; and smoked salmon with scrambled eggs. More substantial are braised shin of beef with oxtail ravioli; crispy pork and tiger prawn Thai broth; and spicy bean burger.

Open all day all wk Closed 25-26 Dec **Food** Lunch Mon-Fri 12-2.30, Sat-Sun 12-4 Dinner all wk 6.30-9.30 Av main course £12 ⊕ PUNCH TAVERNS ◀ Rebellion IPA ♂ Westons Stowford Press. **Facilities** Non-diners area ♦♦ Children's portions Garden ⋔ Parking WiFi ☎ (notice required)

LONG CRENDON — Map 5 SP60

The Angel Inn ⊛ — PICK OF THE PUBS

tel: 01844 208268 **47 Bicester Rd HP18 9EE**
email: info@angelrestaurant.co.uk
dir: *M40 junct 7, A418 to Thame, B4011 to Long Crendon. Inn on B4011*

Great food in an exceptional village inn

Nestled in the Vale of Aylesbury and close to the rippling Chiltern Hills, Long Crendon was a medieval centre for lace-making. Much olde-worlde atmosphere remains to beguile visitors, including the old Courthouse, picturesque rows of cottages and the gabled Angel Inn. This old coaching stop retains much of its character, with original fireplaces and wattle-and-daub walls alongside modern features including an airy conservatory, dressed with tasteful natural materials and fabrics throughout. Choice of refreshment centres around ales such as Vale Wychert and Morrells Oxford Blue; 18 wines are sold by the glass. Turning to the AA Rosette

menu, sharing tapas platters may suffice at lunchtime – choose between seafood, meat or vegetarian. Daily fish specials are written on the blackboard. A typical three-course dinner could include crispy duck and bacon on oriental vegetable salad; roast local lamb chump on cassoulet of summer beans; and warm treacle tart with honeycomb ice cream.

Open all day Closed 1-2 Jan, Sun eve **Food** Lunch all wk 12-2.30 Dinner Mon-Sat 7-9.30 Set menu available Restaurant menu available all wk ⊕ FREE HOUSE ◀ Morrells Oxford Blue, Vale Wychert, Brakspear. ♥ 18 **Facilities** Non-diners area ♦♦ Children's portions Garden ⋔ Parking WiFi ☎ (notice required)

MARLOW — Map 5 SU88

The Hand & Flowers ⊛⊛⊛⊛ — PICK OF THE PUBS

tel: 01628 482277 **126 West St SL7 2BP**
email: reservations@thehandandflowers.co.uk
dir: *M4 junct 9, A404 to Marlow, A4155 towards Henley-on-Thames. Pub on right*

Multi-award winning gastronomic hotspot

Tom Kerridge and his sculptor wife Beth continue to run this highly successful, 18th-century pub on the town's outskirts. Tom continues to gather accolades at a rapid rate, and such is the popularity of his restaurant, booking well in advance to eat here is essential. Acclaim notwithstanding, it remains a relaxed and unpretentious place, with flagstone floors, old beams and timbers, log fires and striking modern art. Fans of Greene King will be familiar with the real ale line-up, except perhaps for the guest beer, Marlow Brewery's curiously-named Rebellion Roasted Nuts. Tom's cooking is broadly modern British with rustic French backing, resulting in seasonal menus featuring perhaps Wiltshire pork tenderloin with pickled mustard leaf, malt-glazed cheek and garlic sausage; spiced fillet of Cornish brill with roasted cauliflower and peanut crumble; and Essex lamb 'bun' with sweetbreads and salsa verde.

Open 12-2.45 6.30-9.45 (Sun 12-3.15) Closed 24-26 Dec, 1 Jan Dinner, Sun eve **Food** Lunch Mon-Sat 12-2.30, Sun 12-3.15 Dinner Mon-Sat 6.30-9.30 Av main course £30 Set menu available ⊕ GREENE KING ◀ Abbot Ale, Morland Old Speckled Hen, Rebellion Roasted Nuts ♂ Aspall & Perronelle's Blush. ♥ 17 **Facilities** Non-diners area ♦♦ Children's portions Outside area ⋔ Parking

The Kings Head

tel: 01628 484407 **Church Rd, Little Marlow SL7 3RZ**
email: clive.harvison@sky.com
dir: *M40 junct 4, A4040 S, then A4155 towards Bourne End. Pub 0.5m on right*

Good range of real ales close to the Thames Path

This charming 16th-century pub with a large garden is only a few minutes' walk from the Thames Path. The open-plan interior features original beams and log fires. A great selection of ales awaits visitors to The Kings Head, including a couple from the Rebellion Brewery in Marlow. As well as sandwiches, baguettes, paninis and jacket potatoes, the food includes substantial salads, steaks, grilled salmon, chilli con carne, wholetail scampi and pumpkin and red onion tagine. Tell staff you've parked the car, go for a walk and return for a meal.

Open all day all wk Closed 26 Dec **Food** Lunch Mon-Sat 12-2.15, Sun 12-7 Dinner Mon-Sat wk 6.30-9.30, Sun 12-7 ⊕ ENTERPRISE INNS ◀ Fuller's London Pride, Timothy Taylor Landlord, Adnams Broadside, Rebellion IPA & Smuggler ♂ Thatchers Gold. ♥ 13 **Facilities** Non-diners area ♦♦ Children's menu Children's portions Garden ⋔ Parking WiFi ☎ (notice required)

MILTON KEYNES
Map 11 SP83

The Swan Inn

tel: 01908 665240 **Broughton Rd, Milton Keynes Village MK10 9AH**
email: info@theswan-mkvillage.co.uk
dir: *M1 junct 14 towards Milton Keynes. Pub off V11 or H7*

Rustic rural charm with orchard garden

In the heart of the original Milton Keynes village, the beautiful 13th-century Swan Inn offers everything you could wish for from an ancient thatched pub. The interior is an eclectic mix of traditional charm and contemporary chic; it has flagstone floors, an open fire in the inglenook in winter keeps things cosy, and an orchard garden for those warmer days. The open-plan kitchen creates simple yet creative dishes such as ham hock terrine with spiced pear chutney, piccalilli dressing and toasted ciabatta, followed by slow-roasted pork belly with truffle mash and creamed wild mushroom, with banoffee crème brûlée and coconut shortbread for pudding.

Open all day all wk Mon-Thu 11-11 (Fri-Sat 11-mdnt Sun 12-10.30) **Food** Lunch Mon-Thu 12-3, Fri-Sat 12-10, Sun 12-8 Dinner Mon-Thu 6-9.30, Fri-Sat 12-10, Sun 12-8 ⊕ FRONT LINE INNS ◀ Wells Bombardier, Young's, Guest ales ⭮ Symonds. ♒ 34 **Facilities** Non-diners area ☘ (Bar Garden) ♦ Children's portions Garden ⊼ Parking WiFi ☷ (notice required)

MOULSOE
Map 11 SP94

The Carrington Arms

tel: 01908 218050 **Cranfield Rd MK16 0HB**
email: enquiries@thecarringtonarms.co.uk
dir: *M1 junct 14, A509 to Newport Pagnell 100yds, turn right signed Moulsoe & Cranfield. Pub on right*

Traditional countryside inn which is all about customer choice

Only a short hop from the rush and noise of the M1, the family-run Carrington in the pretty village of Moulsoe combines tradition with modern hospitality. Real ales and a good wine list are a given, but the pub is most famous for its fresh meat counter where customers can talk through their selection with the chef; locally-raised Bedfordshire beef is a highlight. The choice starts with sandwiches and pub favourites, but other options are a modern take on a prawn cocktail, then pink Woburn venison loin with smoked venison boudin, fondant potato with a red wine and port jus. The large garden hosted a beer and cider festival in mid June.

Open all day all wk 12-11 **Food** Lunch all wk 12-10 Dinner all wk 12-10 Av main course £15-£18 Restaurant menu available all wk ⊕ FREE HOUSE ◀ Fuller's London Pride, Marston's Pedigree, Guest ales ⭮ Aspall, Westons. ♒ 15 **Facilities** Non-diners area ♦ Children's portions Garden ⊼ Beer festival Cider festival Parking WiFi ☷ (notice required)

NEWTON BLOSSOMVILLE
Map 11 SP95

NEW The Old Mill ★★★ INN

tel: 01234 881273 **MK43 8AN**
email: enquiries@oldmill.uk.com **web:** www.oldmill.uk.com
dir: *A509 N of Milton Keynes. Right to village. Or A428 from Bedford. In Turvey left to village*

Much loved village local with reliable cuisine

A handsome stone inn in a village of thatched cottages tucked away in the tranquil Ouse Valley; The Old Mill is an ideal base to stay-over in its attractive bedrooms. The beer range changes with the seasons, whilst the choice on the menu relies heavily on what's available from local suppliers. There's a solid base of pub

favourites, complemented by daily special; perhaps home-made lamb and mint pie or the Friday fish dish. There's a peaceful, dog-friendly grassy garden, whilst a wood-burner flickers in the cosy bar. Regulars keep warm playing skittles in the local league.

Open all wk 12-3 5-11 (Fri-Sun 12-11) **Food** Lunch Mon-Sat 12-2.30, Sun 12-4 Dinner Mon-Sat 6-9 Restaurant menu available all wk ⊕ FREE HOUSE ◀ Black Sheep Best, Guest ale. **Facilities** Non-diners area ☘ (Bar Garden) ♦ Children's menu Children's portions Garden ⊼ WiFi ☷ (notice required) **Rooms** 5

PENN
Map 6 SU99

The Old Queens Head
PICK OF THE PUBS

See Pick of the Pubs on page 54

NEW The Red Lion

tel: 01494 813107 **Elm Rd HP10 8LF**
email: redlionpub@btconnect.com
dir: *Phone for detailed directions*

Traditional village pub popular with Chiltern walkers

Set in the pretty village of Penn, this 16th-century pub is an ideal base for exploring the beautiful Chiltern Hills and nearby Penn Wood. For those in need of more leisurely exploits, sit on the sunny front terrace overlooking the village green with a pint of Chiltern Beechwood Bitter and watch the world go by. Inside, log fires warm the cosy, antique-strewn bar in winter as good conversation abounds. The food here is home-cooked and hearty with traditional dishes including liver and bacon with creamy mash and onion gravy; moules et frites; or vegetarian cassoulet.

Open all day all wk **Food** Lunch all day Dinner all day Av main course £12 Restaurant menu available all wk ⊕ ENTERPRISE INNS ◀ Penn Village Ale, Chiltern Beechwood Bitter ⭮ Westons Mortimers Orchard. ♒ 11 **Facilities** Non-diners area ☘ (Bar Restaurant Garden) ♦ Children's menu Children's portions Garden ⊼ Parking WiFi ☷ (notice required)

RADNAGE
Map 5 SU79

The Three Horseshoes Inn

tel: 01494 483273 **Horseshoe Rd, Bennett End HP14 4EB**
email: threehorseshoe@btconnect.com
dir: *M40 junct 5, A40 towards High Wycombe, after unrestricted mileage sign turn left signed Radnage (Mudds Bank). 1.8m, 1st left into Bennett End Rd, inn on right*

European flavours in a renovated pub

When chef-patron Simon Crawshaw bought this beautiful old building, he knew it would be something special. Down a leafy lane, it is truly traditional — worn flagstones, blackened beams and original inglenook fireplace. On his modern English and European menus he typically offers rillette of poached and smoked Scottish salmon with home-made Hovis-style loaf, then roast rump of lamb with ratatouille, Suffolk kale and gratin potatoes and red wine jus. Enjoy Marlow's Rebellion ale in the bar or in the lovely garden.

Open 12-3 6-11 (Mon 6-11 Sat all day Sun 12-6) Closed Sun eve, Mon L **Food** Lunch Tue-Sat 12-2.30, Sun 12-3 Dinner Mon-Thu 6-9, Fri-Sat 6-9.30 ⊕ FREE HOUSE ◀ Rebellion, Brakspear Oxford Gold. ♒ 12 **Facilities** Non-diners area ☘ (Bar Garden) ♦ Children's portions Garden ⊼ Parking WiFi ☷ (notice required)

PICK OF THE PUBS

The Old Queens Head

PENN   Map 6 SU99

tel: 01494 813371
Hammersley Ln HP10 8EY
email: info@oldqueensheadpenn.co.uk
web: www.oldqueensheadpenn.co.uk
dir: *B474 into School Rd, 500yds, left into Hammersley Ln*

Appetising food and well-kept ales

Between the delightful villages of Penn and Tylers Green and with lovely walks in beech woodland on its doorstep, this old pub has bags of character and atmosphere. It's one of the well regarded Salisbury Pubs mini-empire in and around the Chilterns.* The timber built dining room dates from 1666 (word of the Great Fire of London clearly hadn't reached here) when it was constructed as a barn, and although it has seen several additions since then, the cosy corners, undulating floors and real fires are reminders of its history. The owners have spent time at local auctions carefully selecting old furniture and pictures in keeping with the age of the pub. A sunny terrace overlooks the village church, and there's a large garden in which to eat and drink or you could settle by the fire with a pint of Ruddles County or a mug of hot chocolate. The kitchen team has created a modern British menu with starters of honey and fennel cured Scottish salmon, choucroute fritters and horseradish

cream; and potted pork rillettes with warm oak-smoked bacon brioche bun and piccalilli. Main course options are similarly mouth watering - spaghetti with Cornish clams, garlic, chilli and parlsey; or Chiltern lamb faggot with slow-roasted garlic mash and minted gravy. For pudding, consider rhubarb and custard crème brûlée with almond biscotti or a plate of English cheeses. The wine list includes 24 by the glass and a separate pudding wine selection.

*Alford Arms, Hemel Hempstead, Hertfordshire; and in Buckinghamshire, The Swan Inn, Denham; The Royal Oak, Bovingdon Green.

Open all day all wk 11-11 (Sun 12-10.30) Closed 25-26 Dec **Food** Lunch Mon-Fri 12-2.30, Sat 12-3, Sun 12-9 Dinner Mon-Thu 6.30-9.30, Fri-Sat 6.30-10 Av main course £14.75
⊕ SALISBURY PUBS LTD ◧ Greene King Ruddles County & IPA, Guinness
♻ Thatchers Gold. ♟ 24
Facilities Non-diners area ♥ (Bar Garden) ♦♦ Children's portions Garden
♐ Parking WiFi

SEER GREEN

Map 6 SU99

The Jolly Cricketers ⊛

tel: 01494 676308 **24 Chalfont Rd HP9 2YG**
email: amanda@thejollycricketers.co.uk
dir: *M40 junct 2, A355 signed Beaconsfield A40, Amersham. At Pyebush rdbt 1st exit, A40 signed Beaconsfield, Amersham, A355. At rdbt, A355 signed Amersham. Right into Longbottom Ln signed Seer Green. Left into Bottom Ln, right into Orchard Rd, left into Church Rd, right into Chalfont Rd*

Top notch food in a homely setting

Chris Lillitou and Amanda Baker's 19th-century, wisteria-clad free house in the heart of the picture-perfect Seer Green appeals to all-comers: locals chatting over pints of Marlow's Rebellion IPA, quiz addicts on Sunday nights, live jazz fans, beer festival-goers, dog-walkers. The modern, AA-Rosette menu could include crispy Cornish squid with chilli and lemon sauce; spicy chorizo and razor clams with shallots, tomatoes and black-eye beans as typical starters. Follow with pan-fried stone bass, wild mushrooms, braised fennel in orange and saffron. For dessert, maybe vanilla cheesecake with rhubarb and rhubarb sorbet. Beer festivals on Easter weekend and Summer Bank Holiday.

Open all day all wk Mon-Thu 12-11.30 (Fri-Sat 12-12 Sun 12-10.30) **Food** Lunch Mon-Fri 12-2.30, Sat 12-3 Dinner Mon-Sat 6.30-9 Av main course £8.50 Restaurant menu available Mon-Sat ⊕ FREE HOUSE ◖ Rebellion IPA, Fuller's London Pride, Chiltern Beechwood Bitter, Vale VPA ☼ Millwhites, Artisan bottle selection. ☗ 16 **Facilities** Non-diners area ✿ (Bar Garden) ♦️ Children's menu Children's portions Garden ⋒ Beer festival Parking WiFi

SKIRMETT

Map 5 SU79

The Frog
PICK OF THE PUBS

tel: 01491 638996 **RG9 6TG**
email: info@thefrogatskirmett.co.uk
dir: *Exit A4155 at Mill End, pub in 3m*

Quality choices in both refreshment and food

An 18th-century coaching inn within the Chilterns Area of Outstanding Natural Beauty, with the Hamble Brook flowing gently behind. In summer the garden is a relaxing place to be, perhaps after a ramble to the famous windmill on nearby Turville Hill. Winter warmth is guaranteed in the charming public bar where oak beams, bare floorboards and leather seating combine with colourful textiles to create a welcoming atmosphere. Where better to settle with a pint of Leaping Frog or Henry's Original IPA? Alternatively 15 wines are sold by the glass, or push the boat out and share a sparkler from the Hambleden vineyard just down the road. Head chef and co-owner Jim Crowe uses superb ingredients in flavoursome dishes to satisfy the most discerning of palates. Specials may offer a starter of avocado and quail's egg salad with warm crispy bacon. Roast rump of Oxfordshire lamb in port and redcurrant jus is typical of the main courses.

Open 11.30-3 6-11 Closed 25 Dec, Sun eve (Oct-Apr) **Food** Lunch all wk 12-2.30 Dinner all wk 6.30-9.30 ⊕ FREE HOUSE ◖ Leaping Frog, Rebellion IPA, Sharp's Doom Bar, Wadworth Henry's Original IPA ☼ Thatchers. ☗ 15 **Facilities** Non-diners area ✿ (Bar Garden) ♦️ Children's menu Children's portions Family room Garden ⋒ Parking 🚐

STOKE MANDEVILLE

Map 5 SP81

NEW The Bell

tel: 01296 612434 **29 Lower Rd HP22 5XA**
email: info@bellstokemandeville.co.uk **web:** www.bellstokemandeville.co.uk
dir: *From S & E follow signs from Stoke Mandeville towards Stoke Mandeville Hospital, pub on left in 200yds after primary school. From N & W pass Stoke Mandeville Hospital on left, pub approx 1m on right*

An honest-to-goodness great British dining pub

A sign saying 'Dogs, children and muddy boots welcome' sets the friendly tone of a visit to this traditional country village pub. Physiotherapists caring for those with spinal injuries at nearby Stoke Mandeville hospital have been known to set The Bell as an objective for their newly mobile patients. The reward could be a pint of Wells Bombardier or Scrumpy Jack cider, with a plate of fresh seasonal food. James Penlington has some star kitchens on his CV, so expect proper bar snacks and hearty full-flavoured meals – typical are bubble-and-squeak with smoked bacon, poached egg and hollandaise; and desserts like apple and berry crumble with vanilla custard.

Open all day all wk Closed 25-26 Dec **Food** Lunch Mon-Sat 12-6.30 Restaurant menu available all wk ⊕ CHARLES WELLS ◖ Eagle IPA & Bombardier, Guest ale ☼ Symonds Scrumpy Jack. ☗ 16 **Facilities** Non-diners area ✿ (Bar Restaurant Garden) ♦️ Children's menu Children's portions Garden ⋒ Parking WiFi 🚐 (notice required)

PICK OF THE PUBS

The Bull & Butcher

TURVILLE Map 5 SU79

tel: 01491 638283
RG9 6QU
email: info@thebullandbutcher.com
web: www.bullandbutcher.com
dir: *M40 junct 5, follow Ibstone signs. Right at T-junct. Pub 0.25m on left*

A quintessentially English pub in the Chilterns

Built in 1550, Turville's village pub received its first licence in 1617 after workmen building the nearby church refused to continue without refreshments. Originally known as the 'Bullen Butcher' – a reference to Henry VIII and his second wife Anne Boleyn – the name was later adapted to its current form. Its picturesque setting in the Hambleden Valley a few miles outside Henley-on-Thames yields some beautiful vistas, including a windmill which appeared in the film *Chitty Chitty Bang Bang;* many episodes of *Midsomer Murders* have been set here. You'll soon feel at home in the relaxed atmosphere of the Windmill Lounge or the Well Bar, where a 50-foot well discovered in 1999 now features as a table. Original beams and large open fires add to the pub's charm. There's also a large garden and patio area, as well as a function room well suited for family occasions – children and dogs are welcome. Reliable Brakspear and guest ales along with Symonds cider are the bar's major thirst quenchers; oenophiles will be delighted by the choice of wines sold by the glass, of which there are three dozen. When it comes to choosing from the menu of popular dishes, the kitchen prides itself on the seasonality and freshness of ingredients. A typical three-course choice could start with creamy garlic mushrooms; continue with treacle-baked ham with two eggs, thick-cut chips and minted peas; and finish with apple and berry crumble with custard. The children's menu embraces their favourites too, such as home-made chicken goujons or bangers and mash with gravy. Sunday lunches are popular: will it be roast beef and Yorkshire pudding? Slow roast pork loin with crackling? Try the wild boar and apple sausages with wholegrain mustard mash for a change.

Open all wk summer 12-11 (Sat noon-1am) winter 12-3 5.30-11 **Food** Lunch Mon-Sat 12-2.30, Sun 12-3 Dinner Mon-Sat 6-9.30 BRAKSPEAR Bitter & Oxford Gold, Guest ales Symonds. 36 **Facilities** Non-diners area (Bar Garden) Children's menu Garden Parking WiFi (notice required)

TURVILLE
Map 5 SU79

The Bull & Butcher
PICK OF THE PUBS

See Pick of the Pubs on opposite page

WEST WYCOMBE
Map 5 SU89

The George and Dragon Hotel

tel: 01494 535340 **High St HP14 3AB**
email: georgeanddragon@live.co.uk
dir: *On A40*

Delightful timber-framed hotel reached through a cobbled archway

After a hard day touring the West Wycombe Caves, and stately houses at Cliveden and Hughenden, relax at this traditional coaching inn located in a National Trust village. The 14th-century inn was once a hideout for highwaymen stalking travellers between London and Oxford; indeed, one unfortunate guest, robbed and murdered here, is rumoured still to haunt its corridors. Reliable real ales include St Austell Tribute and Skinner's Smugglers. The varied menu offers freshly-prepared dishes cooked to order such as beef and ale pie; beer-battered haddock; a button mushroom, brie and cranberry filo parcel; and succulent rib-eye steaks.

Open all day all wk 12-12 (Fri-Sat noon-1am Sun 12-11.30) **Food** Lunch Mon-Sat 12-2.30, Sun 12-3 Dinner Mon-Thu 6-9, Fri-Sat 6-9.30 Restaurant menu available all wk ⊕ ENTERPRISE INNS ◀ St Austell Tribute, Skinner's Smugglers Ale ♂ Symonds. ₹ 9 **Facilities** Non-diners area ❖ (Bar Restaurant Garden) ♦♦ Children's menu Children's portions Play area Family room Garden ⋒ Parking WiFi ▭ (notice required)

WHEELER END
Map 5 SU89

The Chequers Inn

tel: 01494 883070 **Bullocks Farm Ln HP14 3NH**
email: landlord@chequerswheelerend.co.uk
dir: *4m N of Marlow*

Families welcome at this Fuller's pub

This picturesque 16th-century inn, with its low-beamed ceilings, roaring winter fires and two attractive beer gardens, is ideally located for walkers on the edge of Wheeler End Common (families and dogs are welcome). Lunchtime dishes include pub favourites such as spaghetti bolognaise or bangers and mash with gravy; and there's a sandwich menu too. Typical evening choices are spicy chicken wings with blue cheese dressing; bacon and Stilton beefburger with chips; or pie of the day.

Open 12-3 6-11 (Sat 12-11 Sun 12-6) Closed Sun eve, Mon L **Food** Lunch Tue-Thu 12-2, Fri-Sun 12-3 Dinner Tue-Thu & Sat 6-9, Fri 6-9.30 ⊕ FULLER'S ◀ London Pride & ESB, George Gale & Co Seafarers, Guest ale ♂ Aspall. ₹ 12 **Facilities** Non-diners area ❖ (Bar Garden) ♦♦ Children's menu Children's portions Garden ⋒ Parking WiFi ▭ (notice required)

WOOBURN COMMON
Map 6 SU98

Chequers Inn ★★★ HL ❀❀
PICK OF THE PUBS

tel: 01628 529575 **Kiln Ln HP10 0JQ**
email: info@chequers-inn.com **web:** www.chequers-inn.com
dir: *M40 junct 2, A40 through Beaconsfield towards High Wycombe. Left into Broad Ln, signed Taplow/Burnham/Wooburn Common. 2m to pub*

Pub grub meets fine dining in the Chilterns

The heart of this 17th-century coaching inn is still firmly rooted in the past, especially in the open-fired bar, where the hand-tooled oak beams and posts, and timeworn flagstone and wooden floors shrug off the passage of time. Contrast then the 21st-century chic lounge, with leather sofas and chairs, low tables and

greenery while outside, sheltering the patio and flowery garden, stands a magnificent old oak tree. Beers are from Marlow's Rebellion and the St Austell breweries, and 14 wines are by the glass. In the bar, tempura prawns with chilli sauce; and lamb kofta are examples of small plates, with pan-fried calves' liver as a special. The two-AA Rosette restaurant menu features ever-changing dishes such as beef fillet with beef cheek ravioli, roasted baby onion jus and salsify; and hake with crushed new potatoes, baby artichokes and saffron butter sauce. Accommodation comprises 17 designer rooms.

Open all day all wk 12-12 **Food** Lunch Mon-Fri 12-2.30, Sat 12-10, Sun 12-9.30 Dinner Mon-Thu 6-9.30, Fri 6-10, Sat 12-10, Sun 12-9.30 Set menu available Restaurant menu available all wk ⊕ FREE HOUSE ◀ Rebellion IPA & Smuggler, St Austell Tribute ♂ Westons Stowford Press. ₹ 14 **Facilities** Non-diners area ♦♦ Children's menu Children's portions Garden ⋒ Parking WiFi **Rooms** 17

CAMBRIDGESHIRE

ABBOTS RIPTON
Map 12 TL27

NEW The Abbot's Elm ★★★★ INN ❀❀

tel: 01487 773773 **PE28 2PA**
email: info@theabbotselm.co.uk **web:** www.theabbotselm.co.uk
dir: *From A141 or Huntingdon follow Abbots Ripton signs*

Thatched village inn restored after major fire

After a devastating fire, The Abbot's Elm rose from the ashes of what was the 17th-century Three Horseshoes in the delightful village of Abbots Ripton. From the outside, this thatched inn looks pretty much the same as it always did but the new open-plan bar and restaurant are bathed in natural light. Owners John and Julia Abbey are genial hosts and visitors are welcome whether it's for coffee or a seven-course tasting dinner. A chalkboard menu of pub classics runs alongside a carte featuring ham hock and game terrine; and fillet of wild sea bass with crab and pea risotto.

Open all day Closed Sun eve **Food** Lunch all wk 12-2.15 Dinner Mon-Sat 6-9 Av main course £10 Set menu available Restaurant menu available all wk ⊕ FREE HOUSE ◀ Oakham Ales JHB, Guest ales ♂ Symonds. ₹ 50 **Facilities** Non-diners area ❖ (Bar Garden) ♦♦ Children's menu Children's portions Garden ⋒ Parking WiFi **Rooms** 3

BALSHAM
Map 12 TL55

The Black Bull Inn ★★★★ INN ❀

tel: 01223 893844 **27 High St CB21 4DJ**
email: info@blackbull-balsham.co.uk **web:** www.blackbull-balsham.co.uk
dir: *From S: M11 junct 9, A11 towards Newmarket, follow Balsham signs. From N: M11 junct 10, A505 signed Newmarket (A11), onto A11, follow Balsham signs*

Transformed inn for excellent food and a good night's sleep

An AA Rosette for food and four AA stars for accommodation are just two of the awards acquired by this 16th-century pub, run by the same team as The Red Lion in nearby Hinxton. The bar serves East Anglian real ales and ciders, sandwiches, baguettes, hot meals and four types of shortcrust pastry pie. The restaurant is in an adjoining converted barn, where main dishes, depending on the season, may include grilled trout fillet with new potatoes, leek and prawn and caper nut butter; artichoke risotto; or slow braised breast of lamb with champ mash and red cabbage. Out front is a tree-lined sandstone patio, and at the back a south-facing beer garden.

Open all day all wk **Food** Lunch Mon-Thu 12-2, Fri-Sun 12-2.30 Dinner Mon-Thu 6.30-9, Fri-Sat 6.30-9.30, Sun 7-9 Av main course £12 Restaurant menu available all wk ⊕ FREE HOUSE ◀ Woodforde's Wherry, Adnams Southwold Bitter, Red & Black, Brandon Rusty Bucket, Nethergate ♂ Aspall & Harry Sparrow. ₹ 12 **Facilities** Non-diners area ❖ (Bar Garden) ♦♦ Children's menu Children's portions Garden ⋒ Beer festival Parking WiFi ▭ (notice required) **Rooms** 5

The Royal Oak

tel: 01223 870791 **31 West Green CB22 7RZ**
email: info@royaloakbarrington.co.uk
dir: *From Barton off M11, S of Cambridge*

Quintessential English pub by village green

One of the oldest thatched and timbered pubs in England, this rambling 16th-century building overlooks a 30-acre village green. With a pretty 'chocolate-box' image on the outside, the smart interior is now contemporary in design; the menu lists the classic dishes for which the pub has long been known, such as pie of the day, toad-in-the-hole, beer battered haddock, and aubergine parmigana. Alongside this is a collection of salads and sandwiches, and a choice of ales that includes Buntingford Twitchell and Adnams.

Open all wk 12-3 6-11 (Sun 12-11) **Food** Lunch all wk 12-2 Dinner all wk 6-9.30 Av main course £10.50 ⊕ FREE HOUSE ◄ Woodforde's, Buntingford Twitchell, Adnams, O'Hanlon's Royal Oak ♂ Aspall, Thatchers Gold. ♀ 8 **Facilities** Non-diners area ❤ (Bar Garden) ♦❙ Children's menu Children's portions Garden ⋈ Parking WiFi ⛟ (notice required)

The Willow Tree

tel: 01954 719775 **29 High St CB23 2SQ**
email: contact@thewillowtreebourn.com
dir: *From Royston on A1188, right on B1046 signed Bourn. Pub in village on right*

Shabby chic candlelit restaurant and bar serving East Anglian ales

A certain chemistry is at work in this village pub just off Ermine Street, the old Roman road from London to York. Head chef Craig Galvin-Scott, you see, is married to front-of-house manager, Shaina, and after they bought it in late 2012 they set about creating the shabby-chic (their word) interior, with a candlelit restaurant and bar. It soon began attracting attention. Seasonal menus feature lamb rump with braised Savoy cabbage, cream and bacon; sea bass with Jerusalem artichoke; and roulade with chard, ricotta and root vegetable. In the garden stands a graceful willow tree from which the inn takes its name.

Open all day all wk **Food** Lunch all wk 12-3 Dinner all wk 5.30-9.30 Av main course £12 Set menu available ⊕ FREE HOUSE ◄ Milton Pegasus, Woodforde's Wherry ♂ Addlestones, Aspall. ♀ 49 **Facilities** Non-diners area ❤ (Garden) ♦❙ Children's menu Children's portions Garden ⋈ Beer festival Cider festival Parking WiFi ⛟ (notice required)

The Crown Inn

tel: 01487 824428 **Bridge Rd PE28 3AY**
email: info@thecrowninnrestaurant.co.uk
dir: *A141 from Huntingdon towards Warboys. Left to Broughton*

Picturesque inn at the heart of the community

In the mid-19th century, this village inn incorporated a saddler's shop, thatched stables and piggeries. Today it focuses on being a popular pub and restaurant in a thriving local community. The bar offers real ales from Suffolk and national breweries, and you'll also find Aspall cider. The restaurant combines a traditional pub look with contemporary design, and it's here you'll be able to eat modern European dishes cooked using the best sustainable fish caught by day boats, the highest quality meats and excellent seasonal vegetables. Menus change regularly, so you may find one offering seared pigeon breast; roast cod on a bed of sautéed celeriac; and cappuccino and hazelnut praline gâteau.

Open all wk Mon-Sat 11.30-3 6.30-11 (Sun 11.30-8) **Food** Lunch Mon-Sat 12-2.15, Sun 12-3.30 Dinner Mon-Sat 6.30-9.15 ⊕ FREE HOUSE ◄ Rotating Local ales ♂ Aspall. ♀ 10 **Facilities** Non-diners area ❤ (Bar Garden) ♦❙ Children's menu Children's portions Play area Garden ⋈ Parking

The Anchor Pub, Dining & River Terrace

tel: 01223 353554 **Silver St CB3 9EL**
email: info@anchorcambridge.com
dir: *Phone for detailed directions*

New hands on the tiller at this popular riverside pub

Bordering Queens' College is a medieval lane, at the end of which stands this attractive pub, right by the bridge over the River Cam. Head for the riverside patio with a local real ale, such as Fellows or BlackBar, or a Hazy Hog cider, and watch rookie punters struggling with their tricky craft - another definition of pole position, perhaps. A good choice of food includes sea bass fillet with pumpkin and sage risotto; honey-glazed Barbary duck leg with parsnip mash; and beer-battered fish and chips. Sandwiches, sausage rolls and Scotch eggs are available too.

Open all day all wk Mon-Thu & Sun 11-11 (Fri-Sat 11am-mdnt) **Food** Lunch all wk 11.30-4.30 Dinner all wk 5.30-9.30 Av main course £14 Restaurant menu available all wk ⊕ METROPOLITAN PUBS ◄ Fellows, BlackBar Bitter, Oakham Ales, Nethergate ♂ Aspall, Hogs Back Hazy Hog. ♀ 12 **Facilities** Non-diners area ♦❙ Children's menu Outside area ⋈ WiFi ⛟ (notice required)

The Old Spring

tel: 01223 357228 **1 Ferry Path CB4 1HB**
email: theoldspring@hotmail.co.uk
dir: *Just off Chesterton Rd, (A1303) in city centre, near Midsummer Common*

Neighbourhood pub with a lengthy and varied menu

You'll find this bustling pub in the leafy suburb of De Freville, just a short stroll from the River Cam and its many boatyards. The bright and airy interior offers rug-covered wooden floors, comfy sofas and large family tables. Sip a pint of Abbot Ale, one of the five real ales on tap, or one of 20 wines by the glass while choosing from over a dozen main courses plus specials, perhaps red Thai black tiger prawn curry; steak frites; corned beef hash; pan-seared halibut steak; a platter of cured meat; smoked salmon and crayfish; or pan-fried gnocchi.

Open all day all wk 11.30-11 (Sun 12-10.30) **Food** Lunch Mon-Fri 12-2.30, Sat 12-4, Sun 12-9.30 Dinner Mon-Sat 6-9.30, Sun 12-9.30 ⊕ GREENE KING ◄ IPA & Abbot Ale, Elgood's Cambridge Bitter, Guest ales ♂ Aspall. ♀ 20 **Facilities** Non-diners area ♦❙ Children's menu Children's portions Outside area ⋈ Parking WiFi ⛟

The Punter

tel: 01223 363322 **3 Pound Hill CB3 0AE**
email: info@thepuntercambridge.co.uk
dir: *Phone for detailed directions*

Seasonal food and a great atmosphere

Two minutes' walk from the city centre, this former coaching house is popular with post-grads, locals and dog lovers alike who create a happy mood with their chatter and laughter. The interior is an eclectic mix of previously loved hand-me-downs, comfy sofas, sturdy school chairs, and an assortment of pictures and painting jostling for space on the walls. Drinkers can enjoy local ales but it seems it's the food that draws people in. Be certain to look out for roasted loin of cod with bulgar wheat, Alsace bacon and onion textures.

Open all day all wk Closed 25 Dec **Food** Lunch all day ⊕ PUNCH TAVERNS ◄ Punter ale, Punter Blonde, Guest ales ♂ Addlestones. ♀ 13 **Facilities** Non-diners area ❤ (Bar Restaurant Outside area) ♦❙ Children's portions Outside area ⋈ WiFi

COTON
Map 12 TL45

NEW The Plough

tel: 01954 210489 **2 High St CB23 7PL**
email: info@theploughcoton.co.uk
dir: M11 juncts 12 or 13. Follow Coton signs

Fine food in Cambridge-edge countryside

Nudging the cricket pitches and grassy recreation ground, this much upgraded village pub caters for savvy diners escaping the hubbub of nearby Cambridge. The cool, chic interior is a model of contemporary decor, with colourful rugs, leather sofa and colourwashed walls producing a relaxing atmosphere in which to enjoy the modern, gastro-style menu. Sharing 'planks' of cured meats and cheeses; inspired upmarket pizzas or mains like pan-fried loin of pollock with oyster fritter; or Jerusalem artichoke, truffle and almond risotto typify an evening's repast. The wine list features around 30 bins; beers are from East Anglian breweries and there's a summer beer festival.

Open all day all wk **Food** Contact pub for details Av main course £12 Set menu available Restaurant menu available all wk ⊕ ENTERPRISE INNS ◀ Sharp's Doom Bar, Adnams Lighthouse, Greene King Ruddles Best, Woodforde's Wherry. ♥ **Facilities** Non-diners area ✿ (Garden) ♦️ Children's menu Children's portions Play area Garden ⊐ Beer festival Parking WiFi ▦

DRY DRAYTON
Map 12 TL36

The Black Horse

tel: 01954 782600 **35 Park St CB23 8DA**
email: deniseglover@hotmail.co.uk
dir: A14 junct 30, follow signs for Dry Drayton. In village turn right to pub. Signed

Renowned for its ales and good food

Just five miles from Cambridge, The Black Horse has been at the heart of this quiet village for more than 300 years. Gary and Denise Glover and chef Daniel Walker have built a reputation for notable food. Many local ales are showcased in the bar, and local suppliers dominate the menu in the restaurant. A starter of pan-seared pigeon breast, black pudding and game jus might be followed by Aldeburgh stone bass with green lentils, spinach and mussel sauce. The pub holds an annual beer festival over the St George's Day weekend in April.

Open 12-3 6-11 (Sun 12-4) Closed Mon **Food** Lunch Tue-Sat 12-2, Sun 12-4 Dinner Tue-Sat 6-9.30 ⊕ FREE HOUSE ◀ Black Horse, Adnams, Guest ale Ō Aspall. **Facilities** Non-diners area ✿ (Bar Garden) ♦️ Children's portions Garden ⊐ Beer festival Parking WiFi

DUXFORD
Map 12 TL44

The John Barleycorn
PICK OF THE PUBS

tel: 01223 832699 **3 Moorfield Rd CB2 4PP**
email: info@johnbarleycorn.co.uk
dir: Exit A505 into Duxford

Traditional and comfortable village pub

If you need somewhere to relax after a day's racing at Newmarket, head for this thatched and whitewashed former coach house built in 1660. It took the name John Barleycorn in the mid-19th century and during World War II was a favourite watering hole for the brave young airmen of Douglas Bader's Duxford Wing. Step through the door into the softly lit bar with a rustic mix of country furniture, large brick fireplace, old tiled floor, cushioned pews and hop-adorned low beams. It's a cosy place in which to enjoy a hearty home-cooked meal, washed down with a refreshing pint of Greene King IPA or Abbot Ale. You can nibble on a bowl of olives or share a charcuterie board while making your menu selections: kipper and whisky pâté perhaps, followed by Dingley Dell maple-glazed rump of pork. Summer alfresco eating can be enjoyed on the flower-festooned rear patio.

Open all day all wk **Food** Lunch Mon-Thu 12-3, Fri-Sat 12-10, Sun 12-8.30 Dinner Mon-Thu 5-9.30, Fri-Sat 12-10, Sun 12-8.30 ⊕ GREENE KING ◀ Greene King IPA, Abbot Ale, Ruddles Best & Ruddles County, Morland Old Speckled Hen Ō Thatchers. ♥ 12 **Facilities** Non-diners area ✿ (Bar Restaurant Garden) ♦️ Children's menu Children's portions Play area Garden ⊐ Parking WiFi ▦ (notice required)

ELTON
Map 12 TL09

The Crown Inn ★★★★★ INN
PICK OF THE PUBS

tel: 01832 280232 **8 Duck St PE8 6RQ**
email: inncrown@googlemail.com **web:** www.thecrowninn.org
dir: A1(M) junct 17, W on A605 signed Oundle/Northampton. In 3.5m right to Elton, 0.9m left signed Nassington. Inn 0.3m on right

Thatched stone inn oozing character and charm

The 17th-century Crown is tucked away behind a towering chestnut tree in the heart of the unspoilt village of Elton. Click open the door latch to reveal oak beams and natural stone aplenty, with a crackling winter fire in the inglenook. Golden Crown Bitter — locally brewed by the Tydd Steam brewery — takes pole position amongst the real ales at the bar, supported by Westons Old Rosie and Glebe Farm ciders. Chef-patron Marcus Lamb places great emphasis on the food, with the finest local ingredients forming the basis for the freshly prepared traditional British favourites and dishes with a twist. Bar lunches feature sandwiches, baguettes and omelettes, as well as pub classics such as a trio of home-made sausages. In the evening, pan-fried breast of pigeon with glazed figs, confit shallot and smoked bacon might herald slow-roasted belly of rare-breed pork, fondant potato, braised red cabbage and chicory, and a Calvados jus. Annual treats include a May Day party.

Open all day all wk 12-11 **Food** Lunch Mon-Sat 12-2, Sun 12-3 Dinner Mon-Sat 6.30-9 ⊕ FREE HOUSE ◀ Tydd Steam Golden Crown Bitter, Greene King IPA, Phipps IPA, Guest ales Ō Westons Old Rosie, Glebe Farm. ♥ 8 **Facilities** Non-diners area ✿ (Bar) ♦️ Children's menu Children's portions Outside area ⊐ Parking WiFi ▦ (notice required) **Rooms** 5

ELY
Map 12 TL58

The Anchor Inn ★★★★ INN ⊛
PICK OF THE PUBS

See Pick of the Pubs on page 60

FEN DITTON
Map 12 TL46

Ancient Shepherds

tel: 01223 293280 **High St CB5 8ST**
email: ancientshepherds@hotmail.co.uk
dir: From A14 take B1047 signed Cambridge/Airport

Popular pub in a peaceful riverside village

Three miles from Cambridge, this heavily beamed pub is a popular dining destination away from the bustle of the city. Built as three cottages in 1540, it was named after the ancient order of Shepherds who once met here. The pub is free of music, darts and pool, and is a cosy place to sup a pint of London Pride beside one of the inglenook fires. The bar lunch menu offers an extensive range of filled baguettes as well as jackets and snacks. In the restaurant, follow marinated crayfish tails with braised lamb shank in a minted red wine and rosemary gravy, and apple strudel for dessert. Specials could include fishcakes, lasagne or cannelloni.

Open 12-2.30 6-11 Closed 25-26 Dec, 1 Jan, Sun eve & Mon **Food** Lunch Tue-Sat 12-2, Sun 12-2.30 Restaurant menu available Tue-Sat ⊕ PUNCH TAVERNS ◀ Adnams Southwold Bitter, Greene King IPA, Fuller's London Pride Ō Aspall. ♥ 8 **Facilities** Non-diners area ✿ (Bar Garden) ♦️ Children's portions Garden ⊐ Parking WiFi

PICK OF THE PUBS

The Anchor Inn ★★★★ INN 🌹

ELY Map 12 TL58

tel: 01353 778537
Sutton Gault CB6 2BD
email: anchorinn@popmail.bta.com
web: www.anchorsuttongault.co.uk
dir: *From A14, B1050 to Earith, take B1381 to Sutton. Sutton Gault on left*

Riverside inn beneath big Fenland skies

The Fens were lawless and disease-ridden until, in 1630, the Earl of Bedford commissioned Dutch engineer Cornelius Vermuyden to drain them. By digging the Old and New Bedford Rivers, the Dutchman ended the constant danger of flooding and began the process that created today's rich agricultural landscape. Using thick gault clay, he built raised river banks and beside the New Bedford (or 'The Hundred Foot Drain') constructed the Anchor for his workforce; it has been a pub ever since. Today, low beams, dark wood panelling, scrubbed pine tables, gently undulating tiled floors, antique prints and log fires create the intimate character of this family-run free house. Ten wines by the glass and East Anglian real ales BlackBar and Nethergate Growler will be found in the bar. The modern British cuisine is strong on local produce, including hand-dressed crabs from Cromer, Brancaster oysters and mussels, samphire, fresh asparagus, and venison from the Denham Estate. In

the winter there'll be pheasant, partridge, pigeon and wild duck. Making an interesting starter is seared scallops with chorizo jam, Bloody Mary semi-gel and apple crisp; this could be followed by poached fillet of skrei cod (a high-quality, sustainable Norwegian variety) with crispy duck egg, wholegrain mustard mash, Swiss chard and tomato hollandaise sauce; or pea and leek risotto with parmesan waffle. Desserts may include Madeira-poached pear with orange paté de fruit, chocolate soil and Amaretto ice cream; and apple and blackberry crumble with apple ice cream and blackberry jelly. Sunday roasts - indeed, any meal - may be enjoyed on the terrace overlooking the river. The cathedral cities of Ely and Cambridge are both within easy reach.

Open all wk Mon-Fri 12-2.30 7-10.30 (Sat 12-3 6.30-11 Sun 12-4 6.30-10) Closed 25-26 Dec eve **Food** Lunch Mon-Fri 12-2, Sat-Sun 12-2.30 Dinner Mon-Fri 7-9, Sat-Sun 6-9 Set menu available 🌐 FREE HOUSE 🛢 Nethergate Old Growler, BlackBar Bitter. 🍷 10 **Facilities** Non-diners area 🍴 Children's portions Garden 🎋 Parking WiFi 🚌 (notice required) **Rooms** 4

FENSTANTON
Map 12 TL36

King William IV

tel: 01480 462467 **High St PE28 9JF**
email: kingwilliamfenstanton@btconnect.com
dir: *On A14 between Hunstanton & Cambridge follow Fenstanton signs*

Rustic village inn with good food

This rambling 17th-century village pub features oak beams, old brickwork and a wonderful central fireplace. Lunchtime offerings include a range of hot and cold sandwiches but also light bites such as sliced ham, fried egg and hand-cut chips; or minute steak and French fries. Diners looking for something more substantial can choose from the restaurant or classics menus - seared duck breast, potato rösti, braised red cabbage and balsamic glaze; liver, bacon, greens, mash and gravy or butternut squash and garlic risotto. Occasionally, there's live music on a Sunday afternoon.

Open all wk Mon-Thu 12-3 5-11 (Fri-Sun all day) **Food** Lunch all wk 12-2.30 Dinner Mon-Thu 6-9, Fri-Sat 6-9.30 Restaurant menu available ⊕ GREENE KING ◀ IPA, Guest ales ♂ Aspall. ♟ 13 **Facilities** Non-diners area ✿ (Bar Garden) ♦♦ Children's portions Garden ⌁ Parking WiFi ⛟ (notice required)

FORDHAM
Map 12 TL67

White Pheasant ◉◉
PICK OF THE PUBS

tel: 01638 720414 **CB7 5LQ**
email: whitepheasant@live.com
dir: *From Newmarket A142 to Ely, approx 5m to Fordham. Pub on left in village*

Carefully constructed menu of select options

This 18th-century building stands in a fenland village between Ely and Newmarket. In recent years its considerable appeal has been subtly enhanced by improvements that preserve its period charm – a heritage now in the care of new owners. While enjoying a pint of Adnams or glass of wine, choose between the dishes of good English fare on the menu. Cooking continues to be taken seriously here, with quality, presentation and flavour taking top priority; specials change daily. Starters may include king scallop with pressed chicken wing, apple and celeriac; or venison cottage pie, baked potato cream, and pickled cabbage flavoured with dark chocolate. Follow with slow-roasted belly pork, ham hock, pistachio, black pudding and ham liquor; or plaice with brown shrimp, turnip, chicory, tomato and truffle dressing. Desserts follow more conventional lines with the likes of apple and plum crumble; and sticky toffee pudding.

Open Tue-Sat 12-2.30 6.30-9.30 (Sun 12-2.30) **Food** Lunch Tue-Sun 12-2.30 Dinner Tue-Sat 6.30-9.30 Restaurant menu available Tue-Sat ⊕ FREE HOUSE ◀ Adnams ♂ Aspall Harry Sparrow. ♟ 12 **Facilities** Non-diners area ♦♦ Children's portions Garden ⌁ Parking WiFi ⛟ (notice required)

GREAT WILBRAHAM
Map 12 TL55

The Carpenters Arms

tel: 01223 882093 **10 High St CB21 5JD**
email: contact@carpentersarmsgastropub.co.uk
web: www.carpentersarmsgastropub.co.uk
dir: *From A11 follow "The Wilbraham" signs. Into Great Wilbraham, right at junct, pub 150yds on left*

Traditional free house, microbrewery and French-inspired food

A beer house since 1729, this smart pub restaurant is still brewing – today they're called Crafty Beers, such as Carpenter's Cask and Sauvignon Blonde. Landlords Rick and Heather Hurley previously ran an award-winning restaurant in France, so expect French - eg tartiflette - Catalan, Italian and even Thai dishes on the menus. Other possibilities include slow roast belly pork with crackling, cinnamon and apple sauce; roast chicken breast stuffed with mushrooms, brandy cream sauce; fish of the day; and fillet steak with spiced cocoa sauce, triple cooked chips and vanilla scented beans, while Sunday roasts remain decidedly English. A Suffolk white features among the world-sourced wine list.

Open 11.30-3 6.30-11 Closed 26 Dec, 1 Jan, 1wk Nov & 1wk Feb, Sun eve & Tue **Food** Lunch Wed-Mon 12-2.30 Dinner Wed-Sat & Mon 7-9 Av main course £10.95 Restaurant menu available Wed-Sun ⊕ FREE HOUSE ◀ Crafty Carpenter's Cask & Sauvignon Blonde ♂ Aspall. **Facilities** Non-diners area ♦♦ Children's menu Children's portions Garden Outside area ⌁ Parking ⛟ (notice required)

See advert on page 62

PICK OF THE PUBS

The Cock Pub and Restaurant

HEMINGFORD GREY Map 12 TL27

tel: 01480 463609
47 High St PE28 9BJ
email: cock@cambscuisine.com
web: www.cambscuisine.com
dir: *Between A14 juncts 25 & 26, follow village signs*

Confident cooking in a pretty village close to the River Ouse

A handsome 17th-century pub on the main street of the charming village of Hemingford Grey, The Cock stands among thatched, timbered and brick cottages. Although it's only a mile away from the busy A14, it feels like a world away and it's the ideal place to relax with peaceful views across the willow-bordered Great Ouse. Other than the peaceful location, the detour is well worth taking as the food on offer is excellent – the set lunch menu is a steal. The stylishly revamped interior comprises a contemporary bar for drinks only, and a restaurant with bare boards, dark or white-painted beams, wood-burning stoves, and church candles on an eclectic mix of old dining tables. Cooking is modern British, with the occasional foray further afield, and fresh local produce is used in preparing the short, imaginative carte, while daily deliveries of fresh fish dictate the chalkboard menu choice. A typical meal might kick off with smoked chicken and black pepper tian with roast lemon salad; pork, pigeon and prune terrine

with chutney and toast; or beetroot and apple rösti with celeriac remoulade and poached egg. Follow with braised beef cheek with garlic mash, black pudding, creamed Savoy cabbage and red wine sauce; pheasant wrapped in bacon with roast sweet potato, celeriac, sweet onion purée and port sauce; or hake fillet with butterbean, chorizo and tomato stew; then round off with chocolate terrine with stewed cherries and Chantilly cream; warm poached pear with pear and chocolate ice cream and mulled wine syrup, or a plate of unusual cheeses. The wine list specialises in the Languedoc-Roussillion area and the choice of real ales favours local microbreweries, perhaps Nethergate IPA or Brewster's Hophead. A beer festival every Summer Bank Holiday weekend.

Open all wk 11.30-3 6-11 **Food** Set menu (Mon-Fri) & Restaurant menu (all wk) 🛢 FREE HOUSE 🍺 Brewster's Hophead, Great Oakley Wagtail, Oldershaw Best Bitter, Nethergate IPA 🍏 Cromwell. 🍷 18 **Facilities** Non-diners. area 👶 Children's portions Garden 🪑 Beer festival Parking 🚌 (notice required)

HEMINGFORD GREY — Map 12 TL27

The Cock Pub and Restaurant — PICK OF THE PUBS

See Pick of the Pubs on page 63

HILTON — Map 12 TL26

The Prince of Wales

tel: 01480 830257 **Potton Rd PE28 9NG**
email: bookings@thehiltonpow.co.uk
dir: *On B1040 between A14 & A428 S of St Ives*

Popular inn in the heart of rural Cambridgeshire

The Prince of Wales is a traditional, 1830s two-bar village inn. To drink, choose from Adnams, Timothy Taylor Landlord or a guest ale. Food options range from bar snacks to full meals, among which are grills, fish, curries brought in from a local Indian restaurant, and daily specials, such as lamb hotpot. Home-made puddings include crème brûlée and sherry trifle. The village's 400-year-old grass maze was where locals used to escape the devil.

Open 12-2.30 6-11 Closed Mon L **Food** Lunch Tue-Sun 12-2 Dinner all wk 7-9 ⊕ FREE HOUSE ◀ Timothy Taylor Landlord, Adnams, Guest ales ♂ Aspall. ⬤ 9 **Facilities** Non-diners area ✿ (Bar Garden) ♦️ Children's menu Children's portions Garden ⊅ Parking WiFi 🚍

HINXTON — Map 12 TL44

The Red Lion Inn ★★★★ INN ◉ — PICK OF THE PUBS

tel: 01799 530601 **32 High St CB10 1QY**
email: info@redlionhinxton.co.uk **web:** www.redlionhinxton.co.uk
dir: *N'bound only: M11 junct 9, towards A11, left onto A1301. Left to Hinxton. Or M11 junct 10, A505 towards A11/Newmarket. At rdbt take 3rd exit onto A1301, right to Hinxton*

Country pub, restaurant and B&B with super garden

With many awards for what goes on inside, this 16th-century, pink-washed free house and restaurant has much going for it outside too, with a pretty walled garden and dovecote, and a patio that overlooks the church. Four local real ales stand by in the low-ceilinged, wooden-floored bar, three of which - Woodforde's Wherry, Crafty Sauvignon Blonde and the house Red & Black - are fixtures, the fourth a local microbrew. Over 20 wines are sold by the glass. It's good to eat in the bar, but you might prefer the high-raftered, L-shaped restaurant, where high-backed settles, similar to those in the bar, make another appearance. Modern British menu options include locally sourced maple-glazed goose breast with parsnip fondants, purple broccoli and blood orange tuile; pan-fried turbot with potato gnocchi, steamed leeks and moules marinière; and wild mushroom risotto with spring onions and Stilton. A beer festival is held in late summer.

Open all day all wk **Food** Lunch Mon-Thu 12-2, Fri-Sun 12-2.30 Dinner Mon-Thu 6.30-9, Fri-Sat 6.30-9.30, Sun 7-9 Av main course £12 Restaurant menu available all wk ⊕ FREE HOUSE ◀ Crafty Sauvignon Blonde, Woodforde's Wherry, Brandon Rusty Bucket, Adnams, Red & Black, Guest ales ♂ Aspall Harry Sparrow. ⬤ 22 **Facilities** Non-diners area ✿ (Bar Garden) ♦️ Children's menu Children's portions Garden ⊅ Beer festival Cider festival Parking WiFi 🚍 (notice required) **Rooms** 8

HISTON — Map 12 TL46

Red Lion

tel: 01223 564437 **27 High St CB24 9JD**
dir: *M11 junct 14, A14 towards. Exit at junct 32 onto B1049 for Histon*

Village pub with good choice of real ales

A pub since 1836, this popular village local on Cambridge's northern fringe has been run by Mark Donachy for almost two decades. A dyed-in-the-wool pub man, Mark's real ales include Oakham Bishops Farewell, as well as Pickled Pig Porker's

Snout cider. There are also over 30 different bottled beers from around the world. Typical dishes are goats' cheese, beetroot and roasted red onion salad; and pan-fried snapper fillet with new potatoes, chorizo and sauce vièrge. Expect cheerful service, winter log fires and a good-sized neat garden. Time a visit for the Easter or early September beer and cider festivals.

Open all day all wk 10.30am-11pm (Fri 10.30am-mdnt Sun 12-11) **Food** Lunch Mon-Fri 12-2.30, Sat 10.30-9.30, Sun 12-5 Dinner Tue-Thu 6-9.30, Sat 10.30-9.30 Av main course £10 ⊕ FREE HOUSE ◀ Oakham Bishops Farewell, Batemans Yella Belly, Adnams Ghost Ship, Tring Side Pocket for a Toad ♂ Pickled Pig Porker's Snout, Westons Perry. **Facilities** Non-diners area ♦️ Children's portions Family room Garden ⊅ Beer festival Cider festival Parking WiFi 🚍 (notice required)

HORNINGSEA — Map 12 TL46

The Crown & Punchbowl

tel: 01223 860643 **CB5 9JG**
email: info@thecrownandpunchbowl.co.uk
dir: *Phone for detailed directions*

Friendly coaching inn with seasonal menus

Dating back to 1764, the tiled and whitewashed Crown & Punchbowl stands in a little one-street village. Soft colours and wooden floors create a warm atmosphere, while in the low-beamed restaurant innovative influences are at play in dishes created with the finest, locally sourced ingredients: pan-seared scallops with curried parsnip purée, pineapple, chilli jam and curry tuile; and herb-crusted cod supreme, Brancaster mussel and vegetable chowder, parsley and pine nut pesto. The pudding menu is equally appealing, with the likes of blood orange and almond Battenberg, spiced orange and cardamom ice cream; and Bramley apple and sultana samosa, milk purée, apple sorbet, apple crisps and crushed hazelnuts.

Open Mon-Sat 12-3 6.30-9.30 (Sun 12-3) Closed Sun eve & BHs eve **Food** Contact pub for details ⊕ FREE HOUSE ◀ Thwaites Original. **Facilities** Non-diners area ♦️ Children's portions Garden ⊅ Parking WiFi

KEYSTON — Map 11 TL07

Pheasant Inn ◉◉ — PICK OF THE PUBS

tel: 01832 710241 **Village Loop Rd PE28 0RE**
email: info@thepheasant-keyston.co.uk
dir: *0.5m from A14, clearly signed, 10m W of Huntingdon, 14m E of Kettering*

Sixteenth-century village inn with excellent food

In 1964, long before the term gastro-pub had been coined, the Hoskins family bought The Pheasant and started serving top-quality food. Maintaining the policy are today's owners, Simon Cadge and Gerda Koedijk, while John Hoskins, a Master of Wine, is still involved, compiling the wine list. In a sleepy farming village, the pub is thatched and very pretty, with a large, oak-beamed bar serving Adnams, Nene Valley and Digfield Barnwell Bitter. At the rear the Garden Room surveys a sunny patio and herb garden. Simon relies greatly on local produce for his menus, but not so much that he can't offer Shetland mussels; braised Cornish lamb shank; and Uig Lodge smoked salmon from the Isle of Lewis. His comprehensive menu also lists glazed Barbary duck breast; skate croquette; steak and ale casserole; and home-made black pudding. A dessert to catch the eye is rhubarb trifle with passionfruit custard.

Open 12-3 6-11 (Sun 12-5) Closed Mon & Sun eve **Food** Lunch Tue-Sat 12-2 Dinner Tue-Sat 6.30-9.30 Set menu available ⊕ FREE HOUSE ◀ Adnams Broadside, Nene Valley NVB, Digfield Ales Barnwell Bitter ♂ Aspall. ⬤ 16 **Facilities** Non-diners area ✿ (Bar Restaurant Garden) ♦️ Children's menu Children's portions Garden ⊅ Parking WiFi 🚍 (notice required)

LITTLE WILBRAHAM — Map 12 TL55

Hole in the Wall 🏆🏆 — PICK OF THE PUBS

tel: 01223 812282 **2 High St CB21 5JY**
email: info@holeinthewallcambridge.com
dir: Phone for detailed directions

Enjoyable food from an award-winning chef

The name of this 16th-century village pub and restaurant between Cambridge and Newmarket comes from the days when farm workers used to collect their jugs of beer through a hole in the wall so as not to upset the gentry in the bar. The heavily timbered pub is owned by former BBC MasterChef finalist Alex Rushmer who has created an award-winning enterprise. Customers can drink ales from the Milton Brewery and the Indian Summer Brewing Company in the hop-adorned bar. The first-class modern British cooking is prepared from fresh local produce and includes turkey, bacon and leek pie; and local venison sausages, mash and red cabbage at lunch and, in the evening, Keen's Cheddar and onion rarebit tart; or Blythburgh pork chop with potato and butternut mash, cider and mustard sauce. Finish with passionfruit posset or rice pudding, apple compôte and crumble.

Open 11.30-3 6.30-11 Closed 2wks Jan, 25 Dec, Mon, Tue L, Sun eve **Food** Lunch Wed-Sun 12-2 Dinner Tue-Sat 7-9 Set menu available ⊕ FREE HOUSE ◀ Milton Brewery, Indian Summer Brewing Co ♂ Aspall. ♀ 10 **Facilities** Non-diners area ◆▮ Children's portions Garden ⌒ Parking WiFi

MADINGLEY — Map 12 TL36

The Three Horseshoes — PICK OF THE PUBS

tel: 01954 210221 **High St CB23 8AB**
email: 3hs@btconnect.com
dir: M11 junct 13, 1.5m from A14

Cutting edge meals in traditional pub

Chimneys of mellow brick pierce the thick thatch of this cute village inn outside Cambridge. Between the reed-roofed main building and the extensive beer garden, a substantial conservatory restaurant bathes in the dappled light cast by mature trees edging this plot in one of the county's most charming villages. With tasty beers from the likes of City of Cambridge brewery and 22 wines by the glass, the wet side of the business attracts a good following. The meals emerging from the kitchen overseen by chef-patron Richard Stokes take the treat to another level again. A meal could start with quail with chestnut cream, king brown mushroom, truffle and parsley crumbs, then mains may continue with pan-fried cod fillet, deep-fried spiced cauliflower ras al hanout, buckwheat, sultanas and almonds; or roast duck breast, smoked beet juice, salt-baked kohlrabi, cicoria, grains and sprouts. Still room, perhaps, for crack pie with passionfruit curd and pomegranate sherbet? Menus change weekly and seasonally; children's portions are available.

Open all wk 11.30-3 6-11 (Sun 11.30-3 6-9.30) **Food** Lunch Mon-Fri 12-2, Sat-Sun 12-2.30 Dinner all wk 6.30-9.30 Restaurant menu available all wk ⊕ FREE HOUSE ◀ Adnams Southwold Bitter, Hook Norton Old Hooky, Smiles Best Bitter, City of Cambridge Hobson's Choice, Guest ales ♂ Westons Stowford Press. ♀ 22 **Facilities** Non-diners area ◆▮ Children's portions Garden Outside area ⌒ Parking WiFi ▭ (notice required)

NEWTON — Map 12 TL44

The Queen's Head

tel: 01223 870436 **Fowlmere Rd CB22 7PG**
dir: 6m S of Cambridge on B1368, 1.5m off A10 at Harston, 4m from A505

No nonsense food and good beer in old fashioned pub

The same family has owned and operated this tiny and very traditional village pub for some 50 years. Unchanging and unmarred by gimmickry, the stone-tiled bars, replete with log fires, pine settles and old school benches, draw an eclectic clientele, from Cambridge dons to local farm workers. They all come for tip-top Adnams ale direct from the barrel, the friendly, honest atmosphere and straightforward pub dishes. Food is simple – at lunch, soup, sandwiches and Aga-baked potatoes. In the evening, just soup, toast and beef dripping, and cold platters. Village tradition is kept alive with time-honoured pub games – dominoes, table skittles, shove ha'penny and nine men's Morris.

Open all wk 11.30-2.30 6-11 (Sun 12-2.30 7-10.30) Closed 25-26 Dec **Food** Lunch all wk 12-2.15 Dinner all wk 7-9.30 ⊕ FREE HOUSE ◀ Adnams Southwold Bitter, Broadside, Fisherman, Regatta ♂ Crones. ♀ 9 **Facilities** Non-diners area ♣ (Bar Outside area) ◆▮ Children's portions Family room Outside area ⌒ Parking **Notes** ⊗

OFFORD D'ARCY — Map 12 TL26

The Horseshoe Inn

tel: 01480 810293 **90 High St PE19 5RH**
email: info@theoffordshoe.co.uk
dir: Between Huntingdon & St Neots. 1.5m from Buckden on A1

Inventive cooking at inn close to the river

Built by a yeoman farmer in 1626, this spruced up pub-restaurant (aka The Offord Shoe) stands close to the River Ouse in a sleepy village just off the A1. Famished travellers keen to escape the faceless services will find two comfortable bars serving good local real ales – try a pint of Nethergate Old Growler – and an imaginative changing menu. Chef-patron Richard Kennedy offers lunchtime pub classics like beer-battered haddock and hand-cut chips or seasonal dishes such as braised rabbit with mustard and button mushrooms; slow cooked pork belly with haricot bean stew; and pan-roasted hake with spiced lentils and coriander yogurt. A midsummer beer festival is held on the green.

Open all wk **Food** Lunch Mon-Sat 12-2.30 Dinner Mon-Sat 6-9.30 Set menu available Restaurant menu available all wk ⊕ FREE HOUSE ◀ Adnams Southwold Bitter, Nethergate Old Growler, Sharp's Doom Bar. ♀ 17 **Facilities** Non-diners area ♣ (Bar Garden) ◆▮ Children's portions Play area Garden ⌒ Beer festival Parking WiFi ▭ (notice required)

PETERBOROUGH — Map 12 TL19

The Brewery Tap

tel: 01733 358500 **80 Westgate PE1 2AA**
email: brewerytap.manager@oakagroup.com
dir: Opposite bus station

Award-winning brewpub with American style and local ales

Located in the old labour exchange on Westgate, this striking American-style pub is home to the multi-award winning Oakham Brewery and it is one of the largest brewpubs in Europe. Visitors can see the day-to-day running of the brewery through a glass wall spanning half the length of the bar. As if the appeal of the 12 real ales and the vast range of bottled beers was not enough, Thai chefs beaver away producing delicious snacks, soups, salads, stir-fries and curries. Look out for live music nights, and DJs on Saturday nights.

Open all day all wk Closed 25-26 Dec, 1 Jan **Food** Lunch Mon-Thu 12-2.30, Fri-Sat 12-10.30, Sun 12-3.30 Dinner Mon-Thu 5.30-10.30, Fri-Sat 12-10.30, Sun 5.30-9.30 ⊕ FREE HOUSE ◀ Oakham Inferno, Citra, JHB & Bishops Farewell, Guest ales ♂ Westons Old Rosie, Rosie's Pig & Wyld Wood Vintage, Oakham Opale. ♀ 10 **Facilities** Non-diners area ♣ (Bar) ◆▮ WiFi ▭

PETERBOROUGH *continued*

Charters Bar & East Restaurant

tel: 01733 315700 & 315702 (bkgs) **Upper Deck, Town Bridge PE1 1FP**
email: charters.manager@oakagroup.com
dir: *A1/A47 towards Wisbech, 2m to city centre & town bridge (River Nene). Barge moored at Town Bridge (west side)*

Moored barge on the River Nene

The largest floating real ale emporium in Britain can be found moored in the heart of Peterborough. The 176-foot converted barge motored from Holland across the North Sea in 1991, and is now a haven for real-ale and cider-lovers. Twelve hand pumps dispense a continually changing repertoire of cask ales, while entertainment, dancing, live music and an Easter beer festival are regular features. The 'East' part of the name applies to the oriental restaurant on the upper deck which offers a comprehensive selection of pan-Asian dishes.

Open all day all wk 12-11 (Fri-Sat noon-2am) Closed 25-26 Dec, 1 Jan **Food** Lunch all wk 12-2.30 Av main course £5.95 Set menu available Restaurant menu available all wk ⊕ FREE HOUSE ◁ Oakham JHB, Bishops Farewell, Citra, Inferno & Scarlet Macaw, Guest ales ♂ Westons Old Rosie & Traditional. ☕ 10 **Facilities** Non-diners area ✿ (Bar Garden) ◆◆ Garden ⊼ Beer festival Cider festival Parking WiFi ═ (notice required)

| **REACH** | Map 12 TL56 |

Dyke's End

tel: 01638 743816 **CB25 0JD**
dir: *Phone for detailed directions*

At the heart of village life

Located in the centre of the village, overlooking the green, this pub was saved from closure by villagers in the 1990s. They ran it as a co-operative until 2003, when it was bought by Frank Feehan, who further refurbished and extended it. Frank's additions included the Devil's Dyke microbrewery, which continues to be run by owners Catherine and George Gibson. The pub has a strong local following for its food and beers. The menu is seasonal with daily-changing specials, although pub favourites like beer-battered haddock and steak frites are always popular.

Open 12-2.30 6-11 (Sat-Sun 12-11) Closed Mon L **Food** Lunch Tue-Sun 12-2 Dinner all wk 7-9 ⊕ FREE HOUSE ◁ Devil's Dyke, Thwaites Wainwright, Adnams Southwold Bitter ♂ Aspall. ☕ 8 **Facilities** Non-diners area ✿ (Bar Restaurant Garden) ◆◆ Children's portions Play area Family room Garden ⊼ Parking WiFi

---

| **SPALDWICK** | Map 12 TL17 |

The George

tel: 01480 890293 **5-7 High St PE28 0TD**
email: info@thegeorgespaldwick.co.uk
dir: *In village centre. Just off A14 junct 18. 5m W of Huntingdon*

Village centre inn gaining high praise

Dating from 1679, this former coaching inn is today a successful pub and restaurant with 21st-century credentials, yet which has retained its rustic charm and character. Proving the point is the bar, with its low ceilings and wooden floor, serving local real ales and snacks from sandwiches to light meals, such as home-made chilli with wild rice. In the restaurant, dishes similarly making use of free-range or organic meats, seasonal vegetables and other locally supplied produce include chargrilled Aberdeenshire steak; pan-fried sea bass; and Mediterranean Wellington. Tables on the lawns and a terraced patio are popular on fine days.

Open all wk 11.30-3 5.30-11 (Sat 11.30am-mdnt Sun 12-10.30) **Food** Lunch Mon-Sat 12-2.30, Sun 12-7 Dinner Mon-Sat 6-9, Sun 12-7 Restaurant menu available all wk ⊕ PUNCH TAVERNS ◁ Woodforde's Wherry, Timothy Taylor Landlord, Black Sheep. ☕ 9 **Facilities** Non-diners area ✿ (Bar Garden Outside area) ◆◆ Children's menu Children's portions Garden Outside area ⊼ Beer festival Cider festival Parking WiFi ═ (notice required)

| **STAPLEFORD** | Map 12 TL45 |

The Rose at Stapleford

tel: 01223 843349 **81 London Rd CB22 5DG**
email: info@rose-stapleford.co.uk
dir: *Phone for detailed directions*

Great home-cooked food and accredited ales

Paul and Karen Beer have weaved some magic at The Rose, a traditional village pub close to Cambridge and Duxford Imperial War Museum. Expect a stylish interior, replete with low beams and inglenook fireplaces, and extensive menus that draw on local Suffolk produce, particularly meat, with fish from Lowestoft. As well as a good selection of seafood appetisers, typical main dishes include home-made vegetable curry; warm Cajun chicken salad; wild mushroom Stroganoff; and beef lasagne.

Open all wk 12-3 5.30-11 (Sun 12-10.30) **Food** Lunch Mon-Sat 12-2, Sun 12-8.30 Dinner Mon-Sat 5.30-9.30, Sun 12-8.30 Set menu available Restaurant menu available Mon-Sat ⊕ CHARLES WELLS ◁ Wells Bombardier, Courage Directors, Young's ♂ Symonds. ☕ 12 **Facilities** Non-diners area ◆◆ Children's menu Children's portions Garden ⊼ Parking ═ (notice required)

| **STILTON** | Map 12 TL18 |

The Bell Inn Hotel ★★★ HL ⊛ | PICK OF THE PUBS |

tel: 01733 241066 **Great North Rd PE7 3RA**
email: reception@thebellstilton.co.uk **web:** www.thebellstilton.co.uk
dir: *From A1(M) junct 16 follow signs for Stilton. Hotel on main road in village centre*

Handsome stone inn with historic Stilton pedigree

A Bell Inn has stood here since 1500, although this one is mid-17th century and it is reputedly the oldest coaching inn on the old Great North Road, with an impressive stone façade, a splendid inn sign and a fine original interior with an upbeat feel. It once welcomed (or maybe not!) highwayman Dick Turpin, as well as Lord Byron and Clark Gable, who was stationed nearby in 1943. Modern British dishes in the Bar/Bistro include confit of pheasant; and home-cured salt beef, sour cream and gherkins; Dingley Dell pork belly, pearl barley broth, mash and kale; and beef and Guinness casserole with Stilton dumplings. Famous as the birthplace of Stilton cheese, the pub is again making their own, called Bell Blue, and the Stilton cheese sampler is a must to try. All the en suite bedrooms are round the old courtyard — two have four-posters.

Open all wk 12-2.30 6-11 (Sat 12-3 6-12 Sun 12-11) Closed 25 Dec **Food** Lunch Mon-Sat 12-2.30, Sun 12-3 Dinner all wk 6-9.30 ⊕ FREE HOUSE ◁ Greene King IPA, Oakham Bishops Farewell, Digfield Fool's Nook, Guest ales ♂ Aspall. ☕ 11 **Facilities** Non-diners area ✿ (Garden) ◆◆ Children's menu Children's portions Garden ⊼ Parking WiFi ═ (notice required) **Rooms** 22

STRETHAM Map 12 TL57

The Lazy Otter ★★★★ INN

tel: 01353 649780 **Cambridge Rd CB6 3LU**
email: thelazyotter@btconnect.com **web:** www.lazy-otter.com
dir: *Phone for detailed directions*

Welcoming waterside focal point amidst the Fens

A pub here has served fenland watermen for several centuries; today's bustling incarnation is popular with leisure boaters on the River Ouse, which glides past the extensive beer garden, from which are cracking views over the rich farmland. Barley from these acres goes into the good range of East Anglian beers, including the house ale from Milton Brewery; an annual beer and cider festival is also held. The contemporary restaurant has modern dishes like gnocchi in Stilton, spinach and pea creamy sauce; traditionalists can savour rich home-made pies or smoked haddock and poached egg.

Open all day all wk 7am-11pm (Sun 8.30am-10.30pm) **Food** Contact pub for details Restaurant menu available all wk ⊕ FREE HOUSE ◀ Adnams Broadside, Milton Lazy Otter, Milton Tiki, Oakham JHB, Woodforde's Wherry, Guest ales ♂ Westons Stowford Press & Old Rosie. ♟ 10 **Facilities** Non-diners area ✿ (All areas) ♦♦ Children's menu Children's portions Play area Garden Outside area ⋈ Beer festival Cider festival Parking WiFi ⋙ **Rooms** 3

The Red Lion

tel: 01353 648132 **47 High St CB6 3LD**
email: redlion@charnwoodpubco.co.uk
dir: *Exit A10 between Cambridge & Ely into Stretham. Left into High St, pub on right*

Busy local with traditional food

In the village of Stretham ten miles north of Cambridge, this former coaching inn has a busy locals' bar where you can enjoy a pint of Adnams beer or Pickled Pig cider with bar meals such as a chicken fajita wrap with chips and salad or a whole baked camembert with crusty bread. Alternatively, head to the conservatory-style restaurant for traditional home-made favourites such as battered fish and chips; lasagne; steak and ale pie; home-cooked ham, eggs and chips; or one of the steaks from the grill, served with chips and salad.

Open all day all wk **Food** Lunch all wk 12-2.30 Dinner all wk 6-9 ⊕ CHARNWOOD PUB CO ◀ Greene King IPA, Wychwood Hobgoblin, Adnams, Marston's ♂ Pickled Pig. ♟ 8 **Facilities** Non-diners area ✿ (Bar Garden) ♦♦ Children's menu Children's portions Garden ⋈ Parking WiFi ⋙ (notice required)

UFFORD Map 12 TF00

The White Hart ★★★★ INN

tel: 01780 740250 **Main St PE9 3BH**
email: info@whitehartufford.co.uk **web:** www.whitehartufford.co.uk
dir: *From Stamford take B1443 signed Barnack. Through Barnack, follow signs to Ufford*

Creative menus, local ales and a warm welcome

Salvaged cast-iron railway signs and old agricultural tools embellish the bar of this 17th-century country inn, serving Aspall Suffolk Cyder and four real ales. An extensive wine list reflects the help of Master of Wine, John Atkinson. Locally sourced produce including game finds its way onto the seasonal menus, perhaps alongside traditional Lincolnshire sausages, mash and onion gravy; Thai-style seafood casserole; and wild mushroom, spinach and smoked Lincolnshire Poacher cheese risotto. Four individually styled bedrooms are in the main building, two in the converted cart shed.

Open all day all wk Mon-Thu 9am-11pm (Fri-Sat 9am-mdnt Sun 9-9) **Food** Lunch Mon-Sat 12-2.30, Sun 12-6 Dinner Mon-Sat 6-9.30 ⊕ FREE HOUSE ◀ Black Sheep, Sharp's Doom Bar, Castle Rock Harvest Pale, Adnams ♂ Aspall. ♟ 10 **Facilities** Non-diners area ✿ (Bar Garden) ♦♦ Children's menu Children's portions Play area Garden ⋈ Parking WiFi ⋙ (notice required) **Rooms** 6

WHITTLESFORD Map 12 TL44

NEW The Tickell Arms

tel: 01223 833025 **North Rd CB22 4NZ**
email: tickell@cambscuisine.com
dir: *M11 junct 10, A505 towards Saffron Walden. Left signed Whittlesford*

Food prepared and served by a knowledgeable team

Part of the Cambscuisine (that's cuisine from Cambridgeshire) group, this blue-washed village pub stands behind a neat, white picket fence. The car park is entered through wrought-iron gates. Inside the pub are elegant fireplaces, gilt mirrors and whimsical bowler hat-shaped lampshades. Among the four local real ales is Pegasus from Milton Brewery in Cambridge, and from Hemingford Grey comes Cromwell cider. The restaurant serves seasonal modern British and European food from a regularly-changing menu. Examples are slow-cooked ox cheek; pan-fried duck breast; and fresh fish from Peterhead. The garden room and terrace overlook a pond. The beer festival is in May.

Open all wk **Food** Lunch Mon-Fri 12-2.30, Sat-Sun 12-5 Dinner Mon-Fri 6-11, Sat-Sun 5-11 Av main course £17 Set menu available Restaurant menu available all wk ⊕ FREE HOUSE ◀ Milton Pegasus, Brewster's Hophead ♂ Cromwell. ♟ 16 **Facilities** Non-diners area ✿ (Bar Garden) ♦♦ Children's menu Children's portions Garden ⋈ Beer festival Parking WiFi ⋙ (notice required)

CHESHIRE

ALDFORD Map 15 SJ45

The Grosvenor Arms PICK OF THE PUBS

tel: 01244 620228 **Chester Rd CH3 6HJ**
email: grosvenor.arms@brunningandprice.co.uk
dir: *On B5130, S of Chester*

Freshly cooked food with broad appeal

With its red brick and black and white timbering, this higgledy-piggledy Brunning & Price pub was designed by Victorian architect John Douglas, who designed around 500 buildings, many of them in Cheshire. The spacious, open-plan interior includes an airy conservatory and a panelled, book-filled library. The range of real ales from small breweries around the country changes all the time so it's no wonder the locals are fond of it. On the bistro-style menu, starters may feature potted mackerel and shrimp with horseradish butter, potato cakes and pickled cucumber, which might precede main courses of Red Leicester, potato and onion pie; or pan-fried duck breast with confit carrot, roasted beetroot, dauphinoise potato, redcurrant and balsamic jus. Leave room for glazed lime tart with passionfruit sauce, mascarpone and citrus fruit salad. A terrace leads into a small but pleasing garden, and on out to the village green.

Open all day all wk **Food** Lunch Mon-Thu 12-9.30, Fri-Sat 12-10, Sun 12-9 Dinner Mon-Thu 12-9.30, Fri-Sat 12-10, Sun 12-9 Av main course £12.95 ⊕ FREE HOUSE/ BRUNNING & PRICE ◀ Original Bitter, Weetwood Eastgate Ale, Phoenix, Guest ales ♂ Westons Stowford Press, Aspall. ♟ 20 **Facilities** Non-diners area ✿ (Bar Garden) ♦♦ Children's menu Children's portions Garden ⋈ Parking WiFi

---

Find out more about the AA's accommodation rating schemes on page 8

PICK OF THE PUBS

The Bhurtpore Inn

ASTON   Map 15 SJ64

tel: 01270 780917
Wrenbury Rd CW5 8DQ
email: simonbhurtpore@yahoo.co.uk
web: www.bhurtpore.co.uk
dir: *Just off A530 between Nantwich &*
Whitchurch. Follow Wrenbury signs at
x-rds in village

Friendly traditional inn with real community spirit

A pub since at least 1778, when it was called the Queen's Head. It subsequently became the Red Lion, but it was Lord Combermere's success at the Siege of Bhurtpore in India in 1826 that inspired the name that has stuck. Simon and Nicky George came across it in 1991, boarded-up and stripped out. Simon is a direct descendant of Joyce George, who leased the pub from the Combermere Estate in 1849, so was motivated by his family history to take on the hard work of restoring the interior. Since then, 'award winning' hardly does justice to the accolades heaped upon this hostelry. In the bar, 11 ever-changing real ales are always available, mostly from local microbreweries, as are real ciders, continental draught lagers and around 150 of the world's bottled beers. An annual beer festival, reputedly Cheshire's largest, is in its 18th year, with around 130 real ales. The pub has also been shortlisted five times for the 'National Whisky Pub of the Year' award,

and there is a long soft drinks menu. Recognition extends to the kitchen too, where unfussy dishes of classic pub fare are prepared. Among the hearty British ingredients you'll find seasonal game, such as venison haunch on cabbage with smoked bacon and cream; and rabbit loin with a pork and black pudding stuffing. Curries and balti dishes are always on the blackboard. Vintage vehicles bring their owners here on the first Thursday of the month, and folk musicians play on the third Tuesday.

Open all wk 12-2.30 6.30-11.30, Fri-Sat 12-12, Sun 12-11 Closed 25-26 Dec, 1 Jan **Food** Mon-Fri 12-2 6.30-9.30 Sat 12-9.30 Sun 12-9 Av main course £10.95 ⊕ FREE HOUSE ◖ Salopian

Golden Thread, Abbeydale Absolution, Weetwood Oast-House Gold, Hobsons Twisted Spire ♻ Thatchers Cheddar Valley, Wrenbury. **Facilities** ✤ (Bar Garden Outside area) ⁙ Children's portions Garden Outside area Beer festival Parking WiFi ☷ (notice required)

ALLOSTOCK
Map 15 SJ77

The Three Greyhounds Inn

tel: 01565 723455 **Holmes Chapel Rd WA16 9JY**
email: info@thethreegreyhoundsinn.co.uk **web:** www.thethreegreyhoundsinn.co.uk
dir: *S from Allostock on A50. Right on B5082 signed Northwich. Over M6, pub on right*

A real find at a rural crossroads

This 300-year-old former farmhouse is now a stylishly eclectic dining pub. Inside is a warren of atmospheric rooms, replete with exposed beams, rugs on wooden floors, crackling log fires in brick fireplaces, fat candles on old dining tables, and a host of quirky touches to make you smile. Go there for a choice of five local ales and over 50 brandies behind the bar, and some cracking pub food – seafood sharing plate; potted beef with stout piccalilli; cod loin with shrimp butter; duck leg and haricot bean stew; apple and Calvados crumble, and an imaginative choice of sandwiches. Book ahead for the memorable Sunday lunches. Dogs are welcome in the snug and the garden.

Open all day all wk **Food** Lunch all wk 12-9.30 Dinner all wk 12-9.30 ⊕ FREE HOUSE ◼ Almighty Allostock Ale, Byley Bomber, Merlins Gold, Three Greyhound Bitter, Weetwood Ales Cheshire Cat. ☻ 15 **Facilities** Non-diners area ❄ (Bar Garden) ⧫ Children's portions Garden ⧉ Parking WiFi ▭ (notice required)

ASTON
Map 15 SJ64

The Bhurtpore Inn
PICK OF THE PUBS

See Pick of the Pubs on opposite page

BROXTON
Map 15 SJ45

Egerton Arms

tel: 01829 782241 **Whitchurch Rd CH3 9JW**
email: egertonarms@woodwardandfalconer.com
dir: *On A41 between Whitchurch & Chester*

Spacious pub with sun-trap garden

This elegant, eye-catching Victorian roadhouse is part of a small group of quality dining pubs bringing together excellent local beers with top-notch food from the generous larders of the area. It's handy for active visitors making the most of Cheshire's hilly sandstone spine, with its castles, hill fort and countless byways. Wind down in the extensive garden, enjoying a glass of Weetwood beer and discerning your choices from the well-balanced, regularly updated menu which is strong on seafood (lobster thermidor is a signature dish) and generous with both meat and vegetarian options. There's an airy country-house feel to the inside, where myriad local photos add interest.

Open all day all wk 12-11 (Sun 12-10.30) Closed 25 Dec & 31 Dec eve **Food** Contact pub for details ⊕ WOODWARD & FALCONER PUBS LTD ◼ Piffle & Balderdash, Weetwood Ales. ☻ 16 **Facilities** Non-diners area ⧫ Children's menu Children's portions Play area Family room Garden ⧉ Parking WiFi ▭

BUNBURY
Map 15 SJ55

The Dysart Arms
PICK OF THE PUBS

tel: 01829 260183 **Bowes Gate Rd CW6 9PH**
email: dysart.arms@brunningandprice.co.uk
dir: *Between A49 & A51, by Shropshire Union Canal*

Well defined English hostelry

A classic English village pub with open fires, lots of old oak, full-height bookcases and a pretty garden with views to two castles and the neighbouring parish church. Built as a farmhouse in the mid-18th century and licensed since the late 1800s, it once functioned simultaneously as a farm, an abattoir and a pub; the abattoir building was demolished by a German bomber on its way home from 'rearranging' the Liverpool docks. The hostelry is named after local landowners, the Earls of Dysart, whose coat of arms is above the door. An ever-changing line-up of ales is served in the central bar, around which are several airy rooms perfect for drinking and eating. Snacks include a home-made fish finger butty; starters may list venison carpaccio with candied red cabbage; and main courses range from breast of pheasant with bacon and chestnut hash cake, to a pine nut-encrusted hake fillet.

Open all day all wk 11.30-11 (Sun 12-10.30) **Food** Lunch Mon-Sat 12-9.30, Sun 12-9 Dinner Mon-Sat 12-9.30, Sun 12-9 Av main course £12.50 ⊕ BRUNNING & PRICE ◼ Original Bitter, Weetwood Best Cask, Guest ales ♂ Aspall. ☻ 18 **Facilities** Non-diners area ❄ (Bar Garden Outside area) ⧫ Children's menu Children's portions Garden Outside area ⧉ Parking WiFi

PICK OF THE PUBS

The Pheasant Inn ★★★★★ INN 🏵

BURWARDSLEY   Map 15 SJ55

tel: 01829 770434
CH3 9PF
email: info@thepheasantinn.co.uk
web: www.thepheasantinn.co.uk
dir: *A41 (Chester to Whitchurch) left signed Tattenhall. Through Tattenhall to Burwardsley. In Burwardsley follow Cheshire Workshops signs*

Newly refurbished pub with magnificent views

High on the sandstone ridge known as the Peckforton Hills stands Beeston Castle. Enjoying a similarly lofty position on its west-facing slopes overlooking the Cheshire Plain, is this 300-year-old former farmhouse and barn, where only five families have been licensees since it became an alehouse. Such is its elevation that you can see the Welsh hills and two cathedrals, Liverpool's 23 miles away and, much nearer, Chester's. Particularly familiar with the Pheasant are walkers and hikers on the Sandstone Trail long-distance footpath that links Frodsham on the Mersey with Whitchurch in Shropshire. On a fine day the obvious place to be is in the flower-filled courtyard or on the terrace, but when the weather dictates otherwise grab a space by the big open fire in the wooden-floored, heftily-beamed bar. Here you'll find four real ales, three from the Weetwood Brewery near Tarporley,

The kitchen makes extensive use of local produce, while much of the seafood comes from Fleetwood in Lancashire. With the daily-changing restaurant menu offering a wide choice of modern British and European dishes, think about starting with crispy beef hash cake with beetroot ketchup, fried egg and Wirral watercress; or Loch Duart smoked salmon with shallots and capers. Follow with slow-braised blade of Ridings Reserve beef bourguignon; sizzling tiger prawns and monkfish in sweet chilli sauce; or coriander and chilli gnocchi with tomato fondue, caramelised orange and pesto. And don't miss the choices on the specials board. Comfortable en suite accommodation is available.

Open all day all wk **Food** Lunch Mon-Thu 12-9.30, Fri-Sat 12-10, Sun 12-9 Dinner served Mon-Thu 12-9.30, Fri-Sat 12-10, Sun 12-9 ⊕ FREE HOUSE ◾ Weetwood Old Dog Premium Bitter, Eastgate Ale & Best Bitter, Guest ale ○ Kingstone Press. ♟ 12
Facilities Non-diners area ❤ (Bar Restaurant Garden) ♦♦ Children's menu Children's portions Garden ⋒ Parking 🚌 (notice required) WiFi **Rooms** 12

BURLEYDAM
Map 15 SJ64

The Combermere Arms

tel: 01948 871223 **SY13 4AT**
email: combermere.arms@brunningandprice.co.uk
dir: *From Whitchurch take A525 towards Nantwich, at Newcastle/Audlem/Woore sign, turn right at junct. Pub 100yds on right*

Classic coaching inn with impressive menu

Local shoots, walkers and town folk frequent this classic 17th-century country inn. Full of character and warmth, it has three roaring fires and a wealth of oak, nooks and crannies, pictures and old furniture. Food options range from light bites such as a rump steak sandwich to full meals – maybe garlic wild mushrooms on toasted brioche followed by steak and kidney pudding with mash, buttered greens and gravy. You could finish with chocolate and chilli tart with an orange and mint salad. There is a great choice of real ales and ciders, an informative wine list and impressive cheese board.

Open all day all wk 11.30-11 **Food** Lunch Sun-Thu 12-9, Fri-Sat 12-10 Dinner Sun-Thu 12-9, Fri-Sat 12-10 ⊕ FREE HOUSE/BRUNNING & PRICE ◀ Original Bitter, Weetwood Cheshire Cat, Wadworth 6X, Guest ales Ö Westons Stowford Press, Thatchers Green Goblin, Aspall. ♀ 20 **Facilities** Non-diners area ♦♦ Children's menu Children's portions Garden ⊼ Parking WiFi

BURWARDSLEY
Map 15 SJ55

The Pheasant Inn ★★★★★ INN ⊛   PICK OF THE PUBS

See Pick of the Pubs on opposite page

CHELFORD
Map 15 SJ87

NEW Egerton Arms

tel: 01625 861366 **Knutsford Rd SK11 9BB**
email: jeremy@chelfordegertonarms.co.uk **web:** www.chelfordegertonarms.co.uk
dir: *On A537 (Knutsford to Macclesfield road)*

Family-run and family welcoming pub/restaurant

Sited in Cheshire's best countryside in the affluent area known as the 'golden triangle', the Egerton Arms is efficiently and enthusiastically run by Jeremy Hague. Low beams, large fireplaces, eccentric antiques and a long bar with brass pumps characterise the interior of this 16th-century building, whose history is closely tied to Lord Egerton and his Tatton Park estate near by. Six local real ales are briskly served in the bar, while the 100-seat restaurant caters to hungry families with a menu full of pub classics, including deli boards, grills, and pizzas from the stone-baked oven. There is now a deli adjoining to the pub which sells a wide choice of artisan produce from all over the country.

Open all day all wk **Food** Lunch all day Dinner all day Av main course £11 Restaurant menu available all wk ⊕ FREE HOUSE ◀ Wells Bombardier, Copper

Dragon, 4 Local ales. ♀ 9 **Facilities** Non-diners area ♣ (All areas) ♦♦ Children's menu Children's portions Play area Garden Outside area ⊼ Parking WiFi ▥ (notice required)

CHESTER
Map 15 SJ46

The Brewery Tap

tel: 01244 340999 **52-54 Lower Bridge St CH1 1RU**
email: drink@the-tap.co.uk
dir: *From B5268 in Chester into Lower Bridge St towards river*

Great ale in historic city surroundings

This historic pub is situated in part of Gamul House, named after Sir Francis Gamul, a wealthy merchant and mayor of Chester who built it in 1620. It is reputedly where Charles I stayed when his troops were defeated at Rowton Moor, shortly before the king's final flight to Wales. Relax with a Thirstquencher ale and enjoy the pub's numerous period details, then choose from a menu of hearty pub favourites such as smoked mackerel, beetroot and horseradish; braised beef and Old Wavertonian pie, pickled red cabbage and fat chips.

Open all day all wk Closed 25-26 Dec **Food** Lunch Mon-Sat 12-9.30, Sun 12-9 Dinner Mon-Sat 12-9.30, Sun 12-9 ⊕ FREE HOUSE/SPITTING FEATHERS ◀ Thirstquencher, Old Wavertonian Stout Ö Gwynt y Ddraig Black Dragon, Guest ciders. ♀ 14 **Facilities** Non-diners area ♦♦ WiFi

Old Harkers Arms

tel: 01244 344525 **1 Russell St CH3 5AL**
email: harkers.arms@brunningandprice.co.uk
dir: *Close to railway station, on canal side*

A buzzy city watering hole

Housed in a former Victorian chandler's warehouse beside the Shropshire Union Canal, the tall windows, lofty ceilings, wooden floors and bar constructed from salvaged doors make this one of Chester's more unusual pubs. The bar offers over 100 malt whiskies and ales from a range of breweries. The daily-changing menu from light dishes such as crab linguine through to main courses like lamb shoulder, dauphinoise potatoes and sticky red cabbage; cauliflower and chickpea tagine; and honey-glazed ham. The pub holds events such as 'Pudding, Pie and Great British Beers Week' in February or March time, where over 20 award-winning ales can be tried, plus a 'Pie and Champion Ale' week in October.

Open all day all wk 10.30am-11pm (Sun 12-10.30) Closed 25 Dec **Food** Lunch all wk 12-9.30 Dinner all wk 12-9.30 Av main course £11.95 ⊕ FREE HOUSE/BRUNNING & PRICE ◀ Brunning & Price Original Bitter, Weetwood Cheshire Cat, Flowers Original, Salopian, Derby, Facer's North Star Porter Ö Westons Country Perry, Gwynt y Ddraig Black Dragon. ♀ 15 **Facilities** Non-diners area ♣ (Bar Outside area) Outside area ⊼ Beer festival Cider festival WiFi

NEW The Stamford Bridge

tel: 01829 740229 **CH3 7HN**
email: stamfordbridge@woodwardandfalconer.com
dir: *A51 from Chester towards Tarporley, left at lights, pub on left*

Relaxing country-edge inn with fine menu and beers

Close to the little River Gowy, Chester's fabulous heritage and fine zoo, this out-of-town country inn has nice views across the Cheshire Plain from its beer garden. Inside, country-house meets cottage with grand log fires, library shelves and a comfy mix of leather and rustic furnishings scattered beneath heavy beams. Real ales from Cheshire and Conwy vie for attention at the bar; diners can anticipate a generous fish menu alongside mains like venison hotpot or creamed leek and chickpea cannelloni, with an all-day menu change every six weeks to add spice to the mix.

continued

CHESTER *continued*

Open all day all wk 12-11 (Sun 12-10.30) Closed 25 Dec & 31 Dec eve **Food** Contact pub for details ⊕ WOODWARD & FALCONER PUBS LTD ◼ Piffle, Balderdash, Weetwood, Conwy. ♀ 14 **Facilities** Non-diners area ◀ Children's menu Children's portions Play area Family room Garden ⌐ Parking WiFi ▭

CHOLMONDELEY	Map 15 SJ55

The Cholmondeley Arms   PICK OF THE PUBS

See Pick of the Pubs on opposite page

CHRISTLETON	Map 15 SJ46

Ring O'Bells

tel: 01244 335422 **Village Rd CH3 7AS**
email: info@ringobellschester.co.uk **web:** www.ringobellschester.co.uk
dir: *3m from Chester between A51 towards Nantwich & A41 towards Whitchurch*

A welcoming Chester-fringe pub

Wine tastings, live music and lunchtime networking meetings are among the events that draw drinkers and diners to this spruced-up village pub. And therein lies much of the appeal. The bar stocks real ale from Chester's Spitting Feathers brewery, as well as representatives from Mobberley Ales and Weetwood. Take your pick of outdoor dining areas - perhaps the decked suntrap terrace. Good use of local produce is evident on seasonal menus; beer-battered fish and hand-cut chips is always a favourite choice.

Open all day all wk **Food** Lunch Mon-Fri 12-3, Sat-Sun 12-5 Dinner Mon-Thu 5-9, Fri-Sat 5-9.30, Sun 5-8 ⊕ TRUST INNS ◼ Spitting Feathers, Weetwood, Big Hand, Mobberley. ♀ **Facilities** Non-diners area ❤ (Bar Restaurant Garden) ◀ Children's menu Children's portions Play area Garden ⌐ Parking WiFi ▭ (notice required)

See advert below

CONGLETON	Map 16 SJ86

Egerton Arms Country Inn ★★★★ INN

tel: 01260 273946 **Astbury Village CW12 4RQ**
email: egertonastbury@totalise.co.uk **web:** www.egertonarms.com
dir: *1.5m SW of Congleton off A34, by St Mary's Church*

Good pub food in delightful village

A buzzing, family-run village local with a good name for dependable real ales and freshly prepared fodder. Set at the edge of one of Cheshire's picture-perfect villages, near the ancient church and flowery green, the Egerton Arms enjoys views from the peaceful beer garden onto the nearby Bosley Cloud Hill. Take a stroll along the paths there or stroll along the Macclesfield Canal towpath. The restaurant offers a good selection including steak and kidney suet pudding; fresh sardines with lime and coriander butter; and a variety of baguettes and sandwiches. Stay awhile in the comfortable accommodation and you may meet the ghost, a local lady murdered next door in 1922. Dogs are welcome outside and children inside and out until 9pm.

Open all day all wk **Food** Lunch Mon-Sat 11.30-2, Sun 12-8 Dinner Mon-Sat 6-9, Sun 12-8 Av main course £10.50 Set menu available Restaurant menu available all wk ⊕ ROBINSONS ◼ Unicorn, Dizzy Blonde, Double Hop, Seasonal ales. ♀ 12 **Facilities** Non-diners area ❤ (Garden) ◀ Children's menu Children's portions Play area Garden ⌐ Parking WiFi **Rooms** 6

PICK OF THE PUBS

The Cholmondeley Arms

CHOLMONDELEY   Map 15 SJ55

tel: 01829 720300 **SY14 8HN**
email: info@cholmondeleyarms.co.uk
web: www.cholmondeleyarms.co.uk
dir: *On A49, between Whitchurch &*
Tarporley

Friendly inn with imaginative menus and 140 gins

Set in rolling Cheshire countryside virtually opposite Cholmondeley Castle on the A49, and still part of the Vicount's estate, is this red-brick former schoolhouse (closed 1982). Quirky and eclectic, it's surely one of England's more unique pubs, the decor and artefacts, including family heirlooms, educational memorabilia, bell tower without and blackboards within add tremendously to the atmosphere of the cavernous interior. No longer a draughty institute, owners Tim and Mary Bird have created a warm and inviting interior, with fat church candles on old school desks, fresh flowers, glowing log fires and a relaxing atmosphere. After exploring the local countryside, visiting nearby Cholmondeley Castle, country seat of Lord and Lady Cholmondeley or the fabulous ruins at Beeston, stapled to Cheshire's hilly sandstone spine, it's the perfect place to unwind, sup a pint of Shropshire Gold or Cholmondeley Best (only microbrewery beers from a 30-mile radius can be found on the five hand pumps), or delve into the mindboggling

list of over 140 different gins behind the bar. Allow time to taste some of the best produce from Cheshire's burgeoning larder, including seasonal game from the estate. Nibble and natter over little potted shrimps on toast, or home-made venison Scotch egg, then start with a trawler's seafood board; pan-fried devilled lamb's kidneys; or Mr Bourne's little Cheshire cheesecakes with smoked pear. The 'Old School Favourites' mains take in wild boar faggots with cider and Puy lentil stew; their 'legendary' steak and kidney pie, chips and 'not so mushy' peas; and fish pie with crispy mash and spiced cauliflower; leaving room for steamed Yorkshire rhubarb and ginger pudding – school meals were never like this! There's a gin festival each year.

Open all day all wk **Food** Lunch all wk 12-9.30 Dinner all wk 12-9.30 Av main course £14 ⊕ FREE HOUSE
◀ Cholmondeley Best Bitter, Salopian Shropshire Gold, Tatton Best, Headmasters Ale, Teachers Tipple ♻ Westons Old Rosie. ♈ 16
Facilities Non-diners area ♣ (Bar Restaurant Garden) ⋔ Children's portions Garden ♒ Parking WiFi 🚌 (notice required)

CONGLETON *continued*

The Plough At Eaton ★★★★ INN

tel: 01260 280207 **Macclesfield Rd, Eaton CW12 2NH**
email: enquiries@theploughinncheshire.com **web:** www.theploughinncheshire.com
dir: *On A536 (Congleton to Macclesfield road)*

Popular inn with barn restaurant

Set well back from the main road in the hamlet of Eaton, this 400-year-old Cheshire-brick inn is a far cry from its genesis as a farmers' local in a farmhouse. It's now a popular destination dining-pub with a wide-ranging menu, available throughout the very traditional interior or in the restaurant housed in a remarkable cruck barn moved here from Wales. The kitchen team are dedicated to sourcing their produce locally, resulting in 90% of the food being purchased within a 30-mile radius. On the menu you might find hot leek and Shropshire Blue tart; or Bantry Bay steamed mussels steamed in cider with bacon as starters, then there's a choice of chargill dishes, such as a mixed grill or BBQ-basted chicken breast; the 'main event' dishes include Butter Cross Farm bangers and mash; and deep-fried, pale ale battered haddock, hand-cut chips and mushy peas.

Open all day all wk 11am-mdnt **Food** Lunch Mon-Fri 12-2.30, Sat 12-9, Sun 12-8 Dinner Mon-Fri 6-9.30, Sat 12-9, Sun 12-8 ⊕ FREE HOUSE ◀ Storm, Flowers, Tatton, Local Guest ales ○ Thatchers. ♀ 10 **Facilities** Non-diners area ♦ Children's menu Garden ⋒ Parking ▥ **Rooms** 17

Fox & Barrel

tel: 01829 760529 **Foxbank CW6 9DZ**
email: info@foxandbarrel.co.uk **web:** www.foxandbarrel.co.uk
dir: *On A49, 2.8m N of Tarporley*

Countryside pub offering a warm welcome and excellent food

The rather cute explanation for the pub's name is that a fox being chased by the local hunt ran into the cellar, where the landlord gave it sanctuary. And who's to say otherwise? Restored and refreshed features include a huge open log fire, old beams and half-panelled walls; the snug bar is the perfect spot for a pint of Weetwood. Classic pub food with an adventurous angle includes whole grilled flounder with tenderstem broccoli and new potatoes; crispy belly pork with creamed celeriac and black pudding; and steak burger topped with mozzarella, served with hand-cut chips. Outside is a secluded landscaped garden surrounded by unspoilt Cheshire countryside.

Open all day all wk Closed 25-26 Dec pm, 31 Dec am, 1 Jan pm **Food** Lunch Mon-Sat 12-9.30, Sun 12-9 Dinner Mon-Sat 12-9.30, Sun 12-9 ⊕ FREE HOUSE ◀ Weetwood Eastgate Ale, Caledonian Deuchars IPA. ♀ 20 **Facilities** Non-diners area ☻ (Bar Garden) ♦ Children's portions Garden ⋒ Parking WiFi

The Fishpool Inn

tel: 01606 883277 **Fishpool Rd CW8 2HP**
email: info@thefishpoolinn.co.uk
dir: *Phone for detailed directions*

Striking gastro-pub making a name for itself

Until 2013, this 17th-century country pub was rather quaint, but it's changed a bit since family-owned Nelson Hotels spent several million on a refit. The interior is something else, really impressive; in parts it's downright quirky, especially the gaily-coloured, antlered stags' heads. A newly-built cellar keeps Cheshire real ales and Herefordshire cider in tip-top condition. From an open kitchen comes seasonal, regionally sourced, modern British and European cooking, including pies and Bowland beef steaks; chargrilled Scottish salmon; sizzling tiger prawns and monkfish in sweet chilli sauce; ox-tail, ox-cheek and blue cheese suet pudding; and oven-fired, thin-crust pizzas.

Open all day all wk **Food** Lunch Mon-Thu 12-9.30, Fri-Sat 12-10, Sun 12-9 Dinner Mon-Thu 12-9.30, Fri-Sat 12-10, Sun 12-9 ⊕ FREE HOUSE ◖ Weetwood Ales Best Bitter & Eastgate, Guest ales ♂ Herefordshire Cider. ☗ 14 **Facilities** Non-diners area ♣ (Bar Garden Outside area) ◆ Children's menu Children's portions Garden Outside area ⊞ Parking WiFi ▭ (notice required)

◼ FARNDON Map 15 SJ45

The Farndon ★★★★ INN

tel: 01829 270570 **High St CH3 6PU**
email: enquiries@thefarndon.co.uk **web:** www.thefarndon.co.uk
dir: From Wrexham take A534 towards Nantwich. Follow signs for Farndon on left

Fine food in the tranquil Dee Valley

This most imposing magpie inn commands Farndon's High Street as it winds down to the ancient, haunted stone bridge across the River Dee, which forms the England/Wales border. Coaches stopped here en route between the Midlands and Holyhead; centuries of hospitality are continued in the contemporary, comfy interior, a relaxing mix of colour-washed walls and modern furnishings all warmed by a seasonal roaring fire. Cheshire beers such as Weetwood accompany an impressive menu; a ballottine of pheasant starter followed by local venison and red wine casserole a typical choice from the regularly changing fare. Five boutique guest bedrooms complete the picture.

Open all wk 5-11 (Sat 12-11 Sun 12-10.30) **Food** Lunch Sat-Sun 12-9.30 Dinner Mon-Fri 6-9, Sat-Sun 12-9.30 Restaurant menu available all wk ⊕ FREE HOUSE ◖ Timothy Taylor Landlord, Weetwood Cheshire Cat & Eastgate Ale, Spitting Feathers Thirstquencher, Sandstone, Big Hand. **Facilities** Non-diners area ♣ (Bar Garden) ◆ Children's menu Children's portions Garden ⊞ Parking WiFi ▭ (notice required) **Rooms** 5

◼ GAWSWORTH Map 16 SJ86

Harrington Arms

tel: 01260 223325 **Church Ln SK11 9RJ**
dir: From Macclesfield take A536 towards Congleton. Turn left for Gawsworth

Lovely pub on a working farm

Part farmhouse, part pub, the little-changed interior comprises a main bar serving Robinsons real ales and quirky rooms with open fires and rustic furnishings. Memorable for its impression of timelessness, it dates from 1664 and has been licensed since 1710. On offer is good pub food made extensively from the wealth of local produce, including home-made pies; rib-eye, sirloin and gammon steaks; fish and chips; vegetarian sausage and mash; hot sandwiches; roast turkey crown and daily specials. Early October sees the annual conker championship here.

Open all wk 12-2.30 5-11.30 (Fri 12-2.30 4.30-12 Sat 12-11.30 Sun 12-11) Closed 25 Dec **Food** Lunch Mon-Fri 12-2.30, Sat 12-9, Sun 12-8 Dinner Mon-Thu 5-8.30, Fri 5-9, Sat 12-9, Sun 12-8 Av main course £10.95 ⊕ ROBINSONS ◖ Unicorn, 1892, Dizzy Blonde & Seasonal ale, Guinness ♂ Westons Stowford Press. ☗ 8 **Facilities** Non-diners area ♣ (Bar Garden) ◆ Children's portions Garden ⊞ Parking ▭ (notice required)

◼ GOOSTREY Map 15 SJ77

The Crown

tel: 01477 532128 **111 Main Rd CW4 8DE**
email: info@thecrowngoostrey.co.uk **web:** www.thecrowngoostrey.com
dir: In village centre. Follow Goostrey signs either from A50, or from A535 in Tremlow Green

Charming village local with good food and local ales

A traditional pub set in the heart of the Cheshire farming village of Goostrey, The Crown has been an integral part of community life since the 18th century. Beyond its red-bricked façade, the pub has been sympathetically refurbished but retains much charm with oak beams and real fireplaces. Local breweries including Weetwood and Dunham Massey are well represented, perhaps accompanied by home-made crackling. The extensive modern menu takes in slow-roasted lamb shank with roasted root vegetables, parsley mash and minted gravy; and salmon and cod fishcakes. Check with the pub for details of its summer beer festival and its annual gooseberry-growing competition.

Open all wk 11.30-11 **Food** Lunch Mon-Sat 12-9, Sun 12-8 Dinner Mon-Sat 12-9, Sun 12-8 Av main course £12 ⊕ FREE HOUSE ◖ Weetwood Ales, Dunham Massey Ales, Tatton Ales White Queen. **Facilities** Non-diners area ♣ (Bar Garden Outside area) ◆ Children's menu Children's portions Garden Outside area ⊞ Beer festival Parking WiFi ▭ (notice required)

GREAT BUDWORTH
Map 15 SJ67

George and Dragon

tel: 01606 892650 **High St CW9 6HF**
email: thegeorge-dragon@btinternet.com
dir: From M6 junct 19 or M56 junct 10 follow signs for Great Budworth

Village local steeped in history

Painstakingly restored three years ago, this charming inn's many original features include a stone tablet in the bar dated 1722 and inscribed 'Nil nimium cupito' ('I desire nothing to excess'). Also visible is a verse above a door written by local Astley Hall estate-owner, Rowland Egerton-Warburton, who had the inn remodelled in 1875. Regular real ales are Lees Bitter from Manchester and the pub's own Great Budworth Best Bitter, the latter used to flavour the home-made steak, ale and mushroom pie. Other dishes include 'hot off the griddle' steaks, ribs and mixed grills; lamb rogan josh; and traditional fish and chips.

Open all day all wk **Food** Lunch Mon-Sat 11.30-3, Sun 12-8.30, snacks 3-5 Dinner Mon-Sat 5-9.30, Sun 12-8.30 Restaurant menu available all wk ⊕ J W LEES ⬛ Lees Bitter, Great Budworth Best Bitter. ⚑ 12 **Facilities** Non-diners area ⬤ Children's menu Children's portions Outside area ⌗ Parking WiFi ⬛ (notice required)

HANDLEY
Map 15 SJ45

The Calveley Arms

tel: 01829 770619 **Whitchurch Rd CH3 9DT**
email: calveleyarms@btconnect.com
dir: 5m S of Chester, signed from A41. Follow signs for Handley & Aldersey Green Golf Course

Old inn, old beams, great beer

The spruced-up old coaching inn, first licensed in 1636, stands opposite the church with views of the distant Welsh hills. Chock full of old timbers, jugs, pots, pictures, prints and ornaments, the rambling bars provide an atmospheric setting in which to sample some cracking beers and decent pub food. Typically, tuck into lunchtime filled baguettes (hot beef), steak and kidney pie, sirloin steak with pepper sauce, speciality salads, and a good selection of pasta dishes. There are spacious gardens to enjoy in summer.

Open all wk 12-3 6-11 (Sun 12-3 7-11) **Food** Lunch all wk 12-3 Dinner Mon-Sat 6-9, Sun 7-9 ⊕ ENTERPRISE INNS ⬛ Castle Eden Ale, Marston's Pedigree, Theakston Black Bull Bitter, Wells Bombardier, Greene King IPA, Black Sheep Ŏ Aspall. **Facilities** Non-diners area ⬤ Children's portions Play area Garden Parking ⬛

HAUGHTON MOSS
Map 15 SJ55

The Nags Head

tel: 01829 260265 **Long Ln CW6 9RN**
email: enquiries@nagsheadhaughton.co.uk
dir: Exit A49 S of Tarporley at Beeston/Haughton sign into Long Ln. 2.75m to pub

Secluded country inn with finest Cheshire produce

Deep in the Cheshire countryside near to a dramatic wooded sandstone ridge, this half-timbered country inn has seen a comprehensive refurbishment by new owners, Ribble Valley Inns. There's no hiding the near-400-year heritage of the place, though; the huge cruck frame and crackling fire ooze rustic character and charm, which set-off nicely the light, conservatory-inspired dining extension which overlooks the tranquil garden and increasingly rare bowling green. The riches of the northern Welsh Marches are liberally mined, with great beers from Cheshire's Weetwood and Tatton breweries matched by the wide-ranging menu which always guarantees a selection of steaks, classic pub pies and a decent net of seafood options.

Open all day all wk **Food** Contact pub for details ⊕ FREE HOUSE ⬛ Weetwood Ales, Tatton, Salopian. ⚑ **Facilities** ❀ (Bar Garden) ⬤ Children's menu Children's portions Garden ⌗ Parking WiFi

KERRIDGE
Map 16 SJ97

NEW The Lord Clyde

tel: 01625 562123 **SK10 5AH**
email: hello@thelordclyde.co.uk
dir: From Macclesfield A523 towards Poynton. At rdbt follow Bollington sign onto B5090. 1st right into Clark Ln

Very good country dining

Tables outside this converted terrace of weavers' cottages look out to the wood-dappled Kerridge Edge, the fringe of the Peak District. With choice beers from the north-west to sit and sup there's room for lovers of the hop; but it's for the restrained and interesting menu that diners beat a route to the door of this gastro-pub just outside Macclesfield. Chef-proprietor Ernst van Zyl has worked in some of the world's top restaurants; his seasonally changing menu reflects the very best of Cheshire's benevolent larder. Quail breast, leg and egg may feature as a starter, and a main of loin and leg of rabbit with parsnip, buckwheat and plum showcase the thoroughly modern approach that's championed here. The wine list is both extensive and impressive.

Open all wk 12-3 5-11 (Fri-Sun all day) **Food** Lunch all wk 12-3 Dinner all wk 6.30-9 Set menu available Restaurant menu available Tue-Sun ⊕ PUNCH TAVERNS ⬛ Morland Old Speckled Hen, Weetwood Ales Cheshire Cat, Moorhouse's Pride of Pendle Ŏ Westons Stowford Press. ⚑ 12 **Facilities** Non-diners area ❀ (Bar Outside area) ⬤ Children's portions Outside area ⌗ Parking WiFi ⬛ (notice required)

KETTLESHULME
Map 16 SJ97

Swan Inn

tel: 01663 732943 **SK23 7QU**
email: the.swan.kettleshulme@googlemail.com
dir: On B5470 between Whaley Bridge (2m) & Macclesfield (5m)

Charming village pub renowned for its beer and seafood dishes

Huddled in the shadow of the craggy Windgather Rocks in the Cheshire Peak District, The Swan is a glorious yet tiny 15th-century village inn, saved from closure when a consortium of locals bought the place eight years ago. Now safe and thriving in private hands again, the eclectic and international menu has interesting dishes such as Greek-style rabbit stew slow-cooked with red wine, cinnamon, shallots and currants; and an extensive seafood menu including bouillabaisse and scallops Thermidor. Local craft ales such as Thornbridge keep ramblers and locals very contented, especially at the pub's beer festival on the first weekend in September.

Open all wk Mon 5-11 Tue-Sun all day Closed 25-26 Dec, 1 Jan, Mon L **Food** Lunch Tue 12-8.30, Wed & Sat 12-9, Thu-Fri 12-7, Sun 12-4 Dinner Tue 12-8.30, Wed & Sat 12-9, Thu-Fri 12-7, Sun 12-4 ⊕ FREE HOUSE ⬛ Marston's, Marble, Thornbridge, Phoenix. **Facilities** Non-diners area ❀ (Bar Garden Outside area) ⬤ Children's portions Garden Outside area ⌗ Beer festival Parking WiFi

KNUTSFORD
Map 15 SJ77

The Dog Inn
PICK OF THE PUBS

See Pick of the Pubs on opposite page

PICK OF THE PUBS

The Dog Inn

KNUTSFORD   Map 15 SJ77

tel: 01625 861421
Well Bank Ln, Over Peover WA16 8UP
email: info@thedogpeover.co.uk
web: www.thedogpeover.co.uk
dir: *S from Knutsford take A50. Turn into Stocks Ln at The Whipping Stocks pub. 2m to inn*

Friendly inn with good food and local ales

This inn started life as a row of cottages and then became a grocer's, shoemaker's and farmstead, which were later united as a public house in 1860. Before you go in, enjoy the pub sign, because there cannot possibly be another in Britain featuring a boxer dog with a turquoise ice-pack on its head! Colourful flowerbeds, tubs and hanging baskets create quite a display in summer, while year-round appeal derives from the cask-conditioned Cheshire ales from Hydes in Manchester and Weetwood in Tarporley, and an array of malt whiskies. There's an interesting choice of food too, prepared from produce sourced largely within Cheshire and which might appear on the menu as scallops with carrot purée, vanilla ice cream and crisp bacon; poached rabbit ragout on tagliatelle; grilled lamb cutlets, rosemary polenta chips and spiced tomato and minted yogurt dips; and curried crab fritters with avocado and sun-blushed tomato salad. The ever-popular desserts include strawberry cheesecake, sticky toffee pudding and Cheshire dairy ice creams. For something lighter, choose from the excellent range of sandwiches or go for a slice of home-made pork pie with a pickled egg and piccalilli. On the first Sunday in August the pub is the venue for the Over Peover Gooseberry Show, when you can find out what possesses grown men and women to try and grow Cheshire's biggest gooseberry. Given the pub's name, it should come as no surprise to learn that dogs are welcome, except of course in the restaurant.

Open all day all wk ⊕ FREE HOUSE 🍺 Weetwood Best Bitter & Cheshire Cat, Hydes. **Facilities** 🐾 (Bar Garden) ⁑ Children's menu Children's portions Garden Parking WiFi 🚍

PICK OF THE PUBS

The Bulls Head

MOBBERLEY   Map 15 SJ77

tel: 01565 873395 **Mill Ln WA16 7HX**
email: info@thebullsheadpub.com
web: www.thebullsheadpub.com
dir: *From Knutsford take A537, then A5085 to Mobberley*

A 200-year-old pub with lots going on

Sister pub to the Cholmondley Arms near Malpas, this little gem thrives as both a village local and as a destination pub. One attraction is the real ales from Cheshire microbreweries all within a radius of 30-35 miles - Dunham Massey, Merlin, Mobberley, Redwillow, Storm, Tatton and Wincle - but you'll need to spread your visits to make acquaintance with them all. Yet another, Weetwood, brews Mobberley Wobbly (aka Mobb Wobb) exclusively for the pub; it's a pint of this that comes with the 'legendary' handcrafted steak and ale pie with chips and 'not so mushy' peas. Smart, traditionally-styled rooms provide a comfortable and convivial setting for wholesome home-cooked food, including delicious Sunday roasts; slow-cooked ox casserole in rich caramelised port gravy with celery, carrot, onion and celeriac; local organic pork sausages with creamy mash, red cabbage and shallot gravy; pan-fried Old Winchester cheese-breadcrumbed chicken with fresh tomato, basil sauce and salad; and smoked fish pie with haddock, salmon, trout, and carrot and celeriac mash. One of the home-made

puddings is Irish whiskey sticky toffee pudding with vanilla ice cream. Wheat-free and gluten-free dishes are also available. The pub hosts two car clubs: The 3p, which stands for 'Pub, Porsche and Pint', and for which you have to own, borrow or regularly hire said German vehicle; and The Goodfellows, for which you must own anything but a Porsche. (Membership isn't quite that simple - see the pub website for details.) There's a garden and a June beer festival. Finally, you may be interested to know that, just after the First World War, the Bulls Head was run by the parents of a young man who later established the Umbro sportswear chain - his stock room was a cupboard in the pub.

Open all day all wk **Food** Contact pub for details ⊕ FREE HOUSE ◀ Bulls Head Bitter, Mobberley Wobbly Ale, 1812 Overture Ale, White Bull. ♟ 16 **Facilities** Non-diners area ☙ (Bar Restaurant Garden) ◑ Children's portions Garden ☴ Beer festival Parking 🚐 (notice required) WiFi

LACH DENNIS
Map 15 SJ77

The Duke of Portland

tel: 01606 46264 **Penny's Ln CW9 7SY**
email: info@dukeofportland.com
dir: *M6 junct 19, A556 towards Northwich. Left onto B5082 to Lach Dennis*

Recommended for the use of local produce

This family-run pub continues to make a name for itself through a committed use of local and regional produce from across the Cheshire and Lancashire area. In the bar, enjoy a pint of Jennings Cocker Hoop or Cumberland Ale or one of the 10 wines by the glass. The kitchen's top-drawer local suppliers are listed on the menus, which might include beef, Guinness and mushroom pie; risotto of smoked haddock with lemon, mint and pea; and classic coq au vin. A sunny, landscaped garden complements the attractive building.

Open all day all wk **Food** Lunch all wk 12-5.30 Dinner all wk 5.30-9.30 ⊕ MARSTON'S ◀ Banks's Original, Brakspear Oxford Gold, Jennings Cocker Hoop & Cumberland Ale, Marston's Pedigree ♂ Thatchers Gold. ♣ 10 **Facilities** Non-diners area ♣ (Bar Garden) ♦♦ Children's menu Children's portions Garden ⚘ Parking WiFi ▬

MARTON
Map 16 SJ86

The Davenport Arms `PICK OF THE PUBS`

tel: 01260 224269 **Congleton Rd SK11 9HF**
email: info@thedavenportarms.co.uk
dir: *2m from Congleton on A34*

Charming pub with pleasing home-made dishes

Dating back to the 18th century, this former farmhouse is steeped in history and enjoys a picturesque location opposite the oldest half-timbered church still in use in Europe. Inside, many period details make for a comfortable atmosphere. Pull up a leather armchair or sofa clad with cushions to the roaring fire in the traditional bar, and choice from the good selection of real ales and nine wines by the glass. In warmer times, the large garden is a big draw. There's something for everyone on the crowd-pleasing menu, all freshly made on the premises using local ingredients. You could start with home-made fishcake, citrus mayonnaise and sweet chilli dip; or black pudding stack with creamed leeks and bacon before trying perhaps chicken breast stuffed with haggis, Skirlie potatoes, fresh vegetables and whisky and thyme sauce. There are also regularly changing chef's specials and curry nights on Tuesdays.

Open 12-3 6-12 (Fri-Sun 12-12) Closed Mon L (ex BHs) **Food** Lunch Tue-Fri 12-2.30, Sat 12-9, Sun 12-8 Dinner Tue-Fri 6-9, Sat 12-9, Sun 12-8 ⊕ FREE HOUSE ◀ Copper Dragon, Storm, Theakston, Beartown, Courage Directors, Wincle, Moorhouses. ♣ 9 **Facilities** Non-diners area ♣ (Bar Garden) ♦♦ Children's menu Play area Garden ⚘ Parking WiFi ▬ (notice required)

MOBBERLEY
Map 15 SJ77

The Bulls Head `PICK OF THE PUBS`

See Pick of the Pubs on opposite page

NEW The Church Inn `PICK OF THE PUBS`

See Pick of the Pubs on page 80

MOULDSWORTH
Map 15 SJ57

The Goshawk

tel: 01928 740900 **Station Rd CH3 8AJ**
email: goshawk@woodwardandfalconer.com
dir: *A51 from Chester onto A54. Left onto B5393 towards Frodsham. Into Mouldsworth, pub on left*

Old railway inn popular with cyclists and walkers

This sturdy inn has a hint of Edwardian grandeur whilst benefiting from contemporary comforts; print-clad walls and dado rails, comfy sofas and open fires. Its village setting makes the most of the area's delights, including the many miles of footpaths, cycle trails and meres of nearby Delamere Forest; Chester is just one stop away on the train. Local ales from Weetwood draw an appreciative crowd, whilst the wide-ranging menu is matched by an extensive wine list. The menus, that include good fish and vegetarian choices, change every six weeks. The terrace and large grassy beer garden offer views across the heart of Cheshire.

Open all day all wk 12-11 (Sun 12-10.30) Closed 25 Dec & 1 Jan **Food** Contact pub for details ⊕ WOODWARD & FALCONER PUBS LTD ◀ Piffle, Weetwood Eastgate Ale & Best Bitter, Guest ales. ♣ 14 **Facilities** Non-diners area ♦♦ Children's menu Children's portions Play area Family room Garden ⚘ Parking WiFi ▬

NANTWICH
Map 15 SJ65

The Thatch Inn

tel: 01270 524223 **Wrexham Rd, Faddiley CW5 8JE**
dir: *Follow signs for Wrexham from Nantwich, inn on A534 in 4m*

Pretty inn with plenty of beams and fires

Believed to be the oldest (and one of the prettiest) pubs in south Cheshire, the black-and-white Thatch Inn has a three-quarter acre garden, while inside there are plentiful oak beams, and open fires in winter. Starters might be black pudding and streaky bacon stack with creamy wholegrain mustard sauce, or traditional prawn cocktail with a mixed leaf salad. For your main course, maybe oven roasted pork fillet with carrot and parsnip mash, Parmentier potatoes and carrot and orange scented jus. Finish with chocolate praline and vanilla cheesecake with Cheshire Farm ice cream. Children have their own menu.

Open Mon-Tue 5.30-11, Wed-Thu 12-3 5.30-11, Fri-Sat 12-11, Sun 12-10.30 Closed Mon L & Tue L **Food** Lunch Wed-Fri 12-3, Sat 12-9, Sun 12-8.30 Dinner Mon-Fri 5.30-9, Sat 12-9, Sun 12-8.30 ⊕ ENTERPRISE INNS ◀ Weetwood Eastgate Ale, Salopian Shropshire Gold. **Facilities** Non-diners area ♦♦ Children's menu Play area Garden ⚘ Parking WiFi ▬

NORTHWICH
Map 15 SJ67

The Red Lion ★★★ INN

tel: 01606 74597 **277 Chester Rd, Hartford CW8 1QL**
email: cathy.iglesias@tesco.net **web:** www.redlionhartford.com
dir: *From A556 take Hartford exit. Red Lion at 1st junct on left next to church*

Popular village inn with stylish accommodation

This engaging inn was the village fire station until a century or so ago, and many artefacts remain from that time. Hunker down with a pint of Black Sheep, tuck in to hearty pub grub like home-made lamb hotpot, or take on the locals at darts or dominoes. This is a thriving community local where visitors to the nearby Delamere Forest or Oulton Park motor-racing circuit can also bed down in the en suite accommodation here. Log fires in winter, and at the back there is an enclosed beer garden.

Open all day all wk **Food** Lunch Mon-Sat 12-2 Dinner Mon-Sat 6-8 ⊕ FREE HOUSE ◀ Marston's Pedigree, Black Sheep, John Smith's Cask. ♣ 9 **Facilities** Non-diners area ♣ (Bar Garden) ♦♦ Family room Garden ⚘ Parking WiFi **Rooms** 3

PICK OF THE PUBS

The Church Inn

MOBBERLEY Map 15 SJ77

tel: 01565 873178 **WA16 7RD**
email: info@churchinnmobberley.co.uk
web: www.churchinnmobberley.co.uk
dir: *From Knutsford take B5085 towards Wilmslow. In Mobberley left into Church Ln. Pub opposite church*

Local produce drives the menu of this stylish village pub

When Tim Bird and Mary McLaughlin acquired this brick-built 18th-century village pub in 2013, it was in a near-derelict state and in desperate need of some TLC. Now fully restored and refurbished after significant investment from the couple, who also have The Bulls Head in the village, The Church Inn is a stylish country pub that appeals to locals and destination diners alike. On the edge of the village and opposite the 12th-century St Wilfrid's church, it is ideally situated between the bustling towns of Wilmslow and Knutsford and only eight miles from Manchester Airport. Surrounded by rolling Cheshire countryside, the rear garden and attractive summer dining terrace leads down to an old bowling green that boasts panoramic views across neighbouring fields. In the bar and boot room, a range of locally sourced ales includes Mallory's Mobberley Best, named after Mobberley-born mountaineer George Mallory, who is buried at St Wilfrid's. A choice of intimate dining areas offers a relaxed

and comfortable setting for the extensive food offering, which takes in pub classics (shepherd's pie; lamb burgers; fish and chips) alongside the main menu. A starter of Cumbrian pig's cheek slow cooked in cider and served with braised barley, herb salad and brown butter vinaigrette might be followed by roast breast of Goosnargh duck with cherry and red wine sauce, chicory and shallot tart, kale and creamed celeriac. Nutmeg-topped baked egg custard with poached vanilla rhubarb is a typical dessert, although the board of Cheshire artisan cheeses changes daily. Canines are more than welcome in the bar and the boot room and there is a bowl of dog biscuits on the bar, as well as dog 'beer' (meat-based stock) for them to drink.

Open all day all wk **Food** Lunch & dinner all day all wk Av main course £13 Restaurant menu available all wk. 🍺 Dunham Massey Mallory's Mobberley Best, Tatton Brewery Ale-Alujah, Guest ales 🍎 Ty Gwyn. 🍷
Facilities Non-diners area 🐾 (Bar) 👶 Children's portions Garden 🪑 Parking WiFi 🚐 (notice required)

PARKGATE
Map 15 SJ27

The Boat House

tel: 0151 336 4187 **1 The Parade CH64 6RN**
email: boathouse@woodwardandfalconer.com
dir: On B5135, 3m from Heswall

Hard-to-beat location on the edge of a nature reserve

Once a thriving Deeside port, Parkgate's silted-up waters are now a nature reserve, although exceptionally high tides do still reach the walls of this striking black-and-white-timbered pub. The salt marshes begin right in front of it, so there's nothing to spoil the views of North Wales across the estuary. Real ales include Piffle and Balderdash, while for food stay in one of the modernised bars, or head for the Dee-facing dining room. Menus, always with a good fresh fish and seafood selection, change six-weekly, offering perhaps seared scallops and haggis; trio of sausages; slow-roasted shoulder of lamb; and chicken tikka masala.

Open all day all wk 12-11 (Sun 12-10.30) Closed 25 Dec, 1 Jan **Food** Contact pub for details ⊕ FREE HOUSE ◀ Morland Old Speckled Hen, Woodward & Falconer Piffle & Balderdash Weetwood Eastgate Ale, Theakstons Best, West Ales. ☗ 16 **Facilities** Non-diners area ♦ Children's menu Children's portions Outside area ⌂ Parking WiFi ▭ (notice required)

The Ship Hotel

tel: 0151 336 3931 **The Parade CH64 6SA**
email: info@the-shiphotel.co.uk
dir: A540 (Chester towards Neston) left then immediately right onto B5136 (Liverpool Rd). In Neston town centre, left onto B5135. Follow to The Parade in Parkgate, hotel 50yds on right

Free house with fine views of the Welsh mountains

Parkgate's port is now silted up, but the views from The Parade across what is now the RSPB's Dee Estuary bird reserve to the Welsh coast don't change. With 18th-century origins, The Ship was regularly visited by Lord Nelson and his mistress Lady Hamilton, who had been born in nearby Neston. Real ale names to conjure with in the contemporary bar include Trapper's Hat from Wirral brewery Brimstage and Weetwood Oast-House Gold, also from Cheshire. Enjoy home-made food by the fire, with options such as pheasant wrapped in pancetta; Cumberland sausage and mash; surf and turf; Thai green curry, and specials.

Open all day all wk **Food** Lunch all wk 12-9 Dinner all wk 12-9 ⊕ FREE HOUSE ◀ Brimstage Trapper's Hat, Weetwood Oast-House Gold, Jennings Cumberland Ale, Tatton Gold. ☗ 15 **Facilities** Non-diners area ♦ Children's menu Children's portions Outside area ⌂ Parking WiFi ▭ (notice required)

PRESTBURY
Map 16 SJ87

The Legh Arms

tel: 01625 829130 **The Village SK10 4DG**
email: legharms@hotmail.co.uk
dir: On A538 (New Road)

Serving good food all day every day

Trendy Prestbury is popular with premiership footballers and they're lucky to have the gabled and part-timbered Legh Arms on their doorstep. Fine ales from Robinsons Brewery nearby are dispensed at the bar with its oak beams and roaring fires and where simpler fare is on offer, such as salads, sharing platters, sandwiches and pub favourites. For a celeb-spotting special dinner, eat in the restaurant, where dishes use herbs from the pub's own walled garden. Pork chop served with Dijon and cider sauce and a leek and potato cake might fit the bill. The beer garden has a wood-burning stove for cooler nights.

Open all day all wk **Food** Lunch all wk 12-10 Dinner all wk 12-10 Set menu available Restaurant menu available all wk ⊕ ROBINSONS ◀ Robinsons 1892, Robinsons Hatters, Unicorn. ☗ **Facilities** Non-diners area ♣ (Garden) ♦ Children's portions Garden ⌂ Parking WiFi

SPURSTOW
Map 15 SJ55

The Yew Tree Inn

tel: 01829 260274 **Long Ln CW6 9RD**
email: info@theyewtreebunbury.com
dir: 400mtrs from A49

Beer is taken seriously at this village pub

Built by the Earl of Crewe, this is a sympathetically refurbished 19th-century pub. Inside, the original beams and open fires are a reminder of the pub's history, while the terrace is a more modern addition and perfect for summer dining. Up to eight real ales are available and the Easter beer festival, from Good Friday to Easter Monday, shouldn't be missed. As well as Westons Stowford Press, there is a guest cider on handpump. A seasonal menu is driven by local produce and might include leek, mushroom and blue cheese rarebit; rib-eye steak; grilled smoked haddock with buttered spinach, mash, poached egg and mustard sauce; or pie of the day.

Open all day all wk **Food** Lunch Mon-Thu 12-9.30, Fri-Sat 12-10, Sun 12-9 Dinner Mon-Thu 12-9.30, Fri-Sat 12-10, Sun 12-9 Av main course £12 ⊕ FREE HOUSE ◀ Stonehouse Station Bitter, 7 Guest ales ♨ Westons Stowford Press, Guest cider. ☗ 14 **Facilities** Non-diners area ♣ (Bar Garden Outside area) ♦ Children's menu Children's portions Garden Outside area ⌂ Beer festival Parking WiFi ▭ (notice required)

STOAK
Map 15 SJ47

The Bunbury Arms

tel: 01244 301665 **Little Stanney Ln CH2 4HW**
email: bunburyarmschester@gmail.com
dir: From M53/M56 junct 11/15 take A5117. 1st left into Little Stanney Ln

Much loved alehouse with good food

In a small wooded hamlet and with a continuing fine reputation, this traditional alehouse prides itself on good food and the hospitality it offers. Inside, expect an open fire, TV, board games and darts, not forgetting an award-winning selection of real ales and extensive wine list. Typical dishes include black pudding and chorizo sautéed in red wine, on a spicy croûte; steak, ale and mushroom pie; and Thai green curry. The Bunbury Arms is handy for the Cheshire Oaks retail outlet, Chester Zoo and Blue Planet Aquarium.

Open all day all wk **Food** Lunch Mon-Thu 2-9, Fri-Sat 12-9.30, Sun 12-8 Dinner Mon-Thu 2-9, Fri-Sat 12-9.30, Sun 12-8 ⊕ FREE HOUSE ◀ Robinsons Unicorn, JW Lees Coronation Street, Joseph Holt, Cains, Guest ale. ☗ 26 **Facilities** Non-diners area ♣ (Bar Garden) ♦ Children's menu Children's portions Garden ⌂ Beer festival Parking WiFi ▭ (notice required)

STYAL
Map 15 SJ88

NEW The Ship Inn

tel: 01625 444888 **Altrincham Rd SK9 4JE**
email: info@theshipstyal.co.uk **web:** www.theshipstyal.co.uk
dir: From B5166 N of Wilmslow, left signed Styal into Altrincham Rd

All that's good in a pub still casting its spell

Styal's history is closely bound to that of the local cotton industry; many of the Ship's customers call in after visiting nearby Quarry Bank Mill. The 350-year-old building was once a shippon, an ancient term for a farm's cattle shed; it became a pub when the farmer owner started brewing for the locals. Happily craft ales are still high in the pub's attractions, with Weetwood Cheshire Cat and Big Tree Bitter by Dunham Massey usually among the five on offer. There's something for everyone on the menu, with traditional favourites often given a creative spin. Children have their own selection, and are welcome until 8pm. Beer festival in summer.

Open all wk 11.30-11 (Sun 12-10.30) **Food** Lunch all wk 12-9 Dinner all wk 12-9 Av main course £12 ⊕ FREE HOUSE ◀ Weetwood Best & Cheshire Cat, Dunham Massey Big Tree Bitter. ♥ 11 **Facilities** Non-diners area ◀♦ Children's menu Children's portions Garden ⋒ Beer festival Parking WiFi 🚌 (notice required)

SUTTON LANE ENDS
Map 16 SJ97

Sutton Hall
PICK OF THE PUBS

tel: 01260 253211 **Bullocks Ln SK11 0HE**
email: sutton.hall@brunningandprice.co.uk
dir: A523 from Macclesfield. At lights left into Byron's Ln (signed Sutton, Langley & Wincle). Left into Bullock's Ln. Pub on left

Former manor house turned spacious pub

The family seat of the Earls of Lucan, this striking half-timbered and gritstone manor house is surrounded by its own estate. Dating from the 16th century, but considerably added to since, it conceals a wealth of nooks and crannies, a snug, a library and seven different dining areas, with terraces and gardens outside. The Macclesfield Canal runs nearby, while in the other direction are the steeply wooded hills and crags of Macclesfield Forest. As part of the Brunning & Price chain of dining pubs, it offers the company's own Original Bitter alongside Lord Lucan, a local brew whose whereabouts are no mystery; the wine list is well compiled and there are over 100 whiskies. A typical starter is potted smoked mackerel, crayfish, apple and fennel salad. Sample mains include honey-roast duck breast; pan-fried sea bass with chorizo, caper and tomato dressing; and Moroccan spiced pepper with couscous, aubergine and okra salad.

Open all day all wk 11.30-11 (Sun 11-10.30) **Food** Lunch Mon-Sat 12-10, Sun 12-9.30 Dinner Mon-Sat 12-10, Sun 12-9.30 ⊕ FREE HOUSE/BRUNNING & PRICE ◀ Brunning & Price Original Bitter, Flowers Original, Wincle Lord Lucan Ö Aspall, Westons Wyld Wood Organic. ♥ 21 **Facilities** Non-diners area ♣ (Bar Garden) ◀♦ Children's portions Play area Garden ⋒ Parking WiFi

SWETTENHAM
Map 15 SJ86

The Swettenham Arms
PICK OF THE PUBS

tel: 01477 571284 **Swettenham Ln CW12 2LF**
email: info@swettenhamarms.co.uk
dir: M6 junct 18 to Holmes Chapel, then A535 towards Jodrell Bank. 3m right (Forty Acre Lane) to Swettenham (NB do not use postcode for Sat Nav; enter Swettenham Lane)

A sure-fire hit with both drinkers and diners

Remote near the end of a winding no-through-road in the depths of the Cheshire countryside, this ancient inn is ideally situated for taking easy rambles into the tranquil valley of the nearby River Dane. The renowned Lovell Quinta Arboretum - established by the famous astronomer Sir Bernard Lovell of nearby Jodrell Bank - adjoins the inn. The building itself is tucked into a former Tudor nunnery; one of its three working fireplaces said to be haunted by a black-clad nun named Sarah. Those presumably harsh days of yore have been replaced by a comfy pub full of quiet corners where the best of Cheshire food and drink draws an appreciative crowd year-round. In summer the neighbouring lavender meadow is a fragrant location to sit and sup Bollington Bitter, musing on the fine contemporary menu created by talented chef Thomas Lüdecke. Braised Cheshire beef blade bourguignon with smoked mash, or mixed game and wild mushroom pie hit the mark; many dishes benefit from the inn's own-grown vegetables and free-range chickens.

Open all wk 11.30am-close (Closed Mon-Fri 3.30-6 Winter) **Food** Lunch Mon-Fri 12-2.30, Sat-Sun 12-6 Dinner Mon-Sat 6-9.30, Sun 6-8.30 Av main course £12-£15 ⊕ FREE HOUSE ◀ Timothy Taylor Landlord, Sharp's Doom Bar, Bollington Best, Courage Directors, Moorhouse's Pride of Pendle, Slater's Top Totty, Black Sheep, Beartown, Wells Bombardier, Fuller's London Pride, Tatton, Thwaites Wainwright Ö Addlestones, Westons Old Rosie. ♥ 12 **Facilities** Non-diners area ♣ (Bar Garden) ◀♦ Children's menu Children's portions Garden ⋒ Parking WiFi 🚌 (notice required)

PICK OF THE PUBS

The Bear's Paw ★★★★★ INN ❀

WARMINGHAM　　　Map 15 SJ76

tel: 01270 526317
School Ln CW11 3QN
email: info@thebearspaw.co.uk
web: www.thebearspaw.co.uk
dir: *M6 junct 18, A54, A533 towards Sandbach. Follow signs for village*

Refined gastro-pub cooking

With its prominent central gable and some nods towards typical Cheshire black-and-white half-timbering, this stylish 19th-century gastro inn has clearly had a lot of money spent on it. Acres — well it seems like acres — of reclaimed antique oak flooring, leather sofas surrounding two huge open fireplaces, bookshelves offering plenty of choice for a good read, and more than 200 pictures and archive photos lining the oak-panelled walls. The bar, in which stands a carved wooden bear with a salmon in its mouth, offers a half dozen cask ales from local microbreweries, including the somewhat appropriate Beartown in Congleton, Weetwood in Tarporley, and Tatton in Knutsford, as well as Hereford dry cider. Whether you're sitting out front looking across to the churchyard or in the clubby interior, there's plenty of comfortable dining space in which to sample wholesome, locally sourced food from wide-ranging daily menus that expertly blend the classic with the modern. Take, for example, starters like home-made black

pudding with poached duck egg, pea purée and mustard jus; or goats' cheese and pickled beetroot ballotine with balsamic walnuts; and main dishes such as eight-hour braised shin of beef, carrot purée, creamy mash, confit garlic and red wine jus; beer-battered North Sea haddock, mushy peas, tartare sauce and chunky chips; or tomato, chorizo and basil spaghetti. Great for sharing are the imaginative deli boards, which come laden with local cheeses, charcuterie or pickled and smoked fish, and don't miss the Sunday roast lunches. For something lighter, think in terms of a filled baguette or ciabatta, or sandwich. The Bear's Paw offers distinctive, boutique-style en suite bedrooms.

Open all day all wk **Food** Mon-Thu 12-9.30, Fri-Sat 12-10, Sun 12-8 ⊕ FREE HOUSE ◀ Weetwood Best Bitter, Cheshire Cat & Eastgate Ale, Spitting Feathers, Beartown, Tatton ♂ Hereford Dry Cider. ♟ 10 **Facilities** Non-diners area ♣ (Bar Restaurant Garden) ♥ Children's menu Children's portions Garden ⋒ Parking WiFi ▭ (notice required) **Rooms** 17

TARPORLEY
Map 15 SJ56

Alvanley Arms Inn ★★★★ INN

tel: 01829 760200 **Forest Rd, Cotebrook CW6 9DS**
email: info@alvanleyarms.co.uk **web:** www.alvanleyarms.co.uk
dir: *On A49, 1.5m N of Tarporley*

Local produce on the menus

This lovely 16th-century former coaching inn has links to the Cotebrook Shire Horse Centre next door, so expect a horse-themed decor – harnesses and horseshoes – in the traditional oak-beamed bar. Hand-pulled ales complement a range of freshly prepared dishes, based on ingredients from local family businesses; the chef patron makes his own bread from local Walk Mill flour. Dishes range from starters such as goats' cheese, tomato and pesto tart; and chef's soup of the day; and to main courses of game pie; pan-fried lamb's liver on black pudding mash; and steak and Robinson Ale pie. Lighter options such as baguettes and skinny fries are available at lunchtime.

Open all wk 12-3 5.30-11.30 (Sat-Sun 12-11) **Food** Lunch Mon-Fri 12-2, Sat-Sun 12-9 Dinner Mon-Fri 6-9, Sat-Sun 12-9 Set menu available Restaurant menu available all wk ⊕ ROBINSONS ◀ Dizzy Blonde, Trooper, Unicorn, Guest ales ⚲ Westons Stowford Press. ♟ 12 **Facilities** Non-diners area ♦♦ Children's menu Children's portions Garden ♬ Parking WiFi 🚌 (notice required) **Rooms** 7

The Swan, Tarporley

tel: 01829 733838 **50 High St CW6 0AG**
email: info@theswantarporley.co.uk **web:** www.theswantarporley.co.uk
dir: *From junct of A49 & A51 into Tarporley. Pub on right in village centre*

Restored coaching inn serving enjoyable seasonal food

The 16th-century Swan has been the hub of Cheshire's picturesque Tarporley village for over 500 years and was once a convenient resting place for travellers on their way from London to Chester. Tastefully restored by the current owners, this stylish coaching inn serves food all day, from breakfast onwards, although locals can still pop in for a pint of Cheshire Cat. Local produce is the cornerstone of the kitchen and the seasonal menus change weekly. Typical dishes include pan-fried chicken supreme with asparagus and pea risotto; and crayfish and tiger prawn linguine. Look out for the summer beer festival.

Open all wk **Food** Lunch Mon-Fri 7am-9pm, Sat 8am-9pm, Sun 8-8 Dinner Mon-Fri 7am-9pm, Sat 8am-9pm, Sun 8-8 Av main course £12 ⊕ FREE HOUSE ◀ Weetwood Best Bitter & Cheshire Cat, Timothy Taylor Landlord. ♟ 13 **Facilities** Non-diners area ❧ (Bar Garden) ♦♦ Children's menu Children's portions Family room Garden ♬ Beer festival Parking WiFi 🚌 (notice required)

WARMINGHAM
Map 15 SJ76

The Bear's Paw ★★★★★ INN ⊛
PICK OF THE PUBS

See Pick of the Pubs on page 83

WINCLE
Map 16 SJ96

The Ship Inn

tel: 01260 227217 **Barlow Hill SK11 0QE**
email: garybparker@btconnect.com
dir: *From Buxton towards Congleton on A54 left into Barlow Hill at x-rds, follow signs for Wincle (0.75m) & Swythamley, then brown (spoon & fork) signs to pub*

Popular Peak District destination

The adjoining villages of Danebridge and Wincle straddle the River Dane, which here in the western Peak District National Park divides Cheshire from Staffordshire. The park's moors, lush woodland and drystone-walled pastures are a favourite with walkers, many of whom beat a path to this 17th-century, pink-hued pub with a flagstoned taproom serving JW Lees' Manchester-brewed MPA. There's an interesting and regularly-changing menu, perhaps on the day you visit offering vegetable and chickpea Thai curry; smoked cheese stuffed chicken in Cajun spices; pie of the day; or oven-roasted belly pork with black pudding bubble-and-squeak. There are splendid views from the beer garden.

Open Tue-Fri 12-3 5.30-11 (Sat-Sun all day) Closed Mon (ex BHs) **Food** Lunch Tue-Fri 12-2.30, Sat 12-9.30, Sun 12-5 Dinner Tue-Thu 6-9, Fri-Sat 6-9.30 ⊕ J W LEES ◀ MPA, Bitter. ♟ 13 **Facilities** Non-diners area ❧ (Bar Restaurant Garden) ♦♦ Children's menu Children's portions Family room Garden ♬ Parking WiFi 🚌 (notice required)

WRENBURY
Map 15 SJ54

The Dusty Miller

tel: 01270 780537 **CW5 8HG**
email: info@thedusty.co.uk
dir: *Phone for detailed directions*

Transformed former corn mill on Llangollen Canal

This beautifully converted 18th-century corn mill is beside the Llangollen Canal in the rural village of Wrenbury. The pub's large arched windows offer views of passing boats, while a black-and-white lift bridge, designed by Thomas Telford, completes the picture-postcard setting. Alongside a good choice of real ales, the modern British menu, which mainly relies on ingredients from the region, offers frequently changing options to suit everyone.

Open 12-12 Closed Mon in winter **Food** Lunch Mon-Fri 12-3, Sat 12-9.30, Sun 12-8 Dinner Mon-Fri 6-9, Sat 12-9.30, Sun 12-8 Av main course £12 ⊕ ROBINSONS ◖ Robinsons Unicorn, Old Tom & Dizzy Blonde, Guest ales ♂ Westons Stowford Press & Traditional. ♟ 12 **Facilities** Non-diners area ♣ (All areas) ♦ Children's menu Children's portions Garden Outside area ⊫ Parking WiFi ▄▄ (notice required)

CORNWALL & ISLES OF SCILLY

ALTARNUN
Map 2 SX28

Rising Sun Inn

tel: 01566 86636 **PL15 7SN**
email: risingsuninn@hotmail.co.uk
dir: *From A30 follow Altarnun signs onto unclassified road. Through Altarnun & Treween to T-junct. Inn 100yds on left*

Moorland free house worth leaving the A30 for

It's still fine to arrive by horse at this inviting, 18th-century moorland inn – there's a hitching post in the car park. On horseback could be the best way home, too, given the real ales from the village's Penpont brewery (which celebrates its birthday at a beer festival here in mid November), Skinner's Betty Stogs, and also Cornish Orchards and Press Gang ciders. Lunch and dinner dishes include all kinds, from bangers and mash to lobster. The specials board changes daily, but always focuses on seasonal and locally sourced produce. Home of the original 'Boxeater' steak.

Open all wk 12-2.30 5.30-11 (Sat 12-11 Sun & BHs 12-10.30) **Food** Lunch all wk 12-2 Dinner all wk 6-9 ⊕ FREE HOUSE ◖ Penpont St. Nonna's, Skinner's Betty Stogs, Guest ales ♂ Cornish Orchards, Skinner's Press Gang. ♟ 10 **Facilities** Non-diners area ♣ (Bar Garden) ♦ Children's menu Children's portions Garden ⊫ Beer festival Parking WiFi ▄▄ (notice required)

BODINNICK
Map 2 SX15

The Old Ferry Inn ★★★ INN

tel: 01726 870237 **PL23 1LX**
email: info@oldferryinn.co.uk **web:** www.oldferryinn.co.uk
dir: *From Liskeard on A38 to Dobwalls, left at lights onto A390. After 3m left onto B3359 signed Looe. Right signed Lerryn/Bodinnick/Polruan for 5m*

Traditional Cornish pub with splendid estuary views

Daphne du Maurier wrote many of her novels at 'Ferryside', the house next door to this 400-year-old inn by the River Fowey. You can watch people messing about in boats from one of the sun terraces, stay in the bar among the nautical memorabilia, or cosy up in the stone-walled snug. A long list of snacks includes Cornish Pasties, while among the mains are cod in Sharp's ale batter; wholetail scampi and chips; roast chicken breast with local cider, cream and apple sauce; and wild mushroom and thyme penne pasta. The adjacent ferry carries cars over to Fowey town.

Open all day all wk **Food** Lunch all wk 12-3 Dinner all wk 6-9.15 ⊕ FREE HOUSE ◖ Sharp's Cornish Coaster & Own ♂ Haye Farm, Sharp's Orchard Cornish Cider. **Facilities** Non-diners area ♣ (Bar Outside area) ♦ Children's menu Family room Outside area ⊫ Parking WiFi **Rooms** 12

BOLINGEY
Map 2 SW75

NEW Bolingey Inn

tel: 01872 571626 **Penwartha Rd TR6 0DH**
email: michaelsanders@bolingeyinn.co.uk
dir: *From B3285 in Perranporth at rdbt into Station Rd. Approx 0.5m right signed Bolingey. Pub 0.5m on right*

Delightful pub associated with Cornwall's former mining industry

In a previous life, the Bolingey Inn was reputedly a count house for the vicinity's mines; doubtless the money men would have appreciated ale on tap without needing to leave the building. 'More landlords than can be researched', the menu tells us, have served here since its change of use, some making structural changes during their tenure. Today the Bolingey charms its clients with its atmosphere, serves four bitters from the likes of Sharp's and Fuller's, and prepares good home-cooked dishes in the kitchen. Most ingredients are sourced locally, with the specials board listing fresh fish options. Beer festivals in April and October.

Open all day all wk **Food** Lunch all wk 12-2.30 Dinner all wk 6-9.30 Av main course £12 ⊕ PUNCH TAVERNS ◖ Sharp's Doom Bar, Greene King Abbot Ale, Butcombe, St Austell Proper Job, Fuller's London Pride ♂ Thatchers. **Facilities** Non-diners area ♣ (Bar Outside area) ♦ Children's menu Children's portions Outside area ⊫ Beer festival Parking WiFi ▄▄ (notice required)

BOSCASTLE
Map 2 SX09

Cobweb Inn

tel: 01840 250278 **The Bridge PL35 0HE**
email: cobweb.inn@virgin.net
dir: *In village centre*

Freshly prepared food in Cornish tourist spot

Built in the 1600s, this immense, five-storey stone edifice was once a bonded warehouse where customs agents guarded taxable imported goods. Rumour has it that despite this, one could drink illicitly in the beamed, flag-floored back room; today the bottle- and jug-festooned bar, where Cornwall-brewed real ales and farm ciders can be ordered without subterfuge. Eat here or in the charming white-painted restaurant, where seafood, steaks, pasties and a great deal more feature on the extensive menu and daily specials boards.

Open all day all wk **Food** Lunch all wk 11-2.30 Dinner all wk 6-9.30 ⊕ FREE HOUSE ◖ St Austell Tribute, Tintagel Harbour Special, Guest ales ♂ Healey's Cornish Rattler (apple & pear), Westons Stowford Press, Thatchers, Addlestones. **Facilities** Non-diners area ♣ (Bar Garden) ♦ Children's menu Children's portions Family room Garden ⊫ Beer festival Parking WiFi ▄▄ (notice required)

The Wellington Hotel ★★★ HL ◉◉ **PICK OF THE PUBS**

See Pick of the Pubs on page 86
See Pick of the Pubs on page 86

PICK OF THE PUBS

The Wellington Hotel ★★★ HL 🌹🌹

tel: 01840 250202
The Harbour PL35 0AQ
email: info@wellingtonhotelboscastle.com
web: www.wellingtonhotelboscastle.com
dir: *A30/A395 at Davidstow follow Boscastle signs. B3266 to village. Right into New Rd*

Popular pub and fine dining restaurant on the Cornish coast

This listed 16th-century coaching inn with its castellated tower sits on one of England's most stunning coastlines, at the end of a glorious wooded valley where the rivers Jordan and Valency meet; in 1852 it was renamed in honour of the Duke of Wellington. Known affectionately as 'The Welly' by both locals and loyal guests, it was fully restored after devastating floods a few years ago, but retains much of its original charm. The traditional Long Bar, complete with minstrels' gallery, proffers a good selection of Cornish ales, ciders such as Cornish Orchard, and malt whiskies. Bar snacks here embrace sandwiches with or without soup of the day, along with small plates such as smoked chicken terrine with artichoke and pickles; smoked haddock fishcakes; and steamed mussels with house bread. For a proper lunch, look to the blackboard for daily specials or the carte for the likes of crab linguine; sausages and mash; or grilled leg of lamb steak with crispy polenta. Follow

perhaps with an Eton Mess; chocolate brownie with poached cherries and cherry ripple ice cream; or sticky toffee pudding with clotted cream. Children are well catered for with their own menu, and some adult main courses can be served in half-size portions. For fine dining, head to the first floor of the hotel to find the Waterloo Restaurant. The kitchen team prepares fresh local produce — none fresher or more local than the seafood landed by the boats in the harbour a few yards away. Starters may include tortellini of crab and lobster with wild garlic; or mackerel with kohlrabi, clams and celeriac. Continue with lamb cannon, asparagus and gratin potatoes; or an escalopine Normande of Launceston veal cooked with Calvados and Braeburn apples.

Open all day all wk 11-11 **Food** Mon-Fri 12-3, 6-9, Sat-Sun 12-9 Av main course £13 Restaurant menu available Tue-Sat ⊕ FREE HOUSE ◗ St Austell Tribute, Sharp's Doom Bar Ö Cornish Orchards, Healey's Cornish Rattler.
Facilities Non-diners area 😺 (Bar Garden Outside area) 🧒 Children's menu Children's portions Family room Garden Outside area 🪑 Parking WiFi 🚍 (notice required) **Rooms** 14

CADGWITH
Map 2 SW71

Cadgwith Cove Inn

tel: 01326 290513 **TR12 7JX**
email: garryandhelen@cadgwithcoveinn.co.uk
dir: *A3083 from Helston towards Lizard. Left to Cadgwith*

Local seafood and beer in a former smugglers' haunt

A visit to this 300-year-old pub in the largely unspoilt fishing hamlet on the Lizard coastline will illustrate why it once appealed to smugglers. Relics in the atmospheric bars attest to a rich seafaring history; the cove itself is just across the old pilchard cellar from its sunny front patio. Traditional favourites include fish and chips; crab salad and vegetarian trio of the day. Quiz nights are on Mondays, folk music on Tuesdays, the Cadgwith Singers perform every Friday and there are seafood buffets on Saturdays throughout the summer. Time a visit for the October beer and cider festival.

Open all day all wk **Food** Lunch all wk 12-3 Dinner all wk 6-9 Restaurant menu available all wk ⊕ PUNCH TAVERNS ◀ Sharp's, Skinner's, Guest ales ᵭ Westons Stowford Press, Thatchers. ⬙ 9 **Facilities** Non-diners area ❀ (Bar Restaurant Outside area) ◀ Children's menu Children's portions Outside area ♠ Beer festival Cider festival WiFi

CALLINGTON
Map 3 SX36

Manor House Inn

tel: 01579 362354 **Rilla Mill PL17 7NT**
email: jackie.cole67@googlemail.com
dir: *5m from Callington, just off B3257*

Market town inn close to many walks

Standing by the River Lynher on the edge of Bodmin Moor near The Minions and Cheesering Stones, this former granary once supplied the neighbouring mill. Today it offers Cornish real ales and ciders, plus a varied menu that includes pub favourites such as steak and ale pie, and beer battered fish and chips. There's a beer festival in February. There are delightful woodland and riverside walks so this inn is popular with walkers, who will be pleased to know that their dogs are welcome too.

Open Tue-Fri 12-3 5-11 (Sat-Sun all day) Closed Closed Mon Nov-Mar **Food** Lunch Tue-Sun 12-2 Dinner Tue-Sun 6-9 Av main course £9 ⊕ FREE HOUSE ◀ Sharp's Own, Special, Guest ale ᵭ Westons, Healey's Cornish Rattler, Somersby Cider. **Facilities** Non-diners area ❀ (Bar Outside area) ◀ Children's menu Children's portions Outside area ♠ Beer festival Parking WiFi ▦ (notice required)

CHAPEL AMBLE
Map 2 SW97

NEW The Maltsters Arms

tel: 01208 812473 **PL27 6EU**
dir: *A39 from Wadebridge towards Camelford. In 1m left signed Chapel Amble. Pub on right in village*

Traditional home-cooking in charming Cornish village inn

In the pretty Cornish village of Chapel Amble and a short drive from Rock and Port Isaac, The Maltsters Arms oozes old-world charm and character, from slate floors and copper pots to 'mind-your-head' beams and open fires. A pub at the heart of the community with a quiz night and must-book Sunday carvery, the food is home-cooked and traditional. Pub favourites of burgers and beer-battered fish and chips

appear alongside main menu dishes such as roasted cod loin, mussels, prawns and saffron linguine; and local lamb shank with garlic and spring onion mash and redcurrant jus.

Open all wk 11-3 6-11 **Food** Lunch all wk 11-3 Dinner all wk 6-9.30 Set menu available ⊕ FREE HOUSE ◀ Sharp's Doom Bar, St Austell Tribute ᵭ Westons Old Rosie. ⬙ 11 **Facilities** Non-diners area ❀ (Bar Restaurant Outside area) ◀ Children's menu Children's portions Outside area ♠ Parking WiFi ▦ (notice required)

CONSTANTINE
Map 2 SW72

Trengilly Wartha Inn
PICK OF THE PUBS

tel: 01326 340332 **Nancenoy TR11 5RP**
email: reception@trengilly.co.uk
dir: *Follow signs to Constantine, left towards Gweek until 1st sign for inn, left & left again at next sign, continue to inn*

Family pub close to the Helford River

Will and Lisa Lea took over here about eight years ago, and have since transformed it into a popular hostelry. The Cornish name means a settlement above the trees, although it actually lies at the foot of a densely wooded valley. Frequently-changing local real ales are served from the stillage in the black-beamed bar, which they share with Healey's Cornish Rattler and Ty Gwyn ciders, 15 wines by the glass, and over 40 malts. A meal, more than likely sourced from a local farm or fishing boat, could be one of the specials, such as mussels with white wine, onion, garlic and cream sauce; or roasted guinea fowl with creamy chorizo sauce. Alternatively, a pub classic of home-made chicken and leek pie; or vegetarian wild mushroom and cheddar risotto. A pretty beer garden and vine-shaded pergola are surrounded by three meadows, once part of the original smallholding.

Open all wk 11-3 6-12 **Food** Lunch all wk 12-2.15 Dinner all wk 6.30-9.30 Av main course £11 ⊕ FREE HOUSE ◀ Skinner's Cornish Knocker & Betty Stogs, Sharp's Doom Bar & Eden Ale, Penzance Potion No 9, Guest ales ᵭ Healey's Cornish Rattler, Thatchers Gold, Ty Gwyn. ⬙ 15 **Facilities** Non-diners area ❀ (Bar Garden) ◀ Children's menu Children's portions Play area Family room Garden ♠ Beer festival Cider festival Parking WiFi ▦ (notice required)

CRAFTHOLE
Map 3 SX35

The Finnygook Inn

tel: 01503 230338 **PL11 3BQ**
email: eat@finnygook.co.uk
dir: *10m W of Tamar Bridge take A374 S. In 3m right signed Crafthole & follow pub signs. From Torpoint take A374, 5m to Antony. Left in Antony, 1m to T-junct. 3m to Crafthole*

Old coaching inn serving peninsula-brewed beers

They say the ghost of smuggler Silas Finny walks abroad on the cliffs and byways hereabouts; so, too, do ramblers and visitors seeking to share the St Austell and Penpont beers, and tempting fodder available at this 16th-century pub. Located in a hamlet above Portwrinkle's cove-nibbled coast, The Finnygook serves seafood dishes, such as grilled Cornish sardines and crab linguine, backed by a host of reliable pub favourites (sausages with bubble-and-squeak, beefburger, and treacle sponge for dessert) taken by the log fire, in the library room or on the terrace with distant views up the Tamar estuary.

Open all day Closed Mon in Nov-Mar **Food** Lunch all wk 12-9 (Nov-Mar Tue-Sun 12.30-2.30) Dinner all wk 12-9 (Nov-Mar Tue-Sun 6-9) ⊕ FREE HOUSE ◀ Sharp's Doom Bar, St Austell Tribute & Proper Job, Penpont Cornish Arvor, Dartmoor ᵭ Thatchers. ⬙ 10 **Facilities** Non-diners area ❀ (Bar Garden) ◀ Children's menu Children's portions Garden ♠ Parking WiFi ▦ (notice required)

CUBERT
Map 2 SW75

The Smugglers' Den Inn

tel: 01637 830209 **Trebellan TR8 5PY**
email: info@thesmugglersden.co.uk
dir: *From Newquay take A3075 to Cubert x-rds, then right, then left signed Trebellan, 0.5m to inn*

Classic pub selection focusing on Cornish provenance

Look to the blackboard for fish specials in this thatched 16th-century pub situated less than 15 minutes from Newquay; the table d'hôte menu includes catch of the day too. Popular with locals and visitors alike, the pub comprises a long bar, family room, children's play area, courtyards and huge beer garden. Local suppliers are listed at the bottom of the no-nonsense modern menu, where a salt and chilli squid could be followed by a slow-roasted shoulder of Cornish lamb.

Open all wk 11.30-3 6-11 (Sat 11-3 6-12 Sun & summer open all day) Closed 25 Dec 12-3 ⊕ FREE HOUSE ◄ Sharp's Doom Bar, St Austell Tribute, Guest ales ♂ Healey's Cornish Rattler, Thatchers Gold. **Facilities** ❄ (Bar Garden) ❅ Children's menu Play area Family room Garden Parking WiFi

DUNMERE
Map 2 SX06

The Borough Arms

tel: 01208 73118 **PL31 2RD**
email: borougharms@hotmail.co.uk
dir: *From A30 take A389 to Wadebridge, pub approx 1m from Bodmin*

Welcome refreshment in a Cornish valley

One of England's best loved recreational trails, the Camel Trail, skims past this considerably updated Victorian railway pub in the Cornish countryside outside Bodmin. Trains carrying china clay along the old line have been replaced by cyclists and ramblers, accessing the pub car park directly from the trail to indulge in a range of West Country real ales and ever-reliable pub grub. Ploughman's, steaks, curry of the day and freshly battered fish and chips revive flagging lovers of the outdoors, or try the carvery. Families are well catered for, with a children's play area to burn off extra calories.

Open all day all wk **Food** Lunch all wk 12-9 Dinner all wk 12-9 ⊕ ST AUSTELL BREWERY ◄ Tribute, Dartmoor, Bass. **Facilities** Non-diners area ❄ (Bar Garden) ❅ Children's menu & portions Play area Family room Garden ⏴ Parking WiFi

FEOCK
Map 2 SW83

The Punchbowl & Ladle

tel: 01872 862237 **Penelewey TR3 6QY**
email: punchbowlandladle@googlemail.com
dir: *From Truro take A39 towards Falmouth, after Shell garage at Playing Place rdbt follow King Harry Ferry signs. 0.5m, pub on right*

Cornish comforts in a thatched retreat

Flowers adorn the exterior of this gorgeous old pub close to the King Harry Ferry. Local rumour has it that the bar fireplace was used to burn contraband when customs officers dropped by. Head for the suntrap walled garden or patio with a glass of St Austell Proper Job beer or Cornish Rattler cider. Alternatively, settle down on the comfortable sofas in the cosy low-beamed bar and await your choice from the menu, which uses seasonal ingredients sourced from local Cornish suppliers and features great comfort dishes such as baked Cornish camembert; confit belly pork with black pudding mash; smoked haddock risotto; and sticky toffee pudding. Jackets, salads and sandwiches are also on offer.

Open all day all wk **Food** Lunch Mon-Sat 12-2.30, Sun 12-3 Dinner all wk 6-9 ⊕ ST AUSTELL BREWERY ◄ Tribute, Proper Job, Trelawny & HSD ♂ Healey's Cornish Rattler. ♟ 16 **Facilities** Non-diners area ❄ (Bar Garden) ❅ Children's menu Children's portions Garden ⏴ Parking WiFi

FOWEY
Map 2 SX15

The Ship Inn

tel: 01726 832230 **Trafalgar Square PL23 1AZ**
dir: *From A30 take B3269 & A390*

Very old inn situated in Fowey's narrow streets

One of Fowey's oldest buildings, The Ship was built in 1570 by John Rashleigh, who sailed to the Americas with Walter Raleigh. Given Fowey's riverside position, assume a good choice of fish, including River Fowey mussels as a starter or main; grilled sardines in garlic. Other options include Mr Kittow's pork sausages and mash; spinach, asparagus and wild mushroom risotto. St Austell ales, real fires and a long tradition of genial hospitality add the final touches.

Open all day all wk 11am-mdnt (Fri-Sat 11am-1am) **Food** Lunch 12-2.30 Dinner 6-9 ⊕ ST AUSTELL BREWERY ◄ Tribute & Proper Job, Dartmoor IPA ♂ Healey's Cornish Rattler & Pear Rattler. **Facilities** Non-diners area ❄ (Bar) ❅ Children's menu Children's portions Family room WiFi

GUNNISLAKE
Map 3 SX47

The Rising Sun Inn

tel: 01822 832201 **Calstock Rd PL18 9BX**
dir: *From Tavistock take A390 to Gunnislake. Left after lights into Calstock Rd. Inn approx 500mtrs on right*

Charming inn in a lovely Cornish valley

Overlooking the stunning Tamar Valley, this traditional two-roomed picture-postcard pub is a popular stop for walkers, wildlife enthusiasts and cyclists; great walks start and finish from the pub. There's been a change of hands here and at the time of going to press we didn't have any information on the type of food being served.

Open all wk 12-3 5-11 **Food** Contact pub for details ⊕ FREE HOUSE ◄ Skinner's Betty Stogs, St Austell Tribute, Otter, Dartmoor Legend, Dartmoor Jail Ale, Guest ales ♂ Westons Stowford Press, Thatchers. ♟ 25 **Facilities** Non-diners area ❄ (Bar Garden) ❅ Garden ⏴ Parking **Notes** ✉

GUNWALLOE
Map 2 SW62

The Halzephron Inn
`PICK OF THE PUBS`

tel: 01326 240406 **TR12 7QB**
email: enquiries@halzephron-inn.co.uk
dir: *3m S of Helston on A3083, right to Gunwalloe, through village. Inn on left*

Stunning views and lots of local seafood on the menu

The name of the inn derives from Als Yfferin, old Cornish for 'Cliffs of Hell', an appropriate description for this hazardous stretch of Atlantic coastline. Located high above Gunwalloe Fishing Cove, this 500-year-old, rugged stone inn commands an enviable position, with breathtaking views across Mount's Bay. On sunny days grab a front bench and enjoy a pint of St Austell Tribute while looking out to St Michael's Mount. The two interconnecting bars feature cosy log fires, fishing memorabilia, and watercolours of local scenes. The à la carte and daily changing specials utilise the best Cornish produce available, including fresh seafood. Everything is home made, with the likes of Cornish seafood chowder; and local mussels steamed in white wine and cream among the starters. Main courses include steak and Guinness pie; lamb's liver and crispy bacon in onion sauce; and fresh Cornish crab meat baked in Thermidor sauce. Change of hands.

Open all day all wk 11-11 (Sun 12-10.30) **Food** Lunch Mon-Sat 12-2, Sun 12-3 Dinner all wk 6-9 Av main course £10 ⊕ FREE HOUSE ◄ Sharp's Own, Doom Bar & Special, St Austell Tribute, Skinner's Betty Stogs ♂ Symonds Founders Reserve. ♟ 10 **Facilities** Non-diners area ❄ (Bar Garden) ❅ Children's menu Children's portions Play area Family room Garden ⏴ Parking WiFi (notice required)

GWEEK
Map 2 SW72

Black Swan ★★★★ INN

tel: 01326 221502 **TR12 6TU**
email: info@blackswangweek.co.uk **web:** www.blackswangweek.co.uk
dir: *In village centre*

Home-cooked food and Cornish beers

Located in the picturesque village of Gweek on the River Helford, a stone's throw from the popular National Seal Sanctuary, this delightful inn has new landlords. The Black Swan has become famous for their sirloin steaks, but also offers signature dishes of steak and Guinness pie with creamy mash, and Cajun chicken breast, chips and peas. There's a choice of regularly changing specials too to widen the options. Not to be missed is a selection of Cornish ales and guest ales. If you'd like to stay over the pub has stylish bedrooms delightfully named Raspberry, Blackberry, Gooseberry and Mulberry.

Open all day all wk **Food** Lunch all wk, all day Dinner all wk, all day Av main course £8.95 Restaurant menu available all wk ⊕ PUNCH TAVERNS ◀ Sharp's Doom Bar, Bass, St Austell Tribute, Skinner's Betty Stogs. ▼ 9 **Facilities** Non-diners area ❤ (Bar Garden) ♦ Children's menu Children's portions Garden ⊓ Parking WiFi ▥ (notice required) **Rooms** 4

GWITHIAN
Map 2 SW54

The Red River Inn

tel: 01736 753223 **1 Prosper Hill TR27 5BW**
email: louisa.saville@googlemail.com
dir: *Exit A30 at Loggans Moor rdbt, follow Hayle signs. Immediately take 3rd exit at mini rdt onto B3301 signed Gwithian. 2m to pub in village centre*

A village pub that offers something for everyone

The name of this 200-year-old pub recalls the colour of the village river when tin was mined locally. Close by runs the South West Coastal Path, and the beach is popular with surfers who, even in their wetsuits, are warmly welcomed here. Among its attractions are up to five, ever-changing Cornish real ales, an Easter weekend beer and cider festival, and food that ranges from fresh crab sandwiches and haloumi salad to fresh sea bass, steaks and Middle Eastern, Mexican and Indonesian dishes. Burgers are named Firebolt and Stinky Pig. An in-house shop sells artisan bread, pastries and farm produce.

Open 12-11 summer (Tue-Fri 12-2 5.30-11 Sat-Sun 12-11 winter) Closed Mon (winter only) **Food** Lunch 12-2 Dinner 6-9 ⊕ FREE HOUSE ◀ Sharp's Own, Spingo, Cornish Chough, Tintagel Harbour Special ⊘ Sharp's Orchard, Thatchers Gold, Healey's Cornish Rattler, Cornish Orchards. **Facilities** Non-diners area ❤ (Bar Restaurant Garden) ♦ Children's menu Children's portions Garden ⊓ Beer festival Cider festival Parking WiFi ▥ (notice required)

HALSETOWN
Map 2 SW43

NEW The Halsetown Inn

tel: 01736 795583 **TR26 3NA**
email: info@halsetowninn.co.uk
dir: *On B3311, 1m for St Ives*

Smart country gastro-pub showcasing local produce

Built in 1831, The Halsetown Inn is named after the village's architect and benefactor, James Halse. From the outside, little has changed at this stone-built pub, but the interior reveals a more contemporary style although the open fires remain and dogs are welcome. Run by the same team as the award-winning Blas Burgerworks restaurant in St Ives, local produce drives the menus here, typical

mains include Cornish mussels in curried laksa broth; Trevaskis Farm sausages with white bean stew; and rabbit pie. Look out for the August beer festival.

Open 11-3 5.30-close Closed 1st 2wks Jan, Sun eve **Food** Lunch Mon-Sat 12-2, Sun 12-3 Dinner Mon-Sat 6-9 (5.30-9.30 summer) Av main course £13 ⊕ PUNCH TAVERNS ◀ Sharp's Doom Bar, Skinner's Betty Stogs ⊘ Cornish Orchards. **Facilities** Non-diners area ❤ (Bar Outside area) ♦ Children's menu Children's portions Outside area ⊓ Beer festival Parking WiFi ▥ (notice required)

HELFORD PASSAGE
Map 2 SW72

The Ferryboat Inn

tel: 01326 250625 **TR11 5LB**
email: manager@ferryboatinnhelford.com
dir: *In village centre, 1st turn after Trebah Gardens*

Wonderful views and great seafood

There are fabulous views over the Helford estuary from this waterside pub, which dates back 300 years. Whether it's a plate of oysters and a glass of fizz on the sunny, south-facing terrace or Cornish bratwurst, mustard and dill mash, red cabbage and onion gravy by the warmth of the granite fireplace inside, this is a venue for all weathers. Everything is made on the premises and the Ferryboat burger is especially popular. The pub is owned by Wright Brothers, custodians of the Duchy of Cornwall's oyster farm, so the quality of the shellfish and seafood speaks for itself. Try beer battered Cornish haddock with chips, tartare sauce and mushy peas.

Open all day all wk **Food** Lunch 12-3 Dinner 6-9 (summer 6-10) Av main course £10 ⊕ ST AUSTELL ◀ Tribute, Dartmoor, Proper Job ⊘ Healey's Cornish Rattler. ▼ 12 **Facilities** Non-diners area ❤ (Bar Restaurant Outside area) ♦ Children's menu Children's portions Outside area ⊓ Parking WiFi ▥ (notice required)

HELSTON
Map 2 SW62

The Queens Arms

tel: 01326 573485 **Breage TR13 9PD**
email: queensarmsbreage@btconnect.com
dir: *Follow Breage signs from A394 approx 3m W of Helston. Pub adjacent to church*

Ideal base for Cornish coast and country exploration

In an enviable position, this 500-year-old inn sits opposite the church in a stone-built village on The Lizard, just a short hop from fabulous beaches and charming harbours. Inside it's pure village inn, from the convivial bar, all beams, bar stools, banquettes and log-burner, to the busy games room and the pocket-sized beer garden. Beers hail from small Cornish breweries like Tintagel and Harbour; an annual beer festival adds to the range. Dedicated chefs create tantalising dishes with equally peninsula provenance: fish from Newlyn, meats from a butcher in nearby Helston and organic vegetables from local gardens. The new licensees are quickly making their mark.

Open all day all wk **Food** Lunch all wk 12-2.30 Dinner all wk 6.30-8.30 Av main course £9 ⊕ PUNCH TAVERNS ◀ Sharp's Doom Bar, Otter, St Austell Tribute, Tintagel Arthur's Ale & Harbour Special ⊘ Addlestones, Thatchers. **Facilities** Non-diners area ❤ (Bar Restaurant Garden) ♦ Children's menu Children's portions Play area Garden ⊓ Beer festival Parking WiFi ▥ (notice required)

LANLIVERY
Map 2 SX05

The Crown Inn ★★★ INN
PICK OF THE PUBS

tel: 01208 872707 **PL30 5BT**
email: thecrown@wagtailinns.com **web:** www.wagtailinns.com
dir: *Signed from A390. Follow brown sign approx 1.5m W of Lostwithiel*

One of Cornwall's oldest pubs

In a moorland village above a tributary of the Fowey River is this former longhouse, with characteristic thick stone walls, low beams, granite and slate floors, open fires and an unusual bread oven. Much of the present building dates from the 12th century, when it housed the stonemasons constructing the nearby church. The pub has been extensively but sympathetically restored over the years; at one point the work uncovered a deep well, now covered by glass, under the porch. With the sea only a few miles away, expect a menu offering plenty of fresh fish and seafood, as well as other local produce. A popular main course is Cornish ale-battered fish with chips, crushed peas and home-made tartare sauce. At lunchtime in warm weather, enjoy a fresh Fowey crab sandwich or a proper Cornish Pasty and a pint of Skinner's Betty Stogs in the lovely garden.

Open all day all wk **Food** Lunch 12-2.30 Dinner 6-9 ⊕ FREE HOUSE ◀ Harbour Amber Ale, Skinner's Betty Stogs, Guest ales ♂ Healey's Cornish Rattler. **Facilities** Non-diners area ❖ (Bar Garden) ♦ Children's menu Children's portions Garden ⋒ Parking WiFi ➤ (notice required) **Rooms** 9

LOOE
Map 2 SX25

The Ship Inn ★★★ INN

tel: 01503 263124 **Fore St PL13 1AD**
dir: *In town centre*

Busy pub on a narrow street

This lively St Austell Brewery-owned pub stands on a corner in the heart of this charming old fishing town, a minute's walk from the working harbour. Locals and tourists join together in the appreciation of a pint of Tribute, and select their favourites from the menu – a burger or hot baguette for some, while others go for steak and ale pie or hunter's chicken. A quiz is held on Mondays throughout the year, live bands play regularly, and well-equipped bedrooms are available for those wanting to tarry awhile.

Open all day all wk **Food** Contact pub for details ⊕ ST AUSTELL BREWERY ◀ Tribute, Tinners, HSD ♂ Healey's Cornish Rattler. **Facilities** Non-diners area ❖ (Bar) ♦ Children's menu Children's portions Family room **Rooms** 8

LUXULYAN
Map 2 SX05

The Kings Arms

tel: 01726 850202 **Bridges PL30 5EF**
dir: *From A30 at Innis Downs junct take A39 signed St Austell. Left signed Luxulyan. Over railway & river. Inn on right at bottom of hill*

Well-kept beers, good pub grub and a friendly welcome

Walkers, cyclists, families, dog owners - all are most welcome at this traditional stone-built village pub. Owned by St Austell Brewery, it offers their HSD, Trelawny and Tribute real ales, an occasional guest, and Healey's Cornish Rattler cider; wine drinkers have a choice of 12 by the glass. The menu of locally sourced produce offers a selection of no-nonsense home-made snacks and main meals that should leave everybody happy - Trelawny pie; rabbit casserole; fish and chips; and 'build a burger'. A takeaway service includes home-made pizzas.

Open all day all wk Sun-Thu 11-11 (Fri-Sat 11am-mdnt) **Food** Lunch all wk 12-2.30 Dinner all wk 6-9 ⊕ ST AUSTELL BREWERY ◀ HSD, Tribute, Trelawny, Guest ale ♂ Healey's Cornish Rattler. ₹ 12 **Facilities** Non-diners area ❖ (Bar Restaurant Garden) ♦ Children's menu Children's portions Garden ⋒ Parking WiFi ➤ (notice required)

MEVAGISSEY
Map 2 SX04

The Ship Inn

tel: 01726 843324 **Fore St PL26 6UQ**
dir: *7m S of St Austell*

A popular tavern a few steps from the harbour

This 400-year-old inn stands just a few yards from Mevagissey's picturesque fishing harbour, so the choice of fish and seafood dishes comes as no surprise on a menu of home-cooked dishes: moules marinière, beer-battered cod, and oven-baked fillet of haddock topped with prawns and Cornish Tiskey cheese. The popular bar has low-beamed ceilings, flagstone floors and a strong nautical feel.

Open all day all wk 11am-mdnt **Food** Lunch all wk 12-3 Dinner all wk 6-9 ⊕ ST AUSTELL BREWERY ◀ St Austell Tribute & Proper Job, Guest ale ♂ Healey's Cornish Rattler. ₹ 8 **Facilities** Non-diners area ❖ (Bar) ♦ Children's menu WiFi ➤

MITCHELL
Map 2 SW85

The Plume of Feathers ★★★★ INN
PICK OF THE PUBS

tel: 01872 510387 **TR8 5AX**
email: theplume@hospitalitycornwall.com **web:** www.theplumemitchell.co.uk
dir: *From A30 follow Mitchell signs*

Friendly atmosphere in a historic inn

This charming 16th-century coaching inn is set in the quiet leafy village of Mitchell. It has a rich history – John Wesley preached Methodism here while Sir Walter Raleigh lived close by – and is a welcoming place to eat and drink today, thanks to its beamed ceilings, real fires and local artwork. The airy conservatory is also an appealing place to dine while seven stylish bedrooms provide the perfect overnight retreat. Local Cornish produce takes centre stage on the modern British menu and there's always a good showing of fish and locally reared meats. You might find hand rolled ravioli of pheasant, truffle oil and mascarpone to start, followed by a chargrilled Cornish beefburger; or St Austell Bay mussels with white wine, cream, chilli, garlic and parsley. A beer garden, Cornish real ales and a beer festival in May all prove an additional draw.

Open all day all wk 9am-11pm/mdnt (25 Dec 11-4) **Food** Lunch all wk 12-6 Dinner all wk 6-10 ⊕ FREE HOUSE ◀ Sharp's Doom Bar, John Smith's Extra Smooth, Skinner's, St Austell Tribute ♂ Healey's Cornish Rattler. ₹ **Facilities** Non-diners area ❖ (Bar Garden) ♦ Play area Garden ⋒ Beer festival Parking WiFi ➤ (notice required) **Rooms** 7

MITHIAN
Map 2 SW75

The Miners Arms

tel: 01872 552375 **TR5 0QF**
email: minersarms@live.co.uk
dir: *From A30 at Chiverton Cross rdbt take A3075 signed Newquay. At Pendown Cross left onto B3284 signed Perranporth. Left, left again to Mithian*

Fascinating history at centuries' old pub

The curiously light interior of this historic 16th-century pub adds yet another layer of mystery to the legends of its past. Over the centuries it has served as a courthouse, a venue for inquests, a smugglers' lair and even a house of ill repute. Relax beneath the low-beamed ceilings while admiring the wall paintings of Elizabeth I, and choose from the menu of dishes freshly cooked to order from local produce: hake topped with pesto; steak of the day; vegetable tagine; and the Miners fish pie is a must.

Open all day all wk 12-11.30 **Food** Lunch all wk 12-2.30 Dinner all wk 6-9 ⊕ PUNCH TAVERNS ◀ Sharp's Doom Bar, St Austell Tribute & Skinner's Betty Stogs ♂ Westons Stowford Press. **Facilities** Non-diners area ❖ (Bar) ♦ Children's menu Children's portions Garden ⋒ Parking ➤

PICK OF THE PUBS

The Pandora Inn

MYLOR BRIDGE   Map 2 SW83

tel: 01326 372678
Restronguet Creek TR11 5ST
email: info@pandorainn.com
web: www.pandorainn.com
dir: *From Truro/Falmouth follow A39, left at Carclew, follow signs to pub*

Historic waterside inn

Until the early 20th century, the tidal Restronguet Creek played an important part in the export of tin and copper. Overlooking the water is this 13th-century inn, named after the ship sent to Tahiti in 1790 to bring back the mutinous crew of Capt Bligh's HMS *Bounty*. Unfortunately, the Pandora sank with considerable loss of life on the Great Barrier Reef and its captain was eventually court-martialled. He subsequently bought the inn. Thatched, with low-beamed ceilings and flagstone floors, it was badly damaged by fire in 2011, but reopened a year later after careful restoration. The ground floor is largely unchanged, but it's a different story upstairs, where although ugly 1970s additions disappeared for good, a combination of listed building status and the wishes of long-term proprietors John Milan and Steve Bellman ensured the rest was restored using only traditional materials and building methods. An example is the vaulted dining area, where green-oak beams have been wooden-pegged the medieval

way. A few scorched sections of timber serve as reminders of what was lost. In the kitchen chef Tom Milby knows the area like the back of his oven glove and sources the freshest produce from local farmers, growers and fishermen. "What can be better than buying fish and shellfish off the boat as they land it on the Pandora's own pontoon?", he asks. Dine on that very pontoon, at a table by the water's edge, or in one of the series of little rooms inside, perhaps on seared Cornish scallops and langoustines, followed by slow-roasted pork belly, or home-smoked chicken breast. Alternatively, start with Mylor-smoked mackerel fillet, then pan-fried Cornish lamb's liver and bacon. Real ales come from the St Austell Brewery, and the ciders are Cornish Rattler.

Open all day all wk 10.30am-11pm
Food all wk 10.30-9.30 🛢 ST AUSTELL BREWERY ◀ HSD, Tribute, Proper Job & Trelawny Ŏ Healey's Cornish Rattler & Pear Rattler. **Facilities** 🐾 (Bar) 🚻 Children's menu Children's portions Outside area Parking WiFi 🚌 (notice required)

MYLOR BRIDGE
Map 2 SW83

The Pandora Inn
PICK OF THE PUBS

See Pick of the Pubs on page 91

NEWQUAY
Map 2 SW86

The Lewinnick Lodge Bar & Restaurant ★★★★ RR

tel: 01637 878117 **Pentire Headland TR7 1NX**
email: thelodge@hospitalitycornwall.com
web: www.hospitalitycornwall.com/lewinnicklodge
dir: *From Newquay take Pentire Rd 0.5m, pub on right*

Recommended for its fresh seafood and stunning views

Lewinnick Lodge perches on the cliff top of the Pentire Headland, enjoying a timeless panorama of sea views. This is a destination eatery, but real ales, local cider, crisp wines and premium lagers are all on offer in the bar. Wraps and baps and gourmet burgers can be ordered, but fresh seafood, much of it from Cornish waters, is the menu's key attraction; expect the likes of St Austell Bay mussels or Cornish fish pie. Meats from the county include slow-roasted pork and lamb. Leave room for the spiced apple and almond crumble served with Cornish clotted cream.

Open all day all wk **Food** Lunch all wk 12-5 Dinner all wk 5-10 ⊕ FREE HOUSE ◀ Sharp's Doom Bar, Skinner's Betty Stogs, St Austell Tribute ♂ Cornish Orchards. ♟ 8 **Facilities** Non-diners area ♥ (Bar Garden) ♦♦ Children's menu Children's portions Garden ⋒ Parking WiFi ➡ **Rooms** 10

PAR
Map 2 SX05

The Britannia Inn & Restaurant ★★★★ INN

tel: 01726 812889 **St Austell Rd PL24 2SL**
email: info@britanniainn.com web: www.britanniainn.com
dir: *On A390 between Par & St Austell, adjacent to Cornish Market World*

A family-owned inn with large garden

Three generations of the Lafferty family have so far held the keys to this 16th-century free house, where Sharp's Doom Bar and St Austell Tribute real ales, and Healey's Cornish Rattler cider declare its loyalty to the Royal Duchy. The three dining areas do likewise by offering prime-cut Cornish steaks and other locally sourced dishes, typically battered cod and chips; lamb rogan josh with chickpeas and spinach; home-made beef stew with herb dumplings; and pesto chicken with penne pasta and red peppers. Special deals are available on Tuesday grill nights. Guest rooms are named after Cornish locations.

Open all day all wk **Food** Lunch all wk 12-9 Dinner all wk 12-9 ⊕ FREE HOUSE ◀ Sharp's Doom Bar, St Austell Tribute, Bass ♂ Thatchers Gold, Healey's Cornish Rattler. ♟ **Facilities** Non-diners area ♥ (Bar Garden) ♦♦ Children's menu Children's portions Play area Family room Garden ⋒ Parking WiFi ➡ (notice required) **Rooms** 7

The Royal Inn ★★★★ INN

tel: 01726 815601 **66 Eastcliffe Rd PL24 2AJ**
email: info@royal-inn.co.uk web: www.royal-inn.co.uk
dir: *A3082 Par, follow brown tourist signs for 'Newquay Branch line' or railway station. Pub opposite rail station*

Welcoming pub on the Rail Ale Trail

Originally frequented by travellers and employees of the Great Western Railway, this 19th-century inn was named after a visit by King Edward VII to a local copper mine. The pub is now on the Atlantic Coast Line of the 'Rail Ale Trail', and the building is much extended, with an open-plan bar serving a variety of real ales. Leading off are the dining areas which comprise a cosy beamed room and conservatory. The long bar menu offers everything from pizzas and burgers to salads and omelettes. The

restaurant menu includes ham hock terrine, whole lemon sole with spicy prawn butter; and steaks with all the trimmings. Fifteen comfortable rooms are available.

Open all day all wk 11.30-11 (Sun 12-10.30) **Food** Lunch all wk 12-2 Dinner all wk 6.30-9 ⊕ FREE HOUSE ◀ Sharp's Doom Bar & Special, Wells Bombardier, Shepherd Neame Spitfire, Cotleigh Barn Owl, Guest ales ♂ Healey's Cornish Rattler, Thatchers Gold. ♟ 13 **Facilities** Non-diners area ♥ (Bar Garden) ♦♦ Children's menu Children's portions Garden ⋒ Parking WiFi ➡ **Rooms** 15

PENZANCE
Map 2 SW43

The Coldstreamer Inn ★★★ INN ⊛

tel: 01736 362072 **Gulval TR18 3BB**
email: info@coldstreamer-penzance.co.uk web: www.coldstreamer-penzance.co.uk
dir: *From Penzance take B3311 towards St Ives. In Gulval right into School Ln. Pub in village centre*

Expect the best local produce at this traditional village inn

This unassuming inn tucked away in a sleepy village close to Penzance and St Ives makes an ideal setting for chef Andrew Gibsons's simple yet accomplished regional cooking. Produce from local fishermen, farmers and growers is used to good effect in dishes such as Newlyn crab rarebit with bloody Mary dressing; or Cornish Yarg fritters with romanesco and almonds to start; a main course of Terras Farm duck breast with celeriac gratin, black kale and star anise; and yogurt pannacotta, poached rhubarb and apple curd; or sticky toffee pudding, honey and clotted cream ice cream to finish. Well kept local and guest ales, good value home-made bar snacks, a roaring fire and contemporary bedrooms complete the picture.

Open all day all wk **Food** Lunch all wk 12-3 Dinner all wk 6-9.30 (summer), 6-9 (winter) ⊕ PUNCH TAVERNS ◀ Skinner's Ginger Tosser, Bays Topsail, Guest ale. ♟ 12 **Facilities** Non-diners area ♥ (Bar Outside area) ♦♦ Children's menu Children's portions Outside area ⋒ WiFi ➡ (notice required) **Rooms** 3

Dolphin Tavern ★★★ INN

tel: 01736 364106 **Quay St TR18 4BD**
email: dolphin@tiscali.co.uk web: www.dolphintavern.com
dir: *From rail station follow road along harbour. Tavern on corner opposite Scilonian Ferry Terminal*

Interesting history and fish always on the menu

Sir Walter Raleigh is said to have smoked the first pipe of tobacco in England at this lovely 16th-century pub, the central part of which was once used as a courtroom by Judge Jeffreys. These days, the Dolphin serves great home-made food accompanied by a full range of St Austell beers, plus accommodation. Fresh, locally caught fish features on the daily specials board, and the menu offers a tempting selection of meat, vegetarian and children's dishes. A typical menu might feature steak and ale pie or Newlyn crab salad.

Open all day all wk Closed 25 Dec **Food** Contact pub for details ⊕ ST AUSTELL BREWERY ◀ HSD, Tinners Ale, Tribute ♂ Healey's Cornish Rattler. ♟ 10 **Facilities** Non-diners area ♦♦ Children's menu Children's portions Play area Family room Garden WiFi ➡ **Rooms** 2

The Turks Head Inn

tel: 01736 363093 **Chapel St TR18 4AF**
email: turks@fsmail.net
dir: *Phone for detailed directions*

Historic tucked-away town pub

This popular terraced side-street local is the oldest pub in Penzance, dating from around 1233, and was the first in the country to be given the Turks Head name. Sadly, a Spanish raiding party destroyed much of the original building in the 16th century, but an old smugglers' tunnel leading directly to the harbour still exists. Wash down hearty pub food – steaks, burgers, fish pie – or perhaps seafood broth, green Thai monkfish curry or braised lamb shank, with a cracking pint of Sharp's Doom Bar, best enjoyed in the sunny flower-filled garden. Don't miss the annual beer festival.

Open all day all wk **Food** Lunch all wk 12-2.30 Dinner all wk 6-10 ⊕ PUNCH TAVERNS ◀ Sharp's Doom Bar, Turk's Head Ale ♂ Westons Old Rosie. ⚑ 12 **Facilities** Non-diners area ✿ (Bar Restaurant Garden) ⚬∤ Children's menu Children's portions Family room Garden ⚬ Beer festival WiFi ⚬ (notice required)

PERRANUTHNOE   Map 2 SW52

The Victoria Inn ★★★ INN ⊛⊛   PICK OF THE PUBS

tel: 01736 710309 **TR20 9NP**
email: enquiries@victoriainn-penzance.co.uk **web:** www.victoriainn-penzance.co.uk
dir: Exit A394 (Penzance to Helston road), signed Perranuthnoe

Coastal pub with award-winning food

With a history spanning nine centuries, this striking, pink-washed village inn is probably Cornwall's oldest public house. Decorated with seafaring memorabilia, its typically Cornish, stone-walled bar attracts families strolling up from Perran Sands and walkers from the South West Coastal Path. Cornish real ales, lager and cider have a complete monopoly in the wood-fire-warmed, softly lit bar; outside is a Mediterranean-style patio garden. Chef-proprietor Stewart Eddy (who runs the pub with his wife, Anna) cooks AA Rosette-standard local fish, seafood, meats and other quality dishes featuring on a menu listing honey-roasted duck breast and confit leg; slow-cooked pork belly and roasted pork fillet with black pudding; Provençal fish stew; and roasted tomatoes, aubergines and olives with crispy polenta. Lunch possibilities are chargrilled rib-eye steak, St Buryan pork sausages with bubble-and-squeak; and ham, free-range eggs and chips. Overnight guests can stay in smart en suite bedrooms.

Open 12-3 5.30-11 (Jun-Sep all day) Closed 25-26 Dec, 1 Jan, 1wk Jan, Sun eve & Mon (off season) **Food** Lunch Mon-Sat 12-2, Sun 12-2.30 Dinner all wk 6.30-9 ⊕ FREE HOUSE ◀ Sharp's Doom Bar, St Austell Tribute, Skinner's Betty Stogs, Cornish Chough Serpentine ♂ Healey's Cornish Orchards. **Facilities** Non-diners area ⚬∤ Children's menu Children's portions Garden ⚬ Parking WiFi **Rooms** 2

PHILLEIGH   Map 2 SW83

Roseland Inn

tel: 01872 580254 **TR2 5NB**
email: contact@roselandinn.co.uk
dir: From Truro take A39 towards Falmouth. Left onto B3289 towards St Mawes. Left at sharp right bend for Philleigh

Traditional Cornish pub with welcoming, cosy interior

Owner Phil Heslip and chef Brian Green take pride in the quality of the home-prepared modern British cooking at this highly appealing, rural 16th-century inn. The character of the interior owes much to the low-beamed ceilings, brassware, paintings and prints. Phil brews his ornithologically themed Cornish Shag, Chough to Bits and High-as-a-Kite beers on site. So, in winter cosy up to the fire for a drink or a meal of perhaps slow roasted shoulder of Cornish lamb, or oven-baked hake with pan-fried new potatoes; in warmer weather head outside to the picnic tables. Just to the west is the famous King Harry Ferry over the River Fal.

Open all wk 11-3 6-11.30 **Food** Lunch all wk 12-2.30 Dinner all wk 6-9 ⊕ PUNCH TAVERNS ◀ Skinner's Betty Stogs, Roseland Cornish Shag, High-as-a-Kite & Chough to Bits, Sharp's Doom Bar ♂ Westons Stowford Press. **Facilities** Non-diners area ✿ (Bar Garden) ⚬∤ Children's menu Children's portions Garden ⚬ Beer festival Parking WiFi ⚬ (notice required)

POLKERRIS   Map 2 SX05

The Rashleigh Inn

tel: 01726 813991 **PL24 2TL**
email: jonspode@aol.com
dir: From A3082 between Fowey & Par follow Polkerris signs

Right on the beach

Once a coastguard station, this 300-year-old pub at the end of a no-through road to Polkerris beach faces west, so watching the sun set over St Austell Bay is a delight. In the bar there's a good selection of real ales from Cornwall and elsewhere, real cider, local organic soft drinks and a water bowl and Bonio biscuits for visiting dogs. Good, locally sourced food is typically slow-roasted Cornish belly pork; pan-fried fillet of wild sea bass; roasted darnes of gurnard; mushroom ravioli; and tapas, served on a slate platter.

Open all day all wk **Food** Lunch all wk 12-3, snacks 3-5 Dinner all wk 6-9 ⊕ FREE HOUSE ◀ Timothy Taylor Landlord, Skinner's Betty Stogs, St Austell HSD, Otter Bitter, Black Sheep Best Bitter, Young's Special, Guest ales ♂ Westons Stowford Press, Addlestones. ⚑ 11 **Facilities** Non-diners area ✿ (Bar Garden) ⚬∤ Children's menu Children's portions Garden ⚬ Parking WiFi

PORT GAVERNE   Map 2 SX08

Port Gaverne Hotel   PICK OF THE PUBS

tel: 01208 880244 **PL29 3SQ**
email: graham@port-gaverne-hotel.co.uk
dir: Signed from B3314, S of Delabole via B3267, E of Port Isaac

Local fish and seafood drives the menu here

The secluded cove just down from this delightful 17th-century inn is where women once loaded sea-bound ketches with slate from the great quarry at Delabole. After the railway arrived in 1893, sea trade declined and tranquillity returned to the port. Nowadays, walkers from the Heritage Coastal Path pause here for a pint of St Austell Tribute or Cornish Orchard cider in the small beer garden. The bar has slate floors (of course), low wooden beams and the customary log fire. Locally supplied produce includes plenty of fresh fish, destined to appear, for example, as pan-fried monkfish medallions with vegetables, orange and ginger coulis; smoked haddock pancake au gratin or baked wing of skate with brown butter, crayfish tails and capers. Other possibilities include sautéed escalopes of pork with Prosciutto ham, Madeira and white wine; or vegetable Stroganoff. Home-made puddings are supplemented with Cornish ice creams.

Open all day all wk **Food** Lunch all wk 12-2.30 Dinner all wk 6-9 ⊕ FREE HOUSE ◀ Sharp's Doom Bar & Cornish Coaster, St Austell Tribute ♂ Cornish Orchards. ⚑ 9 **Facilities** Non-diners area ✿ (Bar Garden) ⚬∤ Children's menu Children's portions Garden ⚬ Parking WiFi ⚬

PORTHLEVEN   Map 2 SW62

The Ship Inn

tel: 01326 564204 **TR13 9JS**
email: theshipinnporthleven@gmail.com
dir: From Helston follow signs to Porthleven (B3304), 2.5m. On entering village continue to harbour. Follow road to other side of harbour. 1st left to inn

Unspoilt pub in an unspoilt fishing port

Dating from the 17th century, this smugglers' inn is actually built into the cliffs, and is approached by a flight of stone steps. During the winter, two log fires warm the interior, while the flames of a third flicker in the separate Smithy children's room. Expect a good selection of locally caught fish and seafood, such as crab and prawn mornay; pan-fried mackerel with warm salad niçoise; or the smoked fish platter, all smoked in Cornwall. Meat eaters might choose beef and ale pie, or sausage cassoulet. August cider festival.

continued

PORTHLEVEN *continued*

Open all day all wk 11.30-11.30 (Sun 12-10.30) **Food** Lunch all wk 12-2 Dinner all wk 6.30-9 ⊕ FREE HOUSE ◀ Sharp's Doom Bar, Guest ales ♂ Cornish Orchards. ♀ 8 **Facilities** Non-diners area ❤ (Bar Restaurant Garden) ◑ Children's menu Family room Garden ⋒ Cider festival WiFi

---

| **PORT ISAAC** | Map 2 SW98 |

The Slipway

tel: 01208 880264 **Harbour Front PL29 3RH**
email: slipway@portisaachotel.com
dir: *From A39 take B3314 signed Port Isaac. Through Delabole & Pendoggett, right onto B3267. 2m to Port Isaac, pass Co-op on right, 100mtrs into Back Hill (one way) to harbour (NB no parking by hotel; car park at top of village)*

Harbourside pub noted for fish and seafood

With a reputation for seriously good fresh fish and seafood, this 16th-century, one-time ship's chandlery could hardly be closer to Port Isaac's tiny harbour. Cornish Orchards cider, and real ales from Tintagel and Sharp's breweries are on handpump in the bar, while in the heavy-beamed, galleried restaurant locally sourced dishes include bouillabaisse; whole roasted plaice; Cornish sirloin and venison steaks; and wild mushroom and rocket tagliatelle. On summer evenings the covered terrace overlooking the harbour is the perfect place to dine and enjoy music from the local bands.

Open all day all wk Closed 25 Dec **Food** Lunch all wk 12-2.30 Dinner all wk 6.30-8.30 (9 summer) Restaurant menu available all wk ⊕ FREE HOUSE ◀ Tintagel Harbour Special, Sharp's Doom Bar ♂ Cornish Orchards. **Facilities** Non-diners area ❤ (Bar Outside area) ◑ Children's menu Children's portions Outside area ⋒ WiFi

---

| **PORTREATH** | Map 2 SW64 |

Basset Arms

tel: 01209 842077 **Tregea Ter TR16 4NG**
email: bassettarms@btconnect.com
dir: *From Redruth take B3300 to Portreath. Pub on left near seafront*

Local seafood a specialty

Built as a pub to serve harbour workers, at one time this early 19th-century Cornish stone cottage served as a mortuary for ill-fated seafarers, so there are plenty of ghost stories. Tin-mining and shipwreck photographs adorn the low-beamed interior of the bar where you can wash down a meal with a pint of Skinner's real ale. The menu makes the most of local seafood, such as seafood stew; and home-made fish pie, but also provides a wide selection of alternatives, including steak and ale pie; gammon steak with pineapple, egg, chips and peas; and home-made mushroom Stroganoff.

Open all day all wk 11-11 (Fri-Sat 11am-mdnt Sun 11-10.30) **Food** Lunch all wk 12-2, Summer 12-3 Dinner all wk 6-9, Summer 5-9 ⊕ FREE HOUSE ◀ Sharp's Doom Bar, Skinner's, Dartmoor Legend, St Austell Tribute ♂ Thatchers Gold. **Facilities** Non-diners area ❤ (Bar Outside area) ◑ Children's menu Children's portions Play area Outside area ⋒ Parking 🚐 (notice required)

| **RUAN LANIHORNE** | Map 2 SW84 |

The Kings Head

tel: 01872 501263 **TR2 5NX**
email: contact@kings-head-roseland.co.uk
dir: *3m from Tregony Bridge on A3078*

Country pub with delightful summer garden

This traditional country pub set deep in the Roseland countryside has a warm and welcoming atmosphere. Roaring winter fires, beamed ceilings and mulled wine contrast with summer days relaxing on the terrace with a jug of Pimm's, a pint of Betty Stogs or Stowford Press cider. Whatever the time of year, the chef responds with seasonal dishes using the best local produce, including duo of local sausages with red onion and marmalade mash to chicken breast stuffed with prunes and leeks and wrapped in bacon. Look out for the signature dish, too – Ruan duck three ways: confit leg, pan-fried breast and drakes pudding.

Open 12-2.30 6-11 Closed Sun eve, Mon (Oct-Etr) **Food** Contact pub for details ⊕ FREE HOUSE ◀ Skinner's Kings Ruan & Betty Stogs, Keltek Even Keel ♂ Westons Stowford Press. ♀ 9 **Facilities** Non-diners area ◑ Garden ⋒ Parking

---

| **ST AGNES** | Map 3 SW75 |

Driftwood Spars ★★★★ GA | PICK OF THE PUBS

tel: 01872 552428 **Trevaunance Cove TR5 0RT**
email: info@driftwoodspars.co.uk **web:** www.driftwoodspars.co.uk
dir: *A30 onto B3285, through St Agnes, down steep hill, left at Peterville Inn, follow Trevaunance Cove sign*

Coastal path haven with home-brewed beers

With tin-mining heritage all round and a ruined harbour in Trevaunance Cove just down the lane, the inn's location is unmistakeably Cornish. The striking, whitewashed building variously served these industries for centuries; today it caters for enthusiastic locals and tourists at the heart of the rugged north Cornwall coast. It's a warren inside, with rooms on several levels and a terrace with restful views to the Atlantic swells. Ships' wheels and nautical memorabilia recall its time as a chandlers; magpie furnishings, open fires and dressed stone walls add tremendous character. The roof timbers are spars from a local wreck. Beers from the on-site microbrewery lead at the three bars, complemented by locally made cider and English wines from an attractive list of bins. Platters and ciabattas are fulfilling bar snacks; seafood dishes feature strongly on the main menu, along with traditional pub meals such as lamb shank. Some of the bedrooms have sea views, as does the inn's Fitty Pysk bistro. Beer festivals occur in March and May.

Open all day all wk 11-11 (Fri-Sat 11am-1am 25 Dec 11am-2pm) **Food** Lunch all wk 12-2.30 Dinner all wk 6-9.30 (winter 6.30-8.30) Av main course £10 Restaurant menu available Tue-Sat Etr-Sep ⊕ FREE HOUSE ◀ Driftwood Spars, Sharp's Doom Bar, Guest ales ♂ Healey's Cornish Rattler, Thatchers, Touchwood. ♀ 9 **Facilities** Non-diners area ❤ (Bar Garden Outside area) ◑ Children's menu Children's portions Garden Outside area ⋒ Beer festival Parking WiFi 🚐 (notice required) **Rooms** 15

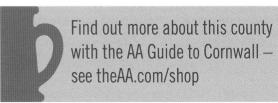

ST BREWARD   Map 2 SX07

The Old Inn & Restaurant

tel: 01208 850711 **Churchtown, Bodmin Moor PL30 4PP**
email: theoldinn@macace.net
dir: *A30 to Bodmin. 16m, right just after Temple, follow signs to St Breward. B3266 (Bodmin to Camelford road) turn to St Breward, follow brown signs*

Ancient inn high on the moor

On the edge of Bodmin Moor, this is not just Cornwall's highest inn (720ft above sea level), it's one of the oldest too, having been built in the 11th century for monks to live in. It's believed to have been a pub since the 15th century, although records only go back to 1806. You can see ancient granite fireplaces and sloping ceilings in the bars, where Sharp's Doom Bar and Orchard cider are in the line-up. The pub is now run by Melvyn and Christine Hooper, who previously owned a pub in Wiltshire, and they are introducing more locally sourced game onto their menus. You'll also find mixed grills, daily changing specials, pie of the day, locally caught fish, and an all-day Sunday carvery are served in the bars, spacious restaurant or large garden. Cream teas are also a speciality.

Open all day 12-11 Closed weekday afternoons out of season **Food** Lunch Mon-Fri 12-2, Sat-Sun 12-9 Dinner Mon-Fri 6-9, Sat-Sun 12-9 ⊕ FREE HOUSE ◀ Sharp's Doom Bar, Tintagel Castle Gold, Guest ales ♂ Cornish Orchards, Westons Stowford Press. ☲ 15 **Facilities** Non-diners area ♣ (Bar Garden) ♦ Children's menu Children's portions Family room Garden Parking WiFi ▭

ST EWE   Map 2 SW94

The Crown Inn

tel: 01726 843322 **PL26 6EY**
email: thecrownstewe@hotmail.co.uk
dir: *From St Austell take B3273. At Tregiskey x-rds turn right. St Ewe signed on right*

Local ales and home-cooking in this pretty village inn

Only a mile away from the famous 'Lost Gardens of Heligan', this attractive 16th-century village inn is the ideal place to refuel, whether it's by the fire in the traditional bar or in the peaceful flower-festooned garden in summer. Quaff a pint of Proper Job ale and tuck into the home-cooked food, perhaps traditional prawn cocktail followed by slow-roasted belly pork with apple sauce and cider gravy; or home-made curry of the day. Lunchtime sandwiches, jacket potatoes and smaller portions of main dishes are also available.

Open all wk 12-3 5.30-close (summer all day) **Food** Lunch all wk 12-2 Dinner Mon-Sat 6-9 Av main course £9 ⊕ ST AUSTELL BREWERY ◀ Tribute, Dartmoor & Proper Job ♂ Healey's Cornish Rattler. **Facilities** Non-diners area ♣ (Bar Garden) ♦ Children's menu Children's portions Play area Family room Garden ⅋ Parking WiFi ▭

ST IVES   Map 2 SW54

The Queens ★★ HL ◉

tel: 01736 796468 **2 High St TR26 1RR**
email: info@queenshotelstives.com **web:** www.queenshotelstives.com
dir: *Phone for detailed directions (5 mins walk from rail station)*

Winning combination of fine food and stylish accommodation

There's an easy-going mix of chic, contemporary design with a nod to times past in this thriving hostelry at the heart of the old town. It's worth the stroll from the harbour or the resort's beaches to discover this solid granite-built, late-Georgian building, where local art works vie for attention with local cider, Cornish beers and a great menu inspired by the wealth of the county's larder. Partridge, scotched quail's egg, tomato and bacon jam could be followed by Cornish duck breast, confit

thigh, hash brown and parsnips; a chalkboard holds much additional promise. Try the tempting butterscotch and sea salt honeycomb. Some of the stylish bedrooms have views to Carbis Bay.

Open all day all wk **Food** Lunch Mon-Sat 12-2.30, Sun 12-4 Dinner Mon-Sat 6.30-9.30 Av main course £10 ⊕ ST AUSTELL BREWERY ◀ Tribute, HSD ♂ Healey's Cornish Rattler. ☲ 16 **Facilities** Non-diners area ♣ (Bar Restaurant) ♦ Children's menu Children's portions WiFi ▭ (notice required) **Rooms** 10

The Sloop Inn ★★★ INN

tel: 01736 796584 **The Wharf TR26 1LP**
email: sloopinn@btinternet.com **web:** www.sloop-inn.co.uk
dir: *On St Ives harbour by middle slipway*

Famous St Ives inn by picturesque harbour

A trip to St Ives wouldn't be complete without visiting this 700-year-old pub perched right on the harbourside. Slate floors, beamed ceilings and nautical artefacts dress some of the several bars and dining areas, whilst the cobbled forecourt is an unbeatable spot for people- and harbour-watching, preferably with a pint of local Doom Bar. The menu majors on local seafood, from line-caught St Ives Bay mackerel and fries to home-made Newlyn cod, smoked haddock and smoked bacon fishcakes. Most of the comfortably appointed bedrooms overlook the pretty bay.

Open all day all wk **Food** Lunch all wk 12-3 Dinner all wk 5-10 ⊕ ENTERPRISE INNS ◀ Sharp's Doom Bar ♂ Thatchers Gold. **Facilities** Non-diners area ♦ Outside area ⅋ WiFi ▭ (notice required) **Rooms** 18

The Watermill

tel: 01736 757912 **Lelant Downs, Hayle TR27 6LQ**
email: watermill@btconnect.com
dir: *Exit A30 at junct for St Ives/A3074, turn left at 2nd mini rdbt*

Converted mill with food to suit everyone

Set in extensive gardens on the old St Ives coach road, with glorious valley views towards Trencrom Hill, The Watermill is a cosy, family-friendly pub and restaurant created in the 18th-century Lelant Mill. The old mill machinery is still in place and the iron waterwheel continues to turn, gravity fed by the mill stream. Downstairs is the old beamed bar and wood-burning stove, while upstairs in the open-beamed mill loft is the atmospheric restaurant where steaks and fish (sea bass, sardines and mackerel perhaps) are specialities. There are beer festivals in June and November with live music all weekend.

Open all day all wk 12-11 **Food** Lunch all wk 12-2.30 Dinner all wk 6-9 ⊕ FREE HOUSE ◀ Sharp's Doom Bar, Skinner's Betty Stogs, Guest ales ♂ Healey's Cornish Rattler. **Facilities** Non-diners area ♣ (Bar Garden) ♦ Children's menu Play area Garden ⅋ Beer festival Parking ▭

ST KEW
Map 2 SX07

St Kew Inn

tel: 01208 841259 **Churchtown PL30 3HB**
email: stkewinn@btconnect.com
dir: *From Wadebridge N on A39. Left to St Kew*

A chocolate-box village pub

In summer, the pretty façade of this 15th-century, stone-built pub is enhanced with flower tubs and creepers. Inside, traditional features include a huge open fire. Cornish St Austell beers and Rattler cider are the prime refreshments, while menus proffer carefully sourced and prepared British dishes (often featuring fish and seafood) with cosmopolitan touches. Choose between four eating areas – five if you include the garden – when ordering your lunchtime snack of potted smoked mackerel with toasted carrot bread. Alternatively, in the evening try the deep-fried salt and pepper squid, follow with pan-fried pollock with sag aloo and curried mussel cream, and finish with lemon tart with mandarin sorbet. Set menus are available.

Open all wk 11-3 5.30-11 (summer all day) **Food** Lunch all wk 12-2, summer all day Dinner all wk 6-9, summer all day ⊕ ST AUSTELL BREWERY ◼ Tribute, HSD, Proper Job Ꝺ Healey's Cornish Rattler. **Facilities** Non-diners area ❦ (Bar Garden) ♦ Children's menu Children's portions Family room Garden ⊓ Parking WiFi

ST MAWES
Map 2 SW83

The Victory Inn
PICK OF THE PUBS

tel: 01326 270324 **Victory Hill TR2 5DQ**
email: contact@victory-inn.co.uk
dir: *A3078 to St Mawes. Pub adjacent to harbour*

Seafood takes top billing on the menus

Named after Nelson's flagship, this friendly fishermen's local near the harbour adopts a modern approach to its daily lunch and dinner menus. You may eat downstairs in the traditional bar, or in the modern and stylish first-floor Seaview Restaurant (white walls, white linen and wicker chairs), with a terrace that looks across the town's rooftops to the harbour and the River Fal. High on the list of ingredients is fresh seafood – all from Cornish waters – the choice changing daily to include crab risotto, fisherman's pie, and beer-battered cod and hand-cut chips, with chicken breast cordon bleu, lamb shank Provençale, and curry or casserole of the day among the other favourites. Wines are all carefully chosen and excellent in quality, as are the real ales from Cornwall's own Roseland, Sharp's and Skinner's breweries. There is outside seating with views over the harbour. Booking for meals is definitely advisable in the summer.

Open all day all wk 11am-mdnt **Food** Lunch all wk 12-2.30 Dinner all wk 6-9.30 Av main course £10.95 ⊕ PUNCH TAVERNS ◼ Skinner's Betty Stogs, Sharp's Doom Bar. **Facilities** Non-diners area ❦ (Bar Garden) ♦ Children's menu Children's portions Garden ⊓ WiFi ⊞

ST MAWGAN
Map 2 SW86

The Falcon Inn ★★★★ INN
PICK OF THE PUBS

See Pick of the Pubs on opposite page

ST MERRYN
Map 2 SW87

The Cornish Arms
PICK OF THE PUBS

tel: 01841 532700 **Churchtown PL28 8ND**
email: reservations@rickstein.com
dir: *From Padstow follow signs for St Merryn then Churchtown*

Simple British pub food the Rick Stein way

In the village of St Merryn, just outside Padstow, this ancient village pub is part of the Stein portfolio. Situated across the road from the parish church and overlooking a peaceful valley, the pub has remained very much the village boozer certainly to happiness of the locals. Replete with slate floors, beams and roaring log fires, the pub oozes character and they have kept the food offering equally traditional. The chalkboard lists simple pub classics prepared from fresh produce: scampi in a basket, mussels and chips, local rump steaks, followed perhaps by apple pie or treacle tart. Wash it down with a glass of Chalky's Bark, named after Rick's much-missed, rough-haired Jack Russell. Check with the pub for details of themed nights and the beer and mussels festival in March.

Open all day all wk 11.30-11 **Food** Lunch all wk 12-2.30 Dinner all wk 6-8.30 ⊕ ST AUSTELL BREWERY ◼ Tribute, Proper Job, Trelawny, Chalky's Bite, Chalky's Bark Ꝺ Healey's Cornish Rattler. ☗ 16 **Facilities** Non-diners area ❦ (Bar Restaurant Garden) ♦ Children's menu Children's portions Garden ⊓ Beer festival Parking WiFi ⊞

ST TUDY
Map 2 SX07

NEW St Tudy Inn

tel: 01208 850656 **PL30 3NN**
email: info@tudyinn.co.uk
dir: *Follow St Tudy signs from A39 between Camelford & Wadebridge. Pub in village centre*

Fine old inn with a tearoom and café

For generations Hope Hall, as this early 16th-century building was once called, was the Balguy family seat. In 1730 it became an inn, The Cross Daggers, then in 1876 it was renamed The Hall Hotel. If you fancy a snack, there are baguettes - hot roast beef and Stilton; and smothered chicken, cheese and Mediterranean vegetables. Main menus promise grills; steak and ale pie; sausages and mash; Scottish salmon linguine; and wild mushroom and oatcake millefeuille. In the 18th century a cattle market was held here; today, on bank holidays, the Hope Valley Beer and Cider Festival draws the crowds.

Open 12-3 6-12 Closed Sun eve & Mon **Food** Lunch Tue-Sun 12-2 Dinner Tue-Sat 6.30-9 Av main course £9.50 ⊕ FREE HOUSE ◼ Sharp's Doom Bar Ꝺ Symonds. ☗ **Facilities** Non-diners area ❦ (Bar Outside area) ♦ Children's portions Outside area ⊓ Parking WiFi

PICK OF THE PUBS

The Falcon Inn ★★★★ INN

ST MAWGAN Map 2 SW86

tel: 01637 860225
TR8 4EP
email: thefalconinnstmawgan@gmail.com
web: www.thefalconinnstmawgan.co.uk
dir: *From A30 (8m W of Bodmin) follow signs to Newquay Airport. Turn right 200mtrs before airport terminal into St Mawgan, pub at bottom of hill*

Traditional Cornish village inn

This wisteria-clad, stone-built inn situated in the Vale of Lanherne is just four miles from Newquay. It can trace its ancestry back as far as 1758, but is thought to be even older. By 1813 the pub had been renamed more than once, and in about 1880 it changed again to The Falcon Inn, an allusion to the nearby estate's coat of arms. Throughout much of the 20th century the inn was run by members of the Fry family; the present innkeepers are David Carbis and Sarah Lawrence. The Falcon's interior is cosy and relaxed, with flagstone floors and log fires in winter; there's a large attractive garden, magnificent magnolia tree and cobbled courtyard for alfresco summer dining. An ever-changing selection of predominantly West Country real ales is augmented by rotating real ciders, and a dozen wines are served by the glass. Lunchtime brings snacks like Cornish pasty and breaded scampi, plus an appetising range of sandwiches. There's also a good choice of hot dishes,

all home made, such as soup of the day, pâté, pie, fish and curry every day. The evening menu is served in the more formal restaurant; main courses include rose veal burger with red onion marmalade, Cornish blue cheese and 'real' chips; Nalli gosht - braised lamb shank cooked with chillies, yogurt and honey, served with coriander rice and naan bread; steak and kidney suet crust pudding with real ale gravy, chips and peas; pan-roasted locally smoked haddock, bubble and squeak and poached duck egg. Three comfortable, individually furnished en suite bedrooms are also available, and events like charity quiz nights run throughout the year. Contact the pub for details of the beer and cider festival.

Open all wk 11-3 6-11 (Jul-Aug all day) Closed 25 Dec (open 12-2) **Food** Lunch all wk 12-2 Dinner all wk 6-9 Av main course £10 ⊕ FREE HOUSE ◀ rotating real ales ♨ rotating real ciders. ♟ 12 **Facilities** Non-diners area ☻ (Bar Garden) ♦♦ Children's menu Children's portions Garden ⌁ Beer festival Cider festival Parking WiFi ➡ **Rooms** 3

SALTASH
Map 3 SX45

The Crooked Inn ★★★★ INN

tel: 01752 848177 **Stoketon Cottage, Trematon PL12 4RZ**
email: info@crooked-inn.co.uk **web:** www.crooked-inn.co.uk
dir: Phone for detailed directions

Family-run inn with good food and great children's facilities

Overlooking the lush Lyher Valley and run by the same family for more than 25 years, this delightful inn once housed staff from Stoketon Manor, whose ruins lie on the other side of the courtyard. It is set in 10 acres of lawns and woodland, yet only 15 minutes from Plymouth. There is an extensive menu including evening specials with plenty of fresh fish and vegetarian dishes. The children's playground has friendly animals, swings, slides, a trampoline and a treehouse. The spacious bedrooms are individually designed.

Open all day all wk 11-11 (Sun 12-10.30) Closed 25 Dec **Food** Lunch all wk 11-2.30 Dinner all wk 6-9.30 ⊕ FREE HOUSE ◀ St Austell HSD, Dartmoor Jail Ale, Guest ales ♂ Thatchers Gold, Addlestones. **Facilities** Non-diners area ♣ (Bar Restaurant Garden) ♦ Children's menu Play area Garden ⊓ Parking WiFi ➡ **Rooms** 18

ISLES OF SCILLY

See Tresco

TORPOINT
Map 3 SX45

Edgcumbe Arms
PICK OF THE PUBS

tel: 01752 822294 **Cremyll PL10 1HX**
dir: Phone for detailed directions

A 15th-century pub with glorious views over the Tamar estuary

Close to the foot ferry from Plymouth, this inn next to Mount Edgcumbe Country Park offers fabulous views from its bow window seats and waterside terrace, which take in Drakes Island, the Royal William Yard and the marina. Real ales from St Austell like Tribute, plus Healey's Cornish Rattler cider, and quality home-cooked food are served in a series of rooms, which are full of character with American oak panelling and flagstone floors. The same extensive menu is offered throughout and dishes are a mixture of international and traditional British pub favourites: garlicky Cornish sardines on toasted ciabatta or shredded duck pancakes with hoi-sin sauce to start, followed by toad-in-the-hole; fish pie; or chilli braised beef. Vegetarian options might include Mediterranean vegetable and nut strudel. Sandwiches, loaded potato skins and platters are also available. The inn has a courtyard garden.

Open all day 11-11 Closed Jan-Feb Mon & Tue eve **Food** Lunch 12-5 Dinner 12-9 ⊕ ST AUSTELL BREWERY ◀ Tribute, Proper Job, Trelawny ♂ Healey's Cornish Rattler. ♟ 10 **Facilities** Non-diners area ♣ (Bar Garden) ♦ Children's menu Children's portions Garden ⊓ Parking WiFi ➡ (notice required)

TREBARWITH
Map 2 SX08

The Mill House Inn
PICK OF THE PUBS

tel: 01840 770200 **PL34 0HD**
email: management@themillhouseinn.co.uk **web:** www.themillhouseinn.co.uk
dir: From Tintagel take B3263 S, right after Trewarmett to Trebarwith Strand. Pub 0.5m on right

Family-friendly inn with good food and live entertainment

Close to Tintagel Castle, The Mill House is half a mile from the surfing beach at Trebarwith Strand, one of the finest in Cornwall. Set in seven acres of woodland on the north Cornish coast, the log fires in this atmospheric stone building – a charming former corn mill dating from 1760 - warm the residents' lounge and slate-floored bar, where wooden tables and chapel chairs help create a relaxed, family-friendly feel. Locally brewed real ales are supplied by Sharp's and Tintagel breweries, and the ciders are Cornish Orchards and Healey's Cornish Rattler. Lunches, evening drinks and barbecues are particularly enjoyable out on the attractive terraces, while a more intimate dinner in the Millstream Restaurant might involve pan-fried tiger prawns, crayfish and poppy seed toast, chilli dressed micro salad, followed by roast chicken in lemon thyme spice, green leaf salad and chips. Regular live events feature local musicians and comedians.

Open all day all wk 11-11 (Fri-Sat 11am-mdnt Sun 12-10.30) **Food** Lunch Mon-Sat 12-2.30, Sun 12-3 Dinner all wk 6.30-8.30 ⊕ FREE HOUSE ◀ Sharp's Doom Bar, Tintagel Cornwall's Pride ♂ Cornish Orchards, Healey's Cornish Rattler. **Facilities** Non-diners area ♣ (Bar Garden) ♦ Children's menu Children's portions Play area Family room Garden ⊓ Parking WiFi ➡ (notice required)

The Port William

tel: 01840 770230 **Trebarwith Strand PL34 0HB**
email: portwilliam@staustellbrewery.co.uk
dir: From A39 onto B3314 signed Tintagel. Right onto B3263, follow Trebarwith Strand signs, then brown Port William signs

Stunning location by the sea

Occupying one of the best locations in Cornwall, this former harbourmaster's house lies directly on the coastal path, 50 yards from the sea, which means the views of the Trebarwith Strand are amazing. There is an entrance to a smugglers' tunnel at the rear of the ladies' toilet! Obviously there's quite an emphasis on fresh fish, but there's no shortage of other options. A typical menu starts with pulled pork with smoky barbecue sauce and toasted crouton, or sautéed Cornish mushrooms with peppercorn sauce and crumbled blue cheese; then moves on to mains such as gourmet burger with chunky chips; ocean pie; local mussels or vegetable red Thai curry. If you've room, check the specials board for the desserts of the day.

Open all day all wk 10am-11pm (Sun 10am-10.30pm) **Food** Lunch all wk 12-3, 3-6 Dinner all wk 6-9 ⊕ ST AUSTELL BREWERY ◀ Tribute & Trelawny, Guest ales ♂ Healey's Cornish Rattler. ♟ 8 **Facilities** Non-diners area ♣ (Bar Restaurant Garden) ♦ Children's menu Children's portions Family room Garden ⊓ Parking WiFi

TREBURLEY
Map 3 SX37

The Springer Spaniel
PICK OF THE PUBS

tel: 01579 370424 **PL15 9NS**
email: enquiries@thespringerspaniel.org.uk
dir: *On A388 halfway between Launceston & Callington*

Developing gastro-pub menu in Cornish village setting

Set above the valley of the River Inny in lush Cornish countryside just a handful of miles south of Launceston, this long-established pub has now been taken on by Anton Piotrowski, a winner of BBC MasterChef 'The Professionals'. A subtle refurbishment has brightened up the pub considerably, with a new range of drinks and a choice menu breathing fresh life into this village local. There's a tree-shaded beer garden to the rear, a pleasant place to relax with a pint of Jail Ale from the increasingly popular Dartmoor Brewery - the pub is about half-way between Dartmoor and Bodmin Moor. It might be a struggle to make a choice from the menu of classics and specials. A robust start could be smoked bacon Guinness mussels with smoked bacon foam and crisp pancetta; whilst mains range from Penrhyn Pork sausages to oxtail and venison suet pudding with horseradish mash and green beans in Parma ham. To finish, Earl Grey tea pannacotta with lemon curd, honeycomb and pistachio nuts.

Open all day Closed 25-26 Dec, Mon **Food** Lunch all day Dinner all day Av main course £10-£15 Restaurant menu available Tue-Sun ⊕ FREE HOUSE ◄ St Austell Tribute & Proper Job, Dartmoor Jail Ale ♂ Thatchers, Cornish Orchards, Healey's Cornish Rattler. **Facilities** Non-diners area ❖ (Bar Garden) ❖❖ Children's portions Garden ⋒ Parking WiFi ⛟ (notice required)

TREGADILLETT
Map 3 SX28

Eliot Arms

tel: 01566 772051 **PL15 7EU**
email: humechris@hotmail.co.uk
dir: *From Launceston take A30 towards Bodmin. Then follow brown signs to Tregadillett*

Creeper covered inn with lots of nostalgia

The extraordinary decor in this charming creeper-clad coaching inn, dating back to 1625, includes Masonic regalia, horse brasses and grandfather clocks. It was believed to have been a Masonic lodge for Napoleonic prisoners, and even has its own friendly ghost. Customers can enjoy real fires in winter and lovely hanging baskets in summer. Food, based on locally sourced meat and fresh fish and shellfish caught off the Cornish coast, is served in the bar or bright and airy restaurant. Expect home-made soups, pie and curry of the day; steak and chips; chargrills; and home-made vegetarian dishes.

Open all day all wk 11.30-11 (Fri-Sat 11.30am-mdnt Sun 12-10.30) **Food** Lunch all wk 12-2 Dinner all wk 6-9 Av main course £5.95-£16.95 ⊕ FREE HOUSE ◄ St Austell Tribute, Wadworth 6X, Wells Bombardier. ☂ 9 **Facilities** Non-diners area ❖ (Bar Outside area) ❖❖ Children's menu Children's portions Family room Outside area Parking WiFi ⛟ (notice required)

TRESCO (ISLES OF SCILLY)
Map 2 SV81

The New Inn ★★★★ INN ⊛
PICK OF THE PUBS

tel: 01720 422849 **New Grimsby TR24 0QQ**
email: newinn@tresco.co.uk **web:** www.tresco.co.uk
dir: *By New Grimsby Quay*

Sub-tropical splendour and local bounty at the edge of Britain

Close to Tresco Abbey Garden's nodding palms and surrounded by white-sand beaches and azure bays and with fabulous birdwatching opportunities, this inn may be the ultimate get-away-from-it-all destination. The New Inn seeps maritime history, the bar is partly created from salvage from local wrecks giving a rustic, instantly welcoming ambience. An AA Rosette recognises the quality of food –

served from the same menu wherever you dine – in the quiet restaurant, the livelier Driftwood Bar, the Pavilion, or alfresco. Scillonian produce forms the backbone of the fare; the signature dish is their take on surf 'n turf featuring Bryher lobster and Tresco beefsteak. The chefs regularly introduce new dishes; Cornish pork and Tresco partridge sausage roll makes an enticing snack to accompany a Tresco Tipple beer. An evening meal of fish stew (locally caught seafish of course) can be helped along by wine from a newly established vineyard on neighbouring St Martin's. There are beer festivals in mid May and early September, and a cider festival in June. Some of the stylish rooms available have ocean views.

Open all day all wk all day (Apr-Oct) phone for winter opening **Food** Lunch all wk 12-2 Dinner all wk 6-9 Av main course £14 ⊕ FREE HOUSE/TRESCO ESTATE ◄ Skinner's Betty Stogs, Tresco Tipple, Ales of Scilly Scuppered & Firebrand, St Austell Proper Job, Tintagel Harbour Special ♂ Healey's Cornish Rattler & Pear Rattler. ☂ 13 **Facilities** Non-diners area ❖❖ Children's menu Children's portions Garden ⋒ Beer festival Cider festival WiFi **Rooms** 16

TRURO
Map 2 SW84

Old Ale House

tel: 01872 271122 **7 Quay St TR1 2HD**
email: jamie@oahtruro.com
dir: *In town centre*

County town bolthole with vibrant atmosphere

At a busy city-centre location close to the old port, warehouses and quays on the Truro River. This eye-catching partly wood-fronted, bare-boarded and heavily beamed pub is Skinners' Brewery tap, so a reliable pint from their range of Cornish ales is guaranteed. The slightly cloudy Skreach cider is also popular with the loyal band of regulars who enjoy the frequent live music nights here. The Old Ale House specialises in freshly made skillet meals; the ever-evolving choices include beef and Stilton; mushroom Stroganoff; and vegetable stir-fry with soy sauce. There's a beer festival here every April or May.

Open all day all wk 11-11 (Fri-Sat 11am-1am Sun 12-10.30) Closed 25-26 Dec, 1 Jan **Food** Lunch all wk 12-2.30 Av main course £6.25 ⊕ ENTERPRISE INNS ◄ Skinner's, Shepherd Neame Spitfire, Greene King Abbot Ale, Fuller's London Pride, Courage, Guest ales ♂ Skreach. ☂ 9 **Facilities** Non-diners area ❖❖ (Bar) ❖❖ Children's portions Beer festival WiFi ⛟ (notice required)

The Wig & Pen

tel: 01872 273028 **Frances St TR1 3DP**
email: wigandpentruro@hotmail.com
dir: *In city centre near Law Courts*

Friendly city centre pub where everything is made in-house

Tim and Georgie Robinson's pub has both an L-shaped ground-floor bar and Quills restaurant in the basement which opens in the evenings. Food is freshly made in-house, and that even includes the crisps and the pork scratchings that go with HSD and Tribute beers. Choose a casual meal in the bar which serves modern pub classics such as beer battered fish and chips and gourmet burgers, or venture downstairs to Quills for a more fine dining experience; here the menu changes weekly and there are jazz nights once a month.

Open all day all wk Closed 25-26 Dec, 1 Jan **Food** Lunch all wk 12-2.30 Dinner all wk 6-9.30 Av main course £10 Restaurant menu available ⊕ ST AUSTELL BREWERY ◄ Tribute, HSD, Trelawny ♂ Healey's Cornish Rattler & Pear Rattler. ☂ 16 **Facilities** Non-diners area ❖❖ (Bar Garden) ❖❖ Children's portions Garden ⋒ ⛟ (notice required)

VERYAN   Map 2 SW93

The New Inn

tel: 01872 501362 **TR2 5QA**
email: info@newinn-veryan.co.uk
dir: *From St Austell take A390 towards Truro, in 2m left to Tregony. Through Tregony, follow signs to Veryan*

Traditional home cooking and good ales

This unspoiled pub started life as a pair of cottages in the 16th-century. In the centre of a pretty village on the Roseland Peninsula, The New Inn has open fires, a beamed ceiling, a single bar serving St Austell ales and a warm, welcoming atmosphere. Sunday lunch is a speciality; other choices during the week might include home-made vegetable chilli; hand-carved Cornish ham; local beer-battered fish; or wholetail breaded scampi. Traditional puddings take in apple crumble, chocolate fudge cake and sticky toffee pudding – some served with Cornish clotted cream.

Open all day all wk 12-3 5.30-11 (Sun 7-11) Closed 25 Dec **Food** Lunch all wk 12-2 Dinner Mon-Sat 6.30-9, Sun 7-9 Av main course £10 Set menu available ⊕ ST AUSTELL BREWERY ◀ Tribute, Proper Job, Dartmoor Ò Healey's Cornish Rattler. ♀ **Facilities** Non-diners area ❄ (Bar Garden) ✦ Children's menu Children's portions Garden ⊟ WiFi ➟ (notice required)

WADEBRIDGE   Map 2 SW97

The Quarryman Inn

tel: 01208 816444 **Edmonton PL27 7JA**
email: thequarryman@live.co.uk
dir: *From A39 (W of Wadebridge) follow Edmonton sign (opposite Royal Cornwall Showground)*

Tucked away in the Cornish countryside

Close to the famous Camel Trail, this friendly 18th-century free house has evolved from a courtyard of cottages once home to slate workers from the nearby quarry. Several bow windows, one of which features a stained-glass quarryman panel, add character to this unusual inn. The pub's menus change everyday but their signature dishes are chargrilled steaks served on sizzling platters and fresh local seafood; puddings are on the blackboard. Meals and drinks can be enjoyed outside in the slate courtyard in summer, or by a roaring fire in colder months.

Open all day all wk 12-11 **Food** Lunch all wk 12-2.30 Dinner all wk 6-9 ⊕ FREE HOUSE ◀ Timothy Taylor Landlord, Sharp's, Skinner's, Otter, Guest ales Ò Westons Stowford Press. **Facilities** Non-diners area ✦ Children's menu Children's portions Garden ⊟ Parking WiFi ➟ (notice required)

WIDEMOUTH BAY   Map 2 SS20

Bay View Inn

tel: 01288 361273 **Marine Dr EX23 0AW**
email: thebayviewinn@aol.com
dir: *Adjacent to beach*

Ocean views and good food

Dating back around 100 years, this welcoming, family-run pub was a guest house for many years before becoming an inn in the 1960s. True to its name, the pub has fabulous views of the rolling Atlantic from its restaurant and the large raised decking area outside. The menu makes excellent use of local produce, as in the signature dish of fish pie; and sea bass fillets with Florentine potatoes and tiger prawn and saffron sauce. Other choices include home-made pies, casseroles and burgers.

Open all day all wk **Food** Lunch Mon-Fri 12-2.30, Sat-Sun 12-9 Dinner Mon-Fri 5.30-9, Sat-Sun 12-9 ⊕ FREE HOUSE ◀ Skinner's Betty Stogs & Spriggan Ale, Sharp's Doom Bar Ò Somersby Cider. ♀ 14 **Facilities** Non-diners area ❄ (Bar Garden) ✦ Children's menu Children's portions Play area Garden ⊟ Parking WiFi ➟ (notice required)

ZENNOR   Map 2 SW43

The Tinners Arms   `PICK OF THE PUBS`

tel: 01736 796927 **TR26 3BY**
email: tinners@tinnersarms.co.uk
dir: *Take B3306 from St Ives towards St Just. Zennor approx 5m*

Timeless village inn with local ales and good food

Its closeness to the South West Coastal Path almost guarantees that muddy-booted walkers will be found among the Tinners Arms' clientele, enjoying the timelessness of its stone floors, low ceilings, cushioned settles, winter open fires and the revivifying Cornish real ales or Burrow Hill cider from Somerset. Built of granite in 1271 for masons working on ancient St Senara's church next door (famous for its richly carved Mermaid Chair), many may welcome the fact that the only pub in the village has no TV, jukebox or fruit machine, nor can a mobile phone signal reach it. Based on ingredients from local suppliers, the dinner menu offers Newlyn crab and prawn cocktail; roast fillet of hake with chorizo and chickpea stew; or a traditional homity pie with chips and salad. Sandwiches and light meals are available at lunchtime. Outside is a peaceful garden and large terrace with sea views.

Open all day all wk **Food** Lunch all wk 12-3 Dinner all wk 6.30-9 (ex Sun & Mon eve winter) ⊕ FREE HOUSE ◀ Zennor Mermaid, St Austell Tinners Ale, Sharp's Own Ò Burrow Hill. ♀ 10 **Facilities** Non-diners area ❄ (Bar Restaurant Garden) ✦ Children's menu Children's portions Garden ⊟ Parking WiFi

CUMBRIA

AMBLESIDE
Map 18 NY30

Drunken Duck Inn
PICK OF THE PUBS

tel: 015394 36347 **Barngates LA22 ONG**
email: info@drunkenduckinn.co.uk
dir: From Kendal on A591 to Ambleside, then follow Hawkshead sign. In 2.5m inn sign on right, 1m up hill

Traditional Lakeland inn with fine views

High above Ambleside, at a lonely crossroads, the 17th-century Duck enjoys wonderful views of the fells towards Lake Windermere. The name dates from Victorian times, when a landlady's ducks overindulged in beer-soaked feed. Beer is still brewed here in the adjoining Barngates Brewery and served on a counter of local black slate in the oak-floored bar, where hops adorn the old beams, and Herdwick wool coverings soften the wooden settles. Add candlelight and a log fire, what more could you ask, except perhaps for locally sourced guinea fowl with sourdough sauce, pearl barley, girolles and wild garlic; brill with cockles, samphire, Jersey royals and sea-purslane; or ricotta gnocchi with chestnut mushrooms, peas, watercress and pine nuts. Then, for dessert, orange and poppy seed cake with orange sorbet and chocolate sauce. The tranquil garden with its own tarn, is home to a rich variety of wildlife.

Open all day all wk Closed 25 Dec **Food** Lunch all wk 12-4 Restaurant menu available ⊕ FREE HOUSE ◀ Barngates Cracker Ale, Chesters Strong & Ugly, Tag Lag, Cat Nap, Brathay Gold. ▼ 17 **Facilities** Non-diners area ◀◀ Children's portions Garden ᴘ Parking WiFi

Wateredge Inn

tel: 015394 32332 **Waterhead Bay LA22 OEP**
email: stay@wateredgeinn.co.uk
dir: M6 junct 36, A591 to Ambleside, 5m from Windermere station

Family-run inn on the shores of Lake Windermere

The Wateredge Inn was converted from two 17th-century fishermen's cottages, and now offers a stylish bar and restaurant. With large gardens and plenty of seating running down to the lakeshore, the inn has been run by the same family for nearly 30 years. The lunch menu offers sandwiches, salads, pub classics and slates – platters of smoked fish, charcuterie or cheese and antipasti. Meanwhile the dinner menu has choices ranging from local Cumberland sausage and mash to seared fillet of salmon with a tomato, chilli and tarragon salsa. Specials and a children's menu are also available.

Open all day all wk 10.30am-11pm Closed 23-26 Dec **Food** Lunch Mon-Fri 12-2.30, Sat-Sun 12-4 Dinner all wk 6-9 ⊕ FREE HOUSE ◀ Theakston, Barngates Tag Lag & Cat Nap, Watermill Collie Wobbles Ö Symonds. ▼ 15 **Facilities** Non-diners area ◀ (Bar Garden) ◀◀ Children's menu Children's portions Garden ᴘ Parking WiFi

APPLEBY-IN-WESTMORLAND
Map 18 NY62

Tufton Arms Hotel
PICK OF THE PUBS

tel: 017683 51593 **Market Square CA16 6XA**
email: info@tuftonarmshotel.co.uk
dir: In town centre

Elegant coaching inn with renowned fish dishes

This imposing, gabled building sits at the foot of Appleby's main street, close to the River Eden below the curvaceous fells of the wild North Pennines. There's an elegant, country house feel to the public rooms, where co-owner Teresa Milsom's design skills shine through, with astonishing attention to detail producing classic atmosphere and contemporary comforts. At the heart of the hotel, overlooking a cobbled mews courtyard, is the Conservatory Fish Restaurant, where David Milsom and his kitchen team's cuisine is complemented by a serious wine list. The menu covers all bases, with lamb shank, belly pork or home-made steak and ale pie as comforting standards. It's for the fresh fish dishes, however, that the Tufton has a particular reputation. Daily deliveries from Fleetwood are crafted into starters like smoked haddock and mushroom hotpot baked in cheese sauce; progressing to mains of seafood tagliatelle, or pan-fried hand picked crab and salmon cake. Beer connoisseurs may enjoy the hotel's own house ale.

Open all day all wk 7.30am-11pm Closed 25-26 Dec **Food** Lunch all wk 12-2 Dinner all wk 6-9 ⊕ FREE HOUSE ◀ Tufton Arms Ale, Cumberland Corby Ale. ▼ 15 **Facilities** Non-diners area ◀ (Bar Outside area) ◀◀ Children's portions Outside area ᴘ Parking WiFi ᴤᴤᴤ

BASSENTHWAITE
Map 18 NY23

The Pheasant ★★★ HL ◉
PICK OF THE PUBS

See Pick of the Pubs on page 102

BEETHAM
Map 18 SD47

The Wheatsheaf at Beetham
PICK OF THE PUBS

tel: 015395 62123 **LA7 7AL**
email: info@wheatsheafbeetham.com
dir: On A6 5m N of junct 35

Family-owned traditional village free house

In the 17th century, this was a farmhouse and the farmer's wife would feed the labourers; it later became a coaching inn. Today its long history of providing refreshment continues with a remarkable offer from owners Jean and Richard Skelton: order a main course and pay just 1p for your starter and dessert. So, having raided the piggy bank, what do your pennies buy? There are five starters, among them chicken and pork pâté with home-made chutney; and goats' cheese and tomato tart. Main courses include pan-fried minute steak with mushroom, onion, potato and red wine ragout; and home-made fish pie with haddock and prawns, mash and melted cheese. Splurging another penny on dessert could get you rich warm chocolate fudge cake and cream. The Old Tap Bar offers Thwaites Wainwright, Tirril Queen Jean and Cross Bay Nightfall real ales, as well as Kingstone Press cider.

Open all day all wk 10am-11pm Closed 25 Dec **Food** Lunch Mon-Sat 12-9, Sun 12-8.30 Dinner Mon-Sat 12-9, Sun 12-8.30 Av main course £12 Restaurant menu available all wk ⊕ FREE HOUSE ◀ Thwaites Wainwright, Tirril Queen Jean, Cross Bay Nightfall Ö Kingstone Press. **Facilities** Non-diners area ◀◀ Children's menu Children's portions Outside area ᴘ Parking WiFi ᴤᴤᴤ (notice required)

PICK OF THE PUBS

The Pheasant ★★★ HL 🏵

BASSENTHWAITE   Map 18 NY23

tel: 017687 76234
CA13 9YE
email: info@the-pheasant.co.uk
web: www.the-pheasant.co.uk
dir: *A66 to Cockermouth, 8m N of Keswick on left*

Accomplished food in peaceful Lake District setting

At the foot of the Sale Fell and close to Bassenthwaite Lake, this 17th-century former coaching inn occupies a peaceful spot in the Lake District and is surrounded by lovely gardens. Once a farmhouse, the pub today combines the role of traditional Cumbrian hostelry with that of an internationally renowned modern hotel. Even so, you still sense the history the moment you walk through the door – the legendary foxhunter John Peel, whose "view halloo would awaken the dead", according to the song, was a regular here. In the warmly inviting bar, with polished parquet flooring, panelled walls and oak settles, hang two of Cumbrian artist and former customer Edward H Thompson's paintings. Here, you can order a pint of Coniston Bluebird or Eden Fuggle, or cast your eyes over the extensive selection of malt whiskies. The high standard of food, recognised by an AA Rosette, is well known for miles around; meals are served in the attractive beamed restaurant, bistro,

bar and lounges overlooking the gardens. Light lunches served in the lounge and bar include open sandwiches, ploughman's and home-made pork pies, as well as main courses such as smoked haddock and salmon fishcakes; chicken supreme with carrot purée and caramelised fennel. A three course dinner in the restaurant could feature broccoli and pea velouté with crème fraîche and toasted pumpkin seeds; seared rump of lamb with lentils, cherry tomatoes and a garlic jus; and hot sticky toffee pudding, sticky sauce, boozy prunes, and vanilla ice cream. Treat the family to afternoon tea with home-made scones and rum butter. The Pheasant can get pretty busy, so booking for meals may be required.

Open all day all wk Closed 25 Dec
Food Lunch all wk 12-4.30 Dinner all wk 6-9 Restaurant menu available Tue-Sun. 🍺 FREE HOUSE 🛢 Coniston Bluebird, Cumberland Corby Ale, Eden Fuggle 🍏 Thatchers Gold. 🍷 12
Facilities Non-diners area 🐾 (Bar Garden) 👨‍👧 Children's menu Children's portions Garden 🎍 Parking WiFi
Rooms 15

BOOT
Map 18 NY10

Brook House Inn ★★★★ INN

tel: 019467 23288 **CA19 1TG**
email: stay@brookhouseinn.co.uk **web:** www.brookhouseinn.co.uk
dir: M6 junct 36, A590 follow Barrow signs. A5092, then A595. Pass Broughton-in-Furness, right at lights to Ulpha. Cross river, next left signed Eskdale to Boot. (NB not all routes to Boot are suitable in bad weather conditions)

Tranquil location for tempting, home-made food

Few locations can rival this: Lakeland fells rise behind the inn to England's highest peak, whilst golden sunsets illuminate tranquil Eskdale. Footpaths wind to nearby Stanley Ghyll's wooded gorge with its falls and red squirrels, and the charming La'al Ratty narrow gauge railway steams to and from the coast. It's a magnet for ramblers and cyclists, so a small drying room is greatly appreciated. Up to seven real ales are kept, including Yates Best Bitter and Langdale from Cumbrian Legendary Ales, and an amazing selection of 175 malt whiskies. Home-made food prepared from Cumbria's finest showcases the menus, so temper the drizzle with a warming bowl of home-made soup, or pigeon and bacon salad, followed by grilled sea bass with sweet chilli jam; belly pork with apple and cider pudding. Chocolate mocha pot, or treacle sponge with custard, make a fine finish. This great community pub also takes a full role in the famous Boot Beer Festival each June.

Open all day all wk Closed 25 Dec **Food** Contact pub for details ⊕ FREE HOUSE ◼ Hawkshead Windermere Pale, Cumbrian Legendary Langdale, Yates Best Bitter, Guest ales ♂ Westons. ♟ 10 **Facilities** Non-diners area ◑ Children's menu Children's portions Family room Garden 🏚 Beer festival Parking WiFi ☞ **Rooms** 8

BORROWDALE
Map 18 NY21

The Langstrath Country Inn

tel: 017687 77239 **CA12 5XG**
email: info@thelangstrath.com
dir: From Keswick take B5289, through Grange & Rosthwaite, left to Stonethwaite. Inn on left after 1m

Picturesque village inn, a favourite with ramblers

Sitting in the stunning Langstrath Valley in the heart of the Lakes and on the coast-to-coast and Cumbrian Way walks, this lovely family-run, 16th-century inn was originally a miner's cottage. It is an ideal base for those attempting England's highest peak, Scafell Pike. The restaurant is ideally positioned to maximise the spectacular views. Here hungry ramblers enjoy high-quality Lakeland dishes based on local ingredients. A typical choice could include steak and ale pie; pork tenderloin medallions with vegetables and mash; or sirloin steak with cracked pepper and whisky sauce. Local cask-conditioned ales include some from the Keswick Brewery.

Open all day 12-10.30 Closed Dec & Jan, Mon **Food** Lunch Tue-Sun 12-2.30 Dinner Tue-Sun 6-9 ⊕ FREE HOUSE ◼ Jennings Bitter & Cocker Hoop, Keswick Thirst Rescue, Theakstons Old Peculier ♂ Thatchers Gold. ♟ 9 **Facilities** Non-diners area ◑ (Bar Garden) ◑ Children's menu Children's portions Garden 🏚 Parking WiFi ☞ (notice required)

BOWLAND BRIDGE
Map 18 SD48

Hare & Hounds Country Inn

tel: 015395 68333 **LA11 6NN**
email: info@hareandhoundsbowlandbridge.co.uk
dir: M6 junct 36, A590 signed Barrow. Right onto A5074 signed Bowness & Windermere. Approx 4m at sharp bend left & follow Bowland Bridge sign

Fabulous views and local produce

Very much at the heart of the community, this 17th-century coaching inn even hosts the Post Office on Tuesday and Thursday afternoons. In the pretty little hamlet of

Bowland Bridge, not far from Bowness, the pub has gorgeous views of Cartmel Fell. Now refurbished, its traditional country-pub atmosphere is fostered by the flagstone floors, stacked logs, wooden tables and mis-matched chairs. Strong links with local food producers result in exclusively reared pork and lamb featuring on the menu alongside Cumbrian brewed beers. Visit at lunchtime and take your pick from sandwiches and salads or hearty meals such as smoked mackerel and celeriac pâté, followed by lamb hotpot, black pudding, whole baby onions, pickled red cabbage, and dauphinoise potatoes. Finish with home-made sticky toffee pudding with butterscotch sauce.

Open all day all wk 12-11 Closed 25 Dec **Food** Lunch Mon-Fri 12-2, Sat 12-9, Sun 12-8.30 Dinner Mon-Fri 6-9, Sat 12-9, Sun 12-8.30 ⊕ FREE HOUSE ◼ Tirril, Coniston, Ulverston, Hawkshead, Kirkby Lonsdale ♂ Cowmire Hall. ♟ 10 **Facilities** Non-diners area ◑ (Bar Garden) ◑ Children's menu Children's portions Garden 🏚 Parking WiFi ☞ (notice required)

BRAITHWAITE
Map 18 NY22

Coledale Inn

tel: 017687 78272 **CA12 5TN**
email: info@coledale-inn.co.uk
dir: M6 junct 40, A66 signed Keswick. Approx 18m. Exit A66, follow Whinlatter Pass & Braithwaite sign, left on B5292. In Braithwaite left at pub sign, over stream bridge to inn

An atmospheric place to finish a walk

Originally a woollen mill, the Coledale Inn dates from around 1824 and had stints as a pencil mill and a private house before becoming the inn it is today. The interior, in part now refurbished, is attractively designed, whilst footpaths leading off from the large gardens make it ideal for exploring the nearby fells. Two homely bars serve a selection of local ales while traditional lunch and dinner menus are served in the dining room. Typical choices include duo of black pudding and haggis; chilli con carne; rosemary and garlic chicken; and hot chocolate and fudge cake; there's further options on the specials board.

Open all day all wk **Food** Lunch all wk 12-2 Dinner all wk 6-9 Av main course £10.95 Set menu available ⊕ FREE HOUSE ◼ Cumberland Corby Ale, Hesket Newmarket, Yates, Keswick, Tirril, Geltsdale, Marston's. ♟ 8 **Facilities** Non-diners area ◑ (Bar Garden) ◑ Children's menu Children's portions Play area Garden 🏚 Parking WiFi ☞ (notice required)

The Royal Oak ★★★★ INN

tel: 017687 78533 **CA12 5SY**
email: tpfranks@hotmail.com **web:** www.royaloak-braithwaite.co.uk
dir: M6 junct 40, A66 towards Keswick, approx 18m (bypass Keswick), exit A66 left onto B5292 to Braithwaite. Pub in village centre

Delightful country pub surrounded by beautiful landscapes

Surrounded by high fells and beautiful scenery, The Royal Oak is set in the centre of the village and is the perfect base for walkers. The interior is all oak beams and log fires, and the menu offers hearty pub food, such as slow-roasted pork belly on apple mash; home-made fish pie; and slow-roasted lamb rump with mint gravy, all served alongside local ales, such as Sneck Lifter or Cumberland Ale. Visitors can extend the experience by staying over in the comfortable en suite bedrooms.

Open all day all wk **Food** Lunch all wk 12-2 Dinner all wk 6-9 Av main course £10 ⊕ MARSTON'S ◼ Jennings Lakeland Stunner, Cumberland Ale, Cocker Hoop, Sneck Lifter. ♟ 8 **Facilities** Non-diners area ◑ Children's menu Children's portions Garden 🏚 Parking WiFi ☞ **Rooms** 10

BRAMPTON
Map 21 NY56

Blacksmiths Arms ★★★★ INN

tel: 016977 3452 **Talkin CA8 1LE**
email: blacksmithsarmstalkin@yahoo.co.uk **web:** www.blacksmithstalkin.co.uk
dir: M6 junct 43, A69 E. 7m, straight on at rdbt, follow signs to Talkin Tarn then Talkin Village

Attractive free house serving good home-cooked food

With cartwheels lined up outside, this former smithy faces a small green by the crossroads in the centre of the village. On its doorstep is northern Cumbria's wildly beautiful countryside. The menu of good, traditional home cooking makes extensive use of fresh local produce for sweet and sour chicken; medallions of beef; rainbow trout; and spinach and ricotta cannelloni. Likely contenders as blackboard specials are lamb chump with redcurrant and port gravy; liver, bacon and onion casserole; and smoked haddock florentine. Two of the real ales come from the Geltsdale Brewery in neighbouring Brampton. There's a beer garden, and out front a couple of tables with seating.

Open all day all wk **Food** Lunch all wk 12-2 Dinner all wk 6-9 Av main course £8.95 ⊕ FREE HOUSE ◄ Geltsdale Cold Fell, Yates, Brampton, Entente Cordiale. ☂ 16 **Facilities** Non-diners area ◄◗ Children's menu Children's portions Garden ⋔ Parking WiFi **Rooms** 8

BROUGHTON-IN-FURNESS
Map 18 SD28

Blacksmiths Arms
PICK OF THE PUBS

tel: 01229 716824 **Broughton Mills LA20 6AX**
email: blacksmiths@aol.com
dir: A593 from Broughton-in-Furness towards Coniston, in 1.5m left signed Broughton Mills, pub 1m on left

Ancient pub surrounded by quiet fells and farms

Originally a farmhouse and then an inn and blacksmith's (hence the name), this whitewashed Lakeland pub dates from 1577 and stands in the secluded Lickle Valley, with miles of glorious walks radiating from the front door. The interior remains largely unchanged, with oak-panelled corridors, slate floors, oak-beamed ceilings and log fires. The Lanes own and run the Blacksmiths, Michael dividing his time between the kitchen and the bar, and Sophie running front of house. The bar is reserved for drinking only, with ales from Barngates and Tirril and Westons Old Rosie cider. The Lanes use only suppliers who guarantee quality produce for their menus. Apart from lunchtime sandwiches, there are options such as Cajun-spiced chicken salad and roasted pork tenderloin. The evening menu typically features honey-roast breast of duck and roasted rump of lamb. The sheltered, flower-filled front patio garden is great for alfresco dining.

Open all wk Mon 5-11 Tue-Fri 12-2.30 5-11 Sat 12-11 Sun 12-10.30 (Summer school hols 12-11 ex Mon) Closed 25 Dec, Mon L **Food** Lunch Tue-Sun 12-2 Dinner Tue-Sun 6-9 ⊕ FREE HOUSE ◄ Barngates Cracker Ale, Dent Golden Fleece, Tirril, Rotating ales ♂ Westons Old Rosie. **Facilities** Non-diners area ◄◗ Children's menu Garden ⋔ Beer festival Parking

CALDBECK
Map 18 NY34

Oddfellows Arms

tel: 016974 78227 **CA7 8EA**
email: info@oddfellows-caldbeck.co.uk
dir: Phone for detailed directions

Hearty Lake District pub food

Caldbeck's famous resident, the huntsman John ("D'ye ken...") Peel lies in the churchyard opposite this 17th-century coaching inn. The pub serves Jennings real

ales, lunchtime snacks – typically jacket potatoes and sandwiches – and offers a menu on which representative dishes include salmon and haddock fishcakes; traditional Cumberland sausage ring; Herdwick lamb cobbler; and cheese ploughman's. From the garden you can admire the dramatic northern fells of the Lake District National Park, before hitting the Cumbrian Way, which passes the front door, or pedalling off to the Reivers cycling route from Whitehaven to Tynemouth two miles away.

Open all day all wk **Food** Lunch Mon-Sat 12-2, Sun 12-8 Dinner Mon-Sat 5.30-9, Sun 12-8 ⊕ MARSTON'S ◄ Jennings Bitter, Cumberland Ale. ☂ 13 **Facilities** Non-diners area ❁ (Bar Garden) ◄◗ Children's menu Children's portions Garden ⋔ Parking WiFi ⬛ (notice required)

CARTMEL
Map 18 SD37

The Cavendish Arms
PICK OF THE PUBS

tel: 015395 36240 **LA11 6QA**
email: info@thecavendisharms.co.uk
dir: M6 junct 36, A590 signed Barrow-in-Furness. Cartmel signed. In village take 1st right

Cosy retreat in a medieval village

A babbling stream flows past the tree-lined garden of this 450-year-old coaching inn situated within Cartmel's village walls, its longest-surviving hostelry. Many traces of its history remain, from the mounting block outside the main door to the bar itself, which was once the stables. Low, oak-beamed ceilings, uneven floors, antique furniture and an open fire create a traditional, cosy atmosphere, and outside. As well as Cumbrian ales, the food owes much to its local origins. The menu changes every six weeks, listing lunchtime sandwiches and starters such as mixed game pâté. Then move on to oven-baked fillet of hake or tagliatelle primavera. Desserts include banoffee crunch sundae and blackcurrant fool. The owners have teamed up with a local company that offers carriage tours of the village. This popular area is ideal for walking, horse riding, and visiting Lake Windermere.

Open all day all wk 9am-11pm Closed 25 Dec **Food** Lunch all wk 12-9 Dinner all wk 12-9 ⊕ STAR PUBS & BARS ◄ Caledonian Golden XPA, Cumberland Corby Ale, Theakston, Guest ales ♂ Symonds. ☂ 8 **Facilities** Non-diners area ❁ (Bar Garden) ◄◗ Children's menu Children's portions Garden ⋔ Beer festival Parking WiFi ⬛

The Masons Arms

tel: 015395 68486 **Strawberry Bank LA11 6NW**
email: info@masonsarmsstrawberrybank.co.uk
dir: M6 junct 36, A590 towards Barrow. Right onto A5074 signed Bowness/Windermere. 5m, left at Bowland Bridge. Through village, pub on right

Attractive inn in a beautiful spot

An atmospheric, charmingly decorated pub with a stunning location overlooking the Winster Valley and beyond, The Masons Arms has an atmospheric interior with low, beamed ceilings, old fireplaces and quirky furniture. Waiting staff manoeuvre through the busy bar, dining rooms and heated, covered terraces carrying popular dishes such as warm pitta bread and home-made houmous to nibble; chicken liver pâté with fig and apple chutney to start; and a main course of creamy chicken, ham and leek pie with buttered peas and a choice of potato. Wash it down with a pint of Thwaites Wainwright.

Open all day all wk 9.30am-11pm **Food** Lunch Mon-Fri 12-2.30, Sat-Sun 12-9 Dinner Mon-Fri 6-9, Sat-Sun 12-9 ⊕ FREE HOUSE/INDIVIDUAL INNS LTD ◄ Thwaites Wainwright, Guest ales ♂ Kingstone Press. ☂ 12 **Facilities** Non-diners area ◄◗ Children's menu Children's portions Garden ⋔ Parking WiFi

PICK OF THE PUBS

The Punch Bowl Inn ★ ★ ★ ★ ★ ★ INN

CROSTHWAITE   Map 18 SD49

tel: 015395 68237
LA8 8HR
email: info@the-punchbowl.co.uk
web: www.the-punchbowl.co.uk
dir: *M6 junct 36, A590 towards Barrow, A5074, follow Crosthwaite signs. Pub by church*

Luxury Lake District inn and restaurant

Very much a destination dining inn, The Punch Bowl stands alongside the village church in the delightfully unspoilt Lyth Valley. The slates on the bar floor were found beneath the old dining room and complement the Brathay slate bar top and antique furniture, while in the restaurant are polished oak floorboards, comfortable leather chairs and an eyecatching stone fireplace. Two rooms off the bar add extra space to eat or relax with a pint and a daily paper in front of an open fire. Head chef Scott Fairweather focuses on the best local and seasonal produce and has two AA Rosettes to show for his expertise. Sourcing extensively from the area's estates, farms and coastal villages, the lunch and dinner menus in both the bar and the restaurant might begin with seared hand-dived scallops with white chocolate and truffle risotto; or loin of venison tartare, juniper, hazelnut, blue cheese, capers and smoked egg yolk. For a main course, possibly roast loin of

rabbit, crayfish mousse, leg croquette, confit potatoes, apricot and chard; salt-baked beetroot risotto, pickled carrot, pistachio and deep-fried brie; or maple glazed duck breast, braised red cabbage, orange, golden raisins, dauphinoise potatoes. And for dessert, round things off with wild strawberry soufflé with basil and lemonade sorbet; or dark chocolate delice, hazelnut, coffee and caramel. The owners are great supporters of Cumbrian microbreweries, witness Westmorland Gold from Barngates, and Bluebird from the Coniston brewery. In addition to a good list of dessert wines, champagne is available by the glass. Individually furnished guest rooms with freestanding roll-top baths are available.

Open all day all wk **Food** Mon-Fri 12-9, Sat-Sun 12-4 5.30-9 ⊕ FREE HOUSE ◀ Barngates Westmorland Gold, Coniston Bluebird Bitter, Winster Valley Old School ♂ Thatchers Gold. ♛ 14 **Facilities** Non-diners area ♨ (Bar Garden) ♦♦ Children's menu Children's portions Garden ⊼ Parking WiFi **Rooms** 9

CARTMEL *continued*

Pig & Whistle

tel: 015395 36482 **Aynsome Rd LA11 6PL**
email: info@pigandwhistlecartmel.co.uk
dir: *M6 junct 36, A590 towards Barrow. Left at Cartmel sign, pub in village centre*

A genuine local with first-class food

The co-landlord here with Penny Tapsell is Simon Rogan, one of the UK's most accomplished chefs. The pub has long been his local, and he likes it that way. His short but perfectly formed menu offers remarkably good value-for-money dishes, starting with mussel curry and cumin breadsticks or quail Caesar salad; move on to venison toad-in-the-hole, fish pie or Cumbrian hogget and black pudding tattiepot with braised red cabbage. Leave room in the pudding department for bread and butter pudding or boozy cherry and chocolate trifle. Real ale drinkers may run into a Dizzy Blonde in the bar – it's one of Robinsons of Stockport's seasonal brews.

Open all wk Summer 12–11 (Winter Mon & Tue 4–11 Fri-Sun 12–11) **Food** Lunch Wed-Sat 12–2, Sun 12–8.30 Dinner Wed-Sat 5.30–8.30, Sun 12–8.30 ⊕ ROBINSONS ◀ Dizzy Blonde, Hartleys Cumbria Way ♂ Westons Stowford Press.
Facilities Non-diners area ✿ (Bar Garden) ♦ Children's menu Garden ⊨ WiFi ▭

COCKERMOUTH continued — CONISTON section

| CLIFTON | Map 18 NY52 |

George and Dragon   PICK OF THE PUBS

tel: 01768 865381 **CA10 2ER**
email: enquiries@georgeanddragonclifton.co.uk
dir: *M6 junct 40, A66 towards Appleby-in-Westmorland, A6 S to Clifton*

Historic pub majoring on local produce

This lovely pub is more peaceful today than it was in 1745, when the retreating army of Bonnie Prince Charlie was defeated in the nearby village of Clifton. Set on the historic Lowther Estate near Ullswater; the ruined castle-mansion is set at the heart of pasture, woodland and fells alongside the rushing River Lowther and pretty village of Askham. Meticulously renovated by owner Charles Lowther, it is a traditional inn with contemporary comforts. The appealing menu majors on the bountiful produce of the estate. Beef is from pedigree Shorthorns; pork from home-reared rare breed stock; game and most fish from local waters. Settle in with a pint of Cumberland Corby Blonde and secure a starter of twice-baked cheese soufflé with spinach and chive cream sauce, followed by minute steak with garlic butter, field mushrooms and seasonal vegetables. Finish with vanilla cheesecake or apple and cinnamon sponge. There is a secluded courtyard and garden.

Open all day all wk Closed 26 Dec **Food** Lunch all wk 12–2.30 Dinner all wk 6–9 Set menu available ⊕ FREE HOUSE ◀ Hawkshead Bitter, Eden Gold, Cumberland Corby Blonde ♂ Westons Stowford Press. ₹ 17 **Facilities** Non-diners area ✿ (Bar Garden) ♦ Children's menu Children's portions Garden ⊨ Parking WiFi

---

| COCKERMOUTH | Map 18 NY13 |

The Trout Hotel ★★★★ HL

tel: 01900 823591 **Crown St CA13 OEJ**
email: enquiries@trouthotel.co.uk web: www.trouthotel.co.uk
dir: *In town centre*

Town-centre hotel overlooking the River Derwent

Until he was eight, the poet William Wordsworth lived next door, although then this 17th-century building was a private house. Much remains to remind us of its heritage: stone walls, exposed beams, marble fireplaces, restored plasterwork, period stained-glass, and a carefully-preserved oak staircase. At the bar ales from town brewery Jennings are joined by Carlisle-brewed guest, Corby Blonde. Fresh, locally sourced ingredients drive the menu, from smoked haddock fishcake, made with Thornby Moor Stumpies goats' cheese, to Cumbrian beef sirloin fajitas. A drink or a meal in the gardens overlooking the River Derwent is an enjoyable way of passing time.

Open all day all wk **Food** Lunch all wk 12–9.30 Dinner all wk 12–9.30 Av main course £12 Restaurant menu available all wk ⊕ FREE HOUSE ◀ Jennings Cumberland Ale, Cooper Hoop, Cumberland Corby Blonde ♂ Thatchers. ₹ 24
Facilities Non-diners area ♦ Children's menu Children's portions Garden ⊨ Parking WiFi ▭ (notice required) **Rooms** 49

| CONISTON | Map 18 SD39 |

The Black Bull Inn & Hotel   PICK OF THE PUBS

tel: 015394 41335 & 41668 **1 Yewdale Rd LA21 8DU**
email: i.s.bradley@btinternet.com
dir: *M6 junct 36, A590. 23m from Kendal via Windermere & Ambleside*

Four-hundred-year-old Lake District heartland pub

Beside a stream, or beck as they say round here, stands this traditional Lakeland pub. Its bare stone walls, oak beams, log-burning stove and part-slate floor all contribute to its appeal, while of further interest, at least to beer drinkers, is its own microbrewery's Bluebird Bitter, commemorating Donald Campbell's attempts on the world water speed record; it also brews Old Man Ale, named for the local 2,634-ft mountain. Those out walking all morning or all day can look forward to sandwiches or filled jacket potatoes. Chances are they'll want something heartier, such as a 10-oz platter of Waberthwaite's Cumberland sausage with creamy mash, green beans and red onion gravy; grilled gammon steak with fried eggs, mushrooms and battered onion rings; or lightly breaded scampi with side salad and coleslaw. Ask about beer festival dates.

Open all day all wk **Food** Lunch all wk 12–9 Dinner all wk 12–9 ⊕ FREE HOUSE ◀ Coniston Bluebird Bitter, Bluebird Premium XB, Old Man Ale, Winter Warmer Blacksmiths Ale, Special Oatmeal Stout ♂ Broadoak Premium Perry & Moonshine, Gwynt y Ddraig Haymaker, Guest ciders. ₹ 10 **Facilities** Non-diners area ✿ (Bar Garden) ♦ Children's menu Children's portions Family room Garden ⊨ Beer festival Parking WiFi ▭ (notice required)

| CROSTHWAITE | Map 18 SD49 |

The Punch Bowl Inn ★★★★★ INN ◉◉ PICK OF THE PUBS

See Pick of the Pubs on page 105

| ELTERWATER | Map 18 NY30 |

The Britannia Inn   PICK OF THE PUBS

tel: 015394 37210 **LA22 9HP**
email: info@britinn.co.uk
dir: *In village centre*

Village inn well placed for Lake District walkers

This free house in the Langdale Valley is a short drive from Ambleside, Grasmere, Windermere, Hawkshead and Coniston, while walks and mountain-bike trails head off in all directions from the front door. Built as a farmhouse and cobbler's more than 500 years ago, the whitewashed building only became an inn some 200 years back and the bar area is essentially a series of small, cosy rooms with low-beamed oak ceilings and winter coal fires. Bar staff pull pints of guest beers nineteen to the dozen, as well as the house special brewed by Coniston. An even wider selection of real ales is available during the two-week beer festival in mid-November. The inn offers a wide choice of fresh, home-cooked food, with an evening meal typically featuring Cumbrian steak, ale and mushroom pie; and vegetable lasagne. Dine alfresco in the garden and take in the views of the village and tarns.

Open all day all wk 10.30am–11pm **Food** Lunch all wk 12–9.30 Dinner all wk 12–9.30 Av main course £13 ⊕ FREE HOUSE ◀ Jennings Bitter, Coniston Bluebird Bitter & Britannia Inn Special Edition, Dent Aviator, Hawkshead Bitter, Guest ales. **Facilities** Non-diners area ✿ (Bar Garden) ♦ Children's menu Children's portions Garden ⊨ Beer festival Parking WiFi ▭ (notice required)

ESKDALE GREEN
Map 18 NY10

Bower House Inn
PICK OF THE PUBS

tel: 019467 23244 **CA19 1TD**
email: info@bowerhouseinn.co.uk
dir: *4m off A595, 0.5m W of Eskdale Green*

Old world charm and Cumbrian favourites

Hidden away in the fabulously unspoilt Eskdale Valley, this traditional Lake District hotel has been serving locals and walkers since the 17th century. Less than four miles from the main Cumbria coast road, it is ideally placed for visitors heading to the western lakes. Inside, oak beams, ticking clocks and crackling log fires create a comfortable setting to enjoy a pint of Bower House bitter in the bar, which opens out on to an attractive enclosed garden. The restaurant is a charming room with candlelit tables, exposed stone, log fires and equestrian pictures. Here, typical starters may include hand-pressed Cumberland terrine with tomato chutney, which might be followed by pan-fried duck breast with burnt orange sauce, fondant potato and vegetables or local Cumberland sausages with mash, peas and onion gravy. Dog-lovers may want to time a visit to coincide with the UK's largest annual meeting of Staffordshires in May.

Open all day all wk 11am-mdnt **Food** Lunch all wk 12-9 Dinner all wk 12-9 ⊕ FREE HOUSE ◀ Bower House Ale, Guest ales. **Facilities** Non-diners area ✿ (Bar Garden) ◀♦ Children's menu Children's portions Play area Garden ♠ Parking WiFi ▩ (notice required)

FAUGH
Map 18 NY55

The String of Horses Inn

tel: 01228 670297 **CA8 9EG**
email: info@stringofhorses.com
dir: *M6 junct 43, A69 towards Hexham. In approx 5m right at 1st lights at Corby Hill/ Warwick Bridge. 1m, through Heads Nook, in 1m sharp right. Left into Faugh. Pub on left down hill*

Traditional coaching inn in historic area

Close to Hadrian's Wall in the peaceful village of Faugh, this traditional 17th-century Lakeland inn may be tucked away but it's just ten minutes from Carlisle. There are oak beams, wood panelling, old settles and log fires in the restaurant, where imaginative pub food is on offer, and in the bar, where you'll find real ales from Brampton Brewery. Local black pudding with apple sauce; vegetable samosas; beef goulash; Cumberland sausage, mash and gravy; or Caribbean chicken admirably represent what's on a typical menu.

Open Tue-Sun 6-11 Closed Mon **Food** Dinner Tue-Sun 6-8.45 ⊕ FREE HOUSE ◀ Allendale Pennine Pale, Brampton Best, Geltsdale Cold Fell ♂ Westons Family Reserve. ▾ 8 **Facilities** Non-diners area ◀♦ Children's menu Outside area Parking WiFi ▩ (notice required)

Looking for a beer or cider festival?
Check our listings at the end of this guide

GRASMERE
Map 18 NY30

The Travellers Rest Inn

tel: 015394 35604 **Keswick Rd LA22 9RR**
email: stay@lakedistrictinns.co.uk **web:** www.lakedistrictinns.co.uk
dir: *A591 to Grasmere, pub 0.5m N of Grasmere*

Old world charm and a mountain backdrop

Located on the edge of picturesque Grasmere and handy for touring and exploring the ever-beautiful Lake District, The Travellers Rest has been a pub for more than 500 years. Inside, a roaring log fire complements the welcoming atmosphere of the beamed and inglenook bar area. Along with ales like Sneck Lifter, an extensive menu of traditional home-cooked fare is offered, ranging from steak and kidney pudding with potatoes and vegetables, to roasted aubergine with haricot bean ratatouille. Leave room for sticky toffee pudding or red berry sundae.

Open all day all wk 12-11 **Food** Lunch all wk 12-9.30 Dinner all wk 12-9.30 ⊕ FREE HOUSE ◀ Jennings Bitter, Cocker Hoop, Cumberland Ale & Sneck Lifter, Guest ales. ▾ 10 **Facilities** Non-diners area ✿ (Bar Garden) ◀♦ Children's menu Children's portions Family room Garden ♠ Parking WiFi ▩

GREAT LANGDALE
Map 18 NY20

The New Dungeon Ghyll Hotel ★★★ HL

tel: 015394 37213 **LA22 9JX**
email: enquiries@dungeon-ghyll.com **web:** www.dungeon-ghyll.com
dir: *From Ambleside take A593 towards Coniston for 3m, at Skelwith Bridge right onto B5343 towards 'The Langdales'*

Spectacularly located walkers' inn

Set in a spectacular spot at the foot of the Langdale Pikes and Pavey Ark, this traditional stone building was once a farmhouse before being transformed into a hotel in 1832. Full of character and charm, the rustic bar is popular with walkers returning from the fells. Local specialities are served in the bar and smart dining room. Typical dishes include game spring rolls with hoi sin and soy dipping sauce; pan-fried venison haunch with parsnip fondant and cranberry, thyme and port sauce; and sticky toffee pudding with ice cream. Real ales include Thwaites Original, Langdale Tup and Wainwright.

Open all day all wk **Food** Lunch all wk 12-9 Restaurant menu available all wk ⊕ FREE HOUSE ◀ Thwaites Original, Langdale Tup, Wainwright ♂ Kingstone Press. ▾ 9 **Facilities** Non-diners area ◀♦ Children's menu Children's portions Garden ♠ Parking WiFi ▩ (notice required) **Rooms** 22

GREAT SALKELD
Map 18 NY53

The Highland Drove Inn and Kyloes Restaurant
PICK OF THE PUBS

tel: 01768 898349 **CA11 9NA**
email: highlanddrove@kyloes.co.uk
dir: M6 junct 40, A66 E'bound, A686 to Alston. 4m, left onto B6412 for Great Salkeld & Lazonby

Convivial village pub deep in the pretty Eden Valley

On an old drove road, this 300-year-old country inn recalls the long-vanished days when hardy Highland cattle were driven across open water from Scotland's Western Isles to markets in England. A reputation for high-quality food might suggest it's a destination pub, as indeed it is, but it's more than that, because locals love it too, one attraction being a cask-conditioned ale called Kyloes Kushie. The attractive brick and timber bar, where snacks are available, is furnished with old tables and settles; the more formal dining takes place upstairs in the hunting lodge-style restaurant, where a verandah offers fine country views. The kitchen depends on locally-sourced game, fish and meat, examples including venison rendang, an Indonesian curry with coconut milk and spices; Cumbrian lamb shank slow-braised in Guinness; duck breast marinated in pineapple, chilli and soy sauce; and baked fillet of halibut.

Open Tue-Fri 12-2 (all wk 6pm-12am Sat 12pm-2am) Closed 25 Dec, Mon L **Food** Lunch Tue-Sun 12-2 Dinner all wk 6-9 ⊕ FREE HOUSE ◗ Theakston Black Bull Bitter, Best & Traditional Mild, John Smith's Cask & Smooth, Eden Brewery Kyloes Kushie, Guest ale ♂ Symonds. ♚ 10 **Facilities** Non-diners area ♣ (Bar Garden) ♦♦ Children's menu Children's portions Garden ⋒ Parking WiFi ▥ (notice required)

GREAT URSWICK
Map 18 SD27

General Burgoyne

tel: 01229 586394 **Church Rd LA12 0SZ**
email: dropusaline@generalburgoyne.com
dir: M6 junct 36, A590 towards Barrow-in-Furness. Through Ulverston, left after Swarthmoor signed Great Urswick, 1.5m to pub

Traditional country pub continuing to make a big impression

Gentleman Johnny was a British army officer, politician and dramatist, infamous for surrendering his men to the enemy during the American War of Independence. A skull – not Burgoyne's – found during renovations in 1995 is displayed in the fire-

warmed bar, where Robinsons beers are served, and the comprehensive menu includes pub classics and sandwiches. In the modern Orangery Restaurant, look for braised featherblade of Lakeland beef; pan-fried rainbow trout; potato and chickpea Dhal with roast chicken breast, or without for vegetarians. For pie 'n' peas night, go on a Wednesday. Walkers, cyclists, bikers and dogs are always welcome.

Open all day Closed 26 Dec & 1st wk Jan, Mon **Food** Lunch Tue-Sun 12-2 Dinner Tue-Sun 6-9 Av main course £12.15 ⊕ ROBINSONS ◗ Dizzy Blonde, Hartleys Cumbria Way. **Facilities** Non-diners area ♣ (Bar Outside area) ♦♦ Children's portions Outside area ⋒ Parking WiFi ▥ (notice required)

HAWKSHEAD
Map 18 SD39

Kings Arms ★★★ INN

tel: 015394 36372 **The Square LA22 0NZ**
email: info@kingsarmshawkshead.co.uk **web:** www.kingsarmshawkshead.co.uk
dir: M6 junct 36, A590 to Newby Bridge, right at 1st junct past rdbt, over bridge, 8m to Hawkshead

Homely inn in Beatrix Potter village

In the charming square at the heart of this virtually unchanged Elizabethan Lakeland village, made famous by Beatrix Potter who lived nearby, this 16th-century inn throngs in summer. In colder weather, bag a table by the fire in the traditional carpeted bar, quaff a pint of Hawkshead Bitter and tuck into lunchtime food such as hot Cumberland sausage with a jacket potato and gravy or evening meals along the lines of smoked trout with cream cheese toasts followed by game and smoked bacon casserole. Look out for the carved figure of a king in the bar. Cosy, thoughtfully equipped bedrooms are available.

Open all day all wk 11am-mdnt **Food** Lunch all wk 12-2.30 Dinner all wk 6-9.30 Av main course £9 ⊕ FREE HOUSE ◗ Hawkshead Gold & Bitter, Coniston Bluebird, Cumbrian Legendary, Guest ales. **Facilities** Non-diners area ♣ (Bar Outside area) ♦♦ Children's menu Children's portions Outside area ⋒ Beer festival WiFi ▥ (notice required) **Rooms** 8

The Queen's Head Inn & Restaurant ★★★★ INN
PICK OF THE PUBS

See Pick of the Pubs on opposite page and advert below

PICK OF THE PUBS

The Queen's Head Inn & Restaurant ★★★★ INN

HAWKSHEAD Map 18 SD39

tel: 015394 36271
Main St LA22 0NS
email: info@queensheadhawkshead.co.uk
web: www.queensheadhawkshead.co.uk
dir: *M6 junct 36, A590 to Newby Bridge,*
1st right, 8m to Hawkshead

Excellent food and hospitality in the southern Lakes

Hawkshead has impressive literary links – William Wordsworth attended the local grammar school, and Beatrix Potter lived just up the road. Now refurbished, the 17th-century Queen's Head is a stone's throw from Esthwaite Water on the village's main street and surrounded by fells and forests. Behind the pub's flower-bedecked exterior, low oak-beamed ceilings, wood-panelled walls, slate floors and welcoming fires create a relaxed, traditional setting. A range of real ales might include Hartleys Cumbria Way or Double Hop and an extensive wine list includes nearly a dozen by the glass, while the menu brims with fresh, quality local produce. At lunchtime, sandwiches served with French fries and salad refuel the ramblers. In the evening you might start with seared scallops with cauliflower purée, pickled cauliflower, crispy ham, lime and vanilla dressing; or black pudding Scotch egg, watercress and apple salad, home-made piccalilli; follow with slow cooked shoulder of

Lakeland lamb with rosemary mash, confit carrots, red wine jus; or roasted fillet of cod with pomme purée, chicory, sweet potato and crayfish dressing. Vegetarians may plump for a dish of butternut squash and cumin risotto, roasted squash, crispy sage leaves, parmesan shavings or wild mushroom, leek and spinach linguine. There is also a range of pizzas available. Puddings are written on the blackboard and could include peanut butter parfait, coffee milkshake, chocolate chilli popcorn, or dark chocolate tart, white chocolate mousse and cassis sorbet, although there is an impressive selection of Cumbrian cheeses with home-made chutney, celery, grapes and biscuits. The en suite guest rooms are individually styled.

Open all day all wk 11am-11.45pm (Sun 12-11.45) **Food** Lunch Mon-Sat 12-3, Sun 12-4 Dinner all wk 6-9 Set menu available ⊕ ROBINSONS ◖ Double Hop, Hartleys Cumbria Way, Guest ale. ♟ 11
Facilities Non-diners area ☙ (Bar Garden) ⦿ Children's menu Family room Garden ⼌ WiFi ⛟ (notice required)
Rooms 13

HAWKSHEAD *continued*

The Sun Inn

tel: 015394 36236 **Main St LA22 ONT**
email: rooms@suninn.co.uk
dir: *N'bound on M6 junct 36, A591 to Ambleside, B5286 to Hawkshead. S'bound on M6 junct 40, A66 to Keswick, A591 to Ambleside, B5286 to Hawkshead*

A popular hostelry in a busy village

This listed 17th-century coaching inn is at the heart of the charming village where Wordsworth went to school. Inside are two resident ghosts – a giggling girl and a drunken landlord – and outside is a paved terrace with seating. The wood-panelled bar has low, oak-beamed ceilings, and hill walkers and others will enjoy the log fires, real ales and locally sourced food. Choices range from steak and vegetable Westmorland pie; vegetable bake; and Lancashire hotpot to venison burger and fillet of plaice.

Open all day all wk 10am-mdnt **Food** Lunch all wk 12-2.30 Dinner all wk 6-9 ⊕ FREE HOUSE ◗ Cumbrian Legendary Loweswater Gold, Jennings, Guest ale. **Facilities** Non-diners area ✿ (Bar Garden) ♦♦ Children's menu Children's portions Garden ⋒ Beer festival WiFi ▱

| KESWICK | Map 18 NY22 |

The George ★★★★ INN

tel: 017687 72076 **3 Saint John's St CA12 5AZ**
email: rooms@thegeorgekeswick.co.uk **web:** www.thegeorgekeswick.co.uk
dir: *M6 junct 40, A66, filter left signed Keswick, pass pub on left. At x-rds left into Station St, inn 150yds on left*

Imposing coaching inn with plenty of character

Keswick's oldest coaching inn is a handsome 17th-century building in the heart of this popular Lakeland town. Restored to its former glory, retaining its traditional black panelling, Elizabethan beams, ancient settles and log fires, it makes a comfortable base from which to explore the fells and lakes. Expect to find local Jennings ales on tap and classic pub food prepared from local ingredients. Typical dishes include trio of Cumbrian pork, seafood pasta, venison casserole, cow (steak) pie, apple crumble cheesecake, and sticky toffee pudding. There are 12 comfortable bedrooms available.

Open all day all wk **Food** Lunch Mon-Thu 12-2.30, Fri-Sun 12-5 Dinner all wk 5.30-9 ⊕ JENNINGS ◗ Bitter, Cumberland Ale, Sneck Lifter & Cocker Hoop, Guest ales. ♛ 10 **Facilities** Non-diners area ✿ (Bar Garden) ♦♦ Children's menu Garden Parking ▱ **Rooms** 12

The Horse & Farrier Inn | PICK OF THE PUBS

tel: 017687 79688 **Threlkeld Village CA12 4SQ**
email: info@horseandfarrier.com
dir: *M6 junct 40, A66 signed Keswick, 12m, right signed Threlkeld. Pub in village centre*

A must for Lakeland walkers

Built in 1688, this lovely Lakeland inn is situated at the foot of Blencathra on the ancient route between Keswick and Penrith. With views across Skiddaw and Helvellyn, it's little wonder that it's a hot spot for serious walkers. Within the thick, whitewashed stone walls of this long, low building you'll find slate-flagged floors, beamed ceilings and crackling log fires, with hunting prints decorating the traditional bars and panelled snug. The inn has an excellent reputation for good food and the chefs make full use of local and seasonal produce. The lunchtime bar menu has all the old favourites, from home-roasted Cumbrian ham sandwiches to chilli con carne. In the restaurant, starters could be a pork, bacon and herb terrine; or hot oak-smoked fillet of Scottish salmon. Main courses take in Whitby scampi and chips; traditional Cumberland sausages and slow-braised lamb shoulder.

Open all day all wk 7.30am-mdnt **Food** Lunch all wk 12-9 Dinner all wk 12-9 ⊕ JENNINGS ◗ Bitter, Cocker Hoop, Sneck Lifter & Cumberland Ale, Guest ale. ♛ 10 **Facilities** Non-diners area ✿ (Bar Garden) ♦♦ Children's menu Children's portions Family room Garden ⋒ Parking WiFi ▱ (notice required)

The Kings Head | PICK OF THE PUBS

tel: 017687 72393 **Thirlspot CA12 4TN**
email: stay@lakedistrictinns.co.uk **web:** www.lakedistrictinns.co.uk
dir: *M6 junct 40, A66 to Keswick then A591, pub 4m S of Keswick*

Lovely valley views south of Keswick

Helvellyn, the third highest peak in England, towers above this 17th-century coaching inn; the long, whitewashed building and its delightful beer garden enjoy great views of the surrounding fells, while indoors the traditional bar features old beams and an inglenook fireplace. In addition to several regulars from the Cumberland brewery, there are guest real ales and a fine selection of wines and malt whiskies. In the bar, paninis, sandwiches and jacket potatoes head the lunchtime options, which also feature a deli board and ploughman's. It's in the restaurant, which looks out to the glacial valley of St Johns in the Vale, that dinner might begin with local Cumberland sausage and mash; and haddock in Jennings beer batter; and end with sticky toffee pudding. From Monday to Saturday chargrilled steaks, ham, pork and salmon extend the daily range.

Open all day all wk 11-11 **Food** Lunch all wk 12-9.30 Dinner all wk 12-9.30 ⊕ FREE HOUSE ◗ Jennings Bitter, Cumberland Ale, Sneck Lifter & Cocker Hoop, Guest ales. ♛ 9 **Facilities** Non-diners area ✿ (Bar Garden) ♦♦ Children's menu Family room Garden ⋒ Parking WiFi ▱

Pheasant Inn

tel: 017687 72219 **Crosthwaite Rd CA12 5PP**
dir: *On A66 Keswick rdbt towards town centre, 60yds on right*

Local food and ales, an ideal stop after a Lakeland walk

An open-fired, traditional Lakeland inn, owned by Jennings Brewery, so expect their regular range on tap, and a monthly guest. For the seasonal menus, the kitchen produces home-cooked, locally sourced food, including starters of whitebait with smoked paprika sauce; and 'gooey' baked camembert with ciabatta dipping sticks and chilli, red onion and tomato relish. Follow with a favourite like red Thai chicken and mango curry, or a chef's speciality, such as prime Cumbrian rump steak; pan-fried swordfish marinated in basil and lemon; or oven-roasted chicken supreme on fettuccine pasta.

Open all day all wk Closed 25 Dec **Food** Lunch all wk 12-4 (12-2 low season) Dinner all wk 6-9 Av main course £11.95 ⊕ JENNINGS ◗ Bitter, Cumberland Ale, Cocker Hoop & Sneck Lifter, Guest ale ♢ Thatchers Gold. ♛ 8 **Facilities** Non-diners area ✿ (Bar Garden) ♦♦ Children's menu Garden ⋒ Parking WiFi

PICK OF THE PUBS

The Royal Oak at Keswick ★★★★ INN

KESWICK   Map 18 NY22

tel: 017687 74584
Main St CA12 5HZ
email: relax@theinnkeswick.co.uk
web: www.theinnkeswick.co.uk
dir: *M6 junct 40, A66 to Keswick town centre to war memorial x-rds. Left into Station St. Inn 100yds*

Popular inn at the heart of walking country

Located on the corner of Keswick's vibrant market square, this large yet friendly 18th-century coaching inn (formerly called The Inn at Keswick) combines contemporary comfort with charming reminders of its place in local history. It is understandably popular with walkers – it's within a few strides of England's three highest peaks; dogs are permitted in the bar and some of the bedrooms, an important consideration for many. Lancaster Bomber is one of the award-winning Thwaites ales on tap, and Kingstone Press cider is popular too. The wine selection is small but perfectly formed, with 12 or more wines by the glass. The kitchen's careful sourcing of ingredients from ethical suppliers ensures sustainability as well as freshness, and local artisans such as Thornby Moor Dairy are supported and named on the menu. The slight price premium for these policies is all but unnoticeable, as the menu represents excellent value for money. From noon until teatime, hot sandwiches such as

tuna savoury with cheddar are available, alongside cold sandwiches, light dishes such as tiger prawn tempura, and home comforts such as beefsteak and ale pie topped with puff pastry. Deli boards showing off a selection of local cheeses or meats are great for sharing. In the evening the chargrill is fired up, producing a delicious range of beef, gammon and chicken main courses. Alternatively, go for the hotpot of Fellside lamb topped with sliced potatoes – the inn's bestselling dish. For those with a nagging sweet tooth, a plate of warm treacle tart with clotted cream should hit the spot. If you book to stay in one of the en suite rooms, a wholesome Cumbrian breakfast will set you up for the ramble you have planned.

Open all day all wk 9am–mdnt **Food** Mon-Sat 11-10, Sun 12-9 Av main course £12.95 Set menu available ⊕ THWAITES INNS OF CHARACTER ◀ Wainwright, Original, Lancaster Bomber ♂ Kingstone Press. ♥ 12 **Facilities** Non-diners area ✿ (Bar Restaurant) ♦ Children's menu Children's portions WiFi 🚌 (notice required) **Rooms** 19

KESWICK *continued*

The Royal Oak at Keswick ★★★★ INN | PICK OF THE PUBS

See Pick of the Pubs on page 111 and advert below

KIRKBY LONSDALE	Map 18 SD67

The Pheasant Inn ★★★★ INN | PICK OF THE PUBS

tel: 01524 271230 **Casterton LA6 2RX**
email: info@pheasantinn.co.uk **web:** www.pheasantinn.co.uk
dir: *M6 junct 36, A65 for 7m, left onto A683 at Devils Bridge, 1m to Casterton centre*

Peaceful inn with lovely views of the fells

Below the fell on the edge of the beautiful Lune Valley is this sleepy hamlet with its whitewashed 18th-century coaching inn. It's perfectly situated for exploring the Dales, the Trough of Bowland and the Cumbrian Lakes. The Wilson family and staff ensure a warm welcome in the bar and stylish oak-panelled dining room. Guest ales and beers from Theakstons can be sampled while perusing the interesting menu. It mixes home-grown seasonal produce from valley farms with favourite recipes from foreign fields: starters, for example, include Chinese-style crispy pork belly; and Moroccan spiced chicken kebabs with warm couscous and chickpea salad. The Pheasant's proper steak and ale pie is served with hand-cut chips and a rich beef gravy. The excellent dessert choice ranges from old fashioned warm treacle tart with clotted cream, to banana fritters in coconut batter, with pineapple parfait and caramel sauce. Food can be served on the lawn in fine weather.

Open all day all wk Closed 2wks mid-Jan **Food** Lunch all wk 12-2 Dinner all wk 6-9 ⊕ FREE HOUSE ◼ Theakstons, Tirril, Guest ales. ₹ 8 **Facilities** Non-diners area ✿ (Bar Garden Outside area) ♦ Children's menu Children's portions Garden Outside area ⊓ Parking WiFi ▦ (notice required) **Rooms** 10

The Sun Inn ★★★★★ RR ◉ | PICK OF THE PUBS

tel: 01524 271965 **Market St LA6 2AU**
email: email@sun-inn.info **web:** www.sun-inn.info
dir: *M6 junct 36, A65 for Kirkby Lonsdale. In 5m left signed Kirkby Lonsdale. Left at next T-junct. Right at bottom of hill*

Terrific period inn with top-notch menu

Beside one of the narrow, twisty streets of the dreamy little Lunesdale town of Kirkby Lonsdale stands The Sun Inn. It burrows back from a pretty pillared frontage into a jigsaw of cosy corners, some splayed around the feature log fire in the most time-honoured, mellow of interiors. The enthusiastic owners are keen supporters of locally produced goods on both wet and food sides; expect beer from the town's microbrewery to accompany the uplifting bill of fare based on the wealth of this hilly country's provender. A new chef in 2014 has refined and tweaked the restaurant's menu, producing an absorbing selection of dishes that are changed every month. Starters may offer braised leg and breast of partridge, leading to saddle of venison with haggis croquette. The bar menu is equally capable - seared calves' liver with Puy lentils, or sea bass with mussel broth and samphire for example. Eleven bedrooms make The Sun an ideal base from which to explore the Lake District and Yorkshire Dales.

Open Mon 3-11, Tue-Sun 10am-11pm Closed Mon L **Food** Lunch Tue-Sun 12-4 Dinner Mon-Sun 6.30-9 Av main course £10.95 Set menu available ⊕ FREE HOUSE ◼ Kirkby Lonsdale Radical, Thwaites Wainwright, Hawkshead Bitter. ₹ 9 **Facilities** Non-diners area ✿ (Bar) ♦ Children's portions WiFi **Rooms** 11

The Whoop Hall ★★ HL

tel: 015242 71284 **Skipton Rd LA6 2GY**
email: info@whoophall.co.uk **web:** www.whoophall.co.uk
dir: *M6 junct 36, A65. Pub 1m SE of Kirkby Lonsdale*

Comfy inn in stunning countryside

Set in the gorgeous Lune Valley with fells rising to over 2,000-ft just up the lane, this considerately modernised 400-year-old coaching inn and hotel is a grand base for exploring the nearby Yorkshire Dales National Park. Yorkshire also provides beers such as Black Sheep and excellent local produce used on the enticing menus in the restaurant and bistro bar. Slow cooked pork belly with braised leeks and cider jus or roasted chump of lamb with bubble-and-squeak satisfy major appetites; or snack on stone baked pizzas or hot deli sandwiches while sitting on the terrace. 24 individually styled rooms encourage a lingering visit.

Open all day all wk **Food** Lunch all wk 12-9 Dinner all wk 12-9 ⊕ FREE HOUSE ◼ Jennings Cumberland Cream & Cumberland Ale, Black Sheep ♉ Thatchers Gold. ₹ 14 **Facilities** Non-diners area ✿ (Bar Garden) ♦ Play area Family room Garden ⊓ Parking ▦ **Rooms** 24

PICK OF THE PUBS

Kirkstile Inn ★★★★★ INN

LOWESWATER Map 18 NY12

tel: 01900 85219 **CA13 0RU**
email: info@kirkstile.com
web: www.kirkstile.com
dir: *From A66 Keswick take Whinlatter Pass at Braithwaite. Take B5292, at T-junct left onto B5289. 3m to Loweswater. From Cockermouth B5289 to Lorton, past Low Lorton, 3m to Loweswater. Left at red phone box*

Traditional pub set among woods, fells and lakes

Stretching as far as the eye can see, the woods, fells and lakes are as much a draw today as they must have been in the inn's infancy some 400 years ago. The beck below meanders under a stone bridge, oak trees fringing its banks with the mighty Melbreak towering impressively above. Tucked away next to an old church, this classic Cumbrian inn stands just half a mile from the Loweswater and Crummock lakes and makes an ideal base for walking, climbing, boating and fishing. The whole place has an authentic, traditional and well-looked-after feel – whitewashed walls, low beams, solid polished tables, cushioned settles, a well-stoked fire and the odd horse harness remind you of times gone by. You can call in for afternoon tea, but better still would be to taste one of the Cumbrian Legendary Ales – Loweswater Gold, Grasmoor Dark Ale, Esthwaite

Bitter – brewed by landlord Roger Humphreys in Esthwaite Water near Hawkshead. Traditional pub food is freshly prepared using local produce and the lunchtime menu brims with wholesome dishes that will satisfy the most hearty appetites. Look for chicken liver pâté; omelette Arnold Bennet; or lamb stew tatie pot. If you're in need of a lighter meal, tuck into sandwiches or ciabatta panini rolls. Evening additions and daily specials may take in guinea fowl supreme with bubble and squeak; wild mushroom risotto; or slow roasted Lakeland lamb shoulder, buttered mash and red wine and orange jus. Leave room for treacle tart and toffee fudge ripple ice cream; or a selection of Cumbrian cheeses.

Open all day all wk Closed 25 Dec
Food Lunch all wk 12-2, light menu 2-4.30 Dinner served all wk 6-9 ⊞ FREE HOUSE ◪ Cumbrian Legendary Loweswater Gold, Esthwaite Bitter, Grasmoor Dark Ale, Langdale ☼ Westons Stowford Press. ☲ 9 **Facilities** Non-diners area ☻ Bar until 6pm ⦿ Children's menu & portions Family room Garden ⊼ Beer festival Parking **Rooms** 10

LITTLE LANGDALE — Map 18 NY30

Three Shires Inn ★★★★ INN — PICK OF THE PUBS

tel: 015394 37215 **LA22 9NZ**
email: enquiry@threeshiresinn.co.uk **web:** www.threeshiresinn.co.uk
dir: *Exit A593, 2.3m from Ambleside at 2nd junct signed 'The Langdales'. 1st left 0.5m. Inn in 1m*

Popular stop-over in a wonderful setting

Comfortably fitting into a break in the drystone walls and thick hedges bordering the winding lane leading to the Wrynose and Hard Knott Passes, is this slate-built Lake District pub. Ian Stephenson and his family have run it since 1983. It's Lakeland through and through, from its Cumbrian-sourced food, and real ales from Hesket Newmarket, Hawkshead and Ennerdale, to its comfortable accommodation. Everyone – including families with children and dogs – is welcome in the beamed bar for a ploughman's, a warm ciabatta, a sandwich, or even a lamb stew. When it's cold there's a fire; when it's warm the place to be is the landscaped garden, views over the fells a bonus. For an evening meal, battered black pudding with herb mash and balsamic onion gravy, followed by grilled fresh Lakeland trout, or marinated pork loin steak, finishing with spiced sultana sponge and vanilla custard.

Open all wk 11-3 6-10.30 Dec-Jan, 11-10.30 Feb-Nov (Fri-Sat 11-11) Closed 25 Dec **Food** Lunch all wk 12-2 (ex 24-25 Dec) Dinner all wk 6-8.45 (ex mid-wk Dec-Jan) ⊕ FREE HOUSE ◀ Cumbrian Legendary Melbreak Bitter, Jennings Bitter & Cumberland Ale, Coniston Old Man Ale, Hawkshead Bitter, Ennerdale Blonde. **Facilities** Non-diners area ❄ (Bar Garden) ◀ Children's menu Garden ⚲ Parking WiFi **Rooms** 10

LOWESWATER — Map 18 NY12

Kirkstile Inn ★★★★ INN — PICK OF THE PUBS

See Pick of the Pubs on page 113

LOW LORTON — Map 18 NY12

The Wheatsheaf Inn

tel: 01900 85199 & 85268 **CA13 9UW**
email: j.williams53@sky.com
dir: *From Cockermouth take B5292 to Lorton. Right onto B5289 to Low Lorton*

Good beers, good food and good views

Occasionally, landlord Mark Cockbain crosses the lane from his white-painted, 17th-century pub to look for salmon and trout in the River Cocker. For visitors it's the panoramic views of the lush Vale of Lorton from the child-friendly beer garden that matter. The quaint, open-fired bar looks like a gamekeeper's lodge: "We like our locals to feel at home," says Mark's wife, Jackie. Real ales from Jennings in Cockermouth also help in that respect. On the menu are cottage pie; gammon and sirloin steaks; chicken, leek and Stilton pie; and vegetable curry. The end of March is beer festival time.

Open Tue-Sun Closed Mon & Tue eve in Jan & Feb **Food** Lunch Fri 12-2, Sat 12-3, Sun 12-8.30 Dinner Tue-Sat 6-8.30, Sun 12-8.30 ⊕ MARSTON'S ◀ Pedigree, Jennings Bitter & Cumberland Ale, Brakspear Oxford Gold ⚬ Scrumpy Jack. **Facilities** Non-diners area ❄ (Bar Garden) ◀ Children's menu Children's portions Family room Garden ⚲ Beer festival Parking ⛟

LUPTON — Map 18 SD58

The Plough Inn ☆☆☆☆☆ INN ◉ — PICK OF THE PUBS

tel: 015395 67700 **Cow Brow LA6 1PJ**
email: info@theploughatlupton.co.uk **web:** www.theploughatlupton.co.uk
dir: *M6 junct 36, A65 towards Kirkby Lonsdale. Pub on right in Lupton*

Affectionately held in the hearts of locals

Below Farleton Knott, a hill from where locals would broadcast warnings of Scottish unrest, stands this apparently simple roadside pub. Any notion of simplicity, however, is quickly dispelled on entering what turns out to be an extensively refurbished 1760s inn. Oak beams, leather sofas, colourful rugs and antique furniture impart a farmhouse feel; Brathay slate tops the bar, and polished oak floors lead into the Farleton Room restaurant, where open fires and wood-burning stoves do a sterling job when needed. Fourteen wines by the glass and local Jennings Cumberland, Kirkby Lonsdale Monumental and Coniston Bluebird beers await weary fell-walkers. After beginning with pan-fried Stornoway black pudding, or prawn and Braeburn apple cocktail, the essentially British, one-AA Rosette menu continues with fisherman's and ploughman's boards; Aberdeen Angus burger; ale-battered fish and hand-cut chips; and wild mushroom risotto. You can see the 'caves' from where your accompanying wine is selected.

Open all day wk **Food** Lunch all wk 12-9 Dinner all wk 12-9 ⊕ FREE HOUSE ◀ Kirkby Lonsdale Monumental, Jennings Cumberland Ale, Coniston Bluebird Bitter ⚬ Thatchers Gold. ▼ 14 **Facilities** Non-diners area ❄ (Bar Garden) ◀ Children's menu Children's portions Garden ⚲ Parking WiFi **Rooms** 6

NEAR SAWREY — Map 18 SD39

Tower Bank Arms — PICK OF THE PUBS

See Pick of the Pubs on opposite page

OUTGATE — Map 18 SD39

Outgate Inn

tel: 015394 36413 **LA22 0NQ**
email: info@outgateinn.co.uk
dir: *M6 junct 36, by-passing Kendal, A591 towards Ambleside. At Clappersgate take B5285 to Hawkshead, Outgate 3m*

Traditional Cumbrian inn with welcoming atmosphere

Once owned by a mineral water manufacturer and now part of Robinsons and Hartleys Brewery, this 17th-century Lakeland inn is full of traditional features including oak beams and a real fire in winter. The secluded beer garden at the rear is a tranquil place to enjoy the summer warmth. Food choices include salads and light bites such as a beefburger or ham, egg and chips; and hearty dishes such as steak and ale pie with hand-cut chips; or braised shoulder of lamb, creamy mash and red wine and rosemary sauce. Typical desserts are sticky toffee pudding, and chocolate and hazelnut brownie. Gluten-free options are available.

Open all day all wk **Food** Lunch all wk 12-5.30 Dinner all wk 5.30-8.45 Av main course £11.50 ⊕ ROBINSONS ◀ Dizzy Blonde, Hartleys XB ⚬ Westons Stowford Press. **Facilities** Non-diners area ❄ (Bar Garden) ◀ Children's menu Children's portions Garden ⚲ Parking WiFi ⛟ (notice required)

PICK OF THE PUBS

Tower Bank Arms

NEAR SAWREY Map 18 SD39

tel: 015394 36334 **LA22 0LF**
email: enquiries@towerbankarms.co.uk
web: www.towerbankarms.co.uk
dir: *On B5285 SW of Windermere.1.5m from Hawkshead. 2m from Windermere via ferry*

Popular rustic pub

This 17th-century village pub on the west side of Lake Windermere is owned by the National Trust (although run independently), as is Beatrix Potter's old home, Hill Top, which can be found just behind the inn. It has been known as the Tower Bank Arms for over a century and Potter illustrated it perfectly in her *Tale of Jemima Puddleduck*, although history fails to record whether she ever slipped in for a drink during a break from sketching. The literary connection brings out the Peter Rabbit fan club in force, particularly in summer, so the delightfully unspoilt rustic charm of this little treasure may be easier to appreciate out of season (check opening times). In the low-beamed slate-floored main bar are an open log fire, fresh flowers and ticking grandfather clock, with local brews on hand-pump from the Cumbrian Legendary and Barngates breweries. Lunch and dinner menus are both served throughout all areas. Hearty country food makes good use of local produce, whether in a midday snack such as a Cumbrian baked ham sandwich with wholegrain honey

mustard; or dishes of traditional Cumberland sausages supplied by Woodall's of Waberthwaite, who hold a royal warrant; or deep-fried beer-battered haddock with mushy peas, chips and tartare sauce. In the evening, try perhaps leg of lamb noisette, black pepper mash and rosemary, garlic and redcurrant sauce. Puds, however, are confirmed favourites: chocolate brownie, vanilla ice cream and black cherry sundae, and lemon sherbert and basil cheesecake with berry coulis are two examples. Alternatively an assorted slate of Cumbrian cheeses is accompanied with red onion marmalade. Food and drink can be served in the garden, where the panorama of farms, fells and fields makes a relaxing vista.

Open all wk (all day Etr-Oct) Closed 1wk Jan **Food** Lunch all wk 12-2 Dinner Mon-Sat 6-9, Sun & BH 6-8 (Mon-Thu Oct-Apr) Av main course £12.95 ⊕ FREE HOUSE ◀ Barngates Tag Lag & Cat Nap, Hawkshead Bitter & Brodie's Prime ♂ Westons Wyld Wood Organic Vintage, Country Perry. ▾ 10 **Facilities** Non-diners area ✿ (Bar Garden) ♦ Children's portions Garden 〒 Parking WiFi 🚌 (notice required)

PICK OF THE PUBS

The Black Swan ★★★★★ INN

RAVENSTONEDALE Map 18 NY70

tel: 015396 23204
CA17 4NG
email: enquiries@blackswanhotel.com
web: www.blackswanhotel.com
dir: *M6 junct 38, A685 E towards Brough; or A66 onto A685 at Kirkby Stephen towards M6*

One of Lakeland's best family-run residential inns

In a pretty conservation village, stands this handsome, multi-gabled Victorian proudly run by enterprising owners Alan and Louise Dinnes. The building has been refurbished to its former glory, and has friendly bars and a lounge warmed by an open fire. In its tranquil riverside gardens below Wild Boar Fell and the headwaters of the River Eden you might spot a red squirrel or two. An acclaimed real ale line-up features regulars from the Black Sheep brewery and guests from Dent, Hawkshead, Hesket Newmarket and Tirril microbreweries. Meals may be eaten in both bar areas, the lounge or in either of the two beautifully restored and decorated restaurants. As with the beers, reliance on local produce is key, which is evident in the names of some of the dishes - warm smoked Penrith pepperpot sausage with tomato, basil and white bean cassoulet; and Brougham Hall smoked tuna with lime and dill potato salad, sesame seed-buttered fine

beans, both starters - for example. Main course favourites include chicken, haggis and cured bacon pie; seared medallions of monkfish with pea purée, and crayfish and Chardonnay cream sauce; and fresh egg spaghetti with Galloway beef bolognese. A children's option is Cumberland sausage with chips and peas. On a memorable day in 2008 HRH Prince Charles opened the Black Swan's on-site village store where essential groceries, stationery and locally-made gifts, crafts and organic soaps and toiletries - as used in the guest rooms - are on sale. A beer festival is held in the garden in the summer. In such a lovely area of the country it is certainly worth considering stopping over in one of the inn's individually designed bedrooms.

Open all day all wk 8am-1am **Food** all day from 8am Dinner all wk 6-9 Av main course £12 Set menu available ⊕ FREE HOUSE ◼ Black Sheep Ale & Best Bitter, John Smith's Cask, Guinness, plus rotating local guest ales Ō Thatchers. ♀ **Facilities** Non-diners area ✤ (Bar Garden) ♦♦ Children's menu Children's portions Play area Garden ⊓ Beer festival Parking 🚌 (notice required) WiFi **Rooms** 15

PENRITH
Map 18 NY53

Cross Keys Inn

tel: 01768 865588 **Carleton Village CA11 8TP**
email: crosskeys@kyloes.co.uk
dir: *From A66 in Penrith take A686 to Carleton Village, inn on right*

Lovely views and traditional food

This much-refurbished old drovers' and coaching inn at the edge of Penrith offers sweeping views to the nearby North Pennines from the upstairs restaurant where timeless, traditional pub meals are the order of the day; Scottish wholetail battered scampi or Cumberland lamb hotpot for example. Kyloes Grill here is particularly well thought of, with only Cumbrian meats used. Beers crafted in nearby Broughton Hall by Tirril Brewery draw an appreciative local clientele, warming their toes by the ferocious log-burner or laying a few tiles on the domino tables.

Open all wk Mon-Fri 12-2.30 5-12 (Sat-Sun all day) **Food** Lunch all wk 12-2.30 Dinner Mon-Thu 6-9, Fri-Sat 5.30-9, Sun 6-8.30 ⊕ FREE HOUSE ◀ Tirril 1823, Guest ale. ♥ 10 **Facilities** Non-diners area ❧ (Bar Garden) ♦♦ Children's menu Children's portions Garden ⊨ Parking WiFi ⊟ (notice required)

RAVENSTONEDALE
Map 18 NY70

The Black Swan ★★★★ INN `PICK OF THE PUBS`

See Pick of the Pubs on opposite page

The Fat Lamb Country Inn ★★★★ INN `PICK OF THE PUBS`

tel: 015396 23242 **Crossbank CA17 4LL**
email: enquiries@fatlamb.co.uk **web:** www.fatlamb.co.uk
dir: *On A683 between Sedbergh & Kirkby Stephen*

Old fashioned hospitality and idyllic countryside

High above the green meadows of Ravenstonedale in the furthest corner of old Westmorland, this 350-year-old stone coaching inn has its own nature reserve – seven acres of open water and wetlands surrounded by flower-rich meadows. From the Fat Lamb's gardens, your gaze will fall on some of England's most precious and remote countryside, so it's no surprise that ramblers and country-lovers call in to quaff pints of Black Sheep and natter with locals by the open fire. Snacks and meals are served both in the traditional Yorkshire bar, and in the relaxed restaurant decorated with old prints and plates. Start with salmon three ways, or a field mushroom baked with crumbled Blacksticks Blue cheese. Classics include air-dried gammon loin with fried duck egg, pineapple relish and chunky chips. Alternatively, check out the day's specials and five-course set menu – all are prepared in the kitchen using the freshest local ingredients.

Open all day all wk **Food** Lunch Mon-Fri 12-2, Sat-Sun 12-6 Dinner all wk 6-9 Set menu available Restaurant menu available all wk ⊕ FREE HOUSE ◀ Black Sheep Best Bitter Ŏ Westons Stowford Press. **Facilities** Non-diners area ❧ (Bar Garden) ♦♦ Children's menu Children's portions Play area Garden ⊨ Parking WiFi ⊟ (notice required) **Rooms** 12

The King's Head

tel: 015396 23050 **CA17 4NH**
email: enquiries@kings-head.com
dir: *M6 junct 38, A685 towards Kirkby Stephen. Approx 7m, right to Ravenstonedale. Pub 200yds on right*

Set in beautiful rolling Cumbrian countryside

It's hard to believe that this old whitewashed pub was, at one time, closed for three years. There are real fires in the restaurant, where a three-course lunch or evening meal might be 'Taste of the Lakes' smoked haddock; venison and cranberry pie, with braised cabbage and chips; and home-made warm treacle tart with vanilla ice cream. Vegetarians will find dishes such as beetroot risotto, and potato and smoked cheese suet pudding. Three regularly-changing real ales and eight wines by the glass are served in the open-plan bar. Cyclists will appreciate the lock-up facility for their bikes.

Open all day all wk Closed 25 Dec **Food** Lunch all wk 12-6 Dinner all wk 6-9 Av main course £13 ⊕ FREE HOUSE ◀ 3 Guest ales regularly changing. ♥ 8 **Facilities** Non-diners area ❧ (Bar Garden) ♦♦ Children's menu Children's portions Garden ⊨ Parking WiFi ⊟ (notice required)

SANTON BRIDGE
Map 18 NY10

Bridge Inn

tel: 019467 26221 **CA19 1UX**
email: info@santonbridgeinn.com
dir: *From A595 at Gosforth follow Eskdale & Wasdale sign. Through Santon to inn on left. Or inn signed from A595 S of Holmkirk*

A "reet good welcome" awaits visitors to this country inn

The Lake District was formed, not by ice or volcanic action, but by large moles and eels. Actually, that's a lie, one of the many told in this comfortable old inn at the annual World's Biggest Liar competition, held every November. No doubt pints of Jennings Sneck Lifter and Cocker Hoop help to inspire such outrageous fibbing. Main courses include home-made steak and kidney pie; deep-fried haddock in Cocker Hoop beer batter; griddled gammon steak; and Kenyan Coast msetto (aubergine moussaka, mozzarella cheese and naan bread). The inn is licensed for civil marriages, when, hopefully, "I do" is not a lie!

Open all day all wk **Food** Lunch all wk 12-2.30 Dinner all wk 5.30-9 Av main course £10 ⊕ JENNINGS ◀ Cumberland Ale, Sneck Lifter & Cocker Hoop. ♥ 10 **Facilities** Non-diners area ❧ (Bar Outside area) ♦♦ Children's menu Children's portions Family room Outside area ⊨ Parking WiFi ⊟ (notice required)

SATTERTHWAITE
Map 18 SD39

NEW The Eagles Head

tel: 01229 860237 **LA12 8LN**
email: theeagleshead@gmail.com
dir: *Phone for detailed directions*

Traditional food and local beers in family-run Lake District pub

More than 400 years old, The Eagles Head occupies a lovely spot in the tiny village of Satterthwaite in the Grizedale Forest. A traditional, family-run Cumbrian inn with a crackling log fire in winter and pretty beer garden for sunnier days, the pub has a good reputation for serving tip-top quality beers from local microbreweries such as Hawkshead and Barngates. Local meat and vegetables, as well as fish from the east coast appear in straightforward, enjoyable dishes. Whole Lakeland trout with new potatoes and salad; and Cumberland sausage, mash and onion gravy are typical main courses.

Open all day all wk **Food** Lunch 12-3 Dinner 6-9 ⊕ FREE HOUSE ◀ Hawkshead Bitter & Red, Cumbrian Legendary Ales Loweswater Gold, Barngates Cracker Ale Ŏ Cowmire Hall. **Facilities** Non-diners area ❧ (Bar Restaurant Garden) ♦♦ Children's menu Children's portions Garden ⊨ Beer festival Parking WiFi ⊟ (notice required)

Follow us on Facebook
www.facebook.com/TheAAUK

Newfield Inn

tel: 01229 716208 **LA20 6ED**
dir: *From Broughton-in-Furness take A595 signed Whitehaven & Workington. Right signed Ulpha. Through Ulpha to Seathwaite, 6m (NB it is advisable not to use Sat Nav)*

Classic walkers' pub with view-filled garden

Tucked away in the peaceful Duddon Valley, Wordsworth's favourite, is Paul Batten's 16th-century cottage-style pub. Hugely popular with walkers and climbers, the slate-floored bar regularly throngs with parched outdoor types quaffing pints of local ales. Served all day, food is hearty and traditional and uses local farm meats; the choice ranges from fresh rolls, salads and lunchtime snacks like double egg and chips, to beef lasagne, grilled T-bone steak, and pear and chocolate crumble. Retreat to the garden in summer and savour cracking southern fells views, or come for the beer festival in October.

Open all day all wk **Food** Lunch all wk 12-9 Dinner all wk 12-9 Av main course £10 ⊕ FREE HOUSE ◀ Cumberland Corby Ale, Jennings Cumberland Ale, Jennings Sneck Lifter, Barngates Cat Nap. ♟ 8 **Facilities** Non-diners area ✿ (Bar Garden) ♦ Children's portions Play area Garden 🎪 Beer festival Parking 🚐

The Strickland Arms

tel: 015395 61010 **LA8 8DZ**
email: thestricklandarms@yahoo.co.uk
dir: *From Kendal A591 S. At Brettargh Holt junct left, at rdbt 3rd exit onto A590 (dual carriageway) signed Barrow. Follow brown signs for Sizergh Castle. Into right lane, turn right across dual carriageway. Pub on left*

Popular spot after exploring the southern lakes

Beside the lane leading to the National Trust's Sizergh Castle and just a stride from paths alongside the lively River Kent, this slightly severe-looking building (also NT-owned) slumbers amidst low hills above the Lyth Valley at the southern fringe of the Lake District National Park. The essentially open-plan interior is contemporary-Edwardian, with high ceilings, flagstoned floors, grand fires and Farrow & Ball finish to the walls, creating an instantly welcoming atmosphere. Expect a menu of good traditional dishes such as chicken liver pâté; seafood risotto; burgers; steaks; steak and ale pie; and vegetable hotpot.

Open all day all wk Closed 25 Dec **Food** Lunch Mon-Fri 12-2, Sat-Sun all day Dinner Mon-Sat 6-9, Sat-Sun all day ⊕ FREE HOUSE ◀ Guest ales ♂ Kingstone Press. ♟ 9 **Facilities** Non-diners area ✿ (Bar Restaurant Garden) ♦ Children's menu Children's portions Garden 🎪 Beer festival Parking WiFi 🚐

The Kings Arms ★★★★ INN

tel: 017683 62944 **CA10 1SB**
email: enquiries@kingsarmstemplesowerby.co.uk
web: www.kingsarmstemplesowerby.co.uk
dir: *M6 junct 40, E on A66 to Temple Sowerby. Inn in town centre*

Hostelry at the heart of the village

This 400-year-old coaching inn, just a few miles from Penrith, was where William Wordsworth and Samuel Coleridge, in 1799, set off for their exploration of the Lake District. The kitchen serves a mix of old pub-grub favourites, including chicken liver parfait; whitebait with bread and butter; and steak and ale pie; plus modern dishes such as bacon and Stilton rarebit; slow roasted pork belly; and mushroom Stroganoff. There is a good choice of vegetarian choice, a children's menu and the desserts are home made.

Open all wk 10-3 6-11 ⊕ FREE HOUSE ◀ Black Sheep, Guest ales ♂ Westons Stowford Press. **Facilities** ✿ (Bar Garden) ♦ Children's menu Children's portions Garden Parking WiFi **Rooms** 8

Queen's Head ★★★★ INN   `PICK OF THE PUBS`

tel: 015394 32174 **Townhead LA23 1PW**
email: reservations@queensheadtroutbeck.co.uk **web:** www.queensheadtroutbeck.co.uk
dir: *M6 junct 36, A590, A591 towards Windermere, right at mini rdbt onto A592 signed Penrith/Ullswater. Pub 2m on left*

Old Lakeland inn with a reputation for international cooking

This 17th-century inn stands in the valley of Troutbeck; bordered by impressive fells and criss-crossed by footpaths, it's a real magnet for ramblers. With nooks and crannies, a log fire throughout the year, and low beams stuffed with old pennies by farmers on their way home from market, this smart coaching inn overflows with traditional ambience; even the bar is made from a four-poster bed which once saw service in Appleby Castle. Check out the carved panelling below bar counter level while ordering a pint of Robinsons Double Hop. The extensive menu is renowned for its international flavours. Typical of first courses is the pan-roasted clam, bacon and chive risotto topped with rocket, crispy pancetta and poached duck egg, followed by a main course of chicken breast stuffed with smoked brie, wrapped in smoked bacon and served with truffle potato and mushroom and tarragon sauce.

Open all day all wk **Food** Lunch all wk 12-6 Dinner Sun-Thu 6-9, Fri-Sat 6-10 Av main course £13.95 ⊕ ROBINSONS ◀ Dizzy Blonde, Old Tom & Double Hop, Hartleys Cumbria Way & XB. ♟ 12 **Facilities** Non-diners area ✿ (Bar Restaurant Outside area) ♦ Children's menu Children's portions Outside area 🎪 Parking WiFi 🚐 **Rooms** 15

Farmers Arms Hotel

tel: 01229 584469 **Market Place LA12 7BA**
email: roger@thefarmers-ulverston.co.uk
dir: *In town centre*

A warm welcome and crowd-pleasing pub grub

Perhaps the oldest inn in the Lake District, there's a hospitable welcome here at the Farmers Arms, whether in the traditionally decorated restaurant with its oak beams and impressive views of the Crake Valley or in the 14th-century stable bar complete with a log fire and original slate floors. The wide-ranging menus include basket meals like quarter chicken with chips; sautéed mushrooms and creamy Stilton hot baguette; a variety of steaks plus lots of crowd-pleasers such as ploughman's lunch and locally sourced Cumberland sausage. Local ales include Hawkshead Bitter and there's both beer and cider festivals annually.

Open all day all wk **Food** Lunch all wk 9-3 Dinner all wk 6-9 ⊕ FREE HOUSE ◀ Hawkshead Bitter, John Smith's, Courage Directors, Yates ♂ Symonds. ♟ 12 **Facilities** Non-diners area ♦ Children's menu Children's portions Garden 🎪 Beer festival Cider festival WiFi 🚐 (notice required)

Old Farmhouse

tel: 01229 480324 **Priory Rd LA12 9HR**
email: oldfarmhouse@hotmail.co.uk
dir: *From A590 in Ulverston take A5087 signed Bardsea. Pub on right*

Community focused pub in a converted barn

Located just south of the town and a short distance from Morecambe Bay, the Old Farmhouse is a busy pub housed within a beautifully converted barn. Its very popular restaurant in the main barn area offers an extensive traditional menu -

choose a classic such as their celebrated Cumberland pie, or pork cutlets with mushroom and pancetta sauce from the grill section. Specials may include lamb rump with redcurrant jus, and leave room for the apple and cinnamon crumble. Local Cumbrian ales, a sun-trap courtyard garden, a big screen for live sports and a function room for private hire complete the picture.

Open all day all wk **Food** Lunch all wk 12-9 Dinner all wk 12-9 Set menu available Restaurant menu available all wk ⊕ FREE HOUSE ◑ Ulverston Harvest Moon, Lancaster Blonde, Cumberland, Sharp's Doom Bar, Copper Dragon. ⁑ 9 **Facilities** Non-diners area ❧ (Bar Garden Outside area) ◑ Children's menu Children's portions Garden Outside area ⌂ Parking WiFi ⎚

The Stan Laurel Inn

tel: 01229 582814 **31 The Ellers LA12 OAB**
email: thestanlaurel@aol.com
dir: M6 junct 36, A590 to Ulverston. Straight on at Booths rdbt, left at 2nd rdbt in The Ellers, pub on left after Ford garage

Local ales and hearty food

When the old market town of Ulverston's most famous son – the comic actor Stan Laurel – was born in 1890, this town-centre pub was still a farmhouse with two cottages surrounded by fields and orchards. Owners Trudi and Paul Dewar serve a selection of locally brewed real ales and a full menu of traditional pub food plus a specials board. Take your pick from starters such as pork, chicken and apricot terrine; Greek salad; or battered black pudding. Among tasty mains are steak and ale pie; vegetable and Stilton crumble; and a selection from the grill.

Open Mon 7pm-11pm Tue-Thu 12-2.30 6-11 Fri-Sat 12-2.30 6-12 Sun 12-11.30 Closed Mon L **Food** Lunch Tue-Sat 12-2, Sun 12-8 Dinner Tue-Sat 6-9, Sun 12-8 ⊕ FREE HOUSE ◑ Thwaites Original, Ulverston, Barngates, Salamander. **Facilities** Non-diners area ❧ (Bar Outside area) ◑ Children's menu Children's portions Outside area ⌂ Parking WiFi

WASDALE HEAD   Map 18 NY10

Wasdale Head Inn ★★★★ INN

tel: 019467 26229 **CA20 1EX**
email: reception@wasdale.com **web:** www.wasdale.com
dir: From A595 follow Wasdale signs. Inn at head of valley

Welcoming inn surrounded by record breakers

Dramatically situated at the foot of England's highest mountain, adjacent to England's smallest church and not far from the deepest lake, this Victorian inn is reputedly the birthplace of British climbing – photographs decorating the oak-panelled walls reflect the passion for this activity. It is also allegedly the home of the World's Biggest Liar, but hopefully that doesn't extend to the menu. Expect local ales and hearty food such as Wasdale Particular (pea and Cumberland ham soup); followed by Wasdale lamb cobbler; or Cumberland sausage. The Wasdale Show on the 2nd Saturday in October is a great reason to hang up the climbing boots for a day and maybe stay over in one of the comfortable bedrooms.

Open all day all wk **Food** Lunch all wk 12-8.30 Dinner all wk 12-8.30 Av main course £10.50 Restaurant menu available Wed-Sun ⊕ FREE HOUSE ◑ Cumbrian Legendary Ales Loweswater Gold & Esthwaite Bitter, Jennings, Hesket Newmarket High Pike ⓞ Westons. **Facilities** Non-diners area ❧ (Bar Restaurant Garden) ◑ Children's menu Children's portions Garden ⌂ Beer festival Parking **Rooms** 20

WINDERMERE   Map 18 SD49

Eagle & Child Inn

tel: 01539 821320 **Kendal Rd, Staveley LA8 9LP**
email: info@eaglechildinn.co.uk
dir: M6 junct 36, A590 towards Kendal then A591 towards Windermere. Staveley approx 2m

Free house with a riverside beer garden

Surrounded by miles of excellent walking, cycling and fishing country in a quiet village, this friendly inn shares the same name with several pubs in Britain, which refers to a legend of a baby found in an eagle's nest during the time of King Alfred. The rivers Kent and Gowan meet at the pub's gardens with its picnic tables for outdoor eating and local-ale drinking. Dishes include ingredients from village suppliers, such as slow-roasted lamb shank, Cumberland sausage or chicken breast wrapped in smoked bacon. Interesting vegetarian choices might be Malaysian vegetable curry or vegetable and chickpea casserole.

Open all day all wk **Food** Lunch Mon-Fri 12-2.30, Sat-Sun 12-9 Dinner Mon-Fri 6-9, Sat-Sun 12-9 ⊕ FREE HOUSE ◑ Hawkshead Bitter, Yates Best Bitter, Tirril, Coniston, Dent, Jennings Cumberland ⓞ Westons, Thatchers Gold, Guest cider. ⁑ 10 **Facilities** Non-diners area ❧ (Bar Restaurant Garden) ◑ Children's menu Children's portions Garden ⌂ Parking WiFi ⎚

WINSTER   Map 18 SD49

The Brown Horse Inn

tel: 015394 43443 **LA23 3NR**
email: steve@thebrownhorseinn.co.uk
dir: On A5074 between Bowness-on-Windermere & A590 (Kendal to Barrow-in-Furness road)

An inn of many talents

The beautiful and tranquil Winster Valley is a perfect location for this 1850s inn full of original features. Despite all the time-worn charm, the decor has a subtly modern edge. The inn is virtually self-sufficient: vegetables and free-range meat come from the owners' surrounding land, and ales are brewed on site. The innovative cooking is a contemporary take on traditional fare and dinner could see a starter of lobster custard, sea salt croûte, pistachio and parmesan; mains range from home-made pie of the week to mixed grill of lamb with fondant potatoes and minted hollandaise.

Open all day all wk **Food** Lunch Mon-Fri 12-2, Sat-Sun, BHs & School Hols 12-4 Dinner all wk 6-9 ⊕ FREE HOUSE ◑ Winster Valley Best Bitter, Old School, Hurdler, Chaser ⓞ Somersby. ⁑ 12 **Facilities** Non-diners area ❧ (Bar Outside area) ◑ Children's menu Children's portions Outside area ⌂ Parking WiFi ⎚ (notice required)

WORKINGTON
Map 18 NY02

The Old Ginn House

tel: 01900 64616 **Great Clifton CA14 1TS**
email: enquiries@oldginnhouse.co.uk
dir: *Just off A66, 3m from Workington & 4m from Cockermouth*

Converted farm building offering good food

When this was a farm, ginning was the process by which horses were used to turn a grindstone that crushed grain. It took place in the rounded area known today as the Ginn Room and which is now the main bar, serving local ales. The dining areas, all butter yellow, bright check curtains and terracotta tiles, rather bring the Mediterranean to mind, although the extensive menu and specials are both cosmopolitan and traditional. The pub has a good reputation for steaks but others options are cod loin with streaky bacon and smoked cheese sauce; whole shoulder of lamb marinated in mint, honey and garlic; pan-fried sea bass fillet with cracked black pepper and lemon butter. A good vegetarian choice is available.

Open all day all wk Closed 24-26 Dec, 1 Jan **Food** Lunch all wk 12-2 Dinner all wk 6-9.30 ⊕ FREE HOUSE ◀ John Smith's, Coniston Bluebird Bitter, Local Guest ales. **Facilities** Non-diners area ◀◀ Children's menu Children's portions Garden ⊟ Parking 🚐 (notice required)

YANWATH
Map 18 NY52

The Yanwath Gate Inn
PICK OF THE PUBS

tel: 01768 862386 **CA10 2LF**
email: enquiries@yanwathgate.com
dir: *Phone for detailed directions*

Known for its Cumbrian craft beers and good food

Well placed for excursions to the shores of Ullswater or the great, scalloped fells of the high Pennines, this one-time tollgate house dates from 1683, evolving into a pub several centuries later. Its favoured location between the fells and lakes, in an area of country estates and the rich pasturelands of the Eden Valley, holds the promise of great food and drink. Long-established proprietor Matt Edwards doesn't fail to impress on this score. Some of the best Cumbrian microbrewery beers from the likes of Yates and Barngates draw guests into the country-style interior with lots of beams, old pine and roaring winter log fire. Lunch and evening menus vary, and content depends on seasonal or specialist availability. A Gate Inn platter of fish, game and cheese gives a great flavour of the area, whilst more heavyweight mains can cover hogget steak with three-bean ragout and onion mash, or lemon and aubergine risotto with thyme crème fraîche. For lighter eaters there's an impressive tapas menu.

Open all day all wk **Food** Lunch all wk 12-2.30 Dinner all wk 6-9 ⊕ FREE HOUSE ◀ Tirril, Barngates, Yates ♻ Westons Old Rosie. ♀ 12 **Facilities** Non-diners area ♣ (Bar Garden) ◀◀ Children's menu Garden ⊟ Parking WiFi

DERBYSHIRE

ASHOVER
Map 16 SK36

The Old Poets Corner

tel: 01246 590888 **Butts Rd S45 0EW**
email: enquiries@oldpoets.co.uk
dir: *From Matlock take A632 signed Chesterfield. Right onto B6036 to Ashover*

Thriving pub with ten real ales

It's no wonder that ale and cider aficionados flock to this traditional village local; it dispenses eight ciders, and ten cask ales including choices from the Ashover Brewery behind the pub. The March and October beer festivals see these numbers multiply. There's live music here twice a week, quizzes, special events and Sunday night curries. Hearty home-cooked pub dishes range from creamy garlic mushrooms on sourdough bread to braised liver and onions in a rich gravy made with the pub's own Coffin Lane Stout. Walk it off in the scenic Derbyshire countryside.

Open all day all wk **Food** Lunch Mon-Fri 12-2, Sat-Sun 12-3 Dinner Mon-Thu 6.30-9, Fri-Sat 6-9.30, Sun 7-9 ⊕ FREE HOUSE ◀ Ashover, Oakham, Guest ales ♻ Broadoak Perry & Moonshine, Westons Old Rosie. **Facilities** Non-diners area ♣ (Bar Restaurant Outside area) ◀◀ Family room Outside area ⊟ Beer festival Parking WiFi 🚐 (notice required)

BAKEWELL
Map 16 SK26

The Monsal Head Hotel
PICK OF THE PUBS

tel: 01629 640250 **Monsal Head DE45 1NL**
email: enquiries@monsalhead.com
dir: *A6 from Bakewell towards Buxton. 1.5m to Ashford. Follow Monsal Head signs, B6465 for 1m*

Extensive range of local ales on draught

Only a few minutes from Chatsworth House and the famous railway viaduct at Monsal Head, the hotel's Stables bar reflects its earlier role as the home of railway horses collecting passengers from Monsal Dale station. It has a rustic ambience with an original flagstone floor, seating in horse stalls and a log fire – the perfect place to enjoy a range of cask ales from microbreweries such as Tollgate and Kelham Island. The Longstone restaurant is spacious and airy with large windows to appreciate the views, again with an open fire in the colder weather. Although the menu has influences from around the world, it demonstrates an extensive use of local produce. Breakfasts and morning coffee are available everyday, and the same menu is offered in the bar, restaurant and the large outdoor seating area.

Open all day all wk 8am-mdnt **Food** Lunch Mon-Sat 12-9.30, Sun 12-9 Dinner Mon-Sat 12-9.30, Sun 12-9 Av main course £13 Restaurant menu available all wk ⊕ FREE HOUSE ◀ Wincle, Pennine Brewery Co, Tollgate Brewery, Welbeck Abbey Brewery, Kelham Island ♻ Addlestones. ♀ 17 **Facilities** Non-diners area ♣ (Bar Garden Outside area) ◀◀ Children's menu Children's portions Garden Outside area ⊟ Beer festival Parking 🚐 (notice required)

BAMFORD
Map 16 SK28

Yorkshire Bridge Inn
PICK OF THE PUBS

See Pick of the Pubs on page 122 and advert below

BARROW UPON TRENT
Map 11 SK32

Ragley Boat Stop

tel: 01332 703919 **Deepdale Ln, Off Sinfin Ln DE73 1HH**
email: pippa@king-henrys-taverns.co.uk
dir: *Phone for detailed directions*

Canalside pub ideal for watching the world go by

This timbered and whitewashed free house features a lovely garden sloping down to the Trent and Mersey Canal. A huge balcony overlooking the canal and the grassy garden complete with picnic benches are both great spots for a quiet drink. The smart, spacious interior is cool and contemporary with muted colours, stripped wood and plenty of comfy sofas. The menu of freshly prepared dishes has choices to suit every appetite. Beef in all its forms is a major attraction; alternatively international flavours abound in dishes such as vegetable fajitas, chicken korma, swordfish steak, and a Cajun chicken and ribs combo.

Open all day all wk 11.30-11 **Food** Lunch all wk 12-10 Dinner all wk 12-10 ⊕ FREE HOUSE/KING HENRY'S TAVERNS ▄ Greene King IPA, Marston's Pedigree, Guinness. ₹ 16 **Facilities** Non-diners area ♦ Children's menu Children's portions Garden Parking ▄▄

BEELEY
Map 16 SK26

The Devonshire Arms at Beeley ★★★★ INN ⊛⊛
PICK OF THE PUBS

tel: 01629 733259 **Devonshire Square DE4 2NR**
email: res@devonshirehotels.co.uk web: www.devonshirebeeley.co.uk
dir: *B6012 towards Matlock, pass Chatsworth House. After 1.5m turn left, 2nd entrance to Beeley*

Up-to-the-minute inn with a rich history

This handsome 18th-century village inn is surrounded by classic Peak District scenery and stands on the Chatsworth Estate. It became a thriving coaching inn; Charles Dickens was a frequent visitor; and it is rumoured that King Edward VII often met his mistress Alice Keppel here. The comfortably civilised and neatly furnished interior comprises three attractive beamed rooms, with flagstone floors, roaring log fires, antique settles and farmhouse tables; the rustic taproom is perfect for walkers with muddy boots. In contrast, the brasserie dining room is modern, bright and colourful, with stripey chairs and bold artwork. Come for beers brewed at Chatsworth's brewery and some sublime modern British food (two AA Rosettes) cooked by chef-patron Alan Hill. Using estate-reared and -grown produce, dishes include classics like beer-battered haddock and chips; beef cobbler; tempura skate wing with lobster sauce; and Chatsworth venison spit-roasted over the fire. There are wonderful walks from the front door.

Open all day all wk **Food** Lunch all wk 12-3 Dinner all wk 6-9.30 Av main course £16 ⊕ FREE HOUSE/DEVONSHIRE HOTELS & RESTAURANTS ▄ Peak Chatsworth Gold, Thornbridge Jaipur, Theakston Old Peculier ♂ Aspall. ₹ 10 **Facilities** Non-diners area ♦ Children's menu Children's portions Garden Parking WiFi **Rooms** 8

BIRCHOVER
Map 16 SK26

The Druid Inn
PICK OF THE PUBS

tel: 01629 653836 **Main St DE4 2BL**
email: info@druidinnbirchover.co.uk
dir: *From A6 between Matlock & Bakewell take B5056 signed Ashbourne. In approx 2m, left to Birchover*

New owners at this ancient pub

This pub, open for business since 1607, has changed hands. Utilising plenty of Peak District produce, there's traditional home-made dishes on the menu, all of which can be enjoyed in one of the four dining areas. Lunch and maybe a pint of Abbeydale Absolution in the bar and snug; a more formal meal in the upper or lower restaurant; or outside on the terrace, from where you can survey the surrounding countryside. The menu includes starters such as chicken liver pâté; and grilled sardines; followed by trio of lamb, pommes Anna and cabbage; beer-battered haddock, chips and mushy peas; and grilled chicken breast with mushroom casserole. To round things off there could be a sharing plate of very tempting desserts. Children and dogs are welcome too.

Open all day all wk noon-late **Food** Lunch Mon-Sat 12-9, Sun 12-8 Dinner Mon-Sat 12-9, Sun 12-8 ⊕ FREE HOUSE ▄ Abbeydale Absolution, Guest ales ♂ Westons Stowford Press. ₹ 10 **Facilities** Non-diners area ♣ (Bar Garden) ♦ Children's menu Children's portions Family room Garden Parking ▄▄ (notice required)

PICK OF THE PUBS

The Yorkshire Bridge Inn

BAMFORD Map 16 SK28

tel: 01433 651361
Ashopton Rd S33 0AZ
email: info@yorkshire-bridge.co.uk
web: www.yorkshire-bridge.co.uk
dir: *From Sheffield A57 towards Glossop,
left onto A6013, pub 1m on right*

In the heart of wonderful Peak District walking country

Named after the old packhorse bridge over the River Derwent, this early 19th-century free house is only a short distance away from the Ladybower Reservoir. Between 1935 and 1943, when it was created, two local villages were drowned and during periods of drought it's possible to see the remains of one of them. It was in 1943 that the RAF's 617 Squadron, known as 'The Dambusters', used Ladybower and two other nearby reservoirs for testing Barnes Wallis's famous bouncing bombs, later to destroy two important German dams. Back inside, views from the beamed and chintz-curtained bars take in the peak of Whin Hill, making it a jolly good spot for enjoying a pint of the unique Bombs Gone specially brewed for the inn at the Bradfield Brewery, and good-quality pub food made with fresh local produce. Sandwiches are all freshly prepared, with fillings from home-baked ham to hot tuna melt. Main meal starters include Thai cod and prawn fishcakes,

and a sharing platter in which nachos with melted cheese, jalapeño peppers and baked spare ribs marinated in barbecue sauce are just a pointer to what will arrive on the plate. Next could come slow-roasted Derbyshire belly pork; roast chicken breast with Yorkshire pudding and sausage; freshly battered catch of the day; or one of the various salad platters. If you've walked to one of the reservoirs and back, look to the grill for a calorie replacing T-bone, sirloin or gammon steak, cooked to your liking without demur from a chef who doesn't insist on doing it his way. Chocolate mousse, and daily-changing hot sponges finish a meal off well. A beer and cider festival is held in mid-May. Nearby attractions include Chatsworth, Haddon Hall, Buxton and Bakewell.

Open all day all wk **Food** Lunch Mon-Sat 12-2, Sun 12-8.30 Dinner Mon-Thu 6-9, Fri-Sat 6-9.30, Sun 12-8.30 Av main course £10.95 ⊕ FREE HOUSE ◀ Peak Ales Bakewell Best Bitter, Bradfield Farmers Blonde, Farmers Bitter & Bombs Gone, Abbeydale Moonshine Ö Thatchers. ♟ 11 **Facilities** Non-diners area ♦♦ Children's menu & portions Garden ⋒ Beer festival Cider festival Parking 🚐 (notice required) WiFi

BIRCHOVER *continued*

Red Lion Inn   PICK OF THE PUBS

tel: 01629 650363 **Main St DE4 2BN**
email: red.lion@live.co.uk
dir: *5.5m from Matlock, off A6 onto B5056*

Good beer plus Sardinian dishes on the menu

Built in 1680, the Red Lion started life as a farmhouse and gained its first licence in 1722; its old well, now glass-covered, still remains in the taproom. Follow a walk to nearby Rowter Rocks, a gritstone summit affording stunning valley and woodland views, cosy up in the oak-beamed bar with its exposed stone walls, scrubbed oak tables, worn quarry-tiled floor, and welcoming atmosphere. Quaff a pint of locally brewed Nine Ladies or one of the other real ales on tap that change weekly, and refuel with a plate of home-cooked food prepared from predominantly local ingredients. Start with a Sardinian speciality from owner Matteo Frau's homeland, perhaps a selection of cured meats, cheese and olives, then follow with pork loin medallions with lemon, caper and sage butter, or field mushroom tart Tatin with Birchover Blue cheese. Don't miss the mid-July beer festival.

Open 12-2.30 6-11.30 (Sat & BH Mon 12-12 Sun 12-11) Closed Mon in winter ex BHs **Food** Lunch Mon-Fri 12-2.30, Sat 12-9, Sun-12-8 Dinner Mon-Fri 6-9, Sat 12-9, Sun-12-8 ⊕ FREE HOUSE ◄ Peak Swift Nick, Nine Ladies, Peakstones Rock, Buxton, Thornbridge, Ichinusa (Sardinian) ♻ Traditional Local ciders.
Facilities Non-diners area ♦♦ Children's portions Garden Beer festival Parking ⛟

■ **BONSALL**   **Map 16 SK25**

The Barley Mow

tel: 01629 825685 **The Dale DE4 2AY**
email: david.j.wragg@gmail.com
dir: *S from Matlock on A6 to Cromford. Right onto A5012 (Cromwell Hill). Right into Water Ln (A5012). Right in Clatterway towards Bonsall. Left at memorial into The Dale. Pub 400mtrs on right*

Good food, real ales and fast fowl

There are several reasons to visit this intimate, former lead miner's cottage: Bonsall is apparently Europe's UFO capital; the pub hosts the World Championship Hen Races; and landlords Colette and David display an unshakeable commitment to Peak District and other regional real ales, as their bank holiday beer festivals help to confirm. The simple menu is all about home-cooked pub grub, such as ham, egg and chips; scampi and chips; extra-mature rump steak; chicken curry; sausages and mash; beef chilli; and gammon steak.

Open 6-11 (Sat-Sun 12-11) Closed Mon (ex BHs) **Food** Lunch Sat-Sun 12-3 Dinner all wk 6-9 Av main course £8.95 ⊕ FREE HOUSE ◄ Thornbridge, Whim, Abbeydale, Blue Monkey ♻ Hecks, Westons Perry. ♈ 10 **Facilities** Non-diners area ♣ (Bar Restaurant Outside area) ♦♦ Children's menu Children's portions Outside area ⌂ Beer festival Cider festival Parking WiFi ⛟

■ **BRADWELL**   **Map 16 SK18**

NEW The Samuel Fox Country Inn ★★★★★ INN ◉◉

tel: 01433 621562 **Stretfield Rd S33 9JT**
email: enquiries@samuelfox.co.uk web: www.samuelfox.co.uk
dir: *M1 junct 29, A617 towards Chesterfield onto A623 (Chapel-en-le-Frith). B6049 to Bradwell. Pub on left*

Fine food and real ales in the Hope Valley

A country inn in the heart of the Peak District National Park close to the Pennine Way. It's named after the villager credited with inventing the steel-ribbed umbrella – hence the pub sign showing a fox sheltering beneath one. Owner and chef, James

Duckett, has the experience of working and running restaurants in several countries and it is he who ensures that there's a warm welcome and pleasant atmosphere for villagers and visitors alike. This is his first pub venture but it's no surprise that contemporary and cosmopolitan notes creep into the food, which otherwise is firmly based on fresh local produce. Expect the likes of spicy chickpea fritters; pan-fried cod fillet and chunky clam casserole; and roast pheasant with fondant potatoes. Farmers Blonde ale is brewed just down the road in Bradfield.

Open 12-3 6-11 Closed 2-29 Jan, Mon all year (Tue winter) **Food** Lunch Summer Wed-Sat 12-2.30, Sun 12-3.30. Winter Fri-Sat 12-2.30, Sun 12-3.30 Dinner Tue-Sat 6-9 Set menu available ⊕ FREE HOUSE ◄ Bradfield ♻ Thatchers Heritage. ♈ 14 **Facilities** Non-diners area ♦♦ Children's menu Children's portions Outside area ⌂ Parking WiFi **Rooms** 4

■ **BRASSINGTON**   **Map 16 SK25**

Ye Olde Gate Inn   PICK OF THE PUBS

tel: 01629 540448 **Well St DE4 4HJ**
email: info@oldgateinnbrassington.co.uk
dir: *2m from Carsington Water exit A5023 between Wirksworth & Ashbourne*

Cosy inn popular with locals and visitors alike

Sitting beside an old London to Manchester turnpike in the heart of Brassington, a hill village on the southern edge of the Peak District, this venerable inn dates back to 1616. Aged beams (allegedly salvaged from the wrecked Armada fleet), a black cast-iron log burner, an antique clock, charmingly worn quarry-tiled floors and a delightful mishmash of polished furniture give the inn plenty of character – as does the reputed ghost. Hand-pumped Jennings Cumberland takes pride of place behind the bar, alongside other Marston's beers and guest ales. As well as the specials the menu offers firm lunchtime favourites such as home-made steak and Guinness or chicken and ham pie; or a range of filled baguettes. In the evening you may find warm goats' cheese en croûte with pear and walnut salad; trio of White Peak sausages, mash and onion gravy; beer battered cod fillet with home-made chips and mushy peas; or pan-fried sea bass with herb and lemon sauce.

Open Tue eve-Sun Closed Mon (ex BHs), Tue L **Food** Lunch Wed-Sat 12-1.45, Sun 12.30-2.45 Dinner Tue-Sat 6.30-8.45 ⊕ MARSTON'S ◄ Pedigree, Jennings Cumberland Ale, Guest ales. **Facilities** Non-diners area ♣ (Bar Garden) ♦♦ Children's portions Family room Garden ⌂ Parking WiFi

---

■ **CASTLETON**   **Map 16 SK18**

The Peaks Hotel

tel: 01433 620247 **How Ln S33 8WJ**
dir: *On A6187 in centre of village*

Plenty on offer at this Peak District magnet

Here's where to aim for after climbing Lose Hill, or walking along the Hope Valley. Standing below Peveril Castle, this 17th-century, stone-built pub is a real magnet, seducing visitors with its leather armchairs, open log fires and locally brewed cask beers, real ciders and wines by the glass; alternative places to recover are the restaurant/coffee shop and raised sun terrace. Regional ingredients are used to good effect. Change of hands.

Open all day all wk **Food** Lunch Mon-Fri 12-3, Sat 12-8.30, Sun 12-4 Dinner Mon-Fri 5.30-8.30, Sat 12-8.30 Av main course £8.50 ⊕ PUNCH TAVERNS ◄ Kelham Island Easy Rider, Castle Rock Harvest Pale, Guest ales ♻ Westons Old Rosie & Stowford Press. ♈ 9 **Facilities** Non-diners area ♣ (Bar Garden) ♦♦ Children's menu Children's portions Garden ⌂ Beer festival Cider festival Parking WiFi ⛟ (notice required)

CASTLETON *continued*

Ye Olde Nags Head

tel: 01433 620248 **Cross St S33 8WH**
email: info@yeoldenagshead.co.uk
dir: *A625 from Sheffield, W through Hope Valley, through Hathersage & Hope. Pub on main road*

A warm welcome and crowd-pleasing food

Situated in the heart of the Peak District National Park, close to Chatsworth House and Haddon Hall, this traditional 17th-century coaching inn continues to welcome thirsty travellers. Miles of wonderful walks and country lanes favoured by cyclists bring visitors seeking a warm welcome and refreshment in the cosy bars warmed by open fires. The interior is a successful mix of contemporary and traditional, a theme also reflected in the menu: expect stone-baked pizzas, beef, ale and potato pie and The Nags mighty mixed grill. There's also a beer festival in the summer.

Open all day all wk **Food** Lunch all wk 12-9 Dinner all wk 12-9 ⊕ FREE HOUSE ◀ Timothy Taylor Landlord, Buxton Kinder Sunset, Kelham Island Riders on the Storm, Black Sheep, Sharp's Doom Bar, Bradfield Farmers Blonde, Guinness ⚬ Westons Old Rosie, Rosie's Pig, Family Reserve. **Facilities** Non-diners area ✿ (Bar) ⚬⚬ Children's menu Children's portions Beer festival Parking WiFi ▭ (notice required)

CHELMORTON	Map 16 SK16

The Church Inn ★★★★ INN

tel: 01298 85319 **SK17 9SL**
email: justinsatur@tiscali.co.uk **web:** www.thechurchinn.co.uk
dir: *From A515 or A6 take A5270 between Bakewell & Buxton. Chelmorton signed*

Superb food and ales down limestone lanes

A narrow no-through-road ends here in secluded Chelmorton amidst a remarkable landscape of tiny medieval walled fields and hidden, wildflower-rich deep limestone dales. The Church Inn, too, is tiny and hidden; take the time discover it to relish the memorable mix of regional and microbrewery beers, and an eclectic menu of pub favourites and home-crafted specials which may include pork Stroganoff; steak and kidney pie; or chickpea tagine. Bag a table in the patio garden to appreciate the exquisite location, opposite Derbyshire's highest church, or chinwag and warm up by the bar's roaring wood-burner.

Open all wk 12-3 6-12 (Fri-Sun 12-12) **Food** Lunch Mon-Thu 12-2.30, Fri-Sun 12-9 Dinner Mon-Thu 6-9, Fri-Sun 12-9 Av main course £9.95 ⊕ FREE HOUSE ◀ Marston's Burton Bitter & Pedigree, Adnams Southwold Bitter, Local ales. **Facilities** Non-diners area ✿ (Bar Garden) ⚬⚬ Children's menu Children's portions Garden ▭ WiFi ▭ (notice required) **Rooms** 4

CHESTERFIELD	Map 16 SK37

Red Lion Pub & Bistro ★★★★ HL ◉◉ PICK OF THE PUBS

tel: 01246 566142 **Darley Rd, Stone Edge S45 0LW**
email: dine@peakedgehotel.co.uk **web:** www.peakedgehotel.co.uk
dir: *Phone for detailed directions*

Innovative food close to good walking country

Dating back to 1788, the Red Lion has seen many changes but it has retained much of its character. Located on the edge of the beautiful Peak District National Park, the original wooden beams and stone walls are complemented by discreet lighting and comfy leather armchairs which add a contemporary edge. Striking black-and-white photographs decorate the walls, whilst local bands liven up the bar on Thursday evenings. Meals are served in the bar and bistro, or beneath

umbrellas in the large garden. Seasonal produce drives the menu and the chefs make everything, from sauces to the chips. Typical choices might start with crab lasagne, or carpaccio of beef with pickled vegetables, followed by stone bass, confit radishes, pak choi and chicken oysters; or poached and roasted rabbit, carrot variations and rabbit bolognese. Leave space for 'The Bakewell' with custard, or one of the home-made ice creams.

Open all day all wk **Food** Lunch Sun-Thu 12-9, Fri-Sat 12-9.30 Dinner Sun-Thu 12-9, Fri-Sat 12-9.30 ⊕ FREE HOUSE ◀ Guest ales. ☐ 12 **Facilities** Non-diners area ⚬⚬ Children's menu Children's portions Garden ▭ Parking WiFi ▭ (notice required) **Rooms** 27

CHINLEY	Map 16 SK08

Old Hall Inn PICK OF THE PUBS

See Pick of the Pubs on opposite page

NEW The Paper Mill Inn

tel: 01663 750529 **Whitehough SK23 6EJ**
email: info@papermillinn.co.uk
dir: *In village centre*

A cosy beer haven with frequently changing menus

Run by the same team as the adjacent Old Hall Inn, the pub is a veritable haven for beer and sport lovers. Flagstone floors, open fires and sporting events on TV combine to create a highly satisfactory ambience for customers enjoying real ales such as Thornbridge, or a world beer from the list of many; the choice peaks at festivals in February and September, with the latter also hosting draught ciders. Food ranges from simple tapas-style small plates, to traditional pub starters such as prawn cocktail or fried haloumi; and mains like Cumberland pork sausages with mash, or 30-day-hung Derbyshire steaks with all the trimmings.

Open all wk 5-11 (Sat-Sun 12-11) **Food** Contact pub for details Av main course £5 ⊕ FREE HOUSE ◀ Thornbridge, Marston's. **Facilities** Non-diners area ✿ (Bar Restaurant Outside area) ⚬⚬ Outside area ▭ Beer festival Cider festival Parking WiFi ▭

DALBURY	Map 10 SK23

The Black Cow ★★★★ INN ◉

tel: 01332 824297 **The Green DE6 5BE**
email: info@blackcow.co.uk **web:** www.theblackcow.co.uk
dir: *From A52 (W of Derby) take B5020 signed Mickleover. On left bend right signed Long Ln & Longford. Left signed Lees Dalbury. Pub on left in village. (NB if using Sat Nav follow directions not postcode)*

Recommended for its hospitality, accommodation and cuisine

Facing the village green and its iconic red telephone box, this free house champions real ales from county-based Dancing Duck, Mansfield and Mr Grundy's breweries. In the one AA-Rosette restaurant, award-winning head chef Jaswant Singh's seasonal menus might feature red Thai vegetable stir-fry; spicy meatballs in tomato parsley sauce with melted cheddar and pasta; and breaded scampi with home-made chips. Since this is Derbyshire, expect Bakewell tart with crème anglaise to make an appearance. Tastefully decorated guest rooms offer free WiFi. A small store/farm shop even sells ramblers' and cyclists' requirements.

Open all wk 12-3 5-close (Sat & Sun 12-close) **Food** Lunch Mon-Fri 12-2, Sat 12-9.30, Sun 12-4 Dinner Mon-Thu 6-9, Fri 6-9.30, Sat 12-9.30 ⊕ FREE HOUSE ◀ Guest real ales. ☐ 10 **Facilities** Non-diners area ⚬⚬ Children's menu Children's portions Play area Family room Garden Outside area ▭ Beer festival Parking WiFi ▭ (notice required) **Rooms** 6

PICK OF THE PUBS

Old Hall Inn

CHINLEY   Map 16 SK08

tel: 01663 750529
Whitehough SK23 6EJ
email: info@old-hall-inn.co.uk
web: www.old-hall-inn.co.uk
dir: *B5470 W from Chapel-en-le-Frith. Right into Whitehough Head Ln. 0.8m to inn*

An ideal stop for serious walkers

Prime Peak District walking country surrounds this family-run 16th-century pub attached to Whitehough Hall. It's within easy reach are the iconic landscape features of Kinder Scout, Mam Tor and Stanage Edge, popular with climbers and fell-walkers who head here for refreshment following their exertions. And no wonder. The drinks list is as long as your arm, with local breweries to the fore; beers from Kelham Island, Red Willow, Thornbridge and many more all have their enthusiasts, which makes for a lively atmosphere in the bar. Sheppy's from Somerset is among the real ciders and perries — a cider festival is held on the third weekend in September. All manner of bottled beers, particularly Belgian wheat, fruit and Trappist varieties, a remarkable choice of malts and gins and around 80 wines round off the excellent drinks range. Food service is busy too; the pub opens into the Minstrels' Gallery restaurant in the old manor house, where a short seasonal menu and daily specials offer freshly made 'small plates' of whitebait with home-made tartare sauce; fried haloumi with home-made houmous and sun-dried tomato pesto; and corned beef hashcake with a fried egg and rocket. Main courses range from Derbyshire steaks hung for one month, served with grilled tomato, mushroom, peas and home-made chips; to pan-roasted salmon steak with buttered mash, green beans and a lemon, dill and caper sauce. Half a dozen desserts, award-winning British cheeses, artisan teas and freshly roasted coffee complete the all-embracing menu.

Open all day all wk **Food** Lunch Mon-Sat 12-2, Sun 12-7.30 Dinner Mon-Thu 5-9, Fri-Sat 5-9.30, Sun 12-7.30 Av main course £10 Set menu available ⊕ FREE HOUSE ◀ Marston's, Thornbridge, Phoenix, Abbeydale, Storm, Kelham Island, Red Willow ♂ Thatchers, Sheppy's, Westons. ♟ 12 **Facilities** Non-diners area ♦♦ Children's menu Children's portions Garden ⋒ Beer festival Cider festival Parking WiFi 🚌

DERBY
Map 11 SK33

The Alexandra Hotel

tel: 01332 293993 **203 Siddals Rd DE1 2QE**
email: alexandrahotel@castlerockbrewery.co.uk
dir: *150yds from rail station*

Victorian railway hotel with an excellent choice of real ales

This small hotel was built in 1871 and is named after the Danish princess who married the Prince of Wales, later Edward VII. It was also known as the Midland coffee house after the Midland Railway company, one of Derby's major employers. It is noted for its real ales with between six and eight pumps on the go at any one time; real ciders, and bottled and draught continental beers complete the line-up at the bar. Simple food offerings include pies and filled rolls.

Open all day all wk 12-11 (Fri 12-12 Sat 11am-mdnt) **Food** Contact pub for details ⊕ CASTLE ROCK ◀ Harvest Pale ♂ Westons Old Rosie. **Facilities** Non-diners area ✿ (Bar Outside area) ♦ Outside area Parking WiFi

The Brunswick Inn

tel: 01332 290677 **1 Railway Ter DE1 2RU**
email: brunswickderby@aol.com
dir: *From rail station turn right. Pub 100yds*

Rich in history and real ales

'A True Ale House and Brewery' it says on the sign outside this Grade II listed pub, which the Midland Railway built in the 1840s. It has no fewer than 16 handpumps, six for Brunswick ales brewed on the premises, the rest for guest beers. Real ciders are brought up from the cellar. Their signature dishes are casseroles made from locally sourced ingredients as much as possible. There's a beer festival during the first weekend in October.

Open all day all wk 11-11 (Fri-Sat 11am-11.30pm Sun 12-10.30) **Food** Lunch Mon-Sat 11.30-2.30, Sun 12-3 ⊕ FREE HOUSE ◀ Brunswick, Guest ales ♂ Westons Old Rosie, Rosie's Pig, Perry. **Facilities** Non-diners area ✿ (Bar Garden) ♦ Children's portions Family room Garden ⌂ Beer festival ▦ Notes ⊛

DOE LEA
Map 16 SK46

Hardwick Inn

tel: 01246 850245 **Hardwick Park S44 5QJ**
email: hardwickinn@hotmail.co.uk
dir: *M1 junct 29, A6175. 0.5m left signed Stainsby/Hardwick Hall. After Stainsby, 2m, left at staggered junct. Follow brown tourist signs*

Step back in time at this village inn

Dating from the 15th century and built of locally quarried sandstone, this striking building was once the lodge for Hardwick Hall (NT) and stands at the south gate of Hardwick Park, not far from Chesterfield. Owned by the Batty family for three generations, the pub has a rambling interior and features period details such as mullioned windows, oak beams and stone fireplaces. Traditional food takes in a popular carvery roast, a salad bar, hearty home-made pies and casseroles, as well as selections of fish and vegetarian dishes. A handy pitstop for M1 travellers.

Open all day all wk **Food** Contact pub for details Av main course £10 Set menu available ⊕ FREE HOUSE ◀ Theakston Old Peculier & XB, Bess of Hardwick, Black Sheep, Peak Ales Chatsworth Gold ♂ Addlestones, Symonds Scrumpy Jack. ▼ 10 **Facilities** Non-diners area ✿ (Bar Garden) ♦ Children's menu Children's portions Play area Family room Garden ⌂ Parking ▦

ELMTON
Map 16 SK57

The Elm Tree

tel: 01909 721261 **S80 4LS**
email: enquiries@elmtreeelmton.co.uk
dir: *M1 junct 30, A616 signed Newart through 5 rdbts. Through Clowne, right at staggered x-rds into Hazelmere Rd to Elmton*

Contemporary dining pub with a passion for local produce

Food is very much the focus at this 17th-century pub tucked away in pretty Elmton. Chef-patron Chris Norfolk is passionate about sourcing seasonal and fully traceable produce from local suppliers, including fruit and vegetables from neighbour's gardens, and everything, from bread, pasta and pastry, is made on the premises. Changing menus (served all day) may deliver game terrine with apple chutney, liver and bacon with thyme gravy, their award-winning burger (topped with Stilton and jalapeño peppers), and blueberry frangipane tart. There's a contemporary feel in the stone-floored bar and 'The Library' private dining room and four real ales on tap.

Open all day Closed Tue **Food** Lunch Mon, Wed-Sat 12-9, Sun 12-6 Dinner Mon, Wed-Sat 12-9, Sun 12-6 ⊕ PUNCH TAVERNS ◀ Black Sheep, Kelham Island Easy Rider, Elm Tree Bitter ♂ Westons Old Rosie & Perry. ▼ **Facilities** Non-diners area ✿ (Bar Garden) ♦ Children's portions Play area Garden ⌂ Parking ▦ (notice required)

EYAM
Map 16 SK27

Miners Arms

tel: 01433 630853 **Water Ln S32 5RG**
dir: *Off B6521, 5m N of Bakewell*

Children, dogs and walkers all welcome

This welcoming 17th-century inn and restaurant was built just before the plague hit Eyam; the village tailor brought damp cloth from London and hung it to dry in front of the fire so releasing the infected fleas. The pub gets its name from the local lead mines of Roman times. Owned by Greene King, there's always the option to pop in for a pint of their IPA or Ruddles Best bitter, or enjoy a meal. A beer festival is held three times a year.

Open all wk Mon 12-3 5.30-12 Tue-Sun 12-12 **Food** Lunch Mon-Sat 12-2, Sun 12-3 Dinner Mon 6-8, Tue-Fri 6-9, Sat 7-9 ⊕ GREENE KING ◀ IPA, Ruddles Best, Guest ales ♂ Westons Old Rosie. **Facilities** Non-diners area ✿ (Bar Garden) ♦ Children's menu Children's portions Garden ⌂ Beer festival Parking WiFi ▦ (notice required)

FENNY BENTLEY
Map 16 SK14

Bentley Brook Inn ★★★ INN
`PICK OF THE PUBS`

tel: 01335 350278 **DE6 1LF**
email: all@bentleybrookinn.co.uk **web:** www.bentleybrookinn.co.uk
dir: *2m N of Ashbourne at junct of A515 & B5056*

Local specialities at the edge of the Peak District

Just a short distance from the glories of Dovedale, this eye-catching black-and-white country property was created over 200 years ago on the footprint of a medieval farmhouse. It became a pub only in the 1970s. Many period features remain, including a splendid central log fireplace, whilst outside are several acres of landscaped garden which play host every summer to the World Toe-Wrestling Championship. It's also home to a popular beer festival each Spring Bank holiday, when the usual range of beers from Leatherbritches Brewery (which originated here) is comprehensively expanded. Participants in both these events can stay at the inn's 11 bedrooms, safe in the knowledge that an excellent repast will be in prospect. With the Peak District's farms and estates as suppliers, food mileage is kept low and is of quality high. Steaks are a favourite, or invest in a local dish like oatcake with smoked salmon and poached egg. A signature dish here is Derbyshire Lobby, a variation on hot pot using minced lamb. Change of hands.

Open all day all wk 12-12 **Food** Lunch all wk 12-9 (Winter Mon-Fri 12-3) Dinner all wk 12-9 (Winter Mon-Fri 6-9) Set menu available ⊕ FREE HOUSE ◀ Leatherbritches Dr Johnson, Falstaff, Marston's Pedigree ♂ Addlestones. ♇ 10
Facilities Non-diners area ✿ (Bar Garden) ♦ Children's menu Children's portions Play area Garden ♈ Beer festival Parking WiFi ➡ **Rooms** 11

The Coach and Horses Inn

tel: 01335 350246 **DE6 1LB**
email: coachandhorses2@btconnect.com
dir: On A515 (Ashbourne to Buxton road), 2.5m from Ashbourne

17th-century coaching inn offering good, honest cooking

A cosy refuge in any weather, this family-run, 17th-century coaching inn stands on the edge of the Peak District National Park. Besides the beautiful location, its charms include stripped wood furniture and low beams, real log-burning fires plus a welcoming and friendly atmosphere. Expect a great selection of real ales and good home cooking that is hearty and uses the best of local produce. Specials could include chicken breast wrapped in bacon with a Stilton sauce; poached salmon fillet with a cream, white wine and seafood sauce; or spicy vegetable and chilli bean casserole on rice, with haloumi. Hot and cold sandwiches and baguettes provide lighter options.

Open all day all wk 11-11 (Sun 12-10.30) **Food** Lunch all wk 12-9 Dinner all wk 12-9 ⊕ FREE HOUSE ◀ Marston's Pedigree, Oakham JHB, Peak Swift Nick, Whim Hartington Bitter, Derby. **Facilities** Non-diners area ♦ Children's menu Family room Garden ♈ Parking ➡ (notice required)

■ **FOOLOW**   Map 16 SK17

The Bulls Head Inn ★★★★ INN

tel: 01433 630873 **S32 5QR**
email: wilbnd@aol.com **web:** www.thebullatfoolow.co.uk
dir: Just off A623, N of Stoney Middleton

Traditional English country pub serving good food

In an upland village surrounded by a lattice-work of dry-stone walls, this 19th-century former coaching inn is the epitome of the English country pub. Well, with open fires, oak beams, flagstone floors, great views and good food and beer, it has to be. The bar serves Black Sheep and Peak Ales, lunchtime snacks and sandwiches, while main meals include Cumberland sausages and Yorkshire pudding; beef Wellington with red wine gravy; sea bream fillets with lemon butter; Mediterranean vegetable hotpot; and even ostrich steak with brandied game gravy. The bedrooms are well equipped.

Open 12-3 6.30-11 (Sun all day) Closed Mon (ex BHs) **Food** Lunch Tue-Sun 12-2 Dinner Tue-Sun 6.30-9 ⊕ FREE HOUSE ◀ Black Sheep, Peak, Adnams, Tetley. **Facilities** Non-diners area ✿ (Bar) ♦ Children's menu Children's portions ♈ Parking ➡ **Rooms** 3

■ **FROGGATT**   Map 16 SK27

The Chequers Inn ★★★★ INN ⊛   **PICK OF THE PUBS**

tel: 01433 630231 **Froggatt Edge S32 3ZJ**
email: info@chequers-froggatt.com **web:** www.chequers-froggatt.com
dir: On A625, 0.5m N of Calver

Hillside village pub offering a warm welcome and excellent food

Hugging the wooded hillside below Froggatt Edge, this traditional, 16th-century country inn was originally four stone cottages. The comfortable interior of wooden floors, antiques and blazing log fires is perfect for a relaxing pint of Bradfield Farmers Blonde or Peak Bakewell Best Bitter, brewed on the nearby Chatsworth Estate. The traditional pub menu includes favourites such as beer-battered haddock; and beef and ale pie, both home made of course. In addition, there's a range of lunchtime sandwiches and an ever-changing selection of blackboard specials, such as poached monkfish wrapped in Parma ham, crab arancini, winter roots and veal jus; braised Scarsdale belly pork, pan-seared scallop, squid and chorizo cabbage, black cider sauce; and mixed bean cassoulet for the vegetarians. Popular with walkers, the gritstone escarpment can be reached by a steep, wild woodland footpath from the pub's elevated secret garden.

Open all day all wk Closed 25 Dec **Food** Lunch Mon-Fri 12-2.30, Sat 12-9.30, Sun 12-9 Dinner Mon-Fri 6-9.30, Sat 12-9.30, Sun 12-9 ⊕ FREE HOUSE ◀ Kelham Island Easy Rider, Peak Bakewell Best Bitter, Bradfield Farmers Blonde, Guest ales. ♇ 10
Facilities ♦ Children's menu Children's portions Garden ♈ Parking WiFi **Rooms** 6

■ **GREAT HUCKLOW**   Map 16 SK17

The Queen Anne Inn ★★★ INN

tel: 01298 871246 **SK17 8RF**
email: angelaryan100@aol.com **web:** www.queenanneinn.co.uk
dir: A623 onto B6049, exit at Anchor pub towards Bradwell, 2nd right to Great Hucklow

Great hospitality in a country setting

The sheltered south-facing garden of this traditional country free house has stunning open views. The inn dates from 1621; a licence has been held for over 300 years, and the names of all the landlords are known. Inside you'll find an open fire in the stone fireplace, good food made using locally sourced produce, and an ever-changing range of cask ales. The inn has an AA Dinner Award in recognition of the quality of the food on offer; popular choices include sea bass fillet with parmesan crust; steak and kidney pudding; and steamed mussels with freshly baked bread. There is a child-friendly south-facing garden and two guest bedrooms are available.

Open 12-2.30 5-11 (Fri-Sun 12-11) Closed Mon **Food** Lunch Tue-Sun 12-2 Dinner Tue-Thu 6-8.30, Fri-Sat 6-9, Sun 6-8 Av main course £9 Set menu available ⊕ FREE HOUSE ◀ Tetley's Cask, Bass, Local guest ales ♂ Westons Stowford Press. ♇ 9
Facilities Non-diners area ✿ (Bar Garden) ♦ Children's menu Children's portions Family room Garden ♈ Parking WiFi ➡ (notice required) **Rooms** 2

PICK OF THE PUBS

The Maynard ★★★ HL @@

tel: 01433 630321
Main Rd S32 2HE
email: info@themaynard.co.uk
web: www.themaynard.co.uk
dir: *M1 junct 30, A619 into Chesterfield, then onto Baslow. A623 to Calver, right into Grindleford*

Imposing Peak District hotel with a fine-dining restaurant

Renowned attractions lie within easy reach of this former coaching inn. Chatsworth House is the family seat of the Dukes of Devonshire, and near Castleton is the Blue John Cavern, where the semi-precious mineral is still mined. Above the pub are the steep, wooded crags of Froggatt Edge, while below is the village of Grindleford and, beyond, the Derwent Valley. Although decorated in a contemporary style, the interior of this stone-built inn retains plenty of original features to make visitors aware of its Edwardian origins. Local artists are invited to display their work around the walls, alongside photographs of Peak District scenes. In the Longshaw Bar, with its leather sofas and log fires, real ales include Abbeydale Moonshine, and Peak Ales Bakewell Best, brewed on the Chatsworth Estate. Here, lime and ginger cod fishcake is offered as a starter, perhaps followed by lamb, shallot and garden pea pie, or teriyaki-

style salmon fillet. The alternative place in which to find out why the Maynard has earned two AA rosettes is the contemporary restaurant overlooking the gardens and countryside, where seasonal menus might offer starters of a pork tasting plate, or crisp sea bass fillet; main courses of 28-day aged Derbyshire rib-eye steak; pan-fried gilt-head bream fillet; or Moroccan-style vegetable and chickpea stew; and desserts of home-made Yorkshire parkin with spiced rum custard, or mulled fruit crumble. The large beer garden offers stunning panoramas across moorland and river valley. Beautifully appointed en suite bedrooms offer a king-size bed and flat-screen TV, tea and coffee facilities and complimentary WiFi. Dogs are most welcome.

Open all day all wk **Food** Lunch all wk 12-2 Dinner all wk 7-9 Restaurant menu available all wk. ⊕ FREE HOUSE ◀ Abbeydale Moonshine, Peak Bakewell Best Bitter. **Facilities** Non-diners area ❄ (Bar) ⭧ Children's menu Garden ⏞ Parking WiFi (public areas only) 🚐 (notice required) **Rooms** 10

GREAT LONGSTONE
Map 16 SK27

NEW The White Lion

tel: 01629 640252 **Main St DE45 1TA**
email: info@whiteliongreatlongstone.co.uk
dir: Take A6020 from Ashford-in-the-Water towards Chesterfield. Left to Great Longstone

Stylish pub in an unspoilt Peak District village

Whether arriving on foot, on two wheels, or on four legs, visitors to Great Longstone's White Lion are sure to recuperate from their exertions. Sitting under the mass of Longstone Edge not far from Bakewell, Greg and Libby Robinson's gastropub has a peaceful outside patio and dog-welcoming snug bar. Very much food focussed, the monthly-changing menus use locally-sourced produce whenever possible. A fixed-price two- or three-course lunch represents excellent value: a starter of grilled haloumi cheese, warm chickpea salad, couscous and sundried tomatoes could be followed by a plate of Spanish-style chicken thighs, with black-eyed bean and chorizo cassoulet and garlic bread.

Open all wk 12-3 6-9 (Sat 12-9 Sun 12-8) **Food** Contact pub for details Set menu available ⊕ ROBINSONS **Facilities** Non-diners area ❀ (Bar Outside area) ⊪ Children's portions Outside area ⋒ Parking WiFi ⥗ (notice required)

GRINDLEFORD
Map 16 SK27

The Maynard ★★★ HL ◉◉   PICK OF THE PUBS

See Pick of the Pubs on opposite page

HARDSTOFT
Map 16 SK46

The Shoulder at Hardstoft ★★★★★ INN ◉◉

tel: 01246 850276 **Deep Ln S45 8AF**
email: info@thefamousshoulder.co.uk **web:** www.thefamousshoulder.co.uk
dir: From B6039 follow signs for Hardwick Hall. 1st right into car park

Top-notch menu in Derbyshire countryside inn

Just ten minutes from the M1, this 300-year-old pub is an ideal base for exploring the Peak District and Sherwood Forest. Peak Ales' Bakewell Best Bitter is one of the local beers available in the bar, with its open log fires. The kitchen sources all ingredients within 15 miles of the pub where possible, with the exception of fish, which is from sustainable sources. In the restaurant (with 2 AA Rosettes), look forward to a pan-seared scallop or basil and spinach gnocchi starter, a taster for mains such as poached salmon fishcakes with poached egg and tartare sauce; or wild mushroom and goats' cheese risotto. 'Perfect puds' include chocolate tart and apple tarte Tatin.

Open all day all wk **Food** Contact pub for details ⊕ FREE HOUSE ◀ Peak Bakewell Best Bitter, Thornbridge Jaipur, Greene King Abbot Ale. ☗ 10 **Facilities** Non-diners area ❀ (Bar Restaurant) ⊪ Children's portions ⋒ Parking WiFi ⥗ (notice required) **Rooms** 4

HARTSHORNE
Map 10 SK32

The Mill Wheel ★★★★ INN ◉

tel: 01283 550335 **Ticknall Rd DE11 7AS**
email: info@themillwheel.co.uk **web:** www.themillwheel.co.uk
dir: From A511 between Burton upon Trent & Ashby-de-la-Zouch take A514 at Woodville signed Derby. 1.8m to Hartshorne

Award-winning food in a lovely setting

Close to the National Trust's remarkable Calke Abbey, many trades have used this old building over the centuries; today it's a feel-good, rustic pub in an attractive setting. The mill wheel, which has powered bellows, grindstones and hoists only

momentarily diverts attention from Colin Brown's enticing menus, which have gained an AA Rosette. A typical dinner might include smoked Scottish salmon with celeriac and horseradish coleslaw; followed by slow braised venison and root vegetable casserole with beetroot mash; or local steaks from the grill. There are modern bedrooms for overnighters.

Open all wk (Sat-Sun all day) **Food** Lunch Mon-Fri 12-2.30, Sat 12-9.15, Sun 12-8 Dinner Mon-Thu 6-9.15, Fri 6-9.30, Sat 12-9.15, Sun 12-8 Av main course £8.95 Set menu available Restaurant menu available all wk ⊕ FREE HOUSE ◀ Greene King Abbot Ale, Hop Back Summer Lightning, Marston's Pedigree, Bass. ☗ 8 **Facilities** Non-diners area ⊪ Children's menu Children's portions Garden ⋒ Parking WiFi ⥗ **Rooms** 4

HASSOP
Map 16 SK27

The Old Eyre Arms

tel: 01629 640390 **DE45 1NS**
email: nick@eyrearms.com
dir: On B6001 N of Bakewell

A perfect Peak District escape

In a plum village-edge location between the formality of Chatsworth's vast estate, bold gritstone edges and the memorable wooded limestone dales of Derbyshire's River Wye, this comfortably unchanging, creeper-clad old inn ticks all the right boxes for beers and food too. Real ales from Peak Ales and Bradfield breweries couldn't be more local, whilst all meals are prepared in-house: kick off with a prawn skewer with chilli and lemon butter, and follow with Old English rabbit pie with cider and bacon, or aubergine and mushroom lasagne to take the chill off a long ramble. Oak beams and furnishing and log fires complete the picture.

Open all wk 11-3 6-11 Closed 25-26 Dec, 2wks in Jan **Food** Lunch Mon-Fri 12-2, Sat-Sun 12-2.30 Dinner all wk 6-9 Set menu available ⊕ FREE HOUSE ◀ Peak Ales Swift Nick & Chatsworth Gold, Black Sheep Ale, Bradfield Farmers Blonde ♂ Westons Stowford Press. ☗ 9 **Facilities** Non-diners area ⊪ Children's menu Children's portions Garden ⋒ Parking

HATHERSAGE
Map 16 SK28

The Plough Inn ★★★★ INN ◉   PICK OF THE PUBS

See Pick of the Pubs on page 130

The Scotsmans Pack Country Inn

tel: 01433 650253 **School Ln S32 1BZ**
email: scotsmans.pack@btinternet.com
dir: From A6187 in Hathersage turn at church into School Lane

A warm welcome for locals and visitors alike

Set in the beautiful Hope Valley on one of the old packhorse trails used by Scottish 'packmen', this traditional inn is a short walk from Hathersage church and Little John's Grave. Weather permitting, head outside onto the sunny patio, next to the trout stream. The pub offers a good choice of hearty daily specials – six starters, ten main and eight desserts – perhaps best washed down with a pint of Jennings Cumberland. This is a perfect base for walking and touring the Peak District.

Open all day all wk **Food** Lunch Mon-Fri 12-6, Sat-Sun 12-9 Dinner Mon-Fri 6-9, Sat-Sun 12-9 ⊕ MARSTON'S ◀ Burton Bitter, EPA & Pedigree, Jennings Cumberland Ale. ☗ 10 **Facilities** Non-diners area ⊪ Children's menu Children's portions Family room Garden ⋒ Parking WiFi ⥗

PICK OF THE PUBS

The Plough Inn ★★★★ INN

HATHERSAGE Map 16 SK28

tel: 01433 650319 & 650180
Leadmill Bridge S32 1BA
email: sales@theploughinn-hathersage.co.uk
web: www.theploughinn-hathersage.co.uk
dir: *M1 junct 29, take A617W, A619, A623, then B6001 N to Hathersage*

Stylish, riverside award-winner with extensive menu choices

The 16th-century Plough stands in nine acres by the River Derwent where the 18th-century, three-arched Leadmill Bridge carries the Derwent Valley Heritage Way over the rapids that disturb the otherwise gently flowing waters. Inside, smart red tartan carpets work well with the open fires and wooden beams of the bar, which serves hand-pulled Adnams, Black Sheep and Timothy Taylor ales. An extensive British menu features locally sourced starters such as mussel and saffron chowder; and rillette of confit salmon and crab, beef tomato, caper berries and lemon with chive oil. Next choose from the best part of 20 main courses, including fillet of British beef with lyonnaise potatoes, slow-roast shallots, spinach and roast garlic cream; chargrilled sea bream with marinated cherry tomatoes, sweet potato, wild rocket and salsa verde; and red pepper couscous with vegetable tagine and grilled haloumi. If you prefer, there's traditional pub grub too, typically

seared lamb's liver with grilled back bacon; and ale-battered cod, with lighter meals served until 5.30pm. Roast meats are only part of the Sunday line-up, with dishes featuring lemon sole, pork medallions, chicken and pissaladière also on offer. The Plough's well-stocked cellar combines Old and New World wines, from France to Chile one way, and New Zealand the other. Guests may stroll through the landscaped grounds before retiring to one of the bedrooms in the inn itself, or in the converted barn across the cobbled courtyard.

Open all day all wk 11-11 (Sun 12-10.30) Closed 25 Dec **Food** please contact the inn for food service times; set menu available ⊕ FREE HOUSE ◀ Adnams, Black Sheep, Timothy Taylor, Bass Extra Smooth, Local ales. ☙ 15 **Facilities** Non-diners area ❖ (Bar Restaurant Garden) ✦ Children's menu Children's portions Garden ⊼ Parking WiFi **Rooms** 5

HAYFIELD
Map 16 SK08

The Royal Hotel

tel: 01663 742721 **Market St SK22 2EP**
email: enquiries@theroyalathayfield.com
dir: *From A624 follow Hayfield signs*

Village centre pub on the Peak District border

Up in the High Peak, below the windswept plateau of Kinder Scout, the hotel dates from 1755. Its period charm still very evident, one place to relax with a pint of Thwaites Original or Happy Valley Kinder Falldown is the oak-panelled, log-fired bar. Others are the Cricket Room, popular with the local cricket team, whose course is next door, and the Ramblers Bar which has hiking boots strung along the beams. The bar menu keeps things simple: sausage and mash; roast beef and Yorkshire pudding; and breaded wholetail scampi. There's also a separate sandwich menu, and on Fridays and Saturdays, a bistro menu. Meals can be served on the patio overlooking the moorland; visit first weekend in October for the beer festival.

Open all day all wk 10am-11pm (Fri-Sat 10am-11.30pm from 11am in Winter) **Food** Lunch Mon-Fri 12-2.30 (Winter), (12-8 Summer), Sat 12-9, Sun 12-7 Dinner Mon-Fri 6-8 (Winter), (12-8 Summer), Sat 12-9, Sun 12-7 Av main course £9.95 Set menu available Restaurant menu available Fri-Sun ⊕ FREE HOUSE ◾ Thwaites Original, Happy Valley Kinder Falldown ♂ Westons Stowford Press, Scrumpy. ▼ **Facilities** Non-diners area ♣ (Bar Outside area) ♦ Children's menu Children's portions Family room Outside area ⋒ Beer festival Parking WiFi ⚌ (notice required)

HOGNASTON
Map 16 SK25

The Red Lion Inn

tel: 01335 370396 **Main St DE6 1PR**
email: enquiries@redlionhognaston.org.uk **web:** www.redlionhognaston.org.uk
dir: *From Ashbourne take B5035 towards Wirksworth. Approx 5m follow Carsington Water signs. Turn right to Hognaston*

Traditional country pub off the beaten track

In a village of old cottages close to the huge Carsington Water, this very traditional pub fronting the main street bursts with antique furniture spread liberally around an open-fire warmed interior originating in the 17th century. Beams, bare brick, old photos and bric-a-brac add further character to this peaceful retreat in fine walking and cycling country. Settle into a settle with a pint of bitter perhaps from Wincle Brewery and home in on a tasty menu crafted from top-notch Derbyshire produce; Barbary duck with new potatoes and brandy and black cherry sauce takes the eye, but freshly baked baguettes with a variety of fillings may be just the ticket. The garden has a boules court.

Open all wk 12-2.30 6-11 **Food** Lunch all wk 12-2.30 Dinner all wk 6.30-9 summer, 6-8.30 winter ⊕ FREE HOUSE ◾ Marston's Pedigree, Greene King Ruddles County, Black Sheep, Wincle, Timothy Taylor Landlord. ▼ 10 **Facilities** Non-diners area ♣ (Bar Garden) ♦ Children's portions Garden ⋒ Parking WiFi

HOPE
Map 16 SK18

Cheshire Cheese Inn

tel: 01433 620381 **Edale Rd S33 6ZF**
email: laura@thecheshirecheeseinn.co.uk
dir: *On A6187 between Sheffield & Castleton, turn at Hope Church into Edale Rd*

Country inn with a rich history

Originally a farm, this 17th-century inn used to provide salt-carriers crossing the Pennines to Yorkshire with overnight lodgings, for which they paid in cheese. In the unspoilt atmosphere of today's pub payment is made the conventional way, but cheese with tomato, onion or pickle makes a good sandwich with a locally brewed real ale. Other home-made food includes main meals such as gammon steak with fried egg and chips; steak and kidney pudding; beer-battered Grimsby haddock; and large Yorkshire pud with local sausages. Dogs are welcome in the inn and beer garden.

Open Tue-Fri 12-3 6-late (Sat 12-late Sun 12-10) Closed Mon (out of season) **Food** Lunch Tue-Fri 12-2, Sat 12-9, Sun 12-7.30 (Sun 12-4 winter) Dinner Tue-Fri 6-9, Sat 12-9, Sun 12-7.30 ⊕ ENTERPRISE INNS ◾ Peak Swift Nick, Bradfield Farmers Blonde, Adnams Ghost Ship, Guest ales ♂ Addlestones. **Facilities** Non-diners area ♣ (Bar Garden) ♦ Children's portions Family room Garden ⋒ Parking WiFi ⚌ (notice required)

NEW The Old Hall Hotel

tel: 01433 620160 **Market Place S33 6RH**
email: info@oldhallhotelhope.com
dir: *In town centre*

For generations Hope Hall, as this early 16th-century building was once called, was the Balguy family seat. In 1730 it became an inn, The Cross Daggers, then in 1876 it was renamed The Hall Hotel. If you fancy a snack, there are baguettes - hot roast beef and Stilton; and smothered chicken, cheese and Mediterranean vegetables. Main menus promise grills; steak and ale pie; sausages and mash; Scottish salmon linguine; and wild mushroom and oatcake millefeuille. In the 18th century a cattle market was held here; today, on bank holidays, the Hope Valley Beer and Cider Festival draws the crowds.

Open all day all wk **Food** Lunch all wk 12-5 Dinner all wk 5-9 Av main course £10 ⊕ HEINEKEN/THEAKSTON ◾ Theakston Best, Old Peculier & XB, Castle Rock Harvest Pale, Adnams, Caledonian ♂ Symonds. **Facilities** Non-diners area ♣ (Bar Garden Outside area) ♦ Children's menu Children's portions Garden Outside area ⋒ Beer festival Cider festival Parking WiFi ⚌ (notice required)

HURDLOW
Map 16 SK16

NEW The Royal Oak

tel: 01298 83288 & 07866 778847 **SK17 9QJ**
email: hello@peakpub.co.uk
dir: *From A515 between Buxton & Ashbourne follow Hurdlow signs*

Popular pitstop for walkers and cyclists on the Tissington Trail

Situated in the southern Peak District, this warm-hearted hostelry welcomes one and all, at any time of day. Tired ramblers and cyclists head straight for the pumps, where five real ales include locals such as Hartington and Thornbridge. Families with children and dogs add to the fun, arriving whenever suits them in the knowledge that generous plates of home-cooked pub food are served throughout the day. Most ingredients are seasonal and sourced within 20 miles of the pub from suppliers with trusted reputations. Whether it's a legendary breakfast bap at 10am, or a full three-course meal in the evening, The Royal Oak caters well.

Open all day all wk **Food** Lunch Mon-Fri 10-9, Sat-Sun 8.30am-9pm Dinner Mon-Fri 10-9, Sat-Sun 8.30am-9pm Av main course £10.95 ⊕ FREE HOUSE ◾ Whim Hartington Bitter, Thornbridge, Buxton, Wincle. **Facilities** Non-diners area ♣ (Bar Restaurant Garden) ♦ Children's menu Children's portions Garden ⋒ Parking WiFi ⚌ (notice required)

INGLEBY
Map 11 SK32

The John Thompson Inn & Brewery

tel: 01332 862469 **DE73 7HW**
email: nick@johnthompsoninn.com
dir: *From A38 between Derby & Burton upon Trent take A5132 towards Barrow upon Trent. At mini rdbt right onto B5008 (signed Repton). At rdbt 1st exit into Brook End. Right into Milton Rd. Left, left again to Ingleby*

Friendly brewpub serving hearty lunches

A pub since 1968, this 15th-century former farmhouse took its name from licensee and owner John Thompson. Now run by son Nick, it is a traditional brewpub set in idyllic countryside beside the banks of the River Trent with views of the neighbouring National Forest. Inside, a wealth of original features make it an atmospheric place to enjoy a pint of home-brewed JTS XXX and tuck into lunches ranging from sandwiches to a roast beef carvery or a trio of cheese and pasta broccoli bake. Finish with home-made bread and butter pudding.

Open Tue-Fri 11-2.30 6-11 (Sat-Sun 11-11 Mon 6-11) Closed Mon L **Food** Lunch Tue-Sun 12-2 ⊕ FREE HOUSE ◄ John Thompson JTS XXX, St Nick's, Gold, Rich Porter. ♀ 9 **Facilities** Non-diners area ♦♦ Children's portions Family room Garden Parking WiFi ━━

KIRK IRETON
Map 16 SK25

Barley Mow Inn

tel: 01335 370306 **DE6 3JP**
dir: *Phone for detailed directions*

Step back in time at this traditional pub

Built on the edge of the Peak District National Park by the Storer family of yeomen farmers in the 16th century, the building became an inn during the early 1700s. The imposing free house has remained largely unchanged over the years. Six nine-gallon barrels of beer stand behind the bar, with cheese and pickle or salami rolls and bar snacks on offer at lunchtime. Tea and coffee is always available. Close to Carsington Water, there are good walking opportunities on nearby marked paths.

Open all wk 12-2 7-11 (Sun 12-2 7-10.30) Closed 25 Dec, 1 Jan **Food** Contact pub for details ⊕ FREE HOUSE ◄ Whim Hartington Bitter, Rotating ales ♂ Thatchers. **Facilities** Non-diners area ♦♦ Garden Parking **Notes** ✉

LITTLE HAYFIELD
Map 16 SK08

Lantern Pike

tel: 01663 747590 **45 Glossop Rd SK22 2NG**
email: tomandstella@lanternpikeinn.co.uk
dir: *On A624 between Glossop & Chapel-en-le-Frith*

Welcoming pub in hilly terrain

Set in a tiny mill village at the edge of the Kinder Scout moors and below the shapely Lantern Pike hill, site of an Armada beacon, the sublime views from the beer garden of the wooded Peak District hills are reason enough to seek out this fine pub. Add a well-considered selection of real ales and an ever-changing menu – perhaps fresh fillet of red snapper, or griddled loin of pork in Stilton sauce – and it's little wonder that this ultra-traditional 170-year-old inn is a highly popular destination for diners and outdoor pursuits enthusiasts alike. Unique 'Coronation Street' ephemera add fascination for the faithful.

Open Mon 5-12, Tue-Fri 12-3 5-12 (Sat-Sun all day) Closed 25 Dec, Mon L **Food** Lunch Tue-Fri 12-2.30, Sat-Sun 12-8.30 Dinner Mon 5-8, Tue-Fri 5-8.30, Sat-Sun 12-8.30 Av main course £10 Restaurant menu available all wk ⊕ ENTERPRISE INNS ◄ Timothy Taylor Landlord, Castle Rock Harvest Pale, Ossett Silver King, Theakston Black Bull. **Facilities** Non-diners area ♦♦ Children's menu Children's portions Garden ⋒ Parking WiFi ━━ (notice required)

LITTON
Map 16 SK17

Red Lion Inn

tel: 01298 871458 **SK17 8QU**
email: theredlionlitton@hotmail.co.uk
dir: *Just off A623 (Chesterfield to Stockport road), 1m E of Tideswell*

Pub paradise beside the village green

A miniature marvel, with mouldering stocks on the timeless green outside to detain those rash enough to leave this engaging Peak District village pub. A range of beamed little rooms spread from the bar, where local microbrewery beers stand out. Prepare for dancing log fires, bric-a-brac, board games and wood panelling; murmuring village chit-chat and happy ramblers returning from nearby limestone gorges. Licensed since 1787, this rake of slim stone cottages invites a lingering visit; doubly so with the homely menu of unfussy pub stalwarts - steak and kidney pie; roasted vegetable hotpot; and cumin and chilli chicken breast fulfil the keenest appetites. The pub's small size mean it's not ideal for children inside.

Open all day all wk **Food** Lunch Mon-Sat 12-9, Sun 12-8 Dinner Mon-Sat 12-9, Sun 12-8 Set menu available Restaurant menu available ⊕ ENTERPRISE INNS ◄ Abbeydale Absolution, 2 Guest ales ♂ Westons Stowford Press. ♀ 10 **Facilities** Non-diners area ✿ (Bar Restaurant) Outside area ⋒

MATLOCK
Map 16 SK35

The Red Lion ★★★ INN

tel: 01629 584888 **65 Matlock Green DE4 3BT**
dir: *From Chesterfield, A632 into Matlock, on right just before junct with A615*

An all rounder in the heart of Derbyshire's county town

This friendly, family-run free house makes a good base for exploring local attractions like Chatsworth House, Carsington Water and Dovedale. Spectacular walks in the local countryside help to work up an appetite for bar lunches, or great tasting home-cooked dishes in the homely restaurant. On Sunday there's a popular carvery with freshly cooked gammon, beef and turkey. In the winter months, open fires burn in the lounge and games room, and there's a boules area in the attractive beer garden for warmer days. Some of the ales from the bar were brewed on the Chatsworth Estate. There are six comfortable bedrooms.

Open all day all wk **Food** Lunch Tue-Fri 12-2 Dinner Tue-Sat 6-9 ⊕ FREE HOUSE ◄ Morland Old Speckled Hen, Peak, Guest ales. **Facilities** Non-diners area Children's menu Children's portions Garden ⋒ Parking WiFi ━━ **Rooms** 6

MIDDLE HANDLEY
Map 16 SK47

Devonshire Arms

tel: 01246 434800 **Lightwood Ln S21 5RN**
email: enquiries@devonshirearmsmiddlehandley.com
dir: *B6052 from Eckington towards Chesterfield. 1.5m*

Great local beers and thoughtful menu

A contemporary dining pub which has not forgotten its roots as a time-honoured local. The stylish interior has original features including a grandfather clock and wood-burning stove, perfect to sit beside in winter with a glass of Sheffield's Kelham Island beer or Aspall cider. Modern, locally-sourced British ingredients form the backbone of the pub classics and inspirations such as Moss Valley belly pork slowly cooked overnight in cloudy cider, with apple and potato terrine. The Devonshire Arms certainly welcomes dogs, just as long as they keep to the tiled floor areas.

Open 12-3 5-9 (Sat 12-10 Sun 12-5) Closed Mon **Food** Lunch Tue-Fri 12-3, Sat 12-10, Sun 12-5 Dinner Tue-Fri 5-9, Sat 12-10, Sun 12-5 ⊕ FREE HOUSE ◄ Bradfield Farmers Blonde, Kelham Island Pride of Sheffield, Peak Chatsworth Gold, Guest ales ♂ Aspall. ♀ 10 **Facilities** Non-diners area ✿ (All areas) ♦♦ Children's menu Children's portions Garden Outside area ⋒ Parking WiFi

MILLTOWN — Map 16 SK36

The Nettle Inn

tel: 01246 590462 **S45 0ES**
email: marcus.sloan@thenettleinn.co.uk
dir: Phone for detailed directions

Local ales and good menu choices at this traditional inn

A 16th-century hostelry on the edge of the Peak District, this inn has all the traditional charm you could wish for, from flower-filled hanging baskets to log fires and a stone-flagged taproom floor. Expect well-kept ales such as Bakewell Best, and impressive home-made food using the best of seasonal produce. Typical bar options are chicken and leek pie or chargrilled pork chop and plenty of sandwiches, while on the restaurant menu dishes such as wild salmon roulade; game cooked three ways; or confit of lamb rump with rosemary jus may tempt.

Open all wk 12-2.30 5.30-11 (Sun 12-10) **Food** Contact pub for details Restaurant menu available Tue-Sat ⊕ FREE HOUSE ◀ Peak Swift Nick, Bakewell Best Bitter, DPA. ♟ 9 **Facilities** Non-diners area ♦♦ Children's menu Children's portions Garden Parking WiFi ▥

PILSLEY — Map 16 SK27

The Devonshire Arms at Pilsley ★★★ INN

tel: 01246 583258 **High St DE45 1UL**
email: res@devonshirehotels.co.uk **web:** www.devonshirepilsley.co.uk
dir: From A619, in Baslow, at rdbt take 1st exit onto B6012. Follow signs to Chatsworth, 2nd right to Pilsley

Traditional inn on the Chatsworth Estate

Here is a fabulous old stone pub in an estate village amidst the rolling parkland surrounding Chatsworth House, the 'Palace of The Peaks'. It's also an ideal base for visiting Matlock Bath and Castleton. There are open fires, Peak Ales from the estate's brewery and meats, game and greens from the adjacent estate shop, all sourced from these productive acres at the heart of the Peak District. A mixed grill, corned beef hash or minted lamb hotpot is a filling repast after a day's exploration of the area. Stop over at the luxurious accommodation designed by the Duchess of Devonshire.

Open all day all wk **Food** Lunch all wk 12-2.30 Dinner all wk 5-9 ⊕ FREE HOUSE ◀ Thornbridge Jaipur, Peak Chatsworth Gold, Guest ales. ♟ 12
Facilities Non-diners area ♦♦ Children's menu Children's portions ▭ Parking WiFi **Rooms** 7

ROWSLEY — Map 16 SK26

The Grouse & Claret

tel: 01629 733233 **Station Rd DE4 2EB**
dir: On A6 between Matlock & Bakewell

Angling connections and a menu for everyone at this popular pub

A venue popular with local anglers, this 18th-century pub takes its name from a fishing fly. Situated at the gateway to the Peak District National Park, it is handy for visits to the stately homes of Haddon Hall and Chatsworth House. After quenching the thirst with a pint of Hobgoblin, the comprehensive menu promises a selection of well-priced and tasty pub meals: warm Caesar salad; towering onion rings with BBQ sauce; golden breaded scampi; and 10oz 28-day aged Oxfordshire rib-eye steak set the style. From the dessert choices are pear and ginger sponge; and Irish cream and caramel cheesecake. Change of hands.

Open all day all wk **Food** Lunch Mon-Sat 11.30-10, Sun 11.30-9 Dinner Mon-Sat 11.30-10, Sun 11.30-9 Av main course £7 Set menu available ⊕ MARSTON'S ◀ Pedigree, Wychwood Hobgoblin, Guest ale. ♟ 16 **Facilities** Non-diners area ♦♦ Children's menu Children's portions Play area Garden ▭ Beer festival Parking WiFi ▥

SHARDLOW — Map 11 SK43

The Old Crown Inn

tel: 01332 792392 **Cavendish Bridge DE72 2HL**
email: jamesvize@hotmail.co.uk
dir: M1 junct 24, A50 signed Stoke (& Shardlow). Take slip road signed B6540. At rdbt right, follow Shardlow sign. Left at Cavendish bridge sign to inn

Traditional inn with regular evening events

Up to nine real ales are served at this family-friendly pub on the south side of the River Trent, where there's a beer festival twice a year. Built as a coaching inn during the 17th century, it retains its warm and atmospheric interior. Several hundred water jugs hang from the ceilings, while the walls display an abundance of brewery and railway memorabilia. Food is lovingly prepared by the landlady; main meals focus on pub classics such as home-made steak and kidney pie; ham, eggs and chips; lasagne; curry; steaks; and daily specials. Monday night is quiz night; folk music on the first and third Tuesday of every month; curry night on Wednesdays.

Open all wk 11am-11.30pm (Mon 3-11 Fri-Sat 11am-12.30am Sun 11-11) **Food** Lunch Tue-Fri 12-2, Sat 12-8, Sun 12-3 Dinner Tue-Fri 5-8, Sat 12-8 Av main course £6.95 ⊕ MARSTON'S ◀ Pedigree & Old Empire, Jennings Cocker Hoop, Guest ales ♂ Thatchers Gold. **Facilities** Non-diners area ♣ (Bar Restaurant) ♦♦ Children's menu Children's portions Play area Garden ▭ Beer festival Parking ▥ (notice required)

SHIRLEY — Map 10 SK24

NEW The Saracen's Head

tel: 01335 360330 **Church Ln DE6 3AS**
email: info@saracens-head-shirley.co.uk
dir: A52 from Ashbourne towards Derby. Right in 4m to Shirley

A gastro-pub where traditional meets contemporary

Overlooking the front garden and village street, the 1791-built Saracen's Head takes its name from the family crest of Sewallis de Scyrle (pronounced Shirley), a Holy Land crusader. In addition to Greene King, it offers a rotating guest ale. All dishes are made on the premises from local, ethical sources. Starting with cream of leek and potato soup, it's an easy move to, say, fresh and spicy Goan-style fish and tiger prawn curry with rice; or slow-roasted shank of lamb with rosemary jus. For a quintessential country pub experience, visit on a Sunday lunchtime.

Open all wk 11-3 6-11 (Sun 11-10.30) **Food** Lunch Mon-Sat 12-2, Sun 12-2.30 Dinner all wk 6-9 Av main course £12.50 ⊕ GREENE KING ◀ IPA, St Edmunds, Morland Old Speckled Hen, Guest ales. **Facilities** Non-diners area ♣ (Bar Garden) ♦♦ Children's portions Garden ▭ Parking WiFi ▥ (notice required)

STANTON IN PEAK — Map 16 SK26

The Flying Childers Inn

tel: 01629 636333 **Main Rd DE4 2LW**
dir: From A6 (between Matlock & Bakewell) follow Youlgrave signs. Onto B5056 to Ashbourne. Follow Stanton in Peak signs

Enchanting old-style village pub

Above this instantly likeable, charmingly old-fashioned village pub looms Stanton Moor, riddled with Neolithic stone monuments. At the heart of a pretty old Peak District estate village, The Flying Childers was named after a champion racehorse owned by the 4th Duke of Devonshire. Little log fires warm the cosy, beamed interior, where settles and magpie-furniture fit an absolute treat. The lunchtime-only menu is small but perfectly formed; hot roast pork filled cobs with stuffing and roast potatoes or maybe a rabbit and vegetable casserole, all with locally sourced ingredients. Local real ales, a beer garden and a great welcome for canine companions, too.

Open all wk 12-2 7-11 (Mon-Tue 7pm-11pm Sat-Sun 12-3 7-11) **Food** Lunch Wed-Sun 12-2 ⊕ FREE HOUSE ◀ Wells Bombardier, Guest ales. **Facilities** ♣ (Bar Garden) ♦♦ Garden Parking **Notes** ▤

TIDESWELL
Map 16 SK17

The George ★★★ INN

tel: 01298 871382 **Commercial Rd SK17 8NU**
email: info@georgeinn.co.uk **web:** www.georgeinntideswell.co.uk
dir: A619 to Baslow, A623 towards Chapel-en-le-Frith, 0.25m

Charming coaching inn with traditional food

Set in the shadow of St John the Baptist's church (known locally as the Cathedral of the Peak), this delightful stone-built coaching inn dates from 1730 and is conveniently placed for exploring the National Park and visiting Buxton, Chatsworth and Eyam. The simple, unfussy menu focuses on traditional pub fare – lunchtime sandwiches and full meals such as mushroom and Stilton crumble followed by traditional rag pudding with gravy, and sticky toffee pudding for dessert. There's also a good selection from the grill, ranging from steaks to a fish medley or Cajun chicken.

Open all day all wk **Food** Lunch all wk 12-3 Dinner all wk 5-9 Set menu available ⊕ GREENE KING ◀ Morland, Ruddles, Guest ale ♂ Aspall. **Facilities** Non-diners area ❤ (All areas) ♦ Children's menu Children's portions Garden Outside area ➤ Parking WiFi ▦ (notice required) **Rooms** 4

Three Stags' Heads

tel: 01298 872268 **Wardlow Mires SK17 8RW**
dir: At junct of A623 (Baslow to Stockport road) & B6465

Pottery and a pint under the same roof

A remarkable survivor, this unspoilt, unchanged and rustic 17th-century moorland longhouse stands in renowned walking country and features a stone-flagged bar and huge range fire. The bar counter, a 1940s addition, sells Abbeydale beers, including the heady Black Lurcher and Brimstone bitter, and several ciders. Hearty food includes pea and ham soup; chicken casserole; roast partridge; and bread-and-butter pudding. Note the restricted opening hours, which allow owners Geoff and Pat Fuller time to make pottery, which you can buy. Sorry, it's not a pub for children.

Open all day Sat-Sun 12-12 (Fri 7-12) Closed Mon-Thu (ex BHs) **Food** Lunch Sat-Sun 12-3.30 Dinner Fri-Sun 6-9.30 ⊕ FREE HOUSE ◀ Abbeydale Matins, Absolution, Black Lurcher, Brimstone ♂ Dunkertons Black Fox, Kingston Black, Gawtkin Yarlington Mill. **Facilities** Non-diners area Parking **Notes** ☺

WOOLLEY MOOR
Map 16 SK36

NEW The White Horse Inn

tel: 01246 590319 **Badger Ln DE55 6FG**
dir: From A61 at Stretton take B6014, then B6036 Woolley Moor

Spick and span bar/restaurant near Matlock

This 200-year-old pub sits in two acres of gardens amidst beautiful countryside; the nearby Ogston Reservoir is where Ellen Macarthur learned her sailing skills. The building's interior has been meticulously updated, with exposed solid stone walls and precisely laid flagstone floors providing the backdrop for an abundance of polished tables and chairs in both the bar area and bright garden conservatory. Peak Ales are well-kept and wines sold by the glass are numerous, but this is primarily a food destination. Crab and prawn ravioli with a shellfish bisque makes a flavoursome starter, to be followed perhaps with lamb's liver, black pudding and smoked bacon mash.

Open all wk 12-3 5.30-11 (Sun 12-5) **Food** Lunch Mon-Sat 12-1.45, Sun 12-4 Dinner Mon-Sat 6-8.45 Set menu available Restaurant menu available all wk ⊕ FREE HOUSE ◀ Peak Ales Bakewell Best & Chatsworth Gold. ☗ 13 **Facilities** Non-diners area ♦ Children's portions Play area Garden ➤ Parking WiFi ▦ (notice required)

DEVON

ASHBURTON
Map 3 SX77

The Rising Sun ★★★ INN

tel: 01364 652544 **Woodland TQ13 7JT**
email: admin@therisingsunwoodland.co.uk **web:** www.therisingsunwoodland.co.uk
dir: From A38 E of Ashburton follow Woodland & Denbury signs. Pub on left, approx 1.5m

Family friendly pub with large garden near Dartmoor

This former drovers' pub is in the hands of the capable Reynolds family who are putting this family – and dog - friendly pub firmly on the map. Surrounded by gorgeous countryside, and with a large garden in which to sup a pint of Dartmoor Jail Ale, you're on the edge of Dartmoor National Park. Renowned for their pies, chips and specials board, they also offer light snacks at lunchtime, and a great children's menu. Sample specials include pork belly with vanilla mashed potatoes, spinach and caramelized apple jus; and braised lamb shoulder with colcannon and black trumpet mushrooms.

Open 12-3 6-11 (Sun 12-3 6.30-11) Closed Mon L Jan-Mar **Food** Lunch Tue-Sat 12-2.15, Sun 12-2.30 Dinner Mon-Thu 6-9, Fri-Sat 6-9.30, Sun 6.30-9 ⊕ FREE HOUSE ◀ Dartmoor Jail Ale, Guest ales ♂ Annings Fruit Cider, Thatchers Gold. **Facilities** Non-diners area ❤ (Bar Restaurant Garden) ♦ Children's menu Children's portions Play area Garden ➤ Parking WiFi ▦ (notice required) **Rooms** 4

AVONWICK
Map 3 SX75

The Turtley Corn Mill
PICK OF THE PUBS

tel: 01364 646100 **TQ10 9ES**
email: eat@turtleycornmill.com
dir: From A38 at South Brent/Avonwick junction, take B3372, then follow signs for Avonwick, 0.5m

Seasonal menus in an idyllic riverside setting

This sprawling old free house is set among six acres of gardens and fields in the South Hams on the edge of Dartmoor and includes a lake complete with ducks and its own small island. Originally a corn mill, it spent many years as a chicken hatchery before being converted to a pub. The interior is light and fresh with old furniture and oak and slate floors. You'll find plenty of newspapers and books to browse through while enjoying a whisky or supping a pint of Summerskills Start Point. The daily-changing modern British menus for breakfast/brunch, lunch and dinner are extensively based on local produce from around the pub's idyllic location. Typical main course choices include pheasant breast with dauphinoise potatoes, seasonal vegetables and rosemary gravy; Scottish salmon fillet topped with Morecambe Bay shrimps, stir-fried noodles and vegetables; pan-fried calves' liver with creamy mash, curly kale and bacon.

Open all day all wk Closed 25 Dec **Food** Lunch all wk 12-10 Dinner all wk 12-10 Set menu available ⊕ FREE HOUSE ◀ St Austell Tribute, Sharp's Doom Bar, Summerskills Start Point, Guest ales ♂ Thatchers. ☗ 10 **Facilities** Non-diners area ❤ (Bar Restaurant Garden) ♦ Children's portions Garden ➤ Parking WiFi

AXMOUTH
Map 4 SY29

The Harbour Inn
PICK OF THE PUBS

tel: 01297 20371 **Church St EX12 4AF**
email: info@theharbour-inn.co.uk
dir: In main street opposite church, 1m from Seaton

Daily-changing blackboard menus of local produce

A pebble's throw from the Axe Estuary in the picturesque village of Axmouth, this cosy, oak-beamed harbourside inn is a popular place for walkers and birdwatchers to refuel. Local ingredients are sourced for the food here and the bar and bistro menu offers comforting classics like local butcher's ham sandwiches; half a pint of king prawns; and smoked haddock and Somerset cheddar fishcakes. From a daily updated blackboard menu, you might want to consider oven-roasted salmon fillet with roasted fennel, caper and lemon butter sauce; breaded plaice fillets with peas and triple-fried chips; or steak and Poachers Ale pie. Leave room for apple and blackberry oat crunch crumble with vanilla custard; or banana Eton Mess with butterscotch sauce, meringue and honeycomb ice cream. The Harbour makes a great stop if you are walking the South West Coastal Path between Lyme Regis and Seaton.

Open all day all wk **Food** Lunch all wk 12-9.30 (Bkfst 9-11.30) Dinner all wk 12-9.30 ⊕ HALL & WOODHOUSE ◀ Badger First Gold, Tanglefoot, K&B Sussex ♂ Badger Applewood, Westons Stowford Press. **Facilities** Non-diners area ✿ (Bar Garden) ⦁ Children's menu Children's portions Play area Garden ⊟ Parking ⊟

| BAMPTON | Map 3 SS92 |

Exeter Inn

tel: 01398 331345 **EX16 9DY**
email: exeter_inn@btconnect.com
dir: From Bampton take B3227 (Brook St) signed Tiverton A396. Approx 1.2m to pub on rdbt (junct with A396)

Historic 15th-century inn and restaurant

Set below wooded hills in the Exe Valley just a short distance from Exmoor National Park, this long, low, white-painted inn was taken on by new owners in 2014. Beer lovers will be heartened by the sight of up to six barrels stillaged behind the snug little old bar here, with West Country ales favoured brews. This timeless scene complements the rest of the interior of the inn which has stood here for around six centuries; you'll find flagstone floors, beams, log fires and cosy corners; there's a well-appointed restaurant, too. The menu changes weekly and offers traditional English favourites, fish specials and a range of dishes with worldwide inspirations.

Open all day all wk **Food** Lunch all wk 12-2.30 Dinner all wk 5.30-9 ⊕ PUNCH TAVERNS ◀ Exmoor, Cotleigh ♂ Thatchers, Addlestones. **Facilities** Non-diners area ✿ (Bar Outside area) ⦁ Children's menu Children's portions Outside area ⊟ Parking WiFi ⊟ (notice required)

NEW The Swan ★★★★ INN

tel: 01398 332248 **Station Rd EX16 9NG**
email: info@theswan.co **web:** www.theswan.co
dir: M5 junct 17, A361 towards Barnstaple. At rdbt NW of Tiverton take A396 to Bampton

Seriously good food at this village gem

The Swan originally accommodated masons and other craftsmen enlarging the church in 1450, from when the oak beams and fireplace certainly date, and maybe the bread oven too. Renovation has endowed the bar with a contemporary-style, yet traditional-looking solid oak counter serving Devon Storm, Otter and Proper Job real ales, Sandford Orchard Devon Red cider and around 40 wines by the glass. Beef faggots, onion purée and gravy get a meal off to a good start, followed by fillet of bass on linguine, chilli and River Exe mussels; or steak, kidney and ale suet pudding.

Open Tue-Thu 12-11 (Fri-Sat 12-12 Sun 12-10.30 Mon 5-11) Closed 25 Dec, Mon L **Food** Lunch Tue-Sat 12-2, Sun 12-2.30 Dinner Tue-Sat 6-9.30 Av main course £12.50 ⊕ FREE HOUSE ◀ Red Rock Devon Storm, Otter, St Austell Proper Job ♂ Sandford Orchards Devon Red. ⦁ **Facilities** Non-diners area ✿ (Bar Outside area) ⦁ Children's menu Children's portions Family room Outside area ⊟ Parking WiFi ⊟ (notice required) **Rooms** 3

| BEER | Map 4 SY28 |

Anchor Inn ★★★★ INN

tel: 01297 20386 **Fore St EX12 3ET**
email: 6403@greeneking.co.uk **web:** www.oldenglish.co.uk
dir: A3052 towards Lyme Regis. At Hangmans Stone take B3174 into Beer. Pub on seafront

Enjoy sea views and sample fresh fish

A traditional inn overlooking the bay in the picture-perfect Devon village of Beer, this pretty colour-washed pub is perfectly situated for walking the Jurassic coastline. Fish caught by local boats features strongly on the menu, and the tempting starters might include a crabmeat pot with mixed leaves and granary bread, followed by home-made steak and Guinness pie; whole sea bass on king prawn and vegetable stir-fry; or wild mushroom and spinach risotto. Six comfortable guest rooms are also available.

Open all day all wk 8am-11pm ⊕ GREENE KING ◀ IPA & Abbot Ale, Otter Ale ♂ Aspall. **Facilities** ✿ (Bar Garden) ⦁ Children's menu Garden WiFi **Rooms** 6

| BEESANDS | Map 3 SX84 |

The Cricket Inn ★★★★ INN ⊛   PICK OF THE PUBS

tel: 01548 580215 **TQ7 2EN**
email: enquiries@thecricketinn.com **web:** www.thecricketinn.com
dir: From Kingsbridge take A379 towards Dartmouth. At Stokenham mini rdbt turn right to Beesands

This seaside inn is a must for seafood-lovers

In a small South Hams fishing village, The Cricket Inn first opened its doors in 1867 and has since survived storms, a World War II bomb and a mudslide. The inn encompasses a dog-friendly bar serving West Country ales, an AA-Rosette restaurant with sea views, and bright and airy accommodation. The Cricket is just metres from the sloping beach and clear waters of Start Bay and the head chef works closely with local fishermen who bring their catch straight to the kitchen door. From the lunch menu, sample diver-caught Beesands scallops with celeriac purée; boneless chicken wings and curried lentils; or hand-picked Start Bay crab sandwiches. Choices at dinner could be chicken and ham hock pie; the 'almost world famous' seafood pancake; and slow-cooked smoked duck, all made with produce from the Devonshire countryside and its waters.

Open all wk 11-3 6-11 (May-Sep all day) **Food** Lunch all wk 12-2.30 Dinner all wk 6-8.30 ⊕ HEAVITREE ◀ Otter Ale & Bitter, St Austell Tribute ♂ Aspall, Heron Valley, Thatchers. ⦁ 12 **Facilities** Non-diners area ✿ (Bar Restaurant) ⦁ Children's menu Children's portions Outside area ⊟ Parking WiFi **Rooms** 8

| BICKLEIGH | Map 3 SS90 |

Fisherman's Cot

tel: 01884 855237 **EX16 8RW**
email: fishermanscot.bickleigh@marstons.co.uk
dir: Phone for detailed directions

Riverside hostelry popular with locals and visitors alike

Well-appointed thatched inn by Bickleigh Bridge over the River Exe with food all day and beautiful gardens, just a short drive from Tiverton and Exmoor. The Waterside Bar is the place for doorstep sandwiches, pies, snacks and afternoon tea, while the restaurant incorporates a carvery (on Sunday) and carte menus. Expect dishes such as goats' cheese tart; seafood tagliatelle; chicken goulash; and for dessert deep dish apple pie.

Open all day all wk 11-11 (Sun 12-10.30) **Food** Contact pub for details ⊕ MARSTON'S ◀ Wychwood Hobgoblin, Ringwood. ⦁ 8 **Facilities** Non-diners area ✿ (Bar Garden) ⦁ Children's portions Garden ⊟ Parking WiFi ⊟ (notice required)

BLACKAWTON
Map 3 SX85

NEW The George Inn ★★★ INN

tel: 01803 712342 **Main St TQ9 7BG**
email: tgiblackawton@yahoo.co.uk **web:** www.blackawton.com
dir: *From Totnes on A381 through Halwell. Left onto A3122 towards Dartmouth, turn right to Blackawton*

Family-friendly village pub close to Dartmouth

In the South Hams village of Blackawton, The George is an ideal base for visitors to nearby Totnes and Dartmouth, as well as Woodlands Leisure Park. The pub gained its name during George III's reign but it was rebuilt after a fire in 1939, after which it became the rallying point for the forced evacuation of the parish in WW2. Now a family-friendly pub with comfortable accommodation, it's a place to relax over a pint of Teignworthy Spring Tide and a traditional menu including pizzas, curries and pub classics.

Open all wk 12-3 5-11 (Sun 12-3 7-10.30) **Food** Lunch all wk 12-2 Dinner Mon-Sat 6-9, Sun 7-9 ⊕ FREE HOUSE ◀ Teignworthy Spring Tide, Guest ales Ö Thatchers Gold, Somersby Cider, Healey's Cornish Rattler. ₸ 12 **Facilities** Non-diners area ❤ (Bar Restaurant Outside area) ♦️ Children's menu Children's portions Play area Garden Outside area ⋒ Beer festival Parking WiFi **Rooms** 4

The Normandy Arms ★★★★ INN ◉ PICK OF THE PUBS

tel: 01803 712884 **Chapel St TQ9 7BN**
email: info@normandyarms.co.uk **web:** www.normandyarms.co.uk
dir: *From Dartmouth take A3122 towards Halwell. Right at Forces Tavern to Blackawton*

Sixteenth-century free house with south-facing garden

Why Normandy? In 1944, soldiers trained for D-Day and the Normandy landings on nearby Slapton Sands, which explains why there's a salvaged Sherman tank in nearby Torcross (but why Blackawton hosts the annual International Festival of Wormcharming, you'll have to ask). The pub's character comes from the clean lines of the slate-floored bar and relaxing dining room, both with log-burners. In the bar, local and regional guest ales support Otter Ale and Thatchers Cheddar Valley cider. Proprietor Andrew West-Letford headed up the kitchens at several other highly-rated establishments before arriving here to earn an AA Rosette for his traditional British bar meals and modern European restaurant dishes. There are beef and lamb from Blackawton farms; roasted cod loin with rösti, roasted shallots and carrots, spinach and jus Parisienne; and Creedy Carver duck breast with confit duck crespelle and Jerusalem artichokes. Among Andrew's desserts is treacle tart with vanilla ice cream.

Open 12-3 5.30-11 Closed 2 Jan-1 Feb, Sun & Mon **Food** Lunch Tue-Sat 12-2.30 Dinner Tue-Sat 6.30-9.30 Av main course £16 Set menu available Restaurant menu available Tue-Sat ⊕ FREE HOUSE ◀ Otter Ale Ö Thatchers Cheddar Valley. ₸ 12 **Facilities** Non-diners area ❤ (Bar Restaurant Garden) ♦️ Garden ⋒ Parking WiFi **Rooms** 4

BRAMPFORD SPEKE
Map 3 SX99

The Lazy Toad Inn with Rooms PICK OF THE PUBS

tel: 01392 841591 **EX5 5DP**
email: thelazytoadinn@btinternet.com
dir: *From Exeter take A377 towards Crediton 1.5m, right signed Brampford Speke*

Excellent food at stylish country inn near Exeter

There's much to commend this 19th-century country inn situated in a thatched village in peaceful countryside with riverside walks. Polished slate tiles surround a bar which dispenses ales from Otter as well as tasty ciders from Sandford Orchards. Behind the pub Clive and Mo Walker's smallholding supplies the soft fruit, herbs, vegetables, lamb and eggs to the kitchen, while meat and fish are cured in the pub smokery. Farming implements jostle with bistro-style art and an eclectic mix of tables and chairs make for a modern country atmosphere. Settle by the fire and study a daily-changing menu that feature starters like ham hock terrine, pickled carrot chutney with brioche; and mains of steak and kidney pie with duck fat roasted potatoes; or seared fillet of Newlyn gurnard with Anna potatoes and wild mushrooms. Excellent vegetarian options too and a pretty cobbled courtyard and garden at the rear.

Open 11.30-2.30 6-11 (Sun 12-3) Closed 3wks Jan, Sun eve & Mon **Food** Lunch Tue-Sun 12-2 Dinner Tue-Sat 6.30-9 ⊕ FREE HOUSE ◀ Otter Bitter, St Austell Tribute Ö Sandford Orchards Devon Red & Devon Mist. ₸ 12 **Facilities** Non-diners area ❤ (Bar Garden Outside area) ♦️ Children's menu Children's portions Family room Garden Outside area ⋒ Parking WiFi

BRANSCOMBE
Map 4 SY18

The Fountain Head

tel: 01297 680359 **EX12 3BG**
email: thefountainhead@btconnect.com
dir: *From Seaton on A3052 towards Sidmouth left at Branscombe Cross to pub*

Often packed with walkers and locals

This 500-year-old forge and cider house is a true rural survivor, tucked away in a peaceful village just a short walk from the coastal path. The traditional worn flagstones, crackling log fires, rustic furnishings, village-brewed beers from Branscombe Vale, and the chatty atmosphere (no intrusive music or electronic games here) charm both locals and visitors. Hearty pub food includes Moroccan-style vegetable stew; chicken supreme stuffed with smoked cheese and bacon; and home-cooked honey-roast ham, double egg and chips. There's a spit-roast and barbecue every Sunday evening between July and September. Don't miss the midsummer beer festival.

Open all wk 11-3 6-11 (Sun 12-10.30) **Food** Lunch all wk 12-2 Dinner all wk 6.30-9 ⊕ FREE HOUSE ◀ Branscombe Vale Branoc, Jolly Geff, Summa That Ö Westons, Pip. **Facilities** Non-diners area ❤ (Bar Restaurant Garden) ♦️ Children's menu Children's portions Family room Garden ⋒ Beer festival Parking 🚌 (notice required)

The Masons Arms PICK OF THE PUBS

tel: 01297 680300 **EX12 3DJ**
email: masonsarms@staustellbrewery.co.uk
dir: *Exit A3052 towards Branscombe, down hill, Masons Arms at bottom of hill*

Ancient pub close to the sea

Located in the picturesque village of Branscombe, the inn is just a 10-minute stroll from the beach; its peaceful gardens have sea views across a picturesque valley. This creeper-clad pub dates from 1360, when it was a cider house squeezed into the middle of a row of cottages. Back then it was a smugglers' haunt and its interior has barely changed since those days: slate floors, stone walls, ships' beams, an old jail railing and a huge open fireplace used for spit roasts on Sundays all add to the time-warp charm. Five real ales such as Otter and Proper Job are always available, including several that are locally brewed, plus ciders such as Healey's Pear Rattler. Food is a serious business here; where possible all ingredients are grown, reared or caught locally, especially lobster and crab. A three-day beer festival is held in the middle of July.

Open all day all wk 11-11 (Sun 12-10.30) **Food** Lunch all wk 12-2.15 Dinner all wk 6.30-9 ⊕ ST AUSTELL BREWERY ◀ Tribute & Proper Job, Otter Ö Thatchers Gold, Healey's Pear Rattler. ₸ 14 **Facilities** Non-diners area ❤ (Bar) ♦️ Children's menu Children's portions Outside area ⋒ Beer festival Parking WiFi

BRAUNTON
Map 3 SS43

The Williams Arms

tel: 01271 812360 **Wrafton EX33 2DE**
email: info@williamsarms.co.uk
dir: *On A361 between Barnstaple & Braunton*

Family owned free house with popular carvery

This postcard-pretty thatched free house beside the popular Tarka Trail dates back to the 16th century and has been owned by the Squire family since the mid-70s. Its prime location sees weary walkers, cyclists and local diners pile in for the pub's famous daily carvery, which always features locally reared meat and seasonal vegetables. Alternatively, you can try Devon scallops in white wine and cream sauce; steak and real ale pie or lighter options like prawn salad or roast turkey ciabatta - perfect when washed down with a pint of Sharp's Doom Bar. The carvery proves very popular.

Open all day all wk 8.45am-11pm **Food** Lunch all wk 12-9 Dinner all wk 12-9
⊕ FREE HOUSE ◀ Worthington's Creamflow, Sharp's Doom Bar, Exmoor Ales Gold, Guinness Ŏ Thatchers. ☂ 10 **Facilities** Non-diners area ◀◀ Children's menu Children's portions Play area Garden ⊟ Parking WiFi ▦ (notice required)

BRENDON
Map 3 SS74

Rockford Inn

tel: 01598 741214 **EX35 6PT**
email: enquiries@therockfordinn.com
dir: *A39 through Minehead follow signs to Lynmouth. Left to Brendon*

Popular Exmoor hideaway

Standing alongside the East Lyn River in the tucked-away Brendon Valley, this traditional 17th-century free house stands in the heart of Exmoor and is handy for several walking routes. Thatchers ciders complement local cask ales such as Barn Owl and Devon Darter, and there's a choice of good home-made pub meals. Honey roasted ham, leek and wild mushroom pie; lamb rogan josh; and venison and pear sausages and mash are typical menu choices; the specials board changes daily. Eat in the garden in warm weather, or head inside to the open fire when the weather changes.

Open all day all wk **Food** Lunch all wk 12-2.30 Dinner all wk 6-8.30 Av main course £11 ⊕ FREE HOUSE ◀ Cotleigh Barn Owl & 25, St Austell Tribute, Clearwater Proper Ansome, Devon Darter & Real Smiler, Exmoor Ŏ Thatchers, Addlestones. **Facilities** Non-diners area ◀◀ (Bar Restaurant Garden) ◀◀ Children's menu Children's portions Garden ⊟ Parking WiFi

Find out about pubs and pigs in Swine and dine on page 12

BRIDFORD
Map 3 SX88

The Bridford Inn

tel: 01647 252250 **EX6 7HT**
email: info@bridfordinn.co.uk **web:** www.bridfordinn.co.uk
dir: *Phone for detailed directions*

Traditional inn with Dartmoor views

Converted from three 17th-century cottages, this elevated Dartmoor village inn and shop is set in the pretty village of Bridford overlooking the stunning Teign Valley. Oak beams, exposed stonework and a huge inglenook fireplace with log-burner retains the pub's original character and the bar serves Dartmoor Brewery Jail Ale alongside three weekly guest beers. The menu changes quarterly but might offer a pie of the day; fish and chips and a veggie-friendly potato gnocchi with Devon blue cheese cream sauce. Look out for the pub's bank holiday beer and cider festivals in May and August.

Open all day all wk **Food** Lunch Mon-Fri 12-2, Sat-Sun 12-3 Dinner Mon-Thu 6.30-8.30, Fri-Sat 6.30-9 Av main course £10 Set menu available Restaurant menu available all wk ⊕ FREE HOUSE ◀ Dartmoor Jail Ale, Guest ales Ŏ Sandford Orchards, Westons. **Facilities** Non-diners area ◀◀ (All areas) ◀◀ Children's menu Children's portions Garden Outside area ⊟ Beer festival Cider festival Parking WiFi ▦ (notice required)

BUCKLAND MONACHORUM
Map 3 SX46

Drake Manor Inn

tel: 01822 853892 **The Village PL20 7NA**
email: drakemanor@drakemanorinn.co.uk
dir: *From A386 (Plymouth) turn left before Yelverton, follow signs to Buckland Monachorum. Left into village, on left next to church*

12th-century inn known for its warm welcome and good food

In the 12th century, when nearby St Andrew's church was being built, the masons needed a house to live in. Today's licensee of that now very old house is Mandy Robinson, who prides herself on running a 'proper pub', with a menu of locally-sourced delights. Start with crispy Chinese duck and hoi sin spring rolls, or whitebait with sweet chilli dip; follow on with a local steak with onion rings; steak and ale pie, or a trio of sausages on mash with peas and gravy. Leave space for some delicious home-made dessert. There's a lovely cottage garden to the side of the pub, and a wood-burner in the winter.

Open all wk Mon-Thu 11.30-2.30 6.30-11 (Fri-Sat 11.30-11.30 Sun 12-11)
Food Lunch Mon-Fri 11.30-2, Sat-Sun 11.30-2.30 Dinner Sun-Thu 6.30-9.30, Fri-Sat 6.30-10 Av main course £10 ⊕ PUNCH TAVERNS ◀ Dartmoor Jail Ale, Sharp's Doom Bar, Otter Bitter Ŏ Thatchers Gold & Heritage. ☂ 9
Facilities Non-diners area ◀◀ (Bar Garden) ◀◀ Children's menu Children's portions Family room Garden ⊟ Parking

BUTTERLEIGH
Map 3 SS90

The Butterleigh Inn

tel: 01884 855433 **EX15 1PN**
email: thebutterleighinn1@btconnect.com
dir: *M5 junct 28, B3181 signed Cullompton. In Cullompton High St right signed Butterleigh. 3m to pub*

Regularly changing real ales and home-made food

Set in a delightful village opposite the 13th-century St Matthew's church and in the heart of the rolling Devon countryside, the 400-year-old Butterleigh is a traditional free house. There is a mass of local memorabilia throughout this friendly local, where customers can choose from a selection of changing real ales including Dartmoor Jail Ale, ciders including Devon Scrumpy from Sandford Orchards, and around 15 malt whiskies. Expect home-made dishes such as turkey and pork pie; curry of the day; lamb chops; broccoli, leek and Stilton bake; and steaks from the grill. On fine days, the garden is very popular.

Open 12-2.30 6-11 (Fri-Sat 12-2.30 6-12 Sun 12-3) Closed Sun eve, Mon L **Food** Lunch Tue-Sat 12-2 Dinner Tue-Sat 7-9 Av main course £10-£11 ⊕ FREE HOUSE ◀ Cotleigh Tawny Ale, Otter Ale & Amber, Dartmoor IPA & Jail Ale, Guest ale ⊙ Sandford Orchards Devon Scrumpy, Sheppy's, Winkleigh Sam's. ▼ 9 **Facilities** Non-diners area ❄ (Bar Garden) ◆ Children's portions Garden ⋒ Parking WiFi

CHAGFORD
Map 3 SX78

Sandy Park Inn
`PICK OF THE PUBS`

tel: 01647 433267 **TQ13 8JW**
email: info@sandyparkinn.co.uk
dir: *From A30 exit at Whiddon Down, left towards Moretonhampstead. Inn 3m*

Lovely thatched pub with a timeless quality

In a beautiful setting near the River Teign on the edge of Dartmoor, this inn attracts locals and travellers alike, while dogs are frequently to be found slumped in front of the fire. Homely horse brasses and sporting prints adorn the walls of the beamed bar, where you can choose from an eclectic wine list and a good range of traditional local ales like Otter Bitter and Dartmoor Jail Ale. Whether you eat in the bar, snug or candlelit dining room, menus of home-made dishes change with the seasons, blending pub classics with modern fusion and vegetarian options; a range of gourmet stone-baked pizzas is especially popular. Sample dishes are honey-glazed goats' cheese; oven-roasted fillet of hake; pan-fried lamb steak; and vanilla cheesecake. Sandwiches and salads are perfect for summer lunchtimes, when they can be served in the garden with its views towards the Castle Drogo estate and deer park.

Open all day all wk **Food** Lunch all wk 12-2.30 Dinner all wk 6-9 Av main course £10 ⊕ FREE HOUSE ◀ Otter Bitter, Dartmoor IPA, Dartmoor Jail Ale ⊙ Thatchers, Westons Old Rosie. **Facilities** Non-diners area ❄ (Bar Garden) ◆ Children's portions Family room Garden ⋒ Parking WiFi ▭

CLAYHIDON
Map 4 ST11

The Merry Harriers

tel: 01823 421270 **Forches Corner EX15 3TR**
email: merryharriers.bookings@gmail.com
dir: *M5 junct 26, A38 signed Wellington. At next rdbt left signed Exeter/A38. Left into Ford St (follow brown pub sign). At next x-rds left signed Merry Harriers 1.5m*

Family- and dog-friendly free house high on the Blackdown Hills

Although not immediately apparent from its black-and-white-timbered, two-storey façade, this delightful pub was built in 1492 as a traditional Devon longhouse. Interior features include beamed ceilings, an inglenook fireplace with wood-burner, and attractive dining areas, where Peter and Angela Gatling's seasonal menus offer

filled baguettes; steak and kidney pie; cod and chips, and other fish fresh from Lyme Bay; and daily specials. The large garden is popular, not least because there's a children's play area. Bar favourites include Exmoor, Cotleigh and Otter real ales, Bollhayes Somerset cider, and 14 wines by the glass. Check for the summer beer festival dates.

Open 12-3 6.30-11 Closed Sun eve & Mon **Food** Lunch Tue-Sat 12-2, Sun 12-2.15 Dinner Tue-Sat 6.30-9 ⊕ FREE HOUSE ◀ Exmoor, Cotleigh & Otter Ales ⊙ Thatchers Gold, Bollhayes. ▼ 14 **Facilities** Non-diners area ❄ (Bar Garden) ◆ Children's menu Children's portions Play area Garden ⋒ Beer festival Cider festival Parking WiFi ▭ (notice required)

CLEARBROOK
Map 3 SX56

The Skylark Inn

tel: 01822 853258 **PL20 6JD**
email: skylvic@btinternet.com
dir: *5m N of Plymouth on A386 towards Tavistock. Take 2nd right signed Clearbrook*

Child-friendly pub set in the Dartmoor National Park

Originally used by miners in the 18th century, The Skylark is just 10 minutes from Plymouth. The village and surrounding area are ideal for cyclists and walkers. Children are welcome at this attractive pub and there is a special play area for them. Local ales and good wholesome food are served in the beamed bar with its large fireplace and wood-burning stove. Dishes include sizzling steaks, Mediterranean-style tuna, prawn salad, spinach and mascarpone lasagne, and classics like breaded scampi and barbecued ribs. Jackets and baguettes are also on offer. There is a beer festival on the Summer Bank Holiday and monthly charity quiz nights.

Open all wk 11.30-3 6-11.30 (Sat-Sun all day) **Food** Lunch Mon-Fri 12-2, Sat-Sun all day Dinner Mon-Fri 6.30-9, Sat-Sun all day ⊕ UNIQUE PUB CO LTD ◀ Otter Ale, St Austell Tribute, Dartmoor. **Facilities** Non-diners area ❄ (Bar Garden) ◆ Children's menu Children's portions Play area Family room Garden ⋒ Beer festival Parking WiFi ▭ (notice required)

CLOVELLY
Map 3 SS32

Red Lion Hotel ★★ HL
`PICK OF THE PUBS`

tel: 01237 431237 **The Quay EX39 5TF**
email: redlion@clovelly.co.uk **web:** www.redlion-clovelly.co.uk/redlionindex.html
dir: *From Bideford rdbt, A39 to Bude, 10m. At Clovelly Cross rdbt right, pass Clovelly Visitor Centre entrance, bear left. Hotel at bottom of hill*

Excellent home-cooked food in unspoilt fishing village

This charming whitewashed hostelry sits right on the quay in Clovelly, the famously unspoilt 'village like a waterfall', which descends down broad steps to a 14th-century harbour. Guests staying in the whimsically decorated bedrooms can fall asleep to the sound of waves lapping the shingle. Originally a beerhouse for fishermen and other locals, the Red Lion has plenty of character and offers Cornish ales such as Sharp's Doom Bar in its snug bar, where you can rub shoulders with the locals. Alternatively, you could settle in the Harbour Bar, and sample the home-cooked food, the modern seasonal menu specialising in fresh seafood, which is landed daily right outside the door. Choose pan-fried John Dory or poached brill with creamy mushroom sauce, or opt for Clovelly Estate venison and game dishes; or pork fillet with smoked bacon, apple purée and red wine jus. There is an annual beer festival at Spring Bank Holiday.

Open all day all wk **Food** Lunch all wk 12-2.30 Dinner all wk 6-8.30 ⊕ FREE HOUSE ◀ Sharp's Doom Bar, Clovelly Cobbler, Guinness ⊙ Thatchers, Winkleigh, Westons Stowford Press. **Facilities** ❄ (Bar) ◆ Children's menu Children's portions Family room Beer festival Parking WiFi ▭ **Rooms** 17

CLYST HYDON
Map 3 ST00

NEW The Five Bells Inn

tel: 01884 277288 **EX15 2NT**
email: info@fivebells.uk.com
dir: *B3181 towards Cullompton, right at Hele Cross towards Clyst Hydon. 2m turn right, then sharp right at left bend at village sign*

Sixteenth-century pub saved by the villagers

The pub and the church were neighbours until early last century, when the rector's objections forced the inn to move into this old thatched farmhouse, its new name intended as a raspberry to the rector. Otter and Butcombe real ales hold sway in the bar - note the original counter. Exposed brick and cream-papered walls are adorned with signed Exeter Chiefs rugby shirts, and there's a German-style 'stammtisch', or regulars' table. Simple pub food includes bangers and mash; Jerusalem artichoke risotto; South Devon Herd rump steak; and fresh fish pie, plus daily specials. Very child friendly. The beer festival is held on the Early Spring Bank Holiday.

Open all wk 12-3 6-12 (Sun 12-10) **Food** Lunch Mon-Sat 12-2, Sun 12-9 Dinner Mon-Thu 6-9, Fri-Sat 6-9.30, Sun 12-9 Av main course £9-£13.50 Set menu available ⊕ FREE HOUSE ◀ Otter Ale, Otter Amber, Butcombe Bitter ♂ Berry Farm. ♟ 9 **Facilities** Non-diners area ✤ (Bar Garden Outside area) ♦♦ Children's menu Children's portions Garden Outside area ⋈ Beer festival Cider festival Parking WiFi ▭ (notice required)

COCKWOOD
Map 3 SX98

The Anchor Inn

tel: 01626 890203 **EX6 8RA**
email: scott.anchor@hotmail.co.uk **web:** www.anchorinncockwood.com
dir: *From A379 between Dawlish & Starcross follow Cockwood sign*

Waterside pub specialising in seafood

Originally a Seamen's Mission, this 450-year-old inn overlooks a small landlocked harbour on the River Exe and was once the haunt of smugglers. There is even a friendly ghost with his dog. In summer, customers spill out onto the verandah and harbour wall, while real fires, nautical bric-a-brac and low beams make the interior cosy in winter. For fish lovers, the comprehensive menu will make decisions difficult – there are over 20 different ways to eat mussels, and plenty of scallop dishes and fish platters. Meat-eaters and vegetarians are not forgotten. Beer festivals twice a year around Easter and Halloween.

Open all day all wk 11-11 (Sun 12-10.30 25 Dec 12-2) **Food** Lunch Mon-Sat 12-10, Sun 12-9.30 Dinner Mon-Sat 12-10, Sun 12-9.30 Av main course £10.95 Restaurant menu available all wk ⊕ HEAVITREE ◀ Otter Ale, St Austell Tribute & Proper Job, Dartmoor Jail Ale, 3 Guest ales. **Facilities** Non-diners area ✤ (Bar Outside area) ♦♦ Children's menu Children's portions Outside area ⋈ Beer festival Parking ▭ (notice required)

COLEFORD
Map 3 SS70

The New Inn ★★★★ INN
PICK OF THE PUBS

tel: 01363 84242 **EX17 5BZ**
email: enquiries@thenewinncoleford.co.uk **web:** www.thenewinncoleford.co.uk
dir: *From Exeter take A377, 1.5m after Crediton left for Coleford, 1.5m to inn*

Local ales and food in secluded Devon valley

The attractive 13th-century building with thatched roof makes a perfect home for this friendly inn. The ancient slate-floored bar with its old chests and polished brass blends effortlessly with fresh white walls, original oak beams and simple wooden furniture in the dining room. Set beside the River Cole, the garden is perfect for alfresco summer dining, when you can ponder on the pub's history: it was used by travelling Cistercian monks long before Charles I reviewed his troops from a nearby house during the English Civil War. Menus change regularly, and special events such as 'posh pies week' or 'sea shanty evening' are interspersed throughout the year. Home-made bar food includes a range of soups, omelettes and platters, while a larger meal might include poached Brixham skate wing with parmesan crust; or sautéed pork tenderloin fillet, black pudding and Madeira sauce. The pub's Amazon Blue parrot, called Captain, has been a famous fixture here for nearly 30 years, greeting bar regulars and guests booking into the six well-appointed bedrooms.

Open all wk 12-3 6-11 (Sun 12-3 6-10.30) **Food** Lunch all wk 12-2 Dinner all wk 6-9.30 ⊕ FREE HOUSE ◀ Sharp's Doom Bar, Otter Ale ♂ Winkleigh Sam's, Thatchers Gold. ♟ **Facilities** Non-diners area ✤ (Bar Garden Outside area) ♦♦ Children's menu Children's portions Garden Outside area ⋈ Parking WiFi ▭ (notice required) **Rooms** 6

DARTMOUTH
Map 3 SX85

Royal Castle Hotel ★★★ HL
PICK OF THE PUBS

See Pick of the Pubs on page 140

DENBURY
Map 3 SX86

The Union Inn

tel: 01803 812595 **Denbury Green TQ12 6DQ**
email: enquiries@theunioninndenbury.co.uk
dir: *2m from Newton Abbot, signed Denbury*

Old and new come together in this village inn

Overlooking the village green, The Union Inn is at least 400 years old and counting. Inside are the original stone walls that once rang to the hammers of the blacksmiths and cartwrights who worked here many moons ago. The bar area has comfy leather sofas while the decor throughout is a mix of traditional and contemporary. Choose from the tapas and bar snack menu, the restaurant menu or the daily specials. Mouth-watering starters could include quail stuffed with pancetta or barbecued chicken wings. Follow with vegetable filo roulade; slow-cooked belly of Devon pork; seafood linguine; or the Union Inn burger.

Open all wk 12-3 6-11.30 (Thu-Sun 12-11) **Food** Lunch all wk 12-2.30 Dinner all wk 6.30-9.30 ⊕ ENTERPRISE INNS ◀ Otter Bitter, Hunter's Denbury Dreamer, Guest ales ♂ Westons. ♟ 10 **Facilities** Non-diners area ✤ (Bar Restaurant Garden) ♦♦ Children's menu Children's portions Garden ⋈ Parking WiFi ▭

PICK OF THE PUBS

Royal Castle Hotel ★★★ HL

DARTMOUTH   Map 3 SX85

tel: 01803 833033
11 The Quay TQ6 9PS
email: enquiry@royalcastle.co.uk
web: www.royalcastle.co.uk
dir: *In town centre, overlooking inner harbour*

Historic pub and hotel with great estuary views

An iconic 17th-century building in the centre of this bustling town, the Royal Castle Hotel commands a prime site overlooking the Dart estuary. Originally four Tudor houses built on either side of a narrow lane, which now forms the lofty hallway, this handsome old coaching inn offers plenty of original features in the shape of period fireplaces, spiral staircases, oil paintings and priest holes. The choice of real ales from local breweries includes Dartmoor Jail Ale and Otter Amber, and there is an impressive number of carefully selected wines served by the glass; a wider range of high quality wines appears on the Castle Collection list. A supporter of Taste of the West's 'buy local' campaign, the kitchen showcases plenty of Devon produce on both the all-day bar menu and the Grill Room restaurant. Typical choices in the pubby Harbour Bar and Galleon Lounge might take in local crab sandwiches; seafood chowder; chargrilled South Devon sirloin steak and chips; or the vegetarian quesadilla

baked with Cheddar cheese, peppers, onion and roasted jalapeño peppers. With its lovely river views, the Grill Room upstairs is a great setting to enjoy starters such as South Devon mussels mariniere or ham hock terrine with duck liver mousse, home-made piccalilli and root vegetable vinaigrette. These might be followed by braised turbot on the bone with wilted spinach, Parisienne potatoes and lemongrass and coriander emulsion; or oven-roasted venison loin with sweet potato gratin, aubergine and courgette cannelloni, slow-roasted celeriac purée and juniper jus. Finish, perhaps, with mascarpone and raspberry trifle terrine, raspberry sorbet and strawberry gremolata; or a board of West Country cheeses with local ale chutney.

Open all day all week 8am-11.30pm
Food Lunch and dinner all week 11.30-10 Set menu; Restaurant menu all week. ⊕ FREE HOUSE ◼ Dartmoor Jail Ale, Otter Amber, Sharp's Doom Bar Ⓞ Thatchers Gold, Orchard's. ☷ 29
Facilities Non-diners area ☙ (Bar) ♦ Children's menu & portions Family room WiFi **Rooms** 25

DODDISCOMBSLEIGH
Map 3 SX88

The Nobody Inn ★★★★ INN ⬡
PICK OF THE PUBS

See Pick of the Pubs on page 142

DOLTON
Map 3 SS51

Rams Head Inn

tel: 01805 804255 **South St EX19 8QS**
email: ramsheadinn@btopenworld.com
dir: *8m from Torrington on A3124*

Traditional pub in Devon's lovely countryside

This 15th-century free house has retained much of its original character with huge old fireplaces, bread ovens and pot stands. The inn's central location places it on many inland tourist routes, whilst the Tarka Trail and Rosemoor Gardens are both nearby. Expect a selection of cask ales on tap, accompanied by popular and traditional meals on the restaurant menu, served at lunchtime and in the evening.

Open 10-3 6-11 (Fri-Sat 12-12 Sun 12-4 6-11) Closed Mon winter **Food** Lunch all wk 12-2.30 Dinner Mon-Sat 6.30-9 Av main course £10 Restaurant menu available Tue-Sat ⬡ FREE HOUSE ◀ Sharp's Own, Guest ales ⭗ Winkleigh. ▾ 14 **Facilities** Non-diners area ☙ (Bar Outside area) ◗◗ Garden Outside area ⅌ Parking WiFi 🚐

EAST ALLINGTON
Map 3 SX74

The Fortescue Arms

tel: 01548 521215 **TQ9 7RA**
email: info@fortescue-arms.co.uk
dir: *Phone for detailed directions*

Pretty free house in a South Hams village

This charming old country inn was taken over by a friendly family in 2013. The flagstone-floored bar now offers two real ales from Dartmoor Brewery as well as a selection of lagers and ciders. The food operation focusses on presenting traditional dishes cooked to order in good sized portions at reasonable prices; look to the boards for fish availability, specials which change weekly, and children's choices. A typical three-course selection could comprise a trio of smoked fish with home-made crusty bread; pan-fried tenderloin of pork with mustard creamed potatoes; and white chocolate cheesecake with raspberry coulis and Devon clotted cream.

Open Tue-Fri 6-11 (Sat-Sun all day) Closed Mon **Food** Contact pub for details Av main course £11 ⬡ FREE HOUSE ◀ Dartmoor Legend, IPA & Jail Ale, Guinness ⭗ Thatchers. ▾ **Facilities** Non-diners area ☙ (Bar Restaurant Garden) ◗◗ Children's menu Children's portions Garden ⅌ Parking WiFi 🚐 (notice required)

EAST PRAWLE
Map 3 SX73

NEW The Pigs Nose Inn

tel: 01548 511209 **TQ7 2BY**
email: info@pigsnoseinn.co.uk
dir: *From Kingsbridge take A379 towards Dartmouth. After Frogmore turn right signed East Prawle. Approx 5m to pub in village centre*

A 500-year-old inn overlooking the village green

Smugglers used to store their shipwreck booty here but, rather than hiding contraband, today's owners Lesley and Peter Webber prefer to demonstrate their adherence to old-fashioned values by banning juke boxes and games machines, and by their provision of a 'knitting corner', games and toys. Devon-sourced real ales are served straight from the barrel in the wonderfully cluttered bar. Food here is never a 'minuscule blob on an oversized square plate', but good helpings of traditional pub grub, such as chicken curry; scampi and chips; cod and chips; and vegetarian Mediterranean pasta. There's also a dog menu!

Open 12-3 6-11.30 Closed Sun (Nov-Mar) **Food** Lunch all wk 12-2 Dinner all wk 6.30-9 Av main course £9 ⬡ FREE HOUSE ◀ The South Hams Eddystone & Devon Pride, Otter ⭗ Thatchers Heritage. **Facilities** Non-diners area ☙ (Bar Restaurant Outside area) ◗◗ Children's menu Children's portions Play area Family room Outside area ⅌ WiFi **Notes** ⬡

EXETER
Map 3 SX99

The Hour Glass

tel: 01392 258722 **21 Melbourne St EX2 4AU**
email: ajpthehourglass@yahoo.co.uk
dir: *M5 junct 30, A370 signed Exeter. At Countess Weir rdbt 3rd exit onto Topsham Rd (B3182) signed City Centre. In approx 2m left into Melbourne St*

Quirky end-of-terrace pub with friendly staff

This distinctively shaped backstreet pub has built up a reputation for its friendly service and inventive food, not to mention its impressive range of local real ales. Expect beams, wood floors, an open fire and resident cats in the bar, where handpulled pints of Otter Bitter or Exeter Avocet; can be enjoyed with curried eggs and watercress; or lamb, quince and Rioja stew with anchovy dumplings.

Open 12-2.30 5-close (Sat-Sun all day Mon 5-close) Closed 25-26 Dec & 2 Jan, Mon L **Food** Lunch Tue-Fri 12-2.15, Sat-Sun 12-3 Dinner Mon-Sat 7-9.30, Sun 6-9 ⬡ ENTERPRISE INNS ◀ Otter Bitter, Exeter Avocet, Bath SPA, Rotating Local ales ⭗ Burrow Hill. ▾ 24 **Facilities** Non-diners area WiFi

Red Lion Inn

tel: 01392 461271 **Broadclyst EX5 3EL**
dir: *On B3181 (Exeter to Cullompton road)*

Tucked away in a quiet corner of the Killerton Estate

You'll find the Red Lion in a 16th-century listed building set at the heart of a delightful village in the National Trust's Killerton Estate. The interior has a wealth of beams and warming open fires, where pints of Tribute and Doom Bar are cheerfully served and supped. The typical menu may offer lamb's liver, onion and bacon casserole; pot roasted lamb shank; grilled sea bass; or Exmoor ale rabbit stew. Treat yourself to a home-made pud afterwards. Vegetarians and coeliacs are catered for, as are the canine contingent, who have their own bar menu.

Open all wk 12-2.30 5.30-11 (Sat-Sun 12-11) **Food** Lunch all wk 12-1.45 Dinner all wk 6-8.45 ⬡ FREE HOUSE ◀ St Austell Tribute, Sharp's Doom Bar, Guest ale ⭗ Thatchers Gold. ▾ 8 **Facilities** Non-diners area ☙ (Bar Garden) ◗◗ Children's menu Children's portions Garden ⅌ Parking 🚐 (notice required)

NEW The Rusty Bike

tel: 01392 214440 **67 Howell Rd EX4 4LZ**
email: tiny@rustybike-exeter.co.uk
dir: *Phone for detailed directions*

Truly unique gastro-pub a stone's throw from Exeter University

Now into their 5th year, The Rusty Bike is a place for the kitchen team to show what they can do with the wealth of local produce available. The pub offers tempting choices ranging from goose, clementine and smoked bacon rillette to blade of Red Ruby beef, parsley and garlic mash with snail popcorn – all locally sourced, or as they say, 'from welly to belly'. Beer and cider aficionados will also enjoy the Fat Pig Brewery's own creations, Pigmalion Ale, John Street Ale and Rusty Pig Cider.

Open all wk 5-11 (Fri-Sat 5-12 Sun 12-7.30) **Food** Lunch Sun 12-7.30 Dinner Mon-Sat 6-10, Sun 12-7.30 Av main course £16 ⬡ FREE HOUSE ◀ Fat Pig Ham 69, John Street Ale & Pigmalion ⭗ Rusty Pig. ▾ 18 **Facilities** Non-diners area ☙ (Bar Restaurant Outside area) ◗◗ Children's portions Outside area WiFi 🚐 (notice required)

PICK OF THE PUBS

The Nobody Inn ★★★★ INN 🌹

tel: 01647 252394
EX6 7PS
email: info@nobodyinn.co.uk
web: www.nobodyinn.co.uk
dir: *3m SW of Exeter Racecourse (A38)*

All the old-world charm you could want

For over 400 years, this old building has stood in the rolling countryside between the Haldon Hills and the Teign Valley. Remodelling over the centuries has reflected its several roles, including a long spell as a centre for parish affairs and meeting place until in 1838 Pophill House, as it was then known, formally became The New Inn. Among the five landlords since was the poor chap in 1952 whose body undertakers mistakenly left in the mortuary, so that his funeral went ahead with an empty coffin - which is how the inn acquired its name. Inside, providing all the expected old-world charm, are low ceilings, blackened beams, an inglenook fireplace and antique furniture. The bar serves 30-odd wines by the glass, selected from a range of more than 250 bins, some quite rare, and the shelves groan under the weight of a mind-boggling 280 whiskies, mostly malts. Branscombe Vale brewery supplies Nobody's Bitter, with guests adding further real ale choice. Crisp white napkins define the restaurant, where

head chef Rob Murray's menus, awarded an AA Rosette, rely extensively on fine Devon produce. A typical lunch or dinner would be rabbit tortellini with carrot purée, and bacon and tarragon foam; followed by sustainably-sourced fish pie topped with creamy mash and cheese, and carrot, beetroot and fennel salad; and, to finish, pumpkin cheesecake with orange flower-water ice cream. Daily specials might be Nobody ale-battered fish and chips; and cumin- and honey-glazed home-cooked ham with free-range eggs. If you want a bar snack, there's homity pie; and ploughman's, featuring Sharpham brie, Devon Blue or Devon oke cheese.

Open all day all wk 11-11 (Sun 12-10.30) Closed 1 Jan **Food** Lunch Mon-Sat 12-2, Sun 12-3 Dinner Mon-Thu 6.30-9, Fri-Sat 6.30-9.30, Sun 7-9 Restaurant menu Tue-Sat. 🍺 FREE HOUSE 🛢 Branscombe Vale Nobody's Bitter, Guest ales ♻ Brimblecombe's, St Austell Copper Press, Thatchers Gold. 🍷 28 **Facilities** Non-diners area 🐾 (Bar Garden) 🚼 Children's portions Garden 🪑 Parking **Rooms** 5

■ EXTON
Map 3 SX98

The Puffing Billy
PICK OF THE PUBS

tel: 01392 877888 **Station Rd EX3 0PR**
email: enquiries@thepuffingbilly.co.uk
dir: *A376 signed Exmouth, through Ebford. Follow signs for pub, right into Exton*

Smart modern setting for seasonal British food

The neighbouring Exe estuary and the distant upwellings of Dartmoor's hills and woods may be glimpsed from the tables set in front of this old whitewashed pub. The building might be 16th century; the name 19th century and referring to the nearby railway line; the food is absolutely 21st century, served in a chic, modern dining pub-restaurant. The traditional exterior disguises the crisp, clean lines and finish within, where reliable West Country beers from the likes of Otter and Sharp's and a zesty menu combine to make The Puffing Billy a favourite destination dining bar, now under new ownership. The menu is energetically English, seasonally changing and based on the best that Devon can provide - and all home cooked. Crab cakes with beetroot and apple relish and watercress salad is a possible starter; continuing then with sage and garlic stuffed West Country belly pork with baked pear and cider sauce. To finish - steamed treacle pudding with, what else, Devon clotted cream.

Open all wk 12-3 6-11 (Apr-Sep all day) **Food** Lunch Mon-Sat 12-2 Dinner Mon-Sat 6-9 Set menu available Restaurant menu available Mon-Sat ⊕ FREE HOUSE ◀ Otter Bitter, Sharp's Doom Bar. ☥ 15 **Facilities** Non-diners area ☙ (Bar Garden) ♦♦ Children's menu Children's portions Garden ⊨ Parking WiFi ☵ (notice required)

■ GEORGEHAM
Map 3 SS43

The Rock Inn

tel: 01271 890322 **Rock Hill EX33 1JW**
email: therockgeorgeham@gmail.com
dir: *From A361 at Braunton follow Croyde Bay signs. Through Croyde, 1m to Georgeham. Pass shop & church. Inn on right*

A mixture of dining options at this popular inn

A great watering hole for walkers and cyclists, this old inn is also handy for the famous surfing beaches at Woolacombe. Its friendly atmosphere, comprising a mix of happy banter from the locals and gentle jazz played at lunchtime, adds to the enjoyment of a pint selected from the five ales on offer. Choose between the traditional bar, the slightly more contemporary lower bar, or a bright conservatory decorated with local art. The tasty menu is hard to resist, extending from a light lunch of Dave Wong's salt and pepper chilli squid, to dinner dishes such as the Rock's fish pie.

Open all day all wk 11am-mdnt **Food** Lunch all wk 12-2.30 Dinner all wk 6-9.30 ◀ Timothy Taylor Landlord, Exmoor Ale, St Austell Tribute, Sharp's Doom Bar, Otter ☥ Thatchers Gold, Addlestones. ☥ 12 **Facilities** Non-diners area ☙ (Bar Garden) ♦♦ Children's menu Children's portions Garden ⊨ Parking WiFi ☵

■ HAYTOR VALE
Map 3 SX77

The Rock Inn ★★★★ INN ⊛
PICK OF THE PUBS

tel: 01364 661305 **TQ13 9XP**
email: info@rock-inn.co.uk **web:** www.rock-inn.co.uk
dir: *A38 from Exeter, at Drum Bridges rdbt take A382 for Bovey Tracey, 1st exit at 2nd rdbt (B3387), 3m left to Haytor Vale*

An oasis of calm and comfort on wild Dartmoor

Sheltering below the Haytor Rocks, this beamed and flagstoned 18th-century coaching inn occupies a stunning location just inside Dartmoor National Park, with wonderful surrounding walks. The traditional interior is full of character with

antique tables, settles, prints and paintings, a grandfather clock, and pieces of china over the two fireplaces, where logs crackle constantly on winter days. After a day walking on the moor, healthy appetites can be satisfied with some solid modern British cooking, using top-notch local produce in attractively presented dishes of steamed River Teign mussels; pan-roasted venison saddle; or rump steak with hand-cut chips. Leave room for a Bakewell tart or iced coffee parfait. Meals can be enjoyed alfresco in the courtyard or in the peaceful garden across the lane. West Country cheese is a particular feature, alongside wine from the Sharpham Vineyard in Totnes and local ales, including Dartmoor Jail Ale or IPA.

Open all day all wk 11-11 (Sun 12-10.30) Closed 25-26 Dec **Food** Lunch all wk 12-2 Dinner all wk 7-9 ⊕ FREE HOUSE ◀ Dartmoor Jail Ale & IPA ☥ Sandford Orchards. ☥ 12 **Facilities** Non-diners area ☙ (Garden) ♦♦ Children's menu Children's portions Family room Garden ⊨ Parking WiFi **Rooms** 9

■ HOLSWORTHY
Map 3 SS30

The Bickford Arms

tel: 01409 221318 **Brandis Corner EX22 7XY**
email: info@bickfordarms.com
dir: *On A3072, 4m from Holsworthy towards Hatherleigh*

Traditional pub with a diverse menu

A pub has stood here, on the Holsworthy to Hatherleigh road, for over 300 years and today's Bickford Arms still retains much period charm, with beams, a welcoming bar and two fireplaces. The bar serves international beers, local real ales and ciders. Choose from the same menu in the bar and restaurant – perhaps free-range Devon duck breast with redcurrant and red wine sauce, or home-made steak and ale pie. All food is prepared with locally sourced ingredients. On Sunday summer evenings, the beer garden hosts popular barbecues.

Open all wk 11-11 **Food** Lunch all wk 12-2.30 Dinner all wk 6-9 ⊕ FREE HOUSE ◀ Sharp's Doom Bar, Dartmoor Legend, St Austell Tribute ☥ Healey's Cornish Rattler. **Facilities** Non-diners area ☙ (Bar Garden) ♦♦ Children's menu Children's portions Garden ⊨ Parking WiFi ☵ (notice required)

■ HONITON
Map 4 ST10

The Holt ⊛⊛
PICK OF THE PUBS

tel: 01404 47707 **178 High St EX14 1LA**
email: enquiries@theholt-honiton.com
dir: *Phone for detailed directions*

A chic pub, restaurant and smokehouse

Brothers Joe and Angus McCaig opened their split-level establishment some ten years ago, just where the High Street crosses a stream called The Gissage. The downstairs bar is stocked with the full range of Otter beers from nearby Luppitt, ciders from Sheppy's and Honiton's own Norcotts, and Joe's wine selection; it's also where the open-plan kitchen is; for the candlelit, two-AA Rosette restaurant, head upstairs. The cooking style is modern British, with regularly changing menus showcasing local suppliers in a big way and making good use of meats and fish from Angus's smokehouse. Tapas are served at lunchtime and in the evening, and daily specials supplement main dishes such as corned duck with toasted brewer's sourdough, celeriac rémoulade and plum dressing; and grilled fillet of sea bream with crisp squid, seared vegetables, soy, ginger and lime sauce. The Holt hosts quarterly musical events, from jazz to rock to reggae to folk.

Open 11-3 5.30-12 Closed 25-26 Dec, Sun & Mon **Food** Lunch Tue-Sat 12-2 Dinner Tue-Sat 6.30-9 ⊕ FREE HOUSE ◀ Otter Bitter, Ale, Bright, Amber, Head ☥ Sheppy's, Thatchers Gold, Norcotts Cider. ☥ 9 **Facilities** Non-diners area ☙ (Bar) ♦♦ Children's portions Beer festival WiFi ☵

HONITON *continued*

NEW The Railway

tel: 01404 47976 **Queen St EX14 1HE**
email: sue@gochef.co.uk
dir: *From High St into New St (Lloyds bank on corner). 1st left into Queen St, follow road around to right. Pub on left before the railway bridge*

Local ale and good food in this friendly town pub

The Railway dates back to 1869, when it was built as a cider house for thirsty GWR workers. Melanie and Jean Sancey have breathed new life into the place, which offers a warm, family-friendly atmosphere. Whether it's in the bar with its cosy log burner and range of real ales or in the restaurant, the appealing menu offers plenty of choice including meze and gourmet pizzas and there is an emphasis on quality local ingredients. A typical starter of creamed Arbroath haddock and gambas prawn chowder might be followed by guinea fowl breast 'schnitzel' with melted Taleggio cheese.

Open 12-3 6-close Closed Sun & Mon **Food** Lunch 12-2 Dinner 6-9 Av main course £10.95 Restaurant menu available all wk ⊕ FREE HOUSE ◼ St Austell Proper Job, Bath Ales Gem, Branscombe Vale Branoc, O'Hanlon's Yellow Hammer ♨ Bath Ciders Bounders, Thatchers. ⬤ 12 **Facilities** Non-diners area ❖ (Bar Outside area) ⬤ Children's portions Outside area 戸 Parking

IDDESLEIGH
Map 3 SS50

The Duke of York
PICK OF THE PUBS

tel: 01837 810253 **EX19 8BG**
email: john@dukeofyorkdevon.co.uk
dir: *Phone for detailed directions*

Picture-perfect Devon pub in secluded village

A thatched Devon cob inn in a tiny village of jaw-droppingly pretty cottages. It was here that local author Michael Morpurgo tentatively started his novel *War Horse*, undisturbed by veterans enjoying the bar's enticing range of West Country cider and ales – Cotleigh Tawny Owl is a favoured brew. He's not the only writer whose pilgrims visit this secluded Torridge Valley; the well-known Tarka Trail, named for the otter in Henry Williamson's novel, passes the pub door. Around 640 years old, the inn oozes that indefinable aura of extreme maturity; huge inglenooks, timeworn wooden tables, ancient beams and pillars characterise the pub, popular with both the scattered local community and visitors tackling the vicinity's fishing and rambling opportunities. A menu of robust Devon fare is on offer, including the locally renowned home-made steak and kidney pudding in suet pastry. Desserts are also hand-crafted, while Dunstable Farm provides the ice cream. There's a beer festival in August.

Open all day all wk 11-11 **Food** Lunch all wk 11-10 Dinner all wk 11-10 Av main course £10 Restaurant menu available all wk ⊕ FREE HOUSE ◼ Adnams Broadside, Cotleigh Tawny Owl, Guest ales ♨ Winkleigh. ⬤ 10 **Facilities** Non-diners area ❖ (Bar Garden) ⬤ Children's menu Children's portions Garden 戸 Beer festival WiFi ⬛

KILMINGTON
Map 4 SY29

The Old Inn

tel: 01297 32096 **EX13 7RB**
email: pub@oldinnkilmington.co.uk **web:** www.oldinnkilmington.co.uk
dir: *From Axminster on A35 towards Honiton. Pub on left in 1m*

Delightful Devon longhouse offering classic pub meals

Duncan and Leigh Colvin's thatched Devon longhouse dates from 1650, when it was a staging house for changing post horses, and stands beside the A35 just west of Axminster. Weary travellers will find a cosy, beamed interior with a relaxed atmosphere, crackling log fires, and a fine range of local ales on tap. Order a pint of Otter to accompany a traditional pub meal, perhaps a Devon beef ploughman's lunch; ham, egg and chips; fish pie; or a daily chalkboard special like sea bass on sweet potato and fennel risotto. The south-facing garden is the venue for the Spring and Summer Bank Holiday beer festivals.

Open all wk 11-3 6-11 Closed 25-26 Dec **Food** Lunch all wk 12-2 Dinner all wk 6-9 ⊕ FREE HOUSE ◼ Otter Bitter, Branscombe Vale Branoc & Drayman's Best ♨ Ashton Still. ⬤ 10 **Facilities** Non-diners area ❖ (Bar Garden) ⬤ Children's menu Children's portions Garden 戸 Beer festival Parking ⬛ (notice required)

KINGSBRIDGE
Map 3 SX74

The Crabshell Inn

tel: 01548 852345 **Embankment Rd TQ7 1JZ**
email: info@thecrabshellinn.com
dir: *A38 towards Plymouth, follow signs for Kingsbridge*

Gourmet pizzas and great views

The Crabshell is a traditional sailors' watering hole on the Kingsbridge estuary – you can moor up to three hours either side of high tide. As you would expect, the views from the outside tables – with a glass of Proper Job or Thatchers Gold in hand – and from the first-floor restaurant are unbeatable. As well as a good selection of salads, meat, poultry and fish dishes using locally sourced ingredients, the pub has introduced a gourmet pizza menu. Made with thin sourdough bases, there are more than a dozen mouthwatering toppings to choose from: quattro formaggi (four cheeses), fiorentina (spinach and egg), and 'go figa' (gorgonzola, fig, pancetta and cherry tomatoes).

Open all day all wk **Food** Lunch all wk 12-3, all day Jul-Aug Dinner all wk 6-9, all day Jul-Aug ⊕ FREE HOUSE ◄ Sharp's Doom Bar, St Austell Proper Job, Tribute, Dartmoor Jail Ale Ö Thatchers Gold, Heron Valley. ᵼ **Facilities** Non-diners area ✿ (Bar Restaurant Garden) ◖◗ Children's menu Children's portions Play area Family room Garden ⌂ Parking WiFi ═

KINGSKERSWELL
Map 3 SX86

Bickley Mill Inn
PICK OF THE PUBS

tel: 01803 873201 **TQ12 5LN**
email: info@bickleymill.co.uk
dir: *From Newton Abbot take A380 towards Torquay. Right at Barn Owl Inn, follow brown tourist signs*

A charming mix of old and new in an old flour mill

A short drive from Torquay and Newton Abbot, this former 14th-century flour mill occupies an enviably secluded location in the wooded Stoneycombe Valley. Now a family-owned free house, the spacious property blends old and new in a fresh contemporary style. It comprises an attractive bar with roaring log fires and comfy sofas, and a restaurant separated into three areas – the Fireside, the Mill Room and the Panel Room. While perusing the appealing menu enjoy a pint from Bays Brewery in Torbay. Dishes are freshly prepared using quality produce from the local area. Expect the likes of creamy garlic mushrooms with toasted ciabatta; rump of lamb with roasted black pudding, red wine shallots and swede purée; and home-made puddings like honeycomb cheesecake with honeycomb pieces and caramel sauce. Decking and a tranquil garden are there to be enjoyed when the sun is shining.

Open all day all wk **Food** Lunch Mon-Sat 12-2.30, Sun 12-3 Dinner Mon-Sat 6-9, Sun 6-8 Av main course £11 ⊕ FREE HOUSE ◄ Otter Ale, Teignworthy, Bays. ᵼ 12 **Facilities** Non-diners area ✿ (Bar Garden) ◖◗ Children's menu Children's portions Garden ⌂ Parking WiFi ═

KINGS NYMPTON
Map 3 SS61

The Grove Inn
PICK OF THE PUBS

tel: 01769 580406 **EX37 9ST**
email: eatdrink@thegroveinn.co.uk
dir: *2.5m from A377 (Exeter to Barnstaple road). 1.5m from B3226 (South Molton road). Follow brown pub signs*

Classic English village pub

The Grove has everything one expects of an English pub: thatched, whitewashed, beamed ceilings, stone walls, rustic furnishings, flagstone floors and winter log fires. It is, of course, a listed building, just like many others in this secluded village. Moreover, the owners work closely with nearby farmers to provide the fresh, seasonal produce we all demand these days – count the local farm names on the various menus. From the well thought out dishes there may be line-caught West Country mackerel rarebit; Deborah's chicken liver pâté; individual North Devon beef Wellington with dauphinoise potatoes; Devon rose veal burger with Taw Valley Cheddar in a brioche roll. An accompanying drink could be one of the 26 wines by the glass, a pint of Hunter's Devon Dreamer or Otter Ale, for example – or a Sam's Dry cider from Winkleigh. Afterwards, investigate the collection of 65 single malts. A beer and cider festival takes place in July.

Open 12-3 6-11 (BH 12-4) Closed Mon L (ex BHs) **Food** Lunch Tue-Sat 12-2, Sun 12-3 Dinner Tue-Sat 6.45-9 Av main course £11 ⊕ FREE HOUSE ◄ Exmoor Ale, Skinner's Betty Stogs, Otter Ale, Chuffin' Ale, Hunter's Devon Dreamer, Exe Valley DOBS Best Bitter Ö Winkleigh Sam's Dry. ᵼ 26 **Facilities** Non-diners area ✿ (Bar Restaurant Outside area) ◖◗ Children's menu Children's portions Outside area ⌂ Beer festival Cider festival WiFi ═ (notice required)

KINGSTON
Map 3 SX64

The Dolphin Inn

tel: 01548 810314 **TQ7 4QE**
email: info@dolphininn.eclipse.co.uk
dir: *From A379 (Plymouth to Kingsbridge road) take B3233 signed Bigbury-on-Sea, at x-rds straight on to Kingston. Follow brown inn signs*

Off the beaten track for precious tranquillity

Church stonemasons lived here in the 15th century, and later it was taken over by fishermen and their families. The inn is close to the beautiful Erme estuary and the popular surfing beaches of the South Hams. Teignworthy's Spring Tide is one of several real ales, alongside Thatchers cider. Home-made food includes pan-set pigeon breast, chocolate, foie gras and cherries; wild mushroom and pesto linguine; pork belly, hogs pudding, scallops and creamed potato; and tiramisù with honeycomb ice cream. A circular walk from the pub takes in woodland, the estuary and the South West Coastal Path.

Open 12-3 6-11 (Sun 12-3 7-10.30) Closed Sun eve & Tue winter **Food** Lunch Mon-Fri 12-2, Sat-Sun 12-2.30 Dinner all wk 6-9 Av main course £10.95 Set menu available Restaurant menu available ⊕ PUNCH TAVERNS ◄ Exmoor Ale, Teignworthy Spring Tide, Sharp's Doom Bar, Otter, Timothy Taylor Landlord Ö Thatchers. **Facilities** Non-diners area ✿ (Bar Restaurant Garden) ◖◗ Children's menu Children's portions Play area Family room Garden ⌂ Parking WiFi

KNOWSTONE
Map 3 SS82

NEW The Masons Arms ◉◉

tel: 01398 341231 **EX36 4RY**
email: enqs@masonsarmsdevon.co.uk
dir: *Follow Knowstone signs from A361*

Village local crossed with a high-end restaurant

A thatched 13th-century inn on the edge of Exmoor, which combines excellent food and drink with a genuinely warm welcome. Villagers mix happily with visiting walkers in the low-beamed bar, where pints of Cotleigh Tawny ale and Sam's Poundhouse cider are supped around the warmth of the huge fireplace. The bright rear dining room offers long views, an extraordinary ceiling mural, and food worthy of two AA Rosettes – chef/owner Mark Dobson can boast cooking under the guidance of Michel Roux. An excellent value fixed-price lunch could comprise guinea fowl terrine with Russian salad; fillet of sea bream with herb risotto; and pannacotta with roasted pineapple.

Open 12-2 6-11 Closed 1st wk Jan, Sun eve & Mon **Food** Lunch Tue-Sun 12-2 Dinner Tue-Sat 6-11 Set menu available Restaurant menu available ⊕ FREE HOUSE ◄ Cotleigh Tawny Owl Ö Winkleigh Sam's Poundhouse. ᵼ 10 **Facilities** Non-diners area ✿ (Bar Garden Outside area) Children's portions Garden Outside area ⌂ Parking

LIFTON
Map 3 SX38

The Arundell Arms
PICK OF THE PUBS

tel: 01566 784666 **PL16 0AA**
email: reservations@arundellarms.com
dir: 1m from A30 dual carriageway, 3m E of Launceston

Renowned for country pursuits

Escape the hurly-burly with a pint of Dartmoor Jail Ale in the Courthouse Bar, a former police station incorporated into this famous hotel, whilst allowing the extraordinary range of country pursuits and activities here detain you further. Walkers and horse-riders can enjoy some of Devon's most unspoilt countryside, Dartmoor's bristling tors are a short drive away whilst the inn's fishing beats on the Tamar and tributaries attract fly-fishers. Local farms and estates host shoots, as well as raising livestock that features across the menus of the three dining areas. The bar meals reflect the care taken in selecting the finest local produce; The Courthouse dishes and regularly-changing specials incorporate the best pub food traditions, with home-made fishcakes; ham, egg and chips or a warming beef Stroganoff just the ticket after a day spent indulging in the great outdoors. Excess energy can be burnt off playing alley skittles.

Open all wk 12-3 6-11 **Food** Lunch all wk 12-2 Dinner all wk 6-9.30 ⊕ FREE HOUSE ◀ St Austell Tribute, Dartmoor Jail Ale, Guest ales ♂ Thatchers, Healey's Cornish Rattler. ♚ 9 **Facilities** Non-diners area ♥ (Bar Garden) ♦♦ Children's menu Children's portions Garden ⇆ Parking WiFi

LUSTLEIGH
Map 3 SX78

The Cleave Public House

tel: 01647 277223 **TQ13 9TJ**
email: ben@thecleavelustleigh.com
dir: From Newton Abbot take A382, follow Bovey Tracey signs, then Moretonhampstead signs. Left to Lustleigh

Delightful thatched pub beside the village cricket pitch

Set on the edge of Dartmoor National Park, and dating from the 16th century, this thatched, family-run pub is the only one in the village and is adjacent to the cricket pitch. It has a traditional snug bar, with beams, granite flooring and log fire; to the rear, formerly the old railway station waiting room, is now a light and airy dining area leading to a lovely cottage garden. The pub/bistro has gained a reputation for an interesting and varied, daily-changing menu. Dishes include Ligurian fish stew; River Teign mussels; sausages in ale gravy with bubble-and-squeak; or hand-made pumpkin ravioli with sage butter and balsamic onions.

Open all day all wk 11-11 (Sun 12-9) **Food** Lunch all wk Dinner all wk Av main course £12 ⊕ HEAVITREE ◀ Otter Ale, Bitter ♂ Aspall. **Facilities** Non-diners area ♥ (Bar Garden) ♦♦ Children's menu Children's portions Garden ⇆ Parking WiFi

What makes a Pick of the Pubs?
See page 5 to find out more

LUTON (NEAR CHUDLEIGH)
Map 3 SX97

The Elizabethan Inn

tel: 01626 775425 **Fore St TQ13 0BL**
email: elizabethaninn@btconnect.com **web:** www.elizabethaninn.co.uk
dir: Between Chudleigh & Teignmouth

Good honest Devon food and drink

Known locally as the Lizzie, this smart, welcoming 16th-century free house attracts diners and drinkers alike. There's a great selection of West Country ales like Dartmoor IPA to choose from, as well as Thatchers Gold and local Reddaway's Farm cider. Sit beside a log fire in winter or in the pretty beer garden on warmer days. The pub prides itself on using the best local ingredients. The bar menu includes salad bowls, omelettes, risottos and traditional dishes, while the daily specials boards might offer River Teign mussels; home-made lamb and mint sausages; and vegetable terrine. A take-away menu is available.

Open all wk 12-3 6-11.30 (Sun all day) (Sat all day BST) Closed 25-26 Dec, 1 Jan ⊕ FREE HOUSE ◀ Fuller's London Pride, Teignworthy Reel Ale, Otter Ale, Dartmoor IPA, St Austell Tribute ♂ Thatchers Gold, Reddaway's Farm. **Facilities** ♥ (Bar Garden) ♦♦ Children's menu Children's portions Garden Parking WiFi

LYMPSTONE
Map 3 SX98

The Globe Inn

tel: 01395 263166 **The Strand EX8 5EY**
email: info@globelympstone.co.uk
dir: Phone for detailed directions

A stone's throw from the river estuary

This friendly beamed village pub in the estuary village of Lympstone has a good local reputation for food and drink. Well-kept Otter and London Pride are the ales on offer in the bar, while the menu offers fresh seafood and seasonal produce in traditional dishes such as lamb's liver, bacon and onion; home-made fish pie and seafood platters to share. On Sundays, the traditional roasts are especially popular. Occasional music nights and Tuesday is quiz night.

Open all day all wk 11-close (12-close winter) **Food** Lunch Mon-Sat 12-9, Sun 12-8 Dinner Mon-Sat 12-9, Sun 12-8 ⊕ HEAVITREE ◀ Fuller's London Pride, Otter, St Austell Tribute , Bass ♂ Taunton Traditional, Thatchers Gold. ♚ 10 **Facilities** Non-diners area ♥ (Bar) ♦♦ WiFi

PICK OF THE PUBS

California Country Inn

MODBURY Map 3 SX65

tel: 01548 821449
California Cross PL21 0SG
email: enquiries@californiacountryinn.co.uk
web: www.californiacountryinn.co.uk
dir: *On B3196 (NE of Modbury)*

A real find in the South Hams area

This centuries-old inn stands in some of the most tranquil countryside in southern England, just a few miles from Dartmoor to the north and the cliffs and estuaries of the coast to the south. In fact, this Area of Outstanding Natural Beauty encompasses the hills and vales which can be seen from the pub's landscaped gardens. Dating from the 14th century, its unusual name is thought to derive from local adventurers in the mid-19th century who heeded the call to 'go west' and waited at the nearby crossroads for the stage to take them on the first part of their journey to America's west coast. They must have suffered wistful thoughts of home when recalling their local pub, with its wizened old beams, exposed dressed stone walls and a fabulous, huge stone fireplace. Old rural prints and photographs, copper kettles, jugs, brasses and many other artefacts add to the rustic charm of the whitewashed pub's atmospheric interior. A family-run free house, the beers on tap are likely to include Sharp's and St Austells', the wine list has award-winning Devon

wines from nearby Sharpham Vineyard, and the good-value house wines come from Chile. Having won accolades as a dining pub, head chef Tim Whiston's food is thoughtfully created and impressively flavoursome. Most ingredients are sourced from the bounty of the local countryside and waters, with meats from a supplier in nearby Loddiswell. Meals can be taken from the bar menu, but why not indulge in the à la carte menu from the inn's dining room? Appetising starters include crispy belly pork, tempura scallop with pickled vegetables and beetroot crisps. The main course selection may include local guinea fowl (leg confit and pan-fried breast) with creamed wild mushrooms, or pan-fried sea bass fillets.

Open all day all week **Food** Lunch Mon-Sat 12-2, Sun 12-2.30 Dinner Mon-Sat 6-9, Sun 6-8.30 Av main course £11 Restaurant menu available Wed-Sun (evening) ⊕ FREE HOUSE ◀ Otter Bitter, Sharp's Doom Bar, St Austell Tribute ℧ Addlestones, Thatchers Gold, Westons Old Rosie. ♀ 8 **Facilities** Non-diners area ✿ (Bar Garden) ♦♦ Children's menu Children's portions Family room Garden ⊨ Parking ▭ WiFi

LYNMOUTH
Map 3 SS74

Rising Sun Hotel ★★ HL ●
PICK OF THE PUBS

tel: 01598 753223 **Harbourside EX35 6EG**
email: reception@risingsunlynmouth.co.uk **web:** www.risingsunlynmouth.co.uk
dir: M5 junct 25 follow Minehead signs. A39 to Lynmouth

Historic inn with literary connections

Overlooking Lynmouth's tiny harbour and bay is this 14th-century thatched smugglers' inn. In turn, overlooking them all, are Countisbury Cliffs, the highest in England. The building's long history is evident from the uneven oak floors, crooked ceilings and thick walls. Literary associations are plentiful: R D Blackmore wrote some of his wild Exmoor romance, *Lorna Doone*, here; the poet Shelley is believed to have honeymooned in the garden cottage, and Coleridge stayed here too. Immediately behind rises Exmoor Forest and National Park, home to red deer, wild ponies and birds of prey. With moor and sea so close, game and seafood are in plentiful supply; appearing in dishes such as braised pheasant with pancetta and quince and Braunton greens; and roast shellfish – crab, mussels, clams and scallops in garlic, ginger and coriander. At night the oak-panelled, candlelit dining room is an example of romantic British inn-keeping at its best.

Open all day all wk 11am-mdnt Closed 25 Dec **Food** Lunch all wk 12-2.30 Dinner all wk 6-9 ⊕ FREE HOUSE ◄ Exmoor Gold, Exmoor Ales Stag ♂ Thatchers Gold, Addlestones. **Facilities** Non-diners area ❤ (Bar) Outside area ⋒ ▄▄ **Rooms** 14

MARLDON
Map 3 SX86

The Church House Inn

tel: 01803 558279 **Village Rd TQ3 1SL**
dir: Take Torquay ring road, follow signs to Marldon & Totnes, follow brown signs to pub

Grade II listed, 18th-century inn with contemporary touches

Built as a hostel for the stonemasons of the adjoining village church, this ancient country inn dates from 1362. It was rebuilt in 1740 and many features from that period still remain, including beautiful Georgian windows; some of the original glass is intact despite overlooking the cricket pitch. These days it has an uncluttered, contemporary feel with additional seating in the garden. As well as sandwiches, the menu might include Cullen skink; wild mushroom and tarragon pâté with walnut bread; monkfish tail, parmesan polenta, tomato and herb dressing; turkey breast paupiette with fennel seed, garlic and sage sausage stuffing; or braised shin of beef with local ale, vegetables and thyme with mashed potato.

Open all wk 11.30-2.30 5-11 (Fri-Sat 11.30-2.30 5-11.30 Sun 12-3 5.30-10.30) **Food** Lunch all wk 12-2 Dinner all wk 6.30-9.30 Av main course £16.50 ⊕ FREE HOUSE ◄ St Austell Dartmoor & Tribute, Teignworthy Gundog. ₱ 12 **Facilities** Non-diners area ❤ (Bar Garden) ♦▮ Children's portions Garden Parking

MEAVY
Map 3 SX56

The Royal Oak Inn

tel: 01822 852944 **PL20 6PJ**
email: info@royaloakinn.org.uk
dir: B3212 from Yelverton to Princetown. Right at Dousland to Meavy, past school. Pub opposite village green

At the heart of the community in Dartmoor village

This traditional 15th-century inn is situated by a village green within Dartmoor National Park. Flagstone floors, oak beams and a welcoming open fire set the scene at this free house popular with cyclists and walkers. Local cask ales, ciders and fine wines accompany the carefully sourced ingredients in a menu ranging from lunchtime light bites to steak and ale pie; home-cooked ham, egg and chips; or local bangers and mash. Look out for cider and beer festivals during the year.

Open all wk Mon-Fri 11-3 6-11 (Sat-Sun & Apr-Oct all wk 11-11) **Food** Lunch Mon-Fri 12-2.30, Sat-Sun 12-3 Dinner all wk 6-9 Av main course £8-£10 ⊕ FREE HOUSE ◄ Dartmoor Jail Ale & IPA, Meavy Oak Ale, Guest ale ♂ Westons Old Rosie, Sandford Orchards Scrumpy & Old Kirton. ₱ 12 **Facilities** Non-diners area ❤ (Bar Garden) ♦▮ Children's menu Children's portions Garden ⋒ Beer festival Cider festival ▄▄ (notice required)

MODBURY
Map 3 SX65

California Country Inn
PICK OF THE PUBS

See Pick of the Pubs on page 147

MORETONHAMPSTEAD
Map 3 SX78

NEW The Horse

tel: 01647 440242 **George St TQ13 8PG**
email: info@thehorsedartmoor.co.uk
dir: In village centre

One for those who enjoy Italian food

Once virtually derelict, The Horse is an object lesson in pub revival, as its beautiful dining room, Mediterranean-style courtyard and stunning barn conversion testify. The chesterfield-furnished bar offers Devon-brewed real ales and ciders, and the same menu as the restaurant, which, with its clear Italian ring, could mean antipasto; hand-rolled gourmet pizzas; or hand-made meatballs in rich tomato sauce, while the courtyard smokery is responsible for smoked pastrami, salmon and salt beef. For dinner, bouillabaisse; crispy Dartmoor lamb breast; or slow-braised Dartmoor beef pie may be on offer. Local folk musicians have a sing-song on the last Monday of every month.

Open 12-3.30 5-12 (Sun-Mon 5-12) Closed 25 Dec, Sun L & Mon L **Food** Lunch Tue-Sat 12.30-2.30 Dinner all wk 6.30-9 (pizza only Sun-Mon) Av main course £13 ⊕ FREE HOUSE ◄ Dartmoor Legend & IPA, Otter Ale ♂ Sandford Orchards Devon Red, Winkleigh Sam's Poundhouse. ₱ 12 **Facilities** Non-diners area ❤ (Bar) ♦▮ Children's menu Children's portions Outside area ⋒ WiFi ▄▄ (notice required)

NEWTON ABBOT
Map 3 SX87

The Wild Goose Inn

tel: 01626 872241 **Combeinteignhead TQ12 4RA**
dir: From A380 at Newton Abbot rdbt take B3195 (Shaldon road) signed Milber, 2.5m to village, right at pub sign

Flying the flag for West Country ales and ciders

Set in the heart of Combeinteignhead at the head of a long valley, this charming free house boasts a sunny walled garden, overlooked by the ancient village church. The former farmstead was originally licensed as the Country House Inn in 1840 and renamed in the 1960s when nearby geese began intimidating the pub's customers. A good range of West Country real ales and ciders accompanies home-made pub food prepared from local ingredients. The lunch menu lists roast hake with a chorizo and white bean cassoulet, while an example from the à la carte is pork belly, braised lentils, choucroute and sage jus. There is a beer festival every Early Spring Bank Holiday weekend.

Open all wk 11-3 5.30-11 (Sun 12-3 7-11) **Food** Lunch all wk 12-2.30 Dinner Mon-Sat 6-9, Sun 7-9 Av main course £10.95 ⊕ FREE HOUSE ◄ Otter Ale, Skinner's Best Bitter, Teignworthy, Branscombe Vale, Exe Valley, Cotleigh, Sharp's ♂ Skinner's Press Gang, Wiscombe Suicider, Milltop Gold. ₱ 10 **Facilities** Non-diners area ❤ (Bar Garden) ♦▮ Children's menu Children's portions Family room Garden ⋒ Beer festival Parking

NEWTON ST CYRES
Map 3 SX89

The Beer Engine

tel: 01392 851282 **EX5 5AX**
email: info@thebeerengine.co.uk
dir: *From Exeter take A377 towards Crediton. Signed from A377 towards Sweetham. Pub opposite rail station, over bridge*

Popular railway brewpub

This pretty whitewashed free house originally opened as a railway hotel in 1852. It sits opposite the Tarka Line on the banks of the River Creedy, much favoured by dogs and their walkers. Home to one of Devon's leading microbreweries, it produces ales with names such as Rail Ale and Sleeper Heavy. Freshly baked bread uses the wort (beer yeast) from the brewery; dishes may include a home-made fishcake with sweet chilli sauce and fresh bread; fresh haddock in Beer Engine batter; and chicken curry with rice. Vegetarians will rejoice in the range of soups and bakes.

Open all day all wk Tue-Sat 11-11 (Sun 12-10.30 Mon 11-10.30) **Food** Lunch all wk 12-2.15 Dinner Tue-Sat 6.30-9.15, Sun-Mon 6.30-8.15 Av main course £9.62 ⊕ FREE HOUSE ◀ The Beer Engine Piston Bitter, Rail Ale, Sleeper Heavy, Silver Bullet ♂ Green Valley Cyder, Dragon Tears. ♟ 9 **Facilities** Non-diners area ❖ (Bar Garden) ♦️ Children's portions Garden ⋒ Parking WiFi 🚐 (notice required)

NORTH BOVEY
Map 3 SX78

The Ring of Bells Inn
PICK OF THE PUBS

tel: 01647 440375 **TQ13 8RB**
email: mail@ringofbells.net
dir: *1.5m from Moretonhampstead off B3212. 7m S of Whiddon Down junct on A30*

Dog-friendly Dartmoor village pub

Dating back to the 13th-century, this thatched Dartmoor pub was originally built to house the stonemasons building the parish church. Overlooking the village green, The Ring of Bells draws Dartmoor visitors and walkers in for good food and regularly changing guest ales. The kitchen uses fresh, locally sourced produce and menus reflect the changing seasons with both traditional and contemporary dishes; suppliers are proudly listed. Served in cosy low-beamed bars, with heavy oak doors, rustic furnishings, crackling winter log fires and evening candlelight, the daily menu may list grilled goats' cheese and onion tart, and local mussels as starters, followed by main dishes such as sweet potato and chickpea falafels with pitta bread and tzatziki; chunky fish soup, saffron rouille, granary bread and chips; and confit duck leg, pak choi, beetroot and Asian-spiced jus. Round off with pineapple tarte Tatin with stem ginger ice cream.

Open all day all wk **Food** Lunch all wk 12-2.30 Dinner all wk 6-9 Av main course £10.95 ⊕ FREE HOUSE ◀ Teignworthy Reel Ale, Dartmoor IPA, Guest ales ♂ Thatchers, Devon Mist. ♟ 12 **Facilities** Non-diners area ❖ (Bar Garden) ♦️ Children's menu Children's portions Family room Garden ⋒ WiFi 🚐 (notice required)

NOSS MAYO
Map 3 SX54

The Ship Inn
PICK OF THE PUBS

tel: 01752 872387 **PL8 1EW**
email: ship@nossmayo.com
dir: *5m S of Yealmpton. From Yealmpton take B3186, then follow Noss Mayo signs*

Waterside free house popular with sailing enthusiasts

Surrounded by wooded hills, Noss Mayo lies on the south bank of the tidal Yealm; opposite is Newton Ferrers. The waterside location means you can, if you wish, sail to this deceptively spacious pub, which has been superbly renovated using reclaimed local stone and English oak. Log fires, wooden floors, old bookcases and dozens of local pictures characterise the interior spaces. The cellar keeps a good range of beers, mostly from brewers that know the Ship well. Whether eating in the

bar, panelled library or by the river, daily-changing home-made dishes include fillet steak with Portobello mushrooms; breast of duck with stir-fried vegetables, egg noodles and fresh plum sauce; and small Dover sole with monkfish tail, crab and pink peppercorn butter. For chicken curry and rice; steak and kidney pie; or ploughman's and baguettes, see the bar menu. Dogs are allowed downstairs.

Open all day all wk **Food** Lunch Mon-Sat 12-9.30, Sun 12-9 Dinner Mon-Sat 12-9.30, Sun 12-9 ⊕ FREE HOUSE ◀ Dartmoor Jail Ale & IPA, St Austell Tribute & Proper Job, Otter, Palmers. ♟ 13 **Facilities** Non-diners area ❖ (Bar Garden) ♦️ Children's portions Garden ⋒ Parking

OTTERY ST MARY
Map 3 SY19

The Talaton Inn

tel: 01404 822214 **Talaton EX5 2RQ**
dir: *A30 to Fairmile, then follow signs to Talaton*

Black and white timbered, traditional inn

This well-maintained, timber-framed 16th-century inn is run by a brother and sister partnership. There is a good selection of real ales (Otter Ale, Otter Amber) and malts, and a fine collection of bar games. The regularly-changing evening blackboard menu might include brie wedges with cranberry dip; surf and turf; tuna steak au poivre; or gammon and egg. At Sunday lunchtimes (booking advisable), as well as the popular roast, there is also a pie and vegetarian choice. Lunchtime special deals available. There is a patio for summer dining and themed food nights.

Open 12-3 7-11 Closed Mon (winter) **Food** Lunch Tue-Sun 12-2 Dinner Wed-Sat 7-9 Set menu available Restaurant menu available all wk ⊕ FREE HOUSE ◀ Otter Ale & Amber, Guest ale ♂ Westons Stowford Press. **Facilities** Non-diners area ❖ (Bar Outside area) ♦️ Children's portions Outside area ⋒ Parking 🚐 (notice required)

PARRACOMBE
Map 3 SS64

The Fox & Goose

tel: 01598 763239 **EX31 4PE**
email: info@foxandgooseinnexmoor.co.uk
dir: *1m from A39 between Blackmoor Gate & Lynton. Follow Parracombe signs*

Laid-back Exmoor inn

This whitewashed Victorian building has been a hotel since 1898, when the Lynton to Barnstaple narrow-gauge railway arrived. Decorating the interior are farm memorabilia, a scarf-wearing stag's head and photographs of villagers. Beer and cider drinkers will find Devon and Somerset well represented. Home-made starters include Greek salad with mixed leaves, cherry tomatoes, cucumber, feta and olives; and duck rillettes with salad garnish and granary toast. Typical mains are sticky barbecue ribs with mild chilli, ginger and bourbon marinade; red-wine-poached brill fillets; and steak and Guinness shortcrust pie. A vegetarian option could be mushroom Stroganoff with cream, mustard and Cognac. To follow are South West cheeses; hot chocolate brownie with ice cream; and walnut and caramel tart. Pizzas are also available to eat in or take away. Children and dogs are welcome and can enjoy themselves in the paved courtyard garden overlooking the river.

Open all wk 12-2.30 6-11 (Sun 12-2.30 7-10.30; summer all day) Closed 25 Dec ⊕ FREE HOUSE ◀ Cotleigh Barn Owl, Exmoor Fox, Otter Ale, Sharp's Doom Bar, Guinness ♂ Winkleigh. **Facilities** ❖ (Bar Outside area) ♦️ Children's menu Children's portions Outside area Parking WiFi

PLYMTREE
Map 3 ST00

The Blacksmiths Arms

tel: 01884 277474 **EX15 2JU**
email: blacksmithsplymtree@yahoo.co.uk
dir: *From A373 (Cullompton to Honiton road) follow Plymtree signs. Pub in village centre*

Well-kept ales and locally-sourced food

Alan and Susie Carter have been at the helm for a numbers of years and the pub has become the hub of this idyllic Devon village. A traditional free house with exposed beams and log fire, it has a reputation for serving quality food using local ingredients, and is known for generous portions of classics like game pie and local steaks, as well as curries, sharing platters and fish dishes. Up to 14 well-kept local ales include Otter Amber, and there is a fine selection of wines. A beer festival is held in July every even-numbered year. A large beer garden and alfresco dining area complete the picture.

Open Tue-Fri 6-11 (Sat 12-11 Sun 12-4) Closed Mon, Tue-Fri L, Sun eve **Food** Lunch Sat-Sun 12-2 Dinner Tue-Sat 6-9 Av main course £10-£11 ⊕ FREE HOUSE ◀ O'Hanlon's Yellow Hammer, Otter Amber, St Austell Proper Job & Tribute, Sharp's Doom Bar ♂ Thatchers Gold. ☻ 8 **Facilities** Non-diners area ✿ (Bar Restaurant Garden) ◀ Children's menu Children's portions Play area Family room Garden ⟞ Beer festival (even numbered years only) Parking WiFi ▭ (notice required)

PORTGATE
Map 3 SX48

The Harris Arms
PICK OF THE PUBS

tel: 01566 783331 **EX20 4PZ**
email: info@theharrisarms.co.uk
dir: *From A30 at Broadwoodwidger/Roadford Lake follow signs to Lifton then Portgate*

Rural pub with a passion for local produce

At the heart of a hamlet snuggled on a ridge between the rivers Lyd and Thrushel, magnificent views are a given from the cosy patio and terrace. With Dartmoor a stunning horizon to the east and the delights of Cornwall just a hop to the west, the capable owners here make the most of their rural hinterland to provide both drinks and food. Devon cider from Winkleigh and reliable beers from local microbreweries like Fry's or Bays complement the outstanding wine list of 60 bins in this 16th-century inn. Cornish seafish, West Country artisan cheeses and game from local farms and estates may all be found on the carte menu and ever-changing specials board. A starter of twice-baked goats' cheese soufflé with tomato fondue and basil foam sets the standard; mains come in with rabbit casserole with creamy mash and seasonal vegetables; or 24-hour slow-roasted local pork with all the trimmings and cider sauce. There's a children's menu, and the inn is very dog-friendly.

Open 12-3 6.30-11 Closed 25, 26 & 31 Dec, Sun eve & Mon **Food** Lunch Tue-Sun 12-2 Dinner Tue-Sat 6.30-9 Av main course £13.95 ⊕ FREE HOUSE ◀ Bays, Fry's Brewery ♂ Winkleigh Sam's Poundhouse Crisp. ☻ 20 **Facilities** Non-diners area ✿ (Bar Garden Outside area) ◀ Children's menu Children's portions Garden Outside area ⟞ Parking WiFi

POSTBRIDGE
Map 3 SX67

Warren House Inn

tel: 01822 880208 **PL20 6TA**
dir: *On B3212 between Moretonhampstead & Princetown*

Timeless Dartmoor pub

Built in 1845 to service the local tin mining industry, the Warren House Inn now stands alone and isolated high on Dartmoor. It has no mains services - it uses generators for electricity and gravity-fed water from a spring - but the fire in the hearth is said to have been burning continuously since the day the pub first opened. Four real ales and scrumpy cider are served, along with a menu of good home-

cooked food: hearty soups, a selection of pies (including rabbit of course), beef and lamb raised on the moor, and vegetables supplied by local farms.

Open all day all wk 11-11 (winter Mon-Tue 11-3) **Food** Lunch Mon-Sat 12-9, Sun 12-8.30, Mon-Tue in winter 12-2.30 Dinner Mon-Sat 12-9, Sun 12-8.30 ⊕ FREE HOUSE ◀ Otter Ale, Sharp's Doom Bar, Guest ales ♂ Countryman Cider, Thatchers Gold. **Facilities** Non-diners area ✿ (Bar Garden) ◀ Children's menu Family room Garden ⟞ Parking ▭

RATTERY
Map 3 SX76

Church House Inn

tel: 01364 642220 **TQ10 9LD**
email: ray.hardy@btconnect.com
dir: *1m from A38 (Exeter to Plymouth Road) & 0.75m from A385 (Totnes to South Brent Road)*

Centuries of conversation and hospitality

Tracing its history as far back as 1028, this venerable inn burgeons with brasses, bare beams, large fireplaces and other historic features. Some customers encounter the wandering spirit of a monk; fortunately he seems to be friendly. In the character dining room, dishes include snow crab cocktail followed by pork loin cutlets in apple and sage sauce. Fresh fish (sea bass; fisherman's pie, grilled plaice or sea bream) features strongly. For dessert, maybe choose spotted dick or apple pie, served with double cream, vanilla ice cream or custard. There is a large lawned beer garden and patio where you can enjoy a pint of Dartmoor Jail Ale in warmer months.

Open all wk 11-2.30 6-11 (Sun 12-3 6-10.30) **Food** Lunch Mon-Sat 11.30-2, Sun 12-2 Dinner all wk 6.30-9 ⊕ FREE HOUSE ◀ Dartmoor Jail Ale & Legend, St Austell Proper Job, Guest ale ♂ Thatchers Gold. ☻ 10 **Facilities** Non-diners area ✿ (Bar Garden) ◀ Children's menu Children's portions Garden ⟞ Parking WiFi ▭ (notice required)

ROCKBEARE
Map 3 SY09

Jack in the Green Inn ◉◉
PICK OF THE PUBS

See Pick of the Pubs on opposite page

SALCOMBE
Map 3 SX73

The Victoria Inn
PICK OF THE PUBS

tel: 01548 842604 **Fore St TQ8 8BU**
email: info@victoriainn-salcombe.co.uk
dir: *In town centre, overlooking estuary*

Friendly town pub with excellent local seafood

Tim and Liz Hore's refurbished pub has something unique among Salcombe's licensed premises - a really big garden with sun terraces. Where better for that glass of Cornish Rattler cider? From the first-floor restaurant you can watch the fishing boats bringing in the catch, destined perhaps to reappear as sauté of mild Thai-spiced monkfish and king prawns with coconut and coriander rice. Other internationally-influenced dishes include chicken souvlaki with tzatziki and salad; and, from a generous vegetarian selection, red lentil, potato and aubergine moussaka. Cottage pie with bacon and cheddar crust helps restore British balance. Treats await well-behaved children and dogs.

Open all day all wk 11.30-11 Closed 25 Dec **Food** Lunch all wk 12-9 Dinner all wk 12-9 ⊕ ST AUSTELL BREWERY ◀ Tribute, Dartmoor, Proper Job ♂ Healey's Cornish Rattler. ☻ 20 **Facilities** Non-diners area ✿ (Bar Garden) ◀ Children's menu Children's portions Play area Garden ⟞ WiFi

PICK OF THE PUBS

Jack in the Green Inn ❀ ❀

ROCKBEARE Map 3 SY09

tel: 01404 822240
London Rd EX5 2EE
email: info@jackinthegreen.uk.com
web: www.jackinthegreen.uk.com
dir: *M5 junct 29, A30 towards Honiton, left signed Rockbeare*

Top notch pub food for everyone

This white-painted, roadside pub has been run for over two decades by rugby aficionado Paul Parnell. The empty plates and contented smiles of diners (and two AA Rosettes) testify to the Jack's well-deserved reputation for upmarket modern pub food, but Paul dislikes the term 'gastro-pub' as he doesn't want people, especially families, to think that it's purely a dining venue, and drive on by. What he offers is good West Country brews on tap and, in the restaurant, a simple philosophy of serving the best Devon produce in stylish surroundings. The smart interior with its low beamed rooms, soft brown leather chairs and a wood-burning stove creates a contemporary pub atmosphere. Local artisan producers underpin chef Matthew Mason's innovative menus with punchy flavours, be it the local shoots which supply the game, or the growers of salad leaves and seasonal vegetables who are just six miles away. Pressed to label the food style, Paul and Matthew would say modern British, exemplified by dishes

like goats' cheese and chilli pineapple cannelloni; and peppered duck breast, Devon honey, five spice and pickled pears. The more traditional pub grub selection offers braised oxtail with celeriac and horseradish; and rump steak with chorizo butter, chunky chips and onion rings. The three course 'Totally Devon' menu is good value, but why not push the boat out and go for the six-course tasting menu? Look to the chalkboard for daily specials like roast pheasant, rösti, seasonal veg and bread sauce. Head pastry chef Harriet Pecover creates the tasty 'sweets and treats' like rose crème brûlée with raspberry sorbet. Dine alfresco in the spacious rear courtyard in summer; dogs are very welcome but only outside.

Open all wk 11-3 5.30-11 (Sun 12-11) Closed 25 Dec-5 Jan **Food** Lunch Mon-Sat 12-2, Sun 12-9 Dinner Mon-Sat 6-9.30, Sun 12-9 Set menu; Restaurant menu available all wk. ⊕ FREE HOUSE ◀ Otter Ale & Amber, Sharp's Doom Bar, Butcombe Bitter ♂ Dragon Tears, Luscombe ♟ 12 **Facilities** Non-diners area ♦♦ Children's menu & portions Family room Outside area ⅂ Parking WiFi 🚐 (notice required)

SANDFORD
Map 3 SS80

The Lamb Inn

tel: 01363 773676 **The Square EX17 4LW**
email: thelambinn@gmail.com **web:** www.lambinnsandford.co.uk
dir: *A377 from Exeter to Crediton. 1st right signed Sandford & Tiverton. Left, left again, up hill. 1.5m left into village square*

A thriving community local

Mark Hildyard has worked hard at making this 16th-century former coaching inn a cracking all-round pub. Set in a sleepy Devon village, the pub's upstairs room is used as an art gallery, skittle alley, cinema (screenings most weekends), theatre, venue for open-mic nights and a meeting room for village groups. Downstairs, expect to find three log fires, candles on scrubbed tables and an imaginative chalkboard menu. Using the best Devon produce, top-notch dishes may include Creedy Carver chicken and bacon salad; and roasted monkfish with Serrano ham and vanilla butter sauce. Everyone is welcome, including dogs and walkers in muddy boots.

Open all day all wk 11am-11.30pm **Food** Lunch all wk 12.30-2.15 Dinner all wk 6.30-9.15 Av main course £12.50 ⊕ FREE HOUSE ◀ Otter Bitter, O'Hanlon's Yellow Hammer, Dartmoor Jail Ale & Legend, Skinner's ♂ Sandford Orchards. ♥ 9 **Facilities** Non-diners area ❤ (Bar Restaurant Garden) ♦♦ Children's portions Garden ⌂ Beer festival WiFi ➡ (notice required)

SHEBBEAR
Map 3 SS40

The Devil's Stone Inn

tel: 01409 281210 **EX21 5RU**
email: churst1234@btinternet.com
dir: *From Okehampton turn right opposite White Hart, follow A386 towards Hatherleigh. At rdbt outside Hatherleigh take Holsworthy road to Highampton. Just after Highampton right, follow signs to Shebbear*

A village pub with an interesting history

A farmhouse before it became a coaching inn some 400 years ago, this inn is reputedly one of England's top dozen most haunted pubs. That does not deter the country sports lovers who use it as a base for their activities; it is especially a haven for fly-fishermen, with beats, some of which the pub owns, on the middle and upper Torridge. The pub's name comes from the village tradition of the turning the Devil's Stone (situated opposite the pub), which happens every year on 5th November. The beamed and flagstone-floored interior has several open fires. Locally sourced and home-cooked food, a selection of real ales and ciders, a games room, separate dining room and large garden complete the picture.

Open all wk 12-3 6-11 (Fri-Sun all day fr 12) **Food** Lunch all wk 12-2.30 Dinner all wk 6-9.30 Restaurant menu available all wk ⊕ FREE HOUSE ◀ Sharp's Doom Bar, St Austell Tribute, Otter Ale, Cottage ♂ Healey's Cornish Rattler, Thatchers Gold. **Facilities** Non-diners area ❤ (Bar Garden) ♦♦ Children's menu Children's portions Play area Garden ⌂ Parking WiFi ➡ (notice required)

SIDBURY
Map 3 SY19

The Hare & Hounds

tel: 01404 41760 **Putts Corner EX10 0QQ**
email: contact@hareandhounds-devon.co.uk **web:** www.hareandhounds-devon.co.uk
dir: *From Honiton take A375 signed Sidmouth. In approx 0.75m pub at Seaton Rd x-rds*

Whitewashed free house serving classic pub dishes

Behind the whitewashed walls of this traditional Devon free house you'll find a comfortable interior with wooden beams and winter log fires. There's also a large garden and an extension which both enjoy fantastic views down the valley to the sea at Sidmouth. Besides the daily carvery, the extensive menu features classic pub dishes and snacks. Main course options include spaghetti bolognaise and steak and kidney pudding, as well as fish dishes and vegetarian options. The permanent cask ales are brewed less than 10 miles away by the Otter Brewery.

Open all day all wk 10am-11pm (Sun 11-10.30) **Food** Lunch Mon-Sat 12-9 Dinner Mon-Sat 12-9 ⊕ FREE HOUSE ◀ Otter Bitter & Ale, Guest ales ♂ Wiscombe Suicider. **Facilities** Non-diners area ❤ (Bar Garden) ♦♦ Children's menu Children's portions Play area Garden ⌂ Parking WiFi

PICK OF THE PUBS

The Tower Inn

SLAPTON Map 3 SX84

tel: 01548 580216
Church Rd TQ7 2PN
email: towerinn@slapton.org
web: www.thetowerinn.com
dir: *Exit A379 S of Dartmouth, left at Slapton Sands*

West Country ales and seasonal menus

Tucked up a narrow driveway behind cottages and the church in this unspoilt Devon village, the ancient ivy-clad tower (which gives this charming 14th-century inn its name) looms hauntingly above the pub. It is all that remains of the old College of Chantry Priests – the pub was built to accommodate the artisans who constructed the monastic college. Six hundred years on and this truly atmospheric village pub continues to welcome guests and the appeal, other than its peaceful location, is the excellent range of real ales on tap and the eclectic choice of modern pub grub prepared from locally sourced ingredients, which include smoked fish from Dartmouth, quality Devon-reared beef, and fresh fish and crab landed at Brixham. Expect hearty lunchtime sandwiches alongside the ploughman's platter laden with pork pie, cheddar cheese, home-made relish and crusty bread; and Thai fishcakes. A typical evening meal may take in carpaccio of Exmoor venison with rocket, olive

tapenade and parmesan; followed by pork belly with curly kale and sage jus; or pan-fried wild sea bass with braised fennel, crab dumplings and a crab bisque. Round off with apple and blueberry crumble with vanilla ice cream and wash down with a pint of Otter or St Austell Proper Job. Stone walls, open fires, low beams, scrubbed oak tables and flagstone floors characterise the welcoming interior, the atmosphere enhanced at night with candlelit tables. There's a splendid landscaped rear garden, perfect for summer alfresco meals. Visitors exploring Slapton Ley Nature Reserve and Slapton Sands should venture inland to seek out this ancient inn.

Open 12-2.30 (12-3 summer) 6-11 Closed 1st 2wks Jan, Sun eve in winter **Food** Lunch all wk 12-2.30 Dinner all wk 6.30-9.30 ⊕ FREE HOUSE ◀ Butcombe Bitter, Otter Bitter, St Austell Proper Job, Sharp's Doom Bar Ὄ Addlestones, Sharp's Orchard. **Facilities** Non-diners area ✿ (Bar Restaurant Garden) ♦♦ Children's menu Children's portions Garden ☶ Beer festival Parking WiFi ▭

SIDMOUTH
Map 3 SY18

Blue Ball Inn
PICK OF THE PUBS

tel: 01395 514062 **Stevens Cross, Sidford EX10 9QL**
email: enquiries@blueballinnsidford.co.uk
dir: M5 junct 30, A3052, through Sidford towards Lyme Regis, inn on left

Family-friendly pub with a warm welcome

Postcard-pretty under its thatched roof, the 14th-century cob-and-flint Blue Ball in Sidford is popular with locals and visitors alike. Lovingly maintained, colourful and attractive gardens surround the inn. A wide selection of freshly prepared food from traditional beer battered fish and chips, and steak and kidney pudding to a wide range of fresh fish including crab, lobster, sole and mussels; in addition there are many other dishes from the regularly changing specials board. The wine list ranges from new world and more traditional choices that will suit all pockets. The real ales include local Otter Bitter, St Austell Tribute, Sharp's Doom Bar and Bass. The inn is within easy reach of the M5, A303 and Exeter, and just minutes from stunning walks inland and along the coast. Families are very welcome here.

Open all day all wk Closed 25 Dec eve **Food** Lunch all wk 12-2.30 Dinner all wk 6-9 Set menu available ⊕ PUNCH TAVERNS ◀ Otter Bitter, St Austell Tribute, Sharp's Doom Bar, Bass, Guest ale ♂ Thatchers Gold. ₹ 13 **Facilities** Non-diners area ♣ (Bar Garden) ♦ Children's portions Garden Outside area ♬ Parking WiFi ﹗

Dukes ★★★★ INN
PICK OF THE PUBS

tel: 01395 513320 **The Esplanade EX10 8AR**
email: dukes@sidmouthinn.co.uk **web:** www.dukessidmouth.co.uk
dir: Exit A3052 to Sidmouth, left onto Esplanade

Relaxed, informal dining on the Regency esplanade

A stone's throw from the sea in Sidmouth's town centre, this contemporary family-friendly inn has a stylish and lively interior, a continental feel in the bar and public areas, and comfortable en suite bedrooms. In fine weather, the patio garden, which overlooks the sea, is a great place in which to bask in the sun with a pint of Otter Ale. If it's chilly, relax inside on one of the comfortable leather sofas, perhaps with an award-winning Christopher Piper wine, all of which are by the bottle or glass. Menu choices feature fresh fish from Brixham and prime meats and game from West Country farms. Lunchtime brings sandwiches and lighter pub favourites, while in the evening expect medallions of tenderloin pork, Puy lentil moussaka, and pan-fried sea bass fillet. Pizzas are also always available. Dukes has received an AA Dinner Award and also holds a green tourism award. A beer festival takes place during the first week of August.

Open all day all wk **Food** Lunch Mon-Fri 12-2.30, Sat 12-9.30, Sun 12-9 Dinner Mon-Thu 6-9, Fri 6-9.30, Sat 12-9.30, Sun 12-9 Av main course £11 ⊕ FREE HOUSE ◀ Branscombe Vale Branoc & Summa That, Otter Ale, ♂ Sandford Orchards, Annings Fruit Cider. ₹ 20 **Facilities** Non-diners area ♣ (Bar Garden) ♦ Children's menu Children's portions Garden ♬ Beer festival Parking WiFi ﹗ (notice required) **Rooms** 13

SLAPTON
Map 3 SX84

The Tower Inn
PICK OF THE PUBS

See Pick of the Pubs on page 153

SOURTON
Map 3 SX59

The Highwayman Inn

tel: 01837 861243 **EX20 4HN**
email: info@thehighwaymaninn.net
dir: On A386 (Okehampton to Tavistock road). From Exeter, exit A30 towards Tavistock. Pub 4m from Okehampton, 12m from Tavistock

One of a kind pub, crammed with objects both eccentric and obscure

The Highwayman is a fascinating and unique place, full of legend, strange architecture, eccentric furniture and obscure bric-à-brac, with roots going back to 1282. John 'Buster' Jones began creating his vision in 1959 — features include part of a galleon, wood hauled from Dartmoor's bogs, and Gothic church arches; the entrance is through the old Okehampton to Launceston coach. The pub is now run by his daughter Sally. Popular with holidaymakers and international tourists, The Highwayman refreshes one and all with drinks that include real farmhouse cider and interesting bottled beers from local breweries; great pasties and pies are always available.

Open 11.30-2 6-10.30 (Sun 12-2 7-10.30) Closed 25-28 Dec, Mon eve it is advisable to check with pub that it is open ⊕ FREE HOUSE ◀ Marston's Pedigree, Wychwood Hobgoblin, Sharp's Doom Bar, Shepherd Neame Spitfire ♂ Grays. **Facilities** ♣ (Bar Restaurant Garden) Family room Garden Parking WiFi **Notes** ⊛

SOUTH POOL
Map 3 SX74

The Millbrook Inn
PICK OF THE PUBS

See Pick of the Pubs on opposite page

SOWTON
Map 3 SX99

The Black Horse Inn

tel: 01392 366649 **Old Honiton Rd EX5 2AN**
email: blackhorseinnexeter@btconnect.com
dir: On old A30 from Exeter towards Honiton, 0.5m from M5 junct 29; 1m from Exeter International Airport. Inn between Sowton & Clyst Honiton

Good food within easy reach of Exeter

This Wadworth-owned village pub has a relaxed atmosphere and is the perfect setting to enjoy a menu that uses plenty of produce from local suppliers. Now under new management and with a new chef, there's a wide ranging menu of fish dishes, grilled steaks, pastas, salads and pub favourites like oven-baked lasagne; chilli con carne; and slow roasted pork belly. Try the local ale while sitting on the terrace on warmer days.

Open all day all wk 11-11 (Sun 11-9 Winter) **Food** Lunch Mon-Thu 11.45-2.30, Fri-Sun 11.45-9.30 (Sun 11.45-8 Winter) Dinner Mon-Thu 6-9.30, Fri-Sun 11.45-9.30 ⊕ WADWORTH ◀ Henry's Original IPA & 6X, Guest ales ♂ Westons Stowford Press. ₹ 11 **Facilities** Non-diners area ♣ (Bar Garden) ♦ Children's menu Garden ♬ Parking WiFi ﹗

PICK OF THE PUBS

The Millbrook Inn

SOUTH POOL   Map 3 SX74

tel: 01548 531581 **TQ7 2RW**
email: info@millbrookinnsouthpool.co.uk
web: www.millbrookinnsouthpool.co.uk
dir: *A379 from Kingsbridge to Frogmore. In Frogmore right signed South Pool. 2m to village*

French country cooking meets good pub grub

This quaint, white-painted 16th-century village pub is little more than a good mooring rope's throw from South Pool creek on the Salcombe estuary. No surprise then that it attracts boat-owners from all along the coast. Being end-on to the village street, its compact courtyard with bench tables is at one side, while at the rear a small terrace overlooks fields. Open fires warm the two traditionally decorated beamed bars, and there's a small dining room, whose charm you may not be able to enjoy if you don't book. A pint of Devon-brewed Red Rock IPA, or a guest ale, usually Otter, will no doubt be uppermost in the minds of arrivals by boat after all that belaying and tacking. Ciders is on draught too. Wines, many from Languedoc-Roussillon, are designed to complement the food, the big draw being chef Jean-Philippe Bidart's auberge-type food, based on French family recipes and the best South Hams meats and fish. A close look at his menus reveals Start Bay crab bisque; escargots with garlic, parsley

and Pernod butter; tenderloin of pork; bouillabaisse; and monkfish and mussel linguine. The lighter bar menu offers pan-fried chorizo with new potatoes, spinach and duck egg; smoked haddock and butterbean cassoulet; and pig's cheeks with mash and apple sauce, known as Bath Chaps. Monsieur Bidart turns out seductive desserts too, such as cardamom pannacotta with mango and berry sorbet; and sticky toffee pudding with toffee sauce and Devon clotted cream. Rural West Country and French cheeses - among them Exmoor Jersey Blue, Cornish Yarg and Tomme de Savoie - are served with celery, quince, apple, grapes and oat cakes. A 24-hour Veg Shed with an honesty box helps to replace a long-lost village shop.

Open all day all wk 12-11 (Sun 12-10.30) **Food** Lunch all wk 12-2 Dinner all wk 7-9 ⊕ FREE HOUSE
◀ Red Rock, Millbrook, Guest ales
♂ Thatchers Heritage & Gold. ♟ 10
Facilities Non-diners area ♣ (Bar Restaurant Garden) ♦ Children's portions Garden Outside area ☿ WiFi

PICK OF THE PUBS

The Treby Arms ❀❀

SPARKWELL Map 3 SX55

tel: 01752 837363
1 Newton Row PL7 5DD
email: trebyarms@hotmail.co.uk
web: www.thetrebyarms.co.uk

Village pub that punches above its weight

Chef-patron Anton Piotrowski and his wife Clare have transformed a humble, 17th-century, end-of-terrace local into a vibrant gastro-pub. Anton's achievement as a BBC MasterChef in 2012 has undoubtedly helped to ramp up interest, so booking is essential if you want to experience his inspired cooking. But first the bar, where Dartmoor Jail and IPA share counter space with St Austell Tribute, Otter Amber, and Symonds and Rekorderlig ciders. The restaurant's achievement of two AA Rosettes acknowledges the passion Anton and his staff have for their food, all, it goes without saying, prepared, cooked and presented to a very high standard. They use fresh seasonal produce, including locally-caught fish, estate game and village allotment vegetables, for the daily carte and set menus. A typical three-course option might be celeriac and smoked garlic soup; venison suet pudding, kale and horseradish mash; and Earl Grey pannacotta with lemon curd and yogurt ice cream. Turn to the carte for sirloin of beef with haggis bonbons, chestnut

mushroom and pancetta; white wine-battered fish and chips with 'chip shop treats'; or honey and mustard pork fillet with smoked ham hock, egg, red pepper ketchup and salad. If your meal isn't complete without a dessert, especially one you may not have come across before, try the chocolate caramel yuzu and date sponge, and also Horlicks. Alternatively, and more conventionally, there's a cheeseboard, on which Miss Muffet from Bude and Sharpham Rustic from Totnes are possible choices. Anton also puts together a six-course taster menu with wines for £100 a head. His monthly Master Class is for 'students' wanting to learn how to prepare pasta, venison, fish and the dishes that form their post-course meal.

Open 12-3 6-11 (Fri-Sun 12-11) Closed 25-26 Dec & 1-2 Jan, Mon **Food** Lunch Tue-Thu 12-3, Fri-Sun 12-9 Dinner served Tue-Thu 6-9, Fri-Sun 12-9 Set menu available, Restaurant menu Tue-Sun. ⊕ FREE HOUSE ◀ St Austell Tribute, Otter Amber, Dartmoor Jail Ale & IPA ♎ Thatchers, Symonds, Rekorderlig. **Facilities** Non-diners area ♥ (Bar Outside area) ♦ Children's portions Outside area ⊼ Parking WiFi

SPARKWELL — Map 3 SX55

The Treby Arms ◉◉ — PICK OF THE PUBS

See Pick of the Pubs on opposite page

SPREYTON — Map 3 SX69

The Tom Cobley Tavern — PICK OF THE PUBS

tel: 01647 231314 **EX17 5AL**
dir: *From A30 at Whiddon Down take A3124 N. 1st right after services, 1st right over bridge*

Fabulous views and a huge range of ales

This whitewashed Dartmoor village pub draws the crowds thanks to its association with the Widecombe Fair. It was from this pub one day in 1802 that Thomas Cobley and his companions set forth for the fair, an event immortalised in song; his cottage still stands in the village. The tavern remains a traditional village local. The unspoilt main bar has a roaring log fire, cushioned settles, and an award-winning range of tip-top real ales straight from the cask. The pub also offers great real ciders, among which are Lilley's Cider Barn and Gwynt y Ddraig's Welsh brew. Food is traditional pub grub, but the Tom Cobley prides itself on its selection of vegetarian, vegan and gluten-free options. Snacks include hot toasted sandwiches and omelettes, home-made pasties, and baked jacket potatoes. Larger dishes range from pies to fishcakes, and grills include a home-made burger smothered in melted Taw Valley cheddar.

Open 12-3 6-11 (Sun 12-4 7-11 Mon 6.30-11 Fri-Sat 12-3 6-1am) Closed Mon L **Food** Lunch Tue-Sun 12-2 Dinner all wk 7-9 ⊕ FREE HOUSE ◂ Cotleigh Tawny Ale, Teignworthy Gundog, Sharp's Doom Bar, St Austell Tribute & Proper Job, Dartmoor Jail Ale & Legend, Holsworthy Tamar Black Ŏ Winkleigh, Westons Stowford Press, Healey's Berry Rattler & Pear Rattler, Sandford Orchards, Gwynt y Ddraig, Lilley's. **Facilities** Non-diners area ☻ (Bar Garden) ◆◆ Children's menu Children's portions Garden ⋒ Parking ▭ (notice required)

STAVERTON — Map 3 SX76

Sea Trout Inn

tel: 01803 762274 **TQ9 6PA**
email: info@theseatroutinn.co.uk
dir: *From A38 take A384 towards Totnes. Follow Staverton & Sea Trout Inn sign*

Long, white-painted pub offering a modern British menu

Apart from the occasional puff of a steam train drifting across the pretty Dart Valley from the South Devon Railway, this character village inn is the epitome of tranquillity. Dating back 600 years, the Sea Trout ticks all the boxes for the authentic country pub, from the delightful locals' bar to the stylish restaurant, where trying to choose from the modern British menu can be agonising; slow-roast pork belly with chorizo bubble-and-squeak, or perhaps Massaman seafood curry, with well-kept Palmers ales the icing on the cake.

Open all day all wk **Food** Lunch Mon-Fri 12-2, Sat 12-2.30, Sun 12-3 Dinner Mon-Thu 6-9, Fri-Sat 6-9.30, Sun 6.30-9 ⊕ PALMERS ◂ 200, Copper Ale, Best Bitter & Dorset Gold Ŏ Thatchers. ☻ **Facilities** Non-diners area ☻ (Bar Garden) ◆◆ Children's menu Children's portions Garden Parking WiFi ▭

STOKE FLEMING — Map 3 SX84

The Green Dragon Inn

tel: 01803 770238 **Church Rd TQ6 0PX**
email: pcrowther@btconnect.com
dir: *From A379 (Dartmouth to Kingsbridge coast road) follow brown pub sign, into Church Rd. Pub opposite church*

A haven of boating memorabilia

Opposite the village church, this South Hams pub has many seafaring connections, being only two miles from Dartmouth. Although there has been a building on this site since the 12th century, the first recorded landlord took charge in 1607. The current landlord has decorated the interior in a seafaring theme with charts and sailing pictures. Local beers such as Otter and Exmoor slake the thirst of walkers, whilst the great-value menu can satisfy the largest of appetites with hearty baguettes, hand-picked crab, cottage pie, Glamorgan sausages, surf 'n' turf burger or a West Country sirloin steak.

Open all wk 11.30-3 5.30-11 (Sun 12-3.30 6.30-10.30) Closed 25-26 Dec **Food** Lunch all wk 12-2 Dinner all wk 6.30-8.30 ⊕ HEAVITREE ◂ Otter Ale, Exmoor Ale, Guest ales Ŏ Aspall, Addlestones. ☻ 10 **Facilities** Non-diners area ☻ (Bar Garden) ◆◆ Children's menu Children's portions Play area Garden ⋒ Parking

TAVISTOCK — Map 3 SX47

NEW The Cornish Arms

tel: 01822 612145 **15-16 West St PL19 8AN**
email: info@thecornisharmstavistock.co.uk
dir: *Phone for detailed directions*

Cosy and welcoming pub on the edge of Dartmoor

Historically the last coaching inn before reaching Cornwall, The Cornish Arms is under the new stewardship of husband and wife team John and Emma Hooker. Whether inside the modern but cosy interior or out in the garden, guests will find an unpretentious menu of pub favourites, from pork pie and piccalilli; steak and kidney pudding, mash and buttered swede to Devon ham, egg and chips. The bar is well stocked with ales including St Austell's Trelawny and ciders such as Cornish Rattler, and the real ale and cider festival in August is a must-attend occasion for visitors.

Open all day all wk **Food** Lunch all wk 12-6 Dinner all wk 6-9.30 ⊕ ST AUSTELL BREWERY ◂ Tribute, Proper Job & Trelawny Ŏ Healey's Cornish Rattler, Symonds. **Facilities** Non-diners area ☻ (Bar Garden Outside area) ◆◆ Children's menu Children's portions Garden Outside area ⋒ Beer festival Cider festival Parking WiFi ▭ (notice required)

Peter Tavy Inn

tel: 01822 810348 **Peter Tavy PL19 9NN**
email: chris@wording.freeserve.co.uk
dir: *From Tavistock take A386 towards Okehampton. In 2m right to Peter Tavy*

Dartmoor inn recommended for its pies

It is thought this inn was originally built in the 15th century as a Devon longhouse for the stonemasons rebuilding the village church. On the western flanks of Dartmoor, it is likely that it became a pub by the early 17th century and a further floor was added. It is now as much a draw for its range of local real ales and ciders as it is for its food, much of it sourced locally. The pies are popular main dishes, while there are always vegetarian and vegan options like spicy African sweet potato and spinach stew. Wash down seafood gumbo with pints of Jail Ale.

Open all wk 12-3 6-11 (Sun 12-3 6-10.30); all day Etr-Autumn Closed 25 Dec **Food** Lunch all wk 12-2 Dinner all wk 6.30-9 ⊕ FREE HOUSE ◂ Dartmoor Jail Ale, Branscombe Vale Drayman's Best Bitter, Tavy Ideal Pale Ale Ŏ Winkleigh Sam's Poundhouse & Crisp. ☻ 9 **Facilities** Non-diners area ☻ (Bar Restaurant Garden) ◆◆ Children's menu Children's portions Garden ⋒ Parking WiFi

PICK OF THE PUBS

The Golden Lion Inn

TIPTON ST JOHN Map 3 SY09

tel: 01404 812881
EX10 0AA
email: info@goldenliontipton.co.uk
web: www.goldenliontipton.co.uk
dir: *Phone for detailed directions*

Mediterranean slant to excellent menus

Michelle and Francois Teissier have been at the helm of this welcoming Devon village pub for over a decade. So many things contribute to its traditional feel – the low wooden beams and stone walls, the winter log fire, the art-deco prints and Tiffany lamps, not to mention the paintings by Devonian and Cornish artists. And there's the bar, of course, where locally brewed Otter ales are the order of the day. Chef-patron Franky (as everyone calls him) trained in classical French cooking at a prestigious establishment in the Loire Valley, a grounding that accounts today for his rustic French, Mediterranean and British menus. Their delights may include home smoked duck salad; crevettes in garlic butter; breast of duck with oriental plum sauce; Breton chicken with smoky bacon and leeks in cream; lobster in garlic butter; or venison pie. Given that the genteel seaside town of Sidmouth is just down the road, the seafood specials depend totally on that day's catch – cod, hake and sea bass are all candidates. Tempting white and granary

bread sandwiches are filled with fresh Lyme Bay crab, mature cheddar or home-cooked ham. The Sunday lunch menu offers roast West Country beef with Yorkshire pudding; roast lamb with mint sauce; and winter vegetable crêpe. As Franky sums up: 'When Michelle and I took over in 2003, our aim was to create a friendly, inviting village pub offering great value, high-quality food made from the freshest ingredients; with our combination of rustic French dishes and traditional British food with a Mediterranean twist, there's something for everyone!' Outside there is a grassy beer garden and walled terrace area with tumbling grapevines. On summer evenings you can listen to jazz.

Open 12-2.30 6-11 (Sun 12-2.30) Closed Sun eve **Food** Lunch all wk 12-2 Dinner Mon-Sat 6.30-8.30 Av main course £12.50 ⊕ HEAVITREE ◼ Bass, Otter Ale & Bitter. ♀ 12 **Facilities** Non-diners area ♦♦ Children's menu Children's portions Garden ⊓ Parking ⟊ (notice required)

THURLESTONE
Map 3 SX64

The Village Inn

tel: 01548 563525 **TQ7 3NN**
email: enquiries@thurlestone.co.uk
dir: *Take A379 from Plymouth towards Kingsbridge, at Bantham rdbt take B3197, right signed Thurlestone, 2.5m*

Popular country pub offering fresh seafood

Just minutes from the beach and coastal path, The Village Inn was built in the 16th century using timbers salvaged from a wrecked Spanish Armada ship. A popular village pub, it is under the same ownership as the nearby Thurlestone Hotel. Expect traditional country pub decor, good service from the Grose family, well-kept ales and decent food. In addition to sandwiches and salads, classic dishes are bangers and mash; and ham, egg and chips. Look to the blackboards for daily specials.

Open all wk 11.30-3 6-11.30 (Sat-Sun & summer all day) **Food** Lunch Mon-Fri 12-2.30, Sat-Sun 12-9 Dinner Mon-Fri 6-9, Sat-Sun 12-9 Av main course £9.95 ⊕ FREE HOUSE ◄ Palmers Best Bitter, Sharp's Doom Bar, Guest ale ♂ Heron Valley. **Facilities** Non-diners area ✿ (Bar Restaurant Outside area) ◄ Children's menu Children's portions Outside area ⌁ Parking WiFi ➡ (notice required)

TIPTON ST JOHN
Map 3 SY09

The Golden Lion Inn
PICK OF THE PUBS

See Pick of the Pubs on opposite page

TOPSHAM
Map 3 SX98

Bridge Inn
PICK OF THE PUBS

tel: 01392 873862 **Bridge Hill EX3 0QQ**
email: tom@cheffers.co.uk
dir: *M5 junct 30 follow Sidmouth signs, in approx 400yds right at rdbt onto A376 towards Exmouth. In 1.8m cross mini rdbt. Right at next mini rdbt to Topsham. 1.2m, cross River Clyst. Inn on right*

True brewing heritage with royal approval

This 'museum with beer' is substantially 16th century, although its constituent parts vary considerably in age. Most of the fabric is local stone, while the old brewhouse at the rear is traditional Devon cob. Four generations of the same family have run it since great-grandfather William Gibbings arrived in 1897, and it remains eccentrically and gloriously old fashioned – mobile phones are definitely out. Usually around 10 real ales from local and further-flung breweries are served straight from their casks, the actual line-up varying by the week. There are no lagers and only a few wines, two from a local organic vineyard. Traditional, freshly prepared lunchtime bar food includes granary ploughman's, pork pies, veggie or meat pasties, and sandwiches, all made with local ingredients. Queen Elizabeth II visited in 1998; it is believed this is the only time she has officially stepped inside an English pub.

Open all wk 12-2 6-10.30 (Fri-Sat 12-2 6-11 Sun 12-2 7-10.30) **Food** Lunch all wk 12-2 ⊕ FREE HOUSE ◄ Branscombe Vale Branoc, Adnams Broadside, Exe Valley, O'Hanlon's, Teignworthy, Jollyboat Plunder. **Facilities** Non-diners area ✿ (Bar Garden) ◄ Garden ⌁ Parking WiFi **Notes** ☺

NEW The Globe

tel: 01392 873471 **34 Fore St EX3 0HR**
email: theglobe@staustellbrewery.co.uk
dir: *M5 junct 30, A379 to Topsham. At rdbt take B3182. In Topsham at mini rdbt straight ahead into Fore St. Pub approx 500yds on left*

Sixteenth-century coaching inn in appealing estuary town

Rich textures and colours meet the eye on entering this newly restored and sympathetically updated old inn, close to the River Exe. Although it's owned by Cornwall's St Austell brewery, you might also find a real ale from Devons' Dartmoor brewery in the comfortable fire-warmed bar. The wood-panelled Elizabethan restaurant makes excellent use of locally grown, reared or caught ingredients for chargrilled Devonshire rump and fillet steaks; whole grilled Cornish sardines; and walnut and gorgonzola tortellini. Daily-changing specials make the most of West Country produce too. Head here on a Monday for 'pie and a pint night'.

Open all day all wk **Food** Lunch all day Dinner all day ⊕ ST AUSTELL ◄ St Austell Tribute, Proper Job & Dartmoor ♂ Thatchers Gold. ☏ 10 **Facilities** Non-diners area ✿ (Bar Outside area) ◄ Children's menu Children's portions Outside area ⌁ Parking WiFi ➡ (notice required)

TORCROSS
Map 3 SX84

Start Bay Inn

tel: 01548 580553 **TQ7 2TQ**
email: clair@startbayinn.co.uk
dir: *Between Dartmouth & Kingsbridge on A379*

Ancient pub serving the very freshest seafood

Located on the beach and with a freshwater reserve on its other side, the patio of this 14th-century inn overlooks the sea. The fishermen working from Start Bay deliver their catch direct to the kitchen; so does a local crabber, who leaves his catch at the back door to be cooked by the pub. The former landlord (father of landladies Clair and Gail) continues to dive for scallops. Be in no doubt therefore about the freshness of the seafood on the specials board. Look also for locally sourced steaks, burgers from the village butcher, and Salcombe Dairy ice creams. Ploughman's, sandwiches and jackets are also available.

Open all day all wk 11.30-11 **Food** Lunch all wk 11.30-2.15 Dinner all wk 6-9.30 winter, 6-10 summer ⊕ HEAVITREE ◄ Bass, Otter Ale & Bitter, St Austell Tribute ♂ Heron Valley. ☏ 8 **Facilities** Non-diners area ◄ Children's menu Children's portions Family room Garden ⌁ Parking

TORQUAY
Map 3 SX96

The Cary Arms ★★★★★ INN
PICK OF THE PUBS

See Pick of the Pubs on page 160

PICK OF THE PUBS

The Cary Arms ★★★★★ INN

TORQUAY   Map 3 SX96

tel: 01803 327110
Babbacombe Beach TQ1 3LX
email: enquiries@caryarms.co.uk
web: www.caryarms.co.uk
dir: *On entering Teignmouth, at bottom of hill at lights, right signed Torquay/ A379. Cross river. At mini rdbt follow Babbacombe signs. Pass Babbacombe Model Village, through lights, left into Babbacombe Downs Rd, left into Beach Rd*

Beachside inn that has it all

Right on the beach, the rambling and whitewashed Cary Arms is a real find in Babbacombe Bay. This 'boutique inn' is so much more than just a pub; unwind in the beamed bar with its original stone walls, perhaps with a pint of Bays Topsail or Otter Ale in hand, contemplating the stunning views across the bay; stay in one of the luxury sea-facing bedrooms; and sample the delicious gastro-inn food from the daily-changing menu. The informal bar is perfect for playing a board game and relaxing after a bracing walk or a day on the beach. If it's a glorious summer's day, you will unquestionably wish to eat in the terraced gardens that lead down to the water's edge; this is when the barbecue and wood-fired oven come into their own. The watchwords in the kitchen are freshness and seasonality, underpinned by a respect for the local

pastures and waters. Catch of the day will be a must for fish-lovers – perhaps pan-fried sea bass with rosemary crust, sauté potatoes and anchovy and tomato butter – but the menu reflects coast and country in equal measure. Hard to resist are Devon crab and crayfish cocktail with pickled lemons; steak and Otter Ale pie; pan-seared Brixham scallops, butternut squash risotto; lamb rump; and their long-standing classic of fish, chips and crushed peas. Gastro evenings are a regular event; the barbecue is often booked by groups, and a menu is available for the 'nippers'. If staying over, the bedrooms are classic and cool with echoes of New England beachside-chic, and most have a private terrace or balcony overlooking the sea.

Open all day all wk 12-11 **Food** Lunch all wk 12-3 Dinner all wk 6.30-9 🍺 FREE HOUSE ◀ Otter Ale, Bays Topsail ☼ Sandford Devon Mist & Devon Red. 🍷 11 **Facilities** Non-diners area 🐾 (Bar Restaurant Garden) 👫 Children's menu Children's portions Family room Garden 🎋 WiFi **Rooms** 8

TOTNES
Map 3 SX86

The Durant Arms
PICK OF THE PUBS

tel: 01803 732240 **Ashprington TQ9 7UP**
email: macwoolly@gmail.com
dir: *From Totnes take A381 towards Kingsbridge, 1m, left for Ashprington*

Refurbished village free house high above the River Dart

In March 2014, this 1725-built village pub reopened following an extensive refurbishment. Among other things, this endowed it with a new bar 'in all its solid-oak glory' and a wood-burning stove, but the original stone-flag floor remains. The bar stocks West Country ales and ciders, and award-winning Luscombe organic soft drinks and wines from Sharpham Vineyard just down the hill (tours are available). Ingredients sourced from in and around Totnes appear on a seasonal menu listing home-cooked dishes such as aubergine parmigiana; steak, kidney and Otter Ale pie; roasted cod with chickpeas, chorizo and courgettes; and lamb rogan josh. Waving the flag for the desserts section might be crème brûlée; sticky toffee pudding; and apple crumble. Simple snacks, sandwiches and salads are available at lunchtime. Doors from the dining room lead to a sheltered courtyard.

Open all day 11-11 Closed Mon (out of season) **Food** Lunch all wk 12-close Dinner all wk 12-close ⊕ FREE HOUSE ◀ Dartmoor, Otter, Guest ales ☼ Sandford Orchards Devon Red. ☘ 22 **Facilities** Non-diners area ♦ Children's menu Children's portions Family room Outside area ⚲ Parking WiFi ▭

Royal Seven Stars Hotel

tel: 01803 862125 **The Plains TQ9 5DD**
email: enquiry@royalsevenstars.co.uk
dir: *From A382 signed Totnes, left at 'Dartington' rdbt. Through lights towards town centre, through next rdbt, pass Morrisons car park on left. 200yds on right*

Town centre favourite

In the heart of Totnes, this Grade II listed property has three character bars and a grand ballroom. In the champagne bar, an addition to the TQ9 brasserie, is where bubbly is served by the glass or bottle from 5pm onwards, along with cocktails and wines. Excellent local brews and ciders are always on tap. Quality food at affordable prices is another strength – expect the likes of Thai marinated beef shortribs with Thai noodle salad; chicken breast in Parma ham filled with seasonal mushrooms, with sautéed potatoes, fine beans and hollandaise sauce; and steaks from the grill.

Open all day all wk **Food** Lunch all wk 11-9.30 Dinner all wk 11-9.30 Set menu available Restaurant menu available Mon-Sat ⊕ FREE HOUSE ◀ Sharp's Doom Bar, Bays Gold, Courage Best, Dartmoor Legend & Jail Ale ☼ Thatchers, Orchard's, Ashridge. ☘ 26 **Facilities** Non-diners area ♣ (Bar Outside area) ♦ Children's menu Children's portions Family room Outside area ⚲ Beer festival Cider festival Parking WiFi

Rumour

tel: 01803 864682 **30 High St TQ9 5RY**
dir: *Follow signs for Totnes castle/town centre. On main street up hill above arch on left. 5 min walk from rail station*

Stylish bar serving exciting European food

Named after Fleetwood Mac's landmark 1977 album, this 17th-century building at the top of the high street has had a chequered history including stints as a milk bar, restaurant and wine bar. Food offerings include an extensive hand-made pizza menu encompassing light bites and brunch-style offerings and a more formal à la carte menu that could proffer rump steak with garlic mushrooms, tomato and French fries, or seared fillet of salmon Sri Lankan curry, pilau rice and cumin flatbread. Typical desserts might include plum Pavlova with cardamom ice cream or a dark chocolate and peanut terrine with caramel and whipped cream.

Open all wk Mon-Sat 10am-11pm (Sun 6-10.30) **Food** Lunch Mon-Sat 12-3 Dinner Mon-Sat 6-10, Sun 6-9 Av main course £15 ⊕ FREE HOUSE ◀ Otter, Dartmoor

Legend, Bays Topsail ☼ South West Orchards Cider, Sheppy's, Ashridge Organic.
☘ 17 **Facilities** Non-diners area ♦ Children's portions WiFi

Steam Packet Inn ★★★★ INN

tel: 01803 863880 **St Peter's Quay TQ9 5EW**
email: steampacket@buccaneer.co.uk web: www.steampacketinn.co.uk
dir: *Exit A38 towards Plymouth, 18m. A384 to Totnes, 6m. Left at mini rdbt, pass Morrisons on left, over mini rdbt, 400yds on left*

Popular inn on the River Dart

Named after the passenger, cargo and mail steamers that once plied the Dart, this riverside pub (alongside which you can moor your boat) with four newly refurbished en suite guest rooms offers great views, particularly from the conservatory restaurant and heated waterside patio, where there is plenty of seating. A real log fire warms the bar in the colder months. The mainly traditional choices at lunch and dinner might include plaice goujons, gammon steak, lamb rump and Mexican fajitas. There are daily fish specials on the blackboard. Look out for the three-day beer festival in mid-May, occasional live music and summer barbecues.

Open all day all wk **Food** Lunch Mon-Fri 12-2.30, Sat 12-3, Sun 12-8 Dinner Mon-Sat 6-9.30, Sun 12-8 Av main course £11 ⊕ FREE HOUSE/BUCCANEER ◀ Sharp's Doom Bar, Dartmoor Jail Ale, Guest ale ☼ Westons Stowford Press & GL, Ashridge. ☘ 11 **Facilities** Non-diners area ♣ (Bar Garden) ♦ Children's menu Garden ⚲ Beer festival Parking WiFi ▭ (notice required) **Rooms** 4

The White Hart Bar & Restaurant
PICK OF THE PUBS

tel: 01803 847111 **Dartington Hall TQ9 6EL**
email: bookings@dartingtonhall.com
dir: *A38 onto A384 towards Totnes. Turn at Dartington church into Dartington Hall Estate*

British tapas in a medieval setting

The White Hart is surrounded by landscaped gardens and is part of the splendid 14th-century Dartington Hall Estate and deer park; it even has its own cinema located in a renovated medieval barn. Ancient tapestries, crackling fires, flagstones, Gothic chandeliers and limed oak settles characterise the interior. Local Devon and Cornish real ales are available in the bar together with Thatchers draught cider, and there's a patio for the warmer weather. The exciting British tapas menu lists regularly changing, creative dishes made from the best local produce: example dishes include mixed game pie; and whole John Dory, stir-fried vegetables, egg noodles and Thai broth. Children are welcome and are encouraged to sample the tapas with the rest of the family. The daily-changing bar and restaurant menu uses fresh, seasonal ingredients from south Devon and the estate itself – single-suckled beef, grass-reared lamb, additive-free and free-range chickens and eggs, and fish.

Open all day all wk 12-11 **Food** Lunch all wk 12-9 Dinner all wk 12-9 Av main course £10 ⊕ FREE HOUSE ◀ St Austell Tribute & Proper Job, Bays Topsail, Local guest ales ☼ Thatchers. **Facilities** Non-diners area ♦ Children's menu Children's portions Garden ⚲ Parking WiFi ▭ (notice required)

TRUSHAM
Map 3 SX88

Cridford Inn
PICK OF THE PUBS

tel: 01626 853694 **TQ13 0NR**
email: reservations@vanillapod-cridfordinn.com
dir: *From A38 exit at junct for Teign Valley, right, follow Trusham signs for 4m*

Historic pub near Dartmoor with great food

Medieval masons' marks are still visible above the bar in this heritage gem of a pub; over a thousand years of history are packed into its rough stone walls and thatched roof. Find a seat on the terrace beneath mature trees for views over the Teign Valley. Ales include Dartmoor Brewery's Dragon's Breath, which was born in the snows of 2010 and is flavoured with black treacle. You can eat in either the bar or the renowned Vanilla Pod restaurant, where food with an excellent local pedigree and seasonal flavours delights locals and visitors alike. Start with lamb Scotch broth, or pan-fried scallops with celeriac purée; follow with a whole Brixham plaice with lemon butter, fresh parsley and shoestring fries – hand-picked Teignmouth crab can be added for a small cost. Hand-crafted desserts include the chef's signature torte; and plum frangipane served with Devon clotted cream. There's a beer festival in June.

Open all wk 11-3 6.15-11 (Sat 11-11 Sun 12-10.30) **Food** Lunch Mon-Fri 12-2.30, Sat & Sun (Mar-Sep) all day, Sun (Oct-Feb) 12-3 Dinner all wk 7-9.30 ⊕ FREE HOUSE ◀ Sharp's Doom Bar, Dartmoor Legend & Dragon's Breath, Teignworthy, Bays ⌂ Thatchers. ♈ 10 **Facilities** Non-diners area ♣ (Bar Garden Outside area) ♦ Children's menu Children's portions Family room Garden Outside area ♫ Beer festival Parking WiFi ➡ (notice required)

TUCKENHAY
Map 3 SX85

The Maltsters Arms

tel: 01803 732350 **TQ9 7EQ**
email: maltsters@tuckenhay.com
dir: *A381 from Totnes towards Kingsbridge. 1m, at hill top turn left, follow signs to Tuckenhay, 3m*

Ideal hostelry for riverside eating and drinking

Once owned by the TV chef Keith Floyd, this is a warm and welcoming riverside pub and restaurant in the picturesque Dart Valley. Steeped in history, the 18th-century inn sits in the village of Tuckenhay, once a hive of activity thanks to abundant water power for the wool and then paper industries. An excellent choice of ales includes Dartmoor's Jail Ale and Bays Topsail; a beer festival is held annually. During the summer months, the outdoor Croc Bar with quayside dining buzzes with locals and visitors tucking into plates of home-cooked food based on seasonal and locally sourced ingredients.

Open all day all wk Mon-Thu & Sun 9am-11pm (Fri-Sat 9am-mdnt) **Food** Lunch Mon-Sat 12-2.30, Sun 12-3 Dinner Sun-Thu 6-9, Fri-Sat 6-9.30 Av main course £12 ⊕ FREE HOUSE ◀ Dartmoor Jail Ale, Otter Ale, Bays Topsail ⌂ Thatchers Gold, Sheppy's. ♈ 10 **Facilities** Non-diners area ♣ (Bar Restaurant Garden) ♦ Children's menu Children's portions Garden ♫ Beer festival Parking WiFi

TYTHERLEIGH
Map 4 ST30

The Tytherleigh Arms

tel: 01460 220214 **EX13 7BE**
email: tytherleigharms@gmail.com
dir: *Equidistant from Chard & Axminster on A358*

Local produce at a smart 16th-century inn

This 16th-century coaching inn on the borders of Devon, Dorset and Somerset still retains plenty of original features, including beamed ceilings and huge fires, which

makes for a lovely setting if you are popping in for a pint of Branoc ale, or making a beeline for the daily-changing menu. Local produce drives the menu, whether it's potted Lyme Bay crab, whole roast partridge or Tytherleigh fish pie topped with Somerset cheddar mash.

Open 11-4 6-12 Closed 25 Dec, Sun eve winter **Food** Lunch Mon-Fri 12-2.30, Sat 12-3, Sun 12-4 Dinner Mon-Fri 6-9.30, Sat 6-10, Sun 6-9 ⊕ FREE HOUSE ◀ Otter Ale & Bitter, Branscombe Vale Branoc ⌂ Thatchers Gold, Westons Wyld Wood Organic. ♈ 10 **Facilities** Non-diners area ♣ (Bar Garden) ♦ Children's portions Garden ♫ Parking WiFi ➡ (notice required)

WIDECOMBE IN THE MOOR
Map 3 SX77

The Old Inn

tel: 01364 621207 **TQ13 7TA**
email: rlynton@btinternet.com
dir: *From Bovey Tracey take B3387 to Widecombe in the Moor*

Country pub for all weathers

This 14th-century pub in the heart of a quintessential village is the start and finishing point for several excellent Dartmoor walks. A pub for all seasons, enjoy the five log fires when the weather turns cold or sit outside in the beer garden with its water features. Cask ales include seasonal guests, with plenty of wines by the glass. Fresh traditional pub food sourced locally and includes Dartmoor farmers beef. Steak and kidney pie is a menu favourite.

Open all day all wk 12-11 **Food** Lunch Mon-Sat 12-9, Sun 12-8 Dinner Mon-Sat 12-9, Sun 12-8 ⊕ FREE HOUSE ◀ Badger, Dartmoor, Guest ales ⌂ Westons Stowford Press. ♈ 23 **Facilities** Non-diners area ♣ (Bar Restaurant Garden) ♦ Children's menu Children's portions Garden ♫ Parking WiFi ➡

The Rugglestone Inn
PICK OF THE PUBS

tel: 01364 621327 **TQ13 7TF**
email: enquiries@rugglestoneinn.co.uk
dir: *From village centre take road by church towards Venton. Inn down hill on left*

Pretty, wisteria-clad Dartmoor pub

Originally a cottage, this unaltered Grade II listed building was converted to an inn around 1832. Set in the picturesque village of Widecombe in the Moor, the pub is surrounded by tranquil moorland and streams; the Rugglestone stream rises behind the pub, and Widecombe's famous church acts as a beacon for ramblers and riders seeking out the inn's rural location. Cosy little rooms and comforting wood-burners encourage appreciative visitors and locals alike to tarry awhile and sup ales such as Dartmoor Legend; farmhouse ciders such as Ashridge are stillaged behind the snug bar and tapped straight from the barrel. The filling fare is a decent mix of classic pub staples and savoury dishes, keeping the cold away in winter or fulfilling a summer evening's promise in the streamside garden. The Rugglestone platter of ham, cheddar and Stilton served with salad, pickles, home-made coleslaw and crusty bread is a great Dartmoor experience.

Open all wk Mon-Thu 11.30-3 6-11.30 Fri 11.30-3 5-12 Sat 11.30am-mdnt Sun & BH 12-11 **Food** Lunch all wk 12-2 Dinner all wk 6.30-9 Av main course £10.50 ⊕ FREE HOUSE ◀ O'Hanlon's Yellow Hammer, Otter Bitter, Teignworthy Rugglestone Moor, Dartmoor Legend ⌂ Ashton Press, Lower Widdon Farm, Ashridge, North Hall Manor. ♈ 10 **Facilities** Non-diners area ♣ (Bar Restaurant Garden) ♦ Children's menu Children's portions Garden ♫ Parking ➡ (notice required)

WOODBURY SALTERTON
Map 3 SY08

The Digger's Rest
PICK OF THE PUBS

See Pick of the Pubs on opposite page

PICK OF THE PUBS

The Digger's Rest

WOODBURY SALTERTON   Map 3 SY08

tel: 01395 232375 **EX5 1PQ**
email: bar@diggersrest.co.uk
web: www.diggersrest.co.uk
dir: *2.5m from A3052. Signed from Westpoint Showground*

Picturesque thatched pub offering the best of seasonal produce

This picturesque free house is just a few minutes' drive from the Exeter junction of the M5, and stands in the delightful east Devon village of Woodbury Salterton. The Digger's Rest is more than 500 years old and with its thatched roof, thick stone and cob walls, heavy beams and log fire was originally a cider house. Today the choice on the bar is much wider but cider is still well represented with Westons Scrumpy and Stowford Press. Real ales feature Otter Bitter from Devon with guest appearances from other West Country brewers such as Bays and Palmers. Wine fans will appreciate the wine list which has been created by the independent Wine Merchant, Tanners of Shrewsbury. The food menus are created to make the best of seasonal produce. Sourcing locally plays a big role in freshness and quality control, and English and West Country organic produce is used wherever possible. The kitchen is also committed to supporting farmers who practise good husbandry. Menus feature

fish landed at Brixham and Looe, West Country beef hung for 21 days and pork from a farm just up the road. As well as the main menu there is a blackboard which features special dishes the chef has created from prime cuts or rarer seasonal ingredients he has sought out. Many of the dishes can be served as smaller portions for children and there is also a children's menu. Whether you want to check your emails (free WiFi), have a drink, snack or a full meal, you will find a warm welcome at The Digger's Rest. It's also worth checking the website for details of food clubs, quizzes and events.

Open all week 11-3 5.30-11 (Sun 12-3.30 5.30-10.30) **Food** Lunch all week 12-2 Dinner Mon-Sat 6-9, Sun 6-8.30 ⊕ FREE HOUSE ◀ Otter Bitter, Bays Topsail, Palmers Copper Ale ♂ Westons & Stowford Press. ♀ 11 **Facilities** Non-diners area ♣ (Bar Garden) ♦♦ Children's menu Children's portions Garden ⋒ Parking ▭ (notice required) WiFi

Rose & Crown   PICK OF THE PUBS

tel: 01752 880223 **Market St PL8 2EB**
email: info@theroseandcrown.co.uk
dir: *Phone for detailed directions*

Classy dining among the enticing countryside

Close to the pretty Yealm Estuary and the seductive wilderness of southern Dartmoor, foodies make a bee-line here to experience Simon Warner's modern British cooking. There's a cool, airy, bistro-like atmosphere in this classy dining pub at the heart of the South Hams. Village locals and beer-lovers can sample beers from the St Austell Brewery stable, perhaps in the walled courtyard garden with its fishpond and fountain, but it is as a destination dining pub that the Rose & Crown shines out. The menu proffers traditional classics with an extra touch of class, allowing the kitchen's focus on quality and local supply to be maintained. A choice of pub favourites such as curry of the day or home-made burger runs alongside a carte that might kick off with crab risotto, roast scallop, fennel and aïoli; and continue with a main course Cornish hake, Jerusalem artichoke, crispy chicken, broccoli and hazelnuts.

Open all day all wk **Food** Lunch all wk 12-2.30 Dinner all wk 6.30-9.30 Set menu available Restaurant menu available all wk ⊕ ST AUSTELL BREWERY ◀ Tribute, HSD & Proper Job ♂ Thatchers Gold, Symonds. **Facilities** Non-diners area ❤ (Bar Garden) ✦ Children's menu Children's portions Garden ♫ Parking WiFi ▭ (notice required)

DORSET

The Spyway Inn ★★★★ INN

tel: 01308 485250 **DT2 9EP**
email: spywayinn@sky.com **web:** www.spyway-inn.co.uk
dir: *From A35 follow Askerswell sign, then follow Spyway Inn sign*

Oak beams, cask ales and stunning views

Handy for Dorchester and Bridport, this old beamed country inn offers magnificent views of the glorious Dorset countryside. Close to West Bay and an ideal base to explore the Jurassic Coast World Heritage Site at nearby West Bay, the pub boasts a landscaped beer garden with a pond, stream and children's play area. It all makes for a lovely setting to enjoy a glass of Otter Ale and sample locally sourced, home-made fare like pie of the day; minted lamb chops with mash and vegetables, or home-made fish pie. Accommodation is also available.

Open all wk 12-3 6-close **Food** Lunch all wk 12-3 Dinner all wk 6-9 Av main course £10 ⊕ FREE HOUSE ◀ Otter Ale, Bitter ♂ West Milton, Kingcombe Cider. ☝ 10 **Facilities** Non-diners area ✦ Children's menu Children's portions Play area Garden ♫ Parking WiFi ▭ (notice required) **Rooms** 3

The Anvil Inn ★★★★ INN

tel: 01258 453431 **Salisbury Rd, Pimperne DT11 8UQ**
email: theanvil.inn@btconnect.com **web:** www.anvilinn.co.uk
dir: *Phone for detailed directions*

Very old inn offering good food and accommodation

A thatched, 16th-century inn with parts dating back even further, whose two bars offer a range of real ales, including Palmers Copper, and light meals. The charming beamed restaurant with log fire offers a full menu using Dorset produce, such as fresh fish landed on the nearby coast. Try the haddock and spring onion fishcakes; the Mediterranean vegetable lasagne; or maybe the home-made steak and ale pie (with shortcrust pastry, of course). The garden's lovely, especially by the fish pond. There are plenty of walks in the surrounding area and the Anvil Inn welcomes dogs.

Open all day all wk **Food** Lunch all wk 12-8.45 Dinner all wk 12-8.45 ⊕ FREE HOUSE ◀ Fuller's London Pride, Palmers Copper Ale, Butcombe Bitter, Guinness ♂ Addlestones, Ashton Press. ☝ 9 **Facilities** Non-diners area ❤ (Bar Garden) ✦ Children's menu Children's portions Garden ♫ Parking WiFi **Rooms** 12

The White Lion Inn

tel: 01747 840866 **High St SP8 5AT**
email: office@whitelionbourton.co.uk
dir: *Off A303, opposite B3092 to Gillingham*

Popular inn with a good choice of dishes and beers

Dating from 1723, The White Lion is a beautiful, stone-built, creeper-clad Dorset inn. The bar is cosy, with beams, flagstones and an open fire, and serves a range of real beers and ciders. Imaginative menus draw on the wealth of quality local produce, and dishes range from twice-baked cheddar soufflé or duck rillette to Moroccan tagine or roast venison. There is a cider festival in July.

Open all day all wk **Food** Lunch Mon-Sat 12-2, Sun 12-4 Dinner all wk 6-9 ⊕ ADMIRAL TAVERNS ◀ Otter Amber, St Austell Tribute ♂ Thatchers, Rich's Farmhouse. **Facilities** Non-diners area ❤ (Bar Garden) ✦ Children's menu Children's portions Garden ♫ Cider festival Parking WiFi ▭ (notice required)

The Shave Cross Inn ★★★★★ INN   PICK OF THE PUBS

tel: 01308 868358 **Shave Cross, Marshwood Vale DT6 6HW**
email: roy.warburton@virgin.net **web:** www.theshavecrossinn.co.uk
dir: *From Bridport take B3162. In 2m left signed 'Broadoak/Shave Cross', then Marshwood*

Caribbean food in the heart of Hardy country

Off the beaten track down narrow lanes in the beautiful Marshwood Vale, deep in Thomas Hardy country, this thatched 14th-century cob-and-flint inn was once a resting place for pilgrims and other monastic visitors on their way to Whitchurch Canonicorum to visit the shrine to St Candida and St Cross. While they were at the inn they had their tonsures trimmed, hence the pub's name. Step inside cosy bar to find low beams, stone floors, a huge inglenook fireplace, rustic furnishings, and local Dorset ale on tap, as well as real farm ciders. The food here is both unusual and inspirational, with a strong Caribbean influence together with dishes originating as far afield as Fiji. A starter of jerk chicken salad with plantain, crispy bacon and aïoli might be followed by a main course of hot and spicy Cuban seafood bouillabaisse or Jamaican jerk pork tenderloin with pineapple compôte.

Open 11-3 6-11.30 Closed Mon (ex BHs) **Food** Lunch Tue-Sun 12-2.30 Dinner Tue-Sat 6-8.30, Sun 6-8 Av main course £10 Set menu available Restaurant menu available Tue-Sun ⊕ FREE HOUSE ◀ Branscombe Vale Branoc, Dorset, Local guest ales ♂ Westons Old Rosie, Thatchers, Pitfield Thunderbolt. ☝ 12 **Facilities** Non-diners area ❤ (Bar Garden) ✦ Children's menu Children's portions Play area Garden ♫ Parking WiFi ▭ (notice required) **Rooms** 7

Stapleton Arms   PICK OF THE PUBS

tel: 01963 370396 **Church Hill SP8 5HS**
email: relax@thestapletonarms.com
dir: *3.5m from Wincanton in village centre*

Imaginative food in a relaxed setting

Clean, modern lines within belie the Georgian exterior of this progressive village inn. It's set at the edge of Blackmoor Vale in Thomas Hardy's rolling Dorset countryside; classic walking country enjoyed by many of the inn's patrons. The stylish, unstuffy pub majors on farmhouse ciders; Orchard Pig and Ashton Press amongst a handful regularly available, complementing real ales from regional microbreweries (there's an annual beer festival here, too) and a tantalising range of earthy apple juices too. Oenophiles will also appreciate the choice of 30 bins by the glass to enjoy with the innovative modern menu, which swings with the seasons and the supply chain from the local farms and markets. At lunchtime there's a good selection of light-bites and sandwiches as well as good, old-fashioned pub grub classics. Evenings see the choice expand considerably. Kick in with Jerusalem artichoke tart with black truffle and parmesan, an hors d'oeuvre for venison fillet with fondant potatoes, tenderstem broccoli and pan jus.

Open all wk 11-3 6-11 (Sun 12-10.30) **Food** Lunch all wk 12-3 Dinner all wk 6-10 ⊕ FREE HOUSE ◀ Moor Revival, Butcombe ♂ Thatchers Cheddar Valley & Gold, The Orchard Pig, Ashton Press, Harry's Farmhouse Cider, Guest ciders. ♟ 30 **Facilities** Non-diners area ✿ (Bar Garden) ♦♦ Children's menu Children's portions Play area Garden ⋒ Beer festival Parking WiFi ▄▄▄ (notice required)

▌CATTISTOCK   Map 4 SY59

Fox & Hounds Inn

tel: 01300 320444 **Duck St DT2 OJH**
email: lizflight@yahoo.co.uk
dir: On A37, between Dorchester & Yeovil, follow signs to Cattistock

Popular inn in pretty Dorset village

Expect a bar full of locals, children, dogs and even chickens under foot at this attractive pub. Situated in a picturesque village, the 17th-century inn has a welcoming and traditional atmosphere engendered by ancient beams, open fires in winter and huge inglenooks, one with an original bread oven. Palmers ales are on tap, along with Taunton cider, while home-made meals embrace Lyme Bay scallop and smoked bacon salad; vine tomato, fennel and basil pie; and lamb shank with redcurrant and rosemary sauce. Regular events include folk music and poetry.

Open 12-2.30 6-11 (Sun 12-10) Closed Mon L **Food** Lunch Tue-Sun 12-2 Dinner Mon-Sat 7-9, Sun 6-8 ⊕ PALMERS ◀ Best Bitter, Copper Ale, 200, Dorset Gold ♂ Taunton Traditional, Thatchers Gold, Sheppy's. **Facilities** Non-diners area ✿ (Bar Restaurant Garden) ♦♦ Children's portions Play area Garden ⋒ Parking WiFi ▄▄▄ (notice required)

▌CERNE ABBAS   Map 4 ST60

NEW The New Inn

tel: 01300 341274 **14 Long St DT2 7JF**
email: info@thenewinncerneabbas.co.uk
dir: Take A352 from Dorchester to Cerne Abbas. Pub in village centre

Refurbished coaching inn serving accomplished cooking

After closing completely for a top-to-toe refurbishment, this 16th-century former coaching inn reopened in 2013 to accolades for both its food and bar management. Palmers ales are much in demand, but it's the mix of contemporary British and pub classic dishes that brings most people here. Who can resist twice-baked Portland crab soufflé? Follow perhaps with pheasant breast wrapped in Serrano ham with fondant potato, carrot, swede and truffle cream. Leave space, though, for panettone bread and butter pudding with blood oranges and stewed kumquats – you can always walk it off afterwards around the nearby Cerne Abbas giant.

Open all wk 12-3 6-close Closed 25-26 Dec **Food** Lunch all wk 12-2.15 Dinner all wk 7-9 Av main course £15 Restaurant menu available all wk ⊕ PALMERS ◀ IPA, Copper, Dorset Gold. ♟ 12 **Facilities** Non-diners area ✿ (Bar Garden) ♦♦ Children's menu Children's portions Garden ⋒ Parking WiFi

▌CHEDINGTON   Map 4 ST40

Winyard's Gap Inn

tel: 01935 891244 **Chedington Ln DT8 3HY**
email: enquiries@winyardsgap.com
dir: 5m S of Crewkerne on A356

Extravagant views, craft ciders and seasonal produce

Situated beside National Trust woodlands in a corner of the Dorset Area of Outstanding Natural Beauty, the old inn's garden commands an extraordinary view across Somerset from the eponymous gap in the sinuous chalk hills. The two counties provide the wherewithal for the August cider festival here, whilst beers from Exmoor and Otter breweries anoint the bar, with its solid rustic seating and tables and a log-burner for the winter nip. The ploughman's lunch takes in the cheeses of the area, or enjoy local crab and sautéed Lyme Bay scallop, avocado, grapefruit and aïoli, then pan-fried calves' liver, bubble-and-squeak with roasted shallot and sage sauce.

Open all wk 11.30-3 6-11 (Sat-Sun 11.30-11) Closed 25-26 Dec **Food** Lunch Mon-Sat 12-2 Dinner all wk 6-9 Set menu available Restaurant menu available all wk ⊕ FREE HOUSE ◀ Sharp's Doom Bar, Dorset Piddle, Exmoor Ale, Otter Ale ♂ Thatchers Gold, Westons Old Rosie & 1st Quality, Dorset Nectar. ♟ 12 **Facilities** Non-diners area ✿ (Bar Garden) ♦♦ Children's menu Children's portions Garden ⋒ Cider festival Parking WiFi ▄▄▄ (notice required)

▌CHETNOLE   Map 4 ST60

The Chetnole Inn

tel: 01935 872337 **DT9 6NU**
email: enquiries@thechetnoleinn.co.uk
dir: A37 from Dorchester towards Yeovil. Left at Chetnole sign

Tranquil village pub with garden overlooking fields

Bright, airy and hung with hop-bines, the interior of snug, bar and restaurant melds well into this flagstone-floored old village-centre inn opposite a pretty church deep in Thomas Hardy country. Plenty of walks thread their way through the rich countryside; it's handy, too, for the historic town of Sherborne. West Country meats and Bridport-landed seafood fill the British menu. Choose perhaps one of the chef's pies or roast fillet of cod with Puy lentils and bacon and enjoy at a table in the tree-shaded garden, home to the pub's two giant rabbits. Otter beers may feature; there's a regular beer festival here.

Open 12-3 6.30-close Closed Sun eve & Mon (Sep-Apr) **Food** Lunch all wk 12-2 Dinner Mon-Sat 6.30-9 ⊕ FREE HOUSE ◀ Sharp's Doom Bar, Otter Ale, Marston's Pedigree ♂ Westons Stowford Press. ♟ 12 **Facilities** Non-diners area ✿ (Bar Garden) ♦♦ Children's menu Children's portions Play area Garden ⋒ Beer festival Parking WiFi ▄▄▄ (notice required)

CHIDEOCK
Map 4 SY49

The Anchor Inn

tel: 01297 489215 **Seatown DT6 6JU**
dir: *On A35 turn S in Chideock opposite church & follow single track road for 0.75m to beach*

Set in a little cove beneath Golden Cap

A former smugglers' haunt, The Anchor (refurbished in 2014) enjoys an incredible setting in a cove surrounded by National Trust land. The large sun terrace and cliffside beer garden overlooking the beach make it a premier destination for throngs of holidaymakers in the summer, while on winter weekdays it is blissfully quiet. The menu starts with snacks and light lunches – three types of ploughman's, salads and a range of sandwiches and baguettes might take your fancy. For something more substantial choose beer-battered catch of the day, bangers and mash, or butternut squash and aubergine curry accompanied with one of the Palmers real ales.

Open all wk 11.30-10.30 ⊕ PALMERS ◀ 200, Best Bitter, Copper Ale ♂ Thatchers Gold. **Facilities** ❀ (Bar Restaurant Garden) ♦♦ Children's menu Children's portions Family room Garden Parking

CHRISTCHURCH
Map 5 SZ19

The Ship In Distress

tel: 01202 485123 **66 Stanpit BH23 3NA**
email: shipindistress@rocketmail.com
dir: *Phone for detailed directions*

Community pub with lots of seafood

The seafood menu at this 300-year-old smugglers' pub reflects the closeness of Mudeford Quay and the English Channel. Nautical memorabilia is everywhere, so bag a seat by the wood-burner with a pint of Ringwood Best Bitter or Fortyniner and traditional fish and chips or cottage pie; alternatively, head into the restaurant for salmon and scallion fishcake; fruits de mer; locally caught lobster; or whole Dorset crab. The full carte, including steaks, is on the blackboard. In summer enjoy the Shellfish Bar on the suntrap terrace.

Open all day all wk 11am-mdnt (Sun 11-11) **Food** Lunch Mon-Fri 12-2, Sat-Sun 12-2.30 Dinner Sun-Thu 6.30-9, Fri-Sat 6.30-9.30 Av main course £6.25 Set menu available Restaurant menu available all wk ⊕ PUNCH TAVERNS ◀ Brains The Rev. James, Dartmoor Jail Ale, Dorset Jurassic, St Austell Tribute, Ringwood Best Bitter & Fortyniner, Adnams Broadside, Sharp's Doom Bar, Wells Bombardier, Guest ales ♂ Westons Stowford Press. **Facilities** Non-diners area ❀ (Bar Garden) ♦♦ Children's portions Garden ⋒ Parking WiFi 🚐 (notice required)

CHURCH KNOWLE
Map 4 SY98

The New Inn

tel: 01929 480357 **BH20 5NQ**
email: maurice@newinn-churchknowle.co.uk
dir: *From Wareham take A351 towards Swanage. At Corfe Castle right for Church Knowle. Pub in village centre*

A warm welcome in charming village pub

The Estop family have run this part-thatched, stone-built, 16th-century village inn for nearly 30 years, and have retained many of the building's original features. Still in place are the old inglenook fireplaces and a brick alcove that used to be the kitchen oven from its days as a farmhouse. Real ales include Jurassic and changing guests, and there are draught ciders too. Wine is kept in the 'wine shack', where customers can browse for the right bottle to accompany their meal. A carvery is available alongside fresh home-cooked food including catch of the day, roasts, traditional pies, steaks, fish, sandwiches and home-made desserts. The Purbeck Lounge is tailor-made for family dining. Booking may be required for Sunday lunches and on some evenings.

Open 10-3 6-11 (10-3 5-11 summer) Closed Mon Jan-Mar **Food** Lunch all wk 12-2.15 Dinner all wk 6-9.15 (5-9.15 summer) Av main course £8.50-£17.95 Set menu available ⊕ PUNCH TAVERNS ◀ Dorset Jurassic, Sharp's Doom Bar, St Austell Tribute, Guest ales ♂ Westons Old Rosie, Stowford Press & Traditional. ☂ 10 **Facilities** Non-diners area ❀ (Garden Outside area) ♦♦ Children's menu Children's portions Family room Garden Outside area ⋒ Parking WiFi 🚐 (notice required)

CRANBORNE
Map 5 SU01

The Inn at Cranborne ★★★★ INN

tel: 01725 551249 **5 Wimborne St BH21 5PP**
email: info@theinnatcranborne.co.uk **web:** www.theinnatcranborne.co.uk
dir: *On B3078 between Fordingbridge & Wimborne Minster*

Hearty food and Dorset ales in a delightful village

Open all day Closed Mon (bar & rest) **Food** Lunch Tue-Fri 12-2, Sat 12-2.30, Sun 12-4 Dinner Tue-Thu 6-9, Fri-Sat 6-9.30 ⊕ HALL & WOODHOUSE ◀ Badger First Gold, The Fleur ⬡ Westons Stowford Press, Badger Pearwood & Applewood. ☂ 10 **Facilities** Non-diners area ❀ (Bar Restaurant Outside area) ❢ Children's portions Outside area ⯂ Beer festival Parking WiFi ☷ (notice required) **Rooms** 9

See advert on opposite page

Jane Gould searched long and hard for somewhere to turn into her vision of a traditional English country pub. Since finding this 17th-century, former coaching inn she has skilfully transformed it into a must-visit destination in Cranborne Chase, nearly 400 square miles of rolling chalk downland. The inn's own Fleur Ale, brewed specially by Hall & Woodhouse, shares bar space with Dorset and Somerset ciders. Choose a table near one of the wood-burning stoves for something hearty from the daily-changing menu, such as seared sea trout with cavolo nero, herb gnocchi and quince jam; slow cooked shin of beef with mash and roasted roots; or wild mushroom and parmesan risotto.

EAST MORDEN
Map 4 SY99

The Cock & Bottle
PICK OF THE PUBS

See Pick of the Pubs on page 168

EVERSHOT
Map 4 ST50

The Acorn Inn ★★★★ INN ⊛
PICK OF THE PUBS

See Pick of the Pubs on page 169 and advert below

PICK OF THE PUBS

The Cock & Bottle

EAST MORDEN Map 4 SY99

tel: 01929 459238
BH20 7DL
email: cockandbottle@btconnect.com
web: www.cockandbottlemorden.co.uk
dir: *From A35 W of Poole right onto B3075, pub 0.5m on left*

Local beer and a menu to suit all

Parts of this old Dorset longhouse were built about 400 years ago; the pub was originally cob-walled and, though it was sheathed in brick some time around 1800, it retained its thatched roof until the mid-60s. Today, the unspoilt interiors with their low-beamed ceilings and a wealth of nooks and crannies are redolent of a bygone age. The lively locals' bar is simply furnished and comfortably rustic, with a large wooden settle on which to while away a winter's evening with a game of dominoes beside the cosy log fire. The fine range of real ales from the nearby Hall & Woodhouse brewery is also available in the lounge bar, and a modern restaurant at the back completes the picture. Fresh game and fish feature strongly on the ever-changing menu, which ranges from light lunches, bar meals and Sunday roasts to pub favourites like steak-and-kidney pudding or lamb shank. The carte menu choices might include a starter of local dressed crab, or deep-fried brie wedges with a Cumberland sauce. Moving on, rabbit pie with root

vegetable and mushroom sauce; and grilled wild sea bass with crushed new potatoes, rocket and horseradish crème fraîche are typical main course options. Home-made desserts like orange and spiced rum crème brûlée; or dark and white chocolate terrine with a fruit coulis make a fitting finale to the meal. Lovely pastoral views over the surrounding farmland include the pub's paddock, which occasionally hosts vintage car and motorcycle meetings during the summer. Well-behaved dogs are welcome.

Open 11.30-2.30 6-11 (Sun 12-3) Closed Sun eve **Food** Lunch all wk 12-1.45 Dinner Mon-Sat 6-8.45 Restaurant menu available all wk. 🍺 HALL & WOODHOUSE ◧ Badger Dorset Best & Tanglefoot, Guest ale. **Facilities** Non-diners area 🐾 (Bar Restaurant Garden) 👫 Children's menu Children's portions Play area Garden 🎪 Parking 🚌

PICK OF THE PUBS

The Acorn Inn ★★★★ INN ❀

EVERSHOT   Map 4 ST50

tel: 01935 83228 **DT2 0JW**
email: stay@acorn-inn.co.uk
web: www.acorn-inn.co.uk
dir: *From A37 between Yeovil & Dorchester, follow Evershot & Holywell signs, 0.5m to inn*

Surrounded by unspoilt rolling countryside

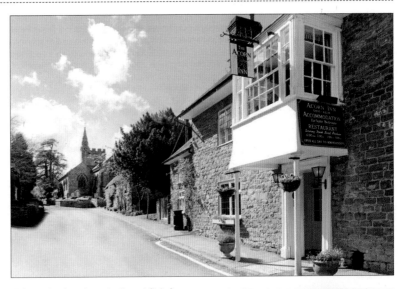

Since the last edition of this guide, landlords Jack and Alex have become a married couple, but although their legal status has changed, nothing changes this pretty 16th-century village inn. Wessex novelist and poet Thomas Hardy called the pub the 'Sow and Acorn' in *Tess of the d'Urbervilles*. Much would still be familiar to him, from the unusual porch to the old beams, low ceilings, oak panelling, flagstone floors and carved Hamstone fireplaces. He'd also recognise the bedroom names, taken from places in his books, such as Kingsbere, his pseudonym for Bere Regis. The lively bar is a big draw for villagers, who enjoy the real ales, quiz nights and the occasional yard-of-ale-drinking challenges. In the softly lit, AA Rosette restaurant you'll find smartly laid tables and terracotta tiles. An elegant stone fireplace is carved with oak leaves and, as it happens, acorns. Sustainability is the watchword for a modern British menu that uses local, seasonal produce for home-made soups,

light and crispy beer-battered fish from the nearby coast, honey-roast beetroot salad and chargrilled sirloin steak. Lunch and bar menus offer sandwiches, twice-baked Somerset cheddar soufflé, deep-fried whitebait, venison sausages and ploughman's. Beer drinkers can choose between Otter and Doom Bar, while 34 wines by the glass, and an impressive stock of malt whiskies, give everyone else plenty of options. The pub also features a lovely old skittle alley and a beer garden, while some of the rooms feature four-poster beds. Good walks radiate from the village, so stick your wellies in the car boot.

Open all day all wk 11am-11.30pm
Food Lunch all wk 12-2 Dinner all wk 7-9 Av main course £9.50 Restaurant menu available all wk. ⊕ FREE HOUSE
◀ Sharp's Doom Bar, Otter ♂ Thatchers Gold & Traditional. ♟ 34
Facilities Non-diners area ♨ (Bar Garden) ♦♦ Children's portions Family room Garden ⊼ Parking WiFi
🚌 (notice required) **Rooms** 10

FARNHAM
Map 4 ST91

The Museum Inn ★★★★ INN ⚜⚜ | PICK OF THE PUBS

tel: 01725 516261 **DT11 8DE**
email: enquiries@museuminn.co.uk web: www.museuminn.co.uk
dir: *From Salisbury take A354 to Blandford Forum, 12m. Farnham signed on right. Pub in village centre*

A great combination of tip-top ales and quality food

This part-thatched country pub lies in Cranborne Chase, where kings used to hunt and where, in the 19th century, General Augustus Pitt Rivers pioneered modern archaeological fieldwork. He built the inn for visitors to a small museum, now gone, where he displayed his finds. The interior features the original inglenook fireplace, flagstone floors, a fashionable mismatch of furniture and a book-filled sitting room. Landlord Gary Brewer is passionate about his ales – a pint of Sixpenny 6D Best, or Orchard Pig cider if you prefer, never tasted better. Head chef Jenny Jones prepares dishes with quality seasonal ingredients, many sourced from local estates and farms. With two AA Rosettes, expect dishes of accomplished cuisine; an entrée such as Dorset snails on cheese rarebit toast with prosciutto crisp could be followed by a sea bream fillet with cockle and saffron sauce. Desserts are no less focussed, and a fine selection of teas and coffees confirms the attention to detail.

Open all day all wk **Food** Lunch Mon-Fri 12-2, Sat 12-2.30, Sun 12-3 Dinner all wk 7-9.30 ⊕ FREE HOUSE ◀ Sixpenny 6D Best, Fuller's London Pride, Guest ale Ö The Orchard Pig. � 12 **Facilities** Non-diners area ❖ (Bar Restaurant Garden) ♦ Children's menu Children's portions Garden ⊞ Parking WiFi ➡ (notice required) **Rooms** 8

FERNDOWN
Map 5 SU00

The Kings Arms

tel: 01202 577490 **77 Ringwood Rd, Longham BH22 9AA**
email: thekingsarmslongham@yahoo.co.uk
dir: *On A348*

Revived free house with top chefs

With pubs failing at a rate of knots, how good to see one go from zero to hero. Open again following a period of closure, it shows what can be done in good hands. Locally, it's known for its British classics, especially beef, and other locally-sourced dishes prepared by chefs Mark Miller and Tim Butler. From their main menu come a variety of steaks, including a 100-day, grain-fed rib-eye, and a 16-18oz Chateaubriand for sharing. Also, pan-roasted cod loin; Dorset home-cooked ham, egg and chips; lamb two ways; and risottos, both chicken and chorizo, and vegetarian. Fresh seared tuna loin on wilted spinach; and wild mushroom, courgette and asparagus ragoût are specials. The bar usually keeps three real ales, among them Ringwood Best, from a few miles east, and various traditional ciders. Some 15 wines are by the glass, the reds chosen very much with the beef dishes in mind.

Open all day all wk **Food** Lunch Sun-Thu 12-9, Fri-Sat 12-9.30 Dinner Sun-Thu 12-9, Fri-Sat 12-9.30 Av main course £10.95 Set menu available ⊕ FREE HOUSE ◀ Ringwood Best, Otter Ale, Fuller's London Pride, Timothy Taylor Ö Westons. � 15 **Facilities** Non-diners area ❖ (Bar Outside area) ♦ Children's portions Outside area ⊞ Parking WiFi ➡ (notice required)

FONTMELL MAGNA
Map 4 ST81

The Fontmell ★★★★ INN

tel: 01747 811441 **SP7 0PA**
email: info@thefontmell.com web: www.thefontmell.com
dir: *Halfway between Shaftesbury & Blandford Forum, on A350*

Smart inn with seasonally inspired menus

On the A350, between Shaftesbury and Blandford Forum is The Fontmell, a stylish and comfortable country pub, complete with a stream flowing between the bar and the dining room. Linger over a pint of Keystone Mallyshag at the bar, or curl up on the sofa and peruse the newspapers. Most visitors and guests cannot resist chef/patron Tom Shaw's frequently changing menus which feature the flavour packed dishes such as crab and Armagnac soup; seafood tapas; duo of lamb; and tandoori-style monkfish and tiger prawn curry. From Monday to Thursday a set menu is available at lunchtime.

Open all day all wk **Food** Lunch Mon-Thu 12-2, Fri-Sun 12-2.30 Dinner Mon-Thu 6-9, Fri-Sat 6-9.30, Sun 6-8.30 Set menu available ⊕ FREE HOUSE ◀ Keystone Mallyshag, Seasonal ale Ö Rotating Guest ciders. � 13 **Facilities** Non-diners area ❖ (Bar Garden) ♦ Children's menu Children's portions Garden ⊞ Parking WiFi **Rooms** 6

GILLINGHAM
Map 4 ST82

The Kings Arms Inn

tel: 01747 838325 **East Stour Common SP8 5NB**
email: nrosscampbell@aol.com
dir: *4m W of Shaftesbury on A30*

Family-run pub with a Scottish flavour

Scottish touches – paintings by artist Mavis Makie, quotes by Robert Burns, the presence of haggis, skirlie and cranachan on the menus, and a wide choice of single malts – reflect the origin of this inn's landlord and landlady. A 200-year-old, family-run village free house where Victorian fireplaces sit comfortably alongside modern wooden furniture and subtly coloured fabrics, it offers an extensive choice of dishes ranging from salmon and hoki fillets with garden pea purée, tempura king prawns and sweet chilli drizzle to slow roast belly pork on bubble-and-squeak with black pudding, cider sauce, apple fritter and crackling. Look out for the £6 pub lunch specials.

Open all wk 12-3 5.30-11.30 (Sat-Sun 12-12) **Food** Lunch Mon-Sat 12-2.30, Sun 12-9.15 Dinner Mon-Sat 5.30-9.15, Sun 12-9.15 Av main course £13 Restaurant menu available all wk ⊕ FREE HOUSE ◀ Sharp's Doom Bar, St Austell Tribute, Worthington's. � **Facilities** Non-diners area ❖ (Bar Garden) ♦ Children's menu Children's portions Family room Garden ⊞ Parking WiFi ➡ (notice required)

GUSSAGE ALL SAINTS
Map 4 SU01

The Drovers Inn

tel: 01258 840084 **BH21 5ET**
dir: *From A31 at Ashley Heath rdbt, take B3081, follow signs*

A warm welcome, real ale in a country setting

There's a new landlord at this rural 16th-century pub that has a fine terrace and wonderful views from its garden. The interior retains plenty of traditional appeal with flagstone floors and oak furniture. Ales from Ringwood include seasonal guests, and the short menu includes baguettes, jacket potatoes; Wiltshire gammon, double free-range eggs, chunky chips and garden peas; shortcrust pie of the week with seasonal veg and a choice of potatoes.

Open all wk 12-3 6-12 (Sat-Sun & BH all day) **Food** Lunch all wk 12-2.30 Dinner all wk 6-9 Av main course £9 ⊕ RINGWOOD BREWERY ◀ Best Bitter, Old Thumper, Fortyniner & Seasonal ales, Guest ales Ö Thatchers Gold & Traditional. � 10 **Facilities** Non-diners area ❖ (Bar Restaurant Garden) ♦ Children's menu Children's portions Garden ⊞ Beer festival Parking WiFi ➡ (notice required)

LYME REGIS
Map 4 SY39

The Mariners ★★★★ INN ⬡

tel: 01297 442753 **Silver St DT7 3HS**
email: enquiries@hotellymeregis.co.uk **web:** www.hotellymeregis.co.uk
dir: A35 onto B3165 (Lyme Rd). The Mariners is pink building opposite road to The Cobb (Pound Rd)

Try the local seafood specials

Once a coaching inn in the 17th century, this restored property in the heart of the town is steeped in Lyme's fossil history, having once been home to the Philpot sisters, famed as collectors in the early 19th century. Beatrix Potter is said to have stayed here too, reputedly writing *The Tale of Little Pig Robinson* – The Mariners is pictured in the book. The building combines traditional character with modern style. Simple menus feature the best of local seafood and other quality ingredients in dishes such as scallops with crispy pancetta, asparagus and watercress pesto; wild mushroom and ricotta tortellini; and mango pannacotta to finish. Only bottled beers are available.

Open all day all wk **Food** Lunch all wk 12-2 Dinner all wk 6.30-9 Restaurant menu available all wk ⊕ FREE HOUSE ◀ Otter Bright, Mighty Hop Mighty Red IPA & Mariners Ale Ò Thatchers Gold. ▼ 9 **Facilities** Non-diners area ✿ (Bar Garden) ♦♦ Children's menu Children's portions Garden ✑ Parking WiFi ☰ **Rooms** 14

MILTON ABBAS
Map 4 ST80

The Hambro Arms

tel: 01258 880233 **DT11 0BP**
email: info@hambroarms.com
dir: From A354 (Dorchester to Blandford road), exit at Milborne St Andrew to Milton Abbas

A community-owned pub in a unique village

Picture-perfect Milton Abbas, including the charming Hambro Arms, was built in 1780. It replaced a nearby medieval hamlet which was demolished by the privacy-seeking landowner, the Earl of Dorchester; thus Milton Abbas may claim to be the first planned village in England. Today the long thatched and whitewashed pub thrives in the ownership of the community. Its two spacious and refurbished bars stock local guest ales, spirits and quality wines. Menus cater for all appetites, from lighter lunchtime bites to full à la carte dining in the elegant Library Restaurant; whatever your choice, the pub's 'real food with real flavours' promise is fulfilled with simply cooked fresh and local produce. A beer festival in July.

Open all wk 11.30-3 6-11 (Sat-Sun 11.30-11.30) **Food** Lunch Mon-Fri 12-2.30, Sat-Sun 12-3 Dinner Mon-Thu 6-9, Fri-Sat 6-9.30 ⊕ FREE HOUSE ◀ Sharp's Doom Bar, Ringwood, Guest ales Ò Westons Stowford Press. ▼ 8 **Facilities** Non-diners area ♦♦ Children's menu Children's portions Garden ✑ Beer festival Parking WiFi ☰

MOTCOMBE
Map 4 ST82

The Coppleridge Inn ★★★ INN

tel: 01747 851980 **SP7 9HW**
email: thecoppleridgeinn@btinternet.com **web:** www.coppleridge.com
dir: Take A350 towards Warminster for 1.5m, left at brown tourist sign. Follow signs to inn

Former farm in beautiful surroundings

Chris and Di Goodinge took over this 18th-century farmhouse and farm about 25 years ago and converted it into the pub you see today. As well as retaining the flagstone floors and log fires, they have kept the farm's 15 acres of meadow and woodland, where they raise their own cattle. The bar offers a wide range of real ales, as well as constantly changing old favourites such as beer battered haddock and chips, or seasonal dishes, perhaps pheasant breast and leg with chestnut and mushroom stuffing, Savoy cabbage and bacon. Ten spacious bedrooms are situated around a converted courtyard and there is a secure children's playground.

Open all wk 11-3 5-11 (Sat 11am-mdnt Sun 12-11) **Food** Lunch all wk 12-2.30 Dinner all wk 6-9 Av main course £10 Set menu available Restaurant menu available all wk ⊕ FREE HOUSE ◀ Butcombe Bitter, Wadworth 6X, Fuller's London Pride, Sharp's Doom Bar, Ringwood Best Bitter Ò Ashton Press, Thatchers. ▼ 10 **Facilities** Non-diners area ✿ (Bar Garden) ♦♦ Children's menu Children's portions Play area Family room Garden ✑ Parking WiFi ☰ (notice required) **Rooms** 10

NETTLECOMBE
Map 4 SY59

Marquis of Lorne

tel: 01308 485236 **DT6 3SY**
email: info@themarquisoflorne.co.uk
dir: From A3066 (Bridport-Beaminster road) approx 1.5m N of Bridport follow Loders & Mangerton Mill signs. At junct left past Mangerton Mill, through West Milton. 1m to T-junct, straight over. Pub up hill, approx 300yds on left

Recommended for its interesting menus and lovely views

In a picturesque hamlet and close to the market town of Bridport, The Marquis of Lorne is surrounded by beautiful views. Built as a farmhouse in the 16th century and converted into a pub in 1871, it is now run by Steve and Tracey Brady. They have renewed the focus on local produce throughout the menus, and locally brewed Palmers ales are on tap. Home-made duck liver pâté spiked with pistachio makes an interesting starter, while international influences are at play in a main course of tenderloin of Dorset pork wrapped in Serrano ham on flageolet bean and spinach ragout. Look out for special dinner evenings. The attractive gardens are family friendly, too.

Open all wk 12-2.30 6-11 **Food** Lunch all wk 12-2 Dinner all wk 6-9 ⊕ PALMERS ◀ Copper Ale, Best Bitter, Dorset Gold. ▼ 9 **Facilities** Non-diners area ✿ (Bar Garden) ♦♦ Children's menu Children's portions Play area Garden ✑ Parking WiFi ☰ (notice required)

NORTH WOOTTON
Map 4 ST61

The Three Elms

tel: 01935 812881 **DT9 5JW**
dir: From Sherborne take A352 towards Dorchester then A3030. Pub 1m on right

Village store, post office...and pub

Incorporating a shop and post office, this family-friendly pub near the beautiful Blackmore Vale has become the heart of the community. The bar is well stocked with weekly changing guest real ales and ciders, and freshly cooked pub classics served at candlelit tables include West Country mixed grill; chilli con carne; and spinach and ricotta cannelloni. Among the 'two for £10' deals are chicken, beef and veggie burgers, fishcakes and lasagne; takeaways are available, too. The large beer garden hosts summer barbecues and beer festivals.

Open all day all wk 11-11 (Sun 12-10.30) Closed 26 Dec **Food** Lunch Mon-Sat 12-2.30, Sun 12-3 Dinner Mon-Sat 6-9.30, Sun 6-9 ⊕ FREE HOUSE ◀ St Austell Tribute, Guest ale Ò Thatchers & Gold, St Austell Copper Press. **Facilities** Non-diners area ✿ (Bar Restaurant Garden) ♦♦ Children's menu Children's portions Play area Garden ✑ Beer festival Parking WiFi ☰

OSMINGTON MILLS   Map 4 SY78

The Smugglers Inn

tel: 01305 833125 **DT3 6HF**
email: smugglersinn.weymouth@hall-woodhouse.co.uk
dir: *7m E of Weymouth towards Wareham, pub signed*

Coastal inn with an interesting past

Set on the cliffs at Osmington Mills with the South Coast Footpath running through the garden, the inn has beautiful views across Weymouth Bay. In the late 18th century (the inn dates back to the 13th century) it was the base of infamous smuggler Pierre La Tour who fell in love with the publican's daughter, Arabella Carless, who was shot dead while helping him to escape during a raid. Things are quieter now and you can enjoy a pint of Tanglefoot or one of the guest ales like Pickled Partridge. On the menu typical dishes are smoked haddock Benedict; venison sausages and mash; and steak and Tanglefoot pie.

Open all day all wk 11-11 (Sun 12-10.30) **Food** Lunch Mon-Sat 12-9.30, Sun 12-9 Dinner Mon-Sat 12-9.30, Sun 12-9 ⊕ HALL & WOODHOUSE ◀ Badger Tanglefoot, Guest ale ⛆ Westons Stowford Press. ▼ 12 **Facilities** Non-diners area ❖ (Bar Restaurant Garden) ◀ Children's menu Children's portions Play area Garden ⊨ Parking ◻

PIDDLEHINTON   Map 4 SY79

The Thimble Inn

tel: 01300 348270 **DT2 7TD**
email: info@thimbleinn.co.uk
dir: *Take A35 W'bound, right onto B3143, Piddlehinton in 4m*

Thatched village local with open fires

French-trained chef Mark Ramsden and his wife Lisa became tenants of this Palmers Brewery-owned, 18th-century pub and restaurant in 2014. It stands between streams in over four acres of grounds; get there early if you want to stake your claim on the patio overlooking the River Piddle. Mark's menus make use of the best local produce for dishes such as rose veal chop with Puy lentils and bacon; wild mushroom risotto with mascarpone and truffle oil; and pub classics such as beer-battered cod; and sirloin steak baguette. Desserts include dark chocolate tart with pistachio ice cream; and rhubarb crème brûlée.

Open 12-3 6-11 Closed Mon **Food** Lunch Tue-Sat 12-2.30, Sun 12-3 Dinner Tue-Sat 6-9 Restaurant menu available Tue-Sun ⊕ PALMERS ◀ Copper Ale, Best Bitter, 200 ⛆ Thatchers Gold. **Facilities** Non-diners area ❖ (Bar Restaurant Garden) ◀ Children's menu Children's portions Garden ⊨ Parking WiFi ◻

PIDDLETRENTHIDE   Map 4 SY79

The Poachers Inn

tel: 01300 348358 **DT2 7QX**
email: info@thepoachersinn.co.uk
dir: *6m N from Dorchester on B3143. At church end of village*

Good range of food and garden with swimming pool

Located in the pretty little village of Piddletrenthide in the heart of Thomas Hardy country, this 17th-century riverside pub is perfectly situated for exploring west Dorset and the Jurassic Coast. The kitchen makes good use of Dorset suppliers to create both classic pub meals (scampi, pie of the day, gourmet burger, lamb cutlets) and contemporary alternatives (butternut squash and Mediterranean vegetable risotto) for the extensive menu. Relax with a glass of Butcombe Bitter in the beer garden, which even has a heated swimming pool to enjoy throughout the summer. Details of three circular walks are available at the bar.

Open all day all wk 8am-mdnt **Food** Lunch all wk 12-2.30 Dinner all wk 6-9.30 Set menu available ⊕ FREE HOUSE ◀ Sharp's Doom Bar, St Austell Tribute, Butcombe Bitter ⛆ Thatchers Gold. ▼ 9 **Facilities** Non-diners area ❖ (Bar Garden) ◀ Children's menu Children's portions Garden ⊨ Parking WiFi ◻ (notice required)

PLUSH   Map 4 ST70

The Brace of Pheasants ★★★★ INN

tel: 01300 348357 **DT2 7RQ**
email: info@braceofpheasants.co.uk **web:** www.braceofpheasants.co.uk
dir: *A35 onto B3143, 5m to Piddletrenthide, then right to Mappowder & Plush*

Village inn popular with walkers

Tucked away in a fold of the hills in the heart of Hardy's beloved county, this pretty 16th-century thatched village inn is an ideal place to start or end a walk. With its welcoming open fire, oak beams and fresh flowers, it is the perfect setting to enjoy a selection of real ales and ciders and 18 wines by the glass. Food options might include pan-fried lamb's kidneys with mustard cream sauce or local venison steak with red wine reduction. The inn offers eight en suite bedrooms, four above the pub and four in the old skittle alley.

Open all wk 12-3 7-11 **Food** Lunch all wk 12-2.30 Dinner all wk 7-9 ⊕ FREE HOUSE ◀ Flack Manor Flack's Double Drop, Palmers, Ringwood Best Bitter, Sunny Republic, Guest ales ⛆ Westons Traditional, Purbeck Dorset Draft, Cider by Rosie. ▼ 18 **Facilities** Non-diners area ❖ (Bar Restaurant Garden) ◀ Children's portions Garden ⊨ Parking WiFi ◻ (notice required) **Rooms** 8

POOLE   Map 4 SZ09

The Rising Sun

tel: 01202 771246 **3 Dear Hay Ln BH15 1NZ**
email: paul@risingsunpoole.co.uk
dir: *On A350 rdbt in town centre (parking adjacent)*

Popular pub in busy town centre

This 18th-century pub just off the High Street in Poole has a warm and relaxing atmosphere, whether you are popping in for a pint of Doom Bar in the elegant lounge bar, or heading for the charming restaurants. The menus successfully combine traditional pub classics with more adventurous dishes and make sound use of fresh local ingredients. Starters might be Thai crab cakes and sweet chilli dip; or smoked mackerel with saffron new potato salad, and to follow beef Madras curry; burgers (including the vegetarian goats' cheese burger); or British shellfish linguine. Specials are chalked on the blackboards daily.

Open all day 11-11 Closed 25-26 Dec, Sun **Food** Lunch Mon-Sat 12-2.30 Dinner Mon-Sat 6-9.30 Set menu available ⊕ FREE HOUSE ◀ Sharp's Doom Bar, Dorset Jurassic, Guest ale ⛆ Westons Stowford Press, Aspall. ▼ 12 **Facilities** Non-diners area Garden ⊨ WiFi

PICK OF THE PUBS

The Kings Arms ★★★★★ INN

SHERBORNE Map 4 ST61

tel: 01963 220281 **North Rd,
Charlton Horethorne DT9 4NL
email:** admin@thekingsarms.co.uk
web: www.thekingsarms.co.uk
dir: *On A3145, N of Sherborne. Pub in
village centre*

Enjoyable food in elegantly converted country pub

On the Somerset and Dorset border, three miles from the historic market towns of Sherborne and Wincanton, this Edwardian building has been transformed into a chic country pub and modern restaurant with boutique-style accommodation. Locals and visitors head to the bar to order local ales which include Wadworths, and Lawrence's cider from nearby Corton Denham. The wine list details 50 bottles, with 13 sold by the glass. Stay in the bar if you're looking for a light snack in relaxed surroundings, otherwise follow a wide walkway past a theatre-style kitchen to the more formal Georgian-mirrored dining room; from here, doors open on to an extensive dining terrace overlooking a croquet lawn. The cooking style is both traditional and modern British; add in influences from around the world and the result is an AA Rosette-winning menu. Everything is made in-house, including bread, pasta and ice creams. Starters range from cream of leek and potato soup; to crab fritters with pickled vegetables, mixed leaves and sweet chilli. The kitchen's specialist charcoal grill oven is kept busy with main courses such as a local rib-eye steak with watercress salad and peppercorn sauce. Alternatively you may find a free-range confit of duck leg served with polenta chips, wok-cooked chard, quince chutney and Madeira jus. Pudding favourites such as rhubarb and apple crumble or steamed jam sponge are both served with custard, while chocolate and cherry brandy torte with hazlenuts, or blueberry frangipane tart with vanilla ice cream, brim with cosmopolitan flavours. A short selection of dishes just for children is prepared to the same high standards. Ten individually designed bedrooms complete the picture.

Open all day all wk **Food** Lunch all wk 12-2.30 Dinner Mon-Thu 7-9.30, Fri-Sat 7-10, Sun 7-9 ⊞ FREE HOUSE ◖ Sharp's Doom Bar, Butcombe, Wadworth 6X Ö Lawrence's. ♇ 13 **Facilities** Non-diners area ☙ (Bar Garden) ♙ Children's menu Children's portions Garden ☵ Parking WiFi ▭ (notice required) **Rooms** 10

POWERSTOCK
Map 4 SY59

Three Horseshoes Inn ★★★★ INN ◉ PICK OF THE PUBS

tel: 01308 485328 **DT6 3TF**
email: threehorseshoespowerstock@live.co.uk **web:** www.threeshoesdorset.co.uk
dir: *3m from Bridport off A3066 (Beaminster road)*

Great reputation for creative cooking

To locals it's known as 'the Shoes', a pretty late-Victorian inn belonging to Palmers, a part-thatched brewery in nearby Bridport. The pub patio and terraced garden look out over the village, above which rises Eggardon Iron Age hill fort. The food, accredited with an AA Rosette, owes much to the kitchen's devotion to seasonal, locally sourced ingredients, some from the garden and some foraged from surrounding hedgerows. Local asparagus, for example, is served with a poached egg, morels, pecorino and wild garlic. Daily-changing menus lean towards game dishes in winter and fresh fish in summer, but inventiveness is present all year round. Your visit may coincide with an entrée of half a dozen café de Paris snails farmed in Dorset. A blade of beef is slow-braised overnight and served with creamed wild mushrooms, bone marrow, chips and cress. For the sweet of tooth, desserts include Eton mess; or baked custard tart with home-made ice cream.

Open 12-3 6.30-11.30 (Sun 12-3 6.30-10.30) Closed Mon L **Food** Lunch Tue-Sat 12-2.30, Sun 12-3 Dinner all wk 6.30-9.30 ⊕ PALMERS ◀ Best Bitter, Copper Ale, Tally Ho!, Palmers 200 ♂ Thatchers Gold & Traditional. **Facilities** Non-diners area ♣ (Bar Garden) ♦ Children's menu Children's portions Garden ⌂ Parking WiFi **Rooms** 3

PUNCKNOWLE
Map 4 SY58

The Crown Inn

tel: 01308 897711 **Church St DT2 9BN**
email: email@thecrowninndorset.co.uk
dir: *From A35, into Bride Valley, through Litton Cheney. From B3157, inland at Swyre*

Chocolate-box thatched inn

This picturesque 16th-century pub was once the haunt of smugglers on their way from nearby Chesil Beach to visit prosperous customers in Bath. There's a traditional, welcoming atmosphere within the rambling, child- and dog-friendly bars with their log fires, comfy sofas and low beams. Home-cooked food ranges from Dorset cream teas, tapas slates, jackets and sandwiches to seasonally changing dishes prepared using local fish and meat. Enjoy a glass of real ale or one of the wines by the glass with a meal, or while playing one of the many traditional board games that dotted around the pub. The lovely garden overlooks the Bride Valley.

Open 11-3 5-11 Closed Sun eve in winter **Food** Lunch Mon-Sat 12-2.30, Sun 12-5 Dinner Mon-Sat 6-9 ⊕ PALMERS ◀ Best Bitter, 200, Copper Ale, Seasonal ales ♂ Thatchers Gold. **Facilities** Non-diners area ♣ (Bar Restaurant Garden) ♦ Children's menu Children's portions Garden ⌂ Parking WiFi **=** (notice required)

SHAPWICK
Map 4 ST90

The Anchor Inn

tel: 01258 857269 **West St DT11 9LB**
email: anchor@shapwick.com
dir: *From Wimborne or Blandford Forum take B3082. Pub signed*

Village-owned pub with great local food

The village owns this welcoming pub lock, stock and barrel. Food-wise there are some surprising 'pub classics' such as pan-fried Irish white pudding with a grain mustard rarebit topping, plus à la carte options like smoked eel with horseradish cream, beetroot coulis and chive and potato salad, and salt and vinegar battered haddock with chips, tartare sauce and pea purée.

Open all day Closed Sun eve **Food** Lunch Mon-Sat 12-3, Sun 12-4 Dinner Mon-Sat 6-9.30 ⊕ FREE HOUSE ◀ Sharp's Doom Bar, Local guest ales ♂ Westons Stowford Press. ¶ 20 **Facilities** Non-diners area ♣ (Bar Restaurant Garden) ♦ Children's menu Children's portions Garden ⌂ Parking WiFi **=** (notice required)

SHERBORNE
Map 4 ST61

The Kings Arms ★★★★★ INN ◉ PICK OF THE PUBS

See Pick of the Pubs on page 173

SHROTON OR IWERNE COURTNEY
Map 4 ST81

The Cricketers PICK OF THE PUBS

See Pick of the Pubs on opposite page

STRATTON
Map 4 SY69

Saxon Arms

tel: 01305 260020 **DT2 9WG**
email: rodsaxonlamont1@yahoo.co.uk
dir: *3m NW of Dorchester on A37. Pub between church & village hall*

Thatched flint-stone pub serving good food

Popular with villagers as much as visiting fishermen, cycling clubs and ramblers, this handsome, thatched flint-stone free house is ideally situated for riverside walks. Flagstone floors, a wood-burning stove and solid oak beams create a comfortable setting for a traditional English inn that offers a friendly welcome, a range of well-kept real ales and simple, carefully cooked food. Menu choices include braised Dorset shoulder of lamb with garlic mash and redcurrant jus; pheasant breast on red cabbage with sweet raspberry vinegar sauce; chargrilled pork tenderloin with bubble-and-squeak; and roasted butternut squash and chargrilled artichoke tagliatelle. There's also a deli counter and a selection of baguettes and jackets.

Open all wk 11-3 5.30-late (Fri-Sun 11am-late) **Food** Lunch Mon-Thu 11-2.15, Fri-Sat 11.30-9.30, Sun 12-9 Dinner Mon-Thu 6-9.15, Fri-Sat 11.30-9.30, Sun 12-9 Set menu available ⊕ FREE HOUSE ◀ Fuller's London Pride, Palmers Best Bitter, Greene King Abbot Ale & Ruddles, Otter, Ringwood, Timothy Taylor, Butcombe, Guest ales ♂ Westons Stowford Press, Guest ciders. ¶ 15 **Facilities** Non-diners area ♣ (Bar Garden) ♦ Children's menu Children's portions Garden ⌂ Parking WiFi **=** (notice required)

STUDLAND
Map 5 SZ08

The Bankes Arms Hotel

tel: 01929 450225 **Watery Ln BH19 3AU**
dir: *B3369 from Poole, take Sandbanks chain ferry, or A35 from Poole, A351 then B3351*

Creeper-clad, 16th-century pub close to Studland Bay

Standing above the wide sweep of Studland Bay, this 16th-century creeper-clad inn was once a smugglers' dive. Nowadays the pub hosts an annual four-day festival in mid-August, featuring live music and some 200 beers and ciders that include award-winning ales from its own Isle of Purbeck brewery. Fresh fish and seafood salads are a speciality, but slow-braised lamb shank with rosemary mash; chilli con carne; and a daily curry are other examples from the menu.

Open all day all wk 11-11 (Sun 11-10.30) Closed 25 Dec **Food** Lunch all wk 12-3 (summer & BH 12-9.30) Dinner Mon-Sat 6-9.30, Sun 6-9 (summer & BH 12-9.30) ⊕ FREE HOUSE ◀ Isle of Purbeck Fossil Fuel, Studland Bay Wrecked, Solar Power, Thermal Cheer, Harry's Harvest ♂ Thatchers Cheddar Valley, Broadoak. **Facilities** Non-diners area ♣ (Bar Restaurant Garden) ♦ Children's menu Garden ⌂ Beer festival WiFi **=**

PICK OF THE PUBS

The Cricketers

SHROTON OR IWERNE COURTNEY Map 4 ST81

tel: 01258 860421 **DT11 8QD**
email: info@thecricketersshroton.co.uk
web: www.heartstoneinns.co.uk
dir: *7m S of Shaftesbury on A350, turn right after Iwerne Minster. 5m N of Blandford Forum on A360, past Stourpaine, in 2m left into Shroton. Pub in village centre*

Award-winning free house in secluded gardens

Under Hambledon Hill, where General Wolfe trained his troops before his assault on Quebec in 1759, lies what maps show as both Iwerne Courtney and Shroton; ask locals for the latter when looking for this early 20th-century pub and you'll be pointed in the right direction. Built to replace a much earlier establishment, over the years it has become not only a real community local, but also a popular pit-stop for walkers on the Wessex Way, who, since the path passes conveniently right by, are rarely so unwise as to wander through without stopping for Joe and Sally Grieves' genuine hospitality. In the light, open-plan interior, where in winter there's a cosy log-burner, the real beers are Salisbury English Ale and Otter Amber, while wine drinkers will find up to nine by the glass; there's no separate restaurant. The menu changes seasonally and makes use of locally

sourced, home-cooked ingredients to offer starters such as Stilton fritters; duck liver pâté, and mussels marinière. Main dishes include pork belly and home-made chorizo cassoulet; pan-fried lambs' liver and bacon, mash and onion gravy; and braised beef brisket and polenta cake. For vegetarians there's cauliflower, sweet potato and aubergine curry; and saffron tagliatelle with spiced butter. Sandwiches are available at lunchtime, and on Sunday a choice of roast meats is always on offer; specials are forever changing. Events include occasional summer barbecues and a beer festival weekend with live music. The pub is proud of its long association with the Shroton Cricket Club, from which it takes its name.

Open all wk 12-3 6-11 (Sun 12-10.30)
Food Lunch all wk 12-2.30 Dinner Mon-Thu 6.30-9, Fri-Sat 6.30-9.30
⊕ FREE HOUSE ◖ Salisbury English Ale, Otter Amber ♻ Westons Stowford Press.
♍ 9 **Facilities** Non-diners area ♦♦
Children's menu Children's portions
Garden ⼐ Beer festival Parking ⛟
(notice required) WiFi

SYDLING ST NICHOLAS — Map 4 SY69

The Greyhound Inn ★★★★ INN — PICK OF THE PUBS

tel: 01300 341303 **DT2 9PD**
email: info@dorsetgreyhound.co.uk web: www.dorsetgreyhound.co.uk
dir: *From A37 (Yeovil to Dorchester road), exit at staggered x-rds signed Sydling St Nicholas & Cerne Abbas*

Good food in the heart of Hardy country

Deep in Thomas Hardy country, this 18th-century pub is tucked away among pastel-hued flint and stone houses in a valley formed by Sydling Water; there are many enjoyable walks on the doorstep. There are four areas to eat in: the bar, with its open fire; the conservatory with oak, fruitwood and scrubbed wood tables and a deep chesterfield; the restaurant and the suntrap front terrace. Relax in the open-plan bar with a pint of Butcombe or a glass of draught Thatchers cider. The food is fresh and menus change every day. Fish, the pub's strength, is ordered the night before from the quaysides in Weymouth and Bridport, and there's usually game in season. Look out for the likes of home-made warm Scotch egg; and Asian glazed seared Lyme Bay scallops to start, then try the Greyhound open fish pie; slow roasted pork belly, parsnip purée, spiced red cabbage and dauphinoise potatoes; or wild mushroom, chestnut, pea and leek herby spaghetti. Accommodation, appointed to a high standard, is available.

Open 11-3 6-11 (Sun 12-5) Closed Sun eve **Food** Lunch Mon-Sat 12-2, Sun 12-4 Dinner Mon-Sat 6-9 ⊕ FREE HOUSE ◀ St Austell Tinners Ale, Butcombe, Guest ales ⌀ Thatchers. ☂ 12 **Facilities** Non-diners area ❤ (Bar Restaurant Garden) ♦♦ Children's menu Children's portions Play area Garden ⊼ Parking WiFi **Rooms** 6

TARRANT MONKTON — Map 4 ST90

The Langton Arms ★★★★ INN — PICK OF THE PUBS

tel: 01258 830225 **DT11 8RX**
email: info@thelangtonarms.co.uk web: www.thelangtonarms.co.uk
dir: *A31 from Ringwood, or A357 from Shaftesbury, or A35 from Bournemouth*

Family-friendly thatched inn with great food and ales

Close to the village church and surrounded by countryside immortalised in Thomas Hardy's novels, this pretty 17th-century thatched inn has two bars: the Farmers and the Carpenters; both are relaxing places to savour a pint from the ever-changing choice of outstanding local ales. Traditional pub dishes are served in the bars, as well as in the Stables restaurant and conservatory. Expect choice West Country traditional fare made based on local produce – sourced in Dorset whenever possible. Children, if you can persuade them to leave the fully-equipped play area, are spoilt for choice with their own menu or smaller portions from the adult carte.

A speciality is the beef from the pub's own herd, served in many ways including steaks, burgers, lasagne, and roasted on Sundays. Desserts are English favourites such as fruit crumble with custard. All the comfortable and well-equipped bedrooms are on the ground floor, situated around an attractive courtyard.

Open all day all wk **Food** Lunch Mon-Fri 12-2.30, Sat-Sun all day Dinner Mon-Thu 6-9.30, Fri 6-10, Sat-Sun all day ⊕ FREE HOUSE ◀ Local guest ales ⌀ Thatchers, Westons Stowford Press. **Facilities** Non-diners area ❤ (Bar Garden) ♦♦ Children's menu Children's portions Play area Family room Garden ⊼ Parking WiFi ⇛ (notice required) **Rooms** 6

TRENT — Map 4 ST51

The Rose and Crown Inn, Trent ★★★★★ INN
PICK OF THE PUBS

tel: 01935 850776 **DT9 4SL**
email: info@theroseandcrowntrent.co.uk web: www.theroseandcrowntrent.co.uk
dir: *Just off A30 between Sherborne & Yeovil*

Modern British food in a timeless village inn

Originally built to house builders of the Saint Andrew's church spire in this conservation village, this idyllic ivy-clad 14th-century inn owes more to its days as a farmhouse in the 18th-century, but you can still enjoy the beams and flagstone floors of this Dorset gem. Located on the Ernest Cook Trust estate that surrounds Trent, the lounge has a large, log-surrounded open fire and comfortable leather sofa; the main bar looks out over the fields, and from the restaurant you can survey the valley. Wadworth keeps the bar supplied with Bishop's Tipple and their other best-sellers, with ciders arriving from Thatchers and Westons. Quality local produce lies behind modern British food such as a starter of warm Dorset crab, spring onion and saffron tart, followed perhaps by venison haunch steak, potato hotpot, wild mushrooms, Savoy cabbage and bacon. Leave room for hot pistachio soufflé with lemon curd ice cream.

Open all day all wk **Food** Lunch Mon-Sat 12-2.30, Sun 12-3 Dinner all wk 6-9 Av main course £12 ⊕ WADWORTH ◀ 6X, Henry's Original IPA, Horizon & The Bishop's Tipple, Guest ale ⌀ Westons Stowford Press, Thatchers Gold. ☂ 8
Facilities Non-diners area ❤ (Bar Restaurant Garden) ♦♦ Children's menu Children's portions Family room Garden ⊼ Parking WiFi ⇛ (notice required) **Rooms** 3

WEST BEXINGTON — Map 4 SY58

The Manor Hotel

tel: 01308 897660 **DT2 9DF**
email: relax@manorhoteldorset.com
dir: *On B3157, 5m E of Bridport. In Swyre turn opposite The Bull Inn into 'No Through Road'*

Cosy old pub overlooking Chesil Beach

Overlooking the Jurassic Coast's most famous feature, Chesil Beach, parts of this 16th-century manor house are thought to date from the 11th century. It offers an inviting mix of flagstones, Jacobean oak panelling, roaring fires and a cosy cellar bar serving Otter ales and locally sourced dishes. Eat in the Manor Restaurant or in the Cellar Bar. With a pint of Otter Ale in hand study the chalkboards displaying modern British dishes; perhaps Italian meatballs followed by a home-made fish or turkey and leek pie. The large free car park is a bonus.

Open all wk 11.30-3 6-10 Closed 1st 2wks Jan **Food** Lunch all wk 12-2 Dinner Mon-Sat 6.30-9, Sun 6-8 ⊕ FREE HOUSE ◀ Otter Ale & Bitter ⌀ Thatchers Gold, Lilley's. ☂ 10 **Facilities** Non-diners area ❤ (Bar Garden) ♦♦ Children's menu Garden ⊼ Parking WiFi ⇛ (notice required)

Lulworth Cove Inn

tel: 01929 400333 **Main Rd BH20 5RQ**
email: lulworthcoveinn@hall-woodhouse.co.uk
dir: *From A352 (Dorchester to Wareham road) follow Lulworth Cove signs. Inn at end of B3070, opposite car park*

A short stroll from Lulworth Cove and the Jurassic Coast

Lulworth Cove's famous horseshoe bay is just steps away from the front door of this inn. It was once a distribution point for the mail service arriving by stagecoach, plus many smugglers stories can be heard. Ramblers can sate their appetites from the extensive menu, which features light bites, filled baguettes and jacket potatoes, as well as main course dishes like the ever popular steak and Tanglefoot ale pie, the Haddock smokie pie and crisp parmesan chicken.

Open all day all wk **Food** Lunch all wk 12-9 Dinner all wk 12-9 Av main course £9 ⊕ HALL & WOODHOUSE ◼ Badger Ŏ Westons Stowford Press. ⼂ 10
Facilities Non-diners area ❖ (Bar Restaurant Garden) ⋈ Children's menu Children's portions Garden ⋔ WiFi ⇐

The Ship Inn

tel: 01747 838640 **SP8 5RP**
email: mail@shipinn-dorset.com
dir: *On A30, 4m W of Shaftesbury (4m from Henstridge)*

Combining old and new in a rural setting

Walkers can explore the footpaths, which pass through the picturesque Dorset countryside surrounding this coaching inn built in 1750. The main bar has a traditional flagstone floor, low ceiling and log fire, while the lounge bar has stripped oak floorboards and chunky farmhouse furniture. Both offer a selection of beers and ciders, with weekly-changing guest ales. An evening menu includes open venison burger with fries and onion rings, wild, mushroom, blue cheese, spinach and hazelnut Wellington; or game pie. Home-made desserts may include dark chocolate and brandy torte. Outside there's a suntrap patio and large child-friendly garden.

Open all wk 12-3 6-11.30 **Food** Lunch all wk 12-2.30 Dinner Mon-Sat 6-9 Set menu available ⊕ FREE HOUSE ◼ Palmers IPA, Sharp's Doom Bar, Ringwood Fortyniner Ŏ Thatchers Cheddar Valley & Heritage, Westons Stowford Press. ⼂ 13
Facilities Non-diners area ❖ (Bar Garden) ⋈ Children's menu Children's portions Garden ⋔ Beer festival Parking WiFi

The Old Ship Inn

tel: 01305 812522 **7 The Ridgeway DT3 5QQ**
email: info@theoldshipupwey.co.uk
dir: *3m from Weymouth town centre, at bottom of The Ridgeway*

Weymouth views and real ales

Thomas Hardy refers to this 400-year-old pub in his novel *Under the Greenwood Tree*, and copper pans, old clocks and a beamed open fire create a true period atmosphere. Expect a good selection of real ales of tap, perhaps Dorset Jurassic, Otter and Sharp's Doom Bar, with Addlestones cloudy cider as an alternative. A frequently changing menu of good home-cooked pub food offers pressed terrine of venison, partridge and pheasant; seared lamb's liver with smoked bacon and onion gravy; home-made pie of the day; and twice cooked blade of beef with horseradish mash. On sunny days bag a bench in the garden and enjoy the views across Weymouth.

Open all wk Mon 5-11 Tue-Fri 12-3 5-11 Sat 12-11 Sun 12-10 **Food** Lunch Tue-Sat 12-2.30, Sun 12-6 Dinner Mon-Sat 6-9 ⊕ PUNCH TAVERNS ◼ Sharp's Doom Bar, Ringwood Best Bitter, Dorset Jurassic, Otter, Guest ales Ŏ Addlestones, Westons Stowford Press. ⼂ 13 **Facilities** Non-diners area ❖ (Bar Garden) ⋈ Children's menu Children's portions Garden ⋔ Parking WiFi ⇐

The Red Lion

tel: 01305 786940 **Hope Square DT4 8TR**
email: info@theredlionweymouth.co.uk **web:** www.theredlionweymouth.co.uk
dir: *Opposite Brewers Quay*

Rums, real ale and extensive food choices

Smack opposite the old Devenish Brewery in the heart of Weymouth, the former brewery tap has long been a famous ale house, popular with locals and visitors, and with strong links with the local RNLI – it's the lifeboat crew's nearest pub. Expect a comfortably rustic feel to the rambling rooms, with wood floors, candles on scrubbed tables, eclectic furnishings, period fireplaces, walls adorned with lifeboat pictures and artefacts, newspapers to peruse, and a cracking bar serving 80 rums, five ales and traditional ciders. To eat, there are platters to share, big bowls of mussels served with crusty bread, fresh dressed crab and classic likes steak and ale pie.

Open all day all wk 11-11 (Fri-Sat 11am-mdnt Sun 12-10.30) **Food** Lunch all wk 12-3, Apr-Sep all day Dinner all wk 6-9, Apr-Sep all day Av main course £9 ⊕ FREE HOUSE ◼ Otter Brewery Life Boat Ale, Dorset Jurassic, Sharp's Doom Bar, Ringwood Best Ŏ Westons Traditional Scrumpy & Country Perry. ⼂ 12
Facilities Non-diners area ❖ (Outside area) ⋈ Children's menu Children's portions Outside area ⋔ WiFi ⇐ (notice required)

WINTERBORNE ZELSTON
Map 4 SY89

Botany Bay Inne

tel: 01929 459227 **DT11 9ET**
dir: *A31 between Bere Regis & Wimborne Minster*

Classic pub food at this main road pub

The pub was built by the Hall & Woodhouse brewery in the 1920s to replace one in the village the local squire found offensive. Initially called the General Allenby, its name was changed in the 1980s in belated recognition of prisoners from Dorchester jail awaiting transportation to Australia. No such threat hangs over today's visitors here for locally sourced pub snacks and main dishes such as breaded wholetail scampi; steak and Stilton pie; slow-roasted lamb shank; butterflied chicken breast; and sweet potato and red pepper cannelloni.

Open 10-3 6-11 Closed Mon eve **Food** Lunch all wk 12-2.15 Dinner Tue-Sun 6-9 Set menu available ⊕ HALL & WOODHOUSE ◼ Badger First Gold & Tanglefoot, Guest ales. **Facilities** Non-diners area ❧ (Bar Garden) ᴪ Children's menu Children's portions Garden ⋤ Parking ⇔ (notice required)

WORTH MATRAVERS
Map 4 SY97

The Square and Compass

tel: 01929 439229 **BH19 3LF**
dir: *Between Corfe Castle & Swanage. From B3069 follow signs for Worth Matravers*

Lovely pub with beer but no bar and limited food

Little has changed at this stone-built pub for the past century, during which time it has been run by the same family. This tucked-away inn boasts a simple interior with no bar, just a serving hatch and an abundance of flagstone floors, oak panels and a museum of local artefacts and fossils from the nearby Jurassic Coast. Award-winning West Country beers and ciders come straight from the barrel and food is limited to just pasties and pies. On the first Saturday in October there's a beer and pumpkin festival, and in early November there's a cider festival.

Open all wk 12-3 6-11 (summer & Fri-Sun 12-11) **Food** Contact pub for details ⊕ FREE HOUSE ◼ Palmers Copper Ale, Wessex Longleat Pride, Hatty Browns Mustang Sally Ŏ Hecks Farmhouse, home-produced. **Facilities** Non-diners area ❧ (All areas) ᴪ Garden Outside area Beer festival Cider festival ⇔ **Notes** ⊛

Find out more about the AA's accommodation rating schemes on page 8

Follow us on twitter
@TheAA_Lifestyle

AYCLIFFE
Map 19 NZ22

The County ✦✦✦✦ RR

tel: 01325 312273 **13 The Green, Aycliffe Village DL5 6LX**
email: info@thecountyaycliffevillage.com **web:** www.thecountyaycliffevillage.com
dir: *A1 (M) junct 59, off A167 into Aycliffe Village*

Picturesque village green setting and celebrity visitors

Prettily perched on the village green, the Hairy Bikers filmed here on location in 2012. The smart restaurant and terrace is a lovely place to eat, as is the homely bar where you can sup a pint of Black Sheep or Cocker Hoop. With superb local produce on the doorstep, expect the likes of warm caramelised red onion and Mordon Farm feta cheese tartlet, then roast pheasant, roast garlic and thyme mashed potato, sautéed cep mushrooms and jus, with spiced treacle sponge with dairy custard to finish.

Open all wk 12-3 5-11 (Sun all day) Closed 25-26 Dec, 1 Jan **Food** Lunch Mon-Sat 12-2, Sun 12-9 Dinner Mon-Sat 5.30-9, Sun 12-9 Av main course £12 Restaurant menu available all wk ⊕ FREE HOUSE ◼ Cocker Hoop, Black Sheep, Yorkshire Dales, Hawkshead Ŏ Kingstone Press. ♟ 10 **Facilities** Non-diners area ᴪ Children's portions Outside area ⋤ Parking **Rooms** 7

BARNARD CASTLE
Map 19 NZ01

The Morritt Arms Hotel
PICK OF THE PUBS

tel: 01833 627232 **Greta Bridge DL12 9SE**
email: relax@themorritt.co.uk
dir: *On A1(m) at Scotch Corner take A66 towards Penrith, in 9m exit at Greta Bridge. Hotel over bridge on left*

Country house atmosphere

This fine building dates from the late 17th century, when it served Carlisle- and London-bound coach travellers. Traditionally a fine-dining venue, the restaurant has been brought bang up to date with vibrant colours, a touch of black leather, comfortable armchairs, silk blinds over window seats and works by local artists. This association with art began in 1946, when local portraitist Jack Gilroy painted the mural of Dickensian characters you'll find in the bar. Here, the menu opens with a seafood platter, before featuring Mediterranean vegetable risotto; Neasham pork and leek sausages; and beer-battered cod. In the restaurant, venison loin with beetroot risotto; butter-fried plaice fillets; and wild mushroom and vegetable Wellington may well appear. Major Morritt beer is named after the hotel's former owner and namesake.

Open all day all wk 7am-11pm (Sun 7am-10.30pm) ⊕ FREE HOUSE ◼ Morritt Arms Major Morritt, Timothy Taylor Landlord, Thwaites. **Facilities** ᴪ Children's menu Children's portions Play area Family room Garden Parking WiFi

NEW Three Horseshoes ★★★★ INN

tel: 01833 631777 **5-7 Galgate DL12 8EQ**
email: info@three-horse-shoes.co.uk **web:** www.three-horse-shoes.co.uk
dir: *In town centre on A67*

Local produce in refurbished family-run pub

In the centre of the historic market town of Barnard Castle, the Three Horseshoes is an ideal base for walkers exploring the nearby Teesdale Valley and the North Pennines. The Green family bought this 17th-century coaching inn in 2010 and they have restored it to its original splendour, completing the refurbishment some three years later. Enjoy a pint of Black Sheep as you scan the menus, which take in sandwiches at lunchtime. The evening menu focuses on local produce – start perhaps with chicken and duck liver parfait before moving on to a curry of Teesdale lamb shoulder with pilaf rice. Accommodation available.

Open all day all wk **Food** Lunch Mon-Sat 11.30-3, Sun 12-4 Dinner Mon-Sat 5.30-9 Set menu available ⊕ FREE HOUSE ◀ Black Sheep Best Bitter, Wychwood Hobgoblin, Ringwood Boondoggle. ♟ 12 **Facilities** Non-diners area ◀ Children's menu Children's portions Garden Outside area ⅀ Parking WiFi ➡ **Rooms** 11

■ CHESTER-LE-STREET Map 19 NZ25

The Moorings Hotel

tel: 0191 370 1597 **Hett Hill DH2 3JU**
email: info@themooringsdurham.co.uk
dir: *A1(M) junct 63 to Chester-le-Street. Take B6313. Hotel on left*

Tranquil Tees Valley setting

Handy both for the fascinating open air museum at Beamish and the historic heart of Chester-le-Street, this thriving hotel bar attracts much custom from ramblers and riders enjoying the glorious countryside along the valley of the River Tees. Thirsts are quenched by beers from the respected microbrewery at the Beamish complex, whilst keen appetites can be sated by dishes created from the freshest local produce. The menu of modern classics ranges across the spectrum, from breaded cod, haddock and crayfish tail fishcakes on ratatouille to sirloin steak with garlic butter tiger prawns, finishing with warm Scotch pancakes with chocolate sauce.

Open all day all wk **Food** Lunch Mon-Sat 11.45-9.30, Sun 11.45-8.30 Dinner Mon-Sat 11.45-9.30, Sun 11.45-8.30 ⊕ FREE HOUSE ◀ The Stables Beamish Hall Bitter, Guest ales. **Facilities** ◀ Children's menu Family room Garden Outside area ⅀ Parking WiFi ➡ (notice required)

■ COTHERSTONE Map 19 NZ01

The Fox and Hounds

tel: 01833 650241 **DL12 9PF**
email: ianswinburn999@btinternet.com
dir: *4m W of Barnard Castle. From A66 onto B6277, signed*

Picturesque village setting

At the heart of beautiful Teesdale and just a stone's throw from the river's wooded gorge, The Fox and Hounds is huddled above one of the village greens in pretty Cotherstone. Beams, open fires and thickly cushioned wall seats tempt you to linger at this 360-year-old coaching inn, admiring the local photographs and country pictures while you sip a pint of Black Sheep or Symonds cider. From the menu, tuck in to dishes made from the best of fresh, local ingredients: Wensleydale and hazelnut pâté with caramelised onion relish; steak, black pudding and Black Sheep ale pie; and pan-fried lamb's liver in rich gravy.

Open 12-2.30 6-11 (Sun 12-2.30 6-10.30) Closed 25-26 Dec, Mon-Wed winter **Food** Lunch all wk 12-2 Dinner all wk 6-8.30 Av main course £9.50 Set menu available ⊕ FREE HOUSE ◀ Black Sheep Best Bitter & Ale, The Village Brewer Bull Premium Bitter, York Yorkshire Terrier, Daleside ☉ Aspall, Symonds. **Facilities** Non-diners area ◀ Children's menu Children's portions Outside area ⅀ Parking WiFi ➡ (notice required)

■ DARLINGTON Map 19 NZ21

NEW Number Twenty 2

tel: 01325 354590 **22 Coniscliffe Rd DL3 7RG**
email: accountsnorthbay@btconnect.com
dir: *In town centre, off A67*

An ale drinkers' heaven in the town centre

Looking just like other shop fronts in the street, the door of Number Twenty 2 opens to reveal a classic Victorian pub. Multiple awards recognise that real ales are the name of the game here – up to 13 being pulled at busy times; expect to find Bull Premium and White Boar. Add to these nine continental beers, wines chosen for easy quaffing, and a select list of fine spirits and you have a drinker's paradise. Whether by popular demand or applied common sense, a seating area known as 'the canteen' is where bar bites, soups and sandwiches are served from midday until 7pm.

Open all day Closed 25-26 Dec, 1 Jan & BH Mon, Sun **Food** Lunch Mon-Sat 12-7 Dinner Mon-Sat 12-7 Av main course £6 ⊕ FREE HOUSE ◀ The Village Brewer White Boar Bitter & Bull Premium Bitter, Thwaites Lancaster Bomber. ♟ 22 **Facilities** Non-diners area ◀ WiFi

---

■ DURHAM Map 19 NZ24

Victoria Inn

tel: 0191 386 5269 **86 Hallgarth St DH1 3AS**
dir: *In city centre*

Traditional red brick, street pub at the heart of the city

This unique listed inn has scarcely changed since it was built in 1899 – not a jukebox, pool table or television to be found. Just five minutes' walk from the cathedral, it has been carefully nurtured by the Webster family for over three decades. Small rooms warmed by coal fires and a congenial atmosphere include the tiny snug, where a portrait of Queen Victoria still hangs above the upright piano. You'll find a few simple snacks to tickle the taste buds, but it's the cracking well-kept local ales, single malts, and over 40 Irish whiskies that are the main attraction.

Open all wk 11.45-3 6-11 **Food** Contact pub for details ⊕ FREE HOUSE ◀ Wylam Gold Tankard, Durham Magus, Big Lamp Bitter, Fyne Ales Jarl, Hill Island, Saltaire Blonde. **Facilities** Non-diners area ❀ (Bar Restaurant) ◀ Family room Parking WiFi ➡

■ FIR TREE Map 19 NZ13

Duke of York Inn

tel: 01388 767429 **DL15 8DG**
email: info@dukeofyorkfirtree.co.uk
dir: *On A68, 12m W of Durham. From Durham take A690 W. Left onto A68 to Fir Tree*

A warm welcome, modern interior and good food

On the tourist route (A68) to Scotland, the Duke of York is a former drovers' and coaching inn dating from 1749. It is appointed inside and out to a high standard, keeping the traditional country feel with contemporary touches. Look for Black Sheep and Camerons beers to accompany the food served all day. There's light bites, sandwiches and omelettes plus main menu choices such as the signature dish of chicken in creamy leek and pancetta sauce with crushed potatoes; or full rack of smokey BBQ baby ribs and hand-cut chips.

Open all day all wk **Food** Lunch all wk 12-9 Dinner all wk 12-9 Av main course £10-£12 Set menu available ⊕ CAMERONS BREWERY ◀ Black Sheep Best Bitter, Camerons Guest ales. **Facilities** Non-diners area ❀ (Bar Garden) ◀ Children's menu Children's portions Garden ⅀ Parking WiFi ➡

FROSTERLEY
Map 19 NZ03

The Black Bull Inn

tel: 01388 527784 **DL13 2SL**
dir: *From A68 onto A689 towards Stanhope. Left into Frosterley. Inn adjacent to railway station*

Great ales with bells on

Uniquely, this family-run, independent country pub has its own church bells – not to mention a great range of real ales to enjoy after a spot of bell-ringing. Located next to Weardale steam railway station, it has cosy, music-free rooms, a stone-flagged bar and open fires in Victorian ranges. The ad hoc beer festivals demonstrate unwavering backing for local microbreweries, while the kitchen is equally supportive of the regional suppliers behind the food. A meal might take in potted North Shields crab; herb crusted lamb shoulder with apricot and walnut stuffing, dauphinoise potatoes and rosemary jus; and raspberry and white chocolate cheesecake.

Open all day Closed 1 Jan for 2wks, Sun eve, Mon, Tue & Wed **Food** Lunch Thu-Sun 12.30-2.30 Dinner Thu-Sat 7-9 ⊕ FREE HOUSE ◀ Allendale, Wylam, Consett, York, Jarrow ♂ Wilkins Farmhouse, Westons. **Facilities** ❤️ (Bar Garden) ♦️ Children's portions Garden ⌐ Beer festival Cider festival Parking WiFi ▭ (notice required)

HURWORTH-ON-TEES
Map 19 NZ30

The Bay Horse

tel: 01325 720663 **45 The Green DL2 2AA**
email: mail@thebayhorsehurworth.com
dir: *From A66 at Darlington Football Club rdbt follow Hurworth sign*

Fine dining in pretty Tees Valley village

Savvy diners may get bitter and twisted at the bar in this sublime gastro-pub; its one of the real ales there to satisfy devotees seeking out the culinary magic conjured up by talented chef-proprietors Jonathan Hall and Marcus Bennett. The ancient pub retains considerable character enhanced by carefully chosen period furnishings. Thoroughly modern cuisine sets this ambience off to a tee; starters based on roasted pigeon breast or smoked eel merely a hint of the creative mains; perhaps daube of beef with colcannon or roasted salmon with creamed clams may satisfy, taken in the bar or restaurant.

Open all day all wk Closed 25-26 Dec **Food** Lunch Mon-Sat 12-2.30, Sun 12-4 Dinner all wk 6-close Set menu available Restaurant menu available Mon-Sat & Sun eve ⊕ FREE HOUSE ◀ Harviestoun Bitter & Twisted, Jennings Cumberland Ale. ▼ 12 **Facilities** Non-diners area ♦️ Children's menu Garden ⌐ Parking WiFi

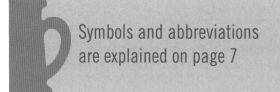
Symbols and abbreviations are explained on page 7

Read all about whisky in our feature on page 18

HUTTON MAGNA
Map 19 NZ11

The Oak Tree Inn ◉◉
PICK OF THE PUBS

tel: 01833 627371 **DL11 7HH**
dir: *From A1 at Scotch Corner take A66 W. 6.5m, right for Hutton Magna*

18th-century, free house offering excellent cooking with a pedigree

At this whitewashed, part 18th-century free house run by Alastair and Claire Ross, expect great food, a superb selection of drinks and a warm welcome. Alastair previously spent 14 years in London working at The Savoy, Leith's and, more recently, a private members' club on The Strand. The AA two-Rosette cuisine in the simply furnished dining room is based around the finest local ingredients, and dishes change daily depending on produce available. The refined cooking style combines classic techniques and modern flavours: you could start with home-cured salmon with crab jelly, beetroot and cream cheese; lamb and black pudding shepherd's pie; cauliflower, parmesan and thyme soup, or smoked haddock and roast squash risotto. After that, maybe fillet of cod with provençale vegetables, pesto potato, aubergine and fennel; seared duck breast with caramelized endive and sweet potato; or sea bass with Shetland mussels and mash. As well as fine real ales, there's a menu of bottled beers from around the globe, and a list of over 20 malt whiskies.

Open 6-11 (Sun 5.30-10.30) Closed Xmas & New Year, Mon **Food** Contact pub for details Restaurant menu available Tue-Sun ⊕ FREE HOUSE ◀ Wells Bombardier, Timothy Taylor Landlord, Copper Dragon. ▼ 10 **Facilities** Non-diners area ❤️ (Bar) Parking

LONGNEWTON
Map 19 NZ31

Vane Arms ★★★★ INN

tel: 01642 580401 **Darlington Rd TS21 1DB**
email: thevanearms@hotmail.com **web:** www.vanearms.com
dir: *W end of village, just off A66 midway between Stockton-on-Tees & Darlington*

Village pub with two beer festivals

This 18th-century pub is now successfully run by villagers Jill and Paul Jackson. There's no jukebox, pool or gaming machine, and the TV is on only for special events; background music plays quietly in the lounge. Sensibly priced home-made restaurant food includes seared king scallops; poached and roasted monkfish tail; pasta marinara; and white chocolate and mascarpone cheesecake. Grill night is Tuesday, French cuisine and tapas are available on alternate Wednesday evenings, roasts on Sunday, and there is a Black Sheep beer festival in October and a mini beer festival in July. A large garden looks towards the Cleveland Hills and the North Yorkshire Moors.

Open all wk Tue-Thu 12-2 5-11 (Mon 5-11 Fri-Sat 12-2 5-12 Sun 12-11) **Food** Contact pub for details Av main course £8.50 Set menu available Restaurant menu available all wk ⊕ FREE HOUSE ◀ Black Sheep Best Bitter, Guest ales ♂ Hereford Dry, Somersby Cider. **Facilities** Non-diners area ❤️ (Garden) ♦️ Children's portions Garden ⌐ Beer festival Parking WiFi ▭ (notice required) **Rooms** 4

PICK OF THE PUBS

The Rose & Crown Hotel ★★★ HL 🌹🌹

tel: 01833 650213
DL12 9EB
email: hotel@rose-and-crown.co.uk
web: www.rose-and-crown.co.uk
dir: *6m NW from Barnard Castle on B6277*

A real rural dining pub with a long pedigree

Overlooking the village's old stocks and water pump, this creeper-clad stone built coaching inn stands on the village green, while next door is the Saxon church known as 'The Cathedral of the Dale'. Step inside the 18th-century pub to be greeted by fresh flowers, varnished oak panelling, old beams, and gleaming copper and brass artefacts, then enter the quirky little bar and you'll encounter oak settles, a vast dog grate, old prints, carriage lamps and rural curios. In the secluded lounge you can retire to a wing-backed chair and be lulled by the ticking of a grandfather clock, with maybe a glass of Thwaites Wainwright or Black Sheep. The chefs rely on produce from Teesdale's farms and sporting estates, and fish from east coast to create their menus. Drop in at lunchtime for just a ham and cheese toasted sandwich; or to satisfy real hunger pangs choose a pork pie with mustard; Whitby caught fish with triple cooked chips; and a seasonal beef bourguignon; or roasted butternut squash and sage risotto with toasted pine nuts. For a meal in the evening perhaps choose a starter of beetroot, hazelnut and orange salad with creamy goats' cheese mousse; or five-spice duck breast and ginger noodle soup. Mains might be cod bouillabaisse with king prawns, mussels, fondant potato and braised courgettes and leeks; or, for two to share, cote de boeuf, roast potatoes, buttered cabbage, baby carrots and red wine sauce. Perhaps round things off with chilled apple tart with Calvados ice cream and warm toffee sauce , or a selection of local cheeses — White Hilton, Cotherstone and Teesdale Blue.

Open all day all wk Closed 24-26 Dec
Food Lunch all wk 12-2.30 Dinner all wk 6.30-9 🌐 FREE HOUSE 🛢 Black Sheep Best Bitter, Thwaites Wainwright ♂ Kingston. ♟ 9
Facilities Non-diners area ✿ (Bar Outside area) ♦ Children's menu Children's portions Outside area ⊟ Parking WiFi **Rooms** 14

MICKLETON
Map 18 NY92

NEW The Crown

tel: 07919 915640 **DL12 OJZ**
email: info@thecrownatmickleton.co.uk
dir: B6277 from Barnard Castle. Approx 6m to Eggleston. Follow Mickleton signs

Tasty treats in memorable countryside

Set in the higher reaches of the magnificent Tees Valley, this old stone inn mellows in a straggling, attractive village beneath the lumpy hills and heather moors of the North Pennines Area of Outstanding Natural Beauty. Candlelight and a log-burning stove illuminate the lovingly updated interior; in summer the dog-friendly garden is a real treat. The owning Rowbotham family are enthusiastic supporters of local craft breweries; perhaps savour a Sonnet 43 brewhouse beer here. The rich, Teesdale-inspired menu may offer pan-roasted breast of pheasant or home-made sausages, with a tasting platter of miniature deserts to follow.

Open all day all wk **Food** Contact pub for details ⊕ FREE HOUSE ◀ Cumberland Corby Ale, Jarrow Rivet Catcher, Sonnet 43 Steam Beer. ♀ 9
Facilities Non-diners area ✿ (All areas) ◀♦ Children's portions Garden Outside area ⊓ Parking WiFi ➡ (notice required)

NEWTON AYCLIFFE
Map 19 NZ22

Blacksmiths Arms

tel: 01325 314873 **Preston le Skerne, (off Ricknall Lane) DL5 6JH**
dir: Exit A167 (dual carriageway) at Gretna Green pub signed Great Stanton, Stillington & Bishopton, into Ricknall Ln. Blacksmiths Arms 0.5m

Large dining pub in a rural setting serving good food

Enjoying an excellent reputation locally as a good dining pub, this former smithy dates from the 1700s, and is still relatively isolated in its farmland setting. The menu offers starters of crispy battered chicken with sweet chilli dip; king prawns with watercress and garlic sautéed potatoes; or potted mushrooms in a Chardonnay cream sauce. Requiring their own page on the menu are fish dishes such as green-lipped mussels, slow-roasted pesto salmon, and grilled swordfish with prawn sauce. There's also a page of chef's specialities, good selection of vegetarian dishes and a gluten-free menu. There is an ever-changing selection of real ales served in the bar.

Open 11.30-2.30 6-11 Closed 1 Jan, Mon **Food** Lunch Tue-Sun 11.30-2 Dinner Tue-Sun 6-9 ⊕ FREE HOUSE ◀ Guest ales. ♀ 10 **Facilities** Non-diners area ◀♦ Children's menu Play area Garden ⊓ Parking ➡ (notice required)

ROMALDKIRK
Map 19 NY92

The Rose & Crown Hotel ★★★ HL ⊚⊚ **PICK OF THE PUBS**

See Pick of the Pubs on page 181

SEAHAM
Map 19 NZ44

The Seaton Lane Inn ★★★★ INN

tel: 0191 581 2036 **Seaton Ln SR7 OLP**
email: info@seatonlaneinn.com **web:** www.seatonlaneinn.com
dir: S of Sunderland on A19 take B1404 towards Houghton-le-Spring. In Seaton turn left for pub

Traditional pub with stylish, contemporary interior and good food

With a traditional bar area as well as a stylish restaurant and lounge, this boutique-type inn offers four real ales to keep the regulars happy, served from the central bar. The menu proffers dishes such as smooth chicken liver parfait; and classic Caesar salad with hot kiln smoked salmon flakes as starters, followed by beef cheeks braised in stout, mash and honey-roasted carrots; fillet of monkfish

cassoulet; Thai vegetable risotto; or Wallington Estate prime rib-eye steak. Bedrooms are modern, spacious and smartly furnished.

Open all day all wk 11am-mdnt **Food** Lunch all wk 7am-9.30pm Dinner all wk 7am-9.30pm Av main course £8 Set menu available Restaurant menu available all wk ⊕ FREE HOUSE ◀ Timothy Taylor Landlord, Wells Bombardier, Caledonian Deuchars IPA, Sharp's Doom Bar. ♀ 10 **Facilities** Non-diners area ✿ (Bar Garden Outside area) ◀♦ Children's menu Children's portions Garden Outside area ⊓ Parking WiFi ➡ **Rooms** 18

STANLEY
Map 19 NZ15

The Stables Pub and Restaurant ★★★★ CHH

tel: 01207 288750 & 233733 **Beamish Hall Hotel, Beamish DH9 OYB**
email: info@beamish-hall.co.uk **web:** www.beamish-hall.co.uk
dir: A693 to Stanley. Follow signs for Beamish Hall Country House Hotel & Beamish Museum. Left at museum entrance. Hotel on left 0.2m after golf club. Pub within hotel grounds

Own-brewed beer and ever popular food

The stone-floored, beamed bar is the perfect spot to sample the pub's own real ales, brewed on site at their microbrewery. The beer festival in the third week of September will get you even more closely acquainted, while a cider festival is held during the second weekend of December. The pub has been creatively moulded from the estate workshops of a stunning country mansion and has excellent accommodation. Regional producers supply the best local ingredients from which are crafted exemplary meals. Snack on open ravioli of smoked haddock, peas, tomato, chervil and fish cream; or sink into pan-fried lamb rump, lentils, fine beans, Chantenay carrots and apple purée.

Open all day all wk Mon-Thu 11-11 (Fri-Sat 11am-mdnt Sun 11-10.30) **Food** Lunch Mon-Thu 12-9, Fri-Sat 12-9.30, Sun 12-8 Dinner Mon-Thu 12-9, Fri-Sat 12-9.30, Sun 12-8 Set menu available Restaurant menu available all wk ⊕ FREE HOUSE ◀ The Stables Beamish Hall Bitter, Beamish Burn Brown Ale, Old Miner Tommy, Silver Buckles ♂ Gwynt y Ddraig Haymaker & Farmhouse Pyder. ♀ **Facilities** Non-diners area ✿ (Garden) ◀♦ Children's menu Children's portions Play area Garden ⊓ Beer festival Cider festival Parking WiFi ➡ **Rooms** 42

THORPE THEWLES
Map 19 NZ32

NEW The Vane Arms

tel: 01740 630458 **TS21 3JU**
email: tom@thevanearms.com
dir: Take A177 from Stockton-on-Tees towards Sedgefield. Left to Thorpe Thewles

Long established village pub

Tables out-front at this handsome pub overlook the green in a peaceful Tees Valley village. The pub's named after the Vane-Tempest family of Raby, higher up the valley, and has served the villagers for over 200 years. Yorkshire beers such as Timothy Taylor Landlord major on the bar, whilst the traditional lunchtime menu – seasonal terrine, sharing platters, pies, steaks – is considerably enhanced in the evenings. Led by talented chef Vanessa Wade, pan-roast duck breast with bean cassoulet, or game pie with celeriac mash typify the quality repast here.

Open 12-2 5-11 (Sat 12-11 Sun 12-5) Closed Sun eve & Mon **Food** Lunch Tue-Sat 12-2, Sun 12-4 Dinner Tue-Sat 5.30-9 ⊕ FREE HOUSE ◀ Black Sheep Bitter, Timothy Taylor Landlord ♂ Aspall. ♀ 12 **Facilities** Non-diners area ◀♦ Children's portions Garden Outside area ⊓ Parking

WINSTON
Map 19 NZ11

The Bridgewater Arms

tel: 01325 730302 **DL2 3RN**
email: paul.p.grundy@btinternet.com
dir: *Exit A67 between Barnard Castle & Darlington, onto B6274 into Winston*

Former schoolhouse serving fresh seafood

Set in a former schoolhouse, this Grade II listed pub is decorated with original photographs of the building and its pupils. It prides itself on offering high quality, simple meals made with local produce, particularly seafood. Chicken liver, black pudding, apple and Stilton salad followed by roast rack of lamb with a leek and potato cake and rosemary gravy is a typical meal, while fishy offerings could include langoustines split and grilled in garlic butter; and monkfish wrapped in bacon on a curried prawn risotto. Afterwards, the historic Winston Bridge and beautiful views to the church are a short stroll away.

Open 12-2.30 6-11 Closed 25-26 Dec, Sun & Mon **Food** Lunch Tue-Sat 12-2 Dinner Tue-Sat 6-9 ⊕ GREENE KING ◀ Timothy Taylor Landlord, Marston's, Cumberland, Mithril Ales ♂ Thatchers. ♟ 15 **Facilities** Non-diners area ♦♦ Children's portions Outside area ⌱ Parking WiFi

---

ESSEX

ARKESDEN
Map 12 TL43

Axe & Compasses
PICK OF THE PUBS

See Pick of the Pubs on page 184

AYTHORPE RODING
Map 6 TL51

Axe & Compasses

tel: 01279 876648 **Dunmow Rd CM6 1PP**
email: axeandcompasses@msn.com
dir: *From A120 follow signs for Dunmow*

Nostalgic pub with great home cooking

The owners of this weather-boarded, 17th-century pub like to create a 'nostalgic pub experience'. In the bar, ales from brewers such as Adnams, are backed by Westons ciders. David Hunt, a skilled self-taught chef, uses the best of seasonal produce and loves to offer dishes such as chicken liver and brandy parfait; pigeon breast with bacon lardons, Savoy cabbage, Puy lentils and game gravy; and a choice of five home-made pies. The pub also serves breakfast daily and offers a great range of bar snacks such as pork crackling with warm apple sauce or a home-made Scotch egg.

Open all day all wk 9am-11.30pm (Sun 9am-11pm) **Food** Bkfst all wk 9am-11.30am Lunch Mon-Sat 12-2.30, Sun 12-8 Dinner Mon-Sat 6-9.30, Sun 12-8 ⊕ FREE HOUSE ◀ Sharp's Doom Bar, Adnams Broadside & Lighthouse, Guest ale ♂ Westons Old Rosie, Rosie's Pig & Cider Twist Raspberry. ♟ 15 **Facilities** Non-diners area ♣ (Bar Garden) ♦♦ Children's menu Children's portions Garden ⌱ Parking WiFi ▭

BLACKMORE
Map 6 TL60

The Leather Bottle
PICK OF THE PUBS

tel: 01277 823538 & 821891 **The Green CM4 0RL**
email: leatherbottle@tiscali.co.uk
dir: *M25 junct 8 onto A1023, left onto A128, 5m. Left onto Blackmore Rd, 2m. Left towards Blackmore, 2m. Right then 1st left*

Enjoyable food in village pub with large beer garden

With its creeper-clad exterior and spacious garden, The Leather Bottle still continues to draw the crowds after 400 years. The stone-floored bar is a cosy,

---

welcoming place to savour East Anglian real ales and cider, while the restaurant is smart, with modern furnishings, and an airy conservatory opens on to the large garden and covered patio. The cuisine is a blend of European and traditional English, prepared with top-quality ingredients mainly from local suppliers. Lunchtime options include home-made beef casserole; wild mushroom and courgette tart; and pie of the day, while typical evening dishes are pan-fried chicken supreme; something from the extensive steak board selection; or smoked haddock with parsley mash and a poached egg. Warm fresh fruit meringue with Chantilly cream and Baileys and white chocolate pannacotta are tasty-sounding desserts. The first Monday of every month is jazz night.

Open all day all wk **Food** Lunch Mon-Sat 12-2, Sun 12-4 Dinner Tue-Sat 7-9 Set menu available Restaurant menu available all wk ⊕ FREE HOUSE ◀ Adnams Southwold Bitter & Broadside, Courage Directors, Sharp's Doom Bar, Woodforde's Wherry, Cottage Cactus Jack, Young's Special ♂ Aspall, Westons Old Rosie. ♟ 9 **Facilities** Non-diners area ♣ (Bar Garden) Children's portions Garden Parking

---

BURNHAM-ON-CROUCH
Map 7 TQ99

Ye Olde White Harte Hotel

tel: 01621 782106 **The Quay CM0 8AS**
email: whiteharte hotel@gmail.com
dir: *Along high street, right before clocktower, right into car park*

Quayside hotel with an olde worlde atmosphere

Situated on the waterfront overlooking the River Crouch, the hotel dates from the 17th century and retains many original features, including beams and fireplaces. It also has its own private jetty. Enjoy fresh local produce and fish in The Waterside Restaurant, or eat in the bar or on the terrace. The dining room offers a wide range of starters, as well as main course options that include vegetarian dishes and a daily roast. The bar menu might feature lasagne and salad; or locally caught skate with new potatoes and vegetables.

Open all day all wk **Food** Lunch all wk 12-2.15 Dinner all wk 6.30-9 Av main course £9 Restaurant menu available all wk ⊕ FREE HOUSE ◀ Adnams Southwold Bitter, Crouch Vale Brewers Gold. **Facilities** ♣ (Bar Outside area) ♦♦ Children's portions Outside area ⌱ Parking WiFi ▭ (notice required)

CASTLE HEDINGHAM
Map 13 TL73

The Bell Inn
PICK OF THE PUBS

See Pick of the Pubs on page 185

CHELMSFORD
Map 6 TL70

Admiral J McHardy

tel: 01245 256783 **37 Arbour Ln CM1 7RG**
email: admiraljmchardy@gmail.com
dir: *Phone for detailed directions*

White clapboard alehouse with a stylish interior

Owned by Fireside Pubs & Restaurants, this late 19th-century pub is named after the first Chief Constable of Essex, who was appointed in 1840. The team's philosophy is 'to provide the best the customer can expect', guaranteeing that all produce is locally sourced and of a high quality. The chic decor is a stylish mix of traditional and contemporary while the menu offers predominantly classic pub dishes and grills - perhaps barbecue rack of ribs, grilled chicken burger in a ciabatta roll, and salmon, chorizo and broad bean fishcakes. There is a front patio and more secluded rear garden for alfresco dining.

Open all day all wk 11-11 (Sun 11-10.30) **Food** Lunch Mon-Fri 12-2, Sat 12-9, Sun 12-5 Dinner Mon-Fri 6-9, Sat 12-9 ⊕ FREE HOUSE ◀ Greene King IPA, Moorland Old Speckled Hen, Guest ales ♂ Somersby. ♟ 12 **Facilities** Non-diners area ♦♦ Children's menu Children's portions Garden ⌱ Beer festival Parking WiFi ▭

PICK OF THE PUBS

Axe & Compasses

ARKESDEN Map 12 TL43

tel: 01799 550272
High St CB11 4EX
email: axeandcompasses@mail.com
web: www.axeandcompasses.co.uk
dir: *From Buntingford take B1038 towards Newport, left for Arkesden*

Lovely inn with Greek dishes on the menus

The Axe & Compasses is the centrepiece of this sleepy, picture-postcard village, whose narrow main street runs alongside gentle Wicken Water, spanned by a succession of footbridges that give access to white, cream and pink washed cottages. The thatched central part of the pub dates from 1650; the right-hand extension was added during the early 19th century and is now the public bar. It's run by Themis and Diane Christou from Cyprus, who between them have knocked up a good few awards for the marvellous things they do here. Easy chairs and settees, antique furniture, clocks and horse brasses fill their comfortable lounge and, in winter, there's an open fire. The pumps of Greene King hold sway in the bar, and it's with a pint of Olde Trip that you can have a sandwich or light meal, such as monkfish served on a roasted red pepper sauce. In the softly lit restaurant area, which seats 50 on various levels, and where agricultural implements adorn the old beams, the slightly Greek-influenced menus offer a

good selection of starters, including flat field mushrooms baked with garlic, thyme, lemon juice and olive oil; and avocado, bacon and blue cheese crostini. There's a good choice of main courses too, examples being moussaka; supreme of chicken Kiev with mushroom duxelles in puff pastry and wholegrain mustard cream; tender rump of lamb with mint and red wine gravy; grilled halibut steak with creamed leeks; and fried spinach and potato cakes with tomato and basil sauce. Rounding off the menu are desserts from the trolley, such as trifle of the day, and summer pudding. The wine list is easy to navigate, with house reds and whites coming in at modest prices. On fine days many drinkers and diners head for the patio.

Open all wk 12-2.30 6-11 (Sun 12-3 6-10.30) **Food** Lunch all wk 12-2 Dinner all wk 6.30-9.15 Av main course £13.95 Restaurant menu available Mon-Sat. ⊕ GREENE KING ◀ IPA, Hardys & Hansons Olde Trip, Guest ale ♂ Thatchers Gold. ♟ 14
Facilities Non-diners area ♦♦ Children's portions Outside area ㅈ Parking WiFi 🚐 (notice required)

PICK OF THE PUBS

The Bell Inn

CASTLE HEDINGHAM Map 13 TL73

tel: 01787 460350
Saint James St CO9 3EJ
web: www.hedinghambell.co.uk
dir: *On A1124 N of Halstead, right to Castle Hedingham*

British and Turkish cooking in a traditional village local

A 15th-century former coaching inn situated in the charming medieval village of Castle Hedingham, The Bell has been run by the Ferguson family for over 40 years. From the late 1700s the pub was a popular stop for coaches en route between Bury St Edmunds and London and it remains a traditional pub serving good quality real ales and honest food using local ingredients including herbs and vegetables from the pub's own allotment at the back. Exposed stone walls, heavy beams and real log fires create a welcoming atmosphere in which to enjoy a Mighty Oak Maldon Gold, Adnams Southwold Bitter or one of the guest ales. The Turkish chef puts his stamp on the menu, with Mediterranean fish nights on Mondays, and Turkish stone-baked pizzas on Wednesdays. In the summer, the wood-fired oven and barbecue is wheeled out for guests to enjoy Middle Eastern dishes and fish specials alfresco in the walled garden and orchard, once home to cock-fighting, croquet and quoits. At lunchtime, Italian

paninis are one option, alongside favourites such as ploughman's. Otherwise, enjoy unpretentious dishes like grilled lamb shish with sweet red pepper in a tortilla wrap with bulgur wheat; salmon and broccoli fishcakes with salad and potato salad; lemon roast chicken with root vegetables; or red bean and roast aubergine chilli; with chocolate truffle torte for afters. Half-size portions of many dishes are available for younger visitors. The annual Easter weekend and July beer festivals that showcase up to 15 ales prove popular, as is live music every Friday night and jazz on the last Sunday of the month.

Open all wk 11.45-3 6-11 (Fri-Sat 12-12 Sun 12-11) Closed 25 Dec eve

Food Lunch Mon-Fri 12-2, Sat 12-2.30, Sun 12-3 Dinner Sun-Mon 7-9, Tue-Sat 7-9.30 Av main course £10 ⊞ GRAY & SONS ◼ Mighty Oak Maldon Gold & IPA, Adnams Southwold Bitter, Guest ale ♉ Aspall, Delvin End **Facilities** Non-diners area ✿ (Bar Restaurant Garden) ♦ Children's menu Children's portions Play area Family room Garden ⊼ Beer festival Parking ⛟ (notice required) WiFi

CHRISHALL
Map 12 TL43

The Red Cow

tel: 01763 838792 **11 High St SG8 8RN**
email: thepub@theredcow.com
dir: *M11 junct 10, A505 towards Royston. 2m, pass pet creamtorium, 1st left signed Chrishall. 3.5m, pub in village centre*

Recommended for their game dishes

Conveniently positioned between Saffron Walden and Royston, this 500-year-old thatched pub is very much the hub of the community in this pretty village. In the bar the real ales and cider are locally brewed or from East Anglia; on the menu are soups, sandwiches, jacket potatoes and other pub favourites. The seasonally changing restaurant carte typically offers coarse game terrine with home-made chutney, which might be followed by beef and venison casserole, blue cheese scone and mash; or roasted root vegetable risotto. Each week there's a pub favourites' night, a steak night and 'the day beef-ore Friday' pie night, and look out for regular beer and music festivals in May.

Open 12-3 6-12 (Sat 12-12 Sun 12-11) Closed Mon **Food** Lunch Tue-Sun 12-3 Dinner Tue-Thu 6-9, Fri-Sat 6-9.30 ⊕ FREE HOUSE ◀ Adnams Southwold Bitter, Woodforde's Wherry & Nelson's Revenge, Morland Old Speckled Hen, Purity Mad Goose, Sharp's Doom Bar, Timothy Taylor Landlord Ō Aspall Harry Sparrow. **Facilities** Non-diners area ♛ (Bar Garden) ♦♦ Children's menu Children's portions Play area Garden ⊟ Beer festival Parking WiFi ⛐ (notice required)

CLAVERING
Map 12 TL43

The Cricketers
PICK OF THE PUBS

tel: 01799 550442 **CB11 4QT**
email: info@thecricketers.co.uk
dir: *M11 junct 10, A505 E, A1301, B1383. At Newport take B1038*

Famous dining pub in rural Essex

The Cricketers lies in the lovely village of Clavering with winding lanes, extensive woodland and thatched cottages. The pub has served the community for almost 500 years; all the signs are here – the beams, a forest of wooden pillars, old fireplaces, while outside a wisteria surrounds the door and tables dot a rose-fringed garden. The seasonally changing dishes are expertly prepared by head chef Justin Greig and his team. Meats are properly hung, the fish is always fresh, and local organic produce is used wherever possible. Jamie Oliver, son of landlords Trevor and Sally (over 30 years here), supplies the vegetables and herbs from his certified organic garden that is nearby. Begin perhaps with roasted local ham hock and candy beetroot, or steamed Scottish mussels with smoked bacon and Adnams ale. A salad or pasta dish might follow, or you could try 30-day hung rib-eye steak, roast sweet cherry bell peppers and blue cheese sauce; or mild venison curry. The extensive wine list changes regularly and features excellent house wines and a popular Connoisseurs' Wine List, while beers are mostly East Anglian. Children are particularly welcome.

Open all day all wk Closed 25-26 Dec **Food** Lunch Mon-Sat 12-2, Sun 12-8 Dinner Mon-Sat 6.30-9.30, Sun 12-8 ⊕ FREE HOUSE ◀ Adnams Broadside & Southwold Bitter, Tetley's Bitter, Greene King IPA, Woodforde's Wherry & Norfolk Nog Ō Aspall. ♟ 17 **Facilities** Non-diners area ♦♦ Children's menu Children's portions Garden ⊟ Parking WiFi ⛐ (notice required)

COLCHESTER
Map 13 TL92

The Rose & Crown Hotel ★★★ HL

tel: 01206 866677 **East St CO1 2TZ**
email: info@rose-and-crown.com **web:** www.rose-and-crown.com
dir: *M25 junct 28, A12 N. Follow Colchester signs*

Ancient, black-and-white oak-framed hotel

Just a few minutes' stroll from Colchester Castle, this beautiful timber-framed building dates from the 14th century and is believed to be the oldest hotel in the oldest town in England. The Tudor bar with its central roaring fire is a great place to relax with a drink. Food is served in the Oak Room or the Tudor Room brasserie, an informal alternative serving classic bar food. Typically, start with ham hock terrine or a sharing platter of shellfish, then follow with pork belly with butterbean, pancetta and chorizo cassoulet. Leave room for warm pear and almond tart.

Open all wk **Food** Lunch all wk 12-2.30 Dinner all wk 6.30-9.30 ⊕ FREE HOUSE ◀ Rose & Crown Bitter, Tetley's Bitter, Adnams Broadside. **Facilities** Non-diners area ♦♦ Children's portions Family room Outside area Parking WiFi ⛐ **Rooms** 39

The Whalebone

Chapel Road, Fingringhoe, Colchester, Essex CO5 7BG • Tel: 01206 729307
Email: info@thewhaleboneinn.co.uk • **Website:** www.thewhaleboneinn.co.uk

If you're looking for a relaxed ambience, superb food, fantastic value and a place you'll return to again and again, The Whalebone fits the bill.

If you're looking for somewhere to indulge your palate, you're certain to find something to delight you on the menu. It takes a really talented chef to serve up the fabulous menus on offer – and The Whalebone has two! There's also a great wine list to complement your choice.

Set in a picturesque village with beautiful surrounding countryside, and stunning views it's no surprise that The Whalebone is a popular place to visit.

DEDHAM
Map 13 TM03

Marlborough Head Inn ★★★ INN

tel: 01206 323250 **Mill Ln CO7 6DH**
email: jen.pearmain@tiscali.co.uk **web:** www.marlborough-head.co.uk
dir: *E of A12, N of Colchester*

Comfortable and cosy inn serving hearty food

Tucked away in glorious Constable Country, this 16th-century building was once a clearing-house for local wool merchants. In 1660, after a slump in trade, it became an inn. Today it is as perfect for a pint, sofa and newspaper as it is for a good home-cooked family meal. Traditional favourites such as steak, Guinness and mushroom pie; and lamb shank with red wine and rosemary appear on the menu, plus fish is given centre stage on Fridays. There is a terrace and walled garden to enjoy in the warmer weather. Three en suite bedrooms are available.

Open all day all wk 11.30-11 **Food** Contact pub for details ⊕ PUNCH TAVERNS ◀ Greene King IPA, Adnams Southwold ⚙ Aspall. ₹ 12 **Facilities** Non-diners area ❤ (Bar Garden) ♦ Children's menu Children's portions Family room Garden ⊞ Parking WiFi ➡ (notice required) **Rooms** 3

The Sun Inn ★★★★★ INN ❀❀ | PICK OF THE PUBS |

tel: 01206 323351 **High St CO7 6DF**
email: office@thesuninndedham.com **web:** www.thesuninndedham.com
dir: *From A12 follow signs to Dedham for 1.5m, pub on High Street*

A centuries-old inn with Mediterranean-influenced cuisine

Independently owned and run, this lovely old inn has a smart yellow-painted exterior. Inside are two informal bars, an open dining room, a snug oak-panelled lounge, three open fires, and exposed timbers; outside is a suntrap terrace and walled garden overlooked by the church tower. So take your pick of where to enjoy your chosen refreshment, be it a pint of Crouch Vale Brewers Gold or Aspall Harry Sparrow cider; for wine drinkers, the choice extends beyond two dozen served by the glass. Locally sourced seasonal ingredients drive the daily-changing menu of traditional Mediterranean-style dishes, many with a strong Italian influence. Two AA Rosettes have been awarded for tastebud-tingling light dishes such as sardine in saòr; tagliatelle with squid bolognese; and salt cod fritte. For a non-traditional Sunday lunch you may find spiedini of Norfolk quail with sausage and bacon; or calves' liver with grilled polenta.

Open all day all wk 11-11 Closed 25-27 Dec **Food** Lunch Mon-Thu 12-2.30, Fri-Sun 12-3 Dinner Sun-Thu 6.30-9.30, Fri-Sat 6.30-10 Set menu available ⊕ FREE HOUSE ◀ Crouch Vale Brewers Gold, Adnams Broadside, 2 Guest ales ⚙ Aspall Harry Sparrow. ₹ 25 **Facilities** Non-diners area ❤ (Bar Garden) ♦ Children's menu Children's portions Garden ⊞ Parking WiFi **Rooms** 7

FEERING
Map 7 TL82

The Sun Inn

tel: 01376 570442 **Feering Hill CO5 9NH**
email: hello@sunninnfeering@.co.uk
dir: *On A12 between Colchester & Witham. Village 1m*

Ancient pub with two annual beer festivals

A pretty pub dating from 1525 with heavily carved beams to prove it, this Grade II listed building has two inglenook fireplaces and a large garden and courtyard. The traditional bar, which sells Shepherd Neame's real ales, has no TV or games machines. Home-cooked pub classics are backed by mains like herb-crusted rump of lamb with celeriac mash, wilted spinach and a rich meat jus. From May to September wood-fired pizzas are available. Three roasts, together with other options, are offered on Sundays. Over 30 real ales and ciders are showcased at June and September festivals.

Open all wk Sat-Sun all day **Food** Lunch Mon-Sat 12-2.30, Sun 12-8 Dinner Mon-Sat 6-9.30, Sun 12-8 Av main course £10 ⊕ SHEPHERD NEAME ◀ Master Brew, Spitfire & Bishops Finger, Whitstable Bay Pale Ale, Guest ales ⚙ Thatchers Heritage. ₹ 12 **Facilities** Non-diners area ❤ (Bar Garden) ♦ Children's menu Children's portions Garden ⊞ Beer festival Cider festival Parking ➡ (notice required)

FINGRINGHOE
Map 7 TM02

The Whalebone

tel: 01206 729307 **Chapel Rd CO5 7BG**
email: info@thewhaleboneinn.co.uk **web:** www.thewhaleboneinn.co.uk
dir: *Phone for detailed directions*

British cuisine and breathtaking views

This Grade II listed 18th-century free house enjoys beautiful views from its position at the top of the Roman River Valley. Its name comes from the bones of a locally beached whale, which were once fastened above the door of the pub. Wooden floors, exposed beams, bespoke furniture, a roaring fire and unique artwork all combine to create a feeling of warmth and character. Hearty British fare is prepared from local ingredients, along with Adnams and Woodforde's ales. A lunchtime snack can be enjoyed in one of the garden pavilions. The carte menu options include pan-fried red snapper to chargrilled rib-eye steak and roast topside of local beef.

Open all wk 12-3 5.30-11 (Sat 12-11 Sun 12-10.30 Winter Sun 12-6) **Food** Lunch Mon-Sat 12-2.30, Sun 12-8, Sun Nov-Mar 12-5 Dinner Mon-Thu 6.30-9, Fri-Sat 6.30-9.30, Sun 12-8, Sun Nov-Mar 12-5 ⊕ FREE HOUSE ◀ Adnams Southwold Bitter, Woodforde's Wherry, 2 Guest ales ⚙ Aspall. ₹ 13 **Facilities** Non-diners area ❤ (Bar Restaurant Garden) ♦ Children's menu Children's portions Play area Family room Garden ⊞ Parking ➡ (notice required)

See advert on opposite page

FULLER STREET

Map 6 TL71

The Square and Compasses

tel: 01245 361477 **CM3 2BB**
email: info@thesquareandcompasses.co.uk **web:** www.thesquareandcompasses.co.uk
dir: *From A131 (Chelmsford to Braintree) take Great Leighs exit, enter village, right into Boreham Rd. Left signed Fuller St & Terling. Pub on left*

A prominent feature of village life

Known locally as The Stokehole, this beautifully restored 17th-century village pub is set in lovely countryside but is just 10 minutes from Chelmsford. Originally two farm cottages, the privately owned and run free house still retains its original beams and inglenook fireplaces, with antique furnishings. The locally sourced food is straightforward, served alongside a good selection of ciders and ales. As well as pub classics, the daily-changing seasonal specials might include Cromer crab cake, 28-day-hung rib-eye steak with chunky chips and roasted tomato, and orange and passionfruit tart. There is a picket fenced front garden affording views of the Essex Way, and Mediterranean-style decking area.

Open all wk 11.30-3 5.30-11 (Sat-Sun 12-11) **Food** Lunch Mon-Fri 12-2, Sat 12-2.30, Sun 12-6 Dinner Mon-Sat 6.30-9.30, Sun 12-6 ⊕ FREE HOUSE ◼ Farmers Ales A Drop of Nelsons Blood, Square and Compasses Stokers Ale, Wibblers Dengie Gold Ö Westons, Aspall. ♀ 14 **Facilities** Non-diners area ❄ (Bar Garden) ♦♦ Children's portions Garden ⊼ Parking

GESTINGTHORPE

Map 13 TL83

AA PUB OF THE YEAR FOR ENGLAND 2014–2015

The Pheasant ★★★★★ INN ⊛   PICK OF THE PUBS

tel: 01787 465010 **Audley End, Church St CO9 3AU**
email: thepheasantpb@aol.com **web:** www.thepheasant.net
dir: *A131 from Sudbury towards Castle Hedingham. Right, follow Castle Hedingham sign, through Gestingthorpe to Audley End*

Gastro-pub with top-notch plot-to-plate cooking

On the Essex and Suffolk border and surrounded by lovely countryside, James and Diana Donoghue have gained a strong reputation at this stylish gastro-pub. James was an award-winning garden designer and he has used his skills to great effect by building the pub's raised vegetable beds, which now provide a steady supply of seasonal organic fruit and vegetables for the restaurant's busy kitchen. The pub's green-fingered owner keeps bees, too, using the honey in dressings and salads. Starters typically include goats' cheese and beetroot mousse with ciabatta crostini and smoked oil leaf salad; and prawn kebab with spicy Thai coleslaw and prawn crackers, followed by mains of Gressingham duck breast with garlic mash, green beans and white wine mushroom sauce; or trio of Newmarket sausages with red cabbage and creamy mashed potato. Poached pears with warm chocolate sauce is one typical dessert.

Open all day all wk Closed 1st 2wks Jan **Food** Lunch all wk 12-2.30 Dinner all wk 6.30-9.30 ⊕ FREE HOUSE ◼ Adnams Southwold Bitter, Sleaford Pleasant Pheasant, Woodforde's Ö Aspall. **Facilities** Non-diners area ❄ (Bar Garden Outside area) ♦♦ Children's portions Garden Outside area ⊼ Parking WiFi ▭ (notice required) **Rooms** 5

GOLDHANGER

Map 7 TL90

The Chequers Inn

tel: 01621 788203 **Church St CM9 8AS**
email: chequersgoldhang@aol.com
dir: *From B1026, 500mtrs to village centre*

'Low' pub in a riverside village

Built in 1410, The Chequers can be found next to the church in picturesque Goldhanger, on the River Blackwater. The pub name comes from a chequerboard used by the tax collector in the pub many, many years ago. At around 30 feet above sea level, it reputedly has the 'lowest' bar in Britain, where you can enjoy a pint of Adnams Ghost Ship. Several rooms decorated with farming and fishing implements surround the bar area. Pride is taken in the preparation and presentation of food, which includes crispy chicken fillets with a lemon and herb butter; and Somerset brie and beetroot chutney tart. There are beer festivals in March and September.

Open all day all wk **Food** Lunch all wk 12-3 Dinner Mon-Sat 6.30-9 Av main course £11 ⊕ PUNCH TAVERNS ◼ Young's Bitter, Crouch Vale Brewers Gold, Sharp's Doom Bar, Adnams Ghost Ship, Fuller's Bengal Lancer Ö Westons Traditional & Perry. ♀ 13 **Facilities** Non-diners area ❄ (Bar Garden) ♦♦ Children's menu Children's portions Garden ⊼ Beer festival Parking WiFi ▭ (notice required)

GREAT TOTHAM

Map 7 TL81

The Bull at Great Totham ★★★★ RR ⊛⊛   PICK OF THE PUBS

tel: 01621 893385 **2 Maldon Rd CM9 8NH**
email: reservations@thebullatgreattotham.co.uk **web:** www.thebullatgreattotham.co.uk
dir: *Exit A12 at Witham junct to Great Totham*

A highly regarded destination gastro-pub and restaurant

The Bull, overlooking the cricket green, is a 16th-century coaching inn and proud holder of two AA Rosettes. It offers not far short of 20 fine wines by the glass, real ales from Adnams and Greene King, and a bar menu of baguettes, sausage and mash, and beer-battered cod tail. Named after the ancient tree in the lavender-filled garden is the fine-dining Willow Room, where you might start with chicken liver parfait with apple and plum chutney and toasted soldiers, then follow with braised lamb shank and parsnip mash; or pan-fried sea bass with tagliatelle and mixed seafood chowder. If you're a vegetarian, the pumpkin ravioli with roasted artichokes, sage butter and toasted pumpkin seeds might take your fancy. Finish in style with orange and cinnamon frangipane with kirsch cherries. Musical and themed dining evenings and other events are held frequently.

Open all day all wk **Food** Lunch Mon-Fri 12-2.30 (light bites till 5.30), Sat 12-10, Sun 12-6.45 Dinner Mon-Thu 5.30-9, Fri 5.30-10, Sat 12-10, Sun 12-6.45 ⊕ FREE HOUSE ◀ Adnams, Greene King. ♀ 17 **Facilities** Non-diners area ☀ (Bar Garden Outside area) ♦ Children's menu Children's portions Play area Garden Outside area ⊨ Parking ⊟ (notice required) **Rooms** 4

| GREAT YELDHAM | Map 13 TL73 |

The White Hart ★★★★ RR ◉◉ 〔PICK OF THE PUBS〕

tel: 01787 237250 **Poole St CO9 4HJ**
email: mjwmason@yahoo.co.uk **web:** www.whitehartweddingvenue.co.uk
dir: On A1017 between Haverhill & Halstead

Character old inn with contemporary cooking

Highwaymen were once locked up in a small prison beneath the stairs of this impressive 500-year-old timber-framed inn. Situated on the border of Essex and Suffolk, The White Hart enjoys a setting within 4.5 acres of gardens, close to Heddingham Castle, the Colne Valley and Newmarket. With its blend of traditional and contemporary, it's a popular wedding venue on the one hand, and a great place to sample Brandon Rusty Bucket on the other. The hard work put in by the establishment's owner, Matthew Mason, has resulted in many awards, including two AA Rosettes for the food. A sample menu lists favourites such as panko coated brie with tomato chutney; grilled sea bass with sautéed potatoes, spinach and cockle cream; pork and leek sausages; vegetable lasagne and sirloin steak. For dessert there's baked cheesecake or vanilla pannacotta. Eleven en suite and fully equipped rooms complete the picture. Please note, dogs are only allowed in the garden.

Open all day all wk **Food** Lunch all wk 12-3 Dinner all wk 6-9 Av main course £12.95 Restaurant menu available Tue-Sat ⊕ FREE HOUSE ◀ Brandon Rusty Bucket, Nethergate Old Growler. ♀ 10 **Facilities** Non-diners area ☀ (Garden) ♦ Children's menu Children's portions Garden ⊨ Parking WiFi ⊟ (notice required) **Rooms** 11

| HASTINGWOOD | Map 6 TL40 |

Rainbow & Dove

tel: 01279 415419 **Hastingwood Rd CM17 9JX**
email: rainbowanddove@hotmail.co.uk
dir: Just off M11 junct 7

Little pub with a varied history

Dating back to at least the 16th century, Rainbow & Dove was a farmhouse, staging post, village shop and post office before it became a pub. English Heritage has given it Grade II historical building status. There are cask-conditioned real ales, a selection of whiskies and a good wine list. Menus revolve around fresh seasonal produce. On the snack menu you'll find ciabattas, baguettes sandwiches, toasties and jacket potatoes, but if its something more substantial that you require then the carte lists dishes such as coarse farmhouse pork pâté; steak, kidney and ale pie; roast chicken breast with Stilton and bacon sauce; and spinach, chickpea and sweet potato curry.

Open 11.30-3.30 6-11 (Sat 12-11 Sun 12-9 Mon 11.30-3.30) Closed Mon eve **Food** Lunch Mon-Sat 12-3, Sun 12-6 Dinner Tue-Sat 6-9, Sun 12-6 Av main course £9.50 Restaurant menu available all wk ⊕ FREE HOUSE ◀ Rainbow & Dove, Adnams Broadside, Sharp's Doom Bar, Guest ales ♂ Aspall. ♀ 10 **Facilities** Non-diners area ☀ (Bar Garden) ♦ Children's menu Children's portions Garden ⊨ Beer festival Parking ⊟ (notice required)

| HATFIELD BROAD OAK | Map 6 TL51 |

The Duke's Head

tel: 01279 718598 **High St CM22 7HH**
email: info@thedukeshead.co.uk **web:** www.thedukeshead.co.uk
dir: M11 junct 8, A120 towards Great Dunmow. Right into B183 to Hatfield Broad Oak. Pub on left at 1st bend in village

Welcoming child- and dog-friendly pub

On a corner, behind a white-painted picket fence, stands this 185-year-old village pub. Spacious, and with two wood-burning fires, it has a large catchment area, with customers drawn particularly by the seasonal British menu devised by chef/proprietor Justin Flodman. Justin's Sunday roasts are not alone in enjoying county-wide fame: among the starters are Seville orange marmalade on sourdough toast, and crispy parmesan chicken liver 'nuggets', while mains include beer-battered haddock with thrice-cooked chips, roast pumpkin and brie lasagne; and maple-cured, hot smoked salmon fishcake. For afters, don't miss the banana and walnut bread and butter pudding.

Open all day all wk Closed 25-26 Dec **Food** Lunch Mon-Fri 12-2.30, Sat 10.30-10, Sun 10.30-9 Dinner Mon-Thu 6.30-9.30, Fri 6.30-10, Sat 10.30-10, Sun 10.30-9 Av main course £11.75 ⊕ ENTERPRISE INNS ◀ Greene King IPA, Sharp's Doom Bar, Timothy Taylor Landlord ♂ Aspall. ♀ 25 **Facilities** Non-diners area ☀ (Bar Garden) ♦ Children's menu Children's portions Play area Garden ⊨ Parking WiFi ⊟ (notice required)

| HATFIELD HEATH | Map 6 TL51 |

The Thatcher's

tel: 01279 730270 **Stortford Rd CM22 7DU**
email: info@thethatcherspub.co.uk
dir: In village on A1060 (Bishop's Stortford road)

Quaint old pub serving home-made food

A pretty, thatched 16th-century pub overlooking the village green with oak beams and a welcoming inglenook wood-burning stove. The dishes are all prepared on the premises and might start with blue shell Shetland mussels, white wine and shallot thyme liquor; butternut squash and vanilla soup; or poached asparagus with duck egg and sun-blushed tomatoes, followed by a sous vide lamb rump with crushed minted peas, potatoes au gratin and Madeira sauce; or Devon skate wing with creamed potatoes, crispy kale with bacon and brown butter. Finish with banoffee soufflé, Tiptree jam and sherry trifle. Also enjoy a pint from the Mighty Oak brewery among others.

Open all wk 11.30-3.30 5.30-11 (Sat-Sun all day) **Food** Lunch all wk 12-2 Dinner all wk 6-9 ⊕ FREE HOUSE ◀ St Austell Tribute, Nethergate, Mighty Oak, Adnams. ♀ 11 **Facilities** Non-diners area ♦ Children's portions Family room Garden ⊨ Parking ⊟ (notice required)

HORNDON ON THE HILL
Map 6 TQ68

Bell Inn & Hill House
PICK OF THE PUBS

tel: 01375 642463 **High Rd SS17 8LD**
email: info@bell-inn.co.uk
dir: M25 junct 30/31 signed Thurrock

Historic family-run inn with plenty of talking points

This 15th-century coaching inn has been in the same family since 1938 but prior to that it had a chequered history including one local landowner being burnt at the stake for heresy. In the wood-panelled bar, regular brews like Crouch Vale Brewers Gold are backed by a selection of changing guest ales. The lunchtime bar menu offers sandwiches and light meals but booking is essential in the popular restaurant, where the daily-changing menu is driven by seasonal produce. A typical meal might be confit rabbit dumpling with Jerusalem artichoke cream, celeriac velouté and apple, followed by oven-roast lamb chump with dauphinoise potatoes, spinach and devilled kidney. You might notice hot cross buns hanging from the original king post that supports the ancient roof timbers. Every year the oldest willing villager hangs another, an unusual tradition that dates back 100 years to when the pub changed hands on a Good Friday.

Open all wk 11-11 (Sun 12-10.30) Closed 25-26 Dec **Food** Lunch all wk 12-1.45 Dinner Mon-Fri 6.30-9.45, Sat 6-9.45, Sun 7-9.45 Restaurant menu available all wk ⊕ FREE HOUSE ◀ Greene King IPA, Crouch Vale Brewers Gold, Sharp's Doom Bar, Bass, Guest ales. ♀ 16 **Facilities** Non-diners area ♣ (Bar Garden) ◀▮ Children's portions Garden ⨅ Parking WiFi

INGATESTONE
Map 6 TQ69

The Red Lion

tel: 01277 352184 **Main Rd, Margaretting CM4 0EQ**
dir: From Chelmsford take A12 towards Brentwood. Margaretting in 4m

A proper English pub

Emphatically a traditional inn and not a restaurant (although it does sell quality food), the 17th-century Red Lion is best described as a 'quintessential English pub'. The bar is decorated in burgundy and aubergine, the restaurant in coffee and cream. From an extensive menu choose prawn tostada; home-made balti curry; or classic moules marinière. Every Thursday you can get two steaks and a bottle of wine for £25. Wash it down with a pint of Greene King IPA or guest ales, and look out for Mr Darcy and Mr Gray, the house donkeys.

Open all wk 12-11 (Sun 12-6) **Food** Lunch all wk 12-3 Dinner Mon-Sat 6-9 Av main course £7.95 ⊕ GREENE KING ◀ IPA, Guest ales Ò Westons Stowford Press. ♀ 14 **Facilities** Non-diners area ◀▮ Children's menu Children's portions Play area Garden ⨅ Parking WiFi (notice required)

LANGHAM
Map 13 TM03

The Shepherd

tel: 01206 272711 **Moor Rd CO4 5NR**
email: info@shepherdlangham.co.uk
dir: A12 from Colchester towards Ipswich, take 1st left signed Langham

Stylish village food pub in Constable Country

In the pretty village of Langham, deep in Constable Country on the Suffolk/Essex border, this Edwardian pub – formerly the Shepherd & Dog - was taken over by Richard and Esther Brunning in May 2013. The new owners have given this family-friendly free house a stylish and contemporary makeover and the pub is open all day. Adnams and Woodforde's are among the ales served at the bar, alongside an extensive list of wines and cocktails. A typical meal could take in salt and pepper calamari with sweet chilli mayonnaise, followed by Suffolk ham, bubble-and-squeak cake, poached eggs and hollandaise.

Open all day all wk **Food** Lunch all wk 12-3 Dinner Tue-Sat 6-9 Av main course £12 Restaurant menu available ⊕ FREE HOUSE ◀ Adnams Southwold & Ghost Ship, Woodforde's Wherry Ò Aspall. **Facilities** Non-diners area ♣ (Bar Garden) ◀▮ Children's menu Children's portions Garden ⨅ Parking WiFi (notice required)

LITTLE BRAXTED
Map 7 TL81

The Green Man

tel: 01621 891659 & 07971 064378 **Green Man Ln CM8 3LB**
email: info@thegreenmanlittlebraxted.com
dir: From A12 junct 22 take unclassified road (Little Braxted Ln) through Little Braxted. Straight ahead into Kelvedon Rd. Right into Green Man Ln

Classic village local in hands of a Masterchef

Take the Kelvedon road northbound from the village centre to find this unspoilt brick-and-tiled, Greene King pub. Dating from the early 1700s, it has a traditional interior with collections of beer tankards, horse brasses and old woodworking tools. The concise menu lists such dishes as lamb shank in red wine and mint gravy; beef lasagne with jacket potato; and Thai green chicken curry. Other attractions are Hydes and guest ales, and beer and cider festivals (please contact the pub for dates). Outside is a tree-shaded rear garden.

Open all wk Mon-Sat 11.30-3 5-11 (Sun 12-7) **Food** Lunch Mon-Sat 12-2.30, Sun 12-6 Dinner Mon-Sat 6-9 ⊕ GREENE KING ◀ IPA, Abbot Ale & Abbot Reserve, Hydes, Guest ales. ♀ 9 **Facilities** Non-diners area ♣ (Bar Garden) ◀▮ Children's menu Children's portions Garden ⨅ Beer festival Cider festival Parking WiFi (notice required)

LITTLE BURSTEAD
Map 6 TQ69

The Dukes Head

tel: 01277 651333 **Laindon Common Rd CM12 9TA**
email: enquiry@dukesheadlittleburstead.co.uk
dir: From Basildon take A176 (Noah Hill Rd) N toward Billericay. Left into Laindon Common Rd to Little Burstead. Pub on left

Welcoming pub known for its themed food events

Smart interiors and a friendly team characterise the atmosphere in this large hostelry between Brentwood and Basildon. Chunky wood tables, leather-upholstered stools and relaxing armchairs surround the open fire in the bar area, where the ales vie for selection with an excellent range of wines served by the glass. Modern British food ranges from pizzas and pastas to the chef's daily specials.

Open all day all wk **Food** Lunch Mon-Thu 12-10, Fri-Sat 12-10.30, Sun 12-9 Dinner Mon-Thu 12-10, Fri-Sat 12-10.30, Sun 12-9 Set menu available ⊕ MITCHELLS & BUTLERS ◀ Fuller's London Pride, Sharp's Doom Bar, Adnams Southwold Bitter Ò Aspall. ♀ 21 **Facilities** Non-diners area ♣ (Bar Garden) ◀▮ Children's menu Children's portions Garden ⨅ Parking WiFi (notice required)

LITTLEBURY
Map 12 TL53

The Queens Head Inn Littlebury

tel: 01799 520365 **High St CB11 4TD**
email: queensheadlittlebury@aol.co.uk
dir: M11 junct 9A, B184 towards Saffron Walden. Right onto B1383, S towards Wendens Ambo

Popular community pub with good home-made food

A beautiful family-run former coaching inn with open fires, exposed beams and one of only two remaining full-length settles in England. Very much at the centre of the local community, the pub runs darts and football teams and pétanque competitions; a large beer garden with bouncy castle confirms its family-friendly credentials. The kitchen aims to produce good home-made pub grub at realistic prices, with a menu of popular favourites from fresh baguettes, fish and chips, a choice of home-made gourmet burgers and curries to the chef's specials.

Open all day all wk Mon 10am-11pm Tue-Thu 8am-11pm Fri 8am-1am Sat 9am-1am Sun 9am-11pm Food Lunch Mon-Sat 12-2.30, Sun 12-4 Dinner Mon-Sat 6-9.30 Set menu available Restaurant menu available Mon-Sat ⊕ GREENE KING ◀ IPA, Morland Old Speckled Hen, Guest ales Ò Westons Stowford Press, Aspall. ▼ 9 Facilities Non-diners area ❀ (Bar Garden) ◆ Children's menu Children's portions Play area Garden ⋒ Beer festival Parking WiFi ▱

LITTLE CANFIELD
Map 6 TL52

The Lion & Lamb

tel: 01279 870257 **CM6 1SR**
email: info@lionandlamb.co.uk
dir: *M11 junct 8, B1256 towards Takeley & Little Canfield*

Perfect for a pre-flight meal

Built as a coaching inn on what used to be the main East Coast road, this traditional country pub and restaurant is ideal for business or leisure. Now bypassed, travellers on the way to Stansted Airport seek it out for a last English pint before their trip, relaxing in the large and well-furnished garden. Inside are oak beams, winter log fires and plenty of real ales. A typical meal might be wild mushroom risotto with pesto and shaved parmesan followed by slow-roasted pork belly stuffed with apricots and sage, mashed sweet potato with a rich wine sauce. Finish with that English classic, spotted dick.

Open all day all wk 11-close (Sun 12-close) Food Lunch all wk 12-10 Dinner all wk 12-10 ⊕ GREENE KING ◀ IPA & St Edmunds, St Austell, Guest ales Ò Aspall. ▼ 11 Facilities Non-diners area ◆ Children's menu Children's portions Play area Garden ⋒ Parking WiFi ▱

LITTLEY GREEN
Map 6 TL71

The Compasses

tel: 01245 362308 **CM3 1BU**
email: compasseslittleygreen@googlemail.com
dir: *Phone for detailed directions*

Unspoilt country local deep in rural Essex

Ridley Brewery's former tap fell on hard times following the closure of the brewery and sale of the pub estate in 2005. Joss Ridley left London and a top job and snapped up the pub in 2008 to revive the family link and hasn't looked back. The traditional inn stands in a sleepy hamlet and thrives selling tip-top ales straight from the barrel, including Bishop Nick, brewed by Joss's brother Nelion, and fresh, hearty pub food. Using local ingredients, the menu and chalkboard specials include filled 'huffer' baps, pea and mushroom risotto, and beer battered cod and chips. The interior is timeless and unspoilt, the garden large and peaceful.

Open all wk 12-3 5.30-11.30 (Thu-Sun all day) Food Lunch Mon-Fri 12-2.30, Sat-Sun 12-5 Dinner Sun-Fri 7-9.30, Sat 5-9.30 ⊕ FREE HOUSE ◀ Adnams, Bishop Nick, Green Jack, Crouch Vale, Mighty Oak Ò Gwynt y Ddraig, Westons, Burnard's. Facilities Non-diners area ❀ (Bar Restaurant Garden) ◆ Children's portions Garden ⋒ Beer festival Parking WiFi ▱ (notice required)

MANNINGTREE
Map 13 TM13

The Mistley Thorn ◉◎
PICK OF THE PUBS

tel: 01206 392821 **High St, Mistley CO11 1HE**
email: info@mistleythorn.co.uk
dir: *From Ipswich A12 junct 31 onto B1070, follow signs to East Bergholt, Manningtree & Mistley. From Colchester A120 towards Harwich. Left at Horsley Cross. Mistley in 3m*

Excellent seafood dishes and estuary views

Outside the Thorn, a hanging sign says 'Oysters', a big clue as to what's in store, those from Mersea Island being available year-round and Colchester natives when in season. This former coaching inn was built in 1723 and overlooks the estuary of

the River Stour. Inside, all the public spaces are light and airy with high ceilings, having received a makeover in 2013. Californian co-owner and executive chef Sherri Singleton also runs the Mistley Kitchen cookery school next door. With seafood a speciality, the two AA Rosette menus change daily to reflect availability: a starter of seared sea scallops with Puy lentils and spinach might be followed by seared local hake fillet with tomato, chorizo, smoked paprika and cannellini bean ragout; or butternut squash, haloumi and oregano tart. And for dessert, perhaps warm coffee and walnut cake with clotted cream. Real ales come from the Adnams and Mersea Island breweries.

Open all wk 12-2.30 6.30-9.30 (Fri 6-9.30 Sat-Sun all day) Food Lunch Mon-Fri 12-2.30, Sat-Sun & BHs 12-5 Dinner Mon-Thu 6.30-9.30, Fri-Sun 6-9.30 Av main course £9.50 Set menu available Restaurant menu available all wk ⊕ FREE HOUSE ◀ Adnams Southwold Bitter, Mersea Island. ▼ 17 Facilities Non-diners area ❀ (Bar Restaurant) ◆ Children's menu Children's portions Parking WiFi

---

MARGARETTING TYE
Map 6 TL60

The White Hart Inn

tel: 01277 840478 **Swan Ln CM4 9JX**
email: liz@thewhitehart.uk.com web: www.thewhitehart.uk.com
dir: *From A12 junct 15, B1002 to Margaretting. At x-rds in Margaretting left into Maldon Rd. Under rail bridge, left. Right into Swan Ln, follow Margaretting Tye signs. Follow to pub on right*

Two popular beer festivals held here

Parts of this pub, sitting proudly on a green known locally as Tigers Island, are 250 years old. Landlady Liz and her team revel in offering a great choice of the best regional and local beers and ciders. The pub's interior, all match boarding, old pictures, brewery memorabilia, dark posts, pillars, beams and fireplaces, oozes character, while the solidly traditional menu and specials board shout quality. Start with an Italian meat platter, and move on to lamb's liver and bacon casserole; grilled extra mature rib-eye steak; or grilled haddock served on creamy spring onion mash with a wild mushroom fricasée.

Open all wk 11.30-3 6-12 (Sat-Sun 12-12) Closed 25 Dec Food Lunch Mon-Fri 12-2, Sat 12-2.30, Sun 12-7.30 Dinner Tue-Thu 6.30-9, Fri-Sat 6-9.30, Sun 12-7.30 ⊕ FREE HOUSE ◀ Adnams Southwold Bitter & Broadside, Mighty Oak IPA & Oscar Wilde Mild Ò Aspall, Rekorderlig. ▼ 10 Facilities Non-diners area ❀ (Bar Garden) ◆ Children's menu Family room Garden ⋒ Beer festival Parking WiFi ▱ (notice required)

MOUNT BURES
Map 13 TL93

The Thatchers Arms

tel: 01787 227460 **Hall Rd CO8 5AT**
email: hello@thatchersarms.co.uk
dir: *From A12 onto A1124 towards Halstead. Right immediately after Chappel Viaduct. 2m, pub on right*

Bustling rural pub with well thought out menus

There's something for all-comers at this cheery country pub in the lovely Stour Valley. Challenge the quoits beds in the large beer garden, or ramble on paths that Constable may once have walked; there's even a small cinema here. Popular with locals and visitors, up to five real ales (and twice-yearly beer festivals) slake the thirst of hop-lovers, whilst diners may choose from a sheaf of enticing menus, perhaps tempting with grilled sardines on toast with tomato and olive tapenade; seared pigeon breast with bubble-and-squeak; home-made sweet potato, kaffir lime, lentil and coconut curry; or slow-cooked salt beef brisket with ale and root broth. Slimmers and food allergy sufferers are also well catered for here.

Open all day Closed Mon **Food** Lunch Tue-Fri 12-2.30, Sat 12-9, Sun 12-8 Dinner Tue-Fri 6-9, Sat 12-9, Sun 12-8 Av main course £10-£12 ⊕ FREE HOUSE ◄ Adnams Southwold Bitter, Crouch Vale Brewers Gold, Guest ales. ₹ 10
Facilities Non-diners area ♣ (Bar Restaurant Garden) ♦ Children's portions Garden ⋒ Beer festival Parking WiFi ⚌ (notice required)

MOUNTNESSING
Map 6 TQ69

The George & Dragon

tel: 01277 352461 **294 Roman Rd CM15 OTZ**
email: enquiry@thegeorgeanddragonbrentwood.co.uk
dir: *In village centre*

Flavoursome food in a laid-back gastro-pub

Spruced-up in true contemporary gastro-pub style, the interior of this 18th-century former coaching inn successfully blends bold artwork, colourful leather chairs and chunky modern tables with preserved original wooden floors, exposed beams and brick fireplaces. In this relaxed and convivial setting tuck into Mediterranean-inspired British dishes from an extensive menu that should please all tastes and palates. There are sharing platters, salads and pasta dishes, a selection of stone-baked pizzas and main courses like calves' liver with champ and red wine jus; and sea bass with sweet potato and aubergine tagine.

Open all day all wk **Food** Lunch all wk 12-10 Dinner all wk 12-10 ⊕ MITCHELLS & BUTLERS ◄ Fuller's London Pride, Adnams Best Ò Aspall. ₹ 21
Facilities Non-diners area ♦ Children's portions Garden ⋒ Parking ⚌ (notice required)

NEWNEY GREEN
Map 6 TL60

The Duck Pub & Dining

tel: 01245 421894 **CM1 3SF**
email: theduckinn1@btconnect.com
dir: *From Chelmsford take A1060 (Sawbridgeworth). Straight on at mini rdbt, 4th left into Vicarage Rd (signed Roxwell & Willingate), left into Hoe St, becomes Gravelly Ln, left to pub*

Peace and quiet at a quintessential country inn

Formed from two agricultural cottages, this 17th-century inn is situated in the tiny hamlet of Newney Green. Fully restored by the current owners, the friendly Duck offers up to six real ales, including weekly guests, and menus that reflect the region's produce. Choose from the extensive menu in the beamed dining room, from classics like steak and ale pie and scampi and chips, to game casserole with dumplings, and lamb shank braised in honey and mint. Soak up the sun in the garden with its children's play area. There is an Summer Bank Holiday beer festival.

Open all day Closed Mon **Food** Lunch Tue-Sun 12-9.30 Dinner Tue-Sun 12-9.30 Av main course £13 ⊕ FREE HOUSE ◄ Woodforde's Wherry, Adnams Broadside, Sharp's Doom Bar, Guest ales. ₹ 14 **Facilities** Non-diners area ♦ Children's menu Children's portions Play area Family room Garden ⋒ Beer festival Parking WiFi ⚌

NORTH FAMBRIDGE
Map 7 TQ89

The Ferry Boat Inn

tel: 01621 740208 **Ferry Ln CM3 6LR**
dir: *From Chelmsford take A130 S, then A132 to South Woodham Ferrers, then B1012. Turn right to village*

Traditional riverside village inn

Believed to have been an inn for at least 200 years, this 500-year-old, weatherboarded inn sits beside a yacht haven on the River Crouch. Known locally as the FBI, it started out as three fishermen's cottages, whose low beams and winter fires add character to the bars selling Greene King ales and Aspall cider. Menu choices include baguettes; jacket potatoes and burgers; steak and kidney pudding; Somerset pork loin steaks; scampi and chips; and vegetarian cheddar pie. Next door is a 600-acre Essex Wildlife Trust nature reserve, a winter feeding ground for flocks of Brent geese.

Open all day all wk **Food** Lunch all wk 12-2 Dinner all wk 7-9.30 ⊕ FREE HOUSE ◄ Greene King IPA & Abbot Ale, Morland Ò Aspall. **Facilities** Non-diners area ♣ (Bar Garden) ♦ Children's menu Children's portions Family room Garden ⋒ Parking ⚌ (notice required)

PATTISWICK
Map 13 TL82

The Compasses at Pattiswick
PICK OF THE PUBS

tel: 01376 561322 **Compasses Rd CM77 8BG**
email: info@thecompassesatpattiswick.co.uk
dir: *A120 from Braintree towards Colchester. After Bradwell 1st left to Pattiswick*

Destination pub, an ideal rural retreat

Years ago, two farm workers' cottages were amalgamated to form this friendly pub, still surrounded by the meadows and pocket woodlands of the Holifield Estate. The pub's owners source some of the raw materials for their menu direct from the estate. Support for local producers is at the centre of the pub's ethos, with minimising food miles being a guiding principle. Hearty rural recipes and uncomplicated cooking allow the dishes to do the talking. The main menu is supplemented by a daily specials board, allowing the chefs to take full advantage of seasonal produce. The dinner menu might feature toad-in-the-hole; Mediterranean vegetable linguine; and roast mutton shepherd's pie. The wine list is very comprehensive and features some exclusive Bordeaux and Burgundies. A roaring log fire makes a welcoming sight in winter after a local walk, while in summer the large garden is inviting. Families are very well catered for here, with a play area and toy box to keep little diners entertained.

Open all wk 11-3 5.30-11 (Sat 11-3 5.30-12 Sun 12-4 5.30-9) **Food** Lunch all wk 12-3 Dinner Mon-Thu 5.30-9.30, Fri-Sat 5.30-9.45, Sun 5.30-9 ⊕ FREE HOUSE ◄ Woodforde's Wherry, Adnams Broadside, St Austell Tribute Ò Aspall. ₹ 13
Facilities Non-diners area ♦ Children's menu Children's portions Play area Garden Parking WiFi

Looking for a beer or cider festival?
Check our listings at the end of this guide

PELDON
Map 7 TL91

The Peldon Rose

tel: 01206 735248 **Colchester Rd CO5 7QJ**
email: enquiries@thepeldonrose.co.uk
dir: On B1025 Mersea Rd, just before causeway

Historic inn, modern food

Contraband was once big business at this early 15th-century inn, understandably given its proximity to The Strood, which bridges the network of channels and creeks separating mainland Essex from Mersea Island. You can easily imagine the smugglers in the original-beamed bar with its leaded windows, but less so in the contemporary conservatory leading to the garden. A well-deserved reputation for good food begins with regularly changing menus offering dishes such as chicken and chorizo terrine; and beetroot-cured salmon as starters, and main courses of Thai-style vegetable linguine; Moroccan-style lamb tagine; and beer-battered fish and chips. Chef's quiche of the day makes an ideal light lunch.

Open all day all wk Closed 25 Dec **Food** Lunch all wk 12-2.30 Dinner all wk 6.30-9 Av main course £9.95 ⊕ FREE HOUSE ◀ Adnams Southwold Bitter, Woodforde's Wherry ♂ Aspall. ▼ 15 **Facilities** Non-diners area ♦♦ Children's menu Children's portions Garden ⋈ Parking ➡ (notice required)

RICKLING GREEN
Map 12 TL52

The Cricketers Arms ★★★ INN

tel: 01799 543210 **CB11 3YG**
email: info@thecricketersarmsricklinggreen.co.uk
web: www.thecricketersarmsricklinggreen.co.uk
dir: M11 junct 10, A505 E. 1.5m, right onto B1301, 2.2m, right onto B1383 at rdbt. Through Newport to Rickling Green. Right into Rickling Green Rd, 0.2m to pub, on left

Classic village green pub - perfect for cricket fans

Well-placed for Saffron Walden and Stansted Airport, this inn enjoys a peaceful position overlooking the village green and cricket pitch in sleepy Rickling Green. The rambling bar and dining rooms have a comfortable, contemporary feel, with squashy sofas by the log fire providing the perfect winter evening refuge for tucking into vegetarian tapas; locally caught rabbit with mustard sauce; Thai fishcake with clam broth; or oven baked whole sea bass with ginger and lemongrass cream. Arrive early on summer weekends to bag a table on the terrace – a popular spot in which to relax with a pint of Doom Bar and watch an innings or two.

Open all day all wk **Food** Lunch Mon-Thu 12-3, Fri-Sat 12-10, Sun 12-8 Dinner Mon-Thu 6-10, Fri-Sat 12-10, Sun 12-8 Av main course £12-£16 Set menu available ⊕ PUNCH TAVERNS ◀ Sharp's Doom Bar, Woodforde's Wherry, Guest ale ♂ Aspall. ▼ 10 **Facilities** Non-diners area ♣ (Bar Outside area) ♦♦ Children's menu Children's portions Outside area ⋈ Parking WiFi ➡ (notice required) **Rooms** 10

SAFFRON WALDEN
Map 12 TL53

NEW The Crown Inn ★★★ INN

tel: 01799 522475 **Little Walden CB10 1XA**
email: pippathecrown@aol.com **web:** www.thecrownlittlewalden.co.uk
dir: 2m from Saffron Walden on B1052

A family-friendly beamed country pub

The Crown's rural situation just outside the pretty market town of Saffron Walden makes it a good choice for local businessmen in need of a change of scene, and for families wanting to tire out children and dogs on one of the many walks in the surrounding countryside. Mums and dads can return for a well-earned glass of Adnams Broadside or a glass of wine, and hungry children can choose from the half dozen options on their dedicated menu. The short but reasonably priced menus embrace all the classic pub grub dishes. There's live jazz on Wednesday evenings.

Open all wk 11.30-2.30 6-11 (Sun 12-10.30) **Food** Lunch Mon-Sat 11.30-2, Sun 12-3 Dinner Mon-Sat 6.30-9 Av main course £9.95 ⊕ FREE HOUSE ◀ Woodforde's Wherry, Adnams Broadside, Greene King Abbot Ale, Guest ales.
Facilities Non-diners area ♣ (Bar Restaurant Outside area) ♦♦ Children's menu Children's portions Outside area ⋈ Parking WiFi ➡ (notice required) **Rooms** 3

Old English Gentleman

tel: 01799 523595 **11 Gold St CB10 1EJ**
email: goodtimes@oldenglishgentleman.com **web:** www.oldenglishgentleman.co.uk
dir: M11 junct 9a, B184 signed Saffron Walden. Left at High St lights into George St, 1st right into Gold St (one-way system)

A warm, friendly town-centre local

Regulars call Jeff and Cindy Leach's 19th-century, town centre pub the OEG, an informality which the top-hatted dandy on the sign over the front door might frown upon. Ancient beer taps line a wall of the central bar area, which extends into a dining space with a log burner and air conditioning, while outside is a heated patio garden. Resident ales Adnams Southwold and Woodforde's Wherry are backed up by changing guests and Aspall cider; a portfolio that earns customers' respect. Hearty main meals include beer-battered catch of the day; OEG pie of the week; and sausages and mash. For a lighter bite try a panini or hand-cut sandwiches.

Open all day all wk **Food** Lunch all wk 12-2.30 ◀ Woodforde's Wherry, Adnams Southwold Bitter, 2 Guest ales ♂ Aspall. ▼ 10 **Facilities** Non-diners area ♣ (Bar Outside area) ♦♦ Outside area ⋈ WiFi

STANSTED AIRPORT

See Little Canfield

STOCK

Map 6 TQ69

The Hoop

tel: 01277 841137 **21 High St CM4 9BD**
email: thehoopstock@yahoo.co.uk **web:** www.thehoop.co.uk
dir: *On B1007 between Chelmsford & Billericay*

Traditional pub with a focus on food

This 15th-century free house on Stock's village green is every inch the traditional country pub, offering a warm welcome, authentic pub interiors and a pleasing absence of music and fruit machines. There's an emphasis on food here, with dishes ranging from traditional toad in the hole with mash and gravy to crispy pig's head with apple celery and Bramley apple purée. You could finish with chocolate fondant. The annual beer festival (late May) has been going from strength to strength for over 30 years; you'll have over 100 real ales to choose from, not to mention fruit beers, perries and more.

Open all day all wk **Food** Lunch Mon-Fri 12-2.30, Sat 12-9.30, Sun 12-5 Dinner Mon-Thu 6-9, Fri 6-9.30, Sat 12-9.30 Av main course £10 Restaurant menu available Tue-Sat ⊕ FREE HOUSE ◼ Adnams Southwold Bitter, Crouch Vale Brewers Gold, Young's, Wibblers, Guest ales Ō Thatchers Gold. ☻ 12
Facilities Non-diners area ☻ (Bar Garden) ♦♦ Children's portions Garden ⊼ Beer festival WiFi

WENDENS AMBO

Map 12 TL53

NEW The Bell

tel: 01799 540382 **Royston Rd CB11 4JY**
email: batesabroad@eircom.net
dir: *Phone for detailed directions*

Traditional old English pub with beams galore

First mentioned in 1576 as a farm, evidence of its great age is everywhere, particularly the fine Elizabethan chimney stack. Other attributes include acres of gardens, a willow-edged pond, a woodland walk, play equipment, open fires and a resident ghost. Then there's the traditional country pub food, such as the hugely popular Bell beef and real ale pie; lamb Marrakesh; battered 'catch of the day'; and roasted vegetable and goats' cheese strudel. Cask ales and real ciders are always on tap. Ambo, incidentally, means 'both' in Latin and reflects a 17th-century merging of parishes.There's a beer festival over the Summer Bank Holiday weekend.

Open all day Closed Mon L (winter) **Food** Contact pub for details Av main course £10 Set menu available ⊕ FREE HOUSE ◼ Woodforde's Wherry, Oakham Ales JHB, Adnams Ō Westons Old Rosie. **Facilities** Non-diners area ☻ (Bar Garden) ♦♦ Children's menu Children's portions Play area Garden ⊼ Beer festival Parking WiFi ▦ (notice required)

WOODHAM MORTIMER

Map 7 TL80

Hurdlemakers Arms

tel: 01245 225169 **Post Office Rd CM9 6ST**
email: info@hurdlemakersarms.co.uk
dir: *From Chelmsford A414 to Maldon/Danbury. 4.5m, through Danbury into Woodham Mortimer. Over 1st rdbt, 1st left, pub on left. Behind golf driving range*

Family-run pub with a great beer festival

Previously two cottages, this 400-year-old listed building in the sleepy village of Woodham Mortimer became a pub in 1837. The beamed interior still retains its open log fire and many original features, and ale-lovers will be delighted by the range of real ales such as Wibblers, Mighty Oak and Farmers. Home-made dishes might include baked skate wing; roast or pie of the day; grilled steaks and beer-battered cod. There are weekend summer barbecues in the large garden, and a beer festival takes place on the last weekend of June, when there are over 25 ales and ciders to sample.

Open all day all wk 12-11 (Sun 12-9) **Food** Lunch Mon-Fri 12-3, Sat 12-9.30, Sun 12-8 Dinner Mon-Fri 6-9.30, Sat 12-9.30, Sun 12-8 ⊕ GRAY & SONS ◼ Mighty Oak, Farmers, Wibblers, Guest ales Ō Westons Old Rosie, Wibblers Dengie Cider. ☻ 8
Facilities Non-diners area ♦♦ Children's menu Children's portions Play area Garden ⊼ Beer festival Parking WiFi ▦

GLOUCESTERSHIRE

ALDERTON

Map 10 SP03

The Gardeners Arms

tel: 01242 620257 **Beckford Rd GL20 8NL**
email: gardeners1@btconnect.com
dir: *M5 junct 6, A46 towards Evesham. At rdbt take B4077 signed Stow. Left to Alderton*

Tapas, fresh fish and seasonal specials

Operating as a pub since the 16th century, this pretty, family-run, thatched free house is popular with walkers, cyclists and car clubs. You can play boules in the large beer garden, and traditional games in the stone-walled bar, where Cotswold Way numbers among the real ales. There's an early bird lunch menu, offering plenty of choice, and the fresh fish and seasonal specials change regularly. Spring Bank Holiday and Boxing Day both kick off five-day beer festivals, while the cider drinkers' turn is on the Summer Bank Holiday.

Open all wk 9-2 5.30-10 (Fri 9-2 5.30-12 Sat 9-2.30 5.30-10.30 Sun 10-9) Closed 3 days in Jan **Food** Lunch all wk 12-2 Dinner all wk 5.30-9 Set menu available ⊕ FREE HOUSE ◼ Sharp's Doom Bar, Butcombe Bitter, Prescott Track Record, Wickwar Cotswold Way, Local guest ales Ō Westons Stowford Press. **Facilities** Non-diners area ☻ (Bar Garden) ♦♦ Children's menu Children's portions Garden ⊼ Beer festival Cider festival Parking ▦ (notice required)

PICK OF THE PUBS

The Old Passage Inn ★★★★★ RR

ARLINGHAM Map 4 SO71

tel: 01452 740547
Passage Rd GL2 7JR
email: oldpassage@btconnect.com
web: www.theoldpassage.com
dir: *A38 onto B4071 through Arlingham. Through village to river*

Famous for its seafood and river views

Overlooking the River Severn and set against the backdrop of the Forest of Dean, this was once the site of the ford across the River. This seafood restaurant-with-rooms on the riverbank once provided refreshment to ferry passengers across the tidal river but now attracts people from afar for its quality food and air of tranquillity. Eating in the open and airy dining room, or on the popular riverside terrace in summer is a delight. A selection of oysters and pre-starters such as soft shell crab with spicy kumquat chutney or North Atlantic prawns and mayonnaise act as a delicious curtain raiser to the main menu. Head chef Mark Redwood uses only the freshest fish and seafood and keeps things simple to let the ingredients shine, whether it's lobster from Cornwall or oysters from Essex. Dishes may include scallop thermidor, spinach, cream

sherry sauce; seared scallops with belly pork, spiced lentils, cauliflower purée, rum soaked raisins and lime syrup; brill fillet poached in red wine, braised gem lettuce, celeriac purée; or lobsters from the pub's own seawater tank — try one grilled with parsley and garlic butter. Carnivores will not be disappointed with seared breast of pigeon, celeriac gratin, pickled wild mushrooms and beetroot salad; and local sirloin of beef, balsamic cherry tomatoes, mushrooms, hand-cut chips and béarnaise sauce. Leave room for the local Cerney Ash goats' cheese or chocolate brownie with yogurt ice cream.

Open 10-3 7-close Closed 25 Dec, Jan-Feb Tue & Wed eve, Sun eve & Mon **Food** Lunch Tue-Sat 12-2 Sun 12-3 Dinner Tue-Sat 7-9 ⊕ FREE HOUSE **Facilities** ♦ Children's portions Garden Parking WiFi **Rooms** 3

ALMONDSBURY
Map 4 ST68

The Bowl

tel: 01454 612757 **16 Church Rd BS32 4DT**
email: bowlinn@sabrain.com
dir: *M5 junct 16 towards Thornbury. 3rd left onto Over Ln, 1st right into Sundays Hill, next right into Church Rd*

Village inn with four ales and fine food

The Bowl sits on the edge of the Severn Vale, hence its name. Part of this pretty, whitewashed building dates from 1147, when monks were building the church, so it was getting on when it became an inn in 1550. It has an atmospheric interior with exposed stonework and a wood-burner for winter warmth. The freshly prepared food includes blue cheese soufflé with sticky fig chutney; pork tenderloin, black pudding and green beans; Moroccan spiced lamb shank with chickpea mash; passionfruit posset with home-made shortbread. There's good charcuterie and cheese boards too. There's Thatchers Gold cider and The Rev. James ale, with more at the beer festival in late summer.

Open all day all wk **Food** Lunch Mon-Fri 12-2.30, Sat 12-9.30, Sun 12-7 Dinner Mon-Fri 6-9.30, Sat 12-9.30, Sun 12-7 ⊕ BRAINS ◀ Bitter & The Rev. James, St Austell Tribute, Butcombe ♂ Thatchers Gold. ♀ 16 **Facilities** Non-diners area ♦️ Children's menu Children's portions Outside area ⊼ Beer festival Parking WiFi

NEW The Swan Hotel

tel: 01454 625671 **14 Gloucester Rd BS32 4AA**
email: garth@swanhotelbristol.com
dir: *M5 junct 16, A38 to Almondsbury*

Comfortable village pub with family-friendly food

On the outskirts of Bristol, parts of this former coaching inn date back to the 16th century and its hilltop position offers views across the Bristol Channel towards Wales. A family-friendly pub where children get their own menu (and half-size Sunday roasts), head chef Nigel Bissett champions local produce and keeps things interesting with Tuesday steak nights and Thursday seafood evenings. The daily menu might offer steak and mushroom suet pudding; honey-glazed ham hock with braised red cabbage and mustard mash; or grilled paneer and peppers with yogurt and spiced couscous. The pub holds a beer and cider festival in July.

Open all day all wk **Food** Lunch all wk 12-4 Dinner Mon-Sat 4-9.30, Sun 4-8.30 Av main course £10.95 ⊕ MARSTONS ◀ Martson's Pedigree, Wychwood Hobgoblin, Brakspear Oxford Gold ♂ Thatchers Gold & Cheddar Valley, Westons Stowford Press. ♀ 12 **Facilities** Non-diners area ♦️ Children's menu Children's portions Play area Garden ⊼ Beer festival Cider festival Parking WiFi 🚐 (notice required)

ARLINGHAM
Map 4 SO71

The Old Passage Inn ★★★★ RR ◉◉ PICK OF THE PUBS

See Pick of the Pubs on page 195

ASHLEWORTH
Map 10 SO82

The Queens Arms
PICK OF THE PUBS

tel: 01452 700395 **The Village GL19 4HT**
dir: *From Gloucester N on A417 for 5m. At Hartpury, right at Broad St to Ashleworth. Pub 100yds past village green*

Free house offering an interesting menu

Set in a rural village between rolling hills and the River Severn, this 16th-century inn is owned by Tony and Gill Burreddu. Although alterations have been made over the years, the original beams and iron fireplaces have been kept, simply complemented with comfortable armchairs, antiques and a gallery of local artists'

work. As a free house, the Queens offers ales from a range of breweries including Brecon Brewing and Shepherd Neame. Tony and Gill have built a loyal customer base and an excellent reputation for imaginative dishes made from the best local produce. Specials board entries may include a starter of crispy whitebait tossed in garlic butter; a main course of fresh monkfish served with parmesan and basil risotto, topped with fresh tomato beurre blanc; and Cape brandy pudding, a South African speciality made with light sponge and brandy-soaked dates.

Open 12-3 7-11 Closed 25-26 Dec & 1 Jan, Sun eve & Mon (ex BHs wknds) **Food** Lunch Tue-Sun 12-2 Dinner Tue-Sat 7-9 Av main course £13.50 ⊕ FREE HOUSE ◀ Timothy Taylor Landlord, Donnington BB, Brains The Rev. James, Shepherd Neame Spitfire, Sharp's Doom Bar, Brecon Brewing Gold Beacons ♂ Westons Stowford Press. ♀ 14 **Facilities** Non-diners area ♦️ Garden ⊼ Parking

BARNSLEY
Map 5 SP00

The Village Pub ★★★★★ INN ◉ PICK OF THE PUBS

tel: 01285 740421 **GL7 5EF**
email: reservations@thevillagepub.co.uk **web:** www.thevillagepub.co.uk
dir: *On B4425 4m NE of Cirencester*

Stylish Cotswold inn with food to match

The Village Pub manages to be both the local and a chic pub-restaurant, without becoming just another Cotswold tourist honeypot. Polished flagstones, oak floorboards, exposed timbers and open fireplaces are all there in spades, and the civilised atmosphere continues in each of the five rambling dining rooms, all sporting an eclectic mix of furniture, rug-strewn floors, oil paintings, cosy settles and warm terracotta walls. Modern British pub food draws a discerning dining crowd, with daily menus featuring quality local ingredients, some organic, like the vegetables from the Barnsley House gardens. Executive head chef Graham Grafton's modern European menus include slow roast pork belly with roast vegetables and apple sauce, and orange steamed pudding and custard. Half portions are available for 'younger clientele'.

Open all wk 11-11 (Sun 11-10) **Food** Lunch Mon-Fri 12-2.30, Sat-Sun 12-3 Dinner Mon-Thu 6-9.30, Fri-Sat 6-10, Sun 6-9 ⊕ FREE HOUSE ◀ Hook Norton Hooky Bitter, Butcombe Gold, Guest ales ♂ Ashton Press. ♀ 10 **Facilities** Non-diners area ♣ (Bar) ♦️ Children's portions Outside area ⊼ Parking WiFi **Rooms** 6

BERKELEY
Map 4 ST69

The Malt House ★★★ INN

tel: 01453 511177 **Marybrook St GL13 9BA**
email: the-malthouse@btconnect.com **web:** www.themalthouse.uk.com
dir: *M5 junct 13/14, A38 towards Bristol. Pub on main road towards Sharpness*

Village charm in the pretty Vale of Berkeley

At the heart of historic Berkeley, close to the remarkable castle and the Edward Jenner (the pioneer immunologist) Museum, this village free house is a popular place with walkers on the spectacular Severn Way along the nearby estuary shoreline; comfy accommodation and good food tempt overnight stops here. Ease into the copiously beamed old bar and consider a menu rich with modern British dishes - steak and ale pie; lamb shank; or halibut steak with sweet chilli dip will satisfy; there's a good vegetarian selection including nut roast and a specials board with a great sausage choice.

Open all wk Mon-Thu 6-11 (Fri 6-12 Sat 12-12 Sun 12-3) **Food** Lunch Sat-Sun 12-2 Dinner Mon-Sat 6.30-8.30 ⊕ FREE HOUSE ◀ Theakston Best Bitter Ö Westons Stowford Press, Thatchers Gold. **Facilities** Non-diners area ♦♦ Children's menu Children's portions Garden ⊨ Parking WiFi ➡ (notice required) **Rooms** 9

◼ BIBURY　　　　　　　　　　　　　　Map 5 SP10

Catherine Wheel ★★★★ INN

tel: 01285 740250 **Arlington GL7 5ND**
email: info@catherinewheel-bibury.co.uk **web:** www.catherinewheel-bibury.co.uk
dir: On B4425, W of Bibury

Welcoming Cotswold stone building offering a pleasing menu

This former blacksmith's has changed hands many times since J Hathaway opened it as an inn in 1856 but a warm welcome, a good selection of accredited ales and quality food remain its hallmarks. The beautiful Cotswold-stone building, stable courtyard and orchard date back to the 15th century and plenty of historical features remain. The appetising menu might include seared scallops with crispy duck confit, squash purée and red wine syrup; pot-roasted chicken with truffle mash, smoked bacon, shallots and peas; and king prawn and mussel spaghetti.

Open all day all wk 9am-11pm **Food** Lunch Mon-Fri 12-3, Sat 12-9.30, Sun 12-9 Dinner Mon-Fri 6-9.30, Sat 12-9.30, Sun 12-9 ⊕ FREE HOUSE/WHITE JAYS LTD ◀ Sharp's Doom Bar, Hook Norton Ö Westons Stowford Press, Aspall. ♀ 9 **Facilities** Non-diners area ♣ (Bar Garden) ♦♦ Children's menu Children's portions Garden ⊨ Beer festival Parking WiFi ➡ **Rooms** 4

◼ BIRDLIP　　　　　　　　　　　　　　Map 10 SO91

The Golden Heart

tel: 01242 870261 **Nettleton Bottom GL4 8LA**
email: info@thegoldenheart.co.uk
dir: On A417 (Gloucester to Cirencester road). 8m from Cheltenham. Pub at base of dip in Nettleton Bottom

Traditional pub with stunning views

A traditional 17th-century Cotswold-stone inn that was once a drovers' resting place, this lovely pub boasts stunning views of the valley from the terraced gardens. The main bar is divided into four cosy areas with log fires and traditional built-in settles. Excellent local ales and ciders are backed by a good selection of

wines, while the extensive menus demonstrate commitment to local produce, particularly prize-winning meat from the region. Perhaps try roast partridge with Parma ham and red wine sauce; bubble-and-squeak with pork sausages or the more exotic kangaroo steak with mushroom and red wine jus. Vegetarian, vegan and gluten-free options are available.

Open all day all wk Closed 25 Dec **Food** Lunch all wk 11-11 Dinner all wk 11-11 Av main course £11.95 ⊕ FREE HOUSE ◀ Otter Bitter, Cotswold Way, Cotswold Lion, Brakspear, Hook Norton Ö Westons, Henney's, Thatchers. ♀ 10 **Facilities** Non-diners area ♣ (Bar Restaurant Garden) ♦♦ Family room Garden ⊨ Parking WiFi ➡

◼ BLAISDON　　　　　　　　　　　　　　Map 10 SO71

The Red Hart Inn

tel: 01452 830477 **GL17 0AH**
dir: Take A40 (NW of Gloucester) towards Ross-on-Wye. At lights left onto A4136 signed Monmouth. Left into Blaisdon Lane to Blaisdon

Village inn with tranquil country views

On the fringe of the Forest of Dean, this old whitewashed pub exudes the charm of a village local, all flagstoned floor, log fire, low beams and friendly pub dog to-boot. Four guest ales whet the whistle of passing ramblers, whilst those dining out will appreciate the quality pork raised by the pub's owners; sampled in the slow roast belly with black pudding, sage mash and cider cream sauce. Specials introduce dishes featuring venison or pheasant to the well-balanced menu, taken in the bar or restaurant. The sunny garden is a good place to sit with a glass of local cider.

Open all wk 12-3 6-11.30 (Sun 12.30-4 7-11) **Food** Lunch all wk 12-2.15 Dinner all wk 6.30-9 Av main course £12 ⊕ FREE HOUSE ◀ 4 Guest ales Ö Westons Stowford Press, Traditional & 1st Quality. **Facilities** Non-diners area ♦♦ Children's menu Children's portions Play area Garden ⊨ Parking WiFi ➡ (notice required)

◼ BLEDINGTON　　　　　　　　　　　　Map 10 SP22

The Kings Head Inn ★★★★ INN ◎　　PICK OF THE PUBS

tel: 01608 658365 **The Green OX7 6XQ**
email: info@kingsheadinn.net **web:** www.kingsheadinn.net
dir: On B4450, 4m from Stow-on-the-Wold

Sublime Cotswolds free house

It's axiomatic that people make pubs - on both sides of the bar. They certainly do here. On one side, long-term owners Archie and Nicola Orr-Ewing; on the other, their customers, drawn by a reputation for well-kept real ales and top-quality, locally sourced food. Facing the village green, this stone-built pub dates back to the 15th century; it's been called the quintessential Cotswolds inn. Original structure survives in the low-beamed ceilings, flagstone floors, exposed stone walls and an inglenook fireplace. On the beer pumps, the labels of Hooky Bitter, Purity Gold and Wye Valley appear alongside local lagers; 11 wines are served by the glass. Among choices in the AA Rosette restaurant are deep-fried Windrush goats' cheese salad; vodka-and-tonic soft-shell crab; wood-pigeon tart; seafood and saffron risotto; and Tamworth pork and black pudding burger. For dessert, how about affogato?

Open all day all wk Closed 25-26 Dec **Food** Lunch Mon-Fri 12-2, Sat-Sun 12-2.30 Dinner Sun-Thu 6.30-9, Fri-Sat 6.30-9.30 Av main course £14 ⊕ FREE HOUSE ◀ Hook Norton Hooky Bitter, Purity Gold, Wye Valley, Butcombe, Butts, Bath Ales Ö Westons Stowford Press. ♀ 11 **Facilities** Non-diners area ♦♦ Children's menu Children's portions Garden ⊨ Parking WiFi **Rooms** 12

BOURTON-ON-THE-HILL
Map 10 SP13

Horse and Groom
PICK OF THE PUBS

tel: 01386 700413 **GL56 9AQ**
email: greenstocks@horseandgroom.info
dir: *2m W of Moreton-in-Marsh on A44*

Elegant Georgian inn with views offering excellent locally-sourced food

The Greenstock brothers have run this handsome Grade II listed Cotswold stone pub for some 10 years, and it is both a serious dining destination and a friendly place for a drink. The building combines a contemporary feel with plenty of original period features and the mature garden is a must-visit in summer with its panoramic hilltop views. The beer selection mixes local brews such as Goffs Jouster and over 20 carefully selected wines are served by the glass. The blackboard menu changes daily, providing plenty of appeal for even the most ardent regulars. With committed local suppliers backed up by the pub's own abundant vegetable patch, the kitchen has plenty of good produce to work with. A typical menu might feature home-cured, glazed Tamworth ham with fried egg and chips, or griddled Longhorn rib-eye steak with green peppercorn, parsley and shallot butter; followed by puds such as damson jam Bakewell tart.

Open 11-3 6-11 Closed 25 Dec, Sun eve **Food** Lunch all wk 12-2 Dinner Mon-Sat 7-9 ⊕ FREE HOUSE ◀ Wye Valley Bitter, Purity Pure UBU, Goffs Jouster, Cotswold Wheat Beer, Stroud Organic ♂ Hogan's. ₹ 21 **Facilities** Non-diners area ♦▮ Children's portions Garden ⊼ Parking WiFi

BROCKHAMPTON
Map 10 SP02

Craven Arms Inn

tel: 01242 820410 **GL54 5XQ**
email: cravenarms@live.co.uk
dir: *From Cheltenham take A40 towards Gloucester. In Andoversford, at lights, left onto A436 signed Bourton & Stow. Left, follow signs for Brockhampton*

Secluded village setting in fine walking country

Inside and out, this set-back, gabled old village inn glows with mellow honeyed stone; log fires, beams and mullioned windows add to the charm of its setting beneath the gently undulating horizon of the Cotswolds themselves. A selection of real ales, plus ciders and perry from regional orchards attract drinkers, who also appreciate the annual July beer festival here. Diners can self-cook their fish and steaks on grill-stones at the table, or appreciate either the good old-fashioned comfort food or modern dishes like pan-fried sea bass with roasted Mediterranean vegetables or wild mushroom, apricot and goats' cheese loaf. There's a gluten free menu too.

Open 12-3 6-11 Closed Sun eve & Mon **Food** Lunch Tue-Sun 12-2.30 Dinner Tue-Thu 6.30-9, Fri-Sat 6.30-9.30 ⊕ FREE HOUSE ◀ Otter, Butcombe ♂ Westons Stowford Press, Dunkertons. ₹ 9 **Facilities** Non-diners area ♥ (Bar Garden) ♦▮ Children's portions Garden ⊼ Beer festival Parking WiFi (notice required)

CHEDWORTH
Map 5 SP01

Hare & Hounds
PICK OF THE PUBS

tel: 01285 720288 **Foss Cross GL54 4NN**
email: stay@hareandhoundsinn.com
dir: *On A429 (Fosse Way), 6m from Cirencester*

Built of mellow Cotswold stone with atmosphere to match

A memorable mix of old-world character and contemporary cuisine; creepers cling to the sharply-pitched roofline of the 14th-century inn, the old inn sign swings beneath a shady oak, and a string of open fires welcomes ramblers from the countless local walks, visitors to the nearby Roman villa complex or fans of the turf breaking away from Cheltenham's racecourse just a few miles distant. The interior is an eclectic marriage of original features and modern chic; the ideal foundation for relaxing with a glass of locally brewed Arkell's bitter to accompany the excellent menu which is strong on seafood dishes with a nod to world cuisine. Grilled fillet of halibut with mildly spiced celeriac; or spiced tofu, grilled haloumi cheese and oriental vegetable stir-fry could be on the regularly updated menu here. In summer eat alfresco in the suntrap garden.

Open all wk Mon-Sat 11.30-2.30 6-close (Sun 11.30-2.30 7-close) **Food** Lunch all wk 12-2.30 Dinner Mon-Sat 6.30-9.30, Sun 7-9 ⊕ ARKELL'S ◀ 3B, Moonlight, Wiltshire Gold ♂ Westons Stowford Press. ₹ 8 **Facilities** Non-diners area ♥ (Bar Restaurant Garden) ♦▮ Children's menu Children's portions Family room Garden ⊼ Parking WiFi

CHELTENHAM
Map 10 SO92

The Gloucester Old Spot

tel: 01242 680321 **Tewkesbury Rd, Piff's Elm GL51 9SY**
email: eat@thegloucesteroldspot.co.uk
dir: *On A4019 on outskirts of Cheltenham towards Tewkesbury*

Traditional pub with enthusiastic owners

Simon and Kate Daws run this free house and it ticks all the boxes with its quarry tile floors, roaring log fires, farmhouse furnishings and real ales such as Wye Valley; they also own another Cheltenham pub, The Royal Oak Inn. Local ciders and perries are on offer at the bar and there is a Early May Bank Holiday cider festival, too. The baronial dining room takes its inspiration from the local manor, and game and rare-breed pork make an appearance on a menu that includes pork mixed grill and slow roasted belly pork with braised pig cheek bourguignon; and Old Spots pork loin steak with hand-cut chips.

Open all day all wk Closed 25-26 Dec **Food** Lunch all wk 12-2 Dinner Mon-Sat 6-9 Av main course £9 Set menu available ⊕ FREE HOUSE ◀ Timothy Taylor Landlord, Purity Mad Goose, Wye Valley HPA ♂ Thatchers, Westons Stowford Press, Black Rat. **Facilities** Non-diners area ♥ (Bar Garden) ♦▮ Children's menu Children's portions Garden ⊼ Beer festival Cider festival Parking WiFi (notice required)

The Royal Oak Inn

tel: 01242 522344 **The Burgage, Prestbury GL52 3DL**
email: eat@royal-oak-prestbury.co.uk
dir: *From town centre follow signs for Winchcombe/Prestbury & Racecourse. In Prestbury follow brown signs for inn from Tatchley Ln*

Welcoming pub recommended for its beer and cider festivals

On the outskirts of Cheltenham and close to the town's famous racecourse, this 16th-century pub was once owned by England cricket legend Tom Graveney. Owners Simon and Kate, who have been here for over a decade, also own The Gloucester Old Spot, Cheltenham. Enjoy well-kept local cask ales, real ciders and delicious food in the snug, the comfortable dining room or the heated patio overlooking a pretty beer garden. Menus include braised lamb shank, pork belly, vegetable curry, pan-fried duck breast and lunchtime filled ciabattas. There is a beer and sausage festival on the Spring Bank Holiday and a cider festival on the Summer Bank Holiday.

Open all day all wk Closed 25 Dec **Food** Lunch Mon-Sat 12-2, Sun 12-9 Dinner Mon-Sat 6-9, Sun 12-9 ⊕ FREE HOUSE ◀ Timothy Taylor Landlord, Purity Mad Goose, Butcombe Bitter ♂ Thatchers, Westons Stowford Press, Black Rat Perry. **Facilities** Non-diners area ♦▮ Children's menu Children's portions Garden ⊼ Beer festival Cider festival Parking WiFi

PICK OF THE PUBS

Seagrave Arms

CHIPPING CAMPDEN   Map 10 SP13

tel: 01386 840192 **Friday St, Weston Subedge GL55 6QH**
email: info@seagravearms.co.uk
web: www.seagravearms.co.uk
dir: *From Moreton-in-Marsh A44 towards Evesham. 7m, right onto B4081 to Chipping Campden. Left at junct with High St. 0.5m, straight on at x-rds to Weston Subedge. Left at T-junct*

Restaurant and country inn under new ownership

Built as a farmhouse around 1740 and Grade II listed, the four-square, Cotswold-stone Seagrave Arms is approached between a display of neatly-trimmed, globe-shaped bushes in stone planters. Sympathetically restored, its previously large restaurant/bar space has been reconfigured so that the bar is, well, just a bar, with real ales from Cotswold, Hook Norton, Purity and Wye Valley breweries, a range of British bottled craft beers, and Hogan's traditional cider from the Malvern Hills. To eat you must head for the Dining Room, the former Games Room, or the sheltered courtyard. Local sourcing and sustainability are the basic tenets of the compact seasonal menus, thus asparagus from Evesham, pork from Gloucester Old Spot pigs, local venison and Dexter beef, and Cotswold lamb, with winter shoots providing pheasant,

wild duck and partridge. You could start with velouté of watercress and slow-cooked hen's egg; or pressed ham hock and chicken terrine with pickled vegetables, and continue with a main course of roast wood-pigeon with crispy leg, pancetta crumbs, leeks and poultry sauce; or Cornish pollock and squid with herb crust, almond purée and braised gem lettuce. Appealing desserts could be Muscovado sugar and star anise parfait with gingerbread ice cream; or a selection of Cotswold cheeses. The Sunday roasts prove to be very popular. A few miles away is Chipping Campden itself, notable for its elegant terraced high street dating from the 14th to the 17th century.

Open all day Closed Mon **Food** Lunch Tue-Sat 12-3, Sun 12-4 Dinner Tue-Sat 6-9 ⊕ FREE HOUSE ◀ Hook Norton, Cotswold, Purity, Wye Valley, Guest ale ☐ 13 ♂ Westons Stowford Press, Hogan's. **Facilities** ✿ (Bar Garden) ⚫ Children's portions Garden Parking WiFi

CHIPPING CAMPDEN
Map 10 SP13

The Bakers Arms

tel: 01386 840515 **Broad Campden GL55 6UR**
email: lutti.asf@live.co.uk
dir: *1m from Chipping Campden*

Sublime Cotswold pub with friendly welcome

Ease into the compact little bar here, squeeze into a space near the eye-catching inglenook and live the Cotswold dream, with local Stanney Bitter mirroring the colour of the mellow thatched stone cottages in this picture-postcard hamlet. The patio, terrace and garden are all ideal on summer evenings in this most tranquil spot, lost amidst lanes and tracks below tree-fringed hilltops. The traditional, well-considered menu may offer a creamy beetroot risotto starter with chicken, ham and leek pie or lamb shank to follow; the intimate dressed-stone walled restaurant area is a peaceful retreat from the popular bar.

Open 11.30-2.30 5.30-11 (Fri-Sat 11.30-11 Sun 12-10.30) Closed 25 Dec, Mon L (ex BH) **Food** Lunch Tue-Fri 12-2, Sat 12-2.30, Sun 12-3 Dinner Mon-Thu 6-8.30, Fri-Sat 6-9 ⊕ FREE HOUSE ◀ Stanway Stanney Bitter, Wickwar, Wye Valley, North Cotswold Windrush ♂ Thatchers Heritage. **Facilities** Non-diners area ♣ (Bar Garden) ♦♦ Children's menu Children's portions Play area Garden ⋈ Parking WiFi ⊶ (notice required)

Eight Bells
PICK OF THE PUBS

tel: 01386 840371 **Church St GL55 6JG**
email: neilhargreaves@bellinn.fsnet.co.uk web: www.eightbellsinn.co.uk
dir: *In town centre*

Tranquil town inn with finest Cotswold hospitality

There's a golden glow both inside and outside of this glorious, hanging basket bedecked Cotswold inn. The mellow Ham stone was recycled about 400 years ago from an earlier inn, which originated in medieval times when the set of church bells was stored here prior to hanging. The cobbled entranceway leads into two beamed bars with open fireplaces and, in the floor of one, a surviving priest's hole; rough-hewn stone walls add further period character. Outside is an enclosed courtyard and terraced garden overlooking the almshouses and church. Beers such as Goffs Jouster and Hook Norton Hooky are sourced from the Cotswolds; in a similar vein the produce of these limestone hills and vales is used in many of the seasonally-adjusted dishes from the kitchen. Anticipate roasted loin of Gloucester Old Spots pork with all the trimmings; or seared lamb's liver on bubble-and-squeak with rich onion gravy. A specials board includes fish and seafood dishes.

Open all day all wk 12-11 (Sun 12-10.30) Closed 25 Dec **Food** Lunch Mon-Thu 12-2, Fri-Sat 12-2.30, Sun 12-9 Dinner Mon-Thu 6.30-9, Fri-Sat 6.30-9.30, Sun 12-9 ⊕ FREE HOUSE ◀ Hook Norton Hooky Bitter, Purity Pure UBU & Gold, Goffs Jouster, Wye Valley HPA ♂ Westons Old Rosie, 1st Quality & Stowford Press. ♚ 8 **Facilities** Non-diners area ♣ (Bar Garden) ♦♦ Children's menu Children's portions Garden ⋈ WiFi ⊶ (notice required)

The Kings ★★★★ RR ◉◉
PICK OF THE PUBS

tel: 01386 840256 **The Square GL55 6AW**
email: info@kingscampden.co.uk web: www.kingscampden.co.uk
dir: *Phone for detailed directions*

Wide choice of dining options in charming town centre pub

Facing the square of one of England's prettiest towns, this sympathetically restored old townhouse is packed with character, the oldest parts including the 16th-century stone mullioned windows on the first floor. The bar offers at least two real ales, including local North Cotswold Windrush, as well as daily papers and traditional pub games, but no noisy gaming machines. Bar snacks include a good range of sandwiches and baguettes, while main meals are served in the informal bar brasserie or more formal two AA-Rosette restaurant overlooking the square. The packed menu offers some imaginative delights: pressed ham hock roulade, pickled vegetables and Scotch quail's egg; fillet of pollock, violet potato gnocchi, samphire, saffron and crab velouté; and chargrilled vegetable tian with mozzarella arancini. The large grassed garden and dining terrace is surprising to find in a town centre pub. Individually decorated bedrooms offer period features with plenty of modern comforts.

Open all day all wk 7am-11pm (Sat-Sun 8am-11pm) **Food** Lunch all wk 12-2.30 Dinner all wk 6.30-9.30 Av main course £10 Set menu available Restaurant menu available all wk ⊕ FREE HOUSE ◀ Hook Norton Hooky Bitter, North Cotswold Windrush ♂ Thatchers Gold. ♚ 10 **Facilities** Non-diners area ♦♦ Children's menu Children's portions Garden Outside area ⋈ Parking WiFi ⊶ (notice required) **Rooms** 19

Noel Arms Hotel
PICK OF THE PUBS

tel: 01386 840317 **High St GL55 6AT**
email: reception@noelarmshotel.com
dir: *On High St, opposite Town Hall*

Delightful inn with its own curry club

The Noel Arms is one of the oldest hotels in the Cotswolds, a place where traditional appeal has been successfully preserved and interwoven seamlessly with contemporary comforts. Charles II reputedly stayed in this golden Cotswold-stone 16th-century coaching inn. It was through the carriage arch that packhorse trains used to carry bales of wool, the source of Chipping Campden's prosperity, to Bristol and Southampton. Absorb these details of the hotel's history while sipping a pint of Butty Bach in front of the log fire in Dover's Bar; read the papers over a coffee and pastry in the coffee shop; and enjoy brasserie-style food in the restaurant. An alternative to the modern English dishes is brought by Indunil Upatissa who creates his trademark curries daily, and enthusiasts arrive for his Curry Club on the last Thursday evening of every month.

Open all day all wk **Food** Lunch all wk 12-2 Dinner all wk 6-9.30 ⊕ FREE HOUSE ◀ Wye Valley Butty Bach, Noel Arms Ale (pub's own), Guest ale ♂ Westons Stowford Press. ♚ **Facilities** Non-diners area ♣ (Bar) ♦♦ Children's menu Children's portions Outside area ⋈ Parking WiFi ⊶

Seagrave Arms
PICK OF THE PUBS

See Pick of the Pubs on page 199

The Volunteer Inn

tel: 01386 840688 **Lower High St GL55 6DY**
email: info@thevolunteerinn.net
dir: *From Shipston on Stour take B4035 to Chipping Campden*

Cotswold character and cuisine with a twist

The beautiful, honey-coloured Cotswold stone glowing beside Chipping Campden's main street continues within; the convivial, log-fire warmed stone floored bar a welcoming retreat for guests hunting through the town's antique shops or pausing on a stroll along the Cotswold Way footpath. Once a recruiting centre for volunteer militia, today's clients sign on for some very interesting dishes from the Maharaja Restaurant located here; Jalali hash is a roasted duck, red onion and peppers combination, or perhaps venison tikka would be the dish to try with a pint of Doom Bar. The grassy beer garden is a quiet town centre retreat.

Open all wk Mon-Thu 3-12 (Fri-Sun 11am-late) **Food** Contact pub for details ⊕ FREE HOUSE ◀ Sharp's Doom Bar ♂ Westons Stowford Press. **Facilities** Non-diners area ♦ Children's portions Play area Family room Garden WiFi ▭

CIRENCESTER
Map 5 SP00

The Crown of Crucis ★★★ HL
PICK OF THE PUBS

tel: 01285 851806 **Ampney Crucis GL7 5RS**
email: reception@thecrownofcrucis.co.uk **web:** www.thecrownofcrucis.co.uk
dir: On A417 to Lechlade, 2m E of Cirencester

Quintessential Cotswolds coaching inn

Five minutes' out of Cirencester, overlooking a cricket green, is this 16th-century former coaching inn, with Ampney Brook meandering past its lawns. It derives its name from the 'crucis' or ancient cross in the churchyard. Although clearly modernised, the interior still feels old, and the traditional beams and log fires help to create a warm, friendly atmosphere, especially in the bar where Crown Bitter and Wickwar are among the real ales, and some 17 wines are sold by the glass. Sandwiches, salads, pastas and grills are served all day here, while in the restaurant the fine-dining evening menu may start with garlic mushrooms on toasted home-made brioche; or scallops, black pudding, pancetta and pine nuts. To follow, try lamb tagine with couscous; pistachio-crusted sea bass fillets with spring onion mash; or broccoli and cream cheese bake. The lunch menu is similar, but has added specials, such as omelettes and ploughman's.

Open all day all wk Closed 25 Dec **Food** Lunch all wk 12-5 Dinner all wk 5-10 ⊕ FREE HOUSE ◀ Crown Bitter, Sharp's Doom Bar & Seasonal ales, Wickwar ♂ Westons Stowford Press. ▾ 17 **Facilities** Non-diners area ♦ (Bar Garden) ♦ Children's menu Children's portions Garden ⊨ Parking WiFi ▭ (notice required) **Rooms** 25

The Fleece at Cirencester ★★★★★ INN

tel: 01285 658507 **41 Dyer St, Market Place GL7 2NZ**
email: relax@thefleececirencester.co.uk **web:** www.thefleececirencester.co.uk
dir: In centre of Cirencester

Cotswolds dining pub with royal links

There has been a change of hands at this 17th-century Cirencester coaching inn, once visited by Charles II. Newly refurbished, the bar, restaurant and lounge retain their original charms with wooden beams, a log fire and an outdoor courtyard for long summer days. A range of Thwaites beers are on offer at the bar, including Lancaster Bomber, and the extensive menu features deli boards; chargrilled steaks; and mains of roasted butternut squash risotto; or blade of beef cooked in ale with parsnip and potato mash. There are 28 bedrooms if you want to extend your visit and explore the Cotswolds.

Open all day all wk **Food** Lunch all wk 12-6 Dinner Mon-Sat 6-9.30, Sun 6-8.30 ⊕ THWAITES INNS OF CHARACTER ◀ Wainwright, Lancaster Bomber & Signature Ales, Cotswold Lion Golden Fleece, Guest ales ♂ Kingstone Press. ▾ 10 **Facilities** Non-diners area ♦ (Bar Outside area) ♦ Children's menu Children's portions Outside area ⊨ Parking WiFi **Rooms** 28

See advert on page 202

CLEARWELL
Map 4 SO50

The Wyndham Arms ★★★ HL ◉

tel: 01594 833666 **The Cross GL16 8JT**
email: dine@thewyndhamhotel.co.uk **web:** www.thewyndhamhotel.co.uk
dir: M4 junct 21 onto M48 for Chepstow. Exit at junct 2 signed A48/Chepstow. At rdbt take A48 towards Gloucester. Take B4228 to Coleford & The Forest of Dean. 10m, through St Briavels, in 2m Clearwell signed on left

Cosy hotel between the Forest of Dean and the Wye Valley

Open log-burners and oak flooring create the sort of rustic charm that's ideal for enjoying a pint of Kingstone's real ales, brewed at nearby Tintern, or Severn Sider Cider from Newnham. In the domed stone vaults of the Old Spot Country Restaurant, the AA has awarded a Rosette for the classic British food, as in smoked fish pâté and potato salad; Wyndham raised Gloucester Old Spots ham and turkey pie; liver and bacon, onion gravy and crushed potatoes; bread and butter pudding; and apple crumble and custard. The Wyndham's accommodation is perfect for Clearwell Castle, a popular wedding venue.

Open all day all wk Closed early Jan **Food** Lunch Mon-Sat 12-2, Sun 12-2.30 Dinner all wk 6.30-9 Av main course £12 Restaurant menu available all wk ⊕ FREE HOUSE ◀ Kingstone Humpty's Fuddle IPA, Kingstone Gold Fine Ale ♂ Severn Sider Cider. ▾ 10 **Facilities** Non-diners area ♦ (Bar Outside area) ♦ Children's menu Children's portions Outside area ⊨ Parking WiFi **Rooms** 18

CLEEVE HILL
Map 10 SO92

The Rising Sun ★★★ INN

tel: 01242 676281 **GL52 3PX**
email: 9210@greeneking.co.uk **web:** www.oldenglish.co.uk
dir: On B4632, 4m N of Cheltenham

Hilltop inn offering stunning vistas

On a clear day you can see south Wales from this Victorian property on Cleeve Hill, which also boasts views across Cheltenham and the Malverns. Whether you are staying overnight or just popping in to relax, settle in the nicely modernised bar or, in summer, out in the garden, which is well furnished with trestle tables and benches. The wide ranging menu includes sandwiches, wraps, ciabattas, steaks and grills, burgers, jacket potatoes and roasts on Sundays.

Open all day all wk **Food** Contact pub for details ⊕ GREENE KING ◀ IPA, Abbot Ale ♂ Aspall. ▾ 15 **Facilities** Non-diners area ♦ Children's menu Children's portions Family room Garden ⊨ Parking WiFi ▭ (notice required) **Rooms** 24

CLIFFORD'S MESNE
Map 10 SO72

The Yew Tree
PICK OF THE PUBS

tel: 01531 820719 **GL18 1JS**
email: unwind@yewtreeinn.com **web:** www.yewtreeinn.com
dir: *From Newent High Street follow signs to Clifford's Mesne. Pub at far end of village on road to Glasshouse*

Hard-to-find pub with stunning views and glorious home cooking

On the slopes of National Trust's May Hill, Gloucestershire's highest point, from where you can see the Welsh mountains, the Malvern Hills and the River Severn, you will find this former cider press tucked away down a little lane. The pub has a quarry-tiled floor and winter log fires, and offers a good choice of local real ales from breweries like Wye Valley and Cotswold Spring, and ciders from Lyne Down and Three Choirs. As for the food, the emphasis is on tasty home cooking using seasonal local produce, with daily-changing menus and specials. Starters could include rustic pork terrine with crusty bread, or goats' cheese with rosemary crostini. For a main course, think about rump of Welsh lamb with dauphinoise potatoes, or perhaps Gloucester Old Spots loin steaks. Home-made desserts include fresh pineapple crumble. Time a visit for the October beer and cider festival.

Open 12-2.30 6-11 (Sun 12-5) Closed Mon, Tue L, Sun eve **Food** Lunch Wed-Sat 12-2, Sun 12-4 Dinner Tue-Sat 6-9 Av main course £15 ⊕ FREE HOUSE ◀ Wye Valley HPA, Cotswold Spring Stunner, Sharp's Own, Gloucester Mariner, Local ales ♂ Westons Stowford Press, Lyne Down, Severn Cider & Perry, Swallowfield Cider & Perry, Three Choirs. ♀ 12 **Facilities** Non-diners area ♣ (Bar Restaurant Garden) ♦♦ Children's menu Children's portions Play area Garden ⌂ Beer festival Cider festival Parking WiFi

COATES
Map 4 SO90

The Tunnel House Inn
PICK OF THE PUBS

See Pick of the Pubs on opposite page

COLESBOURNE
Map 10 SP01

The Colesbourne Inn

tel: 01242 870376 **GL53 9NP**
email: colesbourneinn@wadworth.co.uk
dir: *Midway between Cirencester & Cheltenham on A435*

Georgian country inn full of character

This handsome, stone-built inn is just a short meadow walk from the source of the Thames; you can sit in the two-acre grounds with a pint of Wadworth 6X and savour the glorious country views. Dating back to 1827, the inn oozes historic charm and character with its original beams and roaring log fires aplenty. The seasonal menus combine traditional pub classics, including fish and chips and mushy peas, with modern ideas, perhaps confit duck leg with orange, pomegranate and ginger jus; or naturally smoked haddock and spring onion fishcake with creamed vegetables and fries.

Open all day all wk ⊕ WADWORTH ◀ 6X, Henry's Original IPA, Horizon ♂ Westons Stowford Press. **Facilities** ♦♦ Children's portions Garden Parking WiFi

COWLEY
Map 10 SO91

The Green Dragon Inn ★★★★ INN
PICK OF THE PUBS

See Pick of the Pubs on page 204

PICK OF THE PUBS

The Tunnel House Inn

COATES   Map 4 SO90

tel: 01285 770280
Tarlton Rd GL7 6PW
email: info@tunnelhouse.com
web: www.tunnelhouse.com
dir: *A433 from Cirencester towards Tetbury, 2m, right towards Coates, follow brown inn signs*

Delightful Cotswold village inn

Down an unmade track, this rural inn was built for the navvies who spent five years constructing the two-mile long Sapperton Tunnel on the now-disused Thames and Severn Canal. The inn overlooks the entrance to the tunnel which hasn't been navigated by a barge since 1911. Three winter log fires warm the curio-filled bar, where oddities include an upside-down table suspended from the ceiling. Food, all home cooked, is served every day from noon onwards and you may eat in the bar or restaurant, starting perhaps with pheasant, lardons and plum mixed leaf salad with redcurrant and balsamic reduction; or potted salt beef served with toasted brioche, pickled onions and gherkins. A typical spring menu might offer main courses of goats' cheese and thyme-stuffed chicken breast, wrapped in smoked bacon, with creamy red pesto linguine; baked smoked haddock stuffed with spinach and pine nuts on a bed of lemon and thyme risotto; and wild mushroom, leek and blue cheese puff

pastry pie with sweet potato wedges and parsnip crisps. Apple and red berry crumble with crème anglaise may appear on the desserts list, while Cotswold ice creams almost certainly will. At lunchtime eat more simply with a hot panini or a mature cheddar or Stilton ploughman's. The garden is tailor-made for relaxing with a pint of one of the mostly local real ales — typically from Uley, Wye Valley and Hook Norton breweries — or a Somerset or Herefordshire real cider, while enjoying the views over the fields. A beer and cider festival in August, a children's play area and delightful walks add to the pub's popularity.

Open all day all wk noon-late **Food** 12-9.30 ⊕ FREE HOUSE 🍺 Uley Old Spot & Bitter, Wye Valley Bitter, Stroud Budding Pale Ale, Hook Norton, Butcombe ⚖ Healey's Cornish Rattler, Black Rat, Westons Wyld Wood Organic.
Facilities 🐾 (All areas) 🚻 Children's menu Children's portions Play area Family room Garden Beer festival Cider festival Outside area Parking WiFi 🚐

PICK OF THE PUBS

The Green Dragon Inn ★★★★★ INN

COWLEY	Map 10 SO91

tel: 01242 870271
Cockleford GL53 9NW
email: green-dragon@buccaneer.co.uk
web: www.green-dragon-inn.co.uk
dir: *Phone for detailed directions*

Cotswolds inn featuring Mouseman furniture

With a pretty rose- and creeper-covered Cotswold-stone façade, this building was recorded as an inn in 1675. However, it was 1710 before Robert Jones, a churchwarden, became the first landlord, splitting his time between pew and pump for the next 31 years. In summer the secluded patio garden overlooking a lake is an obvious spot to head for. Step inside the stone-flagged Mouse Bar and you will notice that each piece of English oak furniture features a carved mouse, the trademark of Robert Thompson, the Mouseman of Kilburn. He died in 1955, but North Yorkshire craftsmen continue the tradition. There's even one of the little beggars running along the edge of the bar in front of the Butcombe, Hook Norton and Sharp's beer pumps. Lunchtime light meals and sandwiches can be served on the patio, weather permitting. An evening dinner starter could be warm chicken liver and bacon salad with quail eggs and crispy croûtons; or butternut squash and cranberry risotto with parmesan shavings. Pan-fried tiger king prawns with a crayfish and pancetta risotto and mange-tout could follow; or oven-roasted duck breast with egg noodles and stir-fry vegetables in a plum and ginger sauce. Children are catered for with a range of favourites. The comfortable and individually furnished en suite bedrooms, and the St George's Suite (which has its own sitting room overlooking Cowley lakes), make the Green Dragon an ideal base for exploring the Cotswolds; the local Miserden Gardens and Chedworth Roman Villa should not be missed.

Open all day all wk Closed 25 Dec eve & 1 Jan eve **Food** Lunch Mon-Fri 12-2.30, Sat 12-3, Sun 12-3.30 Dinner all wk 6-10 Av main course £16 ⊕ FREE HOUSE/BUCCANEER 🍺 Hook Norton, Butcombe, Sharp's Doom Bar, Guest ale Ŏ Westons Stowford Press.
Facilities Non-diners area ⁑ Children's menu Outside area 🍴 Parking WiFi 🚐
Rooms 9

CRANHAM
Map 10 SO81

The Black Horse Inn

tel: 01452 812217 **GL4 8HP**
dir: *A46 towards Stroud, follow signs for Cranham*

A great rest-stop for walkers

Near the Cotswold Way and the Benedictine Prinknash Abbey, in a small village surrounded by woodland and commons, this inn is popular with walkers, the cricket team and visiting Morris dancers. Mostly home-cooked traditional pub food includes grilled lamb chops; roast pork, beef or turkey; kleftiko (half-shoulder of slow-cooked lamb in red wine, lemon and herbs); haggis and bacon; fresh trout with garlic and herb butter; and roast vegetable, cranberry and goats' cheese nut roast. Among the real ales are Stroud Tom Long, Sharp's and Otter, and there are good ciders too in the cosy, open-fire-warmed bar.

Open 12-2 6.30-11 (Sun 12-2 8.30-11) Closed 25 Dec, Mon (ex BHs L) **Food** Lunch Tue-Sun 12-2 Dinner Tue-Sat 6.30-9 ⊕ FREE HOUSE ◀ Sharp's Doom Bar, Otter, Stroud Tom Long, Guest ales ♂ Thatchers Gold & Cheddar Valley, Westons Stowford Press & Country Perry. ♟ 8 **Facilities** Non-diners area ♣ (Bar Outside area) ♦♦ Children's portions Outside area ⋈ Parking ⬛ (notice required)

DURSLEY
Map 4 ST79

The Old Spot Inn
PICK OF THE PUBS

tel: 01453 542870 **Hill Rd GL11 4JQ**
email: enquiries@oldspotinn.co.uk
dir: *From Tetbury on A4135 (or Uley on B4066) into Dursley, round Town Hall. Straight on at lights towards bus station, pub behind bus station. Or from Cam to lights in Dursley immediately prior to pedestrianised street. Right towards bus station*

Excellent beer at popular village local

This classic 18th-century free house is a former real ale pub of the year, so it's worth visiting to sample the regularly changing, tip-top real ales on handpump and to savour the cheerful buzzing atmosphere, as The Old Spot is a cracking community local. It sits smack on the Cotswold Way and was once three terraced farm cottages known as 'pig row.' It's apt, then that it should take its name from the Gloucestershire Old Spots pig. As well as organising three real ale festivals a year, landlord Steve Herbert organises a host of events, including brewery visits, cricket matches and celebrity chef nights. Devoid of modern-day intrusions, the rustic and traditional low-beamed bars are havens of peace, with just the comforting sound of crackling log fires and the hubbub of chatting locals filling the rambling little rooms. Food is wholesome and home made, ranging from ploughman's lunches and doorstep sandwiches to a pork and apple burger; haddock and chive fishcakes; or chicken fajitas. Puddings include treacle tart and white chocolate cheesecake. There's also a pretty garden for summer alfresco sipping.

Open all day all wk 11-11 (Sun 12-11) **Food** Lunch all wk 12-3 Dinner Mon only 6-9 ⊕ FREE HOUSE ◀ Old Ric, Butcombe, Otter, Guest ales ♂ Westons 1st Quality & Old Rosie, Pheasant Plucker. ♟ 8 **Facilities** Non-diners area ♣ (Bar Garden) ♦♦ Children's portions Family room Garden ⋈ Beer festival Parking WiFi ⬛

EBRINGTON
Map 10 SP14

The Ebrington Arms ★★★★ INN ⓐⓐ
PICK OF THE PUBS

tel: 01386 593223 **GL55 6NH**
email: reservations@theebringtonarms.co.uk **web:** www.theebringtonarms.co.uk
dir: *From Chipping Campden on B4035 towards Shipston on Stour. Left to Ebrington signed after 0.5m*

Home-brewed ales at this quintessential village pub

Built in 1640, this award-winning Cotswold gem has an abundance of character thanks to the heavy beams and original flagstones in both the bar and Old

Bakehouse dining room; the large inglenook fireplaces recall the building's days as the village bakery. Very much the hub of community life, lucky locals (and visitors too, of course) are spoilt for choice. Now brewing three of its own beers: Yubberton Yubby, Yawnie and YPA, which sit alongside guests such as Stroud and Cotswold Brewing's cider and lagers. Chef James Nixon grew up in the area, so knows where to find freshly harvested, organic produce, some of it from the fields around the pub. Recognised with two AA Rosettes, the pub's carte offers the likes of Cornish crab cake with aïoli, followed by roasted cod with basil mash. Visit in early October for a beer festival, or later in the month for a cider pressing day.

Open all day all wk noon-close **Food** Lunch Mon-Sat 12-2.30, Sun 12-3.30 Dinner Mon-Thu 6-9, Fri-Sat 6-9.30, Sun 6-8.30 ⊕ FREE HOUSE ◀ Stroud Budding Pale Ale, North Cotswold Windrush Ale, Prescott Hill Climb, Yubberton Yubby Bitter, Yawnie & YPA ♂ Cotswold. ♟ 9 **Facilities** Non-diners area ♣ (Bar Garden) ♦♦ Children's menu Children's portions Garden ⋈ Beer festival Parking WiFi ⬛ (notice required) **Rooms** 3

EWEN
Map 4 SU09

The Wild Duck ★★★★ INN

tel: 01285 770310 **GL7 6BY**
email: duckreservations@aol.com **web:** www.thewilдduckinn.co.uk
dir: *From Cirencester take A429 towards Malmesbury. At Kemble left to Ewen. Inn in village centre*

Cotswold pub with an excellent choice of ales

Children and canine companions are welcome at this inn, built from honeyed Cotswold stone in 1563; the source of the Thames and the Cotswold Water Park (where there's lots of walks) are nearby. Family-owned for more than 20 years, the pub has oil portraits, log fires, oak beams and a resident ghost. Deep red walls give the Post Horn bar a warm feel, as does the extensive choice of real ales. The rambling restaurant has a lunch menu of wholesome pub favourites, while dinner may extend to wild duck antipasto, followed by luxury fish bouillabaisse. Enclosed courtyard garden. For details of the summer beer festival contact the inn.

Open all day all wk Closed 25 Dec (eve) **Food** Lunch Mon-Fri 12-2, Sat-Sun all day Dinner all wk 6.30-10 ⊕ FREE HOUSE ◀ The Wild Duck Duckpond Bitter, Butcombe Bitter, Wye Valley Dorothy Goodbody's Country Ale, Greene King Abbot Ale, Morland Old Speckled Hen, Bath Gem ♂ Ashton Press, Westons Stowford Press, Aspall. ♟ 32 **Facilities** Non-diners area ♣ (Bar Garden) ♦♦ Children's menu Children's portions Garden ⋈ Beer festival Parking WiFi ⬛ (notice required) **Rooms** 12

FRAMPTON MANSELL
Map 4 SO90

The Crown Inn ★★★★ INN   PICK OF THE PUBS

tel: 01285 760601 **GL6 8JG**
email: enquiries@thecrowninn-cotswolds.co.uk **web:** www.thecrowninn-cotswolds.co.uk
dir: *A419 halfway between Cirencester & Stroud*

A handsome Cotswold inn perfect for whiling away a few hours

Once a simple cider house, this classic 17th-century Cotswold-stone inn is full of old-world charm, with honey-coloured stone walls, beams and open fireplaces where logs blaze in winter. Right in the heart of the village, it is surrounded by the peace and quiet of the Golden Valley. Plenty of seating in the large garden allows for contemplative supping during the warmer months. Gloucestershire beers, such as Stroud Organic and Laurie Lee's Bitter, are usually showcased alongside others from the region, and a good choice of wines by the glass is served in the restaurant and three inviting bars. Fresh local food with lots of seasonal specials is the carte's promise. A black pudding Scotch egg with home-made brown sauce is a tasty starter, to be followed perhaps by pork tenderloin with a bacon, wholegrain mustard and honey stuffing. For non-meat eaters, the vegetarian cottage pie with lamb's lettuce and pomegranate salad is ideal.

Open all day all wk 12-11 Closed 25 Dec **Food** Lunch Mon-Sat 12-2.30, Sun 12-8.30 Dinner Mon-Sat 6-9.30, Sun 12-8.30 Av main course £10 ⊕ FREE HOUSE ◀ Butcombe Bitter, Uley Laurie Lee's Bitter, Stroud Organic, Guest ales Ö Westons Stowford Press, Cotswold Cider, Sherston. ₸ 16 **Facilities** Non-diners area ✿ (Bar Restaurant Garden) ♦ Children's portions Garden ⊟ Parking WiFi ⚐ **Rooms** 12

GLOUCESTER
Map 10 SO81

Queens Head

tel: 01452 301882 **Tewkesbury Rd, Longford GL2 9EJ**
email: queenshead@aol.com
dir: *On A38 (Tewkesbury to Gloucester road) in Longford*

A cracking line-up at the locals' bar

This pretty 250-year-old half-timbered pub/restaurant is just out of town, but cannot be missed in summer when it is festooned with hanging baskets. Inside, a lovely old flagstone-floored locals' bar proffers a great range of real ales and ciders. The owners believe in giving their diners high-quality, freshly prepared food that is great value for money. Menus tempt with modern British food: duck and orange pâté; braised shoulder of Herefordshire beef; and the ever-popular Longford lamb – slow-roasted in chef's own secret gravy. Smart casual dress and no children under 12 years.

Open all wk 11-3 5.30-11 **Food** Lunch all wk 12-2 Dinner all wk 6.30-9.30 ⊕ FREE HOUSE ◀ Wye Valley Butty Bach, Sharp's Doom Bar, Skinner's Betty Stogs, Otter, Butcombe Gold Ö Ashton Press, Westons Stowford Press. ₸ **Facilities** Non-diners area Parking WiFi

---

GREAT BARRINGTON
Map 10 SP21

The Fox Inn   PICK OF THE PUBS

tel: 01451 844385 **OX18 4TB**
email: info@foxinnbarrington.com
dir: *From Burford take A40 towards Northleach. In 3m right signed The Barringtons, pub approx 0.5m on right*

An owner's dream of a pub come true

Set in the picturesque Windrush Valley, this busy centuries-old former coaching house is popular with race-goers visiting Cheltenham. It's a quintessential Cotswold inn built of mellow local stone proffering a range of well-kept Donnington beers and a concise wine list. Changes made a couple of years ago, including to the menu, have borne fruit, so now the conservatory dining bar, barbecue and alfresco eating area, and the garden all contribute to the friendly and relaxed atmosphere.

Landlord Paul Porter's enthusiasm for tasty food shines through with the menu's descriptions: examples are a 'long and slightly spicy' Greek shish kebab with cooling mint raita; and a 'mega knuckle of Cotswold lamb slow roasted to melting off the bone' with rosemary sautéed potatoes. Regular events include curry buffets, special anniversaries and the Sunday carvery. The garden overlooks the River Windrush; on warm days it's a perfect base for lovely walks and cycle rides.

Open all day all wk 11am-close **Food** Lunch Mon-Fri 12-2.30, Sat-Sun all day Dinner Mon-Fri 6.30-9.30, Sat-Sun all day ⊕ DONNINGTON ◀ BB, SBA Ö Westons Stowford Press & Perry, Addlestones. **Facilities** Non-diners area ✿ (Bar Garden) ♦ Children's portions Garden ⊟ Parking WiFi ⚐

HAM
Map 4 ST69

NEW The Salutation Inn

tel: 01453 810284 **GL13 9QH**
dir: *S of Berkeley towards Stone*

All that a good village free house should be

According to landlord Peter Tiley, "something intangible" makes The Sally special. But to focus on the tangible elements, there's the five, mostly local, real ales, eight real ciders and heritage pub games in the cosy, log-fired bar. Pub grub lunches are of the ham, egg and chips, and faggots and mash variety. Evening meals are served only on Guest Chef Nights (Mondays), when Peter's friends, Polly and Craig, cook a 'whole hog' dish one week, a 'non-pork' dish the next, and on Fridays and Saturdays, when Peter knocks up a beef or perhaps venison stew.

Open 12-2.30 5-11 (Sat 12-11 Sun 12-10.30) Closed Mon L **Food** Lunch Tue-Sun 12-2.30 Dinner Mon 6.30-9.30 ⊕ FREE HOUSE ◀ Butcombe Bitter, Bristol Beer Factory, Cotswold Spring, Severn Vale, Wye Valley Ö Gwatkins, Tom Olivers, Barnes & Adams. **Facilities** Non-diners area Garden ⊟ Parking WiFi ⚐ (notice required)

HINTON
Map 4 ST77

The Bull at Hinton   PICK OF THE PUBS

tel: 0117 937 2332 **SN14 8HG**
email: reservations@thebullathinton.co.uk
dir: *From M4 junct 18, A46 to Bath 1m, turn right 1m, down hill. Pub on right*

Village inn on the southern edge of the Cotswolds

Should you run into a lady in grey in this 17th-century, stone-built former farmhouse and dairy, see if she disappears through the wall before asking for a pint - she might be the resident ghost. Her possible existence is a clue to the pub's character, with beams in the bar and dining room, flagstone floors, inglenook fireplaces, old pews and big oak tables. Meals are freshly prepared from ingredients from carefully chosen, mostly local, producers and suppliers, meaning that a typical candlelit dinner might feature blue cheese soufflé, poached pear and peanut dressing; followed by supreme of chicken with spinach and mozzarella, wrapped in Parma ham; and finally Tia Maria and coffee crème brûlée. A chalkboard offers imaginative specials, such as duo of pheasant with sautéed new potatoes, wilted spinach and rosemary jus. The south-facing terrace and garden is where to be when the sun's out.

Open 12-3 6-12 (Sat-Sun & BH open all day) Closed Mon L (ex BHs) **Food** Lunch Tue-Fri 12-2, Sat 12-9.30, Sun 12-8.30 (BHs 12-8) Dinner Mon-Fri 6-9, Sat 12-9.30, Sun 12-8.30 (BHs 12-8) ⊕ WADWORTH ◀ 6X, Henry's Original IPA, The Bishop's Tipple & Summersault, Guest ale Ö Thatchers Gold, Westons Stowford Press. ₸ 11 **Facilities** Non-diners area ✿ (Bar Garden) ♦ Children's menu Play area Garden ⊟ Parking WiFi ⚐ (notice required)

LECHLADE ON THAMES　　　　　　　Map 5 SU29

The Trout Inn

tel: 01367 252313 **St Johns Bridge GL7 3HA**
email: chefpjw@aol.com
dir: *A40 onto A361 then A417. From M4 junct 15, A419, then A361 & A417 to Lechlade*

Extensive menu served in an ancient inn

When workmen constructed a new bridge over the Thames in 1220, they built an almshouse to live in. It became an inn in 1472, and its flagstone floors and beams now overflow into the old boathouse. The extensive menu features meat, fish and vegetarian options, as well as pizzas, filled jacket potatoes and burgers. This family-friendly pub offers smaller portions for children, who also have their own separate menu. The large garden often hosts live jazz, an annual steam week and a beer festival, both in June, plus a riverfolk festival in July.

Open all wk 10-3 6-11 (summer all wk 10am-11pm) Closed 25 Dec **Food** Lunch all wk 12-2 Dinner all wk 7-10 ⊕ ENTERPRISE INNS ◀ Courage Best, Sharp's Doom Bar & Cornish Coaster, Guest ales. ¶ 15 **Facilities** Non-diners area ❤ (Bar Garden) ❢ Children's menu Children's portions Play area Family room Garden Beer festival Parking WiFi ☞ (notice required)

LEIGHTERTON　　　　　　　　　　　Map 4 ST89

The Royal Oak

tel: 01666 890250 **1 The Street GL8 8UN**
email: info@royaloakleighterton.co.uk
dir: *M4 junct 18, A46 towards Stroud. After Dunkirk continue on A46. Right signed Leighterton*

Majors on local seasonal produce

Set in a picture-postcard Cotswold village, close to Westonbirt Arboretum, Paul and Antonia Whitbread's pub thrives as a popular dining venue. The bright, contemporary bar and dining room successfully blends exposed beams, open fires and antiques with modern furnishings. Enjoy a pint of Bath Ales or Hook Norton ale with a lunchtime sandwich or platter or dive into the main menu. Food is classic British and everything is made on the premises from local ingredients. In addition to pub classics (fish and chips, burgers and pies) typically, tuck into lobster ravioli and vermouth butter sauce; game casserole with juniper berry dumplings; and ginger and cinnamon sponge, warm poached apples and whipped cream.

Open all wk 12-3 5.30-11 (Sat 12-11 Sun 12-10.30) **Food** Lunch Mon-Fri 12-2, Sat 12-2.30, Sun 12-3 Dinner Mon-Thu 6-9, Fri-Sat 6-9.30 Set menu available ⊕ FREE HOUSE ◀ Bath Ales Gem, Hook Norton Hooky Bitter, Guest ales ♂ Westons Stowford Press, Sherston. ¶ 10 **Facilities** Non-diners area ❤ (Bar Garden) ❢ Children's menu Children's portions Garden Beer festival Parking WiFi ☞ (notice required)

LONGHOPE　　　　　　　　　　　　Map 10 SO61

The Glasshouse Inn

tel: 01452 830529 **May Hill GL17 0NN**
email: glasshouseinn@gmail.com
dir: *From A40 approx 8m SE of Ross-on-Wye, follow signs for May Hill. Through May Hill to pub on left*

Gimmick-free traditional pub

The Glasshouse gets its name from Dutch glassmakers who settled locally in the 16th century but its origins can be traced back further, to 1450. A gimmick-free traditional pub, it is located in a fabulous rural setting with a country garden and

an elegant interior. The inn serves a range of real ales including Butcombe and Sharp's Doom Bar, plus home-cooked dishes such as fish pie; cod and chips; beef curry; steak and kidney served in Yorkshire puddings; and chilli. At lunch you can also choose from a range of sandwiches, ploughman's lunches or basket meals of chips with the likes of scampi or sausage. There's a choice of roasts at Sunday lunch – booking advisable.

Open 11.30-3 7-11 (Sun 12-3) Closed Sun eve **Food** Lunch all wk 12-2 (booking required for parties of 6 or more) Dinner Mon-Sat 7-9 (booking required for parties of 6 or more) ⊕ FREE HOUSE ◀ Sharp's Doom Bar, Butcombe ♂ Westons Stowford Press. ¶ 12 **Facilities** Garden ☰ Parking WiFi

---

LOWER ODDINGTON　　　　　　　　Map 10 SP22

The Fox　　　　　　　　　　　▐ PICK OF THE PUBS ▌

tel: 01451 870555 & 870666 **GL56 0UR**
email: info@foxinn.net
dir: *A436 from Stow-on-the-Wold, right to Lower Oddington*

Creeper-clad pub with a delightful garden

Set in a quintessential Cotswold village and dating back to the 17th century, this is a stone-built, creeper-clad free house. The interior boasts polished flagstone floors, beams, log fires and antique furniture that creates a period feel. The daily-changing menus take full advantage of fresh, local produce. Typical starters include spinach and parmesan risotto; baked crab gratin; and beetroot, feta and pine nut salad. Followed by mains of pan-fried calves' liver, mash and onion and bacon gravy; and honey and mustard baked ham with parsley sauce. In summer, there's a terrace for alfresco dining, as well as a pretty, traditional cottage garden.

Open all wk 12-2.30 6-11 or 12 (Sun 12-3.30 7-10.30) Closed 25 Dec **Food** Lunch all wk 12-2.30 Dinner Mon-Fri 6.30-9.30, Sat 6.30-10, Sun 7-9 ⊕ FREE HOUSE ◀ Hook Norton Hooky Bitter, Donnington SBA & Gold, Dark Star The Art of Darkness, Prescott, Wickwar Rite Flanker, Rotating ales ♂ Cotswold. ¶ 15 **Facilities** Non-diners area ❢ Children's portions Garden ☰ Parking WiFi

---

MARSHFIELD　　　　　　　　　　　Map 4 ST77

The Catherine Wheel

tel: 01225 892220 **39 High St SN14 8LR**
email: roo@thecatherinewheel.co.uk
dir: *M4 junct 18, A46 signed Bath. Left onto A420 signed Chippenham. Right signed Marshfield*

Traditional Cotswold inn with sunny patio

On the edge of the Cotswolds, this mainly 17th-century inn has the expected exposed brickwork and large open fireplaces offset by a simple, stylish decor. Menus are also simple and well presented, with favourites at lunchtime including steak and kidney pie; and jacket potatoes. In the evening look forward to potted smoked mackerel, lemon and herb pâté or tomato and goats' cheese tartlets, followed perhaps by venison stew and thyme dumplings or fish pie. A small but sunny patio is a lovely spot for a summertime pint of Butcombe Bitter or Thatchers cider.

Open all day all wk **Food** Lunch Mon-Fri 12-2, Sat-Sun 12-3 Dinner Mon-Thu 6.30-9, Fri-Sat 6.30-9.30, Sun 6-8.30 Set menu available ⊕ FREE HOUSE ◀ Butcombe Bitter, Sharp's Doom Bar, Cotswold Spring Stunner ♂ Ashton Press, Thatchers. ¶ 10 **Facilities** Non-diners area ❤ (Bar Garden) ❢ Children's portions Garden ☰ Parking WiFi ☞ (notice required)

PICK OF THE PUBS

The Weighbridge Inn

MINCHINHAMPTON Map 4 S080

tel: 01453 832520 **GL6 9AL**
email: enquiries@weighbridgeinn.co.uk
web: www.weighbridgeinn.co.uk
dir: *On B4014 between Nailsworth & Avening*

Recommended for its freshly made pies

Parts of this whitewashed free house date back to the 17th century, when it stood adjacent to the original packhorse trail between Bristol and London. While the trail is now a footpath and bridleway, the road in front (now the B4014) became a turnpike in the 1820s. The innkeeper at the time ran both the pub and the weighbridge for the local woollen mills – serving jugs of ale in between making sure tolls were paid. Associated memorabilia and other rural artefacts from the time are displayed around the inn, which has been carefully renovated to retain original features, like exposed brick walls and open fires. Up in the restaurant, which used to be the hayloft, the old roof timbers reach almost to the floor. The inn prides itself on its decent ales and ciders, and the quality of its food, with everything cooked from scratch. Fish lovers could start with potted shrimps or a fish sharing board. Otherwise, the Mediterranean medley is sure to get the taste buds going. The hearty main courses include beef hot pot, broccoli

and cauliflower cannelloni, and chicken chasseur. Lighter meals are available as salads, omelettes, jacket potatoes and filled baguettes. The Weighbridge is also the home of 'the famous 2 in 1 pies', one half containing a filling of your choice from a selection of seven (such as pork, bacon and celery) and topped with pastry, the other half home-made cauliflower cheese – all cooked to order and available to take away or even bake at home. Typical desserts are banana crumble and chocolate cheesecake. From the patios and sheltered, landscaped garden the Cotswolds are in full view.

Open all day all wk 12-11 (Sun 12-10.30) Closed 25 Dec **Food** all wk 12-9.30 Av main course £10 ⊕ FREE HOUSE ◤ Wadworth 6X, Uley Old Spot, Palmers Best Bitter, Box Steam Chuffin Ale, Stroud Budding ⭗ Bath Ciders Bounders, Westons Rosie's Pig. ♟ 15 **Facilities** Non-diners area ❄ (Bar Restaurant Garden) ❤ Children's menu Children's portions Family room Garden ⊟ Parking WiFi ⇔ (notice required)

MARSHFIELD *continued*

The Lord Nelson Inn

tel: 01225 891820 **1 & 2 High St SN14 8LP**
email: enquiries@lordnelsonatmarshfield.com
dir: *M4 junct 18, A46 towards Bath. Left at Cold Ashton rdbt towards Marshfield & Chippenham*

Log fires in winter, patio in summer

In a conservation village on the edge of the Cotswolds and surrounded by wonderful walks, this 16th-century former coaching inn draws a loyal local crowd for good home-made food and quality cask ales. A spacious bar that provides a chance to mix with the locals, a candlelit restaurant, log fires in winter and a patio for summer use complete its attractions. With the food emphasis on simplicity and quality, the varied menus take in light bar lunches (ham, egg and chips), hearty evening dishes like pheasant with red wine and redcurrant gravy, and a very popular Sunday carvery.

Open all wk 12-2.30 5-11 (Fri-Sun 12-11) **Food** Lunch Mon-Sat 12-2, Sun 12-3 Dinner Mon-Sat 6.30-9, Sun 6.30-8.30 ⊕ ENTERPRISE INNS ◀ Bath Gem, Sharp's Doom Bar, Otter ♂ Thatchers Gold, Symonds. ☕ 9 **Facilities** Non-diners area ♦♦ Children's menu Children's portions Play area Garden ⌓ WiFi ☷ (notice required)

MEYSEY HAMPTON — Map 5 SP10

The Masons Arms

tel: 01285 850164 **28 High St GL7 5JT**
email: info@masonsarms.biz
dir: *6m E of Cirencester off A417, beside village green*

At the heart of village life

This is a quintessential 17th-century stone-built Cotswold inn, situated alongside the green in the heart of the village. The hub of the community and welcoming to visitors, it offers something for everyone, from a warming log fire in the large inglenook to the range of well-kept Arkell's ales and Westons cider served in the convivial beamed bar. Good value home-made food could include local smoked trout salad or Gloucestershire pork loin with chips. Worth noting if visiting the Cotswold Water Park nearby.

Open 12-2 5.30-11 (Sat 12-11 Sun 12-2.30 5.30-8.30 winter 12-5) Closed Mon **Food** Lunch all wk 12-2 Dinner all wk 6.30-8.30 ⊕ ARKELL'S ◀ Wiltshire Gold & Hurricane Ale ♂ Westons Stowford Press. **Facilities** Non-diners area ❄ (Bar Garden) ♦♦ Children's portions Garden ⌓ WiFi ☷ (notice required)

MINCHINHAMPTON — Map 4 SO80

The Weighbridge Inn — PICK OF THE PUBS

See Pick of the Pubs on opposite page

MORETON-IN-MARSH — Map 10 SP23

The Red Lion Inn

tel: 01608 674397 **GL56 0RT**
email: info@theredlionlittlecompton.co.uk
dir: *Between Chipping Norton & Moreton-in-Marsh on A44*

A good place to enjoy pub games and seasonal food

A pretty Cotswold-stone building quietly located on the edge of the village, this is one of 15 pubs owned by Donnington Brewery – a family concern that has been brewing since 1865. Set in a large mature garden, the building has exposed stone walls and beams, inglenook fireplaces and real fires. Public bar games include darts, dominoes, a jukebox and pool table. The restaurant offers a seasonal menu and sensibly priced daily-changing specials.

Open all wk 12-3 6-12 **Food** Lunch all wk 12-2 Dinner Mon-Sat 6-9, Sun 7-8.30 ⊕ DONNINGTON ◀ BB, SBA, Gold. ☕ 10 **Facilities** Non-diners area ❄ (Bar Restaurant Garden) ♦♦ Children's portions Garden ⌓ Parking WiFi

NAILSWORTH — Map 4 ST89

The Britannia

tel: 01453 832501 **Cossack Square GL6 0DG**
email: pheasantpluckers2003@yahoo.co.uk
dir: *From A46 S'bound right at town centre rdbt. 1st left. Pub directly ahead*

Former manor house with a brasserie-style menu

Occupying a delightful position on the south side of Nailsworth's Cossack Square, The Britannia is a stone-built, 17th-century building. The interior is bright and uncluttered, while outside you'll find a pretty garden with plenty of tables, chairs and parasols for sunny days. The menu offers an interesting blend of modern British and continental food, with ingredients bought from both local suppliers and London's Smithfield Market. Go lightly with just a starter, perhaps moules marinière; or plunge into hearty mains such as chargrilled rump steak or confit pork belly. Other options include stone-baked pizzas and impressive meat-free options. Great wines, too.

Open all wk 11-11 (Fri-Sat 11am-mdnt Sun 11-10.30) Closed 25 Dec **Food** Lunch Mon-Fri 11-2.45, Sat-Sun 11-10 Dinner Mon-Fri 5.30-10, Sat-Sun 11-10 ⊕ FREE HOUSE ◀ Sharp's Doom Bar, Buckham, Otter, Guest ales ♂ Thatchers Gold, Westons Stowford Press. ☕ 10 **Facilities** ❄ (Bar Garden) ♦♦ Garden ⌓ Parking ☷

NETHER WESTCOTE — Map 10 SP22

The Feathered Nest Country Inn ★★★★★ INN ⊛⊛⊛ — PICK OF THE PUBS

See Pick of the Pubs on page 210

NEWENT — Map 10 SO72

Kilcot Inn ★★★★ INN

tel: 01989 720707 **Ross Rd, Kilcot GL18 1NA**
email: info@kilcotinn.com **web:** www.kilcotinn.com
dir: *M50 junct 3, B4221 signed Newent. Approx 2m to pub on left*

Renovated country inn offering great hospitality

This delightful inn has the best traditions of hospitality, food and drink. From the selection of real ales and local ciders on tap to the high quality produce used in the dishes in the bar and restaurant there is something for everyone. Their menu might include Italian meat antipasti or smoked bacon and chorizo risotto for starters, followed by a home-made pie, chicken and ham or vegetable pie; pan cooked Gloucester Old Spots pork loin, or grilled sirloin steak. Outdoor seating is available, including a pleasant garden area to the rear. The four stylish bedrooms are appointed to a high standard.

Open all day all wk **Food** Lunch all wk 12-2.30 Dinner Mon-Wed 6-9, Thu-Sat 6-9.30 ⊕ FREE HOUSE ◀ Wye Valley Butty Bach, Marston's EPA ♂ Westons Stowford Press, Old Rosie & Country Perry. **Facilities** Non-diners area ❄ (Bar Garden Outside area) ♦♦ Children's menu Children's portions Play area Garden Outside area ⌓ Parking WiFi ☷ (notice required) **Rooms** 4

PICK OF THE PUBS

The Feathered Nest Country Inn ★★★★★ INN ◉◉◉

NETHER WESTCOTE　　Map 10 SP22

tel: 01993 833030 **OX7 6SD**
email: info@thefeatherednestinn.co.uk
web: www.thefeatherednestinn.co.uk
dir: *A424 between Burford &*
Stow-on-the-Wold, follow signs

Award-winning food in a beautiful rural location

In the picturesque village of Nether Westcote on the border of Gloucestershire and Oxfordshire, The Feathered Nest has marvellous views over the Evenlode Valley. Originally an old malthouse, the pub has been updated and thoughtfully furnished whilst retaining the original character, especially in the cosy log-fired bar, where local and award-winning real ales are on offer. Herbs and vegetables are grown in the kitchen garden, with local produce forming the backbone of the menus. As well as bar snacks, the modern British cuisine brings a daily set lunch menu for relaxed eating in the bar, and on the garden terrace (shaded by a sycamore tree) when the weather allows. Dishes could include piccalilli and quail egg terrine with parsley mayonnaise. The seasonal à la carte offers a modern take on classic combinations, such as mutton with root vegetables, potato gnocchi, smoked bacon and curly kale; or stone bass with langoustine, leeks, cauliflower, Avruga caviar and shellfish foam. For simpler tastes there's a selection from the charcoal grill; maybe 28-day aged rib-eye steak with skinny chips, béarnaise or peppercorn sauce and mixed leaf salad. Be sure to leave room for desserts such as passionfruit parfait with caramel sauce and pine nuts. Afternoon tea and Sunday lunch are also served. Individually decorated bedrooms furnished with antiques and comfortable beds are available; the pub makes an excellent base from which to explore the countryside and the quaint and charming villages nearby. Look out for enjoyable events running throughout the year, including a pie and pint tasting evening, live jazz, and a quiz night.

Open all day Closed 25 Dec, Mon
Food Lunch Tue-Sat 12-2.30, Sun 12-3.30 Dinner Tue-Sat 6.30-9.30
⊕ FREE HOUSE ◼ Rotating Local Ales ♂ Thatchers Gold. ♟ 19 **Facilities** Non-diners area ♣ (Bar Garden) ♦ Children's menu Children's portions Family room Garden ⌁ Parking WiFi **Rooms** 4

NEWLAND

Map 4 SO50

The Ostrich Inn

PICK OF THE PUBS

tel: 01594 833260 **GL16 8NP**
email: kathryn@theostrichinn.com
dir: *Follow Monmouth signs from Chepstow (A466), Newland signed from Redbrook*

Huge range of real ales here

On the western edge of the Forest of Dean and adjoining the Wye Valley in a pretty village, the 13th-century Ostrich is thought to have taken its name from the family emblem of the Probyns, local landowners in previous centuries; it retains many of its ancient features, including a priest hole. With its warm welcome, The Ostrich is a thriving social centre for the village. An open log fire burns in the large lounge bar throughout the winter, and customers can relax immediately in the friendly atmosphere with a pint of their chosen brew. And what a choice. Eight cask-conditioned real ales such as Butty Bach are served at any one time; real ciders, too, are strongly represented. Diners settle down in the small and intimate restaurant, in the bar or out in gardens.

Open all wk 12-3 (Mon-Fri 6.30-11.30 Sat 6-11.30 Sun 6.30-10.30) **Food** Lunch all wk 12-2.30 Dinner Sun-Fri 6.30-9.30, Sat 6-9.30 ⊕ FREE HOUSE ◼ Wye Valley Butty Bach, Uley Pigs Ear, Hook Norton Old Hooky, Adnams, Guest ales Ⓒ Westons Stowford Press, Mortimers Orchard & Old Rosie, Ty Gwyn, Severn Cider. **Facilities** Non-diners area ⚘ (Bar Restaurant Garden) ᵢᵢ Garden ⚲

NORTH CERNEY

Map 5 SP00

Bathurst Arms

PICK OF THE PUBS

tel: 01285 831281 **GL7 7BZ**
email: james@bathurstarms.com
dir: *5m N of Cirencester on A435*

Affable Cotswold dining pub

Close to the River Churn on the Earl of Bathurst's estate, this creeper-covered 17th-century pub is hugely appealing to diners and drinkers alike. The flagstoned and beamed bar, even when the log fires aren't lit, is an inviting environment but if the weather's kind the pretty riverside garden is equally pleasant. Prepared from locally sourced ingredients, are grilled sardines with Bloody Mary sauce; and chargrilled beefburger and chips, while dinner suggestions might include home-made ox cheek suet pudding; crispy slow-roasted pork belly with mixed bean cassoulet; or shallot tart Tatin with butternut squash and pearl barley risotto. For those who can manage a dessert, try chocolate and berry trifle with crème Anglaise; or rhubarb and apple crumble with cream. Hooky Bitter and Ramsbury Gold await real ale drinkers, with many more local brews on tap at the January, April, July and October beer festivals.

Open all day all wk **Food** Lunch all wk 12-2 Dinner all wk 6-9 Av main course £14 Set menu available ⊕ FREE HOUSE ◼ Hook Norton Hooky Bitter, Ramsbury Gold Ⓒ Westons Stowford Press, Hogan's. ⚑ 15 **Facilities** Non-diners area ⚘ (Bar Garden) ᵢᵢ Children's menu Children's portions Garden ⚲ Beer festival Parking WiFi ⚌ (notice required)

NORTHLEACH

Map 10 SP11

The Wheatsheaf Inn

tel: 01451 860244 **West End GL54 3EZ**
email: reservations@cotswoldswheatsheaf.com
dir: *Just off A40 between Oxford & Cheltenham*

Stylish pub worth seeking out

A beautiful Cotswold-stone 17th-century inn on the square of the pretty former wool town of Northleach, The Wheatsheaf is everything anyone could wish for, with flagstone floors, beams, log fires and a vibrant, smartened-up feel throughout. It's the perfect place for enjoying bracing walks then chilling out in the bar with the papers or sampling some seriously good food. Monthly menus evolve with the season and may take in duck leg cassoulet with white beans, pancetta and Morteau sausage; calves' liver with sage and balsamic onions; sticky toffee pudding and cheeses from Neal's Yard Dairy.

Open all day all wk **Food** Lunch all wk 12-3 Dinner all wk 6-10 Av main course £15 Set menu available ⊕ FREE HOUSE ◼ Fuller's London Pride, Bath Ales Barnsey, Wye Valley HPA Ⓒ Dunkertons Premium Organic. ⚑ 15 **Facilities** Non-diners area ⚘ (Bar Restaurant Garden) ᵢᵢ Children's menu Children's portions Play area Garden ⚲ Parking WiFi ⚌ (notice required)

OAKRIDGE LYNCH

Map 4 SO90

NEW The Butchers Arms

tel: 01285 760371 **GL6 7NZ**
email: enquiries@butchersarmsoakridge.com
dir: *A419 from Stroud towards Cirencester take Toadsmoor Rd towards Bisley. Through Eastcombe, after dip & left bend follow Oakridge sign, then brown pub signs to Oakridge Lynch*

Picturesque village pub serving excellent food

With its large sunny beer garden for summer supping, and three cosy log fires burning in winter, this pub is a year-round treat for walkers taking their exercise in the stunning countryside around the Golden Valley and Severn Canal. The 18th-century building's neat interior welcomes with stone walls adorned with pictures, and beamed ceilings; dogs are welcome and children well catered for. Michael Bedford's CV as a chef includes several illustrious eateries, so settle down with a Wadworth cask ale and the menu. Home-made Scotch egg with pickled gherkin, and a classic coq au vin with creamy mash, are typical dishes.

Open 12-3 6-11 Closed Mon **Food** Lunch Tue-Sat 12-2.15, Sun 12-2.30 Dinner Tue-Sat 7-9.30 ⊕ WADWORTH ◼ Henry's Original IPA, 6X & Horizon. **Facilities** Non-diners area ⚘ (Bar Restaurant Garden) ᵢᵢ Children's menu Children's portions Garden ⚲ Parking WiFi

OLDBURY-ON-SEVERN

Map 4 ST69

The Anchor Inn

tel: 01454 413331 **Church Rd BS35 1QA**
email: info@anchorinnoldbury.co.uk
dir: *From N A38 towards Bristol, 1.5m then right, village signed. From S A38 through Thornbury*

Homely inn in tranquil Severnside village

Set beside a tree-lined pill (stream) that meanders down to the nearby Severn Estuary, this family-friendly pub is on the Severn Way footpath and a popular stopping place for ramblers. Parts of the stone-built inn are nearly 500 years old, and an olde-worlde welcome is assured for travellers to this charming, out-of-the-way village. Appetite-busters on the good-value bar and dining room menu include pan-fried pheasant breast or crispy pork belly and black pudding with creamed cabbage and bacon. Reliable real ales include guests like Severn Sins, plus there's a good range of bottled cider and perry.

Open all wk Mon-Thu 11.30-2.30 6-11 (Fri-Sat 11.30am-mdnt Sun 12-10.30) **Food** Lunch Mon-Fri 12-2, Sat 12-2.30, Sun 12-3 Dinner all wk 6-9 Av main course £10.50 Set menu available ⊕ FREE HOUSE ◼ Bass, Butcombe Bitter, Otter Bitter, Guest ales Ⓒ Ashton Press & Still, Thatchers. ⚑ 16 **Facilities** Non-diners area ᵢᵢ Children's menu Family room Garden ⚲ Parking ⚌ (notice required)

PAINSWICK
Map 4 SO80

The Falcon Inn ★★★★ INN

tel: 01452 814222 **New St GL6 6UN**
email: info@falconpainswick.co.uk **web:** www.falconpainswick.co.uk
dir: *On A46 in centre of Painswick, opposite St Mary's church*

Historic inn with wide-ranging menus

In the heart of the town and opposite the church with its iconic 99 yew trees, this inn dates from 1554 but spent over 200 years as a courthouse. Expect a good choice of local real ales, including Hook Norton, and tasty, home-cooked meals any time of day. An evening meal might offer apricot and pistachio stuffed pork loin with fruit cider sauce and sweet potato mash; chicken and vegetable tagine with couscous; or grilled turbot bouillabaisse with celeriac and vanilla purée. Leave room for some raspberry and vanilla roulade; or chocolate bread and butter pudding. A blackboard offers daily specials, steaks and pies.

Open all day all wk 10am-11pm **Food** Lunch all wk 12-2.30 Dinner all wk 7-9.30 Av main course £14.95 Restaurant menu available ⊕ PARSNIP INNS LTD ◀ Sharp's Doom Bar, Hook Norton, Wickwar BOB, Guest ale ♂ Westons Stowford Press. ₹ 10 **Facilities** Non-diners area ✿ (All areas) ♦ Children's menu Children's portions Garden Outside area ⊨ Parking WiFi ▭ (notice required) **Rooms** 11

POULTON
Map 5 SP00

The Falcon Inn

tel: 01285 851597 & 850878 **London Rd GL7 5HN**
email: bookings@falconinnpoulton.co.uk **web:** www.falconinnpoulton.co.uk
dir: *From Cirencester 4m E on A417 towards Fairford*

Informal atmosphere and locally brewed cask ales

Owned by husband and wife Gianni Gray and Natalie Birch, this 300-year-old village pub places a welcome emphasis on real ales and good food. Contemporary furnishings blend with original features and log fires to create an informal pub for locals who want to sup a pint of Hooky or one of the rotating guest beers. Diners will be tempted by confit duck leg and rabbit rillette with fig and date chutney and toasted sour dough; fillet of Loch Duart salmon, couscous with almonds, courgette

and raisins, bok choi and saffron sauce; and passionfruit bavarois with caramelised pineapple and meringues to finish.

Open Tue-Sat 12-3 5-11 (Sun 12-4) Closed 25 Dec, Mon **Food** Lunch Tue-Sat 12-2.15, Sun 12-3 Dinner Tue-Sat 6-9 Set menu available ⊕ FREE HOUSE ◀ Hook Norton Hooky Bitter, Guest ale ♂ Westons Stowford Press. ₹ 11 **Facilities** Non-diners area ♦ Children's menu Children's portions Garden ⊨ Parking WiFi

See advert on opposite page

SAPPERTON
Map 4 SO90

The Bell at Sapperton
PICK OF THE PUBS

See Pick of the Pubs on page 214

SHEEPSCOMBE
Map 4 SO81

The Butchers Arms
PICK OF THE PUBS

See Pick of the Pubs on page 215

SOMERFORD KEYNES
Map 4 SU09

The Bakers Arms

tel: 01285 861298 **GL7 6DN**
email: enquiries@thebakersarmssomerford.co.uk
dir: *Exit A419 signed Cotswold Water Park. Cross B4696, 1m, follow signs for Keynes Park & Somerford Keynes*

Chocolate-box Cotswold pub

The beautiful Bakers Arms dates from the 17th century and was formerly the village bakery; it still has its low-beamed ceilings and inglenook fireplace. Only a stone's throw from the Thames Path and Cotswold Way, the pub is a convenient watering hole for walkers. The mature gardens are ideal for alfresco dining, with discreet children's play areas. The home-cooked food on offer runs along the lines of baguettes, specials and pub favourites — pasta bake, marinated rack of pork ribs, quiche of the day and Butcombe ale-battered fish and chips.

Open all day all wk 12-11 (Sun 12-6 BH Sun 12-11) **Food** Lunch Mon-Sat 12-9, Sun 12-4 Dinner Mon-Sat 12-9, Sun BH 6-8 Av main course £12 Set menu available ⊕ ENTERPRISE INNS ◀ Butcombe Bitter, Stroud Budding, Sharp's Doom Bar ♂ Thatchers Gold, Westons Stowford Press. **Facilities** Non-diners area ✿ (Bar Restaurant Garden) ♦ Children's menu Children's portions Play area Garden ⊨ Parking WiFi ▭ (notice required)

STOW-ON-THE-WOLD
Map 10 SP12

NEW The Bell at Stow

tel: 01451 870916 **Park St GL54 1AJ**
email: info@thebellatstow.com **web:** www.thebellatstow.com
dir: *In town centre on A436*

Handsome Cotswold pub with excellent seafood

Taken over by Sue Hawkins and her niece, Rachel, in 2013, this ivy-clad stone pub in lovely Stow offers a warm welcome to all, including dogs. Open-plan with flagstone floors, beamed ceilings and log fires, it's a relaxed setting to enjoy a pint of Old Hooky or one of the 10 wines sold by the glass. Seafood dominates the daily-changing specials boards - typical dishes including smoked haddock and coriander fishcakes; and chargrilled Cajun-spiced swordfish steaks. Non-fish options might be game pie and a vegetarian roast butternut squash, spinach and gorgonzola tagliatelle.

Open all day all wk Closed 25 Dec **Food** Lunch all day Dinner all day Av main course £8 Restaurant menu available all wk ⊕ FREE HOUSE ◀ Fuller's London Pride, Hook Norton Old Hooky. ♀ 10 **Facilities** Non-diners area ✿ (Bar Garden) ♦♦ Garden ⊓ Parking WiFi

The Unicorn

tel: 01451 830257 **Sheep St GL54 1HQ**
email: reception@birchhotels.co.uk
dir: *Phone for detailed directions*

Terrific Cotswold market town setting

In the main square of Stow-on-the-Wold, this eye-catching 17th-century property is built from honey-coloured limestone and bedecked with abundantly flowering window boxes. The interior is stylishly presented with Jacobean pieces, antique artefacts and open log fires. Food is served in the oak-beamed bar, the stylish contemporary restaurant or in the secluded garden if the weather is fine. Typical dishes include duck and port pâté with red onion marmalade; knuckle of lamb braised with root vegetables in a rich sauce; home-made meringue with red berries and cream. Freshly made sandwiches are also available.

Open all day all wk **Food** Lunch all wk 12-2 Dinner all wk 7-9 ⊕ FREE HOUSE ◀ Hook Norton Lion ♂ Westons, Symonds. **Facilities** Non-diners area ♦♦ Children's menu Children's portions Garden ⊓ Parking WiFi ▭

PICK OF THE PUBS

The Bell at Sapperton

SAPPERTON Map 4 SO90

tel: 01285 760298 **GL7 6LE**
email: info@bellsapperton.co.uk
web: www.bellsapperton.co.uk
dir: *From A419 between Cirencester & Stroud follow Sapperton signs*

Village free house, very much part of the community

The Cotswold stone exterior of this village inn has been quietly mellowing for over 300 years; still gently maturing too are the beamed ceilings, unrendered walls, polished flags, bare boards and open fireplaces of the interior. Although most people arrive by car or on foot, horse riders and their mounts are also welcome, and will be able to tie up and water them. Liquid refreshment for humans includes real ales from Butcombe, Hook Norton, Otter and Stroud, and a dozen wines by the glass. Food, from home-made bread to the chocolate truffles that complement an after-dinner coffee, is always freshly prepared. In the garden the chef oversees cultivation of vegetables and salads, while top local suppliers furnish other ingredients. Meals are served throughout four cosy dining areas, each with its own individual character; outside, a secluded rear courtyard and a landscaped front garden make fine-weather dining a pleasure. For lunch or dinner, you might start with Thai spiced mussels, coconut and coriander; or

chicken liver parfait with red onion marmalade and brioche. Main course possibilities include slow-cooked lamb shank with dauphinoise potato and red cabbage; whole Cornish lemon sole with brown shrimp potato cake, braised celery, and caper and lemon butter; and vegetarian leek, wild mushroom and brie filo parcel with new potatoes, rocket and redcurrant syrup. There are specials too, as well as ideas for children. And should you want a dessert, try flourless chocolate indulgence cake with vanilla ice cream and plum purée; or apple and winter berry crumble with custard. Cirencester Park close by, stretches all the way to the town, although it is screened from it by the world's tallest yew hedge.

Open all wk 11-3 6.30-11 (Sun 12-10.30) Closed 25 Dec **Food** Lunch Mon-Sat 12-2.30, Sun 12-4 Dinner served Mon-Sat 6-9.30 ⊕ FREE HOUSE 🍺 Otter Bitter, Hook Norton Hooky Bitter, Butcombe, Stroud Budding Ö Westons Stowford Press. ♟ 12
Facilities Non-diners area 🐾 (Bar Restaurant Garden) 🍴 Children's menu Children's portions Garden 🪑 Beer festival Parking WiFi

PICK OF THE PUBS

The Butchers Arms

SHEEPSCOMBE Map 4 SO81

tel: 01452 812113 **GL6 7RH**
email: mark@butchers-arms.co.uk
web: www.butchers-arms.co.uk
dir: *1.5m S of A46 (Cheltenham to Stroud road), N of Painswick*

Rural Cotswold gem with stunning views

Tucked into the western scarp of the Cotswolds and reached via narrow winding lanes, pretty Sheepscombe radiates all of the mellow, sedate, bucolic charm you'd expect from such a haven. The village pub, dating from 1670 and a favourite haunt of *Cider with Rosie* author Laurie Lee, lives up to such expectations and then some. Views from the gardens are idyllic whilst within is all you'd hope for: log fires, clean-cut rustic furnishings, village chatter backed up by local beers from Prescotts of Cheltenham Brewery. Walkers, riders and locals all beat a path to the door beneath the pub's famous carved sign showing a butcher supping a pint of ale with a pig tied to his leg. The pub takes its name from its association with Henry VIII's Royal Deer Park, which was located nearby, when deer carcasses were hung in what is now the bar. The fulfilling fodder here includes locally sourced meats, including beef from Beech Farm; the beef, ale and mushroom pie is a perennial favourite, as is the homemade

burger – try one with a blue cheese and chorizo topping. Alternative main courses take in ham, egg and chips and specials like seared tuna steak with fresh mango and pineapple salsa, and a smoked bacon chop with sautéed potatoes, warm onion, fennel and apple slaw and apple and sage jus. Nibblers can graze on a delicious bacon, West Country brie and cranberry sandwich, others can share a baked camembert or a huge fish platter, while those thinking of tucking into the memorable Sunday roasts should book well ahead. To drink, there's a cracking range of ales, and a traditional farmhouse scrumpy cider.

Open all wk 11.30-2.30 6.30-11 (Sat 11.30-11.30 Sun 12-10.30)

Food Lunch Mon-Fri 12-2.30, Sat-Sun all day Dinner Mon-Sat 6.30-9.30, Sun all day (ex Sun Jan & Feb) ⊕ FREE HOUSE ◄ Otter Bitter, Butcombe Bitter, St Austell Proper Job, Wye Valley Dorothy Goodbody's Ale ♂ Westons Stowford Press & Traditional Scrumpy.
Facilities Non-diners area ♣ (Bar Garden) ♦♦ Children's menu Children's portions Garden ⊼ Cider festival Parking WiFi

STOW-ON-THE-WOLD *continued*

White Hart Inn

tel: 01451 830674 **The Square GL54 1AF**
email: stay@thewhitehartstow.com
dir: *From A429 into market square. Inn on left*

Cosy bars and warming fires

Some of the mellow stone buildings in this lovely Cotswold town date to the 12th century, including parts of the White Hart. Two cosy bars benefit from open fires, and an atmospheric dining room serves lunchtime snacks such as a Lincolnshire poacher and piccalilli sandwich. For dinner, you could start with Cornish scallops with chorizo; follow with local pheasant cooked with cloves and cinnamon; and round off with chocolate marquis. There's a spacious car park.

Open all day all wk 11-11 (Sun 11-10) Closed 1wk May & 1wk Oct **Food** Lunch all wk 12-2.30 Dinner Mon-Thu 6-9, Fri-Sat 6-9.30, Sun 6.30-9 ⊕ ARKELL'S ◀ 3B, Wiltshire Gold ♂ Westons Stowford Press. ♀ 11 **Facilities** Non-diners area ❤ (Bar) ◀ Children's portions Garden ⋒ Parking WiFi

STROUD   Map 4 SO80

Bear of Rodborough Hotel ★★★ HL   PICK OF THE PUBS

tel: 01453 878522 **Rodborough Common GL5 5DE**
email: info@bearofrodborough.info **web:** www.cotswold-inns-hotels.co.uk/bear
dir: *From M5 junct 13 follow signs for Stonehouse then Rodborough*

Surrounded by 300 acres of National Trust land

Located amidst the rolling, windswept grassland of Rodborough Common with its far-reaching views of the Stroud Valley and Severn Vale, and cattle roaming free in the summer months, this 17th-century former alehouse takes its name from the bear-baiting that used to take place nearby. Head to the bar for a pint of Wickwar before seeking a seat on the York stone terrace or in the gardens with their walled croquet lawn. The bar menu has many delights, such as afternoon tea, sharing platters and ploughman's, and fond favourites: fisherman's pie, cornfed chicken supreme and chargrilled steaks. Look to the Library Restaurant for a more formal affair, where you can try smoked Scottish scallops with butternut squash and chorizo; followed by rump of lamb and braised shoulder, dauphinoise potatoes, wilted spinach and rosemary jus; and lastly raspberry crème brûlée with a cassis smoothie and vanilla, all the while enjoying panoramas of the Cotswold countryside. Guest rooms are distinctively furnished and decorated with rich fabrics.

Open all day all wk 10.30am-11pm **Food** Lunch all wk 12-9.30, light menu all wk 12-9.30 Dinner all wk 6.30-9.30, light menu all wk 12-9.30 Restaurant menu available all wk ⊕ FREE HOUSE ◀ Butcombe, Stroud, Wickwar ♂ Ashton Press. ♀ 10 **Facilities** Non-diners area ❤ (Bar Garden) ◀ Children's menu Children's portions Play area Garden ⋒ Parking WiFi (notice required) **Rooms** 46

The Ram Inn

tel: 01453 873329 **South Woodchester GL5 5EL**
dir: *A46 from Stroud to Nailsworth, right after 2m into South Woodchester, follow brown tourist signs*

17th-century inn with splendid Cotswold views

In winter the warmth from its huge fireplace might prove more appealing than standing on the terrace of this 17th-century Cotswold-stone inn, admiring the splendid views. Originally a farm, it became an alehouse in 1811 and is still full of historic little gems. Typical dishes are starters of black pudding tapas, Scotch egg, chorizo chips or chicken goujons, followed by main courses such as fillet steak, beer-battered cod or haddock, or the Woodchester Whopper burger. Paninis are also served at lunchtime.

Open all day all wk **Food** Lunch Mon-Fri 12-2, Sat-Sun 12-3 Dinner all wk 6-9 ⊕ FREE HOUSE ◀ Butcombe Bitter, Wickwar Cotswold Way, Otter Amber, Gloucester

Gold ♂ Westons Stowford Press, Lilley's Apples & Pears & Bee Sting Pear, Pheasant Plucker. **Facilities** Non-diners area ❤ (Bar Restaurant Garden) ◀ Children's portions Garden ⋒ Parking WiFi (notice required)

TETBURY   Map 4 ST89

Gumstool Inn   PICK OF THE PUBS

tel: 01666 890391 **Calcot Manor GL8 8YJ**
email: reception@calcotmanor.co.uk
dir: *3m W of Tetbury at A4135 & A46 junct*

Stylish gastro-pub with good wine choices

A popular and stylish free house, this stone farmhouse was originally built by Cistercian monks in the 14th century. It is part of Calcot Manor Hotel, the buzzy and comfortable Gumstool Inn has a real country-pub atmosphere and stocks a good selection of ales such as Butcombe Bitter, and local ciders including Ashton Press. An excellent choice of wines is offered by the glass or bottle. The food here is top-notch and there is a pronounced use of local suppliers. Kick off with starters of twice-baked smoked haddock and Montgomery Cheddar cheese soufflé; or warm Cornish tart with rocket and frisée. Among the main courses may be found roasted salmon fillet with crushed sweet potato, fennel and blood orange; and slow-cooked pork belly with haricot beans and chorizo cassoulet. In the summer, grab a table on the pretty, flower-filled sun terrace, while indoor winter evenings are warmed with cosy log fires.

Open all day all wk **Food** Lunch all wk 12-2.30 Dinner Mon-Sat 5.30-9.30, Sun 5.30-9 Av main course £14 ⊕ FREE HOUSE ◀ Butcombe Bitter, Sharp's Doom Bar ♂ Ashton Press. ♀ 23 **Facilities** Non-diners area ◀ Children's menu Children's portions Play area Family room Garden ⋒ Parking WiFi (notice required)

The Priory Inn ★★★ SHL   PICK OF THE PUBS

tel: 01666 502251 **London Rd GL8 8JJ**
email: info@theprioryinn.co.uk **web:** www.theprioryinn.co.uk
dir: *M4 junct 17, A429 towards Cirencester. Left into B4014 to Tetbury. Over mini rdbt into Long St, pub 100yds after corner on right*

Family-friendly Cotswold pub and hotel

An enormous 'walk-around' open log fire greets visitors to this thriving gastro-pub and hotel. Its high exposed beams date from the 16th century, when it was the stable-block and grooms' cottages for the neighbouring priory. Local microbreweries, typically Uley and Cotswold Lion, supply the real ales; a white wine and a sparkling rosé come from a vineyard in Malmesbury; and damson brandy, sloe gin and quince liqueur are made on the banks of the River Severn. Meals in the bare-boarded, beamed bar and more contemporary restaurant use fresh ingredients sourced from within a 30-mile radius for twice-baked Single Gloucester cheese soufflé with pickled beetroot; pan-roasted cannon of lamb with leek and tarragon mousse, celeriac dauphinoise and braised onions; and halibut with pesto topping and toasted pine nuts. Children can create personalised wood-fired pizzas. The Early May Bank Holiday beer and cider festival is a big draw.

Open all day all wk 7am-11pm (Fri 7am-mdnt Sat 8am-mdnt Sun 8am-11pm) **Food** Lunch Mon-Thu 12-3, Fri-Sun & BH all day (bkfst served all wk 7-10.30) Dinner Mon-Thu 5-10, Fri-Sun & BH all day ⊕ FREE HOUSE ◀ Uley Bitter, Cotswold Lion, Guest ale ♂ Thatchers Gold, Cotswold, Guest cider. ♀ 13 **Facilities** Non-diners area ◀ Children's menu Children's portions Play area Family room Garden ⋒ Beer festival Cider festival Parking WiFi (notice required) **Rooms** 14

Snooty Fox Hotel ★★★ SHL

tel: 01666 502436 **Market Place GL8 8DD**
email: res@snooty-fox.co.uk **web:** www.snooty-fox.co.uk
dir: *In town centre opposite covered market hall*

Draw up a chair by the log fire

Occupying a prime spot in the heart of Tetbury, this 16th-century coaching inn and hotel retains many of its original features. Sit in a leather armchair in front of the log fire with a pint of Wadworth 6X and order from the extensive bar menu – eggs Benedict or a bowl of mussels maybe. Alternatively, head for the restaurant and enjoy the likes of pan-fried scallops with cauliflower purée and crisp black pudding followed by slow-roast lamb shank with leeks, bacon, creamed mash and onion sauce. Traditional puddings include Cambridge burnt cream, and rhubarb and apple crumble.

Open all day all wk **Food** Lunch all wk 12-3, snacks 3-6 Dinner all wk 6-9.30 ⊕ FREE HOUSE ◖ Wadworth 6X, Butcombe Bitter ♂ Ashton Press. ☂
Facilities Non-diners area ♦◊ Children's menu Children's portions Outside area ⌷ WiFi ▭ (notice required) **Rooms** 12

■ UPPER ODDINGTON	Map 10 SP22

The Horse and Groom Inn · PICK OF THE PUBS

tel: 01451 830584 **GL56 OXH**
email: info@horseandgroom.uk.com
dir: *1.5m S of Stow-on-the-Wold, just off A436*

Cotswold-stone inn specialising in local beer and food

Situated in a conservation village in the Evenlode Valley, this 16th-century inn has been owner operated for the past decade. The pub boasts polished flagstones, beams and an inglenook log fire – what more could you ask for? Well, you could add the grapevines outside and the pleasure of dining on the terrace or in the walled gardens. Then there's the bar, offering an ever-changing choice of real ales from regional breweries, local cider and over 20 wines by the glass. The kitchen's commitment to local produce is impressive: bread, for instance, is made daily from locally milled flour, meats are from a Chipping Norton butcher, and venison is from the nearby Adlestrop Estate. Peruse the imaginative menus, typically featuring pork and rosemary meatballs, spiced tomato sauce, egg tagliatelle; baked salmon, mustard creamed leeks, lemon and caper mash, wilted spinach; and steamed chocolate and pear sponge, raspberry sorbet and white chocolate Anglaise.

Open all wk 12-3 5.30-11 (Sun 12-3 6.30-10.30) **Food** Lunch all wk 12-2 Dinner Mon-Sat 6.30-9, Sun 7-9 ⊕ FREE HOUSE ◖ Wye Valley Bitter & HPA, Goffs Tournament, Prescott Hill Climb, Cisco Whale's Tale Pale Ale, Otter Bitter, North Cotswold Shagweaver ♂ Cotswold. ☂ 25 **Facilities** Non-diners area ♥ (Bar Restaurant Garden) ♦◊ Children's menu Children's portions Garden ⌷ Parking WiFi ▭ (notice required)

■ WINCHCOMBE	Map 10 SP02

NEW The Lion Inn

tel: 01242 603300 **37 North St GL54 5PS**
email: reception@thelionwinchcombe.co.uk
dir: *In town centre (parking in Chandos St)*

Shabby-chic, friendly and caring town centre hostelry

Following a major spruce-up nearly five years ago, this attractive watering hole in the ancient town of Winchcombe has been buzzing afresh; even the Lion's large sunny garden had a makeover. With 15th-century origins, care had to be taken that the building's quirky charms were retained. The results can be enjoyed in today's

light, spacious and relaxed bar where real ale and wine lovers are spoilt for choice. The menu features good English ingredients in dishes such as partridge and pigeon terrine; quail stuffed with mushrooms; roasted salmon with purple potatoes and Jerusalem artichokes; and apple and pear tarte Tatin with clotted cream.

Open all day all wk **Food** Lunch all wk 12-3 Dinner all wk 6-9.30 ⊕ FREE HOUSE ◖ Brakspear Oxford Gold, Sharp's, Cotswold Lion, Ringwood ♂ Thatchers Gold. ☂ 19 **Facilities** Non-diners area ♥ (Bar Garden) ♦◊ Children's portions Garden ⌷ WiFi

The White Hart Inn and Restaurant

tel: 01242 602359 **High St GL54 5LJ**
email: info@whitehartwinchcombe.co.uk
dir: *In centre of Winchcombe on B4632*

Town pub specialising in wine

Popular with walkers, this 16th-century inn offers the perfect place to unwind in the cosy bar or intimate restaurant. The White Hart is in the heart of Winchcombe just outside Cheltenham, a small historic town set in the Cotswold countryside. There is a wine shop as well as the bar and restaurant. Specialising in an amazing choice of wines, there are also plenty of real ales, and simple and unpretentious British food sourced from local suppliers. Main dishes include Cotswold venison stew, roasted root vegetable tart and steamed sea bream.

Open all day all wk 10am-11pm (Fri-Sat 10am-mdnt Sun 10am-10.30pm) **Food** Lunch all wk 12-3, bar snacks all day Dinner all wk 6-9 ⊕ ENTERPRISE INNS ◖ Wadworth 6X, Butcombe, Otter, Guest ales ♂ Westons Stowford Press, Thatchers Gold. ☂ 8 **Facilities** Non-diners area ♥ (Bar Garden) ♦◊ Children's menu Children's portions Garden ⌷ Parking WiFi

GREATER MANCHESTER	
■ DENSHAW	Map 16 SD91

The Rams Head Inn

tel: 01457 874802 **OL3 5UN**
email: info@ramsheaddenshaw.co.uk
dir: *M62 junct 22, A672 towards Oldham, 2m to inn*

A gastro-pub, farm shop and tea room

At 1,212 feet above sea level, this 450-year-old family-owned country inn has fabulous moorland views and is just two miles from the M62. Log fires and collections of memorabilia are features of the interior, which includes The Pantry, an in-house farm shop, deli, bakery and tea room selling everything from cheeses to chocolates. Game and seafood figure strongly on the menu, with dishes ranging from Boroughbridge breast of pigeon to Scottish salmon Wellington. There are also plenty of vegetarian options. Finish with the inn's 'famed' sticky toffee pudding. There's a garden area to the rear of the inn with bench seating and panoramic views.

Open Tue-Fri 12-2.30 5.30-10 (Sat 12-10.30 Sun 12-8.30) Closed 25-26 Dec, 1 Jan, Mon (ex BHs) **Food** Lunch Tue-Fri 12-2.30, Sat 12-10, Sun 12-8.30 Dinner Tue-Thu 5.30-8.30, Fri 5.30-9.30, Sat 12-10, Sun 12-8.30 Av main course £10.95 Set menu available Restaurant menu available Tue-Sun ⊕ FREE HOUSE ◖ Marston's Burton Bitter, Timothy Taylor Landlord, Black Sheep Best Bitter, Theakston Old Peculier, Thwaites Wainwright. ☂ 16 **Facilities** Non-diners area ♦◊ Children's portions Garden ⌷ Parking WiFi ▭ (notice required)

DIDSBURY
Map 16 SJ89

The Metropolitan

tel: 0161 438 2332 **2 Lapwing Ln M20 2WS**
email: info@the-metropolitan.co.uk
dir: *M60 junct 5, A5103, right into Barlow Moor Rd, left into Burton Rd. Pub at x-rds. Right into Lapwing Ln for car park*

Airy Victorian railway hotel and gastro-pub

A former Victorian railway hotel, 'the Met' is well situated in the leafy suburb of West Didsbury on the old Midland Railway line into Manchester. Today its decorative floor tiling, ornate windows, delicate plasterwork and huge airy interior filled with antique tables, chairs and deep sofas attract a mainly young and cosmopolitan clientele. The drinks choice matches customer demand with nearly 30 wines sold by the glass, and international bottles such as Swedish Rekorderlig cider. The all-day menu proffers the likes of smoked haddock rarebit on toasted ciabatta, and braised beef and kidneys with roasted root vegetables.

Open all day all wk 10am-11.30pm (Fri-Sat 10am-mdnt) Closed 25 Dec **Food** Lunch Mon-Thu 12-9.30, Fri-Sat 12-10, Sun 12-9 (bkfst all wk 10-11.45) Dinner Mon-Thu 12-9.30, Fri-Sat 12-10, Sun 12-9 Set menu available ⊕ ENTERPRISE INNS ◀ Timothy Taylor Landlord, Caledonian Deuchars IPA, Guinness ♂ Westons, Rekorderlig. ♥ 28 **Facilities** Non-diners area ♦ Children's menu Children's portions Outside area ⟫ Parking WiFi ⊜ (notice required)

LITTLEBOROUGH
Map 16 SD91

The White House

tel: 01706 378456 **Blackstone Edge, Halifax Rd OL15 OLG**
dir: *On A58, 8m from Rochdale, 9m from Halifax*

A favourite with walkers and cyclists

Known as The White House for over 100 years, this 17th-century coaching house has been in the same hands for almost 30 of them. On the Pennine Way, 1,300 feet above sea level, it has panoramic views of the moors and Hollingworth Lake far below. Not surprising then, that it attracts walkers and cyclists who rest up and sup on Black Sheep and Theakstons Best Bitter. A simple menu of pub grub ranges from sandwiches and salads, to grills, international and vegetarian dishes, and traditional mains such as home-made steak and kidney pie, and haddock and prawn Mornay.

Open all wk Mon-Sat 12-3 6-10 (Sun 12-10.30) Closed 25 Dec **Food** Lunch Mon-Sat 12-2, Sun 12-9 Dinner Mon-Sat 6.30-9.30, Sun 12-9 ⊕ FREE HOUSE ◀ Theakston Best Bitter, Black Sheep, Guest ales. **Facilities** Non-diners area ♦ Children's menu Parking ⊜

MANCHESTER
Map 16 SJ89

Dukes 92

tel: 0161 839 3522 **14 Castle St, Castlefield M3 4LZ**
email: info@dukes92.com
dir: *In Castlefield town centre, off Deansgate*

Relaxed contemporary dining in restored canalside building

Originally a block of 19th-century stables for horses delivering food from barges to the warehouses opposite, this beautifully restored canalside building reopened as a contemporary bar and grill over 20 years ago. The interior is full of surprises, with minimalist decor downstairs and an upper gallery displaying local artistic talent. At the bar you'll find JW Lees beers, cocktails and wines by the glass. A grill restaurant is supplemented by a lunchtime bar menu and pizza range; choices from the renowned cheese and deli counter, displaying over 40 British and European savoury products, are served with freshly baked granary bread.

Open all day all wk Sun-Wed 11.30-11 (Thu-Sat 11.30-12) Closed 25-26 Dec, 1 Jan **Food** Lunch all wk 12-10 Dinner all wk 12-10 ⊕ FREE HOUSE ◀ JW Lees Bitter, Joseph Holt ♂ Rekorderlig. ♥ 15 **Facilities** Non-diners area ♦ Children's menu Children's portions Garden ⟫ Parking ⊜

Marble Arch

tel: 0161 832 5914 **73 Rochdale Rd M4 4HY**
dir: *In city centre (Northern Quarter)*

Victorian pub popular with ale aficionados

A listed building famous for its sloping floor, glazed brick walls and barrel-vaulted ceiling, the Marble Arch is a fine example of Manchester's Victorian heritage. Part of the award-winning organic Marble Brewery, the pub was built in 1888 by celebrated architect Alfred Darbyshire for Manchester brewery B&J McKenna. An established favourite with beer aficionados and offering six regular ales and eight seasonal house beers, the pub offers a well-considered menu offering traditional bar meals of burgers and hot salt beef bagels to innovative mains including pan-fried halibut with Madras curry sauce and polenta cakes. It hosts its own beer festivals.

Open all day all wk Closed 25 Dec **Food** Lunch Mon-Sat 12-8.45, Sun 12-7.45 Dinner Mon-Sat 12-8.45, Sun 12-7.45 ⊕ FREE HOUSE ◀ Marble Manchester Bitter, Lagonda IPA, Ginger Marble ♂ Moonshine. **Facilities** ♣ (Bar Garden) ♦ Garden ⟫ Beer festival

MARPLE BRIDGE
Map 16 SJ98

Hare & Hounds

tel: 0161 427 4042 **19 Mill Brow SK6 5LW**
email: haremillbrow@gmail.com
dir: *From A626 in Marple Bridge (at lights at river bridge) follow Mellor signs into Town St. 1st left into Hollins Ln. Right at T-junct into Ley Ln. Pub 0.25m on left*

Idyllic rural retreat in lovely countryside

Tucked away in a secluded hamlet in the hills fringing the Peak District, this comfortable community local first opened its doors in 1805. It retains much character of days gone by and is a popular stop with ramblers exploring the countless paths threading the ridges, moors and wooded cloughs hereabouts. Roaring winter fires take away the chill; or settle down outside with a glass of Stockport-brewed Robinsons beer and anticipate freshly cooked mains such as lamb loin with asparagus, peppers, confit tomato and garlic; or cheddar cheese and spring onion pie, with chocolate and mango coulis-topped egg custard to finish.

Open Mon-Tue 5-10 (Wed-Thu 5-12 Fri 12-3 5-12 Sat 12-12 Sun 12-10) Closed Mon-Thu L **Food** Lunch Fri-Sat 12-2, Sun 1-7 Dinner Wed-Sat 6-9.30, Sun 1-7 Av main course £13 ⊕ ROBINSONS ◀ Unicorn, Hatters, Dizzy Blonde, Seasonal Ales ♂ Westons Stowford Press. **Facilities** Non-diners area ♣ (Bar Restaurant Outside area) ♦ Children's portions Outside area ⟫ Parking WiFi

MELLOR
Map 16 SJ98

The Moorfield Arms ★★★★ INN

tel: 0161 427 1580 **Shiloh Rd SK6 5NE**
email: moorfieldarms@gmail.com **web:** www.moorfieldarms.com
dir: *From Marple station down Brabyns Brow to lights. Right into Town St. 3m, left into Shiloh Rd. 0.5m, pub on left*

Lovely views and good food

This old pub dates from 1640 and retains plenty of old-world charm and atmosphere. With stunning views of Kinder Scout and Lantern Pike, The Moorfield Arms makes an ideal Peak District base and is popular with fell walkers. The extensive menu includes fish specials and slow-roasted lamb in mint gravy and finished with fresh rosemary from the pub's own herb garden. When the sun makes an appearance, head for the garden terrace. Situated in a barn conversion, the en suite rooms are comfortable and stylish.

Open Tue-Sat 12-2.30 6-12 (Sun 12-9) Closed Mon **Food** Lunch Tue-Sat 12-2, Sun 12-9 Dinner Tue-Fri 6.30-9, Sat 6-9, Sun 12-9 Set menu available ⊕ FREE HOUSE ◾ Wychwood Hobgoblin, Marston's EPA. ♥ 12 **Facilities** Non-diners area ♦❙ Children's menu Garden ⼝ Parking 🚌 **Rooms** 4

OLDHAM | Map 16 SD90

NEW The Old Bell Inn ★★★★ INN ⊚

tel: 01457 870130 **5 Huddersfield Rd, Delph OL3 5EG**
email: info@theoldbellinn.co.uk **web:** www.theoldbellinn.co.uk
dir: M62 junct 22, A672 to Denshaw junct (signed Saddleworth). Left onto A6052 signed Delph. Through Delph to T-junct. Left onto A62, pub 150yds on left

Historic coaching inn with excellent food

Legend has it that highwayman Dick Turpin was rested here on his way to the gallows; more certain is that a young Queen Victoria stayed when visiting York. Standards are high throughout, whether for a well-kept pint of Black Sheep in the bar, a relaxing snack in the brasserie, a special-occasion dinner in the restaurant, or a night in one of the bedrooms. A typical choice from chef Mark Pemberton's signature menu could commence with Port of Lancaster smoked haddock with cheese and leek fishcake; continue with Round Green Farm venison loin on the bone; and finish grandly with grandma's sticky marmalade pudding.

Open all day all wk **Food** Lunch all wk 12-5 Dinner Mon-Sat 5-9.30, Sun 5-9 Set menu available Restaurant menu available all wk ⊕ FREE HOUSE ◾ Timothy Taylor Landlord & Golden Best, Black Sheep Best Bitter ♂ Thatchers. **Facilities** Non-diners area ♦❙ Children's menu Children's portions Garden Outside area ⼝ Parking WiFi 🚌 **Rooms** 18

The Roebuck Inn

tel: 0161 624 7819 **Strinesdale OL4 3RB**
email: sehowarth1@hotmail.com
dir: From Oldham Mumps Bridge take Huddersfield Rd (A62), right at 2nd lights into Ripponden Rd (A672), 1m right at lights into Turfpit Ln, 1m

Country pub not far from Oldham

A thousand feet up in Strinedale on the edge of Saddleworth Moor, this traditionally styled inn provides a menu with plenty of choice. Starters include Bury black pudding with hot mustard sauce, and smoked salmon and prawns, then comes a long list of main courses, including fillet of beef Stroganoff; fajitas with sour cream and guacamole; roast half-duck with orange stuffing; and deep-fried haddock in batter. Vegetarians could well find an option like spinach and ricotta tortellini with roasted peppers. Beers come from a variety of local breweries.

Open all wk 12-3 5-11 (Fri-Sun 12-11) **Food** Lunch all wk 12-2.15 Dinner all wk 5-9.15 Set menu available Restaurant menu available all wk ⊕ FREE HOUSE ◾ Black Sheep. ♥ 9 **Facilities** Non-diners area ❀ (Bar Garden) ♦❙ Children's menu Children's portions Play area Garden Parking WiFi 🚌

The White Hart Inn ⊚ | PICK OF THE PUBS

tel: 01457 872566 **51 Stockport Rd, Lydgate OL4 4JJ**
email: bookings@thewhitehart.co.uk
dir: From Manchester A62 to Oldham. Right onto bypass, A669 through Lees. In 500yds past Grotton, at brow of hill right onto A6050

Charming dining pub with award-winning gardens

High on the hillside overlooking Oldham and Manchester, The White Hart is owned by Charles Brierley, who converted the ground floor into a smart bar and brasserie, and who also put together the wine list after months of research. There's been a pub on this site since 1788, when its vast cellars were used for brewing beer using water from the well. The inn has retained its period charm of beams, exposed stonework and open fireplaces, blending these with contemporary decor. The kitchen team believe in creating 'meals, not sculptures on a plate' and in making good use of local ingredients to offer cosmopolitan dishes. Sample tuna sashimi, followed by slow-cooked rabbit leg, and vanilla cheesecake in the rustic brasserie. Book the contemporary restaurant for the seven-course chef's choice tasting menu. There's also an intimate library dining area.

Open all day all wk Closed 26 Dec, 1 Jan **Food** Lunch Mon-Sat 12-2.30, Sun 12-8 Dinner Mon-Sat 6-9.30, Sun 12-8 Set menu available Restaurant menu available Wed-Sat eve ⊕ FREE HOUSE ◾ Timothy Taylor Landlord & Golden Best, JW Lees Bitter, Thwaites Wainwright ♂ Westons Stowford Press. ♥ 9 **Facilities** Non-diners area ♦❙ Children's menu Garden ⼝ Beer festival Parking WiFi

---

SALFORD | Map 15 SJ89

The King's Arms

tel: 0161 839 8726 **11 Bloom St M3 6AN**
email: kingsarmssalford@gmail.com
dir: Phone for detailed directions

Impressive Victorian pub with Bohemian atmosphere

Redevelopment has swept away much of old Salford. Fortunately this striking street-corner edifice survives intact amidst the concrete, steel and glass, across the River Irwell from Manchester's gleaming centre. It's a grass-roots venue renowned for arts, festivals and creative exhibitions. Music and theatre feature in the busy function room; co-owner Paul Heaton is a celebrated musician whilst the pub itself features in the cult TV series Fresh Meat. At this wet-led pub (no food except Sunday roasts) you'll find an ever-changing range of up to six beers, mostly from Greater Manchester's renowned microbrewery culture; guest ciders and continental bottled beers add to the lively jigsaw.

Open all wk Mon-Wed 4-close (Thu-Sun 12-close) **Food** Lunch Sun 12-8 Dinner Sun 12-8 Set menu available ⊕ FREE HOUSE ◾ 6 changing guest ales ♂ 2 changing guest ciders. ♥ **Facilities** Non-diners area ❀ (Bar Restaurant Garden) ♦❙ Garden ⼝ Beer festival WiFi 🚌 (notice required)

STOCKPORT | Map 16 SJ89

The Arden Arms

tel: 0161 480 2185 **23 Millgate SK1 2LX**
email: steve@ardenarms.com
dir: M60 junct 27 to town centre. Across mini rdbt, at lights turn left. Pub on right of next rdbt behind Asda

Timeless gem with interesting real ales

In the centre of Stockport, this Grade II listed late-Georgian coaching inn retains its unspoilt multi-roomed layout and original tiled floors. The building was last modernised in 1908, giving drinkers the opportunity to order from the traditional curved bar before settling down by the coal fire or in the tiny snug behind the bar. Outside, the large cobbled courtyard is used for alfresco dining and summer concerts. The lunch menu has an extensive list of hot and cold sandwiches and daily-changing specials, while a cheese and onion pie or pan-fried lamb chops may be dinner options. There's always a traditional Sunday roast, as well as jazz nights and charity quizzes.

Open all wk 12-12 Closed 25-26 Dec, 1 Jan **Food** Lunch Mon-Fri 12-2.30, Sat 12-4, Sun 12-6.30 Dinner Thu-Sat 6-9 Av main course £9.95 ⊕ ROBINSONS ◾ Unicorn, Trooper, 1892, Dizzy Blonde, Seasonal ales ♂ Westons Stowford Press. ♥ 9 **Facilities** Non-diners area ❀ (Bar Restaurant Garden) ♦❙ Garden ⼝ WiFi

STOCKPORT *continued*

The Nursery Inn

tel: 0161 432 2044 **Green Ln, Heaton Norris SK4 2NA**
email: nurseryinn@hydesbrewery.com
dir: *M60 junct 1, A5145 towards Didsbury. At lights right into Bankhall Rd (B5169), 5th right into Green Ln. Pass rugby club. Right onto narrow cobbled road, pub 100yds on right*

1930s pub with its own bowling green

The hub of the community, The Nursery Inn is an unspoilt Grade II listed hostelry, which can be located down a cobbled lane. In the spacious multi-roomed interior, including the oak-panelled lounge, you can drink beers from Hydes and enjoy some good value, home-cooked lunchtime snacks (the kitchen is closed in the evening). Sandwiches, toasties, jacket potatoes and pub-grub mains like gammon, scampi and rib-eye steak are available. The pub's well-used bowling green is to the rear. Eight guest real ales on handpump are served at the three annual beer festivals.

Open all day all wk **Food** Lunch Tue-Fri 12-2.30, Sat-Sun 12-4 ⊕ HYDES BREWERY ◀ Original, Jekyll's Gold & Seasonal ales, Guest ales. **Facilities** Non-diners area ❖ (Bar Garden) ♦ Children's portions Garden ⌁ Beer festival Parking WiFi ▭

■ WALMERSLEY | Map 15 SD81

The Lord Raglan

tel: 0161 764 6680 **Nangreaves BL9 6SP**
dir: *M66 junct 1, A56 to Walmersley. Left into Palatine Drive, left into Ribble Drive, left into Walmersley Old Rd to Nangreaves*

Recommended for its own microbrewery beers

The rambling, stone-built Lord Raglan is set beside a cobbled lane high on the moors above Bury, at the head of a former weaving hamlet, where lanes and tracks dissipate into deep, secluded gorges rich in industrial heritage. Beers brewed at the on-site Leyden microbrewery may be taken in the garden, where the throaty cough of steam engines on the East Lancashire Railway echoes off the River Irwell's steep valley sides below the towering Peel Monument. Reliable, traditional pub grub and changing specials take the edge off walkers' appetites. Try the chicken and mushroom pie, hot steak sandwich, or grilled halibut steak served with a lime and tomato salsa. There are beer festivals in the summer and autumn.

Open all wk 12-2.30 6-11 (Fri 12-2.30 5-11 Sat-Sun all day) **Food** Lunch Mon-Fri 12-2, Sat 12-9, Sun 12-8 Dinner Mon-Thu 6-9, Fri 5-9, Sat 12-9, Sun 12-8 ⊕ FREE HOUSE ◀ Leyden Nanny Flyer, Crowning Glory, Light Brigade, Black Pudding ♂ Wilce's Herefordshire. ♀ 10 **Facilities** ❖ (Bar Garden) ♦ Children's menu Children's portions Garden Beer festival Parking WiFi ▭

■ ALTON | Map 5 SU73

The Anchor Inn ★★★★★ RR ◉◉ PICK OF THE PUBS

tel: 01420 23261 **Lower Froyle GU34 4NA**
email: info@anchorinnatlowerfroyle.co.uk web: www.anchorinnatlowerfroyle.co.uk
dir: *From A31 follow Bentley signs*

Celebrating the traditional English country inn

A 16th-century, tile-hung farmhouse forms the nucleus of the Anchor. It's one of the Miller's Collection of traditional English inns in Hampshire and Berkshire, all four of which focus on fine food and beer and country sports. Low ceilings, wooden floors, exposed beams and open fires suggest that little has changed for decades in the intimate snug and saloon bar, source of local beers Triple fff Alton's Pride, Andwell King John and Bowman Wallops Wood. The restaurant's two AA Rosette award recognises the quality of the regularly changing, locally sourced food that at lunchtime or dinner could be pan-fried cod fillet with potato gnocchi, Jerusalem artichoke, spinach, and mushroom and chestnut sauce; pulled pork with pan haggerty, cabbage and bacon; or butternut squash ravioli with rocket, aged balsamic and toasted pumpkin seeds. Working closely with the kitchen team is French Master Sommelier Vincent Gasnier.

Open all day all wk Closed 25 Dec **Food** Lunch all wk 12-2.30 Dinner all wk 6.30-9.30 ⊕ FREE HOUSE/MILLER'S COLLECTION ◀ Triple fff Alton's Pride, Andwell King John, Bowman Wallops Wood ♂ Westons Stowford Press. ♀ 9 **Facilities** Non-diners area ❖ (Bar Garden) ♦ Children's menu Children's portions Garden ⌁ Parking WiFi ▭ **Rooms** 5

■ AMPFIELD | Map 5 SU42

White Horse at Ampfield

tel: 01794 368356 **Winchester Rd SO51 9BQ**
email: whitehorseinn@hotmail.co.uk
dir: *From Winchester take A3040, then A3090 towards Romsey. Ampfield in 7m. Or M3 junct 13, A335 (signed Chandler's Ford). At lights right onto B3043, follow Chandler's Ford Industrial Estate then Hursley signs. Left onto A3090 to Ampfield*

Traditional village inn once frequented by pilgrims

With roots as a pilgrims' inn in the 16th century, the timber-framed White Horse is the only pub in the village in which The Rev W. Awdry, *Thomas the Tank Engine's* creator, lived as a boy. The building is home to three large inglenooks, the one in the public bar having an iron fireback decorated with the crest of Charles I and hooks on which to hang bacon sides for smoking. Typical dishes are mushroom mille feuille with mixed bean and chickpea cassoulet and pea purée; roast chicken breast with sweet chilli and honey sauce; and smoked trout with new potatoes and salad.

Open all day all wk 11-11 (Sun 12-9) **Food** Lunch Mon-Fri 12-2.30, Sat 12-9, Sun 12-5 Dinner Mon-Fri 6-9, Sat 12-9 ⊕ GREENE KING ◀ IPA, Morland Old Speckled Hen & Original. ♀ 14 **Facilities** Non-diners area ❖ (Bar Garden Outside area) ♦ Children's menu Children's portions Play area Garden Outside area ⌁ Parking WiFi ▭ (notice required)

PICK OF THE PUBS

The Wellington Arms ❀❀

BAUGHURST　　　　Map 5 SU56

tel: 0118 982 0110
Baughurst Rd RG26 5LP
email: hello@thewellingtonarms.com
web: www.thewellingtonarms.com
dir: *From A4, E of Newbury, through Aldermaston. At 2nd rdbt 2nd exit signed Baughurst, left at T-junct, pub 1m*

Drawing discerning diners from miles around

Lost down a maze of lanes in peaceful countryside between Basingstoke and Newbury is the smart, whitewashed 'Welly', a former hunting lodge for the Duke of Wellington. Inside are wooden tables, tiled floors and attractively patterned curtains and blinds. Jason King and Simon Page have worked wonders with the place since taking over some nine years ago. Their ethos is simple: local, well-priced and delicious food. Jason's award-winning, daily chalkboard menus offer plenty of interest and imagination and much of the produce is organic, local or home grown. Salad leaves, herbs and vegetables are grown in the pub's polytunnel and raised vegetable beds, free-range eggs come from their rare-breed and rescue hens, and there are also rare-breed sheep, Tamworth pigs and two beehives. This might translate to a starter of home-reared Tamworth pig pork shoulder potted with seeded

mustard and thyme; or twice-baked Marksbury Cheddar soufflé on buttered zucchini, pine nuts and double cream. Follow with potpie of braised Baughurst venison; or roast line-caught cod fillet with hand gathered mushrooms, veal jus and mash. One of the Wellington's home-made desserts will make the perfect finish - perhaps flourless dark chocolate and walnut torte with caramel ice cream; or jelly of home-made elderflower cordial with Persian fairy floss. The dining room is small so booking is still advisable, or maybe just arrive early to secure a table. The well tended garden is an extension for diners when the sun shines too ; if the weather is on the chilly side, just ask to borrow a cosy mohair rug to keep you warm.

Open 12-3 6-11 (Sun 12-3) Closed Sun eve **Food** Lunch 12-3 Dinner Mon-Sat 6-9 Set menu available Restaurant menu available all wk. ⊕ FREE HOUSE ◪ Wadworth, West Berkshire, Two Cocks, Wild Weather Ales Ö Tutts Clump. ♟ 9 **Facilities** ❧ (Bar Restaurant Garden) ⫼ Children's menu Children's portions Garden ⩍ Parking ▭ (notice required) WiFi

AMPORT
Map 5 SU34

The Hawk Inn

tel: 01264 710371 **SP11 8AE**
email: info@hawkinnamport.co.uk
dir: *Phone for detailed directions*

Both modern and traditional British food

In the light and spacious interior of adjoining rooms, the bar offers Ramsbury Gold real ale, while a meal at one of the widely-spaced tables could feature crispy squid with smoked paprika aïoli, or Jerusalem artichoke soup with truffle oil to start, followed by thyme and garlic roasted whole poussin with caramelised onions and hand-cut chips; or The Hawk Burger with smoked Applewood cheddar, bacon and fries. The terrace area affords great views towards Pill Hill Brook.

Open all day all wk Closed 25 Dec **Food** Lunch all wk 12-2.30 Dinner Mon-Sat 6.30-9.30, Sun 6-9 Av main course £13.95 ⊕ FREE HOUSE ◀ Ramsbury Gold. ♀ 14 **Facilities** Non-diners area ♣ (Bar Outside area) ♦♦ Children's menu Children's portions Outside area ♬ Parking WiFi

ANDOVER
Map 5 SU34

Wyke Down Country Pub & Restaurant

tel: 01264 352048 **Wyke Down, Picket Piece SP11 6LX**
email: info@wykedown.co.uk
dir: *3m from Andover town centre on A303 follow signs for Wyke Down Caravan Park*

Converted barn and conservatory dining

A diversified farm on the outskirts of Andover, this establishment combines a pub/restaurant with a golf driving range, but still raises its own beef cattle. The pub started in a barn over 25 years ago and the restaurant was built some years later. A typical meal might be chef's own chicken liver pâté with onion marmalade and warm toast followed by steamed pudding filled with steak, bacon, onion and London Pride. Other choices include plenty from the grill and international favourites such as curry and Cajun chicken. You might want to time your visit for a summer Sunday car boot sale, held in an adjacent field.

Open all wk 12-3 6-11 Closed 25 Dec-2 Jan **Food** Lunch all wk 12-2 Dinner all wk 6-8 ⊕ FREE HOUSE ◀ Fuller's London Pride ♨ Aspall. **Facilities** Non-diners area ♦♦ Children's menu Children's portions Play area Garden ♬ Parking ◛ (notice required)

BALL HILL
Map 5 SU46

The Furze Bush Inn

tel: 01635 253228 **Hatt Common, East Woodhay RG20 0NQ**
email: info@furzebushinn.co.uk
dir: *From Newbury take A343 (Andover Road), pub signed*

Hearty food in a handy location

A popular rural free house, this is a perfect place for refreshment following a day at the Newbury Races, walking the Berkshire Downs, or visiting Highclere Castle, the location for the TV series *Downton Abbey*. The bar menu features a good range of favourites, such as baked in the box camembert; pork belly with apple mash potato; minted lamb shank and mustard mash; and lemon meringue pie. There's a large front garden, a children's play area and a rear patio with parasols – perfect for summer drinking.

Open all day all wk **Food** Lunch Mon-Fri 12-3, Sat 12-9, Sun 12-8.30 Dinner Mon-Fri 5-9, Sat 12-9, Sun 12-8.30 Restaurant menu available all wk ⊕ FREE HOUSE ◀ Greene King Abbot Ale & IPA, Salisbury English Ale. ♀ 9 **Facilities** Non-diners area ♦♦ Children's menu Play area Garden ♬ Beer festival Parking WiFi ◛

BAUGHURST
Map 5 SU56

The Wellington Arms ◉◉
PICK OF THE PUBS

See Pick of the Pubs on page 221

BEAULIEU
Map 5 SU30

The Drift Inn

tel: 023 8029 2342 **Beaulieu Rd SO42 7YQ**
email: bookatable@driftinn.co.uk
dir: *From Lyndhurst take B3056 (Beaulieu Rd) signed Beaulieu. Cross railway line, inn on left*

Family-friendly New Forest inn

Part of the New Forest Hotels group, the inn is surrounded by the glorious New Forest. The word 'drift' refers to the centuries-old, twice a year, round-up of the 3,000-plus free-wandering ponies. Beers from Ringwood on the western side of the forest and a guest ale are served in the bar, while in the restaurant a competitively priced menu lists chicken linguine with bacon, parsley and garlic; steak and ale pie; mushroom and cherry tomato Stroganoff; and a selection of sandwiches, baguettes and jacket potatoes. Outside are two children's play areas and large gardens, although no one minds if you come inside wearing walking boots and with your dog in tow.

Open all day all wk 10am-11pm (Sat 9am-11pm Sun 9am-10.30pm) **Food** Lunch all wk 12-3 (Etr-Oct 12-9) Dinner all wk 6-9 (Etr-Oct 12-9) Av main course £10.50 ⊕ FREE HOUSE ◀ Ringwood Best Bitter, Old Thumper & Fortyniner, Guest ales ♨ Thatchers. **Facilities** Non-diners area ♣ (Bar Restaurant Garden) ♦♦ Children's menu Children's portions Play area Garden ♬ Beer festival Parking WiFi ◛ (notice required)

BEAUWORTH
Map 5 SU52

The Milburys

tel: 01962 771248 **SO24 0PB**
email: martin1949@gma.co.uk
dir: *A272 towards Petersfield, 6m, turn right for Beauworth*

Popular community pub with great views and traditional pub grub

Dating from the 17th century and taking its name from the Bronze Age barrow nearby, this rustic hill-top pub is noted for its massive, 250-year-old treadmill that used to draw water from the 300-ft well in the bar. In summer, sweeping views across Hampshire can be savoured from the lofty garden. Inside you will find a great selection of real ales which you can enjoy by the warming winter fires. Traditional pub food, such as steak and ale pie and battered cod, is served all week in the bar and restaurant. There's a skittle alley, and car, motor cycle and caravan rallies are held here.

Open all wk **Food** Lunch all wk 12-2 Dinner all wk 6-9 Av main course £10 ⊕ FREE HOUSE ◀ Milburys Best, Goddards Ale of Wight, Hop Back Summer Lightning & Crop Circle ♨ Westons Stowford Press. **Facilities** Non-diners area ♣ (Bar Garden) ♦♦ Children's menu Children's portions Play area Family room Garden ♬ Parking ◛

The Sun Inn

Bentworth, Hampshire GU34 5JT • **Tel:** 01420 562338

Website: www.thesuninnbentworth.co.uk • **Email:** info@thesuninnbentworth.co.uk

Hidden down a lane on the edge of Bentworth Village in Hampshire, *The Sun Inn* is a pretty flower-adorned and unspoilt rural free-house dating back to the 17th century when it was a pair of traditional cottages.

The landlady Mary Holmes has been at *The Sun* for the past 17 years and has ensured the pub has kept its original character. The brick and board floors are laid with a rustic mix of scrubbed pine tables, benches and settles, the original beams are hung with sparkling horse brasses, while the walls are adorned with plates and prints depicting the history of the village of Bentworth.

Nestle in front of one of the three crackling log fires warming each of the interlinked rooms. Peruse a magazine, enjoy the fresh flowers and relax in a cosy candlelit atmosphere with friendly helpful service. A thriving free house, the Sun offers a selection of real ales from around the local Hampshire area all on hand pump. These include *Andwells Resolute, Hogsback T.E.A, Bowman's Swift One* and *Ringwood Best*. As well as local real ales there is a wide range of guest beers including *Fuller's London Pride, Timothy Taylor's Landlord*, and *Sharps Doombar*, plus many more regular favourites.

As well as *The Sun's* charm and extensive range of real ales and lagers, this freehouse really comes into its own by serving hearty home-cooked dishes that make a trip to this pub well worth the visit. Dishes range from ploughman's lunches, home-made soups and sandwiches to more filling options such as beer-battered cod, calves liver and bacon, tiger prawns and scallops in garlic butter, steak and Guinness pie, and half-shoulder of lamb with redcurrant and mint jelly. Game is also served in season including venison, partridge and pheasant.

If that is not enough to fill you up indulge in some of the home-made puddings like apple and rhubarb crumble, warm chocolate brownie, sticky toffee pudding, banoffee pie or strawberry and white chocolate cheesecake. When visiting *The Sun Inn* you will be sure to receive a warm and friendly welcome from Mary and her team.

BENTLEY
Map 5 SU74

The Bull Inn

tel: 01420 22156 **GU10 5JH**
email: enquiries@thebullinnbentley.co.uk
dir: *2m from Farnham on A31 towards Winchester*

Period details and an extensive menu

Exposed beams, real fires and plenty of alfresco seating make this 15th-century coaching inn well worth a visit. There's also a great selection of food. Lunch choices brings The Bull platter, sandwiches, salads and a two-course lunch special; the à la carte menu includes chargrill dishes. There's a good selection of wines, and real ales such as Fuller's London Pride, Ringwood Best Bitter and St Austell Tribute.

Open all day all wk 11-11 (Sun 12-10.30) Closed 1 Jan **Food** Lunch Mon-Sat 12-2.30, Sun 12-4.30 Dinner Mon-Sat 6-9.30 Av main course £15 Set menu available ⊕ ENTERPRISE INNS ◀ Fuller's London Pride, St Austell Tribute, Ringwood Best Bitter ⚆ Aspall. ♟ 9 **Facilities** Non-diners area ❧ (Bar Outside area) ♦ Children's menu Children's portions Outside area ⊞ Parking WiFi ☕ (notice required)

BENTWORTH
Map 5 SU64

The Sun Inn
PICK OF THE PUBS

See Pick of the Pubs on opposite page and advert on page 223

BISHOP'S WALTHAM
Map 5 SU51

The Hampshire Bowman

tel: 01489 892940 **Dundridge Ln SO32 1GD**
email: hampshirebowman@uwclub.net
dir: *From Bishop's Waltham on B3035 towards Corhampton. Right signed Dundridge. 1.2m to Pub*

Rustic rural gem lost down lanes

A true rural local, set in 10 acres beside a country lane in rolling downland, this unassuming Victorian pub remains delightfully old fashioned. In the beamed, simply furnished and brick-floored bar you'll find time-honoured pub games and barrels of beer on racks behind the bar. Ale-lovers come for foaming pints of Bowman Ales Swift One or Wallops Wood, or a glass of heady Black Dragon cider, best enjoyed in the rambling orchard garden. Soak it up with a traditional bar meal, perhaps ham, egg and chips; liver and bacon with mash and shallot jus; or fish and chips. Don't miss the July and December beer festivals.

Open all day all wk **Food** Lunch Mon-Thu 12-2, Fri-Sun 12-9 Dinner Mon-Thu 6-9, Fri-Sun 12-9 Av main course £8.50 ⊕ FREE HOUSE ◀ Bowman Ales Swift One & Wallops Wood, Guest ales ⚆ Gwynt y Ddraig Black Dragon, Lilley's Sunset, Guest ciders. ♟ 10 **Facilities** Non-diners area ❧ (Bar Restaurant Garden) ♦ Children's menu Children's portions Play area Garden ⊞ Beer festival Cider festival Parking WiFi ☕ (notice required)

BOLDRE
Map 5 SZ39

The Hobler Inn

tel: 01590 623944 **Southampton Rd, Battramsley SO41 8PT**
email: hedi@alcatraz.co.uk
dir: *From Brockenhurst take A337 towards Lymington. Pub on main road*

New Forest pub popular with families

On the main road between Brockenhurst and Lymington, The Hobler has a large grassed area and trestle tables ideal for families visiting the New Forest. The Hobler Inn is more London wine bar than local with stylish leather furniture, but still serves a well-kept pint of Ringwood. The food, served all day, is locally sourced and freshly cooked.

Open all day all wk **Food** Contact pub for details Av main course £10 Set menu available ⊕ ENTERPRISE INNS ◀ Ringwood Best Bitter, Timothy Taylor. ♟ 10 **Facilities** Non-diners area ♦ Children's menu Garden Parking WiFi ☕ (notice required)

The Red Lion
PICK OF THE PUBS

tel: 01590 673177 **Rope Hill SO41 8NE**
dir: *M27 junct 1, A337 through Lyndhurst & Brockenhurst towards Lymington, follow Boldre signs*

15th-century pub for all seasons

Mentioned in the Domesday Book, the Red Lion sits at the crossroads in the ancient village of Boldre. The rambling interior contains cosy, beamed rooms, log fires and rural memorabilia; the rooms glow with candlelight on antique copper and brass. Expect a genuinely warm welcome and traditional values, with Ringwood ales on offer at the bar. The kitchen places an emphasis on traditional meals made using the very best of the forest's produce. Typical starters include tea-smoked Hampshire trout with home-made potato salad; and twice baked goats' cheese soufflé. Typical of the Red Lion's traditional favourites are lamb shank slow braised with redcurrant, rosemary and honey, mash and root vegetables; and free-range chicken supreme, crispy bacon, smoked cheese sauce and chunky chips. In the summer, you can enjoy full table service outside on the herb patio.

Open all wk 11-3 5.30-11 (Sun 12-8) (summer Sat 11-11) Closed 25 Dec **Food** Lunch Mon-Sat 12-2.30, Sun 12-8 (summer Sat 12-9.30) Dinner Mon-Sat 6-9.30 Sun 12-8 (summer Sat 12-9.30) Av main course £7.50 Restaurant menu available all wk ⊕ FREE HOUSE ◀ Ringwood Best Bitter & Fortyniner, Brakspear Oxford Gold, Guinness, Guest ales ⚆ Thatchers Gold. ♟ 15 **Facilities** Non-diners area ❧ (Bar Restaurant Garden) ♦ Children's portions Garden ⊞ Parking WiFi ☕ (notice required)

BRANSGORE
Map 5 SZ19

The Three Tuns Country Inn ⊛
PICK OF THE PUBS

tel: 01425 672232 **Ringwood Rd BH23 8JH**
email: threetunsinn@btconnect.com
dir: *1.5m from A35 Walkford junct. 3m from Christchurch & 1m from Hinton Admiral railway station*

Thatched, yet spacious, New Forest pub with a large garden

This chocolate box 17th-century inn is adorned with a riot of flowers in the spring and summer. It's set in a south-facing garden with over 2,500 square metres of lawn surrounded by fields, trees and grazing ponies. Newly re-thatched and refurbished, the Three Tuns' serves excellent food and drink in any of five public areas. The comfortable lounge bar warmed by log fire stocks an admirable range of cask-conditioned real ales and ciders, with mulled wine and cider in winter; an oak-beamed snug, similarly warmed, has biscuits and water for the dog; a large terrace with water feature suits summer alfresco dining; and the 60-seat restaurant serves AA Rosette-quality dishes. Favourites such as shepherd's pie or bangers and mash sit alongside menu specials based on Mudeford fish; roast corn-fed chicken; or local pigeon, rabbit and venison. A cider festival is held during the summer holidays, followed by a beer festival at the end of September.

Open all day all wk 11-11 (Sun 12-10.30) **Food** Lunch Mon-Fri 12-2.15, Sat-Sun 12-9.15 Dinner Mon-Fri 6.30-9.15, Sat-Sun 12-9.15 Set menu available Restaurant menu available all wk ⊕ ENTERPRISE INNS ◀ St Austell Tribute, Ringwood Best Bitter & Fortyniner, Exmoor Gold, Otter Bitter, Timothy Taylor, Skinner's Betty Stogs & Cornish Knocker ⚆ Thatchers Gold & Katy, New Forest Traditional. ♟ 9 **Facilities** Non-diners area ❧ (Bar Garden) ♦ Children's menu Children's portions Garden ⊞ Beer festival Cider festival Parking WiFi ☕ (notice required)

PICK OF THE PUBS

The Sun Inn

BENTWORTH Map 5 SU64

Tel: 01420 562338
Sun Hill GU34 5JT
email: info@thesuninnbentworth.co.uk
web: www.thesuninnbentworth.co.uk
dir: *From A339 between Alton &*
Basingstoke follow Bentworth signs

A step back in time to pretty pub with hearty food

Just as you think you're about to leave the village behind, this pretty, foliage covered, rural free house comes into view. Dating from the 17th century, when it was built as a pair of traditional cottages, little can have changed inside in recent years, which is how landlady Mary Holmes intends things to stay. The floors in the three interlinked rooms are laid with brick and board; the furniture is a mix of scrubbed pine tables, benches and settles; the old ceiling beams are hung with horse brasses; and assorted prints and plates decorate the walls. Log fires may be burning, while tasteful cosmetic touches – magazines, fresh flowers, flickering candlelight – enhance the period feel still further. Apart from The Sun's overall charm, people come here for its good selection of real ales, including from Andwell, Sharp's, Fuller's, Ringwood and Stonehenge breweries, as well as Aspall cider. They come too for the extensive range of hearty home-cooked dishes, which run from ploughman's, home-made soup and sandwiches, to tiger prawns and scallops in garlic butter; chicken breast in Stilton and walnut sauce; steak, mushroom and ale pie; and Yorkshire pudding with vegetable sausages. Game in season includes pheasant, and venison cooked in Guinness with pickled walnuts. The uncomplicated desserts are typically warm chocolate brownie, banoffee pie, and treacle tart. There's a lot to see and do in the area: in Selborne, there's the house where naturalist Gilbert White lived and where the Oates (of Scott's ill-fated 1911-12 Antarctic expedition fame) Collection is now found, and Jane Austen's House at Chawton is an easy drive too. A ride on the Watercress Line from Alton about 15 minutes away takes you on a 10-mile steam train journey through the Hampshire countryside.

Open all wk 12-3 6-11 (Sun 12-10.30)
Food Lunch all wk 12-2 Dinner all wk 7-9.30 ⊞ FREE HOUSE ◀ Andwell Resolute, Ringwood Fortyniner, Sharp's Doom Bar, Stonehenge Pigswill, Fuller's London Pride, Black Sheep Ŏ Aspall.
Facilities ❀ (Bar Garden) ♦♦ Children's menu Children's portions Family room Garden Parking

BROCKENHURST
Map 5 SU30

The Filly Inn ★★★★ INN

tel: 01590 623449 **Lymington Rd SO42 7UF**
email: info@thefillyinn.co.uk **web:** www.thefillyinn.co.uk
dir: *On A337, 1m S of Brockenhurst towards Lymington*

A gem in the heart of the New Forest

Facing the open heathland of the New Forest National Park, this one-time coaching inn goes from strength to strength. On arrival you might be welcomed by the owners' dog, Bob. Seasonal menus list freshly prepared Hampshire-sourced dishes from pickled eggs to home-made puddings, a range that includes ploughman's platters; steak and ale pie; beer-battered fish and chips; and award-winning cheeses and pork pies. Outside, is an enclosed terrace and an ample garden.

Open all day all wk **Food** Lunch Mon-Fri 12-3, Sat-Sun all day Dinner Mon-Fri 5-9, Sat-Sun all day ⊕ PUNCH TAVERNS ◼ Rotating Guest ales ♻ Thatchers & Aspall. ▾11 **Facilities** Non-diners area ♣ (Bar Restaurant Garden) ♦◀ Children's menu Children's portions Garden ⋒ Parking WiFi ☜ (notice required) **Rooms** 5

BURGHCLERE
Map 5 SU46

Marco Pierre White The Carnarvon Arms

tel: 01635 278222 **Winchester Rd, Whitway RG20 9LE**
email: info@thecarnarvonarmshotel.com
dir: *M4 junct 13, A34 S to Winchester. Exit A34 at Tothill Services, follow Highclere Castle signs. Pub on right*

A relaxed country-pub environment

Originally a coaching inn for travellers to neighbouring Highclere Castle, this Grade II listed building constructed in the 1800s is steeped in history. The Carnarvon Arms is now a modern country inn, decorated with an eclectic mix of artefacts and art. At the bar, try The Governor, a British beer created in collaboration with JW Lees, or a cider of the same name from Westons. The kitchen team prepare Marco's culinary creations, including fried duck egg and Stornoway black pudding in brioche; kipper pâté with whisky; caramelised honey-roast belly of pork; and smoked haddock with poached eggs.

Open all day all wk **Food** Lunch all wk 12-2.30 Dinner all wk 6-9 ⊕ FREE HOUSE ◼ Black Sheep Bitter, Greene King London Glory, JW Lees The Governor ♻ Westons Old Rosie, Aspall. ▾15 **Facilities** Non-diners area ♣ (Bar) ♦◀ Children's menu Children's portions Outside area ⋒ Parking WiFi ☜ (notice required)

BURLEY
Map 5 SU20

The Burley Inn

tel: 01425 403448 **BH24 4AB**
email: info@theburleyinn.co.uk
dir: *4m SE of of Ringwood*

Favoured forest village setting

A great base from which to explore the tracks, paths and rides of the surrounding New Forest National Park, this imposing Edwardian edifice, in neat grounds behind picket fencing, is one of a small local chain of dining pubs combining the best of local real ales – Flack Manor and Fuller's breweries often feature - with homely, traditional pub grub from an extensive menu. Toast wintery toes before log fires or relax on the decking patio, looking forward to olde English fish pie or venison casserole, with key lime pie to finish, whilst idly watching free-roaming livestock amble by on the village lanes.

Open all day all wk **Food** Lunch all wk 12-10 Dinner all wk 12-10 ⊕ FREE HOUSE ◼ Flack Manor Double Drop, Fuller's London Pride, Guest ales ♻ Thatchers. ▾10 **Facilities** Non-diners area ♣ (Bar Outside area) Children's menu Children's portions Outside area ⋒ Parking WiFi ☜

CADNAM
Map 5 SU31

Sir John Barleycorn

tel: 023 8081 2236 **Old Romsey Rd SO40 2NP**
email: sjb@alcatraz.co.uk
dir: *From Southampton M27 junct 1 into Cadnam*

The oldest inn in the New Forest

The name of this friendly thatched establishment comes from a folksong celebrating the transformation of barley to beer. It is formed from three 12th-century cottages, one of which was once home to the charcoal burner who discovered the body of King William Rufus. Beers on offer are Fuller's London Pride and HSB, while ciders are represented by Westons Stowford Press. The menu has something for everyone with quick snacks and sandwiches, a children's menu and traditional dishes like New Forest sausages, honey-roast ham, and fillet of sea bass. More inventive options are chicken and pea risotto, and smoked mackerel salad.

Open all day all wk 11-11 **Food** Lunch Mon-Sat 12-late, Sun 12-8 Dinner Mon-Sat 12-late, Sun 12-8 ⊕ FULLER'S ◼ London Pride, George Gale & Co HSB, Guest ales ♻ Westons Stowford Press, Guest cider. ▾10 **Facilities** Non-diners area ♦◀ Children's menu Garden ⋒ Parking ☜ (notice required)

CHALTON
Map 5 SU71

The Red Lion
PICK OF THE PUBS

tel: 023 9259 2246 **PO8 0BG**
email: redlion.chalton@fullers.co.uk
dir: *Just off A3 between Horndean & Petersfield. Follow signs for Chalton*

Traditional English pub with South Downs views

Said to be the oldest pub in Hampshire, dating back to 1147, when it was built to house craftsmen constructing St Michael's church opposite. It retains an olde worlde English charm, from the thatched roof and whitewashed exterior to the brass knick-knacks, timbered beams and roaring fires inside. To one side a large purpose-built dining room is kept busy serving plates of pub grub. The expansive garden gives lovely views of the South Downs. Inside or out, and now under new management, this is a peaceful place to enjoy a Fuller's ale, or a bottle of Kopparberg cider for a change.

Open all day all wk 11.30-11 (Sun 12-10.30) **Food** Lunch Mon-Sat 12-9, Sun 12-8 Dinner Mon-Sat 12-9, Sun 12-8 Av main course £10.95 ⊕ FULLER'S ◼ London Pride, George Gale & Co Seafarers & HSB, Guest ales ♻ Kopparberg, Aspall. ▾20 **Facilities** Non-diners area ♣ (Bar Garden) ♦◀ Children's menu Children's portions Garden ⋒ Beer festival Parking WiFi ☜ (notice required)

CHARTER ALLEY
Map 5 SU55

The White Hart Inn

tel: 01256 850048 **White Hart Ln RG26 5QA**
email: enquiries@whitehartcharteralley.com
dir: *M3 junct 6, A339 towards Newbury. Right signed Ramsdell. Right at church, then 1st left into White Hart Ln*

Good pub food and reliable ales

When this free house opened in 1818, on the northern edge of the village overlooking open farmland and woods – just as today – it must have delighted the woodsmen and coach drivers visiting the farrier next door. Real ale pumps lined up on the herringbone-patterned, brick-fronted bar include Moor Revival, Triple fff Moondance and a couple from Bowman. The menu changes daily to offer typical locally sourced dishes as steak and Stilton pie; pork belly; rump steak burger; traditional cottage pie; and spinach and mushroom penne pasta. A patio leads into an attractive garden. Contact the inn for its occasional beer festival dates.

Open Mon 7-11 (Tue-Wed 12-2.30 7-11 Thu-Fri 12-2.30 5.30-11 Sat 12-3 6.30-11 Sun 12-4 7-10.30) Closed 25-26 Dec, 1 Jan, Mon L **Food** Lunch Tue-Sun 12-2 Dinner Tue-Sat 7-9 Av main course £11 ⊕ FREE HOUSE ◼ Triple fff Moondance, Bowman Swift One & Wallops Wood, Moor Revival. **Facilities** Non-diners area ❤ (Bar Garden) ❤ Children's menu Children's portions Family room Garden ⋒ Beer festival Parking WiFi 🚌 (notice required)

▌CHAWTON — — — — — — — — — — — — — — Map 5 SU73

The Greyfriar
tel: 01420 83841 **Winchester Rd GU34 1SB**
email: hello@thegreyfriar.co.uk **web:** www.thegreyfriar.co.uk
dir: *Just off A31 near Alton. Access to Chawton via A31/A32 junct. Follow Jane Austen's House signs. Pub opposite*

Old fashioned values and family-friendly

Opposite Jane Austen's House Museum stands this 16th-century pub. As well as its friendly atmosphere and delightful village setting, the south-facing suntrap garden is another draw. The pub is Fuller's-owned and offers London Pride and Seafarers along with great food. A sample menu includes Japanese breaded prawns or baked Tunworth cheese for two (Hampshire's answer to camembert) to start, followed by smoked mackerel fishcakes, braised lamb shank, 10-hour roasted belly pork, vegetable linguine, gammon steak or steak and ale pie. Sandwiches and jackets are also available for lunch.

Open all day all wk 12-11 (Sun 12-10.30) **Food** Lunch Mon-Sat 12-2.30, Sun 12-7 Dinner Mon-Sat 6-9.30 Av main course £12 Restaurant menu available all wk ⊕ FULLER'S ◼ London Pride, George Gale & Co Seafarers, Seasonal ales ♂ Aspall. ⍟ **Facilities** Non-diners area ❤ (Bar Garden) ❤ Children's portions Garden ⋒ Parking WiFi 🚌 (notice required)

▌CHERITON — — — — — — — — — — — — — — Map 5 SU52

The Flower Pots Inn
tel: 01962 771318 **SO24 0QQ**
dir: *A272 towards Petersfield, left onto B3046, pub 0.75m on right*

Popular village pub with its own microbrewery

Known almost universally as The Pots, this pub used to be a farmhouse and home to the head gardener of nearby Avington Park. These days, local beer drinkers know the pub well for its award-winning Flower Pots Bitter and Goodens Gold, brewed across the car park in the microbrewery. Simple home-made food includes hearty filled baps, toasted sandwiches, jacket potatoes, cheese and meat ploughman's and different hotpots – chilli con carne, lamb and apricot, steak and ale, spicy mixed bean. A large, safe garden, with a covered patio, allows children to let off steam (under 14s are not allowed in the bar). The pub holds a beer festival in August.

Open all wk 12-2.30 6-11 (Sun 12-3 7-10.30) **Food** Lunch all wk 12-1.45 Dinner Mon-Sat 7-8.45 ⊕ FREE HOUSE ◼ Flower Pots Bitter, Goodens Gold ♂ Westons Old Rosie. **Facilities** Non-diners area ❤ (Bar Garden) ❤ Children's portions Garden Beer festival Parking **Notes** ◉

▌CLANFIELD — — — — — — — — — — — — — — Map 5 SU71

The Rising Sun Inn ★★★ INN
tel: 023 9259 6975 **North Ln PO8 0RN**
email: enquiries@therisingsunclanfield.co.uk **web:** www.therisingsunclanfield.co.uk
dir: *A3(M) then A3 towards Petersfield. Left signed Clanfield. Follow brown inn signs*

Traditional village inn just inside the South Downs National Park

Although it looks two centuries old, the flint-faced Rising Sun was built in 2003. Apparently, in 1960, its predecessor was constructed in one day, even serving its first pint at 6pm. Today the bar sells a variety of real ales and ciders, as well as a selection of single malt whiskies. The menu focuses on pub classics such as liver and bacon, beer battered cod and lasagne, with support from leek and potato bake, tapas, salmon steak in prawn, mushroom and dill sauce, and a choice of baguettes and sandwiches. Tuesday night is steak night, curries are Thursday and it's Friday for music. The B&B accommodation is popular with walkers and cyclists on the South Downs Way.

Open all day all wk **Food** Lunch all wk 12-9 Dinner all wk 12-9 ⊕ ENTERPRISE INNS ◼ George Gale & Co HSB, Ringwood Best Bitter, Sharp's Doom Bar, Guest ales ♂ Westons Old Rosie, Thatchers Gold. **Facilities** Non-diners area ❤ (All areas) ❤ Children's menu Children's portions Garden Outside area ⋒ Beer festival Parking WiFi 🚌 (notice required) **Rooms** 3

▌CRAWLEY — — — — — — — — — — — — — — Map 5 SU43

The Fox and Hounds
tel: 01962 776006 **SO21 2PR**
email: foxandhoundscrawley@hotmail.co.uk
dir: *A34 onto A272 then 1st right into Crawley*

Attractive village pub known for its range of wines

Rebuilt in impressive mock-Tudor style in 1910, this popular inn serves a well-to-do village close enough to affluent Winchester to attract its citizens too. Dining tables grouped round a central bar soon fill up for well prepared chicken with Stilton and mushroom sauce; cod with basil and parmesan crust; home-made pies; and mushroom Stroganoff. To drink, there is an amazing number of wines by the glass and the beers come from Ringwood and Wychwood. Just down the road is a proper village duck pond.

Open all wk 11-3 6-11 (Sun 12-6) ⊕ ENTERPRISE INNS ◼ Ringwood Best Bitter, Salisbury English Ale, Sharp's Doom Bar, Wychwood Hobgoblin, Guest ales ♂ Westons Stowford Press, Symonds. **Facilities** ❤ (Bar Garden) ❤ Children's menu Children's portions Play area Garden Parking

CROOKHAM VILLAGE
Map 5 SU75

The Exchequer

tel: 01252 615336 **Crondall Rd GU51 5SU**
email: bookings@exchequercrookham.co.uk
dir: *M3 junct 5, A287 towards Farnham for 5m. Left to Crookham Village*

Welcoming dining pub with top-notch ales

Amongst the quiet villages of north Hampshire in the beautiful setting of Crookham Village, this whitewashed free house is just a stone's throw from the A287. With a new landlord, The Exchequer serves carefully chosen wines and local ales straight from the cask, and offers a great seasonal menu with dishes featuring the best local produce. Start with a sharing board of meze or perhaps a sweet pepper and goats' cheese tart. Main course dishes include crushed new potato, salmon and smoked haddock fishcake; and roast chicken breast wrapped in Parma ham and stuffed with pâté. Leave room for blackberry and apple crumble with custard. Sandwiches and pub classics are available at lunchtime.

Open all wk 12-3 6-11 (Fri-Sun 12-11) **Food** Lunch Tue-Fri 12-2, Sat 12-2.30, Sun 12-8 Dinner Tue-Fri 6-9, Sat 6-9.30, Sun 12-8 Av main course £9.50 Restaurant menu available all wk ⊕ FREE HOUSE ◀ Andwell, Hogs Back TEA, Ringwood Fortyniner ♂ Addlestones, Hogs Back Hazy Hog. ♚ 10 **Facilities** Non-diners area ◀ Children's menu Children's portions Garden ⩋ Parking WiFi

DROXFORD
Map 5 SU61

The Bakers Arms ◉
PICK OF THE PUBS

tel: 01489 877533 **High St SO32 3PA**
email: enquiries@thebakersarmsdroxford.com
dir: *10m E of Winchester on A32 between Fareham & Alton. 7m SW of Petersfield*

Hampshire food, Hampshire ales

Droxford is a pretty village in the Meon Valley, one of Hampshire's most attractive areas. So that's two reasons to head for this unpretentious, white-painted pub and restaurant. Reasons for going continue: it has plenty of country charm, the staff are friendly and locals clearly love the place, always a good sign. The village's own Bowman Brewery supplies the bar with Swift One and Wallops Wood, named after where it is brewed. Also in the bar you'll find home-made Cornish pasties, pickled eggs and onions, and hot filled baguettes, while over the big log fire a blackboard menu lists the day's AA Rosette-standard main dishes. Among these might be spiced Hyden Farm lamb salad with mint yogurt dressing; whole dressed crab with parmesan and hollandaise; grilled Hampshire rib-eye steak; and courgette, goats' cheese and pine nut parcel. Adam Cordery, the owner, shoots or grows much of the produce himself.

Open 11.45-3 6-11 (Sun 12-3) Closed Sun eve **Food** Lunch all wk 12-2 Dinner Mon-Sat 7-9 Set menu available ⊕ FREE HOUSE ◀ Bowman Swift One, Wallops Wood ♂ Thatchers. ♚ 11 **Facilities** Non-diners area ♣ (Bar Restaurant Garden) ◀ Children's portions Garden ⩋ Parking WiFi

DUMMER
Map 5 SU54

The Queen Inn

tel: 01256 397367 **Down St RG25 2AD**
email: richardmoore49@btinternet.com
dir: *From M3 junct 7 follow Dummer signs*

Country inn just off the M3

You can dine by candlelight in the restaurant at this low-beamed, 16th-century inn with a huge open log fire. The main menu offers a wide choice: steaks and burgers; fillet of beef medallions; teriyaki salmon; curry of the day; and warm bacon, mushroom and asparagus salad. Or at lunchtime there are savouries like Welsh rarebit and flame-grilled chicken ciabatta. Children are encouraged to have small adult portions, but have their own menu if all entreaties fail. There's a good real ale line-up, including Sharp's Doom Bar, Otter Bitter and guests.

Open all wk 11-3 6-11 (Sun 12-3 7-10.30) **Food** Lunch all wk 12-2.30 Dinner Mon-Sat 6.30-9.30, Sun 7-9 ⊕ ENTERPRISE INNS ◀ Otter Bitter, Sharp's Doom Bar, Guest ale ♂ Thatchers Gold, Westons Stowford Press. **Facilities** Non-diners area ◀ Children's menu Children's portions Garden Parking WiFi 🚐

The Sun Inn

tel: 01256 397234 **A30 Winchester Rd RG25 2DJ**
email: thesuninndummer@hotmail.co.uk
dir: *M3 junct 7, A30 (Winchester Rd) towards Basingstoke. Left onto A30 towards Winchester. Inn on right*

Certainly worth a detour from a motorway journey

The Sun has stood for many years alongside the main coaching route from London to Exeter, today's A30. Passing traffic is not a problem since most West Country travellers now use the M3, accessible from nearby junction 7. Moondance from Triple fff takes pole position in the bar, alongside Symonds cider, while in the restaurant the well conceived menu might list oven-roasted duck breast with dauphinoise potatoes; and pan-fried hake with roast red pepper, clams and buttered samphire alongside pub classics such ale-battered fish and triple cooked chips. A lovely garden lies at the back.

Open all wk 12-11 **Food** Lunch all wk 12-3 Dinner Mon-Sat 6-9 ⊕ FREE HOUSE ◀ Triple fff Moondance, Sharp's Doom Bar ♂ Symonds. ♚ 8 **Facilities** Non-diners area ♣ (Bar Garden) ◀ Children's menu Children's portions Play area Garden ⩋ Parking WiFi 🚐

DUNBRIDGE
Map 5 SU32

The Mill Arms ★★★★ INN

tel: 01794 340401 **Barley Hill SO51 0LF**
email: millarms@btconnect.com **web:** www.millarms.co.uk
dir: *From Romsey take A3057 signed Stockbridge & Winchester. Left onto B3084 through Awbridge to Dunbridge. Pub on left before rail crossing*

Smart country pub offering good food not far from the River Test

This attractive 18th-century inn is situated in the heart of the Test Valley and close to the River Test, one of the finest chalk streams in the world. Not surprisingly, the pub is popular with fly fishermen from far and wide. A traditional country inn with wood and stone floors, oak beams and open fires, the menus combine old favourites and contemporary dishes. An excellent grill menu showcases local produce including buffalo and rare-breed pork, and wood-fired pizzas are available to eat in or takeaway. There's also a function room, a skittle alley and large landscaped gardens.

Open 12-2.30 6-11 (Sat 12-11 Sun 12-4) Closed 25 Dec, Sun eve & Mon **Food** Lunch Tue-Fri 12-2.30, Sat 12-9.30, Sun 12-3 Dinner Tue-Thu 6-9, Fri-Sat 6-9.30 Restaurant menu available Tue-Sat ⊕ ENTERPRISE INNS ◀ Flack Manor Flack's Double Drop, Guest ales ♂ Addlestones, Symonds. ♚ 10 **Facilities** Non-diners area ♣ (Bar Garden) ◀ Children's menu Children's portions Garden ⩋ Parking WiFi 🚐 (notice required) **Rooms** 6

EAST BOLDRE
Map 5 SU30

Turfcutters Arms

tel: 01590 612331 **Main Rd SO42 7WL**
email: enquiries.turfcutters@gmail.com
dir: *From Beaulieu take B3055 towards Brockenhurst. Left at Hatchet Pond onto B3054 towards Lymington, turn left, follow signs for East Boldre. Pub approx 0.5m*

Off the beaten track and offering good value food

Five miles south of Beaulieu, this New Forest pub, easily recognised by its white picket fence, attracts cyclists, ramblers, dog-walkers and locals all year round. In winter the open fires warm the cockles, while the lovely garden comes into its own in summer. Good beer including Ringwood and draught ciders such as Thatchers complement a menu of unpretentious pub grub including baguettes, jacket potatoes and main meals such as fish and chips, BBQ belly pork, chicken curry, chicken burger and hommity pie. Children have their own menu, and canine treats are handed out at the bar. Time a visit for the annual beer festival.

Open all day all wk **Food** Lunch all wk 12-3 Dinner all wk 6-9 Av main course £10.50 Set menu available ⊕ ENTERPRISE INNS ◀ Ringwood Best Bitter, Fortyniner, Boondoggle, Young's Special ♂ Thatchers Gold. **Facilities** Non-diners area ✿ (Bar Restaurant Garden) ♦♦ Children's menu Children's portions Play area Garden ♬ Beer festival Parking WiFi ☞ (notice required)

EAST END
Map 5 SZ39

The East End Arms
PICK OF THE PUBS

tel: 01590 626223 **Main Rd SO41 5SY**
email: manager@eastendarms.co.uk
dir: *From Lymington towards Beaulieu (past Isle of Wight ferry), 3m to East End*

Striking all the right notes

Find the East End Arms by threading your way through lanes along the southern edge of the New Forest National Park; the Solent is just a short stroll south, and the delightful village of Bucklers Hard is nearby. It's a happy mix of community village inn and restaurant, with menus drawing on local produce and changing daily. The inviting Foresters Bar is pleasingly old-fashioned, with flagstoned floors and roaring fire adding to the pleasure of a gravity-drawn pint of Andwell's ale or a bottle of Brothers cider. Lunchtime sandwiches are served on granary or white bloomer with French fries or crisps. The bright and airy restaurant is decorated with photographs of musicians, reflecting the pub's ownership by Dire Straits' bass player John Illsley. Starters such as duck egg with Serrano ham, parmesan shavings and slow-roast tomatoes could be followed by bourguignon of New Forest venison.

Open all wk 11.30-3 6-11 (Fri-Sun 11.30-11) **Food** Lunch Mon-Sat 12-2.30 Dinner Mon-Sat 7-9 Av main course £14 Restaurant menu available lunch all wk ⊕ FREE HOUSE ◀ Ringwood Best Bitter & Fortyniner, Andwell's, Jennings, Cottage ♂ Thatchers, Brothers. **Facilities** Non-diners area ✿ (Bar Garden) ♦♦ Children's portions Garden Outside area ♬ Parking WiFi

---

EAST MEON
Map 5 SU62

Ye Olde George Inn

tel: 01730 823481 **Church St GU32 1NH**
email: yeoldegeorge@live.co.uk
dir: *S of A272 (Winchester/Petersfield). 1.5m from Petersfield turn left opposite church*

Medieval inn set in a lovely village

In the beautiful countryside of the Meon Valley, the setting for this delightful 15th-century coaching inn is hard to beat. The village boasts a magnificent Norman church where tapestry designs similar to Bayeux can be found. If you want heavy beams, inglenook fireplaces and wooden floors, look no further – they're all here, creating an ideal atmosphere for a choice of Hall & Woodhouse ales and Westons cider. The monthly changing menus reflect the seasons, with lighter dishes in the summer and hearty, warming food in the winter – such as roast rump of lamb Wellington with sweet potato gratin, pea purée and rosemary jus. There are tables outside on the pretty patio.

Open all wk 11-3 6-11 (Sun 11-10) Closed 25 Dec **Food** Lunch Mon-Sat 12-2.30, Sun 12-3 Dinner Mon-Sat 6.30-9.30, Sun 6.30-9 Restaurant menu available all wk ⊕ HALL & WOODHOUSE ◀ Badger First Gold, K&B Sussex, Tanglefoot ♂ Westons Stowford Press. ☗ 9 **Facilities** Non-diners area ✿ (Bar Outside area) ♦♦ Children's menu Children's portions Outside area ♬ Parking WiFi ☞ (notice required)

EASTON
Map 5 SU53

The Chestnut Horse

tel: 01962 779257 **SO21 1EG**
email: info@thechestnuthorse.com
dir: *M3 junct 9, A33 towards Basingstoke, then B3047. 2nd right, 1st left*

Hidden away in an idyllic Itchen Valley village

This gem of a 16th-century pub has an abundance of traditional English character and atmosphere; old tankards hang from the low-beamed ceilings in the two bar areas, and a large open fire is the central focus through the winter months. Award-winning beers, such as Pickled Partridge and Chestnut Horse Special can be enjoyed in the bar or the garden. Typical à la carte choices are beetroot and goats' cheese risotto; roasted John Dory with fennel, sorrel and lemon cream linguine; and roast saddle of venison. You can walk off any excesses on one of the enjoyable countryside walks that start at the front door.

Open all wk 12-3.30 5.30-11 (Fri-Sat 12-11.30 Sun 12-10.30) **Food** Lunch Mon-Sat 12-2.30, Sun 12-8 Dinner Mon-Sat 6-9.30 Av main course £12 Set menu available ⊕ HALL & WOODHOUSE ◀ Badger First Gold & Pickled Partridge, Chestnut Horse Special ♂ Westons Stowford Press. ☗ **Facilities** Non-diners area ✿ (Bar Garden) ♦♦ Children's menu Children's portions Garden ♬ Parking WiFi ☞

EAST STRATTON
Map 5 SU54

Northbrook Arms

tel: 01962 774150 **SO21 3DU**
email: northbrookarms@hotmail.com
dir: *Follow brown pub sign from A33, 4m S of junct with A303*

Social centre of a small but perfectly formed village

Memo to Hollywood: if you need an English pub location, look no further. Bang opposite the village green and architecturally perfect, it endears itself to local bar-proppers with six or seven real ales and four ciders, a May beer festival and a September cider celebration. The compact menu gets the thumbs up too, with dishes such as spicy duck parcels with chilli and apple purée; wild mushroom and thyme mille feuille; baked lemon and pepper salmon; and buttermilk pudding with cardamom strawberries. There are light bites and deli options such as Indian potato cake, and smoked cod Scotch egg. Landlord Jon Coward plans to open a much-needed village shop.

Open all day all wk **Food** Lunch all wk 12-9.30 Dinner all wk 12-9.30 Av main course £11.50 Restaurant menu available all wk ⊕ FREE HOUSE ◀ Otter, Bowman Swift One, Flower Pots Cheriton Pots, Flack Manor Flack's Double Drop, Amber Sharp's Cornish Coaster, Alfred's Saxon Bronze ♂ Aspall, Westons Old Rosie, Thatchers, Mr Whiteheads. ☗ 12 **Facilities** Non-diners area ✿ (All areas) ♦♦ Children's menu Children's portions Play area Garden Outside area ♬ Beer festival Cider festival Parking WiFi ☞ (notice required)

EMSWORTH
Map 5 SU70

NEW The Sussex Brewery

tel: 01243 371533 **36 Main Rd PO10 8AU**
email: info@sussexbrewery.com
dir: *On A259, E of Emsworth towards Chichester*

Friendly roadside pub with a winning ale-and-sausage combination

No prizes for guessing this pub was once a brewery, and this ethos continues with its pride in offering good honestly-priced food and drink served by friendly staff in a happy atmosphere. Young's ales sit beside guests, with Addlestones and Thatchers ciders served too. Locally made sausages form the backbone of the menu, and have done for over ten years; differing flavours, including a special made with Young's bitter, are served with creamy mash, caramelised onions and gravy. Equally in

continued

EMSWORTH *continued*

demand are light bites such a bucket of whitebait with home-made tartare sauce, and main courses like ale-battered hake with chips.

Open all day all wk **Food** Lunch Mon-Sat 12-2.30, Sun 12-3 Dinner Mon-Sat 6-9, Sun 6.30-9 Av main course £12 Restaurant menu available all wk ⊕ YOUNG'S ◀ London Gold & Special, Wells Bombardier, St Austell Tribute ♻ Addlestones, Thatchers. ♟ 12 **Facilities** Non-diners area ♥ (Bar Outside area) ♦♦ Children's portions Outside area ⋒ Parking WiFi ◪ (notice required)

▌ EVERSLEY — Map 5 SU76

The Golden Pot — PICK OF THE PUBS

tel: 0118 973 2104 **Reading Rd RG27 ONB**
email: info@golden-pot.co.uk
dir: *Between Reading & Camberley on B3272 approx 0.25m from Eversley cricket ground*

Innovative home cooked food and a good range of beers

This well-established free house, now with new owners, dates back to the 1700s and offers a fine selection of real ales and nine wines by the glass. A double-sided warming fire connects the bar and restaurant, while outside the Snug and Vineyard, surrounded by colourful tubs and hanging baskets, are just the ticket for summer relaxation. Tuck into home-cooked food such as steak and ale pies; fish pie; organic salmon Wellington; and calves' liver and bacon with creamed potatoes and red wine sauce. Desserts are all home made too, perhaps chocolate and orange trifle; apple and plum tart with custard; or strawberry and vanilla cheesecake. Dogs are welcome in the bar area and the garden.

Open all day all wk 11.30-11 Closed 25-26 & 31 Dec, 1 Jan **Food** Lunch all wk 12-2.30 Dinner all wk 5.30-10 ⊕ FREE HOUSE ◀ Andwell, Bowman, Ascot, Rebellion, Windsor & Eton, Upham Ale, Church End, Longdog Ales, Hammerpot Ales, Guest ale ♻ Rekorderlig, Aspall, Henney's. ♟ 9 **Facilities** Non-diners area ♥ (Bar Garden) ♦♦ Children's menu Children's portions Garden ⋒ Beer festival Cider festival Parking WiFi

---

▌ EXTON — Map 5 SU62

The Shoe Inn

tel: 01489 877526 **Shoe Ln SO32 3NT**
email: theshoeexton@googlemail.com
dir: *Exton on A32 between Fareham & Alton*

Good food with many ingredients from the pub's own garden

On warmer days, you can enjoy views of Old Winchester Hill from the garden of this popular pub in the heart of the Meon Valley. Food is key – local ingredients include those from its ever-expanding herb and organic vegetable garden. A typical selection of dishes could include local Southdown lamb's liver, bacon, onion gravy and mashed potato; slow-cooked Oxford Sandy belly pork with Savoy cabbage and cider jus. The bar offers well-kept Wadworth ales, weekly changing guest ales, and over a dozen wines served by the glass.

Open all wk 11-3 6-11 (Sat-Sun all day) Closed 25 Dec **Food** Lunch all wk 12-2.15 Dinner all wk 6-9 ⊕ WADWORTH ◀ 6X, Henry's Original IPA, The Bishop's Tipple, Guest ales ♻ Westons Stowford Press. ♟ 13 **Facilities** ♥ (Bar Restaurant Garden) ♦♦ Children's menu Children's portions Garden ⋒ Parking

---

▌ FORDINGBRIDGE — Map 5 SU11

The Augustus John

tel: 01425 652098 **116 Station Rd SP6 1DG**
email: enquiries@augustusjohnfordingbridge.co.uk
dir: *12m S of Salisbury on A338 towards Ringwood*

Good stop off close to the New Forest

After 14 years as a member of staff, Lorraine Smallwood took over this former station pub some five years ago. The Welsh post-impressionist painter Augustus John was a regular here, although today it's the Ringwood real ales and food that continues to attract locals and visitors. A typical menu might include lamb braised with mint; pan-fried pork fillet flamed with brandy and apricots; the chef's casserole of the day; or grilled salmon fillet with lemon and saffron sauce. Time a visit for the May beer festival.

Open all wk 11.30-3 6.30-11.30 (Sun 12-3 7-11.30) **Food** Lunch all wk 12-2.30 Dinner Mon-Sat 6.30-9, Sun 7-9 (booking advised Fri-Sun) ⊕ MARSTON'S ◀ Ringwood Best Bitter & Fortyniner, Guest ale ♻ Thatchers Gold. **Facilities** Non-diners area ♥ (Bar Garden) ♦♦ Children's menu Children's portions Garden ⋒ Beer festival Parking WiFi ◪ (notice required)

▌ HAMBLE-LE-RICE — Map 5 SU40

The Bugle ⊛ — PICK OF THE PUBS

tel: 023 8045 3000 **High St SO31 4HA**
email: manager@buglehamble.co.uk
dir: *M27 junct 8, follow signs to Hamble. In village centre turn right at mini rdbt into one-way cobbled street, pub at end*

Enjoyable food in restored waterside pub with views

Rescued from proposed demolition, this famous waterside pub was taken over by Matthew Boyle who has lovingly refurbished it using traditional methods and materials. Old features include exposed beams and brickwork, natural flagstone floors and the wonderful oak bar, plus there's a large heated terrace with lovely views over the River Hamble - perfect for outdoor dining. A pint of locally brewed Itchen Valley ale makes an ideal partner for one of the 'small plates' (great for sharing), a fish finger, tartare sauce and cucumber sandwich, or pub classics like moules frites or seasonal meat pie. From the dining room menu, go for pressed rabbit and prune terrine to start, then order the bream fillet with creamed leeks, warm kale and potato salad. Round off with apple crumble tart and vanilla ice cream. The Bugle is the sister pub to The White Star Tavern in Southampton.

Open all day all wk Mon-Thu 11-11 (Fri-Sat 11-mdnt Sun 12-10.30) **Food** Lunch Mon-Thu 12-2.30, Fri 12-3, Sat 12-4, Sun 12-9 Dinner Mon-Thu 6-9.30, Fri-Sat 6-10, Sun 12-9 ⊕ FREE HOUSE ◀ Itchen Valley, Rotating local ales. ♟ 10 **Facilities** Non-diners area ♦♦ Children's portions Outside area ⋒ WiFi ◪

▌ HANNINGTON — Map 5 SU55

The Vine at Hannington — PICK OF THE PUBS

tel: 01635 298525 **RG26 5TX**
email: info@thevineathannington.co.uk
dir: *Follow Hannington signs from A339 between Basingstoke & Newbury*

A favourite with walkers and cyclists

Given the nature of North Hampshire's rolling chalk downland, you can expect rambling and cycling devotees to patronise this gabled Victorian inn. It used to be the Wellington Arms because it stands on what was once the Iron Duke's estate, but was renamed in 1960 after the Vine & Craven Hunt, whose kennels are nearby. A wood-burning stove heats the spacious, traditionally furnished bar areas and conservatory, where rural artefacts pop up here and there. Seasonal menus and daily specials feature marinated lamb and vegetable kebab, saffron rice and tomato and chilli sauce; medallions of beef with red wine, tarragon and mushroom sauce; and spinach and ricotta cannelloni. Many of the herbs, salads and vegetables used in the kitchen are grown in the large garden, where there's also a children's play area.

Open 12-3 6-11 (Sat-Sun all day) Closed 25 Dec, Mon Food Lunch Tue-Sat 12-2, Sun 12-7 Dinner Tue-Sat 6-9 ⊕ PUNCH TAVERNS ◀ Sharp's Doom Bar, Guest ales ♂ Thatchers Gold. ♥ 11 Facilities Non-diners area ♣ (Bar Restaurant Garden) ♦♦ Children's menu Children's portions Play area Family room Garden ⋒ Beer festival Parking WiFi ▭ (notice required)

HAWKLEY   Map 5 SU72

The Hawkley Inn ★★★★ INN

tel: 01730 827205 Pococks Ln GU33 6NE
email: info@hawkleyinn.co.uk web: www.hawkleyinn.co.uk
dir: From A3 (Liss rdbt) towards Liss on B3006. Right at Spread Eagle, in 2.5m left into Pococks Ln

New owner, same quirky interior and seriously good food

An inn sign saying 'Free Hoose' owes something to the moose head hanging above one of the fires. It sums up this pub's quirky decor, and any change under the Hawkley's new ownership is likely to be more of the same. With 10 beer engines, the pub is well known to local real ale enthusiasts and cider lovers; a festival takes place over June's first weekend. Menus change daily and proffer the likes of grilled smoked salmon with asparagus; and calves' liver with lentils. These and the vegetarian specials are all locally sourced and freshly prepared on the premises, and any dietary need can be catered for.

Open all wk Mon-Fri 12-3 5.30-11 (Sat-Sun all day) Food Lunch Mon-Sat 12-2.30, Sun 12-4 Dinner Mon-Sat 6-9.30 Av main course £12 ⊕ FREE HOUSE/HAWKLEY MOOSE LIMITED ◀ 7 constantly changing ales, Guest ales ♂ Mr Whitehead's. ♥ 8 Facilities Non-diners area ♣ (Bar Restaurant Garden) ♦♦ Children's portions Garden ⋒ Beer festival WiFi ▭ (notice required) Rooms 5

HERRIARD   Map 5 SU64

The Fur & Feathers

tel: 01256 384170 Herriard Rd RG25 2PN
email: bookings@thefurandfeathers.co.uk
dir: From Basingstoke take A339 towards Alton. After Herriard follow pub signs. Turn left to pub

Bag a table in the garden when the weather allows

Its high-ceilinged Victorian proportions translate into light and airy spaces for drinkers and diners, and comfort too, with log-burning fireplaces at each end of the bar. Purpose-built 120 years ago for local farm workers, The Fur & Feathers has to this day obligations in the upkeep of the church roof. In the bar, a trio of ales are rotated, and menus of modern British cooking are perused. Typical dishes are Hampshire pork loin steaks with apple, celery and sultana compôte; and Indonesian curry made with local venison. A large garden hosts entertainment, and is home to chickens laying eggs for the pub's kitchen.

Open Tue-Thu 12-3 5-11 (Fri-Sat 12-11 Sun 12-6) Closed 1wk end of Dec, Sun eve & Mon Food Lunch Tue-Sat 12-2, Sun 12-3 Dinner Tue-Sat 6.30-9 ⊕ FREE HOUSE ◀ Local ales, rotating Flack Manor Flack's Double Drop, Hogs Back TEA, Sharp's Doom Bar, Itchen Valley Fagins, Wild Weather Ales, Long Dog, Bowman Ales ♂ Hogs Back Hazy Hog, Sharp's Orchard. ♥ 28 Facilities Non-diners area ♦♦ Children's menu Children's portions Garden ⋒ Parking WiFi ▭ (notice required)

HIGHCLERE   Map 5 SU45

NEW The Yew Tree

tel: 01635 253360 Hollington Cross, Andover Rd RG20 9SE
email: info@theyewtree.co.uk
dir: M4 junct 13, A34 S, 4th junct on left signed Highclere/Wash Common, turn right towards Andover A343, inn on right

Delightful 17th-century pub

After visiting nearby Highclere Castle, where *Downton Abbey* is filmed, have lunch here. Or vice versa. Either way, enjoy its high standards of food and service, starting in the newly-refurbished bar with tartan high back seats and comfy leather chairs, which offers 13 wines by the glass, real ales from the Two Cocks and Upham breweries, and Orchard Pig Reveller cider. Admired for his locally sourced fresh fish and game, chef Simon Davis presents frequently-changing menus featuring bar snacks, sharing plates and, typically, salt and pepper Brixham squid with mango, chilli and lime dressing; Laverstoke Park mozzarella crostini with chargrilled aubergine; and wild line-caught black bream with squid and potato chowder.

Open all day all wk Food Lunch Mon-Sat 12-2.30, Sun 12-3.30 Dinner Mon-Sat 6.30-9.30, Sun 7-8.30 Av main course £13.95 ⊕ CIRRUS INNS ◀ Two Cocks Cavalier, Upham Punter ♂ Orchard Pig Reveller. ♥ 13 Facilities Non-diners area ♣ (Bar Restaurant Garden) ♦♦ Children's menu Children's portions Garden ⋒ Parking WiFi ▭ (notice required)

HOLYBOURNE   Map 5 SU74

The White Hart Hotel

tel: 01420 87654 139 London Rd GU34 4EY
dir: M3 junct 5, follow Alton signs (A339). In Alton take A31 towards Farnham. Follow Holybourne signs

Friendly village pub

The village of Holybourne is steeped in history: an old Roman fort lies under the cricket field, and the village also stands on the Pilgrims' Way. Rebuilt in the 1920s on the site of the original inn, The White Hart provides a comfortable, welcoming setting for a well-kept pint of Greene King IPA or a hearty meal. Children are welcome and there's a bouncy castle in the summer.

Open all day all wk Food Lunch Mon-Fri 12-3, Sat 12-9, Sun 12-8 Dinner Mon-Fri 5-9, Sat 12-9, Sun 12-8 ⊕ GREENE KING ◀ Hardys & Hansons, Morland Old Speckled Hen, 3 Guest ales ♂ Mr Whitehead's Holybourne Cider, Aspall, Rekorderlig. ♥ 10 Facilities Non-diners area ♣ (Bar Garden) ♦♦ Children's menu Play area Garden ⋒ Parking WiFi ▭ (notice required)

Follow us on Facebook
www.facebook.com/TheAAUK

HOOK
Map 5 SU75

Crooked Billet

tel: 01256 762118 **London Rd RG27 9EH**
email: richardbarwise@aol.com **web:** www.thecrookedbilletpub.co.uk
dir: *M3 junct 5, B3349 signed Hook. At 3rd rdbt right onto A30 towards London, pub on left 0.5m*

Guest ales and riverside garden

At first sight this family- and dog-friendly free house looks quite old; in fact it dates from only 1935, although a hostelry has been here since the 1600s. Richard and Sally Sanders have owned it for more than 27 years, so keeping their customers happy is second nature. Beer drinkers know they will always be greeted by new guest ales (they count 830 to date), with more at the Summer Bank Holiday beer festival. Food includes favourites like home-made chilli; chicken curry; gammon steak with egg or pineapple; various salads; and some eight to ten specials available at any one time; the pies and casseroles in winter are all home made as well. The lovely riverside garden has a children's play area.

Open all wk Mon-Fri 11.30-3 6-12 (Sat 11.30am-mdnt Sun 12-10) **Food** Lunch Mon-Sat 12-2.30, Sun 12-8 Dinner Mon-Fri 6.30-9.30, Sat 6.30-10 ⊕ FREE HOUSE ◄ Courage Best Bitter, Sharp's Doom Bar, Andwell, Dark Star, Hogs Back, Guest ales Ö Thatchers Green Goblin. **Facilities** Non-diners area ❤ (Bar Garden) ♦ Children's menu Children's portions Play area Garden ㅋ Beer festival Parking WiFi ➡ (notice required)

The Hogget Country Pub & Eating House

tel: 01256 763009 **London Rd, Hook Common RG27 9JJ**
email: home@hogget.co.uk
dir: *M3 junct 5, A30, 0.5m, between Hook & Basingstoke*

Value for money just off the M3

Having passed the five-year milestone, the Hogget's reputation for good food and service continues to grow. Ringwood Best is the session beer, while the stronger candidates are either Ringwood 49er, Marston's Best Bitter or Wychwood Hobgoblin. Carefully prepared English favourites include slow cooked pork belly; gourmet burgers; and ham, egg and chips, but you'll also find seared fresh tuna; pork and sage meatballs with linguine; Shipyard's pale ale battered cod; and Hereford-Angus beef from a friend's farm in Wiltshire.

Open all wk 12-3 5.30-11 (Sat 12-11 Sun 12-10.30) Closed 25-26 Dec **Food** Lunch all wk 12-2.30 Dinner all wk 5.30-9 Av main course £12 ⊕ MARSTON'S ◄ Ringwood Best Bitter, Wychwood Hobgoblin, Guest ales Ö Thatchers Gold. ₸ 12 **Facilities** Non-diners area ❤ (Bar Outside area) ♦ Children's menu Children's portions Outside area ㅋ Parking WiFi

HOUGHTON
Map 5 SU33

NEW The Boot Inn

tel: 01794 388310 **SO20 6LH**
email: bootinnhoughton@btconnect.com
dir: *Phone for detailed directions*

Quality pub dining with fishing by arrangement

Sitting beside the River Test, renowned as one of the world's best fly fishing waters, the Boot's bar hosts well-camouflaged hunters of both the fishing and shooting varieties. Massively refurbished in 2013, the pub's owners have built the kitchen and bar down in the garden. The 18th-century timber-framed bar serves a choice of beers and ciders, while its restaurant strives to serve good food without earning the gastro-pub sobriquet. Expect pub grub of a higher order, therefore, in lunchtime plates of rabbit cassoulet; and evening dishes like stir-fried tiger prawns with garlic and chillies, followed by pork medallions with seasonal vegetables.

Open all wk 10-3 6-11 **Food** Lunch all wk 12-2 Dinner all wk 6.30-9 Av main course £10 Restaurant menu available L all wk, D Tue-Sat ⊕ FREE HOUSE ◄ Sharp's Doom Bar, Ringwood Best Bitter Ö Thatchers. ₸ 9 **Facilities** Non-diners area ❤ (Bar Garden Outside area) ♦ Children's menu Children's portions Garden Outside area ㅋ Parking WiFi ➡ (notice required)

HURSLEY
Map 5 SU42

The Dolphin Inn

tel: 01962 775209 **SO21 2JY**
dir: *Phone for detailed directions*

16th-century coaching inn close to South Downs National Park

Like most of the village, this old coaching inn with magnificent chimneys once belonged to the Hursley Estate, which is now owned by IBM. It was built between 1540 and 1560, reputedly using timbers from a Tudor warship called HMS *Dolphin* (today's less glamorous 'ship' is a shore establishment in Gosport). On tap in the beamed bars are Ringwood Best, Hop Back Summer Lightning, George Gale & Co HSB and Green Goblin oak-aged cider. In addition to sandwiches, baguettes and jacket potatoes, favourites include Hursley-made faggots; lamb's liver and bacon; scampi and chips; and macaroni cheese.

Open all day all wk Mon-Sat 11-11 (Sun 12-10.30) **Food** Lunch Mon-Sat 12-2.30, Sun 12-8.30 Dinner Mon-Thu 6-9, Fri-Sat 6.30-9.30, Sun 12-8.30 Av main course £9.95 ⊕ ENTERPRISE INNS ◄ Hop Back Summer Lightning, George Gale & Co HSB, Ringwood Best Bitter Ö Thatchers & Green Goblin. ₸ 12 **Facilities** Non-diners area ❤ (Bar Garden) ♦ Children's menu Children's portions Play area Family room Garden ㅋ Parking ➡ (notice required)

The Kings Head ★★★★ INN

tel: 01962 775208 **Main Rd SO21 2JW**
email: enquiries@kingsheadhursley.co.uk **web:** www.kingsheadhursley.co.uk
dir: On A3090 between Winchester & Romsey

A winning mix of modernity and tradition

Close to historic Winchester and with pleasant walks nearby, The Kings Head was bought, a few years ago, by five local farming families who extensively refurbished it with decor and furniture to reflect its Georgian origins. The 'Taste of Hampshire Menu', available Monday to Friday lunchtime in addition to sandwiches and pub classics, offers pan-fried fillet of red mullet with tabouleh salad and saffron aïoli to start; followed by braised daube of Hampshire beef, choucroute cabbage and creamed piper potatoes; and bread-and-butter pudding with vanilla custard. The dinner menu includes Shetland mussels, confit belly of pork, and curried monkfish. Two guest ales change on a weekly basis. Beer festivals are held on the Summer Bank Holiday.

Open all day all wk 7.30am-11pm **Food** Lunch all wk 12-9 Dinner all wk 12-9 ⊕ FREE HOUSE ◀ Bowman Ales Wallops Wood, Sharp's Doom Bar, Ringwood, 2 Guest ales ♂ Orchard Pig. ▾ 10 **Facilities** Non-diners area ♣ (Bar Garden) ♦ Children's menu Children's portions Garden ⧖ Beer festival Parking WiFi ☐ (notice required) **Rooms** 8

The Bun Penny

tel: 023 9255 0214 **36 Manor Way PO13 9JH**
email: bar@bunpenny.co.uk **web:** www.bunpenny.co.uk
dir: From Fareham take B3385 to Lee-on-the-Solent. Pub 300yds before High St

Classic country free house a short walk from the water

A short walk from the waterfront, this former farmhouse occupies a prominent position on the road into Lee-on-the-Solent. Every inch a classic country free house, it has a large patio at the front and an extensive back garden that's ideal for summer relaxation, while real fires and cosy corners are welcome in winter. Otter beer is sold direct from the cask, backed by hand-pulls including ales from the local Oakleaf Brewery. A typical meal might be paprika-crusted calamari with garlic mayonnaise and sweet chilli dip followed by fillet of pork Wellington, roasted root vegetables with a light scrumpy sauce.

Open all day all wk 11-11 (Fri-Sat 11am-mdnt Sun 12-10.30) **Food** Lunch Mon-Sat 12-2.30, Sun 12-9 Dinner Mon-Sat 6-9, Sun 12-9 ⊕ FREE HOUSE ◀ Otter Bitter, Oakleaf Hole Hearted, Guest ales ♂ Westons. ▾ 13 **Facilities** Non-diners area ♣ (Bar Garden) ♦ Children's menu Children's portions Garden ⧖ Parking WiFi ☐ (notice required)

The Jolly Drover ★★★★ INN

tel: 01730 893137 **London Rd, Hillbrow GU33 7QL**
email: thejollydrover@googlemail.com **web:** www.thejollydrover.co.uk
dir: From station in Liss at mini rdbt right into Hill Brow Rd (B3006) signed Rogate, Rake, Hill Brow. At junct with B2071, pub opposite

Just out of town at the top of the hill

This pub was built in 1844 by Mr Knowles - a drover - to offer cheer and sustenance to other drovers on the old London road. For 18 years it has been run by Anne and Barry Coe, who welcome all-comers with a large log fire, secluded garden, a covered and heated patio, a choice of real ales such as London Pride, and home-cooked food. The same menu is served in the bar and restaurant. Dishes include local award-winning sausages, gammon steaks, ham and mushroom pie, fried egg and chips, and beef lasagne. Gluten-free and vegetarian choices are also available.

Open all wk 10.30-3 5.30-11 (Sat 10.30-3 5.30-11 Sun 12-4) Closed 25-26 Dec, 1 Jan, Sun eve **Food** Lunch Mon-Sat 12-2.15, Sun 12-2.30 Dinner Mon-Sat 7-9.30 Av main course £12 Restaurant menu available all wk ⊕ ENTERPRISE INNS ◀ Fuller's London Pride, Sharp's Doom Bar, Timothy Taylor Landlord. ▾ 10 **Facilities** Non-diners area ♦ Children's portions Garden ⧖ Parking WiFi ☐ (notice required) **Rooms** 6

The Running Horse ★★★★ INN ⊛⊛   PICK OF THE PUBS

See Pick of the Pubs on page 234

PICK OF THE PUBS

The Running Horse ★★★★ INN 🌹🌹

LITTLETON   Map 5 SU43

tel: 01962 880218
88 Main Rd SO22 6QS
email: info@runninghorseinn.co.uk
web: www.runninghorseinn.co.uk
dir: *3m from Winchester, 1m from Three Maids Hill, signed from Stockbridge Rd*

Upmarket village pub and restaurant

The Running Horse belongs to the Upham Pub Co, a small group of judiciously restored and rejuvenated country pubs. Just outside Winchester's boundary, it's a popular alternative to the city's pubs and restaurants, and all the associated hassle of parking. The interior's tasteful refurbishment shows just what a good designer can achieve: a combination of heritage-red walls, wooden flooring, post-war dining tables whose style many will remember from childhood, bookcases crammed with old volumes, and a large hatch revealing the kitchen. Upham also owns a brewery, set up in 2009 in the village of the same name a few miles the other side of Winchester; cider fans will find Orchard Pig, and wine drinkers a good selection by the glass. Two AA Rosettes prove the quality of the food, all freshly prepared from produce delivered by carefully chosen, often family-run, local suppliers. Breakfasts, lunches and dinners, including daily specials, are available every day of the year. To give

an idea, there are starters of cauliflower pannacotta with Cajun-spiced parmesan crumb, mixed shoots and brioche; and poached salmon and quail's egg salad. Something to follow might be honey-roasted ham, egg and chips; omelette Arnold Bennett with new potatoes and salad; pan-roasted Barbary duck breast with Heritage carrots, pearl barley and spinach; or Upham beer-battered fish and chips with peas and tartare sauce. There are roasts on Sundays. For dessert, welcome back knickerbocker glory, or the more contemporary passion fruit posset with pistachio nuts. An open area at the front features a cosy thatched cabana, and at the rear are tables and benches, beyond which impressive accommodation is arranged around the lawned garden.

Open all day all wk Closed 25 & 26 Dec Evenings **Food** Lunch Mon-Sat 12-2.30 Sun 12-3.30 Dinner Mon-Sat 6.30-9.30 Sun 6.30-9 Restaurant menu available all wk. 🍺 FREE HOUSE/UPHAM PUB CO 🍺 Tipster, Punter & Stakes Ö Orchard Pig. ¶ 12 **Facilities** Non-diners area 🐾 (Bar Garden) ♦ Children's menu Children's portions Garden ☴ Beer festival Parking WiFi 🚌 (notice required) **Rooms** 9

LONGPARISH

Map 5 SU44

The Plough Inn ◎ ◎

PICK OF THE PUBS

tel: 01264 720358 **SP11 6PB**
email: eat@theploughinn.info
dir: M3 junct 8, A303 towards Andover. In approx 6m take B3048 towards Longparish

Traditional country pub with a contemporary feel

A mile or so past this charming, early 18th-century inn runs the A303, so when someone suggests a break on seeing the Longparish turn-off, say 'yes' and head straight here. For Test Way walkers too, it's a good place to stop because the long-distance path runs through the pub car park. Since taking over in 2012, chef James Durrant and his wife Louise have focused on food - already worthy of two AA Rosettes - but not at the expense of its role as a local, with a snug bar offering Timothy Taylor Landlord and Ringwood Best, and continental lagers, draught and bottled ciders and a dozen wines by the glass. A short carte lists Cornish mussels with cider, bacon and crème fraîche; Jerusalem artichoke and Old Winchester cheese risotto; and braised pork belly with cockles, sausages and white beans. The garden is just the ticket for outdoor dining.

Open Mon-Thu 12-3.30 6-11 (Fri-Sat all day Sun 12-6) Closed Sun eve **Food** Lunch Mon-Sat 12-2.30, Sun 12-4.30 Dinner Mon-Sat 6-9.30 Restaurant menu available Mon-Sat ⊕ ENTERPRISE INNS ◀ Timothy Taylor Landlord, Ringwood Best Bitter, Guest ale Ö Aspall, Thatchers, Westons. ♟ 12 **Facilities** Non-diners area ❤ (Bar Garden) ♦♦ Children's menu Children's portions Garden ♒ Parking WiFi ⬛ (notice required)

LOVEDEAN

Map 5 SU61

NEW The Bird in Hand

tel: 023 9259 1055 **269 Lovedean Ln PO8 9RX**
email: enquiries@lovedeanbirdinhand.co.uk
dir: A3(M) junct 2, A3 signed Portsmouth. At next rdbt left (A3/Portsmouth). Right into Lovedean Ln (signed Lovedean). Pub on left

Thatched pub that's moved with the times

Known by locals as 'the Bird', this old pub is coping well with the growth in population along the old London to Portsmouth road. Its thatched roof was a landmark in the 1800s, when it housed a bakery and greengrocer's shop. For the duration of World War II, the FA cup was hidden here under a bed, Portsmouth FC having won it in 1939. The bar stocks an excellent range of real ales from the likes of the Bowman and Havant Breweries. The kitchen too raises the food standard above the norm; expect starters like oxtail and kidney suet pudding, and main courses such as harissa-marinated lamb rump with celeriac.

Open all day all wk **Food** Lunch Mon-Sat 12-3, Sun 12-7.30 Dinner Mon-Sat 6-9.30, Sun 12-7.30 Set menu available ⊕ ENTERPRISE INNS ◀ Ringwood Best Bitter, Bowman Ales Wallops Wood, Havant Finished, Guest ales Ö Westons Stowford Press. ♟ 11 **Facilities** Non-diners area ❤ (Bar Garden) ♦♦ Children's menu Children's portions Garden ♒ Parking WiFi ⬛ (notice required)

LOWER SWANWICK

Map 5 SU40

NEW The Navigator

tel: 01489 572123 **286 Bridge Rd SO31 7EB**
email: info@thenavigatorswanwick.co.uk
dir: M27 junct 8, A3024 signed Bursledon. 1st exit at next rdbt onto A27 (Bridge Rd). Cross river, pub 300yds on left

Food-driven hostelry on the River Hamble

With its prime location on the magnificent marina front at Lower Swanwick, the Navigator's ambience reflects the strong sea-faring traditions of this area. It's one of the Upham Pub Group, so no surprise to find ales from its own brewery behind the bar. Head chef Gareth Longhurst moved here from the Navigator's well-regarded sister pub in West Meon, the Thomas Lord. So food of a higher order can be expected, and the carte does not disappoint. The fixed price lunch menu, for example, details a cauliflower and parmesan tart with smoked onion purée; a poached smoked haddock kedgeree with fennel salad; and caramelised pear and vanilla pannacotta with pecan brittle.

Open all day all wk **Food** Lunch Mon-Sat 12-2.30, Sun 12-3.30 Dinner Mon-Sat 6.30-9.30, Sun 6.30-9 Set menu available ⊕ UPHAM PUB CO ◀ Tipster, Punter & Stakes. ♟ 12 **Facilities** Non-diners area ❤ (Bar Outside area) ♦♦ Children's menu Children's portions Outside area ♒ Parking WiFi ⬛ (notice required)

LOWER WIELD

Map 5 SU64

The Yew Tree

PICK OF THE PUBS

tel: 01256 389224 **SO24 9RX**
dir: A339 from Basingstoke towards Alton. Turn right for Lower Wield

Good selection of fine wines and local ales

The eponymous, 650-year-old yew tree was just getting into its stride when this free house started serving real ale in 1845. Set in wonderful countryside, opposite a picturesque cricket pitch, the popular landlord's simple mission statement promises 'Good honest food; great local beers; fine wines (lots of choice); and, most importantly, good fun for one and all'. Triple fff Moondance is the house beer, with 20 guest ale brewers on rotation, including Bowman Ales and Hogs Back. Most of the food is sourced from Hampshire or neighbouring counties, and the menu reflects the seasons while keeping the regular favourites 'to avoid uproar'. Sample dishes include gorgonzola and crispy bacon salad; smoked mackerel pâté with toast and lime pepper mayo, followed by roasted guinea fowl with balsamic roasted vegetables and new potatoes; or cheesy ham hock, leek and pea pie. There is an annual cricket match and sports day in summer, and quizzes in the winter months.

Open Tue-Sat 12-3 6-11 (Sun all day) Closed 1st 2wks Jan, Mon **Food** Lunch Tue-Sun 12-2 Dinner Tue-Sat 6.30-9, Sun 6.30-8.30 Av main course £10.95 ⊕ FREE HOUSE ◀ Flower Pots Cheriton Pots, Bowman Swift One, Triple fff Moondance, Hogs Back TEA, Hop Back GFB, Andwell Gold Muddler. ♟ 14 **Facilities** Non-diners area ❤ (Bar Garden) ♦♦ Children's menu Children's portions Garden Parking WiFi

LYMINGTON

Map 5 SZ39

Mayflower Inn

tel: 01590 672160 **Kings Saltern Rd SO41 3QD**
email: manager@themayflowerlymington.co.uk
dir: A337 towards New Milton, left at rdbt by White Hart, left to Rookes Ln, right at mini rdbt, pub 0.75m

Mock-Tudor inn serving good food, right next to the yacht haven

A favourite with yachtsmen and dog walkers, this solidly built mock-Tudor inn overlooks the Lymington River, with glorious views to the Isle of Wight. There's a magnificent garden with splendid sun terraces where visitors can enjoy a pint of Goddards Fuggle-Dee-Dum, and an on-going summer barbecue in fine weather. Menu prices are reasonable, with dishes that range from light bites like lemon and pepper monkfish goujons or a sharing platter, to main courses of black bean chicken stir-fry, or sea bass fillet with prawn and saffron risotto.

Open all day all wk **Food** Lunch all wk 12-9.30 Dinner all wk 12-9.30 Av main course £7-£10 Set menu available ⊕ ENTERPRISE INNS/COASTAL INNS & TAVERNS LTD ◀ Ringwood Best Bitter, Fuller's London Pride, Wadworth 6X, Goddards Fuggle-Dee-Dum Ö Thatchers. ♟ 9 **Facilities** Non-diners area ❤ (Bar Garden) ♦♦ Children's menu Children's portions Play area Garden ♒ Parking WiFi ⬛ (notice required)

LYMINGTON *continued*

The Walhampton Arms

tel: 01590 673113 **Walhampton Hill SO41 5RE**
email: enquiries@walhamptonarms.co.uk **web:** www.walhamptonarmslymington.co.uk
dir: *From Lymington take B3054 towards Beaulieu. Pub in 2m*

Order a meal from the popular carvery

Originally a farm building in the early 19th-century that included a model dairy supplying Walhampton Estate, this friendly pub serves real ales from Ringwood, with guest ales from local microbreweries throughout the year. This pub is also known for its excellent value carvery, but the steaks and surf 'n' turf are two other reasons why people flock here. Looking for different options? Then other dishes might include lamb's liver and bacon; steak and ale pie or the chef's curry with rice. Children too will find all their favourites on their own menu.

Open all day all wk 11-11 (Sun 12-10.30) **Food** Lunch Tue-Sat 12-9, Sun-Mon 12-8 Dinner Tue-Sat 12-9, Sun-Mon 12-8 ⊕ FREE HOUSE ◪ Ringwood Best Bitter, Otter Bitter, Guest ales. ♱ 10 **Facilities** Non-diners area ♣ (Bar Outside area) ♦♦ Children's menu Children's portions Outside area ☴ Parking WiFi ▄▄ (notice required)

▌ **LYNDHURST**	Map 5 SU30

New Forest Inn

tel: 023 8028 4690 **Emery Down SO43 7DY**
email: info@thenewforestinn.co.uk
dir: *M27 junct 1 follow signs for A35/Lyndhurst. In Lyndhurst follow signs for Christchurch, turn right at Swan Inn towards Emery Down*

Friendly 18th-century inn with large garden

New Forest ponies occasionally wander into this traditional local, a distraction that only serves to enhance its friendly atmosphere. There's incumbents Fortyniner, Flack's Double Drop and Thatchers Green Goblin cider on tap. The menu showcases a multitude of items – doorstep sandwiches, snacks, chargrills, toasted paninis, vegetarian and chef's choices. In there somewhere are smoked haddock kedgeree with poached egg; pork cutlet with ratatouille and mash; herb crusted salmon fillet on chorizo and pea risotto; and leek and gruyère tart. Beer and cider festivals are, respectively, on July's second weekend and March's last.

Open all day all wk **Food** Contact pub for details ⊕ ENTERPRISE INNS ◪ Ringwood Fortyniner, Flack Manor Flack's Double Drop, Guest ales ♂ Thatchers Gold, Thatchers Green Goblin. ♱ 12 **Facilities** Non-diners area ♣ (Bar Restaurant Garden) ♦♦ Children's menu Children's portions Garden ☴ Beer festival Cider festival Parking WiFi ▄▄ (notice required)

The Oak Inn

tel: 023 8028 2350 **Pinkney Ln, Bank SO43 7FD**
email: oakinn@fullers.co.uk
dir: *From Lyndhurst signed A35 to Christchurch, follow A35 for 1m, left at Bank sign*

Reliable oasis on New Forest trails

At the heart of the National Park, patrons enjoying Gales ales in the garden of this bare-boarded, bric-a-brac full country pub may idly watch local residents' pigs snuffling for acorns, New Forest ponies grazing or even fallow deer fleetingly flitting amidst the trees. It's a popular stop with cyclists and walkers exploring the Forest's tracks, breaking for a while to partake of the enticing menu which is strong on meals prepared using produce of the parish; perhaps a doorstop sandwich with New Forest ham and Looshanger cheese, or cider braised pork belly, celeriac and sage purée, gratin potatoes and spiced apple compôte as a main. Booking for meals is advised.

Open all wk Mon-Fri 11.30-3 6-11 (Sat 11.30-11 Sun 12-10.30) **Food** Lunch Mon-Fri 12-2.30, Sat 12-9.30, Sun 12-9 Dinner Mon-Fri 6-9.30, Sat 12-9.30, Sun 12-9 ⊕ FULLER'S ◪ London Pride, George Gale & Co HSB & Seafarers ♂ Aspall. ♱ 12 **Facilities** Non-diners area ♣ (Bar Restaurant Garden) ♦♦ Children's menu Children's portions Garden ☴ Parking WiFi

---

▌ **MAPLEDURWELL**	Map 5 SU65

The Gamekeepers   `PICK OF THE PUBS`

tel: 01256 322038 & 07786 998994 **Tunworth Rd RG25 2LU**
email: info@thegamekeepers.co.uk
dir: *M3 junct 6, A30 towards Hook. Right across dual carriageway after The Hatch pub. Pub signed*

Weatherboarded pub with a large garden overlooking fields

When, in the mid-19th century, shoemaker Joseph Phillips tired of measuring less-than-fragrant feet, he turned his workshop and home into a pub, calling it The Queen's Head. Just beyond the village, its noteworthy internal features include low beams, flagstone floors and an indoor well. Armed with a drink, settle into a leather sofa and study the daily-changing menu with a view to choosing between, perhaps, a starter of Moroccan meatballs in cumin, paprika, onion, garlic, chilli and tomato sauce with herb linguine; or the charcuterie board of buffalo mozzarella, salami, black olive tapenade, sun-dried tomatoes and pesto. Further thought is then required for whether to choose oven-baked loin of cod with sag aloo, mange-tout, and yogurt and curry oil dressing; slow-cooked venison and Guinness hotpot with wild mushrooms; or pumpkin ravioli cooked in sage butter with rocket and parmesan. Peach and champagne sorbet, or apple crumble with cinnamon ice cream could follow.

Open all wk Mon-Fri 11-2.30 5.30-11 (Sat 11-11 Sun 11-10.30) Closed 31 Dec, 1 Jan **Food** Lunch Mon-Fri 11-2.30, Sat-Sun 11-9.30 Dinner Mon-Fri 5.30-9.30, Sat-Sun 11-9.30 ⊕ FREE HOUSE ◪ Andwell Gold Muddler, Ruddy Darter, Resolute & King John, Fuller's London Pride ♂ Westons Stowford Press. ♱ 10 **Facilities** Non-diners area ♣ (Bar Garden) ♦♦ Children's portions Garden ☴ Parking WiFi ▄▄ (notice required)

▌ **MARCHWOOD**	Map 5 SU31

NEW The Pilgrim Inn

tel: 023 8086 7752 **Hythe Rd SO40 4WU**
email: pilgrim.inn@fullers.co.uk
dir: *M27 junct 2, A326 towards Fawley. Follow brown sign for inn, turn left into Twiggs Lane. At T-junct right into Hythe Rd. Pub on right*

Family-friendly dining on the edge of the New Forest

Only nine miles from Southampton and on the edge of New Forest National Park, The Pilgrim comprises two handsome thatched buildings complete with exposed beams, stone walls and log fire. It all makes for a genial setting to enjoy a pint of ondon Pride in the bar, or to settle down in the dining area and choose from a amily-friendly menu showcasing local produce. Typical mains include faggots, red abbage and mash; and pan-fried cod fillet with celeriac, bacon and mushroom ricassée. Leave room for plum crumble with cinnamon ice cream.

pen all day all wk **Food** Lunch Mon-Fri 12-3, Sat-Sun 12-6 Dinner Mon-Fri 6-9.30, at 6-10, Sun 6-8 Av main course £10.95 ⊕ FULLER'S ⬛ London Pride, Gales HSB. 17 **Facilities** Non-diners area ✿ (Bar Garden) ⧫ Children's menu Children's ortions Garden ⊓ Parking WiFi (notice required)

MICHELDEVER
Map 5 SU53

he Dove Inn

el: 01962 774288 **Andover Rd, Micheldever Station SO21 3AU**
mail: info@doveinn.co.uk
ir: M3 junct 8 merge onto A303, take exit signed Micheldever Station, follow station igns onto Andover Rd, on left

risp Georgian lines and period charm

n imposing, Grade II listed former railway and stagecoach hotel of late-Georgian rigins, with three bars and two restaurants which reflect this heritage, a heady mix f bare-board floors, robust beams to the ceilings, open fires and impressive period urnishings and decor. Constantly changing real ales and a reliable wine list ccompany the diverse choice of home-made dishes; braised wood pigeon with ider sauce and shallot confit to start, teamed with hazelnut and butternut squash avioli or Hampshire venison burger as a main. There's a modest beer garden here, nd a vine-dressed patio.

pen all wk 12-3 5.30-11 (Sat-Sun all day) **Food** Lunch Mon-Fri 12-2, Sat 12-9, Sun 2-8 Dinner Mon-Fri 6-9, Sat 12-9, Sun 12-8 ⊕ FREE HOUSE ⬛ Guest ales. ♀ 9 **acilities** Non-diners area ✿ (Bar Garden) ⧫ Children's menu Children's portions arden ⊓ Parking WiFi (notice required)

Half Moon & Spread Eagle

el: 01962 774339 **Winchester Rd SO21 3DG**
ir: From Winchester take A33 towards Basingstoke. In 5m left after Class tractors. Pub m on right

Traditional pub in pretty village

When Brian Thomas and Sally Agnew took over here in 2013, they knew exactly what hey wanted their first such venture to be: not a gastro-pub, not a destination pub, ut a proper village pub. And that's what it is. The only pub in the country with this name, incidentally, it comprises a large central bar, flanked one side by a pool oom-cum-library, and the other by the restaurant, although many visitors like to at in the convivial bar. A simple menu of home-cooked food starts, for example, with mushrooms in garlic sauce; and deep-fried whitebait, then lists pie of the day, egetables and mashed potato (or fries); deep-fried battered cod with chips and eas; and home-made vegetable curry with rice and poppadom. Thursday steak nights are a hit.

Open 12-2.30 6-10.30 (Fri 12-2.30 6-12 Sat 12-12 Sun 12-8) Closed Mon **Food** unch Tue-Fri 12-2, Sat 12-8.45, Sun 12-3 Dinner Tue-Fri 6-8.45, Sat 12-8.45 ⊕ GREENE KING ⬛ Hardys & Hansons, Guest ales ⚬ Aspall, Westons Old Rosie. **acilities** Non-diners area ✿ (Bar Garden) ⧫ Children's menu Children's portions Play area Garden ⊓ Parking WiFi (notice required)

NEW ALRESFORD
Map 5 SU53

The Bell Inn

tel: 01962 732429 **12 West St SO24 9AT**
email: info@bellalresford.com
dir: In village centre

Small, family-run free house in charming town centre

A well-restored former coaching inn in Georgian Alresford's main street, where Hampshire real ales hold their own against contenders from Cornwall and Devon, and over 18 wines are available by the glass. The bar dining area and candlelit restaurant offer fresh, locally sourced pork, ale and watercress sausages and mash; lamb shank with roast carrots and swede; pan-seared king scallops; and roast Gressingham duck breast. A two-courses-for-£10 meal could begin with grilled goats' cheese salad with walnut dressing, then Thai green chicken curry and basmati rice. Station Road opposite the inn leads to the famous Watercress Line.

Open all day Closed Sun eve **Food** Lunch all wk 12-3 Dinner Mon-Sat 6-9 Set menu available ⊕ FREE HOUSE ⬛ Sharp's Doom Bar, Itchen Valley Winchester Ale, Salisbury English Ale, Upham Ale, Otter ⚬ Aspall. ♀ 18 **Facilities** Non-diners area ✿ (Bar) ⧫ Children's menu Children's portions Outside area ⊓ Parking WiFi (notice required)

NORTHINGTON
Map 5 SU53

The Woolpack Inn
PICK OF THE PUBS

tel: 01962 734184 **Totford SO24 9TJ**
email: info@thewoolpackinn.co.uk
dir: From Basingstoke take A339 towards Alton. Under motorway, turn right (across dual carriageway) onto B3046 signed Candovers & Alresford. Pub between Brown Candover & Northington

Welcoming country inn with cracking food and local ales

Set in stunning Hampshire countryside, this Grade II listed drovers' inn has a sense of calm modernity while still retaining the classic feel of a country pub. Standing in a tiny hamlet in the peaceful Candover Valley, The Woolpack welcomes walkers and their dogs, families, cyclists and foodies. Ales change weekly but include one named after The Woolpack, while an up-market wine list will please the cognoscenti. Eat in the traditional bar, where rugs on tiled or wood floors and a roaring log fire create a relaxing atmosphere; alternatives are the smart dining room or a heated terrace. The bar menu proffers classics such as pie of the day or bangers and mash with onion gravy. Typical dining room main courses are confit pork belly, smoked bacon and potato gratin; or spiced winter vegetable hotpot, carrot and onion fritters and garlic flatbread.

Open all day all wk **Food** Lunch all wk 12-3 Dinner Mon-Sat 6-9, Sun 6-8.30 ⊕ FREE HOUSE ⬛ The Woolpack Ale, Palmers Copper Ale, Weekly changing Guest ale ⚬ Thatchers Gold. ♀ 11 **Facilities** Non-diners area ✿ (Bar Restaurant Garden) ⧫ Children's menu Children's portions Play area Garden ⊓ Parking WiFi (notice required)

NORTH WALTHAM
Map 5 SU54

The Fox
PICK OF THE PUBS

See Pick of the Pubs on opposite page

OLD BASING
Map 5 SU65

The Crown

tel: 01256 321424 **The Street RG24 7BW**
email: sales@thecrownoldbasing.com
dir: *M3 junct 6 towards Basingstoke. At rdbt right onto A30. 1st left into Redbridge Ln, to T-junct. Right into The Street, pub on right*

Village local with well-kept ales

Just outside Basingstoke is the picturesque village of Old Basing, in the heart of which is The Crown. Reliable and popular national ales are backed by local brews like Andwell King John and a good wine list. Here, they take great pride in the fact that every dish is prepared from scratch in the pub's kitchen. Food takes the form of bar snacks like filled rolls, salads and deli boards, and on the main menu, a typical choice could be a starter of crispy breaded Tunworth cheese with Doom Bar chutney, followed by crisp belly of lamb with cauliflower purée and spiced lentils. Lemon posset or warm coffee and walnut sponge both make for a delicious finale. Look out for the August beer festival.

Open all wk 11.30-2.30 5-11 (Fri-Sat 11.30-11.30 Sun 11.30-10) Closed 1 Jan **Food** Lunch Mon-Thu 12-2, Fri-Sun 12-2.30 Dinner Mon-Thu 6-9, Fri-Sat 6-9.30 Restaurant menu available ⊕ ENTERPRISE INNS ◀ Sharp's Doom Bar, Fuller's London Pride, Andwell King John ⏾ Thatchers Gold. ♥ 9 **Facilities** Non-diners area ✿ (Bar Garden) ⬤ Children's menu Children's portions Garden ⊨ Beer festival Parking WiFi ▭ (notice required)

OVINGTON
Map 5 SU53

The Bush
PICK OF THE PUBS

tel: 01962 732764 **SO24 0RE**
email: thebushinn@wadworth.co.uk
dir: *A31 from Winchester towards Alton & Farnham, approx 6m, left to Ovington. 0.5m to pub*

Much-praised, old-world riverside pub

This unspoilt, 17th-century, rose-covered pub tucks itself away down a short approach road that is, in fact, part of the ancient Pilgrim's Way from Winchester to Canterbury. On its other side runs the River Itchen. Small rooms off the bar are characterised by their subdued lighting, dark-painted walls, sturdy tables and chairs, high-backed settles, and fishing and other country artefacts. You can imagine what it's like when the log fire's blazing away. Regularly-changing menus offer food described as "contemporary in style, traditional in origin", including ploughman's, sandwiches, and 'gourmet' burgers, before getting down to the serious business of listing main meals such as pan-seared lamb's liver and crispy bacon; fresh Cornish fish of the day in beer batter; 8oz rump of Hampshire beef; and gnocchi gratin with wild mushroom fricassée. Real ales come from Wadworth and a guest brewery.

Open all wk Mon-Fri 11-3 6-11 Sat 11-11 Sun 12-10.30 (summer hols Mon-Sat 11-11 Sun 12-10.30) **Food** Lunch Mon-Fri 12-2.30, Sat-Sun 12-9.30, summer hols Mon-Sat 12-9, Sun 12-8.30 Dinner Mon-Fri 6-9.30, Sat-Sun 12-9.30, summer hols Mon-Sat 12-9, Sun 12-8.30 ⊕ WADWORTH ◀ 6X, Henry's Original IPA, Horizon, Guest ales ⏾ Thatchers Gold. ♥ 19 **Facilities** Non-diners area ✿ (Bar Restaurant Garden) ⬤ Children's menu Children's portions Family room Garden ⊨ Parking WiFi

PETERSFIELD
Map 5 SU72

The Old Drum ★ ★ ★ ★ INN ⊛

tel: 01730 300544 **16 Chapel St GU32 3DP**
email: info@theolddrum.co.uk **web:** www.theolddrum.co.uk
dir: *From A3 follow town centre signs (Winchester Rd). At mini rdbt, 2nd exit. Over rail crossing, 3rd right into Chapel St. Pub on right*

A contemporary pub in the centre of town

Two school friends, now in their fifties, and their wives have transformed Petersfield's oldest pub, rediscovering en route original 16th-century features, including a superb beamed ceiling and, of perhaps less pulse-racing potential, a tongue-and-groove 60s ceiling. The bar where author H G Wells once sat with a pint of mild now serves five frequently-changing, locally micro-brewed real ales. The food too has moved considerably on from H G's pickled-egg-if-he-was-lucky days to include AA Rosette-standard rabbit pie and home-made pickle; roast partridge, sprouts, chestnuts, boxty potatoes and bread sauce; and pumpkin, pearl barley and couscous risotto with goats' cheese fritters.

Open 10-3 5-11 Closed 25 Dec, 1st wk Jan, Sun eve **Food** Lunch Mon-Sat 12-2, Sun 12-3 Dinner Mon-Sat 6.30-9.30 Av main course £11 Restaurant menu available all wk ⊕ FREE HOUSE ◀ Dark Star Hophead, American Pale Ale & The Art of Darkness, Bowman Ales Wallops Wood, Suthwyk Ales Liberation, Triple fff Moondance ⏾ Westons Bounds. ♥ 12 **Facilities** Non-diners area ✿ (Bar Restaurant Garden) ⬤ Children's portions Garden ⊨ Beer festival WiFi **Rooms** 2

The Trooper Inn
PICK OF THE PUBS

tel: 01730 827293 **Alton Rd, Froxfield GU32 1BD**
email: info@trooperinn.com
dir: *From A3 follow A272 Winchester signs towards Petersfield (NB do not take A272). 1st exit at mini rdbt for Steep. 3m, pub on right*

Ideal for visitors to South Downs National Park

Said to have been a recruiting centre at the outset of the First World War, this 17th-century free house sits in a dip on one of the highest hills in the Hampshire countryside. The inn backs onto Ashford Hangers National Nature Reserve, and is also well positioned for access to the South Downs National Park, Jane Austen's Chawton and Gilbert White's Selborne. Inside the pub can be found winter log fires, a spacious bar and a charming restaurant with vaulted ceiling and wooden settles. Ales such as Ballards are on tap, and dishes with north African notes can be found in the restaurant. In the bar, snack on buckets of calamari or whitebait, or larger plates such as sausage casserole with creamy mash, or curry of the moment. On the carte, expect the likes of chermoula-marinated salmon with saffron and lemon baked risotto; and cherry, almond and marzipan sponge with orange blossom syrup.

Open 12-3 6-11 Closed 25-26 Dec & 1 Jan, Sun eve & Mon L **Food** Lunch Tue-Sat 12-2, Sun 12-2.30 Dinner Mon-Fri 6.30-9, Sat 7-9.30 ⊕ FREE HOUSE ◀ Ringwood Best Bitter, Ballards, Local guest ales. **Facilities** Non-diners area ✿ (Bar Restaurant Garden) ⬤ Children's menu Children's portions Garden ⊨ Parking WiFi ▭ (notice required)

PICK OF THE PUBS

The Fox

NORTH WALTHAM   Map 5 SU54

el: 01256 397288
RG25 2BE
email: info@thefox.org
web: www.thefox.org
dir: *M3 junct 7, A30 towards Winchester. North Waltham signed on right. Take 2nd signed road, then 1st left at Y junct*

Family-friendly pub with a large garden

Built as three farm cottages in 1624, a feature of the bar in this peaceful village pub is its collection of miniatures – over 1,100 so far, and counting. It's an easy place to get to whether travelling on the A303 or the M3. The Fox welcomes families, as you might guess from the children's adventure play area in the extensive beer garden which blazes with colour in summer when the pretty flower borders and hanging baskets are in bloom. In the bar, landlord Rob MacKenzie serves well-looked after real ales from Sharp's, Brakspear, West Berkshire and a guest brewery, and an impressive malt whisky selection among which you'll find the relatively scarce Auchentoshan, Dalmore and Singleton. Bar choices include a ciabatta bacon butty; and steak and beef sausage pie and mash. Rob's wife Izzy is responsible for the monthly menus and daily specials board in the tartan-carpeted restaurant, which list the house specialities of cheese soufflé,

and Hampshire venison served with glazed shallots, field mushrooms, spinach, creamed swede, sauté potatoes and port glaze. Among typical main courses there might be chicken breast stuffed with McSween's haggis, crushed new potatoes, carrots and whisky sauce; or pan-fried pheasant breast and confit leg in apricot and wine sauce with dauphinoise potatoes and steamed green beans. Home-made desserts are tempting too – there's pineapple Alaska; passionfruit crème brûlée; and bread and butter pudding, caramelised apples, toffee sauce and ice cream. The Fox's events calendar features monthly wine tasting dinners, and a beer festival in late April.

Open all day all wk 11-11 Closed 25 Dec
Food Lunch all wk 12-2.30 Dinner all wk 6-9.30 Av main course £7.95 Restaurant menu available all wk. ⊕ FREE HOUSE
◀ West Berkshire Good Old Boy, Brakspear, Sharp's Doom Bar, Guest ale ⏃ Aspall. ♛ 14 **Facilities** Non-diners area ❖ (Bar Garden) ♦♦ Children's menu Children's portions Play area Garden ⊼ Beer festival Parking 🚌 (notice required)

The White Horse Inn

tel: 01420 588387 **Priors Dean GU32 1DA**
email: info@pubwithnoname.co.uk
dir: *From Petersfield through Steep, 5m, right at small x-rds to East Tisted (follow brown pub sign), 2nd right*

Former forge with excellent beers

Originally used as a forge for passing coaches, this splendid 17th-century farmhouse is also known as the 'Pub With No Name' as it has no sign. The blacksmith sold beer to the travellers while their horses were attended to. Today there is an excellent range of beers including No Name Strong. Menus offer the likes of red onion, feta and olive tart; duck breast with red cabbage and pork reduction; and a selection of burgers and sharing platters. The pub holds a beer festival every June and a cider festival in September.

Open all day all wk 12-12 **Food** Lunch Mon-Fri 12-2.30, Sat-Sun all day Dinner Mon-Fri 6-9.30, Sat-Sun all day ⊕ FULLER'S ◄ London Pride, No Name Best & No Name Strong, Ringwood Fortyniner, Guest ales ♂ Aspall. ♥ 10 **Facilities** Non-diners area ✿ (Bar Garden) ♦ Children's menu Children's portions Family room Garden ⊼ Beer festival Cider festival Parking ➡

PRESTON CANDOVER   Map 5 SU64

Purefoy Arms ◉◉

PICK OF THE PUBS

See Pick of the Pubs on opposite page

RINGWOOD   Map 5 SU10

The Star Inn

tel: 01425 473105 **12 Market Place BH24 1AW**
email: thestarringwood@yahoo.co.uk
dir: *From A31 follow market place signs*

Specialising in Thai and Asian cuisine

Ian Pepperell, the landlord of this 470-year-old pub on the square has played a character in BBC Radio 4's *The Archers* for over 15 years. Away from his radio career he pulls pints of Ringwood Best for locals and helps serve the authentic Thai and oriental food that dominates the menu. Typical dishes include salt and pepper squid, deep-fried sea bass with chilli sauce, chicken in black bean sauce, and aromatic crispy duck. At lunch, you can also tuck into rib-eye steak and chips and tuna mayonnaise sandwiches.

Open all day all wk Closed 1 Jan **Food** Lunch all wk 12-2.30 Dinner all wk 6-9.30 Set menu available Restaurant menu available Mon-Sat ⊕ ENTERPRISE INNS ◄ Ringwood Best Bitter, Hop Back Summer Lightning, Fuller's London Pride, Black Sheep, Brains ♂ Black Rat, Thatchers Green Goblin. ♥ 11 **Facilities** Non-diners area ✿ (Bar) ♦ Outside area ⊼ WiFi ➡ (notice required)

ROCKBOURNE   Map 5 SU11

The Rose & Thistle

tel: 01725 518236 **SP6 3NL**
email: enquiries@roseandthistle.co.uk
dir: *Follow Rockbourne signs from either A354 (Salisbury to Blandford Forum road) or A338 at Fordingbridge*

Pretty, quintessentially English pub

Originally two thatched cottages in the 17th century, The Rose & Thistle stands at the top of a fine main street lined with picture-postcard period houses. Long, low and whitewashed, the pub has a stunning rose arch, hanging baskets round the door, and a quaint dovecote in the glorious front garden. The charming beamed bars boast attractive country-style fabrics and two huge fireplaces for blazing winter warmth – perfect after a breezy downland walk. Expect a relaxing

atmosphere, well-kept ale on tap and a selection of quality dishes from lunchtime bar snacks like Welsh rarebit to more formal options such as slow-cooked pork belly or steak and kidney pudding.

Open all wk 11-3 6-11 (Sat 11-11 Sun 12-8) **Food** Lunch all wk 12-2.30 Dinner Mon-Sat 7-9.30 ⊕ FREE HOUSE ◄ Ringwood Best, Sharp's Doom Bar, Butcombe Bitter ♂ Westons, Black Rat. ♥ 12 **Facilities** Non-diners area ♦ Children's portions Garden ⊼ Parking WiFi ➡ (notice required)

ROCKFORD   Map 5 SU10

The Alice Lisle

tel: 01425 474700 **Rockford Green BH24 3NA**
email: alicelisle@fullers.co.uk
dir: *From Ringwood A338 towards Fordingbridge. 1m, turn right into Ivy Ln. At end, left, cross cattle grid. Inn on left*

Child friendly and popular with walkers and cyclists

A picturesque, red-brick pub with a beautiful garden overlooking Blashford Lakes to the rear and Rockford Green to the front. Lady Alice Lisle, who lived down the road, was beheaded in 1685 for harbouring fugitives, following the failure of the Monmouth Rebellion. With the majority of produce sourced from New Forest Marque suppliers, choose from a menu including crab, fennel and chilli linguine; River Test trout fillet; gammon steak, chips and free-range eggs; and tomato and basil gnocchi.

Open all day all wk 10.30am-11pm **Food** Lunch Mon-Fri 12-3, Sat 12-9, Sun 12-8 Dinner Mon-Fri 6-9, Sat 12-9, Sun 12-8 ⊕ FULLER'S ◄ London Pride, George Gale & Co Seafarers & HSB, Guest ale ♂ Cornish Orchards. ♥ 10 **Facilities** ✿ (Bar Garden) ♦ Children's menu Children's portions Play area Garden ⊼ Parking WiFi ➡ (notice required)

ROMSEY   Map 5 SU32

The Cromwell Arms ★★★★ RR

tel: 01794 519515 **23 Mainstone SO51 8HG**
email: info@thecromwellarms.com **web:** www.thecromwellarms.com
dir: *From Romsey take A27 signed Ringwood, Bournemouth, Salisbury. Cross River Test, pub on right*

Offering locally sourced food and ales

With Broadlands, former home of Lord Mountbatten and current home of Lord and Lady Brabourne, as its neighbour, The Cromwell Arms derives its name from Romsey's links with the English Civil War. It offers fresh, home-cooked food and attentive service with some unique twists on traditional gastro-pub favourites. Typical locally sourced dishes are home-made game terrine with spiced apple chutney; and twice-baked cheese and mushroom soufflé with new potatoes and mixed leaves. Its Hampshire-skewed offering of real ales includes Double Drop from the town's Flack Manor brewery, and a diverse selection of wines.

Open all day all wk Closed 25 Dec **Food** Lunch Mon-Fri 12-3 & 3-6 (sandwiches only), Sat 12-9.30, Sun 12-5 Dinner Mon-Fri 6-9.30, Sat 12-9.30, Sun 6-7.30 ⊕ FREE HOUSE ◄ Flack Manor Flack's Double Drop, Guest ale ♂ Thatchers Gold. ♥ 17 **Facilities** Non-diners area ♦ Children's menu Children's portions Garden ⊼ Parking WiFi ➡ (notice required) **Rooms** 10

Find out more about

the AA's awards for food excellence on page 9

PICK OF THE PUBS

Purefoy Arms ✿✿

PRESTON CANDOVER Map 5 SU64

Tel: 01256 389777
Alresford Rd RG25 2EJ
email: info@thepurefoyarms.co.uk
web: www.thepurefoyarms.co.uk
dir: On B3046, S of Basingstoke

Fabulous food in the Candover Valley

Heavy on the bare brick and chunky wooden furnishings, there's nevertheless an air of quiet sophistication to this rural roadside dining pub in one of Hampshire's most appealing valleys. With the possible exception of the real ales, which are down-to-earth and delicious from breweries such as Itchen Valley, the word 'sophisticated' is an appropriate description for the entire operation. Take the wine list and throw caution to the winds with a Kung Fu Girl Riesling from Washington State, USA; if the wallet will not stretch that far, at least one of seventeen wines sold by the glass is bound to appeal. The menus are equally astonishing. Settle into a fireside chesterfield to study the hand-written cartes, perhaps with an appetiser of gordal olives; or Manchego with membrillo, a popular Spanish paste made with quince. Then enjoy trying to decide which of Andres Alemany's creative, two AA Rosette-dishes to sample. Some dishes are more familiar than others: a starter of crispy lambs' tongues and beetroots may be

considered more adventurous than hand-dived scallops with watercress and pata negra. The heavy Spanish accent continues with main courses such as charred secretto Iberico with romesco sauce, patatas al pobre and caramelised chicory. For dessert, you can stay in Spain for the likes of crema Catalana, or move to Italy for affogato with hand-made truffles. If your visit is timed for lunch rather than dinner, the 'simple lunch' is a fixed-price menu offering exceptional value: black pudding hash with duck egg and HP sauce could be followed by slow-cooked rump of Galician beef with dripping chips and salad; finish with queen of puddings. On a lovely summer's evening the garden is a peaceful place to relax with a drink and tapas-style nibbles.

Open 12-3 6-11 (Sun 12-4) Closed 26 Dec & 1 Jan, Sun eve & Mon **Food** Lunch Tue-Sat 12-3, Sun 12-4 Dinner Tue-Sat 6-10 Av main course £14 Set menu available ⊕ FREE HOUSE ◖ Flack Manor Flack's Double Drop, Itchen Valley Ò Westons Bounds. ♟ 17
Facilities Non-diners area ❤ (Bar Restaurant Garden) ♟ Children's menu Children's portions Garden ㅈ Parking WiFi ☷ (notice required)

ROMSEY *continued*

The Three Tuns 🏮

tel: 01794 512639 **58 Middlebridge St SO51 8HL**
email: manager@the3tunsromsey.co.uk
dir: *From Romsey bypass (A27) follow town centre sign. Left into Middlebridge St*

Award-winning, market town pub

A stone's throw from the market square this 300-year-old Grade II listed pub holds an AA rosette. Smart wood panelling, vintage chandeliers and botanical prints blend well with low oak beams and open fireplaces to give a traditional yet upbeat ambience. A simple British menu features many local ingredients for seasonal classics, sharing platters and Sunday roasts: how about choosing a main of lamb kofta with Moroccan couscous, hummous and tzatiki; or haddock and chips, followed by lemon posset with ginger nut crumb? For a quiet fireside pint, there's Ringwood or a guest ale.

Open all wk 12-3 5-11 (Fri-Sun 12-11) summer all day (Sun 11-10.30) **Food** Lunch Mon-Thu 12-2.30, Fri-Sun 12-3 Dinner Mon-Thu 6-9, Fri-Sat 6-9.30 Av main course £11 ⊕ ENTERPRISE INNS ◀ Ringwood Best Bitter, Flack Manor Flack's Double Drop, 2 Guest ales Ŏ Westons Stowford Press. ☂ 11 **Facilities** Non-diners area ❤ (Bar Garden) ♦ Children's portions Garden ⌂ Parking WiFi

ROTHERWICK ▪ Map 5 SU75

The Coach and Horses

tel: 01256 768976 **The Street RG27 9BG**
email: ian027@btinternet.com
dir: *Follow brown signs from A32 (Hook to Reading road)*

A cosy, welcoming and unpretentious atmosphere

Close to the church in Rotherwick – a picturesque village that has appeared in TV's *Midsomer Murders* – parts of this smart, cream-washed inn can be traced back to the 17th century. With log fires in winter, board games, exposed brickwork and red-and-black tiled or wooden floors, the interior is pleasingly traditional. The south-facing garden with views of fields is a draw in the summer as a place for a relaxed pint of ale, an afternoon tea or a sensibly priced meal; in summer wood-fired pizzas are available. Look out for visiting Morris dancers throughout the summer, and visits by vintage tractors and classic cars.

Open 12-3 5-11 (Sat 12-11 Sun 12-6) Closed Sun eve & Mon **Food** Lunch Tue-Sat 12-3, Sun 12-3.30 (booking advisable Sun) Dinner Tue-Sat 6-9 ⊕ HALL & WOODHOUSE ◀ Badger First Gold, Fursty Ferret, Tanglefoot Ŏ Westons Stowford Press & Old Rosie. **Facilities** Non-diners area ❤ (Bar Restaurant Garden) ♦ Children's menu Children's portions Garden ⌂ Parking WiFi (notice required)

SELBORNE ▪ Map 5 SU73

The Selborne Arms

tel: 01420 511247 **High St GU34 3JR**
email: info@selbornearms.co.uk
dir: *From A3 take B3006, pub in village centre*

Microbrewery delights in a friendly village pub

A huge chimney, known as a baffle entry, blocks your way on entering this 17th-century pub. You have to turn left or right, but it doesn't matter which, for either way you'll find homely bars with hop-strewn beams, a huge fireplace, Courage Best, Ringwood Fortyniner, local guest ales and Mr Whitehead's cider. The menu will please those who enjoy, for example, Welsh rarebit with Suthwyk Ale; local hand-made pork sausages and mash; smoked Scottish salmon salad; or Hampshire beefburger. A beer festival takes place on the first weekend in October. Eighteenth-century naturalist Gilbert White lived at The Wakes just up the road.

Open all wk 11-3 6-11 (Sat-11-11 Sun 12-11) **Food** Lunch Mon-Sat 12-2, Sun 12-3 Dinner Mon-Sat 7-9, Sun 7-8.30 ⊕ FREE HOUSE ◀ Courage Best Bitter, Ringwood Fortyniner, Bowman Ales Swift One, Local guest ales Ŏ Mr Whitehead's. ☂ 10 **Facilities** Non-diners area ♦ Children's menu Children's portions Play area Garden ⌂ Beer festival Parking (notice required)

SILCHESTER ▪ Map 5 SU66

Calleva Arms

tel: 0118 970 0305 **Little London Rd, The Common RG7 2PH**
dir: *A340 from Basingstoke, signed Silchester*

Village pub close to a famous archaeological site

Named for the nearby Calleva Atrebatum, a Roman town whose surviving walls are some of the best preserved in Britain, this 19th-century pub overlooking the common is the perfect starting (or finishing) point for walks. Two bar areas, with a log-burner in the middle, lead to a pleasant conservatory and large enclosed garden. A comprehensive menu lists grilled steaks with fries; salads such as chicken Caesar; traditional choices like barbecued pork ribs; and vegetarian options. Baguettes and paninis are added to the lunchtime selection.

Open all wk 11-3 5.30-11 (Sat 11am-11.30pm Sun 12-11) **Food** Lunch all wk 12-2 Dinner all wk 6.30-9 ⊕ FULLER'S ◀ London Pride, George Gale & Co HSB, Guinness Ŏ Aspall, Westons Stowford Press. ☂ 10 **Facilities** Non-diners area ❤ (Bar Garden) ♦ Children's portions Garden ⌂ Parking WiFi (notice required)

SOUTHAMPTON ▪ Map 5 SU41

The White Star Tavern, Dining & Rooms ★★★★★ INN 🏮🏮

tel: 023 8082 1990 **28 Oxford St SO14 3DJ**
email: reservations@whitestartavern.co.uk **web:** www.whitestartavern.co.uk
dir: *M3 junct 13, A33 to Southampton. Follow Ocean Village & Marina signs*

Seasonal cooking amid ocean liner decor

Named after the famous White Star Line shipping company that used to set sail from Southampton, this stylish gastro-pub with rooms is set in cosmopolitan Oxford Street. The restaurant provides modern British cooking typified by bream fillet with chorizo, chickpea, red pepper and tomato; chestnut crusted cod loin with artichoke purée and dauphinoise potato; and sticky toffee pudding with butterscotch sauce and vanilla ice cream. Watch the world go by from the pavement tables, or stay a little longer in one of the smart and comfortable bedrooms.

Open all day all wk 7am-11pm (Fri 7am-mdnt Sat 8.30am-mdnt Sun 8.30am-10.30pm) Closed 25 Dec **Food** Lunch Mon-Thu 7am-11am (bkfst) 12-2.30, Fri-Sat 7am-11am (bkfst) 12-3, Sun 7.30am-11am (bkfst) 12-8 Dinner Mon-Thu & Sat 6-9.30, Fri 6-10, Sun 6-8 Av main course £13 ⊕ ENTERPRISE INNS ◀ Fuller's London Pride, Bowman Swift One, Ringwood. ☂ 11 **Facilities** Non-diners area ♦ Children's menu Children's portions ⌂ WiFi **Rooms** 13

SPARSHOLT ▪ Map 5 SU43

The Plough Inn ▪ PICK OF THE PUBS

See Pick of the Pubs on opposite page

PICK OF THE PUBS

The Plough Inn

SPARSHOLT   Map 5 SU43

tel: 01962 776353
Woodman Ln SO21 2NW
dir: *B3049 from Winchester towards Salisbury, left to Sparsholt, 1m*

Ever popular inn down a country lane

Built as a coach house to serve Sparsholt Manor opposite, this popular village pub just a few miles from Winchester has been a popular local alehouse for more than 150 years. Inside, the main bar and dining areas blend harmoniously together, with farmhouse-style pine tables, wooden and upholstered seats, stone jars, miscellaneous agricultural implements, wooden wine box end-panels and dried hops. Wadworth of Devizes supplies all the real ales, and there's a good wine selection. Lunchtime regulars know that 'doorstep' is a most apt description for the great crab and mayonnaise, beef and horseradish and other sandwiches, plus good soups and chicken liver parfait. The dining tables to the left of the entrance look over open fields to wooded downland, and it's at this end of the pub you'll find a daily changing blackboard offering dishes such as salmon and crab fishcakes with saffron sauce; lamb's liver and bacon with mash and onion gravy; beef, ale and mushroom pie; and whole baked

camembert with garlic and rosemary. The menu board at the right-hand end of the bar offers the more substantial venison steak with celeriac mash and roasted beetroot; roast pork belly with bubble-and-squeak, five spice and sultana gravy; chicken breast filled with goats' cheese mousse; and fillet of sea bass with olive mash. Puddings include sticky toffee pudding and crème brûlée. The Plough is very popular, so it's best to book for any meal. The delightful flower- and shrub-filled garden has plenty of room for children to run around and play in. There's a jazz night on the first Sunday in August and carol singing with Father Christmas on 23rd December.

Open all wk 11-3 6-11 (Sun 12-3 6-10.30) Closed 25 Dec **Food** Lunch all wk 12-2 Dinner served Sun-Thu 6-9, Fri-Sat 6-9.30 ⊕ WADWORTH ◖ Henry's Original IPA, 6X, Old Timer, JCB. ♟ 15 **Facilities** Non-diners area ❄ (Bar Garden) ♯ Children's menu Children's portions Play area Family room Garden ╦ Parking WiFi

STEEP | Map 5 SU72

Harrow Inn `PICK OF THE PUBS`

tel: 01730 262685 **GU32 2DA**
dir: *From A272 in Petersfield to Sheet, left opposite church (School Ln), over A3 by-pass bridge. Inn signed on right*

Real ales, hearty food and serious charity fund raiser

This 16th-century tile-hung gem is situated in a lovely rural location and has changed little over the years. The McCutcheon family has run it since 1929; sisters Claire and Nisa, both born and brought up here, are now the third generation with their names over the door. Tucked away off the road, it comprises two tiny bars - the 'public' is Tudor, with beams, tiled floor, inglenook fireplace, scrubbed tables, wooden benches, tree-trunk stools and a 'library'; the saloon (or Smoking Room, as it is still called) is Victorian. Beers are dispensed from barrels, there is no till and the toilets are across the road. Food is in keeping: ham and pea soup; hot Scotch eggs (some days); cheddar ploughman's; and various quiches. The large garden has plenty of tables surrounded by country-cottage flowers and fruit trees. Quiz nights raise huge sums for charity, for which Claire's partner Tony grows and sells flowers outside. Ask about the Harrow Cook Book, a collection of customers' recipes on sale for charity.

Open 12-2.30 6-11 (Sat 11-3 6-11 Sun 12-3 7-10.30) Closed Sun eve in winter **Food** Lunch all wk 12-2 Dinner all wk 7-9 Av main course £10 ⊕ FREE HOUSE ◀ Ringwood Best Bitter, Hop Back GFB, Bowman, Dark Star Hophead, Flack Manor Flack's Double Drop Ö Thatchers Heritage. **Facilities** Non-diners area ❤ (Bar Garden Outside area) Garden Outside area 禾 Parking **Notes** ⊛

STOCKBRIDGE | Map 5 SU33

Mayfly

tel: 01264 860283 **Testcombe SO20 6AZ**
dir: *Between A303 & A30, on A3057. Between Stockbridge & Andover*

Famous pub on the River Test

Standing right on the banks of the swiftly flowing River Test, the Mayfly is an iconic drinking spot. Inside the beamed old farmhouse with its traditional bar and bright conservatory you'll find a choice of draught ciders and up to six real ales. All-day bar food might include grilled black pudding and poached egg; chicken and five bean chilli; baked sea bream stuffed with fennel and red peppers; or steak and Stilton pie. Arrive early on warm summer days to grab a bench on the large riverside terrace.

Open all day all wk 10am-11pm **Food** Lunch all wk 11.30-9 Dinner all wk 11.30-9 Av main course £12 ⊕ FREE HOUSE ◀ George Gale & Co Seafarers & HSB Ö Aspall, Thatchers Green Goblin & Gold. ☕ 20 **Facilities** Non-diners area ❤ (Bar Restaurant Garden) ◑ Children's portions Garden 禾 Parking WiFi ▭

The Peat Spade Inn ★★★★ INN ⊛ `PICK OF THE PUBS`

tel: 01264 810612 **Longstock SO20 6DR**
email: info@peatspadeinn.co.uk **web:** www.peatspadeinn.co.uk
dir: *Phone for detailed directions*

Timeless inn famous for its fishing connections

Located between Winchester and Salisbury, The Peat Spade is a reminder of a bygone England and its country sport traditions. Perched on the banks of the River Test in a corner of Hampshire countryside famed for being the fly-fishing capital of the world, the unusual paned windows overlook the peaceful village lane and idyllic heavily thatched cottages at this striking, red-brick and gabled Victorian pub. You will find a relaxed atmosphere in the cosy fishing- and shooting-themed bar and dining room; a simple daily-changing menu lists classic English food combined with flavoursome European ingredients. The kitchen uses locally-sourced produce, including allotment-grown fruit and vegetables, and game from the Leckford Estate. To drink there are local cask ales such as Flack Catcher, and a small but

innovative wine list which includes a choice of two champagnes served by the glass. In summer, retire to the super terrace.

Open all day all wk 11-11 (Sun 11-10.30) Closed 25 Dec **Food** Lunch all wk 12-2.30 Dinner all wk 6.30-9.30 ⊕ FREE HOUSE/MILLER'S COLLECTION ◀ Flower Pots Goodens Gold, Flack Manor Flack Catcher, Guest ales. ☕ 11 **Facilities** Non-diners area ❤ (Bar Restaurant Garden) ◑ Children's menu Children's portions Garden 禾 Parking WiFi ▭ (notice required) **Rooms** 8

The Three Cups Inn ★★★★ INN ⊛ `PICK OF THE PUBS`

tel: 01264 810527 **High St SO20 6HB**
email: manager@the3cups.co.uk **web:** www.the3cups.co.uk
dir: *M3 junct 8, A303 towards Andover. Left onto A3057 to Stockbridge*

Charming pub with low beams and a river in the garden

The pub's name apparently comes from an Old English phrase for a meeting of three rivers, although there's only one river here. That river happens to be the Test, generally regarded as the birthplace of modern fly fishing. One of these channels flows through the delightful rear garden of this 15th-century, timber-framed building, where brown trout may be spotted from the patio. The low-beamed bar to the right of the front door can be warmed by the centrally placed log fire; Itchen Valley and Flower Pots - Hampshire real ales - and a guest, are served here. You can eat in the bar, the main, candlelit dining area is at the other end of the building. Modern European and traditional selections blend fresh regional ingredients to create starters such as smoked salmon and crème fraîche terrine with citrus dressing; and main courses of rabbit leg braised in sherry, saffron, Savoy cabbage and wild mushroom tortellini. Suites provide excellent overnight accommodation.

Open all day all wk 10am-11pm (Fri-Sun 8am-11pm) **Food** Lunch all wk 12-2.30 Dinner all wk 6-9.30 ⊕ FREE HOUSE ◀ Itchen Valley Fagins, Young's Bitter, Flower Pots, Guest ales Ö Westons Stowford Press. ☕ **Facilities** Non-diners area ❤ (Bar Garden) ◑ Children's menu Children's portions Garden 禾 Beer festival Cider festival Parking WiFi ▭ **Rooms** 8

SWANMORE | Map 5 SU51

The Rising Sun

tel: 01489 896663 **Hill Pound SO32 2PS**
dir: *M27 junct 10, A32 through Wickham towards Alton. Left into Bishop's Wood Rd, right at x-rds into Mislingford Rd to Swanmore*

Homely, haunted pub

Tucked in the heart of the beautiful Meon Valley, this 17th-century coaching inn has winter fires, low beams, uneven floors and lots of nooks and crannies. In summer, enjoy a pint of Palmers, Dorset Gold or Sharp's Doom Bar in the secluded rear garden. Home-cooked food makes good use of locally sourced ingredients in simple snacks such as sandwiches and salads through to full meals along the lines of home-made chicken liver pâté with Cumberland sauce and melba toast followed by smoked haddock and spring onion fishcakes with salad and new potatoes. Look out for the resident ghost! There's a beer, cider and wine festival on the Summer Bank Holiday Saturday.

Open all wk Mon-Sat 11.30-3 5.30-11 (Sun 12-4 5.30-10.30) **Food** Lunch Mon-Sat 12-2, Sun 12-2.30 Dinner Mon-Sat 6-9, Sun 6-8.30 Av main course £10.50 Set menu available ⊕ FREE HOUSE ◀ Sharp's Doom Bar, Palmers, Dorset Gold, Irving Type 42, Suthwyk Palmerston's Folly Ö Thatchers Gold. ☕ 13 **Facilities** Non-diners area ❤ (Bar Garden) ◑ Children's menu Children's portions Garden 禾 Beer festival Cider festival Parking ▭ (notice required)

TANGLEY
Map 5 SU35

The Fox Inn

tel: 01264 730276 **SP11 0RU**
email: info@foxinntangley.co.uk
dir: *From rdbt (junct of A343 & A3057) in Andover follow station signs (Charlton Rd). Through Charlton & Hatherden to Tangley*

Local ales and spicy treats in rural seclusion

Curiously, a former chef to the Thai Royal Family now dedicates his skills to providing a startling menu to pub-goers who adventure along the country lanes that cross outside this secluded inn in the North Wessex Downs Area of Outstanding Natural Beauty. Their reward is a superb setting beside coppice woodland with relaxing views across sloping arable fields that stretch to the horizons. This 300-year-old brick and flint cottage has been a pub since 1830; inside it is largely furnished in a casual-contemporary style featuring an unusual log-end bar design, where guests may enjoy a wide choice of genuine Thai dishes and some fine local beers.

Open all day all wk 12-11 (Sun 12-10.30) Closed 25 Dec, 1 Jan **Food** Lunch all wk 12-2.30 Dinner Mon-Sat 6-9.30, Sun 6-8 Set menu available Restaurant menu available all wk ⊕ FREE HOUSE ◀ Ramsbury, Flack Manor Flack's Double Drop, Upham Punter Ö Symonds. ₹ 12 **Facilities** Non-diners area ✿ (Bar Restaurant Garden) ♦ Children's menu & portions Garden ⋒ Parking WiFi ☞ (notice required)

THRUXTON
Map 5 SU24

NEW The White Horse Inn & Restaurant ★★★ INN

tel: 01264 772401 **Mullens Pond SP11 8EE**
email: enquiries@whitehorsethruxton.co.uk **web:** www.whitehorsethruxton.co.uk
dir: *S of Thruxton. Phone for detailed directions*

Thatched, 15th-century pub with lovingly-tended garden

Newly refurbished maybe, but there's still plenty of old-time, Grade II listed atmosphere in this Test Valley pub, thought to date from around 1450. The spacious bar does its bit for local breweries by offering Romsey's Flack Manor Double Drop,

and King John from Andwell, near Basingstoke. Australian chef-patron Norelle Oberin shows her hand with sea bass fillet, brown shrimp risotto, tomato and spring onion velouté; Hampshire rib-eye steak and château potatoes, Portobello mushrooms and red wine jus; and smoked paprika with aubergine and courgette risotto. For dessert, rice pudding and blood orange compôte. Baguettes and sandwiches are available at lunchtime.

Open all day all wk **Food** Lunch all wk 12-3 Dinner Mon-Sat 6-9 Av main course £11.50 Set menu available Restaurant menu available all wk ⊕ FREE HOUSE ◀ Sharp's Doom Bar, Andwell King John, Flack Manor Flack's Double Drop Ö Thatchers. ₹ 24 **Facilities** Non-diners area ✿ (Bar Garden) ♦ Children's menu Children's portions Garden ⋒ Parking WiFi **Rooms** 4

TICHBORNE
Map 5 SU53

The Tichborne Arms
PICK OF THE PUBS

tel: 01962 733760 **SO24 0NA**
email: tichbornearms@xln.co.uk
dir: *Follow pub signs from B3046, S of A31 between Winchester & Alresford*

Worth turning off the main road for

The thatched roof suggests it's old, but this is actually a mid-20th century rebuild of its burnt-down predecessor. In fact, it fits so harmoniously into this tucked away settlement that you'd be forgiven for not realising. In the 1870s the village hit the headlines while the lengthy trial took place of a crooked East End butcher pretending to be The Tichborne Claimant, heir to a Tichborne family legacy. He was eventually found guilty. Antiques, prints and other artefacts attractively clutter the rustically furnished, dried hop-strung bar, so there's plenty to look at as you relax with a Downton or Palmers real ale, or Mr Whitehead's local cider. Owner-chef Patrick Roper's short daily menus typically feature fillet of sea bream with creamy prawn sauce; medallions of pork tenderloin with apple and cider sauce; and mushroom tagliatelle. A June beer festival takes place in the tree-shaded garden.

Open all wk 11.45-3 6-11.30 (Sat open all day) **Food** Lunch all wk 12-2 Dinner all wk 6-9 Set menu available Restaurant menu available all wk ⊕ FREE HOUSE ◀ Sharp's, Downton, Hop Back, Palmers, Bowman Ö Mr Whitehead's Cirrus Minor & Strawberry. ₹ 10 **Facilities** Non-diners area ✿ (Bar Restaurant Garden) ♦ Children's portions Garden ⋒ Beer festival Parking WiFi ☞ (notice required)

UPPER FROYLE
Map 5 SU74

The Hen & Chicken Inn

tel: 01420 22115 **GU34 4JH**
email: info@henandchicken.co.uk
dir: *2m from Alton towards Farnham on A31. Adjacent to petrol station. Signed from A31*

Character coaching inn off the A31

Highwaymen, hop-pickers and high clergy have all supped and succoured here in this noble, three-storey Georgian road house. They'd still recognise some of the comfortably traditional interior - timeless panelling, beams, old tables and inglenook; maybe, too, the little wooden barn in a corner of the grassy garden, stood on its painted staddle stones. The reliable country menu is strong on local produce and vegetables from the garden; start with home-made Scotch eggs; then move onto pollock with chorizo and white beans; beef stew with winter vegetables; or sweet pepper and goats' cheese tart. It may be hard to resist the warm Bramley apple pie and custard.

Open all day all wk 11-11 (Sun 12-9) **Food** Lunch all wk 12-9 Dinner all wk 12-9 Av main course £5.95 Set menu available ⊕ HALL & WOODHOUSE ◀ Badger Tanglefoot, K&B Sussex Ö Westons Stowford Press. **Facilities** Non-diners area ✿ (Bar Garden) ♦ Children's menu Children's portions Play area Garden ⋒ Parking WiFi ☞ (notice required)

The George & Falcon ★★★★ INN

tel: 01730 829623 **Warnford Rd SO32 3LB**
email: reservations@georgeandfalcon.com **web:** www.georgeandfalcon.com
dir: *M27 junct 10, A32 signed Alton. Approx 10.5m to Warnford*

Country inn with modern cuisine

The lively little River Meon slides past the garden of this imposing inn, first recorded over 400 years ago. The cosy, fire-warmed snug is the place to settle with a pint of Ringwood Fortyniner and reflect on a grand winter walk on nearby Old Winchester Hill; or discover the terrace and consider the enticing modern British menu. Duck terrine or baked camembert whet the appetite for mains which include lamb shoulder with roasted root vegetables, or The George & Falcon burger topped with mozzarella and onion rings. Six en suite residential rooms complete the scene.

Open all day all wk 11-11 (Oct-Mar 11-3 6-11) **Food** Lunch all wk 11-3 Dinner all wk 6-9 Set menu available ⊕ MARSTON'S ◼ Ringwood Best Bitter, Fortyniner ⚬ Thatchers Gold. ♥ 9 **Facilities** Non-diners area ❖ (Bar Restaurant Garden) ⦁♦ Children's menu Children's portions Family room Garden ⊓ Parking WiFi ⛟ (notice required) **Rooms** 6

The Jolly Farmer Country Inn

tel: 01489 572500 **29 Fleet End Rd SO31 9JH**
email: mail@thejollyfarmer.uk.com
dir: *M27 junct 9, A27 (Fareham), right into Warsash Rd. 2m, left into Fleet End Rd*

Locally caught seafood a speciality

Martin and Cilla O'Grady have been running the show here since 1983, and their enthusiasm is as strong as ever. Old farming implements decorate the rustic-style bars, while outside are a patio, beer garden and children's play area. The comprehensive menu ranges from locally caught seafood dishes, sandwiches, salads, grills and pub favourites, to home-made dishes like confit of duck in orange and black cherry jus; grilled fresh haddock with prawn, garlic and herb sauce; and vegetable tikka masala. Daily chalkboard lunch, dinner and Sunday lunch specials, such as Catch-of-the-Day, and dishes for children, extend the options.

Open all day all wk 11-11 **Food** Lunch Mon-Fri 12-2.30, Sat-Sun all day Dinner Mon-Fri 6-10, Sat-Sun all day Set menu available ◼ Fuller's London Pride, George Gale & Co HSB & Seafarers, Worthington's. ♥ 14 **Facilities** Non-diners area ❖ (Bar Garden) ⦁♦ Children's menu Children's portions Play area Family room Garden ⊓ Parking WiFi ⛟ (notice required)

The Chequers Inn

tel: 01256 862605 **RG29 1TL**
email: thechequers5@hotmail.co.uk
dir: *From Odiham High St into King St, becomes Long Ln. 3m, left at T-junct, pub 0.25m on top of hill*

Locally renowned little cracker

A lovely country pub with a multitude of low beams testifying to its 15th-century origins. In July 2013 Paul and Nichola Sanders took over, bringing a wealth of experience after running a successful restaurant in nearby Farnham. Their forte is preparing classic English dishes and daily specials based on fresh fish, steaks and duck, and serving well-kept pints of Hall & Woodhouse ales. A brasserie menu proffers the likes of salmon and crab fishcakes, while the carte overflows with favourites such as avocado and prawn cocktail, and pan-fried calves' liver with bacon. Eat and drink by a log fire, out front under sheltered grapevines, or in the rear garden overlooking the countryside.

Open all wk 12-3 6-11 (Sat 12-11 Sun 12-10.30 Jun-Sep all day) **Food** Lunch Mon-Fri 12-2, Sat 12-3, Sun 12-6 Dinner Mon-Thu 6.30-9, Fri-Sat 6.30-9.30 Restaurant

menu available all wk ⊕ HALL & WOODHOUSE ◼ Badger First Gold & Tanglefoot, Seasonal ales ⚬ Westons Stowford Press, Badger Applewood & Pearwood. ♥ 12 **Facilities** Non-diners area ❖ (Bar Garden Outside area) ⦁♦ Children's portions Garden Outside area ⊓ Parking WiFi ⛟ (notice required)

The Thomas Lord ⊛⊛   PICK OF THE PUBS

tel: 01730 829244 **High St GU32 1LN**
email: info@thethomaslord.co.uk
dir: *M3 junct 9, A272 towards Petersfield, right at x-roads onto A32, 1st left*

Country inn with impressive cricket connections

This beautifully restored pub in the pretty village of West Meon close to Winchester was named after the founder of Lord's Cricket Ground, who retired to West Meon in 1830 and is buried in the churchyard. The bar is decorated with cricketing memorabilia and well furnished with drinkers' tables and chairs; it's an agreeable setting for a well-kept Ringwood ale, or a chilled glass of white chosen from the sophisticated range of wines. The pub's own garden supplies the kitchen with herbs, salads and vegetables, as do local farms and small-scale producers ;the result is a menu of seasonal delights. A typical meal might start with Portland crab with brown crab custard, treacle bread and kohlrabi remoulade, followed by a kaleidoscope of flavours in the duck breast with duck faggot, rösti potato, honey parsnip purée, celeriac, horseradish, turnip and kale.

Open all day all wk **Food** Lunch Mon-Fri 12-2.30, Sat 12-3, Sun 12-4 Dinner Mon-Thu 6-9.30, Fri-Sat 6-10, Sun 6-9 Av main course £11.50 Set menu available ⊕ FREE HOUSE ◼ Upham Ales, Ringwood Best Bitter ⚬ Thatchers Cheddar Valley. ♥ 15 **Facilities** Non-diners area ❖ (Bar Garden) ⦁♦ Children's portions Garden ⊓ Parking WiFi ⛟

The Black Horse

tel: 01794 340308 **The Village SP5 1NF**
email: info@theblackhorsepublichouse.co.uk
dir: *In village centre*

Ideal spot for walkers and cyclists

This traditional 17th-century former coaching inn is the perfect spot to rest and refuel. Located on the Clarendon Way, the popular walking/cycling trail between Winchester and Salisbury, it's a proper village community pub, replete with skittle alley, regular quiz nights and locals supping pints of Hop Back and Flower Pots ales by the blazing fire in the oak-beamed main bar. Food ranges from lunchtime filled ciabatta sandwiches to curries, pie of the day, burgers and main courses like tarragon chicken or creamy vegetable risotto. There is also a good-value and extensive Sunday lunch menu.

Open 12-3 6-11 (Sun 12-8) Closed 2 days after New Year BHs, Mon L & Tue L **Food** Lunch Wed-Sun Dinner Tue-Sun ⊕ FREE HOUSE ◼ Hop Back, Stonehenge, Bowman, Flower Pots ⚬ Westons 1st Quality. ♥ 8 **Facilities** Non-diners area ❖ (Bar Restaurant Garden) ⦁♦ Children's menu Children's portions Play area Garden ⊓ Parking WiFi ⛟ (notice required)

NEW The White Hart ★★★ INN

tel: 01256 892900 **Newbury St RG28 7DN**
email: thewhitehart.whitchurch@arkells.com **web:** www.whitehartotelwhitchurch.co.uk
dir: *On B3400 in town centre*

Tasty pub grub near the source of the River Test

Strategically located where the old London to Exeter and Oxford to Southampton roads cross, this was Swindon brewery Arkell's first Hampshire pub. Dating from 1461, its rich history includes patronage by the late Lord Denning, Master of the

Rolls, who was born opposite. What he dined on is unknown, but today's menu lists jacket potatoes; steak and ale pie; Somerset pork casserole; beer-battered fish and chips; and sizzling home-made fajitas. For vegetarians, there's three-cheese macaroni, and vegetable Madras. Just over the road is Whitchurch Silk Mill, the oldest of its type in the UK in its original building, and still using 19th-century machinery.

Open all day all wk **Food** Contact pub for details ⊕ ARKELL'S ◄ 3B & Wiltshire Gold ♻ Westons Stowford Press. **Facilities** Non-diners area ♣ (Bar Restaurant Outside area) ◄ Children's menu Family room Outside area ⊟ Parking WiFi **Rooms** 10 **Notes** ⊗

▍ WICKHAM   Map 5 SU51

Greens Restaurant & Bar

tel: 01329 833197 **The Square P017 5JQ**
dir: M27 junct 10, A32 to Wickham

Hardy perennial of the pub world

It's hard to miss Greens' black-and-white timbered building, standing prominently on a corner of Wickham's medieval market square, the second largest in England. Its proprietors for nearly 30 years, Frank and Carol Duckworth still use their original slogan – 'Nothing is too much trouble', a promise evident in the modern British seasonal menus and, more importantly, on the plate. Starters include steamed mussels; and Gressingham duck, apricot and orange terrine; while main dish options are local free-range pork with black pudding mash; Hampshire rib-eye steak; and pan-fried fillet of hake. Bowmans, in nearby Droxford, supplies two of its prize-winning ales.

Open 10-3 6-11 (Sat 11-11 Sun & BH 12-5 May-Sep all day) Closed 19-20 May, Sun eve & Mon **Food** Lunch Tue-Sat 12-2.30, Sun 12-5 Dinner Tue-Sat 6-9.30 ⊕ FREE HOUSE ◄ Bowman Wallops Wood & Swift One. ♟ 12 **Facilities** Non-diners area ◄ Children's portions Garden ⊟

▍ WINCHESTER   Map 5 SU42

The Bell Inn

tel: 01962 865284 **83 St Cross Rd S023 9RE**
dir: M3 junct 11, B3355 towards city centre. Approx 1m pub on right

Community local close to pretty water meadows

Close to the 12th-century Hospital of St Cross & Almshouse of Noble Poverty, this refurbished community local has now changed hands. Expect a warm welcome, good ales, and good value food which is either served in the main bar, lounge or walled garden. Daily specials include pan-fried sirloin steak; oven-roasted chicken supreme stuffed with mozzarella and chorizo; pan-seared salmon fillet; and wild mushroom risotto. There's a children's selection too. A walk through the River Itchen water meadows leads to Winchester College and the city centre.

Open all day all wk 11-11 (Fri-Sat 12-12 Sun 12-10.30) **Food** Lunch Mon-Sat 12-2.30, Sun 12-4 Dinner Mon-Sat 6-9 ⊕ GREENE KING ◄ Ruddles Best, Belhaven Grand Slam, Morland Old Speckled Hen, Timothy Taylor Landlord, IPA Gold ♻ Westons Stowford Press. ♟ 15 **Facilities** Non-diners area ♣ (Bar Garden) ◄ Children's menu Children's portions Play area Garden ⊟ Beer festival Parking WiFi 🚌 (notice required)

The Black Boy

tel: 01962 861754 **1 Wharf Hill S023 9NQ**
email: enquiries@theblackboypub.com
dir: Off Chesil St (B3300)

Traditional pub with the emphasis firmly on local ales

This old fashioned whitewashed pub in the ancient capital of Wessex is a decidedly beer-led hostelry. As well as three regular regional ales from the Cheriton, Ringwood and Hop Back breweries, The Black Boy offers two Hampshire guests, perhaps from Triple fff or Itchen Valley. A small selection of good French wines is also available. The interior features old wooden tables and a quirky decor with all manner of objects hanging from the ceiling, while the short daily menu on the blackboard could include sandwiches, home-made burgers and fish and chips. There is a sheltered garden with patio heaters.

Open all day all wk **Food** Lunch Wed-Sun 12-2 Dinner Tue-Sat 7-9 ⊕ FREE HOUSE ◄ Flower Pots Cheriton Pots, Ringwood Best Bitter, Bowman Ales Swift One, Hop Back Summer Lightning, Guest ales ♻ Westons Stowford Press. **Facilities** Non-diners area ♣ (All areas) ◄ Garden Outside area ⊟ WiFi

The Golden Lion

tel: 01962 865512 **99 Alresford Rd S023 0JZ**
email: bridphelan@me.com
web: www.thegoldenlionwinchester.co.uk
dir: From Union St in town centre follow 'All other routes' sign. At rdbt 1st exit into High St. At rdbt 1st exit into Bridge St (B3404) signed Alton/Alresford, (becomes Alresford Rd)

Charming flower bedecked pub

Winners of Winchester in Bloom awards for multiple years, bedecked with flower baskets, Brid and Derek Phelan's 1932-built, delightfully cottage-style pub is on Winchester's eastern fringe. As well as Irish charm, expect main and specials menus offering plenty of straightforward hearty pub meals. Lasagne, home-baked ham, breaded plaice fillet, steak and ale pie, pork belly and chargrilled lamb cutlets all feature. Soft cushions are provided for those sitting in the large beer garden, or smoking shelter.

Open all wk Mon-Sat 11.30-3 5.30-11 (Sun 12-10.30) **Food** Lunch all wk 12-2.30 Dinner all wk 6-9 ⊕ WADWORTH ◄ 6X, Henry's Original IPA, Seasonal ales ♻ Westons Stowford Press. ♟ **Facilities** Non-diners area ♣ (Bar Restaurant Garden) ◄ Children's menu Children's portions Garden ⊟ Parking WiFi 🚌 (notice required)

See advert on page 248

The Golden Lion

99 Alresford Road, Winchester, Hants SO23 0JZ • **Tel:** 01962 865512
Website: www.thegoldenlionwinchester.co.uk • **Email:** bridphelan@me.com

We warmly invite you to *The Golden Lion Pub*, Winchester, for our cosy vintage style interiors, excellent home cooked food and great Irish welcome! We are located just on the Eastern edge of the city, within very easy reach of the M3, the A272 and the A34, and just a 10 minute walk into the beautiful heart of the city with all of its historic attractions and wealth of independent shops. We have a large car park as well as patio areas and beer gardens to the front and back, including a special enclosed area for doggies to have a run. We also have disabled access and facilities inside. We are a TV and gaming machine free zone so that you can relax in our friendly atmosphere and enjoy our great background music. We also welcome children who are eating with their parents/guardians.

We are very proud to have received many awards for the services that we offer, including 'The Casque Mark' and 'Master Cellerman' for our real ales, the certificate of 'Excellent' for our food hygiene, and we have won many awards for our floral displays and hanging baskets. We were very honoured to have been awarded as the Wadworth Brewery 'Retailer of the Year'. We were also delighted to receive the Quality Assured Award in Hampshire Hospitality Awards 2014 and the 'Certificate of Excellence' from TripAdvisor.

We have regular live music sessions such as Bluegrass music on the last Tuesday evening of the month, and Irish music on the second Thursday evening of the month.

With our newly built extension, we can now cater for private functions, such as weddings, birthdays, wakes or group meetings, and more. You can choose from a formal sit-down meal to a casual buffet style menu, or a summer barbecue in our garden.

Follow us on Facebook at **facebook.com/goldenlionwinchester**

Or on Twitter **@GoldenLionWinch**

We very much look forward to welcoming you very soon!

PICK OF THE PUBS

The Wykeham Arms ★★★★★ INN

WINCHESTER　　　　　Map 5 SU42

tel: 01962 853834
75 Kingsgate St SO23 9PE
email: wykehamarms@fullers.co.uk
web: www.wykehamarmswinchester.co.uk
dir: *Near Winchester College &*
Winchester Cathedral

Sophisticated gastro-pub in Winchester's historic heart

It's quite hard to convey just how much character The Wyk has. For it's more than a pub and a restaurant with accommodation; it's a Winchester institution. Beyond the cathedral from the High Street, with Winchester College as a neighbour, this 270-year-old building is entered from the pavement through curved, etched-glass doors straight into two bars, one dead ahead, the other to your left. Both have open fires and are furnished with old pine tables and redundant college desks. Everywhere, and that's no understatement - are portraits and prints, pewter tankards and miscellaneous ephemera. It all creates a warm feeling - gemütlichkeit as they say in Germany. Perhaps this is why it attracts such a varied clientele - business people, barristers, clergy, college dons, ladies who lunch, tourists and, yes, locals, for this is a desirable residential quarter. You may eat in the bars, but serious dining is done in tucked-away rooms, where wide-

ranging, modern British menus ring the seasonal changes to include ham hock terrine with vegetables à la Grècque and sweet mustard sabayon; and cherry tomato, balsamic gel, red pepper and goats' curd consommé, as typical starters. Equally representative are main dishes of roasted cod fillet with braised pork cheek, pea purée and mini-fish pie; and roasted venison loin with red cabbage ketchup, cocoa gnocchi, beetroot and triple-cooked chips with harissa mayo. 'Home Comforts' include Devon mussels; and confit Gressingham duck leg. Finish off with dark Muscovado sponge with grilled banana, salt caramel butterscotch and banana milkshake. It's one of the Fuller's brewery's flagship pubs, although there's a guest real ale too, perhaps

hoppy Goodens Gold from the nearby Flower Pots microbrewery. The wine list is impressive.

Open all day all wk **Food** Lunch all wk 12-3 Dinner all wk 6-9.30 ⊕ FULLER'S ◀ London Pride, Geoge Gale & Co HSB & Seafarers, Flower Pots Goodens Gold, Guest ales Ŏ Westons. ⬤ 20
Facilities Non-diners area ☙ (Bar) Outside area ⋈ Parking WiFi **Rooms** 14

WINCHESTER *continued*

The Green Man

tel: 01962 866809 **53 Southgate St SO23 9EH**
email: greenmanwinchester@gmail.com
dir: *Phone for detailed directions*

Cool and quirky town centre treasure

Jayne Gillin appears to have the midas touch with pubs in Winchester, sprucing up and reinvigorating fading boozers with style and panache and the Green Man, located opposite the city's tiny cinema, is no exception. Expect a funky retro vibe in the bar – wood floors, comfy chairs and intimate booths – a Gothic-style upstairs dining room with rich fabrics, candelabras and chandeliers, and in the Outhouse, the revamped old skittle alley, a chic and cool venue for private parties with platter suppers, pitchers of wine and buckets of beer served at a huge refectory table. Food in the bar takes in pig's cheeks with lentil and potato stew; macaroni cheese; and platters of charcuterie and cheeses, best washed down with a pint of Morland.

Open all day all wk 12-12 (Sun-Mon 12-10.30) Closed 25-26 Dec **Food** Lunch all wk 12-3 Dinner all wk 6-10 ⊕ GREENE KING ◀ St Edmunds, Morland ♂ Aspall. ☏ 16 **Facilities** Non-diners area WiFi

The Old Vine ★ ★ ★ ★ INN

tel: 01962 854616 **8 Great Minster St SO23 9HA**
email: reservations@oldvinewinchester.com **web:** www.oldvinewinchester.com
dir: *M3 junct 11, follow Saint Cross & City Centre signs. 1m, right at Green Man pub right into St Swithun St, bear left into Symonds St (one-way). Right into Great Minster St (NB for Sat Nav use SO23 9HB)*

Cathedral views and top hospitality

An elderly vine rambles all over the street frontage of this elegant pub, built on Saxon foundations in the 18th century. Directly opposite is Winchester's fine cathedral and the City Museum. There are four guest beers, including local ales, in the oak-beamed bar, where you can eat sandwiches, salads and light meals. Freshly prepared, in the restaurant are, typically, starters like duck confit with potato, apple and thyme croquettes; crab pâté with crème fraiche, horseradish, chives, dill and capers; followed by baked haddock in crispy Japanese panko breadcrumbs; grilled salmon with watercress and crème fraîche sauce; or pumpkin ravioli with garlic butter and chilli sauce. Desserts include apple tart, butterscotch and treacle sponge pudding, and honey and vanilla pannacotta. At the back is a flower-filled patio.

Open all day all wk Closed 25 Dec **Food** Lunch Mon-Thu 12-2.30, Fri-Sun 12-6 Dinner Mon-Sat 6.30-9.30, Sun 6.30-9 ⊕ ENTERPRISE INNS ◀ Guest ales. ☏ 11 **Facilities** Non-diners area ✿ (Bar Outside area) ♦♦ Family room Outside area ⊞ WiFi **Rooms** 6

The Westgate Inn ★ ★ ★ INN

tel: 01962 820222 **2 Romsey Rd SO23 8TP**
email: wghguy@yahoo.co.uk **web:** www.westgateinn.co.uk
dir: *On corner of Romsey Rd & Upper High St, opposite Great Hall & Medieval West Gate*

Top of the hill landmark hostelry

Standing boldly on a street corner, the curving, Palladian-style façade of this 1860s inn overlooks the city's medieval Westgate. A well-known interest in real ales and ciders is backed up by an annual beer festival. Full English breakfasts and mid-morning brunches are followed by made-to-order lunchtime sandwiches, soups and uncomplicated three-egg omelettes with various fillings; bangers and mash, along with many other pub classics. Attractive and good-sized accommodation is available.

Open all day all wk 12-11.30 **Food** Lunch all wk 12-2.30 Dinner all wk 6-9.30 ⊕ MARSTON'S ◀ Jennings Cumberland Ale, Ringwood Best Bitter & Fortyniner, Guest ales ♂ Thatchers Gold, Green Goblin. **Facilities** Non-diners area ✿ (Bar) ♦♦ Children's menu Children's portions Beer festival WiFi **Rooms** 8

The Wykeham Arms ★ ★ ★ ★ INN ◉◉ **PICK OF THE PUBS**

See Pick of the Pubs on page 249

HEREFORDSHIRE

▌AYMESTREY   Map 9 SO46

The Riverside Inn **PICK OF THE PUBS**

tel: 01568 708440 **HR6 9ST**
email: theriverside@btconnect.com
dir: *On A4110, 18m N of Hereford*

Friendly hostelry in countryside setting

Built in 1580, this character inn started catering to the passing sheep drovers in 1700; it's midway along the Mortimer Trail, just by the ford across the River Lugg. All the country pursuits are here: choose between 10 circular walks. Look out for otters, kingfishers, herons and deer on the way. The wood-panelled interior with low beams and log fires makes a cosy setting for the enjoyment of ales such as Wye Valley Butty Bach and Hobsons Best; ciders include Westons and Robinsons. The pub's vegetable, herb and fruit garden is the source of many ingredients for the seasonal menus; a duo of River Lugg trout with pickled beetroot and garden salad is as local as it gets. Herefordshire beef braised in ale; Shropshire pork cooked in cider; and croquettes of Welsh border lamb are also among the mouthwatering dishes on offer.

Open Tue-Sat 11-3 6-11 (Sun 12-3) Closed 26 Dec & 1 Jan, Sun eve, Mon L, Mon eve in winter **Food** Lunch Tue-Sun 12-2.15 Dinner Tue-Sat 7-9 Av main course £10 Restaurant menu available Tue-Sun evening ⊕ FREE HOUSE ◀ Wye Valley Bitter & Butty Bach, Hobsons Best Bitter ♂ Westons Stowford Press, Robinsons Flagon. **Facilities** Non-diners area ✿ (Bar Restaurant Garden) ♦♦ Children's portions Garden ⊞ Parking WiFi ▭ (notice required)

▌BRINGSTY COMMON   Map 10 SO75

Live and Let Live

tel: 01886 821462 **WR6 5UW**
email: theliveandletlive@tiscali.co.uk
dir: *From A44 (Bromyard to Worcester road) turn at pub sign (black cat) onto track leading to common. At 1st fork bear right. Pub 200yds on right*

Ancient cider house offering local ales and ciders

One of the oldest buildings in the area is this 16th-century thatched cider house set amidst bracken and old orchards on Bringsty Common. Local Oliver's cider is joined by beers from Herefordshire breweries. Bar meals and the intimate Thatch Restaurant major on seasonal food from the home area. A typical main course option is chicken breast stuffed with sun-dried tomatoes, topped with melted mozzarella and served with duchess potatoes, fresh vegetables and a home-made cheese sauce.

Open Tue-Thu 12-2.30 6-11 (Fri-Sun & summer all day) Closed Mon (ex BHs) **Food** Lunch Tue-Sun 12-2 (12-4 summer) Dinner Tue-Sun 6-9 (5-9 summer) Av main course £12.75 ⊕ FREE HOUSE ◀ Wye Valley, Hobsons, Ludlow, Otter, Ledbury Ales ♂ Thatchers, Oliver's, Hogan's. **Facilities** Non-diners area ✿ (Bar Garden) ♦♦ Children's menu Children's portions Garden ⊞ Beer festival Parking ▭ (notice required)

CAREY
Map 10 SO53

Cottage of Content

tel: 01432 840242 **HR2 6NG**
dir: *From x-rds on A49 between Hereford & Ross-on-Wye, follow Hoarwithy signs. In Hoarwithy branch right, follow Carey signs*

Cracking inn secluded in Wye Valley

Lost along narrow lanes in bucolic countryside close to the meandering River Wye, this pretty streamside inn has been licensed for 530 years. Now, as then, local ciders and beers flow from the bar in the lovingly updated interior, which boasts log fire and flagged floors, with heavy timbering and pubby furnishings. Making the most of the county's produce, dishes on the concise menu might be twice baked Herefordshire Hop cheese soufflé with basil cream; locally reared beef is served griddled with herb butter and pan-fried field mushrooms and onions; and fruit and suet sponge. From the sloping, family-friendly grassy garden are relaxing views across the tranquil countryside.

Open 12-2 6.30-11 (times vary summer & winter) Closed 1wk Feb, 1wk Oct, Sun eve, Mon (Tue winter only) **Food** Lunch Tue-Sat 12-2 Restaurant menu available Tue-Sun L, Tue-Sat D ⊕ FREE HOUSE ⬤ Wye Valley Butty Bach, Hobsons Best Bitter ♂ Ross-on-Wye, Carey Organic, Westons Stowford Press. **Facilities** Non-diners area ♦♦ Children's menu Children's portions Garden ⊼ Parking ⛟ (notice required)

CLIFFORD
Map 9 SO24

The Castlefields

tel: 01497 831554 **HR3 5HB**
email: info@thecastlefields.co.uk
dir: *On B4352 between Hay-on-Wye & Bredwardine*

Traditional country pub and restaurant in Golden Valley

After hours spent browsing in nearby Hay-on-Wye, the 'Town of Books', a 10-minute drive will get you to this family-run, 16th-century former coach house. The interior is furnished with elegantly modern tables and chairs, although a reminder of the pub's long life is the glass-covered, 39ft-deep well. Home-cooked, locally-sourced food served all day includes roast half-duck with orange sauce; pan-fried liver and crispy bacon; tagliatelle carbonara; wholetail scampi; and lots of grills. Wednesday is curry night and traditional roasts are served on Sundays. The Rev. James and his companions, Doom Bar and Butty Bach, will be in the bar.

Open all day 11.45am-close Closed Mon (Nov-Feb) **Food** Lunch Tue-Sat 12-9, Sun 12-8 Dinner Tue-Sat 12-9, Sun 12-8 ⊕ FREE HOUSE ⬤ Sharp's Doom Bar, Brains The Rev. James, Wye Valley Butty Bach ♂ Westons Stowford Press. ♀ **Facilities** Non-diners area ♦♦ Children's menu Children's portions Play area Garden ⊼ Parking WiFi ⛟ (notice required)

CRASWALL
Map 9 SO23

The Bulls Head

tel: 01981 510616 **HR2 0PN**
email: info@thebullsheadcraswall.co.uk
dir: *From A465 at Pandy follow Walterstone, Oldcastle & Longtown signs. In Longtown follow Craswall sign. Village in 11m*

Weekend only refuelling stop

You'll find this old drovers' inn south of Hay-on-Wye in a remote spot at the foot of the Black Mountains. Only open at weekends, it is popular with walkers and riders, who tie their horses at the rail outside. Real ales and farmhouse ciders are served through the hole in the wall servery in the bar with its flagstone floors and log fires.

There is a Mediterranean feel to the menu, which might take in soup au pistou; Italian style meatballs; ragu of boar with chestnuts and creamed polenta; and clementine cake for dessert.

Open Fri-Sun 12-3 7-late Closed Mon-Thu (phone in Jan & Feb for wknd opening times) **Food** Lunch Fri-Sun 12-2.30 Dinner Fri-Sat 7-8.30 Av main course £15 ⊕ FREE HOUSE ⬤ Wye Valley Butty Bach & Bitter ♂ Gwatkin's Farmhouse, Oliver's, Dunkertons Premium Organic & Black Fox. **Facilities** Non-diners area ✿ (Bar Garden) ♦♦ Garden WiFi

DORSTONE
Map 9 SO34

The Pandy Inn
PICK OF THE PUBS

tel: 01981 550273 **HR3 6AN**
email: info@pandyinn.co.uk
dir: *Exit B4348, W of Hereford. Inn in village centre*

Lovely views from the large garden

Just a few miles from Hay-on-Wye, The Pandy is an ideal stop when touring the Brecon Beacons or the picturesque Golden Valley. Reputed to be one of the oldest inns in the county, Richard de Brito, one of the four Norman knights who murdered Thomas à Becket in 1170, is said to have built The Pandy to house workers. Much later, Oliver Cromwell is known to have taken refuge here during the Civil War. The ancient hostelry is delightfully situated opposite the village green; the large garden has views of Dorstone Hill. The interior retains some original flagstone floors and beams. In the dog-friendly bar you'll find Wye Valley Butty Bach, or a pint of Stowford Press cider if you prefer. Bar food takes the form of baguettes, and pizzas can be ordered in two sizes. In the restaurant, there is a short but excellent range of dishes.

Open Tue-Fri 12-3 6-11 (Sat 12-11 Sun 12-3 6.30-10.30) Closed Mon **Food** Lunch Tue-Sun 12-2 Dinner Tue-Sun 6-9 ⊕ FREE HOUSE ⬤ Wye Valley Butty Bach ♂ Westons Stowford Press. **Facilities** Non-diners area ✿ (Bar Garden) ♦♦ Children's menu Children's portions Play area Garden ⊼ Parking WiFi ⛟

EARDISLEY
Map 9 SO34

The Tram Inn

tel: 01544 327251 **Church Rd HR3 6PG**
email: info@thetraminn.co.uk
dir: *On A4111 at junct with Woodeaves Rd*

Friendly free house with a long tradition of hospitality

This traditional black and white timbered, 16th-century inn has wood-burning stoves to welcome you in the winter and a garden for enjoying a pint and a meal in the warmer months, and the chance for a game of petanque too. The à la carte and set menus offer dishes such as chicken and duck liver pâté; roasted sweet potato soup; spinach and goats' cheese pasty; Herefordshire steak and ale pie; roast topside of Willersley beef (served pink); and pan-roasted hake and salmon fillets. Blackboard specials add to the choices. Desserts are tempting – sticky toffee pudding with butterscotch sauce and cream, or lemon posset with ginger sponge bites. A family and dog friendly pub.

Open 12-3 6-12 (Fri-Sat 12-3 6-12.30 Sun 12-3 7-11) Closed Mon (ex BHs) **Food** Lunch Tue-Sun 12-3 Dinner Tue-Sat 6-9 ⊕ FREE HOUSE ⬤ Wye Valley Butty Bach, Hobsons Best Bitter ♂ Westons Stowford Press, Dunkertons Organic. **Facilities** Non-diners area ✿ (Bar Garden) ♦♦ Children's portions Play area Garden ⊼ Parking WiFi ⛟ (notice required)

GARWAY
Map 9 SO42

Garway Moon Inn ★★★★ INN

tel: 01600 750270 **HR2 8RQ**
email: info@garwaymooninn.co.uk **web:** www.garwaymooninn.co.uk
dir: *From Hereford S on A49. Right onto A466, right onto B4521. At Broad Oak turn right to Garway*

Eat, drink and relax in this privately owned country inn

A family-run freehouse dating back to 1750, overlooking the peaceful and picturesque common. Ask at the bar for three circular walks which will take you to a Knights Templar church of 1180, Stenfrith Castle, and panoramic views of Garway Hill. A good selection of real ales includes Kingstone and Wye Valley, with Westons cider also on tap. Traditional pub food is based on high quality local ingredients – many of the producers are regulars in the bar. A home-made chargrilled beef patty is served with the Garway's secret sauce (and chips, of course); and Guernsey milk and cream from the Kelsmor Dairy are turned into delicious ice creams in the village.

Open Mon-Tue 6-11 (Wed-Fri 12-2.30 5-11 Sat-Sun 11-11) Closed Mon & Tue L **Food** Lunch Wed-Sun 12-2.30 Dinner Tue-Sun 6-9.30 Restaurant menu available Tue-Sun ⊕ FREE HOUSE ◀ Wye Valley Butty Bach & HPA, Butcombe, Kingstone Brewery Ò Westons Stowford Press. **Facilities** Non-diners area ✿ (Bar Garden) ◑ Children's menu Children's portions Family room Garden ⊼ Parking WiFi ▄ (notice required) **Rooms** 3

HOARWITHY
Map 10 SO52

The New Harp Inn

tel: 01432 840900 **HR2 6QH**
email: newharpinn@btinternet.com
dir: *From Ross-on-Wye take A49 towards Hereford. Turn right for Hoarwithy*

A real country pub

The New Harp's slogan reads: 'Kids, dogs and muddy boots all welcome' – and it's certainly popular with locals, fishermen, campers and visitors to the countryside. Situated on the River Wye in an Area of Outstanding Natural Beauty, the pub has extensive gardens and a real babbling brook. Begin your visit with a local real ale or the home-produced cider. The menu includes starters such as chicken liver pâté, and balsamic-glazed goats' cheese on a pesto croûton, then moves on to mains like wild rabbit, bacon and perry pie; or 'a celebration of pork' - roasted, rare breed Mangelitsa pork with ginger and local cider and served with a wild boar faggot. There's also a board for specials. Look out for bank holiday beer festivals and a cider festival on the Summer Bank Holiday.

Open all wk 12-3 6-11 (Fri-Sun all day) **Food** Lunch Mon-Fri 12-3, Sat-Sun all day Dinner Mon-Fri 6-9, Sat-Sun all day Av main course £7.95 Set menu available Restaurant menu available all wk ⊕ FREE HOUSE ◀ Wye Valley Butty Bach & Dorothy Goodbody's Country Ale, Otter Ò Westons Stowford Press & Gold Label, Mortimers Orchard, New Harp Reserve. ₹ 10 **Facilities** Non-diners area ✿ (Bar Garden Outside area) ◑ Children's menu Children's portions Garden Outside area ⊼ Beer festival Cider festival Parking WiFi ▄

KILPECK
Map 9 SO43

The Kilpeck Inn

tel: 01981 570464 **HR2 9DN**
email: booking@kilpeckinn.com **web:** www.kilpeckinn.com
dir: *From Hereford take A465 S. In 6m at Belmont rdbt left towards Kilpeck. Follow church & inn signs*

A warm welcome awaits at this green inn

Kilpeck is renowned for its Romanesque church, a few minutes' walk from this 250-year-old, whitewashed pub now run by chef patron Ross Williams. Commendably green, the pub uses a wood-pellet burner for underfloor heating; rainwater to flush the loos; and solar panels for hot water. Typical dishes on a dinner menu include maple roasted carrot and ginger soup; Brixham mussels, pancetta lardoons and tarragon cream sauce; slow-roasted pork belly, boudin noir stuffed tenderloin, apple mash, red cabbage and cider gravy; and lemon pannacotta, lime curd and orange shortbread. The bar stocks local real ales, and draught cider from Westons in Much Marcle.

Open 12-2.30 5.30-11 (Sun 12-5.30) Closed 25 Dec, Sun eve **Food** Lunch Mon-Sat 12-2, Sun 12-3 Dinner Mon-Sat 6-9 Set menu available Restaurant menu available Mon-Sat ⊕ FREE HOUSE ◀ Wye Valley Butty Bach, Boddingtons, Wye Valley Bitter Ò Westons Stowford Press. ₹ 9 **Facilities** Non-diners area ◑ Children's portions Garden ⊼ Parking WiFi ▄ (notice required)

KIMBOLTON
Map 10 SO56

Stockton Cross Inn

tel: 01568 612509 **HR6 0HD**
email: mb@ecolots.co.uk
dir: *From A49 take A4112 between Leominster & Ludlow*

Chocolate-box pretty, inside and out

Standing at a lonely crossroads where witches were allegedly hanged, this 16th-century, black-and-white former drovers' inn is picture-book pretty, and is regularly photographed by tourists as well as appearing on calendars. There's a good range of ales, including local Wye Valley Butty Bach, and regular guest beers. A typical evening meal could include Thai-style salmon fishcakes; chicken and leek pie; char-grilled swordfish steaks; home-made Shropshire fidget pie; and vegetarian Wellington. Lunchtime choices include sandwiches and salads; in summer, enjoy them in the pretty garden. It is fish night every second Friday of the month. Change of hands.

Open all day all wk 11-11 **Food** Lunch all wk 12-3 Dinner all wk 6-9 Av main course £12 ⊕ FREE HOUSE ◀ Wye Valley Butty Bach & HPA, Guest ales Ò Robinsons Flagon, Westons Stowford Press. **Facilities** Non-diners area ✿ (Bar Restaurant Garden) ◑ Children's portions Garden ⊼ Beer festival Parking WiFi ▄ (notice required)

KINGTON
Map 9 SO25

The Stagg Inn and Restaurant ◉◉   PICK OF THE PUBS

tel: 01544 230221 **Titley HR5 3RL**
email: reservations@thestagg.co.uk
dir: *Between Kington & Presteigne on B4355*

A fusion of village local and child-friendly fine-dining restaurant

Part medieval, part early Victorian and with a bit from the 1970s, this highly acclaimed gastro-pub stands where two sheep-droving roads once met. Then called The Balance because wool was weighed there, it was renamed The Stag's Head by local 19th-century reformer Eliza Greenly after her family crest, the extra 'g' worming its way in later. Locals drink, eat and chat, undisturbed by music, amidst a collection of 200 pub jugs in the small bar and at farmhouse tables in the dining rooms. Real ales are Ludlow Gold and Butty Bach, and top ciders include Dunkertons and Ralph's. Awarded two AA Rosettes, Roux-trained local boy Steve Reynolds creates dishes such as pheasant breast with parsnip purée and white truffle; Madgett's farm duck with fondant potato; and cinnamon pannacotta with mulled wine fruits. Vegetarians have their own menu - perhaps cherry tomato and tarragon risotto, tempura vegetables and salad.

Open 12-3 6.30-11 Closed 25-27 Dec, 2wks Nov, 2wks Jan & Feb, Mon & Tue **Food** Lunch 12-3 Dinner 6.30-9 Av main course £11.50 Restaurant menu available Wed-Sat, Sun D ⊕ FREE HOUSE ◧ Ludlow Gold, Wye Valley Butty Bach ☼ Dunkertons, Westons, Ralph's, Robinsons. ☂ 12 **Facilities** Non-diners area ☀ (Bar Garden) ◖◗ Children's menu Children's portions Garden ⊨ Parking WiFi

LEDBURY
Map 10 SO73

Prince of Wales

tel: 01531 632250 **Church Ln HR8 1DL**
email: pebblewalk@gmail.com
dir: *M50 junct 2, A417 to Ledbury. Pub in town centre behind Market House (black & white building) on cobbled street (parking nearby)*

Character inn with home-made pies and excellent local beers

In an enchanting spot hidden between Ledbury's memorable half-timbered market house and the ancient church, a cobbled alley lined by eye-catching medieval houses hosts this cracking little pub. All low beams with bags of character, folk nights add to the craic at this half-timbered gem, where home-made pies or pork and beef sausages from an award-winning local butcher are firm favourites on the traditional pub menu. The local theme continues, with Westons Rosie's Pig scrumpy from neighbouring Much Marcle and beers from Wye Valley Brewery just down the road complementing a huge range of guest ales.

Open all day all wk **Food** Lunch all wk 12-2.30 Dinner all wk 6-8.30 ⊕ FREE HOUSE ◧ Hobsons Best Bitter, Wye Valley Butty Bach & HPA, Otter Bitter, Ledbury Dark, Guest ales ☼ Westons Rosie's Pig. **Facilities** Non-diners area ◖◗ Children's menu Outside area ⊨ WiFi ◻ (notice required)

The Talbot

tel: 01531 632963 **14 New St HR8 2DX**
email: talbot.ledbury@wadworth.co.uk
dir: *From A449 in Ledbury into Bye St, 2nd left into Woodley Rd, over bridge to junct, left into New St. Pub on right*

Beautiful inn in historic town

This higgledy-piggledy marvel is one of the stars of Ledbury's extensive suite of amazing half-timbered buildings. Parts of it date back to 1550; the interior of the coaching inn oozes the character of great age, with fine beams and panelling in the refined dining room. Holes caused by musket shot fired during a Civil War skirmish are just another quirky talking point of the gabled building, where Wadworth's beers and local organic perry slake the thirst of ramblers fresh from the challenging local

countryside. Indulge in tasty platters, large grills or chicken, ham and leek pie, perhaps sat in the sun-trap courtyard garden.

Open all day all wk **Food** Lunch all wk 12-3 Dinner Mon-Sat 5.30-9, Sun 5-8 Av main course £12 ⊕ WADWORTH ◧ 6X, Henry's Original & Wadworth guest ales, Wye Valley Butty Bach ☼ Westons Stowford Press, Wyld Wood Organic & Perry, Thatchers Gold. ☂ 15 **Facilities** Non-diners area Children's portions Garden ⊨ WiFi

The Trumpet Inn

tel: 01531 670277 **Trumpet HR8 2RA**
email: trumpet@wadworth.co.uk
dir: *4m from Ledbury, at junct of A438 & A417*

Beamed inn dating from the Middle Ages

This former coaching inn and post house takes its name from the days when mail coaches blew their horns on approaching the crossroads. A traditional black and white building, it dates back to the late 14th century. The cosy bars feature a wealth of exposed beams, with open fireplaces and a separate dining area. There is camembert or fisherman's platters to share, and main courses like Mr Waller's trio of sausages with mash and onion gravy; Angus beefburgers; or risotto or pie of the day to choose from.

Open all day all wk 11-11 (Sun 11-10.30) **Food** Lunch Mon-Sat 12-2.30, Sun 12-8 Dinner Mon-Sat 6-9, Sun 12-8 Set menu available Restaurant menu available Mon-Sat ⊕ WADWORTH ◧ 6X, Henry's Original IPA, Guest ales ☼ Westons Stowford Press. **Facilities** Non-diners area ◖◗ Garden Parking WiFi ◻

LEOMINSTER
Map 10 SO45

The Grape Vaults

tel: 01568 611404 **Broad St HR6 8BS**
email: jusaxon@tiscali.co.uk
dir: *Phone for detailed directions*

In the heart of the town centre

This unspoilt, 15th-century pub is so authentic that even its fixed seating is Grade II listed. Its many charms include a small, homely bar complete with a coal fire. A good selection of real ale is a popular feature, and includes microbrewery offerings. The unfussy food encompasses favourites like cottage pie, lasagne, chicken curry and various fresh fish and vegetarian choices. There are also plenty of jackets, baguettes, omelettes and other lighter meals available. No jukebox, gaming machines or alcopops. There is live music every Sunday and in December a beer festival takes place on the same day as the Victorian street market.

Open all day all wk 11-11 **Food** Lunch all wk 12-2 Dinner Mon-Sat 5.30-9 Av main course £6.95 ⊕ FREE HOUSE ◧ Ludlow Best, Mayfields, Wood's, Malvern Hills, Guest ales ☼ Westons Stowford Press. ☂ 10 **Facilities** Non-diners area ☀ (Bar Restaurant) ◖◗ Children's portions Beer festival WiFi **Notes** ◉

MADLEY
Map 9 SO43

The Comet Inn

tel: 01981 250600 **Stoney St HR2 9NJ**
email: thecometinn-madley@hotmail.co.uk
dir: *6m from Hereford on B4352*

Hearty food served in converted cottages with plenty of character

Set at a crossroads deep in rural Herefordshire, the space-age parabolic dishes of the Madley Earth Station and the distant smudge of the Black Mountains provide contrasting skylines visible from the large grounds of this convivial local. Within, it retains much of the character of the old cottages from which it was converted over 100 years ago, including a roaring fire in the winter months. Vicky Willison, the enthusiastic and welcoming owner, serves a select range of Herefordshire- and Worcestershire-brewed beers to accompany simple and hearty home-cooked pub

continued

MADLEY *continued*

food in the conservatory off the main bar, with smaller portions for smaller appetites if required. In summer visitors can enjoy the large garden that has a children's play area.

Open all wk 12-3 6-11 (Fri-Sun & BHs all day) **Food** Lunch all wk 12-3 Dinner Mon-Sat 6-9 (Sun bookings only) Restaurant menu available all wk (Sun eve bookings only) ⊕ FREE HOUSE ◀ Wye Valley, St George's, Hereford ♻ Westons Stowford Press, Gold Label & Vintage. **Facilities** Non-diners area ⊕ Children's menu Children's portions Play area Garden ⋒ Parking WiFi ⛟ (notice required)

MICHAELCHURCH ESCLEY
Map 9 SO33

NEW The Bridge Inn

tel: 01981 510646 **HR2 0JW**
email: thebridgeinn@hotmail.com
dir: *From Peterchurch take B4348 towards Hereford, turn right in Vowchurch to Michaelchurch Escley*

A truly welcoming inn by a river

With its 16th-century origins, traditional wood-burning stoves and friendly atmosphere, this delightful riverside inn exudes a warm welcome. It makes an ideal base for exploring the Golden Valley, the Brecon Beacons National Park and Offa's Dyke. Cask-conditioned ales and a selection of local ciders are bar highlights; over Summer Bank Holiday weekend, a festival celebrates both forms of refreshment. Lunch sees the serving of 'huffers' – open sandwiches made with home-made bread. At the end of the day, heartwarming pub classics may include shoulder of lamb braised with Gwatkin cider and damson vinegar.

Open all wk 12-3 5.30-10 (Sat-Sun all day) **Food** Lunch Tue-Fri 12-2.30, Sat-Sun 12-3 Dinner Mon-Thu 5.30-8.30, Fri-Sat 5.30-9.30, Sun 5.30-8 Restaurant menu available all wk ⊕ FREE HOUSE ◀ Wye Valley Butty Bach ♻ Gwatkin Pyder & Yarlington Mill, Westons Wyld Wood. ♟ 9 **Facilities** Non-diners area ✿ (Bar Garden) ⊕ Children's menu Children's portions Garden ⋒ Beer festival Cider festival Parking WiFi ⛟ (notice required)

ORLETON
Map 9 SO46

The Boot Inn

tel: 01568 780228 **SY8 4HN**
email: hello@thebootinnorleton.co.uk **web:** www.thebootinnorleton.co.uk
dir: *Follow A49 S from Ludlow (approx 7m) to B4362 (Woofferton), 1.5m off B4362 turn left. Inn in village centre*

Atmospheric hostelry with many tall tales

A black and white, half-timbered, 16th-century village inn characterised by a large inglenook fireplace, oak beams, mullioned windows, and exposed wattle-and-daub. Herefordshire real ales and Robinsons cider accompany dishes such as slow-cooked belly pork; line-caught sea bass; and wild mushroom and spinach linguine. In the

back room is a painting from which the figure of one-time regular Joe Vale was obliterated after arguing with the landlord. Occasionally, old Joe's ghost returns.

Open all wk 12-3 5.30-11 (Sat-Sun all day) **Food** Lunch Mon-Sat 12-2, Sun 12-3 Dinner all wk 6.30-9 ⊕ FREE HOUSE ◀ Hobsons Best Bitter, Wye Valley, Local guest ales ♻ Robinsons, Thatchers Gold. **Facilities** Non-diners area ✿ (Bar Garden) ⊕ Children's menu Play area Garden ⋒ Cider festival Parking ⛟

PEMBRIDGE
Map 9 SO35

New Inn

tel: 01544 388427 **Market Square HR6 9DZ**
dir: *From M5 junct 7 take A44 W through Leominster towards Llandrindod Wells*

Traditional inn for good beer and home-cooked food

Formerly a courthouse and jail, and close to the site of the last battle of the War of the Roses, this 14th-century black and white timbered free house has been under the same ownership for 30 years. Worn flagstone floors and winter fires characterise the cosy bar, and in summer customers spill out into the pub's outdoor seating area in the Old Market Square. Don't expect to find any background music or a TV screen. Home-cooked English fare, using local produce, might include seafood stew with crusty bread; beef steak and ale pie; or leek, mushroom and Shropshire Blue cheese croustade with salad.

Open all wk 11-2.30 6-11 (summer 11-3 6-11) Closed last wk Feb **Food** Lunch all wk 12-2 Dinner all wk 6.30-9 ⊕ FREE HOUSE ◀ Hobsons Town Crier, Sharp's Doom Bar, Hook Norton, Three Tuns, Ludlow ♻ Westons Stowford Press & Wyld Wood Organic, Dunkertons. ♟ 10 **Facilities** Non-diners area ⊕ Children's portions Family room Garden Parking

STAPLOW
Map 10 SO64

The Oak Inn
PICK OF THE PUBS

tel: 01531 640954 **HR8 1NP**
email: oakinn@wyenet.co.uk
dir: *M50 junct 2, A417 to Ledbury. At rdbt take 2nd exit onto A449, then A438 (High St). Take B4214 to Staplow*

17th-century pub in the heart of rural Herefordshire

Set in bucolic Herefordshire countryside richly endowed with orchards and hopyards. The Oak enjoys an enviable location close to the lovely old market town of Ledbury, with the striking ridge of the Malvern Hills a sublime horizon. Ramblers can enjoy a walk along the nearby course of the former Herefordshire and Gloucestershire Canal before retiring to the lovingly extended cottage-style pub, complete with log-burning stoves, flagstone floors and old wooden beams adorned with hops. Both the drinks and food menus draw lavishly on the county's larder; beers from Ledbury and Wye Valley breweries adorn the bar, whilst local cider adds interest. Dishes from the starter menu include Madgett's Farm (Wye Valley) chicken liver and brandy parfait, whilst a sharing platter includes Severn and Wye smoked 'Var' salmon. Juniper braised blade of Herefordshire beef with roasted beetroot and carrots and wild berry sauce examples the comfortable mains menu here. Dogs are very welcome both inside and in the orchard-side garden.

Open all day all wk **Food** Lunch Mon-Sat 12-2.30, Sun 12-3 Dinner Mon-Sat 6.30-9.30, Sun 7-8.30 ⊕ FREE HOUSE ◀ Bathams Best Bitter, Ledbury Gold, Wye Valley Bitter, Guest ales ♻ Westons Stowford Press, Robinsons.
Facilities Non-diners area ✿ (Bar Restaurant Garden) ⊕ Children's portions Garden ⋒ Parking WiFi

PICK OF THE PUBS

The Saracens Head Inn ★★★★ INN

SYMONDS YAT (EAST)   Map 10 SO51

tel: 01600 890435 **HR9 6JL**
email: contact@saracensheadinn.co.uk
web: www.saracensheadinn.co.uk
dir: *A40 onto B4229, follow Symonds Yat East signs, 2m*

Former cider mill in an unrivalled location

Occupying a stunning position on the east bank of the River Wye where it flows into a steep wooded gorge on the edge of the Royal Forest of Dean, The Saracens Head can be reached by the inn's own ferry, which still operates by hand, just as it has for the past 200 years. Symonds Yat East ('yat' being the local name for a gate or pass) was named after Robert Symonds, a Sheriff of Herefordshire in the 17th century, and has been designated an Area of Outstanding Natural Beauty. There's a relaxed atmosphere throughout the 16th-century inn, from the bar (serving Wye Valley ales), the cosy lounge and stylish dining room, and two sunny terraces overlooking the Wye. Seasonal menus and daily specials boards offer both the traditional and modern: steamed rope-grown River Teign mussels in Stowford Press cider cream leek sauce could be followed by chargrilled wild boar chop and faggot, stuffed cabbage leaves, fondant potato and candy beetroot purée. If you come at lunchtime, try a Severn and Wye hot-

smoked salmon and dill crème fraîche sandwich, or a free-range local woodland pork hot baguette. Main courses at dinner might include Welsh lamb and rosemary suet pudding, lamp rump and cutlet. Complete your meal with one of the home-made desserts on the blackboard or you might opt for a slate of three local cheeses — Hereford Hop, Per Las and Tintern — served with grapes, crackers, and quince and rose petal jelly. A stay in one of the ten en suite bedrooms is a must if you're exploring this area.

Open all day all wk Closed 25 Dec
Food Lunch all wk 12-2.30 Dinner all wk 6.30-9 Av main course £13.95
⊕ FREE HOUSE ◗ Wye Valley HPA &

Butty Bach, Otley 01, Bespoke Saved by the Bell, Sharp's Doom Bar, Kingstone 1503 Tudor Ale ♨ Westons Stowford Press & Country Perry. ♟ 10
Facilities Non-diners area ♣ (Bar Garden) ♦♦ Children's menu Children's portions Garden ☂ Parking WiFi
Rooms 10

SYMONDS YAT (EAST)　　Map 10 SO51

The Saracens Head Inn ★★★★ INN　PICK OF THE PUBS

See Pick of the Pubs on page 255 and advert below

TILLINGTON　　Map 9 SO44

The Bell

tel: 01432 760395 **HR4 8LE**
email: glenn@thebellinntillington.co.uk
dir: *From A4103 (N Hereford) follow Tillington sign*

Village pub with something for everybody

Amidst blossoming fruit trees (in the spring, that is) this traditional, village pub has been run since 1988 by the Williams family. With two bars, one with an open fire and a screen for sporting events, dining room, extensive gardens, patio and grassed play area, it offers something for everybody. Home-made ciders are served alongside Herefordshire ales and Sharp's Doom Bar. Prepared from locally-sourced ingredients are sandwiches, light lunches, and dishes such as rabbit casserole; seafood chowder; steak, mushroom and ale pie; and peppered duck breast with crushed lemon thyme potatoes, pea and wild mushroom ragout. If you have a sweet tooth, go for the Mars Bar cheesecake. Fish specials are offered every Wednesday night.

Open all day all wk **Food** Lunch Mon-Fri 12-2.30, Sat all day, Sun 12-3 Dinner Mon-Fri 6-9.30, Sat all day Av main course £12 ◣ Sharp's Doom Bar, Hereford Best Bitter, Local ales ♂ Tillington Belle (pub's own). **Facilities** Non-diners area ⁙ Children's menu Play area Garden ⩗ Parking WiFi ▭ (notice required)

WALFORD　　Map 10 SO52

The Mill Race　PICK OF THE PUBS

See Pick of the Pubs on opposite page

WALTERSTONE　　Map 9 SO32

Carpenters Arms

tel: 01873 890353 **HR2 0DX**
email: carpentersarms1@btinternet.com
dir: *Exit A465 between Hereford & Abergavenny at Pandy*

Step back in time inside the cosy Carpenters

Half a mile from the Welsh border, this 300-year-old free house has been owned by the Watkins for three generations. Located on the edge of the Black Mountains and overlooked by Offa's Dyke, there's plenty of character in the pub. You'll find beams, antique settles and a leaded range with open fires that burn all winter; a perfect cosy setting for enjoying a pint of Ramblers Ruin. Popular food options include salmon and leek pie; lamb cutlet with a redcurrant and rosemary sauce; and vegetarian cannelloni. Ask about the large choice of home-made desserts. There are a few tables outside which can be a suntrap in summer.

Open all day all wk 12-11 Closed 25 Dec **Food** Contact pub for details ⊕ FREE HOUSE ◣ Wadworth 6X, Breconshire Golden Valley & Ramblers Ruin ♂ Westons. **Facilities** Non-diners area ⁙ Children's portions Play area Family room Garden Parking ▭ **Notes** ⊛

The Saracens Head Inn

For centuries the *Saracens Head Inn* has occupied its spectacular position on the east bank of the River Wye, where the river flows into a steep wooded gorge. The Inn's own ferry across the river still operates by hand, just as it has for the past 200 years.

There's a relaxed atmosphere throughout the Inn, from the flagstoned bar to the cosy lounge and dining room. The riverside terraces are a great place to watch the world go by.

The Inn has a reputation for high quality food, using fresh local ingredients where possible, with a regularly changing menu and daily specials – not to mention a tempting choice of 6 real ales (featuring local breweries), and freshly-ground coffee.

Symonds Yat East is situated in an Area of Outstanding Natural Beauty on the edge of the Forest of Dean, so a stay in one of the ten guest bedrooms is a must for exploring the unspoilt local countryside.

The Wye Valley Walk passes the Inn, as does the Peregrine cycle trail. Walking, cycling, mountain biking, river cruises, canoeing, kayaking, climbing and fishing are all available nearby.

Symonds Yat East, Ross-on-Wye, Herefordshire HR9 6JL
Tel: 01600 890435
Website: www.saracensheadinn.co.uk • Email: contact@saracensheadinn.co.uk

PICK OF THE PUBS

The Mill Race

WALFORD　　　　Map 10 SO52

tel: 01989 562891
HR9 5QS
email: enquiries@millrace.info
web: www.millrace.info
dir: B4234 from Ross-on-Wye to Walford. Pub 3m on right

The best local produce, direct from its own nearby farm

There's another Walford in the north of the county, so make sure you've put the right postcode into your Sat Nav. It lies on the banks of the River Wye, just upstream from the picturesque gorge at Symonds Yat, and the Forest of Dean. Standing majestically on the other bank is Goodrich Castle, home to 'Roaring Meg', the only surviving Civil War mortar, which the Parliamentarians used to breach its walls. The pub's interior is suitably cosy and welcoming, with a beamed and flagstone-floored bar and rustically furnished dining areas. Warm up in winter by one of the log fires, or in summer relax on the terrace and watch the buzzards drifting overhead. At nearby Bishopwood is the pub's own 1,000-acre farm estate, which together with a dedicated supply chain of local producers, allows landlord Luke Freeman and his team to dedicate their days to producing the food that is highly regarded within the Herefordshire Slow Food movement. Lunch and evening menus vary; a typical midday meal might begin with warm chicken

and bacon Caesar salad with parmesan, cos lettuce and anchovies; with chargrilled steak with confit vine tomato, field mushroom and chips to follow. In the evening, consider a starter of seared scallops and red mullet stew with chorizo; followed by barbeque monkfish with white pork fritter; or braised beef cheek with cauliflower cheese, truffle, salsify and Swiss chard. Wednesday night is fish night, while on Tuesday, Thursday and Sunday evenings the outdoor pizza oven is fired up to produce unusual English-style pizzas, such as Hopcraft Hot One (sweet chilli, jalapeño peppers) and Dorstone Delight (goats' cheese, mozzarella, wilted spinach, caramelised onion, garlic oil). Wines from Herefordshire are on the globe-spanning list.

Open all wk 11-3 5-11 (Sat 11-11 Sun 12-10.30) **Food** Lunch Mon-Fri 12-2, Sat 12-2.30, Sun 12-4 Dinner Mon-Sat 6-9.30 Sun 6-9 Av main course £11 ⊕ FREE HOUSE ◀ Wye Valley Bitter & Butty Bach, Butcombe Rare Breed, Ledbury Gold ♂ Westons Stowford Press, Gwynt y Ddraig Farmhouse Pyder. ♀ 25 **Facilities** Non-diners area ♦♦ Children's menu Children's portions Garden ⊓ Parking WiFi 🚐 (notice required)

WELLINGTON
Map 10 SO44

The Wellington

tel: 01432 830367 **HR4 8AT**
email: info@wellingtonpub.co.uk
dir: *Exit A49 into village centre. Pub 0.25m on left*

Country pub ideal for families

The garden of this pub is sunny and secure, an ideal venue for the beer festival held here in early June. If the weather is inclement, the pub's restaurant and conservatory are also at the disposal of family groups. Here, a typical lunch could comprise potted crab, cottage pie topped with cheddar mash, and sticky toffee pudding. Dinner choices include seared scallops, pancetta and apple and mustard sauce; steak au poivre and chunky chips; and chocolate pudding cake with clotted cream. Ales are local, coming from Wye Valley Brewery in Herefordshire.

Open 12-2.30 5.30-11 Closed Mon **Food** Lunch Tue-Sun 12-3 Dinner Tue-Sat 6-9.30 ⊕ FREE HOUSE ◀ Wye Valley Butty Bach & HPA, Butcombe, Guest ales ♦ Westons. ₹ 9 **Facilities** Non-diners area ❤ (Bar Garden) ♦♦ Children's portions Garden 규 Beer festival Parking WiFi ☕ (notice required)

WEOBLEY
Map 9 SO45

Ye Olde Salutation Inn
PICK OF THE PUBS

tel: 01544 318443 **Market Pitch HR4 8SJ**
email: info@salutation-inn.com
dir: *A44, then A4112, 8m from Leominster*

Timber-framed free house run by a chef-proprietor

Known to locals as 'the Sal', this 17th-century black-and-white pub is in the heart of the medieval village of Weobley. The inn, sympathetically converted from an old alehouse and adjoining cottage, is the perfect base for exploring the Welsh Marches and the Black-and-White Villages Trail. The book capital of Hay-on-Wye and the cathedral city of Hereford are close by, as are the Wye Valley and Black Mountains. Chef-proprietor Stuart Elder took over a few years ago, 12 years after he worked here as a chef for the previous owners. Chef's specials and old favourites are served in the traditional lounge bar with its welcoming atmosphere and cosy inglenook fireplace. The inn's restaurant offers a range of tempting dishes created with the use of locally sourced ingredients. Start, perhaps, with deep-fried artichoke hearts in a light batter, and continue with half a roast duck with orange and ginger sauce, and finish with lemon tart and raspberry sorbet.

Open all day all wk 12-11 (Sun 12-10.30) **Food** Lunch all wk 12-3 Dinner all wk 6-9.30 Set menu available ⊕ FREE HOUSE ◀ Wye Valley Butty Bach, Local Guest ales ♦ Westons Stowford Press, Robinsons. **Facilities** Non-diners area ♦♦ Children's portions Outside area 규 Parking WiFi ☕ (notice required)

WINFORTON
Map 9 SO24

The Sun Inn

tel: 01544 327677 **HR3 6EA**
email: richard23457@btinternet.com
dir: *In village centre on A438 (Hereford to Brecon road)*

Small, intimate pub with a friendly atmosphere

Owners Gail and Richard Greenwood and their chefs have established a network of local Herefordshire food producers in order to create their monthly changing menus. 'Local' really doesn't get much closer than the pork and lamb from the chef's own farm, and beef from less than a mile away; fish travels a little further but is fresh from Cornwall. With that in mind perhaps choose new season Hay-on-Wye lamb loin chop, vodka mint jelly, lamb and mint jus from a spring menu; or on another occasion pan-fried scallops in brandy; slow roasted pork belly and soured apple compôte with crispy crackling.

Open 12-3 6.30-last orders (Sun 12-2 winter) Closed Sun eve & Mon (Tue Oct-Apr) **Food** Lunch Tue-Sat 12-2, Sun 12-3, Wed-Sun 12-2 winter Dinner Tue-Sat 6.30-9, Wed-Sat 6.30-9 winter ⊕ FREE HOUSE ◀ Wye Valley Butty Bach, Brecon Gold Beacons ♦ Gwatkin, Westons Old Rosie, Local cider. **Facilities** Non-diners area ♦♦ Children's menu Children's portions Garden 규 Parking WiFi

WOOLHOPE
Map 10 SO63

The Crown Inn

tel: 01432 860468 **HR1 4QP**
email: menu@crowninnwoolhope.co.uk
dir: *B4224 to Mordiford, left after Moon Inn. Pub in village centre*

Locally sourced food and great choice of ciders and perries

A traditional village free house with large gardens, The Crown Inn is popular with walkers and well supported by locals and visitors alike. Excellent food and drink are a priority here, with good ales as well as 24 local ciders and perries. Daily specials include trout fishcakes with garlic mayonnaise; cider-braised ham with free-range eggs and chunky chips; pheasant Kiev with sweet potato mash and stir-fried cabbage. There is an outside summertime bar in the garden on Saturday nights and a Early May Bank Holiday beer and cider festival.

Open all wk 12-2.30 6-11 (Sat-Sun all day) **Food** Lunch all wk 12-2 Dinner all wk 6-9 ⊕ FREE HOUSE ◀ Wye Valley HPA, Ledbury Bitter, Guest ales ♦ Westons Stowford Press, Country Perry & Bounds, Local ciders. ₹ 8 **Facilities** Non-diners area ♦♦ Children's menu Children's portions Garden 규 Beer festival Cider festival Parking WiFi ☕ (notice required)

HERTFORDSHIRE

ALDBURY
Map 6 SP91

The Greyhound Inn

tel: 01442 851228 **19 Stocks Rd HP23 5RT**
email: greyhound@aldbury.wanadoo.co.uk
dir: *Phone for detailed directions*

A traditional village inn offering good food in a relaxed atmosphere

The village's ancient stocks and duck pond are popular with film-makers who frequently use Aldbury as a location, allowing the pub's customers the chance to witness every clap of the clapperboard. In the oak-beamed restaurant, the comprehensive menu includes salads and platters, as well as king prawn and crab linguine; roasted duck breast with lime scented rice and sweet pepper and aubergine jam; or confit of pork belly on mash and bok choi. Among the desserts are baked figs with mascarpone cheese, and warm almond and treacle tart with custard. The bar snacks are a local legend, especially when accompanied by Badger Dorset Best or Tanglefoot ale.

Open all day all wk 11.30-11 (Sun 12-10.30) Closed 25 Dec **Food** Lunch all wk 12-2.30 Dinner all wk 6.30-9.30 ⊕ HALL & WOODHOUSE ◀ Badger Dorset Best, Tanglefoot, K&B Sussex. ₹ 13 **Facilities** Non-diners area ❤ (Bar Garden) ♦♦ Family room Garden Parking WiFi ☕ (notice required)

The Valiant Trooper

tel: 01442 851203 **Trooper Rd HP23 5RW**
email: valianttrooper@gmail.com
dir: *A41 at Tring junct, follow rail station signs 0.5m, at village green turn right, 200yds on left*

Delicious dishes in the Chilterns

Named in honour of the Duke of Wellington who allegedly discussed strategy with his troops here, this old pub has been enjoyed by lucky locals for centuries. Located in the quintessential Chilterns' village of Aldbury, beneath the beech woods of

Ashridge Park, the Trooper's bar proffers six real ales and beer festivals usually take place on Bank Holidays. Bar food encompasses jackets, sandwiches, ploughman's and pub favourites. The restaurant menu features more creative dishes like braised spring vegetable medley with shredded ham hock, parmesan, cheddar scones and wholegrain mustard.

Open all day all wk 12-11 (Sun 12-10.30) **Food** Lunch Mon-Fri 12-3, Sat 12-9, Sun 12-4 Dinner Mon-Fri 6-9, Sat 12-9 Av main course £10.95 Set menu available Restaurant menu available Wed-Sun ⊕ FREE HOUSE ◀ Fuller's London Pride, Tring Side Pocket for a Toad, Chiltern Beechwood, Guest ales Ở Lilley's Apples & Pears, Millwhites Hedge Layer, Westons. **Facilities** Non-diners area ♣ (Bar Garden) ♦ Children's menu Children's portions Play area Family room Garden Beer festival Parking WiFi ▬ (notice required)

ARDELEY
Map 12 TL32

Jolly Waggoner

tel: 01438 861350 **SG2 7AH**
email: adrian@churchfarmardeley.co.uk
dir: *From Stevenage take B1037, through Walkern, in 2m right to Ardeley*

Ancient village pub with a 'one-mile menu'

All meat on the Jolly Waggoner's menu, including heritage varieties and rare breeds, is traditionally reared at Church Farm across the road, together with over 100 different vegetables, fruits and herbs. As Church Farm runs this 500-year-old pub, the food on offer is truly local, being sourced from within a one-mile radius. Start with garlic mushrooms or smoked duck breast, and continue with pan-roasted partridge breast or bean, tomato and caramelised onion pie from the market menu. Regular beers are Buntingford and Fuller's London Pride. The annual beer festival takes place in August.

Open all day all wk 12-11.30 (Fri-Sat noon-12.30am) **Food** Lunch Mon-Fri 12-2, Sat 12-9, Sun 12-7 Dinner Mon-Fri 6.30-9, Sat 12-9, Sun 12-7 ⊕ FREE HOUSE ◀ Thwaites Highwayman, Fuller's London Pride, Adnams Broadside, Dark Star, Buntingford, Red Squirrel RSX Ở Aspall. ♀ 13 **Facilities** Non-diners area ♣ (Bar Garden) ♦ Children's menu Children's portions Garden ⋒ Beer festival Parking WiFi ▬

AYOT GREEN
Map 6 TL21

The Waggoners ◉

tel: 01707 324241 **Brickwall Close AL6 9AA**
email: laurent@thewaggoners.co.uk
dir: *Ayot Green on unclassified road off B197, S of Welwyn*

Modern French cuisine in the Hertfordshire countryside

Close to the large, traditional village green and with good English real ales flowing in the beamed bar, it comes as a surprise that the menu has a strong French bent to it. Cue the Gallic owners, whose culinary skills have gained an AA Rosette for their inspired cuisine at this former waggoners' and coaching stop in the low Hertfordshire hills. Menus may include sweet chilli foccacia with crayfish and aïoli; Toulouse sausages with braised lentils and chorizo; or pan-fried turbot with celeriac, samphire, pea and truffle sauce. The wine list stretches to 50 bins.

Open all day all wk **Food** Lunch all wk 12-2.45 Dinner all wk 6.30-9.30 Av main course £7 Set menu available Restaurant menu available all wk ⊕ PUNCH TAVERNS ◀ Fuller's London Pride, St Austell Tribute, Adnams Broadside, Greene King Abbot Ale & IPA, Sharp's Doom Bar Ở Westons Stowford Press. ♀ 50 **Facilities** Non-diners area ♣ (Bar Garden Outside area) ♦ Children's portions Garden Outside area ⋒ Parking WiFi ▬ (notice required)

BARLEY
Map 12 TL43

The Fox & Hounds

tel: 01763 849400 **High St SG8 8HU**
email: foxandhoundsbarley@hotmail.co.uk
dir: *A505 onto B1368 at Flint Cross, pub 4m*

Historic pub with a reputation for good microbrewery ales

This 16th-century former hunting lodge is set in a beautiful and historic village in north Hertfordshire. Expect a wealth of exposed beams, fireplaces, wood-burners, original flooring and more nooks and crannies than you can shake a stick at. The pub has made a name for itself by serving top-quality real ales from microbreweries and offering home-cooked food in the dedicated restaurant. A typical menu might include home-made beef lasagne and chicken curry. A child- and dog-friendly pub.

Open all day all wk 12-11 (Fri-Sat 12-12) **Food** Lunch all wk 12-2 Dinner all wk 6-9 ⊕ FREE HOUSE ◀ Adnams Southwold Bitter, Flowers IPA, Woodforde's Wherry, Falstaff Phoenix, Greene King Abbot Ale Ở Lyne Down Roaring Meg. ♀ 12 **Facilities** Non-diners area ♣ (Bar Garden) ♦ Children's menu Children's portions Play area Garden Beer festival Parking WiFi ▬

BERKHAMSTED
Map 6 SP90

The Old Mill

tel: 01442 879590 **London Rd HP4 2NB**
email: oldmill@peachpubs.com
dir: *At east end of London Rd in town centre*

Historic waterside pub buzzing throughout the week

Occupying a plum spot on the Grand Union Canal, this is a great place to enjoy a pint of Bring Me Sunshine and a deli board, either while relaxing on big leather sofas in the low-beamed bar or outside in the canal-side garden. The restored pub retains many of its original Georgian and Victorian features; a reclaimed millstone and historic photographs of mill machinery reflect the building's past. Menus in the comfortable dining room showcase the best seasonal ingredients – perhaps pan-fried cod fillet with a lobster spring roll, spring vegetables and garlic and ginger broth. From the sheltered courtyard you can watch the mill-race crashing over the weir.

Open all day all wk Closed 25 Dec **Food** Lunch all wk 12-6 Dinner all wk 6-10 Av main course £14.50 ⊕ PEACH PUBS ◀ Red Squirrel Conservation Bitter, Tring Side Pocket for a Toad & Bring Me Sunshine, Sharp's Doom Bar Ở Aspall. ♀ 16 **Facilities** Non-diners area ♣ (Bar Garden) ♦ Children's portions Garden ⋒ Parking WiFi ▬ (notice required)

Find out about pubs and pigs in Swine and dine on page 12

BRAUGHING | Map 12 TL32

The Golden Fleece

tel: 01920 823555 **2O Green End SG11 2PG**
email: pub@goldenfleecebraughing.co.uk **web:** www.goldenfleecebraughing.co.uk
dir: A10 N from Ware. At rdbt right onto B1368 signed Braughing. Approx 1m to village

Lovingly restored village inn on the way to Cambridge

This Grade II-listed Georgian coaching inn was closed for a decade until Peter and Jessica Tatlow bought it at auction and reopened it after a major renovation. Their hard work has clearly paid off as the pub has quickly gained a good reputation for its local real ales and ciders, but also its food, which specialises in gluten- and dairy-free dishes. Carrot and orange soup followed by venison, apple and thyme burger are typical choices and the monthly tapas night is a popular fixture on the last Wednesday of each month.

Open all wk 11.30-3 5.30-11 (Fri 11.30-3 5.30-12 Sat 11.30am-mdnt Sun 12-10) Closed 25 Dec **Food** Lunch Mon-Sat 12-2.30, Sun 12-6 Dinner Mon-Thu 6-9, Fri-Sat 7-10, Sun 12-6 Set menu available ⊕ FREE HOUSE ◀ Adnams, Nethergate, Buntingford, Mauldons, Church End, Cottage ♂ Aspall Harry Sparrow. ♟ 15 **Facilities** Non-diners area ♦♦ Children's menu Children's portions Play area Garden ⊟ Parking WiFi ➡ (notice required)

BROOKMANS PARK | Map 6 TL20

NEW Brookmans

tel: 01707 664144 **Bradmore Green AL9 7QW**
email: brookmans@peachpubs.com
dir: A1000 from Hatfield towards Potters Bar. Right signed Brookmans Park. Through Bradmore Green. Pub on right

Enjoyable local food in a buzzy village hub

Built as a hotel in the 1930s, Brookmans may no longer offer a bed for the night but it remains the social hub of the village. Racing Green leather upholstery and silk lampshades add a touch of class to the bar, where a rotating choice of guest ales is complemented by 15 wines by the glass. Local produce and named suppliers drive the modern British menu and daily specials, which might include chilli and lime crab cake with wasabi mayo; Cornish lamb casserole and creamy mash, finishing off with Valrhona white chocolate cheesecake and Baileys cream.

Open all day all wk Closed 25 Dec **Food** Lunch all wk 12-6 Dinner Mon-Sat 6-10, Sun 6-9 Av main course £12-£14 ⊕ FREE HOUSE ◀ Sharp's Doom Bar & Cornish Coaster, Guest ales ♂ Aspall. ♟ 15 **Facilities** Non-diners area ♣ (Bar Garden) ♦♦ Children's portions Play area Garden ⊟ Parking WiFi ➡ (notice required)

BUNTINGFORD | Map 12 TL32

The Sword Inn Hand ★★★★ INN

tel: 01763 271356 **Westmill SG9 9LQ**
email: welcome@theswordinnhand.co.uk **web:** www.theswordinnhand.co.uk
dir: Off A10 1.5m S of Buntingford

Welcoming travellers since the 14th century

Midway between London and Cambridge, this old inn provides an excellent stopping off point. Inside are the original oak beams, flagstone floors and open fireplace; outside is a large garden and pretty patio. As a free house, there is a varied selection of real ales from the likes of Greene King, Sharp's and Young's. Fresh produce is delivered daily for a good selection of bar snacks including salads, omelettes, sandwiches and light dishes. Taken from a typical evening menu are mozzarella-stuffed peppers with couscous; basil-crusted salmon fillet with Mediterranean vegetables; and calves' liver and bacon. Luxury accommodation is available.

Open all wk 12-3 5-11 (Fri-Sat all day, Sun 12-7) **Food** Lunch Mon-Sat 12-2.30, Sun 12-4 Dinner Mon-Sat 6.30-9.30 ⊕ FREE HOUSE ◀ Greene King IPA, Young's Bitter, Sharp's Doom Bar, Guest ales ♂ Westons Stowford Press. ♟ 9 **Facilities** Non-diners area ♦♦ Children's menu Children's portions Play area Garden ⊟ Parking WiFi ➡ **Rooms** 4

COTTERED | Map 12 TL32

The Bull at Cottered

tel: 01763 281243 **SG9 9QP**
email: darren.perkins@tiscali.co.uk
dir: On A507 in Cottered between Buntingford & Baldock

Charming, traditional village local

Low beams, antique furniture, cosy fires and teamwork – four key things that sum up this member of the Greene King portfolio. Then, of course, there's the food. You can eat in one of two traditional bars with open fires, in the pretty beamed dining room, or in the large, well-kept gardens. Everything that can be is home-made, the brasserie-style cooking typified by starters of fresh Devon crab salad, warm goats' cheese or smoked salmon and prawn parcel; then calves' liver with sage, butter and bacon; beef sirloin with smoked bacon and Roquefort sauce, or sea bass fillet with scallops and chive cream.

Open all wk 11.30-3 6.30-11 (Sun 12-10.30) **Food** Lunch Mon-Sat 12-2, Sun 12-4 Dinner Mon-Sat 6.30-9.30, Sun 6-9 Av main course £12.50 Restaurant menu available all wk ⊕ GREENE KING ◀ IPA & Abbot Ale, Morland Old Speckled Hen. **Facilities** Non-diners area ♦♦ Children's portions Garden ⊟ Parking WiFi ➡ (notice required)

PICK OF THE PUBS

The Bricklayers Arms 🌹

FLAUNDEN Map 6 TL00

Tel: 01442 833322
Hogpits Bottom HP3 0PH
email: goodfood@bricklayersarms.com
web: www.bricklayersarms.com
dir: *M25 junct 18, A404 (Amersham road). Right at Chenies for Flaunden*

Country inn with Anglo-French cuisine

The creeper-clad Bricklayers Arms is a low, cottagey tiled pub formed from a pair of 18th-century cottages. It was in 1832 that Benskin's brewery converted the first of the cottages into an alehouse; the other joined it in the 1960s. Lost down leafy Hertfordshire lanes in a peaceful and inviting location, the pub has featured in many fictional films and TV programmes, and is a favourite with locals, walkers, horse-riders and, well, just about everyone. In summer, the flowerfestooned garden is the perfect place to savour an alfresco pint or meal. An ivy covered façade gives way to an immaculate interior, complete with low beams, exposed brickwork, candlelight and open fires. The award-winning restaurant is housed in a converted outbuilding and barn. Here you'll find a happy marriage of traditional English and French cooking. The Gallic influence comes from experienced head chef, Claude Pallait, and his team who use fresh organic produce from local

suppliers to create seasonal lunch and dinner menus, plus daily specials. For starters try venison coarse terrine with Kentish pear chutney; or charcuterie for two to share. To follow pan-fried duck breast with duck leg confit marinated in salt and duck fat, with sweet and sour cranberry jus; or roast breast of guinea fowl with pheasant sausage and a liver mousse feuillete. But don't stop there, from the puddings perhaps choose sticky toffee pudding with a date mascarpone and vanilla ice cream, or lemon tart with pannacotta and raspberry ice cream. Opt for one of the 120 wines from all corners of the world and, in the summer, enjoy it with your lunch in the terraced garden.

Open all day all wk 12-11.30 (Sun 9.15am-10.30pm 25 Dec 12-3)
Food Lunch Mon-Sat 12-2.30, Sun 12-3.30 Dinner Mon-Sat 6.30-9.30, Sun 6.30-8.30 ⊕ FREE HOUSE ◀ Tring Jack O'Legs, Sharp's Doom Bar, Rebellion ♻ Aspall, Thatchers Gold. ♟ 20
Facilities Non-diners area ❤ (Bar Garden) ♦ Children's portions Garden ⊼ Parking WiFi

DATCHWORTH
Map 6 TL21

The Tilbury ◉

tel: 01438 815550 **Walton Rd SG3 6TB**
email: info@thetilbury.co.uk
dir: A1(M) junct 7, A602 signed Ware & Hertford. At Bragbury End right into Bragbury Ln to Datchworth

Elegant country pub serving varied menus

A change of hands at The Tilbury means you'll now find varied menus that include popular pub classics such as venison cottage pie, and an à la carte of refined British dishes. The three new owners and their head chef have created tempting choices such as potted rabbit and carrot cake; salt and pepper squid with lemon mayo; braised hogget bun and loin with greens and mint sauce; roast sea trout, crab mash, samphire and tomato butter sauce; and cereal milk pannacotta with honey ice cream. The large terrace and garden is perfect for enjoying a drink or meal on sunny days, and with several dining areas, The Tilbury can offer private dining options. A set menu menu is available at both lunch and dinner.

Open all day Closed Sun eve & Mon **Food** Lunch Tue-Sun 12-2 Dinner Tue-Sat 6-9.30 Set menu available Restaurant menu available Tue-Sun ⊕ BRAKSPEAR ◀ Bitter ☼ Westons Wyld Wood Organic, Symonds. ☗ 20 **Facilities** Non-diners area ♦♦ Children's menu Children's portions Garden ⋒ Parking WiFi ▬

EPPING GREEN
Map 6 TL20

The Beehive

tel: 01707 875959 **SG13 8NB**
email: squirrell15@googlemail.com
dir: B158 from Hertford towards Hatfield. Left signed Little Berkhamsted. Left at war memorial signed Epping Green

Countryside pub with emphasis on fish dishes

This family-run free house has held its liquor licence for over 200 years and featured in the *Catweazel* TV series in the 1970s. These days it retains plenty of traditional charms including exposed beams, a real fire in winter and decked and grassed areas for sunnier days. The kitchen specialises in fresh fish from Billingsgate Market – maybe poached fish pie or sea bass fillets with basil pesto. Alternatives include steak, mushroom and ale pudding, Thai green chicken curry and a wide range of vegetarian choices. A constantly changing special board adds to the choices. At the bar you'll find two permanent ales and a changing guest.

Open all wk Mon-Sat 11.30-3 5.30-11 (Sun 12-10.30) **Food** Lunch Mon-Sat 12-2.30, Sun 12-4 Dinner Mon-Sat 6-9.30, Sun 6-8.30 Restaurant menu available all wk ⊕ FREE HOUSE ◀ Greene King IPA, Abbot Ale, Guest ale. ☗ 12 **Facilities** Non-diners area ♦♦ Children's portions Garden ⋒ Parking WiFi ▬ (notice required)

FLAUNDEN
Map 6 TL00

The Bricklayers Arms ◉
PICK OF THE PUBS

See Pick of the Pubs on page 261

HEMEL HEMPSTEAD
Map 6 TL00

Alford Arms
PICK OF THE PUBS

See Pick of the Pubs on opposite page

HERONSGATE
Map 6 TQ09

The Land of Liberty, Peace and Plenty

tel: 01923 282226 **Long Ln WD3 5BS**
email: beer@landoflibertypub.com
dir: M25 junct 17, follow Heronsgate signs. 0.5m, pub on right

Top quality beers and ciders in single-bar pub

Named after a Chartist settlement established in Heronsgate in 1847, this inn is believed to have the second longest pub name in the British Isles. A traditional pub with a large garden and covered decked area, the cosy single bar has a buzz of conversation from locals. The focus here are the real ales and real ciders, all of which can be enjoyed with bar snacks of pork pies, pasties and pots of nuts. Please note that no children or the use of mobile phones are allowed in the bar. Regular events and beer festivals are held during the year.

Open all wk 12-11 (Fri-Sat 12-12) **Food** Contact pub for details ⊕ FREE HOUSE ◀ 8 Guest ales. **Facilities** Non-diners area ♣ (Bar Garden) Garden ⋒ Beer festival Parking WiFi ▬ (notice required)

HEXTON
Map 12 TL13

The Raven

tel: 01582 881209 **SG5 3JB**
email: theraven@emeryinns.com
dir: 5m W of Hitchin. 5m N of Luton, just outside Barton-le-Clay

Family friendly pub

This neat 1920s pub is named after Ravensburgh Castle in the neighbouring hills. Comfortable bars witness the serving of four weekly-changing guest ales, perhaps Fuller's London Pride or Greene King IPA, while outside a large garden with heated terrace and a play area ensure family friendliness. Extensive menus and blackboard specials embrace pub classics, salads, jackets, baguettes and wraps, vegetarian options, fish dishes and 'combination' meat plates like ribs and/or steak with Cajun chicken, and surf 'n' turf. So a three-course meal could see loaded potato skins, fillet of salmon salad, and chocolate and honeycomb sundae.

Open all day all wk **Food** Lunch 12-9 Dinner 12-9 ⊕ FREE HOUSE ◀ Greene King IPA, Morland Old Speckled Hen, Fuller's London Pride, Timothy Taylor Landlord, Sharp's Doom Bar. ☗ 24 **Facilities** Non-diners area ♦♦ Children's menu Children's portions Play area Garden ⋒ Parking WiFi ▬ (notice required)

HITCHIN
Map 12 TL12

NEW Hermitage Rd.

tel: 01462 433603 **20-21 Hermitage Rd SG5 1BT**
email: reservations@hermitagerd.co.uk
dir: From lights on B656 in town centre into Hermitage Rd

A bar, restaurant and coffee house

This one-time ballroom and then nightclub is no typical town-centre pub. With a revamped interior, costing well over half a million pounds in 2011, the effect is knockout, although original features survive, like the high vaulted ceiling, arched windows and stage, now a dining area, where many a Sixties pop star rocked the night away. Also part of the transformation is the open-plan kitchen, from which come north Norfolk oysters and mussels; venison and beef meatballs with fettuccine; pan-fried sea trout; and aubergine, feta and basil bake. On a globe-trotting wine list appears a sparkling white from East Sussex.

Open all day all wk **Food** Lunch Mon-Sat 12-9.30, Sun 12-8 Dinner Mon-Sat 12-9.30, Sun 12-8 Av main course £12 Restaurant menu available all wk ⊕ FREE HOUSE ◀ Adnams Southwold Bitter, Caledonian Deuchars IPA, Sharp's Doom Bar, Brancaster Oyster Catcher ☼ Symonds Founders Reserve. ☗ 13 **Facilities** Non-diners area ♦♦ Children's menu Children's portions WiFi ▬ (notice required)

PICK OF THE PUBS

Alford Arms

HEMEL HEMPSTEAD   Map 6 TL00

tel: 01442 864480
Frithsden HP1 3DD
email: info@alfordarmsfrithsden.co.uk
web: www.alfordarmsfrithsden.co.uk
dir: *A4146 from Hemel Hempstead 2nd left at Water End. 1m, left at T-junct, right in 0.75m. Pub 100yds on right*

Professional but relaxed pub with understated style

With a flower-filled garden overlooking the green in the untouched hamlet of Frithsden, this pretty Victorian pub is surrounded by National Trust woodland and has historic Ashridge Park on its doorstep. It's one of four in the well regarded Salisbury Pubs mini-empire in and around the Chilterns.* Cross the threshold and you'll immediately pick up on the warm and lively atmosphere, derived from the buzz of conversation, some soft jazz in the background, and from the rich colours and eclectic mix of old furniture and antique pictures in the dining room and bar from Tring's well known salerooms. Also from Tring is real ale called Side Pocket for a Toad, which shares bar space with Rebellion IPA and Sharp's Doom Bar. The seasonal menus and daily specials are a balance of modern British with more traditional dishes, all prepared from fresh local produce whenever possible. There's a great choice of light dishes or 'small plates', from slow-dried tomato,

spinach and wild garlic tart with herb tabouleh, to crisp smoked salmon kedgeree fritters with soft boiled quail's egg and Indian spiced aïoli. Equally imaginative main meals include roast Chiltern Hills leg of lamb, onion sauce and all the trimmings; pan-roast coley fillet, saffron dauphinoise potatoes, shrimp bisque and crispy seaweed; and classic Potash Farm coq au vin with parsley mash and parsnip crisps. White chocolate pot with shortbread and blueberry jam is one way to finish, or there's also the plate of British cheeses or home-made sorbets and ice creams.

*The Swan Inn, Denham; The Royal Oak, Bovingdon Green; and The Old Queens Head, Penn (all in Buckinghamshire).

Open all day all wk 11-11 (Sun 12-10.30) Closed 25-26 Dec **Food** Lunch Mon-Fri 12-2.30, Sat 12-3, Sun all day Dinner Mon-Thu 6.30-9.30, Fri-Sat 6.30-10, Sun all day Av main course £14.75 ⊕ SALISBURY PUBS LTD
🛢 Rebellion IPA, Sharp's Doom Bar
🍺 Westons Mortimers Orchard. ♟ 24
Facilities Non-diners area 🐾 (Bar Garden) ♦ Children's portions Garden ⊓ Parking WiFi

HUNSDON
Map 6 TL41

The Fox and Hounds
PICK OF THE PUBS

See Pick of the Pubs on opposite page

LITTLE HADHAM
Map 6 TL42

The Nags Head

tel: 01279 771555 **The Ford SG11 2AX**
email: paul.arkell@virgin.net
dir: *M11 junct 8, A120 towards Puckeridge & A10. Left at lights in Little Hadham. Pub 1m on right*

Along the country byways just south of Little Hadham

This warm and relaxed country pub was built in 1595 and still retains its traditional atmosphere, with an old bakery oven and a good range of real ales at the bar. Fish dishes such as poached skate wing with black butter and capers feature strongly on the full à la carte menu, which also includes a choice of steaks and vegetarian meals. At lunchtime, sandwiches and jacket potatoes offer a lighter alternative to hot main courses. Sit out the front on a good day and enjoy the countryside.

Open all wk 11.30-2.30 6-11 (Sun 12-10.30) **Food** Lunch Mon-Sat 12-2, Sun all day Dinner Mon-Sat 6-9, Sun all day Set menu available Restaurant menu available all wk ⊕ GREENE KING ◀ Abbot Ale, Ruddles County & IPA, Morland Old Speckled Hen, Marston's Pedigree. ♈ 12 **Facilities** Non-diners area ◑▮ Children's menu Children's portions Garden ⋒ WiFi ➡

NORTHAW
Map 6 TL20

The Sun at Northaw

tel: 01707 655507 **1 Judges Hill EN6 4NL**
email: reservations@thesunatnorthaw.co.uk
dir: *M25 junct 24, A111 to Potters Bar. Right onto A1000, becomes High Street (B156). Follow to Northaw, pub on left*

Pretty inn with a skilled chef patron

A Grade II listed inn on a picturesque village green, The Sun has gained a reputation for its real ale, with up to seven available at any time. There is also an excellent wine list to complement cooking from chef and owner Oliver Smith, whose menus are driven by local, seasonal produce. An appetiser of smoked sprats and horseradish might precede a starter of potted beef, pickled prunes and Yorkshire pudding, followed by a main course of venison saddle, swede, haggis mash, wild cabbage and sloe gin. Finish with salted caramel rice pudding, rum and raisins.

Open 12-4 5-11 Closed Sun eve & Mon **Food** Lunch Tue-Sun 12-4 Dinner Tue-Sat 5-11 Set menu available ⊕ FREE HOUSE ◀ Adnams, Buntingford, Saffron, Nethergate, Red Squirrel RSX ♨ Millwhites, Aspall. ♈ 13 **Facilities** Non-diners area ✿ (Bar Garden) ◑▮ Children's menu Children's portions Garden ⋒ Parking WiFi

PERRY GREEN
Map 6 TL41

The Hoops Inn

tel: 01279 843568 **SG10 6EF**
email: reservations@hoops-inn.co.uk
dir: *From Ware on B1004 towards Bishop's Stortford right onto unclassified road to Perry Green*

Stylish inn with links to famous sculptor

Once home to Henry Moore, Perry Green is dotted with his famous sculptures. This comfortable dining inn is part of the estate and it boasts a chic country decor, contemporary furnishings and Moore-inspired artefacts. The food here draws a crowd thanks to dishes such as five-spice battered soft shell crab with oriental

salad; and seared haunch of venison with carrot and horseradish purée. Excellent Sunday roasts can be walked off by visiting the Moore Foundation's estate just across the village green. There is a large front terrace and back garden to enjoy in the warmer weather.

Open all day 11.30-11 Closed Mon **Food** Lunch Tue-Sat 12-3, Sun 12-6 Dinner Tue-Sat 5-9.30 Set menu available Restaurant menu available Wed-Sun ⊕ FREE HOUSE ◀ Adnams Southwold Bitter, Guinness ♨ Aspall. **Facilities** ◑▮ Children's menu Children's portions Garden ⋒ Beer festival Cider festival Parking ➡ (notice required)

POTTEN END
Map 6 TL00

Martins Pond

tel: 01442 864318 **The Green HP4 2QQ**
dir: *A41 onto A416 signed Chesham, follow signs to Berkhamsted town centre. At lights straight over into Lower Kings Rd. Pass station, into Station Rd. Left at pub on opposite side of village green*

Innovative food and good walks directly from the pub

The unusual name refers to the village green where this welcoming pub is located. A section of Grim's Dyke, an ancient bank-and-ditch earthwork, is clearly visible nearby. By comparison the pub – dating from 1924 – is relatively new, but there's been a public house here since the 17th century. These days it's a good destination for home-cooked food such as crispy duck and filo parcels with spiced plums and red chard, followed by venison and smoked bacon meatballs with buttered Savoy cabbage and a red wine and cranberry gravy.

Open all day all wk Closed 26 Dec **Food** Lunch Mon-Sat 12-2.30, Sun 12-4 Dinner Mon-Sat 6-9 ⊕ FREE HOUSE ◀ Fuller's London Pride, Red Squirrel. ♈ 13 **Facilities** Non-diners area ✿ (Bar Garden) ◑▮ Children's portions Garden ⋒ Parking WiFi

POTTERS CROUCH
Map 6 TL10

The Holly Bush

tel: 01727 851792 **AL2 3NN**
email: info@thehollybushpub.co.uk
dir: *Village accessed from A4147 & A405*

Country pub with old-world charm

Tucked away in a hamlet, The Holly Bush is a picturesque 17th-century pub with a large enclosed garden complete with wooden benches and tables. There is a delightfully welcoming atmosphere, with antique dressers, log fires and exposed beams setting the interior style. Traditional and modern pub fare is offered. At lunch there's ploughman's, baked potatoes, garden salads, deli platters, burgers and toasted sandwiches; while on the evening menu there might be smoked haddock fishcake with poached egg and wilted spinach; or lamb koftas with feta cheese salad, grilled pittas, tzatziki and olives. The pub is close to St Albans with its Roman ruins and good local walks.

Open all wk 12-2.30 6-11 (Sun 12-3) **Food** Lunch Mon-Sat 12-2, Sun 12-2.30 Dinner Wed-Sat 6-9 ⊕ FULLER'S ◀ London Pride, ESB, George Gale & Co Seafarers, Seasonal ales. **Facilities** Non-diners area Garden ⋒ Parking WiFi ➡ (notice required)

PICK OF THE PUBS

The Fox and Hounds

HUNSDON   Map 6 TL41

tel: 01279 843999
2 High St SG12 8NH
email: info@foxandhounds-hunsdon.co.uk
web: www.foxandhounds-hunsdon.co.uk
dir: *From A414 between Ware & Harlow take B180 in Stanstead Abbotts N to Hunsdon*

Mediterranean inspired menu in a relaxed pub

Owned and run by chef James Rix and wife Bianca, this renowned gastro-pub is set in a sleepy Hertfordshire village, but attracts food lovers from afar. The easy-going atmosphere is thanks to a cosy winter fire warming the old bar, liberally supplied with Victorian-style furnishings. There's no pressure to do anything other than enjoy a glass of Adnams, but resistance is futile when you see James's imaginative, Mediterranean-inspired menu, which changes daily and with the seasons. There's no doubt that the food side of the pub is the main draw here, and lunch and dinner can be taken in the bar or elegant, chandeliered dining room. James successfully combines traditional pub favourites (with a twist) with French and Italian influences, and his simply described dishes champion local produce. Expect interesting combinations of ingredients, bold flavours and difficulty in deciding. Kick off with Palourde clams and Nduja

(spicy Calabrian salami), or burrata, wild treviso, blood orange and mint; then calves' liver persillade and duck fat potato cake; roast fillet of cod, wild garlic, brown shrimps and mash; or a dish from the charcoal oven, perhaps Scotch Black Angus côte de boeuf. Finish with hot chocolate pudding with espresso ice cream and hot chocolate sauce, or apple tart fine, caramel sauce and vanilla ice cream. In winter the menus will include shot game such as partridge, venison, hare and pheasant and in the summer months, crab and native lobster straight from the Cornish coast. The tree shaded garden, together with the covered terrace is popular with drinkers and alfresco diners. Booking for meals is advised.

Open 12-4 6-11 Closed 26 Dec, Sun eve, Mon & BHs eve (Tue after BHs)
Food Lunch Tue-Sat 12-2.30, Sun 12-3.30 Dinner Tue-Sat 6-9.30 Set menu available 🛢 FREE HOUSE 🍺 Adnams Southwold Bitter & Broadside, Local ales Ö Aspall. 🍷 9
Facilities Non-diners area 🐾 (Bar Garden) 🚸 Children's menu Children's portions Play area Garden 🎪 Parking WiFi

---

The Cock Inn

tel: 01923 282908 **Church Ln WD3 6HH**
email: enquiries@cockinn.net
dir: *M25 junct 18, A404 signed Chorleywood, Amersham. Right follow signs to Sarratt. Pass church on left, pub on right*

Welcoming rustic pub oozing character and charm

A warm and friendly welcome is guaranteed at this traditional village inn standing opposite Sarratt's Norman church. Originally called the Cock Horse, the 17th-century pub is in the heart of the Chess Valley, an area favoured by walkers. It has head-cracking low beams, an inglenook fireplace and Hall & Woodhouse ales at the bar, while the ancient timbered barn houses the restaurant. Expect classic pub dishes such as cottage pie; pork and leek sausages; or liver and bacon casserole. Light bites and sandwiches are served in the bar or garden.

Open all day all wk **Food** Lunch Mon-Sat 12-2.30, Sun 12-6 Dinner Mon-Sat 6-9, Sun 12-6 Restaurant menu available Tue-Sun ⊕ HALL & WOODHOUSE ◀ Badger Tanglefoot, K&B Sussex ⌕ Westons Stowford Press & Rosie's Pig.
Facilities Non-diners area ✿ (Bar Garden) ◖ Children's menu Children's portions Play area Garden 🚐 Parking WiFi ⇔ (notice required)

The White Horse, Shenley

tel: 01923 853054 **37 London Rd WD7 9ER**
email: enquiry@whitehorseradlett.co.uk
dir: *M25 junct 22, B556 then B5378 to Shenley*

Village pub with an interesting menu

The White Horse belies its 170-year-old foundation as a village pub, offering contemporary comforts and dining at the fringe of this green-belt village, with country walks to the Hertfordshire Way from the door. Bright, light and cheerful inside, with some quirky decor, it's an ideal place to sup a Sharp's Doom Bar bitter over a Sunday roast or crack a bottle from the extensive wine list and indulge in soft shell crab with crispy calamari, soy, ginger and chilli dip followed by pork fillet wrapped in sage and prosciutto with pistachio and blue cheese sauce, with white chocolate brûlée for dessert. There's also a children's menu.

Open all day all wk 11-11 **Food** Lunch Mon-Sat 12-10, Sun 12-9 Dinner Mon-Sat 12-10, Sun 12-9 ⊕ FREE HOUSE/MITCHELLS & BUTLERS ◀ Sharp's Doom Bar, Young's ⌕ Aspall. ☗ 12 **Facilities** Non-diners area ✿ (Bar Garden) ◖ Children's menu Children's portions Garden 🚐 Parking ⇔ (notice required)

Papillon Woodhall Arms ★★★ INN

tel: 01992 535123 **17 High Rd SG14 3NW**
email: info@papillonrestaurant.co.uk **web:** www.papillonrestaurant.co.uk
dir: *On A119, between A602 & Hertford*

Reliable and popular rural fringe inn

Nudging the fringe of Hertfordshire's pleasant countryside of pasture and copses, this handsome roadhouse has a long-established reputation as a destination dining pub. Good, pubby bar meals like beef Stroganoff or chicken, ham and leek pie accompany beers such as St Austell Tribute in the comfortably appointed, fire-warmed bar, whilst the thriving Papillon Restaurant side of the business pushes the culinary boat out. Anticipate a hot avocado starter with prawns and cheese fondue; then fresh skate wing with beurre noir, or saddle of venison with cinnamon black cherry sauce. Good value accommodation makes this ideal for a short break.

Open all wk 12-2 6.30-10.30 (Sun 12-2.30 6.30-10.30) **Food** Lunch all wk 12-2 Dinner Sun-Sat 6.30-10 Set menu available Restaurant menu available all wk ⊕ FREE HOUSE ◀ Greene King IPA, Young's Special, St Austell Tribute, Black Sheep

---

⌕ Aspall. ☗ 10 **Facilities** Non-diners area ✿ (Garden) ◖ Children's menu Children's portions Family room Garden 🚐 Parking WiFi ⇔ (notice required) **Rooms** 10

The Cow Roast Inn

tel: 01442 822287 **Cow Roast, London Rd HP23 5RF**
email: cowroastinn@btconnect.com
dir: *Between Berkhamstead & Tring on A4251*

Old coaching inn with an oriental twist

The classic interior of this venerable inn threads through a forest of timber posts, splaying out on timeworn flagstone floors to comfy asides with horse-brass bedecked log fire and drinking areas with pub games. In past centuries it was frequented by local farmers driving cattle to the London markets and navvies building the nearby Grand Union Canal. Today's guests appreciate beers from the local Tring Brewery and a restaurant specialising in Thai meals, whilst those with a less adventurous palate savour pub staples like fish pie or rack of ribs. There's a grand garden, and a beer festival is held.

Open all day all wk 12-close **Food** Lunch Tue-Sun 12-9 Dinner Tue-Sun 12-9 ◀ Greene King Abbot Ale, Tring Side Pocket for a Toad, Sharp's Doom Bar, Guest ales ⌕ Addlestones, Westons Stowford Press. **Facilities** Non-diners area ✿ (Bar Garden) ◖ Children's menu Children's portions Garden 🚐 Beer festival Parking WiFi ⇔ (notice required)

NEW The Bull

tel: 01920 831032 **High St SG14 3SB**
email: info@thebullwatton.co.uk
dir: *A602 from Stevenage towards Ware. At rdbt follow Watton-at-Stone sign. Right at mini rdbt (Datchworth & Walkern) into High St. Pub on right*

Village pub infused with love and vitality by local family

The Bramley family were living in this pretty village when The Bull became available. Using their experience in managing gastro-pubs, this inn is once again extending warm hospitality to all-comers. Families gather for Christmas carols around the huge inglenook fireplace, Morris dancers entertain in summer, and beer and cider festivals are hosted in May and October. Seasonality is also key to the kitchen's work, together with the provenance of high-grade ingredients; rare breed meats, for example, are reared just outside the village. So expect menus of hearty British fare such as Earl Grey smoked venison; Tamworth gammon steak with fat chips and fried duck egg; and salt marsh rack of lamb.

Open all day all wk **Food** Lunch Mon-Sat 12-3, Sun 12-6 Dinner Mon-Sat 6-10, Sun 12-6 Av main course £14.50 Set menu available ⊕ PUNCH TAVERNS ◀ Sharp's Doom Bar, Adnams Southwold, Guest ale ⌕ Aspall. ☗ 10 **Facilities** Non-diners area ◖ Children's menu Children's portions Play area Garden Outside area 🚐 Beer festival Cider festival Parking WiFi ⇔ (notice required)

NEW The Wellington ★★★★★ INN ⊛

tel: 01438 714036 **High St AL6 9LZ**
email: info@wellingtonatwelwyn.co.uk **web:** www.wellingtonatwelwyn.co.uk
dir: *A1(M) junct 6 to Welwyn*

Stylish village pub with notable food

Opposite the Saxon church in the attractive village of Welwyn, this 13th-century coaching inn has been completely restored and now offers six comfortable bedrooms alongside its one AA-Rosette food. When the weather allows, grab a table on the terrace or enjoy a drink by the river at the bottom of the garden. There is plenty of choice when it comes to food, from lunchtime wraps to ambitious modern

British specials such as crab and apple salad, roasted walnuts, pickled leeks, watercress and vanilla oil; and roast loin of lamb with aubergine purée, feta and pine nut dolma and mint jus.

Open all day all wk **Food** Lunch Mon-Fri 12-3, Sat-Sun 12-10 Dinner Mon-Fri 5.30-10, Sat-Sun 12-10 Set menu available Restaurant menu available all wk ⊕ GREENE KING ◀ Morland Old Speckled Hen, Wellington Ale Ⓐ Aspall. ♀ 37 **Facilities** Non-diners area ♦♦ Children's menu Children's portions Garden ⨅ Parking WiFi ▭ (notice required) **Rooms** 6

The White Hart ★★★★ INN

tel: 01438 715353 **2 Prospect Place AL6 9EN**
email: bookings@thewhitehardhotel.net **web:** www.thewhiteharthotel.net
dir: A1(M) junct 6. On corner of Prospect Place (just past fire station), at top of High St

Elegant former coaching inn

Once on the A1 trunk road, long ago rerouted well to the east, this 17th-century coaching inn today stands in a much quieter Welwyn. Its old beams, stone flags and inglenook fireplace blend easily with contemporary wood floors, leather chairs and numerous framed pictures and prints. The restaurant's monthly menus mix modern and traditional British styles to offer a range of burgers or fish and chips (in the bar); pan-fried salmon with garlic new potatoes; roast duck breast with chilli rösti and braised red cabbage; pan-fried stone bass and Mediterranean vegetable and feta in filo pastry with tomato fondue. A Charles Wells pub, so expect Bombardier and Young's bitter and regular guests, with Aspall cider too.

Open all day all wk 7am-mdnt (Sun 9am-10.30pm) **Food** Lunch all wk 12-2.30 Dinner Mon-Sat 6.30-9.30, Sun 6-8.30 ⊕ CHARLES WELLS ◀ Bombardier, Young's, Guest ale Ⓐ Westons Stowford Press, Aspall. ♀ 15 **Facilities** Non-diners area ♦♦ Children's menu Children's portions Parking WiFi **Rooms** 13

▌ WELWYN GARDEN CITY   Map 6 TL21

The Brocket Arms

tel: 01438 820250 & 07867 537718 **Ayot St Lawrence AL6 9BT**
email: bookings@brocketarms.com
dir: A1(M) junct 4 follow signs to Wheathampstead, then Shaw's Corner. Pub past Shaw's Corner on right

Great ales in a traditional setting

Encircled by a picturesque village that was once home to George Bernard Shaw, The Brocket Arms dates in parts to 1378 when it was built as a monks' hostel; it became a tavern in the 1630s. Huge oak beams and hefty hearths greet you along with a great range of real ales and wines. Food options range from snacks such as a Scotch egg with home-made chutney through to full meals such as pan-seared scallops with caramelised cauliflower purée and parsnip crisp followed by pan-fried pork loin with black pudding mash, thyme jus and creamed leeks. Change of hands.

Open all day all wk 12-11 (Sun 12-10.30) **Food** Lunch all wk 12-2.30 Dinner Mon-Sat 6-9 ⊕ FREE HOUSE ◀ Nethergate Brocket Bitter, Greene King IPA & Abbot Ale, Sharp's Doom Bar, 3 Brewers, Guest ales Ⓐ Aspall, Westons Mortimers Orchard. ♀ 18 **Facilities** Non-diners area ♣ (Bar Garden) ♦♦ Children's menu Children's portions Play area Garden ⨅ Parking WiFi ▭

▌ WILLIAN   Map 12 TL23

The Fox ⊛   PICK OF THE PUBS

tel: 01462 480233 **SG6 2AE**
email: info@foxatwillian.co.uk
dir: A1(M) junct 9 towards Letchworth, 1st left to Willian, pub 0.5m on left

Fine dining pub with a smart, contemporary interior

An imposing Georgian building sitting opposite the village pond and right next to the church, the 18th-century Fox is an award-winning destination, attracting

locals, walkers and cyclists. It's overseen by Cliff Nye, known for his Norfolk pubs, so it's no surprise to discover that East Anglian ales and fresh fish are brought in from Norfolk, while other produce is sourced locally. A clean, crisp look defines the interior, while the laid-back bar, restaurant atrium, enclosed courtyard and two beer gardens are all pleasant places to settle down with the modern British menus. There's plenty of choice on the menus – from bar snacks such as Thai fishcakes, lemongrass and black sesame mayo; a starter of duck leg and venison terrine with shallot purée and balsamic roasted figs, to a main course of truffle, pea and wild mushroom risotto, or shellfish tagliatelle, mussels, clams and crayfish with crispy pancetta. Look out for wine of the month deals and the popular themed food nights that take place throughout the year.

Open all day all wk **Food** Lunch Mon-Fri 12-2, Sat 12-6, Sun 12-3 Dinner Mon-Fri 7-9 Restaurant menu available Mon-Sat & Sun L ⊕ FREE HOUSE ◀ Adnams Southwold Bitter, Woodforde's Wherry, Sharp's Doom Bar, Brancaster Best. ♀ 15 **Facilities** Non-diners area ♣ (Bar Garden Outside area) ♦♦ Children's portions Garden Outside area ⨅ Beer festival Parking WiFi ▭ (notice required)

▌ ISLE OF WIGHT

▌ ARRETON   Map 5 SZ58

The White Lion

tel: 01983 528479 **Main Rd PO30 3AA**
email: whitelioniow@gmail.com
dir: On A3056 (Blackwater to Shanklin/Sandown road)

Traditional pub food and reliable real ales

A 200-year-old coaching inn in the heart of Arreton village, now under new management. Reliable ales like Doom Bar and Timothy Taylor Landlord are the top refreshments, while prices on the short wine list are commendably affordable. Food ranges from paninis and sandwiches to light bites and children's choices, and then on to classic starters, favourites main courses, and traditional desserts. A typical choice could kick off with blue cheese and Ventnor Bay crab beignets served with a port and Stilton sauce. Next may come the short-crust pie of the day from the blackboard, with a home-made berry Pavlova with crème Chantilly to finish.

Open all day all wk **Food** Lunch all wk 12-9.30 Dinner all wk 12-9.30 ⊕ ENTERPRISE INNS ◀ Sharp's Doom Bar, Timothy Taylor Landlord. **Facilities** Non-diners area ♣ (Bar Garden) ♦♦ Children's menu Children's portions Family room Garden ⨅ Parking

▌ BEMBRIDGE   Map 5 SZ68

The Crab & Lobster Inn ★★★★ INN

tel: 01983 872244 **32 Forelands Field Rd PO35 5TR**
email: info@crabandlobsterinn.co.uk **web:** www.crabandlobsterinn.co.uk
dir: From High St in Bembridge, 1st left after Boots into Forelands Rd. At right bend, left into Lane End Rd, 2nd right into Egerton Rd. At T-junct left into Howgate Rd. Road bears right & becomes Forelands Field Rd, follow brown inn signs

Great sea views and seafood at beamed inn

This inn is bedecked with flower baskets in summer and the stunning coastal location beside Bembridge Ledge means the raised deck and patio is a perfect place to sup locally brewed Goddards Fuggle-Dee-Dum bitter whilst watching yachts and fishing boats out in the eastern approach to the Solent. Locally caught seafood is one of the pub's great attractions, with dishes such as baked crab ramekin, moules marinière, seafood tagliatelle and lobster salad. There are meat and vegetarian dishes too, and sandwiches at lunchtime. Some of the light and airy bedrooms have outstanding sea views.

Open all day all wk 11-11 (Sun 11-10.30) **Food** Lunch all wk 12-2.30 (summer Sat-Sun & BH 2.30-5.30 limited menu) Dinner Sun-Thu 6-9, Fri-Sat 6-9.30 ⊕ ENTERPRISE INNS ◀ Sharp's Doom Bar, Goddards Fuggle-Dee-Dum, Greene King IPA, John Smith's Ⓐ Westons Stowford Press. ♀ 12 **Facilities** Non-diners area ♣ (Bar Garden) ♦♦ Children's menu Children's portions Garden ⨅ Parking WiFi **Rooms** 5

BEMBRIDGE *continued*

NEW The Pilot Boat Inn

tel: 01983 872077 **Station Rd PO35 5NN**
email: george@thepilotboatinn.com
dir: *Follow B3395 (Embankment Rd) around harbour. Pub on junct with Station Rd*

Welcoming harbourside local beside coastal footpath

With a startling, quirky look of a beached ark, this lively pub makes the most of its setting beside Bembridge Harbour, with an ever-varying choice of daily seafood specials progressing straight from creel to galley. Slow cooked lamb shank with all the trimmings is another staple at this accommodating local in what is said to be England's largest village, where beers from the Isle of Wight's own Goddards Brewery keep seafarers old and new in chatty mode. A winter fire warms the brightly appointed interior, dressed with nautical and other flags, whilst morris dancers may enliven a summer's afternoon.

Open all day all wk **Food** Lunch all wk 12-2.30 Dinner all wk 6-8.30 Av main course £11 Restaurant menu available all wk ⊕ FREE HOUSE ◀ Goddards Ale of Wight ♂ Westons Old Rosie. **Facilities** Non-diners area ♣ (Bar Restaurant Garden) ♦♦ Children's menu Children's portions Garden ⊟ Parking WiFi ▦ (notice required)

▌ **BONCHURCH**	Map 5 SZ57

The Bonchurch

tel: 01983 852611 **Bonchurch Shute PO38 1NU**
email: gillian@bonchurch-inn.co.uk **web:** www.bonchurch-inn.co.uk
dir: *Signed from A3055 in Bonchurch*

Family-run free house with an Italian emphasis

Tucked away in a secluded Dickensian-style courtyard, this small inn is in a quiet, off-the-road location. In fact, little has changed here since this former coaching inn and stables was granted a licence in the 1840s. Food is available lunchtime and evenings in the bar; choices range from sandwiches and salads to plenty of daily-fresh fish (sea bass, pollock and crab among the choices) and traditional meat dishes. Italian specialities are a prominent feature on account of the owners' heritage; try one of the pizzas, the tagliatelle carbonara, or the king prawn portofino (mushrooms, Pernod, cream and rice). Desserts also have an Italian bias – perhaps zabaglione, tiramisù or cassata.

Open all wk 12-3 6.30-11 Closed 25 Dec **Food** Lunch all wk 12-2 Dinner all wk 6.30-9 Av main course £12 ⊕ FREE HOUSE ◀ Courage Best Bitter, Wells Bombardier. **Facilities** Non-diners area ♣ (Bar) ♦♦ Children's menu Children's portions Family room Outside area ⊟ Parking WiFi

---

▌ **COWES**	Map 5 SZ49

Duke of York Inn ★★★ INN

tel: 01983 295171 **Mill Hill Rd PO31 7BT**
email: bookings@dukeofyorkcowes.co.uk **web:** www.dukeofyorkcowes.co.uk
dir: *In town centre*

Inn with a seafaring theme and seafood on the menu

This former coaching inn has been run by the same friendly family for over 40 years. Situated close to the centre of Cowes and the marina, the informal pub has a nautical theme running throughout. Everyone is made welcome here, even soggy, wet yachtsmen. Fuggle-Dee-Dum from the island's Goddards Brewery is just one real ale on offer. Quality home-cooked food with an emphasis on fresh seafood is available in the bar and restaurant and includes grilled sardines, seafood mixed grill, moules marinière, bangers and mash, and half a roast chicken, as well as daily blackboard specials and Sunday roasts. There are comfortable, individually decorated bedrooms.

Open all day all wk **Food** Lunch all wk 12-2.30 Dinner all wk 6-10 ⊕ ENTERPRISE INNS ◀ Goddards Fuggle-Dee-Dum, Sharp's Doom Bar, Ringwood Best Bitter

♂ Westons 1st Quality & Old Rosie. **Facilities** Non-diners area ♣ (Bar Restaurant Outside area) ♦♦ Children's menu Children's portions Outside area ⊟ Parking WiFi ▦ **Rooms** 13

The Fountain Inn ★★★ INN

tel: 01983 292397 **High St PO31 7AW**
email: 6447@greeneking.co.uk **web:** www.oldenglish.co.uk
dir: *Adjacent to Red Jet passenger ferry in town centre*

Quayside contentment at the heart of Cowes

An imposing foursquare Georgian building built to cater for travellers awaiting the mainland ferry that still plies from the dock behind the inn. Character oozes from the nooks and crannies peppering the public areas, where French King Charles X and family also took sustenance in 1830. The decking patio overlooking the bustling West Cowes Quay is a fine base at which to appreciate the Greene King beers or chow down on a robust menu of pub favourites like roasted cod loin, pan-seared black pearl scallops or Suffolk pork sausages with cheddar mash. Some of the en suite bedrooms have sea views.

Open all day all wk **Food** Lunch all wk 11-10 Dinner all wk 11-10 ⊕ GREENE KING ◀ IPA, Ruddles County, Morland Old Golden Hen. ♥ **Facilities** Non-diners area ♣ (Bar Outside area) ♦♦ Children's menu Children's portions Outside area ⊟ WiFi **Rooms** 20

▌ **FISHBOURNE**	Map 5 SZ59

The Fishbourne ★★★★ INN

tel: 01983 882823 **Fishbourne Ln PO33 4EU**
email: info@thefishbourne.co.uk **web:** www.thefishbourne.co.uk
dir: *From East Cowes ferry terminal to rdbt. 3rd exit signed Ryde & Newport. At T-junct left onto A3021 signed Ryde & Newport. At next rdbt 1st exit signed Newport. At next rdbt 1st exit onto A3054 signed Ryde. Left at lights into Fishbourne Ln signed Portsmouth. Pass ferry terminal to pub*

Top quality eating in a pub environment

Time your ferry crossing to Portsmouth carefully and, since it's down the same cul-de-sac as the Wightlink terminal, you'll be able to visit this mock-Tudor dining pub. A design-savvy approach to furnishing is apparent in the spacious bar, where there are smart leather sofas, and in the elegant dining area, where lunchtime sees sandwiches, baguettes, seafood specialities, deli boards and sharing platters, as well as old favourites like fish and chips, and sausages and mash. Daily-changing blackboard specials may include local shellfish, halibut wrapped in Parma ham; and slow-roasted pork belly. The en suite bedrooms are stylishly decorated with light and airy decor and modern amenities.

Open all day all wk **Food** Lunch all wk 12-2.30 Dinner all wk 6-9.30 (varies with season) ⊕ ENTERPRISE INNS ◀ Goddards Fuggle-Dee-Dum, Sharp's Doom Bar ♂ Westons Stowford Press. ♥ 11 **Facilities** Non-diners area ♦♦ Children's portions Garden ⊟ Parking WiFi **Rooms** 5

▌ **FRESHWATER**	Map 5 SZ38

The Red Lion   PICK OF THE PUBS

tel: 01983 754925 **Church Place PO40 9BP**
dir: *In Old Freshwater follow signs for All Saints Church*

Friendly village pub ideally located for harbour walks

Walkers, golfers and yachtsmen beat a path to the door of the Red Lion, which is located next to one of the oldest churches on the Isle of Wight. This welcoming pub can trace its origins back to the 11th century and the local stories flow over pints of Goddards Special and Fuggle-Dee-Dum. The bar has settles and sofas around well-scrubbed pine tables and polished flagstones. Many ingredients used are from the island and herbs and vegetables are grown in the pub's large garden. Mull over whether to start with herring roes on toast or scrambled egg and smoked salmon; then ponder a main of calves' liver with bacon and onion gravy or roasted pork belly with apple sauce. Old favourites include fish pie and gammon steak with parsley sauce. Finish with treacle tart or jam roly-poly and you'll be ready for snooze in front of the log fire.

Open all wk 11.30-3 5.30-11 (Sun 12-3 7-10.30) **Food** Lunch all wk 12-2 Dinner Mon-Sat 6.30-9, Sun 7-9 ⊕ ENTERPRISE INNS ◖ Goddards Special Bitter & Fuggle-Dee-Dum, Sharp's Doom Bar Ö Thatchers. **Facilities** Non-diners area ❀ (Bar Garden) Garden ⊟ Parking

GODSHILL
Map 5 SZ58

The Taverners
PICK OF THE PUBS

tel: 01983 840707 **High St PO38 3HZ**
dir: *Phone for detailed directions*

Village pub incorporating its own local food shop

A village pub with its own shop selling home-made foods from the kitchen, fine wines, and local products, The Taverners is run with an impressive commitment to keeping food and drink miles low. Meats and dairy products all come from Isle of Wight farmers, fish are from local waters, island fruit and vegetables are used when in season, and much else is locally caught, shot or foraged. Ten wines by the glass, Taverners Own real ale and Godshill cider are sold in the bar. Pub favourites and classics include lamb burger, beetroot, feta cheese, red onion and mint salad; triple baked cheese macaroni with cherry tomatoes; and ham, egg and chips. Daily specials have included grilled ox tongue with balsamic lentil salad and gremolata; and Brownrigg duck breast, duck hot pot, swede purée and sprout tops. In the garden, adjoining the vegetable plots, is a toddlers' play area.

Open all day all wk Closed 1st 3wks Jan **Food** Lunch all wk 12-3 Dinner Mon-Thu 6-9, Fri-Sat 6-9.30 Av main course £12 ⊕ PUNCH TAVERNS ◖ Taverners Own, Sharp's Doom Bar, Brains The Rev. James, Black Sheep, Butcombe Ö Westons Stowford Press, Godshill. ☗ 10 **Facilities** Non-diners area ❀ (Bar Garden) ♦ Children's menu Children's portions Play area Garden ⊟ Parking WiFi ▤ (notice required)

HULVERSTONE
Map 5 SZ38

The Sun Inn at Hulverstone

tel: 01983 741124 **Main Rd PO30 4EH**
email: info@sun-hulverstone.com
dir: *Between Mottistone & Brook on B3399*

Village-edge inn in stunning location

All flagstones, floorboards, beams, settles and fires, this lovely ancient thatched pub occupies an enviable position in the gently rolling countryside towards the western tip of the island. With English Channel views from the pleasant garden here, customers can indulge in Wight-brewed beers from Goddards and choose from a menu almost entirely sourced from the island's own producers. The village bakery, farm shop, local fishmongers and cheesemaker ensure the produce is the freshest possible. Cue beer-battered cod; or chicken breast with bacon and Isle of Wight Blue cheese, whilst the specials board details the home-made pie of the day. Different diets can be catered for, please ask. Restaurant booking is advised.

Open all day all wk **Food** Lunch all wk 12-9 Dinner all wk 12-9 ⊕ ENTERPRISE INNS ◖ Ringwood Fortyniner, Goddards Fuggle-Dee-Dum, Adnams Southwold Bitter, Otter Ale, Island Ales, Rotating ales Ö Westons Stowford Press. **Facilities** Non-diners area ❀ (Bar Garden) ♦ Children's portions Garden ⊟ Parking WiFi ▤ (notice required)

NEWPORT
Map 5 SZ48

NEW The Stag ★★★★ INN

tel: 01983 522709 **Stag Ln PO30 5TW**
email: info@thestagiow.co.uk **web:** www.thestagiow.co.uk
dir: *On A3020 between Cowes & Newport*

Quality dining at the heart of the island

Opened by new owners in May 2013 after refurbishment, The Stag belongs to the island-based Inns of Distinction group of pubs. Pale-coloured wood predominates in the attractive long bar, where Sharp's Doom Bar is on tap and sandwiches and baguettes come with dressed salad and home-made vegetable crisps. The island is the prime source of ingredients for dishes such as hand-sliced ham; sausages and mash; rump steak; and lobster and crab salads. From the specials board there's fried corn-fed chicken with chorizo and sweet potato Parmentier; and grilled sea bream with samphire and fennel purée.

Open all day all wk **Food** Lunch all wk 12-2.30 Dinner all wk 6-9.30 Set menu available ⊕ PUNCH TAVERNS ◖ Sharp's Doom Bar Ö Westons Stowford Press. ☗ 12 **Facilities** Non-diners area ♦ Children's portions Garden ⊟ Parking WiFi **Rooms** 4

NINGWOOD
Map 5 SZ38

Horse & Groom

tel: 01983 760672 **Main Rd PO30 4NW**
email: info@horse-and-groom.com
dir: *On A3054 (Yarmouth to Newport road)*

Great for families with young children

Just a couple of miles west of Yarmouth on the Newport road, this large landmark pub is certainly family-friendly. There's a pleasant garden with a large children's play area, and an extensive and well-priced kids' menu. Food is served daily from noon until 9pm, and the offering ranges from jacket potatoes and light bites to pub favourites like home-made lasagne; chargrilled pork loin with English mustard sauce; and sticky toffee pudding plus a specials board offering seasonal specialities. Four-footed family members are also welcome on the stone and wood-floor indoor areas.

Open all day all wk **Food** Lunch all wk 12-9 Dinner all wk 12-9 ⊕ ENTERPRISE INNS ◖ Ringwood, Sharp's Doom Bar Ö Westons Stowford Press, Somersby Cider. ☗ 13 **Facilities** Non-diners area ❀ (Bar Garden) ♦ Children's menu Children's portions Play area Garden ⊟ Parking WiFi ▤ (notice required)

NITON
Map 5 SZ57

Buddle Inn

tel: 01983 730243 **St Catherines Rd PO38 2NE**
email: sayhi@buddleinn.co.uk
dir: *From Ventnor take Whitwell Rd (signed Niton). In Whitwell left after church into Kemming Rd (signed Niton). In Niton, left opposite Norris (shop), right into St Catherines Rd*

Popular with hikers and ramblers

With the English Channel on one side and the coastal path on the other, this 16th-century, former cliff-top farmhouse and smugglers' inn is one of the island's oldest hostelries. The interior has the full traditional complement - stone flags, oak beams and a large open fire, great real ales on tap, and muddy boots are welcome. Expect hearty home-made food, deep-filled Buddle pies, a large specials board full of seasonal dishes, and a great variety of freshly caught local fish. Two beer festivals a year take place - in June and September.

Open all day all wk 12-10.30 (Wed 12-11 Fri-Sat 12-11.30) **Food** Lunch all wk 12-9 Dinner all wk 12-9 ⊕ ENTERPRISE INNS ◖ Goddards Fuggle-Dee-Dum, Ale of Wight & Winter Warmer, Sharp's Doom Bar, Greene King Abbot Ale Ö Westons Stowford Press. ☗ 12 **Facilities** Non-diners area ❀ (All areas) ♦ Children's menu Children's portions Garden Outside area ⊟ Beer festival Parking ▤ (notice required)

PICK OF THE PUBS

The New Inn

SHALFLEET Map 5 SZ48

tel: 01983 531314
Main Rd PO30 4NS
email: info@thenew-inn.co.uk
web: www.thenew-inn.co.uk
dir: *6m from Newport to Yarmouth on A3054*

Recommended for their seafood

One of the island's best-known dining pubs, The New Inn's name refers to how it rose phoenix-like from the charred remains of an older inn, which burnt down in 1743. Set on the National Trust owned Newtown River estuary, this charming whitewashed pub is an absolute mecca for sailing folk. Original inglenook fireplaces, flagstone floors and low-beamed ceilings give the place bags of character. The waterside location sets the tone for the menu; the pub has a reputation for excellent seafood dishes, with lobster and cracked local crab usually available. Daily specials are chalked on blackboards around the place. Further fish options may include whole local mackerel with roasted fennel and tomato balsamic; mussels cooked in cider, shallots and cream, or fish pie. Meat lovers could try slow cooked pork belly with rainbow chard and rich port sauce; or locally made pork and chive sausages with wholegrain mustard mash. Vegetarians can enjoy the likes of Mediterranean stuffed butternut squash

topped with Isle of Wight soft cheese. There's also a list of dishes for 'smaller appetites', including beer-battered fish and chips; local 5oz rump steak and chips with peas or gnocchi with sautéed kale, almonds, cream and parmesan – but if it's a light lunch you're seeking, be sure to consider the best-selling hand-picked crabmeat sandwiches and baguettes or the ploughman's featuring local cheeses. At the bar you'll find Goddards Fuggle-Dee-Dum and Doom Bar among others, Westons scrumpy cider and over 60 worldwide wines comprise one of the island's most extensive selections.

Open all day all wk **Food** Lunch all wk 12-2.30 Dinner all wk 6-9.30 (varies with season) ⊕ ENTERPRISE INNS ◨ Goddards Fuggle-Dee-Dum, Sharp's Doom Bar ♨ Westons Stowford Press & Traditional Scrumpy. ♞ 11 **Facilities** ❧ (Bar Garden) ⅋ Children's portions Garden ⊨ Parking WiFi

---

■ NORTHWOOD   Map 5 SZ49

Travellers Joy

tel: 01983 298024 **85 Pallance Rd PO31 8LS**
email: thetravellersjoy@hotmail.co.uk
dir: *Phone for detailed directions*

Family-friendly haven for ale lovers

A little way inland from Cowes, this 300-year-old alehouse is well-known for its eight real ales on handpump all year round. Happily new owners Ashley and Katie are continuing this tradition, and planning beer festivals in the months of July and September. Menus of classic pub food are improving too, with the addition of fresh fish and locally farmed produce; daily specials change with the seasons and availability. The appeal is to all-comers — from walkers and cyclists to locals and tourists, especially families with children and dogs. A kiddies' play area and bicycle racks have already been installed in the large garden, and the pétanque terrain with a pint in hand is a great attraction on a summer's evening.

Open all day all wk 12-12 **Food** Lunch all wk 12-9 Dinner all wk 12-9 Av main course £8.95 ⊕ FREE HOUSE ◀ Island Wight Gold, Courage Directors, Caledonian Deuchars IPA, St Austell Tribute, Timothy Taylor Landlord Ö Biddenden Bushels, Scrumpy. **Facilities** Non-diners area ❖ (Bar Garden) ♦ Children's menu Children's portions Play area Garden ⊟ Beer festival Parking WiFi 🚐 (notice required)

■ ROOKLEY   Map 5 SZ58

The Chequers

tel: 01983 840314 **Niton Rd PO38 3NZ**
email: richard@chequersinn-iow.co.uk
dir: *Phone for detailed directions*

A country pub at the heart of the island

While possessing many modern facilities, this family-friendly country free house with log fires and a large garden still retains a traditional character that recalls its days as a customs and excise house in the 18th century. Current landlords Richard and Sue Holmes know the names of all their predecessors back to 1799. A reputation for good food at reasonable prices can be attributed to a repertoire of bar snacks, children's dishes, sandwiches, cold platters, grilled meats and main menu items like fresh seafood specials; Godshill game sausage; chicken and seafood stir-fry; and home-made vegetable curry.

Open all day all wk 11-11 (Sun 11.30-11) **Food** Lunch Mon-Sat 12-9.30, Sun 12-9 Dinner Mon-Sat 12-9.30, Sun 12-9 ⊕ FREE HOUSE ◀ Ringwood Best Bitter & Fortyniner, Guest ales Ö Thatchers. ❧ **Facilities** Non-diners area ❖ (Bar Garden) ♦ Children's menu Children's portions Play area Family room Garden ⊟ Parking WiFi

---

■ SEAVIEW   Map 5 SZ69

The Boathouse ★★★★ INN

tel: 01983 810616 **Springvale Rd PO34 5AW**
email: info@theboathouseiow.co.uk **web:** www.theboathouseiow.co.uk
dir: *From Ryde take A3055. Left onto A3330, left into Puckpool Hill. Pub 0.25m on right*

Watch the ocean liners from this seaside location

At the rather chic and certainly aptly-named Seaview, the powder-blue-painted Boathouse overlooks the eastern Solent. The setting really is spectacular. Well-kept ales and an extensive global wine listing complement specials boards that make the most of freshly landed local fish. Other choices include lunchtime baguettes and sandwiches; Isle of Wight rump and sirloin steaks; whole cracked crab salad; and macaroni cheese with ale, melted Gallybagger cheese and garlic bread. Children might like dishes such as sausages with chips and peas; and baked penne pasta with wild mushrooms, roast vegetables and goats' cheese topping. Sea views are available in some of the stylish en suite bedrooms.

Open all day all wk 9am-11pm (varies with season) **Food** Lunch all week 12-2.30 Dinner all week 6-9.30 (varies with season) ⊕ PUNCH TAVERNS ◀ George Gale & Co Seafarers, Sharp's Doom Bar Ö Westons Stowford Press. ❧ 11 **Facilities** Non-diners area ♦ Children's portions Garden ⊟ Parking WiFi **Rooms** 4

The Seaview Hotel & Restaurant ★★★ HL ⊛

PICK OF THE PUBS

tel: 01983 612711 **High St PO34 5EX**
email: reception@seaviewhotel.co.uk **web:** www.seaviewhotel.co.uk
dir: *B3330 from Ryde, left signed Puckpool, along seafront, hotel on left*

Great combination of coastal views and island produce

One of life's great pleasures has to be sitting on the terrace outside this ivy-clad hotel, sipping beer from Wight brewers like Yates and drinking in the views over racing dinghies to one of the Solent's remarkable sea forts. Warm and welcoming, The Pump Bar is a hidden gem at the heart of the hotel and perfect for ladies who lunch, old friends spinning yarns or families chilling out; its decor reflects the seaside location with a quirky selection of lobster pots, oars, masts and other nautical memorabilia. Fittingly, seafood features strongly on the one AA Rosette menu, with soup de poisson starter or pan-fried skate wing served with wild garlic ticking all the right boxes. The owners raise deer, highland cattle and pigs on their farm, ensuring traceability and top quality for the carte and specials. Pork belly with Savoy cabbage and bacon; cottage pie; or pork sausages with mash and caramelised onion gravy are typical of the traditionally-styled choices. Comfy accommodation is the icing on the cake here.

Open all wk 10-3 6-11 **Food** Lunch all wk 12-2.30 Dinner all wk 6.30-9.30 Av main course £10.95 Restaurant menu available all wk ⊕ FREE HOUSE ◀ Goddards, Island Ales, Yates Ö Westons Stowford Press. **Facilities** Non-diners area ❖ (Bar Restaurant Outside area) ♦ Children's menu Children's portions Outside area ⊟ Parking WiFi **Rooms** 29

■ SHALFLEET   Map 5 SZ48

The New Inn   PICK OF THE PUBS

See Pick of the Pubs on opposite page

■ SHORWELL   Map 5 SZ48

The Crown Inn   PICK OF THE PUBS

See Pick of the Pubs on page 272

■ WHIPPINGHAM   Map 5 SZ59

The Folly

tel: 01983 297171 **Folly Ln PO32 6NB**
dir: *Phone for detailed directions*

Extensive menus and a large beer garden

The Folly stands beside the River Medina and you can, if you wish, travel here from Cowes on the pub's own waterbus. In the bar are timbers from the hull of an old barge, and even the restaurant tables are named after boats. The menus offer a wide choice of lighter bites — sandwiches, wraps, jacket potatoes and salads — as well as gourmet burgers, steaks and grills, and classic pub grub. In addition, there are sharing plates, daily specials and international mains such as aubergine gratin; chicken fajitas; and sweet potato, apricot, chickpea and red pepper skewers. Wednesday evening is 'Get Spicy' curry night.

Open all day all wk **Food** Lunch all wk 12-5 Dinner all wk 5-10 ⊕ GREENE KING ◀ IPA, Morland Old Speckled Hen Ö Aspall. ❧ 11 **Facilities** ❖ (All areas) ♦ Children's menu Children's portions Garden Outside area ⊟ Parking WiFi 🚐

PICK OF THE PUBS

The Crown Inn

SHORWELL   Map 5 SZ48

tel: 01983 740293
Walkers Ln PO30 3JZ
email: enquiries@crowninnshorwell.co.uk
web: www.crowninnshorwell.co.uk
dir: *Left at top of Carisbrooke High
Street. Shorwell approx 6m*

Family-friendly village pub beside a delightful stream

A traditional country pub in the pretty
village of Shorwell, a short hop south-
west from Newport. After World War II,
the Crown was one of the first pubs to
boast an island-wide trade thanks to
the entertainment value of its then
landlord, Vivian 'Nutty' Edwards, who
entertained customers nightly with his
music hall approach to tales from his
army days; Nutty retired in the 1960s to
become the island's last Chelsea
Pensioner. Today's owners, Nigel and
Pamela Wynne, are continuing this
heritage of welcoming hospitality, with
a family-friendly approach throughout
the all-day operation. The rear garden
boasts a children's play area, bounded
by a spring-fed stream where trout,
ducks and moorhens can be spotted.
Parts of the Crown date from the 17th
century, although its varying floor levels
suggest many subsequent alterations.
The most recent building work has
increased the floor area significantly,
but the pub's character has been
preserved with log fires burning and

antique furniture in abundance. Real
ales include Goddards that's brewed on
the island, while cider comes from
Healey's Farm in Cornwall. If you
overindulge, you might glimpse the
female ghost who is friendly but shows
her disapproval of customers playing
cards by throwing them on the floor (the
cards, that is, not the customers). The
kitchen makes good use of locally
sourced lamb, beef, game and fish in
daily specials. Otherwise pub staples
include lasagne, curries, scampi or
beer-battered fish with chips, a range of
pizzas, and sausages with mash.
Steaks, gammon and burgers from the
chargrill are understandably popular,
but vegetarian choice is good too with
dishes such as wild mushroom and
spinach gratin.

Open all day all wk **Food** all wk 12-9.30
Av main course £11 ⊕ ENTERPRISE INNS
◀ Sharp's Doom Bar, Adnams
Broadside, Goddards, St Austell Tribute
Ⓞ Westons Stowford Press, Healey's.
♟ 12 **Facilities** Non-diners area ❖ (Bar
Restaurant Garden) ⁙ Children's menu
Children's portions Play area Garden ⊓
Parking WiFi ▭ (notice required)

KENT

BEARSTED
Map 7 TQ85

The Oak on the Green

tel: 01622 737976 **Bearsted Green ME14 4EJ**
email: headoffice@villagegreenrestaurants.com
dir: *In village centre*

Beefy treats beside the village green

Half a Kentish hop garden drapes the beams in this lively old pub, known for its thoughtful, quality menu and the sometimes unusual real ales. The oak-shaded terrace of this eye-catching gabled pub, which dates from 1665, overlooks a corner of the immense village green and cricket pitch, great for those long summer evenings. The kitchens were once the village goal; escaping from them today are freshly-prepared dishes with a distinct nod towards Scottish beef - the range of gastro-burgers is notable, or plump for a chicken Cordon Bleu, whilst seafood lovers should go for the whole, grilled local plaice perhaps.

Open all day all wk Closed 25 Dec **Food** Lunch Mon-Sat 12-10.30, Sun 12-10 Dinner Mon-Sat 12-10.30, Sun 12-10 Av main course £10 ⊕ FREE HOUSE ◀ Harvey's Sussex Best Bitter, Old Dairy Red Top & Guest ale ♂ Biddenden. ☂ **Facilities** Non-diners area ♣ (Bar Restaurant) ♦♦ Children's menu Children's portions Outside area ⨅ Parking WiFi ☞

BENENDEN
Map 7 TQ83

The Bull at Benenden
PICK OF THE PUBS

tel: 01580 240054 **The Street TN17 4DE**
email: enquiries@thebullatbenenden.co.uk
dir: *From A229 onto B2086 to Benenden. Or from Tenterden take A28 S towards Hastings. Right onto B2086*

One for all the family

Missing out on 16th-century origins by a whisker - it was built in 1601 - The Bull overlooks the village green and cricket pitch. Hard-to-miss features include the unusual chinoiserie windows, the huge brick inglenook fireplace, the rounded wooden bar, and the antique furniture collection. Dark Star, Harvey's and Larkins breweries man the pumps, with Biddenden's own Bushels cider also ready for duty. The traditional pub menu offers steak and kidney pudding; fresh cod in beer batter; wild rabbit stew; and Mrs Bull's home-made pies and suet puddings "with a top, bottom and side". Mr Bull lends his name to a range of burgers, including Moroccan spiced lamb; chickpea and bean; and American beef with Monterey Jack cheese. For children there's wholetail scampi, home-cooked ham with free-range eggs, and pasta pomodoro. Colouring pens and paper, and high chairs are also provided (for kids, that is). Outside is a 'secret' garden.

Open all day all wk noon-mdnt **Food** Lunch Mon-Sat 12-2.30, Sun 12-4 Dinner Mon-Sat 6-9.20 Av main course £11.50 ⊕ FREE HOUSE ◀ Dark Star Hophead, Larkins, Harvey's, Guest ales ♂ Biddenden Bushels. ☂ 9 **Facilities** Non-diners area ♣ (Bar Garden) ♦♦ Children's menu Children's portions Garden ⨅ Parking ☞ (notice required)

BIDDENDEN
Map 7 TQ83

The Three Chimneys
PICK OF THE PUBS

tel: 01580 291472 **Biddenden Rd TN27 8LW**
dir: *From A262 midway between Biddenden & Sissinghurst, follow Frittenden signs. (Pub visible from main road). Pub immediately on left*

Pretty village pub with excellent food

With an original, small-roomed layout and old-fashioned furnishings, this 15th-century timbered pub is a classic. Further atmosphere is provided by low beams, wood-panelled walls, worn brick floors, log fires, evening candlelight and nothing electronic except the till. From the Garden Room and conservatory customers can head for the secluded, heated patio and huge shrub-filled garden. A good idea of the locally sourced food, all chalked up daily, can be had from examples such as pan-roasted breast of guinea fowl with baby onions, mushrooms and pancetta; sweet chilli-glazed fillet of salmon with spicy courgette and aubergine ragout; and fresh herb and pine nut pesto couscous with grilled goats' cheese on balsamic roasted vegetables. Harvey's Sussex Old and Adnams ales and the heady (8.4 per cent ABV) Biddenden cider are tapped direct from cask. The village sign depicts the Biddenden Maids, Siamese-twins that were born here in 1100.

Open all wk 11.30-3 5.30-11 (Sat-Sun 11.30-4 5.30-11) Closed 25 Dec **Food** Lunch all wk 12-2.30 Dinner all wk 6.30-9.30 ⊕ FREE HOUSE ◀ Harvey's Sussex Old Ale, Adnams ♂ Biddenden. ☂ 10 **Facilities** Non-diners area ♣ (Bar Garden) ♦♦ Children's portions Garden ⨅ Parking

BOSSINGHAM
Map 7 TR14

The Hop Pocket

tel: 01227 709866 **The Street CT4 6DY**
dir: *Phone for detailed directions*

A warm welcome at this family-friendly village inn

Birds of prey and an animal corner for children are among the more unusual attractions at this family pub in the heart of Kent. Canterbury is only five miles away and the county's delightfully scenic coast and countryside are within easy reach. As this is a free house there is a good range of ales to accompany dishes like fish pie, supreme of chicken, spicy salmon, Cajun beef, chilli nachos and fish platter. There is also an extensive range of sandwiches and omelettes.

Open all wk 11-3 6-12 (Sat & Sun all day) **Food** Lunch all wk 12-2.30 Dinner Mon-Sat 7-9.30 ⊕ FREE HOUSE ◀ Fuller's London Pride, Wadworth 6X, Adnams, Purity, Local Ales. **Facilities** Non-diners area ♣ (Bar Restaurant Garden) ♦♦ Children's portions Play area Garden ⨅ Parking WiFi ☞

BRABOURNE
Map 7 TR14

The Five Bells Inn

tel: 01303 813334 **The Street TN25 5LP**
email: visitus@fivebellsinnbrabourne.com
dir: *5m E of Ashford*

Blowing the trumpet for fine Kent produce

Environmental responsibility is important to the owners of this old village inn which trims the North Downs. Locally sourced wood supplies 25% of the energy here, whilst most of the food and drink is traceable locally. Thus the beers travel the few miles from Goacher's Maidstone brewery, wines are from Biddenden, meats arrive from Kent's Romney Marsh or the Alkham Valley, and seafood from boats at Hythe. Tempting in ramblers from the popular walking country hereabouts may be sea marsh lamb's liver and Brabourne pork sausage, or Dungeness catch of the day with a herb and oat crust, cooked in the wood-fired oven. The on-site deli/shop is a trove of all things comestible and Kentish.

Open all day all wk **Food** Contact pub for details ⊕ FREE HOUSE ◀ Goacher's, Hopdaemon, Brabourne Stout, Guest ales ♂ Biddenden. **Facilities** Non-diners area ♣ (All areas) ♦♦ Children's portions Garden Outside area ⨅ Parking WiFi ☞ (notice required)

CANTERBURY
Map 7 TR15

The Chapter Arms

tel: 01227 738340 **New Town St, Chartham Hatch CT4 7LT**
email: info@chapterarms.com
dir: *A28 from Canterbury towards Ashford. Right signed Chartham Hatch. 1m to pub*

An acre of gardens and a talented kitchen team

This charming and picturesque free house was once three cottages owned by Canterbury Cathedral's Dean and Chapter – hence the name. It sits on the North Downs Way overlooking apple orchards and oast houses. The à la carte menu includes ballotine of salmon with smoked salmon and beetroot and spinach salad; and deep-fried whitebait to start, followed by spatchcock Gressingham poussin with Parmentier potatoes, or sea bass with basil with spinach red pepper butter. Look out for the Spoofers' Bar, where you can enjoy a game of spoof; The Chapter Arms hosted the World Spoofing Championships in 2010 and was featured in Rory McGrath and Will Mellor's TV programme *Champions of the World* in 2013. A barbecue is available for special events.

Open all wk 11-3 6-11 (Sun 12-5) **Food** Lunch all wk 12-2.30 Dinner Mon-Sat 6.30-9 Set menu available Restaurant menu available all wk ⊕ FREE HOUSE ◀ Greene King IPA & London Glory, Seasonal Ales ☼ Thatchers. ☗ 10 **Facilities** Non-diners area ❤ (Bar Garden) ◀❙ Children's menu Children's portions Play area Garden ⊨ Parking WiFi ▥

The Dove Inn ◉
PICK OF THE PUBS

tel: 01227 751360 **Plum Pudding Ln, Dargate ME13 9HB**
email: bookings@thedovedargate.co.uk
dir: *6m from Canterbury; 4m from Whitstable. Phone for detailed directions*

Friendly village pub with great food

Just inland from the old port of Whitstable, this classic village inn slumbers in a tranquil landscape of wooded hills and the fruit orchards for which Kent is widely renowned. New hands on the handpumps here have settled seamlessly into this Shepherd Neame pub, with its matchboarding, stripped-wood floors and log-burning stove. Rustic, candlelit tables welcome diners keen to sample the menu, drawing on quality local ingredients which are soundly handled, offering a balanced choice of contemporary country dishes. It is a moveable feast, so featured dishes will change; a selection may include starter beetroot carpaccio of pickled baby beetroot, glazed goats' cheese and micro herbs, leading to roast fillet of beef, broccoli and Stilton purée, chive mash, wild mushrooms and red wine jus. Outside is a gorgeous cottage garden where, appropriately, a dovecote and doves present an agreeably scenic backdrop for an alfresco meal or quiet pint, or to wonder at the intriguing pub game known as bat and trap.

Open 12-3 6-12 (Fri 12-12 Sun 12-5) Closed Mon **Food** Lunch Wed-Sat 12-2.30 Dinner Wed-Sat 6.30-9 ⊕ SHEPHERD NEAME ◀ Master Brew, Spitfire, Whitstable Pale Ale, Seasonal ales. ☗ 10 **Facilities** Non-diners area ❤ (Bar Garden) ◀❙ Children's portions Garden ⊨ Parking WiFi ▥ (notice required)

The Granville

tel: 01227 700402 **Street End, Lower Hardres CT4 7AL**
email: thegranville.canterbury@gmail.com
dir: *On B2068, 2m from Canterbury towards Hythe*

Ever-changing art at pub with contemporary character

As well as a striking feature central fireplace/flue, this light and airy pub not far from Canterbury displays an interesting series of roll-over art exhibitions and installations (lino cuts, photographs, sculptures). Ample parking, a patio and large beer garden where summer barbecues take place make this Shepherd Neame pub good for families and dogs, whilst locals head for the public bar. The kitchen team has a confident approach to utilising the best that Kent and the enfolding seas can provide. You could start with warm salad of teal, beetroot and orange, followed

perhaps by roast venison haunch with celeriac and wild mushrooms; or roast cod fillet with tartare sauce. Finish with roast plums on French toast with cinnamon ice cream.

Open all wk 12-3.30 5.30-11 Closed 26 Dec **Food** Lunch Tue-Sat 12-2.30 Dinner Tue-Sat 6.30-9 Av main course £15.95 Set menu available Restaurant menu available Tue-Sun ⊕ SHEPHERD NEAME ◀ Master Brew, Seasonal ale ☼ Thatchers. **Facilities** Non-diners area ❤ (Bar Garden) ◀❙ Children's portions Garden ⊨ Parking WiFi

The Red Lion
PICK OF THE PUBS

tel: 01227 721339 **Stodmarsh CT3 4BA**
email: info@theredlionstodmarsh.com
dir: *From Canterbury take A257 towards Sandwich, left into Stodmarsh Rd to Stodmarsh*

Modern British food in a pretty Kent village

An inn full of character on the edge of the renowned Stodmarsh National Nature Reserve, where rare raptors and waterbirds co-exist amidst tidal creeks and reedy marshland. The Red Lion is also ideally placed for explorers keen to escape the busy medieval streets of nearby Canterbury. Kent-boarding and hang-tiling catch the eye outside; the inside is busy with ephemera, boarded flooring and beams dressed with hop-bines, with gravity-dispensed beers stillaged behind the bar. Add cracking log fires in winter and a secluded, flowery beer garden for long summer days; the scene is completed by a menu of solidly British dishes with a modern twist. New owners have retained both the quirkiness of the pub and the high quality of the food; typically a starter of sloe gin cured salmon with rye bread and dill cream, followed by a mains choice of braised shin of veal with celeriac, saffron and tomato risotto; or oxtail slow cooked in ale for eight hours. Tuesday is pie night.

Open all day 11.30-11 (Sat 11.30-11.30 Sun 12-5) Closed Sun eve **Food** Lunch Mon-Sat 12-2.15, Sun 12-2.30 Dinner Mon-Sat 6.30-9.15 Av main course £15 ⊕ FREE HOUSE ◀ Greene King IPA, Shmaltz Brewing company He'Brew Genesis Ale ☼ Thatchers. **Facilities** Non-diners area ❤ (Bar Restaurant Garden) ◀❙ Children's menu Children's portions Play area Family room Garden ⊨ Parking WiFi ▥

CHARING
Map 7 TQ94

The Bowl Inn

tel: 01233 712256 **Egg Hill Rd TN27 0HG**
email: rooms@bowl-inn.co.uk
dir: *M20 junct 8/9, A20 to Charing, then A252 towards Canterbury. Left at top of Charing Hill into Bowl Rd, 1.25m*

Popular inn especially with walkers and cyclists

Standing high on top of the North Downs in an Area of Outstanding Natural Beauty, this popular pub was originally built as a farmhouse in 1512. For over 20 years it has been run by the Paine family, who have retained the old-world charm courtesy of warming winter fires in the large inglenook fireplace. The well-priced menu includes bar snacks of spinach and feta cheese goujons, plus a main menu featuring cheese and ham ploughman's, sausage sandwiches and steak baps. An annual beer festival takes place in mid-July.

Open all wk Mon-Thu 4-11.30 (Fri-Sat 12-12 Sun 12-11) **Food** Lunch Fri-Sun 12-9.30 Dinner Mon-Thu 4-9.30, Fri-Sun 12-9.30 ⊕ FREE HOUSE ◀ Fuller's London Pride, Adnams Southwold Bitter, Harvey's Sussex Best Bitter, Whitstable East India Pale Ale, Young's Bitter. **Facilities** Non-diners area ❤ (Bar Garden) ◀❙ Garden ⊨ Beer festival Parking WiFi ▥ (notice required)

PICK OF THE PUBS

Castle Inn

CHIDDINGSTONE   Map 6 TQ54

Tel: 01892 870247

TN8 7AH

email: info@castleinn-kent.co.uk

web: www.castleinn-kent.co.uk

dir: *1.5m S of B2027 between Tonbridge & Edenbridge*

Historic inn in film-set village

Arguably one of England's prettiest villages, Chiddingstone is a fine example of a Tudor one-street village. To ensure its preservation, the National Trust bought it in 1939, part of the deal included the Castle Inn, built in 1420 when it was known as Waterslip House. It was over three centuries later that two brothers opened it as the Five Bells. Timber-framed and tile-hung, the inn — indeed, the whole village — may seem familiar, because it has been the backdrop to numerous films requiring scenes of a rural England now largely vanished. The heavily beamed saloon bar serves beers from Larkins, brewed a few hundred yards away, and Harvey's from Lewes in neighbouring East Sussex; about 150 wines are on the wine list. Although chef John McManus is also the proprietor, it's really because of what he and his team do in the kitchen and restaurant that attracts the most attention. For a start, they ensure a good lunchtime range of bar snacks and main and light meals, from a ploughman's to smoked haddock

fishcake, and specials too. There's also plenty of choice at dinner: start maybe with mosaic of free-range chicken with tarragon, wild mushrooms and artichoke; follow with cottage pie, pickled red cabbage and cheddar mash; or rump steak, grilled mushroom, vine tomatoes, triple cooked chips and peppercorn sauce; and finish with Baileys crème brûlée. On Sundays a set three-course lunch might feature crayfish cocktail; sirloin of Kentish beef with crispy roast potatoes, Yorkshire pudding and pan gravy; and lemon posset with home-made shortbread. Behind the inn is a vine-hung courtyard with its own bar, then over a bridge are a beautifully tended lawn and flowerbeds.

Open all day all wk 11-11 (Sun 12-10.30) **Food** Lunch Mon-Fri 12-2, Sat-Sun 12-4 Dinner Mon-Sat 7-9.30 ⊕ FREE HOUSE ◀ Larkins Traditional, Porter & Platinum Blonde, Harvey's Sussex Ö Westons Stowford Press. ₹ 9 **Facilities** Non-diners area ✿ (Bar Garden) ♦️ Children's menu Children's portions Garden ⋒ WiFi 🚌 (notice required)

CHARING continued

The Oak

tel: 01233 712612 **5 High St TN27 0HU**
email: info@theoakcharing.co.uk
dir: *M20 junct 9, A20 towards Maidstone. 5m to Charing. Right into High St*

Contemporary cuisine in a picturesque inn

This gabled old inn in one of Kent's prettiest villages makes the most of its location, sourcing beers from Nelson, across the North Downs in Chatham, and harvesting produce from the bountiful surrounding acres of the 'Garden of England'. High-quality ingredients are sourced for the robust modern English menus. Fish from Hythe and Rye, pork and lamb from downland farms, and vegetables from local growers feature in dishes such as pan-seared fillet of smoked haddock on sautéed leeks with crème fraîche mash.

Open all wk 11-11 (Sun 12-10.30) **Food** Lunch Mon-Sat 12-2.30, Sun 12-4 Dinner Mon-Thu 6-9, Fri-Sat 6-9.30 Restaurant menu available all wk ⊕ FREE HOUSE ◀ Shepherd Neame Master Brew, Guest ales. **Facilities** Non-diners area ❄ (Bar Outside area) ♦♦ Children's menu Children's portions Outside area Parking WiFi

---

| CHIDDINGSTONE | Map 6 TQ54 |

Castle Inn   PICK OF THE PUBS

See Pick of the Pubs on page 275

| CHILHAM | Map 7 TR05 |

The White Horse

tel: 01227 730355 **The Square CT4 8BY**
email: thewhitehorsechilham@outlook.com
dir: *Take A28 from Canterbury then A252, in 1m turn left*

One of the most photographed pubs in Britain

The White Horse is situated opposite the 15th-century village square where the annual May Fair is held; the square is a delightfully haphazard mix of gabled, half-timbered houses, shops, and inns dating from the late Middle Ages, with the North Downs Way passing through. This flint and stone inn, now with new landlords, offers a traditional atmosphere and a wide selection of real ales from breweries like Sharp's, White Horse and Shepherd Neame. The modern cooking is based on fresh local produce. The bar menu offers sandwiches, ploughman's and dishes like pie of the week; mushroom Wellington; and chilli con carne. An evening menu could easily tempt with chicken cake and home-made lemon mayo; lamb rack chops, mustard mash, greens and red wine jus; and rich chocolate tart with raspberry compôte.

Open all day all wk noon-close Closed 25 Dec eve **Food** Lunch Mon-Fri 12-3, Sat-Sun all day Dinner Mon-Fri 6-9, Sat-Sun all day Av main course £10 Set menu available Restaurant menu available all wk ⊕ ENTERPRISE INNS ◀ Shepherd Neame Master Brew, Sharp's Doom Bar, White Horse Ale, Guest ale ♂ Thatchers Gold. ☂
Facilities Non-diners area ❄ (Bar Restaurant Garden) ♦♦ Children's menu Children's portions Garden ⊼ Beer festival Parking WiFi ⛟ (notice required)

| CHILLENDEN | Map 7 TR25 |

The Griffins Head   PICK OF THE PUBS

See Pick of the Pubs on opposite page

| CHIPSTEAD | Map 6 TQ55 |

George & Dragon

tel: 01732 779019 **39 High St TN13 2RW**
email: info@georgeanddragonchipstead.com
dir: *Phone for detailed directions*

Sincerity in everything is the watchword here

The delights of this 16th-century village gastro-pub are easily summarised: the welcoming open fires, the heavy oak beams and solid furnishings; the splendidly beamed upstairs restaurant; and the tree-house-inspired private dining room. Then there's Westerham Brewery's specially-produced George's Marvellous Medicine ale; and finally, the food, using top free-range or organic meats from farms in Kent and neighbouring counties, and sustainable fish from south-east coastal waters. Daily-changing menus might list grilled skate wing with lemon and caper butter; seared haunch of Chart Farm venison with Jerusalem artichoke and truffle; and beetroot and goats' cheese risotto.

Open all day all wk 11-11 Closed 1 Jan **Food** Lunch Mon-Fri 12-3, Sat-Sun 12-4 Dinner Mon-Sat 6-9.30, Sun 6-8.30 ⊕ FREE HOUSE ◀ Westerham George's Marvellous Medicine & Grasshopper ♂ Westons Stowford Press. ☂ 18 **Facilities** Non-diners area ❄ (Bar Garden) ♦♦ Children's menu Children's portions Play area Garden ⊼ Parking WiFi ⛟ (notice required)

| CRANBROOK | Map 7 TQ73 |

The George Hotel

tel: 01580 713348 **Stone St TN17 3HE**
email: georgehotel@shepherd-neame.co.uk
dir: *From A21 follow signs to Goudhurst. At large rdbt take 3rd exit to Cranbrook (A229). Hotel on left*

Former courthouse offers brasserie and restaurant dining

One of Cranbrook's landmark buildings, the 14th-century George Hotel traditionally served visiting buyers of locally made Cranbrook cloth. Magistrates held court here for over 300 years, and today the sophisticated interior mixes period features with contemporary decor. Two separate menus have been created; the brasserie offers a take on classic English cuisine – grilled veal escalope with crushed sweet potatoes, grilled vegetables and a port jus, perhaps, while in the restaurant diners can sample modern English dishes like pan-roasted lamb noisettes with dauphinoise potatoes, chicory, red onion and apricot Tatin and rosemary jus.

Open all day all wk **Food** Lunch all wk 12-3 Dinner Mon-Sat 6-9.30, Sun 6-9 Restaurant menu available ⊕ SHEPHERD NEAME ◀ Master Brew, Spitfire, Whitstable Bay, Guinness ♂ Symonds. ☂ 16 **Facilities** Non-diners area ❄ (Bar Outside area) ♦♦ Children's menu Children's portions Outside area ⊼ Parking WiFi ⛟ (notice required)

PICK OF THE PUBS

The Griffins Head

CHILLENDEN   Map 7 TR25

tel: 01304 840325 **CT3 1PS**
web: www.griffinsheadchillenden.co.uk
dir: *A2 from Canterbury towards Dover,*
then B2046. Village on right

Ancient inn with imaginative food

Dating from 1286, when Edward I was on the English throne, this fine black-and-white, half-timbered Wealden hall house is an architectural gem. It was once part of the estate of John de Chillenden and for centuries was a farm and brewhouse, until in 1766 it was granted a full licence to serve travellers on what then was the main road from Canterbury to Deal, although it's hard to believe today. The building you see is Tudor, constructed around the original wattle-and-daub walls, some of which can be seen in one of the three mercifully unspoilt flagstone-floored rooms. Here you can sit at old scrubbed pine tables and on recycled church pews and take in the exposed brick walls and beams above your head. Owned by Shepherd Neame, it has been managed for nearly 30 years by Jerry and Karen Copestake, who have won awards as testament to how well they do things here. The constantly changing seasonal menu is typically English and specialises in game from local estates and locally caught fish, especially haddock, cod, sea bass and sea bream. Typical dishes might include red wine marinated shoulder of lamb; warm salads with steak and roasted vegetables; chicken and ham pie; beef bourguignon; and traditional pub favourites like lambs' or calves' liver and bacon. Desserts include apple crumble, and home-made ice creams flavoured with passionfruit, ginger, raspberry or strawberry. The pretty garden, full of rambling roses and clematis, is especially popular during summer weekend barbecues. On the first Sunday of every month vintage and classic car enthusiasts turn up in their Armstrong Siddeleys, Austin 7s, MG TCs and other venerable vehicles. Local cricketers like to meet here too. Children are not allowed indoors.

Open all day Closed Sun pm
Food Lunch all wk 12-2
Dinner Mon-Sat 7-9.30
⊕ SHEPHERD NEAME ◖ Shepherd
Neame. ♟ 10
Facilities Non-diners area Garden
Outside area ⋒ Parking WiFi

DARTFORD

Map 6 TQ57

The Rising Sun Inn ★★★ INN

tel: 01474 872291 **Fawkham Green, Fawkham, Longfield DA3 8NL**
web: www.risingsun-fawkham.co.uk
dir: *0.5m from Brands Hatch Racing Circuit & 5m from Dartford*

Traditional 16th-century pub opposite the village green

Standing on the green in a picturesque village not far from Brands Hatch, The Rising Sun is a 16th-century building, which has been a pub since 1702. Inside you will find a bar full of character, complete with inglenook log fire, and Inglenooks restaurant where home-made traditional house specials and a large fresh fish menu, using the best local produce, are served. Among the mains you may find a selection of steaks; pork fillet with Stilton, bacon and chives wrapped in Parma ham; veal with paprika sauce; and lamb shank with a redcurrant jus. There is also a front patio and garden for alfresco dining in warmer weather, plus comfortable en suite bedrooms if you would like to stay over.

Open all day all wk **Food** Contact pub for details Av main course £8.90 Set menu available Restaurant menu available all wk ⊕ FREE HOUSE ◄ Courage Best & Directors, Fuller's London Pride, Sharp's Doom Bar. ♥ 9 **Facilities** Non-diners area ♦♦ Children's portions Garden ⋈ Parking WiFi ⛟ (notice required) **Rooms** 5

FAVERSHAM

Map 7 TR06

Albion Taverna

tel: 01795 591411 **29 Front Brents ME13 7DH**
email: contact@albiontaverna.com
dir: *Phone for detailed directions*

Mexican and English cook house on the waterfront

Located next to the Shepherd Neame Brewery near the Faversham swing bridge, the Albion Taverna looks directly onto the attractive waterfront area. The colourful menu is a combination of Mexican and English dishes. On the Mexican side are fajitas and quesadillas with a choice of fillings, nachos, buffalo wings, marinated ribs, chipotle meatballs and beef or bean chilli pots. English options include a lamb, mint and chilli burger; chargrilled steak and crab cake salad. Other treats are mussels cooked country style, Thai style or Mexican style. For dessert, try churros with dark chocolate fondue. There is an annual hop festival in early September.

Open all wk 12-3 6-11.30 (Sat-Sun 12-11.30) **Food** Contact pub for details ⊕ SHEPHERD NEAME ◄ Master Brew, Whitstable Bay, Early Bird, IPA ⛊ Thatchers Gold. ♥ **Facilities** Non-diners area ❄ (Garden) ♦♦ Children's menu Children's portions Play area Garden ⋈ Beer festival Parking WiFi ⛟ (notice required)

Shipwright's Arms

tel: 01795 590088 **Hollowshore ME13 7TU**
dir: *A2 through Ospringe then right at rdbt. Right at T-junct then left opposite Davington School, follow signs*

Walk in the footsteps of pirates, smugglers and sailors

The creekside Shipwright's Arms was first licensed in 1738, when the brick and weatherboarded pub's remote location on the Swale marshes made it a popular haunt for briny ne'er-do-wells; it's been a favoured watering hole for sailors and fishermen ever since. Best reached on foot or by boat, the effort in getting here is well rewarded, as this charming and unspoilt tavern oozes historic character. Step back in time in the relaxed and comfortable bars, which boast nooks and crannies, original timbers, built-in settles, well-worn sofas, wood-burning stoves, and a wealth of maritime artefacts. Locally-brewed Hopdaemon and Goacher's ales are tapped straight from the cask, and make for a perfect match with simple, traditional bar food such as baguettes and jacket potatoes. Alternatively look to the specials board for fresh fish, or the carte for the likes of steak and Merlot pie, and roast chicken. In summer come and support the pub's Bat and Trap team.

Open 11-3 6-10 (Sat-Sun 11-4 6-11 in winter; Sat 11-11 Sun 12-10.30 in summer) Closed Mon (Oct-Mar) **Food** Lunch Mon-Sat 11-2.30, Sun 12-2.30 Dinner Tue-Sat 7-9 (no food Tue-Thu eve in winter) ⊕ FREE HOUSE ◄ Goacher's, Hopdaemon, Whitstable, Local ales. ♥ 12 **Facilities** Non-diners area ♦♦ Children's menu Children's portions Family room Garden ⋈ Parking ⛟

GOODNESTONE

Map 7 TR25

The Fitzwalter Arms

tel: 01304 840303 **The Street CT3 1PJ**
email: thefitzwalterarms@hotmail.co.uk
dir: *From A2 & B2046 follow Goodnestone Park Garden signs*

Stunning inn in memorable estate village

This charming village inn has been catering for travellers crossing north Kent since 1589. A true community local; loyal regulars welcome today's visitors heading for the renowned Goodnestone Gardens nearby, where Jane Austen was a regular guest at the great house. This attractive, brick-built inn boasts log fires, bar billiards, a tranquil church-side garden and some great beers from the nearby Shepherd Neame brewery; ample themes around which to plot a visit and investigate the seasonally-tilted menu of home-cooked fare. Mushroom risotto to start, and then pork belly, caramelised apple, black pudding and mustard seed jus are good menu examples; special diets can be accommodated.

Open Tue-Thu 12-3 6-11 (Fri-Sat noon-1am Sun 12-11) Closed Mon (Tue L in winter) **Food** Lunch Wed-Sun 12-3 Dinner Wed-Sat 6.30-8.30 ⊕ SHEPHERD NEAME ◄ Master Brew, Spitfire, Early Bird, Late Red, Kent's Best. **Facilities** Non-diners area ❄ (Bar Garden) ♦♦ Children's portions Garden ⋈ WiFi ⛟ (notice required)

GOUDHURST

Map 6 TQ73

The Goudhurst Inn

tel: 01580 212605 **Cranbrook Rd TN17 1DX**
email: enquiries@thegoudhurstinn.com
dir: *From A21 (or A228) take A262, follow Goudhurst signs. Pub on A262 in village*

Revitalised village pub with stunning views

The Goudhurst Inn's bar and dining area have a comfortable contemporary feel, perfect for a relaxing with a pint of Harvey's and a classic lunchtime bar meal – ham, egg and chips, Scotch egg with mustard mayonnaise, or Moroccan spiced lamb burger. Come in the evening for Rye bay scallops, lamb shoulder with truffle cream potato and port sauce, and baked chocolate tart. Dine alfresco and savour glorious Wealden views.

pen all day all wk 11-11 (Sun 12-10) Food Lunch Mon-Thu 12-2.30, Fri 12-3, Sat 2-9.30, Sun 12-8 Dinner Mon-Fri 6-9.30, Sat 12-9.30, Sun 12-8 ⊕ ENTERPRISE NNS ◼ Harvey's, Timothy Taylor Landlord, Sharp's Doom Bar ♂ Symonds. ♍ acilities Non-diners area ♣ (Bar Restaurant Garden) ♦ Children's menu Children's ortions Play area Family room Garden ㅈ Parking WiFi ▭ (notice required)

reen Cross Inn

el: 01580 211200 TN17 1HA
ir: A21 from Tonbridge towards Hastings left onto A262 towards Ashford. 2m, Goudhurst n right

ining pub specialising in seafood

n an unspoiled corner of Kent, close to Finchcocks Manor, and originally built to erve the Paddock Wood to Goudhurst railway line, this thriving dining pub pecialises in fresh seafood. Arrive early to bag a table in the dining room, prettily ecorated with fresh flowers, and tuck into grilled skate wing, halibut with cream nd spinach sauce; or seafood paella or go for the slow roasted pork belly with rackling, gravy and apple sauce, followed by pineapple sorbet or lemon chiffon; all reshly prepared by the chef-owner who is Italian and classically trained.

pen all wk 12-3 6-11 Closed Sun eve Food Lunch all wk 12-2.30 Dinner Mon-Sat -9.45 Restaurant menu available all wk ⊕ FREE HOUSE ◼ Harvey's Sussex Best itter, Guinness ♂ Biddenden. Facilities ♦ Children's portions Garden ㅈ Parking iFi ▭ (notice required)

he Star & Eagle ★★★★ INN `PICK OF THE PUBS`

ee Pick of the Pubs on page 280

ee Pick of the Pubs on page 280

GRAVESEND Map 6 TQ67

he Cock Inn

el: 01474 814208 Henley St, Luddesdowne DA13 0XB
mail: andrew.r.turner@btinternet.com
ir: Phone for detailed directions

dults-only pub with cask conditioned English ales

ating from 1713, this whitewashed free house in the beautiful Luddesdowne Valley as two traditional beamed bars with wood-burning stoves and open fires. Always vailable are eight well-kept real ales, Köstritzer and other German beers, and not a ruit machine, jukebox or television in sight. All food is ordered at the bar: expect lled submarine rolls, basket meals and home-made cod and chips; steak, ushroom and Irish stout pie; and spinach and ricotta ravioli. As an adults-only ub, no-one under 18 is allowed in.

pen all day all wk 12-11 (Sun 12-10.30) Food Lunch all wk 12-3 Dinner all wk 5-8 FREE HOUSE ◼ Adnams Southwold Bitter, Broadside & Lighthouse, Goacher's eal Mild Ale, St Austell Trelawny, Truman's Swift. Facilities Non-diners area ♣ (Bar estaurant Garden) Garden ㅈ Parking

HALSTEAD Map 6 TQ46

ose & Crown

el: 01959 533120 Otford Ln TN14 7EA
mail: info@roseandcrownhalstead.co.uk
r: M25 junct 4, A21, London (SE)/Bromley/Orpington signs. At Hewitts Rdbt 1st exit onto 224 signed Dunton Green. At rdbt 3rd exit into Shoreham Ln. In Halstead left into Station d, left into Otford Ln

ustling community local

his handsome Grade II listed pub, situated in the lee of the North Downs, is all a ood village pub should be; traditional pub games including bat and trap, family

---

friendly, supporting local microbreweries such as Tonbridge and Westerham (with no less than three beer festivals held each year) and a welcoming base for walks into the peaceful countryside on the doorstep. With lively bar, peaceful lounge, Stables Restaurant and tranquil garden to suit all tastes, home-made pub grub is the icing on the cake, from home-made chilli con carne to breaded fruits de mer with salad, chips and peas.

Open all day all wk Food Lunch all wk 12-11 Dinner all wk 12-11 Set menu available ⊕ FREE HOUSE ◼ Larkins Traditional, Guest ales ♂ Westons. ♍ Facilities Non-diners area ♣ (Bar Garden Outside area) ♦ Children's menu Children's portions Play area Garden Outside area ㅈ Beer festival Parking WiFi ▭

HAWKHURST Map 7 TQ73

The Black Pig at Hawkhurst

tel: 01580 752306 Moor Hill TN18 4PF
email: enquiries@theblackpigathawkhurst.co.uk
dir: On A229, S of Hawkhurst

Local produce to the fore

An inviting roadside inn on the outskirts of Hawkhurst in the High Weald Area of Outstanding Natural Beauty, the pub's owners make the most of this favoured location by specialising in food and drink sourced from suppliers in Kent and Sussex. Settle in to the cosy interior or secluded garden with a beer from Larkins, cider from Biddenden or a Kentish wine and indulge in a dish such as butternut squash, aubergine and toasted pine nut-filled pancake with Sussex Blue cheese gratin. The signature dish here is home-made pie of the day with mash, vegetables and lashings of gravy; or perhaps a vegetarian sharing platter will appeal.

Open all day all wk 11am-mdnt Food Lunch Mon-Sat 12-2.30, Sun 12-4 Dinner all wk 6.30-9.30 ⊕ FREE HOUSE ◼ Dark Star Hophead, Larkins Traditional, Old Dairy Copper Top, Harvey's ♂ Biddenden. Facilities Non-diners area ♣ (Bar Garden) ♦ Children's menu Children's portions Garden ㅈ ▭

The Great House `PICK OF THE PUBS`

tel: 01580 753119 Gills Green TN18 5EJ
email: enquiries@thegreathouse.net
dir: Just off A229 between Cranbrook & Hawkhurst

Family-friendly free house in the heart of the Kentish Weald

A wonderfully atmospheric 16th-century free house with a mix of exposed beams, log fires and stone floors. In addition to ales, the bar stocks a real cider from nearby Biddenden; 70 world wines include 20 sold by the glass. Three dining areas are complemented by an orangery opening on to a Mediterranean-style terrace furnished with Italian designer chairs; a lychgate leads through to a manicured garden. Traditional English food with cosmopolitan touches starts with a British tapas menu, which includes venison and boar pudding Scotch egg; Lamberhurst chipolatas; and crispy fried squid. A proper lunch could start with seared scallops, piquillo pepper purée, chorizo and pickled cucumber; follow with a hearty game pie comprising venison, partridge, wild duck and rabbit served with seasonal vegetables. The children's dedicated menu has more than a dozen options to choose from. A beer festival with food and fun is held each year.

Open all day all wk 11.30-11 Food Lunch Mon-Fri 12-3, Sat-Sun 12-9.45 Dinner Mon-Fri 6-9.45, Sat-Sun 12-9.45 Av main course £15 ⊕ FREE HOUSE ◼ Harvey's, Sharp's Doom Bar, Guinness ♂ Biddenden, Aspall. ♍ 20 Facilities Non-diners area ♣ (Bar Restaurant Garden) ♦ Children's menu Children's portions Garden ㅈ Beer festival Parking WiFi

PICK OF THE PUBS

The Star & Eagle ★★★★ INN

GOUDHURST　　　　Map 6 TQ73

tel: 01580 211512
High St TN17 1AL
email: starandeagle@btconnect.com
web: www.starandeagle.co.uk
dir: *Just off A21 towards Hastings. Take A262 into Goudhurst. Pub at top of hill*

Outstanding views, historic interiors, and cooking with a European twist

If a visit to the old spa town of Royal Tunbridge Wells is in your plans, or perhaps a stroll around the gardens at Sissinghurst Castle, the Star & Eagle in Goudhurst's High Street would make an ideal port of call. Its 14th-century origins can be seen in vaulted stonework that suggests that this rambling, big-beamed building may once have been a monastery; the tunnel from the cellars probably surfaces beneath the neighbouring parish church. In the 18th century it was a base for the infamous Hawkhurst gang, who hatched smuggling plans over their ales and terrorised the surrounding area with their thieving. Standing 400 feet above sea level, the Star & Eagle's breathtaking views survey the orchards and hop fields that have earned Kent the accolade 'The Garden of England'. Harvey's, Wychwood Hobgoblin and a guest ale are always on offer, and a good selection of wine is served by the glass. While quaffing, unwind and enjoy choosing between fine traditional and continental dishes prepared by head

chef Scott Smith and his team under the watchful eyes of proprietors Karin and Enrique Martinez. Tapas-style starters such as deep-fried whitebait sprinkled with Spanish paprika, or large pan-fried Portuguese sardines, can be served in large portions for sharing. The blackboard displays daily specials, or look to the house specialities for the likes of roast guinea fowl with Chantenay carrots, bubble and squeak cake, orange and ginger sauce. For fish lovers, a lemon-spiced fillet of salmon, or a whole lemon sole with prawn and lemon butter sauce, are typical choices. Desserts follow English favourite lines: apple and blackberry crumble and sticky toffee sponge pudding are both served with vanilla custard; or choose a selection of Kentish cheeses served with grapes and chutney.

Open all day all wk 11-11 (Sun 12-3 6.30-10.30) **Food** Lunch all wk 12-2.30 Dinner all wk 7-9.30 ⊕ FREE HOUSE ◾ Harvey's, Brakspear Oxford Gold, Wychwood Hobgoblin Ô Biddenden. ♀ 14 **Facilities** Non-diners area ♦♦ Children's menu Children's portions Family room Outside area ♠ Parking WiFi ⛟ **Rooms** 10

HERNHILL

Map 7 TR06

The Red Lion

tel: 01227 751207 **Crockham Ln ME13 9JR**
email: enquiries@theredlion.org **web:** www.theredlion.org
dir: *M2 junct 7, A299 signed Whitstable, Herne Bay & Ramsgate. Follow Fostall sign, up slip road. Right, signed Fostall & Hernhill. In Hernhill pub on left*

Historic pub by pretty village green

An eye-catching mix of crucks and half-timbering outside; within, a forest of hop-adorned beams and pillars characterise this rambling, medieval, flagstone floored inn next to the village green. The beer garden has views to distant wooded hills, a sheltered base in which to sup real ales from regional breweries, complemented by a Summer Bank Holiday beer festival. Fine, fulfilling pub grub such as pan-fried salmon fillet with caper and spinach butter; and Thai chicken and rice might appear on the weekly-changing specials board. There's a pensioner's special lunchtime menu on Wednesdays.

Open all wk 11.30-3 6-11 (Fri-Sat 12-11 Sun 12-10.30) **Food** Lunch Mon-Sat 12-3, Sun 12-8 Dinner Mon-Sat 6-9, Sun 12-8 Set menu available ⊕ FREE HOUSE ◀ Sharp's Doom Bar, Fuller's London Pride, Adnams Broadside. ⬥ 12 **Facilities** Non-diners area ✿ (Bar Garden) ♦♦ Children's menu Children's portions Play area Family room Garden ⌁ Beer festival Parking WiFi 🚐

See advert on page 282

HODSOLL STREET

Map 6 TQ66

The Green Man

tel: 01732 823575 **TN15 7LE**
email: the.greenman@btinternet.com
dir: *On North Downs between Brands Hatch & Gravesend off A227*

Recommended for its fish dishes

This 300-year-old, family-run pub is loved for its decent food and real ales. It stands in the picturesque village of Hodsoll Street on the North Downs, surrounded by beautiful Kent countryside, with a large garden for warmer weather. Sharp's Doom Bar and Timothy Taylor Landlord are a couple of the four real ales on tap. Food is prepared to order using fresh local produce, and the evening menu includes a wide variety of fish, such as smoked haddock, whole sea bass, halibut steak and crab and prawn salad, as well as dishes like duck and bacon salad; steak and kidney filo parcel; and vegetable and Stilton crumble.

Open all wk 11-2.30 6-11 (Fri-Sun all day) **Food** Lunch Mon-Thu 12-2, Fri-Sun all day Dinner Mon-Thu 6.30-9.30, Fri-Sun all day Av main course £12 Set menu available ⊕ HAYWOOD PUB COMPANY LTD ◀ Timothy Taylor Landlord, Harvey's, Sharp's Doom Bar, Guest ale ⭕ Thatchers Gold. **Facilities** Non-diners area ✿ (Bar Restaurant Garden) ♦♦ Children's menu Children's portions Play area Garden ⌁ Parking WiFi 🚐

HOLLINGBOURNE

Map 7 TQ85

The Dirty Habit

PICK OF THE PUBS

tel: 01622 880880 **Upper St ME17 1UW**
email: enquiries@thedirtyhabit.net
dir: *M20 junct 8, follow A20 signs, then Hollingbourne signs on B2163. Through Hollingbourne, pub on hill top on right*

Historic watering hole on the Pilgrims Way

There's been a pub on this site since the 11th century, when monks brewed ale here for pilgrims plodding from Winchester to the shrine of Thomas à Becket at Canterbury. Renovation has done wonders for the building, without losing any of its period charm. Look, for instance, at the long Georgian oak bar and panelling, and the Victorian furniture, all beautifully restored by skilled local craftsmen. Harvey's of Lewes is one of the real ales on tap, and there's cider from Biddenden too. The Monks Corner, with oak beams to the apex and a bread oven in the corner, is ideal for private dining, while outside is a quiet terrace. The kitchen prepares traditional favourites such as steak and kidney pie, and fish and chips, as well as 21-day-matured Kentish beef fillet; braised and roasted partridge; pan-fried salmon; wild mushroom risotto, and specialities including langoustines and lobster.

Open all day all wk **Food** Lunch Mon-Sat 12-3, Sun all day Dinner Mon-Sat 6-9.45, Sun all day Av main course £14 ⊕ ENTERPRISE INNS ◀ Harvey's, Old Dairy Red Top, Timothy Taylor Landlord ⭕ Biddenden, Aspall. ⬥ 28 **Facilities** ✿ (Bar Restaurant Outside area) ♦♦ Children's menu Children's portions Outside area ⌁ Parking WiFi

Red Lion

Crockham Lane, Hernhill, Kent
Tel: 01227 751207
Website: www.theredlion.org
Email: enquiries@theredlion.org

A picturesque 14th century pub situated in a small village near the town of Faversham. Surrounded in history the pub dates back to the 1300s and still contains many original features. The pub offers a selection of traditional English food alongside the frequently changing seasonal specials. Facilities include an upstairs restaurant, available for dining or large functions, a front patio overlooking the church and village green, and a well-established pub garden with many historical features and a large play area for children.

ICKHAM
Map 7 TR25

The Duke William

tel: 01227 721308 & 721244 **The Street CT3 1QP**
email: goodfood@dukewilliam.biz
dir: *A257 Canterbury to Sandwich. In Littlebourne left opposite The Anchor, into Nargate St. 0.5m right into Drill Ln, right into The Street*

Child-friendly village inn recommended for its Sunday lunches

This family-friendly, whitewashed free house is in the heart of Ickham village. Traditional, locally sourced and home-cooked food is the keynote here; the Sunday lunches are particularly popular. Menu choices might include fresh fish, venison or slow-roast pork, all served with local vegetables. Chicken liver pâté and rabbit casserole could appear on the daily specials menu. The lovely garden features a covered patio, as well as a children's play area with a swing and slide.

Open all day all wk all day **Food** Lunch Mon-Sat 12-3, Sun 12-8 Dinner Mon-Sat 6-10, Sun 12-8 Restaurant menu available Mon-Sat ⊕ FREE HOUSE ◀ Shepherd Neame Whitstable Bay, Sharp's Doom Bar, Old Dairy Gold Top, Guest ale ♂ Aspall. ♀ 9 **Facilities** Non-diners area ❤ (Bar Garden) ♦♦ Children's menu Children's portions Play area Garden ⋒ WiFi ▄▄ (notice required)

IDEN GREEN
Map 6 TQ73

The Peacock

tel: 01580 211233 **Goudhurst Rd TN17 2PB**
dir: *A21 from Tunbridge Wells to Hastings, onto A262, pub 1.5m past Goudhurst*

Family friendly inn

Dating from the 14th century, this Grade II listed former smugglers' haunt has exposed brickwork, low beams, an inglenook fireplace, and ancient oak doors. Kent Best and Bishops Finger can be found among several ales in the convivial bar. Popular with families, The Peacock offers a wide range of traditional pub food made using produce from local farmers; maybe garlic tiger prawns on toast followed by ham, egg and chips; steak and ale pie; chicken and bacon salad; or liver and bacon. In summer enjoy the large enclosed garden with fruit trees and picnic tables on one side of the building. Beer festivals are held at varying times in the year.

Open all day all wk 12-11 (Sun 12-6) **Food** Lunch Tue-Fri 12-2.30, Sat all day, Sun 12-3 Dinner Tue-Fri 6-8.45, Sat all day Av main course £10 ⊕ SHEPHERD NEAME ◀ Master Brew, Kent, Bishops Finger, Seasonal ales. **Facilities** Non-diners area ❤ (Bar Garden) ♦♦ Children's menu Children's portions Family room Garden ⋒ Beer festival Parking WiFi ▄▄ (notice required)

IGHTHAM
Map 6 TQ55

The Harrow Inn
PICK OF THE PUBS

tel: 01732 885912 **Common Rd TN15 9EB**
dir: *1.5m from Borough Green on A25 to Sevenoaks, signed Ightham Common, left into Common Rd. Inn 0.25m on left*

Worth seeking out for imaginative food

Tucked away down country lanes, yet easily accessible from both the M20 and M26, this creeper-clad, stone-built free house dates back to at least the 17th century. The two-room bar area has a great brick fireplace, open to both sides and piled high with logs, while the restaurant's vine-clad conservatory opens on to a terrace that's ideal for a pint of Loddon Hoppit or Gravesend Shrimpers and warm weather dining. Menus vary with the seasons, and seafood is a particular speciality: fish lovers can enjoy dishes such as crab and ginger spring roll; swordfish with Cajun spice and salsa; or pan-fried fillets of sea bass with lobster cream and spinach. Other main courses may include baked sausage with gammon, fennel, red onions and garlic; and tagliatelle with wild mushroom, fresh herb, lemongrass and chilli ragout. The car park is fairly small, although there's adequate street parking.

Open 12-3 6-11 Closed 1wk between Xmas & New Year, Sun eve & Mon-Wed **Food** Lunch Thu-Sun 12-2 Dinner Thu-Sat 6-9 Av main course £13.50 Restaurant menu available Thu-Sun ⊕ FREE HOUSE ◀ Loddon Hoppit, Gravesend Shrimpers. ♀ 9 **Facilities** Non-diners area ♦♦ Children's portions Family room Outside area ⋒ Parking

IVY HATCH
Map 6 TQ55

The Plough at Ivy Hatch
PICK OF THE PUBS

See Pick of the Pubs on page 284

LAMBERHURST
Map 6 TQ63

The Vineyard
PICK OF THE PUBS

tel: 01892 890222 **Lamberhurst Down TN3 8EU**
email: enquiries@thevineyard.com
dir: *From A21 follow brown Vineyard signs onto B2169 towards Lamberhurst. Left, continue to follow Vineyard signs. Straight on at x-rds, pub on right*

Robust Anglo-French cooking with good ale and wines to match

Built more than 300 years ago, original elements of this country roadside pub are reflected in the quirky stuffed boar's head mounted above the huge brick-built fireplace. Leather sofas, wingback and parlour chairs mix easily with the rustic look and chunky wooden furniture, whilst the eye is taken by a mural illustrating the well-established winemaking craft in the area. The pub is next door to one of England's oldest vineyards and there's a carefully chosen wine list and 20 served by the glass. Fans of the hop are rewarded with firkins from microbreweries such as Old Dairy. From the kitchen comes a pleasing mix of top-notch traditional English and regional French brasserie dishes: seared scallops, apple and vanilla purée, black pudding to start, then guinea fowl breast, thyme mash, braised red cabbage, curly kale and Bourguignon sauce, finishing with warm pear and almond tart.

Open all day all wk 11.30-11 **Food** Lunch Mon-Fri 12-6, Sat-Sun 12-9.30 Dinner Mon-Fri 6-9.45, Sat-Sun 12-9.30 Av main course £14 ⊕ FREE HOUSE ◀ Sharp's Doom Bar, Harvey's, Old Dairy ♂ Aspall. ♀ 20 **Facilities** Non-diners area ❤ (Bar Garden) ♦♦ Children's portions Garden ⋒ Parking

LEIGH
Map 6 TQ54

The Greyhound Charcott

tel: 01892 870275 **Charcott TN11 8LG**
email: ghatcharcott@aol.com
dir: *From Tonbridge take B245 N towards Hildenborough. Left onto Leigh road, right onto B2027 (Stocks Green Rd). Through Leigh, right then left at T-junct, right into Charcott (Camp Hill)*

True pub traditions at the heart of the village

This cosy pub has been welcoming locals and visitors for around 120 years and you can expect a traditional atmosphere in which music, pool table and fruit machine have no place. Winter brings log fires, while in summer you can relax in the garden with a pint of Adnams Lighthouse. From a changing menu begin with home-made pork and brandy pâté with apple chutney followed by braised lamb shank, mash and rosemary, garlic and red wine gravy, or plaice fillet with lemon, caper and shrimp butter. Snacks include ploughman's, sandwiches and classics like cod and chips.

Open 12-3 5.30-11 (Sat all day) Closed Sun Eve & Mon L **Food** Lunch Tue-Sat 12-2, Sun 12-3 Dinner Mon-Sat 6.30-9.30 ⊕ ENTERPRISE INNS ◀ Harvey's, Otter, Adnams Lighthouse ♂ Westons Stowford Press. ♀ 12 **Facilities** Non-diners area ♦♦ Children's portions Garden Parking WiFi ▄▄ (notice required)

PICK OF THE PUBS

The Plough at Ivy Hatch

IVY HATCH   Map 6 TQ55

tel: 01732 810100
High Cross Rd TN15 0NL
email: info@theploughivyhatch.co.uk
web: www. theploughivyhatch.co.uk
dir: *Exit A25 between Borough Green & Sevenoaks, follow Ightham Mote signs*

Village pub near the National Trust's Ightham Mote

This 17th-century, tile-hung pub in the picturesque village of Ivy Hatch is but a short walk from the National Trust's Ightham Mote, Britain's best-preserved medieval manor house. From spring to autumn, The Plough keeps its own pigs and chickens in a cobnut coppice in the back garden. During the week it's open for breakfast and a wide range of teas and coffees. In the bar, the real ales come from a select roster of Kentish breweries, and food includes sandwiches with chips or soup; 100 per cent rump steak beefburgers; and wild boar and apple sausages with mash, red onion marmalade and jus. On the daily-changing restaurant menus are British- and European-style dishes featuring seafood, game and, courtesy of those pigs, country pork terrines; home-made bacon, pork and apple burgers; and mouth-watering, slow-cooked legs and shoulders. A starter of Shetland mussels with shallots, garlic, white wine and cream might be followed by a main course of confit duck leg with

Toulouse sausage and white bean cassoulet; braised ox-cheek with garlic mash, cavolo nero and braising reduction; or pan-fried grey mullet with home-cured bacon and mussel stew. Desserts include chocolate and salt caramel delice with white chocolate fudge and honeycomb ice cream; and pistachio sponge with spiced apricots and home-made nougat. There are many excellent walks through the countryside surrounding The Plough, and the road- and mountain-biking opportunities are excellent too. Muddy boots and cycling gear, if not necessarily de rigueur, are definitely not frowned upon and wearers caught in the rain will be able to dry off either in front of the winter open fire, or, if the sun's out, on the terrace.

Open all wk 9-3 6-11 (Sat 10am-11pm Sun 10-6) Closed 26 Dec **Food** Lunch Mon-Sat 12-2.45, Sun 12-6 Dinner Mon-Sat 6-9.30 ⊕ FREE HOUSE ◼ Tonbridge Coppernob, Tonbridge Rustic ♂ Thatchers Gold. ♟ 10
Facilities Non-diners area ♦ Children's menu Children's portions Garden ⅀ Parking WiFi ᗜ (notice required)

LEYSDOWN-ON-SEA
Map 7 TR07

The Ferry House Inn ★★★★ INN

tel: 01795 510214 **Harty Rd ME12 4BQ**
email: info@theferryhouseinn.co.uk **web:** www.theferryhouseinn.co.uk
dir: From A429 towards Sheppey. At rdbt take B2231 to Eastchurch. From Eastchurch High St into Church Rd. At rdbt into Rowetts Way signed Leysdown. Right into Harty Ferry Rd to village

In remotest Sheppey, but well worth finding

On the edge of the Swale estuary, this 16th-century pub stands in three acres of terraced lawns offering views over the water to Faversham, Whitstable and the North Downs. Even major refurbishment has not upset its character and charm - the open log fires, the wooden beams, the solid oak floors. For many years it has been a popular rendezvous for yachtsmen, and with AA-rated accommodation holidaymakers find it too. Membership of 'Produced in Kent' means locally sourced food, such as fisherman's catch of the day; Ferry burger, using beef from the pub's own farm, chips and salad; and crispy mushroom risotto cake.

Open Tue-Fri & Mon (Apr-Sep) 11-3 6.30-11 (Sat all day Sun 11-5) Closed 24-31 Dec, Mon (Oct-Mar) **Food** Lunch Mon-Fri 12-2.30, Sat & Sun 12.30-4 Dinner Mon-Sat 6.30-9 ⊕ FREE HOUSE ◀ Shepherd Neame Spitfire, Young's Special ♂ Sheppy's, Hush Heath Jake's Orchard. **Facilities** Non-diners area ☺ (Garden) ♦ Children's menu Children's portions Play area Family room Garden ♫ Parking WiFi ▭ (notice required) **Rooms** 4

LINTON
Map 7 TQ75

The Bull Inn

tel: 01622 743612 **Linton Hill ME17 4AW**
email: food@thebullatlinton.co.uk
dir: S of Maidstone on A229 (Hastings road)

Rural pub ideal for alfresco eating and drinking

Built in 1674, this part-timbered former coaching inn stands high on the Greensand Ridge, with wonderful views and sunsets over the Weald. The award-winning garden includes two oak gazebos and a large decked area for alfresco bistro dining and afternoon tea. Inside there is an imposing inglenook fireplace, lots of beams and a bar serving Shepherd Neame ales. The wide-ranging menu offers hearty sandwiches and pub classics – perfect sustenance for walkers tackling the Greensand Way. You might also find seafood linguine, Thai green curry, and rocky road cheesecake, as well as a carvery on Sundays.

Open all day all wk 11am-11.30pm (Sun 12-10.30) **Food** Lunch all wk 12-9 Dinner all wk 12-9 Av main course £9.95 Set menu available ⊕ SHEPHERD NEAME ◀ Shepherd Neame Master Brew, Kent's Best, Late Red ♂ Thatchers Gold. **Facilities** Non-diners area ☺ (Bar Garden) ♦ Children's menu Children's portions Garden ♫ Parking WiFi ▭

LOWER HALSTOW
Map 7 TQ86

The Three Tuns

tel: 01795 842840 **The Street ME9 7DY**
email: info@thethreetunsrestaurant.co.uk
dir: From A2 between Rainham & Newington turn left, follow Lower Halstow sign. At T-junct right signed Funton & Iwade. Pub on right

Quality dining, pub grub and Kentish real ales

Built in 1468 and licensed to sell ale since 1764, Chris and Carol Haines's traditional fire-warmed bar is paradise for lovers of local real ales and cider. They stock Millis Kentish Best, Goacher's Real Mild and Dudda's Tun cider, while Summer Bank Holiday sees the Kentish Ale and Cider Festival, with a hog-roast, seafood and live music. Farms supply much of the food on the ever-changing restaurant menu, where items might include pan-fried pheasant breast; Dover sole; and grilled sirloin steak. A large beer garden with decking flanks a stream that soon flows into nearby Halstow Creek.

Open all day all wk **Food** Lunch 12-9 Restaurant menu available Mon-Sat ⊕ FREE HOUSE ◀ Millis Brewing Co Kentish Best, Goacher's Real Mild Ale, Guest ales ♂ Dudda's Tun Kentish Cider, Core Fruit Products Hard Core. ₹ 10 **Facilities** Non-diners area ☺ (Bar Garden) ♦ Children's menu Children's portions Garden ♫ Beer festival Cider festival Parking WiFi ▭ (notice required)

MAIDSTONE
Map 7 TQ75

The Black Horse Inn ★★★★ INN

tel: 01622 737185 **Pilgrim's Way, Thurnham ME14 3LD**
email: info@wellieboot.net **web:** www.wellieboot.net
dir: M20 junct 7, A249, right into Detling. Turn opposite Cock Horse Pub into Pilgrim's Way

Charming free house on the Pilgrim's Way

Tucked beneath the North Downs on the Pilgrim's Way, this 18th-century former forge welcomes guests with an open log fire in the colder months. Dine in the conservatory restaurant that has stunning countryside views or in the cosy candlelit restaurant. Real ales change weekly and the kitchen uses local ingredients in fish or meat sharing plates, or in mains like haunch of Chart Farm venison with tomato relish, chunky chips and garlic mushrooms; a daily-changing specials board adds to the choices.

Open all day all wk **Food** Lunch all wk 12-6 Dinner all wk 6-10 ⊕ FREE HOUSE ◀ Greene King IPA, Wychwood Hobgoblin, Westerham Grasshopper, Harvey's Sussex Best Bitter, Black Sheep ♂ Biddenden. ₹ 21 **Facilities** Non-diners area ☺ (Bar Garden) ♦ Children's menu Children's portions Garden ♫ Parking ▭ (notice required) **Rooms** 27

MARKBEECH
Map 6 TQ44

The Kentish Horse

tel: 01342 850493 **Cow Ln TN8 5NT**
dir: 3m from Edenbridge & 7m from Tunbridge Wells. 1m S of Hever Castle

Popular free house in the Garden of England

Britain's only Kentish Horse honours Invicta, the county's prancing white stallion. Popular with ramblers and cyclists, the locals rate it too, partly because Chiddingstone-brewed Larkins and Lewes-brewed Harvey's are available, with guest ales on high days and holidays. New owners Trevor and Tina Dobson serve home-cooked, traditional food, such as pan-fried lamb's liver and onions; beer-battered fresh fillet of haddock; and tagliatelle with Stilton and mushroom cream sauce. Nearly four acres of land incorporate an extensive garden and a children's play area. And you also get a terrific view over Winnie the Pooh's home, Ashdown Forest.

Open all day all wk **Food** Lunch Mon-Sat 12-2.30, Sun 12-3 Dinner Mon-Sat 7-9.30 ⊕ FREE HOUSE ◀ Harvey's, Larkins ♂ Westons Stowford Press, Symonds. **Facilities** Non-diners area ☺ (Bar Garden) ♦ Children's menu Children's portions Play area Garden Parking ▭ (notice required)

MATFIELD

Map 6 TQ64

NEW The Poet at Matfield

tel: 01892 722416 **Maidstone Rd TN12 7JH**
email: info@thepoetatmatfield.co.uk **web:** www.thepoetatmatfield.co.uk
dir: *From Tonbridge on A21 towards Hastings left onto B2160 signed Paddock Wood. Approx 1.5m to pub on left in Matfield*

Smart village inn with impressive literary links

Named after poet Siegfried Sassoon, who was born in this quintessentially English village just outside Tunbridge Wells, this Grade II listed pub is more than 350 years old. The pub retains its original character with the beams and antiques, but comfortable leather chesterfield sofas and armchairs add an elegant edge. Provenance is the cornerstone of the menu, which lists local suppliers including the Old Dairy Brewery responsible for the Red Top ale served at the bar. The concise carte could kick off with smoked haddock risotto and move on to Kentish pork belly with boudin noir, carrots, sprouts and apple.

Open all day all wk **Food** Lunch Mon-Sat 12-2.30, Sun 12-3 Dinner all wk 6.30-9 Av main course £13 Restaurant menu available all wk ⊕ ENTERPRISE INNS ◖ Old Dairy Red Top, Tonbridge Coppernob. ☂ 12 **Facilities** Non-diners area ✿ (Bar Garden) ♦ Children's portions Garden ⊼ Parking WiFi ⚌ (notice required)

See advert below

PENSHURST

Map 6 TQ54

The Bottle House Inn

PICK OF THE PUBS

See Pick of the Pubs on opposite page

The Spotted Dog

PICK OF THE PUBS

tel: 01892 870253 **Smarts Hill TN11 8EE**
email: thespotteddogpub@gmail.com
dir: *Off B2188 between Penshurst & Fordcombe*

Sitting in the folds of the Weald

This independently run, weatherboarded inn started life as a row of cottages in the 15th century, and is now a rambling building with open fires, a forest of low beams and oak-board floors. There are tiered beer gardens to the front and rear, the latter offering fantastic views in the summer. Kentish ales from Larkins and cider from Chiddingstone are just another excellent reason to stop here, along with the bang up-to-date menu, making the most of the produce grown in this richly endowed countryside. Sample a starter of deep-fried crispy duck rolls drizzled with hoi sin sauce, precursor to Thai green chicken curry; steak and kidney pie; or loin of lamb with a red wine, rosemary and redcurrant jus. These are enhanced by a daily-changing specials board and lunchtime baguettes, sandwiches and ploughman's. The Spotted Dog is close to two magnificent stately homes, Penshurst Place and Hever Castle.

Open all day all wk 11.30-11 (Sun 12-8 Mon 11.30-9) **Food** Lunch Mon-Fri 12-2.30, Sat-Sun 12-4 Dinner Mon-Sat 6-9 ⊕ FREE HOUSE ◖ Larkins Traditional, Harvey's, Guest ale ♨ Chiddingstone, Thatchers Gold. **Facilities** Non-diners area ✿ (Bar Garden Outside area) ♦ Children's menu Children's portions Garden Outside area ⊼ Parking WiFi ⚌ (notice required)

PICK OF THE PUBS

The Bottle House Inn

PENSHURST Map 6 TQ54

tel: 01892 870306
Coldharbour Rd TN11 8ET
email: info@thebottlehouseinnpenshurst.co.uk
web: www.thebottlehouseinnpenshurst.co.uk
dir: *A264 W from Tunbridge Wells onto B2188 N. After Fordcombe left towards Edenbridge & Hever. Pub 500yds after staggered x-rds*

Historic pub off the beaten track

Built as a farmhouse in 1492, this historic building formed part of a local estate during Henry VII's reign. A handsome, weatherboarded inn set down a country lane, it wasn't until 1806 that it was granted a licence to sell ales and ciders, later diversifying to function as a shop, farrier's and cobbler's too. Refurbishment in 1938 unearthed hundreds of old bottles, which inspired its unusual name. Later improvements included ancient oak beams sandblasted back to their natural colour, brickwork exposed and walls painted in neutral shades. At the copper-topped bar counter choose between Harvey's of Lewes and Chiddingstone-brewed Larkins handpumped beers, or a wine from one of the 19 served by the glass, then settle at a table on the patio or on the terrace. The menus in the stylish dining room change regularly to capitalise on the availability of seasonal produce, and the chef's recommendations change frequently. Light bites might include croque-monsieur and skinny fries; or rosemary and garlic studded camembert. Starters are equally enticing – Madras crusted tuna, cucumber salad, soy and chilli dipping sauce, for instance. Among the main courses are beef and Guinness suet pudding, horseradish mash and winter vegetables; grilled sea bass fillets, chorizo, basil and red pepper salsa, tempura zuccini and crushed new potatoes; and falafel burger, halloumi, sweet potato wedges and fennel coleslaw. From the home-made desserts, you're likely to find coconut pannacotta, caramelised mango and peach salad.

Open all day all wk 11-11 (Sun 11-10.30) Closed 25 Dec **Food** Mon-Sat 12-10, Sun & BH 12-9 FREE HOUSE Harvey's Sussex Best Bitter, Larkins Traditional, Guest ales from Westerham Brewery. 19 **Facilities** Non-diners area (Bar Outside area) Children's menu & portions Outside area Parking (notice required)

PLUCKLEY
Map 7 TQ94

The Dering Arms
PICK OF THE PUBS

tel: 01233 840371 **Station Rd TN27 0RR**
email: jim@deringarms.com
dir: M20 junct 8, A20 to Ashford. Right onto B2077 at Charing to Pluckley

Great selection of seafood dishes

Creeper-clad stone gables and arched windows mark out this imposing building as something special. There's a touch of Victorian Gothic and 'Hammer' films about this eye-catching pub, built originally as a hunting lodge. The grandeur remains inside, with open fires, bare boards, scrubbed old tables and a hop-bine dressed bar groaning with venerable handpumps. The separate clubroom has comfy settees, log-burner and a baby grand just itching to be played. It's a popular destination for seafood lovers, with ever-changing dishes filling the specials board. A starter of mackerel fillet with beetroot and orange salsa could be followed by fillet of sea bass, minted leeks, bacon and red wine sauce or pan-fried scallops with basil spaghetti and saffron sauce. The non-fish dishes are equally inspiring; venison steak with potato celeriac purée and port sauce might tempt. Drinkers are rewarded with a fine cellar, plus a selection of Kentish ales and ciders.

Open Mon-Fri 11.30-3.30 6-11 (Sat 9am-11pm Sun 12-4) Closed 26-27 Dec, Sun eve **Food** Lunch Mon-Fri 12-2.30, Sat 12-3, Sun 12-4 Dinner Mon-Sat 6.30-9 Av main course £15 Restaurant menu available all wk ⊕ FREE HOUSE ◀ Goacher's Best Dark Ale, Gold Star Ale, Old Ale, Dering Ale Ö Biddenden. 🍷 8
Facilities Non-diners area 🐾 (Bar Garden) ♦️ Children's portions Family room Garden ⌒ Parking WiFi

ROLVENDEN
Map 7 TQ83

The Bull

tel: 01580 241212 **1 Regent St TN17 4PB**
email: thebullinnkent@yahoo.com
dir: Just off A28, approx 3m from Tenterden

The beer garden overlooks the village cricket pitch

This handsome, tile hung village inn dates, in part, back to the 13th century and is located close to the walled garden that inspired Frances Hodgson Burnett's classic tale *The Secret Garden*. Handy, too, for steam trains of the Kent and East Sussex Railway, there's a welcome focus on local beers and produce, with a heart-warming, pubby menu enhanced by modern dishes like tempura prawns served with sweet chilli dipping sauce, followed by Moroccan lamb tagine and Mediterranean couscous or home-roasted ham with free-range eggs and hand-cut chips. There's a lovely beer garden overlooking the village cricket ground.

Open all day all wk **Food** Lunch all wk 12-3 Dinner all wk 6-10 ⊕ FREE HOUSE ◀ Red Top, Harvey's, Old Dairy Gold Top Ö Westons Stowford Press. 🍷 12
Facilities Non-diners area 🐾 (Bar Garden) ♦️ Children's menu Children's portions Garden ⌒ Beer festival Parking WiFi

ST MARGARET'S BAY
Map 7 TR34

The Coastguard
PICK OF THE PUBS

tel: 01304 853176 **CT15 6DY**
email: bookings@thecoastguard.co.uk **web:** www.thecoastguard.co.uk
dir: A258 between Dover & Deal follow St Margaret's at Cliffe signs. 2m, through village towards sea

Splendid coastal views and market-fresh food

The popular Heritage Coast footpath passes the door of this convivial waterside pub, whilst the watersport fans beach their kayaks here to indulge in a half of Gadds' The Ramsgate No 5 bitter or a sip of Biddenden cider. Sitting on the suntrap terrace here, the hazy smudge on the horizon is likely to be the French coast, shimmering beyond the silently passing ferries and freighters. Crane your neck

upwards and the view of Blighty's fine countryside is cut off by – well – Blighty's most famous natural feature, the White Cliffs of Dover. The food is renowned for its wonderful flavours, and all freshly made on the premises from local produce as far as possible. Many dishes have a story behind them: they might be based on an old Roman recipe, a reworked classic dish, or perhaps an original creation. Remarkably, the menus change twice daily, depending on what's available.

Open all day all wk 11-11 (Sun 11-10.30) **Food** Lunch all wk 12.30-2.45 Dinner all wk 6.30-8.45 ⊕ FREE HOUSE ◀ Gadds' The Ramsgate No 5, Fyne, Adnams Ö Biddenden, Westons. **Facilities** Non-diners area ♦️ Children's portions Garden ⌒ Parking WiFi

SANDWICH
Map 7 TR35

George & Dragon Inn

tel: 01304 613106 **Fisher St CT13 9EJ**
email: enquiries@georgeanddragon-sandwich.co.uk
dir: Between Dover & Canterbury (park at Quay Car Park, walk through Fisher Gate to Fisher St)

Charming family run pub serving modern British food

Built in 1446, ale was first sold here in 1549, but was only licensed under the name of George & Dragon in 1615. This town centre pub oozes charm and character, with its wood floors and open fires, and makes a welcome pit stop when exploring historic Sandwich on foot. Run by two brothers, you can refuel with a pint of well-kept Shepherd Neame Master Brew or a guest ale. On the monthly-changing evening menu, you might find butterbean and mushroom pâté with bread and onion marmalade, followed by pork loin on cabbage and leeks, bacon and cheddar mash and roasted apple sauce. Head outside to the picturesque suntrap courtyard in summer.

Open all day 11-11 (Sun 12-4) Closed Sun eve **Food** Lunch all wk 12-2 Dinner Mon-Sat 6-9 Av main course £8-£13 Set menu available ⊕ ENTERPRISE INNS ◀ Shepherd Neame Master Brew, Wantsum, Guest ales Ö Aspall. 🍷 9 **Facilities** Non-diners area 🐾 (Bar Garden) Garden ⌒ WiFi

SELLING
Map 7 TR05

The Rose and Crown

tel: 01227 752214 **Perry Wood ME13 9RY**
email: info@roseandcrownperrywood.co.uk
dir: From A28 right at Badgers Hill, left at end. 1st left signed Perry Wood

Pretty country pub with a long history

Goldings hops are draped around this rambling, low-beamed 16th-century inn, with exposed brickwork, inglenooks, horse brasses, corn dollies and a bar offering Harvey's and Adnams real ales and Biddenden cider. Descend to the restaurant, where the ghost of Hammond Smith, murdered after a boozy day in 1889, may join you, but don't let his presence detract from the pleasure of home-cooked Kent fish pie; lamb shank; chicken and carrot casserole; or brie, bacon and walnut jacket potato. The flower-festooned garden is made for summer eating and drinking.

Open 12-3 6.30-11 Closed 25-26 Dec eve, 1 Jan eve, Mon eve **Food** Lunch all wk 12-2 Dinner Tue-Sat 6.30-9 ⊕ FREE HOUSE ◀ Adnams Southwold Bitter, Harvey's Sussex Best Bitter, Guest ale Ö Westons Stowford Press, Biddenden.
Facilities Non-diners area 🐾 (Bar Restaurant Garden) ♦️ Children's menu Children's portions Play area Garden ⌒ Parking 🚌 (notice required)

SHIPBOURNE
Map 6 TQ55

The Chaser Inn

tel: 01732 810360 **Stumble Hill TN11 9PE**
email: enquiries@thechaser.co.uk
dir: *N of Tonbridge take A227 towards Shipbourne. Pub on left*

Popular pub with famous connections

Once a haunt for stars such as Richard Burton and Elizabeth Taylor, The Chaser Inn is an informal, relaxed village inn, next to the church and overlooking the common. Well-kept real ales and plenty of wines by the glass are complemented by an extensive menu of sandwiches, light bites and main courses such as whole grilled plaice, caper and citrus butter; or steak and vegetable suet pudding. There is a lovely beer garden and the covered courtyard comes into its own in the winter months. The pub takes its name from its long association with the nearby Fairlawne racing stables.

Open all day all wk **Food** Contact pub for details ⊕ WHITING AND HAMMOND ◀ Greene King IPA & Abbot Ale, Morland Old Speckled Hen, Guest ales. ♥ 16
Facilities Non-diners area ❤ (Bar Garden) ♦ Children's portions Garden ⋒ Parking WiFi ⬛ (notice required)

SMARDEN
Map 7 TQ84

The Chequers Inn
PICK OF THE PUBS

tel: 01233 770217 **The Street TN27 8QA**
email: spaldings@thechequerssmarden.com
dir: *Through Leeds village, left signed Sutton Valence & Headcorn, left for Smarden. Pub in village centre*

Ancient pub with courtyard and lovely gardens

The former weavers' village of Smarden has around 200 buildings of architectural and historical interest, one of which is the clapboarded 14th-century Chequers Inn. Its beautiful landscaped garden features a large carp pond and an attractive south-facing courtyard. Ales brewed by Sharp's, Fullers, Wadworth and the Old Dairy Brewery are served in the low-beamed bars. Seasonal ingredients are sourced locally for the menus of traditional and modern food. Typical of the restaurant choices are starters of mussels and squid in a spicy sauce with garlic bread; and main courses like pan-fried chicken stuffed with goats' cheese and wrapped in bacon. The bar menu, carte and children's menu are all served on Sundays too, when traditional beef, lamb and pork roasts are joined by gammon and turkey.

Open all day all wk **Food** Lunch all wk 12-3 Dinner all wk 6-9 ⊕ FREE HOUSE ◀ Sharp's Doom Bar, Fuller's London Pride, Wadworth 6X, Old Dairy ♂ Westons Stowford Press. **Facilities** Non-diners area ♦ Children's menu Children's portions Garden ⋒ Parking WiFi ⬛

SPELDHURST
Map 6 TQ54

George & Dragon
PICK OF THE PUBS

tel: 01892 863125 **Speldhurst Hill TN3 0NN**
email: julian@speldhurst.com
dir: *Phone for detailed directions*

Kentish ales, wine and fare in ancient timber-framed inn

Set in a part of Kent dappled with architectural gems like Penshurst Place and Hever Castle, this wonderful village inn more than holds its own. Much of the heavy tiled roof, vast chimneys and ancient timbers have been here since the pub was built over 800 years ago; the interior is equally mature with log fires and rippling oak beams creating a timeless setting for guests keen to savour the wet and dry sides of the inn. The wine list is extensive (including a Kent sparkling white), whilst lovers of the hop will appreciate beers from some of the area's burgeoning microbrewery sector. The seasonal menu promises organic, free-range and GM-free produce whenever possible. Provenance is king, with rare-breed pork and venison coming from named farms nearby, fish from a Kentish fishmonger and vegetables from local suppliers. A starter of seared local pigeon breast with smoked bacon and watercress walnut salad sets a high standard; mains cover Ashdown Forest venison rump and chop with hand-cut chips and aïoli, or seared fillet of sea bass with samphire and mussels.

Open all day all wk **Food** Lunch all wk 12-2.30 Dinner Mon-Sat 7-9.45 Av main course £10.50 Set menu available ⊕ FREE HOUSE ◀ Harvey's Sussex Best Bitter, Westerham George's Marvellous Medicine, Larkins ♂ Westons Stowford Press. ♥ 11
Facilities Non-diners area ❤ (Bar Garden) ♦ Children's portions Family room Garden ⋒ Parking WiFi ⬛

STALISFIELD GREEN
Map 7 TQ95

The Plough Inn

tel: 01795 890256 **ME13 0HY**
email: info@theploughinnstalisfield.co.uk
dir: *From A20 (dual carriageway) W of Charing follow Stalisfield Green signs. Approx 2m to village*

Downland pub with a passion for Kentish produce

The Plough Inn is a splendid, 15th-century Wealden hall house situated by the green in an unspoilt hamlet high up on the North Downs. A real country pub, it enjoys far-reaching views across the Swale estuary and is worth seeking out for the array of Kentish drinks - microbrewery beers, ciders and juices - and modern pub food prepared from ingredients sourced from local farms and artisan producers. The menus evolve with the seasons; there's a bar snack menu plus a set menu at lunchtime and on Tuesday, Wednesday and Thursday evenings.

Open 12-3 6-11 (Sat 12-11 Sun 12-6) Closed Mon **Food** Lunch Tue-Sat 12-2, Sun 12-3.30 Dinner Tue-Sat 6-9 Set menu available Restaurant menu available Tue-Sun ⊕ FREE HOUSE ◀ Local Guest ales ♂ Biddenden Bushels. ♥ 9 **Facilities** Non-diners area ❤ (Bar Restaurant Garden) ♦ Children's menu Children's portions Family room Garden ⋒ Beer festival Parking ⬛ (notice required)

STOWTING
Map 7 TR14

The Tiger Inn

tel: 01303 862130 **TN25 6BA**
email: info@tigerinn.co.uk
dir: *Phone for detailed directions*

Classic village pub with rustic charm and hearty food

Lost down winding lanes in a scattered North Downs hamlet, the 250-year-old Tiger Inn oozes traditional character and rural charm. The front bar is delightfully rustic and unpretentious, with stripped oak floors, two warming wood-burning stoves, old cushioned pews and scrubbed old pine tables. Mingle with the locals at the bar with a pint of Master Brew or the pub's own Tiger Top, then order a hearty meal from the inviting chalkboard menu — perhaps Romney Marsh rack of lamb with redcurrant jus; whole Dover sole; and chicken, ham and leek pie with shortcrust pastry. In summer dine alfresco on the suntrap front terrace. There are super walks all around.

Open all day Closed Mon & Tue **Food** Lunch Wed-Sun 12-9 Dinner Wed-Sun 12-9 Av main course £13 ⊕ FREE HOUSE ◀ Shepherd Neame Master Brew, Harvey's, Old Dairy, Gadds', Hop Fuzz, Tiger Inn Tiger Top ♂ Biddenden. ♥ 10
Facilities Non-diners area ❤ (Bar Garden) ♦ Children's menu Children's portions Garden ⋒ Parking WiFi ⬛

TENTERDEN
Map 7 TQ83

White Lion Inn

tel: 01580 765077 **57 High St TN30 6BD**
email: info@whateliontenterden.com
dir: *On A28 (Ashford to Hastings road)*

Spruced up town centre inn

Beside the broad tree-lined street in Tenterden, 'the Jewel of the Weald', stands this renovated and rejuvenated inn, which combines many original features with a contemporary look and feel. Reasonably priced fresh food ranges from starters of baked camembert with onion jam to share, or salmon and crab cakes with tartare sauce, to mains such as steak, mushroom and ale pie; battered haddock and fat chips; or grilled salmon Niçoise. Look out for special offers on pub classics served all day. Reliable Marston's and Wychwood Hobgoblin ales are the mainstay in the bar.

Open all wk 10am-11pm (wknds 10am-mdnt) **Food** Lunch Mon-Sat 12-10, Sun 12-9 Dinner Mon-Sat 12-10, Sun 12-9 ⊕ MARSTON'S ◀ Marston's EPA, Old Dairy, Ringwood Best Bitter, Wychwood Hobgoblin, Guest ales ♂ Symonds. **Facilities** Non-diners area ♦ Children's menu Children's portions Outside area ⊓ Parking WiFi ➡ (notice required)

TONBRIDGE
Map 6 TQ54

See also Penshurst

The Little Brown Jug

tel: 01892 870318 **Chiddingstone Causeway TN11 8JJ**
email: enquiries@thelittlebrownjug.co.uk
dir: *On B2027 between Tonbridge & Bough Beech*

Warm and welcoming village favourite

With three open fires on cold days, this village treasure always feels as warm as toast; even the Polynesian-style Little Brown Huts in the garden are heated, each seating up to ten for lunch or dinner (booking advised). Amenities of a more conventional kind include the bar, dispensing Chiddingstone-brewed Larkins beers, and the restaurant, which does a particularly good line in moules and frites; Stargazy fish pie; Highfield Farm shoulder of lamb; coq au vin; and vegetable Wellington. Events are a big thing here, with sausage and pie weeks, and the May and October three-day beer festivals.

Open all day all wk **Food** Contact pub for details ⊕ WHITING AND HAMMOND ◀ Greene King IPA & Abbot, Larkins, Guest ale ♂ Thatchers. ☘ 16 **Facilities** ☘ (Bar Garden) ♦ Children's portions Play area Garden ⊓ Beer festival Parking WiFi ➡

TUDELEY
Map 6 TQ64

The Poacher & Partridge

tel: 01732 358934 **Hartlake Rd TN11 0PH**
email: enquiries@thepoacherandpartridge.com
dir: *A21 S onto A26 E, at rdbt turn right. After 2m turn sharp left into Hartlake Rd, 0.5m on right*

Stylish rural pub with good food

Set amongst Kentish orchards, this pretty country pub was taken over by new owners in 2014 and refurbished to a high standard. The Poacher & Partridge has a rustic, down-to-earth feel with sturdy old wood furniture and unique features such as a beautiful old wine cellar and deli kitchen. Outside, you'll discover a large garden with a children's play area, ideal for a refreshing summer pint of Harveys

from the wide selection of local ales and ciders. Traditional English cuisine and regional French brasserie-style fare feature on the pub's well-considered menu, perhaps smoked haddock bake, followed by beef brisket stew.

Open all day all wk **Food** Lunch all wk 12-3 Dinner all wk 6-9.45 Av main course £14 ⊕ FREE HOUSE ◀ Sharp's Doom Bar, Shepherd Neame Spitfire, Tonbridge, Harvey's, Old Dairy ♂ Thatchers Gold, Aspall, Biddenden. ☘ 30 **Facilities** Non-diners area ☘ (Bar Garden) ♦ Children's menu Children's portions Play area Garden ⊓ Parking WiFi ➡ (notice required)

TUNBRIDGE WELLS (ROYAL)
Map 6 TQ53

The Beacon
PICK OF THE PUBS

See Pick of the Pubs on opposite page

The Crown Inn

tel: 01892 864742 **The Green, Groombridge TN3 9QH**
email: crown.inn.groombridge@gmail.com
dir: *Take A264 W of Tunbridge Wells, then B2110 S*

Good food and bags of character

In the 18th century this charming free house was the infamous headquarters for a gang of smugglers who hid their casks of tea in the passages between the cellar and Groombridge Place, later home to Sir Arthur Conan Doyle. Doyle made this 16th-century pub his local and today, its low beams and an inglenook fireplace are the setting for some great food and drink. Favourites include lamb's liver with crispy bacon and mash; beer battered fish and chips, peas and home-made tartare sauce, and daily specials based on fresh local produce. Eat alfresco during the summer months.

Open all day all wk **Food** Lunch Mon-Fri 12-2.30, Sat 12-9, Sun 12-6 Dinner Mon-Fri 6-9, Sat 12-9, Sun 12-6 ⊕ FREE HOUSE ◀ Harvey's Sussex Best Bitter, Black Cat, Larkins ♂ Westons Stowford Press. **Facilities** Non-diners area ☘ (Bar Garden) ♦ Children's menu Children's portions Play area Garden ⊓ Parking ➡ (notice required)

The Hare on Langton Green
PICK OF THE PUBS

tel: 01892 862419 **Langton Rd, Langton Green TN3 0JA**
email: hare@brunningandprice.co.uk
dir: *From Tunbridge Wells take A264 towards East Grinstead. Pub on x-rds at Langton Green*

Imaginative daily-changing menus

In a well-to-do suburb of equally well-to-do Tunbridge Wells, overlooking the village green, the 'brewers-Tudor-style' Hare opened in 1901, replacing an 18th-century predecessor demolished a year earlier after a fire. Pub group Brunning & Price lease it from Greene King, so expect the usual Bury St Edmunds range, plus Biddenden Bushel and Aspall ciders. The extensive menu changes daily: an interesting way to start is with crispy duck egg, shredded duck, pickled mushrooms, asparagus and sherry vinaigrette; or vegetable pakora, coconut and mango salad with raita. Equally off the beaten menu track are mains of Malaysian fish stew (king prawns, cod, salmon, haddock and mussels) with sticky rice; and chilli and herb gnocchi with roasted pepper, grilled courgette, sweet potato and Bloody Mary dressing. For something closer to home, try braised shoulder of lamb with dauphinoise potato, baby carrots, parsnips and mint jus. There are also light bites and sandwiches.

Open all day all wk **Food** Lunch Sun-Thu 12-9.30, Fri-Sat 12-10 Dinner Sun-Thu 12-9.30, Fri-Sat 12-10 ⊕ BRUNNING & PRICE ◀ Greene King IPA, Ruddles Best & Abbot Ale, Morland Original, Hardys & Hansons Olde Trip ♂ Westons Old Rosie & Wyld Wood Organic, Aspall, Biddenden Bushel. ☘ 20 **Facilities** Non-diners area ☘ (Bar Garden) ♦ Children's menu Children's portions Garden ⊓ Parking WiFi

PICK OF THE PUBS

The Beacon

TUNBRIDGE WELLS (ROYAL) Map 6 TQ53

tel: 01892 524252
Tea Garden Ln TN3 9JH
email: info@the-beacon.co.uk
web: www.the-beacon.co.uk
dir: *From Tunbridge Wells take A264 towards East Grinstead. Pub 1m on left*

Extensive grounds, great views, good food

As the address suggests, there were tea gardens here in an area called Happy Valley. They were created about 1820, but the late Victorians presumably lost interest, because in 1895 Sir Walter Harris was able to buy the land and build a house, Rusthall Beacon, here. After a wartime spell as a hostel for Jewish refugees, in 1950 it became a hotel. Standing in nearly 17 acres, the building is jam-packed with impressive architectural features – moulded plaster ceilings and stained glass windows in particular. The bar offers a trinity of real ales – Harvey's Best, Larkins Traditional and Timothy Taylor Landlord, as well as Stowford Press draught cider and Westons Organic bottled pear cider. Take a pint out to the terrace and enjoy the terrific views. Food is served in the bar, the restaurant, or in one of three private dining rooms, where the menus take full advantage of local produce, not least the fruit, vegetables and herbs from The Beacon's own kitchen garden. Start perhaps with

confit duck with an Asian pomegranate dressing and poached pear; a sharing charcuterie plate with home-made pickle and rustic bread. For a main course, select from a list containing pan-seared sea bass fillet with red risotto, confit cherry tomatoes and a deep-fried quail's egg; pan-seared pork fillet with celeriac purée, croquette potatoes, buttered spinach and blackberry sauce. There are plenty of others to choose from, as well as the daily specials board. A good wine list offers plenty of choice by the glass.

Open all day all wk 11-11 (Sun 12-10.30) **Food** Lunch Mon-Thu 12-2.30, Fri-Sun 12-9.30 Dinner Mon-Thu 6.30-9.30, Fri-Sun 12-9.30 Set menu available ⊕ FREE HOUSE

🛢 Harvey's Sussex Best Bitter, Timothy Taylor Landlord, Guest ales ♂ Westons Stowford Press ♟ 12
Facilities Non-diners area 👪 Children's menu Children's portions Garden 🎪 Beer festival Parking WiFi 🚌 (notice required)

WESTERHAM
Map 6 TQ45

The Fox & Hounds

tel: 01732 750328 **Toys Hill TN16 1QG**
email: hickmott1@hotmail.com
dir: *From A25 in Brasted follow brown signs for pub into Chart Lane. 2m to pub*

Great ale house, especially for dog owners

Chartwell, where Sir Winston Churchill lived, is not far from this late 18th-century alehouse surrounded by National Trust land high on Kent's Greensand Ridge. All food served in the bar and traditionally styled restaurant is made on the premises from locally sourced produce. A starter might be anchovy and red onion shortcrust tartlet, followed by roasted pork tenderloin, sauté potatoes, black pudding, vegetables and apple sauce. Their signature dish is a 'fish pot' – a French-style bouillabaisse served with crusty bread. Lunchtime filled rolls are available Tuesdays to Saturdays and there are hog roasts in summer. The landlord describes the pub as very dog friendly.

Open all day all wk 11-11 Closed 25 Dec **Food** Lunch all wk 12-9 Dinner all wk 12-9 ⊕ GREENE KING ◀ IPA, Abbot Ale, Morland Original. ₹ 10 **Facilities** Non-diners area ❤ (Bar Garden Outside area) ◑ Children's menu Garden Outside area ⋒ Parking WiFi ▭ (notice required)

Grasshopper on the Green

tel: 01959 562926 **The Green TN16 1AS**
email: info@grasshopperonthegreen.com
dir: *M25 junct 5, A21 towards Sevenoaks, then A25 to Westerham. Or M25 junct 6, A22 towards East Grinstead, A25 to Westerham*

Local brews and modern home-cooked cuisine

Overlooking Westerham's pretty green, the 700-year-old Grasshopper takes its name from the arms of local merchant Thomas Gresham, founder of London's Royal Exchange in 1565. The bar's low-beamed ceilings, hung with antique jugs, and its winter log fire are particularly appealing, as are Westerham brewery's Grasshopper and British Bulldog real ales. House specials include spicy chicken wrap; and home-made roasted vegetable lasagne, while regular cast members include grilled fresh tuna, lemon butter and capers; and slow-roasted lamb shank with red wine and rosemary jus. Ask long-term hosts Neale and Anne Sadlier for directions to Chartwell, Sir Winston Churchill's former home.

Open all day all wk **Food** Lunch all wk 12-9 Dinner all wk 12-9 Av main course £9 ⊕ FREE HOUSE ◀ Adnams Broadside, Harvey's Sussex Best Bitter, Courage Best Bitter, Westerham British Bulldog BB & Grasshopper ♻ Symonds. ₹ 12 **Facilities** Non-diners area ❤ (Bar Garden) ◑ Children's menu Children's portions Play area Garden ⋒ Parking WiFi ▭ (notice required)

WEST MALLING
Map 6 TQ65

The Farm House
`PICK OF THE PUBS`

tel: 01732 843257 **97 The High St ME19 6NA**
email: enquiries@thefarmhouse.biz
dir: *M20 junct 4, S on A228. Right to West Malling. Pub in village centre*

Elegant gastro-pub adding a French accent to local ingredients

Well positioned in the heart of the Kentish market town of West Malling, with a pretty walled garden overlooking 15th-century stone barns. The handsome Elizabethan building offers a friendly welcome, whether stopping for refreshment in the stylish bar or eating in one its two dining areas. Local seasonal ingredients are expertly used in menus with a strong French influence. So a glass of wine may be

called for – choose from 20 sold by the glass. A typical starter is sticky pork cheek with pak choi, ginger and garlic. Main courses vary from pub favourites such as Harvey's beer battered fish and chips; to seared sea bass with Kentish new potatoes, roasted Jerusalem artichokes and crayfish beurre blanc. The choice for children is impressively varied and sophisticated, with dishes like lamb koftas with flatbread, salad and dip. Beer festival in early May.

Open all day all wk 10am-11pm **Food** Lunch Mon-Thu 10-3, Fri-Sat 10-9.45, Sun 10-9.30 Dinner Mon-Thu 6-9.45, Fri-Sat 10-9.45, Sun 10-9.30 Av main course £16 ⊕ ENTERPRISE INNS ◀ Harvey's, Sharp's Doom Bar, Guinness ♻ Biddenden, Aspall. ₹ 20 **Facilities** Non-diners area ◑ Children's portions Garden ⋒ Beer festival Parking WiFi

WHITSTABLE
Map 7 TR16

NEW Pearson's Arms

tel: 01227 773133 **Sea Wall CT5 1BT**
email: info@pearsonsarmsbyrichardphillips.co.uk
dir: *In town centre. On one-way system, left at end of High St*

Relaxed seafront hostelry serving the county's best

Once owned by the Kray twins, this beach-facing pub was built to accommodate workers building the railway line between the town and Canterbury – now a popular rambling route called the Crab and Winkle Way. Today this friendly pub proffers all good Kentish things, including ales such as Gadds Seasider, and Aspalls cider; drinks can be served in plastic cups for taking to the beach. Chef Richard Phillips' flavoursome food is fresh and also sourced as locally as possible: fried Whitstable rock oysters with celeriac remoulade could precede a plate of Griggs of Hythe smoked haddock with poached egg and bubble-and-squeak.

Open all day all wk **Food** Lunch Mon-Sat 12-9.30 Dinner Mon-Sat 12-9.30 Av main course £7 Set menu available Restaurant menu available all wk ⊕ ENTERPRISE INNS ◀ Timothy Taylor Landlord, Whitstable IPA, Gadds Seasider ♻ Aspall. ₹ 10 **Facilities** Non-diners area ❤ (Bar) ◑ Children's menu Children's portions WiFi ▭ (notice required)

WROTHAM
Map 6 TQ65

The Bull ★★★★ INN ◉

tel: 01732 789800 **Bull Ln TN15 7RF**
email: info@thebullhotel.com **web:** www.thebullhotel.com
dir: *M20 junct 2, A20 (signed Paddock Wood, Gravesend & Tonbridge). At rdbt 3rd exit onto A20 (signed Wrotham, Tonbridge, Borough Green, M20 & M25). At rdbt take 4th exit into Bull Ln (signed Wrotham)*

Ancient pub featuring micro-beers and an aircraft theme

In a quiet country location, this attractive three-storey building can be traced to 1385; it was first licensed under Henry VII in 1495. More recently, World War II pilots relaxed here; stamps on the restaurant ceiling mark downed German planes, and dozens of pictures of Spitfires decorate the place. Ales from the award-winning Dark Star microbrewery are supported by a vast wine list. Food follows classic lines, but as much as possible is sourced from local growers and suppliers: Hartley Bottom lamb's liver and bacon with creamy mash, spring onions and an onion jus; or Woods Farm egg and cheese omelette are just two examples. Why not stay over in one of the bedrooms and try the circular walk from the pub?

Open all day all wk **Food** Lunch Mon-Sat 12-2.30 Dinner Mon-Sat 6-9 ⊕ FREE HOUSE ◀ Dark Star Partridge Best Bitter, Hophead ♻ Westons Stowford Press. ₹ 8 **Facilities** Non-diners area ❤ (Bar Garden) ◑ Children's portions Garden ⋒ Parking WiFi ▭ (notice required) **Rooms** 11

WYE
Map 7 TR04

The New Flying Horse

tel: 01233 812297 **Upper Bridge St TN25 5AN**
email: newflyhorse@shepherd-neame.co.uk
dir: *Phone for detailed directions*

Charming inn with an award-winning garden

With a 400-year-old history, this village inn charms with its low ceilings, black beams, open brickwork and large open fireplace. In winter snuggle up by the fire, savour a pint of Late Red and select a couple of classics from the menu, such as sea bass with fennel and red pepper risotto; and roast pheasant with fondant potato and parsnip crisps. Very much the village local it has a rare bat and trap game, and a stunning World War II 'Soldier's Dream of Blighty' garden which won an award at the Chelsea Flower Show a few years ago.

Open all day all wk ⊕ SHEPHERD NEAME ◀ Master Brew, Spitfire & Late Red, Guest ales. **Facilities** ◀ Children's menu Children's portions Play area Garden Parking

LANCASHIRE

ALTHAM
Map 18 SD73

The Walton Arms

tel: 01282 774444 **Burnley Rd BB5 5UL**
email: walton-arms@btconnect.com
dir: *M65 junct 8, A678, pub between Accrington & Padiham*

Popular pub serving good pub food

A long-established way-station on an ancient highway linking Yorkshire and Lancashire, this sturdy, stone-built dining pub oozes history. Pilgrims to Whalley Abbey called at an inn here when Henry VII was king. Beams and brasses, rustic furniture and slabbed stone floors welcome today's pilgrims intent on sampling the comprehensive menu, either as a bar meal or in the atmospheric dining room. Typical choices include sea bass fillets, crayfish, chorizo and lemon risotto; spinach, cherry tomato and mozzarella suet pudding; or the inn's signature dish - shoulder of local lamb with roasted vegetables.

Open 12-2.30 5.30-11 (Sun 12-10.30) Closed Mon **Food** Lunch Tue-Sat 12-2, Sun 12-8.30 Dinner Tue-Sat 6-9, Sun 12-8.30 Set menu available Restaurant menu available Tue-Sun ⊕ J W LEES ◀ Bitter. ⚑ 16 **Facilities** Non-diners area ◀ Children's menu Children's portions Outside area ⊼ Parking ▭ (notice required)

BARROW
Map 18 SD73

The Eagle at Barrow

tel: 01254 825285 **Clitheroe Rd BB7 9AQ**
email: info@theeagleatbarrow.co.uk
dir: *Off A59, N of Whalley. Phone for detailed directions*

Successful pub with great interior

At the heart of The Eagle is the oak-panelled public bar with a log fire, antique pews and chairs, and a baby grand piano providing lively entertainment on Friday and Saturday evenings. Taylor's champagne bar is for those after a little more privacy. The wide choice of food in the Brasserie, sourced from the very best local produce, includes beef bourguignon; steamed suet steak pudding; fish pie; and spiced aubergine. Buy take-away award-winning sausages and other regional treats from the in-house Berkins Deli.

Open all day all wk 12-11 (Fri-Sat noon-1am) **Food** Lunch Mon-Sat 12-2.30, Sun 12-8 Dinner Mon-Sat 6-9 Set menu available ⊕ FREE HOUSE ◀ Courage Directors, Caledonian Deuchars IPA, Local Guest ales ♂ Old Mout. ⚑ **Facilities** Non-diners area ♣ (Bar Outside area) ◀ Children's menu Children's portions Outside area ⊼ Parking WiFi

BILSBORROW
Map 18 SD53

Owd Nell's Tavern

tel: 01995 640010 **Guy's Thatched Hamlet, Canal Side PR3 0RS**
email: info@guysthatchedhamlet.com
dir: *M6 junct 32 N on A6. In approx 5m follow brown tourist signs to Guy's Thatched Hamlet*

Old-world charm and family fun by the canal

Run by the Wilkinson family for over 30 years this country-style tavern forms part of Guy's Thatched Hamlet, a cluster of eating and drinking venues beside the Lancaster Canal. Expect excellent ales, such as Owd Nell's Canalside Bitter or Black Sheep, and an authentic country pub ambience enhanced by flagged floors, fireplaces and low ceilings. All-day fare is typified by Connemara mussels and home-made soups; followed by steak and kidney pudding (also made in the pub's kitchen) or dry-cured gammon steak; and finishing with banoffee pie. Children's menus are available. There are beer, cider, wine and oyster festivals in summer.

Open all day all wk 7am-2am Closed 25 Dec **Food** Lunch all wk 12-9 Dinner all wk 12-9 Av main course £10 Restaurant menu available all wk ⊕ FREE HOUSE ◀ Moorhouse's Premier Bitter & Pendle Witches Brew, Owd Nell's Canalside Bitter, Bowland, Copper Dragon, Black Sheep, Thwaites, Hart ♂ Thatchers Heritage & Cheddar Valley. ⚑ 20 **Facilities** Non-diners area ♣ (Bar Garden Outside area) ◀ Children's menu Children's portions Family room Garden Outside area ⊼ Beer festival Cider festival Parking WiFi ▭ (notice required)

BLACKBURN
Map 18 SD62

Clog and Billycock ⊛
PICK OF THE PUBS

tel: 01254 201163 **Billinge End Rd, Pleasington BB2 6QB**
email: enquiries@theclogandbillycock.com
dir: *M6 junct 29 to M65 junct 3, follow Pleasington signs*

Fully refurbished landmark village pub

The Bay Horse Inn was the more prosaic name the mid-Victorians bestowed on this popular village pub; today's handle celebrates the favourite attire of an early 20th-century landlord, a billycock being a felt hat. The Ribble Valley Inns group, which owns it, has upgraded the decor to include wall lights fashioned from old weaving shuttles, lamps from cobblers' shoe stretchers, and artwork by north-west artist, Nicholas Saunders. Background music is played in some parts of the building. The real ales are from Thwaites of Blackburn, while the award-winning wine list is compiled by leading authority, Craig Bancroft. All contributing towards its AA Rosette are Nigel Haworth's Lancashire hotpot; cheese and onion pie; chicken kebab and curried lentil sauce; pan-roasted sea bass with yellow beets; Garstang Blue, pear and walnut salad; and smoked fish pie. If the weather's good, eat and drink outdoors. Out on Blackburn's western fringes, the pub is well placed for walks through pleasantly wooded countryside.

Open all wk 12-11 (Sun 12-10) **Food** Lunch Mon-Fri 12-2, Sat & BHs 12-9, Sun 12-8.30, (afternoon bites Mon-Fri 2-5.30) Dinner Mon-Thu 5.30-8.30, Fri 5.30-9, Sat & BHs 12-9, Sun 12-8.30 Set menu available ⊕ RIBBLE VALLEY INNS ◀ Thwaites Original, Wainwrights & Nutty Black ♂ Kingstone Press. ⚑ 11 **Facilities** Non-diners area ♣ (Bar Outside area) ◀ Children's menu Outside area ⊼ Parking WiFi

See advert on page 303

PICK OF THE PUBS

The Millstone at Mellor ★★★★★ INN

BLACKBURN   Map 18 SD62

tel: 01254 813333
Church Ln, Mellor BB2 7JR
email: relax@millstonehotel.co.uk
web: www.millstonehotel.co.uk
dir: *M6 junct 31, A59 towards Clitheroe, past British Aerospace. Right at rdbt signed Blackburn/Mellor. Next rdbt 2nd left. At top of hill on right*

Country-edge inn with superb cuisine

This handsome coaching inn stands in an old village at the edge of Mellor Moor above Blackburn. With the beautiful Ribble Valley and Forest of Bowland Area of Natural Beauty to the north, Pendle Hill nearby and the half timbered wonder that is Samlesbury Hall just along the lanes, it's little wonder that this inn is a popular place. It's very much a village inn at the heart of the community, presided over by chef-patron Anson Bolton, whose culinary skills have repeatedly gained two AA Rosettes in recognition of his innovative take on classic dishes. Warm up by the log fire in the well-appointed bar or relax in the oak-panelled Miller's restaurant, perhaps picking at the nibbles board - black pudding fritters, bhajis and chipolatas with dips and pondering the attractive menu options. The selection of starters ranges from duck spring rolls to omelette Arnold Bennett; or settle for the fishmongers

deli board featuring smoked Scottish salmon, smoked mackerel pâté, soused herrings, fish fingers and peeled prawns. Mains reflect the strong tradition of good pub food, with a sturdy fish pie a popular option, whilst the Bowland steak, kidney and Thwaites Wainwright Ale suet pudding is a great winter warmer. Let your eyes drift to the 'Inn Season' specials board, drawing on the extravagant produce for which the Ribble Valley is widely renowned; 28-day aged Bowland steaks are also a favourite. Walkers passing from the local footpath network can expect beers from the local Thwaites brewery, founded over 200 years ago by Daniel Thwaite, who is buried in the church yard near this, one of his first pubs.

Open all day all wk **Food** Mon-Sat 12-9.30, Sun 12-9 ⊞ THWAITES INNS OF CHARACTER ◀ Lancaster Bomber, Original, Wainwright ♻ Kingstone Press. ♟ 10 **Facilities** Non-diners area ♦♦ Children's menu Children's portions Outside area ⋈ Parking WiFi **Rooms** 23

BLACKBURN *continued*

The Millstone at Mellor ★★★★★ INN @@

See Pick of the Pubs on opposite page and advert below

BLACKO
Map 18 SD84

Moorcock Inn

tel: 01282 614186 **Gisburn Rd BB9 6NG**
email: moorcockinn@gmail.com
dir: *M65 junct 13, A682, inn halfway between Blacko & Gisburn*

Country pub with many walks around

Beyond the folly of Blacko Tower, high on the road towards Gisburn on the Upper Admergill area, lies this family-run, 18th-century inn with traditional log fires, splendid views towards the Pendle Way and locally brewed cask ales in the bar. There's a wide choice on the menu and specials board including salads and sandwiches, and vegetarian and children's meals. Main dishes are hearty and include home-made pies, steaks, salads, sandwiches and specials that might include beef hash, bratwursts and schnitzels. Vegetarian options are available too.

Open 12-2 6-9 (Sat 12-9 Sun 12-6) Closed Mon eve **Food** Lunch Mon-Fri 12-2, Sat 12-9, Sun 12-6 Dinner Tue-Fri 6-9, Sat 12-9, Sun 12-6 Av main course £8 Set menu available ⊕ FREE HOUSE ◀ Reedley Hallows Ò Kingstone Press.
Facilities Non-diners area ✿ (Bar Restaurant Outside area) ♦️ Children's menu Children's portions Outside area ⊓ Parking ▄ (notice required)

BURROW
Map 18 SD67

The Highwayman @

tel: 01524 273338 **LA6 2RJ**
email: enquiries@highwaymaninn.co.uk
dir: *M6 junct 36, A65 to Kirkby Lonsdale. A683 S. Burrow approx 2m*

In a picturesque corner of Lancashire

The Highwayman is a Ribble Valley Inn, part of chef-patron Nigel Haworth's and wine expert Craig Bancroft's expanding Northcote Restaurants group. An 18th-century coaching inn, it features craggy stone floors, warm wooden furniture and log fires. Thwaites of Blackburn supply the real ales, Kingstone Press its draught Malvern cider, and Craig chooses the extensive wine list, with eleven by the glass. Inspired by Nigel, all Ribble Valley Inn menus pick up local and regional favourites, such as the reassuringly predictable Lancashire hotpot and Wainwright real ale-infused Goosnargh chicken breast. Other possibilities are Cartmel Valley pork and black pudding Scotch egg; smoked fish pie; 21-day-aged Cumbrian fell-bred sirloin steak; and cheese and onion pie. There are seasonal alternatives, a good children's menu and a gluten-free one too. Butterflies and birds love the terraced gardens, where there is comfortable seating and outdoor heating.

Open all day all wk 12-11 (Sun 12-10.30) **Food** Lunch Mon-Sat 12-2, Sun 12-8.30 Dinner Mon-Thu 5.30-8.30, Fri-Sat 5.30-9, Sun 12-8.30 Av main course £12 Set menu available ⊕ RIBBLE VALLEY INNS ◀ Thwaites Original, Lancaster Bomber & Wainwright Ò Kingstone Press. ♟ 11 **Facilities** ✿ (Bar Garden) ♦️ Children's menu Garden ⊓ Parking

See advert on page 303

CARNFORTH
Map 18 SD47

The Longlands Inn and Restaurant

tel: 01524 781256 **Tewitfield LA6 1JH**
email: info@longlandshotel.co.uk
dir: *Phone for detailed directions*

Confident cooking of local produce

Although very much Lancastrian, this traditional country inn is only minutes away from the Cumbria border. With its nooks and crannies, old beams and uneven floors, this family-run dog-friendly inn stands next to Tewitfield locks on the Lancaster Canal and is an ideal base for the Lake District. The bar, with Tirril ales on tap, rocks to live bands on Mondays while hungry music lovers consume plates of stone-baked pizzas and pasta. Otherwise look to the restaurant for good country cooking and local produce, with Lakeland steaks and Morecambe Bay shrimps on the appetising menu. Children are well catered for.

Open all day all wk 11-11 **Food** Lunch Mon-Fri 12-2.30, Sat 12-4, Sun 12-9 Dinner Mon-Sat 6-9.30, Sun 12-9 ⊕ FREE HOUSE ◀ Tirril Old Faithful, Black Sheep, Bowland Hen Harrier, Old School Brewery. ♟ 9 **Facilities** Non-diners area ✿ (Bar Garden) ♦️ Children's menu Garden ⊓ Parking WiFi ▄ (notice required)

CHIPPING
Map 18 SD64

Dog & Partridge

tel: 01995 61201 **Hesketh Ln PR3 2TH**
dir: *M6 junct 31A, follow Longridge signs. At Longridge left at 1st rbdt, straight on at next 3 rdbts. At Alston Arms turn right. 3m, pub on right*

Tudor pub with a restored barn restaurant

Dating back to 1515, this pleasantly modernised rural pub in the Ribble Valley enjoys delightful views of the surrounding fells. The barn has been transformed into a welcoming dining area, where home-made food on the comprehensive bar snack menu is backed by a specials board featuring fresh fish and game dishes. A typical menu shows a starter of deep-fried garlic mushrooms; and chilled melon with cream curry sauce; then mains of braised pork chops with home-made apple sauce and stuffing; poached salmon with prawn sauce; or home-made steak and kidney pie.

Open 11.45-3 6.45-11 (Sat 11.45-3 6-11 Sun 11.45-10.30) Closed Mon **Food** Lunch Tue-Sat 12-1.45 ⊕ FREE HOUSE ◀ Black Sheep, Tetley's, Guest ales. ♀ 8 **Facilities** Non-diners area ♦♦ Children's menu Children's portions Parking ▭

CHORLTON CUM HARDY
Map 15 SJ89

NEW The Horse & Jockey

tel: 0161 860 7794 **Chorlton Green M21 9HS**
email: info@horseandjockeychorlton.com
dir: *M60 junct 7, A56 towards Stretford. Right onto A5145 towards Chorlton. After lights, 2nd right into St Clements Rd. Pub on left on green*

Facing Chorlton's wooded town green

Assuming this Tudor pub's interior designers had a free hand when it was last refurbished, they certainly made the most of it. Wherever you look - the bar, the restaurant, the rooms, the beer garden - the results are impressive. The pub doubles as the home of the Bootleg Brewery, run by an all-too-rare female head brewer. Meet her perhaps at the Jocktoberfest, held over the last weekend in September. Home-made 'gourmet' pies; Lancashire lamb hotpot; seafood platter; pearl barley and beetroot risotto; mussels frites; Thai-style aubergine curry with coconut rice; and burger boards all feature on a comprehensive menu.

Open all day all wk **Food** Lunch all wk Dinner all wk Av main course £9.50 Restaurant menu available all wk ⊕ JOSEPH HOLT ◀ Bootleg Chorlton Pale Ale, Mammoth Real McCoy, Prohibition Lawless IPA ♂ Westons Stowford Press. ♀ **Facilities** Non-diners area ♣ (Bar Outside area) ♦♦ Children's menu Children's portions Outside area ▭ Beer festival WiFi

CLAUGHTON
Map 18 SD54

NEW The Fenwick Seafood Pub

tel: 01524 221157 **Hornby Rd LA2 9LA**
email: info@fenwickarms.co.uk
dir: *M6 junct 34, A683. Follow Kirkby Lonsdale signs. Approx 5m to pub on left*

Specialist seafood pub

Joycelyn Neve founded her Seafood Pub Company on the back of her family's long-standing maritime associations. One of her several pubs, this 250-year-old inn, with open fires, low-beamed ceilings and oak-planked floors, combines its traditional role with that of specialist fish and seafood restaurant. Top quality produce arrives daily from the family business in Fleetwood, to emerge from the kitchen perhaps as haddock goujons with pea purée; monkfish Stroganoff; or Malaysian seafood curry. Other attractions include rabbit and pheasant pie with bubble-and-squeak; and cauliflower cheese with hazelnut and spring onion crumble. In the bar there's Black Sheep and Dark Horse Hetton Pale Ale.

Open all day all wk **Food** Lunch Mon-Sat 12-3, Sun 12-8.30 Dinner Mon-Thu 5-9, Fri-Sat 5-10, Sun 12-8.30 ⊕ FREE HOUSE ◀ Black Sheep, Dark Horse Hetton Pale Ale. ♀ 14 **Facilities** Non-diners area ♣ (Bar Outside area) ♦♦ Children's menu Children's portions Outside area ▭ Beer festival Parking WiFi ▭ (notice required)

CLITHEROE
Map 18 SD74

The Assheton Arms
`PICK OF THE PUBS`

tel: 01200 441227 **Downham BB7 4BJ**
email: info@asshetonarms.com
dir: *A59 to Chatburn, then follow Downham signs*

Historic north west inn focusing on seafood

Originally a farmhouse brewing beer just for its farm workers, this pub became the George and Dragon in 1872, then in 1950 was renamed in honour of the contribution Ralph Assheton, Lord Clitheroe, made to the war effort during World War II. Just a few years ago the inn was taken over by the family-owned and operated Seafood Pub Company who made sweeping changes. At the bar you'll find a great choice of real ales, as well as cider from Thatchers. Local sourcing is a priority here and the fish- and seafood-oriented menu is full of interest, with typical choices including lobster and salmon momos with tomato and leaf broth; smoked haddock tart; piri piri swordfish, herb and citrus quinoa, smoked peppers and crispy chickpeas; and Goan king prawn curry. Besides the regular menu there are daily specials, and plenty of choice for those who aren't so keen on fish. The inn hosts a seafood festival in September.

Open all day all wk 12-10.30 (Fri-Sat 12-12) **Food** Lunch Mon-Sat 12-3, Sun 12-8 Dinner Mon-Thu 6-8.30, Fri-Sat 6-9, Sun 12-8 ⊕ FREE HOUSE ◀ Thwaites Wainwright, Black Sheep, Hawkshead, Timothy Taylor ♂ Thatchers Gold, Kopparberg. ♀ 10 **Facilities** Non-diners area ♣ (Bar Garden) ♦♦ Children's menu Children's portions Garden ▭ Parking WiFi ▭ (notice required)

ELSWICK
Map 18 SD43

The Ship at Elswick

tel: 01995 672777 **High St PR4 3ZB**
email: mail@theshipatelswick.co.uk
dir: *M55 junct 3, A585 signed Fleetwood. Right onto Thistleton Rd (B5269)*

Former farmhouse in a quiet village, offering hearty food

In a quiet village on the Fylde and handy both for Blackpool and the quieter resorts of Cleveleys and Fleetwood, this former farmhouse is now a reliable village local and dining inn. From Fleetwood come some of the fish inhabiting the very traditional menu here; beef and Guinness pie is another favourite or start with a plate of Bury black pudding with poached egg hollandaise, chorizo and rocket. There are also pasta choices, salads and a Sunday roast. The owners are proud to use Lancashire produce in most of their dishes, although the standard beer is Yorkshire's Black Sheep.

Open all day all wk **Food** Contact pub for details ⊕ PUNCH TAVERNS ◀ Jennings Cumberland Ale, Black Sheep, Guest ales. ♀ 8 **Facilities** Non-diners area ♦♦ Children's menu Children's portions Play area Garden ▭ Parking WiFi ▭

FENCE
Map 18 SD83

Fence Gate Inn

tel: 01282 618101 **Wheatley Lane Rd BB12 9EE**
email: info@fencegate.co.uk
dir: *From M65 junct 13 towards Fence, 1.5m, pub set back on right opposite T-junct for Burnley*

Village inn with a bustling brasserie

Once a private house, this imposing 300-year-old building next to the village church only became an inn as recently as 1982. At the edge of beautiful open countryside, the pub's brasserie and dining suites reveal its function as a foodie destination, but drinkers aren't forgotten, with a wood-panelled bar featuring a grand log fire and high-quality furnishings, where Lancashire-brewed beers are the order of the day. The Lancashire theme continues with the locally sourced food going into dishes such as Bowland beef steak burger, pulled pork sandwich, chicken schnitzel, lamb kofta salad and vegetable Thai green curry.

Open all day all wk noon-close **Food** Lunch Mon-Sat 12-2.30, Sun 12-8 Dinner Mon-Sat 6-9, Sun 12-8 ⊕ FREE HOUSE ◼ Courage Directors, Caledonian Deuchars IPA, Theakston, Moorhouse's, Bowland, Guest ales. ♛ 10 **Facilities** Non-diners area ♣ (Bar Garden) ♦♦ Children's menu Children's portions Garden Parking WiFi ▄

FENISCOWLES
Map 18 SD62

Oyster & Otter
PICK OF THE PUBS

tel: 01254 203200 **631 Livesey Branch Rd BB2 5DQ**
email: info@oysterandotter.co.uk
dir: *M65 junct 3, right at lights, right at mini rdbt into Livesey Branch Rd*

A family-owned, seafood-led gastro-pub with global influences

This Blackburn-fringe pub has more of a New England look than mill-town Lancashire, thanks to the clapboard and stone exterior. Successful ex-Fleetwood fish wholesaler Chris Neve, its owner, comes from a long line of North Sea and Irish Sea trawlermen; his daughter Joycelyn studied the coastal food industry in South America before becoming head of operations here. The third lynch-pin is executive chef Antony Shirley, formerly head chef at Raffles in the West Indies. You might try fish starters such as crispy katsu prawns with Japanese curry dip, while main courses include roast hake with bacon and brioche crumb. Alternatively, there's Indian slow roast lamb shank; or baby back ribs with orange, rosemary and chilli, apple slaw and sea salt fries. A typical dessert is chocolate and cherry mousse with almond cookie crush. In addition to the menu, the specials board regularly features the best fish straight from Fleetwood, complemented by locally sourced produce.

Open all day all wk **Food** Lunch all wk 12-5 Dinner Sun-Thu 5-9, Fri-Sat 5-10 ⊕ THWAITES ◼ Wainwright, Lancaster Bomber, Original ♂ Kingstone Press. ♛ 9 **Facilities** Non-diners area ♦♦ Children's menu Children's portions Garden Parking WiFi ▄ (notice required)

FORTON
Map 18 SD45

The Bay Horse Inn
PICK OF THE PUBS

tel: 01524 791204 **LA2 0HR**
email: yvonne@bayhorseinn.com
dir: *M6 junct 33 take A6 towards Garstang, turn left for pub, approx 1m from M6*

Stylish family-run inn with imaginative menu

Tucked down a country lane on the edge of the Forest of Bowland, the Wilkinson family has been at the helm of this charming 18th-century pub for over 20 years. They have continued to develop and improve the pub and its extended gardens, which lead to open fields where pheasants and deer can often be spotted. Mismatched furniture and a handsome stone fireplace with roaring log burner

characterise the inn, which offers Moorhouse's Pendle Witches Brew among the cask-conditioned real ales; the wine list is worth a look too. Chef Craig Wilkinson specialises in simple, fresh and imaginative dishes. A sample menu offers starters such as prawn and hot-smoked salmon cocktail; or smoked mackerel terrine with malt whisky, beetroot and horseradish. The short list of main courses may feature roast chump of Lancashire lamb with crushed potatoes; or slow-cooked Goosnargh duck with creamy mash and red wine-soaked prunes.

Open 12-3 6-12 Closed Mon (ex BHs L) **Food** Lunch Tue-Sat 12-1.45, Sun 12-3 Dinner Tue-Sat 6-9 ⊕ FREE HOUSE ◼ Moorhouse's Pendle Witches Brew, Black Sheep, Guest ale. ♛ 11 **Facilities** Non-diners area ♣ (Bar Garden) ♦♦ Children's portions Garden ⚏ Parking WiFi

GREAT ECCLESTON
Map 18 SD44

NEW Farmers Arms

tel: 01995 672018 **Halsalls Square PR3 0YE**
email: info@greatecclestonpub.co.uk
dir: *M55 junct 3, A585, A586 to Great Eccleston. From High St into Chapel St, pub on left*

Definitely one for all the family

This two-storey pub-restaurant, just off the main Garstang to Blackpool road, belongs to the Seafood Pub Company. This was set up in 2010 by Joycelyn Neve who, after studying the coastal food industry in South America, decided to capitalise on her family's long-standing involvement with deep-sea fishing. Naturally, there's plenty of fish and seafood on the menu, from devilled crab, salmon and brown shrimp with country toast, radish and cress salad, to seaside fritto misto with proper chips and Bloody Mary ketchup. Szechuan cod is baked in a clay pot with Chinese sherry, crispy shallots, garlic, ginger and chilli, while a Japanese-style grill is, perhaps a little strangely, the piece of kit behind Persian chicken with jewelled rice, pomegranates, almonds and yogurt dressing. No chicken nuggets for children, but the more adventurous ones can go off-piste with mushroom and roast squash patties with salad, or sticky ribs with rice and coleslaw.

Open all day all wk **Food** Lunch all wk 12-5 Dinner Sun-Thu 5-9, Fri-Sat 5-10 ⊕ FREE HOUSE ◼ Timothy Taylor Landlord, Thwaites Wainwright, Lancaster Blonde ♂ Thatchers Gold. ♛ 12 **Facilities** Non-diners area ♣ (Bar Garden Outside area) ♦♦ Children's menu Children's portions Garden Outside area ⚏ Parking WiFi ▄

GRINDLETON
Map 18 SD74

Duke of York

tel: 01200 441266 **Brow Top BB7 4QR**
email: info@dukeofyorkgrindleton.com
dir: *From A59 N of Clitheroe left to Chatburn. In Chatburn right into Ribble Ln. Over river, right at T-junct. Pub at brow of hill on left*

A leading Ribble Valley dining pub

Built of local stone, with an interior characterised by low ceilings, stone-flagged floors and little nooks and crannies, this creeper-clad village pub is at least 150 years old. Food takes the lead, although the bar still gets its fair share of Lancaster Blonde real ale drinkers. Driving things from the kitchen is chef/proprietor Michael Heathcote, on whose daily menu appears a short, but carefully chosen, choice of dishes, such as crispy duck and chorizo salad; Lancashire cheese and caramelised onion soufflé; steamed steak and ale pudding with triple cooked chips; and lobster thermidor. There's a lovely garden too.

Open 12-3 6-11 (Sun 12-3 5-11) Closed 25 Dec, Mon (ex BHs, closed Tue following BHs) **Food** Lunch Tue-Sun 12-2 Dinner Tue-Sat 6-9, Sun 5-7.30 Av main course £16.95 Set menu available ⊕ PUNCH TAVERNS ◼ Timothy Taylor Landlord, Lancaster Blonde. ♛ 20 **Facilities** Non-diners area ♣ (Bar Garden) ♦♦ Children's menu Children's portions Garden ⚏ Parking WiFi ▄ (notice required)

HESKIN GREEN
Map 15 SD51

Farmers Arms

tel: 01257 451276 **85 Wood Ln PR7 5NP**
email: andy@farmersarms.co.uk
dir: *On B5250 between M6 & Eccleston*

Handsome family-run pub

This fine 17th-century pub used to be called the Pleasant Retreat, but in 1902 the name was changed. Never mind, because this long, creeper-covered building is still pleasant, very pleasant actually, and its flagstone Vault Bar is still a retreat. Malcolm and Ann Rothwell have been here for a quarter of a century, although son Andrew and his wife Sue are slowly taking over the helm. The menu may include minted lamb cutlets or baked haddock gratin, while the main menu features Cumberland sausage, lasagne verdi, grills and steaks, and a selection of salads, jacket potatoes and sandwiches. Hand-pulled real ales include Silver Tally, named after the token that miners would exchange for a lamp.

Open all day all wk **Food** Contact pub for details ⊕ ENTERPRISE INNS ◼ Timothy Taylor Landlord, Marston's Pedigree, Prospect Silver Tally, Black Sheep, Tetley's. **Facilities** Non-diners area ❄ (Bar Garden) ♦ Children's menu Children's portions Play area Garden Parking WiFi

HEST BANK
Map 18 SD46

Hest Bank Inn

tel: 01524 824339 **2 Hest Bank Ln LA2 6DN**
email: chef.glenn@btinternet.com
dir: *From Lancaster take A6 N, after 2m left to Hest Bank*

Historic inn with lots to offer

First licensed in 1554, this former coaching inn is awash with history: it was occupied by Cromwell's officers in the Civil War and later became the haunt of highwaymen. Comedian Eric Morecambe used to drink at the canalside Hest Bank, which offers cask ales and a wide selection of meals all day, with local suppliers playing an important role in maintaining food quality. The good value menu ranges from piri piri chicken to steamed venison and beef pudding. Enjoy a pint of Thwaites Wainwright in the terraced garden. Wednesday evening is quiz night, while steak night is every Thursday. Call the pub for details of their beer festival.

Open all day all wk 11.30-11.30 (Sun 11.30-10.30) **Food** Lunch Mon-Sat 12-9, Sun 12-8 Dinner Mon-Sat 12-9, Sun 12-8 ⊕ PUNCH TAVERNS ◼ Thwaites Wainwright, Black Sheep Best Bitter, Lancaster Blonde, Guest ales. **Facilities** Non-diners area ❄ (Bar Garden) ♦ Children's menu Children's portions Play area Garden ⋒ Beer festival Parking WiFi ⛟ (notice required)

LANCASTER
Map 18 SD46

The Borough

tel: 01524 64170 **3 Dalton Square LA1 1PP**
email: jodie@theboroughlancaster.co.uk **web:** www.theboroughlancaster.co.uk
dir: *Phone for detailed directions*

Superb Lancashire produce in town house pub

This Grade II Georgian pub, in the city centre, with a Victorian frontage continues to go from strength to strength. Wooden floors, chunky tables, chesterfield sofas, warm green hues and masses of light from a huge bay window create a friendly, relaxed vibe for enjoying their own microbrewery's Borough pale, dark and bitter and a quality food offering. Using top-notch ingredients from local suppliers, including meat and eggs from surrounding farms, the seasonal menu may take in salt and pepper calamari, minted locally reared lamb Henry and summer berry jelly. Steaks from the grill and a real value 'school dinners' menu are also available.

Open all wk 12-11 (Fri noon-12.30am Sat 9am-12.20am) Closed 25 Dec **Food** Lunch Sun-Thu 12-9, Fri-Sat 12-9.30 Dinner Sun-Thu 12-9, Fri-Sat 12-9.30 Set menu available ⊕ FREE HOUSE ◼ Lancaster Amber, Young's Bitter, Wells Eagle IPA, Bowland Hen Harrier, Borough Brewery Bitter, Pale & Dark. ☗ 11 **Facilities** Non-diners area ❄ (Bar Garden) ♦ Children's menu Garden ⋒ WiFi ⛟ (notice required)

Penny Street Bridge ★★★★ INN
PICK OF THE PUBS

See Pick of the Pubs on opposite page and advert below

PICK OF THE PUBS

Penny Street Bridge ★★★★ INN

LANCASTER Map 18 SD46

tel: 01524 599900 **Penny St LA1 1XT**
email: relax@pennystreetbridge.co.uk
web: www.pennystreetbridge.co.uk
dir: *In city centre*

Quirkily elegant, canal-side, city centre townhouse offering the best of Lancashire produce

Right in the centre of the city, the listed Penny Street Bridge was once a Corporation Toll House. Demolished in 1901, it was then rebuilt as two separate pubs, which Thwaites Brewery joined together again in 2007 to create a smart town-house, bar and brasserie. Its wonderfully high ceilings make it feel light and modern, although retained period features can be seen everywhere, from the listed staircase to the servant bell hooks, and from the stained-glass windows to the rather special wardrobe in one of the bedrooms that the owners can't, and wouldn't ever want to, move. The atmosphere is quirkily elegant, with wooden floors in the brasserie, mismatched tables and tub chairs in the traditional bar and grill, and a stylish, contemporary feel in the refurbished bedrooms. Chef Andrew Nixon and his team prepare all food on the premises. Served all day, their seasonal menus make the most of the excellent Lancashire produce available locally, from smoked haddock fishcakes

or tempura tiger prawns for a starter, to main courses such as steamed steak and ale pudding; Lancashire cheese, onion and potato pie; or lamb hotpot. Steaks aged for 28 days are seared on the charcoal grill and served with thick cut chips and a Caesar side salad. Stone-baked pizzas made with fresh dough come with all the popular toppings, like pepperoni, or goats' cheese and red onion. For pudding, try the banoffee sundae, apple and blackberry crumble, or sticky toffee pudding. Opposite the pub is Penny Street Bridge itself, under which runs the Lancaster Canal on its 42-mile journey from Tewitfield to Kendal.

Open all day all wk 9am-mdnt **Food** all wk 11.30-9 Av main course £12
⊕ THWAITES INNS OF CHARACTER
◀ Wainwright, Lancaster Bomber, Original ♂ Kingstone Press. ♞ 11
Facilities Non-diners area ♦️ Children's menu Children's portions Garden ☵ Parking WiFi 🚐 (notice required)
Rooms 28

LANCASTER *continued*

The Stork Inn

tel: 01524 751234 **Conder Green LA2 0AN**
email: tracy@thestorkinn.co.uk
dir: *M6 junct 33 take A6 N. Left at Galgate & next left to Conder Green*

Traditional coaching inn with South African influences

The Stork is a white-painted coaching inn spread along the banks of the tidal Lune estuary, with a colourful 300-year-history that includes several name changes. The quaint sea port of Glasson Dock is a short walk along the Lancashire Coastal Way. In the bar you will find local ales such as Lancaster Black, Amber and Blonde. Seasonal specialities join home-cooked English and South African food like pan-fried chicken breast topped with Lancashire cheese and bacon; Boerewors - lightly spiced pure beef sausage, served with sweet potato mash and balsamic, red onion and tomato relish; and Cape Malay Kerrie - slow braised mutton and apricots in Cape Malay spices.

Open all day all wk 7.30am-11pm **Food** Sun-Mon 7.30am-8pm, Tue-Thu 7.30am-8.30pm, Fri-Sat 7.30am-9pm ⊕ ENTERPRISE INNS ◀ Timothy Taylor Landlord & Golden Best, Black Sheep, Lancaster Blonde, Amber & Black. ☗ 10
Facilities Non-diners area ✿ (Bar Restaurant Garden) ♦♦ Children's portions Play area Garden ⋒ Parking WiFi ▥

The Sun Hotel and Bar ▐ PICK OF THE PUBS

tel: 01524 66006 **LA1 1ET**
email: info@thesunhotelandbar.co.uk
dir: *6m from M6 junct 33*

Famous for its hospitality over the centuries

The oldest building in Lancaster, The Sun was first licensed as 'Stoop Hall' in 1680 as the town's premier coaching inn. Generals from the occupying Jacobean Army lodged here in 1745, and the artist JMW Turner stayed whilst making sketches of Heysham in 1812. Original features include a bottomless well and beautiful old door. Owned by the Lancaster Brewery, the pub has a wide selection of cask ales, world beers and wines. The bar is frequented throughout the day; from hotel guests and business breakfasters, to shoppers enjoying mid-morning coffee or brunch, and customers tucking into the locally sourced food at lunch and dinner, as well as wine and ale connoisseurs. The experienced kitchen brigade prepares sea bass Niçoise; baby carrot and fennel risotto; and sausages and mash. The extensive cheese board menu is especially popular, and also includes cold meats, pâtés and fish. There is a patio for alfresco dining in warmer weather, regular quiz nights and an annual beer festival in the summer.

Open all day all wk from 7.30am-late **Food** Lunch Mon-Sat 12-3, Sun 12-8 Dinner Mon-Thu 4-9, Fri 4-8, Sat 4-7, Sun 12-8 ⊕ FREE HOUSE ◀ Lancaster Amber & Blonde ♻ Kingstone Press. ☗ 23 **Facilities** Non-diners area ♦♦ Children's menu Children's portions Garden ⋒ Beer festival WiFi ▥ (notice required)

The White Cross

tel: 01524 33999 **Quarry Rd LA1 4XT**
email: twcpub@yahoo.co.uk
dir: *S on one-way system, left after Town Hall. Over canal bridge, on right*

Enjoy good food as canal boats go by

Set in a 130-year-old former cotton mill warehouse on the edge of the Lancaster Canal, The White Cross is a short stroll from the city centre. A regularly changing selection of up to 14 cask ales includes beers from Copper Dragon, Timothy Taylor and Theakston breweries, but food is an equal draw at this popular waterfront venue. Home-made pork pies; lamb, mint and rosemary burgers; lasagne al forno; and deli boards to share are typical menu choices. A beer and pie festival takes place in late April.

Open all day all wk **Food** Contact pub for details ⊕ ENTERPRISE INNS ◀ Copper Dragon Golden Pippin, Timothy Taylor Landlord, Theakston Old Peculier ♻ Westons Stowford Press & Old Rosie, Ribble Valley Gold. ☗ 13 **Facilities** Non-diners area ♦♦ Children's menu Children's portions Garden ⋒ Beer festival Parking WiFi ▥ (notice required)

▐ **LANESHAW BRIDGE**   Map 18 SD94

The Alma Inn ★★★★ INN

tel: 01282 857830 **Emmott Ln BB8 7EG**
email: reception@thealmainn.com **web:** www.thealmainn.com
dir: *M65, A6068 towards Keighley. At Laneshaw Bridge left into Emmott Ln. 0.5m, pub on left*

Country inn serving local produce

Deep in Pendle's magnificent countryside, this 18th-century inn has been lovingly restored to preserve original features such as stone floors, original beams and real fires. It offers a relaxed and welcoming setting for drinking or dining. The menu is built around local produce including steak (served with a choice of sauces) and Pendle Forest lamb cutlets, maybe pan fried and served with sweet potato fondant, tomato fondue and smoked Lancashire cauliflower cheese. Other options include sandwiches and filled crusty ciabattas. Finish with home-churned ice cream or vanilla rice pudding with home-made jam.

Open all day all wk **Food** Lunch all wk 12-9 Dinner all wk 12-9 ⊕ FREE HOUSE ◀ Moorhouse's Pride of Pendle, Lancaster Blonde, Guest ales ♻ Rekorderlig. ☗ 10
Facilities Non-diners area ✿ (Bar Restaurant Garden) ♦♦ Children's menu Children's portions Garden ⋒ Parking WiFi ▥ **Rooms** 9

▐ **LITTLE ECCLESTON**   Map 18 SD44

The Cartford Inn ▐ PICK OF THE PUBS

See Pick of the Pubs on opposite page

▐ **NEWTON-IN-BOWLAND**   Map 18 SD65

Parkers Arms ▐ PICK OF THE PUBS

tel: 01200 446236 **BB7 3DY**
email: enquiries@parkersarms.co.uk
dir: *From Clitheroe take B6478 through Waddington to Newton-in-Bowland*

Imaginative cooking and delightful countryside views

In a beautiful hamlet amidst the rolling hills of the Trough of Bowland, this Georgian dining inn is just yards from the River Hodder and enjoys panoramic views over Waddington Fell. It celebrates its rural location by serving the best of Lancashire produce. This includes ales from the local breweries, meats raised on nearby moorland, vegetables from Ribble Valley farms and fresh fish from nearby Fleetwood. French chef-patron Stosie Madi even forages for ingredients herself. The simple, but elegant, modern dishes on the daily-changing, seasonal menu include Goosnargh corn-fed chicken and leek pie; slow-braised shin of Bowland beef in ale with creamed mash; and fillet of sea bass with pea gnocchi and a lemon reduction. For pudding could be 'Wet Nelly', a classic north-west dessert originally created for Lord Nelson in Liverpool and reworked by co-owner Kathy Smith.

Open 12-3 6-close (Sat-Sun & BH 12-close) Closed Mon **Food** Lunch Tue-Sun 12-3 Dinner Tue-Sun 6-8.30 ⊕ FREE HOUSE/ENTERPRISE LEASE ♻ Westons Stowford Press.
Facilities Non-diners area ✿ (Bar Restaurant Garden) ♦♦ Children's menu Children's portions Garden ⋒ Parking WiFi ▥ (notice required)

PICK OF THE PUBS

The Cartford Inn

LITTLE ECCLESTON   Map 18 SD44

tel: 01995 670166 **PR3 0YP**
email: info@thecartfordinn.co.uk
web: www.thecartfordinn.co.uk
dir: N of A586 (W of Great Eccleston)

17th-century inn with eclectic interiors and excellent food

Set in an idyllic location adjoining a toll bridge across the tidal Rive Wyre, this award-winning 17th-century coaching inn enjoys extensive views over the countryside towards the Trough of Bowland and the Lake District. Owners Julie and Patrick Beaume have created a relaxed family-run inn: the stylish and contemporary interior is an appealing blend of striking colours, natural wood and polished floors, whilst the smart open fireplace and an eclectic selection of furniture adds a comfortable and relaxed feel to the bar lounge. There's a choice of eating areas - the Riverside Lounge, Fire Lounge and alcove, and outside on the terrace - where you can enjoy an imaginative range of dishes based on quality ingredients from local suppliers. Lunchtime sandwiches like cold poached salmon or Cumbrian cured ham and chutney come on Pebby's fresh bread and are served with organic crisps, whilst wooden platters are the showcase for local antipasti, Fleetwood

seafood, and organic crudités. Cartford favourites include venison Wellington with purple potato mash; and the ever popular Cartford cassoulet. Other main course options range from roast pork belly, gratin potatoes, buttered Savoy cabbage, apple and black pudding fritter, to fish stew and moules frites. Blackberry curd tart, and brioche bread and butter pudding are just two of the choices for dessert. The Cartford Inn makes an ideal spot from which to explore the surrounding area; Lancaster, the Royal Lytham Golf Club, and Blackpool with its Winter Gardens and Grand Theatre are all within easy reach.

Open all day Closed 25 Dec, Mon L
Food Lunch Tue-Sat 12-2, Sun 12-8.30
Dinner Mon-Thu 5.30-9, Fri-Sat 5.30-10
🍺 FREE HOUSE 🍺 Moorhouse's Pride of Pendle, Hawkshead Lakeland Gold, Theakston Old Peculier, Giddy Kipper
🍏 Westons Stowford Press.
Facilities Non-diners area 👪 Children's menu Children's portions Garden 🅿 Parking WiFi

PARBOLD

Map 15 SD41

The Eagle & Child

PICK OF THE PUBS

tel: 01257 462297 **Maltkiln Ln, Bispham Green L40 3SG**

dir: *M6 junct 27, A5209 to Parbold. Right onto B5246. 2.5m, Bispham Green on right*

Excellent alfresco dining potential in summer

A country dining pub in a pretty and peaceful location, The Eagle & Child's outside seating is ideally positioned to enjoy bowling on the green during the summer months. The bar maintains its traditional atmosphere by offering a choice of real ciders and regularly-changing guest ales from a dozen nearby microbreweries; the annual Early May Bank Holiday beer festival attracts up to 2,000 people to a huge marquee in the pub grounds. Menus for both bar and restaurant hinge on locally sourced and organic produce when possible. Typical starters of sticky chicken wings with lemon, thyme and garlic or crispy duck salad might be followed by traditional Lancashire hotpot or chicken and mushroom pie. The pub's unusual name derives from a local legend that Lord Derby's illegitimate son was discovered in an eagle's nest; a more prosaic local title is the Bird and Bastard.

Open all day all wk 12-11 (Sun 12-10.30) **Food** Lunch all wk 12-2 Dinner Sun-Thu 5.30-8.30, Fri-Sat 5.30-9 ⊕ FREE HOUSE ◀ Moorhouse's Black Cat, Thwaites Original, Southport Golden Sands, Guest ales Ò Kingstone Press, Farmhouse Cider Scrumpy. **Facilities** Non-diners area ✿ (Bar Restaurant Garden) ✦ Children's menu Children's portions Family room Garden ⊨ Beer festival Parking ▨ (notice required)

PENDLETON

Map 18 SD73

The Swan with Two Necks

tel: 01200 423112 **BB7 1PT**

email: swanwith2necks@yahoo.co.uk

dir: *Exit A59 between Whalley & Chatburn follow Pendleton signs, 0.5m to pub*

Charming inn set in a beautiful stone-built Lancashire village

Hidden away in the pretty village of Pendleton, The Swan with Two Necks is a traditional village inn dating back to 1722. Pendleton sits under Pendle Hill, which is famous for its witches, and that's not the only curious piece of history attached to this place; the inn's name refers to the tradition of marking the necks of swans belonging to the Worshipful Company of Vintners with two 'nicks' to distinguish them from swans belonging to the king or queen. Of course you won't find swan on the menu here, but this pub is renowned for its ales and ciders, so be sure to try the likes of Phoenix Wobbly Bob or Ribble Valley Gold.

Open 12-3 6-11 (Sun 12-10.30) Closed 25 Dec, Mon L **Food** Lunch Tue-Sat 12-1.45, Sun 12-6 Dinner Mon 6-8, Tue-Sat 6-8.30 Av main course £10 ⊕ FREE HOUSE ◀ Phoenix Wobbly Bob, Copper Dragon Golden Pippin, Prospect Nutty Slack, Marble, Salamander Ò Westons Traditional & Country Perry, Ribble Valley Gold. ♟ 14 **Facilities** Non-diners area ✦ Children's menu Children's portions Garden ⊨ Parking WiFi ▨ (notice required)

SAWLEY

Map 18 SD74

The Spread Eagle

PICK OF THE PUBS

tel: 01200 441202 **BB7 4NH**

email: spread.eagle@zen.co.uk

dir: *Just off A159 between Clitheroe & Skipton, 4m N of Clitheroe*

Well-appointed trendy pub focusing on modern dishes

This handsome old stone inn stands on a quiet lane in the glorious Ribble Valley, flanked on one side by the ruins of Sawley Abbey, and on other by the River Ribble. Inside, choose between the elegant, light-filled dining room with its lush river views through picture windows, or the charming 17th-century bar, where you'll find

traditional stone-flagged floors, old oak furniture and roaring fires alongside trendy wallpaper, painted settles strewn with bright cushions, colourful upholstered chairs, eclectic objets d'art and cool Farrow & Ball hues. All this adds up to a cosy and relaxing setting for savouring a pint of something from the Black Horse Brewery and some decent modern pub food. Served throughout the inn and changing daily, the menu may include black pudding Scotch egg with piccalilli mayonnaise; fish pie with cheesy mash; spiced cauliflower and chickpea terrine; and warm chocolate brownie with maple ice cream. Don your boots and walk it all off in the Bowland Hills.

Open all day all wk 11-11 (Sun 12-10.30) **Food** Lunch Mon-Sat 12-2, Sun 12-7 Dinner Mon-Fri 5.30-9, Sat 6-9.30, Sun 12-7 Set menu available ⊕ INDIVIDUAL INNS ◀ Thwaites Wainwright, Moorhouse's, Black Horse Brewery Ò Kingstone Press. ♟ 16 **Facilities** Non-diners area ✿ (Bar Garden) ✦ Children's menu Children's portions Garden ⊨ Parking ▨

TOCKHOLES

Map 15 SD62

The Royal Arms

tel: 01254 705373 **Tockholes Rd BB3 0PA**

dir: *M65 junct 4 follow Blackburn signs. Right at lights, 1st left. Up hill left at 3B's Brewery into Tockholes Rd. Pub in 1m on left*

Rich with pickings from Lancashire microbreweries

High in the West Pennine Moors is this appealing old stone pub situated in a tiny fold of mill-workers' cottages. Walks from the door drop into Roddlesworth Woods or climb to the imposing Jubilee Tower on nearby Darwen Hill. There's an engaging hotchpotch of furnishings in the fire-warmed, flagstoned and beamed rooms together with fascinating old photos of the local villages in their mill-town heyday. Take a glass of ale out to tables on the lawn and study the regularly changing menu of home-cooked goodies, including giant Yorkshire pudding with a roast beef dinner inside and some great spicy dishes. Dogs and muddy boots welcome.

Open all day Closed Mon **Food** Lunch Tue-Fri 12-2, Sat 12-3, Sun 12-6 Dinner Wed-Sat 6-8.45, Sun 12-6 Av main course £7 Restaurant menu available Tue-Sun ⊕ FREE HOUSE ◀ Banks's Bitter, Copper Dragon Golden Pippin, Moorhouse's Pendle Witches Brew, Three B's, York Dark Knight, Guest ales. **Facilities** Non-diners area ✿ (Bar Garden) ✦ Children's menu Children's portions Garden ⊨ Beer festival Parking WiFi ▨ (notice required)

TUNSTALL

Map 18 SD67

The Lunesdale Arms

tel: 015242 74203 **LA6 2QN**

email: info@thelunesdale.co.uk

dir: *M6 junct 36. A65 Kirkby Lonsdale. A638 Lancaster. Pub 2m on right*

Welcoming pub showcasing locally sourced produce

Set in a small rural village in the beautiful Lune Valley, this bright and cheery pub has quite a reputation for its food, wines and regional ales. It's early days for new owner Nigel Bridgestock, but he aims to continue drawing diners from far and wide with a daily-changing chalkboard menu; highlights include bread baked on the premises, meat from local farms and organically grown vegetables and salads. Depending on the season, you could start with a twice-baked Lancashire cheese and leek soufflé; and continue with roast rump of Lune Valley lamb with mini lamb faggot, dauphinoise potatoes, cauliflower cheese purée and green beans.

Open 11-3 6-12 (Sat Sun & BH 11-4 6-1am) Closed 25-26 Dec, Mon (ex BHs) **Food** Lunch Tue-Fri 12-2, Sat-Sun 12-2.30 Dinner Tue-Sun 6-9 ⊕ FREE HOUSE ◀ Dent Aviator, Black Sheep, Brysons, Guinness Ò Westons Stowford Press. **Facilities** Non-diners area ✿ (Bar Outside area) ✦ Children's portions Family room Outside area ⊨ Parking ▨ (notice required)

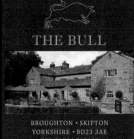

LOCAL HEROES

This part of the world attracts millions of visitors every year thanks, in no small part, to its magnificent scenery. But it's now also recognised as the food capital of Great Britain...home to the country's most gifted artisan producers and a group of famous pubs that has picked up a hatful of the nation's most coveted awards.

Ribble Valley Inns really puts the 'local' into locals. On the menu... traditional dishes with a contemporary twist, created by a Michelin Star chef using the finest, freshest ingredients sourced from the pick of the local farmers and suppliers.

This is food with roots, served in warm and welcoming surroundings...with log fires crackling in the winter, sprawling terraces to dine alfresco in the summer, and an impressive line-up of fine wines and guest beers to complete the picture.

Four stunning pubs...three in Lancashire and a fourth in Yorkshire. And just one promise. Whichever you choose you'll enjoy the real taste of the North!

RIBBLE VALLEY INNS...PUBS WITH A SERIOUS PEDIGREE

The multi award-winning RVI concept is the creation of
Northcote's Craig Bancroft and Nigel Haworth, Michelin Starred chef and
winner of BBC2's Great British Menu.

RVI
RIBBLE
VALLEY
INNS

WADDINGTON
Map 18 SD74

NEW The Lower Buck

tel: 01200 423342 **Edisford Rd BB7 3HU**
email: thelowerbuck@aol.com
dir: *From A671 at rdbt onto B6478 (Well Terrace) signed Waddington. In Waddington at x-rds left into Waddow View. At T-junct right signed Bashall Eaves. At next T-junct right, pub on left*

Easily missed gem in a 'Best Kept Village'

In the chocolate box village of Waddington, winner of 'Best Kept Village' on several occasions, look for St Helen's church and you'll find The Lower Buck just behind it. The 250-year-old pub has been affectionately run by Andrew Warburton for ten years now, without music or fruit machines disturbing the peace. The emphasis is on warmth of welcome, four excellent ales – with Bowland Hen Harrier among them – and a classic pub menu of quality dishes. Snacks include superior sandwiches such as hot topside of beef with fried onions, while the fisherman's salad overflows with smoked salmon, prawns, poached salmon and cockles.

Open all day all wk **Food** Lunch Mon-Fri 12-2.30, Sat-Sun 12-9 **Dinner** Mon-Fri 6-9, Sat-Sun 12-9 ⊕ FREE HOUSE ◀ Bowland Hen Harrier, Timothy Taylor Landlord, Guest ales Ö Ribble Valley Gold. ♀ 12 **Facilities** Non-diners area ❤ (Bar Outside area) ♦♦ Children's menu Children's portions Outside area ⌁ WiFi ▭

Waddington Arms

tel: 01200 423262 **West View, Waddington Rd BB7 3HP**
email: info@waddingtonarms.co.uk
dir: *In village centre*

Menu featuring local specialities

There's some doubt about the age of James Warburton's imposing establishment, although knowing that it was a coaching inn points one in the right direction. In the bar and outside a nice touch is the cushioned wickerwork chairs, perfect for relaxing with a pint of Bowland Hen Harrier. Dining is available throughout, including in two cosy side rooms off the main bar. Strong on local specialities, the menu offers Lancashire hotpot with pickled red cabbage; pork loin with black-pudding-crushed potatoes; pan-fried salmon fillet with sautéed potatoes and prawns; and wild mushroom risotto.

Open all day all wk **Food** Lunch Mon-Fri 12-2.30, Sat 12-9.30, Sun 12-9 **Dinner** Mon-Fri 6-9.30, Sat 12-9.30, Sun 12-9 ⊕ FREE HOUSE ◀ Bowland Hen Harrier, Tirril, Lancaster Blonde Ö Ribble Valley Gold. ♀ 14 **Facilities** Non-diners area ❤ (Bar Garden) ♦♦ Children's menu Children's portions Play area Family room Garden ⌁ Parking WiFi ▭ (notice required)

WHALLEY
Map 18 SD73

The Three Fishes ◉

PICK OF THE PUBS

See Pick of the Pubs on opposite page
See advert on page 303

WHEELTON
Map 15 SD62

The Dressers Arms

tel: 01254 830041 **Briers Brow PR6 8HD**
email: info@dressersarms.co.uk
dir: *M61 junct 8, A674 to Blackburn. Follow sign for pub on right*

Dog-friendly, welcoming fires and good pub grub

Until the 1960s, this was the smallest pub in Lancashire. The long, low, creeper-festooned old gritstone building is crammed with local photos, collectables and artefacts spread through a clutch of separate drinking areas; partly flagged floors are warmed by roaring fires in winter. Its appeal is enhanced by the choice of ales and a reliable raft of home-made pub grub: perhaps a hot tuna melt sandwich, a salad or a jacket potato will hit the spot; otherwise look to the main for lamb Henry, gammon steak, chilli con carne, Cumberland sausage or poached salmon.

Open all day all wk **Food** Lunch all wk 12-9 **Dinner** all wk 12-9 Av main course £5 ⊕ FREE HOUSE ◀ The Dressers Arms Dressers Bitter, Black Sheep Ö Westons. ♀ 20 **Facilities** Non-diners area ❤ (Bar Restaurant Garden) ♦♦ Children's menu Children's portions Family room Garden ⌁ Parking WiFi ▭

WHITEWELL
Map 18 SD64

The Inn at Whitewell ★★★★★ INN ◉ PICK OF THE PUBS

tel: 01200 448222 **Forest of Bowland BB7 3AT**
email: reception@innatwhitewell.com **web:** www.innatwhitewell.com
dir: *From B6243 follow Whitewell signs*

Historic inn with spectacular valley views

This must be one of the most enchantingly-sited inns in England. The River Hodder swirls by verdant meadows abutting wooded clefts in the glorious Forest of Bowland. The partly 13th-century inn slumbers by a tiny Georgian chapel here; paths slide to stepping stones through the torrent, whilst all around the high moors, pastures and estates burst with provender for the inn's renowned kitchens. The engaging, multi-roomed interior is liberally spread with antiques, ephemera and pictures; there's also an art gallery and a wine merchant. All-in-all ample to detain residential guests booked in to some of the 23 individually designed, luxury period bedrooms. Jamie Cadman oversees the kitchen; an AA Rosette qualifies the fine cuisine, typified by a starter of home-made black pudding with Lancashire cheese mash. Locally sourced dishes abound, such as shoulder of Lonk lamb slow-roast with rosemary and garlic. Ramblers dropping in from the heights will delight in beers from Hawkshead or Moorhouse's, enjoyed on a terrace overlooking the fabulous Bowland Fells, the very centre of the Great Britain.

Open all day all wk 10am-1am **Food** Lunch all wk 12-2 **Dinner** all wk 7.30-9.30 Restaurant menu available all wk evenings only ⊕ FREE HOUSE ◀ Timothy Taylor Landlord, Bowland, Copper Dragon, Moorhouse's, Hawkshead Ö Dunkertons Premium Organic. ♀ 16 **Facilities** Non-diners area ❤ (Bar Garden) ♦♦ Children's portions Garden ⌁ Parking WiFi ▭ (notice required) **Rooms** 23

PICK OF THE PUBS

The Three Fishes

WHALLEY Map 18 SD73

tel: 01254 826888
Mitton Rd, Mitton BB7 9PQ
email: enquiries@thethreefishes.com
web: www.thethreefishes.com
dir: *M6 junct 31, A59 to Clitheroe.*
Follow Whalley signs, B6246, 2m

State-of-the-art hostelry championing local food and drink

With Pendle Hill forming one horizon and Longridge Fell another, the Three Fishes at Mitton sits in a landscape that inspired parts of JRR Tolkien's *Lord of the Rings* trilogy. For more than four centuries travellers have stopped for refreshment at this fork in the road; its 200th anniversary as a licensed hostelry has just been celebrated. But times and tastes change, so current owners Ribble Valley Inns closed it for a top-to-toe refurbishment; many thousands of pounds later, it re-opened to high praise from locals and visitors alike. Gone is the traditional dark wood interior, replaced with a contemporary and relaxing decor that reflects customers' evolving attitudes to hospitality in the 21st century. Certainly the focus is still on AA Rosette-standard food, but Bowland and Thwaites ales in the bar are reassuringly consistent. As you settle with your refreshment of choice, you'll notice black-and-white photographs of local award-winning food producers on the walls. Some new cooking techniques have been introduced in the quest to keep pace with trends, but chef-patron Nigel Haworth has retained many classics, and even reinstated old favourites such as the prawn cocktail, steak Diane and Black Forest cheesecake. Well-trained staff are adept at friendly and professional service, ushering plates of potted Goosnargh livers or warm Flookburgh shrimps from kitchen to table. Next may come Nigel's Lancashire hotpot; North Sea fish pie; or a chargrilled steak with chips cooked in dripping. Dessert choices may include lemon meringue pie; or Leagrams day-old curd tart. If you're not driving you may be tempted by the post-dinner drinks list of single malt whiskies and Somerset cider brandy.

Open all day all wk 12-11 (Sun 12-10.30) **Food** Lunch Mon-Fri 12-2, Sat 12-9, Sun 12-8.30 Dinner served Mon-Thu 5.30-8.30, Fri 5.30-9, Sat 12-9, Sun 12-8.30 Av main course £12 Set menu available ⊞ FREE HOUSE
◀ Bowland Hen Harrier, Thwaites Wainwright ♻ Westons Stowford Press.
🍷 11 **Facilities** Non-diners area
🐾 (Bar Garden) ✚ Children's menu Garden ⋈ Parking WiFi

LEICESTERSHIRE

BIRSTALL
Map 11 SK50

The White Horse

tel: 0116 267 1038 **White Horse Ln LE4 4EF**
email: info@thewhitehorsebirstall.co.uk
dir: *M1 junct 21A, A46 towards Newark 5.5m. Exit A46 at Loughborough towards Leicester, follow brown signs for White Horse*

Delivering the very best expected of a village inn

A former canal-worker's beerhouse whose tranquil garden was once a coal wharf serving the village of Birstall, The White Horse (formerly The Mulberry Tree) overlooks Watermead Country Park. Rebuilt in the 1920s, the pub has matured over the years into today's restful retreat offering reliable beers, good company and a sought-after range of dishes. Boaters and ramblers alike look forward to classic main courses such as a hand-made burger with chips and onion rings; gammon with egg and chips; or beef lasagne with dressed salad and garlic bread. Or follow the locals' lead and tuck in to the pie of the week with all the trimmings.

Open all wk winter 12-3 5.30-11 (Sun 12-10.30); summer all day all wk
Food Lunch Mon-Sat 12-2.30, Sun 12-4 Dinner Mon-Sat 6-9 Av main course £9
⊕ TRUST INNS ◀ Timothy Taylor Landlord, Jennings Cumberland Ale, Guest ale. ☂ 8
Facilities Non-diners area ❖ (Bar Garden) ♦ Children's menu Children's portions Play area Garden ⚲ Parking WiFi ⛟ (notice required)

BREEDON ON THE HILL
Map 11 SK42

The Three Horseshoes

tel: 01332 695129 **Main St DE73 8AN**
email: ian@thehorseshoes.com
dir: *5m from M1 junct 23a. Pub in village centre*

Welcoming old pub with a chocolate workshop next door

Originally a farrier's, the buildings here are around 250 years old; the pub has been here for at least a century, while the main kitchen, a farm shop and a chocolate workshop now occupy the smithy and stables in the courtyard. Inside, numerous original features and old beams are supplemented by antique furniture, and sea-grass matting completes the warm and welcoming atmosphere. Typical dishes start with grilled goats' cheese with piccalilli, or fish and spinach pancake with cheese, followed by beef, red wine and mushroom casserole, or duck breast with cabbage and whisky. Try lemon cheesecake or chocolate whisky trifle for dessert.

Open 11.30-2.30 5.30-11 (Sun 12-3) Closed 25-26 & 31 Dec-1 Jan, Sun eve & Mon
Food Lunch Tue-Sat 12-2, Sun 12-3 Dinner Tue-Sat 6-9 Restaurant menu available Tue-Sun ⊕ FREE HOUSE ◀ Marston's Pedigree, Guest ales.
Facilities Non-diners area ❖ (Bar Garden) ♦ Children's portions Garden ⚲ Parking

BRUNTINGTHORPE
Map 11 SP68

The Joiners

tel: 0116 247 8258 **Church Walk LE17 5QH**
email: stephen@thejoinersarms.co.uk
dir: *4m from Lutterworth*

Food-led village gastro-pub

Yesteryear's modest village pub is today's popular eating place, thanks to Stephen and Tracy Fitzpatrick. You'll find stripped oak beams, flagstone floors, an open fire and candles. Menus change constantly, with ingredients sourced from wherever Stephen thinks best – beef from Scotland, seafood from Cornwall, black pudding from Clonakilty. A typical example lists monkfish in Parma ham, cherry tomato and basil gnocchi; Barbary duck breast with black cherry and brandy sauce; supreme of chicken with pea and smoked bacon risotto; and aubergine stuffed with ratatouille

and mozzarella. Every Tuesday there's a three-course fixed-price 'Auberge Supper'. Booking is advisable.

Open 12-2 6.30-11 Closed Mon **Food** Lunch Tue-Sun 12-2 Dinner Tue-Sat 6.30-9.30 Av main course £15 Set menu available ⊕ FREE HOUSE ◀ Sharp's Doom Bar. ☂ 16
Facilities Non-diners area Outside area ⚲ Parking WiFi ⛟ (notice required)

BUCKMINSTER
Map 11 SK82

Tollemache Arms

tel: 01476 860477 **48 Main St NG33 5SA**
email: info@tollemache-arms.co.uk
dir: *4m from A1, between Colsterworth & Melton Mowbray on B676*

Comfy village pub at the heart of the community

This striking 18th-century building on the Tollemache Estate is situated in the beautiful village of Buckminster. Those looking to enjoy a drink are welcomed by the big oak bar which serves local Oakham Ales, while diners can get comfy in the stylish, oak-floored dining room and library and enjoy the good modern British food. Using local seasonal produce, daily menus may feature celeriac, mushroom and thyme soup; duck breast, sweet potato chips and watercress and beetroot salad; and Bakewell tart. Thursday evening is lobster night (when in season). This is a community focused pub where dogs and children are welcome.

Open Tue-Sat 12-3 6-11 (Sun 12-4.30) Closed 25, 27-29 Dec, Sun eve, Mon
Food Lunch Tue-Sun 12-2 Dinner Tue-Sat 6.30-9 ⊕ FREE HOUSE ◀ Oakham Ales JHB, Guest ale. **Facilities** Non-diners area ❖ (Bar Garden Outside area) ♦ Children's menu Children's portions Garden Outside area ⚲ Parking WiFi ⛟ (notice required)

COLEORTON
Map 11 SK41

George Inn

tel: 01530 834639 **Loughborough Rd LE67 8HF**
email: janice@jwilkinson781.orangehome.co.uk
dir: *A42 junct 13 onto A512*

Relaxing country pub in National Forest

A comfortable old local bristling with homely touches, with crackling log-burners in the main rooms and a tree-shaded beer garden looking over the rich pasturelands of this corner of Leicestershire. It's at the heart of extensive National Forest, whilst Calke Abbey is a leisurely drive away. Bright and airy inside, with colourwash and panelled walls and nooks and crannies to explore, Marston's Pedigree complements the sturdy menu. Kick in with goats' cheese and poached pear, following up with wild boar sausages or steak and ale pie with Stilton; some gluten-free options, too.

Open 12-3 5.30-11 (Fri-Sat 12-11 Sun 12-4) Closed Sun eve, Mon **Food** Lunch Tue-Sat 12-2.30, Sun 12-2 Dinner Tue-Thu 6-9, Fri-Sat 6-9.30 Av main course £12
⊕ FREE HOUSE ◀ Marston's Pedigree, Guest ales Ø Thatchers Gold. ☂ 12
Facilities Non-diners area ♦ Children's menu Children's portions Play area Garden ⚲ Parking WiFi

EVINGTON
Map 11 SK60

The Cedars

tel: 0116 273 0482 **Main St LE5 6DN**
email: pippa@king-henrys-taverns.co.uk
dir: *From Leicester take A6 towards Market Harborough. Left at lights, onto B667 to Evington. Pub in village centre*

'Something for everyone' menus

At The Cedars you can choose to eat in the restaurant with its panoramic windows overlooking the fountain and pond, dine alfresco in the gardens, or just enjoy a drink in the lounge bar with its leather sofas and relaxed atmosphere. The menu of freshly prepared dishes offers something for everyone — small and large appetites alike. Choose from steaks, grills and burgers, as well as traditional favourites such as fish pie, vegetarian options and international dishes like lamb rogan josh. Smaller plates include paninis, salads and jackets. For dessert, the chocolate fudge cake or pecan pie is a treat for those with a sweet tooth.

Open all day all wk 11.30-11 **Food** Lunch all wk 12-10 Dinner all wk 12-10 ⊕ FREE HOUSE/KING HENRY'S TAVERNS ◀ Greene King IPA, Marston's Pedigree, Guinness. **Facilities** Non-diners area ♦♦ Children's menu Children's portions Garden ⌐ Parking WiFi ➡

GRIMSTON — Map 11 SK62

The Black Horse

tel: 01664 812358 **3 Main St LE14 3BZ**
email: amanda.wayne@sky.com
dir: *Phone for detailed directions*

Family pub in the countryside

The address of Amanda Sharpe's 16th-century coaching inn may well be Main Street, but Grimston's main street isn't even a B road. The pub overlooks the village green, and beyond that to the Vale of Belvoir, which locals pronounce 'Beaver', a tip that may help if ordering Belvoir Star Mild in the bar; real ales from Adnams, Marston's and St Austell should present no problem. Traditional main courses include sirloin, fillet and gammon steaks; chicken with Stilton and bacon; salmon supreme; and vegetarian specials. A daily-changing board lists fresh fish specials and more unusual dishes. The outdoor eating area is popular.

Open all wk 12-3 6-11 (Sun 12-6) ⊕ FREE HOUSE ◀ Marston's Pedigree, St Austell Tribute, Belvoir Star Mild, Adnams, Guest ales ♂ Thatchers Gold. **Facilities** ❖ (Bar Garden) ♦♦ Children's menu Children's portions Garden Outside area ⌐

KNOSSINGTON — Map 11 SK80

The Fox & Hounds

tel: 01664 452129 **6 Somerby Rd LE15 8LY**
dir: *4m from Oakham in Knossington*

Cosy, inviting interior and good food

High quality food and helpful, friendly service are the hallmarks of this 500-year-old pub. Set in the leafy village of Knossington close to Rutland Water, the building retains lots of traditional features, and the large rear garden and sitting area are ideal for alfresco summer dining. All food is freshly cooked to order and comes with fresh vegetables and potatoes of the day.

Open Tue-Fri 6-11 (Sat 6.30-11, Sun 12-4) Closed 10 days in summer, Sun eve & Mon **Food** Dinner Tue-Sat 6.30-9 ⊕ ENTERPRISE INNS ◀ Fuller's London Pride. **Facilities** Non-diners area ❖ (Bar Garden Outside area) Children's portions Garden Outside area ⌐ Parking WiFi ➡ (notice required)

LEICESTER — Map 11 SK50

NEW The Rutland & Derby

tel: 0116 262 3299 **Millstone Ln LE1 5JN**
email: rutlandandderby@ssoosh.co.uk
dir: *Phone for detailed directions*

City centre pub which pleases on many levels

Everything here seems carefully considered, and nothing is without some special quality. Handy for city-centre attractions, and not far from the city's rugby ground, the pub is worth seeking out for a craft ale such as Everards, a glass of wine from the 20 on offer, or a carefully prepared cocktail. Attention to detail is evident too in the food. Ethically sourced ingredients feature in quirky but flavoursome dishes such as sticky chilli chicken wings with Cropwell Blue cheese sauce. Hand-stretched and stone-cooked flatbreads are a speciality: Tamworth pulled pork, Brooklyn barbecue sauce, shallots, and fiordilatte mozzarella makes a winning combination.

Open all day Closed Sun **Food** Contact pub for details ⊕ FREE HOUSE ◀ Adnams Broadside, Everards Tiger ♂ Westons. ♀ 20 **Facilities** Non-diners area ♦♦ Children's portions Garden ⌐ WiFi ➡ (notice required)

LONG WHATTON — Map 11 SK42

The Falcon Inn ★★★ INN

tel: 01509 842416 **64 Main St LE12 5DG**
email: enquiries@thefalconinnlongwhatton.com **web:** www.thefalconinnlongwhatton.com
dir: *Phone for detailed directions*

Mediterranean spice in classic British pub

There's a taste of the Middle East to this traditional country inn in the shape of Lebanese-born proprietor Jad Otaki; the Mezzeh is akin to a tasting menu of some half dozen starters and four main courses. If spice is not your thing, you can plump for familiar bar meals such as home-made steak and ale pie; or salmon fillet in a cream, mushroom and seafood sauce. However, The Falcon is at heart an English pub, decked out with flower displays and hosting real ale drinkers on the striking heated rear terrace. Accommodation is available.

Open all day all wk **Food** Lunch Mon-Sat 12-2, Sun 12-4 Dinner Mon-Sat 6.30-9 ⊕ EVERARDS ◀ Tiger & Original, Guest ale. **Facilities** Non-diners area ♦♦ Children's portions Family room Garden Outside area ⌐ Parking WiFi ➡ (notice required) **Rooms** 11

The Royal Oak ★★★★ INN ⊛ — PICK OF THE PUBS

tel: 01509 843694 **26 The Green LE12 5DB**
email: enquiries@theroyaloaklongwhatton.co.uk **web:** www.theroyaloaklongwhatton.co.uk
dir: *M1 junct 24, A6 to Kegworth. Right into Whatton Road (becomes Kegworth Ln) to Long Whatton. From Loughborough, A6 towards Kegworth. Left onto B5324, right into Hathern Rd leading to The Green*

Stylish village inn with rooms

The Royal Oak is ideally situated in a picturesque village close to Loughborough and East Midlands Airport. An award-winning gastro-pub, offering high quality, locally sourced food, The Royal Oak features popular brews in the smart bar, and the carefully selected wine list proffers nine by the glass. In the stylish restaurant diners can expect some tough decisions: will it be pan-fried fillet of sea bass with crab cannelloni in crab bisque; Moroccan spiced chicken 'one pot'; an individual rabbit suet pudding; or a pub classic such as ham, egg and chips? Leave room for desserts like sticky toffee pudding and banoffee ice cream sandwich, or almond tart with black cherry compôte. An annual summer beer festival offers 30 real ales and 10 ciders. The impeccably furnished guest bedrooms are in a separate building.

Open all day all wk **Food** Lunch Mon-Sat 12-2.30, Sun 12-4 Dinner Mon-Sat 5.30-9.30 ⊕ FREE HOUSE ◀ St Austell Tribute, Bass, Blue Monkey, Sharp's Doom Bar, Guest ales ♂ Westons Old Rosie, Thatchers. ♀ 9 **Facilities** Non-diners area ♦♦ Children's menu Children's portions Garden ⌐ Beer festival Cider festival Parking WiFi **Rooms** 7

Visit theAA.com/shop
for the latest Hotel, B&B and Restaurant Guides

LUTTERWORTH
Map 11 SP58

The Man at Arms

tel: 01455 552540 **The Green, Bitteswell LE17 4SB**
email: pippa@king-henrys-taverns.co.uk
dir: *From Lutterworth take Lutterworth Rd towards Ullesthorpe. Turn left at small white cottage. Pub on left after college on village green*

Contemporary decor and hearty pub grub

Close to the market town of Lutterworth, this large village pub is named after a bequest by the Dowse Charity to the nearby village of Bitteswell in return for providing a 'man at arms' for times of war. It was the first pub bought by the King Henry's Taverns group; now, 28 years later, it has a smart, contemporary interior, all clean lines, wooden floorboards and high-backed leather seats, and shares a common menu with its sister pubs. Along with traditional favourites, there are international, fish and vegetarian dishes. Sizeable options include the Titanic challenge – a rump steak weighing some three pounds.

Open all day all wk 11.30-11 **Food** Lunch all wk 12-10 Dinner all wk 12-10 ⊕ FREE HOUSE/KING HENRY'S TAVERNS ◀ Greene King IPA, Wells Bombardier, Guinness, Bass. ☂ 16 **Facilities** Non-diners area ♦♦ Children's menu Children's portions Garden Parking ⛟

MOUNTSORREL
Map 11 SK51

The Swan Inn

tel: 0116 230 2340 **10 Loughborough Rd LE12 7AT**
email: danny.harwood@hotmail.com
dir: *On A6 between Leicester & Loughborough*

17th-century cottage beside the river

Originally built as two terraced cottages in 1688, this Grade II listed free house stands on the banks of the River Soar and has a secluded riverside garden, ideal for summer sipping and dining. Exposed beams, flagstone floors and roaring winter log fires characterise the cosy bar and dining areas. Fine wines and cask-conditioned beers from Theakston and Black Sheep accompany a varied, weekly-changing menu of British and European classics, as well as light lunches and snacks: smoked haddock and mustard fishcakes, followed by pan-fried trout fillet with balsamic beetroot and horseradish yogurt, or maybe a steak chimmichurri.

Open all wk 12-2.30 5.30-11 (Fri 12-2.30 4.30-12 Sat 12-12 Sun 12-10.30) **Food** Lunch Mon-Sat 12-2, Sun 12-5 Dinner Mon-Sat 6.30-9.30 Set menu available Restaurant menu available ⊕ FREE HOUSE ◀ Black Sheep Best Bitter, Theakston XB, Morland Old Speckled Hen, Castle Rock Harvest Pale, Guest ales Ö Westons Stowford Press, Guest ciders. **Facilities** Non-diners area ❀ (Bar Garden) ♦♦ Children's portions Garden ⋔ Beer festival Parking

MOWSLEY
Map 11 SP68

The Staff of Life
PICK OF THE PUBS

tel: 0116 240 2359 **Main St LE17 6NT**
dir: *M1 junct 20, A4304 to Market Harborough. Left in Husbands Bosworth onto A5199. In 3m turn right to pub*

Fresh look for a charming village inn

Tucked away in the countryside, this pub has been in the same hands for over a decade during which time it has been very well maintained. Were they to return, the former residents of this well-proportioned Edwardian house would surely be amazed by the transformation of their home into such an appealing community local. The bar has high-backed settles, a flagstone floor and large wood-burning stove. Look up to see not only a fine wood-panelled ceiling but also, not quite where you'd expect it, the wine cellar. The dining area overlooking the garden sees the serving of

dishes using the best of British seasonal produce, with a strong emphasis on local game: Bruntingthorpe wild rabbit with a black pudding and bacon salad; and seared wood pigeon breast wrapped in smoked bacon with parsnip purée are typical starters. Follow with Cotesbach partridge escalope; or roast leg of lamb with apricot and rosemary stuffing.

Open Mon-Fri 6-close (Sat 12-3 6-close Sun 12-10.30) Closed Mon-Fri L **Food** Lunch Sat 12-2.15, Sun 12-3 Dinner Tue-Sat 6-9.15 Set menu available ⊕ FREE HOUSE ◀ Thwaites Wainwright, Okells, Sharp's Doom Bar. ☂ 19 **Facilities** Non-diners area ♦♦ Children's portions Garden ⋔ Parking ⛟ (notice required)

OADBY
Map 11 SK60

The Cow & Plough
PICK OF THE PUBS

tel: 0116 272 0852 **Gartree Rd, Stoughton Farm LE2 2FB**
email: cowandplough@googlemail.com
dir: *From Leicester on A6 towards Oadby. Left at hospital sign at lights. At next rdbt follow Spire Hospital sign into Gartree Rd*

Former farm building famous for its pies

Housed in old Victorian farm buildings, The Cow & Plough continues to thrive, hosting functions and events including quarterly beer festivals. The pub also brews its own award-winning Steamin' Billy beers, named in honour of the owners' Jack Russell terrier. The interior is decorated with historic inn signs and brewing memorabilia, providing a fascinating setting in which to enjoy food from the regularly changing menus. Typical choices include terrine of prawn and smoked salmon, or quail Scotch egg with pig's head croquettes followed by confit duck leg with celeriac pomme Anna, green beans and red cabbage, or a vegetarian-friendly chargrilled vegetable tarte Tatin. A separate list of 'traditional dishes' offers the likes of lamb's liver and crispy bacon or a pie of the day (Thursday is pie night). Puddings continue in a traditional vein with the likes of lemon posset or baked blueberry and white chocolate cheesecake.

Open all day all wk **Food** Lunch Mon-Fri 12-2.30, Sat 12-9, Sun 12-5 Dinner Mon-Fri 6-9, Sat 12-9 ⊕ FREE HOUSE ◀ Steamin' Billy Bitter & Skydiver, Fuller's London Pride, Batemans Dark Mild, Abbeydale, Belvoir & Guest ales Ö Steamin' Billy Country Cider, Moonshine, Rekorderlig, Thatchers, Westons. ☂ 10 **Facilities** Non-diners area ❀ (Bar Outside area) ♦♦ Children's menu Children's portions Family room Outside area ⋔ Beer festival Parking WiFi ⛟

SILEBY
Map 11 SK61

The White Swan

tel: 01509 814832 **Swan St LE12 7NW**
email: tamiller56@googlemail.com
dir: *From Leicester A6 towards Loughborough, right for Sileby; or take A46 towards Newark-on-Trent, left for Sileby*

A reputation for home-cooked food

Behind the unassuming exterior of this 1930s building, you'll find a free house of some character, with a book-lined restaurant and a homely bar with an open fire and pictures and knick-knacks adorning the walls. Menus change weekly, and there are blackboard specials, too. Their pub nights prove popular – home-made pie night; sausage and burger night; and spicy night. Typical dishes are duck and vegetable pancake rolls; and twice-baked cheddar and chive soufflé for starters, followed by beef cobbler; orzo pasta with Mediterranean vegetables and feta; and roast leg of lamb with butternut squash and potato cake.

Open Wed-Fri & Sun 12-2 Tue-Sat 6-11 Closed 27 Dec & 1 Jan, Sat & Tue L, Sun eve & Mon **Food** Lunch Wed-Fri & Sun 12-1.30 Dinner Tue-Sat 7-8.30 Av main course £8.95 ⊕ FREE HOUSE ◀ Fuller's London Pride, Guest ales. ☂ 8 **Facilities** Non-diners area ♦♦ Children's menu Children's portions Outside area ⋔ Parking WiFi

■ SOMERBY
Map 11 SK71

Stilton Cheese Inn

tel: 01664 454394 **High St LE14 2QB**
web: www.stiltoncheeseinn.co.uk
dir: *From A606 between Melton Mowbray & Oakham follow signs to Pickwell & Somerby. Enter village, 1st right to centre, pub on left*

Great for real ales and whiskies

Customers say that entering this inn is like stepping back in time. An attractive 17th-century building made from mellow local sandstone, it stands in the centre of the village surrounded by beautiful countryside. Nearby is Melton Mowbray, famous for its pork pies and Stilton cheese – hence the pub's name. It enjoys a good reputation for its food, and for its great selections of real ales, wines and malt whiskies. A typical meal might include home-made pâté followed by tuna steak in tomato and olive sauce or another pub classic such as steak and kidney with chips, or Somerby sausages with mash and onion gravy. There's an ever-changing blackboard for further choices.

Open all wk 12-3 6-11 (Sun 12-3 7-11) **Food** Lunch all wk 12-2 Dinner Mon-Sat 6-9, Sun 7-9 ⊕ FREE HOUSE ◄ The Grainstore Ten Fifty, Brewster's Hophead, Belvoir Star, Oakham Ales JHB, Newby Wyke Kingston Topaz Ö Westons Old Rosie & Bounds. ♟ 15 **Facilities** Non-diners area ♦♦ Children's menu Children's portions Family room Garden ♠ Parking ▥ (notice required)

■ STATHERN
Map 11 SK73

Red Lion Inn
PICK OF THE PUBS

tel: 01949 860868 **Red Lion St LE14 4HS**
email: info@theredlioninn.co.uk
dir: *From A1 (Grantham), A607 towards Melton, turn right in Waltham, right at next x-rds then left to Stathern*

An inn for all the seasons

Located in the beautiful Vale of Belvoir, details like the flagstone bar, the elegant dining room and the comfortable lounge (complete with plenty of reading material) make this establishment stand out. The Red Lion has plenty to offer all year round: logs crackling in the stove in winter, 'country cocktails' in summer, Sunday lunches, cookery demonstrations and wine evenings. There's a great line-up of regional ales, farmhouse ciders and local fruit beers at the bar. Menus change seasonally in accordance with locally supplied produce, and offer a mix of classic pub food and innovative country cooking. Typical of chef Sean Hope's dishes are cauliflower soup

with truffle sabayon; red snapper, saffron and chilli, crushed potatoes, lemon grass and ginger velouté; and braised lamb shoulder, pearl barley, honey roast parsnip and garlic. Desserts reflect an attention to detail and are listed with suggested wines, ports and beers: try vanilla and blood orange pannacotta; or pistachio and honey cheesecake. There are good value set meals too.

Open 12-3 6-11 (Fri-Sat 12-11 Sun 12-7) Closed Sun eve & Mon **Food** Lunch Tue-Sat 12-2, Sun 12-3 Dinner Tue-Thu 6-9, Fri 5.30-9.30, Sat 7-9.30 Set menu available ⊕ FREE HOUSE/RUTLAND INN COMPANY LTD ◄ The Grainstore Red Lion Ale, Brewster's Marquis, Fuller's London Pride, Castle Rock Harvest Pale Ö Aspall, Sheppy's, Westons. ♟ 8 **Facilities** Non-diners area ✿ (Bar Garden) ♦♦ Children's menu Children's portions Garden Outside area ♠ Parking WiFi ▥ (notice required)

■ SWITHLAND
Map 11 SK51

The Griffin Inn

tel: 01509 890535 **174 Main St LE12 8TJ**
email: thegriffininn@swithland.info
dir: *From A46 into Anstey. Right at rdbt to Cropston. Right at x-rds, 1st left, 0.5m to Swithland. Follow brown signs for inn*

Unpretentious food in a traditional walker's inn

Parts of this welcoming, traditional, family-run country inn date back to the 15th century. There are three cosy bar areas serving a range of real ales, two dining rooms, a skittle alley, large patio and 'secret' garden with a stream. Menus and a wide range of specials offer unfussy, good-value internationally inspired food including moules marinière; chicken and chorizo linguine; traditional Spanish paella; and rhubarb and ginger sponge, lemon curd and vanilla ice cream. Dogs are only allowed in one room near the bar. The area is popular with walkers heading for Swithland Woods, Beacon Hill and the Old John folly. There's also a steam railway nearby.

Open all day all wk **Food** Lunch Mon-Thu 12-2, Fri-Sun 12-9 Dinner Mon-Thu 6-9, Fri-Sun 12-9 Set menu available ⊕ EVERARDS ◄ Tiger & Original, Adnams Southwold Bitter, 2 Guest ales Ö Symonds, Guest cider. ♟ 15 **Facilities** Non-diners area ♦♦ Children's portions Garden ♠ Parking WiFi ▥

■ THORPE LANGTON
Map 11 SP79

The Bakers Arms

tel: 01858 545201 **Main St LE16 7TS**
dir: *Take A6 S from Leicester then left signed 'The Langtons', at rail bridge continue to x-rds. Straight on to Thorpe Langton. Pub on left*

Intimate thatched pub with great fish nights

A pretty thatched pub set in an equally pretty village, The Bakers Arms has the requisite low beams, rug-strewn quarry-tiled floors, large pine tables and open fires. Its weekly-changing menu of modern pub food has gained it a keen local following. Expect dishes like pan-fried scallops with Clonakilty black pudding and orange sauce; confit of duck with red pepper and ginger marmalade; and crêpes with apple and cinnamon. Fish lovers should be sure to visit on a Thursday, when fish specials might include hake with asparagus cream sauce. The area is popular with walkers, riders and mountain bikers.

Open 6.30-11 (Sat 12-2.30 6.30-11 Sun 12-2.30) Closed 1-7 Jan, Sun eve, Mon **Food** Contact pub for details Av main course £16 Restaurant menu available all wk ⊕ FREE HOUSE ◄ Langton Bakers Dozen Bitter. ♟ 9 **Facilities** Non-diners area Garden ♠ Parking WiFi

WELHAM

Map 11 SP79

The Old Red Lion

tel: 01858 565253 **Main St LE16 7UJ**
email: pippa@king-henrys-taverns.co.uk
dir: *NE of Market Harborough take B664 to Weston by Welland. Left to Welham*

Tranquil setting in rolling countryside

The airy, split-level, contemporary interior of today's pub blends well with vestiges of its origins as a coaching inn. Polished floorboards, leather seating and open fire are a welcome retreat for ramblers drifting in from the area's popular walking routes. Views from the windows stretch across this rural corner of Leicestershire where the River Welland meanders through rich pastureland. One of a small chain of local dining pubs; the menu covers all bases, from British classics such as steak and ale pie to a select choice of international dishes, with vegetarian options including mushroom, cranberry and brie Wellington. Beers include Marston's Pedigree.

Open all day all wk 11.30-11 **Food** Lunch all wk 12-10 Dinner all wk 12-10 Av main course £3.50 ⊕ FREE HOUSE/KING HENRY'S TAVERNS ◄ Greene King IPA, Marston's Pedigree, Fuller's London Pride, Guinness. ₹ 15 **Facilities** Non-diners area ♦ Children's menu Children's portions Outside area ⌢ Parking WiFi ▭

WOODHOUSE EAVES

Map 11 SK51

The Wheatsheaf Inn ★★★★ INN

tel: 01509 890320 **Brand Hill LE12 8SS**
email: richard@wheatsheafinn.net **web:** www.wheatsheafinn.net
dir: *M1 junct 22, follow Quorn signs*

Old village inn at heart of Charnwood Forest

A rambling, creeper dressed stone inn (it was a quarrymen's watering hole 200 years ago) with contemporary bed and breakfast accommodation, a comfortably traditional bar and 'The Mess' dining area based on RAF connections. Charnwood Forest's stirring countryside is all around and the Great Central Railway (steam) is close-by. Explorers may choose to sit in the flowery courtyard garden, indulging in Timothy Taylor Landlord bitter and select from an ever-changing menu; haddock in beer batter with mushy peas, fries and home-made tartare sauce or perhaps forest mushroom tagliatelle with parmesan and pine nuts. There's a decent list of wines to accompany.

Open all wk Closed Sun eve in winter **Food** Lunch Mon-Fri 12-2.30, Sat 12-2.30, Sun 12-3.30 Dinner Mon-Sat 6.30-9.15 Av main course £12 ⊕ FREE HOUSE ◄ Greene King Abbot Ale, Timothy Taylor Landlord, Adnams Broadside, Tetley's Smoothflow, Marston's Pedigree, Guest ale ○ Thatchers. ₹ 16 **Facilities** Non-diners area ♥ (Bar Garden) ♦ Children's menu Children's portions Garden ⌢ Parking WiFi ▭ (notice required) **Rooms** 2

WYMESWOLD

Map 11 SK62

The Windmill Inn

tel: 01509 881313 **83 Brook St LE12 6TT**
email: info@thewindmillwymeswold.com
dir: *From A46 N of Six Hills left onto A606 signed Wymeswold. In village left into Church Ln, left into Brook St. Or from M1 junct 24, A6 signed Loughborough & Kegworth, A6006 to Wymeswold*

Spruced up local that loves families

Step over the threshold of The Windmill Inn to find a fresh, contemporary feel in the rambling bar and dining areas, with wood or stone tiled floors, wood-burning stoves, warm Farrow & Ball hues and comfortable seating setting the informal scene. Monthly menus combine pub classics and grills with modern British dishes, perhaps mussels, leek and bacon broth followed by thyme-roasted chicken with garlic crushed potatoes and lemon sauce, and rhubarb crumble. Dogs and children (toy box in evidence) are really welcome here and there's a gorgeous garden for summer dining.

Open all wk 12-3 5.15-11.30 (Mon 12-3 5.15-11 Fri-Sat 12-12 Sun 12-9) **Food** Lunch Mon-Thu 12-2.30, Fri-Sat 12-9.30, Sun 12-5 Dinner Mon 5.30-9, Tue-Thu 5.30-9.30, Fri-Sat 12-9.30 Set menu available ⊕ FREE HOUSE ◄ Sharp's Doom Bar, Castle Rock Harvest Pale, Guest ale ○ Symonds. ₹ **Facilities** Non-diners area ♥ (Bar Garden Outside area) ♦ Children's menu Children's portions Family room Garden Outside area ⌢ Parking WiFi

WYMONDHAM

Map 11 SK81

The Berkeley Arms

tel: 01572 787587 **59 Main St LE14 2AG**
email: info@theberkeleyarms.co.uk
dir: *In town centre*

Locally sourced, freshly prepared meals and fine wines

Having fulfilled their long-held ambition to own a pub, Neil and Louise Hitchen have seen their appealing, stone-built Berkeley Arms go from strength to strength. They are dedicated to sourcing fresh, local produce for the daily-changing menus. So a winter menu may offer chargrilled rare local wood pigeon breast with a Waldorf salad; haunch of local sika deer with swede purée, poached pear and caramelised walnuts; and David Cox of Strathern Lincolnshire sausages, mash and red onion gravy. Leave a little room for poached pear with chocolate sauce and vanilla ice cream. Well thought out two- and three- course lunches are served on Sundays.

Open 12-3 6-11 (Sun 12-5) Closed 1st 2wks Jan & 1wk summer, Sun eve & Mon **Food** Lunch Tue-Sat 12-2 Dinner Tue-Sat 6.30-9.30 Set menu available ⊕ FREE HOUSE ◄ Castle Rock Harvest Pale, Batemans XB, Marston's Pedigree ○ Westons Stowford Press. ₹ 10 **Facilities** Non-diners area ♥ (Bar Garden) ♦ Children's portions Garden ⌢ Parking

LINCOLNSHIRE

BARNOLDBY LE BECK — Map 17 TA20

The Ship Inn

tel: 01472 822308 **Main Rd DN37 OBG**
email: the_ship_inn@btinternet.com
dir: *M180 junct 5, A18 past Humberside Airport. At Laceby Junction rdbt (A18 & A46) straight over follow Skegness/Boston signs. Approx 2m turn left signed Waltham & Barnoldby le Beck*

Traditional village pub with coal fires and great seafood

Set in a picturesque village on the edge of the Lincolnshire Wolds, this 300-year-old inn has always attracted an interesting mix of customers, from Grimsby's seafarers to aviators from the county's World War II airstrips. The bar is filled with maritime bric-à-brac and serves a grand choice of ales such as Black Sheep or Tom Wood's, and there's also a beautiful garden. Seafood is a speciality so tuck into pan-fried cod cheeks with pea purée and chorizo, and then whole salt-crusted sea bass, coriander and chilli rice and stir-fried vegetables.

Open 12-3 6-11 (Fri-Sat 12-3 6-12 Sun 12-5) Closed 25 Dec, Sun eve **Food** Lunch Mon-Sat 12-2, Sun 12-5 Dinner Mon-Sat 6-9 Av main course £12 ⊕ FREE HOUSE/INNOVATIVE SIGHT LTD ◀ Black Sheep Best Bitter, Tom Wood's, Guinness Ö Thatchers Gold. ♀ 9 **Facilities** Non-diners area ♣ (Garden) ♦♦ Children's portions Garden ⋒ Parking WiFi ⛵ (notice required)

BELCHFORD — Map 17 TF27

The Blue Bell Inn

tel: 01507 533602 **1 Main Rd LN9 6LQ**
email: bluebellbelchford@gmail.com
dir: *From Horncastle take A153 towards Louth. Right signed Belchford*

In the heart of the Lincolnshire Wolds

Pantiles on the roof, white walls reflecting the sun, this family-run free house stands on the Viking Way long-distance path from the Humber to Rutland Water. Diners from all over the county are attracted by its many culinary temptations, among them local wild fallow venison and red wine pie; Lincolnshire sausages and mash; lamb chump marinated in garlic and rosemary; guinea fowl au vin; and smoked haddock, salmon and prawn fish pie. Anyone just after a glass of wine or pint of Wainfleet-brewed Batemans XXXB, Greene King IPA or a guest beer, will find plenty of armchairs to sink into.

Open all wk 11.30-2.30 6.30-11 (Sun 12-10.30) Closed 2nd & 3rd wk Jan **Food** Lunch all wk 12-2 Dinner all wk 6.30-9 ⊕ FREE HOUSE ◀ Batemans XXXB, Greene King IPA, Guest ale. **Facilities** Non-diners area ♣ (Bar Garden) ♦♦ Children's menu Children's portions Garden ⋒ Parking WiFi

CONINGSBY — Map 17 TF25

The Lea Gate Inn

tel: 01526 342370 **Leagate Rd LN4 4RS**
email: theleagateinn@hotmail.com
dir: *From Coningsby take A153 towards Horncastle. Right onto B1192 signed Boston. Pub on left*

The oldest licensed premises in the county

Dating from 1542, this was the last of the Fen Guide Houses that provided shelter before the treacherous marshes were drained. Among the oak-beamed pub's features are a priest's hole, low ceilings, a very old inglenook fireplace, extensive gardens and a yew tree dating from the 1600s. The same family has been running the pub for 30 years and they source their produce locally (including game in

season). All food is home made, and dishes on the seasonal menu could include wild game pie, slow roasted blade of beef, fisherman's pie and double-dipped full rack of BBQ ribs. Wednesday night is steak night.

Open all wk 11.30-3 6-11 (Sun 12-10.30) **Food** Lunch Mon-Sat 11.45-2, Sun 12-9 Dinner Mon-Sat 6-9, Sun 12-9 ⊕ FREE HOUSE ◀ Wells Bombardier, Black Sheep, Guest ales Ö Thatchers Gold. ♀ 10 **Facilities** Non-diners area ♣ (Bar Garden) ♦♦ Children's menu Children's portions Play area Garden ⋒ Parking WiFi ⛵

DRY DODDINGTON — Map 11 SK84

Wheatsheaf Inn

tel: 01400 281458 **NG23 5HU**
email: wheatsheafdrydoddington@hotmail.co.uk
dir: *From A1 between Newark-on-Trent & Grantham. Turn into Doddington Ln for Dry Doddington*

Village inn with a good selection of ales on tap

The church, with its leaning tower, faces this pantile-roofed inn across the village green. No one's sure of the inn's age, but they can date the pre-Jurassic era stones used to build it as 200 million years old. Abbot Ale, Batemans XB and Timothy Taylor Landlord are the regular real ales, with Lincolnshire easily the biggest contributor of produce on the menus. Enjoy a starter of pea, mint and crème fraîche risotto, followed by slow-braised shoulder of lamb; fish of the day; or honey-roasted pepper and goats' cheese tart, in the bar, restaurant or sheltered garden.

Open 12-3 5-11 (Sat-Sun 12-11) Closed Mon **Food** Lunch Tue-Fri 12-2, Sat 12-2.30, Sun 12-3 Dinner Tue-Fri 6-9, Sat 6-9.30 ⊕ FREE HOUSE ◀ Timothy Taylor Landlord, Greene King Abbot Ale, Batemans XB Ö Hogan's. ♀ 12 **Facilities** Non-diners area ♣ (Bar Garden) ♦♦ Children's menu Children's portions Garden ⋒ Parking WiFi ⛵ (notice required)

FULBECK — Map 17 SK95

The Hare & Hounds

tel: 01400 273322 **The Green NG32 3JJ**
email: harefulbeck@yahoo.co.uk
dir: *On A607, N of Grantham*

Village pub with imaginative food

Overlooking an attractive village green, this is a 17th-century, Grade II listed pub where a log fire does the business in winter; on warmer days, an outside eating area awaits. The beer pumps in the bar announce Jennings Cumberland, and a couple from the Marston's stable. The chef and his team work with only the best locally sourced ingredients, producing a typical three-course dinner of curried smoked haddock risotto with poached egg and crispy pancetta; breast of chicken with pan haggerty, green beans and wild mushroom sauce; and Baileys crème brûlée. Pub classics include Lincolnshire sausages with mash and onion gravy; and barbecued sticky ribs.

Open 12-2 5.30-11 (Sun 12-4) Closed Sun eve **Food** Lunch Mon-Sat 12-2, Sun 12-3 Dinner Mon-Sat 6-9 ⊕ MARSTON'S ◀ Pedigree, Jennings Cumberland Ale. ♀ 11 **Facilities** Non-diners area ♦♦ Children's menu Children's portions Family room Outside area ⋒ Parking WiFi

GEDNEY DYKE

Map 12 TF42

NEW The Chequers

tel: 01406 366700 **PE12 0AJ**
email: info@the-chequers.co.uk **web:** www.the-chequers.co.uk
dir: *From A17 between Holbeach & Sutton Bridge left at rdbt onto B1359 (signed Gedney Dyke)*

Destination eatery with beguiling warmth

Real ales such as Old Speckled Hen rotate regularly behind the Chequers' spotless bar, but chances are most people arriving here will have booked a table. The contemporary decor, crisp white napery and smartly dressed front of house staff all indicate a quality food destination. That said, dogs are welcome in the bar, children have their own menu, and the staff's welcome matches the warmth of the atmosphere. So choose your refreshment and settle down to enjoy the labours of a highly-qualified kitchen brigade - confit of duck ravioli; braised ox tongue with horseradish; pan-fried Lowestoft plaice with chestnuts; and blood orange trifle are indicative dishes.

Open 11.30-3 5-11 Closed Mon & Tue **Food** Lunch Wed-Sat 12-2.30, Sun 12-3 Dinner 6-9 Set menu available Restaurant menu available Wed-Sun ⊕ FREE HOUSE ◀ Woodforde's Wherry, Wells Bombardier, Morland Old Speckled Hen, Guest ales Ò Aspall. ♚ 12 **Facilities** Non-diners area ♣ (Bar Garden) ♠ Children's menu Children's portions Garden ⚲ Parking WiFi ▄

GOSBERTON

Map 12 TF23

The Black Horse

tel: 01775 840995 **66 Siltside, Gosberton Risegate PE11 4ET**
dir: *From Spalding take A16 towards Boston. Left onto A152. At Gosberton take B1397 to Gosberton Risegate. Pub set back from road*

Fenland pub championing local food

Tucked away in a village amidst the Fens outside Spalding, this lovely creeper-clad pub is a showcase for Lincolnshire's wealth of food producers. Huddle up to the wood-burning stove or catch the summer rays in the beer garden, sipping Black Sheep or Fuller's London Pride. The menu changes fortnightly and has Italian and Asian influences. Tuck into beef parmagiana; herb crusted salmon fillet; mushroom and red pepper Stroganoff; and rib-eye steak with hand-cut chips and all the trimmings. Finish with sticky toffee pudding, or a chocolate and almond brownie.

Open Tue-Thu 5.30-10.30 (Fri-Sat 12-2 5.30-10.30 Sun 12-10.30) Closed Mon **Food** Lunch Fri-Sat 12-2, Sun 12-5 Dinner Tue-Sat 6-9 Av main course £12 Restaurant menu available ⊕ FREE HOUSE ◀ Black Sheep, Fuller's London Pride. **Facilities** Non-diners area ♣ (Bar Garden) ♠ Children's portions Garden ⚲ Parking WiFi ▄

HOUGH-ON-THE-HILL

Map 11 SK94

The Brownlow Arms ★★★★★ INN ⊛

tel: 01400 250234 **High Rd NG32 2AZ**
email: armsinn@yahoo.co.uk **web:** www.thebrownlowarms.com
dir: *From A607 (Grantham to Sleaford road), Hough-on-the-Hill signed from Barkston*

Country-house-style village inn

Following a full refurbishment early in 2014, this 17th-century stone inn is firing on all cylinders. Named after former owner Lord Brownlow, it still looks, inside and out, every inch the country house it once was. Enjoy a pint of Timothy Taylor Landlord or Black Sheep in the convivial bar, while browsing the menu for AA-Rosette standard dishes such as whole baked sea bass; butter-poached supreme of chicken; and Moroccan sweet potato and aubergine tagine. The landscaped terrace invites outdoor drinking and dining, although please note that children must be eight or over to be allowed in the pub.

Open Tue-Sat 6pm-11pm, Sun L Closed 25-27 Dec, 31 Dec-1 Jan, Mon, Sun eve **Food** Contact pub for details Restaurant menu available ⊕ FREE HOUSE ◀ Timothy Taylor Landlord, Black Sheep. ♚ 10 **Facilities** Non-diners area Garden ⚲ Parking WiFi **Rooms** 6

INGHAM

Map 17 SK98

Inn on the Green

tel: 01522 730354 **34 The Green LN1 2XT**
email: enquiries@innatthegreeningham.co.uk **web:** www.innonthegreeningham.co.uk
dir: *From Lincoln take A15 signed Scunthorpe. Left into Ingham Ln signed Ingham, Cammeringham. Right onto B1398 (Middle St), left to Ingham*

Village pub offering some excellent pub food

Its name tells you all you need to know about the position of this charming, ever popular Grade II listed country pub. In addition to the choice of real ales, seasonal dishes using local produce are served throughout the pub's three bars — cosy entrance bar with sofas, front bar with roaring log fire, and another upstairs; restaurant seating is at the rear on the ground and first floors. A typical meal may start with Portobello mushroom soup with wild mushroom cornettos, or sweetcorn fingers with avocado salsa; then follow with roasted butternut squash risotto with Cote Hill red bon bons and sage crisps, or braised blade of beef with bubble-and-squeak. Super desserts include warm treacle tart with ice cream. Booking for meals is recommended.

Open 11.30-3 6-11 (Sat 11.30-11 Sun 12-10.30) (Sat 11.30-3 6-11 in winter) Closed Mon **Food** Lunch Tue-Sat 12-2, Sun 12-4 Dinner Tue-Sat 6-9 ⊕ FREE HOUSE ◀ Batemans XB, Adnams, Sharpe's Doom Bar & Special ♂ Westons Stowford Press, Thatchers. ☻ 10 **Facilities** Non-diners area ◀◀ Children's portions Garden ⊼ Beer festival Parking ➡ (notice required)

KIRKBY LA THORPE

Map 12 TF04

Queens Head

tel: 01529 305743 & 307194 **Church Ln NG34 9NU**
email: clrjcc@aol.com **web:** www.thequeensheadinn.com
dir: *Pub signed from A17 (dual carriageway)*

Offering ales brewed in a windmill

Heavy beams, open log fires, antique furnishings and original watercolours - this destination dining pub ticks all the boxes when it comes to original features and traditional character. The French-trained chef-proprietor prepares everything on site, from breads to desserts, and local ingredients get star billing on the extensive seasonal menus. A smoked duck, chicken and avocado salad might make way for grilled sea bass or three nut, parsnip and sweet potato cakes. Wash it down with Lincolnshire ales from the 8 Sail Brewery, brewed in Heckington Windmill, or wines from a well-considered list.

Open all wk 12-3 6-11 (Sun 12-11) **Food** Lunch Mon-Sat 12-2.30, Sun 12-8.30 Dinner Mon-Fri 6-9.30, Sat 6-10, Sun 12-8.30 Av main course £8.95 Set menu available Restaurant menu available all wk ⊕ FREE HOUSE ◀ Batemans XB, 8 Sail Brewery, Guest ales. ☻ 9 **Facilities** Non-diners area ◀◀ Children's menu Children's portions Outside area ⊼ Parking WiFi ➡ (notice required)

See advert on page 314

KIRTON IN LINDSEY
Map 17 SK99

The George

tel: 01652 640600 **20 High St DN21 4LX**
email: enquiry@thegeorgekirton.co.uk
dir: *From A15 take B1205, turn right onto B1400*

Country inn near Ermine Street

Lincoln and the Wolds are within easy reach of this extensively restored yet traditional pub. The 18th-century former coaching inn serves locally brewed ales and seasonally changing menus. Customers can dine in the comfortable bar area or in the informal restaurant. Favourite starters such as prawn cocktail, and bar meals such as lasagne with salad and hand-cut chips, are topped by regularly changing specials such as chicken schnitzel with a brandy and mushroom sauce; and game and blackcurrant pie.

Open all wk 5–11 (Sun 12–2.30) **Food** Lunch Sun 12–2 Dinner Mon-Sat 5–9 ⊕ FREE HOUSE ◼ Rotating Guest ales. **Facilities** Non-diners area ⁑ Children's menu Children's portions Play area Garden Outside area ⊟

LINCOLN
Map 17 SK97

The Pyewipe

tel: 01522 528708 **Fossebank, Saxilby Rd LN1 2BG**
email: enquiries@pyewipe.co.uk
dir: *From Lincoln on A57 past Lincoln/A46 Bypass, pub signed in 0.5m*

Waterside inn with home-made food

There's a great view of nearby Lincoln Cathedral from the grounds of this waterside inn, which takes its name from the local dialect for lapwing. Set in four wooded acres beside the Roman-built Fossedyke Navigation, it serves real ales and home-made, locally sourced food. Expect dishes such as partridge and black pudding stack with a red wine sauce; pork belly with a cider and grain mustard sauce and mash; or loin of cod poached in Thai broth with noodles and stir-fried vegetables. There is a beer garden and riverside patio where you can enjoy your meal and a cold beer.

Open all day all wk 11–11 **Food** Lunch all wk 12–9.30 Dinner all wk 12–9.30 ⊕ FREE HOUSE ◼ Guest ales. **Facilities** Non-diners area ⁑ Children's portions Garden ⊟ Parking WiFi ⊟

The Victoria

tel: 01522 541000 **6 Union Rd LN1 3BJ**
email: jonathanjpc@aol.com
dir: *From city outskirts follow signs for Cathedral Quarter. Pub 2 mins' walk from all major up-hill car parks. Adjacent to West Gate of Lincoln Castle*

Good real ales in the city

Situated right next to the West Gate entrance of the castle and a short stroll from Lincoln Cathedral, a long-standing drinkers' pub with a range of real ales, including three changing guest beers, ciders and perries. As well as the fantastic views of the castle, the pub also offers great meals made from home-prepared food including hot baguettes and filled rolls. House specials include sausage and mash, various pies, chilli con carne and home-made lasagne. Facilities include a large beer garden with children's play area. There are Halloween and winter beer festivals.

Open all day all wk 11am-mdnt (Fri-Sat 11am-1am Sun 12-12) **Food** Lunch all wk 12–2.30 Av main course £6.95 ⊕ BATEMANS ◼ XB & Yella Belly Gold, Timothy Taylor Landlord, Castle Rock Harvest Pale, Guest ales ⚙ Westons. **Facilities** Non-diners area ⁑ (Bar Garden) ⁑ Children's portions Play area Garden ⊟ Beer festival WiFi ⊟ (notice required)

The Queens Head

Kirkby La Thorpe, Sleaford, Lincolnshire NG34 9NU
Tel: 01529 305743 or 01529 307194 • **Website:** www.thequeensheadinn.com

John and Paul, proprietors for over 18 years, are delighted to welcome you to the Queens Head, Kirkby-La-Thorpe, one of Lincolnshire's finest traditional dining experiences.

Visitors to the Queens Head will experience the best in traditional English cuisine with a touch of modern flair and local theme. We offer local cask conditioned ales, a comprehensive wine list and many other drinks all set in luxurious informal surroundings.

We pride ourselves on the fact that all produce is sourced locally guaranteeing freshness, variety and choice. All food is homemade on the premises including many different types of bread, succulent sweets and with a fresh fish, meat & vegetable delivery every day.

We also have a large covered patio area which on a hot summer night is the perfect place for some alfresco dining under the stars or just to relax and have a drink with your friends.

We strongly advise that you pre-book your table (evenings in particular) as we do get very busy and don't like to disappoint customers.

We hope that every visit will be a pleasant surprise & look forward to welcoming you very soon!

Open Monday-Saturday 12pm-3pm & 6pm-11pm (Last meals served at 2.30pm & 9.30pm)

Sunday open all day from 12 noon (meals served all day)

Wig & Mitre   PICK OF THE PUBS

tel: 01522 535190 **32 Steep Hill LN2 1LU**
email: email@wigandmitre.com
dir: *At top of Steep Hill, adjacent to cathedral & Lincoln Castle car parks*

Old fashioned values and contemporary cuisine

Ideally located between the castle and the cathedral in the upper part of the medieval city, the Wig & Mitre is a mix of architectural styles from the 14th century onwards. Owned and operated by the Hope family, it's a music-free zone, instead you'll find a reading room and, since it's not tied to a brewery, real ales from Oakham, Black Sheep and Young's. Food includes English breakfasts served until noon, all-day hot and cold sandwiches, and light meals. Turning to the main menu, you might start with ham hock, black pudding and mustard pie; then slow-cooked lamb breast stuffed with anchovies and capers; or beer-battered salmon with tartare potato salad and green beans. Under 'puds' the menu lists lemon posset and ginger parkin with toffee sauce. Popular gourmet food and wine evenings are held regularly (booking essential).

Open all day all wk 8.30am-mdnt Closed 25 Dec **Food** Lunch all wk 8.30am-10pm Dinner all wk 8.30am-10pm Set menu available Restaurant menu available all wk ⊕ FREE HOUSE ◖ Oakham Ales JHB, Young's London Gold, Black Sheep ♻ Aspall. ♟ 24 **Facilities** Non-diners area ⚘ (Bar) ♦ Children's menu Children's portions WiFi

◼ LITTLE BYTHAM   Map 11 TF01

The Willoughby Arms

tel: 01780 410276 **Station Rd NG33 4RA**
email: info@willoughbyarms.co.uk
dir: *B6121 (Stamford to Bourne road), at junct follow signs to Careby/Little Bytham, inn 5m on right*

Former railway property now a traditional inn

This beamed, traditional stone country inn started life as the booking office and waiting room for Lord Willoughby's private railway line. These days it has a fresher look whilst retaining its traditional charms. Expect a good selection of real ales - including several from local microbreweries - with great, home-cooked food available every lunchtime and evening. Dishes range from home-made steak and kidney pie to spiced haddock. As well as a cosy bar with open fire, and a light and airy sun lounge, there is also a large beer garden with stunning views to enjoy on warmer days. Summer holiday beer festival.

Open all day all wk 12-11 **Food** Lunch Mon-Sat 12-2, Sun 12-3 Dinner all wk 6-9 Av main course £8.50 ⊕ FREE HOUSE ◖ Hopshackle Simmarillo, Abbeydale Absolution ♻ Aspall, Westons Stowford Press, Guest cider. ♟ 10 **Facilities** Non-diners area ⚘ (Bar Garden) ♦ Children's menu Children's portions Garden ⌂ Beer festival Parking WiFi 🚌 (notice required)

◼ MARKET RASEN   Map 17 TF18

NEW The Advocate Arms ★★★★★ RR ◉

tel: 01673 842364 **2 Queen St LN8 3EH**
email: info@advocatearms.co.uk **web:** www.advocatearms.co.uk
dir: *In town centre*

Convenient town-centre location

A full refurbishment has given this 18th-century, three-storey corner property in the town centre a contemporary veneer. Until 11am there's a wide choice of breakfasts, including kippers, then for lunch there are sandwiches, omelettes, salads and light meals, such as penne carbonara, and maybe a more substantial steak and ale pie with mash. Taken from a sample evening carte are fillet of brill with stuffed pancetta roll; roasted prime rib of Lincolnshire beef with braised ox cheek; spiced duck breast with celeriac rösti; and tomato, pepper and goats' cheese tian.

Open all day all wk **Food** Lunch all wk 12-6 Dinner all wk 6-9.30 Av main course £8 Restaurant menu available Mon-Sat ⊕ FREE HOUSE ◖ Wells Bombardier, Greene King IPA ♻ Aspall, Westons Rosie's Pig. ♟ 8 **Facilities** Non-diners area ♦ Children's menu Children's portions Outside area ⌂ Parking WiFi 🚌 (notice required) **Rooms** 10

◼ PARTNEY   Map 17 TF46

Red Lion Inn

tel: 01790 752271 **PE23 4PG**
email: enquiries@redlioninnpartney.co.uk
dir: *On A16 from Boston, or A158 from Horncastle*

Sound reputation for good, home-cooked food

Here is a welcoming village inn especially to walkers and cyclists due to its location, just below the Lincolnshire Wolds; many inevitably more than ready for pint of Black Sheep, or a glass of chilled wine. The pub's solid reputation for home-cooked food can be attributed to dishes such as sweet and sour chicken with rice; moussaka; pheasant, venison and rabbit pie; and cod and prawns in cheese sauce. A formidable selection of desserts includes puddings, sponges, sundaes and tarts.

Open 12-2 6-11 (Sun 12-2 6-10.30) Closed Mon **Food** Lunch Tue-Sun 12-2 Dinner Tue-Sun 6-9 ⊕ FREE HOUSE ◖ Black Sheep, Tetley's, Guinness, Guest ales. **Facilities** Non-diners area ♦ Children's menu Children's portions Parking WiFi 🚌 (notice required)

◼ RAITHBY   Map 17 TF36

Red Lion Inn

tel: 01790 753727 **PE23 4DS**
dir: *A158 from Horncastle, through Hagworthingham, right at top of hill signed Raithby*

Quiet village setting, cosy in winter, garden in summer

This traditional beamed village pub, parts of which date back 300 years, is situated on the edge of the Lincolnshire Wolds, a great place for walking and cycling. Inside is a wealth of character with log fires providing a warm welcome in winter. Dine in one of the four bars or on the comfort of the restaurant. A varied menu of home-made dishes is prepared using fresh local produce - sea bass with stir-fried vegetables; roast guinea fowl with tomato, garlic and bacon; and medallions of beef with peppercorn sauce. Meals can be taken in the garden in the warmer months.

Open 12-2 6-11 (Mon 7-11) Closed Mon L **Food** Lunch Tue-Sun 12-2 Dinner Tue-Sat 7-8.30 ⊕ FREE HOUSE ◖ Thwaites, Batemans ♻ Thatchers Gold. **Facilities** Non-diners area ♦ Children's menu Children's portions Outside area ⌂ Parking 🚌 (notice required)

Looking for a beer or cider festival?
Check our listings at the end of this guide

SOUTH RAUCEBY
Map 11 TF04

The Bustard Inn & Restaurant ◉ | PICK OF THE PUBS

tel: 01529 488250 **44 Main St NG34 8QG**
email: info@thebustardinn.co.uk
dir: *A15 from Lincoln. Right onto B1429 for Cranwell, 1st left after village, straight across A17 to South Rauceby*

Grade II listed pub with its own house ale

Situated above Lincoln Edge, this imposing building dates from 1860 and sits at the heart of a pretty stone-built estate village. The pub's name is based on the legend that the last indigenous great bustard was shot nearby in 1845 by the local lord of the manor. In the beer garden and courtyard, locals indulge in the house beer Cheeky Bustard, brewed by a local micro. The renovated, light and airy interior is divided between the bar and an elegant restaurant, with dressed stone walls, beamed ceiling and tapestry chairs; an ornate oriel window looks out on to the lovely garden. Head chef Phil Lowe's AA Rosette cooking draws on local produce where possible. The menu for bar and restaurant is one and the same: tempura squid with baby chorizo and micro cress makes an appetising starter, followed perhaps by Belton Park venison and mushroom stew.

Open 12-3 5.30-11 (Sun 12-3.30) Closed 1 Jan, Sun eve, Mon **Food** Lunch Tue-Sat 12-2.30, Sun 12-3 Dinner Tue-Sat 6-9.30 Set menu available ⊕ FREE HOUSE ◀ Riverside Cheeky Bustard, Batemans Yella Belly Gold, Guinness, Guest ale ♻ Aspall. ☗ 13 **Facilities** Non-diners area ♦ Children's menu Children's portions Garden ⊟ Parking WiFi ➡ (notice required)

SOUTH WITHAM
Map 11 SK91

Blue Cow Inn & Brewery

tel: 01572 768432 **High St NG33 5QB**
email: enquiries@bluecowinn.co.uk
dir: *Between Stamford & Grantham on A1*

Own-brewed real ale and pub classics

Licensee Simon Crathorn has been brewing the award-winning Blue Cow Best Bitter at the small brewery here for more than ten years – ask for a free viewing, subject to availability. The pub was renamed 'blue' by erstwhile owner the Duke of Buckminster nearly 400 years ago, on account of his political allegiance to his king. Low beams, flagstone floors and dressed-stone walls characterise the ancient interior, with crackling log fires to take the edge off the fenland breezes; any remaining chill may be generated by the pub's ghosts – a lady and a dog. Snacks, salads and sandwiches are offered, as well as mains like gammon steak, sausages and scampi.

Open all day all wk 11-11 **Food** Lunch all wk 12-2.30 Dinner all wk 6-9.30 Av main course £8 ⊕ FREE HOUSE ◀ Blue Cow Best Bitter, Sharp's Doom Bar. ☗ 10 **Facilities** Non-diners area ♦ (Bar Restaurant Garden) ♦ Children's menu Children's portions Family room Garden ⊟ Parking WiFi ➡ (notice required)

STAMFORD
Map 11 TF00

NEW The Bull & Swan at Burghley ★★★★ INN ◉

tel: 01780 766412 **High St, St Martin's PE9 2LJ**
email: enquiries@thebullandswan.co.uk **web:** www.thebullandswan.co.uk
dir: *A1 onto B1081 (Carpenters Lodge junct). Signed Stamford & Burghley. 1m, pub on right*

Memorable meals in a magnificent market town setting

Commanding a prime position on one of historic Stamford's most stunning streets, this gabled coaching inn is recognised by the AA for both its top-notch accommodation and its good food. Tucked behind the mellow stone façade is a comfily-appointed, traditional destination which appeals to all-comers, where dining is to the fore but beer lovers aren't short-changed. Local brewers Grainstore are one reliable supplier to the bar, whilst produce from this corner of the East Midlands plump out the enticing menu. Smoked eel risotto with scorched baby leeks comes as starter or main; or try a taste of Old England with Lincoln Red beef, ale and parsnip steamed pudding.

Open all day all wk **Food** Lunch all wk 12-2.30 Dinner all wk 6-9 Av main course £14 Set menu available ⊕ FREE HOUSE ◀ Nene Valley Blond Session BSA, Adnams Southwold Bitter, The Grainstore Triple B ♻ Westons Stowford Press. ☗ 10 **Facilities** Non-diners area ♦ (Bar Outside area) ♦ Children's menu Children's portions Outside area ⊟ Parking WiFi **Rooms** 7

The George of Stamford ★★★★ HL ◉ | PICK OF THE PUBS

tel: 01780 750750 **71 St Martins PE9 2LB**
email: reservations@georgehotelofstamford.com **web:** www.georgehotelofstamford.com
dir: *From Peterborough take A1 N. Onto B1081 for Stamford, down hill to lights. Hotel on left*

Perhaps one of England's most famous coaching inns

The Great North Road was one of Britain's premier highways, which was why Lord Burghley, Elizabeth I's Lord High Treasurer, built an inn here in 1597. A much older hostelry predated it and its long history is evident throughout: for example, there's a medieval crypt, and a walled 'Monastery Garden', where Crusaders relaxed. In the York Bar northbound passengers waited while horses were changed; the London Room fulfilled the same purpose for those heading south. Today's, usually motorised, visitors can have a snack or light meal in the bar, lounge, Garden Room or cobbled courtyard. The George holds an AA Rosette for traditional English food such as roast sirloin of beef carved at the table; trio of lamb with deep-fried sweetbreads; and grilled Dover sole. Additionally, there are shellfish, pastas and cold buffets. Above the road outside is the gallows sign that warned highwaymen to stay away. Surely, it still does.

Open all day all wk 11-11 (Sun 12-11) **Food** Lunch all wk 12-2.30 Set menu available Restaurant menu available all wk ⊕ FREE HOUSE ◀ Adnams Broadside, The Grainstore, Bass, Guest ales ♻ Aspall. ☗ 24 **Facilities** Non-diners area ♦ Children's portions Garden Outside area ⊟ Parking WiFi **Rooms** 47

The Tobie Norris

PICK OF THE PUBS

tel: 01780 753800 **12 Saint Pauls St PE9 2BE**
email: info@tobienorris.com
dir: *From A1 to Stamford on A6121, becomes West St, then East St. After right bend right into Saint Pauls St*

Lively pub in award-winning restored medieval building

A medieval hall house built in 1280, this splendidly restored and renovated building is named after Tobias Norris, who bought it in 1617 for use as a bell foundry. Adnams Southwold Bitter and Castle Rock Harvest Pale are permanent fixtures in the wood-floored bar, while national and regional guest ales are rotated regularly. Having started maybe with a plate of antipasti, your main course, from the rather imaginative menu, could be wild game, ale and brown sugar pie; chickpea burger with patatas bravas; spiced cod and cockle korma; and harissa-roasted chicken breast with spiced Moroccan salad. Stone-baked pizzas are cooked in ovens imported from Italy, their toppings ranging from anchovies to Tallington (the pub's own farm) meatballs. Puddings include treacle tart and clotted cream ice cream, and apple and cinnamon crumble. A large enclosed patio appeals on warmer days. Note that, lunchtimes apart, there's a strict over-21s only policy.

Open all day all wk **Food** Lunch all wk 12-2.30 Dinner Mon-Sat 6-9 Av main course £13.95 ⊕ FREE HOUSE ◀ Adnams Southwold Bitter, Castle Rock Harvest Pale, Guest ales ♨ Aspall, Guest cider. ♥ 18 **Facilities** Non-diners area ❖ (Bar Garden) Garden ⚲ WiFi

SUSWORTH

Map 17 SE80

The Jenny Wren Inn

tel: 01724 784000 **East Ferry Rd DN17 3AS**
email: info@jennywreninn.co.uk
dir: *Phone for detailed directions*

Italian dishes a specialty here

With an upstairs function room overlooking the River Trent, this beamed and wood-panelled former farmhouse has buckets of character. No better place then for the sampling of special cocktails and nibbles now served every evening; ale lovers can stick to the likes of Morland Old Speckled Hen. The pub gains much praise for its food, especially for dishes involving line-caught fresh fish. Otherwise the Italian head chef and his team create both traditional pub favourites and authentic pasta, to be enjoyed in the ground-floor lounge with open fire. Chicken Bologna and smoked haddock with mash and leek sauce are typical main courses.

Open all wk 12-3 5.45-10.30 (Sat-Sun 11.30-10.30) **Food** Lunch Mon-Fri 12-2, Sat 12-9, Sun 12-8 Dinner Mon-Fri 5.45-9, Sat 12-9, Sun 12-8 ⊕ FREE HOUSE ◀ Morland Old Speckled Hen, Sharp's Doom Bar. **Facilities** Non-diners area ❖ (Bar Garden) ⊶ Children's menu Children's portions Family room Garden Parking WiFi ⚌

TEALBY

Map 17 TF19

NEW The Kings Head

tel: 01673 838347 **11 Kingsway LN8 3YA**
email: sol.newunion@googlemail.com **web:** www.thekingsheadtealby.co.uk
dir: *At lights in Market Rasen take B1203 (Jameson Bridge St) to Tealby*

The oldest thatched pub in Lincolnshire

Dating from around 1367, The Kings Head stands in an ample garden in a pretty village where former resident and songwriter Bernie Taupin was apparently inspired by the colour of the Lincolnshire stone to pen *Goodbye Yellow Brick Road* for his mate, Elton John. Dogs are welcome in the bar, where the line-up includes real ales from Marston's, Ringwood, Jennings and Wychwood plus ciders. Lincolnshire lamb's liver and bacon appears on the bar menu, while in the converted barn restaurant the main listing includes pressed belly pork with smoked black pudding mash; pan-fried salmon with basil and tomato risotto; and Mediterranean vegetable strudel.

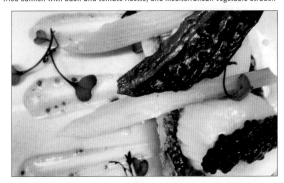

Open all day all wk **Food** Lunch Tue-Sat 12-9, Sun-Mon 12-7 Dinner Tue-Sat 12-9, Sun-Mon 12-7 Av main course £10 Set menu available Restaurant menu available all wk ⊕ MARSTON'S ◀ Pedigree, Ringwood Boondoggle, Jennings Cumberland, Wychwood Hobgoblin ♨ Thatchers Gold, Rekorderlig. ♥ 9 **Facilities** Non-diners area ❖ (Bar Garden) ⊶ Children's portions Garden ⚲ Parking WiFi ⚌

See advert on page 318

THEDDLETHORPE ALL SAINTS

Map 17 TF48

Kings Head Inn

tel: 01507 339798 **Mill Rd LN12 1PB**
email: lordandladyhutton@hotmail.co.uk
dir: *From A1031 between Mablethorpe & Theddlethorpe, turn left into Mill Rd. Pub on right*

Ultra low ceilings and old world charm

Two miles from the beach and close to a nature reserve, this thatched 16th-century inn is a sight for sore eyes. Inside are charming bars with traditional furnishings and very low ceilings. All food is locally sourced and vegetables are home grown. Fish is a speciality in the summer; game in the winter. Dishes range from chicken satay, or Welsh rarebit as starters to a rich game pie; steaks, burgers and grills; or oven crisp pork belly with apple and brandy gravy for mains.

Open 12-3 6-11 (Sat 12-11 Sun 12-10.20 summer; Sun 12-5 winter) Closed Mon (winter) **Food** Lunch Sun-Fri 12-2.30, Sat all day Dinner Sun-Fri 6-9, Sat all day Restaurant menu available ⊕ FREE HOUSE ◾ Batemans XB ○ Thatchers Gold, Skidbrooke. **Facilities** Non-diners area ✿ (Bar Garden) ♦♦ Children's portions Family room Garden ⋒ Beer festival Parking WiFi ▆ (notice required)

WOODHALL SPA

Map 17 TF16

Village Limits Country Pub, Restaurant & Motel

tel: 01526 353312 **Stixwould Rd LN10 6UJ**
email: info@villagelimits.co.uk
dir: *At rdbt on main street follow Petwood Hotel signs. Motel 500yds past Petwood Hotel*

Tranquil location beside country park

Handily placed for the southern hills of the Lincolnshire Wolds and the Battle of Britain Flight aircraft heritage at nearby RAF Coningsby, the heart of the old Edwardian spa town is just a short walk away. This little country inn excels at offering beers from Tom Wood's and Dixon's and meals which champion the best of locally sourced ingredients. Lincolnshire Poacher cheese rarebit sets the scene for steamed mussels with tomato and chilli sauce or a creamy leek and Stilton crumble. Keep an eye on the specials board for the latest dishes.

Open 11.30-3 6.30-11 Closed 26 Dec-2 Jan, Mon L **Food** Lunch Tue-Sun 11.30-2 Dinner all wk 6.30-9 Av main course £12-£15 ⊕ FREE HOUSE ◾ Batemans XB, Tom Wood's Best Bitter, Dixon's Major Bitter ○ Thatchers. ☕ 8 **Facilities** Non-diners area ♦♦ Children's menu Children's portions Garden ⋒ Parking WiFi

WOOLSTHORPE

Map 11 SK83

The Chequers Inn ★★★★ INN ⊛ — PICK OF THE PUBS

tel: 01476 870701 **Main St NG32 1LU**
email: justinnabar@yahoo.co.uk **web:** www.chequersinn.net
dir: *Approx 7m from Grantham. 3m from A607, follow heritage signs to Belvoir Castle*

Country dining pub with charming interior

Leicestershire, Lincolnshire and Nottinghamshire all meet not far from this 17th-century coaching inn overlooking the village cricket pitch. From here you can see Belvoir Castle, a mile or so away. Five real fires warm the interior, and a well-stocked bar does a good line in real ales and cider, including Milestone Loxley Ale from Newark and Aspall; there are draught Belgian beers too. Dine in the Snug & Bar, the contemporary Dining Room or the Bakehouse Restaurant, which still features the oven from village bakery days. On the menu may be chargrilled rib-eye steak with hand-cut chips; pavé of venison with celeriac purée; rosette of plaice with rösti potato and brown shrimp and crayfish velouté; and butternut squash and aubergine tagine. Representing the pub classics category are home-made pie; beer-battered cod; and Thai green curry. Typical puddings are apple and berry crumble with custard, and lemon meringue pie with raspberry sorbet.

Open all day all wk **Food** Lunch Mon-Sat 12-2.30, Sun 12-4 Dinner Mon-Sat 6-9.30, Sun 6-8.30 Set menu available ⊕ FREE HOUSE ◾ Timothy Taylor Landlord, Sharp's Doom Bar, Milestone Loxley Ale ○ Aspall. ☕ 30 **Facilities** Non-diners area ✿ (Bar Garden) ♦♦ Children's menu Children's portions Garden ⋒ Parking WiFi ▆ (notice required) **Rooms** 4

LONDON

E1

Town of Ramsgate PLAN 2 G3

tel: 020 7481 8000 **62 Wapping High St E1W 2NP**
email: peter@townoframsgate.co.uk
dir: *Nearest tube: Wapping*

River Thames gem full of history

Close to The City, this Grade II listed building dates back 500 years and is steeped in history. Press gangs used to work the area, imprisoning men overnight in the cellar, and Judge Jeffreys was caught here while trying to flee the country. The pub retains much of its original character with bric-à-brac and old prints. The owners serve a range of real ales and more than a dozen wines by the glass. Enjoy dishes such as cottage pie in the bar or on the terrace overlooking the River Thames.

Open all day all wk 12-12 (Sun 12-11) **Food** Lunch all wk 12-4 Dinner all wk 5-9 Av main course £9 ⊕ FREE HOUSE ◼ Fuller's London Pride, Adnams, Young's ♂ Aspall. ☻ 13 **Facilities** Non-diners area ❖ (Bar Garden) ♦♦ Garden ⊓ WiFi 🚐 (notice required)

E8

The Cat & Mutton PLAN 2 G4

tel: 020 7249 6555 **76 Broadway Market, Hackney E8 4QJ**
dir: *Phone for detailed directions*

Popular food pub

Used by workers on their way to London's livestock markets in the 17th century, this revamped pub was once known as the 'Cattle & Shoulder of Mutton'. Today (under new ownership), the building has been reinvented as one of East London's busiest food pubs. At scrubbed tables in trendy, gentrified surroundings, order a 'small plate' of burnt broccoli, yogurt, pickled mustard seeds and almonds; onglet steak with chimichurri; or octopus, potatoes and black garlic crème fraîche. For bigger appetites there's 'large plates' of jerk chicken and mango coleslaw; lamb belly with smoked aubergine; and a bucket of mutton chops, bean salad and mint sauce. Blood orange sorbet with a glass of prosecco finishes a meal nicely.

Open all day all wk Mon 12-11 Tue-Thu 12-12 Fri noon-1am Sat 11am-1am Sun 12-11.30 **Food** Lunch Sat 12-11, Sun 12-9 Dinner Mon-Thu 6-10, Fri 6-11, Sat 12-11, Sun 12-9 Restaurant menu available all wk ⊕ THE COLUMBO GROUP ◼ Adnams Southwold Bitter, Shepherd Neame Spitfire, Caledonian Deuchars IPA, Harvey's Sussex ♂ Westons, Addlestones, Aspall. ☻ 12 **Facilities** Non-diners area ❖ (Bar Restaurant Outside area) ♦♦ Children's portions Outside area ⊓ WiFi

E9

The Empress ◉ PLAN 2 G4   PICK OF THE PUBS

tel: 020 8533 5123 **130 Lauriston Rd, Victoria Park E9 7LH**
email: info@empresse9.co.uk
dir: *From Mile End Station turn right into Grove Rd, leads into Lauriston Rd*

Café, bar and restaurant pleasing a Bohemian clientele

A classic mid-Victorian East End corner pub, with Gothic revival windows at first-floor level and lofty ceilings. A long bar serves ale from that venerable East End brewer, Truman's, and Aspall Harry Sparrow cider. Neighbourhood suppliers are important to The Empress, with meats and fish from Victoria Park suppliers Ginger Pig and Jonathan Norris respectively, and coffee from Climpson & Sons. Head chef Elliott Lidstone's great value bar snacks include crispy pig's ear with apple sauce; crispy ox tongue with mustard mayo; and squid with smoked paprika aïoli. Equally well priced are mains such as guinea fowl with celeriac, wild mushroom and bacon; and cod served with lentils and salsa verde. The short list of sweet things may include a vanilla pannacotta with poached rhubarb. The weekend brunch menu's

Full Empress – two eggs, bacon, black pudding, beans, mushrooms, slow-roasted tomatoes and toast – is as popular as ever.

Open all day all wk Closed 25-26 Dec **Food** Lunch all wk 12-3.30 Dinner all wk 6-10.15 ⊕ FREE HOUSE ◼ East London Foundation Bitter, Truman's Swift ♂ Aspall Harry Sparrow. ☻ 19 **Facilities** Non-diners area ❖ (Bar Outside area) ♦♦ Children's menu Children's portions Outside area ⊓ WiFi 🚐

E14

The Grapes PLAN 2 G3   PICK OF THE PUBS

tel: 020 7987 4396 **76 Narrow St, Limehouse E14 8BP**
email: info@thegrapes.co.uk
dir: *Phone for detailed directions*

Dickensian pub on the Thames

In *Our Mutual Friend*, Charles Dickens immortalised this old Thames-side pub as the Six Jolly Fellowship Porters. While he might recognise the wood-panelled, Victorian long bar and The Dickens Snug, where as a child he reputedly danced on a table, much of surrounding Limehouse has changed beyond recognition. So too has the Isle of Dogs, as looking east from the small terrace over the river at the back to the skyscrapers of Canary Wharf proves. Cask-conditioned ales in the bar include Adnams, Marston's Pedigree, Timothy Taylor Landlord and guests, while in the tiny upstairs dining room the fresh seafood includes pan-seared scallops, chorizo and smoked chilli; grilled or crispy battered haddock fillet; and whole roasted sea bass. If you'd prefer steak and chips, or shepherd's pie, they're on the menu too. Salads, sandwiches and bar meals are always available, and there are traditional roasts on Sundays.

Open all day all wk 12-11 (Mon-Wed 12-3 5.30-11) Closed 25-26 Dec, 1 Jan **Food** Lunch Mon-Fri 12-2.30, Sat 12-9.30, Sun 12-3.30 Dinner Mon-Fri 6.30-9.30, Sat 12-9.30 Restaurant menu available all wk ⊕ SPIRIT LEASED ◼ Marston's Pedigree, Timothy Taylor Landlord, Adnams, Guest ales ♂ Aspall. **Facilities** Non-diners area ❖ (Bar Outside area) Outside area

The Gun ◉ PLAN 2 G3   PICK OF THE PUBS

tel: 020 7515 5222 **27 Coldharbour, Docklands E14 9NS**
email: info@thegundocklands.com
dir: *From South Quay DLR, east along Marsh Wall to mini rdbt. Turn left, over bridge then 1st right*

A surviving riverside gem

Once a dockers', stevedores' and boatmen's local, this old Thames-side pub was named after the cannon fired to celebrate the opening of West India Docks in 1802. In the main bar Adnams and Jugged Hare Pale Ale sit alongside regularly changing guest beers. There is also a restaurant, two private dining rooms (one where Lord Nelson and Lady Hamilton secretly met), two snugs and a riverside terrace overlooking the O2 Arena. Snacks include Colchester rock oysters; devilled whitebait; and black pudding Scotch eggs, while the dining room menu offers dishes such as pan-fried fillet of sea bass with clams, saffron potato purée, sea shore vegetables, and fennel cream; or smoked loin of wild Suffolk venison, with braised leg shepherd's pie, turnip tops and parsnip purée. Croatian, Greek and Lebanese wines feature among the 100-or-so listed.

Open all wk 11am-mdnt (Sun 11-11) Closed 25-26 Dec **Food** Lunch Mon-Sat 12-3, Sun 12-4 Dinner Mon-Sat 6-10.30, Sun 6.30-9.30 ⊕ ETM GROUP ◼ Adnams Southwold Bitter, Jugged Hare Pale Ale, Guest ales ♂ Symonds. ☻ 22 **Facilities** Non-diners area ♦♦ Children's portions Outside area ⊓ WiFi 🚐 (notice required)

EC1

The Bleeding Heart Tavern ⊚   PLAN 1 E4   PICK OF THE PUBS

tel: 020 7242 8238 **19 Greville St EC1N 8SQ**
email: bookings@bleedingheart.co.uk
dir: *Close to Farringdon tube station, at corner of Greville St & Bleeding Heart Yard*

City pub specialising in French cuisine

The tavern dates from 1746, when its distinctly non-pc slogan invited customers to get 'drunk for a penny and dead drunk for twopence'. In the hardly surprising absence of a 21st-century equivalent, the tavern wisely promotes its Full English breakfasts, with croissants and baguettes from its own bakery, and its Bistro fare, such as traditional French dishes, perhaps coq au vin; lapin à la moutarde; and steak hâché. Holding court in the bar are traditional ales from Adnams, and Aspall cider; of the 450 wines, nearly 20 are by the glass. Downstairs in the wood-panelled restaurant are spit-roasted suckling pig; grilled lamb burger from the Bleeding Heart's own organic herd; and game and poultry. Other dishes include grilled south coast mackerel with beetroot and crispy curly kale; roast maize-fed chicken with autumn vegetable risotto; and gnocchi Parisienne with fricassée of garden vegetables. Desserts include chocolate tart with clementine sauce.

Open all day 7am-11pm Closed BHs, 10 days at Xmas, Sat-Sun **Food** Contact pub for details Av main course £10.50 Set menu available Restaurant menu available Mon-Fri ⊕ FREE HOUSE ◀ Adnams Southwold Bitter, Broadside, Fisherman, May Day ♂ Aspall. ⛾ 17 **Facilities** Non-diners area WiFi

The Coach & Horses   PLAN 1 E5   PICK OF THE PUBS

tel: 020 7278 8990 **26-28 Ray St, Clerkenwell EC1R 3DJ**
email: info@thecoachandhorses.com
dir: *From Farringdon tube station right into Cowcross St. At Farringdon Rd turn right, after 500yds left into Ray St. Pub at bottom of hill*

Archetypal Victorian gastro-pub in Clerkenwell

This restored, wood-panelled, late 19th-century pub was built to serve the myriad artisans, many of them Italian, who once lived in this area. At one time a secret passage led to the long-buried River Fleet, which still runs beneath the pub and is audible from a drain outside the entrance. Unsurprisingly, there are a few ghosts, including an old man and a black cat. Typical 'small plates' include gin cured salmon with pickled cucumber; and rabbit, foie gras and prune terrine, while in the Eduardo Paolozzi-artwork-decorated dining room the modern British menu lists reasonably priced dishes such as venison shoulder casserole, porcini, pancetta and thyme dumplings; ale battered haddock with triple cooked chips; and whole Cornish mackerel, warm potato salad with beetroot relish. Enticing desserts could include lavender brûlée with a chocolate cookie. Enjoy with a pint of Portobello Star, Doom Bar or Symonds cider, or a glass of wine from the well-balanced list.

Open all wk 12-11 (Sat 6-11 Sun 12.30-5) Closed 24 Dec-1st Mon in Jan, BHs **Food** Lunch Mon-Fri 12-3, Sun 1-4 Dinner Mon-Sat 6-10 Av main course £12 ⊕ PUNCH TAVERNS ◀ Woodforde's Wherry, Brentwood BBC 2, Sharp's Doom Bar, Portobello Star ♂ Symonds. ⛾ 17 **Facilities** Non-diners area ❖ (Bar Restaurant Outside area) ♦ Children's portions Outside area ⌂ WiFi 🚐 (notice required)

The Eagle   PLAN 1 E5

tel: 020 7837 1353 **159 Farringdon Rd EC1R 3AL**
dir: *Nearest tube station: Angel or Farringdon. Pub at north end of Farringdon Rd*

One of trendy Clerkenwell's top establishments

Blazing a trail in the early 1990s and paving the way for what we now except as stylish gastro-pubs, The Eagle is still going strong – despite considerable competition. The lofty interior includes a wooden-floored bar and dining area, a mishmash of vintage furniture, and an open-to-view kitchen that produces a creatively modern, twice-daily changing menu and tapas selection which revel in bold, rustic flavours. Typical of the range are parsnip soup; smoked haddock and clam chowder; and braised whole partridge with borlotti beans, pancetta and sage.

Open all day 12-11 (Sun 12-5) Closed BHs L (1wk Xmas), Sun eve **Food** Lunch Mon-Fri 12-3, Sat 12-3.30, Sun 12.30-4 Dinner Mon-Sat 6.30-10.30 ⊕ FREE HOUSE ◀ Wells Eagle IPA & Bombardier, Hackney Ales ♂ Westons, Addlestones. ⛾ 15 **Facilities** Non-diners area ❖ (Bar) ♦ Children's portions

The Jerusalem Tavern   PLAN 1 E4   PICK OF THE PUBS

tel: 020 7490 4281 **55 Britton St, Clerkenwell EC1M 5UQ**
email: thejerusalemtavern@gmail.com
dir: *100mtrs NE of Farringdon tube station; 300mtrs N of Smithfield*

Historic inn with St Peter's Brewery cask and bottled beers

Owned by Suffolk's St Peter's Brewery, this historic tavern has close links to Samuel Johnson, Oliver Goldsmith, David Garrick and the young Handel, who used to drink here on his visits to London. Named after the Priory of St John of Jerusalem, founded in 1140, the pub can be traced back to the 14th century, having occupied several sites in the area including part of St John's Gate. The current premises date from 1720 although the shop frontage dates from about 1810, when it was a workshop for Clerkenwell's various watch and clock craftsmen. Its dimly lit Dickensian bar, with bare boards, rustic wooden tables, old tiles, candles, open fires and cosy corners, is the perfect film set - which is what it has been on many occasions. A classic pub in every sense, it offers the full range of cask and bottled beers from St Peter's Brewery, as well as a range of simple pub fare.

Open all day 11-11 Closed 25 Dec-1 Jan, Sat-Sun **Food** Lunch Mon-Fri 12-3 Av main course £8 ⊕ ST PETER'S BREWERY ◀ St Peter's (full range) ♂ New Forest Traditional, Oliver's, Once Upon a Tree Tumpy Ground. **Facilities** Non-diners area ❖ (Bar) Outside area WiFi

The Peasant   PLAN 1 E5   PICK OF THE PUBS

tel: 020 7336 7726 **240 Saint John St EC1V 4PH**
email: eat@thepeasant.co.uk
dir: *Nearest tube: Farringdon. Pub on corner of Saint John St & Percival St*

Restored Victorian pub with reputation for good food

One of the first gastro-pubs, this dining institution stands opposite tree-shaded gardens in the heart of Clerkenwell. With imposing brickwork and a balustrade outside, the eye-catching interior emphasises the Victorian grandeur of the pub with its decorative tiling, plasterwork ceiling, mosaic floor and great horseshoe mahogany bar. The first-floor restaurant continues the theme, with bold chandeliers and a quirky collection of arty circus memorabilia. Beer hounds will not be disappointed by the selection of real ales, including beers from Crouch Vale brewery, whilst Orchard Pig cider quenches a sharper thirst. A twice-yearly beer festival adds to the choices. The good value bar menu indulges most tastes, kicking in with starters typified by confit duck leg with white bean and Morteau sausage cassoulet. Mains impress with braised shoulder of venison and caramelised onion pie with mash and vegetables; or pan-fried fillet of sea bream with chilli, tomato, capers and garlic linguine. The restaurant has a set menu of modern European-inspired dishes; roast herb-crusted cod with mussel stew catches the eye.

Open all day all wk Closed 24 Dec-2 Jan **Food** Lunch all wk 12-11 Dinner all wk 12-11 Restaurant menu available ⊕ FREE HOUSE ◀ Wells Bombardier, Crouch Vale Brewers Gold, Truman's Runner, Guest ales ♂ Thatchers Pear & Katy, Aspall, The Orchard Pig. ⛾ 15 **Facilities** Non-diners area ♦ Children's portions Garden Beer festival 🚐 (notice required)

Ye Olde Mitre PLAN 1 E4

tel: 020 7405 4751 **1 Ely Court, Ely Place EC1N 6SJ**
email: yeoldemitre@fullers.co.uk
dir: *From Chancery Lane tube station exit 3 walk downhill to Holborn Circus, left into Hatton Garden. Pub in alley between 8 & 9 Hatton Garden*

Historic, hidden away pub

Built in 1546, extended in 1781, in the shadow of the palace of the Bishops of Ely, this quirky historic corner pub is in Ely Court, off Hatton Garden. It is often used as a film location. Choose from at least six real ales in the magnificent wood-panelled rooms, with a range of bar snacks or 'English tapas' that includes toasted sandwiches, pork pies, Scotch eggs, sausage rolls, olives and picked eggs. Please note that this pub, without music and bar TVs, is closed at weekends and Bank Holidays. Beer festivals are held in May, August and December.

Open all day Closed 25 Dec, 1 Jan, BHs, Sat-Sun (ex 1st wknd Aug) **Food** Lunch Mon-Fri 11.30-9.30 Dinner Mon-Fri 11.30-9.30 ⊕ FULLER'S ◀ London Pride, George Gale & Co Seafarers, Caledonian Deuchars IPA, Adnams Broadside, Guest ales Ò Biddenden Bushels, The Orchard Pig Philosopher, Gwynt y Ddraig Black Dragon. ☗ 8 **Facilities** Non-diners area Garden ♫ Beer festival WiFi

EC2

The Fox PLAN 1 F4

tel: 020 7729 5708 **28-30 Paul St EC2A 4LB**
email: info@thefoxpublichouse.co.uk
dir: *Nearest tube: Old Street. Take exit 4 for City Road South, into City Rd. 2nd left into Epworth St, 500yds, pub on corner at junct with Paul St*

Chill out with good food in this Shoreditch retreat

Not long ago, few visited Shoreditch for pleasure. Now, together with neighbouring Hoxton and Spitalfields, it is one of the capital's buzziest districts, with Victorian pubs like this thriving once more. Carefully selected wines and real ales - Harvey's Sussex and Otter, for example - and simple, straightforward food help to make it the place to head for after the shops and flower market of Columbia Road, the Asian bustle of Brick Lane, or a hard day at the office. Typically on the regularly changing menu are devilled whitebait with tahini; Toulouse sausage, mash and onion gravy; and roasted red onion, fennel and chicory tart with feta.

Open all day all wk Closed 25-28 Dec & BHs **Food** Lunch all wk 12-3 Dinner all wk 5-10 Av main course £13 ⊕ ENTERPRISE INNS ◀ Harvey's Sussex Best Bitter, Sharp's Doom Bar, Otter Bitter Ò Addlestones. ☗ 13 **Facilities** Non-diners area ❀ (Bar Outside area) ♦♦ Outside area ♫ WiFi

Old Dr Butler's Head PLAN 1 F4

tel: 020 7606 3504 **Mason's Av, Coleman St, Moorgate EC2V 5BT**
email: olddoctorbutlers@shepherdneame.co.uk
dir: *Phone for detailed directions*

Traditional pub in the heart of the City

Physician to James I, Dr Butler was actually an old fraud whose home-brewed medicinal ale could only be sold at inns displaying his portrait on their sign. Although the pub is old, the wooden façade is probably Victorian and certainly older than the mock-Tudor buildings opposite. A Shepherd Neame house, it stocks their real ales in the bar, where you can tuck into steak and kidney suet pudding. Restaurant dishes include ale-battered cod and chips; 10oz mature rump steak; pan-fried calves' liver; and sausages and mash. Please note that, like some other City pubs, the ODBH closes at weekends.

Open all day Closed Sat-Sun ⊕ SHEPHERD NEAME ◀ Spitfire, Bishops Finger, Master Brew, Kent's Best, Seasonal ale. **Facilities** Outside area WiFi

The Princess of Shoreditch PLAN 1 F4

tel: 020 7729 9270 **76-78 Paul St EC2A 4NE**
email: info@theprincessofshoreditch.com
dir: *Nearest tube: Old Street*

Well-known City gastro-pub

A pub since 1742, the former Princess Royal acquired its new name in 2010 following a major refurbishment that, say owners Scott and Maria Hunter, "made the old girl look better than ever". In the lively ground-floor bar beers change weekly, with regular supplies from London Fields brewery in Hackney, and real cider from Hogan's in Warwickshire. Food is served too, although for more formal dining (booking is recommended), climb the spiral staircase to the restaurant for dishes such as pan-fried pollock with cherry tomato and cannellini bean ragout; trio of lamb; and butternut squash, spinach and wild mushroom pie.

Open all day all wk Closed 25-27 Dec **Food** Lunch Mon-Fri 12-3, Sat 12-4, Sun 12-8 Dinner Mon-Sat 6.30-10, Sun 12-8 Av main course £14 Restaurant menu available Mon-Sat ⊕ ENTERPRISE INNS ◀ Sharp's, London Fields, Hackney, Redemption Ò Hogan's. ☗ 9 **Facilities** Non-diners area ♦♦ Children's portions Outside area WiFi

EC4

The White Swan ⊛ PLAN 1 E4   PICK OF THE PUBS

tel: 020 7242 9696 **108 Fetter Ln, Holborn EC4A 1ES**
email: info@thewhiteswanlondon.com
dir: *Nearest tube: Chancery Lane. From station towards St Paul's Cathedral. At HSBC bank left into Fetter Ln. Pub on right*

Handsome pub on legal London's eastern fringe

This exquisitely fitted-out City pub comprises a traditional ground-floor bar, a galleried mezzanine, and a first-floor dining room. For its cosmopolitan selection of bottled beers and lagers, Adnams on tap, Addlestones cider and a dozen wines by the glass, it has to be the bar, of course, whose cream-coloured walls provide the backdrop for leather-covered stools and assorted tables, chairs and banquettes. Modern British dishes here include roast Peterhead cod; and artichoke and sprout-top ravioli with duck egg and wild mushrooms. Upstairs is the beautifully restored dining room with mirrored ceiling and linen-clad tables, where the day's choices might include wild Brixham sea bass (fish comes in daily from Billingsgate), fennel and Pernod velouté; pan-fried loin and slow-cooked neck of Herdwick mutton with braised shallot, truffle gnocchi and anchovy jus; or Cumbrian veal cheek with spätzle, roast pumpkin and January King cabbage. Finish with pineapple soufflé and coconut sorbet.

Open all day Closed 25-26 Dec, wknds & BHs, Sat-Sun **Food** Lunch Mon-Fri 12-3 Dinner Mon-Fri 6-10 Av main course £14 Set menu available Restaurant menu available Mon-Fri ⊕ PUNCH TAVERNS ◀ Adnams Ò Addlestones. ☗ 12 **Facilities** Non-diners area ♦♦ WiFi

Find out more about
the AA's awards for food excellence on page 9

N1

The Albion   PLAN 2 F4

tel: 020 7607 7450 **10 Thornhill Rd, Islington N1 1HW**
email: info@the-albion.co.uk
dir: *From Angel tube station, cross road into Liverpool Rd past Sainsbury's, continue to Richmond Ave. Left. At junct with Thornhill Rd turn right. Pub on right*

Spacious walled garden for alfresco drinking

There has been a change of hands at this Georgian gem of a pub in the Barnsbury conservation area of Islington. New licensee Ann Haagensen continues to build on the pub's previous reputation for serving good food using top-notch British produce as well as a seasonal cocktail menu. In winter, log fires warm the pub's tastefully furnished interior, with the large walled garden and wisteria-covered pergola drawing the crowds in summer. The daily-changing menu includes slow-roast Hampshire pork belly with Lyonnaise potatoes, roasted roots and wholegrain mustard sauce; and goats' cheese pearl barley, artichokes, parsnips, wild mushrooms and truffle oil.

Open all day all wk **Food** Lunch Mon-Fri 12-3, Sat 12-4, Sun 12-9 Dinner Mon-Sat 6-10, Sun 12-9 Av main course £17 ⊕ PUNCH TAVERNS ◀ Ringwood Best Bitter, Caledonian Deuchars IPA ♂ Addlestones. ₹ 12 **Facilities** Non-diners area ❤ (Bar Garden) ●◀ Children's menu Children's portions Garden ⨍ WiFi ▭ (notice required)

The Barnsbury   PLAN 2 F4

tel: 020 7607 5519 **209-211 Liverpool Rd, Islington N1 1LX**
email: thebarnsburypub@gmail.com
dir: *Phone for detailed directions*

Popular north London pub with relaxing walled garden

In the heart of Islington, The Barnsbury changed hands in June 2013 but remains a reliable pub on the London scene. Food and drink are well conceived here and its walled garden is a secluded and sought-after summer oasis. Up to five guest ales are backed by an in-depth wine list. The food is cooked from daily supplies of fresh ingredients. Starter dishes range from buffalo chicken wings with blue cheese sauce to fried brie with apple and date chutney. Tempting mains include asparagus and pea ravioli; and sirloin steak with chips and béarnaise sauce. Desserts can include home-made cheesecake.

Open all wk 4.30-11 (Fri-Sat 12-11 Sun 12-10.30) Closed Mon-Thu L **Food** Lunch Fri-Sat 12-4, Sun 12-5 Dinner Mon-Sat 6-9.30, Sun 6-8.30 ⊕ FREE HOUSE ◀ Dark Star Hophead, rotating guest ales. ₹ **Facilities** Non-diners area ❤ (Bar Restaurant Garden) ●◀ Children's portions Garden ⨍ WiFi

The Charles Lamb   PLAN 2 F4

tel: 020 7837 5040 **16 Elia St, Islington N1 8DE**
email: food@thecharleslambpub.com
dir: *From Angel station turn left, at junct of City Rd turn left. Pass Duncan Terrace Gdns, left into Colebrooke Row. 1st right*

A really friendly London local

Named after a local writer who lived in Islington in the 1830s, this cracking neighbourhood pub thrives thanks to the hard work and dedication of Camille and MJ Hobby-Limon. Locals beat a path to the door for microbrewery ales and the hearty, home-cooked comfort food listed on the daily chalkboard menu. With inspiration from the Mediterranean, dishes may include Basque fish stew, wild mushroom and pearl barley risotto, and a rustic cassoulet. The pub hosts an annual Bastille Day event complete with petanque competition, and a Spring Bank Holiday beer festival.

Open all wk Mon & Tue fr 4 Wed-Sun fr noon Closed 23 Dec-1 Jan **Food** Lunch Wed-Fri 12-3, Sat 12-4, Sun 12-6 Dinner Mon-Sat 6-9.30, Sun 7-9 ⊕ FREE HOUSE ◀ Dark Star Hophead, Triple fff Alton's Pride, Guest ales ♂ Thatchers, Orchard Pig. ₹ 9 **Facilities** Non-diners area ❤ (Bar Restaurant Outside area) ●◀ Outside area ⨍ Beer festival WiFi

The Drapers Arms ◉   PLAN 2 F4   `PICK OF THE PUBS`

tel: 020 7619 0348 **44 Barnsbury St N1 1ER**
email: nick@thedrapersarms.com
dir: *Turn right from Highbury & Islington station, into Upper St. Barnsbury St on right opposite Shell service station*

Neighbourhood pub in trendy Islington

The Drapers' Company, one of the City of London's oldest guilds, built this handsome pub in the 1830s. Peppermint green paintwork, timber floors, squashy sofas and wooden tables give the ground floor bar a very pleasing look. Here, a trio of London brews, Portobello Star, Sambrook's Wandle and Truman's Runner, accompany out-of-towners Cornish Crown and Harvey's Sussex, while for cider drinkers there's Westons Wyld Wood Organic and Orchard Pig. Upstairs in the chequerboard-floored dining room, the daily-changing, AA Rosette menu might pose a question or two: will lunch be steak, Guinness and oyster pie; or confit duck leg cassoulet? In the evening another quandary: pheasant and hazelnut butter Kiev with braised Savoy cabbage and bacon; or cuttlefish, chorizo, potato and mussel stew with aïoli? Neal's Yard cheeses, and lemon curd doughnuts with vanilla ice cream are dessert options. A good crowd fills the pretty garden during the August beer festival.

Open all day all wk Closed 25-26 Dec **Food** Lunch Mon-Sat 12-3, Sun 12-8.30 Dinner Mon-Sat 6-11, Sun 12-8.30 ⊕ FREE HOUSE ◀ Harvey's Sussex, Sambrook's Wandle, Truman's Runner, Dark Star Hophead, Windsor & Eton Windsor Knot, Cornish Crown Bitter, Portobello Star ♂ Westons Stowford Press & Wyld Wood Organic, The Orchard Pig. ₹ 18 **Facilities** Non-diners area ❤ (Bar Garden) ●◀ Children's portions Garden ⨍ Beer festival WiFi

The Duke of Cambridge   PLAN 2 F4   `PICK OF THE PUBS`

tel: 020 7359 3066 **30 Saint Peter's St N1 8JT**
email: duke@dukeorganic.co.uk
dir: *Phone for detailed directions*

Organic pub advocating sustainable and ethical values

Geetie Singh's obsession with achieving the lowest possible carbon footprint possible at her remarkable Islington gastro-pub, the first certified organic pub in Britain, has reached new heights. Everything possible is re-used or recycled and even the electricity is wind and solar generated. Sustainable, ethically-produced ingredients are approved by the Soil Association and Marine Conservation Society, and items such as bread, ice cream and pickles are all made on site. Beers from local microbreweries, real ciders such as Luscombe, and organic wines go hand-in-hand with a mouthwatering seasonal menu that may change twice daily, with 80 per cent of ingredients sourced from the Home Counties. A spring choice could be mussels in tomato, chorizo and ale sauce, followed by Dover sole with Savoy cabbage, pancetta and sautéed potatoes. The winter menu may offer beetroot and cumin seed soup with crème fraîche, followed by rabbit and red wine stew with bubble-and-squeak. To finish, there could be rhubarb fool with coconut macaroon.

Open all day all wk Closed 24-26 & 31 Dec, 1 Jan **Food** Lunch all wk 12-5 Dinner Mon-Sat 6.30-10.30, Sun 6.30-10 ⊕ FREE HOUSE ◀ Pitfield SB Bitter, East Kent Goldings, Shoreditch Stout, Eco Warrior & Duke of Cambridge ♂ Westons, Dunkertons, Luscombe. ₹ 12 **Facilities** Non-diners area ❤ (Bar) ●◀ Children's portions ▭

NEW The Pig and Butcher   PLAN 2 F4

tel: 020 7226 8304 **80 Liverpool Rd, Islington N1 0QD**
email: crackling@thepigandbutcher.co.uk
dir: *Nearest tube: Angel*

Lovely ales and food 'like Granny used to make'

Before The Pig and Butcher was built in the mid-1800s, the fields here grazed by livestock on its way to Smithfield. Owner Jack Ross embraces this concept by receiving carcasses direct from the farm and then butchering on site. Rare breeds such as White Park cattle, Iron Age pigs and Hebridean lamb are specialities, along with game and vegetables from Kent and south coast fish. In winter, meats are brined, cured, smoked and braised, while summer sees the specially built charcoal grill glowing. Ales from the likes of Sambrook's and Bath complete the ethos behind this pub's carefully considered operation.

Open all wk 5-11 (Thu 5-12 Fri-Sat noon-1am Sun 12-11) Closed 24-26 Dec **Food** Lunch Fri 12-3.30, Sat 12-4, Sun 12-9 Dinner Mon-Sat 6.30-10, Sun 12-9 ◀ Bath Gem, Sharp's Doom Bar, Sambrook's Wandle. ☂ **Facilities** Non-diners area ✿ (Bar Outside area) ◀ Children's portions Outside area ⊟ WiFi

Smokehouse ◉◉   PLAN 2 F4

tel: 020 7354 1144 **63-69 Canonbury Rd N1 2DG**
email: info@smokehouseislington.co.uk
dir: *Phone for directions*

A historic house in leafy Islington, offering a seasonal British menu

Situated in Islington's prestigious Canonbury district but moments away from the hustle and bustle of Upper Street, this successful gastro-pub has featured in a celebrity cookbook and garnered plenty of praise since it opened its doors a few years ago. Expect a thoroughly modern, seasonal British menu at lunch and dinner. Typical dishes include almond crust brie cheese with cranberry compôte and pitta bread, or Poole mussels with Somerset cider and parsley to start; followed by venison pie with root vegetable mash, roast guinea fowl breast with sweet potato fondant, or pan-fried sea bass with caramelised Jerusalem artichoke and langoustine bisque. Leave room for rice pudding with autumn fruits and sloe gin, or baked vanilla cheesecake.

Open Mon-Wed 5-11 (Thu & Fri 5-mdnt Sat 11am-mdnt Sun & BHs 12-10.30) Closed Mon-Thu L (ex BHs) **Food** Lunch Sat 11-4, Sun 12-9 Dinner Mon-Fri 6-10, Sat 6-10, Sun 12-9 ⊕ NOBLE INNS ◀ Rotating Craft ales ⚬ Bath Ciders Bounders, Lilley's Apples & Pears. ☂ 15 **Facilities** Non-diners area ✿ (Bar Garden) ◀ Children's menu Children's portions Garden ⊟ WiFi ▭

N6

The Flask   PLAN 2 E5   PICK OF THE PUBS

tel: 020 8348 7346 **77 Highgate West Hill N6 6BU**
email: theflaskhighgate@london-gastros.co.uk
dir: *Nearest tube: Archway or Highgate*

Landmark gastro-pub with links to Dick Turpin

This Grade II listed pub, dating back to 1663 and made famous by Byron, Keats, Hogarth and Betjeman, has become a London landmark. High on Highgate Hill, it may now be a gastro-pub with a big reputation but its name was made long ago when Dick Turpin frequented it. It retains much of its character and cosy atmosphere and a maze of small rooms is served by two bars, one of which houses the original sash windows. Fuller's and guest real ales from newer London breweries are on offer alongside two dozen bottled ales and ciders, and some sensibly priced wines. Starters include smoked duck and celeriac remoulade, while typical mains are gammon, hispi, colcannon and parsley sauce; and whole sea bass with fennel and sauce vièrge. For dessert, try chocolate and Guinness cake. The large front garden is especially popular in the summer.

Open all day all wk 12-11 (Sun 12-10.30) Closed 25 Dec **Food** Lunch all wk 12-4 Dinner Mon-Sat 6-10, Sun 6-9 Av main course £11 ⊕ FULLER'S ◀ London Pride, ESB, George Gale & Co Seafarers, Guest ales ⚬ Cornish Orchards Gold. ☂ 13 **Facilities** Non-diners area ✿ (Bar Restaurant Garden) ◀ Garden ⊟ WiFi ▭ (notice required)

NW1

The Chapel   PLAN 1 B4

tel: 020 7402 9220 **48 Chapel St NW1 5DP**
email: thechapel@btconnect.com
dir: *By A40 Marylebone Rd & Old Marylebone Rd junct. Off Edgware Rd by tube station*

A popular child-friendly gastro-pub

The Chapel has a bright, open-plan interior of stripped floors and pine furniture, and boasts one of central London's largest enclosed pub gardens – great for the children to let off steam. Owners Alison McGrath and Lakis Hondrogiannis take delivery of the freshest produce for daily-changing menus featuring internationally influenced dishes, as well as Mediterranean antipasti and canapés. A sample dinner menu lists baked egg cocotte with mushrooms and speck, gruyère cream; chargrilled onglet steak with chips, green salad and mustard sauce; pan-roast chicken breast with mushroom and ricotta ravioli. Many wines are served by the glass.

Open all day all wk Closed 25-26 Dec, 1 Jan, Etr **Food** Lunch Mon-Sat 12-2.30, Sun 12-3 Dinner all wk 7-10 Av main course £13 Set menu available ⊕ FREE HOUSE/ GREENE KING ◀ Adnams Southwold Bitter, Black Sheep ⚬ Somersby Cider. ☂ 15 **Facilities** Non-diners area ✿ (Bar Restaurant Garden) ◀ Children's menu Children's portions Garden ⊟ ▭ (notice required)

The Engineer   PLAN 2 E4   PICK OF THE PUBS

tel: 020 7483 1890 **65 Gloucester Av, Primrose Hill NW1 8JH**
email: enquiries@theengineerprimrosehill.co.uk
dir: *Phone for detailed directions*

World beers and eclectic dishes in a relaxed atmosphere

Built by Isambard Kingdom Brunel in 1841, this unassuming street corner pub stands tucked away in a residential part of Primrose Hill close to Camden Market. It attracts a discerning dining crowd who relish its imaginative and well-prepared food and friendly, laid-back atmosphere. There is a spacious bar area, wood floors, sturdy wooden tables with candles, simple decor and cosy upstairs private dining rooms. A walled, paved and heated garden to the rear is popular in fine weather. In addition to cosmopolitan beers, the drinks list includes hand-crafted teas, freshly ground coffees, interesting wines, and a variety of whiskies. Regularly changing menus feature an eclectic mix of inspired home-made dishes using organic and free-range products. A typical Sunday lunch menu may feature rabbit terrine with piccalilli to start, followed by roast duck with plums and braised red cabbage, or lamb shoulder with confit garlic and mint sauce. Leave room for bitter chocolate pudding with malt ice cream.

Open all day all wk 12-11 (Sat 10-11 Sun 12-10.30) **Food** Lunch all wk 12-10 Dinner all wk 12-10 ⊕ MITCHELLS & BUTLERS ◀ Redemption, Sharp's Doom Bar ⚬ Aspall Harry Sparrow. ☂ 19 **Facilities** Non-diners area ✿ (Bar Garden) ◀ Children's menu Children's portions Family room Garden ⊟ Beer festival Cider festival WiFi ▭

LONDON NW1 *continued*

The Prince Albert PLAN 2 F4

tel: 020 7485 0270 **163 Royal College St NW1 0SG**
email: info@princealbertcamden.com
dir: *From Camden tube station follow Camden Rd. Right into Royal College St, 200mtrs on right*

Organic food at character pub

Picnic tables furnish the small paved courtyard, while The Prince Albert's wooden floors and bentwood furniture make a welcoming interior for customers and their four-legged friends. Real ales there are, but you may fancy a refreshing glass of wine and there's plenty of choice. Bar snacks range from home-made baba ganoush to Mediterranean vegetables and haloumi sandwiches; these can be followed by confit Barbary duck leg, burgers and relish, or fish and chips. Two or three times a year the pub holds a three-day real ale festival.

Open all day all wk **Food** Lunch all wk 12-3 Dinner all wk 6-10 Av main course £11 Set menu available ⊕ FREE HOUSE ◀ Dark Star, Sambrook's, Adnams, Redemption. ♟ 14 **Facilities** Non-diners area ♣ (Bar Garden) ♦♦ Children's portions Garden ⌂ Beer festival Cider festival WiFi ▰ (notice required)

▌ NW3

The Holly Bush PLAN 2 E4

tel: 020 7435 2892 **Holly Mount, Hampstead NW3 6SG**
email: hollybush@fullers.co.uk
dir: *Nearest tube: Hampstead. Exit tube station into Holly Hill, 1st right*

Historic pub serving hearty food

Once the stables belonging to the home of English portraitist George Romney, The Holly Bush became a pub after his death in 1802. The building has been investigated by 'ghost busters', but more tangible 21st-century media celebrities are easier to spot these days. The pub has undergone a refurbishment in 2014. Depending on your appetite, the menu offers beef, ale and mushroom pie; seared duck breast with red cabbage, new potatoes and fennel; and bar snacks of sausage rolls and Scotch eggs – perfect with a pint of London Pride or Seafarers.

Open all day all wk 12-11 (Sun 12-10.30) ⊕ FULLER'S ◀ London Pride & ESB, Butcombe, George Gale & Co Seafarers Ŏ Aspall. **Facilities** ♣ (Bar Restaurant) ♦♦ Children's portions Outside area WiFi

▌ NW5

The Bull and Last PLAN 2 E5

tel: 020 7267 3641 **168 Highgate Rd NW5 1QS**
email: info@thebullandlast.co.uk
dir: *From Kentish Town tube station N into Highgate Rd (4 mins walk from Gospel Oak Station)*

Tempting menus and many wines by the glass

A historic free house in a Grade II listed building, a stone's throw from Hampstead Heath. Children and dogs are welcome too, so this really is a relaxing place to sample a pint of Redemption Big Chief or one of the wines sold by the glass. Wondering whether to eat? A glance at the home-made dishes on the menu will make up your mind – who can resist mouth watering starters like confit rabbit, smoked eel and ham hock terrine with sour apple purée? Move on to roast cod, hazelnut pesto, Roscoff onions, monk's beard and white kale; or Denham Vale aged côte de boeuf for two if you're determined to push the boat out. Summer picnic hampers and take-away ice creams are available too.

Open all day all wk 12-11 (Fri-Sat 12-12 Sun 12-10.30 Sat-Sun 9am-11am) Closed 24-25 Dec **Food** Bkfst Sat-Sun 9am-11am Lunch Mon-Fri 12-3, Sat-Sun 9am-11am (bkfst) 12.30-4 Dinner Mon-Sat 6.30-10, Sun 6.30-9 ⊕ FREE HOUSE/ETIVE PUBS LTD ◀ Dark Star Partridge Best Bitter, ELB So Solid Brew, Redemption Big Chief,

Red Squirrel London Porter Ŏ Addlestones, Snails Bank Tumbledown. ♟ 17 **Facilities** Non-diners area ♣ (Bar Outside area) ♦♦ Children's menu Children's portions Outside area ⌂ WiFi

The Lord Palmerston PLAN 2 E5

tel: 020 7485 1578 **33 Dartmouth Park Hill NW5 1HU**
email: lordpalmerston@geronimo-inns.co.uk
dir: *From Tufnell Park Station turn right. Up Dartmouth Park Hill. Pub on right, on corner of Chetwynd Rd*

Pub with a focus on quality

A stylish London pub in the Dartmouth Park conservation area where food is taken seriously. Expect dishes such as pork rillettes with cornichons and toast; wood pigeon with pearl barley, bacon, peas and red wine jus; and apple crumble with fresh cream. Other choices range from ale battered cod and chips to pickled walnut, Oxfordshire Blue, chicory and pear salad. As well as beer festivals, the pub holds weekly quiz nights and film screenings.

Open all day all wk 12-11 (Sun 12-10.30) **Food** Lunch Mon-Fri 12-3, Sat 12-10, Sun 12-9 Dinner Mon-Fri 6-10, Sat 12-10, Sun 12-9 ⊕ GERONIMO INNS LTD ◀ Sharp's Doom Bar, Young's, Guest ales Ŏ Aspall. ♟ 24 **Facilities** Non-diners area ♣ (Bar Restaurant Garden) ♦♦ Children's portions Garden Beer festival Cider festival WiFi ▰

▌ NW6

The Salusbury Pub and Dining Room PLAN 2 D4

tel: 020 7328 3286 **50-52 Salusbury Rd NW6 6NN**
email: thesalusburypub@btconnect.com
dir: *100mtrs left from Queen's Park tube & train station (5 mins walk from Brondesbury station)*

A community local serving good value fare

A stone's throw from Queen's Park tube, this pub serves the local community well, admitting dogs and children and serving kiddy-sized portions from the uncomplicated menu. Small plates come cold (Dorset crab, quail's egg and watercress) or hot (devilled lamb's kidneys on toast), while main dishes are robust and classically British: grilled Barnsley chop with grain mustard mash and broccoli; or Guinness-braised ox cheek with pearl barley. Desserts may feature Bramley apple and quince crumble with clotted cream. Along with the food, ales from St Austell and Greene King, Aspall's cider and a good range of wines can all be served on the outside patio.

Open all day all wk 12-11 (Thu-Sat 12-12 Sun 12-10.30) Closed 25-26 Dec **Food** Lunch all wk 12-4 Dinner Mon-Sat 6-10, Sun 6-9 Av main course £12.50 ⊕ FREE HOUSE ◀ St Austell Tribute, Greene King Abbot Ale, Moorland Old Speckled Hen Ŏ Aspall. ♟ 15 **Facilities** Non-diners area ♣ (Bar Outside area) ♦♦ Children's portions Family room Outside area ⌂ WiFi ▰ (notice required)

▌ NW8

The New Inn PLAN 2 E4

tel: 020 7722 0726 **2 Allitsen Rd, St John's Wood NW8 6LA**
email: thenewinn@gmail.com
dir: *Exit A41 by St John's Wood tube station into Acacia Rd, last right, to end on corner*

British favourites meet international tapas

Colourful flower baskets and troughs break the lines of this street-corner pub, where pavement tables are a popular retreat for locals supping Abbot Ale, Aspall cider or a choice from the extensive wine list. This convivial Regency inn is well-placed for nearby Regent's Park and Lord's Cricket Ground. In the elegant restaurant, diners indulge in the sharing boards, the global tapas selection, fresh salads or a traditional main like bangers and mash or rack of ribs. Desserts include a tiramisù and home-made ice creams. There is also a 'Little People's' menu.

Open all day all wk 7.30am-11pm (Fri 7.30am-mdnt Sat 8am-mdnt Sun 8.30am-10.30pm) **Food** Lunch all day Dinner all day Restaurant menu available all wk ⊕ GREENE KING ◀ Abbot Ale, IPA, London Glory Ŏ Aspall, Kopparberg, Rekorderlig. ♟ 14 **Facilities** Non-diners area ♣ (Bar Restaurant) ♦♦ Children's menu Children's portions WiFi ▭

SE1

The Garrison   PLAN 1 G2 PICK OF THE PUBS

tel: 020 7089 9355 **99-101 Bermondsey St SE1 3XB**
email: info@thegarrison.co.uk
dir: From London Bridge tube station, E towards Tower Bridge 200mtrs, right into Bermondsey St. Pub in 100mtrs

Friendly neighbourhood gastro-pub

No doubt this green-tiled, street-corner pub was once a popular local for generations of Surrey Docks stevedores. The docks are no more and Bermondsey has gone up-market, but were those old boys to return they'd no doubt be amazed by the pub's 21st-century restyling, based around an idiosyncratic mix of decorative themes and antique knick-knacks. The place pulsates from breakfast through to the evening, when the downstairs room doubles as a mini-cinema. Start the day with a 'full and proper' or 'full vegetarian' breakfast, or maybe smoked haddock with poached egg, potato pancake and hollandaise; for lunch, there's pan-roasted coley with Jerusalem artichoke and chervil root purée; or Somerset brie with roasted pepper and pesto sandwich. In the evening, check out smoked salmon kedgeree; braised ox cheek with roasted parsnips; or the day's steak special. Drinks include beers from Adnams, and Munich's Spaten-Franziskaner, as well as Breton ciders.

Open all day all wk 8am-11pm (Fri 8am-mdnt Sat 9am-mdnt Sun 9am-10.30pm) Closed 25-26 Dec **Food** Lunch Mon-Fri 12-3, Sat-Sun 12.30-4 Dinner all wk 6-10.30 ⊕ FREE HOUSE ◀ Spaten-Franziskaner-Bräu Franziskaner Hefe-Weisse, Adnams, Samuel Adams Ŏ Thatchers Old Rascal, Cidre Breton. ♟ 17 **Facilities** Non-diners area WiFi

The George Inn   PLAN 1 F3

tel: 020 7407 2056 **77 Borough High St SE1 1NH**
email: 7781@greeneking.co.uk
dir: From London Bridge tube station, take Borough High St exit, left. Pub 200yds on left

Unique former haunt of Charles Dickens

The coming of the nearby railway meant demolition of part of what is now London's sole surviving example of a 17th-century, galleried coaching inn, but what's left is impressive. National Trust-owned, it still features some very old woodwork, like the simple wall seats. Serving thirsty Londoners for centuries, the pub is mentioned in Dickens's *Little Dorrit*. As well as Greene King ales and rotating guests, George Inn Ale is the house beer. The pub grub includes a sharing fish slate, potted mackerel, chicken casserole, shepherd's pie, roasted vegetable and cheese filo parcel, and Toulouse sausages. There are various beer festivals throughout the year.

Open all day all wk 11-11 (Sun 12-10.30) Closed 25-26 Dec **Food** Lunch Mon-Sat 11-10, Sun 12-9 Dinner Mon-Sat 11-10, Sun 12-9 ⊕ GREENE KING ◀ IPA, George Inn Ale, Guest ales Ŏ Aspall. **Facilities** Non-diners area ♦♦ Children's portions Garden ♫ Beer festival WiFi ▭

The Market Porter   PLAN 1 F3

tel: 020 7407 2495 **9 Stoney St, Borough Market, London Bridge SE1 9AA**
dir: Close to London Bridge Station

A real ale pub with a Harry Potter connection

With as apt a name as you could wish for, this Borough Market pub is blessed with a really good atmosphere, especially on Thursdays, Fridays and Saturdays, when the retail market operates. Harry Potter fans will surely know that the inn became the 'Third Hand Book Emporium' in one of the films. The exceptional choice of real ales

includes the resident Harvey's, others changing up to nine times a day along with some international sidekicks. Apart from sandwiches and bar snacks there's dishes such as Scottish salmon and crab remoulade; Harvey's ale and mushroom pie; tempura cod and chips with caramelised lemon; and for vegetarians, wild garlic and parsley risotto with Cashel Blue. On weekdays the pub opens its doors at 6am. Children are welcome before 6pm.

Open all day all wk 6am-9am, 11-11 (Sat 12-11 Sun 12-10.30) Closed 25-26 Dec, 1 Jan **Food** Lunch Mon-Thu 12-3, Fri-Sun 12-5 Av main course £10.50 Set menu available Restaurant menu available all wk ⊕ FREE HOUSE ◀ Harvey's Sussex Best Bitter, wide selection of international ales Ŏ Traditional Scrumpy. ♟ 10 **Facilities** Non-diners area ♦♦ Children's portions Outside area ♫ ▭ (notice required)

SE5

The Crooked Well   PLAN 2 F3

tel: 020 7252 7798 **16 Grove Ln, Camberwell SE5 8SY**
email: info@thecrookedwell.com
dir: Nearest tube: Denmark Hill

Neighbourhood restaurant and bar is a Camberwell beauty

Set up and run by three friends, each with stacks of restaurant experience in the kitchen or front of house, this Victorian, street corner pub has rapidly earned some worthy plaudits for its food. A penchant for home-cooked British classics, such as rabbit and bacon pie (for two), still allows continental influences to not so much creep in as enter with brio – for example, roast lamb with spiced aubergine and tzatziki; rose-harissa-toasted couscous; and coley with tagliatelle and salsa verde. Regularly involved with community events, it holds mums' (and dads') mornings and jazz nights.

Open all day all wk Closed 25-27 Dec **Food** Lunch Tue-Sat 12.30-3, Sun 12.30-4 Dinner Mon-Sat 6.30-10.30, Sun 7-9.30 Set menu available Restaurant menu available all wk ⊕ PUNCH TAVERNS ◀ Sharp's Doom Bar Ŏ Westons Wyld Wood Organic. ♟ 10 **Facilities** Non-diners area ♣ (Bar Restaurant Outside area) ♦♦ Children's menu Children's portions Outside area ♫ WiFi ▭ (notice required)

SE10

Greenwich Union Pub   PLAN 2 G3

tel: 020 8692 6258 **56 Royal Hill SE10 8RT**
email: theunion@meantimebrewing.com
dir: From Greenwich DLR & main station exit by main ticket hall, turn left, 2nd right into Royal Hill. Pub 100yds on right

A beer-drinker's idea of heaven

In the heart of Greenwich's bustling Royal Hill, this pub's comfortable leather sofas and flagstone floors help to keep its original character intact. Interesting craft beers from the award-winning Meantime Brewing Co, along with lagers from around the world and a beer garden, make this a popular spot. The food is an eclectic range of traditional and modern dishes drawn from around the world. Everything is freshly prepared and sourced locally where possible: fish comes straight from Billingsgate Market, while bread comes from the Greenwich itself. The lunch menu includes sandwiches, and favourites like home-made 28-day-aged Aberdeen Angus beefburger, while at dinner you could opt for Welsh rarebit followed by kedgeree or three bean chilli. All courses, including dessert, can be accompanied by a recommended beer, so you could round off with sticky toffee pudding and a glass of Meantime Chocolate Porter.

Open all day all wk 12-11 (Fri-Sat 9-11 Sun 9-10.30) **Food** Lunch all wk 12-10 Dinner all wk 12-10 ⊕ FREE HOUSE ◀ Meantime Pale Ale, Pilsner, Yakima Red, Cotswold Wheat Beer Ŏ Sheppy's. **Facilities** ♣ (Bar Restaurant Garden) ♦♦ Garden ♫ WiFi

LONDON SE10 *continued*

North Pole Bar & Restaurant   PLAN 2 G3 PICK OF THE PUBS

tel: 020 8853 3020 **131 Greenwich High Rd, Greenwich SE10 8JA**
email: info@northpolegreenwich.com
dir: *Right from Greenwich rail station, pass Novotel. Pub on right*

The complete package in Greenwich

Dating from 1849, the name originated with the Victorian obsession for polar exploration, and North Pole Road adjoins the pub. It's a stylish, contemporary venue, offering a complete night out under one roof, with a bar, restaurant and basement club. Outside in the beer garden (which is also home to a shisha pipe lounge) is seating for well over 100 people. Refreshments range from international beers such as Staropramen to cocktails, while the all-day bar menu features tapas, platters, sandwiches, grills and salads. The Piano restaurant attracts both visitors and loyal locals with its seasonally changing, modern European à la carte and brasserie menus: baked fillet of Loch Dock salmon; rolled belly of pork stuffed with mixed herbs, vegetable lentils, apple purée and pear cider sauce; and grilled chicken supreme with sautéed potatoes, green beans and cep mushroom sauce. Desserts range from star anise crème brûlée to treacle pudding.

Open all day all wk noon-2am **Food** Lunch all wk 12-10 Dinner all wk 12-10 Av main course £9 Set menu available Restaurant menu available all wk ⊕ FREE HOUSE ◀ Staropramen, Greene King IPA, Guinness ⚬ Aspall. ♟ 9 **Facilities** Non-diners area ❄ (All areas) ♦ Children's menu Children's portions Garden Outside area ⊼ WiFi 🚌 (notice required)

NEW The Old Brewery   PLAN 2 G3

tel: 020 3327 1280 **The Pepys Building, Old Royal Naval College, Greenwich SE10 9LW**
email: benjamin@oldbrewerygreenwich.com
dir: *Nearest tube: Cutty Sark*

Buzzy pub housing the only brewery in a World Heritage Site

By day, the stuccoed façade of The Pepys Building in the grounds of The Old Royal Naval College house a convivial pub/café; in the evening it becomes a vibrant pub/restaurant. It's home also to the Meantime Brewery Company, whose real ales accompany Dark Star, Adnams and fifty-plus bottled world classics. No wonder there are four beer festivals a year. Pub food is served in the bar and courtyard during the day, while an evening meal amidst the copper tuns and suspended bottles in the main hall might be barbecued ribs marinated in Meantime wheat beer; fisherman's pie; or mushroom and Jerusalem artichoke risotto.

Open all day all wk Closed 26 Dec **Food** Lunch all wk 12-5 Dinner all wk 6-10 Av main course £10-£12 Restaurant menu available all wk ⊕ MEANTIME BREWING CO ◀ Meantime Brewing Co beer, Dark Star Hophead, Adnams Southwold ⚬ Thatchers Gold. **Facilities** Non-diners area ❄ (Bar Garden) ♦ Children's menu Children's portions Garden ⊼ Beer festival WiFi 🚌 (notice required)

■ SE21

The Crown & Greyhound   PLAN 2 F2

tel: 020 8299 4976 **73 Dulwich Village SE21 7BJ**
email: enquiry@thecrownandgreyhound.co.uk
dir: *Nearest station: North Dulwich*

A warm welcome in Dulwich

With a history reaching back to the 18th century, The Crown & Greyhound (nicknamed The Dog) counts Charles Dickens and John Ruskin amongst its celebrated patrons. In the olden days, the pub was split in two - The Crown served

the gentry while The Greyhound housed the labourers. Modern day customers will find three bars and a restaurant in the heart of peaceful Dulwich Village. The ever-changing menu might feature Shropshire roast chicken with herb butter and fries, and sticky toffee pudding for dessert. There are daily salads, pasta and fish dishes, as well.

Open all day all wk 11-11 (Thu-Sat 11am-mdnt Sun 11-10.30) **Food** Lunch Mon-Sat 12-10, Sun 12-9 Dinner Mon-Sat 12-10, Sun 12-9 ⊕ MITCHELLS & BUTLERS ◀ Harvey's Sussex Best Bitter, Sharp's Doom Bar, Guest ales ⚬ Aspall Harry Sparrow, Gaymers. ♟ 20 **Facilities** Non-diners area ❄ (Bar Garden) ♦ Children's menu Children's portions Garden ⊼ 🚌 (notice required)

The Rosendale   PLAN 2 F2

tel: 020 8761 9008 **65 Rosendale Rd, West Dulwich SE21 8EZ**
email: info@therosendale.co.uk
dir: *Nearest station: West Dulwich*

Transformed mid-Victorian coach house

Owned by three former schoolmates who also run other South London pubs, The Rosendale, just like the other pubs in the group, has been totally transformed. The owners like keeping things simple but interesting, so the formidably-stocked bar might include Moor Nor' Hop, a Somerset brew, but also North American-style, pale ale, several real ciders, and a mind-boggling range of rums, tequilas and vodkas. Traditional British food, using top-quality ingredients such as meats from the boys' own farm in Hampshire, includes bar snacks like Welsh rarebit, and the more substantial honey-spiced Goosnargh duck; and roast butternut and ricotta ravioli.

Open all day all wk Closed 26 Dec **Food** Lunch Mon-Fri 12-3.30, Sat 12-4, Sun 12-9 Dinner Mon-Thu 6-10, Fri-Sat 6-10.30, Sun 12-9 ⊕ RENAISSANCE PUBS ◀ Moor Nor' Hop, Adnams Ghost Ship, Harvey's Sussex Best Bitter, Timothy Taylor Landlord ⚬ Wilkins Farmhouse, Hecks, Sandford Orchards, Wilcox. ♟ 27 **Facilities** Non-diners area ❄ (Bar Garden) ♦ Children's menu Children's portions Play area Garden ⊼ WiFi 🚌

■ SE22

The Palmerston ⊛   PLAN 2 F2

tel: 020 8693 1629 **91 Lordship Ln, East Dulwich SE22 8EP**
email: info@thepalmerston.co.uk
dir: *2m from Clapham, 0.5m from Dulwich Village (10 mins walk from East Dulwich station)*

Smart London corner pub serving excellent modern food

A striking gastro-pub, heavy on the wood panelling, with much stripped floorboard and some great floor tiling. Occasional installations of photographic exhibitions add to the flair of this corner-plot destination dining pub in leafy Dulwich. Chef Jamie Younger's AA Rosette award results from his modern British menu with a Mediterranean twist. Start with slow braised lamb, spring vegetable and oregano broth; follow with braised suckling pork belly or whole baked royal bream with sauce vierge and crème fraîche; and finish with iced zabaglione or orange marmalade and almond tart. Affable locals pop in for some flavoursome beers, too, from the likes of Sharp's and Harvey's.

Open all day all wk Closed 25-26 Dec, 1 Jan **Food** Lunch Mon-Fri 12-2.30, Sat-Sun 12-3.30 Dinner Mon-Sat 7-10, Sun 7-9.30 Av main course £19 Set menu available ⊕ ENTERPRISE INNS ◀ Sharp's Doom Bar, Harvey's, Timothy Taylor Landlord, Sambrook's Wandle ⚬ Westons Stowford Press. ♟ 16 **Facilities** Non-diners area ♦ Children's portions Outside area ⊼ WiFi

SE23

The Dartmouth Arms   PLAN 2 G2

tel: 020 8488 3117 **7 Dartmouth Rd, Forest Hill SE23 3HN**
email: dartmouth@innpublic.com
dir: *800mtrs from Horniman Museum*

Smart Georgian pub with modern British cuisine

The long-vanished Croydon Canal once ran behind this pub dating from 1815, and you can still see the towpath railings at the bottom of the car park. Behind the smart façade, bars serve snacks, traditional real ales, continental lagers, cocktails, coffees and teas, while the restaurant might offer grilled haloumi skewers or duck liver parfait as starters, and mains might be Shetland mussels in a cider, leek and cream sauce or pan-fried salmon with sun-dried tomato risotto and watercress. Puddings include vanilla pannacotta. There's a small, secluded garden.

Open all wk Closed 25-26 Dec, 1 Jan **Food** Lunch Mon-Fri 12-3.30, Sat 12-9.30, Sun 12-4 Dinner Mon-Fri 6-9.30, Sat 12-9.30, Sun 5-9 ⊕ ENTERPRISE INNS ◀ St Austell Tribute, Brockley Golden, Guest ale Ò Addlestones. **Facilities** Non-diners area ◈ Garden ⊟ Parking WiFi ▥

SW1

The Buckingham Arms   PLAN 1 D2

tel: 020 7222 3386 **62 Petty France SW1H 9EU**
email: buckinghamarms@youngs.co.uk
dir: *Nearest tube: St James's Park*

Forever popular for good beer and top pub food

This elegant Young's pub was known as the Black Horse until 1903 and retains much of its old charm including etched mirrors and period light fittings in the bar. Close to Buckingham Palace, it is popular with pretty much everyone: tourists, business people, politicians, media types and real ale fans. Expect a good range of simple pub food, including grazers (perhaps breaded brie with raspberry and rosemary dip), sandwiches and hearty favourites such as sausages and mash, steak and ale pie and West Country beef burgers.

Open all day 11-11 (Sat 12-6 Sun 12-6 summer) Closed 25-26 Dec, Sun (winter) **Food** Lunch all wk 12-3 Dinner Mon-Fri 3-8, Sat-Sun 3-5 Av main course £10 ⊕ YOUNG'S ◀ Bitter, Wells Bombardier, Young's Special, London Gold, Guest ales Ò Aspall. ▼ 15 **Facilities** Non-diners area ◈ (Bar) ◈ WiFi

The Nags Head   PLAN 1 B2 | PICK OF THE PUBS |

tel: 020 7235 1135 **53 Kinnerton St SW1X 8ED**
dir: *Phone for detailed directions*

Seek out this mews pub and step back in time

This pub was built in the early 19th century to cater for below-stairs staff and stable hands working in this quiet Belgravia mews near Harrods. With its Dickensian frontage and an interior like a well-stocked bric-à-brac shop, The Nags Head stubbornly resists any contemporary touches. It's a mobile-free zone, and you are politely requested to hang coats and bags on the hooks provided. Compact and bijou, its front and back bars are connected by a narrow stairway and boast wooden floors, low ceilings and panelled walls covered with photos, drawings, and mirrors; other adornments include helmets, model aeroplanes, and even penny-slot machines. The atmosphere is best described as 'entertaining' if you're in the right mood. The waist-high bar is another oddity, but the full Adnams range is served, along with a good value menu of traditional pub grub. Jazz Sunday specials include lamb stew with Irish brown soda bread.

Open all day all wk 11-11 **Food** Lunch all wk 11-9.30 Av main course £7.50 ⊕ FREE HOUSE ◀ Adnams Southwold Bitter, Broadside, Fisherman, Regatta & Old Ale Ò Aspall. **Facilities** Non-diners area ◈ (Bar) ◈ ⊟

The Orange Public House & Hotel   PLAN 1 C1

tel: 020 7881 9844 **37 Pimlico Rd SW1W 8NE**
email: reservations@theorange.co.uk
dir: *Nearest tube: Victoria or Sloane Street*

An ornate corner building offering rustic and uncomplicated food

Recognised for its approach to sustainability, The Orange comprises a number of light and airy adjoining rooms, which have a rustic Tuscan feel with their muted colours and potted orange trees on stripped wooden boards. Well-heeled locals quaff Adnams ales and Italian wines while selecting from menus of modern European dishes. Wood-fired pizzas and oven roasts lead the way, but the carte is full of good things: grilled English rose veal chop; line-caught cod with celeriac, apple, Puy lentils, kale and Madeira jus; and steak, ale and cheddar pie, to list but a few.

Open all day all wk 8am-11.30pm (Sun 8am-10.30pm) **Food** Lunch all wk 12-6 Dinner all wk 6-10 ⊕ FREE HOUSE ◀ Adnams, Meantime Wheat & Pale Ale Ò Aspall. ▼ 15 **Facilities** Non-diners area ◈ Children's menu Children's portions WiFi

The Thomas Cubitt   PLAN 1 C2

tel: 020 7730 6060 **44 Elizabeth St SW1W 9PA**
email: reservations@thethomascubitt.co.uk
dir: *Nearest tube: Victoria or Sloane Square*

Distinguished pub in fashionable district

Norfolk-born builder Thomas Cubitt developed Belgravia as a stuccoed rival to swanky Mayfair. This exclusive, white-painted corner pub draws a discerning crowd to its country-house-style interior featuring open fireplaces, detailed panelling and a superb hand-made, oak counter. Floor-to-ceiling glass doors open out on to tables and chairs on the street. In the bar, where Adnams and Deuchars real ales are resident, enjoy Carlingford rock oysters; and corn-fed chicken Caesar salad: upstairs the dining room offers Highland venison Wellington; Isle of Gigha halibut fillet; and Fivemiletown goats' cheese and spinach pie. Booking is essential for the memorable Sunday roast.

Open all day all wk 12-11 (Sun 12-10.30) Closed Xmas **Food** Lunch all wk all day Dinner all wk all day ⊕ FREE HOUSE ◀ Caledonian Deuchars IPA, Adnams Ò Aspall. ▼ **Facilities** Non-diners area ◈ Children's menu Children's portions ⊟ ▥ (notice required)

The Wilton Arms   PLAN 1 B2

tel: 020 7235 4854 **71 Kinnerton St SW1X 8ED**
email: wilton@shepherd-neame.co.uk
dir: *Between Hyde Park Corner & Knightsbridge tube stations*

Cosy pub serving Shepherd Neame ales

Known locally as The Village Pub, this early 19th-century hostelry's other name is a reference to the 1st Earl of Wilton. In summer it is distinguished by fabulous flower-filled baskets and window boxes. High settles and bookcases create cosy, individual seating areas in the air-conditioned interior, and a conservatory covers the old garden. Shepherd Neame ales, including Spitfire, accompany traditional pub fare: ploughman's, toasted sandwiches, burgers, sausages and mash with onion gravy; and a smoked salmon platter with brown bloomer bread are typical options. There's also a good choice of chicken dishes including garlic battered chicken goujons.

Open all day all wk Closed 25-26 Dec, BHs **Food** Lunch Mon-Fri 12-4, Sat 12-3 Dinner Mon-Fri 5.30-9 Av main course £6.50 ⊕ SHEPHERD NEAME ◀ Spitfire & Bishops Finger, Oranjeboom. **Facilities** Non-diners area ◈ (Bar Outside area) ◈ Children's portions Outside area ⊟ WiFi ▥

SW3

The Builders Arms PLAN 1 B1 `PICK OF THE PUBS`

tel: 020 7349 9040 **13 Britten St SW3 3TY**
email: thebuildersarms@geronimo-inns.co.uk
dir: *From Sloane Square tube station into King's Rd. Right into Chelsea Manor St, at end right into Britten St, pub on right*

Modern English food with a twist

The Builders Arms is a stylish three-storey Georgian pub tucked away in the back streets of Chelsea, just off the King's Road. It was built by the same crew that constructed St Luke's church over the way. Inside, leather sofas dot the spacious informal bar area, where you can enjoy a pint of Bombardier or Doom Bar. The Geronimo team are committed to using seasonal food, and have also developed a bespoke cheese, Stithians, which is only available in their pubs. The menu offers a wide range, from chicken liver parfait with tomato and apple chutney to a fillet steak open sandwich served with fries and red onion marmalade. Starters include wild mushrooms, brioche and truffle cream sauce, while a sample main course is mussels steamed with beer, celery and Oxford Blue sauce. There is an impressive number of wines by the glass. When the sun shines the outdoor terrace is hugely popular.

Open all wk Mon-Wed 11-11 Thu-Sat 11am-mdnt (Sun 12-10.30) **Food** Contact pub for details ⊕ GERONIMO INNS ◼ Wells Bombardier, Sharp's Doom Bar, Builders and Monks ♂ Aspall. ♀ 36 **Facilities** Non-diners area ♥ (Bar Restaurant) ♦♦ Children's portions Outside area ⊟ WiFi 🚌

Coopers Arms PLAN 1 B1

tel: 020 7376 3120 **87 Flood St, Chelsea SW3 5TB**
email: coopersarms@youngs.co.uk
dir: *From Sloane Square tube station, into King's Rd. Approx 1m W, opposite Waitrose, turn left. Pub half way down Flood St*

Classy Chelsea pub offering a genial welcome

Just off the King's Road and close to the river, this pub sees celebrities rubbing shoulders with the aristocracy and blue collar workers. The stuffed Canadian moose brings a character of its own to the bar, where at least five real ales grace the pumps. Food is served both in the main bar area and in the first-floor Albert Room, which also plays host to private dinners and parties. The menu offers a range of modern British classics, including beef and bone marrow burger and a pie of the day. There is a weekly Tuesday quiz night, as well as a May beer festival.

Open all day all wk 12-11 (Sun 12-10.30) **Food** Lunch Mon-Fri 12-3, Sat 12-10, Sun 12-7 Dinner Mon-Fri 5-10, Sat 12-10, Sun 12-7 Av main course £12 Set menu available ⊕ YOUNG'S ◼ Special & Bitter, Wells Bombardier, Sambrook's Wandle, Guinness ♂ Aspall. ♀ 15 **Facilities** Non-diners area ♥ (Bar Garden) ♦♦ Children's menu Children's portions Garden Beer festival WiFi

SW4

The Abbeville PLAN 2 F2

tel: 020 8675 2201 **67-69 Abbeville Rd SW4 9JW**
email: info@theabbeville.co.uk
dir: *Nearest tube: Clapham South*

Smart Clapham neighbourhood pub

The one-time Huguenot enclave around Abbeville Road lacked its own pub until local boys Nick Fox, Tom Peake and Mark Reynolds transformed a former restaurant into the pioneering member of today's Renaissance group of south London pubs; Massimo Tebaldi joined later as group executive chef. In style terms we're talking eccentric 16th-century paintings and mismatched furniture, although the long-legged bar chairs are clearly members of the same family. Timothy Taylor Landlord bitter hits the spot with the locals, and dishes include tandoori spiced plaice with

chilli and mint couscous; roasted lamb rump with tapenade, chickpeas and tomatoes; and wild mushroom risotto with parmesan, rocket and truffle oil.

Open all day all wk **Food** Contact pub for details ⊕ FREE HOUSE ◼ Timothy Taylor Landlord ♂ Aspall. ♀ 14 **Facilities** Non-diners area ♥ (Bar Restaurant Outside area) ♦♦ Children's menu Children's portions Outside area ⊟ WiFi

The Stonhouse PLAN 2 E2

tel: 020 7819 9312 **165 Stonhouse St SW4 6BJ**
email: info@thestonhouse.co.uk
dir: *Nearest tube: Clapham Common*

Modern local on a residential side street

Tucked discreetly away between Clapham's Old Town and its busy High Street is this impressively transformed corner local. In the elegant bar, Sambrook's Wandle and Timothy Taylor Landlord vie for real ale drinkers' attention, while cider fans can choose Aspall. In the log-fire-warmed dining area, the brasserie-style menu is skewed towards modern British food, in particular steaks, dishes featuring free-range chicken and pork from the pub's Hampshire farm, and sustainably sourced fish. Starters include hake, smoked salmon and prawn fishcake, lemon and basil mayonnaise; and foie gras ballotine, while mains might be Parma ham wrapped guinea fowl breast, spiced lentils, curly kale with tarragon cream sauce. A partially-covered paved garden area lies outside.

Open all day all wk Closed 25-26 Dec **Food** Lunch Mon-Fri 12-3.30, Sat 11-4, Sun 11-9 Dinner Mon-Sat 6-10.30, Sun 11-9 Av main course £13 ⊕ PUNCH TAVERNS ◼ Timothy Taylor Landlord, Sambrook's Wandle ♂ Aspall. ♀ 19
Facilities Non-diners area ♥ (Bar Garden) ♦♦ Children's menu Children's portions Garden ⊟ WiFi 🚌 (notice required)

SW6

The Atlas PLAN 2 E3 `PICK OF THE PUBS`

tel: 020 7385 9129 **16 Seagrave Rd, Fulham SW6 1RX**
email: reservations@theatlaspub.com
dir: *2 mins walk from West Brompton tube station*

Traditional London pub with a walled garden

Just around the corner from West Brompton tube, The Atlas is one of only a handful of London pubs to have a walled garden. Located in a trendy part of town where a great many pubs have been reinvented to become diners or restaurants, here is a traditional, relaxed local that remains true to its cause with a spacious bar area split into eating and drinking sections. Typical menus might feature starters such as roast butternut squash soup with orange and sour cream; or crispy soft shell crab with guacamole and red pepper slaw. Tempting mains demonstrate some European influences in dishes such as roast guinea fowl with crispy polenta, cherry tomato and basil; and linguine alla 'genovese', green beans, potato, pesto and parmesan. There are good choices on the wine list, and The London Wine Academy holds wine workshops here.

Open all day all wk 12-12 Closed 24-31 Dec **Food** Lunch Mon-Fri 12-2.30, Sat 12-4, Sun 12-10 Dinner Mon-Sat 6-10, Sun 12-10 ⊕ FREE HOUSE ◼ Fuller's London Pride, Guest ales ♂ Symonds. ♀ 15 **Facilities** Non-diners area ♦♦ Children's portions Garden ⊟ WiFi 🚌 (notice required)

The Harwood Arms ◉◉ PLAN 2 E3 `PICK OF THE PUBS`

tel: 020 7386 1847 **Walham Grove SW6 1QP**
email: admin@harwoodarms.com
dir: *Phone for detailed directions*

Tip-top dining pub in leafy Fulham

The combined talents of chef Brett Graham and TV chef Mike Robinson, who also owns the Pot Kiln in Berkshire, have transformed this neighbourhood pub in leafy Fulham into top dining venue. There's inspired British cooking but the Harwood remains a proper pub, with microbrewery ales on tap, a vibrant, friendly atmosphere, and a quiz night on Tuesdays. The kitchen's passion about provenance and seasonality of food is key to its success, and the pub is renowned for its game and wild food, predominantly from Berkshire, where Mike Robinson shoots on various estates. The short, ever-changing menu delivers warm salad of wood pigeon; roe deer haunch with tarragon, mustard and garlic potatoes; bream with cucumber, sea purslane and mussels; and fig tart with honey and thyme. Be sure to book ahead.

Open all day 12-11 (Mon 5.30-11) Closed 24-27 Dec, 1 Jan, Mon until 5.30pm **Food** Lunch Tue-Sat 12-3, Sun 12-4 Dinner Mon-Sat 6.15-9.30, Sun 7-9 ⊕ ENTERPRISE INNS ◀ Sambrook's Wandle, Bath Ales Gem, Guest ales. ☻ 20 **Facilities** Non-diners area ❤ (Bar Restaurant) ⬥ Children's portions WiFi ⬛ (notice required)

The Jam Tree PLAN 2 E3

tel: 020 3397 3739 **541 King's Rd SW6 2EB**
email: chelsea@thejamtree.com
dir: Nearest tube: Imperial Wharf or Fulham Broadway

Quirky gastro-pub with a vibrant night life

Number two in The Jam Tree gastro-pub family, this Chelsea sibling echoes the quirkiness of its Clapham sister. Antique mirrors, personalised artworks, old chesterfields and mismatched furniture give the interior a decidedly individual look. The modern British menu with colonial undertones offers curries; thali, an Indian tasting platter; chicken or vegetable Madras; and beef rang dang. Other possibilities are slow-roasted duck leg; and seared scallops with Malay potato cake. A long cocktail list, barbecue, plasma screen and resident DJs could be additional reasons for visiting.

Open all day all wk **Food** Lunch Mon-Fri 12-3, Sat-Sun 11-5 Dinner Mon-Fri 6-10, Sat 5-10, Sun 5-9 ⊕ FREE HOUSE ◀ Timothy Taylor Landlord ♂ Symonds. ☻ 9 **Facilities** Non-diners area ❤ (Bar Restaurant Garden) ⬥ Children's menu Children's portions Garden ⌰ WiFi

NEW The Malt House PLAN 2 E3

tel: 020 7084 6888 **17 Vanston Place, Fulham SW6 1AY**
email: reservations@malthousefulham.co.uk
dir: Nearest tube: Fulham Broadway

A quietly situated, upmarket Fulham pub

Opened in 2013 by Mayfair restaurateur Claude Bosi and his brother Cedric, the former Jolly Maltster - its old name still appears on a gable-end - is a Brakspear pub, with Marston's Pedigree in support. Kitchen policy is to source the ingredients for the classic British dishes served here from independent local suppliers. To convey an idea of the style, starters include rare Cumbrian beef with Jerusalem artichokes; partridge sausage with lentils; and slow-cooked salmon with celery and pickled turnips. And for main courses, salsify fritters with wild mushroom ragout; and pan-fried skate with fishcake and celeriac purée.

Open all day all wk Closed 25 Dec **Food** Lunch Mon-Sat 12-3, Sun 12-9 Dinner Mon-Sat 6-10 Av main course £16 ⊕ BRAKSPEAR ◀ Brakspear Bitter, Marston's Pedigree ♂ Symonds. **Facilities** Non-diners area ❤ (Bar Restaurant Garden) ⬥ Children's menu Children's portions Garden ⌰ WiFi ⬛ (notice required)

The Sands End Pub PLAN 2 E3

tel: 020 7731 7823 **135-137 Stephendale Rd, Fulham SW6 2PR**
email: thesandsend@hotmail.co.uk
dir: From Wandsworth Bridge Rd (A217) into Stephendale Rd. Pub 300yds at junct with Broughton Rd

Local, seasonal produce drives the menu here

A stylish country pub in the city is how fashionable Fulham foodies regard this much-loved neighbourhood gem. Expect to find scrubbed farmhouse tables, wooden

floors, locals quaffing pints of Harvery's Sussex Best, chalkboard menus listing terrific bar snacks (the Scotch eggs are legendary) and a food philosophy built around the 'Field to Fork' mantra. The British seasonal cooking makes use of foraged produce and even vegetables from the pub's allotment, resulting in hearty and honest dishes like glazed Barbary duck breast, Savoy cabbage, pancetta and duck fat chips, and home-made vanilla yogurt with rhubarb and ginger compôte.

Open all day all wk Closed 25 Dec **Food** Lunch Mon-Fri 12-3, Sat 12-4, Sun 12-9, snacks all day Dinner Mon-Sat 6-10, Sun 12-9 Av main course £16 Set menu available ⊕ FREE HOUSE ◀ Harvey's Sussex Best Bitter, Greene King IPA, Upham Punter ♂ Aspall. ☻ 24 **Facilities** Non-diners area ❤ (Bar Restaurant Outside area) ⬥ Children's portions Outside area ⌰ WiFi

The White Horse PLAN 2 E3 PICK OF THE PUBS

tel: 020 7736 2115 **1-3 Parson's Green, Fulham SW6 4UL**
email: bookings@whitehorsesw6.com
dir: 140mtrs from Parson's Green tube

Beer Academy at the 'Sloaney Pony'

With a triangular walled front terrace overlooking Parson's Green, the former late 18th-century coaching inn and Victorian gin palace is a substantial sandstone pub. It's a destination for lovers of British pub food and interesting real ales and wines, with a restaurant in the former coach house, an upstairs bar, and a luxurious private dining area. The interior is a pleasing blend of polished mahogany and wooden and flagstone floors, open fires and contemporary lighting. Every dish on the menu comes with a recommended beer to drink, such partnering forming part of the pub's Beer Academy Courses. For instance, a starter of scotched hen's egg is paired with Rocky Head Session; and a main of free-range orchard sausages, mash and spring veg should be washed down with a pint of Adnams Broadside. It's good for Sunday brunch, summer barbecues and its four annual beer festivals – American, European, British and Old Ale.

Open all day all wk **Food** Lunch all wk 12-10.30 Dinner all wk 12-10.30 Av main course £14 Set menu available Restaurant menu available all wk ⊕ MITCHELLS & BUTLERS ◀ Adnams Broadside, Oakham JHB, Harvey's Sussex Best Bitter ♂ Aspall. ☻ 20 **Facilities** Non-diners area ❤ (Bar Garden) ⬥ Children's portions Garden ⌰ Beer festival WiFi

▐ SW10

The Hollywood Arms PLAN 1 A1 PICK OF THE PUBS

tel: 020 7349 7840 **45 Hollywood Rd SW10 9HX**
email: hollywoodarms@youngs.co.uk
dir: From Chelsea & Westminster Hospital in Fulham Rd into Hollywood Rd opposite, 200mtrs on right

Gem of a pub with a considered approach to cooking

In the heart of Chelsea, this listed building dates back to the mid-17th century when it was the home of landowner Henry Middleton, who owned land in England, Barbados and America. The interior of this hidden treasure is elegantly appointed, its original charm complemented by rich natural woods, pastel shades and modern fabrics. The large upstairs lounge has elegant mouldings around the ceiling and large open fires, whilst the ground-floor pub and restaurant retains much of its traditional atmosphere. Here the chefs lovingly create dishes from scratch using high-quality ingredients. Small plates will produce diver-caught scallop gratin or potted Wiltshire rabbit on sourdough, while main courses offer game pie; Gressingham duck breast with rösti and spiced red cabbage; or whole baked sea bass with fennel, orange and caper salad. Classic puddings include treacle tart and apple crumble with custard.

Open all day all wk 12-11.30 (Thu-Sat 12-12 Sun 12-10.30) ⊕ YOUNG'S ◀ Wells Bombardier, Young's, Meantime ♂ Aspall. **Facilities** ❤ (Bar Restaurant) ⬥ Children's portions WiFi

SW11

The Bolingbroke Pub & Dining Room PLAN 2 E2

tel: 020 7228 4040 **172-174 Northcote Rd SW11 6RE**
email: info@thebolingbroke.com
dir: *Nearest tube: Clapham South or Clapham Junction*

Family-friendly dining pub

This refined dining pub stands in a road known colloquially as 'Nappy Valley', due to its popularity with well-heeled young families. Named after the first Viscount Bolingbroke, who managed to be both brilliant politician and reckless rake, the pub caters admirably for children and adults alike. Expect modern British fare along the lines of beetroot and goats' cheese tarte Tatin with balsamic glaze followed by braised beef cheeks with haggerty potatoes and red cabbage. Weekend brunch includes boiled egg and soldiers for the very young.

Open all day all wk Closed 25-26 Dec **Food** Lunch Mon-Fri 12-3.30, Sat 10-4, Sun 12-9 Dinner Mon-Sat 6-10.30, Sun 12-9 Av main course £13.50 ⊕ FREE HOUSE ◀ Timothy Taylor Landlord, Sambrook's Junction ♂ Aspall. �$ 13 **Facilities** Non-diners area ♣ (Bar Restaurant Outside area) ♦ Children's menu Children's portions Outside area ⋔ WiFi ▦ (notice required)

The Fox & Hounds PLAN 2 E2   **PICK OF THE PUBS**

tel: 020 7924 5483 **66 Latchmere Rd, Battersea SW11 2JU**
email: foxandhoundsbattersea@btopenworld.com
dir: *From Clapham Junction exit into High St turn left, through lights into Lavender Hill. After post office, left at lights. Pub 200yds on left*

Known for its international wine list and Mediterranean food

This is one of those archetypal Victorian corner pubs that London still has in abundance but from the moment you step through the door you'll feel like one of the locals. Its style is simple: with bare wooden floors, an assortment of furniture, walled garden, extensive patio planting and a covered and heated seating area. Regulars head here for the good selection of real ales and an international wine list; the menu suggests the 'Wine of the Moment' with tasting notes, and Ales of the Week. Fresh ingredients are delivered daily from the London markets, enabling the Mediterranean-style menu and specials to change accordingly; all prepared in the open-to-view kitchen. So, you might start with saffron potato soup or squid and chorizo with prawns. Follow with roast spatchcock chicken with Parma ham; spinach and roast garlic risotto; rib-eye steak, roast potatoes and salsa verde; or pan-roasted salmon. A traditional British lunch is served on Sundays.

Open 12-3 5-11 (Mon 5-11 Fri-Sat 12-11 Sun 12-10.30) Closed 24-30 Dec, Mon L **Food** Lunch Fri 12.30-3, Sat 12.30-4, Sun 12.30-10.30 Dinner Mon-Sat 6.30-10, Sun 12.30-10 ⊕ FREE HOUSE ◀ St Austell Tribute, Dark Star, Sambrook's, Guest ales ♂ Cornish Orchards. �$ 14 **Facilities** Non-diners area ♣ (Bar Restaurant Garden) ♦ Children's portions Garden ⋔ WiFi ▦ (notice required)

SW12

The Avalon PLAN 2 E2

tel: 020 8675 8613 **16 Balham Hill SW12 9EB**
email: info@theavalonlondon.com
dir: *Nearest tube: Clapham South*

Elegant, comfortable and relaxing

Named after the mythical isle of Arthurian legend, the attractions of this Balham member of the Renaissance group of south London pubs are far from fairytale. For example, there's a three-tiered rear garden that comes alive on summer days, the bar stocks Timothy Taylor Landlord, Sharp's Doom Bar and Aspall cider, and the wine list offers many by the glass. On top of that, house policy is to serve beef aged in-house, sustainable fish from English waters, and free-range pork and chicken from the group's own farm. Bar meals include meze platter; Welsh rarebit; fish and chips; and croque monsieur.

Open all day all wk Closed 26 Dec **Food** Lunch Mon-Fri 12-3.30, Sat 12-4, Sun 12-9 Dinner Mon-Sat 6-10.30, Sun 12-9 Av main course £6 Set menu available ⊕ ENTERPRISE INNS ◼ Timothy Taylor Landlord, Sharp's Doom Bar ♂ Aspall. ♟ 15 **Facilities** Non-diners area ♨ (Bar Garden) ♦ Children's menu Children's portions Family room Garden ⌂ WiFi

SW13

NEW The Brown Dog   PLAN 2 D2

tel: 020 8392 2200 **28 Cross St, Barnes SW13 0AP**
email: info@thebrowndog.co.uk
dir: *Phone for detailed directions*

Pleasant family oasis a short detour from the Thames

Given the pub's name, it would be odd if The Brown Dog did not welcome canines, albeit that the resident dog is black. The pub also welcomes children, which is perhaps surprising given its location in the exclusive back streets of Barnes and the gastro nature of its operation. However cask ales such as Truman's testify to its drinking credentials, along with a wine list designed to match an enticing menu. Here you'll find oysters among the starters, main courses boasting Tamworth pork or aged Scottish beef, and traditional sweets such as apple and rhubarb crumble with vanilla ice cream. A granite-slabbed terrace furnished with bench tables and parasols completes this altogether rather pleasant establishment.

Open all day all wk **Food** Lunch Mon-Fri 12-3, Sat-Sun 12-4 Dinner Mon-Fri 6.30-10, Sat 6-10, Sun 6-9 Av main course £14 ⊕ FREE HOUSE ◼ Hackney Pale Ale, Truman's Runner, Twickenham Original ♂ Westons Stowford Press, Cidre Breton. ♟ 18 **Facilities** Non-diners area ♨ (Bar Restaurant Garden) ♦ Children's menu Family room Garden ⌂ WiFi

The Idle Hour   PLAN 2 D2   PICK OF THE PUBS

tel: 020 8878 5555 **62 Railway Side, Barnes SW13 0PQ**
email: theidlehour@aol.com
dir: *From Mortlake High St (A3003) into White Hart Ln. 5th left into Railway Side (at rail crossing). Pub just past school*

A good place for celebrity spotting

Being a little tricky to find doesn't fox the locals, nor apparently does it deter the custom of 'names' from music, film and TV, who frequent this mid 19th-century, Barnes-backwater free house. Although designed with a nod to tradition, that is, lots of candles and fresh flowers everywhere and a real fire in the winter, it's still modern and stylish. A bit quirky too - for proof, check any of the wrong-time-telling clocks. What confirms its pub status is that there are always at least ten draught beers, many more in bottles, a 'mind-boggling' array of spirits, and a carefully selected, almost entirely organic, wine list, many by the glass. The small, frequently changing menu makes use of mainly organic ingredients. A secluded garden doubles as a suntrap during the day and a romantic, candlelit spot for evening dining.

Open 5-12 (Sat noon-1am Sun 12-10.30) Closed 25 Dec, Mon-Fri L **Food** Lunch Sat 12.30-10.30, Sun 12.30-9 Dinner Mon-Fri 6-10, Sat 12.30-10.30, Sun 12.30-9 ⊕ FREE HOUSE ◼ Guest ales ♂ Addlestones. ♟ 15 **Facilities** Non-diners area ♨ (Bar Restaurant Garden) ♦ Garden ⌂ WiFi

SW14

The Victoria ★★★★ RR   PLAN 2 C2

tel: 020 8876 4238 **10 West Temple Sheen, East Sheen SW14 7RT**
email: bookings@thevictoria.net **web:** www.thevictoria.net
dir: *Nearest tube: Richmond*

Family-friendly and a real charmer

Close to Richmond Park, The Victoria offers something for everyone, with a large conservatory dining room and a leafy garden with a safe children's play area. TV chef Paul Merrett and restaurateur Greg Bellamy are at the helm, so you can expect

top culinary delights. Small plates for sharing and grazing prove popular such as goats' curd with honey and figs, and roasted bone marrow with chicory and apple. The dining room menu reveals such choices as spiced lamb and pistachio kofta; pollock roasted in Serrano; and seasonal dishes like slow-cooked Yorkshire rhubarb, buttermilk and vanilla pannacotta with almond tozzetti biscuit.

Open all day all wk Closed 1 Jan **Food** Lunch Mon-Fri 12-2.30, Sat 8.30-10.30 (bkfst) 11-3 (brunch), Sun 12-4 Dinner Mon-Fri 6-10, Sat 5-10, Sun 5-8 Set menu available Restaurant menu available ⊕ ENTERPRISE INNS ◼ Fuller's London Pride, Timothy Taylor Landlord, Guest ale ♂ Aspall. ♟ 28 **Facilities** Non-diners area ♨ (Bar Garden) ♦ Children's menu Children's portions Play area Garden ⌂ Parking WiFi **Rooms** 7

SW15

NEW Prince of Wales   PLAN 2 D2

tel: 020 8788 1552 **138 Upper Richmond Rd, Putney SW15 2SP**
email: princeofwales@foodandfuel.co.uk **web:** www.princeofwalesputney.co.uk
dir: *From East Putney station turn left, pub on right. From Putney Station, left into High St, left into Upper Richmond Rd; pub on left*

Victorian pub serving good beer and interesting food

Just two minutes from East Putney tube station, this Victorian corner pub attracts a mix of drinkers and foodies. In the cosy front bar, you can enjoy pints of Sambrook's Wandle and Timothy Taylor Landlord with the locals or head to the rear dining room with its skylight and eclectic country-style decor of stuffed animals and wall-mounted antlers. The food here is not lacking ambition – a starter of crispy pig's cheeks with spicy sweet and sour sauce might be followed by pan-seared brill, squid ink risotto, crab-stuffed cucumber and red wine reduction.

Open all day all wk **Food** Lunch all wk 12-3 Dinner all wk 6.30-10 Set menu available ⊕ PUNCH TAVERNS/FOOD & FUEL ◼ Purity Mad Goose, Timothy Taylor Landlord, Sambrook's Wandle ♂ Aspall, Addlestones. ♟ 30 **Facilities** Non-diners area ♨ (Bar Outside area) ♦ Children's portions Outside area ⌂ WiFi ⚌ (notice required)

See advert on opposite page

LONDON SW15 *continued*

The Spencer   PLAN 2 D2   PICK OF THE PUBS

See Pick of the Pubs on opposite page and advert on page 334

The Telegraph   PLAN 2 D2

tel: 020 8788 2011 **Telegraph Rd, Putney Heath SW15 3TU**
email: info@thetelegraphputney.co.uk
dir: *Nearest tube: East Putney. Nearest rail station: Putney High St*

A 'country pub' just minutes from the busy streets

This pub was close to an Admiralty telegraph station between London and Portsmouth, and has been involved in the sale of beer since before 1856. Although it's only five minutes from the hustle and bustle of Putney High Street, The Telegraph feels more like a country pub. Certainly the focus on well-kept real ales cannot be faulted, with St Austell Tribute and Courage Directors always available. The menu, with its pub fare and contemporary European dishes, includes grazing boards and chicken, chorizo and haloumi skewers to start, and mains of braised lamb shank, roast duck breast, steaks and burgers.

Open all day all wk 11-mdnt **Food** Lunch Mon-Sat 12-9.30, Sun 12-9 Dinner Mon-Sat 12-9.30, Sun 12-9 ⊕ FREE HOUSE ◀ Sharp's Doom Bar, St Austell Tribute, Courage Directors ♂ Thatchers Gold. **Facilities** ♣ (Bar Restaurant Garden) ♦♦ Children's menu Children's portions Garden Parking ▦

▮ SW18

The Earl Spencer   PLAN 2 E2   PICK OF THE PUBS

tel: 020 8870 9244 **260-262 Merton Rd, Southfields SW18 5JL**
dir: *Exit Southfields tube station, into Replingham Rd, left at junct with Merton Rd, to junct with Kimber Rd*

Sophisticated Edwardian gastro-pub

A forecourt enclosed by a brick walls distances this grand Edwardian gastro-pub from the street. It's a popular drinking and dining venue, especially during 'Wimbledon Fortnight', but that still leaves 50 other weeks for its attractions to work their magic. The log fires and polished wood furnishings make their contribution, of course, but for many it's the Sambrook's Wandle, Otter Amber and other real ales and ciders, and then there's South London's very own Merton Mule, a cocktail of vodka, ginger beer, ginger ale and crushed lime. Another big draw is the daily-changing menu on which everything is home made, including the bread. Start with lamb, mint and potato croquettes and yogurt and cucumber; and for a main course, roast skate wing with buttered new potatoes, tenderstem broccoli and salsa verde. Finish with a plate of Époisses, Stilton, Brillat-Savarin and other cheeses with toast and apple chutney.

Open all wk 4-11 (Fri-Sat 11am-mdnt Sun 12-10.30) Closed 25 & 26 Dec **Food** Lunch Fri-Sat 12.30-3, Sun 12.30-4 Dinner Mon-Sat 7-10.30, Sun 7-9.30 ⊕ ENTERPRISE INNS ◀ Adnams Broadside, Sambrook's Wandle, Otter Amber, Harvey's Sussex Best Bitter, Sharp's Cornish Coaster, Timothy Taylor Landlord, Guest ales ♂ Aspall, Westons Old Rosie & Wyld Wood Organic. ♟ 17
Facilities Non-diners area ♣ (Bar Restaurant Garden) ♦♦ Garden Outside area ☂ WiFi

The Roundhouse   PLAN 2 E2

tel: 020 7326 8580 **2 Northside, Wandsworth Common SW18 2SS**
email: info@theroundhousewandworth.com
dir: *Phone for detailed directions*

Recommended for its London microbrewery ales

Between Clapham Junction and Wandsworth, The Roundhouse has the ambience of a friendly local, with a round black walnut bar, open kitchen, and eclectic art on the walls. Ales come from two local microbreweries, including Sambrook's Wandle - an ale named after a nearby river. The short, daily-changing menu may take in roast beetroot, feta, apple and caramelised pecan salad; pan-fried pollock, Jerusalem artichoke, purple sprouting broccoli and carrots; or roasted vegetable lasagne with a mixed leaf salad. Finish with chocolate cheesecake brownie and popcorn ice cream.

Open all day all wk Mon-Thu 12-11 (Fri-Sat 12-12 Sun 12-10.30) Closed 25-26 Dec **Food** Lunch Mon-Fri 12-3, Sat 12-4, Sun 12-4.30 Dinner Mon-Sat 6-10, Sun 6.30-9 ⊕ FREE HOUSE ◀ Sambrook's Wandle, Guest ales ♂ Symonds. ♟ 15
Facilities Non-diners area ♣ (Bar Garden) ♦♦ Children's portions Garden ☂ WiFi ▦ (notice required)

▮ SW19

NEW Fox & Grapes ⊛   PLAN 2 D1

tel: 020 8619 1300 **9 Camp Rd, Wimbledon Common SW19 4UN**
email: reservations@foxandgrapeswimbledon.co.uk
dir: *Just off Wimbledon Common*

Premium gastro-pub on a secluded edge of Wimbledon Common

Opened nearly five years ago, the Fox & Grapes' success from day one was more or less assured by the pedigree of its chefs. Step inside to an large open-plan interior of parquet flooring, wood panelling, scrubbed wooden tables. Certainly you can enjoy a pint of Doom Bar or Wye Valley, as many dog-walkers do; or consult the wine carte for the small selection of sustainable, organic and biodynamic wines. But AA Rosette-standard cooking based on ingredients from small producers remains the prime attraction; booking is advisable, especially if you have Sunday lunch in mind, when roast rump of Highland beef, Duroc pork belly, or Goosnargh chicken are typical of the choice roasts on offer.

Open all day all wk Closed 25 Dec **Food** Lunch Mon-Sat 12-3, Sun 12-9 Dinner Mon-Sat 6-9.30, Sun 12-9 Av main course £16 ⊕ ENTERPRISE INNS ◀ Sharp's Doom Bar, Wye Valley ♂ Symonds. **Facilities** Non-diners area ♣ (Bar Restaurant) ♦♦ Children's menu Children's portions WiFi ▦ (notice required)

▮ W1

Duke of Wellington   PLAN 1 B4

tel: 020 7723 2790 **94a Crawford St W1H 2HQ**
email: theduke@hotmail.co.uk
dir: *5 mins' walk from Baker Street Station*

Stylish decor and fine food

A refreshing mix of street-corner local and cosmopolitan restaurant is found here at the busy heart of Marylebone, amidst Georgian-style terraces close to leafy Bryanston Square. Inspired interior design raises The Duke's profile, with gilt mirrors and an eye-catching Roman-style mural acting as foils to the dark-wood bar, rustic tables and fittings. The bright, first-floor restaurant is a tranquil escape and shares many dishes with the bar menu; smoked haddock with quails' eggs a starter before artichoke, sweet potato, chestnut and tomato crumble or chargrilled Galloway onglet steak with béarnaise sauce. Outside tables are popular with drinkers supping Doom Bar.

Open all day all wk Closed 25 Dec-2 Jan **Food** Lunch Mon-Fri 12-3, Sat-Sun 12-4.30 Dinner all wk 6.30-10 ◀ Sharp's Doom Bar, Fuller's London Pride, Black Sheep ♂ Addlestones. ♟ **Facilities** Non-diners area ♣ (Bar) ♦♦ Children's portions ☂ WiFi ▦ (notice required)

PICK OF THE PUBS

The Spencer

SW15　　　　　　　　**PLAN 2 D2**

tel: 020 8788 0640
**237 Lower Richmond Rd, Putney
SW15 1HJ**
email: info@thespencerpub.com
web: www.thespencerpub.com
dir: *Corner of Putney Common & Lower
Richmond Rd, opposite Old Putney
Hospital*

Well kept ales and family-friendly food

Formerly known as The Spencer Arms, this landmark pub occupies a lofty position on green and leafy Putney Common and its close proximity to the Thames Embankment makes it one of the best vantage points for watching the annual Oxford and Cambridge boat race. The beer garden here is part of the common and the pub's 25 picnic benches are hotly contested in the summer by those in search of an alfresco lunch. A light, bright and airy interior belies the rather traditional look of the place; revamped a few years ago, the emphasis is on good dining in a stylish environment where locals are still welcomed to sup at the bar, with Timothy Taylor Landlord and Fuller's London Pride among the pick of the beers. Meals, in the bar or restaurant area, are a modern take on traditional favourites, such as a starter of potted salmon with lemon, dill and chives, or classic prawn cocktail with Marie Rose sauce. Mains take on a seasonal look to reflect the desire to use only the freshest ingredients; look for a ravioli of rocket and ricotta with sage butter; monkfish, butterfly prawns and chorizo brochettes with rice; or venison and juniper berry casserole with wild mushrooms and butternut squash. Typical desserts might include spiced apple and sultana crumble and custard or mango and passion fruit cheesecake. Sunday roasts and rotisserie free-range chickens are a favourite with families, and children get to choose from their own well-priced menu. An extensive breakfast menu (available 9am-noon from Monday to Saturday) is a popular option with early morning dog walkers and cyclists.

Open all day all wk **Food** Mon-Sat 9am-mdnt Sun 11-11 🛢 FREE HOUSE
🍺 Fuller's London Pride, Sharp's Doom Bar, Guinness, Timothy Taylor Landlord
🍏 Aspall Draught & Peronelle's Blush.
Facilities 🐾 (Bar Restaurant Garden)
👫 Children's menu Children's portions Play area Garden WiFi

237 Lower Richmond Rd, Putney, London SW15 1HJ
Tel: 020 8788 0640 **Fax:** 01455 221 296
Website: www.thespencerpub.com
Email: info@thespencerpub.com

We at *The Spencer* pride ourselves on serving good food, excellent drinks and having friendly staff going above and beyond, to make your experience a truly memorable one. Our menu is full of British pub classics but also has a few contemporary dishes which makes for a mouth watering selection. We handpick the wines to complement the menu and our knowledgeable staff are always on hand to give you advice.

Our focus is on you, our customer, and we try to ensure that your experience is an enjoyable one. The food is great value for money and the beers and wine are possibly some of the best selected in the area.

The Spencer is situated in the leafy backstreets of Putney, off the beaten track with a beautiful view of the common. There is plenty of space for all the family; children and dogs included. You can relax outside with a Pimm's in the all day sun or toast your feet during those cold winter evenings in front of our fire.

LONDON W1 *continued*

French House   PLAN 1 D4

tel: 020 7437 2477 **49 Dean St, Soho W1D 5BG**
dir: *Nearest tube: Piccadilly Circus; Tottenham Court Road; Covent Garden. Pub at Shaftesbury Avenue end of Dean St*

The rich and famous beat a path to this Soho spot

2014 sees the centenary year for this legendary Soho watering hole – it was known as the Maison Francais a hundred years ago. It was patronised by General de Gaulle during the Second World War, and later by Dylan Thomas, Francis Bacon, Dan Farson and many other louche Soho habitués. Run by Lesley Lewis for over 20 years, the small, intimate and very atmospheric bar only serves half pints of Meteor, Kronenbourg and Guinness. The upstairs is a second bar, offering more informal drinking space; this area is also used as an art gallery. Only lunchtime bar food is served.

Open all day all wk 12-11 (Sun 12-10.30) Closed 25 Dec **Food** Lunch Mon-Fri 12-4 Av main course £15 ⊕ FREE HOUSE ◀ Budweiser Budvar, Kronenbourg, Leffe, Meteor, Guinness. ♚ 22 **Facilities** Non-diners area WiFi

The Grazing Goat   PLAN 1 B4

tel: 020 7724 7243 **6 New Quebec St W1H 7RQ**
email: reservations@thegrazinggoat.co.uk
dir: *Behind Marble Arch tube station, off Seymour St*

Stylish London dining pub with plenty of character

Just minutes away from Oxford Street and Marble Arch, this classy, six-storey pub is full of period features including open fireplaces, oak floors and solid oak bars. The name is not mere whimsy; goats did once graze around here because the first Lady Portman was allergic to cow's milk. Expect modern British, seasonal cooking – maybe roasted celeriac soup or wild mushroom and spinach tart to start; followed by Petley Farm pork and ham hock pie or Highland game venison, with pear and hazelnut tart or rhubarb trifle for dessert. Floor-to-ceiling glass doors are opened in warmer weather for alfresco dining.

Open all day all wk 7.30am-11.30pm (Sun 7.30am-10.30pm) **Food** Contact pub for details ⊕ FREE HOUSE ◀ Sharp's Doom Bar, Caledonian Deuchars IPA Ò Aspall. ♚ 20 **Facilities** Non-diners area ◆ Children's portions 🅿 WiFi 🚌 (notice required)

The Only Running Footman ◉   PLAN 1 C3

tel: 020 7499 2988 **5 Charles St, Mayfair W1J 5DF**
email: manager@therunningfootmanmayfair.com
dir: *Nearest tube: Green Park*

Smart Mayfair pub - popular all year round

This central Mayfair pub's full name is 'I Am The Only Running Footman', recalling the manservants who would precede their aristocrat master's carriage, clearing riff-raff out of the way and paying tolls. By the early 1800s, only the 4th Duke of Queensbury's footman remained in service, so His Grace renamed this, their once-favourite pub, after him. The ground floor is traditionally pub-like, with removable windows to create an inside/outside feel in summer, but upstairs is an elegant restaurant serving slow-roast pork belly; fillet of wild halibut; fish stew; and venison loin from Holcot Estate, the pub's game farm in Northamptonshire.

Open all day all wk **Food** Contact pub for details Set menu available Restaurant menu available all wk ⊕ THE MEREDITH PUB GROUP ◀ Wells Bombardier, Greene King IPA, Young's Special Ò Aspall. ♚ 20 **Facilities** Non-diners area ♣ (Bar Outside area) ◆ Children's menu Children's portions Outside area 🅿 WiFi 🚌 (notice required)

The Portman   PLAN 1 B4

tel: 020 7723 8996 **51 Upper Berkeley St W1H 7QW**
email: manager@theportmanmarylebone.com
dir: *From Marble Arch into Great Cumberland Place, 3rd left into Upper Berkeley St*

Stylish central London pub with a seasonal British menu

Tucked between the hustle of Oxford Street and the elegant shops of Marylebone, prisoners once stopped here for a final drink on their way to the gallows at Tyburn Cross. These days, this friendly central London pub is the perfect place for weary shoppers to refuel on a St Austell or Timothy Taylor beer and seasonal British classics served all day, 365 days a year. Beer battered fish and chips and the pie of the day are popular choices in the ground-floor pub but for a fine dining experience there's a restaurant upstairs where meals are served by way of an unpretentious silver service.

Open all day all wk **Food** Lunch all day Dinner all day Av main course £15 Set menu available Restaurant menu available all wk ⊕ FREE HOUSE ◀ St Austell Proper Job, Timothy Taylor, Guest ale Ò Aspall. ♚ 15 **Facilities** Non-diners area ♣ (Bar Outside area) ◆ Children's menu Children's portions Outside area 🅿 WiFi 🚌 (notice required)

W4	Map 6 TQ27

The Swan   PLAN 2 D3   `PICK OF THE PUBS`

tel: 020 8994 8262 **1 Evershed Walk, 119 Acton Ln, Chiswick W4 5HH**
email: reservations@theswanpub.com
dir: *At end of Evershed Walk*

Mediterranean cuisine accompanied by recommended ales

A friendly gastro-pub, The Swan is the perfect spot for all seasons with its welcoming wood-panelled interior and a large lawned garden and patio for summertime refreshments. Good food is at the heart of the operation, and you can sit and eat wherever you like. The menu of modern, mostly Mediterranean cooking has a particular Italian influence, and vegetarians are not forgotten. Start perhaps with octopus salad with samphire and paprika potatoes or roast beetroot and balsamic soup. Next comes the main course: pan-fried guinea fowl with roasted artichoke, chilli greens and pancetta; or pea and broad bean risotto with mint and parmesan. If you still have an appetite, then finish off with pear and almond tart, or home-made ice cream. Real ale recommendations are shown on the menu.

Open all wk 5-11.30 (Sat 12-11.30 Sun 12-11) Closed 24-28 Dec **Food** Lunch Sat 12.30-3, Sun 12.30-10 Dinner Mon-Thu 6-10, Fri-Sat 6-10.30 Av main course £13 ⊕ FREE HOUSE ◀ Fuller's London Pride, St Austell Tribute, Dark Star, Hopback Ò Aspall. ♚ 12 **Facilities** Non-diners area ♣ (Bar Garden) ◆ Children's portions Garden 🅿 WiFi

Follow us on twitter
@TheAA_Lifestyle

W6

Anglesea Arms ® PLAN 2 D3

tel: 020 8749 1291 **35 Wingate Rd W6 0UR**
email: anglesea.events@gmail.com
dir: *Phone for detailed directions*

Cosy London pub

This traditional corner pub is reputed to be where the Great Train Robbery was hatched back in the 1960s. Today, real fires and a relaxed atmosphere are the attraction of this intimate pub, together with a terrace where drinks and food can be served. Behind the Georgian façade, well-kept ales are dispensed from breweries as far apart as Suffolk and Cornwall, and the place positively buzzes with people eagerly seeking out the unashamedly gastro-pub food. Perhaps try starters such as split pea and smoked ham soup, and mains of slow roast pork belly with mashed potato and red cabbage. Custard tart with white chocolate ice cream could be a pudding option.

Open all day all wk 11-11 (Sun 12-10.30) Closed 25-27 Dec ⊕ ENTERPRISE INNS ◄ Ringwood Fortyniner, St Austell Tribute, Sharp's Cornish Coaster, Otter Ale & Bitter, Woodforde's Wherry Ò Westons Wyld Wood Organic, Gaymers, Aspall. **Facilities** ✿ (Bar Garden) ♦♦ Children's portions Garden

The Dartmouth Castle PLAN 2 D3 `PICK OF THE PUBS`

tel: 020 8748 3614 **26 Glenthorne Rd, Hammersmith W6 0LS**
email: dartmouth.castle@btconnect.com
dir: *Nearest tube: Hammersmith. 100yds from Hammersmith Broadway*

Corner pub with a reputation for imaginative cooking

While it's very much a place to relax over a pint or two, the food is proving a great attraction at this corner pub. Choices on the menu include Mediterranean dishes such as bruschetta di pomodoro; and Crespelle Italian pancakes; or an antipasti platter to share for starters, then caldeirada fish stew; kofta lamb meatballs with harissa and couscous salad; or penne with Italian sausage ragu. But if you prefer a grilled rib-eye steak and roast potatoes, that's available too. Vegetarians aren't forgotten either, with choices like linguine alla genovese or slow-roast tomato and saffron risotto. Typical desserts are apple and rhubarb crumble and home-made ice creams. The range of beers includes at least two real ales on tap at any one time, and there's a well-chosen international wine list with 15 available by the glass. There's also a beer garden for the summer months.

Open all day 12-11 (Sat 5-11 Sun 12-10.30) Closed Etr, 23 Dec-2 Jan, Sat L **Food** Lunch Mon-Fri 12-2.30, Sun 12-9.30 Dinner Mon-Fri 6-10, Sat 6-10, Sun 12-9.30 ⊕ FREE HOUSE ◄ Sharp's Doom Bar, Sambrook's Wandle, Otter Bitter, Guest ales Ò Aspall. ♀ 15 **Facilities** Non-diners area ✿ (Bar Restaurant Garden) ♦♦ Garden ⋒ WiFi

The Hampshire Hog PLAN 2 D3

tel: 020 8748 3391 **225-227 King St W6 9JT**
email: info@the-hog.com
dir: *Nearest tube: Hammersmith*

Passion and flair in downtown Hammersmith

Externally Victorian, right down to its street corner location, the interior of this stylish gastro-pub is impressively contemporary, with wood floors, lots of white paint, quirky crockery and a conservatory. Typifying the carefully sourced food are pear and daikon salad with curly endive, dandelion, cashew nut cheese and pomegranate; tarragon and dried fruit-stuffed pork neck with celeriac purée, kale and lardons; and poached hake with chilli, coriander and lemongrass broth, corn and udon noodles. Brunch is served until midday and you can buy home-made food from the pub's pantry.

Open all day all wk Closed 25-26 Dec **Food** Lunch Mon-Sat 12-4, Sun & BHs 12.30-5 Dinner Mon-Sat 6.30-10.30 ⊕ STAR PUBS & BARS ◄ Caledonian 80/- & Deuchars IPA Ò Symonds. ♀ 14 **Facilities** Non-diners area ✿ (Bar Garden) ♦♦ Children's menu Children's portions Garden ⋒ WiFi ➡ (notice required)

The Stonemasons Arms PLAN 2 D3

tel: 020 8748 1397 **54 Cambridge Grove W6 0LA**
email: stonemasonsarms@london-gastros.co.uk
dir: *From Hammersmith tube station into King St, 2nd right into Cambridge Grove, pub at end*

Creative cooking and a tempting alfresco area

Fascinating menu options make this imposing corner pub, just a short hop from Hammersmith tube station, well worth finding; London Porter hot-smoked salmon, pickled cucumber and horseradish remoulade might be a good place to start before 35-day hung, grass-fed Hampshire rump steak, house chips with pepper sauce, or choose one of the seasonal specials. The tasty eating options make the Stonemasons popular with local residents and business people alike. During warmer months a decking area can be used for alfresco dining, and there's a secluded, intimate restaurant area. The pub carries an ever-changing display of works by a local artist, and there are weekly quiz nights.

Open all day all wk 11-11 (Sun 12-10.30) Closed 25-26 Dec **Food** Lunch Mon-Fri 12-3, Sat 12-10, Sun 12-9.30 Dinner Mon-Fri 6-10, Sat 12-10, Sun 12-9.30 ⊕ FULLER'S ◄ London Pride & Organic Honey Dew, Guinness, Peroni Ò Westons Stowford Press. ♀ 20 **Facilities** Non-diners area ♦♦ Children's portions Outside area ⋒ WiFi ➡ (notice required)

W8

The Mall Tavern ®® PLAN 2 E3

tel: 020 7229 3374 **71-73 Palace Gardens Ter, Notting Hill W8 4RU**
email: info@themalltavern.com
dir: *Nearest tube: Notting Hill*

Stylish pub at the heart of Notting Hill life

A Victorian pub built in 1856 midway between Notting Hill and Kensington, The Mall was, and remains, a true locals' tavern – albeit a rather stylish, upmarket one. With two AA Rosettes, expect a hearty, playful and modern take on pub food – maybe gala pie with Hawaiian salad or chicken liver pâté with pickled onion to start; followed by fried kitchari with Indian onions and nigella seeds; or pollock fillet with cloud mushrooms, scorched shallots and oyster leaves. Finish off with cranberry cheesecake, warm chocolate 'finger of fudge' cake with clementines for dessert. Besides regular beers such as Sharp's Doom Bar, there's an impressive list of wines, with many available by the glass. Also on offer is a 'secret' kitchen table that allows up to 10 diners an interactive dining experience.

Open all day all wk Closed 25-26 Dec **Food** Lunch all wk 12-10 Dinner all wk 12-10 ⊕ ENTERPRISE INNS ◄ Sharp's Doom Bar, Hackney Brewery, Moncada Notting Hill Blonde Ò Aspall. ♀ 10 **Facilities** Non-diners area ✿ (Bar Restaurant Garden) ♦♦ Children's portions Garden ⋒ WiFi ➡ (notice required)

The Scarsdale PLAN 2 E3

tel: 020 7937 1811 **23A Edwardes Square, Kensington W8 6HE**
email: scarsdale@fullers.co.uk
dir: *From Kensington High Street tube station turn left. 0.5m (10 mins' walk) left into Edwardes St after Odeon Cinema*

19th-century character pub in quiet area

The Scarsdale is a 19th-century free-standing building with colourful hanging baskets and window boxes spilling into the small terraced patio, in a leafy road just off Kensington High Street. The Frenchman who developed the site was supposedly one of Bonaparte's secret agents, but more recently - the 1970s and 80s - the

Scarsdale played a role as the local watering hole for Bodie and Doyle, in ITV's *The Professionals*. A typical restaurant menu offers duck leg confit with apple compôte; fillet of beef Wellington in puff pastry with pâté and red wine sauce; and spinach and ricotta tortellini with sundried tomato sauce. There is also an equally tempting bar menu, and an impressive wine list.

Open all day all wk 12-11 (Sun 12-10.30) Closed 25-26 Dec **Food** Contact pub for details ⊕ FULLER'S ◄ London Pride & Bengal Lancer, George Gale & Co Seafarers, Butcombe. ☞ 20 **Facilities** Non-diners area ☺ (Bar Garden) Garden ⌂ WiFi

---

NEW **The Windsor Castle** PLAN 2 E3

tel: 020 7243 8797 **114 Campden Hill Rd W8 7AR**
email: enquiry@thewindsorcastlekensington.co.uk
web: www.thewindsorcastlekensington.co.uk
dir: *From Notting Hill tube station into Bayswater Rd towards Holland Park. Left into Campden Hill Rd*

Eccentric and therefore not to be missed

One legend has it that Windsor Castle could be seen from the upstairs windows when the pub was built in the 1830s; another, that the skeleton of Thomas Paine (Rights of Man) was buried in the cellar after his son sold it to settle a beer debt. Such stories add to the fascination of this pub, where wood panelling separates three areas inexplicably called Campden, Private and Sherry. Read the menu before choosing your refreshment – it matches a beer with each dish: Devon crab is paired with Curious Brew, for example; or perhaps you fancy chicken hotpot with a pint of Hop Back's Winter Lightning. Beer and cider festival in July.

Open all wk 12-11 (Sun 12-10.30) **Food** Lunch all wk 12-6 Dinner Mon-Sat 6-10, Sun 6-9 Av main course £17 Restaurant menu available Mon-Sat ⊕ MITCHELLS & BUTLERS ◄ Timothy Taylor Landlord, Windsor & Eton Knight of the Garter Ö Westons Old Rosie, Addlestones, Aspall Harry Sparrow. ☞ 21 **Facilities** Non-diners area ☺ (Bar Garden) ●● Children's menu Children's portions Garden ⌂ Beer festival Cider festival WiFi ▭ (notice required)

W9

The Waterway PLAN 2 E4

tel: 020 7266 3557 **54 Formosa St W9 2JU**
email: info@thewaterway.co.uk
dir: *From Warwick Avenue tube station into Warwick Av, turn left into Formosa St*

Canalside pub with a great range of drinks

Enjoying a lovely setting in Maida Vale, The Waterway offers great alfresco opportunities with is outdoor terrace, where popular barbecues are held in summer. In colder weather, the bar is a great place to relax with its sumptuous sofas and open fires. There is a good choice of drinks, including many wines and a couple of champagnes by the glass, as well as draught beers and non-alcoholic cocktails. The menus offer British and European food – goats' cheese fritters with apricot and chilli chutney; seared scallops, Jerusalem artichoke purée, wilted kale and hazelnut beurre noisette; and pear, almond and Amaretto tart to finish.

Open all day all wk 11am-mdnt (Sat 10-mdnt Sun 10am-11pm) **Food** Lunch all day Dinner all day Av main course £14 Set menu available Restaurant menu available all wk ⊕ ENTERPRISE INNS ◄ Sharp's Doom Bar, Fuller's London Pride, Skinner's Cornish Knocker, Red Squirrel Redwood American IPA Ö Aspall. ☞ 16 **Facilities** Non-diners area ●● Children's menu Children's portions Garden ⌂ WiFi ▭

W11

Portobello Gold PLAN 2 E3

tel: 020 7460 4900 **95-97 Portobello Rd, Notting Hill W11 2QB**
email: reservations@portobellogold.com
dir: *From Notting Hill Gate tube station follow signs to Portobello Market*

A touch of gold in Notting Hill

In the heart of famous Portobello Road Market, this quirky Notting Hill pub/wine bar/brasserie has opened a new oyster bar and has added more seating; menus always list game and seafood, including sashimi, British mussels and Irish oysters. All dishes (pasta, tortillas, seafood, burgers, bangers and steaks) are prepared from scratch on the premises. With the landlord's wife, Linda Bell, an established wine writer, 18 wines by the glass should be no surprise. The pub also offers an interesting range of British ales and European beers (including a gluten-free choice) and cocktails. Former US President Bill Clinton dropped into Portobello Gold with an entire motorcade, stayed an hour and left without paying! Many other famous visitors have called in or become regulars.

Open all day all wk Closed 25-31 Dec **Food** Lunch all day Dinner all day Av main course £10-£11 ⊕ ENTERPRISE INNS ◄ Brakspear Oxford Gold, Harvey's Sussex, Freedom, Guinness, Meantime Yakima Red Ö Thatchers Gold, Katy & Spartan. ☞ 18 **Facilities** Non-diners area ☺ (Bar) ●● Children's portions WiFi ▭ (notice required)

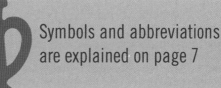
Symbols and abbreviations are explained on page 7

W14

The Albion PLAN 2 D3

tel: 020 7603 2826 **121 Hammersmith Rd, West Kensington W14 0QL**
email: info@thealbionpub.com
dir: *Near Kensington Olympia & Barons Court tube stations*

Old pub with a great atmosphere

If you've been wandering around Olympia all day head across the road to The Albion for a pint of London Pride, St Austell Tribute or one of the many wines by the glass. A fine old pub that takes its name from HMS *Albion*, it has the look and feel of an old ship, with bare floor boards and long, scrubbed wooden tables. The menu features a selection of burgers and salads, with jackets, sandwiches and omelettes available at lunchtime. Other choices are sausages, mash, rich onion gravy; Cajun chicken; home-made steak and ale pie; and battered fish and chips. August beer festival.

Open all day all wk **Food** Lunch Mon-Fri 12-3 Dinner all wk 5-10 Av main course £10 ⊕ HEINEKEN ◖ Fuller's London Pride, St Austell Tribute ♂ Symonds. ♟ 13 **Facilities** Non-diners area ⚹ (Bar Restaurant Outside area) Outside area ⊫ Beer festival WiFi ⬛ (notice required)

The Cumberland Arms PLAN 2 D3 **PICK OF THE PUBS**

tel: 020 7371 6806 **29 North End Rd, Hammersmith W14 8SZ**
email: thecumberlandarmspub@btconnect.com
dir: *From Kensington Olympia tube station turn left. At T-junct right into Hammersmith Rd. 3rd left into North End Rd, 100yds pub on left*

Gastro-pub with a locals' atmosphere

At the heart of cosmopolitan Hammersmith and handy for Olympia, this eye-catching gastro-pub, generously dressed with colourful summer hanging baskets and boxes, is a popular place for people-watching. Bag a bench beside the adjacent flowery enclave on sunny days, or head inside where mellow furniture and stripped floorboards characterise the interior. Friendly staff, a comprehensive wine list and well-kept ales (St Austell Tribute, Skinner's Betty Stogs, Exmoor Gold) are the draw for those seeking after-work refreshment. But it's also a great place for sampling enticing cuisine with an Italian accent from a regularly updated menu and specials selection. Starters embrace Tuscan minestrone; bruschetta al pomodoro; and ham hock, broad bean and pea tart. Among the mains are grilled Italian sausages; stuffed squid with prawns and chorizo; and home-made ravioli with chicken, spinach and ricotta. Desserts are few but sweet: sticky date pudding with caramel, perhaps, or chocolate brownie with ice cream.

Open all day all wk 12-11 (Sun 12-10.30 Thu-Fri 12-12) Closed 24 Dec-1 Jan **Food** Contact pub for details ⊕ FREE HOUSE ◖ Exmoor Gold, Sharp's Doom Bar, Skinner's Betty Stogs, St Austell Tribute. ♟ 16 **Facilities** Non-diners area ⚹ (Bar Restaurant Garden) ♦ Children's portions Garden ⊫ WiFi ⬛ (notice required)

WC1

The Bountiful Cow PLAN 1 E4 **PICK OF THE PUBS**

tel: 020 7404 0200 **51 Eagle St, Holborn WC1R 4AP**
email: manager@roxybeaujolais.com
dir: *230mtrs NE from Holborn tube station, via Procter St. Walk through 2 arches into Eagle St. Pub between High Holborn & Red Lion Square*

Homage to the cow

Pub cookbook author Roxy Beaujolais runs this 'public house devoted to beef', her second pub venture following the delightful Seven Stars in WC2. Two floors are crowded with framed pictures of cows, bullfights, cowgirls, diagrams of meat cuts and posters of cow-themed films; jazzy but discreet music adds to an atmosphere halfway between funky bistro and stylish saloon. The well kept ales are from Adnams and Dark Star, and the short but estimable wine list includes several gutsy reds. The value-priced menu features Bountyburgers and perfectly grilled and

tender aged steaks; the meat is sourced from a trusted Smithfield Market supplier. Starters of garlic fried prawns or octopus salad, and desserts like Belgian apple tart with vanilla ice cream might open and close the proceedings, with an oak steak board platter for two in between. Booking for all meals is advisable.

Open all day 11-11 (Sat 12-11) Closed 25-26 Dec, 1 Jan, some BHs, Sun **Food** Lunch Mon-Sat 12-10.30 Dinner Mon-Sat 12-10.30 ⊕ FREE HOUSE ◖ Adnams Southwold Bltter, Dark Star Hophead ♂ Aspall. ♟ **Facilities** Non-diners area ♦ Outside area ⊫ WiFi ⬛ (notice required)

NEW The Easton PLAN 1 E5

tel: 020 7278 7608 **22 Easton St WC1X 0DS**
email: info@theeastonpub.co.uk
dir: *Nearest tube stations: Farringdon; Angel; Kings Cross*

Dog-friendly gastro-pub in deepest Clerkenwell

Near the famous Sadlers Wells Theatre a short distance from Farringdon tube, this gastro-pub with pavement benches is also just a stroll away from EC1's Exmouth Market. Timothy Taylor, Truman's and Hackney Pale Ale are the top real ales, backed by Bretonne cider and 16 wines served by the glass. A dozen tasty bar snacks tempt with the likes of porcini arancini; mini smoked haddock fishcakes with tartare sauce; and smoked ham croquettes with aïoli. These indicate the modern approach to cosmopolitan ingredients found on the seasonally-changing main menu, in dishes such as rabbit ravioli with parmesan; pan-fried pollock fillet; and asparagus, tarragon and goats' cheese pie.

Open all day all wk **Food** Lunch Mon-Fri 12-3, Sat 12-4, Sun 12-5 Dinner Mon-Sat 6-10, Sun 6-9 Av main course £12.50 ⊕ ENTERPRISE INNS ◖ Timothy Taylor Landlord, Truman's Runner, Hackney Pale Ale ♂ Westons Stowford Press, Cidre Breton. ♟ 16 **Facilities** Non-diners area ⚹ (Bar Restaurant Outside area) ♦ Children's menu Outside area ⊫ WiFi ⬛ (notice required)

The Lady Ottoline PLAN 1 E4

tel: 020 7831 0008 **11A Northington St WC1N 2JF**
email: info@theladyottoline.com
dir: *Nearest tube: Chancery Lane*

Smart Bloomsbury set piece

Scott and Maria Hunter (also owners of the Princess of Shoreditch) have made a real success here. Named after Bloomsbury society hostess Lady Ottoline Morrell, this attractive corner pub, complete with log fire, serves four local ales, including Sambrook's, bottled craft beers and ciders, and nine wines by the glass. In the upstairs dining rooms, head chef Alan Irwin prepares simple, but awfully good, seasonally-based food such as Kentish pork rillettes, Braeburn apple piccalilli, followed by globe artichoke pie, toasted chestnuts and sheep's curd; or braised pork belly, black pudding and potato pan haggerty. Well-behaved children (until 6pm) are welcome in the pub.

Open all day all wk Closed 25 Dec-2 Jan **Food** Lunch Mon-Fri 12-3, Sat 12-4, Sun 12-8 Dinner Mon-Sat 6.30-10, Sun 12-8 Set menu available Restaurant menu available ⊕ PUNCH TAVERNS ◖ Sharp's Doom Bar, Sambrook's, Redemption Pale Ale. ♟ 9 **Facilities** Non-diners area ♦ Children's portions Outside area ⊫ WiFi

Norfolk Arms PLAN 1 D5

tel: 020 7388 3937 **28 Leigh St WC1H 9EP**
email: info@norfolkarms.co.uk
dir: *Nearest tube: Russell Square; King's Cross St Pancras; Euston*

Classic London corner pub offering international tapas choices

Located on a busy street corner in Bloomsbury, within five minutes' walk of St Pancras International, the Norfolk Arms is a London gastro-pub. Behind its Victorian frontage, the main bar and dining area are at ground level, with private dining on the first floor. The extensive and eclectic bar menu features British, European and Middle Eastern tapas: typical choices are stuffed vine leaves, Scotch egg, Valencian carrots and Serrano ham. The main menu includes oxtail stew and spicy Italian sausages. A great choice of beers and ten wines by the glass complete the picture.

Open all day all wk Closed 25-26, 31 Dec & 1 Jan **Food** Contact pub for details ⊕ STAR PUBS & BARS ◾ Theakston XB, Greene King IPA. ⚑ 10 **Facilities** Non-diners area ⬤ Children's portions ⌁ WiFi

WC2

The Seven Stars PLAN 1 E4
PICK OF THE PUBS

tel: 020 7242 8521 **53 Carey St WC2A 2JB**
email: roxy@roxybeaujolais.com
dir: *From Temple tube station turn right. 1st left into Arundel St. Right into Strand (walking). Left into Bell Yard. 1st left into Carey St*

A real one off - stylish saloon style and market driven dishes

The Seven Stars may never have seen better days in its 413 years of existence. Since Roxy Beaujolais took over this Grade II listed pub behind the Royal Courts of Justice 15 years ago, delicate and undisruptive priming has produced nothing but accolades. Look out for the mullioned glass dumbwaiter, designed by Roxy's architect husband, that looks tactfully historic, and the new cat, named Ray Brown, who wears a ruff just as his predecessor did. Strengthened by its personalities and ambience, The Seven Stars is considered the ideal pub – the food is simple but well executed, the ales are kept perfectly, the wines are few but very good, and the staff are welcoming and efficient. Roxy cooks most of the time here. The day's dishes, listed on the blackboard, change according to what's best in the market and what tickles Roxy's fancy. Examples are dill cured herring with potato salad; pheasant and pork pie with cranberries; and Spanish scramble - eggs, chorizo, potatoes, garlic, saffron and parsley.

Open all day all wk 11-11 (Sat 12-11 Sun 12-10.30) Closed 25-26 Dec, 1 Jan, Etr Sun, some BHs **Food** Lunch Mon-Fri 12-9.30, Sat-Sun 1-9.30 Dinner Mon-Fri 12-9.30, Sat-Sun 1-9.30 Av main course £11 ⊕ FREE HOUSE ◾ Adnams Southwold Bitter & Broadside, Sambrook's Wandle, Sharp's Cornish Coaster Ò Aspall. **Facilities** Non-diners area WiFi

The Sherlock Holmes PLAN 1 D3

tel: 020 7930 2644 **10 Northumberland St WC2N 5DB**
email: 7967@greeneking.co.uk
dir: *From Charing Cross tube station into Villiers St. Through 'The Arches' (runs underneath Charing Cross station) straight across Craven St into Craven Passage to Northumberland St*

Themed pub serving comforting pub grub

Painted black with etched glass windows and colourful hanging baskets, this traditional corner pub is chock-full of Holmes memorabilia, including photographs of Conan Doyle, mounted pages from manuscripts, and artefacts and pieces recording the adventures of the Master Detective. There's even a replica of Holmes' and Watson's sitting room and study. This split-level establishment has a bar on the ground floor and on the first floor an intimate covered roof garden and the restaurant. There's Sherlock Holmes Ale to drink, hot and cold bar food plus an à la carte menu offering traditional roast dinners, ham, egg and chips and home-made steak and mushroom in ale pie with cheesecake of the day for afters.

Open all day all wk Closed 25 Dec **Food** Lunch all wk 9am-10pm Dinner all wk 11-10 Restaurant menu available all wk ⊕ GREENE KING ◾ Sherlock Holmes Ale & Abbot Ale, Morland Old Speckled Hen Ò Aspall. ⚑ 14 **Facilities** Non-diners area ⬤ Outside area ⌁ WiFi ▭ (notice required)

GREATER LONDON

CARSHALTON
Map 6 TQ26

The Sun

tel: 020 8773 4549 **4 North St SM5 2HU**
email: thesuncarshalton@googlemail.com
dir: *From A232 (Croydon Rd) between Croydon & Sutton, turn into North St signed Hackbridge (B277). Pub on right at x-rds*

Stylish gastro-pub with excellent real ales

This imposing corner-plot pub stands close to the heart of Carshalton village. The enclosed walled garden area houses a wood-fired pizza oven, whilst a newly developed private dining room is ideal for small group gatherings. Both wet and food sides of the business are increasingly popular; six real ales, such as Rudgate Ruby Mild, attract beer lovers - there's a June beer festival, too - whilst a gastro-style menu encourages diners to tarry a while in the modish interior. Commence with a warm salad of wood pigeon with roast beetroot, orange and walnut dressing, leaving room for mains such as pan-fried grey mullet with king prawns and herb Puy lentils with caper and Pernod sauce.

Open all day Closed Mon until 5pm **Food** Lunch Tue-Fri 12-3, Sat 12-10, Sun 12-9 Dinner Mon Fri 6-9.30, Sat 12-10, Sun 12-9 Set menu available ⊕ FREE HOUSE ◾ Timothy Taylor Landlord, Rudgate Ruby Mild, Sharp's Doom Bar Ò Westons, Addlestones. ⚑ 14 **Facilities** Non-diners area ❀ (Bar Restaurant Garden) ⬤ Children's menu Children's portions Play area Family room Garden ⌁ Beer festival WiFi ▭ (notice required)

CHELSFIELD
Map 6 TQ46

NEW The Bo-peep

tel: 01959 534457 **Hewitts Rd BR6 7QL**
dir: *M25 junct 4 (Bromley exit). At rdbt follow Well Hill sign. Pub approx 500yds on right*

Traditional home cooking close to the M25

Just five minutes from the M25, this 16th-century inn was originally known as The White Hart, changing its name to The Bo-peep as recently as 1971. The low timber beams and inglenook in the bar offer plenty of original character in the bar, where Westerham ales are on tap. Everything here is home cooked and typical dishes include belly of pork with cider jus; and fillet of sea bass with ratatouille. On sunny days, bag a table in the large garden surrounded by fields of horses.

Open all day all wk **Food** Contact pub for details Av main course £10.95 ⊕ ENTERPRISE INNS ◾ Adnams, Sharp's Doom Bar, Westerham's Beers on rotation Ò Thatchers. ⚑ 12 **Facilities** ❀ (Bar Garden) ⬤ Children's portions Garden ⌁ Parking WiFi

Who are the AA's award-winning pubs? For details see pages 10 & 11

CHELSFIELD *continued*

The Five Bells

PICK OF THE PUBS

tel: 01689 821044 **BR6 7RE**
dir: *M25 junct 4, A224 towards Orpington. In approx 1m turn right into Church Rd. Pub on left*

Country pub with live music and open mic nights

This whitewashed family-run pub is a Grade II listed building conveniently located just inside the M25, but also situated in a protected conservation village, with many lovely walks in the area. Dating from 1680, The Five Bells takes its name from the magnificent bells at the St Martin of the Tours church just up the road. There are two bars: one is a dog-friendly front bar boasting an original inglenook fireplace; the other houses the restaurant area. This in turn leads to the patio and extensive garden, which comes complete with a children's swing and play area. The seasonal menu, backed by daily-changing chef's specials, complements the real ales and wines on offer: home-made steak and ale pie; slow-braised cider and apple pulled pork with roast new potatoes and apple sauce; and goats' cheese and beetroot tart are examples from a winter menu. Sandwiches, baguettes, ciabattas and home-made pizzas are available too, and beer festivals take place at Easter and in October along with regular live music, quizzes and other events.

Open all day all wk **Food** Lunch all wk 12-2.45 Dinner Thu-Sat 6.30-8.45 Av main course £9 Restaurant menu available Thu-Sat eve ⊕ ENTERPRISE INNS ◀ Courage Best, Sharp's Doom Bar, Otter, Jennings Cumberland. ♀ 13
Facilities Non-diners area ✿ (Bar Garden) ♦ Children's menu Children's portions Play area Garden ⊞ Beer festival Parking WiFi ➡ (notice required)

KINGSTON UPON THAMES

The Boaters Inn PLAN 2 C1

tel: 020 8541 4672 **Canbury Gardens, Lower Ham Rd KT2 5AU**
email: enquiries@boaterskingston.com
dir: *Just off Lower Ham Rd*

Thames-side favourite for jazz, food and ale

Arrive early to bag one of the prized balcony seats at this stunning riverside pub and savour the view across the Thames, which is best enjoyed at sunset. The place heaves at weekends and on sunny days, with Thames-path walkers and cyclists, and boaters jostling with local diners for a table on the impressive alfresco terrace. The draw, other than the river, are the seven microbrewery ales on tap in the airy, wood-floored bar, the famous Sunday evening jazz sessions, and the fresh, modern pub food on offer. Daily menus may list rabbit ragout on toast; a ploughman's board to share; salmon and squid linguine; venison with orange marmalade; and sticky toffee pudding.

Open all day all wk **Food** Lunch Mon-Fri 12-4, Sat 11-9.30, Sun 12-9.30 Dinner Mon-Fri 5-9.30, Sat 11-9.30, Sun 12-9.30 ⊕ GREENE KING ◀ Sambrook's Wandle, Dark Star American Pale Ale & Hophead, Surrey Hills Shere Drop, Twickenham Brewery ⚬ Westons Stowford Press, Mortimers. ♀ 10 **Facilities** Non-diners area ✿ (Bar Garden) ♦ Children's menu Children's portions Garden ⊞ Beer festival Cider festival WiFi ➡ (notice required)

PINNER

NEW The Queens Head PLAN 2 B5

tel: 020 8868 4607 **31 High St HA5 5PJ**
email: info@queensheadpinner.co.uk **web:** www.queensheadpinner.co.uk
dir: *Nearest tube station: Pinner*

Pinner's oldest, maybe spookiest, inn

In 1872, Admiral Nelson's only daughter, Eleanor, was killed by a bolting horse outside this ancient inn. They say her ghost still roams its rooms, but she's

supposedly benevolent and with five permanent and two weekly-changing guest real ales to choose from she might even join you for a pint. On the lunch menu are cod, spinach and Mendip Hills Cheddar fishcakes; scampi, chips and mushy peas; gammon steak with egg and pineapple; and hand-made beefburger, while on Sundays there's a traditional roast. Although dinner is not served, bar snacks are available until 9pm. Beer festivals are held in the spring.

Open all day all wk **Food** Lunch all wk 12-3 Av main course £9.50 ⊕ SPIRIT PUB COMPANY ◀ Young's Special, Rebellion Mutiny, Greene King Abbot Ale, Adnams, Wells Bombardier, Guest ales ⚬ Aspall. ♀ 13 **Facilities** Non-diners area ✿ (Bar Restaurant Garden) Garden ⊞ Beer festival Parking WiFi

RICHMOND UPON THAMES

NEW The White Swan PLAN 2 C2

tel: 020 8940 0959 **26 Old Palace Ln TW9 1PG**
email: info@whiteswanrichmond.co.uk
dir: *Nearest tube: Richmond*

Excellent food in the heart of Richmond

Tucked away from Richmond's bustling high street, The White Swan dates back to 1777. Whether it's for a pint of Otter Bitter in the cosy bar with its open fire or a meal in the upstairs dining room or suntrap garden, this is a pub to suit every occasion. The kitchen has gained a good reputation for its daily-changing menus. A typical meal might feature apple, parsnip and cinnamon soup, followed by venison and thyme sausages, mash and onion gravy. Look out for pub dog Jake, a friendly Springer Spaniel.

Open all day all wk **Food** Lunch Mon-Fri 12-3, Sat-Sun 12-4 Dinner Mon-Fri 6.30-9, Sat-Sun 6.30-10 Av main course £13 ⊕ FREE HOUSE ◀ Sharp's Doom Bar, Timothy Taylor Landlord, Otter Bitter ⚬ Westons Stowford Press, Aspall. ♀ 18 **Facilities** Non-diners area ✿ (Bar) ♦ Children's portions Outside area WiFi

MERSEYSIDE

BARNSTON

Map 15 SJ28

Fox and Hounds

tel: 0151 648 7685 **107 Barnston Rd CH61 1BW**
email: info@the-fox-hounds.co.uk
dir: *M53 junct 4, A5137 to Heswall. In Heswell at rdbt onto A551 signed Barnston*

Home-cooked food in friendly village pub

In the quaint village of Barnston, the Fox and Hounds was built in 1911 and the pub's Edwardian character is preserved via leaded windows, pitch-pine woodwork and open fire. In the Snug, the original bar, are collections of bric-à-brac including brewery clocks and flying ducks. A good variety of real ales includes Brimstage Trapper's Hat, and there is a huge range of malts. Pub classics like curry of the day, game pie, and sausage and mash are supplemented at lunchtime by sandwiches, light meals, baked potatoes and salad platters. The traditional Sunday roasts feature Welsh Black beef and Welsh lamb.

Open all day all wk **Food** Lunch Mon-Sat 12-2, Sun 12-3 Dinner Tue-Fri 5-8.30 Av main course £9.50 ⊕ FREE HOUSE ◀ Theakston Best Bitter & Old Peculier, Brimstage Trapper's Hat, Timothy Taylor ⚬ Aspall, Rosie's Llandegla. **Facilities** Non-diners area ✿ (Bar Garden) ♦ Children's portions Garden ⊞ Parking ➡ (notice required)

GREASBY
Map 15 SJ28

Irby Mill

tel: 0151 604 0194 **Mill Ln CH49 3NT**
email: info@irbymill.co.uk
dir: *M53 junct 3, A552 signed Upton & Heswall. At lights onto A551 signed Upton & Greasby. At lights left into Arrowe Brook Rd. At rdbt 3rd exit into Mill Ln*

Former miller's cottage serving local produce

An eye-catching, solid, sandstone-block built old miller's cottage (the windmill was demolished in 1898, the pub opened in 1980) just a short jog from the airy heights of Thurstaston Common at the heart of The Wirral Peninsula. One of the area's best choices of real ales meets an exceptional, very pubby menu strong on Wirral produce – 'Muffs' sausage and mash comes with black pudding, peas, mushrooms, gravy and onion rings and could be followed by Nicholls of Parkgate ice cream or Belgian waffles. Popular with ramblers and Sunday diners, there's a suntrap grassy garden for summer; a log fire for the winter.

Open all day all wk **Food** Lunch Mon-Sat 12-9, Sun 12-8 Dinner Mon-Sat 12-9, Sun 12-8 ⊕ STAR PUBS & BARS ◀ Wells Bombardier, Greene King Abbot Ale, Jennings Cumberland Ale, 5 Guest ales. ▮ 12 **Facilities** ❤ (Bar Garden) ♦ Children's menu Children's portions Garden ⚲ Parking WiFi ▬

HESWALL
Map 15 SJ28

NEW The Jug and Bottle

tel: 0151 342 5535 **Mount Av CH60 4RH**
email: info@the-jugandbottle.co.uk
dir: *From A540 in Heswall. At lights into The Mount, 1st left into Mount Ave*

Good locally-sourced food on the Wirral Peninsula

In the heart of Heswall, on the spectacular Wirral Peninsula with its views towards Liverpool and North Wales, 'The Jug' (as the locals call it) is tucked away off the main road but convenient for the M56. With two open fires and surrounded by gardens, this traditional country pub offers a warm welcome all year round, serving good food in the dining room and a range of real ales including local Brimstage Trapper's Hat. Locally-sourced food is served lunchtimes and evenings, typical choices being fisherman's pie with spring greens; and braised oxtail suet pudding with horseradish mash and ale gravy.

Open all day all wk **Food** Lunch Mon-Sat 12-2.30, Sun 12-8 Dinner Mon-Thu 5.30-9, Fri-Sat 5.30-9.30, Sun 12-8 Av main course £12 ⊕ FREE HOUSE ◀ Brimstage Trapper's Hat, Theakston Best Bitter, St Austell Tribute. **Facilities** Non-diners area ❤ (Bar Garden) ♦ Children's menu Children's portions Garden ⚲ Parking WiFi ▬

HIGHTOWN
Map 15 SD30

The Pheasant Inn

tel: 0151 929 2106 **20 Moss Ln L38 3RA**
email: enquiry@thepheasanthightown.co.uk
dir: *From A565 take B5193, follow signs to Hightown*

A different event every day of the week

This attractive pub with a whitewashed wooden exterior is a former alehouse with a sunny garden. It's just minutes from Crosby Beach, where sculptor Antony Gormley's famous 100 cast-iron figures gaze out to sea. Surrounded by fields and golf courses, the pub retains an original brick in the restaurant wall dated 1719. In the bar these days you'll find Thwaites Wainwright alongside Aspall ciders. The menu is changed twice a year so expect dishes like pulled beef and bacon pie or a minted lamb burger. There are also the legendary Sunday platter, fish suppers on 'Fin and Fizz' Fridays, retro dining evenings and a menu just for ladies on Wednesday nights.

Open all day all wk 12-11 (Sun 12-10.30) **Food** Lunch all wk 12-6 Dinner all wk 6-9.30 ⊕ MITCHELLS & BUTLERS ◀ Thwaites Wainwright ౧ Aspall Draught & Organic. ▮ 30 **Facilities** Non-diners area ❤ (Bar Garden) ♦ Children's menu Garden ⚲ Parking WiFi ▬

LIVERPOOL

Map 15 SJ39

The Monro

tel: 0151 707 9933 **92 Duke St L1 5AG**
email: mail.monro@themonrogroup.com web: www.themonro.com
dir: *Phone for detailed directions*

Elegant gastro-pub offering fresh, locally sourced food

In 1746, merchant John Bolton built himself a finely-proportioned house, which today is this popular city gastro-pub. Bolton later entered history as a combatant in Liverpool's last recorded duel (he was the victor). The elegance of the interior would make him feel very nostalgic, although he might struggle with the concept of naming beers Boondoggle (Ringwood), Cocker Hoop (Jennings) and GingerBeard (Wychwood). Examples from a monthly-changing menu include duck bourgignon with pancetta lardons and port-wine-glazed silverskin onions; poached salmon and sea bass with pea linguine and garlic cream sauce; and vegetable Wellington. The Early Doors menu is for those short of time.

Open all day all wk Closed 25-26 Dec, 1 Jan **Food** Lunch all wk 12-9.30 Dinner all wk 12-9.30 Set menu available Restaurant menu available Mon-Sat ⊕ FREE HOUSE 🍺 Ringwood Boondoggle, Jennings Cocker Hoop, Wychwood GingerBeard ♂ Thatchers Katy. 🍷 10 **Facilities** Non-diners area ♦ Children's menu Children's portions Garden 🌳 WiFi 🚐 (notice required)

See advert on page 341

NORFOLK

BAWBURGH

Map 13 TG10

Kings Head

PICK OF THE PUBS

tel: 01603 744977 **Harts Ln NR9 3LS**
email: anton@kingshead-bawburgh.co.uk
dir: *From A47 take B1108 W towards Walton. Right signed Bawburgh*

Worth finding after exploring nearby Norwich

Old English roses and lavender fragrance the lanes in front of this low, rambling 17th-century pub, set in a cosy village of flint and brick cottages beside the River Yare. Behind the roadside brick house rambles an eyecatching half-timbered cottage, complete with bulging walls, wooden floors and log fires. Leather sofas and a vaguely rustic mix of furnishings add to the charm which attracts customers keen to engage with Pamela and Anton Wimmer's enticing menu of pub favourites and something that little bit special. The busy kitchen team relies on East Anglian suppliers for virtually all the ingredients; pan-fried Norfolk quail, confit leg, wild mushroom duxelle and celeriac a typically uplifting starter. There's plenty of seafood on the monthly-changing menu - witness the Norfolk moules frites with bacon, celery, garlic, white wine and cream. Gluten free options and daily specials add to the choices.

Open all day all wk **Food** Lunch Mon-Sat 12-2, Sun 12-4, summer Sun 12-3 Dinner Mon-Sat 5.30-9, summer Sun 6-9 Av main course £14 ⊕ FREE HOUSE 🍺 Adnams Southwold Bitter & Broadside, Woodforde's Wherry, Guest ale ♂ Aspall. 🍷 15 **Facilities** Non-diners area ♥ (Bar Garden) ♦ Children's menu Children's portions Garden 🌳 Parking WiFi 🚐 (notice required)

BLAKENEY

Map 13 TG04

The Blakeney White Horse

PICK OF THE PUBS

tel: 01263 740574 **4 High St NR25 7AL**
email: hello@blakeneywhitehorse.co.uk
dir: *From A148 (Cromer to King's Lynn road) onto A149 signed to Blakeney*

Popular pub in fishing village

Since the 17th century, this former coaching inn has been tucked away among Blakeney's flint-built fishermen's cottages, a short, steepish amble up from the small tidal harbour. The tastefully appointed, Adnams-stocked bar is stylish yet informal, the conservatory is naturally bright – both are eating areas, where the same menu and daily specials apply. Locally sourced food is a given, especially the lobster, crab and mussels from village fishermen, meats and game from Norfolk estates, soft fruit, salads, asparagus and free-range eggs from local smallholders, while rod- and line-caught mackerel and sea bass find their way through the kitchen door in summer. On the lunch menu there'll be filled bagels, baguettes and pie of the day. In the evening maybe smoked haddock fishcakes with beetroot rémoulade and poached egg; braised beef brisket with horseradish mash, wilted spinach, sautéed garlic, wild mushrooms and red wine jus; and gooseberry jam crème brûlée.

Open all day all wk 10.30am-11pm Closed 25 Dec **Food** Lunch Mon-Sat 12-2, Sun 12-2.30 Dinner all wk 6.30-9 ⊕ ADNAMS 🍺 Southwold Bitter, Broadside, Adnams, Guest ales ♂ Aspall. 🍷 14 **Facilities** Non-diners area ♥ (Bar Restaurant) ♦ Children's menu Children's portions Family room Outside area 🌳 Parking WiFi

The Kings Arms

tel: 01263 740341 **Westgate St NR25 7NQ**
email: kingsarmsnorfolk@btconnect.com
dir: *From Holt or Fakenham take A148, then B1156 for 6m to Blakeney*

Very old pub in lovely seaside village

Tucked away in a popular fishing village close to north Norfolk's coastal path (Peddars Way), this thriving free house is the perfect refreshment stop following an invigorating walk, time spent birdwatching, or a boat trip to the nearby seal colony. Open all day and run by the same family for almost 40 years, it serves an excellent selection of real ales, including Norfolk-brewed Woodforde's Wherry that is backed by menus featuring locally caught fish and seasonal seafood. Perhaps cod, prawn and bacon chowder; mussels in garlic cream sauce – together with braised pheasant with bacon jus; steak and Adnams ale suet pudding; and home-made lasagne.

Open all day all wk Closed 25 Dec eve **Food** Lunch 8.30am-9.30pm Dinner 8.30am-9.30pm Av main course £8.50 ⊕ FREE HOUSE ◀ Morland Old Speckled Hen, Woodforde's Wherry, Marston's Pedigree, Adnams Southwold Bitter. ₱ 10 **Facilities** Non-diners area ❖ (Bar Restaurant Garden) ◀ Children's menu Children's portions Play area Family room Garden ⊨ Parking WiFi ▭

■ **BRANCASTER** Map 13 TF74

The Ship Hotel

tel: 01485 210333 **Main Rd PE31 8AP**
email: thebar@shiphotelnorfolk.co.uk
dir: *On A149 in village centre*

Nautical pub serving cracking food

Set in a prime coastal location close to Brancaster beach, TV chef and hotelier Chris Coubrough's stylish gastro-pub continues to attract walkers, beach bums and families with its appealing menus of modern pub food prepared from fresh produce sourced from local farmers and fisherman. Be tempted by smoked haddock, cockles and leek chowder or local venison casserole. Wash it down with a pint of Bitter Old Bustard and relax in the gorgeous bar and dining rooms, where you can expect rug-strewn wood floors, wood-burning stoves, shelves full of books, quirky antiques, scrubbed wooden tables and a distinct nautical feel.

Open all day all wk **Food** Lunch 12-2.30 (school holidays, menu available 3-6) Dinner 6.30-9.30 ⊕ FREE HOUSE/FLYING KIWI INNS ◀ Jo C's Norfolk Kiwi & Bitter Old Bustard, Adnams Southwold Bitter ⓝ Aspall. ₱ 19 **Facilities** Non-diners area ❖ (Bar Outside area) ◀ Children's menu Children's portions Outside area ⊨ Parking WiFi

---

■ **BRANCASTER STAITHE** Map 13 TF74

The Jolly Sailors

tel: 01485 210314 **PE31 8BJ**
email: info@jollysailorsbrancaster.co.uk
dir: *On A149 (coast road) midway between Hunstanton & Wells-next-the-Sea*

Children, muddy boots and dogs welcome

Focal point of the village, the 18th-century 'Jolly' is the brewery tap for the Brancaster microbrewery, both being run by father and son team, Cliff and James Nye. In the Harbour Snug you can look out over the water, read local books, and play darts and board games. The Nyes' Brancaster ales aren't obligatory – you'll also find Woodforde's and Adnams, and newly added a selection of 34 rums. Pub food is typified by open-fired pizzas (including gluten-free choices), plus from the blackboard, lamb curry; steak and ale pie; and vegetarian falafel burgers. The beach-themed ice cream hut in the garden is an attraction in the summer. A beer and music festival is held in June.

Open all day all wk **Food** Lunch (winter) Mon-Fri 12-2 (all day spring & summer), Sat-Sun 12-9 Dinner (winter) Mon-Fri 6-9 (all day spring & summer), Sat-Sun 12-9 Av main course £9.95 ⊕ FREE HOUSE ◀ Brancaster Best, The Wreck & Oyster Catcher, Woodforde's Wherry, Adnams, Guest ales ⓝ Symonds. ₱ 12 **Facilities** Non-diners area ❖ (Bar Restaurant Garden) ◀ Children's menu Children's portions Play area Garden ⊨ Beer festival Cider festival Parking WiFi ▭ (notice required)

The White Horse ★★★ HL ◉◉ PICK OF THE PUBS

tel: 01485 210262 **PE31 8BY**
email: reception@whitehorsebrancaster.co.uk web: www.whitehorsebrancaster.co.uk
dir: *A149 (coast road), midway between Hunstanton & Wells-next-the-Sea*

Stylish inn on marshland coastline

From the airy conservatory restaurant, summer sun deck and elegant bedrooms at The White Horse, there are stunning vistas over glorious tidal marshes to Scolt Head Island, a four-mile long sandbar that's home to a nature reserve rich in birdlife. Reflecting the view, colours are muted and natural, and beach-found objects are complemented by contemporary artworks. Scrubbed pine tables and high-backed settles in the bar create a welcoming atmosphere, while alfresco dining in the sunken front garden is a popular warm-weather option, accompanied by local Brancaster Oyster Catcher. While the bar menu lists grills, salads and sandwiches, the extensive, daily-changing restaurant menu (with two AA Rosettes) champions the freshest local seafood, including seasonal fish and shellfish gathered at the foot of the garden. Typically, follow curried fish and sweetcorn chowder; pan-fried hake, Marsh pig chorizo with mussel and bean stew; local venison and orange sausages, thyme mash and textures of onion; or sage and butternut squash risotto. There are also good puddings – perhaps try the lemon tart with raspberry sorbet.

Open all day all wk 11-11 (Sun 11-10.30) (open from 9am for breakfast) **Food** Lunch all wk 9-9 Dinner all wk 9-9 Restaurant menu available all wk ⊕ FREE HOUSE ◀ Adnams Explorer, Woodforde's Wherry, Brancaster Best, Malthouse Bitter & Oyster Catcher, Guest ales ⓝ Aspall. ₱ 14 **Facilities** Non-diners area ❖ (Bar Garden Outside area) ◀ Children's menu Children's portions Garden Outside area ⊨ Parking WiFi ▭ (notice required) **Rooms** 15

■ **BURNHAM MARKET** Map 13 TF84

The Hoste ★★★★ HL ◉◉ PICK OF THE PUBS

tel: 01328 738777 **The Green PE31 8HD**
email: reception@thehoste.com web: www.thehoste.com
dir: *Signed from B1155, 5m W of Wells-next-the-Sea*

One of Norfolk's most popular dining inns

North Norfolk's endless sandy beaches and beautiful countryside are within easy reach of this cream-painted and pantiled old village manor house. A hotel since 1651, it has also been a courthouse, livestock market, brothel and Horatio Nelson's Saturday morning local. Today, The Hoste combines top-notch two-AA Rosette food with boutique accommodation. Of the three restaurants there is one at the back, which on fine days, opens seamlessly onto the sheltered walled garden area, so bringing the outdoors indoors. The East Anglian real ale line-up includes Woodforde's Wherry and Abbot Ale, while Aspall cider doesn't have far to travel either; 24 of the 150-bin wine list can be served by the glass. The seasonal modern British menus embrace dressed Cromer crab, baked halibut, grilled hake, and Aberdeen Angus steaks. Delightful vegetarian options include grilled Mediterranean vegetables; and a potato galette with Puy lentils and woodland mushrooms. Finish with Mrs Temple's Norfolk cheeses, or stem ginger cheesecake with lime sorbet.

Open all day all wk **Food** Lunch all wk 12-2.15 Dinner all wk 6-9.15 ⊕ FREE HOUSE ◀ Woodforde's Wherry & Nelson's Revenge, Abbot Ale ⓝ Aspall. ₱ 24 **Facilities** Non-diners area ❖ (Bar Garden) ◀ Children's menu Children's portions Garden Parking WiFi **Rooms** 37

BURNHAM THORPE
Map 13 TF84

The Lord Nelson
PICK OF THE PUBS

tel: 01328 738241 **Walsingham Rd PE31 8HN**
email: enquiries@nelsonslocal.co.uk **web:** www.nelsonslocal.co.uk
dir: *B1355 (Burnham Market to Fakenham road), pub 9m from Fakenham & 1.75m from Burnham Market*

Soak up over 370 years of atmosphere

This pub started life in 1637 as The Plough and was renamed The Lord Nelson in 1798, to honour Horatio Nelson who was born in the village. Located opposite the delightful village cricket ground and bowling green, it has an atmospheric interior that has changed little over the past 370 plus years; you can even sit on Nelson's high-backed settle. Drinks are served from the taproom, with real ales drawn straight from the cask. In the cosy bar you can also partake in unique rum-based tipples such as Nelson's Blood. The kitchen aims to cook dishes with balance between flavours, so that the quality of the ingredients shines. A typical meal is farmhouse pâté with toast and red onion marmalade followed by pan-fried salmon in a green herb crust with beurre blanc and duchess potatoes, with apple pie and vanilla ice cream for dessert. Children will enjoy the huge garden. From May to September, weekend walking tours of Nelson's village are available.

Open all wk 12-3 6-11 (Jul-Aug & BHs 12-11) **Food** Lunch all wk 12-2.30 Dinner all wk 6-9 ⊕ GREENE KING ◀ Abbot Ale, Woodforde's Wherry ♻ Aspall. ♟ 12 **Facilities** Non-diners area ♣ (Bar Garden) ♦♦ Children's menu Play area Garden ♠ Parking WiFi ➡

BURSTON
Map 13 TM18

The Crown

tel: 01379 741257 **Mill Rd IP22 5TW**
email: enquiries@burstoncrown.com
dir: *NE of Diss*

Very much a locals' pub serving inventive food

Steve and Bev Kembery have transformed their 16th-century pub by the green into a cracking community pub, drawing locals in for top-notch ale and food, organising the village fête, hosting three beer festivals a year, and offering a weekly busker's night and regular theme nights. As well as a decent pint of Adnams, you can tuck into goats' cheese, red onion marmalade and Parma ham bruschetta or 'a very Norfolk platter' charcuterie board. From the à la carte, moules marinière or fresh oysters to start perhaps, followed by poached skate wing, capers and blackened butter; or lamb shank braised in red wine and redcurrant with garlic mash. A pub well worth seeking out.

Open all day all wk **Food** Lunch Tue-Sat 12-2, Sun 12-4 Dinner Tue-Sat 6.30-9 Av main course £11 Restaurant menu available Tue-Sun ⊕ FREE HOUSE ◀ Adnams Southwold Bitter & Old Ale, Elmtree Burston's Cuckoo, Greene King Abbot Ale, Elgood's ♻ Aspall. **Facilities** Non-diners area ♣ (Bar Garden) ♦♦ Children's menu Children's portions Garden ♠ Beer festival Parking WiFi ➡ (notice required)

CLEY NEXT THE SEA
Map 13 TG04

The George Hotel
PICK OF THE PUBS

See Pick of the Pubs on opposite page

CROMER
Map 13 TG24

The Red Lion Food and Rooms ★★★★ INN

tel: 01263 514964 **Brook St NR27 9HD**
email: info@redlion-cromer.co.uk **web:** www.redlion-cromer.co.uk
dir: *From A149 into Cromer, on one-way system, pass church on left. 1st left after church into Brook St. Pub on right*

Top-notch seafood is a real draw

Built in the 19th century, when Cromer was fast becoming a popular seaside resort, The Red Lion overlooks the pier and Blue Flag beach. Although used by the armed forces during World War II, it mercifully retains much of its Victorian interior. For real ale drinkers, the bar is heaven, with Bees Wobble, Humpty Dumpty Railway Sleeper and Adnams Broadside in the line-up (many more at the autumn beer festival). Coastal waters provide treats like Cromer crab thermidor and Morston mussels; others are Norfolk sausages and venison; braised lamb shank; and wild mushroom Stroganoff. Many of the bedrooms have sea views.

Open all day all wk **Food** Lunch Mon-Fri 12-2.30, Sat-Sun 12-9.30 Dinner Mon-Fri 6-9.30, Sat-Sun 12-9.30 Av main course £9 ⊕ FREE HOUSE ◀ Bees Wobble, Green Jack Lurcher Stout, Woodforde's Nelson's Revenge, Humpty Dumpty Railway Sleeper, Adnams Broadside ♻ Westons. ♟ 14 **Facilities** Non-diners area ♣ (Bar) ♦♦ Children's menu Children's portions Beer festival Parking WiFi ➡ (notice required) **Rooms** 15

EAST RUSTON
Map 13 TG32

The Butchers Arms

tel: 01692 650237 **Oak Ln NR12 9JG**
email: info@thebutchersarms.biz
dir: *From A149 SE of North Walsham follow signs for Briggate, Honing & East Ruston. Oak Ln off School Rd*

Local ale and traditional food

A timeless village pub, without jukebox or pool table but with 'Mavis', a 1954 Comma fire engine, parked outside, this quintessential beamed pub started life as three terraced cottages in the early 1800s. Landlady Julie Oatham has been here for over 23 years, and ensures a welcoming atmosphere. Changing guest ales are offered alongside traditional favourites such as home-made cottage pie; beef chilli and a roast of the day. The desserts change daily but are of the comforting, traditional type. There is a beer garden and vine-covered patio for summer dining.

Open 12-2.30 6.30-11 Closed Mon (Sep-Jun) **Food** Lunch all wk 12-2 Dinner all wk 7-8.30 ⊕ FREE HOUSE ◀ Guest ales ♻ Somersby. **Facilities** Non-diners area ♣ (Bar Garden) ♦♦ Children's menu Children's portions Garden ♠ Parking WiFi ➡ (notice required) **Notes** ⊜

PICK OF THE PUBS

The George Hotel

CLEY NEXT THE SEA Map 13 TG04

tel: 01263 740652 **High St NR25 7RN**
email: info@thegeorgehotelatcley.co.uk
web: www.thegeorgehotelatcley.co.uk
dir: *On A149 through Cley next the Sea,
approx 4m from Holt*

Village hostelry popular with birdwatchers

The George's beer garden backs on to the salt marshes of the north Norfolk coast, a renowned paradise for birdwatchers. Indeed, this old hotel has been an ornithological focal point for many years – it is well-known for its 'bird bible' which records sightings by visiting twitchers. In the capable hands of new owners Polina and Steve Cleeve since late 2013, the George is as welcoming as always, proffering several real ales at the bar, including Yetman's from just along the coast at Holt. You can snack in the lounge bar or dine in the light, painting-filled restaurant. At the time of writing, a new head chef is being appointed, so additions to the menu are anticipated. Meanwhile the daily-changing dishes offer the best of local fresh ingredients, and fish and seafood is a real strength. Starters which can also be served as main courses include tempura tiger prawns with sweet chilli dipping sauce; Cley smoked haddock chowder with pancetta, sweet corn and rustic bread; and Mrs Temple's cheeses and leek tart with beetroot and walnut salad.

Alternatively choose a plate from the list of pub favourites: typical of these are the George's home-made beefburger with toasted bun, baby gem lettuce, red onion, tomato, gherkin and relish, fries and salad; pan-seared lamb's liver with cured treacle-and-ale bacon, herb mash and shallot jus; and wild mushroom Stroganoff, basmati rice, rocket, truffle oil and toasted pine nuts. Desserts like the triple chocolate brownie with banana ice cream and chocolate sauce keep the birdwatchers coming back. They can even bring in their dogs, which are welcome in the bar and front restaurant. With a great choice for children and a roaring open fire in winter, the George's welcome is warm at any time of year. The village's famous mill and Blakeney Harbour are just a mile away.

Open all day all wk 10.30am-11.30pm
Food Lunch Mon-Sat 12-2.30, Sun 12-3
Dinner Mon-Sat 6-9, Sun 6-8.30 ⊕ FREE
HOUSE ◀ Greene King IPA, Woodforde's
Wherry, Winter's, Yetman's, Guest ales
Ŏ Aspall. ♀ 11 **Facilities**
Non-diners area ❤ (Bar Restaurant
Garden) ♦♦ Children's menu Garden 🨄
Parking WiFi ➡ (notice required)

EATON
Map 13 TG20

The Red Lion

tel: 01603 454787 **50 Eaton St NR4 7LD**
email: admin@redlion-eaton.co.uk
dir: *Off A11, 2m S of Norwich city centre*

The menus offer a seemingly endless choice

This heavily beamed 17th-century coaching inn has bags of character, thanks to its Dutch gable ends, panelled walls, suit of armour and inglenook fireplaces. The covered terrace enables customers to enjoy one of the real ales or sample a glass from the wine list outside during the summer months. Everyone will find something that appeals on the extensive menus, which include plenty of fish options: pan-fried mackerel with a roast beetroot and feta salad; Cromer crab cakes with sweet chilli and lime mayonnaise; and Swannington lamb cutlets with chargrilled courgettes, tomatoes and basil butter. There's a light meals and snack menu too.

Open all day all wk **Food** Lunch all wk 12-2.15 Dinner all wk 6.30-9 🍺 Adnams Southwold Bitter, Woodforde's Wherry, Fuller's London Pride ♂ Aspall. ☻ 10 **Facilities** Non-diners area ♦♦ Children's portions Garden Parking WiFi

FAKENHAM
Map 13 TF92

The Wensum Lodge Hotel

tel: 01328 862100 **Bridge St NR21 9AY**
email: enquiries@wensumlodge.fsnet.co.uk
dir: *In town centre*

Delightful riverside hostelry

Idyllically located by the River Wensum just three minutes' walk from Fakenham, this lovely place has a stream flowing through its garden and offers guests free fishing on the river. The building dates from around 1700, and was originally the grain store for the adjoining mill. Fine ales are complemented by home-cooked food prepared from locally supplied ingredients, with baguettes, jacket potatoes and an all-day breakfast on the light bite menu, and a carte menu for heartier fare. An ideal base for cycling, birdwatching, fishing and horseracing.

Open all wk **Food** Lunch all wk 12-3 Dinner all wk 6.30-9 Set menu available ⊕ FREE HOUSE 🍺 Greene King Abbot Ale & IPA, Old Mill Traditional Bitter, Adnams, Elmtree Beers ♂ Thatchers Gold. **Facilities** Non-diners area 🐾 (Bar Garden Outside area) ♦♦ Children's portions Garden Outside area ⊟ Parking WiFi ▭

GREAT MASSINGHAM
Map 13 TF72

The Dabbling Duck ★ ★ ★ INN

tel: 01485 520827 **11 Abbey Rd PE32 2HN**
email: info@thedabblingduck.co.uk **web:** www.thedabblingduck.co.uk
dir: *From King's Lynn take either A148 or B1145 then follow Great Massingham signs. Or from Fakenham take A148 signed King's Lynn. Or from Swaffham take A1065 towards Cromer, then B1145 signed King's Lynn*

Stylish village-owned inn

Resurrected, after a period of closure, as The Dabbling Duck by a consortium of local businessmen and a tireless campaign by the local authority, the pub on Great Massingham's glorious green thrives as a community local and a stylish inn. Head for the high-backed settles by the raised log fire to peruse the papers with a pint of Woodforde's Wherry or Adnams Broadside, or tuck into a steak and bone marrow

burger, bacon jam and thrice cooked beef dripping chips, and then buffalo milk bread and butter pudding, salted beer caramel with clotted cream at a scrubbed table in one of the comfortably rustic dining areas. There are shelves groaning with books and board games, rugs on tiled floors and the atmosphere is informal and relaxed. The result is a cracking village pub.

Open all day all wk 12-11 **Food** Lunch all wk 12-2.30 Dinner all wk 6.30-9 Av main course £12 ⊕ FREE HOUSE 🍺 Woodforde's Wherry, Beeston Worth the Wait, Adnams Broadside ♂ Aspall. **Facilities** Non-diners area 🐾 (Bar Garden Outside area) ♦♦ Children's menu Children's portions Play area Garden Outside area ⊟ Parking WiFi ▭ (notice required) **Rooms** 6

GREAT RYBURGH
Map 13 TF92

The Blue Boar Inn ★ ★ ★ INN

tel: 01328 829212 **NR21 0DX**
email: eat@blueboar-norfolk.co.uk **web:** www.blueboar-norfolk.co.uk
dir: *From Fakenham take A1067 towards Norwich. Approx 4m right to Great Ryburgh*

Good food in pretty Wensum Valley inn

Lots to see at this character, listed village inn; beyond the beer garden is a notable round-towered medieval church (once linked to the pub by a secret tunnel), whilst inside are quarry-tile floors, beams and a vast inglenook, spread through a jumble of levels marking alterations to this popular local pub over the centuries. It was used as a recruiting station during the Napoleonic Wars; all that's required of today's visitors is to enjoy the local Yetman's beers and indulge the richly varied, Norfolk-based menu, which may include cassoulet of chicken leg and sausage, or pot roast half guinea fowl.

Open 6-11 (Sun 12-6) Closed Tue **Food** Lunch Sun 12-4.30 Dinner Wed-Sat & Mon 6.30-9 ⊕ FREE HOUSE 🍺 Adnams Southwold Bitter, Winter's Golden & Revenge, Staropramen, Yetman's, Guinness ♂ Addlestones, Westons Stowford Press, Aspall. ☻ 8 **Facilities** Non-diners area ♦♦ Children's menu Children's portions Play area Family room Garden ⊟ Parking WiFi ▭ **Rooms** 6

HEVINGHAM
Map 13 TG12

Marsham Arms Coaching Inn

tel: 01603 754268 **Holt Rd NR10 5NP**
email: info@marshamarms.co.uk
dir: *On B1149 N of Norwich airport, 2m through Horsford towards Holt*

Charming inn serving ales from the taproom

Victorian philanthropist and landowner Robert Marsham built the Marsham Arms as a roadside hostel for poor farm labourers, and some original features, including the wooden beams and large open fireplace are still evident. Real ales are served straight from the barrel. The seasonal menu uses fresh local produce and there are always vegetarian and gluten-free options; Wednesday evenings are fish nights and there are regular music evenings too. There is a spacious garden with a paved patio. The inn holds a Green Tourism award.

Open all day all wk **Food** Lunch Mon-Fri 12-2.30, Sat-Sun all day Dinner Mon-Fri 6-9, Sat-Sun all day ⊕ FREE HOUSE 🍺 Adnams Southwold Bitter & Broadside, Woodforde's Wherry, Mauldons, Grain Best Bitter, Humpty Dumpty ♂ Aspall. ☻ **Facilities** Non-diners area 🐾 (Bar Restaurant Garden) ♦♦ Children's menu Children's portions Garden ⊟ Parking WiFi ▭ (notice required)

PICK OF THE PUBS

The Pigs

HOLT Map 13 TG03

tel: 01263 587634 **Norwich Rd, Edgefield NR24 2RL**
email: info@thepigs.org.uk
web: www.thepigs.org.uk
dir: *On B1149*

Bustling village local with pig-inspired menus

Bought by three ambitious co-owners in 2006, this 17th-century country inn on the edge of a lovely village has been transformed into a thriving local and celebration of all things Norfolk, both on the plate and in the glass. The lovely tranquil setting at the fringe of the village allows for a peaceful garden, whilst locals barter their fresh fruit and vegetables over the bar for a pint or two, practise darts or bar billiards and quaff the Old Spot bitter brewed by local Wolf Brewery — what else. An impressively versatile menu emerges from the kitchen, utilising forgotten cuts of locally sourced meat and produce from the pub's adjoining allotment. If it's genuine 'nose to tail' dining you're looking for, the Honey, Colman's mustard and marmalade glazed pork ribs, followed by the slow-cooked belly of pork with smoky bacon beans, apple chutney, black pudding and crackling should fit the bill. Tapas-style starters called 'Iffi ts' also include devilled whitebait with gentleman's relish and lemon, thyme and garlic chicken wings

and are ideal for sharing. If pork-based treats aren't your thing, then venison and port casserole with honey and sage roasted root vegetables, Colman's mustard mash and cinnamon spiced red cabbage may tempt, along with fish options such as deep-fried line-caught haddock, mushy peas, beef dripping chips and tartare sauce. Leek, wild mushroom and pine nut pot barley stew is one of the meat-free choices. Leave room for one of the tempting desserts, perhaps sticky date pudding with toffee sauce and vanilla ice cream. A children's cookery school proves popular.

Open all day all wk 8am-11pm
Food Mon-Sat 12-2.30 6-9 Sun & BH 12-9 ⊞ FREE HOUSE ◀ Woodforde's Wherry, Greene King Abbot Ale, Wolf Old Spot, Adnams Broadside & Southwold Bitter Ò Aspall. **Facilities** ❀ (Bar) ♦♦ Children's menu Children's portions Play area Family room Outside area Parking WiFi 🚌 (notice required)

HEYDON
Map 13 TG12

Earle Arms

tel: 01263 587376 **The Street NR11 6AD**
email: theearlearms@gmail.com
dir: *Signed between Cawston & Corpusty on B1149 (Holt to Norwich road)*

One for fans of the turf

"H", the landlord and chef, is responsible for the horseracing memorabilia throughout this 16th-century, Dutch-gabled free house on the village green. As part-owner of a racehorse, he will gladly give you a tip, but says it's probably best not to go nap on it. The privately owned conservation village of Heydon is often used for filming, and many a star of the big and small screen has enjoyed the Earle's off-the-pier-fresh seafood; fillet of beef Marchand de Vin with vegetables; mixed bean chilli with rice; and game stew. A beer festival is held on St George's Day (23rd April).

Open 12-3 6-11 (Sun all day) Closed Mon **Food** Lunch Tue-Sun 12-2 Dinner Tue-Sun 6-8.30 ⊕ FREE HOUSE ◀ Woodforde's Wherry, Adnams, Guest ales Ö Addlestones. ♀ 16 **Facilities** Non-diners area ♦♦ Children's menu Children's portions Garden ⋤ Beer festival Parking WiFi ▄▄

HINGHAM
Map 13 TG00

The White Hart Hotel

tel: 01953 850214 **3 Market Place NR9 4AF**
email: whitehart@flyingkiwiinns.co.uk
dir: *In market square on B1108*

A gastro-pub drawing on the larder of East Anglia

A considered mix of chic contemporary design and a nod to the rustic, coaching origins of this upmarket village inn characterises this imposing Georgian building at the heart of pretty Hingham. Quirky additions - note the antler chandelier - add a colourful twist to this, one of celebrity chef Chris Coubrough's stable of inns. Chris's wife Jo adds further to this eclectic mix with tasty beers from her microbrewery near Fakenham. The menu is equally diverse; start with Asian-style duck rillette and follow with grilled fish of the day with étuvée of leeks and courgettes.

Open all day all wk **Food** Lunch all wk 12-2.30 Dinner all wk 6.30-9.30 Av main course £12 Set menu available Restaurant menu available ⊕ FREE HOUSE ◀ Adnams Southwold Bitter, Jo C's Norfolk Kiwi, Guest ale Ö Aspall. ♀ **Facilities** ♣ (Bar) ♦♦ Children's menu Children's portions Outside area ⋤ WiFi

HOLT
Map 13 TG03

The Pigs
PICK OF THE PUBS

See Pick of the Pubs on page 347

HUNSTANTON
Map 12 TF64

The Ancient Mariner Inn ★★★★ HL

tel: 01485 536390 **Golf Course Rd, Old Hunstanton PE36 6JJ**
email: conference@lestrangearms.co.uk **web:** www.traditionalinns.co.uk
dir: *Exit A149, 1m N of Hunstanton. Turn left at sharp right bend by pitch & putt course*

Coastal setting with great views and local walks

Summer evenings can be spectacular here; when the sun sets across the sands of The Wash, the light matches the straws and golds of the real ales enjoyed by drinkers in the peaceful gardens, up to seven beers may be on tap. Equally enticing is the menu of modern pub classics such as 10oz gammon steak or chilli con carne;

daily fish specials boost the choice. The appealing flint and brick inn is creatively incorporated into the stable block of a Victorian hotel, the stylish rooms of which are popular with visitors to the beautiful Norfolk Coast Area of Outstanding Natural Beauty.

Open all day all wk **Food** Lunch all wk 12-9 Dinner all wk 12-9 ⊕ FREE HOUSE ◀ Adnams, Theakston, Wychwood, Shepherd Neame, Sharp's, Woodforde's Ö Symonds. ♀ 10 **Facilities** Non-diners area ♣ (Bar Garden) ♦♦ Children's menu Children's portions Play area Family room Garden ⋤ Beer festival Parking WiFi ▄▄ (notice required) **Rooms** 43

The King William IV Country Inn & Restaurant

tel: 01485 571765 **Heacham Rd, Sedgeford PE36 5LU**
email: info@thekingwilliamsedgeford.co.uk
dir: *A149 to Hunstanton, right at Norfolk Lavender in Heacham onto B1454, signed Docking. 2m to Sedgeford*

Food and drink to please all tastes

Tucked away in the village of Sedgeford, this free house has been an inn for over 175 years. It's conveniently close to the north Norfolk coastline and the Peddars Way. Made cosy by winter log fires, it has four dining areas, plus a covered alfresco terrace where you may enjoy a local crab salad in the summer months. You'll find five real ales on tap, and extensive menus (including gluten free and vegetarian) to please everyone: spicy chicken strips or sautéed lamb's kidneys for starters, and parmesan-crusted sea bass in pesto sauce, and stuffed guinea fowl breast to follow. Events include quiz Mondays, curry Tuesdays and piano Fridays.

Open all day 11-11 (Sun 12-10.30) Closed Mon L (ex BHs) **Food** Lunch Tue-Sat 12-2, Sun 12-2.30 Dinner all wk 6.30-9 Av main course £12 Set menu available ⊕ FREE HOUSE ◀ Woodforde's Wherry, Adnams Southwold Bitter, Greene King Abbot Ale, Morland Old Speckled Hen, Guest ale Ö Aspall Harry Sparrow. ♀ 9 **Facilities** Non-diners area ♣ (Bar Garden) ♦♦ Children's menu Children's portions Family room Garden ⋤ Parking WiFi ▄▄ (notice required)

HUNWORTH
Map 13 TG03

The Hunny Bell
PICK OF THE PUBS

tel: 01263 712300 **The Green NR24 2AA**
email: hunnybell@animalinns.co.uk
dir: *From Holt take B1110. 1st right to Hunworth*

Tranquil and charming old pub

A lovely location just a handful of miles from the fabulous heritage coastline at Blakeney. This 18th-century gem of a village pub is far enough from the popular marshland nature reserves and beaches to offer a blissful dose of serenity. In-the-know visitors can retreat to the cosy snug and the rustic-chic beamed main bar, which successfully blend historic charm with a contemporary feel. On sublime summer days the colourful garden or the terrace overlooking the strung-out village green are ideal spots in which to enjoy Adnams beers and contemplate meals which make the most of north Norfolk's seafood and agricultural largesse. A tempting starter might bring pan-seared pigeon breast with popcorn, game chips, charred sweetcorn and corn purée to the table. Mains, augmented by an ever-changing specials board, come in with cod fillet and potato cake; or 6-hour braised venison shoulder with horseradish mash and red cabbage, whilst local Aberdeen Angus beef features severally. Each August a popular beer festival is held here.

Open all wk 12-3 6-11 **Food** Lunch all wk 12-2.30 Dinner all wk 6-9 Av main course £12.95 Set menu available ⊕ FREE HOUSE/ANIMAL INNS ◀ Woodforde's Wherry, Adnams, Greene King, Marston's Pedigree Ö Aspall. ♀ 10 **Facilities** Non-diners area ♣ (Bar Garden) ♦♦ Children's menu Children's portions Garden ⋤ Beer festival Parking ▄▄ (notice required)

INGHAM
Map 13 TG32

The Ingham Swan ★★★★ RR 🏵🏵 | PICK OF THE PUBS

tel: 01692 581099 **Swan Corner, Sea Palling Rd NR12 9AB**
email: info@theinghamswan.co.uk **web:** www.theinghamswan.co.uk
dir: *From A149 through Stalham to Ingham*

Picture-postcard dining inn

This ancient, flint-built pub and the majestic church it adjoins are all that survive of the once-flourishing Ingham Priory. Lanes from the tiny village of Ingham meander to the nearby Norfolk Coast Area of Outstanding Natural Beauty and a string of broadland nature reserves renowned for rare birds. The Swan itself, slumbering beneath trim thatch, was carefully transformed into a destination dining pub and restaurant a few years back whilst retaining the aura of a pub. Drinkers are always welcome at the bar for real ales from the local Grain Brewery. Chef-patron Daniel Smith trained at Le Gavroche in London and Blakeney's Morston Hall, and he sticks to his Norfolk roots with a creative, modern menu packed with seasonal local produce. A lazy lunch could start with peppered venison carpaccio with chicken liver mousse and pulled pork cake, followed by pan-fried sea bass with buttered spinach, saffron fennel, crispy crab cakes and brown shrimps. Matching wines are suggested on the menu.

Open all wk 11-3 6-11 Closed 25-26 Dec **Food** Lunch Mon-Sat 12-2, Sun 12-3 Dinner all wk 6-9 ⊕ FREE HOUSE 🍺 Woodforde's Wherry, Nelson's Revenge, Grain Oak & Redwood ♂ Aspall. ☗ 10 **Facilities** Non-diners area ⢷ Children's portions Garden ⊟ Parking 🚌 (notice required) **Rooms** 4

ITTERINGHAM
Map 13 TG13

The Walpole Arms

tel: 01263 587258 **NR11 7AR**
email: info@thewalpolearms.co.uk **web:** www.thewalpolearms.co.uk
dir: *From Aylsham towards Blickling. After Blickling Hall take 1st right to Itteringham*

Dining pub with inventive food

Owned by a local farming family, this renowned rural dining venue is tucked away down narrow lanes on the edge of sleepy Itteringham, close to the National Trust's Blickling Hall. Its oak-beamed bar offers local Woodforde's and Adnams ales on tap, while menus champion top-notch meats and produce from the farm and local artisan producers. Typical dishes include fried duck egg with black pudding and chorizo, spinach and toast; free-range chicken and ham hock pie with mash and greens; and cauliflower and lentil curry with pilau rice and a carrot and onion bhaji.

Open all wk 12-3 6-11 (Sat 12-11 Sun 12-5) **Food** Lunch Mon-Sat 12-2.30, Sun 12-3 Dinner Mon-Sat 6.30-9.15 ⊕ FREE HOUSE 🍺 Adnams Broadside & Southwold Bitter, Woodforde's Wherry, Guest ales ♂ Aspall. ☗ 20 **Facilities** Non-diners area ⢷ (Bar Garden) ⢷ Children's menu Children's portions Garden ⊟ Parking WiFi 🚌 (notice required)

KING'S LYNN
Map 12 TF62

The Stuart House Hotel, Bar & Restaurant ★★★ HL

tel: 01553 772169 **35 Goodwins Rd PE30 5QX**
email: reception@stuarthousehotel.co.uk **web:** www.stuarthousehotel.co.uk
dir: *Follow signs to town centre, pass under Southgate Arch, immediate right, in 100yds turn right*

Small independent hotel and free house

In a central, but nevertheless quiet location, this hotel and bar in attractive grounds is one of the town's favoured eating and drinking places. Top-notch East Anglian ales and traditional snacks are served in the bar, and there's a separate restaurant menu typically featuring Norfolk sausages with creamy mash and red onion gravy; pan-fried fillet of sea bass with herbed sauté potatoes; sweet chilli beef with noodles; and vegetable Kiev with garlic butter sauce. Daily specials, like everything else, are home cooked from fresh local produce. Events include regular live music, murder mystery dinners and a July beer festival.

Open all wk 5-11 **Food** Dinner all wk 6-9.30 ⊕ FREE HOUSE 🍺 Oakham JHB, Timothy Taylor Landlord, Adnams, Woodforde's ♂ Aspall. **Facilities** Non-diners area ⢷ (Bar Garden) Children's portions Play area Garden Beer festival Parking WiFi 🚌 (notice required) **Rooms** 18

LARLING
Map 13 TL98

Angel Inn | PICK OF THE PUBS

tel: 01953 717963 **NR16 2QU**
email: info@angel-larling.co.uk
dir: *5m from Attleborough, 8m from Thetford. 1m from station*

Family-run inn with a range of ales and enjoyable food

On the edge of Breckland and Thetford Forest Park, this 17th-century former coaching inn has been run for more than 80 years by three generations of the Stammers family and has a good local feel and warm welcome. In the beamed public bar, a jukebox, dartboard and fruit machine add to the traditional feel, while the oak-panelled lounge bar has dining tables with cushioned wheel-back chairs, a wood burner and a collection of water jugs. Five ales, including Crouch Vale Brewers Gold, are served, as well as more than a hundred whiskies. Menus make good use of local ingredients, with lighter snacks including sandwiches, jacket potatoes, ploughman's, burgers and salads. Typically among the mains are home-made steak and kidney pie; sweet and sour pork with rice; smoked haddock Mornay; and vegetarian broccoli and cream cheese bake. Look out for the August festival, with over 100 real ales and ciders.

Open all day all wk 10am-mdnt **Food** Lunch Sun-Thu 12-9.30, Fri-Sat 12-10 Dinner Sun-Thu 12-9.30, Fri-Sat 12-10 Av main course £10.95 ⊕ FREE HOUSE 🍺 Adnams Southwold Bitter, Crouch Vale Brewers Gold, Timothy Taylor Landlord, Mauldons, Hop Back ♂ Aspall. ☗ 10 **Facilities** Non-diners area ⢷ Children's menu Children's portions Play area Garden ⊟ Beer festival Parking WiFi 🚌

Who are the AA's award-winning pubs? For details see pages 10 &11

LETHERINGSETT
Map 13 TG03

The Kings Head
PICK OF THE PUBS

tel: 01263 712691 **Holt Rd NR25 7AR**
email: info@kingsheadnorfolk.co.uk
dir: *On A148, 1m from Holt. Pub on corner*

Vintage-chic gastro-pub recommended for its outdoor areas

From the outside this looks to be a grand, manor-like building, but step through the door to find elegant, rustic-chic decor throughout the rambling dining areas that radiate from the central bar, with warm heritage hues, rugs on terracotta tiles, feature bookcases, an eclectic mix of old dining tables, and squashy sofas and leather chairs fronting blazing winter log fires. The atmosphere is informal, the beer on tap is Woodforde's Wherry, and the modern British food is prepared from top-notch ingredients supplied by local farmers, fisherman and artisan producers. This translates to pub favourites such as Allard's red onion and black pepper sausages; an 8oz beefburger with hand-cut chips and tomato relish; and an 8oz rib-eye steak, slow roast tomatoes, mushrooms, béarnaise sauce and, of course, those hand-cut chips. This gastro-pub has superb alfresco areas including an excellent children's garden and a gravelled front terrace with benches and brollies. Change of hands.

Open all day all wk 11-11 **Food** Lunch all wk 12-2.30, BHs all day Dinner Mon-Sat 6.30-9.30, Sun 6.30-8, BHs all day ⊕ FREE HOUSE ◀ Adnams, Norfolk Moon Gazer, Woodforde's Wherry, Guest ales Ö Aspall. ▼ 14 **Facilities** Non-diners area ✿ (Bar Restaurant Garden) ♦ Children's menu Children's portions Play area Garden ⊟ Parking WiFi ◰

MARSHAM
Map 13 TG12

The Plough Inn
PICK OF THE PUBS

tel: 01263 735000 **Norwich Rd NR10 5PS**
email: enquires@ploughinnmarsham.co.uk
dir: *On A140, 10m N of Norwich, 1m S of Aylsham*

Countryside inn specialising in gluten- and wheat-free dishes

Whether you're touring the Norfolk Broads or on your way to Norwich Airport six miles away, the welcome at this 18th-century country hostelry will be warm, and experienced staff will ensure you enjoy your visit. Greene King IPA and Adnams are the ales on offer, together with a good range of wines. The restaurant uses local and seasonal produce if possible; the varied menus of modern British favourites are prepared in house, and wheat- and gluten-free meals are a speciality. The range of lunchtime sandwiches, jacket potatoes and omelettes offer fillings to suit every palate. Tasty starters are home-made focaccia with olives, and chicken liver pâté. Main courses range from sirloin steak Stroganoff to fillet of salmon with a leek and potato cake, vegetables and a white wine sauce. Children are well catered for with their own menu. The carvery is popular on Sundays.

Open all wk 12-11 **Food** Lunch all wk 12-2.30 Dinner all wk 6-9 Set menu available ⊕ FREE HOUSE ◀ Greene King IPA, Adnams, John Smith's Ö Aspall. ▼ 10 **Facilities** Non-diners area ♦ Children's menu Children's portions Garden ⊟ Parking WiFi ◰ (notice required)

MUNDFORD
Map 13 TL89

Crown Hotel

tel: 01842 878233 **Crown Rd IP26 5HQ**
email: info@the-crown-hotel.co.uk **web:** www.the-crown-hotel.co.uk
dir: *A11 to Barton Mills onto A1065 through Brandon to Mundford*

Formerly a hunting lodge, now a great pub with two restaurants

Originally a hunting lodge, this historic hillside inn on the edge of Thetford Forest dates back to 1652. Traditional, home-cooked food is served in the bars and two restaurants; perhaps roasted rump of lamb on minted leeks with port and redcurrant gravy or seafood penne made with prawns, scallops, crayfish, mussels, cockles and smoked salmon in garlic and herb cream. In addition to the real ales and wines, there is a choice of over 50 malt whiskies. Being on a hill, the garden is on the first floor.

Open all day all wk 10.30am-mdnt **Food** Lunch all wk 12-3 Dinner all wk 6.30-10 ⊕ FREE HOUSE ◀ Courage Directors, Greene King Ruddles County, Hardys & Hansons Olde Trip, Woodforde's Wherry, Guest ales. ▼ 9 **Facilities** Non-diners area ✿ (Bar Garden) ♦ Children's portions Garden ⊟ Parking WiFi ◰

NORWICH
Map 13 TG20

Adam & Eve

tel: 01603 667423 **Bishopsgate NR3 1RZ**
email: theadamandeve@hotmail.com
dir: *Behind Anglican Cathedral, adjacent to Law Courts*

Historic city-centre bolt hole

This enchanting, brick-and-flint built inn sits beneath trees at the fringe of the grounds of Norwich's Anglican Cathedral, the builders of which lodged at the pub, licensed since 1249. It's a refreshing step back in time, free of electronic diversions whilst rich with beers from Woodforde's and Wolf breweries; spirits here include ghosts of lingering, long-gone former locals. Who can blame them when the food is as rewarding as the ales; visitors resting on a tour of Norwich's finest can expect no-nonsense quality pub classics like filled large Yorkshire pudding, trawlerman's pie, home-made curry or chilli. The hanging basket displays are stunning.

Open all day all wk 11-11 (Sun 12-10.30) Closed 25-26 Dec, 1 Jan **Food** Lunch Mon-Sat 12-7, Sun 12-5 Av main course £8.95 ⊕ ENTERPRISE INNS ◀ Adnams Southwold Bitter, Theakston Old Peculier, Wolf Straw Dog, Woodforde's Sundew Ö Aspall. ▼ 11 **Facilities** Outside area ⊟ Parking WiFi ◰

The Mad Moose Arms
PICK OF THE PUBS

tel: 01603 627687 **2 Warwick St NR2 3LD**
email: madmoose@animalinns.co.uk
dir: *1m from A11*

Ambitious cooking in a gastro-pub popular with the locals

Dating back to the late 1800s, this bustling neighbourhood pub offers the best of both worlds, with a welcoming ground-floor bar and an elegant upstairs dining room. Regulars know they can expect well-kept real ales and a seasonal menu served in both the bar and the fairytale themed upstairs restaurant. Look out for crispy chilli chicken with sesame stir-fried noodles; chicken and bacon burger; fish and chips; and a selection of wraps and paninis. There is a stylish outdoor patio for alfresco dining and beer festivals in May and October.

Open all day all wk 12-12 **Food** Lunch all wk 12-5 Dinner all wk 5-9 Av main course £10 ⊕ FREE HOUSE/ANIMAL INNS ◀ Banks's Bitter & Sunbeam, Ringwood Boondoggle Ö Aspall. ₹ 10 **Facilities** Non-diners area ❤ (Bar Garden) ▪️ Children's portions Garden ⋒ Beer festival WiFi ⇔ (notice required)

NEW The Reindeer Pub & Kitchen

tel: 01603 612995 **10 Dereham Rd NR2 4AY**
email: enquiries@thereindeerpub.co.uk
dir: *Phone for detailed directions*

Gastro-pub where real ales share star billing with food

Dan and Katie Searle took over here at the end of 2011 and the emphasis is now as much on the food as the beer. Chef Stuart Pegg previously worked in a number of notable restaurants and his seasonal, locally sourced dishes include such temptations as scallops, potato purée and sautéed leeks; black treacle pork belly, leek and mustard mash, spiced red cabbage; and whisky and marmalade bread and butter pudding with vanilla sauce. Wash it all down with one of several real ales from breweries such as Dark Star and Magic Rock. Look out for the summer beer festival.

Open all day Closed Mon **Food** Lunch Tue-Sat 12-3, Sun 12-5 Dinner Tue-Sat 6-10 Av main course £10-£15 ⊕ ELGOOD'S & SONS ◀ Elgood's, Dark Star, Thornbridge, Green Jack, Humpty Dumpty, Magic Rock Ö Westons & Bounds, The Orchard Pig. ₹ 12 **Facilities** Non-diners area ▪️ Children's menu Children's portions Garden ⋒ Beer festival Parking WiFi ⇔ (notice required)

Ribs of Beef

tel: 01603 619517 **24 Wensum St NR3 1HY**
email: roger@cawdron.co.uk
dir: *From Tombland (in front of cathedral) turn left at Maids Head Hotel. Pub 200yds on right on bridge*

City centre local with cask ales and river views

Originally an alehouse back in the 18th century, between the 1960s and 1980s, this building was used variously as an antiques shop, electrical store and fashion boutique before Roger and Anthea Cawdron relicensed in the mid 80s. They continue to welcome locals and holidaymakers cruising The Broads. The pub is valued for its comfy leather seats, range of cask ales, excellent wines and traditional English food using locally sourced produce. Breakfast is available until midday, whilst hearty choices like sausage, beans and chips; salmon and dill fishcakes; and nut and vegetable roast rub shoulders with sandwiches, burgers and jacket potatoes on the varied main menu. Sit outside on the jetty during the warmer months with its fabulous river views.

Open all day all wk 11-11 (Fri-Sat 11am-1am) **Food** Lunch Mon-Fri 12-2.30, Sat-Sun 12-5 Av main course £7.95 ⊕ FREE HOUSE ◀ Woodforde's Wherry, Adnams Southwold Bitter, Elgood's Black Dog, Oakham JHB, Fuller's London Pride Ö Kingfisher Norfolk Cider. ₹ 9 **Facilities** Non-diners area ▪️ Children's menu Children's portions Family room Garden Outside area ⋒ WiFi ⇔ (notice required)

SALTHOUSE
Map 13 TG04

The Salthouse Dun Cow

tel: 01263 740467 **Coast Rd NR25 7XA**
email: salthouseduncow@gmail.com
dir: *On A149 (coast road). 3m E of Blakeney, 6m W of Sheringham*

An ideal retreat overlooking salt marsh scenery

In a quiet coastal village within an Area of Outstanding Natural Beauty, this traditional brick and flint pub probably originated as a cattle barn built around 1650. Today it overlooks some of Britain's finest salt marshes, so expect to share it, particularly the front garden, with birdwatchers and walkers. The interior decor seems to reflect the surrounding farmland and seascapes with brick walls, bare floorboards and a wood-burning stove. Local suppliers provide high quality produce for select menus prepared from scratch, especially fresh shellfish and game from local shoots. Samphire, asparagus and soft fruit are all sourced within five miles.

Open all day all wk **Food** Lunch all wk 12-9 Dinner all wk 12-9 Av main course £13 ⊕ PUNCH TAVERNS ◀ Woodforde's Wherry, Adnams, Greene King Abbot Ale, Guest ales Ö Aspall. ₹ 19 **Facilities** Non-diners area ❤ (Bar Restaurant Garden) ▪️ Children's menu Children's portions Garden ⋒ Parking WiFi ⇔ (notice required)

SHERINGHAM
Map 13 TG14

NEW The Two Lifeboats

tel: 01263 823144 **2 High St NR26 8JR**
email: bridget@thetwolifeboats.co.uk
dir: *In town centre*

Traditional pub a few yards from the beach

Once the local Fisherman's Mission building and a coffee shop, this seafront pub was named in honour of the two lifeboats that rescued a crew of eight from a Norwegian brig in the late 19th century. Newly refurbished, this is a traditional pub where you can either quaff pints of Adnams Broadside alongside the locals or grab a table to enjoy home-cooked dishes such as creamy smoked salmon and dill linguine; lamb's liver and bacon with mustard mash; or roasted butternut squash and red pepper risotto.

Open all day all wk **Food** Lunch all wk 12-3, summer all day Dinner all wk 6-9, summer all day ⊕ PUNCH TAVERNS ◀ Adnams Broadside & Ghost Ship, Woodforde's Wherry, Sharp's Doom Bar Ö Aspall. ₹ **Facilities** Non-diners area ❤ (Bar Outside area) ▪️ Children's menu Children's portions Outside area ⋒ WiFi ⇔ (notice required)

SNETTISHAM
Map 12 TF63

The Rose & Crown ★★★★ INN ⊛
PICK OF THE PUBS

tel: 01485 541382 **Old Church Rd PE31 7LX**
email: info@roseandcrownsnettisham.co.uk **web:** www.roseandcrownsnettisham.co.uk
dir: *10m N from King's Lynn on A149 signed Hunstanton. At Snettisham rdbt take B1440 to Snettisham. Left into Old Church Rd, inn on left*

Roses round the door, fresh seafood and beef from the salt marshes

Anthony and Jeannette Goodrich's splendid 14th-century inn was originally built as accommodation for craftsmen working on the beautiful church up the road. It offers everything you'd expect from a Norfolk village inn – even the pretty walled garden was once the hamlet's bowling green. Within the rose-festooned façade lie twisting passages and hidden corners. Three charming bars are replete with heavy oak beams, uneven red-tiled floors, inglenook fireplaces, tip-top Adnams ale on tap, and an informal atmosphere. Locally supplied produce includes beef from cattle that graze the nearby salt marshes; fishermen, still in waders, deliver Brancaster mussels; seasonal strawberries and asparagus are abundant. The no-nonsense carte of good English favourites proffers starters such as devilled lamb's kidneys on

continued

SNETTISHAM *continued*

toasted sourdough; main courses may feature local mallard à l'orange with goose-fat fondant potatoes; and, if you cannot manage a full dessert, try a mini-pud of crème brûlée with shortbread biscuit.

Open all day all wk **Food** Lunch Mon-Fri 12-2, Sat-Sun 12-5.30 Dinner Sun-Thu 6.30-9, Fri-Sat 6.30-9.30 Av main course £13 ⊕ FREE HOUSE ◀ Adnams Southwold Bitter & Broadside, Bass, Fuller's London Pride, Greene King IPA. ☂ 12 **Facilities** Non-diners area ❤ (Bar Restaurant Garden) ◗◀ Children's menu Children's portions Play area Family room Garden ☂ Parking WiFi **Rooms** 16

■ STIFFKEY — Map 13 TF94

The Stiffkey Red Lion

tel: 01328 830552 **44 Wells Rd NR23 1AJ**
email: redlion@stiffkey.com
dir: *On A149, 4m E of Wells-next-the-Sea; 4m W of Blakeney*

A perfect spot for walkers and birdwatchers

Dating from the 17th century, this comfortable inn has been a house and even a doctor's surgery in its long life. Located on the north Norfolk coast, it is now a popular bolt-hole for walkers and birdwatchers stepping off the nearby salt marshes. Grab an old pew by one of the four log fires and warm up over a glass of Nelson's Revenge and locally sourced seasonal dishes such as salmon and crab fishcakes with home-made tartare sauce; home honey-roasted ham with egg and chips; and classic spotted dick for dessert. Children's meals are available.

Open all day all wk 12-12 **Food** Lunch Mon-Sat 12-2.30, Sun 12-9 Dinner Mon-Sat 6-9, Sun 12-9 ⊕ FREE HOUSE ◀ The Stiffkey Red Lion Stewkey Brew, Woodforde's Wherry & Nelson's Revenge ♺ Aspall. ☂ 12 **Facilities** Non-diners area ❤ (Bar Restaurant Garden) ◗◀ Children's menu Children's portions Garden ☂ Parking WiFi

---

■ STOKE HOLY CROSS — Map 13 TG20

The Wildebeest — PICK OF THE PUBS

tel: 01508 492497 **82-86 Norwich Rd NR14 8QJ**
email: wildebeest@animalinns.co.uk
dir: *From A47 take A140, left to Dunston. At T-junct turn left, pub on right*

Perfect retreat from city hustle and bustle

Very much a destination dining pub, with tables ready set out to cater for such, there's nevertheless a warm welcome for thirsty travellers. Quenchers include Marston's Burton Bitter and Thatchers cider; the newly refurbished terrace may be the place to sit and sup. Inside it's a slightly quirky scene that greets, with a select collection of African artefacts and some dazzling wall-hung tapestry rugs breaking up the colourwashed walls. Oak beams sew the ceiling, whilst rustic, hand-carved oak tables tempt diners to relax and consider the contemporary menus. The latter promises starters such as oven-baked pigeon breast Wellington with braised Puy lentils and pickled shiitake mushrooms. Advance then to mains typified by pistachio stuffed pork tenderloin wrapped in Parma ham with Parmentier potatoes, apricot and thyme purée; or herb potato gnocchi with Jerusalem artichokes, wild mushrooms and roasted butternut squash. Fish dishes depend on the daily-changing availability of the freshest catch.

Open all wk all day (Etr-Sep) phone for winter opening **Food** Lunch all wk 12-2.30 Dinner all wk 6-9 ⊕ FREE HOUSE ◀ Adnams, Marston's Burton Bitter ♺ Thatchers Gold. ☂ 10 **Facilities** Non-diners area ◗◀ Children's menu Children's portions Garden ☂ Parking

---

■ STOW BARDOLPH — Map 12 TF60

The Hare Arms — PICK OF THE PUBS

tel: 01366 382229 **PE34 3HT**
email: trishmc@harearms222.wanadoo.co.uk
dir: *From King's Lynn take A10 to Downham Market. After 9m village signed on left*

Handsome country pub with a good vegetarian selection

Expect to see peacocks in the garden of this ivy-clad pub named after the Hare family, who have resided at Stow Hall since 1553. Trish and David McManus have run the pub for the past four decades and they ensure that no music drowns out the conversations in the L-shaped bar and adjoining conservatory, which are both full of fascinating bygones the landlords have collected along the way. A seasonally changing menu is supplemented by daily specials of, say, duck breast with noodles, chilli, spring onion, garlic and soy sauce. Starters could be spicy Thai fishcakes; classic 70s-style prawn cocktail or vegetable spring rolls with hoi sin dip. Sample main courses include chicken breast with creamy mushroom and bacon sauce or pork steak with apricot, pistachio and tarragon breadcrumb topping. There is a separate vegetarian menu with a good choice of dishes, from nut cutlets to Moroccan vegetable tagine.

Open all wk 11-2.30 6-11 (Sat & BH Mon 11-11 Sun 12-10.30) Closed 25-26 Dec **Food** Lunch Mon-Fri 12-2, Sat-Sun & BH Mon 12-10 Dinner Mon-Fri 6.30-10, Sat-Sun & BH Mon 12-10 Av main course £11 ⊕ GREENE KING ◀ Abbot Ale & IPA, Morland Old Speckled Hen, Guest ales ♺ Aspall. ☂ 9 **Facilities** Non-diners area ◗◀ Children's menu Children's portions Family room Garden ☂ Parking WiFi ➡ (notice required)

■ THOMPSON — Map 13 TL99

Chequers Inn — PICK OF THE PUBS

See Pick of the Pubs on opposite page

■ THORNHAM — Map 12 TF74

Marco Pierre White The Lifeboat Inn — PICK OF THE PUBS

tel: 01485 512236 **Ship Ln PE36 6LT**
email: reception@lifeboatinn.co.uk
dir: *A149 from Hunstanton for approx 4m. 1st left after Thornham sign*

Different dining areas and Marco inspired dishes

This rambling, 16th-century smugglers' inn, situated on the edge of a vast expanse of salt marsh, is a short stroll from sweeping beaches, renowned bird reserves and bracing coastal path walks. The ramble of old rooms retain their original character, boasting low-beamed ceilings, rug-strewn tiled floors, low doors, half-panelled walls, five log-burning fires, and a rustic array of furniture, from carved oak tables to antique settles and pews. Antique oil lamps suspended from the ceiling and a wealth of nautical bric-à-brac enhance the charm, while the adjoining conservatory is renowned for its ancient vine and there's an adjacent walled patio garden. Food includes starters like corned beef hash with poached duck egg and sauce béarnaise, salt and pepper calamari, or potted shrimps on toast; mains such as rib-eye steak and all the trimmings, hickory pork ribs, or the hot and cold Lifeboat fish platter. A selection of sandwiches is also available.

Open all day all wk **Food** Lunch all wk 12-2.30, 3-5.30 Dinner all wk 6-9.30 ⊕ VICTORY INNS ◀ Greene King Abbot Ale & IPA, Woodforde's Wherry, Adnams, JW Lees The Governor, Guest ales ♺ Aspall, Westons Stowford Press, Governor. ☂ 10 **Facilities** Non-diners area ❤ (Bar Garden) ◗◀ Children's menu Children's portions Play area Garden ☂ Parking WiFi ➡ (notice required)

The Orange Tree — PICK OF THE PUBS

See Pick of the Pubs on page 354

PICK OF THE PUBS

Chequers Inn

THOMPSON Map 13 TL99

tel: 01953 483360 **Griston Rd IP24 1PX**
email: richard@thompsonchequers.co.uk
web: www.thompsonchequers.co.uk
dir: *Exit A1075 between Watton &*
Thetford

Breckland pub well off the beaten track

If you can't place Breckland, it's that region of gorse-covered sandy heath straddling south Norfolk and north Suffolk. Within its boundaries you'll find this splendid, long and low, thatched 17th-century inn, and worth finding it is for its peaceful location and unspoilt charm. In the 18th century manorial courts were held here, dealing with rents, letting of land, and petty crime. It's more fun here today. Beneath its steeply-raked thatch lies a series of low-ceilinged, interconnecting rooms served by a long bar at which the principal real ales are Adnams Southwold Bitter, Greene King IPA and Wolf Ale. The overall impression of the interior is of skew-whiff wall timbers, squat doorways, open log fires, rustic old furniture and farming implements. Although not long, the main menu more than adequately covers most bases, with starters of pan-fried mushrooms in Stilton and cream sauce; local asparagus with crispy pancetta and hollandaise sauce; and Cranworth smoked salmon with dill and lemon

mayonnaise. Its seven or eight main dishes may well include seafood tagliatelle with tomato and herb sauce; Chinese-spiced roast belly of pork with stir-fried vegetables and noodles; and roast vegetable and Portobello mushroom puff pastry pie. To add to one's choice, there are specials - typically breast of chicken stuffed with smoked salmon, and steak and kidney pudding. Finally, the desserts, perhaps home-made apple crumble; treacle and almond tart; or chocolate profiteroles. You'll find picnic tables in the large rear garden, where dogs are welcome. The inn is an ideal base for walking the Peddars Way and the Great Eastern Pingo Trail, which follows a string of lakelets (the pingos) left behind after the Ice Age.

Open all wk 11.30-3 6.30-11
Food Lunch all wk 12-2 Dinner all wk 6.30-9 ⊕ FREE HOUSE ◀ Adnams Southwold Bitter, Wolf Ale, Greene King IPA ♂ Thatchers, Aspall. ♟ 8
Facilities Non-diners area ♥ (Bar Garden) ♦♦ Children's menu Children's portions Garden ☴ Beer festival Parking WiFi ▭ (notice required)

PICK OF THE PUBS

The Orange Tree

THORNHAM   Map 12 TF74

tel: 01485 512213
High St PE36 6LY
email: email@theorangetreethornham.co.uk
web: www.theorangetreethornham.co.uk
dir: *Phone for detailed directions*

Contemporary dining pub in a coastal village

Standing in the centre of the village opposite the church, this family-run pub makes a useful stop for walkers on the ancient Peddars Way. Formerly a smugglers' haunt, the 400-year-old whitewashed inn has evolved over the years into the stylish country pub it is today. Develop an appetite with a stroll to the local staithe, where working fishing boats still come and go through the creeks of Brancaster Bay, before returning for meal and a pint of East Anglian-brewed ale. Chef Philip Milner makes the most of freshly landed local seafood, with innovative dishes like pan-fried lemon sole with a lemon, fennel and caper salad, anchovy and roasted red pepper aïoli. But it's not just the seafood that justifies his claim that the restaurant is the jewel in The Orange Tree's crown; the pub has a long-established relationship with local suppliers, and most of the meat is sourced from the Sandringham Estate. Typically found on the restaurant menu are Capricorn goats' cheese and red pepper crème caramel; and rump of salt

marsh lamb, aubergine kofta, spiced vegetable tagine, rose water Israeli couscous. Meanwhile, dishes on the bar classics menu could include Moroccan chickpea, preserved lemon and feta burger with a bucket of chips; or the OT balti with a choice of two heat and spice levels. Look to the board for the daily sandwich selection. Leave space to sample the appetising selection of desserts, the delightfully themed 'Fairground': bubblegum pannacotta, baby toffee apples, candyfloss, butterscotch popcorn and chocolate covered honeycomb. Traditionalists might opt for lemon cheesecake or a home-made ice cream or sorbet. Dogs get their own beer and menu, while children will love the climbing frame in the pub's garden.

Open all day all wk **Food** Lunch all wk 12-9.30 Dinner all wk 12-9.30 Av main course £12 ⊕ PUNCH TAVERNS 🛢 Woodforde's Wherry, Adnams Southwold Bitter, Crouch Vale Brewers Gold Ŏ Aspall. ₹ 29 **Facilities** Non-diners area 🐾 (Bar Garden) ⏸ Children's menu Children's portions Play area Garden ⊼ Parking WiFi 🚐

TITCHWELL
Map 13 TF74

Titchwell Manor Hotel ★★★ HL ◉◉◉ PICK OF THE PUBS

tel: 01485 210221 **PE31 8BB**
email: margaret@titchwellmanor.com **web:** www.titchwellmanor.com
dir: A149 between Brancaster & Thornham

Sublime sea views and extraordinary cuisine

The north Norfolk coast fragments into a series of sandbank islands and marshes creating a memorable landscape, home for 200 bird species. Ramblers and twitchers work up healthy appetites here; which may be sated at the comfy mix of dining opportunities at Titchwell Manor. Once a marshland farmhouse, over 25 years Margaret and Ian Snaith have tastefully modernised it, while their son Eric and his team are responsible for the three AA-Rosette cuisine in the elegant Conservatory overlooking the walled garden, the Eating Rooms and the bar; in summer the sea-view terrace is popular. The modern European menus feature starters like crispy ham hock with piccalilli and crackling; and buttermilk quail, sorrel mayonnaise. Time then for the mains of 'Mac and Cheese' – gruyère, mushrooms, vegetarian black pudding; or beef dripping fish and chips, minted mushy pies. From the barbeque options perhaps choose spicy Kansas City pork ribs with miso coleslaw; or a 40-day matured sirloin steak. Puddings take in chocolate sundae. Some of the luxurious suites have sea views.

Open all day all wk **Food** Lunch all wk 12-5.30 Dinner all wk 6-9.30 ⊕ FREE HOUSE ◀ Abbot Ale, Woodforde's Wherry ♂ Aspall. ♟ 17 **Facilities** Non-diners area ♣ (Bar Garden) ♦ Children's menu Children's portions Garden ⤢ Parking WiFi ▄▄ (notice required) **Rooms** 27

WARHAM ALL SAINTS
Map 13 TF94

Three Horseshoes
PICK OF THE PUBS

tel: 01328 710547 **NR23 1NL**
email: mail@warhamhorseshoes.co.uk
dir: From Wells A149 to Cromer, then right onto B1105 to Warham

Memorable heritage pub with great pies and ales

In a row of brick-and-flint stands this timeless village pub. Its rambling, quarry-tile floored, period-piece rooms recall long-gone taverns; the bar is lit by gas mantles and beers from the likes of Wolf and Woodforde breweries are often gravity-served from barrels stillaged behind the servery. Vintage posters, clay pipes, photographs and memorabilia adorn the walls, whilst a curious green and red dial in the ceiling turns out to be a rare example of Norfolk Twister, an ancient drinking game. As befits such a rural pub, robust artisan food is the order of the day and generous home-made pies the undoubted stalwarts of the chalkboard menu. Mushroom and nut, or pork and apricot varieties may stand out, or perhaps a bowl of game and vegetable broth will disperse a winter chill. As the coast is only a short hop away, fish dishes are well represented. Alfresco enjoyment can be taken in a rose-bedecked courtyard or grassy garden, whilst dog-lovers can treat their pooch to the doggy-biscuit menu.

Open all wk 12-2.30 6-11 **Food** Lunch all wk 12-2 Dinner all wk 6-8 Av main course £9.80 ⊕ FREE HOUSE ◀ Woodforde's Wherry, Nelson's Revenge, Wolf Ale, Moon Gazer ♂ Whin Hill. **Facilities** Non-diners area ♣ (Bar Garden) ♦ Children's portions Family room Garden ⤢ Parking ▄▄ (notice required)

WELLS-NEXT-THE-SEA
Map 13 TF94

The Crown Hotel
PICK OF THE PUBS

tel: 01328 710209 **The Buttlands NR23 1EX**
email: reception@crownhotelnorfolk.co.uk
dir: 10m from Fakenham on B1105

Boutique inn on the coast

This 17th-century former coaching inn overlooks the tree-lined green known as The Buttlands. The Crown's striking contemporary decor blends effortlessly with its old-world charm and beneath the bar's ancient beams, East Anglian ales and Aspall real cider are on tap. Whether you eat in the bar, more formally in the restaurant, in the cheerful Orangery, or outside with its great views, the menus offer traditional favourites, the best of modern British cuisine and internationally influenced dishes. Perhaps opt for baked feta polenta with a ratatouille sauce; or roast salmon fillet on a prawn, chickpea and broccoli broth from the main menu. The Crown Classics set menu changes every two weeks and could feature Holkham venison casserole or honey and mustard marinated goats' cheese salad. Desserts might include honey and thyme brûlée. A good few wines are available by the glass and there are a few half-bottles. Tuesday evening is seafood night.

Open all day all wk **Food** Lunch all wk 12-2.30 Dinner all wk 6.30-9.30 ⊕ FREE HOUSE/FLYING KIWI INNS ◀ Adnams Southwold Bitter, Jo C's Norfolk Kiwi, Guest ale ♂ Aspall. ♟ 14 **Facilities** Non-diners area ♣ (Bar Garden) ♦ Children's menu Children's portions Garden ⤢ Parking WiFi

WINTERTON-ON-SEA
Map 13 TG41

Fishermans Return

tel: 01493 393305 **The Lane NR29 4BN**
email: enquiries@fishermansreturn.com **web:** www.fishermansreturn.com
dir: 8m N of Great Yarmouth on B1159

Just round the corner from sandy beaches

This dog-friendly, 350-year-old brick and flint built free house stands close to long beaches and National Trust land, making it the ideal spot to finish a walk. Guest ales support Woodforde's Norfolk Nog and Wherry behind the bar, whilst the menus range from popular favourites like fish and chips; and chicken, bacon and cheese burger to sirloin steak and three bean chilli. Look out for fish and seafood specials on the daily-changing blackboard, where freshly caught mackerel or sea bass may be on offer. The pub hosts a beer festival on Summer Bank Holiday.

Open all wk 11-2.30 5.30-11 (Sat-Sun 11-11) **Food** Lunch all wk 12-2.30 Dinner all wk 6-9 ⊕ FREE HOUSE ◀ Woodforde's Wherry & Norfolk Nog, Greene King Skippers Tipple & IPA, Guest ales ♂ Westons Stowford Press & Old Rosie Scrumpy, Local ciders. ♟ 9 **Facilities** Non-diners area ♣ (Bar Restaurant Garden) ♦ Children's menu Children's portions Play area Family room Garden Beer festival Cider festival Parking WiFi ▄▄

PICK OF THE PUBS

Wiveton Bell ❀

WIVETON	Map 13 TG04

tel: 01263 740101
Blakeney Rd NR25 7TL
email: wivetonbell@me.com
web: www.wivetonbell.com
dir: *From Blakeney take A149 towards Cley next the Sea. Right to Wiverton*

Tranquil country pub championing local fish and game

Immaculately spruced-up though it is, and while rightly renowned for its cuisine, the Bell remains faithful to its roots as a traditional village pub. This means that, even in full walking gear (dog in tow) you are welcome to drift in for just a pint of Woodforde's Wherry, or Norfolk Moon Gazer, and nobody will suggest you should be better dressed, or have left Rex in his basket. In a village pub so close to the unspoilt salt marshes of the North Norfolk coast - an Area of Outstanding Natural Beauty - and just ten minutes' walk from Blakeney nature reserve, that's a wise approach. Built in the 18th century, it features earthy, heritage-coloured walls, stripped beams, chunky tables and oak-planked floors, with further character imbued by local artworks lining the walls of the bar and conservatory dining room. On a winter's evening head for the tables close to the inglenook fireplace, where, by the light of the masses of candles, your meal might begin with pan-fried mackerel,

cauliflower purée, peppered walnut brittle and caper crisps; or smoked ham hock terrine with soft-boiled, free-range egg and parsley emulsion. For a main course try the 'Wivvy Bell' salt marsh-grazed beefburger, topped with Norfolk Dapple smoked cheese, served with onion rings, hand-cut chips and home-made relish; or roasted local pigeon crown with cherry-braised red cabbage, fondant potato and pea fricassée. Petit pois, baby spinach and Binham Blue cheese risotto is a vegetarian option. On a Sunday there's an excellent choice of roasts, but booking is essential. Two sample desserts to give you a good idea of the Wivvy style are treacle-dipped ginger parkin with vanilla ice cream; and orange and star anise blancmange with candied orange and roast almonds.

Open all day all wk Closed 25 Dec
Food Lunch all wk 12-2.15 Dinner all wk 6-9 ⊕ FREE HOUSE ◧ Woodforde's Wherry, Norfolk Moon Gazer, Yetman's ○ Aspall. ⏺ 14 **Facilities** Non-diners area ᵻ Children's menu Children's portions Garden ⊼ Parking WiFi

WIVETON
Map 13 TG04

Wiveton Bell ⊚
PICK OF THE PUBS

See Pick of the Pubs on opposite page

WOODBASTWICK
Map 13 TG31

The Fur & Feather Inn

tel: 01603 720003 **Slad Ln NR13 6HQ**
dir: *From A1151 (Norwich to Wroxham road), follow brown signs for Woodforde's Brewery. Pub adjacent to brewery*

An idyllic thatched country pub ideal for beer lovers

Eight real ales from Woodforde's Brewery next door are served straight from the cask here, with no jukebox, TV or pool table to disturb the peace. The pub was originally two farm cottages, and now boasts three cosy bar areas and a smart restaurant. Here you can enjoy traditional home-made English fare, with a great selection of pies, burgers and grills: venison and Merlot pie; sirloin steak with trimmings; and steamed steak and kidney pudding. A selection of vegetarian and gluten-free options complete the picture.

Open all day all wk **Food** Lunch 10-9 Dinner 10-9 Av main course £11 Woodforde's Wherry, Bure Gold, Sundew, Norfolk Nog, Nelson's Revenge, Once Bittern, Headcracker, Mardler's Mild. ♥ 12 **Facilities** Non-diners area ♦ Children's menu Garden ⌐ Parking WiFi (notice required)

NORTHAMPTONSHIRE

ASHBY ST LEDGERS
Map 11 SP56

The Olde Coach House Inn ★★★★ INN

tel: 01788 890349 **CV23 8UN**
email: info@oldecoachhouse.co.uk **web:** www.oldecoachhouse.co.uk
dir: *M1 junct 18 follow A361/Daventry signs. Village on left*

Good food in a memorable village setting

This mellow stone inn sits amidst thatched cottages in the lovely estate village here; until a century ago it was a farmhouse. Today it's an engaging mix of contemporary and rustic, with a strong emphasis on comfort; deep leather furnishings tempt you to linger by log fires, wondering at the function of the archaic rural artefacts on display. The courtyard dining area is a popular place to sample the extensive fare which ranges from home-made, stone-fired pizzas and 'design your own' grazing boards to dishes such as Ashby-reared rare breed pork cutlet, grain mustard mash and creamy cider jus. Boutique-style accommodation is available.

Open all day all wk **Food** Lunch Mon-Sat 12-2.30, Sun 12-8 Dinner Mon-Sat 6-9.30, Sun 12-8 Av main course £14 Set menu available Restaurant menu available all wk CHARLES WELLS Bombardier, Young's. ♥ 12 **Facilities** Non-diners area ♥ (Bar Garden Outside area) ♦ Children's menu Children's portions Play area Garden Outside area ⌐ Parking WiFi (notice required) **Rooms** 15

ASHTON
Map 11 SP74

The Old Crown

tel: 01604 862268 **1 Stoke Rd NN7 2JN**
email: bex@theoldcrownashton.co.uk
dir: *M1 junct 15, A508 to Roade. 1m, left to Ashton*

Dining pub with innovative menus

A well-appointed homely village local in the small rural community of Ashton. A pub for over 300 years, its pretty, sheltered gardens are a popular choice for summer dining, or settle in to the beamed bar room and look forward to choosing from the well-thought-out, balanced menus while sipping a pint of well-kept ale. Perhaps

start with deep-fried squid with aïoli, followed by ginger and soy marinated chicken breast with sticky coconut rice; or trio of lamb (cutlet, mini shepherd's pie and slow cooked shoulder); then spiced pecan and chocolate tart. There are regular events held throughout the year.

Open 12-3 6-11 (Sat 12-11.30 Sun 12-10.30) Closed Mon **Food** Lunch Tue-Fri 12-2.30, Sat 12-9.30, Sun 12-4 Dinner Tue-Fri 6-9.30 CHARLES WELLS Eagle IPA, Courage Directors, Young's. ♥ 10 **Facilities** Non-diners area ♥ (Bar Restaurant) ♦ Children's portions Garden Parking WiFi (notice required)

AYNHO
Map 11 SP53

The Great Western Arms

tel: 01869 338288 **Station Rd OX17 3BP**
email: info@great-westernarms.co.uk
dir: *From Aynho take B4031 (Station Road) W towards Deddington. Turn right to pub*

Run by a young and friendly bunch

The Great Western Railway company disappeared in 1948, but its name lives on in this foliage-covered inn between the line it built to Birmingham, and the Oxford Canal. It's a Hook Norton pub, so the brewery's range of ales is well represented; ten wines are sold by the glass, and there's a packed whisky and spirit shelf. Good things on chef-patron René Klein's menus include his creamy chicken curry; venison, pheasant, cranberry and port pie; Cajun-dusted salmon fillet; and leek and cheese sausages. The pretty courtyard and garden has won Hook Norton's top award.

Open all day all wk 11-11 Closed 25 Dec **Food** Lunch Mon-Sat 12-3, Sun 12-9 Dinner Mon-Sat 6-9, Sun 12-9 HOOK NORTON Old Hooky, Guest ales Westons Perry, Old Rosie & Stowford Press. ♥ 10 **Facilities** Non-diners area ♥ (Bar Garden) ♦ Children's menu Children's portions Garden ⌐ Parking WiFi (notice required)

BULWICK
Map 11 SP99

The Queen's Head
PICK OF THE PUBS

tel: 01780 450272 **Main St NN17 3DY**
email: info@thequeensheadbulwick.co.uk
dir: *Just off A43, between Corby & Stamford*

Village free house supporting local breweries

A 17th-century stone-built free house overlooking the village church, parts of The Queen's Head date back to 1400. The pub is a warren of small rooms with exposed wooden beams, four open fireplaces and flagstone floors. Relax by the fire or on the patio with a pint of real ale from the local Oakham or Rockingham breweries. Local shoots supply seasonal game such as teal, woodcock and partridge, and other ingredients often include village-grown fruit and vegetables brought in by customers and friends. Lunchtime brings a good selection of sandwiches, snacks and main dishes. The evening menu might feature local pork sausages with mash and white onion and grainy mustard sauce. The menu is backed by a comprehensive wine list; there's an outdoor oven for outside dining.

Open 12-3 6-11 (Sun 12-7) Closed Mon **Food** Lunch Tue-Sat 12-2, Sun 12-3 Dinner Tue-Sat 6-9 FREE HOUSE Rockingham, Oakham, Digfield Ales, Shepherd Neame Aspall, Hogan's Scrumpy. ♥ 9 **Facilities** Non-diners area ♥ (Bar Outside area) ♦ Children's portions Outside area ⌐ Parking

CRICK

Map 11 SP57

The Red Lion Inn

tel: 01788 822342 **52 Main Rd NN6 7TX**
dir: M1 junct 18, A428, 0.75m, follows signs for Crick from rdbt

Village inn in the same hands for many years

An old gabled, thatched, coaching inn of mellow ironstone standing beside the pretty main street just a stone's throw from Crick's ancient church. Exposed beams, low ceilings and open fires characterise this village free-house, family-run for the past 34 years. Beers from Adnams or Wells example the varied range of real ales available here, with classic pub meals the order of the day.

Open all wk 11-2.30 6.15-11 (Sun 12-3 7-11) **Food** Lunch all wk 12-2 Dinner Mon-Sat 6.30-9 Av main course £5-£8 ⊕ FREE HOUSE ◀ Adnams Southwold Bitter, Wells Bombardier, Morland Old Speckled Hen, Guest ale. **Facilities** Non-diners area ❄ (Bar Restaurant Garden) ♦ Children's menu Children's portions Garden ⊼ Parking WiFi

EAST HADDON

Map 11 SP66

The Red Lion

PICK OF THE PUBS

tel: 01604 770223 **Main St NN6 8BU**
email: nick@redlioneasthaddon.co.uk
dir: Just off A428

Top gastro-pub with its own cookery school

Since taking over, former Gary Rhodes chef Adam Gray and his partner Nick Bonner have put The Red Lion firmly on the map as a top destination gastro-pub. Such is the pub's reputation for culinary excellence that it even runs its own cookery school. Expect a high standard of food at this village pub, whether in snacks such as free-range pork Scotch egg, or crispy onion bhajis to begin; main dishes like confit pork belly with a root vegetable gratin, Stilton mash and gravy; or seared king scallops with crushed peas, crispy bacon and creamy mash; and puddings along the lines of banana fool with toffee sauce. Accompany your meal with one of 14 wines served by the glass or a pint of Courage Directors. The landscaped gardens offer good views over rolling countryside.

Open all day all wk 11-11 **Food** Lunch Mon-Fri 12-2.30, Sat-Sun all day Dinner Mon-Fri 6-9, Sat-Sun all day Av main course £12 ⊕ CHARLES WELLS ◀ Young's, Courage Directors. ♔ 14 **Facilities** Non-diners area ♦ Children's menu Children's portions Garden ⊼ Parking WiFi ▄ (notice required)

FARTHINGHOE

Map 11 SP53

The Fox

tel: 01295 713965 **Baker St NN13 5PH**
email: enquiries@foxatfarthinghoe.co.uk
dir: M40 junct 11, A422, towards Brackley. Approx 5.5m to Farthinghoe

Relaxed and friendly village pub that's close to Silverstone

Only 12 miles from Silverstone, this Charles Wells pub brings its customers fresh, locally sourced food with friendly service and a relaxing village atmosphere. In practice this translates as a varied menu offering pub favourites such as glazed Cotswold ham, sticky BBQ ribs, kedgeree smoked haddock, and chef's fish pie, along with more exotic options such as chicken and chorizo linguine. Sandwiches and wraps are also available, and there is even a take-out menu. Ladies' Night on Wednesdays means three courses and a glass of wine for £16.50. A roast is offered every Sunday lunch.

Open all wk 12-3 6-11 (Fri-Sun 12-11) **Food** Lunch all wk 12-2.30 Dinner all wk 6-9.30 ⊕ CHARLES WELLS ◀ Courage Directors, Young's, Erdinger, Guinness, Guest ale Ò Aspall. ♔ 12 **Facilities** Non-diners area ❄ (Bar Garden) ♦ Children's portions Garden ⊼ Parking WiFi ▄ (notice required)

FARTHINGSTONE

Map 11 SP65

The Kings Arms

PICK OF THE PUBS

tel: 01327 361604 **Main St NN12 8EZ**
email: paul@kingsarms.fsbusiness.co.uk
dir: M1 junct 16, A45 towards Daventry. At Weedon take A5 towards Towcester. Turn right signed Farthingstone

Attractive village pub with wildlife loving garden

Close to the National Trust's Elizabethan mansion at Canon's Ashby, this 300-year-old stone free house is tucked away in perfect walking country. Paul and Denise Egerton grow their own salads and herbs in the pub's quirky garden, which is full of interesting recycled items, decorative trees and shrubs, and secluded corners; it is a haven for wildlife with 200 species of moths, 20 of butterflies, and 50 different types of birds all noted. The terrace is the place to enjoy alfresco drinking on warmer days with red kites and buzzards wheeling overhead; in winter, real fires warm the stone-flagged interior. The Kings Arms is mainly a drinkers' pub, with up to five real ales and Westons Old Rosie cider on tap. But bar lunches, available at weekends, feature quality fine food,s and platters are served on request in the evening. Sample their Loch Fyne fish platter; local game casserole; or Yorkshire pudding filled with steak and kidney; desserts include raspberry meringue; and hot gingerbread with maple syrup.

Open 7-11.30 (Fri 6.30-12 Sat-Sun 12-4 7-11.30) Closed Mon **Food** Lunch Sat-Sun 12-2.30 Dinner last Fri in month Av main course £8.95 ⊕ FREE HOUSE ◀ Skinner's Betty Stogs, Vale VPA, St Austell Trelawny, Sharp's Doom Bar Ò Westons Old Rosie. **Facilities** Non-diners area ❄ (Bar Restaurant Garden) ♦ Children's portions Family room Garden ⊼ Parking WiFi

FLORE

Map 11 SP66

NEW White Hart

tel: 01327 341748 **High St NN7 4LW**
email: thewhitehartflore@gmail.com
dir: M1 junct 16, A45 towards Daventry. Pub on left in village

A much cared-for oasis within a stone's throw of the M1

The White Hart is not only Flore's oldest purpose-built pub but also the village high street's sole surviving hostelry. Newly refurbished and run with dedication by the McCue family, customer satisfaction is all important, as much for the community as for travellers passing through. Welcoming staff serve real ales such as Timothy Taylor Landlord and Theakston Old Peculier, or a glass of wine from a dozen on the carte. The kitchen prepares competitively-priced dishes based on seasonally fresh ingredients: braised lamb neck with spring vegetable broth and herb gnocchi; and roast pumpkin risotto with toasted pumpkin seeds are typical examples.

Open 12-3 5-11 (Sat-Sun 12-11 Mon 5-11) Closed Mon L **Food** Lunch Tue-Sat 12-3, Sun 12-5 Dinner Tue-Sat 6-9.30 Av main course £6.95 Restaurant menu available Tue-Sun ⊕ ENTERPRISE INNS ◀ Sharp's Doom Bar, Timothy Taylor Landlord, Theakston Old Peculier. ♔ 12 **Facilities** Non-diners area ❄ (Bar Outside area) ♦ Children's menu Children's portions Outside area ⊼ Parking WiFi ▄ (notice required)

FOTHERINGHAY
Map 12 TL09

The Falcon Inn
PICK OF THE PUBS

tel: 01832 226254 **PE8 5HZ**
email: info@thefalcon-inn.co.uk **web:** www.thefalcon-inn.co.uk
dir: *From A605 between Peterborough & Oundle follow Fotheringhay signs*

Popular locals' inn with designer garden

First the history: it was in this sleepy village that Richard III was born in 1452, and 115 years later Mary, Queen of Scots was beheaded. The attractive 18th-century, stone-built pub stands in gardens redesigned by award-winning landscape architect Bunny Guinness. It's a real local, the Tap Bar regularly used by the village darts team, their throwing arms lubricated by pints of Fool's Nook ale and Aspall cider. The menus in both the bar and charming conservatory restaurant rely extensively on locally sourced ingredients. In the winter, offerings from the restaurant are Portland crab; crayfish and saffron tart; and ham hock terrine to start. Mains might be rack of lamb with dauphinoise potato, baby vegetables and red wine jus. The bar menu has sandwiches and a selection of starters and mains, such as sautéed king prawns, and shin of beef. For dessert, there's lemon meringue pie or chocolate nemesis.

Open all day 12-11 (Mon-Sat 12-11 Sun 12-4 Jan-Mar) Closed Sun eve Jan-Mar **Food** Lunch Mon-Sat 12-2, Sun 12-3 (Sun 12-4 Jan-Mar) Dinner Mon-Sat 6-9, (Sun 6-8 Apr-Dec) ⊕ FREE HOUSE ◀ Greene King IPA, Digfield Fool's Nook, Fuller's London Pride ♂ Aspall. ☐ 14 **Facilities** Non-diners area ☺ (Bar Restaurant Garden) ♦♦ Children's menu Children's portions Garden ☐ Beer festival Parking WiFi ☐ (notice required)

GRAFTON REGIS
Map 11 SP74

The White Hart

tel: 01908 542123 **Northampton Rd NN12 7SR**
email: alan@pubgraftonregis.co.uk
dir: *M1 junct 15, A508 towards Milton Keynes*

Thatched pub offering a friendly welcome

This thatched, stone-built property dating from the 16th century is the focal point for a friendly village with around 100 residents. In 1464 Edward IV married Elizabeth Woodville in this historic place. The pub has been run by the same family for since 1996 and Alan the owner, is also the chef. Menus change frequently according to available produce. Typical choices include salmon and monkfish mornay with pesto tagliatelle; lasagne; steak, Stilton and mushroom pie; and a selection of steaks. Well-kept ales and 14 wines by the glass complete the picture. The garden has a gazebo/band stand.

Open 12-2.30 6-11 Closed Mon **Food** Lunch Tue-Sun 12-2 Dinner Tue-Sun 6-9.30 Av main course £10 ⊕ FREE HOUSE ◀ Greene King, Abbot Ale, IPA ♂ Aspall. ☐ 14 **Facilities** Non-diners area ☺ (Garden) ♦♦ Children's portions Garden ☐ Parking WiFi

GREAT HOUGHTON
Map 11 SP75

NEW The Old Cherry Tree

tel: 01604 761399 **Cherry Tree Ln NN4 7AT**
email: info@theoldcherrytree.co.uk
dir: *From A45 SE of Northampton take A428 towards Bedford. Right to Great Houghton. Left in The Cross, left into Cherry Tree Ln. Pub at end*

Traditional food and relaxing beer garden

East of Northampton and close to the A428 towards Bedford, this tucked away 16th-century thatched pub is a popular country rendezvous for families, and it's dog-friendly too. Enjoy a pint of Charles Wells Eagle IPA by the real log fire, or head to the tranquil beer garden if the weather allows. At lunchtime, soups, jacket potatoes, burgers and baguettes offer a light option but the evening menu moves up a gear with the likes of chicken supreme served with mushroom, thyme and bacon, or beef and Stilton pie. Leave room for the ginger pudding with custard.

Open all wk 11-3 5.30-11 (Sun 12-7) **Food** Lunch all wk 12-2.30 Dinner Tue-Sat 6.30-9 Restaurant menu available Tue-Sat (dinner only) ⊕ CHARLES WELLS ◀ Eagle IPA, Young's London Gold, Courage Directors. ☐ 15 **Facilities** Non-diners area ☺ (Bar Garden) ♦♦ Children's menu Children's portions Garden ☐ Parking WiFi ☐ (notice required)

GREAT OXENDON
Map 11 SP78

The George Inn

tel: 01858 465205 **LE16 8NA**
email: info@thegeorgegreatoxendon.co.uk
dir: *A508 towards Market Harborough*

Village inn with an attractive conservatory restaurant

On the edge of the little village of Great Oxendon stands this old pub run by new chef-patron Allan Wiseman. At the welcoming bar, beers from Marston's are supplemented by regular guest ales. The inn has been lovingly restored and refurbished over the years, retaining much character, with beams, open log fires and comfy furnishings. Choose the airy conservatory overlooking the gardens or sit outside on the sun-warmed patio in summer, and start with a smoked salmon platter or mushroom ragout on a toasted muffin with béarnaise sauce. Mains offer up steaks, sausages, breaded haddock, slow-braised shoulder of lamb and supreme of chicken.

Open 12-3 5.30-11 (Sun 12-3) Closed 25 Dec, Sun eve **Food** Lunch all wk 12-2 Dinner Tue-Sat 6-9.30 ⊕ FREE HOUSE ◀ Marston's Pedigree, Guest ales. ☐ 10 **Facilities** Non-diners area ☺ (Bar) ♦♦ Children's portions Garden ☐ Parking WiFi ☐ (notice required)

HARRINGWORTH
Map 11 SP99

The White Swan

tel: 01572 747543 **Seaton Rd NN17 3AF**
email: thewhiteswanharringworth@gmail.com
dir: *From A47 between Uppingham & Duddington take B672 signed Coldacott & Seaton. Under Harringworth Viaduct to T-junct. Left signed Harringworth. Under viaduct again. Pub in village centre on left*

Sixteenth-century coaching inn on the county border

Now fully refurbished, this handsome ironstone inn overlooks the village centre. A little farther north is England's longest masonry viaduct, carrying a now-closed railway line over the Welland Valley. At lunchtime an Adnams Southwold Bitter or Somersby cider might be followed by mini-toad-in-the-hole with mash, peas and gravy (vegetarian version also available); or a home-made pie. In the evening, possibilities include Moroccan braised sirloin steak, sweet potato chips and creamed coleslaw; golden-breaded scampi, hand-cut chips and tartare sauce; and quiche of the day.

Open all wk Mon-Thu 12-3 5.30-11 (Fri-Sun all day) **Food** Lunch Tue-Fri 12-2, Sat 12-3, Sun 12-7 Dinner Mon-Fri 5.30-9, Sat 12-9.30, Sun 12-8 Set menu available Restaurant menu available all wk ⊕ FREE HOUSE ◀ The Grainstore Ten Fifty, Marston's Pedigree, Moorland Old Speckled Hen, Shepherd Neame Spitfire, Guinness, Guest ales ♨ Westons Stowford Press, Somersby Cider.
Facilities Non-diners area ♦️ Children's menu Children's portions Garden Parking 🚐

KILSBY
Map 11 SP57

The George

tel: 01788 822229 **Watling St CV23 8YE**
dir: *M1 junct 18, follow A361/Daventry signs. Pub at rdbt junct of A361 & A5*

A great local with home-cooked food

A warm welcome and great local atmosphere characterise this village pub, which has a traditional public bar and a high-ceilinged wood-panelled lounge opening into a smarter but relaxed area with solidly comfortable furnishings. The lunch bar menu includes sandwiches, filled baguettes, faggots with spring onion mash and mushy peas; and home-made fishcakes. The evening menu majors on home-made, hearty dishes such as beef and real ale shortcrust pie; lasagne; and the generous chicken and bacon Caesar salad. A children's menu is always available. There is an attractive garden for sunny days.

Open all wk 11.30-3 5.30-11.30 (Sun 12-5 6-11) **Food** Lunch Mon-Sat 12-2, Sun 12-4 Dinner all wk 6-9 ⊕ PUNCH TAVERNS ◀ Fuller's London Pride, Adnams Southwold Bitter, Timothy Taylor Landlord. ♀ 8 **Facilities** Non-diners area ♦️ Children's menu Children's portions Garden Parking WiFi 🚐

LITTLE BRINGTON
Map 11 SP66

NEW The Saracens Head

tel: 01604 770640 **Main St NN7 4HS**
email: info@thesaracensatbrington.co.uk
dir: *M1 junct 16, A45 to Flore. In Flore 1st right signed the Bringtons. Straight on at x-rds to Little Brington, pub on left*

Old village inn with smallholding produce

Barrel tables and beams; quarry tile and bareboard floors; leaded windows and a fierce wood-burner; The Saracens has character in droves. This 17th-century building of mellow ironstone slumbers in a tiny village where lucky locals enjoy a changing range of beers that may include local micros like Gun Dog Ales. It's a

popular stop too, for horseriders using the network of local bridleways, who can hitch-up in the garden for more sedate views of the countryside. The exceptional menu here has a modern twist; witness the confit pigs' cheeks starter or main of roast loin of cod wrapped in pancetta, whilst coeliacs and the gluten-intolerant have a good choice of dishes, cooked on the premises.

Open all day all wk **Food** Lunch Tue-Sat 12-2.30, Sun 12-5 Dinner Tue-Sat 6-9.30 ⊕ FREE HOUSE ◀ Greene King IPA, Timothy Taylor Landlord, Guest ale. ♀ 14 **Facilities** Non-diners area ♣ (Bar Garden) ♦️ Children's portions Garden Parking WiFi 🚐 (notice required)

LITTLE HOUGHTON
Map 11 SP85

NEW Four Pears

tel: 01604 890900 **28 Bedford Rd NN7 1AB**
email: info@thefourpears.com
dir: *From Northampton take A428 towards Bedford. Left signed Little Houghton*

Smartly renovated village inn with appealing menu

In a peaceful, ironstone-built village just outside Northampton, this 400-year-old hostelry was rescued from closure by local residents in 2010. The fresh, contemporary design owes little to the past. Rather; tip-top real ales are supped in the smart, light bar area, where dog-walkers straying from the nearby Nene Valley lakes will find a warm welcome. The refined, soft-furnishing rich lounge captures the essence of the dining pub; a comfy retreat where bistro meets pub-grub. Start with crispy pig with cured ham and apple chutney, or go straight for spiced salmon and crayfish linguine in the bright restaurant area popular with families.

Open all day all wk **Food** Lunch all wk 12-3 Dinner Mon-Sat 6-9 Av main course £14 Set menu available Restaurant menu available Mon-Sat ⊕ FREE HOUSE ◀ St Austell Tribute, Oakham Ales Bishops Farewell ♨ Westons Stowford Press. ♀ **Facilities** Non-diners area ♣ (Bar Outside area) ♦️ Children's portions Outside area 🌳 WiFi 🚐 (notice required)

NASSINGTON
Map 12 TL09

The Queens Head Inn ★★★★ INN 🏵🏵

tel: 01780 784006 **54 Station Rd PE8 6QB**
email: info@queensheadnassington.co.uk web: www.queensheadnassington.co.uk
dir: *Exit A1 at Wansford, follow Yarwell & Nassington signs. Through Yarwell. Pub on left in Nassington*

Traditional inn with great food

A stone-built inn with exposed beams and traditional furnishings, The Queens Head's name nods to the beheading of Mary, Queen of Scots at nearby Fotheringhay Castle in 1587. Proud of its AA Rosettes, it offers favourites old and new, including pressed ham hock and foie gras terrine with quail's egg, piccalilli and baby onions; slow braised shin of venison with carrot and cinnamon purée, and boulangère potatoes; and banana and tonka bean pannacotta with toffee sauce, banana wafer and peanut brittle. Dine outdoors in warmer weather. Stay in one of the nine en suite bedrooms.

Open all day all wk 11-11 (Sat 11-12 Sun 12-11) **Food** Lunch Mon-Sat 12-2.30, Sun 12-8 Dinner all wk 6-9 ⊕ FREE HOUSE ◀ Greene King IPA, Oakham JHB. ♀ 8 **Facilities** Non-diners area ♣ (Bar Garden) ♦️ Children's menu Children's portions Garden Parking WiFi 🚐 (notice required) **Rooms** 9

NORTHAMPTON

Map 11 SP76

Althorp Coaching Inn

tel: 01604 770651 **Main St, Great Brington NN7 4JA**
email: althorpcoachinginn@btconnect.com
dir: From A428 pass main gates of Althorp House, left before rail bridge. Great Brington 1m

Thatched pub with old world charm and locally sourced food

Occupying a lovely position in the pretty village of Great Brington on the Althorp Estate, this 16th-century stone coaching inn has original decor throughout. The cellar restaurant specialises in traditional English cooking based on locally sourced ingredients. Look out for dishes such as venison casserole; and fillet of sea bass on garlic infused fennel. A brick and cobbled courtyard is surrounded by stable rooms, and the enclosed flower garden is a peaceful spot in which to sample one of the real ales from a wide selection that includes five guest ales. Contact the pub for details of its beer festival.

Open all day all wk 11-11 (wknds 11am-mdnt) **Food** Lunch Mon-Sat 12-3, Sun 12-5 Dinner Mon-Thu 6.30-9.30, Fri-Sat 6.30-10 Av main course £8-£18 Restaurant menu available all wk ⊕ FREE HOUSE ◀ Greene King IPA & Abbot Ale, Fuller's London Pride, Cottage Puffing Billy, Tunnell Sweet Parish Ale, 5 Guest ales ⚬ Farmhouse, Thatchers Heritage. ♀ 10 **Facilities** Non-diners area ♣ (Bar Garden) ♦♦ Children's menu Children's portions Garden ⊟ Beer festival Parking WiFi ➡ (notice required)

OUNDLE

Map 11 TL08

The Chequered Skipper

tel: 01832 273494 **Ashton PE8 5LD**
email: enquiries@chequeredskipper.co.uk
dir: A605 towards Oundle, at rdbt follow signs to Ashton. 1m, turn left into Ashton

Well known for their pizzas

Destroyed by fire in 1997, The Chequered Skipper has been restored to its traditional thatched exterior complemented by a contemporary interior. Located opposite the green in the model village of Ashton, built for the estate workers in the 1880s, the pub plays its part well, with timeless oak floor and beams, and a collection of butterfly display cases diverting attention from a bar stocking locally brewed beers (two beer festivals a year). The menu mixes speciality pizzas and traditional English and European dishes — pork and liver pâté might be followed by braised shoulder of lamb with dauphinoise potatoes.

Open all wk 11.30-3 6-11 (Sat 11.30-11 Sun 11.45-11) **Food** Lunch Mon-Fri 12-2, Sat 12-2.30, Sun 12-3 Dinner Mon-Sat 6.30-9.30, Sun 6.30-9 ⊕ FREE HOUSE ◀ Rockingham Ale, Brewster's Hophead, Oakham. ♀ 8 **Facilities** Non-diners area ♣ (Bar Garden) ♦♦ Children's portions Garden Beer festival Parking WiFi ➡ (notice required)

SIBBERTOFT

Map 11 SP68

The Red Lion

PICK OF THE PUBS

tel: 01858 880011 **43 Welland Rise LE16 9UD**
email: andrew@redlionwinepub.co.uk
dir: From Market Harborough take A4304, through Lubenham, left through Marston Trussell to Sibbertoft

A real passion for good wine

The interior of this friendly 300-year-old free house is an appealing blend of contemporary and classic decor, with oak beams, leather upholstery and a smartly turned-out dining room. Andrew and Sarah Banks have built a loyal following here thanks to their special passion for wine: over 200 bins appear on the ever-growing list, 20 labels are served by the glass, and an annual wine festival is a high point in the pub's busy calendar. After tasting, all wines can be bought at take-home prices, avoiding the guesswork of supermarket purchases. The monthly-changing and reasonably priced menu is served in both bar and restaurant, and helps customers choose their refreshment by matching wines, beers or ciders with the dishes on offer. Goats' cheese with Sibbertoft honey is paired with Chardonnay, for example, whilst a Merlot goes well with a main of blackened Cajun chicken with rice, peas and mango sauce.

Open 5-11 (Sat 12-3 6-11 Sun 12-6) Closed Mon-Fri L & Sun eve **Food** Lunch Sat 12-3, Sun 12-6 Dinner Mon-Sat 5-11 Av main course £10 ⊕ FREE HOUSE ◀ St Austell Tribute, Green King Abbot Ale ⚬ Aspall, Westons. ♀ 20 **Facilities** Non-diners area ♣ (Garden) ♦♦ Children's menu Children's portions Play area Garden ⊟ Parking WiFi ➡ (notice required)

STAVERTON

Map 11 SP56

NEW The Countryman

tel: 01327 311815 **Daventry Rd NN11 6JH**
email: thecountrymanstaverton@gmail.com web: www.thecountrymanstaverton.co.uk
dir: On A425 between Daventry & Southam

Quality modern cooking in traditional village coaching inn

Dating from the 17th century, this lovely coaching inn is built in traditional Northamptonshire ironstone and retains plenty of original character courtesy of log fires and beamed ceilings. A range of ales from local microbreweries such as Great Oakley and Gun Dog keep beer fans happy, whilst the seasonal menu showcases regional produce in dishes such as beer-braised ox cheek with artichoke purée, chive mash and kale; and chicken and wild mushroom tagliatelle. Dark chocolate pistachio cake with salted caramel and vanilla ice cream is certainly one reason to stay for dessert.

Open all wk 12-3 6-11 (Sun 12-10.30) Closed 5-15 Jan 2015 **Food** Lunch Mon-Sat 12-2.30, Sun 12-9 Dinner Mon-Sat 6-9.30, Sun 12-9 Set menu available ⊕ FREE HOUSE ◀ Gun Dog Ales, Church End, Great Oakley. ♀ 9 **Facilities** Non-diners area ♣ (Bar Outside area) ♦♦ Children's portions Outside area ⊟ Parking WiFi ➡ (notice required)

STOKE BRUERNE
Map 11 SP74

The Boat Inn

tel: 01604 862428 **NN12 7SB**
email: info@boatinn.co.uk **web:** www.boatinn.co.uk
dir: *In village centre, just off A508 & A5*

Family-run free house on the Grand Union Canal

Just across the lock from the National Waterways Museum, the busy Boat Inn has been run by the Woodward family since 1877. Take your pick from the selection of beers: Marston's Pedigree, Wychwood Hobgoblin and Jennings Cumberland Ale are just a few. The all-day bar menu lists hot baguettes, light bites, burgers, and main courses such as vegetable tart, chicken Bruerne and steak and ale pie. For a more formal experience overlooking the peaceful waters, the Woodwards Restaurant offers à la carte and set menus, including salmon goujons with coriander mayonnaise; mushroom and tarragon strudel; and lemon curd ice cream terrine.

Open all day all wk 9.30am-11pm (Sun 9.30am-10.30pm) **Food** Lunch all wk 9.30-9.30 Dinner all wk 9.30-9.30 Set menu available Restaurant menu available all wk ⊕ FREE HOUSE ◼ Banks's Bitter, Marston's Pedigree & Old Empire, Wychwood Hobgoblin, Jennings Cumberland Ale, Ringwood Best ⭗ Thatchers Traditional. ♟ 10 **Facilities** Non-diners area ❀ (Bar Garden) ♦� Children's menu Children's portions Garden ⊟ Parking ▦ (notice required)

THORNBY
Map 11 SP67

The Red Lion

tel: 01604 740238 **Welford Rd NN6 8SJ**
email: enquiries@redlionthornby.co.uk
dir: *A14 junct 1, A5199 towards Northampton. Pub on left in village*

An oasis just off the A14

Weary A14 travellers should take note of this 400-year-old traditional pub, as it's just a mile from junction 1 in tiny Thornby. Rest and refuel in the glorious summer garden, or bag a seat by the log fire in the comfortable bar on cold winter days. Simon and Louise Cottle have slowly refurbished the interior, and offer four ales on handpump and a regularly changing menu of freshly prepared dishes. Menus change every month but they always include the ever popular home-made steak and Stilton pie; another choice might be pan-fried lamb's liver, smoked bacon and colcannon, caramelised onion gravy; sandwiches are available at lunchtime. Annual beer festivals are held.

Open all wk 12-3 5-11 (Mon 5-10 Sat-Sun 12-11) **Food** Contact pub for details ⊕ FREE HOUSE ◼ Adnams, Black Sheep, The Grainstore, Purity, Nobby's ⭗ Westons Stowford Press. **Facilities** Non-diners area ❀ (Bar Garden) ♦◆ Children's portions Garden ⊟ Beer festival Parking ▦ (notice required)

TITCHMARSH
Map 11 TL07

The Wheatsheaf at Titchmarsh

tel: 01832 732203 **1 North St NN14 3DH**
email: enquiries@thewheatsheafattitchmarsh.co.uk
dir: *A14 junct 13, A605 towards Oundle, right to Titchmarsh. Or from A14 junct 14 follow signs for Titchmarsh*

Pretty village pub with smart, modern interior

This stone-built village pub is a mix of traditional and contemporary styles that are in perfect balance. A wide selection of real ales is on offer in the bar and can be enjoyed beside one of the two real fires. Freshly prepared dishes might include black olive risotto cakes with roasted tomato chutney as a starter followed by a slow cooked venison, mushroom and red wine pie. Among the lighter dishes are deep-fried breaded whitebait, and prime strips of rump steak on toasted ciabatta. Greene King real ales are backed by others from Sharp's, Butcombe and regularly changing guests.

Open all wk 12-3 6-11 (Sat 12-11 Sun 12-8) **Food** Lunch Mon-Thu 12-2, Fri-Sat 12-2.30, Sun 12-5 Dinner Mon-Sat 6-9.30 Restaurant menu available all wk ⊕ FREE HOUSE ◼ Greene King IPA, Sharp's Doom Bar, Fuller's London Pride, Butcombe, Guest ales ⭗ Aspall. ♟ 11 **Facilities** Non-diners area ❀ (Bar Garden) ♦◆ Children's menu Children's portions Garden ⊟ Parking WiFi ▦ (notice required)

TOWCESTER
Map 11 SP64

The Saracens Head ★★★ INN

tel: 01327 350414 **219 Watling St NN12 6BX**
email: saracenshead.towcester@greeneking.co.uk
web: www.saracenshead-towcester.co.uk
dir: *M1 junct 15A, A43 towards Oxford. Take A5 signed Towcester*

400 years old and immortalised by Charles Dickens

This imposing building dates back over 400 years, and is featured in Charles Dickens' first novel, *The Pickwick Papers*. The same home comforts that Dickens enjoyed when visiting Towcester have been updated to modern standards, and discerning customers will find excellent service in the restored pub. Starters might be potted smoked mackerel; or shredded duck and hoi sin spring rolls, followed by a main course of Suffolk-farmed pork sausages with mature cheddar mash and sautéed red onion gravy; or vegetable and cashew nut paella. Sandwiches, jackets, wraps and ciabattas are all available too.

Open all day all wk 11-11 (Fri-Sat 11am-mdnt) **Food** Lunch all wk 11-5 Dinner all wk 5-10 ⊕ GREENE KING/OLD ENGLISH INNS ◼ Abbot Ale & IPA, Morland Old Speckled Hen, Guest ale. ♟ 13 **Facilities** Non-diners area ♦◆ Children's menu Children's portions Garden ⊟ Beer festival Parking WiFi ▦ **Rooms** 21

Read all about whisky
in our feature on page 18

WADENHOE
Map 11 TL08

The King's Head
PICK OF THE PUBS

tel: 01832 720024 **Church St PE8 5ST**
email: aletha@wadenhoekingshead.co.uk
dir: *From A605, 3m from Wadenhoe rdbt. 2m from Oundle*

Pretty pub featuring a shaded riverside garden

Set in the unspoilt village of Wadenhoe, alongside the picturesque River Nene, this stone-built, partially thatched inn has been serving travellers since the 17th century. In the summer, grab a seat in extensive riverside gardens in the shade of the ancient willow trees and watch the colourful narrow boats over a pint of King's Head Bitter. In winter, head for the comfortable bar with its quarry-tiled and bare-boarded floors, heavy oak-beamed ceilings, pine furniture and open log fires. The pub offers the most modern facilities but has lost none of its old world charm. The lunchtime menu offers sandwiches, pies and light bites such as home-made burger topped with cheddar cheese and chips or a ploughman's. In the evening you can feast like a king on warm pork and black pudding terrine with apple sauce, or roast chicken, tarragon and shallot pot pie, minted new potatoes and purple sprouting broccoli.

Open all day all wk 11-11 (Sun 12-10 winter 11-2.30 5.30-11 Sun 12-6) Closed Sun eve in winter **Food** Lunch all wk 12-2.30 Dinner all wk 6-9 ⊕ FREE HOUSE ◖ King's Head Bitter, Digfield Barnwell Bitter, Hogs Back BSA. ☋ 15 **Facilities** Non-diners area ◖◗ Children's portions Garden ☴ Beer festival Parking ⛟

WESTON
Map 11 SP54

The Crown
PICK OF THE PUBS

tel: 01295 760310 **Helmdon Rd NN12 8PX**
email: mike.foalks@live.co.uk
dir: *Accessed from A43 or B4525*

Community-focused village pub with an interesting legend

If the fugitive Lord Lucan is still alive, he would probably consider it unwise to return to this delightful 16th-century inn. That's because the day after the murder of his children's nanny in 1974, he was allegedly spotted here knocking back a pint. But were he to come back, he'd see the huge difference the extensive remodelling has made. Now under new ownership, it fulfils a role as a true community pub, with a reputation for its family- and dog-friendly attitude, its excellent beers and a range of high-quality, locally-sourced, 'nothing-out-of-a-packet' dishes. A seasonal menu might well feature the following appetite sharpeners: cider and thyme mussels; peppered duck breast; Tuscany fish stew; and aubergine with spicy tomato coulis. Regular events include Fish and Folk Nights, and Ruby Tuesdays, the rhyming-slang explanation making sense only to those who remember a Northern Irish singer called Ruby Murray, thus curry.

Open all wk 12-3 5-11 (Fri-Sat 12-11 Sun 12-10.30) Closed Mon L **Food** Lunch Tue-Sat 12-3, Sun 12-6 Dinner Mon-Sat 6-9.30 Av main course £12-£15 ⊕ FREE HOUSE ◖ Hooky, Fuller's London Pride, St Austell Tribute, Sharp's Doom Bar ⌀ Thatchers Gold. **Facilities** Non-diners area ❖ (Bar Garden) ◖◗ Children's menu Children's portions Garden ☴ Parking WiFi ⛟ (notice required)

WOODNEWTON
Map 11 TL09

NEW The White Swan

tel: 01780 470944 **22 Main St PE8 5EB**
web: whiteswanwoodnewton.co.uk
dir: *Phone for detailed directions*

Popular village pub with contemporary interior

When Ian Simmons bought this 19th-century, stone-built pub in 2010 it was in a bad way, with heavy shutters on the windows and doors, having closed down no less than three times in five years. But with his dedication and strong local support, The White Swan really is making a name for itself. Beer drinkers will find Digfield Ale from Barnwell, as well as Woodforde's Wherry and Fuller's London Pride. On the menu, pub classics include chef's fish pie; and chargrilled beefburger; other mains are pan-fried sea bass fillet; braised sticky beef; and butternut squash and pine nut tagliatelle.

Open all wk 12-3 6-11 (Fri-Sat 12-11 Sun 12-10.30) **Food** Lunch Mon-Sat 12-3, Sun 12-6 Dinner Mon-Thu 6-9, Sat 6-9.30 Av main course £11 Set menu available ⊕ FREE HOUSE ◀ Woodforde's Wherry, Fuller's London Pride ♾ Jollydale.
Facilities Non-diners area ❤ (Bar Garden) ⬤ Children's menu Children's portions Garden ⋒ Parking WiFi 🚐 (notice required)

See advert on page 363

YARDLEY HASTINGS
Map 11 SP85

NEW Rose & Crown

tel: 01604 696276 **4 Northampton Rd NN7 1EX**
email: info@roseandcrownbistro.co.uk **web:** www.roseandcrownbistro.co.uk
dir: *A428 from Northampton. 1st left to Yardley Hastings*

Great food, good ale and live music

Andrew and Melissa Dunkley's stone-built village pub has been a hostelry since at least 1748, but the Bistro is their own creation. It's here that Andrew's daily-changing menu blends traditional British cuisine with more distant influences to produce dishes such as rich venison casserole; red Thai monkfish curry; pan-fried lamb's liver; and fresh beer-battered Atlantic haddock. An old favourite among the desserts is sticky toffee pudding with clotted cream, while a good selection of cheeses includes Wodehill Blue from Bedfordshire. Hart Family Brewers in Wellingborough supplies its India Pale Ale. The pub stages regular live jazz, rock and blues events.

Open all day Closed Mon L **Food** Lunch Tue-Sat 12-11, Sun 12-10 Dinner all wk 6-9 Set menu available Restaurant menu available all wk ⊕ FREE HOUSE ◀ Hart Brewery The Local, Phipps IPA, Greene King Abbot Ale ♾ Aspall, Thatchers. 🍷 20
Facilities Non-diners area ❤ (Bar Restaurant Garden) ⬤ Children's portions Garden ⋒ Parking WiFi

NORTHUMBERLAND

ALNWICK   Map 21 NU11

NEW The Hogs Head Inn ★★★ INN

tel: 01665 606576 **Hawfinch Dr NE66 2BF**
email: info@hogsheadinnalnwick.co.uk web: www.hogsheadinnalnwick.co.uk
dir: *From S: A1 onto A1068 signed Alnwick. 3rd exit at rdbt. Under A1, right at BP garage. From N: A1 onto A1068 signed Alnwick. 1st left, right at BP garage (NB older Sat Nav systems may not recognise pub's postcode)*

Notable local food served at this Harry Potter-inspired pub

Named after the pub featured in the Harry Potter books, this inn is just minutes from Alnwick Castle, which was used as Hogwarts in the first two films. Close to Alnwick Garden, The Hog's Head is an ideal base for exploring Northumberland and food at this family-friendly pub is served all day. North East produce appears throughout the menu; a deep-fried North Shields crab claws with honey and ginger dipping sauce might be followed by Cumberland sausage and mash. Wash it down with a pint of Hadrian Border Tyneside Blonde.

Open all day all wk **Food** Contact pub for details Av main course £10 ⊕ FREE HOUSE ◀ Black Sheep Best Bitter, Hadrian Border Tyneside Blonde. ♥
Facilities Non-diners area ♦♦ Children's menu Children's portions Play area Garden Outside area ⊟ Parking WiFi ▄ (notice required) **Rooms** 53

BARRASFORD   Map 21 NY97

The Barrasford Arms ◉

tel: 01434 681237 **NE48 4AA**
email: contact@barrasfordarms.co.uk
dir: *From A69 at Hexham take A6079 signed Acomb & Chollerford. In Chollerford by church turn left signed Barrasford*

A destination food pub

Chef Tony Binks's village inn stands close to Hadrian's Wall deep in the glorious Northumbrian countryside, with spectacular views of the Tyne Valley. Despite the emphasis on food, it retains a traditional pub atmosphere, with local Wylam and Hadrian Border ales on tap in the time-honoured bar, which fills with locals and passing walkers and cyclists. Most beat a path to the door for Tony's short, imaginative, one-AA Rosette menus. For dinner, tuck into twice-baked cheddar soufflé; seared fillet of wild sea trout, shrimp, tomato and saffron broth; soft pistachio meringue, orange and vanilla mascarpone and strawberries. His set and Sunday lunches are great value.

Open 12-3 6-11 (Sat-Sun all day) Closed 1st wk Jan, Mon L **Food** Lunch Tue-Sun 12-2.30 Dinner Tue-Sat 6.30-9 Set menu available ⊕ FREE HOUSE ◀ Wylam Gold Tankard, Hadrian Border Gladiator. **Facilities** Non-diners area ♦♦ Children's portions Garden ⊟ Parking WiFi ▄ (notice required)

BEADNELL   Map 21 NU22

The Craster Arms ★★★★ INN

tel: 01665 720272 **The Wynding NE67 5AX**
email: michael@crasterarms.co.uk web: www.crasterarms.co.uk
dir: *Exit A1 at Brownieside signed Preston. Left at T-junct signed Seahouses. Right signed Beadnell village. Pub on left*

Within walking distance of beautiful beaches

In the 15th century, the English in this neck of the woods built small fortified watch towers to warn of Scottish invasions – this was one of them. Since becoming a pub in 1818 its role has widened to offer not just food, drink and accommodation, but a

programme of live entertainment, the Crastonbury music festival, and a beer and cider festival (last weekend in July). Sandwiches, baguettes, paninis, salads and hot meals are available at lunchtime; in the evening there's braised lamb shank; Thai green chicken curry; seasonal blackboard specials; crab fishcake and other local seafood.

Open all day all wk **Food** Contact pub for details ⊕ PUNCH TAVERNS ◀ Camerons Strongarm, Black Sheep, Mordue Workie Ticket Ò Westons Traditional Scrumpy & Old Rosie. **Facilities** Non-diners area ♣ (Bar Garden) ♦♦ Children's menu Children's portions Garden ⊟ Beer festival Cider festival Parking WiFi ▄ **Rooms** 3

BELFORD   Map 21 NU13

Blue Bell Hotel

tel: 01668 213543 **Market Place NE70 7NE**
email: enquiries@bluebellhotel.com
dir: *From A1 halfway between Berwick-upon-Tweed & Alnwick follow Belford signs*

Worth leaving the busy A1 for

At one time a busy coaching inn in the village centre on the old London to Edinburgh road, the hotel and its fine gardens still attract many a traveller. Unquestionably, the food has much to do with its appeal, with starters that include bacon, brie and black pudding salad; smoked salmon and dill fishcake; and local Adderstone Scotch egg, while the roll-call of main dishes includes chicken Kiev; pan-fried liver, red onions and bacon; Eyemouth fish pie; rib-eye and sirloin steaks; and tagliatelle pesto. A little further north, over a causeway, is Holy Island, but do be sure to check the times of the tides before visiting.

Open all day all wk 11am-mdnt **Food** Lunch all wk 12-2.30 Dinner all wk 6-9 ⊕ FREE HOUSE ◀ Tetley's Smoothflow, Black Sheep, Guinness.
Facilities Non-diners area ♦♦ Children's menu Children's portions Play area Garden ⊟ Parking WiFi ▄ (notice required)

BLANCHLAND   Map 18 NY95

NEW The Lord Crewe Arms

tel: 01434 675469 **DH8 9SP**
dir: *10m S of Hexham via B6306*

Memorable village inn with unfussy, reliable menu

Refurbished in 2014 with a close eye on its venerable heritage, this visually striking inn stands at the heart of the exquisite little estate village of Blanchland, high in the Durham Dales. The inn was the Abbot's Lodge and guest house to a Norman abbey; the 800 years catering for visitors shines through in today's incarnation. The vaulted Crypt Bar offers local ales, including a golden house beer from Wylam Brewery; from the kitchen equally parochial dishes vary by the season and aim at offering old fashioned nostalgic grub in the bar and two restaurants. Anticipate fulfilling fish dishes; chops; Goosnargh duck, or a great range of 'Day Bait' snack dishes enjoyed alfresco in the beautiful gardens.

Open all day all wk 11-11 **Food** Contact pub for details ⊕ FREE HOUSE ◀ Allendale Golden Plover, Wylam Gold Tankard, Lord Crewe Brewe (pub's own) Ò Westons Stowford Press. ♥ 9 **Facilities** Non-diners area ♣ (Bar Garden) ♦♦ Children's menu Children's portions Garden ⊟ Parking WiFi

PICK OF THE PUBS

The Pheasant Inn ★★★★ INN

FALSTONE   Map 21 NY78

tel: 01434 240382
Stannersburn NE48 1DD
email: stay@thepheasantinn.com
web: www.thepheasantinn.com
dir: *A69, B6079, B6320, follow signs for Kielder Water*

Perfect base for Northumbrian adventures

In the early 17th century, long, long before nearby Kielder Water and Kielder Forest were created, agricultural workers drank at a beer-house in Stannersburn. This ivy-clad country inn is that beer-house, now finding itself where the Northumberland National Park meets the Border Forest Park, and surrounded by verdant valleys, high moors and tranquil woodlands. It's well positioned too for cycle tracks, a sculpture trail, an observatory, endless walks and wildlife watching, including red squirrels. What you see today is what Irene and Robin Kershaw have achieved since they acquired it, then rather run down, in 1985. Most spaces in the two bars have been filled with historic Northumberland memorabilia, and on the exposed stone walls that support the blackened beams are photos of yesteryear's locals working at forgotten trades like blacksmithing and coalmining. In winter, log fires cast flickering shadows across the furniture. The restaurant, with terracotta-coloured

walls and furnished in mellow pine, looks out over the countryside. Self evidently it's where to enjoy Irene and Robin's daily-changing, traditional British food, all making the most of what Northumbria has to offer, such as slow-roasted local lamb with rosemary and redcurrant jus; grilled fresh salmon with hot pepper marmalade and crème fraîche; fresh dressed crab from the Northumberland coast; and Stilton and vegetable crumble with salad. Excellent beers from Wylam Brewery and Timothy Taylor might cloud the mind, but not the dark night skies, which make the area a mecca for astronomers. There is a tranquil stream-side garden.

Open 12-3 6.30-11 Closed 25-27 Dec, Mon-Tue (Nov-Mar) **Food** Lunch Mon-Sat 12-2.30 Dinner all wk 6-9 (Etr-Oct 6-8.30) ⊕ FREE HOUSE ◪ Timothy Taylor Landlord, Wylam Gold Tankard, Rocket, Red Kite, Red Shot & Angel. **Facilities** Non-diners area ♦♦ Children's menu Children's portions Play area Family room Garden Outside area ♫ Parking WiFi **Rooms** 8

CARTERWAY HEADS
Map 19 NZ05

The Manor House Inn
PICK OF THE PUBS

tel: 01207 255268 **DH8 9LX**
email: themanorhouseinn@gmail.com
dir: A69 W from Newcastle, left onto A68 then S for 8m. Inn on right

Head out of town for this popular all-rounder

When shopping in Newcastle or Durham palls and you fancy a drink or meal out of town, a 30-minute drive will get you to this former coaching inn. As the stone walls, low-beamed ceiling and massive timber support in the bar might suggest, it was built in the mid 18th century. From its lofty position, there are great views of both the Derwent Valley and reservoir. Jostling for real ale drinkers' attention are five contenders, among them Robinsons Dizzy Blonde and Copper Dragon's Golden Pippin. The restaurant is divided into two, the larger area welcoming families with children. Most produce is local and includes game and wild fish from hereabouts. Suggested dishes include Northumbrian black pudding with apple, soft poached egg and salad; rolled shoulder of Minsteracres lamb with rich redcurrant jus; tandoori rabbit legs; and North Sea haddock in crispy beer batter. Beer festivals are held throughout the year.

Open all day all wk 11-11 (Sun 12-10.30 Mon 12-11) Closed 26 Dec, 1st Mon in Jan **Food** Lunch Mon-Sat 12-9, Sun 12-8 Dinner Mon-Sat 12-9, Sun 12-8 Av main course £13 ⊕ ENTERPRISE INNS ◀ Morland Old Speckled Hen, Local guest ales ⊙ Westons Old Rosie. ♟ 12 **Facilities** Non-diners area ☻ (Bar Garden) ◀ Children's menu Children's portions Garden ⟗ Beer festival Cider festival Parking WiFi ⛟ (notice required)

CORBRIDGE
Map 21 NY96

The Angel of Corbridge

tel: 01434 632119 **Main St NE45 5LA**
email: info@theangelofcorbridge.com
dir: 0.5m off A69, signed Corbridge

Prime location in historic town

In the scenic Tyne Valley and handy for Hadrian's Wall, this reinvigorated old coaching inn has made a success in each area of its operation; there's a striking restaurant offering a solid English menu drawing on the producers of Northumbria (including their own lambs) and a traditional locals' bar, where beers from the local brewery are in evidence; the Angel also has a Martini bar. Typical dishes on the menu are a starter of black pudding, poached egg and pancetta; a main course of pan-seared lamb's liver with bacon, champ mashed potato and onion gravy. Tempting sandwiches (sliced local ham with home-made pease pudding) and strong puddings complete the deal.

Open all day all wk 11-11 (Fri-Sat 11am-mdnt Sun 11-10.30) **Food** Lunch Mon-Sat 12-9, Sun 12-5 Dinner Mon-Sat 12-9 ⊕ FREE HOUSE ◀ Hadrian Border Tyneside Blonde, Wylam Angel, Local ales. ♟ 12 **Facilities** Non-diners area ◀ Children's menu Children's portions Outside area ⟗ Parking WiFi ⛟ (notice required)

CRASTER
Map 21 NU21

The Jolly Fisherman

tel: 01665 576461 **Haven Hill NE66 3TR**
email: info@thejollyfishermancraster.co.uk
dir: Exit A1 at Denwick. Follow Seahouses signs, then 1st sign for Craster

Fine harbourside location

The charm of this historic stone-flagged, low-beamed pub remains undimmed. When it's cold, relax by an open fire; at any time admire impressive Dunstanburgh Castle from the delightful beer garden. When the pub opened in 1847, Craster was a thriving fishing village; now only a few East Coast cobles leave harbour, mostly for the herring that, once smoked, become the famous kippers. House specialities are fresh fish stew; whole line-caught sea bass; breast of chicken in Serrano ham; and slow-roasted pepper with butternut squash and celeriac risotto. At the bar are Black Sheep and Mordue Workie Ticket bitter.

Open all day all wk 11-11 **Food** Lunch Mon-Sat 11-3, Sun 12-3 Dinner Mon-Sat 5-8.30 winter, 5-9 Summer, Sun 5-9 ⊕ PUNCH TAVERNS ◀ Mordue Workie Ticket, Black Sheep, Timothy Taylor Landlord, Guest ale ⊙ Symonds Scrumpy Jack. ♟ 12 **Facilities** Non-diners area ☻ (Bar Garden) ◀ Children's menu Children's portions Garden ⟗ Parking WiFi ⛟ (notice required)

FALSTONE
Map 21 NY78

The Pheasant Inn ★★★★ INN
PICK OF THE PUBS

See Pick of the Pubs on opposite page

HAYDON BRIDGE
Map 21 NY86

The General Havelock Inn

tel: 01434 684376 **Ratcliffe Rd NE47 6ER**
email: generalhavelock@aol.com
dir: On A69, 7m W of Hexham

Free house overlooking the River Tyne

Built in the 1760s, this riverside inn is named after a 19th-century British Army officer. The pub, with its restaurant in a converted stone barn, is a favourite with local showbusiness personalities. The real ales are all sourced from a 15-mile radius: Mordue Workie Ticket and Big Lamp Bitter are but two. Owner and chef Gary Thompson makes everything by hand, including the bread and ice cream. Local ingredients are the foundation of his dishes, which include steamed lemon sole in a crisp pasty pillow; chicken and mushroom pie; and warm walnut tart. In summer, the patio area is covered by a marquee.

Open 12-2.30 7-12 (Sun 12-10.30) Closed Mon **Food** Lunch Tue-Sun 12-3.30 Dinner Tue-Sat 7-9 ⊕ FREE HOUSE ◀ High House Farm Nel's Best, Geltsdale Cold Fell, Big Lamp Bitter, Mordue Workie Ticket, Cumberland Corby Blonde. ♟ 15 **Facilities** Non-diners area ☻ (Bar Garden) ◀ Children's portions Family room Garden ⟗ WiFi ⛟ (notice required)

HEDLEY ON THE HILL
Map 19 NZ05

The Feathers Inn
PICK OF THE PUBS

See Pick of the Pubs on page 368

PICK OF THE PUBS

The Feathers Inn

HEDLEY ON THE HILL   Map 19 NZ05

tel: 01661 843607 **NE43 7SW**
email: info@thefeathers.net
web: www.thefeathers.net
dir: *A695 towards Gateshead. In Stocksfield right into New Ridley Rd. Left at Hedley on the Hill sign to village*

Microbrewery ales and cracking food

This small, 200-year-old stone-built free house is set high above the Tyne Valley with splendid views across the Cheviot Hills. Once frequented by lead miners and cattle drovers, all visitors are charmed by the friendly and relaxed atmosphere created by owners Rhian Cradock and Helen Greer. It's also worth the detour for its rotating choice of microbrewery ales; relax and sup Wylam Red Kite or Northumberland Pit Pony beside a welcoming wood-burning stove. Old oak beams, rustic settles and stone walls decorated with local photographs set the informal scene. There's a good selection of traditional pub games like shove ha'penny and bar skittles and you'll find a good collection of cookery books to browse through. Rhian's impressive daily menu makes sound use of the freshest local ingredients – including game from local shoots, rare breed local cattle and Longhorn beef – to create great British classics as well as regional dishes from the north east. You could start with

cornfed Goosnargh chicken liver parfait, toasted brioche and pickles, or Craster kipper and whisky pâté. Typical main courses include Cranston's Cumberland sausage, creamy mash and real ale gravy; and local haggis, bashed neeps and tatties. Leave room for rice pudding and poached quince, or steamed marmalade pudding with vanilla custard. Families are welcome, and a small side room can be booked in advance if required. The annual beer and food festival takes place over Easter and includes a barrel race, egg jarping, barbecue and a farmers' market, while the cider festival is on Summer Bank Holiday in August.

Open all wk 12-11 (Mon 6-11 Sun 12-10.30) **Food** Lunch Tue-Sat 12-2,

Sun 12-4.30 Dinner Tue-Sat 6-8.30 Av main course £13 Set menu available No food 1st 2wks Jan ⊕ FREE HOUSE ◀ Mordue Workie Ticket, Northumberland Pit Pony, Orkney Red MacGregor, Wylam Red Kite, The Consett Ale Works Red Dust ♂ Westons 1st Quality & Old Rosie. ♥ **Facilities** Non-diners area ♦♦ Children's portions Outside area ⋈ Beer festival Cider festival Parking WiFi

HEXHAM

Map 21 NY96

Battlesteads Hotel & Restaurant

PICK OF THE PUBS

tel: 01434 230209 **Wark NE48 3LS**
email: info@battlesteads.com
dir: 10m N of Hexham on B6320 (Kielder road)

Utterly charming pub, hotel and restaurant

Just a few miles north of Hadrian's Wall, and surrounded by some of the country's finest livestock herds, game shooting and fishing, this converted 18th-century farmhouse is renowned for its food. There are three dining options: in the relaxed bar area, serving Durham Magus and other local real ales; the conservatory, overlooking the walled garden, source of herbs, salads, vegetables and fruit; and the softly-lit main restaurant, decorated with old railway travel posters. Among head chef Eddie Shilton's primarily modern British dishes are Northumbrian fillet steak, coated with mustard powder and pepper and topped with blue cheese; Louisiana chicken, marinated in Cajun spices, with red onions, bacon and prawns in cream sauce; and wild mushroom and haloumi stack. Desserts include gooseberry and apple crumble tart. Owner Richard Slade is always pleased to show visitors the hotel's extensive 'green' features.

Open all day all wk **Food** Lunch all wk 12-3 Dinner all wk 6.30-9.30 Set menu available Restaurant menu available all wk ⊕ FREE HOUSE ◀ Durham Magus, High House Farm Nel's Best, Guest ales ♂ Sandford Orchards. ♚ 25
Facilities Non-diners area ♣ (Bar Garden) ♦ Children's portions Garden ♬ Beer festival Parking WiFi ☞ (notice required)

Dipton Mill Inn

PICK OF THE PUBS

tel: 01434 606577 **Dipton Mill Rd NE46 1YA**
email: ghb@hexhamshire.co.uk
dir: 2m S of Hexham on HGV route to Blanchland, B6306, Dipton Mill Rd

Converted mill that now brews its own beer

Surrounded by farmland and woods with footpaths for pleasant country walks, and Hadrian's Wall and other Roman sites, this former farmhouse was rebuilt some 400 years ago and has a pretty millstream running right through the gardens. The Dipton Mill is home to Hexhamshire Brewery ales, which include Devil's Water, Old Humbug and Whapweasel, plus Blackhall English Stout. All dishes are freshly prepared from local produce where possible. Start with tomato and vegetable soup, followed by mince and dumplings; duck breast with orange and cranberries; or haddock baked with tomatoes and basil. A decent selection of vegetarian options includes cheese and onion flan with salad. Dessert brings comforting favourites such as creamy lemon tart; and syrup sponge and custard, plus a good selection of Northumberland and Durham cheeses. Salads and an extensive selection of sandwiches and ploughman's are always available.

Open 12-2.30 6-11 (Sun 12-3) Closed 25 Dec, Sun eve **Food** Lunch all wk 12-2 Dinner Mon-Sat 6.30-8 Av main course £8 ⊕ FREE HOUSE ◀ Hexhamshire Shire Bitter, Old Humbug, Devil's Water, Devil's Elbow, Whapweasel, Blackhall English Stout ♂ Westons Old Rosie, Guest cider. ♚ 17 **Facilities** Non-diners area ♣ (Garden) ♦ Children's portions Garden ♬ ☞ (notice required) **Notes** ☺

Miners Arms Inn

tel: 01434 603909 **Main St, Acomb NE46 4PW**
email: minersarms2012@gmail.com
dir: 2m W of Hexham on A69

Traditional food in peaceful family-run village pub

The Greenwell family took over this 18th-century village pub near Hadrian's Wall a few years ago, and it's very much a family business with David and Elwyn helped by their son and two daughters. Among the choice of ales, local Wylam Gold Tankard is always available, with guest beers available every week. Mainly locally sourced dishes, including haggis and black pudding with peppercorn sauce; and home-made steak and ale pie typify the traditional food. Visitors can enjoy the open-hearth fire, the sunny beer garden, or simply sit out front soaking up life in this peaceful village. Beer festivals are held occasionally.

Open all wk 4-12 (Sat-Sun 12-12) **Food** Contact pub for details ⊕ FREE HOUSE ◀ Wylam Gold Tankard, Yates Best Bitter, Guest ale. **Facilities** Non-diners area ♣ (Bar Garden) ♦ Children's menu Children's portions Garden ♬ Beer festival

Rat Inn

PICK OF THE PUBS

tel: 01434 602814 **NE46 4LN**
email: info@theratinn.com
dir: 2m from Hexham, Bridge End (A69) rdbt, take 4th exit signed Oakwood. Inn 500yds on right

Passionate about local food and beer

Opposite the handkerchief-sized green in a tiny hamlet of stone-built cottages and farms, this convivial pub commands a shoulder of land above the River Tyne, looking out over the historic town of Hexham spread below. The tree-shaded terraced garden unlocks these great views; indulge in a pint of beer from local microbreweries like High House Farm and contemplate that the pub itself may be built from stone liberated from nearby Hadrian's Wall. The stone theme continues within, with grand open fires and flagstone floors in the superbly traditional old bar of this one-time drovers' inn. Join in lively conversation with locals by the fine carved-oak bar, consider their opinions on the origin of the pub's name and contemplate a fine menu of proudly Northumbrian delicacies. Kick in with rillette of Craster kipper; or straight to a main of fried leek and thyme risotto with local pigeon and Woodalls black pudding. The Sunday roast is phenomenal value.

Open all day all wk **Food** Lunch Tue-Sat 12-2, Sun 12-3 Dinner Tue-Sat 6-9 ⊕ FREE HOUSE ◀ Cumberland Corby Ale, High House Farm Nel's Best, Hexhamshire Shire Bitter, Timothy Taylor Landlord, Wylam Gold Tankard. ♚ **Facilities** Non-diners area ♦ Children's portions Garden ♬ Parking WiFi

LONGFRAMLINGTON

Map 21 NU10

The Anglers Arms

PICK OF THE PUBS

tel: 01665 570271 & 570655 **Weldon Bridge NE65 8AX**
email: info@anglersarms.com
dir: Take A697 N of Morpeth signed Wooler & Coldstream. 7m, left to Weldon Bridge

Still welcoming visitors after 250 years

Since the 1760s, this part-battlemented, three-storey, former coaching inn on the road to and from Scotland has commanded the picturesque Weldon Bridge over the River Coquet. It belongs to John and Julie Young, whose knick-knacks and curios, pictures and fishing memorabilia are liberally distributed within. On the bar top pump badges declare the availability of Timothy Taylor Landlord, Theakston Best Bitter and a trio of Greene King brews. A comprehensive menu suggests, for example, trio of Coquetdale lamb cutlets; Whitby wholetail scampi; Northumberland pork and leek sausage; steak, ale and onion pie; and green pea and mushroom risotto. The carefully tended half-acre of garden is perfect for outdoor dining and includes a children's play park. It is possible to fish for brown trout, salmon and sea trout on the pub's own one-mile stretch of the Coquet.

Open all day all wk 11-11 (Sun 12-10.30) **Food** Lunch all wk 12-9.30 Dinner all wk 12-9.30 Av main course £10.95 ⊕ FREE HOUSE ◀ Timothy Taylor Landlord, Morland Old Speckled Hen, Greene King Abbot Ale, Theakston Best Bitter.
Facilities Non-diners area ♣ (Bar Garden Outside area) ♦ Children's portions Play area Family room Garden Outside area ♬ Parking ☞ (notice required)

LONGHORSLEY
Map 21 NZ19

Linden Tree ★★★★ HL ⊕⊕

tel: 01670 500033 **Linden Hall NE65 8XF**
email: lindenhall@macdonald-hotels.co.uk **web:** www.macdonald-hotels.co.uk/lindenhall
dir: *From A1 onto A697, 1m N of Longhorsley*

The 19th-hole after a round of golf

The friendly and informal Linden Tree pub stands within the 450-acres surrounding of Linden Hall, the impressive Georgian mansion that is now a popular golf and country club. A sunny patio makes for a relaxed setting for lunch in summer and the brasserie-style menu makes good use of Scottish beef and lamb. Dishes might include Thai green curry mussels; 21-day aged Scottish beefburger with tomato relish and beef dripping chips; leg of lamb steak; battered haddock with chips and mushy peas or steak and ale pie. Round off a long day with a nightcap in the golfers' lounge.

Open all day all wk Mon-Sat 11-11 (Sun 11-10.30) **Food** Lunch all wk 12-9.30 ⊕ FREE HOUSE ◀ Mordue, Guest ale. **Facilities** Non-diners area ✿ (Bar Garden) ❙❙ Children's menu Children's portions Play area Garden ⊓ Parking ☐ (notice required) **Rooms** 50

LOW NEWTON BY THE SEA
Map 21 NU22

The Ship Inn

tel: 01665 576262 **The Square NE66 3EL**
email: forsythchristine@hotmail.com
dir: *NE from A1 at Alnwick towards Seahouses*

Good, simple food and home-brewed beers

There's a very salty tang about this pretty, late-1700s inn - of course there is, since it overlooks Newton Haven's sandy beach. Then there are the names of the real ales: Sea Coal, Sea Wheat, Ship Hop Ale and Sandcastles at Dawn, all in fact, with Dolly Day Dream brewed next door. The barrels then have to be rolled all of 15ft to the cellar; from here they are pumped to the small bar, where you can expect plenty of locally caught fresh and smoked fish; Peelham Farm free-range bacon, mushroom and tomato stottie (flat loaf); vegetarian options, and old-fashioned possets and crumbles.

Open all wk seasonal variations, please telephone for details Closed 24, 25 & 26 Dec **Food** Lunch all wk 12-2.30 Dinner Wed-Sat 7-8 ⊕ FREE HOUSE ◀ The Ship Inn Sea Coal, Dolly Day Dream, Sea Wheat, Ship Hop Ale, Sandcastles at Dawn. **Facilities** ✿ (Bar Restaurant Garden) ❙❙ Garden **Notes** ⊜

MILFIELD
Map 21 NT93

The Red Lion Inn

tel: 01668 216224 **Main Rd NE71 6JD**
email: redlioninn@fsmail.net **web:** www.redlionmilfield.co.uk
dir: *On A697, 9m S of Coldstream (6m N of Wooler)*

Historic inn serving comfort food and guest ales

Dating back to the 1700s, sheep drovers from the northern counties stayed at this stone building before it was used as a stopover for the mail stagecoach en route from Edinburgh and London. Well placed for salmon and trout fishing on the River Tweed and for shooting on the Northumberland estates, the Red Lion offers a relaxing atmosphere, good guest beers and wholesome food. Start with breaded chicken goujons with sweet chilli or garlic mayonnaise before enjoying home-made steak and ale suet crust pie with chips and peas; for pudding choose vanilla crème brûlée or Eton Mess. There's also a beer festival in June.

Open all wk 11-2 5-11 (Sat 11-11 Sun 11-10.30) (Apr-Nov all day) **Food** Lunch all day all wk Apr-Nov, Dec-Mar Mon-Fri 11-2, Sat-Sun 11-9 Dinner all day all wk Apr-Nov, Dec-Mar Mon-Fri 5-9, Sat-Sun 11-9 ⊕ FREE HOUSE ◀ Black Sheep, Guinness, Guest ales ♂ Thistly Cross, Westons, Guest cider. **Facilities** Non-diners area ❙❙ Children's menu Children's portions Garden ⊓ Beer festival Parking WiFi ☐

NETHERTON
Map 21 NT90

The Star Inn

tel: 01669 630238 **NE65 7HD**
dir: *7m from Rothbury*

Old fashioned inn, tip-top cask ales but no food

Little has changed at this timeless gem since the Wilson-Morton family took over in 1917. Lost in superb remote countryside north of Rothbury, The Star retains many period features and the bar is like stepping into someone's living room, comfortable and quiet, with no intrusive fruit machines or piped music. Don't expect any food, just cask ales in the peak of condition, served from a hatch in the entrance hall. This inn is a real find - just check the days of the week that it's open.

Open Tue-Wed & Sun 7.30pm-10.30pm (Fri-Sat 7.30pm-11pm) Closed Mon, Thu **Food** Contact pub for details ⊕ FREE HOUSE ◀ Guest ales. **Facilities** Non-diners area Outside area Parking ☐ (notice required) **Notes** ⊜

NEWTON
Map 21 NZ06

Duke of Wellington Inn

tel: 01661 844446 **NE43 7UL**
email: info@thedukeofwellingtoninn.co.uk
dir: *From Corbridge A69 towards Newcastle. 3m to village*

Hillside, traditional country pub

Just off the A69 near Corbridge, this early 19th-century coaching inn overlooks the Tyne Valley and has stunning views, and is a handy base for exploring the National Park and Hadrian's Wall. The building's original oak and stone construction is complemented by modern furniture and fabrics that create a comfortable pub. On offer are local ales, a comprehensive wine list and enjoyable dishes such as smoked haddock and asparagus risotto; and braised feather blade of beef with mustard mash and honey roast vegetables. The stone floored bar has a roaring log fire during the colder months but when the sun shines there is ample space on the terrace to enjoy refreshments. Dogs are welcome in the bar and garden.

Open all day all wk **Food** Lunch 12-9 ⊕ FREE HOUSE ◀ Hadrian Border Tyneside Blonde, Timothy Taylor Landlord. ♀ 11 **Facilities** Non-diners area ❤ (Bar Garden) ♦♦ Children's menu Children's portions Garden ⋒ Parking WiFi ▦ (notice required)

NEWTON-ON-THE-MOOR
Map 21 NU10

The Cook and Barker Inn ★★★★ INN   PICK OF THE PUBS

tel: 01665 575234 **NE65 9JY**
email: info@cookandbarkerinn.co.uk **web:** www.cookandbarkerinn.co.uk
dir: *0.5m from A1 S of Alnwick*

International food in traditional Northumbrian inn with amazing views

A traditional, stone-built inn clad in creepers and flower baskets, The Cook and Barker enjoys spectacular views of the Northumberland coast and the Cheviot Hills. Phil Farmer's long-established family business goes way beyond simply providing 'pub grub with rooms', thanks to his deployment of expert front-of-house and skilled kitchen teams. As he also runs Hope House Farm eight miles away, he has no trouble sourcing the organic beef, lamb and pork that feature on the wide-ranging bar and restaurant menus. These offer modern European cuisine focusing on seafood and 'forest and field' with the occasional influence from Asia. Typically, start with Thai shredded pork and noodle salad with ginger and lemongrass, continue with fillet of sea bass and crab and shrimp risotto; or grilled lamb's liver, onions, black pudding and bacon. The cosy en suite bedrooms are smartly furnished, some with traditional features such as exposed beams.

Open all day all wk 12-11 **Food** Lunch all wk 12-2 Dinner all wk 6-9 Set menu available Restaurant menu available all wk ⊕ FREE HOUSE ◀ Timothy Taylor Landlord, Black Sheep, Bass ☓ Kopparberg. **Facilities** Non-diners area ♦♦ Children's portions Garden ⋒ Parking WiFi ▦ (notice required) **Rooms** 18

SEAHOUSES
Map 21 NU23

The Bamburgh Castle Inn ★★★ INN

tel: 01665 720283 **NE68 7SQ**
email: enquiries@bamburghcastleinn.co.uk **web:** www.bamburghcastleinn.co.uk
dir: *A1 onto B1341 to Bamburgh, B1340 to Seahouses, follow signs to harbour*

Harbourside inn with superb Farne Islands views

With its prime location on the quayside giving wraparound sea views as far as the Farne Islands, this is surely one of the best positioned pubs anywhere along Northumberland's stunning coast. Dating back to the 18th century, the inn has been transformed in more recent times to offer superb bar and dining areas plus seating outside. A beer festival is held in the garden every year, children and dogs are welcomed, and pub dishes of locally sourced food represent excellent value. Typical of these are venison and chilli pâté; home-made fishcakes; and Moroccan lamb steak.

Open all day all wk **Food** Contact pub for details ⊕ FREE HOUSE ◀ Hadrian Border Farne Island. ♀ 11 **Facilities** Non-diners area ❤ (Bar Restaurant Garden) ♦♦ Children's menu Children's portions Family room Garden ⋒ Beer festival Parking WiFi ▦ (notice required) **Rooms** 29

The Olde Ship Inn ★★★★ INN   PICK OF THE PUBS

tel: 01665 720200 **9 Main St NE68 7RD**
email: theoldeship@seahouses.co.uk **web:** www.seahouses.co.uk
dir: *Lower end of main street above harbour*

Family-owned inn with a nautical theme

Built on farmland around 1745, this stone-built inn with rooms has been in the present owners' family for the past century. Set above the bustling old harbour of Seahouses, The Olde Ship interior is lit through stained-glass windows and the main saloon bar is full of character, its wooden floor made from ships' decking. A range of whiskies is supplemented by a selection of real ales, such as Hadrian Border Farne Island and Black Sheep. The inn's corridors and boat gallery are an Aladdin's cave of antique nautical artefacts, ranging from a figurehead to all manner of ship's brasses and dials. Bar foods include locally caught seafood and home-made soups. In the evenings, starters like a crab and prawn ramekin or home-made meatloaf with apple and apricot chutney might be followed by smoked fish chowder; BBQ spare ribs and chips or seafood platter. Some of the bedrooms have views of the Farne Islands.

Open all day all wk 11-11 (Sun 12-11) **Food** Lunch all wk 12-2.30 Dinner all wk 7-8.30 (no D late Nov-late Jan) ⊕ FREE HOUSE ◀ Greene King Ruddles, Courage Directors, Hadrian Border Farne Island, Morland Old Speckled Hen, High House Farm Nel's Best, Black Sheep, Theakston ☓ Westons Old Rosie & Family Reserve. ♀ 10 **Facilities** Non-diners area ♦♦ Children's menu Children's portions Family room Garden ⋒ Parking WiFi **Rooms** 18

SLAGGYFORD
Map 18 NY65

The Kirkstyle Inn

tel: 01434 381559 **CA8 7PB**
email: mail@andrewmarkland.plus.com
dir: *Just off A689, 6m N of Alston*

Wonderful views of the South Tyne Valley

Slaggyford has no shop or school, but when the South Tynedale Railway, currently being restored, reaches the village it will again have a station and its first trains since 1976. Thankfully, it already has the 18th-century Kirkstyle Inn, named after the stile into the adjacent churchyard and blessed with wonderful views of the river. In winter a log fire heats the bar, where among the real ales are Yates Best Bitter and a summer brew named after the inn. On the menu are local sausages with Alston honey mustard; shepherd's suet pudding; and breaded scampi. Fridays and Saturdays are steak nights.

Open 12-3 6-11 Closed Mon (Tue in winter) **Food** Lunch Tue-Sun 12-2 Dinner Tue-Sat 6-8.30 ⊕ FREE HOUSE ◀ Kirkstyle Ale, Yates Best Bitter, Guinness. **Facilities** Non-diners area ✿ (Bar Outside area) ◀ Children's portions Outside area ⅁ Parking WiFi ⇔ (notice required)

WARDEN
Map 21 NY96

The Boatside Inn

tel: 01434 602233 **NE46 4SQ**
email: sales@theboatsideinn.com **web:** www.theboatsideinn.com
dir: *From A69 W of Hexham, follow signs to Warden Newborough & Fourstones*

A traditional haven for walkers and cyclists

Standing beneath Warden Hill at the confluence of the North and South Tyne rivers, The Boatside is surrounded by woodland footpaths and bridleways, and has fishing rights on the river. The name of this stone-built country free house harks back to the days when a rowing boat ferried people across the river before the bridge was built. Black Sheep, Wylam and Mordue ales are on offer in the bar with its log fire and dart board. Meals are served in the conservatory, restaurant or snug, and include curry of the day, seasonal game casserole, seafood pie, Japanese stir-fry and mushroom Stroganoff. The Boatside welcomes children too.

Open all day all wk 11-11 (Sun 11-10.30) **Food** Lunch Mon-Sat 11-9, Sun 12-8 Dinner Mon-Sat 11-9, Sun 12-8 Av main course £9.95 ⊕ FREE HOUSE ◀ Black Sheep, Caffrey's Irish Ale, John Smith's, Mordue, Wylam. **Facilities** Non-diners area ✿ (Bar Garden) ◀ Children's menu Children's portions Garden ⅁ Parking WiFi ⇔ (notice required)

WARENFORD
Map 21 NU12

The White Swan ◉

tel: 01668 213453 **NE70 7HY**
email: dianecuthbert@yahoo.com
dir: *100yds E of A1, 10m N of Alnwick*

Award-winning cuisine just off the main road

This 200-year-old coaching inn stands near the original toll bridge over the Waren Burn. Formerly on the Great North Road, the building is now just a stone's throw from the A1. Inside, you'll find thick stone walls and an open fire for colder days; in summer, there's a small sheltered seating area outside, with further seats in the adjacent field. The Dukes of Northumberland once owned the pub, and its windows and plasterwork still bear the family crests. Visitors and locals alike enjoy the welcoming atmosphere, fine wines and Northumbrian ales. The modern British dishes are created in-house from the county's produce; the bread, preserves and desserts are home made too. Try perhaps pheasant and black pudding terrine with black grape, apricot and cumin chutney; and seared duck breast, apple and hazelnut fricassée, anise velouté. Vegetarians are well catered for, with interesting dishes like baked tower of aubergine, courgette, onion, sweet pepper and mushroom, beetroot sorbet and blue cheese.

Open all wk Mon-Sat 12-2.30, 5.30-10 (Sun all day) **Food** Lunch all wk 12-2.30 Dinner all wk 6-9 Av main course £14.50 ⊕ FREE HOUSE ◀ Caledonian Flying Scotsman, Hadrian Border Tyneside Blonde, Greene King IPA. Ⓐ 10 **Facilities** Non-diners area ✿ (Bar Garden) ◀ Children's menu Children's portions Garden ⅁ Parking WiFi ⇔

NOTTINGHAMSHIRE

BEESTON
Map 11 SK53

The Victoria

tel: 0115 925 4049 **Dovecote Ln NG9 1JG**
email: victoriabeeston@btconnect.com
dir: *M1 junct 25, A52 E. Turn right at Nurseryman PH, right opposite Rockaway Hotel into Barton St, 1st left, adjacent to railway station*

Excellent range of beers, ciders and whiskies

This free house combines a welcoming atmosphere with great food and a wide choice of traditional ales and ciders, continental beers and lagers, many wines by the glass and single malt whiskies. The Victoria dates from 1899 when it was built next to Beeston Railway Station, and the large, heated patio garden is still handy for a touch of train-spotting. Main courses could include chicken souvlaki; smoked haddock, fresh spinach and prawn lasagne, or cottage pie with bacon and cheddar crust. There are just as many options for vegetarians. Check out the dates of the four annual beer festivals – end of January, Easter, last two weeks in July, and October.

Open all day all wk 10.30am-11pm (Sun 12-11) Closed 26 Dec **Food** Lunch Sun-Tue 12-8.45, Wed-Sat 12-9.30 ⊕ FREE HOUSE ◀ Batemans XB, Castle Rock Harvest Pale, Everards Tiger, Holden's Black Country Bitter, Blue Monkey, Kelham Island Best Bitter, Guest ales ⒹThatchers Traditional, Broadoak, Biddenden Bushels. Ⓐ 25 **Facilities** Non-diners area ✿ (Bar Garden) ◀ Children's portions Garden ⅁ Beer festival Parking WiFi

BLIDWORTH   Map 16 SK55

Fox & Hounds

tel: 01623 792383 **Blidworth Bottoms NG21 0NW**
email: info@foxandhounds-pub.com **web:** www.foxandhounds-pub.com
dir: *From Ravenshead towards Blidworth on B6020, right to Blidworth*

Revitalised country pub with theatrical leanings

A fusion of blues, creams, reds and a change of furniture and fabrics have revitalised the pub without damaging the traditional country-style character that stem from its early 19th-century origins. For nearly 100 years the locals have performed a 'Plough Play' in the pub every January, recalling the days when Blidworth Bottoms was a larger community with shops and a post office. The Greene King ales are reliable as ever, and the refreshed menu still delivers well-priced dishes of popular home-made favourites, such as beef casserole and herb dumplings or cottage pie.

Open all day all wk 11.30-11.30 (Fri-Sat 11.30am-mdnt) **Food** Lunch all wk 11.30-9 Dinner all wk 11.30-9 ⊕ GREENE KING ◀ Morland Old Golden Hen, Hardys & Hansons Best Bitter & Olde Trip, Black Sheep, Seasonal guest ales Ŏ Thatchers Gold. ☗ 9 **Facilities** Non-diners area ❄ (Bar Garden) ♦ Children's menu Children's portions Play area Garden ⊟ Parking ▄

CAR COLSTON   Map 11 SK74

The Royal Oak

tel: 01949 20247 **The Green NG13 8JE**
email: rich-vicky@btconnect.com
dir: *From Newark-on-Trent on A46 follow Mansfield, then Car Colston signs. From rdbt N of Bingham on A46 follow Car Colston sign. Left at next rdbt signed Car Colston*

Good pub food and an intriguing past

Some experts attribute origins as a hosiery factory to this 200-year-old inn, citing as evidence its unusual vaulted brick ceiling, undoubtedly capable of supporting any weighty textile machinery above. Much older is the centurion, perhaps from the nearby Roman-British town of Margidunum, whose ghost you may run into. Normally on duty in the bar is owner Richard Spencer, dispensing his carefully tended Marston's, Brakspear and Wychwood real ales, while Vicky, his wife (a dab hand chef) is in the kitchen preparing dishes such as fresh beer-battered or oven-baked haddock; shepherd's pie; and her very popular steak pies.

Open all wk 11.30-3 5.30-11 (Fri-Sat 11.30-11 Sun 12-10.30) **Food** Lunch Mon-Sat 12-2.15, Sun 12-4 Dinner Mon-Sat 6-8.45 ⊕ MARSTON'S ◀ Marston's EPA & Burton Bitter, Brakspear Bitter, Wychwood Hobgoblin. ☗ 13 **Facilities** Non-diners area ❄ (Bar Garden) ♦ Children's portions Garden ⊟ Parking WiFi ▄ (notice required)

CAUNTON   Map 17 SK76

Caunton Beck   `PICK OF THE PUBS`

tel: 01636 636793 **NG23 6AB**
email: email@cauntonbeck.com
dir: *6m NW of Newark on A616 to Sheffield*

A village pub-restaurant open early until late

The eponymous stream charts a willow-lined course behind this engaging village dining pub, which stands close to the impressive St Andrew's church. An imposing rose arbour created by a former vicar features at the pantile-roofed, much extended 16th-century cottages at the core of the pub. Fans of the hop can expect a glass of Oakham Ales JHB alongside three further real ales; wine-lovers have a sturdy choice of 24 by the glass. Like its sister establishment the Wig & Mitre in Lincoln, meals begin with breakfast and continue throughout the day until late evening, and can be taken outside on the terrace. The seasonally changing menus tempt with a range of modern European and solidly British dishes. A starter of Cornish sardines panzenella sets the scene for mains like pot roast guinea fowl jardinière with smokey bacon and tarragon broth, with an exemplary cheeseboard to finish. Blackboard specials extend the choice, whilst their regular gourmet evenings prove very popular.

Open all day all wk 9am-10.30pm Closed 25 Dec **Food** Lunch all wk 9am-10pm Dinner all wk 9am-10pm Av main course £12.50 Set menu available Restaurant menu available all wk ⊕ FREE HOUSE ◀ Black Sheep, Oakham Ales JHB, Guinness, Guest ales Ŏ Westons Stowford Press. ☗ 24 **Facilities** Non-diners area ❄ (Bar Garden Outside area) ♦ Children's menu Children's portions Garden Outside area ⊟ Parking WiFi

COLSTON BASSETT

Map 11 SK73

The Martin's Arms

PICK OF THE PUBS

See Pick of the Pubs on opposite page

EDWINSTOWE

Map 16 SK66

Forest Lodge ★★★★ INN

tel: 01623 824443 **4 Church St NG21 9QA**
email: reception@forestlodgehotel.co.uk **web:** www.forestlodgehotel.co.uk
dir: *A614 towards Edwinstowe, onto B6034. Inn opposite church*

Lovingly restored coaching inn at the edge of Robin Hood's Sherwood

This 18th-century coaching inn stands on the edge of Sherwood Forest opposite the church where Robin Hood reputedly married Maid Marian. Sympathetically restored by the Thompson family over the past decade, it includes stylish accommodation and a comfortable restaurant and bar. Award-winning cask ales are always on tap in two beamed bars warmed by open fires. An impressive baronial-style dining hall is an ideal setting for wholesome fare such as roast rabbit loin, baby leeks, braised lettuce and red wine essence; followed by oak-smoked haddock with champ potato, black pudding and cauliflower pureé; or confit leg of guinea fowl with goose fat roast potatoes and Savoy cabbage.

Open all wk 11.30-3 5.30-11 (Fri 11.30-3 5-11 Sun 12-3 6-10.30) Closed 1 Jan **Food** Lunch all wk 12-2.30 Dinner all wk 6-9.30 ⊕ FREE HOUSE ◀ Wells Bombardier, Kelham Island Pale Rider, Forest Lodge English Pale Ale, Ossett Silver King. **Facilities** Non-diners area ♦♦ Children's menu Children's portions Garden ⊨ Parking WiFi ➡ (notice required) **Rooms** 13

FARNDON

Map 17 SK75

The Farndon Boathouse ⊛

PICK OF THE PUBS

tel: 01636 676578 **Off Wyke Ln NG24 3SX**
email: info@farndonboathouse.co.uk
dir: *From A46 rdbt (SW of Newark-on-Trent) take Fosse Way signed Farndon. Right into Main St signed Farndon. At T-junct right into Wyke Ln, follow Boathouse signs*

Riverside pub serving award-winning food

Superbly located on the banks of the River Trent, this modern bar and eatery is styled on an old boathouse and many customers prefer to arrive in style by cruiser. Whichever mode of transport you take, the extensively glazed frontage is a lovely spot to watch sunsets. Clad in wood, with chunky exposed roof trusses, stone floors and warehouse-style lighting, it makes for a relaxed setting for the food, which has won an AA Rosette. Head chef Dan Garner champions local sourcing and home preparation, with home-smoked meats, fish and cheeses, for example, and herbs and leaves grown in the kitchen garden. Exciting dishes include Asian duck salad; chargrilled Barnsley lamb chop, creamed mash, buttered curly kale, salsa verde and minted redcurrant jus; and shallot and walnut tart Tatin. Cask-conditioned real ales change frequently and there are some 46 wines by the glass. Live music is played every Sunday evening.

Open all day all wk 10am-11pm **Food** Lunch Mon-Fri 12-2.30, Sat-Sun 12-3 Dinner all wk 6-9.30 Set menu available Restaurant menu available all wk ⊕ FREE HOUSE ◀ Greene King IPA, Guest ales Ö Thatchers. ♥ 46 **Facilities** Non-diners area ♦♦ Children's menu Children's portions Garden Parking WiFi ➡ (notice required)

HARBY

Map 17 SK87

Bottle & Glass

tel: 01522 703438 **High St NG23 7EB**
email: email@bottleandglassharby.com
dir: *S of A57 (Lincoln to Markham Moor road)*

Village inn with historic links

Just seven miles west of Lincoln, this lovely old free house is situated in the peaceful village of Harby – famous for being where Edward I's wife Eleanor is said to have died in 1290. Compact and convivial, with flagged floors and heavy beams, the pub offers great food, beginning with full English breakfast and with sandwiches and light meals available all day. Seasonal main dishes include baked cheese soufflé with purple sprouting broccoli and beetroot; or line-caught cod with spinach, new potatoes and pink grapefruit rind sauce. There's also a wide selection of tapas dishes. Inevitably, the terrace is popular on sunny days.

Open all day all wk 10am-11pm Closed 25 Dec **Food** Lunch Mon-Fri & Sun 10-9.30, Sat 10-10 Dinner Mon-Fri & Sun 10-9.30, Sat 10-10 Set menu available Restaurant menu available all wk ⊕ FREE HOUSE ◀ Young's Bitter & London Gold, Black Sheep, Guinness Ö Thatchers Gold. ♥ 24 **Facilities** Non-diners area ♥ (Bar Garden) ♦♦ Children's menu Children's portions Play area Garden ⊨ Parking WiFi

HOVERINGHAM

Map 11 SK74

NEW The Reindeer Inn

tel: 0115 966 3629 **Main St NG14 7JR**
email: reindeer@castlerockbrewery.co.uk
dir: *NE of Nottingham. Phone for detailed directions*

Reliable village inn close to lakeside walks

Piles of logs by the door beneath a flowery pergola signal the warm and friendly welcome offered at this traditionally furnished and decorated village pub in the Trent Valley lakeland. Set back from a main street lined with attractive cottages, it has a beer garden that overlooks the cricket ground, where trays of beers from Nottingham's Castle Rock Brewery slake a summer thirst. The quality pub-food menus change daily, but always include the signature dishes of Scotch egg with soft poached egg, leeks and cheese sauce; and dry-aged rib of Nottinghamshire beef. Themed dining nights - fish and lobster or food and wine - extend the dining choices.

Open 12-close (Mon-Tue 5-close Wed 12-3 5-close) Closed Mon L & Tue L **Food** Lunch Wed-Sat 12-2, Sun 12-3.30 Dinner Tue-Sat 6.30-9 Av main course £9.95-£19.95 Set menu available ⊕ FREE HOUSE ◀ Castle Rock Harvest Pale, Black Sheep Best Bitter Ö Westons Stowford Press. ♥ 12 **Facilities** Non-diners area ♥ (Bar Garden Outside area) ♦♦ Children's portions Garden Outside area ⊨ Parking ➡ (notice required)

PICK OF THE PUBS

The Martin's Arms

COLSTON BASSETT   Map 11 SK73

tel: 01949 81361
School Ln NG12 3FD
email: martins_arms@hotmail.com
web: www.themartinsarms.co.uk
dir: *Exit A46 between Leicester & Newark*

Traditional 18th-century pub with seasonally inspired menus

In the pretty village of Colston Bassett in the Vale of Belvoir, this striking Grade-II listed building occupies a quintessentially English spot on the corner of a leafy cul-de-sac close to an old cross. At the heart of village life since the 18th century, the pub takes its name from Henry Martin, MP for Kinsale in County Cork, who was the local squire in the early 19th century. Close to National Trust land, the pub is surrounded by ancient trees in the estate parkland to which it belonged until 1990, when the current owners, Jack Inguanta and Lynne Strafford Bryan, bought it, undertaking to maintain its character and unique atmosphere. This they have clearly managed to do, since much of the interior will transport you straight back in time, especially the Jacobean fireplaces and the period furnishings. The bar has an impressive range of real ales, with Castle Rock Harvest Pale waving the flag for the county, while another local 'brew' is elderflower pressé from Belvoir Fruit Farms. Bread,

preserves, sauces, terrines, soups, pasta and much, much more are all made on site. Classic pub dishes include a pie of the day; fish and chips and a beef burger teamed with Colston Bassett's famous Stilton, while mains from the à la carte might include rolled pork loin, pork pie purée and cripsy black pudding nuggets; or pan-fried Gressingham duck breast with roasted carrot purée, orange and coriander caramel, sweet potato fondant and escabech salad. Among the desserts are textures of forced Yorkshire rhubarb, granola, pannacotta and refresher merangue; and hot and cold jam sandwich, liquid peanut butter and roasted peanut milk. Overlooked by the church spire, the one-acre garden incorporates a croquet lawn.

Open all wk 12-3 6-11 (Sun 12-4 7-11) Closed 25 Dec eve & 26 Dec eve **Food** Lunch Mon-Sat 12-2, Sun 12-2.30 Dinner Mon-Sat 6-9.30 Restaurant menu available all wk. ⊕ FREE HOUSE ◀ Marston's Pedigree, Bass, Greene King IPA, Timothy Taylor Landlord, Castle Rock Harvest Pale ♻ Aspall. ♀ **Facilities** Non-diners area ♦ Children's portions Family room Garden ⇥ Parking WiFi 🚌 (notice required)

KIMBERLEY
Map 11 SK44

The Nelson & Railway Inn

tel: 0115 938 2177 **12 Station Rd NG16 2NR**
dir: *M1 junct 26, A610 to Kimberley*

Family-run former railway inn

This popular village pub has been run by the same family for nearly 45 years. Originally 17th-century with Victorian additions, it sits next door to the Hardys & Hansons Brewery that supplies many of the beers. Sadly the two nearby railway stations that once made it a railway inn are now derelict. Interesting brewery prints and railway signs decorate the beamed bar and lounge. A hearty menu of pub favourites includes ploughman's and hot rolls, as well as grills and pub classics like lasagne, scampi and chips and home-made steak and ale pie.

Open all day all wk 11am-mdnt **Food** Lunch Mon-Fri 12-2.30, Sat 12-9, Sun 12-6 Dinner Mon-Fri 5.30-9, Sat 12-9 ⊕ GREENE KING ◀ Hardys & Hansons Best Bitter, Cool & Dark Mild, Guest ales. **Facilities** Non-diners area ⊪ Children's menu Children's portions Family room Garden Beer festival Parking WiFi ▭

LAXTON
Map 17 SK76

The Dovecote Inn

tel: 01777 871586 **Cross Hill NG22 OSX**
email: dovecote_inn@btconnect.com
dir: *Exit A1 at Tuxford through Egmanton to Laxton*

Superb local produce features on the menus

This family-run, 18th-century pub has a delightful beer garden with views of the church, while the interior has a bar as well as three cosy wining and dining rooms. Like most of the village of Laxton, it is Crown Estate property, belonging to the Royal Family. The seasonal, home-cooked dishes could include duck liver and brandy parfait with red onion compôte, Madeira jelly and toasted sourdough; smoked haddock with poached egg and creamy saffron and chive risotto; and cinnamon poached pear with cocoa meringue, chocolate sauce and pear sorbet. There's a country day every March, which includes beer, a hog roast, and plenty of country pursuits.

Open all wk 11.30-3 5.30-11 (Sun 12-10.30) **Food** Lunch Mon-Sat 11.30-3, Sun all day Dinner Mon-Sat 5.30-11, Sun all day Av main course £11 Set menu available ⊕ FREE HOUSE ◀ Castle Rock Harvest Pale, Black Sheep Best Bitter, Timothy Taylor Landlord, Guest ales. ▼ 11 **Facilities** Non-diners area ⊪ Children's menu Children's portions Garden Parking WiFi ▭ (notice required)

MORTON
Map 17 SK75

The Full Moon Inn
`PICK OF THE PUBS`

tel: 01636 830251 **Main St NG25 OUT**
email: bookings@thefullmoonmorton.co.uk
dir: *A617 from Newark towards Mansfield. Past Kelham, left to Rolleston & follow signs to Morton*

Pretty red-brick pub with year-round appeal

Big flavours, no frills is the motto at this ivy-clad Trent Valley free house with a charming summer garden. William and Rebecca White have transformed the place into a contemporary and comfortable pub, exposing the old beams and brickwork from the original 18th-century cottages, and bringing in reclaimed panelling and furniture. The choice on hand-pull shows that William takes his real ales seriously, whilst Rebecca's forte is cooking. Her kitchen produces farm-fresh dishes based on locally sourced ingredients for finely judged and competitively priced menus. Typical of the starters is a generous ham hock salad with new potatoes, green beans, soft boiled egg and honey mustard dressing. Follow this with a braised blade of beef with celeriac remoulade, watercress, capers and red wine jus. The pub is truly

family-friendly, with prompt service for hungry children to ensure their parents enjoy a relaxing experience; dogs are welcome too.

Open all wk fr 11am **Food** Lunch Mon-Fri 12-2, Sat 12-2.30, Sun 12-4 Dinner Mon-Fri 5.30-9, Sat 6-9.30 Av main course £10 ⊕ FREE HOUSE ◀ Black Sheep, Navigation Pale, Sharp's Doom Bar, Timothy Taylor. ▼ 9 **Facilities** Non-diners area ❧ (Bar Garden) ⊪ Children's menu Children's portions Play area Family room Garden Parking WiFi ▭ (notice required)

NEWARK-ON-TRENT
Map 17 SK75

The Prince Rupert

tel: 01636 918121 **46 Stodman St NG24 1AW**
email: info@theprincerupert.co.uk
dir: *5 mins walk from Castle on entry road to Market Sq*

Brimming with character and charm

The 15th-century Prince Rupert oozes character and charm and is one of Newark's most historic pubs. Expect old beams, wood floors, crackling log fires and cosy corners in the series of small downstairs rooms; make sure you explore upstairs, as the ancient architectural features are stunning. To drink, Oakham Ales JHB and Brains The Rev. James take pride of place alongside constantly changing choices while menus take in pub classics and excellent stone-baked pizzas. There are regular live music events and beer and cider festivals in the summer months.

Open all day all wk 10am-mdnt (Fri-Sat 10am-1am Sun 12-12) Closed 25 Dec **Food** Lunch Sun-Fri 12-2.30, Sat 12-5 Dinner all wk 6-9 ⊕ FREE HOUSE ◀ Brains The Rev. James, Oakham Ales JHB ♂ Westons Wyld Wood Organic Vintage. ▼ 16 **Facilities** Non-diners area ⊪ Outside area Beer festival Cider festival WiFi ▭

NOTTINGHAM
Map 11 SK53

Fellows Morton & Clayton

tel: 0115 950 6795 **54 Canal St NG1 7EH**
email: office@fellowsmortonandclayton.co.uk
dir: *Phone for detailed directions*

Britain's canal heritage on a plate

The pub used to be the headquarters of FM&C, until 1948 the largest canal transportation company in England. From the Castle Wharf complex, the pub's cobbled courtyard overlooks the Nottingham Canal. A giant plasma screen might be showing a big sporting event while you tuck into a salad, pasta, burger, light meal or more substantial dish, such as hand-made pork faggots with Irish champ potato, peas and carrots; rolled and stuffed pork belly with crispy crackling, sweet potato mash and green beans; or beef and ale gravy pie. Nottingham EPA is one of the real ales.

Open all day all wk **Food** Lunch all wk 10-3 Dinner Thu-Sun 3-9 ⊕ ENTERPRISE INNS ◀ Timothy Taylor Landlord, Fuller's London Pride, Nottingham EPA, St Austell Trelawny ♂ Westons Scrumpy. **Facilities** Non-diners area Children's portions Garden Parking WiFi ▭ (notice required)

Ye Olde Trip to Jerusalem
`PICK OF THE PUBS`

tel: 0115 947 3171 **1 Brewhouse Yard, Castle Rd NG1 6AD**
email: 4925@greeneking.co.uk
dir: *In town centre*

Medieval gem with history aplenty

Castle Rock, upon which stands Nottingham Castle, is riddled by caves and passageways cut into the sandstone. The builders of this unusual pub made the most of this, incorporating some of the caves into the design of the inn, one of Britain's oldest- founded in AD1189. The name recalls that soldiers, clergy and penitents gathered here before embarking on the Crusade to the Holy Land – doubtless they drank to their quest at the castle's beerhouse before their trip to

Jerusalem. Centuries of service impart instant appeal, from the magpie collection of furnishings in the warren of rooms to the unique Rock Lounge, and quirks such as the cursed galleon and the fertility chair. Beers from the Nottingham Brewery feature strongly, accompanying a reliable menu of old favourites like slow-cooked pork belly and Scottish scampi, to tapas style dishes, sharing plates, lighter mains and fish such as oven-baked cod, crayfish and spinach fishcakes. Several annual beer festivals.

Open all day all wk 11-11 (Fri-Sat 11am-mdnt) Closed 25 Dec **Food** Dinner all wk 11-10 ⊕ GREENE KING ◾ IPA & Abbot Ale, Hardys & Hansons Olde Trip, Nottingham guest ales ♂ Aspall. ▼ 13 **Facilities** Non-diners area ◀ Garden Beer festival WiFi ▭ (notice required)

TUXFORD	Map 17 SK77

NEW The Fountain

tel: 01777 872854 **155 Lincoln Rd NG22 OJQ**
email: icthefountain@gmail.com
dir: *Phone for detailed directions*

Family-oriented pub with a good local reputation

Sir Walter Scott called the Great North Road "the dullest road in the world". Today, as the A1(M), it's even duller, so turn off into Tuxford and find this rejuvenated pub. After being closed for a while, it reopened in 2013, with its beams, exposed stone, and little nooks and crannies all intact. On tap are beers from Welbeck Abbey Brewery and cider from the Scrumpy Wasp company in East Markham. If you want food that's more than basic pub grub without being pretentious, this is the place: for example, home-made Scotch egg with crispy pancetta salad and red pepper piperade; shank of lamb braised in red wine with mashed potatoes, root vegetables and mint; and smoked salmon with dill and penne pasta in cream and white wine sauce. Pies come with various fillings - game, fish or roasted root vegetables, and there are steaks and a mixed grill.

Open all day all wk **Food** Contact pub for details Set menu available ⊕ FREE HOUSE ◾ Welbeck Abbey Brewery ♂ Scrumpy Wasp. ▼ **Facilities** Non-diners area ◀ Children's menu Children's portions Play area Garden ▭ Parking WiFi ▭ (notice required)

The Mussel & Crab

tel: 01777 870491 **Sibthorpe Hill NG22 OPJ**
email: musselandcrab1@hotmail.com **web:** www.musselandcrab.com
dir: *From Ollerton/Tuxford junct of A1 & A57. N on B1164 to Sibthorpe Hill. Pub 800yds on right*

A huge choice of seafood dishes

Landlocked Nottinghamshire may not offer sea views but Bruce and Allison Elliott-Bateman have turned this quirky pub into a renowned seafood restaurant since taking over in the late 1990s. Beautifully fresh fish and seafood dominate the menu, with food served in a multitude of rooms; the piazza room is styled as an Italian courtyard and the beamed restaurant is big on rustic charm. Over a dozen blackboards offer ever-changing fish dishes, as well as 'things that don't swim'. You could select rock oysters, chargrilled swordfish and a mini Baileys cheesecake, or whole camembert, duo of pork and crème brûlée.

Open all wk 11-3 6-11 **Food** Lunch Mon-Sat 11-2.30, Sun 11-3 Dinner Mon-Sat 6-10, Sun 6-9 Av main course £15 Set menu available ⊕ FREE HOUSE ◾ Tetley's Smoothflow & Cask, Guinness ♂ Somersby. ▼ 16 **Facilities** Non-diners area ◀ (Bar Garden) ◀ Children's menu Family room Garden ▭ Parking

---

OXFORDSHIRE

ADDERBURY	Map 11 SP43

Red Lion ★★★ INN

tel: 01295 810269 **The Green OX17 3LU**
email: 6496@greeneking.co.uk
dir: *S of Banbury on A4260*

Historic inn overlooking the village green

A fine stone-built coaching inn overlooking the village green. Dating back to English Civil War times, it was once owned by the Royalists who, a tad sycophantically, called it The King's Arms. A list of landlords since 1690 is displayed inside, where age-blackened 'duck or grouse' beams, oak panelling and great big fireplaces set the scene for daily newspapers, real ales and good wines. Classic dishes include British beef and Ruddles ale pie; slow-cooked lamb shank; chicken tikka masala; and grilled sea bass fillets. Accommodation is provided in 12 individually designed rooms.

Open all day all wk Mon-Thu 7am-11pm (Fri 7am-11.30pm Sat 8am-11.30pm Sun 8am-10.30pm) ⊕ GREENE KING ◾ Rotating ales. **Facilities** ◀ Children's menu Children's portions Garden Parking WiFi **Rooms** 12

BAMPTON	Map 5 SP30

The Romany

tel: 01993 850237 **Bridge St OX18 2HA**
email: theromanyinnbampton@yahoo.co.uk
dir: *Phone for detailed directions*

A warm welcome and live entertainment

This 18th-century building of Cotswold stone was a shop until a couple of decades ago. Now a pretty inn, The Romany counts a beamed bar, log fires and intimate dining room among its many charms. The choice of food ranges from bar snacks and bar meals to a full carte, with home-made specials like lasagne, chicken Romany, or chilli and chips. There is also a good range of vegetarian choices. The garden might be just the spot to enjoy a pint of Hooky Bitter or London Pride. Regional singers provide live entertainment a couple of times a month.

Open all day all wk 12-12 **Food** Lunch Fri-Sat 12-9, Sun 12-3 Dinner Tue-Thu 4-9, Fri-Sat 12-9 Av main course £8.50 ⊕ PUNCH TAVERNS ◾ Hook Norton Hooky Bitter, Fuller's London Pride, Guest ales. **Facilities** Non-diners area ◀ Children's menu Children's portions Play area Garden ▭ WiFi ▭ (notice required)

BANBURY
Map 11 SP44

The Wykham Arms

tel: 01295 788808 **Temple Mill Rd, Sibford Gower OX15 5RX**
email: info@wykhamarms.co.uk **web:** www.wykhamarms.co.uk
dir: *Between Banbury & Shipston-on-Stour off B4035*

Attractive village inn with modern menu

A beautiful thatched, mellow stone pub in a hilly village of venerable, reed-roofed cottages at the edge of The Cotswolds. With roses round the door and a cosy courtyard for long summer evenings, it's the idyllic rural inn. With a brace and more of real ales, including one from local brewers Whale, proprietors and classically trained chefs Damian and Debbie Bradley skilfully balance the wet side of the pub with a regularly changing menu of contemporary dishes. Snack on a chicken satay light-bite or plump for mains like lentil, mushroom and spinach cottage pie, or pavé of fresh cod with smoked salmon and prawn potato cake, roast fennel and pea cream.

Open 12-3 6-11 Closed 25 Dec, Mon (ex BHs) **Food** Lunch Tue-Sun 12-2.30 Dinner Tue-Sat 6-9.30 Av main course £17.50 Restaurant menu available Tue-Sat ⊕ FREE HOUSE ◀ Wye Valley HPA, St Austell Trelawny, Whale Ale Brewery, Guinness ♂ Guest ciders. 🍷 20 **Facilities** Non-diners area ❤ (Bar Garden Outside area) ♦️ Children's portions Family room Garden Outside area ⏚ Parking WiFi

See advert on opposite page

Ye Olde Reindeer Inn

tel: 01295 270972 **47 Parsons St OX16 5NA**
email: thereindeerbanbury@gmail.com
dir: *1m from M40 junct 11, in town centre just off market square. Car park access via Bolton Rd*

Town pub with interesting history

Cotswold-brewed beers from the renowned Hook Norton Brewery draw in a lively local clientele to this historic pub right at the core of old Banbury, just a stone's throw from the Cross of nursery-rhyme fame. Its origins go back to Tudor times, whilst from here in the Civil War Oliver Cromwell himself is believed to have directed his commanders in the richly panelled Globe Room. Weekly events include live music, steak nights and quizzes. Enjoy good, solid pub grub in the traditional, time-worn, classic interior or indulge in a game of Aunt Sally in the flower-decked courtyard.

Open all day all wk Mon-Thu 11am-11pm (Fri-Sat 11am-mdnt Sun 12-10.30) Closed 25 Dec **Food** Lunch all wk 12-3 Dinner Mon-Sat 6-9 ⊕ HOOK NORTON ◀ Hooky Bitter, Old Hooky, Hooky Lion, Hooky Mild ♂ Westons Stowford Press. **Facilities** Non-diners area ❤ (All areas) ♦️ Children's menu Children's portions Family room Garden Outside area ⏚ Beer festival Parking 🚌 (notice required)

BARNARD GATE
Map 5 SP41

The Boot Inn
PICK OF THE PUBS

tel: 01865 881231 **OX29 6XE**
email: info@theboot-inn.com
dir: *Off A40 between Witney & Eynsham*

Where footwear is king

The Cotswolds start just west of ancient Eynsham, where Adelaide-born chef Craig Foster runs the low-beamed, stone-flagged Boot. His inn has a renowned celebrity footwear collection, among which are boots formerly worn by Kevin Pietersen, Stirling Moss and three Jeremys - that's Clarkson, Irons and Paxman; no women seem to be represented. Inside, two open fires set the scene, while outside is a pleasant garden. Otter Ale from Devon and Young's London Gold from Bedford are on tap, as is Symonds cider from Hereford. The wine list is good, too – look for those marked "Landlord's Choice". The lunch menu offers salads, omelettes and sandwiches, while main menu options include Loch Duart gravad lax; braised and pressed blade of beef; and courgette and feta cheese spring roll. Make a booking under the "Roll a Dice" promo and get up to 35 per cent off your bill.

Open all wk 12-3 6-11 (Sun 12-10) **Food** Lunch Mon-Sat 12-2.30, Sun 12-9 Dinner Mon-Sat 7-9.30, Sun 12-9 ⊕ FREE HOUSE ◀ Young's London Gold, Otter Ale, Wells Bombardier ♂ Symonds. 🍷 8 **Facilities** Non-diners area ♦️ Children's menu Children's portions Garden ⏚ Parking WiFi 🚌 (notice required)

BLACK BOURTON
Map 5 SP20

The Vines
PICK OF THE PUBS

See Pick of the Pubs on page 380

BLOXHAM
Map 11 SP43

The Elephant & Castle

tel: 01295 720383 **OX15 4LZ**
email: bloxhamelephant1@btconnect.com
dir: *Take A361 from Banbury towards Chipping Norton, 1st left after shops in Bloxham*

Traditional Cotswold stone coaching inn

Locals play Aunt Sally or shove-ha'penny in this 15th-century coaching inn's big wood-floored bar, whilst the lounge boasts a bar-billiards table and a large inglenook fireplace. External features include an arch that used to straddle the former Banbury to Chipping Norton turnpike; at night the gates of the pub were closed, and no traffic could get over the toll bridge. Today the menu offers toasties and baguettes, and favourites like scampi, crispy cod and vegetarian shepherd's pie. The bar serves seasonal and guest ales as well as Westons ciders. The beer festival in May is part of the Bloxfest Music Festival.

Open all wk 10-3 6-12 (Fri 10-3 5-2am Sat 10am-2am Sun 10am-mdnt) **Food** Lunch Mon-Sat 12-2 ⊕ HOOK NORTON ◀ Hooky Bitter & Seasonal ales, Guest ales ♂ Westons 1st Quality, Old Rosie, Wyld Wood, Perry & Rosie's Pig, Thatchers, Hogan's Picker's Passion & Panking Pole. **Facilities** Non-diners area ❤ (Bar Restaurant Garden) ♦️ Children's menu Children's portions Family room Garden ⏚ Beer festival Cider festival Parking WiFi 🚌

| **BRIGHTWELL BALDWIN** | Map 5 SU69 |

The Lord Nelson Inn

PICK OF THE PUBS

tel: 01491 612497 **OX49 5NP**
email: ladyhamilton1@hotmail.co.uk
dir: *Off B4009 between Watlington & Benson*

Pretty garden for alfresco dining

In Nelson's day the pub was simply known as the Admiral Nelson, but when, in 1797, the great man was elevated to the peerage, the pub's name was elevated too. In 1905, the inn was closed following complaints about over-indulgent estate workers but several years later, the building was bought by a couple who gave it a complete makeover, and The Lord Nelson finally reopened on Trafalgar Day, 1971. Now full of fresh flowers, candlelight and a splendid inglenook fireplace, it's just the place to relax after a country walk or a day at the office. And, during the summer, the pretty terraced garden with its weeping willow is popular for alfresco eating and drinking. All the food is freshly cooked, using local produce where possible. Starters might include twice baked soufflé with wilted spinach, while main course options include pork fillet medallions, creamy leek and apple sauce and champ mash.

Open all wk 12-3 6-11 (Sun 12-10.30) (Summer 11-3 6-11) Closed 25 Dec **Food** Lunch Mon-Sat 12-2.30, Sun 12-3.30 Dinner Mon-Sat 6-10, Sun 7-9.30 Set menu available ⊕ FREE HOUSE ◀ Rebellion IPA, Loose Cannon, Black Sheep ♂ Westons Stowford Press. ⬤ 20 **Facilities** Non-diners area ☻ (Bar Garden Outside area) ♦️ Children's portions Garden Outside area ⋈ Parking WiFi 🚍 (notice required)

| **BRIGHTWELL-CUM-SOTWELL** | Map 5 SU59 |

The Red Lion

tel: 01491 837373 **The Street OX10 0RT**
dir: *From A4130 (Didcot to Wallingford road) follow Brightwell-cum-Sotwell signs. Pub in village centre*

Friendly village pub

This picture-postcard thatched and timbered 16th-century village pub is not only pretty but also a cracking community local. Hearty, traditional pub food is freshly prepared from local produce. Look to the chalkboard for the famous short-crust pastry pies of the day, or the main menu for things like lasagne, pork tenderloin with black pudding and caramelised apple, or vegetable chilli. Don't miss the Sunday roast lunches. The pub holds a beer festival (with live music) for two days every summer. Behind the bar, beers come from the likes of West Berkshire, Loddon and Appleford breweries, while a choice of wine comes from the very local Brightwell Vineyard.

Open all wk 12-3 6-11 **Food** Lunch all wk 12-2 Dinner Tue-Sat 6.30-9 ⊕ FREE HOUSE ◀ West Berkshire Good Old Boy, Loddon Hoppit ♂ Symonds Founders Reserve, Tutts Clump. **Facilities** Non-diners area ☻ (Bar Garden) ♦️ Children's menu Children's portions Garden ⋈ Beer festival Parking WiFi

| **BRITWELL SALOME** | Map 5 SU69 |

NEW The Red Lion

tel: 01491 613140 **OX49 5LG**
dir: *M40 junct 6, B4009 signed Watlington. Through Watlington, follow Benson & B480 signs to Britwell Salome*

Relaxed village inn with confident cooking of local produce

After a spell as a fine dining restaurant, The Red Lion has returned to its pub roots under new owners Eilidh Ferguson and Andrew Hill. With real ales from West Berkshire brewery and a good number of wines by the glass, the pub has reclaimed the locals from this peaceful village, which is also a good base for walkers out exploring the Chilterns. Produce doesn't get more local than pork and beef from the adjacent farm and the menu changes daily. Pheasant and prune terrine might be followed by pork loin steak, Hen of the Wood mushrooms, January King cabbage and mash.

Open 12-3 6-11 (Fri-Sat 12-3 5.30-11 Sun 12-5) Closed 1st wk Jan, 1wk after Etr, 1wk after Summer BH, Sun eve, Mon & Tue L **Food** Lunch 12-2 Dinner 6-9 Restaurant menu available all wk ⊕ FREE HOUSE ◀ West Berkshire Mr Chubb's Lunchtime Bitter, Loose Cannon Bombshell & Dark Horse ♂ Westons Stowford Press. ⬤ 18 **Facilities** Non-diners area ☻ (Bar Restaurant Outside area) ♦️ Children's portions Outside area ⋈ Parking WiFi

PICK OF THE PUBS

The Vines

BLACK BOURTON   Map 5 SP20

tel: 01993 843559
Burford Rd OX18 2PF
email: info@vineshotel.com
web: www.vinesblackbourton.co.uk
dir: *A40 at Witney onto A4095 to Faringdon, 1st right after Bampton to Black Bourton*

Stylish village retreat with modern British food

Ahdy and Karen Gerges bought The Vines, already a highly regarded restaurant and bar, in 2002, and have never looked back. Built of Cotswold stone, as virtually everywhere is round here, it has been an inn since only the 1940s, when it apparently helped relieve pressure on the village local caused by the influx of American servicemen based around here. But beyond the Cotswold stone façade, nowhere else has an interior like it. The striking murals and reliefs in the restaurant and bar are the legacy of John Clegg, who created it for a BBC television programme. Take it all in over a pint of Old Hooky in the spacious and comfortably furnished lounge, or make for the patio, where you can stop playing art critic and play a challenging game of Aunt Sally. The menus list an imaginative choice of internationally influenced modern British dishes, all freshly prepared using locally sourced produce. Typical examples from the starters listed on the

carte include hoi sin duck spring rolls with hoi sin dip; chorizo and chicken skewers with BBQ glaze; or pan-seared scallops with lobster medallions, bresaola, roasted pepper, pistachio and lemon vinaigrette. Then among the mains could be chargrilled aged rib-eye steak with roasted vine tomatoes and triple cooked chips; pan-fried sea bass with vermouth poached mussels, saffron mash, samphire and lemon caraway sauce; or sun-dried tomato and spinach tart Tatin with goats' cheese parmesan tuille, seasonal salad and roasted figs. For dessert try lemon crème brûlée with poached mango and home-made shortbread. There's always a good selection of Old and New World wines.

Open all wk **Food** Dinner Mon-Sat 6-9, Sun 7-9 Restaurant menu available all wk. ⊕ FREE HOUSE ◖ Hook Norton Old Hooky, Tetley's Smoothflow ♂ Westons Stowford Press.**Facilities** Non-diners area ❤ (Garden) ♦♦ Children's menu Children's portions Garden ☐ Parking WiFi ⛟ (notice required)

BROUGHTON
Map 11 SP43

Saye and Sele Arms

tel: 01295 263348 **Main Rd OX15 5ED**
email: mail@sayeandselearms.co.uk
dir: *From Banbury Cross take B4035 to Broughton. Approx 3m*

Peaceful retreat in historic village

Named after the family who own the astonishing, moated Broughton Castle at the edge of this attractive village; this charming, ironstone-built pub is itself over 400 years old. Beams in the cosy restaurant and bar sag with the weight of over 200 collectable water jugs; at the bar, beer lovers will find ales from Vale, Cottage and other micros, pleasing to quaff in the tree-shaded garden. There's a very strong, wide-ranging menu, featuring home-made shortcrust pies from chef-patron Danny McGeehan, typically alongside mains like sea bass, vegetable lasagne, sausage and mash or grilled rump steak. Danny's desserts are also popular, especially the souffléd bread and butter pudding.

Open 11.30-2.30 7-11 (Sat 11.30-3 7-11 Sun 12-5) Closed 25 Dec, Sun eve **Food** Lunch Mon-Sat 12-2 Dinner Mon-Sat 7-9.30 ⊕ FREE HOUSE ◄ Adnams Southwold Bitter, Sharp's Doom Bar, 2 Guest ales Ò Westons Stowford Press, Thatchers Dry. ♀ 9 **Facilities** Non-diners area ¶¶ Children's portions Garden 戸 Parking ⇔ (notice required)

BURCOT
Map 5 SU59

The Chequers

tel: 01865 407771 **OX14 3DP**
email: enquiries@thechequers-burcot.co.uk
dir: *On A415 (Dorchester to Abingdon road) between Clifton Hampden & Dorchester*

Serious but unpretentious British classic food

Steven Sanderson's 400-year-old, thatched and timber-framed pub was once a staging post for boats on the river locals call the Isis, but which everyone else knows as the Thames. As chef, he devises straightforward British classics for his seasonal menus, using carefully chosen meats, fish from Devon and Cornwall markets, mussels from the Norfolk coast, and oysters from Loch Ryan in Scotland and from Jersey. Locals supply game during the winter, and neighbours' gardens and allotments also yield their bounty. Try skate wing with burnt butter, capers, heritage potatoes and samphire; or the rib-eye with triple cooked chips; the wine list reflects his passionate oenological interest.

Open all day all wk 12-11 **Food** Lunch all wk 12-3 Dinner all wk 6.30-9.30 Set menu available Restaurant menu available Tue-Sun ⊕ FREE HOUSE ◄ St Austell Tribute, Young's, Cottage, Loose Cannon Abingdon Bridge, Guest ales Ò Aspall. ♀ 20 **Facilities** Non-diners area ¶¶ Children's menu Children's portions Garden 戸 Parking WiFi ⇔ (notice required)

BURFORD
Map 5 SP21

NEW The Angel at Burford ★★★★ INN ⊛

tel: 01993 822714 **14 Witney St OX18 4SN**
email: enquiries@theangelatburford.co.uk **web:** www.theangelatburford.co.uk

Upmarket 16th-century coaching inn

Refurbishment of the interior was planned as this guide went to press, so the results have yet to be discovered. The exterior, of course, is integral to the timeless Cotswold-stone streetscape and is unlikely to change. Since it's a Hook Norton house, real ale drinkers know where they stand, and what they'll drink when they do. In terms of food, the available-at-all-times (except Sunday lunch) menu offers supreme of corn-fed chicken with chorizo and artichoke hearts; cod fillet with quinoa, cauliflower two ways, capers and pomegranate; and wild mushroom risotto with poached quail's egg and parmesan.

Open all day all wk **Food** Lunch all wk 12-3 Dinner all wk 6-9.30 Av main course £13 Set menu available Restaurant menu available ⊕ HOOK NORTON BREWERY ◄ Hooky Ò Westons Stowford Press. **Facilities** Non-diners area ♣ (Bar Restaurant Garden) ¶¶ Children's menu Children's portions Garden 戸 Beer festival WiFi ⇔ (notice required) **Rooms** 3

The Highway Inn

tel: 01993 823661 **117 High St OX18 4RG**
email: info@thehighwayinn.co.uk
dir: *From A40 onto A361*

Charming pub in a picturesque Cotswold town

An attractive inn of medieval origin at the heart of pretty Burford; the secluded courtyard garden to the rear is a blissful retreat from the hurly-burly of this ancient town. Beers from the likes of Hook Norton, together with local cider are the order of the day; a June beer festival tradition is being continued by new owners here. The relaxing interior, with lots of dressed stone, open fire, bric-a-brac and cosy corners is popular with diners drawn to the unfussy, high-quality menu of seasonal dishes. Cotswold largesse is exampled by mains like oven-roasted breast of pheasant with game jus; home-made pies and the renowned rack of ribs.

Open all day all wk 12-11 Closed 1st 2wks Jan **Food** Lunch all wk 12-2.30 Dinner all wk 6-9 Av main course £12 Set menu available Restaurant menu available all wk ⊕ FREE HOUSE ◄ Hook Norton Hooky Bitter, Guest ale Ò Westons Stowford Press, Cotswold. **Facilities** Non-diners area ♣ (Bar Outside area) ¶¶ Children's menu Children's portions Outside area 戸 Beer festival WiFi

The Inn for All Seasons ★★★ INN   PICK OF THE PUBS

tel: 01451 844324 **The Barringtons OX18 4TN**
email: sharp@innforallseasons.com
dir: *3m W of Burford on A40*

Excellent fresh fish specials and extensive wine list

The Sharp family took over in the mid-1980s, but this 17th-century inn has a long history and once witnessed the dispatch of Cotswold stone for buildings like St Paul's Cathedral. The pub's unusual name comes from former owner Jeremy Taylor, who renamed the pub after *A Man for All Seasons*, a film he had worked on as a horse choreographer. Within lies a treasure trove of ancient oak beams, leather chairs and interesting memorabilia. The bar offers Wadworth ales and guests, as well as an extensive wine list. Matthew Sharp selects seasonal local produce for his British-continental cuisine, and he also offers one of the best fresh fish boards in the area. Meat options include terrine of local pheasant and rabbit; and braised beef, garlic potatoes, Hereford snails in red wine, root vegetable gratin and sautéed wild mushrooms. Meals can also be taken in the lovely beer garden.

Open all wk 11-2.30 6-11 (Fri-Sat 11-11) **Food** Lunch all wk 12-2.30 Dinner all wk 6.30-9.30 ⊕ FREE HOUSE ◄ Wadworth 6X & Horizon, Sharp's Doom Bar Ò Sharp's Orchard. ♀ 16 **Facilities** Non-diners area ♣ (Bar Garden) ¶¶ Children's menu Children's portions Play area Family room Garden 戸 Parking WiFi ⇔ **Rooms** 10

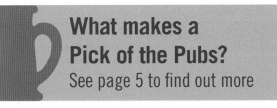

What makes a Pick of the Pubs? See page 5 to find out more

BURFORD *continued*

The Lamb Inn ★★★ SHL ◉◉ | PICK OF THE PUBS

tel: 01993 823155 **Sheep St OX18 4LR**
email: info@lambinn-burford.co.uk **web:** www.cotswold-inns-hotels.co.uk/lamb
dir: *M40 junct 8, follow A40 & Burford signs, 1st turn, down hill into Sheep St*

Cotswold charm and style

In a grass-verged, tranquil side street in this attractive Cotswolds town, the 15th-century Lamb is a dyed-in-the-wool award winner, including two AA Rosettes. A welcoming atmosphere is generated by the bar's flagstone floor, log fire, cosy armchairs, gleaming copper, brass and silver and, last but not least, Hook Norton and Wickwar real ales. In fact, old-world charm and stylish interiors are a feature throughout. Take, for example, the elegant columns and mullioned windows of the courtyard-facing restaurant, where chef Sean Ducie presents contemporary English cooking, based extensively on local produce. Starters such as scallops, black pudding and creamed mash set you up for mains such as West Country farmed, 21-day aged steaks; and whole dressed crab with skinny chips; after that, if you have room, desserts including chocolate tart and peanut butter ice cream; or apple and cinnamon crumble with custard may tempt you. An extensive cellar offers over 100 wines.

Open all day all wk **Food** Lunch all wk 12-9.30 Dinner all wk 12-9.30 Av main course £10-£20 Set menu available Restaurant menu available all wk ⊕ FREE HOUSE ◀ Hook Norton Hooky Bitter, Wickwar Cotswold Way. ⬦ 16 **Facilities** Non-diners area ❀ (Bar Garden Outside area) ◀ Children's menu Children's portions Garden Outside area ⊫ Parking WiFi **Rooms** 17

NEW The Maytime Inn ★★★★ INN

tel: 01993 822068 **Asthall OX18 4HW**
email: info@themaytime.com **web:** www.themaytime.com
dir: *Phone for detailed directions*

Pleasing combination of traditional ambience and eclectic food

Dominic Wood heads up the young and passionate team in this freshly refurbished countryside pub; dating from the 17th century, it once had its own smithy. You'll find it in the pretty Cotswold village of Asthall, where the Mitford sisters were raised. The church is worth a visit, and the manor often hosts public events. Real ales are a strength, and ciders include Black Dragon from Wales. The ambitious kitchen seeks to impress with eclectic dishes such as gravad lax with dukkah-topped poached egg, saffron sauce, Avruga caviar and sweet potato crisp. Excellent value Sunday lunches follow more conventional lines.

Open all day all wk **Food** Lunch all wk 12-3 Dinner all wk 6-9.30 Av main course £14.95 Restaurant menu available all wk ⊕ FREE HOUSE ◀ Otter Amber, Loose Cannon Abingdon Bridge, North Cotswold Windrush, Hook Norton Hooky Bitter ⬦ Gwynt y Ddraig Black Dragon & Haymaker, Westons Old Rosie. ⬦ 12 **Facilities** Non-diners area ❀ (All areas) ◀ Children's portions Garden Outside area ⊫ Parking WiFi ⛟ (notice required) **Rooms** 6

▌ CASSINGTON | Map 5 SP41

The Chequers Inn

tel: 01865 882620 **6 The Green OX29 4DG**
email: info@chequersoxford.co.uk
dir: *From Oxford take A40 towards Witney. Right to Cassington*

Smart village inn not far from Oxford

Turn off the busy A40, and you'll find this imposing Cotswold-stone inn next to the church at the end of the village road. The interior is cosy yet stylish, with polished flagstone floors, winter log fires and wooden furniture adorned with pretty candles. Freshly prepared meals include starters of goats' cheese and caramelised plum crostini, or parsnip and sweet potato soup; followed by main courses of Thai chicken curry; honey and cider ham; and rib-eye steak with peppercorn sauce. There is a beautiful orangery, perfect for private parties and functions.

Open all wk Mon-Fri 12-2.30 4.30-11 (Sat 12-11 Sun 12-10.30) **Food** Lunch Mon-Fri 12-2, Sat 12-2, Sun 12-4 Dinner Mon-Sat 6-9 ⊕ FREE HOUSE ◀ Hook Norton Hooky Bitter ⬦ Westons Stowford Press. ⬦ 10 **Facilities** Non-diners area ◀ Children's menu Children's portions Outside area ⊫ Parking WiFi ⛟ (notice required)

▌ CHALGROVE | Map 5 SU69

The Red Lion Inn | PICK OF THE PUBS

tel: 01865 890625 **The High St OX44 7SS**
dir: *B480 from Oxford ring road, through Stadhampton, left then right at mini rdbt. At Chalgrove Airfield right into village*

Historic pub overlooking the village green

Other than the occasional quack of inquisitive ducks, the medieval village of Chalgrove may be tranquil these days but that wasn't the case in 1643 when Prince Rupert clashed with John Hampden's Parliamentarian forces during the first Civil War. The stream-side beer garden of this old inn overlooks the compact green at the heart of the village, where thatched cottages slumber not far from the church which is, unusually, owner of the pub. In the bar, select from the great range of draught beers complementing the appealing menu created from the best local ingredients by chef-patron Raymond Sexton. The choice may include roulade of smoked salmon with cream cheese and chives, an appetiser for lemon sole fillets simply grilled in a little butter, or slow cooked pork belly with braised vegetables and roast gravy.

Finish with sticky toffee pudding or warm treacle tart courtesy of Suzanne Sexton, an accomplished pastry chef.

Open all wk 11-3 6-12 (Fri-Sat 6-1am Sun all day) **Food** Lunch all wk 11-3 Dinner Mon-Thu 6-12, Fri-Sat 6-1am ⊕ FREE HOUSE ◀ Fuller's London Pride, Butcombe, Guest ale ♂ Westons Stowford Press, Local cider. ♟ 11 **Facilities** Non-diners area ❖ (Bar Garden) ♦ Children's menu Children's portions Play area Garden ⋈ ⛬ (notice required)

CHARLBURY
Map 11 SP31

The Bull Inn
PICK OF THE PUBS

tel: 01608 810689 **Sheep St OX7 3RR**
email: info@bullinn-charlbury.com
dir: M40 junct 8, A40, A44 follow Woodstock/Blenheim Palace signs. Through Woodstock take B4437 to Charlbury, pub at x-rds in town

Imaginative cooking and Cotswold ales

A short hop from Woodstock, Blenheim Palace and the attractions of the Cotswolds, this handsome stone-fronted 16th-century free house presides over Charlbury's main street. Log fires burning in the inglenook fireplaces and the beamed interior add to the charming period character, as does the wooden-floored bar that offers a range of Cotswold ales by Goffs. A tastefully furnished lounge and dining room add to the relaxing space, while outside the vine-covered terrace is a lovely backdrop for a drink or meal in summer. Sandwiches served at lunchtime from Tuesday to Saturday may suffice, but the main menu may prove tempting with a starter of roast celeriac and Stilton salad with caramelised hazelnut dressing and main courses like rump of lamb with crispy polenta, braised celery and carrots or sausages and mash. Leave room for the baked vanilla cheesecake with poached rhubarb or selection of local cheeses.

Open 12-2.30 6-11 Closed 25-26 Dec & 1 Jan, Sun eve & Mon **Food** Lunch Tue-Fri 12-2, Sat-Sun 12-2.30 Dinner Tue-Sat 6.30-9 Av main course £13 ⊕ FREE HOUSE ◀ Goffs, Marston's ♂ Thatchers Gold. ♟ 10 **Facilities** Non-diners area ♦ Children's portions Garden ⋈ Parking

CHECKENDON
Map 5 SU68

The Highwayman ❀
PICK OF THE PUBS

tel: 01491 682020 **Exlade St RG8 0UA**
email: thehighwaymaninn@btconnect.com
dir: On A4074 (Reading to Wallingford road)

Desirable food below Chiltern beech woods

The wooded hills of the Chilterns, criss-crossed by bridleways and footpaths, form a constant horizon drifting above the rural location of this attractive old building. Just a stone's throw away is the remarkable Maharaja's Well at nearby Stoke Row, a bracing circular ramble from the inn. Bare brick and beams predominate in the airy interior, interspersed by alcoves and warmed by log-burning stoves in this much updated 16th-century inn, where contented regulars sup beers supplied from the nearby Loddon brewery. The AA Rosette menu is eclectic and strong on locally sourced raw materials. A speciality here is the pies; wild boar pie or venison cottage pie may tempt as a follow-up to a smoked mackerel pâté and whisky jelly starter. Alternatively a crisp snowy walk is well-rewarded with roasted chestnut and winter vegetable hotpot with potato rösti, whilst the steaks here are from the Royal Windsor Estate. A peaceful rear garden and suntrap terrace make for laid-back summer drinking.

Open 12-3 6-11 (Sun 12-6) Closed Mon **Food** Lunch Tue-Sat 12-2, Sun 12-3 Dinner Tue-Sat 6-9 ⊕ FREE HOUSE ◀ Fuller's London Pride, Loddon Hoppit, Butlers, Guest ale ♂ Aspall. ♟ 11 **Facilities** Non-diners area ❖ (Bar Garden) ♦ Children's portions Garden ⋈ Parking WiFi ⛬ (notice required)

CHINNOR
Map 5 SP70

The Sir Charles Napier ❀❀❀
PICK OF THE PUBS

tel: 01494 483011 **Spriggs Alley OX39 4BX**
dir: M40 junct 6, B4009 to Chinnor. Right at rdbt to Spriggs Alley

Outstanding cooking in the Chilterns

Elegant red kites soar over this sublime flint-and-brick dining inn, which is just 10 minutes from the M40. High amidst the beech woods of the Chiltern Hills in an Area of Outstanding Natural Beauty, the pub makes the most of this secluded locale, seasonal forays to the hedgerows and woods produce herbs, fungi and berries used in the inventive menus, whilst the plump local game finds its way into some of the extraordinary three AA-Rosette winning dishes here. Diners distribute themselves amidst a most eclectically furnished suite of rooms, or in summer lunch on the vine-covered terrace or under cherry trees on the lawn. Wood pigeon with beetroot risotto and hazelnuts gives a flavour of things to come; then pork belly, Toulouse sausage and confit duck leg cassoulet; or lemon sole with pak choi, violet artichokes, cockles and grapes for example are accompanied by an excellent wine list. In autumn the inn runs popular 'fungi forays' into the woods and the head chef cooks soups and risottos from gathered produce.

Open 12-4 6-12 (Sun 12-6) Closed 25-26 Dec, Mon, Sun eve **Food** Lunch Tue-Fri 12-2.30 Dinner Tue-Fri 6.30-9 Av main course £15.50 Set menu available Restaurant menu available Tue-Sun ⊕ FREE HOUSE ◀ Wadworth 6X, Henry's Original IPA. ♟ 12 **Facilities** Non-diners area ♦ Children's menu Children's portions Garden ⋈ Parking WiFi

CHISELHAMPTON
Map 5 SU59

Coach & Horses Inn

tel: 01865 890255 **Watlington Rd OX44 7UX**
email: enquiries@coachhorsesinn.co.uk
dir: From Oxford on B480 towards Watlington, 5m

Peace and quiet aplenty at this charming pub

This delightful 16th-century inn is set in peaceful countryside six miles south-east of Oxford. Inside you'll find roaring log fires, original exposed beams, an old bread oven and furniture styles that enhance the character of the building. A wide range of imaginative food is served, including a daily specials fish board; grills, poultry and game dishes are also perennial favourites.

Open all day all wk 11-11 (Sun 12-3.30 7-10.30) **Food** Lunch all wk 12-2 ⊕ FREE HOUSE ◀ Hook Norton Hooky Bitter & Old Hooky, Sharp's Doom Bar, Loddon, Guest ales ♂ Westons Stowford Press. ♟ 10 **Facilities** Non-diners area ♦ Children's menu Children's portions Garden ⋈ Parking WiFi

Find out more about
the AA's awards for food
excellence on page 9

PICK OF THE PUBS

Bear & Ragged Staff

CUMNOR   Map 5 SP40

tel: 01865 862329
28 Appleton Rd OX2 9QH
email: enquiries@bearandraggedstaff.com
web: www.bearandraggedstaff.com
dir: *A420 from Oxford, right onto B4017 signed Cumnor*

Old World charm and modern menus

In typically tranquil Oxfordshire countryside, this 16th-century, stonebuilt dining pub has a rich history, not least having served as a billet for troops during the English Civil War. While the soldiers were here, Richard Cromwell, son of Oliver and Lord Protector of England, allegedly chiselled away the Royal Crest that once adorned the lintel above one of the doors in the bar, and Sir Walter Scott mentions this very Bear & Ragged Staff in his novel, *Kenilworth*. The chefs here take full advantage of the fresh, seasonal game available from local estates and shoots, since the surrounding woods and farmland teem with pheasant, partridge, deer, muntjac, rabbit, duck and pigeon. From the kitchen come hearty, country-style casseroles, stews, steaks, bangers and mash and other pub classics. Install yourself in one of the traditional bar rooms, all dressed stone and warmed by log fires, relax on the stone-flagged patio, or settle in the comfortable restaurant and ask for the

eminently manageable menu. Start with meze, charcuterie, crispy duck leg pancakes or home-made soup; then choose vegetable tagine; pork and wild boar faggots; chargrilled venison steak; market fish of the day; or butternut squash, brown cap mushrooms and spinach risotto. Pizzas from an authentic oven are another option. If, to follow, upside-down apple pudding with Calvados crème anglaise, or creamy rice pudding with red plum compôte fail to tick the right box, call for the cheeseboard, full of British classics with crackers, celery, chutney and grapes. The Bear has a climbing frame for children and dogs are welcome in the bar area.

Open all day all wk ⊞ GREENE KING ◀ Guest ales, Guinness Ō Aspall, Hogan's. **Facilities** ❀ (Bar Garden) ♦♦ Children's menu Children's portions Play area Garden Outside area Parking WiFi ▭ (notice required)

CHURCH ENSTONE
Map 11 SP32

The Crown Inn
PICK OF THE PUBS

tel: 01608 677262 **Mill Ln OX7 4NN**
dir: *From A44 at Enstone (15m N of Oxford) onto B4030 signed Church Enstone*

Charming pub with all the right ingredients

Your hosts at this 17th-century village inn are Tony and Caroline Warburton, who have built up a formidable reputation for their cuisine, especially for fish, Tony's speciality. There's a traditional rustic bar, with log fires in the inglenook and old photos of long-departed villagers, a comfortable environment therefore in which to enjoy Hook Norton Hooky Bitter, Wychwood Hobgoblin, or perhaps local Cotswold cider. Equally appealing are the beamed dining room and slate-floored conservatory, where the compact menu might offer Cornish bacon and scallop salad; or Parma ham with poached pear, rocket and blue cheese to begin, then perhaps steak and Hooky pie, chips and peas; roast belly of Cotswold pork with cider gravy and apple sauce; or poached smoked haddock with cheddar mash and soft egg. Sunny days can be spent in the sheltered cottage garden, or on the terrace admiring the village's thatched, honey-coloured stone cottages.

Open all wk 12-3 6-11 (Sun 12-4) Closed 26 Dec, 1 Jan **Food** Lunch all wk 12-2 Dinner Mon-Sat 7-9 Av main course £12 Set menu available ⊕ FREE HOUSE ◀ Hook Norton Hooky Bitter, Timothy Taylor Landlord, Wychwood Hobgoblin Ö Cotswold. ♀ 8 **Facilities** Non-diners area ♦♦ Children's portions Garden ⋒ Parking

CLIFTON
Map 11 SP43

Duke of Cumberland's Head

tel: 01869 338534 **OX15 OPE**
email: enquiries@cliftonphm.com
dir: *A4260 from Banbury, then B4031 from Deddington*

Lovely old inn with popular dishes

Believed to be Elizabethan, this thatched stone pub commemorates Prince Rupert of the Rhine, who fought alongside his uncle, Charles I, at the nearby Battle of Edge Hill in 1642. Many old features survive, including the inglenook fireplace and low exposed beams. Three real ales are always on tap, as is Addlestones cider, and the whisky bar needs no explanation. Largely traditional pub favourites, sourced from local farmers, gamekeepers and suppliers, include pie of the day; slow-cooked pork belly; seafood linguine; and roasted butternut squash and sage risotto.

Open all wk 11-3 6-11 Closed 25 Dec **Food** Lunch Mon-Sat 12-2.30, Sun 12-3 Dinner Mon-Thu 6.30-9, Fri-Sat 6.30-9.30 ⊕ FREE HOUSE ◀ Hook Norton, Tring, Vale, Sharp's Doom Bar, Ramsbury Ö Addlestones. ♀ 11 **Facilities** Non-diners area ♣ (Bar Restaurant Garden) ♦♦ Children's menu Children's portions Garden ⋒ Parking WiFi

CUMNOR
Map 5 SP40

Bear & Ragged Staff
PICK OF THE PUBS

See Pick of the Pubs on opposite page

The Vine Inn

tel: 01865 862567 **11 Abingdon Rd OX2 9QN**
dir: *A420 from Oxford, right onto B4017*

Well kept ales and a large garden

A vine does indeed clamber over the whitewashed frontage of this 18th-century village pub. In 1560, nearby Cumnor Place was the scene of the suspicious death of the wife of Lord Robert Dudley, favourite of Elizabeth I; the house was pulled down in 1810. There's a selection of rotating real ales in the carpeted bar, and a typical starters include traditional prawn cocktail; whitebait; or calamari and salad; followed by a meat, fish or oven-baked camembert sharing plate; or perhaps chilli con carne or one of the burger choices. Children love the huge garden.

Open all wk 12-3 6-11.30 (Fri-Sun all day) **Food** Lunch Mon-Sat 12-2.30, Sun 12-6 Dinner Mon-Sat 6-9 Av main course £10 ⊕ PUNCH TAVERNS ◀ Sharp's Doom Bar, Brakspear, Hobgoblin, Guest ales Ö Somersby. **Facilities** Non-diners area ♣ (Bar Garden) ♦♦ Children's menu Children's portions Play area Garden ⋒ Beer festival Parking WiFi ⬛ (notice required)

DEDDINGTON
Map 11 SP43

Deddington Arms ★★★ HL ◉
PICK OF THE PUBS

tel: 01869 338364 **Horsefair OX15 OSH**
email: deddarms@oxfordshire-hotels.co.uk **web:** www.deddington-arms-hotel.co.uk
dir: *M40 junct 11 to Banbury. Follow signs for hospital, then towards Adderbury & Deddington, on A4260*

Good country pub fare in a 16th-century inn

Overlooking Deddington's pretty market square, this striking 16th-century former coaching inn boasts a wealth of timbering, flagstone floors, numerous nooks and crannies, crackling winter log fires and sought-after window seats in the beamed bar. Here you can savour a pint of Hook Norton or Adnams ale while perusing the great value set lunch menu or the imaginative carte. Eat in the bar or head for the elegant dining room and kick off a one AA-Rosette meal with Thai-style prawn and cod fishcakes, followed by pork cutlet with bubble-and-squeak, apple fondant and carrot purée, or a freshly-made pizza, finishing with stem ginger crème brûlée. From the market lunch menu perhaps choose chickpea falafel with mint yogurt, and seared lamb's liver and bacon with mash and onion gravy. Accommodation includes 27 en suite bedrooms with cottage suites and four-poster luxury.

Open all day all wk 11am-mdnt (Sun 11-11) **Food** Lunch all wk 12-2.30 Dinner all wk 6.30-9.30 ⊕ FREE HOUSE ◀ Adnams, Hook Norton Lion, 2 Guest ales Ö Westons Stowford Press. ♀ 8 **Facilities** Non-diners area ♦♦ Children's menu Children's portions Parking WiFi ⬛ (notice required) **Rooms** 27

PICK OF THE PUBS

The George ★★★ HL

DORCHESTER (ON THAMES)   Map 5 SU59

tel: 01865 340404
25 High St OX10 7HH
email: georgedorchester@relaxinnz.co.uk
web: www.thegeorgedorchester.co.uk
dir: *From M40 junct 7, A329 S to A4074 at Shillingford. Follow Dorchester signs. From M4 junct 13, A34 to Abingdon then A415 E to Dorchester*

Take a step back in time at this friendly inn

The multi-gabled, 15th-century George stands in the old town's picturesque high street, opposite the 12th-century Dorchester Abbey. Believed to be one of the country's oldest coaching inns, it has been a welcome haven for many an aristocrat, including Sarah Churchill, the first Duchess of Marlborough, while much later the non-aristocratic author D H Lawrence favoured it with his presence. Oak beams and inglenook fireplaces characterise the interior, while the elevated restaurant offers a secret garden with a waterfall. The Potboys Bar, apparently named after the Abbey bell-ringers, is a traditional taproom and therefore unquestionably the right place to enjoy a pint from one of the six breweries that make up The George's roll of honour while tucking into pasta carbonara with garlic bread; bangers and mash with gravy; or an 8oz rump steak with fat chips from the bar menu. Food is all locally sourced: the

Abbey gardens, for example, supply all the herbs, customers contribute the occasional home-grown vegetables, and local shoots provide pheasants. In Carriages Restaurant the menu offers confit of crisp belly pork with Puy lentils, local Toulouse sausages and crushed new potatoes; coq au vin with roasted garlic croûtons and celeriac mash; fresh and smoked fish pie with potato and cheddar cheese glaze; and butternut squash risotto with red onion, fresh herbs, white truffle oil and parmesan shavings. Expect white chocolate and marmalade bread-and-butter pudding with Disaronno custard, and Eton Mess for dessert. There are well-equipped bedrooms some with views of either the extensive gardens or the Abbey.

Open all day all wk 7am-mdnt
Food all wk 12-3 6-9 ⊕ CHAPMANS GROUP ◢■ Wadworth 6X, Skinner's Betty Stogs, Fuller's London Pride, Sharp's Doom Bar, Butcombe, Hook Norton Ö Westons Stowford Press.
Facilities ♦♦ Children's menu Children's portions Garden Outside area Parking WiFi 🚐 **Rooms** 24

DORCHESTER (ON THAMES) Map 5 SU59

The George ★★★ HL PICK OF THE PUBS

See Pick of the Pubs on opposite page

The White Hart ★★★ HL PICK OF THE PUBS

tel: 01865 340074 **High St OX10 7HN**
email: whitehart@oxfordshire-hotels.co.uk **web:** www.oxfordshire-hotels.co.uk
dir: *On A4074 (Oxford to Reading road)*

Smart hotel with a claim to fame

If this picture-perfect hotel looks familiar, that could be because it has played a starring role in the TV series *Midsomer Murders*. Set seven miles from Oxford in heart of historic Dorchester, it has welcomed travellers for around 400 years, and the bars attract locals, residents and diners alike. There is a great choice of real beers available. Log fires and candlelight create an intimate atmosphere for the enjoyment of innovative dishes prepared from fresh ingredients. A good-value fixed-price lunch is available Monday to Saturday, with a choice of three starters, mains and desserts. The carte menu doubles your choice and includes imaginative dishes such as pumpkin risotto or Thai-style fishcakes, followed by roasted loin of pork with braised red cabbage, caramelised apple and sweet potato crisps; fish and chips in beer-batter with crushed minted peas and hand-cut chips; or grilled peppered rump steak.

Open all day all wk 11am-mdnt (Sun 11-11) **Food** Lunch all wk 12-2.30 Dinner all wk 6.30-9.30 ⊕ FREE HOUSE ◀ Adnams, Brakspear, Hook Norton Lion ♂ Somersby. ⚑ 12 **Facilities** Non-diners area ◷ Children's portions Garden ⅁ Parking ⛟ **Rooms** 28

EAST HENDRED Map 5 SU48

Eyston Arms

tel: 01235 833320 **High St OX12 8JY**
email: info@eystonarms.co.uk
dir: *Just off A417 (Wantage to Reading road)*

A family-owned local favourite

Owned, appropriately, by the Eyston family, who have lived in the village since 1443, this old inn stands just north of the prehistoric track known as The Ridgeway. With some of its original look revealed by renovations, the pub greets its customers with a huge log fire, flagstone floor, simple polished tables, leather chairs and cartoons of its regulars. The bar stocks real ales from Wadworth and Oxfordshire neighbour, Hook Norton. Chef Maria Jaremchuk's ever-changing menus may feature cock-a-leekie pie; chargrilled rib-eye steak; and vegetarian pad Thai, while carefully cultivated contacts with south coast fishermen mean excellent fish specials.

Open all wk 11-3 6-11 (Fri-Sat 11-11 Sun 11-9) **Food** Lunch Mon-Sat 12-2, Sun 12-4 Dinner Mon-Sat 6.30-9.30 ⊕ FREE HOUSE ◀ Hook Norton, Wadworth 6X ♂ Westons Stowford Press. **Facilities** Non-diners area ◷ (Bar Outside area) ⅁ Children's portions Outside area ⅁ Parking WiFi

FARINGDON Map 5 SU29

The Lamb at Buckland PICK OF THE PUBS

tel: 01367 870484 **Lamb Ln, Buckland SN7 8QN**
email: thelambatbuckland@googlemail.com
dir: *Just off A420, 3m E of Faringdon*

Welcoming country pub and restaurant

Down a little cul-de-sac, the 17th-century Lamb forms part of a cluster of similar-vintage Cotswold-stone cottages. Richard and Shelley Terry, and Christopher Green, all trained chefs, run it, although it's the two men who wear the chef's check trousers, allowing Shelley to look after front of house. They still share an objective, though: to offer good food, relaxed and friendly service in a pub atmosphere. Localness is important too, so the real ales come from Oxfordshire and Berkshire, and many of the vegetables grow beside the suntrap patio in the kitchen garden. Typical dishes include tempura squid with sweet chilli dip; chargrilled sirloin, rump and rib-eye steaks; pan-roasted belly of pork, apple and onion purée and sage mash; and grilled smoked haddock with leek and mustard potato cake, pancetta crisp and poached egg. There's also vegetarian pan-fried crispy tarragon gnocchi with watercress, chicory, Oxford Blue cheese and pine nut salad.

Open all wk 11.30-3 6-11 Closed Sun eve, Mon **Food** Lunch Tue-Sat 12-2, Sun 12-3 Dinner Tue-Sat 7-9 Av main course £12-£15 ⊕ FREE HOUSE ◀ Brakspear Bitter, Ramsbury Gold, West Berkshire Good Old Boy, Loose Cannon Abingdon Bridge. ⚑ 12 **Facilities** Non-diners area ◷ (Bar Restaurant Garden) ⅁ Children's portions Garden ⅁ Parking WiFi

The Trout at Tadpole Bridge ★★★★ INN ⊛
PICK OF THE PUBS

tel: 01367 870382 **Buckland Marsh SN7 8RF**
email: info@troutinn.co.uk **web:** www.troutinn.co.uk
dir: *A415 from Abingdon signed Marcham, through Frilford to Kingston Bagpuize. Left onto A420. 5m, right signed Tadpole Bridge. Or M4 (E'bound) junct 15, A419 towards Cirencester. 4m, onto A420 towards Oxford. 10m, left signed Tadpole Bridge*

Award-winning free house by the River Thames

Just twenty minutes from Oxford, this lovely stone pub by an ancient bridge over the River Thames is popular with boaters, and ramblers from the Thames Path threading along the bank. Up the road is Kelmscott Manor, the remarkable home of 19th-century artist and designer, William Morris. Stretching down to the water is a secluded garden, clearly designed for just lolling about with a pint of Ramsbury Bitter, Loose Cannon Abingdon Bridge, or Cotswold real cider. To the restaurant or bar (or outside, if you prefer) for Gareth and Helen Pugh's well balanced, AA Rosette-awarded cooking, all based on the best produce - fish and seafood up daily from Cornwall, game from area shoots, and local fruit, herbs and vegetables. Try carpaccio of venison with quince purée; confit rabbit Wellington with roasted salsify and smoked garlic spinach; and good old beer-battered haddock and chips. The sensible children's menu is chicken nugget free.

Open all wk 11.30-3 6-11 (Sat-Sun all day May-Sep all wk all day) Closed 25-26 Dec **Food** Lunch all wk 12-2 Dinner all wk 7-9 ⊕ FREE HOUSE ◀ Ramsbury Bitter, Young's Bitter, White Horse Wayland Smithy, Loose Cannon Abingdon Bridge ♂ Westons Stowford Press, Cotswold. ⚑ 12 **Facilities** Non-diners area ◷ (Bar Restaurant Garden) ⅁ Children's menu Children's portions Garden ⅁ Parking WiFi **Rooms** 6

FERNHAM
Map 5 SU29

The Woodman Inn

tel: 01367 820643 **SN7 7NX**
email: enquiries@thewoodmaninn.net
dir: M4 junct 15, A419 towards Swindon. Right onto A420 signed Oxford/Shrivenham. Straight on at next 2 rdbts. At x-rds left onto B4508 to Fernham

Old inn near famous landmark

An enticing mix of ultra-traditional old village bar wrapped around a tempting stillage, plus an eye-opening Tudor-style banqueting hall welcome guests to this pretty 400-year old pub. In a peaceful village in the Vale of White Horse, the famous Uffington white horse chalk figure is just a handful of miles away; the inn's reputation for fine ales and good food draws visitors from this notable landmark. Beers from the likes of Oakham breweries are richly supplemented in the annual beer festival here. Great lite-bite snacks satisfy; or indulge in dishes such as honey roasted breast of duck, spring onion mash and cherry sauce.

Open all day all wk **Food** Lunch Mon-Fri 12-2, Sat-Sun 12-2.30 Dinner all wk 6.30-9.30 ⊕ FREE HOUSE ◀ Timothy Taylor Landlord, Wadworth 6X, Sharp's Doom Bar, Greene King Old Speckled Hen, Guest ales ♂ Aspall, Thatchers. **Facilities** Non-diners area ❤ (Bar Restaurant Garden) ♦ Children's menu Children's portions Family room Garden ⌂ Beer festival Parking WiFi ━

FILKINS
Map 5 SP20

The Five Alls
`PICK OF THE PUBS`

tel: 01367 860875 **GL7 3JQ**
email: info@thefivealsfilkins.co.uk
dir: Between Lechlade & Burford, just off A361

A class act in the Cotswolds

Respected restaurateurs Sebastian and Lana Snow have been successfully running The Five Alls, in picture-postcard Filkins, for a few years now. The pub's the interior oozes warmth and style, with rugs on stone floors, flickering candles on old dining tables, and a leather chesterfield fronting the log fire – the perfect spot to relax with a pint and the papers. The bar bustles with locals, walkers and cyclists supping pints of Wychwood Hobgoblin or Brakspear Oxford Gold and tucking into proper bar snacks, while the concise modern British menu bristles with quality, locally sourced ingredients, draws diners from far and wide across the Cotswolds. Typically, you'll find line-caught salmon sashimi with wasabi, pickled ginger and soy; caramelised onion, sage and gruyère tart; and Thai steamed mussels to start, then skillet roast whole lemon sole with brown butter and capers, spinach and fries; lamb sweetbread fritters with tartare sauce; or breast of chicken saltimbocca with a cheese soufflé.

Open all day Closed 25 Dec, Sun eve **Food** Lunch all wk 12-2.30 Dinner Mon-Sat 6-9.30 Set menu available Restaurant menu available all wk ⊕ BRAKSPEAR ◀ Ringwood, Brakspear Oxford Gold, Wychwood Hobgoblin ♂ Thatchers. **Facilities** Non-diners area ❤ (Bar Restaurant Garden) ♦ Children's menu Children's portions Play area Garden ⌂ Parking WiFi ━

FRINGFORD
Map 11 SP62

The Butchers Arms

tel: 01869 277363 **OX27 8EB**
email: tg53@sky.com
dir: 4m from Bicester on A4421 towards Buckingham

Charming pub next to the village green

Lark Rise to Candleford author Flora Jane Thompson was born at Juniper Hill, a couple of miles from this pretty, creeper-covered pub, and her first job was in the Post Office in Fringford. In her writings, Juniper Hill became Lark Rise, Fringford became Candleford Green, and Buckingham and Banbury metamorphosed into Candleford. Handpumps dispense Doom Bar, Adnams and Brakspear Bitter, while the menu offers a good traditional selection, including pie of the day; lemon sole; home-made curry; and liver, bacon and onions. You can watch the cricket from the patio and in July there's a beer festival.

Open all day all wk **Food** Lunch all wk 12-2.30 Dinner Tue-Sat 6.30-9 Av main course £10.95 ⊕ PUNCH TAVERNS ◀ Sharp's Doom Bar, Adnams, Brakspear ♂ Thatchers Katy, Westons Stowford Press. **Facilities** Non-diners area ❤ (Bar) ♦ Children's menu Children's portions ⌂ Beer festival Parking WiFi ━ (notice required)

FULBROOK
Map 10 SP21

The Carpenters Arms

tel: 01993 823275 **Fulbrook Hill OX18 4BH**
email: carpentersarms@ymail.com
dir: From rdbt on A40 at Burford take A361 signed Chipping Norton. Pub on right 150mtrs from mini rdbt just after bridge

Stylish pub with seasonally changing menus

Expect oodles of charm and character from this 17th-century stone pub; the warren of cosy, beautifully decorated and furnished rooms draws a cosmopolitan crowd, many of whom stop to enjoy the modern British cooking. Choices range from bar snacks such as game pie with mash and carrots to more ambitious dishes such as goats' cheese tian with tomato, basil and olives followed by rack of lamb with sautéed potatoes, asparagus, lemon and rosemary.

Open Tue 6-11.30 Wed-Sat 12-3 6-11.30 Sun 12-5 Closed Sun eve, Mon, Tue L (winter) **Food** Lunch Wed-Fri 12-2.30, Sat-Sun 12-3 Dinner Tue-Thu 6-9, Fri-Sat 6-9.30 ⊕ GREENE KING ◀ Abbot Ale, Guest ales ♂ Aspall. ♛ 10 **Facilities** Non-diners area ❤ (Bar Restaurant Garden) ♦ Children's portions Garden ⌂ Parking WiFi

FYFIELD
Map 5 SU49

The White Hart ◉◉
`PICK OF THE PUBS`

See Pick of the Pubs on opposite page

GORING
Map 5 SU68

Miller of Mansfield
`PICK OF THE PUBS`

tel: 01491 872829 **High St RG8 9AW**
email: mary.galer@millerofmansfield.com
dir: From Pangbourne take A329 to Streatley. Right on B4009, 0.5m to Goring

A beautiful focal point for the village

Creepers cover the front of this 18th-century coaching inn, now in new hands. In an upmarket riverside village, surrounded by the rolling Berkshire and Oxfordshire countryside, it's just a hop, step and a jump from the River Thames. Shiny wooden floors, fat candles on scrubbed tables, log fires and local ales Good Old Boy, Old Hooky and Rebellion IPA sum up the newly-refurbished bar, while a restaurant overview must mention its Philippe Starck-influenced design. Virtually everything on the menu is home made, such as the warm salmon bradan rost with horseradish; and cauliflower lasagne with cumin, raisin and hazelnuts starters. Mains include pan-roasted fillet of brill with summer mushrooms and asparagus; shepherd's pie with peas, grain mustard and confit garlic; chargrilled Black Angus bavette steak with fries, shallot wine sauce and watercress salad; and pearl barley porridge with mint pesto, soya beans and rocket salad. Typical desserts are chocolate custard, and rhubarb sundae.

Open all day all wk **Food** Lunch Mon-Sat 12-2.30, Sun 12-4 Dinner Mon-Thu 6-9, Fri-Sat 6-9.30, Sun 6-8 Av main course £15 ⊕ ENTERPRISE INNS ◀ Hook Norton Old Hooky, West Berkshire Good Old Boy, Rebellion IPA ♂ Westons, Thatchers. ♛ 11 **Facilities** Non-diners area ❤ (Bar Outside area) ♦ Children's menu Children's portions Outside area ⌂ Parking WiFi ━ (notice required)

PICK OF THE PUBS

The White Hart 🌹🌹

FYFIELD Map 5 SU49

tel: 01865 390585
Main Rd OX13 5LW
email: info@whitehart-fyfield.com
web: www.whitehart-fyfield.com
dir: *7m S of Oxford, just off A420 (Oxford to Swindon road)*

Confident cooking in picturesque village inn

Mark and Kay Chandler's 500-year-old former chantry house is steeped in history and has been a pub since 1580 when St John's College in Oxford leased it to tenants but reserved the right to 'occupy it if driven from Oxford by pestilence' – so far this has not been invoked! The building is breathtaking and boasts a grand hall with a 15th-century arch-braced roof, original oak beams, flagstone floors, and huge stone-flanked windows. For a table with a view there's still a splendid 30ft high minstrels' gallery overlooking the restaurant. Study the wonderful history and architecture over a pint of local Loose Cannon Abingdon Bridge or Sharp's Doom Bar, or one of the 14 wines served by the glass in the character bar – in winter arrive early to bag the table beside the roaring fire. Awarded two AA Rosettes for his food, chef/owner Mark is steadfast in his pursuit of fresh, seasonal food from trusted local suppliers and their own kitchen garden provides a regular

supply of fruit and vegetables. Mark's cooking reveals a high level of technical skill and his menus change daily, perhaps featuring chicken and duck liver parfait, apple and vanilla chutney; or beetroot cured salmon, salmon pâté, root vegetable slaw and thyme crisps among the starters. To follow, try roast haunch of venison, little venison cottage pie, creamed juniper cabbage and girolles; or fillet of sea bass, Brixham crab, crushed new potatoes, samphire and crab bisque; then rhubarb and ginger tart, rhubarb sorbet and stem ginger custard. Fish, antipasti or meze sharing boards are great for nibbles. The lunchtime set menu is great value.

Open 12-3 5.30-11 (Sat 12-11 Sun 12-10.30) Closed Mon (ex BHs)

Food Lunch Tue-Sat 12-2.30, Sun 12-3 Dinner Tue-Sat 7-9.30 Set menu available ⊕ FREE HOUSE 🛢 Sharp's Doom Bar, Purity UBU, Loose Cannon Abingdon Bridge, Guest ales
Ö Thatchers Cheddar Valley & Gold.
🍷 14 **Facilities** Non-diners area
👪 Children's menu Children's portions Play area Garden 🪑 Beer festival Parking 🚌 WiFi

GREAT TEW
Map 11 SP42

The Falkland Arms
PICK OF THE PUBS

tel: 01608 683653 **OX7 4DB**
email: falklandarms@wadworth.co.uk
dir: *Off A361, 1.25m, signed Great Tew*

Ancient inn replete with English character

Named after Lucius Carey, 2nd Viscount Falkland, who inherited the manor of Great Tew in 1629, this 500-year-old creeper-clad inn can be found at the end of a charming row of Cotswold-stone cottages. The Falkland Arms is a classic: wooden floors, exposed beams, high-backed settles and low stools and an inglenook fireplace characterise the intimate bar, where a huge collection of beer and cider mugs and jugs hangs from the ceiling. Wadworth and guest ales, together with a meal, can be enjoyed in the bar or the lovely pub garden. Sharing plates, pork pie, baked camembert and home-made soup supplement the lunchtime menu of thick-cut bloomer sandwiches. In the evening, booking is essential for dinner in the small dining room. Expect pan-fried potato gnocchi with wild mushrooms and spinach; honey-roast Wiltshire ham; and chef's pie of the day. Being a genuine English pub, clay pipes and snuff are always on sale!

Open all day all wk 8am-11pm **Food** Lunch all wk 12-2.30 Dinner all wk 6.30-9.30 ⊕ WADWORTH ◀ 6X, Henry's Original IPA & Horizon, Guest ales Ò Westons Traditional & Stowford Press. ▼ 14 **Facilities** Non-diners area ❤ (Bar Restaurant Garden) ♦ Children's portions Garden ⌐ Beer festival WiFi ▭ (notice required)

HAMPTON POYLE
Map 11 SP51

The Bell
PICK OF THE PUBS

tel: 01865 376242 **OX5 2QD**
email: contactus@thebelloxford.co.uk
dir: *From N: exit A34 signed Kidlington, over bridge. At mini rdbt turn right, left to Hampton Poyle (before slip road to rejoin A34). From Kidlington: at rdbt (junct of A4260 & A4165) take Bicester Rd (Sainsbury's on left) towards A34. Left to Hampton Poyle*

Good food and welcoming, professional staff

A centuries-old inn that is independent and privately owned. Its conveniently sited for Oxford, Bicester Village shopping outlet and Blenheim Palace. The charms of its oak beams and time-worn flagstone floors are complemented by the dining area with an open kitchen featuring an eye-catching wood-burning oven, from which are produced rustic pizzas and other dishes. These, along with burgers and salads, are served in the bar at any time, while in the restaurant a meal might start with pork, duck and pigeon terrine and celeriac remoulade; or twice-baked cheese soufflé, pear and walnut salad; continue with 'a gentleman's lunch' of cold, rare rib of beef, string chips and salad; chilli seafood linguine; or slow roast Tamworth pork belly, apple sauce and creamy mash. Finish with ginger and lemon syrup sponge with rhubarb compôte and custard. Should you have a well-behaved dog, it will be welcome to join you in the bar or out on the delightful south-facing terrace.

Open all day all wk 7am-11pm **Food** Lunch Mon-Sat 12-2.30, Sun 12-3 Dinner Sun-Thu 6-9, Fri-Sat 6.30-9.30 Set menu available ⊕ FREE HOUSE ◀ Hook Norton Hooky Bitter, Wye Valley Butty Bach Ò Westons Stowford Press. ▼ 10
Facilities Non-diners area ❤ (Bar Garden Outside area) ♦ Children's portions Family room Garden Outside area ⌐ Parking WiFi ▭ (notice required)

HARWELL
Map 5 SU48

The Hart of Harwell

tel: 01235 834511 **High St OX11 0EH**
email: info@hartofharwell.com **web:** www.hartofharwell.com
dir: *In village centre, accessed from A417 & A4130*

Village pub with unusual wells and great food

Several old wells were found during renovations of this 15th to 16th-century pub, and one now serves as a dining table. You can peer down it while eating – an unusual diversion. The modern bar's stable of Greene King real ales is supplemented by regularly-changing guests. Sandwiches are served at lunchtime only, while the main menu covers both lunch and dinner, so either meal could feature a pulled pork, pickles and toast starter, followed by, say, treacle baked ham with egg, chips and peas; or perhaps beef and Guinness pie with cabbage and mash; and, to end, ginger pear and black cherry crumble with vanilla custard.

Open all wk 12-3 5.30-11 (Fri-Sat 12-12 Sun 12-11) **Food** Lunch all wk 12-2.30 Dinner all wk 6-9.30 ⊕ GREENE KING ◀ Morland Old Speckled Hen & Original, Hardys & Hansons Best Bitter Ò Aspall. ▼ 24 **Facilities** Non-diners area ❤ (Bar Garden) ♦ Children's menu Children's portions Garden ⌐ Parking WiFi

The Cherry Tree Inn
Stoke Row South Oxfordshire

PUB | RESTAURANT | ROOMS

The Cherry Tree Inn is your quintessential English country pub at its very best. Beautifully situated in the Chiltern's in the picturesque South Oxfordshire village of Stoke Row, it is surrounded by the most enchanting beech woods & a slice of the country life.

With miles of walks, cycling, riding & outdoor pursuits & with four AA 4* letting rooms, a vibrant & busy bar & some of the best pub food around, it is a firm favourite in the area.

Just 10 minutes west of the historic town of Henley on Thames, it is perfectly positioned for those wanting a day trip, as part of a holiday in the area & most definitely for the well kept ales, wines & innovative food that delivers fresh pub classics alongside more foodie treats. They have a seasonally changing menu, daily scrummy specials, cracking bar bites & attract, businesses, couples, groups & locals alike.

Definitely worth a visit, especially in the spring & summer in their glorious garden. BBQ's, Live Music, Sporting Events & more will be found on their events calendar. This is a lovely pub!

OPEN EVERY DAY | DRINKS | LUNCH | DINNER
CASK ALES | WINES | CHAMPAGNE
SEASONAL MENU | DAILY SPECIALS BOARDS | SUNDAY ROASTS

www.thecherrytreeinn.co.uk | 01491 680 430

HENLEY-ON-THAMES　　　　　　　　　　**Map 5 SU78**

The Cherry Tree Inn ★★★★ INN ◉　PICK OF THE PUBS

See Pick of the Pubs on opposite page and advert on page 391

The Five Horseshoes　　　　　　　PICK OF THE PUBS

tel: 01491 641282 **Maidensgrove RG9 6EX**
email: admin@thefivehorseshoes.co.uk
dir: *From Henley-on-Thames take A4130, 1m, take B480 signed Stonor. In Stonor left, through woods, over common, pub on left*

Popular for its summer hog roasts and barbecues

There's every chance of seeing red kites wheeling around above this 16th-century, brick and flint pub overlooking the Chiltern Hills. Its two snug bar areas are characterised by beams, wrought iron, brasswork, open fires, traditional pub games and Brakspear's real ales on the handpumps. To dine in the large conservatory restaurant is to enjoy an approach to traditional English dishes that often involves tweaking them to intensify the flavours, thus a menu typically begins with Cornish oysters and Bloody Mary sorbet; and whole baked camembert stuffed with almonds and rosemary. Of appeal to follow might be a main course of roast haunch of muntjac venison; herb-crusted fillet of wild sea bass; goats' cheese and ratatouille ravioli; or even a Chateaubriand for two. Pub classics include beer-battered haddock and chips and doorstep sandwiches. Dogs are welcome in the bar and two large beer gardens.

Open 12-3.30 6-11 (Sat 12-11 Sun 12-6) Closed Mon **Food** Lunch Tue-Fri 12-2.30, Sat 12-3, Sun 12-4 Dinner Tue-Sat 6.30-9.30 ⊕ BRAKSPEAR ◂ Ordinary, Oxford Gold ♂ Symonds. **Facilities** Non-diners area ♣ (Bar Garden) ♦♦ Children's portions Garden Parking ▭

The Little Angel

tel: 01491 411008 **Remenham Ln RG9 2LS**
email: enquiries@thelittleangel.co.uk **web:** www.thelittleangel.co.uk
dir: *M4 juncts 8 & 9, A404, A4130 to Henley, then towards Maidenhead. Pub on left*

Spacious and busy pub with an inviting interior

This large whitewashed pub just over Henley's famous bridge from the town gets pretty packed, especially at weekends. The chic interior features wooden floorboards, duck-egg blue tones with warming accents, an open fire, and spacious bar and dining areas. Other attractions are the well-compiled wine list, the Brakspear ales, and the exceptional modern menu, which is changed quarterly. Try game pasty with spiced potato and parsnip relish; baked pollock fillet on Puy lentil and sun-blushed tomato cassoulet; and banana tart Tatin with vanilla ice cream to finish. Sundays are 'unbelievably busy' so booking is essential, but don't worry, lunch is served all day.

Open all day all wk 11-11 (Fri-Sat 11am-mdnt Sun 12-10) **Food** Lunch Mon-Fri 12-3, Sat-Sun all day Dinner Mon-Fri 7-10, Sat-Sun all day Av main course £12.50 Set menu available Restaurant menu available all wk ⊕ BRAKSPEAR ◂ Brakspear, Oxford Gold, Guinness, Seasonal ales ♂ Symonds. ♀ 11 **Facilities** Non-diners area ♣ (Bar Restaurant Garden) ♦♦ Children's menu Children's portions Garden ▭ Parking WiFi ▭ (notice required)

See advert on page 394

The Three Tuns

tel: 01491 410138 **5 The Market Place RG9 2AA**
email: info@threetunshenley.co.uk
dir: *In town centre. Parking nearby*

Known for its warm and friendly service

Mark and Sandra Duggan turned this formerly run-down pub into a bustling drinking and dining spot. One of the oldest pubs in town, the cosy, matchboarded front bar has scrubbed tables, an open fire and Brakspear Brewery prints from a bygone era. From the adjacent cosy and intimate dining room, a passageway leads to the suntrap terrace garden. Freshly sourced local produce (the butcher is only next door) underpins menus both traditional and modern: goats' cheese soufflé, confit duck leg, and roast loin of cod, for example. There is live music every Sunday evening and live comedy acts on the first Thursday each month. Private dining for up to 30.

Open all day 11.30-11 (Sat 11am-mdnt Sun 11-10) Closed 25 Dec, Mon **Food** Lunch Tue-Sat 12-3, Sun 12-4 Dinner Tue-Sat 6-9.45 Set menu available ⊕ BRAKSPEAR ◂ Special, Oxford Gold & Bitter ♂ Symonds. ♀ 20 **Facilities** Non-diners area ♣ (Bar Garden Outside area) ♦♦ Children's portions Garden Outside area ▭

PICK OF THE PUBS

The Cherry Tree Inn ★★★★ INN ✿

HENLEY-ON-THAMES　　Map 5 SU78

tel: 01491 680430
Stoke Row RG9 5QA
email: enquiries@thecherrytreeinn.co.uk
web: www.thecherrytreeinn.co.uk
dir: *B481 towards Reading & Sonning Common 2m, follow Stoke Row sign*

British and European food at smart inn

Originally three flint cottages, the 400-year-old Cherry Tree's interior has strong colours and modern, comfortable furnishings that look good alongside the original flagstone floors, beamed ceilings and fireplaces. Brakspear's Bitter and Special and seasonal ales are on hand-pump in the bar, where there is also a good range of malt whiskies, chilled vodkas and wines by the glass. An eat-anywhere policy means freedom to enjoy any of the British and European dishes in the bar, restaurant or large garden. Local produce is used throughout the menu, with items such as lobster, oysters and game available in season. Try and decide between a starter of rabbit and black pudding terrine with cherry chutney; or salmon and green bean Thai fishcakes with a green onion salad perhaps, before moving onto red pepper marinated sea bass fillet, crushed potatoes and coriander oil; Barbary duck breast, braised red cabbage and dauphinoise potatoes; or spiced bean goulash, deep

fried courgette and tomato bulgar wheat. Desserts are no less tempting — mocha profiteroles dipped in white chocolate; and kiwi and lime cheesecake to name just two. Chalkboards offer daily specials, and Sunday roasts feature Scottish prime beef, Yorkshire pudding, roast potatoes, fresh vegetables and home-made horseradish. Children may eat in the dining rooms until 8pm, choosing from a menu that includes grilled fresh chicken and chips; pork and leek sausages and mash; and fish and chips. The large south-facing garden makes fine-weather dining a pleasure. All around is the Chilterns Area of Outstanding Natural Beauty.

Open all day all wk **Food** Lunch Mon-Fri 12-3, Sat-Sun all day Dinner Mon-Fri 6.30-10 Av main course £11.50 ⊕ BRAKSPEAR ◀ Brakspear & Special, Guest ale Ö Symonds. ☐
Facilities Non-diners area ♦♦ Children's menu Children's portions Garden ⋒ Beer festival Parking WiFi **Rooms** 4

THE LITTLE ANGEL
Henley on Thames

Henley on Thames, South Oxfordshire is just an hour from London & home to the famous Little Angel Pub. Just 80 yards from Henley Bridge & the famous Royal Regatta course on the River Thames, it is renowned the world over. One of the largest & most individual pubs in the area, the focus here is a cracking bar, fantastic food & good times. Open every day, all day & serving only the best local & seasonal food, this award winning pub is one of the busiest in the region & is as happy hosting thousands during regatta week in July, as it is a romantic table for two! A uniquely designed pub, it has several individual areas that can cater for parties of all sizes & with a large car park for its patrons, is highly prized in the town. Daily specials boards deliver delicious foodie treats, as does the daily bar food offer, including enormous home made Scotch eggs that are superb. Cosy in the winter but equally loved for its large patio garden for al fresco dining or drinks. Overlooking the quintessential Henley Cricket Club grounds, you could do worse than while away an afternoon with a good lunch, chilled bottle of rosé & good company. Whether you are enjoying a day trip, passing through or partaking in one of the large annual events in the town, you would not want to pass The Little Angel & not pop in. Their friendly & efficient staff will take great care of you.

THE LITTLE ANGEL REMENHAM LANE HENLEY ON THAMES BERKS RG9 2LS
01491 411 008 ENQUIRIES@THELITTLEANGEL.CO.UK WWW.THELITTLEANGEL.CO.UK

HENLEY-ON-THAMES *continued*

The White Hart `PICK OF THE PUBS`

tel: 01491 641245 **High St, Nettlebed RG9 5DD**
email: whitehart@tmdining.co.uk
dir: *On A4130 between Henley-on-Thames & Wallingford*

History and tradition blend with stylish modernity

Royalist and parliamentary soldiers frequently lodged in taverns during the English Civil War; this 15th-century inn reputedly billeted troops loyal to the King. During the 17th and 18th centuries the area was plagued by highwaymen, including the notorious Isaac Darkin who was eventually caught, tried and hung at Oxford Gaol. Today the beautifully restored property is favoured by a stylish crowd who appreciate the chic bar and restaurant. Heading the beer list is locally-brewed Brakspear, backed by popular internationals and a small selection of cosmopolitan bottles. Food comprises typically English dishes interspersed with South African offerings such as boerewors served as a starter with bread and a spicy dipping sauce. Half a spit-roasted chicken can be cooked either with garlic lemon butter or basted with piri piri sauce. The dessert choice includes stalwarts such as banoffee pie, and sticky toffee pudding with custard.

Open all day all wk 7am-11pm (Sun 8am-10pm) **Food** Lunch Mon-Sat 12-3, Sun 12-8 Dinner Mon-Sat 6-10 ⊕ BRAKSPEAR ◀ Brakspear, Guinness Ö Symonds. ♀ 20 **Facilities** Non-diners area ❖ (Bar Garden) ♦ Children's menu Children's portions Garden ⋒ Parking ▭

| HETHE | Map 11 SP52 |

The Muddy Duck `PICK OF THE PUBS`

See Pick of the Pubs on page 396 and advert below

| HIGHMOOR | Map 5 SU78 |

Rising Sun

tel: 01491 640856 **Witheridge Hill RG9 5PF**
email: info@risingsunwitheridgehill.co.uk
dir: *From Henley-on-Thames take A4130 towards Wallingford. Take B481, turn right to Highmoor*

Intimate, cottagey pub in the Chilterns

Next to the green in a Chilterns' hamlet, you approach this 17th-century pub through the garden. Inside, you'll notice the richly coloured walls, low-beamed ceilings, boarded floors and open fires. Chalkboards tell you which guest ales are accompanying regulars Brakspear's Ordinary and Oxford Gold, and Wyld Wood Organic, the incumbent cider. A tapas menu offers Cajun crayfish, black pudding, battered calamari rings and other appetisers. The three-section restaurant is a cosy place to dine on slow-cooked belly pork with black pudding mash; button mushroom and sweet potato curry; or roast sea bass fillet with rösti. Check dates of outdoor music events.

Open all wk Mon-Fri 12-3 5-11 (Sat 12-11 Sun 12-7) **Food** Lunch Mon-Fri 12-2, Sat-Sun 12-3 Dinner Mon-Sat 6.30-9 ⊕ BRAKSPEAR ◀ Ordinary, Oxford Gold Ö Westons Wyld Wood Organic. ♀ 10 **Facilities** Non-diners area ❖ (Bar Garden) ♦ Children's menu Children's portions Family room Garden ⋒ Parking WiFi ▭ (notice required)

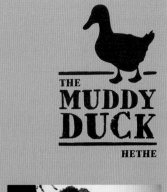

PICK OF THE PUBS

The Muddy Duck

HETHE   Map 11 SP52

Main St **OX27 8ES**
tel: 01869 278099
email: dishitup@themuddyduckpub.co.uk
web: www.themuddyduckpub.co.uk
dir: *From Bicester towards Buckingham on A4421 left signed Fringford. Through Fringford, right signed Hethe, left signed Hethe*

Family-run rural pub and restaurant

The Harris family, who run this stone-built village pub, have made sure the new areas sit harmoniously alongside the old. The refurbished part is where to enjoy a pint by the fire and have a snack, or an uncomplicated meal like ale-battered fish and chips. For the full dining experience you'll want the Malthouse restaurant, which incorporates a restored hop oven. Between these two areas is an open kitchen, which the Harrises believe illustrates their honest and passionate approach to cooking, and their championing of free-range, high welfare and sustainability. For them, obtaining the best local or British produce is paramount, and they do so extensively. The food is all fresh - as they say, there's "No ping-and-ding, no frozen." A rich offering of starters includes sticky barbecue beef rib; honey-baked Cerney Ash goats' cheese with beetroot and hazelnuts; Cornish squid with merguez

sausage, smashed avocado and tomato salsa; and devilled duck livers. A similarly big-hearted selection of mains offers steak of the day; 'much loved' Provençale fish stew; slow-roasted and stuffed pork belly; natural-smoked haddock, and other fish specials; and spiced sweet potato and red pepper frittata. The tomato and shallot tarte Tatin may appeal to vegetarians. For dessert, don't overlook baked vanilla seed cheesecake; or zesty orange posset. On the heated terrace overlooking the beer garden stands a traditional wood-fired oven, made high in the Tuscan hills. The real ales are likely to include old favourites Hooky, Landlord and Tribute, from a cellar looked after by Ian, a former innkeeper.

Open all wk 11-11 **Food** Lunch Mon-Sat 12-2.30, Sun 12-4 Dinner Mon-Sat 6-9 Restaurant menu available all wk. ⊕ FREE HOUSE ◀ Timothy Taylor Landlord, St Austell Tribute, Hook Norton Hooky Bitter Ŏ Westons Stowford Press. **Facilities** Non-diners area ❖ (Bar Garden) ♦ Children's portions Garden ⊓ Parking WiFi

KELMSCOTT
Map 5 SU29

The Plough Inn

tel: 01367 253543 **GL7 3HG**
email: josie.plough@hotmail.co.uk
dir: *M4 junct 15, A419 towards Cirencester, then right onto A361 to Lechlade. A417 towards Faringdon, follow signs to Kelmscott*

Picturesque village pub and River Thames walks

Dating from 1631, this attractive Cotswold-stone inn stands on the Thames Path a mere 600 yards from the river and midway between Radcot and Lechlade, making it a haven for walkers and boaters – own moorings for customers. It's also just a short walk from Kelmscott Manor, once home to William Morris. Exposed stone walls and flagstone floors set the scene for real ales and an extensive, hearty menu. Dishes range from slow cooked pork belly with wholegrain mustard mash, fine beans and a cider jus to tomato tart Tatin with new potatoes and salad. There's a beer, cider and music festival in August.

Open all day all wk 11.30-11 (Sun 11-11) **Food** Lunch all wk 12-3 Dinner all wk 7-10 Av main course £12.95 Restaurant menu available all wk ⊕ FREE HOUSE ◀ Wye Valley, Hook Norton, Box Steam, Wickwar, Guest ales ♂ Thatchers, Westons Stowford Press. **Facilities** Non-diners area ♦ Children's menu Children's portions Garden ⋈ Beer festival Cider festival WiFi ▭ (notice required)

KINGHAM
Map 10 SP22

The Kingham Plough ★ ★ ★ ★ INN ◉◉ `PICK OF THE PUBS`

tel: 01608 658327 **The Green OX7 6YD**
email: book@thekinghamplough.co.uk **web:** www.thekinghamplough.co.uk
dir: *B4450 from Chipping Norton to Churchill. 2nd right to Kingham, left at T-junct. Pub on right*

Relaxed and upmarket village pub with an imaginative menu

On the green of this quintessential Cotswold village, The Kingham Plough has a relaxing bar where you can enjoy one of the local real ales and daily-changing bar snacks like hand-raised pork pie with ploughman's pickle, or beetroot cured Bibury trout and rye toast. In the restaurant, chef-proprietor Emily Watkins changes the short menu daily to accommodate the deliveries from local farms, smallholdings and game estates. Expect innovative two AA-Rosette dishes like Crown Prince pumpkin soufflé; or parsley soup with garlic snails and wild mushrooms; followed by slow-cooked pork belly with pheasant boudin, kale and mash; or venison Wellington with clapshot, purple sprouting leaves and cranberry jelly. For dessert have a spoon ready for apple charlotte with cinnamon ice cream or go for the exemplary local cheeseboard. Look out for events such as the annual farmers' market and food tasting evenings.

Open all day all wk Closed 25 Dec **Food** Lunch Mon-Sat 12-9, Sun 12-8 Dinner Mon-Sat 12-9, Sun 12-8 Restaurant menu available all wk ⊕ FREE HOUSE ◀ Wye Valley HPA, Purity Mad Goose, Cotswold Wheat Beer, Hook Norton ♂ Ashton Press. **Facilities** Non-diners area ♣ (Bar Garden) ♦ Children's menu Children's portions Garden ⋈ Parking WiFi **Rooms** 7

KIRTLINGTON
Map 11 SP52

NEW The Oxford Arms

tel: 01869 350208 **Troy Ln OX5 3HA**
email: enquiries@oxford-arms.co.uk **web:** www.oxford-arms.co.uk
dir: *Take either A34 or A44 N from Oxford, follow Kirlington signs*

Homely village pub serving unpretentious good food

Dating from 1862, this attractive stone-built village inn prides itself on providing a warm welcome mirrored by its real log fire. In summer, head to the patio for alfresco dining near the kitchen garden that produces a supply of herbs, salad leaves and soft fruits. Inside, freshly-cut flowers and wax-encrusted church candles on the tables adds a rustic touch to proceedings. Everything in the kitchen is made from scratch from local produce, although the fish arrives from Devon every day. Start perhaps with cream of spicy pumpkin and chilli soup before a fillet of sea bass with lemon risotto.

Open all wk 12-3 6-11 **Food** Lunch all wk 12-2.30 Dinner Mon-Sat 6.30-9.30 ⊕ PUNCH TAVERNS ◀ St Austell Tribute, Hook Norton Hooky Bitter ♂ Westons Old Rosie. ☒ 12 **Facilities** Non-diners area ♣ (Bar Restaurant Garden) ♦ Children's portions Garden ⋈ Parking ▭ (notice required)

LOWER SHIPLAKE
Map 5 SU77

The Baskerville ★ ★ ★ ★ INN
`PICK OF THE PUBS`

tel: 0118 940 3332 **Station Rd RG9 3NY**
email: enquiries@thebaskerville.com **web:** www.thebaskerville.com
dir: *Just off A4155, 1.5m from Henley-on-Thames towards Reading, follow signs at War Memorial junct*

Variety and a relaxed atmosphere are key here

On the popular Thames Path is this modern-rustic pub of real quality. Walkers remove their muddy boots at the door before heading to the bar that's adorned with sporting memorabilia, and where pints of Loddon Hoppit, brewed two miles away,

continued

LOWER SHIPLAKE *continued*

await. There is plenty of choice food-wise; whether it's the bar menu or the à la carte, the objective is to serve great food at reasonable prices in an unpretentious atmosphere. Modern British describes the kitchen's approach, with continental and Eastern influences evident in the sustainably sourced ingredients. For lunch, you could go for an open sandwich or savour seafood linguine. Typical evening choices might be rope-grown mussels steamed in a fragrant Thai sauce; and slow-cooked Oxfordshire pork belly. The wine list extends to 50 bins, and owner Allan Hannah betrays his origins with 40 malt whiskies. The pub boasts an attractive garden, where summer Sunday barbecues are a common fixture.

Open all day all wk 11-11 (Sun 12-10.30) Closed 25 Dec, 1 Jan **Food** Lunch Mon-Sat 12-6, Sun 12-3.30 Dinner Mon-Thu 6-9.30, Fri-Sat 6-10 Set menu available Restaurant menu available all wk ◼ Loddon Hoppit, Timothy Taylor Landlord, Sharp's Doom Bar, Marlow Rebellion IPA ♂ Thatchers. ♟ 12
Facilities Non-diners area ❄ (Bar Garden) ♦♦ Children's menu Children's portions Play area Garden ⊓ Parking WiFi **Rooms** 4

■ LOWER WOLVERCOTE **Map 5 SP40**

The Trout Inn

tel: 01865 510930 **195 Godstow Rd OX2 8PN**
dir: *From A40 at Wolvercote rdbt (N of Oxford) follow signs for Wolvercote, through village to pub*

Utterly captivating waterside inn

Threaded into the structure of a very old building, The Trout was already ancient when Lewis Carroll, and later CS Lewis took inspiration here; centuries before it had been a hospice for Godstow Nunnery, on the opposite bank of the Thames. It featured in several episodes of *Inspector Morse*, and has long been a favourite with undergraduates. Its leaded windows, great oak beams, flagged floors and glowing fireplaces make it arguably the area's most atmospheric inn. On a summer day bag a table on the terrace by the fast flowing water to enjoy the comprehensive menu that has distinct Mediterranean lineage; there's a wide range of freshly made pastas and pizzas backed up by reliable modern British fare to choose from.

Open all day all wk 9am-close **Food** Lunch all wk 12-10 Dinner all wk 12-10 Set menu available ⊕ FREE HOUSE ◼ Brakspear Bitter, Sharp's Doom Bar, Guest ales ♂ Aspall. ♟ 21 **Facilities** Non-diners area ❄ (Bar Garden) ♦♦ Children's menu Children's portions Garden ⊓ Parking WiFi ⊞

■ MARSH BALDON **Map 5 SU59**

Seven Stars

tel: 01865 343337 **The Green OX44 9LP**
email: info@sevenstarsonthegreen.co.uk
dir: *From Oxford ring road onto A4074 signed Wallingford. Through Nuneham Courtenay. Left, follow Marsh Baldon signs*

Thriving community-owned pub

After several closures the exasperated Marsh Baldon residents dug deep into their pockets and bought the historic 350-year-old pub on the pretty village green. Today the restyled Seven Stars has a smart interior, local ales on tap and a modern pub menu offering a good range of dishes prepared from fresh local ingredients. Typical dishes include pea, spinach and mint risotto, sausages and mash, classic Sunday roasts, and specials like fish pie and sticky toffee pudding. For summer, there's a gorgeous garden and an August beer festival, and the new restaurant in a converted barn is proving a great success.

Open all day all wk **Food** Lunch Mon-Fri 12-9, Sat-Sun 10-9 Dinner Mon-Fri 12-9, Sat-Sun 10-9 Av main course £9.95 ⊕ FREE HOUSE ◼ Fuller's London Pride, Loose Cannon Abingdon Bridge, Shotover Prospect, Village Idiot, White Horse ♂ Aspall. ♟ 9
Facilities Non-diners area ❄ (Bar Restaurant Garden) ♦♦ Children's menu Children's portions Garden ⊓ Beer festival Parking WiFi ⊞ (notice required)

■ MIDDLETON STONEY **Map 11 SP52**

Best Western The Jersey Arms ★★ HL

tel: 01869 343234 **OX25 4AD**
email: jerseyarms@bestwestern.co.uk **web:** www.jerseyarms.com
dir: *3m from junct 9/10 of M4. 3m from A34 on B430*

British food in a historic property

Until 1951, when a family called Ansell bought it, this 13th-century country inn belonged to the Jersey Estate. In 1985 the Ansells sold it to Donald and Helen Livingston, making them only its third set of owners since 1243. It is just three minutes from Bicester Shopping Village. Food can be taken in the Bar & Grill where the British menu is supplemented by daily specials. Start with king-size prawns in hot garlic oil, then move onto confit of duck with caramelised orange, parsnip mash and orange sauce; classic spaghetti bolognaise; or red Thai curry. Puddings like warm apple pancake and vanilla ice cream round things off nicely.

Open all day all wk **Food** Lunch all wk 12-2 Dinner all wk 6.30-9 Restaurant menu available all wk ⊕ FREE HOUSE ◼ Flowers. ♟ 9 **Facilities** Non-diners area ♦♦ Children's menu Garden ⊓ Parking WiFi **Rooms** 20

■ MILCOMBE **Map 11 SP43**

The Horse & Groom Inn ★★★★ INN

tel: 01295 722142 **OX15 4RS**
email: horseandgroominn@gmail.com **web:** www.thehorseandgroominn.co.uk
dir: *From A361 between Chipping Norton & Bloxham follow Milcombe signs. Pub at end of village*

A traditional Cotswold pub with daily-changing menus

The 17th-century Horse & Groom still signs of the traditional elements such as the stone floor, wood-burning stove, and snug area but is right in the 21st century otherwise. The contemporary dining room seats 50, and the daily-changing menus are bursting with dishes created from local produce. Start off with Wye Valley smoked salmon and mackerel pâté; followed by a steak from Long Compton, or crispy roasted confit leg of Barbary duck with sautéed potatoes, vegetables and onion gravy. Vegetarians have interesting choices too – grilled goats' cheese crouton with red onion marmalade; or falafel burger with chips and salad, perhaps.

Open 12-3 6-11 (Sun 12-5) Closed 25 Dec eve & 26 Dec, Sun eve **Food** Lunch Mon-Sat 12-2.30, Sun 12-4 Dinner Mon-Sat 6-9 Av main course £11 ⊕ PUNCH TAVERNS ◼ Sharp's Doom Bar, Hook Norton Hooky Bitter, Young's Bitter, Black Sheep. ♟ 11
Facilities Non-diners area ❄ (Bar Outside area) ♦♦ Children's menu Children's portions Outside area ⊓ Parking WiFi ⊞ (notice required) **Rooms** 4

■ MILTON **Map 5 SU49**

NEW The Plum Pudding

tel: 01235 834443 **44 High St OX14 4EJ**
email: jez@theplumpuddingmilton.co.uk
dir: *From A34 (Milton Interchange) follow Milton signs. 1st left (signed Milton) into High St*

Proper village free house serving old breed pork

Previously known as the Admiral Benbow, the Plum Pudding was so christened by new owners Mandy and Jez Hill in 2013. The name derives from the nickname of the Oxford Sandy and Black Pig, one of the oldest of British breeds and bred in this area. The dog-friendly bar stocks local and regional ales such as Loose Cannon, and Plum Pudding pork specialities may include slow-roast belly with wholegrain mustard mash, and different flavours of specially made sausages. Alternatives such as filled baguettes, battered cod with mushy peas, and Oxfordshire sirloin steak complete a menu of confirmed pub favourites. Beer festivals in April and October.

Open all wk 11.30-2.30 5-11 (Fri-Sun all day) Food Lunch Mon-Sat 12-2, Sun 12-3 Dinner Mon-Sat 6-9 ⊕ FREE HOUSE ◀ Loose Cannon, Brakspear, Ringwood, Guest ales. Facilities Non-diners area ✿ (Bar Garden) ◀ Children's portions Garden ⩕ Beer festival Parking WiFi ▬

MURCOTT
Map 11 SP51

The Nut Tree Inn ◉◉
PICK OF THE PUBS

tel: 01865 331253 **Main St OX5 2RE**
dir: *M40 junct 9, A34 towards Oxford. Left onto B4027 signed Islip. At Red Lion turn left. Right signed Murcott, Fencott & Charlton-on-Otmoor. Pub on right in village*

Destination dining venue successfully doubling as village local

Murcott is one of the 'Seven Towns' (think villages) encircling the semi-wetland bird sanctuary of Otmoor. For Mike and Imogen North, the acquisition of this thatched, 15th-century free house overlooking the pond was a long-held dream fulfilled. Oak beams, wood-burners and unusual carvings are the setting for a pint of something rather good from local breweries, Vale or Oxfordshire Ales. The Norths raise rare-breed pigs and grow their own fruit and veg, as well as buying in from villagers. Mike's and his sister Mary's award-winning modern British food has earned two AA Rosettes for dishes such as pavé of home-smoked Loch Duart salmon with horseradish cream and Avruga caviar; grilled fillet of aged Charolais beef with triple-cooked chips, baked tomato, onion rings and tarragon butter; and hot passionfruit soufflé. There are two seven-course tasting menus, one for vegetarians. Light meals and sandwiches are served at lunchtime.

Open all day Closed 1wk from 27 Dec, Sun eve & Mon Food Lunch Tue-Sat 12-2.30, Sun 12-3 Dinner Tue-Sat 7-9 Av main course £10 Set menu available Restaurant menu available Tue-Sun ⊕ FREE HOUSE ◀ Vale Best Bitter, Fuller's London Pride, Brains The Rev. James, Shepherd Neame Spitfire, Oxfordshire Ales Pride of Oxford. ⏺ 13 Facilities Non-diners area ◀ Children's portions Garden ⩕ Parking ▬ (notice required)

NORTH HINKSEY VILLAGE
Map 5 SP40

The Fishes

tel: 01865 249796 **OX2 0NA**
email: fishes@peachpubs.com
dir: *From A34 S'bound (dual carriageway) left at junct after Botley Interchange, signed North Hinksey & Oxford Rugby Club. From A34 N'bound exit at Botley Interchange & return to A34 S'bound, then follow as above*

Victorian pub with a tranquil garden

A short walk from the centre of Oxford, this attractive tile-hung pub sits in three acres of wooded grounds running down to a stream. Delightfully tranquil and with lots of shade, this is an ideal place for a picnic (complete with rug and Pimm's) ordered at the bar or one of their regular barbecues. There is also a generously proportioned decking area and a lovely playground for the children. Real ales can be enjoyed in the cosy snug, which is often used for book clubs and dance classes, but you may well be tempted to eat the modern British food in the conservatory. Choices include free-range Cotswold chicken with potato rösti, wilted spinach and morel cream.

Open all day all wk Closed 25 Dec Food Lunch all wk 12-6 Dinner all wk 6-10 ⊕ PEACH PUBS ◀ Morland Old Speckled Hen, St Austell Proper Job, Timothy Taylor Landlord, Guest ales ♂ Aspall. ⏺ 16 Facilities Non-diners area ✿ (Bar Garden) ◀ Children's portions Garden ⩕ Parking WiFi ▬ (notice required)

NORTHMOOR
Map 5 SP40

The Red Lion

tel: 01865 300301 **OX29 5SX**
dir: *A420 from Oxford. At 2nd rdbt take 3rd exit onto A415. Left after lights into Moreton Ln. At end turn right, Pub on right*

A pretty pub with a new lease of life

A pretty 17th-century pub with a large garden set on the skew in the middle of the village; experts have deduced from the positioning of its wooden beams and open fireplaces that it was originally two cottages. After re-opening the pub in the spring of 2014 following a community buy-out from a brewery chain, the experienced new publicans Ian Neale and Lisa Lyn are breathing fresh life into the place. Hook Norton and Brakspear are on tap along with Thatchers Gold and Cotswold cider.

Open 10-3 6-11 (Sat all day Sun 12-4) Closed Sun eve & Mon Food Lunch Mon-Sat 12-2.30, Sun 12-3.30 Dinner Mon-Sat 6.30-9.30 ⊕ FREE HOUSE ◀ Wychwood Hobgoblin, Brakspear, Hook Norton Lion, Guest ale ♂ Thatchers Gold, Cotswold. Facilities Non-diners area ✿ (All areas) ◀ Children's menu Children's portions Garden Outside area ⩕ Beer festival Parking WiFi ▬ (notice required)

OXFORD
Map 5 SP50

The Magdalen Arms

tel: 01865 243159 **243 Iffley Rd OX4 1SJ**
email: info@magdalenarms.co.uk
dir: *On corner of Iffley Rd & Magdalen Rd*

Busy food pub with a boho vibe

Just a short stroll from Oxford city centre, this bustling food pub is run by the same team as Waterloo's hugely influential Anchor & Hope gastro-pub. There is a similar boho feel to the place with its dark red walls and vintage furniture and the nose-to-tail menu will be familiar to anybody who knows the pub's London sibling. Expect the likes of chicken and bacon terrine with cornichons and toast; Swiss chard with semolina gnocchi and goats' curd; and plum Bakewell tart and vanilla ice cream. Real ales are complemented by a vibrant modern wine list.

Open 11-11 (Mon 5-11 Sun 12-10.30) Closed BHs, 24-26 Dec, Mon L Food Lunch Tue-Sat 12-2.30, Sun 12-3 Dinner Mon-Sat 6-10, Sun 6-9.30 ⊕ STAR PUBS & BARS ◀ Caledonian XPA & Deuchars IPA, Theakston Black Bull, Guest ale ♂ Symonds. ⏺ 16 Facilities Non-diners area ✿ (Bar Garden) ◀ Children's portions Garden ⩕ Beer festival WiFi ▬ (notice required)

The Oxford Retreat

tel: 01865 250309 **1-2 Hythe Bridge St OX1 2EW**
email: info@theoxfordretreat.com
dir: *In city centre. 200mtrs from rail station towards centre*

Perched on the river close to the city centre

Smack beside the River Isis, the decked, tree-shaded waterside garden at this imposing gabled pub is the place to be seen and is best enjoyed after a day exploring the city of dreaming spires. Arrive early and relax, start by sipping cocktails or quaffing a pint of London Pride, then order from the eclectic pub menu, tucking into baked goats' cheese with roasted pepper and chickpea cassoulet; beer battered cod and chips; tomato pesto penne; or bavette steak with grilled Portobello mushroom, confit tomato, fries, watercress and red wine jus. In winter, retreat inside and cosy up around the log fire.

Open all day all wk Closed 25-26 Dec & 1 Jan Food Lunch Mon-Thu 12-3, Fri-Sat 12-10, Sun 12-6 Dinner Mon-Thu 6-10, Fri-Sat 12-10, Sun 12-6 Set menu available ⊕ FREE HOUSE ◀ Fuller's London Pride, Guinness, Staropramen ♂ Westons Wyld Wood Organic. ⏺ 10 Facilities Non-diners area ✿ (Bar Garden) ◀ Children's portions Garden ⩕ WiFi ▬ (notice required)

PICK OF THE PUBS

The Crown Inn

PISHILL Map 5 SU78

tel: 01491 638364
RG9 6HH
email: enquiries@thecrowninnpishill.co.uk
web: www.thecrowninnpishill.co.uk
dir: *A4130 from Henley-on-Thames,
right onto B480 to Pishill*

Coaching inn with thatched barn

A pretty 15th-century brick and flint former coaching inn, The Crown has had a colourful history. The building began life in medieval times, serving ale to the thriving monastic community, then providing refuge to Catholic priests escaping Henry VIII's tyrannical rule. It contains possibly the country's largest priest hole, in which one Father Dominique met his end, and whose ghost is occasionally seen around the premises. Before going any further, how should Pishill be pronounced? Old maps show a second 's' in the name, supporting the theory that farm-waggon drivers used to stop at the inn having made the long climb out of Henley-on-Thames, and while the men topped themselves up in the bar, the horses would relieve themselves. Fast-forward to the Swinging 60s, and the neighbouring thatched barn housed a nightclub hosting George Harrison, Dusty Springfield and other big names from the world of pop. Nowadays, the barn is licensed for civil ceremonies, as well as serving as a function room. In

the pub itself, the bar is supplied by mostly local breweries, typically Brakspear, Loddon, Rebellion, Vale and West Berkshire. The menu always includes sandwiches and ploughman's at lunchtimes, and features fresh local produce cooked to order. Lunch and dinner are served every day and may be enjoyed inside, where there are three log fires, or in the picturesque garden overlooking the valley. Depending on the season, you might find lamb and kidney hotpot with cauliflower cheese gratin; fish brandade with vegetable and chestnut crumble, and pink peppercorn and dill hollandaise sauce; and red onion, pine nut and blue cheese parcel with roasted new potatoes, poached pear and rocket salad. In late September, there's a beer festival.

Open all wk 12-3 6-11 (Sun 12-3 7-10) Closed 25-26 Dec **Food** Lunch all wk 12-2.30 Dinner Mon-Thu 6.30-9, Fri-Sat 6.30-9.30, Sun 7-9 Av main course £12.50 ⊕ FREE HOUSE ◀ Brakspear, West Berkshire, Loddon, Rebellion, Branscombe Vale. **Facilities** Non-diners area ✿ (Bar Garden) ♦♦ Children's portions Garden ⋒ Beer festival Parking 🚐 (notice required) WiFi

OXFORD *continued*

The Punter

tel: 01865 248832 **7 South St, Osney Island OX2 0BE**
email: info@thepunteroxford.co.uk
dir: *Phone for detailed directions*

Quirky Thames-side treasure

If feeling famished on your tour of the Dreaming Spires, then seek out this rustically-cool pub on Osney Island in the heart of the city – it enjoys a magnificent and very tranquil spot beside the River Thames. The decor is eclectic and interesting, with much to catch the eye, from rugs on flagstone floors and mismatched tables and chairs to bold artwork on whitewashed walls. Come for a relaxing pint of Punter Ale by the river or refuel on something tempting from the daily menu – potted crayfish with pickled cucumber and radish salad; chilli with rice and garlic chive crème fraîche; vine wrapped sea bass with Parisien potatoes, samphire and sauce vièrge; or steak and chips.

Open all day all wk **Food** Lunch Mon-Fri 12-3, wknds all day Dinner Mon-Fri 6-10, wknds all day ◄ The Punter Ale ♂ Addlestones. ♀ 12 **Facilities** Non-diners area ♦ Children's portions Garden ✦ WiFi

NEW The Rickety Press

tel: 01865 424581 **67 Cranham St OX2 6DE**
email: info@thericketypress.com
dir: *Phone for detailed directions*

In the heart of historic Jericho

The Rickety Press is run by the same three old school friends as The Rusty Bicycle in east Oxford. Deceptively spacious, there's a large conservatory restaurant, a snug and a bar serving Arkell's real ales, handpicked wines, coffees and teas, while the spicy aroma of mulled wine fills the winter air. Big hits on winter-into-spring menus include radicchio and taleggio risotto; treacle-cured Loch Duart salmon; crispy soft-shell crab with tamarind; and Thai green monkfish curry with macadamia nuts. One particularly tempting bar snack is Cornish rock oysters with triple-cooked chips and béarnaise sauce.

Open all day all wk **Food** Lunch Mon-Sat 12-2.30, Sun 12-3 Dinner Sun-Thu 6-9.30, Fri-Sat 6-10 Av main course £15 Set menu available Restaurant menu available all wk ⊕ ARKELL'S ◄ 3B, Moonlight, Kingsdown. **Facilities** Non-diners area ♣ (Bar) ♦ Children's menu Children's portions WiFi

NEW The Rusty Bicycle

tel: 01865 435298 **28 Magdalen Rd OX4 1RB**
email: info@therustybicycle.com
dir: *From Oxford ring road (A4142) take A4158 (Iffley Rd) towards city centre. Right into Magdalen Rd*

Great community local with fine pies

You can't miss the hanging sign for this quirky suburban pub - look for a 1950's grocer's bike swinging high above Magdalen Road's pavement. It's a community pub in a very cosmopolitan part of the city, established just five years ago with the ambition of catering for all-comers. The plan appears to work well, with grand beers from owners Arkell's Brewery and carefully chosen guests coupled with a decidedly traditional menu of favourites like pies (albeit unusual varieties like pumpkin, chickpea and coconut), burgers and filling snacks, all created from scratch. Bareboard floors, real fires and eclectic furnishing, this is one to discover and savour at length.

Open all day all wk Closed 25 Dec **Food** Lunch all wk 12-2.30 Dinner all wk 6-9 Av main course £10 ⊕ ARKELL'S ◄ 3B, Moonlight, Kingsdown ♂ Westons Old Rosie. **Facilities** Non-diners area ♣ (Bar Garden) ♦ Children's menu Children's portions Garden ✦ Beer festival WiFi

Turf Tavern

tel: 01865 243235 **4 Bath Place, off Holywell St OX1 3SU**
email: 8004@greeneking.co.uk
dir: *Phone for detailed directions*

The hidden haunt of dons and students over many centuries

A jewel of a pub, and consequently one of Oxford's most popular, although it's not easy to find, as it is approached through hidden alleyways, which, if anything, adds to its allure. Previously called the Spotted Cow, it became the Turf in 1842, probably in deference to its gambling clientele; it has also had brushes with literature, film and politics. The Turf Tavern is certainly one of the city's oldest pubs, with some 13th-century foundations and a 17th-century low-beamed front bar. Three beer gardens help ease overcrowding, but the 11 real ales and reasonably priced pub grub keep the students, locals and visitors flowing in.

Open all day all wk 11-11 Closed 25 Dec **Food** Lunch all wk 11-9 Dinner all wk 11-9 ⊕ GREENE KING ◄ Guest ales ♂ Westons Old Rosie, Guest ciders. **Facilities** ♣ (Bar Garden) ♦ Garden ✦ WiFi ▭

PISHILL	Map 5 SU78

The Crown Inn
PICK OF THE PUBS

See Pick of the Pubs on opposite page

RAMSDEN	Map 11 SP31

The Royal Oak
PICK OF THE PUBS

See Pick of the Pubs on page 402

ROTHERFIELD PEPPARD	Map 5 SU78

The Unicorn

tel: 01491 628674 **Colmore Ln, Kingwood RG9 5LX**
email: enquiries@unicornkingwood.co.uk
dir: *Exit A4074 (Reading to Wallingford), follow Sonning Common & Peppard signs. Left in Peppard Common signed Stoke Row. Right into Colmore Ln at Unicorn sign*

Popular, smart village pub

A village local set in the Chilterns, The Unicorn is five miles from Henley-on-Thames and Reading. Petitioning villagers saved the pub from closure and change of use. Now, with children and dogs welcome, expect to have to fight your way in on a Friday or Saturday evening, or during the summer beer festival, such is The Unicorn's reputation as a friendly pub and the heart of the community. It's certainly worth a long look at the menu – perhaps share a warm whole camembert with red onion chutney before moving onto pan-fried mackerel fillet with warm horseradish potato salad, then pressed pork belly with black pudding mash, braised red cabbage and apple cider jus. Puddings are no less tempting, salted toffee popcorn, with strawberry milkshake and vanilla marshmallows makes a fun finish. There's a garden to enjoy in the summer and great walks all around.

Open all wk 11-3 5.30-11 (Fri-Sat 11am-11pm Sun 12-10) **Food** Lunch Mon-Fri 12-3, Sat 12-4, Sun 12-5 Dinner Mon-Sat 7-10, Sun 7-9 Av main course £11.50 Set menu available Restaurant menu available all ek ⊕ BRAKSPEAR ◄ Brakspear & Special. **Facilities** Non-diners area ♣ (Bar Garden) ♦ Children's menu Children's portions Garden ✦ Beer festival Parking WiFi ▭ (notice required)

PICK OF THE PUBS

The Royal Oak

RAMSDEN Map 11 SP31

tel: 01993 868213 **High St OX7 3AU**
email: jonoldham57@gmail.com
web: www.royaloakramsden.com
dir: B4022 from Witney towards
Charlbury, right before Hailey, through
Poffley End

Award-winning pub near many lovely walks

Built of Cotswold stone and facing
Ramsden's fine parish church, this
former 17th-century coaching inn is a
popular refuelling stop for walkers
exploring nearby Wychwood Forest and
visitors touring the pretty villages and
visiting Blenheim Palace. Whether you
are walking or not, the cosy inn oozes
traditional charm and character, with
its old beams, warm fires and stone
walls, and long-serving landlords John
and Jo Oldham provide a very warm
welcome. A free house, it dispenses
beers sourced from local breweries,
such as Hook Norton Hooky Bitter and
Old Hooky, alongside Adnams Broadside
and Young's Special. Somerset's Original
Cider Company supplies the bar with
Pheasant Plucker cider, alongside
Westons Old Rosie from Herefordshire.
With a strong kitchen team, the main
menu, built on the very best of fresh
local and seasonal ingredients,
regularly features a pie of the week
topped with puff pastry, or the popluar
steak and kidney suet pudding; there

are popular choices such as starters of
oven baked baby brie; devilled lambs'
kidneys with Dijon mustard sauce; or
chargrilled aubergine, sundried feta
cheese and piquant tomato sauce.
Typical mains are confit of duck, Puy
lentils, garlic potatoes, red berry and
quince sauce; seafood pot au feu;
Gymkhana Club curry, a traditional Sri
Lankan dish, served with rice and
pickles; and a choice of Aberdeen Angus
steaks and burgers. Carefully selected
by the owner, the wine list has over 200
wines, specialising in those from
Bordeaux and Languedoc, with 30 of
them served by the glass. Every
Thursday evening there is a special offer
of steak, with a glass of wine and
dessert included.

Open all wk 11.30-3 6.30-11 (Sun
11.30-3 7-10.30) Closed 25 Dec
Food Lunch all wk 12-2 Dinner Mon-Sat
7-9.45, Sun 7-9 ⊕ FREE HOUSE ◀ Hook
Norton Old Hooky & Hooky Bitter,
Adnams Broadside, Young's Special,
Wye Valley Ŏ Westons Old Rosie,
Pheasant Plucker. ♀ 30
Facilities Non-diners area ❖ (Bar
Garden) Children's portions Garden
Parking

SHILTON
Map 5 SP20

Rose & Crown

tel: 01993 842280 **OX18 4AB**
dir: *From A40 at Burford take A361 towards Lechlade on Thames. Right, follow Shilton signs on left. Or from A40 E of Burford take B4020 towards Carterton*

Well-supported village local and destination food pub

A traditional Cotswold-stone inn dating back to the 17th century, whose two rooms retain their original beams and are warmed by a winter log fire. In the bar, Hook Norton Old Hooky might well partner Young's Bitter and Ashton Press cider. As their pedigrees might lead you to expect, chef-landlord Martin Coldicott, who trained at London's Connaught Hotel, and head chef Jamie Webber, from The Ivy, prepare above average, but simply presented food, typically partridge with braised haricot beans, bacon and garlic; smoked haddock, salmon and prawn pie; and baked aubergine parmigiana with mozzarella. You may eat and drink in the garden if you prefer.

Open all wk 11.30-3 6-11 (Fri-Sun & BH 11.30-11) **Food** Lunch Mon-Fri 12-2, Sat-Sun & BH 12-2.45 Dinner all wk 7-9 Av main course £13 ⊕ FREE HOUSE ◄ Butcombe, Hook Norton Old Hooky, Loose Cannon, Wye Valley, Young's Bitter ♂ Ashton Press, Westons Wyld Wood Organic. ☂ 10 **Facilities** Non-diners area ☺ (Bar Garden) ♦♦ Garden ⋒ Parking WiFi

SHIPLAKE
Map 5 SU77

NEW The Plowden Arms

tel: 0118 940 2794 **Reading Rd RG9 4BX**
email: info@doffandbow.co.uk
dir: *On A4155, 4m from Reading (2m from Henley-on-Thames)*

Family-welcoming hostelry proposing refreshments from a bygone era

Equidistant between Henley-on-Thames and Reading, The Plowden Arms takes its name from the family who occupied Shiplake Court (now Shiplake College) in the 17th century. Period features, original beams and a working fireplace are the setting for Brakspear beers, draught ciders, and a menu that takes its inspiration from forgotten dishes of bygone times. The recipe for John Bull's steamed steak and onion pudding, for example, dates from 1845; herrings in oatmeal with a sweet lemon salad is even older. Puddings of the dessert variety include steamed carrot with brown sugar sauce; and tipsy cake made with a brioche-type dough served with grilled pineapple.

Open 11-2.30 5-11 (Sun 12-4 7-10.30) Closed Mon **Food** Lunch Tue-Sat 12-2, Sun 12-3.30 Dinner Tue-Sat 6-10, Sun 7-9 Av main course £16 ⊕ BRAKSPEAR ◄ Bitter, Ringwood Boondoggle ♂ Addlestones, Thatchers Heritage. ☂ 13
Facilities Non-diners area ☺ (Bar Garden) ♦♦ Children's menu Children's portions Family room Garden ⋒ Parking

SHIPTON-UNDER-WYCHWOOD
Map 10 SP21

The Shaven Crown Hotel

tel: 01993 830500 **High St OX7 6BA**
email: relax@theshavencrown.co.uk
dir: *On A361, halfway between Burford & Chipping Norton*

Historic inn overlooking the picturesque village green and church

This 14th-century coaching inn was built by the monks of Bruern Abbey as a hospice for the poor. Following the Dissolution of the Monasteries, Elizabeth I used it as a hunting lodge before giving it to the village in 1580, when it became the Crown Inn. Thus it stayed until 1930, when a brewery with a sense of humour changed the name as homage to the familiar monastic tonsure. Its interior is full of original architectural features, like the Great Hall. Light meals and real ales are served in the bar, while the restaurant offers modern English dishes. Change of hands.

Open all wk 11-3 5-11 (Sat-Sun 11-11) **Food** Lunch Mon-Fri 12-2, Sat 12-9.30, Sun 12-9 Dinner Mon-Fri 6-9.30, Sat 12-9.30, Sun 12-9 ⊕ FREE HOUSE ◄ Hook Norton, Wye Valley, Goffs, Cottage ♂ Westons Stowford Press. ☂ 10
Facilities Non-diners area ☺ (Bar Garden) ♦♦ Children's menu Children's portions Garden ⋒ Parking WiFi ⛁ (notice required)

STANDLAKE
Map 5 SP30

The Bell Inn

tel: 01865 300784 **21 High St OX29 7RH**
email: info@thebellstandlake.co.uk
dir: *From A415 in Standlake into High St, pub 500yds on right*

Thriving village pub close to the Thames

Experienced landlord Craig Foster, who also owns the Boot in Barnard Gate, runs this pub which stands tucked away in a sleepy village close to the River Thames. Appointed in a comfortably rustic style, it draws drinkers and diners in for its relaxed atmosphere, four real ales on tap, and the short imaginative lunch and dinner menus. Typically, tuck into mussels steamed with white wine, shallots and cream; braised blade of beef; and chicken, leek and mushroom pie, with decent sandwiches (rare roast beef and mustard) on offer at lunchtimes.

Open all day all wk **Food** Lunch Wed-Sat 12-2.30, Sun 12-3 Dinner Tue-Thu 6.30-9.30, Fri-Sat 6.30-10 ⊕ FREE HOUSE ◄ Skinner's Betty Stogs, West Berkshire Good Old Boy, Guest ales ♂ Thatchers Gold. ☂ 8 **Facilities** Non-diners area ☺ (Bar Restaurant Garden) ♦♦ Children's menu Children's portions Family room Garden ⋒ Beer festival Parking WiFi ⛁ (notice required)

STEEPLE ASTON
Map 11 SP42

The Red Lion

tel: 01869 340225 **South Side OX25 4RY**
email: redlionsa@aol.com
dir: *0.5m off A4260 (Oxford Rd). Follow brown tourist signs for pub*

Unspoilt 18th-century pub popular with walkers

In an elevated position in the village, this newly refurbished Hook Norton brewery pub offers a number of options: in front of the fire in the bar; in the comfortably furnished, oak-beamed Garden Room; or head for the pretty suntrap terrace, not least for its view of the delightful Cherwell Valley. In addition to generous Sunday roasts, other locally sourced dishes include salads; thin-crust, stone-baked pizzas; Aberdeen Angus burgers; risottos; roast rump of lamb with redcurrant and rosemary; and fresh haddock with or without batter, triple-cooked chips and mushy peas. Children and dogs are welcome.

Open all wk 12-3 5.30-11 (Sat 12-11 Sun 12-5) (Jun-Oct all day) Closed Sun eve from 5pm **Food** Lunch all wk 12-2.30 Dinner Mon-Sat 6-9 ⊕ HOOK NORTON ◄ Hooky Bitter, Lion & Seasonal ales ♂ Westons Stowford Press. ☂ 11
Facilities Non-diners area ☺ (Bar Outside area) ♦♦ Children's portions Outside area ⋒ Parking WiFi ⛁ (notice required)

STOKE ROW
Map 5 SU68

Crooked Billet
PICK OF THE PUBS

tel: 01491 681048 **RG9 5PU**
dir: *From Henley towards Oxford on A4130. Left at Nettlebed for Stoke Row*

17th-century pub with plenty of character and an excellent menu

Built in 1642, the Crooked Billet was once the hideout of notorious highwayman Dick Turpin. Tucked away down a single track lane in deepest Oxfordshire, this charmingly rustic pub is now a popular hideaway for the well-heeled and the well known. Many of its finest features are unchanged, including the low beams, tiled floors and open fires that are so integral to its character. Brakspear ales are well kept, while local produce and organic fare are the mainstays of the kitchen; the chef-proprietor will even exchange a lunch or dinner for locals' excess vegetables. A set lunch starter and main course could kick off with tartare of Loch Duart salmon with celeriac slaw and pickled cucumber; and continue with local pheasant breast, soft herb polenta, spiced lentils, kale and parsnip crisps. Finish with a pud such as plum Bakewell with cinnamon cream for a small additional cost.

Open all wk 12-3 7-12 (Sat-Sun 12-12) **Food** Lunch Mon-Fri 12-2.30, Sat 12-10.30, Sun 12-10 Dinner Mon-Fri 7-10, Sat 12-10.30, Sun 12-10 Set menu available ⊕ BRAKSPEAR ◀ Organic Best Bitter. ☕ 10 **Facilities** Non-diners area ◀ Children's portions Garden ⊟ Parking

STONOR
Map 5 SU78

NEW The Quince Tree

tel: 01491 639039 **RG9 6HE**
email: home@thequincetree.com
dir: *From Henley-on-Thames take A4130 towards Wallingford. Right on B480 to Stonor*

Pub, café, shop and more in a pretty Chilterns village

With Henley-on-Thames nearby and Stonor Park's scenic grounds on the doorstep, The Quince Tree is well placed for walkers, cyclists and wildlife lovers. Lots on offer too, within this sensitively restored 17th-century coaching inn – a welcoming mix of pub, café, shop, bakery, pâtisserie and deli. The menus range from bruschettas for starters to main courses like poached sea bream with morels, linguine and broad beans. The bakery works through the night to supply unbeatably fresh breads and pastries. As for liquid refreshments, Marston's and guest ales on tap are accompanied by a terrific range of bottled craft ales and ciders.

Open 12-3 5-11 (Sun 12-4) Closed Sun eve **Food** Lunch Mon-Fri 12-2.30, Sat-Sun 12-3 Dinner Mon-Thu 6.30-9, Fri-Sat 6.30-9.30 Av main course £15 Set menu available ⊕ FREE HOUSE ◀ Marston's EPA, Guest ales Ŏ Cotswold Cider. ☕ **Facilities** Non-diners area ◀ (Bar Garden) ◀ Children's menu Children's portions Garden ⊟ Parking WiFi ▭ (notice required)

SWERFORD
Map 11 SP33

The Mason's Arms

tel: 01608 683212 **Banbury Rd OX7 4AP**
email: admin@masons-arms.com
dir: *Between Banbury & Chipping Norton on A361*

Large beer garden ideal for families

Jamie Bailey and Louise Robertson arrived at The Mason's Arms after running pubs in Shropshire. A 300-year-old, stone-built former Masonic lodge, this pub in the Cotswolds has retained its traditional, informal feel. Jamie's modern European cooking concentrates on local produce where possible and there is an emphasis on fish on the specials board, which might offer pan-fried tiger prawns with chilli and

chorizo followed by pan-fried red mullet on crab meat and samphire linguine. Non-fish options include coq au vin or venison Wellington. The large garden has stunning views of the surrounding area.

Open all wk 10-3 6-11 (Sun 12-dusk) **Food** Lunch Mon-Sat 12-2.30, Sun 12-dusk Dinner Mon-Sat 7-9, Sun 12-dusk ⊕ FREE HOUSE ◀ Wychwood Hobgoblin, Brakspear. ☕ 20 **Facilities** Non-diners area ◀ (Bar Garden) ◀ Children's menu Children's portions Garden ⊟ Parking WiFi ▭

SWINBROOK
Map 5 SP21

The Swan Inn ★★★★ INN ֎֎
PICK OF THE PUBS

tel: 01993 823339 **OX18 4DY**
email: info@theswanswinbrook.co.uk **web:** www.theswanswinbrook.co.uk
dir: *A40 towards Cheltenham, left towards Swinbrook, pub 1m before Burford*

Tranquility and class at Cotswold boutique inn

Hidden in the Windrush Valley you will find the idyllic village of Swinbrook where time stands still. Owners Archie and Nicola Orr-Ewing took on the lease of this dreamy, wisteria-clad stone pub from the Dowager Duchess of Devonshire, the last surviving Mitford sister. The Swan is the perfect English country pub – it stands by the River Windrush near the village cricket pitch, overlooking unspoilt Cotswold countryside. It gets even better inside: the two cottage-style front rooms, replete with worn flagstones, crackling log fires, low beams and country furnishings, lead through to a cracking bar and classy conservatory extension. First-class pub food ranges from simple bar snacks to more substantial main courses of guinea fowl, apricot and chickpea tagine; and Cornish hake with a casserole of butter beans, tomato and chorizo. You won't want to leave, so book one of the stunning en suite rooms in the restored barn.

Open all wk 11.30-11 (Closed afternoons Nov-Feb) Closed 25 Dec **Food** Lunch Mon-Fri 12-2, Sat 12-2.30, Sun 12-3 Dinner Mon-Thu & Sun 7-9, Fri-Sat 7-9.30 ⊕ FREE HOUSE ◀ Hook Norton, Guest ales Ŏ Aspall, Westons Wyld Wood Organic & Stowford Press. ☕ 9 **Facilities** Non-diners area ◀ (Bar Restaurant Garden) ◀ Children's menu Children's portions Garden ⊟ Parking WiFi **Rooms** 6

SYDENHAM
Map 5 SP70

The Crown Inn
PICK OF THE PUBS

tel: 01844 351634 **Sydenham Rd OX39 4NB**
email: swancraft@hotmail.com
dir: *M40 junct 6, B4009 towards Chinnor. Left onto A40. At Postcombe right to Sydenham*

Delightful village inn very much part of the community

In a small village below the scarp slopes of the Chilterns, this pretty 16th-century inn shows how careful refurbishment can successfully incorporate both traditional and modern styles. Old photographs, for example, hang contentedly alongside contemporary paintings. The menu is short – barely a dozen items are featured – but expect good things of those that are, such as main courses of slow-roasted Moroccan spiced lamb shank pie with baked potato mash; seafood and chorizo risotto; and pan-fried pork escalope with avocado, mature cheddar and cream. Desserts include chocolate fondant and apple and almond tart. In the bar, a pint of IPA would go well with a ploughman's, omelette, baguette or pizza. The pub also hosts quizzes and live music.

Open 12-3 5.30-11 (Sat 12-11 Sun 12-3) Closed Mon **Food** Lunch Thu-Sun 12-2.30 Dinner Thu-Sat 7-9.30 ⊕ FREE HOUSE/THE SYDENHAM PUB CO ◀ Rebellion IPA & Zebedee, Sharp's Doom Bar, Bath Ales Barnsey, Black Sheep Ŏ Thatchers Gold. **Facilities** Non-diners area ◀ (Bar Restaurant Garden) ◀ Children's portions Garden ⊟ ▭

TETSWORTH
Map 5 SP60

The Old Red Lion

tel: 01844 281274 **40 High St OX9 7AS**
email: info@theoldredliontetsworth.co.uk
dir: *From Oxford ring road at Headington take A40. Follow A418 signs (over M40). Right onto A40 signed Milton Common & Tetsworth*

Village pub ideal for early birds

An airy, contemporary pub with traditional flourishes, ideal for trippers heading for the nearby Chilterns. Open for breakfast from 7am, birdwatchers pursuing red kites can stop by before hitting the hills, whilst cricketers inspecting the wicket on the adjacent village green pitch can take a leisurely mid-morning Full-English. Not content with two restaurant areas and a bustling bar to run, the owners also host a village shop here. Beers from local microbreweries hit the spot, whilst timeless pub grub meals like sausage and mash fill the gap. Summer barbecues are popular. There's a mini beer festival every Easter.

Open all day all wk Mon-Thu & Sat 7am-10pm (Fri 7am-mdnt Sun 8am-4.30pm) **Food** Lunch Mon-Thu & Sat 11-10, Fri 11-mdnt, Sun 12-3.30 (open for breakfast 7am-11.30am) Dinner Mon-Thu & Sat 11-10, Fri 11-mdnt Av main course £8.50 ⊕ FREE HOUSE ◀ Loose Cannon Brewery, White Horse ♂ Thatchers Gold. **Facilities** Non-diners area ❖ (Bar Outside area) ♦ Children's menu Children's portions Garden Outside area ⊨ Beer festival Parking WiFi ▭

THAME
Map 5 SP70

The James Figg

tel: 01844 260166 **21 Cornmarket OX9 2BL**
email: thejamesfigg@peachpubs.com
dir: *In town centre*

Buzzing market place pub with secret garden

An attractive 18th-century pub whose name celebrates England's first undisputed champion boxer who lived here 300 years ago. A traditional interior with dark wood floors, a double-sided open fire and a curving bar stocking ales such as Mad Goose and Vale Best Bitter. A list of snacks offers Scotch eggs, pork pies and breaded camembert, while light options include sandwiches and a hot roast bap. If you're seeking something more substantial, look to a range of burgers, pizzas and classics such as honey-roasted ham, egg and chips. Beyond The Stables function room, you'll find a private garden.

Open all day all wk 11am-mdnt Closed 25 Dec ⊕ FREE HOUSE/PEACH PUBS ◀ Vale Best Bitter, Purity Mad Goose, Sharp's Doom Bar ♂ Aspall. **Facilities** ❖ (Bar Restaurant Garden) ♦ Children's portions Garden Parking WiFi

The Thatch

tel: 01844 214340 **29-30 Lower High St OX9 2AA**
email: thatch@peachpubs.com
dir: *From rdbt on A418 into Oxford Rd signed town centre. Follow into Thame High St. Pub on right*

Half-timbered pub with a sunny courtyard garden

In the heart of Thame's high street, the striking Thatch (thatched, of course) was originally a row of 16th-century cottages. It remains a cosy warren of rooms with inglenook fireplaces and antique furniture. If you make it past the bar without being tempted by coffee, cakes or a pint of Doom Bar, you'll find yourself in the restaurant overlooking the garden. The kitchen focuses on the best seasonal and responsibly sourced ingredients – a cold cuts deli board to share might be followed by guinea fowl confit, chestnut and bacon salad, and cranberry dressing; mulled Cornish lamb casserole and mash; or sweet potato lasagne with jalapeño pesto. There is a beer festival during National Cask Ale Week.

Open all day all wk Closed 25 Dec **Food** Lunch all wk 12-10 Dinner all wk 12-10 Av main course £14.50 ⊕ PEACH PUBS ◀ Vale Wychert, Sharp's Doom Bar ♂ Aspall. ☻ 16 **Facilities** Non-diners area ❖ (Bar Garden) ♦ Children's portions Garden ⊨ Beer festival Parking WiFi ▭ (notice required)

TOOT BALDON
Map 5 SP50

The Mole Inn ◉◉
PICK OF THE PUBS

tel: 01865 340001 **OX44 9NG**
email: info@themoleinn.com
dir: *5m SE from Oxford city centre off B480*

A foodie destination with great service

The 300-year-old, Grade II listed Mole Inn has put the amusingly named village of Toot Baldon on the map with the exciting, two AA-Rosette culinary output of chef and host Gary Witchalls. His dedication in the kitchen is matched by the front-of-house professionalism of his wife, Jenny. Drinks are also a strength: try a pint of Hook Norton, Shepherd Neame Spitfire or The Mole's Pleasure - an ale developed together with Moodley's microbrewery, which is particularly suited to the pub's dry-aged steaks from Aberdeenshire. Pick from rib-eye, rump, sirloin or fillet steaks and then choose your sauce. Other options could include bubble-and-squeak with a poached egg, cheddar sauce and a crunchy vegetable and sesame salad; fish mixed grill, lime aïoli, rocket, cherry tomato salad with frites; and mango and passionfruit Pavlova. Leather sofas, stripped beams, solid white walls and terracotta floors provide the perfect background for a leisurely meal.

Open all day all wk 12-12 (Sun 12-11) Closed 25 Dec **Food** Lunch all wk 12-2.30 Dinner all wk 7-9.30 Set menu available Restaurant menu available all wk ⊕ FREE HOUSE ◀ The Mole's Pleasure, Fuller's London Pride, Shepherd Neame Spitfire, Hook Norton, Guinness ♂ Westons Stowford Press. ☻ 11 **Facilities** Non-diners area ♦ Children's menu Children's portions Garden ⊨ Parking WiFi

UFFINGTON
Map 5 SU38

NEW The Fox & Hounds ★★★★ INN

tel: 01367 820680 **High St SN7 7RP**
email: enquiries@uffingtonpub.co.uk **web:** www.uffingtonpub.co.uk
dir: *From A420 (S of Faringdon) follow Fernham or Uffington signs*

Traditional food and good beer in timeless village inn

Amidst the thatched cottages and 13th-century church in the charming village of Uffington, The Fox & Hounds boasts unrivalled views of The Ridgeway and the Uffington White Horse. Writer John Betjeman once lived across the road from the pub and Tolkein was a frequent visitor – legend has it that St George slew the dragon at nearby Dragon Hill. A traditional free house with a range of well-kept real ales, the home-cooked food is simple and takes in such pub favourites as pie of the day; wholetail scampi with chips; and home-made burgers. Contact the pub for details of its beer festivals.

Open all day all wk **Food** Lunch Mon-Fri 12-2, Sat-Sun & BHs 12-3 (ex 25 Dec) Dinner Mon-Sat 6-9 ⊕ FREE HOUSE ◀ Local ales ♂ Thatchers. **Facilities** Non-diners area ❖ (Bar Restaurant Garden) ♦ Children's menu Children's portions Garden ⊨ Beer festival Parking WiFi ▭ (notice required) **Rooms** 2

WEST HANNEY
Map 5 SU49

Plough Inn

tel: 01235 868674 **Church St OX12 OLN**
email: info@theploughwesthanney.co.uk
dir: *From Wantage take A338 towards Oxford. Inn in 1m*

Friendly village free house

Thatched with four 'eyebrows', the Plough dates from around 1525, when it was a row of cottages. Steve Cadogan took over in 2013 and enjoys executive responsibility for such things as ensuring there are logs for the fires, choosing the six rolling real ales, and organising the Easter, spring and summer bank holiday beer festivals. From the kitchen come home-cooked, seasonal dishes such as king prawns in tomato sauce with garlic and chilli; Dews Farm pork and gammon with black pudding; and wild mushroom tart with Oxford Blue cheese. For a treat, dine in the pretty walled garden.

Open all wk 12-3 6-12 (Sat-Sun all day) **Food** Lunch all wk 12-3 Dinner all wk 6-9 Av main course £10.95 ⊕ FREE HOUSE ◄ Adnams, Bass, Marston's, Timothy Taylor ♂ Westons, Thatchers Gold. ♟ 10 **Facilities** Non-diners area ❖ (Bar Garden) ♦ Children's menu Children's portions Play area Garden ⊓ Beer festival Parking WiFi ⛟

WHEATLEY
Map 5 SP50

Bat & Ball Inn

tel: 01865 874379 **28 High St, Cuddesdon OX44 9HJ**
email: info@batball.co.uk
dir: *Through Wheatley towards Garsington, turn left signed Cuddesdon*

Cricket themed village pub

No surprise that the bar here is packed to the gunnels with cricketing memorabilia, but the charm of this former coaching inn extends to beamed ceilings, flagstone floors and solid wood furniture warmed by an open log fire. The house ale, Oxford Gold, is flanked by Marston's beers. A comprehensive seasonal menu, supplemented by daily specials, is likely to include the Bat burger, home made from steak and with a choice of toppings; and slow-braised shoulder of lamb. Look out for clay pigeon shoots, pig roasts, steak nights and sausage and mash evenings. The pub is in an ideal spot for walkers, and dogs are welcome too.

Open all day all wk **Food** Lunch Mon-Fri 12-2.30, Sat all day, Sun 12-8 Dinner Mon-Fri 6-9.30, Sat all day, Sun 12-8 Av main course £10.95 ⊕ MARSTON'S ◄ Pedigree, Brakspear Oxford Gold, Guinness, Guest ale ♂ Thatchers Gold. **Facilities** Non-diners area ❖ (Bar Garden) ♦ Children's menu Children's portions Garden ⊓ Parking WiFi ⛟ (notice required)

WITNEY
Map 5 SP31

The Fleece

tel: 01993 892270 **11 Church Green OX28 4AZ**
email: fleece@peachpubs.com
dir: *In town centre*

Flexible dining in an ex-brewery

Overlooking the village's beautiful church green in the heart of picturesque Witney, this fine Georgian building was once the home of Clinch's brewery. Nowadays, it serves food and drink from lunch through the afternoon to dinner plus well-kept ales are a big draw. Share an inventive deli board or spiced chickpea, red pepper and feta pitta and cumin crème fraîche roll or dig into mains like sea trout fishcake, spinach and chive butter sauce; or free-range chicken breast, seasonal greens, cauliflower purée, roasted garlic and basil dressing.

Open all day all wk ⊕ PEACH PUBS ◄ Greene King IPA, Morland Old Speckled Hen, Guest ale ♂ Aspall. **Facilities** ❖ (Bar) ♦ Children's portions Parking WiFi

WOODSTOCK
Map 11 SP41

The Kings Arms ★★★ HL ⊛
PICK OF THE PUBS

See Pick of the Pubs on opposite page

WOOLSTONE
Map 5 SU28

The White Horse

tel: 01367 820726 **SN7 7QL**
email: info@whitehorsewoolstone.co.uk
dir: *Exit A420 at Watchfield onto B4508 towards Longcot signed Woolstone*

Olde-worlde thatched Elizabethan pub

Following an invigorating Ridgeway walk across White Horse Hill, this black-and-white timbered village pub is the perfect rest and refuelling stop. Upholstered stools line the traditional bar, where a fireplace conceals two priest holes, visible to those who don't mind getting their knees dirty. Accompany a pint of Arkell's ale with a trio of hand-made sausages and buttered mash, or lamb two ways – roast rump and crispy belly with sweet potato and roast beetroot. Bailey's crème brûlée proves an excellent finish. The pub has a garden, and children and dogs are welcome throughout.

Open all day all wk 11-11 **Food** Lunch all wk 12-2.30 Dinner Mon-Sat 6-9 Set menu available Restaurant menu available all wk ⊕ ARKELL'S ◄ Moonlight & Wiltshire Gold, Arkell's 3B, Guinness ♂ Westons Stowford Press. **Facilities** Non-diners area ❖ (Bar Restaurant Garden) ♦ Children's portions Garden ⊓ Parking WiFi ⛟ (notice required)

WYTHAM
Map 5 SP40

White Hart

tel: 01865 244372 **OX2 8QA**
email: whitehartwytham@wadworth.co.uk
dir: *Just off A34 NW of Oxford*

Smart gastro-pub that's been on TV

In a sleepy hamlet west of Oxford, this Cotswold-stone pub was featured in the *Inspector Morse* TV series. The pub is more 'smart gastro-pub' than traditional village local, the bold interior blending flagged floors and big stone fireplaces with a contemporary style. You can pop in for a pint but this is predominantly a place to eat, and boasts an extensive wine list. In summer, dine alfresco on the Mediterranean-style terrace.

Open all wk 12-3 6-11 (Sat-Sun 12-11, all day everyday Apr-Oct) **Food** Lunch Mon-Fri 12-2.30, Sat 12-9, Sun 12-8 Dinner Mon-Fri 6-9, Sat 12-9, Sun 12-8 ⊕ WADWORTH ◄ Henry's IPA & 6X, Guest ales ♂ Westons Stowford Press. ♟ 15 **Facilities** Non-diners area ❖ (Bar Garden) ♦ Children's menu Garden ⊓ Beer festival Cider festival Parking WiFi

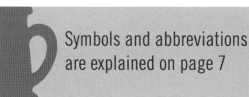

Symbols and abbreviations are explained on page 7

PICK OF THE PUBS

The Kings Arms ★★★ HL 🌹

WOODSTOCK Map 11 SP41

tel: 01993 813636 **19 Market St OX20 1SU**
email: stay@kingshotelwoodstock.co.uk
web: www.kingshotelwoodstock.co.uk
dir: *In town centre, on corner of Market St & A44*

Smart hotel with bags of style

This imposing Georgian free house and hotel is in the middle of the charming, historic town of Woodstock, less than five minutes' walk from Blenheim Palace, home of the Dukes of Marlborough and birthplace of Winston Churchill. The comfortable bar areas have stripped wooden floors, a log-burning stove and marble-topped counters, where a guest real ale accompanies regulars Brakspear Bitter, North Cotswold Brewery's Cotswold Best and Loose Cannon Gunners Gold. The all-day bar menu lists sandwiches, sharing boards and cream teas. For rather more stylish surroundings, go to the Atrium Restaurant with its black-and-white tiled flooring and high-backed leather chairs, where the AA has awarded a Rosette for the modern and classic English cuisine. You might begin with potted mackerel with crispy capers; chicken and tarragon terrine with raisin and walnut toast; or cream of cauliflower and chive soup. A good choice of main dishes includes baked cod, buttered cockles, pea mayonnaise

and hand-cut chips; pork belly with pear and cider gravy, spring Savoy and black pudding croquettes; and slow cooked Cornish lamb shank, crushed pink fir potatoes and herb roasted beets. And there are enough desserts to keep anyone happy: dark chocolate almond cake with salted nut brittle; lemon curd posset with semolina shortbread; an old fashioned treacle tart with Upper Norton Jersey cream; and a range of natural ice creams and sorbets. It makes a good base from which to explore Oxfordshire and the Cotswolds.

Open all day all wk **Food** Lunch Mon-Fri 12-2.30, Sat 12-3, Sun all day Dinner Mon-Sat 6.30-9, Sun all day Set menu available Restaurant menu available all wk. ⊕ FREE HOUSE ◀ Brakspear Bitter, Loose Cannon Gunners Gold, North Cotswold Brewery Cotswold Best ⚫ Thatchers Green Goblin. ▾ 15 **Facilities** Non-diners area ♦♦ Children's portions Outside area ⋒ WiFi 🚌 (notice required) **Rooms** 15

RUTLAND

BARROWDEN
Map 11 SK90

Exeter Arms
PICK OF THE PUBS

tel: 01572 747247 **LE15 8EQ**
email: enquiries@exeterarmsrutland.co.uk
dir: *From A47 turn at landmark windmill, village 0.75m S. 6m E of Uppingham & 17m W of Peterborough*

Cracking country pub boasting a vast garden

In the heart of pretty Barrowden, overlooking the village green, duck pond and open countryside. The 17th-century stone building has played many roles in its long life, including a smithy, a dairy and a postal collection point. Landlord Martin Allsopp brews ales called Beech, Pilot, Owngear, Hop Gear and Blackadder in his on-site microbrewery, and also offers a range of 10 wines by the glass. Expect a traditional feel to the spacious bar and an informal atmosphere in which to enjoy your drink and good pub food. At lunchtime, tuck into sandwiches or pub classics such as Barrowden steak and ale puff pastry pie with hand-cut chips. An equally hearty dinner could begin with BBQ glazed ribs and wings with coleslaw; and continue with mint marinated lamb served with mixed salad and new potatoes. The huge garden has a pétanque piste for lazy summer days, or settle on the front patio for alfresco eating.

Open 12-2.30 6-11 Closed Sun eve, Mon L **Food** Lunch Tue-Sat 12-2 Restaurant menu available all wk ⊕ FREE HOUSE ◖ Exeter Arms Beech, Owngear, Hop Gear, Pilot, Blackadder. ⭑ 10 **Facilities** Non-diners area ⛲ (Bar Garden) ⊪ Garden ⋒ Parking WiFi ▭ (notice required)

BRAUNSTON
Map 11 SK80

The Blue Ball

tel: 01572 722135 **6 Cedar St LE15 8QS**
email: blueballbraunston@gmail.com
dir: *From Oakham N on B640. Left into Cold Overton Rd, 2nd left into West Rd, into Braunston Rd (becomes Oakham Rd). In village 2nd left into Cedar St. Pub on left opposite church*

A warm welcome at the oldest inn in Rutland

The 17th-century thatched Blue Ball, only a few miles from Rutland Water, makes an excellent stopping-off point for cyclists and walkers. Landlord Dominic Way looks after his ales, as locals in the beamed and cosy bar will testify. Seasonal and local ingredients go into pub classics like steak and kidney pie and risottos plus modern dishes such as goats' cheese, roasted beetroot and caramelised onion tart; oven-baked sea bass with pan-fried chorizo; and a tempting dessert like almond treacle pudding with toffee ice cream. There is a Sunday roast menu and young diners are welcome to order small portions of most dishes, confirming the pub's family-friendly credentials.

Open 12-2.30 6-11 (Sat 12-11 Sun 12-8) Closed 25 Dec, Mon **Food** Lunch Tue-Fri 12-1.45, Sat 12-2, Sun 12-3 Dinner Tue-Sun 6.30-9 Set menu available ⊕ MARSTON'S ◖ EPA & Burton Bitter, Jennings Cumberland Ale ⚬ Thatchers. ⭑ 10 **Facilities** Non-diners area ⊪ Children's portions Outside area ⋒ WiFi ▭ (notice required)

CLIPSHAM
Map 11 SK91

The Olive Branch ★ ★ ★ ★ INN ◉◉
PICK OF THE PUBS

tel: 01780 410355 **Main St LE15 7SH**
email: info@theolivebranchpub.com **web:** www.theolivebranchpub.com
dir: *2m from A1 at B664 junct, N of Stamford*

Award-winning hostelry on the fringe of the Wolds

Investigate the bar here for its range of bottled beers, ales from the Grainstore brewery in nearby Oakham, and Sheppy's cider. Note the unusual nurdling chair – used for an archaic pub game when coins are thrown into a hole in the seat. The chair is just one of a range of artefacts enriching the interior of this one-time terrace of farmworkers' cottages. The pub's name originated when a local squire made a peace offering by opening the inn in 1890 after closing another in the village. It boasts two AA Rosettes for chef and co-owner Sean Hope, whose well-balanced menus are fiercely local in provenance. Set lunch and dinner menus are backed by the carte which proffers the likes of twice-baked cheese soufflé with red wine poached pear and walnut salad; smoked haddock kedgeree with curried rice and soft-boiled egg; and winter berry Charlotte with clotted cream.

Open all wk 12-3.30 6-11 (Sat 12-11 Sun 12-10.30) Closed 25 Dec eve **Food** Lunch Mon-Sat 12-2, Sun 12-3 Dinner Mon-Sat 7-9.30, Sun 7-9 Set menu available Restaurant menu available all wk ⊕ FREE HOUSE/RUTLAND INN COMPANY LTD ◖ The Grainstore Olive Oil, Timothy Taylor Landlord ⚬ Sheppy's Cider with Honey. ⭑ 15 **Facilities** Non-diners area ⛲ (Bar Garden) ⊪ Children's menu Children's portions Garden ⋒ Parking WiFi **Rooms** 6

COTTESMORE
Map 11 SK91

The Sun Inn

tel: 01572 812321 **25 Main St LE15 7DH**
email: suninncottesmore@btinternet.com
dir: *Take B668 from Oakham to Cottesmore, or from A1 at Stretton take B668 to Cottesmore*

Good looks inside and out

With its well-trimmed thatched roof, whitewashed walls, hanging baskets and flagstoned courtyard, the 17th-century Sun is as pretty as the proverbial picture. The interior lends its weight too, thanks especially to the beamed ceilings and stone-flagged floors. Despite being The Who's former drinking haunt, there are no pinball wizards in the bar, just Everard ales and a wide range of meals, such as hot filled baps; lamb and chickpea curry; and local pork and herb sausages with mash. Other home-cooked possibilities include venison and forest fruits in game gravy; fish pie; and wild mushroom risotto.

Open all day all wk 11-11 (Sun 11-10.30) **Food** Lunch Mon-Fri 12-3, Sat 12-9, Sun 12-8 Dinner Mon-Fri 6-9, Sat 12-9, Sun 12-8 ⊕ EVERARDS ◖ Everards Tiger, Beacon, Sunchaser & Original, Guinness & Guest ales. **Facilities** Non-diners area ⛲ (Bar Garden) ⊪ Children's menu Children's portions Garden ⋒ Parking WiFi ▭ (notice required)

EMPINGHAM
Map 11 SK90

The White Horse Inn

tel: 01780 460221 **Main St LE15 8PS**
email: info@whitehorserutland.co.uk
dir: *From A1 take A606 signed Oakham & Rutland Water. From Oakham take A606 to Stamford*

Stone-built pub on the shores of Rutland Water

A stylish refurbishment at this 17th-century former courthouse brought the interior right into the 21st century yet retained period features such as wooden floors and open fireplaces. The beamed bar, good selection of real ales and friendly staff makes it an ideal place to relax after a walk or cycle ride. The pub works closely with local suppliers to ensure high-quality seasonal ingredients for the menu of pub classics and more sophisticated choices, such as sausages and mash, and honey-roast duck breast with braised red cabbage.

Open all day all wk Closed 25 Dec **Food** Lunch Mon-Fri 12-2.30, Sat 12-9, Sun 12-5 Dinner Mon-Fri 6-9, Sat 12-9 ⊕ ENTERPRISE INNS ◀ Timothy Taylor Landlord, The Grainstore Rutland Bitter, Oakham Ales JHB, Castle Rock Harvest Pale ♂ Symonds. ♀ 10 **Facilities** Non-diners area ♣ (Bar Garden) ♦ Children's menu Children's portions Garden ⊼ Parking WiFi ▄

EXTON
Map 11 SK91

Fox & Hounds
`PICK OF THE PUBS`

tel: 01572 812403 **19, The Green LE15 8AP**
email: sandra@foxandhoundsrutland.co.uk
dir: *Take A606 from Oakham towards Stamford, at Barnsdale turn left, after 1.5m turn right towards Exton. Pub in village centre*

Perfect place to unwind and enjoy quality food

Traditional English and Italian food is the hallmark of this imposing 17th-century free house, which stands opposite the green amid the charming stone and thatched cottages in the village centre. There's a delightful walled garden, making this former coaching inn a perfect spot for a sunny day. The pub has a reputation for good food and hospitality, and is an ideal stopping-off point for walkers and cyclists exploring nearby Rutland Water and the surrounding area. Its menu is the work of Italian chef-proprietor Valter Floris and his team, and in the evenings there's an impressive list of authentic, thin-crust pizzas. In addition, the main menu features coq au vin with bacon, chestnut mushrooms, Savoy cabbage and new potatoes; roasted pumpkin and goats' cheese filo tartlets; and calves' liver with mash and onion gravy. Good beers include Grainstore Ten Fifty.

Open all wk 11-3 6-11 (Sat-Sun all day) **Food** Lunch Mon-Fri 12-2, Sat-Sun 12-9 Dinner Mon-Fri 6-9, Sat-Sun 12-9 ⊕ FREE HOUSE ◀ Grainstore Ten Fifty, Phipps IPA ♂ Thatchers Gold. ♀ 10 **Facilities** Non-diners area ♦ Children's menu Children's portions Family room Garden ⊼ Parking WiFi ▄

GREETHAM
Map 11 SK91

The Wheatsheaf

tel: 01572 812325 **1 Stretton Rd LE15 7NP**
email: enquiries@wheatsheaf-greetham.co.uk
dir: *From A1 follow signs for Oakham onto B668 to Greetham, pub on left*

Homely refuge with an emphasis on locally sourced food

Set sideways to the road, this 18th-century, stone-built village pub is lovingly run by Carol and Scott Craddock. Carol notched up more than 20 years working in several renowned kitchens before coming to put her wide experience to excellent use

here. She changes her modern British menu weekly, and cooks using locally sourced meats and high quality sustainable fresh fish; she makes bread daily, too. A typical dinner might feature smoked sprats on toast, or home-made black pudding, soft egg and apple sauce for starters, then line-caught cod fillet with chorizo, tomato and bean stew for the main course. Rutland-brewed real ales are served in the bar.

Open 12-3 6-close (Fri-Sun all day) Closed 1st 2wks in Jan, Mon (ex BHs) **Food** Lunch Tue-Fri 12-2, Sat 12-2.30, Sun 12-3 Dinner Tue-Sat 6.30-9 Set menu available ⊕ PUNCH TAVERNS ◀ Greene King IPA, Oldershaw Newton's Drop, Brewsters Decadence, Oakham Ales Inferno, Grainstore Triple B. ♀ 11 **Facilities** Non-diners area ♣ (Bar Garden) ♦ Children's menu Children's portions Garden ⊼ Parking WiFi

LYDDINGTON
Map 11 SP89

The Marquess of Exeter ★★★★ INN ◉

tel: 01572 822477 **52 Main St LE15 9LT**
email: info@marquessexeter.co.uk **web:** www.marquessexeter.co.uk
dir: *A1(N) exit towards Leicester/A4. At rdbt onto A47 towards Leicester. At Uppingham rdbt onto A6003/Ayston Rd. Through Uppingham to Stoke Rd. Left into Lyddington, left into Main St. Pub on left*

Smart village inn with great food

Run by renowned local chef Brian Baker, this old village inn fits seamlessly into Lyddington's long, yellow-brown ironstone streetscape. Stylish, contemporary design works well together with traditional pub essentials, to wit, beams, flagstone floors and winter fires. Modern British menus offer starters like devilled crab beignets with lemon aïoli; or salt and chilli squid, and main courses such as grilled swordfish loin; ricotta and spinach stuffed chicken breast; and Brian's signature sharing dish of grilled rib of Derbyshire beef with frites and béarnaise sauce. Add a shady garden and the mix is complete for an enjoyable overnight stay, especially now that guest rooms have been given the luxury treatment.

Open all day all wk **Food** Lunch Mon-Sat 12-2.30, Sun 12-3 Dinner Mon-Sat 6.30-9.30, Sun 6-9 Set menu available Restaurant menu available ⊕ MARSTON'S ◀ Pedigree, Brakspear ♂ Thatchers. ♀ 14 **Facilities** Non-diners area ♦ Children's menu Children's portions Garden ⊼ Parking WiFi ▄ (notice required) **Rooms** 17

Old White Hart ★★★★ INN

tel: 01572 821703 **51 Main St LE15 9LR**
email: mail@oldwhitehart.co.uk **web:** www.oldwhitehart.co.uk
dir: *From A6003 between Uppingham & Corby take B672. Pub on main street*

17th-century inn in a rural conservation village

Owners Stuart and Holly East have been running this free house opposite the village green for over 14 years. It is constructed from honey-coloured sandstone like the surrounding cottages, and has original beamed ceilings and stone walls. On warm days customers take their pint of Great Oakley bitter (this and more at the summer beer festival), or Aspall cider out into the gardens or onto the covered patio. Dishes served in the restaurants include ham hock terrine, rib-eye steak, grilled pork chop, and vegetarian choices. Half-price menu offers are available Monday to Thursday. The inn also has a floodlit petanque pitch. Accommodation is in converted cottages alongside the pub.

Open all wk 12-3 6.30-11 (Sun 12-3 7-10.30) Closed 25 Dec, 26 Dec eve **Food** Lunch Mon-Sat 12-2, Sun 12-2.30 Dinner all wk 6.30-9 ⊕ FREE HOUSE ◀ Greene King IPA, Timothy Taylor Landlord & Golden Best, The Grainstore, Great Oakley ♂ Aspall. ♀ 10 **Facilities** Non-diners area ♦ Children's portions Play area Garden ⊼ Beer festival Parking WiFi ▄ (notice required) **Rooms** 10

MANTON

Map 11 SK80

The Horse and Jockey

tel: 01572 737335 **2 St Marys Rd LE15 8SU**
email: enquiries@horseandjockeyrutland.co.uk
dir: *Exit A6003 between Oakham & Uppingham signed Rutland Water South Shore. 1st left in Manton into St Marys Rd*

Handy refuelling stop by Rutland Water

Cyclists and ramblers investigating the recreational tracks around Rutland Water can expect treats in the form of fine Rutland-brewed beers – including one created for the pub - and some robust pub food at this pleasing, stone-built village free house. Privately owned, the innate charm of the traditional, stone-floored, beamed interior complements the wholesome home-cooked menu which is strong on produce with local provenance. Steaks, curries, baked fish or roast loin of pork are amongst the pub favourites helping refuel visitors to the vast reservoir. Vegetarian options may include mushroom and red onion confit pudding and a specials board is also available.

Open all day all wk **Food** Lunch all wk 12-9 (Apr-Sep) all wk 12-2.30 (Oct-Mar) Dinner all wk 12-9 (Apr-Sep) all wk 6-9 (Oct-Mar) ⊕ FREE HOUSE ◗ The Grainstore Cooking & Ten Fifty (Fall At The First), Guest ales ♂ Jollydale, Kopparberg. ♥ 12 **Facilities** Non-diners area ♣ (Bar Garden) ♦ Children's portions Garden ⌁ Parking WiFi ▄▄ (notice required)

MARKET OVERTON

Map 11 SK81

NEW The Black Bull

tel: 01572 767677 **2 Teigh Rd LE15 7PW**
email: enquiry@blackbullrutland.co.uk **web:** www.blackbullrutland.co.uk
dir: *From Oakham take B668 to Cottesmore. Left signed Market Overton*

Convivial village local with good food

Just six miles from Rutland Water nature reserve and a short drive from Stamford and Nottingham, The Black Bull occupies a lovely spot in the picturesque village of Market Overton. Once a coach house, the thatched pub offers a traditional atmosphere with real fires and sumptuous sofas, although walking boots, children and dogs are as welcome as diners. Local produce fills the menu here, including steaks from a local farm and lamb from Launde Abbey. Try the Goosnargh chicken breast with white wine, thyme and leek sauce or a pub classic of steak and Guinness pie.

Open 12-3 6-12 (Sun 12-6) Closed Sun eve & Mon **Food** Lunch Tue-Sat 12-2.30, Sun 12-3 Dinner Tue-Sat 6-9.30 Av main course £10 ⊕ FREE HOUSE ◗ Black Sheep, Grainstore Rutland Bitter ♂ Thatchers Gold, Westons Old Rosie, Scrambler. **Facilities** Non-diners area ♣ (Bar Outside area) ♦ Children's menu Children's portions Outside area Parking WiFi ▄▄ (notice required)

OAKHAM

Map 11 SK80

The Grainstore Brewery

tel: 01572 770065 **Station Approach LE15 6RE**
email: enquiries@grainstorebrewery.com
dir: *Adjacent to Oakham rail station*

The largest brewery in the smallest county

One of the best brew pubs in Britain, the Grainstore Brewery is housed in a three-storey Victorian grain store next to Oakham railway station. Founded in 1995, Davis's brewing company uses the finest quality hops and ingredients to make the beers that can be sampled in the pub's taproom. Food is wholesome and straightforward, with the ales playing an important part in recipes for Rutland Panther chilli con carne and pork and Ten Fifty sausages. A full diary of events includes live music, the annual Summer Bank Holiday Rutland beer festival and the Early May Bank Holiday cider and sausage festival. Tours of the brewery can be arranged.

Open all day all wk Mon-Fri 11-mdnt (Sat-Sun 8.30am-mdnt) **Food** Lunch Mon-Fri 11-9, Sat 9am-9pm, Sun 9-6 Dinner Mon-Fri 11-9, Sat 9am-9pm, Sun 9-6 ⊕ FREE HOUSE ◗ The Grainstore Rutland Panther, Triple B, Ten Fifty, Rutland Beast, Nip, Cooking, Seasonal beers ♂ Sheppy's. **Facilities** Non-diners area ♣ (Bar Garden) ♦ Children's portions Garden ⌁ Beer festival Cider festival Parking WiFi ▄▄ (notice required)

SOUTH LUFFENHAM

Map 11 SK90

The Coach House Inn

tel: 01780 720166 **3 Stamford Rd LE15 8NT**
email: thecoachhouse123@aol.com
dir: *On A6121, off A47 between Morcroft & Stamford*

Former stables serving well-kept real ales

Horses were once stabled here while weary travellers enjoyed a drink in what is now a private house next door. This elegantly appointed, attractive stone inn offers a comfortable 40-cover dining room and a cosy bar serving Adnams, Morland and Greene King beers. A short, appealing menu in the Ostler's Restaurant might feature chicken liver pâté with orange and cranberry chutney; and lamb shank with garlic mash, root vegetables and redcurrant jus. In the bar tuck into roast cod with hand-cut chips and pea purée; or beef and ale casserole.

Open 12-2 5-11 (Sat all day) Closed 25 Dec, 1 Jan, Sun eve, Mon L **Food** Lunch Tue-Sat 12-2 Dinner Mon-Sat 6.30-9 ⊕ FREE HOUSE ◗ Morland Old Speckled Hen, Adnams, Greene King IPA, St Austell Tribute, The Grainstore Triple B, Guinness ♂ Aspall. **Facilities** Non-diners area ♣ (Bar Garden Outside area) ♦ Children's portions Garden Outside area ⌁ Parking WiFi ▄▄ (notice required)

Find out about pubs and pigs in Swine and dine on page 12

PICK OF THE PUBS

Kings Arms ★★★★ INN 🌸🌸

WING　　　　　　　Map 11 SK80

tel: 01572 737634 **Top St LE15 8SE**
email: info@thekingsarms-wing.co.uk
web: www.thekingsarms-wing.co.uk
dir: *1m off B6003 between Uppingham & Oakham*

Seventeenth century inn with its own smokehouse

David and Gisa Goss have run this attractive, stone-built free house for some 10 years now; son James is the chef and Kathy Goode looks after front of house. Dating from 1649, the pub's flagstone floors, low-beamed ceilings and two open fires are original. In the bar an adventurous snack-buying policy means you might want to consider whether to nibble salami or biltong, then decide which goes best with home-made sloe gin, elderflower vodka or Zermatter mulled wine, all made with locally foraged berries or neighbour-donated fruits. There are real ales too, of course, Grainstore's Cooking among them and from the real cider line-up Jollydale demands attention, not least for its name. Lunchtime bar meals are supplemented in the restaurant by a carte that reflects the Gosses' close links with local farmers, millers, smallholders, hunters and fishermen. Such alliances lead to the likes of roast woodcock, fallow deer fillet and gamebird hotpot, while from the pub's own smokery come trout, herring, eels,

bacon, hams and venison, the meats forming the basis of Rutland smokehouse platter. For items like these one has to thank James's skilled Swiss and Danish curing, smoking and air-drying techniques. Fish dishes include halibut loin served with herbed crab bisque linguine, and sea bass supreme with saffron, spring onion, parmesan and tomato risotto. At lunchtime only can you get freshly baked cobs filled with home-made beef dripping chips, roast Hambleton beef, Colston Basset Stilton, or pork loin with apple compôte. Home-made too are the ice creams and sorbets, often derived from seasonal windfall fruits and locally grown flowers. The eight spacious letting rooms are set away from the pub.

Open Tue-Sun 12-3 6.30-11 (times vary) Closed Sun eve, Mon, Tue L (Oct-Mar), Sun eve, Mon L (Apr-Sep) **Food** Lunch Tue-Sun 12-2.30 Dinner Tue-Sat 6.30-8.30 Restaurant menu Tue-Sun. 🍺 FREE HOUSE 🍺 Shepherd Neame Spitfire, The Grainstore Cooking, Marston's Pedigree 🍏 Sheppy's, Jollydale. 🍷 33 **Facilities** Non-diners area 🐾 (Bar) 🚼 Children's menu & portions Outside area 🎋 Parking WiFi 🚐 (notice required) **Rooms** 8

STRETTON
Map 11 SK91

The Jackson Stops Country Inn `PICK OF THE PUBS`

tel: 01780 410237 **Rookery Rd LE15 7RA**
email: info@thejacksonstops.com
dir: *From A1 follow Stretton signs*

Timeless pub with seasonal dishes

The long, low, stone-built partly thatched building dates from 1721, and has plenty of appeal: stone fireplaces with log fires, exposed stone, quarry-tiled floors, scrubbed wood tables and five intimate dining rooms. In the timeless and beamed snug bar, the choice of real ales lifts the heart, boding well for the excellent value to be had from the dishes on the seasonally changing menu, all freshly prepared and cooked by the kitchen staff. Children can choose from their own menu or take smaller portions from the adult choice. And, if you were wondering about the pub's name: there can be few pubs in the country that have acquired their name by virtue of a 'For Sale' sign. One was planted outside the pub for so long during a previous change of ownership that the locals dispensed with the old name in favour of the name of the estate agent on the board.

Open 12-3.30 6-11 (Sun 12-5) Closed Sun eve, Mon **Food** Lunch Tue-Sat 12-3, Sun 12-5 Dinner Tue-Sat 6.30-9.30 ⊕ FREE HOUSE ◀ The Grainstore Cooking. ▼ 48 **Facilities** Non-diners area ❖ (Bar Garden) ♦ Children's menu Children's portions Garden ⌗ Parking ▬ (notice required)

WHITWELL
Map 11 SK90

The Noel @ Whitwell ★★★ INN

tel: 01780 460347 **Main Rd LE15 8BW**
email: info@thenoel.co.uk web: www.thenoel.co.uk
dir: *Between Oakham & Stamford on A606, N shore of Rutland Water*

North shore village pub for everyone

The part-thatched village inn stands just a 15-minute stroll from the north shore of Rutland Water, so worth noting if you are walking or pedalling the lakeside trail and in need of refreshment. The friendly, spruced-up bar and dining room have a stylish modern feel and feature flagstone floors, heritage colours and a warming winter log fires. Expect to find local Grainstore ales on tap and a wide-ranging menu listing pasta and salad dishes alongside shoulder of lamb with red wine gravy; beef bourguignon; and Cajun salmon with chilli dressing.

Open 12-3 6-close Closed Mon **Food** Lunch Tue-Sat 12-2, Sun 12-3 Dinner Tue-Sat 6.30-9 Av main course £11 Restaurant menu available Tue-Sat ⊕ ENTERPRISE INNS ◀ The Grainstore Rutland Bitter Ŏ Westons Stowford Press. ▼ 10 **Facilities** Non-diners area ❖ (Bar Garden) ♦ Children's menu Children's portions Garden ⌗ Parking WiFi ▬ (notice required) **Rooms** 8

WING
Map 11 SK80

Kings Arms ★★★★ INN ◉◉ `PICK OF THE PUBS`

See Pick of the Pubs on page 411

See Pick of the Pubs on page 411

SHROPSHIRE

ADMASTON
Map 10 SJ61

The Pheasant Inn at Admaston

tel: 01952 251989 **TF5 OAD**
email: info@thepheasantadmaston.co.uk
dir: *M54 junct 6 towards Whitchurch then follow B5063 towards Shawbirch & Admaston. Pub is on left of main road*

Stylish country inn with good children's menu

Dating from the 19th century, this lovely old country pub offers a stylish interior decor and real fire, which add character to the dining areas. The large enclosed garden is ideal for families and there is a good menu for children under ten. Grown-ups certainly aren't overlooked, either – the kitchen uses the best local produce in dishes such as Shropshire Blue and caramelised onion horn, which might be followed by Wickstead aged sirloin steak with balsamic tomatoes, watercress salad and chips. Steamed chocolate pudding, and banana and pecan tart are just two options for dessert.

Open all day all wk 11-11 (Thu 11am-11.30pm Fri-Sat 11am-mdnt) **Food** Lunch Mon-Fri 12-2, Sat 12-9.15, Sun 12-7 Dinner Mon-Fri 6-9 ⊕ ENTERPRISE INNS ◀ Salopian Shropshire Gold, Greene King IPA, Guinness. ▼ 10 **Facilities** Non-diners area ❖ (Garden Outside area) ♦ Children's menu Children's portions Play area Garden Outside area ⌗ Parking WiFi ▬

BASCHURCH
Map 15 SJ42

The New Inn

tel: 01939 260335 **Church Rd SY4 2EF**
email: eat@thenewinnbaschurch.co.uk
dir: *8m from Shrewsbury, 8m from Oswestry*

Shropshire beers plus the best local produce on the menus

Near the medieval church, this stylishly modernised old whitewashed village pub is a focal point for all things Welsh Marches, with beers from nearby Oswestry's Stonehouse brewery amongst five ales stocked, meats from the village's Moor Farm or Shrewsbury's renowned market, and cheeses from a Cheshire supplier. In addition to the interesting sandwich menu, the tempting fare might include a pre-starter 'nibble' of home-made Scotch egg with wholegrain mustard mayonnaise; then salmon and sweet potato fishcakes. The perhaps choose a main course of pan-fried, parmesan crusted sea bass fillet with lemon crayfish cream sauce.

Open Tue-Fri 11-3 6-11 (Sat 11-11 Sun 12-6) Closed 26 Dec, 1 Jan, Mon **Food** Lunch Tue-Sat 12-2, Sun 12-3 Dinner Tue-Sat 6-9 ⊕ FREE HOUSE ◀ Banks's Bitter, Stonehouse Station Bitter, Hobsons Best Bitter, Guest ales Ŏ Thatchers Gold. ▼ **Facilities** Non-diners area ♦ Children's menu Children's portions Garden ⌗ Parking WiFi

BISHOP'S CASTLE · Map 15 SO38

The Three Tuns Inn · PICK OF THE PUBS

tel: 01588 638797 **Salop St SY9 5BW**
email: timce@talk21.com
dir: *From Ludlow take A49 through Craven Arms, then left onto A489 to Lydham, then A488 to Bishop's Castle, inn at top of the town.*

Historic inn famed for its microbrewery ales

One of England's most renowned inns fronts the country's oldest brewery. The picture-perfect enclave of compact tower brewery and adjoining inn snuggles beside the top of the steep main street of a pretty hill-town deep in the Welsh Marches. For over 350 years the pub and brewery were a single business, and although ownership has now split, they continue to work together, producing the enticing array of Three Tuns real ales sold here, including 1642, commemorating the date of the inn's first brewing licence. The engaging warren of rooms is generally music and games machine free, although regular live jazz, rock, classical music and morris dancing events prove very popular. An airy dining room overlooks the brewing tower; test out a menu by choosing courgette bhajis or pan-seared scallops for starters. Progressing to the mains, the choice may include grilled hake with chorizo and roasted pepper sauce; or loin of venison. A dynamic beer festival over the second weekend of July involves all the town's pubs.

Open all day all wk **Food** Lunch all wk 12-3 Dinner Mon-Sat 7-9 ⊕ STAR PUBS & BARS ◀ Three Tuns XXX, Solstice, Old Scrooge, Cleric's Cure, 1642. ♟ 12 **Facilities** Non-diners area ✿ (Bar Restaurant Outside area) ♦♦ Children's menu Children's portions Outside area Beer festival

BRIDGNORTH · Map 10 SO79

Halfway House Inn ★★★ INN

tel: 01746 762670 **Cleobury Rd, Eardington WV16 5LS**
email: info@halfwayhouseinn.co.uk **web:** www.halfwayhouseinn.co.uk
dir: *M54 junct 4, A442 to Bridgnorth. Or M5 junct 4, A491 towards Stourbridge. A458 to Bridgnorth. Follow tourist signs on B4363*

An olde-worlde coaching inn

This 17th-century coaching inn was renamed in 1823 after the very young Princess Victoria stopped here en route between Shrewsbury and Worcester; when she asked where she was, came the diplomatic reply, 'halfway there ma'am'. An original Elizabethan mural has been preserved behind glass for all to enjoy, and the pub is renowned for a good selection of regional real ales, 40 malts, and around 100 wines. The weekend lunch menu ranges from light bites to home-cooked pub classics, while the dinner menu has steaks from the grill, deep-fried breaded brie, and chicken curry. Finish with warm chocolate fudge cake.

Open all day 6-11.30 (Fri-Sat 11am-11.30pm Sun 11-9) Closed Sun eve Nov-Mar **Food** Lunch Fri-Sun 12-2 Dinner Mon-Sat 6-9 Set menu available Restaurant menu available all wk ⊕ FREE HOUSE ◀ Holden's Golden Glow, Wood's Shropshire Lad, Guinness ☼ Westons Stowford Press. ♟ 10 **Facilities** Non-diners area ✿ (Bar Garden) ♦♦ Children's menu Children's portions Play area Garden ⊼ Parking WiFi ⬛ (notice required) **Rooms** 10

CARDINGTON · Map 10 SO59

The Royal Oak

tel: 01694 771266 **SY6 7JZ**
email: inntoxicated@gmail.com
dir: *N of Church Stretton right to Cardington; or from Much Wenlock take B4371, 2m to Cardington*

Historic pub in a conservation village

Set in a conservation village and reputedly the oldest continuously licensed pub in Shropshire, this free house can trace its roots to the 15th century. The rambling low-beamed bar with vast inglenook (complete with cauldron, black kettle and pewter jugs) and comfortable beamed dining room are refreshingly undisturbed by music, TV or games machines. Choose from the excellent cask ales and ponder your choice of sustenance: good-value home-made fare includes fried black pudding and bacon on mixed leaves; fish pie; and good meat-free options such as vegetable tagine with chickpeas.

Open 12-2.30 (Sun 12-3.30) Tue-Sat 6.30-11 (Sun 7-11 Apr-Oct) Closed Mon (closed Sun eve Nov-Mar) **Food** Lunch Tue-Sat 12-2, Sun 12-2.30 Dinner Tue-Sat 6.30-9 (Sun 7-9 Apr-Oct) Av main course £10.95 ⊕ FREE HOUSE ◀ Ludlow Best, Three Tuns XXX, Wye Valley Butty Bach, Salopian Hop Twister, Sharp's Doom Bar. **Facilities** Non-diners area ✿ (Bar Outside area) ♦♦ Children's menu Outside area ⊼ Parking WiFi ⬛ (notice required)

CHURCH STRETTON · Map 15 SO49

The Bucks Head ★★★★ INN

tel: 01694 722898 **42 High St SY6 6BX**
email: lnutting@btinternet.com **web:** www.the-bucks-head.co.uk
dir: *12m from Shrewsbury & Ludlow*

Traditional pub in the Shropshire Hills

The small market town of Church Stretton is sandwiched between the Long Mynd and Wenlock Edge, and the charming old Bucks Head is without doubt where to stay to explore these impressive landscape features. The pub is known for several essential things: its comfortable, AA four-star accommodation, its well-kept Banks's, Marston's and guest ales, and its restaurant. Where possible, the kitchen uses local fresh meat, poultry and vegetables for rib-eye, sirloin and rump steaks; Cajun chicken with sour cream; plaice fillet in breadcrumbs; beef or roasted vegetable lasagne; and cream cheese and broccoli bake.

Open all day all wk **Food** Lunch all wk 12-2.30 Dinner all wk 6-9 ⊕ MARSTON'S ◀ Pedigree, Banks's Original & Bitter, 2 Guest ales. ♟ 9 **Facilities** Non-diners area ♦♦ Children's menu Children's portions Garden ⊼ WiFi ⬛ (notice required) **Rooms** 4

CLAVERLEY · Map 10 SO79

The Woodman

tel: 01746 710553 **Danford Ln WV5 7DG**
email: enquiries@thewoodmanclaverley.com
dir: *On B4176 (Bridgnorth to Dudley road)*

In open countryside with a warm welcome

Village farms, butcher and baker supply much of the produce used in the well-respected dishes here at this sibling-run, three-storey Victorian inn. Outside a picturesque settlement deep in the east Shropshire countryside, the beer, too, comes from just down the lane in Enville, whilst the wine list spreads its wings worldwide. The contemporary interior is a comfy mix of village local and bistro, where dishes such as smoked duck breast terrine with plum and hoi sin dressing; and braised lamb shank, Savoy cabbage mash, and red wine and mint gravy could appear on the menus. Alfresco dining is a popular summer option, indulging in grand rural views to the ridge of Abbot's Castle Hill.

Open 12-2.30 6-11 (Sun 12-4) Closed 1st 2wks Jan, Sun eve, Mon **Food** Lunch Tue-Sun 12-2.30 Dinner Tue-Sat 6-9 ⊕ PUNCH TAVERNS ◀ Black Sheep, Enville Ale. ♟ 10 **Facilities** Garden ⊼ Parking WiFi

The Crown Inn   PICK OF THE PUBS

tel: 01299 270372 **Hopton Wafers DY14 0NB**
dir: On A4117 8m E of Ludlow, 2m W of Cleobury Mortimer

Delightful old coaching inn with three restaurants

The exterior of this 16th-century coaching inn pushes the description 'creeper-clad' to its limit, and delightful it looks as a result. Birmingham to Ludlow mail coaches used to take on extra horses here for the steep climb up the hill. Much of its period past is evident inside - in the bar, for example, and in Poachers Dining Area, where you'll find exposed beams, stonework and a large inglenook fireplace. The two other eating areas are the Shropshire Restaurant, overlooking the countryside, and the Rent Room, with pine kitchen-style seating, sofas and more rural views. A typical three-course meal might be warm smoked salmon with salad and horseradish, followed by braised shank of local lamb with red wine, rosemary and redcurrant jus; or home-made meat or vegetarian curry with jasmine rice; and finally, Eton mess. The wine list, selected by a local merchant, includes a range of fine ports, Armagnacs and Cognacs.

Open all day all wk **Food** Lunch all wk 12-2.30 Dinner all wk 6-9 Set menu available Restaurant menu available all wk ⊕ FREE HOUSE ◼ Hobsons Best Bitter, Guest ales. ♟ 25 **Facilities** Non-diners area ❤ (Bar Garden) ♦️ Children's menu Children's portions Play area Garden Parking ➡️

The White Horse Inn

tel: 01588 640305 **The Square SY7 8JA**
email: pub@whi-clun.co.uk **web:** www.whi-clun.co.uk
dir: On A488 in village centre

Home to the Clun Brewery

In the beautiful Shropshire Hills, this gloriously unspoilt and unpretentious village inn oozes character with beams, wizened wood and slab floors. Three beers brewed in their own microbrewery, the Clun, together with others selected from Shropshire's many craft breweries provide the line-up at the bar. This 'green' pub offers visitors drawn to AE Housman's 'Quietest place under the sun' heart-warming pub grub, derived from very local suppliers. Main courses may include Cajun chicken fillet, cauliflower gratin, and beer-battered haddock. The traditional suet puddings are a speciality. Regular events take place here, including the Clun Valley beer festival on the first weekend in October.

Open all day all wk **Food** Lunch Mon-Sat 12-2, Sun 12.30-2.30 Dinner all wk 6.30-8.30 Av main course £9.95 ⊕ FREE HOUSE ◼ Clun Pale Ale, Citadel & Loophole, Wye Valley Butty Bach, Hobsons Best Bitter, Guest ales ♂ Westons 1st Quality, Robinsons Flagon. **Facilities** Non-diners area ❤ (Bar Garden) ♦️ Children's menu Children's portions Garden ⊟ Beer festival WiFi ➡️ (notice required)

The Sun Inn

tel: 01584 861239 **Corfton SY7 9DF**
email: normanspride@btconnect.com
dir: On B4368, 7m N of Ludlow

Family-run pub with an innovative microbrewery

Close to the towns of Ludlow and Bridgnorth, and the ramblers' paradise of Clee Hill and Long Mynd, this historic pub was first licensed in 1613. It has been run by the Pearce family since 1984 and since 1997 landlord Norman Pearce has been brewing the Corvedale ales in what was the pub's old chicken and lumber shed, using local borehole water; Herefordshire's Gwatkin cider is another thirst-quenching option. Teresa Pearce uses local produce in a delicious array of traditional dishes – lamb hotpot, battered cod, lamb curry. There are also vegetarian and some vegan options. The pub holds a beer festival in May.

Open all wk 12-2.30 6-11 (Sun 12-3 7-11) **Food** Lunch Mon-Sat 12-2, Sun 12-2.45 Dinner Mon-Sat 6-9, Sun 7-9 ⊕ FREE HOUSE ◼ Corvedale Norman's Pride & Golden Dale, Dark & Delicious ♂ Gwatkin. ♟ 8 **Facilities** Non-diners area ❤ (Bar Garden Outside area) ♦️ Children's menu Children's portions Play area Garden Outside area ⊟ Beer festival Parking WiFi ➡️ (notice required)

The Riverside Inn

tel: 01952 510900 **Cound SY5 6AF**
email: info@theriversideinn.net
dir: On A458 7m from Shrewsbury, 1m from Cressage

Great river views from the conservatory and garden

This inn sits in three acres of gardens alongside the River Severn, offering customers delightful river views both outdoors and from a modern conservatory. Originally a vicarage for St Peter's church in the village, the building also housed a girls' school and a railway halt before becoming a pub in 1878. The pub is popular with anglers. The monthly-changing menu might open with roast parsnip soup or seafood pancake, followed by perhaps oven baked herb crusted hake; minced steak pie; or vegetarian chilli. Comforting desserts include Bakewell tart and cream. Their own brew, Riverside Inn Bitter, is available in the cosy bar.

Open all wk Sat-Sun all day May-Sep **Food** Lunch all wk 12-2.30 Dinner all wk 6.30-9 Av main course £11 ⊕ FREE HOUSE ◼ Riverside Inn Bitter, Guest ales. ♟ **Facilities** Non-diners area ❤ (Bar Garden Outside area) Garden Outside area ⊟ Parking WiFi

HODNET
Map 15 SJ62

The Bear at Hodnet

tel: 01630 685214 **TF9 3NH**
email: reception@bearathodnet.co.uk
dir: At junct of A53 & A442 turn right at rdbt. Inn in village centre

Haunted, historic, former coaching inn

With old beams, open fireplaces and secret passages leading to the church, this black-and-white-timbered, former coaching inn was once known for its bear-baiting pit. In the 1680s, a landlord threw Jasper, a regular down on his luck, out into a bitterly cold night. Within hours both were dead, Jasper from hypothermia, the landlord from fright, as if he'd seen a ghost, which legend suggests was Jasper. Food includes crispy cod cheeks with pea purée and Maynard's black pudding; pork and tarragon mustard pie, buttered mash and allotment greens; and pan-fried black bream, chilli and lemongrass risotto cake, pak choi and sweet potato broth.

Open all day all wk 12-11 (Sun 12-10.30) **Food** Lunch Mon-Thu 12-3, Fri-Sat 12-9.30, Sun 12-6 Dinner Mon-Thu 6-9, Fri-Sat 12-9.30, Sun 12-6 Av main course £10.95 ⊕ FREE HOUSE ◀ Salopian Shropshire Gold, Three Tuns ♂ Westons Stowford Press. ♟ 10 **Facilities** Non-diners area ♣ (Bar Garden) ♦♦ Children's menu Children's portions Play area Garden ♠ Parking WiFi ⛨ (notice required)

IRONBRIDGE
Map 10 SJ60

The Malthouse

tel: 01952 433712 **The Wharfage TF8 7NH**
email: info@themalthouse.co.uk
dir: Phone for detailed directions

Live music and good food

In the Severn Gorge, within a mile of the famous Iron Bridge, the 18th-century Malthouse is known for its Friday and Saturday night live music. But for a different way to spend the evening try the restaurant, where candlelit tables and an extensive menu feature home-made steak and Guinness pie; king prawn linguine; braised shoulder of Shropshire lamb; and mushroom, pepper and spinach Stroganoff. There's pubbier grub too, such as thick pork sausages with black pudding mash. Brakspear, Wood's and Wychwood make up the real ale portfolio.

Open all day all wk 11.30-11 **Food** Lunch all wk 11.30-10 Dinner all wk 11.30-10 ⊕ FREE HOUSE ◀ Wychwood Hobgoblin, Wood's Shropshire Lad, Brakspear Oxford Gold, Sharp's Doom Bar ♂ Thatchers Gold, Somersby. ♟ 10 **Facilities** Non-diners area ♦♦ Children's menu Children's portions Garden ♠ Parking WiFi ⛨

LITTLE STRETTON
Map 15 SO49

The Ragleth Inn

tel: 01694 722711 **Ludlow Rd SY6 6RB**
email: wendyjd65@hotmail.com
dir: From Shrewsbury take A49 towards Leominster. At lights in Church Stretton turn right. 3rd left into High St. Continue to Little Stretton. Inn on right

Country inn serving home-cooked favourites

This 17th-century country inn sits midway between Shrewsbury and Ludlow in beautiful countryside at the foot of the Long Mynd hills. The pretty, traditional exterior includes a large beer garden with plenty of wooden benches and a children's play area, matched within by two bars and a restaurant with oak beams, antiques and inglenook fireplaces. A good range of ales accompanies classic pub dishes such as breaded brie wedge with cranberry sauce; creamy fish pie; vegetable lasagne; and a selection of baguettes and jacket potatoes. Specials include squid filled with mussels, mushroom and garlic; followed by sea bass fillet on stir-fry vegetables with oyster sauce or lamb's liver and bacon on mash with onion gravy. All diets can be catered for.

Open all wk **Food** Lunch Mon-Sat 12-2.15, Sun all day Dinner Mon-Sat 6.30-9, Sun all day Av main course £11 Set menu available ⊕ FREE HOUSE ◀ Greene King Abbot Reserve, Wye Valley Butty Bach, Hobsons, Three Tuns, Sharp's Doom Bar ♂ Westons Stowford Press, Thatchers Gold. **Facilities** Non-diners area ♣ (Bar Garden) ♦♦ Children's menu Children's portions Play area Garden Outside area ♠ Parking WiFi ⛨ (notice required)

LLANFAIR WATERDINE
Map 9 SO27

The Waterdine
PICK OF THE PUBS

tel: 01547 528214 **LD7 1TU**
email: info@waterdine.com
dir: 4.5m W of Knighton off B4355, turn right opposite Lloyney Inn, 0.5m into village, last on left

Excellent food in an extravagant landscape

Just yards from the Welsh border and close to Offa's Dyke in the magnificent Shropshire Hills, the compact riverside inn offers sublime views along the deep Teme Valley. It originated as a Welsh longhouse, becoming a drovers' inn 450 years ago. The family of Lord Hunt, of Everest expedition fame, lived in the village, and some of the planning reputedly took place in the lounge bar. Today it serves an appealing range of real ales, ciders and wines; wood-burning stoves create a cosy atmosphere in winter. There are two dining rooms: the Garden Room looks out over the river, and the beamed Taproom has a massive oak mantle which displays burn marks from long-extinguished candles. The fixed-price menus change with the seasons and local availability of game and meats; start with devilled Cornish mackerel, or spiced duck confit and red onion croquette, continuing with sautéed wild boar fillet with slow roasted pork belly with beetroot mash leading to lavender crème brûlée with damson compôte. Booking is essential.

Open 12-3 7-11 Closed 1wk winter, 1wk spring, Sun eve & Mon (ex BHs), Tue-Sat L **Food** Lunch Sun 12-1.30 Set menu available Restaurant menu available Tue-Sat D & Sun L ⊕ FREE HOUSE ◀ Wood's Shropshire Legends, Parish Bitter, Shropshire Lad ♂ Brook Farm. **Facilities** Non-diners area ♦♦ Children's portions Garden Parking

LUDLOW
Map 10 SO57

The Church Inn ★★★ INN

tel: 01584 872174 **Buttercross SY8 1AW**
web: www.thechurchinn.com
dir: In town centre, behind Buttercross

Real ales and pies in a narrow town centre street

The inn stands on one of the oldest sites in Ludlow town centre, dating back some seven centuries, and through the ages has been occupied by a blacksmith, saddler, apothecary and barber-surgeon. These days it enjoys a reputation for providing a good range of up to ten real ales in the cosy bar areas alongside the pies for which it has become well known - there's a choice of 30 different pies at any one time. There are 10 comfortable en suite bedrooms with smart modern bathrooms.

Open all day all wk **Food** Lunch Mon-Fri 12-2.30, Sat-Sun 12-3 Dinner Mon-Sat 6.30-9, Sun 6.30-8.30 ⊕ FREE HOUSE ◀ Hobsons Town Crier & Hobsons Mild, Weetwood, Wye Valley Bitter, Ludlow Gold & Boiling Well, Guest ales ♂ Stowford, Aspall, Robinsons. **Facilities** Non-diners area ♦♦ Children's menu ⛨ **Rooms** 10

LUDLOW *continued*

The Clive Bar & Restaurant with Rooms ★ ★ ★ ★ ★ RR ☺☺

PICK OF THE PUBS

tel: 01584 856565 **Bromfield SY8 2JR**
email: info@theclive.co.uk **web:** www.theclive.co.uk
dir: *2m N of Ludlow on A49, between Hereford & Shrewsbury*

Handsome Georgian building with classy bar and restaurant

Clive of India lived on the Earl of Plymouth's estate, which included this former farmhouse; in the early 1900s it became the Clive Arms to cater for thirsty estate workers. Untouched until 1997, a refurbishment introduced contemporary style while retaining original features. The bar comprises two areas: an 18th-century lounge with log fire and Clive's original coat of arms; and a more contemporary upper part that leads out to a courtyard with tables and parasols. Now under new management, you'll find Hobsons ales at the bar, plus ciders such as Robinsons Flagon, and nine wines served by the glass. Lunchtime bar snacks served with home-cut chips proffer the likes of a smoked salmon, chive cream cheese and cucumber bagel; or a baguette of cured local bacon and Shropshire Blue cheese. A three-course choice in the evening could comprise fillet of mackerel with beetroot terrine; rolled saddle of Welsh lamb with rosemary fondant potatoes; and hot coffee soufflé with biscotti. Tastefully converted period outbuildings provide accommodation.

Open all day all wk Closed 25-26 Dec **Food** Lunch Mon-Fri 12-3, Sat-Sun 12-6.30 Dinner Mon-Sat 6.30-10, Sun 6.30-9.30 Restaurant menu available all wk ⊕ FREE HOUSE ◀ Hobsons Best Bitter, Ludlow Gold Ò Dunkertons, Thatchers Old Rascal, Robinsons Flagon. ♚ 9 **Facilities** Non-diners area ♦ Children's portions Garden ⊼ Parking WiFi ⛟ (notice required) **Rooms** 15

| MARTON | Map 15 SJ20 |

The Lowfield Inn

tel: 01743 891313 **SY21 8JX**
email: lowfieldinn@tiscali.co.uk
dir: *From Shrewsbury take B4386 towards Montgomery. Through Westbury & Brockton. Pub on right in 13m just before Marton*

Successful modern interpretation of old village inn

In a stunning location below the crinkly west Shropshire Hills, this pub is a modern replacement for an old inn demolished in 2007. Although the ambience has altered, the atmosphere of a friendly village local is retained, with fierce dedication to supporting microbreweries dotted along the England/Wales border – Monty's and Three Tuns beers are regularly stocked, as are a range of decent ciders. Modern British pub grub is the order of the day; black and white pudding with fried egg and

Cumberland sauce starter, followed by chicken Wellington with mushroom stuffing is a typical choice. The eye-catching brick bar, comfy seating, slab floor, log-burner and duck pond add to the developing character of this fast becoming village favourite.

Open all day all wk **Food** Lunch all wk 12-9.30 Dinner all wk 12-9.30 Av main course £11 Set menu available ⊕ FREE HOUSE ◀ Three Tuns XXX & 1642, Monty's Moonrise & Mojo, Wood's Shropshire Lad, Salopian Shropshire Gold Ò Inch's Stonehouse, Westons Old Rosie, Gwynt y Ddraig Dog Dancer. ♚ 18 **Facilities** Non-diners area ♣ (Bar Restaurant Garden) ♦ Children's menu Children's portions Garden ⊼ Parking WiFi ⛟

The Sun Inn

tel: 01938 561211 **SY21 8JP**
email: suninnmarton@googlemail.com
dir: *On B4386 (Shrewsbury to Montgomery road), in centre of Marton*

Convivial free house respected for its food

Probably about 300 years old, the attractive, stone-built Sun stands on a corner in a quiet hamlet. The Gartell family runs it very much as a convivial local, with darts, dominoes, regular quiz nights and Hobsons real ales from Cleobury Mortimer. It's well respected as a dining venue, with the Gartells offering modern British dishes such as goats' cheese, fig and honey tart; braised local venison with juniper and thyme; sticky roast belly of pork; and blackboard fish specials. Offa's Dyke Path runs nearby on its 177-mile route from Sedbury Cliffs on the Severn estuary to Prestatyn.

Open 12-3 7-12 Closed Sun eve, Mon, Tue L **Food** Lunch Wed-Sat 12-2.30 Dinner Tue-Fri from 7pm Set menu available Restaurant menu available Tue-Sat ⊕ FREE HOUSE ◀ Hobsons Best Bitter, Guest ales. ♚ 8 **Facilities** Non-diners area ♣ (Bar Garden) ♦ Children's portions Garden ⊼ Parking ⛟ (notice required)

| MUCH WENLOCK | Map 10 SO69 |

The George & Dragon

tel: 01952 727312 **2 High St TF13 6AA**
email: thegeorge.dragon@btinternet.com
dir: *On A458 halfway between Shrewsbury & Bridgnorth, on right of the High Street*

Good pub food and choice of ales

If you are looking for somewhere dog-friendly, with five cask ales and several draught ciders, and where newspapers are provided, this early 18th-century inn should do nicely. Over the fireplace in the bar, an oak beam features the initials of the Yates family, innkeepers from 1834 to 1958. On the menu are baguettes and light lunches, while in the evening choose from deep-fried breaded scampi; chicken breast wrapped in bacon, stuffed with garlic mushrooms; a selection of pies – beef in ale, traditional fish and Shropshire fidget (pork and apple) – and vegetarian options. Beer festivals through the year.

Open all day all wk 12-11 (Fri-Sat 12-12) **Food** Lunch all wk 12-2.30 Dinner Mon-Tue, Thu-Sat 6-9 ⊕ PUNCH TAVERNS ◀ Greene King Abbot Ale, Hobsons Best Bitter, St Austell Tribute, Guest ales Ò Westons Wyld Wood Organic, Thatchers Gold. **Facilities** Non-diners area ♣ (Bar Outside area) ♦ Children's menu Children's portions Outside area ⊼ Beer festival WiFi ⛟

| MUNSLOW | Map 10 SO58 |

The Crown Country Inn ★★★★ INN ☺☺ **PICK OF THE PUBS**

See Pick of the Pubs on opposite page

PICK OF THE PUBS

The Crown Country Inn ★★★★ INN

MUNSLOW   Map 10 SO58

tel: 01584 841205
SY7 9ET
email: info@crowncountryinn.co.uk
web: www.crowncountryinn.co.uk
dir: *On B4368 between Craven Arms &*
Much Wenlock

Dedication to serving excellent food

The Grade II listed Crown has stood in its lovely setting below the limestone escarpment of Wenlock Edge since Tudor times. An impressive three-storey building, it served for a while as a Hundred House, a type of court, where the infamous 'Hanging' Judge Jeffreys sometimes presided over proceedings. Could it be that the black-swathed Charlotte, whose ghost is sometimes seen in the pub, once appeared before him? The main bar retains its sturdy oak beams, flagstone floors and prominent inglenook fireplace, and on offer are beers from the Three Tuns Brewery. Owners Richard and Jane Arnold are well known for their strong commitment to good food, Richard being not only head chef but Shropshire's only Master Chef of Great Britain, a title he has cherished for many years. Meals based on top-quality local produce from trusted sources are served in the main bar, the Bay dining area, and the Corvedale restaurant, the former court room. These may include dishes such as flaked ham hock and tomato terrine with hazelnut and paprika dressing; roast wood pigeon breast, warm beetroot chutney, rosemary polenta fritter and port wine syrup; and griddled rib-eye or Hereford sirloin steak. Sundays here are deservedly popular, when a typical lunch might start with cream and coriander soup; followed by roast fore rib of beef and Yorkshire pudding, or pavé of Shetland salmon, with red wine and crayfish butter sauce; and to finish, Limoncello cheesecake, or Seville orange pannacotta. Three large bedrooms are in a converted Georgian stable block.

Open Tue-Sat 12-3.30 6.45-11 (Sun 12-3.30) Closed Xmas, Sun eve, Mon **Food** Lunch Tue-Sun 12-2 Dinner Tue-Sat 6.45-8.45 Restaurant menu available Tue-Sat. ⊕ FREE HOUSE ◀ Three Tuns 1642, Corvedale Golden Dale, Ludlow Best.
Facilities Non-diners area ♦ Children's portions Play area Garden ⊼ Parking WiFi ⛟ (notice required) **Rooms** 3

NORTON
Map 10 SJ70

The Hundred House ★★★★ INN PICK OF THE PUBS

tel: 01952 580240 **Bridgnorth Rd TF11 9EE**
email: reservations@hundredhouse.co.uk **web:** www.hundredhouse.co.uk
dir: On A442, 6m N of Bridgnorth, 5m S of Telford centre

Award-winning pub with quirky features

Surrounded by rolling Severn Valley countryside and just a 10-minute drive from Ironbridge Gorge, this historic 14th-century inn has been run by the Phillips family for over 25 years. Downstairs is an amazing interconnecting warren of lavishly decorated bars and dining rooms with old quarry-tiled floors, exposed brickwork, beamed ceilings and Jacobean oak panelling. The gardens are also an enchanting place to spend some time. Stuart Phillips continues to head kitchen operations, producing a mix of innovative new dishes and pub favourites. Choices from the à la carte include starters like black pudding, apple and chorizo stack with smoked cheese sauce, and Stilton stuffed mushrooms wrapped in bacon with tomato chutney; mains such as roast rack of lamb on creamed garlic mash of baked chicken breast stuffed with ricotta, spinach and pine nuts. Cookery classes are also available.

Open all day all wk 10am-11pm Closed 25 Dec eve **Food** Lunch all wk 12-2.30 Dinner all wk 6-9.30 ⊕ FREE HOUSE ◀ Ironbridge, Three Tuns, Ludlow ♻ Rosie's. ♟ 10 **Facilities** Non-diners area ☻ (Bar Garden) ♦♦ Children's menu Children's portions Family room Garden ⌁ Parking WiFi 🚐 (notice required) **Rooms** 9

OSWESTRY
Map 15 SJ22

The Bradford Arms

tel: 01691 830582 **Llanymynech SY22 6EJ**
email: robinbarsteward@tesco.net
dir: 5.5m S of Oswestry on A483 in Llanymynech

Tip-top ales at Welsh Borders pub

Once part of the Earl of Bradford's estate, between Oswestry and Welshpool, this 17th-century coaching inn is ideally situated for golfing, fishing and walking. It is well known as a community pub serving first-class real ales. Eating in the spotless, quietly elegant bar, dining rooms and conservatory is a rewarding experience, with every taste catered for. For lunch try oven-roast chicken supreme, giant filled Yorkshire pudding, or steak and kidney pudding; while a typical dinner menu features Stilton chicken, beef Stroganoff, fisherman's pie, and leek, mushroom and onion pancake.

Open all day all wk 11.30-3 5.30-12 **Food** Lunch all wk 11.30-2 Dinner all wk 5.30-9 Av main course £8.95 Set menu available Restaurant menu available all wk ⊕ FREE HOUSE ◀ Black Sheep Best Bitter, 2 Guest ales ♻ Westons Stowford Press. **Facilities** Non-diners area ☻ (Bar Outside area) ♦♦ Children's menu Children's portions Outside area ⌁ Parking WiFi 🚐 (notice required)

PAVE LANE
Map 10 SJ71

The Fox

tel: 01952 815940 **TF10 9LQ**
email: fox@brunningandprice.co.uk
dir: 1m S of Newport, just off A41

Grand Edwardian pub offering Shropshire ales

Behind The Fox's smart exterior are spacious rooms and little nooks wrapped around a busy central bar, where there is an original wooden fireplace and plenty of Shropshire real ales demanding attention. The menu offers sandwiches and light meals (camembert quiche, goats' cheese rarebit), as well as grilled smoked haddock kedgeree, honey-glazed ham, falafel burger, and pork schnitzel. To finish, choose from ice cream, sorbet, cheese or traditional puddings like chocolate brownie. Enjoy the gently rolling countryside and wooded hills from the lovely south-facing terrace with its patio tables and large grassy area.

Open all day all wk 11-11 (Sun 11-10.30) **Food** Lunch all day Dinner all day Av main course £12.50 ⊕ FREE HOUSE/BRUNNING & PRICE ◀ Wood's Shropshire Lad, Titanic Mild, Holden's Golden Glow, Three Tuns XXX, Purple Moose Snowdonia. ♟ 12 **Facilities** Non-diners area ☻ (Bar Garden) ♦♦ Children's menu Children's portions Play area Garden ⌁ Parking WiFi

SHIFNAL
Map 10 SJ70

Odfellows Wine Bar

tel: 01952 461517 **Market Place TF11 9AU**
email: odfellows@gmail.com
dir: M54 junct 4, 3rd exit at rdbt, at next rdbt take 3rd exit, past petrol station, round bend under rail bridge. Bar on left

Quirky and good value

No letters please, telling us we can't spell. The single 'd' is because Odley Inns own this slate-floored, town-centre café bar and restaurant, one of its three in Shropshire. And beer drinkers should not misinterpret the rest – a wine bar, yes, but there are six real ales, including its own brew and a good Belgian selection. Lunch in the elevated dining area and attractive conservatory includes sandwiches and light meals, and the evening menu lists grills; leek and mushroom gratin; Od fish pie; and bacon-wrapped pheasant breast. There's regular live music, and beer and cider festivals are in May and September.

Open all day all wk Closed 25-26 Dec, 1 Jan **Food** Lunch Mon-Thu 12-2.30, Fri-Sun 12-9 Dinner Mon-Thu 6-9, Fri-Sun 12-9 ⊕ FREE HOUSE ◀ Salopian Shropshire Gold, Best Odley Bitter (pub's own), Guest ale ♻ Thatchers, Addlestones. ♟ 11 **Facilities** Non-diners area ♦♦ Children's menu Children's portions Garden ⌁ Beer festival Parking WiFi

SHREWSBURY
Map 15 SJ41

The Armoury

tel: 01743 340525 **Victoria Quay, Victoria Av SY1 1HH**
email: armoury@brunningandprice.co.uk
dir: Phone for detailed directions

Great beers and food in converted warehouse

Smack beside the River Severn, this former armoury building was converted by Brunning & Price and makes an impressive, large-scale pub with its vast warehouse windows. Inside, huge bookcases dominate the bar and restaurant area, where the modern monthly-changing menu is accompanied by a great range of real ales such as Salopian Shropshire Gold, local cider and a well-considered wine list. Typical dishes are scallops with pea purée; local venison with redcurrant and rosemary gravy; excellent sandwiches (roast beef, rocket and horseradish), and glazed lemon tart with mixed berry coulis for pudding.

Open all day all wk 10.30am-11pm (Sun 10.30am-10.30pm) **Food** Lunch Mon-Sat 12-10, Sun 12-9.30 Dinner Mon-Sat 12-10, Sun 12-9.30 ⊕ FREE HOUSE/BRUNNING & PRICE ◀ Salopian Shropshire Gold, Wood's Shropshire Lad, Hobsons Twisted Spire, Phoenix, Brunning & Price Original Bitter ♻ Westons Rosie Pig. ♟ 12 **Facilities** Non-diners area ♦♦ Children's menu Children's portions Garden Outside area ⌁ WiFi

NEW The Boat House

tel: 01743 231658 **New St SY3 8JQ**
email: info@boathouseshrewsbury.co.uk **web:** www.boathouseshrewsbury.co.uk
dir: *From A458 & A488 rdbt (N of River Severn) follow A488 (Porthill & Bishops Castle). 1st left into New St. Pub on left by suspension footbridge*

Riverside ambience and serious Shropshire fare

Paths from the medieval heart of the town drift through Quarry Park and across a footbridge to this half-timbered retreat beside a great loop of the River Severn at Shrewsbury. Lounge on the huge riverside terrace or make a base in the beamed, rambling, airy interior where real ales from Shropshire's best microbreweries, including Three Tuns and Ludlow Gold should delight the most discerning beer-lover. Start with fig and blue cheese tart, then tuck in to Bourbon BBQ pulled pork or Moroccan spiced lamb with apricot and almond couscous. Dishes from the grill are specialities of the house, using meats with a largely Welsh Marches provenance.

Open all day all wk **Food** Lunch Mon-Sat 12-2.30, Sun 12-9 Dinner Mon-Sat 6-10, Sun 12-9 Av main course £12 ⊕ ENTERPRISE INNS ◀ Salopian Shropshire Gold, Three Tuns, Wood's Shropshire Lad, Purity Mad Goose, Ludlow Gold. ⚲
Facilities ⚫ Children's portions Garden Outside area ⋒ Parking WiFi

Lion & Pheasant Hotel ★★★ TH ⊛⊚

tel: 01743 770345 **50 Wyle Cop SY1 1XJ**
email: info@lionandpheasant.co.uk **web:** www.lionandpheasant.co.uk
dir: *From S & E: pass abbey, cross river on English Bridge to Wyle Cop, hotel on left. From N & W: follow Town Centre signs onto one-way system to Wyle Cop. Hotel at bottom of hill on right*

Boutique hotel luxury in historic market town

The handsome façade of this family-owned hotel and free house graces medieval Wyle Cop, shortly before the street becomes English Bridge over the River Severn. A coolly elegant look is evident throughout, from the ground floor public areas to the spacious, well-equipped bedrooms upstairs. Just off the reception is the wood-floored café-style bar, which leads to the flagstoned Inglenook Bar, serving snacks and a full range of main meals. On the first floor is the split-level restaurant, where Cumbrian rose veal with onion soubise; seafood stew with spicy mussel and saffron sauce; and parmesan gnocchi help to maintain their two AA Rosette status.

Open all day all wk Closed 25-26 Dec **Food** Lunch 12-2.30 Dinner 6-9.30 Av main course £14 Restaurant menu available Tue-Sat ⊕ FREE HOUSE ◀ Ludlow Gold, Salopian Shropshire Gold, Wye Valley HPA, 3 Guest ales ♂ Robinsons, Westons Stowford Press. ⚲ 13 **Facilities** Non-diners area ⚫ Children's menu Children's portions Garden ⋒ Parking WiFi ⟺ (notice required) **Rooms** 22

The Mytton & Mermaid Hotel   PICK OF THE PUBS

tel: 01743 761220 **Atcham SY5 6QG**
email: reception@myttonandmermaid.co.uk
dir: *M54 junct 7, follow Shrewsbury signs, at 2nd rdbt take 1st left signed Ironbridge & Atcham. In 1.5m hotel on right after bridge*

Attractive riverside coaching inn

Opposite the entrance to the National Trust's palatial Attingham Park, this magnificent part creeper-clad Georgian mansion stands beside a graceful bridge across the River Severn. Dating from 1735, the inn is tastefully appointed throughout; the lovingly updated interior reflects the essence of long-past mail-coach days. There's a relaxed feel about the place, especially the bar which features a wood floor, scrubbed tables, comfy sofas and an open log fire. Real ales from small Welsh Marches breweries predominate at the bar, but it's for the reliable menus that diners beat a path to the door. Take the edge off with a starter of Ragstone goats' cheese, beetroot and red onion marmalade tart, looking then to pheasant and smoked bacon Kiev with chestnut and thyme butter, gruyère mash and wilted spinach; or carrot, roasted nut and parmesan sausages with port wine and chestnut jus, finishing with chocolate torte.

Open all day all wk 7am-11pm Closed 25 Dec **Food** Brunch 9-12, Lunch 12-2.30, Afternoon 2.30-6 Dinner Mon-Sat 6-10, Sun 6-9 ⊕ FREE HOUSE ◀ Wood's Shropshire Lad, Salopian Shropshire Gold, Hobsons Best Bitter, Wye Valley. ⚲ 12 **Facilities** Non-diners area ⚫ Children's menu Garden ⋒ Parking WiFi ⟺ (notice required)

STOTTESDON   Map 10 SO68

Fighting Cocks

tel: 01746 718270 **1 High St DY14 8TZ**
email: sandrafc_5@hotmail.com
dir: *11m from Bridgnorth off B4376*

Deep-in-the-countryside pub and shop

According to a framed newspaper cutting on the pub wall, 'Nipper Cook' drank 30 pints of cider each night at this unassuming 18th-century rural free house. Today, this lively local hosts regular music nights, as well as an apple day each October and an annual beer festival in November. The menus change daily but expect home-made pâtés, curries, pies and puddings on the menu. The owners' neighbouring shop supplies local meats, home-made pies, sausages, and produce from the gardens.

Open all wk 6pm-mdnt (Fri 5pm-1am Sat 12-12 Sun 12-10.30) **Food** Lunch Sat-Sun 12-2.30 ⊕ FREE HOUSE ◀ Hobsons Best Bitter, Town Crier & Mild, Wye Valley HPA & Bitter, Ludlow Gold ♂ Westons Stowford Press, Robinsons Flagon.
Facilities Non-diners area ⚫ Children's menu Garden Outside area ⋒ Beer festival Parking WiFi

WELLINGTON
Map 10 SJ61

The Old Orleton Inn

tel: 01952 255011 **Holyhead Rd TF1 2HA**
email: aapub@theoldorleton.com
dir: *From M54 junct 7 take B5061 (Holyhead Rd), 400yds on left on corner of Haygate Rd & Holyhead Rd*

Grand views and wide-ranging menus

The old and new blend effortlessly throughout this 17th-century former coaching inn. Overlooking the famous Wrekin Hill, it is popular with walkers exploring the Shropshire countryside. Expect a relaxed and informal atmosphere, local Hobsons ales on tap and modern British food prepared from scratch. At lunch in the brasserie taking in soup, sandwiches, salad platters, chef's dish of the day and more. Evening choices include Bar Bites for a just a snack or three- course meals that might include pan-seared, 16oz Border County T-bone steak; and guinea fowl and oyster mushroom hot pot.

Open 12-3 5-11 Closed 1st 2wks Jan, Sun eve **Food** Lunch Mon-Sat 12-2.30, Sun 12-4 Dinner Mon-Sat 6-9.30 Av main course £14.95 ⊕ FREE HOUSE ◀ Hobsons Best Bitter, Town Crier Ŏ Westons Stowford Press. ♟ 10 **Facilities** Non-diners area Garden ⊼ Parking WiFi ➡ (notice required)

WENTNOR
Map 15 SO39

The Crown Inn

tel: 01588 650613 **SY9 5EE**
dir: *From Shrewsbury A49 to Church Stretton, follow signs over Long Mynd to Asterton, right to Wentnor*

A lovely village pub set in a beautiful landscape

Deep amid the Shropshire Hills, this inviting 16th-century timbered inn is popular with walkers who warm themselves at wood-burning stoves in winter and on the outside decking in the summer; here you can sup Three Tuns bitter and gaze at the Long Mynd's lofty ridge. The pub's homely atmosphere, enhanced by beams and horse brasses, makes eating and drinking here a pleasure. Meals are served in the bar or separate restaurant; expect pub classics like garlic mushrooms and chicken balti with rice, chips and naan bread.

Open all day all wk **Food** Lunch all wk 12-9.30 Dinner all wk 12-9.30 ⊕ FREE HOUSE ◀ Brains The Rev. James, Hobsons Old Henry, Three Tuns, Wye Valley Butty Bach Ŏ Westons Scrumpy. ♟ 8 **Facilities** Non-diners area ✿ (Bar Garden) ◀ Children's menu Children's portions Play area Garden ⊼ Beer festival Parking WiFi ➡ (notice required)

WHITCHURCH
Map 15 SJ54

Willeymoor Lock Tavern

tel: 01948 663274 **Tarporley Rd SY13 4HF**
dir: *2m N of Whitchurch on A49 (Warrington to Tarporley road)*

Canalside pub ideal for families and walkers

Watch narrow boats negotiating the lock from this much-extended former lock-keeper's cottage on the attractive and busy Llangollen Canal. In the bar, Shropshire Gold represents the county, teapots hang from low beams and there are open log fires. Competitively priced food includes plenty of fish and veggie dishes, as well as pub classics and meats from the grill: beef and onion pie, wholetail scampi, and vegetable chilli. The children's play area and large beer garden make this an ideal warm weather location, and it's a popular refreshment spot for walkers exploring the nearby Sandstone Trail and the Bishop Bennett Way.

Open all wk 12-2.30 6-11 (Sun 12-2.30 6-10.30) Closed 25 Dec **Food** Lunch all wk 12-2 Dinner all wk 6-9 ⊕ FREE HOUSE ◀ Weetwood Eastgate Ale, Timothy Taylor Landlord, Greene King IPA, Morland Old Speckled Hen, Salopian Shropshire Gold, Stonehouse Ŏ Aspall, Westons. ♟ 9 **Facilities** Non-diners area ◀ Children's menu Play area Garden Outside area ⊼ Parking ➡ (notice required)

SOMERSET

ASHCOTT
Map 4 ST43

Ring O'Bells

tel: 01458 210232 **High St TA7 9PZ**
email: info@ringobells.com
dir: *M5 junct 23 follow A39 & Glastonbury signs. In Ashcott turn left, at post office follow church & village hall signs*

Traditional family-run village free house

Successfully run by the same family for over 25 years, this independent free house dates in parts from 1750, and the interior reflects this with beams, split-level bars, an old fireplace and a collection of bells and horse brasses. The pub is close to the Somerset Levels, the RSPB reserve at Ham Wall and the National Nature Reserve at Shapwick Heath. Local ales and ciders are a speciality, while all food is made on the premises. Expect good-value dishes and daily specials such as chicken pie with chorizo; pork tenderloin in creamy scrumpy and apple sauce; or African beef and peanut curry. Treat yourself to an ice cream sundae or sherry trifle for dessert.

Open all wk 12-3 7-11 (Sun 7-10.30) Closed 25 Dec **Food** Lunch all wk 12-2 Dinner all wk 7-10 Av main course £10 ⊕ FREE HOUSE ◀ Rotating Local Guest ales Ŏ Wilkins Farmhouse, The Orchard Pig. ♟ 8 **Facilities** Non-diners area ✿ (Bar Garden) ◀ Children's menu Children's portions Play area Garden ⊼ Parking WiFi ➡ (notice required)

ASHILL
Map 4 ST31

Square & Compass ★★★★ INN

tel: 01823 480467 **Windmill Hill TA19 9NX**
email: squareandcompass@tiscali.co.uk **web:** www.squareandcompasspub.com
dir: *Exit A358 at Stewley Cross service station onto Wood Rd. 1m to pub in Windmill Hill*

Friendly rural pub with high-quality accommodation

Beautifully located overlooking the Blackdown Hills, this traditional family-owned country pub has been a labour of love for owners Chris and Janet Slow for over 15 years. A warm and friendly atmosphere pervades the bar with its hand-made settles and tables. Exmoor and St Austell ales head the refreshments list, while reasonably priced and freshly made meals are prepared in the state-of-the-art kitchen. In addition to classic pub dishes, grills and omelettes, the chef's specials may tempt with sea bass fillets on crushed new potatoes and tomato and basil vinaigrette; and breast of duck with a wild berry sauce. The inn offers AA rated accommodation, and the barn next door hosts weddings and regular live music.

Open 12-3 6.30-late (Sun 7-late) Closed 25-26 Dec, Tue-Thu L **Food** Lunch Fri-Mon 12-2 Dinner all wk 7-9.30 ⊕ FREE HOUSE ◀ St Austell Tribute & Trelawny, Exmoor Ŏ Burrow Hill. **Facilities** Non-diners area ✿ (Bar Garden) ◀ Children's menu Children's portions Garden ⊼ Parking WiFi **Rooms** 8

AXBRIDGE

Map 4 ST45

Lamb Inn

tel: 01934 732253 **The Square BS26 2AP**
dir: *10m from Wells & Weston-Super-Mare on A370*

Plenty of pub favourites at this old inn

Parts of this rambling 15th-century building were once the guildhall, but when a new town hall was opened in 1830 it became an inn. Opposite is the medieval King John's Hunting Lodge, so christened in 1905 by an owner who chose to ignore the fact that John died over two centuries before it was built. The bars are heated by log fires and offer Butcombe ales; there's also a skittle alley and large terraced garden. Examples of pub favourites are beef and ale pie; chicken parmigiani; home-made curries; and salmon fillet supreme. Jacket potatoes, baguettes and sandwiches are available too. As we went to press we learnt that there had been a change of hands.

Open all wk 11-3 6-11 (Thu-Sat 11am-11.30pm Sun 12-10.30) **Food** Lunch all wk 12-2.30 Dinner Mon-Sat 6-9 Av main course £9.75 ⊕ BUTCOMBE ◀ Bitter & Gold, Guest ales Ŏ Thatchers, Ashton Press. **Facilities** Non-diners area ❅ (Bar) Children's menu Children's portions Garden ⊓ WiFi ⊑ (notice required)

BABCARY

Map 4 ST52

Red Lion ★★★★ INN

tel: 01458 223230 **TA11 7ED**
email: redlionbabcary@btinternet.com **web:** www.redlionbabcary.co.uk
dir: *NE of Yeovil. Follow Babcary signs from A303 or A37*

Pretty pub with a great range of food

Rich colour-washed walls, heavy beams and simple wooden furniture characterise this beautifully appointed, thatched free house. The bar offers a great selection of real ales, and you can dine there, in the restaurant or in the garden. The daily menus run from pub favourites such as steak and kidney suet pudding or chargrilled steak with all the trimmings through to grilled fillet of bream, chard, leeks, saffron potatoes, samphire with mussel and clam cream broth; and slow roasted belly pork with braised red cabbage, mustard mash and apple sauce. All bread is baked on the premises and local suppliers are used whenever possible.

Open all wk 12-3 6-12 **Food** Lunch all wk 12-2.30 Dinner Mon-Sat 7-9.30 Av main course £11 ⊕ FREE HOUSE ◀ Teignworthy, Otter, Bays, Yeovil Ales Ŏ Thatchers, Lilleys. ♟ 12 **Facilities** Non-diners area ❅ (Bar Garden) ♦↑ Children's portions Play area Garden ⊓ Parking WiFi ⊑ **Rooms** 6

BATH

Map 4 ST76

NEW The Blathwayt Arms

tel: 01225 421995 **Lansdown BA1 9BT**
email: info@blathwaytarms.co.uk **web:** www.blathwaytarms.co.uk
dir: *2m N of Bath*

Classic country pub serving traditional fare and interesting ales

Named after William Blathwayt, a 17th-century politician who established the War Office as an official government department and effectively became the country's first Minister for War; his National Trust country house a few miles from the pub is known for its deer park. With its welcoming approach to dogs, children and muddy boots, this is a proper pub for anything from a pint of Chuffin to a plate of ham, egg and chips. Mulled wine is supped around log fires in winter, while barbecues in summer are prepared in the large garden, which has a children's play area and overlooks Bath Racecourse.

Open all day all wk **Food** Lunch Mon-Thu 12-9, Fri-Sat 12-9.30, Sun 12-7.30 Dinner Mon-Thu 12-9, Fri-Sat 12-9.30, Sun 12-7.30 Av main course £10-£12 Set menu available Restaurant menu available all wk ⊕ FREE HOUSE/HEARTSTONE INNS LTD ◀ Otter Bitter, Box Steam Chuffin Ale. ♟ 9 **Facilities** Non-diners area ❅ (Bar Garden) ♦↑ Children's menu Children's portions Play area Garden ⊓ Parking WiFi

BATH *continued*

The Chequers ◎◎

tel: 01225 360017 **50 Rivers St BA1 2QA**
email: info@thechequersbath.com **web:** www.thechequersbath.com
dir: *In city centre, near the Royal Crescent and The Circus*

Smart city gastro-pub

A beautifully appointed gastro-pub that's been serving customers since sedan-chair carriers first quenched their thirst here in 1776. A short walk from The Circus and the Royal Crescent, The Chequers' reputation for excellent ales and great food has made it a firm favourite with city locals and visitors alike; booking is advisable. The refurbished upstairs restaurant has been aligned with the look and feel of the ground floor; a large window into the kitchen introduces an air of modern theatricality to the enjoyment of a lamb Scotch egg with Jerusalem artichoke and mint vinaigrette, or pigeon pie with chips.

Open all day all wk 12-11 Closed 25 Dec **Food** Lunch Mon-Sat 12-2.30, Sun 12-6 Dinner Mon-Sat 6-9.30, Sun 12-6 Av main course £13 Restaurant menu available all wk ⊕ ENTERPRISE INNS ◀ Butcombe Bitter, Bath Gem ♂ Westons Wyld Wood Organic, Addlestones, Symonds Founders Reserve. ₹ 26 **Facilities** ◆ Children's portions Outside area ⌱ WiFi ⛟ (notice required)

The Garricks Head

tel: 01225 318368 **7-8 St John's Place BA1 1ET**
email: info@garricksheadpub.com
dir: *Adjacent to Theatre Royal. Follow Theatre Royal brown tourist signs*

City centre pub with a dining room and outside terrace

Once the home of Beau Nash, the celebrated dandy who put the spa city on the map, The Garricks Head is named after 18th-century theatrical powerhouse David Garrick, and is adjacent to the Theatre Royal, for whose customers it provides pre-show dining facilities. The bar has a lot to commend it: a selection of natural wines from Europe, four real ales, five Somerset ciders, and the largest selection of single malt whiskies in Bath. The food, locally sourced as far as possible, includes pub classics such as liver and bacon, and fish and chips, while the carte features salmon mousse with shaved fennel and pickled cucumber; braised ox cheek with onion purée, kale and mash; and apple crumble with custard.

Open all day all wk Closed 25-26 Dec **Food** Lunch Mon-Sat 12-3, Sun 12-4 Dinner Mon-Sat 5.30-10, Sun 5.30-9 Av main course £12.50 Set menu available Restaurant menu available all wk ⊕ FREE HOUSE ◀ Otter Bitter, Palmers, Milk Street Funky Monkey ♂ The Orchard Pig, Honey's Midford Cider. ₹ 20 **Facilities** Non-diners area ♣ (Bar Restaurant Garden) ◆ Children's portions Garden ⌱ WiFi ⛟ (notice required)

NEW The Hare & Hounds ◎

tel: 01225 482682 **Lansdown Rd BA1 5TJ**
email: info@hareandhoundsbath.com **web:** www.hareandhoundsbath.com
dir: *Phone for detailed directions*

Visit for the view, stay to eat and drink

Only a mile from Bath city centre, the Hare & Hounds sits high on Lansdown Hill with stunning views over the valley to Solsbury Hill. Happily the feast for the eyes extends to the pub's food and drink – so tarry awhile with an eponymous pint of ale or one of over 30 wines served by the glass. The welcome is warm, the staff and service friendly, and the food unpretentiously good. In summer the terrace is much sought after for alfresco dining: typical dishes are cod and crab fishcakes with pineapple salsa; chargrilled pork chop with bacon, potato fondant and cabbage; and rhubarb and Madeira doughnut with white chocolate.

Open all day all wk Open from 8.30am every day **Food** Contact pub for full details Av main course £12.50 Restaurant menu available all wk ⊕ STAR PUBS ◀ St Austell Tribute, Caledonian Hare & Hounds (pub's own) ♂ Symonds. ₹ 31 **Facilities** Non-diners area ♣ (Bar Restaurant Garden) ◆ Children's menu Children's portions Play area Garden ⌱ Parking WiFi ⛟ (notice required)

PICK OF THE PUBS

The Marlborough Tavern ❀❀

BATH   Map 4 ST76

tel: 01225 423731
35 Marlborough Buildings BA1 2LY
email: info@marlborough-tavern.com
web: www.marlborough-tavern.com
dir: *200mtrs from W end of Royal Crescent*

Agreeable hostelry well placed for Bath's best attractions

Just round the corner from the famous Royal Crescent, this 18th-century pub once refreshed foot-weary sedan-chair carriers. Today's clientele is more likely to need a break from the rigours of traipsing around Bath's shops, for which the Marlborough is handily placed. The interior is contemporary yet retro, with an abundance of mismatched chairs, sturdy solid wood tables and scrubbed floorboards. At the rear is a walled and trellised courtyard terrace, a secluded little spot ideal for whiling away a warm summer's evening. Butcombe and Box Steam Brewery's Piston Broke are the prime ales dispensed in the spotless bar, with Orchard Pig cider also very popular; the wine selection comprising 26 sold by the glass offers something for everyone. The lunch menu pleases too by not straying far from popular and traditional pub classics, such as Cornish haddock in Piston Broke batter with triple cooked chips, mushy peas and tartare. Other light bites range from sandwiches served with fries and salad; a venison

and beef burger with caramelised red onion and winter slaw; to a Thai curried carrot soup with vegetable pakoras. This is one of the starters on the excellent value set lunch menu, which could be followed by Exmouth mussels in a cider, sage and smoked bacon sauce; conclude sweetly with a mocha brûlée served with chocolate biscotti and hazlenut cream. A typical three-course dinner may start with a trio of Brixham crab - crab bisque, chilli crab cake with salsa, and crab rillettes on toast with crab mayonnaise. Next may come a slow-cooked beef shin and ox kidney pudding, with pan-seared fillet, horseradish mash, squash purée, purple sprouting broccoli and confit shallots. Finish with a dark and white chocolate brownie with vanilla ice cream.

Open all day all wk 8am-11pm (Sat-Sun 9am-11pm) Closed 25 Dec **Food** Lunch 12-3 Dinner 6-9.30 Av main course £13 Set menu available; Restaurant menu available all wk. ⊕ FREE HOUSE ⬛ Butcombe Bitter, Box Steam Piston Broke Ꝺ The Orchard Pig. ⏍ 26 **Facilities** Non-diners area 👪 Children's menu Children's portions Garden 🜉 WiFi 🚌 (notice required)

BATH *continued*

The Hop Pole | PICK OF THE PUBS

tel: 01225 446327 **7 Albion Buildings, Upper Bristol Rd BA1 3AR**
email: hoppole@bathales.co.uk
dir: *On A4 from city centre towards Bristol. Pub opposite Royal Victoria Park*

An oasis of calm plus top notch beer and food

Just off the River Avon towpath, opposite Royal Victoria Park, sits this delightful pub. Described as both a country pub in the heart of a city, and as a secret oasis, it has a stripped-down, stylish interior and a lovingly restored, spacious beer garden, which has been refreshed with a grapevine canopy. Bath Ales, now elevated from microbrewery to regional brewery status, supplies many beers from its stable – here you'll find Barnsey, Gem and SPA. All food is home cooked, from the bar snacks to the main meals such as River Fowey mussels with cider and saffron sauce; honey and clove ham hock, piccalilli and cauliflower cheese; grilled cod with chorizo and haricot cassoulet; and grilled vegetable tart with rocket, parmesan shavings and potato salad. Children can be served smaller portions from the main menu.

Open all day all wk 12-11 (Fri-Sat 12-12) **Food** Lunch Mon-Sat 12-9.30, Sun 12-8 Dinner Mon-Sat 12-9.30, Sun 12-8 Set menu available ⊕ BATH ALES ◀ Gem, SPA, Barnsey, Guest ales ♻ Bath Ciders Bounders & Traditional. ♥ 16 **Facilities** Non-diners area ♥ (Bar Garden Outside area) ♥♦ Children's menu Children's portions Garden Outside area ⊨ WiFi ━━ (notice required)

King William | PICK OF THE PUBS

tel: 01225 428096 **36 Thomas St BA1 5NN**
email: info@kingwilliampub.com
dir: *At junct of Thomas St & A4 (London Rd), on left from Bath towards London. 15 mins walk from Bath Spa main line station*

Modern British cooking and well-kept local ales

A short stroll from the city centre on a busy main road, this unassuming Bath stone building offers a happy mix of destination dining inn and locals' pub. In the cosy snug and traditional bar, real ale buffs will generally find a regular Palmers ale, supplemented by guest beers from local microbreweries such as Stonehenge, Milk Street and Yeovil. The kitchen creates traditional dishes, with a contemporary twist, from locally produced seasonal ingredients. The bar menu offers lighter dishes such as a ploughman's or a good beef, pickle and horseradish sandwich, but serious diners will seek out the inspiring daily-changing menu served in the elegant upstairs dining room. A starter of scallops, Jerusalem artichokes and apple might precede a main course of chicken, broccoli cheese, Puy lentils and wild mushrooms. Ginger and treacle sponge is one highly comforting end to an evening, matched by a carefully chosen wine list.

Open all wk 12-3 5-close (Sat-Sun 12-close) Closed 25 Dec **Food** Lunch Mon-Sun 12-3 Dinner Mon-Sat 6-10, Sun 6-9 Av main course £11 Set menu available Restaurant menu available Wed-Sat ⊕ FREE HOUSE ◀ Stonehenge Danish Dynamite, Palmers Dorset Gold, Milk Street Funky Monkey, Yeovil Ales Star Gazer ♻ Pheasant Plucker, Westons Wyld Wood Organic, The Orchard Pig, Honey's Midford Cider. ♥ 14 **Facilities** Non-diners area ♥ (Bar) ♥♦ Children's portions WiFi ━━ (notice required)

The Marlborough Tavern ◉◉ | PICK OF THE PUBS

See Pick of the Pubs on page 423

The Star Inn

tel: 01225 425072 **23 Vineyards BA1 5NA**
email: landlord@star-inn-bath.co.uk
dir: *On A4, 300mtrs from centre of Bath*

The city's oldest pub offering ales from its only brewery

Set amid glorious Georgian architecture and first licensed in 1760, the impressive Star Inn is one of Bath's oldest pubs and is of outstanding historical interest, with a rare and totally unspoiled interior. Original features in the four drinking areas include 19th-century Gaskell and Chambers bar fittings, a barrel lift from the cellar, and even complimentary pinches of snuff found in tins in the smaller bar. Long famous for its pints of Bass served from the jug, these days Abbey Ales from Bath's only brewery are also popular. Fresh filled rolls are available and free snacks on Sundays. A beer festival focusing on Cornish beers is held twice a year.

Open all wk 12-2.30 5.30-12 (Fri-Sat noon-1am Sun 12-12) **Food** Contact pub for details ⊕ PUNCH TAVERNS ◀ Abbey Bellringer, Bath Star, Twelfth Night & White Friar, Bass ♻ Abbey Ales Hells Bells. **Facilities** Non-diners area ♥ (Bar Restaurant) ♥♦ Beer festival WiFi ━━

◼ BAWDRIP   **Map 4 ST33**

The Knowle Inn

tel: 01278 683330 **TA7 8PN**
email: toby@theknowleinn.co.uk
dir: *M5 junct 23 or A39 from Bridgwater towards Glastonbury*

A true community pub with amazing views

This 16th-century pub on the A39 nestles beneath the Polden Hills and has far-reaching views across Sedgemoor to the Quantocks and Blackdown Hills. The live music, skittles and darts are popular with locals, while the seafood specials and Mediterranean-style garden attract visitors from further afield for summer alfresco meals. A full range of sandwiches and light meals is backed by pub favourites such as creamy garlic mushrooms; deep-fried plaice fillet; celery and cashew nut roast; smoked haddock with cheese and tomato topping; grilled steak with all the trimmings; and Malteser cheesecake.

Open all day all wk **Food** Lunch all wk 11-3 Dinner all wk 6-9 ⊕ ENTERPRISE INNS ◀ Otter, Guest ales ♻ Thatchers. **Facilities** Non-diners area ♥ (Bar Garden) ♥♦ Children's menu Children's portions Garden ⊨ Parking WiFi ━━ (notice required)

◼ BECKINGTON   **Map 4 ST85**

Woolpack Inn ★★★★ INN

tel: 01373 831244 **BA11 6SP**
email: 6534@greeneking.co.uk **web:** www.oldenglish.co.uk
dir: *Just off A36 near junct with A361*

Former coaching inn with smart interior

This charming, stone-built coaching inn dates back to the 1500s. Standing in the middle of the village and a short drive from Bath, inside there's an attractive, flagstone floor in the bar and outside at the back, a delightful terraced garden. The lunch menu offers soup and sandwich platters, and larger dishes such as sausages and mash; burger; pies; steaks; and beer-battered cod and chips. The evening menu is extensive. Twelve e-suite bedrooms, including one four-poster room and one family room, are available.

Open all day all wk 11-11 (Sun 11-10) **Food** Lunch Mon-Fri 12-3, Sat-Sun 12-10 Dinner Mon-Fri 6-10, Sat-Sun 12-10 ⊕ OLD ENGLISH INNS & HOTELS ◀ Greene King IPA & Abbot Ale, Butcombe, Guest ale ♻ Westons Stowford Press, Thatchers. ♥ 14 **Facilities** Non-diners area ♥ (Bar Garden) ♥♦ Children's menu Children's portions Garden Parking WiFi ━━ **Rooms** 12

BISHOP SUTTON
Map 4 ST55

NEW The Red Lion

tel: 01275 333042 **Sutton Hill BS39 5UT**
email: redlionbishopsutton@aol.com
dir: *Between Pensford & Clutton on A37 take A368 to Bishop Sutton*

Simple food the village pub way

Having taken over here early in 2014, Duncan Ferguson has quickly built up a sound reputation. Early visitors were quick to comment on its friendliness, the efficiency of its staff and how much they had enjoyed eating and drinking here. In the bar, Bath Ales Gem single-handedly raises the flag for Somerset. Nothing too adventurous on the menu, just good old, home-made pub grub like pork faggots with mash, red cabbage and onion gravy; beef, ale and vegetable pie with new potatoes and peas; and beer-battered cod with chips, peas and tartare sauce.

Open 12-2.30 4.30-11 (Fri-Sun 12-12 Mon 4.30-11) Closed Mon L **Food** Contact pub for full details Av main course £8 Set menu available ⊕ PUNCH TAVERNS ◄ Courage Best, Fuller's London Pride, Sharp's Doom Bar, Bath Ales Gem ♂ Thatchers Dry & Gold. ♥ **Facilities** Non-diners area ✿ (All areas) ✦ Children's menu Children's portions Play area Garden Outside area ⌂ Beer festival Parking WiFi ▦ (notice required)

BISHOPSWOOD
Map 4 ST21

Candlelight Inn

tel: 01460 234476 **TA20 3RS**
email: info@candlelight-inn.co.uk
dir: *From A303 SW of Newtown, right a x-rds signed Bishopswood & Churchinford. Pub on right in village*

Remote pub with excellent food

Debbie Lush and Tom Warren run this rustic rural local tucked away deep in the Blackdown Hills. A 17th-century flint-built inn with wooden floors, crackling log fires and a warm and friendly atmosphere, locals gather here for tip-top pints of Exmoor or Branscombe ale drawn straight from the cask. Food will not disappoint, with everything made on the premises, including vegetables grown in the pub's garden. Follow creamy cauliflower soup or devilled lamb's kidney on toast with venison haunch with mash and vegetables, plaice fillets with brown crab mousse, or smoked cheddar and leek cannelloni, leaving room for sticky toffee pudding with toffee sauce and double cream. Occasionally there are beer festivals.

Open 12-3 6-11 (Sun all day) Closed 25-27 Dec, Mon **Food** Lunch Tue-Fri 12-2, Sat-Sun 12-2.30 Dinner Tue-Thu & Sun 7-9, Fri-Sat 7-9.30 Set menu available ⊕ FREE HOUSE ◄ Otter Bitter, Bass, Exmoor, Branscombe ♂ Thatchers, Sheppy's, Tricky. ♥ 9 **Facilities** Non-diners area ✿ (Bar Garden) ✦ Children's portions Garden ⌂ Beer festival Parking WiFi ▦ (notice required)

CATCOTT
Map 4 ST33

The Crown Inn

tel: 01278 722288 **1 The Nydon TA7 9HQ**
email: catcottcrownin@aol.com
dir: *M5 junct 23, A39 towards Glastonbury. Turn left to Catcott*

Venerable ale house with good home-cooked food

Originally a beer house serving local peat-cutters, this low-beamed, flagstoned pub in the Somerset levels is perhaps 400 years old. The winter log fire takes the chill off Bristol Channel winds; in summer the half-acre beer garden is great for families and sun worshippers. Food is plentiful, imaginative and home made; typical options include spicy battered chilli beef; lasagne; and cheesecake. Look out for specials

such as fish pie au gratin; game casserole; or teriyaki belly pork. A good range of cask ales and ciders from regional suppliers completes the picture.

Open 12-2.30 6-late Closed Mon L **Food** Lunch Tue-Sun 12-2 (booking advisable Sun) Dinner all wk 6-9 ⊕ FREE HOUSE ◄ Sharp's Doom Bar, St Austell Proper Job, Molegrip Core ♂ Pheasant Plucker, Thatchers Gold. ♥ 10 **Facilities** Non-diners area ✿ (Bar Garden) ✦ Children's menu Children's portions Play area Garden ⌂ Parking WiFi ▦

CHEW MAGNA
Map 4 ST56

The Bear and Swan
PICK OF THE PUBS

tel: 01275 331100 **South Pde BS40 8SL**
dir: *A37 from Bristol. Turn right signed Chew Magna onto B3130. Or from A38 turn left on B3130*

Much loved by locals and visitors alike

The Victorians clearly didn't like the frontage of this early 18th-century pub, so they gave it one of their own. Inside, the oak-beamed rooms with scrubbed wooden floors and diverse collection of reclaimed tables, chairs and assorted artefacts all contribute to its warm and friendly atmosphere. It's owned by Fuller's, so expect London Pride, but you'll also find Butcombe Bitter, local real ciders and a list of well selected wines. The restaurant offers daily one-, two- and three-course menus with good choices of fish, game, seafood, meats and vegetarian dishes. You might care to start with wasabi tuna and tiger prawn satay with pepper salad; before moving on to aubergine rarebit with tomato, caper and pesto risotto; or baked cod with pancetta crust, fennel and rocket linguine and sweet roasted garlic velouté. Spring into summer beer and cider festival. Change of hands.

Open all day all wk 9am-mdnt Closed 25 Dec **Food** Lunch 9am-10pm Dinner 9am-10pm ⊕ FULLER'S ◄ London Pride, Butcombe Bitter ♂ Ashton Press, Aspall, Symonds. ♥ 12 **Facilities** Non-diners area ✿ (Bar Restaurant Garden) ✦ Children's menu Children's portions Garden ⌂ Beer festival Cider festival Parking WiFi ▦ (notice required)

The Pony and Trap ◉◉

tel: 01275 332627 **Knowle Hill, Newton BS40 8TQ**
email: info@theponyandtrap.co.uk
dir: *Take A37 S from Bristol. After Pensford turn right at rdbt onto A368 towards Weston-Super-Mare. In 1.5m right signed Chew Magna & Winford. Pub 1m on right*

Country cottage pub-restaurant with award-winning cuisine

This 200-year-old building benefits from a stunning location, enjoying fantastic views across the Chew Valley. The Pony and Trap still feels like a rural local despite the acclaim it has achieved with its food. Committed to sourcing all ingredients as locally as possible, everything on the menu is made on the premises, right down to the bread and the butter. Try fillet of lamb, braised shoulder, devilled kidney, potato cake and turnip tops, followed by chocolate fondant with beetroot sorbet. A seven-course tasting menu is also available. Fine wines, local real ales and a local cider sum up its appeal.

Open 12-3 6.30-12 (Sun all day) Closed Mon (ex BHs & Dec) **Food** Lunch Tue-Sat 12-2.30, Sun 12-3.30 Dinner Tue-Fri & Sun 7-9.30, Sat 6-9.30 Av main course £16 ⊕ FREE HOUSE ◄ Butcombe Bitter, Sharp's Doom Bar, Guest ale ♂ Ashton Press. ♥ 26 **Facilities** Non-diners area ✦ Children's portions Garden ⌂ Parking WiFi

CHURCHILL   Map 4 ST45

The Crown Inn

tel: 01934 852995 **The Batch BS25 5PP**
dir: *From Bristol take A38 S. Right at Churchill lights, left in 200mtrs, up hill to pub*

Rural village pub with lovely gardens

This gem of a pub was once a stop on what was then the Bristol to Exeter coach road. A good selection of real ales is served straight from the cask in the two flagstone-floored bars, where open fires blaze on cold days. The freshly prepared bar lunches include sandwiches, soups, salads and ploughman's, all made from the best local ingredients. In fact the beef comes straight from the fields that can be seen from the pub's windows. You can enjoy a meal in the beautiful gardens in warmer weather, perhaps beef casserole; chilli; or cauliflower cheese.

Open all day all wk 11-11 (Fri 11am-mdnt) **Food** Lunch all wk 12-2.30 ⊕ FREE HOUSE ◀ Palmers IPA, Bass, RCH PG Steam & Hewish IPA, Bath Gem, St Austell Tribute, Butcombe ᷍ Thatchers, Ashton Press, Healey's Cornish Rattler, Bath Ciders Bounders. **Facilities** Non-diners area ❄ (Bar) ◈ Children's portions Garden Outside area ⊟ Parking WiFi ▭ Notes ☺

CLAPTON-IN-GORDANO   Map 4 ST47

The Black Horse   PICK OF THE PUBS

tel: 01275 842105 **Clevedon Ln BS20 7RH**
email: theblackhorse@talktalkbusiness.net
dir: *M5 junct 19, 3m to village. 2m from Portishead, 10m from Bristol*

Real ales, short lunchtime menu, families welcome

The bars on one of the windows of this attractive, whitewashed inn near Bristol are a reminder that the Black Horse's Snug Bar was once the village lock-up. Built in the 14th century, the traditional bar of this pub features low beams, flagstone floors, wooden settles, and old guns above the big open fireplace. Real ales served straight from the barrel include local Butcombe Bitter and Bath Ales Gem, whilst cider fans will rejoice at the sight of Thatchers Heritage and Dry. The small kitchen in this listed building limits its output to traditional pub food served lunchtimes only (Monday to Saturday). The repertoire includes hot and cold filled baguettes and rolls; home-made soup of the day; pies and seasonal specials. The large rear garden includes a children's play area, and there's a separate family room.

Open all day all wk **Food** Lunch Mon-Sat 12-2.30 ⊕ ENTERPRISE INNS ◀ Courage Best Bitter, Bath Ales Gem, Butcombe Bitter, Exmoor Gold, Otter Bitter ᷍ Thatchers Heritage & Dry. ☖ 8 **Facilities** Non-diners area ❄ (Bar) ◈ Play area Family room Garden Parking WiFi

CLUTTON   Map 4 ST65

The Hunters Rest ☆☆☆☆ INN   PICK OF THE PUBS

See Pick of the Pubs on opposite page

COMBE HAY   Map 4 ST75

The Wheatsheaf Combe Hay ★★★★ INN ◉

PICK OF THE PUBS

tel: 01225 833504 **BA2 7EG**
email: info@wheatsheafcombehay.co.uk **web:** www.wheatsheafcombehay.co.uk
dir: *From Bath take A369 (Exeter road) to Odd Down, left at park & ride & immediately right towards Combe Hay. 2m to thatched cottage, turn left*

Grab a table in the tranquil garden

The Wheatsheaf was built in 1576 as a farmhouse, but not until the 18th century did it begin its life as an alehouse, and today its old persona rubs shoulders companionably with the new, country-chic interior. A long, whitewashed free house with a pantiled roof, the pub stands on a peaceful hillside. The building is decorated with flowers in summer, when the gorgeous south-facing garden makes an ideal spot for outdoor drinking and dining. In the stylishly decorated, rambling bar with its massive wooden tables, sporting prints and open fires, the resident real ale is Butcombe Bitter and the ciders are Cheddar Valley and Ashton Press. The garden is home to free-range chickens and ducks, blissfully unaware of the importance of their various contributions to the daily menus prepared by head chef, Eddy Rains, who is wholly committed to the use of the freshest seasonal ingredients.

Open 10.30-3 6-11 (Sun 11-5.30) Closed 25-26 Dec & 1st wk Jan, Sun eve, Mon (ex BHs) **Food** Lunch Tue-Sat 12-2 Dinner Tue-Sat 6.30-9.30 ⊕ FREE HOUSE ◀ Butcombe Bitter, Otter, Guest ale ᷍ Thatchers & Cheddar Valley, Honey's Midford Cider Honey & Daughter, Ashton Press. ☖ 13 **Facilities** Non-diners area ❄ (Bar Restaurant Garden) ◈ Garden ⊟ Parking WiFi **Rooms** 3

COMPTON DANDO   Map 4 ST66

The Compton Inn

tel: 01761 490321 **Court Hill BS39 4JZ**
email: paul@huntersrest.co.uk
dir: *From A368 between Chelwood & Marksbury follow Hunstrete & Compton Dando signs*

Confident cooking in a picturesque location

A former farmhouse, the Grade II listed Compton Inn has only been a pub since World War II, but it has been sympathetically restored. Located in picturesque Compton Dando, with its imposing church and hump-backed bridge crossing the River Chew, it is only a few miles from the bustling city of Bristol. It's an ideal bolt-hole to enjoy local ale and cider, and well-cooked dishes like herb-crusted hake, lemon and chorizo crushed potatoes and ratatouille or Somerset faggots in onion gravy, mustard and spring onion mash and vegetables. For pudding try Bakewell tart and blackberry ice cream.

Open all day all wk **Food** Lunch Mon-Sat 12-2.15, Sun 12-6 Dinner Mon-Sat 6.15-9.15 Restaurant menu available all wk ⊕ PUNCH TAVERNS ◀ Bath Ales Gem, Sharp's Doom Bar, Butcombe Bitter ᷍ Thatchers Traditional & Dry. ☖ 10 **Facilities** Non-diners area ❄ (Bar Restaurant Garden) ◈ Children's menu Children's portions Garden ⊟ Parking WiFi ▭ (notice required)

PICK OF THE PUBS

The Hunters Rest ★★★★★ INN

CLUTTON   Map 4 ST65

tel: 01761 452303
King Ln, Clutton Hill BS39 5QL
email: info@huntersrest.co.uk
web: www.huntersrest.co.uk
dir: *On A37 follow signs for Wells through Pensford, at large rdbt left towards Bath, 100mtrs right into country lane, pub 1m up hill*

Traditional country inn with excellent views

Dating from 1750, The Earl of Warwick's former hunting lodge offers far-reaching views across the Cam Valley to the Mendip Hills and the Chew Valley towards Bristol. When the estate was sold in 1872, the building became a tavern serving the growing number of coal miners working in the area, but all the mines closed long ago and the place has been transformed into a popular and attractive inn. Paul Thomas has been running the place for more than 25 years, during which time he has established a great reputation for good home-made food, real ales – typically Butcombe, Bath Gem and Otter – and a well-stocked wine cellar. The menu includes warm chicken and bacon salad; coarse chicken liver pâté on warm granary toast; giant pastries called oggies, which might come with a variety of fillings, such as beef steak and Stilton, mixed smoked fish, cauliflower cheese, and not for the faint

hearted they say - the Welsh Dragon, casseroled beef with fiery chillies, peppers and tomatoes. Other dishes may include chilli burritos; and lamb's liver and bacon with onion gravy; and from the specials blackboard a selection of daily delivered, Brixham-landed sea bass and other fish; smoked duck and blood orange salad; beef steak kebab, garlic and chilli butter, lemon thyme rice and Greek salad; and game casserole with herb dumplings. Finish with a popular dessert such as blackcurrant cheesecake; Bakewell tart; or sticky toffee pudding. In summer you can sit out in the landscaped grounds, and if a longer visit is on the cards the inn has very stylish en suite bedrooms.

Open all day all wk **Food** Lunch all wk 12-9.45 Dinner all wk 12-9.45 ⊕ FREE HOUSE ◀ Bath Gem, Otter Ale, Butcombe ð Broadoak, Thatchers. ☻ 10 **Facilities** Non-diners area ✿ (Bar Restaurant Garden) ✦ Children's menu Children's portions Play area Family room Garden Parking WiFi ☁ (notice required) **Rooms** 5

CORTON DENHAM
Map 4 ST62

The Queens Arms ★★★★ INN ⊛
PICK OF THE PUBS

tel: 01963 220317 **DT9 4LR**
email: relax@thequeensarms.com **web:** www.thequeensarms.com
dir: *A303 follow signs for Sutton Montis, South Cadbury & Corton Denham. Through South Cadbury, 0.25m, left, up hill signed Corton Denham. Left at hill top to village, approx 1m. Pub on right*

Relaxing country pub where the food is worth a detour

Three miles from Sherborne, this late 18th-century, stone-built former cider house is set in a web of lanes meandering through stunning countryside on the Somerset/Dorset border. Beneath the old beams in the bar and separate dining room are old scrubbed tables set with designer china, grand open fireplaces, and leather chairs and sofas. Outside, the sheltered terrace and sunny garden are perfect for outdoor eating and drinking. Owners Gordon and Jeanette Reid provide over 30 bottled beers, draught ales from Pitney's microbrewery Moor, and local farm ciders. There's a great wine list, too. They champion high-quality local produce, measuring food in metres rather than miles. A starter of leek, parmesan and mustard seed tart with beetroot purée sets the scene for mains of local venison Wellington, or pan-fried cod with Devon crab mash, brown shrimps and cockle butter. Events include a beer festival. Spacious guest rooms overlook the rolling countryside.

Open all day all wk **Food** Lunch all wk 12-3 Dinner Mon-Sat 6-10, Sun 6-9 Av main course £12.50 Restaurant menu available all wk ⊕ FREE HOUSE ◀ Moor Revival & Nor'Hop, Otter Ale, Bath Ales Gem, Guest ales Ŏ Thatchers Gold, Hecks, Wilkins Farmhouse, Burrow Hill, The Orchard Pig. ₹ 14 **Facilities** Non-diners area ✿ (Bar Garden) ♦♦ Children's menu Children's portions Garden ☐ Beer festival Parking WiFi **Rooms** 8

CRANMORE
Map 4 ST64

Strode Arms

tel: 01749 880450 **BA4 4QJ**
email: info@strodearms.co.uk
dir: *S of A361, 3.5m E of Shepton Mallet, 7.5m W of Frome*

Country pub in pretty setting

On warm days the terrace of this handsome stone coaching inn overflows with happy punters clutching well kept pints of Strong in the Arm or Henry's Original IPA as they gaze over the village duck pond. Inside all is reassuringly traditional with a spacious bar and a cosy country character with log fires. Starters include warm salad of black pudding, smoked bacon and crispy potatoes with dressed leaves and poached egg; mains include slow roasted feather blade of beef, roasted shallots, buttery garlic potato cake, local spinach and thyme jus. There are several price conscious offers and a good value menu for children as well.

Open all wk 11.30-3 6-11 **Food** Lunch all wk 12-2 Dinner Mon-Sat 6-9 Av main course £9 Set menu available ⊕ WADWORTH ◀ Horizon, Henry's Original IPA, 6X, The Bishop's Tipple, Strong in the Arm Ŏ Westons Traditional. ₹ **Facilities** Non-diners area ✿ (Bar Garden) ♦♦ Children's menu Children's portions Play area Family room Garden ☐ Parking WiFi ➡ (notice required)

CREWKERNE
Map 4 ST40

The George Inn ★★★ INN

tel: 01460 73650 **Market Square TA18 7LP**
email: georgecrewkerne@btconnect.com **web:** www.thegeorgehotelcrewkerne.co.uk
dir: *Phone for detailed directions*

400 years of hospitality in busy market town

Situated in the heart of Crewkerne, The George has been welcoming travellers since 1541, though the present hamstone building dates from 1832, and the current

landlord has held sway since 1994. Thatchers Gold cider sits alongside the real ales in the bar, while the kitchen produces an array of popular dishes for bar snacks and more substantial meals from the daily specials board. Vegetarian and vegan meals are always available. Comfortable en suite bedrooms are traditionally styled and include four-poster rooms.

Open all day all wk **Food** Lunch all wk 12-2 Dinner all wk 7-9 Restaurant menu available all wk ⊕ FREE HOUSE ◀ St Austell Trelawny, Dartmoor Legend, Boddingtons Ŏ Thatchers Gold. ₹ 8 **Facilities** Non-diners area ♦♦ Children's menu Children's portions Outside area ☐ WiFi ➡ **Rooms** 13

The Manor Arms

tel: 01460 72901 **North Perrott TA18 7SG**
email: bookings@manorarms.net
dir: *From A30 (Yeovil/Honiton) take A3066 towards Bridport. North Perrott 1.5m*

A bastion of tradition in the country

On the Dorset/Somerset border, this 16th-century Grade II listed pub and its neighbouring hamstone cottages overlook the green in the conservation village of North Perrott. The inn has been lovingly restored and an inglenook fireplace, flagstone floors and oak beams are among the charming features inside. Dogs and children are welcome, there's a good beer garden for warmer days, and there are plenty of rambling opportunities on the doorstep. To accompany ales like Butcombe, and Ashton Press cider, expect wholesome traditional food such as steak and ale pie, pan-fried lamb's liver and beer-battered cod. There is also a specials board, and every month sees a different theme night.

Open 12-3 6-11 Closed Sun eve **Food** Lunch all wk 12-2 Dinner Mon-Sat 6.30-9 ⊕ FREE HOUSE ◀ Butcombe, St Austell Trelawny, Fuller's London Pride Ŏ Ashton Press. **Facilities** Non-diners area ✿ (Bar Garden) ♦♦ Children's menu Children's portions Garden ☐ Parking WiFi

CROSCOMBE
Map 4 ST54

The George Inn

tel: 01749 342306 & 345189 **Long St BA5 3QH**
email: pg@thegeorgeinn.co.uk
dir: *On A371 midway between Shepton Mallet & Wells*

Renovated pub with traditional food and two beer festivals

This 17th-century village pub has received ongoing renovations since the Graham family bought it 14 years ago and is now a great place to enjoy local ales such as Moor Revival in the bar with its real hops, large inglenook fireplace and family grandfather clock. There are real ciders too, including Orchard Pig and Thatchers Gold, and diners can enjoy locally sourced quality food, with daily specials complementing old favourites such as smoked haddock fishcakes; steak and ale pie; and local rump steaks. The garden terrace incorporates an all-weather patio and children's area next to a function room and wood-fired pizza oven. There are beer festivals on the Spring Bank Holiday and in October, and a curry buffet the last Thursday of each month.

Open all wk 12-3 6-11 **Food** Lunch Mon-Sat 12-2.15, Sun 12-2.30 Dinner all wk 6-9 ⊕ FREE HOUSE ◀ Butcombe Bitter, Moor Revival, Blindmans, Hop Back Summer Lightning, Cheddar Ales Potholer Ŏ Thatchers Cheddar Valley & Gold, The Orchard Pig, Bittersweet. ₹ 9 **Facilities** Non-diners area ✿ (Bar Garden) ♦♦ Children's menu Children's portions Play area Family room Garden ☐ Beer festival Parking WiFi

DINNINGTON
Map 4 ST41

Dinnington Docks

tel: 01460 52397 **TA17 8SX**
email: hilary@dinningtondocks.co.uk
dir: S of A303 between South Petherton & Ilminster

Traditional locals' pub in a small hamlet

Formerly known as the Rose & Crown, this traditional village pub on the old Fosse Way has been licensed for over 250 years and has no loud music, pool tables or fruit machines to drown out the conversation. Inside you will find pictures, signs and memorabilia of its rail and maritime past. Good-quality cask ales and farmhouse cider are served, and freshly prepared food including the likes of crab cakes, faggots, snapper, steak, and lamb shank for two feature on the menu. There's a carvery every Sunday, and the pub is located in an ideal place for cycling and walking.

Open all wk 11.30-3 6-12 (Sat-Sun all day) **Food** Lunch all wk 12-2 Dinner all wk 7-9 Set menu available ⊕ FREE HOUSE ◀ Butcombe Bitter, Guest ales ♂ Burrow Hill, Westons, Thatchers Gold. **Facilities** Non-diners area ✿ (Bar Garden) ♦♦ Children's menu Children's portions Play area Family room Garden ⋈ Parking ⋙

DITCHEAT
Map 4 ST63

The Manor House Inn
PICK OF THE PUBS

tel: 01749 860276 **BA4 6RB**
email: landlord@manorhouseinn.co.uk
dir: From Shepton Mallet take A371 towards Castle Cary, in 3m turn right to Ditcheat

Local ales complement fine food in lovely Mendips setting

In the pretty village of Ditcheat, between Shepton Mallet and Castle Cary, this handsome red-brick, 17th-century free house belonged to the lord of the manor about 150 years ago when it was known as the White Hart. Convenient for the Royal Bath and West Showground and the East Somerset Steam Railway, it is also boasts views of the Mendips. Flagstone floors and warming log fires in winter add to the charm of the friendly bar, which serves local Butcombe Bitter and regular guest ales, Orchard Pig cider and up to nine wines by the glass. The seasonal menu may offer starters such as home-baked ratatouille with rich provençale sauce; and scallops in shells with lemon and lime dressing; followed by main courses of braised brisket of beef with creamy horseradish mash and rich Guinness sauce; or guinea fowl breast with spinach, fondant potato and Marsala sauce.

Open all day all wk Mon-Sat 12-11 (Sun 12-9) **Food** Lunch all wk 12-9 Dinner all wk 12-9 ⊕ FREE HOUSE ◀ Butcombe Bitter, Guest ales ♂ Ashton Press, The Orchard Pig Reveller & Philosopher. ♀ 9 **Facilities** Non-diners area ♦♦ Children's portions Garden ⋈ Parking WiFi ⋙ (notice required)

DULVERTON
Map 3 SS92

NEW The Bridge Inn

tel: 01398 324130 **20 Bridge St TA22 9HJ**
email: info@thebridgeinndulverton.com
dir: M5 junct 27, A361 towards Barnstaple. In Tiverton take A396 signed Dulverton. Left onto B3222 to Dulverton. Pub by river in village

Walkers' choice on the southern edge of Exmoor

'Chris from the pet shop' supplies this early-Victorian pub with gravy bones for 'all those visiting dogs'. Indeed, well-behaved dogs are welcome, as is everyone seeking award-winning cask ales, worldwide craft beers, sensibly priced wines and traditional pub food. Classics include West Country ploughman's, made with Devon Blue and Somerset cheddar; fish pie, with cod, haddock, salmon and prawns; and

home-cooked ham with free-range eggs and chips. Grazing plates of meats, and River Exe mussels are designed as both main courses or for sharing. Check out the pies too. A beer festival is held over the Spring Bank Holiday.

Open all wk 12-11 summer (Mon 12-3 Tue-Thu 12-3 6-11 Fri-Sun 12-11 winter) Closed 25 Dec **Food** Lunch all wk 12-2.30 Dinner all wk 6-9 Av main course £10 ⊕ FREE HOUSE ◀ Exmoor Ale, St Austell Proper Job, Otter Ale ♂ Thatchers Gold, Addlestones. ♀ 12 **Facilities** ✿ (Bar Restaurant Garden) ♦♦ Children's menu Children's portions Garden ⋈ Beer festival Parking WiFi ⋙ (notice required)

Woods Bar and Restaurant ◉

tel: 01398 324007 **4 Bank Square TA22 9BU**
email: woodsdulverton@hotmail.com
dir: From Tiverton take A396 N. At Machine Cross take B3222 to Dulverton. Establishment adjacent to church

Serious food and a friendly atmosphere

In the rural town of Dulverton on the edge of Exmoor, this is a bar and restaurant where food and drink are taken seriously, but without detriment to its friendly atmosphere. It's run by owners with a passion for wine — every bottle on the comprehensive list (up to £25) can be opened for a single glass. The cosy bar crackles with conversation while dishes of modern British cooking with a French accent leave the kitchen. Typical of these one AA-Rosette dishes are roast chicken supreme with rösti potato, Savoy cabbage, pancetta and Jerusalem artichoke and wild mushroom fricassée.

Open all wk 11-3 6-11.30 (Sun 12-3 7-11) **Food** Lunch all wk 12-2 Dinner all wk 6-9.30 ⊕ FREE HOUSE ◀ St Austell Tribute, HSD, Dartmoor ♂ Thatchers, Winkleigh Sam's Poundhouse. ♀ **Facilities** Non-diners area ✿ (Bar Restaurant Garden) ♦♦ Children's menu Children's portions Garden

DUNSTER
Map 3 SS94

The Luttrell Arms
PICK OF THE PUBS

tel: 01643 821555 **High St TA24 6SG**
email: enquiry@luttrellarms.co.uk
dir: From A39 (Bridgwater to Minehead), left onto A396 to Dunster (2m from Minehead)

Memorable setting for a drink or meal

Picture-postcard Dunster has featured in countless films and television series; the imposing sandstone-built Luttrell Arms plays a pivotal role at the heart of the quaint village. The inn has stood here, just a couple of miles from the beaches of the Bristol Channel, for over 700 years. One of Britain's oldest post-houses, it retains its galleried courtyard, stone-mullioned windows, wood-panelled walls and open fireplaces; from here Oliver Cromwell directed the siege of Dunster Castle, ancestral home of the Luttrells, during the Civil War. You can see the castle from the inn's hidden garden; relax here with a pint of Exmoor Ale and ponder a selection of classic English dishes from the bar menu, including perhaps a Somerset brie ploughman's lunch; or trio of sausages featuring venison and bramble jelly, herb and pork, and pork and apple sauce varieties. The restaurant menu extends into a range of steaks, slow braised shin of beef or fillets of lemon sole.

Open all day all wk 8am-11pm **Food** Lunch all wk 10-9.30 Dinner all wk 10-9.30 Av main course £10.95 Restaurant menu available all wk ⊕ FREE HOUSE ◀ Exmoor Ale, Sharp's Doom Bar, Guest ale ♂ Thatchers Cheddar Valley. ♀ 12 **Facilities** Non-diners area ✿ (Bar Restaurant Garden) ♦♦ Children's menu Children's portions Family room Garden ⋈ WiFi ⋙

PICK OF THE PUBS

The White Horse at Haselbury

HASELBURY PLUCKNETT   Map 4 ST41

tel: 01460 78873
North St TA18 7RJ
email: whitehorsehaselbury@hotmail.co.uk
web: www.thewhitehorsehaselbury.com
dir: *Just off A30 between Crewkerne & Yeovil on B3066*

Rural pub offering French and British classics

Until opening here in 2012, Rebecca and Richard Robinson were part of the London restaurant scene but, being a Dorset girl, Rebecca couldn't resist the pull of the West Country. A look at the surrounding countryside - both Dorset and Somerset - is enough to tell you why. The pub used to be a rope works and flax store, then a cider house, and now proves amenable to a repertoire that, in addition to the French and British classics prepared by chef-proprietor Richard, and chef Jonathan. Real ales are from Otter, Palmers, Teignworthy and other breweries, with ciders from Burrow Hill. The excellent local produce, particularly the abundant fine seafood from West Bay and the Dorset coast, inspires dishes that social media commentators enthuse about. You'll get an idea of the cooking style from dishes such as a starter of Dorset snails with mixed wild mushrooms, Alsace bacon on toast and bordelaise sauce, followed by ragout of brill, clams and mussels with new potatoes, lemon

oil and chives. An alternative pairing might be salad of whipped goats' cheese with beetroot, walnuts and pear, then grilled tranche of calves' liver with flat mushrooms, bacon and caramelised onions. A third course might be Agen prunes marinated in Armagnac with crème anglaise, or a selection of cheeses with home-made chutney and biscuits, perhaps accompanied by a glass of Churchill's Finest Reserve port. Given Richard and Rebecca's pledge that the "great British pub experience is important to them", they equally welcome those who just want something simple, like Saxon Splendour sausages with mash and onion gravy, for example, or Stornoway black pudding with apple and celeriac.

Open 12-2.30 6.30-11 Closed Sun eve, Mon **Food** Lunch Tue-Sun 12-2.30 Dinner Tue-Sat 6.30-9.30 Set menu; Restaurant menu Tue-Sun. ⊕ FREE HOUSE ◼ Palmers Best Bitter, Otter Ale, Teignworthy, Wadworth 6X, Sharp's Doom Bar ♨ Thatchers, Burrow Hill.♟ 10 **Facilities** Non-diners area ❖ (Garden) ♟ Children's menu & portions Garden ☰ Beer festival Cider festival Parking WiFi ▦ (notice required)

DUNSTER *continued*

The Stags Head Inn

tel: 01643 821229 **10 West St TA24 6SN**
email: info@stagsheadinnexmoor.co.uk
dir: *From A39 take A396 to Dunster. Pub on right*

Cosy, welcoming pub on edge of Exmoor

Dunster Castle dominates this historic village, the Gateway to Exmoor National Park. The inn itself is 16th century, as a fresco in a bedroom depicting Henry VIII as the devil confirms. The bar stocks Somerset real ciders and ales, including Wills Neck, named after the highest point in the Quantocks. Club sandwiches are served at lunchtime, while the main menu presents hake, salmon, prawn and smoked haddock pie; chicken rogan josh; chargrilled West Country sirloin steak; and baked venison and butternut squash in shortcrust pastry. This small inn has limited seating, so reservations for dinner and Sunday lunch are recommended.

Open 11.45-3.30 5.45-11 Closed Wed L **Food** Lunch Thu-Tue 12-2.30 Dinner all wk 6-9 ⊕ FREE HOUSE ◾ Exmoor Ale, Otter Ale, Quantock Wills Neck ⚬ Thatchers Gold. **Facilities** Non-diners area ✿ (Bar Garden) ᛭ Children's menu Garden ♫ Cider festival WiFi ▬ (notice required)

| | EAST BOWER | Map 4 ST33 |

The Bower Inn

tel: 01278 422926 **Bower Ln TA6 4TY**
email: enquiries@thebowerinn.co.uk
dir: *M5 junct 23, A39 signed Glastonbury & Wells. Right at lights signed Bridgwater. Under motorway, left into Bower Ln to pub on right*

Attractive 18th-century building in a picturesque cottage garden

The Bower Inn was converted from a private family home to a restaurant in the 1980s, then following two years of closure, it attracted the attention of Peter and Candida Leaver, who purchased and renovated it. Business is good, both in the bar (mind the tiger!), where Somerset's Butcombe and Devon's Otter real ales are served, and in the contemporary restaurant, renowned for home-made food such as grilled pork loin steak with black pepper and cider sauce; fresh battered cod with pea purée; and spinach and ricotta tortellini in white wine cream sauce.

Open 12-3 6-11 Closed Mon L **Food** Lunch Tue-Sun 12.30-2.30 Dinner Mon-Sat 6.30-9, Sun 6.30-8 ⊕ FREE HOUSE ◾ Otter, Butcombe. **Facilities** Non-diners area ✿ (Bar Garden) ᛭ Children's menu Children's portions Garden ♫ Parking WiFi ▬ (notice required)

| | EAST COKER | Map 4 ST51 |

The Helyar Arms   PICK OF THE PUBS

tel: 01935 862332 **Moor Ln BA22 9JR**
email: info@helyar-arms.co.uk
dir: *3m from Yeovil. Take A57 or A30, follow East Coker signs*

Sublime inn in idyllic Somerset village

Named after Archdeacon Helyar, a chaplain to Queen Elizabeth I, the inn sits at heart of a truly picturesque village of thatched houses trimmed by colourful cottage gardens. Peek through the stone mullioned windows of this partly 15th-century building and you'll glimpse a traditional village-style old bar warmed by open fires. Step inside to enjoy a beer from one of a number of West Country breweries regularly stocked; settle in and look forward to a menu which makes full use of local produce, including Somerset game and fish from the south Devon coast which often feature on the specials board. A la carte starters include pan-fried crab cakes with chilli and lime mayonnaise; the main event may be a classic Brixham fish, chips, crushed

peas and tartare sauce, whilst 28-day hung Somerset beef makes for excellent steaks. A popular spot for ramblers exploring the tranquil countryside or visiting the NT's remarkable Montacute House.

Open all wk 11-3 6-11 Closed 25 Dec eve **Food** Lunch all wk 12-2.30 Dinner all wk 6.30-9.30 ⊕ PUNCH TAVERNS ◾ Butcombe Bitter, Sharp's Doom Bar, Exmoor ⚬ Thatchers Gold, Taunton Original. **Facilities** Non-diners area ✿ (Bar Restaurant Garden) ᛭ Children's portions Family room Garden ♫ Parking WiFi ▬ (notice required)

| | EXFORD | Map 3 SS83 |

The Crown Hotel ★★★ HL ◉   PICK OF THE PUBS

tel: 01643 831554 **TA24 7PP**
email: info@crownhotelexmoor.co.uk **web:** www.crownhotelexmoor.co.uk
dir: *From M5 junct 25 follow Taunton signs. Take A358 then B3224 via Wheddon Cross to Exford*

Dedicated to produce from the South West

A family-run 17th-century coaching inn in the heart of Exmoor National Park, the Crown is a comfortable mix of elegance and tradition. With three acres of its own grounds and a tributary of the infant River Exe flowing through its woodland, it's popular with visiting outdoor pursuit enthusiasts. But the cosy bar is also very much the social hub of the village, where many of the patrons enjoy the range of Exmoor Ales from Wiveliscombe just down the road. The AA-Rosette cuisine promises much, especially with Exmoor's profuse organic produce on the doorstep and the kitchen's close attention to sustainable sources. A typical selection from the bar menu could include steamed Cornish mussels in cider, onion, garlic and cream served with crusty parmesan and onion bread; South West beef and ale pie with bubble-and-squeak cake and vegetable panaché; and warm chocolate brownie with vanilla ice cream, chocolate sauce and toasted nuts.

Open all day all wk 12-11 **Food** Lunch all wk 12-2.30 Dinner all wk 5.30-9.30 Restaurant menu available all wk ⊕ FREE HOUSE ◾ Exmoor Ale & Gold, Guest ales ⚬ Thatchers Gold, St Austell Copper Press. ♟ 10 **Facilities** Non-diners area ✿ (Bar Garden Outside area) ᛭ Children's portions Garden Outside area ♫ Parking WiFi ▬ (notice required) **Rooms** 16

| | FAULKLAND | Map 4 ST75 |

Tuckers Grave

tel: 01373 834230 **BA3 5XF**
dir: *From Bath take A36 towards Warminster. Right onto A366, through Norton St Philip towards Faulkland. In Radstock, left at x-rds, pub on left*

The smallest pub in Somerset in a lovely countryside setting

Tapped Butcombe ale and Cheddar Valley cider draw local aficionados to this unspoilt rural gem, which was threatened with permanent closure a few years ago. Somerset's smallest pub has a tiny atmospheric bar with old settles but no counter, or music, television or jukebox either. Lunchtime sandwiches are available, and a large lawn with flower borders makes an attractive outdoor seating area, with the countryside adjacent. The 'grave' in the pub's name is the unmarked one of Edward Tucker, who hung himself here in 1747.

Open 11.30-3 6-11 (Sun 12-3 7-10.30) Closed 25 Dec, Mon L **Food** Contact pub for details ⊕ FREE HOUSE ◾ Fuller's London Pride, Butcombe Bitter ⚬ Thatchers Cheddar Valley. **Facilities** ᛭ Family room Garden ♫ Parking **Notes** ◉

| | HASELBURY PLUCKNETT | Map 4 ST41 |

The White Horse at Haselbury   PICK OF THE PUBS

See Pick of the Pubs on opposite page

HINTON BLEWETT
Map 4 ST55

Ring O'Bells

tel: 01761 452239 **BS39 5AN**
email: ringobellshinton@butcombe.com
dir: *11m S of Bristol on A37 towards Wells. Turn right from either Clutton or Temple Cloud to Hinton Blewett*

A great walkers' pub with a welcoming atmosphere

On the edge of the Mendips, this 200-year-old inn describes itself as the 'archetypal village green pub' and offers good views of the Chew Valley. An all-year-round cosy atmosphere is boosted by a log fire in winter, and a wide choice of well-kept real ales. An extra dining area/function room has been added. There's always something going on, whether it's a tour of the brewery, pig racing night or fishing competitions. Good-value dishes include beer-battered haddock fillet with chips; pie of the day with mashed potato; or Ashton cider-braised pork belly and pork cheek on a black pudding mash. Baguettes, sandwiches, jacket potatoes and ploughman's are also available.

Open all day all wk **Food** Lunch Fri-Sat 12-2.30, Sun 12-3 Dinner all wk 6-9 ⊕ BUTCOMBE ◀ Fuller's London Pride, Butcombe, Guest ales Ö Ashton Press & Still. ☕ 8 **Facilities** Non-diners area ❀ (Bar Outside area) ♦♦ Children's menu Children's portions Garden Outside area Parking WiFi ▨

HINTON ST GEORGE
Map 4 ST41

The Lord Poulett Arms
PICK OF THE PUBS

See Pick of the Pubs on opposite page

HOLCOMBE
Map 4 ST64

The Holcombe Inn ★★★★★ INN ◉

tel: 01761 232478 **Stratton Rd BA3 5EB**
email: bookings@holcombeinn.co.uk **web:** www.holcombeinn.co.uk
dir: *On A367 to Stratton-on-the-Fosse, take concealed left turn opposite Downside Abbey signed Holcombe, take next right, pub 1.5m on left*

Known for great food and glorious sunsets

From the lovely gardens of this 17th-century, Grade II listed country inn you can see Downside Abbey, home of a community of Benedictine monks. Log-fired, flagstone-floored and with tucked-away corners, this is where to find some of the county's top locally-produced food, represented on the AA Rosette menus. Typically there might be Brixham crab fritters, guacamole and pink grapefruit; breaded Stinking Bishop, salad and hot onion jam; pan-fried hake, samphire, fishcake and pesto cream sauce; pan-seared venison steak, fondant potatoes, red cabbage and forester sauce. Otter and Bath Gem real ales, and Thatchers and Orchard Pig real ciders are on tap and wines by the glass are plentiful. Catch a sunset – they can be rather special here.

Open all wk 12-3 6-11 (Fri-Sun all day) **Food** Lunch Mon-Thu 12-2.30, Fri-Sun all day Dinner Mon-Thu 6.30-9.30, Fri-Sun all day ⊕ FREE HOUSE ◀ Otter Ale, Bath Gem Ö Thatchers, The Orchard Pig, Hecks. ☕ 17 **Facilities** Non-diners area ❀ (Bar Garden) ♦♦ Children's menu Children's portions Garden ⏝ Parking WiFi ▨ **Rooms** 8

HOLTON
Map 4 ST62

The Old Inn

tel: 01963 32002 **BA9 8AR**
email: enquiries@theoldinnrestaurant.co.uk
dir: *From W into village, pub on left*

Convivial village inn with eclectic menu

At the heart of a small village outside Wincanton, this sympathetically restored modest coaching inn is now in the safe hands of locally renowned chef Tim Cordall

and co-owner Sue Bloxham. With Wessex produce to the fore, you'll be assured of tip-top beers from popular microbrewers Glastonbury Ales; an ideal accompaniment to a considered selection of tapas choices or a dish from the dependable modern European menu. Seared Dorset scallops with black pudding and chorizo, or confit duck leg with a sticky shallot sauce give a flavour of the range. Weekly steak nights and a Wednesday lunchtime OAP VIP menu both prove popular.

Open all wk 12-3 6-11 (Sat 12-11 Sun 12-10.30) **Food** Lunch Tue-Sat 12-2.30, Sun 12-3 Dinner Tue-Sat 6.30-9 Av main course £12 Set menu available Restaurant menu available Tue-Sat ⊕ FREE HOUSE ◀ Glastonbury Ales Lady of the Lake, Butcombe Ö Thatchers. ☕ 10 **Facilities** Non-diners area ❀ (Bar) ♦♦ Children's menu Children's portions Outside area ⏝ Parking WiFi ▨ (notice required)

HUISH EPISCOPI
Map 4 ST42

Rose & Crown (Eli's)

tel: 01458 250494 **TA10 9QT**
dir: *M5 junct 25, A358 towards Ilminster. Left onto A378. Huish Episcopi in 14m (1m from Langport). Pub near church in village*

The pub with no bar, but plenty of real ales

Locked in a glorious time-warp, this 17th-century thatched inn, affectionately known as Eli's, (named after the current licensee's grandfather) has been in the same family for over 150 years. Don't expect to find a bar counter, there's just a flagstoned taproom where customers congregate among the ale and farmhouse cider casks. In the four side rooms you'll find an upright piano, time-honoured pub games, books and old family photographs. Home-made food includes popular steak and ale pie; pork, apple and cider cobbler, cauliflower cheese, home-made soups and ploughman's lunches. There's a pool table, jukebox, children's play area, skittle alley and regular live music nights.

Open all wk 11.30-3 5.30-11.30 (Fri-Sat 11.30-11.30 Sun 12-10.30) Closed 25 Dec eve **Food** Lunch all wk 12-2 Dinner Mon-Sat 5.30-7.30 ⊕ FREE HOUSE ◀ Teignworthy Reel Ale, Glastonbury Mystery Tor, Hop Back Summer Lightning, Butcombe Bitter, Otter Bright, Exmoor Gold, Palmers 200 Ö Burrow Hill, Thatchers Gold, Westons Stowford Press, Harry's Cider. **Facilities** Non-diners area ❀ (Bar Garden) ♦♦ Play area Family room Garden ⏝ Parking WiFi ▨ **Notes** ◉

ILCHESTER
Map 4 ST52

NEW The Bull Inn

tel: 01935 840400 **The Square BA22 8LH**
dir: *From A303 between Sparkford & Ilminster take A37 signed Ilchester. At rdbt left onto B3151. Pub in village on left*

Unpretentious town centre watering hole for sports fans

Sitting in the heart of Ilchester's town square, the Bull is a traditional free house serving Yeovil ales and Doom Bar, along with Thatchers and Brothers Pear ciders. If the two large television screens are switched off, other amusements available are a pool table, bar football, and a skittle alley. The menu is an unpretentious choice of favourite pub grub plates, but meats are supplied by local butchers and fresh fish is delivered daily from Brixham. It's properly child-friendly too, but note that the Bull opens at 2pm, serves food from 3pm, and stays open until way after bedtime.

Open all wk 2pm-mdnt Closed 25 Dec **Food** Dinner Mon-Sat 3-9 ⊕ FREE HOUSE ◀ Sharp's Doom Bar, Yeovil Ales Ö Thatchers Gold, Brothers Pear. ☕ **Facilities** Non-diners area ❀ (Bar Restaurant Garden) ♦♦ Children's menu Children's portions Garden ⏝ WiFi ▨

PICK OF THE PUBS

The Lord Poulett Arms

HINTON ST GEORGE Map 4 ST41

tel: 01460 73149 **High St TA17 8SE**
email: reservations@lordpoulettarms.com
web: www.lordpoulettarms.com
dir: *2m N of Crewkerne, 1.5m S of A303*

Award-winning pub between the A30 and A303

A pub since 1680, there's that certain something about this handsome stone village inn that we do so well in Britain: thatched roof, secluded garden; wisteria-draped pergola tucked in next to an old Fives court. Then inside, a magpie-mix of polished antique furniture distributed judiciously across timeworn boarded floors, shiny flagstones and a vast fireplace pumping out the heat into tastefully decorated rooms. The feel is so quintessentially, dare we say it, English. The inner bar is popular with locals, not least because it dispenses pints of Branscombe Vale, Hop Back and Otter ales, and West Country ciders straight from the cask. Such a traditional interior does not mean you'll necessarily get traditional food, although if you want fish and triple cooked chips with tartare sauce, it could well be waiting for you to ask. Just as likely, though, are cured wild duck breast, pickled beets and red cabbage; or goats' cheese 'cheesecake' with red onion jam to start; venison and bacon meat loaf, soft parmesan polenta, green beans and truffle; or pan-seared sea

bream with locally foraged wild garlic risotto as a main course; then poached Yorkshire rhubarb and tonka bean pannacotta; or a fine selection of West Country cheeses served with home-made oat cakes and chutney to round things off. The set two- and three-course Sunday lunches are good value, as is the Supper Club comfort food menu served from 5-7pm each evening. There's a decent wine list, too, and a summer weekend beer festival. For outdoor dining there are white metalwork tables and chairs in a lavender-fringed gravelled area reminiscent of somewhere French, and picnic-sets in a wild flower meadow.

Open all day all wk 12-11 Closed 26 Dec, 1 Jan **Food** Lunch all wk 12-2.30, bar menu 3-6.30 Dinner served all wk 7-9.15 Av main course £14 ⊕ FREE HOUSE ◀ Hop Back, Branscombe Vale, Otter, Dorset ☼ Thatchers Gold, Burrow Hill. ♀ 14 **Facilities** Non-diners area ♦♦ Children's portions Garden ⊨ Beer festival Cider festival Parking WiFi

ILCHESTER *continued*

Ilchester Arms

tel: 01935 840220 **The Square BA22 8LN**
email: mail@ilchesterarms.com
dir: *From A303 take A37 signed Ilchester & Yeovil, left at 2nd Ilchester sign. Pub 100yds on right*

Smart hostelry close to A303

An elegant Georgian-fronted house with lots of character, this establishment was first licensed in 1686; attractive features include warming open fires and a lovely walled garden. Between 1962 and 1985 it was owned by the man who developed Ilchester cheese, and its association with good food continues: chef-proprietor Brendan McGee takes pride in producing modern British dishes such as black pudding with apricot and ginger chutney; venison steak with gin, juniper berry and redcurrant sauce; beef Stroganoff; and wild boar sausages with mustard mash and onion gravy. Bank holiday beer and cider festivals are held - contact the pub for details.

Open all day all wk 7am-11pm Closed 26 Dec **Food** Lunch Mon-Sat 12-2.30 Dinner Mon-Sat 7-9 Av main course £10.50 Set menu available Restaurant menu available Mon-Sat ⊕ FREE HOUSE ◀ Yeovil Ales, Local Ales ⋓ Westons Mortimers Orchard. ⬤ 14 **Facilities** Non-diners area ⛄ (Bar Garden) ⬤ Children's portions Play area Family room Garden ⟰ Beer festival Cider festival Parking WiFi 🚐

█ **ILMINSTER** Map 4 ST31

New Inn ★★★★ INN

tel: 01460 52413 **Dowlish Wake TA19 0NZ**
email: newinn-ilminster@btconnect.com **web:** www.newinn-llminster.co.uk
dir: *From Ilminster follow Kingstone & Perry's Cider Museum signs, in Dowlish Wake follow pub signs*

Recommended for its home-cooked food and local cider

Deep in rural Somerset, this 350-year-old stone-built pub is tucked away in the village of Dowlish Wake, close to Perry's thatched Cider Mill and Museum. Inside are two bars (serving Perry's Cider, of course) with wood-burning stoves and a restaurant, where menus of home-cooked food capitalise on the quality and freshness of local produce. You could opt for a signature dish such as fillet of salmon in a prawn and butter glaze; or perhaps stick to pub favourites like a giant Yorkshire pudding filled with pork sausages, new potatoes, vegetables and gravy. There are four guest rooms situated in an annexe overlooking the large secluded garden.

Open all wk 11.30-3 6-11 **Food** Lunch all wk 12-2.30 Dinner all wk 6-8.45 ⊕ FREE HOUSE ◀ Butcombe Bitter, Otter Ale ⋓ Thatchers Gold, Perry's. ⬤ 10 **Facilities** Non-diners area ⛄ (All areas) ⬤ Children's menu Children's portions Garden Outside area ⟰ Parking WiFi 🚐 (notice required) **Rooms** 4

█ **KILVE** Map 3 ST14

The Hood Arms

tel: 01278 741210 **TA5 1EA**
email: info@thehoodarms.com
dir: *From M5 junct 23/24 follow A39 to Kilve. Village between Bridgwater & Minehead*

Enjoyable food and beer betwixt the sea and the hills

Just an ammonite's throw from Kilve's fossil-rich beach, the Quantock Hills rise up behind this family-run 17th-century coaching inn. Real ales to enjoy in the beamed bar or in the garden include Exmoor Gold and Otter Head, plus local ciders, any of which will happily accompany a ciabatta roll, jacket potato or something from the main menu, such as pan-fried sea bass with saffron and shellfish broth; slow-

roasted belly pork with black pudding, mashed potato, roasted pear and cider jus; or classic cod and chips. Specials are chalked up daily.

Open all day all wk **Food** Lunch Mon-Sat 12-2, Sun 12-3 Dinner Mon-Sat 6-9, Sun 6-8 ⊕ FREE HOUSE ◀ Otter Head, Exmoor Gold, Fuller's London Pride, Guinness, Guest ales ⋓ Thatchers Gold. ⬤ 12 **Facilities** Non-diners area ⛄ (Bar Restaurant Garden) ⬤ Children's menu Children's portions Play area Family room Garden ⟰ Parking WiFi

---

█ **KINGSDON** Map 4 ST52

Kingsdon Inn

tel: 01935 840543 **TA11 7LG**
email: enquiries@kingsdoninn.co.uk
dir: *A303 onto A372, right onto B3151, right into village, right at post office*

Former cider house with very good food

Once a cider house, this pretty thatched pub is furnished with stripped pine tables and cushioned farmhouse chairs, and there are enough open fires to keep everywhere well warmed. The three charmingly decorated, saggy-beamed rooms have a relaxed and friendly feel. Hosts Adam Cain and Cinzia Iezzi have a wealth of experience in some of the UK's most respected hotels and restaurants, and they have made food a key part of the Kingsdon's appeal. Menus make excellent use of seasonal, local and often organic produce - maybe seared pigeon with pearl barley and cep risotto followed by pan-fried turbot with pea tortellini, baby vegetables and light shellfish bisque.

Open all wk 12-3 6-11 (Sun 12-3 7-10.30) **Food** Lunch all wk 12-2 Dinner all wk 6.30-9 Set menu available Restaurant menu available Mon-Sat ⊕ FREE HOUSE/ GAME BIRD INNS ◀ Sharp's Doom Bar, Butcombe, Otter ⋓ Thatchers, Ashton Press. ⬤ 10 **Facilities** Non-diners area ⛄ (Bar Garden) ⬤ Children's menu Children's portions Garden ⟰ Parking WiFi 🚐 (notice required)

█ **LANGLEY MARSH** Map 3 ST02

The Three Horseshoes

tel: 01984 623763 **TA4 2UL**
email: mark_jules96@hotmail.com
dir: *M5 junct 25 take B3227 to Wiveliscombe. Turn right up hill at lights. From square, turn right, follow Langley Marsh signs, pub in 1m*

Traditional pub values with home-cooked food

Surrounded by beautiful countryside, this handsome 17th-century red sandstone pub has had only four landlords during the last century. It remains a free house, with traditional opening hours, a good choice of ales straight from the barrel and a warm, friendly welcome. The landlord's wife prepares home-cooked meals that incorporating local ingredients. Popular with locals, walkers and cyclists, there's outdoor seating for use in warmer weather.

Open 7pm-11pm (Sun 12-2.30) Closed Sun eve, Mon, Tue-Sat L **Food** Lunch Sun 12-1.45 Dinner Tue-Sat 7-9 Av main course £9.95 ⊕ FREE HOUSE ◀ Otter Bitter, St Austell Tribute, Butcombe Rare Breed ⋓ Thatchers Gold. **Facilities** Non-diners area ⬤ Children's portions Outside area ⟰ Parking

---

█ **LONG SUTTON** Map 4 ST42

The Devonshire Arms ★★★★ INN ◉ PICK OF THE PUBS

tel: 01458 241271 **TA10 9LP**
email: mail@thedevonshirearms.com **web:** www.thedevonshirearms.com
dir: *Exit A303 at Podimore rdbt onto A372. 4m, left onto B3165*

Exceptional food and beers in a former hunting lodge

The small palm trees in front of this handsome, three-gabled inn by the village green must have looked a trifle incongruous in early 2014. At that time, the Somerset Levels, known locally as the Moors, were so devastatingly flooded that

Moor Revival, a pub regular real ale, must have seemed a highly optimistic name. (In fact, the name predates the floods and commemorates the rebirth of its nearby brewery). Other bar regulars are Merlin's Magic and Cheddar Potholer, while Burrow Hill and village-pressed Harry's are the draught ciders. Locally sourced dishes helping the Devonshire to an AA Rosette are pheasant breast with pancetta stuffing, and mash and curried parsnip purée; home-smoked chicken Caesar salad with marinated anchovies and parmesan; and gilt head bream with Jerusalem artichoke, fennel and Italian speck. Wisteria, acers and lavender surround the walled courtyard; croquet, boules and Jenga can be played on the terraced lawns.

Open all wk 12-3 6-11 Closed 25-26 Dec, 1 Jan **Food** Lunch all wk 12-2.30 Dinner all wk 7-9.30 ⊕ FREE HOUSE ◀ Cheddar Potholer, Moor Revival, Merlin's Magic, Otter Bitter ♂ Burrow Hill, Harry's Cider. ₹ 10 **Facilities** Non-diners area ⚓ (Bar Outside area) ⚫ Children's menu Play area Garden Outside area ⌂ Parking WiFi **Rooms** 9

LOWER GODNEY
Map 4 ST44

NEW The Sheppey

tel: 01458 831594 **BA5 1RZ**
email: hi@thesheppey.co.uk
dir: From Wells towards Wedmore on B3139. Through Bleadney. Left into Tilleys Drove to Godney. From Glastonbury & Street take B3151 to Meare, follow Godney signs

Enticing combination of ales, ciders, art and music

On the Somerset Levels and only a hippy's dance away from Glastonbury, the Sheppey sits beside its eponymous river like a cider barn crossed with a private members' club. But the ales and craft beers are reassuringly real – around a dozen to tease the taste buds. Serious ciders too – six barrels sit atop the bar, so there's no danger of running out as happened in 1976; only recently has the pub been reopened, revamped and restored. Tasty dishes from the Spanish charcoal oven include lamb tagine with apricots; and braised ox cheek in red wine. Live music, cider and beer festivals in August, and decorative artworks complete the unique picture.

Open 12-2.30 5.30-12 (Sat-Sun all day) **Food** Lunch all wk 12-2.30 Dinner all wk 6.30-9.30 Av main course £10 Set menu available Restaurant menu available all wk ⊕ FREE HOUSE ◀ Glastonbury, Cheddar Ales, Arbor ♂ Wilkins, Sheppeys own, Hecks, Harry's Cider, Tricky. **Facilities** Non-diners area ⚓ (all areas) ⚫ Children's menu Children's portions Family room Garden Outside area ⌂ Beer festival Cider festival Parking WiFi ▦ (notice required)

LOWER LANGFORD
Map 4 ST46

The Langford Inn ★★★★ INN

tel: 01934 863059 **BS40 5BL**
email: langfordinn@aol.com **web:** www.langfordinn.com
dir: M5 junct 21, A370 towards Bristol. At Congresbury turn right onto B3133 to Lower Langford. Village on A38

Traditional and international food

This acclaimed Mendip's pub and restaurant is owned by the Cardiff brewery, Brains, so expect a decent pint of SA in the bar. Brains beers are joined by local Butcombe ales in the bar, which is adorned with local memorabilia. The daily-changing menu proffers traditional dishes such as crispy whitebait, steak and chips or beef and ale pie; but masala chicken curry; sizzling beef and oyster sauce; and sizzling vegetable fajitas offer something different. There's a good choice of 24 wines by the glass to accompany your meal. The inn also offers accommodation in converted 17th-century barns.

Open all day all wk **Food** Lunch 12-9 Dinner 12-9 ⊕ BRAINS ◀ SA, Butcombe, Guinness ♂ Thatchers Gold & Katy. ₹ 24 **Facilities** Non-diners area ⚓ (Bar Garden) ⚫ Children's menu Children's portions Garden Parking WiFi ▦ (notice required) **Rooms** 7

LOWER VOBSTER
Map 4 ST74

Vobster Inn ★★★★ INN ◉◉
PICK OF THE PUBS

tel: 01373 812920 **BA3 5RJ**
email: info@vobsterinn.co.uk **web:** www.vobsterinn.co.uk
dir: 4m W of Frome

Historic village pub with Spanish twist

Set in four acres of glorious countryside in the pretty hamlet of Lower Vobster, it is believed the inn originated in the 16th century and was used by King James II and his army of Royalists prior to the battle of Sedgemoor in 1685. For lunch, choose a filled baguette, ploughman's, or a steak. On the main menu you'll find rabbit pie; Cornish hake with salsa verde and Palourde clams; and a mixed grill comprising rib-eye, gammon, black pudding, sausage, hen's egg, onion rings and French fries. The tapas menu offers roast Catalan tomato bread and Spanish meatballs. All desserts are home made, with choices like chocolate pannacotta and orange and mango sorbet. Special events like paella night and pudding night are popular. Individually furnished bedrooms are available.

Open 12-3 6.30-11 Closed Sun eve & Mon **Food** Lunch Tue-Sun 12-2 Dinner Tue-Thu & Sat 7-9, Fri 6.30-9 ⊕ FREE HOUSE ◀ Butcombe Bitter, Morland Old Golden Hen ♂ The Orchard Pig, Thatchers Gold. ₹ 10 **Facilities** Non-diners area ⚓ (Bar Garden) ⚫ Children's menu Children's portions Family room Garden ⌂ Parking WiFi ▦ (notice required) **Rooms** 4

MARTOCK
Map 4 ST41

The Nag's Head Inn

tel: 01935 823432 **East St TA12 6NF**
dir: Phone for detailed directions

Hamstone former cider house offering good grub, skittles and beer

This 16th-century former cider house is set in a lovely hamstone street in a picturesque south Somerset village. The large rear garden is partly walled and has pretty borders and trees. Ales, wines and home-cooked food are served in both the public and lounge/diner bars, where crib, dominoes, darts and pool are available. The pub also has a separate skittle alley. There's a poker evening on Thursday, and Sunday evening is quiz night.

Open all wk 12-3 6-11 (Fri-Sun 12-12) **Food** Lunch all wk 12-2 Dinner Mon-Tue 6-8, Wed-Sat 6-9 ⊕ FREE HOUSE ◀ Yeovil Ruby, Local Guest ales ♂ Thatchers Gold, Westons Stowford Press. **Facilities** Non-diners area ⚓ (Bar Restaurant Garden) ⚫ Children's menu Children's portions Family room Garden ⌂ Parking ▦ (notice required)

MELLS
Map 4 ST74

The Talbot Inn

tel: 01373 812254 **Selwood St BA11 3PN**
email: info@talbotinn.com
dir: A362 from Frome towards Radstock. Left signed Mells, Hapsford & Great Elm. Right at T-junct in Mells. Inn on right

Traditional yet stylish coaching inn

In coaching days, this 15th-century inn was the stop before Wells. Perhaps some passengers mistakenly alighted here in Mells, a bonus for the innkeepers of the day. It has a main bar, snug and map rooms, all open for classic pub food and Talbot Ale. Across a cobbled courtyard is the Coach House Grill Room, where chef Pravin Nayar's fish and meats are grilled over a charcoal fire and, on Sundays, whole roast chickens and suckling pigs are carved at table. His bar snacks – including deep-fried rabbit legs, and duck hearts on toast – are clearly no ordinary bar snacks.

Open all day all wk **Food** Lunch all wk 12-3 Dinner all wk 6-9.30 Av main course £14 ⊕ FREE HOUSE ◀ Butcombe, Talbot Ale ♂ Ashton Press, The Orchard Pig, Westons Wyld Wood Organic. ₹ 10 **Facilities** Non-diners area ⚓ (Bar Restaurant Garden) ⚫ Children's menu Children's portions Garden ⌂ Parking WiFi

The Globe ★ ★ ★ INN ◉   PICK OF THE PUBS

tel: 01823 400534 **Fore St TA4 1JX**
email: info@theglobemilverton.co.uk **web:** www.theglobemilverton.co.uk
dir: *On B3187*

Contemporary inn close to the Quantocks

The Globe is very much part of the local community, thanks to Mark and Adele Tarry, who bought the freehold of this old coaching inn, with its clean-lined, contemporary interior sitting comfortably within the Grade II listed building. Local artists display their paintings on the walls of the restaurant and bar area, whilst a wood-burning stove and a sun terrace provide for all seasons. Expect tip-top local ales like Exmoor and Otter and heady cider from Sheppy's. The extensive menu makes good use of West Country produce and ranges from traditional steak and kidney pie and home-made burgers at lunchtime, to roasted vegetable and feta tart; roast lamb with garlic, fennel and redcurrant sauce; and lemon tart with raspberry cream. Everything is home made, including the bread and there is a carefully thought-out children's menu too. Stay over in one of the comfortable bedrooms and explore the Quantock Hills and Exmoor.

Open 12-3 6-11 (Fri-Sat 12-3 6-11.30) Closed Sun eve, Mon **L Food** Lunch Tue-Sun 12-2 Dinner Mon-Sat 6.30-9 ⊕ FREE HOUSE ◀ Exmoor Ale, Butcombe Bitter, Otter Bitter, Guest ales Ö Sheppy's. ♜ 9 **Facilities** Non-diners area ♠ Children's menu Outside area ⋈ Parking WiFi **Rooms** 3

Wheelwrights Arms

tel: 01225 722287 **BA2 7HB**
email: bookings@wheelwrightsarms.co.uk
dir: *SE of Bath*

Lovely valley and village setting for old pub

Sit in the lavender-scented garden with an Otter beer, or cosy up to the snug's log fire with a glass of Honey's cider in this attractive village inn set on the slopes of the Avon Valley just outside Bath. Handy for ramblers straying from the Kennet and Avon Canal towpath walk, the accomplished menu of home-prepared, locally sourced dishes mean it's also a popular dining inn. Start with lamb raviolo and wild garlic broth or consider a sharing plate of whole oven baked camembert. Mains may stretch to seared fillet of bream with salsify, mussels and clams, whilst desserts such as Jerusalem artichoke cheesecake make a memorable finale. The extensive wine list is equally satisfying.

Open all day all wk **Food** Lunch Mon-Fri 12-2, Sat-Sun 12-3 Dinner all wk 6-10 Set menu available Restaurant menu available all wk ⊕ FREE HOUSE ◀ Butcombe, Otter Ö Honey's Midford Cider Honey & Daughter. ♜ 10 **Facilities** ♠ Children's portions Garden ⋈ Parking WiFi ▬ (notice required)

The Kings Arms Inn

tel: 01935 822255 **49 Bishopston TA15 6UU**
email: info@thekingsarmsinn.co.uk
dir: *From A303 onto A3088 at rdbt signed Montacute. Hotel in village centre*

17th-century village pub with cosy bar and good food

The hamstone-built Kings Arms has stood in this picturesque village, at the foot of Mons Acutus (thus, supposedly, Montacute) since 1632. Along with cask ales and fine wines, you can eat in several places as there are two restaurant areas, a bar/lounge, and a large beer garden which has games for both adults and children. Seasonal dishes based on locally sourced produce are offered on both the traditional bar menu and the à la carte. Perhaps try smoked trout with roast beetroot and horseradish salad; and venison steak, dauphinoise potatoes and red wine jus. There are plenty of events to watch out for.

Open all day all wk 7.30am-11pm **Food** Lunch all wk 12-3 Dinner all wk 6-9 Restaurant menu available all wk ⊕ GREENE KING ◀ Ruddles Best & IPA, Morland Old Speckled Hen, Timothy Taylor Landlord Ö Thatchers. ♜ 11
Facilities Non-diners area ♠ (Bar Garden Outside area) ♠ Children's menu Children's portions Garden Outside area ⋈ Parking WiFi ▬

The Phelips Arms

tel: 01935 822557 **The Borough TA15 6XB**
email: thephelipsarms@hotmail.com
dir: *From Cartgate rdbt on A303 follow signs for Montacute*

Pub classics in a classic setting

About 1598 Sir Edward Phelips, Master of the Rolls and the prosecutor during the Gunpowder Plot trial, built Montacute House, now owned by the National Trust. Next door, overlooking the village square, stands this 17th-century hamstone building, offering well-kept Palmers beers and Thatchers Old Rascal cider. The main menu features chef's pie of the day; honey and mustard roasted ham and free-range eggs; Somerset sausage and creamy apple mash; and pasta arrabbiata. Sandwiches, baguettes and jacket potatoes are available too. The pub, with its beautiful walled garden, featured in the 1995 film *Sense and Sensibility*.

Open all wk 12-2.30 6-11 (Sun 12-6) Closed 25 Dec **Food** Lunch Mon-Sat 12-2, Sun 12-4 Dinner Mon-Sat 6.30-9 ⊕ PALMERS ◀ Best Bitter, 200, Copper Ale, Tally Ho! & Dorset Gold Ö Thatchers Gold & Old Rascal. ♜ 10 **Facilities** Non-diners area ♠ (Bar Restaurant Garden) ♠ Children's menu Children's portions Garden Parking WiFi ▬

The Bird in Hand

tel: 01823 490248 **1 Queen Square TA3 6LT**
dir: *M5 junct 25, A358 towards Ilminster, left onto A378 towards Langport. Left to North Curry*

Low beams, warming fires, friendly service

Cheerful staff provide a warm welcome to this friendly 300-year-old village inn, which boasts large inglenook fireplaces, flagstone floors, exposed beams and studwork. The place is very atmospheric at night by candlelight, and the daily-changing blackboard menus feature local produce, including game casserole, curries and bubble-and-squeak with sausage, bacon, eggs and mushrooms. The à la carte menu always has three or four fresh fish dishes, steaks and home-made desserts.

Open all wk 12-3 6-11 (Fri 12-3 5.30-12 Sat 12-3 6-12) Closed 25 Dec eve **Food** Lunch Mon-Sat 12-2, Sun 12-3 Dinner Sun-Thu 6.45-9, Fri-Sat 7-9.30 Restaurant menu available all wk ⊕ FREE HOUSE ◀ Otter Bitter & Ale, Exmoor Gold, Cotleigh Barn Owl, Butcombe Gold, North Curry Gold Ö Parsons Choice, Ashton Press, Thatchers Gold. ♜ 9 **Facilities** Non-diners area ♠ (Bar Outside area) ♠ Children's portions Outside area ⋈ Parking WiFi

George Inn   PICK OF THE PUBS

tel: 01373 834224 **High St BA2 7LH**
email: georgeinn@wadworth.co.uk
dir: *A36 from Bath to Warminster, 6m, right onto A366 to Radstock, village 1m*

Historic pub with a far-reaching reputation

Grade I listed, this truly remarkable building was built, so historians believe, in 1223 as temporary accommodation for Carthusian monks while they constructed Hinton Priory two miles away. In 1397, the Prior granted it a licence to sell ale, making it one of the country's oldest continuously licensed inns. When Wadworth, the Devizes brewery, carried out a major restoration, it uncovered medieval wall paintings, which are now preserved, as are other interesting features like the stone-tiled roof, massive doorway, turreted staircase, cobbled courtyard and open-air gallery. There are two menus, the carte and the more pocket-friendly and informal Monmouth's. For a lighter option, a selection of ciabattas is served until 6pm. Outside, you can eat in the ancient and atmospheric courtyard and from the beer garden watch cricket on the Mead.

Open all day all wk 10-11 (Sun 12-10.30) **Food** Lunch Mon-Sat 12-2.30, Sun 12-9 Dinner Mon-Thu 6-9, Fri-Sat 6-9.30, Sun 12-9 ⊕ WADWORTH ◀ 6X, Henry's Original IPA, The Bishop's Tipple Ŏ Westons Stowford Press, Thatchers Gold. ♀
Facilities Non-diners area ❤ (Bar Garden) ♦♦ Children's menu Children's portions Play area Garden ⊓ Parking WiFi ▭

NUNNEY   Map 4 ST74

The George at Nunney

tel: 01373 836458 **Church St BA11 4LW**
email: info@thegeorgeatnunney.co.uk
dir: 0.5m N off A361, Frome/Shepton Mallet

The hub of the village's lively community

With views of 14th-century moated castle ruins, and a babbling brook and waterfall directly opposite, this rambling inn has the added attractions of landscaped gardens and a winter log fire. Run by the Hedges family, the stylish interior merges contemporary with traditional. The beamed bar has a choice of Wadworth ales, Thatchers cider and fine wines. The extensive à la carte menu changes with the seasons and mixes modern British dishes with Asian and Mediterranean influences: Greek meze, ham hock terrine, Somerset pork belly, stone-baked pizzas, king prawn linguine. Sandwiches are available at lunchtime and there are roasts on Sundays.

Open all day all wk **Food** Lunch all wk 12-2.30 Dinner all wk 7-9.30 ⊕ WADWORTH ◀ Wadworth 6X, Henrys IPA & The Bishop's Tipple Ŏ Thatchers Gold. ♀ 8
Facilities Non-diners area ❤ (Bar Restaurant Garden) ♦♦ Children's menu Children's portions Family room Garden ⊓ Parking WiFi ▭ (notice required)

OAKHILL   Map 4 ST64

The Oakhill Inn ★★★★ INN ◉   PICK OF THE PUBS

tel: 01749 840442 **Fosse Rd BA3 5HU**
email: info@theoakhillinn.com **web:** www.theoakhillinn.com
dir: On A367 between Stratton-on-the-Fosse & Shepton Mallet

Mendips inn with a coveted AA Rosette

Spacious yet cosy, old but contemporary, this smart stone-built inn stands on a corner in the middle of the village. From the landscaped garden you can see the village church and the Mendip Hills; inside, the duck-egg blue interior features a display of over 20 clocks. Real ales from Butcombe and Palmers keep bar-top company with Pheasant Plucker and Lilley's Sunset ciders. Head chef Neil Creese's award-winning food conforms to free-range, organic and local-sourcing principles so, even though the menus are brief, the dishes are certainly not short on quality. Consider a three-course meal of honey-roast beetroot, goats' cheese truffles and toasted sesame seeds; pot-roast beef with Yorkshire pudding and horseradish cream; and hot chocolate pot with Midway Farm cream. The bar menu offers a good choice of steaks, as well as ploughman's, fish and chips, and sandwiches. Accommodation is available.

Open all wk 12-3 5-11 (Sat-Sun 12-12) **Food** Lunch all wk 12-3 Dinner all wk 6-9 Av main course £13 Restaurant menu available all wk ⊕ FREE HOUSE ◀ Butcombe Bitter, Palmers, Guest ale Ŏ Pheasant Plucker, Lilley's Sunset. ♀
Facilities Non-diners area ❤ (Bar Restaurant Garden) ♦♦ Children's menu Children's portions Garden ⊓ Parking WiFi ▭ (notice required) **Rooms** 5

OVER STRATTON   Map 4 ST41

The Royal Oak

tel: 01460 240906 **TA13 5LQ**
email: info@the-royal-oak.net
dir: Exit A303 at Hayes End rdbt (South Petherton). 1st left after Esso garage signed Over Stratton

Real ales and home-cooked food

With X-shaped tie-bar ends securing its aged hamstone walls, a thatched roof, blackened oak beams, flagstones, log fires, old church pews and settles, this 17th-century former farmhouse certainly looks like a textbook example of an English country pub. First licensed in the 1850s, the bar dispenses real ales from Hall & Woodhouse in Blandford, Dorset. With different prices for small or normal appetites, home-cooked dishes on the menu range from chicken tikka lahoori, via salmon en croûte, to beef and bacon pie. Added attractions are the good value two-course set lunch menu, large patio, children's play area and barbecue.

Open Tue-Sun Closed Mon **Food** Lunch Tue-Sun 12-2 Dinner Tue-Sun 6-9 Set menu available ⊕ HALL & WOODHOUSE ◀ Badger Dorset Best, Tanglefoot, K&B Sussex.
Facilities Non-diners area ❤ (Bar Garden) ♦♦ Children's menu Children's portions Play area Family room Garden Parking

PITNEY   Map 4 ST42

The Halfway House

tel: 01458 252513 **TA10 9AB**
dir: On B3153, 2m from Langport & Somerton

One for lovers of real ales and ciders

A delightfully old fashioned rural pub, The Halfway House has three homely rooms boasting open fires, books and traditional games, but no music or electronic games. This free house is largely dedicated to the promotion of quality brews, with an annual beer festival in March and cider festival in August. Eight to twelve top ales and ciders are served, including Otter Ale, Teignworthy and Kingston Black cider. The home-cooked rustic fare is made using local ingredients. Sandwiches, jacket potatoes, ploughman's and soups are served at lunchtimes, while a great range of curries and specials are available for dinner. Sundays lunches stretch from 1 until 5.

Open all wk 11.30-3 4.30-11 (Fri 11.30-3 4.30-12 Sat-Sun all day) **Food** Lunch Mon-Sat 12-2.30, Sun 1-5 Dinner Mon-Sat 7-9.30 Av main course £8.95 ⊕ FREE HOUSE ◀ Butcombe Bitter, Otter Ale, Hop Back Summer Lightning, Moor Northern Star, Teignworthy Ŏ Kingston Black, Burrow Hill, Wilkins Farmhouse, Gold Rush. ♀ 8
Facilities Non-diners area ❤ (Bar Garden) ♦♦ Children's portions Play area Garden Beer festival Cider festival Parking WiFi

PORLOCK   Map 3 SS84

The Bottom Ship

tel: 01643 863288 **Porlock Weir TA24 8PB**
email: enquiries@shipinnporlockweir.co.uk
dir: Phone for detailed directions

Thatched inn at lovely Porlock Weir location

Enjoy superb views across the Bristol Channel to south Wales from the suntrap terrace at this thatched waterside pub, best enjoyed following a coastal path stroll. Exmoor ales are the mainstay in the beamed bar, with a couple of real ciders also on tap. Home-made food using fresh local produce includes most pub favourites, from deep-fried whitebait to steak and ale pie. Children have their own menu and dogs are welcome. Don't miss the music and ale festival in early July.

Open all day all wk **Food** Lunch all wk 12-2.45 Dinner all wk 6-8.45 ⊕ FREE HOUSE ◀ Exmoor Ale & Stag, Otter Amber, St Austell Trelawny, Sharp's Doom Bar Ŏ Thatchers.
Facilities Non-diners area ❤ (Bar Garden) ♦♦ Children's menu Children's portions Garden ⊓ Beer festival Cider festival Parking ▭

PORLOCK *continued*

The Ship Inn

tel: 01643 862507 **High St TA24 8QD**
email: enquiries@shipinnporlock.co.uk
dir: *A358 to Williton, then A39 to Porlock. 6m from Minehead*

Picture-postcard inn with sea-faring tales to tell

Reputedly one of the oldest inns on Exmoor, this 13th-century free house stands at the foot of Porlock's notorious hill, where Exmoor tumbles into the sea. In the past it's attracted the sinister attentions of Nelson's press gang, but now its thatched roof and traditional interior provide a more welcoming atmosphere. Regularly changing menus include an appealing selection of hot and cold baguettes, and hot dishes from home-made beef casserole with dumplings to risotto of the day. There's also a beer garden and children's play area.

Open all day all wk **Food** Lunch all wk 12-2.30 Dinner all wk 6-9 ⊕ FREE HOUSE ◀ St Austell Tribute & Proper Job, Exmoor Ale, Cotleigh Tawny Owl, Otter ♂ Thatchers & Cheddar Valley. **Facilities** Non-diners area ✿ (Bar Garden) ♦♦ Children's menu Children's portions Play area Garden ☴ Parking WiFi ▰

RODE ▐   Map 4 ST85

The Mill at Rode

tel: 01373 831100 **BA11 6AG**
email: mill@butcombe.com
dir: *6m S of Bath*

Impressive riverside building with alfresco eating terrace

A converted grist mill on the banks of the beautiful River Frome, this magnificent multi-storeyed Georgian building sits in its own landscaped grounds in the rural hinterland south of Bath. The dining-terrace overhangs the rushing waters, a great location in which to indulge in local beers or select from the West Country-based menu; maybe terrine of local game with apple chutney and warm toast, followed by fillets of Cornish plaice stuffed with mushrooms and spinach and topped with vintage cheddar sauce. A children's playroom offers grown-ups the chance of escape and have a peaceful chinwag.

Open all day all wk 11-11 (Sun 12-10.30) **Food** Lunch Mon-Sat 11-9, Sun 12-8 Dinner Mon-Sat 11-9, Sun 12-8 ⊕ FREE HOUSE ◀ Butcombe Bitter, Fuller's London Pride, Guest ales ♂ Ashton Press, Thatchers Cheddar Valley. ☗ 35 **Facilities** Non-diners area ♦♦ Children's menu Children's portions Play area Family room Garden Parking WiFi ▰

RUDGE ▐   Map 4 ST85

The Full Moon at Rudge ★★★ INN

tel: 01373 830936 **BA11 2QF**
email: info@thefullmoon.co.uk web: www.thefullmoon.co.uk
dir: *From A36 (Bath to Warminster road) follow Rudge signs*

Cosy interior, good ales and ciders

Just seven miles from Longleat, this venerable 16th-century old cider house is located at the crossing of two old drove roads and enjoys great views of Westbury White Horse. Sympathetically updated, the pub retains its stone-floored rooms furnished with scrubbed tables. The modern menus change to reflect the seasons, with Barnsley lamb chop with rosemary jus or Somerset sirloin steak being examples of the fare. There is a large garden with a play area, and 17 comfortable bedrooms for those wishing to stay longer.

Open all day all wk 11.30-11 (Sun 12-10.30) **Food** Lunch Sun-Thu 12-2, Fri-Sat 12-9 Dinner Mon-Thu 6-9, Fri-Sun 12-9 ◀ Butcombe Bitter, Otter, Guest ale ♂ Thatchers Gold, Rich's Farmhouse. **Facilities** Non-diners area ✿ (Bar) ♦♦ Children's menu Play area Garden Parking WiFi ▰ Rooms 17

SHEPTON BEAUCHAMP ▐   Map 4 ST41

Duke of York

tel: 01460 240314 **North St TA19 OLW**
email: sheptonduke@tiscali.co.uk
dir: *N of A303 between Ilchester & Ilminster*

Traditional village pub with plenty of reasons to visit

Husband and wife team Paul and Hayley Rowlands have now been at the helm of this 17th-century free house for more than a decade. The bar stocks good West Country ales and local ciders, and the restaurant's traditional menu pleases locals and tourists alike with home-made pie of the day, baked belly pork in apple and cider sauce, vegetable curry, beef lasagne, chargrilled steaks and lunchtime sandwiches. Gardens, a skittle alley, two steak nights a week, a Sunday carvery and a beer festival in September round off the attractions of this homely pub.

Open all day Mon 5.30-11 Tue-Sun 12-12 (Sep-Apr Mon 5.30-11 Tue-Wed 4-12 Thu-Sun 12-12) Closed Mon L **Food** Lunch Tue-Sun 12-2 (Sep-Apr Thu-Sun 12-2) Dinner Tue-Sat 6.45-9 ⊕ FREE HOUSE ◀ Teignworthy Reel Ale, Otter Ale ♂ Thatchers Gold. ☗ 9 **Facilities** Non-diners area ✿ (Bar Garden) ♦♦ Children's menu Children's portions Family room Garden Beer festival Parking WiFi ▰ (notice required)

SHEPTON MALLET ▐   Map 4 ST64

The Three Horseshoes Inn   `PICK OF THE PUBS`

tel: 01749 850359 **Batcombe BA4 6HE**
email: info@thethreehorseshoesinn.com
dir: *Take A359 from Frome to Bruton. Batcombe signed on right. Pub by church*

Local produce drives the enjoyable menu here

Squirrelled away in the rural Batcombe Vale, this honey-coloured stone inn enjoys a peaceful position with a lovely rear garden overlooking the old parish church. The long and low-ceilinged main bar has exposed stripped beams, a huge stone inglenook with log fire, and is tastefully decorated, with pale blue walls hung with old paintings. From gleaming handpumps on the bar come pints of local brews including Plain Ales Innocence. Menus draw on the wealth of fresh seasonal produce available, including surplus vegetables from local allotments. Lunches take in broccoli and Dorset Blue Vinney soup; and beer battered fish and chips. Choice at dinner extends to steamed Cornish mussels in chilli, shallot, ginger and lemongrass cream; or a more traditional home-made beefburger. Desserts include chocolate fondant with salted caramel ice cream or a board of local cheeses. Look out for beer festivals at Easter and the Summer Bank Holiday.

Open all wk Mon-Fri 11-3 6-11 (Sat 11-11 Sun 12-10.30) **Food** Lunch all wk 12-2.30 Dinner Mon-Sat 6-9.30, Sun 6-9 Av main course £10 ⊕ FREE HOUSE ◀ Butcombe Bitter, Plain Ales Innocence, Wild Beer ♂ Rich's Farmhouse, Ashton Press. ☗ 8 **Facilities** Non-diners area ✿ (Bar Garden) ♦♦ Children's menu Children's portions Garden ☴ Beer festival Cider festival Parking WiFi ▰ (notice required)

The Waggon and Horses   `PICK OF THE PUBS`

tel: 01749 880302 **Old Frome Rd, Doulting Beacon BA4 4LA**
email: waggon.horses09@googlemail.com
dir: *1.5m NE of Shepton Mallet. From Shepton Mallet take A37 N towards Bristol. At x-rds right into Old Frome Rd (follow brown pub sign)*

Traditional home-cooked dishes in the Mendips

Sitting high in the Mendip Hills with views over Glastonbury is this pretty, whitewashed building with leaded windows. Once a coaching inn in the 18th century, it is now a family-run pub with a large enclosed garden, where drinks and meals can be enjoyed outside in fine weather. A varying range of local real beers and ciders are served alongside traditional home-cooked dishes. You could begin with prawns in filo pastry; or a pot of mushrooms, bacon and cheese, followed by scampi and chips; lasagne; faggots in onion gravy; or chicken breast in a tarragon or mushroom sauce. Baguettes, jacket potatoes, ploughman's and other light bites are available at lunchtime. Children are most welcome, and the building is accessible for wheelchairs. There are regular (motor) bike nights and Italian food every Thursday evening.

Open all wk Mon-Sat 12-2.30 6-11 (Sun 12-3 6-10) **Food** Lunch Mon-Sat 12-2.30, Sun 12-3 Dinner Mon-Sat 6-9, Sun 6-8 ⊕ FREE HOUSE ◙ Butcombe, Box Steam Brewery Chuffin' Ale ⚲ Wilkins Farmhouse, Ashton Press. **Facilities** Non-diners area ❤ (Bar Garden) ♦ Children's menu Children's portions Garden ⚲ Parking WiFi ▭

■ SHEPTON MONTAGUE
Map 4 ST63

The Montague Inn
PICK OF THE PUBS

tel: 01749 813213 **BA9 8JW**
email: info@themontagueinn.co.uk
dir: *From Wincanton take A371 towards Castle Cary, right signed Shepton Montague. Or from A359, S of Bruton left signed Shepton Montague*

A treasure amongst the country lanes of Somerset

Located in rolling unspoilt Somerset countryside on the edge of sleepy Shepton Montague, this 18th-century stone-built village inn is hidden down winding country lanes. Tastefully decorated throughout, with the homely bar featuring old dark pine and an open log fire, and a cosy, yellow-painted dining room, the focus and draw of this rural dining pub is the careful sourcing of local foods from artisan producers and the kitchen's imaginative seasonal menus. Expect to find cask ales from Bath Ales; salads, fruit and vegetables from local farms, and free-range eggs from Blackacre Farm. This translates to lunchtime dishes like duck liver parfait and orange jelly; smoked haddock soufflé; and devilled chicken livers on toast. Evening specials might include rump of lamb with roasted garlic and parsley mash, ending with strawberry parfait and berry compôte. The attractive rear terrace with rural views is perfect for summer sipping. Families are most welcome.

Open 12-3 6-11.30 Closed Sun eve & BHs eve **Food** Lunch all wk 12-2.30 Dinner Mon-Sat 7-9 ⊕ FREE HOUSE ◙ Bath Ales Gem, Guest ales ⚲ Thatchers Gold, Lilley's Apples & Pears, Local cider. ♟ **Facilities** Non-diners area ❤ (Bar Garden) ♦ Children's portions Family room Garden ⚲ Cider festival Parking WiFi

---

■ SOMERTON
Map 4 ST42

NEW The White Hart

tel: 01458 272273 **Market Place TA11 7LX**
email: info@whitehartsomerton.com
dir: *In village centre*

Reliable stone inn set beside pretty market place

A major renovation in 2013 brought this 500-year-old historic town inn tastefully up to date. Chic modern lines blend easily with old beams, wooden flooring, matchboarding and other timeless features to produce a quality dining pub where beer drinkers aren't left on the back foot and children and dogs are welcome. Bath Ales and Cheddar beers, together with farmhouse ciders ensure the place is a thriving local; a great place to sup is the sheltered beer garden here. Diners can revel in a fine choice of dishes using West Country ingredients; Wiltshire rabbit with chorizo, or a platter of pickled, smoked, tartare and potted fish may tempt.

Open all day all wk **Food** Lunch all wk 12-3 Dinner all wk 6-10 Restaurant menu available all wk ⊕ FREE HOUSE ◙ Cheddar Ales Potholer, Bath Ales Gem, Guest ales ⚲ Thatchers Gold, The Orchard Pig, Harry's Cider. ♟ **Facilities** Non-diners area ❤ (Bar Garden) ♦ Children's menu Children's portions Garden ⚲ WiFi ▭ (notice required)

■ STANTON WICK
Map 4 ST66

The Carpenters Arms
PICK OF THE PUBS

See Pick of the Pubs on page 440

■ STOGUMBER
Map 3 ST03

The White Horse

tel: 01984 656277 **High St TA4 3TA**
email: info@whitehorsestogumber.co.uk
dir: *From Taunton take A358 to Minehead. In 8m left to Stogumber, 2m into village centre. Right at T-junct & right again. Pub opposite church*

Village local off the beaten track

This traditional free house on the edge of the Quantock Hills is ideally situated for walkers and visitors travelling on the West Somerset Steam Railway and who alight at Stogumber station. Formerly the village's Market Hall and Reading Room, the dining room is now the place to study a menu of home-cooked dishes such as Caribbean pork with apple, mango and ginger; steak and kidney pudding; or local gammon steak, egg and chips. Enjoy local ales such as Otter Bitter in the courtyard garden.

Open all day all wk **Food** Lunch all wk 12-2 Dinner all wk 7-9 Av main course £9.50 ⊕ FREE HOUSE ◙ St Austell Proper Job, Otter Bitter, Local & Guest ales ⚲ Thatchers, Healey's Cornish Rattler, Lilley's Apples & Pears. **Facilities** Non-diners area ❤ (Bar Restaurant Garden) ♦ Children's menu Children's portions Garden ⚲ Parking WiFi ▭ (notice required)

■ STOKE ST GREGORY
Map 4 ST32

Rose & Crown

tel: 01823 490296 **Woodhill TA3 6EW**
email: info@browningpubs.com
dir: *M5 junct 25, A358 towards Langport, left at Thornfalcon, left again, follow signs to Stoke St Gregory*

Family-run showcase for local food and ales

Bought by Ron and Irene Browning back in the late 1970s, this Somerset Levels pub is now run by sons Stephen and Richard and their other halves, making it very much a family-run concern. The brothers are also the chefs, responsible for its well-deserved reputation for good food, while partners Sally and Leonie look after front of house. Classic pub dishes appear alongside the more modern such as warm dressed lemon pepper chicken salad, which might be followed by crispy pressed Somerset pork belly with tangy orange sauce. Sandwiches, burgers and paninis are also on offer. There's West Country real ales aplenty and farmhouse ciders in the bar include Exmoor Ale and Thatchers.

Open all wk 11-3 6-11 **Food** Lunch all wk 12-2 Dinner Mon-Sat 7-9, Sun 7-8.30 ⊕ FREE HOUSE ◙ Exmoor Ale, Fox & Stag, Otter Ale, Butcombe, Wickwar, Guest ales ⚲ Thatchers Gold, Local cider. **Facilities** Non-diners area ♦ Children's menu Children's portions Garden ⚲ Parking WiFi ▭ (notice required)

PICK OF THE PUBS

The Carpenters Arms

STANTON WICK   Map 4 ST66

tel: 01761 490202
BS39 4BX
email: carpenters@buccaneer.co.uk
web: www.the-carpenters-arms.co.uk
dir: *From A37 at Chelwood rdbt take A368 signed Bishop Sutton. Right to Stanton Wick*

Good food and local ale in peaceful hamlet

The Carpenters Arms is well placed for visiting Bath, Bristol and the smaller cathedral city of Wells, but if you're already in one of these cities, then this quiet hamlet is equally well situated if you fancy pointing the car the other way and heading for somewhere rural. If you have your walking boots, nearby Chew Valley Lake is an established wildlife haven, where you can walk the Grebe and Bittern nature trails. A charming stone-built, pantile-roofed free house overlooking the Chew Valley, the pub was converted from a row of miners' cottages. Beyond the flower-hung exterior, in the rustic bar, you'll find low beams, old pews, squashy sofas, and precision-cut logs stacked neatly from floor to ceiling in the large fireplace. It all adds up to an appealing, music-free, chatty atmosphere. For a pint of local Butcombe Bitter, the bar is where you need to be, although you can always take it outside to the attractively

landscaped patio. The menus are changed regularly to make the best of West Country, seasonal produce, incorporated into a menu that might feature king prawn stir-fry with crisp vegetables and sweet chilli sauce; pork loin steak with fondant potato and spinach with cider apple cream sauce; and sauté of mushrooms, leeks, red onion and spinach in tarragon cream sauce topped with puff pastry. And then there are the delicious home-made desserts, especially the treacle tart with clotted cream, and the chocolate and hazelnut brownie with vanilla ice cream. The extensive wine list combines New and Old World favourites, with a lovely Chilean pudding wine available by the half bottle.

Open all day all week 11-11 (Sun 12-10.30) Closed 25-26 Dec **Food** Bar Meals Lunch Mon-Sat 12-2.30, Sun 12-9 Dinner Mon-Thu 6-9.30, Fri-Sat 6-10, Sun 12-9 Av main course £13.95 Restaurant menu available all week. ⊕ FREE HOUSE ◀ Butcombe Bitter, Sharp's Doom Bar. ☙ 10 **Facilities** Non-diners area ♦♦ Children's menu Children's portions Outside area ☂ Parking 🚐 (notice required) WiFi

STREET

Map 4 ST43

The Two Brewers ★★★★ INN

tel: 01458 442421 **38 Leigh Rd BA16 OHB**
email: richardwpearce@btinternet.com web: www.thetwobrewers.co.uk
dir: *In town centre*

A country pub in a town

This stone inn successfully achieves a balance between town local and country pub. Behind the bar, which serves cask-conditioned ales like Courage Best bitter, is a collection of unusual pump-clips. Both alley skittles and boules in the enclosed garden are taken seriously. Guests staying over in the converted stable accommodation may plan visits to nearby Glastonbury Tor over a meal of freshly home-cooked goodies, such as crispy golden whitebait; the bestselling Ohio meat pie; steak and chips; or a simple jacket potato. Children's portions are available. Puddings include Somerset apple cake and hot chocolate fudge cake.

Open all wk 11-3 6-11 (Sun 11.30-3 6-10.30) Closed 25-26 Dec **Food** Lunch all wk 12-2 Dinner all wk 6-9 ⊕ FREE HOUSE ◀ St Austell Tribute, Courage Best, 2 Guest ales Ŏ Westons Stowford Press. **Facilities** Non-diners area ♦♦ Children's menu Children's portions Garden ⋒ Parking WiFi **Rooms** 3

TAUNTON

Map 4 ST22

The Hatch Inn

tel: 01823 480245 **Village Rd, Hatch Beauchamp TA3 6SG**
email: carl@thehatchinn.com
dir: *M5 junct 25, S on A358 for 3m. Left to Hatch Beauchamp, pub in 1m*

A good reputation for quality pub food and ales

Surrounded by splendid Somerset countryside, the pub dates back to the mid-1700s and has its share of ghostly occupants. The inn prides itself on its friendly, community atmosphere and the quality of its wines and West Country beers, including St Austell and Butcombe. Wholesome home-made food is served, prepared from seasonally changing, local produce, with a good choice of snacks and meals such as breaded whitebait, vegetable chilli, chicken korma and gammon steak. There's a takeaway menu as well.

Open all day all wk 12-3 5-11 (Thu 12-3 5-12 Fri-Sat 12-12 Sun 12-10.30) **Food** Lunch all wk 12-3 Dinner all wk 6-9.30 Av main course £10 Restaurant menu available Mon-Sat ⊕ FREE HOUSE ◀ Yeovil Summerset, St Austell Tribute, Butcombe Ŏ Westons Stowford Press, Thatchers Gold. ⬤ 9 **Facilities** Non-diners area ❤ (Bar Restaurant Outside area) ♦♦ Children's menu Children's portions Outside area ⋒ Parking WiFi (notice required)

TINTINHULL

Map 4 ST41

The Crown and Victoria Inn ★★★★ INN ⊛
PICK OF THE PUBS

tel: 01935 823341 **14 Farm St BA22 8PZ**
email: info@thecrownandvictoria.co.uk web: www.thecrownandvictoria.co.uk
dir: *1m S of A303. Adjacent to Tintinhull Garden (NT)*

Excellent food served in this family-friendly inn

Three hundred years old, and run by Isabel Thomas and Mark Hilyard, this lovely pub occupies an enviable position amidst the sweeping willow trees in its tranquil beer garden. The beer pumps belong exclusively to West Country real ales, such as Butcombe, Cheddar and Yeovil, while from the wine list, 10 are sold by the glass. Locally-sourced food, much of it organic and free-range, feature on the AA Rosette menus. Typical starters might include fried duck egg and foie gras with toasted brioche; and half a pint of prawns with garlic mayonnaise. Mains could include pan-fried chicken breast with wild mushroom sauce, potato hash brown and crispy proscuitto ham; chuck and brisket burger with smoked cheddar, bacon and chips; or mushroom Wellington with cranberry and port sauce. Finish with blueberry crumble tart with crème anglaise or a board of West Country cheeses. Five spacious, well-equipped bedrooms complete the picture.

Open all wk 10-4 5.30-late **Food** Lunch all wk 12-2.30 Dinner Mon-Sat 6.30-9.30 ⊕ FREE HOUSE ◀ Sharp's Doom Bar, Butcombe, Cheddar, Cotleigh, Yeovil Ŏ Ashton Press. ⬤ 10 **Facilities** Non-diners area ♦♦ Children's menu Children's portions Garden ⋒ Parking WiFi **Rooms** 5

TRISCOMBE

Map 4 ST13

The Blue Ball Inn
PICK OF THE PUBS

tel: 01984 618242 **TA4 3HE**
email: enq@blueballinn.info
dir: *From Taunton take A358 past Bishops Lydeard towards Minehead*

Inventive dishes with top quality, traceable ingredients

Although the 18th-century Blue Ball is still down the same narrow lane in the Quantock Hills, some years ago it moved across the road to the pretty thatched barn, which was converted into a pub. The inn looks south to the Brendon Hills and serves regional ales such as Quantock Nightjar and Box Steam Chuffin, plus Thatchers and Mad Apple ciders. Here, they care a lot about the produce they buy, "reliably sourced, fully traceable and cooked to order" they say. Lunch might consist of Blapas (Blue Ball tapas), followed by braised pork chop, and dark chocolate pudding to finish; or a filled country roll. The frequently changing dinner menu could offer carpaccio of venison, shaved fennel salad and blackberry dressing; breasts of Quantock pigeon, cabbage Charlotte, truffle potato purée and a little pigeon pie; and steamed treacle sponge, rhubarb and clotted cream. There is a separate Somerset cheese menu.

Open 12-3 6-11 (Fri-Sat 12-11 Sun 12-6) Closed 25 Dec, 26 Dec eve, 1 Jan eve, Mon, Sun eve (winter only) **Food** Lunch Mon-Sat 12-2, Sun 12-3 Dinner all wk 6-8.45 ⊕ FREE HOUSE ◀ Box Steam Chuffin Ale, Exmoor Stag, Quantock Nightjar, Guest ale Ŏ Thatchers Gold, Mad Apple. **Facilities** Non-diners area ❤ (Bar Garden) ♦♦ Children's portions Garden ⋒ Parking WiFi (notice required)

WATERROW

Map 3 ST02

The Rock Inn
PICK OF THE PUBS

See Pick of the Pubs on page 442

WEDMORE

Map 4 ST44

The George Inn ★★★★ INN

tel: 01934 712124 **Church St BS28 4AB**
email: info@thegeorgewedmore.co.uk web: www.thegeorgewedmore.co.uk
dir: *M5 junct 22, follow Bristol/Cheddar signs (A38). From dual carriageway right, follow signs for Mark, then Wedmore. Pub in village centre*

Home-from-home philosophy at pretty village inn

Owner Gordon Stevens has overseen a superb refurbishment at this former coaching inn, and in so doing original features, artwork, old and new furniture all blend seamlessly. There are four different dining areas, each with a warming open fire lit in the winter months. As it's a free house, expect cask ales from Butcombe and Sharp's, and Wilkins Farmhouse real cider. As you might hope, food is sourced as locally as possible and a winter menu reveals pheasant, apple and Calvados pâté, onion confit; venison and winter root vegetable stew, wilted spinach and home-made chips; home-made beef dupiaza; and sea bass, cod, lime and ginger fishcakes.

Open all day all wk **Food** Lunch Mon-Fri 12-2, Sat-Sun 12-3 Dinner Mon-Sat 6-9 Av main course £10 ⊕ FREE HOUSE ◀ Butcombe, Sharp's Doom Bar Ŏ Thatchers, Symonds, Wilkins Farmhouse. **Facilities** Non-diners area ❤ (Bar Garden Outside area) ♦♦ Children's menu Children's portions Play area Garden Outside area ⋒ Beer festival Cider festival Parking WiFi (notice required) **Rooms** 4

PICK OF THE PUBS

The Rock Inn

WATERROW   Map 3 ST02

tel: 01984 623293
TA4 2AX
email: enquiries@rockinn.co.uk
web: www.rockinn.co.uk
dir: *From Taunton take B3227. Waterrow approx 14m W. Or from M5 junct 27, A361 towards Tiverton, then A396 N, right to Bampton, then B3227 to Waterrow*

Traditional food with a contemporary edge

A back-road between Taunton and South Molton brings you to this 400-year-old, half-timbered former smithy and coaching inn, built into the rock-face beside the River Tone. Newly arrived in 2013, but now well and truly established, are husband and wife team Daren and Ruth Barclay, whose business philosophy is "to offer a more modern approach to dining… and to dispense with the set restaurant format". This doesn't mean there isn't a restaurant, because there is: it's up a few steps, with an open fire, scrubbed tables and a flexible menu. And, of course, there's a bar - dogs on leads welcome - where locals congregate on the well-worn floors in front of the log fire drinking real ales with appropriate West Country names like St Austell Proper Job and Cotleigh Tawny Owl, or Sheppy's Oakwood cider. Both eating areas share the same menu, which

Daren changes according to whatever fine local produce he can source. Far from untypical are lamb hotpot with roasted vegetables; Aberdeen Angus grilled sirloin steak with mushroom, tomato, hand-cut chips and truffle butter; pigs' cheeks braised in cider with greens and black pudding; and falafel with halloumi cheese, raita sauce, roasted butternut and pine kernels. Other dishes feature Brixham's best fish, delivered daily, such as deep-fried, beer-battered Cornish plaice. Local shoots provide the game, perhaps venison haunch steak with horseradish mash and braised red cabbage; and wild rabbit pie with woodland mushroom, truffle mash and roasted vegetables. A private dining room caters for up to 14 people.

Open all wk Mon-Tue 6-11 Wed-Sun 12-3 6-11 **Food** Lunch Wed-Sun 12-2 Dinner Mon-Sat 6.30-9.30, Sun 6.30-8 Av main course £12.50 ⊕ FREE HOUSE ◀ Cotleigh Tawny Owl, St Austell Proper Job & Tribute Ö Sheppy's Oakwood, Thatchers Gold. ♑ 10
Facilities Non-diners area ✿ (Bar Outside area) ♦♦ Children's menu Outside area ⩎ Parking WiFi 🚐 (notice required)

WEDMORE continued

NEW The Swan

tel: 01934 710337 **Cheddar Rd BS28 4EQ**
email: info@theswanwedmore.com
dir: In village centre

Busy village pub with all day food

Open fires, stripped wood floors and big mirrors now greet visitors to what in the early 1700s was a beer house, then by the mid 19th century had developed into a hotel. It's a free house, which allows boss Richard Hamblin to stock the bar with Cheddar Ales Potholer, Bath Ales Gem and Thatchers Gold cider. In the kitchen, head chef Tom Blake, ex-River Cottage Canteen, is now in charge of a team producing cider-steamed Dorset clams with watercress, soy and peanut dressing; merguez-spiced chickpea and butternut stew; and chargrilled Somerset rib-eye steak, roasted garlic and parsley butter, and hand-cut chips.

Open all day all wk **Food** Contact pub for details Av main course £10 Restaurant menu available all wk ⊕ FREE HOUSE ◼ Cheddar Ales Potholer, Bath Ales Gem ⚬ Thatchers Gold. ♟ 12 **Facilities** Non-diners area ❀ (Bar Garden) ♦ Children's menu Children's portions Garden ⌁ Parking WiFi

---

▐ WELLS   Map 4 ST54

The City Arms

tel: 01749 673916 **69 High St BA5 2AG**
email: cityofwellspubcoltd@hotmail.com
dir: On corner of Queen St & Lower High St

Cathedral city gem with a colourful past

Once the city jail, this pink-washed pub then became an abattoir. Owner Penny Lee says some people would argue that it was therefore only a matter of time before it became a hostelry. A true free house, it offers seven real ales, some rarely encountered outside Somerset, three draught ciders, and a good choice of wines and champagnes by the glass. Fresh local produce is paramount, with the menu offering creamy fish pie; lean-cut steak and ale pie; home-cooked honey- and mustard-glazed ham; and vegetarian options. The weekly-changing specials board incorporates fresh fish and speciality dishes, such as Somerset chicken casserole.

Open all wk 9am-11pm (Fri-Sat 9am-mdnt Sun 10am-11pm) **Food** Lunch all wk 12-9.30 Dinner all wk 12-9.30 ⊕ FREE HOUSE ◼ Cheddar Potholer, Quantock Ale & Rorke's Drift, Glastonbury Hedge Monkey & Golden Chalice ⚬ Ashton Press, Addlestones, Soap Dodger. ♟ 10 **Facilities** Non-diners area ❀ (Bar Garden) ♦ Children's menu Children's portions Family room Garden WiFi ⌁

The Crown at Wells ★★★★ INN

tel: 01749 673457 **Market Place BA5 2RP**
email: eat@crownatwells.co.uk **web:** www.crownatwells.co.uk
dir: On entering Wells follow signs for Hotels & Deliveries. Left at lights into Sadler St, left into Market Place. For hotel car park pass Bishop's Palace entrance, post office & town hall into car park

15th-century coaching inn with famous links

Overlooking the Market Place at Wells and a stone's throw from the magnificent cathedral, the exterior of this 15th-century inn will be familiar to movie buffs as it featured in Hot Fuzz. The inn's comfortable Penn Barr was named after William Penn, a Quaker who preached from The Crown and who later gave his name to Pennsylvania. Menu choices include honey-glazed Somerset ham, eggs and chips; local steaks and home-made burgers, plus vegetarian options of spelt risotto with pumpkin, butternut squash and sunblushed tomatoes. A restaurant, Anton's Bistrot, is also on site and there are 15 en suite bedrooms.

Open all day all wk Closed 25 Dec **Food** Lunch all wk fr noon Dinner Mon-Sat 6-9.30, Sun 6-9 Restaurant menu available all wk ⊕ FREE HOUSE ◼ Sharp's Doom Bar,

Glastonbury Holy Thorn, Butcombe ⚬ Ashton Press. ♟ 11 **Facilities** Non-diners area ♦ Children's menu Children's portions Parking WiFi ⌁ (notice required) **Rooms** 15

The Fountain Inn   PICK OF THE PUBS

tel: 01749 672317 **1 Saint Thomas St BA5 2UU**
email: eat@fountaininn.co.uk
dir: In city centre, at A371 & B3139 junct. Follow signs for The Horringtons. Inn on junct of Tor St & Saint Thomas St

Well placed for visiting this gem of a city

Wells Cathedral is a short walk away from this attractive blue-shuttered pub with pretty window boxes. The interior is just as enticing, with a large open fire in the big, comfortable bar, interesting bric-à-brac, discreet music and board games. Head chef Julie Pearce, along with co-owner Tessa Hennessey, maintains her winning repertoire of high quality, home-cooked food. Among the dinner favourites are 'Priddy (a nearby village) Good' steaks and sausages; slow-roasted lamb shank with fresh mint and port-wine jus; pan-fried escalope of salmon topped with saffron and dill cream sauce; and wild mushroom, pecan nut, blue cheese and cream tagliatelle. Some of these you'll also find at lunchtime, alongside baked local ham, duo of eggs and hand-cut chips. Finish on either occasion with apricot and almond tart with local clotted cream. Parking is available opposite.

Open all wk 12-3 6-11 (Sun 12-2.30 7-11) Closed 26 Dec **Food** Lunch Tue-Sat 12-2, Sun 12-2 Dinner Mon-Sat 6-9, Sun 7-11 ⊕ PUNCH TAVERNS ◼ Butcombe Bitter, Sharp's Doom Bar, Bath Ales Gem, Guest ales. ♟ 23 **Facilities** Non-diners area ♦ Children's menu Children's portions Parking ⌁ (notice required)

▐ WEST BAGBOROUGH   Map 4 ST13

The Rising Sun Inn

tel: 01823 432575 **TA4 3EF**
email: jon@risingsuninn.info
dir: Phone for detailed directions

Family-run pub serving West Country ales

This traditional, 16th-century village pub lies in the picturesque Quantock Hills and is run by the Brinkman family. After a fire the inn was rebuilt around the cob walls and magnificent door; the decor is both bold and smart. A good choice of ales and food, both sourced from local suppliers, is on offer. Main courses include venison in a port and plum sauce; and oven-roasted lemon sole topped with shrimp butter. Among the many puddings are banoffee pie, and vanilla and passionfruit cheesecake. A gallery restaurant above the bar is ideal for private functions.

Open all wk 10.30-3 6-11 **Food** Lunch all wk 12-2 Dinner all wk 6.30-9.30 ⊕ FREE HOUSE ◼ Exmoor Ale, St Austell Proper Job, Butcombe. ♟ **Facilities** Non-diners area ❀ (Bar) ♦ Children's portions WiFi

---

▐ WEST CAMEL   Map 4 ST52

The Walnut Tree   PICK OF THE PUBS

tel: 01935 851292 **Fore St BA22 7QW**
email: info@thewalnuttreehotel.com
dir: Exit A303 between Sparkford & Yeovilton Air Base at x-rds signed West Camel

Family-run village pub with good reputation for food

Just half a mile from the A303, this family-run country inn makes for an ideal pit stop for those weary travellers driving to and from the West Country. The eponymous tree provides the terrace with welcoming dappled shade on warm sunny days, while inside the black-beamed, part-oak, part-flagstone-floored bar sets the scene. As well as a carefully chosen wine list, Devon-brewed Otter real ales and Thatchers Gold cider from Somerset can accompany owner/chef Peter Ball's seasonal, locally sourced dishes in the comfortable, wood-panelled Rosewood restaurant. Typical starters of Cornish scallops with chorizo, bacon and pasta, or filo parcel filled with cheddar cheese and red onion marmalade with tomato and basil sauce might

continued

WEST CAMEL *continued*

precede main courses of smoked haddock with parmesan cream sauce, or duck breast on stir-fry noodles with soy sauce. Leave room for one of the 10 home-made desserts.

Open 11-3 5.30-11 Closed 25-26 Dec, 1 Jan, Sun eve, Mon L, Tue L **Food** Lunch Wed-Sun 12-2 Dinner Mon-Sat 6-9 Av main course £9-£20 Restaurant menu available Tue-Sat FREE HOUSE Otter Ale, Bitter Thatchers Gold. **Facilities** Non-diners area Children's portions Garden Parking WiFi

WEST HATCH — Map 4 ST22

The Farmers Arms

tel: 01823 480980 **TA3 5RS**
email: info@fawh.co.uk
dir: *M5 junct 25, A358 towards Ilminster. Approx 2m follow West Hatch & RSPCA Centre signs. Continue following RSPCA signs & brown pub sign (ignore West Hatch sign). Pub at brow of hill on left*

Traditional pub that's a walker's favourite retreat

A converted farmhouse dating from the 16th century in the countryside just a five-minute drive from Taunton. Walkers and riders are frequent visitors as the pub is on the 13.5 mile Neroche Staple Fitzpaine Herepath (meaning people's path). Either sit in the light and airy restaurant or in the beer garden to enjoy well kept Otter and Butcombe beers and food such as a starter of pork and wholegrain mustard terrine and apple purée, or tuna Thai fishcake. Then choose perhaps a main dish of bouillabaisse with grilled salmon, new potatoes, smoked paprika remoulade; or braised pork belly with bubble-and-squeak, honey roast beetroot, braised greens and cider sauce.

Open all day all wk 11am-11.30pm **Food** Lunch Mon-Sat 12-2, Sun 12-3, cream teas 3-5.30 Dinner Mon-Sat 6-9 FREE HOUSE Otter, Sharp's Doom Bar, Butcombe Ashton Press. **Facilities** Non-diners area (Bar Garden Outside area) Children's portions Garden Outside area Parking WiFi (notice required)

WEST HUNTSPILL — Map 4 ST34

Crossways Inn ★★★★ INN — PICK OF THE PUBS

See Pick of the Pubs on opposite page

WEST MONKTON — Map 4 ST22

The Monkton Inn — PICK OF THE PUBS

tel: 01823 412414 **Blundells Ln TA2 8NP**
dir: *M5 junct 25 to Taunton, right at Creech Castle for 1m, left into West Monkton, right at Procters Farm, 0.5m on left*

Pretty little pub offering hearty meals

A little bit tucked away on the edge of the village, this convivial pub is run by Peter and Val Mustoe who, for many years, lived in South Africa. Once inside you'll undoubtedly be struck by the polished floorboards, stone walls, log fire, leather sofas, smart dining furniture, in fact, by the whole set-up. At the bar you'll be able to order Exmoor and Sharp's real ales, as well as your food, but meals are served only in the restaurant or on the patio. Lunch could be springbok burger and hand-cut chips, or lamb's liver and mash, while the dinner menu offers tapas to share; grilled kingclip fillet with lemon butter; Thai-style chicken and prawn curry; chicken chasseur; or vegetarian choices of risotto, fresh tagliatelle and vegetable curry. Gluten free dishes are available too. On Sundays expect roasts, fish and chips, a curry and chargrills. Peter and Val say they are child, dog and horse friendly.

Open all wk 12-3 6-11 **Food** Lunch all wk 12-2 Dinner Mon-Sat 6-9, Sun 6-8 Restaurant menu available all wk ENTERPRISE INNS Sharp's Doom Bar, Exmoor Ale, Otter Ale Thatchers Gold, Aspall. 10 **Facilities** Non-diners area (Bar Garden Outside area) Children's menu Children's portions Play area Garden Outside area Parking WiFi (notice required)

WHEDDON CROSS — Map 3 SS93

The Rest and Be Thankful Inn ★★★★ INN

tel: 01643 841222 **TA24 7DR**
email: stay@restandbethankful.co.uk **web:** www.restandbethankful.co.uk
dir: *5m S of Dunster*

Traditional pub on Exmoor's heights

Almost 1,000 feet up in Exmoor National Park's highest village, this early 19th-century coaching inn blends old-world charm with friendly hospitality. Today's travellers are welcomed with log fires warming the bar in winter; traditional entertainments of skittle alley and pool table are at the disposal of the energetic. Menus of carefully prepared pub favourites may include deep-fried brie wedges; Exmoor sausages in red onion gravy; a 'taste of the West' cheeseboard; and Somerset farmhouse ice creams. The popular Sunday carvery represents excellent value.

Open all wk 10-3 6-close **Food** Lunch all wk 12-2 Dinner all wk 6.30-9 FREE HOUSE Exmoor Ale, St Austell Proper Job & Tribute, Sharp's Own, Guinness Thatchers & Gold, St Austell Copper Press. 9 **Facilities** Non-diners area Children's menu Children's portions Garden Beer festival Parking WiFi (notice required) **Rooms** 8

WINSFORD — Map 3 SS93

Royal Oak Inn ★★★★ INN

tel: 01643 851455 **TA24 7JE**
email: enquiries@royaloakexmoor.co.uk **web:** www.royaloakexmoor.co.uk
dir: *Follow Winsford signs from A396 (Minehead to Tiverton road)*

Local ales and seasonal produce in a delightful setting

Previously a farmhouse and dairy, the Royal Oak is a stunningly attractive thatched inn in one of Exmoor's prettiest villages, huddled beneath the rising moors beside the River Exe. Inside its all big fires, comfy chairs, restrained paraphernalia and restful decor, all the better to enjoy the twin treats of good honest Exmoor beers and rich local produce on the seasonal bar and restaurant menus, including slow-braised lamb shank with pan-fried gnocchi and red wine jus; butternut squash risotto cake; and deep-fried scampi in stout batter and chips.

Open all wk 11-3 6-11 **Food** Lunch all wk 12-2 Dinner all wk 6-9 ENTERPRISE INNS Exmoor Ale, Stag, Gold Thatchers, Addlestones. **Facilities** Non-diners area Children's menu Children's portions Garden Parking WiFi **Rooms** 10

PICK OF THE PUBS

Crossways Inn ★★★★ INN

WEST HUNTSPILL Map 4 ST34

tel: 01278 783756
Withy Rd TA9 3RA
email: info@crosswaysinn.com
web: www.crosswaysinn.com
dir: M5 juncts 22 or 23 on A38

Good beer and cider choices plus classic pub food

A family-run 17th century, tile-hung coaching inn ideally positioned for visitors to the Somerset Levels or walkers looking for a cosy respite from the rigours of the Mendip Hills. The Crossways Inn has benefited from major renovation work in recent years, including the revamped skittle alley and state-of-the-art kitchen. Warmed by two open log fireplaces, the cosy, wavy-beamed interior has an array of fine old photos of the area. Draw close to the bar to inspect the ever-rotating selection of excellent beers, often from microbreweries in Somerset, such as Moor and RCH. The beer choice increases significantly during the pub's popular Summer Bank Holiday beer festival. Cider drinkers are spoiled for choice, too, with Thatchers on tap and Rich's Cider created at a local farm just a couple of miles away. The classic food here also tends to be very locally sourced, like Somerset rump and sirloin steaks, which come with home-made peppercorn, Stilton or white wine and mushroom sauce. Cottage pie, sausages

and mash, curry of the day, and scampi and chips are all popular options, but you will need to check the specials board for the daily pie. The pasta section of the menu offers lasagne, spaghetti bolognese and, for vegetarians, roasted vegetable and four-cheese bake. Lighter meals include sandwiches, baguettes, ploughman's and jacket potatoes. Interesting desserts are toffee and Dime Bar crunch pie, and Alabama chocolate fudge cake. Under-10s can have a menu of their own. In summer, the large enclosed beer garden and children's play area comes into its own, as does the heated gazebo.

Open all day all wk Closed 25 Dec
Food Lunch all wk 12-2.30 Dinner all wk 6-9 ⊕ FREE HOUSE ◀ Exmoor Stag,

Cotleigh Snowy, Sharp's Doom Bar, Otter Ale, RCH Double Header, Moor, Butcombe, Cheddar Gorge Best Ö Thatchers Gold, Dry & Heritage, Rich's. ♉ 16 **Facilities** Non-diners area ⚘ (Bar Restaurant Garden) ⋔ Children's menu Children's portions Play area Family room Garden ⨝ Beer festival Parking WiFi 🚌 (notice required) **Rooms** 7

WITHYPOOL

Map 3 SS83

NEW The Royal Oak Inn ★★★★ INN

tel: 01643 831506 **TA24 7QP**
email: enquiries@royaloakwithypool.co.uk **web:** www.royaloakwithypool.co.uk
dir: *Phone for detailed directions*

Local food and ales in village pub with literary links

Only four miles from the historic Tarr Steps, The Royal Oak Innhas been the hub of the pretty Exmoor village of Withypool for over 300 years. During that time, the pub has welcomed some notable guests including RD Blackmore, who stayed here whilst writing *Lorna Doone*. In the two bars with their real fires and wheelback chairs, join the locals over a pint of Exmoor Gold, or head to the restaurant for seasonal dishes such as roasted stuffed crown of pheasant with juniper jus; or steak and Exmoor Ale pie.

Open all day all wk **Food** Lunch all wk 12-3 Dinner all wk 6.30-9 Av main course £12.95 ⊕ FREE HOUSE ◀ Exmoor Ale & Gold, Guest ale ♨ Sheppy's, Thatchers. ☗ 10 **Facilities** Non-diners area ✿ (Bar Outside area) ✪ Children's menu Children's portions Outside area ⋔ Parking WiFi ▄ (notice required) **Rooms** 8

WOOKEY

Map 4 ST54

The Burcott Inn

tel: 01749 673874 **Wells Rd BA5 1NJ**
email: ian@burcottinn.co.uk
dir: *2m from Wells on B3139*

Homely stone-built inn offering a friendly welcome

On the edge of a charming village just two miles from the cathedral city of Wells, the age of this 300-year-old pub is confirmed by the low-beamed ceilings, flagstone floors and log fires. Another notable feature is its copper-topped bar with five real ales and Thatchers Gold on hand-pull. Here, you can have a snack or a daily special, while in the restaurant typical dishes include chicken and basil fusilli, apricot chicken breast, sweet pepper and tomato tartlet and grilled trout fillets with prawn and white wine cream sauce. There are also specials board choices. The large enclosed garden enjoys views of the Mendip Hills.

Open 11.30-2.30 6-11 (Sun 12-3) Closed 25-26 Dec, 1 Jan, Sun eve **Food** Lunch all wk 12-2 Dinner Tue-Sat 6.30-9 Restaurant menu available Tue-Sun ⊕ FREE HOUSE ◀ Teignworthy Old Moggie, RCH Pitchfork, Hop Back Summer Lightning, Cheddar Potholer, Butts Barbus barbus ♨ Thatchers Gold. **Facilities** Non-diners area ✪ Children's menu Children's portions Family room Garden ⋔ Parking ▄ (notice required)

WOOKEY HOLE

Map 4 ST54

Wookey Hole Inn

tel: 01749 676677 **High St BA5 1BP**
email: mail@wookeyholeinn.com
dir: *Opposite Wookey Hole caves*

A top selection of beers and noteworthy cuisine

Located opposite the famous caves, this family-run hotel, restaurant and bar is outwardly traditional, although the interior looks and feels very laid-back. Somerset and continental draught and bottled beers include Glastonbury Love Monkey and fruity Belgian Früli; local Wilkins tempts cider-heads. There are plenty of lunchtime snacks and dishes such as wild boar burger, Greek salad and sweet chilli chicken stir-fry. The evening restaurant menu could see fillet of Elm's Farm beef with triple cooked chips; and winter vegetable and cheese pithivier with gnocchi, tomato and sweet chilli sauce, and rocket, parmesan and toasted seed salad.

Open all day Closed 25-26 Dec, Sun eve **Food** Lunch all wk 12-2.30 Dinner Mon-Sat 7-9.30 ⊕ FREE HOUSE ◀ Glastonbury Love Monkey, Cheddar, Yeovil, Cottage ♨ Wilkins Farmhouse. **Facilities** Non-diners area ✿ (Bar Garden) ✪ Children's menu Children's portions Garden ⋔ Parking WiFi ▄ (notice required)

YEOVIL

Map 4 ST51

The Half Moon Inn ★★★ INN

tel: 01935 850289 **Main St, Mudford BA21 5TF**
email: enquiries@thehalfmooninn.co.uk **web:** www.thehalfmooninn.co.uk
dir: *A303 at Sparkford onto A359 to Yeovil, 3.5m on left*

Long menu with something for everyone

The exposed beams and flagstone floors retain the character of this painstakingly restored 17th-century village pub just north of Yeovil. Local East Street Cream ale is one of the beers on tap and there are 10 wines by the glass to accompany the extensive menu of home-cooked food, which includes pub classics and main meals such as braised lamb shank, redcurrant and rosemary jus; seafood Thermidor; and broccoli, Stilton and mushroom lasagne. The large cobbled courtyard is ideal for alfresco dining and spacious, well-equipped bedrooms are also available.

Open all day all wk Closed 25-26 Dec **Food** Lunch all wk 12-9.30 Dinner all wk 12-9.30 ⊕ FREE HOUSE ◀ RCH Pitchfork, East Street Cream ♨ Thatchers, Westons Wyld Wood Organic. ☗ 10 **Facilities** Non-diners area ✪ Children's menu Children's portions Outside area ⋔ Parking WiFi ▄ (notice required) **Rooms** 14

The Masons Arms ★★★★ INN   PICK OF THE PUBS

tel: 01935 862591 **41 Lower Odcombe BA22 8TX**
email: paula@masonsarmsodcombe.co.uk **web:** www.masonsarmsodcombe.co.uk
dir: *A3088 to Yeovil, right to Montacute, through village, 3rd right after petrol station to Lower Odcombe*

Strong green credentials and a microbrewery

Once a cider house and bolt-hole for local quarry workers, Paula and Drew's thatched, 16th-century pub serves an exclusive clutch of real ales - Odcombe No 1, Spring and Roly Poly - all brewed for it by Drew. The couple are big on green initiatives and grow many of their own vegetables and fruit, and offer organic, vegetarian, biodynamic and Fairtrade wines. Another string to Drew's bow is the modern British cooking that lies behind the dishes on his seasonal and daily-changing menus. Typically, these include honey and rosemary lamb rump with ratatouille and minted gnocchi; red wine-poached brill, herbed cream potatoes and braised cavolo nero with smoked bacon; and sweet potato, okra and spinach pasanda, Peshwari pilau rice and mushroom bhaji. Finish with sticky toffee pudding, butterscotch sauce and vanilla ice cream. The comfortable en suite letting rooms are set back from the road, overlooking the pretty garden.

Open all wk 12-3 6-12 **Food** Lunch all wk 12-2 Dinner all wk 6.30-9.30 ⊕ FREE HOUSE ◀ Odcombe No 1, Spring, Roly Poly, Winters Tail, Half Jack ♨ Thatchers Gold & Heritage. ☗ 8 **Facilities** Non-diners area ✿ (Bar Restaurant Garden) ✪ Children's menu Children's portions Garden ⋔ Parking WiFi **Rooms** 6

STAFFORDSHIRE

ALSTONEFIELD
Map 16 SK15

The George
PICK OF THE PUBS

tel: 01335 310205 **DE6 2FX**
email: emily@thegeorgeatalstonefield.com
dir: *7m N of Ashbourne, signed Alstonefield to left off A515*

A pretty Peak District National Park pub

In a village above Dovedale, this attractive, stone-built pub offers a bar with a homely fire, historic artefacts, portraits of locals and a good choice of real ales. To one side is the snug, which, as the dining room, has lime-plastered walls and farmhouse furniture, with candlelight and fresh flowers adding an elegant touch. Emily Brighton, whose family has run The George for three generations, warmly welcomes all-comers, although asks walkers to leave their muddy boots at the door. The kitchen's passion for using locally sourced food has prompted the pub to create its own organic garden, which now produces abundant vegetables, salad leaves and herbs. A winter lunch menu might offer chicken liver parfait with toasted brioche; and trio of local sausages with onion marmalade, while dinner might start with Stilton beignet, sautéed mushrooms and spinach velouté; then market fish of the day with shrimps, mussels and Parmentier potatoes.

Open all wk Mon-Fri 11.30-3 6-11 (Sat 11.30-11 Sun 12-9.30) Closed 25 Dec **Food** Lunch all wk 12-2.30 Dinner Mon-Sat 7-9, Sun 6.30-8 ⊕ MARSTON'S ◀ Burton Bitter & Pedigree, Jennings Cumberland Ale, Brakspear Oxford Gold, Guest ale, Banks's Sunbeam ♂ Thatchers. ♟ 10 **Facilities** Non-diners area ♣ (Bar Garden) ♦♦ Children's portions Garden Parking

ALTON
Map 10 SK04

Bulls Head Inn

tel: 01538 702307 **High St ST10 4AQ**
email: janet@thebullsheadalton.co.uk
dir: *M6 junct 14, A518 to Uttoxeter. Follow Alton Towers signs. Onto B5030 to Rocester, then B5032 to Alton. Pub in village centre*

Family-run inn with a varied menu

This 18th-century coaching inn is handy for the Peak District, and Alton Towers theme park, which is less than a mile away. Oak beams and an inglenook fireplace set the scene for the old-world bar, where a rotating selection of real ales from three handpumps, and Addlestones cider are on offer. In the country-style dining room with its pine furniture and slate floor, the evening menu might include smoked salmon and pesto tagliatelle; oven-roasted lemon and thyme chicken leg; vegetable fajitas; pan-fried sea bass with stir-fried noodles; and curry or pie of the day.

Open all day all wk 11.30-close **Food** Lunch all wk 12-2.30 Dinner all wk 6-9 ⊕ FREE HOUSE ◀ Greene King Abbot Ale & Ruddles County, Sharp's Doom Bar, Guest ales ♂ Addlestones. ♟ 8 **Facilities** Non-diners area ♦♦ Children's menu Children's portions Garden ⊨ Parking WiFi

BARTON-UNDER-NEEDWOOD
Map 10 SK11

The Waterfront

tel: 01283 711500 **Barton Marina DE13 8DZ**
email: info@waterfrontbarton.co.uk **web:** www.waterfrontbarton.co.uk
dir: *Exit A38 onto B5016 towards Barton-under-Needwood. 1st left signed Barton Turn. 1st right into Barton Marina*

Large modern pub overlooking a marina

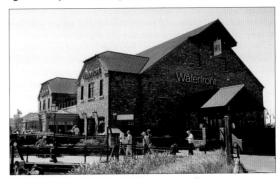

This pub is part of a purpose-built marina complex, and is constructed with reclaimed materials to resemble a Victorian canalside warehouse. Overlooking busy moorings, it offers beers specially brewed for the pub and a fair few cocktails. Dine in the contemporary conservatory from an extensive menu of snacks, oven-fired pizzas, and old favourites like chicken tikka, Barnsley lamb chop, Caesar salad, rib-eye steak and Cajun chicken burger. A walk along the Trent & Mersey towpath leads to the nearby National Memorial Arboretum, the UK's Centre of Remembrance.

Open all day all wk Sun-Thu 10am-11pm (Fri-Sat 10am-2am) **Food** Lunch 12-9.30 Dinner 12-9.30 ⊕ FREE HOUSE ◀ Waterfront Barton Pale & Marina Bitter, St Austell Tribute, Marston's Pedigree ♂ Thatchers. ♟ 20 **Facilities** Non-diners area ♦♦ Children's menu Children's portions Garden ⊨ Parking WiFi ⛟ (notice required)

CAULDON
Map 16 SK04

Yew Tree Inn

tel: 01538 309876 **ST10 3EJ**
email: info@yewtreeinncauldon.co.uk
dir: *From either A52 or A523 follow Cauldon signs. Village approx 5m from Alton Towers*

Family-run pub with an eclectic decor

Alan East has now been joined by his stepson Dan to help run this 400-year-old pub, which has been in the family for over 50 years. An Aladdin's cave of antiques and curios - including an ancient Grecian urn, penny-farthings and a pair of Queen Victoria's stockings - the Yew Tree is affectionately known as the 'junk shop with a bar'. A modest but hearty menu offers locally made pies and pasties; and made-to-order sandwiches, all ready to be accompanied by a pint of Rudgate Ruby Mild. Time a visit for the July beer festival.

Open all wk 6-11 (Fri 6-mdnt Sat 12-12 Sun 12-11) **Food** Lunch Sat-Sun 12-9 Dinner Mon-Fri 6-9, Sat-Sun 12-9 Av main course £5 ⊕ FREE HOUSE ◀ Burton Bridge, Rudgate Ruby Mild, Guest ales ♂ Westons, Thatchers. ♟ 9 **Facilities** Non-diners area ♣ (Bar Garden Outside area) ♦♦ Children's portions Play area Family room Garden Outside area ⊨ Beer festival Parking ⛟ Notes ⊛

CHEADLE

Map 10 SK04

The Queens At Freehay

tel: 01538 722383 **Counslow Rd, Freehay ST10 1RF**
email: mail@queensatfreehay.co.uk
dir: *From Cheadle take A552 towards Uttoxeter. In Mobberley left, through Freehay to pub at next rdbt. Freehay also signed from B5032 (Cheadle to Denstone road)*

Family-run pub tucked away in a quiet village

Surrounded by mature trees and well-tended gardens, this 18th-century, family-run pub and restaurant has a refreshing, modern interior and it's just four miles from Alton Towers. Ringwood Fortyniner and the more local Alton Abbey are among the beers on handpump in the bar. With a good reputation for food, its main menu is supplemented by daily chef's specials on the fresh fish and meat boards. Expect crayfish salad or Staffordshire black pudding topped with cheese and bacon to start, followed by Moroccan lamb tagine; beef and Merlot pie; or royal mixed grill. Crusty rolls and light bites are lunchtime options.

Open all wk 12-3 6-11 (Sun 12-4 6.30-11) Closed 25-26, 31 Dec-1 Jan **Food** Lunch Mon-Sat 12-2, Sun 12-2.30 Dinner Mon-Sat 6-9.30, Sun 6.30-9.30 Av main course £12.95 Restaurant menu available all wk ⊕ FREE HOUSE ◼ Peakstones Rock Alton Abbey, Guinness, Marstons Pedigree, Ringwood Fortyniner. ⬤
Facilities Non-diners area ⬤ Children's portions Garden ⌁ Parking WiFi

COLTON

Map 10 SK02

The Yorkshireman

PICK OF THE PUBS

tel: 01889 583977 **Colton Rd WS15 3HB**
email: theyorkshireman@wine-dine.co.uk
dir: *From A51 rdbt in Rugeley follow rail station signs, under rail bridge, to pub*

Try real ales from the local microbrewery

The pub's name comes from a scion of the White Rose county who was once landlord here although the heritage of this edge-of-town pub opposite Rugeley's Trent Valley railway station is lost in the mists of time. Many believe it may have been established as a tavern to serve the new railway in the 19th century and it's certainly seen a lot of life since those days, including a meeting place for farmers and soldiers. Walk through the doors today to find a panelled, wood-floored dining pub specialising in dishes using top Staffordshire produce and offering beers from a local microbrewery including, unusually, a lager. The eclectic furnishings are part of the charm, and the faux Stubbs paintings attract much comment. The seasonal menu is updated regularly, but a good range covering all the bases is assured.

Open all wk 12-2.30 5.30-10 (Sat 12-11 Sun 12-6) ⊕ FREE HOUSE ◼ Blythe ⬤ Westons Stowford Press. **Facilities** ⬤ (Bar Garden) ⬤ Children's portions Garden Parking WiFi

ECCLESHALL

Map 15 SJ82

The George

tel: 01785 850300 **Castle St ST21 6DF**
email: vicki@slatersales.co.uk
dir: *From M6 junct 14 take A5013 to Eccleshall (6m)*

Slater's beers the big attraction here

Effectively this pub is the taphouse for the family microbrewery, whose Top Totty bitter received much media coverage in 2012 when it was withdrawn as a guest ale from a House of Commons bar, because its pump badge upset the Shadow Equalities Minister. Dog-friendly and welcoming, The George serves snacks and light meals in both the open-fired bar and restaurant; among the choices could be grilled steaks; pork medallions in whisky and mushroom sauce; battered coley and hand-cut chips; and roast beetroot and asparagus risotto. A beer festival is held in the spring.

Open all day all wk 11am-1.30am (Fri-Sat 11am-2.30am Sun 12-12) **Food** Lunch Mon-Fri 12-3, Sat 12-9, Sun 12-6 Dinner Mon-Fri 6-9, Sat 12-9, Sun 12-6 ⊕ SLATER'S ALES ◼ Slater's Ales ⬤ Symonds. ⬤ 10 **Facilities** Non-diners area ⬤ (Bar Restaurant) ⬤ Children's menu Children's portions ⌁ Beer festival Parking WiFi ⬤

GREAT BRIDGEFORD

Map 10 SJ82

The Mill at Worston

tel: 01785 282710 **Worston Ln ST18 9QA**
email: info@themillatworston.co.uk **web:** www.themillatworston.co.uk
dir: *M6 junct 14, A5013 signed Eccleshall. 2m to Great Bridgeford. Turn right signed Worston Mill. Or from Eccleshall on A5013 towards Stafford. 3m to Great Bridgeford, turn left to Mill*

A restored corn mill now serving good food

Documents can trace a mill on this site from 1279. The building that now occupies this rural spot beside the River Sow dates from 1814, when it was in daily use as a corn mill. Visitors can still see the original wheel and gearing that powered the mill stone. Drop in for meals that range from ciabatta or baguette sandwiches, jacket potatoes and grills to home-made steak and ale pie, wild mushroom carbonara and roasted field mushrooms with Welsh rarebit, all washed down with a pint of Joule's Slumbering Monk perhaps? The pretty gardens, with duck pond, make a great place for alfresco eating in the warmer months.

Open all day all wk Closed 26 Dec **Food** Lunch all wk 12-6 Dinner Sun-Thu 6-9, Fri-Sat 6-10 Av main course £10 Set menu available Restaurant menu available ⊕ FREE HOUSE ◼ Morland Old Speckled Hen, Joule's Slumbering Monk. ⬤ 12 **Facilities** Non-diners area ⬤ Children's menu Children's portions Play area Garden ⌁ Parking WiFi ⬤ (notice required)

See advert on opposite page

The Mill at Worston

Worston Lane, Great Bridgeford, Staffordshire ST18 9QA • **Tel:** 01785 282710
Website: www.themillatworston.co.uk • **Email:** info@themillworston.co.uk

It is quite rare to stumble across a hidden gem as unique as *The Mill at Worston*. Nestled in some of our best Staffordshire countryside it sits beside the River Sow and has spectacular grounds, yet it is easily accessible, being just five minutes from junction 14 of the M6. The building itself is a 200 year old watermill and it has been tastefully converted retaining many features from its milling days. Thus, the lounge is dominated by the impressive original 10 foot pit wheel and full of character with enormous original beams spanning the ceiling and log burning stoves providing warmth on autumn and winter evenings. *The Mill at Worston* is cask marque accredited and has four cask ales on rotation, featuring beers from many local micro-breweries including Titanic, Lymestone and Peakstones.

The Mill at Worston is an avid supporter of local sourcing, and nearby farms and suppliers feature strongly on their menu. Starters include grilled black pudding topped with poached egg laced with a mustard dressing and oven baked field mushroom filled with welsh rarebit and served with rustic bread. For your main course their weekly specials currently feature such temptations as salmon au poivre with sauté potatoes, chargrilled vegetables and chervil hollandaise and mint glazed lamb cutlets with leek and potato cake, roast beetroot and spinach. If you've still got room desserts start from £4.25 and include the highly recommended sticky toffee pudding made to The Mill's own recipe, or for those wanting something more adventurous why not try the raspberry and basil cheesecake? Alternatively, the cheeseboard features traditional favourites, along with more local produce. Service is friendly and attentive without being too formal, making *The Mill at Worston* the perfect place to relax with family and friends.

The Mill at Worston serves food all day, seven days a week from 12pm. The venue's restaurant is open Wednesday to Saturday evenings from 6pm, and 12pm–4pm on Sundays when customers can enjoy a traditional Sunday carvery. Reservations are advisable, especially at peak times.

Directions to *The Mill at Worston* and further information can be downloaded
from www.themillatworston.co.uk.

PICK OF THE PUBS

The Holly Bush Inn

STAFFORD Map 10 SJ92

tel: 01889 508234 **Salt ST18 0BX**
email: geoff@hollybushinn.co.uk
web: www.hollybushinn.co.uk
dir: *From Stafford on A518 towards Weston. Left signed Salt. Pub on left in village*

Ancient pub with second oldest licence in England

This thatched inn is situated in the village of Salt, which has been a settlement since the Saxon period. It is thought to be only the second pub in the country to receive, back in Charles II's reign, a licence to sell alcohol, although the building itself may date from 1190; and when landlord Geoff Holland's son Joseph became a joint licensee at the age of 18 years and 6 days, he was the youngest person ever to be granted a licence. The pub's comfortably old fashioned interior contains all the essential ingredients: heavy carved beams, open fires, attractive prints and cosy alcoves. The kitchen has a strong commitment to limiting food miles by supporting local producers, and to ensuring that animals supplying meat have lived stress-free lives. The main menu features traditional dishes such as steak and ale pie; battered cod with mushy peas; and beefburger with beer battered onion rings; but also included are the still-traditional-but-less-well-known, such as grilled pork chop with

cheese, beer and mustard topping; and free range supreme of chicken with Guinness. Specials change every session, but usually include Staffordshire oatcakes stuffed with bacon and cheese; hand-made pork, leek and Stilton sausages with fried eggs and chips; roast topside of beef; or ham with sweet Madeira gravy. Evening specials may offer home-smoked fillet of Blythe Field trout with horseradish sauce; warm pan-fried duck and pear salad; Scottish mussels steamed with cider and cream; rabbit casserole with dumplings; or slow-cooked mutton with caper sauce. Seasonal puddings include traditional bread-and-butter pudding, and apple crumble. During the warmer months hand-made pizzas are cooked in a wood-fired brick oven.

Open all day all wk 12-11 (Sun 12-10.30) Closed 25-26 Dec
Food Lunch Mon-Sat 12-9.30, Sun 12-9
⊕ FREE HOUSE ◖ Marston's Pedigree, Adnams, Guest ales. ♟ 12
Facilities Non-diners area ♦♦ Children's menu Children's portions Garden ⊼ Beer festival Cider festival Parking WiFi

LEEK — Map 16 SJ95

Three Horseshoes Inn ★★★ HL ◉◉

tel: 01538 300296 **Buxton Rd, Blackshaw Moor ST13 8TW**
email: enquiries@3shoesinn.co.uk **web:** www.3shoesinn.co.uk
dir: *On A53, 3m N of Leek*

Award-winning food at a well known inn

A family-run inn and country hotel in the Peak District National Park, the Three Horseshoes offers breathtaking views of the moorlands, Tittesworth reservoir and rock formations from the attractive gardens. Inside this creeper-covered inn are ancient beams, gleaming brass, rustic furniture and wood fires in the winter, with a good selection of real ales. Using the best Staffordshire produce, visitors can choose from wide ranging lunch and dinner menus: locally-reared roast meat in the bar carvery, the relaxed atmosphere of the brasserie offering modern British and Thai dishes, or Kirks Restaurant. Delicious afternoon teas are also available.

Open all day all wk **Food** Contact pub for details Av main course £11 Set menu available ⊕ FREE HOUSE ◼ Theakston XB, Courage Directors, Morland Old Speckled Hen, John Smith's. ❢ 12 **Facilities** Non-diners area ◆◆ Children's menu Children's portions Play area Garden ⊓ Parking WiFi ◼◼ **Rooms** 26

ONNELEY — Map 15 SJ74

The Wheatsheaf Inn

tel: 01782 751581 **Bar Hill Rd CW3 9QF**
email: pub@wheatsheafpub.co.uk
dir: *On A525 between Madeley & Woore*

Attractive inn offering good regional ales

Starting life as a coaching inn in the 18th century, this whitewashed pub with flower-filled window boxes lies in the hamlet of Onneley. Although it has been modernised, the old beams and fires are still in place, making for a cosy setting to enjoy real ales from Staffordshire breweries like Titanic and Peakstones. Meat from the local farm appears on the menu, which includes whole baby chicken glazed with honey and mustard, beefburger and lamb steak.

Open all day all wk **Food** Lunch Mon-Sat 12-9, Sun 12-8 Dinner Mon-Sat 12-9, Sun 12-8 ⊕ FREE HOUSE ◼ Wells Bombardier, Joule's, Titanic, Salopian, Peakstones, 2 Guest ales Ὄ Westons. ❢ 8 **Facilities** Non-diners area ❀ (Bar Garden) ◆◆ Children's menu Children's portions Play area Family room Garden ⊓ Parking WiFi

STAFFORD — Map 10 SJ92

The Holly Bush Inn

PICK OF THE PUBS

See Pick of the Pubs on opposite page

STOURTON — Map 10 SO88

The Fox Inn

tel: 01384 872614 & 872123 **Bridgnorth Rd DY7 5BL**
email: foxinnstourton@gmail.com
dir: *5m from Stourbridge town centre. On A458 (Stourbridge to Bridgnorth road)*

Forty-plus years behind the bar

Stefan Caron has been running this late 18th-century inn for more than 40 years. In unspoilt countryside on an estate once owned by Lady Jane Grey, it retains the style of an old country pub, with church pews in the bar, where Black Country brewers Bathams and Wye Valley put on a double act. Menus variously offer chicken balti; fresh tagliatelle; Tex Mex, a rib-eye steak with chilli and mozzarella; pie of the day

with peas and chunky chips; and beer-battered cod with mushy peas. A large garden with weeping willow, gazebo and attractive patio area are the external attractions.

Open all wk 10.30-3 5-11 (Sat-Sun 10.30am-11pm) **Food** Lunch Mon-Sat 12-2.30, Sun 12.30-7 Dinner Tue-Sat 7-9.30, Sun 12.30-7 ⊕ FREE HOUSE ◼ Bathams, Wye Valley HPA, Guinness Ὄ Robinsons, Thatchers. **Facilities** Non-diners area ❀ (Garden) ◆◆ Children's menu Children's portions Garden ⊓ Parking WiFi ◼◼ (notice required)

SUMMERHILL — Map 10 SK00

Oddfellows in the Boat

tel: 01543 361692 **The Boat, Walsall Rd WS14 0BU**
email: info@oddfellowsintheboat.com
dir: *A461 (Lichfield towards Walsall). At rdbt junct with A5 (Muckley Corner) continue on A461. 500mtrs, U-turn on dual carriageway back to pub*

An ale lover's dream

Just four miles from Lichfield, this light and airy pub with country pine furnishings once served bargees on the now-disused 'Curly Wyrley' Canal to the rear. Real ale lovers can enjoy what amounts to a rolling beer festival all year thanks to an ever-changing choice from local microbreweries. Locally sourced dishes are prepared in an open kitchen and chalked up daily. Typical choices include spicy sausage and white bean cassoulet; roasted Nile perch with crushed potato and pineapple salsa; and toffee and banana crumble. There is a large, attractive beer garden to enjoy on sunny days.

Open all wk 11-3 6-11 (Sun 12-11) Closed 25 Dec **Food** Lunch Mon-Sat 12-2.15, Sun 12-8.15 Dinner Mon-Sat 6-9.30, Sun 12-8.15 Restaurant menu available all wk ⊕ FREE HOUSE ◼ Backyard The Hoard, Blythe Staffie, 3 Guest ales. ❢ 13 **Facilities** Non-diners area ◆◆ Garden ⊓ Beer festival Parking WiFi

TAMWORTH — Map 10 SK20

The Globe Inn ★★★ INN

tel: 01827 60455 **Lower Gungate B79 7AT**
email: info@theglobetamworth.com **web:** www.theglobetamworth.com
dir: *Phone for detailed directions*

Restored early 20th-century pub with a hearty menu of favourites

A popular meeting place in the 19th century, The Globe was rebuilt in 1901. The restored exterior shows off its original appearance, while interior decoration has followed design styles of the era – the elegant carved bar and fireplaces reinforce its period character; air conditioning in public areas and satellite TV are two concessions to 21st-century living. Beers from large breweries, menus of pub grub, a function room, and en suite accommodation complete the picture. Food-wise expect wraps, ciabattas, sandwiches, burgers, and jackets as well as chicken curry, scampi and chips, chilli beef nachos, and vegetable lasagne.

Open all day all wk 11-11 (Thu-Sat 11am-mdnt Sun 12-11) Closed 25 Dec, 1 Jan **Food** Lunch Mon-Sat 11-2, Sun 12-4 Dinner Mon-Sat 6-9 Av main course £8.50 Set menu available Restaurant menu available Mon-Sat ⊕ FREE HOUSE ◼ Bass, Worthington's, Holden's Black Country Mild. **Facilities** Non-diners area ◆◆ Children's menu Children's portions Parking WiFi ◼◼ (notice required) **Rooms** 18

PICK OF THE PUBS

The Crown Inn

WRINEHILL   Map 15 SJ74

tel: 01270 820472 **Den Ln CW3 9BT**
email: info@thecrownatwrinehill.co.uk
web: www.thecrownatwrinehill.co.uk
dir: *On A531, 1m S of Betley. 6m S of Crewe; 6m N of Newcastle-under-Lyme*

Great ales and food at this family-run village pub

In the picturesque village of Wrinehill, The Crown is just six miles south of Crewe and the same distance from Newcastle-under-Lyme so it's well located for visitors crossing the borders of Staffordshire and Cheshire. The Davenhill family bought this 19th-century former coaching inn back in 1977 and it is now run by Anna and Mark Condliffe, the daughter and son-in-law of long-serving licensee Charles Davenhill. With an open-plan layout the pub retains its oak beams and famously large inglenook fireplace, always a welcome feature. The bar does a good line in well-kept real ales, with always a choice of seven, two each from Jennings and Marston's, one from Salopian Ales and every week two microbrewery guests including their own 'Legend' ale; 15 wines are offered by the glass. Food is a major reason for the success of The Crown, not just for its consistent quality but for the generosity of the portions. Regularly changing menus are jam-packed with choice: from modestly priced light meals, such as home-made

veggie chilli and rice; or marinated chicken tikka kebabs with onions, mushrooms and red and green peppers, to head chef Steve's trademark minced beef or vegetable lasagne al forno or his 'legendary' beef and ale pie with a hint of Stilton. Anna, a vegetarian herself, recognises that choice should extend beyond mushroom Stroganoff, so alternatives such as Cheddar cheese and onion pasty with balsamic roasted cherry tomatoes, caramelised onion chutney and potatoes will always make a showing on the menus. For pudding, try home-made raspberry Bakewell with cream; or a slice of Bramley apple pie with hot custard. On their own menu, children will find locally produced pork and leek sausage with mash, peas and gravy; or scampi, chips and peas.

Open 12-3 6-11 (Sun 12-4 6-10.30) Closed 25-26 Dec, Mon L **Food** Lunch Tue-Fri 12-2, Sat-Sun 12-3 Dinner Sun-Thu 6-9, Fri 6-9.30, Sat 6-10 Av main course £11 ⊕ FREE HOUSE ◼ Marston's Pedigree & Burton Bitter, Jennings Sneck Lifter, Legend, Salopian, Guest ales ᗧ Hogan's, Lyme Bay. ⦅ 15 **Facilities** Non-diners area ⁑ Children's menu Children's portions Outside area ⊓ Parking WiFi 🚌 (notice required)

WALL
Map 10 SK10

NEW The Trooper

tel: 01543 480413 **Watling St WS14 OAN**
email: info@thetrooperwall.co.uk
dir: *Phone for detailed directions*

Free house on a hillside overlooking Roman Letocetum

The Trooper was built in Victorian times, on Roman Watling Street's original line, now superseded by the A5. The bar, big enough to justify two large open fireplaces, is homely and comfortable. Black Country brewer Holden's supplies one of its real ales, alongside big hitters Pedigree and Black Sheep. On offer in the modern rustic restaurant might be Peroni-battered haddock with beef-dripping chips and mushy peas; dandelion and burdock-braised pork belly; and fennel and lemongrass risotto. A large rear garden has plenty of room for children to play and, should it interest them, admire Lichfield cathedral's lofty spire.

Open all day all wk **Food** Lunch all wk 12-5 Dinner all wk 5-9.30 Av main course £12-£15 ⊕ FREE HOUSE ◀ Marston's Pedigree, Holden's Golden Glow, Black Sheep Ŏ Aspall, Westons Stowford Press. ⬤ 13 **Facilities** Non-diners area ✤ (Bar Garden) ♦️ Children's menu Children's portions Garden ⊓ Beer festival Parking WiFi ▭

WETTON
Map 16 SK15

Ye Olde Royal Oak

tel: 01335 310287 **DE6 2AF**
email: ian.lett@yahoo.co.uk
dir: *A515 from Ashebourne towards Buxton, left in 4m signed Alstonfield. In Alstonfield follow Wetton sign*

Old pub in astonishing Peak District countryside

Set in a pretty village in the White Peak; this comfortably traditional pub has been here for over 250 years. Lanes plummet into the chasm of the nearby Manifold Valley with its famous ash woods and Thor's Cave, whilst byways thread through a landscape revealing the area's fascinating lead and copper mining heritage. Beers from microbreweries like Wincle help pass the time in the peaceful beer garden or sun lounge, where ravenous walkers and cyclists can look forward to home-cooked pub grub. Sausage of the day, and freshly caught trout from the Rivers Dove and Minifold are particularly popular.

Open 12-3 6-close (Sat-Sun & BHs 12-close) Closed Mon-Tue in winter **Food** Lunch Wed-Fri 12-2.30, Sat-Sun & BHs 12-8.30 Dinner Wed-Fri 6-8.30, Sat-Sun & BHs 12-8.30 ⊕ FREE HOUSE ◀ Wincle Sir Philip, Whim Ales Hartington Bitter, Worthington M and B Mild, Local Guest ale Ŏ Thatchers Gold. **Facilities** Non-diners area ✤ (Bar Garden) ♦️ Children's menu Family room Garden ⊓ Parking ▭ (notice required)

WRINEHILL
Map 15 SJ74

The Crown Inn
PICK OF THE PUBS

See Pick of the Pubs on opposite page

The Hand & Trumpet

tel: 01270 820048 **Main Rd CW3 9BJ**
email: hand.and.trumpet@brunningandprice.co.uk
dir: *M6 junct 16, A351, follow Keele signs, 7m, pub on right in village*

Smart pub with alfresco area overlooking the water

A deck to the rear of this relaxed country pub overlooks sizeable grounds, which include a large pond. The pub has a comfortable interior with original floors, old furniture, open fires and rugs. Six cask ales and over 70 malt whiskies are offered, along with a locally sourced menu. Typical dishes on the comprehensive menu are

char sui belly pork and warm noodles salad; Cheshire Blue cheesecake with pear jelly; sharing platters; steak and ale pie; Moroccan roasted cod with spiced taboulleh; and dark chocolate and Bailey's torte. There is a cider festival and a hog roast in August.

Open all day all wk 11.30-11 (Sun 11.30-10.30) **Food** Lunch all wk 12-10 Dinner all wk 12-10 ⊕ BRUNNING & PRICE ◀ Brunning & Price Original, Caledonian Deuchars IPA, Salopian Oracle Ŏ Aspall. ⬤ 12 **Facilities** Non-diners area ✤ (Bar Garden) ♦️ Children's portions Garden ⊓ Cider festival Parking

SUFFOLK

ALDRINGHAM
Map 13 TM46

The Parrot and Punchbowl Inn & Restaurant

tel: 01728 830221 **Aldringham Ln IP16 4PY**
dir: *On B1122, 1m from Leiston, 3m from Aldeburgh, on x-rds to Thorpeness*

Former smugglers' haunt, now a welcoming pub and restaurant

If you thought bizarre pub names were a late 20th-century fad, think again. Originally called The Case is Altered, this 16th-century pink-washed smugglers' inn became The Parrot and Punchbowl in 1604 when Aldringham was a centre for smuggled contraband. East Anglian-brewed ales from Adnams and Woodforde's, and Suffolk's Aspall cider all feature in the bar line-up. The good-value menu offers chicken liver pâté with chutney and toast; steak and kidney pudding; lasagne; bangers and mash; and steaks. Daily specials and vegetarian meals also have very reasonable price tags. There are roasts on Sundays and quiz nights.

Open all wk 12-2.30 6-11 (Sun 12-4) **Food** Lunch all wk 12-2 Dinner Mon-Sat 6.30-9 Av main course £9 Restaurant menu available Tue-Sun ⊕ ENTERPRISE INNS ◀ Woodforde's Wherry, Adnams, Guest ale Ŏ Aspall. **Facilities** Non-diners area ✤ (Bar Garden) ♦️ Children's menu Children's portions Play area Family room Garden ⊓ Parking WiFi ▭

BRANDESTON
Map 13 TM26

The Queens Head ◉
PICK OF THE PUBS

tel: 01728 685307 **The Street IP13 7AD**
dir: *From A14 take A1120 to Earl Soham, then S to Brandeston*

Family- and dog-friendly hostelry in a sleepy village

Created from four cottages and first opened in 1811, this smart Adnams pub stands slightly off the beaten track deep in peaceful Suffolk countryside. A detour is well worthwhile to sample one of the cracking Southwold ales, or a meal prepared to AA-Rosette standard. Outside is a well-furnished summer garden, while inside the warm and richly coloured decor complements the traditional homely features of wood panelling, quarry-tiled floors and open log fires. The modern British menu, described as 'pub food with a twist', is based on local produce where possible, and bristles with interest. How often do you come across fricassée of golden beetroot, pak choi, russet apples and parmesan cream? Or mushroom ravioli, braised oxtail, pickled mushrooms and shallot purée? Sunday lunches are always popular and family-based events are organised throughout the year, including barbecues in the garden and a beer festival in June to coincide with the village fête.

Open 12-3 5-12 (Sun 12-6 Mon 5-12) Closed Sun eve, Mon lunch **Food** Lunch Tue-Sat 12-2, Sun 12-2.30 Dinner Tue-Sat 6-9 ⊕ ADNAMS ◀ Broadside, Southwold Bitter, Guest ales Ŏ Aspall. **Facilities** Non-diners area ✤ (Bar Garden) ♦️ Children's menu Children's portions Garden ⊓ Beer festival Parking WiFi ▭

BROMESWELL
Map 13 TM35

The British Larder ◉◉

tel: 01394 460310 **Orford Rd IP12 2PU**
email: info@britishlardersuffolk.co.uk
dir: *From A12 take A1152 signed Orford, Rendlesham, Woodbridge & Melton. Over railway line, approx 1m to pub on left*

A pub passionate about Suffolk produce

Put firmly on Suffolk's culinary map by chef Madalene Bonvini-Hamel and named after her hugely successful recipe blog, The British Larder champions local and seasonal produce sourced from Suffolk farms and artisan suppliers. Daily menus are brim full of fresh ingredients - pan-fried Iken partridge and salad, or Orford smokehouse platter as a starter, then Blaxhall venison loin, shoulder croquette and choucroute, or slow cooked beef and ale pie with onion and celeriac topping for mains. Baked white chocolate and forced rhubarb cheesecake might round things off. The seasonal seven-course tasting menu could prove too tempting to ignore. To drink, there's ale from Woodforde's and cider from Aspall, and the atmosphere throughout the contemporary bar and dining rooms is relaxed and informal.

Open 12-4 6-10 (Sat 12-11 Sun 12-10 (6pm winter)) Closed Sun eve & Mon (Jan-mid Apr) **Food** Lunch all wk 12-3 Dinner all wk 6-9 Av main course £16 Set menu available ⊕ PUNCH TAVERNS ◀ Woodforde's Wherry, Adnams ♂ Aspall. ☂ 28 **Facilities** Non-diners area ♣ (Bar Garden Outside area) ♦ Children's menu Children's portions Play area Garden Outside area ⋈ Parking WiFi ▭ (notice required)

BURY ST EDMUNDS
Map 13 TL86

The Nutshell

tel: 01284 764867 **17 The Traverse IP33 1BJ**
dir: *Phone for detailed directions*

Officially the smallest pub in Britain

Measuring just 15ft by 7ft, this unique pub has been confirmed as Britain's smallest by *Guinness World Records*; and somehow more than 100 people and a dog managed to fit inside in the 1980s. It has certainly become a tourist attraction and there's lots to talk about while you enjoy a drink – a mummified cat and the bar ceiling, which is covered with paper money. There have been regular sightings of ghosts around the building, including a nun and a monk who apparently weren't praying! No food is available, though the pub jokes about its dining area for parties of two or fewer.

Open all day all wk **Food** Contact pub for details ⊕ GREENE KING ◀ IPA & Abbot Ale, Guest ales. **Facilities** Non-diners area WiFi ▭ (notice required) **Notes** ☺

The Old Cannon Brewery ★★★ INN   PICK OF THE PUBS

See Pick of the Pubs on opposite page

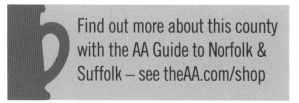

Find out more about this county with the AA Guide to Norfolk & Suffolk – see theAA.com/shop

The Three Kings

tel: 01284 766979 **Hengrave Rd, Fornham All Saints IP28 6LA**
email: thethreekings@keme.co.uk
dir: *A14 junct 42, B1106 to Fornham All Saints*

Family-run village pub and restaurant

An 18th-century coaching inn in Greene King's heartland, just two miles north of its Bury St Edmunds brewery. In 1173, Fornham was the site of the only documented pitched battle to have been fought in Suffolk. Family run, the pub has all the essentials – wood-panelled bars, restaurant, conservatory and courtyard. Bar food is mainly baguettes, sandwiches, wraps, salads and burgers, while the more adventurous main menu offers braised steak in red onion and balsamic jus; grilled smoked haddock; and Quorn chilli con carne. Pies and a vegetarian curry of the day feature as specials.

Open all day 12-11 (Sun 12-5) Closed 26 Dec, 1 Jan, Sun eve **Food** Lunch all wk 12-2.30 Dinner Mon 6-8, Tue-Sat 6-9.30 ⊕ GREENE KING ◀ Rotating Ales ♂ Aspall. ☂ 18 **Facilities** ♦ Children's menu Children's portions Outside area ⋈ Parking WiFi ▭ (notice required)

CAVENDISH
Map 13 TL84

Bull Inn

tel: 01787 280245 **High St CO10 8AX**
email: knaffton@btinternet.com
dir: *A134 (Bury St Edmunds to Long Melford), right at green, pub 3m on right*

Warming fires, oak beams, good beers and good food

A fine double-fronted, probably Victorian façade masks the splendid 15th-century beamed interior of this pub in one of Suffolk's prettiest villages. The atmosphere's good, the beers are from Adnams and a guest brewery, and the food's jolly decent too, with a menu listing perhaps rustic steak, mushroom and Irish ale pie; beer-battered fish and chips; smoked salmon and crayfish tagliatelle; and Mediterranean vegetable lasagne. Sunday roast may be selected from joints of beef, pork, lamb, chicken and turkey. Dogs are welcome downstairs in the public bar and in the patio garden.

Open all wk 11-3 6.30-11 **Food** Lunch all wk 12-3 Dinner all wk 6.30-9 ⊕ ADNAMS ◀ Southwold Bitter & Broadside, Guest ales ♂ Aspall. **Facilities** Non-diners area ♣ (Bar Garden) ♦ Children's menu Children's portions Garden ⋈ Parking ▭ (notice required)

CHILLESFORD
Map 13 TM35

The Froize Inn ◉   PICK OF THE PUBS

tel: 01394 450282 **The Street IP12 3PU**
email: dine@froize.co.uk
dir: *On B1084 between Woodbridge (8m) & Orford (3m)*

Foodie heaven near heritage coastline

This noble old pantiled building harbours a superb dining pub developed by the enthusiastic and skilled chef-patron David Grimwood. He puts his green credentials to the fore when creating dishes that have gained him an AA one-Rosette award here, deep in the Suffolk countryside just inland from Orford Ness. Local produce goes into the fresh Orford crab cakes starter, whilst mains might include stuffed breast of local pheasant with pumpkins and redcurrants from the innovative hot buffet. The Froize Inn champions the great British pudding, so leave room for a traditional favourite, or perhaps a helping of chocolate, prune and Armagnac pâté will tempt.

Open Tue-Sun Closed Mon **Food** Contact pub for details Restaurant menu available Tue-Sun ⊕ FREE HOUSE ◀ Adnams ♂ Aspall. ☂ 12 **Facilities** ♦ Children's portions Garden ⋈ Parking WiFi ▭ (notice required)

PICK OF THE PUBS

The Old Cannon Brewery ★★★ INN

BURY ST EDMUNDS   Map 13 TL86

tel: 01284 768769
86 Cannon St IP33 1JR
email: info@oldcannonbrewery.co.uk
web: www.oldcannonbrewery.co.uk
dir: *A14 junct 43 follow signs to Bury St Edmunds town centre, 1st left at 1st rdbt into Northgate St, 1st right into Cadney Ln, left at end into Cannon St*

A free house with long brewing history

Brewing started at this Victorian pub over 160 years ago. Today it's brewing still, the only independent brewpub in Suffolk where you can see beer being brewed on a regular basis. Indeed, dominating the bar are two giant stainless steel brewing vessels, fount of Old Cannon Best Bitter, Gunner's Daughter and seasonal and special occasion beers, augmented by ever-rotating regular and other guest ales. In keeping with having a brewery inside the bar-cum-dining room, the decor and furnishings are easy on the eye, with rich, earth-coloured walls, wooden floors and scrubbed tables. Exploiting the obvious pun, the menu is headed 'Cannon Fodder', among which, all freshly prepared from local produce, are starters and light dishes of deep-fried whitebait and smoked ham hock, and main meals of home-made beef and smoked oyster pie; winter chicken and goats' cheese pasta; pan-fried sea bass with chorizo and cherry tomatoes; and moules marinière. And the daily-changing specials board offers at least three more options. The possibility of a home-made pudding or a British cheeseboard is worth planning ahead for; otherwise, try a lighter locally produced ice cream. For the really keen, the pub offers a Brew Day experience giving two people the opportunity to work alongside the brewer, loading the malt, creating the wort and adding the hops, all during normal production hours. A Summer Bank Holiday beer festival and tours of the brewery are added attractions. Overnight guests stay in the converted old brewery, just across the courtyard. Since the pub is tucked away in the back streets, follow the website directions carefully.

Open all day all wk 12-11 (Sun 12-10.30) **Food** Lunch Mon-Sat 12-9, Sun 12-3 Dinner Mon-Sat 12-9 Set menu available ⊕ FREE HOUSE ◀ The Old Cannon Best Bitter & Gunner's Daughter & Seasonal ales, Adnams Southwold Bitter, Guest ales Ö Aspall. ⬤ 12 **Facilities** Non-diners area Garden ⌱ Beer festival Parking WiFi **Rooms** 7

CRATFIELD

Map 13 TM37

The Cratfield Poacher

tel: 01986 798206 **Bell Green IP19 0BL**
email: cratfieldpoacher@yahoo.co.uk
dir: *B1117 from Halesworth towards Eye. At Laxfield right, follow Cratfield signs. Or, A143 from Diss towards Bungay. Right at Harleston onto B1123 towards Halesworth. Through Metfield, 1m, right, follow Cratfield signs*

Family-run free house in rural location

A pub for the past 350 years, this handsome longhouse in deepest rural Suffolk is off the beaten track but well worth the detour. Boasting some impressive exterior plasterwork pargeting, it is just as charming inside, with low beams and tiled floors. There's always six draught beers available, often from the Adnams and Oakham breweries, plus local Aspall cider. Home-cooked food, such as smoked mackerel salad and shepherd's pie, with daily-changing specials complete the pleasing picture at this proper village local, which is the hub of the community.

Open 12-2.30 6-12 (Sat-Sun all day) Closed Mon, Tue L **Food** Lunch Fri 12-2.30 (Sat-Sun all day) Dinner Tue-Fri 6-9 (Sat-Sun all day) Av main course £9 Set menu available ⊕ FREE HOUSE ◀ Crouch Vale Brewers Gold, Oakham JHB, Earl Soham Victoria Bitter & Gannet Mild, Adnams Ò Aspall. **Facilities** Non-diners area ❤ (Bar Garden) ♦♦ Children's menu Children's portions Garden ⋈ Parking ▭ (notice required)

DENNINGTON

Map 13 TM26

Dennington Queen

tel: 01728 638241 **The Square IP13 8AB**
email: denningtonqueen@yahoo.co.uk
dir: *From Ipswich A14 to exit for Lowestoft (A12). Then B1116 to Framlingham, follow signs to Dennington*

Village centre pub worth seeking out

A 16th-century inn with bags of old-world charm including open fires, a coffin hatch, a bricked-up tunnel to the neighbouring church and a ghost. Locally brewed Aspall cider accompanies real ales from Adnams, plus rotating ales Black Sheep, Timothy Taylor and, from Woodbridge, Earl Soham. Suggestions from the modern British menu include Thai fishcakes with sweet chilli jam; calves' liver with champ mash, Bramfield bacon and red onion jus; and wild mushroom and smoked cheddar risotto. A typical daily special is spinach and pea linguine with salsa verde.

Open all wk 12-3 6.30-10.30 **Food** Lunch all wk 12-2 Dinner all wk 6.30-9 ⊕ FREE HOUSE ◀ Adnams, Guest ale Ò Aspall. **Facilities** Non-diners area ♦♦ Children's menu Children's portions Garden ⋈ Parking ▭ (notice required)

DUNWICH

Map 13 TM47

The Ship at Dunwich ★★ SHL ◉   PICK OF THE PUBS

See Pick of the Pubs on opposite page

EARL SOHAM

Map 13 TM26

Victoria

tel: 01728 685758 **The Street IP13 7RL**
dir: *From A14 at Stowmarket take A1120 towards Yoxford*

Microbrewery beers at their best

This friendly, down-to-earth free house is a showcase for Earl Soham beers, which for many years were produced from a microbrewery behind the pub. Some ten years ago the brewery moved to the Old Forge building a few yards away, where

production still continues. Inside this traditional pub, simple furnishings, bare floorboards and an open fire set the scene for traditional home-cooked pub fare, including ploughman's, jacket potatoes and macaroni cheese. Heartier meals include a variety of curries and casseroles, local sausages and mash, and gammon and eggs, followed by home-made desserts. A specials board and vegetarian dishes add to the choices.

Open all wk 11.30-3 6-11 **Food** Lunch all wk 12-2 Dinner all wk 7-10 ⊕ FREE HOUSE/EARL SOHAM BREWERY ◀ Earl Soham Victoria Bitter, Albert Ale, Brandeston Gold, Sir Roger's Porter Ò Aspall. **Facilities** Non-diners area ❤ (Bar Garden) ♦♦ Children's portions Garden ⋈ Parking WiFi ▭ (notice required)

ELVEDEN

Map 13 TL88

Elveden Inn ★★★★★ INN   PICK OF THE PUBS

tel: 01842 890876 **Brandon Rd IP24 3TP**
email: enquiries@elvedeninn.com **web:** www.elvedeninn.com
dir: *From Mildenhall take A11 towards Thetford. Left onto B1106, pub on left*

Award-winning inn showcasing produce from the estate

Located on the Elveden Estate, home to a direct descendent of the Guinness family, this village inn has a relaxed and contemporary bar, several dining areas, and four luxury bedrooms. Expect a family-friendly atmosphere, blazing log fires in winter, a range of guest ales on tap, and a modern pub menu that brims with produce sourced from the estate farm and surrounding area. Whether eating inside, or outside on the large patio area, a meal could kick off with a mixed antipasti sharing platter; salmon and chive fishcake on a bed of red chard and baby spinach; or winter greens and gruyère cheese tart. Next might be duet of suet puddings with gravy and vegetables; baked guinea fowl on confit red onions and duchess potato; or chickpea and banana curry. Children can choose from their own selection of 'fawn-size' portions. A previous winner of AA Pub of the Year for England.

Open all day all wk **Food** Lunch all wk 7.30am-9pm Dinner all wk 7.30am-9pm Restaurant menu available all wk ⊕ FREE HOUSE ◀ Adnams Southwold, Guest ales Ò Aspall. ▾ 14 **Facilities** Non-diners area ❤ (Bar Restaurant Garden) ♦♦ Children's menu Children's portions Play area Garden ⋈ Beer festival Cider festival Parking WiFi ▭ (notice required) **Rooms** 4

EYE

Map 13 TM17

The White Horse Inn ★★★★ INN

tel: 01379 678222 **Stoke Ash IP23 7ET**
email: mail@whitehorse-suffolk.co.uk **web:** www.whitehorse-suffolk.co.uk
dir: *On A140 between Ipswich & Norwich*

Family run inn with good food

Midway between Norwich and Ipswich, this 17th-century coaching inn is set amid lovely Suffolk countryside. The heavily timbered interior accommodates an inglenook fireplace, two bars and a restaurant. An extensive menu is supplemented by lunchtime snacks, grills and daily specials from the blackboard. Try salmon pâté or smoked duck salad to start. Main courses include red pepper and goats' cheese lasagne; honey and mustard chicken; venison casserole; chicken Madras; and baked salmon with a sage and parmesan crust. There are 11 spacious motel bedrooms in the grounds, as well as a patio and secluded grassy area.

Open all day all wk 7am-11pm (Sat 8am-11pm Sun 8am-10.30pm) **Food** Contact pub for details ⊕ FREE HOUSE ◀ Greene King Abbot Ale, Adnams, Woodforde's Wherry Ò Aspall. **Facilities** Non-diners area ♦♦ Children's menu Children's portions Garden Parking WiFi ▭ **Rooms** 11

PICK OF THE PUBS

The Ship at Dunwich ★★ SHL 🌹

DUNWICH Map 13 TM47

tel: 01728 648219
Saint James St IP17 3DT
email: info@shipatdunwich.co.uk
web: www.shipatdunwich.co.uk
dir: *N on A12 from Ipswich through Yoxford, right signed Dunwich*

Coastal pub renowned for its fish and chips

Dunwich was at one time a medieval port of some size and importance, but then the original village was virtually destroyed by a terrible storm in 1326. Further storms and erosion followed and now the place is little more than a hamlet beside a shingle beach. Two minutes' stroll from the beach, The Ship at Dunwich is a well-loved old smugglers' inn overlooking the salt marshes and sea, and is popular with walkers and birdwatchers visiting the nearby RSPB Minsmere reserve. The Ship keeps Dunwich on the map with hearty meals and ales from Adnams, Woodforde's and St Peter's – to name just a few. Its delightful unspoilt public bar offers nautical bric-à-brac, a wood-burning stove in a huge fireplace, flagged floors and simple wooden furnishings. Sympathetically spruced up in recent years, with the addition of clean, comfortable and contemporary style bedrooms, it is locally renowned for its fish and chips, which include a choice of cod, whiting, plaice or hake.

Other dishes plough a traditional furrow. You could start with twice-baked Binham Blue soufflé with chicory, pear and hazelnuts, or salt cod fishcakes, crispy capers and home-made tartare sauce, followed perhaps by slow-braised Bramfield ox cheeks and bone marrow fritter with creamy mash, curly kale and cauliflower cheese; or grilled Suffolk lamb Barnsley chop with anchovy and rosemary dressing, pan-hagerty potatoes, braised red cabbage, carrot and swede purée. Desserts continue in a similar vein – maybe spiced apple crumble and custard, or a knickbocker glory. Look for the ancient fig tree in the garden, and take note of the inn's beer festivals that take place on Bank Holiday Sundays.

Open all day all wk **Food** Lunch all wk 12-3 Dinner all wk 6-9 Av main course £11.95 🍽 FREE HOUSE 🛢 Adnams Southwold Bitter, Humpty Dumpty, Brandon Rusty Bucket, Earl Soham, Green Jack, Grain Norfolk Brewery, Woodforde's, St Peter's Ö Aspall. ⏺ 9 **Facilities** Non-diners area ✿ (Bar Restaurant Garden) ⬢ Children's menu Children's portions Family room Garden ☷ Beer festival Parking WiFi **Rooms** 15

Map 13 TM15

NEW The Shepherd & Dog

tel: 01449 711685 **IP14 5HN**
email: info@theshepherdanddog.com
dir: *From Stowmarket (A14 junct 50) take A1120 signed Stowupland. Through Stowupland, approx 2m to pub*

A country bar, contemporary lounge and modern eatery

On the edge of the village, looking out over a field, this pub is very much part of the community. Bar meals include a half lobster with warm toast and roast garlic butter, and cauliflower risotto, but if you'd prefer the restaurant, its menu lists Suffolk lamb loin with salsify purée, slow-roast root vegetables and roast garlic polenta; pan-fried pork belly with pork croquette, roast pear and Brussels sprouts; and herb-crusted cod fillet with smoked eel gnocchi, whitebait, wilted greens and crispy kale. You don't have to be vegetarian to enjoy roasted Jerusalem artichoke with red cabbage.

Open all day Closed 1-15 Jan, Mon-Tue **Food** Lunch Wed-Sun 12-9 Dinner Wed-Sun 12-9 Av main course £10 Restaurant menu available Wed-Sun ⊕ FREE HOUSE ◀ Greene King IPA Ö Aspall. ❣ 12 **Facilities** Non-diners area ❖ (Bar Outside area) ♦ Children's menu Children's portions Outside area ⋒ Parking WiFi

Map 13 TM26

The Station Hotel

tel: 01728 723455 **Station Rd IP13 9EE**
email: framstation@btinternet.com
dir: *Bypass Ipswich towards Lowestoft on A12. Approx 6m, left onto B1116 to Framlingham*

Known for its bold and flavoursome dishes

Built as part of the local railway in the 19th century, The Station Hotel has been a pub since the 1950s, outliving the railway which closed in 1962. Inside, you will find scrubbed tables and an eclectic mix of furniture. During the last decade it has established a fine reputation for its gutsy and earthy food listed on the ever-changing blackboard menu. A typical lunch could be kedgeree; dinner might include pot-roasted rabbit and bean stew; pan-fried mullet with linguine clam chowder, or something cooked in wood-fired pizza oven. Several of the beers are supplied by Suffolk brewery, Earl Soham and there is a beer festival in mid July.

Open all wk 12-2.30 5-11 (Sun 12-3 7-10.30) **Food** Lunch all wk 12-2 Dinner Sun-Thu 6.30-9, Fri-Sat 6.30-9.30 ⊕ FREE HOUSE ◀ Earl Soham Victoria Bitter, Albert Ale & Gannet Mild, Veltins, Crouch Vale, Guinness Ö Aspall. **Facilities** Non-diners area ❖ (Bar Garden) ♦ Children's portions Family room Garden Beer festival Parking ⟳

Map 13 TM15

The Dobermann Inn

tel: 01473 890461 **The Street IP14 6HG**
dir: *S off A1120 (Stowmarket to Yoxford road). 10m from Ipswich on B1077 towards Debenham*

Thatched village inn with popular food

This pretty country pub was named by its current proprietor who is a prominent breeder and judge of Dobermanns. The thatched roofing, gnarled beams, open fire and assorted furniture reflect its 16th-century origins. With a selection of Adnams ales on offer and Mauldons Dickens bitter, food ranges from sandwiches, hearty ploughman's and salads to main courses featuring plenty of fish and vegetarian choices. Reliable favourites include chilli con carne, spicy nut loaf, Dover sole, and steak and mushroom pie.

Open 12-3 7-11 Closed 25-26 Dec, Sun eve, Mon **Food** Lunch Tue-Sun 12-2 Dinner Tue-Sat 7-9 ⊕ FREE HOUSE ◀ Adnams Southwold Bitter, Old Ale & Broadside, Mauldons Dickens Ö Aspall. **Facilities** Non-diners area Garden ⋒ Parking ⟳ (notice required) **Notes** ⊛

Map 13 TM05

The Veggie Red Lion PICK OF THE PUBS

tel: 01473 657799 **Green Street Green IP7 7DD**
email: janwise@fsmail.net
dir: *4.5m from Needham Market on B1078*

Smart country inn with innovative approach to meals

After several years as standard bearer in the field of specialist vegetarian and vegan destination dining pubs, Jan Wise's inspirational business continues to thrive. You'll find the Veggie deep in the Suffolk countryside, surrounded by rich farmland. Guest ales change weekly in the bar, but it's the innovative menu that draws the discerning diner well off the beaten track. Jan's unfailing commitment to developing exquisite dishes has won accolades – you'll find barely a hint of anything that once grazed, swam or pecked. Special diets are usually no problem either, and many dishes are gluten free. Settle down in the rustic beamed and colour-washed interior to experience the delightful difficulty of deciding just what treats to try. Smoked tofu and mushroom skewers are marinated with garlic and herbs, while the lentil, carrot and coriander burger is blended with spices, sweet potato and pumpkin seeds. Daily changing specials guarantee there's always something new to try.

Open 12-3 6-11 Closed Sun eve & Mon **Food** Lunch Tue-Sun 12-2 Dinner Tue-Sat 6-9 Av main course £9.90 ⊕ GREENE KING ◀ IPA, Morland Old Speckled Hen, Rotating Guest ales Ö Aspall. **Facilities** Non-diners area ❖ (Bar Garden) ♦ Children's menu Children's portions Play area Garden ⋒ Parking WiFi

Map 13 TM37

The Queen's Head PICK OF THE PUBS

tel: 01986 784214 **The Street, Bramfield IP19 9HT**
email: info@queensheadbramfield.co.uk
dir: *2m from A12 on A144 towards Halesworth*

Local produce gets pride of place on an ever-changing menu

In the centre of Bramfield on the edge of the Suffolk Heritage Coast near Southwold, the enclosed garden of this lovely Grade II listed pub is overlooked by the thatched village church with its unusual separate round bell tower. The pub's interior is welcoming, with scrubbed pine tables, a vaulted ceiling in the bar and enormous fireplaces. In the same hands for two decades, the pub's landlord enthusiastically supports local and organic producers, reflected by a constantly evolving menu which proudly names the farms and suppliers. Sample dishes include sweet-cured marinated herring fillets; twice-baked goats' cheese soufflé; home-made Thai fishcakes with sweet chilli sauce. In addition there's a big choice of sandwiches, filled baguettes and filled ciabatta, ploughman's and hamburgers. Look out for the live music events.

Open all wk 12-2.30 6.30-11 (Sun 12-4 7-10.30) **Food** Lunch Mon-Sat 12-2, Sun 12-4 Dinner Mon-Fri 6.30-9, Sat 6.30-9.30, Sun 7-9 Restaurant menu available all wk ⊕ ADNAMS ◀ Southwold Bitter, Broadside Ö Aspall. ❣ 8 **Facilities** Non-diners area ❖ (Bar Restaurant Garden) ♦ Children's menu Children's portions Family room Garden ⋒ Parking WiFi ⟳ (notice required)

HAWKEDON   Map 13 TL75

The Queen's Head   PICK OF THE PUBS

tel: 01284 789218 **Rede Rd IP29 4NN**
dir: *From A143 at Wickham St, between Bury St Edmunds & Haverhill, follow Stansfield sign. At junct left signed Hawkedon. 1m to village*

Thriving village local with a butcher's shop

Off-the-beaten track by the green in a picture-book village deep in rural Suffolk, The Queen's Head is worth seeking out for its classic 15th-century character and charm – inglenook fireplace, stone floors, head-cracking timbers, scrubbed pine tables – and top-notch hearty pub food prepared from the best local ingredients. The pub rears its own livestock (Suffolk sheep and Dexter cattle) and, like the pork, venison, poultry and wild boar sourced from local farms, they are hung and butchered at the butcher's shop in the pub grounds. This may translate to venison carpaccio; pork chops with Stilton, pear and sage; and pot-roasted beef with red wine and red onion marmalade; with butterscotch and almond pudding among the desserts. Sunday roast lunches, traditional bar snacks, and pizzas baked in the stone oven complete the culinary picture. A thriving community local, it also offers live music, a beer and cider festival in July, and game and wine tasting dinners.

Open 5-11 (Fri-Sun 12-11) Closed Mon-Thu L **Food** Lunch Fri-Sun 12-2.30 Dinner Wed-Thu 6-9, Fri-Sun 6.30-9 ⊕ FREE HOUSE ◀ Woodforde's Wherry, Adnams, Guest ales ♂ Westons Old Rosie & Country Perry, Guest cider. **Facilities** Non-diners area ✿ (Bar Garden) ⚬ Children's portions Garden ⩩ Beer festival Cider festival Parking WiFi

HITCHAM   Map 13 TL95

The White Horse Inn

tel: 01449 740981 **The Street IP7 7NQ**
email: lewis@thewhitehorse.wanadoo.co.uk
dir: *13m from Ipswich & Bury St Edmunds, 7m Stowmarket, 7m Hadleigh*

Friendly pub in the heart of the countryside

A blacksmith's forge was once attached to this 400-year-old inn, originally a staging post for London and Norwich coaches. In the late 17th century a notorious highwayman was arrested and tried in what nowadays is the public bar, found guilty and hanged from a nearby tree. Today, the bar is for more for hanging out, drinking Rattlesden Best and other Suffolk real ales, and playing traditional pub games. Freshly prepared meals include jacket potatoes; ham or cheese ploughman's; butterflied chicken breast; salmon steak; and vegetarian Italian layer bake.

Open all wk 12-3 6-11 **Food** Lunch all wk 12-2.30 Dinner all wk 6-9 Restaurant menu available all wk ⊕ FREE HOUSE ◀ Adnams Southwold Bitter & Fisherman, Rattlesden Best, Cox and Holbrook Stowmarket Porter ♂ Aspall. ☂
Facilities Non-diners area ✿ (Bar Garden) ⚬ Children's menu Children's portions Garden ⩩ Parking WiFi ⬛ (notice required)

HOLBROOK   Map 13 TM13

The Compasses

tel: 01473 328332 **Ipswich Rd IP9 2QR**
email: jayne.gooding@hotmail.co.uk
dir: *From A137 S of Ipswich, take B1080 to Holbrook, pub on left. From Ipswich take B1456 to Shotley. At Freston Water Tower right onto B1080 to Holbrook. Pub 2m right*

Proudly not a gastro-pub

On the spectacular Shotley peninsula bordered by the rivers Orwell and Stour, this traditional 17th-century country pub offers a simple, good-value menu. There's nothing self-consciously primped and styled about its interior or its food offerings; it prides itself on not being a gastro-pub but offering good value and plenty of choice. Typical starters include prawn cocktail and breaded mushrooms with garlic mayo. Follow this with minced beef and onion pie; crispy chicken mornay; or local sausages with egg and chips. There's a separate kids' menu and some good vegetarian choices such as Cajun five bean chilli.

Open 11.30-2.30 6-11 (Sun 12-3 6-10.30) Closed 26 Dec, Tue eve **Food** Lunch all wk 12-2.15 Dinner Wed-Mon 6-9.15 ⊕ PUNCH TAVERNS ◀ Adnams Southwold Bitter, Sharp's Doom Bar ♂ Aspall. ☂ 12 **Facilities** Non-diners area ⚬ Children's menu Children's portions Play area Garden ⩩ Parking WiFi ⬛ (notice required)

HONEY TYE   Map 13 TL93

The Lion

tel: 01206 263434 **CO6 4NX**
email: info@thelioncolchester.com
dir: *On A134 midway between Colchester & Sudbury*

Good food in dining pub with alfresco options

Under new owners since October 2013, this traditional country dining pub occupies an enviable spot in an Area of Outstanding Natural Beauty. The spacious restaurant is decorated in a modern, comfortable style and the bar has low-beamed ceilings and wood burner. The reasonably priced food here is sourced locally and the menu changes with the seasons. Start with twice-baked goats' cheese soufflé, perhaps, before a main course of oven-roasted rump of new season lamb with pearl barley risotto and salsa verde. The Lion has a walled beer garden for alfresco eating and drinking in the summer.

Open all day 11-11 Closed Mon **Food** Lunch Tue-Sun 12-9 Dinner Tue-Sun 12-9 Set menu available ⊕ FREE HOUSE ◀ Adnams ♂ Westons. ☂ 9
Facilities Non-diners area ⚬ Children's menu Children's portions Garden ⩩ Parking WiFi ⬛ (notice required)

INGHAM   Map 13 TL87

The Cadogan ★★★★ INN ◉

tel: 01284 728443 **The Street IP31 1NG**
email: info@thecadogan.co.uk **web:** www.thecadogan.co.uk
dir: *A14 junct 42, 1st exit onto B1106. At rdbt take 1st exit (A134). 3m to Ingham. Pub on left*

A welcoming place to stay or dine

A friendly and inviting pub with seven en suite bedrooms for those who want to stay longer, The Cadogan sits just four miles from the centre of Bury St Edmunds. The kitchen places an emphasis on seasonality and local produce; for something lighter there's grazing boards at both lunch and dinner (cheese; seafood; deli and puds). Dinner menu options could be winter spiced mackerel fillets and granary bread; or confit guinea fowl and wild mushroom terrine to start, followed by Norfolk turkey ballotine with potato fondant, roast carrots and bread sauce; or herb crust hake, roast butternut squash and pearl barley risotto. Open all day, the pub has a large garden, with a children's play area, perfect for alfresco dining.

Open all day all wk Closed 25-26 Dec & 31 Jan eve **Food** Lunch Mon-Sat 12-2.30, Sun 12-8.30 Dinner Mon-Sat 6-9.30, Sun 12-8.30 Av main course £11 ⊕ GREENE KING ◀ Abbot Ale, Brewshed Pale Ale ♂ Aspall. ☂ 14 **Facilities** Non-diners area ⚬ Children's menu Children's portions Play area Garden ⩩ Parking WiFi ⬛ (notice required) **Rooms** 7

IPSWICH
Map 13 TM14

The Fat Cat

tel: 01473 726524 **288 Spring Rd IP4 5NL**
email: fatcatipswich@btconnect.com
dir: *From A12 take A1214 towards town centre, becomes A1071 (Woodbridge Road East). At mini rdbt 2nd left into Spring Rd*

One for the beer lover

Good beer and conversation are the two main ingredients in this no-frills free house. The Fat Cat is a mecca for beer aficionados, with a friendly atmosphere in two homely bars and a raft of real ales served in tip-top condition from the taproom behind the bar. The head-scratching choice – up to 22 every day – come from Dark Star, Elgood's, Green Jack and a host of local microbreweries. Soak up the beer with simple bar snacks like beef and Guinness pasties, sausage rolls, pork pies and baguettes.

Open all day all wk **Food** Contact pub for details ⊕ FREE HOUSE ◀ Adnams Old Ale, Dark Star Hophead, Elgood's Black Dog, Green Jack Gone Fishing, Crouch Vale Brewers Gold, Guest ales Ò Aspall. ☗ 8 **Facilities** Garden ☚ (notice required) **Notes** ⊛

LAXFIELD
Map 13 TM27

The Kings Head (The Low House)   PICK OF THE PUBS

tel: 01986 798395 **Gorams Mill Ln IP13 8DW**
email: lowhouse@keme.co.uk
dir: *On B1117*

Discover a real old pub with authentic atmosphere

This unspoilt thatched 16th-century alehouse is a rare Suffolk gem that oozes charm and character. Locals know it as The Low House because it lies in a dip below the churchyard. Tip-top Adnams ales are served straight from the cask in the original taproom – this is one of the few pubs in Britain which has no bar. Order a pint of Broadside and retire to an ancient fireplace with a horseshoe of high-backed settles with an oak table in the middle. Traditional lunchtime fare includes sandwiches and baguettes, perhaps a BLT or roast beef and horseradish. Home-cooked dishes range from classics like sausages with mash and onion gravy to slow-roasted Dingley Dell pork, and lamb shank cooked in Guinness. Beer festivals in May and September are unforgettable occasions thanks to the beautiful situation of the pub overlooking the river; its grounds, now with rose gardens and an arbour, were formerly the village bowling green.

Open all wk 11am-close (winter 12-3 6-close) **Food** Lunch all wk 12-3 Dinner Mon-Sat 6.30-9 ⊕ ADNAMS ◀ Southwold Bitter, Broadside & Ghost Ship ales, Guest ales Ò Aspall. ☗ 11 **Facilities** Non-diners area ❤ (Bar Garden) ♦ Children's portions Play area Family room Garden ☞ Beer festival Parking WiFi ☚ (notice required)

LIDGATE
Map 12 TL75

The Star Inn   PICK OF THE PUBS

tel: 01638 500275 **The Street CB8 9PP**
dir: *From Newmarket clocktower in High St follow signs towards Clare on B1063. Lidgate 7m*

Mediterranean dishes at horseracing fraternity favourite

Quintessential English pub dating back to the 14th century. An important meeting place for local residents, the pub is popular with Newmarket trainers on race days, and with dealers and agents from all over the world during bloodstock sales. Originally two cottages, the two traditionally furnished bars still fit the old-world bill with heavy oak beams, log fires, pine tables and antique furniture, but the dishes on the menu are a mix of Spanish and British. On the Spanish side are starters like whole baby squid with garlic and chilli or fish soup, which might be followed by bean and chorizo stew. British tastes are also catered for, with dishes

such as warm chicken liver salad; venison steaks in port; and pigs' cheeks. There's an extensive wine list, too, with a number of well-priced Riojas jostling for position alongside the real ales on tap.

Open 12-3 6-12 Closed Mon **Food** Lunch Tue-Sat 12-2.30, Sun 12-3 Dinner Tue-Sat 6.30-9.30 ⊕ FREE HOUSE ◀ Black Sheep, Marston's Pedigree, Timothy Taylor, Woodforde's Wherry Ò Aspall, Thatchers. **Facilities** Non-diners area ❤ (Bar) ♦ Children's portions Garden ☞ Parking ☚

LINDSEY TYE
Map 13 TL94

The Lindsey Rose

tel: 01449 741424 **IP7 6PP**
email: thelindseyrose@hotmail.co.uk
dir: *From A12 between Ipswich & Sudbury take A1141 signed Lavenham. Ignore 1st sign for Lindsey, follow 2nd sign, then pub sign*

Lindsey's local for over half a millennium

Set in the beautiful Suffolk countryside between Ipswich and Sudbury, The Lindsey Rose has been the village local for over 500 years. The region's produce is celebrated on the menu, which might include their famous Red Poll beefburger with blue cheese, bacon and home-made chips; Thai green vegetable curry; haddock and chips; and sticky toffee pudding. Children are very welcome here and get their own menu and activity area outside.

Open all wk 11-3 5-11 (Sat-Sun 11-11) **Food** Lunch Mon-Sat 12-2.30, Sun 12-3 Dinner Mon-Sat 5-9, Sun 7-9 ⊕ FREE HOUSE ◀ Adnams Southwold Bitter, Mauldons Ò Aspall. ☗ 11 **Facilities** Non-diners area ❤ (Bar Restaurant Garden) ♦ Children's menu Children's portions Play area Garden ☞ Parking WiFi ☚ (notice required)

MILDENHALL
Map 12 TL77

The Bull Inn ★★★★★ INN ⊛   PICK OF THE PUBS

See Pick of the Pubs on opposite page

NAYLAND
Map 13 TL93

Anchor Inn   PICK OF THE PUBS

tel: 01206 262313 **26 Court St CO6 4JL**
email: info@anchornayland.co.uk
dir: *Follow A134 from Colchester towards Sudbury for 3.5m through Great Horkesley, at bottom of hill right into Horkesley Rd. Pub on right after bridge*

Eclectic modern dining in Constable Country

The inn, which enjoys a placid setting beside the alder-fringed meadows of the River Stour, is reputedly the last remaining place from which press-gangs recruited their 'volunteers' in this area. Today's customers can rest easy here, recovering from strolls around the idyllic village, which is close to the heart of 'Constable Country'. Having undergone a comprehensive yet sensitive refurbishment, the Anchor is a light, airy destination where local and regional ales change monthly (there are also twice-yearly beer festivals), with the riverside decking and garden the ideal spot to tarry a while. Head chef Ross Armstead presides over a progressive menu of pub favourites and modern European dishes, so anticipate fish and chips or beefburger in brioche; or have a go at roast chicken breast with celeriac purée, new potatoes and baby carrots; or slow cooked pork belly with potato fondant, apple purée, three way crackling and red wine jus. The inn has a smokehouse, and meals on the à la carte menu often reflect this.

Open all wk Tue-Sun all day (Mon 11-3 5-11) **Food** Lunch Mon-Fri 12-2, Sat 12-2.30, Sun 12-4 Dinner Mon-Fri 6.30-9, Sat 6.30-9.30 Av main course £11 Set menu available Restaurant menu available all wk ⊕ FREE HOUSE/EXCLUSIVE INNS ◀ Greene King IPA, Adnams, Local & Guest ales Ò Aspall, Carter's. ☗ 10 **Facilities** Non-diners area ❤ (Bar Garden) ♦ Children's menu Children's portions Garden ☞ Beer festival Parking WiFi ☚ (notice required)

PICK OF THE PUBS

The Bull Inn ★★★★★ INN

MILDENHALL Map 12 TL77

tel: 01638 711001
The Street, Barton Mills IP28 6AA
email: reception@bullinn-bartonmills.com
web: www.bullinn-bartonmills.com
dir: *Exit A11 between Newmarket & Mildenhall, signed Barton Mills*

An independent, quirky inn with something to suit everyone

With its fine roofline, dormer windows and old coaching courtyard, this rambling 16th-century building certainly looks like a traditional roadside inn. Stepping inside you'll be wowed by a contemporary sprucing-up that successfully blends original oak beams, wooden floors and big fireplaces with funky fabrics, designer wallpapers and bold colours. This, along with their dedication, is how family owners Cheryl, Wayne and Sonia breathed new life into an old inn, making the bar, with scrubbed pine tables and cosy seats by a winter fire, the hub of the building (and indeed the village). Here you can study the menus, perhaps with one of the eleven wines by the glass, or an East Anglian real ale from Adnams, Wolf or Humpty Dumpty. Menus evolve with the seasons, with every effort made to reduce 'food miles' by sourcing locally. In the AA Rosette dining rooms a meal might begin with marinated king scallops, black pudding, crispy bacon and apple purée; followed by rump of Denham Estate lamb with gratin potato

and red wine and thyme jus; or the signature dish of fillet steak tower. Options continue with fresh Lowestoft haddock or cod in beer batter with double-cooked chips and pea purée; roast breast of Gressingham duck, potato and thyme rösti, piccolo parsnips, sautéed spinach and port and onion jus; and the Bull's 'famous' MOO pie filled with slow-cooked fillet steak in Brandon-brewed Rusty Bucket ale, with creamy mash and roasted root vegetables. Bar meals include classics like Newmarket sausages with mash and caramelised red onion gravy; and chicken curry with basmati rice. Sandwiches too, if you prefer. Accommodation available.
Winner of the AA Funky B&B of the Year 2014-15.

Open all day all wk 8am-11pm Closed 25 Dec **Food** Lunch Sun-Thu 12-9, Fri-Sat 12-9.30 (bkfst 8-12) Dinner Sun-Thu 12-9, Fri-Sat 12-9.30 Av main course £13 Restaurant menu all wk. ⊕ FREE HOUSE ◄ Adnams Broadside, Greene King IPA, Brandon Rusty Bucket, Humpty Dumpty, Wolf ♂ Aspall. ♀ 11 **Facilities** Non-diners area ♦♦ Children's menu & portions Garden ⊟ Parking ▭ (notice required) WiFi **Rooms** 15

NEWMARKET
Map 12 TL66

NEW The Packhorse Inn ★★★★★ INN ◉◉
PICK OF THE PUBS

tel: 01638 751818 **Bridge St, Moulton CB8 8SP**
email: info@thepackhorseinn.com web: www.thepackhorseinn.com
dir: *A14 junct 39, B1506 signed Newmarket. Left onto B1085 to Moulton*

Stylish country pub near Newmarket

As a resident of the village, former banker Philip Turner soon recognised the untapped potential of his local pub, formerly the King's Head, located on the green in peaceful Moulton. Philip reopened this Suffolk pub in October 2013 after a six-month refurbishment; its new name reflects the adjacent medieval bridge across the River Kennet. Just two miles from Newmarket Racecourse, it is now a stylish, family-friendly country pub that attracts locals, racegoers and also London professionals looking for somewhere to unwind. Run by experienced husband-and-wife team Chris and Hayley Lee, the emphasis is on quality food and drink, much of it sourced locally, including beers from Adnams and Woodforde's breweries, and Aspall cider. The appealing menus might start with seared scallops with cumin, chicken wings, cauliflower and apple; followed by braised Suffolk ox cheek with bacon and bubble-and-squeak. Leave room for coconut rice pudding with passionfruit jelly.

Open all day all wk **Food** Lunch all wk 12-2.30 Dinner all wk 7-9.30 Av main course £15 ⊕ FREE HOUSE ◀ Woodforde's Wherry, Adnams Broadside, Fuller's London Pride, Guest ales ♂ Aspall Harry Sparrow. ☘ 19 **Facilities** Non-diners area ♣ (Bar Restaurant Garden) ♦ Children's portions Garden ⌁ Parking WiFi ⛟ (notice required) **Rooms** 4

REDE
Map 13 TL85

The Plough

tel: 01284 789208 **IP29 4BE**
dir: *On A143 between Bury St Edmunds & Haverhill*

Interesting menus in Suffolk's highest spot

Tucked away in the village on the green is this part-thatched, 16th-century pub easily identified by an old plough and a weeping willow at the front. On long-standing landlord Brian Desborough's ever-changing blackboard menu look for diced Highland beef in cream with wholegrain mustard and whisky sauce; minted local venison in chilli sauce with potato and cheese topping; and sea bass fillets in cream with bacon, butterbean and sweetcorn sauce. The bar serves Fuller's, Adnams, Ringwood and Sharp's ales and 10 wines by the glass. At 128 metres above sea level, Rede is Suffolk's highest point - verified by the *Guinness Book of World Records*.

Open all wk 11-3 6-12 (Sun 12-3) **Food** Lunch all wk 12-2 Dinner Mon-Sat 6-9 ⊕ ADMIRAL TAVERNS ◀ Fuller's London Pride, Ringwood Best Bitter, Sharp's Cornish Coaster, Adnams ♂ Aspall. ☘ 10 **Facilities** Non-diners area ♦ Children's portions Garden ⌁ Parking WiFi ⛟ (notice required)

SIBTON
Map 13 TM36

Sibton White Horse Inn ★★★★ INN ◉ PICK OF THE PUBS

See Pick of the Pubs on opposite page

SNAPE
Map 13 TM35

The Crown Inn
PICK OF THE PUBS

tel: 01728 688324 **Bridge Rd IP17 1SL**
email: snapecrown@tiscali.co.uk
dir: *A12 from Ipswich towards Lowestoft, right onto A1094 towards Aldeburgh. In Snape right at x-rds by church, pub at bottom of hill*

Ancient village inn with home-raised menu mains

Getting on for 600 years old and once the haunt of smugglers using the nearby River Alde, this character village stalwart shelters beneath a most extraordinary saltbox pantile roof. Inside, the public area threads beneath vast old beams and across mellow brick floors to cosy corners and an inglenook enclosed by the arms of a huge double settle. Folk musicians regularly take over this area for informal gigs; far more renowned is the nearby Snape Maltings complex where international performers are the order of the day. Pre- or post-concert meals are available for such concert goers. The Crown's owners Teresa and Garry Cook run their own livestock smallholding behind the pub, ensuring a very local supply chain. This is enhanced by locally sourced Limousin beef, seafood from Orford boats, game from nearby shoots, village vegetables and foraged specialities. Menus change frequently and a specials board adds spice to the mix - pheasant breast stuffed with prunes; smoked fish platter with lemon mayonnaise or their own rare-breed pork sausages may feature.

Open all wk 12-3 6-11 **Food** Lunch all wk 12-2.30 Dinner all wk 6-9.30 ⊕ ADNAMS ◀ Southwold Bitter, Broadside, Seasonal ales ♂ Aspall. ☘ 12 **Facilities** Non-diners area ♣ (Bar Garden) ♦ Children's portions Garden ⌁ Parking ⛟ (notice required)

The Golden Key
PICK OF THE PUBS

tel: 01728 688510 **Priory Ln IP17 1SA**
email: info@goldenkeysnape.co.uk
dir: *Phone for detailed directions*

Dog-friendly, 16th-century, cottage-style pub

This delightful village pub is a five-minute walk from Snape Maltings, home of the well-known Concert Hall, one of the focal points of the annual Aldeburgh Festival. The pub's low beamed ceilings and log fires not only attest to its age, but also help to generate its comfortable feel, especially in the quarry-tiled main bar, where you'll find villagers enjoying their pints of Southwold-brewed Adnams Broadside and Explorer. The food, both in the bar and in the pine-furnished dining room, owes much to the immediate locality, with fish delivered daily from Aldeburgh, lamb from a neighbouring farm and game supplied by the Benhall Shoot. Among the typical dishes are Richardson Smokehouse Suffolk ham with egg and chips; lamb curry with braised rice, tomato and coriander salad; and vegetable moussaka. Pre- and post-concert dining is available, but please book. Annual beer festival.

Open all wk 12-3 5.30-11 (wknds all day) **Food** Lunch all wk 12-2.30 Dinner all wk 6-9 ⊕ ADNAMS ◀ Southwold Bitter, Broadside, Explorer, Old Ale, Ghost Ship ♂ Aspall. ☘ 15 **Facilities** Non-diners area ♣ (All areas) ♦ Children's portions Garden Outside area ⌁ Beer festival Parking WiFi ⛟ (notice required)

PICK OF THE PUBS

Sibton White Horse Inn ★★★★★ INN

SIBTON Map 13 TM36

tel: 01728 660337
Halesworth Rd IP17 2JJ
email: info@sibtonwhitehorseinn.co.uk
web: www.sibtonwhitehorseinn.co.uk
dir: *A12 at Yoxford onto A1120, 3m to Peasenhall. Right opposite butchers, inn 600mtrs*

Delightful, award-winning inn

Off the beaten track in the heart of the Suffolk countryside, but just five minutes from the A12 at Yoxford and ten miles from the coast, this rustic 16th-century inn retains much of its Tudor charm and incorporates stone floors, exposed brickwork and ships' timbers believed to have come from Woodbridge shipyard. A genuine free house, the bar with its raised gallery is the place to enjoy pints of Green Jack Trawlerboys or Woodforde's Once Bittern. There is a choice of dining areas to sample the award-winning food, while the secluded courtyard has a Mediterranean feel when the sun comes out. Owners Neil and Gill Mason are committed to producing high-quality food from fresh local ingredients – and, to prove it, they grow many of their own vegetables behind the pub. At lunch, you can order from the set menu or from the selection of light bites and sandwiches. The à la carte, available at both lunch and dinner, offers old favourites like smoked mackerel pâté

with sweet pickled cucumber and Emmerdale 28-day-hung sirloin steak with thrice cooked, hand-cut chips. For something a little more special, there's lightly seared wood pigeon breast, thyme rösti potato, spinach and red wine jus; venison suet pudding, Parmentier potato, wilted greens and red onion gravy; or twice baked Binham Blue cheese soufflé, with Bramley apple, pear and red wine compôte. Finish, perhaps, with ginger sponge, toffee sauce and vanilla ice cream. Well behaved children are welcome; only those over six are permitted in the evening.

Open 12-2.30 6.30-11 (Sun 12-3.30 6.45-10.30) Closed 26-27 Dec, Mon L **Food** Lunch Tue-Sat 12-2, Sun 12-2.30

Dinner served Mon-Sat 6.30-9, Sun 7-8.30 Set menu available Restaurant menu available Mon-Sat. 🍺 FREE HOUSE 🍺 Adnams Southwold Bitter, Woodforde's Once Bittern, Green Jack Trawlerboys Best Bitter Ď Aspall. 🍷 9 **Facilities** Non-diners area 🐾 (Bar Garden) 👫 Children's menu children's portions (lunch only) Garden 🎪 Beer festival Parking WiFi **Rooms** 6

SNAPE *continued*

Plough & Sail

tel: 01728 688413 **Snape Maltings IP17 1SR**
dir: *On B1069, S of Snape. Signed from A12*

Drawing in the crowds in Snape

Local twins, Alex (front of house) and Oliver (chef) Burnside own this pink, pantiled old inn at the heart of the renowned Snape Maltings complex; it's handy for cultural and shopping opportunities and close to splendid coastal walks. The interior is a comfy mix of dining and avant-garde destination pub; local ales and a good bin of wines accompany a solid menu, featuring a Mediterranean fish soup with rouille, gruyère and crostini, and home-made potted shrimps on toast to start; followed by seasonal fish pie; Gressingham duck breast, braised red cabbage, sweet potato purée and jus; or Adnams beer battered fish and chip with crushed minted peas. Leave room for coffee crème brûlée with white chocolate and nut biscotti; or date and toffee pudding with caramelised bananas, toffee sauce and mascarpone.

Open all day all wk **Food** Lunch all wk 12-2.30 Dinner all wk 6-9 ⊕ FREE HOUSE ◀ Adnams Broadside, Southwold Bitter, Ghost Ship, Guest ale Ö Aspall. ▼ 10 **Facilities** Non-diners area ✿ (Bar Garden) ▪ Children's menu Children's portions Garden ⋈ Parking WiFi 🚃 (notice required)

SOMERLEYTON   **Map 13 TM49**

The Duke's Head

tel: 01502 733931 & 730281 **Slug's Ln NR32 5QR**
email: dukeshead.somerleyton@googlemail.com
dir: *From A143 onto B1074 signed Lowestoft & Somerleyton. Pub signed from B1074*

Rural estate-owned gastro-pub

Owned by and overlooking the Somerleyton Estate, this newly refurbished pub stands tucked away down Slug's Lane on the edge of the village. Renowned locally for its imaginative seasonal menus, which champion game and meats reared on estate farms, it thrives as a gastro-pub and the rambling and very relaxed bar and dining areas fill early with diners in the know. Savour the views over a pint of Wherry in the garden in summer.

Open all day all wk **Food** Lunch Mon-Sat 12-2.30, Sun 12-5 Dinner Mon-Sat 6.30-9 ⊕ FREE HOUSE ◀ Adnams, Woodforde's Wherry, Guest ales in summer Ö Aspall. ▼ 12 **Facilities** Non-diners area ✿ (Bar Garden) ▪ Children's menu Children's portions Play area Garden ⋈ Beer festival Cider festival Parking WiFi 🚃 (notice required)

SOUTHWOLD   **Map 13 TM57**

The Crown Hotel   `PICK OF THE PUBS`

tel: 01502 722275 **The High St IP18 6DP**
email: crown.hotel@adnams.co.uk
dir: *A12 onto A1095 to Southwold. Hotel in town centre*

The flagship hotel for the Adnams Brewery

Centrally located in the seaside town of Southwold, The Crown dates back to the 18th century, when it was a coaching inn. Buzzing with lively informality, it is now a hotel owned by the Adnams Brewery (also based in Southwold), and offers a range of excellent ales on tap, as well as local Aspall cider. The location brings seafood options such as roulade of lemon sole, pan-fried sea bream fillet, and roasted scallops. Other choices from 'land' and 'garden' might include confit Gressingham duck leg, roast rack of lamb, goats' cheese risotto, and savoury pear tarte Tatin. Warm chocolate and peanut butter brownie is among the excellent puddings.

Open all wk 8am-11pm (Sun 8am-10.30pm) **Food** Lunch Mon-Fri 12-2, Sat-Sun 12-2.30 Dinner Sun-Fri 6-9, Sat 6-9.30 (5.30-9.30 summer) ⊕ ADNAMS ◀ Adnams Ö Aspall. ▼ 20 **Facilities** Non-diners area ▪ Children's menu Children's portions Garden ⋈ Parking WiFi

The Randolph   `PICK OF THE PUBS`

tel: 01502 723603 **41 Wangford Rd, Reydon IP18 6PZ**
email: reception@therandolph.co.uk
dir: *A12 onto A1095 towards Southwold. Left into Wangford Rd*

Striking village pub just outside Southwold

Built in 1899 by the town's well-known Adnams Brewery, this hotel was named after Lord Randolph Churchill, Sir Winston's father and a keen huntsman like the brewery's directors. The light and airy lounge bar, with contemporary high-backed chairs and comfortable sofas, overlooks a sunny, enclosed garden. In the bar and restaurant a concise modern British menu offers starters of ham hock fritters with English mustard mayonnaise; and smoked mackerel and leek tart with pickled beetroot and rocket salad. Mains include a trio of venison sausages with grain mustard mash; traditional breaded scampi and chips; chargrilled 10oz sirloin steak; and winter vegetable, goats' cheese and lentil crumble. Children are welcome and have their own menu. The Randolph could be just the place to call into after a day exploring Suffolk's Heritage Coast, although it is advisable to book a table.

Open all day all wk **Food** Lunch all wk 12-2 Dinner all wk 6.30-9 Restaurant menu available all wk ⊕ ADNAMS ◀ Southwold Bitter, Explorer, Old Ale, Adnams Ghost Ship Ö Aspall. **Facilities** Non-diners area ▪ Children's menu Children's portions Garden ⋈ Parking WiFi 🚃 (notice required)

STOKE-BY-NAYLAND   **Map 13 TL93**

The Angel Inn ★★★★ INN   `PICK OF THE PUBS`

tel: 01206 263245 **CO6 4SA**
email: info@angelinnsuffolk.co.uk **web:** www.angelinnsuffolk.co.uk
dir: *From Colchester take A134 towards Sudbury, 5m to Nayland. Or from A12 between juncts 30 & 31 take B1068, then B1087 to Nayland*

Charming coaching inn in Constable's country

The church in this idyllic Suffolk village appears in several of Constable's paintings, although apparently not always in the right place. The Angel occupies a 16th-century building that has been an inn for most of its existence, and the modern facilities, like the air-conditioned conservatory, patio and sun terrace, harmonise happily with the ancient charm of its beamed bars, log fires and snug areas. The Well Room, with its lofty, timbered ceiling and 52-ft deep well, is a popular place for a meal, with modern British main course options of confit duck leg, rice noodles, pak choi, mushroom, ginger and chilli broth; pan-roasted salmon, black pudding mash, sautéed cavolo nero, crispy boiled egg and hollandaise sauce; and roasted vegetable and camembert strudel with tomato pesto and rocket salad. The 35-bin wine list offers up to 12 by the glass, and real ales come mostly from small regional breweries.

Open all day all wk 11-11 (Sun 11-10.30) **Food** Lunch Mon-Fri 12-3.30, Sat 12-9.30, Sun 12-9 Dinner Mon-Fri 6-9.30, Sat 12-9.30, Sun 12-9 Set menu available Restaurant menu available all wk ⊕ FREE HOUSE/EXCLUSIVE INNS ◀ Adnams Southwold Bitter, Greene King, Nethergate, 2 Guest ales Ö Aspall, Thatchers. ▼ 12 **Facilities** Non-diners area ✿ (Bar Garden) ▪ Children's menu Children's portions Family room Garden Outside area ⋈ Parking WiFi 🚃 (notice required) **Rooms** 6

The Crown ★★★ SHL ◉◉   `PICK OF THE PUBS`

tel: 01206 262001 **CO6 4SE**
email: info@crowninn.net **web:** www.crowninn.net
dir: *Exit A12 signed Stratford St Mary & Dedham. Through Stratford St Mary 0.5m, left, follow signs to Higham. At village green left, left again, 2m, pub on right*

Delightful combination of village pub and boutique hotel

In the heart of Constable country and within easy reach of the timeless villages of Lavenham, Kersey and Long Melford, this 16th-century free house sits above the Stour and Box valleys on the Suffolk and Essex border. The dining areas are stylish yet informal, while the contemporary bar presents an excellent array of local ales. These are matched by an award-winning cellar of some 250 bins; over 30 of them can be bought by the glass. Tasty seasonal and local produce underpins a modern British menu. Typical starters are Godminster cheddar twice-baked soufflé; and pan-fried gnocchi with wild garlic pesto and parmesan chips. Children are welcome but dining is for adults only after 8pm. This is when the kitchen team produces the likes of venison and prune casserole with herb dumplings; and roasted lamb rump with cockles and purple sprouting broccoli. Eleven luxury en suite bedrooms complete the jewels in this crown.

Open all day all wk 7.30am-11pm (Sun 8am-10.30pm) Closed 25-26 Dec **Food** Lunch Mon-Sat 12-2.30, Sun 12-9 Dinner Mon-Thu 6-9.30, Fri-Sat 6-10, Sun 12-9 ⊕ FREE HOUSE ◀ Adnams Southwold Bitter, Crouch Vale Brewers Gold, Woodforde's Wherry, Guest ales Ō Aspall. ♟ 32 **Facilities** Non-diners area ♦♦ Children's menu Children's portions Outside area ⊓ Parking WiFi **Rooms** 11

The Buxhall Crown

tel: 01449 736521 **Mill Rd, Buxhall IP14 3DW**
email: mail@thebuxhallcrown.co.uk
dir: B1115 from Stowmarket, through Great Finborough to Buxhall

Charming rural pub with exceptional menu

A fetching mix of cosy 17th-century cottage and Georgian artisan's house, this lavishly-beamed, wood-framed gastro-pub manages to retain the atmosphere of a traditional old village inn, complete with log fire and timeworn quarry tiles. There's a large, pergola-lined patio with restful views across the rich farmland, where Adnams beers are the order of the day. Light lunches include a sharing cured meat meze; the carte menu is eye-opening. A starter of smoked pork belly croquettes with infused apple and sage purée might go down well before seared queen scallops with black and white pudding. Local provenance is assured; breads, chutneys and sweets are made at the pub.

Open 12-3 7-11 (Sat 12-3 6.30-11) Closed Sun eve & Mon **Food** Lunch Tue-Sun 12-2 Dinner Tue-Fri 7-9, Sat 6.30-9 ⊕ FREE HOUSE ◀ Adnams Southwold Bitter & Broadside Ō Aspall. ♟ 12 **Facilities** Non-diners area ♣ (Bar Restaurant Garden) ♦♦ Children's portions Garden Parking WiFi ⟲ (notice required)

The Ivy House

tel: 01379 384634 **Wilby Rd IP21 5JN**
email: stensethhome@aol.com
dir: Phone for detailed directions

Interesting ales and wines in a pretty pub

Around the corner from Stradbroke's main street, this Grade II listed thatched pub with wooden beams dates from the Middle Ages. Real ales on handpump and wine from the Adnams wine cellar are the draw here. The weekly-changing menu makes good use of local and seasonal produce to offer both British and Asian-style dishes, and in warmer weather you can sit outside at the front or in the garden. Typical options include teriyaki-marinated chicken skewers with salsa to start; and pan-fried calves' liver with Suffolk dry-cured bacon, mash and onion gravy as a main course. Leave room for dark chocolate cake with praline ice cream. Curries and other dishes are available to take away.

Open all wk 12-3 6-11 **Food** Contact pub for details ⊕ FREE HOUSE ◀ Adnams, Woodforde's, Buffy's Ō Aspall. **Facilities** Non-diners area ♣ (Bar Garden) Garden ⊓ Parking WiFi

Moon & Mushroom Inn

tel: 01473 785320 **High Rd IP6 9LR**
email: moonandmushroom@gmail.com
dir: Take B1077 (Westerfield road) from Ipswich. Approx 6m right to Swilland

Tranquil escape in deepest Suffolk

The delightful sight of several firkins of East Anglian beer still aged enticingly behind the bar welcomes drinkers to this 400-year-old free-house in the Suffolk countryside. Diners, too, relish the prospect of indulging in home-cooked specials such as Suffolk fish pie with salmon, cod, haddock and prawns; or slow roasted breast of lamb with lamb croquettes and redcurrant gravy. The pub was reputedly a staging post for the dispatch of convicts to Australia, and the records at Ipswich Assizes do indeed show that a previous landlord was deported for stealing two ducks and a pig. Today's guests are able to linger longer in the colourful, cottagey interior or the fragrant rose garden here.

Open Tue-Sat & Sun L Closed Sun eve & Mon **Food** Lunch Tue-Sat 12-2, Sun 12-2.30 Dinner Tue-Sat 6.30-9 Av main course £8.95 Set menu available Restaurant menu available Tue-Sat ⊕ FREE HOUSE ◀ Nethergate Suffolk County, Woodforde's Wherry & Admiral's Reserve, Wolf Ale & Golden Jackal, Earl Soham Brandeston Gold & Victoria Bitter Ō Aspall. **Facilities** Non-diners area ♣ (Bar Garden) ♦♦ Children's portions Garden ⊓ Beer festival Parking ⟲ (notice required)

The Dolphin Inn

tel: 01728 454994 **Peace Place IP16 4NA**
email: dolphininn@hotmail.co.uk **web:** www.thorpenessdolphin.com
dir: A12 onto A1094 & follow Thorpeness signs

At the community's heart and close to never ending beaches

A stone's throw from the shingle of Suffolk's Heritage Coast and in a conservation area, this community-focused free house replaced a 1910 predecessor, destroyed by fire in 1995. At the bar are real ales from Adnams and Earl Soham, nearly 20 wines by the glass, and bourbons and single malts in abundance. Look forward to dressed crab salad; potted brown shrimps; seared Gressingham duck breast with sweet potato mash; grilled sea bass fillet; and lemon and elderflower cheesecake. After a bracing walk on the beach sit beside the fire and enjoy a pint of the local brew; in summer barbecues are held in the huge garden.

Open 11-3 6-11 (Sat all day Sun 11-5) Closed Sun eve & Mon in winter **Food** Lunch all wk 12-2.30 Dinner all wk 6.30-9.30 Set menu available ⊕ FREE HOUSE ◀ Adnams Southwold Bitter & Broadside, Brandon Rusty Bucket, Mauldons Midsummer Gold, Woodforde's Wherry Ō Aspall. ♟ 18 **Facilities** Non-diners area ♣ (Bar Garden) ♦♦ Children's menu Children's portions Garden ⊓ Parking WiFi ⟲

PICK OF THE PUBS

The Westleton Crown ★★★ HL 🏵️🏵️

WESTLETON   Map 13 TM46

tel: 01728 648777   **The Street IP17 3AD**
email: info@westletoncrown.co.uk
web: www.westletoncrown.co.uk
dir: *A12 N, turn right for Westleton just
after Yoxford. Hotel opposite on entering
Westleton*

Classic dishes with a twist and and fine local ales

Standing opposite the parish church in a peaceful village close to the RSPB's Minsmere, this traditional coaching inn dates back to the 12th century and provides a comfortable base for exploring Suffolk's glorious Heritage Coast. The pub retains plenty of character and rustic charm, complemented by all the comforts of contemporary living. On winter days you'll find three crackling log fires, local real ales including Brandon Rusty Bucket and Adnams Southwold Bitter, as well as a good list of wines (with 11 available by the glass). There's also an extensive menu that includes innovative daily specials and classic dishes with a twist, freshly prepared from the best local produce. Eat in the cosy bar, in the elegant dining room, or in the garden room. Sandwiches are made with a choice of The Crown's own breads, and served with sea-salted crisps and a dressed salad. More substantial

appetites might choose from starters like orange and cumin stuffed quail ballotine, raisin purée and carrot salad; or Norfolk crab risotto, spring onions and crème fraîche. Follow up with main course choices such as pan-fried sea bass fillet, herb potato cake, wild mushroom fricassée; or chargrilled, marsh-fed sirloin, chips, confit tomato, with béarnaise or Diane sauce. Save some space for accomplished desserts like dark chocolate and ale cake with muscavado ice cream; or caramelised set stem ginger crème brûlee and orange sorbet. Retire to one of the 34 comfortably and individually styled bedrooms. Outside, the large terraced gardens are floodlit in the evening.

Open all day all wk 7am-11pm (Sun 7.30am-10.30pm) **Food** Lunch all wk 12-2.30 Dinner all wk 6.30-9.30 Av main course £16.50 🌐 FREE HOUSE 🍺 Adnams Southwold Bitter, Brandon Rusty Bucket Ď Aspall Harry Sparrow. 🍷 11 **Facilities** Non-diners area 🐾 (Bar Garden) 🧒 Children's menu Children's portions Garden 🚪 Parking WiFi 🚌 (notice required) **Rooms** 34

TUDDENHAM   Map 13 TM14

The Fountain

tel: 01473 785377 **The Street IP6 9BT**
email: fountainpub@btconnect.com
dir: *From Ipswich take B1077 (Westerfield Rd) signed Debenham. At Westerfield turn right for Tuddenham*

Informal bistro-style eating in a 16th-century country pub

In the lovely village of Tuddenham St Martin, only three miles north of Ipswich, this 16th-century country pub combines old fashioned pub hospitality with an informal bistro-style restaurant. The menu changes frequently and there is an emphasis on local produce in dishes such as twice baked Cromer crab soufflé; wild mushroom and tarragon risotto; and chocolate and pecan brownie with vanilla ice cream and caramel sauce. Wash it all down with pints of Adnams ale or Aspall cider.

Open all wk 12-3 6-11 **Food** Lunch Mon-Sat 12-2, Sun 12-3 Dinner Mon-Fri 6-9, Sat 6-9.30 Set menu available Restaurant menu available all wk ⊕ FREE HOUSE ◄ Adnams ◊ Aspall. ⦿ 9 **Facilities** Non-diners area ⧫ Children's menu Children's portions Garden ⇱ Parking WiFi

UFFORD   Map 13 TM25

The Ufford Crown

tel: 01394 461030 **High St IP13 6EL**
email: max@theuffordcrown.com
dir: *Just off A12 between Woodbridge & Wickham*

Friendly, family-run village pub and restaurant

Step though the doors of Max and Polly Durrant's handsome property and you'll find a spacious restaurant, cosy bar, stylish lounge area and, at the rear, a terrace and garden, where there's plenty to keep children amused. Adnams, Earl Soham badges adorn the real ale pumps, with Aspall cider alongside. A glass of sloe gin fizz would make a great intro for lunch or dinner here. Gifted chef Will Hardiman has a reputation for using all cuts of meat, including sweetbreads and ox cheeks, and Lowestoft-landed fish. Heavily reliant on seasonal produce from local suppliers, his menus feature harissa pork rillettes with fried quails's egg; grilled Ramsholt herring, caper buerre noisette and new potatoes; and BBQ short rib of beef, dauphinoise potatoes and greens.

Open 12-3 5-11 (Sat-Sun all day) Closed Tue **Food** Lunch Wed-Mon 12.30-2 Dinner Wed-Mon 6.30-9 ⊕ FREE HOUSE ◄ Adnams Southwold Bitter, Earl Soham Brandeston Gold & Victoria Bitter ◊ Aspall. ⦿ 15 **Facilities** Non-diners area ⧫ (Bar Garden) ⧫ Children's menu Children's portions Play area Garden Outside area ⇱ Parking WiFi ⤮ (notice required)

WALBERSWICK   Map 13 TM47

The Anchor ◉◉   PICK OF THE PUBS

tel: 01502 722112 **Main St IP18 6UA**
email: info@anchoratwalberswick.com
dir: *A12 onto B1387, follow Walberswick signs*

A family-friendly retreat with first-class food

Mark and Sophie Dawber are responsible for ensuring this striking Arts and Crafts pub on the Suffolk coast is more than just a village local. Mark, who oversees the drinks side, used to run a highly rated London pub, while Sophie, who once provided the catering on *Star Wars* film-sets, and whose family has long-standing local connections, runs the kitchen. The menu suggests a beer or wine to accompany each dish, thus Belgian Westmalle Tripel or Pinot Grigio are teamed with scallops, parsnip purée and pancetta salad; and Adnams Broadside or Sesti Grangiovese are recommended as accompaniments to Anchor pie with mustard mash. Similarly,

partnerships are also proposed for West Mersea oysters; rib-eye steak; and saffron, tomato and fennel linguine. Dessert of treacle tart is paired with a Muscat. The adjoining wild flower meadow is perfect for a picnic, especially during the mid-August beer festival.

Open all day all wk 11-11 **Food** Lunch 12-3 Dinner 6-9 ⊕ ADNAMS ◄ Southwold Bitter, Broadside & Seasonal ales, Meantime Helles & Pale Ale, Bitburger, Guest ales ◊ Aspall. ⦿ 22 **Facilities** Non-diners area ⧫ Children's menu Children's portions Family room Garden ⇱ Beer festival Parking WiFi

The Bell Inn

tel: 01502 723109 **Ferry Rd IP18 6TN**
email: info@bellinnwalberswick.co.uk
dir: *From A12 take B1387 to Walberswick, after village green right down track*

Old inn where the menu captures top Suffolk produce

Six centuries old and going stronger than ever, the Bell stands close to the Southwold ferry, the Suffolk Coastal Path and the marshes. Character is certainly not in short supply, with oak-beamed ceilings, hidden alcoves, worn flagstone floors and open fires. Firm favourites on the menu are Suffolk smokies with granary toast; fish pie; and lamb moussaka with Greek-style salad. Out back is a family-friendly garden overlooking a creek and the beach; here too is the Barn Café, offering everything for a picnic. Well-behaved dogs are welcome.

Open all day all wk 12-3 Dinner all wk 6-9 Av main course £12 ⊕ ADNAMS ◄ Southwold Bitter, Broadside, Spindrift, Ghost Ship ◊ Aspall. ⦿ 15 **Facilities** Non-diners area ⧫ (Bar Garden) ⧫ Children's menu Children's portions Family room Garden ⇱ Parking ⤮ (notice required)

WESTLETON   Map 13 TM46

The Westleton Crown ★★★ HL ◉◉   PICK OF THE PUBS

See Pick of the Pubs on opposite page

WHEPSTEAD   Map 13 TL85

The White Horse ◉   PICK OF THE PUBS

See Pick of the Pubs on page 468

WOODBRIDGE   Map 13 TM24

NEW Cherry Tree Inn ★★★★ INN

tel: 01394 384627 **73 Cumberland St IP12 4AG**
email: andy@thecherrytreepub.co.uk **web:** www.thecherrytreepub.co.uk
dir: *Phone for detailed directions*

Classically appealing hostelry with a caring approach

Winner of an AA Dinner Award and recognised for the sustainability of its operation, the Cherry Tree Inn features a large central counter, and several distinct seating areas amidst the twisting oak beams. The year sees around eight guest ales rotate, with Adnams and Aspall's cider in permanent residence; a beer festival in early July confirms the pub's ale credentials. The focus on customer care manifests subtly in many ways: the availability of board games; play equipment for children in the large enclosed garden; wheelchair access; dog friendliness; free WiFi; and many gluten-free options among the locally-sourced and home-cooked menu dishes.

Open all day all wk 10.30am-11pm **Food** Lunch Mon-Sat 12-9, Sun 12-8 Dinner Mon-Sat 12-9, Sun 12-8 Av main course £10 ⊕ ADNAMS ◄ Adnams ales, Guest ales ◊ Aspall. ⦿ 11 **Facilities** Non-diners area ⧫ (Bar Outside area) ⧫ Children's menu Children's portions Play area Garden Outside area ⇱ Beer festival Parking WiFi ⤮ (notice required) **Rooms** 3

PICK OF THE PUBS

The White Horse 🏵

WHEPSTEAD   Map 13 TL85

tel: 01284 735760
Rede Rd IP29 4SS
web: www.whitehorsewhepstead.co.uk
dir: *From Bury St Edmunds take A143
towards Haverhill. Left onto B1066 to
Whepstead. In Whepstead right into
Church Hill, leads into Rede Rd*

Delightful East Anglian pub with a loyal following

This village pub was built as a
farmhouse in the early 17th century and
extended during the Victorian era. As it
is surrounded by rural public footpaths,
many people take advantage of pub's
short walk guides and then return here
for lunch or dinner. The bright, spacious
interior makes it a great space for the
display and sale of artworks by local
painters. The large, copper-topped bar,
open fire and comfortable wooden chairs
make you feel instantly at home, while
nostalgic touches like the Tuck Shop
– which sells ice cream, sweets and
chocolate – appeal to adults and
children alike. As well as reliable Suffolk
ales and real cider behind the bar, the
award-winning menus change on a
daily basis. Owner Gary Kingshott
oversees the kitchen, and his passion
for great, uncomplicated food is evident
in every dish. Quality seasonal
ingredients are locally sourced where
possible and always fresh; meat comes
from the butcher in the next village.

Starters could include pressed ham
hock terrine with home-made piccalilli;
or deep-fried sweet peppers with ginger
and garlic relish. Main course options
might be an open pie filled with chicken,
mushrooms, tarragon and wine;
Madras-style fish curry, braised basmati
and warm naan bread; or slow braised
shoulder of Ickworth lamb, black olives
and creamy mash. For a lighter snack
choose perhaps roast pumpkin risotto or
camembert, gruyère and roasted tomato
tart. For pudding the baked apricot
cheesecake will go down well. Front of
house is run by Di Kingshott and her
years of experience ensure quick and
friendly service. Skye, the dog, can be
found snoozing in a corner when he is
not gently greeting customers.

Open 11.30-3 7-11 Closed 25-26 Dec,
Sun eve **Food** Lunch all wk 12-2 Dinner
Mon-Sat 7-9.30 Av main course £12.95
🌐 FREE HOUSE 🍺 Adnams Southwold
Bitter & Broadside, Guest Ale 🍏 Aspall.
🍷 10 **Facilities** Non-diners area 🐾 (Bar
Garden) 🚼 Children's portions Garden
Parking 🚐

WOODDITTON
Map 12 TL65

NEW The Three Blackbirds

tel: 01638 731100 **36 Ditton Green CB8 9SQ**
email: info@thethreeblackbirdswoodditton.co.uk
dir: *From Newmarket High Street (Cambridge end) take B1061 opposite Total garage. In 300yds turn left, 2.5m to Woodditton. At x-rds turn right, pub 300yds on right.*

Exciting food and local ales in beautiful thatched village inn

Just three miles from Newmarket, the beautiful village of Woodditton was mentioned in the Domesday Book. The thatched Three Blackbirds dates from 1642 and it reopened in 2013 after an 18-month renovation restoring it to its original splendour. The two cosy oak-beamed bars offer a range of real ales and diners can choose between the restaurant and private dining room to sample a daily-changing menu packed with local produce. Denham Estate venison with chocolate and red wine sauce; and Barbary duck with curly kale and celeriac mash are typical dishes.

Open 12-3 5-11 (Fri 12-3 5-mdnt Sat 12-3 5.30-12 Sun 12-7) Closed Sun eve **Food** Lunch Mon-Sat 12-2.30, Sun 12-4 Dinner Mon-Sat 6.30-9.15 Set menu available Restaurant menu available all wk ⊕ FREE HOUSE ◀ Adnams Best Bitter, Woodforde's Wherry, Sharp's Doom Bar ♂ Aspall. ♀ 17 **Facilities** Non-diners area ✿ (Bar Garden Outside area) ♦ Children's menu Children's portions Garden Outside area ⊞ Beer festival Cider festival Parking WiFi ▄ (notice required)

SURREY

ABINGER
Map 6 TQ14

NEW The Abinger Hatch

tel: 01306 730737 **Abinger Ln RH5 6HZ**
email: manager@theabingerhatch.com
dir: *A25 from Dorking towards Guildford. Left to Abinger Common*

Quintessentially English pub with something for everyone

It's been a couple years now since Andy and Sarah took over this lovely pub, aiming to please families with their special brand of hospitality. Lots of variety is the key, from the children's choices to menus of dishes based on fresh locally sourced produce. Traditionally English from its beams to its flagstone floors, the pub enjoys a light and airy atmosphere. There's lots of space outside too, with capacious car parking and a huge garden where a summer barbecue, wood-burning oven and outdoor bar make for a truly relaxing experience. Ringwood and guest ales head the refreshments list, with plenty of wines to choose from.

Open all day all wk **Food** Lunch all wk 12-6 Dinner Mon-Sat 6-10, Sun 6-9 ⊕ FREE HOUSE ◀ Ringwood Best & Fortyniner, Cottage, Guest ales. ♀ 14 **Facilities** Non-diners area ✿ (Bar Restaurant Garden) ♦ Children's menu Children's portions Garden ⊞ Parking WiFi ▄ (notice required)

The Stephan Langton
PICK OF THE PUBS

tel: 01306 730775 & 737129 **Friday St RH5 6JR**
email: info@stephanlangtonpub.co.uk
dir: *Exit A25 between Dorking & Guildford at Hollow Ln. 1.5m, left into Friday St*

A popular stop for walkers

This is prime Surrey walking country and a popular pitstop is The Stephan Langton, a 1930s building named after the first archbishop of Canterbury, who was supposedly born in Friday Street. Undulating mixed woodland surrounds this secluded hamlet at the base of Leith Hill, the highest summit in south-east England. Langton helped draw up the Magna Carta and a copy of the document is pinned to a wall in the rustic, bare-boarded bar. Equally unpretentious is the adjoining dining room, with its cream-washed walls, simple wooden tables and chairs, and open fires. Having conquered Leith Hill, relax on the suntrap patio and savour a thirst-quenching pint of locally brewed Hogs Back TEA. Peruse the short, inviting menu that hits the spot with lunchtime sandwiches and hearty main dishes. Changing daily specials make the most of local produce, much of it sourced from the surrounding Wooton Estate.

Open 11.30-3 5.30-11 (Sat 11-11 Sun 12-9) Closed Mon L **Food** Lunch Tue-Sat 12-2.30, Sun 12-4 Dinner Tue-Sat 6.30-9.30 ⊕ FREE HOUSE ◀ Hogs Back TEA, Sharp's Doom Bar, Fuller's London Pride, Guest ales ♂ Thatchers Gold. **Facilities** Non-diners area ✿ (Bar) ♦ Children's portions Outside area ⊞ Parking ▄ (notice required)

The Volunteer

tel: 01306 730985 **Water Ln, Sutton RH5 6PR**
email: volunteer247@btinternet.com
dir: *Between Guildford & Dorking, 1m S of A25*

Good spot for tip-top beer and good food

Enjoying a delightful rural setting with views over the River Mole, this popular village pub was originally farm cottages and first licensed about 1870. Under the ownership of Hall & Woodhouse, it remains an ideal watering hole for walkers who want to relax over a pint in the attractive three-tier pub garden, or in the bustling bar with its two fireplaces. Typical dishes include red Thai curry; chicken and asparagus pie; and the renowned Volunteer fish pie. Sandwiches, baguettes, melts, toasted sandwiches and jacket potatoes are all available too.

Open all wk 12-3 6-11 (Sat 12-11 Sun 12-4) **Food** Lunch Mon-Fri 12-2.30, Sat 12-9, Sun 12-3 Dinner Mon-Fri 6.30-9.30, Sat 12-9 ⊕ HALL & WOODHOUSE ◀ Badger Tanglefoot, K&B Sussex, Guest ales ♂ Westons Stowford Press. ♀ 9 **Facilities** Non-diners area ✿ (Bar Restaurant Garden) ♦ Children's menu Children's portions Garden ⊞ Parking WiFi ▄ (notice required)

ALBURY
Map 6 TQ04

The Drummond at Albury ★★★ INN

tel: 01483 202039 **The Street GU5 9AG**
email: drummondarms@aol.com **web:** www.thedrummondarms.co.uk
dir: *6m from Guildford on A248*

Riverside pub in the heart of the Surrey Hills

This eye-catching village inn, which has hanging flower baskets outside in summer, was reopened a few years ago by the Duke of Northumberland whose family have historic links to the pub. Its pleasant beer garden backs onto River Tillingbourne. Expect a comforting mix of great local (from Hogs Back) and national real ales. In the conservatory restaurant, the best of modern and traditional British cooking is on offer – herb-roasted chicken breast, trout from the Albury Estate lakes, and the popular home-made Drummond pies. Individually appointed letting rooms make the pub a good base from which to explore the North Downs.

Open all day all wk 11-11 (Fri-Sat 11am-mdnt Sun 12-10.30) **Food** Lunch Mon-Fri 12-3, Sat 12-6, Sun 12-8 Dinner Mon-Sat 6-9.30, Sun 12-8 ⊕ FREE HOUSE ◀ Courage Best Bitter, Fuller's London Pride, Hogs Back TEA, Adnams. ♀ 10 **Facilities** Non-diners area ✿ (Bar Garden) ♦ Children's portions Garden ⊞ Parking WiFi **Rooms** 9

ALBURY *continued*

William IV

tel: 01483 202685 **Little London GU5 9DG**
dir: *Off A25 between Guildford & Dorking (for detailed directions contact pub)*

16th-century free house on a quiet country lane

Deep in the wooded Surrey Hills yet only a few miles from Guildford, this 16th-century free house provides 'proper pub food' made from mostly local produce. Sometimes it's the free-range pork raised by landlord Giles written on the blackboards, but more usually it's liver and bacon, beer-battered cod and chips, or pan-fried Cajun chicken, all served in the bar and dining room. Young's and two Surrey breweries supply the real ales. It is great walking and riding country, and the attractive garden is ideal for post-ramble relaxation.

Open all wk 11-3 5.30-11 (Sat 11-11 Sun 12-11) **Food** Lunch all wk 12-2 Dinner Mon-Sat 7-9 ⊕ FREE HOUSE ◀ Young's, Hogs Back, Surrey Hills ♂ Westons Stowford Press, Addlestones. **Facilities** Non-diners area ♣ (Bar Garden) ♦♦ Children's portions Garden ⋒ Parking WiFi ☎ (notice required)

BETCHWORTH   Map 6 TQ25

The Red Lion

tel: 01737 843336 **Old Rd, Buckland RH3 7DS**
email: info@redlionbetchworth.com
dir: *Phone for detailed directions*

A favourite with walkers and cyclists

Set in 18 acres next to a cricket ground, the family-run Red Lion dates back to the 18th century, is home to a wisteria thought to be around 250 years old. Although only 15 minutes from Gatwick, the pub enjoys lovely rolling countryside views - the area is ideal for walkers. Sandwiches are listed on the bar menu, while starters from the à la carte menu could include crab spring rolls with sweet chilli dip; pasta topped with ratatouille; roasted salmon fillet with tarragon cream sauce; or home-cooked ham, free eggs and hand-cut chips. There are two unusual function areas: a fully air-conditioned cellar, and an outdoor area covered with a cedar shingle roof.

Open all day all wk 11am-11.30pm (Fri-Sat 11am-mdnt) **Food** Lunch Sun-Fri 12-2.30, Sat 12-4 ⊕ PUNCH TAVERNS ◀ Harvey's, Ringwood, Sharp's Doom Bar ♂ Addlestones, Westons Stowford Press. ♥ 9 **Facilities** Non-diners area ♣ (Bar Restaurant Garden) ♦♦ Children's menu Children's portions Garden ⋒ Parking WiFi ☎ (notice required)

BRAMLEY   Map 6 TQ04

Jolly Farmer Inn

tel: 01483 893355 **High St GU5 0HB**
email: enquiries@jollyfarmer.co.uk
dir: *From Guildford take A281 (Horsham road). Bramley 3.5m S of Guildford*

Welcoming and friendly pub

A 16th-century coaching inn steeped in character and history, this friendly family-run free house clearly has a passion for beer. Besides the impressive range of Belgian bottled beers, you'll always find up to eight constantly-changing cask real ales on the counter. The pub offers a high standard of food all freshly cooked, with daily specials board featuring Scottish sirloin and vegetable stir-fry; home-made lasagne; Caesar salad and a full rack of barbecue pork ribs with chips and salad.

Open all day all wk 11-11 **Food** Lunch all wk 12-2.30 Dinner all wk 6-9.30 Av main course £10 ⊕ FREE HOUSE ◀ 8 Guest ales ♂ Westons Stowford Press, Aspall. ♥ 16 **Facilities** Non-diners area ♣ (Bar Garden Outside area) ♦♦ Children's menu Garden Outside area ⋒ Parking WiFi ☎ (notice required)

BUCKLAND   Map 6 TQ25

The Jolly Farmers Eatery + Farm Shop

tel: 01737 221355 **Reigate Rd RH3 7BG**
email: info@thejollyfarmersreigate.co.uk
dir: *On A25 approx 2m from Reigate & 4m from Dorking*

Delightful deli, farm shop and pub combo

Beside the A25 between Reigate and Dorking, this unique free house may look like a traditional pub but step inside and you'll find a cracking deli and farm shop that showcases local foods and artisan producers smack next to the comfortable, wood-floored bar and restaurant. Choose from deli snacks such as a hand-made sausage roll with onion marmalade or Jolly Farmer pickled eggs, or plump for a full meal – maybe deep-fried baby squid followed by a gourmet burger with Jolly Farmers relish and real chips. Wash it down with a pint of Dark Star Hophead or WJ King Horsham Best.

Open all day all wk **Food** Lunch all wk all day Dinner all wk all day Av main course £9.95 ⊕ FREE HOUSE ◀ Dark Star Hophead, WJ King Horsham Best, Dorking DB Number One, Pilgrim Surrey Bitter. ♥ 14 **Facilities** Non-diners area ♣ (Bar Garden) ♦♦ Children's menu Children's portions Play area Garden ⋒ Parking WiFi ☎ (notice required)

CHIDDINGFOLD   Map 6 SU93

The Crown Inn ★★★★★ INN

tel: 01428 682255 **The Green GU8 4TX**
email: enquiries@thecrownchiddingfold.com web: www.thecrownchiddingfold.com
dir: *On A283 between Milford & Petworth*

Historic timbered inn, more than 700 years old

Set by the village green and church, this beautifully appointed inn is one of the county's oldest buildings. It oozes charm and character, featuring ancient panelling, open fires, distinctive carvings, huge beams, and eight comfortable bedrooms. In addition to the house beer, Crown Bitter, ales come from Surrey, Hampshire and London breweries. Food ranges from decent snacks like a seafood platter and smoked salmon ciabatta sandwich, to Crown favourites such as corned beef hash, and imaginative dishes, perhaps confit leg and roast breast of guinea fowl with Puy lentils and spinach; or sweet potato, chickpea and shallot tagine.

Open all day all wk **Food** Lunch Mon-Sat 12-2.30, Sun 12-3 Dinner Mon-Sat 6.30-10, Sun 6.30-9 ⊕ FREE HOUSE/FGH INNS ◀ Crown Bitter, Fuller's London Pride, Triple fff Moondance, Hop Back Summer Lightning. **Facilities** Non-diners area ♦♦ Children's menu Children's portions Garden ⋒ WiFi ☎ **Rooms** 8

The Swan Inn ★★★★ INN ⊛   PICK OF THE PUBS

See Pick of the Pubs on opposite page

Follow us on twitter
@TheAA_Lifestyle

PICK OF THE PUBS

The Swan Inn ★★★★ INN

tel: 01428 684688
Petworth Rd GU8 4TY
email: info@theswaninnchiddingfold.com
web: www.theswaninnchiddingfold.com
dir: *From A3 follow Milford/Petworth/*
A283 signs. At rdbt 1st exit onto A283.
Slight right onto Guildford & Godalming
bypass. Right into Portsmouth Rd, left
(continue on A283), to Chiddingfold

Cosmopolitan food and drink in stylish village inn

The owners of The Swan Inn ran a pub in fashionable Knightsbridge for 20 years before taking over here and they have added luxurious boutique-style accommodation to this lovely old village inn. Nestling among the Surrey Hills in the village of Chiddingfold between Guildford and Petworth, The Swan is typical of the coaching inns that used to serve customers travelling to or from the south coast. Rebuilt in the 1880s and refurbished to a high standard in 2010, The Swan today offers weary travellers a friendly and relaxed welcome. In the bar, temptations include local ales such as Shere Drop brewed by the Surrey Hills Brewery, and from an international list, there are 16 wines served by the glass. The menu also has broad appeal, with top-notch produce such as Scottish salmon, Parma ham and foie gras. A typical meal might kick off with an appetiser of vegetable chowder with

toasted corn bread; a classic Caesar salad; or lamb koftas with cucumber and mint raita. They might be followed by main course choices of rack of lamb, celeriac gratin, crispy lamb belly, buttered spinach and rosemary jus; calves' liver with mustard mash and onion gravy; beer battered haddock, shoestring fries, pea purée and tartare sauce; or Moroccan chickpea and vegetable tagine, tabbouleh, chargrilled aubergine and rocket pesto. For dessert perhaps choose date sponge pudding with caramel sauce and vanilla ice cream; or for something a little different, sweetcorn pannacotta with popcorn croquant, madeleine sponge and popcorn ice cream.

Open all day all wk 11-11 (Sun 12-10.30) **Food** Lunch all wk 12-3 Dinner Mon-Sat 6.30-10, Sun 6.30-9 Av main course £13.50 ⊕ FREE HOUSE ◀ Adnams Southwold Bitter, Surrey Hills Shere Drop, Guest ale ♂ Hogan's, Aspall. ♥ 16 **Facilities** Non-diners area ☘ (Bar Garden) ⼧ Children's menu Children's portions Garden ⼂ Beer festival Parking WiFi **Rooms** 10

COLDHARBOUR
Map 6 TQ14

The Plough Inn
PICK OF THE PUBS

tel: 01306 711793 **Coldharbour Ln RH5 6HD**
email: theploughinn@btinternet.com
dir: *M25 junct 9, A24 to Dorking. A25 towards Guildford. Coldharbour signed from one-way system*

Well established pub in pretty village

Known to date from 1641, the Abrehart family's old coaching inn gets much of its footfall from walkers and cyclists scaling nearby 965-ft Leith Hill, the highest point in south-eastern England. Earlier visitors were smugglers en route from the south coast to London, which may be why the resident ghost is a sailor. Another high point is the landlord's own microbrewery, producing Tallywhacker porter, Crooked Furrow bitter and the lighter Beautiful South, as well as Biddenden cider. The Abreharts' 26-year residency has produced a family-friendly place with big fires, a pretty garden and an evening steakhouse with a malt whisky bar serving 21-day, dry-aged local Aberdeen Angus steaks and other chargrills. On the menus expect lamb, mint and coriander sausages and mash with Merlot gravy; cod, haddock, prawn and salmon pie; and Mediterranean vegetable and goats' cheese tart. Home-made puddings include spotted dick and a daily crumble.

Open all day all wk 11.30am-close Closed 25 Dec **Food** Lunch Mon-Fri 12-2.30, Sat-Sun 12-3 Dinner Mon-Sat 7-9.30 ⊕ FREE HOUSE ◀ Leith Hill Crooked Furrow, Tallywhacker & The Beautiful South, Guest ale Ö Biddenden.
Facilities Non-diners area ◀◀ Children's menu Children's portions Garden Parking WiFi ⬛ (notice required)

COMPTON
Map 6 SU94

The Withies Inn

tel: 01483 421158 **Withies Ln GU3 1JA**
dir: *Phone for detailed directions*

Eclectically furnished old village inn

This low-beamed inn has slumbered beside the wooded common for five centuries, maturing into a popular, cosy village local enhanced by an intimate restaurant area, where home-made pâté can lead in to poached halibut with prawns and brandy sauce. Seasonal specials tumble from the menu; asparagus, grouse or wild duck may be available here. Comfort-food bar snacks range from filled jacket potatoes to fisherman's broth or a hot salt beef sandwich; tuck into sausage, mash and onion gravy after a stroll in the lovely surrounding countryside, or relax in the garden with a pint of TEA from the local Hogs Back Brewery.

Open 11-3 6-11 (Fri 11-11) Closed Sun eve **Food** Lunch all wk 12-2.30 Dinner Mon-Sat 6-10 Restaurant menu available all wk ⊕ FREE HOUSE ◀ Hogs Back TEA, Greene King IPA, Adnams, Sharp's Doom Bar Ö Aspall. ▼ 12
Facilities Non-diners area ◀◀ Children's portions Garden ⌂ Parking WiFi ⬛ (notice required)

CRANLEIGH
Map 6 TQ03

The Richard Onslow

tel: 01483 274922 **113-117 High St GU6 8AU**
email: hello@therichardonslow.co.uk
dir: *From A281 between Guildford & Horsham take B2130 to Cranleigh, pub in village centre*

A grand old tile-hung pub

In the heart of the village, this smart pub maintains its traditional character in the original brick inglenook and other carefully restored features while also benefiting from contemporary decor. Enjoy pints of ale from local independent breweries like Surrey Hills and take advantage of the fact that food is served all day starting with breakfast – to eat in or take away. The emphasis is firmly on seasonal produce, as

much as possible being sourced locally. Just some of the options are deli boards, chargrilled steaks, the roast of the day and mains such as roasted monkfish fillet.

Open all day all wk Closed 25 Dec **Food** Lunch Mon-Sat 12-3, Sun 12-9 Dinner Mon-Sat 6-10, Sun 12-9 ⊕ PEACH PUBS ◀ Surrey Hills Shere Drop, Sharp's Doom Bar Ö Hogs Back Hazy Hog. ▼ 16 **Facilities** Non-diners area ◀◀ Children's portions Garden ⌂ Beer festival Cider festival WiFi ⬛ (notice required)

DUNSFOLD
Map 6 TQ03

The Sun Inn

tel: 01483 200242 **The Common GU8 4LE**
email: suninn@dunsfold.net
dir: *A281 through Shalford & Bramley, take B2130 to Godalming. Dunsfold on left after 2m*

Bags of traditional charm

A traditional 17th-century inn opposite the cricket green and village pond in a chocolate-box village, The Sun Inn delivers a warm welcome, blazing fires and an array of real ales from the likes of Adnams, Harvey's and Sharp's. The home-made healthy eating dishes use produce from the inn's own vegetable garden. Typical starters include porcini mushroom soup, and breaded king prawns with chilli dip and nachos. Among the main courses you'll find Mexican salsa burger; salmon fishcakes; and butternut squash and spinach lasagne. Enjoy the quiz every Sunday evening, the pies on Wednesdays and curries on Fridays.

Open all day all wk **Food** Lunch all wk 12-2.30 Dinner Mon-Sat 7-9.15, Sun 7-8.30 Av main course £8.95 ⊕ PUNCH TAVERNS ◀ Sharp's Doom Bar, Harvey's Sussex, Adnams, Guest ales Ö Westons Scrumpy. ▼ 10 **Facilities** Non-diners area ❦ (Bar Garden) ◀◀ Children's menu Children's portions Garden ⌂ Parking WiFi ⬛ (notice required)

EASHING
Map 6 SU94

The Stag on the River

tel: 01483 421568 **Lower Eashing GU7 2QG**
email: bookings@stagontherivereashing.co.uk
dir: *From A3 S'bound exit signed Eashing, 200yds over river bridge. Pub on right*

A good meeting place by the river

The river is the Wey, and this comfortable, well-appointed village inn on its banks takes full advantage, with a large beer garden and separate patio. Fixtures on handpump in the bar are Hogs Back TEA (Traditional English Ale) and Surrey Hills Shere Drop, named after a nearby village; others rotate. A seasonal menu might begin with duck and truffle parfait with fig chutney, or a charcuterie sharing plate. Main courses include wild boar sausages, roasted parsnip purée and red currant jus; or a classic fish pie. For dessert try white chocolate and pistachio pannacotta with poached rhubarb.

Open all day all wk Closed 25 Dec **Food** Lunch Mon-Sat 12-3, Sun 12-8.30 Dinner Mon-Sat 6-9, Sun 12-8.30 Set menu available ⊕ FREE HOUSE ◀ Hogs Back TEA, Surrey Hills Shere Drop, Guest ales. ▼ 12 **Facilities** Non-diners area ❦ (Bar Garden) ◀◀ Children's menu Children's portions Garden ⌂ Parking WiFi

EAST CLANDON
Map 6 TQ05

The Queens Head

tel: 01483 222332 **The Street GU4 7RY**
email: bookings@queensheadeastclandon.co.uk
dir: *4m E of Guildford on A246. Signed*

Smart village pub - eat and drink in or out

This bustling brick-built village pub close to the North Downs Way is a haven for ramblers and locals seeking the best local produce. Beer is courtesy of the nearby

Surrey Hills Brewery, while the food majors on locally sourced seasonal produce including meat from a 100-acre farm. A hearty plate of British steak, real ale and mushroom pie with seasonal vegetables and chunky chips will revive after a long winter walk, or share a fish board, including crayfish, Devon crab and smoked mackerel, in the tree-shaded garden.

Open all wk 12-3 6-11 (Sat 12-11 Sun 12-9) **Food** Lunch Mon-Fri 12-2.30, Sat 12-9.30, Sun 12-8 Dinner Mon-Thu 6-9, Fri 6-9.30, Sat 12-9.30, Sun 12-8 ⊕ FREE HOUSE ◀ Surrey Hills Shere Drop, Hogs Back TEA, Brakspear Oxford Gold, Shepherd Neame Spitfire, Sharp's Doom Bar. ♥ 13 **Facilities** Non-diners area ♦♦ Children's menu Children's portions Garden ⋈ Parking WiFi ▥

EFFINGHAM
Map 6 TQ15

The Plough

tel: 01372 458121 **Orestan Ln KT24 5SW**
dir: Between Guildford & Leatherhead on A246

Hidden gem in the Surrey Hills

Decorated with neutral tones, in a light and airy atmosphere, this pub probably dates from the mid-1870s, judging by the beamed interior. The Plough also acquired a beautiful orchard garden; there are plenty of tables in the garden and terrace, and Surrey Hills ramblers are often to be found here enjoying a pint of Young's. Monthly-changing, freshly prepared contemporary and traditional British favourites include mussel, spinach and bacon gratin; glazed cauliflower cheese with toasted garlic and rosemary foccacia; beer battered haddock and chips; and pan-roasted guinea fowl with kale, bread sauce and goose fat roasted potatoes. Sunday roasts come with huge Yorkshire puds. The Plough is near Polesden Lacey, an opulent National Trust country house.

Open all wk 11.30-3 5.30-11 (Sun 12-7) Closed 25-26 Dec & 31 Dec eve **Food** Lunch Mon-Sat 12-2.30, Sun 12-5 Dinner Mon-Sat 7-10 Av main course £12.95 ⊕ YOUNG'S ◀ Special, Twickenham Fine Ales, Redhead, Naked Ladies & Grandstand ♂ Aspall. ♥ 16 **Facilities** Non-diners area ♦♦ Children's menu Children's portions Garden Parking WiFi

ELSTEAD
Map 6 SU94

The Woolpack

tel: 01252 703106 **The Green, Milford Rd GU8 6HD**
email: info@woolpackelstead.co.uk
dir: A3 S, take Milford exit, follow signs for Elstead on B3001

Village local with an Italian flavour

Originally a wool exchange dating back to the 17th century, the attractive tile-hung Woolpack continues to display weaving shuttles and other artefacts relating to the wool industry. You'll also find open log fires, low beams, high-backed settles, comfortable window seats and cask-conditioned ales including local Hogs Back TEA and Ringwood Fortyniner. On the menu which features Italian dishes from the owners' home country, you might find starters such as fried nutty brie wedge with sweet cranberry sauce, followed by fish pie; rib-eye steak with chunky chips and peppercorn sauce; or creamy goats' cheese and roasted pepper carbonara. There is also a sandwich menu and obviously a wide selection of stone-baked pizzas. The surrounding common land attracts ramblers galore, especially at lunchtime.

Open all wk 12-3 5.30-late (Sun 12-late) **Food** Lunch all wk 12-3 Dinner Mon-Sat 6-9, Sun 6-8 Restaurant menu available all wk ⊕ PUNCH TAVERNS ◀ Ringwood Fortyniner, Hogs Back TEA, Sharp's Doom Bar ♂ Westons Stowford Press. ♥ 9 **Facilities** Non-diners area ♣ (Bar Garden) ♦♦ Children's menu Children's portions Play area Garden ⋈ Parking WiFi ▥ (notice required)

ENGLEFIELD GREEN
Map 6 SU97

The Fox and Hounds

tel: 01784 433098 **Bishopsgate Rd TW20 0XU**
email: marketing@thefoxandhoundsrestaurant.com
dir: M25 junct 13, A30 signed Basingstoke & Camberley. Right at lights onto A328 signed Englefield Green. With village green on left, left into Bishopsgate Rd

Upmarket dining close to Windsor Great Park

Dating back to 1780, this pub is ideally situated next to the Bishopsgate entrance to Windsor Great Park in the village of Englefield Green. Enjoy a pint of Brakspear bitter in the stylish bar or enjoy a slap-up meal in the light and elegant conservatory restaurant. A starter of gin cured gravad lax or fennel and chilli dusted squid might be followed by goats' cheese papperdelle; belly of pork; or lemon and garlic spatchcock poussin. Leave room for dark chocolate and walnut tart or the tasting plate of puddings to share.

Open all day all wk 8am-11pm **Food** Lunch all wk 12-9.30 Dinner all wk 12-9.30 Av main course £10-£12 Set menu available ⊕ FREE HOUSE/BRAKSPEAR ◀ Brakspear Bitter & Oxford Gold ♂ Symonds. ♥ 14 **Facilities** Non-diners area ♣ (Bar Garden) ♦♦ Children's menu Children's portions Garden ⋈ Parking WiFi ▥ (notice required)

FARNHAM
Map 5 SU84

The Bat & Ball Freehouse
PICK OF THE PUBS

tel: 01252 792108 **15 Bat & Ball Ln, Boundstone GU10 4SA**
email: info@thebatandball.co.uk
dir: From A31 (Farnham bypass) onto A325 signed Birdworld. Left at Bengal Lounge. At T-junct right, immediately left into Sandrock Hill Rd. 0.25m left into Upper Bourne Ln. Follow signs.

A mid-Victorian free house well worth seeking out

A little tricky to find - it's down a long cul-de-sac - but you'll be pleased you persevered. It's a real community pub, the interior featuring terracotta floors, oak beams, a warming fire and cricketing memorabilia, while in the garden you'll find a patio with picnic tables, a vine-topped pergola and a children's fort. Six frequently-changing real ales come from regional microbreweries, the cider is Aspall and plenty of wines are by the glass. Lizzy, daughter of owners Kevin and Sally Macready, masterminds a menu comprising both modern and traditional dishes. After, for instance, a devilled whitebait starter, main courses include roasted duck legs with red wine and bacon-braised Puy lentils, shallot purée and watercress pesto; beef shin osso buco with gremolata; and crab samosa with Indian salad. A huge choice of ales and ciders is laid on during the beer, cider and music festival during the second weekend in June.

Open all day all wk 11-11 (Sun 12-10.30) **Food** Lunch Mon-Sat 12-2.15, Sun 12-3 Dinner Mon-Sat 7-9.30, Sun 6-8.30 ⊕ FREE HOUSE ◀ Hogs Back TEA, Triple fff, Bowman, Ballards, Andwell, Arundel, Weltons, Itchen Valley ♂ Westons Stowford Press, Aspall. ♥ 8 **Facilities** Non-diners area ♣ (All areas) ♦♦ Children's menu Children's portions Play area Family room Garden Outside area ⋈ Beer festival Cider festival Parking WiFi

FARNHAM *continued*

The Spotted Cow at Lower Bourne

tel: 01252 726541 **Bourne Grove, Lower Bourne GU10 3QT**
email: thespottedcow@btinternet.com **web:** www.thespottedcowpub.com
dir: *From Farnham town centre, cross rail line, onto B3001. Right into Tilford Rd, up hill, at lights straight on, Bourne Grove 3rd right*

Idyllic woodland and garden setting

Set in four acres of secluded, woodland-shaded grounds and two gardens, one of which is enclosed and especially suitable for young children, the Spotted Cow is a perfect place to unwind. Indulge in some of the great TEA beer from nearby Hogs Back Brewery and consider the ever-changing menu of tried-and-tested favourites, all made fresh on the premises. Sandwiches and jackets are on the bar lunch menu, while regularly-changing specials could include home-made spiced parsnip soup with chunky bread or breast of duck on crushed new potatoes with a port and cranberry sauce.

Open all wk 12-3 5.30-11 (Sat 12-11 Sun 12-10.30) **Food** Lunch Mon-Sat 12-2.30 Dinner Mon-Sat 6-9.15 Av main course £12 ⊕ FREE HOUSE ◀ Timothy Taylor Landlord, Hogs Back TEA, Sharp's Doom Bar ♂ Addlestones. ♥
Facilities Non-diners area ❖ (Bar Restaurant Garden) ♦♦ Children's portions Play area Garden ⊨ Parking WiFi

■ FETCHAM　　　　　　　　　　　　　Map 6 TQ15

The Bell

tel: 01372 372624 **Bell Ln KT22 9ND**
email: bellfetcham@youngs.co.uk
dir: *From A245 in Leatherhead take Waterway Rd (B2122). At rdbt 2nd exit into Guildford Rd (B2122). At mini rdbt right into Cobham Rd. Straight on at next 2 mini rdbts. Left into School Ln, left into Bell Ln*

Something for everyone whether inside or outdoors

The striking 1930s building in the pretty Mole Valley is one of the Young's Brewery's 'flagship' dining pubs. Expect a smart terrace for alfresco drinking and dining, a light and airy wood-panelled restaurant, and a comfortable bar, replete with leather sofas and chairs. Using quality, seasonal produce, including vegetables from Secretts Farm and pork from Dingley Dell Farms, everything on the menus is cooked from scratch. The traditional British cuisine includes the likes roast Gressingham duck leg, and pan-fried sea bream on the main menu. Booking is essential for Sunday roasts.

Open all day all wk **Food** Lunch Mon-Thu 12-3, Fri-Sat 12-9.30, Sun 12-8.30 Dinner Mon-Thu 6-9.30, Fri-Sat 12-9.30, Sun 12-8.30 ⊕ YOUNG'S ◀ Bitter & Special, Guest ales ♂ Aspall. ♥ 22 **Facilities** Non-diners area ♦♦ Children's portions Garden ⊨ Beer festival Parking WiFi ▦ (notice required)

■ FOREST GREEN　　　　　　　　　　Map 6 TQ14

The Parrot Inn　　　　　　`PICK OF THE PUBS`

tel: 01306 621339 **RH5 5RZ**
email: drinks@theparrot.co.uk
dir: *B2126 from A29 at Ockley, signed Forest Green*

Inviting 17th-century country pub with its own farm

Overlooking the village green and cricket pitch up here in the Surrey Hills is Linda Gotto's and Lucinda Parks' tile-hung country pub. Their traditional bar, with low-beamed ceilings, flagstone floor and huge brass fireplace is so typically English it could have been transported straight from a film set. From it, French doors lead to a sheltered, paved terrace. At Linda's farm in nearby Dorking with her customers very much in mind, she raises rare-breed pigs, Shorthorn cattle and Dorset sheep. Now fast-forward to your plate, on which could appear coarse pork and pistachio terrine; sirloin steak with beef tomato; pork, cider and mustard pie; or chargrilled hogget chops with butterbean mash. Some dishes need to be sourced from beyond Dorking, such as mussel chowder, and grilled lemon sole. Butchers Hall, an on-site farm shop, opens daily and sells, well, let's just say it does the job of a well-stocked village store.

Open all day all wk Closed 25 Dec **Food** Lunch Mon-Sat 12-3, Sun 12-5 Dinner Mon-Sat 6-10 ⊕ FREE HOUSE ◀ Ringwood Best Bitter & Old Thumper, Timothy Taylor Landlord, Dorking DB Number One, Young's ♂ Aspall, Hogs Back Hazy Hog. ♥ 14
Facilities Non-diners area ❖ (Bar Garden) Children's portions Garden ⊨ Beer festival Parking WiFi

■ GUILDFORD　　　　　　　　　　　Map 6 SU94

NEW The Weyside

tel: 01483 568024 **Millbrook GU1 3XJ**
email: weyside@youngs.co.uk
dir: *From Guildford take A281 towards Shalford. Pub on right*

When in Guildford, definitely one to head for

Overlooking the River Wey, this is one humdinger of a pub. The decor, the furnishings, the accessorising - all have been conceived and applied by people who understand good interior design. There are plenty of places to eat and drink, not least on the waterside decking (first grab some bread from the bowl on bar to feed the ducks). There's even a 'dog corner', with beds, treats and towels. Typical menu items are an 8oz hand-cut sirloin of Surrey Angus beef; coriander-dusted Dorset lamb rump; beer-battered North Sea cod and rustic chips; and purple sprouting broccoli and cauliflower bake.

Open all day all wk **Food** Lunch Mon-Sat 12-10, Sun 12-9.30 Dinner Mon-Sat 12-10, Sun 12-9.30 Av main course £10 ⊕ YOUNG'S ◀ Bitter & Special ♂ Aspall. ♥ 15
Facilities Non-diners area ❖ (Bar Garden) ♦♦ Children's menu Children's portions Garden ⊨ Parking WiFi ▦ (notice required)

■ HASCOMBE　　　　　　　　　　　Map 6 TQ03

The White Horse

tel: 01483 208258 **The Street GU8 4JA**
email: pub@whitehorsehascombe.co.uk
dir: *From Godalming take B2130. Pub on left 0.5m after Hascombe*

Village pub with many walks around

Surrounded by prime walking country, this 16th-century pub's flower-filled garden is a summer stunner. Other selling points include its traditional interior, impressive tally of real ales and ciders, popular family room and ample outdoor seating; then there's the high standard of food, with meats coming from organic pedigree breeds

A meal might take in ribollita (a rich Tuscan soup); Angus beef and ale pie, curly kale and chips; or baked cod, chickpea and chorizo stew; and lemon polenta cake.

Open all day all wk 11-11 (Fri-Sat 11am-1am Sun 11-10.30) **Food** Lunch Mon-Fri 12-3, Sat 12-10, Sun 12-4 Dinner Mon-Fri 6-10, Sat 12-10, Sun 6-9 ⊕ FREE HOUSE ◀ Rotating ales ♂ Hogan's. ♉ 11 **Facilities** Non-diners area ✿ (Bar Garden) ♦♦ Children's menu Children's portions Play area Family room Garden ⊨ Parking WiFi ▄ (notice required)

■ **HASLEMERE**   Map 6 SU93

The Wheatsheaf Inn ★★★ INN
----

tel: 01428 644440 **Grayswood Rd, Grayswood GU27 2DE**
email: thewheatsheaf@aol.com **web:** www.thewheatsheafgrayswood.co.uk
dir: Exit A3 at Milford, A286 to Haslemere. Grayswood approx 7.5m N

Woodland-edge setting in the Surrey Hills

A most distinctive part hang-tiled Edwardian pub with enough vegetation to give Kew a run for its money. The hanging-basket festooned verandah, creeper-covered pergola and patio and colourful garden just invite a lingering visit with a pint of Langham Hip Hop bitter to hand, relaxing after a walk in the enfolding Surrey Hills beloved by Tennyson. There's opportunity to stay overnight here in one of the comfy rooms so creating an added excuse to engage with a wide-ranging menu of pub classics and thoughtful specials. Kick in on warmed brie with Cumberland sauce, leaving room for slow-braised pork belly on colcannon with cider and sage gravy.

Open all wk 11-3 6-11 (Sun 12-3 7-10.30) **Food** Lunch all wk 12-2 Dinner all wk 7-9.45 ⊕ FREE HOUSE ◀ Fuller's London Pride, Sharp's Doom Bar, Greene King Abbot Ale, Langham Hip Hop ♂ Aspall. **Facilities** Non-diners area ✿ (Bar Garden) ♦♦ Children's menu Children's portions Garden Parking WiFi **Rooms** 7

■ **LEIGH**   Map 6 TQ24

The Plough
----

tel: 01306 611348 **Church Rd RH2 8NJ**
email: sarah@theploughleigh.wanadoo.co.uk
dir: Phone for detailed directions

Ramblers' retreat in the Surrey countryside

Some parts of this appealing, architecturally mixed building are known to date from the 15th century, whilst the popular locals' bar with its fire and traditional pub games is somewhat younger. Situated by a large green bordered by old houses and the medieval church, The Plough today is a cracking village pub. Beers from the Hall & Woodhouse list slake the thirst of walkers enjoying exploration of the Surrey Weald, whilst the popular pub grub menu of bangers and mash or fish and chips is supplemented by chicken fillet, Black Forest ham or lamb steak dishes. The home-made pies also prove very popular.

Open all wk 11-11 (Sun 12-11) **Food** Lunch Mon-Sat 12-10, Sun 12-9 Dinner Mon-Sat 12-10, Sun 12-9 ⊕ HALL & WOODHOUSE ◀ Badger Dorset Best, Tanglefoot, K&B Sussex ♂ Westons Rosie's Pig. ♉ 11 **Facilities** Non-diners area ✿ (Bar Garden) ♦♦ Children's menu Children's portions Garden ⊨ Parking WiFi ▄

The Seven Stars   PICK OF THE PUBS
----

tel: 01306 611254 **Bunce Common Rd, Dawes Green RH2 8NP**
email: info@7starsleigh.co.uk
dir: S of A25 (Dorking to Reigate road)

Timeless tavern with high quality food

Tucked away in the rural southern reaches of the Mole Valley, the charm of this early 17th-century, tile-hung tavern is enhanced by the absence of games machines, TV screens and piped music. The older bar is centred on an inglenook fireplace at one end and a log-burning stove at the other. It's a peaceful spot to enjoy a pint of

Young's or Fuller's London Pride real ale and a glass of Aspall cider. The restaurant has its own bar, which is always available to use when open. The food served is of high quality and is prepared by a team of three chefs using local produce whenever possible. At the front is a garden for those with a drink, at the side a patio and garden for diners, and there's plenty of parking space.

Open all wk 12-11 (Sun 12-10) **Food** Lunch Mon-Sat 12-9.30, Sun 12-6 Dinner Mon-Sat 12-9.30, Sun 12-6 ⊕ PUNCH TAVERNS ◀ Fuller's London Pride, Young's, Sharp's Doom Bar, Guest ales ♂ Aspall. ♉ 12 **Facilities** Non-diners area ✿ (Bar Garden) ♦♦ Children's portions Garden ⊨ Parking

---

■ **LINGFIELD**   Map 6 TQ34

Hare and Hounds   PICK OF THE PUBS
----

tel: 01342 832351 **Common Rd RH7 6BZ**
email: info@hareandhoundspublichouse.co.uk
dir: From A22 follow Lingfield Racecourse signs into Common Rd

Delightful country pub with excellent modern and classic food

Standing alone in open countryside, this 18th-century, pale-blue-washed country pub is a delight. Upholstered banquettes, leopard-spot-patterned fabrics, wooden tables and assorted chairs all come together pleasingly in the bar. In the dining room, a herring-bone parquet floor and a 'ceiling' of red ochre-coloured fabric swagging, reminiscent perhaps of a Bedouin tent. The pub's good name for modern and classic food stems from dishes such as stuffed rabbit Wellington with chorizo and chive mash; roast stone bass with artichoke and cherry tomato marmalade, and deep-fried olive dumpling; and pan-fried Sussex rib-eye steak with triple-cooked chips and red wine sauce. A brunch and light lunch selection offers creamed mushroom soup with croûtons; and cos lettuce salad with blue cheese mayonnaise, poached pear and toasted walnut. Barbecues and pizzas extend the choices. The decked patio is a good spot for a glass of wine, from a selection by a village-based merchant vintners' company.

Open all day Closed 1-5 Jan, Sun eve **Food** Lunch Mon-Sat 12-2.30, Sun 12-3 Dinner Mon-Sat 7-9.30 Set menu available ⊕ PUNCH TAVERNS ◀ Harvey's Sussex, Sharp's Doom Bar, Guinness ♂ Westons Stowford Press. ♉ 12 **Facilities** Non-diners area ✿ (Bar Garden) ♦♦ Children's portions Garden ⊨ Parking

---

■ **LONG DITTON**   Map 6 TQ16

The Ditton
----

tel: 020 8339 0785 **64 Ditton Hill Rd KT6 5JD**
email: goodfood@theditton.co.uk
dir: Phone for detailed directions

Suburban local not far from Hampton Court

With its large, south-facing beer garden, The Ditton is clearly a popular community local. Playing their part of course are beers from Sambrook's, Surrey Hills and Truman's and lots of wines by the glass. A typical menu offers ciabattas, wraps and jacket potatoes; potato skins topped with Stilton and bacon; toad-in-the-hole with bubble-and-squeak, fried onions and gravy; and vegetable lasagne with garlic bread and dressed salad. Fish dishes are there too, such as breaded wholetail scampi; as well as beef and Cajun chicken burgers; and home-made, hand-stretched pizzas. Children's main courses arrive with an ice lolly. Those irresistible old favourites, sticky date and toffee pudding, and chocolate and caramel tart, both with Yorvale vanilla ice cream, are characteristic desserts. Skittle alley league nights are every Monday, and quiz nights are Tuesday. Summer barbecues are held in the garden and live music backs a June beer and cider festival.

Open all day all wk 12-11 **Food** Lunch Mon-Sat 12-9, Sun 12-5 Dinner Mon-Sat 12-9, Sun 12-5 ⊕ ENTERPRISE INNS ◀ Sharp's Doom Bar, Sambrook's Wandle, Surrey Hills Shere Drop, Truman's Swift, Otter Bitter. ♉ 10 **Facilities** Non-diners area ✿ (Bar Garden) ♦♦ Children's menu Children's portions Play area Garden ⊨ Beer festival Cider festival Parking WiFi ▄ (notice required)

MICKLEHAM · Map 6 TQ15

The Running Horses

tel: 01372 372279 **Old London Rd RH5 6DU**
email: info@therunninghorses.co.uk
dir: *M25 junct 9, A24 towards Dorking. Left signed Mickleham/B2209*

Lovely country inn below Box Hill

Built in the 16th century, the inn had an important role as a coaching house, but it also sheltered highwaymen - a tiny ladder leading to the roof space was discovered during alterations. The inn acquired its name in 1825 after two horses, Colonel and Cadland, running in the Derby at Epsom, passed the post together. They appear on the inn sign, and the bars are named after them. Food includes sausage, mash and onion gravy; smoked haddock and salmon fishcakes; Rosary Ash goats' cheese and caramelised red onion quiche; pan-fried calves' liver with grilled bacon, wilted spinach, mash and rich onion jus; and pearl barley and Somerset brie risotto. Chunky sandwiches are available at lunchtime.

Open all day all wk 12-11 (Sun 12-10.30) Closed 25, 26 & 31 Dec eve, 1 Jan eve **Food** Lunch Mon-Fri 12-2.30, Sat-Sun 12-3 Dinner Mon-Sat 7-9.30, Sun 6.30-9 Av main course £15 Restaurant menu available all wk ⊕ BRAKSPEAR ◀ Bitter & Special, Fuller's London Pride, Ringwood ♻ Symonds. ☂ 9 **Facilities** Non-diners area ♣ (Bar Garden) •↑ Children's portions Garden ⋈ WiFi

NEWDIGATE · Map 6 TQ14

The Surrey Oaks

tel: 01306 631200 **Parkgate Rd RH5 5DZ**
email: ken@surreyoaks.co.uk
dir: *From A24 follow signs to Newdigate, at T-junct turn left, pub 1m on left*

Excellent beers in lovely country pub

Creepers wind up this partly hang-tiled little pub set amidst copses at the village edge in deepest Surrey. It's over 440 years old; until the 1850s it was the wheelwright's shop, but today's visitors can build muscle playing boules in the large garden or alley skittles. Loads of character invests the interior, including a fine inglenook and flagged floors in the bars. Regular beer festivals complement the enticing, ever-changing selection of real ales. Booking is highly recommended for both restaurant and bar meals here, where enticing dishes on the specials board may include pork fillet in pear and cider sauce.

Open all wk 11.30-2.30 5.30-11 (Sat 11.30-3 6-11 Sun 12-9) **Food** Lunch Mon-Sat 12-2, Sun 12-2.30 Dinner Tue-Sat 6.30-9 ⊕ ADMIRAL TAVERNS ◀ Harvey's Sussex Best, Surrey Hills Ranmore Ale, Guest ales ♻ Moles Black Rat, Westons Country Perry. **Facilities** Non-diners area ♣ (Bar Garden) •↑ Children's menu Children's portions Play area Garden ⋈ Beer festival Parking WiFi ▭ (notice required)

OCKLEY · Map 6 TQ14

Bryce's The Old School House ◉ · PICK OF THE PUBS

tel: 01306 627430 **RH5 5TH**
email: fish@bryces.co.uk
dir: *8m S of Dorking on A29*

Smart country inn championing seafood

This Grade II listed former boarding school dates back to 1750, and owner Bill Bryce has been at the helm for over 20 years now. He is passionate about fresh fish and offers an appealing range, despite the land-locked location in rural Surrey. These days, it's more of a restaurant than a pub, although there is a bar with a choice of real ales including those from WJ King at Horsham, and a dozen select wines sold

by the glass. The dishes on the restaurant menu are nearly all fish, but the specials for non-piscivores such as calves' liver with bacon, black pudding and bubble-and-squeak; or parmesan breaded chicken breast with tomato and basil risotto are more than likely to please. If seafood is your thing, dive into Dorset crab cakes with mango and tomato salsa, followed by roast cod fillet with herb crust, creamed cabbage and chorizo. Puddings are all home made.

Open 12-3 6-11 Closed 25-26 Dec, 1 Jan, Sun pm & Mon Nov, Jan-Feb **Food** Lunch all wk 12-2.30 Dinner all wk 6-9.30 Av main course £14.95 ⊕ FREE HOUSE ◀ Fuller's London Pride, WJ King Horsham Best ♻ Westons. ☂ 13 **Facilities** Non-diners area ♣ (Bar Outside area) •↑ Children's portions Outside area ⋈ Parking WiFi ▭ (notice required)

SOUTH GODSTONE · Map 6 TQ34

Fox & Hounds

tel: 01342 893474 **Tilburstow Hill Rd RH9 8LY**
email: info@foxandhounds.org.uk
dir: *4m from M25 junct 6*

Haunted country pub serving home-cooked food

Dating in part to 1368, the Fox & Hounds has been a pub since 1601, and it is said that 17th-century pirate and smuggler John Trenchman haunts the building; he died in the building after being fatally wounded in an ambush nearby. A large inglenook in the restaurant and a real fire in the lower bar add to the old-world charm. Food-wise there's plenty to choose from, including a starter of crayfish and smoked salmon salad; baguettes; and mains ranging from applewood-smoked ham to whole sea bass. The ever-changing specials board might include beef Wellington and bouillabaisse, and a choice of roasts every Sunday. The large garden offers rural views and home-grown vegetables; marquees are erected in summer for alfresco dining.

Open all day all wk **Food** Lunch all wk 12-9 Dinner all wk 12-9 Av main course £9.95 ⊕ GREENE KING ◀ Abbot Ale & IPA, Guest ales. ☂ 12 **Facilities** Non-diners area ♣ (Bar Garden) •↑ Children's menu Children's portions Garden ⋈ Parking WiFi ▭ (notice required)

STOKE D'ABERNON · Map 6 TQ15

The Old Plough

tel: 01932 866419 **2 Station Rd KT11 3BN**
email: info@oldploughcobham.co.uk
dir: *From A245 into Station Rd. Pub on corner*

Friendly, smart and independently-owned community pub

This 300-year-old pub is where Sherlock Holmes and Dr Watson stayed in one of Sir Arthur Conan Doyle's novels. In reality, you'll find a charming bar and a light, bright restaurant overlooking the garden. The kitchen prepares fresh food all day, including fresh sandwiches and light lunch options (until 5.30pm in the bar), with starters such as seafood gratin; and duck and spring onion potato hash, oriental coriander salad and hoi sin sauce heading the menu before sharing dishes and mains that include rotisserie chicken, sautéed new potatoes and roasted shallots; Conisbee's free-range Cumberland sausages, colcannon mash and onion gravy; and wild mushroom, baby spinach and poached egg risotto with truffle oil. Children are welcome in the restaurant area until 7.30pm.

Open all day all wk **Food** Contact pub for details Av main course £12 ⊕ FULLER'S ◀ London Pride, Surrey Hills Shere Drop, George Gale & Co Seafarers ♻ Aspall. ☂ 18 **Facilities** Non-diners area ♣ (Bar Garden) •↑ Children's menu Children's portions Garden ⋈ Parking WiFi ▭

PICK OF THE PUBS

The Inn @ West End

WEST END Map 6 SU96

tel: 01276 858652
42 Guildford Rd GU24 9PW
email: greatfood@the-inn.co.uk
web: www.the-inn.co.uk
dir: *On A322 towards Guildford. 3m from M3 junct 3, just beyond Gordon's School rdbt*

Pub and restaurant that punches above its weight

Gerry and Ann Price have created an establishment that out-manoeuvres many a competitor, with weekly fish nights, monthly quizzes and special events linked to their expanding wine business. This has now launched its first own-label wine, Labradouro, a brand created by Labrador-owning Gerry, who also has a big thing about the Douro region of Portugal. But this serious interest in wine needn't dissuade anyone from popping in for a simple pint of Dark Star Hophead, Fuller's London Pride or Butcombe Rare Breed with a newspaper in the bar, or out on the clematis-adorned terrace overlooking the garden and boules pitch. The modern interior is open plan with wooden floors, yellow walls, crisp linen-clothed tables and an open fire. Charley Dingley and his kitchen team make great use of the pub's fruit and vegetable garden, and game comes from Windsor Great Park or is shot by Gerry himself. Such bounty later

appears on the menu as, perhaps, shallot, rabbit and fallow terrine with apple and walnut salad; or game casserole with mash. Other main dishes likely to make an appearance include monkfish and red onion risotto; rack of lamb with salsa verde; corn-fed chicken wrapped in Parma ham; and seared calves' liver with caramelised onion jus and crispy bacon. At lunchtime, consider pairing kedgeree with a glass of white Rioja. The comprehensive bar menu includes field mushrooms on toast; fish stew; and home-made burger. Also home-made are the desserts, such as rice pudding with caramelised apples; and a selection of English cheeses, maybe accompanied by an Italian sweet red Recioto.

Open all wk 11-3 5-11 (Sat 11-11 Sun 12-10.30) **Food** Lunch Mon-Sat 12-2.30 Sun 12-3 Dinner Mon-Sat 6-9.30 Sun 6-9 ⊕ FREE HOUSE ◀ Fuller's London Pride, Dark Star Hophead, Andwell, George Gale & Co Seafarers, Guest ales ♂ Aspall. ♀ 16 **Facilities** ❖ (Bar Garden) Children's portions Garden ⟞ Parking WiFi

TILFORD

Map 5 SU84

The Duke of Cambridge

tel: 01252 792236 **Tilford Rd GU10 2DD**
email: amy.corstin@redmistleisure.co.uk
dir: *From Guildford on A31 towards Farnham follow Tongham, Seale, Runfield signs. Right at end, follow Eashing signs. Left at end, 1st right (signed Tilford St). Over bridge, 1st left, 0.5m*

Family-friendly pub offering wholesome local fodder

Set among pine trees with a lovely garden and terrace, this attractive pub in the Surrey countryside welcomes all, children and dogs included. Expect Surrey ales and hearty local food with much of the seasonal produce on the menu coming from the neighbouring farm. Typical of the menu are deli boards; pan-seared rump of venison; pesto and butternut squash tagliatelle; and bangers and mash. In May fundraising for a local charity is just one excuse for a beer and music festival. The Garden Bar & Grill is a summer feature (weather permitting), as well as garden parties and hog roasts.

Open all wk 11-3 5-11 (Sat 11-11 Sun 12-10.30) Closed 25 Dec & 31 Dec eve **Food** Lunch Mon-Thu 12-2.30, Sat 12-3.30, Sun 12-8.30 Dinner Mon-Thu 6-9.30, Sat 6-9.30, ⊕ FREE HOUSE/RED MIST LEISURE LTD ◀ Hogs Back, Ringwood, Marston's ♂ Addlestones, Hogs Back Hazy Hog. ₹ 15 **Facilities** ✿ (Bar Restaurant Garden) ♦️ Children's menu Children's portions Play area Garden ⧥ Beer festival Parking WiFi

WEST CLANDON

Map 6 TQ05

The Onslow Arms

tel: 01483 222447 **The Street GU4 7TE**
email: info@onslowarmsclandon.co.uk
dir: *On A247, S of railway line*

Eye-catching village pub with cosmopolitan appeal

Cyclists and ramblers; drinkers and diners all mix seamlessly at this vibrant and smart community local. Totally refurbished a couple of years ago, the visually striking building retains much character, with a wealth of beams, huge open fire, squashy sofas and chairs set in a light, cool interior. Relax within or on the sheltered terrace with a glass of Tillingbourne Brewery bitter and choose from an all-day menu which offers a great mix of comfort meals and contemporary dishes. Stilton, spinach and avocado sandwiches with chips or soup is a grand filler, or perhaps fillet of sea bream with potato cake, pak choi and king prawns.

Open all day all wk Closed 26 Dec **Food** Contact pub for details ⊕ FREE HOUSE ◀ Surrey Hills Shere Drop, Sharp's Cornish Coaster, Tillingbourne Brewery Ales ♂ Westons Stowford Press. ₹ 18 **Facilities** Non-diners area ✿ (Bar Garden) ♦️ Children's menu Children's portions Garden ⧥ Parking WiFi ━

WEST END

Map 6 SU96

The Inn @ West End

PICK OF THE PUBS

See Pick of the Pubs on page 477

WEST HORSLEY

Map 6 TQ05

The King William IV

PICK OF THE PUBS

tel: 01483 282318 **83 The Street KT24 6BG**
dir: *Off A246 (Leatherhead to Guildford road)*

Relaxed and homely atmosphere in leafy Surrey

Named in honour of the monarch who relaxed England's brewing laws, this popular gastro-pub is situated in a leafy Surrey village. The business was started by a miller, Edmund Collins, who knocked two cottages together to create an alehouse. Many of the original Georgian features have been preserved, but there is also an airy conservatory restaurant and a large garden and terrace to the rear, with colourful tubs and floral baskets. It's popular with walkers and is close to the Royal Horticultural Society's Wisley Gardens. Local beers include Surrey Hills Shere Drop and Courage Directors, plus a guest ale of the month, and a dozen wines are offered by the glass. The well-priced menu ranges from burgers and fish pie to platters, oven-baked salmon fillet and rump steak. Leave room for banoffee pie, chocolate fudge cake or crème brûlée. Quiz nights and bingo nights are held (check with the pub for details).

Open all day all wk 11.30am-mdnt (Sun 12-10.30) **Food** Lunch Mon-Fri 12-3, Sat-Sun 12-4 Dinner Mon-Thu 6-9, Fri-Sat 6-9.30 ⊕ ENTERPRISE INNS ◀ Surrey Hills Shere Drop, Courage Best & Directors, Guest ales. ₹ 12 **Facilities** Non-diners area ✿ (Bar Garden) ♦️ Children's menu Children's portions Family room Garden ⧥ Parking WiFi ━

WINDLESHAM

Map 6 SU96

The Half Moon

tel: 01276 473329 **Church Rd GU20 6BN**
email: c@sturt.tv
dir: *M3 junct 3, A322 follow Windlesham signs into New Rd; right at T-junct into Church Rd, pub on right*

Old-fashioned values and friendly service

Family-owned since 1909, Helga and Conrad Sturt's slate-floored, low-beamed, 17th-century free house offers the traditional country pub experience, including locally brewed Hogs Back real ale and Lilley's Bee Sting Pear cider from Somerset. There's plenty of choice at lunchtime, while dinner options include Cumberland sausage with creamed potatoes, crispy leeks and onion jus; grilled fillet of sea bass with spicy tomato and king prawn sauce; ricotta, spinach and wild mushroom cannelloni; and local game in season. Go past the patio terrace into the well-kept beer garden with a children's play area. Check with the pub for beer festival dates.

Open all day all wk 9am-11pm **Food** Lunch all wk 9.30-9.30 Dinner all wk 9.30-9.30 ⊕ FREE HOUSE ◀ Sharp's, Theakston, Fuller's, Timothy Taylor, Hogs Back, Palmers, Dark Star ♂ Lilley's Bee Sting Pear, Westons Old Rosie. ₹ 10 **Facilities** ✿ (Bar Garden Outside area) ♦️ Children's menu Children's portions Play area Garden Outside area ⧥ Beer festival Parking WiFi ━ (notice required)

EAST SUSSEX

ALCISTON — Map 6 TQ50

Rose Cottage Inn — PICK OF THE PUBS

tel: 01323 870377 **BN26 6UW**
email: ian@alciston.freeserve.co.uk
dir: Off A27 between Eastbourne & Lewes

Home-cooked food in a pretty cottage

Expect a warm welcome at this traditional village pub, housed in a 17th-century flint cottage complete with roses round the door and a lovely front garden. At the foot of the South Downs, ramblers will find it a good base for long walks in unspoilt countryside, especially along the old traffic-free coach road to the south. With its oak beams, and sloping walls and ceilings, the inn has been in the same family for over 40 years, and is well known for its good, home-cooked food, including organic vegetables and local meats, poultry and game. You might choose from the wide selection of fish — perhaps the 'jolly posh' fish pie, or opt for Keralan chicken curry; home-made steak and ale shortcrust pie; or wild Alciston rabbit casserole from the daily specials. Classic pub dishes, salads and light bites are also available. When in season, fresh mussels are delivered from Scotland every Friday, and are then cooked in French or Italian style. The inn sells a number of items from local suppliers for customers to buy, including honey and eggs.

Open 11.30-3 6.30-11 Closed 25-26 Dec, Sun eve **Food** Lunch all wk 12-2 Dinner Mon-Sat 7-9.30 Restaurant menu available Mon-Sat evening ⊕ FREE HOUSE ◀ Harvey's Sussex Best Bitter, Burning Sky Plateau ♂ Biddenden. ♀ 8 **Facilities** Non-diners area ❤ (Bar Garden Outside area) Children's portions Garden Outside area ♬ Parking WiFi

ALFRISTON — Map 6 TQ50

George Inn

tel: 01323 870319 **High St BN26 5SY**
email: info@thegeorge-alfriston.com
dir: Phone for detailed directions

Period inn in a lovely location

First licensed to sell beer as far back as 1397, this splendid Grade II listed flint and half-timbered inn is set in a picturesque village with the South Downs Way passing its front door. The heavy oak beams and ancient inglenook fireplace add plenty of character to the bar, whilst the kitchen serves delights such as rustic boards to share; honey roast ham hock terrine; Thai-style chicken balls; braised shoulder of beef with spring onion mash; chicken supreme stuffed with spinach, feta and pine nuts with wild mushroom linguine; and sticky toffee pudding with butterscotch sauce and vanilla ice cream to finish. A network of smugglers' tunnels leads from the pub's cellars.

Open all day all wk Closed 25-26 Dec **Food** Lunch Sun-Thu 12-9, Fri-Sat 12-10 Dinner Sun-Thu 12-9, Fri-Sat 12-10 ⊕ GREENE KING ◀ Abbot Ale, Hardys & Hansons Olde Trip, Dark Star Hophead ♂ Aspall. ♀ 14 **Facilities** Non-diners area ❤ (Bar Restaurant Garden) ♦ Children's menu Children's portions Garden ♬ WiFi

ASHBURNHAM PLACE — Map 6 TQ61

Ash Tree Inn

tel: 01424 892104 **Brownbread St TN33 9NX**
email: ashtreeinn@gmail.com
dir: From Eastbourne take A271 at Boreham Bridge towards Battle. Next left, follow pub signs

Popular country pub that welcomes walkers

Deep in the Sussex countryside on the delightfully named Brownbread Street, the 400-year-old Ash Tree is a hub of local activity, hosting everything from quiz nights to cricket club meetings. It boasts a warm and bright interior, replete with stripped wooden floors, four fireplaces (two of them inglenooks), exposed beams and a friendly local atmosphere. Expect to find Harvey's ale on tap and traditional home-cooked meals such as breaded tiger prawns with sweet chilli dip; or soup of the day followed by steak and kidney pudding; tagliatelle with bacon, mushroom and garlic cream sauce; or ham, free-range eggs and chips. Walkers and dogs are welcome.

Open 12-4 7-11 (Sat-Sun 11.30am-mdnt) Closed Mon pm (Sun pm winter) **Food** Lunch Tue-Sun 12-3 (Summer Sun 12-5) Dinner Tue-Sat 7-9 (Summer Fri-Sat 6-9.30) ⊕ FREE HOUSE ◀ Harvey's Sussex Best Bitter, Guest ales ♂ Westons Stowford Press. **Facilities** Non-diners area ❤ (Bar Restaurant Garden) ♦ Children's portions Garden ♬ Parking WiFi ➔ (notice required)

BERWICK — Map 6 TQ50

The Cricketers Arms — PICK OF THE PUBS

tel: 01323 870469 **BN26 6SP**
email: pbthecricketers@aol.com
dir: At x-rds on A27 (between Polegate & Lewes) follow Berwick sign, pub on right

Popular with South Downs walkers

Previously two farmworkers' cottages dating from the 16th century, this flintstone building was an alehouse for 200 years, until around 50 years ago Harvey's of Lewes, Sussex's oldest brewery, bought it and turned it into a 'proper' pub. The Grade II listed building, in beautiful cottage gardens, is close to many popular walks - the South Downs Way runs along the crest of the chalk scarp between here and the sea. Three beamed, music-free rooms with stone floors and open fires are simply furnished with old pine furniture. A short menu of home-made food includes king prawns in chilli oil, and peppered mackerel with horseradish mayonnaise as starters. Their home-made burger is an ever-popular main course, as are ham, egg and chips; and fresh dressed crab salad. Nearby is Charleston Farmhouse, the country rendezvous of the Bloomsbury Group of writers, painters and intellectuals, and venue for an annual literary festival.

Open all wk Mon-Fri 11-3 6-11 Sat 11-11 Sun 12-9 (May-Sep Mon-Sat 11-11 Sun 12-10.30) Closed 25 Dec **Food** Lunch Oct-Apr Mon-Fri 12-2.15, Sat-Sun 12-9, May-Sep all wk 12-9 Dinner Oct-Apr Mon-Fri 6.15-9, Sat-Sun 12-9, May-Sep all wk 12-9 Av main course £10 ⊕ HARVEYS OF LEWES ◀ Sussex Best Bitter, Armada Ale ♂ Thatchers. ♀ 12 **Facilities** ❤ (Bar Garden) ♦ Children's portions Family room Garden ♬ Parking ➔ (notice required)

BLACKBOYS

Map 6 TQ52

The Blackboys Inn

tel: 01825 890283 **Lewes Rd TN22 5LG**
email: info@theblackboys.co.uk
dir: *From A22 at Uckfield take B2102 towards Cross in Hand. Or from A267 at Esso service station in Cross in Hand take B2102 towards Uckfield. Village 1.5m*

Hamlet pub known for its Sunday roasts

This inn was named after the local charcoal-burners, or the soot-caked 'blackboys', with whom the 14th-century pub was once a favourite. Today's well-scrubbed visitors enjoy beers from Harvey's of Lewes in one of two bars, and in the restaurant, vegetables from the garden, game from local shoots, and fish from Rye and Hastings. Typical dishes include grilled mackerel, slow-braised lamb shank, and wild mushroom risotto. A function room is available for larger parties to hire. Outside are rambling grounds with resident ducks and an orchard. There are quiz nights and live music every month, as well as an annual beer festival — contact the pub for details.

Open all day all wk 12-11 (Sun 12-10) **Food** Lunch Mon-Thu 12-2.30, Fri-Sat 12-9.30, Sun 12-8 Dinner Mon-Thu 6-9.30, Fri-Sat 12-9.30, Sun 12-8 Restaurant menu available all wk ⊕ HARVEY'S OF LEWES ◀ Sussex Best Bitter, Sussex Hadlow Bitter, Sussex Old Ale, Seasonal ales. ☂ 12 **Facilities** Non-diners area ☺ (Bar Restaurant Garden) •♦ Children's menu Children's portions Garden ♬ Beer festival Parking WiFi ▄

BRIGHTON & HOVE

Map 6 TQ30

The Basketmakers Arms

tel: 01273 689006 **12 Gloucester Rd BN1 4AD**
email: bluedowd@hotmail.co.uk
dir: *From Brighton station main entrance 1st left (Gloucester Rd). Pub on right at bottom of hill*

Leave The Lanes to the tourists and find this cracker

Peter Dowd has run his Victorian back-street local, tucked away in the bohemian North Laine area, with passion and pride for over 25 years. Quirky customer messages left in vintage tins on the walls have made the pub a local legend. Expect to find a splendid selection of Fuller's and guest real ales, around 100 malt whiskies and rarely seen vodkas, gins and bourbons. Food is all prepared from locally sourced produce, such as the fish which comes in daily from Sussex fishermen. Hot mains include venison and pheasant stew; rib-eye and rump steaks; and authentic beef or vegetarian Mexican chilli.

Open all day all wk 11-11 (Fri-Sat 11am-mdnt Sun 12-11) **Food** Lunch all wk 12-8.30 Dinner all wk 12-8.30 ⊕ FULLER'S ◀ London Pride, ESB, Discovery & Bengal Lancer, George Gale & Co HSB & Seafarers, Guest ales. **Facilities** ☺ (Bar Restaurant) •♦ Outside area ♬ WiFi

The Bell

tel: 01273 770773 **15-17 Belfast St BN3 3YS**
email: info@thebellhove.co.uk
dir: *From A259 (coast road) into Hove St (A2023). Right into Blatchington Rd at lights. 4th right into Haddington St, right into Malvern St, left into Belfast St to pub (one-way system)*

Popular side-street pub, known for friendly service

Once you find the side street, the vermillion- and white-painted façade of this smart, late-Victorian community pub quickly reveals its location. Another clue, when it's warm, is the customers at the tables out front, and on further

investigation more are sitting in the secret rear garden. A guest ale accompanies Bass and Lewes-brewed Harvey's in the bar, where happy hour lasts all day on Mondays, and from 4-6pm on other weekdays. The food is described as 'stylish without pretence'; the chefs produce freshly made traditional pub dishes with a modern twist, such as Jamaican jerk whole chicken breast burger with Reggae Reggae mayo. Look out for the lunchtime meal deal for two.

Open all day all wk **Food** Lunch all wk 12-3 Dinner all wk 6-9.30 ⊕ ENTERPRISE INNS ◀ Harvey's Sussex Best Bitter, Bass, Guest ale. **Facilities** Non-diners area ☺ (Bar Restaurant Garden) •♦ Children's portions Garden ♬ WiFi ▄ (notice required)

NEW The Foragers ⊛

tel: 01273 733134 **3 Stirling Place BN3 3YU**
email: info@theforagerspub.co.uk
dir: *At lights on A259 (seafront road) onto A2023. Right into Stirling Place*

Smart Victorian corner pub

Since it reopened, this has been Paul Hutchinson's baby, one he has nurtured to become a much-loved Hove local. He likes to stock Harvey's Best straight from its brewery in Lewes, and Sharp's Doom Bar from Cornwall, as well as the 14 wines he offers by the glass. Behind the AA Rosette lies food sourced extensively from Sussex and Kent for dishes such as confit chicken with warm couscous and date, fig and watercress salad; mutton suet pudding with cavalo nero, buttered turnips and red cabbage purée; and pan-roasted cod with confit potatoes and crab and anchovy croquette.

Open all day all wk **Food** Contact pub for details Set menu available Restaurant menu available ⊕ PUNCH TAVERNS ◀ Harvey's Best, Sharp's Doom Bar ♂ Westons Stowford Press. ☂ 14 **Facilities** Non-diners area ☺ (Bar Garden) •♦ Children's menu Children's portions Garden ♬ WiFi

CHELWOOD GATE

Map 6 TQ43

The Red Lion

tel: 01825 740265 **Lewes Rd RH17 7DE**
email: david@redlionchelwoodgate.co.uk
dir: *On A275*

Popular Ashdown Forest destination

An attractive pub built in the early 1800s that includes among its famous visitors Prime Minister Harold Macmillan and President John F Kennedy. Although it is owned by Kent brewer Shepherd Neame, Harvey's of Lewes also gets a look in on the bar. A full menu is served in the conservatory dining room and on the patio, while a more limited selection applies at tables in the extensive gardens. Typical dishes are pan-fried sirloin of Sussex beef; skate wing with fresh winkles and beurre noisette; and herby couscous-stuffed pepper with roasted vegetables. For a special, maybe rump of lamb with lentils.

Open all day summer all day (winter 12-3 5.30-11) Closed Mon in winter **Food** Lunch all day summer ⊕ SHEPHERD NEAME ◀ Spitfire, Harvey's Sussex Best Bitter ♂ Thatchers Gold. **Facilities** Non-diners area ☺ (Bar Garden) •♦ Children's menu Children's portions Garden ♬ Parking

PICK OF THE PUBS

The Coach and Horses

DANEHILL　　Map 6 TQ42

tel: 01825 740369 **RH17 7JF**
email: coachandhorses@danehill.biz
web: www.coachandhorses.danehill.biz
dir: *From East Grinstead, S through Forest Row on A22 to A275 junct, right on A275, 2m to Danehill, left into School Ln, 0.5m, pub on left*

Family-run country pub offering more than just beer

On the edge of Ashdown Forest, the Coach and Horses opened in 1847 when it was a simple alehouse with stabling. Today it ticks all the boxes for an attractive countryside inn. If you fancy a ramble to work up a thirst or an appetite, ask about the three routes that start at the pub door. Upon your return, you'll find a sunny child-free terrace at the rear dominated by an enormous maple tree; children can play in the peaceful front garden, where the undulating South Downs dominate the horizon. Understated and unspoilt, the pub's interior has retained the typical twin bar layout, with vaulted ceilings, wood-panelled walls and stone and oak flooring lending their quiet charm. The pub's dog lazing on a bar rug sets a friendly tone, along with locals supping weekly-changing guest ales from the likes of Isfield Brewery and Dark Star; local Danehill Black Pig cider is also popular, and English sparkling wines come from the Bluebell vineyard just up

the road. Relax with your drink or settle with a menu in the dedicated eating area. Dishes are traditionally English, but the cooking scores highly with the freshness of ingredients sourced as locally as possible. Lamb raised on the farm opposite makes one of the shortest trips from meadow to pot, in a lighter lunch of Danehill lamb stew served with crusty bread; other light options include baguettes and omelettes. For those of good appetite, a starter of carpaccio of salt-cured Ashdown Forest venison with juniper mayonnaise could be followed by butter-roasted loin of cod with braised spring vegetables, crab tortellini and crab bisque. English desserts may include roasted pear and almond tart, honeycomb and crème fraîche.

Open all wk 11.30-3 6-11 (Sat-Sun 12-11) Closed 26 Dec **Food** Lunch Mon-Fri 12-2, Sat 12-2.30, Sun 12-3 Dinner Mon-Thu 6.30-9, Fri-Sat 6.30-9.30 ⊕ FREE HOUSE ◀ Harvey's, Hammerpot, Dark Star, Isfield Brewery, Turners Brewery, Long Man Best Bitter ♂ Westons Stowford Press, Black Pig. ♟ 8 **Facilities** Non-diners area ♣ (Bar Garden) ♦ Children's menu & portions Play area Garden ⊨ Parking WiFi

CHIDDINGLY
Map 6 TQ51

The Six Bells

tel: 01825 872227 **BN8 6HE**
dir: *E of A22 between Hailsham & Uckfield. Turn opposite Golden Cross pub*

Popular pub with vintage car, music and jazz events

Inglenook fireplaces and plenty of bric-à-brac are to be found at this large free house, which is where various veteran car and motorbike enthusiasts meet on club nights. The jury in the famous 1852 Onion Pie Murder trial sat and deliberated in the bar before finding the defendant, Sarah Ann French, guilty. This is a popular pub with walkers who are out on the many great routes round here including the Vanguard Way. Enjoy live music on Tuesday, Friday and Saturday evenings plus jazz at lunchtime on Sundays. Weekly car and motorcycle meets and events.

Open all wk 10-3 6-11 (Fri-Sun all day) **Food** Lunch all wk 12-2.30, Fri-Sun all day Dinner all wk 6-10, Fri-Sun all day Av main course £8 ⊕ FREE HOUSE ◀ Courage Directors, Harvey's Sussex Best Bitter, Guest ales. **Facilities** Non-diners area ◀❙ Children's portions Family room Garden Parking ▭

DANEHILL
Map 6 TQ42

The Coach and Horses
PICK OF THE PUBS

See Pick of the Pubs on page 481

DITCHLING
Map 6 TQ31

The Bull ★★★★ INN
PICK OF THE PUBS

See Pick of the Pubs on opposite page

EAST CHILTINGTON
Map 6 TQ31

The Jolly Sportsman ◉◉

tel: 01273 890400 **Chapel Ln BN7 3BA**
email: info@thejollysportsman.com
dir: *From Lewes take A275, left at Offham onto B2166 towards Plumpton, into Novington Ln, after approx 1m left into Chapel Ln*

Award-winning rustic food and local ales to match

Isolated but well worth finding, Bruce Wass's dining pub enjoys a lovely garden setting on a peaceful dead-end lane looking out to the South Downs. The bar retains some of the character of a Victorian alehouse, with Dark Star and Harvey's on tap, while the dining room strikes a cool, modern-rustic pose. Well-sourced food shines on daily-changing, two AA-Rosette menus, served throughout the pub, from calves' liver in bacon and shallot sauce with colcannon, broccoli and potatoes to Thai chickpea cakes with crispy aubergine and tofu kofta, garlic spinach, mint yogurt and pepper coulis. Good value fixed-price and children's menus are also available.

Open Tue-Fri 12-3 6-11 (Sat all day Sun 12-5) Closed 25 Dec, Sun eve & Mon **Food** Lunch Tue-Sat 12-2.30, Sun 12-3.30 Dinner Tue-Thu 6.30-9.30, Fri-Sat 6.30-10 Set menu available Restaurant menu available Tue-Sun ⊕ FREE HOUSE ◀ Dark Star Hophead, Harvey's Sussex Best Bitter ♂ Thatchers. ♟ 14
Facilities Non-diners area ❤ (Bar Garden) ◀❙ Children's menu Children's portions Play area Garden ▭ Parking WiFi

EAST DEAN
Map 6 TV59

The Tiger Inn
PICK OF THE PUBS

tel: 01323 423209 **The Green BN20 0DA**
email: tiger@beachyhead.org.uk
dir: *From A259 between Eastbourne & Seaford. Pub 0.5m*

Village inn with splendid downland views

Beside a village green lined with picture-postcard cottages and wonderful downland views, The Tiger Inn is just down from the famous Beachy Head. Hidden up a tranquil side valley, the pub was once the base for smugglers using the now-popular beach at Birling Gap. The interior is quintessentially English too, with log fires, beams, stone floors and ancient settles. As brewery tap for the nearby Beachy Head microbrewery, the best of local beers are guaranteed, supplemented by an annual beer festival. Ramblers from the nearby coastal path join diners in seeking out the fulsome meals on the solid menu of pub favourites like slow-roasted belly of pork with black pudding mash, or perhaps the seasonal risotto of the day, complemented by an ever-changing specials board. Comforting desserts include golden syrup pudding with custard or the daily-changing cheesecake. A traditional ploughman's and classic pub dishes are available at lunchtime.

Open all day all wk **Food** Lunch all wk 12-3 Dinner all wk 6-9 ⊕ FREE HOUSE/ BEACHY HEAD BREWERY ◀ Legless Rambler & Original Ale, Harvey's ♂ Kingstone Press. ♟ 10 **Facilities** Non-diners area ❤ (Bar Garden) ◀❙ Children's portions Garden ▭ Beer festival Parking WiFi

ERIDGE GREEN
Map 6 TQ53

The Nevill Crest and Gun

tel: 01892 864209 **Eridge Rd TN3 9JR**
email: nevill.crest.and.gun@brunningandprice.co.uk
dir: *On A26 between Tunbridge Wells & Crowborough*

Intriguingly named pub with over 500 years of history

This uniquely named, tile-hung pub was built on land owned by the Nevill family, the Earls of Abergavenny, which explains the 'Crest'; a cannon that once stood outside accounts for the 'Gun'. The hamlet's balancing act on the Kent-Sussex border is reflected in the low-beamed, wooden-floored bar where Larkins and Black Cat real ales come from the former, Harvey's from the latter. A springtime daily-changing menu advocates pan-fried thyme polenta with mushrooms, parmesan and pine nut salad; roast leg of pork; harissa-baked salmon with lemon and coriander couscous; and roasted aubergine, goats' cheese and red pepper lasagne.

Open all day all wk 11.30-11 (Sun 12-10.30) **Food** Lunch Mon-Thu 12-9.30, Fri-Sat 12-10, Sun 12-9 Dinner Mon-Thu 12-9.30, Fri-Sat 12-10, Sun 12-9 ⊕ FREE HOUSE ◀ Brunning & Price Original Bitter, Harvey's, Larkins, Black Cat ♂ Aspall, Biddenden. ♟ 16 **Facilities** Non-diners area ❤ (Bar Garden Outside area) ◀❙ Children's portions Play area Garden Outside area ▭ Beer festival Cider festival Parking WiFi ▭ (notice required)

PICK OF THE PUBS

The Bull ★★★★★ INN

DITCHLING   Map 6 TQ31

tel: 01273 843147   **2 High St BN6 8TA**
email: info@thebullditchling.com
web: www.thebullditchling.com
dir: *From Brighton on A27 take A23,*
follow Pyecombe/Hassocks signs, then
Ditchling signs, 3m

Old inn with contemporary feel

This venerable 450-year-old inn started life as monks' lodgings but today's cosy retreat is a far cry from those spartan days. The Bull's memorable interior pushes all the right buttons with open fires, wavy beams, leather sofas, cosy corners, candlelight, bare floorboards, scrubbed tables and a locals' bar brimming with a great selection of 13 craft beers and local ales. Owner Dominic Worrall has toiled tirelessly to create the archetypal English village inn with a refreshing contemporary edge. The monks' draughty rooms are now individually designed guest bedrooms, each newly refurbished and with a range of hand-made products – perfect for visitors to the South Downs National Park within which The Bull stands. The rounded tops of the hills rise steeply beyond the village to the commanding Ditchling Beacon; a self-guided walk from the pub will take you there, and the South Downs Way National Trail also crosses the Beacon; Brighton is just 15 minutes away by car. Sussex farms and

estates provide the chefs with a panoply of delights with which to create their refreshingly modern gourmet British dishes. Typical 'small plate' starters could include braised oxtail with gnocchi horseradish crème fraîche, and main courses take the form of monkfish with chorizo crust and spiced beans; and venison loin, celeriac and potato dauphinoise, sautéed Brussels sprout leaves and toasted nut crumble. Vegetarian options are no less flavoursome, and desserts include Sussex pond pudding and home-made ice creams. Wine lovers will delight in a generous list which includes 23 served by the glass.

Open all day all wk 11-11 (Sat 8.30am-11pm Sun 8.30am-10.30pm)

Food Mon-Fri 12-2.30, 6-9.30 Sat 12-9.30, Sun 12-9 (bkfst Sat-Sun 8.30-10.30am) FREE HOUSE Harvey's Sussex Best Bitter, Timothy Taylor Landlord, Hop Back Summer Lightning, Dark Star Westons Traditional, Cornish Orchards. 23
Facilities Non-diners area Children's menu Children's portions Play area Garden Parking WiFi **Rooms** 4

EWHURST GREEN
Map 7 TQ72

The White Dog

tel: 01580 830264 **Village St TN32 5TP**
email: info@thewhitedogewhurst.co.uk
dir: *On A21 from Tonbridge towards Hastings, left after Hurst Green signed Bodiam. Straight on at x-rds, through Bodiam. Over rail crossing, left for Ewhurst Green*

Family-run country inn overlooking Bodiam Castle

This tile-hung village pub is either the first in, or the last out of the village, depending on which way you are travelling. Its age is more apparent from the interior, particularly the huge fireplace, old oak beams and stone floors. Four hand-pumps dispense regularly-changing, mostly Sussex real ales and some 20 wines are available by the glass. The seasonal menus show how dependent the kitchen is on the local area: for example, pan-fried mushrooms in white wine and garlic sauce, or seared scallops with stir-fry vegetables to start, followed by pork fillet on creamy celeriac mash with asparagus and brandy and paprika sauce, or baked duck breast with dauphinoise potatoes, seasonal vegetables and glazed shallots.

Open all wk 12-3 5-11 (Fri-Sun 12-11) **Food** Lunch all wk 12-2.30 Dinner all wk 6.30-9.30 Av main course £12 Restaurant menu available Tue-Sat ⊕ FREE HOUSE ◀ Harvey's, Growler Brewery Top Dog, Rother Valley Level Best. ☂ 20
Facilities Non-diners area ❄ (Bar Garden Outside area) ◄ Children's menu Children's portions Play area Garden Outside area ⋒ Beer festival Cider festival Parking WiFi ☎ (notice required)

FLETCHING
Map 6 TQ42

The Griffin Inn
PICK OF THE PUBS

tel: 01825 722890 **TN22 3SS**
email: info@thegriffininn.co.uk
dir: *M23 junct 10 to East Grinstead, then A22, then A275. Village signed on left*

Popular for its huge gardens and lovely country views

The unspoilt village of Fletching overlooks the Ouse Valley. This imposing Grade II listed inn has landscaped gardens with views over Ashdown Forest, the Sussex Downs and 'Capability' Brown-designed Sheffield Park Gardens. You might just hear a steam whistle, for the heritage Bluebell Railway is little more than a mile away. The 16th-century interior simply oozes charm from its beams, panelling, settles and log fires. The bar's handles dispense the best of local ales, while the already generous wine list has grown since the introduction of the pub's highly popular wine club, which organises tastings, special dinners and excursions. Walkers and cyclists arriving to join destination diners will revel in the terrific menu, created from the freshest of local produce such as Rye Bay seafood and Sussex beef. On fine summer days the barbecue is fired up and food can be served on the terrace.

Open all day all wk 12-11 (Sat 12-12) Closed 25 Dec **Food** Lunch Mon-Fri 12-2.30, Sat-Sun 12-3 Dinner all wk 7-9.30 Av main course £14 Set menu available Restaurant menu available all wk (ex Sun eve) ⊕ FREE HOUSE ◀ Harvey's Sussex Best Bitter, WJ King, Hepworth & Co, Hogs Back ♉ Westons Stowford Press. ☂ 16
Facilities Non-diners area ❄ (Bar Garden) ◄ Children's menu Children's portions Play area Garden ⋒ Parking WiFi

GUN HILL
Map 6 TQ51

The Gun
PICK OF THE PUBS

tel: 01825 872361 **TN21 0JU**
email: enquiries@thegunhouse.co.uk
dir: *5m S of Heathfield, 1m off A267 towards Gun Hill. 4m off A22 between Uckfield & Hailsham*

First-class food in a charming setting

Lost amidst lanes in the lovely, wooded countryside of the Sussex Weald, many hideyholes and corners pepper the rambling rooms of this half-timbered treasure, parts of which date back to the 15th century. The timber theme continues inside, where lots of beams, wooden floors and open log fireplaces picked out in old brick characterise an interior dressed with rustic furnishings. An elegant new dining room and a stunning terrace offer additional choices for enjoying beers from the long-established Harvey's Brewery in nearby Lewes, or Kentish cider from the Biddenden estate. The substantial menu includes a finger-buffet of British tapas, whilst seared scallops may be a starter or main. Seafood features strongly here; seared sea bass with roasted Jerusalem artichoke and crayfish beurre blanc is a favourite. For vegetarians the choice may include sweet and sour pumpkin risotto with pickled ginger; whilst meat-eaters can look forward to traditional pies and steaks from local suppliers.

Open all wk 11.30-3 5.30-11 (Sun 11.30-10.30) **Food** Lunch Mon-Sat 12-3, Sun 12-9.30 Dinner Mon-Sat 6-9.45, Sun 12-9.30 Av main course £14 ⊕ FREE HOUSE ◀ Sharp's Doom Bar, Harvey's, Guinness ♉ Biddenden, Aspall. ☂ 14
Facilities Non-diners area ❄ (All areas) ◄ Children's menu Children's portions Play area Garden Outside area ⋒ Parking WiFi

HARTFIELD
Map 6 TQ43

Anchor Inn

tel: 01892 770424 **Church St TN7 4AG**
email: info@anchorhartfield.com
dir: *On B2110*

Friendly free house in the Ashdown Forest

This family-orientated pub is in the heart of 'Winnie the Pooh' country. It was built in 1465 and was at one time a workhouse before it became a pub in the late 19th century. Locals meet in the front bar with its stone floors and heavy wooden beams, plus the inglenook fireplace and library area give the back bar a more intimate feel. As well as hot and cold snacks, main courses such as Cumberland sausages and mash or battered haddock, chips and peas satisfy heartier appetites. Friday evening is steak night. The front verandah and large garden are a bonus on warm sunny days. Look out for the early May beer festival.

Open all day all wk **Food** Lunch Mon-Fri 12-3, Sat 12-9, Sun 12-6 Dinner Mon-Thu 6-9, Fri 6-9.30, Sat 12-9, Sun 12-6 Av main course £10 ⊕ FREE HOUSE ◀ Harvey's Sussex Best Bitter, Larkins ♉ Westons Stowford Press. **Facilities** Non-diners area ❄ (Bar Garden) ◄ Children's menu Children's portions Play area Garden ⋒ Beer festival Parking WiFi ☎ (notice required)

The Hatch Inn
PICK OF THE PUBS

See Pick of the Pubs on opposite page

PICK OF THE PUBS

The Hatch Inn

HARTFIELD Map 6 TQ43

tel: 01342 822363
Coleman's Hatch TN7 4EJ
email: nickad@mac.com
web: www.hatchinn.co.uk
dir: *A22 at Forest Row rdbt, 3m to Coleman's Hatch, right by church*

Award-winning pub in the heart of Ashdown Forest

If AA Milne could populate Ashdown Forest with a bear called Winnie the Pooh, a tiger called Tigger and a kangaroo called Kanga, why shouldn't llamas and reindeer live here? Well, they do, on a farm in nearby Wych Cross, not far from this eye-catching old inn at the site of one of the medieval gates into what was then dense woodland with valuable iron and timber reserves. Built around 1430, the part-weatherboarded building may have been cottages for iron workers, although it has been a pub for nearly 300 years, it was no doubt much appreciated by the dry-throated charcoal burners who used to work in these parts, and even passing smugglers. Classic beams and open fires draw an appreciative crowd to sample beers from Fuller's, Larkins and Harvey's, and the food, a fusion of classic and modern, for which proprietor Nicholas Drillsma and partner Sandy Barton have built an enviable reputation. Their daily changing menus are complemented by an extensive wine

list, including 10 by the glass. With plenty of local suppliers to draw on, there is fresh seasonal produce features in just about everything. Lunchtime mains include pan-fried calves' liver with braised red cabbage, griddled bacon and onion gravy; smoked salmon and crayfish risotto; and penne pasta in a roasted red pepper and sun-blushed tomato sauce. A reservation is essential for evening dining where choices may include pork spring roll with cucumber salad and hoi sin sauce, or French onion soup followed by slow roasted shank of lamb with roasted root vegetables, or pan-fried black pudding, quails' eggs and pancetta salad. Finish with lemon possett; apple and cinnamon crumble; or dark rum pannacotta with shortbread.

Open all wk 11.30-3 5.30-11 (Sat-Sun all day) Closed 25 Dec (drinks only) **Food** Lunch all wk 12-2.15 Dinner Mon-Thu 7-9.15, Fri-Sat 7-9.30 Av main course £14 ⬡ FREE HOUSE ◪ Harvey's & Sussex Old Ale, Fuller's London Pride, Larkins, Black Cat ⬠ Westons Stowford Press. ♟ 10 **Facilities** Non-diners area ✿ (Bar Restaurant Garden) ♦♦ Children's portions Play area Garden WiFi

HEATHFIELD

Map 6 TQ52

Star Inn

tel: 01435 863570 **Church St, Old Heathfield TN21 9AH**
email: susiechappelle@aol.co.uk
dir: *Old Heathfield SE of Heathfield accessed from B2096*

Stonemasons' inn with great views and a welcoming interior

Built as an inn for the stonemasons who constructed the 14th-century church, this creeper-clad stone building has a stunning summer garden that affords impressive views across the High Weald; a view once painted by Turner. Equally appealing is the atmospheric, low-beamed main bar with its rustic furnishings and huge inglenook fireplace — all very cosy and welcoming in winter. Note the unusual barrel-vaulted ceiling in the upstairs dining room and the regularly-changing chalkboard menu that lists fresh fish and seafood direct from the day boats in Hastings; the pub uses only local and seasonal ingredients.

Open all day all wk **Food** Lunch Mon-Sat 12-2.30, Sun 12-3 Dinner Mon-Sat 7-9.30, Sun 6-8.30 Av main course £12 ⊕ FREE HOUSE ◂ Harveys, Young's, Whitstable Bay Pale Ale, John Smith's, Guest ale ♂ Thatchers. ♀ 10 **Facilities** Non-diners area ❀ (All areas) ♦ Children's menu Children's portions Garden Outside area 🚲 Parking WiFi ➡ (notice required)

ICKLESHAM

Map 7 TQ81

The Queen's Head

tel: 01424 814552 **Parsonage Ln TN36 4BL**
dir: *Between Hastings & Rye on A259. Pub in village at x-rds near church*

A must for real ale lovers

This 17th-century tile-hung and oak-beamed pub enjoys magnificent views from its gardens of the Brede Valley and as far as the coast at Rye, and has been in the same hands for some 30 years. The traditional atmosphere has been preserved, with vaulted ceilings, large inglenook fireplaces, split-level floors, church pews, antique farm implements, and a bar from the old Midland Bank in Eastbourne. Customers are kept happy with up to 10 real ales, an annual beer festival on the first weekend in October, and menus ranging from salads, sandwiches and ploughman's to a comprehensive main menu selection which includes pan-fried soft herring roe; Thai vegetable curry; minted lamb fillet; and steak and kidney pudding.

Open all wk 11-11 (Sun 11-10.30) Closed 25 & 26 Dec (eve) **Food** Lunch Mon-Fri 12-2.30, Sat-Sun 12-9.30 Dinner Mon-Fri 6-9.30, Sat-Sun 12-9.30 Av main course £9.95 ⊕ FREE HOUSE ◂ Rother Valley Level Best, Greene King Abbot Ale, Harvey's Sussex Best Bitter, Ringwood Fortyniner, Dark Star ♂ Biddenden, Westons Old Rosie. ♀ 12 **Facilities** Non-diners area ❀ (Bar Restaurant Garden) ♦ Children's menu Children's portions Play area Garden 🚲 Beer festival Parking WiFi ➡ (notice required)

LANGNEY

Map 6 TQ60

The Farm @ Friday Street

tel: 01323 766049 **15 Friday St BN23 8AP**
email: enquiries@farmfridaystreet.com
dir: *From A22 onto B2247, left onto B2104. Approx 1m to pub on left*

Excellent find in Eastbourne's outer reaches

Although surrounded by the ever-expanding town, this Whiting & Hammond Group pub still looks like the elegant farmhouse it once was. Fishmongers call the kitchen daily to tell them what's looking good from the day's catch, while other possibilities

are chicken, mushroom and ham shortcrust pastry pie; fillet of beef Stroganoff with pilau rice; braised oxtail suet pudding with black pudding mash; and gnocchi with quinoa, chestnut mushrooms, soft herbs and truffle cream. Desserts include sorbets; banoffee pie; and chocolate brownie. Sunday lunches, with live music, are hugely popular and beer festivals are held in June and August.

Open all day all wk 9am-11pm **Food** Lunch Mon-Sat 12-9.30, Sun 12-9 Dinner Mon-Sat 12-9.30, Sun 12-9 ⊕ ENTERPRISE INNS ◂ Fuller's London Pride, Sharp's Doom Bar, Timothy Taylor, Long Man ♂ Aspall. ♀ **Facilities** Non-diners area ❀ (Bar Restaurant Garden) ♦ Children's portions Garden 🚲 Beer festival Parking WiFi

LEWES

Map 6 TQ41

NEW The Snowdrop Inn

tel: 01273 471018 **119 South St BN7 2BU**
email: tony@thesnowdropinn.com
dir: *From A26 (Tesco) rdbt into South St. Pub on left*

Thriving ale house in memorable town setting

Home to one of Lewes' famous bonfire societies, the pub also has renown as the location for an immense snow avalanche which buried buildings here in 1836. Sitting below chalk cliffs, today's pub offers a very warm welcome and is particularly known for its wide range of craft ales, many such as Dark Star, Harvey's or Burning Sky sourced very locally. Equally local are many of the ingredients included on a very accomplished, wide-ranging menu. Over a dozen starters may appeal before a main like rabbit, morcilla and chorizo paella detains; traditional pub-grub favourites are also stalwarts on the list. Vegetarian options include a very popular Sunday nut roast. An October beer festival is held each year.

Open all day all wk **Food** Lunch all wk 12-9 Dinner all wk 12-9 Av main course £10.50 ◂ Harvey's Best, Dark Star American Pale Ale, Burning Sky Plateau & Aurora ♂ Gwynt y Ddraig Black Dragon, Westons Rosie's Pig. ♀ 15 **Facilities** ♦ Children's portions Garden 🚲 Beer festival WiFi

MAYFIELD

Map 6 TQ52

The Middle House

PICK OF THE PUBS

See Pick of the Pubs on opposite page

MILTON STREET

Map 6 TQ50

The Sussex Ox

tel: 01323 870840 **BN26 5RL**
email: mail@thesussexox.co.uk
dir: *Off A27 between Wilmington & Drusillas. Follow brown signs to pub*

Views of the Long Man of Wilmington from the beer garden

A former slaughterhouse and butcher's dating from 1900, this pub retains its church pew seating and wood panelling. Drink deeply of old Sussex here, with the wonderful, matchboarded old bar rooms serving local ales and oozing character. Dine in the bar, the Garden Room, or the more formal Dining Room; the daily-changing menu relies on the best local ingredients - beef (pedigree purebred Sussex Cattle) is sourced from Jevington Place Farm. Ox burgers and steaks are available every day.

Open all wk 11.30-11 (Sun 12-10.30) Closed 25 Dec **Food** Lunch Mon-Fri 12-2, Sat-Sun 12-2.30 Dinner all wk 6-9 ⊕ FREE HOUSE ◂ Harvey's Sussex Best Bitter, Long Man, Local Guest ales. ♀ 17 **Facilities** Non-diners area ❀ (Bar Restaurant Garden) ♦ Children's portions Family room Garden 🚲 Parking WiFi

PICK OF THE PUBS

The Middle House

MAYFIELD　　　　　　Map 6 TQ52

tel: 01435 872146　**High St TN20 6AB**
email: info@themiddlehousemayfield.co.uk
web: www.themiddlehousemayfield.co.uk
dir: *E of A267, S of Tunbridge Wells*

Historic timber-framed hostelry

Once described as 'one of the finest examples of a timber-framed building in Sussex', this Grade I listed, 16th-century village inn dominates Mayfield's High Street. It has been here since 1575, when it was built for Sir Thomas Gresham, Elizabeth I's Keeper of the Privy Purse and founder of the London Stock Exchange. The entrance hall features a large ornately carved wooden fireplace by master carver Grinling Gibbons, wattle-and-daub infill, a splendid oak-panelled restaurant and secret priest holes. A private residence until the 1920s, it is now a family-run business. Real ale drinkers do well here, with a handsome choice, including Harvey's Sussex Best Bitter from Lewes and Sharp's Doom Bar. As in all good kitchens, the meats, poultry, game and vegetables come from local farms and producers. The bar menu includes classic dishes of home-cooked smoked gammon with two free-range fried eggs; deep-fried wholetail scampi with chunky chips; home-made sausages of the day; fresh salads, vegetarian options and children's healthy-eating options. For something a little less traditional, try pot-roast shank of local lamb tagine, or roast boneless quail filled with mixed forest mushrooms. The carte offers whole large grilled Cornish sardines with garlic butter; fanned marinated duck breast with chorizo and sunblushed tomato risotto; and corn fritter and harissa-roasted vegetable stack with toasted feta cheese. And of the desserts, special mention goes to pine nut and maple pannacotta with roasted blueberries, pistachio ice cream and lavender honeycomb. It isn't just the building that has been described in superlative terms – the private chapel in the restaurant is regarded as 'one of the most magnificent in England'. Step outside onto the lovely terraced gardens to enjoy views of the rolling countryside.

Open all day all wk **Food** Lunch Mon-Fri 12-2.15, Sat 12-2.30 Dinner Mon-Sat 6.30-9.30, Sun all day Restaurant menu Tue-Sat ⊕ FREE HOUSE ◖ Harvey's Sussex Best Bitter, Greene King Abbot Ale, Black Sheep Best Bitter, Theakston Best Bitter, Adnams Southwold Bitter, Sharp's Doom Bar ♂ Thatchers Gold. ♟ 9 **Facilities** Non-diners area ♦♦ Children's menu Children's portions Play area Garden ☂ Parking WiFi

The Blacksmiths Arms ★★★★ INN

tel: 01273 472971 **London Rd BN7 3QD**
email: blacksmithsarms@shineadsl.co.uk **web:** www.theblacksmithsarms-offham.co.uk
dir: *2m N of Lewes on A275*

Many reasons to visit this friendly inn

A hostelry since the mid-18th century, this free house in the South Downs National Park is just two miles from the lovely old town of Lewes. So that makes two reasons to visit, or even stay in the charming, high-quality accommodation. A third reason is Bernard and Sylvia Booker's flavoursome cooking using the best sustainably sourced local produce for lemon sole Walewska; steak and kidney pie; and spinach and ricotta cannelloni. And a fourth is Harvey's real ales in a bar with a log fire in the inglenook.

Open 12-3 6.30-10.30 Closed Sun eve, Mon winter, Mon L summer **Food** Lunch Tue-Sun 12-2 Set menu available Restaurant menu available Tue-Sun ⊕ FREE HOUSE ◀ Harvey's, Bitburger. ♥ 10 **Facilities** Non-diners area ♦ Children's portions Garden ⧟ Parking WiFi **Rooms** 4

The Cock

tel: 01273 812040 **Uckfield Rd BN8 5RX**
email: matt@cockpub.co.uk **web:** www.cockpub.co.uk
dir: *Just off A26 approx 2m N of Lewes just outside Ringmer*

Step back in time at this historic pub

This 16th-century inn takes its name from a bygone era when a cock horse was a spare horse used by coachmen to pull heavy loads – immortalised in the nursery rhyme *Ride a Cock Horse to Banbury Cross*. Once a mustering point during the Civil War, the interior of the main bar is pretty much unaltered since Cromwell's time, including oak beams, flagstone floors and a blazing fire in the inglenook. Harvey's, and two local guest ales accompany a truly extensive menu of favourites and plenty of home-made vegetarian and fish dishes, such as chicken goujons, steak and ale pie, Greek salad, smoked haddock, and mushroom and red pepper Stroganoff.

Open all wk 11-3 6-11.30 (Sun 11-11) Closed 26 Dec **Food** Lunch Mon-Fri 12-2, Sat 12-2.30, Sun 12-9.30 Dinner Mon-Sat 6-9.30, Sun 12-9.30 ⊕ FREE HOUSE ◀ Harvey's Sussex Best Bitter, Hogs Back, Hammerpot Guest ales, Local Guest ales. ♥ 10 **Facilities** Non-diners area ♣ (Bar Garden) ♦ Children's menu Children's portions Play area Garden ⧟ Parking ▬ (notice required)

See advert on opposite page

Horse & Groom

tel: 01435 830320 **TN21 9QE**
email: info@horseandgroomrushlakegreen.co.uk
dir: *Phone for detailed directions*

An appealing pub-restaurant with rustic character

At the edge of the enormous green that gives the village its name, the Horse & Groom has a huge garden offering a grand prospect over the pretty East Sussex countryside, a much sought-after spot for summertime refreshment. Residents have supped here for over 230 years and the pub retains its heavy beams, hearth, brass and copper, and a restaurant complete with antique firearms. Drinkers delight in Harvey's and guest ales, whilst a fulfilling menu of home-cooked fare rewards diners. Typical choices include belly of Old Spots pork; rack of Southdown lamb; and locally caught cod fillet and chips.

Open all day all wk **Food** Lunch Mon-Fri 12-3, Sat 12-9, Sun 12-8 Dinner Mon-Fri 5.30-9.30, Sat 12-9, Sun 12-8 ⊕ SHEPHERD NEAME ◀ Harvey's Sussex Best Bitter, Guest ales ♂ Thatchers Gold. **Facilities** Non-diners area ♣ (Bar Garden) ♦ Children's portions Garden ⧟ Parking WiFi ▬ (notice required)

The Cock

This is a 16th century family run dining pub where the landlords still find time to personally greet both new and returning customers. Walk into the pub and you are met by a huge blackboard that seems to list every pub dish that has ever existed! Should that not be enough choice then this is supplemented by a daily Specials Board and at lunchtimes (ex Sundays) sandwiches, rolls & Ploughman's – we try to offer something for all tastes, appetites and budgets and are also able to cater for Coeliacs and Vegans. The pub is well renowned for its wide choice of homemade dishes featuring locally produced ingredients, such as Steak & Ale Pie, Venison Sausages and Chicken Florentina. Vegetarians are well catered for with 6 regular Vegetarian dishes, 3 of which are prepared to Vegan standards. A variety of fish and steaks are always featured and a favourite is Val's Purse (named after the Landlady!) – Sirloin Steak stuffed with Stilton and with a Creamy Mushroom Sauce. There is always a choice of Sunday Roast with all the 'Trimmings' and if you still have room there are lovely homemade traditional puddings like Rhubarb Crumble, Sticky Toffee & Date Sponge with our own Butterscotch Sauce, Eton Mess or award winning Ice Creams from Downsview Farm (Toffee-Apple as featured on The Apprentice) available every day. And, if there is a dish that you particularly want, with a bit of notice, we will try to provide it.

The Specials Board is always well stocked with locally produced fare, representing the seasons – asparagus in Spring, Game in Autumn/Winter (Venison, Pheasant, Partridge, Guinea Fowl, etc), Winter warmers (Sausage casserole, Lamb's Hearts, Oxtail etc) and fresh salads and quiches in the Summer.

There is a well-stocked bar that always features Harvey's Best Bitter, together with two locally produced seasonal guests from The Hogsback Brewery, Hammerpot, WJ King, together with a number of locally emerging micro-breweries – details of which can be found on the pub's continually updated website at www.cockpub.co.uk. In addition, there is a choice of 12 wines by the glass, including Pinot Grigio, Sauvignon Blanc, Shiraz and Merlot, all at £4.20 per 175 ml glass plus Hot Mulled Wine in the winter and a wide selection of liqueurs, together with a selection of 12 Malt Whiskies.

There are three dining areas, which can accommodate up to 65 covers, plus the Bar area that can seat a further twelve people. The bar is a wonderful unspoilt area with original oak beams, a flagstone floor and an Inglenook fireplace, where a log fire can be found from October to April. Well-behaved children are welcomed in the restaurant and garden, keeping the bar for those who would like a quiet drink or bite to eat.

The garden has plenty of space to enjoy fine weather with patio areas and grass and views to the South Downs and if you are lucky spectacular sunsets on clear evenings. The pub welcomes dogs in the garden and bar area with dog chews and water bowls. The pub's own spaniels Tally & Bailey can often be seen returning through the bar after a walk on the nearby Wellingham Walk.

The Cock Inn takes its name from the bygone era when a spare horse (The Cock Horse) was kept ready at the foot of a steep hill to assist another horse with a heavy load up the hill. Old maps show that there was stabling in the car park area up until the later 1800's. The Cock Horse, of course, was immortalised in the favourite children's nursery rhyme that depicted Queen Elizabeth 1 riding into Banbury Cross aboard a large white stallion, after the Queen's carriage had broken a wheel on the steep climb up the hill.

Built in the mid-16th Century, The Cock has always been a thriving Coaching Inn. Although none of the original stables remain, it was once a mustering point during The Civil War, prior to the siege of Arundel.

The main bar and interior has changed little since Cromwell's time, with low oak beams and Inglenook fireplace. In its earliest days, four rooms within the building were licensed separately, each room identified by a small porcelain plate bearing a number. Two of these plates can still be seen in the main bar.

Uckfield Road, Ringmer, Lewes, East Sussex BN8 5RX • Tel: 01273 812040 • **Email:** matt@cockpub.co.uk
Website: www.cockpub.co.uk • **Twitter:** @CockInnRingmer • **Facebook:** TheCockInnRingmer

RYE

Map 7 TQ92

The George Tap ★★★★ HL ⊛

tel: 01797 222114 **98 High St TN31 7JT**
email: stay@thegeorgeinrye.com **web:** www.thegeorgeinrye.com
dir: M20 junct 10, A2070 to Brenzett, A259 to Rye

16th-century inn in pretty Sussex town

This town centre inn can trace its origins back to 1575. Inside it offers a
fascinating mix of old and new, with an exquisite original Georgian ballroom and
plenty of antique and contemporary furnishings and locally produced art. In the bar,
the draw is beers from Dark Star and Harvey's breweries and a tasty, light bar
menu. Diners taking the one AA-Rosette meals can enjoy fruits of the sea from local
boats; perhaps sweetcorn chowder or salt and pepper squid, followed by classic fish
and chips with mushy peas. Alternatively, try grilled lamb from the wood charcoal
oven or classic steak frites.

Open all day all wk **Food** Lunch all wk 12-6 Dinner all wk 6-10 Av main course £14
Set menu available Restaurant menu available all wk ⊕ FREE HOUSE ◀ Dark Star
American Pale Ale, Harvey's Sussex Best Bitter. ♀ 18 **Facilities** Non-diners area
⬩◀ Children's menu Children's portions Garden ♫ WiFi ➡ **Rooms** 34

Mermaid Inn ★★★ HL ⊛⊛

PICK OF THE PUBS

tel: 01797 223065 **Mermaid St TN31 7EY**
email: info@mermaidinn.com **web:** www.mermaidinn.com
dir: A259, follow signs to town centre, into Mermaid St

Memorable seafood dishes in historic smugglers' inn

The aura of the smugglers' inn remains at the Mermaid, which is one of the most
famous and photographed of England's ancient pubs. This venerable black and
white timber-fronted building was a haunt of seafarers from the Cinque Port
harbour. Its colourful history is reflected in ships' timbers for beams and huge open
fireplaces carved from French stone ballast dredged from Rye harbour. A vast
inglenook where the infamous Hawkshurst gang warmed themselves also has a
hidden priest hole. British and French-style food is served in the bar, restaurant
and under sunshades on the patio. Seafood and local lamb feature strongly on all
menus; a chunky smoked fish chowder can be ordered for one hungry diner or two
people to share, whilst other main courses include steak and kidney pudding or
haddock in beer batter. Superb wines, local Harvey's beer and comfortable
bedrooms complete the package.

Open all day all wk 12-11 **Food** Lunch all wk 12-2.30 Dinner all wk 6-9 Av main
course £9.75 Restaurant menu available all wk ⊕ FREE HOUSE ◀ Fuller's London
Pride, Harvey's ♂ Kingstone Press. ♀ 15 **Facilities** Non-diners area ⬩ (Garden)
◀ Children's menu Children's portions Garden ♫ Parking WiFi ➡ (notice required)
Rooms 31

The Ypres Castle Inn

PICK OF THE PUBS

tel: 01797 223248 **Gun Garden TN31 7HH**
email: info@yprescastleinn.co.uk
dir: Behind church & adjacent to Ypres Tower

A best-kept secrets in the ancient town of Rye

The pretty Ypres Castle Inn, known locally as 'The Wipers', sits beneath the castle's
ramparts and has been providing hospitality since 1640. Under new ownership, the
inn's atmosphere is as relaxed and friendly as ever, and the reading room is still
stocked with an eclectic literary mix and children's games. The bar, featuring the
original timber frame of the building, serves Larkins and Harvey's, plus Biddenden
cider, all to be savoured around the log fire. From the garden there are magnificent
views of Romney Marsh and the River Rother; the Rye Bay fishing fleet moors close
by. Light bites include baguettes, ciabattas and bruschettas; popular traditional
plates include a classic prawn cocktail, and slow-roast belly pork served with
roasted garlic mash. Booking is advisable for the traditional Sunday roasts. The
pub hosts live music on Friday nights, Sundays and in the garden in summer.

Open all day all wk **Food** Lunch all wk 12-3 Dinner Mon-Sat 6-9 Av main course £14
⊕ FREE HOUSE ◀ Harvey's Sussex Best Bitter, Timothy Taylor Landlord, Larkins Best
Bitter, Adnams, Guest ales ♂ Biddenden Bushels. ♀ 12 **Facilities** Non-diners area
⬩ (Bar Garden) ◀ Children's menu Children's portions Garden ♫ WiFi

SALEHURST

Map 7 TQ72

Salehurst Halt

PICK OF THE PUBS

tel: 01580 880620 **Church Ln TN32 5PH**
dir: 0.5m from A21 (Tunbridge Wells to Hastings road). Exit at Robertsbridge rdbt to
Salehurst

Free house with hop growing connections

Built in the 1860s, when it was known as the Old Eight Bells. Legend puts the name
change down to a church organist who commuted to the village from Bodiam,
necessitating a new halt on the Robertsbridge to Tenterden line. Despite use by
many a hop-picker thereafter, the steam railway eventually closed. Today the hop
crop is sold to Harvey's in Lewes, and returned as one of the ales sold by the pub –
its traditional cellar is much prized for maintaining ale in top condition. The hop-
growing farm also supplies the pub's meats, including Buster's burgers; note that
evening meals are only served from Wednesday to Saturday; the menus reflect the
seasons. The landscaped garden has a wonderful terrace with beautiful views over
the Rother Valley; here a wood-fired pizza oven (and outdoor griddle weather
permitting) runs almost continually during the summer, with orders taken at the
garden counter. Before leaving, have a stroll around this picturesque hamlet and
the 12th-century church.

Open Tue-Wed 12-3 6-11 (Thu-Sun 12-11) Closed Mon **Food** Lunch Tue-Sun 12-2.30
Dinner Wed-Sat 7-9 Av main course £9-£15 ⊕ FREE HOUSE ◀ Harvey's Sussex Best
Bitter, Dark Star, Old Dairy, Guest ales ♂ Biddenden Bushels, East Stour.
Facilities Non-diners area ⬩ (Bar Restaurant Garden) ◀ Children's portions
Garden ♫

SHORTBRIDGE

Map 6 TQ42

The Peacock Inn

PICK OF THE PUBS

tel: 01825 762463 **TN22 3XA**
email: enquiries@peacock-inn.co.uk
dir: Just off A272 (Haywards Heath to Uckfield road) & A26 (Uckfield to Lewes road)

Pretty black and white pub with seasonally inspired menus

Mentioned in Samuel Pepys' diary, The Peacock Inn dates from 1567 but is these
days more renowned for its food and its warm welcome. This traditional inn is full
of old-world charm, both inside and out. Long Man Best and a guest ale keep beer-

lovers happy, and there are eight wines by the glass. For the hungry there are starters such as sweet chilli chicken and crispy bacon salad; chicken liver pâté; Sussex smokie, smoked haddock, cream and mustard sauce; followed by poached filled of hake, confit potatoes, clam chowder, buttered spinach and caramelised salsify; or pomegranate glazed duck breast, potato torte, baby leeks, spring greens and jus. Leave room for desserts such as blueberry cheesecake with honeycomb parfait, or toffee sponge pudding and apple ripple ice cream . The large rear patio garden is a delightful spot in summer.

Open all wk 11-3 6-11 Closed 25-26 Dec **Food** Lunch Mon-Sat 12-3, Sun 12-8 Dinner Mon-Sat 6-9.30, Sun 12-8 Av main course £11 ⊕ FREE HOUSE ◄ Harvey's Sussex Best Bitter, Long Man Best Bitter, Guest ale. ♟ 8 **Facilities** Non-diners area ♨ (Bar Garden) ♦ Children's menu Children's portions Garden ⊞ Parking

THREE LEG CROSS
Map 6 TQ63

The Bull

tel: 01580 200586 **Dunster Mill Ln TN5 7HH**
email: enquiries@thebullinn.co.uk
dir: From M25 exit at Sevenoaks toward Hastings, right at x-rds onto B2087, right onto B2099 through Ticehurst, right for Three Leg Cross

Home-cooked food and large family-friendly garden

The Bull started life as a 14th-century Wealden Hall House, reputedly one of the oldest dwelling places in the country, and is set in a hamlet close to Bewl Water. The interior features oak beams, inglenook fireplaces, quarry-tiled floors, and a mass of small intimate areas in the bar. The extensive gardens are popular with families who enjoy the duck pond, petanque pitch, aviary and children's play area. Menus offer pub favourites ranging from freshly baked baguettes and bar snacks to hearty dishes full of comfort, such as bangers and mash and treacle tart. Change of hands.

Open all day all wk 12-12 **Food** Lunch Mon-Fri 12-2.30, Sat 12-3, Sun 12-8 Dinner Mon-Sat 6.30-9, Sun 12-8 Restaurant menu available all wk ⊕ FREE HOUSE ◄ Harvey's Sussex Best Bitter & Armada Ale, Timothy Taylor Landlord, Guest ales Ŏ Westons Stowford Press, Symonds. ♟ 9 **Facilities** Non-diners area ♨ (Bar Garden) ♦ Children's menu Children's portions Play area Garden ⊞ Beer festival Parking WiFi 🚌 (notice required)

TICEHURST
Map 6 TQ63

The Bell
PICK OF THE PUBS

tel: 01580 200234 **High St TN5 7AS**
email: info@thebellinticehurst.com
dir: From A21 follow signs for Ticehurst. Pub in village centre

A village inn to make you smile

Following serious investment and a full-scale refurbishment nearly five years ago, the doors of the new-look Bell opened to reveal a quirky but comfortable pub. The authentic 16th-century charm of the building has been preserved in the bar, with its rustic wooden floors, sagging beams, and a blazing log fire in the huge brick inglenook. A cosy snug next door is furnished with leather chesterfields and shelves of books. Beyond, the Stable with a Table is an inspired function room with long sunken table and benches, perfect for the pub's regular debate evenings and demonstration dinners. Funky design touches abound, from the top hat lampshades and pillar of books in the bar, to the tubas for urinals in the Gents and the stuffed squirrel that appears to hold up a ceiling. Settle in with a smile and a pint of Old Dairy before ordering from the short but perfectly formed menu.

Open all day all wk **Food** Lunch all wk 12-6 Dinner all wk 6-9.30 Av main course £15 Set menu available ⊕ FREE HOUSE ◄ Harvey's, Old Dairy, Seasonal Guest ales Ŏ Symonds. ♟ 12 **Facilities** Non-diners area ♨ (Bar Garden) ♦ Children's menu Garden ⊞ Parking WiFi 🚌 (notice required)

WILMINGTON
Map 6 TQ50

The Giants Rest

tel: 01323 870207 **The Street BN26 5SQ**
email: giantsrest@hotmail.com
dir: 2m from Polegate on A27 towards Brighton

Perfect after a long country walk

This family-owned Victorian free house has the famous chalk figure of the Long Man of Wilmington standing guard further up the lane and proves to be just the place to leave muddy boots at the door after a steep hill walk. The rustic wooden-floored bar is decorated with Beryl Cook prints. Take a seat at a pine table, each with its own wooden puzzle, and order some home-prepared food: baked Normandie camembert with cranberry sauce; Sussex Downs rabbit, bacon, apple and prune pie; and traditional fruit crumble are typical choices. Wash it down with beers from the Long Man Brewery at Litlington just three miles down the road.

Open all wk 11-3 6-11 (Sat-Sun all day) **Food** Lunch Mon-Fri 11.30-2, Sat-Sun all day Dinner Mon-Fri 6.30-9, Sat-Sun all day Av main course £12 ⊕ FREE HOUSE ◄ Long Man Best Bitter, Long Blonde, Old Man, American Pale Ale, Sussex Pride & Copper Hop Ŏ Westons Stowford Press. ♟ 10 **Facilities** Non-diners area ♨ (Bar Restaurant Garden) ♦ Children's portions Garden ⊞ Parking WiFi 🚌

WITHYHAM
Map 6 TQ43

The Dorset Arms
PICK OF THE PUBS

tel: 01892 770278 **TN7 4BD**
email: enquiries@dorsetarms.co.uk
dir: 4m W of Tunbridge Wells on B2110 between Groombridge & Hartfield

Packed with historical features

The picture-postcard perfection of this centuries-old building is a jigsaw of ages and styles - slender chimney stacks, sharp gables, gleaming white weatherboarding and careworn tiles. Licensed some 200 years ago when it took the name of the local landowning family, once Earls of Dorset, the interior doesn't disappoint, with a comfy, period mix of flagstoned and oak-boarded floors, a vast open fireplace, undulating beams, and magpie furniture. It remains at heart a true village local, with darts, good Sussex ales from Harvey's and a vibrant community atmosphere. The produce of the kitchen is also a major draw, with an extensive, daily-changing specials board complementing the respectable carte menu. Starters include goats' cheese crostini; and whitebait with salad. The main course options might be Thai green chicken curry; chargrilled pork chops, wholegrain mustard mash and cider reduction; and beer battered skinless cod fillet and triple cooked hand-cut chips. All desserts are home made. Tables on the green outside allow summertime alfresco dining.

Open all day all wk 12-11 (Sun 12-10.30) **Food** Lunch Mon-Sat 12-2.30, Sun 12-4 Dinner Mon-Sat 6-9 ⊕ FREE HOUSE ◄ Harvey's Sussex Best Bitter, Hepworths, Larkins, Guest ales. **Facilities** Non-diners area ♨ (Bar Garden) ♦ Children's menu Children's portions Garden ⊞ Parking WiFi

WEST SUSSEX

AMBERLEY

Map 6 TQ01

The Bridge Inn

tel: 01798 831619 **Houghton Bridge BN18 9LR**
email: bridgeamberley@btinternet.com **web:** www.bridgeinnamberley.com
dir: *5m N of Arundel on B2139. Adjacent to Amberley rail station*

Reliable old inn in National Park village

Visiting the fascinating Amberley Museum and Heritage Centre, just over the road from this mellow free-house, is a good way of working up an appetite before investigating this charming period pub close to the River Arun. People are drawn in to the candlelit bar and log fires on cold winter evenings for real ales from the likes of Ballards and Harvey's, and in summer to seek shade in the sheltered garden; from here they can appreciate the delightful countryside of the South Downs and contemplate meals from the solid pubby menu, with classics like battered cod fillet and chips. Mediterranean-inspired dishes often feature on the specials board.

Open all day all wk 11-11 (Sun 12-10.30) **Food** Lunch Mon-Fri 12-2.30, Sat-Sun 12-4 Dinner Mon-Sat 6-9, Sun 5.30-8 ⊕ FREE HOUSE ◀ Skinner's Betty Stogs, Harvey's Sussex Best Bitter, Ballards Golden Bine, Langham Hip Hop, Guest ales ♂ Westons Stowford Press. **Facilities** Non-diners area ♣ (Bar Garden) ♠ Children's menu Children's portions Garden Outside area ⋈ Parking ▨ (notice required)

ASHURST

Map 6 TQ11

The Fountain Inn

PICK OF THE PUBS

tel: 01403 710219 **BN44 3AP**
email: manager@fountainashurst.co.uk
dir: *On B2135 N of Steyning*

Traditional English pub with some famous admirers

Acting legend Laurence Olivier was a regular at this lovely 16th-century listed building and Paul McCartney loved the place so much he filmed part of the video for *Wonderful Christmas Time* here. The South Downs and the village duck pond can be seen from the terrace of the pub, which comes complete with wonky floorboards, inglenook fireplaces, beams and skittle alley. Local beers from Harvey's accompany the freshly cooked pub food that attracts walkers, cyclists, locals and those from further afield. At lunchtime there are light bites, or at lunch or dinner you could opt for the full three courses; maybe smoked salmon and prawn cannelloni with herb salad and beetroot followed by pressed belly of Sussex pork, herb mash, roasted Braeburn apple, black pudding and red wine jus. If you still have space, finish with chocolate brownie with morello cherry ice cream. Look out for events including live music.

Open all day all wk 11-11 (Sun 11-10.30) **Food** Lunch Mon-Fri 12-2.30, Sat-Sun 12-9.30 Dinner Mon-Fri 6-9.30, Sat-Sun 12-9.30 Av main course £14 Set menu available ⊕ ENTERPRISE INNS ◀ Harvey's Sussex, Sharp's Doom Bar, Fuller's, Seasonal & Guest ales ♂ Westons Stowford Press. **Facilities** Non-diners area ♣ (Bar Garden) ♠ Children's menu Children's portions Garden ⋈ Parking WiFi ▨ (notice required)

BOSHAM

Map 5 SU80

The Anchor Bleu

tel: 01243 573956 **High St PO18 8LS**
dir: *From A27 SW of Chichester take A259. Follow Fishbourne signs, then Bosham signs*

Harbourside pub with plenty of real ales

If you park your car opposite The Anchor Bleu, check the tide times at this 17th-century inn, as that area floods during most high tides. Flagstone floors, low beams, an open log fire, an upstairs dining room with views and two terraces, one overlooking Chichester Harbour, add to the charm of this popular pub. A good choice of real ales is on offer, including Ringwood Fortyniner. Dishes are based on locally sourced, seasonal ingredients, such as Blackdown venison steak, salt and pepper squid, and brie and artichoke tartlet. Reservations are recommended. Meals can be taken on the terraces during warmer weather.

Open all wk all day (Mon-Thu 11.30-3 6-11 Nov-Mar) **Food** Lunch Mon-Sat 12-3, Sun all day Dinner all wk 6.30-9.30 ⊕ ENTERPRISE INNS ◀ Sharp's Cornish Coaster & Doom Bar, Ringwood Fortyniner, Otter Ale, Hop Back Summer Lightning, Anchor Springs Riptide ♂ Westons Stowford Press. ♀ 10 **Facilities** Non-diners area ♠ Children's menu Children's portions Garden ⋈ ▨ (notice required)

BURGESS HILL

Map 6 TQ31

The Oak Barn

tel: 01444 258222 **Cuckfield Rd RH15 8RE**
email: enquiries@oakbarnrestaurant.co.uk **web:** www.oakbarnrestaurant.co.uk
dir: *Phone for detailed directions*

British produce in a restored barn

As its name suggests, this popular pub-restaurant occupies a 250-year-old barn that has been lovingly restored using salvaged timbers from wooden ships. Brimming with charm, the interior is rich in oak flooring, authentic wagon wheel chandeliers, and fine stained glass. Lofty raftered ceilings, a galleried restaurant, and leather chairs fronting a huge fireplace add to the atmosphere. Sup a pint of Harvey's and tuck into dishes constructed from seasonal British ingredients: smoked pancetta with Savoy and leek hash or whole baked camembert to start; followed by chorizo and sunblushed tomato crusted cod or mixed mushroom pasta; and sticky toffee pudding to finish. Outside is an enclosed courtyard and patios, with water features.

Open all day all wk 10am-11pm (Sun 11-11) **Food** Lunch all wk 12-2.30 Dinner all wk 6-9.30 Av main course £10 Set menu available Restaurant menu available all wk ⊕ FREE HOUSE ◀ Dark Star, Harvey's, Fuller's London Pride, Guinness. ♛ 8 **Facilities** Non-diners area ♦ Children's portions Garden Outside area ⊓ Parking WiFi

See advert below

PICK OF THE PUBS

The Fox Goes Free ★★★★ INN

CHARLTON　　　　Map 6 SU81

tel: 01243 811461 **PO18 0HU**
email: enquiries@thefoxgoesfree.com
web: www.thefoxgoesfree.com
dir: *A286, 6m from Chichester towards Midhurst*

Friendly pub with William III, racing world and WI connections

Standing in unspoiled countryside at the foot of the South Downs, this lovely old brick and flint free house was a favoured hunting lodge of William III. With its three huge fireplaces, old pews and brick floors, the 15th-century building simply exudes charm and character. The pub, which hosted the first English Women's Institute meeting in 1915, lies close to the Weald and Downland Open Air Museum, where 50 historic buildings from around southern England have been reconstructed. Goodwood Estate is also close by, and The Fox attracts many customers during the racing season and the annual Festival of Speed. Away from the high life, you can watch the world go by from the solid timber benches and tables to the front, or relax under the apple trees in the lawned rear garden. Lest all this sounds rather extravagant, you'll find that The Fox is a friendly and welcoming drinkers' pub with a good selection of real ales that includes the eponymous Fox Goes Free bitter. Everything from the chips to the ice cream is home-made

and, whether you're looking for a quick bar snack or something more substantial, the daily-changing menus offer something for every taste. Bar meals include Cumberland sausages with caramelised onion and wholegrain mustard mash, and wild mushroom pasta with parmesan; as well as a selection of ciabattas. Further choices may be a meze platter of the day, or smoked pigeon breast, pancetta and white bean cassoulet. Continue with a main course such as chorizo, scallop and spinach risotto; or braised shoulder of lamb, balsamic and mint jus reduction with Lyonnaise potatoes. Salads can be prepared for both small and large appetites, and there are some appealing vegetarian options, too.

Open all day 11-11 (Sun 12-11) Closed 25 Dec eve **Food** Lunch Mon-Fri 12-2.30, Sat-Sun 12-10 Dinner Mon-Fri 6.30-10, Sat-Sun 12-10 Av main course £12.50 Restaurant menu all wk. ⊕ FREE HOUSE ◀ The Fox Goes Free, Ballards Best Bitter, Otter ♂ Addlestones, Symonds ♀ 10 **Facilities** Non-diners area ♣ (Bar Garden) ♦ Children's menu & portions Garden ⋒ Parking WiFi 🚐 (notice required) **Rooms** 5

BURPHAM
Map 6 TQ00

The George at Burpham
PICK OF THE PUBS

tel: 01903 883131 **BN18 9RR**
email: info@georgeatburpham.co.uk
dir: *Exit A27 1m E of Arundel signed Burpham, 2.5m, pub on left*

Saved by the locals, now a thriving community pub

It's thought that this delightful village pub opposite a Saxon church was built in 1736. Sadly its longevity was no guarantee of its future and, like so many others throughout the country, it succumbed to the recession and closed in 2013. Step forward a trio of local businessmen, all regulars, who organised finance, bought the freehold, and offered shares to Burpham villagers and two other local communities – with amazingly supportive results. The pub was refurbished, renamed, and reopened with the simple aim of welcoming all-comers with real ales, good wine and excellent food. So settle in with a pint of Arundel, and choose from the seasonal, locally sourced and fresh specials. Pan-seared scallops with cauliflower purée and prosciutto is a great way to start, with more fish to follow perhaps: beer-battered hake and chips; fish pie with garden peas; or fish broth with mussels, clams and monkfish, served with warm bread.

Open all wk 12-3 6-11 **Food** Lunch Mon-Fri 12-2, Sat-Sun 12-3 Dinner all wk 6-9 ⊕ FREE HOUSE ◀ Arundel, Guest ales ♂ Aspall. **Facilities** Non-diners area ♦◊ Children's menu Garden ⊟ Parking WiFi ▄

CHARLTON
Map 6 SU81

The Fox Goes Free ★★★★ INN
PICK OF THE PUBS

See Pick of the Pubs on opposite page

CHICHESTER
Map 5 SU80

The Bull's Head ★★★★ INN

tel: 01243 839895 **99 Fishbourne Road West PO19 3JP**
email: enquiries@bullsheadfishbourne.net web: www.bullsheadfishbourne.net
dir: *A27 onto A259, 0.5m on left*

Good range of well-kept real ales

Only three minutes' walk from Chichester harbour, this traditional roadside pub with large open fire has been a hostelry since some time in the 17th century, and before that it was a farmhouse. Its position just outside Chichester is perfect for visiting Fishbourne Roman Palace and Bosham Harbour. Traditional home-cooked food is based on locally sourced ingredients and baguettes and jacket potatoes are on offer as a lighter option. The pub serves five real ales all in tip-top condition. Live music and special events are hosted throughout the year. The comfortable accommodation is light and airy with modern decor and furnishings.

Open all wk 11-3 5.30-11 (Sat 11-11 Sun 12-11) **Food** Lunch Mon-Sat 12-2, Sun 12-3 Dinner Mon-Thu 6-9, Fri-Sat 6-9.30, Sun 6-8 ⊕ FULLER'S ◀ London Pride, ESB & George Gale & Co HSB, Guest ales ♂ Aspall. ▾ 10 **Facilities** Non-diners area ♣ (Bar Outside area) ♦◊ Children's menu Children's portions Outside area ⊟ Parking WiFi ▄ (notice required) **Rooms** 4

The Earl of March ◉
PICK OF THE PUBS

tel: 01243 533993 **Lavant Rd, Lavant PO18 0BQ**
email: info@theearlofmarch.com
dir: *On A286, 1m N of Chichester*

Lots of style at former coaching inn

Named after the local landowning dynasty, The Earl sits at the foot of the South Downs National Park and is an inspirational place to visit. William Blake wrote the words to *Jerusalem* whilst sitting in the east-facing bay window here in 1803; today's visitors can enjoy much the same views that prompted his outpourings. The excellent choice of dishes is prepared from the bounty of local estates and the nearby Channel. A winter menu might have perhaps pan-seared scallops, langoustines, pork belly, pea purée, Selsey bisque; followed by whole roasted partridge, pommes Anna, mulled plums, quail's egg, cep broth and pickled mushroom. Such dishes are crafted by Giles Thompson, former Executive Chef at London's Ritz Hotel and now proprietor of this delightful 18th-century coaching inn appointed in 'country plush' style.

Open all day all wk **Food** Lunch all wk 12-2.30 winter, 12-9 summer Dinner all wk 12-9 summer Set menu available Restaurant menu available all wk ⊕ ENTERPRISE INNS ◀ Harvey's, Fuller's London Pride, Timothy Taylor Landlord, Guest ale ♂ Westons Stowford Press, Aspall. ▾ 24 **Facilities** Non-diners area ♣ (Bar Garden) ♦◊ Children's menu Children's portions Garden ⊟ Parking WiFi

NEW The George & Dragon Inn ★★★ INN

tel: 01243 785660 **51 North St PO19 1NQ**
email: info@thegeorgeanddragoninn.co.uk web: www.georgeanddragoninn.co.uk
dir: *Near Chichester Festival Theatre. Phone for detailed directions*

Refurbished inn with rooms in the heart of Chichester

Dating from the early 18th century, The George & Dragon stands next to the site of the original north walls gatehouse in historic Chichester, and is well positioned near the Old Town Cross and cathedral. Landlord Lee Howard has refurbished the place in the last eight or so years – today you'll find open fires, comfortable sofas and a heated courtyard to enhance the family-friendly feel. In the light and airy conservatory dining room, the menus reveal traditional pub favourites alongside the likes of wild mushroom and pearl barley risotto; and lemongrass and thyme skewered chicken with roasted vegetables.

Open all day all wk Closed 25-26 Dec & 1 Jan **Food** Lunch Mon-Fri & Sun 12-3, Sat 12-5 Dinner Mon-Sat 5-9 Restaurant menu available all wk ⊕ PUNCH TAVERNS ◀ Sharp's Doom Bar, Timothy Taylor Landlord. ▾ 18 **Facilities** Non-diners area ♣ (Bar Outside area) ♦◊ Children's portions Outside area ⊟ WiFi ▄ (notice required) **Rooms** 10

Royal Oak Inn ★★★★★ INN ◉
PICK OF THE PUBS

See Pick of the Pubs on page 496

COMPTON
Map 5 SU71

Coach & Horses

tel: 023 9263 1228 **The Square PO18 9HA**
dir: *On B2146 S of Petersfield, to Emsworth, in centre of Compton*

Appealing South Downs honeypot

David and Christiane Butler have run their 17th-century coaching inn in this pretty South Downs village since 1985. Popular with walkers, cyclists and, let's face it, anyone looking for good food and drink, its unspoiled Victorian bar, with two open fires, is widely known for championing local microbreweries like Ballards Dark Star and Langham. The oldest part of the pub, with many exposed beams, is the restaurant, where David, who trained at The Ritz, serves chicken mushroom and tarragon pie; avocado and spinach bake; and crackling pork belly, and makes good use of local game and South Downs lamb.

Open Tue-Sun 11.30-3 6-11 Closed Mon **Food** Lunch Tue-Sun 12-2 Dinner Tue-Sun 7-9 ⊕ FREE HOUSE ◀ Ballards Best Bitter, Bowmans, Guest ales ♂ Thatchers, Appledram. **Facilities** Non-diners area ♣ (Bar Outside area) ♦◊ Children's portions Outside area ⊟ WiFi ▄ (notice required)

PICK OF THE PUBS

Royal Oak Inn ★★★★★ INN 🏵

CHICHESTER   Map 5 SU80

tel: 01243 527434
Pook Ln, East Lavant PO18 0AX
email: info@royaloakeastlavant.co.uk
web: www.royaloakeastlavant.co.uk
dir: *2m N of Chichester. Exit A286 to East Lavant centre*

A smart dining pub with luxury accommodation

Starting life two centuries ago as a farmhouse, the Royal Oak is set within the South Downs National Park and is just up the hill from Goodwood racecourse; it is also perfectly situated for the nearby cathedral city of Chichester. The creeper-clad Georgian inn is at the heart of the beautiful, historic village of East Lavant and is known for offering great food to visitors and locals alike. The brick-lined restaurant and beamed bar achieve a crisp, rustic brand of chic: details include chunky wooden tables, leather chairs, open fires, fresh flowers, candles, and wine attractively displayed in alcoves set into the walls; local Sussex Gold and Horsham Best ales, whiskies and Gospel Green Champagne cider are among the thirst-quenchers on offer. The seasonal menu is an easy mix of modern European dishes and English classics with a twist, and much of the produce is grown by villagers in return for pints. The lovely patio is the perfect place to enjoy pavé of salmon, or

supreme of corn fed chicken with tomato, chorizo and mixed bean cassoulet perhaps accompanied by one of the 20 wines by the glass. The specials board features the fish and meat dishes of the day, while the autumn à la carte could list sage and honey glazed pork cheeks with lightly curried parsnip purée; slow cooked venison, roast root vegetables, dauphinoise potatoes and redcurrant jus; mini baked Alaska with warm rum custard; or Madagascan vanilla seed crème brûlee. There are luxury guest rooms with large, comfortable beds and en suite bathrooms.

Open all day all wk 7am-11.30pm
Food Lunch all wk 11.30-3.30 Dinner all wk 5.30-9.30 Set menu available Restaurant menu available all wk.
🍺 FREE HOUSE 🍺 Skinner's Betty Stogs, Sharp's Doom Bar, Arundel Sussex Gold, WJ King Horsham Best 🍏 Gospel Green Champagne & Cidermakers, Thatchers Gold. 🍷 20 **Facilities** Non-diners area 👶 Children's portions Garden 🎍 Parking WiFi **Rooms** 8

CUCKFIELD
Map 6 TQ32

The Talbot

tel: 01444 455898 **High St RH17 5JX**
email: info@thetalbotcuckfield.co.uk
dir: B2036 into village centre

Smart village pub showcasing the local larder

Once a staging post for travellers on the road between London and Brighton, The Talbot is still the hub in the historic village of Cuckfield. It's now a contemporary pub and restaurant that prides itself on making the most of the local larder, whether it's Dark Star ales or seasonal dishes such as lamb rump with basil crust, bubble-and-squeak, butternut squash purée, garlic sautéed beans and red wine jus; or potato gnocchi, roasted squash, wilted spinach, tarragon cream sauce and parsnip crisps. There is a local producers' market in the courtyard on the second Saturday of the month.

Open all day all wk **Food** Lunch Mon-Sat 12-2.30, Sun 12-5 Dinner Mon-Sat 6-9.30 Av main course £11 ⊕ FREE HOUSE ◆ Harvey's Sussex Best Bitter, Dark Star, Guest ales ♂ Symonds. ▼ 14 **Facilities** Non-diners area ✿ (Bar Garden) ◆◆ Children's menu Children's portions Garden ⼝ WiFi ⛟ (notice required)

DIAL POST
Map 6 TQ11

The Crown Inn

tel: 01403 710902 **Worthing Rd RH13 8NH**
email: crowninndialpost@aol.com
dir: 8m S of Horsham, off A24

Family heritage at real ale gastro-pub

The Crown Inn is owned by Penny and James Middleton-Burn; Penny's grandparents were the previous owners, in the late 60s and early 70s, of this tile-hung free house overlooking the village green . Penny's sister and husband rear the pigs and lambs that end up in the kitchen, strengthening the family involvement. Although it is food-led, if you just want a pint of bitter from Bedlam, Devil's Dyke or Harvey's brewery, that's absolutely fine. Chef James and his team makes nearly everything on the premises, including chicken liver and pork pâté; Crown burgers; chicken tikka masala; steak, steak pies; and rhubarb, ginger and peach crumble with custard.

Open all wk 11-3 6-11 (Sun 12-4) **Food** Lunch all wk 12-2.15 Dinner Mon-Sat 6-9.15 Av main course £13 ⊕ FREE HOUSE ◆ Harvey's Sussex Best Bitter, Guest ales ♂ Thatchers Gold. **Facilities** Non-diners area ✿ (Bar Restaurant Garden) ◆◆ Children's portions Garden ⼝ Parking WiFi ⛟ (notice required)

DUNCTON
Map 6 SU91

The Cricketers

tel: 01798 342473 **GU28 OLB**
email: info@thecricketersduncton.co.uk
dir: On A285, 3m from Petworth, 8m from Chichester

Ideal rest stop when exploring the South Downs

Named to commemorate its one-time owner John Wisden, the first-class cricketer and creator of the famous sporting almanac, this attractive whitewashed pub sits in beautiful gardens behind Goodwood. Dating to the 16th century, with an inglenook fireplace, the inn has hardly changed over the years. Well-kept real ales include Arundel Sussex Gold, while the blackboard menu offers lunchtime sandwiches and traditional favourites, home-cooked from locally sourced ingredients. Look for the likes of crackling pork hock, toad-in-the-hole, herb-crusted rack of lamb, crab salad, and Sussex Slipcote cheese risotto. Children are welcome and there's a menu to suit younger tastes.

Open all day all wk **Food** Lunch Mon-Thu 12-2.30, Fri-Sun 12-9 Dinner Mon-Thu 6-9, Fri-Sun 12-9 ⊕ FREE HOUSE ◆ Triple fff Moondance, Dark Star Partridge Best Bitter, Arundel Sussex Gold, Guest ale ♂ Thatchers & Heritage. **Facilities** Non-diners area ✿ (Bar Restaurant Garden) ◆◆ Children's menu Children's portions Garden ⼝ Parking

EAST ASHLING
Map 5 SU80

Horse and Groom ★★★★ INN

tel: 01243 575339 **PO18 9AX**
email: info@thehorseandgroomchichester.co.uk
web: www.thehorseandgroomchichester.co.uk
dir: 3m from Chichester on B1278 towards Rowland's Castle

Traditional inn with suntrap beer garden

This 400-year-old village inn with rooms retains much of its heritage; timber frames, oak beams and flagstone floors offer a comfy retreat. The pub has long been popular with visitors exploring Bosham Harbour, and the South Downs National Park to the north. In the bar, try ales such as Dark Star Hophead and Sharp's Doom Bar accompanied by a toasted ciabatta or baked potato, while in the restaurant, enjoy the extensive menu of mains and fish dishes. Choices include steaks, shoulder of lamb, stir-fried duck, salmon fishcakes and grilled sea bass. If ordering from the set menu for ten people or more, pre-booking is required.

Open all day 12-11 (Sun 12-6) Closed Sun eve **Food** Lunch Mon-Sat 12-2.15, Sun 12-2.30 Dinner Mon-Sat 6.30-9.15 Av main course £13 ⊕ FREE HOUSE ◆ Hop Back Summer Lightning, Brewster's Hophead, Dark Star Hophead, Sharp's Doom Bar, Young's ♂ Westons Stowford Press, Addlestones. **Facilities** Non-diners area ✿ (Bar Garden) ◆◆ Children's menu Children's portions Garden ⼝ Parking WiFi **Rooms** 11

EAST DEAN
Map 6 SU91

The Star & Garter
PICK OF THE PUBS

tel: 01243 811318 **PO18 OJG**
email: info@thestarandgarter.co.uk
dir: On A286 between Chichester & Midhurst. Exit A286 at Singleton. Village in 2m

Situated in charming downland village

Built as a pub from traditional Sussex flint in about 1740, The Star & Garter stands close to the village pond in the pretty downland village of East Dean. The interior is open and gives a light and airy atmosphere with original brickwork, antique panelling, scrubbed tables and a wood-burning stove. In the bar, two locally brewed real ales are served from the barrel alongside two ciders and a range of wines by the glass. Locally renowned for an excellent selection of fish and shellfish, the menu also includes fine meat and vegetarian dishes, plus sharing platters. Typical choices include roasted guinea fowl with creamy Shropshire Blue sauce; couscous-crusted goats' cheese with red onion salad; and dishes of Selsey crab and lobster. A sunny sheltered patio, an original well and attractive lawned gardens complete the picture. Goodwood racecourse and motor racing venues are just a short hop by car.

Open all wk 11-3 6-11 (Fri 11-3 5-11 Sat-Sun all day) **Food** Lunch Mon-Fri 12-2.30, Sat-Sun 12-4 Dinner Mon-Fri 6.30-9.30, Sat-Sun 6-10 ⊕ FREE HOUSE ◆ Arundel Castle & Sussex Gold, Guest ales ♂ Westons 1st Quality & Stowford Press. ▼ 11 **Facilities** Non-diners area ✿ (Bar Garden) ◆◆ Children's menu Children's portions Garden ⼝ Parking WiFi ⛟

EAST GRINSTEAD   Map 6 TQ33

The Old Dunnings Mill

tel: 01342 326341 **Dunnings Rd RH19 4AT**
email: enquiries@theolddunningsmill.co.uk
dir: *From High St into Ship St. At mini rdbt right into Dunnings Rd. Pub on right*

Old meets new – and works

There are two parts to this pub: the original 16th-century flour mill, and the stylistically sympathetic 1970s addition, with wooden floors and a bar with an open fire. The front garden is fenced, and a stream, which powers a working water-wheel, runs under the covered decking with tables, chairs, gas-burners and potted plants. As it's a Harvey's of Lewes pub, you'll find their Best and Hadlow real ales in the bar, while on the menu look for braised half-shoulder of lamb with honey, mustard and herb crumb; home-made burgers; and wild mushroom risotto. The ODM holds beer festivals in June and September.

Open all day all wk **Food** Lunch all wk 12-9.30 Dinner all wk 12-9.30 Av main course £11.95 ⊕ HARVEYS OF LEWES ◀ Sussex Best Bitter, Sussex Hadlow Bitter Ō Thatchers Gold Apple & Pear. ☻ 27 **Facilities** Non-diners area ❀ (Bar Garden) ♦❶ Children's portions Garden ⋒ Beer festival Parking WiFi ▄

ELSTED   Map 5 SU81

The Three Horseshoes

tel: 01730 825746 **GU29 0JY**
dir: *A272 from Midhurst towards Petersfield, left in 2m signed Harting & Elsted, 3m to pub on left*

Game is a speciality here

With views across fields and woods, this 16th-century former drovers' alehouse is one of those quintessential English country pubs that Sussex specialises in. Tucked below the steep scarp slope of the South Downs National Park, expect unspoilt cottage-style bars, worn stone-flagged floors, low beams, latch doors, a vast inglenook, and a mix of antique furnishings. On fine days the extensive rear garden, with roaming bantams, is hugely popular. Tip-top real ales, including local Ballards, are drawn from the cask, and a daily-changing blackboard menu offers classic country cooking with game abundant in season and treacle tart being a typical dessert.

Open all wk **Food** Lunch all wk 12-2 Dinner Mon-Sat 6.30-9, Sun 7-8.30 ⊕ FREE HOUSE ◀ Ballards Best Bitter, Hop Back Summer Lightning, Bowman Wallops Wood, Flower Pots Ō Westons Stowford Press. **Facilities** Non-diners area ❀ (Bar Garden) ♦❶ Children's portions Garden ⋒ Parking

FERNHURST   Map 6 SU82

The Red Lion

tel: 01428 643112 **The Green GU27 3HY**
dir: *Just off A286 midway between Haslemere & Midhurst*

Tempting menu in South Downs village

In the dimpled shade of a huge maple, this attractive stone-and-whitewashed inn overlooks a corner of the green in this peaceful village set in the wooded hills of the South Downs National Park. Cricketers from the nearby ground amble here to enjoy Fuller's beers and guest ales, settling in the oak-beamed, fire-warmed heart of the 16th-century building to select from a menu finely balanced between good pub grub (fish and chips, grills) and enticing diversions such as lamb shank, or fillet of salmon with hollandaise. Finish with home-made bread and butter pudding perhaps. Change of hands.

Open all day all wk 11.30-11 (Sun 11.30-10.30) **Food** Lunch all wk 12-3 Dinner all wk 6-9.30 ⊕ FULLER'S ◀ ESB, Chiswick Bitter & London Pride, Guest ale Ō Westons Stowford Press. ☻ 8 **Facilities** Non-diners area ❀ (Bar Garden) ♦❶ Children's menu Children's portions Garden ⋒ Parking WiFi ▄

GRAFFHAM   Map 6 SU91

The Foresters Arms   `PICK OF THE PUBS`

tel: 01798 867202 **The Street GU28 0QA**
email: info@forestersgraffham.co.uk
dir: *From Midhurst S on A285, left to Heyshott, straight on to Graffham. From Petworth S on A286, turn right to Graffham, left fork into village centre*

A rural gem beneath the hills

The South Downs aren't far away, so this charming pub attracts its fair share of walkers and cyclists, as well as those who enjoy browsing nearby Petworth's and Arundel's antique shops. Join them in the bar, where old beams, exposed stone walls and a large, smoke-blackened fireplace set the scene for a pint of Sussex-brewed Harvey's, Langham or Dark Star, or Westons Mortimers Orchard cider. On the short but imaginative menu, as a starter, is beef fillet carpaccio with Egyptian dukkah spices, parmesan shavings and rocket, then, as main courses, roasted belly of pork with rösti, pan-fried black pudding, and honey and ginger jus; and goats' cheese tarte Tatin with caramelised red onions, sun-blushed tomatoes and oregano. Pie and a pint evenings are on Mondays and it's steak on Thursdays, when two can dine with a carafe of wine for under £30. Don't miss the monthly Saturday live jazz evenings.

Open 12-3 6-late Closed Sun eve Nov-Mar **Food** Lunch all wk 12-2.30 Dinner Mon-Sat 6-9.15, Sun 6-8 (Apr-Oct) Av main course £12 Set menu available ⊕ FREE HOUSE ◀ Harvey's Sussex Best Bitter, Dark Star Hophead, Langham seasonal ale Ō Westons Mortimers Orchard. ☻ 17 **Facilities** Non-diners area ❀ (Bar Restaurant Garden) ♦❶ Children's menu Children's portions Garden ⋒ Parking WiFi

HALNAKER   Map 6 SU90

The Anglesey Arms at Halnaker   `PICK OF THE PUBS`

tel: 01243 773474 **PO18 0NQ**
email: info@angleseyarms.co.uk
dir: *From centre of Chichester 4m E on A285 (Petworth road)*

Country pub with extensive gardens and fine dining

Standing on the Goodwood Estate, is this charming, red-brick Georgian country pub. The village name, in which the 'l' is silent, comes from the Old English for 'half an acre'. The Anglesey is set in its own two acres of landscaped grounds, which include a lovely tree-shaded beer garden. The kitchen team makes skilful use of meats from traceable and organically raised animals, including meat from the estate's farm, as well as locally caught sustainable fish and organic vegetables. The Anglesey has built a special reputation for its Sussex steaks, hung for at least 21 days. Hand-cut sandwiches and ploughman's are available at lunchtime along with a full menu including dressed Selsey crab salad and home-baked ham. For dinner try a starter of duck and pork rillettes, follow with Thai-style red king prawn curry with basmati rice; or an organic beefburger served with blue cheese, onion rings and fries. At both lunch and dinner, blackboards list daily specials.

Open all wk 11-3 5.30-11 (Fri-Sun 11-11) ⊕ PUNCH TAVERNS ◀ Young's Bitter, Bowman Swift One, Black Sheep Best Bitter Ō Westons Stowford Press. **Facilities** ❀ (Bar Restaurant Garden) ♦❶ Children's portions Garden Parking WiFi

Read all about whisky
in our feature on page 18

HENLEY
Map 6 SU82

Duke of Cumberland Arms

tel: 01428 652280 **GU27 3HQ**
email: info@thedukeofcumberland.com
dir: *Between Haslemere & Midhurst, just off A286 S of Fernhurst*

'Pretty as a picture' inn with good beers and good food

Many fine words have been written about this beautiful, 15th-century pub perched on a wooded hillside in the South Downs National Park. Inside are flagstones, brick floors, scrubbed tables, and ales served straight from the barrels Harvey's and Langham breweries deliver them in. The first-rate menus impress at lunchtime with Sussex venison ragout, and pan-seared scallop salad, and again in the evening with confit free-range pork belly with apple and Calvados glaze, and whole roasted Sussex partridge with black pudding mash.

Open all day all wk **Food** Lunch all wk 12-2 Dinner Tue-Sat 7-9 ⊕ FREE HOUSE ◀ Harvey's Sussex, Langham Best Bitter & Hip Hop Ò Westons Stowford Press. ♀ **Facilities** Non-diners area ❀ (Bar Garden) ♦♦ Children's portions Garden ⋒ Beer festival Parking WiFi

HEYSHOTT
Map 6 SU81

Unicorn Inn
`PICK OF THE PUBS`

tel: 01730 813486 **GU29 0DL**
email: unicorninnheyshott@hotmail.co.uk
dir: *Phone for detailed directions*

A favourite with walkers and cyclists plus great views

Jenni Halpin's 18th-century free house stands in a sleepy Sussex village and enjoys stunning views of the South Downs from its beautiful, south-facing rear garden, the perfect spot to relax on sunny day with a pint of Adnams. Being within a National Park, it's a fair bet that you'll share the pub with walkers and cyclists (and, of course, some locals) seeking out the home-cooked food listed on seasonal menus that make splendid use of locally sourced produce. The bar, with beams and a large log fire, is particularly atmospheric, while the subtly lit, cream-painted restaurant is where you can sample fresh fish from Selsey – try wild sea bass fillet with white wine and chive sauce – or dishes like slow-roasted lamb shank with mash and redcurrant and rosemary sauce; or confit duck leg with elderberry and balsamic sauce. Good sandwiches (perhaps roast beef and horseradish) and popular Sunday lunches complete the pleasing picture.

Open all day Tue-Sat all day (Sun 12-4) Closed 2wks Jan (contact pub for details), Sun eve & Mon (except BHs & Summer) **Food** Lunch Tue-Sat 11.30-2, Sun 12-2.30 Dinner Tue-Sat 6-9.30 Av main course £10 Restaurant menu available Tue-Sun ⊕ FREE HOUSE ◀ Adnams, Sharp's Doom Bar, Triple fff Ò Westons Stowford Press. **Facilities** Non-diners area ❀ (Bar Garden) ♦♦ Children's menu Children's portions Garden ⋒ Parking ⛟ (notice required)

HORSHAM
Map 6 TQ13

The Black Jug

tel: 01403 253526 **31 North St RH12 1RJ**
email: black.jug@brunningandprice.co.uk
dir: *Phone for detailed directions*

Recommended for its eclectic menu

This handsome, tile-hung and gabled pub has served the discerning clientele of Horsham town centre for around 200 years. With a trim garden and copious flower displays outside; the interior is a delightful mix of panelling, classic time-worn pub

furniture and a warm atmosphere free of music and gaming machines. Up to six beers and some cracking traditional ciders slake the thirst, whilst an indulgent, quality menu may feature seared pigeon breast and beetroot risotto; five spiced duck leg with crispy pork wontons or a light bite roasted red pepper and mozzarella quiche. There's a children's menu too, and a tempting range of puddings. Please note that although dogs are welcome they are not allowed in the conservatory area.

Open all day all wk **Food** Contact pub for details Av main course £12.95 ⊕ BRUNNING & PRICE ◀ Harvey's, Caledonian Deuchars IPA, Rotating Guest ales Ò Aspall, Westons Stowford Press, Rotating Guest ciders. ♀ 19 **Facilities** Non-diners area ❀ (Bar Garden Outside area) ♦♦ Children's portions Garden Outside area ⋒ Beer festival Cider festival WiFi

HURSTPIERPOINT
Map 6 TQ21

NEW The New Inn

tel: 01273 834608 **76 High St BN6 9RQ**
email: info@thenewinnhurst.com
dir: *In village centre*

Bustling village local with large beer garden

Despite its name, The New Inn actually dates back as far as 1450 and it has been a hub of the village ever since. Just off the A23 to the north of the South Downs National Park, this bustling village is also a short hop from Brighton. Whether it's one of the four areas in the pub or in the pretty beer garden, The New Inn is an ideal pitstop to enjoy local Harvey's ales or one of the 10 wines by the glass with dishes such as tiger prawn and coconut curry or honey-glazed pheasant with Savoy cabbage and bacon.

Open all day all wk **Food** Lunch all wk 12-3 Dinner all wk 6-9 Av main course £12 Restaurant menu available all wk ⊕ PUNCH TAVERNS ◀ Harvey's Ò Brothers. ♀ 10 **Facilities** Non-diners area ❀ (Bar Garden) ♦♦ Children's menu Children's portions Play area Garden ⋒ WiFi ⛟

KINGSFOLD
Map 6 TQ13

The Dog and Duck

tel: 01306 627295 **Dorking Rd RH12 3SA**
email: info@thedoganduck.fsnet.co.uk
dir: *On A24, 3m N of Horsham*

Children and dogs very welcome

The Dog and Duck is a 16th-century family-run and family-friendly country pub. There's plenty of children's play equipment in the huge garden (but please note dogs mustn't venture into this area), and three very large fields that encourage dogs and energetic owners to stretch their legs. In the summer a native American camp is set up, complete with tipis and camp fire. The rest of the year sees the diary chock-full of celebratory events, including the charity fundraising beer festival and the halloween party and firework display- contact the pub for details.

Open all wk 12-3 6-11 (Fri 12-3 6-12 Sat 12-12 Sun 12-10) **Food** Lunch all wk 12-2 (3pm Sun) Dinner Mon-Sat 6-9 Av main course £7.95-£9.95 ⊕ HALL & WOODHOUSE ◀ Badger K&B Sussex, Dorset Best, Seasonal ales Ò Westons Stowford Press. **Facilities** Non-diners area ❀ (Bar Garden) ♦♦ Children's menu Children's portions Play area Garden ⋒ Beer festival Cider festival Parking ⛟ (notice required)

KINGSFOLD *continued*

The Owl at Kingsfold

tel: 01306 628499 **Dorking Rd RH12 3SA**
email: info@theowl-kingsfold.co.uk **web:** www.theowl-kingsfold.co.uk
dir: *On A24, 4m N of Horsham*

In a hamlet just 20 minutes from the sea

A traditional country free house with wooden beams, flagstone floors and log burners. It occupies a prominent roadside site in the village, with plenty of parking and a garden with views to the Surrey Hills; composer Ralph Vaughan Williams reputedly arranged the hymn *Kingsfold* here. There are three real ales to choose from, while the frequently changing lunch menu might include West Sussex smokie or home-made liver pâté to start, followed by slow roasted shoulder of lamb; home-made stout and Stilton pie, or half a roast sticky lime chicken and chips; a specials board adds to the choices.

Open all day all wk **Food** Contact pub for details ⊕ FREE HOUSE ◢ Hogs Back TEA, St Austell Tribute, Harvey's Sussex ⚬ Westons. 💡 12 **Facilities** Non-diners area ⬩♦ Children's menu Children's portions Garden ⋔ Parking WiFi

| KIRDFORD | Map 6 TQ02 |

The Half Moon Inn   PICK OF THE PUBS

tel: 01403 820223 **RH14 OLT**
email: info@halfmoonkirdford.co.uk **web:** www.halfmoonkirdford.co.uk
dir: *Exit A272 at Wisborough Green, follow Kirdford signs*

Log fires and serious dining in an unspoilt village

A bit off the beaten track, this red-tiled 16th-century village inn opposite the church is covered in climbing roses. The interior consists of an attractive bar with adjoining wooden-floored restaurant area, oak beams, tiled floors and several log fires in winter. Although drinkers are welcome, this is mainly a dining pub and the

chef serves honest wholesome food with the menus reflecting the best of the season's ingredients. Try starters the likes of pan-fried pigeon breast with home-made plum chutney, before tucking into moules à la crème and frites; or chicken breast stuffed with goats' cheese and wrapped in pancetta. Private dining is available and there are gardens to front and rear.

Open 12-3 6-11 Closed Sun eve, Mon **Food** Lunch Tue-Sun 12-3 Dinner Tue-Sat 6-10 Av main course £12.95 Restaurant menu available Tue-Sun ⊕ ENTERPRISE INNS ◢ Rotating Guest ales. **Facilities** Non-diners area ⬩♥ (Bar Garden) ⬩♦ Children's menu Children's portions Play area Garden ⋔ Parking WiFi ⬚ (notice required)

| LAMBS GREEN | Map 6 TQ23 |

The Lamb Inn

tel: 01293 871336 & 871933 **RH12 4RG**
email: lambinnrusper@yahoo.co.uk
dir: *6m from Horsham between Rusper & Faygate. 5m from Crawley*

Unspoilt village local with a long list of ciders and beers

Landlords Ben and Chris run a successful modern business within the ancient framework of their unspoilt, rustic country pub. They serve some great local beers and ciders in the beamed bar – too many to list, sadly, but there's Weltons Old Cocky for one, while from Kent comes Biddenden real cider. As much as possible, menus feature locally sourced produce, typical dishes being roasted Suffolk duck with green peppercorn and orange sauce; chargrilled gammon steak; and king prawns in crispy filo pastry. Regulars often bring game in for the pot. The annual August beer festival draws a good crowd.

Open all wk Mon-Thu 11.30-3 5.30-11 (Fri-Sat 11.30-11 Sun 12-10.30) Closed 25-26 Dec **Food** Lunch Mon-Thu 12-2, Fri-Sat 12-9.30, Sun 12-9 Dinner Mon-Thu 6.30-9.30, Fri-Sat 12-9.30, Sun 12-9 ⊕ FREE HOUSE ◢ WJ King Kings Old Ale, Weltons Old Cocky, Langham LSD, Dark Star Hophead & Partridge Best Bitter ⚬ Westons Stowford Press, Biddenden, Rekorderlig. 💡 12 **Facilities** Non-diners area ⬩♥ (Bar Outside area) ⬩♦ Children's menu Children's portions Outside area ⋔ Beer festival Parking WiFi ⬚ (notice required)

| LODSWORTH | Map 6 SU92 |

The Halfway Bridge Inn ★★★★★ INN ⊛ PICK OF THE PUBS

tel: 01798 861281 **Halfway Bridge GU28 9BP**
email: enquiries@halfwaybridge.co.uk **web:** www.halfwaybridge.co.uk
dir: *Between Petworth & Midhurst, adjacent to Cowdray Estate & Golf Club on A272*

Excellent food on South Downs National Park's doorstep

A pretty road, the A272 has many attractions, one being this renovated, 17th-century traditional pub and contemporary dining inn. It stands roughly equidistant from Midhurst, home of the Cowdray Estate and British polo, and Petworth, with its huge 17th-century, National Trust mansion. Travellers stopping here will find tastefully furnished rooms with beamed ceilings, log fires and peaceful patio and garden. Those seeking a truly local pint will find real ales from Langham, brewed a mile away; Sharp's Doom Bar, on the other hand, travels up from Cornwall. Bar meals include tagliatelle carbonara; crisp-fried wholetail scampi with hand-cut chips; and chargrilled chicken Caesar salad, while main menus regularly change to offer crab, crayfish and smoked salmon parcel; wild boar and apple sausage with creamed potatoes and caramelised onion gravy; and pearl barley, porcini mushroom and wilted spinach risotto and soft-poached duck egg. Daily specials are listed on a blackboard.

Open all day all wk 8am-11pm **Food** Lunch Mon-Fri 12-2.30, Sat-Sun 12-6 Dinner Mon-Thu 6-9.30, Fri-Sat 6-10, Sun 6-9 Av main course £15 Restaurant menu available all wk ⊕ FREE HOUSE ◢ Sharp's Doom Bar, Langham ⚬ Thatchers. 💡 25 **Facilities** Non-diners area ⬩♥ (Bar Garden) ⬩♦ Children's menu Children's portions Garden ⋔ Parking WiFi **Rooms** 7

The Hollist Arms

PICK OF THE PUBS

tel: 01798 861310 **The Street GU28 9BZ**
email: info@thehollistarms.com
dir: *Between Midhurst & Petworth, exit A272, follow brown pub signs*

Charm and character in an idyllic setting

The Hollist Arms overlooks the green in a picturesque village within the South Downs National Park. Outside this family- and dog-friendly 15th-century pub stands a grand old tree ringed by a bench. Within, inglenook fireplaces, low beams and a blissful absence of games machines imbue it with traditional pub charm and character. After refurbishment and with new management and head chef, this pub's reputation for quality and value continues unabated. Some dishes can be served as starters or in larger portions – pan-fried soft herring roes on sourdough bread, for example. Main courses tempt with the likes of cassoulet of confit duck with Toulouse sausages and cannellini beans. To finish, ask about the tart of the day or the range of ice creams – home made with 100% cream. Real ales are supplied by Langham, the village brewery, and Dark Star. On the first Saturday in October, a cider festival brings the village together to press apples.

Open all day all wk 11-11 **Food** Lunch Tue-Sat 12-3, Sun 12-4 Dinner Tue-Sat 6-9 ⊕ FREE HOUSE ◀ Dark Star Hophead, Langham Best Bitter Ò Westons Stowford Press, Hogan's. ▾ 9 **Facilities** Non-diners area ❤ (Bar Restaurant Garden) ◆ Children's menu Children's portions Garden ⋒ Cider festival Parking WiFi ▬ (notice required)

The Crabtree

tel: 01403 892666 **Brighton Rd RH13 6PT**
email: info@crabtreesussex.com
dir: *On A281 between Cowfold & Horsham, opposite South Lodge Hotel*

Family run pub in lovely Sussex countryside

Call in at The Crabtree and you'll be following in the footsteps of author and poet Hilaire Belloc who was often to be found here. The inn, originally built in 1539, is located in beautiful countryside which is where the pub sources 90% of their produce. Trusty local companies supply meat from high welfare farms and the daily caught fish and shellfish come via the harbour at nearby Shoreham. Start perhaps with scallop ravioli, octopus and mussels followed by local wild venison, smoked celeriac, buttered kale, potato, juniper and port; or Brookland White free-range chicken with duck-fat potatoes. Extensive bar snacks range from Carlingford oysters to Scotch egg with curried mayo.

Open all day all wk **Food** Lunch all wk 12-9 Dinner all wk 12-9 Av main course £12 Set menu available Restaurant menu available all wk ⊕ HALL & WOODHOUSE ◀ Badger Tanglefoot, K&B Sussex Ò Westons Stowford Press. ▾ 20 **Facilities** Non-diners area ❤ (Bar Garden) ◆ Children's portions Garden ⋒ Parking WiFi

THE NOAH'S ARK INN
The Green, Lurgashall, West Sussex GU28 9ET

The Noah's Ark is a beautiful 16th century Inn situated in the picturesque village of Lurgashall, overlooking the cricket green and nestled beneath Blackdown Hill on the borders of Surrey and West Sussex.

Under the ownership of Henry Coghlan and Amy Whitmore, *The Noah's Ark* has become an established venue having achieved the happy balance between 'proper' village pub with a kitchen serving excellent British food.

From the very beginning they have stayed true to their ethos and continue to source only the best local ingredients alongside their budding collection of home grown produce. The menu is built around the English seasons and wherever possible they only use ingredients that can be sourced within a 50 mile radius of Lurgashall. Everything you eat will be prepared to order and onsite by our kitchen team.

Alongside their menus they have a specials board – a daily changing choice of dishes focusing on fish and "unexpected" produce just delivered.

Tel: 01428 707346 • Website: www.noahsarkinn.co.uk • Email: amy@noahsarkinn.co.uk

LURGASHALL
Map 6 SU92

The Noah's Ark

tel: 01428 707346 **The Green GU28 9ET**
email: amy@noahsarkinn.co.uk **web:** www.noahsarkinn.co.uk
dir: *B2131 from Haslemere follow signs to Petworth/Lurgashall. A3 from London towards Portsmouth. At Milford take A283 signed Petworth. Follow signs to Lurgashall*

16th-century inn at the height of country chic

In a picturesque village beneath Blackdown Hill, this attractive 16th-century inn overlooks the cricket green. The pretty, shabby-chic interior is full of warmth thanks to the charm of old beams, a large inglenook fireplace, muted colours, pale wooden furniture, fresh flowers and the enthusiasm of its owners. In addition to the Greene King ales is a regularly changing guest, and the traditional British food with a contemporary twist uses seasonal ingredients carefully sourced from the best local suppliers. The menu is concise but enticing: Scotch egg with spicy apple sauce may precede a main course of pan-fried fillet of hake with swede fondant, mussel, leek and truffle broth.

Open all day all wk 11-11 (Sun 12-10 summer Sun 12-8 winter) **Food** Lunch Mon-Sat 12-2.30, Sun 12-3 Dinner Mon-Sat 7-9.30 Av main course £14.50 ⊕ GREENE KING ◀ IPA & Abbot Ale, Guest ale Ꝺ Westons Stowford Press. **Facilities** Non-diners area ♣ (Bar Garden) ♦ Children's menu Children's portions Garden ⊼ Parking WiFi ⟺ (notice required)

See advert on page 501

MAPLEHURST
Map 6 TQ12

The White Horse

tel: 01403 891208 **Park Ln RH13 6LL**
dir: *5m SE of Horsham, between A281 & A272*

Village-brewed cider and local ales prove a draw

This rural free house has been under the same family ownership for over 30 years and lies deep in the Sussex countryside. It offers a welcome haven free from music and fruit machines. Hearty home-cooked pub food and an enticing selection of five real ales are served over what is reputed to be the widest bar counter in Sussex. Sip a pint of Harvey's Sussex Best Bitter or Welton's Pridenjoy whilst admiring the rolling countryside from the large, quiet, south-facing garden. Village-brewed cider is a speciality.

Open 12-2.30 6-11 (Sun 12-3 7-11) Closed Mon L **Food** Lunch Tue-Sun 12-2 Dinner Mon-Sat 6-9, Sun 7-9 Av main course £7 ⊕ FREE HOUSE ◀ Harvey's Sussex Best Bitter, Weltons Pridenjoy, Dark Star Espresso Ꝺ JB, Local cider. ₹ 11 **Facilities** Non-diners area ♣ (Bar Garden) ♦ Children's menu Children's portions Play area Family room Garden ⊼ Parking WiFi ⟺ (notice required) **Notes** ⊕

OVING
Map 6 SU90

The Gribble Inn

tel: 01243 786893 **PO20 2BP**
dir: *From A27 take A259. After 1m left at rdbt, 1st right to Oving, 1st left in village*

Pub and microbrewery with added extras

This charming 16th-century inn now contains a village store, coffee shop and microbrewery, as well as a pub, within its walls. It is a peaceful spot to sup any of the own-brewed real ales plus a choice of five or six seasonal extras; takeaway polypins are also sold. Named after local schoolmistress Rose Gribble, the inn has large open fireplaces, wood burners, low beams and no background music. From the daily-changing menu, enjoy traditional pub food such as beer-battered haddock or slow-roast pork belly. The inn hosts summer and winter beer festivals, and there is also a skittle alley, enjoyed by parties and works' social functions.

Open all day all wk 11-11 **Food** Lunch all wk 12-2 Dinner all wk 6.30-9.30 ⊕ HALL & WOODHOUSE ◀ Gribble Ale, Reg's Tipple, Pig's Ear, Fuzzy Duck, Plucking Pheasant, & Sussex Quad Hopper, Gribble Wobbler & Pukka Mild Ꝺ Westons Stowford Press & Rosie's Pig. ₹ 20 **Facilities** Non-diners area ♣ (Bar Garden) ♦ Children's menu Children's portions Family room Garden ⊼ Beer festival Parking ⟺

PETWORTH
Map 6 SU92

The Angel Inn ★★ HL

tel: 01798 344445 & 342153 **Angel St GU28 0BG**
email: enquiries@angelinnpetworth.co.uk **web:** www.angelinnpetworth.co.uk
dir: *From Petworth centre take A283 E towards Fittleworth, pub on left*

A real gem in a delightful town

Bowed walls, exposed beams, head-cracking doorways and sloping floors all testify to the Angel's medieval origins, especially in the bedrooms. So too do the ships' beams and three open fireplaces, one of which is used to spit-roast joints of meat. Petworth's Langham Brewery supplies real ales, as does the one in Arundel, alongside guests. The modern British menu changes four times a year; there are also fortnightly and daily specials. Expect dishes such as crispy confit of duck with cherry liqueur sauce; Sussex wild venison casserole; The Angel fish pie; and warm Thai beef salad. The walled patio garden can be a real sun-trap.

Open all day all wk 10.30am-11pm (Sun 11.30-10.30) **Food** Lunch all wk 12-2.30 Dinner Mon-Sat 6.30-9.30, Sun 6-9 ⊕ FREE HOUSE ◀ Arundel, Langham, Guest ales Ꝺ Aspall, Addlestones. ₹ 25 **Facilities** Non-diners area ♣ (Bar Garden) ♦ Children's menu Children's portions Garden ⊼ Parking WiFi **Rooms** 6

PICK OF THE PUBS

The Countryman Inn

SHIPLEY   Map 6 TQ12

tel: 01403 741383
Countryman Ln RH13 8PZ
email: countrymaninn@btinternet.com
web: www.countrymanshipley.co.uk
dir: *A272 at Coolham into Smithers Hill Ln. 1m, left at T-junct*

A real old fashioned, traditional pub that ticks all the boxes

Alan Vaughan and his family, who have been successfully running this traditional rural free house for nearly thirty years, have certainly found the recipe for pleasing their customers. Surrounding the inn is the Knepp Castle Estate, 3,500 acres devoted to nature conservation through regeneration and restoration projects. In the pub's log fire-warmed bar, you'll find cask-conditioned beers from Sussex-brewed Harveys, Langham and Long Man, Shepherd Neame from Kent. Making their way to the kitchen are fish landed at Shoreham and Newhaven, the two closest ports, free-range meats from local farms; game from the Knepp estate, vegetables and salads grown in the pub's own half-acre garden, and through a 'swop shop' arrangement with villagers something unusual often appears on the menu, such as quince, kohlrabi or romanesco. Any surplus garden produce can be purchased in the bar. Country baguettes and flatbreads come filled with prawn and crayfish;

sausage and onion; and brie and redcurrant, while an alternative might be the all-day breakfast. Regular starters and sharing plates are hoi sin lamb wrap; rustic Greek salad; and smörgåsbord of fish, which might be followed by slow-roast pork belly with bubble and squeak; Harveys beer-battered fish and chips; smoked bacon and onion roly poly with colcannon, mushy peas and red wine jus; or pea and broad bean risotto with parmesan shavings. Children are welcome in the restaurant, although the inn doesn't have a separate play area or family dining room. In the garden, weather permitting, an open-air kitchen serves grills, ploughman's and other snacks. In the pub's own farm shop you can buy

free-range eggs and home-made preserves, pickles and relishes.

Open all wk 10-4 6-11 **Food** Lunch all wk 11.30-3.30 Dinner served all wk 6-9.30 Restaurant menu available all wk. ⊕ FREE HOUSE ◼ Harvey's, Langham, Shepherd Neame, Long Man, Guest ales Ŏ Thatchers Gold. ♀ 18 **Facilities** Non-diners area ♦♦ Children's portions Garden ⨓ Parking WiFi

POYNINGS
Map 6 TQ21

Royal Oak
PICK OF THE PUBS

tel: 01273 857389 **The Street BN45 7AQ**
email: ropoynings@aol.com
dir: *From A23 onto A281 signed Henfield & Poynings*

Dining pub in downland village

In a pretty South Downs National Park village and close to the remarkable Devil's Dyke, this pub occupies a lovely spot that's handy for glorious downland walks. In summer, the wonderful garden boasts excellent barbecue facilities, serene rural views. Beyond the handsome exterior, the contemporary decor inside is an effortless blend of solid oak floors, old beams hung with hop bines and sumptuous sofas. In the bar, Sussex brewed Harvey's Sussex Best Bitter sits alongside Westons cider and perry, and the accessible wine list includes New and Old World wines with up to 14 by the glass. The menu changes seasonally and is driven by local produce. Gregarious grazers will appreciate the shared fish platter, offering peppered smoked mackerel, prawns, smoked salmon and marinated anchovies with warm ciabatta; then mains could be braised shin of beef, Guinness and wild mushroom pie with horseradish mash; or chargrilled chicken breast with chorizo, herb and mixed bean stew. Booking ahead for meals is advised.

Open all day all wk 11-11 (Sun 12-10.30) **Food** Lunch all wk 12-9.30 Dinner all wk 12-9.30 ⊕ FREE HOUSE ◀ Harvey's Sussex Best Bitter, Wild Hop, Guest ale ♂ Westons Country Perry, Family reserve. ☍ 14 **Facilities** Non-diners area
◀▮ Children's menu Children's portions Play area Garden ☴ Parking WiFi ☷ (notice required)

ROWHOOK
Map 6 TQ13

The Chequers Inn ⊛
PICK OF THE PUBS

tel: 01403 790480 **RH12 3PY**
email: thechequersrowhook@googlemail.com
dir: *From Horsham A281 towards Guildford. At rdbt take A29 signed London. In 200mtrs left, follow Rowhook signs*

Award-winning food in delightful country pub

A striking, 400-year-old higgledy-piggledy pub with a classic interior of flagstone floor, low beams and blazing fire in the inglenook, The Chequers Inn is run by Master Chef Tim Neal, also the holder of an AA Rosette. The bar offers Harvey's Sussex and Long Man Best Bitter on tap and an impressive wine list to partner the extensive bar menu (home-made sausages and mash; roast beef baguette; steak and chips), which may also be eaten in the inn's restaurant. Tim delights in using only the best local produce, often sourcing seasonal wild mushrooms and even truffles from the generous woodlands near the hamlet of Rowhook. From the restaurant menu (also served in the bar), begin with risotto of king prawns, followed perhaps by crispy confit duck on beer mustard mashed potatoes, buttered Savoy cabbage and thyme jus; or blue cheese and leeks tartlet with spinach, asparagus and chive butter sauce.

Open 11.30-3.30 6-11.30 (Sun 12-3.30) Closed 25 Dec, Sun & BHs eve **Food** Lunch all wk 12-2 Dinner Mon-Sat 7-9 Av main course £9.50 Restaurant menu available all wk ⊕ FREE HOUSE ◀ Harvey's Sussex, Long Man Best Bitter, Firebird Heritage XX ♂ Thatchers Gold. ☍ 10 **Facilities** Non-diners area ♨ (Bar Garden) Children's portions Garden ☴ Parking

SHIPLEY
Map 6 TQ12

The Countryman Inn
PICK OF THE PUBS

See Pick of the Pubs on page 503

SINGLETON
Map 5 SU81

The Partridge Inn

tel: 01243 811251 **PO18 0EY**
email: info@thepartridgeinn.co.uk
dir: *Phone for detailed directions*

Delightful country pub run by a former top London chef

Set within the picturesque Goodwood Estate in a South Downs' village, this pub dates back to the 16th century when the huge hunting park was owned by the Fitzalan Earls of Arundel. Today, the pub is popular with walkers enjoying the rolling Sussex countryside and visitors to Goodwood's motor sports and horseracing events. Run by Giles Thompson, former executive head chef of The Ritz London, you can expect a friendly welcome, great ales from the likes of Hop Back, and food firmly based in the English pub tradition: ploughman's, ramblers' soup, and honey-roasted ham, egg and chips are typical light bites. For something filling and seasonal, pork belly rillettes with toasted soda bread could be followed by braised venison in red wine with mustard mash and buttered kale. Sticky toffee pecan pie with double cream heads the short list of desserts. Pie-and-a-pint and music nights every week.

Open all wk Mon-Fri 12-3 6-11 (Sat-Sun all day) **Food** Lunch Mon-Fri 12-2.30, Sat-Sun 12-3 Dinner Mon-Thu & Sun 6-9, Fri-Sat 6-9.30 Av main course £10.80 ⊕ ENTERPRISE INNS ◀ Fuller's London Pride, Harvey's Sussex, Hop Back Summer Lightning ♂ Westons Stowford Press. ☍ 19 **Facilities** Non-diners area ♨ (Bar Garden) ◀▮ Children's menu Children's portions Garden ☴ Parking WiFi

SLINDON
Map 6 SU90

The Spur

tel: 01243 814216 **BN18 0NE**
email: thespurslindon@btinternet.com
dir: *From A27 take A29 signed Slindon*

Pretty pub with lovely garden for alfresco drinking and eating

Set just outside the village of Slindon on top of the rolling South Downs, this 17th-century pub is a an ideal stopping-off point on a day out in the country. It has been praised for its friendly atmosphere and for generous portions of food. Outside are large pub gardens and a courtyard, inside are an open-plan bar and restaurant, warmed by crackling log fires. Daily-changing bar meals are on the blackboard, and may include lamb cutlets, steak and kidney pie, and fresh fish and shellfish. A skittle alley and function room are also available.

Open all wk 11.30-3 6-11 (Sun 12-10) **Food** Lunch Mon-Sat 12-2, Sun 12-8 Dinner Mon-Tue 7-9, Wed-Sat 7-9.30, Sun 12-8 ⊕ FREE HOUSE ◀ Sharp's Doom Bar, Courage Directors ♂ Thatchers Gold. ☍ 10 **Facilities** Non-diners area ♨ (Bar Garden) ◀▮ Children's menu Children's portions Garden ☴ Beer festival Parking ☷

SOUTH HARTING
Map 5 SU71

NEW The White Hart

tel: 01730 825124 **The Street GU31 5QB**
email: info@the-whitehart.co.uk
dir: *From Petersfield take B2146 to South Harting*

A new look for this cosy inn

An engaging mix of beams and timber framing, log-burners, rustic furnishings, deep leather chairs and an eye-catching stone fireplace set the scene at this 16th-century inn at the heart of a pretty village in the South Downs. The painstaking refurbishment has created an inn of much charm. Ramblers diverting from the nearby long-distance footpath sup beers from Upham Brewery's tasty range, kept well by new licensees who also tempt with a fine menu. Home cooking and local producers ensure that both standard dishes and ever-changing specials have something for all tastes. Pan-roasted cod cassoulet, Toulouse sausage, white beans and chorizo is an heroic starter, or anticipate a main of roast local venison haunch with blackberries, salsify, boulangère potatoes and red cabbage. Restful views from the garden encompass the rolling downland edges.

Open all day all wk **Food** Lunch all wk 12-2.30 Dinner all wk 6-9.30 Set menu available Restaurant menu available all wk ⊕ FREE HOUSE ◖ Upham Punter & Tipster ☼ Somersby. ☗ 9 **Facilities** Non-diners area ✿ (Bar Garden Outside area) ◖◗ Children's menu Children's portions Garden Outside area ⊟ Parking WiFi

---

STEDHAM Map 5 SU82

Hamilton Arms/Nava Thai Restaurant

tel: 01730 812555 **Hamilton Arms, School Ln GU29 0NZ**
email: hamiltonarms@hotmail.com **web:** www.thehamiltonarms.co.uk
dir: Follow Stedham sign from A272 between Midhurst & Petersfield. Pub on left in village

Well known for the excellent Thai food

Smiling Thai staff serve authentic Thai food and beers in this whitewashed free house opposite the village common — but if you prefer you can opt for English bar snacks and ales, including the Hamilton's own draught Armless. Thai food devotees will be spoilt for choice - the extensive menu ranges from soups, salads and curries through to the vegetarian menu. For £10 on Sundays (£6 for children), eat as much as you want from the Thai or English-roast buffets. Takeaways are available too. The pub is home to the Mudita Trust, which helps abused and underprivileged children in Thailand.

Open all day Closed Mon (ex BHs) **Food** Lunch Tue-Sun 12-2.30 Dinner Tue-Sun 6-10 Set menu available Restaurant menu available Tue-Sun ⊕ FREE HOUSE ◖ Fuller's London Pride, Triple fff Alton's Pride, Hamilton Armless, Dark Star Hophead. ☗ 8 **Facilities** Non-diners area ✿ (Bar Garden) ◖◗ Children's menu Children's portions Play area Garden ⊟ Parking WiFi

---

SUTTON Map 6 SU91

The White Horse Inn PICK OF THE PUBS

tel: 01798 869221 **The Street RH20 1PS**
email: mail@whitehorse-sutton.co.uk
dir: From Petworth follow signs for Roman villa then to Sutton

Stylish pub deep in the countryside

In a sleepy village tucked beneath the South Downs amid a maze of the narrow lanes, this 250-year-old pub has been transformed into a stylish modern country inn. Being so handy for polo at Cowdray Park and racing at Goodwood, it makes a great watering hole at the end of a hard day's entertainment. Handpumps in the smart wooden-floored bar dispense the likes of local Harvey's and Wadworth ales, while menus make good use of seasonal produce from local suppliers to create some imaginative and good-value dishes. Perhaps start with mussels grilled with garlic and herb butter, then follow with confit duck with dauphinoise, green beans and red wine jus, and round off with sticky toffee pudding with butterscotch sauce

and vanilla ice cream. Lighter options include Sussex cheddar and pickle sandwiches; ham, egg and chips; and smoked chicken, avocado, chorizo and tomato salad. There's a super terrace and garden for summer alfresco meals.

Open 11-3 6-11 Closed Mon **Food** Lunch Tue-Sun 12-2 Dinner Tue-Sun 6.30-9 ⊕ ENTERPRISE INNS ◖ Harvey's, Sharp's Doom Bar, Wadworth 6X ☼ Somersby. **Facilities** Non-diners area ✿ (Bar Garden) ◖◗ Children's portions Garden Parking WiFi

---

TILLINGTON Map 6 SU92

The Horse Guards Inn ★★★★ INN ◉ PICK OF THE PUBS

tel: 01798 342332 **GU28 9AF**
email: info@thehorseguardsinn.co.uk **web:** www.thehorseguardsinn.co.uk
dir: From Petworth towards Midhurst on A272. 1m, right signed Tillington. Inn 300mtrs up hill opposite church

Country comforts and character in a South Downs village

Beneath its steeply-pitched roof The Horse Guards Inn looks out over the landscaped acres of Petworth Park. The National Trust's most impressive art collection is held in Petworth House, across the parkland where the Horse Guards Regiment grazed their steeds. Inside the 350-year-old inn is a series of tastefully appointed rooms with sagging beams, stripped floorboards, open fires (you can roast chestnuts on one), antique and pine furnishings, fresh flowers and candles. The rustic, tree-shaded garden, complete with chickens and straw bales, is popular with families. The restrained, seasonally-changing menu, often dressed with locally foraged hedgerow specialities, has gained an AA Rosette award. An opening gambit may be new seasons asparagus, poached egg and hollandaise sauce, setting the scene for roast Blackdown Estate venison rack, Boston baked beans and Savoy cabbage. Comfy, country-style bedrooms complete the village idyll.

Open all day all wk **Food** Lunch Mon-Fri 12-2.30, Sat 12-3, Sun 12-3.30 Dinner all wk 6.30-9 Av main course £16 ⊕ ENTERPRISE INNS ◖ Harvey's Sussex Best Bitter, Skinner's Betty Stogs, Staropramen, Guinness ☼ Westons Stowford Press & Old Rosie. ☗ 16 **Facilities** Non-diners area ✿ (Bar Restaurant Garden) ◖◗ Children's menu Children's portions Garden ⊟ WiFi (notice required) **Rooms** 3

TROTTON Map 5 SU82

The Keepers Arms ◉ PICK OF THE PUBS

tel: 01730 813724 **GU31 5ER**
email: sharonmcgrath198@btinternet.com
dir: 5m from Petersfield on A272 towards Midhurst, pub on right just after narrow bridge

Fabulous views of the South Downs

Perched above the A272, one of England's most delightful cross-country roads, this charming 17th-century free house is owned by Salvinia McGrath. Low ceilings, wooden floorboards and an open log fire greet you on entering the convivial bar, where the line-up of ales includes Dark Star, Ringwood, Uphams and Langham. Oak dining tables and comfortable upholstered chairs furnish the restaurant, whose look was inspired by a Scottish hunting lodge, thus the rich tartan fabrics. Real effort is made to source locally for the menus and blackboards that are likely to offer caramelised onion and goats' cheese tart; Parma ham, fig and rocket with parmesan; spiced Gressingham duck breast with Puy lentils and watercress salad; and pan-fried fillets of sea bass with truffle oil, crushed new potatoes, spinach and vanilla butter. There are views of the South Downs from both the restaurant and terrace.

Open 12-3.30 6-11 Closed Mon (until mid May) **Food** Lunch all wk 12-2 Dinner all wk 7-9.30 ⊕ FREE HOUSE ◖ Dark Star Hophead, Ringwood Best Bitter & Fortyniner, Ballards Best Bitter, Otter Ale, Uphams Ale, Langham ☼ Thatchers Gold. ☗ 8 **Facilities** Non-diners area ✿ (Bar Restaurant Garden) ◖◗ Children's portions Garden Outside area ⊟ Parking WiFi

WALDERTON
Map 5 SU71

The Barley Mow

tel: 023 9263 1321 **PO18 9ED**
email: info@thebarleymowpub.co.uk
dir: *B2146 from Chichester towards Petersfield. Turn right signed Walderton, pub 100yds on left*

Popular carvery and pretty garden

A favourite with walkers, cyclists and horse-riders out exploring the Kingley Vale National Nature Reserve, this 18th-century pub was used by the local Home Guard as its HQ in World War II. It is famous locally for its skittle alley, which can be hired in combination with a buffet. The secluded, stream-bordered garden is a real sun trap, perfect for a pint of Ringwood Fortyniner; in winter months the log fires crackle. The menu encompasses grills, fish dishes, salads and pub classics, as well as steaks served sizzling hot 'on the stone' for you to cook to your liking at your table. The Sunday carvery is very popular (booking advised).

Open all wk 11-3 6-11 (Sat 11-11 Sun 12-10.30) **Food** Lunch Mon-Fri 12-2.30, Sat-Sun all day Dinner Mon-Fri 6-9.30 Av main course £9.50 Restaurant menu available all wk ⊕ FREE HOUSE ◀ Ringwood Fortyniner, Fuller's London Pride, Harvey's Sussex Best Bitter, Sharp's Doom Bar & Cornish Coaster, Adnams, Otter Ŏ Westons Stowford Press, Thatchers. ▼ 10
Facilities Non-diners area ✿ (Bar Garden) ◀◀ Children's menu Children's portions Garden ⊟ Parking WiFi ⇌ (notice required)

WARNINGLID
Map 6 TQ22

The Half Moon

tel: 01444 461227 **The Street RH17 5TR**
email: info@thehalfmoonwarninglid.co.uk
dir: *1m from Warninglid & Cuckfield junct on A23 & 6m from Haywards Heath*

Family-owned country inn that's welcoming whatever the season

This picture-perfect Grade II listed building dates from the 18th century and has been sympathetically extended to preserve its traditional feel. Look out for the glass-topped well as you come in. Enjoy a pint of Harvey's or a real cider while perusing the menu, which offers specials and pub classics. Try pan-fried calves' liver with smoked bacon, bacon potato cake, Savoy cabbage and onion gravy; a chicken piri piri burger; or beer battered haloumi with tomato fondue, pea purée, tartare, salad and chips. The pub garden is home to a 250-year-old cider press.

Open all wk 11.30-2.30 5.30-11 (Sat 11.30-11 Sun 11.30-10.30) **Food** Lunch Mon-Sat 12-2, Sun 12-3 Dinner Mon-Sat 6-9.30 Av main course £14 ⊕ FREE HOUSE ◀ Harvey's Sussex & Old Ale, Dark Star Ŏ The Orchard Pig. ▼ 12
Facilities Non-diners area ✿ (Bar Garden) ◀◀ Children's menu Children's portions Family room Garden ⊟ Parking WiFi ⇌ (notice required)

WEST ASHLING
Map 5 SU80

NEW The Richmond Arms ◉

tel: 01243 572046 **Mill Rd PO18 8EA**
email: richmondarms@gmail.com
dir: *Phone for detailed directions*

Raising the beer and pizza game

Thatched flint cottages and a quiet millpond characterise this old village. The Richmond Arms is young by comparison, but this welcoming pub is drawing custom from far afield with its attractive combination of happy interiors, Harvey's beers, sumptuous wine carte, and menus overflowing with tasty ingredients. Outside is a

vintage Citroën van housing a wood-fired pizza oven which is stoked up on Friday and Saturday evenings. Local meats such as partridge and salt marsh rib-eye are charcoal grilled. A newly opened skittle alley bar is a relaxed family-friendly space where dogs are welcome too.

Open 11-3 6-11 Closed 23 Dec-12 Jan, 23-30 Jul, Sun eve, Mon & Tue **Food** Lunch 12-2.30 Dinner 6-9.30 Av main course £16 ⊕ FREE HOUSE ◀ Harvey's Sussex Hadlow Bitter, Star of Eastbourne, Armada Ale & Tom Paine Ale Ŏ Aspall. ▼ 14
Facilities Non-diners area ✿ (Bar Outside area) ◀◀ Children's menu Children's portions Outside area ⊟ Parking WiFi ⇌

WEST CHILTINGTON
Map 6 TQ01

The Queens Head

tel: 01798 812244 **The Hollow RH20 2JN**
email: info@queensheadsussex.co.uk
dir: *Phone for detailed directions*

Sixteenth-century country pub with royal associations

Anne of Cleves, after whom this pub is named, was Henry VIII's fourth wife for merely six months, and acquired some local land in her divorce settlement; she was also able to keep her head. Having taken over the reins here in 2013, Caleb and Kate Burton offer a good selection of regular and guest ales in the beamed, low-ceilinged, open-fired bars. Their locally sourced meals include cider-battered cod and hand-cut, triple-cooked chips; parmesan- and parsley-crusted chicken schnitzel with roast garlic mash and mango chutney; and red pepper and goats' cheese salad. The lunchtime offering is boosted by sandwiches and ploughman's.

Open all day all wk 12-11 (Mon 12-3 6-10.30 ex BH 12-11 Sun 12-10.30) Closed 25 Dec & 1 Jan **Food** Lunch Mon-Fri 12-2.30, Sat 12-9.30, Sun & BH 12-4 Dinner Mon-Fri 6-9.30, Sat 12-9.30 ⊕ ENTERPRISE INNS ◀ Harvey's Sussex Best Bitter, Fuller's London Pride, Timothy Taylor Landlord Ŏ Aspall. **Facilities** Non-diners area ✿ (Bar Restaurant Garden) ◀◀ Children's menu Children's portions Garden ⊟ Parking WiFi ⇌ (notice required)

WEST DEAN
Map 5 SU81

NEW The Dean Ale & Cider House ★★★★ INN

tel: 01243 811465 **Main Rd PO18 0QX**
email: thebar@thedeaninn.co.uk **web:** www.thedeaninn.co.uk
dir: *Between Chichester & Midhurst on A286*

Contemporary community pub with harbour views

In a village of flint and thatch properties between the South Downs and Chichester Harbour, this 200-year-old inn has been transformed into a contemporary country dining inn, complete with eye-catching banqueting hall and airy conservatory. Its community pub ethos remains unaffected, with drinkers revelling in the choice of up to six real ales and a draught traditional cider. With a home-based smokery preserving meat, fish and cheese, the kitchen team produce an arresting range of pub stalwarts and modern dishes, using materials derived from the local catchment area. Smartly converted barns skirting the courtyard house the contemporary B&B accommodation, handy for race-goers to nearby Goodwood.

Open all day all wk **Food** Lunch Sun-Fri 12-3, Sat 12-5 Dinner Mon-Sat 5-9 Restaurant menu available all wk ⊕ FREE HOUSE ◀ Sharp's Doom Bar, Dark Star Hophead Ŏ Westons Old Rosie. ▼ 11 **Facilities** Non-diners area ✿ (Bar Garden) ◀◀ Children's menu Children's portions Garden ⊟ Beer festival Parking WiFi ⇌ (notice required) **Rooms** 6

WEST HOATHLY
Map 6 TQ33

The Cat Inn
PICK OF THE PUBS

tel: 01342 810369 **North Ln RH19 4PP**
email: thecatinn@googlemail.com **web:** www.catinn.co.uk
dir: *From East Grinstead centre take A22 towards Forest Row. Into left lane, into B2110 (Beeching Way) signed Turners Hill. Left into Vowels Ln signed Kingscote & West Hoathly. Left into Selsfield Rd, forward into Chapel Row, right into North Ln*

Village hospitality at its best

Regional and county awards, and a top-to-bottom, inside-and-out paint makeover have been added to the CV of this 16th-century tile-hung pub. In the old bar you'll find two inglenook fireplaces, oak beams, fine wooden panelling and floors, and the sort of buzzy atmosphere village pubs are so good at generating. Local breweries in Groombridge (Black Cat), Partridge Green (Dark Star), Lewes (Harveys) and Chiddingstone (Larkins) deliver the excellent beers. The well-lit dining rooms are furnished with wooden dining chairs and tables on pale wood-strip flooring, and hops, china platters and brass and copper ornaments decorate the walls in homely style. Glass doors from the contemporary garden room open on to a terrace. The kitchen makes good use of South Downs lamb, Sussex coast fish and seafood, estate game and other locally-sourced produce, in addition to quality ingredients from further afield such as Shetland mussels, Hereford rib-eye steaks, and Loch Duart salmon.

Open all day 12-11.30 Closed Sun eve **Food** Lunch Mon-Thu 12-2, Fri-Sun 12-2.30 Dinner Mon-Thu 6-9, Fri-Sat 6-9.30 ⊕ FREE HOUSE ◀ Harvey's Sussex Best Bitter, Black Cat, Larkins, Dark Star ♂ Westons Stowford Press. ♀ 10
Facilities Non-diners area ❤ (Bar Garden) ♦ Children's portions Garden ☂ Parking WiFi

WINEHAM
Map 6 TQ22

The Royal Oak

tel: 01444 881252 **BN5 9AY**
email: theroyaloakwineham@sky.com
dir: *Between A272 (Cowfold to Bolney road) & B2116 (Hurst to Henfield road)*

Quintessential English country inn

Tucked away on a quiet country lane near Henfield, this part-tiled, black-and-white timbered cottage is a classic alehouse, a true rural survivor that has been serving the locals for hundreds of years. Dating from the 14th century, it has head-cracking low beams, a huge inglenook with warming winter fire, brick and stone-flagged floors, rustic furnishings and time-honoured pub games. Bedlam and Dark Star ales are drawn straight from the drum and home-cooked pub food ranges from ploughman's boards to hearty Sussex beef, stout and mushroom pie with new potatoes and baby carrots. Extensive gardens are just the spot for summer alfresco drinking.

Open all wk 11-3 5.30-close (Sat 11-3 6-close Sun 11-3 7-close) **Food** Lunch all wk 12-2.30 Dinner all wk 7-9.30 ⊕ FREE HOUSE ◀ Bedlam Brewery, Dark Star, Harvey's, Guest ales ♂ Wobblegate. ♀ 20 **Facilities** Non-diners area ❤ (Bar Garden) ♦ Children's portions Garden Beer festival Parking WiFi 🚌

ALCESTER
Map 10 SP05

The Holly Bush
PICK OF THE PUBS

tel: 01789 762482 **37 Henley St B49 5QX**
email: thehollybushpub@btconnect.com
dir: *M40 junct 15, A46 signed Warwick & Stratford. From Stratford take A46 to Redditch, follow Alcester signs*

Independent pub in a Roman market town

You wouldn't know it today, but Tracey-Jane Deffley's 16th-century town-centre pub used to have just one bar. Not that there's anything wrong with that, but look at it now, with two bars serving eight beers, including a couple from Purity Brewing in nearby Great Alne, and Hogan's cider, made in the Malvern Hills. Then there's the two dining rooms, and an award-winning, vegetable- and salad-producing garden. Among the contemporary and traditional dishes on offer are roasted Cajun chicken; rump of Warwickshire lamb; braised pork faggots; Irish sausage and mash; and butternut squash and spring greens risotto. Sandwich and fresh fish ideas appear on the specials board. Choosing a wine from the well-priced selection is simplified by refreshingly factual descriptions. Not only are the food and drink good, but the service is friendly too. Regular live music nights and beer and cider festivals in June and October.

Open all day all wk 12-12 (Fri-Sat noon-1am) **Food** Lunch Tue-Sat 12-2.30, Sun 12-3 Dinner Tue-Sat 6-9.30 ⊕ FREE HOUSE ◀ Hook Norton Lion, Purity Gold, Black Sheep, Hobsons Town Crier, Guest ales ♂ Hogan's, Local cider. ♀ 9
Facilities Non-diners area ❤ (Bar Garden) ♦ Children's menu Children's portions Garden ☂ Beer festival Cider festival Parking 🚌 (notice required)

ALDERMINSTER
Map 10 SP24

The Bell ★★★★ INN
PICK OF THE PUBS

See Pick of the Pubs on page 508

ALVESTON
Map 10 SP25

The Baraset Barn
PICK OF THE PUBS

tel: 01789 295510 **1 Pimlico Ln CV37 7RJ**
email: barasetbarn@lovelypubs.co.uk
dir: *Phone for detailed directions*

200-year old history with contemporary refinements

Barn is what it's called, because barn is what it was. Not any more, though. True, the original flagstones reflect its 200-year existence, but it is now a light and modern gastro-pub with a dramatic interior styled in granite, pewter and oak. Stone steps lead from the bar to the main dining area with brick walls and high oak beams, while the open mezzanine level offers a good view of the glass-fronted kitchen. The luxurious lounge is furnished with comfortable sofas for whiling away the morning with a coffee and the papers. The menu successfully blends classic British with Mediterranean ideas, such as sharing plates of tapas; starters of vodka- and beetroot-cured salmon, capers, sieved egg and horseradish crème fraîche; and spiced pumpkin and cauliflower fritters. Follow with Purity real ale-battered fish, chips, minted pea purée and sauce gribiche; or calves' liver and onions. The continental-style patio garden is made for outdoor dining.

Open all day 11-11 (Fri-Sat 11am-mdnt Sun 12-6) Closed 1 Jan, Sun eve **Food** Lunch Mon-Sat 12-2.30, Sun 12-3.30 Dinner Mon-Sat 6.30-9.30 ⊕ FREE HOUSE ◀ Purity Gold. **Facilities** Non-diners area ❤ (Bar Garden) ♦ Children's portions Garden ☂ Parking WiFi 🚌

PICK OF THE PUBS

The Bell ★★★★ INN

ALDERMINSTER Map 10 SP24

tel: 01789 450414
CV37 8NY
email: info@thebellald.co.uk
web: www.thebellald.co.uk
dir: On A3400, 3.5m S of Stratford-upon-Avon

Country pub chic with great food

Part of the Alscot Estate, this striking Georgian coaching inn is set in the heart of a picturesque village between Stratford-upon-Avon and Shipston on Stour. The interior is a refreshing mix of contemporary comforts and rustic charm, with the historic core of beamed ceilings, blazing log fires and flagged floors combining well with bold colours and stylish fabrics and the modern dining courtyard. The inn is located beside a grassy garden and a riverside meadow that ripples down to the River Stour is perfect for enjoying summer picnics. The restaurant oozes charm and is cunningly designed into quirky zones, each with its own distinct atmosphere. Time to enjoy a pint of Hook Norton or the inn's locally-brewed Alscot Ale and nibble on a self-selected grazing platter, perhaps laden with hams, olives, mozzarella, pesto, balsamic shallots, vine tomatoes and garlic focaccia, before considering the indulgent daily-changing menu. Typically, begin with potted duck liver and orange pâté, carpaccio of smoked duck and pink

grapefruit salad, then follow with slow roasted pork stuffed with pepperoni and sage, with crackling and pearl barley risotto. Round off with warm dark chocolate and fudge tart with strawberry ice cream, or a plate of local cheeses with home-made chutney. In the bar, sandwiches are served with hand-cut chips and salad, or you can try a Bell classic, perhaps the beef and thyme burger, or bangers and mash. Much of the produce is local, with vegetables and herbs harvested from Alscot's historic kitchen garden, and game and venison is reared on the estate.

Open all wk 9.30-3 6-11 (Fri-Sat 9.30am-11pm) **Food** Lunch Mon-Fri 12-2, Sat 12-2.30, Sun 12-3 Dinner Mon-Thu 7-9, Fri-Sat 6-9 Set menu available Restaurant menu available all wk. ⊕ FREE HOUSE ◀ Hook Norton, Alscot Ale ♂ Robinsons. ♟ 12
Facilities Non-diners area ♦♦ Children's menu Children's portions Garden Outside area ⊼ Parking WiFi 🚌 (notice required) **Rooms** 9

ARDENS GRAFTON

Map 10 SP15

The Golden Cross

PICK OF THE PUBS

tel: 01789 772420 **Wixford Rd B50 4LG**
email: info@thegoldencross.net
dir: Phone for detailed directions

Pretty pub with prized faggots

This traditional 18th-century country inn is the place to come if you like faggots, because an old recipe that went walkabout was rediscovered, much to the delight of locals. With other traditional favourites the faggots appear on the single menu served throughout, listing starters and light bites such as chicken liver pâté with onion marmalade and toasted farmhouse-style bread; or smoked haddock and prawn risotto, perhaps followed by slow-roasted pork belly with mash, red cabbage and a roast shallot and cider gravy; or spinach and feta filo pie. If you eat in the pastel-toned dining room take a good look at the attractive plasterwork on the ceiling, or if you prefer to stay in the rug-strewn, flagstone-floored bar, the hefty beams are worth more than a cursory glance. The real ales here come from Wells, Purity or a guest. The garden is large and safe, and the patio area is covered.

Open all wk Mon-Thu 12-3 5-11 (Fri-Sat 12-12 Sun 12-10.30) **Food** Lunch Mon-Fri 12-2.30, Sat 12-9, Sun 12-8 Dinner Mon-Fri 5-9, Sat 12-9, Sun 12-8 Set menu available ⊕ CHARLES WELLS ◼ Bombardier, Purity, Guest ales Ŏ Thatchers Heritage. ☕ 10 **Facilities** Non-diners area ❀ (Bar Garden) ◼◦ Children's menu Children's portions Garden ⊐ Parking WiFi ☐ (notice required)

ARMSCOTE

Map 10 SP24

NEW The Fuzzy Duck ★★★★ INN ⊚ PICK OF THE PUBS

tel: 01608 682635 **Ilmington Rd CV37 8DD**
email: info@fuzzyduckarmscote.com **web:** www.fuzzyduckarmscote.com
dir: From A429 (Fosse Way) N of Moreton-in-Marsh follow Armscote signs

Innovative modern cooking in stylish village pub

In the picturesque hamlet of Armscote, a few miles south of historic Stratford-upon-Avon, this building once housed the local blacksmith before becoming a coaching inn in the 18th century. Saved from closure and refurbished, the pub is now owned by the family behind the Baylis & Harding toiletries company; its range of luxury products take pride of place in the stylish bedrooms. In the buzzy bar, contemporary furnishings combine with exposed beams, flagstone floors and original fireplaces to create a relaxed setting to enjoy local ales such as Purity Mad Goose. The seasonal menu majors on local produce and robust, innovative dishes. Jerusalem artichoke soup with Herefordshire snails, parsley and sunflower seeds might be followed by hay-smoked fallow deer, parsnip purée and braised red cabbage. An attractive courtyard garden is a peaceful spot for alfresco dining but if the weather turns, you might be able to make use of the pub's quirky Hunter welly loan service.

Open 12-4 6-close Closed Mon **Food** Lunch 12-2.30 Dinner 6.30-9 Av main course £14 Set menu available Restaurant menu available Tue-Fri L ⊕ FREE HOUSE ◼ Purity Mad Goose, Guest ales Ŏ Westons Mortimers Orchard. **Facilities** Non-diners area ❀ (Bar Restaurant Garden) ◼◦ Children's menu Children's portions Family room Garden ⊐ Parking WiFi **Rooms** 4

ASTON CANTLOW

Map 10 SP16

The King's Head

tel: 01789 488242 **21 Bearley Rd B95 6HY**
email: info@thekh.co.uk **web:** www.thekh.co.uk
dir: Exit A3400 between Stratford-upon-Avon & Henley-in-Arden, and follow Aston Cantlow signs

Rustic Tudor pub steeped in history

Flanked by a huge spreading chestnut tree and oozing historic charm, this impressive black-and-white timbered Tudor building has been appointed in a modern style. Tastefully rustic inside, with lime-washed low beams, huge polished flagstones, painted brick walls, old scrubbed pine tables and crackling log fires, it draws diners for innovative pub food. Tuck into pan-fried sea bass with crab, chilli and coriander risotto; roast strip loin of beef with Yorkshire pud, roast potatoes and thyme jus; or chargrilled Lashford's sausages and mash with onion gravy. There's a smart rear terrace and a cider bar serving up to seven traditional ciders. If you don't want alcohol, try one of the specialist teas on offer.

Open all day all wk **Food** Lunch Mon-Sat 12-9.30, Sun 12-9 Dinner Mon-Sat 12-9.30, Sun 12-9 ⊕ ENTERPRISE INNS ◼ Purity Gold & Pure UBU, Greene King Abbot Ale, M&B Brew XI Ŏ Thatchers. ☕ 12 **Facilities** Non-diners area ❀ (Bar Garden) ◼◦ Children's menu Children's portions Garden ⊐ Parking WiFi ☐ (notice required)

See advert on page 510

BARFORD

Map 10 SP26

The Granville @ Barford

`PICK OF THE PUBS`

tel: 01926 624236 **52 Wellesbourne Rd CV35 8DS**
email: info@granvillebarford.co.uk
dir: *M40 junct 15, A429 signed Stow, left to Barford*

Friendly and stylish village dining pub

Situated in the heart of Shakespeare country, this impressive brick building dates back to Georgian times. The comfortable dining pub benefits from stylish decor and warm, friendly service, which has made it a firm favourite with locals and visitors alike. Relax on the leather sofas in the lounge with a drink - a pint of Pure UBU perhaps, or choose from the accessible wine list. The Granville's ever-changing seasonal menus offer varied, interesting choices and good value. At lunch, the offering ranges from doorstep sandwiches and wraps to starters like linguine in a lightly spiced crab broth with spring onion, lime and coriander. An evening meal might begin with salmon and haddock fishcakes, wilted spinach, lemon and butter sauce, followed by North African spiced lamb patties, winter fruit saffron couscous, mint and cucumber yogurt. Enjoy alfresco dining in the spacious patio garden.

Open all wk Mon-Thu 12-3 5-11 (Fri close 11.30 Sat 12-11.30 Sun 12-11) ⊕ ENTERPRISE INNS ◧ Hook Norton Hooky Bitter, Fuller's London Pride, Pure UBU ⚬ Thatchers Gold, Guest ciders. **Facilities** ❀ (Bar Garden) ◑ Children's portions Play area Garden Parking WiFi

BROOM

Map 10 SP05

NEW The Broom Tavern

tel: 01789 778199 **32 High St B50 4HL**
email: enquiries@thebroomtavern.co.uk
dir: *From A46 onto B439 towards Bidford-on-Avon. Left into Victoria Rd to Broom. In Broom left into High St. Pub on right*

Historic food pub with links to Shakespeare

A timeless timber-framed, 16th-century pub in the pretty village of Broom, this is reputed to have been one of Shakespeare's drinking haunts. Reopened by new owners in 2013, this venerable inn has great charm and character, with log fires in winter and a sunny beer garden for alfresco drinking in the summer. Chef patron Fritz Ronnenburg showcases the best local produce and offers locally-brewed ales including Purity Mad Goose. Everything is made on the premises and a typical meal

might include wild mushroom ravioli and Madeira cream, followed by shin of Herefordshire beef, creamed mash and port jus.

Open all wk 12-3 5-11 (Sat-Sun all day) **Food** Lunch all wk 12-2.30 Dinner all wk 6-9.30 Av main course £12.50 ⊕ FREE HOUSE ◧ Sharp's Doom Bar, Wye Valley Butty Bach, Purity Mad Goose & Pure Gold ⚬ Hogan's. ♟ 10 **Facilities** Non-diners area ❀ (Bar Garden) ◑ Children's menu Children's portions Garden ⋒ Beer festival Cider festival Parking WiFi 🚍 (notice required)

EARLSWOOD

Map 10 SP17

NEW Bull's Head

tel: 01564 700368 **7 Limekiln Ln B94 6BU**
email: relax@bullsheadearlswood.co.uk **web:** www.bullsheadearlswood.co.uk
dir: *M42 junct 4, A34 signed Birmingham & Solihull. Left signed Chiswick Green. Through Chiswick Green, straight on at x-rds into Vicarage Rd. Left at T-junct signed Earlswood. On right bend turn left into Salter St. Pub on left*

Village food pub with large sun terrace

In the charming rural setting of Earlwood, near Solihull, the Bull's Head was built in the 18th century to house navvies building the Stratford-upon-Avon canal. Rumoured to be haunted by the ghost of a lime kiln worker, it comprises a cluster of whitewashed cottages and became a pub in 1832. Popular with walkers, the pub is owned by the Daniel Thwaites Brewery and retains much of its original charm courtesy of log fires and a large sun terrace. Enjoy a glass of Lancaster Bomber as

you choose from an extensive menu offering pizzas, deli boards, salads and chargrilled steaks.

Open all day all wk Food Lunch Sun-Thu 12-10, Fri-Sat 12-10.30 (Bkfst 9am-11.45am) Dinner Sun-Thu 12-10, Fri-Sat 12-10.30 Restaurant menu available all wk ⊕ THWAITES INNS OF CHARACTER ◀ Lancaster Bomber, Wainwright, Nutty Black, Guest ales. ♀ 11 Facilities Non-diners area ✿ (Bar Garden) ♦ Children's menu Children's portions Garden ⋒ Parking WiFi ☗ (notice required)

See advert below

EDGEHILL
Map 11 SP34

Castle at Edgehill

tel: 01295 670255 **OX15 6DJ**
email: enquiries@castleatedgehill.co.uk
dir: *M40 junct 11, A422 towards Stratford-upon-Avon. 6m to Upton House, next right, 1.5m to Edgehill*

A most unusual country pub

In 1742, a man called Sanderson Miller built this curious, castellated property on top of Edgehill to mark the centenary of the English Civil War's first major skirmish. In 1822 it became an alehouse; fast-forward a hundred years and it was acquired by the Hook Norton Brewery, whose real ales you'll find to this day in the two bars. A major refit completed in the spring of 2014 resulted in a new restaurant and a

glass-protected balcony with panoramic views. At the time of going to press the food here ranged from sandwiches, light bites and bar snacks to fine dining.

Open all day all wk Food Lunch all week 12-2.30 Dinner all wk 6-9 Av main course £12 Restaurant menu available all wk ⊕ HOOK NORTON ◀ Hooky Bitter, Old Hooky ☗ Westons Old Rosie. Facilities Non-diners area ✿ (Bar Garden) ♦ Children's menu Children's portions Garden ⋒ Beer festival Cider festival Parking WiFi ☗ (notice required)

ETTINGTON
Map 10 SP24

The Chequers Inn
PICK OF THE PUBS

tel: 01789 740387 **91 Banbury Rd CV37 7SR**
email: hello@the-chequers-ettington.co.uk
dir: *Take A422 from Stratford-upon-Avon towards Banbury. Ettington in 5m, after junction with A429*

Tastefully decorated country inn serving classic fare

Thought to have been a courthouse and probably named after the old chequer tree that used to stand in front of the building, this locals' pub is an elegant place to eat and drink. Cotswold Lion ales are a popular choice in the bar. The dining room is decorated in French style with ornate mirrors and chairs, rich tapestries and comfortable armchairs, while the spacious garden looks out over the kitchen's vegetable patch. A fish finger sandwich with tartare sauce and lettuce will suffice for some, while others will look to the Chequers' classics such as lightly-battered fish with hand-cut chips; or the Chequers cheeseburger with gherkins. For a more extensive meal, kick off proceedings with ham and leek terrine with apple jelly; and follow with beef bourguignon, horseradish mash and braised red cabbage. Puddings along traditional lines may include apple and cherry crumble with custard and vanilla ice cream.

Open 12-3 5-11 (Sat 12-11 Sun 12-6) Closed Sun eve, Mon Food Lunch Tue-Sat 12-2.30, Sun 12.30-3.30 Dinner Tue-Sat 6.30-9.30 ⊕ FREE HOUSE ◀ Greene King IPA, Hook Norton Lion, St Austell Tribute ☗ Thatchers Gold. ♀ 8
Facilities Non-diners area ✿ (Bar Garden) ♦ Children's menu Children's portions Garden ⋒ Parking WiFi ☗ (notice required)

FARNBOROUGH
Map 11 SP44

The Inn at Farnborough
PICK OF THE PUBS

tel: 01295 690615 **OX17 1DZ**
email: enquiries@theinnfarnborough.co.uk
dir: M40 junct 11 towards Banbury. Right at 3rd rdbt onto A423 signed Southam. 4m onto A423. Left onto single track road signed Farnborough. Approx 1m, right into village, pub on right

Stylish pub with excellent food

This Grade II listed, 16th-century property used to be the Butcher's Arms, having once belonged to the butcher on the now National Trust-owned Farnborough Park Estate. Built of locally quarried, honey-coloured Hornton stone, tasteful restoration has ensured the retention of a fine inglenook fireplace and other original features. The bar serves Hook Norton real ales, locally made Hogan's cider, and plenty of wines served by the glass. The concise menu lists British pub classic dishes, and others with a Mediterranean influence, but quality ingredients and high culinary skills ensure impressive results whatever your choice. Starters include shellfish bisque or seared king scallops; and among the mains are chargrilled fillet of sea bass with butter bean and coriander mash, spinach and fennel salad; and bangers and mash with onion gravy. Parents of small children will be glad to see the Little Gourmets menu. Enjoy good coffee in the terraced garden or on the covered decking area.

Open all wk 10-3 6-11 (Sat-Sun all day) **Food** Lunch all wk 12-3 Dinner all wk 6-10 Set menu available Restaurant menu available all wk ⊕ FREE HOUSE ◀ Hook Norton Hooky Bitter Ö Hogan's, Local ciders. ⬥ 14 **Facilities** Non-diners area ✿ (Bar Garden) ♦ Children's menu Children's portions Play area Garden ⋒ Parking WiFi ➡ (notice required)

GAYDON
Map 11 SP35

The Malt Shovel

tel: 01926 641221 **Church Rd CV35 OET**
email: malt.shovel@btconnect.com
dir: M40 junct 12, B4451 to Gaydon

Village pub that gets it right

Richard and Debi Morisot's 16th-century village pub has a reputation for being friendly and reliable, qualities that have helped to make their venture a success. Another plus is the range of real ales, usually from Sharp's Doom Bar, Everards, Fuller's, Hook Norton, Timothy Taylor or Wadworth. Menu options include steak and kidney suet pudding; wild boar and apple sausages; battered haddock; and four-cheese ravioli. If all you want is a lunchtime snack, there are chunky granary sandwiches, baguettes and hot paninis. Well-behaved children and dogs are welcome and can play with Molly, the Morisot's Jack Russell.

Open all wk 11-3 5-11 (Fri-Sat 11-11 Sun 12-10.30) **Food** Lunch all wk 12-2 Dinner all wk 6.30-9 Av main course £10 ⊕ ENTERPRISE INNS ◀ Fuller's London Pride, Timothy Taylor Landlord, Everards Tiger, Wadworth 6X, Hook Norton, Sharp's Doom Bar Ö South West Orchards Cider, Thatchers Gold. ⬥ 11 **Facilities** Non-diners area ✿ (Bar Outside area) ♦ Children's portions Outside area ⋒ Parking WiFi ➡ (notice required)

HENLEY-IN-ARDEN
Map 10 SP16

The Bluebell ◉◉

tel: 01564 793049 **93 High St B95 5AT**
email: info@bluebellhenley.co.uk
dir: Opposite police station on A3400 in town centre

Innovative food in pub with plenty of character

Since taking over The Bluebell seven years ago, Leigh and Duncan Taylor have worked tirelessly to update and improve this 500-year-old former coaching inn on Henley-in-Arden's picturesque high street. Be wowed by the stylish interior design, which combines original beams, worn flagstones and open fireplaces with bold colours and an eclectic mix of furnishings and fabrics. The bar and dining room ooze style and atmosphere and both throng with drinkers and diners choosing from seasonal menus brimming with local or home-grown produce. Typically, tuck into Warwickshire lamb faggot, pearl barley, pickled red cabbage or a tapas board for two to start; then choose confit Creedy Carver duck leg, orange braised chicory, bacon and apple gravy.

Open all day Closed Mon (ex BHs) **Food** Lunch Tue-Sat 12-2.30, Sun 12-3.30 Dinner Tue-Sat 6-9.30 Set menu available ⊕ FREE HOUSE ◀ Purity Pure UBU & Mad Goose, Church End What The Fox's Hat, Hook Norton Hooky Bitter, Wye Valley HPA Ö Hogan's. ⬥ 16 **Facilities** Non-diners area ✿ (Bar Restaurant Garden) ♦ Children's portions Garden ⋒ Parking WiFi

HUNNINGHAM
Map 11 SP36

The Red Lion, Hunningham
PICK OF THE PUBS

tel: 01926 632715 **Main St CV33 9DY**
email: redllionhunningham@aol.com
dir: From Leamington Spa take B4453, through Cubbington to Weston under Wetherby. Follow Hunningham signs (turn sharp right as road bends left towards Princethorpe)

Comic book decoration but a serious approach to food

Set in the heart of rural Warwickshire and beside a 14th-century bridge, this quirky country pub's beer garden leads down to the River Leam and offers views of sheep and cows grazing. The real fires, original features and an eclectic mix of tables and chairs are enhanced by contemporary touches such as framed vintage comic book covers; look out for the additional comments on the menus that should make you smile! Once settled in one of dining areas peruse the appealing, well-executed menu then pop up to the bar to place your order. Locally sourced produce drives the generous dishes - a winter menu included ham and lentil soup; potted chicken pâté with 'too much toast' as starters, followed by Buttercross Farm pork chop with bubble-and-squeak and parsley sauce; spicy Hatton sausage and chickpea casserole; smoked haddock and Thai red curry fishcakes and mixed salad.

Open all day all wk 11-11 (Fri-Sat 11am-mdnt) **Food** Lunch Mon-Sat 12-9, Sun 12-8 Dinner Mon-Sat 12-9, Sun 12-8 ⊕ GREENE KING ◀ IPA, Guest ales Ö Thatchers Gold. ⬥ 28 **Facilities** Non-diners area ✿ (Bar Restaurant Garden) ♦ Children's portions Garden ⋒ Beer festival Parking WiFi

ILMINGTON
Map 10 SP24

The Howard Arms
PICK OF THE PUBS

tel: 01608 682226 **Lower Green CV36 4LT**
email: info@howardarms.com
dir: Exit A429 or A3400, 9m from Stratford-upon-Avon

A popular base for walkers

A stunning 400-year-old Cotswold-stone inn on Ilmington's picturesque village green. The Howard Arms is a popular start and finish to some fabulous circular walks; a detailed guide can be bought at the bar for a small donation to church funds. The flagstoned bar and open-plan dining room create a civilised yet informal atmosphere, all imbued with the warmth of a log fire that burns for most of the year. Award-winning ales come from famous local names such as Purity and Hook Norton, wine drinkers can choose from a list of 30 sold by the glass, and cider lovers can indulge in a bottle or two of The Orchard Pig. Equally serious is the inn's kitchen. Typical starters are boxed baked baby camembert; and game terrine with cranberry and onion confit. Main dishes may include steak, oxtail and mushroom pudding with creamed potatoes. Round off with baked Ilmington apple with mincemeat filling, granola crumble and vanilla custard.

Open all day all wk **Food** Lunch Mon-Sat 12-3, Sun 12-8 Dinner Mon-Sat 6-9.30, Sun 12-8 Av main course £15 ⊕ FREE HOUSE ◄ Wye Valley Bitter, Hook Norton Old Hooky, Purity, Timothy Taylor ☼ The Orchard Pig. ♀ 30 **Facilities** Non-diners area ❤ (Bar Garden) ♦♦ Children's portions Garden ⏚ Parking WiFi ▭ (notice required)

■ KENILWORTH   Map 10 SP27

The Almanack

tel: 01926 353637 **Abbey End North CV8 1QJ**
email: hello@thealmanack-kenilworth.co.uk
dir: *Exit A46 at Kenilworth & brown Castle sign, towards town centre. Left into Abbey Hill (B4104) signed Balsall Common. At rdbt into Abbey End. Opposite Holiday Inn*

Modern British gastro-pub

Inspired by the 1960s Kinks' hit *Autumn Almanac*, the stylish interior harks back to the 60s with its retro Danish teak and rosewood furniture and original album covers on the walls. The huge island bar separates the lounge from the eatery and open kitchen. The pub is open all day for breakfast, coffee and cake, lunch and dinner; menu choices include deli boards, a daily roast, a selection from the chargrill, and full meals such as superfood salad followed by Cornish lamb medallions, dauphinoise potatoes, crushed carrots and pea shoots; with chocolate-glazed mini doughnuts for dessert. There's a special kids' menu, too.

Open all day all wk Closed 25 Dec **Food** Lunch all wk 12-6 Dinner all wk 6-10 Av main course £14 ⊕ FREE HOUSE/PEACH PUBS ◄ Purity Pure UBU & Mad Goose, Sharp's Doom Bar ☼ Aspall. ♀ 16 **Facilities** Non-diners area ❤ (Bar Outside area) ♦♦ Children's portions Outside area ⏚ WiFi ▭ (notice required)

■ LAPWORTH   Map 10 SP17

The Boot Inn   `PICK OF THE PUBS`

tel: 01564 782464 **Old Warwick Rd B94 6JU**
email: thebootinn@lovelypubs.co.uk
dir: *Phone for detailed directions*

Stylish country pub by canal

Precision-cut logs and soft modern furnishings meet the eye in this convivial, 16th-century former coaching inn beside the Grand Union Canal. Beyond its smart interior is an attractive garden, on cooler days under a canopied patio with heaters. Free-house status means a good choice of real ales in the shape of Purity Pure UBU, Sharp's Doom Bar and Marston's EPA. But for many the draw is the brasserie-style food, and there's lots to choose from. For example, the first course could be Thai chicken patties with papaya salad, miso aïoli and black pepper crackers; mains include chargrilled 28-day-matured Hereford rib-eye steak with roast tomato, crispy onions, skin-on chips and béarnaise sauce; and South Indian spiced spit chicken with sweet potato and coconut curry with saffron and cashew pilaf. All wines are half price on Thursdays, Fish Market Night. Children and well-behaved dogs are welcome.

Open all day all wk 11-11 (Thu-Sat 11am-mdnt Sun 12-10.30) **Food** Lunch Mon-Sat 12-2.30, Sun 12-3 Dinner Mon-Fri 7-9.30, Sat 6.30-9.30, Sun 7-9 ⊕ FREE HOUSE ◄ Purity Pure UBU, Marston's EPA, Sharp's Doom Bar ☼ Thatchers Gold, Westons Stowford Press. ♀ 9 **Facilities** Non-diners area ❤ (Bar Restaurant Garden) ♦♦ Children's menu Children's portions Garden ⏚ Parking WiFi ▭ (notice required)

■ LEAMINGTON SPA (ROYAL)   Map 10 SP36

The Moorings at Myton

tel: 01926 425043 **Myton Rd CV31 3NY**
email: info@themoorings.co.uk
dir: *M40 junct 14 or 13, A452 towards Leamington Spa. At 4th rdbt after crossing canal, pub on left*

Anglo-French cuisine in waterside location

This food-led pub beside the Grand Union Canal is a popular stop for boaters on England's arterial waterway. Diners may look forward to dishes created by Raymond Blanc protégés Charles Harris and Nigel Brown, whose ever-evolving Anglo-French menu relies on local suppliers for the ingredients. A sharing charcuterie board is a substantial starter; mains include 28-day dry-aged Aberdeenshire steaks, or perhaps free-range pork collar with pine nut and apricot crust, creamy mash, spinach and red wine jus. Fruit ciders, a decent wine list and beer from Warwickshire craft brewery slip down easily on the waterside terrace.

Open all day all wk **Food** Lunch all wk 12-2.30 Dinner all wk 6-9.30 ⊕ CHARLES WELLS ◄ Bombardier, Young's London Gold, Courage Directors, Warwickshire Darling Buds. ♀ 13 **Facilities** Non-diners area ❤ (Bar Garden) ♦♦ Children's menu Children's portions Family room Garden ⏚ Parking WiFi ▭ (notice required)

■ LONG COMPTON   Map 10 SP23

The Red Lion ★★★★ INN ⊛   `PICK OF THE PUBS`

tel: 01608 684221 **Main St CV36 5JS**
email: info@redlion-longcompton.co.uk web: www.redlion-longcompton.co.uk
dir: *On A3400 between Shipston on Stour & Chipping Norton*

Cotswold character and award-winning cuisine

Squeezed into the northern part of The Cotswolds Area of Outstanding Natural Beauty, this village-edge coaching inn has catered for passing trade since 1748. It's handy for the mysterious Rollright Stones, a stone circle created, so legend has it, from an ancient king and his knights cursed by a witch. A bracing exploration of this enigmatic site works up an appetite that can be well sated from The Red Lion's AA one-Rosette awarded menu. Settle in to the pub's appealing mix of beams, stone-flags and dressed honey-coloured stone, matchboarded walls and log fires and make the difficult choice from the regionally sourced fare. Free-range pork and chicken terrine with apple chutney is a typical starter, leading to chargrilled lamb Barnsley chop with crushed cannellini beans, maple roast shallots and rosemary jus. There's a children's menu too, and even man's best friend can chew on a 'piggy ear' here. Top-notch B&B is on hand for those keen to make a break of it.

Open all wk Mon-Thu 10-2.30 6-11 (Fri-Sun all day) **Food** Lunch Mon-Thu 12-2.30, Fri-Sun 12-9.30 Dinner Mon-Thu 6-9, Fri-Sun 12-9.30 Av main course £14.75 Set menu available ⊕ FREE HOUSE ◄ Hook Norton Hooky Bitter, Adnams, Timothy Taylor. ♀ 11 **Facilities** Non-diners area ❤ (Bar Restaurant Garden) ♦♦ Children's menu Children's portions Play area Garden ⏚ Parking WiFi **Rooms** 5

MONKS KIRBY
Map 11 SP48

The Bell Inn

tel: 01788 832352 **Bell Ln CV23 0QY**
email: belindagb@aol.com
dir: *From B4455 (Fosse Way) follow Monks Kirby signs*

Timbered inn offering menus with strong Spanish influences

This quaint, timbered inn was once the gatehouse of a Benedictine priory and then a brewhouse cottage. The pine bar top came from a tree grown in Leire churchyard nearby. The Spanish owners describe their pub as "a corner of Spain in the heart of England". Mediterranean and traditional cuisine play an important role on the truly extensive menu. Enjoy a glass of Ruddles while taking time to make your choices. Lobster Zarzuela, monkfish al horno, solomillo Andalucia and grilled halibut all make a showing. Grills, pasta dishes and paella are readily available too.

Open 12-3 6.30-10.30 Closed 26 Dec, 1 Jan, Mon L **Food** Lunch Tue-Sun 12-3 Dinner Tue-Sun 6.30-10.30 ⊕ FREE HOUSE ◀ Greene King IPA, Ruddles. **Facilities** Non-diners area ❅ (Garden) ♦◀ Children's portions Garden Outside area Parking WiFi 🚌

OFFCHURCH
Map 11 SP36

The Stag at Offchurch

tel: 01926 425801 **Welsh Rd CV33 9AQ**
email: info@thestagatoffchurch.com
dir: *From Leamington Spa take A425 towards Southam. At Radford Semele left into Offchurch Ln to Offchurch*

Picturesque pub with progressive menu

The Stag is a charming thatched pub in a classic English village. Considerately modernised, it balances the feel of times long-gone with contemporary flourishes; diners, ramblers and locals all flock to the restaurant and bar. The imaginative menu offers plenty of choice – sautéed king scallop, crisp pork belly with roasted white onion purée; roast rack of lamb, slow roast shoulder cannelloni, olive oil mash and green beans; and dark chocolate torte, caramelised banana, and salted almond brittle. The head chef specialises in locally raised, 28-day, dry-aged Aberdeenshire beef steaks.

Open all day all wk **Food** Lunch all wk 12-2.30 Dinner all wk 6-9.30 ⊕ FREE HOUSE ◀ Hook Norton, Warwickshire ♂ Somersby Cider. ▼ 13 **Facilities** Non-diners area ❅ (Bar Garden) ♦◀ Children's menu Children's portions Garden ⋈ Parking WiFi

OXHILL
Map 10 SP34

The Peacock

tel: 01295 688060 **Main St CV35 0QU**
email: info@thepeacockoxhill.co.uk
dir: *From Stratford-upon-Avon take A422 towards Banbury. Turn right to Oxhill*

Destination pub in picturesque village

Yvonne Hamlett and Pam Farrell's objective is to run a classic English country pub. They can tick that one off, then. Their 16th-century, stone-built pub effortlessly combines its historic past with a relaxed modern atmosphere. Hand-pulled ales come from St Austell, Marston's and Wye Valley, and the popular food reflects the kitchen's focus on meats and vegetables from local farms, and fresh fish from Devon and Cornwall. Meal ideas include pie of the day; pan-fried duck breast with port and summer berry sauce; marinated salmon kebabs with stir-fry; and Moroccan spiced lamb chump on fruit couscous with curried mint mayo.

Open all day all wk 12-11 **Food** Lunch Mon-Sat 12-2, Sun 12-8 Dinner Mon-Sat 6-9, Sun 12-8 ⊕ FREE HOUSE ◀ Marston's Pedigree, St Austell Tribute, Sharp's Doom Bar, Wye Valley HPA ♂ Thatchers Pear & Gold, Healey's Cornish Rattler. ▼ 12 **Facilities** Non-diners area ❅ (Bar Garden) ♦◀ Children's menu Children's portions Garden ⋈ Parking WiFi 🚌

PRESTON BAGOT
Map 10 SP16

The Crabmill

tel: 01926 843342 **B95 5EE**
email: thecrabmill@lovelypubs.co.uk
dir: *M40 junct 16, A3400 towards Stratford-upon-Avon. Take A4189 at lights in Henley-in-Arden. Left, 1.5m pub on left*

Richly varied menu in converted cider mill

Handy for a pre-prandial stroll in superb countryside alongside the Stratford-upon-Avon Canal, this carefully renovated former rural mill, where crab apples were perhaps mashed into cider, is a fine destination gastro-pub presented in a modern rustic style. Colourwash, comfy seating and light beams offer an airy, informal interior. Contemporary dishes shine out from the extensive menu; commence with twice baked gruyère cheese soufflé, apple, chicory, candied walnuts and cider honey dressing before tucking into a main of bouillabaisse; or slow cooked Guinness and marmalade lamb shoulder with colcannon and fresh mint dressing.

Open all day 11-11 Closed Sun eve **Food** Lunch Mon-Thu 12-3, Fri-Sat 12-5, Sun 12-4 Dinner Mon-Sat 6.30-9.30 ⊕ FREE HOUSE ◀ Greene King Abbot Ale, Purity Gold & UBU, St Austell Tribute, Fuller's London Pride, Sharp's Doom Bar, Pale Whale ♂ Westons Stowford Press. ▼ 14 **Facilities** Non-diners area ❅ (Bar Garden) ♦◀ Children's menu Children's portions Garden ⋈ Parking WiFi

SALFORD PRIORS
Map 10 SP05

The Bell at Salford Priors

tel: 01789 772112 **Evesham Rd WR11 8UU**
email: info@thebellatsalfordpriors.com
dir: *From A46 (Bidford Island) towards Salford Priors. Through village. Pub on left*

High-quality yet informal dining

This black-and-white timber-framed pub draws diners for its rural location and the daily-changing menu that champions local seasonal produce. It is within striking distance of Stratford-upon-Avon, the Cotswolds and the NEC at Birmingham. Expect a warm welcome, glowing fires and three real ales on tap, including Purity Mad Goose. The dining room is decorated in the contemporary style and you can also eat alfresco, weather permitting. Typically, start with a whole baked camembert studded with walnuts, and follow with chicken escalope served with a garlic, lemon and herb crème fraîche, and then passionfruit crème brûlée. There is a set lunch menu, roasts on Sunday and fish night every Friday.

Open all wk 12-3 6-close (Sat-Sun all day) **Food** Lunch all wk 12-2.30 Dinner all wk 6-9 Set menu available ⊕ ENTERPRISE INNS ◀ Wye Valley HPA, Purity Mad Goose, Wickwar BOB ♂ Westons Old Rosie. ▼ 10 **Facilities** Non-diners area ❅ (Bar Garden) ♦◀ Children's menu Children's portions Garden ⋈ Parking WiFi 🚌 (notice required)

SHREWLEY
Map 10 SP26

The Durham Ox Restaurant and Country Pub
PICK OF THE PUBS

tel: 01926 842283 **Shrewley Common CV35 7AY**
email: 8616@greeneking.co.uk
dir: *M40 junct 15, A46 towards Coventry. 1st exit signed Warwick, left onto A4177. After Hatton Country World, pub signed, 1.5m*

Superior dining in a village pub

Named after an ox of epic proportions, this 300-year-old pub-restaurant (now in new hands) is situated in the peaceful village of Shrewley, just four miles from Warwick and Leamington. Warm and inviting, its old beams, tiled floor, oak panelling, roaring fire and traditional hospitality combine with a city chic to give it that competitive edge. Success is in no small measure due to the restaurant, where impressive, seasonally changing classic and contemporary dishes are prepared.

A meal might consist of a pigeon, spinach and mushroom pasty; slow-braised venison and Black Sheep ale casserole with braised red cabbage and thyme dumplings; and dark chocolate fondant. Potted kippers with cucumber pickle could appear on the specials list. For a real treat, your table could opt for the gourmet experience menu. Bar food includes snacks, sandwiches and hearty pub classics, such as spicy and sticky pork ribs.

Open all wk 11-11 (Sun 12-10) **Food** Lunch all wk 11am-10pm Dinner all wk 11am-10pm ⊕ GREENE KING ◄ Greene King Durham Ox, Purity, Guest ales Ŏ Aspall. ♈ 21 **Facilities** Non-diners area ❖ (Bar Garden Outside area) ♦ Children's menu & portions Play area Garden Outside area ⅋ Parking WiFi ⊟ (notice required)

STRATFORD-UPON-AVON   Map 10 SP25

The One Elm   PICK OF THE PUBS

tel: 01789 404919 **1 Guild St CV37 6QZ**
email: theoneelm@peachpubs.com
dir: *In town centre*

Quirky decor and a Mediterranean-style courtyard

Named after the elm tree that used to be a boundary marker of Stratford-upon-Avon, The One Elm occupies a prime location in the town centre not far from the river and theatre. It mirrors the chic, contemporary look and style of menus to be found at other Peach Pubs, the innovative small pub group. Opening at 9.30am for coffee and breakfast, there's an informal, almost continental feel about the place, especially in the stylish front lounge area with its wood floor, bright painted walls, leather sofas and low tables displaying the day's newspapers. Beyond the central, open-to-view kitchen is a more formal dining area, while the upstairs seating area has an even grander feel. The menu is an eclectic list of modern pub food. Try herb pancakes with spinach and mushroom stuffing and gruyère cream sauce; Aberdeenshire cheeseburger with chips, onion rings and coleslaw; or a deli board to share. The secluded terrace gives you a feeling of being abroad.

Open all day all wk 9.30am-11pm (Thu 9.30am-mdnt Fri-Sat 9.30am-1am Sun 9.30am-10.30pm) Closed 25 Dec **Food** Lunch all wk 12-6 Dinner all wk 6-10 ⊕ FREE HOUSE/PEACH PUBS ◄ Purity Pure UBU & Gold, Sharp's Doom Bar, Guest ales Ŏ Aspall. ♈ 14 **Facilities** Non-diners area ❖ (Bar Garden) ♦ Children's menu Children's portions Garden ⅋ Parking WiFi ⊟

TANWORTH IN ARDEN   Map 10 SP17

The Bell Inn

tel: 01564 742212 **The Green B94 5AL**
email: thebell@realcoolbars.com
dir: *M42 junct 8, A435 signed Evesham. Left signed Portway & Tanworth (Penn Ln). To T-junct, left signed Tanworth. 1st right signed Tanworth. Inn in village centre*

A popular village pub of both real and TV vintage

Older visitors might remember (or perhaps try to forget) a TV soap called *Crossroads*, many of whose outdoor scenes were shot in Tanworth, doubling as 'Kings Oak'. The pub overlooks the small village green and war memorial, and has stood here since the 17th century, so the cool grey tones of the thoroughly modern bar area might come as a surprise. Starters include liver, brandy and mushroom pâté and goats' cheese with parsley mousse on ciabatta; mains might be grilled sea bass on marinated peppers; tagliatelle with broccoli and pine nuts; or pub classics like Cumberland sausage and mash.

Open all day all wk **Food** Lunch Mon-Sat 12-2.30, Sun 12-8 Dinner Mon-Sat 6.30-9, Sun 12-8 ⊕ ENTERPRISE INNS ◄ Timothy Taylor Landlord Ŏ Sandford Orchards Devon Mist. ♈ **Facilities** Non-diners area ❖ (Bar Outside area) ♦ Children's menu Children's portions Outside area ⅋ Parking WiFi ⊟ (notice required)

TEMPLE GRAFTON   Map 10 SP15

The Blue Boar Inn ★★★ INN

tel: 01789 750010 **B49 6NR**
email: info@theblueboar.co.uk **web:** www.theblueboar.co.uk
dir: *From A46 (Stratford to Alcester) turn left to Temple Grafton. Pub at 1st x-rds*

Historic inn with Cotswolds views

The oldest part of this former ale house and now thriving village inn dates back to the early 1600s and includes a 35-foot deep well, now glassed over and illuminated, set into a flagstoned floor and home to goldfish. Warmth in the bar and restaurant comes from four open fires, while in the summer there is a patio garden with views of the Cotswold Hills. Extensive menus include steak from local Freeman's Farm, pork belly with cider jus, pub classics like chilli and coriander beefburger, and a steak and onion sandwich. Wash it down with a pint of Jennings or Wychwood Hobgoblin. There are 14 attractive bedrooms.

Open all day all wk 12-11.30 **Food** Lunch Mon-Fri 12-3, Sat 12-10, Sun 12-9 Dinner Mon-Fri 6-10, Sat 12-10, Sun 12-9 ⊕ MARSTON'S ◄ Pedigree, Wychwood Hobgoblin, Banks's Bitter, Jennings Ŏ Thatchers Gold. ♈ 10 **Facilities** Non-diners area ❖ (Bar Garden) ♦ Children's menu Children's portions Garden ⅋ Parking WiFi ⊟ (notice required) **Rooms** 14

WARWICK   Map 10 SP26

The Rose & Crown   PICK OF THE PUBS

tel: 01926 411117 **30 Market Place CV34 4SH**
email: roseandcrown@peachpubs.com
dir: *M40 junct 15 follow signs to Warwick. Pass castle car park entrance, up hill to West Gate, left into Bowling Green St, 1st right, follow one-way system to T-junct, right into Market Place, pub visible ahead*

A vibrant and stylish gastro-pub

The flagship venture of the innovative Peach Pub Company created over a decade ago, The Rose & Crown continues to thrive. In a corner of Warwick's market place, there are a few tables outside to enjoy a spot of people-watching. The laid-back vibe and contemporary look sit well with period features and homely touches such as comfy leather sofas. The pub opens early for breakfast and offers a modern pub menu that's served all day. Deli boards have a selection of small tapas-style portions, and the seasonal menu displays a wide range of dishes to suit the occasion and time of day. There are sandwiches, salads, grills and roasts, and mains like herb-crusted Cornish lamb leg cannon with crushed minted potatoes, peas and baby onion jus. Puddings may include mixed berry knickerbocker glory. A beer festival is usually held at the end of May.

Open all day all wk Mon-Wed 7am-11pm (Thu 7am-11.30pm Fri 7am-12.30am Sat 8am-12.30am Sun 8am-10pm) Closed 25 Dec **Food** Lunch all wk 12-6 Dinner Mon-Sat 6-10, Sun 6-9.30 Av main course £14.50 ⊕ FREE HOUSE/PEACH PUBS ◄ Purity Pure UBU & Gold, Sharp's Doom Bar Ŏ Aspall. ♈ 16 **Facilities** Non-diners area ❖ (Bar Outside area) ♦ Children's portions Outside area ⅋ Beer festival WiFi ⊟ (notice required)

WELFORD-ON-AVON

Map 10 SP15

The Bell Inn

PICK OF THE PUBS

tel: 01789 750353 **Binton Rd CV37 8EB**
email: info@thebellwelford.co.uk
dir: *Phone for detailed directions*

An enjoyably civilised pub

The interior of this appealing, early 16th-century pub is chock-full of signs of its age. Each distinct space displays its own character, with flagstones in one, and oak flooring in another; there's antique wood panelling in the bar, and three open fires, one an inglenook. Legend has it that William Shakespeare, having been drinking here with the dramatist Ben Jonson, contracted fatal pneumonia after returning to Stratford-upon-Avon in the pouring rain. It's a matter owners Colin and Teresa Ombler leave others to debate, while they focus on providing quality drink and food. For example, there are always five real ales, including at least two local brews, and 16 wines served by the glass. Starters and light meals include smoked salmon with red onion and potato salad; and deep-fried brie with apricot and ginger compôte. Main courses include breaded garlic chicken breast stuffed with smoked cheddar with sweet potato mash and wilted spinach; shellfish paella topped with aïoli; or harissa and yogurt roasted salmon fillet on cucumber, watercress and baby spinach salad. Don't miss the hot-cross bun bread and butter pudding dessert.

Open all wk 11.30-3 6-11 (Sat 11.30-11 Sun 12-10.30) **Food** Lunch Mon-Fri 11.30-2.30, Sat-Sun all day Dinner Mon-Thu 6-9.30, Fri 6-10, Sat-Sun all day Av main course £14 ⊕ ENTERPRISE INNS ◀ Wells Bombardier, Hobsons Best Bitter, Flowers Best Bitter & IPA, Purity Gold & Pure UBU, Hook Norton, Greene King IPA. ☷ 16 **Facilities** Non-diners area ◀◀ Children's menu Children's portions Garden ⩊ Parking WiFi ▭ (notice required)

WITHYBROOK

Map 11 SP48

The Pheasant

tel: 01455 220480 **Main St CV7 9LT**
email: thepheasant01@hotmail.com **web:** www.thepheasanteatinghouse.com
dir: *7m NE of Coventry, on B4112*

Crowd-pleasing pub grub in an idyllic location

A warm welcome awaits you at this 17th-century inn, idyllically situated beside the brook where withies were once cut for fencing, hence the village's name, Withybrook. The Pheasant is a popular free house, cosy and full of character with an inglenook fireplace, farm implements and horse-racing photographs on display. The chalkboard flags up daily and seasonal specials, complementing a wealth of food choices from the extensive main menu. Take your pick from chef's special curry,

---

fresh venison pie, sizzling skillets including Cajun chicken, Japanese breaded king prawns or broccoli and walnut lasagne. Save room for chocolate lumpy bumpy for afters. Outside, the benches on the patio area overlooking the Withy Brook can accommodate 100 people – perfect for a leisurely lunch or a thirst-quenching pint of real ale after a walk in the beautiful surrounding countryside.

Open all wk 11-3 6-11.30 (Sun & BH 11-11) Closed 25-26 Dec **Food** Lunch Mon-Sat 12-2, Sun 12-9 Dinner Mon-Sat 6.30-10, Sun 12-9 ⊕ FREE HOUSE ◖ Courage Directors, Theakston Smooth Dark, John Smith's Extra Smooth, Young's Bitter. ▼ 16 **Facilities** Non-diners area ✿ (Garden Outside area) ᶖ Children's menu Children's portions Garden Outside area ⊫ Parking WiFi ⚌ (notice required)

See advert on opposite page

WEST MIDLANDS

BARSTON
Map 10 SP27

The Malt Shovel at Barston
`PICK OF THE PUBS`

See Pick of the Pubs on page 518 and advert below

BIRMINGHAM
Map 10 SP08

The Old Joint Stock

tel: 0121 200 1892 **4 Temple Row West B2 5NY**
email: oldjointstock@fullers.co.uk
dir: *Opposite main entrance to St Philip's Cathedral, just off Colmore Row*

Great for pies and pre-theatre drinks

Originally a library and later a bank, this impressively colonnaded building was designed by the same architect as part of St Philip's Cathedral opposite. Now a pub with its own theatre and art gallery, its high-Victorian Gothic interior incorporates an immense domed ceiling, stately-home fittings and towering mahogany island bar. Pies take up a chunk of the menu, which also features ham hock and parsley sauce; and curried sweet potato and lentil stew; and evening snacks such as cheese straws. Beer festivals are held in both May and October.

Open all day (Sun 12-5) Closed Sun eve **Food** Lunch all wk 12-5 Dinner Mon-Sat 5-10 Av main course £12 ⊕ FULLER'S ◖ London Pride, ESB, Chiswick Bitter. ▼ 16 **Facilities** Non-diners area ᶖ Family room Outside area ⊫ Beer festival WiFi ⚌ (notice required)

PICK OF THE PUBS

The Malt Shovel at Barston

BARSTON Map 10 SP27

tel 01675 443223
Barston Ln B92 0JP
email themaltshovelatbarston@gmail.com
web www.themaltshovelatbarston.com
dir *M42 junct 5, A4141 towards Knowle. Left into Jacobean Ln, right at T-junct (Hampton Ln). Left into Barston Ln, 0.5m*

Smart, busy inn down the country lanes

The Malt Shovel is an airy, well designed free house with modern soft furnishings and interesting artefacts. An early 20th-century, stylishly converted mill building, it sits comfortably in the countryside outside Solihull. Natural wood and pastel colours characterise the interiors and flowers decorate the unclothed tables in the tiled dining area. The bar is cosy and relaxed with winter log fires, and there's an attractive garden for outdoor dining; at weekends the restaurant in the adjacent converted barn is opened. The extensive choice of modern British dishes makes the best of fresh seasonal ingredients, and, predictably, the daily fish specials board is popular with lovers of seafood. A look through the imaginative menu finds starters such as chicken and chorizo patties; and wild pigeon breast with grapefruit jelly. Main course dishes are just as appetising: there could be grilled plaice, roast sweet potato with crab and

black Tuscan olive dressing; roast venison, spinach, buttered courgette, pepperdew and walnut jus; pork fillet stuffed with black pudding, prunes and pistachios, maple and cider jus; and risotto arancini. As for desserts, you won't often come across a tea cup of rose pannacotta, raspberry compôte and lemon curd brioche; or fig, cinnamon and honey tart with hazelnut ice cream, so tuck in. A board of English and European cheeses with grapes, celery, apple and sultana chutney and crisp-bread will fill any remaining corners.

Open all day all wk **Food** Lunch Mon-Sat 12-2.30, Sun 12-4 Dinner Mon-Sat 6-9.30 ⊕ FREE HOUSE ◀ St Austell Tribute, M&B Brew XI, Sharp's Doom Bar, Black Sheep. ₱ 15 **Facilities** Non-diners area ♦♦ Children's menu Children's portions Garden ⊭ Parking WiFi

CHADWICK END
Map 10 SP27

The Orange Tree
PICK OF THE PUBS

tel: 01564 785364 **Warwick Rd B93 0BN**
email: theorangetree@lovelypubs.co.uk
dir: *3m from Knowle towards Warwick*

Informal modern pub with a diverse menu

The Orange Tree is part of the small Lovely Pubs chain. It fits the brand with its wooden floors, unclothed tables, neutral-toned walls and light modern interiors coupled with old beams, antique mirrors and a relaxed pubby vibe. Outside, landscaped gardens are perfect for dining in the sunshine. On the extensive menu, (of which there is a separate vegetarian one, almost as long) comfort food options sit alongside globally influenced dishes and there's a plat du jour and 'pud de jour' during the week. So try perhaps, gambas pil pil; pan-fried king prawns in garlic, chilli, saffron, paprika and parsley with aïoli crostini; or a sharing plate, then pizza or pasta or chargrilled pork cutlet, pumpkin, wild mushroom and sage, fondant potato and cider sauce. Finish with a retro banana split, brought up to date with dulce de leche and amaretti biscuits.

Open all day all wk 11-11 **Food** Lunch Mon-Sat 12-2.30, Sun 12-7 Dinner Mon-Sat 6-9.30, Sun 12-7 Av main course £10-£12 ⊕ FREE HOUSE ◀ Fuller's London Pride, Purity Pure UBU. ♀ 10 **Facilities** Non-diners area ❖ (Bar Garden) ◆◆ Children's menu Children's portions Play area Garden ㅈ Parking WiFi ➡ (notice required)

HAMPTON IN ARDEN
Map 10 SP28

The White Lion Inn
PICK OF THE PUBS

tel: 01675 442833 **10 High St B92 0AA**
email: info@thewhitelioninn.com
dir: *M42 junct 6, A45 towards Coventry. At rdbt take A452 towards Leamington Spa. At rdbt take B4102 towards Solihull. Approx 2m to Hampton in Arden*

Classic English, simple French and a bit of Jamaican

Once a farmhouse, this 17th-century, timber-framed pub first acquired a drinks licence in the early 1800s. Its bright, modern interior is today furnished with wicker chairs and decorated with fresh flowers. Landlord Chris Roach and his partner FanFan draw on their considerable experience of working in or visiting restaurants, bistros and gastro-pubs throughout England and France to present an ever-appealing combination of classic English pub grub and simple French bistro-style food. Black pudding St Malo would make a good starter, as would whitebait and Dijon mustard mayonnaise; a main of moules marinière à la crème and frites could continue the Gallic approach, or go Jamaican with curried goat and rice. An alternative to a traditional roast on Sunday could be two-cheese penne pasta, or fillet of cod. There are also specials, jacket potatoes and toasted sandwiches. Real ales include Pure UBU (named after the brewery's dog), Bank's Sunbeam and Castle Rock Harvest Pale.

Open all day all wk noon-12.30am (Sun 12-10.30) **Food** Lunch Mon-Sat 12-2.30, Sun 12-4 Dinner all wk 6.30-9.30 ⊕ PUNCH TAVERNS ◀ M&B Brew XI, Purity UBU, Sharp's Doom Bar, Hobsons Best, Banks's Sunbeam, Castle Rock Harvest Pale ♂ Westons Stowford Press, Aspall. ♀ 11 **Facilities** Non-diners area ❖ (Bar Restaurant Garden) ◆◆ Children's menu Children's portions Garden ㅈ Parking WiFi ➡ (notice required)

SEDGLEY
Map 10 SO99

Beacon Hotel & Sarah Hughes Brewery
PICK OF THE PUBS

tel: 01902 883380 **129 Bilston St DY3 1JE**
dir: *Phone for detailed directions*

Enjoy a pint of ale brewed on the premises

Home of the Sarah Hughes Brewery and the famous Dark Ruby Mild, the Beacon Hotel is a restored Victorian tap house that has barely changed in 150 years. Proprietor John Hughes reopened the adjoining Sarah Hughes Brewery in 1987, 66 years after his grandmother became the licensee. The rare snob-screened island bar serves a simple taproom, with its old wall benches and a fine blackened range; a super cosy snug replete with a green-tiled marble fireplace, dark woodwork, velvet curtains and huge old tables; and a large smoke-room with an adjoining, plant-festooned conservatory. On a tour of the brewery you can see the original grist case and rare open-topped copper that add to the Victorian charm and give unique character to the brews. Flagship beers are Sarah Hughes Dark Ruby, Sedgley Surprise & Amber, with seasonal bitter and two guest beers from small microbreweries also available. Food in the pub is limited to filled cob rolls but there is a designated children's room and play area, as well as a large garden.

Open all wk 12-2.30 5.30-11 (Sat-12-3 6-11 Sun 12-3 7-10.30) **Food** Contact pub for details ⊕ FREE HOUSE ◀ Sarah Hughes Dark Ruby, Sedgley Surprise & Amber, Guest ales. **Facilities** Non-diners area ◆◆ Play area Family room Garden Outside area ㅈ Parking ➡ (notice required) **Notes** ⊛

WEST BROMWICH
Map 10 SP09

The Vine

tel: 0121 553 2866 **Roebuck St B70 6RD**
email: bharat@thevine.co.uk
dir: *M5 junct 1, follow West Bromwich/A41 signs. 1st left into Roebuck St. Pub at end on corner*

Spicy meals near West Brom's football ground

Certainly not the most attractive approach road to this pub, but keep going. Beers from reliable well-loved stalwarts such as Bathams and Holden's help this thriving, edge-of-town free house shine out. Equally adept at attracting customers to fill the surprisingly large open-plan interior and conservatory-style dining area is the remarkable menu created by Suki Patel, based around a pick 'n mix of firm Indian favourites. Goat jalfrezi with massala chips – no problem; chicken, lamb and prawn bhuna and bullet naan – take a seat. The indoor barbecue is extremely popular, with chicken tikka particularly favoured. There's also a range of traditional pub grub dishes and some wonderful spicy vegetarian choices, like mutter paneer.

Open all wk 11.30-2.30 5-11 (Fri-Sat 12-11 Sun 12-10) **Food** Lunch Mon-Fri 11.30-2.30, Sat-Sun 12-10 Dinner Mon-Fri 5-10, Sat-Sun 12-10 Av main course £5.95 ⊕ FREE HOUSE ◀ Bathams, Holden's, Wye Valley, Burton Bridge. **Facilities** Non-diners area ◆◆ Garden ㅈ WiFi ➡ (notice required)

WILTSHIRE

ALDBOURNE
Map 5 SU27

The Blue Boar

tel: 01672 540237 **20 The Green SN8 2EN**
email: theblueboar@mail.com
dir: *From Salisbury take B4192 to Aldbourne. Or M4 junct 14 take A338 to Hungerford, B4192 to Aldbourne & follow brown signs*

The sort of pub to dream about when abroad

This Wadworth-owned, 16th-century pub stands on the village green, itself distanced from traffic, with views of pretty houses, the church and a Celtic cross. It couldn't wish for a better location, so outdoor drinking and eating are a particular pleasure, although there will be times when the two open fires inside beckon. Home-prepared food includes sandwiches and baguettes; pan-fried lamb's liver and bacon; home-cooked Wiltshire ham; and pumpkin and parmesan ravioli. New landlords Michael and Joanne Hehir uphold the April and October beer festival tradition, while local enthusiasts periodically relive wartime days when an American parachute regiment was billeted locally.

Open all wk 11.30-3 5.30-11 (Fri-Sun 11.30-11) **Food** Lunch Mon-Fri 12-2, Sat 12-2.30, Sun 12-4 Dinner Mon-Sat 6.30-9 ⊕ WADWORTH ◀ 6X & Henry's Original IPA, Guest ales ♂ Westons Stowford Press. **Facilities** Non-diners area ♣ (Bar Garden) ♦♦ Children's menu Children's portions Garden ⋒ Beer festival WiFi 🚌 (notice required)

The Crown Inn ★★★ INN

tel: 01672 540214 **The Square SN8 2DU**
email: bookings@thecrownaldbourne.co.uk **web:** www.thecrownaldbourne.co.uk
dir: *M4 junct 15, N on A419, signed Aldbourne*

Classic village-square inn in popular rambling area

This imposing coaching inn has served the village for over 400 years, and retains much period feel in the well-beamed old bar. In the Second World War, American NCO's made it their mess-room and enjoyed local beers and food; today's regulars and visitors may indulge in White Horse or Bryden ales, whilst the home-prepared food majors on ingredients sourced from local suppliers. Hunters chicken and ham, egg and chips are favourites, as are the burgers and home-made stone-baked pizzas. There are beer festivals each May and September and a cider festival is held in July.

Open all day all wk 12-12 **Food** Lunch all wk, all day Dinner all wk, all day Av main course £6 Restaurant menu available all wk ⊕ ENTERPRISE INNS ◀ Shepherds Neame Spitfire, Ramsbury Gold, Sharp's Doom Bar, Guest ales ♂ Westons Stowford Press, Aspall. ♥ 16 **Facilities** Non-diners area ♣ (Bar Garden) ♦♦ Children's menu Children's portions Play area Garden ⋒ Beer festival Cider festival Parking WiFi 🚌 (notice required) **Rooms** 4

AXFORD
Map 5 SU27

Red Lion Inn
PICK OF THE PUBS

tel: 01672 520271 **SN8 2HA**
email: info@redlionaxford.com
dir: *M4 junct 15, A346 to Marlborough centre. Left, follow Ramsbury signs. Inn 3m*

Eye-catching dining inn

This old inn has been welcoming travellers for over 400 years. From the flower-bedecked terrace (perfect for alfresco summer dining), divine views percolate to the river and this peaceful stretch of countryside. It's located in the North Wessex Downs Area of Outstanding Natural Beauty and close to the popular walks in the

ancient Savernake Forest; ample opportunity to work up an appetite. Tables and chairs constructed from half-barrels and squashy sofas dot the timeworn parquet flooring of the convivial bar, at the heart of which is a huge inglenook fireplace. Settle in with a vintage from the wine list or a glass of Good Old Boy, and consider a menu which is strong on seasonal game and fish dishes with a contemporary European flavour. Choices include whole grilled trout with lemon and almonds with a stir-fry; braised rabbit with mustard; and roast beef salad.

Open all wk 12-3 6-11 **Food** Lunch Tue-Sat 12-2 Dinner Tue-Fri 6-9 ⊕ FREE HOUSE ◀ Timothy Taylor Landlord, West Berkshire Good Old Boy ♂ Westons Stowford Press. **Facilities** Non-diners area ♦♦ Children's portions Garden Parking WiFi 🚌

BERWICK ST JAMES
Map 5 SU03

NEW The Boot Inn

tel: 01722 790243 **High St SP3 4TN**
email: food@bootatberwick.co.uk
dir: *From either A303 (Deptford to Winterbourne Stoke) or A36 (Deptford to Salisbury) take B3083 to Berwick St James. Pub in village centre*

Worth a short detour if on a A303 journey

Here in their picturesque 18th-century former coaching inn, formally trained chefs and landlords Giles and Cathy Dickinson aim to provide 'traditional British food', all home-made or locally sourced as far as possible. It's a Wadworth house which, as all the Devizes brewery's disciples know, means 6X and Henry's IPA. The Dickinson's say you won't find curry, chilli, lasagne or 'expensive gastro-pub concoctions'; instead, dishes like potted shrimps, devilled kidneys on toast, smoked eel and soused herrings; pies, namely Gloucestershire squab, Shropshire fidget and beef and oyster; rabbit casserole; and old-fashioned apple crumble with custard, fruit fools, and knickerbocker glory.

Open 12-3 6-11 (Fri-Sat 12-3 6-12 Sun 12-4) Closed 1-3 Feb, Sun eve & Mon **Food** Lunch 12-2.15 Dinner 6.30-9.15 ⊕ WADWORTH ◀ Henry's Original IPA & 6X. ♥ 9 **Facilities** Non-diners area ♣ (Bar Restaurant Garden) ♦♦ Children's menu Children's portions Garden ⋒ Parking

BERWICK ST JOHN
Map 4 ST92

The Talbot Inn

tel: 01747 828222 **The Cross SP7 0HA**
dir: *From Shaftesbury take A30 towards Salisbury. Right to Berwick St John. Pub 1.5m*

Traditional pub with lots of character

The Talbot Inn used to be three cottages, one of them the village shop, before becoming an alehouse in 1835. This typical old English country free house in the beautiful Chalke Valley dates from the 17th century and has the beams, low ceilings and huge inglenook fireplace so typical of its kind. Real ales plus good home-cooked food shown on the menus and specials board are on offer; try the crumbed butterfly prawns with sweet chilli dipping sauce or garlic mushrooms to start; followed by cooked ham, egg and chips; home-made lasagne or salmon and broccoli mornay.

Open 12-2.30 6.30-11 (Sun 12-4) Closed Sun eve & Mon **Food** Lunch Tue-Sun 12-2 Dinner Tue-Sat 6.30-9 ⊕ FREE HOUSE ◀ Ringwood Best Bitter, Wadworth 6X, Sixpenny Handley IPA ♂ Westons Stowford Press. **Facilities** ♣ (Bar Garden) ♦♦ Children's portions Garden Parking

---

BISHOPSTONE
Map 5 SU28

The Royal Oak

tel: 01793 790481 **Cues Ln SN6 8PP**
email: royaloak@helenbrowningorganics.co.uk
dir: *M4 junct 15, A419 towards Swindon. At rdbt right into Pack Hill signed Wanborough. In Bishopstone left into Cues Ln. Pub on right*

Rustic, relaxed and friendly pub with its own farm

Organic farmer Helen Browning OBE rescued the delightful Royal Oak from closure. It stands tucked away in a glorious village below the Wiltshire Downs, and you can expect a cracking community atmosphere, Arkell's ales, Westons ciders, roaring logs fires and daily-changing menus. Almost 60 per cent of produce comes from Helen's own farm, with the rest sourced from three other local organic farms and allotments. A three-course dinner could be curried pumpkin soup; pan-fried beef rump with tomato, mushrooms and fries; and doughnuts with smoked plum custard. The child-friendly garden has a Wendy house and rope swing.

Open all wk 12-3 6-11 (Sat 12-12 Sun 12-10) **Food** Lunch all wk 12-3 Dinner all wk 6-9.30 ⊕ ARKELL'S ◀ Moonlight & 3B, Donnington SBA Ŏ Westons Old Rosie, Wyld Wood Organic & Perry. ☻ 12 **Facilities** Non-diners area ♚ (All areas) ♦♦ Children's menu Children's portions Play area Garden Outside area ⋒ Parking WiFi ▨ (notice required)

BOX
Map 4 ST86

The Northey ★★★★ INN

tel: 01225 742333 **Bath Rd SN13 8AE**
email: thenorthey@ohhcompany.co.uk **web:** www.ohhcompany.co.uk
dir: *A4 from Bath towards Chippenham, 4m. Between M4 juncts 17 & 18*

Contemporary inn close to Bath

The former station hotel, built by Brunel for his workers who were building Box Tunnel, was transformed from a shabby roadside drinking pub to a stylish inn by Mark Warburton. The contemporary interior makes good use of wood and flagstone flooring, high-backed oak chairs, leather loungers and handcrafted tables around the bar, where inviting sandwiches (smoked salmon with lemon and chive mayonnaise) and pub classics like ham, egg and chips hold sway. The main menu ranges from potted duck with quince jelly; and rack of lamb with rosemary and olive crust to the pub's speciality fish dishes and great steaks. Swish bedrooms complete the picture.

Open all day all wk Closed 25 Dec **Food** Lunch all wk 12-9.30 Dinner all wk 12-9.30 ⊕ FREE HOUSE ◀ Butcombe & Wadworth 6X, Guest ale Ŏ Ashton Press, Thatchers Dry. ☻ 16 **Facilities** Non-diners area ♚ (Bar Garden) ♦♦ Children's menu Children's portions Garden ⋒ Parking WiFi **Rooms** 3

The Quarrymans Arms

tel: 01225 743569 **Box Hill SN13 8HN**
email: pub@quarrymans-arms.co.uk
dir: *Phone for detailed directions*

Former miners' pub with excellent views

Superb views of the Box Valley can be enjoyed from this 300-year-old pub, from where you can also see Solsbury Hill. A display of Bath stone mining memorabilia bears witness to the years Brunel's navvies spent driving the Great Western Railway through Box Tunnel (spot the bar's replica fireplace) deep beneath the pub. The resultant honeycomb of Bath stone workings attract potholers and cavers, who slake their thirsts on local ales and ciders, and replace lost calories with local faggots; home-made curry; calves' liver, or something from the comprehensive vegetarian selection. 'Mini ale weeks' are held throughout the year.

Open all day all wk 11am-11.30pm **Food** Lunch all wk 11-3 Dinner all wk fr 6 ⊕ FREE HOUSE ◀ Butcombe Bitter, Wadworth 6X, Moles Best, Local Guest ales Ŏ Black Rat, Ashton Press. ☻ 13 **Facilities** Non-diners area ♚ (All areas) ♦♦ Children's portions Family room Garden Outside area ⋒ Beer festival Cider festival Parking WiFi ▨ (notice required)

BRADFORD-ON-AVON
Map 4 ST86

The Dandy Lion

tel: 01225 863433 **35 Market St BA15 1LL**
email: Dandylion35@aol.com
dir: *Phone for detailed directions*

In bustling town near bridge over the River Avon

In the centre of the lovely market town of Bradford-on-Avon, this 18th-century inn was once a boot and shoe shop and a grocery. It is now a popular bar and restaurant offering well-kept Wadworth ales and continental lagers, together with a mix of traditional English and rustic European food. The bar menu offers hot filled flatbreads, light bites and salads, whilst the choice in the upstairs restaurant menu might include chicken Kiev, flash-fried hanger steak, seafood pot pie, nut and seed roast, or home-baked Wiltshire ham, free-range eggs and triple cooked chips.

Open all wk 11-3 6-11 (Fri-Sat 11-11 Sun 11.30-10.30) Closed 25 Dec **Food** Lunch Mon-Thu 12-2.15, Fri-Sat all day, Sun all day till 8.30 Dinner Mon Thu 6-9.30, Fri-Sat all day, Sun all day till 8.30 Av main course £9.95 Restaurant menu available Fri-Sat eve ⊕ WADWORTH ◀ 6X, Henry's Original IPA, Seasonal ales Ŏ Westons Rosie's Pig. ☻ 21 **Facilities** Non-diners area ♚ (Bar) ♦♦ Children's portions

---

The Tollgate Inn ★★★★ INN   `PICK OF THE PUBS`

tel: 01225 782326 **Holt BA14 6PX**
email: laura@tollgateinn.co.uk **web:** www.tollgateinn.co.uk
dir: *M4 junct 18, A46 towards Bath, then A363 to Bradford-on-Avon, then B3107 towards Melksham, pub on right*

Country inn with 16th-century origins

One part of this stone-built village inn used to be a weaving shed, another was the weavers' chapel. Only five minutes by car from the Georgian market town of Bradford-on-Avon, its oak-floored, sofa-furnished main bar serves Ashton Press and Toodle Pip ciders, real ales from small local breweries like Box Steam, and nigh on 20 wines by the glass. The two dining rooms, one upstairs in the old chapel, offer a seasonal menu featuring meats from the farm opposite, and fresh fish from Brixham and Lyme Bay. A pan-seared pigeon breast starter comes with red onion and black pudding compôte; and slow-roasted pork and pea fritter with spiced apple sauce. Main courses include home-made faggots and mash; vegetarian pie of the day; chargrilled steaks; and daily specials, any of which dishes could be enjoyably complemented by lightly spiced crème brûlée with cinnamon sugar, shortbread and ice cream.

Open all day 9am-11.30pm (Sun 9-4.30) Closed Sun eve, Mon **Food** Lunch Tue-Sat 12-2, Sun 12-2.30 Dinner Tue-Sat 6.30-9 ⊕ FREE HOUSE ◀ Box Steam Golden Bolt & Tunnel Vision, St Austell Tribute Ŏ Ashton Press, Toodle Pip. ☻ 19 **Facilities** Non-diners area ♦♦ Children's menu Children's portions Garden ⋒ Parking WiFi ▨ (notice required) **Rooms** 4

BRINKWORTH
Map 4 SU08

The Three Crowns
PICK OF THE PUBS

tel: 01666 510366 **SN15 5AF**
email: info@threecrownsbrinkworth.co.uk
dir: *From Swindon take A3102 to Royal Wootton Bassett, take B4042, 5m to Brinkworth*

Traditional village inn serving non-traditional food

The village sits in rich farming countryside on a low ridge above the River Avon; glimpses of Daunstey Vale catch the eye from the pub's secluded beer garden and tree-shaded patio, where heaters bring additional comfort as the evenings draw in. Lots of greenery inside and out here, with the little village green at the front and the conservatory restaurant hosting some large pot-plants. It's a thriving community pub, welcoming locals and their dogs, the local hunt when it meets, and families set on celebrating a special occasion. Amiable staff greet you in the beamed, fire-warmed old bar, where ales include Sharp's Doom Bar. The menu has long been recognised for its ambition and variety. Expect starters like beef tartare with raw quail's yolk and matchstick fries. If your tastes are more traditional, try the pork fillet with pork belly, black pudding, sauerkraut, apple mash and scallops.

Open all day all wk 10am-mdnt **Food** Lunch Mon-Sat 12-2.30, Sun 12-9 Dinner Mon-Sat 6-9.30, Sun 12-9 Av main course £9.95 Set menu available ⊕ PRESTIGIOUS RESTAURANTS ◀ Sharp's Doom Bar, Fuller's London Pride ⏃ Westons Stowford Press. ⏱ 27 **Facilities** Non-diners area ✿ (Bar Garden) ♦ Children's menu Children's portions Play area Garden ⋒ Beer festival Cider festival Parking WiFi ➡ (notice required)

BROUGHTON GIFFORD
Map 4 ST86

The Fox

tel: 01225 782949 **The Street SN12 8PN**
email: alexgeneen@gmail.com
dir: *From Melksham take B3107 towards Holt. Turn right to Broughton Gifford. Pub in village centre*

Showing a commitment to home-grown and home-reared produce

The excellent ales at this village pub are augmented in the summer months when it hosts a beer and cider festival. Food standards are high too. The owners raise their own chickens, ducks and pigs, tend an extensive vegetable and herb garden, and barter with villagers for wildfowl and other produce. Bread is either baked in the kitchen or provided by the ethical Thoughtful Bread Company. Plans are afoot to build a smokehouse in the grounds, as the pub already produces cured hams, charcuterie and sausages from its pigs. Typical dishes on the menus are Cornish crab quiche; roasted pheasant crown; goats' cheese pesto ravioli; and lamb suet pudding.

Open 12-3 5-9.30 Closed 26 Dec, 1 Jan, Mon **Food** Lunch Tue-Sun 12-2.30 Dinner Mon-Sat 6-9.30 Av main course £13.95 Set menu available ⊕ FREE HOUSE ◀ Bath Gem, Butcombe Bitter, Fuller's London Pride. ⏱ 18 **Facilities** Non-diners area ✿ (Bar Restaurant Garden) ♦ Children's menu Children's portions Garden ⋒ Beer festival Cider festival Parking ➡ (notice required)

BURCOMBE
Map 5 SU03

The Ship Inn

tel: 01722 743182 **Burcombe Ln SP2 0EJ**
email: theshipburcombe@mail.com
dir: *In Burcombe, off A30, 1m from Wilton & 5m W of Salisbury*

Riverside village pub run by passionate foodies

A 17th-century village pub with low ceilings, oak beams and a large open fire. In summer the riverside garden is where you'd enjoy a leisurely meal in the company of the resident ducks. Seasonal menu examples include starters like crab toasties with smoked chilli jam; or pork, mustard and pistachio terrine with balsamic

chutney, followed by mains of pressed pork belly with mash and red cabbage; confit duck leg with gratin dauphinoise and green beans; or home-made fishcakes with herbed fries. In the bar Wadworth 6X, Hop Back Summer Lightning and Butcombe hold the fort on hand-pull.

Open 11-3 6-11 Closed Sun eve in winter **Food** Lunch all wk 12-2.30 Dinner all wk 6-9 ⊕ ENTERPRISE INNS ◀ Wadworth 6X, Hop Back Summer Lightning, Butcombe ⏃ Thatchers Gold. ⏱ 9 **Facilities** Non-diners area ✿ (Bar Garden) ♦ Children's menu Children's portions Garden ⋒ Parking WiFi ➡ (notice required)

BURTON
Map 4 ST87

The Old House at Home ★★★★★ INN

tel: 01454 218227 **SN14 7LT**
email: office@ohhcompany.co.uk web: www.ohhcompany.co.uk
dir: *On B4039 NW of Chippenham*

Family-run, traditional ivy-clad free house offering a warm welcome

This ivy-clad, stone built free house dates from the early 19th century and is one of two run by the Warburton family (the other is The Northey Arms in Box). Dad David has been here for years and still happily pulls pints of Maiden Voyage, Wadworth 6X and Thatchers Gold in the low-beamed bar. The finest seasonal ingredients are used to create impressive menu favourites like venison casserole; peppered smoked haddock pilaf; lasagne verdi or home cooked, honey-glazed ham. The beautifully landscaped gardens feature a waterfall. Six high quality bedrooms are available in a stylish annexe.

Open all day all wk **Food** Lunch all wk 12-9.30 Dinner all wk 12-9.30 ⊕ FREE HOUSE ◀ Ales of Scilly Maiden Voyage, Wadworth 6X, Guest ales ⏃ Thatchers Gold & Traditional. ⏱ 12 **Facilities** Non-diners area ✿ (Bar Restaurant Garden) ♦ Children's menu Children's portions Garden ⋒ Parking WiFi ➡ (notice required) **Rooms** 6

CALNE
Map 4 ST97

NEW The Lansdowne ★★★ INN

tel: 01249 812488 **The Strand SN11 0EH**
email: lansdowne@arkells.com web: www.lansdownestrand.co.uk
dir: *On A4 in town centre*

Traditional food and local ales close to the M4

In the heart of Calne, just 15 minutes from the M4, this 16th-century former coaching inn was once home to the local brewery and the courtyard still retains the medieval brew house. Now owned by Arkell's, the bar showcases that brewery's beers including Wiltshire Gold, alongside monthly guest ales. The straightforward and appealing food menu focuses on traditional pub meals and old favourites. Typical dishes include curry of the week; home-made stew and mash; mushroom carbonara; and gammon steak, eggs and chips. At lunchtime, there is also a well-priced choice of sandwiches and jacket potatoes.

Open all day all wk **Food** Lunch all wk 9-9 Dinner all wk 9-9 Set menu available ⊕ ARKELL'S ◀ 3B, Wiltshire Gold & Guest ale ⏃ Westons Stowford Press. **Facilities** Non-diners area ✿ (Bar Outside area) ♦ Children's menu Children's portions Outside area ⋒ Parking WiFi ➡ **Rooms** 25

NEW The White Horse Inn ★★★★ INN ◉

tel: 01249 813118 **Compton Bassett SN11 8RG**
email: info@whitehorse-comptonbassett.co.uk
web: www.whitehorse-comptonbassett.co.uk
dir: *M4 junct 16 onto A3102, after Hilmarton turn left to Compton Bassett*

Civilised drinking and dining

A stone-built, whitewashed village pub, named after the equine figure cut out of the chalk on a nearby hillside in 1870. The bar's log-burner keeps customers warm in winter, while a year-round attraction is the ever-changing roster of local and national real ales. The kitchen relies on seasonal ingredients - the closer to home their source the better - for home-made Valdosta chicken with Parma ham, and cheese and tomato gratin; braised shoulder of Wiltshire lamb with curly kale and ratatouille; and fillet of Cornish hake with risotto nero. Pecan tart with organic vanilla ice cream makes for a good finish.

Open all day Closed Sun eve & Mon **Food** Lunch Tue-Sun 12-2.15 Dinner Tue-Sat 6-9 Av main course £15 Restaurant menu available ⊕ FREE HOUSE ◀ Bath Ales Gem, Sharp's Doom Bar, Wadworths 6X, Adnams Ò Westons Old Rosie. ☕ 11 **Facilities** Non-diners area ❧ (Bar Garden) ◀↑ Children's menu Children's portions Garden ⊨ Parking WiFi ▄▄ (notice required) **Rooms** 8

COATE
Map 5 SU18

NEW The Sun Inn ★★★★ INN

tel: 01793 523292 **Marlborough Rd SN3 6AA**
email: sun-inn@arkells.com **web:** www.suninn-swindon.co.uk
dir: *M4 junct 15, A419 towards Swindon. At 1st rdbt take A459 signed Swindon & hospital. Left lane at lights. Pub on left before next rdbt*

Ideal watering hole for families

The third Sun public house on this site since 1685, today's pre-war building is close to Arkell's Swindon brewery, which bought its predecessor in 1891. With a large garden and playground, and with Coate Water Country Park nearby, it is understandably popular with families, for whom the menus have clearly been designed. For example, there are takeaway fish and chips, sandwiches and hot drinks; chicken nuggets; giant fish fingers; cheeseburgers; and filled deli rolls. Main dishes include home-made three-cheese macaroni; Wiltshire pork sausages and mash; and scampi, chips and peas. An ever-changing specials board adds to the wide-ranging tally.

Open all day all wk **Food** Lunch all wk 12-9 Dinner all wk 12-9 Av main course £8.95 ⊕ ARKELL'S ◀ 3B, Kingsdown & Wiltshire Gold Ò Westons Stowford Press & Old Rosie. ☕ 10 **Facilities** Non-diners area ❧ (Bar Restaurant Garden) ◀↑ Children's menu Play area Garden ⊨ Parking WiFi ▄▄ (notice required) **Rooms** 10

COLLINGBOURNE DUCIS
Map 5 SU25

The Shears Inn

tel: 01264 850304 **The Cadley Rd SN8 3ED**
email: info@theshears.co.uk
dir: *Just off A338 between Marlborough & Salisbury*

Delightful thatched pub with modern British menu

Dating from the 18th century, this traditional family-run country inn was once a shearing shed for market-bound sheep. The original part of the building is thatched, while inside you'll find wooden and slate floors, low-beamed ceilings and a large inglenook dominating the restaurant. Typical choices from the tasty modern British menu may include beer-battered haggis and black pudding; smoked haddock kedgeree and soft egg; slow roast belly pork with beetroot apples and celeriac mash, and lemon posset with raspberry shortbread or poached pear and honeycomb ice cream for afters. The enclosed sunny garden is an ideal venue for the annual cider festival held in late summer.

Open 11-3 6-11 (Sat 11-11 summer, Sun fr 12) Closed Sun eve **Food** Lunch Mon-Sat 12-2, Sun 12-3.30 Dinner Mon-Sat 6-9.30 Av main course £11.50 Restaurant menu available Mon-Sat ⊕ BRAKSPEAR ◀ Brakspear, Ringwood, Local Guest ales Ò Addlestones, Aspall. ☕ 12 **Facilities** Non-diners area ❧ (Bar Restaurant Garden) ◀↑ Children's menu Children's portions Garden ⊨ Cider festival Parking WiFi ▄▄ (notice required)

CORTON
Map 4 ST94

The Dove Inn ★★★★ INN ◉ `PICK OF THE PUBS`

tel: 01985 850109 **BA12 0SZ**
email: info@thedove.co.uk **web:** www.thedove.co.uk
dir: *5m SE of Warminster. Exit A36 to Corton*

Pub in the heart of the countryside

Squirreled away in the delightful Wylye Valley, this bustling 19th-century pub guarantees a warm welcome. Many original features are still in evidence such as the striking central fireplace and flagstone and oak floors. The appealing menu is based firmly on West Country produce, with many ingredients coming from just a few miles away. Popular lunchtime bar snacks give way to a full evening carte featuring well-made and hearty pub classics. Typical starters include asparagus wrapped with Parma ham, topped with mozzarella and balsamic glaze; and classic prawn cocktail sundae. These might be followed by chicken Caesar salad or beef Stroganoff. Fish and chips, and the famous Dove burger and chips are available to take away, traditionally wrapped in newspaper. Children get to choose from their own menu. The spacious garden is the perfect spot for barbecues or a drink on summer days while the bedrooms arranged around a courtyard make The Dove an ideal touring base.

Open all day all wk **Food** Lunch all wk 12-2.30 Dinner all wk 6-9 Restaurant menu available all wk ⊕ FREE HOUSE ◀ Otter Bitter, Timothy Taylor Landlord, Sharp's Doom Bar, Guest ale Ò Aspall. **Facilities** Non-diners area ❧ (Bar Garden) ◀↑ Children's menu Children's portions Garden ⊨ Parking WiFi ▄▄ (notice required) **Rooms** 13

CRICKLADE
Map 5 SU09

The Red Lion Inn ★★★★ INN ◉

tel: 01793 750776 **74 High St SN6 6DD**
email: info@theredlioninncricklade.co.uk **web:** www.theredlioninncricklade.co.uk
dir: *M4 junct 15, A419 towards Cirencester. Left onto B4040 into Cricklade. Right at T-junct (mini rdbt) into High St. Inn on right*

On-site microbrewery and Saddleback pigs

Just off the Thames Path as it passes through historic Cricklade, this early 17th-century pub retains many historic features. Hop Kettle microbrewery in a barn behind the pub adds to the line-up of real ales and ciders, including Wadworth 6X and Mates Jackdaw. Home-prepared restaurant food is noteworthy for using locally foraged and wild ingredients, rare-breed meats and sustainable fish. Customers can even swap fruit and veg from their gardens for vouchers towards food and drink. Opt for chicken liver parfait, breast of Cold Aston pheasant, and rhubarb and pistachio Eton Mess.

Open all day all wk **Food** Lunch Mon-Sat 12-2.30, Sun 12-3 Dinner Mon-Thu 6.30-9 Restaurant menu available Tue-Sat evenings ⊕ FREE HOUSE ◀ Hop Kettle North Wall, Wadworth 6X, Ninkasi Tricerahops Double IPA Ò Mates Ravens Roost & Jackdaw. ☕ 9 **Facilities** Non-diners area ❧ (Bar Garden) ◀↑ Children's menu Children's portions Garden ⊨ Beer festival WiFi **Rooms** 5

PICK OF THE PUBS

The Fox and Hounds

EAST KNOYLE   Map 4 ST83

tel: 01747 830573
The Green SP3 6BN
email: fox.hounds@virgin.net
web: www.foxandhounds-eastknoyle.
co.uk
dir: *From A303 follow Blandford/East
Knoyle signs onto A350, follow brown
pub signs*

Traditional pub with lovely views

This partly thatched and half-timbered,
rustic 15th-century inn makes the most
of its stunning Blackmore Vale location.
There are exceptional views from the
patio beer garden and nearby East
Knoyle village green across these
Wiltshire and Dorset boundary-lands,
where Sir Christopher Wren was born
and the family of Jane Seymour (Henry
VIII's third wife) were based. Hidden in a
timeless village on a greensand ridge,
the engaging exterior is well matched by
the atmospheric interior, with lots of
flagstone flooring, wood-burning fires
and restful stripped wood furniture.
Locals eager to partake of Thatchers
Cheddar Valley cider or Hop Back Crop
Circle rub shoulders with diners keen to
make the acquaintance of the eclectic
menu. Blackboard menus increase the
choice, dependant entirely on the
availability of the freshest local fare.
Starters might include deep-fried
rosemary and garlic-crusted brie
wedges with cranberry jelly or tempura

battered king prawns with sweet chilli
dip. When it comes to main courses,
good, wholesome pub grub like fish pie;
chicken pie with chips and vegetables
and home-made sausages, mash and
gravy share the board with lamb shank
braised in red wine; slow-roasted belly
pork with an apple and cider sauce;
duck breast with damson sauce and
spring onion mash; or Thai green curry
with lemongrass-scented jasmine rice.
Stone-baked pizzas from a clay oven
and a comprehensive children's menu
add to the fray, whilst desserts include
fresh Dorset apple cake with golden
syrup and cream or chocolate and
raspberry tart with mascarpone cream.
There is also a gluten-free chocolate
fondant and ice cream.

Open all wk 11.30-3 5.30-11 **Food** all
wk 12-2.30 6-9 ⊕ FREE HOUSE ◀ Hop
Back Crop Circle & Summer Lightning,
Plain Ales Sheep Dip, Adnams
Broadside, Palmers Dorset Gold, St
Austell Tribute, Butcombe ⓞ Thatchers
Cheddar Valley. **Facilities** ✿ (Bar
Restaurant Garden)
👫 Children's menu Garden Parking WiFi
🚐 (notice required)

CRUDWELL
Map 4 ST99

The Potting Shed

tel: 01666 577833 **The Street SN16 9EW**
email: bookings@thepottingshedpub.com
dir: On A429 between Malmesbury & Cirencester

A warm welcome awaits at this dining pub

Dogs and children are welcome at this Cotswold dining pub, which prides itself on offering good bitter, interesting wine and a mix of creative and British food. Light pastel shades and beams scrubbed down to their natural hue characterise the appealing interior, where typical dishes include guinea fowl goujons, garlic aïoli, blood orange and hazelnut salad; venison and juniper meatballs, rosemary flatbread and herb citrus couscous; home-made chocolate fudge cake and blueberry ice cream. Food and drink can be served outside; two acres of grounds allow plenty of space for lawns, fruit trees and vegetable plots which supply fresh produce for the kitchen.

Open all day all wk **Food** Lunch Mon-Sat 12-2.30, Sun 12-3 Dinner Mon-Sat 7-9.30, Sun 7-9 ⊕ ENTERPRISE INNS ◀ Butcombe Bitter, Bath Ales Gem, Timothy Taylor Landlord ♂ Thatchers, Bath Ciders Bounders. ₱ 25 **Facilities** Non-diners area ✿ (Bar Restaurant Garden) ♦ Children's portions Garden ⊨ Beer festival Parking WiFi ➡ (notice required)

DEVIZES
Map 4 SU06

The Raven Inn

tel: 01380 828271 **Poulshot Rd SN10 1RW**
email: theraveninnpoulshot@yahoo.co.uk
dir: A361 from Devizes towards Trowbridge, left at Poulshot sign

A warm welcome and ever changing menus of home-cooked food

Worth noting if walking the Kennet & Avon Canal towpath or visiting the famous Caen Hill flight of locks, as this half-timbered 18th-century pub is just a short walk away. Divert for tip-top Wadworth ales and the weekly-changing menu, which offers a mixture of modern pub classics and more imaginative dishes. Expect to find ham, egg and chips; steak and kidney pie; and the Raven burger alongside Nasi Goreng and grilled sole with lemon and parsley butter. Leave room for warm sticky toffee pudding or pear and almond tart. The pub is dog friendly.

Open 11.30-2.30 6-11 (Sun 12-3 6-10) Closed Sun eve & Mon (Oct-Etr) **Food** Lunch all wk 12-2 Dinner all wk 6.30-9 Av main course £10.95 ⊕ WADWORTH ◀ 6X, Henry's Original IPA, Horizon, Old Timer ♂ Thatchers Gold. ₱ 12 **Facilities** Non-diners area ✿ (Bar Garden) ♦ Children's menu Children's portions Garden ⊨ Beer festival Parking WiFi ➡ (notice required)

DONHEAD ST ANDREW
Map 4 ST92

The Forester
PICK OF THE PUBS

tel: 01747 828038 **Lower St SP7 9EE**
email: possums1@btinternet.com
dir: From Shaftesbury on A30 towards Salisbury. In approx 4.5m left, follow village signs

Traditional pub specialising in West Country seafood

Describing itself as very dog friendly, this lovely 15th-century pub is an ideal place to put your feet up after a long walk with your best friend. Close to Wardour Castle in a pretty village, The Forester has warm stone walls, a thatched roof, original beams and an inglenook fireplace. An extension houses a restaurant plus a restaurant/meeting room, with double doors opening on to the lower patio area. The pub has a reputation for excellent cuisine at reasonable prices, and for its use of fresh West Country ingredients, especially seafood. Dishes are constructed with a mix of traditional and cosmopolitan flavours, so expect the likes of grilled Brixham sardine fillets with toast, olives, tomatoes and chorizo; zuppa de pescatore of

Brixham and Cornish fish with aïoli; and Style Farm beef in a stew with herb dumplings. An artisan cheeseboard, in-house ice creams and sorbets, and traditional desserts complete the mouthwatering menu.

Open 12-2 6.30-11 Closed 25-26 Dec, Sun eve **Food** Lunch all wk 12-2 Dinner Mon-Sat 7-9 Av main course £7.50-£13.50 Set menu available ⊕ FREE HOUSE ◀ Butcombe, Otter ♂ Westons Wyld Wood Organic. ₱ 15 **Facilities** Non-diners area ✿ (Bar Restaurant Garden) ♦ Children's menu Children's portions Garden ⊨ Parking WiFi ➡ (notice required)

EAST CHISENBURY
Map 5 SU15

Red Lion Freehouse ★★★★★ INN

tel: 01980 671124 **SN9 6AQ**
email: enquiries@redlionfreehouse.com **web:** www.redlionfreehouse.com
dir: From A303 take A345 N. Exit at Enford. Left at T-junct towards East Chisenbury. Pub 1m on right

Excellent food in rural village pub

A thatched building dating back to Tudor times, the Red Lion started life as a beer house run by Mrs Weeks. On the edge of Salisbury Plain and with fishing rights on the River Avon, the pub attracts country sports enthusiasts, not to mention locals tempted by guest ales and excellent food. Owned by two chefs with a background in top restaurants, everything is made on the premises using prime seasonal ingredients. You could start with warm crab tart; continue with roast rib of Wiltshire beef and end with Valrhona chocolate terrine. Early May Bank Holiday beer festival.

Open all day all wk **Food** Lunch all wk 12.30-2.30 Dinner Mon-Sat 6.30-9, Sun 6-8 Set menu available ⊕ FREE HOUSE ◀ Guest ales ♂ Ty Gwyn, Black Rat, Perry's. ₱ 10 **Facilities** Non-diners area ✿ (Bar Restaurant Garden) ♦ Children's portions Garden ⊨ Beer festival Parking WiFi **Rooms** 5

EAST KNOYLE
Map 4 ST83

The Fox and Hounds
PICK OF THE PUBS

See Pick of the Pubs on opposite page

EBBESBOURNE WAKE
Map 4 ST92

The Horseshoe
PICK OF THE PUBS

tel: 01722 780474 **Handley St SP5 5JF**
dir: Phone for detailed directions

Well-kept beers and home-made food

Dating from the 17th century, the family-run Horseshoe is a genuine old English pub in the pretty village of Ebbesbourne Wake. The original building has not changed much, except for a conservatory extension to accommodate more diners, and there's a lovely flower-filled garden. Beyond the climbing roses are two rooms adorned with simple furniture, old farming implements and country bygones, linked to a central servery where well-kept cask-conditioned ales are dispensed straight from their barrels – Bowman Swift One, Otter Bitter and Palmers Copper – plus real ciders too. Good-value traditional bar food is offered from a varied menu. Freshly prepared from local produce, dishes include local faggots in onion gravy; ham, egg and chips; lamb hotpot; and lunchtime sandwiches. The home-made pies are a firm favourite – venison and mushroom; chicken, ham and mushroom; steak and kidney; and game. Ice creams are provided by Buttercup Ice Cream in Wardour.

Open 12-3 6.30-11 (Sun 12-4) Closed 26 Dec, Sun eve & Mon L **Food** Lunch Tue-Sat 12-2 Dinner Tue-Sat 7-9 Set menu available Restaurant menu available Tue-Sat evening ⊕ FREE HOUSE ◀ Otter Bitter, Bowman Ales Swift One, Palmers Copper Ale, Guest ales ♂ Thatchers Gold, Wessex Cider. **Facilities** Non-diners area ✿ (Bar Garden) ♦ Children's portions Play area Garden ⊨ Parking

EDINGTON
Map 4 ST95

The Three Daggers ★★★★★ INN

tel: 01380 830940 **Westbury Rd BA13 4PG**
email: hello@threedaggers.co.uk **web:** www.threedaggers.co.uk
dir: *A36 towards Warminster, A350 to Westbury, A303 to Edington*

Where locally sourced meals are kept simple

Opened as the Paulet Arms in 1750 by Harry Paulet, the Lord of Edington Manor, locals quickly christened it the Three Daggers, after the family's coat of arms. It has always been well known for its friendly atmosphere, for enjoying a good meal, and for its accommodation, as today's five AA stars and a Dinner Award demonstrate. In the evening look for fish pie; roast halibut; butternut squash and goats' cheese tart; or bacon cheeseburger with pickled cucumber chutney. Next door there is a farm shop selling locally sourced products, and also a microbrewery with a viewing gallery.

Open all day all wk 8am-11pm **Food** Lunch Mon-Sat 12-2.30, Sun 12-8.30 Dinner Mon-Thu 6-9, Fri-Sat 6-9.30, Sun 12-8.30 ⊕ FREE HOUSE ◀ Daggers Ale, Blonde, Stab & Edge ♂ Lilley's Apples & Pears, Pheasant Plucker, Westons Stowford Press. ♀ 14 **Facilities** Non-diners area ♣ (Bar Garden) ♦️ Children's menu Children's portions Play area Garden ⋒ Beer festival Cider festival Parking WiFi ⇌ (notice required) **Rooms** 3

FONTHILL GIFFORD
Map 4 ST93

The Beckford Arms
PICK OF THE PUBS

See Pick of the Pubs on opposite page

FOXHAM
Map 4 ST97

NEW The Foxham Inn ★★★★ INN ❀

tel: 01249 740665 **SN15 4NQ**
email: info@thefoxhaminn.co.uk **web:** www.thefoxhaminn.co.uk
dir: *M4 junct 17, B4122 (signed Sutton Benger). Onto B4069, through Sutton Benger. Right signed Foxham*

Excellent Wiltshire countryside dining inn

This compact brick-built inn stands in a rural village close to the resurgent Wiltshire and Berkshire Canal. Real ales from the local Ramsbury brewery flow from the bar, but it's for the excellent cuisine created by Neil Cooper that customers beat a path to the door. The accomplished menu has received one AA-Rosette; the extensive range of dishes sweeps from Cornish smoked haddock chive and parmesan omelette starter to mains such as saddle of rabbit, rabbit shoulder strudel, curly kale and creamy Marlborough sauce, with equally fulfilling sweets to finish. Accommodation allows diners to rest easy after a classy repast.

Open 12-3 7-11 (Sun 12-3 7-10.30) Closed 1st 2wks Jan, Mon **Food** Lunch Tue-Sun 12-2 Dinner Tue-Sun 7-9.30 Av main course £12 Set menu available ⊕ FREE HOUSE ◀ Butcombe, Ramsbury ♂ Ashton Press. ♀ 10 **Facilities** ♣ (Bar Outside area) ♦️ Children's menu Children's portions Outside area ⋒ Parking WiFi ⇌ (notice required) **Rooms** 2

FROXFIELD
Map 5 SU26

The Pelican Inn

tel: 01488 682479 **Bath Rd SN8 3JY**
email: enquiries@pelicaninn.co.uk **web:** www.pelicaninn.co.uk
dir: *On A4 midway between Marlborough & Hungerford*

Fresh food cooked well at this A4 inn

This 17th-century, roadside inn has been serving the needs of locals and travellers alike for over three centuries. Being only 300 yards from the Kennet & Avon Canal, it is also a popular refuelling stop for walkers, cyclists and the boating fraternity. Expect Otter Bitter and local guest ales on tap, a raft of wines by the glass, and locally sourced food. The menu offers traditional pub favourites such as steak and ale pie; roasted chicken breast filled with mushrooms and pancetta; local pork sausages and mash.

Open all day all wk 11-11 (Sun 12-10) **Food** Lunch all wk 12-9 Dinner all wk 12-9 ⊕ FREE HOUSE ◀ Otter Bitter, Guest ales. ♀ 9 **Facilities** Non-diners area ♣ (Bar Garden) ♦️ Children's menu Garden ⋒ Parking WiFi ⇌ (notice required)

GREAT CHEVERELL
Map 4 ST95

The Bell Inn
PICK OF THE PUBS

tel: 01380 813277 **High St SN10 5TH**
email: gary06weston@aol.com
dir: *From Salisbury take A360 towards Devizes, through West Lavington, 1st left after black & yellow striped bridge onto B3098. Right to Great Cheverell*

A very popular community pub

Apparently mentioned in the Domesday Book, in far more recent times – namely the 18th century – The Bell became a drovers' inn. Free-house status enables Gary and Lou Weston to offer Sharp's Doom Bar, Wadworth 6X and a guest ale in the log-fired bar, while home-cooked food is served in the elegant, oak-beamed restaurant. Starters include two types of meze – Mediterranean, with marinated olives, roasted artichoke and sun-dried tomatoes; and seafood, with breaded king prawns, whitebait and calamari. Main courses include pan-fried halibut; slow-roasted lamb shank; and local venison sausages. Finish a 24oz rump steak and earn a free dessert, most likely Marshfield Farm ice cream, rather than sticky toffee pudding. Pub classics like chicken tikka masala, and wholetail scampi also feature on the menu. The secluded garden and patio are well provided with seating.

Open all wk 12-2 6-9 **Food** Lunch all wk 12-2 Dinner all wk 6-9 ⊕ FREE HOUSE ◀ Wadworth 6X, IPA, Sharp's Doom Bar, Guest ale ♂ Westons Stowford Press. ♀ 16 **Facilities** Non-diners area ♦️ Children's menu Children's portions Garden Parking WiFi ⇌

PICK OF THE PUBS

The Beckford Arms

FONTHILL GIFFORD　　　**MAP 4 ST93**

tel: 01747 870385 **SP3 6PX**
email: info@beckfordarms.com
web: www.beckfordarms.com
dir: *From A303 follow Fonthill Bishop sign. At T-junct in village right, 1st left signed Fonthill Gifford. Through Fonthill Estate arch to pub*

Excellent food in elegant coaching inn with lovely garden

Just three minutes from the A303, this handsome 18th-century coaching inn is set on the edge of the beautiful rolling parkland of Lord Margadale's 10,000-acre Fonthill Estate. Once a stopping point for weary travellers on the way from London to the South West, this elegant dining pub is now a destination in its own right. You can eat wherever you want, either in the main bar with its huge fireplace and parquet floor or in the separate restaurant. In summer, head out into the rambling garden where hammocks hang between the trees, you can play pétanque and children can do what children do. In winter the huge open fire in the bar is used to spit-roast suckling pigs and warm mulled wine. Whatever the season, Keystone's Beckford Phoenix real ale is a permanent fixture in the bar, with other beers on tap including Dorset Piddle's Jimmy Riddle. Sheppy's is one of the real ciders on draught and there are 12 wines available by the

glass including the Fonthill Glebe, a local crisp white wine. Choosing from the daily-changing menu could prove pleasantly tricky: for example, do you start with salad of Wiltshire pigeon, mushrooms, smoked bacon and hazelnuts, or Homewood ewes' cheese and beetroot salad with a port glaze? Then there are the mains: pan-fried Skrei cod with saffron and crab risotto, samphire and chorizo butter; Creedy Carver duck breast, braised salsify, Russian kale and sautéed potatoes; or pearl barley risotto with blushed tomatoes and Rosary goats' cheese. Among the bar meals are a ploughman's and the signature Beckford beef burger. Either way, leave room for the vanilla rice pudding and raspberry jam.

Open all day all wk **Food** Lunch all wk 12-2.30 Dinner served all wk 6-9.30 Av main course £12 ⊞ FREE HOUSE ◀ Keystone Beckford Phoenix, Dorset Piddle Jimmy Riddle, Butcombe, Erdinger Ö Ashton Press, Westons Wyld Wood Organic, Sheppy's. ♈ 12 **Facilities** Non-diners area ♣ (Bar Restaurant Garden) ♙ Children's menu Children's portions Play area Garden ♬ Parking WiFi

HANNINGTON
Map 5 SU19

The Jolly Tar

tel: 01793 762245 **Queens Rd SN6 7RP**
email: jolly.tar@sky.com
dir: *M4 junct 15, A419 towards Cirencester. At Bunsdon/Highworth sign follow B4109. Towards Highworth, left at Freke Arms, follow Hannington & Jolly Tar pub signs*

Local ales and a spacious garden

It may be far from the sea, but there's a nautical reason for this former farmhouse's name – a retired sea captain married into the Freke family, who once owned it. Old timbers and locally brewed Arkell's ales are served in its two bars, making this pretty inn an appealing destination. All food on the daily menu is freshly prepared; a meal could take in crispy chilli squid with garlic mayo followed by home-made steak and ale pie with chunky chips. The conservatory restaurant overlooks the sun terrace and spacious garden, replete with a children's play area.

Open 12-2 6-11 (Sun 12-3 7-11) Closed Mon L (ex BHs) **Food** Lunch Tue-Sun 12-2 Dinner Mon-Sat 6.30-9, Sun 7-9 (closed 1st Sun every month for village quiz) ⊕ ARKELL'S ◄ 3B, Wiltshire Gold, Bees Organic, Guest ales ♂ Westons Stowford Press. ♀ 9 **Facilities** Non-diners area ❤ (Bar Garden) ⦁♦ Children's menu Play area Garden ⊭ Parking WiFi

HEYTESBURY
Map 4 ST94

The Angel
PICK OF THE PUBS

tel: 01985 840330 **High St BA12 0ED**
email: admin@angelheytesbury.co.uk
dir: *A303 onto A36 towards Bath, 8m, Heytesbury on left*

Dining pub in an upmarket village

In the valley of the River Wylye, Heytesbury was where First World War poet Siegfried Sassoon once lived. The Angel, a 17th-century coaching inn, is today very much a dining destination, where you can eat at a scrubbed pine table in the main, log fire-warmed, beamed bar, or relax in the lounge with a pint of Morland, or one of eight wines by the glass. In addition, there's a more modern restaurant and secluded courtyard garden. The lunch menu offers eggs Benedict and Florentine; smoked salmon and crayfish tartine; and cauliflower cheese with smoked bacon. Daily-changing main menus typically propose starters of devilled lamb's kidneys on toast; and scallop, bacon and gruyère gratin; followed by whole lemon sole, crayfish scampi and skinny chips; seared Creedy Carver duck breast stir-fry with plum sauce; and pie of the day.

Open all day all wk 11.30-11 (Sun 11.30-8) **Food** Lunch Mon-Sat 12-2.30, Sun 12-3 Dinner Mon-Sat 6.30-9.30 ⊕ GREENE KING ◄ IPA, Morland Old Speckled Hen ♂ Thatchers Gold. ♀ 8 **Facilities** Non-diners area ❤ (Bar Outside area) ⦁♦ Children's portions Outside area ⊭ Parking WiFi ▭

HINDON
Map 4 ST93

Angel Inn
PICK OF THE PUBS

tel: 01747 820696 **High St SP3 6DJ**
email: info@angel-inn-at-hindon.co.uk
dir: *1.5m from A303, on B3089 towards Salisbury*

Rustic charm meets urbane sophistication

Just minutes from the ancient mounds and henges of Salisbury Plain, this beautifully restored 18th-century coaching inn offers many original features: wooden floors, beams and a huge stone fireplace. Outside is an attractive paved courtyard with garden furniture, where food can be served in fine weather. Behind the bar are Sharp's and Timothy Taylor ales. The pine country-style tables and chairs, together with the day's newspapers, lend a friendly and relaxed atmosphere, while an eclectic mix of traditional and modern British dishes characterises the brasserie-style menu. Dishes are based on quality seasonal ingredients and prepared using classical French techniques. A typical starter is pheasant and bacon terrine; main courses could be Loch Duart salmon en croûte, or chicken supreme with white bean and chorizo stew. Lunchtime snacks are a ploughman's or Cajun chicken and cheese melt ciabatta. Desserts are on the blackboard, as are the day's specials.

Open all day all wk 11-11 (Sun 12-10.30) **Food** Lunch all wk 12-2.30 Dinner Mon-Sat 6-9.30, Sun 6-9 ⊕ FREE HOUSE ◄ Timothy Taylor Landlord, Sharp's, Harvey's ♂ Thatchers Gold. ♀ 14 **Facilities** Non-diners area ❤ (Bar Garden Outside area) ⦁♦ Children's portions Garden Outside area ⊭ Parking WiFi

The Lamb at Hindon ★★★★ INN ⊛
PICK OF THE PUBS

tel: 01747 820573 **High St SP3 6DP**
email: info@lambathindon.co.uk **web:** www.lambathindon.co.uk
dir: *From A303 follow Hindon signs. At Fonthill Bishop right onto B3089 to Hindon. Pub on left*

Traditional, warm and welcoming historic coaching inn

The stone-built Lamb began trading as a beer house in the 12th century; by the late 18th it had become a coaching inn and even in 1870 was still providing 300 horses daily for long-distance coaches. These days the inn retains plenty of old-time character, thanks to its inglenook fireplaces, flagstone floors, heavy beams, and period furnishings and paintings. Where better then for a pint of Butcombe, or a malt whisky from one of Wiltshire's largest selections? Lunch and dinner menus, recognised with an AA Rosette, are broadly similar, the main difference being sandwiches on the former. Otherwise, it's a case of choosing between, for example, main courses of chicken casserole with red wine, shallots, and salt pork and sage dumplings; 21-day-aged rib-eye steak; mushroom and three cheese Wellington; and treacle, orange and thyme roasted Wiltshire ham. Travellers caught in slow-moving traffic on the A303 nearby could easily be tempted to turn off for breakfast, morning coffee or lunch. The accommodation includes four-poster bedrooms.

Open all day all wk 7.30am-11pm **Food** Lunch all wk 12-2.30 Dinner all wk 6.30-9.30 ⊕ BOISDALE ◄ Young's Bitter, St Austell Tribute, Butcombe, Guest ale ♂ Westons Stowford Press. ♀ 10 **Facilities** Non-diners area ❤ (Bar Garden) ⦁♦ Children's menu Children's portions Garden ⊭ Parking WiFi ▭ (notice required) **Rooms** 19

HORNINGSHAM   Map 4 ST84

The Bath Arms at Longleat ★★★★ INN ◎◎
PICK OF THE PUBS

tel: 01985 844308 **BA12 7LY**
email: enquiries@batharms.co.uk **web:** www.batharms.co.uk
dir: Off B3092 S of Frome

Quirky but stylish country inn within the Longleat Estate

Built in the 17th century, The Bath Arms occupies a prime position at one of the entrances to Longleat Estate and the famous Safari Park. The building became a public house with rooms in 1732 called the New Inn; it was later renamed the Weymouth Arms, and became the Marquess of Bath Arms in 1850. An ivy-clad stone inn, it features two fine beamed bars – one traditional with settles, old wooden tables and an open fire, and a bar for dining. The Wessex Brewery furnishes the public bar with its much-cherished Horningsham Pride ale, while most food is sourced within 50 miles of the pub. Simple menus focus on quality produce, with minimal use of international influences and an emphasis on traditional preserving methods – smoking, curing, potting and pickling. The lunchtime menu has traditional favourites such as traditional fish and chips, chicken Caesar salad and rib-eye steak, but these belie the kitchen team's culinary expertise which has won two AA Rosettes - revealed in dinner dishes such as pan-fried fillet of sea bass, brown shrimps and white bean cassoulet; and roasted guinea fowl with fondant potato, mushrooms and bacon. Stylish accommodation is available.

Open all day all wk 10am-11pm (Sun 10am-10.30pm) **Food** Lunch Sun-Thu 12-9, Fri-Sat 12-9.30 Dinner Sun-Thu 12-9, Fri-Sat 12-9.30 ⊕ WESSEX BREWERY ◀ Horningsham Pride & Golden Apostle, Guest ales Ŏ Westons Stowford Press, Addlestones. ₹ 9 **Facilities** Non-diners area ❀ (Bar Garden) ♦ Children's menu Children's portions Garden ♬ Beer festival Parking WiFi ⬛ (notice required) **Rooms** 16

LACOCK   Map 4 ST96

The George Inn

tel: 01249 730263 **4 West St SN15 2LH**
email: thegeorgelacock@wadworth.co.uk
dir: M4 junct 17, A350, S, between Chippenham & Melksham

Step back in time at this historic gem

Steeped in history and much used as a film and television location, the beautiful National Trust village of Lacock includes this atmospheric inn. The George dates from 1361 and boasts a medieval fireplace, a low-beamed ceiling, mullioned windows, flagstone floors, plenty of copper and brass, and an old tread wheel by which a dog would drive the spit. Locals and visitors discuss the merits of the ale selection at the bar, while menus proffer a selection of steaks and flavoursome pies, with fish options among the summertime specials; finish with home-made bread-and-butter pudding.

Open all wk 11-3 6-11 (Fri-Sat 11-11 Sun 11-10.30) **Food** Lunch all wk 12-2.30 Dinner all wk 6-9 ⊕ WADWORTH ◀ 6X, Henry's Original IPA, Farmers Glory, The Bishop's Tipple, Blunderbuss, Horizon, Old Timer, Guest ales Ŏ Westons Stowford Press. ₹ 9 **Facilities** Non-diners area ❀ (Bar Garden) ♦ Children's menu Children's portions Play area Garden Parking ⬛

LOWER CHICKSGROVE   Map 4 ST92

Compasses Inn ★★★★ INN ◎   **PICK OF THE PUBS**

tel: 01722 714318 **SP3 6NB**
email: thecompasses@aol.com **web:** www.thecompassesinn.com
dir: On A30 (1.5m W of Fovant) 3rd right to Lower Chicksgrove. In 1.5m left into Lagpond Ln, pub 1m on left

Charming thatched inn amid beautiful rolling countryside

Situated in a tiny hamlet, an old cobbled path leads to the low latched door of this 14th-century inn. Step inside and you walk into a delightful bar with worn flagstones, exposed stone walls and old beams. Snuggle up to the large inglenook fireplace or relax in the intimate booth seating, perfect on a winter's evening. You can be certain to find three or four local real ales on tap, perhaps from Wiltshire breweries Plain or Stonehenge, and the wine list is comprehensive. Be sure to try the food: the kitchen team has won an AA Rosette for their seasonal dishes; these are chalked up on a blackboard because they change so frequently. Examples of starters are pan-fried pigeon breast salad, croutons and balsamic glaze. Main dishes could be pan-fried pollock with mussel and saffron linguine; or steamed vegetable pudding with parsley mash and mushroom gravy. Five bedrooms are also available.

Open 12-3 6-11 (Sun 12-3 7-10.30) Closed 25-26 Dec, Mon L Jan-Mar **Food** Lunch all wk 12-2 Dinner all wk 6.30-9 Av main course £15 ⊕ FREE HOUSE ◀ Keystone Large One, Stonehenge Spire Ale, Plain Inntrigue, Butcombe Ŏ Ashton Press & Still. **Facilities** Non-diners area ❀ (Bar Restaurant Garden) ♦ Children's menu Children's portions Garden ♬ Parking WiFi ⬛ **Rooms** 5

MALMESBURY   Map 4 ST98

NEW Kings Arms ★★★ INN

tel: 01666 823383 **29 High St SN16 9AA**
dir: M4 junct 17, A429 to Malmesbury. Follow town centre signs. Pub on left in town centre

Sixteenth-century coaching inn in a historic Cotswolds town

Close to Malmesbury Abbey, which was founded as a Benedictine monastery in the 7th century, the inn offers two very different bars, separated by a covered walkway: one is the residents' bar, within the Elmer Restaurant, while the other is the more contemporary Bar 29. The latter serves home-cooked meals throughout the day, including sausages and mash; pie of the day; fish and chips; omelettes; and the house speciality, double egg, Wiltshire ham and chips. There's live entertainment in the bar at weekends. The real ales - 3B and Wiltshire Gold - are from Arkell's, which owns the pub.

Open all day all wk **Food** Lunch all wk 12-2.30 Dinner all wk 6-9 Av main course £12 Restaurant menu available all wk ⊕ ARKELL'S ◀ 3B & Wiltshire Gold. **Facilities** Non-diners area ♦ Children's menu Children's portions Outside area ♬ Beer festival Cider festival Parking WiFi **Rooms** 12

MALMESBURY *continued*

The Smoking Dog

tel: 01666 825823 **62 The High St SN16 9AT**
email: smokindog@sabrain.com
dir: *5m N of M4 junct 17*

Peaceful town centre beer-garden retreat

At the foot of Malmesbury's pretty high street and handy for visiting the famous abbey here, this is a favourite with families, who appreciate the secure beer garden. The Cotswold stone inn is draped with hanging baskets, whilst inside the bar boasts a fine open fire, just the place to hunker down with a glass of Bath Ales Gem beer and consider a fulfilling menu boasting starters such as dolcelatte and walnut tortellini leading to mains covering most bases, from pork loin chop with sticky harissa sauce to roasted fig, blue cheese and prosciutto salad. A popular beer and sausage festival enlivens the Summer Bank Holiday weekend.

Open all day all wk 12-11 (Fri-Sat 12-12 Sun 12-10.30) **Food** Lunch Mon-Fri 12-3, Sat 12-9, Sun 12-8.30 Dinner Mon-Fri 6-9, Sat 12-9, Sun 12-8.30 ⊕ BRAINS ◀ The Rev. James, Bath Ales Gem, Guest ales Ⓞ Symonds. ☻ 11 **Facilities** Non-diners area ☻ (Bar Garden) ♦♦ Children's menu Children's portions Garden ☊ Beer festival WiFi

The Vine Tree   `PICK OF THE PUBS`

tel: 01666 837654 **Foxley Rd, Norton SN16 0JP**
email: tiggi@thevinetree.co.uk
dir: *M4 junct 17, A429 towards Malmesbury. Turn left for village, after 1m follow brown signs*

Former mill with great home cooking

This atmospheric pub used to be a mill; workers apparently passed beverages out through front windows to passing carriages - an early drive-through it would seem. These days, it is well worth seeking out for its interesting modern pub food and memorable outdoor summer dining. In the central bar a large open fireplace burns wood all winter, and there's a wealth of old beams, flagstone and oak floors. Ramblers and cyclists exploring Wiltshire's charms are frequent visitors, and the inn is situated on the official county cycle route. Cooking is modern British in style; you could nibble on marinated olives while making your choice of perhaps devilled lamb's kidneys with fried bread; boeuf bourguignon, creamed potatoes and parsley croutons; or salmon fillet en papillote with lemon beurre blanc. Many dishes are cooked on one of the Big Green Egg barbecues, such as the home maple-wood smoked duck breast. There are also great real ales and a terrific stock of wines, with a high number by the glass. In addition to the suntrap terrace, there's a two-acre garden.

Open 12-3 6-12 (Sun 12-4) Closed Sun eve **Food** Lunch Mon-Sat 12-2.30, Sun 12-3.30 Dinner Mon-Thu 7-9.30, Fri-Sat 7-10 ⊕ FREE HOUSE ◀ St Austell Trelawny & Tribute, Uley Bitter, Stonehenge Pigswill, Flying Monk, Guest ales Ⓞ Westons Stowford Press. ☻ 40 **Facilities** Non-diners area ☻ (Bar Restaurant Garden) ♦♦ Children's menu Children's portions Play area Garden ☊ Parking WiFi ⬛ (notice required)

| **MARDEN** | Map 5 SU05 |

The Millstream

tel: 01380 848490 **SN10 3RH**
email: themillstreammarden@gmail.com
dir: *6m E of Devizes, N of A342*

Peaceful alfresco options here

Set in the heart of the Pewsey Vale, The Millstream is an attractive village pub near Devizes. The large garden is a wonderfully peaceful spot for an alfresco drink or meal. Inside, the three fireplaces make for a cosy and romantic atmosphere in

which to sip a regional Thatchers cider and refuel with a bar snack or a light lunch of traditional ploughman's, or a cold roast beef and horseradish baguette. More substantial meal options include 8oz rib-eye steak, onion rings and peppercorn sauce; or wholetail Cornish scampi with salad and home-made tartare sauce.

Open all wk 12-3 6.30-11 **Food** Lunch all wk 12-2.30 Dinner all wk 6.30-9.30 Set menu available Restaurant menu available Mon-Sat ⊕ WADWORTH ◀ 6X, IPA, Horizon Ⓞ Thatchers Gold. **Facilities** Non-diners area ☻ (Bar Garden) ♦♦ Children's portions Play area Family room Garden ☊ Parking WiFi ⬛ (notice required)

| **MARLBOROUGH** | Map 5 SU16 |

The Lamb Inn ★★★ INN

tel: 01672 512668 **The Parade SN8 1NE**
email: thelambinnmarlboro@fsmail.net **web:** www.thelambinnmarlborough.com
dir: *E along High St (A4) turn right into The Parade, pub 50yds on left*

Flower-bedecked pub with home-cooked food

Overlooking Marlborough's impressively wide main street, this coaching inn dates from 1673. It's a dog-friendly and welcoming hostelry today, but the dining room, converted from the stable, is reputed to be haunted since a woman was killed when pushed down the stairs. Landlady and chef Jackie Scott uses prime local ingredients including Wiltshire beef, pork from farms close by, game in season, and herbs and berries from the hedgerows. Expect the likes of pigeon and wild mushroom pâté; and a home-made cassoulet of smoked ham, garlic sausage, lamb and duck.

Open all day all wk 12-12 **Food** Lunch all wk 12-2.30 Dinner Mon-Thu 6.30-9 ⊕ WADWORTH ◀ 6X, Guest ales. ☻ 10 **Facilities** ☻ (Bar Restaurant Garden) ♦♦ Children's portions Garden ☊ WiFi **Rooms** 6

| **MINETY** | Map 5 SU09 |

Vale of the White Horse Inn   `PICK OF THE PUBS`

tel: 01666 860175 **SN16 9QY**
email: info@valeofthewhitehorseinn.co.uk
dir: *On B4040 (3m W of Cricklade, 6m E of Malmesbury)*

Popular with the local community

An eye-catching and beautifully restored inn overlooking a large pond. Built in the early 1800s, the building's true history is something of a mystery, but it was registered by its current name in the 1881 census. Today, sitting under a parasol on the large raised terrace, it's hard to think of a better spot. The village bar is popular with the local community, drawn by a good selection of real ales and events such as skittles evenings, live music and quizzes. The ethos is to serve good home-cooked food at sensible prices. Upstairs, lunch and dinner are served in the stone-walled restaurant with its polished tables and bentwood chairs. The bar menu offers baguettes, ploughman's, nachos and daily specials. Most pub favourites will be found on the à la carte, ranging from chicken Caesar salad to home-made cottage pie and rib-eye steak. Mint chocolate chip cheesecake might tempt for dessert.

Open all wk 11.45-2.45 4.45-11 (Thu-Sat 11.45-11 Sun 11.45-10.30) **Food** Lunch all wk 12-2.30 Dinner all wk 6-9.15 ⊕ FREE HOUSE ◀ Cotswold Spring Stunner, Otter Bitter, Moles Best Ⓞ Westons Stowford Press, Pheasant Plucker, Broadoak. ☻ 10 **Facilities** Non-diners area ☻ (Bar Garden) ♦♦ Children's menu Children's portions Family room Garden ☊ Parking WiFi ⬛

NEWTON TONY
Map 5 SU24

The Malet Arms

tel: 01980 629279 **SP4 OHF**
email: info@maletarms.com
dir: *8m N of Salisbury on A338, 2m from A303*

Riverside inn ideal for a peaceful pint

Off the beaten track, in a quiet village on the River Bourne, this 17th-century inn was originally built as a dwelling house. Much later it became The Malet Arms after lord of the manor Sir Henry Malet. The pub is free of fruit machines and piped music, creating a peaceful atmosphere in which to enjoy local real ale, draught cider or a whisky. All the food on the ever-changing blackboard menu, from scampi to Thai chicken curry, is home cooked. Game is plentiful in season, often courtesy of the landlord. In fine weather you can sit in the garden where there is a children's play area. Look out for the beer festival in July.

Open all wk 11-3 6-11 (Sun 12-3 6-10.30) Closed 25-26 Dec, 1 Jan **Food** Lunch all wk 12-2.30 Dinner all wk 6.30-9.30 ⊕ FREE HOUSE ◀ Butcombe, Ramsbury, Stonehenge, Triple fff, Palmers, Andwell, Guest ales ♂ Westons Old Rosie & Stowford Press, Ashton Press. ⌾ 9 **Facilities** Non-diners area ♦️ Children's menu Play area Garden Beer festival Parking

NUNTON
Map 5 SU12

The Radnor Arms

tel: 01722 329722 **SP5 4HS**
dir: *From Salisbury ring road take A338 to Ringwood. Nunton signed on right*

South of Salisbury, popular with locals and visitors alike

Not far from Salisbury this is a popular pub in the centre of Nunton dating from around 1750. In 1855 it was owned by the local multi-talented brewer/baker/grocer, and bought by Lord Radnor in 1919. Bar snacks are supplemented by an extensive fish choice and daily specials, which might include braised lamb shank, pan-fried sea bass or Scotch rib-eye fillet, all freshly prepared. There is a summer garden with rural views to enjoy.

Open all wk 12-11 **Food** Lunch all wk 12-9 Dinner all wk 12-9 ⊕ FREE HOUSE ◀ Sharp's Doom Bar, Downton Quadhop, Rotating ales ♂ Thatchers Gold, Symonds. **Facilities** Non-diners area ♣ (Bar Restaurant Garden) ♦️ Children's portions Play area Family room Garden ⊼ Parking WiFi ▭

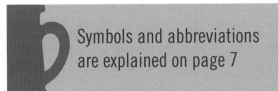

Symbols and abbreviations are explained on page 7

OGBOURNE ST ANDREW
Map 5 SU17

Silks on the Downs

tel: 01672 841229 **Main Rd SN8 1RZ**
email: silks@silksonthedowns.co.uk **web:** www.silksonthedowns.co.uk
dir: *M4 junct 15, A346 towards Marlborough. Approx 6m to Ogbourne St Andrew. Pub on A346*

Village pub with a horseracing theme

A mile north of the bustling market town of Marlborough can be found this pub, tucked away in rolling downland. The free house's name reflects the racing heritage of the Berkshire Downs (whose western boundary is on the border with Wiltshire). Framed silks of leading racehorse owners and jockeys adorn the walls and the pub offers local Ramsbury ales, fine wines and an informal dining experience. There are light meal options at lunchtime or classics like beer-battered fish and chips; and local rib-eye steaks. Sea trout gravad lax, and rump of lamb with colcannon are among the evening additions.

Open 12-3 6.30-11 Closed 25 & 26 Dec, Sun eve **Food** Lunch Mon-Tue 12-2, Wed-Sun 12-2.30 Dinner Mon-Tue 7-9, Wed-Sat 7-9.30 ⊕ FREE HOUSE ◀ Ramsbury Gold, Wadworth 6X, Smooth as Silk (pub's own) ♂ Aspall. ⌾ 11 **Facilities** Non-diners area ♦️ Children's menu Children's portions Garden ⊼ Parking WiFi

---

PEWSEY Map 5 SU16

The Seven Stars Inn

tel: 01672 851325 **Bottlesford SN9 6LW**
email: info@thesevenstarsinn.co.uk
dir: *From A345 follow Woodborough sign. Through North Newton. Right to Bottlesford. Pub on left*

Handsome thatched inn with seven acres of gardens

Close to two of Wiltshire's famous white horses, this 16th-century free house lies in the heart of the Vale of Pewsey between Salisbury Plain and the Marlborough Downs, and is a 15-minute drive from the stone circles of Avebury. The bar maintains its original character with low beams and oak panelling, and you can expect local Wadworth 6X, Ramsbury Gold and guest ales on tap. The menu of home-made, no-frills classics could list warm goats' cheese with beetroot, and walnut salad; followed by roast pork belly, ale-battered haddock, or grilled haloumi with summer vegetable salad.

Open 12-3 6-11 Closed Mon & Tue L **Food** Lunch Wed-Sun 12-3 Dinner Tue-Sat 6-9 Restaurant menu available Tue-Sun ⊕ FREE HOUSE ◼ Wadworth 6X, Ramsbury Gold, Guest ales ð Westons Stowford Press. **Facilities** Non-diners area ❖ (Bar Restaurant Garden) ⊙♦ Children's menu Children's portions Garden ⊼ Parking WiFi ◻ (notice required)

PITTON Map 5 SU23

The Silver Plough   PICK OF THE PUBS

tel: 01722 712266 **White Hill SP5 1DU**
email: info@silverplough-pitton.co.uk
dir: *From Salisbury take A30 towards Andover, Pitton signed. Approx 3m*

Friendly village pub on the fringes of the Salisbury Downs

Close to the cathedral city of Salisbury and ideally situated for visitors to Stonehenge, there's a timeless atmosphere to this English country inn. At its heart is an elaborately moulded old dark-wood bar from which diverge rooms and a snug with rustic furniture, ancient beams, log fires and rustic country-style decor, whilst hop festoons are a reminder that this is the place to get a reliable pint of First Gold or K&B Sussex from Hall & Woodhouse's Dorset brewery. Local produce is to the fore in the menu of pub favourites given a modern twist, such as a half rack of ribs slow-cooked with BBQ sauce or garlic and tarragon king prawns with hot ciabatta. Mains may feature oven-baked salmon fillet with herbed new potatoes, sautéed baby spinach and lemon butter sauce. There's a traditional skittles alley here, too, and the gardens offer views over the villages' thatched roofs.

Open all wk 12-3 6-11 (Sun all day) **Food** Lunch Mon-Sat 12-2, Sun 12-8 Dinner Mon-Sat 6-9, Sun 12-8 Av main course £10.95 ⊕ HALL & WOODHOUSE ◼ Badger Tanglefoot, First Gold & K&B Sussex, Guest ale ð Westons Stowford Press. ♀ 15 **Facilities** Non-diners area ❖ (Bar Garden) ♦ Children's menu Children's portions Family room Garden ⊼ Parking WiFi ◻ (notice required)

RAMSBURY Map 5 SU27

The Bell at Ramsbury ★★★★ INN ◉   PICK OF THE PUBS

See Pick of the Pubs on opposite page

ROWDE Map 4 ST96

The George & Dragon ★★★★ RR ◉◉   PICK OF THE PUBS

tel: 01380 723053 **High St SN10 2PN**
email: thegandd@tiscali.co.uk **web:** www.thegeorgeanddragonrowde.co.uk
dir: *1m from Devizes, take A342 towards Chippenham*

Fish and seafood a speciality

Narrowboaters from the nearby Kennet & Avon Canal enjoy coming here for a pint of Bath Gem, especially after navigating through the 29 locks of the Caen Flight. In 1917 the writer Edward Hutton said that Rowde had a 'curious inn'; since this Wiltshire village possessed four at the time, it's not known whether he meant this 16th-century hostelry. It is certainly interesting to note the Tudor Rose of Elizabeth I carved on the old beams in the cosy interior, where large open fireplaces, wooden floors, antique rugs and candlelit tables create a wonderful ambience. The two AA-Rosette restaurant specialises in fresh fish and seafood delivered daily from Cornwall: expect to find a starter like a simply grilled kipper with hot buttered toast, followed by the likes of whole grilled lemon sole; mackerel; or grilled skate wing with caper butter. Quality accommodation is provided in individually designed bedrooms.

Open 12-3 6.30-10 (Sat 12-4 6.30-10 Sun 12-4) Closed Sun eve **Food** Lunch Mon-Fri 12-3, Sat-Sun 12-4 Dinner Mon-Sat 6.30-10 Av main course £16.50 Set menu available Restaurant menu available all wk ⊕ FREE HOUSE ◼ Butcombe Bitter, Sharp's Doom Bar, Bath Gem, Fuller's ESB & London Pride, Ringwood Fortyniner ð Ashton Press. ♀ 10 **Facilities** Non-diners area ♦ Children's menu Children's portions Garden Parking WiFi ◻ **Rooms** 3

ROYAL WOOTTON BASSETT Map 5 SU08

NEW The Angel ★★★★ INN

tel: 01793 851161 **47 High St SN4 7AQ**
email: theangel.wbassett@arkells.com
dir: *M4 junct 16, A3102 towards Royal Wootton Bassett. At 2nd rdbt left signed Royal Wootton Bassett. Pub on right after lights*

Historic coaching inn with good food and local ales

Slap bang on the high street in Royal Wootton Bassett, this former coaching inn is now a contemporary establishment with traditional bar serving a range of Arkell's ales and an oak-panelled dining room showcasing local produce. Meat from named local farms and South Coast fish delivered daily are cooked on a charcoal grill that is the workhorse of the kitchen. Other options might be five-bean chilli; seafood tagliatelle; or cheese, spinach and parsnip roulade, with sandwiches served at lunchtime and throughout the afternoon, and Sunday roasts so popular that booking is recommended. Time a visit for the September beer festival.

Open all day all wk Closed 26 Dec & 1 Jan **Food** Lunch all wk 12-9.30 Dinner all wk 12-9.30 Av main course £9 Set menu available ⊕ ARKELL'S ◼ 3B, Moonlight & Wiltshire Gold ð Westons Old Rosie. ♀ **Facilities** Non-diners area ❖ (Garden Outside area) ♦ Children's menu Children's portions Garden Outside area ⊼ Beer festival Cider festival WiFi ◻ **Rooms** 17

PICK OF THE PUBS

The Bell at Ramsbury ★★★★★ INN

RAMSBURY Map 5 SU27

tel: 01672 520230
The Square SN8 2PE
email: thebell@thebellramsbury.com
web: www.thebellramsbury.com
dir: *M4 junct 14, A338 to Hungerford. B4192 (Swindon). Left to Ramsbury*

Village-centre pub in the picturesque Kennet Valley

Newly refurbished, this 17th-century coaching inn looks straight down Ramsbury's old High Street. Just outside, a lovely old tree provides shade for a couple of benches; on the wall of a building opposite, one of the AA's pre-war enamel road signs informs motorists that Marlborough is seven miles away, London 68. The bar - shown a photo you'd think it was someone's comfortable living room - serves Ramsbury real ales, brewed in nearby Aldbourne, and Lilley's cider, from Bath. The bar menu offers Mediterranean-style nibbles, and meals such as fish and triple-cooked chips, and a daily pie. The restaurant is led by head chef Duncan Jones, formerly running the kitchen at one of Marco Pierre-White's flagship restaurants, and now guardian of the Bell's AA Rosette for its modern British fine-dining heritage. Among the dishes you may well find on Duncan's concise but inventive menus are haunch and braised shoulder of Ramsbury Estate venison with celeriac and carrot

rösti, parsnip purée and seasonal vegetables; free-range tenderloin of pork with apple and black pudding hash, Savoy cabbage and bacon; and roasted fillet of plaice with tenderstem broccoli, capers, lemon and beurre noisette. It might continue with, say, blackberry Eton mess; cherry chocolate torte with caramelised croûtons and cherry ice cream; or plum sponge with ginger crème anglaise and caramelised plum. Children can have a half portion or even a dish without sauce if they want, although they do have their own small menu. High-chairs are available for toddlers. Breakfast, lunch, coffee and tea are served in the Bell's Shaker-influenced Café Bella. A mud room with welly washer declares the pub's popularity with ramblers.

Open all day all wk 12-11 (Sun 12-10)
Food Lunch Mon-Sat 12-2.30 Dinner Mon-Sat 6-9, Sun 6-8 ⊞ FREE HOUSE
◖ Ramsbury Bitter, Gold ◌ Thatchers Gold, Lilley's Apples & Pears. ◉ 12
Facilities Non-diners area ♥ (Bar Garden) ♦♦ Children's menu Children's portions Garden ⋈ Parking WiFi
Rooms 9

SALISBURY
Map 5 SU12

The Cloisters

tel: 01722 338102 **83 Catherine St SP1 2DH**
email: thecloisters83@gmail.com
dir: *In city centre, near cathedral*

A reputation for good honest food

Near the cathedral, the appropriately named Cloisters is a mid 18th-century pub. Its Victorian windows look into a beamed interior warmed by a pair of open fires. The choice of ales includes Hop Back Summer Lightning and a weekly changing guest ale. Thanks to a well-qualified chef, the menu will please everyone with its popular pub plates, from traditional fish and chips to ratatouille bake and the popular Cloisters beefburger, and the more modern dishes of penne pasta with chicken and pesto, and sea bass with mint, white wine and garlic. Booking is advised for the Sunday carvery.

Open all day all wk 11-10 (Thu-Sat 11am-mdnt Sun 12-10) **Food** Lunch Mon-Fri 11-3, Sat 11-9, Sun 12-9 Dinner Mon-Fri 6-9, Sat 11-9, Sun 12-9 ⊕ ENTERPRISE INNS ◀ Sharp's Doom Bar, Hop Back Summer Lightning, Guest ales. ♟
Facilities Non-diners area ◀ Children's menu Children's portions WiFi ➡ (notice required)

The Wig and Quill

tel: 01722 335665 **1 New St SP1 2PH**
email: theofficialwigandquill@yahoo.com
dir: *On approach to Salisbury follow brown Old George Mall Car Park signs. Pub opposite car park*

Charming old pub close to the cathedral

New Street is very close to the cathedral, whose superlative spire soars skywards just behind this traditional city pub. In the roomy, beamed bar with its open fires, flagstone and wooden floored, enjoy a pint of 6X or a guest cider. From the menu choose between trio of local sausages and mash; warm chicken and bacon salad; and scampi and chips. Try apple pie or hot chocolate fudge cake for dessert. Lying behind the pub is a sheltered courtyard garden for the summer months.

Open all wk 11am-close **Food** Lunch Sun-Fri 12-2.30, Sat all day Dinner Sun-Fri 5.30-9, Sat all day ⊕ WADWORTH ◀ 6X, The Bishop's Tipple, Henry's Original IPA & Horizon, Guest ales ♂ Westons Old Rosie, Thatchers, Aspall. ♟ 14
Facilities Non-diners area ♣ (Bar Restaurant Outside area) ◀ Children's menu Children's portions Outside area ➡

SEEND
Map 4 ST96

Bell Inn

tel: 01380 828338 **Bell Hill SN12 6SA**
dir: *On A361 between Devizes & Semington*

Historic village pub serving a wide range of food

This lovely red-brick pub in the pretty village of Seend has panoramic views of Salisbury plain and the Westbury Valley. The restaurant offers pub classics alongside an à la carte that could include slow-cooked sticky belly pork with stir-fried vegetables; local venison sausages and mash; or roasted butternut and sweet potato curry. Oliver Cromwell and his troops reputedly enjoyed breakfast at this inn in 1645 before attacking nearby Devizes Castle. Its other claim to fame is that John Wesley opened the chapel next door and preached against the 'evils' of drink outside the pub.

Open all wk 12-2.30 5.30-11.30 **Food** Lunch all wk 12-2 Dinner all wk 5.30-9 ⊕ WADWORTH ◀ 6X, Henry's Original IPA ♂ Westons Stowford Press.
Facilities Non-diners area ♣ (Bar Garden) ◀ Children's menu Children's portions Play area Garden Parking WiFi ➡

SEMINGTON
Map 4 ST86

The Lamb on the Strand

tel: 01380 870263 **99 The Strand BA14 6LL**
email: info@thelambonthestrand.co.uk
dir: *1.5m E on A361 from junct with A350*

Craft brews and interesting tapas

This popular dining pub began life as a farmhouse in the 18th-century, later developing into a beer and cider house. Today, customers can choose a real ale from the Wiltshire craft brewery Box Steam, or a cider from Westons. Food is freshly prepared from locally sourced ingredients, with an appetising choice of hot dishes and open sandwiches at lunchtime. The Wiltshire tapas menu offers an interesting mix of British and global treats: Downland's pigs in blankets; deep-fried calamari with garlic aïoli; and crispy spiced free-range chicken goujons being just three. Noisette of lamb, red wine and redcurrant reduction with creamy mash is typical of the modern British fare on the evening menu. Contact the pub for details of the beer festival.

Open all wk 12-3 6-11 **Food** Lunch all wk 12-3 Dinner all wk 6-9.30 Av main course £10 Set menu available Restaurant menu available all wk ⊕ FREE HOUSE ◀ Box Steam ♂ Westons Stowford Press, Thatchers. ♟ 15 **Facilities** Non-diners area ♣ (Bar Restaurant Garden) ◀ Children's menu Children's portions Play area Family room Garden ♬ Beer festival Parking WiFi ➡ (notice required)

SHERSTON
Map 4 ST88

The Rattlebone Inn

tel: 01666 840871 **Church St SN16 0LR**
email: eat@therattlebone.co.uk
dir: *M4 junct 17, A429 to Malmesbury. 2m after passing petrol station at Stanton St Quentin, turn left signed Sherston*

Lots of events and country bistro dining

Named after the legendary Saxon warrior John Rattlebone, who is said to haunt this 16th-century Cotswolds inn. A lively drinkers' pub with bags of character, it serves real ales from Butcombe, and Westons Wyld Wood organic cider. A bar snack highlight is the Rattlebone steak sandwich, while the carte proffers such starters as potted smoked haddock with cream, cheddar and a poached egg; and mains like braised chicken with lemon, smoked garlic mash and broccoli. Outside are three boules pistes, a beautiful skittle alley, and two gardens which host summer barbecues. Paella nights, a cider festival in July, an authentic curry festival, fish and game weeks in winter, and monthly live music are all fixtures in the pub's busy calendar.

Open all wk 12-3 5-11 (Fri-Sat 12-12 Sun 12-11) **Food** Lunch Mon-Sat 12-2.30, Sun 12-3 Dinner Mon-Sat 6-9.30 Av main course £11 Set menu available ⊕ YOUNG'S ◀ Bitter, Butcombe Bitter, St Austell Tribute ♂ Westons Stowford Press & Wyld Wood Organic, Thatchers Gold, Pheasant Plucker. ♟ 14 **Facilities** Non-diners area ♣ (Bar Garden) ◀ Children's menu Children's portions Garden ♬ Cider festival WiFi ➡ (notice required)

SOUTH WRAXALL
Map 4 ST86

NEW The Longs Arms

tel: 01225 864450 **BA15 2SB**
email: info@thelongarms.com
dir: *From Bradford-on Avon take B3109 towards Corsham. Approx 3m, left to South Wraxall. Left, pub on right*

Character pub in lovely village location

There are big stone flags on the floor of the bar, stools at the counter and wheelback chairs at tables all around. The overall effect is homely, the sort of place where you'd be happy to spend time with a Wadworth real ale or maybe a glass of prosecco. Among the modern British classics on the daily menus are duck leg with pink fir apple potatoes and samphire; game pie with mash and spring greens; and purple sprouting broccoli with Blue Monday cheese (made by Blur's Alex James), crispy polenta and brazil nuts. Relax in the walled garden, overlooked by ancient fruit trees.

Open 12-3.30 5.30-11.30 (Fri-Sun 12-11.30) Closed Closed 3wks Jan/Feb, Mon **Food** Lunch Tue-Thu 12-2.30, Fri-Sat 12-9.30, Sun 12-5 Dinner Tue-Thu 5.30-9.30, Fri-Sat 12-9.30 ⊕ WADWORTH ◀ 6X, Henry's Original IPA, Guest ales ♂ Thatchers. ♟ 8 **Facilities** ♣ (Bar Garden) ♦♦ Children's portions Garden ⊓ Parking WiFi ⊟ (notice required)

STOURTON
Map 4 ST73

Spread Eagle Inn ★★★★ INN
PICK OF THE PUBS

tel: 01747 840587 **BA12 6QE**
email: enquiries@spreadeagleinn.com **web:** www.spreadeagleinn.com
dir: *N of A303 off B3092*

In the beautiful setting of the Stourhead Estate

This charming 19th-century inn is in an enviable position right at the heart of the 2,650-acre Stourhead Estate, one of the country's most loved National Trust properties. Before or after a walk through the magnificent gardens and landscapes, there is plenty on offer here, including real ales brewed in a nearby village and traditional countryside cooking using produce from local specialists in and around north Dorset, west Wiltshire and south Somerset. Even the simple ploughman's is prepared with local bread with a Dorset Blue cheese or Keene's mature cheddar served with home-made chutney. In the restaurant, expect oven-baked Cornish sea bass fillets with parmesan mash; free-range tarragon-stuffed chicken suprême with Parmentier potatoes; and chef's crème brûlée to finish. The interior is smartly traditional, and in the bedrooms, antiques sit side by side with modern comforts.

Open all day all wk 9.30am-11pm **Food** Lunch all wk 12-3 Dinner all wk 7-9 ⊕ FREE HOUSE ◀ Wessex Kilmington Best, Butcombe, Guest ales ♂ Ashton Press. ♟ 8 **Facilities** ♦♦ Outside area ⊓ Parking ⊟ **Rooms** 5

SWINDON
Map 5 SU18

NEW The Runner

tel: 01793 523903 **Wootton Bassett Rd SN1 4NQ**
email: runninghorse@arkells.com
dir: *M4 junct 16, A3102 towards Swindon. At 2nd rdbt right signed town centre. Pub on right*

Popular edge-of-town family pub

Arkell's Brewery completely renovated the late 19th-century Running Horse in 2013, streamlining its name at the same time. Every Monday here is Steak Day, while lovers of chicken tikka masala, beef Madras and vegetable Thai curry should make a diary note for Tuesdays - Curry Day. A Lighter Bites menu offers filled baguettes, jacket potatoes and salads, while on Sundays two roasts are always available, as well as a selection of home-made desserts. There's a children's play area and plentiful parking, while on the River Rey, opposite the pub, Swindon's annual Duck Race is held at the end of May.

Open all day all wk **Food** Lunch all wk 12-8.30 Dinner all wk 12-8.30 Av main course £8.95 ⊕ ARKELL'S ◀ 3B & Kingsdown, Guest ale ♂ Westons Stowford Press. ♟ **Facilities** Non-diners area ♣ (Garden) ♦♦ Children's menu Children's portions Play area Family room Garden ⊓ Parking WiFi ⊟ (notice required)

The Weighbridge Brewhouse

tel: 01793 881500 **Penzance Dr SN5 7JL**
email: info@weighbridgebrewhouse.co.uk
dir: *M4 junct 16, follow Swindon Centre signs, then Outlet Car Park West signs*

Striking pub and brewery in former railway building

Built in 1906, the former Great Western Railway Weighhouse was transformed by experienced operator Anthony Windle into a stunning pub-restaurant concept, replete with microbrewery. Many original features have been retained and the old railway building boasts brick walls and lofty ceilings, with a vast bar at one end, dispensing the six home-brewed ales and 25 wines by the glass, and an airy, smart and very comfortable dining room at the other. Extensive monthly menus may deliver rack of lamb with red wine and rosemary sauce various home-made, seasonal fresh fish dishes; and interesting vegetarian options. Portions are very generous, so don't expect starters but, if you have room, there's chocolate fondant pudding to finish.

Open all day all wk Closed 25-26 Dec **Food** Lunch Mon-Sat 12-2.30, Sun 12-8.30 Dinner Mon-Sat 6-9.30, Sun 12-8.30 Av main course £15-£20 Restaurant menu available all wk ⊕ FREE HOUSE ◀ Brinkworth Village, Weighbridge Best, Antsally's, Pooley's Golden, Seasonal ales. ♟ 25 **Facilities** Non-diners area ♦♦ Children's menu Children's portions Outside area ⊓ Parking WiFi

TOLLARD ROYAL
Map 4 ST91

King John Inn
PICK OF THE PUBS

tel: 01725 516207 **SP5 5PS**
email: info@kingjohninn.co.uk
dir: *On B3081 (7m E of Shaftesbury)*

Stylish country pub with innovative modern menus

This handsome brick-built Victorian inn luxuriates in its location on Cranborne Chase, the heart of Thomas Hardy's Wessex deep in stunning countryside outside Shaftesbury. Named after the original hunting lodge built here for King John its airy, open-plan bar and dining areas have a fresh, crisp country feel, featuring rugs on quarry tile flooring, old pine tables, snug alcoves, warming winter log fires and a solid oak bar. Beers from Butcombe may feature, whilst the striking wine list offers 20 by the glass. Lunchtime dining offers a great choice of small-plate sharing options, akin to tapas. Dip in to green kale, clams and chorizo; or venison chop, beetroot and cavolo nero. In favourable weather an intriguing outdoor kitchen operates in the terraced garden. The inspiring, contemporary dinner menu ranges from starters like roast quail and mushroom sauce to mains of brill fillet with potato and bacon chowder, or venison and steak meatball linguine. Just room, perhaps, for apple doughnuts with toffee sauce and mulled cider to finish.

Open all wk 12-3 6-11 **Food** Lunch Mon-Fri 12-2.30, Sat-Sun 12-3 Dinner all wk 7-9.30 ⊕ FREE HOUSE ◀ Butcombe Bitter, Wadworth 6X, Guest ales ♂ Ashton Press. ♟ 20 **Facilities** Non-diners area ♣ (Bar Restaurant Garden) ♦♦ Children's portions Garden ⊓ Parking WiFi

UPPER WOODFORD

Map 5 SU13

The Bridge Inn

tel: 01722 782323 **SP4 6NU**
email: enquiries@thebridgewoodford.co.uk
dir: *From Salisbury take A360. Turn right for Middle Woodford & Upper Woodford. (Village between A360 & A345 5m N of Salisbury)*

Quiet riverside pub with large garden and modern British menus

On a quiet lane running along the west side of the broad Wiltshire Avon, this charming pub has a large, grassy garden running down to the wide sweep of the river. Seasonal starter choices might include crab toasties with smoked chilli jam; or smoked salmon, cream cheese and chive pâté. Appearing among the half-dozen winter menu mains could be butternut squash and spinach risotto with gremolata; fish pie with cheesy mash; home-made fishcakes with herbed fries; and 28-day-aged Stokes Marsh Farm rib-eye steak with chips. Diners can now watch the kitchen in action through the Theatre Kitchen window.

Open all wk 11-3 6-11 **Food** Lunch all wk 12-2.30 Dinner all wk 6-9 ⊕ ENTERPRISE INNS ◼ Hop Back Summer Lightning, Wadworth 6X, Butcombe Bitter ♂ Thatchers Gold. ☗ 10 **Facilities** Non-diners area ❤ (Bar Garden) ◗◗ Children's menu Children's portions Garden ⋈ Parking WiFi ▦ (notice required)

UPTON LOVELL

Map 4 ST94

Prince Leopold Inn ★★★ INN

tel: 01985 850460 **BA12 0JP**
email: info@princeleopold.co.uk **web:** www.princeleopold.co.uk
dir: *From Warminster take A36 towards Salisbury 4.5m, left to Upton Lovell*

Idyllic stream-side setting

Tucked away at the fringe of Salisbury Plain and named after Queen Victoria's youngest son, whose country retreat was nearby, this bustling village inn luxuriates in its enviable position beside the Wylye trout-stream and tree-dappled water

meadows. Those in the know sup on local microbrewery beers in the peaceful waterside garden, or perhaps repair to the traditional, part-panelled interior, period snug or airy contemporary lounge, where a well-balanced menu of pub favourites may include pork and mushroom pie, slow roast belly pork with cider sauce or wild mushroom and spinach lasagne. The restaurant room has relaxing views over the river.

Open all wk 12-3 6-11 Sat-Sun 12-11 summer (12-3 6-11 Sun 12-3 winter) **Food** Lunch Mon-Thu 12-2.30, Fri-Sat 12-3, Sun 12-4 Dinner Mon-Sat 6.30-9, Sun 6-8.30 ⊕ FREE HOUSE ◼ Butcombe, Fuller's London Pride, Otter Amber ♂ Thatchers Dry, Ashton Press. ☗ **Facilities** Non-diners area ❤ (Bar Garden) ◗◗ Children's menu Children's portions Garden Parking WiFi ▦ (notice required) **Rooms** 6

See advert on opposite page

WANBOROUGH

Map 5 SU28

NEW The Harrow Inn ★★★ INN

tel: 01793 791792 **SN4 0AE**
web: www.theharrowwanborough.co.uk
dir: *M4 junct 15, A419 towards Cirencester. Exit at next junct signed Cirencester & Oxford. Follow Wanborough sign from rdbt*

Great local produce showcased on the menu here

This handsome thatched inn retains plenty of original character including exposed beams and inglenook fire, the grate of which is Grade II listed. Parts of The Harrow date back to 1747 and beer was brewed on site for the next century. Brewing ceased in 1863 but the pub still offers a range of ales such as Otter Bitter, which can be enjoyed with enticing dishes such as spiced duck breast, cabbage and bacon, roasted apple and pomegranate jus; or rib of beef braised in ale and red wine with dauphinoise potatoes.

Open all day all wk **Food** Lunch all day Dinner all day ⊕ ENTERPRISE INNS ◼ Timothy Taylor Landlord, Otter Bitter ♂ Westons Stowford Press. ☗ 9 **Facilities** Non-diners area ❤ (Bar Garden) ◗◗ Children's menu Children's portions Garden ⋈ Parking WiFi ▦ (notice required) **Rooms** 3

WARMINSTER

Map 4 ST84

The Bath Arms

tel: 01985 212262 **Clay St, Crockerton BA12 8AJ**
email: batharms@aol.com
dir: *From Warminster on A36 take A350 towards Shaftesbury then left to Crockerton, follow signs for Shearwater*

Family- and dog-friendly pub on the Longleat Estate

Set on the Longleat Estate close to Shearwater Lake, this whitewashed country pub attracts locals, walkers and tourists. The garden has been landscaped to provide a pleasant spot for outdoor drinking and dining, and the Garden Suite, with views across the lawn, provides additional seating on busy weekends. Expect stylish food such as sticky beef with braised red cabbage; grilled salmon with fennel and rocket salad; and pork loin, parsnip mash and chorizo. Baguettes are also available.

Open all day all wk 11-3 6-11 (Sat-Sun 11-11) **Food** Lunch all wk 12-2 Dinner all wk 6.30-9 ⊕ FREE HOUSE ◼ Wessex Crockerton Classic & Potters Ale, Guest ales. **Facilities** Non-diners area ❤ (Bar Garden) ◗◗ Children's menu Children's portions Play area Garden ⋈ Beer festival Parking WiFi ▦ (notice required)

Prince Leopold Inn

Upton Lovell, Warminster, Wiltshire BA12 0JP • **Tel:** 01985 850460
Website: www.princeleopold.co.uk • **Email:** info@princeleopold.co.uk

The Prince Leopold is continuing to build on its stylish recent refurbishment & excellent reputation for great food and hospitable, welcoming service. The uniquely situated Riverside Restaurant facing directly onto the floodlit Wylye River offers a tranquil and delightful setting for any occasion, whether an

elegant meal or a wedding. The garden is very popular in warmer weather for pub meals or drinks in the sunshine, watching the trout jump, and sometimes even for guests to dangle their toes in the clear water! The bedrooms are clean, quiet and tastefully furnished, perfect for an overnight stay or restful break.

WARMINSTER *continued*

The George Inn

tel: 01985 840396 **Longbridge Deverell BA12 7DG**
email: info@the-georgeinn.co.uk
dir: *Phone for detailed directions*

A very popular spot on fine days

A 17th-century coaching inn overlooking the grassy banks of the River Wylye, The George Inn is a very popular spot on fine days. Food served in the traditional, oak-beamed Smithy Bar and in the two restaurants reflects the seasons, so beef and vegetable stew with horseradish dumplings, for example, is a typical winter dish. Other possibilities include black pudding Scotch egg with gooseberry and coriander chutney; pork, leek and chive sausages, mash and onion gravy; and game suet pudding; there's also a dedicated steak menu and Sunday carvery. One of the real ales – Deverill's Advocate – is brewed in the village and is always in demand at the pub's August beer festival.

Open all day all wk 11-11 (Sun 12-10.30) Closed 25 Dec fr 3, 26 Dec (1 Jan open 11-3) **Food** Lunch Mon-Thu 12-2.30, Fri-Sat 12-9.30, Sun 12-9 Dinner Mon-Thu 6-9.30, Fri-Sat 12-9.30, Sun 12-9 ◖ Wadworth 6X, Wessex Deverill's Advocate, John Smith's ♂ Thatchers Cheddar Valley. ♟ 11 **Facilities** ❧ (Bar Garden) ♦ Children's menu Children's portions Play area Garden ⊓ Beer festival Parking WiFi ▨ (notice required)

WHITLEY   Map 4 ST86

Marco Pierre White The Pear Tree Inn   PICK OF THE PUBS

tel: 01225 709131 **Top Ln SN12 8QX**
email: info@wheelerspeartree.com
dir: *A365 from Melksham towards Bath, at Shaw right onto B3353 to Whitley, 1st left*

Chic country pub big on steaks

From the flagstone floors to the grand open fires and quirky collection of agricultural artefacts, the farmhouse character of this village pub remains. The wisteria-clad stone inn epitomises the best of modern interior design, from the beautifully crafted furniture to the positioning of the stone ginger beer jars. Like other inns belonging to the celebrity chef, it offers a carefully selected worldwide wine list and The Governor ale, named after Marco's greyhound. Dine in the bar, restaurant or peaceful gardens and order from the newly-launched steakhouse-style menu, with 28-day aged grass-fed Scottish cattle providing a range of cuts, from 8oz fillet to a hearty 16oz T-bone. There is also a selection of enticing other main courses from the grill including breast of Gressingham duck; half a free-range chicken; and fillet of organic Severn & Wye salmon. Finish with Sicilian lemon sorbet or honeycomb ice cream

Open all day all wk bkfst-11pm **Food** Lunch Mon-Sat 12-2.30, Sun all day Dinner Mon-Sat 6-9.30, Sun all day ◖ JW Lees The Governor, Wadworth 6X, ♂ Thatchers Gold, Governor. ♟ **Facilities** Non-diners area ♦ Children's menu Garden Parking WiFi

WOOTTON RIVERS   Map 5 SU16

Royal Oak   PICK OF THE PUBS

tel: 01672 810322 **SN8 4NQ**
email: royaloak35@hotmail.com
dir: *3m S from Marlborough*

Pretty thatched pub, a favourite with walkers

This much expanded 16th-century thatched and timbered pub is perfectly situated for Stonehenge, Bath and Winchester and for exploring the ancient oaks of Savernake Forest. Only 100 yards from the Kennet & Avon Canal and the Mid-Wilts Way, it has an interior as charming as the setting, with low, oak-beamed ceilings, exposed brickwork and wide open fireplaces. In the bar you'll find Wadworth 6X and

perhaps guest local ale, Ramsbury Bitter. The menus cover all manner of pubby favourites, including home-made chicken liver and brandy pâté; roast topside of beef; and Wiltshire gammon, eggs and mushrooms. Other options include a starter of Iberico ham with artichokes and olives; followed perhaps by beef and Merlot casserole with dauphinoise potatoes; spicy bean tagine; or Savernake game and port pie. To finish, maybe peach and Amaretto trifle.

Open all wk 12-2.30 6-11 (Sun 12-10) **Food** Lunch Mon-Sat 12-2.30, Sun 12-8 Dinner Mon-Sat 6-9, Sun 12-8 Av main course £11 Set menu available ⊕ FREE HOUSE ◖ Ramsbury Bitter, Wadworth 6X, Local Guest ales ♂ Westons Stowford Press. **Facilities** Non-diners area ❧ (Bar Restaurant Outside area) ♦ Children's menu Children's portions Outside area ⊓ Parking WiFi ▨ (notice required)

WORCESTERSHIRE

BECKFORD   Map 10 SO93

The Beckford ★★★★ INN

tel: 01386 881532 **Cheltenham Rd GL20 7AN**
email: enquiries@thebeckford.com **web:** www.thebeckford.com
dir: *M5 junct 9, A46 towards Evesham, 5m to Beckford*

Cotswold country inn just off the A46

Midway between Tewkesbury and Evesham, this rambling Georgian country inn has the Cotswolds beckoning just to the east and shapely Bredon Hill rising immediately to the north. The Beckford is an enticing mix of contemporary comforts and traditional fixtures throughout the public areas and the comfortable bedrooms. A typical meal might include wild mushroom, herb and goats' cheese risotto; chicken fillet with creamy Dijon and shallot sauce with bubble-and-squeak; and sticky toffee pudding with fudge sauce and cream. Steaks and burgers are also on the menu.

Open all day all wk **Food** Lunch all wk 12-3 Dinner all wk 6-9.30 Av main course £10 ⊕ FREE HOUSE ◖ Fuller's London Pride, Courage Best Bitter, Wye Valley, Wickwar, Prescott, Goffs ♂ Westons Stowford Press. ♟ 14 **Facilities** Non-diners area ❧ (Bar Garden) ♦ Children's menu Children's portions Garden ⊓ Beer festival Parking WiFi ▨ (notice required) **Rooms** 10

BEWDLEY   Map 10 SO77

Little Pack Horse

tel: 01299 403762 **31 High St DY12 2DH**
email: enquiries@littlepackhorse.co.uk
dir: *From Kidderminster follow ring road & Safari Park signs. Then follow Bewdley signs over bridge, turn left, then right, right at top of Lax Ln. Pub in 20mtrs*

Homely old inn offering local beers and fabled pies

Close to an old ford through the River Severn, this timber framed inn tucked away in Bewdley's web of lanes has been catering for passing trade for over 480 years. It was a base for jaggers and their packhorses; the inside retains much character from those long-gone days, with cosy log fires and wizened beams. Today's time travellers can indulge in fine beers from the town's brewery and a range of ciders. Fulfilling fodder includes a wealth of pies - Desperate Dan Cow Pie with best Herefordshire beef for example - and savoury suet puddings: venison, port, cranberry and Shropshire Blue a feast in itself. Light bites cater for the less ravenous.

Open all wk 12-2.30 6-11.30 (Sat-Sun 12-12) **Food** Lunch Mon-Fri 12-2.15, Sat-Sun 12-4 Dinner Mon-Thu 6-9, Fri 6-9.30, Sat-Sun 5.30-9.30 Restaurant menu available all wk ⊕ PUNCH TAVERNS ◖ St Austell Tribute, Bewdley Worcestershire Way, Hobsons Town Crier, Holden's Black Country Special ♂ Thatchers Katy, Westons Stowford Press & Mortimers Orchard. ♟ 16 **Facilities** Non-diners area ❧ (Bar Garden Outside area) ♦ Children's menu Children's portions Family room Garden Outside area ⊓ Beer festival WiFi ▨ (notice required)

PICK OF THE PUBS

The Mug House Inn & Angry Chef Restaurant ★★★★ INN

BEWDLEY　　　　Map 10 SO77

tel: 01299 402543
12 Severnside North DY12 2EE
email: drew@mughousebewdley.co.uk
web: www.mughousebewdley.co.uk
dir: *A456 from Kidderminster to Bewdley. Pub in town on river*

Unrivalled riverside location

Although unusual as a pub name today, a 'mug house' was a popular term for an alehouse in the 17th century. The Severnside address is a strong clue to its location – right on that river, with just a narrow cobbled road and some river's edge seating between it and the pub's flower-decked frontage. Bewdley Brewery's Severn Way may be on duty at the bar alongside guest ales and regulars Timothy Taylor Landlord and Wye Valley HPA. Rosie's Pig cider offers a refreshing alternative, even during the May Day Bank Holiday beer festival held in the rear garden. The lunch time set menu comprises a tummy-filling range of crusty cobs, chunky sarnies such as the Mug Club (chicken, bacon, lettuce and tomato with garlic mayo), and doorstep butties overflowing with fish-and-chips or just chips. A range of Mug House platters is served with salad, coleslaw, sweet pickled onion rings, Mug House pickle and a warm cut baguette: choose between the likes of house-cooked roast beef; hot pork bangers; and smoked salmon with citrus and

chive mayonnaise. For those who enjoy a proper lunch, look to the list of mains and desserts, which all follow classic pub lines. The AA Rosette-standard Angry Chef (provenance unknown) restaurant comes into its own in the evening, offering seasonally-based dishes such as pan-fried pigeon breast with boxty pancakes; beetroot and pumpkin risotto; or spiced lamb rump with minted couscous, roasted shallots and butternut squash. Desserts may include the likes of apple and blackberry parcels; or steamed chocolate and pear sponge.

Open all day all wk 12-11 **Food** Lunch Mon-Sat 12-2.30, Sun 12-5 Set menu available Restaurant menu available Mon-Sat evening. ⊕ PUNCH TAVERNS ◀ Bewdley Worcestershire Way, Timothy Taylor Landlord, Wye Valley HPA, Guest ales ♂ Westons Rosie's Pig. ♀ 10 **Facilities** Non-diners area ♚ (Bar Garden) Garden ⋒ Beer festival WiFi **Rooms** 7

BEWDLEY *continued*

The Mug House Inn & Angry Chef Restaurant ★★★★ INN ⊛

PICK OF THE PUBS

See Pick of the Pubs on page 539

See Pick of the Pubs on page 539

Woodcolliers Arms ★★★ INN

tel: 01299 400589 **76 Welch Gate DY12 2AU**
email: roger@woodcolliers.co.uk **web:** www.woodcolliers.co.uk
dir: *3m from Kidderminster on A456*

17th-century free house with a Russian flavour

If you've never tried atbivnaya, you can at this 17th-century, family-run free house built into a hillside just across the river from the Severn Valley steam railway. Battered pork steak, it's one of the several dishes Russian chef Boris Rumba serves alongside largely locally sourced more traditional pub favourites, such as beef, chicken or mushroom Stroganoff (actually, this too is Russian in origin), sea bass fillet or steak. There's always a weekly-changing roll-call of local real ales on offer, and Herefordshire ciders. Comfortable accommodation includes the Secret Room, once blocked off and 'lost' for years.

Open all wk 5pm-12.30am (Sat 12.30-12.30 Sun 12.30-11) **Food** Lunch Sat-Sun 12.30-3 Dinner all wk 5-9 Av main course £12 Restaurant menu available all wk ⊕ FREE HOUSE/OLIVERS INNS LTD ◼ Ludlow Gold, Three Tuns 1642, Kinver Edge ○ Thatchers Gold & Heritage, Westons Old Rosie & Country Perry. ♇ 20
Facilities Non-diners area ♦ Outside area ⋒ Parking WiFi ➡ **Rooms** 5

▌ BRANSFORD

Map 10 SO75

The Bear & Ragged Staff

tel: 01886 833399 **Station Rd WR6 5JH**
email: mail@bearatbransford.co.uk
dir: *3m from Worcester or Malvern, clearly signed from A4103 or A449*

Continuing to build a good reputation for good food

Easily reachable from both Malvern and Worcester, this lovely old free house was built in 1861 as an estate rent office and stables. The current owners have created a reputation for good food and beers, such as Hobsons Twisted Spire (named after Cleobury Mortimer's parish church) and Sharp's Doom Bar. A typical meal might involve white crabmeat and crayfish tails, followed by braised brisket of Herefordshire beef. Blackboard specials include roast fillet of red bream. In addition to the bar and restaurant menus, there are weekend barbecues.

Open 11.30-2.30 6-10.30 (Fri-Sat 11.30-2.30 6-11 Sun 12-2.30) Closed 25 Dec eve, 1 Jan eve, Sun eve **Food** Lunch all wk 12-2 Dinner Mon-Sat 6.30-9 ⊕ FREE HOUSE ◼ Hobsons Twisted Spire, Sharp's Doom Bar ○ Westons Stowford Press. ♇ 10
Facilities Non-diners area ❀ (Bar Garden) ♦ Children's menu Children's portions Garden ⋒ Parking WiFi ➡ (notice required)

▌ BRETFORTON

Map 10 SP04

The Fleece Inn

PICK OF THE PUBS

tel: 01386 831173 **The Cross WR11 7JE**
email: info@thefleeceinn.co.uk **web:** www.thefleeceinn.co.uk
dir: *From Evesham follow signs for B4035 towards Chipping Campden. Through Badsey into Bretforton. Right at village hall, past church, pub in open parking area*

Ancient village inn with seasonal menus

The first pub to be owned by the National Trust, the Fleece was built as a longhouse in Chaucer's time and was owned by the same family until the death in 1977 of Lola Taplin – a direct descendant of the farmer who built it. A quintessentially English pub, the beautiful timbered building was nearly lost in a fire some 10 years ago; a massive renovation followed when its features and integrity were restored. Real ale devotees will admire one of England's oldest pewter collections as they order a pint of Uley Pigs Ear or Wye Valley Bitter; and cider lovers can try the home-brewed Ark cider. Families enjoy summer sunshine in the apple orchard while children let off steam in the play area. Food is well priced yet notches above pub grub, when treats such as asparagus feature in seasonal menus; wintertime sees the likes of game pudding; pork and leek casserole; and pan-fried lamb's liver. Ale and cider festival in October.

Open all day all wk Food Lunch Mon-Sat 12-2.30, Sun 12-4 Dinner Mon-Sat 6.30-9, Sun 6.30-8.30 ⊕ FREE HOUSE ◼ Uley Pigs Ear, Wye Valley Bitter ♂ Thatchers Heritage, The Ark. ☗ 20 Facilities Non-diners area ❀ (Bar Garden) ♦ Children's menu Children's portions Play area Garden ⊟ Beer festival Cider festival WiFi ▦ (notice required)

BROADWAY
Map 10 SP03

Crown & Trumpet

tel: 01386 853202 14 Church St WR12 7AE
email: info@cotswoldholidays.co.uk
dir: From High St follow Snowshill sign. Pub 600yds on left

Ideally placed for exploring the Cotswolds

Just behind the green in this internationally-known picture-postcard village is the Crown & Trumpet, a traditional, 17th-century, mellow-stone inn. The classic beamed bar is just the place for a pint of Cotswold Spring Codrington Codger, or Stanway Cotteswold Gold bitter, or you can take it out into the peaceful patio garden; a winter alternative is a glass of mulled wine or a hot toddy by the fire. Classic, home-made pub food is available at lunch and dinner - try devilled whitebait; venison sausages and mash; home-made Worcester pie; or faggots and chips. There's musical entertainment every Saturday evening, and weekly jazz and blues evenings. Booking for meals is recommended.

Open all wk 11-3 5-11 (Fri-Sat 11am-mdnt Sun 12-11) Food Lunch Mon-Fri 12-2.30, Sat-Sun 12-5 Dinner Mon-Fri 6-9.30, Sat-Sun 5-9.30 Set menu available ⊕ ENTERPRISE INNS ◼ Stroud Tom Long, Cotswold Spring Codrington Codger, Stanway Cotteswold Gold ♂ Black Rat, Black Rat Perry. ☗ 9 Facilities Non-diners area ❀ (Bar Garden) ♦ Children's menu Children's portions Garden ⊟ Beer festival Parking WiFi ▦ (notice required)

CLENT
Map 10 SO97

The Bell & Cross

PICK OF THE PUBS

tel: 01562 730319 Holy Cross DY9 9QL
dir: Phone for detailed directions

Good food near famous country park

Standing at the heart of a peaceful Worcestershire village, this character pub is the ideal culmination of a visit to the remarkable Clent Hills which rumble across the horizon just a mile from The Bell & Cross. Exploring the bald hills, wooded dingles and fabulous viewpoints can work up a healthy appetite; who better to help sate this than the former chef to the England football squad, host-patron Roger Narbett. Head for the bar for a rolling selection of hand-pulled beers and an inviting log fire in winter; the extensive garden, or the covered and heated patio for comfortable alfresco dining on cooler nights. The imaginative menu opens with a substantial range of starters and lite-bites such as Loch Fyne oak-smoked salmon with vodka chantilly, or farmhouse confit duck rillette with pineapple and cracked black pepper salsa. Enticing mains include slow cooked free-range belly pork with smashed apples, spring cabbage and cider sauce; or tandoori spiced salmon fillet, cucumber salad and lime mayo. Booking is recommended.

Open all wk 12-3 6-11 (Sun 12-10.30) Closed 25 Dec, 26 Dec eve, 1 Jan eve Food Lunch all wk 12-2 Dinner Mon-Sat 6.30-9.15 Set menu available Restaurant menu available all wk ⊕ ENTERPRISE INNS ◼ Marston's Pedigree & Burton Bitter, Timothy Taylor Landlord, Guest ales ♂ Thatchers Gold. ☗ 15 Facilities Non-diners area ❀ (Bar Garden) ♦ Children's menu Children's portions Garden ⊟ Parking ▦ (notice required)

NEW The Vine Inn

tel: 01562 882491 Vine Ln DY9 9PH
email: info@vineinnclent.com web: www.vineinnclent.com
dir: Phone for detailed directions

Cracking pub secluded in marvellous hill country

Tucked into one of the sharp valleys which cleave the glorious Clent Hills, The Vine started life as a watermill at the dawn of the Industrial Revolution. Reborn as a pub in 1851, beers from Adnams, supplemented by cider and perry fresh from the Malvern Hills reward ramblers challenging the mini-mountain range that are the Clents. Recover in the tranquil wood-side gardens behind the flowerbasket-hung pub and consider a tempting menu offering the likes of game pie; creamy champagne and chorizo chicken or a fish dish from the specials board, with fruit and nut crumble to finish.

Open all day all wk Food Lunch Mon-Fri 12-3, Sat 12-9.30, Sun 12-8 Dinner Mon-Fri 6-9, Sat 12-9.30, Sun 12-8 Av main course £11 Set menu available ⊕ PUNCH TAVERNS ◼ Thwaites Wainwright, Adnams Southwold Bitter ♂ Hogan's & Hogan's Perry, Thatchers Traditional. Facilities Non-diners area ♦ Children's portions Garden ⊟ Parking WiFi ▦ (notice required)

See advert on opposite page

DROITWICH

Map 10 SO86

The Chequers

PICK OF THE PUBS

tel: 01299 851292 **Kidderminster Rd, Cutnall Green WR9 OPJ**
dir: *Phone for detailed directions*

Charming pub run by ex-England soccer chef

Roger Narbett used to be the England football team chef; his soccer memorabilia can be found in the Players Lounge of this charming pub he now runs with wife Joanne. Its traditional look comes from the cranberry-coloured walls, open fire, church-panel bar and richly hued furnishings. Indeed, some might also make a case for including the range of real ales, such as Enville, Wye Valley HPA and Hook Norton in the bar, adjoining which is the country-style Garden Room with plush sofa and hanging tankards. The menus offer a wide choice, from sandwiches, deli platters and 'bucket food' to pub classics like faggots, mushy peas and cheesy mash. Among the top performers are grilled fillet of sea bream; Merlot-braised blade of Scottish beef; Malaysian chicken curry with sweet potato; and roasted pepper filled with parmesan risotto and Tuscan vegetables. How sorry England's finest must have been to see Roger go.

Open all day all wk Closed 25 Dec, 26 Dec eve & 1 Jan eve **Food** Lunch Mon-Sat 12-2, Sun 12-2 (light bites 2-5.30) Dinner all wk 6.30-9.15 Set menu available Restaurant menu available all wk ⊕ FREE HOUSE ◀ Enville Ale, Greene King Ruddles, Wye Valley HPA, Timothy Taylor, Hook Norton, Otter Bitter, Marston's EPA ♻ Thatchers Gold. ☗ 15 **Facilities** Non-diners area ♣ (Bar Garden) ♦♦ Children's menu Children's portions Family room Garden ⊼ Parking WiFi ▄▄ (notice required)

The Honey Bee

tel: 01299 851620 **Doverdale Ln, Doverdale WR9 OQB**
email: honey@king-henrys-taverns.co.uk
dir: *From Droitwich take A442 towards Kidderminster. Left to Dovedale*

Spacious, modern and friendly pub

Set in four and half acres of grounds, you can go fishing for carp in this pub's two lakes – and even have your meal brought to you. The garden also has a great play area for children and there is a patio for outdoor drinking and dining. The contemporary interior has plenty of areas in which to enjoy freshly prepared dishes which will satisfy small and large appetites alike. Choose from a good selection of steaks and grills, fish and seafood options like swordfish steak, traditional favourites such as half a roast chicken, and international and vegetarian dishes, perhaps vegetable fajitas.

Open all day all wk 11.30-11 **Food** Lunch all wk 12-10 Dinner all wk 12-10 Set menu available Restaurant menu available all wk ⊕ FREE HOUSE/KING HENRY'S TAVERNS ◀ Greene King Abbot Ale, Fuller's London Pride, Sharp's Doom Bar, Guinness. ☗ 15 **Facilities** Non-diners area ♦♦ Children's menu Children's portions Play area Garden Parking ▄▄

The Old Cock Inn

tel: 01905 770754 **Friar St WR9 8EQ**
email: pub@oldcockinn.co.uk
dir: *M5 junct 5, A449 to Droitwich. Pub in town centre opposite theatre*

Town centre pub with unusual stained-glass windows

Three stained-glass windows, rescued from a church destroyed during the Civil War, are a feature of this charming pub, first licensed during the reign of Queen Anne. The stone carving with a frog emerging from its mouth above the front entrance is believed to portray Judge Jeffreys, who is said to have held one of his assizes here. A varied menu, including snacks, platters and more substantial dishes – salmon with a sweet chilli coating; pasta with roasted vegetables and pesto; lamb chop trio; and bacon, egg and chips - is supplemented by the daily specials.

Open 12-11 (Mon 6-11 Fri-Sat 12-12) Closed 26 Dec & 1 Jan, Mon L **Food** Lunch Tue-Sat 12-2.30 Dinner Tue-Sat 6-9 ⊕ MARSTON'S ◀ EPA, Wychwood Hobgoblin,

Guest ales ♻ Thatchers Heritage. **Facilities** Non-diners area ♣ (Bar Garden) ♦♦ Children's portions Garden ⊼ WiFi ▄▄ (notice required)

ELDERSFIELD

Map 10 SO73

The Butchers Arms

tel: 01452 840381 **Lime St GL19 4NX**
dir: *A417 from Gloucester towards Ledbury. After BP garage take B4211. In 2m take 4th left into Lime St*

A real beer-lovers' pub with a concise menu

Dating from the 16th century this is a pub which values its beer-drinking customers. The low-ceilinged, wooden-floored bar offers a good choice of regional beers served from the cask and is the hub of local life (although, sorry, it's not for the under-10s). The seasonal menu may be small, but it sure offers diversity: for example, cider-braised pig's cheek with fried bantam egg and crackling to start; then turbot roasted on the bone with lobster ravioli, fried green beans and buttered chard; and Seville orange marmalade pudding and Drambuie custard to finish. A spacious garden adds to its charm.

Open 12-2 7-11 Closed 1wk Jan, 1 wknd Aug, 24-26 Dec, Sun eve & Mon (incl BHs) **Food** Lunch Fri-Sun 12-1 Dinner Tue-Sat 7-9 Av main course £25 ⊕ FREE HOUSE ◀ Wye Valley Dorothy Goodbody's Golden Ale, St Austell Tribute, Wickwar Sunny Daze. ☗ 11 **Facilities** Non-diners area Garden Parking

FAR FOREST

Map 10 SO77

The Plough Inn

tel: 01299 266237 **Cleobury Rd DY14 9TE**
email: info@nostalgiainns.co.uk
dir: *From Kidderminster take A456 towards Leominster. Right onto A4117 towards Cleobury Mortimer. Approx 0.5m to pub on left*

Top notch carvery operation in lovely countryside setting

The location in beautiful rolling countryside, the excellent range of locally brewed real ales, and one of the best carvery dining operations for miles draw local foodies to this family-owned, 18th-century coaching inn. It's also popular with walkers and cyclists, so arrive early to get the pick of the four roasted joints, perhaps leg of lamb, Far Forest venison, local pork and Scottish beef, all served with a choice of 12 vegetables. The gorgeous summer garden comes with its own bar.

Open all wk 12-3 6-11 (Fri-Sat 12-11 Sun 12-10) **Food** Lunch Mon-Fri 12-2, Sat 12-9, Sun 12-6 Dinner Mon-Fri 6-9, Sat 12-9, Sun 12-6 ⊕ FREE HOUSE ◀ Greene King Abbot Ale, Morland Old Speckled Hen & Old Golden Hen, Guest ales ♻ Aspall, Westons Stowford Press, Robinsons Flagon. **Facilities** Non-diners area ♦♦ Children's menu Children's portions Garden ⊼ Parking WiFi ▄▄ (notice required)

FLADBURY

Map 10 SO94

Chequers Inn

tel: 01386 861854 **Chequers Ln WR10 2PZ**
email: tspchef85@gmail.com
dir: *Off A44 between Evesham & Pershore*

River Avon walkers can refuel here

With its beams and open fire, this lovely old inn has bags of rustic charm. Tucked away in a pretty village with views of the glorious Bredon Hills, local produce from the Vale of Evesham provides the basis for home-cooked dishes such as jumbo crayfish and prawn cocktail; boiled ham with two eggs and chunky chips; and a range of home-made desserts. There is also a traditional Sunday roast. The pretty walled garden enjoys outstanding views – a great setting for drinking or dining – and the nearby River Avon is ideal for walking and fishing.

Open all wk 12-3 5-11 (Sat 12-11 Sun 12-late) **Food** Lunch Tue-Sat 12-2.30, Sun 12-4 Dinner Tue-Sat 6-9 Av main course £10.95 Restaurant menu available Tue-Sat

⊕ ENTERPRISE INNS ◂ Sharp's Doom Bar, Wye Valley HPA ○ Westons Stowford Press. ▾ **Facilities** Non-diners area ✿ (Bar Garden) ◆ Children's menu Children's portions Play area Family room Garden ⌒ Parking WiFi

---

FLYFORD FLAVELL | Map 10 S095

The Boot Inn ★★★★ INN | PICK OF THE PUBS

See Pick of the Pubs on page 544

HARTLEBURY | Map 10 S087

NEW The Tap House @ The Old Ticket Office

tel: 01299 253275 **DY11 7YJ**
email: skdiprose@fsmail.net
dir: *From A449 follow station signs*

Good pub grub in converted railway building

Flagship for the Worcestershire Brewing Company, whose Attwood Ales range of draught and bottled beers are brewed across from the pub. Until not long ago, it was Hartlebury's station building, a purpose recalled by the lounge bar's bench seating and railway-style signs. Meat, fish, Indian and dairy deli-boards and pub meals are served in the oak-panelled restaurant, where typical mains include roast breast of Gressingham duck with orange sauce; 28-day-matured Hereford steaks; fresh and smoked shellfish pie; and Portobello mushroom and spinach crumble. Tables on the outside terrace overlook the valley. A quiz on Mondays, beer club on Tuesdays and poker on Wednesdays.

Open all day all wk **Food** Lunch Wed-Sun 12-2.30 Dinner Wed-Sun 6-9 Av main course £5-£10 Set menu available Restaurant menu available Wed-Sun ⊕ WORCESTERSHIRE BREWING COMPANY ◂ Attwood Nectar Bitter, Pale Ale & Gold. **Facilities** Non-diners area ✿ (Bar Outside area) ◆ Children's menu Outside area ⌒ Beer festival Parking WiFi 🚌 (notice required)

The White Hart

tel: 01299 250286 **The Village DY11 7TD**
email: skdiprose@fsmail.net
dir: *From Stourport-on-Severn take A4025 signed Worcester & Hartlebury. At rdbt take B4193. Pub in village centre*

At the community's centre and with really good food

Owner and top chef Simon Diprose runs this traditional country pub which has gone from strength to strength since his arrival. The concise menus might begin with lightly curried cauliflower soup; whole baked camembert, rustic bread and caramelised onions; or goats' cheese and beetroot galette and walnut salad. Moving onto something more substantial there's spinach and ricotta tortellini; Mr Gough's honey roast ham and free-range eggs; poached fillet of sea bass with tomato, chilli and ginger sauce; English rib eye steak, dauphinoise potatoes, fresh vegetables and barlotti bean and thyme sauce. At lunchtime you could opt for just filled baps, a ploughman's or a burger and chunky chips.

Open all day all wk **Food** Lunch all wk 12-3 Dinner all wk 6-9 Av main course £7.50 Set menu available Restaurant menu available all wk (ex Sun eve) ⊕ PUNCH TAVERNS ◂ Timothy Taylor Landlord, Wye Valley HPA, Purity Mad Goose. **Facilities** Non-diners area ✿ (Bar Garden) ◆ Children's menu Children's portions Garden ⌒ Parking WiFi

---

KEMPSEY | Map 10 S084

Walter de Cantelupe Inn ★★★ INN | PICK OF THE PUBS

tel: 01905 820572 **Main Rd WR5 3NA**
email: info@walterdecantelupe.co.uk **web:** www.walterdecantelupe.co.uk
dir: *4m S of Worcester city centre on A38. Pub in village centre*

Village pub known for its personal service

Just four miles from the centre of Worcester, this privately-owned free house commemorates a 13th-century bishop of that city, although he was strongly opposed to his parishioners brewing and selling ales to raise money for church funds. Whitewashed walls are bedecked with flowers in the summer, while the interior's wooden beams and stone floor testify to the inn's 17th-century origins. The daily menu on the blackboard testifies to the freshness of ingredients, with some produce being supplied by villagers. Worcestershire rare titbit is a Welsh rarebit with a twist; the gammon steak is plate-sized and served with fried free-range egg, pineapple and chips. The walled and paved garden has been fragrantly planted with clematis, roses and honeysuckle, and its south-facing aspect can be a real suntrap. Cask ales include a particularly well-kept Timothy Taylor Landlord, and a beer festival is held in April.

Open Tue-Fri 5.30-11 Sat 12-2.30 5.30-11 Sun 12-9 Closed 25-26 Dec, 1 Jan, Mon (ex BHs) **Food** Lunch Sun 12-5 Dinner Tue-Sat 6-9.30 ⊕ FREE HOUSE ◂ Timothy Taylor Landlord ○ Westons Stowford Press. **Facilities** Non-diners area ✿ (Bar Outside area) ◆ Children's portions Outside area ⌒ Beer festival Parking WiFi **Rooms** 3

KNIGHTWICK | Map 10 S075

The Talbot | PICK OF THE PUBS

tel: 01886 821235 **WR6 5PH**
email: info@the-talbot.co.uk
dir: *A44 (Leominster road) through Worcester, 8m W right onto B4197 at River Teme bridge*

Family-run inn and brewery

Run by the Clift family for the past 30 years, The Talbot is a traditional 14th-century coaching inn on the bank of the River Teme. Surrounded by hop yards and meadows, this peaceful inn is also home to the Teme Valley Brewery, which uses locally grown hops in a range of curiously named cask-conditioned ales called This, That, T'Other and Wot. Nearly everything on the menus is made in-house, including bread, preserves, black pudding and raised pies. Salads, herbs and vegetables are grown in the large organic kitchen garden, and everything else comes from a local source, with the exception of fish, which arrives from Cornwall and Wales. The bar menu offers ploughman's, filled rolls and hot dishes, whilst in the restaurant, starters might include warm pigeon salad, followed by slow-roasted pork belly, griddle black pudding and apple fritters. Leave space for the treacle hollygog (a 19th-century Cambridge University recipe). Three beer festivals a year.

Open all day all wk 7.30am-11.30pm **Food** Lunch all wk 12-9 Dinner all wk 12-9 Restaurant menu available all wk ⊕ FREE HOUSE ◂ Teme Valley This, That, T'Other & Wot, Hobsons Best Bitter ○ Kingstone Press, Robinsons. ▾ 12 **Facilities** Non-diners area ✿ (Bar Restaurant Garden) ◆ Children's portions Garden ⌒ Beer festival Parking WiFi 🚌

PICK OF THE PUBS

The Boot Inn ★★★★ INN

FLYFORD FLAVELL　　　Map 10 SO95

tel: 01386 462658
Radford Rd WR7 4BS
email: enquiries@thebootinn.com
web: www.thebootinn.com
dir: *A422 from Worcester towards Stratford. Turn right to village*

Friendly, family-run old coaching inn

Parts of this family-run, award-winning, traditional coaching inn can be traced back to the 13th century, and for evidence you need only to look at the heavy beams and slanting doorways. Keep an eye out too for the friendly ghost, age uncertain. The large bar area is comfortable, the pool table and TV having been banished to a separate room, while regulars like London Pride and Black Sheep, and an extensive wine list complement the varied and imaginative menus which change every six weeks. You can eat from the lunchtime sandwich and bar snack menu, from the extensive specials board, or from the full à la carte, but no matter which you choose, or indeed where – including the conservatory – only the best and freshest, mostly county-sourced, produce is used. A sample menu therefore may include starters of Portobello mushroom stuffed with crispy bacon and goats' cheese,

and mango and crayfish salad; followed by something from the griddle, such as Aberdeen Angus steaks hung for 21 days; sea bass fillets with sizzled ginger, chilli, spring onion and hoi sin; pork rib-eye steak with walnut crust and cider apple sauce; roasted lamb shank with redcurrant and rosemary gravy; or chive savoury pancakes filled with roasted vegetables and melted brie. Sundays are devoted to roasts – beef, pork and turkey are served, along with the specials menu. Gardens and a shaded patio area are especially suited to summer dining. The comfortable en suite bedrooms in the converted coach house are furnished in antique pine and equipped with practical goodies.

Open all day all wk **Food** Lunch all wk 12-2 Dinner all wk 6.30-10 Set menu (lunch only) and Restaurant menu available all wk. ⊕ PUNCH TAVERNS ◄ Fuller's London Pride, Black Sheep, Sharp's Doom Bar ♨ Westons Stowford Press. ⬚ 8 **Facilities** Non-diners area ♣ (Bar Garden) ♦ Children's menu Children's portions Garden ⋒ Parking ⛐ (notice required) WiFi **Rooms** 5

■ MALVERN Map 10 SO74

The Inn at Welland

tel: 01684 592317 **Drake St, Welland WR13 6LN**
email: info@theinnatwelland.co.uk
dir: *M50 junct 1, A38 follow signs for Upton upon Severn. Left onto A4104, through Upton upon Severn, 2.5m. Pub on right*

Stylish inn with panoramic views

This 17th-century country inn close to the Three Counties Showground is appointed to a high standard with an eclectic mix of smart, contemporary furnishings and rustic chic. There are spectacular views of the Malvern Hills from the stylish terrace, where you can dine alfresco in the warmer months; and the pub has a wood-burner and open fire for the winter. Food centres around seasonal local produce accompanied by Wye Valley or Malvern Hills ales, plus guests. Typical dishes might be goats' cheese and potato terrine, marinated artichokes and truffle vinaigrette; followed by marmalade glazed woodland pork tenderloin, potato croquette and carrot and ginger purée. There is a good children's menu.

Open 12-3.30 6-11 (Sun 9.30-6) Closed Sun eve & Mon **Food** Lunch Tue-Sun 12-2.30 Dinner Tue-Sat 6.30-9.30 Av main course £14 ⊕ FREE HOUSE ◀ Otter Bitter, Wye Valley, Malvern Hills, Guest ales ♂ Westons Stowford Press & Mortimers Orchard. ♛ 17 **Facilities** Non-diners area ✦ Children's menu Children's portions Garden ☴ Parking WiFi

The Nag's Head

tel: 01684 574373 **19-21 Bank St WR14 2JG**
email: enquiries@nagsheadmalvern.co.uk
dir: *Off A449*

An excellent choice of real ales

From this pub's garden, the looming presence of North Hill, northernmost top of the stunning Malvern Hills, takes the eye - if only momentarily - away from the panoply of delights at this enterprising free house. 'Real ale, real food, real people' is the motto at The Nag's Head. Fifteen real ales, many from local breweries, adorn the bar; eight are permanent fixtures and include three from the pub's own St George's microbrewery. The annual beer festival on St George's Day (23rd April) offers even more choice. The interior is dotted with snugs, log fires and a magpie's nest of artefacts to create a cosy atmosphere, and the marvellous menu features grilled Wiltshire trout and butternut squash and pepper tart.

Open all day all wk **Food** Lunch all wk 12-2 Restaurant menu available all wk 6.30-8.30 ⊕ FREE HOUSE ◀ St George's Friar Tuck, Charger & Dragon's Blood, Bathams, Banks's, Wood's Shropshire Lad, Ringwood Fortyniner ♂ Thatchers Gold, Westons Family Reserve. **Facilities** Non-diners area ✦ (Bar Restaurant Garden) ✦ Children's portions Garden ☴ Beer festival Parking WiFi ☁ (notice required)

The Wyche Inn ★★★★ INN

tel: 01684 575396 **74 Wyche Rd WR14 4EQ**
email: thewycheinn@googlemail.com **web:** www.thewycheinn.co.uk
dir: *1.5m S of Malvern. On B4218 towards Malvern & Colwall. Off A449 (Worcester to Ross/Ledbury road)*

Spectacular views and home-cooked food

Start or end a walk in the Malvern Hills in this traditional, dog-friendly country inn, probably the highest in Worcestershire. Indeed, the views from various nearby high points are quite something; from Malvern Beacon, for instance, you can see seven counties. Beers come from Wye Valley among others, while home-cooked dishes include pie of the day, chicken curry and battered cod. Themed food nights feature sirloin steak (Tuesday/Saturday) and mixed grill (Wednesday), and roast lunches are served on Sundays. Well-behaved pets are welcome in the six rooms.

Open all day all wk **Food** Lunch Mon-Fri 12-2.30, Sat 12-8.30, Sun 12-6 (winter Sat 12-2.30, Sun 12-3.30) Dinner Mon-Fri 6-8.30, Sat 12-8.30 (winter Sat 5-8.30) ⊕ FREE HOUSE ◀ Hobsons Best Bitter, Wye Valley HPA, Guest ales ♂ Robinsons. ♛ 9 **Facilities** Non-diners area ✦ (Bar Garden) ✦ Children's menu Children's portions Garden ☴ Parking WiFi **Rooms** 6

■ PERSHORE Map 10 SO94

The Defford Arms

tel: 01386 750378 **Upton Rd, Defford WR8 9BD**
dir: *From Pershore take A4104 towards Upton upon Severn. Pub on left in village*

Revitalised village pub with much charm

Rescued from dereliction by Neil and Sue Overton, The Defford Arms today stands testament to their efforts: they have eschewed music, gambling machines and TV in favour of old fashioned values. It's in a great location too, so days out at Croome Park, the Three Counties Showground at Malvern, Cheltenham Racecourse or Pershore's plum festival could all include a welcome break here. Expect traditional home-made food such home-made shepherd's pie; oven braised lamb shank, mash with red wine and rosemary gravy; cheesy fish pie; and lemon meringue pie.

Open Mon 12-2 Tue 12-2.30 5.30-9 Wed 12-2.30 5.30-9.30 Thu 12-2.30 5.30-10 Fri 12-2.30 5.30-11 Sat 12-11 Sun 12-4 Closed Sun eve & Mon eve **Food** Lunch Mon 12-1.30, Tue-Sun 12-2 Dinner Tue-Sat 6-8 Restaurant menu available Tue-Sat ⊕ FREE HOUSE ◀ Guest ales ♂ Thatchers Gold. **Facilities** Non-diners area ✦ (Bar Garden) ✦ Children's menu Children's portions Garden ☴ Parking ☁ (notice required)

■ POWICK Map 10 SO85

The Halfway House Inn

tel: 01905 831098 **Bastonford WR2 4SL**
email: contact@halfwayhouseinnpowick.co.uk
dir: *M5 junct 7, A4440 then A449*

A warm welcome at this village pub

Standing halfway between Worcester and Malvern on the main road, this aptly named Georgian free house boasts winter log fires and a mature shady garden at the side. Steaks and seafood are a speciality, but the menu also features a good choice of fresh, locally sourced hot dishes such as pork medallions and black pudding on mashed potatoes with creamy, coarse-grain mustard. The extensive lunchtime menu offers salads, sandwiches and jacket potatoes, as well as hot dishes and a range of ploughman's.

Open 12-3 6-11 Closed Mon-Tue **Food** Lunch Wed-Sun 12-2 Dinner Wed-Sat 6-9 Restaurant menu available Tue-Sun ⊕ FREE HOUSE ◀ Greene King Abbot Ale, Fuller's London Pride, St George's, Timothy Taylor ♂ Westons Stowford Press. **Facilities** Non-diners area ✦ Children's menu Children's portions Garden ☴ Parking WiFi ☁ (notice required)

TENBURY WELLS   Map 10 SO56

NEW Pembroke House

tel: 01584 810301 **Cross St WR15 8EQ**
dir: *Phone for detailed directions*

Modern menus and shoot dinners

Pembroke House was built as a farmhouse in the 16th century, but by 1600 had become a cider house. When Andrew Mortimer bought this classic black and white timbered property he created the two intimate restaurants, where today lunch might be home-made beef lasagne; grilled salmon steak; or brie-topped Tuscan vegetable tart. For dinner, spicy pan-fried pork faggots to start; then griddled fillet steak in pancetta with Stilton sauce; or darne of smoked haddock in tarragon milk with green-lipped mussels and prawns. Cider these days comes from Robinsons of Tenbury, the 'Town in the Orchard'; the real ales all come from hereabouts too. Their shoot dinners are popular.

Open 12-3 5-close (Mon 5-close Sat-Sun all day) Closed Mon L **Food** Lunch Tue-Sat 12-2, Sun 12-2.30 Dinner Tue-Sat 7-9.15 Av main course £8 Restaurant menu available Tue-Sat evening ⊕ FREE HOUSE ◀ Hobsons, Wye Valley, Three Tuns, Wood's, Cannon Royall, Ludlow ⊙ Robinsons. ♠ 9 **Facilities** Non-diners area ❁ (Garden) ♦♦ Children's portions Garden ♫ Parking WiFi ☞ (notice required)

NEW Talbot Inn

tel: 01584 781941 **Newnham Bridge WR15 8JF**
email: info@talbotinnnewnhambridge.co.uk
dir: *3m E of Tenbury Wells*

Restored coaching inn in the Teme Valley

Set amidst beautiful countryside in the Teme Valley, this 19th-century coaching inn was painstakingly restored by its current owners and its contemporary rustic style makes for a relaxed base to explore local market towns such as Ludlow and Leominster. Sup a pint of Wye Valley ale in the bar or bag a table and tuck into enjoyable dishes such as local game terrine with pickled wild mushrooms and winter berries; or slow-cooked ham hock, buttered mash, root vegetables and parsley sauce.

Open all day all wk **Food** Lunch Mon-Sat 12-2.30, Sun 12-5 Dinner Mon-Thu 6-9, Fri-Sat 6-9.30 Av main course £13 ⊕ FREE HOUSE ◀ Wye Valley HPA, Hobsons Best Bitter ⊙ Robinsons Cider, Westons Stowford Press. ♠ 11 **Facilities** Non-diners area ❁ (Bar Restaurant Garden) ♦♦ Children's menu Children's portions Garden ♫ Parking WiFi ☞ (notice required)

EAST RIDING OF YORKSHIRE

BARMBY ON THE MARSH   Map 17 SE62

The King's Head

tel: 01757 630705 **High St DN14 7HT**
email: rainderpubcoltd@tiscali.co.uk
dir: *M62 junct 37 follow A614/Bridlington/York/Howden signs. Left at A63. At rdbt 1st exit onto A614/Booth Ferry Rd towards Goole. At rdbt 4th exit on B1228/Booth Ferry Rd. Left, through Asselby to Barmby on the Marsh*

Look out for their Yorkshire tapas menu

In the 17th century this pub served a ferry that crossed the Rivers Ouse and Derwent. Nowadays this family-run village pub is a place that appeals to all tastes; from the beamed bar through a bright, modern lounge to the cosy, intimate restaurant. Several members of the family are trained chefs and make the most of Yorkshire's burgeoning larder; braised beef with clementines and ginger wine served with herb cobbler and mash is just one of the tempting mains here. Their innovative Yorkshire tapas menu features haddock goujons, confit lamb croquettes, and baked mussels. There are great open sandwiches and a take-away deli menu (including ice creams), too.

Open Wed-Thu 12-2 5-11 (Mon-Tue 5-11 Fri 12-2 5-12 Sat 12-12 Sun 12-11) Closed Mon L, Tue L **Food** Lunch Wed-Fri 12-2, Sat-Sun all day Dinner Wed-Thu 5-8.30, Fri 5-9, Sat-Sun all day Set menu available Restaurant menu available Wed-Mon ⊕ FREE HOUSE ◀ Black Sheep Best Bitter, 3 Guest ales.
Facilities Non-diners area ♦♦ Children's menu Children's portions Outside area ♫ Parking WiFi ☞ (notice required)

BEVERLEY   Map 17 TA03

The Ferguson Fawsitt Arms & Country Lodge

tel: 01482 882665 **East End, Walkington HU17 8RX**
email: admin@fergusonfawsitt.com
dir: *M62 junct 38 onto B1230, left on A1034, right onto B1230, on left in centre of Walkington*

Well-positioned traditional inn where time stands still

Three miles from Beverley in the picturesque village of Walkington, there is a timeless quality to this Victorian pub named after two important local families. Parts of the pub used to form the village blacksmith's shop where carriage wheels were repaired. Open fires, dark-wood panelling, carved settles, beams and some decent tiling to the floor welcomes those set on sampling a pint of Black Sheep, or diners intent on a good Sunday roast, home-made steak pie from the carvery or a traditional pub meal from the bar food menu.

Open all day all wk 11-11 (Sun 12-11) **Food** Lunch all wk 12-9 Dinner all wk 12-9 Av main course £8.50 Restaurant menu available all wk ⊕ FREE HOUSE ◀ Courage Directors, Greene King Abbot Ale, Black Sheep, Guest ales. ♠ 10
Facilities Non-diners area ♦♦ Children's menu Children's portions Outside area ♫ Beer festival Parking WiFi ☞ (notice required)

FLAMBOROUGH
Map 17 TA27

The Seabirds Inn

tel: 01262 850242 **Tower St** YO15 1PD
email: philip.theseabirds@virgin.net **web:** www.theseabirds.com
dir: On B1255 E of Bridlington

Village pub that keeps it simple

Just east of this 200-year-old village pub is the famous chalk promontory of Flamborough Head and its equally famed lighthouse. With the North Sea so close you'd expect plenty of fish, and there is, namely, spicy Whitby creel king prawns; deep-fried dusted whitebait; salmon steak Mornay; and battered haddock fillet. This is not a menu to overreach itself, instead keeping to staples like a good choice of steaks; chicken breast with bacon, barbecue sauce and cheese; gammon with egg and pineapple; and steamed suet pudding with spinach, pine nuts, mozzarella cheese and cherry tomatoes. Guest ales are on tap in the bar.

Open 12-3 6-11 Closed Mon (winter) **Food** Lunch all wk 12-2 Dinner Sun-Fri 6-8.30, Sat 6-9.30 Set menu available ⊕ FREE HOUSE ◀ John Smith's, Tetley's Smoothflow, Guest ales. ♥ 9 **Facilities** Non-diners area ♣ (Bar Garden) Children's menu Children's portions Garden ⊓ Parking ᗑ

HUGGATE
Map 19 SE85

The Wolds Inn ★★★ INN

tel: 01377 288217 YO42 1YH
email: woldsinn@gmail.com **web:** www.woldsinn.co.uk
dir: S off A166 between York & Driffield

Yorkshire Wolds inn with hearty home-made food

Sixteenth century in origin, this family-run hostelry is, at 525 feet above sea level, the highest in the Yorkshire Wolds. Copper pans and gleaming brassware fill the wood-panelled interior, where the open fires still burn good old-fashioned coal. The restaurant is widely known for serving large portions of, among other things, locally sourced Barnsley chops; crispy fresh farm duckling; fillet of plaice; chicken breast stuffed with spinach; Wolds Topper, 'the mixed grill to remember' and their celebrated home-made steak pie. The overnight accommodation is particularly popular with those exploring the countryside and coast.

Open 12-2 6-11 (Sun 12-10.30) Closed Mon (ex BHs) **Food** Lunch Tue-Sat 12-2, Sun 12-8 Dinner Tue-Sat 6-9, Sun 12-8 Set menu available Restaurant menu available Tue-Sun ⊕ FREE HOUSE ◀ Timothy Taylor Landlord, Blacksheep, York Guzzler ♂ Kingstone Press. ♥ **Facilities** Non-diners area ♦ Children's menu Children's portions Garden ⊓ Parking WiFi ᗑ (notice required) **Rooms** 3

LOW CATTON
Map 17 SE75

The Gold Cup Inn

tel: 01759 371354 YO41 1EA
dir: 1m S of A166 or 1m N of A1079, E of York

Attractive, family-run country pub

A charming, family-run free house that is 300 years old but may not look it at first glance. Giveaways are the low beams and open fireplaces in the bar, now complemented by wooden floors, modern fabrics and wall-mounted coach-lamps. Bar meals are served every lunchtime (except Monday) and evening from the extensive menu. Equally extensive is the carte, whose options include roast loin of pork or beef with Yorkshire pudding; hot and spicy Cajun chicken with mint yogurt dip; and breaded Whitby scampi. A paddock adjoining the large beer garden runs down to the River Derwent.

Open 12-2.30 6-11 (Sat-Sun 12-11) Closed Mon L **Food** Lunch Tue-Fri 12-2.30, Sat-Sun 12-6 Dinner all wk 6-9 Av main course £11 ⊕ FREE HOUSE ◀ Theakston Black Bull. ♥ 11 **Facilities** Non-diners area ♣ (Bar Garden) ♦ Children's menu Children's portions Play area Garden ⊓ Parking ᗑ (notice required)

LUND
Map 17 SE94

The Wellington Inn

tel: 01377 217294 **19 The Green** YO25 9TE
email: tellmemore@thewellingtoninn.co.uk
dir: On B1248 NE of Beverley

Exciting food in quintessential village inn

Occupying a wonderfully rural location, this country pub is popular with locals and visitors alike, whether for a pint of real ale, a glass of wine, or a plate of decent food. Nicely situated opposite the picture-postcard village green, inside is a unique blend of old and new where you can choose from the traditional pub menu or from the carte in the more formal restaurant. Expect mouthwatering dishes like pulled pork terrine, pea shoot and endive salad and prune jam, followed perhaps by grilled wild sea bass fillet with sweet pepper, rocket and chorizo risotto. Leave space for rhubarb sponge and custard or banana cheesecake.

Open 12-3 6.30-11 Closed Mon L **Food** Lunch Tue-Sun 12-2 Dinner Tue-Sat 6.30-9 Restaurant menu available Tue-Sat evenings ⊕ FREE HOUSE ◀ Timothy Taylor Landlord, Black Sheep Best Bitter, Copper Dragon, Regular guest ale. ♥ 11 **Facilities** Non-diners area ♦ Children's menu Children's portions Outside area ⊓ Parking WiFi

SANCTON
Map 17 SE83

The Star

tel: 01430 827269 **King St YO43 4QP**
email: benandlindsey@thestaratsancton.co.uk
dir: *2m SE of Market Weighton on A1034*

Traditional local serving top-notch pub food

This stylishly modernised and extended old village pub stands at the heart of charming Sancton, past which the Wolds Way recreational footpath threads across the tranquil Yorkshire landscape. Beers from local microbreweries tempt ramblers to linger longer; more leisurely visits are rewarded by a reliable bar menu considerably enhanced by an evening restaurant choice. Smoked haddock risotto may start the repast; seared rib-eye steak from village-reared stock, or white onion tart with lovage pesto and Yorkshire cheddar example the satisfying mains which chef-proprietor Ben Cox crafts from local produce. A forced rhubarb and parkin dessert seals the Yorkshire theme of the very capable bill of fare.

Open 12-3 6-11 (Sun all day) Closed 1st wk Jan, Mon **Food** Lunch 12-2 Dinner 6-9.30 Av main course £13.95 Set menu available Restaurant menu available all wk ⊕ FREE HOUSE ◄ Black Sheep, Copper Dragon, Wold Top ⓧ Moorlands Farm. ☻ 14 **Facilities** Non-diners area ♦♦ Children's menu Children's portions Garden Outside area ⌁ Parking

SOUTH DALTON
Map 17 SE94

The Pipe & Glass Inn ⊚⊚
PICK OF THE PUBS

tel: 01430 810246 **West End HU17 7PN**
email: email@pipeandglass.co.uk
dir: *Just off B1248 (Beverley to Malton road). 7m from Beverley*

Smart inn serving quality food and ales

Part 15th-century, part 17th, the inn occupies the site of the original gatehouse to Dalton Hall, family seat of Lord Hotham. James and Kate Mackenzie's transformation of their inn has helped to earn it two AA Rosettes, but it still feels like the village local, with Copper Dragon, Cropton, Wold Top and other locally brewed ales, and Moorlands Farm cider in the bar. The restaurant is more contemporary in style and the conservatory looks out over the garden. James sources top-notch local and seasonal produce for modern British menus, which at lunchtime may feature fillet of English beef with roast shallots; and beetroot and Yellison Farm (in the Yorkshire Dales) goats' cheese tart. Evening possibilities include slow-cooked crispy lamb with mutton and kidney faggot; and a special of turbot fillet with monkfish cheek fritter and braised oxtail and horseradish sauce. The Hotham Room has its own kitchen for private dining.

Open all day 12-11 (Sun 12-10.30) Closed 2wks Jan, Mon (ex BHs) **Food** Lunch Tue-Sat 12-2, Sun 12-4 Dinner Tue-Sat 6.30-9.30 ⊕ FREE HOUSE ◄ Wold Top, Copper Dragon, Black Sheep, Cropton, York ⓧ Moorlands Farm. ☻ 15 **Facilities** ♦♦ Children's menu Children's portions Garden ⌁ Parking WiFi

NORTH YORKSHIRE

AKEBAR
Map 19 SE19

The Friar's Head

tel: 01677 450201 & 450591 **Akebar Park DL8 5LY**
email: info@akebarpark.com
dir: *From A1 at Leeming Bar onto A684, 7m towards Leyburn. Entrance at Akebar Park*

Stone-built Dales pub with a lovely conservatory

This 200-year-old pub lies in the heart of Wensleydale, known for its castles, abbeys and waterfalls. Located next to an 18-hole golf course and at the entrance to Akebar Holiday Park, The Friar's Head overlooks beautiful countryside and has grounds where you can play bowls or croquet. Inside you'll find exposed beams and stonework, and hand-pulled Yorkshire ales at the bar. The lush plants and vines of the Cloister conservatory dining room give it a tropical appearance; in the evening it looks magical in the candlelit. From the frequently changing menu, typical dishes include twice baked spinach and gruyère soufflé; slow braised lamb shank; Yorkshire farmed venison steak served pink with caramelised onions and juniper sauce.

Open 10-3 6-11.30 (Fri-Sun 10am-11.30pm Jul-Sep) Closed 25 Dec, 26 Dec eve, Mon Jan-Feb **Food** Lunch all wk 12-2.30 Dinner all wk 6-9.30 ⊕ FREE HOUSE ◄ John Smith's, Theakston Best Bitter, Black Sheep Best Bitter, Timothy Taylor Landlord, Guinness. ☻ 12 **Facilities** Non-diners area ♦♦ Children's portions Garden ⌁ Parking WiFi

ALDWARK
Map 19 SE46

The Aldwark Arms ⊚⊚

tel: 01347 838324 **YO61 1UB**
email: peter@aldwarkarms.co.uk
dir: *From York ring road take A19 N. Left into Warehill Ln signed Tollerton & Helperby. Through Tollerton, follow Aldwark signs*

Warm welcomes abound at this family-run community pub

Newly acquired and renovated by local boys the Hardisty brothers, this friendly free house has an inviting atmosphere. Keen to include locally sourced, season produce on his menus the chef offers the likes of smooth duck liver and port pâté; Cumberland sausages and pepper mash; pan-seared Dutch calves' liver; and sea bass fillets with Moroccan chickpea, courgette and spinach ragu. On tap you'll find Black Sheep and Copper Dragon ales, as well as several wines by the glass. On warmer days food and drink can be enjoyed in the pub garden if you prefer.

Open all day Closed Mon **Food** Lunch Tue-Fri 12-2, Sat all day, Sun 12-4 Dinner Tue-Fri 5.30-9, Sat all day Set menu available Restaurant menu available Tue-Sat ⊕ FREE HOUSE ◄ Black Sheep, Copper Dragon. ☻ **Facilities** Non-diners area ♦♦ Children's menu Children's portions Play area Garden ⌁ Parking WiFi ▄▄ (notice required)

PICK OF THE PUBS

Charles Bathurst Inn ★★★★ INN

ARKENGARTHDALE   Map 18 NY90

tel: 01748 884567 **DL11 6EN**
email: info@cbinn.co.uk
web: www.cbinn.co.uk
dir: *A1 onto A6108 at Scotch Corner, through Richmond, left onto B6270 to Reeth. At Buck Hotel right signed Langthwaite, pass church on right, inn 0.5m on right*

Spectacular dale scenery at remote country inn

This 18th-century inn sits in possibly one of the North's finest dales, and takes its name from the son of Oliver Cromwell's physician who built it for his workers in what was once a busy lead mining area. In winter, it caters for serious ramblers tackling The Pennine Way and the Coast to Coast route, and it offers a welcome escape from the rigours of the moors and many a tale has been swapped over pints of Black Sheep or Theakston ale. The 'Terrace Room' features handcrafted tables and chairs from Robert Thompson's craftsmen in nearby Kilburn with their unique hand carved mouse on every item, watch out for them! English classics meet modern European dishes on a menu written up on the mirror hanging above the stone fireplace and the provenance is impeccable: Cogden Hill beef and Black Sheep Ale casserole, suet dumpling and leek mash; roasted globe artichoke and goats' cheese

risotto; and lemon posset with winter berries and shortbread biscuit. Choose the cheeseboard for the chance to taste local specialities such as mature and oak-smoked Wensleydale, and Shepherd Purse cheeses - Mrs Bell's Blue, Yorkshire Ryedale and Monk's Folly. The wine list is also excellent with well-written tasting notes. From April to September the local outdoor game of quoits can be played. The bedrooms have fabulous views overlooking the Stang and Arkengarthdale and are finished to a high standard with exposed beams, cast iron bed frames and warm colours.

Open all day all week 11am-mdnt Closed 25 Dec **Food** Lunch Mon-Fri 12-2.30, Sat-Sun12-6 Dinner all wk 6-9

Restaurant menu available all week (evening) ⊕ FREE HOUSE ◧ Black Sheep Best Bitter, Black Sheep Golden Sheep, Black Sheep Riggwelter, Rudgate Jorvik Blonde, Theakston ○ Symonds. ☜ 12 **Facilities** Non-diners area 🐾 (Bar Garden) ♦♦ Children's menu Children's portions Play area Garden ⊼ Parking 🚌 (notice required) WiFi **Rooms** 19

APPLETON-LE-MOORS
Map 19 SE78

The Moors Inn

tel: 01751 417435 **YO62 6TF**
email: enquiries@moorsinn.co.uk
dir: On A170 between Pickering & Kirbymoorside

Moors village pub with enjoyable home-cooked food

Situated in the North York Moors National Park, this 18th-century Grade II listed inn is a good choice for its location and home-cooked food. Run by the Frank family, the pub is set in a small village with lovely scenery in every direction; in summer you can sit in the garden and enjoy the splendid views. Dishes include braised lamb shank with mint gravy; beef and mushroom pie; and Whitby scampi. Many of the vegetables are grown by the landlord.

Open all day all wk **Food** Lunch Mon-Sat 12.2.30 (light snacks all day) Dinner all wk 6.30-8.30 ⊕ FREE HOUSE ◀ Brass Castle, Great Newsome, Rudgate Viking, York Guzzler, Yorkshire Heart, Theakston ♂ Westons Stowford Press. **Facilities** Non-diners area ❖ (Bar Garden Outside area) ◀▮ Children's portions Garden Outside area ⌒ Parking ▰

APPLETREEWICK
Map 19 SE06

The Craven Arms

tel: 01756 720270 **BD23 6DA**
email: info@craven-cruckbarn.co.uk
dir: 2m E of Burnsall off B6160. 5m N of Bolton Abbey

Interesting blackboard menus

Originally part of a farm, this 16th-century Dales pub has spectacular views of the Wharfedale and Simon's Seat. The building retains its original beams, flagstone floors, gas lighting and magnificent fireplace; the village stocks are still outside. Traditional real ales are served and there's a beer festival every October. The blackboard menu changes daily and offers plenty of choice. A heather-thatched cruck barn to the rear provides additional dining space and a function room for events, wedding receptions and concerts.

Open all day all wk **Food** Lunch Mon-Thu 12-2, Fri-Sun 12-5 Dinner Mon-Sat 6.30-9, Sun 6.30-8.30 Restaurant menu available all wk ⊕ FREE HOUSE ◀ Dark Horse Cruck Barn Bitter & Hetton Pale Ale, Saltaire Raspberry Blonde, Moorhouse's Blond Witch & Black Witch, Ilkley Mary Jane ♂ Kingstone Press, Ampleforth Abbey, Welsh Scrumpy, Cornish Orchards. **Facilities** Non-diners area ❖ (Bar Garden) ◀▮ Children's menu Children's portions Play area Garden ⌒ Beer festival Parking WiFi

ARKENGARTHDALE
Map 18 NY90

Charles Bathurst Inn ★★★★ INN ⊛   PICK OF THE PUBS

See Pick of the Pubs on page 549

ASKRIGG
Map 18 SD99

The King's Arms

tel: 01969 650113 **Main St DL8 3HQ**
email: info@kingsarmsaskrigg.co.uk
dir: From A1 exit at Scotch Corner onto A6108, through Richmond, right onto B6270 to Leyburn. Follow Askrigg signs to Main St

Stone-built Wensleydale inn on the Herriot Trail

Owned by North Yorkshire hotelier Charles Cody, this elegant, 18th-century coaching inn used to double as the fictional Drover's Arms, vet James Herriot's favourite watering hole in the BBC drama *All Creatures Great and Small*. There's a big Yorkshire inglenook fireplace in the oak-panelled bar, where photographs show cast members relaxing between takes. The food, written up daily on an impressive mirror behind the bar, is based on top quality produce, such as game from the surrounding

moors, and fish fresh from Hartlepool. Look also for loin of local lamb; pan-fried salmon; and wild mushroom risotto.

Open all day all wk **Food** Lunch all wk 12-2.30 Dinner Mon-Sat 5.30-9, Sun 5.30-8 ⊕ FREE HOUSE ◀ Black Sheep, Theakstons, Yorkshire Dales ♂ Thatchers Gold. ☗ 13 **Facilities** Non-diners area ❖ (Bar Outside area) ◀▮ Children's menu Children's portions Outside area WiFi ▰ (notice required)

AYSGARTH
Map 19 SE08

The George & Dragon Inn   PICK OF THE PUBS

tel: 01969 663358 **DL8 3AD**
email: info@georgeanddragonaysgarth.co.uk
dir: On A684 midway between Leyburn & Hawes. Pub in village centre

Perfect location for exploring Wensleydale

The George & Dragon Inn is a 17th-century Grade II listed building in a superb location in the Yorkshire Dales National Park, near the beautiful Aysgarth Falls. The area is perfect for walking, touring and visiting the many attractions, including Forbidden Corner, the Wensleydale Railway, and the cheese factory. The owners are proud to continue a centuries-long tradition of Yorkshire hospitality at the inn, with customers keeping cosy in winter by the fireside, and in summer enjoying their drinks and meals out on the furnished flower-filled patio. Well-kept real ales are served, and the inn has a great reputation for its traditional food, including steak pie and fish and chips. In the early evening a fixed-price menu meets the needs of ravenous walkers, while broader à la carte choices come into force after 7pm. Choices could be home-made chicken liver pâté with apple chutney; Wensleydale pork sausages and mash; or braised pork belly, mash, choucroute and cider reduction.

Open all wk 12-close Closed Jan **Food** Lunch all wk 12-2 Dinner all wk 6-8.30, May-Sep 5.30-9 ⊕ FREE HOUSE ◀ Black Sheep Best Bitter, Theakston's Best Bitter, Yorkshire Dales, Guest ales ♂ Thatchers Gold. ☗ 16 **Facilities** Non-diners area ❖ (Bar Garden) ◀▮ Garden ⌒ Parking ▰

BEDALE
Map 19 SE28

The Castle Arms Inn

tel: 01677 470270 **Meadow Ln, Snape DL8 2TB**
email: castlearmsinn@gmail.com
dir: From A1 (M) at Leeming Bar take A684 to Bedale. At x-rds in town centre take B6268 to Masham. Approx 2m, turn left to Thorp Perrow Arboretum. In 0.5m left for Snape

Great base for walking or cycling

In the sleepy village of Snape, this family-run 18th-century pub is a good starting point for walking and cycling, and visiting local stately homes, castles and film locations. The homely interior has exposed beams and horse brasses and a real fire in the bar, home to Ringwood and Brakspear real ales. A meal in the restaurant selected from the ever-changing menu might feature smoked salmon salad; beer battered king prawns with hand-cut chunky chips; and apple crumble for dessert. Afterwards, there is a range of liqueur coffees to tempt you.

Open all wk 12-3 6-12 (Sun 12-4, Apr-Sep open all day) **Food** Lunch Mon-Sat 12-3, Sun 12-4 Dinner Mon-Sat 6-9 Av main course £10 ⊕ MARSTON'S ◀ Ringwood Best, Brakspear Oxford Gold. **Facilities** Non-diners area ❖ (Bar Garden) ◀▮ Children's menu Children's portions Garden ⌒ Parking WiFi

BOROUGHBRIDGE
Map 19 SE36

The Black Bull Inn   PICK OF THE PUBS

See Pick of the Pubs on opposite page

Crown Inn Roecliffe ★★★★★ RR ⊛   PICK OF THE PUBS

See Pick of the Pubs on page 552

PICK OF THE PUBS

The Black Bull Inn

BOROUGHBRIDGE   Map 19 SE36

tel: 01423 322413
6 St James Square YO51 9AR
web: www.blackbullboroughbridge.co.uk
dir: A1(M) junct 48, B6265 E for 1m

Traditional inn offering true Yorkshire hospitality

Using a false name, highwayman Dick Turpin stayed at this ancient inn which stands in a quiet corner of the market square and was one of the main stopping points for travellers on the long road between London and the North. Today you have to turn off the A1(M), but it's well worth it to discover an inn built in 1258 that retains its ancient beams, low ceilings and roaring open fires, not to mention one that also gives houseroom to the supposed ghosts of a monk, a blacksmith, a cavalier and a small boy. Tony Burgess is the landlord and the man responsible for high standards that exclude anything electronic which makes a noise. The hot and cold sandwich selection in the bar is wide, while in the dining room expect a good choice of traditional pub food on menus offering lamb shank on creamy mash in port and honey gravy; salmon steak on fried noodles with spicy oriental sauce; Barnsley chop and other grills; and Sizzlers, such as Mexican spiced vegetables in a hot sweet salsa sauce; and pan-fried duck breast topped with peppers, mushrooms,

bamboo shoots and sweet and sour sauce. Frequently changing blackboard specials widen the choice to include halibut steak with smoked salmon and fresh prawns in white wine sauce; and wild button mushroom ragout with fresh salad. Possible followers are apple pie and custard; citrus lemon tart; or mixed ice creams, brandy snaps and fruit purées. In the bar, real ale drinkers will find favourites from Timothy Taylor, Cottage Brewery and Theakston, while the wine list shows all the signs of careful compilation.

Open all day all wk 11-11 (Fri-Sat 11am-mdnt Sun 12-11) **Food** Lunch all wk 12-2 Dinner served all wk 6-9 Restaurant menu available all wk. ⊕ FREE HOUSE ◀ John Smith's, Timothy Taylor Best Bitter, Wells Bombardier, Theakston, Cottage, Guest ale. ⬤ 11 **Facilities** Non-diners area ✿ (Bar Restaurant) ⬤ Children's menu Children's portions Parking 🚌 WiFi

PICK OF THE PUBS

Crown Inn Roecliffe ★★★★★ RR

BOROUGHBRIDGE   Map 19 SE36

tel: 01423 322300 **Roecliffe YO51 9LY**
email: info@crowninnroecliffe.co.uk
web: www.crowninnroecliffe.co.uk
dir: *A1(M) junct 48, follow Boroughbridge signs. At rdbt to Roecliffe*

Wonderful village just off the A1

Karl and Amanda have worked wonders on this handsome 16th-century former coaching inn beside Roecliffe's neatly trimmed green. The striking green-painted pub has been lovingly restored, with stone-flagged floors, oak beams and crackling log fires featuring prominently in the civilised bar and dining rooms. Children and dogs are welcome, and food and drink can be served in the garden during the summer months. The bar's beer handles tempt with some top Yorkshire brewers (Timothy Taylor, Theakston, Ilkley), but it's the wine list which may catch the eye – it's 20 pages long with a massive choice of 30 wines sold by the glass. An AA Rosette is well deserved for the pub's enthusiastic use of fresh and local produce, from salad and vegetables to farm meats and game – all put to fine use on a clearly focused modern British menu. The bar lunch choice is a strong indicator of the pub's commitment to excellence: sandwiches made with Boroughbridge seven seed granary cob are served with a little bowl of soup;

fillings include rare roasted beef with horseradish, fresh watercress and parmesan. A short selection of hot dishes includes a Yorkshire fish pie (smoked haddock, salmon and king prawns topped with Wensleydale and fresh mussels); and a hand-made Yorkshire Dales gourmet steak burger. Everything that can be is home made, from the black pudding, roasted parsnip purée and Russet apple crisps cuddling the king scallops, to the fresh Yorkshire ale batter embracing the haddock and the tartare sauce on the side. In the evening, settle down to fresh Whitby crab soup, followed by eight-hour braised ox cheek. Delicious puddings may include golden apple crumble with 'lashings' of custard.

Open all wk 12-3.30 5-12 (Sun 12-7) **Food** Lunch Mon-Sat 12-2.30, Sun 12-7 Dinner Mon-Sat 6-9.30, Sun 12-7 Set menu available ⊕ FREE HOUSE
◄ Timothy Taylor Landlord, Ilkley Gold & Mary Jane, Theakston, Black Sheep.
☐ 30 **Facilities** Non-diners area ❀ (Bar Garden) ♦♦ Children's menu Children's portions Garden ⊟ Parking WiFi
🚌 (notice required) **Rooms** 4

■ BROUGHTON
Map 18 SD95

The Bull
PICK OF THE PUBS

tel: 01756 792065 **BD23 3AE**
email: enquiries@thebullatbroughton.com
dir: *3m from Skipton on A59, on right*

Destination dining and free house in an estate setting

The Bull is part of the historic Broughton Estate, 3,000 acres of prime Yorkshire parkland and countryside, owned by the Tempests for nine centuries. Their family seat, Broughton Hall, is close by. While essentially a dining pub, The Bull still loves to see beer drinkers, as its good selection of real ales proves - Dark Horse, Moorhouses and Thwaites - and a real cider line-up of Ampleforth Abbey, Fanny's Bramble and Pure North. With an AA Rosette to their credit, the chefs rely on carefully chosen local producers for modern English dishes such as seafood, game or ham sharing platters; Lancashire hotpot; Herdwick mutton with black pea suet pudding and bubble-and-squeak; North Sea fish pie; a range of chargrills; and Wensleydale cheese and onion pie. A comprehensive gluten-free menu includes battered line-caught haddock with marrowfat peas and dripping-fried chips.

Open all day all wk 12-11 (Sun 12-10) **Food** Lunch Mon-Sat 12-2, Sun 12-8.30, BHs 12-9 (afternoon bites Mon-Sat 2-5.30) Dinner Mon-Thu 5.30-8.30, Fri-Sat 5.30-9, Sun 12-8.30, BHs 12-9 Av main course £12-£20 Set menu available ⊕ FREE HOUSE ◀ Dark Horse Hetton Pale Ale, Moorhouses Black Witch, Thwaites Wainwright ♂ Westons Stowford Press, Ampleforth Abbey, Pure North Cider, Sandford Orchards Fanny's Bramble. ♥ 11 **Facilities** Non-diners area ♣ (Bar Outside area) ♦♦ Children's menu Outside area ⋒ Parking

See advert on page 303

■ BURNSALL
Map 19 SE06

The Devonshire Fell ★★★★ RR ◉◉
PICK OF THE PUBS

tel: 01756 729000 **BD23 6BT**
email: manager@devonshirefell.co.uk **web:** www.devonshirefell.co.uk
dir: *On B6160, 6m from Bolton Abbey rdbt, A59 junct*

Stylish inn with breathtaking views and superb food

This former Victorian club for gentlemen mill-owners sits on the edge of the Duke of Devonshire's estate with unparalleled views of the river, the picturesque village of Burnsall and the Yorkshire Dales. Given the lineage and the stunning setting, one would expect polished antiques and a classic country-house feel. But the decor is bright with vibrant colours, floorboards are polished, and bold, contemporary works of art adorn the relaxing, open-plan lounge bar and conservatory restaurant. Equally bang up-to-date are the modern British dishes, which have been awarded two AA Rosettes. A three-course treat for that special occasion could start with Cornish crab, avocado, mango, radish and fennel ice cream. Next may come a Goosnargh duck breast with smoked celeriac, caramelised figs, griottine cherries and red wine gravy. Leave room for sticky toffee pudding with vanilla ice cream and caramel sauce.

Open all day all wk **Food** Lunch Mon-Sat 12-2, Sun 12-3 Dinner all wk 7-9 ⊕ FREE HOUSE/DEVONSHIRE HOTELS & RESTAURANTS ◀ Copper Dragon Scotts 1816 & Golden Pippin, Truman's. ♥ 10 **Facilities** Non-diners area ♣ (Bar Garden) ♦♦ Children's menu Children's portions Garden ⋒ Parking WiFi ▬ (notice required) **Rooms** 12

The Red Lion
PICK OF THE PUBS

tel: 01756 720204 **By the Bridge BD23 6BU**
email: info@redlion.co.uk
dir: *From Skipton take A59 E, then B6160 towards Bolton Abbey, Burnsall 7m*

Popular 16th-century pub by the river

This 16th-century ferryman's inn overlooks the River Wharfe as it gently curves under a magnificent five-arch bridge. Large gardens and terraces make it an ideal spot for sunny days; while for refuge on chillier days the interior is welcoming with its creaky sloping floors and beamed ceilings. The original 'one-up, one-down' structure, which is now the oak-panelled main bar, is the focal point. Bar food includes lunchtime sandwiches and light meals such as ham hock terrine with shallot compôte, and shepherd's pie or pork belly with a spring vegetable and smoked bacon jardinière in the evening. The main menu ups the ante with the likes of Thai-style fish fritters, followed by oxtail and potato pie.

Open all day all wk 8am-11.30pm **Food** Lunch Mon-Fri 12-2.30, Sat 12-9.30, Sun 12-9 Dinner Mon-Fri 6-9.30, Sat 12-9.30, Sun 12-9 ⊕ FREE HOUSE ◀ Timothy Taylor Best, Theakston Best Bitter, Thwaites ♂ Thatchers. ♥ 14 **Facilities** Non-diners area ♣ (Bar) ♦♦ Play area Family room Garden ⋒ Parking

■ CALDWELL
Map 19 NZ11

Brownlow Arms

tel: 01325 718471 **DL11 7QH**
email: bookings@brownlowarms.co.uk
dir: *From A1 at Scotch Corner take A66 towards Bowes. Right onto B6274 to Caldwell. Or from A1 junct 56 take B6275 N. 1st left through Mesonby to junct with B6274. Right to Caldwell*

Family friendly country inn

Set in delightful rolling countryside between Barnard Castle and Darlington, this stone inn in the tiny village of Caldwell is a great place to seek out. With 10 wines by the glass, plenty more bins and reliable Yorkshire real ales, time passes easily here. A blend of traditional and modern rooms is the setting for unpicking a phenomenally comprehensive, globally inspired menu. Start perhaps with whole baked camembert to share; then follow with smoked haddock and parsnip mash, poached egg and mustard cream; roast chicken breast on pomme purée; rib-eye steak with béarnaise sauce; or trio of lamb roasted cannon, mini shepherd's pie and lamb shank.

Open all wk 5.30pm-10.30pm (Sat-Sun 12-11) **Food** Lunch Sat 12-9, Sun 12-8 Dinner Mon-Fri 5.30-9 ⊕ FREE HOUSE ◀ Timothy Taylor Landlord, Black Sheep, Caffrey's Irish Ale, Sharp's Doom Bar, Guinness. ♥ 10 **Facilities** Non-diners area ♦♦ Children's menu Children's portions Garden Parking WiFi

PICK OF THE PUBS

Ye Old Sun Inn

COLTON **MAP 16 SE54**

tel: 01904 744261
Main St LS24 8EP
email: yeoldsuninn@hotmail.co.uk
web: www.yeoldsuninn.co.uk
dir: *Approx 3.5m from York, off A64*

Country pub that goes from strength to strength

Ashley and Kelly McCarthy took over this 17th-century country pub ten years ago and have worked hard to transform it into a thriving inn. They added a bar area and extended the dining area, allowing them more space to increase the excellent themed events and cookery demonstrations and classes that have proved so popular. In the dining room they have a deli where freshly baked bread, home-made jams and chutneys, fresh fish and daily essentials can be bought. A marquee in the garden overlooks rolling countryside and is used for large functions, which includes a summer beer festival and regular farmers' markets. Ashley takes pride in sourcing food and ale from small local producers and suppliers, including salads from his own polytunnel, and his menus are innovative and exciting. Lunches include light bites such as sandwiches, salads and wraps, plus there's an excellent Sunday lunch menu featuring locally sourced roasted meats, chef's specials and a dinner menu. Expect Yorkshire-style main courses

such as braised beef cheeks with horseradish mash and casseroled vegetables; steak and Black Sheep Bitter pie with shortcrust pastry; or rack of Yorkshire lamb with bubble-and-squeak and red wine jus. Precede with roasted tomato and pesto soup and finish with upside-down plum sponge with home-made plum sorbet, or tuck into Ashley's tasting platter of desserts. All dishes come with a wine recommendation, or look to the handpumps - Rudgate Battle Axe and Timothy Taylor Landlord are among the choice of seven real ales.

Open all wk 12-2.30 6-11 (Sun 12-10.30) **Food** Lunch Mon-Sat 12-2, Sun 12-7 Dinner Mon-sat 6-9 ⊕ FREE HOUSE ◼ Timothy Taylor Landlord & Golden Best, Rudgate Battle Axe, Black Sheep, Ossett, Moorhouse's, Guest ale ♂ Aspall. **Facilities** ♦ Children's menu Children's portions Garden Parking WiFi

CARTHORPE · Map 19 SE38

The Fox & Hounds · PICK OF THE PUBS

tel: 01845 567433 **DL8 2LG**
dir: *Off A1, signed on both N'bound & S'bound carriageways*

Vegetarians have their own extensive menu

In the sleepy village of Carthorpe, the cosy Fox & Hounds has been a country inn for over 200 years, and the old anvil and other tools from its time as a smithy are still evident. Landlady Helen Talyor's parents bought the pub over thirty years ago, and in the her hands and that of her husband Vincent's, they have certainly established an excellent reputation for their food which comes from named suppliers and the daily delivery of fresh fish. A typical dinner could begin with grilled black pudding with roasted apple, followed by half roasted Gressingham duckling with orange sauce, parsley and thyme stuffing and apple sauce, and finish with bramble and almond tart. There is a separate vegetarian menu of dishes that can be chosen as a starter or a main, such as caramelised onion and goats' cheese tart. Beers include local Black Sheep, while the wine choice is global in scope. Home-made produce such as jams and chutneys are available to purchase.

Open Tue-Sun 12-3 7-11 Closed 25 Dec & 1st 2wks Jan, Mon **Food** Lunch Tue-Sun 12-2 Dinner Tue-Sun 7-9.30 ⊕ FREE HOUSE ◀ Black Sheep Best Bitter, Worthington's, Guest ale ♂ Thatchers Gold. **Facilities** ♦ Children's portions Parking

CHAPEL LE DALE · Map 18 SD77

The Old Hill Inn

tel: 015242 41256 **LA6 3AR**
dir: *From Ingleton take B6255 4m, pub on right*

An ancient Dales inn of great character

Beautiful views of the Dales await visitors to this former farmhouse, later a drovers' inn, parts dating from 1615, the rest from 1835. When Winston Churchill stayed here on huntin', shootin', fishin' holidays, he no doubt enjoyed the bar, which these days serves eminent Yorkshire real ales like Black Sheep and Dent Aviator. A family of four chefs run the inn (one of whom makes sculptures from sugar) producing lunchtime snacks of sandwiches and home-made burgers, and typical main dishes of beef and ale casserole; smoked haddock fishcakes; and specials of pan-fried fillet of sea bass; and venison steak.

Open Tue-Sun Closed 24-25 Dec, Mon (ex BHs) **Food** Lunch Tue-Sat 12-2.30, Sun 12-3 Dinner Tue-Fri & Sun 6.30-8.45, Sat 6-8.45 Av main course £13 ⊕ FREE HOUSE ◀ Black Sheep Best Bitter, Theakston Best Bitter, Dent Aviator, Guest beer ♂ Thatchers Gold, Aspall. **Facilities** Non-diners area ❧ (Bar Garden) ♦ Children's menu Children's portions Garden Parking WiFi

COLTON · Map 16 SE54

Ye Old Sun Inn · PICK OF THE PUBS

See Pick of the Pubs on opposite page

CRAYKE · Map 19 SE57

The Durham Ox · PICK OF THE PUBS

See Pick of the Pubs on page 556

CROPTON · Map 19 SE78

The New Inn

tel: 01751 417330 **YO18 8HH**
email: phil@thegreatyorkshirebrewery.co.uk
dir: *Phone for detailed directions*

Microbrewery on site draws many real ale enthusiasts

On the edge of the North York Moors National Park, this family-run free house is fortunate to have the acclaimed Cropton microbrewery at the bottom of the garden. Popular with locals and visitors alike, the pub is a draw to ale lovers and there are beer festivals in May and November. Meals are served in the restored village bar and in the elegant Victorian restaurant: choices could include Yorkshire coast fishcakes or crisp belly pork with dauphinoise potatoes; an extensive range from the grill; plus lunchtime sandwiches and ciabatta rolls.

Open all day all wk 11-11 (Sun 11-10.30) **Food** Lunch all wk 12-2 Dinner all wk 5.30-9 ⊕ FREE HOUSE ◀ Cropton Yorkshire Classic, Yorkshire Golden, Yorkshire Pale, Yorkshire Warrior, Blackout & Monkmans Slaughter ♂ Yorkshire cider. **Facilities** Non-diners area ❧ (Bar Garden) ♦ Children's menu Children's portions Play area Family room Garden ⋒ Beer festival Parking WiFi ⚏ (notice required)

EAST WITTON · Map 19 SE18

The Blue Lion · PICK OF THE PUBS

tel: 01969 624273 **DL8 4SN**
email: enquiries@thebluelion.co.uk
dir: *From Ripon take A6108 towards Leyburn*

Smart 18th-century hostelry with imaginative food

This well maintained 18th-century coaching inn, tucked away in an unspoilt estate village close to Jervaulx Abbey, once catered to drovers and travellers journeying through Wensleydale. Ably run today by Paul and Helen Klein, it has built a reputation as one of North Yorkshire's finest inns. The interior is best described as rural chic, oozing stacks of atmosphere and charm. The classic bar with its open fire and flagstone floor is a beer drinker's haven, where the best of the county's breweries present a pleasant dilemma for the ale lover. A blackboard displays imaginative but unpretentious bar meals, while diners in the candlelit restaurant can expect culinary treats incorporating a variety of Yorkshire ingredients, notably seasonal game. A memorable meal may comprise Whitby crab and spinach raviolone with a shellfish bisque; whole roasted local partridge with sarladaise potatoes, bread sauce and game chips; and dark chocolate torte with passionfruit and coconut.

Open all day all wk 11-11 Closed 25 Dec **Food** Lunch all wk 12-2.15 Dinner all wk 7-9.30 Set menu available ⊕ FREE HOUSE ◀ Black Sheep Best Bitter & Riggwelter, Theakston Best Bitter, Worthington's ♂ Thatchers Gold. ⟟ 12 **Facilities** Non-diners area ❧ (Bar Garden) ♦ Children's portions Garden ⋒ Parking WiFi

PICK OF THE PUBS

The Durham Ox

CRAYKE　　　　　　　**Map 19 SE57**

tel: 01347 821506
Westway YO61 4TE
email: enquiries@thedurhamox.com
web: www.thedurhamox.com
dir: *From A19 through Easingwold to Crayke. From market place left up hill, pub on right*

Free house in the beautiful Howardian Hills

They don't do things by halves here. Not only is this 300-year-old, hilltop pub-restaurant named after a 189-stone ox that was exhibited all over the country, but it also features a steel and cast-iron, charcoal-fired oven nicknamed Big Bertha, weighing in at over a ton. The ox was born in 1796 and, as the pub sign shows, he was a hefty beast; his first owner was the Rt Hon Lord Somerville, a print of whom hangs in the bottom bar. Before entering the pub you somehow just know that inside you'll find flagstone floors, exposed beams, oak panelling and winter fires - and indeed you do. Also, this being Yorkshire, that the real ales will come from nowhere else, thus Timothy Taylors Landlord from Keighley, and Black Sheep Best from Masham. Sandwiches and pub classics like East Coast fish pie, and 'Ox' burger meet the need for something quick and easy, or if time is less of an issue you might want to work through the menu. Smoked salmon with capers, shallots,

gherkins and horseradish cream is one starter option; another is twice-baked Cryer & Stott (a Castleford cheesemaker) cheddar soufflé tart with red onion marmalade. For a main course, there might be Yorkshire duck breast and confit leg with orange sauce, fondant potato and pak choi; wild sea bass with crab and pea risotto and crispy arancini; or Moroccan vegetable tagine with couscous and minted yogurt. So where does Big Bertha come in? Two contenders are roasted rib of beef and Chateaubriand, both with chunky chips, onion rings and a choice of béarnaise, Diane or peppercorn sauce. Desserts are no less appealing, typically rhubarb Bakewell tart, and crêpe Suzette.

Open all day all wk 12-11.30 (Sun 12-10.30) **Food** Lunch Mon-Sat 12-2.30, Sun 12-3 Dinner Mon-Sat 5.30-9.30, Sun 5.30-8.30 ⊕ FREE HOUSE ◀ Timothy Taylor Landlord, Black Sheep Best Bitter. ♟ 10 **Facilities** Non-diners area ✿ (Garden) ⁑ Children's menu Children's portions Garden ⊼ Parking WiFi

EAST WITTON *continued*

The Cover Bridge Inn

tel: 01969 623250 **DL8 4SQ**
email: enquiries@thecoverbridgeinn.co.uk
dir: *On A6108 between Middleham & East Witton*

Welcoming Wensleydale pub with well-kept draught ales

The Harringtons have now owned this magnificent little pub at one end of a venerable arched bridge on the River Cover for some 17 years. The pub's oldest part was probably built around 1670, to cater for the increasing trade on the drovers' route from Coverdale. Watch out for the cunning door-latch, which befuddles many a first-time visitor. The ancient interior rewards with wrinkled beams, a vast hearth and open log fires, settles and wholesome fodder, including home-made pies, daily specials, and their famous ham and eggs. Relax in the riverside garden with your choice from eight ales on tap, three of which are rotating guests.

Open all day all wk **Food** Lunch all wk 12-2 Dinner all wk 6-9 FREE HOUSE Guest ales Westons Old Rosie, Gwynt y Ddraig Happy Daze & Two Trees Perry. **Facilities** Non-diners area (Bar Garden) Children's menu Children's portions Play area Garden Parking WiFi (notice required)

EGTON **Map 19 NZ80**

The Wheatsheaf Inn

PICK OF THE PUBS

tel: 01947 895271 **YO21 1TZ**
email: info@wheatsheafegton.com
dir: *Off A169, NW of Grosmont*

Handsome pub at the centre of the community

This modest old pub is very popular with fishermen, as the River Esk runs along at the foot of the hill, and is a big draw for fly-fishers in particular. The pub sits back from the wide main road and it would be easy to drive past it, but that would be a mistake as the welcoming main bar is cosy and traditional, with low beams, dark green walls and comfy settles. The menu offers sandwiches, soup and hot focaccia rolls at lunchtime, as well as a range of light lunches, including wholetail Whitby scampi. In the evening, the supper menu might include a starter of lamb's kidneys with bacon, Madeira and redcurrant gravy and main courses such as chicken and smoked bacon puff pastry pie. There's a locals' bar too, but it only holds about a dozen people, so get there early.

Open 11.30-3 5.30-11.30 (Sat 11.30-11.30 Sun 11.30-11) Closed Mon **Food** Lunch Tue-Sun 12-2 Dinner Tue-Sat 6-9 FREE HOUSE Black Sheep Best Bitter & Golden Sheep, John Smith's, Timothy Taylor Landlord, Guest ales Thatchers Gold. **Facilities** Non-diners area Garden Parking WiFi

EGTON BRIDGE **Map 19 NZ80**

Horseshoe Hotel

tel: 01947 895245 **YO21 1XE**
email: horseshoehotel@yahoo.co.uk
dir: *From Whitby take A171 towards Middlesborough. Village signed in 5m*

Riverside hotel champions local ingredients and ales

The Horseshoe is an 18th-century country house set in beautiful grounds by the River Esk, handy for visiting Whitby, Robin Hood's Bay, the North Yorkshire Moors Railway and TV's *Heartbeat* country. Inside the welcoming bar are oak settles and tables, local artists' paintings, and plates around the picture rails. Along with some great beers, such as Durham Brewery ale, local ingredients are used to create the varied menu, try wholetail scampi and chips or medallion of pork fillet with woodchopper sauce.

Open all wk 11.30-3 6.30-11 (Sat 11.30-11 Sun 12-10.30) **Food** Lunch all wk 12-2 Dinner all wk 6-9 FREE HOUSE John Smith's Cask, Durham, Black Sheep, Theakston, Guest ales. **Facilities** Non-diners area Children's menu Children's portions Family room Garden Parking WiFi (notice required)

The Postgate

tel: 01947 895241 **YO21 1UX**
dir: *Phone for detailed directions*

Walkers, families and dogs are very welcome

Set in the Esk Valley within a stone's throw of the river, The Postgate is a typical North York Moors country inn; it played the part of the Black Dog in TV's *Heartbeat*. Being on the coast-to-coast trail, and becoming known as a food destination, the pub is popular with walkers who chat amiably with locals in the bar over their pints of Black Sheep. The menu offers an array of locally sourced fresh fish and seafood from Whitby fish market, excellent local meats, and game in season.

Open all wk 12-3 5.30-12 **Food** Lunch all wk 12-2.30 Dinner all wk 6-9 PUNCH TAVERNS Timothy Taylor Landlord, Black Sheep Bitter. **Facilities** Non-diners area (Bar Garden) Children's menu Children's portions Garden Parking WiFi (notice required)

FELIXKIRK **Map 19 SE48**

The Carpenters Arms

tel: 01845 537369 **YO7 2DP**
email: enquiries@thecarpentersarmsfelixkirk.com **web:** www.carpentersarmsfelixkirk.com
dir: *From Thirsk take A170 towards Helmsley. Left signed Felixkirk, 2.25m to village*

Unpretentious village pub with lovely views

Felixkirk, in the Vale of Mowbray, has no shops, making this Provenance Inns owned pub the village's only retail establishment. To the east are the Hambleton Hills and the North Yorks Moors National Park, while west are the Yorkshire Dales. Bare stonework, slate flooring and rich red walls characterise the interior, and there are open fires in the dining areas and the bar. The restaurant and tiered terrace offer the best views. Menu descriptions are simple: pan-seared salmon fillet; braised pork cheeks; gourmet burgers; steak ciabattas; herb crusted haddock; devilled chicken livers; and fish and chips. Check out the Magnificent Seven – seven main courses, each £7.

Open all day all wk **Food** Lunch Mon-Sat 12-2.30, Sun 12-3 Dinner Mon-Sat 6-9.30, Sun 6-8.30 PROVENANCE INNS Black Sheep Best Bitter, Timothy Taylor Landlord Symonds. **Facilities** Non-diners area (Bar Garden) Children's menu Children's portions Garden Parking WiFi (notice required)

GIGGLESWICK
Map 18 SD86

Black Horse Hotel

tel: 01729 822506 **32 Church St BD24 OBE**
email: theblackhorse-giggle@tiscali.co.uk
dir: *Phone for detailed directions*

Village centre inn with pub favourites on the menu

Set next to the church and behind the market cross in the 17th-century main street, this traditional free house is as charming as Giggleswick itself. Down in the warm and friendly bar you'll find a range of hand-pulled ales. The menu of freshly prepared pub favourites ranges from home-made pizzas to main course dishes like home-made steak and ale pie; haddock and chips; and horseshoe of gammon with either eggs, pineapple, or both.

Open 12-2.30 5.30-11 (Sat-Sun 12-11) Closed Mon **Food** Lunch Tue-Sun 12-2 Dinner Tue-Thu 6.30-9, Fri-Sun 6-9 ⊕ FREE HOUSE ◼ Timothy Taylor Landlord & Golden Best, John Smith's, Tetley's, Guest ale. **Facilities** Non-diners area ◗◖ Children's menu Children's portions Garden ⋒ Parking WiFi

GOATHLAND
Map 19 NZ80

Birch Hall Inn

tel: 01947 896245 **Beck Hole YO22 5LE**
email: glenys@birchhallinn.fsnet.co.uk
dir: *9m from Whitby on A169*

One of the smallest bars in the country

Beck Hole is a tiny hamlet of nine cottages and a pub hidden in the steep Murk Esk Valley close to the North Yorkshire Moors (steam) Railway. This delightful little free house has just two tiny rooms separated by a sweet shop; no more than 30 people plus two small dogs have ever fitted inside with the door closed! The main bar offers well-kept local ales to sup beside an open fire in winter, including the pub's house ale, Beckwatter. In warm weather, food and drink can be enjoyed in the large garden, which has peaceful views. The local quoits team play on the village green on summer evenings. The pub has been under the same ownership for over 30 years and the simple menu features the local butcher's pies, old-fashioned flatcakes filled with ham, cheese, corned beef or farmhouse pâté, and home-made scones and buttered beer cake.

Open 11-3 7.30-11 (11-11 summer) Closed Mon eve & Tue in winter **Food** Served during all opening hours ⊕ FREE HOUSE ◼ Birch Hall Inn Beckwatter, Black Sheep Best Bitter, Durham Black Velvet, York Guzzler. **Facilities** ❖ (Bar Garden) ◗◖ Family room Garden ⋒ **Notes** ◎

GRASSINGTON
Map 19 SE06

Grassington House ★★★★★ RR ◉◉

tel: 01756 752406 **5 The Square BD23 5AQ**
email: bookings@grassingtonhousehotel.co.uk web: www.grassingtonhousehotel.co.uk
dir: *A59 into Grassington, in town square opposite post office*

A destination pub and restaurant with rooms

Whoever commissioned this private house in 1760 chose the site well, for this elegant Georgian pub and restaurant stands imposingly in Grassington's cobbled square. Fresh local produce underpins a two AA-Rosette menu offering starters of taster slates of tapas-style nibbles; seared potted hog roast wrapped in Parma ham, toffee apple jus; and cream of leek and fennel soup. Mains might be pumpkin and chestnut lasagne; or pan-fried Pateley lamb best end and loin with artichokes, aubergine and rosemary Anna potatoes. For lighter options there's an interesting

range of open and closed sandwiches, perhaps glazed Blackstick blue cheese, mushrooms and caramelised onions will appeal. Thwaites Original and Wainwright, and Dark Horse Hetton Pale Ale are bar staples.

Open all day all wk **Food** Lunch Mon-Fri 12-2.30, Sat 12-4, Sun 12-8 Dinner Mon-Sat 6-9.30, Sun 12-8 Set menu available ⊕ FREE HOUSE ◼ Dark Horse Hetton Pale Ale, Thwaites Original & Wainwright. ♟ 14 **Facilities** Non-diners area ◗◖ Children's menu Children's portions Garden ⋒ Parking WiFi ◼ (notice required) **Rooms** 9

GREAT HABTON
Map 19 SE77

The Grapes Inn

tel: 01653 669166 **YO17 6TU**
email: info@thegrapes-inn.co.uk
dir: *From Malton take B1257 towards Helmsley. In Amotherby right into Amotherby Ln. After Newsham Bridge right into Habton Ln & follow pub signs. 0.75m to pub*

Enjoyable food in a busy community pub

Adam and Katie Myers have celebrated their tenth year at The Grapes, a welcoming village pub between the Howardian Hills and the North Yorkshire Moors near the bustling market town of Malton. Enjoy a pint of Marston's EPA with the locals in the lively taproom, separated from the dining room – once the village post office – by a double-sided log burner. Chef-proprietor Adam has gained an enviable reputation in Ryedale for his chargrilled steaks, but other hearty options are venison sausages on horseradish and thyme mash with red wine gravy; and monkfish, scallop and chorizo tagliatelle.

Open Tue-Fri 6pm-close (Sat 12-2 6-close Sun open all day) Closed fr 2 Jan for 2wks, Mon **Food** Lunch Sat-Sun 12-2 Dinner Tue-Sat 6-8.30, Sun 6.30-8.30 ⊕ MARSTON'S ◼ EPA, Wychwood Hobgoblin ♂ Thatchers Gold. **Facilities** Non-diners area ◗◖ Children's menu Children's portions Outside area ⋒ Parking

GREEN HAMMERTON
Map 19 SE45

The Bay Horse Inn

tel: 01423 330338 **York Rd YO26 8BN**
email: enquiry@bayhorsegreenhammerton.co.uk
dir: *A1 junct 47 follow signs for A59 towards York. After 3m, turn left into village, on right opposite post office*

Hearty food in the Vale of York

This traditional inn is part of the original settlement of Green Hammerton, positioned on the old Roman road from York to Aldborough. The pub has served travellers and villagers for over 200 years; many features from those days remain in the beamed, fire-warmed interior. Reliable Yorkshire cask beers accompany home-made meals strong on local produce; excellent matured steaks, gammon and chicken grilled to order are always available. Daily-changing dishes include haunch of venison steak with blackberry port sauce; and pork fillet with cider and apple sauce. Outside is a garden and patio area.

Open all wk 11.30-2.30 5.30-12 (Sat 11.30am-mdnt Sun 11.30-8) **Food** Lunch Mon-Sat 12-2.30, Sun 12-7.30 Dinner Mon-Fri 6-9, Sat 12-9, Sun 12-7.30 Av main course £9.50 ⊕ GREENE KING ◼ IPA, Timothy Taylor, Black Sheep, Guest ale. **Facilities** Non-diners area ❖ (Bar Garden) ◗◖ Children's menu Children's portions Garden ⋒ Parking WiFi ◼ (notice required)

GRINTON
Map 19 SE09

The Bridge Inn
PICK OF THE PUBS

See Pick of the Pubs on opposite page

PICK OF THE PUBS

The Bridge Inn

GRINTON Map 19 SE09

tel: 01748 884224
DL11 6HH
email: atkinbridge@btinternet.com
web: www.thebridgeinn-grinton.co.uk
dir: *Exit A1 at Scotch Corner onto A6108, through Richmond. Left onto B6270 towards Grinton & Reeth*

A favourite with ramblers and discerning diners

A 13th-century riverside pub close to one of Yorkshire's finest old churches, known as the Cathedral of the Dales, The Bridge is located in Grinton, which has stood here for almost 1,000 years. Two of the Yorkshire Dales' wildest and prettiest dales meet in Grinton; Arkengarthdale and Swaledale collide in a symphony of fells, moors, waterfalls and cataracts. Lanes and tracks slope down from the heights, bringing ramblers and riders to appreciate the good range of northern beers that Andrew Atkin matches with his fine foods; York Brewery's Yorkshire Terrier being a case in point. Locals enjoy the bustling games room and beamed old bar serving baguettes and rye squares, whilst a more tranquil restaurant area caters for those after a more intimate meal experience. Resident chef Michael Ogden is in charge of the food, his menu inspired by carefully chosen seasonal local game, meats, fish and other produce, including herbs plucked from

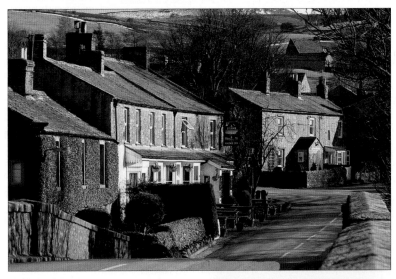

the garden. Expect traditional English dishes with a modern twist, enhanced by daily-changing specials. Starters range from hot smoked salmon fillet with red chard, pickled cucumber, dill salad, poppy seed blinis and chive crème fraîche, to chicken tikka kebabs with a pepper, mixed bean and mint salad and a mango chutney dressing. Mains reflect a similar scope, running from homely slow-roasted pork belly or trio of Swaledale lamb to smoked haddock, salmon and king prawns in a creamy sauce and wrapped in a savoury pancake. Finish with Liz's ginger pudding and vanilla ice cream; blueberry and white chocolate cheesecake; or a selection of Swaledale cheeses with savoury biscuits and chutney.

Open all day all wk **Food** Lunch all wk 12-9 Dinner all wk 12-9 Av main course £12 Restaurant menu available all wk. JENNINGS Cumberland Ale & Cocker Hoop, Caledonian Deuchars IPA, York Yorkshire Terrier, Adnams.
Facilities Non-diners area ✿ (Bar Garden) ♦ Children's menu Children's portions Garden Parking WiFi

HARDRAW
Map 18 SD89

The Green Dragon Inn

tel: 01969 667392 **DL8 3LZ**
email: info@greendragonhardraw.com
dir: *From Hawes take A684 towards Sedbergh. Right to Hardraw, approx 1.5m*

If you're in the area, don't miss this one

Entering the Bar Parlour is like stepping into a Tudor film-set, although parts of the inn are much older – 13th century in fact. Gravestones, forming part of the floor, were washed away from the neighbouring churchyard during floods. In a wooded site behind is Hardraw Force, England's highest single-drop waterfall, which JMW Turner painted while staying here in 1816. The choice of real ales is good, and pub food includes home-made steak pie; giant Yorkshire pudding; and local game casserole. Beer festivals in June and July, a third with cider in October, and regular live folk music are all big draws.

Open all day all wk **Food** Lunch all wk 11.30-3 Dinner all wk 6-10 Av main course £9.95 ⊕ FREE HOUSE ◀ Timothy Taylor Landlord, Theakston Best Bitter & Old Peculier, Wensleydale, Yorkshire Dales ♻ Olivers, Gwatkins, Dunkertons, Ralph's. **Facilities** Non-diners area ♣ (Bar Garden) ♦♠ Children's menu Children's portions Family room Garden ♬ Beer festival Cider festival Parking WiFi ☕ (notice required)

HAROME
Map 19 SE68

The Star Inn ◉◉ | PICK OF THE PUBS

tel: 01439 770397 **YO62 5JE**
email: reservations@thestarinnatharome.co.uk
dir: *From Helmsley take A170 towards Kirkbymoorside 0.5m. Turn right for Harome*

Renowned gastro-pub in prime walking country

On the fringe of the North Yorkshire Moors National Park, this 14th-century thatched gem sits in a idyllic village surrounded by wonderful local walks. Although renowned as a foodie destination, the genuinely pubby bar is worth the journey alone and both locals and visitors can revel in well-kept pints of Copper Dragon or Black Sheep whilst eagerly awaiting the call to dine. Chef/patron Andrew Pern's daily-changing seasonal menu crafted largely from local produce has made this one of the jewels in England's culinary crown and people travel from far and wide to sample his innovative cooking. Treat yourself to 'Mulligatawny' of Harome pheasant with Indian spiced raisins, cucumber and onion bhaji with curry oil before moving on to mulled wine-braised ox cheek with smoked bacon, hedgehog mushrooms, Blue Wensleydale mash, carrots and cooking juices. Finish with Star Inn Orchard apple, sultana and roast hazelnut crumble with elderberry ripple ice cream.

Open all wk 11.30-3 6.30-11 (Mon 6.30-11 Sun 12-11) Closed Mon L **Food** Lunch Tue-Sat 11.30-2, Sun 12-6 Dinner Mon-Sat 6.30-9.30 Av main course £20 Set menu available ⊕ FREE HOUSE ◀ Theakston Best Bitter, Black Sheep, Copper Dragon, Hambleton, Cropton ♻ Westons Stowford Press, Ampleforth Abbey. ₹ 24 **Facilities** Non-diners area ♦♠ Children's menu Children's portions Garden ♬ Parking ☕ (notice required)

HARROGATE
Map 19 SE35

NEW The Fat Badger

tel: 01823 505681 **The White Hart Hotel, Cold Bath Rd HG2 0NF**
email: dominicjackson@btconnect.com

Victorian-style grandeur in the heart of Harrogate

Just around the corner from Harrogate's Royal Pump Rooms in the heart of the spa town's Montpellier Quarter, The Fat Badger has the lofty ceilings and dark wood fixtures reminiscent of the grand gin palaces of more than a century ago. Animal-themed oil paintings, faux gas lamps and leather chesterfields give the place an elegant, clubby feel and makes for a relaxed setting to enjoy a pint of Black Sheep or York Guzzler. The food menu offers plenty of choice, with sharing dishes, sandwiches and main meals such as steak and ale pie; barbecued ribs and spicy chorizo and tomato pasta.

Open all day all wk **Food** Lunch all wk 12-9 Dinner all wk 12-9 Av main course £12 ⊕ FREE HOUSE ◀ York Guzzler, Black Sheep. **Facilities** Non-diners area Garden WiFi ☕ (notice required)

HAWES
Map 18 SD88

The Moorcock Inn

tel: 01969 667488 **Garsdale Head LA10 5PU**
email: admin@moorcockinn.com
dir: *On A684, 5m from Hawes, 10m from Sedbergh at junct with B6259 for Kirkby Stephen*

Old inn surrounded by open countryside

At the tip of Wensleydale, this 18th-century inn stands alone in open countryside, although it is only three-quarters of a mile from Garsdale Station. Inside is a traditional blend of original stonework, bright colours and comfortable sofas. Savour a glass of local real ale from the Tirril Brewery, draught lager or one of the 50 malt whiskies, and enjoy the spectacular views from the garden. Home-cooked lunches include jackets, sandwiches and pub classics. For dinner, start with whitebait, brown bread, lemon and aïoli, then tuck into steak, mushroom and ale pie or a vegetarian choice of sweet potato and aubergine curry.

Open 12-12 Mar-Oct (Mon-Fri 12-3 6-12 Sat-Sun 12-12 Nov-Feb) Closed 25 Dec Mon & Wed in Nov & Jan **Food** Lunch all wk 12-3 Dinner all wk 6.30-8.30 Av main course £10 ⊕ FREE HOUSE ◀ Copper Dragon, Theakston, Tirril Ales, Nine Standards Brewery, Cumberland Corby Ale, Dent, Wensleydale, Guest ales ♻ Symonds. ₹ 12 **Facilities** Non-diners area ♣ (Bar Restaurant Garden) ♦♠ Children's menu Children's portions Garden ♬ Parking WiFi ☕ (notice required)

HAWNBY
Map 19 SE58

The Inn at Hawnby ★★★★ INN ◉ | PICK OF THE PUBS

tel: 01439 798202 **YO62 5QS**
email: info@innathawnby.co.uk **web:** www.innathawnby.co.uk
dir: *From Helmsley take B1257 towards Stokesley. Follow Hawnby signs*

Stunning views and first-rate food

In the midst of the North Yorkshire Moors on top of a hill, this charming 19th-century former drovers' inn rewards customers with panoramic country views. Run by hands-on and welcoming proprietors Kathryn and David Young, it stocks some great Yorkshire-brewed ales, including Great Newsome Brewery's Arden ale and quaffable Hawnby Hops brewed specially for the pub. Head chef Jason Reeves prides himself on use of local and seasonal produce, with his accomplished dishes served either in the Mexborough restaurant or in the cosy bar. Typical of dinner starters are broccoli and Yorkshire Blue soup; and scallops with black truffle, parsnip and apple. These may be followed by chicken breast with Worcestershire ham, baked potato risotto and wild mushrooms; or venison shank with cavalo nero cabbage, mash and kibbled onions. A lunchtime plate of gammon with creamed spinach, fried egg and chips, followed by carrot cake with mascarpone will recharge the batteries nicely.

Open all wk 10-3 6-11 (Fri-Sun all day) Closed 25 Dec & Mon-Tue Feb-Mar **Food** Lunch all wk 12-2 Dinner all wk 7-9 Av main course £14 ⊕ FREE HOUSE ◑ Timothy Taylor Landlord, Black Sheep, Hawnby Hops, Great Newsome Arden ale ⍥ Westons Stowford Press. ♟ 8 **Facilities** Non-diners area ♣ (Bar Garden) ⁑ Children's menu Children's portions Garden ⊓ Parking WiFi ⇛ (notice required) **Rooms** 9

HELPERBY
Map 19 SE46

The Oak Tree Inn

tel: 01423 789189 **Raskelf Rd YO61 2PH**
email: enquiries@theoaktreehelperby.com **web:** www.theoaktreehelperby.com
dir: *A19 from York towards Thirsk. After Easingwold left signed Helperby. Approx 5m to village*

No-nonsense pub food at the village inn

Depending on how you approach the village, the signs say either Helperby Brafferton or Brafferton Helperby, an apparent confusion which to locals probably makes perfect sense. Major refurbishment has revived this member of the Provenance Inns group, giving it a spacious new bar for informal dining, and a barn extension overlooking the rear courtyard for more formal meals. You'll find there's a similar menu to those at the sister pubs in Felixkirk and Marton, offering unfussy mains such as slow-braised venison; Moroccan spiced chicken supreme; Yorkshire steaks; and Black Sheep beer-battered fish and chips.

Open all day all wk **Food** Lunch Mon-Sat 12-2.30, Sun 12-3 Dinner Mon-Sat 5.30-9.30, Sun 5.30-8.30 ⊕ PROVENANCE INNS ◑ Black Sheep Best Bitter, Timothy Taylor Landlord ⍥ Symonds. **Facilities** Non-diners area ♣ (Bar Outside area) ⁑ Children's menu Children's portions Outside area ⊓ Parking WiFi ⇛ (notice required)

HIGH GRANTLEY
Map 19 SE26

The Grantley Arms

tel: 01765 620227 **HG4 3PJ**
email: vsails2@aol.com
dir: *From Ripon on B6265 towards Pateley Bridge (pass Fountains Abbey) take 2nd right signed Grantley. 0.5m pub on left*

Pretty inn not far from Ripon

On the edge of the Yorkshire Dales National Park, three miles from Fountains Abbey and five from the market town of Ripon, is this 17th-century inn that Valerie Sails

and Eric Broadwith have run for some 14 years. They can usually be found front-of-house, either in the bar, home of some excellent Yorkshire real ales, or in the intimate restaurant, where crisp linen cloths cover the tables. With virtually everything made in the pub's own kitchen, start with smoked haddock fillet, diced vegetables, parsley and potato chowder, then rare-breed belly pork with apple sauce and red wine jus, and coconut mousse to finish.

Open 12-3 5.30-11 (Sun 12-3.30 5.30-11) Closed 2wks Nov, Mon ⊕ FREE HOUSE ◑ Theakston, Hambleton, Great Newsome, Old Mill ⍥ Thatchers Gold. **Facilities** ⁑ Children's menu Children's portions Outside area Parking WiFi

HOVINGHAM
Map 19 SE67

The Malt Shovel

tel: 01653 628264 **Main St YO62 4LF**
email: info@themaltshovelhovingham.com
dir: *18m NE of York, 5m from Castle Howard*

Friendly roadside village pub

Tucked away in the Duchess of Kent's home village, the stone-built 18th-century Malt Shovel offers a friendly atmosphere with well-kept ales and food prepared from quality local ingredients. There are two dining rooms where you can enjoy starters of whitebait with lime and chilli mayonnaise, chicken liver pâté with chutney, or black pudding and apple fritters, followed by swordfish with tomato and anchovy sauce, mustard chicken, or chickpea curry. There is also a large beer garden at the rear of the pub where you can sit and enjoy a pint or two in lovely surroundings.

Open all wk winter 11.30-2 6-11 (summer 11.30-2.30 5.30-11) Sun all day **Food** Lunch Mon-Sat 11.30-2 (winter) 11.30-2.30 (summer), Sun 12-2.30 Dinner Mon-Sat 6-9 (winter) 5.30-9 (summer), Sun 5.30-7.45 Set menu available ⊕ PUNCH TAVERNS ◑ Copper Dragon Golden Pippin, Theakston Best Bitter, Black Sheep, Guest ale ⍥ Thatchers. **Facilities** Non-diners area ♣ (Bar Garden) ⁑ Children's menu Children's portions Garden ⊓ Parking WiFi ⇛ (notice required)

The Worsley Arms Hotel
PICK OF THE PUBS

tel: 01653 628234 **Main St YO62 4LA**
email: enquiries@worsleyarms.co.uk
dir: *On B1257 between Malton & Helmsley*

A magnificent base for exploring North Yorkshire

Built by Sir William Worsley in 1841, this village hotel and pub form part of the Worsley family's historic Hovingham Hall Estate, birthplace of the Duchess of Kent, and currently home to her nephew. Hambleton Stallion from nearby Thirsk, and Black Sheep from Masham are on tap in the Cricketers' Bar (the local team has played on the village green for over 150 years). You can eat here or in the restaurant; lunch and afternoon tea are also served in the large walled garden. Lunchtime choices could include traditional mains like Wensleydale gammon steak, and a selection of sandwiches; while the à la carte lists pan-fried sea bass with a crab and king prawn risotto; and confit of braised lamb shank. A short drive from the market town of Pickering, the hotel is also well placed for visiting York, the Dales and Castle Howard. The pub hosts regular wine evenings, monthly quizzes and a supper club.

Open all day all wk **Food** Lunch Mon-Sat 12-2, Sun 12-2.30 Dinner all wk 6.30-9 ⊕ FREE HOUSE ◑ Hambleton Stallion, Black Sheep. ♟ 20 **Facilities** Non-diners area ♣ (Bar Garden) ⁑ Garden ⊓ Parking ⇛ (notice required)

HUBBERHOLME
Map 18 SD97

The George Inn

tel: 01756 760223 **BD23 5JE**
email: visit@thegeorge-inn.co.uk
dir: *From Skipton take B6265 to Threshfield. B6160 to Buckden. Follow signs for Hubberholme*

Dales inn with bags of charm

Stunningly located beside the River Wharfe in the Yorkshire Dales National Park, this pub, now in new hands, was built in the 1600s as a farmstead and still has flagstone floors, stone walls, mullioned windows and an open fire. To check if the bar is open, look for a lighted candle in the window. Beers are local, coming from the Black Sheep and Yorkshire Dales breweries. Enjoy your pint on the terrace in the summer months. For lunch there's soup, sandwiches and baskets of chips; but the traditional choices for an evening meal are based on locally sourced produce such as lamb chops with potatoes, seasonal vegetables and rich gravy.

Open 12-3 6-10.30 (Summer all day 12-11 check website) Closed last 3 wks Jan, Tue **Food** Lunch Wed-Sun 12-2.30 Dinner Wed-Mon 6-8 ⊕ FREE HOUSE ◀ Black Sheep, Yorkshire Dales, Tetley's, Local Guest ales ♂ Thatchers Gold. **Facilities** ✿ (Bar Outside area) ◀♦ Children's portions Outside area ☴ Parking **Notes** ◉

KILBURN
Map 19 SE57

The Forresters Arms Inn

tel: 01347 868386 **The Square YO61 4AH**
email: admin@forrestersarms.com
dir: *From Thirsk take A170, after 3m turn right signed Kilburn. At Kilburn Rd junct, turn right, inn on left in village square*

Sturdy coaching inn with hearty food

Next door to the famous Robert Thompson craft carpentry workshop, The Forresters Arms has fine examples of his early work, with the distinctive trademark mouse evident in both bars. A sturdy stone-built former coaching inn still catering for travellers passing close by the famous White Horse of Kilburn on the North York Moors, it has log fires, cask ales and good food. Dishes include salmon fishcakes with salad and herb mayonnaise; a home-made burger with crispy bacon and Applewood cheese; and traditional fish and chips. There's also a specials board and a selection of lunchtime snacks.

Open all day all wk 9am-11pm **Food** Lunch Mon-Fri 12-3, off season 12-2.30, Sat-Sun all day Dinner all wk 6-9, off season 6-8 ⊕ ENTERPRISE INNS ◀ John Smith's Cask, Guest ales ♂ Addlestones, Westons Stowford Press. **Facilities** Non-diners area ✿ (Bar Outside area) ◀♦ Children's menu Children's portions Outside area ☴ Beer festival Parking WiFi ⬚ (notice required)

KIRBY HILL
Map 19 NZ10

The Shoulder of Mutton Inn

tel: 01748 822772 **DL11 7JH**
email: info@shoulderofmutton.net
dir: *From A1 (Scotch Corner junct) take A66. In approx 6m follow signs for Kirby Hill on left*

Picture-postcard village inn

Most buildings in this pretty hamlet are clustered round the green, diagonally opposite the ivy-clad, 18th-century inn. From its garden and sheltered patio the views over Holmedale are alone worth coming here for, while other obvious attractions are the open log fires warming the traditional bar, the local Daleside ales, and the stone-walled, beamed restaurant. Here seasonal, home-cooked food includes smoky haddock linguine; Gressingham duck breast with plum, orange and ginger sauce; and game pie with mushrooms and black pudding bubble-and-squeak. Hearty bar snacks are a good alternative.

Open all wk 6-11 (Sat-Sun 12-3 6-11) **Food** Lunch Sat-Sun 12-2 Dinner Wed-Sun 6.30-9 ⊕ FREE HOUSE ◀ Daleside, Guest ales ♂ Thatchers. **Facilities** Non-diners area ◀♦ Garden Beer festival Parking

KIRKBY FLEETHAM
Map 19 SE29

The Black Horse Inn ★★★★★ RR ◉◉

tel: 01609 749010 **Lumley Ln DL7 0SH**
email: gm@blackhorsekirkbyfleetham.com web: www.blackhorsekirkbyfleetham.com
dir: *Signed from A1 between Catterick & Leeming Bar*

Charming and successful inn

Legend has it that Dick Turpin eloped with his lady from this village pub in the Swale Valley, just off the vast village green; the inn was named after the outlaw's steed in celebration. The pub garden adjoins fields, and the interior, including the seven character bedrooms, is appointed to create a pleasing mix of tradition and comfort. No surprise then that locals and visitors are encouraged to tarry a while, to sup a grand Yorkshire pint and enjoy accomplished two AA-Rosette food that covers all the bases. Look for signature starters such as chef's black pudding, crunchy hen's egg, with parsnip purée and caramelised apple, and main courses like braised Yorkshire pork belly, black pudding, grain mustard mash and cider jus, or a vegetarian choice of pea and mint risotto.

Open all day all wk **Food** Lunch Mon-Sat 12-2.30, Sun 12-7 Dinner Mon-Sat 5-9.30, Sun 12-7 Av main course £14.50 Set menu available Restaurant menu available all wk ⊕ FREE HOUSE ◀ Black Sheep, Copper Dragon, Timothy Taylor Landlord. ♟ 10 **Facilities** Non-diners area ✿ (Bar Garden) ◀♦ Children's menu Children's portions Garden ☴ Parking WiFi ⬚ (notice required) **Rooms** 7

KIRKBYMOORSIDE
Map 19 SE68

George & Dragon Hotel
PICK OF THE PUBS

tel: 01751 433334 **17 Market Place YO62 6AA**
email: reception@georgeanddragon.net
dir: *Just off A170 between Scarborough & Thirsk. In town centre*

Charming, family-owned favourite

Walk into the G&D, as it is affectionately called, and you'll know instantly that you've made the right decision. The undoubted charm of this family-owned, whitewashed coaching inn is due to many things – the log fire in the bar, the collection of sporting paraphernalia, the fountain in the sheltered courtyard... for some it'll be the five well-kept, hand-pulled real ales, including an in-house brew. At lunchtime, enjoy a baguette or panini in the bar or, if you fancy contemporary decor and leather seats, Knight's Restaurant's short menu offers deep-fried brie with red onion marmalade; haddock, salmon, scallop and prawns in mature cheddar sauce topped with creamed potatoes; and shank of Yorkshire lamb with bubble-and-squeak, spring greens, and minted port and redcurrant sauce. Home-made steak and Stilton pie, and Cajun chicken burgers are listed as pub classics. The traditional Sunday carvery is hugely popular.

Open all day all wk 10.30am-11pm **Food** Lunch all wk 12-2 Dinner all wk 6-9 Restaurant menu available ⊕ FREE HOUSE ◀ Greene King Abbot Ale, Copper Dragon, Black Sheep, House Bitter, Guest ales. ♟ 12 **Facilities** Non-diners area ◀♦ Children's menu Children's portions Garden ☴ Parking WiFi ⬚

KNARESBOROUGH
Map 19 SE35

The General Tarleton Inn ★★★★★ RR ◉◉
PICK OF THE PUBS

See Pick of the Pubs on opposite page

PICK OF THE PUBS

The General Tarleton Inn ★★★★★ RR 🌹🌹

KNARESBOROUGH   Map 19 SE35

tel: 01423 340284
Boroughbridge Rd, Ferrensby HG5 0PZ
email: gti@generaltarleton.co.uk
web: www.generaltarleton.co.uk
dir: *A1(M) junct 48 at Boroughbridge, take A6055 to Knaresborough. Inn 4m on right*

Local produce drives the menu here

Renamed in honour of General Banastre Tarleton who fought in the American War of Independence, this 18th-century coaching inn just north of Knaresborough is an ideal base for exploring the Yorkshire Dales. The renovated interior retains its old beams and original log fires, while the sofas encourage guests to settle down with a pint of Black Sheep Best Bitter and peruse the seasonal menus that have helped chef-proprietor John Topham and his team earn two AA Rosettes. Championing local produce, East Coast fish is delivered daily, local vegetables arrive the day they've been picked, and the game comes from nearby shoots when in season. The 'Food with Yorkshire Roots' menu is available in the Bar Brasserie, fine-dining restaurant, and terrace garden and courtyard. Typical starters include roast wood pigeon salad with blue cheese beignet and roast hazelnuts; Provencal fish soup with rouille, gruyére and

croutons; or seared king scallops with crispy squid, celeriac purée and pomegranate salsa. These might precede mains of haunch of venison, potato terrine, plum ketchup and celeriac; or white wine poached halibut with mussels, new potatoes and red pepper in a saffron broth. Pub classics such as fish and chips; seafood thermidor; and chargrilled rib-eye steak with hand-cut chips, sherry glazed onion, watercress and béarnaise sauce are also available. Leave a space for treacle tart with clotted cream ice cream and salted peanut butter; or apple tart Tatin with apple pannacotta and vanilla ice cream. Accompanying wines can be selected from a list of 150, with eleven served by the glass.

Open all wk 12-3 5.30-11 **Food** Lunch all wk 12-2 Dinner all wk 5.30-9.15 Av main course £18.50 Set menu available ⊞ FREE HOUSE ◧ Black Sheep Best Bitter, Timothy Taylor Landlord ♺ Aspall. ☙ 11 **Facilities** Non-diners area ∮ Children's menu Children's portions Garden ⊓ Parking WiFi **Rooms** 13

LANGTHWAITE
Map 19 NZ00

The Red Lion Inn

tel: 01748 884218 **DL11 6RE**
email: rlionlangthwaite@aol.com **web:** www.redlionlangthwaite.co.uk
dir: *From A6108 between Richmond & Leyburn follow Reeth signs. In Reeth follow Langthwaite sign*

Often used as a film and TV location

The Red Lion Inn is a traditional country pub owned by the same family for 50 years. It hosts two darts teams in winter, a quoits team in summer, and bar snacks are served all year round. There are some wonderful walks in this part of the Dales and relevant books and maps are on sale in the bar. In the tiny snug there are photographs relating to the various films and TV programmes filmed at this unusually photogenic pub (including *All Creatures Great and Small*, *A Woman of Substance* and *Hold the Dream*). Ice cream, chocolates and sweets are also available.

Open all wk 11-3 7-11 **Food** Lunch all wk 11-3 ⊕ FREE HOUSE ◀ Black Sheep Best Bitter, Riggwelter & All Creatures, Guinness Ö Thatchers Gold. **Facilities** Non-diners area Family room Outside area 🚗 Parking

LASTINGHAM
Map 19 SE79

Blacksmiths Arms

tel: 01751 417247 **YO62 6TN**
email: pete.hils@blacksmithslastingham.co.uk
dir: *7m from Pickering & 4m from Kirkbymoorside. A170 (Pickering to Kirkbymoorside road), follow Lastingham & Appleton-le-Moors signs*

Well loved pub on the southern fringe of the North Yorks Moors

With a cottage garden and decked outdoor seating area, this stone-built, 17th-century free house has a wonderful atmosphere. In the small front bar pewter mugs and beer pump clips hang from the low beams, and copper cooking pans decorate the open range. A snug and two delightful dining rooms complete the interior. Home-cooked dishes prepared from local supplies include Yorkshire hotpot; lamb and mint pie; and Whitby breaded scampi (also in takeaway form). Enjoy the food with Theakston Best Bitter or a guest ale. St Mary's Church, opposite the pub, is renowned for its Saxon crypt.

Open all day all wk **Food** Lunch all wk 12-5 Dinner all wk 6.30-8.45 ⊕ FREE HOUSE ◀ Theakston Best Bitter, 2 Guest ales. **Facilities** Non-diners area ▪♦ Children's menu Children's portions Family room Garden 🚗 WiFi 🚌 (notice required)

LEVISHAM
Map 19 SE89

Horseshoe Inn ★★★★ INN

tel: 01751 460240 **Main St YO18 7NL**
email: info@horseshoelevisham.co.uk **web:** www.horseshoelevisham.co.uk
dir: *A169, 5m from Pickering. 4m, pass Fox & Rabbit Inn on right. In 0.5m left to Lockton. Follow steep winding road to village*

Family-run pub in tranquil village

On the edge of the North York Moors National Park, here is this village pub where you can stay overnight while touring the area, perhaps by steam train from Levisham station. Charles and Toby Wood have created an inviting atmosphere that's especially apparent in the beamed and wooden-floored bar, where a gilt-edged mirror hangs above the open fire, and the real ales are from Black Sheep and Cropton. Local suppliers play a big part behind the scenes so that the kitchen can prepare hearty plates of sausage and mash, sirloin steak with home-made chips, and deep-fried Whitby haddock and chips.

Open all day all wk **Food** Lunch all wk 12-2 Dinner all wk 6-8.30 ⊕ FREE HOUSE ◀ Black Sheep Best Bitter, Cropton Yorkshire Moors, Two Pints, Yorkshire Warrior & Endeavour, Wold Top Headland Red, Brass Castle Cliffhanger Ö Thatchers Gold. ♟12 **Facilities** Non-diners area ❀ (Bar Garden) ▪♦ Children's menu Children's portions Garden 🚗 Parking WiFi **Rooms** 9

LEYBURN
Map 19 SE19

The Queens Head ★★★★ INN

tel: 01677 450259 **Westmoor Ln, Finghall DL8 1QZ**
email: enquiries@queensfinghall.co.uk **web:** www.queensfinghall.co.uk
dir: *From Bedale follow A684 W towards Leyburn, just after pub & caravan park turn left signed Finghall*

Dales produce is high on the list

This pretty 18th-century country inn with beams and open fires is set on a hillside above Wensleydale and there are stunning views of the countryside from the terrace. The dining room overlooks Wild Wood – believed to be one of the inspirations for Kenneth Grahame's *Wind in the Willows*. Drinkers can quaff a pint of Theakson XB by the fire and diners can create their own deli board while considering the menu, which demonstrates the kitchen team's passion for Dales produce. As well as sandwiches and pub favourites there are contemporary dishes like Goan spiced fish cakes with creamy lentils; pan-fried venison steak with port and blueberry sauce and hand-cut chips. Spacious accommodation is located in the adjacent annexe.

Open 12-3 6-close Closed 26 Dec & 1 Jan, Mon-Thu L Nov-Feb unless booked in advance **Food** Lunch all wk 12-2 Dinner all wk 6-9 Av main course £7.50 Set menu available ⊕ FREE HOUSE ◀ Theakston XB & Black Bull. ♟10 **Facilities** Non-diners area ▪♦ Children's menu Children's portions Garden 🚗 Parking WiFi 🚌 (notice required) **Rooms** 3

Sandpiper Inn
PICK OF THE PUBS

tel: 01969 622206 **Market Place DL8 5AT**
email: hsandpiper99@aol.com
dir: *A1 onto A684 to Leyburn*

Wensleydale market town inn

Leyburn's oldest building is this 17th-century, ivy-clad inn, although it has been a pub for only 30 years or so. Run by Jonathan and Janine Harrison, its bar and snug offers real ales from a small army of Yorkshire breweries, and some 100 single malts. The restaurant, distinguished by a huge stone lintel above an open fireplace, oak floors and candlelit tables is where Jonathan has built on his already excellent reputation for modern British food. Such reputations, of course, require using the finest ingredients, which he does for traditional and international dishes such as Swinton Park venison with pearl barley and vegetable risotto; sea bass with shellfish sausage and light curry and apple sauce; and potato rösti with glazed balsamic tomatoes and roasted red onions. Lunch offers coq au vin; and house rib-burger. For dessert, why not one of the Sandpiper's own ice creams or sorbets?

Open 11.30-3 6.30-11 (Sun 12-2.30 6.30-10.30) Closed Mon & occasionally Tue **Food** Lunch Tue-Sun 12-2.30 Dinner Tue-Thu & Sun 6.30-9, Fri & Sat 6.30-9.30 ⊕ FREE HOUSE ◗ Black Sheep Best Bitter, Daleside, Copper Dragon, Archers, Yorkshire Dales, Rudgate Brewery Ö Thatchers Gold. ♗ 10 **Facilities** Non-diners area ♦♦ Children's menu Family room Garden ⋒ WiFi

---

LITTON
Map 18 SD97

Queens Arms ★★★ INN

tel: 01756 770096 **BD23 5QJ**
email: info@queensarmslitton.co.uk **web:** www.queensarmslitton.co.uk
dir: From Skipton N on B6265, through Threshfield & Kilnsey. Left signed Arncliffe & Litton

Whitewashed gem in a secret sylvan dale

Secluded Littondale is the Dales of yesteryear; the Queens radiates character and charm from its idyllic hamlet setting amidst wildflower meadows and limestone

crags in one of the most secret of dales. Bag a table out-front and sip a Chinook Blonde whilst drinking in the views across the River Skirfare's valley - the on-site microbrewery is scheduled to re-open. Inside is classical and compact, with open fire, slate floor and beams, all enhanced by contemporary fittings and fabrics. The dishes reflect the inn's setting and change daily; home-made beef, smoked bacon and Black Sheep ale pie a good example. Six rooms may tempt a restful stay-over.

Open 11-3 6-11 Closed Mon (winter) **Food** Lunch all wk 12-2 Dinner all wk 6-8 Av main course £11 ⊕ FREE HOUSE ◗ Thwaites Original, Black Sheep, Goose Eye Chinook Blonde Ö Thatchers. **Facilities** Non-diners area ✿ (All areas) ♦♦ Children's portions Garden Outside area ⋒ WiFi ➾ (notice required) **Rooms** 6

See advert below

The Punch Bowl Inn ★★★★ INN

tel: 01748 886233 **DL11 6PF**
email: info@pbinn.co.uk **web:** www.pbinn.co.uk
dir: *A1 from Scotch Corner take A6108 to Richmond. Through Richmond then right onto B6270 to Low Row*

Lots on offer at this Yorkshire Dales inn

With Wainwright's Coast to Coast Walk on the doorstep, this Grade II listed Swaledale pub dates back to the 17th century. As well as open fires and antique furniture, the bar and bar stools were hand-crafted by Robert 'The Mouseman' Thompson's company during an extensive refurbishment a few years ago (see if you can spot the mice around the bar). Typical food choices include chicken liver and orange pâté; beef and ale casserole with herb dumplings and horseradish mash;

and Yorkshire parkin with apple compôte. Local cask-conditioned ales also feature. If you would like to stay over for the Swaledale festivals, the 11 bedrooms all have spectacular views.

Open all day all wk 11am-mdnt Closed 25 Dec **Food** Lunch Mon-Sat 12-2.30, Sun 12-3 Dinner all wk 6-9 Restaurant menu available all wk ⊕ FREE HOUSE ◀ Theakston Best Bitter, Black Sheep Best Bitter & Riggwelter, Timothy Taylor Landlord ♂ Thatchers Gold. ♛ 13 **Facilities** Non-diners area ♣ (Bar) ◀ Children's menu Children's portions Outside area ♬ Parking WiFi ➡ (notice required) **Rooms** 11

The Lister Arms ★★★★ INN PICK OF THE PUBS

See Pick of the Pubs on opposite page and advert below

PICK OF THE PUBS

The Lister Arms ★★★★ INN

MALHAM   Map 18 SD96

tel: 01729 830330
BD23 4DB
email: relax@listerarms.co.uk
web: www.listerarms.co.uk
dir: *In village centre*

Gorgeous inn and village amidst spectacular scenery

This handsome old stone coaching inn sits amongst some of the county's most impressive limestone scenery which is riddled with caverns. Being right on the village green makes it a good place to stop for morning coffee, a pint of one of the guest ales, or Thwaites Wainwright bitter, named after Blackburn-born Alfred Wainwright, famous for his Lakeland Fells guides. History is visible wherever you look: outside, there's a traditional mounting block for horse riders, and a beautiful tiled entrance way; inside, the renovated ground floor is divided into little nooks, with original beams, flagged floors and wood burning stoves. The kitchen team serve up food that is seasonal, local and always freshly prepared with an Inn Season menu (that changes monthly) available from 5pm. For lunch try honey baked ham and home-made piccalilli sandwich with hand-cut chips; or an old faithful Thwaites Ale battered haddock and chips. The Lister Arms is famous for

their home-made pies - cheddar cheese and onion is always on the menu along with a daily special such as steak and ale pie, served with creamy mash and mushy peas. Alternatively, the grill section offers steaks and chops sourced from local farms in the surrounding Dales; options include an 8oz sirloin, 9oz rib-eye or 10oz rump. Puddings and cake are home made too, with sticky toffee pudding being a firm favourite. The children's menu includes all the little ones' favourite dishes and healthy options, of course. Well-behaved dogs, muddy boots and cycles are also happily welcomed.

Open all day all wk ⊕ THWAITES INNS OF CHARACTER ◀ Wainwright, Original ⊘ Kingstone Press. **Facilities** ✿ (Bar Garden) ⋔ Children's menu Children's portions Garden Parking WiFi **Rooms** 15

MALTON
Map 19 SE77

NEW The New Malton

tel: 01653 693998 **2-4 Market Place YO17 7LX**
email: info@thenewmalton.co.uk
dir: *In town centre opposite church*

Family-friendly pub overlooking the market place

Overlooking the market place in Malton, this prominent 18th-century building has had an interesting history including a time as a 1930s tea room and as a tapas bar. A refurbishment has restored much of its original character, including opening up the fireplaces. Beer drinkers are spoilt for choice, with the range of local ales changing weekly. An extensive menu features a mix of pub classics and more ambitious dishes such as poached cod loin with chorizo and king prawn cassoulet and lime butter; and chicken Kiev with thyme polenta chips.

Open all day all wk Closed 25-26 Dec, 1 Jan **Food** Lunch Mon-Sat 12-9.30, Sun 12-9 Dinner Mon-Sat 12-9.30, Sun 12-9 Av main course £10.50 ⊕ FREE HOUSE ◀ Wold Top Bitter, Great Newsome Pricky Back Otchan, Rudgate Ruby Mild ♂ Westons Stowford Press & Wyld Wood Organic. ₹ 10 **Facilities** ☸ (Bar Restaurant Outside area) ♦◊ Children's portions Outside area ⌱ Parking WiFi

MARTON (NEAR BOROUGHBRIDGE)
Map 19 SE46

The Punch Bowl Inn

tel: 01423 322519 **YO51 9QY**
email: enquiries@thepunchbowlmartoncumgrafton.com
web: www.thepunchbowlmartoncumgrafton.com
dir: *In village centre*

Village pub with six eating areas

A Provenance Inns group member, the 16th-century Punch Bowl commands a central location in the village. Its beamed, wood-floored bar and tap-room's generous seating includes a settle, and there's a log fire in each of the six eating areas. The Yorkshire Plate starter features Harrogate Blue cheese, black pudding fritter, duck rillettes, beetroot salsa, Malham chorizo and griddled sourdough. Typical main dishes are a seafood platter; confit shoulder of lamb; and mushroom, spinach and ricotta Wellington, with roasts and baked Cajun salmon on Sundays. Summer barbecues are held in the courtyard.

Open all day all wk **Food** Lunch Mon-Sat 12-2.30, Sun 12-3 Dinner Mon-Sat 5.30-9.30, Sun 5.30-8.30 ⊕ PROVENANCE INNS ◀ Black Sheep Best Bitter, Timothy Taylor Landlord ♂ Aspall. **Facilities** Non-diners area ☸ (Bar Garden) ♦◊ Children's menu Children's portions Garden ⌱ Parking WiFi ▭ (notice required)

MASHAM
Map 19 SE28

The Black Sheep Brewery

tel: 01765 680101 & 680100 **Wellgarth HG4 4EN**
email: sue.dempsey@blacksheep.co.uk
dir: *Off A6108, 9m from Ripon & 7m from Bedale*

Famous brewery site for over 20 years

Set up by Paul Theakston, a member of Masham's famous brewery family, in the former Wellgarth Maltings in 1992, the complex includes an excellent visitor centre and a popular bar-cum-bistro. Go on a fascinating tour of the brewery. Next take in the wonderful views over the River Ure and surrounding countryside as you sup tip-top pints of Riggwelter and Golden Sheep; then tuck into a good plate of food, perhaps braised beef, fish pie, pan-fried lamb's liver with black pudding, mash and rich onion gravy, or a roast beef sandwich.

Open all wk 10-5 (Thu-Sat 10am-late) Closed 25-26 Dec **Food** Contact pub for details ⊕ BLACK SHEEP BREWERY ◀ Best Bitter, Riggwelter, Ale, Golden Sheep. **Facilities** Non-diners area ☸ (Garden) ♦◊ Children's menu Children's portions Garden ⌱ Parking WiFi ▭ (notice required)

The White Bear

tel: 01765 689319 **Wellgarth HG4 4EN**
email: sue@whitebearmasham.co.uk
dir: *Signed from A1 between Bedale & Ripon*

Theakston's flagship pub in bustling market town

Theakston Brewery's flagship inn stands just a short stroll from the legendary brewhouse and market square in this bustling market town and provides the perfect base for exploring the Yorkshire Dales. Handsome and stylish, there's a snug taproom for quaffing pints of Old Peculier by the glowing fire, oak-floored lounges with deep sofas and chairs for perusing the daily papers, and an elegant dining room. Menus take in pork fillet wrapped in bacon filled with black pudding served with parsnip and English mustard purée; butternut squash and spinach curry; sausage and mash with onion gravy; and mushroom and sweet pepper risotto with parmesan crisps. Expect regular live music and 30 cask ales at the late June beer festival.

Open all day all wk **Food** Lunch all wk 12-9 Dinner all wk 12-9 ⊕ FREE HOUSE/THEAKSTON ◀ Best Bitter, Black Bull Bitter, Lightfoot & Old Peculier, Caledonian Deuchars IPA. **Facilities** Non-diners area ☸ (Bar Garden) ♦◊ Children's menu Children's portions Garden ⌱ Beer festival Parking WiFi ▭ (notice required)

MIDDLEHAM
Map 19 SE18

The White Swan

tel: 01969 622093 **Market Place DL8 4PE**
email: enquiries@whiteswanhotel.co.uk
dir: *From A1, take A684 towards Leyburn then A6108 to Ripon, 1.5m to Middleham*

Popular and attractive inn

Paul Klein's Tudor coaching inn stands in the cobbled market square in the shadow of Middleham's ruined castle and, like the village, is steeped in the history of the turf, with several top horseracing stables located in the area. Expect to find oak beams, flagstones and roaring log fires in the atmospheric bar, where you can quaff tip-top Black Sheep or Wensleydale ales and enjoy modern British pub food. Using quality Yorkshire produce the menu might feature shredded confit of crispy duck leg with bacon salad; chicken breast stuffed with mozzarella and sun-dried tomato, with pesto risotto; and glazed lemon tart with raspberry sauce to finish.

Open all day all wk 8am-11pm (mdnt at wknds) **Food** Contact pub for details ⊕ FREE HOUSE ◀ Black Sheep Best Bitter, John Smith's, Theakston, Wensleydale ♂ Thatchers Gold. ₹ 9 **Facilities** Non-diners area ☸ (Bar Outside area) ♦◊ Children's menu Children's portions Family room Outside area ⌱ Parking WiFi ▭ (notice required)

PICK OF THE PUBS

The Black Swan at Oldstead ★★★★★ RR ⬡⬡⬡

OLDSTEAD   Map 19 SE57

tel: 01347 868387
Main St YO61 4BL
email: enquiries@blackswanoldstead.co.uk
web: www.blackswanoldstead.co.uk
dir: *A1 junct 49, A168, A19S, after 3m left to Coxwold then Byland Abbey. In 2m left for Oldstead, pub 1m on left*

Outstanding food in rural Yorkshire

Dating back to the 16th century and set in a sleepy hamlet below the North York Moors, The Black Swan is owned and run by the Banks family, who have farmed in the village for generations. In the bar you'll find a stone-flagged floor, an open log fire, original wooden window seats, soft cushions, and fittings by Robert 'Mousey' Thompson who, in the 1930s, was a prolific maker of traditional handcrafted English oak furniture. Expect tip-top real ales, cracking wines by the glass, malt whiskies and vintage port, while the first-class food on offer changes with the seasons, being sourced mainly from local farms. The same award-winning menus are offered in the bar and in the comfortable restaurant where Persian rugs line an oak floor, the furniture is antique, and candles in old brass holders create light soft enough to be romantic, but bright enough to read the innovative modern country menus by. Start perhaps with langoustine soup,

crab and cheddar croûton; or butternut squash cannelloni, langoustine, tomato and basil; move on to ox cheek, cauliflower cheese, macaroni, truffle and salsify; or halibut, Jerusalem artichoke, squid, pink fir potato and samphire; and finish with dark chocolate, vanilla and pear. The bedrooms have solid oak floors and are furnished with quality antiques, classy soft fabrics, and paintings. Bathrooms are fitted with an iron roll-top bath and a walk-in wet room shower, which sounds like just the place to head for after one of the pleasant walks radiating from the front of the building (route details are available at the bar).

Open 12-3 6-11 Closed 1wk Jan, Mon L, Tue L, Wed L **Food** Lunch Thu-Sun 12-2 Dinner all wk 6-9 Set menu available Restaurant menu available all wk.
⊕ FREE HOUSE ◼ Black Sheep. ♟ 12
Facilities Non-diners area ⁑ Children's menu Children's portions Garden ⌱ Parking WiFi **Rooms** 4

MIDDLESMOOR
Map 19 SE07

Crown Hotel

tel: 01423 755204 **HG3 5ST**
dir: *Phone for detailed directions*

Family run hotel at the top of the valley

There are great views towards Gouthwaite Reservoir from this breezy 900-ft high hilltop village with its cobbled streets. This family-run traditional free house dates back to the 17th century and is in an ideal spot for anyone following the popular Nidderdale Way. Visitors can enjoy a good pint of local beer and food by the cosy, roaring log fire, or in the sunny pub garden. A large selection of malt whiskies is also on offer.

Open Nov-Apr Tue-Thu 7-11 Fri-Sun all day (May-Oct Tue-Thu 12-2 7-11 Fri-Sun all day) Closed all day Mon, Tue-Thu L (winter) **Food** Lunch Tue-Sun 12-2 Dinner Tue-Sun 7-8.30 ⊕ FREE HOUSE ◀ Black Sheep Best Bitter, Wensleydale Bitter, Guinness Ô Thatchers Gold. **Facilities** ❖ (Bar Restaurant Garden) ◀ Children's portions Garden ⌒ Parking WiFi **Notes** ⊕

NEWTON ON OUSE
Map 19 SE55

The Dawnay Arms

tel: 01347 848345 **YO30 2BR**
email: dine@thedawnay.co.uk
dir: *From A19 follow Newton on Ouse signs*

Great riverside location with a large garden

Right in the middle of a picture-perfect village, The Dawnay Arms dates back to Georgian times. It sits on the banks of the River Ouse, and its large rear garden runs down to moorings for those arriving by boat. The interior, all chunky beams and tables, hosts a great array of cask ales including Treboom, a relatively recent addition to York's renowned microbreweries; the well-chosen wine list also deserves mention. Food, British in style, might include wood pigeon 'Wellington' with celeriac, mushrooms and Madeira; baked Whitby cod with a parmesan and herb crust, and prawn and saffron risotto; pear and almond tart with custard could round things off.

Open 12-3 6-11 (Sat all day Sun 12-8) Closed Mon **Food** Lunch Tue-Sat 12-2.30, Sun 12-6 Dinner Tue-Sat 6-9.30, Sun 12-6 ⊕ FREE HOUSE ◀ Black Sheep, Guest ales Ô Westons Stowford Press. ▾ 12 **Facilities** Non-diners area ❖ (Bar Garden) ◀ Children's portions Garden ⌒ Parking WiFi 🚐 (notice required)

NUN MONKTON
Map 19 SE55

NEW The Alice Hawthorn
PICK OF THE PUBS

tel: 01423 330303 **The Green YO26 8EW**
email: info@theforagerskitchen.com
dir: *From A59 between York & Harrogate follow Nun Monkton signs. Pub 2m on right*

Village pub going the extra mile for local sourcing

At the heart of village life in Nun Monkton for more than 200 years, The Alice Hawthorn was taken over in late 2013 by The Foragers' Kitchen, a team of chefs with an uncompromising passion for local sourcing. All the meat and vegetables used in the kitchen are from local farmers and all fish arrives from the east coast. The chefs have even joined forces with locals who knock on the kitchen door with apples from nearby orchards and just-caught trout – all of it destined for the 'foragers' specials board'. A smokehouse, chicken run and trio of pub pigs complete the sustainable picture at the pub, where only local ales and ciders are served in the friendly bar. A lunchtime sandwich selection and set menu run alongside a

carte that might include crispy belly pork Asian salad; steak and ale pie with honey-roasted root vegetables; finishing with ginger and treacle tartlet.

Open all wk 12-3 5-11 (Sat-Sun all day) **Food** Lunch 12-3 Dinner 5-9 Av main course £11.95 ⊕ FREE HOUSE ◀ Weekly changing local ales Ô Rekorderlig, Local ciders. ▾ 12 **Facilities** Non-diners area ❖ (Bar Garden) ◀ Children's menu Children's portions Garden ⌒ Parking WiFi 🚐

NUNNINGTON
Map 19 SE67

The Royal Oak Inn

tel: 01439 748271 **Church St YO62 5US**
dir: *From A170, S of Helmsley, take B1257 towards Malton. Left to Nunnington (also follow brown Nunnington Hall sign). 1st left at church, pub on left*

Good food, real ales, and cosy real fires in winter

This Grade II listed, 18th-century solid stone country inn welcomes with an open-plan bar furnished with scrubbed pine and decorated with farming memorabilia, open fires in winter and fresh flowers in summer. True to this promise, head chef Ed Woodhill uses the best local produce to create innovative interpretations of traditional dishes. Typical choices include wild mushroom and Yorkshire Blue cheese tart with crispy shallot salad; topside of beef steak pie and rich beef gravy; and apple and plum gratin, apple brandy sabayon and chestnut ice cream.

Open 12-2.30 6.30-11 Closed Mon (ex BHs 12-2) & Tue **Food** Lunch Wed-Sun 12-2 (booking required Sun) Dinner Wed-Sun 6.30-9 (summer) Av main course £13.50 ⊕ FREE HOUSE ◀ Wold Top, John Smith's, Rudgate. ▾ 10 **Facilities** Non-diners area ❖ (Bar Restaurant Garden) ◀ Children's menu Children's portions Garden ⌒ Parking

OLDSTEAD
Map 19 SE57

The Black Swan at Oldstead ★ ★ ★ ★ ★ RR ⊚ ⊚ ⊚
PICK OF THE PUBS

See Pick of the Pubs on page 569

OSMOTHERLEY
Map 19 SE49

The Golden Lion
PICK OF THE PUBS

tel: 01609 883526 **6 West End DL6 3AA**
email: goldenlionosmotherley@yahoo.co.uk
dir: *Phone for detailed directions*

Recommended for its interesting dishes

Standing in Osmotherley, the 'Gateway to the North Yorkshire Moors', The Golden Lion is a 250-year-old sandstone building. The atmosphere is warm and welcoming with open fires, a wooden bar, bench seating, whitewashed walls, mirrors and fresh flowers. As well as some 60 single malt whiskies, there are always three real ales on offer. The extensive menu ranges through basic pub grub to more refined dishes. Starters might include smoked salmon and prawn roulade; grilled aubergines filled with ratatouille; and fresh mussels in a white wine and cream sauce. Mains are along the lines of home-made chicken Kiev; sirloin steak, and fillets of plaice, supplemented by specials such as turkey roulade; duck, chestnut and thyme risotto; and sea bass with a samphire, crayfish and basil sauce. Popular desserts are raspberry ripple cheesecake, ginger sponge and crème brûlée.

Open 12-3 6-11 Closed 25 Dec, Mon L, Tue L ⊕ FREE HOUSE ◤ Timothy Taylor Landlord, York Guzzler, Salamander, Wall's Brewing Co Ō Herefordshire.
Facilities ☼ (Bar Restaurant Outside area) ◖ Children's menu Children's portions Outside area WiFi

■ PICKERING   Map 19 SE78

Fox & Hounds Country Inn ★★★★ INN ⊛
PICK OF THE PUBS

tel: 01751 431577 **Sinnington YO62 6SQ**
email: fox.houndsinn@btconnect.com **web:** www.thefoxandhoundsinn.co.uk
dir: 3m W of town, off A170 between Pickering & Helmsley

Great country pub atmosphere with award-winning food

This friendly, 18th-century coaching inn on the edge of the North York Moors is run by resident proprietors Andrew and Catherine Stephens. In the wood-panelled bar, under oak beams and, depending on the temperature, warmed by a double-sided log-burner called Big Bertha, a pint of Copper Dragon Best, or Black Sheep Best, could be waiting, or maybe a rarely encountered whisky. Making full use of locally farmed produce, light lunches and early suppers (except Saturdays) include fish pie; tempura king prawns with chilli dipping sauce; and beer battered haddock and chips. Differing only in part, the main menu also lists slow-cooked shoulder of lamb, braised beans, sunblush tomatoes, sautéed greens and pesto dumplings; roast guinea fowl breast with confit leg fritters and sauté apples; and steamed steak suet pudding. Turn right along the village street past the village green to an ancient packhorse bridge over the gentle River Seven (yes, Seven).

Open all wk 12-2 5.30-11 (Sat 12-2 6-11 Sun 12-2.30 6-10.30) Closed 25-27 Dec
Food Lunch all wk 12-2 Dinner Mon-Fri 5.30-9, Sat-Sun 6-9 ⊕ FREE HOUSE ◤ Copper Dragon Best Bitter, Black Sheep Best Bitter Ō Thatchers Gold. ▾ 9
Facilities Non-diners area ☼ (Bar Garden) ◖ Children's menu Children's portions Garden ⊨ Parking WiFi ▭ Rooms 10

The Fox & Rabbit Inn

tel: 01751 460213 **Whitby Rd, Lockton YO18 7NQ**
email: info@foxandrabbit.co.uk
dir: From Pickering take A169 towards Whitby. Lockton in 5m

Reliable stop near Dalby Forest

The archetypical North Yorkshire Moors pub, all heavy orange pantiles and honey limestone covered with creepers, set on a secluded junction at the fringe of Dalby Forest. The owning Wood brothers are keen supporters of local microbreweries, with beers from Cropton and Wold Top brewers slaking the thirst of the cyclists and ramblers with whom the pub is a favourite stop after their exertions in the National Park. For the inner man, good solid Yorkshire pub grub like steak and Black Sheep ale pie or Whitby scampi and chips are ideal; or divert to winter butternut squash and pea risotto.

Open all day all wk **Food** Lunch Mon-Thu 12-2.30, Fri-Sun 12.30-4 Dinner all wk 5-8.30 ⊕ FREE HOUSE ◤ Black Sheep Best Bitter, Marston's Oyster Stout, Cropton, Wold Top Ales, Tetley's Smooth Flow, Guest ales Ō Thatchers Gold. ▾ 13
Facilities Non-diners area ☼ (Bar Garden) ◖ Children's menu Children's portions Garden ⊨ Parking ▭ (notice required)

The White Swan Inn ★★★ HL ⊛⊛   PICK OF THE PUBS

tel: 01751 472288 **Market Place YO18 7AA**
email: welcome@white-swan.co.uk **web:** www.white-swan.co.uk
dir: From N: A19 or A1 to Thirsk, A170 to Pickering, left at lights, 1st right onto Market Place. Pub on left. From S: A1 or A1(M) to A64 to Malton rdbt, A169 to Pickering

Elegant market town inn with fine dining

At the heart of pretty Pickering, The White Swan Inn fronts the steep main street dropping to the beck and steam railway station. With open fires, flagstone floors, panelling and eclectic furnishings, this sturdy coaching inn oozes character. Far from being a period piece, the owners have skilfully combined good contemporary design to produce a stylish destination dining inn. A creeper-clad courtyard snuggles behind, where browsers can enjoy Timothy Taylor Landlord bitter. It's for the exceptional menus, however, that guests travel to savour. Garnering two AA Rosettes, the team led by Derren Clemmit scour the Riding for the best ingredients. Rare breed meats from the Ginger Pig Farm at Levisham; and lobster and fish from Whitby are crafted into a fine dining experience. A starter of poached asparagus with pancetta and hollandaise sauce is an appetiser for roasted venison saddle with château potatoes, beetroot and berry sauce; or perhaps a chargrilled Longhorn rib-eye. A local cheeseboard is an ample conclusion, whilst the wine list has 65 bins.

Open all day all wk **Food** Lunch all wk 12-2 Dinner all wk 6.45-9 Av main course £13.95 ⊕ FREE HOUSE ◤ Black Sheep, Timothy Taylor Landlord Ō Westons Stowford Press. ▾ 19 **Facilities** Non-diners area ☼ (Bar Outside area) ◖ Children's menu Children's portions Outside area ⊨ Parking WiFi ▭ (notice required) **Rooms** 21

■ PICKHILL   Map 19 SE38

Nags Head Country Inn ★★★★ INN ⊛⊛ PICK OF THE PUBS

tel: 01845 567391 **YO7 4JG**
email: enquiries@nagsheadpickhill.co.uk **web:** www.nagsheadpickhill.co.uk
dir: A1(M) junct 50, A61 towards Thirsk. Left onto B6267 signed Masham. Right signed Pickhill

Renowned for excellent food, fine wines and real ales

For over 40 years the Boynton family have been welcoming visitors to their extended, former 17th-century coaching inn set in a peaceful village just off the A1 north of Thirsk. Synonymous with Yorkshire hospitality at its best, notably among weary travellers and the local racing fraternity, the inn comprises a beamed lounge and a traditional taproom bar with flagged and tiled floors, beams adorned with ties and a magpie selection of tables and chairs tucked around open fires. A terrific menu is the icing on the cake here; a small but perfectly formed taproom menu offers sandwiches and simple meals such as steak and chips with all the trimmings or Thai chicken, vegetable and noodle stir-fry. In the lounge or elegant restaurant, order mushroom and roasted garlic risotto to start, followed perhaps by corn-fed chicken with a small wing Kiev, buttered cabbage, potato dumplings and pearl barley broth. Tempting, calorific puddings seal the deal, perhaps forced Yorkshire rhubarb pithivier with frangipane and ewe's milk ice cream. If all this leaves you feeling too full to move, consider staying in one of the inn's comfortably furnished bedrooms.

Open all wk 11-11 (Sun 11-10.30) Closed 25 Dec (drinks only available) **Food** Lunch Mon-Sat 12-2, Sun 12-3 Dinner Mon-Sat 6-9.30, Sun 5.30-8 ⊕ FREE HOUSE ◤ Black Sheep Best Bitter, Theakston Old Peculier & Best Bitter, Rudgate Viking Ō Westons Stowford Press. ▾ 8 **Facilities** Non-diners area ◖ Children's menu Children's portions Garden ⊨ Parking WiFi ▭ (notice required) **Rooms** 13

RIPON
Map 19 SE37

The George at Wath ★★★★ INN ⊚

tel: 01765 641324 **Main St, Wath HG4 5EN**
email: reception@thegeorgeatwath.co.uk **web:** www.thegeorgeatwath.co.uk
dir: *From A1 (dual carriageway) N'bound turn left signed Melmerby & Wath. From A1 S'bound exit at slip road signed A61. At T-junct right (signed Ripon). Approx 0.5m turn right signed Melmerby & Wath*

Welcoming free house with very good food

The George at Wath, a brick-built double-fronted free house dating from the 18th century, is just three miles from the cathedral city of Ripon. This traditional Yorkshire pub retains its flagstone floors, log-burning fires and cosy atmosphere, while the contemporary dining room proffers seasonal and locally sourced ingredients for its mix of classic and bistro-style dishes: salt cod fritters could be followed by glazed gammon with chips cooked in dripping; finish with a chocolate tart, or rhubarb and custard. The George is child and dog friendly.

Open 12-3 5-11 (Sat-Sun all day) Closed Mon L & Tue L **Food** Lunch Wed-Sun 12-2 Dinner Mon-Sat fr 5.30 ⊕ FREE HOUSE ◀ Theakston, Rudgate, Guest ale Ổ Westons Stowford Press. ☥ 14 **Facilities** Non-diners area ☙ (Bar Garden) ♦ Children's menu Children's portions Garden 﨟 Beer festival Parking WiFi ▨ (notice required) **Rooms** 5

The Royal Oak ★★★★ INN ⊚

tel: 01765 602284 **36 Kirkgate HG4 1PB**
email: info@royaloakripon.co.uk **web:** www.royaloakripon.co.uk
dir: *In town centre*

Excellent ales and good food in this smart coaching inn

Built in the 18th-century, this beautifully renovated coaching inn in the centre of Ripon changed hands in 2013; it is an ideal base for exploring nearby Harrogate and York. Well-kept local cask ales from Timothy Taylor and Saltaire breweries can be enjoyed in the bar, as well as wines from a carefully chosen list. Sandwiches and 'pub classics' appear on the menu alongside local steaks and signature dishes such as pheasant en croûte with potato gratin; sticky Ripon beef; and crispy skinned sea trout with Whitby crab cake.

Open all day all wk **Food** Lunch Mon-Sat 12-9, Sun 12-8 Dinner Mon-Sat 12-9, Sun 12-8 Set menu available ◀ Timothy Taylor Landlord, Best Bitter & Golden Best, Saltaire Blonde, Guest ales Ổ Westons Stowford Press. ☥ 14
Facilities Non-diners area ☙ (Bar Garden) ♦ Children's menu Children's portions Garden Parking WiFi ▨ **Rooms** 6

ROBIN HOOD'S BAY
Map 19 NZ90

Laurel Inn

tel: 01947 880400 **New Rd YO22 4SE**
dir: *Phone for detailed directions*

On the winding street towards the sea

Given its location it's hardly surprising that this was once the haunt of smugglers who used a network of underground tunnels and secret passages to bring the booty ashore. Nowadays it's the haunt of holidaymakers and walkers, and the setting for this small, traditional pub which retains lots of character features, including beams and an open fire. The bar is decorated with old photographs, and an international collection of lager bottles. This popular free house serves Adnams and Theakston Old Peculier and Best Bitter.

Open all wk **Food** Contact pub for details ⊕ FREE HOUSE ◀ Theakston Best Bitter & Old Peculier, Adnams. **Facilities** ☙ (Bar) ♦ Family room WiFi **Notes** ⊛

SAWDON
Map 17 SE98

The Anvil Inn
PICK OF THE PUBS

tel: 01723 859896 **Main St YO13 9DY**
email: info@theanvilinnsawdon.co.uk
dir: *1.5m N of Brompton-by-Sawdon, on A170 8m E of Pickering & 6m W of Scarborough*

Natural affinity between fine ale and fine dining

There's something of the medieval castle about the internal stone walls of this former blacksmith's forge, although actually it dates from the early 1700s. Blacksmithing finished here in 1985, but all the old essentials remain - the furnace, the bellows, the tools and, of course, the anvil itself. In the steeply-pitched, timber-ceiling bar, weekly-changing Yorkshire beers proliferate and at least 11 wines are sold by the glass. Locally-farmed beef and pork, game from Dalby Forest, and Whitby-landed fresh fish all appear on the menu, which does duty in both the bar and the dining room. So perhaps try black treacle-cured salmon with sesame sushi rice roll, coriander-marinated avocado and beans; roast Mediterranean vegetable moussaka; or outdoor-reared belly pork, slow roasted with Chinese five spices, orange and chilli-glazed king prawns, sautéed pak choi and spring onions and crispy scratchings.

Open 12-2.30 6-11 Closed 25 & 26 Dec, 1 Jan & varying annual holiday, Mon-Tue **Food** Lunch Wed-Sat 12-2, Sun 12-2.30 Dinner Wed-Sat 6.30-9, Sun 6-8 ⊕ FREE HOUSE ◀ Daleside, Wold Top, Leeds, Guest ale Ổ Westons Stowford Press. ☥ 11 **Facilities** Non-diners area ☙ (Bar Garden) ♦ Children's portions Garden 﨟 Parking

SCARBOROUGH
Map 17 TA08

NEW Downe Arms Country Inn ★★★★ INN

tel: 01723 862471 **Main Rd, Wykeham YO13 9QB**
email: info@downearmshotel.co.uk **web:** www.downearmshotel.co.uk
dir: *On A170*

Hospitable stone-built hostelry with country-house interiors

A converted 17th-century farmhouse on the edge of the North Yorkshire Moors, within easy reach of the Scarborough coastline and Ryedale. Inside are lovely high ceilings, and large sash windows look down to the attractive stone village of Wykeham. Yorkshire ales populate the bar, and lunchtime plates represent excellent value. In the evening the charming restaurant is transformed into an intimate candle-lit dining room, where a Whitby smoked herring fishcake could precede the pork loin steak matador (served with Spanish-style patatas bravas). If a hazlenut and mochachino Pavlova cannot be resisted, one of the inn's 10 en suite and sumptuously furnished bedrooms may also prove tempting.

Open all day all wk **Food** Lunch 12-2 Dinner 6-9 Av main course £10.50 Restaurant menu available Mon-Sat ⊕ FREE HOUSE ◀ Black Sheep, Theakston Best Bitter, Wold Top Bitter. **Facilities** Non-diners area ☆ (Bar Garden) •♦ Children's menu Children's portions Garden ⋈ Parking WiFi ➡ (notice required) **Rooms** 10

SCAWTON
Map 19 SE58

The Hare Inn
PICK OF THE PUBS

tel: 01845 597769 **YO7 2HG**
email: liz@thehare-inn.com
dir: *Exit A170 towards Rievaulx Abbey & Scawton. Pub 1m on right*

Historic inn near idyllic moorland dales

Local lore has it that in medieval times a witch lived here. Shape-shifting into a wandering hare, she was pursued home by the hunt, breathing her last in the cottage after changing back into a witch. Other legends and tales - including a resident ghost - abound at this pretty, pantiled pub, which may have been a brewhouse for local abbeys at Rievaulx and Byland. Things are more relaxed today at this dining inn, secluded along lanes between the Hambleton Hills and Rye Dale in the North York Moors National Park. You'll find low-beamed ceilings and flagstone floors, a wood-burning stove offering a warm welcome in the bar, with beers coming from Rudgate and other Yorkshire breweries. An old-fashioned kitchen range features in the dining area. A classy menu from chef-patron Paul Jackson relies on seasonal specialities; a breast and leg of partridge starter may precede fillet and shoulder of venison with truffle, pecorino, port and chanterelle mushrooms.

Open Tue-Sat 12-2 6-9 (Sun 12-6) summer; Wed-Sat 12-2 6-9 (Sun 12-4) winter Closed 2wks end of Jan beg of Feb, Sun eve & Mon (ex BHs) summer; Sun eve, Mon-Tue winter **Food** Contact pub for details Set menu available ⊕ FREE HOUSE ◀ Black Sheep, Rudgate Viking, Guest ales ☼ Thatchers. ♀ 10 **Facilities** Non-diners area ☆ (Bar Garden) •♦ Children's portions Garden ⋈ Parking WiFi ➡ (notice required)

SETTLE
Map 18 SD86

The Lion at Settle ★★★★ INN

tel: 01729 822203 **Duke St BD24 9DU**
email: relax@thelionsettle.co.uk **web:** www.thelionsettle.co.uk
dir: *Phone for detailed directions*

Revamped Dales coaching inn

Owned by Thwaites and set in the heart of Settle's 17th-century market place, this inn's interior oozes history and atmosphere, with original inglenook fireplaces, wooden floors and a grand staircase lined with pictures that trace back through the town's history. It's a comfortable base for exploring the Dales or the spectacular Settle to Carlisle railway line. Expect decent cask ales and a classic pub menu offering freshly prepared pub favourites. Typical examples include Settle beefsteak and ale pudding; Drake & Macefield Three Peaks burger; one of the deli boards - butcher's or fish maybe, and for dessert sticky toffee pudding or blueberry sundae. There's a cider festival in August.

Open all day all wk 11-11 (Fri-Sat 11am-11.30pm Sun 12-10.30 Bkfst served from 7.30-11am) **Food** Lunch Mon-Sat 12-9, Sun 12-8 Dinner Mon-Sat 12-9, Sun 12-8 Av main course £10 ⊕ THWAITES INNS OF CHARACTER ◀ Original, Lancaster Bomber & Wainwright, Guest ales ☼ Kingstone Press. ♀ 9 **Facilities** Non-diners area ☆ (Bar Garden) •♦ Children's menu Children's portions Garden ⋈ Cider festival WiFi ➡ (notice required) **Rooms** 14

See advert on opposite page

SKIPTON
Map 18 SD95

Devonshire Arms at Cracoe

tel: 01756 730237 **Grassington Rd, Cracoe BD23 6LA**
email: info@devonshirecracoe.co.uk
dir: *Phone for detailed directions*

Old beams and warming fires in traditional inn

Close to the famous village of Grassington at the gateway to the Dales, and famed for its association with the Rhylstone Ladies WI calendar. This convivial and lovingly renovated 17th-century inn is favoured by Three Peaks ramblers who enjoy a rotating selection of real ales; the drinks list also offers a generous choice of wines sold by the glass, and an eclectic collection of rare bottled refreshments. Now in the experienced hands of David Tobitt and his team, the inn's menus of gastro-pub-standard dishes feature rare breed meats alongside pub classics. After a field mushroom fricassée, Mr Jackson's pork bangers with creamy mash and onion gravy go down well; or try succulent short-rib of beef and Burgundy stew with horseradish dumplings. The provenance of all ingredients is reassuringly identified on the menu; if you would like to pre-order something special, it can be sourced for you with just a few days' notice.

Open all day all wk 8.30am-11pm **Food** Lunch all wk 12-3 Dinner all wk 6-9 Av main course £10.50 Set menu available Restaurant menu available all wk ⊕ MARSTON'S ◀ EPA & Burton Bitter, Jennings Bitter, Ringwood Old Thumper, Rotating Guest ales Ö Thatchers Gold. ♟ 12 **Facilities** Non-diners area ♣ (Bar Garden) ♦ Children's portions Garden ⌒ Parking WiFi ▄ (notice required)

STARBOTTON
Map 18 SD97

Fox & Hounds Inn

tel: 01756 760269 & 760367 **BD23 5HY**
email: starbottonfox@aol.com
dir: *Phone for detailed directions*

Traditional family-run pub in the glorious Yorkshire Dales

Built as a private house some 400 years ago, this pub has been serving this picturesque limestone Yorkshire Dales village since the 1840s. Make for the bar, with its large stone fireplace, oak beams and flagged floor to enjoy a pint of Black Sheep, something from the local Yorkshire Dales brewery, or one of the wide selection of malts. Head to the dining room for home cooking such as duck liver and orange pâté; steak and ale pie; brie and mushroom Wellington; and balti chicken and rice. The area is renowned for its spectacular walks.

Open 12-3 6-11 (Sun 12-3.30 5.30-10.30) Closed 1-22 Jan, Mon **Food** Lunch Tue-Sun 12-2.30 Dinner Tue-Sat 6-9, Sun 5.30-8 Av main course £10.50 ⊕ FREE HOUSE ◀ Timothy Taylor Landlord, Black Sheep, Moorhouse's, Yorkshire Dales, Guest ales Ö Thatchers Gold. ♟ 10 **Facilities** Non-diners area ♦ Children's menu Garden Outside area ⌒ Parking ▄ (notice required)

SUTTON-ON-THE-FOREST
Map 19 SE56

The Blackwell Ox Inn ★★★★ INN ⊚

tel: 01347 810328 **Huby Rd YO61 1DT**
email: enquiries@blackwelloxinn.co.uk web: www.blackwelloxinn.co.uk
dir: *A1237 onto B1363 to Sutton-on-the-Forest. Left at T-junct, 50yds on right*

Blending period charm with modern elegance

This inn's name celebrates a shorthorn Teeswater Ox that stood 6ft high at the crop and weighed 1,033 kilos. When the beast was slaughtered in 1779 its meat fetched £110, about £7,000 today. Built around 1823 as a private house, the pub's well-stocked bar offers Yorkshire ales like Timothy Taylor Landlord. The simple cooking style owes much to a North Yorkshire-focused sourcing policy for lunchtime hot and cold sandwiches, alongside dishes such as home-cured gravad lax with horseradish crème fraîche, Asian root vegetable casserole; venison en croûte, braised red cabbage and dauphinoise potatoes. The inn has a terrace for alfresco dining.

Open all wk 12-2 5.30-11 (Sun 12-10.30) Closed 25 Dec, 1 Jan **Food** Lunch Mon-Sat 12-2, Sun 12-4 Dinner Mon-Sat 6-9.30 Av main course £11 ⊕ FREE HOUSE ◀ Timothy Taylor Landlord, York Guzzler, Guinness. ♟ 14 **Facilities** Non-diners area ♦ Children's menu Children's portions Garden ⌒ Parking WiFi ▄ (notice required) **Rooms** 7

THORNTON LE DALE
Map 19 SE88

The New Inn

tel: 01751 474226 **Maltongate YO18 7LF**
email: enquire@the-new-inn.com
dir: *A64 N from York towards Scarborough. At Malton take A169 to Pickering. At Pickering rdbt right onto A170, 2m, pub on right*

Warm welcome at a Yorkshire favourite

Standing at the heart of a picturesque village complete with stocks and a market cross, this family-run Georgian coaching house dates back to 1720. The old-world charm of the location is echoed inside the bar and restaurant, with real log fires and exposed beams. Enjoy well-kept Theakston Best Bitter and guest ales, bitters, lagers and wines and tuck into beef and ale stew with herb scones; slow-braised lamb shoulder and minted gravy; and traditional beer battered fish and fat-cut chips. Change of hands.

Open all day all wk **Food** Lunch Mon-Sat 12-2, Sun 12-3 Dinner Mon-Sat 6-8.30, Sun 5-8 ⊕ STAR PUBS & BARS ◀ Theakston Best Bitter, Guest ales. **Facilities** Non-diners area ♣ (Bar Garden) ♦ Children's menu Children's portions Garden ⌒ Parking WiFi ▄ (notice required)

THORNTON WATLASS
Map 19 SE28

The Buck Inn
PICK OF THE PUBS

tel: 01677 422461 **HG4 4AH**
dir: *From A1 at Leeming Bar take A684 to Bedale, B6268 towards Masham. Village in 2m*

Plenty of choice for real ale fans

This traditional pub has no trouble offers a welcoming and relaxed atmosphere. The inn doesn't just overlook the village green and cricket pitch; players score four runs for hitting the pub wall, and six if the ball goes over the roof! Thornton Watlass is very much the quintessential village, and where Wensleydale, gateway to the Yorkshire Dales National Park, begins; this glorious area is where much of the TV series *Heartbeat* was filmed. There are three separate dining areas and the menu ranges from traditional, freshly prepared pub fare to exciting modern cuisine backed by daily changing blackboard specials. Beer drinkers have a choice of five real ales, including Masham-brewed Black Sheep. There's live jazz music most Sunday lunchtimes.

Open all wk 11am-mdnt Closed 25 Dec eve **Food** Lunch Mon-Sat 12-2, Sun 12-3 Dinner Mon-Sat 6-9, Sun 6-8.30 ⊕ FREE HOUSE ◀ Black Sheep Best Bitter, 4 Guest ales Ö Thatchers Gold. **Facilities** Non-diners area ♦ Children's menu Children's portions Play area Family room Garden ⌒ Parking ▄

WASS — Map 19 SE57

Wombwell Arms — PICK OF THE PUBS

tel: 01347 868280 **YO61 4BE**
email: info@wombwellarms.co.uk
dir: From A1 take A168 to A19 junct. Take York exit, then left after 2.5m, left at Coxwold to Ampleforth. Wass 2m

Enjoyable home cooking in friendly family-run village inn

Dating from 1620, this white-painted village pub in the shadow of the Hambleton Hills was built as a granary using stones from the ruins of nearby Byland Abbey. There are two oak-beamed, flagstone-floored bars, one with a huge inglenook fireplace, the other with a wood-burning stove, and the atmosphere is relaxed and informal; locals, walkers and cyclists can be found here quaffing pints of Black Sheep Best Bitter. High quality, modern British meals with a South African twist are prepared from local produce as far as possible. Tuck into decent sandwiches for lunch and choose one of the Wombwell classics for dinner - perhaps the Masham pork and apple sausages with mash and gravy - or try pork fillet medallions with mushrooms and baby onions in brandy and mustard sauce. Leave room for one of the comforting home-made desserts, or a plate of local cheeses.

Open all wk 12-3 6-11 (Sat 12-11 Sun 12-10.30) **Food** Lunch Mon-Fri 12-2, Fri-Sat 12-2.30, Sun 12-3 Dinner Mon-Thu 6-8.30, Fri-Sat 6-9, Sun 6-8 Av main course £12 Set menu available ⊕ FREE HOUSE ◀ Black Sheep Best Bitter, Guest ales. ♀ 10 **Facilities** Non-diners area ❖ (Bar Outside area) ◑ Children's menu Children's portions Outside area ⊨ Parking WiFi ⊜ (notice required)

WELBURN — Map 19 SE76

NEW The Crown and Cushion

tel: 01653 618777 **YO60 7DZ**
email: enquiries@thecrownandcushionwelburn.com
web: www.thecrownandcushionwelburn.com
dir: A64 from York towards Malton. 13m left to Welburn

Traditional stone-built inn serving quality Yorkshire produce

Exposed stone walls and open log fires characterise the comfortable interior of this spacious yet homely village inn. It boasts a traditional tap room, a bar serving Rudgate ales, and three separate dining areas. Menus are based on carefully sourced local produce, including Waterford Farm Limousin and Charolais beef hung for 40 days. So expect top quality steaks and the likes of oxtail cottage pie; four-hour rotisserie pork with apricot and raisin stuffing; and 'Toad in the Hole' Cumberland sausages. At the rear, a tiered terrace offers superb views. An ideal stop before or after visiting Castle Howard a mile down the road.

Open all wk 12-3 5-11 (Fri-Sun all day from noon) **Food** Lunch Mon-Sat 12-2.30, Sun 12-4 Dinner Mon-Sat 5.30-9.30, Sun 4-8 Av main course £12.95 ⊕ FREE HOUSE ◀ Black Sheep, Rudgate Ales ☼ Symonds. **Facilities** Non-diners area ◑ Children's menu Children's portions Garden ⊨ Parking WiFi ⊜ (notice required)

WEST TANFIELD — Map 19 SE27

The Bruce Arms — PICK OF THE PUBS

tel: 01677 470325 **Main St HG4 5JJ**
email: halc123@yahoo.co.uk
dir: On A6108 between Ripon & Masham

Peaceful village inn with enticing home cooking

This homely pub sits at the heart of the pretty village of West Tanfield, which stands beside a languorous loop of the River Ure. The cathedral city of Ripon, Fountains Abbey and the famous spa at Harrogate are within easy reach and it's also handy for the glorious, undiscovered countryside of nearby Nidderdale Area of Outstanding Natural Beauty. The stone-built inn's interior is a comfy mix of traditional village pub, complete with beams, log fires and good Yorkshire-brewed ales such as Black Sheep. The contemporary bistro complements the stylish, modern European cooking of highly experienced chef-patron Hugh Carruthers. There's a regularly changing menu, formulated to make the most of locally available seasonal produce; home in on a starter of smoked haddock and prawn fishcake with cucumber, yogurt and mint, leading to coq au vin with mash and spring greens; or ham hock, Savoy cabbage, white beans, boiled potatoes and parsley.

Open 12-2.30 6-9.30 (Sun 12-3.30) Closed 2wks Feb, Mon **Food** Lunch Tue-Sat 12-2.30 Dinner Tue-Sat 6-7.30 Av main course £14 Set menu available Restaurant menu available Tue-Sun ⊕ FREE HOUSE ◀ Black Sheep Best Bitter, Guest ales ☼ Aspall. ♀ 10 **Facilities** Non-diners area ❖ (Bar Outside area) ◑ Children's portions Outside area ⊨ Parking

WEST WITTON — Map 19 SE08

The Wensleydale Heifer ★★★★★ RR ⊛ PICK OF THE PUBS

tel: 01969 622322 **Main St DL8 4LS**
web: www.wensleydaleheifer.co.uk
dir: A1 to Leeming Bar junct, A684 towards Bedale for approx 10m to Leyburn, then towards Hawes, 3.5m to West Witton

Stylish boutique restaurant with rooms

In the heart of the Yorkshire Dales National Park, between Leyburn and Hawes, is this white-painted coaching inn, built in 1631. For a morning coffee, head for the Whisky Lounge, where you can indeed also enjoy a malt whisky, or a pint of Heifer Gold or Black Sheep real ale, if you prefer. Of the two dining areas the Fish Bar, with sea-grass flooring, wooden tables and rattan chairs, is the less formal, while the restaurant, which leads to the garden, is furnished with chocolate leather chairs and linen table cloths, and decorated with distinctive artworks by international artist, Doug Hyde. Whichever room you choose, the food is AA Rosette-quality, including roast barn-fed Yorkshire chicken with mustard mash, sauté of pancetta, baby onions and spinach, and Madeira jus; 'Classic Heifer' fish pie; and, as a special, 'banana leaf' baked bream fillets with Whitby white crab and Thai-style satay coconut cream.

Open all day all wk **Food** Lunch all wk 12.30-2.30 Dinner all wk 6-9.30 Set menu available Restaurant menu available all wk ⊕ FREE HOUSE ◀ Heifer Gold, Black Sheep ☼ Aspall. ♀ **Facilities** Non-diners area ❖ (Bar Garden) ◑ Children's menu Children's portions Garden ⊨ Parking WiFi ⊜ **Rooms** 13

WHITBY
Map 19 NZ81

The Magpie Café

tel: 01947 602058 **14 Pier Rd YO21 3PU**
email: ian@magpiecafe.co.uk
dir: *Phone for detailed directions*

Fish focussed café

The acclaimed Magpie Café has been the home of North Yorkshire's 'best-ever fish and chips' since the late 1930s. You could pop in for just a pint of Cropton, but the excellent views of the harbour from the dining room, together with the prospect of fresh seafood, could prove too much of a temptation. An exhaustive list of fish and seafood dishes is offered daily; perhaps Whitby crab pâté with French bread and home-made chutney and then seafood paella, or your choice of fish simply battered and served with chips. Desserts include classics like sherry trifle or spotted dick.

Open all day all wk 11-9 summer (11-8 winter) Closed 25 Dec, 6-31 Jan
Food Contact pub for details ⊕ FREE HOUSE ◀ Bradfield Farmers Blonde, Brown Cow, Cropton Blackout & Scoresby Stout, The Captain Cook Slipway. ♥ 10
Facilities ♦♦ Children's menu Children's portions WiFi ▭

YORK
Map 16 SE65

Blue Bell
`PICK OF THE PUBS`

tel: 01904 654904 **53 Fossgate YO1 9TF**
email: robsonhardie@aol.com
dir: *In city centre*

Tucked away, quaint city pub

Its slimline frontage is easy to miss, but don't walk past this charming pub – the smallest in York – which has been serving customers in the ancient heart of the city for 200 years. In 1903 it was given a typical Edwardian makeover, and since then almost nothing has changed – so the Grade II listed interior still includes varnished wall and ceiling panelling, cast-iron tiled fireplaces, and charming old settles. The layout is original too, with the taproom at the front and the snug down a long corridor at the rear, both with servery hatches. The only slight drawback is that the pub's size leaves no room for a kitchen, so don't expect anything more complicated than lunchtime sandwiches. However, there's a good selection of real ales: no fewer than seven are usually on tap, including rotating guests. The pub has won awards for its efforts in fund-raising.

Open all day all wk **Food** Lunch Mon-Sat 12-2.30 ⊕ PUNCH TAVERNS ◀ Timothy Taylor Landlord, Bradfield Farmers Blonde, Roosters Yankee Ŏ Thatchers Heritage. ♥ 21
Facilities Non-diners area ❤ (Bar) WiFi **Notes** ⊜

NEW The Judges Lodgings

tel: 01904 638733 **9 Lendal YO1 8AQ**
web: www.judgeslodgingsyork.co.uk
dir: *Phone for detailed directions*

Seasonal menu amidst period splendour

Completely renovated during 2014, this 300-year-old town house stands just a stone's throw from York Minster in one direction and the riverside Museum Gardens in the other. Originally built for a wealthy doctor, until 1976 it was used as accommodation for visiting assizes judges. The heart of the building is the Cellar Bar, where beers from owners Thwaites' Brewery may accompany a confident, ever-changing seasonal menu of traditional Yorkshire fare. Platters are a favourite, or home-made beef and ale pie to ward off those winter day chills.

Open all day all wk **Food** Lunch Mon-Sat 12-11, Sun 12-10 Dinner Mon-Sat 12-11, Sun 12-10 Av main course £10 Set menu available ⊕ THWAITES INNS OF CHARACTER ◼ Wainwright & Lancaster Bomber. ♈ 15 **Facilities** Non-diners area ⬥ Children's menu Children's portions Garden ⊼ WiFi

See advert on opposite page

Lamb & Lion Inn ★★★★ INN ◉

tel: 01904 612078 **2-4 High Petergate YO1 7EH**
email: gm@lambandlionyork.com **web:** www.lambandlionyork.com
dir: *From York Station, turn left. Stay in left lane, over Lendal Bridge. At lights left (Theatre Royal on right). At next lights pub on right under Bootham Bar (medieval gate)*

Right in the historical centre of York

This rambling Georgian inn has unrivalled views of nearby York Minster from its elevated beer garden. Conjoined to the medieval Bootham Bar gateway, it is furnished and styled in keeping with its grand heritage. A warren of snugs and corridors radiate from a bar offering a challenging array of beers, including Great Heck Golden Mane, brewed for the inn. Equally enticing is the AA-Rosette menu, offering comforting classics ranging from a fish finger butty and steak pie to moules frites, slow-cooked lamb shank and a Yorkshire platter. Finish with chocolate brownie or knickerbocker glory. Accommodation is available.

Open all day all wk **Food** Contact pub for details Av main course £11.95 Set menu available ⊕ FREE HOUSE ◼ Great Heck Golden Mane, Black Sheep Best Bitter, Copper Dragon Golden Pippin, Timothy Taylor Landlord. ♈ 10 **Facilities** Non-diners area ❧ (Bar Restaurant Garden) ⬥ Children's menu Children's portions Garden ⊼ WiFi **Rooms** 12

Lysander Arms

tel: 01904 640845 **Manor Ln, Shipton Rd YO30 5TZ**
email: christine@lysanderarms.co.uk
dir: *Phone for detailed directions*

British menu and Yorkshire hospitality

This pub stands on a former RAF airfield where No. 4 Squadron's Westland Lysander aircraft were based early in World War II. Still relatively modern, which accounts for the contemporary feel of the interior, it has a long, fully air-conditioned bar with up-to-date furnishings, brick-built fireplace and large-screen TV. Brasserie restaurant meals range from 'light bites' such as Yorkshire Blue cheese and chive rarebit with pickled red cabbage to hearty meals such as steak, mushroom and ale pie or slow-cooked belly pork with crispy crackling, black pudding, creamed potatoes and roasted apple.

Open all day all wk **Food** Lunch Tue-Sat 12-2, Sun 12-3 Dinner Tue-Sat 5.30-9 Restaurant menu available Tue-Sat ⊕ FREE HOUSE ◼ Sharp's Doom Bar, York Guzzler, Wychwood Hobgoblin, Copper Dragon, Black Sheep, Theakston, Roosters ⚬ Rekorderlig. ♈ 8 **Facilities** Non-diners area ❧ (Bar Garden) ⬥ Children's menu Children's portions Play area Garden ⊼ Beer festival Cider festival Parking WiFi

---

SOUTH YORKSHIRE

BRADFIELD
Map 16 SK29

The Strines Inn

tel: 0114 285 1247 **Bradfield Dale S6 6JE**
email: thestrinesinn@yahoo.co.uk
dir: *N off A57 between Sheffield & Manchester*

Popular free house overlooking a reservoir

Although built as a manor house in 1275, most of the structure is 16th century; it has been an inn since 1771, the public rooms containing artefacts from its bygone days. The name apparently means 'meeting of waters' in Old English. Locally brewed Bradfield Farmers Bitter shares bar space with ambassadors from the further-flung Marston's, Jennings and Wychwood. Traditional home-made food begins with sandwiches and salads, then by way of pies and giant Yorkshire puddings arrives at the mammoth mixed grill; lasagne verdi; macaroni cheese; and home-made butter bean stew. A play area and an enclosure for peacocks, geese and chickens are outside.

Open all wk 10.30-3 5.30-11 (Sat-Sun 10.30am-11pm; all day Apr-Oct) Closed 25 Dec **Food** Lunch Mon-Fri 12-2.30, Sat-Sun 12-9 (summer all wk 12-9) Dinner Mon-Fri 5.30-9, Sat-Sun 12-9 (summer all wk 12-9) Av main course £9.25 ⊕ FREE HOUSE ◼ Marston's Pedigree, Jennings Cocker Hoop, Bradfield Farmers Bitter, Wychwood Hobgoblin. ♈ 10 **Facilities** Non-diners area ❧ (Bar Garden) ⬥ Children's menu Children's portions Play area Garden ⊼ Parking ⇝ (notice required)

CADEBY
Map 16 SE50

NEW The Cadeby Pub & Restaurant

tel: 01709 864009 **Main St DN5 7SW**
email: info@cadebyinn.co.uk
dir: *A1(M) junct 37, A635 towards Rotherham. Follow Cadeby signs*

Mid 18th-century village destination pub

Under new management following a refit, the former Cadeby Inn stands well back, buffered from the village's main street by a lovely long lawn with tables. Yorkshire-brewed real ales are usually Timothy Taylor Landlord and Black Sheep, while Old Rosie is on cider duty. Snacks and light meals are available at lunchtime, while pub classics on the main menu are typified by steak and kidney pudding; smoked haddock chowder; and large or small Cadeby burgers. For vegetarians, there are feta and pimento pastries, and house risotto. Hard-to-resist desserts might there be pear frangipane, or lavender custard pot.

Open all day all wk **Food** Contact pub for details Av main course £9 Set menu available Restaurant menu available ⊕ FREE HOUSE ◼ Timothy Taylor Landlord, Black Sheep ⚬ Westons Old Rosie. ♈ **Facilities** Non-diners area ❧ (Bar Garden) ⬥ Children's portions Garden ⊼ Beer festival Cider festival Parking WiFi ⇝

PENISTONE
Map 16 SE20

Cubley Hall
PICK OF THE PUBS

tel: 01226 766086 **Mortimer Rd, Cubley S36 9DF**
email: info@cubleyhall.co.uk
dir: *M1 junct 37, A628 towards Manchester, or M1 junct 35a, A616. Hall just S of Penistone*

Impressive building with ornate, elegant decor and excellent food

Built as a farm in the 1700s, Cubley Hall was a gentleman's residence in Queen Victoria's reign and later became a children's home before being transformed into a pub in 1982. In 1990 the massive, oak-beamed bar was converted into the restaurant and furnished with old pine tables, chairs and church pews, and the building was extended to incorporate the hotel, which was designed to harmonise with the original mosaic floors, ornate plaster ceilings, oak panelling and stained glass. On the edge of the Peak District National Park, the hall is reputedly haunted by Florence Lockley, who married there in 1904 and is affectionately known as Flo. Food-wise, take your pick from light bites, chalkboard specials and an extensive main menu listing pub classics and home-made pizzas. Typically, choose from a Crawshaw beefburger with all the trimmings; fish and chips; pork and leek sausages; mash and onion gravy; and chicken and mushroom carbonara.

Open all day all wk 7am-11.30pm **Food** Lunch all wk 12-9 Dinner all wk 12-9 ⊕ FREE HOUSE ◀ Tetley's Bitter, Black Sheep Best Bitter. **Facilities** Non-diners area ◑ Children's menu Children's portions Play area Family room Garden ⋒ Parking WiFi 🚌 (notice required)

SHEFFIELD
Map 16 SK38

The Fat Cat
PICK OF THE PUBS

tel: 0114 249 4801 **23 Alma St S3 8SA**
email: info@thefatcat.co.uk
dir: *Phone for detailed directions*

Own Kelham Island beers in Victorian pub

Built in 1832, it was known as The Alma Hotel for many years, then in 1981 it was the first Sheffield pub to introduce guest beers. The policy continues, with constantly changing, mainly microbrewery, guests from across the country, two handpumped ciders, unusual bottled beers, Belgian pure fruit juices and British country wines. The pub's own Kelham Island Brewery accounts for at least four of the 11 traditional draught real ales. The smart interior is very much that of a traditional, welcoming back-street pub, with real fires making it feel very cosy, while outside is an attractive walled garden with Victorian-style lanterns and bench seating. Except on Sunday evenings, typical home-cooked food from a simple weekly menu is broccoli cheddar pasta; Mexican mince and nachos; and savoury bean casserole. Events include the Monday quiz and curry night. Annual beer festival.

Open all wk 12-11 (Fri-Sat 12-12) Closed 25 Dec **Food** Lunch Mon-Fri & Sun 12-3, Sat 12-8 Dinner Mon-Fri 6-8, Sat 12-8 Av main course £4.50 ⊕ FREE HOUSE ◀ Timothy Taylor Landlord, Kelham Island Best Bitter & Pale Rider, Guest ales Ở Thatchers Gold. **Facilities** Non-diners area ◑ (Bar Garden) ◑ Children's portions Family room Garden Beer festival Parking WiFi 🚌

Kelham Island Tavern
PICK OF THE PUBS

tel: 0114 272 2482 **62 Russell St S3 8RW**
email: lewiskelham@gmail.com
dir: *Just off A61 (inner ring road). Follow brown tourist signs for Kelham Island*

City pub with good reputation for its real ales

Over the last decade and a bit, Lewis Gonda and Trevor Wraith have transformed this tavern into a 'small gem'. The pub is in a conservation and popular walking

area, with old buildings converted into stylish apartments, and The Kelham Island Museum round the corner in Alma Street telling the story of the city's industrial heritage. This 1830s backstreet pub was built to quench the thirst of steelmakers who lived and worked nearby. The real ale list is formidable: residents Barnsley Bitter and Bradfield Farmers Blonde are joined by 10 ever-changing guests, as well as Westons Old Rosie cider, and a midsummer beer festival is held every year at the end of June. The blackboard menu changes daily but typical choices might include home-made pies, stews, soups, pâtés and various bar snacks. Great in the summer, the pub has won awards for its beer garden and floral displays.

Open all day all wk 12-12 **Food** Lunch Mon-Sat 12-3 Av main course £6 ⊕ FREE HOUSE ◀ Barnsley Bitter, Bradfield Farmers Blonde, Pictish Brewers Gold, 10 Guest ales Ở Westons Old Rosie & Country Perry. **Facilities** Non-diners area ◑ (Bar Garden) ◑ Children's portions Family room Garden ⋒ Beer festival Cider festival Parking 🚌 (notice required)

The Sheffield Tap

tel: 0114 273 7558 **Platform 1B, Sheffield Station, Sheaf St S1 2BP**
email: info@sheffieldtap.com
dir: *Access from Sheaf St & from Platform 1B. (NB limited access from Platform 1B on Fri & Sat)*

Very much on track to serve the best beers

For more than 30 years disused and derelict, the former Edwardian refreshment room and dining rooms of Sheffield Midland Railway Station have become a much praised Grade II listed free house. Painstakingly restored to its former glory by the current custodians, with help from the Railway Heritage Trust, The Sheffield Tap is now a beer mecca with its own on-site microbrewery allowing customers to view the complete brewing process while supping a pint or two in comfort. There's ten real ales, one real cider, 12 keg products and more than 200 bottled beers from around the world. Food is limited to bagged bar snacks, and children are welcome until 8pm every day.

Open all day all wk Closed 25-26 Dec, 1 Jan **Food** Contact pub for details ⊕ FREE HOUSE ◀ Tapped Brew Company Ở Thistly Cross. **Facilities** Non-diners area ◑ (Bar Restaurant Outside area) ◑ Outside area WiFi 🚌 (notice required)

TOTLEY
Map 16 SK37

The Cricket Inn
PICK OF THE PUBS

tel: 0114 236 5256 **Penny Ln S17 3AZ**
email: cricket@brewkitchen.co.uk
dir: *Follow A621 from Sheffield, 8m. Right into Hillfoot Rd, 1st left into Penny Ln*

Popular gastro-pub well known for seafood and game dishes

Down a country lane bordered by wooded hills and pastures, this former farmhouse became a pub for the navvies building the nearby Totley railway tunnel in the late 1880s. Walkers and cyclists flock here, while dogs and children are made to feel welcome too. Chef Richard Smith co-runs it with the Thornbridge Brewery in Bakewell, which naturally enough provides the real ales. Richard's kitchen team under Marco Caires produces crab spring roll with home-made sweet red chilli and tomato jam; overnight-cooked shoulder of Peak District lamb; black and white linguine with garlic prawns and salsa verde; and espetada, Marco's Portuguese signature dish featuring herby pieces of chargrilled sirloin steak. They also smoke their own fish and meats. For dessert, try a whole baked Barncliffe Yorkshire Brie - it's enough for two. Summer barbecues are held in the field behind the pub and cricket is played next door.

Open all day all wk 11-11 **Food** Lunch all wk 12-9.30 Dinner all wk 12-9.30 Set menu available ⊕ BREWKITCHEN LTD ◀ Thornbridge Wild Swan, Lord Marples, Jaipur Ở Thatchers Gold. ☗ 10 **Facilities** Non-diners area ◑ (Bar Restaurant Garden) ◑ Children's menu Children's portions Garden ⋒ Parking WiFi 🚌 (notice required)

WEST YORKSHIRE

ADDINGHAM
Map 19 SE04

The Fleece
PICK OF THE PUBS

tel: 01943 830491 **154 Main St LS29 OLY**
email: info@fleeceinnaddingham.co.uk
dir: Between Ilkley & Skipton

Friendly service and real character

Chef-proprietor Craig Minto established a small group of successful gastro-pubs before taking over this 17th-century coaching inn from his father. Located where several well-tramped footpaths meet, it attracts lots of walkers, who can usually be found on the front terrace or in the stone-flagged bar. Here are wooden settles, an enormous fireplace and real ales from, among others, Skipton's Copper Dragon brewery, and Mary Jane from Ilkley (whose bottled range is available from the pub's deli next door). As far as possible, the modern British food is prepared from local and organic ingredients, with noteworthy dishes being grilled Isle of Skye queenie scallops with gruyère cheese; Waberthwaite dry-cured gammon steak with poached egg and proper chips; and posh fish pie, featuring fresh salmon, haddock and coley. Roast leg of lamb with Yorkshire pudding, dripping potatoes and real gravy is a firm Sunday favourite.

Open all day all wk 12-11 (Sun 12-10.30) **Food** Lunch Mon-Sat 12-2.15, Sun 12-8 Dinner Mon-Sat 5-9, Sun 12-8 Set menu available ⊕ PUNCH TAVERNS ◗ Timothy Taylor Landlord, Black Sheep, Copper Dragon, Ilkley Ŏ Westons Stowford Press. ▼ 30 **Facilities** Non-diners area ♣ (Bar Garden) ◗ Children's menu Children's portions Play area Garden ⋒ Parking WiFi ▭ (notice required)

BRADFORD
Map 19 SE13

New Beehive Inn

tel: 01274 721784 **171 Westgate BD1 3AA**
email: newbeehiveinn+21@btinternet.com
dir: Phone for detailed directions

Step back in time at an inn with lots of character

Dating from 1901 and centrally situated with many tourist attractions nearby, this classic Edwardian inn retains its period Arts and Crafts atmosphere with five separate bars and gas lighting. It is on the national inventory list of historic pubs. Outside, with a complete change of mood, you can relax in the Mediterranean-style courtyard. The pub offers a good range of unusual real ales, such as Salamander Mudpuppy and Abbeydale Moonshine, and a selection of over 100 malt whiskies, served alongside some simple bar snacks. Music fans should attend the cellar bar, which is open at weekends and features regular live bands.

Open all day all wk **Food** Contact pub for details ⊕ FREE HOUSE ◗ Kelham Island Best Bitter, Abbeydale Moonshine, Salamander Mudpuppy, Ilkley Mary Jane, Saltaire Cascade Pale Ale Ŏ Westons Old Rosie. **Facilities** Non-diners area ◗ Family room Garden ⋒ Parking WiFi ▭

CALVERLEY
Map 19 SE23

NEW Calverley Arms

tel: 0113 255 7771 **Calverley Ln LS28 5QQ**
email: calverleyarmspudsey@vintageinn.co.uk
dir: Phone for detailed directions

Victorian country house in landscaped grounds

Pleasantly located in the gently rolling countryside of the Aire Valley, with the popular Leeds & Liverpool Canal just across the fields. This very substantial village-edge inn makes the most of its situation, with restful views from the leafy

beer garden. The rustic theme continues inside, with lots of wood, brick and fireplaces, where Leeds Pale or York Yorkshire Terrier are the beers of choice. Part of the Vintage Inns group, the fare reflects their quality menus. Aromatic braised pork belly or slow-cooked game and blackberry pie should take the chill off a bracing Yorkshire day. There's a beer festival here every July.

Open all day all wk **Food** Lunch all wk 12-10 Dinner all wk 12-10 Av main course £10 Set menu available Restaurant menu available all wk ⊕ MITCHELLS & BUTLERS ◗ Leeds Pale, York Yorkshire Terrier. ▼ **Facilities** Non-diners area ◗ Children's menu Children's portions Garden Outside area ⋒ Beer festival Parking WiFi ▭ (notice required)

EMLEY
Map 16 SE21

The White Horse

tel: 01924 849823 **2 Chapel Ln HD8 9SP**
dir: M1 junct 38, A637 towards Huddersfield. At rdbt left onto A636, then right to Emley

The hub of the community

On the old coaching route to Huddersfield and Halifax on the edge of the village, this 18th-century pub has views towards Emley Moor Mast and the surrounding countryside. The pub is popular with walkers, cyclists and locals – walking maps are available from the bar, which is warmed by a working Yorkshire range. Of the eight cask ales, four are permanent (including their own Ossett Brewery ales), and four are ever-rotating guests featuring microbreweries. A simple menu offers the likes of cod goujons; creamy garlic mushrooms; steak and ale pie; and mixed grill. Look to the blackboards for daily specials and desserts.

Open all day all wk 12-11 **Food** Lunch all wk 12-9 Dinner all wk 12-9 ⊕ FREE HOUSE ◗ Ossett Excelsior & Silver King, Emley Cross, Yorkshire Blonde, Guest ales Ŏ Rotating guest ciders. ▼ 9 **Facilities** Non-diners area ♣ (Bar Garden) ◗ Children's portions Family room Garden ⋒ Parking ▭ (notice required)

HALIFAX
Map 19 SE02

Shibden Mill Inn ★★★★ INN ⊛⊛
PICK OF THE PUBS

See Pick of the Pubs on page 581 and advert on page 582

HARTSHEAD
Map 16 SE12

The Gray Ox

tel: 01274 872845 **15 Hartshead Ln WF15 8AL**
email: grayox@hotmail.co.uk
dir: M62 junct 25, A644 signed Dewsbury. Take A62, branch left signed Hartshead & Moor Top/B6119. Left to Hartshead

Hillside inn with great views and fine food

This rural inn seems to grow out of the dark gritstone hills overlooking the deep-cut Calder Valley at the fringe of the West Yorkshire Pennines. Timeless reminders of the old farmhouse it once was flicker in shadows cast from the huge log fire that warms the beamed bar where locals enjoy beers from Jennings. Rooms ramble through the old building, where the six chefs have built a grand reputation for producing fine locally-sourced dishes. Indulge in a starter of seared pigeon breast with braised celeriac, progressing then to Moroccan spiced rump of Yorkshire lamb with fragrant couscous. Booking ahead is advisable.

Open all wk 12-3.30 6-12 (Sun 12-10.30) **Food** Lunch Mon-Sat 12-2, Sun 12-7 Dinner Mon-Fri 6-9, Sat 6-9.30, Sun 12-7 Set menu available ⊕ MARSTON'S ◗ Jennings Cumberland Ale, Cocker Hoop, Sneck Lifter. ▼ 12 **Facilities** Non-diners area ♣ (Garden) ◗ Children's menu Children's portions Garden ⋒ Parking WiFi ▭

HAWORTH
Map 19 SE03

The Old White Lion Hotel

tel: 01535 642313 **Main St BD22 8DU**
email: enquiries@oldwhitelionhotel.com
dir: *A629 onto B6142, 0.5m past Haworth Station*

Charming inn in Brontë country

This traditional family-run 300-year-old coaching inn looks down onto the famous cobbled Main Street of the famous Brontë village of Haworth. In the charming bar the ceiling beams are supported by timber posts, and locals appreciatively quaff their pints of guest ale. Food is taken seriously and 'dispensed with hospitality and good measure'. Bar snacks include baguettes, salads and jackets, while a meal in the Gimmerton Restaurant might include duck parcels with plum, spring onion and hoi sin chutney, followed by chicken and butternut squash roulate or pan-fried duck breast on fondant potato with brandy, orange and cherry sauce. Vegetarians are well catered for.

Open all day all wk 11-11 (Sun 12-10.30) **Food** Lunch Mon-Fri 12-2.30, Sat-Sun all day Dinner Mon-Fri 6-9.30, Sat-Sun all day Set menu available Restaurant menu available all wk evenings only ⊕ FREE HOUSE ◀ Tetley's Bitter, John Smith's, Local guest ales. �troph9 **Facilities** Non-diners area ◀ Children's menu Children's portions Parking WiFi ▅

HOLMFIRTH
Map 16 SE10

Farmers Arms

tel: 01484 683713 **2-4 Liphill Bank Rd HD9 2LR**
email: farmersarms2@gmail.com
dir: *From Holmfirth take A635 (Greenfield Rd) on right signed Manchester. Left at Compo's Café. 2nd right into Liphill Bank Rd*

Great ales and home-cooked food

A small village pub run with pride by Sam Page and Danielle Montgomery, the Farmers Arms sits in typical *Last of the Summer Wine* country. There is a welcome emphasis on real ales, with an annual beer festival every autumn and regulars that include Timothy Taylor Landlord, Greene King IPA and Bradfield Farmers Blonde. The menu appeals too; settle by the log fire and enjoy fresh dishes prepared from scratch such as chicken liver and cognac parfait; braised blade of beef with roast garlic, mashed potatoes, red wine gravy and savoury parsley porridge; and apple crumble with custard.

Open Tue-Thu 12-3 5-12 (Fri-Sun 12-12 Mon 5-12) Closed Mon L **Food** Lunch Tue-Thu 12-2, Fri-Sat 12-3, Sun 12-8 Dinner Tue-Thu 6-9.30, Sat 5-9.30, Sun 12-8 Av main course £10 ⊕ PUNCH TAVERNS ◀ Timothy Taylor Landlord, Bradfield Farmers Blonde, Greene King IPA, Guest ales ♂ Thatchers Gold, Westons Wyld Wood Organic. ♥ 13 **Facilities** Non-diners area ◀ (Bar Garden) ◀ Children's portions Garden ▱ Beer festival Cider festival Parking WiFi ▅ (notice required)

Follow us on Facebook
www.facebook.com/TheAAUK

ILKLEY
Map 19 SE14

NEW The Crescent Inn

tel: 01943 811250 **Brook St LS29 8DG**
email: manager@thecrescentinn.co.uk
dir: *On corner of A65 (Church St) & Brook St*

Vast range of local real ales here

Part of a hotel dating back to 1861, The Crescent is a landmark building in the centre of Ilkley and it shares the site with its French sister restaurant next door. The pub blends original Victorian features such as an open fire with contemporary interiors including handcrafted furniture upholstered in local cloth. Choose from an ever-changing range of eight real ales from local breweries such as Saltaire or pick one of the 15 wines by the glass. Unpretentious and enjoyable dishes on the menu include pie of the day, home-made curry and steak-frites.

Open all day all wk **Food** Lunch Mon-Fri 12-3, Sat-Sun all day Dinner Mon-Fri 5.30-9, Sat-Sun all day Av main course £8.95 ⊕ FREE HOUSE ◀ Saltaire Blonde, Black Sheep Ale, Crescent Ale. ♥ 15 **Facilities** Non-diners area ◀ (Bar Restaurant Outside area) ◀ Children's menu Children's portions Outside area ▱ WiFi ▅ (notice required)

Ilkley Moor Vaults

tel: 01943 607012 **Stockeld Rd LS29 9HD**
email: info@ilkleymoorvaults.co.uk
dir: *From Ilkley on A65 towards Skipton. Pub on right*

Stylish pub at the start of the Dales Way

Known locally as The Taps, it sits at the start of the Dales Way and near the 'old bridge' that crosses the River Wharfe. A popular and stylish establishment, it is equally good for a pint of Timothy Taylor Landlord or traditional dishes such as smoked sausage and pepper omelette; smoked haddock with mustard sauce, spinach and mash; Spanish pork, chicken and chickpea soup or sticky toffee pudding with vanilla ice cream. There's an impressive children's menu, and a great value early bird set menu if you arrive between 5.30pm and 6.30pm.

Open 12-3 5-11 (Sat-Sun all day) Closed Mon (ex BHs) **Food** Lunch Tue-Sat 12-2.30, Sun 12-7 Dinner Tue-Sat 6-9, Sun 12-7 ⊕ STAR PUBS & BARS ◀ Timothy Taylor Landlord, Theakston Best Bitter, Caledonian Deuchars IPA. ♥ 9 **Facilities** Non-diners area ◀ (Bar Garden) ◀ Children's menu Children's portions Garden ▱ Parking ▅ (notice required)

KIRKBURTON
Map 16 SE11

NEW The Woodman Inn ★★★★ INN

tel: 01484 605778 **Thunderbridge Ln HD8 0PX**
email: chris@woodman-inn.com **web:** www.woodman-inn.com
dir: *1.4m SW of Kirkburton. From Huddersfield take A629 towards Sheffield. Follow brown Woodman Inn signs*

Smart gastro-pub with proud Yorkshire provenance

Hidden in a charming hamlet of weavers' cottages in a secluded wooded valley, The Woodman Inn comes up trumps in any search for the perfect Yorkshire inn. Real ales are from county breweries, including the sublime Bradfield Farmers Blonde. Sup this in a long, cosy, log-fire warmed beamed room wrapped around the bar or in the refurbished restaurant, where rustic gastro-food makes the most of Yorkshire's produce. Featherblade and oxtail duo of beef hits the spot, or try the Yorkshire tapas sharing plate. Should you be loathe to leave, 10 boutique-style bedrooms provide the perfect excuse for stopping over.

Open all day all wk **Food** Lunch Mon-Fri 12-2.30, Sat 12-4, Sun 12-7 Dinner Mon-Sat 5-9, Sun 12-7 Av main course £12.95 ⊕ FREE HOUSE ◀ Timothy Taylor Landlord, Black Sheep, Bradfield Farmers Blonde. ♥ 14 **Facilities** Non-diners area ◀ (Bar Garden Outside area) ◀ Children's menu Children's portions Garden Outside area ▱ Parking WiFi ▅ (notice required) **Rooms** 10

PICK OF THE PUBS

Shibden Mill Inn ★★★★★ INN

HALIFAX   Map 19 SE02

tel: 01422 365840
Shibden Mill Fold HX3 7UL
email: enquiries@shibdenmillinn.com
web: www.shibdenmillinn.com
dir: *From A58 into Kell Ln. 0.5m, left into Blake Hill*

Award-winning food in renovated corn mill

The Shibden Valley used to be an important wool production area, the waters of Red Beck powering this 17th-century, former spinning mill until the industry collapsed in the late 1800s. Now it's a charming inn, with open fires, oak beams, small windows and heavy tiles, happily enjoying a more civilised existence below overhanging trees in a wooded glen that makes Halifax just down the road seem a thousand miles away. The beer garden is extremely popular, not least with beer fans who come here to sample a real ale called Shibden Mill, brewed specially for the inn, Black Sheep or one of the three guest ales. With two AA Rosettes, the restaurant attracts those who enjoy food prepared from trusted local growers and suppliers, and a seasonal menu offering newly conceived dishes and old favourites. Two starters to consider might be crispy Denshaw duck eggs, sweet cauliflower purée, truffle and purple broccoli; or roasted quail, white polenta and parmesan, walnut, pear,

grape jelly and black pudding wantons. Turn over the page for possibilities such as an open fish pie of cod, wild salmon, mackerel and grilled langoustine; or mallard and curried pigeon Wellington, duck leg potatoes, green beans and sweetcorn. Among the old favourites mentioned earlier are hand-made 8oz minced Yorkshire beef burger; battered haddock sandwich; and grilled goats' cheese English muffin. There's also a gourmet menu of Yorkshire artisan cheeses served with home-made chutney, oat biscuits, celery and Eccles cakes, ideally accompanied by a glass of vintage port. Stay overnight in one of the individually designed luxury bedrooms, with a full Yorkshire breakfast to look forward to next morning.

Open all day all wk Closed 25-26 Dec eve,1 Jan eve **Food** Bkfst Mon-Fri 7-10 Sat-Sun 8-10; Lunch Mon-Thu 12-2, Fri-Sat 12-2.30, Sun 12-7.30; Dinner Mon-Thu 5.30-9, Fri 5.30-9.30, Sat 6-9.30 Set menu, Restaurant menu all wk ⊕ FREE HOUSE ◖ John Smith's, Black Sheep, Shibden Mill, 3 Guest ales. ♟ 22 **Facilities** Non-diners area ♦ Children's menu & portions Garden ⊼ Parking WiFi **Rooms** 11

Shibden Mill Inn

Shibden Mill Fold, Shibden, Halifax, West Yorkshire HX3 7UL • **Tel:** 01422 365840 • Fax: 01422 362971
Website: www.shibdenmillinn.com • **Email:** enquiries@shibdenmillinn.com

For over 350 years *The Shibden Mill Inn* has been at the heart of life in West Yorkshire's Shibden Valley. It's a magical place where generation after generation of locals have enjoyed time well spent with friends and family, sharing in life's special moments and shaping memories to last a life time.

The Inn's reputation for warm hospitality, premier gastro dining and first class accommodation draws people to the Shibden Valley from far and wide, and the Mill has naturally become a popular choice for those wishing to savour a sumptuous weekend break or mid-week stay.

Stunning countryside walks are in easy reach, as too the bright lights and city centre shopping on offer in Leeds. From its unique location, *The Shibden Mill Inn* offers easy access to the very best to be found in this delightful part of West Yorkshire. However there are those who during their stay simply wish to relax and unwind in the beautiful surrounds of this 17th Century property, where once you've arrived and unpacked, there's no reason to leave.

Whatever the occasion *The Shibden Mill Inn* combines first class service and accommodation of the highest order, to ensure a memorable experience that delivers everything you ask of it, and more.

Crowned Yorkshire's Favourite Pub • UK Food Pub of the Year

Inn of the Year • Sunday Lunch Pub of the Year

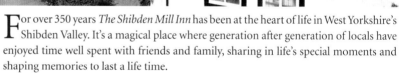

LEEDS
Map 19 SE23

The Cross Keys
PICK OF THE PUBS

tel: 0113 243 3711 **107 Water Ln LS11 5WD**
email: info@the-crosskeys.com
dir: 0.5m from Leeds Station: right into Neville St, right into Water Ln. Pass Globe Rd, pub on left

Robust food in a historic city centre pub

Hard to believe now but this historic landmark from the peak of Leeds' industrial history was closed in the 1980s and used as a tyre storage depot until it was restored in 2005. Built in 1802, The Cross Keys was a watering hole for local foundry workers and it's where steam engine inventor James Watt reputedly hired a room to spy on his competitor Matthew Murray. To learn Murray's trade secrets Watt bought drinks for foundry workers relaxing here after work. This city centre pub has a country pub atmosphere, with hand-pulled pints from local microbreweries complementing food recreated from long lost recipes for traditional British dishes. The best seasonal produce goes into dishes such as braised pig's cheek, mash, braised fennel and cider sauce, which might precede a main course of lamb belly with celeriac purée, celeriac fondant and roasted shallots.

Open all day all wk 12-11 (Fri-Sat 12-12 Sun 12-10.30) Closed 25-26 Dec, 1 Jan **Food** Lunch Mon-Sat 12-3, Sun 12-5 Dinner Mon-Sat 5.30-9.30 Av main course £14.95 ⊕ FREE HOUSE ◀ Kirkstall, Magic Rock, Thornbridge Ö Aspall. ₹ 12 **Facilities** Non-diners area ❤ (Bar Restaurant Garden) ❤ Children's menu Children's portions Garden ⋒ WiFi ▭

North Bar

tel: 0113 242 4540 **24 New Briggate LS1 6NU**
email: info@northbar.com
dir: From rail station towards Corn Exchange, left into Briggate (main shopping area). At x-rds with The Headrow straight on into New Briggate. Bar 100mtrs on right

Beers from around the world in upbeat atmosphere

This pioneering beer bar in the heart of Leeds is heaven for ale aficionados as it offers up to 130 bottled beers from around the globe at any one time, plus 16 draught beers. Yet, pride of place on the vast bar are hand-pumped beers from local microbreweries, notably Roosters ales. It's a trendy European-style bar, full of characters and great conversation, as well as a venue for music and local art exhibitions. Don't miss the regular beer festivals.

Open all day all wk 11am-2am (Sun 11am-mdnt, Mon-Tue 11am-1am) Closed 25 Dec **Food** Lunch all wk 12-10 Dinner all wk 12-10 ⊕ FREE HOUSE ◀ Kirkstall, Roosters, Thornbridge, Buxton, Magic Rock Ö Pure North. **Facilities** Non-diners area ❤ (Bar) ❤ Beer festival Parking WiFi

LINTHWAITE
Map 16 SE11

The Sair Inn

tel: 01484 842370 **Lane Top HD7 5SG**
dir: From Huddersfield take A62 (Oldham road) for 3.5m. Left just before lights at bus stop (in centre of road) into Hoyle Ing & follow sign

Own brewed ales and welcoming atmosphere

You won't be able to eat here, but this old hilltop alehouse has enough character in its four small rooms to make up for that; three are heated by hot Yorkshire ranges in winter. Landlord Ron Crabtree has brewed his own beers for over 32 years and they are much sought after by real ale aficionados. Imported German lagers are available, too. In summer the outside drinking area catches the afternoon sun and commands views across the Colne Valley.

Open all wk 5-11 (Sat 12-11 Sun 12-10.30) **Food** Contact pub for details ⊕ FREE HOUSE ◀ Linfit Bitter, Special Bitter, Gold Medal, Autumn Gold, Old Eli Ö Pure North Original. **Facilities** Non-diners area ❤ (Bar) ❤ WiFi ▭ (notice required)

LINTON
Map 16 SE34

The Windmill Inn

tel: 01937 582209 **Main St LS22 4HT**
email: enquiries@thewindmillinnlinton.co.uk
dir: From A1 exit at Tadcaster/Otley junct, follow Otley signs. In Collingham follow Linton signs

Historic pub with a diverse menu

Once the home of a long forgotten miller, this pleasant village pub is made up of small beamed rooms that have been stripped back to bare stone, presumably the original 14th-century walls. A coaching inn since the 18th century, polished antique settles, log fires, oak beams and copper-topped cast-iron tables set the scene in which to enjoy good food in the bar or restaurant. Dishes on offer include mushroom and shallot fondue; tempura prawns; Cajun steak 'n' ribs or surf 'n' turf; and Ripon City sausages and mash. A beer festival is held in July.

Open all wk 11-3 5.30-11 (Fri-Sat 11-11 Sun 12-10.30) Closed 1 Jan **Food** Lunch Mon-Fri 12-2, Sat 12-9, Sun 12-5.45 Dinner Sat 12-9 Av main course £10 ⊕ HEINEKEN ◀ Theakston Best Bitter, Caledonian, John Smith's. ₹ 12 **Facilities** Non-diners area ❤ (Bar Garden) ❤ Children's menu Children's portions Garden ⋒ Beer festival Parking WiFi ▭ (notice required)

MARSDEN
Map 16 SE01

The Olive Branch

tel: 01484 844487 **Manchester Rd HD7 6LU**
email: eat@olivebranch.uk.com
dir: On A62 between Marsden & Slaithwaite, 6m from Huddersfield

Highly regarded brasserie-style food

Enter this traditional 19th-century inn on a former packhorse route above the River Colne and the Huddersfield Canal and you'll find yourself in a rambling series of rooms, fire-warmed in winter. The restaurant's brasserie-style food is exemplified by starters of parfait of chicken livers, and wood pigeon with garlic risotto and chocolate sauce, while typical main dishes include Gressingham duck breast, Chateaubriand to share, and pan-fried medallions of venison. Enjoy a pint of Greenfield Dobcross Bitter from Saddleworth on the sun deck and admire the views of Marsden Moor Estate.

Open all wk Tue-Sat 5.30pm-11pm (Sun 12-10.30) Closed Mon eve **Food** Lunch Sun 12-8 Dinner Tue-Sat 6.30-9, Sun 12-8 ⊕ FREE HOUSE ◀ Greenfield Dobcross Bitter & Ale. ₹ 12 **Facilities** Non-diners area ❤ Children's menu Children's portions Garden ⋒ Parking WiFi

RIPPONDEN
Map 16 SE01

Old Bridge Inn

tel: 01422 822595 **Priest Ln HX6 4DF**
web: www.theoldbridgeinn.co.uk
dir: *In village centre by church*

Probably West Yorkshire's oldest hostelry

An inn has stood by Ripponden's old bridge, and even earlier ford, since at least 1307. The lower bar is of cruck-frame construction, and the top bar retains its wattle and daub walls, partly later encased in stone. In addition to Timothy Taylor real ales, including Dark Mild and two guests, 14 wines are offered by the glass. Expect main courses like smoked haddock and spinach pancakes; pan-fried chicken on a chorizo, red onion and sweet pepper cassoulet; and crisp belly pork roulade on colcannon mash, with parsnip and cider gravy. Seating outside overlooks the River Ryburn. Booking for meals is recommended.

Open all wk 12-3 5.30-11 (Fri-Sat 12-11.30 Sun 12-10.30) Closed 25 Dec
Food Lunch Mon-Sat 12-2, Sun 12-4 Dinner Mon-Sat 6.30-9.30 Av main course £10.25 ⊕ FREE HOUSE ◀ Timothy Taylor Landlord ,Golden Best, Best Bitter & Dark Mild, Rotating Guest ales ♂ The Orchard Pig. ▾ 14 Facilities Non-diners area ▸♦ Children's portions Garden Outside area ⟑ Parking WiFi

SHELLEY
Map 16 SE21

The Three Acres Inn
PICK OF THE PUBS

tel: 01484 602606 **HD8 8LR**
email: info@3acres.com
dir: *From Huddersfield take A629 then B6116, turn left for village*

Welcoming old drovers' inn with a reputation for good food

Established in the late 1960s by the Ormes and Trueloves, this old drovers' inn is tucked away in the rolling green countryside of the Pennines. An ideal stopping off place for travellers heading north to the Yorkshire Dales, the pub has built a reputation for good quality food and a welcoming atmosphere. The inn's spacious interior has a traditional feel with exposed beams and large fireplaces. On summer evenings, sit out on the deck with a pint of Black Sheep (to remind you of the drovers) or a glass of wine and soak up the fabulous views. The food served in both bar and restaurant successfully fuses traditional English with international influences. A typical three-course meal might be devilled lamb's kidneys; beef

Stroganoff; and peanut butter and chocolate tart. A wide range of lighter meals, grills, rotisserie chickens and sandwiches makes a great lunchtime alternative.

Open all wk 12-3 6-11 (Fri-Sat 12-3 5-11) Closed 25-26 Dec eve, 1 Jan eve
Food Lunch all wk 12-2 Dinner Sun-Thu 6.30-9.30, Fri-Sat 5.30-9.30 Av main course £16 Set menu available Restaurant menu available all wk ⊕ FREE HOUSE ◀ Timothy Taylor Landlord, Black Sheep, Copper Dragon, Bradfield Farmers Blonde. ▾ 19 Facilities ▸♦ Children's portions Garden ⟑ Parking WiFi

SOWERBY BRIDGE
Map 16 SE02

The Alma Inn

tel: 01422 823334 **Cotton Stones HX6 4NS**
email: info@almainn.com
dir: *Exit A58 at Triangle between Sowerby Bridge & Ripponden. Follow signs for Cotton Stones*

Country inn with home-cooked Italian food

An old stone inn set in a dramatically beautiful location at Cotton Stones with stunning views of the Ryburn Valley. Outside seating can accommodate 200 customers, while the interior features stone-flagged floors and real fires. The cosy bar serves several ales including a guest, and a vast selection of Belgian bottled beers, each with its individual glass. The appeal of the restaurant area revolves around the wood-burning pizza oven which is on on display, the only one in the Calderdale area.

Open all day all wk 12-10.30 Food Lunch Mon-Thu 12-10, Fri-Sat 12-10.30, Sun 12-9 Dinner Mon-Thu 12-10, Fri-Sat 12-10.30, Sun 12-9 ⊕ FREE HOUSE ◀ Timothy Taylor Landlord & Golden Best, Tetley's Bitter, Guest ales. ▾
Facilities Non-diners area ♣ (Bar Garden) ▸♦ Children's portions Garden ⟑ Beer festival Parking WiFi ▭ (notice required)

THORNTON
Map 19 SE03

Ring O'Bells Country Pub & Restaurant
PICK OF THE PUBS

tel: 01274 832296 **212 Hilltop Rd BD13 3QL**
email: enquiries@theringobells.com
dir: *From M62 take A58 for 5m, right onto A644. 4.5m follow Denholme signs, into Well Head Rd into Hilltop Rd*

Dining pub in Wuthering Heights country

The Brontë Sisters were born, christened and lived for a while in Thornton – their father was the rector. With 40-mile views over the Pennines, the pub was once a Wesleyan chapel, attended by weavers; today's rather more secular function has been in Ann and Clive Preston's hands for more than 20 accolade-full years. The wood-panelled walls are decorated with prints of the village in the 1920s, while contemporary art is on display in the Brontë Restaurant, a full-length conservatory with glorious valley views. From a traditional British and European menu, a starter might be pan-seared king scallops with crispy Parma ham, pea purée and tomato and shallot dressing; a main course, Black Sheep beer-battered Whitby haddock with hand-cut chips and mushy peas; a dessert, raspberry and white chocolate cheesecake with mango sorbet. Splashing out? Try a luxury surf and turf for two. The wine list features over 100 bins.

Open all wk 11.30-4 5.30-11.30 (Sat-Sun 11.30-4 6.15-11.30) Closed 25 Dec
Food Lunch all wk 12-2 Dinner Mon-Fri 5.30-9.30, Sat-Sun 6.15-9.30 Set menu available ⊕ FREE HOUSE ◀ John Smith's, Courage Directors, Black Sheep, Copper Dragon. ▾ 12 Facilities Non-diners area ▸♦ Children's menu Children's portions Parking WiFi ▭ (notice required)

CHANNEL ISLANDS
GUERNSEY

CASTEL
Map 24

Fleur du Jardin
PICK OF THE PUBS

tel: 01481 257996 **Kings Mills GY5 7JT**
email: info@fleurdujardin.com
dir: 2.5m from town centre

Gastro-pub food with strong Island provenance

This magnificent granite and golden stone hotel has slumbered in the peaceful Guernsey countryside for over 500 years. Curiously, its name comes from a long-gone Guernsey champion cow. The hotel's heritage is long and the ambience of past centuries remains with wooden beams, old fireplaces and stone features as well as a low-ceiling, character bar area. Such seasoned charm is matched by contemporaryazaz attention to decor and design, producing a chic, destination for those seeking the best of Channel Island dining. As an island establishment, fresh seafood features strongly on the menu, with catch of the day perhaps included in the fish pie. Meat eaters are not short-changed either; the pork dishes may derive from pigs that are played soothing music during their local farm upbringing! Sun worshipers making the short walk from Vazon Bay can refresh themselves with beers from both Island and mainland microbreweries or hand-crafted cider from a local farm producer.

Open all day all wk **Food** Lunch all wk 12-2 Dinner all wk 6-9 Av main course £10 Set menu available Restaurant menu available all wk ⊕ FREE HOUSE ◀ Arundel, Liberation Guernsey Sunbeam, Fuller's London Pride, Goose Eye Wonkey Donkey, Sharp's Doom Bar, Guest ales ♂ Rocquette. ₱ 12 **Facilities** Non-diners area ♣ (Bar Restaurant Garden) ♦ Children's menu Children's portions Garden ♯ Parking WiFi ▬ (notice required)

ST PETER PORT
Map 24

The Admiral de Saumarez ★★★ HL

tel: 01481 721431 **Duke of Normandie Hotel, Lefebvre St GY1 2JP**
email: enquiries@dukeofnormandie.com **web:** www.dukeofnormandie.com
dir: From harbour rdbt into St Julians Av, 3rd left into Anns Place, continue to right, up hill, left into Lefebvre St, archway entrance on right

Maritime theme and good pub dishes

Part of the Duke of Normandie Hotel, this thoughtfully restored bar attracts a happy mix of Guernsey locals and hotel residents. It is full of architectural salvage, including old timbers (now painted with well-known amusing sayings) and maritime memorabilia. Details of the great naval victories of the admiral himself are engraved on the tables. You can be served your refreshments out in the suntrap beer garden in warmer weather. The lunch and dinner menus proffer traditional pub favourites, plus the likes of risotto with tiger prawns and chorizo, or spicy chicken wings, straw fries with a BBQ dip.

Open all day all wk 11am-11.30pm **Food** Lunch all wk 12-2 Dinner all wk 6-9 Av main course £10 Restaurant menu available all wk ⊕ FREE HOUSE ◀ Liberation, Randall's of Guernsey Patois ♂ Rocquette. **Facilities** Non-diners area ♦ Children's menu Children's portions Outside area ♯ Parking ▬ (notice required) **Rooms** 37

The Ship & Crown, Crow's Nest Brasserie

tel: 01481 728994 **The Quay GY1 2NB**
email: ship_crown@hotmail.com
dir: Opposite Crown Pier

Waterfront pub with magnificent views

This busy Guernsey town pub and stylish brasserie occupies a historic building and boasts stunning views across the Victoria Marina to the neighbouring Channel Islands. Run by the same family for well over 30 years, The Ship & Crown offers one of the widest ranges of beers and ciders on the island, but it is equally well known for its all-day bar meals. The friendly Crow's Nest Brasserie specialises in fish and seafood dishes, such as king prawn and crab risotto, but there are plenty of salad and meat options too.

Open all day all wk **Food** Lunch all wk 11-9 Dinner all wk 11-9 Set menu available Restaurant menu available all wk ⊕ FREE HOUSE ◀ Fuller's London Pride, Sharp's Doom Bar, Liberation, St Austell Tribute, Brains The Rev. James, Timothy Taylor Landlord ♂ Rocquette. ₱ 8 **Facilities** Non-diners area ♦ Children's portions Parking WiFi ▬

JERSEY

ST AUBIN
Map 24

Old Court House Inn

tel: 01534 746433 **St Aubin's Harbour JE3 8AB**
email: info@oldcourthousejersey.com
dir: From Jersey Airport, right at exit, left at lights, 0.5m to St Aubin

Harbour-side location on Jersey's stunning south coast

At low tide a path snakes across the foreshore to St Aubin's Fort, guarding the harbour overlooked by this old inn. Wizened beams and mellow stone walls testify to the building's medieval origins; its cellars were allegedly used to secrete contraband. A strong suite of seafood options feature on the menus available at the several bars and restaurant rooms here; local oysters grilled with cheese a prelude to asparagus and tiger prawn filled baked breast of chicken, or a locally caught plaice. Jersey-brewed Liberation Ale is a favoured tipple; there's a beer festival too.

Open all day all wk Closed 25 Dec, Mon (Jan-Mar) **Food** Lunch all wk 12.30-2.30, all day May-Aug Dinner Mon-Sat 7.30-10, all day May-Aug Set menu available Restaurant menu available all wk ⊕ FREE HOUSE ◀ Courage Directors, Theakston, John Smith's, Liberation. ₱ 9 **Facilities** Non-diners area ♦ Children's menu Children's portions Outside area ♯ Beer festival WiFi ▬ (notice required)

ST BRELADE
Map 24

The Portelet Inn

tel: 01534 741899 **La Route de Noirmont JE3 8AJ**
email: portelet@randalls.je
dir: Phone for detailed directions

Family-friendly with carvery

Belonging to Jersey's Randalls group of privately owned public houses, the Portelet is a family-friendly pub a short walk from the coast. Since 1948, when it was transformed from a 17th-century farmhouse into the Portelet, much has changed - children can play in Pirate Pete's, while adults relax in the bar. Although kids have their own menu, the Carvery restaurant is ideal for family dining, with a menu offering Southern-fried chicken burger; prime Harmony Farm steaks; beef and dumplings; pan-roasted salmon; and Thai red chicken (or vegetable) curry. There's live entertainment on Fridays and some Saturday nights.

Open all day 11-11 Closed Tue (Jan-Mar) **Food** Lunch Mon-Sat 12-2.30, Sun 12-8 Dinner Mon-Thu 4.30-8.30, Fri-Sat 4.30-9, Sun 12-8 ⊕ RANDALLS ◀ Wells Bombardier, Guest ale. **Facilities** Non-diners area ♦ Children's menu Children's portions Play area Family room Garden ♯ Parking WiFi ▬ (notice required)

ST MARTIN
Map 24

Royal Hotel

tel: 01534 856289 **La Grande Route de Faldouet JE3 6UG**
email: johnbarker@jerseymail.co.uk
dir: *2m from Five Oaks rdbt towards St Martin. Pub on right next to St Martin's Church*

Log fires in winter, beer garden in summer

A friendly local in the heart of St Martin, this former coaching inn prides itself on offering quality food and drink. Landlord John Barker has been welcoming guests for many years. A roaring log fire in the spacious lounge warm winter visitors, and there's a sunny beer garden to enjoy during the summer months. On the menu are traditional home-made favourites such as steak and ale pie, chicken curry, beef burgers, pizzas and jacket potatoes, as well as local seafood available according to season and availability. Children's choices are on offer, too.

Open all day all wk **Food** Lunch all wk 12-2.15 Dinner Mon-Sat 6-8.30 Av main course £9.95-£11.50 ⊕ RANDALLS ◀ Ringwood Best Bitter, Bass Cask, Guest ales ♂ Westons Stowford Press. ☘ 9 **Facilities** Non-diners area ◀ Children's menu Children's portions Play area Garden ♬ Parking WiFi ▭ (notice required)

ST MARY
Map 24

St Mary's Country Inn

tel: 01534 482897 **La Rue des Buttes JE3 3DS**
email: stmarys@liberationpubco.com
dir: *Phone for detailed directions*

Smart inn with island brewed ale and global menu

Jersey's Liberation Brewery owns this appealing country inn with smart, contemporary interior. The menu offers imaginative food at reasonable prices, including roasts and grills; espetadas (Portuguese chargrilled skewered meats and fish); and ale-battered cod with chunky chips. There are just three prices on the wine list, but choice extends to half-litre carafes and plenty by the glass. In the bar you'll find continental lagers, island-brewed Mary Ann and flagship cask-conditioned Liberation Ale. There's a delightful seating area outside.

Open all day all wk **Food** Lunch Mon-Sat 12-2.30, Sun 12-7 Dinner Mon-Sat 6-9, Sun 12-7 Av main course £9 ⊕ LIBERATION GROUP ◀ Liberation Ale, Mary Ann Special, Guest ales. ☘ 19 **Facilities** Non-diners area ♣ (Bar Garden) ◀ Children's menu Children's portions Garden ♬ Parking WiFi ▭ (notice required)

ISLE OF MAN

PEEL
Map 24 SC28

The Creek Inn

tel: 01624 842216 **Station Place IM5 1AT**
email: thecreekinn@manx.net
dir: *On quayside opposite House of Manannan Museum*

A must for ale lovers

The family-run Creek Inn occupies a plum spot on the quayside overlooked by Peel Hill. A real ale drinkers' paradise, it has locally brewed Okells ales with up to five changing guests. Bands play every weekend, and nightly during the TT and Manx Grand Prix, when the pub becomes the town's focal point. There's a huge selection of dishes on the menu, from local fish, steaks and burgers, to vegetarian options and salads, alongside sandwiches, hot baguettes and toasties. A typical meal might be chilli and garlic crab claws followed by steak and Rory's ale pie with chips and peas.

Open all day all wk **Food** Lunch all wk 11-9.30 Dinner all wk 11-9.30 ⊕ FREE HOUSE ◀ Okells Bitter & Seasonal ales, Bushy's, 4 Guest ales ♂ Thatchers Green Goblin, St Helier, Manx Apple. ☘ 12 **Facilities** Non-diners area ♣ (Garden) ◀ Children's menu Children's portions Garden ♬ Parking WiFi ▭

PORT ERIN
Map 24 SC26

Falcon's Nest Hotel

tel: 01624 834077 **The Promenade, Station Rd IM9 6AF**
email: falconsnest@enterprise.net
dir: *Follow coast road S from airport or ferry. Hotel on seafront, immediately after steam railway station*

Family-run pub-hotel with an emphasis on seafood

In the centre of Port Erin, this magnificent building overlooks a beautiful sheltered harbour and sandy beach. Head for the saloon bar, Ophidian's Lair, or the residents' lounge, also open to the public, to sample local ales from Okells and Bushy's, among others, and over 70 whiskies. The former ballroom has been restored and turned into a Victorian-style dining room, where local seafood dishes include local scallops known as 'queenies'. The menu also offers a roast of the day; honey-roast Manx ham; vegetable lasagne; and many gluten-free options. The carvery here is very popular too. A beer festival is held in early May.

Open all day all wk 11am-mdnt (Fri-Sat 11am-12.45am) **Food** Lunch all wk 12-9 Dinner all wk 12-9 ⊕ FREE HOUSE ◀ John Smith's, Okells, Bushy's, Guinness, Guest ales. **Facilities** Non-diners area ◀ Children's menu Children's portions Family room Beer festival Parking WiFi ▭ (notice required)

Scotland

CITY OF ABERDEEN

ABERDEEN — Map 23 NJ90

Old Blackfriars

tel: 01224 581922 **52 Castle St AB11 5BB**
email: oldblackfriars.aberdeen@belhavenpubs.net
dir: *From rail station right into Guild St left into Market St, at end right into Union St. Pub on right on corner of Marishal St*

Historic Castlegate area pub with music nights

Situated in Aberdeen's historic Castlegate, this traditional split-level city centre pub stands on the site of property owned by Blackfriars Dominican monks, hence the name. Inside you'll find stunning stained glass, plus well-kept real ales (five handpumps) and a large selection of malt whiskies. The pub is also renowned for good food and an unobtrusive atmosphere. The wide-ranging menu has all the pub favourites and more – haggis bon bons; chicken satay skewers; black bean and jalapeño burger; and chilli burritos. There's a weekly quiz on Tuesdays and live music every Thursday.

Open all day all wk 10am-mdnt (Fri-Sat 10am-1am Sun 10-11) Closed 25 Dec, 1 Jan **Food** Lunch all wk 10-9 Dinner all wk 10-9 Av main course £8.99 ⊕ BELHAVEN ◀ IPA, Inveralmond Ossian, Old Blackfriars. ⬙ 9 **Facilities** Non-diners area ◆� Children's menu Family room Outside area ☞ WiFi

ABERDEENSHIRE

BALMEDIE — Map 23 NJ91

The Cock & Bull Bar & Restaurant ◉

tel: 01358 743249 **Ellon Rd, Blairton AB23 8XY**
email: info@thecockandbull.co.uk
dir: *11m N of city centre, on left of A90 between Balmedie junct & Foveran*

Country inn with great food of impeccable provenance

A cast-iron range warms the bar in this creeper-clad, stone-built coaching inn, standing quite alone in open farmland north of Aberdeen. Conversaation is easily stimulated by local artist Irene Morrison's paintings, assorted hanging artefacts and good beer. Affordably priced food in the AA-Rosette restaurant uses Marine Stewardship Council-approved white fish and Peterhead-landed shellfish, and beef and pork from the region's stock farms. A seasonal menu might list pork and black pudding burger; seafood medley tagliatelle; Grampian braised lamb shank; and half-roasted aubergine filled with a Mediterranean vegetable casserole. Great wines and whiskies as well.

Open all day all wk 10am-11.30pm (Sun 12-7.30) Closed 26-27 Dec, 2-3 Jan **Food** Lunch Mon-Sat 10-8.45, Sun 12-7.30 Dinner Mon-Sat 10-8.45, Sun 12-7.30 Av main course £13.95 ⊕ FREE HOUSE ◀ Burnside 3 Bullz Bitter Ale, Guinness. **Facilities** Non-diners area ◆� Children's menu Play area Garden ☞ Parking WiFi ☞ (notice required)

MARYCULTER — Map 23 NO89

Old Mill Inn

tel: 01224 733212 **South Deeside Rd AB12 5FX**
email: info@oldmillinn.co.uk
dir: *5m W of Aberdeen on B9077*

A family-run inn with a warm welcome

This delightful family-run 200-year-old country inn stands on the edge of the River Dee, five miles from Aberdeen city centre. A former mill house, the 18th-century granite building has been tastefully modernised to include a restaurant where the finest Scottish ingredients feature on the menu: start with marinated herring salad or black pudding parcel, then continue with pan-roasted lamb cutlets, roast vegetable and pesto tagliatelle, or grilled salmon fillet on sweet potato mash. Food and drink can be enjoyed outside in the warmer months.

Open all day all wk **Food** Lunch all wk 12-2 Dinner all wk 5.30-9 ⊕ FREE HOUSE ◀ Caledonian Deuchars IPA, Timothy Taylor Landlord, Fuller's London Pride. **Facilities** Non-diners area ◆� Children's menu Children's portions Outside area ☞ Parking WiFi ☞

NETHERLEY — Map 23 NO89

The Lairhillock Inn — PICK OF THE PUBS

tel: 01569 730001 **AB39 3QS**
email: info@lairhillock.co.uk
dir: *From Aberdeen take A90. Right towards Durris on B9077 then left onto B979 to Netherley*

A bustling country inn serving seasonal food

Nooks and crannies pepper the rambling interior of this generously-beamed inn that has stood in rural Deeside for over 200 years. Rustic furnishings on quarry tile floors; woodsmoke drifting off the highly unusual slab-mounted central firegrate, reliable real ales and a regularly updated food offering from the country kitchen ensure that it's a popular spot for Aberdonians escaping the nearby Granite City. The confident menu majors on Scottish produce, with robust starters such as hot smoked venison fillet or seared guinea fowl breast a meal in themselves. Unsurprisingly, grilled Aberdeen Angus steaks feature as mains, whilst fish dishes include smoked haddock, pancetta and Applewood cheddar fishcakes with a mild curry mayonnaise. The wider choice stretches to Lairhillock's lasagne, layered with pork, venison and beef and topped with a wild mushroom sauce. There's a light, bright conservatory with garden views, or hunker down at candlelit tables beside gleaming brass and copper lamps, and bric-a-brac.

Open all day all wk Closed 25-26 Dec, 1-2 Jan **Food** Lunch all wk 12-2 Dinner all wk 6-9.30 ⊕ FREE HOUSE ◀ Timothy Taylor Landlord, Caledonian Deuchars IPA, Guest ales. **Facilities** Non-diners area ❄ (Bar Garden) ◆� Children's menu Children's portions Garden ☞ Parking ☞ (notice required)

OLDMELDRUM — Map 23 NJ82

The Redgarth

tel: 01651 872353 **Kirk Brae AB51 0DJ**
email: redgarth1@aol.com
dir: *From A947 (Oldmeldrum bypass) follow signs to Golf Club/Pleasure Park. Inn E of bypass*

Friendly, family-run inn with attractive garden

The Redgarth looks more like a house than a pub, because that's what it was built as in 1928. It became the Redgarth Cocktail Bar in the 1970s and has been further altered since, but not too much. A cask-conditioned ale, such as Highland Scapa Special or Kelburn Pivo Estivo, or a malt whisky from Glen Garioch, the village distillery, might precede chicken Maryland; roast beef and Yorkshire pudding; Hungarian pork goulash; or catch of the day. Grills are well represented and vegetarians will very likely find a vegetable strudel or roast butternut squash and potato flan on the menu.

Open all wk 11-3 5-11 (Fri-Sat 11-3 5-11.45) Closed 25-26 Dec, 1-3 Jan **Food** Lunch all wk 12-2 Dinner Sun-Thu 5-9, Fri-Sat 5-9.30 Av main course £10-£14 ⊕ FREE HOUSE ◀ Inveralmond Thrappledouser, Timothy Taylor Landlord, Highland Scapa Special & Orkney Best, Kelburn Pivo Estivo. **Facilities** Non-diners area ❄ (Garden) ◆� Children's menu Children's portions Garden ☞ Parking WiFi ☞

STONEHAVEN
Map 23 NO88

NEW The Ship Inn ★★★ INN

tel: 01569 762617 **5 Shorehead AB39 2JY**
email: enquiries@shipinnstonehaven.com **web:** www.shipinnstonehaven.com
dir: *From A90 follow signs to Stonehaven, then signs to harbour*

Fresh seafood a speciality

Overnight guests will surely testify that the Ship is in one of the best locations in town, for it overlooks the almost circular harbour, once an important centre of the herring trade. In the blue-carpeted bar you'll find real ales from Inveralmond,

Orkney and elsewhere, as well as a hundred-plus malts. Seafood is served in the bar, the air-conditioned restaurant, and on the open-air terrace, all with harbour views. Cullen skink, and North Sea mussels in white wine and garlic sauce are typical starters, while main dishes include sea bass with herb risotto; salmon and dill fishcakes; steak and Guinness pie; and game hotpot.

Open all day all wk **Food** Lunch Mon-Fri 12-2.15, Sat-Sun 12-9 Dinner Mon-Fri 5.30-9, Sat-Sun 12-9 ⊕ FREE HOUSE ◀ Inveralmond Thrappledouser, Orkney, Guest ales. **Facilities** ✿ (Bar Outside area) ♦♦ Children's menu Children's portions Outside area ⌱ WiFi **Rooms** 11

See advert below

ARGYLL & BUTE

Chartroom II Bistro ★★★ HL ◉◉ PICK OF THE PUBS

tel: 01852 200233 **Loch Melfort Hotel PA34 4XG**
email: reception@lochmelfort.co.uk **web:** www.lochmelfort.co.uk
dir: *On A816, midway between Oban & Lochgilphead*

Fabulous local seafood with stunning views to match

Part of the Loch Melfort Hotel, this modern bar and bistro is located on the path to the NTS Arduaine Gardens with spectacular views over Asknish Bay towards Jura and beyond. Previously the Campbell family's home, it's an ideal spot for garden enthusiasts, sailors or simply those looking for a bit of peace and quiet. The Chartroom II is the place to enjoy local real ales, as well as light lunches and suppers. It has some of the finest views on the West Coast and serves home-made Scottish fare including plenty of locally landed langoustines and shellfish; burgers; steaks, pizzas and salads. You can sit outside and enjoy a drink watching bewitching sunsets or gather around the fire in winter and watch the waves crashing against the rocks. The Chartroom II is family friendly and serves children's meals or smaller portions from the main menu, plus there is a playground.

Open all wk 11-10 Closed Nov-Etr **Food** Lunch all wk 12-2.30 Dinner all wk 6-9 Av main course £12 ⊕ FREE HOUSE ◀ Belhaven, Fyne, Tennent's. ▾ 8 **Facilities** Non-diners area ♦️ Children's menu Children's portions Play area Garden ⊼ Parking WiFi ▭ **Rooms** 25

Cairndow Stagecoach Inn ★★★ INN

tel: 01499 600286 **PA26 8BN**
email: enq@cairndowinn.com **web:** www.cairndowinn.com
dir: *N of Glasgow take A82, left on A83 at Arrochar. Through Rest and be Thankful to Cairndow. Follow signs for inn*

An old coaching inn set in glorious scenery

On the upper reaches of Loch Fyne, this old coaching inn offers plenty of fine views of mountains, magnificent woodlands and rivers. Sample one of many malt whiskies in the friendly bar by the roaring fire, or idle away the time in the loch-side garden watching the oyster-catchers while sipping the local Fyne Ales. The menu in the candlelit Stables Restaurant offers steak and Fyne Ale pie; chicken breast stuffed with smoked Scottish cheddar and ham, wrapped in pancetta; roasted pepper, courgette and wild mushroom risotto; and pan-fried venison steak with shallot, mushroom and smoked bacon red wine sauce. Meals are also served all day in the bar and lounges. Accommodation is available if you would like to stay over and explore the area. On your way to the pub you should look out for Britain's tallest tree (Ardkinglas Grand Fir), which is taller than Nelson's Column.

Open all day all wk **Food** Lunch all wk 12-6 Dinner all wk 6-9 ⊕ FREE HOUSE ◀ Fyne Hurricane Jack, Avalanche, Piper's Gold, Maverick, Jarl. **Facilities** Non-diners area ❤️ (Bar Garden) ♦️ Children's menu Children's portions Family room Garden ⊼ Parking WiFi ▭ (notice required) **Rooms** 18

The Oyster Inn PICK OF THE PUBS

tel: 01631 710666 **PA37 1PJ**
email: stay@oysterinn.co.uk
dir: *Phone for detailed directions*

Excellent local seafood against a backdrop of views to Mull

This 18th-century inn once served ferry passengers, the cannier among them knowing they could be 'stuck' here between ferries and thus evade Oban's Sunday licensing laws. The stone-walled Ferryman's Bar next door is known as the Glue Pot, a reminder that the neighbouring blacksmith once boiled horses' hooves for glue. The pots still hang from the ceiling and tradition requires that on entering or leaving the pub, gentlemen touch the hanging glue pot, whilst ladies wink at the Ferryman. Overlooking the tidal whirlpools and white water of the Falls of Lora, the ferry is long gone, superseded by a modern road bridge, but seafood lovers will find plenty to enjoy on the menu here, with West Coast mussels, oysters and scallops in abundance. In addition, a starter of haggis, neeps and tatties with whisky cream sauce might be followed by chargrilled Scottish steaks.

Open all day all wk 11am-mdnt **Food** Lunch all wk 12-9.30 Dinner all wk 12-9.30 ⊕ FREE HOUSE ◀ Caledonian Deuchars IPA. ▾ 9 **Facilities** Non-diners area ❤️ (Bar Garden) ♦️ Children's menu Children's portions Family room Garden ⊼ Parking WiFi ▭ (notice required)

Crinan Hotel PICK OF THE PUBS

tel: 01546 830261 **PA31 8SR**
email: reservations@crinanhotel.com
dir: *From M8, at end of bridge take A82, at Tarbert left onto A83. At Inveraray follow Campbeltown signs to Lochgilphead, follow signs for A816 to Oban. 2m, left to Crinan on B841*

Stunning views and the freshest West Coast seafood

This romantic retreat enjoys a stunning location with fabulous views across the Sound of Jura. The hotel stands at the north end of the Crinan Canal, which connects Loch Fyne to the Atlantic Ocean. For over two hundred years this hostelry has been caring for the community needs of this tiny fishing village, and welcoming travellers. This sense of continuity has been lovingly provided by Nick and Frances Ryan for over 40 years. Relax with a drink in the Gallery Bar on a summer's evening, or settle in the Mainbrace, a wood-panelled seafood bar which extends to the patio overlooking the fishing boats. The Westward Restaurant's cuisine is firmly based on the freshest seafood – it's landed daily just 50 metres from the hotel. Look out for pan-seared Loch Crinan scallops with roast bacon; whole Loch Crinan langoustines with garlic aïoli; and – if meat is preferred – roast pork sausages with mustard mash.

Open all day all wk 11-11 Closed 25 Dec **Food** Lunch all wk 12-2.30 Dinner all wk 6-8.30 Av main course £13 Restaurant menu available Tue-Sun ⊕ FREE HOUSE ◀ Fyne, Tennent's, Caledonian, Guinness. ▾ 8 **Facilities** Non-diners area ❤️ (Bar Garden) ♦️ Children's menu Children's portions Garden ⊼ Parking WiFi ▭ (notice required)

DUNOON
Map 20 NS17

Coylet Inn

tel: 01369 840426 **Loch Eck PA23 8SG**
email: reservations@coylet-locheck.co.uk web: www.coyletinn.co.uk
dir: *N of Dunoon on A815*

Local produce in pub with loch views

Run by Craig Wilson, this charming, beautifully appointed 17th-century coaching inn has a timeless quality. Located on Loch Eck's shores you wouldn't want a television or games machines to disturb your drink or meal. Well, they won't, at least not in where you can relax with a glass of wine or a pint of Fyne Ales Highlander in peace by a real log fire. An appealing menu offers local favourites such as home-made Cullen skink soup and smoked salmon with rocket and caper salad, which might be followed by peat-smoked battered haddock and chips.

Open all day all wk **Food** Lunch all wk 12-2.30 Dinner all wk 6-8.30 ⊕ FREE HOUSE ◀ Fyne Ales Highlander & Jarl, Guest ales. **Facilities** Non-diners area 😺 (Bar Garden) ⁙ Children's menu Children's portions Garden ⊨ Beer festival Cider festival Parking WiFi 🚍 (notice required)

INVERARAY
Map 20 NN00

George Hotel

tel: 01499 302111 **Main Street East PA32 8TT**
email: info@thegeorgehotel.co.uk
dir: *On A83*

Family-owned gem offering many whiskies, and more

Built in 1776 and in the ownership of the Clark family since 1860, The George occupies a prime spot in the centre of a historic conservation town. Although there have been sensitive additions over the years, nothing detracts from the original flagstone floors and four roaring log fires. More than 100 whiskies and a range of Fyne Ales are complemented by an extensive bar menu that includes traditional haggis, neeps and tatties. The restaurant showcases local produce; try the fresh potted crab followed by slow-braised lamb shank in Loch Fyne ale. The George holds beer and music festivals on bank holidays in May and August.

Open all day all wk 11am-1am Closed 25 Dec **Food** Lunch all wk 12-6 Dinner all wk 6-9 ⊕ FREE HOUSE ◀ Fyne Ales. ⁌ 9 **Facilities** Non-diners area 😺 (Bar Restaurant Garden) ⁙ Children's menu Children's portions Garden ⊨ Beer festival Parking WiFi 🚍 (notice required)

LOCHGILPHEAD
Map 20 NR88

Cairnbaan Hotel ★★★ HL
PICK OF THE PUBS

tel: 01546 603668 **Cairnbaan PA31 8SJ**
email: info@cairnbaan.com web: www.cairnbaan.com
dir: *A816 from Lochgilphead, in approx 2m take B841*

Historic hotel beside the Crinan Canal

Built in 1801 to coincide with the opening of the Crinan Canal, which it overlooks, this historic hotel has been run by Darren and Christine Dobson for the past decade and a bit. Lighter meals are served from the bistro-style menu in the relaxed atmosphere of the bar, conservatory lounge, or alfresco. For a more formal occasion dine in the serene restaurant, where the carte specialises in the use of fresh local produce, notably seafood and game. Look for starters of Tarbet landed langoustines with bread, salad and mayonnaise. Mains might include Sound of Jura scallops wrapped in pancetta with garlic butter and new potatoes. Round off, perhaps, with sticky toffee pudding with vanilla ice cream. From nearby Oban there are sailings to the islands of Mull, Coll and Tiree. Inveraray Castle is also well worth a visit, as is Dunadd Fort where the ancient kings of Scotland were crowned.

Open all wk 8am-11pm Closed 25 Dec **Food** Lunch all wk 12-2.30 Dinner all wk 6-9.30 ⊕ FREE HOUSE ◀ Local ales. ⁌ 8 **Facilities** 😺 (Bar) ⁙ Children's menu Children's portions Garden Parking WiFi **Rooms** 12

LUSS
Map 20 NS39

The Inn on Loch Lomond ★★★★ INN

tel: 01436 860201 **G83 8PD**
email: inverbeg.reception@loch-lomond.co.uk web: www.innonlochlomond.co.uk
dir: *12m N of Balloch*

Scottish hospitality and great views

Today a good road skirts Loch Lomond's western shore, but it wouldn't have been so good in 1814, when this wayside inn opened its doors. Today it incorporates Mr C's Fish & Whisky Restaurant and Bar where the menu might feature haggis, neeps and tatties; Cullen skink; breaded wholetail scampi; and for dessert, cranachan or deep-fried Mars bars with ice cream. More than 200 whiskies are available, but if you prefer ale, there's Deuchars IPA, Fyne Highlander and Houston Killellan. Live folk music is played nightly throughout the summer.

Open all day all wk 11-11 (Fri-Sat 11am-mdnt) **Food** Lunch all wk 12-9 Dinner all wk 12-9 ⊕ FREE HOUSE ◀ Houston Killellan, Fyne Highlander, Caledonian Deuchars IPA. ⁌ 30 **Facilities** Non-diners area 😺 (Outside area) ⁙ Children's menu Children's portions Outside area ⊨ Parking WiFi 🚍 (notice required) **Rooms** 33

OBAN
Map 20 NM83

NEW The Lorne

tel: 01631 570020 **Stevenson St PA34 5NA**
email: lornebar@maclay.co.uk
dir: *Phone for detailed directions*

A place for refreshment before train or ferry

The Lorne is close to both Oban's train station and its terminal for the Mull ferry. It's a family-friendly haven with a sheltered and heated beer garden – an ideal spot to enjoy a pot of freshly brewed coffee or a pint Deuchars IPA before departing the town. From May to September the kitchen serves delicious plates of locally-caught seafood. At other times the menu of pub grub ranges from warm tortilla wraps, toasted paninis and baked potatoes, to pizzas, house burgers, and curries. If you can tarry awhile, the Lorne offers a busy programme of pub quizzes, DJ nights and live music, when the party continues into the early hours.

Open all day all wk **Food** Lunch all wk 12-3 Dinner all wk 5-9 Av main course £7.95 ⊕ MACLAY ◖ Caledonian Deuchars IPA. ⬨ 12 **Facilities** ❤ (Garden Outside area) ⦿ Children's menu Children's portions Garden Outside area ⼏ WiFi ➤ (notice required)

PORT APPIN
Map 20 NM94

The Pierhouse Hotel & Seafood Restaurant ★★★ SHL ◉
PICK OF THE PUBS

tel: 01631 730302 **PA38 4DE**
email: reservations@pierhousehotel.co.uk **web:** www.pierhousehotel.co.uk
dir: *A828 from Ballachulish to Oban. In Appin right at Port Appin & Lismore ferry sign. After 2.5m left after post office, hotel at end of road by pier*

Delicious seafood on the shores of Loch Linnhe

With breathtaking views to the islands of Lismore and Mull, it would be hard to imagine a more spectacular setting for this family-run hotel and renowned seafood restaurant; an AA Rosette is one its many awards, another recognises its green credentials. Once home to the piermaster (hence the name), the distinctive whitewashed building houses a popular bar stocked with Belhaven beers and 50 malt whiskies; a pool room; and a dining area where the finest of Scottish seasonal seafood, meat, game and vegetables are served. Overlooking the pier, the Ferry Bar serves burgers and seafood dishes, plus ciabattas at lunchtime. An evening three-course meal in the restaurant could commence with the Pierhouse seafood chowder, followed by roasted loin of venison. For dessert, try a traditional home-made clootie dumpling served warm with fresh custard. Twelve individually designed bedrooms include some with king-size beds and superb loch views, and a couple of family rooms.

Open all wk 11-11 Closed 25-26 Dec **Food** Lunch all wk 12.30-2.30 Dinner all wk 6.30-9.30 Av main course £20 Restaurant menu available all wk ⊕ FREE HOUSE ◖ Belhaven Best & Export, Guinness. **Facilities** Non-diners area ❤ (Bar Garden) ⦿ Children's menu Garden ⼏ Parking WiFi ➤ **Rooms** 12

STRACHUR
Map 20 NN00

Creggans Inn ★★★ HL ◉◉ PICK OF THE PUBS

tel: 01369 860279 **PA27 8BX**
email: info@creggans-inn.co.uk **web:** www.creggans-inn.co.uk
dir: *A82 from Glasgow, at Tarbet take A83 towards Cairndow, left onto A815 to Strachur*

Award-winning, family-run inn on loch shores

Since the days of Mary, Queen of Scots, this comfortable former coaching inn on Strachur Bay has enjoyed the glorious views across Loch Fyne to Inveraray. Today's hosts, Archie and Gillian MacLellan, offer two dining options: there's bistro-style MacPhunn's for a menu featuring fresh, locally sourced produce, including the loch's famed oysters, salmon and scallops. The other option is the pistachio-coloured, two-AA Rosette dining room, hung with antique prints, offering a daily-changing, fixed-price menu with main courses of caramelised rib-eye steak with garlic and green peppercorn sauce; Aberdeen Angus beefburger; and butternut squash and sun-dried tomato risotto. After dinner, as the sun sets over the waters, you may (if you can) play the baby grand piano, or simply relax with a glass of malt whisky, port, or Scottish real ale, such as Fyne Highlander. A formal terraced garden and patio both make the most of the hard-to-beat view.

Open all day all wk 11am-mdnt **Food** Lunch all wk 12-2.30 Dinner all wk 6-8.30 ⊕ FREE HOUSE ◖ Fyne Highlander, Atlas Latitude, Caledonian Deuchars IPA, Harviestoun Bitter & Twisted. **Facilities** Non-diners area ❤ (Bar Garden) ⦿ Children's menu Children's portions Garden Parking WiFi **Rooms** 14

TAYVALLICH
Map 20 NR78

Tayvallich Inn

tel: 01546 870282 **PA31 8PL**
email: info@tayvallichinn.com
dir: *From Lochgilphead take A816 then B841, B8025*

Popular loch-side pub at the heart of a vibrant community

Established for over 30 years, the inn stands in a picturesque fishing village overlooking the natural harbour of Tayvallich Bay at the head of Loch Sween. There are unrivalled views, particularly from the outside area of decking, where food and a great selection of real ales can be enjoyed. Not surprisingly given the location, fresh seafood features strongly – the catch is landed from the boats right outside the front door! Lobster, crab and langoustine are available in the summer, while typical dishes in winter might be fragrant oven-baked salmon fillet with prawn and caper sauce or line-caught Tarbert haddock in batter with chips.

Open all wk all day in summer (closed 3-6 Tue-Fri in winter) Closed 25-26 Dec, Mon (Nov-Mar) **Food** Lunch all wk 12-2.30 Dinner all wk 6-9 ⊕ FREE HOUSE ◖ Caledonian Best, Loch Ness, Guinness. ⬨ 8 **Facilities** Non-diners area ❤ (Bar Garden) ⦿ Children's menu Children's portions Garden ⼏ Parking ➤ (notice required)

EAST AYRSHIRE

DALRYMPLE
Map 20 NS31

The Kirkton Inn

tel: 01292 560241 **1 Main St KA6 6DF**
email: kirkton@cqm.co.uk
dir: *6m SE from centre of Ayr just off A77*

Welcoming village local with wholesome food

In the heart of the village of Dalrymple, this inn was built in 1879 as a coaching inn and has been providing sustenance to travellers ever since; the welcoming atmosphere makes it easy to feel at home. It's a stoutly traditional setting, with open fires and polished brasses. Eat traditional and wholesome dishes in the Coach Room in the oldest part of the building, and perhaps choose chicken and leek pie, or Kirkton burger, followed by hot chocolate fudge cake. Lighter options are soup and sandwiches. Dining is also available in another room which overlooks the River Doon.

Open all day all wk **Food** Lunch all wk 12-2.30 Dinner all wk 5-8 ◾ John Smith's, Guinness. ⬤ 20 **Facilities** Non-diners area ❧ (Bar Garden) ✦ Children's menu Children's portions Play area Family room Garden ⊨ Parking WiFi ⬛ (notice required)

SORN
Map 20 NS52

The Sorn Inn
PICK OF THE PUBS

tel: 01290 551305 **35 Main St KA5 6HU**
email: craig@sorninn.com
dir: *A70 from S; or A76 from N onto B743 to Sorn*

A fusion of fine dining and brasserie-style food

The whitewashed Sorn Inn dates back to the 18th century when it was a coaching inn on the old Edinburgh to Kilmarnock route; today it's a smart gastro-pub that serves ales that include Corncrake from the Orkney Brewery. Menus offer the best of Scottish and seasonal ingredients. A terrine of local pheasant to start is served with pickled wild mushrooms. Chargrilled beef steaks have been hung for 36 days, and can be enhanced with a slice of Stornaway black pudding, a slice of MacSween's haggis, or an organic egg from Corrie Main. Even the burgers are made with aged mince. Half a dozen classic dishes include smoked Ayrshire bacon carbonara, which can be served as a starter or a main; and smoked haddock and parsley fishcakes with an Isle of Mull cheddar sauce. Finish with a raspberry Bakewell tart served with whipped cream and raspberry compôte.

Open 12-2.30 6-10 (Fri 12-2.30 6-12 Sat 12-12 Sun 12-10) Closed 2wks Jan, Mon **Food** Lunch Tue-Fri 12-2.30, Sat 12-9, Sun 12-8 Dinner Tue-Fri 6-9, Sat 12-9, Sun 12-8 ⬤ FREE HOUSE ◾ John Smith's, Orkney Corncrake, Guinness. ⬤ 12 **Facilities** Non-diners area ❧ (Bar) ✦ Children's menu Children's portions Outside area ⊨ Parking WiFi ⬛ (notice required)

SOUTH AYRSHIRE

SYMINGTON
Map 20 NS33

Wheatsheaf Inn

tel: 01563 830307 **Main St KA1 5QB**
email: thompson676@btinternet.com
dir: *Off A77 between Ayr & Kilmarnock*

Village free house with friendly service

Close to the Royal Troon Golf Course and one of Scotland's oldest churches, this charming 17th-century free house has been run by Martin and Marnie Thompson for over 25 years. Log fires burn in every room of the former coaching inn and the interior is decorated with the work of local artists. The varied menu offers plenty of choice, with dishes like pan-fried sea bass fillet on salsa verde, and Kirsch and cherry glazed duck breast contrasting with more homely favourites such as breaded scampi with fries; desserts include fruit Pavlova. The two-course set menu is a steal.

Open all day all wk 11-11 (Fri-Sat 11am-mdnt) Closed 1 Jan **Food** Lunch all wk 12-9 Dinner all wk 12-9 ⬤ FREE HOUSE ◾ Belhaven Best, Morland Old Speckled Hen, Guinness. **Facilities** Non-diners area ✦ Children's menu Children's portions Garden ⊨ Parking ⬛ (notice required)

DUMFRIES & GALLOWAY

BARGRENNAN
Map 20 NX37

House O'Hill Hotel

tel: 01671 840243 **DG8 6RN**
email: enquiries@houseohill.co.uk
dir: *From Newton Stewart take A714 towards Girvan, 8m. Hotel signed*

Secluded location in Galloway's forested hills

At the fringe of loch-speckled Galloway Forest and beautiful Glen Trool, this contemporary, homely little hotel makes the most of its setting in Europe's first 'Dark Sky' Park. Totally renovated four years ago, the former crofter's cottage attracts cyclists and ramblers on the Southern Upland Way by offering an exceptional combination of local microbrewery beers such as Sulwath and a wide-ranging menu strong on Galloway produce. Chicken stuffed with pork and black pudding on smoked garlic mash, and red wine-braised venison shank are just two of the fine dishes on the hit list. There are themed world-food evenings and beer festivals occur in April and September.

Open all day all wk Closed 3-25 Jan **Food** Lunch all wk 12-2.45 Dinner all wk 5.30-8.30 Av main course £11 Restaurant menu available all wk ⬤ FREE HOUSE ◾ Sulwath, Stewart's, Ayr, Fyne, Houston. **Facilities** Non-diners area ❧ (Bar Restaurant Garden) ✦ Children's menu Children's portions Family room Garden ⊨ Beer festival Parking WiFi ⬛

BLADNOCH
Map 20 NX45

The Bladnoch Inn

tel: 01988 402200 **DG8 9AB**
email: thebladnochinn@hotmail.co.uk
dir: *A714 S of Wigtown to Bladnoch. Inn at rdbt by river bridge*

Perfect stop for book lovers and whisky drinkers

This traditional country inn is in the heart of the Machars peninsula. A mere hip-flask's throw away is Scotland's most southerly distillery, and just down the road is Wigtown, home to some 20 bookshops. At lunchtime there are paninis, freshly baked baguettes and filled baked potatoes, while main courses include chef's signature Irish stew, wholetail scampi, gammon steak, macaroni cheese and roast of the day. Evening favourites are trio of sticky honey and mustard sausages; and haddock in beer batter, or from the bistro menu, chicken breast stuffed with haggis; curry of the day; and steamed salmon fillet.

Open all day all wk **Food** Lunch all wk 12-3 Dinner all wk 6-9 Av main course £10 ⊕ FREE HOUSE ◀ Greene King & IPA, Timothy Taylor Landlord ⊘ Kopparberg. ♚ 15 **Facilities** Non-diners area ✿ (Bar Outside area) ♦♦ Children's menu Children's portions Play area Outside area ⋒ Parking WiFi ☎ (notice required)

ISLE OF WHITHORN
Map 20 NX43

The Steam Packet Inn

tel: 01988 500334 **Harbour Row DG8 8LL**
email: steampacketinn@btconnect.com
dir: *From Newton Stewart take A714, then A746 to Whithorn, then to Isle of Whithorn*

Local seafood a specialty

Personally run by the Scoular family for over 30 years, this lively quayside pub stands in a picturesque village at the tip of the Machars peninsula. Sit in one of the comfortable bars and enjoy a real ale, a malt whisky or a glass of wine. Glance out of the picture windows and watch the fishermen at work, then look to the menu to sample the fruits of their labours. Extensive seafood choices - perhaps isle-landed scallops or mussels in white wine and cream - are supported by the likes of steak pie and chicken curry.

Open all day all wk 11-11 (Sun 12-11) Closed 25 Dec, winter Tue-Thu 2.30-6 **Food** Lunch all wk 12-2 Dinner all wk 6.30-9 ⊕ FREE HOUSE ◀ Timothy Taylor Landlord, Guest ales. ♚ 12 **Facilities** Non-diners area ♦♦ Children's menu Children's portions Garden Outside area ⋒ Parking WiFi ☎

KIRKCUDBRIGHT
Map 20 NX65

Selkirk Arms Hotel

tel: 01557 330402 **Old High St DG6 4JG**
email: reception@selkirkarmshotel.co.uk
dir: *M74 & M6 to A75, halfway between Dumfries & Stranraer on A75*

Choice of two bars and two restaurants

In 1794, when dining at what today is a tastefully refurbished town house, Robert Burns reputedly penned and delivered *The Selkirk Grace*, which famously begins "Some hae meat and canna eat". In the bar, Sulwath Brewery's eponymous ale celebrates the occasion. A good choice of dishes is offered in both the homely lounge and bistro, with comfy sofas and a living-flame fire, and the more intimate Artistas Restaurant. Locally sourced specialities include duo of Galloway beef; fillet of plaice with king scallops; and, for those who canna eat meat, carrot and cashew nut flan. Finish with poached pear in mulled wine.

Open all day all wk **Food** Lunch all wk 12-2 Dinner all wk 6-9 ⊕ FREE HOUSE ◀ Timothy Taylor Landlord, Sulwath Selkirk Grace, Dark Horse Hetton Pale Ale, Caledonian Deuchars IPA. **Facilities** Non-diners area ♦♦ Children's menu Children's portions Garden ⋒ Parking WiFi ☎

NEW GALLOWAY
Map 20 NX67

Cross Keys Hotel

tel: 01644 420494 **High St DG7 3RN**
email: enquiries@thecrosskeys-newgalloway.co.uk
dir: *At N end of Loch Ken, 10m from Castle Douglas on A712*

Great selection of real ales and malts

This 17th-century coaching inn sits in a stunning location at the top of Loch Ken on the edge of Galloway Forest Park, a superb area for walking, fishing, birdwatching, golf, watersports and photography. Part of the hotel was once the police station and in the beamed period bar the food is served in restored, stone-walled cells. Scottish ales are supplied by the Houston and Sulwath breweries, among others. The lunch menu includes sandwiches, pizzas, pastas and burgers, while the weekly-changing dinner specials feature the likes of soy, ginger and honey beef strips with steamed egg noodles. A grill menu and early supper menu are also available.

Open 6-11.30 Closed Sun eve winter **Food** Dinner all wk 6.30-8.30 ⊕ FREE HOUSE ◀ Houston, Sulwath, Guest ales ⊘ Westons Stowford Press. ♚ 9 **Facilities** Non-diners area ✿ (Bar Garden) Children's menu Children's portions Garden WiFi ☎ (notice required)

NEWTON STEWART
Map 20 NX46

Creebridge House Hotel

tel: 01671 402121 **Minnigaff DG8 6NP**
email: info@creebridge.co.uk
dir: *From A75 into Newton Stewart, turn right over river bridge, hotel 200yds on left*

Great Scottish food in a tremendous setting

In a bucolic, tranquil location between Galloway Forest Park's looming mountain and forest landscape and exquisite Wigtown Bay, patrons at this imposing 250-year-old former shooting lodge can expect to live well on the produce of this bounteous setting. Haddock and salmon arrive from the local smokery; Galloway meats from estate farms and scampi from nearby Newton Stewart all feature on the extensive menu in the elegant restaurant or Bridge's Brasserie-bar, where 30 malt whiskies and Creebridge Golden Ale are also stocked. A short walk through the 3-acre garden brings you to the River Cree, after which the hotel is named.

Open all wk 12-2 6-11.30 (Fri-Sat 12-2 6-1am) Closed 1st 3wks Jan **Food** Lunch all wk 12-2 Dinner all wk 6-9 ⊕ FREE HOUSE ◀ Caledonian Deuchars IPA, Guinness, Local Guest ales. **Facilities** Non-diners area ✿ (Bar Garden) ♦♦ Children's menu Children's portions Garden ⋒ Parking WiFi ☎ (notice required)

SANDHEAD
Map 20 NX04

Tigh Na Mara Hotel

tel: 01776 830210 **Main St DG9 9JF**
email: mail@tighnamarahotel.co.uk
dir: *A75 from Dumfries towards Stranraer. Left onto B7084 to Sandhead. Hotel in village centre*

Bracing sea air and long sandy beaches

Tigh na Mara means 'house by the sea', which seems appropriate for this family-run village hotel is set in the tranquil seaside village of Sandhead and boasts breathtaking views of the Sands of Luce. A menu created from top-quality local ingredients might include crispy beer battered camembert with cranberry relish; breaded whitebait with garlic mayonnaise; slow roasted sirloin of beef, Yorkshire pudding and gravy; and home-made steak and ale pie. Relax with a glass of Morland Old Speckled Hen in the garden, comfortable lounge or beside the fire in the public bar.

Open all day all wk **Food** Lunch all wk 12-2.30 Dinner all wk 6-9 Av main course £9.95-£15.95 Set menu available ⊕ BELHAVEN ◀ Best, Morland Old Speckled Hen, Belhaven IPA, Seasonal Specials. **Facilities** Non-diners area ✿ (Bar Garden) ♦♦ Children's menu Children's portions Family room Garden ⋒ Parking WiFi

CITY OF DUNDEE

BROUGHTY FERRY
Map 21 NO43

The Royal Arch Bar

tel: 01382 779741 **285 Brook St DD5 2DS**
dir: *On A930, 3m from Dundee at Broughty Ferry rail station*

Convivial local by the Tay Estuary

This long established street-corner inn is a pleasing mix of local's saloon bar, complete with stained-glass windows and an eye-catching Victorian gantry, and a well-maintained art deco lounge long ago converted from the inn's stables. The Royal Arch itself was a monument built to commemorate Queen Victoria's Dundee visit in 1863; a fragment survives on display in the bar. Dispensed from this bar are quality Scottish beers such as from local micro MòR, as well as over 50 malt whiskies; satisfying pub meals can include lamb shank in red wine or prime Scottish steak pie. There's a new pavement terrace canopy for all-weather, alfresco eating and drinking. Regular beer and cider festivals are held.

Open all day all wk **Food** Lunch Mon-Fri 11.30-2.30, Sat 11.30-8, Sun 12.30-7 Dinner Mon-Fri 5-8, Sat 11.30-8, Sun 12.30-7 Av main course £7.50 Set menu available ⊕ FREE HOUSE ◀ McEwan's 80/-, Belhaven St Andrews, Caledonian Deuchars IPA, MòR Tea, Vicar?, Black Isle Blonde Ö Addlestones. ▾ 30
Facilities Non-diners area ◀▮ Children's portions Family room Garden Beer festival Cider festival WiFi ▭

DUNDEE
Map 21 NO43

Speedwell Bar

tel: 01382 667783 **165-167 Perth Rd DD2 1AS**
dir: *From A92 (Tay Bridge), A991 signed Perth/A85/Coupar Angus/A923. At Riverside rdbt 3rd exit (A991). At lights left into Nethergate signed Parking/South Tay St. Becomes Perth Rd. Pass university. Bar on right*

Edwardian gem with unspoilt interior

This fine example of an unspoiled Edwardian art deco bar is worth visiting for its interior alone; all the fitments in the bar and sitting rooms are beautifully crafted mahogany – gantry, drink shelves, dado panelling and fireplace. Internal doors are all glazed with etched glass. The same family owned it for 90 years, until the present landlord's father bought it in the mid 90s. As well as the cask-conditioned ales, 157 whiskies and imported bottles are offered. A kitchen would be good, but since the pub is listed this is impossible. Visitors are encouraged to bring their own snacks from nearby bakeries. This community pub is home to several clubs and has live Scottish music from time to time on a Tuesday.

Open all day all wk 11am-mdnt **Food** Contact pub for details ⊕ FREE HOUSE ◀ Caledonian Deuchars IPA, Harviestoun Bitter & Twisted, Williams Bros Seven Giraffes Ö Addlestones. ▾ 18 **Facilities** Non-diners area ✿ (Bar) ⊐ Beer festival WiFi ▭ **Notes** ⊛

CITY OF EDINBURGH

EDINBURGH
Map 21 NT27

The Bow Bar

tel: 0131 226 7667 **80 The West Bow EH1 2HH**
dir: *Phone for detailed directions*

A whisky and beer connoisseurs' delight

If there is one free house that reflects the history and traditions of Edinburgh's Old Town, it is The Bow Bar. With some 220 malt whiskies, eight real ales poured from traditional tall founts and 30 bottled beers, the focus may be on liquid refreshment but the range of snacks includes haggis, cheese and chilli pies and bridies (meat pastries). Tables from old train carriages and a church gantry add to the unique feel of a bar where the sound of conversation makes up for the lack of gaming machines and music. Twice a year in January and July, the pub holds ten-day long beer festivals.

Open all day all wk Closed 25-26 Dec **Food** Lunch Mon-Sat 12-3, Sun 12.30-3 ⊕ FREE HOUSE ◀ Alechemy, Tryst Ales, Stewart Edinburgh No 3 & Pentland IPA, Harviestoun Bitter & Twisted, Atlas Latitude, Fyne Avalanche & Jarl, Cairngorm Black Gold, Tempest, Thornbridge Ö Westons Stowford Press.
Facilities Non-diners area ✿ (Bar Restaurant) Beer festival WiFi

The Café Royal ⊛
PICK OF THE PUBS

tel: 0131 556 1884 **19 West Register St EH2 2AA**
dir: *Off Princes St, in city centre*

Hearty Scottish fare in historic building

Designed by local architect Robert Paterson, The Café Royal is a glorious example of Victorian and Baroque, with an interior seemingly frozen in time. Elegant stained glass and fine late Victorian plasterwork dominate the building, as do irreplaceable Doulton ceramic murals in the bar and restaurant. The whole building and its interior were listed in 1970 so future generations can enjoy the unique building which still sticks to its early 19th-century roots by serving local ales such as Harviestoun Bitter & Twisted, wine, coffee and fresh oysters in the bar and restaurant. Scottish produce dominates the menu, from starters of black pudding with king scallops to mains of Balmoral chicken wrapped in bacon and stuffed with haggis. Please note children are allowed in the restaurant but there are no changing facilities for babies.

Open all day all wk **Food** Lunch all wk 11-9.45 Dinner all wk 11-9.45 Av main course £11.95 Restaurant menu available all wk ⊕ SPIRIT PUB COMPANY ◀ Ayr, Edinburgh Pale Ale, Kelburn Ca'Canny & Goldihops, Harviestoun Bitter & Twisted, Cairngorm Ales, Williams Bros, Stewart Ö Aspall. ▾ 9 **Facilities** Non-diners area WiFi ▭ (notice required)

EDINBURGH *continued*

Doric Tavern

PICK OF THE PUBS

tel: 0131 225 1084 **15-16 Market St EH1 1DE**
email: info@the-doric.com
dir: *In city centre opposite Waverly Station & Edinburgh Dungeons*

Edinburgh's oldest gastro-pub

Housed in a 17th-century building, the Doric claims to be Edinburgh's oldest food-serving hostelry; certainly records show a pub on this site since 1823. Its name is taken from an old language once spoken in north-east Scotland, mainly Aberdeenshire. Conveniently located for Waverley Station, the pub is just a short walk from Princes Street and Edinburgh Castle. Public rooms include a ground-floor bar, and a wine bar and bistro upstairs. In these pleasantly informal surroundings, a wide choice of fresh, locally sourced food is prepared by the chefs on site. While supping a pint, you can nibble on marinated olives or haggis spring rolls. Mains from the grill include a Border beef rib-eye, while a chef's specials might be a home-made game pie with chargrilled asparagus. Seafood is delivered fresh each morning: haddock is deep-fried in the pub's own beer-batter and served with hand-cut chips and home-made tartare sauce.

Open all day all wk Sat-Thu 11.30-11 (Fri 11am-1am) Closed 25-26 Dec **Food** Lunch all wk 12-10 Dinner all wk 12-10 ⊕ FREE HOUSE ◀ Caledonian Deuchars IPA, Guest ales ♂ Symonds. **Facilities** Non-diners area ♦♦ Children's menu Children's portions Family room 🚌

The Guildford Arms

tel: 0131 556 4312 **1-5 West Register St EH2 2AA**
email: guildfordarms@dmstewart.com
dir: *Opposite Balmoral Hotel at E end of Princes St*

Celebrated free house and galleried restaurant

Very much a destination pub, particularly during the Edinburgh Fringe; although simply missing one's train at Waverley Station is reason enough to pop into this late-Victorian classic. Study the public bar's magnificent Jacobean-style ceiling at close quarters from the galleried restaurant. Here, dine on creamy fish chowder; mushroom and tarragon pâté; haggis, neeps and tatties; Crombie's sausage of the day, mash and onion gravy. Ten handpumps, their blue porcelain handles bearing the logo of the Stewart family, the pub's owners since 1896, declare a near-religious zeal for real ales, accentuated by two 11-day beer festivals, each featuring over 50 brews, and monthly brewery weekends. Please note children under five are not allowed in the bar area.

Open all day all wk Closed 25-26 Dec, 1 Jan **Food** Lunch all wk 12-3, snacks 3-9 Dinner Sun-Thu 5.30-9.30, Fri-Sat 5.30-10 Av main course £11 Restaurant menu available all wk ⊕ FREE HOUSE ◀ Orkney Dark Island, Cairngorm Wild Cat, Highland Island Hopping, Wells Bombardier, Rotating Guest ales ♂ Thistly Cross, Westons 1st Quality. ♀ 12 **Facilities** Non-diners area ✿ (Bar) ♦♦ Children's portions Family room Beer festival

Halfway House

tel: 0131 225 7101 **24 Fleshmarket Close EH1 1BX**
email: stevewhiting@straitmail.co.uk
dir: *From Royal Mile (close to x-rds with North & South bridges) into Cockburn St. Into Fleshmarket Cl, or take flight of steps off Cockburn St on right*

Edinburgh's smallest pub is an iconic institution

Hidden down one of the Old Town's 'closes' (a narrow alleyway, often with a flight of steps and enclosed by tall buildings), the cosy interior of this pub is adorned with railway memorabilia and throngs with locals, tourists, lawyers, students and beer aficionados supping interesting ales from Scottish microbreweries, perhaps Houston Peter's Well and Cairngorm Trade Winds. Mop up the ale with some traditional Scottish bar food made from fresh produce: Cullen skink is a house speciality. Look out for the regular beer festivals, but if beer is not your thing, then perhaps sample a few of the 40 or so whiskies displayed behind the bar.

Open all day all wk **Food** Lunch all wk all day Dinner all wk all day Av main course £6.75 ⊕ FREE HOUSE ◀ Stewart Pentland IPA, Harviestoun Bitter & Twisted, Cairngorm Trade Winds, Houston Peter's Well, Cromarty, Alechemy ♂ Addlestones. **Facilities** Non-diners area ✿ (Bar) ♦♦ Outside area ⊟ Beer festival WiFi **Notes** ⊛

The Sheep Heid Inn ⊛

PICK OF THE PUBS

tel: 0131 661 7974 **43-45 The Causeway, Duddingston EH15 3QA**
email: enquiry@thesheepheidedinburgh.co.uk
dir: *A1 from city centre towards Musselburgh, at lights into Duddingston Road West, 4th right or 5th right into The Causeway*

Oldest pub in Edinburgh

There's so much history associated with Edinburgh's, and possibly Scotland's, oldest surviving pub – it was established in 1360 – that it could do with its own guidebook. The name itself is a matter of conjecture, but it probably stems from King James VI of Scotland's gift of a ram's head snuff box in 1580. Harviestoun Bitter & Twisted, from the foot of the Ochil Hills, and Caledonian Deuchars IPA occupy the real ale pumps, while food ranges from light meals and tapas-style

sharers to modern British classics. The 'From the Sea' section of the menu offers smoked loin of cod; and beer-battered haddock; 'From the Land' suggests marinated sticky chicken with lemon, honey and chilli sauce; pulled beef and bacon pie with orange- and cardamom-infused carrots; and 'From the Garden' lists crispy potato, squash, olive and truffle cake. The inn is also home to Scotland's oldest skittle alley.

Open all day all wk 11-11 (Fri-Sat 11am-mdnt Sun 12-11) **Food** Lunch Mon-Sat 12-10, Sun 12-9.30 Dinner Mon-Sat 12-10, Sun 12-9.30 ⊕ MITCHELLS & BUTLERS ◀ Caledonian Deuchars IPA, Harviestoun Bitter & Twisted ♂ Aspall. ♟ 20 **Facilities** Non-diners area ♦♦ Children's menu Children's portions Garden ⊼ Beer festival Parking WiFi ☞ (notice required)

The Shore Bar & Restaurant

tel: 0131 553 5080 **3 Shore, Leith EH6 6QW**
email: theshorebar@fishersrestaurantgroup.co.uk
dir: *Phone for detailed directions*

Enjoyable food at Edinburgh's bustling port

Centuries ago, a lighthouse guiding seafarers to the safety of Edinburgh's port is believed to have shared the site of this redoubtable old pub at the heart of Leith's bustling waterfront. A memorable wood-boarded interior welcomes guests keen to sample the excellent Scottish seafood for which the place is widely recognised. Monkfish cheeks with curried parsnip and pickled carrots make a fascinating entrée, coupled with mains like pork belly and scallops with butternut squash purée or perhaps a warming venison casserole. Scottish-brewed real ales are the heart of the liquid fare here. Outside seating looks out on the promenade beside the Water of Leith.

Open all wk noon-1am (Sun 12.30pm-1am) Closed 25-26 Dec, 1 Jan **Food** Lunch all wk 12-6 Dinner all wk 6-10.30 Set menu available Restaurant menu available all wk ⊕ FREE HOUSE ◀ Caledonian Deuchars IPA, Orkney Dark Island, Tennent's, Guinness ♂ Kopparberg, Thistly Cross. ♟ 14 **Facilities** Non-diners area ♣ (Bar Outside area) ♦♦ Children's portions Outside area ⊼ WiFi ☞

Whiski Bar & Restaurant

tel: 0131 556 3095 **119 High St EH1 1SG**
email: info@whiskibar.co.uk web: www.whiskibar.co.uk
dir: *Phone for detailed directions*

Whisky, music and food galore on the Royal Mile

If you find yourself on Edinburgh's famous Royal Mile and in need of sustenance and a 'wee' dram, then seek out this highly acclaimed bar at number 119. Choose from over 300 malt whiskies (all available by the nip) and tuck into some traditional Scottish food. Served all day, the menu makes good use of Scottish Border beef and daily deliveries of seafood from local fishermen. Typically, try Cullen skink; Haggis tower with 'neeps' and mash or smoked salmon penne pasta; then cranachan (a blend of whisky, oatmeal, cream honey and raspberries) for pudding.

Come for the traditional Scottish music in the evening – The Whiski is famous for its fiddle music.

Open all day all wk Closed 25 Dec **Food** Lunch Mon-Thu 10-10, Fri-Sun 10am-10.30pm Dinner Mon-Thu 10-10, Fri-Sun 10am-10.30pm ⊕ FREE HOUSE ◀ Innis & Gunn ♂ Thistly Cross. ♟ 9 **Facilities** Non-diners area ♦♦ Children's menu Children's portions Outside area ⊼ WiFi ☞ (notice required)

See advert on opposite page

RATHO	Map 21 NT17

AA PUB OF THE YEAR FOR SCOTLAND 2014–2015

The Bridge Inn ★★★★ INN — PICK OF THE PUBS

tel: 0131 333 1320 **27 Baird Rd EH28 8RA**
email: info@bridgeinn.com web: www.bridgeinn.com
dir: *From Newbridge at B7030 junct, follow signs for Ratho & Edinburgh Canal Centre*

Canal-side inn offering restaurant cruises

The tree-lined Union Canal between Edinburgh and the Falkirk Wheel runs past this waterside inn, once used by the early 19th-century navvies who dug the cut. In both the bar and restaurant the menu offers dishes based on local produce, including from the pub's kitchen garden, and from its own chickens, ducks and Saddleback pigs, the latter providing a rich supply of pork loin, fillet, belly and sausages. Bar favourites are fresh haddock with hand-cut chips, and pie of the week, while the restaurant features Buccleuch sirloin and fillet steaks; caramelised shoulder of hogget; smoked coley risotto; and hand-dived scallops. Guest Scottish cask ales may include Trade Winds from Cairngorm Brewery, Dark Island from Orkney and beers from Arran. The pub's two renovated barges provide Sunday lunch and dinner cruises. Children and dogs love the big grassy area outside.

Open all day all wk 11-11 (Fri-Sat 11am-mdnt) Closed 25 Dec **Food** Lunch Mon-Fri 12-3, Sat 12-9, Sun 12-8.30 Dinner Mon-Fri 5.30-9, Sat 12-9, Sun 12-8.30 ⊕ FREE HOUSE ◀ Belhaven, rotating Alechemy Ales, Guest ales ♂ Aspall. ♟ 40 **Facilities** Non-diners area ♣ (Bar Garden) ♦♦ Children's menu Children's portions Play area Garden ⊼ Beer festival Parking WiFi ☞ (notice required) **Rooms** 4

FIFE

Burntisland Sands Hotel

tel: 01592 872230 **Lochies Rd KY3 9JX**
email: mail@burntislandsands.co.uk
dir: *Towards Kirkcaldy, Burntisland on A921. Hotel on right before Kinghorn*

Family-run hotel just a hop from the beach

Once a highly regarded girls' boarding school, this small, family-run hotel stands only 50 yards from an award-winning sandy beach. Visitors can expect reasonably priced meals throughout the day, including internationally themed evenings. Typical dishes served in the three dining areas include deep fried breaded mushrooms or king prawns to start; mains like seared tuna steak with lemon butter, or haggis, neeps and tatties; and bread and butter pudding or mint paradise for dessert. Relax and enjoy a Scottish ale in the bar and lounge area, perhaps on a live music night. There is also a patio garden and children can play with the rabbits in the activity area.

Open all day all wk **Food** Lunch Mon-Fri 12-2.30, Sat-Sun all day Dinner Mon-Fri 5-8.30, Sat-Sun all day Av main course £9 Set menu available Restaurant menu available all wk ⊕ FREE HOUSE ◂ Caledonian Deuchars IPA, Tennent's, Belhaven Best, Guinness, Guest ales. **Facilities** Non-diners area ✿ (Garden) ◗◗ Children's menu Children's portions Play area Garden ⋈ Parking WiFi ▥ (notice required)

The Golf Tavern

tel: 01333 330610 **5 Links Rd KY9 1AW**
email: richard@ship-elie.com
dir: *From Lundin Links take A915, then A917 towards Elie. Turn right signed Earlsferry, through golf course to T-junct. Right into one-way system, pub on right near 4th tee*

Free house focusing on sport and traditional food

Known to locals as the '19th', although it is close to the fourth tee on the Elie Golf Course, this pub has become the hub of Earlsferry since Richard and Jill Philip (who also run The Ship Inn, Elie) took over five years ago. Although sport is the draw here, whether it's golf, pool or live rugby on the TV, it offers something for everybody. Enjoy a pint of Deuchars IPA and order from the traditional menu that includes antipasti platters, pâté of the day, steak burger, and chicken curry. Check the blackboard for the daily specials and vegetarian options.

Open all day all wk Closed 25 Dec **Food** Lunch Mon-Sat 12-2.30, Sun 12.30-3 Dinner Sun-Thu 6-9, Fri-Sat 6-9.30 ⊕ FREE HOUSE ◂ Caledonian Deuchars IPA. ♟ 9 **Facilities** Non-diners area ✿ (Bar) ◗◗ Children's menu Children's portions WiFi

The Ship Inn

tel: 01333 330246 **The Toft KY9 1DT**
email: info@ship-elie.com
dir: *A915 & A917 to Elie. From High Street follow signs to Watersport Centre & The Toft*

Community favourite with lots going on

Sitting right on the waterfront at Elie Bay, The Ship has been a pub since 1838. The enthusiastic Philip family (who also run The Golf Tavern, Earlsferry) has run this lively free house for over 20 years. Charity and celebratory events take place throughout the year, including an Easter egg hunt. The pub has its own cricket team, which plays regular fixtures on the beach. Live music is staged, and barbecues are held in the beer garden during the summer. Together with Scottish ales, the best of local produce features on the concise menu that offers the likes of smoked haddock crêpe, and chicken and bacon salad.

Open all day all wk Closed 25 Dec **Food** Lunch Mon-Sat 12-2.30, Sun 12.30-3 Dinner Mon-Thu 6-9, Fri-Sat 6-9.30 ⊕ FREE HOUSE ◂ Caledonian Deuchars IPA & 80/-,

Belhaven Best. **Facilities** Non-diners area ✿ (Bar Garden) ◗◗ Children's menu Children's portions Play area Family room Garden ▥

NEW Hams Hame Pub & Grill

tel: 01334 474371 **The Old Course Hotel, Golf Resort & Spa KY16 9SP**
email: reservations@oldcoursehotel.co.uk **web:** www.oldcoursehotel.co.uk
dir: *M90 junct 8, A91 to St Andrews*

Finest Scottish produce at St Andrews' famous links

There's a hint of art deco in this stylish new addition to the complex of facilities clustered at The Old Course Hotel. The Hams Hame is set by the 18th green at the home of golf, so you might easily find that your fellow drinker or diner is a golfing legend. Here, at this 19th hole you'll discover menus showcasing fine Scottish produce and seafood freshly landed from North Sea fishing boats, plus excellent beers from some of Scotland's best breweries - Black Isle Organic Blonde being a grand example. Local farm ham hock terrine, and East Neuk fish and chips hint at Fife's bountiful larder.

Open all day all wk **Food** Lunch all wk Dinner all wk 5.30-9.30 ⊕ FREE HOUSE ◂ Local ales. **Facilities** Non-diners area ◗◗ Children's menu Children's portions WiFi ▥ (notice required)

The Inn at Lathones ★★★★ INN ⊛⊛ | PICK OF THE PUBS

tel: 01334 840494 **Largoward KY9 1JE**
email: stay@innatlathones.com **web:** www.innatlathones.com
dir: *5m from St Andrews on A915*

Old coaching inn that's big on music

The footprint of this late 17th-century coaching inn takes up most of the hamlet of Lathones in the East Neuk (meaning corner) of Fife. In 1718, at this inn, a minister blessed a young couple's marriage and their wedding stone has served as the lintel over a fireplace ever since. The oldest part, the stone-walled Stables, is home to The Grey Lady, a friendly ghost, and her equally spectral horse. More practically, it's also the bar and frequent live music venue, with its own menu and real ales from nearby St Andrews. For the past 15 years the AA has awarded the restaurant two Rosettes for its innovative cooking of well-sourced local ingredients that, on a winter menu, might appear as smoked ham hough (hock) with piccalilli, quail's egg and Anster cheese; oven-roasted partridge with red cabbage, Puy lentils, fondant potato and red wine jus; and lavender-infused crème brûlée with home-made shortbread.

Open all day all wk 10-10 Closed 2wks Jan **Food** Lunch all wk 12-3 Dinner all wk 6-9 Av main course £13 Restaurant menu available all wk ⊕ FREE HOUSE ◂ Belhaven Best, Eden Ales. **Facilities** Non-diners area ◗◗ Children's menu Children's portions Garden ⋈ Parking WiFi ▥ **Rooms** 21

The Jigger Inn | PICK OF THE PUBS

tel: 01334 474371 **The Old Course Hotel, Golf Resort & Spa KY16 9SP**
email: reservations@oldcoursehotel.co.uk **web:** www.oldcoursehotel.co.uk

dir: *M90 junct 8, A91 to St Andrews*

Possibly golf's best-known 19th hole

Golfing history is an all-embracing experience at this former stationmaster's lodge on the now long-disused railway line to Leuchars. It's now in the grounds of The Old Course Hotel, the course in question being the world-famous Royal & Ancient Golf Club of St Andrews. Belhaven brewery supplies the appropriately named St Andrews real ale, and Jigger, brewed exclusively for both the pub and its sister golfing resort in Wisconsin, USA. Available all day is seafood landed in nearby fishing villages, carefully selected pork, lamb, beef, game and poultry reared by award-winning Scottish producers, and seasonal fruit and vegetables from local farms. Main courses include rib-eye steak with grilled Portobello mushrooms and béarnaise sauce; and tabouleh and Mediterranean vegetable fusilli pasta.

Open all day all wk 11-11 (Sun 12-11) Food Lunch all wk 12-9.30 ⊕ FREE HOUSE ◀ The Jigger Inn Jigger Ale, St Andrews, Guinness. ♥ 8 Facilities Non-diners area ♦ Garden ⌁ Parking 🚌

CITY OF GLASGOW

GLASGOW   Map 20 NS56

Bon Accord

tel: 0141 248 4427 153 North St G3 7DA
email: paul.bonaccord@ntlbusiness.com
dir: M8 junct 19 merge onto A804 (North Street) signed Charing Cross

An unmissable destination for malt whisky lovers

Tourists from all over the world come to the 'Bon', Paul McDonagh and son Thomas's acclaimed alehouse and malt whisky bar. The reason? To sample some of the annual tally of a thousand-plus different beers, over 40 ciders (maybe at one of the four beer and cider festivals), or the 350-strong malts collection (a far cry from the original five on offer). Menus display all-day breakfasts, baguettes, giant Yorkshire puddings, chilli con carne, fish and chips, grilled steaks, chicken salads, macaroni cheese and vegetarian Glamorgan sausage (made with leek and Caerphilly).

Open all day all wk Food Lunch all wk 12-8 Dinner all wk 12-8 Av main course £5.95 Set menu available ⊕ FREE HOUSE ◀ Over 1,000 real ales per year ♂ Over 40 ciders per year. ♥ 11 Facilities Non-diners area ♦ Garden Outside area ⌁ Beer festival Cider festival WiFi 🚌

Rab Ha's

tel: 0141 572 0400 83 Hutchieson St G1 1SH
email: management@rabhas.com
dir: Phone for detailed directions

A blend of Victorian character and contemporary Scottish decor

This hotel, restaurant and bar in the heart of Glasgow's revitalised Merchant City takes its name from Robert Hall, a local 19th-century character known as 'The Glasgow Glutton' who would earn a living by taking bets on the amount of food he could consume. The kitchen team prides itself on the extensive use of carefully sourced Scottish produce to create hearty Scottish dishes like breaded Scottish brie; smoked Loch Fyne trout and salmon rillette; Cullen skink; haggis, neeps and tatties; Angus sirloin steak and hand-cut chips; Rab's tomato and seafood broth; and Ailsa Craig cheese salad. The bar menu even lists haggis nachos.

Open all day all wk 12-12 (Sun 12.30-12) Food Lunch Mon-Thu 12-9, Fri-Sat 12-10, Sun 12.30-9 Dinner Mon-Thu 12-9, Fri-Sat 12-10, Sun 12.30-9 Av main course £9 Set menu available Restaurant menu available Wed-Sat ⊕ FREE HOUSE ◀ Tennent's, Blue Moon, West Brewery St Mungos, Budweiser Budvar, Belhaven Best, Guest ales ♂ Addlestones. Facilities Non-diners area ❄ (Bar Outside area) ♦ Children's portions Outside area ⌁ WiFi 🚌 (notice required)

Stravaigin ◉◉   PICK OF THE PUBS

tel: 0141 334 2665 26-30 Gibson St G12 8NX
email: stravaigin@btinternet.com
dir: Phone for directions

Encouraging a policy of culinary curiosity

'Stravaig' is an old Scots' word meaning 'to wander aimlessly with intent' which fits the Stravaigin's 'think global, eat local' philosophy perfectly. Located in a busy street close to the university, this popular bar/restaurant has picked up two AA Rosettes for the food, and also an environmental award. The modern split-level basement restaurant draws the crowds with its contemporary decor, modern art and quirky antiques. The bar offers an extensive wine list and real ales like Fyne Chip 71. Expect innovative and exciting fusion food cooked from top-notch, seasonal Scottish ingredients – the same menu is served throughout. Embracing the flavours

of the world are dishes of Nasi Goreng; crispy aubergine bitterballen with beetroot and quinoa tabouleh; Korean braised ox cheek with brown rice cake, kimchi, tempura oyster and sesame dressed cucumber; haggis, neeps and tatties (veggie version available too); and coconut sponge and black sesame ice cream for afters (wines are recommended with each dessert).

Open all day all wk Closed 25 Dec, 1 Jan Food Lunch all wk 11-5 Dinner all wk 5-11 Restaurant menu available all wk ⊕ FREE HOUSE ◀ Caledonian Deuchars IPA, Belhaven Best, Fyne Chip 71 ♂ Westons Wyld Wood Organic Classic, Addlestones. ♥ 19 Facilities Non-diners area ❄ (Bar) ♦ Children's menu Children's portions ⌁ WiFi

Ubiquitous Chip ◉◉   PICK OF THE PUBS

tel: 0141 334 5007 12 Ashton Ln G12 8SJ
email: mail@ubiquitouschip.co.uk
dir: In West End of Glasgow, off Byres Rd. Beside Hillhead subway station

Iconic city pub with buzzing atmosphere and memorable menus

One of the city's most intriguing pubs stands hidden down a cobbled lane in Glasgow's Bohemian, trendy West End. Here, this mews property has morphed over four decades into a jigsaw of eating and drinking spaces to savour. The main dining area opens into a vine-covered courtyard, while upstairs is the brasserie-style, two AA-Rosette restaurant. There are three drinking areas: the traditional Big Pub, serving real ales such as Loch Fyne (there's a twice-yearly beer festival here too), nearly 30 wines by the glass and more than 150 malt whiskies; the Wee Bar, which lives up to its name by being possibly the 'wee-est' bar in Scotland; and the Corner Bar, which serves cocktails across a granite slab reclaimed from a mortuary. The menu is a Pandora's Box of delights and draws lavishly on Scotland's generous larder. Lead in with smoked haddock fishcake with Arbroath smokie mayonnaise; then turn attention to Ayrshire mallard breast, confit leg, roast celeriac, Savoy cabbage and bacon with mead gravy.

Open all day all wk 11am-1am Closed 25 Dec, 1 Jan Food Lunch Mon-Sun 11-5 Dinner all wk 5-11 Av main course £13.95 Restaurant menu available all wk ⊕ FREE HOUSE ◀ Caledonian Deuchars IPA, Fyne Chip 71 ♂ Addlestones. ♥ 29 Facilities Non-diners area ❄ (Bar Outside area) ♦ Children's menu Children's portions Outside area ⌁ Beer festival WiFi 🚌 (notice required)

WEST Brewery   PICK OF THE PUBS

tel: 0141 550 0135 Templeton Building, Glasgow Green G40 1AW
email: info@westbeer.com
dir: Phone for detailed directions

German-style brewpub in converted carpet factory

'Glaswegian heart, German head' is the strapline this buzzy brewpub/restaurant uses as the only UK brewery producing beers in accordance with Germany's Purity Law of 1516, which means no additives, colourings or preservatives. It occupies the old Winding House of a former carpet factory, modelled by its Victorian architect on the Doge's Palace in Venice. Look down into the brewhouse from the beer hall and watch the brewers making artisanal lagers and wheat beers, including St Mungo, Dunkel, Munich Red and Hefeweizen. Brewery tours are conducted on selected days of the week. The all-day menu offers roll-mops; pork knuckle; Bavarian pan-fried bread dumplings; and Nuremburg sausages with sauerkraut, but you can also choose from grills, burgers and other British pub grub. For dessert are Viennese apple strudel; pear tarte Tatin; and, in a nod to the past, Black Forest gâteau. Brunch is available at weekends. October's Fridays are Oktoberfest beer festival days.

Open all day all wk Closed 25-26 Dec, 1-2 Jan Food Lunch all wk 12-5 Dinner all wk 5-9 Av main course £9.95 Set menu available Restaurant menu available all wk ⊕ FREE HOUSE ◀ WEST Munich Red, Guest ale. Facilities Non-diners area ❄ (Bar Restaurant Garden) ♦ Children's menu Children's portions Garden ⌁ Beer festival 🚌 (notice required)

HIGHLAND

ACHILTIBUIE
Map 22 NC00

Summer Isles Hotel & Bar
PICK OF THE PUBS

tel: 01854 622282 **IV26 2YG**
email: info@summerisleshotel.com
dir: Take A835 N from Ullapool for 10m, Achiltibuie signed on left, 15m to village. Hotel 1m on left

Tranquil hotel with local seafood and fabulous views

Wonderful is the only word for the views out to Badentarbat Bay and the Summer Isles from this highly praised hotel, set against a backdrop of wild and largely untouched landscape, where the weather can change in days from Arctic to Aegean. Where once crofters gathered to drink, today's guests are mostly locals (some of whom may well be crofters) from the scattering of houses along this remote road, plus tourists, of course. Those old farmers are remembered in Crofters' Pale, one of the bar's three An Teallach Ale Company's brews. The informal all-day bar serves fresh ground coffee, snacks, lunch, afternoon tea and evening meals. Nearly everything you eat is home produced, locally caught or at least Scottish – hand-picked scallops, lobster, langoustines, crab, halibut, turbot, salmon, venison, quail, and Shetland lamb. But note that restaurant food is not served between November and March

Open all wk 11-11 Closed 31 Oct-3 Apr **Food** Lunch all wk 12-3, soup & snacks till 5 Dinner all wk 6-9.30 Restaurant menu available all wk ⊕ FREE HOUSE ◀ An Teallach Crofters' Pale Ale, Beinn Deorg. **Facilities** Non-diners area ✿ (Garden) ♦ Children's menu Children's portions Garden ♠ Parking WiFi ☞ (notice required)

CAWDOR
Map 23 NH85

Cawdor Tavern
PICK OF THE PUBS

See Pick of the Pubs on opposite page

FORTROSE
Map 23 NH75

The Anderson
PICK OF THE PUBS

tel: 01381 620236 **Union St IV10 8TD**
email: info@theanderson.co.uk
dir: From Inverness take A9 N signed Wick. Right onto B9161 signed Munlochy, Cromarty & A832. At T-junct right onto A832 to Fortrose

Coastal conservation village on the Black Isle

On the beautiful Black Isle to the north of Inverness, this striking black-and-white painted pub enjoys a tranquil seaside setting; a short walk from its door passes the gaunt, ruined cathedral before happening on the picturesque harbour at Fortrose, with sweeping views across the Moray Firth. Nearby Chanonry Point lighthouse is renowned as one of the best places from which to watch the dolphins in the Firth. But why leave an inn famed for its classic range of finest Scottish microbrewery beers, vast array of Belgian beers and 230 single malts selected by American proprietor Jim Anderson? The 'global cuisine' created with freshest Scottish produce is equally comprehensive. Aberdeen beef, West Coast seafood and Highland game are amongst ingredients on the daily-changing menu: seafood chowder or fried ravioli are typical starters, followed perhaps by Stornoway guinea fowl stuffed with Munro's white pudding and served with a creamy leek and cider sauce. You could finish with apple rhubarb crumble tartlet with vanilla ice cream.

Open all wk 4pm-11pm Closed mid Nov-mid Dec **Food** Dinner all wk 6-9.30 ⊕ FREE HOUSE ◀ Rotating ales ♂ Addlestones. ♒ 13 **Facilities** Non-diners area ✿ (Bar Garden) ♦ Children's menu Garden ♠ Beer festival Parking WiFi

FORT WILLIAM
Map 22 NN17

Moorings Hotel ★★★★ HL

tel: 01397 772797 **Banavie PH33 7LY**
email: reservations@moorings-fortwilliam.co.uk **web:** www.moorings-fortwilliam.co.uk
dir: From A82 in Fort William follow signs for Mallaig, left onto A830 for 1m. Cross canal bridge, 1st right signed Banavie

Canalside spot with panoramic views

The historic Caledonian Canal and Neptune's Staircase, the famous flight of eight locks, runs right beside this modern hotel and pub. On clear days it has panoramic views towards Ben Nevis, best savoured from the Upper Deck lounge bar and the bedrooms. Food, served in the lounge bar and the fine-dining Neptunes Restaurant, features local fish and seafood, with other choices such as steak and ale pie, and rib-eye of Highland beef. There is access to the canal towpath from the gardens.

Open all day all wk Closed 24-26 Dec **Food** Lunch all wk 12-9.30 Dinner all wk 12-9.30 Av main course £10 Restaurant menu available ⊕ FREE HOUSE ◀ Tetley's Bitter, Caledonian Deuchars IPA, Guinness. ♒ 8 **Facilities** Non-diners area ✿ (Garden) ♦ Children's menu Children's portions Garden ♠ Parking WiFi ☞ (notice required) **Rooms** 27

GAIRLOCH
Map 22 NG87

The Old Inn
PICK OF THE PUBS

tel: 01445 712006 **IV21 2BD**
email: info@theoldinn.net
dir: Just off A832, near harbour at south end of village

Traditional coaching inn with its own brewery

Built in 1750, it was once a changing post for horses but now attracts herds of outdoor enthusiasts, especially walkers. Gairloch's oldest hostelry enjoys a fabulous setting at the foot of the Flowerdale Valley with views of the Outer Hebrides. Owner Alastair Pearson operates the pub's own on-site microbrewery, so expect the pints of The Slattadale, The Flowerdale and Blind Piper to be in tip-top condition at the bar. It's not just the beer that's home made: the pub has its own smokery producing smoked meats, fish and cheese, and bread is baked in-house. Local fish and game feature strongly on menus that run from simple grills and hearty pies to pizza and pasta dishes. Typical mains include smoked haddock risotto and vegetable tagine. Picnic tables on the large grassy area by the stream make an attractive spot for eating and enjoying the views. Dogs are welcome.

Open all day all wk 11am-mdnt (Sun 12-12) Closed 21 Nov-Feb **Food** Lunch all wk 12-2.30, summer 12-4.30 Dinner all wk 5-9.30 Restaurant menu available all wk evening ⊕ FREE HOUSE ◀ The Old Inn The Erradale, The Flowerdale, The Slattadale, Three Sisters & Blind Piper, Adnams Southwold Bitter, An Teallach Crofters' Pale Ale, Cairngorm Trade Winds. **Facilities** Non-diners area ✿ (Bar Garden) ♦ Children's menu Children's portions Garden ♠ Parking WiFi ☞ (notice required)

Read all about whisky in our feature on page 18

PICK OF THE PUBS

Cawdor Tavern

CAWDOR   **Map 23 NH85**

tel: 01667 404777
The Lane IV12 5XP
email: enquiries@cawdortavern.co.uk
web: www.cawdortavern.co.uk
dir: *A96 onto B9006, follow Cawdor Castle signs. Tavern in village centre*

Scottish innkeeping at its best

The Tavern is tucked away in the heart of Cawdor's pretty conservation village; near by is the castle where Macbeth held court. Pretty wooded countryside slides away from the pub, offering umpteen opportunities for rambles and challenging cycle routes. Exercise over, repair to this homely hostelry to enjoy the welcoming mix of fine Scottish food and island micro-brewery ales that makes the pub a destination in its own right. There's an almost baronial feel to the bars, created from the Cawdor Estate's joinery workshop in the 1960s. The lounge bar's wonderful panelling came from Cawdor Castle's dining room as a gift from a former laird; log fires and stoves add winter warmth, as does the impressive choice of Orkney Brewery beers and Highland and Island malts. An accomplished menu balances meat, fish, game and vegetarian options, prepared in a modern Scottish style with first class Scottish produce. Settle in the delightful restaurant beneath wrought iron Jacobean chandeliers and contemplate starting with a trio of

Scottish puddings – black pudding, prize haggis and white pudding layered together and served with home-made chutney. Next maybe a venison burger from the grill, topped with smoked bacon, tomato relish and melting mozzarella. Classic sweets include sticky toffee pudding, and chocolate brownie with warm chocolate sauce. Alfresco drinking and dining is possible on the colourful patio area at the front of the Tavern during the warm summer months. Excellent value is a Sunday high tea starting at 4.30pm.

Open all wk 11-3 5-11 (Sat 11am-mdnt Sun 12.30-11) all day in summer Closed 25 Dec, 1 Jan

Food Lunch Mon-Sat 12-2 Sun 12.30-3 Dinner 5.30-9 (food served all day in summer) ⊕ FREE HOUSE ◀ Orkney Red MacGregor, Raven Ale, Clootie Dumpling & Dark Island, Atlas Latitude Highland Pilsner, Three Sisters, Nimbus & Wayfarer ♂ Thatchers Gold.
Facilities ❤ (Bar Outside area)
❖ Children's menu Children's portions Outside area Parking WiFi 🚌 (notice required)

GLENCOE
Map 22 NN15

Clachaig Inn

tel: 01855 811252 **PH49 4HX**
email: frontdesk@clachaig.com
dir: *Follow Glencoe signs from A82. Inn 3m S of village*

Real craic at this legendary Highland inn

In the heart of Glencoe, against a backdrop of spectacular mountains, this famous Highland inn has welcomed climbers, hill-walkers, skiers, kayakers and regular travellers for over 300 years. Real ales (sometimes as many as 15), nearly 300 malt whiskies, good food and fresh coffee are served in all three bars, each with its own distinctive and lively character. Local dishes on offer include Stornoway black pudding; oak-smoked West Coast salmon; Highland venison burger; and vegetarian haggis, neeps 'n' tatties. As well as beer and whisky tastings, the pub also holds a Hogmanay beer festival, and two others – FebFest and OctoberFest.

Open all day all wk Closed 24-26 Dec **Food** Lunch all wk 12-9 Dinner all wk 12-9 ⊕ FREE HOUSE ◀ Rotating Guest ales ♂ Westons. **Facilities** Non-diners area ♣ (Bar Garden) ♦ Children's menu Children's portions Play area Family room Garden ⍺ Beer festival Parking WiFi ⊨

GLENUIG
Map 22 NM67

Glenuig Inn

tel: 01687 470219 **PH38 4NG**
email: bookings@glenuig.com
dir: *From Fort William on A830 towards Mallaig through Glen Finnan. Left onto A861, 8m to Glenuig Bay*

A more spectacular setting you couldn't wish for

Retaining walls dating back to around 1746 and Bonnie Prince Charlie's time, the Glenuig Inn is a popular base for sea-kayakers drawn to the stunning beaches in the Sound of Arisaig. The emphasis here is 'as local as we can get it' and this philosophy applies to the bar, where only local real ale from Cairngorm is served, and the kitchen, where menus are prepared using organic seasonal ingredients wherever possible. A typical selection might include Glenuig hot smoked salmon, followed by Skye lamb tagine or home-made venison burger, and chocolate and chilli tart to finish. The inn is committed to 'going green' in everything they do.

Open all day all wk **Food** Lunch all wk 12-9 Dinner all wk 12-9 ⊕ FREE HOUSE ◀ Cairngorm Trade Winds, Black Gold & Wild Cat ♂ Thistly Cross. ⏺ 9 **Facilities** Non-diners area ♣ (Bar Restaurant Garden) ♦ Children's menu Children's portions Play area Family room Garden ⍺ Parking WiFi

INVERGARRY
Map 22 NH30

The Invergarry Inn

tel: 01809 501206 **PH35 4HJ**
email: info@invergarryhotel.co.uk
dir: *At junct of A82 & A87*

In a tranquil spot, ideal for walking

A real Highland atmosphere pervades this roadside inn set in glorious mountain scenery between Fort William and Fort Augustus. Welcoming bars make it a great base from which to explore Loch Ness, Glencoe and the West Coast. Relax by the crackling log fire with a wee dram or a pint of Garry Ale, then tuck into a good meal.

Perhaps try Lochaber haggis, bashit neeps and tatties to start; followed by sea bream en papillote or a succulent 10oz rib-eye Scottish beefsteak and hand-cut chips. There are, of course, excellent walks from the front door. Booking is required for dinner.

Open all day all wk **Food** Lunch all wk 8am-9.30pm Dinner all wk 8am-9.30pm Av main course £13.95 ⊕ FREE HOUSE ◀ The Invergarry Inn Garry Ale. **Facilities** Non-diners area ♦ Children's menu Children's portions Family room Garden ⍺ Parking

KYLESKU
Map 22 NC23

Kylesku Hotel
`PICK OF THE PUBS`

tel: 01971 502231 **IV27 4HW**
email: info@kyleskuhotel.co.uk
dir: *A835, A837 & A894 to Kylesku. Hotel at end of road at Old Ferry Pier*

Waterside inn with wonderful seafood

At the centre of the North West Highlands Global Geopark – 2,000 square kilometres of lochs, mountains and wild coast – and close to Britain's highest waterfall, this 17th-century coaching inn enjoys a glorious location. Views from the bar and restaurant are truly memorable – you may catch sight of seals, dolphins, otters, eagles and terns. The fishing boats moor at the old ferry slipway to land the creel-caught seafood that forms the backbone of the daily-changing chalkboard menu. So settle down with a pint of An Teallach Beinn Dearg, and ponder your choice of the morning's catch. You could start with local rope-grown mussels, either in classic marinière style or in a Thai coconut broth with lime and coriander. Next, Loch Glendhu langoustines can be served hot with garlic butter and chips, or cold with mayonnaise and salad. To finish with another range of local flavours, look to the platter of Scottish cheeses.

Open all day all wk Closed Nov-Feb **Food** Lunch all wk 12-6 Dinner all wk 6-9 Av main course £14 ⊕ FREE HOUSE ◀ An Teallach & Beinn Dearg Ale, Isle of Skye. ⏺ 12 **Facilities** Non-diners area ♣ (Bar Restaurant Garden) ♦ Children's menu Children's portions Garden ⍺ WiFi

LEWISTON
Map 23 NH52

NEW The Loch Ness Inn

tel: 01456 450991 **IV63 6UW**
email: info@staylochness.co.uk
dir: *Phone for detailed directions*

Comfy village inn in the famous Great Glen

A brisk stroll from here on the waymarked Great Glen Way heads towards the shoreline of the renowned loch. Try a few jars of the locally brewed Inndiginess bitter at the inn's bustling bar and who knows what you'll see in the shimmering waters? The place is a hive of activity, with music events hosted and as base for the local shinty team. With flambéed haggis tart as a starter; then slow cooked belly pork with apple and celeriac remoulade to follow, that appetite-building loch-side ramble to famous Urquhart Castle looks more and more desirable. Unusually, a range of Scottish distilled gins is available at the bar.

Open all day all wk **Food** Lunch all wk breakfast-9pm Dinner all wk breakfast-9pm Av main course £8.95 Set menu available Restaurant menu available all wk ⊕ FREE HOUSE ◀ Loch Ness LightNess, LochNess & Inndiginess ♂ Thistly Cross. ⏺ 10 **Facilities** Non-diners area ♦ Children's menu Children's portions Garden ⍺ Parking WiFi ⊨ (notice required)

PICK OF THE PUBS

The Plockton Hotel

PLOCKTON　　Map 22 NG83

tel: 01599 544274
Harbour St IV52 8TN
email: info@plocktonhotel.co.uk
web: www.plocktonhotel.co.uk
dir: *A87 towards Kyle of Lochalsh. At Balmacara follow Plockton signs, 7m*

Award-winning local seafood served here

Dating from 1827, the original black fronted building is thought to have been a ships' chandlery before it was converted to serve as the village inn. Set with the mountains on one side and the deep blue waters of Loch Carron on the other, this lovely village is well known for its white-washed cottages and, of all things, palm trees. Alan Pearson happily runs this award-winning harbourside hotel, inheriting a successful legacy from his parents who were in charge for two decades. The hotel specialises in seafood – including freshly landed fish and locally caught langoustines (mid afternoon you can watch the catch being landed) – supplemented by Highland steaks and locally reared beef. Lunchtime features light bites, warm bloomers and toasted paninis, as well as a good range of hot dishes. Evening dishes might include Talisker whisky pâté; sweet pickled herring and prawns; or grilled goats' cheese with beetroot chutney to start, followed by casserole of Highland venison cooked in red wine,

herbs, juniper berries and redcurrant jelly; fillet of monkfish wrapped in bacon; chargrilled Aberdeen Angus steak with whisky sauce; or pan-fried medallions of pork with brandied apricots and cream sauce. Daily specials, written up on the blackboard, add to the tempting choices. A fine range of malts is available to round off that perfect Highland day, perhaps accompanied by one of the 'basket' meals served every evening from 9pm-10pm – try the breaded scampi tails.

Open all day all wk 11am-mdnt (Sun 12.30-11) Closed 25 Dec, 1 Jan **Food** Lunch Mon-Sat 12-2.15, Sun 12.30-2.15 Dinner all wk 6-10 Av main course £12 ⊕ FREE HOUSE ◀ Inveralmond Ossian, Highland Seafire, Amarillo & Orkney Best. **Facilities** Non-diners area ♦♦ Children's menu Children's portions Family room Garden ⊼ Beer festival WiFi

PICK OF THE PUBS

Plockton Inn & Seafood Restaurant

PLOCKTON Map 22 NG83

tel: 01599 544222
Innes St IV52 8TW
email: info@plocktoninn.co.uk
web: www.plocktoninn.co.uk
dir: *A87 towards Kyle of Lochalsh. At Balmacara follow Plockton signs, 7m*

Friendly inn offering great seafood

Located in Plockton which is on Loch Carron in the West Highlands, this inn is owned and run by Mary Gollan, her brother Kenny and his partner Susan Trowbridge. The Gollans were born and bred in the village and it was actually their great-grandfather who built the attractive stone free house as a manse. The beautiful views can be enjoyed from seats on the decking outside. The ladies double up in the role of chef, while Kenny manages the bar, where you'll find winter fires, Plockton real ales from the village brewery, and a selection of over 50 malt whiskies. A meal in the reasonably formal Dining Room or more relaxed Lounge Bar is a must, with a wealth of freshly caught local fish and shellfish, West Highland beef, lamb, game and home-made vegetarian dishes on the menu, plus daily specials. The Plockton prawns (called langoustines here), which Martin the barman catches in the sea loch, are taken to Kenny's smokehouse to the rear of the building to be cured along with other seafood – the results can be

sampled in the seafood platter starter. Other starters include salad niçoise; moules marinière; and haggis and clapshot with home-made pickled beetroot. Among the main dishes are langoustines, served hot with garlic butter or cold with Marie Rose sauce; pan-fried hand-dived king scallops with bacon, garlic and cream; spicy Puy lentil bake with sweet potato topping; and slow roasted pork belly with onion and cider gravy. Desserts include chocolate cheesecake, and Scottish cheeses served with Orkney oatcakes. The public bar is alive on Tuesdays and Thursdays with music from local musicians, who are often joined by talented youngsters from the National Centre of Excellence in Traditional Music in the village.

Open all day all wk **Food** Lunch 12-2.30 Dinner 6-9 Av main course £10
⊕ FREE HOUSE ◨ Greene King Abbot Ale, Fuller's London Pride, Young's Special, Plockton Crags Ale & Bay.
Facilities Non-diners area ❧ (Bar Garden) ❢ Children's menu Children's portions Play area Garden ⊼ Parking WiFi 🚌 (notice required)

NORTH BALLACHULISH
Map 22 NN06

Loch Leven Hotel

tel: 01855 821236 **Old Ferry Rd PH33 6SA**
email: reception@lochlevenhotel.co.uk
dir: *Off A82, N of Ballachulish Bridge*

A hotel with one of Scotland's most idyllic views

The slipway into Loch Leven at the foot of the garden recalls the origins of this 17th-century inn as one of the Road to The Isles staging points linked to the old ferry. Sip beers from Cairngorm Brewery or a wee dram from a choice of over 60 malts while enjoying the warmth of the open fire, or make the most of the terrace and garden when the sun's out. The extraordinary location, near the foot of Glencoe and with horizons peppered by Munro peaks rising above azure sea lochs, is gifted with superb seafood from the local depths. Indulge in Atlantic prawn and grilled aubergine timbale; and pork medallions, melted brie, sautéed potatoes, seasonal vegetables and creamy sage sauce. Adjoining the traditional bar are family and games rooms. A change of hands in late 2013.

Open all day all wk 11-11 (Thu-Sat 11am-mdnt Sun 12.30-11) **Food** Lunch all wk 12-2.30 Dinner all wk 5.30-9.30 ⊕ FREE HOUSE ◀ Cairngorm, Atlas, River Leven. **Facilities** Non-diners area ❤ (Bar Garden) ◀ Children's menu Children's portions Play area Family room Garden ⊼ Parking WiFi ▭ (notice required)

PLOCKTON
Map 22 NG83

The Plockton Hotel
PICK OF THE PUBS

See Pick of the Pubs on page 605

Plockton Inn & Seafood Restaurant
PICK OF THE PUBS

See Pick of the Pubs on opposite page

SHIELDAIG
Map 22 NG85

Shieldaig Bar & Coastal Kitchen
PICK OF THE PUBS

tel: 01520 755251 **IV54 8XN**
email: tighaneilean@keme.co.uk
dir: *Exit A896*

Lochside bar and restaurant in a tiny village

In a remote and peaceful location is the famous Tigh an Eilean Hotel, of which the Shieldaig Bar & Coastal Kitchen is part. Here, the magnificent Torridon Mountains meet the western seas; offshore is Shieldaig Island, while Upper Loch Torridon is just round the corner. An abundance of wildlife is visible from this extraordinary waterside setting — otters and seals, white-tailed sea eagles, oyster catchers, pine martens to name but a few. An Teallach Brewery supplies the traditional bar, where live music and ceilidhs add a weekend buzz. The sea provides much of what appears on the menu, especially the shellfish landed daily by fishermen who employ environmentally responsible creel-fishing and hand-diving techniques. Ways of sampling this local bounty include seafood stew and fisherman's pie, while among the other dishes are home-made beefburgers and wood-fired hand-made pizzas. Outside by the loch is a courtyard with benches and tables where you can watch the spectacular sunsets.

Open all day all wk 11-11 **Food** Lunch all wk 12-2.30 (all day summer) Dinner all wk 6-9 (all day summer) ⊕ FREE HOUSE ◀ An Teallach. ☂ 8 **Facilities** Non-diners area ◀ Children's menu Children's portions Garden ⊼ Parking WiFi ▭ (notice required)

TORRIDON
Map 22 NG95

The Torridon Inn ★★★★ INN
PICK OF THE PUBS

tel: 01445 791242 **IV22 2EY**
email: info@thetorridon.com **web:** www.thetorridon.com/inn
dir: *From Inverness take A9 N, then follow signs to Ullapool. Take A835 then A832. In Kinlochewe take A896 to Annat. Pub 200yds on right after village*

Idyllic location and definitive Scottish menus

The island-fringed, azure waters of Loch Torridon and the striking mountains across the water are neighbours to this bustling inn. It makes it a convenient base to walk, mountaineer, kayak or rock climb, but its cosy comfortable atmosphere and good home-cooked food very much appeal to the less active too. Painstakingly converted from old farm buildings, a stable block and buttery, there's a good range of Highlands and Islands beer on tap, often from Cairngorm and An Teallach breweries, supplemented by an annual October beer festival. A cosy interior with wood fires and bright decor as well as an airy conservatory-diner is a restful place to consider a fine Scottish menu, much of it from the West Coast area. Pan-seared scallops with butternut squash risotto is a filling starter; or plump for crispy braised collar of pork with cider and sage cream sauce, or perhaps Wester Ross salmon fillet.

Open all day all wk Closed Jan **Food** Lunch all wk 12-2 Dinner all wk 6-9 ⊕ FREE HOUSE ◀ Isle of Skye Red Cuillin, Torridon Ale, Cairngorm Trade Winds, An Teallach & Crofters Pale Ale, Cromarty Happy Chappy. **Facilities** Non-diners area ❤ (Bar Garden) ◀ Children's menu Children's portions Play area Garden ⊼ Beer festival Parking WiFi ▭ (notice required) **Rooms** 12

NORTH LANARKSHIRE

CUMBERNAULD
Map 21 NS77

Castlecary House Hotel

tel: 01324 840233 **Castlecary Rd G68 OHD**
email: enquiries@castlecaryhotel.com
dir: *A80 onto B816 between Glasgow & Stirling. 7m from Falkirk, 9m from Stirling*

Friendly, family-run hotel

Castlecary House Hotel is located close to the historic Antonine Wall and the Forth and Clyde Canal. Meals in the four lounge bars plough a traditional furrow with options such as deep-fried black pudding balls; bangers and mash; and baked gammon. Home-made puddings include sticky toffee pudding and profiteroles. More formal fare is available in Camerons Restaurant, where high tea is served on Sundays. There is an excellent selection of real ales on offer, including Arran Blonde and Harviestoun Bitter. A beer festival is held once or twice a year — contact the hotel for details.

Open all day all wk Closed 1 Jan **Food** Lunch 12-9 Dinner 12-9 ⊕ FREE HOUSE ◀ Arran Blonde, Harviestoun Bitter & Twisted, Inveralmond Ossian's Ale, Houston Peter's Well, Caledonian Deuchars IPA. ☂ 8 **Facilities** Non-diners area ◀ Children's menu Children's portions Garden Beer festival Parking WiFi ▭

EAST LOTHIAN

GULLANE
Map 21 NT48

The Old Clubhouse

tel: 01620 842008 **East Links Rd EH31 2AF**
dir: *A198 into Gullane, 3rd right into East Links Rd, pass church, on left*

Pub favourites overlooking the Gullane Links

Established in 1890 as the home of Gullane Golf Club, this building had a chequered past after the golfers moved on to larger premises, including stints as a disco and as tea rooms. In the late 1980s the Campanile family took the reins and it hasn't looked back. Roaring winter fires and walls crammed with golfing memorabilia make a good first impression, and the menu delivers a lengthy list of pub classics including regional specialities such as Cullen skink or Hornings haggis with Stornoway black pudding. For dessert, maybe home-made ice cream.

Open all day all wk Closed 25 Dec & 1 Jan **Food** Lunch all wk 12-9.30 Dinner all wk 12-9.30 ⊕ FREE HOUSE ◀ Timothy Taylor Landlord, Caledonian Deuchars IPA ♂ Thistly Cross. ₹ 9 **Facilities** Non-diners area ♣ (Bar Garden) ♦♦ Children's menu Children's portions Garden ♬ WiFi ▬ (notice required)

HADDINGTON
Map 21 NT57

NEW The Waterside

tel: 01620 825674 **EH41 4AT**
email: robin@watersidebistro.co.uk
dir: *Phone for detailed directions*

Sublime riverside location and great beers

Huddled right beside the ancient sandstone Nungate bridge across the River Tyne, The Waterside enjoys an unrivalled setting in this peaceful Lothian town. With some memorable beers from Scottish microbreweries, plus a huge selection of bottled beers, Gavin Ferguson sets out his stall as a true beer connoisseur. The food pulls no punches either, with a seasonally influenced menu drawing on Scotland's boundless larder for inspiration. Salmon and mussels feature, and Scottish beef is a given; more engaging meals may include Jerusalem artichoke, truffle and pearl barley risotto. Settle into a wingback chair in the carved oak 'The Office' bar and chill out in this welcoming pub-bistro.

Open 12-3 5.30-close (Sat 12-close Sun 12.30-close) Closed Mon in Winter **Food** Lunch Tue-Sun 12-3 Dinner Tue-Sat 6-9, Sun 6-8 Av main course £10.50 Set menu available Restaurant menu available all wk ⊕ FREE HOUSE ◀ Tempest Long White Cloud, Alechemy, Magic Rock Ringmaster, Stewart, Fyne Ales, Knops, Inveralmond ♂ Thistly Cross. ₹ 10 **Facilities** Non-diners area ♣ (Bar Outside area) ♦♦ Children's menu Children's portions Family room Outside area ♬ Beer festival Parking WiFi ▬ (notice required)

LONGNIDDRY
Map 21 NT47

The Longniddry Inn

tel: 01875 852401 **Main St EH32 0NF**
email: info@longniddryinn.com
dir: *On A198 (Main St), near rail station*

Comprehensive menu choices in historic buildings

This combination of a former blacksmith's forge and four cottages on Longniddry's Main Street continues to be a popular spot. Held in high esteem locally for friendly service and good food, it offers an extensive menu featuring the likes of Stornoway

black pudding and poached egg; haggis, neeps and tatties; chef's stir-fry; macaroni cheese; and chicken and combo sizzlers from the grill. In warmer weather take your pint of Belhaven Best, glass of wine or freshly ground coffee outside.

Open all day all wk Closed 26 Dec, 1 Jan **Food** Lunch Mon-Sat 12-8.30, Sun 12.30-7.30 Dinner Mon-Sat 12-8.30, Sun 12.30-7.30 Av main course £9.95 ⊕ PUNCH TAVERNS ◀ Belhaven Best. **Facilities** Non-diners area ♦♦ Children's menu Children's portions Garden Parking WiFi ▬

WEST LOTHIAN

LINLITHGOW
Map 21 NS97

Champany Inn - The Chop and Ale House ◉◉
PICK OF THE PUBS

tel: 01506 834532 **Champany EH49 7LU**
email: reception@champany.com
dir: *2m NE of Linlithgow at junct of A904 & A803*

Renowned inn within striking distance of Edinburgh

Buildings here comprise a former mill-house, a farmer's bothy and some buildings dating from the 16th century. A talking point in the luxurious bar is a rock pond where oysters and lobsters fresh from the Western Isles consider their future, while you, your glass of Caledonia Best, or perhaps own-label South African pinotage in hand, consider your meal. Starters include smoked salmon rillettes; Highland black pudding; and, in winter, Cullen skink. The menu also makes it clear that they're big on Aberdeen Angus steaks here, but among alternatives to steak are roast breast of chicken; grilled salmon; and deep-fried cod and chips. Quite a lot of fruit is grown in Scotland, so that's what dessert could be. The Chop and Ale House, a separate operation from the restaurant, offers Scottish lamb chops and a range of burgers.

Open all wk 12-2 6.30-10 (Fri-Sun 12-10) Closed 25-26 Dec, 1 Jan **Food** Lunch all wk 12-2 Dinner all wk 6.30-10 Restaurant menu available Mon-Sat ⊕ FREE HOUSE ◀ Caledonia Best ♂ Thistly Cross. **Facilities** ♦♦ Children's portions Garden ♬ Parking

The Four Marys

tel: 01506 842171 **65/67 High St EH49 7ED**
email: fourmarys.linlithgow@belhavenpubs.net
dir: *M9 junct 3 or junct 4, A803 to Linlithgow. Pub in town centre*

Real ale paradise in historic town setting

This eye-catching building at the heart of Linlithgow became a pub only in 1981; its pedigree stretches back a further 500 years to when royalty lived at the nearby palace and the town's movers and shakers lived at the house. The eponymous Marys were ladies-in-waiting to Linlithgow-born Mary, Queen of Scots; amongst the bevvy of artefacts in the pub are materials connected to that ill-fated monarch. With striking dressed-stone walls, period and antique furnishings, the pub has forged ever higher standards for real ales in Scotland; twice-yearly beer festivals are held, whilst robust pub grub includes venison and haggis dishes.

Open all day all wk **Food** Lunch all wk 12-5 Dinner all wk 5-9 Av main course £5.95 ⊕ BELHAVEN/GREENE KING ◀ Belhaven 80/- & Four Marys, Belhaven St Andrews, Morland Old Speckled Hen, Caledonian Deuchars IPA, Stewart Edinburgh Gold, St Andrews. ₹ 9 **Facilities** Non-diners area ♦♦ Children's menu Children's portions Garden Outside area Beer festival WiFi ▬

MIDLOTHIAN

DALKEITH
Map 21 NT36

The Sun Inn ★★★★ INN @
PICK OF THE PUBS

tel: 0131 663 2456 **Lothian Bridge EH22 4TR**
email: thesuninn@live.co.uk **web:** www.thesuninnedinburgh.co.uk
dir: On A7 towards Galashiels, opposite Newbattle Viaduct

A thoroughly modern gastro-pub

This family-run former coaching inn stands in wooded grounds close to the banks of the River Esk. The owners have blended the original fireplace, oak beams and exposed stone walls with wooden floors and feature wallpapers. Scottish cask ales have pride of place behind the bar, which also offers an extensive wine list. Food in the more formal restaurant is modern British with a strong Scottish accent, masterminded by owner and head chef Ian Minto and his son Craig. Locally sourced ingredients feature in lunch dishes such as Scottish smoked haddock and leek risotto with soft-poached hen's egg and Arran mustard cream; this can be served as either a starter or a main course. In the evening, settle down to half-shell queenie scallops topped with garlic butter and melting gruyère cheese; and Drum Farm pheasant breast stuffed with chicken and tarragon mousse, sprouts with bacon, and sage and onion croquettes. High teas are served on weekday afternoons.

Open all day all wk Closed 26 Dec, 1 Jan **Food** Lunch Mon-Sat 12-2, Mon-Fri High Tea 2.30-5.30, Sun 12-7 Dinner Mon-Sat 6-9, Sun 12-7 Set menu available ⊕ FREE HOUSE ◀ Caledonian Deuchars IPA, Belhaven Best, Inveralmond ♂ Addlestones. ♥ 28 **Facilities** Non-diners area ♦ Children's menu Children's portions Garden ⊼ Parking WiFi ⇔ (notice required) **Rooms** 5

PENICUIK
Map 21 NT25

The Howgate Restaurant

tel: 01968 670000 **Howgate EH26 8PY**
email: peter@howgate.com
dir: 10m N of Peebles. 3m E of Penicuik on A6094 between Leadburn junct & Howgate

Fine food and ales in a former dairy

Formerly the home of Howgate cheeses, this beautifully converted farm building has a fire-warmed bar offering bistro-style meals, while the candlelit restaurant serves a full carte. The kitchen uses the finest Scottish produce, especially beef and lamb, which are cooked in the charcoal grill; other options might include pheasant stuffed with haggis on chive mash with honey roast root vegetables; chicken and leek risotto; venison, pheasant and Stilton pie, and white chocolate and vanilla cheesecake with hazelnut ice cream to finish. There are fine beers to enjoy and an impressively produced wine list roams the globe.

Open all wk 12-2 6-9.30 Closed 25-26 Dec, 1 Jan **Food** Lunch all wk 12-2 Dinner all wk 6-9.30 Av main course £9.95 ⊕ FREE HOUSE ◀ Belhaven Best, Broughton Ales Greenmantle Ale. ♥ 14 **Facilities** ♦ Children's menu Children's portions Garden ⊼ Parking ⇔ (notice required)

ROSLIN
Map 21 NT26

The Original Rosslyn Inn ★★★★ INN

tel: 0131 440 2384 **2-4 Main St EH25 9LE**
email: enquiries@theoriginalhotel.co.uk **web:** www.theoriginalhotel.co.uk
dir: Off city bypass at Straiton for A703

A perfect city escape that's a stone's throw from Rosslyn Chapel

Just eight miles from central Edinburgh and a short walk from Rosslyn Chapel, this family-run village inn has been in the Harris family for 39 years. Robert Burns, the famous Scottish poet, stayed here in 1787 and wrote a two verse poem for the landlady about his visit. Today you have the chance to catch up with the locals in the village bar, or relax by the fire in the lounge whilst choosing from the menu.

Soups, jackets and paninis are supplemented by main course options like haggis with tatties and neeps; breaded haddock and chips; and vegetarian harvester pie. Alternatively, the Grail Restaurant offers more comprehensive dining options. There are well-equipped bedrooms, four with four-posters.

Open all day all wk **Food** Lunch all wk 12-9.15 Dinner all wk 12-9.15 Restaurant menu available Fri & Sat ⊕ FREE HOUSE ◀ Belhaven Best. ♥ 14 **Facilities** Non-diners area ✿ (Bar Garden) ♦ Children's menu Children's portions Garden ⊼ Parking WiFi ⇔ **Rooms** 7

MORAY

FORRES
Map 23 NJ06

The Old Mill Inn

tel: 01309 641605 **Brodie IV36 2TD**
dir: Between Nairn & Forres on A96

Spacious, family-friendly pub and restaurant

Situated on the Scottish Riviera, officially recorded as one of the sunniest and drierest places in the UK, this inn, a former watermill, has somehow managed to acquire windows, panelling and a beautiful door from a demolished stately home across the Moray Firth. There's a wide choice of food, from chargrills to oven steamed mussels; and haggis wontons, and from Szechuan marinated duck breast to citrus grilled sea bass fillets. There's an ever-changing selection of Scottish real ales at the bar; over 30, all through handpumps, can be tried during the June beer festival.

Open all day all wk Closed 25-26 Dec, 1 Jan **Food** Lunch all wk 11.30-5 Dinner all wk 5-9 Restaurant menu available Tue-Sun ⊕ FREE HOUSE ◀ Rotating Guest ales. ♥ 9 **Facilities** ♦ Children's menu Children's portions Garden ⊼ Beer festival Parking WiFi ⇔ (notice required)

PERTH & KINROSS

KILLIECRANKIE
Map 23 NN96

Killiecrankie House Hotel ★★★ SHL @@
PICK OF THE PUBS

tel: 01796 473220 **PH16 5LG**
email: enquiries@killiecrankiehotel.co.uk **web:** www.killiecrankiehotel.co.uk
dir: Take B8079 N from Pitlochry. Hotel in 3m

Historic venue in stunning location

This white-painted Victorian hotel gleams amidst woodland at the Pass of Killiecrankie, the gateway to The Highlands. It is a magnificent gorge, famed for the battle in 1689 when the Jacobites routed the forces of King William III; today it is a stronghold for red squirrels and a renowned birdwatching area. There are walks bedside rivers and lochs, and countless hill walks, including on the majestic Ben Vrackie that rises behind the hotel. Standing in a four-acre estate, the hotel retains much of its old character and successfully blends it with modern comforts. The cosy, panelled bar is a popular haunt, while the snug sitting room opens on to a small patio. Arm yourself with a Scottish beer as you study a menu that makes the most of Scotland's diverse produce and which has gained the restaurant two AA Rosettes.

Open all day all wk Closed Jan & Feb **Food** Lunch all wk 12.30-2 Dinner all wk 6.30-8.30 ⊕ FREE HOUSE ◀ Orkney Red MacGregor, Caledonian Best, Belhaven Best ♂ Thistly Cross. ♥ 8 **Facilities** Non-diners area ♦ Children's menu Garden ⊼ Parking **Rooms** 10

MEIKLEOUR
Map 21 NO14

NEW Meikleour Arms ★★★★ INN

tel: 01250 883206 **PH2 6EB**
email: contact@meikleourarms.co.uk **web:** www.meikleourarms.co.uk
dir: *From A93 N of Perth, approx 12m take A984 signed Caputh & Dunkeld to Meikleour*

A small country inn set in the heart of a conservation village

Although no longer called a hotel, overnight guests are still welcome at this former mail-coach stopover on the old Edinburgh to Inverness road. The flagstone-floored bar offers Perth-brewed Lure of Meikleour, and Meikleour Gold Bead pilsner from Glasgow. Eat in the bar, the wood-panelled dining room, on the terrace or in the garden and enjoy vegetables, trout and game from the pub's own farm; seafood arrives daily from Aberdeen. Menus feature haggis, clapshot and whisky sauce; Scottish haddock deep fried in ale batter; and wild mushroom carbonara. A beer and cider festival is held in August.

Open all day all wk 11-11 **Food** Contact pub for details Av main course £12 ⊕ FREE HOUSE ◀ Inveralmond Lure of Meikleour, Orkney Dark Island Ö Aspall.
Facilities Non-diners area ❖ (Bar Restaurant Garden) ❖❖ Children's menu Garden ☴ Beer festival Cider festival Parking WiFi ☒ **Rooms** 9

PITLOCHRY
Map 23 NN95

Moulin Hotel
PICK OF THE PUBS

tel: 01796 472196 **11-13 Kirkmichael Rd, Moulin PH16 5EH**
email: enquiries@moulinhotel.co.uk
dir: *From A9 at Pitlochry take A924. Moulin 0.75m*

Hearty local food in prime walking country

Dating from 1695, this welcoming inn located on an old drovers' road at the foot of Ben Vrackie is a popular base for walking and touring. Locals are drawn to the bar for the excellent home-brewed beers, with Moulin Ale of Atholl, Braveheart and Light, and Belhaven Best served on handpump. The interior boasts beautiful stone walls and lots of cosy niches, with blazing log fires in winter; while the courtyard garden is lovely in summer. Menus offer the opportunity to try something local such as mince and tatties; venison Braveheart (strips of local venison pan-fried with mushrooms and Braveheart beer); and Vrackie Grostel (sautéed potatoes with smoked bacon lightly herbed and topped with a fried egg). You might then round off your meal with Highland honey sponge and custard. A specials board broadens the choice further. 25 wines by the glass and more than 30 malt whiskies are available.

Open all day all wk 11-11 (Fri-Sat 11am-11.45pm Sun 12-11) **Food** Lunch all wk 12-9.30 Dinner all wk 12-9.30 ⊕ FREE HOUSE ◀ Moulin Braveheart, Old Remedial, Ale of Atholl & Light, Belhaven Best. ☎ 25 **Facilities** Non-diners area ❖❖ Children's menu Children's portions Garden ☴ Parking WiFi ☒ (notice required)

SCOTTISH BORDERS

ALLANTON
Map 21 NT85

Allanton Inn

tel: 01890 818260 **TD11 3JZ**
email: info@allantoninn.co.uk
dir: *From A1 at Berwick take A6105 for Chirnside (5m). At Chirnside Inn take Coldstream Rd for 1m to Allanton*

Informal dining in family-run Borders pub

Wooden floors, contemporary furnishings, artworks, subtle lighting and that all-important log fire characterise this 18th-century coaching inn. A huge silver spoon and fork dominate one wall of the modern bar, a subtle hint perhaps to study the menu, while enjoying that pint of Inveralmond Ossian. Beef may come from the family farm and the fish is fresh from Eyemouth, while receiving the garden smokehouse treatment are pork, salmon, chicken and even cheeses. Daily blackboard specials add to a regularly changing menu that typically features steamed Shetland mussels; beer battered Eyemouth haddock and hand-cut chips; and vanilla crème brûlée with lavender shortbread. A large garden with fruit trees overlooks open countryside.

Open all day all wk 12-11 Closed 2wks Feb (dates vary) **Food** Lunch all wk 12-3 Dinner all wk 6-9 ⊕ FREE HOUSE ◀ Inveralmond Ossian, Scottish Borders Game Bird, Harviestoun Bitter & Twisted, Fyne Piper's Gold. ☎ 10 **Facilities** Non-diners area ❖❖ Children's menu Children's portions Garden ☴ WiFi

GALASHIELS
Map 21 NT43

Kingsknowes Hotel ★★★ HL

tel: 01896 758375 **1 Selkirk Rd TD1 3HY**
email: enquiries@kingsknowes.co.uk **web:** www.kingsknowes.co.uk
dir: *Exit A7 at Galashiels/Selkirk rdbt*

Traditional food on banks of the Tweed

An imposing Scots baronial mansion dating from 1869, the Kingsknowes is set in over three acres of grounds on the banks of the Tweed with lovely views of the Eildon Hills and Abbotsford House, Sir Walter Scott's ancestral home. Meals are served in two restaurants and the Courtyard Bar, where fresh local or regional produce is used as much as possible. Typical choices include haggis on potato rösti topped with quails' eggs; and pan-fried salmon with chive and king prawn risotto. The impressive glass conservatory is the ideal place to enjoy a glass of McEwan's 70/- or John Smith's.

Open all day all wk Mon-Wed & Sun 12-11 (Thu-Sat noon-1am) Closed 1-3 Jan **Food** Lunch Mon-Fri 12-2, Sat 12-9.30, Sun 12-8.30 Dinner Mon-Fri 5.45-9, Sat 12-9.30, Sun 12-8.30 ⊕ FREE HOUSE ◀ McEwan's 70/-, John Smith's.
Facilities Non-diners area ❖❖ Children's menu Play area Garden Parking ☒ (notice required) **Rooms** 12

INNERLEITHEN
Map 21 NT33

Traquair Arms Hotel

tel: 01896 830229 **Traquair Rd EH44 6PD**
email: info@traquairarmshotel.co.uk
dir: *From A72 (Peebles to Galashiels road) take B709 for St Mary's Loch & Traquair*

A taste of Italy in the Scottish Borders

Amidst heather-covered hills stands this imposing pub-hotel with a tranquil beer garden. Expect to share it with muddy mountain bikers – downhill and cross-country trails are right on the doorstep. It's one of only two places where you can drink Traquair Bear Ale, brewed a stone's throw away at Traquair House. The bar menu has dishes such as chicken and haggis with clapshot mash and whisky sauce; Aberdeen Angus sirloin; and fish pie. In the restaurant, an unusual combination of Scottish and Italian food is prepared by the resident Italian chef. Sample dishes include Italian sausage with borlotti beans, cherry tomatoes, toasted focaccia and salad; and roast haunch of Tweed Valley venison with garlic baby potatoes, root vegetables and a redcurrant jus.

Open all day all wk Closed 25 Dec **Food** Lunch Mon-Fri 12-2.30, Sat-Sun all day Dinner Mon-Fri 5-9, Sat-Sun all day ⊕ FREE HOUSE ◀ Caledonian Deuchars IPA, Timothy Taylor Landlord, Traquair Bear Ale. **Facilities** Non-diners area ❖ (Bar Garden) ❖❖ Children's menu Children's portions Garden ☴ Parking WiFi ☒

KELSO
Map 21 NT73

The Cobbles Freehouse & Dining ◉
PICK OF THE PUBS

See Pick of the Pubs on opposite page

PICK OF THE PUBS

The Cobbles Freehouse & Dining

KELSO   Map 21 NT73

tel: 01573 223548
7 Bowmont St TD5 7JH
email: info@thecobbleskelso.co.uk
web: www.thecobbleskelso.co.uk
dir: *A6089 from Edinburgh to Kelso, right at rdbt into Bowmont St. Pub in 0.3m*

Accomplished food and well-kept beers

Tucked away in a corner of the town's rather fine square stands this modernised 19th-century coaching inn. For the last few years it has taken on a new role as the brewery tap for proprietor Gavin Meiklejohn's Tempest Brewing Co established in Kelso in 2010. Gavin is married to Annika, Cobbles' landlady, and his real ales are always perfectly on song as they flow from the pumps in the log fire-warmed bar. The restaurant's AA Rosette was awarded for its mix of cuisines - British gastro-pub classics, Pacific Rim and modern European. Available in the bar are home-cured salmon, beetroot mayonnaise, caper and raisin purée with toasted wholemeal bread as well as daily blackboard specials. Dishes on the frequently changing restaurant menu feature Scottish fish and shellfish, local lamb, beef and pork, and game in season, thus starters may be Hardiesmill beef haggis bon bon, or Gouda gnocchi with spiced carrot purée; and possible main courses could be

crispy-skin fillet of sea bream, lemongrass and crab risotto; handmade burger of Borders wild roe deer, Standhill blue cheese and green peppercorn mayonnaise. Not far away in Galashiels is Overlangshaw Farmhouse, whence come the dessert ice creams, flavoured with butterscotch, pistachio and chocolate; alternatives include dark chocolate fondant, Tempest mocha ice cream and cherry purée; and apple pie parfait with hazelnut crumb and cinnamon doughnut. On Friday nights, starting at 10pm, the Kelso Folk & Live Music Club holds its weekly sessions in the restaurant. Acoustic guitarists are the mainstay, but pipes, accordion, bouzouki and many other instruments are also likely to appear. There is a private dining and function room.

Open all day all wk 11.30-11 Closed 25-26 Dec **Food** Lunch all wk 12-2.30 Dinner Mon-Sat 5.45-9, Sun 5.30-8.30 Av main course £9.95 Restaurant menu available Tue-Sat. ⊕ FREE HOUSE ◀ Tempest ♂ Thistly Cross.
Facilities Non-diners area ¶ Children's menu Children's portions Outside area ⊼ WiFi ▄▄▄ (notice required)

PICK OF THE PUBS

Burts Hotel ★★★ HL 🏵🏵

tel: 01896 822285
Market Square TD6 9PL
email: enquiries@burtshotel.co.uk
web: www.burtshotel.co.uk
dir: *From A68 N of St Boswells take A6091 towards Melrose. approx 2m right signed Melrose & B6374, follow to Market Sq*

Family-owned, town-centre stalwart

The Henderson family has owned this 18th-century hotel for some 40 years. Built overlooking the market square in 1722 by a local dignitary as a comfortable home for himself, its age dictates listed-building status, which restoration, extension and upgrading have all respected in the Hendersons' quest to provide all the refinements of a modern, first-class hotel. After a day out, perhaps visiting Sir Walter Scott's Abbotsford home, or the ruins of Melrose Abbey, where Robert the Bruce's heart lies buried, settle down with one of the 90 single malts, or a pint of Game Bird from the Scottish Borders Brewery on the Chesters Estate, near Hawick. Lying in the shadow of the Eildon Hills, the town is surrounded by the rich countryside and waters which provide much of the produce used in the kitchen. For lunch or dinner there's the Bistro Bar, where the menu may offer crayfish and smoked salmon cocktail;

and spiced lamb kebabs with pilau rice. The restaurant has held two AA Rosettes since 1995, thanks to dishes such as wild venison with haggis, neeps and tattie dauphinoise, confit butternut squash, and truffle shiitake mushroom jus; and roast halibut with spinach purée, samphire and olive salad, salsa verde and lemon croutons. Desserts too, including Borders soft berry bavarois with iced lavender parfait; and passion fruit mousse with caramelised pineapple and clementine sorbet. Even a quick look at the wine list reveals a wide choice from all over the world, and well-written tasting notes. Bedrooms, all with en suites, are appointed to a high standard.

Open all wk 12-2.30 5-11 **Food** Lunch all wk 12-2 Dinner served all wk 6-9.30 Av main course £13.95 Restaurant menu available Lunch Sat-Sun, Dinner all wk. 🍺 FREE HOUSE ◾ Caledonian Deuchars IPA & 80/-, Timothy Taylor Landlord, Fuller's London Pride, Scottish Borders Game Bird. 🍷 10
Facilities 🐾 (Bar Garden) 👨‍👧 Children's menu Children's portions Garden 🪑 Parking WiFi **Rooms** 20

KIRK YETHOLM
Map 21 NT82

The Border Hotel

tel: 01573 420237 **The Green TD5 8PQ**
email: borderhotel@aol.com
dir: *From A698 in Kelso take B6352 for 7m to Kirk Yetholm*

A homely place to stop awhile

Standing at the end of the 268-mile-long Pennine Way walk, this 18th-century former coaching inn is a welcoming and most hospitable place to revive after any journey, be it on foot or by car. Cracking pints of their own brew will slake parched throats and the traditional British menu, which features local game and farm meats, will satisfy healthy appetites. Try a Cullen skink, or breaded brie with redcurrant, port and orange coulis ahead of chicken, ham and wild mushroom pudding; or sausage and mash. Leave space for banoffee pie or apple crumble. The stone-flagged bar has a blazing winter log fire, and the conservatory dining room looks over the patio and beer garden.

Open all day all wk Closed 25-26 Dec **Food** Lunch all wk 12-2 Dinner all wk 6-8.30 (Winter), 6-9 (Summer) ⊕ FREE HOUSE ◀ Timothy Taylor Landlord, Greene King Abbott Ale, Border Brewery Pennine Pint (pub's own). **Facilities** Non-diners area ❀ (Bar Garden) ♦ Children's menu Children's portions Play area Garden ⅀ Parking WiFi 🚌 (notice required)

MELROSE
Map 21 NT53

Burts Hotel ★★★ HL ⊚⊚
PICK OF THE PUBS

See Pick of the Pubs on opposite page

NEWCASTLETON
Map 21 NY48

Liddesdale ★★★★ INN

tel: 01387 375255 **17 Douglas Square TD9 0QD**
email: reception@theliddesdalehotel.co.uk **web:** www.theliddesdalehotel.co.uk
dir: *In village centre*

Set amidst beautiful countryside

This inn, under new ownership, sits in Douglas Square at the heart of Newcastleton (sometimes referred to as Copshaw Holm), a 17th-century village planned by the third Duke of Buccleuch. An ideal base for exploring the unspoiled countryside in this area, the inn has a bar stocked with over 20 malt whiskies and a different cask-conditioned ale every week in the summer. The menu is full of pub favourites – steak and ale pie; beef, chicken or prawn curry; breaded Whitby scampi; and apple and cinnamon crumble.

Open all day all wk **Food** Lunch all wk 12-2 Dinner Mon-Thu 5-8, Fri-Sun 5-8.30 Av main course £9.95 Set menu available Restaurant menu available Fri-Sun ⊕ FREE HOUSE ◀ Samuel Smith's ○ Samuel Smith's Organic. ⚑ 9 **Facilities** Non-diners area ❀ (Bar Garden) ♦ Children's menu Children's portions Garden ⅀ Beer festival Parking WiFi 🚌 (notice required) **Rooms** 6

ST BOSWELLS
Map 21 NT53

Buccleuch Arms Hotel

tel: 01835 822243 **The Green TD6 0EW**
email: info@buccleucharms.com
dir: *On A68, 10m N of Jedburgh. Hotel on village green*

Friendly hotel serving local food

Originally an inn catering for the fox-hunting aristocracy, this smart and friendly country-house hotel dates from the 16th century. Set beside the village cricket pitch, it's an attractive brick and stone building with an immaculate garden. Inside, the large and comfortable lounge is warmed by a log fire in winter, while the spacious enclosed garden comes into its own during the warmer months. Extensive menus are served in the Blue Coo Bistro, where the focus is on local meat dishes, and in particular steaks from local farms.

Open all day all wk 12-11 Closed 25 Dec **Food** Lunch all wk 12-2.30 Dinner Sun-Thu 5.30-9, Fri-Sat 5.30-9.30 Restaurant menu available all wk ⊕ FREE HOUSE ◀ Scottish Borders Brewery Ales, Belhaven Best. ⚑ **Facilities** Non-diners area ❀ (Bar Garden) ♦ Children's menu Children's portions Play area Garden ⅀ Parking WiFi 🚌 (notice required)

SWINTON
Map 21 NT84

The Wheatsheaf at Swinton
PICK OF THE PUBS

See Pick of the Pubs on page 614

TIBBIE SHIELS INN
Map 21 NT22

Tibbie Shiels Inn
PICK OF THE PUBS

tel: 01750 42231 **St Mary's Loch TD7 5LH**
email: tibbieshiels@hotmail.com
dir: *From Moffat take A708. Inn 14m on right*

Superbly located famous old inn

The first thing any first-time visitor to this lovely white-painted old inn between two lochs wants to know is: who was Tibbie Shiels? She was a young widow who, determined to support herself and her six bairns, took in lodgers and became the first licensee, catering in due course to Sir Walter Scott, Thomas Carlyle and Robert Louis Stevenson. Her spirit still keeps watch over the bar, which serves a real ale named after her, together with over 50 malt whiskies. The majority of the ingredients used in the kitchen are local, including venison, pheasant, partridge, hill-raised lamb and garden-grown herbs. Sandwiches, salads, ploughman's and paninis are all on offer, while the main menu lists Scottish smoked salmon on toasted crumpet; chicken, leek and smoked bacon pie; battered haddock and chips; and macaroni cheese. Evening events, including live music, take place throughout the year.

Open all day 8am-mdnt Closed Wed **Food** Lunch Thu-Tue 12-3.30 Dinner Thu-Tue 5.30-9 Av main course £10 ⊕ FREE HOUSE ◀ Belhaven 80/-, Broughton Greenmantle Ale, Tibbie Shiels Ale & The Reiver ○ Westons Stowford Press. **Facilities** Non-diners area ❀ (Bar Garden) ♦ Children's menu Children's portions Play area Garden ⅀ Parking WiFi 🚌 (notice required)

PICK OF THE PUBS

The Wheatsheaf at Swinton

Main St TD11 3JJ
tel: 01890 860257
email: reception@wheatsheaf-swinton.co.uk
web: www.wheatsheaf-swinton.co.uk
dir: *From Edinburgh A697 onto B6461. From East Lothian A1 onto B6461*

Scottish hospitality and locally sourced food

Husband and wife team Chris and Jan Winson have built up an impressive reputation for their dining destination in this attractive village. Whether you choose to eat in the Sun Room or the Dining Room, the latter overlooking the village green, the menus feature homemade food using locally sourced produce, including daily delivered fresh seafood from Eyemouth 12 miles away, and beef from livestock raised on the surrounding Borders pastures. Also likely to appear, according to the season, are wild salmon, venison, partridge, pheasant, woodcock and duck. The bar and garden menu is likely to offer a club sandwich, steak-and-ale pie and beefburger. A restaurant meal might start with pan-seared woodland pigeon breast, Stornoway black pudding purée, crispy apple and light game jus; or home-made Thai crab cake with sweet chilli sauce. Head chef John Forrestier, from Nancy in France, specialises in fish, so a main course definitely worth considering is his baked

Dover sole with scallop mousse, clams, beurre blanc and pickled cockle salad. Alternatives might include roast Scottish venison with celeriac purée, seared poached pears, rösti potato and light beetroot and chocolate sauce; or pan-seared goats' cheese gnocchi and morel mushroom fricassée, buttered kale and truffle oil. Other regular meat dishes include oven-roast pork fillet, and slow-braised Borders beef blade. Finally, a couple of the desserts: glazed pomegranate tart and lemon sorbet; and baked Malteser cheesecake with passionfruit coulis. The bar stocks Belhaven IPA, draught Peroni, plus Stewart Brewery and Scottish Borders Brewery bottled beers. Here too is a whisky map and tasting notes to study before choosing your single malt.

Open 4-11 (Sat 12-12 Sun 12-11) Closed 23-24 & 26 Dec, 2-3 Jan, Mon-Fri L **Food** Sat 12-3 Mon-Sat 6-9 Sun 12-4 6-8.30 ⊕ FREE HOUSE ◖ Belhaven IPA, Belhaven, Scottish Borders Gamebird & Foxy Blonde, Stewart Brewing Hollyrood, Peroni.
Facilities ⊪ Garden Parking

STIRLING

CALLANDER
Map 20 NN60

The Lade Inn

tel: 01877 330152 **Kilmahog FK17 8HD**
email: info@theladeinn.com
dir: *From Stirling take A84 to Callander. 1m N of Callander, left at Kilmahog Woollen Mills onto A821 towards Aberfoyle. Pub immediately on left*

Warming fires in winter, a garden in summer

In the heart of the Trossachs National Park, the stone-built Lade Inn is part of the surrounding Leny Estate, built as a tearoom in 1935. The family-owned and run inn is known for its own real ales and for its 10-day beer festival in late August/early September. There is also an on-site real ale shop selling bottled ales from microbreweries throughout Scotland. The home-cooked menu offers many smaller portions and allergen-free dishes. A typical menu offers crispy battered haggis balls with creamy whisky sauce; vegetable lasagna; pork and leek sausages; and steak and ale pie. The beer garden with its three ponds and bird-feeding station is great for families.

Open all day all wk **Food** Lunch Mon-Sat 12-9, Sun 12.30-9 Dinner Mon-Sat 12-9, Sun 12.30-9 Set menu available ⊕ FREE HOUSE ◖ Waylade, LadeBack & LadeOut, Belhaven Best, Tennent's ☼ Thistly Cross. ⚑ 9 **Facilities** Non-diners area ❤ (Bar Garden) ♦ Children's menu Children's portions Play area Family room Garden ⊫ Beer festival Parking WiFi ▭ (notice required)

DRYMEN
Map 20 NS48

The Clachan Inn

tel: 01360 660824 **2 Main St G63 0BG**
email: info@clachaninndrymen.co.uk
dir: *Phone for detailed directions*

Scottish hospitality stretching back over the years

Established in 1734, The Clachan Inn is believed to be the oldest licensed pub in Scotland; this quaint white-painted cottage on the West Highland Way was once owned by Rob Roy's sister. Family-run for over 30 years the bar stocks frequently changing guest ales while a warming log fire keeps things cosy. More comfort comes with the food – choose from pub favourites such as deep-fried potato skins with dips; jumbo sausage with baked beans and chips; and home-made toffee sponge pudding.

Open all day all wk 11am-mdnt (Fri-Sat 11am-1am Sun 12-12) Closed 25 Dec & 1 Jan **Food** Lunch Mon-Sat 12-3.45, Sun 12.30-3.45 Dinner Mon-Sat 6-9.45, Sun 5-9.45 ⊕ FREE HOUSE ◖ Harviestoun Bitter & Twisted, Cairngorm Trade Winds, Guinness. ⚑ 9 **Facilities** Non-diners area ❤ (Bar) ♦ Children's menu Children's portions WiFi ▭ (notice required)

KIPPEN
Map 20 NS69

Cross Keys Hotel

tel: 01786 870293 **Main St FK8 3DN**
email: info@kippencrosskeys.co.uk
dir: *10m W of Stirling, 20m from Loch Lomond off A811*

Warming fires in winter, a garden in summer

The 300-year-old Cross Keys stands on Kippen's Main Street and offers seasonally changing menus and a good pint of cask ale. The pub's welcoming interior, warmed by three log fires, is perfect for resting your feet after a walk in nearby Burnside Wood, or you can sit in the garden when the weather permits. The menu takes in chestnut mushroom and pea risotto with toasted pumpkin seeds; squash, spinach and chickpea curry; steak and cheese sour dough sandwich with rocket and sweet onion, and a good range of pub classics, perhaps steak and ale pie, burger and chips, and bangers and mash. Dogs are welcome in the top bar.

Open all wk 12-3 5-11 (Fri 12-3 5-1am Sat noon-1am Sun 12-12) Closed 25 Dec & 1 Jan **Food** Lunch Mon-Fri 12-3, Sat 12-9, Sun 12-8 Dinner Mon-Fri 5-9, Sat 12-9, Sun 12-8 ⊕ FREE HOUSE ◖ Belhaven Best, Harviestoun Bitter & Twisted, Fallen Brewing Co 1703 Archie's amber, Guinness, Guest ales ☼ Addlestones. ⚑ 10 **Facilities** Non-diners area ❤ (Bar Garden) ♦ Children's menu Children's portions Play area Family room Garden ⊫ Parking WiFi ▭ (notice required)

The Inn at Kippen
PICK OF THE PUBS

tel: 01786 870500 **Fore Rd FK8 3DT**
email: info@theinnatkippen.co.uk
dir: *From Stirling take A811 to Loch Lomond. 1st left at Kippen station rdbt, 1st right into Fore Rd. Inn on left*

Welcoming pub with quality approach to local ales and food

A traditional white-painted free house in a picturesque village at the foot of the Campsie Hills; views across the Forth Valley to the Highlands are stunning. Now in the capable hands of new owners Mark Silverwood and Alice Lethbridge, the inn is enjoying a resurgent popularity based on its Fallen Brewing Company and Loch Lomond ales, and a menu that combines classic simplicity with high-quality ingredients and fair prices. Beef, pork and lamb all come from Cairnhill farms, game from local estates, and seafood from Scottish waters. In the winter months you'll be warmed by lovely wood fires and entertained by the locals in the stylish bar. If you're a summer visitor, settle in the pretty garden while choosing from the likes of Cullen skink; Kinloch Rannoch charcuterie of smoked venison, cured duck and smoked beef; and beer battered haddock landed at Scrabster. On the dinner specials list, look out for Ayrshire pork three ways.

Open all day all wk **Food** Lunch all wk 12-2.30 Dinner all wk 5-9 ⊕ FREE HOUSE ◖ Fallen, Loch Lomond ☼ Addlestones. ⚑ 9 **Facilities** Non-diners area ❤ (Bar Garden) ♦ Children's menu Children's portions Garden ⊫ Parking WiFi ▭ (notice required)

SCOTTISH ISLANDS

ISLE OF COLL

ARINAGOUR
Map 22 NM25

Coll Hotel
PICK OF THE PUBS

tel: 01879 230334 **PA78 6SZ**
email: info@collhotel.com
dir: *Ferry from Oban. Hotel at head of Arinagour Bay, 1m from Pier (collections by arrangement)*

Great for local seafood

With stunning views over the sea to Jura and Mull Being the Isle of Coll's only inn it is, naturally, the hub of the island community. Come to this hotel to mingle with the locals, soak in the atmosphere, and enjoy pints of Fyne Ale and malt whiskies. In the summer months the fabulous garden acts as an extension to the bar or the Gannet Restaurant; watch the yachts coming and going while enjoying a glass of Pimm's or something from the global wine selection. Fresh produce is landed and delivered from around the island every day and features on the specials board. Famed for its seafood, you'll find it in dishes such as seared Coll crab cakes with wasabi mayonnaise, and a pot of Connel mussels in garlic and cream. Among the non-fish options, try the venison fillet in redcurrant sauce or steak and ale pie.

Open all day all wk **Food** Lunch all wk 12-2 Dinner all wk 6-9 Av main course £13 ⊕ FREE HOUSE ◀ Fyne Ales. **Facilities** Non-diners area ◀ Children's menu Children's portions Play area Garden ⋒ Parking WiFi ▭ (notice required)

ISLE OF ISLAY

PORT CHARLOTTE
Map 20 NR25

The Port Charlotte Hotel

tel: 01496 850360 **Main St PA48 7TU**
email: info@portcharlottehotel.co.uk
dir: *From Port Askaig take A846 towards Bowmore. Right onto A847, through Blackrock. Take unclassified road to Port Charlotte*

Beachside hotel displaying Scottish art

In an attractive conservation village, this sympathetically restored Victorian hotel is perfectly positioned on the west shore of Loch Indaal. A large conservatory opens out into the garden and directly onto the beach. Lovers of Scottish art will enjoy the work on display in the lounge and public bar. Islay ales and whiskies make a great way to warm up before enjoying menus focusing on local seafood – perhaps half an Islay lobster or oven-baked wild halibut steak. From the restaurant menu, try the lavender crème brûlée for dessert.

Open all day all wk Closed 24-26 Dec **Food** Lunch all wk 12-2 Dinner all wk 6-9 Restaurant menu available all wk ⊕ FREE HOUSE ◀ Islay ♂ Somersby Cider. ₹ 9 **Facilities** Non-diners area ◀ (Garden) ◀ Children's menu Children's portions Play area Family room Garden ⋒ Parking WiFi ▭

ISLE OF MULL

DERVAIG
Map 22 NM45

The Bellachroy Hotel

tel: 01688 400225 **PA75 6QW**
email: info@thebellachroy.co.uk
dir: *Take ferry from Oban to Craignure. A849 towards Tobermory. Left at T-junct onto B8073 to Dervaig*

Oldest inn on Mull specialising in local seafood

Near the foot of a hill road over from Mull's capital, Tobermory, and yards from the pretty sea loch Loch a' Chumhainn, the island's oldest hotel can trace its roots back to 1608. Today's visitors come to experience the wildlife including white-tailed sea eagles, which may well fly overhead as a pint of Fyne Avalanche is being enjoyed on the terrace in front of the inn. The new owners, who arrived in 2013, ensure that the chefs here take full advantage of the generous bounty from Mull's coastal waters and moors. Crab, mackerel and locally smoked haddock all feature on the menus, as does their very popular seafood chowder. Venison and juniper casserole; Ulva lamb shank or a vegetarian platter cater for non-seafood fans.

Open all day all wk **Food** Lunch all wk 12-2.30 Dinner all wk 6-8.30 ⊕ FREE HOUSE ◀ Fyne Avalanche, Highlander. **Facilities** Non-diners area ◀ (Bar Garden) ◀ Children's menu Children's portions Garden ⋒ Parking WiFi ▭ (notice required)

ORKNEY

STROMNESS
Map 24 HY20

Ferry Inn

tel: 01856 850280 **John St KW16 3AD**
email: info@ferryinn.com
dir: *Opposite ferry terminal*

Enjoy island ales overlooking the harbour

With its prominent harbour-front location, the Ferry Inn has long enjoyed a reputation for local ales. The pub has racking for a further ten island ales on top of the five handpulls on the bar and although the beers change regularly look out for the island's own Dark Island and Skull Splitter. If beer isn't your thing, there are plenty of wines and malt whiskies to choose from, as well as an appealing menu that can include haggis and clapshot with whisky sauce or an Orkney seafood platter.

Open all day all wk 9am-mdnt (Thu-Sat 9am-1am Sun 9.30am-mdnt) Closed 25 Dec & 1 Jan **Food** Lunch all wk 11.45-5 Dinner all wk 5-9.30 Av main course £9.95 Restaurant menu available all wk ⊕ FREE HOUSE ◀ Highland Scapa Special & Orkney IPA, Orkney Corncrake, Dark Island & Skull Splitter. **Facilities** Non-diners area ◀ Children's menu Children's portions Outside area ⋒ Parking WiFi ▭

ISLE OF SKYE

ARDVASAR
Map 22 NG60

Ardvasar Hotel ★★★ SHL

tel: 01471 844223 **IV45 8RS**
email: richard@ardvasar-hotel.demon.co.uk web: www.ardvasarhotel.com
dir: *From ferry terminal, 50yds & turn left*

Homely, welcoming and serving excellent Skye produce

Beside the road towards the southern tip of Skye, sit out front to drink in the extraordinary views to the rocky foreshore, Sound of Sleat and the mountains of the Knoydart Peninsula, a ferry ride away via Mallaig. Once you've sipped your Skye-brewed beer or local malt, retire to the comfy lounge bar or dining room to indulge in some of Skye's most renowned seafood meals; the local boats may land salmon, crab, lobster or scallops. Estate venison and Aberdeen Angus beef extend the choice. Residents in the individually designed rooms can look to a fine Scottish breakfast to set another day in paradise off to a good start.

Open all day all wk 11am-mdnt (Sun 12-11) **Food** Lunch all wk 12-2.30 Dinner all wk 5-9 ⊕ FREE HOUSE ◀ Isle of Skye Red Cuillin. **Facilities** Non-diners area ◀ Children's menu Children's portions Garden ⋒ Parking **Rooms** 10

■ CARBOST   Map 22 NG33

The Old Inn and Waterfront Bunkhouse PICK OF THE PUBS

tel: 01478 640205 **IV47 8SR**
email: enquiries@theoldinnskye.co.uk **web:** www.theoldinnskye.co.uk
dir: *From Skye Bridge follow A87 N. Take A863, then B8009 to inn*

Free house attracting locals, tourists and hill walkers

The Old Inn and Waterfront Bunkhouse, on the shores of Loch Harport near the Talisker distillery, is a charming, 200-year-old island cottage very popular among the walking and climbing fraternity. Arrive early for a table on the waterside patio and savour the breathtaking views of the Cuillin Hills with a pint of Hebridean ale in hand. Inside, open fires welcome winter visitors, and live Highland music is a regular feature most weekends. The menu includes daily home-cooked specials with numerous fresh fish dishes such as local prawns and oysters, and mackerel from the loch. A typical choice could start with crispy confit duck leg salad or hot smoked salmon with Achmore crème fraîche; continue with a chargrilled Highland sirloin steak or Thai green vegetable curry; and finish with home-made rice pudding with dried apricots, raisins and toasted almonds.

Open all day all wk Mon-Fri 11am-1am (Sat 11am-12.30am Sun 12.30-11.30) **Food** Lunch all wk 12-9 Dinner all wk 12-9 ⊕ FREE HOUSE ◀ Isle of Skye Red Cuillin & Black Cuillin, Cuillin Skye Ale & Pinnacle Ale, Hebridean. **Facilities** Non-diners area ✿ (Bar Restaurant Garden) ◀ Children's portions Family room Garden ☶ Parking WiFi ▭

■ ISLEORNSAY   Map 22 NG71

Hotel Eilean Iarmain ★★★ SHL ◉◉   PICK OF THE PUBS

tel: 01471 833332 **IV43 8QR**
email: hotel@eilean-iarmain.co.uk **web:** www.eilean-iarmain.co.uk
dir: *A851, A852 right to Isleornsay harbour*

Hebridean charm in spectacular setting

There's masses of Highland character at this well known hotel with its own pier overlooking Sleat Sound and the Knoydart Hills beyond. Step inside to find tartan carpets and stag antlers in the hallway, whilst elsewhere the decor is mainly cotton and linen chintzes with traditional furniture. More a small private hotel than a pub, the bar and restaurant ensure that the standards of food and drinks served here are exacting – the Gaelic Whiskies company is based here so sample a 'wee dram' or two. The head chef declares, 'We never accept second best, it shines through in the standard of food served in our restaurant'. Here you can try dishes like haggis pakora, cumin yogurt, orbost leaves; venison burger, caramelised onions, tomato relish, chips and cabbage slaw; and goats' cheese and orange salad. Half portions are served for children.

Open all day all wk 11am-11.30pm (Thu 11am-12.30am Fri 11am-1am Sat 11am-12.30am Sun 12-11.30) **Food** Lunch all wk 12-2.30 Dinner all wk 5.30-9 Av main course £15.95 Restaurant menu available all wk ⊕ FREE HOUSE ◀ McEwan's 80/-, Isle of Skye, Guinness. **Facilities** Non-diners area ◀ Children's menu Children's portions Garden ☶ Parking WiFi ▭ (notice required) **Rooms** 16

■ STEIN   Map 22 NG25

Stein Inn

tel: 01470 592362 **Macleod's Ter IV55 8GA**
email: angus.teresa@steininn.co.uk **web:** www.steininn.co.uk
dir: *A87 from Portree. In 5m take A850 for 15m. Right onto B886, 3m to T-junct. Turn left*

Skye's oldest inn amid beautiful scenery

If your travels take you to Skye, then you just have to visit the Waternish peninsula and the island's oldest inn, for slap-bang in front of it, across a grassy foreshore, are the beautiful waters of Loch Bay. The wood-panelled bar, with peat fire a-smouldering, stocks 125 malts and Reeling Deck beer from the Isle of Skye Brewery. Daily-changing menus take full advantage of the abundant fresh fish and shellfish, sheep, wild deer and Highland cattle, with choices including peat smoked Scottish salmon; 6oz Highland venison burger; and home-braised steak in ale casserole. Home-made apple and blueberry crumble and custard makes a great finish to a meal.

Open all day all wk 11am-mdnt Closed 25 Dec, 1 Jan **Food** Lunch all wk 12-4 Dinner all wk 6-9.30 ⊕ FREE HOUSE ◀ Isle of Skye Red Cuillin & Reeling Deck, Cairngorm Trade Winds, Caledonian Deuchars IPA, Orkney Dark Island. ♟ 9
Facilities Non-diners area ✿ (Bar Garden) ◀ Children's menu Children's portions Play area Family room Garden Parking WiFi ▭

SOUTH UIST

■ LOCHBOISDALE   Map 22 NF71

The Polochar Inn

tel: 01878 700215 **Polochar HS8 5TT**
email: polocharinn@aol.com
dir: *W from Lochboisdale, take B888. Hotel at end of road*

Cosy island pub overlooking the Sound

Standing virtually alone overlooking the Sound of Eriskay and a prehistoric standing stone, this white-painted inn is the former change-house, where travellers waited for the ferry to Barra. Owned by sisters Morag MacKinnon and Margaret Campbell, it serves Hebridean real ales and specialises in local seafood and meats, as well as pasta dishes, all made with fresh, seasonal ingredients and served in a dining room with outstanding views of the sea. The beer garden is the ideal spot for dolphin watching and for admiring the beautiful sunsets. On summer Saturday nights the sound of live music fills the bar.

Open all day all wk 11-11 (Fri-Sat 11am-1am Sun 12.30pm-1am) **Food** Lunch Mon-Sat 12.30-8.30, Sun 1-8.30 (winter all wk 12-2.30) Dinner Mon-Sat 12.30-8.30, Sun 1-8.30 (winter all wk 5-8.30) ⊕ FREE HOUSE ◀ Hebridean, Guest ales.
Facilities Non-diners area ◀ Children's menu Children's portions Family room Garden ☶ Parking WiFi ▭ (notice required)

Wales

ISLE OF ANGLESEY

BEAUMARIS — Map 14 SH67

Ye Olde Bulls Head Inn ★★★★★ INN ◉◉◉

PICK OF THE PUBS

tel: 01248 810329 **Castle St LL58 8AP**
email: info@bullsheadinn.co.uk **web:** www.bullsheadinn.co.uk
dir: *From Britannia Road Bridge follow A545. Inn in town centre*

Historic and award-winning inn on the island's coast

This 15th-century pub started life as a staging post and inn on the route to Ireland; it's just a stone's throw from the gates of Beaumaris' medieval castle. The bar transports drinkers back to Dickensian times (the man himself stayed here) with settles and antique furnishings; artefacts include the town's old ducking stool. The Bull's location in the midst of a rich larder of seafood and Welsh livestock farms has inspired the multi-talented kitchen team to produce exceptional menus, well deserving of three AA Rosettes. The light and airy Brasserie, moulded from the former stables, serves a good range of modern global dishes such as hotpot of smoked haddock, tomatoes, cream and parmesan; and grilled fillets of rainbow trout with black pasta. Push the boat out in the intimate Loft Restaurant with roast crown of quail with parmesan gnocchi, followed by pan-fried monkfish with split yellow peas, fondant potato, black kale, brown shrimp and capers.

Open all day all wk Closed 25 Dec **Food** Lunch Mon-Sat 12-2, Sun 12-3 Dinner 6-9 Av main course £14 Set menu available Restaurant menu available all wk ⊕ FREE HOUSE ◀ Bass, Hancock's, Guest ales. ▼ 20 **Facilities** Non-diners area ❤ (Bar) ◀◀ Children's menu Children's portions Parking WiFi **Rooms** 26

LLANFAETHLU — Map 14 SH38

NEW The Black Lion Inn

tel: 01407 730718 **LL65 4NL**
email: blacklion.admin@blacklionanglesey.co.uk
dir: *From A55 junct 3, A5 signed Valley. In Valley at lights right (A5025), 5m to pub on right*

An object lesson in pub restoration

Derelict in 2011 when they bought this mid-terrace pub, locals Leigh and Mari Faulkner restored it using slate and reclaimed oak, then filled it with auction-bought furniture. Even an old water trough found a new home. Now it has a snug, a patio, a bar with Welsh guest ales, and a dining room with views of Snowdonia. Sourcing all food on Anglesey can be tricky, but luckily Mari's father and uncle raise livestock, mussels dwell in the Menai Strait, and fruit and vegetables do grow here. Mains (prif gwrs) include double-cooked slow-roasted pork belly; and salmon, dill and natural-smoked haddock fishcakes.

Open all day in holiday season Closed 10 days Jan, Mon & Tue Nov-Mar **Food** Lunch 12-2.30, Sat all day, Sun 12-4 Dinner 6-8.30, Sat all day Av main course £13 Set menu available ⊕ FREE HOUSE ◀ Marston's Pedigree & EPA, Local guest ales ♻ Thatchers Gold. **Facilities** Non-diners area ❤ (Bar Outside area) ◀◀ Children's menu Children's portions Outside area ➤ Parking WiFi ➡ (notice required)

RED WHARF BAY — Map 14 SH58

The Ship Inn — PICK OF THE PUBS

tel: 01248 852568 **LL75 8RJ**
dir: *Phone for detailed directions*

A walkers' favourite with lovely views

Wading birds flock here to feed on the extensive sands of Red Wharf Bay, making the Ship's waterside beer garden a birdwatcher's paradise on warm days. In the Kenneally family's hands for over 40 years, the pub faces east on the lee side of a hill, sheltered from prevailing winds and catching the morning and afternoon sun

perfectly. Before the age of steam, sailing ships landed cargo here from all over the world; now the boats bring fresh Conwy Bay fish and seafood to the kitchens of this traditional free house. Real ales are carefully tended and a single menu applies to both bars and restaurant. Typical starters include a charred bundle of asparagus with a balsamic and honey dressing; and frittata of locally reared duck egg with curried mayonnaise and seasonal salad. Move on to bangers and mash with onion gravy or a minted lamb burger with sour cream, chips and a Greek-style side salad. Other options include lunchtime sandwiches and wraps and a separate children's menu.

Open all day all wk **Food** Lunch all wk 12-2.30 Dinner all wk 6-9 ⊕ FREE HOUSE ◀ Conwy Rampart, Adnams, Guest ales ♻ Westons Wyld Wood Organic. **Facilities** Non-diners area ❤ (Bar Garden) ◀◀ Children's menu Children's portions Play area Family room Garden ➤ Parking WiFi

BRIDGEND

KENFIG — Map 9 SS88

Prince of Wales Inn

tel: 01656 740356 **CF33 4PR**
email: prince-of-wales@btconnect.com
dir: *M4 junct 37 into North Cornelly. Left at x-rds, follow signs for Kenfig & Porthcawl. Pub 600yds on right*

Inn with an intriguing history

Thought to be one of the most haunted pubs in Wales, this 16th-century stone-built free house was formerly the seat of local government for the lost city of Kenfig. Just as remarkably, it is also the only pub in Britain to have held a Sunday school continuously from 1857 to 2000. Welsh brunch, and beef and traditional Welsh ale pie are amongst the local dishes on the menu, and the daily blackboard specials are also worth attention. In the summer of 2013, HRH The Prince of Wales visited his namesake pub, which is part of his The Pub is the Hub organisation, and enjoyed half a pint.

Open all day all wk **Food** Lunch Tue-Sat 12-2.30, Sun 12-3 Dinner Tue-Sat 6-8.30 ⊕ FREE HOUSE ◀ Bass, Sharp's Doom Bar, Worthington's, Local Guest ales ♻ Gwynt y Ddraig Happy Daze, Tomos Watkin Taffy Apples. **Facilities** Non-diners area ❤ (Bar Garden) ◀◀ Children's menu Children's portions Garden ➤ Beer festival Parking WiFi ➡ (notice required)

CARDIFF

CREIGIAU — Map 9 ST08

Caesars Arms — PICK OF THE PUBS

tel: 029 2089 0486 **Cardiff Rd CF15 9NN**
email: info@caesarsarms.co.uk
dir: *M4 junct 34, A4119 towards Llantrisant/Rhondda. Approx 0.5m right at lights signed Groesfaen. Through Groesfaen, past Dynevor Arms pub. Next left, signed Creigiau. 1m, left at T-junct, pass Creigiau Golf Course. Pub 1m on left*

Country dining inn and farm shop handy for Cardiff

'Stumps' were called on the former village cricket pitch some time ago here in the rolling countryside northwest of Cardiff. Polytunnels, vegetable gardens and a smallholding now populate the site, supplying a huge variety of greens, rare breed pork, honey, smoked meats and fish to the adjoining thriving farm shop (the former cricket pavilion) as well as the enterprising country pub itself. The chefs here pride themselves in offering a progressive, modern menu combined with some old favourites, with seafood and exotic fish creating a good range of signature dishes which vary depending on the catch available. Sea bream, turbot or red mullet may feature, whilst a particular favourite is sea bass baked in rock salt then filleted at your table. Welsh game, beef and lamb satisfy the more traditional demands on the menu, whilst free-range chicken and duck come from Madgetts Farm in the Wye

Valley. An extensive, quality wine list ensures that finding the perfect companion to your chosen main meal will be a breeze.

Open 12-2.30 6-10 (Sun 12-4) Closed 25-26 Dec, 1 Jan, Sun eve **Food** Lunch Mon-Sat 12-2.30 ⊕ FREE HOUSE ◀ Felinfoel Double Dragon, Brains Smooth, Guinness ⌂ Gwynt y Ddraig Orchard Gold. **Facilities** Non-diners area ⬩ Children's menu Children's portions Garden ⋒ Parking ▰ (notice required)

GWAELOD-Y-GARTH   Map 9 ST18

Gwaelod-y-Garth Inn

tel: 029 2081 0408 & 07855 313247 **Main Rd CF15 9HH**
email: gwaeloinn@outlook.com
dir: From M4 junct 32, N on A470, left at next exit, at rdbt turn right 0.5m. Right into village

Friendly pub in good walking country with own ales

This stone-built hillside cottage enjoys a wonderful position on the thickly wooded flank of Garth Hill, high above Taffs Well, with great walking and stunning views such as the fairytale Victorian sham castle of Castell Coch across the vale. At the bar guest ales from as far afield as Essex and Derbyshire rub shoulders with local brews, including some from their own microbrewery Violet Cottage, along with a farm cider from Pontypridd. A pleasing selection of home-cooked pub food produces dishes of grilled sea bass fillets on braised fennel, and Welsh Black steak and ale pie with puff pastry.

Open all day all wk 11am-mdnt (Sun 12-11) **Food** Lunch Mon-Thu 12-2, Fri-Sat 11-9, Sun 12-3.30 Dinner Mon-Thu 6.30-9, Fri-Sat 11-9 ⊕ FREE HOUSE ◀ Wye Valley Bitter, Swansea Three Cliffs Gold, RCH Pitchfork, Crouch Vale Brewers Gold, Thornbridge Jaipur, Gower Brewery Co, Tiny Rebel, Violet Cottage Shine On, Total Eclipse & Zig Zag ⌂ Local cider, Gwynt-y-Ddraig. ▾ 10 **Facilities** Non-diners area ⬩ (Bar Garden) ⬩ Children's menu Children's portions Garden ⋒ Parking WiFi ▰

PENTYRCH   Map 9 ST18

Kings Arms

tel: 029 2089 0202 **22 Church Rd CF15 9QF**
email: kingsarmspentyrch@gmail.com
dir: M4 junct 32, A470 (Merthyr Tydfil). Left onto B4262 signed Radyr then Pentyrch. Right at rdbt for Pentyrch. Or M4 junct 34, A4119 (dual carriageway) signed Llantrisant & Rhondda. Into right lane, right at lights signed Groes Farm. Left to Pentyrch

Traditional Welsh longhouse pub

In a leafy village on the outskirts of Cardiff, this Grade II listed pub is full of traditional features, from the flagstoned snug to the exposed lime-washed walls and log fire of the lounge. The restaurant opens out onto the lovely landscaped gardens. Local brewery Brains supplies the real ales while there is also a choice of New and Old World wines. Promoting seasonal Welsh produce, the menus and daily blackboard specials could include a Severn and Wye Valley smoked mackerel foccacia sandwich; confit leg of free-range duck; and loin of pork with a sage and black pudding crust. The Sunday roasts are very popular.

Open all day all wk **Food** Lunch Mon-Fri 12-3, Sat all day, Sun 12-4 Dinner Mon-Fri 5.30-9.30, Sat all day Set menu available Restaurant menu available Tue-Sun ◀ Brains Bitter, Guest ales ⌂ Symonds. **Facilities** Non-diners area ⬩ (Bar Garden) ⬩ Children's menu Children's portions Garden ⋒ Parking WiFi ▰ (notice required)

CARMARTHENSHIRE

ABERGORLECH   Map 8 SN53

The Black Lion

tel: 01558 685271 **SA32 7SN**
email: georgerashbrook@hotmail.com
dir: A40 E from Carmarthen, then B4310 signed Brechfa & Abergorlech

Cosy black and white pub in charming Welsh countryside

A drive through the pretty Cothi Valley brings you to this attractive, 16th-century village pub run by George and Louise Rashbrook. Louise does all the cooking and George wisely gives her generous credit for doing so. You can eat from an extensive menu in the flagstoned bar, while the evening menu in the more modern, candlelit dining room offers beef, almond, mint and lemon casserole; mustard-stuffed chicken in bacon; scampi and chips; and mushroom, brie and cranberry Wellington. The lovely beer garden overlooks a Roman bridge.

Open 12-3 7-11 (Sat-Sun & BH all day) Closed Mon (ex BHs) **Food** Lunch Tue-Sun 12-2.30 Dinner Tue-Sun 7-9 ⊕ FREE HOUSE ◀ Rhymney ⌂ Westons Stowford Press, Gwynt-y-Ddraig. **Facilities** Non-diners area ❀ (Bar Garden Outside area) ⬩ Children's menu Children's portions Garden Outside area ⋒ Parking WiFi ▰ (notice required)

LLANDDAROG   Map 8 SN51

Butchers Arms

tel: 01267 275330 **SA32 8NS**
email: b5dmj@aol.com
dir: From A48 between Carmarthen & Cross Hands follow Llanddarog/B4310 signs. Pub adjacent to church

Pretty pub with longstanding, enthusiastic owners

Well into their third decade here, David and Mavis James's success story continues. David runs his kitchen with unconcealed enthusiasm, making good use of locally sourced ingredients to provide pleasing home-made food. Admire the Toby jug collection, order a pint of Felinfoel Cambrian Bitter or Celtic Pride, then contemplate a traditional lunch of beef and ale pie with chips, or in the evening honey-roast boneless duck with orange and Grand Marnier sauce; a sizzling platter of king tiger prawns in garlic butter; or mushroom Stroganoff. Most children's dishes include chips and some of the ice creams come with a novelty toy.

Open 12-3 6-11 Closed 24-26 Dec, Sun & Mon **Food** Lunch Tue-Sat 12-2.30 Dinner Tue-Sat 6-9.30 Av main course £10 Restaurant menu available Tue-Sat ⊕ FREE HOUSE ◀ Felinfoel Cambrian Bitter, Double Dragon, Celtic Pride. ▾ 10 **Facilities** Non-diners area ❀ (Garden) ⬩ Children's menu Garden ⋒ WiFi ▰ (notice required)

Find out more about this country with the AA Guide to Wales see – theAA.com/shop

LLANDEILO
Map 8 SN62

The Angel Hotel

tel: 01558 822765 **Rhosmaen St SA19 6EN**
email: capelbach@hotmail.com
dir: *In town centre adjacent to post office*

Reliable base in idyllic Welsh market town

This gabled inn commands a position near the crest of the long hill rising from Llandeilo's old bridge across the Towy, at the fringe of the Brecon Beacons National Park. Popular as both a locals' pub, with some reliable Welsh real ales and a good range of wines, and as an intimate place to dine in Y Capel Bach Bistro, an 18th-century gem tucked away at the rear of the hotel. Most diets are catered for on the ever-changing specials board and fixed price menu; perhaps tomato and pesto crostini to start, followed by bacon steak with salsa and cheese, or lentil loaf with cracked pepper cream. There's jam roly-poly and custard if you've left room.

Open 11.30-3 6-11 (Sun 11.30-4) Closed Sun eve **Food** Lunch Mon-Sat 11.30-2.30, Sun 12-3 Dinner Mon-Sat 6-9 Av main course £4.95 Set menu available Restaurant menu available Mon-Sat evening ⊕ FREE HOUSE ◀ Evan Evans, Tomos Watkin, Wye Valley ⚬ Gwynt y Ddraig. ♀ 10 **Facilities** Non-diners area ✿ (Bar Garden) ♦♦ Children's menu Children's portions Garden ⊼ WiFi ➡ (notice required)

LLANDOVERY
Map 9 SN73

The Kings Head

tel: 01550 720393 **1 Market Square SA20 0AB**
email: info@kingsheadcoachinginn.co.uk
dir: *M4 junct 49, A483 through Ammanford, Llandeilo onto A40 to Llandovery. Pub in town centre opposite clock tower*

Former coaching inn with family-friendly food

Once the home of the Llandovery Bank, this 17th-century inn overlooks the town's cobbled market square. Step inside and the exposed beams and crooked floors are a reminder of the pub's heritage, with beers from the Gower Brewery representing the Principality. A good few menus are offered here, including lunchtime specials (all at £5, weekdays), light bites and children's. For your lunchtime fiver you could enjoy quality food from a menu that changes daily, perhaps a Welsh Black steak and onion sandwich. Choices from the à la carte menu include local Welsh lamb rack; or wild mushroom and parmesan linguine.

Open all day all wk 10am-mdnt Closed 25 Dec **Food** Lunch all wk 12-2.30 Dinner all wk 6-9.30 Av main course £8 Restaurant menu available all wk ⊕ FREE HOUSE ◀ Sharp's Doom Bar, Tomos Watkin, Gower Gold ⚬ Kopparberg. **Facilities** Non-diners area ✿ (Bar Outside area) ♦♦ Children's menu Children's portions Outside area ⊼ Parking WiFi ➡ (notice required)

LLANLLWNI
Map 8 SN43

Belle @ Llanllwni

tel: 01570 480495 **SA40 9SQ**
email: food@thebelle.co.uk
dir: *Midway between Carmarthen & Lampeter on A485*

Well cooked food at this cosy roadside inn

Surrounded by countryside and with stunning views, this cosy and welcoming roadside inn sits on the A485 between Carmarthen and Lampeter. Head this way on a sunny day and dine alfresco. There are two rotating ales here to enjoy along with Weston Stowford Press and local Welsh ciders. In the dining room, Welsh Black beef lasagne with triple cooked chips; sweet potato, pea and goats' cheese risotto; or roast, free-range duck leg with crushed new potatoes and wine gravy could precede

Bailey's bread and butter pudding; or rich chocolate truffle cup. Expect excellent ingredients including locally reared meats.

Open 12-3 5.30-11 Closed 25-26 Dec, Mon (ex BHs) **Food** Lunch Wed-Sat 12-3 Dinner Tue-Sun 6-9.30 Set menu available Restaurant menu available ⊕ FREE HOUSE ◀ Peroni, Guinness, Guest ales ⚬ Westons Stowford Press, Gwynt y Ddraig. ♀ 9 **Facilities** Non-diners area ♦♦ Children's menu Children's portions Outside area ⊼ Parking ➡ (notice required)

NANTGAREDIG
Map 8 SN42

Y Polyn ◉◉
PICK OF THE PUBS

tel: 01267 290000 **SA32 7LH**
email: ypolyn@hotmail.com
dir: *From A48 follow signs to National Botanic Garden of Wales. Then follow brown signs to Y Polyn*

Stylish but never stuffy, worth seeking out

With a trout fishery nearby, bracing walks in the Towy Valley just down the hill and the inspiring National Botanic Garden of Wales a mile or so up the road, this former tollhouse outside the attractive county town of Carmarthen is an established destination pub for lovers of Welsh food. The bounty of West Wales is to the forefront in the tempting dishes that come from the modest kitchen here. "Fat equals Flavour. Live with it" is the unapologetic ethos here. Starters include Carmarthen ham with fennel and red onion slaw, and chicken liver parfait with Y Polyn gooseberry chutney; then continue with woodland reared pork and leek pie or carbonnade of Welsh black beef and Otleys ale. Warm plum and frangipane tart or egg custard tart with honey roast plums seal the deal. All this has gained the inn two AA Rosettes for its accomplished country-pub cooking. The excellent beers come from Pontypridd.

Open all wk 12-4 7-11 Closed Mon, Sun eve **Food** Contact pub for details Set menu available Restaurant menu available Tue-Sun ⊕ FREE HOUSE ◀ Otley 01, 03 Boss. ♀ 12 **Facilities** Non-diners area ♦♦ Children's portions Garden ⊼ Parking WiFi

PUMSAINT
Map 9 SN64

NEW The Dolaucothi Arms

tel: 01558 650237 **SA19 8UW**
email: info@thedolaucothiarms.co.uk **web:** www.thedolaucothiarms.co.uk
dir: *On A482 between Lampeter & Llandovery. From Llandeilo or Llandovery take A40*

An authentic taste of Wales in an ancient village hostelry

Set in the rolling green Cothi Valley, the Dolaucothi Arms is a Grade II listed building owned by the National Trust. After closing for five years, it reopened in 2013 with David Joy and Esther Hubert at the helm; both are passionate about

Welsh food and drink. Choose an armchair in the cosy lounge bar, or sit at a large table in the main bar where Welsh real ales and ciders are on tap. Head for the separate dining room with wood-burning stove and eclectic mix of mismatched furniture to enjoy Dinewfr venison sausages; slow-cooked shin of beef; or partridge with cabbage and bacon. Beer and cider festival over the Summer Bank Holiday weekend.

Open all day Closed 25 Dec, Mon & Tue L winter **Food** Lunch 12.30-3 Dinner 6.30-9 Av main course £10 ⊕ FREE HOUSE ◖ Evan Evans Cwrw, Purple Moose Snowdonia Ale, Wye Valley Butty Bach ⍾ Gwynt y Ddraig Black Dragon. ☼ 9
Facilities Non-diners area ☺ (Bar Garden) ♦ Children's menu Children's portions Garden ⌂ Beer festival Cider festival Parking WiFi ☎ (notice required)

CEREDIGION

ABERAERON
Map 8 SN46

The Harbourmaster
PICK OF THE PUBS

tel: 01545 570755 **Pen Cei SA46 OBT**
email: info@harbour-master.com
dir: In Aberaeron follow Tourist Information Centre signs. Pub adjacent

Delightful quayside hotel overlooking Cardigan Bay

The deep mauve external walls of this three-storey, former harbourmaster's house ensure it stands out on the Georgian quayside. Its neighbour, a former grain store, is now the bar, today home to Purple Moose Glaslyn Ale, HM Best Bitter, Hallets Real cider and plenty of wines by the glass. Interior decoration throughout is exquisite: look at how the beautiful spiral staircase and other original features have been enhanced. The bilingual, gastro-pubby breakfast and lunch menus offer modern Welsh dishes such as scrambled eggs with Rhydlewis smoked salmon; Welsh mussels marinières; and Talsarn pork faggots with mash and peas. For dinner consider rib of Welsh beef on the bone with béarnaise sauce; lobster and crab (which you can watch being landed); Montgomery chicken supreme with black pudding mash; or winter vegetable cassoulet.

Open all day all wk 10am-11.30pm Closed 25 Dec **Food** Lunch all wk 12-2.30 Dinner all wk 6-9 Av main course £13 Restaurant menu available all wk ⊕ FREE HOUSE ◖ Purple Moose Glaslyn Ale, HM Best Bitter ⍾ Hallets Real. ☼ 15
Facilities Non-diners area ♦ Children's menu Children's portions ⌂ Parking WiFi

ABERYSTWYTH
Map 8 SN58

NEW The Glengower Hotel

tel: 01970 626191 **3 Victoria Ter SY23 2DH**
email: info@glengower.co.uk
dir: Phone for detailed directions

Local ales and enjoyable food overlooking the bay

Literally a stone's throw from the beach, the sun terrace at 'The Glen' – as it's affectionately known by the locals – offers fabulous views across Cardigan Bay and you might even spot one of the friendly local dolphins. A traditional free house serving a wide range of home-made food all day, from sandwiches and paninis to local butchers' sausages and mash; and home-made chilli con carne. The Glen has a good local reputation for its real ales, including beers from award-winning North Wales brewery Purple Moose. Look out for the pub's bank holiday beer festival in late May.

Open all day all wk **Food** Lunch Mon-Sat 12-8, Sun 12-6 Dinner Mon-Sat 12-8, Sun 12-6 Av main course £8.50 ⊕ FREE HOUSE ◖ Wye Valley, Purple Moose.
Facilities Non-diners area ☺ (Bar Outside area) ♦ Children's menu Children's portions Outside area ⌂ Beer festival WiFi

LLANFIHANGEL-Y-CREUDDYN
Map 9 SN67

y Ffarmers
PICK OF THE PUBS

tel: 01974 261275 **SY23 4LA**
email: bar@yffarmers.co.uk
dir: From Aberystwyth take B4340 towards Trawsgoed. After New Cross left signed Llanfihangel-y-Creuddyn

Excellent local food in the Welsh hills

Since Rhodri and Esther Edwards took over this traditional local and spruced the place up with a contemporary feel, it has become an oasis for tip-top Welsh beer and quality food. Found down winding narrow lanes through stunning countryside the pub is tucked away in Llanfihangel's gorgeous open square alongside listed whitewashed cottages and an imposing church. Expect to find a buzzy community vibe and the place packed with local drinkers supping pints of Wye Valley or potent Gwynt y Ddraig cider, farmers from the hills and local foodies in the know. There's distinct Welsh flavour to the short monthly menus (written in Welsh and English, naturally), which champion produce from local farms and artisan producers. Typically, tuck into cockle fritters with lemon mayonnaise; Welsh lamb tagine with fresh herb couscous, and bara brith bread and butter pudding. Don't miss the Sunday roasts.

Open 12-2 6-11 Closed 2-12 Jan, Mon **Food** Lunch Wed-Sun 12-2 Dinner Tue-Sat 6-9 Av main course £11.50 ⊕ FREE HOUSE ◖ Wye Valley, Evan Evans, Felinfoel ⍾ Gwynt y Ddraig. **Facilities** Non-diners area ☺ (Bar Garden) ♦ Children's menu Children's portions Garden ⌂ WiFi ☎ (notice required)

LLWYNDAFYDD
Map 8 SN35

The Crown Inn & Restaurant

tel: 01545 560396 **SA44 6BU**
email: thecrowninnandrestaurant@hotmail.co.uk
dir: Follow Llwyndafydd signs from, A487 NE of Cardigan

Time a visit for the popular carvery

Outside this traditional Welsh longhouse is a delightful, award-winning garden, while it's an easy walk down the lane leads to a cove with caves and National Trust cliffs. Dating from 1799, the pub has original beams, fireplaces and a pretty restaurant. There's a carvery every Sunday and a varied menu with a good selection of dishes, including chicken liver and cognac pâté, which might be followed by home-grown belly pork with root vegetables and mash. Blackboard specials, a children's menu, light snacks and bar food are also available.

Open all day all wk **Food** Lunch all wk 12-3 Dinner all wk 6-9 Av main course £10 ⊕ FREE HOUSE ◖ Buckleys Best Bitter, Evan Evans, Cottage, Guest ales. ☼ 9
Facilities Non-diners area ☺ (Bar Garden) ♦ Children's menu Children's portions Play area Family room Garden ⌂ Parking ☎ (notice required)

TREGARON
Map 9 SN65

Y Talbot ★★★★ INN

tel: 01974 298208 **The Square SY25 6JL**
email: info@ytalbot.com **web:** www.ytalbot.com
dir: *On B4343 in village centre. (NB take caution in winter on mountain road from Beulah)*

Timeless village inn with great Welsh beer and food

An arresting inn which dominates the compact square at the heart of Tregaron. Surrounded by a web of footpaths, bridleways and drovers' roads, the tiny town bustles with outdoor activity. This idyllic location also guarantees first class provender from local farms, lakes and the Afon Teifi which flows through the town at the fringe of the little-known Cambrian Mountains. Past customers here include the Victorian travel writer George Borrow and former US President Jimmy Carter; perhaps they, too, enjoyed fare such as slow-cooked Cambrian Mountain lamb shoulder from a contemporary Welsh menu. Beers are usually from local craft breweries, augmented by an October beer festival.

Open all day all wk **Food** Lunch all wk 12-2.30 Dinner all wk 6-9 Restaurant menu available all wk ⊕ FREE HOUSE ◄ Purple Moose Glaslyn Ale, Felinfoel Double Dragon, Wye Valley HPA, Buckley's Best ♂ Gwynt y Ddraig Happy Daze, Welsh Mountain Cider. **Facilities** Non-diners area ♣ (Bar Garden) ♦♦ Children's menu Children's portions Garden ⌱ Beer festival Parking WiFi ➟ (notice required) **Rooms** 13

CONWY

BETWS-Y-COED
Map 14 SH75

Ty Gwyn Inn
PICK OF THE PUBS

tel: 01690 710383 & 710787 **LL24 0SG**
email: mratcl1050@aol.com
dir: *At junct of A5 & A470, 100yds S of Waterloo Bridge*

Local, seasonal food drive the menus

Located on the old London to Holyhead road, the Ty Gwyn was welcoming travellers long before Thomas Telford built his impressive cast iron Waterloo Bridge over the River Conwy in 1815. The Ratcliffe family has owned and run this former coaching for the past 28 years, and now Martin (the chef for all that time) and his wife Nicola are in charge. Much of the original 17th-century character is evident inside. Real ales come from as near as Conwy's Great Orme brewery, as well as from much further afield. Martin's cooking relies heavily on quality local produce including home-grown vegetables. Typical dishes include a starter of creamy scrambled free-range goose egg with smoked salmon and wild garlic, and main courses such as slow-roasted suckling pig with black pudding and hazelnut stuffing and thyme-scented roast root vegetables.

Open all wk 12-2 6.30-11 Closed 24, 25 & 26 Dec, 1wk Jan **Food** Lunch all wk 12-2 Dinner all wk 6.30-9 ⊕ FREE HOUSE ◄ Brains The Rev. James, Great Orme. **Facilities** ♦♦ Children's menu Children's portions Outside area ⌱ Parking WiFi ➟

CAPEL CURIG
Map 14 SH75

Bryn Tyrch Inn ★★★★ INN ⊛

tel: 01690 720223 **LL24 0EL**
email: info@bryntyrchinn.co.uk **web:** www.bryntyrchinn.co.uk
dir: *On A5, 6m from Betws-y-Coed*

Smart inn with wonderful Snowdon views

Occupying an idyllic position in the heart of the Snowdonia National Park with breathtaking views of Snowdon and Moel Siabod, this remote inn is an ideal base for exploring the stunning mountains of the region. Welsh produce dominates the menu, which can be enjoyed in the informal bar or the terrace restaurant. Seared wood pigeon, chestnut and bacon tart, poached egg with port reduction; chargrilled

rib-eye Welsh steak with hand-cut chips; and fish of the day are typical choices. Look out for the hog roast that occasionally takes place in the garden during the summer.

Open 4-11 (Fri-Sun all day) Closed mid Dec-27 Dec, 3-21 Jan, Mon-Thu L (excluding holidays) **Food** Lunch Fri-Sun & hols 12-9 Dinner Mon-Thu 5-9, Fri-Sun & hols 12-9 ⊕ FREE HOUSE ◄ Conwy Rampart, Welsh Pride & Clogwyn Gold ♂ Symonds. **Facilities** Non-diners area ♦♦ Children's menu Children's portions Garden ⌱ Parking WiFi **Rooms** 11

Cobdens Hotel ★★ SHL

tel: 01690 720243 **LL24 0EE**
email: info@cobdens.co.uk **web:** www.cobdens.co.uk
dir: *On A5, 5m W of Betws-y-Coed*

Mecca for those enjoying all that Snowdonia has to offer

This 250-year-old inn sits at the foot of Moel Siabod in a beautiful mountain village deep in Snowdonia, with Snowdon itself a couple of miles down the valley. No surprise then that it's a haven for outdoor pursuit enthusiasts of all descriptions taking refreshment, rebuilding their strength or enjoying live music in the famous Mountain Bar built into the rock face. Typical dishes include pear and endive salad with gorgonzola and walnuts; halibut steak Provençale with fine salad and new potatoes; and hearty meat options such as Welsh rib-eye steak with peppercorn sauce.

Open all day all wk 12-11 (Sun 12-10.30) Closed 21-28 Dec, 6-20 Jan **Food** Lunch all wk 12-2 Dinner all wk 6-9 ⊕ FREE HOUSE ◄ Conwy Rampart & Clogwyn Gold, Cobdens Ale, Honey Fayre, Telford Porter, Guest ales ♂ Rosie's Perfect Pear, Triple D & Wicked Wasp. **Facilities** Non-diners area ♣ (Bar Garden) ♦♦ Children's menu Children's portions Garden ⌱ Parking WiFi ➟ (notice required) **Rooms** 17

COLWYN BAY
Map 14 SH87

Pen-y-Bryn
PICK OF THE PUBS

tel: 01492 533360 **Pen-y-Bryn Rd LL29 6DD**
email: pen.y.bryn@brunningandprice.co.uk
dir: *1m from A55. Follow signs to Welsh Mountain Zoo. Establishment at top of hill*

Character interior and friendly atmosphere

Looks can be deceiving. This unprepossessing 1970s building may look like a medical centre but step inside to find a handsome interior, where you'll find a friendly and chatty atmosphere with local ales and cracking pub food served throughout the day. The interior has character in spades, with oak floors, open fires, rugs, bookcases and old furniture, whilst the stunning rear garden and terrace enjoy panoramic views over the sea and the Great Orme headland. The modern British menu offers a great choice of sandwiches and lighter meals, perhaps Welsh rarebit on thick toast with chutney, or you might opt for mussels cooked in white wine, garlic and cream. Main course options range from chargrilled chicken, tagliatelle and spiced saffron butter sauce, to braised shoulder of lamb and crushed new potatoes with rosemary gravy. Chocolate brownie with chocolate sauce and ice cream, or lemon tart with fruit compôte will round things off nicely.

Open all day all wk 12-11 (Sun 12-10.30) **Food** Lunch Mon-Sat 12-9.30, Sun 12-9 Dinner Mon-Sat 12-9.30, Sun 12-9 ⊕ BRUNNING & PRICE ◄ Original, Purple Moose Snowdonia Ale, Guest ales ♂ Aspall. ♥ 14 **Facilities** Non-diners area ♦♦ Children's menu Children's portions Garden ⌱ Beer festival Parking

PICK OF THE PUBS

The Queens Head

LLANDUDNO JUNCTION   Map 14 SH77

tel: 01492 546570
Glanwydden LL31 9JP
email: enquiries@
queensheadglanwydden.co.uk
web: www.queensheadglanwydden.co.uk
dir: *A55 onto A470 towards Llandudno.
At 3rd rdbt right towards Penrhyn Bay,
2nd right into Glanwydden, pub on left*

**A warm welcome, effortless
charm and excellent service**

A former AA Pub of the Year for Wales,
this charming country pub is located in
a pretty rural village just a five-minute
drive from the Victorian seaside town of
Llandudno. Once the storehouse of the
Llangwestennin Parish, this early
18th-century pub is perfectly situated
for country walks, cycling, or a day on
the beach. The Queens Head continues
to attract discerning customers with its
warm welcome, effortless charm and
excellent service. The stylish terrace is
great for summer evenings, whilst on
colder nights the relaxed atmosphere in
the bar is perfect for a pre-dinner drink
by the log fire; real ales include Great
Orme brews, and the lip-smacking wine
list with description notes on the back
of the menu has plenty of choice. The
dedicated kitchen makes excellent use
of local produce in varied menus that
might include a starter of Conwy fish
soup finished with brandy and tomato;

crispy lamb and feta salad; or deep-
fried Welsh brie with home-made
cranberry and orange chutney. Local fish
and seafood is the cornerstone of the
menu and typical examples are home-
made salmon and coriander fishcakes;
seared Anglesey king scallops with pea
purée, pancetta and rocket or monkfish
and king prawn curry in a light mango
and coconut sauce. Meat-lovers and
vegetarians are certainly not overlooked,
with the likes of home-made steak,
mushroom and ale pie; grill pork loin
steak in a soused prune and Armagnac
jus; or roasted half of Barbary duck with
stir fry and noodles. Pasta, salads and
vegetarian choices are also available.

Open all day all wk 12-10.30
Food Contact pub for details of serving
times ⊕ FREE HOUSE ◖ Great Orme.
⬤ 10 **Facilities** Non-diners area
Children's portions Garden ⋒ Parking
🚍 (notice required)

CONWY
Map 14 SH77

The Groes Inn ★★★★★ INN ⊛
PICK OF THE PUBS

tel: 01492 650545 **Ty'n-y-Groes LL32 8TN**
email: reception@groesinn.com **web:** www.groesinn.com
dir: Exit A55 to Conwy, left at mini rdbt by Conwy Castle onto B5106, 2.5m inn on right

Historic pub with views of Snowdonia

Views from tables set out-front of this 450-year-old creeper-clad inn sweep down the widening estuary of the Afon Conwy; whilst from the tree-shaded patio and garden the eye is taken by the profile of nearby Tal y Fan, at 2001-ft the shortest true mountain in Wales. Rambling rooms, beamed ceilings, careworn settles, log fires, military hats, historic cooking utensils – this inn has plenty to point out but don't expect a jukebox or pool table. It's a place to linger over a leisurely beer of Great Orme Welsh Black and face the challenge of choosing from the well-balanced menu. Start off with warm rabbit salad with watercress, rocket and sweet onion dip, progressing then to mains exampled by pan-fried duck breast with brandy plum sauce and buttered cabbage; or pan-fried Scottish salmon with green pea and dill risotto. The inn's renowned steaks are from dry-aged premium Welsh beef. A previous winner of AA Pub of the Year for Wales, the inn has luxurious accommodation and is a popular location for weddings.

Open all wk 12-3 6-11 **Food** Lunch all wk 12-2 Dinner all wk 6.30-9 Av main course £11 ⊕ FREE HOUSE ◀ Groes Ale, Great Orme Welsh Black, Orme, Tetley's Ŏ Westons Stowford Press. ☻ 14 **Facilities** Non-diners area ❀ (Bar Garden) Children's menu Children's portions Family room Garden ☴ Parking WiFi ➡ (notice required) **Rooms** 14

DOLWYDDELAN
Map 14 SH75

Elen's Castle Hotel

tel: 01690 750207 **LL25 OEJ**
email: stay@hotelinsnowdonia.co.uk
dir: 5m S of Betws-y-Coed, follow A470

Relaxed and welcoming atmosphere at this village hostelry

Elen's Castle was once owned by the Earl of Ancaster, who sold it to his gamekeeper. The latter opened it as a coaching inn around 1880, specialising in hunting parties. Now a family-run free house, it boasts an old-world bar with a wood-burning stove and an intimate restaurant with breathtaking views of the mountains and the Lledr River. Sample dishes include chicken Cymru (chicken breast, leek, mushroom, cream and Caerphilly cheese sauce with seasonal vegetables); and Welsh Black beefburger served with chunky chips. Water from the on-site Roman well is said to have healing properties.

Open vary by season Closed 1st 2wks Jan, wk days in quiet winter periods **Food** Dinner 6.30-9 Av main course £9.95 ⊕ FREE HOUSE ◀ Shepherd Neame Spitfire, Wychwood Hobgoblin, Brains, Worthington's, Black Sheep Ŏ Westons Stowford Press. **Facilities** Non-diners area ❀ (Bar) ❶❶ Children's menu Children's portions Play area Family room Garden ☴ Parking WiFi ➡ (notice required)

LLANDUDNO
Map 14 SH78

NEW The Cottage Loaf

tel: 01492 870762 **Market St LL30 2SR**
email: thecottageloaf@hotmail.co.uk
dir: From A55 onto A470, then A456. Into Mostyn St, left into Market St

Quirky seaside pub with good food and local ales

For years a bakery, this whitewashed building in the heart of Llandudno only became a pub in 1981 and much of its quirky interior is made up of salvaged materials from a ship-wrecked coal schooner. With a log fire for winter and a large garden and sun terrace for summer, this welcoming pub attracts visitors all year round. Local Conwy Welsh Pride is one of several ales on rotation, alongside a large range of whiskies and wines. Home-made Indian mutton curry; steak and ale pie; and roasted pepper, chickpea and mozzarella burger are typical choices from the extensive food menu.

Open all day all wk **Food** Lunch all wk 12-9 Dinner all wk 12-9 Av main course £11.50 ⊕ FREE HOUSE ◀ Courage Directors, Conwy Welsh Pride, Guest ales Ŏ Gwynt y Ddraig Black Dragon, Firey Fox, Dog Dancer & Happy Daze, Westons Old Rosie. **Facilities** Non-diners area ❶❶ Children's menu Children's portions Garden ☴ WiFi ➡ (notice required)

LLANDUDNO JUNCTION
Map 14 SH77

The Queens Head
PICK OF THE PUBS

See Pick of the Pubs on page 625

LLANELIAN-YN-RHÔS
Map 14 SH87

The White Lion Inn

tel: 01492 515807 **LL29 8YA**
email: info@whitelioninn.co.uk
dir: A55 junct 22, left signed Old Colwyn, A547. At rdbt 2nd exit onto B5383 signed Betwys-yn-Rhos. In 1m turn right into Llanelian Rd, follow to village. Pub on right

One of the oldest country inns in north Wales

Parts of this attractive family-run inn are reputed to date back over 1,200 years. It still retains its original slate floor and oak-beamed ceiling, and there is an old salt cellar by the inglenook fireplace. The Cole family have been running the inn for around 25 years and have restored and preserved many aspects of traditional village life revolving around the pub, including reinstating the snug next to the bar (dogs are allowed in here). The food is traditional, home cooked, and wherever possible locally sourced, including of course, shoulder of Welsh lamb. Other dishes on the comprehensive main menu and specials board include fish stew and grilled gammon steak.

Open Tue-Fri 11.30-3 6-11 (Sat 11.30-4 6-11.30 Sun 12-10.30) Closed Mon (ex BHs & school summer hols) **Food** Lunch Tue-Sat 12-2, Sun 12-9 Dinner Tue-Sat 6-9, Sun 12-9 Av main course £10.95 ⊕ FREE HOUSE ◀ Marston's Pedigree & Burton Bitter, Guest ale. ☻ 11 **Facilities** Non-diners area ❶❶ Children's menu Children's portions Garden ☴ Parking WiFi ➡ (notice required)

LLANNEFYDD
Map 14 SH97

The Hawk & Buckle Inn

tel: 01745 540249 **LL16 5ED**
email: garethandsiwen@googlemail.com
dir: Phone for detailed directions

Old inn situated high in the hills of north Wales

From high in the north Wales hills, this lovingly restored 17th-century coaching inn enjoys spectacular views across the local countryside to Blackpool Tower and beyond. The real ale selection includes Heavy Industry and Purple Moose Glaslyn Ale and fresh local produce is used wherever possible to create dishes such as black pudding and goats' cheese stack with apple chutney; slow roasted lamb chump with mint and cranberry gravy; the 8oz Hawk burger topped with Welsh cheese and smoked bacon; or red snapper fillet with citrus butter.

Open all wk Mon-Fri 6-11 Sat-Sun 12-12 **Food** Lunch Sat-Sun 12-8 Dinner Mon-Fri 6-8.30, Sat & Sun 12-8 ⊕ FREE HOUSE ◀ Heavy Industry, Purple Moose Glaslyn Ale, Guest ales. **Facilities** Non-diners area Outside area Parking WiFi

TREFRIW	Map 14 SH76

The Old Ship

tel: 01492 640013 **High St LL27 0JH**
email: rhian.barlow@btopenworld.com
dir: From A470 between Tal-y-Bont & Betws-y-Coed follow Trefriw signs

A great place to end a walk

A perfect refuelling stop following a tramp in the hills, this traditional inn is situated in a peaceful village in the wooded eastern edge of the Snowdonia National Park. Warm up by the log fire with a refreshing pint of Purple Moose Glaslyn Ale and peruse the daily chalkboard menu. Using locally sourced ingredients, freshly prepared dishes take in pea and ham soup; coq au vin with dauphinoise potatoes and green beans; and pub classics such as fish and chips, or sausages with garlic mash and red wine gravy. For dessert, maybe dark and white chocolate cheesecake.

Open 12-3 6-11 (Sat-Sun 12-11) Closed Mon (ex BHs) **Food** Lunch Tue-Fri 12-2.30, Sat-Sun 12-9 Dinner Tue-Fri 6-9, Sat-Sun 12-9 ⊕ FREE HOUSE ◀ Banks's Bitter, Purple Moose Glaslyn Ale, Bragdyr Nant Cwrw Coryn, Great Orme. ♚
Facilities Non-diners area ♦ Children's menu Children's portions Garden ⊨ Parking

DENBIGHSHIRE

LLANELIDAN	Map 15 SJ15

The Leyland Arms

tel: 01824 750822 **LL15 2PT**
email: info@leylandarms.co.uk
dir: Midway between Ruthin & Gwyddelwern on A494, left to Llanelidan

Village community pub overlooking the cricket pitch

Adjacent to St Elidan church and overlooking the cricket pitch in sleepy Llanelidan, deep in the Clwydian Hill, The Leyland Arms is the heart and soul of the village. A true community pub, it's the home of the cricket team and the annual nativity play is held in the stables at the back of the pub. In summer enjoy the views from the terraced garden and hunker down by the fire in winter with a pint of Thwaites Original. Food is prepared from locally sourced ingredients and the menu may include Welsh cockle, mussel and crabmeat chowder; warm creamed camembert, leek and chive tartlet; gammon steak, egg and pineapple; Greek moussaka and Greek salad; and Thwaites beer battered haddock fillet.

Open 12-3 6-11 Closed Mon **Food** Lunch Tue-Sun 12-3 Dinner Tue-Sat 6-9 Av main course £5.50 Restaurant menu available Tue-Sun ⊕ FREE HOUSE ◀ Thwaites Original, Timothy Taylor Landlord, Guest ale Ö Kingstone Press. ♚ 12
Facilities Non-diners area ♣ (Bar Garden) ♦ Children's portions Garden ⊨ Parking WiFi ▦ (notice required)

ST ASAPH	Map 15 SJ07

The Plough Inn

tel: 01745 585080 **The Roe LL17 0LU**
email: ploughsa@gmail.com
dir: Exit A55 at Rhyl & St Asaph signs, left at rdbt, pub 200yds on left

A former coaching inn combining modern and traditional

In Simon Rodenhurst's 13 or so years at this 18th-century coaching inn, his first-floor open kitchen has prepared more than half a million meals. The bar is a quirky blend of modern and traditional, with open fires, blackboard menus, an unusual trompe l'oeil bar and real ales from north Wales; the restaurant, though very modern, retains a vaulted ceiling from its days as a ballroom. Dine here on chicken fillet with chicken mousse, mushrooms, spinach with leek and potato mash; grilled

gammon steak with egg, pineapple, peas and chips; or braised lamb shank, dauphinoise potatoes, honey-glazed carrots and rosemary jus, and help Simon towards his millionth meal. There's live music on Friday and Saturday nights, as well as a cocktail bar and a wine shop.

Open all day all wk **Food** Lunch all wk 10-9 Dinner all wk 10-9 Av main course £7.95 Set menu available ⊕ FREE HOUSE ◀ Conwy, Great Orme, Facer's Brewery Flintshire, Heavy Industry Brewery, Weetwood Ales, Coach House Brewing Company. ♚ 10 **Facilities** Non-diners area ♣ (Garden Outside area) ♦ Children's menu Children's portions Garden Outside area ⊨ Parking WiFi ▦

FLINTSHIRE

BABELL	Map 15 SJ17

Black Lion Inn

tel: 01352 720239 **CH8 8PZ**
email: theblacklioninn@btinternet.com
dir: A55 junct 31 to Caerwys. Left at x-rds signed Babell. In 3m turn right

Ancient coaching inn with ghostly residents

Surely no building can survive for 700 years without acquiring ghosts – and this former coaching inn has plenty, including that of a Canadian man forever asking to come in. From its rural location, it commands mind-blowing views across an Area of Outstanding Natural Beauty. Comfy sofas and an open fire distinguish the bar, where locally-brewed cask ales complement an appealing modern British menu featuring slow-poached chicken supreme, wild mushroom risotto and crisp leek ribbons; pan-seared rack of lamb; and sirloin steak with flat field mushroom and onion rings. Every Wednesday is pie night, Thursday night is grill night, and there's a September beer festival.

Open all day Closed Mon & Tue **Food** Lunch Wed-Sun 12-9 Dinner Wed-Sun 12-9 Av main course £13.95 Restaurant menu available ⊕ FREE HOUSE ◀ Purple Moose Myrica Gale, Black Lion Bitter, Great Orme Celtica. ♚ 8 **Facilities** Non-diners area ♦ Children's menu Children's portions Play area Garden ⊨ Beer festival Parking WiFi ▦ (notice required)

CILCAIN	Map 15 SJ16

White Horse Inn

tel: 01352 740142 **CH7 5NN**
email: christine.jeory@btopenworld.com
dir: From Mold take A541 towards Denbigh. After approx 6m turn left

Traditional inn, the hub of the village life

This 400-year-old pub is the last survivor of five originally to be found in this lovely hillside village, probably because it was the centre of the local gold-mining industry in the 19th century. Today, the White Horse is popular with walkers, cyclists and horse-riders. Food here is home made by the landlord's wife using the best quality local ingredients, and is accompanied by a good range of real ales. A typical meal might start with garlic and ginger breaded prawns with curry mayonnaise, followed by home-made steak and kidney pie or, for a vegetarian option, or vegetable biriyani topped with an omelette.

Open all wk 12-3 6-11 (Sat 12-11 Sun 12-10.30) **Food** Lunch all wk 12-2.15 Dinner all wk 7-9 Av main course £9 ⊕ FREE HOUSE ◀ Timothy Taylor Landlord, The Kite Ales, Banks's Ö Thatchers Gold. ♚ 9 **Facilities** Non-diners area ♣ (Bar Garden) Garden ⊨ Parking WiFi

MOLD
Map 15 SJ26

Glasfryn
PICK OF THE PUBS

tel: 01352 750500 **Raikes Ln, Sychdyn CH7 6LR**
email: glasfryn@brunningandprice.co.uk
dir: *From Mold follow signs to Theatr Clwyd, 1m from town centre*

Hill views, heavenly ales and great menus

With magical views from the gardens over the Alyn Valley towards the rippling hills of the Clwydian Range Area of Outstanding Natural Beauty; this imposing dining pub was converted from a judge's country residence some years ago by the Brunning & Price group. Their hallmark style of polished wood, country and quirky prints, quality antiquey furnishings and largely wood flooring complements the Arts and Crafts style of the original building. Locals wouldn't dream of missing its two beer festivals: the first, in March, celebrates Welsh food and drink; in October it's the turn of British Pie Week together with Champion Beers of Britain. The pub's 12 real ale pumps are the tip of the refreshment iceberg – the wine and malt whisky lists are comprehensive too. Fine pub grub is a given; there's a great range of starters and light bites, or investigate mains like slow cooked shoulder of lamb with cinnamon, cumin and chickpeas, apricot and date couscous.

Open all day all wk **Food** Lunch Mon-Sat 12-9.30, Sun 12-9 Dinner Mon-Sat 12-9.30, Sun 12-9 Av main course £10.95 ⊕ BRUNNING & PRICE ◀ Purple Moose Snowdonia Ale, Flowers Original ♂ Aspall. ♚ 16 **Facilities** Non-diners area ♣ (Bar Garden) ♦♦ Garden ♬ Beer festival Parking WiFi

NORTHOP
Map 15 SJ26

Stables Bar Restaurant ★★★ CHH

tel: 01352 840577 **CH7 6AB**
email: info@soughtonhall.co.uk **web:** www.soughtonhall.co.uk
dir: *From A55, take A119 through Northop*

Stable block conversion makes an excellent eatery

This unusual free house dates from the 18th century and was created from Soughton Hall's stable block, and original features like the cobbled floors and roof timbers remain intact; the magnificent main house was built as a bishop's palace. The selection of real ales includes Stables Bitter, or diners can browse the wine shop for a bottle to accompany their meal. Examples from a winter carte menu include ham hock, baby leek and mustard terrine with pineapple piccalilli; and roast loin of cod, pan-fried scallops, creamed cauliflower, vine tomatoes and apple and cumin sauce. Enjoy the gardens in summer.

Open all day all wk Closed Mon-Tue in Winter **Food** Lunch all wk 12-9.30 Dinner all wk 12-9.30 ⊕ FREE HOUSE ◀ Coach House Honeypot Best Bitter & Dick Turpin Premium Bitter, Plassey Bitter, Stables Bitter. **Facilities** Non-diners area ♦♦ Children's menu Children's portions Family room Garden ♬ Parking WiFi ⬛ **Rooms** 15

GWYNEDD

ABERDYFI
Map 14 SN69

Penhelig Arms Hotel & Restaurant
PICK OF THE PUBS

See Pick of the Pubs on opposite page

BEDDGELERT
Map 14 SH54

Tanronnen Inn ★★★★ INN

tel: 01766 890347 **LL55 4YB**
email: guestservice@tanronnen.co.uk **web:** www.tanronnen.co.uk
dir: *In village centre opposite river bridge*

Great hospitality at the heart of Snowdonia

Originally part of the Beddgelert Estate, this stone-built building was the stables for the passing coach trade in 1809; after conversion to a cottage, it opened as a beer house in 1830. By the end of the 19th century, it had two letting bedrooms and was serving meals for visitors. Badly damaged by flooding in 1906, the shop at the back was incorporated to provide more accommodation. Today's inn has two attractive small bars serving Robinsons ales, a large lounge with open fire, a dining room open to non-residents in which to enjoy home-cooked meals, and attractive accommodation.

Open all day all wk **Food** Lunch all wk 12.30-2 Dinner all wk 7-8 ⊕ ROBINSONS ◀ Unicorn, Dizzy Blonde. **Facilities** Non-diners area ♦♦ Children's menu Children's portions Outside area ♬ Parking **Rooms** 7

BRITHDIR
Map 14 SH71

Cross Foxes

tel: 01341 421001 **LL40 2SG**
email: hello@crossfoxes.co.uk
dir: *At junct of A470 & A487, 4m from Dolgellau*

Rejuvinated inn, certainly worth finding

How fortunate that Nicol and Dewi Gwynne bought an abandoned pub, then brilliantly transformed it. Grade II listed it may be, but what an interior! True, they've used traditional Welsh materials like slate and stone, but the effect is light years from being Welsh Traditional. In the impressive bar you'll find regional real ales and ciders, and in the café a multiplicity of teas (including one from Wales), fresh coffees and finger sandwiches; here they also serve a traditional Welsh cream tea and a champagne afternoon tea. A meal in The Grill dining room might be lamb cawl with Caerphilly cheese; Snowdonia Ale-battered sea bass; and strawberry meringue roulade. Gaze at Cader Idris from the large decked area.

Open all day all wk **Food** Lunch all wk 12-9 Dinner all wk 12-9 Av main course £11.95 ⊕ FREE HOUSE ◀ Cader Ales, Evan Evans ♂ Kingstone Press. **Facilities** Non-diners area ♣ (Bar Garden) ♦♦ Children's menu Children's portions Garden ♬ Parking WiFi ⬛ (notice required)

PICK OF THE PUBS

Penhelig Arms Hotel & Restaurant

ABERDYFI   Map 14 SN69

tel: 01654 767215
Terrace Rd LL35 0LT
email: info@penheligarms.com
web: www.penheligarms.com
dir: *On A493, W of Machynlleth*

Small hostelry with a big reputation

This popular waterside inn has been serving travellers and locals since 1870 and offers spectacular views over the mountain-backed tidal Dyfi Estuary, a nature reserve rich in birdlife. Aberdyfi is a charming little resort with a championship golf course, and sandy beach and harbour, making it a favourite with golfers and watersports enthusiasts; the Penhelig Arms is also perfectly situated for visitors to Cader Idris, the Snowdonia National Park and several historic castles in the area. Music and TV-free, the wood-panelled and log-fire-warmed Fisherman's Bar is a cosy and friendly bolt-hole to enjoy Brains real ales and bar meals such as smoked salmon salad, roast supreme of chicken, chargrilled rump steak burger and bloomer sandwiches. The waterfront restaurant offers a more brasserie-style experience with views over the estuary and menus showcasing the abundant Welsh seafood (a Penhelig speciality) and Welsh beef and lamb. The kitchen team emphasise the freshness of ingredients and fuse local and

cosmopolitan influences in a style of cooking that allows natural flavours to shine through. A typical menu might include seared scallops, chorizo and citrus dressing; roast rack of lamb, creamed potatoes, mange-tout, port and red wine sauce; or wild mushroom raviolini with truffle oil. Leave room for apple pie with clotted cream; orange and cardamom pannacotta; or a Welsh cheese slate with biscuits, fruit cake and honey. On Sundays, expect a set menu featuring a traditional roast. Daily specials are listed on the blackboard. The short wine list is attractively priced and complements the excellent food. In warmer weather, you can sit outside on the sea wall terrace.

Open all day all wk **Food** Lunch all wk 12-2.30 Dinner all wk 6-9 Av main course £12.50 ⊕ BRAINS ◼ Bitter & The Rev. James, Guest ale ♉ Symonds. ♟ 25 **Facilities** Non-diners area ❖ (Bar Outside area) ⦁♦ Children's menu Children's portions Outside area Parking WiFi

CAERNARFON

Map 14 SH46

Black Boy Inn ★★★★ INN

tel: 01286 673604 **Northgate St LL55 1RW**
email: reception@black-boy-inn.com **web:** www.black-boy-inn.com
dir: *A55 junct 9 onto A487, follow signs for Caernarfon. Within town walls between castle & Victoria Dock*

Old fashioned values in the shadow of Caernarfon Castle

Character oozes from the very fabric of this ancient gabled inn, one of the oldest in Wales (built 1522). Relax with a pint of local Snowdonia Ale in the fire-warmed, low-ceilinged rooms strewn amidst beams and struts rescued from old ships. Meat and other products are generally local, and dishes from the long menu include field mushrooms and red onion compôte; vegetable cobbler; black pudding-stuffed chicken breast; and braised lamb shank. The well-proportioned bedrooms are ideal for those wishing to explore Mount Snowdon, the Lleyn Peninsula or catch the Welsh Highland Railway.

Open all day all wk **Food** Lunch 12-9 Dinner 12-9 ⊕ FREE HOUSE ◀ Purple Moose Snowdonia Ale, Brains The Rev. James, Hancock's. **Facilities** Non-diners area ♦♦ Children's menu Children's portions Play area Garden ⊼ Parking WiFi ▦ **Rooms** 26

See advert on opposite page

LLANBEDR

Map 14 SH52

Victoria Inn ★★★★ INN

tel: 01341 241213 **LL45 2LD**
email: vicinn@chessmail.co.uk **web:** www.vic-inn.co.uk
dir: *On A496 between Barmouth and Harlech*

Close to the beach and many mountain walks

Fascinating features for pub connoisseurs are the circular wooden settle, ancient stove, grandfather clock and flagged floors in the atmospheric bar of the Victoria. Home-made food is served in the lounge bar and restaurant, complemented by a range of Robinsons traditional ales. A children's play area has been incorporated into the well-kept garden, with a playhouse, slides and swings. Situated beside the River Artro, the Rhinog mountain range and the famous Roman Steps are right on the doorstep. If you would like to explore the area, there are five spacious and thoughtfully furnished bedrooms to stay in.

Open all day all wk 11-11 (Sun 12-10.30) **Food** Lunch Mon-Fri 12-3, Sat-Sun 12-9 (all wk 12-9 summer) Dinner Mon-Fri 5-9, Sat-Sun 12-9 (all wk 12-9 summer) ⊕ ROBINSONS ◀ Unicorn, Guest ales ♂ Westons Stowford Press. ▾ 10 **Facilities** Non-diners area ♦♦ Children's menu Children's portions Play area Garden ⊼ Parking ▦ (notice required) **Rooms** 5

PENNAL

Map 14 SH60

Glan yr Afon/Riverside

tel: 01654 791285 **Riverside Hotel SY20 9DW**
email: info@riversidehotel-pennal.co.uk
dir: *3m from Machynlleth on A493 towards Aberdovey. Pub on left*

Stylish 16th-century inn between sea and mountains

In the glorious Dyfi Valley close to Cader Idris and Cardigan Bay this family-run inn has slate floors, modern light oak furnishings and bold funky fabrics. There's a wood-burning stove pumping out heat in winter, Dark Side of the Moose ale on tap, and a good range of modern pub food. Relax and opt for a starter of Welsh rarebit or baked camembert infused with rosemary and garlic, then shepherd's pie; or salmon, spinach and cheese en croûte with asparagus and new potatoes. There's a riverside garden, with views to the hills, for summer enjoyment.

Open 12-3 6-11 Closed 25-26 Dec, 2wks Jan, Mon (Nov-Mar) **Food** Lunch all wk 12-2 Dinner all wk 6-9 Av main course £10 Set menu available ⊕ FREE HOUSE ◀ Cwrw Cader, Tiny Rebel, Purple Moose Dark Side of the Moose & Snowdonia Ale, Salopian Golden Thread, Stonehouse, Brewdog ♂ Kingstone Press. ▾ 12 **Facilities** Non-diners area ❤ (Bar Garden) ♦♦ Children's menu Children's portions Garden ⊼ Parking WiFi ▦ (notice required)

TREMADOG

Map 14 SH53

The Union Inn

tel: 01766 512748 **7 Market Square LL49 9RB**
email: mail@union-inn.com
dir: *From Porthmadog follow A487 & Caernarfon signs; then Tremadog signs. Inn on right before T-junct in village centre*

Freehold, family-run pub in historic setting

Hefty local stones were used to build this early 19th-century pub, part of a row of cottages facing the main square of Wales' first planned town. Customers can thank these stones for the snugness of the interior, not least the bar, which offers such a good choice of Welsh real ales and ciders. Home-made food is fresh, locally sourced and seasonal, with Welsh lamb and beef dishes held in particularly high regard. You'll also find authentic curries, steak and ale pie, fresh fish, scampi and vegetarian dishes, such as mushroom Stroganoff, and daily specials.

Open all wk 12-2 5.30-11.30 **Food** Lunch all wk 12-2 Dinner all wk 5.30-9 ⊕ FREE HOUSE ◀ Purple Moose Snowdonia Ale & Madog's Ale, Great Orme, Big Bog ♂ Gwynt y Ddraig Happy Daze, Dog Dancer & Farmhouse Scrumpy. **Facilities** Non-diners area ☙ (Bar Outside area) ♦♦ Children's menu Children's portions Outside area ⋒ Parking WiFi 🚐 (notice required)

TUDWEILIOG
Map 14 SH23

Lion Hotel

tel: 01758 770244 **LL53 8ND**
email: martlee.lion@gmail.com
dir: A487 from Caernarfon onto A499 towards Pwllheli. Right onto B4417 to Nefyn, through Edern to Tudweiliog

Family-run pub offering good value dining

Standing at a tangent to the road, fronted by a garden with tables and chairs, the 300-year-old Lion has been run by the Lee family for the past 40 years. The bar

features an extensive list of whiskies, alongside real ales from Big Bog, Cwrw Llyn and Purple Moose breweries, all Welsh of course. Typical pub meals include spare ribs in barbecue sauce; lamb or chicken balti; sweet chilli, prawn and cod fishcakes; and leek and mushroom crumble. Ample parking and a children's play area both help to make it popular with the many families holidaying in the beautiful Lleyn Peninsula.

Open all wk 11-3 6-11 (summer all day) **Food** Lunch all wk 12-2 Dinner all wk 6-9 Av main course £9.50 ⊕ FREE HOUSE ◀ Cwrw Llyn Brenin Enlli, Big Bog, Purple Moose, Guinness. **Facilities** Non-diners area ♦♦ Children's menu Children's portions Play area Family room Garden ⋒ Parking WiFi 🚐 (notice required)

WAUNFAWR
Map 14 SH55

Snowdonia Parc Brewpub & Campsite

tel: 01286 650409 & 650218 **LL55 4AQ**
email: info@snowdonia-park.co.uk
dir: Phone for detailed directions

Own microbrewery and wholesome food

In the heart of Snowdonia, a short drive from Mount Snowdon, this popular walkers' pub is located at Waunfawr Station on the Welsh Highland Railway. There are steam trains on site (the building was originally the stationmaster's house), plus a microbrewery and campsite. Home-cooked food ranges from chicken, leek and ham pie to vegetable curry or roast Welsh beef with all the trimmings. Naturally the pub serves its own Welsh Highland Bitter along with other ales. The Welsh Highland Railway Rail Ale Festival is held in mid-May.

Open all day all wk 11-11 (Fri-Sat 11am-11.30pm) **Food** Contact pub for details ⊕ FREE HOUSE ◀ Snowdonia Welsh Highland Bitter, Summer Ale, Carmen Sutra, Cais, Gwyrfai & Theodore Stout, Corvedale Dark & Delicious, John Thompson Gold. **Facilities** Non-diners area ☙ (Bar Garden) ♦♦ Children's menu Play area Family room Garden ⋒ Beer festival Parking WiFi 🚐 (notice required)

MONMOUTHSHIRE

ABERGAVENNY
Map 9 SO21

Clytha Arms
PICK OF THE PUBS

tel: 01873 840206 **Clytha NP7 9BW**
email: theclythaarms@btinternet.com
dir: *From A449 & A40 junction (E of Abergavenny) follow Old Road Abergavenny & Clytha signs*

Excellent beers and stunning views

This converted dower house on the old Abergavenny to Raglan road stands on the edge of parkland dotted with small woods. From the large garden, there are captivating views across the lush and shapely Vale of Gwent. The main bar is full of character, with old pews, tables and rustic furnishings, as well as posters and a wood-burning stove. The pub is renowned for its range of real ales, with Rhymney Bitter and some great artisan ciders and perrys. Grazers can enjoy tapas or tuck into a full restaurant meal accompanied by a choice of over 100 wines. Starters like cockles, bacon, leeks and black pasta might precede a main course of pork and wild mushroom faggots with black pudding mash. Time a visit for the Welsh Cider Festival, or the Welsh Beer, Cheese and Music festival, held over the late May and Summer Bank Holiday weekends respectively.

Open 12-3 6-12 (Fri-Sun 12-12) Closed 25 Dec, Mon L **Food** Lunch Tue-Sun 12.30-2.30 Dinner Mon-Sat 7-9.30 ⊕ FREE HOUSE ◀ The Kite CPA, Rhymney Bitter, Wye Valley Bitter, 4 Guest ales (300+ per year) Ò Gwynt y Ddraig Black Dragon, Ragan Perry, Clytha Perry. ₹ 12 **Facilities** Non-diners area ♦♦ Children's menu Children's portions Play area Garden Beer festival Cider festival Parking WiFi ▦

LLANGYBI
Map 9 ST39

The White Hart Village Inn ◉◉
PICK OF THE PUBS

tel: 01633 450258 **NP15 1NP**
email: enquiries@thewhitehartvillageinn.com
dir: *M4 junct 25 onto B4596 (Caerleon road), through Caerleon High St, straight over rdbt into Usk Rd, continue to Llangybi*

Historic inn serving excellent food

The welcome is literally 'warm' at this picturesque historic inn in the beautiful Usk Valley, where no fewer than 11 fireplaces can be counted. Oliver Cromwell based himself here during local Civil War campaigns; so add a priest hole, exposed beams, precious Tudor plasterwork and a mention in T S Eliot's poem *Usk* and this is a destination to savour. Chef-patron Michael Bates offers reliable ales from the likes of Wye Valley Butty Bach, as well as unusual ciders such as Gwynt y Ddraig Farmhouse Scrumpy. Using fresh local produce, and combining exciting ingredients with complementary flavours, head chef Adam Whittle prepares dishes with the utmost attention to detail in his two-AA Rosette menus. Representative choices could include scorched mackerel and whitebait with pepper, asparagus and leek; Cwrw Pentref battered cod with chips and peas; and lemon and clove crème brûlée with warm doughnuts. Extensive seating is available outside.

Open all day 12-11 (Sun 12-10) Closed Mon **Food** Lunch Tue-Sat 12-3, Sun 12-4 Dinner Tue-Sat 6-7 Av main course £16.75 Set menu available Restaurant menu available Tue-Sat ⊕ FREE HOUSE ◀ Wye Valley Butty Bach, Wychwood Hobgoblin Ò Thatchers Gold, Ty Gwyn, Gwynt y Ddraig Farmhouse Scrumpy. ₹ 15 **Facilities** Non-diners area ♦♦ Children's menu Children's portions Garden ⋒ Parking WiFi ▦ (notice required)

LLANTRISANT
Map 9 ST39

The Greyhound Inn
PICK OF THE PUBS

tel: 01291 672505 & 673447 **NP15 1LE**
email: enquiry@greyhound-inn.com
dir: *M4 junct 24, A449 towards Monmouth, exit at 1st junct signed Usk. 2nd left for Llantrisant. Or from Monmouth A40, A449 exit for Usk. In Usk left into Twyn Sq follow Llantrisant signs. 2.5m, under A449 bridge. Inn on right*

Halt awhile at this gateway to Wales

Standing alone, this 18th-century Welsh longhouse, an inn since 1845, has been owned and run by the Davies family for over 30 years. Free-house status ensures a range of real ales, and ciders from Gwynt y Ddraig and Kingstone Press, in the log-fire-warmed Stable Bar, where you can play darts, crib and dominoes. Nick Davies heads the highly-praised kitchen team, whose skills you can enjoy in either the candlelit restaurant, or one of three other dining areas. Among the starters are farmhouse pâté with hot toast; and deep-fried breaded brie wedges with cranberry, orange and red wine sauce. Grills are served with peas and a choice of potatoes or salad; in addition there's steak and kidney pie; chicken curry; lasagne; fresh grilled local trout; cauliflower cheese, and daily specials. Outside are two acres of award-winning gardens and a large paddock.

Open all day 11-11 Closed 25 & 31 Dec, 1 Jan, Sun eve **Food** Lunch all wk 12-2.15 Dinner Mon-Sat 6-10 ⊕ FREE HOUSE ◀ Greene King Abbot Ale, Guest ale Ò Gwynt y Ddraig, Kingstone Press. ₹ 10 **Facilities** Non-diners area ♣ (Bar Garden) ♦♦ Children's menu Children's portions Family room Garden ⋒ Parking WiFi ▦ (notice required)

LLANVAIR DISCOED
Map 9 ST49

The Woodlands Tavern Country Pub & Dining
PICK OF THE PUBS

tel: 01633 400313 **NP16 6LX**
email: info@thewoodlandstavern.co.uk
dir: *5m from Caldicot & Magor*

Family-run free house serving modern British food and Welsh beers

Below Gray Hill, near the Roman fortress town of Caerwent, this friendly pub is popular with walkers, cyclists and fishermen. They like it, not just because it's close to the Wentwood Forest and local rivers, but also because it has a good selection of Welsh real ales, such as Wye Valley, Rhymney Bevan's Bitter and regularly changing guests. In addition, there's its modern British food, with baguettes, all-day breakfasts, jacket potatoes and sausage and mash in the bar, and a main menu inviting you to try Parma and Serrano ham with feta and ricotta-stuffed bell peppers; extra-mature sirloin steak with tomato and mushrooms; steak and ale shortcrust pastry pie; or chicken curry with rice, mango chutney and a poppadom. Dressed Devon crab and prawn salad and other daily fish specials appear on a blackboard; vegetarian options are available too. Sunday roasts are always well received, especially out on the patio.

Open 12-3 6-12 (Sun 12-4) Closed 1 Jan, Sun eve, Mon **Food** Lunch Tue-Fri 12-2, Sat 12-2.30, Sun 12-4 Dinner Tue-Fri 6-9, Sat 6-9.30 ⊕ FREE HOUSE ◀ Rhymney Bevan's Bitter, Felinfoel, Marston's & Pedigree, Wye Valley Butty Bach, Guest ales Ò Westons Old Rosie, Thatchers Gold. ₹ 10 **Facilities** Non-diners area ♣ (Bar Outside area) ♦♦ Children's menu Children's portions Outside area ⋒ Parking WiFi ▦ (notice required)

PICK OF THE PUBS

The Inn at Penallt ★★★★ INN ❀

PENALLT   Map 4 SO51

tel: 01600 772765 **NP25 4SE**
email: enquiries@theinnatpenallt.co.uk
web: www.theinnatpenallt.co.uk
dir: *From Monmouth B4293 to Trellech. Approx 2m, left at brown sign for inn. At next x-rds left. Right at war memorial*

An inn with a fast-growing collection of accolades

Originally a farmhouse in the 17th century, the inn stands between the village green and colourful wildflower meadows that head in the direction of the famous, thickly-wooded Wye Gorge. Owners Andrew and Jackie Murphy, having rescued what was then The Bush from closure, took only a few short years to get it into such good shape that it was a winner of the AA Pub of the Year for Wales, as well as winning other awards. For some, the reasons for its success start in the slate-floored bar, where monopolising the pumps are Welsh and border real ales Wye Valley Butty Bach, Kingstone Bitter and Cwrw Gorslas. The ciders are Welsh too, with Ty Gwyn and Gwynt y Ddraig Black Dragon. Another AA award is a Rosette for the Murphys' cooking repertoire, which you can look forward to while nibbling olives and home-made bread with olive oil, before beginning with chicken liver and truffle parfait with chilli jam; or seared smoked salmon with sweet and sour pickled beetroot,

Lilliput capers and horseradish crisp. For an entrée, pan-roasted monkfish tail with spiced brown shrimp ravioli, prawn velouté and parsley potatoes; or home-made faggots with Herefordshire creamed potato, pea purée, crispy smoked Welsh bacon and red wine jus. Vegetarians often plump for spinach, butternut squash and pine nut cannelloni with lightly spiced tomato sauce, buffalo mozzarella and roasted garlic. Desserts not meant to be overlooked include bitter chocolate and almond tart with almond praline ice cream; and Welsh and Welsh Border cheeses. There are regular gourmet evenings with tasting menus and wine matching. Children and dogs are welcome.

Open Tue 6-11 Wed-Sat 12-11 Sun 12-5 Closed Mon (ex BHs), 5-22 Jan, Wed-Fri 3-6 (Nov-end Apr) **Food** Lunch Wed-Sun 12-2.30 Dinner Tue-Sat 6-9 Set menu ⊞ FREE HOUSE ◼ Wye Valley Butty Bach, Kingstone Bitter, Cwrw Gorslas ♂ Ty Gwyn, Gwynt y Ddraig Black Dragon. ♛ **Facilities** Non-diners area ❧ (Bar Garden) ♦ Children's menu Children's portions Play area Garden ⋒ Parking WiFi ⛺ **Rooms** 4

PANTYGELLI
Map 9 SO31

The Crown

tel: 01873 853314 **Old Hereford Rd NP7 7HR**
email: crown@pantygelli.com
dir: *Phone for detailed directions*

Family-run free house with fine views

A charming family-run free house dating from the 16th century, The Crown has fine views of Skirrid, in Welsh Ysgyrid Fawr, known also as Holy Mountain. Walkers and cyclists love it, but it's a genuine community pub too, serving Bass, Rhymney Bitter, Wye Valley HPA and guest real ales as well as Gwatkin cider, all ideal before or with garlic mushrooms on crostini or deep-fried squid with harissa mayo and rocket; venison sausages with mash, green beans and red onion gravy or tenderloin pork with mange tout and Calvados sauce; and a dessert of sticky toffee pudding with butterscotch sauce or poached pear with vanilla ice cream.

Open 12-2.30 6-11 (Sat 12-3 6-11 Sun 12-3 6-10.30) Closed Mon L **Food** Lunch Tue-Sun 12-2 Dinner Tue-Sat 7-9 ⊕ FREE HOUSE ◀ Rhymney Bitter, Wye Valley HPA, Bass, Guest ales ♂ Westons Stowford Press, Gwatkin Yarlington Mill, Kingstone Press. **Facilities** Non-diners area ✿ (Bar Garden) ⬥ Children's portions Garden ☶ Parking WiFi

PENALLT
Map 4 SO51

The Inn at Penallt ★★★★ INN ⊛ PICK OF THE PUBS

See Pick of the Pubs on page 633

RAGLAN
Map 9 SO40

The Beaufort Arms Coaching Inn & Brasserie ★★★ HL ⊛
PICK OF THE PUBS

tel: 01291 690412 **High St NP15 2DY**
email: enquiries@beaufortraglan.co.uk **web:** www.beaufortraglan.co.uk
dir: *0.5m from junct of A40 & A449 Abergavenny/Monmouth, midway between M50 & M4, signed Raglan*

Excellent hostelry with a rich history

This grandly proportioned former coaching inn has always had strong links with nearby Raglan Castle; during the Civil War Roundhead soldiers frequented the bar during the siege of 1646. Nowadays, the place is equally popular when re-enactments are held at the castle, so it's not unusual to see men in full medieval armour tucking into a full Welsh breakfast in the brasserie. The inn has been beautifully appointed with many delightful design features, while holding strong to its traditional roots. A handsome display of fishing trophies dominates the country bar, where locals and visitors gather and chat over pints of Fuller's London Pride. The inn offers well-kept real ales, ciders such as Westons Stowford Press and Thatchers Gold. Food is served in the lounge, with its carved bar, deep leather settees, and large stone fireplace ('lifted', some say, from the castle), as well as in the private dining room and brasserie. Enjoy skilfully presented modern dishes from a regularly changing menu, such as starters of confit duck leg with braised Puy lentils; and St Illtyd traditional Welsh rarebit, followed by seared sea bass, tiger prawn and mussel tagliatelle, white wine and dill cream; or honey and black pepper duck breast, red cabbage, dauphinoise potatoes and red wine jus. For dessert perhaps cherry cheesecake with cherry and brandy compôte; or trio of home-made ice creams or sorbets.

Open all day all wk **Food** Lunch Mon-Thu 12-3, Fri-Sat 12-5 Dinner all wk 6-9.30 Set menu available ⊕ FREE HOUSE ◀ Fuller's London Pride, Wye Valley Butty Bach, IPA ♂ Westons Stowford Press, Thatchers Gold. ☗ 16 **Facilities** Non-diners area ⬥ Children's menu Children's portions Garden ☶ Parking WiFi ▭ (notice required) **Rooms** 15

RHYD-Y-MEIRCH
Map 9 SO30

Goose and Cuckoo Inn

tel: 01873 880277 **Upper Llanover NP7 9ER**
email: llanovergoose@gmail.com
dir: *From Abergavenny take A4042 towards Pontypool. Turn left after Llanover, follow signs for inn*

Walkers' haven with food from the Aga

Popular with walkers, this friendly, whitewashed pub in the Brecon Beacons National Park has a garden with views of the Malvern Hills and a traditional interior with flagstoned bar area and a wood-burning stove. So, the perfect setting for a pint of well-kept Rhymney Bitter or one of the 85 single malt whiskies. All the food is home made on the Aga by landlady Carol Dollery; typical dishes include parsnip soup; steak and ale pie; lasagne; quiche; and treacle tart. The pub hosts two beer festivals – in May and August.

Open Tue-Thu 11.30-3 7-11 (Fri-Sun all day) Closed Mon (ex BHs) **Food** Lunch Tue-Sun 11.30-3 Dinner Tue-Sun 7-9 ⊕ FREE HOUSE ◀ Rhymney Bitter, Celt Iron Age ♂ Kingstone Press. **Facilities** Non-diners area ✿ (Bar Garden) ⬥ Children's portions Family room Garden ☶ Beer festival Parking **Notes** ⊛

SKENFRITH
Map 9 SO42

The Bell at Skenfrith ★★★★★ RR ⊛⊛ PICK OF THE PUBS

tel: 01600 750235 **NP7 8UH**
email: enquiries@skenfrith.co.uk **web:** www.skenfrith.co.uk
dir: *M4 junct 24 onto A449. Exit onto A40, through tunnel & lights. At rdbt take 1st exit, right at lights onto A466 towards Hereford road. Left onto B4521 towards Abergavenny, 3m on left*

Continuing to build a reputation

In lush countryside overlooking the River Monnow, with splendid views of Skenfrith Castle, stands the 17th-century Bell, now with Jon van Niekerk and Nori Tegyei at the helm. Thoughtful restoration and decoration has safeguarded its heritage, not least its polished flagstone floors and oak beams, while antique furniture and comfortable sofas and chairs add to its allure. Pump regulars in the bar are Wye Valley Bitter, Hereford Pale Ale, Kingstone Classic Bitter and Ty Gwyn cider. The restaurant's regularly-changing dishes feature vegetables, herbs and fruits from the organic kitchen garden. Tempting starters could be Cardigan Bay mussels marinière; and pan-fried local pigeon breast with warm beetroot, black pudding and port reduction. For a main course, try marinated spatchcock poussin with french fries; or seafood linguine with white crab, prawns and mussels. The acclaimed wine list offers a well-chosen world selection. The WiFi's free, but the mobile phone signal comes and goes.

Open all day Closed Tue Nov-Mar **Food** Lunch all wk 12-2.30 Dinner Mon-Sat 7-9.30, Sun 7-9 Av main course £5.95 ⊕ FREE HOUSE ◀ Wye Valley Bitter & HPA, Kingstone Classic Bitter ♂ Westons Stowford Press, Ty Gwyn, Local cider. ☗ 13 **Facilities** Non-diners area ⬥ Children's menu Garden ☶ Parking WiFi ▭ (notice required) **Rooms** 11

Find out more about the AA's accommodation rating schemes on page 8

PICK OF THE PUBS

Newbridge on Usk ★★★★ RR

TREDUNNOCK Map 9 ST39

tel: 01633 410262 **NP15 1LY**
email: bookings@celtic-manor.com
web: www.celtic-manor.com
dir: *M4 junct 24 follow Newport signs. Right at Toby Carvery, B4236 to Caerleon. Right over bridge, through Caerleon to mini rdbt. Straight ahead onto Llangibby/Usk road*

Two hundred-year-old inn, now a smart gastro-pub

The pub really is called this. It sounds like a town or village name, but apart from the pub, there's hardly even a hamlet. What there is, right in front, is a bridge over the River Usk that could only have been considered new several centuries ago. Roman Caerleon and the medieval town of Usk are nearby, as is the pub's parent, the famous Celtic Manor Resort. All of which means this, is exceedingly well located. The interior is a pleasing blend of traditional beamed ceilings, snug corners and open fires, with some modern touches. On a warm day, the riverside garden is the place for slipping into a pint of The Rev. James, or a glass of Tomos Watkin Taffy Apples cider. Catch the right time, and while you do so you could watch the golden light of the setting sun bathe the Monmouthshire hills. Entirely worthy of its AA Rosette is the food, with starters of pumpkin velouté with Welsh goats' cheese and truffle; and glazed belly of woodland pork with black pudding and cider apple salad. Equally so are the mains, including free-range Wye Valley chicken breast with twice-cooked hand-cut chips, Portobello mushrooms and grilled plum tomato; pan-fried wild sea bass with globe artichokes, Parma ham and watercress; and vegetable gratin with herb panko crumbs. Two very hungry people can share fillet of Welsh beef with 24-hour-braised cheek, Perl Las Blue cheese, shin and ale pie, corned beef croquette with greens, creamed mushrooms, red wine shallots and beef jus. A sensible dessert to follow all that would be home-made ice cream and sorbet; those still with room could go for the malt cheesecake. On Sundays a jazz band plays at lunchtimes.

Open all wk 12-mdnt **Food** Lunch all wk 12-2.30 Dinner all wk 5-10 Av main course £19.95 Set menu available ⊕ FREE HOUSE ◀ Brains The Rev. James & Smooth, Guest ale Ö Tomos Watkin Taffy Apples. ♟ 12
Facilities Non-diners area ♦♦ Children's menu Children's portions Garden ⋒ Parking WiFi 🚌 **Rooms** 6

TINTERN PARVA
Map 4 SO50

Fountain Inn

tel: 01291 689303 **Trellech Grange NP16 6QW**
email: fountaininntrellech@btconnect.com
dir: *From M48 junct 2 follow Chepstow then A466 & Tintern signs. In Tintern turn by George Hotel for Raglan. Bear right, inn at top of hill, 2m from A466*

Good food and well-kept ales at this village pub

A fine old inn dating from 1611 in lovely countryside, with a garden overlooking the Wye Valley. The pub offers several curries, including chicken Kashmiri, and fruit and vegetable Jalfrezi; and Welsh Black beef, Welsh lamb and roasted ham, all with fresh vegetables, roast potatoes, Yorkshire pudding and beer gravy. There is also a fresh fish menu with whole griddled flounder; sizzling crevettes; and beer-battered cod and chips. The owners' passion for real ales and ciders is evident both in the great bar line-up, and at the September beer festival.

Open all wk Tue-Sun all day (Mon 4-8) **Food** Lunch Tue-Sun 12-2.30 Dinner all wk 6-8 ⊕ FREE HOUSE ◀ Wychwood Hobgoblin, Brains The Rev. James, Kingstone Classic Bitter, Whittingtons Cats Whiskers, Butcombe, Mayfields, Rhymney, Hook Norton, Hereford, Ring O'Bells, Bass, Guest ales ○ Thatchers Gold & Traditional. ☻ 9 **Facilities** Non-diners area ♣ (Bar Garden) ♦ Children's menu Children's portions Family room Garden ⋒ Beer festival Parking WiFi ☞ (notice required)

TREDUNNOCK
Map 9 ST39

Newbridge on Usk ★ ★ ★ ★ RR ◉
PICK OF THE PUBS

See Pick of the Pubs on page 635

TRELLECH
Map 4 SO50

The Lion Inn
PICK OF THE PUBS

tel: 01600 860322 **NP25 4PA**
email: debs@globalnet.co.uk
dir: *From A40 S of Monmouth take B4293, follow Trellech signs. From M8 junct 2, straight across rdbt, 2nd left at 2nd rdbt, B4293 to Trellech*

A traditional inn with nautical links

Built in 1580 as a brewhouse and inn by a former sea captain, the Lion consists of two rooms, both with open fires; one is a traditional bar, the other a restaurant. Although best known for its food and drink, the pub also once showed true versatility by providing the best-dressed entry in the Monmouth raft race. Debbie Zsigo has run it for the past 20 years and knows instinctively what works. In the bar the answer is Wye Valley Butty Bach, and a number of local ciders including Raglan Cider Mill Snowy Owl. In the restaurant Debbie provides bar snacks, pizzas, light meals and a range of main dishes, typically home-made cottage pie; breaded whole tail scampi; home-cooked ham, egg and chips; and pasta carbonara. There's a stream and an aviary in the garden, and beautiful views from the suntrap courtyard. Time a visit for the beer festival in June.

Open 12-3 6-11 (Mon 12-3 7-11 Thu 12-3 6-12 Fri-Sat 12-12 Sun 12-4.30) Closed Sun eve **Food** Lunch Mon-Fri 12-2, Sat-Sun 12-2.30 Dinner Mon 7-9.30, Tue-Sat 6-9.30 Av main course £15 Restaurant menu available all wk ⊕ FREE HOUSE ◀ Butcombe Bitter, Felinfoel Double Dragon, Wye Valley Butty Bach ○ Springfield Red Dragon, Raglan Cider Mill Snowy Owl Sweet Perry. **Facilities** Non-diners area ♣ (Bar Garden) ♦ Children's portions Garden ⋒ Beer festival Cider festival Parking ☞ (notice required)

USK
Map 9 SO30

The Nags Head Inn

tel: 01291 672820 **Twyn Square NP15 1BH**
email: keynags@tiscali.co.uk
dir: *On A472*

Bustling old town hostelry in the Vale of Gwent

Fronting the old town square mid-way between the castle and fine priory church, parts of the inn date from the 15th century. Saunter around the old town before sampling the largely Welsh real ales here, where the same family has held-sway for over 45 years, lovingly caring for the highly-traditional interior that's all beams and polished tables, rural artefacts and horse-brasses. The tempting menu draws on the wealth of produce the fertile Vale of Gwent can offer; seasonal game dishes are a speciality, whilst there's a good vegetarian selection; try the cheese and leek Glamorgan sausage perhaps.

Open all wk 10.30-2.30 5-11 Closed 25 Dec **Food** Lunch all wk 11.45-1.45 Dinner all wk 5.30-9.30 Av main course £10 Restaurant menu available all wk ⊕ FREE HOUSE ◀ Brains Bitter, Buckley's Bitter, The Rev. James & Bread of Heaven, Sharp's Doom Bar ○ Westons Stowford Press. ☻ 9 **Facilities** Non-diners area ♣ (Bar Restaurant Garden) ♦ Children's menu Children's portions Garden Outside area ⋒ Parking WiFi ☞

The Raglan Arms ◉
PICK OF THE PUBS

tel: 01291 690800 **Llandenny NP15 1DL**
email: raglanarms@gmail.com
dir: *From Monmouth take A449 to Raglan, left in village. From M4 take A449 exit. Follow Llandenny signs on right*

Peaceful setting for great food in the Vale of Gwent

At the heart of a small village tucked between Tintern Forest and the rich agricultural lands of the Usk Valley, this neat, stone-built 19th-century pub gains plaudits for its ever-varying, oft-changing menu. The high quality local produce and culinary skills of the team here have gained an AA Rosette for the compact, thoughtfully-balanced menu which mixes the best of Welsh with a more international reach. Indulge with a starter of grilled mackerel fillet with choucroute, mussels and juniper and clear the palate with one of 18 wines by the glass; then launch in to rabbit cooked in Marsala with linguine, or perhaps roast fillet of cod with tomato fondant, herb crust, salsify and olive oil mash. Local pork and lamb also feature, together with village-grown vegetables and home-cured bacon. Customers popping in for a fireside pint will appreciate the real ales form the respected Wye Valley Brewery.

Open Tue-Fri 12-2 6.30-9 (Sat 12-2.30 6.30-9.30 Sun 12-2.30) Closed 25-27 Dec, Sun eve & Mon **Food** Lunch Tue-Fri 12-2, Sat-Sun 12-2.30 Dinner Tue-Fri 6.30-9, Sat 6.30-9.30 ⊕ FREE HOUSE ◀ Wye Valley Bitter ○ Thatchers Gold. ☻ 18 **Facilities** Non-diners area ♣ (Bar Garden) ♦ Children's portions Garden ⋒ Parking

NEWPORT

CAERLEON
Map 9 ST39

The Bell at Caerleon

tel: 01633 420613 **Bulmore Rd NP18 1QQ**
email: thebellinn@hotmail.co.uk
dir: *M4 junct 25, B4596 signed Caerleon. In Caerleon before river bridge right onto B4238 signed Christchurch. Left into Bulmore Rd (follow brown pub sign)*

Superb range of ciders and ales

For more than 400 years this 17th-century coaching inn has stood in ancient Caerleon on the banks of the River Usk. Situated close to an ancient Roman burial ground (also believed by some to be the location of King Arthur's Camelot), the pub is particularly well known for its range of local ciders and perrys. It holds annual real ale and cider festivals with barbecues and free entertainment. Local produce drives the menu, which might include ham hock terrine with home-made chutney; seafood gratin; and venison steak with fondant potato, celery, leek and celeriac ragout and a red wine and port jus.

Open all day all wk **Food** Lunch Mon-Sat 12-2.30, Sun 12-4 Dinner all wk 6-9.30 Set menu available ⊕ ENTERPRISE INNS ◀ Wye Valley HPA, Timothy Taylor Landlord, Tiny Rebel Cwtch Ö Gwynt y Ddraig Black Dragon & Happy Daze, Hallets Real. ♥ 10 **Facilities** Non-diners area ♣ (Bar Garden) ♦♦ Children's portions Garden ⊨ Beer festival Cider festival Parking WiFi ➠ (notice required)

PEMBROKESHIRE

ABERCYCH
Map 8 SN24

Nags Head Inn

tel: 01239 841200 **SA37 OHJ**
email: samnags@hotmail.co.uk
dir: *On B4332 (Carmarthen to Newcastle Emlyn road)*

Classic Welsh riverside pub

Situated at the entrance to the enchanted valley in the famous Welsh folk tales of *Mabinogion*, this famous old inn is the first building you see over the county boundary when crossing into Pembrokeshire from the Teifi Falls at Cenarth. In one of the outbuildings the old forge still remains where the blacksmith crafted the first horse-drawn ploughs for export to America. Old Emrys ale is brewed on the premises ready for consuming in the beamed bars and riverside gardens. The fine fare includes home-made cawl with cheese and crusty bread; steak, Guinness and mushroom pie; and Cardigan Bay lobster.

Open Tue-Sun Closed Mon **Food** Lunch Tue-Sun 12-2 Dinner Tue-Sun 6-9 Set menu available ⊕ FREE HOUSE ◀ Cych Valley Old Emrys. **Facilities** Non-diners area ♣ (Bar Garden) ♦♦ Children's menu Children's portions Play area Garden Parking WiFi ➠

AMROTH
Map 8 SN10

The New Inn

tel: 01834 812368 **SA67 8NW**
email: paulluger@hotmail.com
dir: *A48 to Carmarthen, A40 to St Clears, A477 to Llanteg then left, follow road to seafront, turn left. 0.25m on left*

Old inn specialising in Welsh beef dishes

Originally a farmhouse, this 16th-century inn belongs to Amroth Castle Estate and has been family run for some 38 years. The pub has old-world charm with beamed ceilings, a Flemish chimney, a flagstone floor and an inglenook fireplace. It is close to the beach, with views towards Saundersfoot and Tenby from the dining room upstairs. Along with Welsh beef, home-made dishes include broccoli and cream cheese bake; pork and leek sausages; Greek salad; and minted lamb steak. There is even a toddlers' menu in addition to the children's menu. Enjoy food or drink outside on the large lawn complete with picnic benches.

Open all day all wk Mar-Oct 11-11 (Oct-Mar eve & wknds only) **Food** Contact pub for details ⊕ FREE HOUSE ◀ Sharp's Doom Bar, Hancock's, Preseli Ales, Guinness, Guest ales. **Facilities** Non-diners area ♣ (Bar Garden) ♦♦ Children's menu Children's portions Family room Garden ⊨ Parking ➠

ANGLE
Map 8 SM80

The Old Point House

tel: 01646 641205 **East Angle Bay SA71 5AS**
email: croeso@theoldpointhouse.co.uk
dir: *From Pembroke take B4320 signed Monkton & Hundleton. Right signed Angle. At T-junct left signed West Angle Bay. 1st right at pub sign on wall into narrow lane. Follow lane round bay to pub*

Remote but well worth tracking down

It's all angles round here – Angle village, Angle Bay, Angle RNLI... Indeed, the 15th-century Old Point has been the lifeboatmen's local since 1868, when their boathouse was built nearby. At its uneven-floored heart is the snug, its walls covered in old photos and memorabilia, Felinfoel Best is on handpump, and real cider comes from Honey's in Somerset. Pub food includes sandwiches, jacket potatoes, pan-fried John Dory, curried chicken, Pembrokeshire rib-eye steak, pasta bolognese and daily specials. Picnic tables at the front look across Angle Bay. The track from the village skirts the foreshore, occasionally getting cut off by high spring tides.

Open all day Jul-Sep (12-3 6-10 autumn & winter) Closed 10-31 Jan, Mon & Tue 5 Nov-1 Mar **Food** Lunch 12-2.30 (Mar-5 Oct) Dinner 6.30-8.30 (Mar-5 Oct) ⊕ FREE HOUSE ◀ Felinfoel Best Bitter Ö Honey's Midford Cider, Gwynt y Ddraig. **Facilities** Non-diners area ♣ (Bar Garden Outside area) ♦♦ Children's portions Garden Outside area ⊨ Parking WiFi ➠ (notice required)

CAREW
Map 8 SN00

Carew Inn

tel: 01646 651267 **SA70 8SL**
email: mandy@carewinn.co.uk
dir: *From A477 take A4075. Inn 400yds opposite castle*

One of Wales' best kept secrets

Opposite the Carew Celtic cross and Norman castle, this traditional stone-built country inn is a great place to finish the one-mile circular walk around the castle and millpond. Mandy and Rob Scourfield have celebrated 25 years here, during which time they have built a strong reputation for quality ales and home-cooked food. A meal might include home-made smoked mackerel pâté with toast; pork tenderloin with chorizo sausage in a spicy sauce, served with crispy potatoes; and home-made lemon cheesecake. There's a children's play area in the garden, which also hosts regular barbecues in the summer.

Open all day all wk 11-11 (Sun 12-12) Closed 25 Dec **Food** Lunch all wk 12-2.30 Dinner all wk 6-9 ⊕ FREE HOUSE ◀ Worthington's, Brains The Rev. James, Sharp's Doom Bar Ö Westons Stowford Press. ♥ 9 **Facilities** Non-diners area ♦♦ Children's menu Children's portions Play area Garden ⊨ Parking WiFi ➠ (notice required)

DALE
Map 8 SM80

Griffin Inn

tel: 01646 636227 **SA62 3RB**
email: info@griffininndale.co.uk
dir: *From end of M4 onto A48 to Carmarthen. A40 to Haverfordwest, B4327 to Dale. In Dale (with sea on left) pub on corner by slipway*

By the sea in a hidden corner of west Wales

Standing opposite the sea wall in a pretty coastal village, the Griffin offers the pleasure of roaring log fires in the winter and, in the summer, the joy of eating out on the water's edge, looking across Dale Bay. On tap in the bar you'll find Buckleys Best, The Rev. James and Evan Evans Cwrw Haf (koo-roo - it's Welsh for beer). The kitchen's sourcing policy demands that produce is both local and sustainable: for example, two village fishermen supply fresh fish and seafood from the bay. Arrive there when they land and you can choose from the catch.

Open all wk 12-3 6-11 (Apr-Sep all day) Closed Nov **Food** Lunch all wk 12-2.30 (winter Thu-Sun only) Dinner all wk 5-9 summer, Thu-Sat 6-8.30 winter ⊕ FREE HOUSE ◀ Brains The Rev. James, Evan Evans Cwrw Haf, Buckleys Best Bitter ♂ Westons Stowford Press, Somersby. **Facilities** Non-diners area ♦♦ Children's menu Children's portions Outside area ⊼ Parking WiFi ⊟ (notice required)

LETTERSTON
Map 8 SM92

The Harp Inn

tel: 01348 840061 **31 Haverfordwest Rd SA62 5UA**
email: info@theharpatletterston.co.uk
dir: *On A40, 10m from Haverfordwest, 4m from Fishguard*

Modernised hostelry in the heart of Pembrokeshire

Formerly a working farm and home to a weekly market, this 15th-century free house remained largely unchanged for 500 years. Owned by the Sandall family for over 30 years, the building has a stylish conservatory restaurant where diners can enjoy local favourites like Welsh fillet steak; venison Roquefort; and whole sea bass. Alternatively, the bar lunch menu offers classic pub meals including crispy battered cod and chips. Enjoy lunch in all areas with your children.

Open all day all wk **Food** Lunch all wk 12-9 Dinner all wk 12-9 Av main course £14 Set menu available ⊕ FREE HOUSE ◀ Tetley's, Greene King Abbot Ale ♂ Thatchers Gold. **Facilities** Non-diners area ♦♦ Children's menu Children's portions Play area Garden ⊼ Parking WiFi ⊟ (notice required)

LITTLE HAVEN
Map 8 SM81

St Brides Inn

tel: 01437 781266 **St Brides Rd SA62 3UN**
dir: *From Haverfordwest take B4341 signed Broad Haven. Through Broad Haven to Little Haven*

Great walkers' refuelling stop

An ideal stop for walkers on the nearby Pembrokeshire coastal path as it runs through the seaside village of Little Haven, the St Brides Inn has the added attraction of an indoor ancient well, as well as a pretty floral beer garden. Food-wise expect the likes of deep-fried breaded camembert with warm cranberry sauce; black pudding-stuffed pork loin with cider sauce; and home-made rhubarb and ginger crumble. Lunchtime light bites include a bacon and black pudding bap; and pork and apple sausage and mushroom bap with fried potatoes.

Open all day all wk **Food** Lunch all wk 12-2 Dinner all wk 6-9 ⊕ FREE HOUSE ◀ Brains The Rev. James, Hancock's HB, Pembrokeshire Guest ales ♂ Westons Stowford Press. ♥ 9 **Facilities** Non-diners area ♣ (Bar Garden) ♦♦ Children's menu Children's portions Garden ⊼ WiFi ⊟ (notice required)

The Swan Inn

tel: 01437 781880 **Point Rd SA62 3UL**
email: enquiries@theswanlittlehaven.co.uk
dir: *B4341 from Haverfordwest. In Broad Haven follow seafront & Little Haven signs. 0.75m to inn*

Popular spot in an idyllic setting

Arrive early to bag a window table and savour one of the best views in Pembrokeshire from this 200-year-old pub perched above a rocky cove overlooking St Brides Bay. This free house buzzes with chatter and contented visitors enjoying well-kept real ales and a good choice of wines in the comfortably rustic bar, furnished with old settles, polished oak tables and leather armchairs. There's also an intimate dining room, with an elegant contemporary-style restaurant upstairs; cooking is modern British, with a commitment to seasonal and local produce.

Open all day all wk 11am-mdnt Closed early Jan-mid Feb **Food** Lunch all wk 12-2 Dinner all wk 6-9 ⊕ FREE HOUSE ◀ Brains The Rev. James, Bass. **Facilities** Non-diners area ♣ (Bar) ♦♦ Children's menu Children's portions Garden ⊼ WiFi ⊟ (notice required)

NEWPORT
Map 8 SN03

Salutation Inn

tel: 01239 820564 **Felindre Farchog, Crymych SA41 3UY**
email: johndenley@aol.com **web:** www.salutationcountryhotel.co.uk
dir: *On A487 between Cardigan & Fishguard*

Top local produce served in former coaching inn

This tastefully modernised, 16th-century coaching inn stands on the River Nevern in the Pembrokeshire Coast National Park. Owners since 2000 are John Denley, a veteran of 20 years in restaurants in North Africa and the Middle East, and his wife Gwawr, born two miles away on the slopes of Carningli Mountain. There is an emphasis on fresh locally sourced produce for the menu, which lists pork liver pâté with home-made chutney; paprika chicken breast with tagliatelle; and grilled fillet of fresh salmon with lemon butter. Felinfoel, Brains and a local guest are on tap.

Open all day Closed Tue in winter **Food** Lunch all wk 12.30-2.30 Dinner all wk 6.30-9 Av main course £10 ⊕ FREE HOUSE ◀ Felinfoel, Brains, Local guest ales ♂ Thatchers Gold. **Facilities** Non-diners area ♣ (Bar Garden) ♦♦ Children's menu Children's portions Garden ⊼ Parking WiFi ⊟ (notice required)

PICK OF THE PUBS

The Stackpole Inn

STACKPOLE Map 8 SR99

tel: 01646 672324
SA71 5DF
email: info@stackpoleinn.co.uk
web: www.stackpoleinn.co.uk
dir: *From Pembroke take B4319, follow Stackpole signs, approx 4m*

A real find in beautiful Pembrokeshire

This traditional inn is a walker's delight, set in pristine gardens at the heart of the National Trust's Stackpole Estate and close to the spectacular Pembrokeshire coastal path. There's a rare George V postbox in the mellow stone wall outside, a survival from the time when one of the two original stone cottages was a post office. Nowadays the pub offers facilities for walkers, cyclists, fishermen and climbers, as well as those who simply prefer to relax and do nothing. Once inside, you'll find a slate bar, ceiling beams made from ash trees grown on the estate, and a woodburning stove set within the stone fireplace. The pub's free house status means that there's always a guest beer from around the UK to accompany three Welsh ales, a couple of real ciders and a varied wine list. Local produce from the surrounding countryside and fish from the coast play a major part in the homecooked menu. A lighter lunch menu

offers freshly baked Couronne loaves with an appetising selection of fillings that includes Welsh brie with locally cured bacon, and tuna with tarragon mayonnaise. Three-course appetites might begin with creamy Welsh blue cheese on bitter leaf salad with pickled walnuts and poached grapes, or smoked salmon on potato blini with herb crème fraîche. Main course options range from seared Welsh lamb with Moroccan couscous and tomato jus with seasonal vegetables; to wild sea bass fillet with fennel and saffron risotto. Round things off with caramelised lemon tart and passionfruit sorbet, or creamy rice pudding with cinnamon and apple.

Open all wk 12-3 6-11 Closed Sun eve (winter) **Food** Lunch Mon-Sat 12-2 Sun 12-2.30 Dinner all wk 6.30-9 ⊕ FREE HOUSE ◀ Brains The Rev. James, Felinfoel Double Dragon, Guest ale ♂ Gwynt y Ddraig. **Facilities** ♦♦ Children's menu Children's portions Garden Parking WiFi 🚐

PORTHGAIN
Map 8 SM83

The Sloop Inn

tel: 01348 831449 **SA62 5BN**
email: matthew@sloop-inn.freeserve.co.uk
dir: Take A487 NE from St Davids for 6m. Left at Croesgooch for 2m to Porthgain

Cosy pub with a maritime history

Possibly the most famous pub on the north Pembrokeshire coast, The Sloop Inn is located in beautiful quarrying village of Porthgain and is especially enticing on a cold winter's day. The walls and ceilings are packed with pictures and memorabilia from nearby shipwrecks. The harbour is less than 100 yards from the door and there is a village green to the front, a large south-facing patio and a children's football pitch. With ales like Felinfoel and The Rev. James on the pump, a varied menu includes breakfasts, snacks, pub favourites, steaks and home-caught fish. Just the place to call into when out for one of the amazing nearby walks.

Open all day all wk 9.30am-11pm (winter 11.30-10) Closed 25 Dec eve **Food** Lunch all wk 12-2.30 Dinner all wk 6-9.30 Restaurant menu available all wk ⊕ FREE HOUSE/B G BETTERSPOONS LTD ◀ Hancock's HB, Felinfoel, Brains The Rev. James ♂ Gwynt y Ddraig. **Facilities** Non-diners area ♣ (Garden Outside area) ♦♦ Children's menu Children's portions Garden Outside area ᚛ Parking WiFi ⬛

ROSEBUSH
Map 8 SN02

Tafarn Sinc

tel: 01437 532214 **Preseli SA66 7QT**
email: briandavies2@btconnect.com
dir: Phone for detailed directions

Free house maintaining its nostalgic originality

Built to serve the railway that no longer exists, this large red corrugated-iron free house stands testament to its rapid construction in 1876. This idiosyncratic establishment refuses to be modernised and boasts wood-burning stoves, a sawdust floor, and a charming garden. Set high in the Preseli Hills amid stunning scenery, it is popular with walkers, who can refuel on traditional favourites like local lamb burgers; prime Welsh sirloin steak; home-cooked ham; and Glamorgan sausages with chutney.

Open all day 12-11 Closed Mon (ex BHs & summer) **Food** Lunch Tue-Sat 12-2 Dinner Tue-Sat 6-9 ⊕ FREE HOUSE ◀ Worthington's, Tafarn Sinc, Guest ale. **Facilities** Non-diners area ♦♦ Children's menu Children's portions Garden ᚛ Parking ⬛ (notice required)

ST DOGMAELS
Map 8 SN14

The Teifi Netpool Inn

tel: 01239 612680 **SA43 3ET**
email: pclock101@gmail.com
dir: From A487 follow St Dogmaels signs (B4546). Left signed St Dogmaels, Llandudoch & Poppit (B4546). Left into Maeshfryd St, to end, pub on left

Wide choice of Welsh beers and good food

Historically used by the local fishermen and the place where they sold their daily catch, this traditional pub is family run and family friendly. A little off the beaten track on the banks of the River Teifi near the village green it is worth seeking out. Beers from the Kite microbrewery near Carmarthen feature along with several Welsh guest ales. Sunday lunches are very popular and booking is recommended.

Open all day all wk ⊕ FREE HOUSE ◀ Wye Valley Butty Bach, Kite Brewery ales ♂ Thatchers. **Facilities** ♦♦ Children's menu Children's portions Play area Outside area Parking WiFi

Webley Waterfront Inn & Hotel

tel: 01239 612085 **Poppit Sands SA43 3LN**
email: webleyhotel@btconnect.com
dir: A484 from Carmarthen to Cardigan, then to St Dogmaels, right in village centre to Poppit Sands on B4546

Seafood in a magnificent setting

This long-established family business is spectacularly situated at the start of the Pembrokeshire Coast National Park, a haven for birdwatchers and watersports enthusiasts. The inn offers outstanding views across the River Teifi and Poppit Sands to Cardigan Bay, which supplies the daily catch for the menu. King scallops with crispy bacon and carrot purée, perhaps to start, followed by pan-seared salmon and sautéed new potatoes. The specials board might feature dressed lobster and crab. Other dishes include rump steak and five bean chilli. The bar serves Gwynt y Ddraig Welsh cider together with a selection of ales.

Open all day all wk **Food** Lunch all wk 12-2.30 Dinner all wk 6-8.30 ⊕ FREE HOUSE ◀ Brains Buckley's Bitter, Felinfoel, Guest ales ♂ Gwynt y Ddraig. ♥ 8 **Facilities** Non-diners area ♣ (Bar Garden) ♦♦ Children's menu Children's portions Family room Garden ᚛ Parking WiFi ⬛

STACKPOLE
Map 8 SR99

The Stackpole Inn
PICK OF THE PUBS

See Pick of the Pubs on page 639

TENBY
Map 8 SN10

Hope and Anchor

tel: 01834 842131 **Saint Julians St SA70 7AX**
dir: A478 or A4139 into Tenby. Into High St, becomes Saint Julians St. Pub on left

A popular pub with a good choice of fish dishes

Heading down towards the harbour and the beach at Tenby and you can't miss the blue Hope and Anchor pub. Traditionally a fishing pub it has remained popular with locals for years and years. They offer seven real ales that change throughout the week and the menus and special boards feature lots of fish. Tenby mackerel, pan fried in butter or with a Cajun seasoning; sea bass with rocket and couscous salad; or mussels cooked with bacon, onions, cider and cream; even locally caught lobster is featured. Meat eaters might choose peppered pork steaks; steak and ale pie; or rosemary and garlic chicken.

Open all day all wk Closed 25 Dec L **Food** Contact pub for details Av main course £10 ⊕ FREE HOUSE ◀ Sharp's Doom Bar, Brains The Rev. James, Felinfoel Double Dragon ♂ Westons Scrumpy, Old Rosie, Vintage Cloudy, Welsh ciders. ♥ 13 **Facilities** Non-diners area ♦♦ Children's menu Children's portions Garden ᚛ ⬛ (notice required)

POWYS

The Usk Inn — PICK OF THE PUBS

tel: 01874 676251 **Talybont-on-Usk LD3 7JE**
email: stay@uskinn.co.uk
dir: 6m E of Brecon, just off A40 towards Abergavenny & Crickhowell

An ideal stop for Brecon Beacon visitors

The Usk Inn enjoys an enviable position about 300 metres from the village centre at Talybont-on-Usk on the picturesque Abergavenny to Brecon road. Attracting locals and visitors to the Brecon Beacons National Park in equal number, the inn opened in the 1840s just as the Brecon to Merthyr railway line was being built alongside it. Another source of custom is the Brecon to Monmouthshire canal that passes through the village. Over the years The Usk Inn has been transformed from an ordinary pub into a country inn with a restaurant. Expect a choice of guest ales at the bar, along with ciders and popular wines. Its reputation for good cooking and good value is based on the kitchen's selection of carefully sourced ingredients, served in a blend of traditional and modern dishes.

Open all day all wk 11am-11.30pm (Sun 11-10.30) Closed 25-26 Dec eve ⊕ FREE HOUSE ◀ Guinness, Guest ales Ò Thatchers, Robinsons. **Facilities** ◆◆ Children's portions Garden Parking

The Old Hand and Diamond Inn

tel: 01743 884379 **SY5 9AR**
email: moz123@aol.com **web:** www.oldhandanddiamond.co.uk
dir: From Shrewsbury take A458 towards Welshpool. Right onto B4393 signed Four Crosses. Coedway approx 5m

One for all the family

On the Powys/Shropshire border, this 17th-century inn retains much of its original character, with exposed beams and an inglenook fireplace. Its reputation for good quality food owes much to local farmers who supply excellent meats, including lamb and mutton from rare-breed Jacob sheep. Enjoy local Shropshire Lad and guest real ales in the bar, while choosing from an extensive menu that lists slow roasted lamb Henry; home-made curry; fish of the day; and a daily vegetarian dish. Among the desserts are sticky toffee pudding and ginger and lime cheesecake. The beer garden has plenty of seating and a children's play area.

Open all day all wk 11am-1am **Food** Lunch Mon-Thu 12-2.30, Fri-Sun 12-9.30 Dinner Mon-Thu 6-9.30, Fri-Sun 12-9.30 Restaurant menu available all wk ⊕ FREE HOUSE ◀ Worthington's, Wood's Shropshire Lad, Guest ales. **Facilities** Non-diners area ❀ (Bar Garden) ◆◆ Children's portions Play area Garden ⋈ Parking WiFi 🚌

The Bear ★★★★ INN ⊛ — PICK OF THE PUBS

tel: 01873 810408 **Brecon Rd NP8 1BW**
email: bearhotel@aol.com **web:** www.bearhotel.co.uk
dir: On A40 between Abergavenny & Brecon

Quintessential market town coaching inn

Probably built for a wealthy 15th-century merchant to live in, this imposing white-painted inn has been run by the Hindmarsh family for over 35 years. Their rug-strewn, antique-laden bar offers sandwiches and baguettes on top of the main menu, and Welsh real ales take the lead at the pumps. Alternatively, dine in the original D Restaurant, intimately dressed with linen and fresh cut flowers, or at a table in the restored former kitchen. The cuisine, holder of an AA Rosette, makes good use of Welsh produce, as in Black Mountain smoked salmon with quail egg and horseradish Chantilly; slow-braised Welsh lamb shank with spring onion mash; and Bwlch venison sausages with colcannon. For vegetarians, perhaps spaghetti with tomatoes, peppers and capers. Finish with local cheeses, or apple and whinberry crumble and custard. Bring your dog, there are lots of good walks in the area.

Open all day all wk Closed 25 Dec **Food** Lunch all wk 12-2 Dinner Mon-Sat 6-10, Sun 7-9.30 Av main course £11-£12 Restaurant menu available Mon-Sat ⊕ FREE HOUSE ◀ Brains The Rev. James, Wye Valley Butty Bach, Hancock's HB, Guest ales Ò Westons Stowford Press. ♟ 10 **Facilities** Non-diners area ❀ (Bar Garden) ◆◆ Children's menu Children's portions Family room Garden ⋈ Parking WiFi 🚌 (notice required) **Rooms** 34

The Tanners Arms

tel: 01874 638032 **LD3 8SF**
email: info@tannersarmspub.com
dir: From Brecon take A40 towards Llandovery. Left onto A4067 to Defynnog

Old inn not far from the glorious Brecon Beacons

In a tiny village and overlooking open countryside, this 17th-century inn derives its name from the tannery that was once in business up the road. In the foothills of the Brecon Beacons National Park it makes a good stopping point for those setting off to explore this mountain area. The pub has real ales and ciders changing very regularly and the menus offer breaded crab claws; home-made pâté on toast as starter choices, then there's brie and artichoke quiche with roasted vegetables; 8oz gammon steak with all the trimmings; and a variety of curries ranging from vegetable korma to beef vindaloo. Lunchtime quick bites and sandwiches are offered too.

Open all wk 5-12 (Fri 4-12 Sat-Sun 12-12) **Food** Lunch Sat-Sun 12-2 Dinner all wk 6-9 Restaurant menu available all wk ⊕ FREE HOUSE ◀ Constantly changing ales Ò Constantly changing ciders. **Facilities** Non-diners area ❀ (Bar Garden) ◆◆ Children's menu Children's portions Garden ⋈ Beer festival Parking WiFi 🚌 (notice required)

GLANGRWYNEY
Map 9 SO21

The Bell

tel: 01873 811115 **NP8 1EH**
email: thebellinncrickhowell@gmail.com
dir: *On A40 halfway between Abergavenny & Crickhowell*

A warm retreat in a small rural village

Real ale lovers should visit this lovely Brecon Beacons National Park pub during the Easter or Summer Bank Holiday beer and cider festivals. In fact, at any time it's the perfect destination for anyone who wants somewhere comfortable for a decent pint and something to eat. In addition to a constantly-changing selection of local ales and ciders — Symonds, for example — the menu draws extensively on local produce for dishes such as the creamy cockles, bacon and laverbread on granary toast; home-made steak and real Welsh ale pie; and oven-baked cod parcel with creamy white wine and cucumber sauce.

Open 12-3 6-11.30 (Sat 12-12 Sun 12-10.30) Closed Mon (ex holiday periods) **Food** Lunch Tue-Fri 12-2.30, Sat-Sun 12-4 Dinner Tue-Sat 6-9 Av main course £10 ⊕ BRAINS ◼ Bitter & The Rev. James ♂ Gwynt y Ddraig Orchard Gold, Symonds. **Facilities** Non-diners area ☙ (Bar Garden) ♦ Children's menu Children's portions Garden ⌁ Beer festival Cider festival Parking WiFi ▰ (notice required)

GLASBURY
Map 9 SO31

The Harp Inn

tel: 01497 847373 **HR3 5NR**
email: info@theharpinn.co.uk **web:** www.theharpinn.co.uk
dir: *In village centre on B4350, approx 3.5m from Hay-on-Wye*

Country pub with a long history

A pub since the 17th century, this comfortable inn overlooks the River Wye and is just a few miles from Hay-on-Wye itself. In the bar, grab a table and enjoy a pint of one of several local real ales, including Mayfields Glasbury Undaunted specially brewed for the pub. The tempting menu offers classics of home-made steak and Wye Valley stout pie, trio of Brian George's pork sausages and Thai green curry. Regular music events include monthly folk and Irish sessions and occasional jazz nights.

Open 12-3 6-12 Closed Mon **Food** Lunch Tue-Sun 12-2 Dinner Tue-Sun 6.30-9 ⊕ FREE HOUSE ◼ Wye Valley Dorothy Goodbody's Golden Ale & Butty Bach, Mayfields Glasbury Undaunted ♂ Westons Stowford Press. **Facilities** Non-diners area ☙ (Bar Garden) ♦ Children's menu Children's portions Garden ⌁ Parking WiFi ▰ (notice required)

HAY-ON-WYE
Map 9 SO24

The Old Black Lion ★★★★ INN ◉   PICK OF THE PUBS

tel: 01497 820841 **HR3 5AD**
email: info@oldblacklion.co.uk **web:** www.oldblacklion.co.uk
dir: *From B4348 in Hay-on-Wye into Lion St. Inn on right*

Historic inn with award-winning food

Close to Lion Gate, one of the original entrances to the old walled town of Hay-on-Wye, parts of this charming whitewashed inn date from the 1300s, although structurally most of it is 17th-century. The oak-timbered bar is furnished with scrubbed pine tables, comfy armchairs and a log-burner — perfect for savouring a pint of Wye Valley bitter. The inn has a long-standing reputation for its food — witness the AA Rosette — and the pretty dining room overlooking the garden terrace is where to enjoy grilled mackerel and rhubarb chutney followed by roast pork chop, bubble-and-squeak and Calvados gravy; or roast fillet of salmon, crushed potatoes, mushroom and white wine sauce. Hay, of course, has bookshops at every turn, and it is also home to a renowned annual literary festival. Please note that only children over eight are permitted in the pub.

Open all day all wk 8am-11pm Closed 24-26 Dec **Food** Lunch Mon-Fri 12-2, Sat-Sun 12-2.30 Dinner Sun-Thu 6.30-9, Fri-Sat 6.30-9.30 ⊕ FREE HOUSE ◼ Old Black Lion Ale, Wye Valley Bitter ♂ Westons Stowford Press. ♀ 8 **Facilities** Non-diners area ♦ (8yrs) Children's portions Garden ⌁ Parking WiFi **Rooms** 10

The Three Tuns

tel: 01497 821855 **4 Broad St HR3 5DB**
email: info@three-tuns.com
dir: *In town centre*

Stylish town pub with a warm welcome

Despite a devastating fire a few years ago, this 16th-century, possibly older, pub has attracted an eclectic roll-call of famous, even infamous, visitors, from Jools Holland to the Great Train Robbers. In the bar is an old settle, reclaimed from the fire and restored for that welcome pint of Wye Valley Bitter or Butty Bach. The menus range from a home-made pizza, baked ciabatta or beer battered haddock and chips to choices such as Welsh rarebit, Caerphilly cheese, smoked bacon salad; mixed olive and fennel risotto, deep-fried poached egg, pecorino crackling; and lamb and apricot tagine, lemon couscous and mint yogurt.

Open 11-3 6-11 Closed 25 Dec, Mon & Tue (winter) **Food** Lunch all wk 11-2 Dinner all wk 6-9 ⊕ FREE HOUSE ◼ Wye Valley Bitter, Butty Bach ♂ Westons Old Rosie. **Facilities** Non-diners area ♦ Children's portions Garden ⌁ WiFi ▰

LLANDRINDOD WELLS
Map 9 SO06

The Laughing Dog

tel: 01597 822406 **Howey LD1 5PT**
dir: *From A483 between Builth Wells & Llandrindod Wells follow Howey signs. Pub in village centre*

Village centre inn with adventurous cooking

All you'd expect from a thriving village local, from pub games in the fire-warmed bar to real ales from respected Welsh microbreweries such as Rhymney and The Celt Experience. Originating as a drovers' stopover some 300 years ago and reputedly haunted; the pub's eclectic menu combines the best of Welsh cooking with spicy dishes from around the world. Moroccan lamb and mint meatballs with couscous; or roast Welsh beef topside with red wine gravy are just two of the temptations; spicier options include Malaysian fishballs in yellow coconut curry. The pub is in superb walking country.

Open 6-11 (Fri 5.30-11 Sat-Sun all day) Closed Mon May-Aug except Royal Welsh wk **Food** Lunch Sun 12-2 Dinner Fri-Sat 6.30-9 ⊕ FREE HOUSE ◼ Wye Valley Bitter &

Butty Bach, The Celt Experience Celt-Bronze Ale, Felinfoel Double Dragon, Rhymney Bevan's Bitter. **Facilities** Non-diners area 🐾 (Bar Garden) 🍴 Children's portions Garden 🏕 🚌 (notice required)

Cain Valley Hotel

tel: 01691 648366 **High St SY22 5AQ**
email: info@cainvalleyhotel.co.uk
dir: *From Shrewsbury & Oswestry follow signs for Lake Vyrnwy onto A490 to Llanfyllin. Hotel on right*

Traditional food in long-established hotel

A watering hole since the 17th century, this hotel offers the choice of an oak-panelled lounge bar and a heavily beamed restaurant. A full bar menu is available at lunchtime and in the evening typically offers Thai fishcakes; prawns with Marie Rose sauce, which might be followed by grilled lamb double chop with redcurrant and rosemary sauce; home-made steak and ale pie; chicken in a creamy garlic mushroom sauce. Lovers of mild ale will find Ansell's in the bar, alongside The Rev. James and Westons Stowford Press cider.

Open all day all wk 11.30am-mdnt (Sun 12-11) Closed 25 Dec **Food** Lunch all wk 12-2 Dinner all wk 7-9 Av main course £10 Restaurant menu available all wk ⊕ FREE HOUSE 🍺 Worthington's, Ansell's Mild, Guinness, Brains The Rev. James ♨ Westons Stowford Press. **Facilities** Non-diners area 🍴 Children's menu Children's portions 🏕 Parking WiFi 🚌 (notice required)

The Coach & Horses

tel: 01874 730245 **Cwmcrawnon Rd NP8 1LS**
email: info@coachandhorses.org
dir: *Take A40 from Abergavenny towards Brecon. At Crickhowell left onto B4558 to Llangynidr (NB narrow river bridge), or from Beaufort take B4560 through Brynmawr to Llangynidr*

Enjoy local ales close to the Brecon Beacons

Just two minutes' walk from the nearby canal moorings and surrounded by the Brecon Beacons, this early 18th-century free house is also a popular meeting place for car club members - the car park can accommodate over 70 vehicles. Changing real ales are sourced from a 40-mile radius, and the talented chefs prepare the likes of deep-fried brie followed by home-made venison faggots with horseradish mash and a red wine sauce, finishing with chilled banana terrine. The beer garden has lovely views over the countryside.

Open all day 12-12 Closed Mon in winter **Food** Lunch all wk 12-2 Dinner all wk 6-9 ⊕ FREE HOUSE 🍺 Wye Valley Butty Bach, Sharp's Doom Bar, Bass. **Facilities** Non-diners area 🐾 (Bar Garden) 🍴 Children's menu Children's portions Garden 🏕 Parking WiFi 🚌 (notice required)

Wynnstay Hotel   PICK OF THE PUBS

tel: 01654 702941 **SY20 8AE**
email: info@wynnstay-hotel.com
dir: *At junct A487 & A489. 5m from A470*

Strong commitment to flavoursome Welsh produce

The Romans called it Maglona; today locals abbreviate this busy market town's name to 'Mach'. It was here in the late 18th century that politician Sir Watcyn Williams-Wynne built his pied-à-terre. Now just named the Wynnstay (historically 'the Wynnstay, Herbert Arms and Unicorn Hotel'), the bar tempts with real ales from the Celt Experience Brewery in Caerphilly. The child- and dog-friendly operation is

run by Paul Johns and his brother Gareth, a Master Chef of Great Britain dedicated to sourcing ingredients, as far as is practicable, from within a 50-mile radius. So should you decide to eat only dishes declaring their Welsh origin, you could choose Clywedog trout pâté; Mathafarn pheasant strips with lentils, smoked bacon, red cabbage and mash; rare Gwarcwm beef salad; or line-caught Aberdyfi mullet with roast vegetables. Local cheeses and ice creams can be sampled to complete your taste of Wales.

Open all wk 12-2.30 6-11 Closed 1wk over New Year **Food** Contact pub for details Set menu available ⊕ FREE HOUSE 🍺 Greene King IPA, The Celt Experience Celt-Golden Ale, Monty's Moonrise, Evan Evans Warrior, Guinness. 🍷 10 **Facilities** Non-diners area 🐾 (Bar Outside area) 🍴 Children's menu Children's portions Outside area 🏕 Parking WiFi 🚌 (notice required)

The Harp   PICK OF THE PUBS

tel: 01544 350655 **LD8 2RH**
email: mail@harpinnradnor.co.uk
dir: *Old Radnor signed from A44 between Kington & New Radnor*

Enjoyable food in a Welsh longhouse with lovely views

With magnificent views across the Radnor Valley, this stone-built Welsh longhouse dates from the 15th century. Open the plain wooden door and you step into a cosy lounge and bars with original oak beams, crackling log fires, semi-circular wooden settles and slate floors; books, board games and hop bines complete the warmly traditional appeal. The food focus is on fresh and seasonal produce, and local sourcing is highlighted on the concise, refreshingly no-frills menu. Leek, mushroom and smoked cheddar tart with slow-roasted tomatoes and dressed leaves makes for a tasty starter. Welsh lamb and beef will probably feature in the main course, alongside a pie or risotto, with grilled fillets of sea bream for fish lovers. Finish with a selection of Welsh cheeses; or warm ginger cake, caramel sauce, vanilla ice cream. Real ales from Shropshire and Herefordshire breweries are rotated, and an annual June beer festival is hugely popular.

Open Tue-Fri 6-11 (Sat-Sun 12-3 6-11) Closed Mon (ex BHs) **Food** Lunch Sat-Sun 12-2.30 Dinner Tue-Sat 6-9 Av main course £12-£14 ⊕ FREE HOUSE 🍺 Three Tuns, Wye Valley, Hobsons, Ludlow, Salopian ♨ Dunkertons. **Facilities** Non-diners area 🐾 (Bar Garden) 🍴 Children's portions Garden 🏕 Beer festival Parking WiFi

The Roast Ox Inn

tel: 01497 851398 **LD2 3JL**
dir: *From Hay-on-Wye take B4351, through Clyro to Painscastle*

Classic pub food in restored rural local

In stunning countryside close to Hay-on-Wye and Brecon, the Roast Ox is traditional country pub and one that was fully restored using traditional building materials and methods. Expect rustic brick floors, stone walls, old fireplaces and a classic pub atmosphere, alongside comfortable furnishings and local Wye Valley Butty Bach ale tapped straight from the barrel. The dining room was originally a blacksmith's workshop, which served the drovers on their way to market with oxen and cattle. Menus feature classic pub dishes and the Sunday roast lunches are famous locally – so it's best to book.

Open Contact pub for opening hours **Food** Lunch all wk 12-2 Dinner all wk 6-9 ⊕ FREE HOUSE 🍺 Sharp's Doom Bar, Wye Valley Butty Bach, Guest ale ♨ Thatchers. 🍷 8 **Facilities** Non-diners area 🐾 (Bar Outside area) 🍴 Children's portions Outside area 🏕 Parking WiFi 🚌 (notice required)

PICK OF THE PUBS

The Castle Coaching Inn

TRECASTLE   Map 9 SN82

tel: 01874 636354
LD3 8UH
email: reservations@castle-coaching-inn.co.uk
web: www.castle-coaching-inn.co.uk
dir: On A40, W of Brecon

Ideal for base for walking in the Brecon Beacons

Privately owned and run by the Porter family, this Georgian coaching inn sits on the old London to Carmarthen route in the northern part of the Brecon Beacons National Park. It makes an ideal base for the pursuit of outdoor activities or, for the less energetic, the simple appreciation of mountain views, lakes, waterfalls and wildlife. The inn has lovely old fireplaces and a remarkable bow-fronted window looking out from the bar, where an open log fire burns throughout the winter. The focus on customer satisfaction makes this a relaxing hostelry, even at weekends when it becomes especially lively. Two real ales on tap change weekly, ensuring a pint in tip-top condition; wines and a good selection of Scottish and Irish whiskies are also served. While settling back to enjoy your drink and the pub's great atmosphere, take a look at the menu and specials board. Some guests prefer to stay in the bar to eat; the menu is the same both here and in the restaurant, although additional bar food includes fresh sandwiches, jackets,

seafood or steak and ale pie, lamb casserole. Starters range from homemade soup of the day with crusty bread, to duck and orange pâté; deep-fried camembert; and a salmon, cod and prawn fishcake served with home-made tartare sauce. Main courses typically include Welsh sirloin steak cooked to your liking with mushrooms, cherry tomatoes and onion rings; supreme of chicken stuffed with Stilton, wrapped in bacon, with a white wine and cream sauce; and slow-roasted Welsh lamb. Desserts press all the right buttons with the likes of Belgian triple chocolate praline torte with vanilla ice cream; and lemon posset with shortbread. Outside, the peaceful terrace and garden beckon on sunny days.

Open all wk Sat-Sun 12-3 Mon-Sat 6-11 Sun 7-11 **Food** Sat-Sun 12-2 Mon-Sat 6.30-9 Sun 7-9 ⊕ FREE HOUSE ◀ Guest ales. **Facilities** ❖ (Bar Garden) ♦♦ Children's menu Children's portions Garden Parking WiFi

TALYBONT-ON-USK — Map 9 SO12

Star Inn

tel: 01874 676635 **LD3 7YX**
email: anna@starinntalybont.co.uk
dir: Exit A40 from Brecon towards Crickhowell, inn in 6m

An astonishing number of beers at Brecon Beacons' pub

In the National Park, with a garden right next to the Monmouthshire & Brecon Canal, and an ever-changing choice of real ales – over 500 guests a year – Ian and Anna Bell's village pub is extremely popular, and even that could be an understatement. Beer festivals pull in even more fans in mid-June and mid-October. But, of course, there's food too, in the shape of Welsh lamb shank with chive mash and rosemary and redcurrant jus; fresh fish and chips in beer batter; and butternut squash and mushroom pie. Under-12s have their own selection and the under-2s can have mash, vegetables and gravy – free.

Open all wk 11.30-3 5-11 Fri-Sun 11.30-11 (summer Mon-Thu 11.30-11)
Food Lunch Mon-Fri 12-2, Sat-Sun 12-2.30 Dinner all wk 6-9 (no food Sun eve Nov-Mar) ⊕ PUNCH TAVERNS ◖ Wye Valley, Brecon Brewing, Guest ales ♂ Gwynt y Ddraig, Guest ciders. **Facilities** Non-diners area ♣ (Bar Restaurant Garden) ♦ Children's menu Children's portions Garden ⊟ Beer festival WiFi

TRECASTLE — Map 9 SN82

The Castle Coaching Inn — PICK OF THE PUBS

See Pick of the Pubs on opposite page

RHONDDA CYNON TAFF

AA PUB OF THE YEAR FOR WALES
2014–2015

PONTYPRIDD — Map 9 ST08

Bunch of Grapes — PICK OF THE PUBS

tel: 01443 402934 **Ynysangharad Rd CF37 4DA**
email: info@bunchofgrapes.org.uk
dir: From A470 onto A4054 (Pentrebach Rd to Merthyr road) into Ynysangharad Rd

Excellent beers and good local food in The Rhondda

The fact there are eight hand pumps on the bar is the first clue that this pub is owned by the award-winning Otley Brewery, which is located in the valley nearby. The brewery's flagship O2 Croeso is one of four regular Otley ales on offer here, alongside guests from other UK microbreweries and imported bottles and kegs from Europe and America. Surrounded by the striking, wooded landscapes of the Rhondda Valley, this 160-year-old market town pub also showcases Welsh draught ciders and the best of the region's food. A true taste of south Wales is the starter of sautéed Welsh mussels marinière-style, maybe followed by chargrilled Breconshire sirloin steak with hand-cut chips; or roasted butternut squash stuffed with pearl barley spinach and Gorwydd Caerphilly cheese with toasted seeds salad. Beer festivals are held here every two months and there's also a well-stocked deli selling local produce.

Open all day all wk **Food** Lunch Mon-Fri 12-2.30, Sat 12-3, Sun 12-3.30 Dinner Mon-Sat 6-9.30 Av main course £9 Restaurant menu available all wk ⊕ FREE HOUSE ◖ Otley Ales, Guest ales ♂ Gwynt y Ddraig, Blaengawney. **Facilities** Non-diners area ♣ (Bar Garden) ♦ Children's menu Children's portions Garden ⊟ Beer festival Parking WiFi

---

SWANSEA

LLANGENNITH — Map 8 SS49

Kings Head ★★★★ INN

tel: 01792 386212 **SA3 1HX**
email: info@kingsheadgower.co.uk **web:** www.kingsheadgower.co.uk
dir: M4 junct 47, follow signs for Gower A483, 2nd exit at rdbt, right at lights onto B495 towards Old Walls, left at fork to Llangennith, pub on right

A pub with it all, near glorious coastline

A lane to Rhossili Bay's magnificent beach starts just along from this 17th-century village inn, which still displays plenty of old beams, exposed stonework and a large open fire. The bar serves a weekly rotating schedule of real ales from the Gower Brewery, which pub landlord Chris Stevens co-founded. Expect much praised home-made food using local produce that includes Vietnamese, Goan and Thai curries; pizzas; gourmet burgers; salt marsh lamb; and Welsh beef and venison. Comfortable and stylish accommodation is available. A beer and cider festival is held during the last weekend of October.

Open all day all wk 9am-11pm (Sun 9am-10.30pm) **Food** Lunch all wk 9am-9.30pm Dinner all wk 9am-9.30pm ⊕ FREE HOUSE ◖ Gower Gold, Lighthouse & Power, Guinness ♂ Gwynt y Ddraig Black Dragon. **Facilities** Non-diners area ♣ (Bar Garden) ♦ Children's menu Children's portions Garden ⊟ Beer festival Cider festival Parking ⇌ **Rooms** 27

REYNOLDSTON — Map 8 SS48

King Arthur Hotel

tel: 01792 390775 **Higher Green SA3 1AD**
email: info@kingarthurhotel.co.uk
dir: Just N of A4118, SW of Swansea

A warm welcome and a delightful setting

Sheep graze on the village green opposite this charming inn set in a pretty village at the heart of the beautiful Gower Peninsula. Inside you'll find real log fires, bare wood floors and walls decorated with nautical memorabilia. Eat in the restaurant, main bar or family room, where choices range from pub favourites such as fillet of cod in a lager batter with home-made tartare sauce, or a Welsh Celtic Pride steak through to healthy salads (maybe Greek, ham or chicken Caesar). Enjoy the food with a choice of well-kept local ales, or one of 11 wines served by the glass.

Open all day all wk Closed 25 Dec **Food** Contact pub for details ⊕ FREE HOUSE ◖ Felinfoel Double Dragon, Tomos Watkin OSB, Cottage King Arthur, Worthington's, Bass. ♀ 11 **Facilities** Non-diners area ♦ Children's menu Children's portions Family room Garden Parking ⇌

VALE OF GLAMORGAN

COWBRIDGE
Map 9 SS97

Cross Inn
PICK OF THE PUBS

See Pick of the Pubs on opposite page

Victoria Inn

tel: 01446 773943 **Sigingstone CF71 7LP**
email: oleary445@aol.com
dir: *From Llantwit Major N on B4270. Right to Sigingstone*

Bright and welcoming village inn with extensive menu

Standing near the top of an old village tucked away along country lanes in the Vale of Glamorgan, the captivating coastline of the Bristol Channel is just a short hop away. The eye-catching white-painted tiling outside beckons villagers and explorers into a cottagey, beamed interior with lots of prints, brass and antiques. At the bar will be found a range of south Wales real ales including bitter from Evan Evans and beers from breweries in nearby Cardiff. Walkers on the popular Valeways Millennium Heritage Trail pop in to revive on ale and the tempting, locally sourced menu which is strong on seafood dishes and proffers modern twists on traditional mains like port and mushroom braised steak.

Open all wk 9.30-3 6-11.30 **Food** Lunch all wk 11.45-2.30 Dinner all wk 6-9 Set menu available Restaurant menu available Mon-Sat ⊕ FREE HOUSE ◖ Hancocks HB, Worthington's Creamflow, Evan Evans. ⦿ 10 **Facilities** Non-diners area ⦿ Children's menu Garden Outside area ⊓ Parking WiFi ⚏ (notice required)

EAST ABERTHAW
Map 9 ST06

Blue Anchor Inn
PICK OF THE PUBS

tel: 01446 750329 **CF62 3DD**
email: blueanchor@gmail.com
dir: *From Barry take A4226, then B4265 towards Llantwit Major. Follow signs, turn left for East Aberthaw. 3m W of Cardiff Airport*

14th-century pub run by the same family for over 70 years

The grandfather of the present owners, Jeremy and Andrew Coleman, acquired this pretty, stone-built and heavily thatched inn in 1941, when he bought it from a large local estate. The inn has been trading almost continuously since 1380. The interior is warmly traditional; a warren of small rooms with low, beamed ceilings and open fires, including a large inglenook. A selection of well-kept real ales, including Wye Valley, is always on tap. An enticing range of food is offered in both the bar and the upstairs restaurant. Choose pub classics like haddock with chips and mushy peas or more upmarket offerings such as bocconcini mozzarella and tomato arrancini followed by roasted venison with sweet potato purée, sautéed smoked pancetta and curly kale. A good choice is offered for Sunday lunch.

Open all day all wk 11-11 (25 Dec 12-2) **Food** Lunch Mon-Sat 12-2 Dinner Mon-Sat 6-9 Set menu available ⊕ FREE HOUSE ◖ Theakston Old Peculier, Wadworth 6X, Wye Valley HPA, Brains Bitter. ⦿ 9 **Facilities** Non-diners area ⦿ (Bar Restaurant Garden) ⦿ Children's menu Garden ⊓ Parking WiFi ⚏ (notice required)

PENARTH
Map 9 ST17

NEW The Pilot

tel: 029 2071 0615 **67 Queens Rd CF64 1DJ**
email: pilot@knifeandforkfood.co.uk
dir: *Phone for detailed directions*

Contemporary community pub with harbour views

Set on a hillside overlooking the watery wonder that is Cardiff Bay, The Pilot has seen immense changes since it originated as a dock-workers' pub. Like the harbour and docklands at its feet, the pub has been totally transformed into a popular destination where drinkers and diners are equally welcome. With craft beers from the respected Otley Brewery in Pontypridd and ciders from Gwynt y Ddraig to slake a thirst, attention can turn to the ever-changing fare outlined on the chalkboard. Pub classics mix with modern British dishes on a pleasing choice that may feature pan-roasted cod with Jerusalem artichoke purée. A beer and cider festival is held twice a year.

Open all day all wk **Food** Lunch all day Dinner all day Av main course £12 ⊕ BRAINS ◖ Otley, Roosters, Local & guest ales ⦿ Gwynt y Ddraig, Guest ciders. ⦿ 17 **Facilities** Non-diners area ⦿ Children's menu Children's portions Outside area ⊓ Beer festival Cider festival WiFi ⚏ (notice required)

WREXHAM

ERBISTOCK
Map 15 SJ34

The Boat Inn

tel: 01978 780666 **LL13 0DL**
email: info@boatondee.com
dir: *A483 Whitchurch/Llangollen exit, towards Whitchurch on A539. After 2m turn right at signs for Erbistock & The Boat Inn*

Local ales and modern food at riverside gem

A dead-end lane past the Victorian church leads to the 13th-century Boat, in an unrivalled position on the banks of the River Dee; there was once a ferry crossing here. Expect to find a cosy flagstoned and oak beamed bar and several rambling rooms with open fires, stone walls and charming nooks and crannies. It's a fine spot for a pint of local Weetwood Cheshire Cat and some modern pub food, best enjoyed in the glorious riverside garden. From the extensive menu choose sticky pork ribs; duck spring rolls; or The Boat seafood platter to start; follow with mains like fish and chips; Cajun chicken and beefburgers; lasagne; linguine carbonara; pie of the day; veal Milanese; steaks or sea bass.

Open all day all wk **Food** Contact pub for details ⊕ FREE HOUSE ◖ Weetwood Best & Cheshire Cat, Black Sheep ⦿ Hereford Dry. ⦿ 10 **Facilities** Non-diners area ⦿ (Bar Garden Outside area) ⦿ Children's menu Children's portions Garden Outside area ⊓ Parking WiFi

GRESFORD
Map 15 SJ35

Pant-yr-Ochain
PICK OF THE PUBS

tel: 01978 853525 **Old Wrexham Rd LL12 8TY**
email: pant.yr.ochain@brunningandprice.co.uk
dir: *From Chester towards Wrexham on A483 take A5156 signed Nantwich (dual carriageway). 1st left into Old Wrexham Rd. Pub 500yds on right*

Accomplished food in elegant setting

The Pant (its full name means Ochain's hollow) is a picture-postcard manor house at the end of a long sweeping drive lined by majestic trees, overlooking a small lake and award-winning gardens. A building has been here since the 13th century, although today's structure is Tudor, as confirmed by the timbers and wattle-and-daub walls behind the inglenook fireplace in the snug. Brunning & Price, the pub's owners, brew their own real ale, so you'll find this in the bar alongside Flowers, Purple Moose and Weetwood. A daily-changing menu may start with treacle-cured sea trout, pickled cucumber and radish salad; then perhaps crab linguine with ginger, lime and chilli; seared calves' liver, buttered mash, roast shallots and Madeira sauce; or tandoori haloumi, roast vegetable kebab, couscous and coriander yogurt. Chocolate bread and butter pudding with apricot compôte and vanilla cream is one of the dessert options.

Open all day all wk 11.30am-11pm (Sun 11.30-10.30) **Food** Lunch all wk 12-5 Dinner Mon-Sat 5-9.30, Sun 5-9 Av main course £12.95 ⊕ FREE HOUSE/BRUNNING & PRICE ◖ Flowers Original, Brunning & Price Original Bitter, Purple Moose, Weetwood Ales Eastgate Ale ⦿ Tomas Watkin Taffy Apples, Aspall. ⦿ 22 **Facilities** Non-diners area ⦿ (Bar Garden) ⦿ Children's menu Children's portions Play area Garden ⊓ Parking WiFi

PICK OF THE PUBS

Cross Inn

COWBRIDGE   Map 9 SS97

tel: 01446 772995
Church Rd, Llanblethian CF71 7JF
email: artherolry@aol.com
web: www.crossinncowbridge.co.uk
dir: *Take B4270 from Cowbridge towards Llantwit Major, pub 0.5m on left*

Ever popular country pub

Much loved by visitors, this 17th-century former coaching inn is set in a picturesque corner of the Vale of Glamorgan's countryside on the fringe of the ancient town of Cowbridge, just a few miles from the splendid Heritage Coast. A family-run pub, Cross Inn has a cosy restaurant and comfortable, character bar with welcoming log fires and a convivial atmosphere. The chefs take great pride in developing daily menus of essentially British food with European influences. Fresh produce is sourced from local farmers and other reliable suppliers, with fish, prime Welsh steaks, poultry and other ingredients delivered every day to supply the bar meals, children's meals and the frequently changing restaurant menu. Expect choices to include pub favourites such as home-made curried chicken, beer battered fillet of cod, wholetail scampi, pies and steaks, local pork and leek sausages and mash. The regularly changing specials board features a variety of fish, meat and game dishes,

and the traditional Sunday lunch are always popular. There is a good wine list of regularly selected, quality wines. On arriving at Cross Inn particularly noticeable are the lovely hanging flower baskets which have won the pub several awards. Dogs are very welcome, and the pub, with a good sized car park, is an ideal starting and finishing point for walkers who enjoy exploring the many delightful country walks the area has to offer.

Open all day all wk 11-11 **Food** Tue-Fri 12-2.30, 5.30-9 Sat 12-9, Sun 12-4
⊕ FREE HOUSE ◧ Hancock's HB, Wye Valley Butty Bach, Evan Evans Crwr, Shepherd Neame Bishops Finger, Thornbridge Jaipur ♂ Westons & Stowford Press, Gwynt y Ddraig.
Facilities Non-diners area ♨ (Bar Garden) ♦ Children's menu Children's portions Garden ⋈ Beer festival Parking WiFi 🚌 (notice required)

LLANARMON DYFFRYN CEIRIOG — Map 15 SJ13

The Hand at Llanarmon ★★★★ INN ● PICK OF THE PUBS

tel: 01691 600666 **LL20 7LD**
email: reception@thehandhotel.co.uk **web:** www.thehandhotel.co.uk
dir: *Exit A5 at Chirk follow B4500 for 11m. Through Ceiriog Valley to Llanarmon Dyffryn Ceiriog . Pub straight ahead*

Imaginative food and well-kept local ales

Make the journey up the remote Ceiriog Valley in the shadow of the Berwyn Mountains, and you'll find this classic country inn with its unique dining room and 13 comfortable en suite bedrooms. Still very much at the heart of the local community, this 16th-century free house was once a stopping place for drovers and their flocks on the old road from London to Anglesey. Original oak beams, burnished brass and large fireplaces set the scene in the bar, where travellers and locals mingle over pints of Weetwood Cheshire Cat. The pub has established a strong reputation for no-nonsense dishes, cooked from scratch with flair and imagination. Typical examples are Szechuan spiced butternut squash pakoras with beetroot purée followed by roasted skate wing with peas, leeks, lettuce and white wine butter sauce. The same menu is served in the bar, the restaurant and on the sunny patio garden.

Open all day all wk 11-11 (Sun 12-10.30) Closed 25 Dec **Food** Lunch Mon-Sat 12-2.20, Sun 12.30-2.45 Dinner all wk 6.30-8.45 Set menu available ⊕ FREE HOUSE ◀ Weetwood Cheshire Cat, Conwy Rampart. **Facilities** Non-diners area ❀ (Bar Garden) ♦♦ Children's portions Garden ⊐ Parking WiFi ☲ (notice required) **Rooms** 13

ROSSETT — Map 15 SJ35

NEW The Golden Lion

tel: 01244 571020 **Chester Rd LL12 0HN**
email: goldenlion@woodwardandfalconer.com
dir: *From Chester take A483 towards Wrexham, left onto B5102 signed Rossett, left onto B5445, pub on left in Rossett*

Attractive village inn with interesting heritage

Haunted by the mischievous ghost of a murderous ploughman, this village-centre pub in the northern Welsh Marches is an engaging mix of old and new. Lots of beams, trusses and wooden flooring offer great character within, melding seamlessly with tasteful decor, countless prints and framed ephemera amidst eclectic furnishings. Outside is an immense, tree-shaded beer garden where a pint of Piffle from Wirral's Brimstage Brewery is amongst the choice brews to sample. The regularly changing fare has much for seafood fans, a good vegetarian choice and may feature meaty mains like venison bourguignon pie; an impressive wine list includes 16 by the glass.

Open all day all wk 12-11 (Sun 12-10.30) Closed 25 Dec & 1 Jan **Food** Contact pub for details ⊕ WOODWARD & FALCONER PUBS LTD ◀ Piffle, Theakston Best Bitter, Guest ales. ♉ 16 **Facilities** Non-diners area ♦♦ Children's menu Children's portions Play area Family room Garden ⊐ Parking WiFi ☲

Beer festivals

Beer festivals, or their equivalent, are as old as the hills. The brewing of hops goes back to the beginning of human civilisation, and the combination of a common crop and a fermenting process that results in alcoholic liquid has long been a cause of celebration. Beer festivals officially began in Germany with the first Munich Oktoberfest in 1810. Wherever in the world beer is brewed, today and for the last few millennia, admirers, enthusiasts, aficionados – call them what you will – have gathered together to sample and praise its unique properties. It happens throughout Europe, in Australia, New Zealand, America and Canada, and annual events are held in pubs all over Britain.

Beer festivals are often occasions for the whole family, when entertainment is laid on for children as well as adults. Summer is naturally a popular season for festivals, when the action can take place outdoors, but many are held in October, traditionally harvest time. Beer festivals are sometimes large and well-advertised gatherings that attract a wide following and last several days; or they might be local but none the less enthusiastic neighbourhood get-togethers. For up-to-date information, please check directly with the pub.

Abbreviations

Etr Easter; Early May BH (1st Monday in May); Spring BH (last Monday in May); Summer BH (last Monday in August); wk week; wknd weekend

Public Holidays 2015

New Year's Day January 1; Good Friday April 3; Easter Monday April 6; Early May Bank Holiday May 4; Spring Bank Holiday May 25; Summer Bank Holiday (August Bank Holiday) August 31 (August 3 Scotland only); St Andrew's Day November 30 (Scotland only); Christmas Day December 25; Boxing Day December 26

ENGLAND

BEDFORDSHIRE

LINSLADE
The Globe Inn
01525 373338

STUDHAM
The Bell in Studham
01582 872460
Summer

BERKSHIRE

CURRIDGE
The Bunk Inn
01635 200400
Jun-Jul

HERMITAGE
The White Horse of Hermitage
01635 200325
Jun

KNOWL HILL
Bird In Hand Country Inn
01628 826622
Jun & Nov

MONEYROW GREEN
The White Hart
01628 621460
Summer

READING
The Flowing Spring
0118 969 9878
Midsummer & Autumn

WALTHAM ST LAWRENCE
The Bell
0118 934 1788
Annually (30 real ales, 10 ciders)

WOKINGHAM
The Broad Street Tavern
0118 977 3706
4 times a year

WOOLHAMPTON
The Rowbarge
0118 971 2213
Contact pub for details

BRISTOL

The Alma Tavern & Theatre
0117 973 5171
Jul (summer fayre)

BUCKINGHAMSHIRE

AMERSHAM
Hit or Miss Inn
01494 713109
Mid Jul wknd

AYLESBURY
The King's Head
01296 718812

BEACONSFIELD
The Red Lion
Knotty Green
01494 680888
Sep

The Royal Standard of England
01494 673382
Summer BH

CHESHAM
The Black Horse Inn
01494 784656

The Swan
01494 783075
Summer BH

CUBLINGTON
The Unicorn
01296 681261
May & Summer BHs

DENHAM
The Falcon Inn
01895 832125
Contact pub for details

DORNEY
The Palmer Arms
01628 666612

FARNHAM ROYAL
The Emperor
01753 643006

GERRARDS CROSS
The Three Oaks
01753 899016
Summer

GREAT HAMPDEN
The Hampden Arms
01494 488255
Summer

HEDGERLEY
The White Horse
01753 643225
Etr, Spring BH & Summer BH

LACEY GREEN
The Whip Inn
01844 344060
May & Sep

LITTLE KINGSHILL
The Full Moon
01494 862397
Mid Jul

MOULSOE
The Carrington Arms
01908 218050
Jun

SEER GREEN
The Jolly Cricketers
01494 676308
Etr wknd & Summer BH

CAMBRIDGESHIRE

BALSHAM
The Black Bull Inn
01223 893844
Contact pub for details

BOURN
The Willow Tree
01954 719775
Summer

COTON
The Plough
01954 210489
Summer

DRY DRAYTON
The Black Horse
01954 782600
Apr (St George's Day wknd)

HEMINGFORD GREY
The Cock Pub and Restaurant
01480 463609
Summer BH wknd

HINXTON
The Red Lion Inn
01799 530601

HISTON
Red Lion
01223 564437
Etr & 1st wk Sep

OFFORD D'ARCY
The Horseshoe Inn
01480 810293
Midsummer

PETERBOROUGH
Charters Bar & East Restaurant
01733 315700
Etr Thu-Etr Mon

SPALDWICK
The George
01480 890293

STRETHAM
The Lazy Otter
01353 649780
Jul

WHITTLESFORD
The Tickell Arms
01223 833025
May

CHESHIRE

ASTON
The Bhurtpore Inn
01270 780917
Jul (130 beers)

CHESTER
Old Harkers Arms
01244 344525
Mar (Pie & Champion Ale Wk)

GOOSTREY
The Crown
01477 532128
Summer

KETTLESHULME
Swan Inn
01663 732943
1st wknd Sep

KNUTSFORD
The Dog Inn
01625 861421

MOBBERLEY
The Bulls Head
01565 873395
Jun

SPURSTOW
The Yew Tree Inn
01829 260274
Etr wknd

STOAK
The Bunbury Arms
01244 301665

STYAL
The Ship Inn
01625 444888
Summer

TARPORLEY
The Swan, Tarporley
01829 733838
Summer

CORNWALL & ISLES OF SCILLY

ALTARNUN
Rising Sun Inn
01566 86636
Mid-late Nov

BOLINGEY
Bolingey Inn
01872 571626
Apr & Oct

BOSCASTLE
Cobweb Inn
01840 250278

CADGWITH
Cadgwith Cove Inn
01326 290513
Oct

CALLINGTON
Manor House Inn
01579 362354
Feb

CONSTANTINE
Trengilly Wartha Inn
01326 340332

CUBERT
The Smugglers' Den Inn
01637 830209
Early May BH wknd

GWITHIAN
The Red River Inn
01736 753223
Etr wknd

HALSETOWN
The Halsetown Inn
01736 795583
Aug

HELSTON
The Queens Arms
01326 573485

MITCHELL
The Plume of Feathers
01872 510387
May

PENZANCE
The Turks Head Inn
01736 363093

PHILLEIGH
Roseland Inn
01872 580254
1st wknd Sep

ST AGNES
Driftwood Spars
01872 552428
Mid Mar (mini beer festival) & Early May BH wknd

ST IVES
The Watermill
01736 757912
Jun & Nov

ST MAWGAN
The Falcon Inn
01637 860225
Jul (last full wknd)

ST MERRYN
The Cornish Arms
01841 532700
Mar (beer & mussel festival)

TRESCO (ISLES OF SCILLY)
The New Inn
01720 422849
Mid May & early Sep

TRURO
Old Ale House
01872 271122

CUMBRIA

BOOT
Brook House Inn
019467 23288
Early Jun

BROUGHTON-IN-FURNESS
Blacksmiths Arms
01229 716824
1st wknd Oct

CARTMEL
The Cavendish Arms
015395 36240

CONISTON
The Black Bull Inn & Hotel
015394 41335

ELTERWATER
The Britannia Inn
015394 37210
2wks mid Nov

HAWKSHEAD
Kings Arms
015394 36372
Jul & Dec

The Sun Inn
015394 36236

LOW LORTON
The Wheatsheaf Inn
01900 85199
Late Mar

LOWESWATER
Kirkstile Inn
01900 85219
Contact pub for details

RAVENSTONEDALE
The Black Swan
015396 23204
Summer

SATTERTHWAITE
The Eagles Head
01229 860237

SEATHWAITE
Newfield Inn
01229 716208
Oct

SIZERGH
The Strickland Arms
015395 61010
Contact pub for details

ULVERSTON
Farmers Arms Hotel
01229 584469

WASDALE HEAD
Wasdale Head Inn
019467 26229

DERBYSHIRE

ASHOVER
The Old Poets Corner
01246 590888
Mar & Oct (Thu-Sun, 40 beers & ciders, live music)

BAKEWELL
The Monsal Head Hotel
01629 640250
Sep

BAMFORD
Yorkshire Bridge Inn
01433 651361
May

BIRCHOVER
Red Lion Inn
01629 650363
Mid Jul

BONSALL
The Barley Mow
01629 825685
BHs (3-4 times a year)

CASTLETON
The Peaks Hotel
01433 620247
Etr

Ye Olde Nags Head
01433 620248
Summer

CHINLEY
Old Hall Inn & The Paper Mill Inn
01663 750529
3rd wknd Feb, 3rd wknd Sep

DALBURY
The Black Cow
01332 824297

DERBY
The Brunswick Inn
01332 290677
1st wknd Oct

EYAM
Miners Arms
01433 630853
3 each year

FENNY BENTLEY
Bentley Brook Inn
01335 350278
Spring BH

HAYFIELD
The Royal Hotel
01663 742721
1st wknd Oct

HOPE
The Old Hall Hotel
01433 620160
BHs

ROWSLEY
The Grouse & Claret
01629 733233

SHARDLOW
The Old Crown Inn
01332 792392
Apr & Oct

DEVON

BLACKAWTON
The George Inn
01803 712342
Early May BH & Summer BH

BRANSCOMBE
The Fountain Head
01297 680359
Mid Jun

The Masons Arms
01297 680300
Jul (30 ales & ciders, live music, BBQ)

BRIDFORD
The Bridford Inn
01647 252250
May & Aug

CLAYHIDON
The Merry Harriers
01823 421270
Summer

CLEARBROOK
The Skylark Inn
01822 853258
Summer BH

CLOVELLY
Red Lion Hotel
01237 431237
Spring BH

CLYST HYDON
The Five Bells Inn
01884 277288
Early May BH

COCKWOOD
The Anchor Inn
01626 890203
Etr, Halloween

HONITON
The Holt
01404 47707

IDDESLEIGH
The Duke of York
01837 810253
Aug

KILMINGTON
The Old Inn
01297 32096
Spring BH Sat & Summer BH Sat

KINGS NYMPTON
The Grove Inn
01769 580406
Jul

MEAVY
The Royal Oak Inn
01822 852944
Summer BH

NEWTON ABBOT
The Wild Goose Inn
01626 872241
Early May BH wknd

PLYMTREE
The Blacksmiths Arms
01884 277474
Biannually

SANDFORD
The Lamb Inn
01363 773676
Contact pub for details

SIDMOUTH
Dukes
01395 513320
1st wk Aug

Beer festivals *continued*

SLAPTON
The Tower Inn
01548 580216
Contact pub for details

TAVISTOCK
The Cornish Arms
01822 612145
Summer BH wknd

TOTNES
Royal Seven Stars Hotel
01803 862125
Contact pub for details

Steam Packet Inn
01803 863880
Mid May (3 days)

TRUSHAM
Cridford Inn
01626 853694

TUCKENHAY
The Maltsters Arms
01803 732350
Contact pub for details

DORSET

BUCKHORN WESTON
Stapleton Arms
01963 370396

CHETNOLE
The Chetnole Inn
01935 872337

CRANBORNE
The Inn at Cranborne
01725 551249
Jun

GUSSAGE ALL SAINTS
The Drovers Inn
01258 840084
Etr

IWERNE COURTNEY OR
SHROTON
The Cricketers
01258 860421

MILTON ABBAS
The Hambro Arms
01258 880233
Jul

NORTH WOOTTON
The Three Elms
01935 812881

STUDLAND
The Bankes Arms Hotel
01929 450225
Mid Aug

WEST STOUR
The Ship Inn
01747 838640
Jun or Jul

WORTH MATRAVERS
The Square and Compass
01929 439229
1st Sat Oct (beer & pumpkin
festival)

COUNTY DURHAM

BARNARD CASTLE
The Morritt Arms Hotel
01833 627232

FROSTERLEY
The Black Bull Inn
01388 527784

LONGNEWTON
Vane Arms
01642 580401
Jul (mini beer festival), Oct
(Blacksheep wknd)

STANLEY
The Stables Pub and
Restaurant
01207 288750
3rd wknd Sep

ESSEX

CASTLE HEDINGHAM
The Bell Inn
01787 460350
Etr wknd, 3rd wknd Jul

CHELMSFORD
Admiral J McHardy
01245 256783

CHRISHALL
The Red Cow
01763 838792
Spring BH

FEERING
The Sun Inn
01376 570442
End of Jun & Sep

GOLDHANGER
The Chequers Inn
01621 788203
Mar & Sep

HASTINGWOOD
Rainbow & Dove
01279 415419
Sep

LITTLE BRAXTED
The Green Man
01621 891659

LITTLEBURY
The Queens Head Inn
Littlebury
01799 520365
Etr

LITTLEY GREEN
The Compasses
01245 362308
2nd last wknd Aug

MARGARETTING TYE
The White Hart Inn
01277 840478
Jul & Nov

MOUNT BURES
The Thatchers Arms
01787 227460
May & Oct

NEWNEY GREEN
The Duck Pub & Dining
01245 421894
Summer BH

STOCK
The Hoop
01277 841137
Spring BH

WENDENS AMBO
The Bell
01799 540382
Summer BH

WOODHAM MORTIMER
Hurdlemakers Arms
01245 225169
Last wknd Jun (25+ real ales
& ciders)

GLOUCESTERSHIRE

ALDERTON
The Gardeners Arms
01242 620257
Spring BH & late Dec (both 5
days)

ALMONDSBURY
The Bowl
01454 612757

The Swan Hotel
01454 625671
Jul

BIBURY
Catherine Wheel
01285 740250

BROCKHAMPTON
Craven Arms Inn
01242 820410
2nd wknd Jul

CHELTENHAM
The Gloucester Old Spot
01242 680321
3 times a year

The Royal Oak Inn
01242 522344
Spring BH

CLIFFORD'S MESNE
The Yew Tree
01531 820719
Oct

COATES
The Tunnel House Inn
01285 770280
1st wknd Aug

DURSLEY
The Old Spot Inn
01453 542870
3 times a year

EBRINGTON
The Ebrington Arms
01386 593223
Early Oct

EWEN
The Wild Duck
01285 770310
Summer

LECHLADE ON THAMES
The Trout Inn
01367 252313
Jun

LEIGHTERTON
The Royal Oak
01666 890250
Contact pub for details

NORTH CERNEY
Bathurst Arms
01285 831281
Jan, Apr, Jul & Oct

SAPPERTON
The Bell at Sapperton
01285 760298

TETBURY
The Priory Inn
01666 502251
Early May BH (real ale & cider)

GREATER MANCHESTER

MANCHESTER
Marble Arch
0161 832 5914
Aug

OLDHAM
The White Hart Inn
01457 872566
Contact pub for details

SALFORD
The King's Arms
0161 839 8726
Sep

STOCKPORT
The Nursery Inn
0161 432 2044
3 times a year (8 guests on
handpump)

WALMERSLEY
The Lord Raglan
0161 764 6680
Summer & Autumn

HAMPSHIRE

BALL HILL
The Furze Bush Inn
01635 253228
Xmas

BEAULIEU
The Drift Inn
023 8029 2342

BISHOP'S WALTHAM
The Hampshire Bowman
01489 892940
Jul & Dec

BRANSGORE
The Three Tuns Country Inn
01425 672232
Last wk Sep

CHALTON
The Red Lion
023 9259 2246
End Jul-beginning Aug

CHARTER ALLEY
The White Hart Inn
01256 850048
Contact pub for details

CHERITON
The Flower Pots Inn
01962 771318
Aug

CLANFIELD
The Rising Sun Inn
023 9259 6975
Sep

EAST BOLDRE
Turfcutters Arms
01590 612331
Aug

EAST STRATTON
Northbrook Arms
01962 774150
Early May BH

EVERSLEY
The Golden Pot
0118 973 2104

FORDINGBRIDGE
The Augustus John
01425 652098
Early May BH

HANNINGTON
The Vine at Hannington
01635 298525
Jun

HAWKLEY
The Hawkley Inn
01730 827205
1st wknd Jun

HOOK
Crooked Billet
01256 762118
Summer BH

HURSLEY
The Kings Head
01962 775208
Summer BH

LITTLETON
The Running Horse
01962 880218

LYNDHURST
New Forest Inn
023 8028 4690
2nd wknd Jul

NORTH WALTHAM
The Fox
01256 397288
Late Apr

OLD BASING
The Crown
01256 321424
Aug

PETERSFIELD
The Old Drum
01730 300544
1st wknd in Aug

The White Horse Inn
01420 588387
Jun

SELBORNE
The Selborne Arms
01420 511247
1st wknd Oct

STOCKBRIDGE
The Three Cups Inn
01264 810527
Contact pub for details

SWANMORE
The Rising Sun
01489 896663
Summer BH (Sat)

TICHBORNE
The Tichborne Arms
01962 733760
Jun

WINCHESTER
The Bell Inn
01962 865284
Summer

The Westgate Inn
01962 820222

HEREFORDSHIRE
BRINGSTY COMMON
Live and Let Live
01886 821462
Etr wknd

HOARWITHY
The New Harp Inn
01432 840900
BHs

KIMBOLTON
Stockton Cross Inn
01568 612509

LEOMINSTER
The Grape Vaults
01568 611404
2nd Sat Dec (Victorian Street Market day)

MICHAELCHURCH ESCLEY
The Bridge Inn
01981 510646
Summer BH

ORLETON
The Boot Inn
01568 780228
Last wknd Jul

WELLINGTON
The Wellington
01432 830367
Jun

WOOLHOPE
The Crown Inn
01432 860468
Early May BH

HERTFORDSHIRE
ALDBURY
The Valiant Trooper
01442 851203
BHs

ARDELEY
Jolly Waggoner
01438 861350
Aug

BARLEY
The Fox & Hounds
01763 849400
BH wknds

HERONSGATE
The Land of Liberty, Peace and Plenty
01923 282226
Etr, Summer BH, Xmas

PERRY GREEN
The Hoops Inn
01279 843568
Aug

TRING
The Cow Roast Inn
01442 822287

WATTON-AT-STONE
The Bull
01920 831032
May & Oct

WILLIAN
The Fox
01462 480233

ISLE OF WIGHT
NITON
Buddle Inn
01983 730243
Jun & Sep

NORTHWOOD
Travellers Joy
01983 298024
Jul & Sep

KENT
CHARING
The Bowl Inn
01233 712256
Mid Jul

CHILHAM
The White Horse
01227 730355
Summer

FAVERSHAM
Albion Taverna
01795 591411
Early Sep, annual Hop Festival

HALSTEAD
Rose & Crown
01959 533120
Spring, Summer & Autumn

HAWKHURST
The Great House
01580 753119

HERNHILL
The Red Lion
01227 751207
Summer BH

IDEN GREEN
The Peacock
01580 211233

LOWER HALSTOW
The Three Tuns
01795 842840
Summer BH

ROLVENDEN
The Bull
01580 241212

STALISFIELD GREEN
The Plough Inn
01795 890256

SMARDEN
The Chequers Inn
01233 770217

TONBRIDGE
The Little Brown Jug
01892 870318
May & Oct

TUNBRIDGE WELLS (ROYAL)
The Beacon
01892 524252
3 in summer

WEST MALLING
The Farm House
01732 843257

LANCASHIRE
BILSBORROW
Owd Nell's Tavern
01995 640010
1st wknd Jul (American Beer Festival); 1st wk Sep (Oyster Festival); last wk Oct (Oktoberfest)

CHORLTON CUM HARDY
The Horse & Jockey
0161 860 7794
Last wknd Sep

CLAUGHTON
The Fenwick Seafood Pub
01524 221157

HEST BANK
Hest Bank Inn
01524 824339

LANCASTER
The Sun Hotel and Bar
01524 66006
Summer

The White Cross
01524 33999
Late Apr (beer & pie festival)

PARBOLD
The Eagle & Child
01257 462297
Early May BH

TOCKHOLES
The Royal Arms
01254 705373

LEICESTERSHIRE
LONG WHATTON
The Royal Oak
01509 843694
Summer BH

MOUNTSORREL
The Swan Inn
0116 230 2340
May & Summer BHs

OADBY
The Cow & Plough
0116 272 0852
Quarterly

LINCOLNSHIRE
INGHAM
Inn on the Green
01522 730354
Summer

LINCOLN
The Victoria
01522 541000
Halloween & Winter

LITTLE BYTHAM
The Willoughby Arms
01780 410276
Summer BH

THEDDLETHORPE ALL SAINTS
Kings Head Inn
01507 339798
Jul

LONDON
EC1
The Peasant
020 7336 7726
Apr & Nov

Ye Olde Mitre
020 7405 4751
May, Aug & Dec

N1
The Charles Lamb
020 7837 5040
Spring BH

The Drapers Arms
020 7619 0348
Aug

NW1
The Engineer
020 7483 1890

The Prince Albert
020 7485 0270
BHs

NW3
The Holly Bush
020 7435 2892

NW5
The Lord Palmerston
020 7485 1578

SE1
The George Inn
020 7407 2056

SE10
The Old Brewery
020 3327 1280
4 times a year

SW3
Coopers Arms
020 7376 3120
May

SW6
The White Horse
020 7736 2115
4 times a year (American, Great British, Old Ale & European)

SW10
The Hollywood Arms
020 7349 7840

W8
The Windsor Castle
020 7243 8797

W14
The Albion
020 7603 2826
Aug

Beer festivals *continued*

LONDON, GREATER

CHELSFIELD
The Five Bells
01689 821044
Etr & Oct

KINGSTON UPON THAMES
The Boaters Inn
020 8541 4672
Mar

PINNER
The Queens Head
020 8868 4607
Spring/Summer

NORFOLK

BRANCASTER STAITHE
The Jolly Sailors
01485 210314
Mid-late Jun (Norfolk Ale & Music Festival)

BURSTON
The Crown
01379 741257
2 or 3 a year

CROMER
The Red Lion Food and Rooms
01263 514964
Autumn

HEYDON
Earle Arms
01263 587376
23 Apr (St George's Day)

HUNSTANTON
The Ancient Mariner Inn
01485 536390
Summer

HUNWORTH
The Hunny Bell
01263 712300
Aug

KING'S LYNN
The Stuart House Hotel, Bar & Restaurant
01553 772169
Jul

LARLING
Angel Inn
01953 717963
Early Aug

NORWICH
The Mad Moose Arms
01603 627687
May & Oct

The Reindeer Pub & Kitchen
01603 612995
Summer

THOMPSON
Chequers Inn
01953 483360

WINTERTON-ON-SEA
Fishermans Return
01493 393305
Summer BH

NORTHAMPTONSHIRE

FOTHERINGHAY
The Falcon Inn
01832 226254

NORTHAMPTON
Althorp Coaching Inn
01604 770651

OUNDLE
The Chequered Skipper
01832 273494
Twice a year

THORNBY
The Red Lion
01604 740238
Last wknd Jul

TOWCESTER
The Saracens Head
01327 350414
Contact pub for details

WADENHOE
The King's Head
01832 720024
Aug

NORTHUMBERLAND

BEADNELL
The Craster Arms
01665 720272
Last wknd Jul

CARTERWAY HEADS
The Manor House Inn
01207 255268
Last wknd Aug

HEDLEY ON THE HILL
The Feathers Inn
01661 843607
Etr wknd

HEXHAM
Battlesteads Hotel & Restaurant
01434 230209
Summer

Miners Arms Inn
01434 603909

MILFIELD
The Red Lion Inn
01668 216224
Last wknd Jun

SEAHOUSES
The Bamburgh Castle Inn
01665 720283
Contact pub for details

NOTTINGHAMSHIRE

BEESTON
The Victoria
0115 925 4049
End Jan; Etr; last 2wks Jul (beer & music) & Oct

KIMBERLEY
The Nelson & Railway Inn
0115 938 2177
Each BH

NEWARK-ON-TRENT
The Prince Rupert
01636 918121
Mid May & Late Jun

NOTTINGHAM
Ye Olde Trip to Jerusalem
0115 947 3171
2 or 3 times a year

OXFORDSHIRE

BANBURY
Ye Olde Reindeer Inn
01295 270972

BLOXHAM
The Elephant & Castle
01295 720383
Early May (part of Bloxfest Music Festival)

BRIGHTWELL-CUM-SOTWELL
The Red Lion
01491 837373
Summer, 2 days (local beer & musicians)

BURFORD
The Angel at Burford
01993 822714

The Highway Inn
01993 823661
End Jun

CUMNOR
The Vine Inn
01865 862567

DORCHESTER
The George
01865 340404

FERNHAM
The Woodman Inn
01367 820643
Contact pub for details

FRINGFORD
The Butchers Arms
01869 277363
Jul

FYFIELD
The White Hart
01865 390585
Contact pub for details

GREAT TEW
The Falkland Arms
01608 683653

HENLEY-ON-THAMES
The Cherry Tree Inn
01491 680430

KELMSCOTT
The Plough Inn
01367 253543

MARSH BALDON
Seven Stars
01865 343337
Summer BH

MILTON
The Plum Pudding
01235 834443
Apr & Oct

NORTHMOOR
The Red Lion
01865 300301

OXFORD
The Magdalen Arms
01865 243159
Contact pub for details

The Rusty Bicycle
01865 435298

PISHILL
The Crown Inn
01491 638364
Late Sep

ROTHERFIELD PEPPARD
The Unicorn
01491 628674
Summer

STANDLAKE
The Bell Inn
01865 300784
Contact pub for details

TETSWORTH
The Old Red Lion
01844 281274
Etr (mini festival)

THAME
The Thatch
01844 214340
Late Sep-early Oct (National Cask Ale Week)

UFFINGTON
The Fox & Hounds
01367 820680

WEST HANNEY
Plough Inn
01235 868674
Etr, Spring BH, Summer BH

WYTHAM
White Hart
01865 244372
Etr

RUTLAND

LYDDINGTON
Old White Hart
01572 821703
Summer

OAKHAM
The Grainstore Brewery
01572 770065
Summer BH

SHROPSHIRE

BISHOP'S CASTLE
The Three Tuns Inn
01588 638797
2nd wknd Jul (town festival)

CLUN
The White Horse Inn
01588 640305
1st wknd Oct

CRAVEN ARMS
The Sun Inn
01584 861239
Early May BH

MUCH WENLOCK
The George & Dragon
01952 727312
23 April (St George's Day); late Sep-early Oct (National Cask Ale Week)

SHIFNAL
Odfellows Wine Bar
01952 461517
May & Sep

STOTTESDON
Fighting Cocks
01746 718270
Early Nov

WENTNOR
The Crown Inn
01588 650613
Jul

SOMERSET

BATH
The Star Inn
01225 425072
Twice a year

BISHOP SUTTON
The Red Lion
01275 333042

BISHOPSWOOD
Candlelight Inn
01460 234476

CHEW MAGNA
The Bear and Swan
01275 331100
Spring/Summer

CORTON DENHAM
The Queens Arms
01963 220317

CROSCOMBE
The George Inn
01749 342306
Spring BH wknd, Oct

DULVERTON
The Bridge Inn
01398 324130
Spring BH

HASELBURY PLUCKNETT
The White Horse at Haselbury
01460 78873

HINTON ST GEORGE
The Lord Poulett Arms
01460 73149

ILCHESTER
Ilchester Arms
01935 840220
BHs

LOWER GODNEY
The Sheppey
01458 831594
Aug

PITNEY
The Halfway House
01458 252513
Mar

PORLOCK
The Bottom Ship
01643 863288
1st wknd Jul

SHEPTON BEAUCHAMP
Duke of York
01460 240314
Sep

SHEPTON MALLET
The Three Horseshoes Inn
01749 850359
Etr, Summer BH

WEDMORE
The George Inn
01934 712124

WEST HUNTSPILL
Crossways Inn
01278 783756
Summer BH

WHEDDON CROSS
The Rest and Be Thankful Inn
01643 841222
Contact pub for details

STAFFORDSHIRE

CAULDON
Yew Tree Inn
01538 309876
Jul

ECCLESHALL
The George
01785 850300
Etr wknd

STAFFORD
The Holly Bush Inn
01889 508234
Jun & Sep

SUMMERHILL
Oddfellows in the Boat
01543 361692

WALL
The Trooper
01543 480413

SUFFOLK

BRANDESTON
The Queens Head
01728 685307
Jun

BURY ST EDMUNDS
The Old Cannon Brewery
01284 768769
Summer BH wknd

DUNWICH
The Ship at Dunwich
01728 648219
BH Sundays

ELVEDEN
Elveden Inn
01842 890876
Mid Jun

FRAMLINGHAM
The Station Hotel
01728 723455
Mid Jul

HAWKEDON
The Queen's Head
01284 789218
3rd wknd Jul

LAXFIELD
The Kings Head (The Low House)
01986 798395
May & Sep

NAYLAND
Anchor Inn
01206 262313
Father's Day (Jun), Sep Octoberfest

SIBTON
Sibton White Horse Inn
01728 660337
Jun & Aug

SNAPE
The Golden Key
01728 688510

SOMERLEYTON
The Duke's Head
01502 733931

SWILLAND
Moon & Mushroom Inn
01473 785320
Summer

WALBERSWICK
The Anchor
01502 722112
Mid Aug

WOODBRIDGE
Cherry Tree Inn
01394 384627
Early Jul

WOODDITTON
The Three Blackbirds
01638 731100

SURREY

CARSHALTON
The Sun
020 8773 4549
Jun

CHIDDINGFOLD
The Swan Inn
01428 684688
Sep

CRANLEIGH
The Richard Onslow
01483 274922
Apr (Surrey & Sussex Ales Festival)

FARNHAM
The Bat & Ball Freehouse
01252 792108
2nd wknd Jun

FETCHAM
The Bell
01372 372624
Late Sep-early Oct (National Cask Ale Week)

FOREST GREEN
The Parrot Inn
01306 621339

LONG DITTON
The Ditton
020 8339 0785

NEWDIGATE
The Surrey Oaks
01306 631200
Spring BH & Summer BH

TILFORD
The Duke of Cambridge
01252 792236
May (CherryFest, charity beer & music festival)

WEST END
The Inn @ West End
01276 858652

WINDLESHAM
The Half Moon
01276 473329

SUSSEX, EAST

BLACKBOYS
The Blackboys Inn
01825 890283
Contact pub for details

EAST DEAN
The Tiger Inn
01323 423209

ERIDGE GREEN
The Nevill Crest and Gun
01892 864209

EWHURST GREEN
The White Dog
01580 830264

HARTFIELD
Anchor Inn
01892 770424
Early May

ICKLESHAM
The Queen's Head
01424 814552
Last wknd Oct

LANGNEY
The Farm @ Friday Street
01323 766049
Jun & Aug

LEWES
The Snowdrop Inn
01273 471018
1st or 2nd wknd Oct

THREE LEG CROSS
The Bull
01580 200586

SUSSEX, WEST

EAST GRINSTEAD
The Old Dunnings Mill
01342 326341
Jun & Sep

HENLEY
Duke of Cumberland Arms
01428 652280
Midsummer (biannually)

HORSHAM
The Black Jug
01403 253526
Sep

KINGSFOLD
The Dog and Duck
01306 627295
Annual charity event; contact pub for details

LAMBS GREEN
The Lamb Inn
01293 871336
Aug

OVING
The Gribble Inn
01243 786893
Summer & Winter

SLINDON
The Spur
01243 814216

WEST DEAN
The Dean Ale & Cider House
01243 811465

WINEHAM
The Royal Oak
01444 881252

WARWICKSHIRE

ALCESTER
The Holly Bush
01789 762482
Jun & Oct

BROOM
The Broom Tavern
01789 778199
Summer BH

EDGEHILL
Castle at Edgehill
01295 670255
Summer BH

HUNNINGHAM
The Red Lion, Hunningham
01926 632715
Jul

WARWICK
The Rose & Crown
01926 411117
May

WEST MIDLANDS

BIRMINGHAM
The Old Joint Stock
0121 200 1892
May & Oct

WILTSHIRE

ALDBOURNE
The Blue Boar
01672 540237
Apr & Oct

The Crown Inn
01672 540214
3rd wknd May & 3rd wknd Sep

BOX
The Quarrymans Arms
01225 743569
6 times a year

BRINKWORTH
The Three Crowns
01666 510366

Beer festivals *continued*

BROUGHTON GIFFORD
The Fox
01225 782949
Spring BH

CRICKLADE
The Red Lion Inn
01793 750776
Last wknd Feb & Jun

CRUDWELL
The Potting Shed
01666 577833
Summer BH

DEVIZES
The Raven Inn
01380 828271
Early Aug (Wadworth Shire
Horses' holiday weeks)

EAST CHISENBURY
Red Lion Freehouse
01980 671124
May

EDINGTON
The Three Daggers
01380 830940
Contact pub for details

HORNINGSHAM
The Bath Arms at Longleat
01985 844308
Mid Jun

MALMESBURY
Kings Arms
01666 823383

The Smoking Dog
01666 825823
Spring BH

NEWTON TONY
The Malet Arms
01980 629279
Jul

ROYAL WOOTTON BASSETT
The Angel
01793 851161
Sep

SEMINGTON
The Lamb on the Strand
01380 870263

WARMINSTER
The Bath Arms
01985 212262

The George Inn
01985 840396
Aug

WORCESTERSHIRE

BECKFORD
The Beckford
01386 881532
Oct

BEWDLEY
Little Pack Horse
01299 403762

The Mug House Inn & Angry
Chef Restaurant
01299 402543
Early May BH wknd

BRETFORTON
The Fleece Inn
01386 831173
Mid-late Oct

BROADWAY
Crown & Trumpet
01386 853202
Xmas & New Year

HARTLEBURY
The Tap House @ The Old
Ticket Office
01299 253275

KEMPSEY
Walter de Cantelupe Inn
01905 820572
Etr & Oct

KNIGHTWICK
The Talbot
01886 821235
Apr, Jun & Oct

MALVERN
The Nag's Head
01684 574373
23 April (St George's Day)

YORKSHIRE, EAST RIDING OF

BEVERLEY
The Ferguson Fawsitt Arms &
Country Lodge
01482 882665

YORKSHIRE, NORTH

APPLETREEWICK
The Craven Arms
01756 720270
Oct (over 25 beers)

COLTON
Ye Old Sun Inn
01904 744261
Summer

CROPTON
The New Inn
01751 417330
Nov

HARDRAW
The Green Dragon Inn
01969 667392
Jun, Jul & Oct

KILBURN
The Forresters Arms Inn
01347 868386

KIRBY HILL
The Shoulder of Mutton Inn
01748 822772

MASHAM
The White Bear
01765 689319
Late Jun

RIPON
The George at Wath
01765 641324

YORK
Lysander Arms
01904 640845

YORKSHIRE, SOUTH

CADEBY
The Cadeby Pub & Restaurant
01709 864009

SHEFFIELD
The Fat Cat
0114 249 4801
Aug

Kelham Island Tavern
0114 272 2482
Late Jun wknd

YORKSHIRE, WEST

CALVERLEY
Calverley Arms
0113 255 7771
Jul

HOLMFIRTH
Farmers Arms
01484 683713
Autumn

LEEDS
North Bar
0113 242 4540
Spring (Belgian & Dutch beers),
Summer (USA beers), Autumn/
Winter (German beers)

LINTON
The Windmill Inn
01937 582209
Jul

SOWERBY BRIDGE
The Alma Inn
01422 823334
Late Sep (Oktoberfest)

CHANNEL ISLANDS

JERSEY

ST AUBIN
Old Court House Inn
01534 746433
Nov

ISLE OF MAN

PORT ERIN
Falcon's Nest Hotel
01624 834077
Early May

SCOTLAND

ARGYLL & BUTE

DUNOON
Coylet Inn
01369 840426
Contact pub for details

INVERARAY
George Hotel
01499 302111
Early May BH & Summer BH

CITY OF DUNDEE

BROUGHTY FERRY
The Royal Arch Bar
01382 779741
1st wknd Oct (charity event)

DUNDEE
Speedwell Bar
01382 667783
1st wknd Oct (Rotary Charity
Oktoberfest)

CITY OF EDINBURGH

EDINBURGH
The Bow Bar
0131 226 7667
End Jan & end Jul (plus German
Beer Festival)

The Guildford Arms
0131 556 4312
Apr & Oct (plus monthly brewery
wknds)

Halfway House
0131 225 7101
Contact pub for details

The Sheep Heid Inn
0131 661 7974

RATHO
The Bridge Inn
0131 333 1320

CITY OF GLASGOW

GLASGOW
Bon Accord
0141 248 4427
4 times a year (90 beers & ciders)

Ubiquitous Chip
0141 334 5007
Twice a year (times vary)

WEST Brewery
0141 550 0135
Oct Fridays OktoberFest

DUMFRIES & GALLOWAY

BARGRENNAN
House O'Hill Hotel
01671 840243
Apr & Sep

HIGHLAND

CAWDOR
Cawdor Tavern
01667 404777

FORTROSE
The Anderson
01381 620236
Jan (Burns Weekend Real Ale
Festival), monthly mini-festivals

GLENCOE
Clachaig Inn
01855 811252
Hogmanay, Feb Fest & OctoberFest

PLOCKTON
The Plockton Hotel
01599 544274
May

TORRIDON
The Torridon Inn
01445 791242
1st wknd Oct

LANARKSHIRE, NORTH

CUMBERNAULD
Castlecary House Hotel
01324 840233
Contact pub for details

LOTHIAN, EAST

HADDINGTON
The Waterside
01620 825674
Nov

LOTHIAN, WEST

LINLITHGOW
The Four Marys
01506 842171
Last wknd May & Oct

MORAY

FORRES
The Old Mill Inn
01309 641605
Jun

PERTH & KINROSS

MEIKLEOUR
Meikleour Arms
01250 883206
Aug

SCOTTISH BORDERS

NEWCASTLETON
Liddesdale
01387 375255
1st wknd Jul

STIRLING

CALLANDER
The Lade Inn
01877 330152
Aug/Sep

WALES

BRIDGEND

KENFIG
Prince of Wales Inn
01656 740356

CARMARTHENSHIRE

PUMSAINT
The Dolaucothi Arms
01558 650237
Summer BH wknd

CEREDIGION

ABERYSTWYTH
The Glengower Hotel
01970 626191
Spring BH

TREGARON
Y Talbot
01974 298208
Early Oct

CONWY

COLWYN BAY
Pen-y-Bryn
01492 533360
Contact pub for details (beer &
bangers week; pie & ale week)

FLINTSHIRE

BABELL
Black Lion Inn
01352 720239
April & Sep (Annual Ale Trail)

MOLD
Glasfryn
01352 750500
Mar (Welsh Food & Drink week);
Oct (Great British Pie & Cham-
pion Beers of Britain week)

GWYNEDD

WAUNFAWR
Snowdonia Parc Brewpub &
Campsite
01286 650409
Etr wk & mid May (Welsh
Highland Railway Festival)

MONMOUTHSHIRE

ABERGAVENNY
Clytha Arms
01873 840206
Spring BH

RHYD-Y-MEIRCH
Goose and Cuckoo Inn
01873 880277
End May & end Aug

TINTERN PARVA
Fountain Inn
01291 689303
Etr & Sep

TRELLECH
The Lion Inn
01600 860322
Jun

NEWPORT

CAERLEON
The Bell at Caerleon
01633 420613

POWYS

DEFYNNOG
The Tanners Arms
01874 638032

GLANGRWYNEY
The Bell
01873 811115
Etr & Summer BH

OLD RADNOR
The Harp
01544 350655
Jun

TALYBONT-ON-USK
Star Inn
01874 676635
Mid Jun & mid Oct

RHONDDA CYNON TAFF

PONTYPRIDD
Bunch of Grapes
01443 402934
Every 2 months (20+ ales)

SWANSEA

LLANGENNITH
Kings Head
01792 386212
Last wknd Nov

VALE OF GLAMORGAN

COWBRIDGE
Cross Inn
01446 772995
Late Apr & Sep (mini Beer &
cider festival)

PENARTH
The Pilot
029 2071 0615
Twice a year

Cider festivals

ENGLAND

BEDFORDSHIRE

LINSLADE
The Globe Inn
01525 373338

STUDHAM
The Bell in Studham
01582 872460
Summer

BERKSHIRE

HERMITAGE
The White Horse of
Hermitage
01635 200325

MONEYROW GREEN
The White Hart
01628 621460
Summer

READING
The Flowing Spring
0118 969 9878
Midsummer & Autumn

BRISTOL

The Albion
0117 973 3522
Early May BH

The Alma Tavern & Theatre
0117 973 5171
Late Dec (Xmas fayre)

BUCKINGHAMSHIRE

BEACONSFIELD
The Royal Standard of
England
01494 673382
Summer BH

BRILL
The Pheasant Inn
01844 239370
Spring BH

DENHAM
The Falcon Inn
01895 832125
Contact pub for details

MOULSOE
The Carrington Arms
01908 218050
Jun

CAMBRIDGESHIRE

BOURN
The Willow Tree
01954 719775
Summer

HINXTON
The Red Lion Inn
01799 530601

HISTON
Red Lion
01223 564437
Etr & 1st wk Sep

PETERBOROUGH
Charters Bar & East
Restaurant
01733 315700
Etr Thu-Etr Mon

SPALDWICK
The George
01480 890293

STRETHAM
The Lazy Otter
01353 649780

CHESHIRE

CHESTER
Old Harkers Arms
01244 344525
Mar (Pie & Champion Ale Wk)

CORNWALL & ISLES OF SCILLY

CADGWITH
Cadgwith Cove Inn
01326 290513
Oct

CONSTANTINE
Trengilly Wartha Inn
01326 340332

GWITHIAN
The Red River Inn
01736 753223
Etr wknd

PORTHLEVEN
The Ship Inn
01326 564204
Aug

ST MAWGAN
The Falcon Inn
01637 860225
Jul (last full wknd)

TRESCO (ISLES OF SCILLY)
The New Inn
01720 422849
Jun

Cider festivals *continued*

CUMBRIA

ULVERSTON
Farmers Arms Hotel
01229 584469

DERBYSHIRE

BAMFORD
The Yorkshire Bridge Inn
01433 651361
May

BONSALL
The Barley Mow
01629 825685
BHs (3-4 times a year)

CASTLETON
The Peaks Hotel
01433 620247
Etr

CHINLEY
Old Hall Inn &
The Paper Mill Inn
01663 750529
3rd wknd Sep

HOPE
The Old Hall Hotel
01433 620160
BHs

DEVON

BRIDFORD
The Bridford Inn
01647 252250
May & Aug

CLAYHIDON
The Merry Harriers
01823 421270
Summer

CLYST HYDON
The Five Bells Inn
01884 277288
Early May BH

KINGS NYMPTON
The Grove Inn
01769 580406
Jul

MEAVY
The Royal Oak Inn
01822 852944
Summer BH wknd, Mid Nov
(cider & bean festival)

TAVISTOCK
The Cornish Arms
01822 612145
Summer BH wknd

TOTNES
Royal Seven Stars Hotel
01803 862125
Contact pub for details

DORSET

BOURTON
The White Lion Inn
01747 840866
Jul

CHEDINGTON
Winyard's Gap Inn
01935 891244
Aug

WORTH MATRAVERS
The Square and Compass
01929 439229
1st Sat Nov

DURHAM, COUNTY

FROSTERLEY
The Black Bull Inn
01388 527784

STANLEY
The Stables Pub and
Restaurant
01207 288750
2nd wknd Dec

ESSEX

FEERING
The Sun Inn
01376 570442
End of Jun & Sep

LITTLE BRAXTED
The Green Man
01621 891659

GLOUCESTERSHIRE

ALDERTON
The Gardeners Arms
01242 620257
Aug BH

ALMONDSBURY
The Swan Hotel
01454 625671
Jul

CHELTENHAM
The Gloucester Old Spot
01242 680321
Contact pub for details

The Royal Oak Inn
01242 522344
Summer BH

CLIFFORD'S MESNE
The Yew Tree
01531 820719
Oct

COATES
The Tunnel House Inn
01285 770280

SHEEPSCOMBE
The Butchers Arms
01452 812113

TETBURY
The Priory Inn
01666 502251
Early May BH (cider & real ale)

HAMPSHIRE

BISHOP'S WALTHAM
The Hampshire Bowman
01489 892940
Jul & Dec

BRANSGORE
The Three Tuns Country Inn
01425 672232
Summer holidays (contact pub
for details)

EAST STRATTON
Northbrook Arms
01962 774150
Sep

EVERSLEY
The Golden Pot
0118 973 2104

LYNDHURST
New Forest Inn
023 8028 4690
Last wknd Mar

PETERSFIELD
The White Horse Inn
01420 588387
Sep

STOCKBRIDGE
The Three Cups Inn
01264 810527
Contact pub for details

SWANMORE
The Rising Sun
01489 896663
Summer BH (Sat)

HEREFORDSHIRE

HOARWITHY
The New Harp Inn
01432 840900
Summer BH

MICHAELCHURCH ESCLEY
The Bridge Inn
01981 510646
Summer BH

ORLETON
The Boot Inn
01568 780228
Last wknd Jul

WOOLHOPE
The Crown Inn
01432 860468

HERTFORDSHIRE

PERRY GREEN
The Hoops Inn
01279 843568
Aug

WATTON-AT-STONE
The Bull
01920 831032
May & Oct

KENT

LOWER HALSTOW
The Three Tuns
01795 842840
Summer BH

LANCASHIRE

BILSBORROW
Owd Nell's Tavern
01995 640010
Last wk Jul

LEICESTERSHIRE

LONG WHATTON
The Royal Oak
01509 843694
Summer BH

LONDON

NW1
The Engineer
020 7483 1890
Contact pub for details

The Prince Albert
020 7485 0270
BHs

NW5
The Lord Palmerston
020 7485 1578

SW10
The Hollywood Arms
020 7349 7840

W8
The Windsor Castle
020 7243 8797
Jul

LONDON, GREATER

KINGSTON UPON THAMES
The Boaters Inn
020 8541 4672
Apr

NORFOLK

BRANCASTER STAITHE
The Jolly Sailors
01485 210314

WINTERTON-ON-SEA
Fishermans Return
01493 393305

NORTHUMBERLAND

BEADNELL
The Craster Arms
01665 720272
last wknd Jul

CARTERWAY HEADS
The Manor House Inn
01207 255268
Last wknd Aug

HEDLEY ON THE HILL
The Feathers Inn
01661 843607
Summer BH

NOTTINGHAMSHIRE

NEWARK-ON-TRENT
The Prince Rupert
01636 918121
Summer BH

OXFORDSHIRE

BLOXHAM
The Elephant & Castle
01295 720383
Early May (part of Bloxfest Music
Festival)

KELMSCOTT
The Plough Inn
01367 253543
Aug

WYTHAM
White Hart
01865 244372
Etr

RUTLAND

OAKHAM
The Grainstore Brewery
01572 770065
Early May BH

SOMERSET

CHEW MAGNA
The Bear and Swan
01275 331100
Spring/Summer

DUNSTER
The Stags Head Inn
01643 821229
Dec

HASELBURY PLUCKNETT
The White Horse at
Haselbury
01460 78873

HINTON ST GEORGE
The Lord Poulett Arms
01460 73149

ILCHESTER
Ilchester Arms
01935 840220

LOWER GODNEY
The Sheppey
01458 831594
Aug

PITNEY
The Halfway House
01458 252513
Aug

PORLOCK
The Bottom Ship
01643 863288
1st wknd Jul

SHEPTON MALLET
The Three Horseshoes Inn
01749 850359
Etr, Summer BH

SHEPTON MONTAGUE
The Montague Inn
01749 813213
Contact pub for details

WEDMORE
The George Inn
01934 712124

STAFFORDSHIRE

STAFFORD
The Holly Bush Inn
01889 508234
Jun & Sep

WRINEHILL
The Hand & Trumpet
01270 820048
Aug

SUFFOLK

ELVEDEN
Elveden Inn
01842 890876
Mid Jun

HAWKEDON
The Queen's Head
01284 789218
3rd wknd Jul

SOMERLEYTON
The Duke's Head
01502 733931

WOODDITTON
The Three Blackbirds
01638 731100

SURREY

CRANLEIGH
The Richard Onslow
01483 274922
Apr (Surrey & Sussex Ales Festival)

FARNHAM
The Bat & Ball Freehouse
01252 792108

LONG DITTON
The Ditton
020 8339 0785

SUSSEX, EAST

ERIDGE GREEN
The Nevill Crest and Gun
01892 864209

EWHURST GREEN
The White Dog
01580 830264
Late Sep (book & cider festival)

SUSSEX, WEST

HORSHAM
The Black Jug
01403 253526
Summer

KINGSFOLD
The Dog and Duck
01306 627295
Annual charity event; contact pub for details

LODSWORTH
The Hollist Arms
01798 861310
1st Sat in Oct

WARWICKSHIRE

ALCESTER
The Holly Bush
01789 762482
Jun & Oct

BROOM
The Broom Tavern
01789 778199
Summer BH

EDGEHILL
Castle at Edgehill
01295 670255
Aug/Sep

ALDBOURNE
The Crown Inn
01672 540214
2nd week Jul

BOX
The Quarrymans Arms
01225 743569Jul

BRINKWORTH
The Three Crowns
01666 510366

BROUGHTON GIFFORD
The Fox
01225 782949

COLLINGBOURNE DUCIS
The Shears Inn
01264 850304
Late summer

EDINGTON
The Three Daggers
01380 830940
Sep

MALMESBURY
Kings Arms
01666 823383

ROYAL WOOTTON BASSETT
The Angel
01793 851161
Sep

SHERSTON
The Rattlebone Inn
01666 840871
Jul

WORCESTERSHIRE

BRETFORTON
The Fleece Inn
01386 831173
Mid-late Oct

YORKSHIRE, NORTH

HARDRAW
The Green Dragon Inn
01969 667392
Oct

SETTLE
The Lion at Settle
01729 822203
Aug

YORK
Lysander Arms
01904 640845

YORKSHIRE, SOUTH

CADEBY
The Cadeby Pub & Restaurant
01709 864009

SHEFFIELD
Kelham Island Tavern
0114 272 2482
Late Jun wknd

YORKSHIRE, WEST

HOLMFIRTH
Farmers Arms
01484 683713
Summer BH

SCOTLAND

ARGYLL & BUTE

DUNOON
Coylet Inn
01369 840426
Contact pub for details

CITY OF DUNDEE

BROUGHTY FERRY
The Royal Arch Bar
01382 779741
Last wknd Apr

CITY OF GLASGOW

GLASGOW
Bon Accord
0141 248 4427

PERTH & KINROSS

MEIKLEOUR
Meikleour Arms
01250 883206
Aug

WALES

CARMARTHENSHIRE

PUMSAINT
The Dolaucothi Arms
01558 650237
Summer BH wknd

MONMOUTHSHIRE

ABERGAVENNY
Clytha Arms
01873 840206

TRELLECH
The Lion Inn
01600 860322
Aug

NEWPORT

CAERLEON
The Bell at Caerleon
01633 420613

POWYS

GLANGRWYNEY
The Bell
01873 811115

SWANSEA

LLANGENNITH
Kings Head
01792 386212
Last wknd Oct

VALE OF GLAMORGAN

PENARTH
The Pilot
029 2071 0615
Twice a year

How to find a pub in the atlas section

Pubs are shown in the gazetteer under the name of their nearest town or village. If a pub is in a very small village, or in a remote rural area, it may appear under a larger town that is within five miles of its actual location.

The black dots in the atlas section match the location name in the gazetteer.

The county map shown opposite will help you identify the counties within each country. The county names are shown at the top of each page in the gazetteer.

The atlas section and the index that follow will help you find the towns featured in the guide.

Key to County Map

England

1 Bedfordshire
2 Berkshire
3 Bristol
4 Buckinghamshire
5 Cambridgeshire
6 Greater Manchester
7 Herefordshire
8 Hertfordshire
9 Leicestershire
10 Northamptonshire
11 Nottinghamshire
12 Rutland
13 Staffordshire
14 Warwickshire
15 West Midlands
16 Worcestershire

Scotland

17 City of Glasgow
18 Clackmannanshire
19 East Ayrshire
20 East Dunbartonshire
21 East Renfrewshire
22 Perth & Kinross
23 Renfrewshire
24 South Lanarkshire
25 West Dunbartonshire

Wales

26 Blaenau Gwent
27 Bridgent
28 Caerphilly
29 Denbighshire
30 Flintshire
31 Merthyr Tydfil
32 Monmouthshire
33 Neath Port Talbot
34 Newport
35 Rhondda Cynon Taff
36 Torfaen
37 Vale of Glamorgan
38 Wrexham

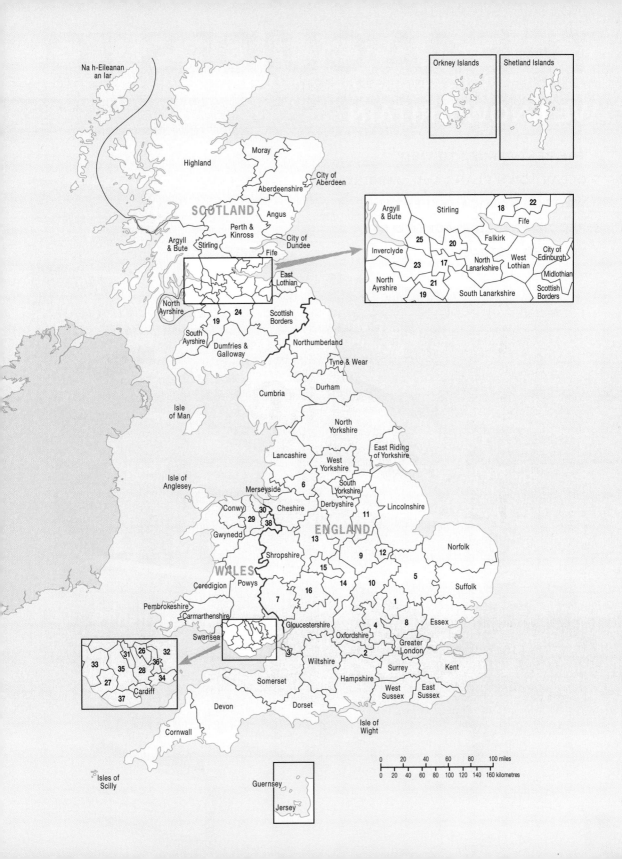

THE AA GUIDES TO

WE KNOW BRITAIN

▸ THE BEST PLACES TO VISIT

▸ CLEAR TOWN PLANS AND MAPPING

▸ WRITTEN BY LOCAL EXPERTS

▸ RECOMMENDED PLACES TO EAT

▸ TRUSTED LISTINGS

🐦 Follow @TheAA_Lifestyle

KEY TO ATLAS

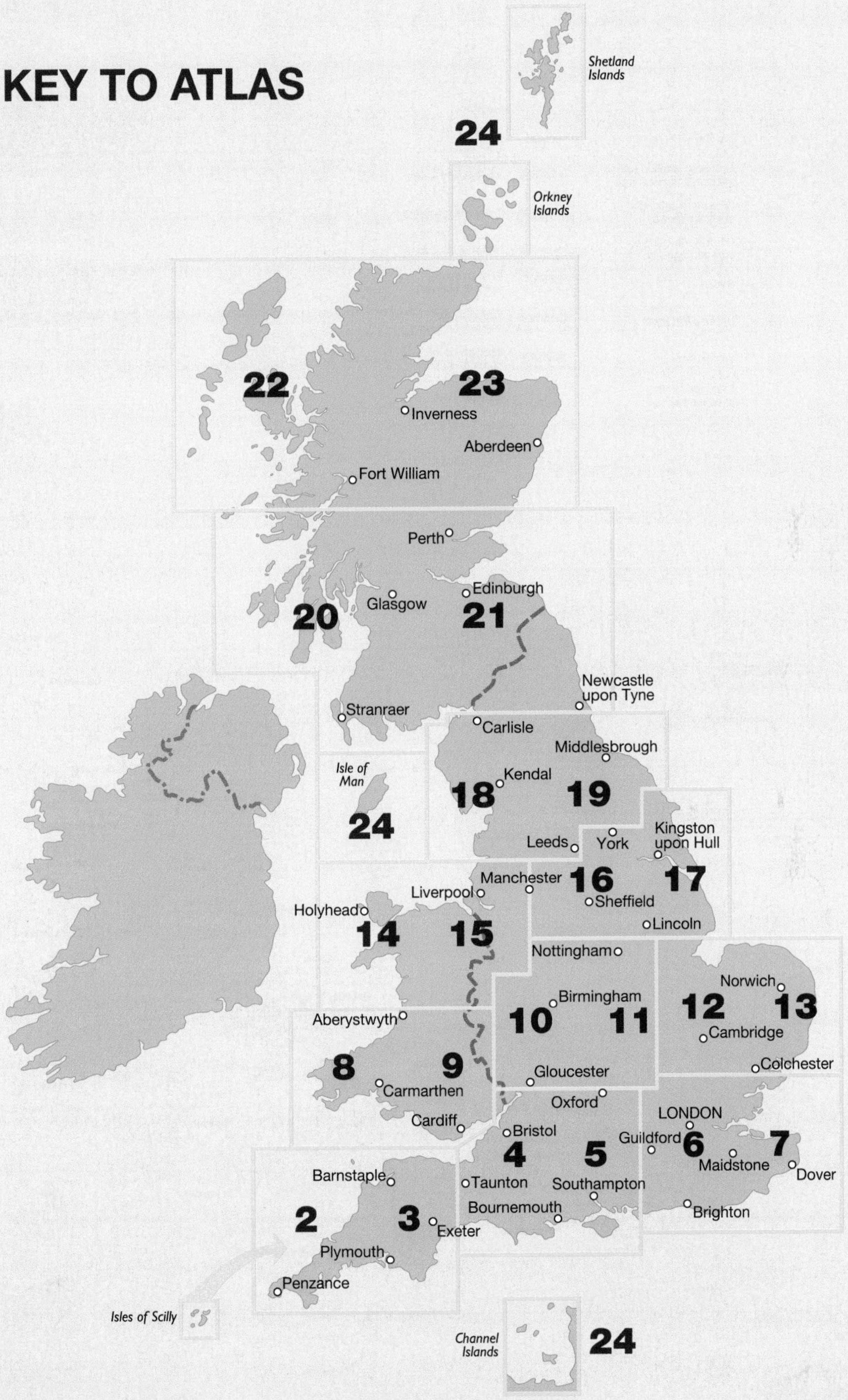

Shetland Islands

24

Orkney Islands

22

23

Inverness

Aberdeen

Fort William

Perth

Edinburgh

20

Glasgow

21

Newcastle upon Tyne

Stranraer

Carlisle

Middlesbrough

Isle of Man

Kendal

18

19

24

Leeds

York

Kingston upon Hull

Manchester

16

17

Holyhead

Liverpool

Sheffield

Lincoln

14

15

Nottingham

Aberystwyth

Birmingham

Norwich

12

13

10

11

Cambridge

8

9

Gloucester

Colchester

Carmarthen

Oxford

LONDON

Cardiff

Bristol

Guildford

6

7

Barnstaple

4

5

Maidstone

Dover

2

3

Taunton

Southampton

Bournemouth

Brighton

Exeter

Plymouth

Penzance

Isles of Scilly

Channel Islands

24

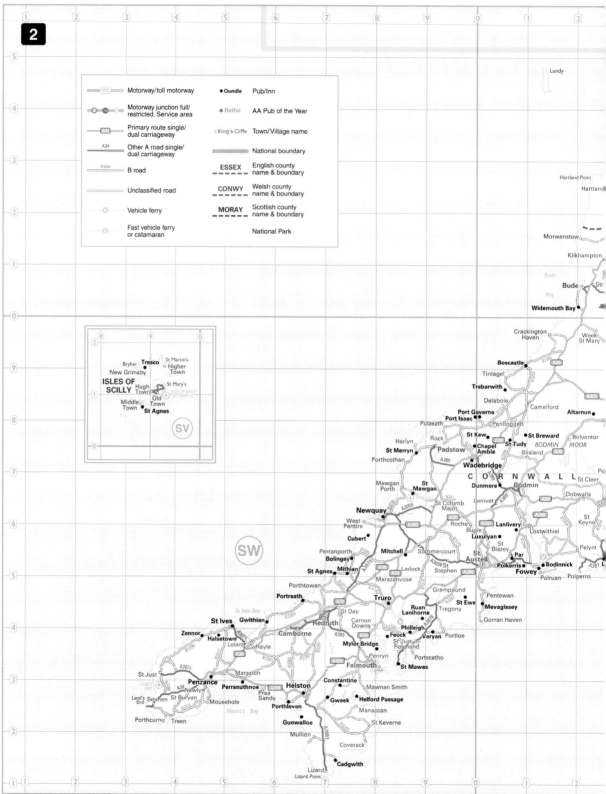

2

Motorway/toll motorway	● **Oundle** Pub/Inn
Motorway junction full/restricted. Service area	○ Ratho AA Pub of the Year
Primary route single/dual carriageway	○ King's Cliffe Town/Village name
Other A road single/dual carriageway	National boundary
B road	**ESSEX** English county name & boundary
Unclassified road	**CONWY** Welsh county name & boundary
Vehicle ferry	**MORAY** Scottish county name & boundary
Fast vehicle ferry or catamaran	National Park

ISLES OF SCILLY

Bryher • **Tresco** • St Martin's ○ Higher Town
New Grimsby
Hugh Town • St Mary's
Middle Town • Old Town
• **St Agnes**

SV

Lundy

Hartland Point
Hartland

Morwenstow ○
Kilkhampton
Bude
Bay
Bude • Str
Widemouth Bay •
Crackington Haven
Week St Mary
Boscastle •
Tintagel
Trebarwith •
Delabole ○
Camelford
Altarnun
Port Gaverne •
Port Isaac •
Pendoggett
Polzeath
St Kew • **St Breward** • Bolventor
Harlyn
Rock ○ **Chapel** • **St Tudy** BODMIN MOOR
St Merryn • **Padstow** Amble Blisland
Porthcothan
Wadebridge •
Po
SW
Mawgan Porth
St Cleer
St Mawgan
C O R N W A L L
Dunmere **Bodmin**
St Columb Major
Lanivet ○ Dobwalls
Newquay
West Pentire
Roche ○ **Lanlivery** St Keyne
Bugle ○ Lostwithiel
Cubert **Luxulyan**
St Blazey
Perranporth **Mitchell** Summercourt **Par** Pelynt
Bolingey ○ Ladock **St** **Polkerris** • **Bodinnick**
St Agnes • **Mithian** Marazanvose St Stephen **Austell** **Fowey** L
Porthtowan Polruan Polperro
Grampound
Portreath • Pentewan
St Day **St Ewe**
St Ives Bay **Gwithian** • **Truro** **Ruan** Tregony **Mevagissey**
St Ives • Carnon **Lanihorne** Gorran Haven
Zennor • Downs **Phillegh** ○
Halsetown • **Redruth** **Feock** • **Veryan** Portloe
Lelant **Camborne** A393 ○ St Just-
Hayle **Mylor Bridge** • Roseland Portscatho
Penryn
St Just Marazion **Falmouth** ○ **St Mawes** •
Penzance **Falmouth**
Newlyn **Constantine** Mawnan Smith
Land's **Perranuthnoe** **Helston** ○
End Sennen St Buryan Praa **Gweek** • **Helford Passage**
Mousehole Sands Manaccan
Porthcurno Treen **Porthleven** • St Keverne
Mount's Bay
Gunwalloe •
Mullion ○
Coverack
Lizard ○ **Cadgwith**
Lizard Point

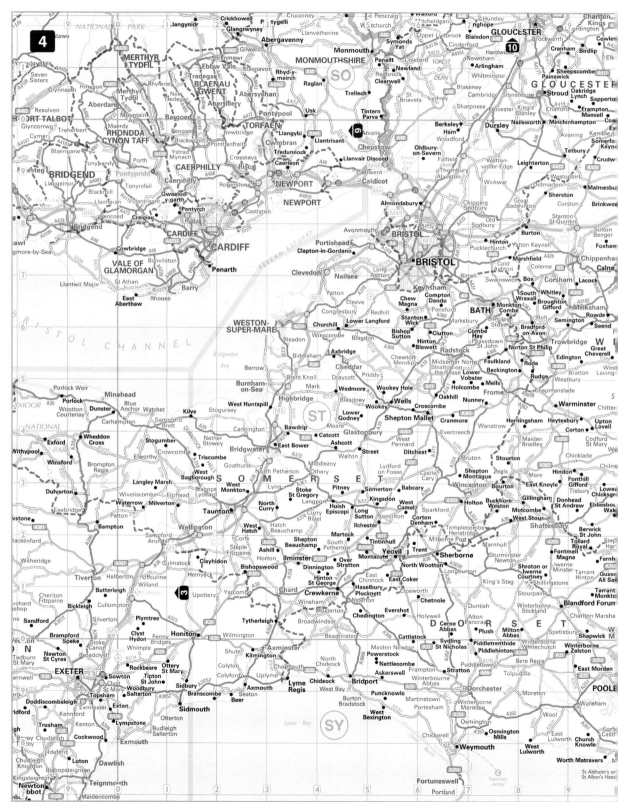

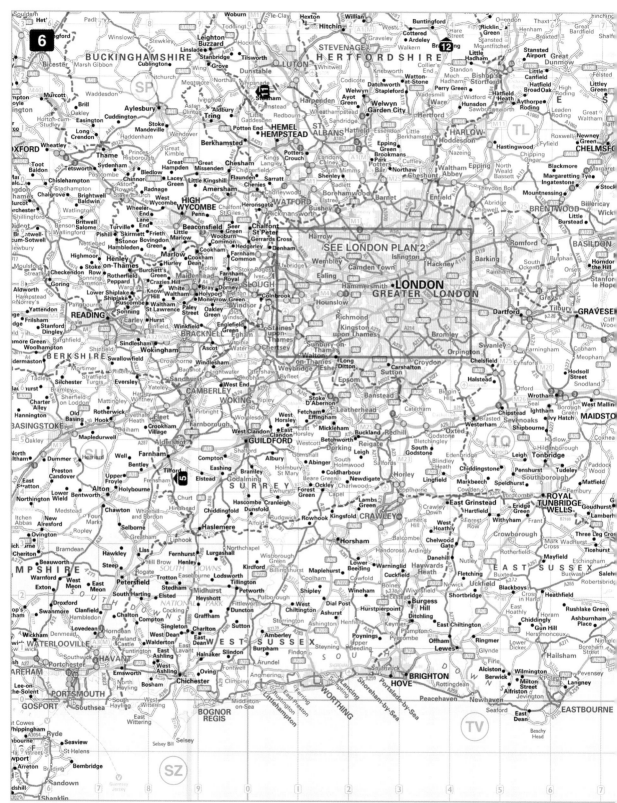

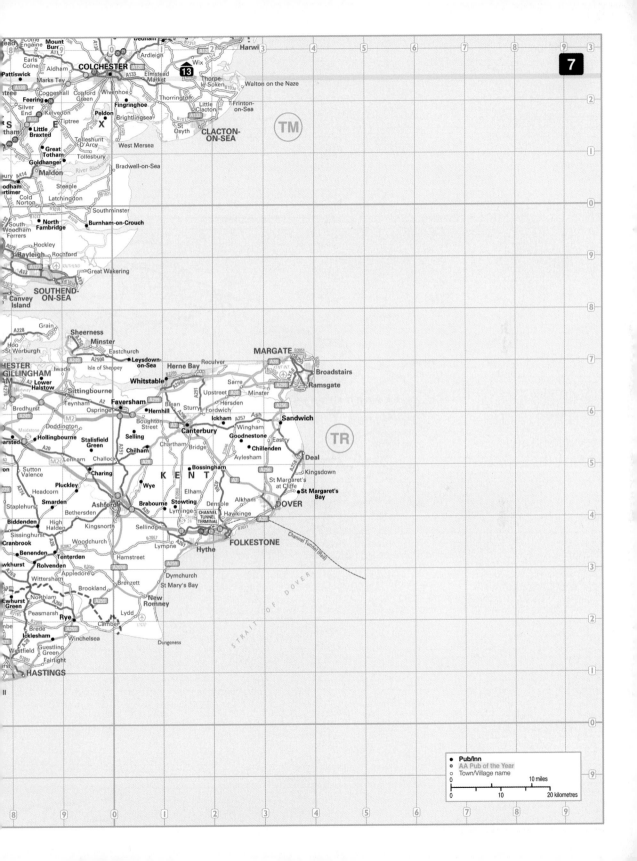

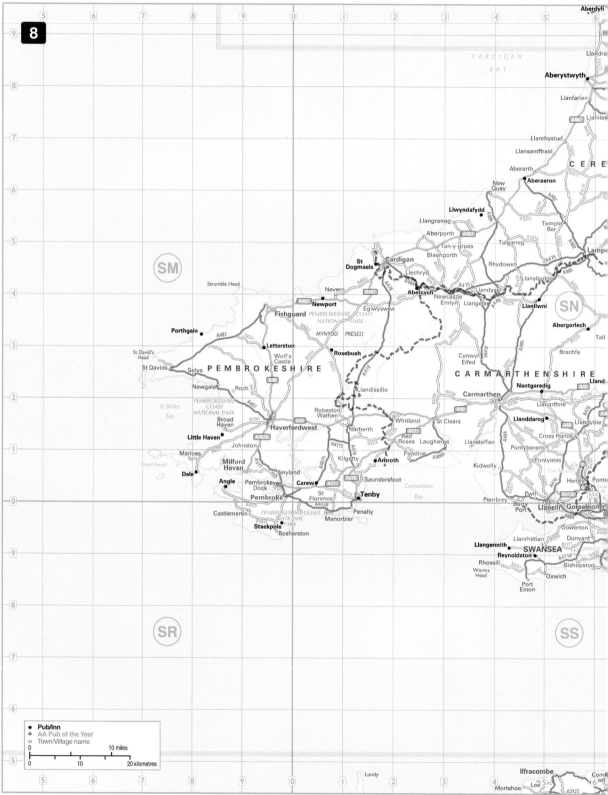

CARDIGAN BAY

Aberdyfi

Aberystwyth

Llanfarian

Llanilar

Llanrhystud

Llansantffraid

Aberarth

New Quay

Aberaeron

CERE

Llwyndafydd

Llangranog

Aberporth

Tan-y-groes

Blaenporth

Talgarreg

Temple Bar

Rhydowen

Lamp

Llanybydder

St Dogmaels

Cardigan

Llechryd

Abercych

Newcastle Emlyn

Llangeler

Llandysul

Llanllwni

Abergorlech

SN

Nevern

Eglwyswrw

Newport

Fishguard

PEMBROKESHIRE COAST NATIONAL PARK

MYNYDD   PRESELI

Strumble Head

Letterston

Rosebush

Cynwyl Elfed

Brechfa

Porthgain

St David's Head

St Davids

Solva

PEMBROKESHIRE

CARMARTHENSHIRE

Wolf's Castle

Llandissilio

Nantgaredig

Lland

Newgale

Roch

St Brides Bay

PEMBROKESHIRE COAST NATIONAL PARK

Broad Haven

Haverfordwest

Robeston Wathen

Narberth

Whitland

St Clears

Carmarthen

Llanarthne

Llanddarog

Llangybie

Cross Hands

Pontyberem

Pontyates

Marloes

Johnston

Kilgetty

Red Roses

Laugharne

Llansteffan

Kidwelly

Broad Sound

Little Haven

Milford Haven

Neyland

Amroth

Pendine

Hendy

Pont

Dale

Angle

Pembroke Dock

Carew

St Florence

Saundersfoot

Carmarthen Bay

Pembrey

Burry Port

Llanelli

Gorseinon

M4

Pembroke

Tenby

Pwll

Castlemartin

PEMBROKESHIRE COAST NATIONAL PARK

Penally

Manorbier

Gowerton

Dunvant

Stackpole

Bosherston

Llangennith

Llanrhidian

Reynoldston

SWANSEA

Bishopston

Rhossili

Worms Head

Oxwich

SM

SR

SS

Port Einon

Ilfracombe

Lundy

Mortehoe   Lee

A3123

Com art

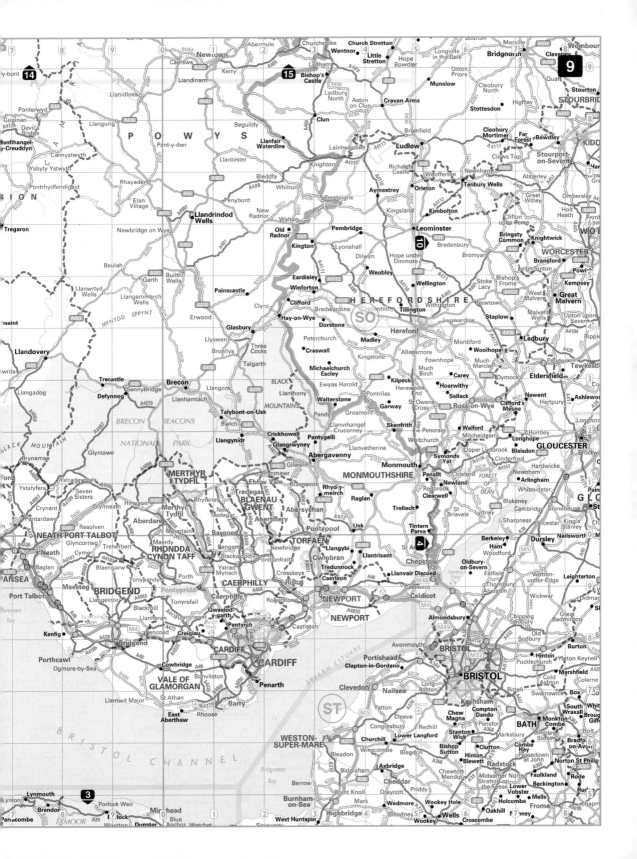

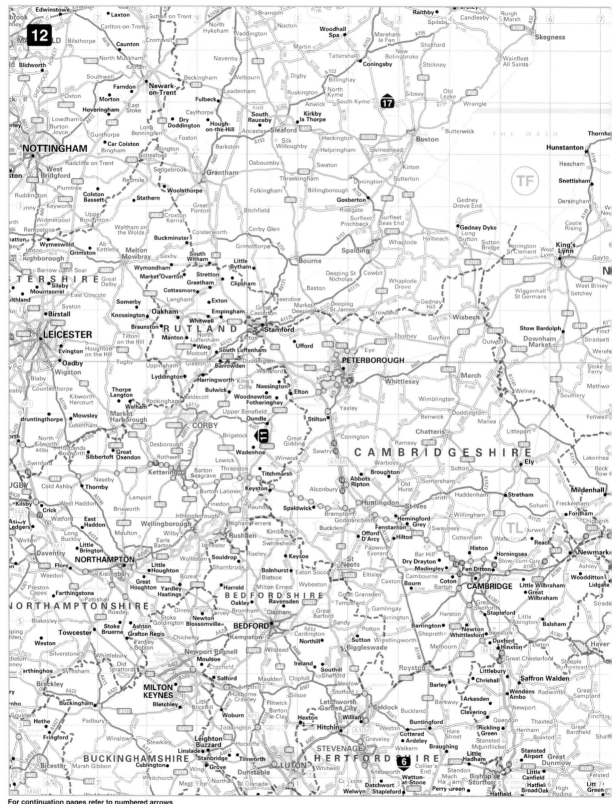

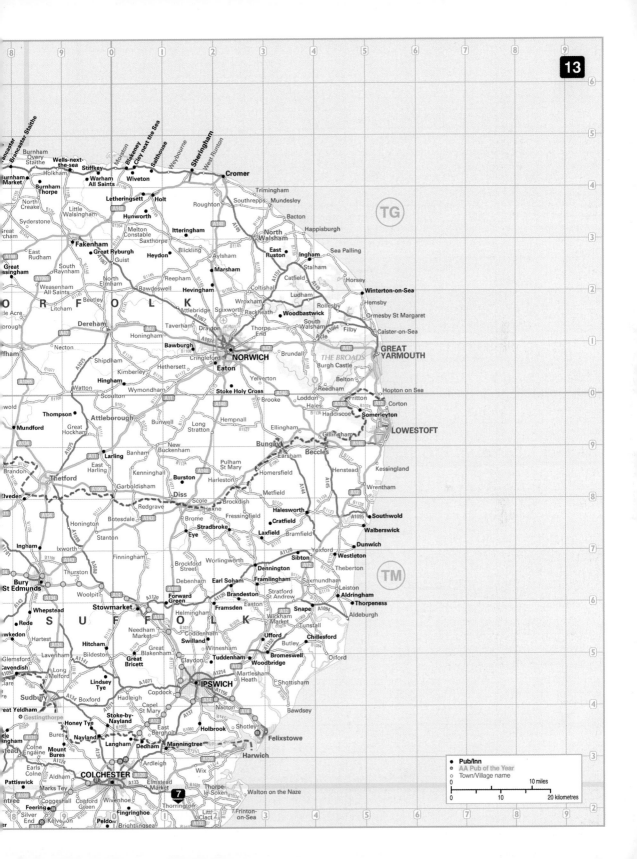

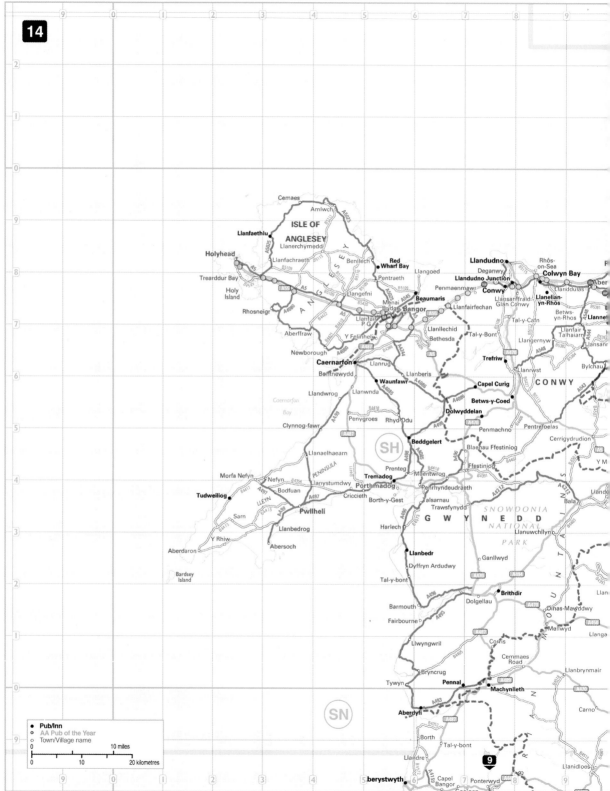

ISLE OF
ANGLESEY

Cemaes
Amlwch

Llanfaethlu
Llanerchymedd

Holyhead
Llanfachraeth
Benllech

Trearddur Bay
Pentraeth

Holy
Island
Llangefni

Rhosneigr

Aberffraw

Newborough

Red
Wharf Bay

Llangoed

Menai
Bridge
Beaumaris

Llanfair
PG
Bangor

Llanfairfechan

Y Felinheli

Llandudno
Deganwy
Llandudno Junction
Conwy

Rhôs-
on-Sea
Colwyn Bay

Llanddulas

Llanelian-
yn-Rhôs

Llansanffraid-
Glan Conwy

Tal-y-Cafn

Betws-
yn-Rhos

Llanfair
Talhaiarn

Llanne

Llansanr

Caernarfon

Llanrug

Bontnewydd

Llanberis

Waunfawr

Llandwrog

Llanwnda

Penygroes

Clynnog-fawr

Morfa Nefyn
Nefyn
Bodfuan

Tudweiliog

LLEYN

Sarn

Y Rhiw

Aberdaron

Bardsey
Island

berystwyth

Bryncrug

Tywyn

Aberdyfi

Borth

Llandre

Llanllechid
Bethesda

Tal-y-Bont

Capel Curig

Betws-y-Coed

Dolwyddelan

Penmachno

Blaenau Ffestiniog

Ffestiniog

Beddgelert

Prenteg

Tremadog
Maentwrog

Porthmadog
Penrhyndeudraeth

Borth-y-Gest
Talsarnau
Trawsfynydd

Harlech

Llanbedr

Dyffryn Ardudwy

Tal-y-bont

Barmouth

Fairbourne

Llwyngwril

Pennal

Trefriw

Llanrwst

Llangernyw

CONWY

Pentrefoelas

Cerrigydrudion

SNOWDONIA

NATIONAL

PARK

Ganllwyd

Brithdir

Dolgellau

Dinas-Mawddwy

Mallwyd

Corris

Cemmaes
Road

Machynlleth

Tal-y-bont

Capel
Bangor

Ponterwyd

Rhyd-Ddu

Penmaenmawr

Llangoed

Llanfairfechan

Llanuwchllyn

GWYNEDD

Bala

Llanbrynmair

Carno

Llanidloes

Llanga

Bylchau

SH

SN

Coernarfon
Bay

Criccieth

Llanystumdwy

Pwllheli

Llanbedrog

Abersoch

PENINSULA

| Pub/Inn |
| AA Pub of the Year |
| Town/Village name |

0   10 miles
0   10   20 kilometres

9

For continuation pages refer to numbered arrows

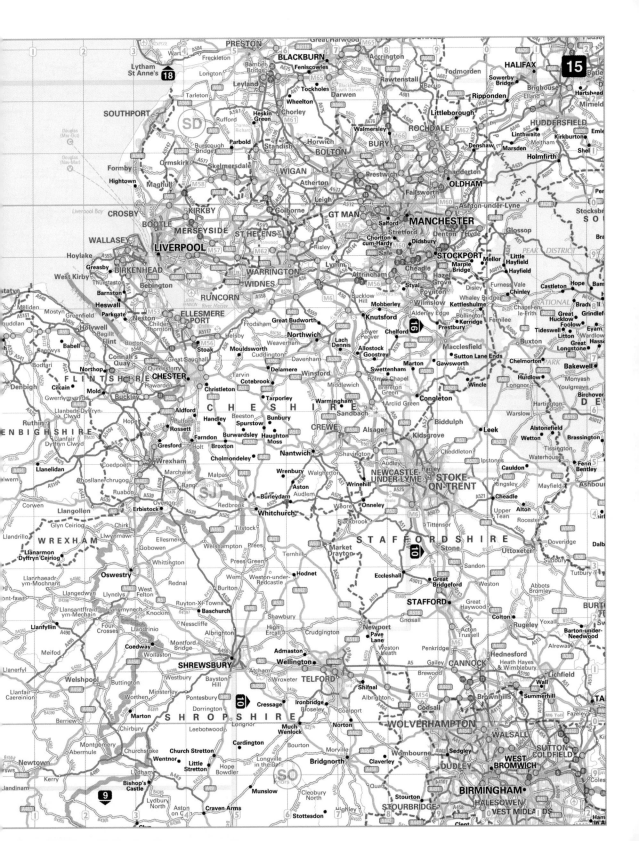

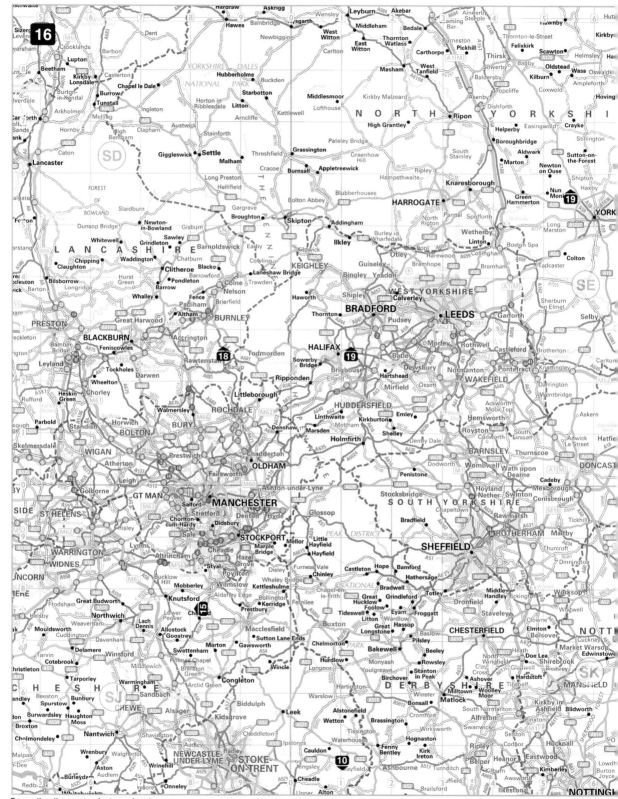

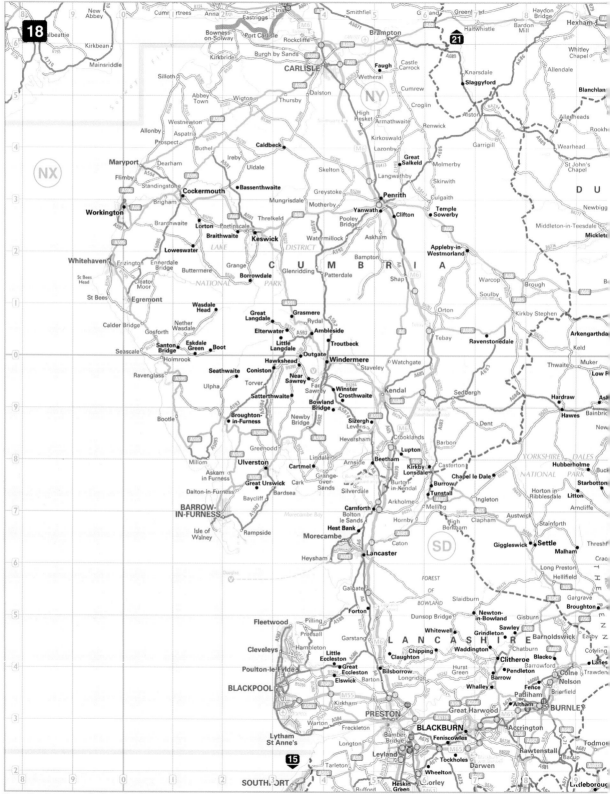

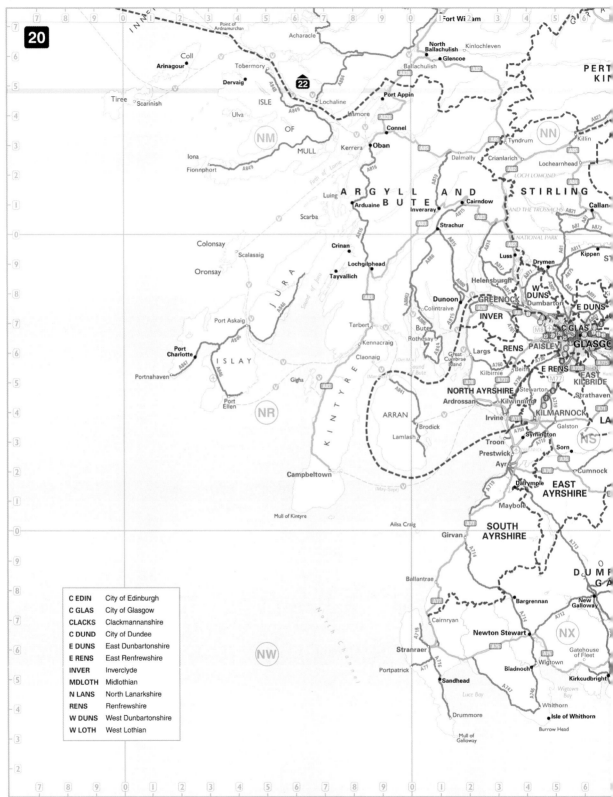

C EDIN | City of Edinburgh
C GLAS | City of Glasgow
CLACKS | Clackmannanshire
C DUND | City of Dundee
E DUNS | East Dunbartonshire
E RENS | East Renfrewshire
INVER | Inverclyde
MDLOTH | Midlothian
N LANS | North Lanarkshire
RENS | Renfrewshire
W DUNS | West Dunbartonshire
W LOTH | West Lothian

For continuation pages refer to numbered arrows

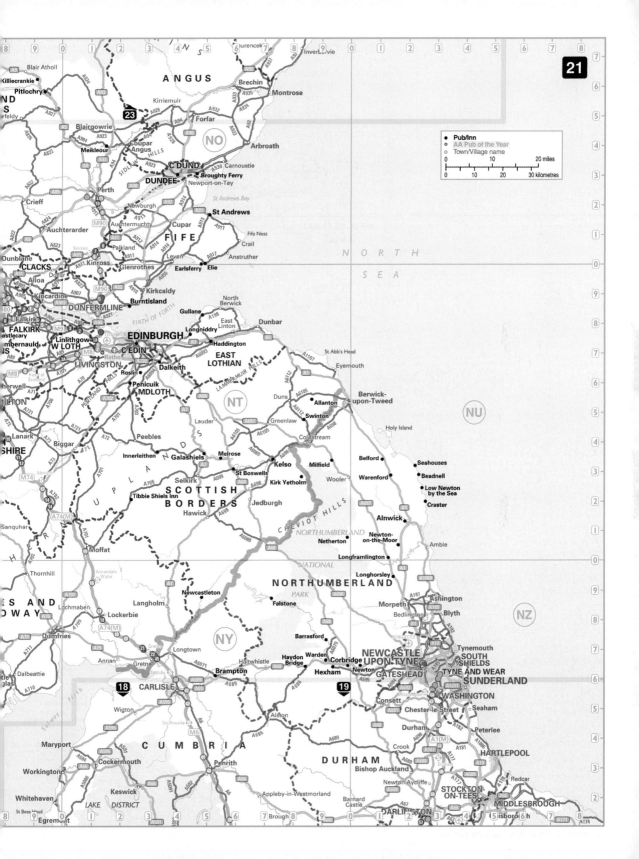

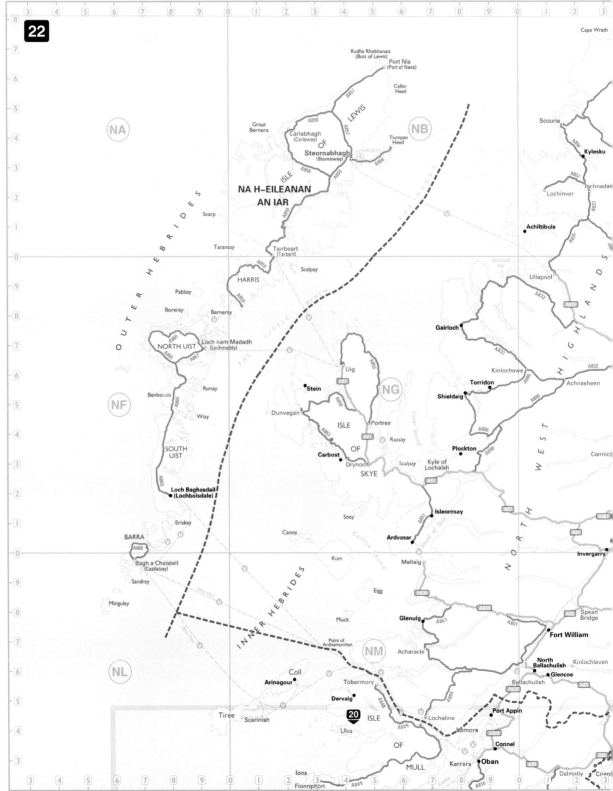

NA

NB

Cape Wrath

Rudha Rhobhanais
(Butt of Lewis)
Port Nis
(Port of Ness)

Cellar
Head

Scourie

LEWIS

Great
Bernera

Carlabhagh
(Carloway)

Tiumpan
Head

Kylesku

OF

Steornabhagh
(Stornoway)

Inchnada

Lochinver

ISLE

NA H–EILEANAN
AN IAR

Scarp

Achiltibuie

OUTER

Taransay

Tairbeart
(Tarbert)

Scalpay

HEBRIDES

Ullapool

HARRIS

Gruinard
Bay

Pabbay

Boreray

Berneray

Gairloch

HIGHLANDS

NORTH UIST

Loch nam Madadh
(Lochmaddy)

Uig

Kinlochewe

Achnasheen

Torridon

NF

Benbecula

Ronay

Stein

NG

Shieldaig

Wiay

Dunvegan

Portree

Raasay

Inner Sound

SOUTH
UIST

ISLE

Plockton

Carbost

OF

Drynoch

Scalpay

Kyle of
Lochalsh

Cannic

Loch Baghasdail
(Lochboisdale)

SKYE

WEST

Eriskay

Soay

Isleornsay

BARRA

Canna

Ardvasar

Bagh a Chaisteil
(Castlebay)

Sandray

Rùm

Mallaig

Invergarry

NORTH

Mingulay

Eigg

INNER

Muck

Glenuig

Spean
Bridge

HEBRIDES

Point of
Ardnamurchan

NM

Acharacle

Fort William

NL

Coll

Tobermory

North
Ballachulish

Kinlochleven

Arinagour

Dervaig

Glencoe

Ballachulish

Tiree

Scarinish

20

ISLE

Lochaline

Port Appin

Ulva

OF

Iasmore

Connel

Kerrera

Oban

Iona

MULL

Dalmally

Crian

Fionnphort

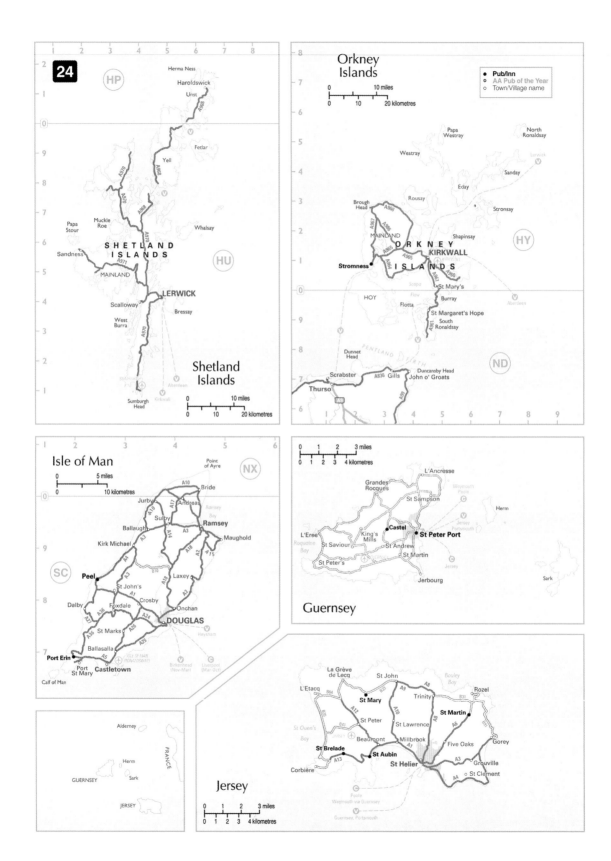

24

Orkney Islands

Shetland Islands

Isle of Man

Guernsey

Jersey

Central London

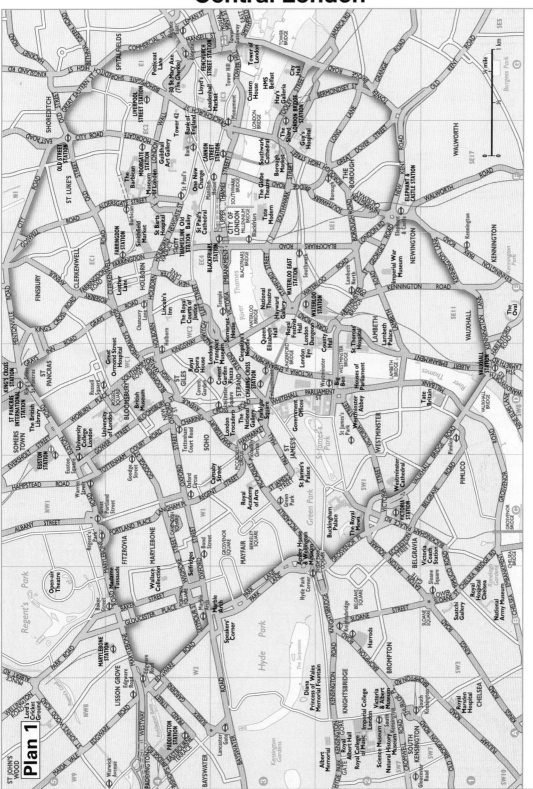

Plan 1

Index

Red entries are Pick of the Pubs

Acknowledgments

The Automobile Association would like to thank the following photographers, companies and picture libraries for their assistance in the preparation of this book.

Abbreviations for the picture credits are as follows – (t) top; (b) bottom; (c) centre; (l) left; (r) right; (AA) AA World Travel Library

Front Cover: © Aleksandr Bryliaev / Alamy

England Opener AA/John Wood;
Scotland Opener AA/Sue Anderson;
Wales Opener AA/Colin Molyneux

003 Courtesy of The Fox, Hampshire; 004 © Anne-Marie Palmer / Alamy;
008 Courtesy of The Green Dragon Inn, Gloucestershire; 009 Courtesy of The Muddy Duck, Oxfordshire; 010-011 AA/Clive Sawyer 010; Courtesy of The Pheasant, Essex; 011l Courtesy of The Bridge Inn, Ratho; 011r Courtesy of Bunch of Grapes, Rhondda Cynon Taff; 012 © imageBROKER / Alamy; 015 © Paul Lilley/Digitalshot / Alamy 016-017 Courtesy of The Bridge Inn, Ratho; 018-019 © Paul Bock / Alamy; 022-023 AA/John Wood; 587 © Eyebyte / Alamy; 588-589 AA/Sue Anderson; 618-619 AA/Colin Molyneux; 648-649 AA/James Tims.

Every effort has been made to trace the copyright holders, and we apologise in advance for any unintentional omissions or errors. We would be pleased to apply any corrections in a following edition of this publication

Readers' Report Form

Please send this form to:–
The Editor, The AA Pub Guide,
AA Lifestyle Guides,
13th Floor,
Fanum House,
Basingstoke RG21 4EA

e-mail: lifestyleguides@theAA.com

Please use this form to tell us about any pub or inn you have visited, whether it is in the guide or not currently listed. We are interested in the quality of food, the selection of beers and the overall ambience of the establishment.

Feedback from readers helps us to keep our guide accurate and up to date. However, if you have a complaint to make during a visit, we do recommend that you discuss the matter with the pub management there and then, so that they have a chance to put things right before your visit is spoilt.

Please note that the AA does not undertake to arbitrate between you and the pub management, or to obtain compensation or engage in protracted correspondence.

Date

Your name (BLOCK CAPITALS)

Your address (BLOCK CAPITALS)

Post code

E-mail address

Name of pub

Location

Comments

(please attach a separate sheet if necessary)

Please tick here ☐ if you DO NOT wish to receive details of AA offers or products

PTO

Readers' Report Form *continued*

Have you bought this guide before? ☐ YES ☐ NO

Do you regularly use any other pub, accommodation or food guides? ☐ YES ☐ NO
If YES, which ones?

What do you find most useful about The AA Pub Guide?

Do you read the editorial features in the guide? ☐ YES ☐ NO

Do you use the location atlas? ☐ YES ☐ NO

Is there any other information you would like to see added to this guide?

What are your main reasons for visiting pubs (tick all that apply)

Food ☐   Business ☐   Accommodation ☐
Beer ☐   Celebrations ☐   Entertainment ☐
Atmosphere ☐   Leisure ☐
Other

How often do you visit a pub for a meal?
more than once a week ☐
once a week ☐
once a fortnight ☐
once a month ☐
once in six months ☐

Readers' Report Form

Please send this form to:–
The Editor, The AA Pub Guide,
AA Lifestyle Guides,
13th Floor,
Fanum House,
Basingstoke RG21 4EA

e-mail: lifestyleguides@theAA.com

Please use this form to tell us about any pub or inn you have visited, whether it is in the guide or not currently listed. We are interested in the quality of food, the selection of beers and the overall ambience of the establishment.

Feedback from readers helps us to keep our guide accurate and up to date. However, if you have a complaint to make during a visit, we do recommend that you discuss the matter with the pub management there and then, so that they have a chance to put things right before your visit is spoilt.

Please note that the AA does not undertake to arbitrate between you and the pub management, or to obtain compensation or engage in protracted correspondence.

Date

Your name (BLOCK CAPITALS)

Your address (BLOCK CAPITALS)

Post code

E-mail address

Name of pub

Location

Comments

(please attach a separate sheet if necessary)

Please tick here ☐ if you DO NOT wish to receive details of AA offers or products   PTO

Readers' Report Form *continued*

Have you bought this guide before? ☐ YES ☐ NO

Do you regularly use any other pub, accommodation or food guides? ☐ YES ☐ NO
If YES, which ones?

_____

_____

What do you find most useful about The AA Pub Guide?

_____

_____

_____

Do you read the editorial features in the guide? ☐ YES ☐ NO

Do you use the location atlas? ☐ YES ☐ NO

Is there any other information you would like to see added to this guide?

_____

_____

_____

What are your main reasons for visiting pubs (tick all that apply)

Food ☐	Business ☐	Accommodation ☐
Beer ☐	Celebrations ☐	Entertainment ☐
Atmosphere ☐	Leisure ☐	
Other		

How often do you visit a pub for a meal?
more than once a week ☐
once a week ☐
once a fortnight ☐
once a month ☐
once in six months ☐